Peterson's
How to Get Money for College

Financing Your Future Beyond Federal Aid

2010

PETERSON'S

A nelnet COMPANY

About Peterson's

To succeed on your lifelong educational journey, you will need accurate, dependable, and practical tools and resources. That is why Peterson's is everywhere education happens. Because whenever and however you need education content delivered, you can rely on Peterson's to provide the information, know-how, and guidance to help you reach your goals. Tools to match the right students with the right school. It's here. Personalized resources and expert guidance. It's here. Comprehensive and dependable education content—delivered whenever and however you need it. It's all here.

For more information, contact Peterson's, 2000 Lenox Drive, Lawrenceville, NJ 08648; 800-338-3282; or find us on the World Wide Web at www.petersons.com/about.

Previous editions published as *Peterson's College Money Handbook* © 1983, 1984, 1985, 1986, 1987, 1988, 1989, 1990, 1991, 1996, 1997, 1998, 1999, 2000, 2001 2002, 2003, 2004, 2005, 2006, 2007, 2008 and as *Paying Less for College* © 1992, 1993, 1994, 1995

Stephen Clemente, President; Bernadette Webster, Director of Publishing; Mark D. Snider, Editor; Ward Brigham, Research Project Manager; Jim Ranish, Research Associate; Phyllis Johnson, Programmer; Ray Golaszewski, Manufacturing Manager; Linda M. Williams, Composition Manager

ISSN 1089-831X
ISBN-13: 978-0-7689-2799-3
ISBN-10: 0-7689-2799-4

Printed in the United States of America

10 9 8 7 6 5 4 3 2 1 11 10 09

Twenty-seventh Edition

By producing this book on recycled paper (40% post consumer waste) 249 trees were saved.

Other Recommended Titles

Peterson's Scholarships, Grants & Prizes

Peterson's Paying for College: Answers to All Your Questions About Financial Aid, Scholarships, Tuition Payment Plans, and Everything Else You Need to Know

Contents

A Note from the Peterson's Editors

The news media seem to constantly remind us that a college education is expensive. It certainly appears to be beyond the means of many Americans. The sticker price for four years at state-supported colleges can be more than $45,000, and private colleges and universities can cost more than $150,000. And these numbers continue to rise.

But there is good news. The system operates to provide the needed money so that most families and students are able to afford a college education while making only a reasonable financial sacrifice. However, because the college financial aid system is complex, finding the money is often easier said than done. That is why the process demands study, planning, calculation, flexibility, filling out forms, and meeting deadlines. Fortunately, for most people, it can produce positive results. There are many ways to manage college costs and many channels through which you can receive help. Be sure to take full advantage of the opportunities that have been opened up to students and their families by the many organizations, foundations, and businesses that have organized to help you with the burden of college expenses.

For nearly forty years, Peterson's has given students and parents the most comprehensive, up-to-date information on how to get their fair share of the financial aid pie. *Peterson's How to Get Money for College* is both a quick reference and a comprehensive resource that puts valuable information about college costs and financial aid opportunities at your fingertips.

- **The ABCs of Paying for College** provides insight into federal financial aid programs that are available, offers an overview of the financial aid landscape, walks you through the process of filing for aid, and provides proven tips on how to successfully navigate the financial aid process to obtain the federal, state, and institutional aid you deserve.
- The **Quick-Reference Chart** offers a snapshot comparison of the financial aid programs available at more than 2,100 four-year institutions across the country.
- The **Profiles of College Financial Aid Programs** provide unbiased financial aid data for each of the more than 2,100 four-year institutions listed.
- The **Appendix** lists the state scholarship and grant programs offered by all fifty states and the District of Columbia.
- The six **Indexes** included in the back of the book allow you to search for specific award programs based on a variety of criteria, including merit-based awards, athletic grants, ROTC programs, and much more.

Peterson's publishes a full line of resources to guide you and your family through the admissions process. Peterson's publications can be found at your local bookstore or library and at your high school guidance office; you can access us online at **www.petersons.com**.

We welcome any comments or suggestions you may have about this publication and invite you to complete our online survey at **www.petersons.com/booksurvey**.

Your feedback will help us make your education dreams possible. The editors at Peterson's wish you the best of luck during the financial aid process!

The ABCs of Paying for College

A Guide to Financing Your Child's College Education

Don Betterton

Given the lifelong benefit of a college degree (college graduates are projected to earn in a lifetime $1 million more than those with only a high school diploma), higher education is a worthwhile investment. However, it is also an expensive one made even more difficult to manage by cost increases that have outpaced both inflation and gains in family income. This reality of higher education economics is that paying for a child's college education is a dilemma that shows no sign of getting easier.

Because of the high cost involved (even the most inexpensive four-year education at a public institution costs about $10,000 a year), good information about college budgets and strategies for reducing the "sticker price" is essential. You have made a good start by taking the time to read *Peterson's How to Get Money for College*. In the pages that follow, you will find valuable information about the four main sources of aid—federal, state, institutional, and private. Before you learn about the various programs, however, it will be helpful if you have an overview of how the college financial aid system operates and what long-range financing strategies are available.

Financial Aid

Financial aid refers to money that is awarded to a student, usually in a "package" that consists of gift aid (commonly called a scholarship or grant), a student loan, and a campus job.

College Costs

The starting point for organizing a plan to pay for your child's college education is to make a good estimate of the yearly cost of attendance. You can use the **College Cost Worksheet** on the next page to do this.

To estimate your college costs for 2010–11, refer to the tuition and fees and room and board figures shown in the **College Costs At-a-Glance** chart starting on page 41. If your child will commute from your home, use $2500 instead of the college's room and board charges and $900 for transportation. We have used $800 for books and $1500 for personal expenses. Finally, estimate the cost of two round trips if your home is more than a few hundred miles from the college. Add the items to calculate the total budget. You should now have a reasonably good estimate of college costs for 2010–11. (To determine the costs for later years, adding 4 percent per year will probably give you a fairly accurate estimate.)

Do You Qualify for Need-Based Aid?

The next step is to evaluate whether or not you are likely to qualify for financial aid based on need. This step is critical, since more than 90 percent of the yearly total of $128 billion in student aid is awarded only after a determination is made that the family lacks sufficient financial resources to pay the full cost of college on its own. To judge your chance of receiving need-based aid, it is necessary to estimate an Expected Family Contribution (EFC) according to a government formula known as the Federal Methodology (FM). You can estimate how much you will be expected to contribute by referring to the EFC Calculator at http://www.finaid.org/calculators/quickefc.phtml.

Applying for Need-Based Aid

Because the federal government provides about 67 percent of all aid awarded, the application and need evaluation process is controlled by Congress and the U.S. Department of Education. The application is the Free Application for Federal Student Aid, or FAFSA. In addition, nearly every state that offers student assistance uses the federal government's system to award its own aid. Furthermore, in addition to arranging for the payment of federal and state aid, many colleges use the FAFSA to award their own funds to eligible students. (Note: In addition to the FAFSA, some colleges also ask the family to complete the CSS/Financial Aid PROFILE® application.)

The FAFSA is your "passport" to receiving your share of the billions of dollars awarded annually in need-based aid. Even if you're uncertain as to whether or not you qualify for need-based aid, everyone who might need assistance in financing an

College Cost Worksheet

	College 1	College 2	College 3	Commuter College
Tuition and Fees	______	______	______	______
Room and Board	______	______	______	$2,500
Books	$ 800	$ 800	$ 800	$ 750
Personal Expenses	$1,500	$1,500	$1,500	$1,500
Travel	______	______	______	$ 900
Total Budget	______	______	______	______

education should pick up a FAFSA from the high school guidance office after mid-November 2009. This form will ask for 2009 financial data, and it should be filed after January 1, 2010, in time to meet the earliest college or state scholarship deadline. Within two to four weeks after you submit the form, you will receive a summary of the FAFSA information, called the Student Aid Report, or SAR. The SAR will give you the EFC and also allow you to make corrections to the data you submitted.

You can also apply for federal student aid via the Internet using FAFSA on the Web. FAFSA on the Web can be accessed at www.fafsa.ed.gov. Both the student and at least one parent should apply for a federal PIN number at www.pin.ed.gov. The PIN number serves as your electronic signature when applying for aid on the Web. (Note: Many colleges provide the option to apply for early decision or early action admission. If you apply for this before January 1, 2010, which is prior to when the FAFSA can be used, follow the college's instructions. Many colleges use either PROFILE or their own application form for early admission candidates.)

Awarding Aid

About the same time you receive the SAR, the colleges you list will receive your FAFSA information so they can calculate a financial aid award in a package that typically includes aid from at least one of the major sources—federal, state, college, or private. In addition, the award will probably consist of a combination of a scholarship or a grant, a loan, and a campus job. These last two pieces—loan and job—are called self-help aid because they require effort on your child's part (that is, the aid must be either earned through work or paid back later). Scholarships or grants are outright gifts that have no such obligation.

How Need Is Calculated and Aid Is Awarded

	College 1	College 2
Total Cost of Attendance	$10,000	$ 24,000
– Expected Family Contribution	– 5,500	– 5,500
= Financial Need	$ 4,500	$ 18,500
– Grant Aid Awarded	– 675	–14,575
– Campus Job (Work-Study) Awarded	– 1,400	– 1,300
– Student Loan Awarded	– 2,425	– 2,625
= Unmet Need	0	0

Note: Sometimes an institution is unable to meet all need. The amount of unmet need is called "the gap."

Comparing Financial Aid Awards and Family Contribution Worksheet

	College 1	College 2	College 3
Cost of Attendance	________	________	________
Aid Awarded	________	________	________
Grant/Scholarship	________	________	________
Loan	________	________	________
Job	________	________	________
Total Aid	________	________	________
Expected Family Contribution	________	________	________
Student Contribution	________	________	________
Parent Contribution	________	________	________

It is important that you understand each part of the package. You'll want to know, for example, how much does gift aid provide, the interest rate and repayment terms of the student loan, and how many hours per week the campus job requires. There should be an enclosure with the award letter that answers these questions. If not, make a list of your questions and call or visit the financial aid office.

Once you understand the terms of each item in the award letter, you should turn your attention to the "bottom line"—how much you will have to pay at each college where your child was accepted. In addition to understanding the aid award, this means having a good estimate of the college budget so you can accurately calculate how much you and your child will have to contribute. (Often, an aid package does not cover the entire need.) Colleges differ in how much detail they include in their award notifications. Many colleges provide full information—types and amounts of aid, yearly costs, and the EFC for the parent and student shares. If these important items are missing or incomplete, you can do the work on your own. (See the **Comparing Financial Aid Awards and Family Contribution Worksheet** on this page.) For example, if only the college's direct charges for tuition, room, and board are shown on the award letter, make your own estimate of indirect costs like books, personal expenses, and travel. Then subtract the total aid awarded from the yearly cost to get the EFC. A portion of that amount may be your child's contribution (35 percent of student assets and 50 percent of student earnings over $2200) and the remainder is the parental share. If you can afford this amount at your child's first-choice college, the financial aid system has worked well for you, and your child's college enrollment plans can go forward.

But if you think your EFC is too high, you should contact the college's financial aid office and ask whether additional aid is available. Many colleges, private high-cost colleges in particular, are enrollment-oriented—they are willing to work with families to help make attendance at their institutions possible. Most colleges also allow applicants to appeal their financial aid awards, the budget used for you, or any of the elements used to determine the family contribution, especially if there are extenuating circumstances or if the information has changed since the application was submitted. Some colleges may also reconsider an award based on a "competitive appeal," the submission of a more favorable award letter from another college.

If your appeal is unsuccessful and there is still a gap between the expected family contribution and what you feel you can pay from income and savings, you are left with two choices. One option is for your child to attend a college where paying your share of the bill will not be a problem. (This assumes that an affordable option was included on your child's original list of colleges, a wise admission application strategy.) The second is to look into alternate methods of financing. At this stage, parental loans and tuition payment plans are the best financing options. A parental loan can bring the yearly cost down to a manageable level by spreading payments over a number of years. This is the type of financing that families use when purchasing a home or automobile. A tuition payment plan is essentially a short-term loan and allows you to pay the costs over ten to twelve months. It is an option for families who have the resources available but need help with managing their cash flow.

Non-Need-Based Aid

Regardless of whether you might qualify for a need-based award, it is always worthwhile to look into merit, or non-need, scholarships from sources such as foundations, agencies, religious groups, and service organizations. For a family that isn't eligible for need-based aid, merit scholarships are the only form of gift aid available. If your child later qualifies for a need-based award, a merit scholarship can be quite helpful in providing additional resources if the aid does not fully cover the costs. Even if the college meets 100 percent of need, a merit scholarship reduces the self-help (loan and job) portion of an award.

In searching for merit-based scholarships, keep in mind that there are relatively few awards (compared to those that are need-based), and most of them are highly competitive. Use the following checklist when investigating merit scholarships.

- Take advantage of any scholarships for which your child is automatically eligible based on parents' employer benefits, military service, association or church membership, other affiliations, or student or parent attributes (ethnic background, nationality, etc.). Company or union tuition remissions are the most common examples of these awards.
- Look for other awards for which your child might be eligible based on the previous characteristics and affiliations but where there is a selection process and an application is required. Free computerized searches are available on the Internet. (You should not pay a fee for a scholarship search.) Peterson's free scholarship search can be accessed by logging on to www.petersons.com/finaid. Scholarship directories, such as *Peterson's Scholarships, Grants & Prizes*, which details more than 4,000 scholarship programs, are useful resources and can be found in bookstores, high school guidance offices, or public libraries.
- See if your state has a merit scholarship program.
- Look into national scholarship competitions. High school guidance counselors usually know about these scholarships. Examples of these awards are the National Merit® Scholarship Program, the Coca-Cola Scholarship, Gates Millennium Scholars, Intel Science Talent Search, and the U.S. Senate Youth Program.
- ROTC (Reserve Officers' Training Corps) scholarships are offered by the Army, Navy, Air Force, and Marine Corps. A full ROTC scholarship covers tuition, fees, textbook costs and, in some cases, a stipend. Acceptance of an ROTC scholarship entails a commitment to take military science courses and to serve for a specific number of years as an officer in the sponsoring branch of the service. Competition is heavy, and preference may be given to students in certain fields of study, such as engineering, languages, science, and health professions. Application procedures vary by service. Contact an armed services recruiter or high school guidance counselor for further information.
- Investigate community scholarships. High school guidance counselors usually have a list of these awards, and announcements are published in local newspapers. Most common are awards given by service organizations like the American Legion, Rotary International, and the local women's club.
- If your child is strong academically (for example, a National Merit Commended Student or better) or is very talented in fields such as athletics or performing/creative arts, you may want to consider colleges that offer their own merit awards to gifted students they wish to enroll. Refer to the Non-Need Scholarships for Undergraduates index.

In addition to merit scholarships, there are loan and job opportunities for students who do not qualify for need-based aid. Federal loan programs include the unsubsidized Federal Stafford Student

Note

A point of clarification about whether to put college savings in your name or your child's: If you are certain that your child will not be a candidate for need-based aid, there may be a tax advantage to accumulating money in his or her name. However, when it comes to maximizing aid eligibility, it is important to understand that student assets are assessed at a 20 percent rate and parental assets at about 5 percent. Therefore, if your college savings are in your child's name, it may be wise to reestablish title to these funds before applying for financial aid. You should contact your financial planner or accountant before making any modifications to your asset structure.

What Is CSS/Financial Aid PROFILE®?

There are many complexities in the financial aid process: knowing which aid is merit-based and which aid is need-based; understanding the difference between grants, loans, and work-study; and determining whether funds are from federal, state, institutional, or private sources.

In addition, the aid application process itself can be confusing. It can involve more than the Free Application for Federal Student Aid (FAFSA) and the Federal Methodology (FM). Many colleges feel that the federal aid system (FAFSA and FM) does not collect or evaluate information thoroughly enough for them to award their own institutional funds. These colleges have made an arrangement with the College Scholarship Service, a branch of the College Board, to establish a separate application system.

The application is called the CSS/Financial Aid PROFILE®, and the need-analysis formula is referred to as the Institutional Methodology (IM). If you apply for financial aid at one of the colleges that uses PROFILE, the admission material will state that PROFILE is required in addition to the FAFSA. You should read the information carefully and file PROFILE to meet the earliest college deadline. Before you can receive PROFILE, however, you must register, either by phone or through the Web (https://profileonline.collegeboard.com/index.jsp), providing enough basic information so the PROFILE package can be designed specifically for you. The FAFSA is free, but there is a charge for PROFILE. As with the FAFSA, PROFILE can be submitted via the Internet.

In addition to the requirement by certain colleges that you submit both the FAFSA and PROFILE (when used, PROFILE is always in addition to the FAFSA; it does not replace it), you should understand that each system has its own method for analyzing a family's ability to pay for college. The main differences between PROFILE's Institutional Methodology and the FAFSA's Federal Methodology are:

- PROFILE includes equity in the family home as an asset; the FAFSA doesn't.
- PROFILE takes a broader look at assets not included on the FAFSA.
- PROFILE expects a minimum student contribution, usually in the form of summer earnings; the FAFSA has no such minimum.
- PROFILE may collect information on the noncustodial parent; the FAFSA does not.
- PROFILE allows for more professional judgment than the FAFSA. Medical expenses, private secondary school costs, and a variety of special circumstances are considered under PROFILE, subject to the discretion of the aid counselor on campus.
- PROFILE includes information on assets not reported on the FAFSA, including life insurance, annuities, retirement plans, etc.

To summarize: PROFILE's Institutional Methodology tends to be both more complete in its data collection and more rigorous in its analysis than the FAFSA's Federal Methodology. When IM results are compared to FM results for thousands of applicants, IM will usually come up with a somewhat higher expected parental contribution than FM.

and Direct Loans. Some of the organizations that sponsor scholarships—for example, the Air Force Aid Society—also provide loans.

Work opportunities during the academic year are another type of assistance that is not restricted to aid recipients. Many colleges will, after assigning jobs to students on aid, open campus positions to all students looking for work. In addition, there are usually off-campus employment opportunities available to everyone.

Creditworthiness

If you will be borrowing to pay for your child's college education, making sure you qualify for a loan is critical. For the most part, that means your credit record must be free of default or delinquency. You can check your credit history with one or more of the following three major credit bureaus and clean up any adverse information that appears. The numbers below will offer specific information on what you need to provide to obtain a report. All of the credit bureaus accept credit report requests over their Web sites. You will usually be asked to provide your full name, phone number, social security number, birth date, and addresses for the last five years. You are entitled to a free report from each bureau.

Equifax Credit Information
P.O. Box 740241
Atlanta, GA 30374
800-685-1111
http://www.equifax.com

Trans Union
800-888-4213
http://www.transunion.com

Experian
888-397-3742
http://www.experian.com

Financing Your Child's College Education

"Financing" means putting together resources to pay the balance due the college over and above payments from the primary sources of aid—grants, scholarships, student loans, and jobs. Financing strategies are important because the high cost of a college education today often requires a family, whether or not it receives aid, to think about stretching its college payment beyond the four-year period of enrollment. For high-cost colleges, it is not unreasonable to think about a 10-4-10 plan: ten years of saving; four years of paying college bills out of current income, savings, and borrowing; and ten years to repay a parental loan.

Savings

Although saving for college is always a good idea, many families are unclear about its advantages. Some families do not save because after normal living expenses have been covered, they do not have much money to set aside. An affordable but regular savings plan through a payroll deduction is usually the answer to the problem of spending your entire paycheck every month.

The second reason why saving for college is not a high priority is the belief that the financial aid system penalizes a family by lowering aid eligibility. The Federal Methodology of need determination is very kind to families that save. In fact, savings are ignored completely for most families that earn less than $50,000. Savings in the form of home equity, retirement plans, and most annuities are excluded from the calculation. And even when savings are counted, a maximum of 5 percent of the total is expected each year. In other words, if a family has $40,000 in savings after an asset protection allowance is considered, the contribution is no greater than $2000. Given the impact of compound interest it is easy to see that a long-term savings plan can make paying for college much easier.

A sensible savings plan is important because of the financial advantage of saving compared to borrowing. The amount of money students borrow for college is now greater than the amount they receive in grants and scholarships. With loans becoming so widespread, savings should be carefully considered as an alternative to borrowing. Your incentive for saving is that a dollar saved is a dollar not borrowed.

Borrowing

Once you've calculated your "bottom-line" parental contribution and determined that the amount is not affordable out of your current income and assets, the most likely alternative is borrowing. First determine if your child is eligible for a larger subsidized Federal Stafford Student or Direct Loan. Because no interest is due while your child attends college, these are the most favorable loans. If this is not possible, look into the unsubsidized Federal Stafford Student or Direct Loan, which is not based on need but the interest accrues each year. The freshman year limit (either subsidized or unsubsidized) is $3500.

After your child has taken out the maximum amount of student loans, the next step is to look into parental loans. The federal government's parent loan program is called PLUS and is the standard against which other loans should be judged. A local bank that participates in the PLUS program can give you a schedule of monthly repayments per $1000 borrowed. Use this repayment figure to compare other parental loans available from commercial lenders (including home equity loans), state programs, or colleges themselves. Choose the one that offers the best terms after all up-front costs, tax advantages, and the amount of monthly payments are considered. Be sure to check with your financial aid office before making a final decision. Often, the financial aid office will have reviewed the various programs that are available and can help direct you to the best choice.

Make Financial Aid Work for You

If you are like millions of families that benefit from financial aid, it is likely that your child's college plans can go forward without undue worry about the costs involved. The key is to understand the financial aid system and to follow the best path for your family. The result of good information and good planning should be that you will receive your fair share of the billions of dollars available each year and that the cost of college will not prevent your child from attending.

Don Betterton is a former Director of Undergraduate Financial Aid at Princeton University.

Federal Financial Aid Programs

There are a number of sources of financial aid available to students: federal and state governments, private agencies, and the colleges themselves. In addition, there are three different forms of aid: grants, earnings, and loans.

The federal government is the single largest source of financial aid for students. For the 2005–06 academic year, the U.S. Department of Education's student financial aid programs made more than $80 billion available in loans, grants, and other aid to 14 million students. At present, there are four federal grant programs—Federal Pell Grant, Federal Supplemental Educational Opportunity Grant (FSEOG), Academic Competitiveness Grant (ACG), and National Smart Grant (SMART). There are three federal loan programs: Federal Perkins Loan Program, Direct Loan Program, and Federal Family Education Loan Program (FFELP). The federal government also has a job program, Federal Work-Study Program (FWS), which helps colleges provide employment for students. In addition to the student aid programs, there are also tuition tax credits and deductions. They are the Hope Credit for freshmen and sophomores, the Lifetime Learning Credit for undergraduate students after their second year, the Tuition and Fees Tax Deduction, and the Student Loan Interest Tax Deduction. Also, there is AmeriCorps. AmeriCorps will pay the interest that is accrued on qualified student loans for members who complete the service program.

The majority of federal higher education loans are made either in the Direct Loan Program or the FFELP. The difference between these loans is the lending source, but, for the borrower, the terms and conditions are essentially the same. Both Direct and FFEL programs make available two kinds of loans: loans to students and PLUS loans to parents or to graduate or professional students. These loans are either subsidized or unsubsidized. Subsidized loans are made on the basis of demonstrated student need, and the interest is paid by the government during the time the student is in school. For the unsubsidized (non-need-based) loans and PLUS loans, interest begins to accrue as funds are disbursed.

To qualify for the Federal Pell Grant, ACG, SMART, FSEOG, FWS, and Federal Perkins Loan Program and the subsidized Federal Stafford Student Loan, you must demonstrate financial need.

Federal Pell Grant

The Federal Pell Grant is the largest grant program; more than 6 million students receive Pell Grants annually. This grant is intended to be the starting point of assistance for lower-income families. Eligibility for a Pell Grant is based on the Expected Family Contribution. The amount you receive will depend on your EFC and the cost of education at the college you will attend. The highest award depends on how much funding the program receives from the government. The maximum for 2008–09 is $4731.

To give you some idea of your possible eligibility for a Pell Grant, the table on page 10 may be helpful. The amounts shown are based on a family of four, with one student in college, no emergency expenses, no contribution from student income or assets, and college costs of at least $4050 per year. Pell Grants range from $400 to $4731.

Federal Supplemental Educational Opportunity Grant (FSEOG)

As its name implies, Federal Supplemental Educational Opportunity Grants provide additional need-based federal grant money to supplement the Federal Pell Grant Program. Each participating college is given funds to award to especially needy students. The maximum award is $4000 per year, but the amount you receive depends on the college's awarding policy, the availability of FSEOG funds, the total cost of education, and the amount of other aid awarded.

Federal Financial Aid Programs

Name of Program	Type of Program	Maximum Award Per Year
Federal Pell Grant	need-based grant	$4731
Federal Supplemental Educational Opportunity Grant (FSEOG)	need-based grant	$4000
Academic Competitiveness Grant (ACG)	need/merit	$750 (first year) $1300 (second year)
National Smart Grant (SMART)	need/merit/program	up to $4000 (third- and fourth-year undergraduate)
Federal Work-Study Program (FWS)	need-based part-time job	no maximum
Federal Perkins Loan Program	need-based loan	$5000
Subsidized Federal Stafford Student Loan/Direct Loan	need-based student loan	$3500 (first year)
Unsubsidized Federal Stafford Student Loan/Direct Loan	non-need-based student loan	$5500 (first year, dependent student)

Academic Competitiveness Grant (ACG)

U.S. citizens who are Pell Grant–eligible and who attended a "rigorous" high school program, as defined by the U.S. Secretary of Education, can receive up to $750 in their first year and $1300 in their second year if they have a minimum 3.0 GPA. More information about this program is available from the high school or college financial aid office.

National Smart Grant (SMART)

Third- and fourth-year undergraduates who are Pell Grant–eligible and major in math, science, technology, or certain foreign languages and have a minimum 3.0 in their major can qualify for a grant of up to $4000. More information about this program is available from the high school or college financial aid office.

Federal Work-Study Program (FWS)

This program provides jobs for students who demonstrate need. Salaries are paid by funds from the federal government as well as the college. Students work on an hourly basis on or off campus and must be paid at least the federal minimum wage. Students may earn only up to the amount awarded in the financial aid package.

Federal Perkins Loan Program

This is a low-interest loan for students with exceptional financial need. Perkins Loans are made through the college's financial aid office with the college as the lender. Students can borrow a maximum of $4500 per year for up to five years of undergraduate study. Borrowers may take up to ten years to repay the loan, beginning nine months after they graduate, leave school, or drop below half-time status. No interest accrues while they are in school, and, under certain conditions (e.g., they teach in low-income areas, work in law enforcement, are full-time nurses or medical technicians, serve as Peace Corps or VISTA volunteers, etc.), some or all of the loan can be cancelled. In addition, payments can be deferred under certain conditions such as unemployment.

Federal Stafford Student and Direct Loans

Federal Stafford Student and Direct Loans generally have the same interest rates, loan maximums, deferments, and cancellation benefits. A Stafford loan may be borrowed from a commercial lender, such as a bank or a credit union. A Direct Loan is borrowed directly from the U.S. Department of Education through the college's financial aid office.

The unsubsidized Direct and Federal Stafford Student Loan Programs carry a fixed 6.8 percent interest rate. The interest rate for subsidized Federal Stafford Student and Direct Loans is fixed at a 5.6 percent interest rate. If a student qualifies for a need-based subsidized Federal Stafford Student or Direct Loan, the interest is paid by the federal government while he or she is enrolled in college, during grace, and during periods of deferment. Over a four-year period beginning July 1, 2008, the fixed interest rate on subsidized Direct and Federal Stafford Student Loans made to undergraduate students who purchased a loan made before July 1, 2006, will be reduced in phases. For loans first disbursed on or after

- July 1, 2009, and before July 1, 2010, the interest rate will be fixed at 5.60 percent;
- July 1, 2010, and before July 1, 2011, the interest rate will be fixed at 4.50 percent;
- July 1, 2011, and before July 1, 2012, the interest rate will be fixed at 3.40 percent.

The maximum amount dependent students may borrow in any one year is $5500 for freshmen, $6500 for sophomores, and $7500 for juniors and seniors, with a maximum of $31,000 for the total undergraduate program (of which not more than $23,000 can be subsidized). The maximum amount independent students can borrow is $9500 for freshmen (of which no more than $3500 can be subsidized), $10,500 for sophomores (of which no more than $4500 can be subsidized), and $12,500 for juniors and seniors (of which no more than $5500 can be subsidized). Independent students can borrow up to $57,500 (of which no more than $23,000 can be subsidized) for the total undergraduate program. Borrowers may be charged a small origination fee, which is deducted from the loan proceeds. Some lenders offer reduced or no-fee loans.

To apply for a Federal Stafford Student Loan, you must first complete the FAFSA to determine eligibility for a subsidized loan and then complete a separate loan application that is submitted to a lender. The financial aid office can help in selecting a lender, but students are free to select any lender they choose. The lender will send a master promissory for completion. The proceeds of the loan, less the origination fee, will be sent to the college to be either credited to your account or released to you directly. Direct loans are processed by the financial aid office as part of the overall financial aid package.

Once the repayment period starts, borrowers of both subsidized and unsubsidized Federal Stafford Student or Direct Loans have to pay a combination of interest and principal monthly for up to a ten-year period. There are a number of repayment options as well as opportunities to consolidate federal loans. There are also provisions for extended repayments, deferments, and repayment forbearance, if needed.

Federal PLUS and Direct PLUS Loans

PLUS loans are for parents of dependent students to help families with the cost of education. There is no needs test to qualify. A Federal PLUS Loan has a fixed interest rate of 8.5 percent. A Direct PLUS Loan has a fixed interest rate of 7.9 percent. There is no yearly limit; you can borrow up to the cost of your child's education, less other financial aid received. Repayment begins sixty days after the funds are disbursed. A small origination fee (usually about 3 percent or less) may be subtracted from the proceeds. Parent borrowers must generally have a good credit record to qualify. PLUS loans may be processed under either the Direct Loan or FFELP system, depending on the type of loan program for which the college has contracted.

Hope Credit and Lifetime Learning Credit

Tuition tax credits allow families to reduce their tax bill by the out-of-pocket college tuition expense. Unlike a tax deduction, which is modified according to your tax bracket, a tax credit is a dollar-for-dollar reduction in taxes paid.

There are two programs: the Hope Credit and the Lifetime Learning Credit. As is true of many federal programs, there are numerous rules and restrictions that apply. You should check with your tax preparer, financial adviser, or IRS Publication 970 for information about your own particular situation.

Hope Credit

The Hope Credit offsets some of the expense for the first two years of college or vocational school. Students or the parents of dependent students can claim an annual income tax credit of up to $1800—100 percent of the first $1200 of tuition and required fees and 50 percent of the second $1200. Grants, scholarships, and other tax-free educational assistance must be deducted from the total tuition and fee payments.

This credit can be claimed for students who are in their first two years of college and who are enrolled on at least a half-time basis in a degree or certificate program for any portion of the year. This credit phases out for joint filers who have an income between $96,000 and $116,000 and for single filers who have between $48,000 and $58,000 of income. Parents may claim credits for more than one qualifying student. (The income figures are subject to change and can be found in each year's IRS Publication 970.)

Lifetime Learning Credit

The Lifetime Learning Credit is the counterpart of the Hope Credit; it is for college juniors, seniors, graduate students, and part-time students pursuing lifelong learning to improve or upgrade their job skills. The qualifying taxpayer can claim an annual tax credit of up to $2000—20 percent of the first $10,000 of tuition. The credit is available for net tuition and fees, less grant aid. The total credit available is limited to $2000 per year per taxpayer (or joint-filing couple), and is phased out at the same income levels as the Hope Credit. (The income figures are subject to change and can be found in each year's IRS Publication 970.)

Tuition and Fees Tax Deduction

The Tuition and Fees Tax Deduction could reduce taxable income by as much as $4000. This deduction is taken as an adjustment to income, which means you can claim this deduction even if you do not itemize deductions on Schedule A of Form 1040. This deduction may benefit taxpayers who do not qualify for either the Hope Credit or Lifetime Learning Credit.

Up to $4000 may be deducted for tuition and fees required for enrollment or attendance at an eligible postsecondary institution. Personal living and family expenses, including room and board, insurance, medical, and transportation, are not deductible expenses.

The exact amount of the Tuition and Fees Tax Deduction depends on the amount of qualified tuition and related expenses paid for one's self, spouse, or dependents, and your Adjusted Gross Income. Consult the IRS or your tax preparer for more information.

Student Loan Interest Tax Deduction

If you made student loan interest payments in 2009, you may be able to reduce your taxable income by up to $2500. You should check with your lender with regards to the amount of interest you paid if you did not receive an IRS Form 1098-E and your tax preparer or IRS Publication 970 for additional information.

AmeriCorps

AmeriCorps is a national umbrella group of service programs for students. Participants work in a public or private nonprofit agency and provide service to the community in one of four priority areas: education, human services, the environment, and public safety. In exchange, they earn a stipend (for living expenses), health insurance coverage, and $4725 per year for up to two years to apply toward college expenses. Many student-loan lenders will postpone the repayment of student loans during service in AmeriCorps, and AmeriCorps will pay the interest that is accrued on qualified student loans for members who complete the service program. Participants can work before, during, or after college and can use the funds to either pay current educational expenses or repay federal student loans. For more information, visit www.americorps.org.

Analyzing Financial Aid Award Letters

Richard Woodland

You have just received the financial aid award letters. Now what? This is the time to do a detailed analysis of each college's offer to help you pay for your child's education. Remember, accepting financial aid is a family matter. More often than not, parents need to borrow money to send their dependent children to college. You need to clearly understand the types of aid you and your child are being offered. How much is "free" money in the form of grants and/or scholarships that does not have to be repaid? If your financial aid award package includes loans, what are the terms and conditions for these loans? A good tool to have with you is the federal government's most recent issue of *Funding Education Beyond High School: The Guide to Federal Student Aid,* available from the school's financial aid office or at http://studentaid.ed.gov/students/publications/student_guide/index.html. This publication is very helpful in explaining the federal grant and loan programs that are usually a part of the aid package.

Let's take a minute to explain what is meant by "financial aid award package." A college will offer an aid applicant a combination of aid types, "packaged" in the form of grants and scholarships, loans, and a work-study job, based on the information provided on the FAFSA and/or another application. Many schools use a priority filing date, which guarantees that all applications received by this date will be considered for the full range of institutional aid programs available. Late applicants (by even one day!) often are only awarded the basic aid programs from state and federal sources. *It is important to apply on time.*

Evaluate Each Letter

As each award letter comes in, read it through carefully. The following are some critical points to consider:

- **Does the Cost of Attendance (COA) include all projected costs?** Each award letter should state the school's academic year COA. Tuition, fees, room, board, books, transportation, and personal expenses are what normally make up the COA. Does the award letter itemize all these components? Or does it omit some? This is crucial because this is what you will need to budget for. If you need additional information, be sure to contact the financial aid office. They will be glad to provide you with information or answer any questions you may have about their costs.
- **What is your Expected Family Contribution (EFC)?** Is the school's—not just the federal government's—EFC listed on the award letter? Some schools may require a higher EFC than you expected. Be aware that the EFC may increase or decrease each year depending on the information you provide on the renewal FAFSA or other financial aid application.
- **Is there unmet need?** Does the aid package cover the difference between the COA and the EFC? Not every school can cover your full need. If the aid package does not cover your full need, does the information with the award letter provide you with alternative loan options? If not, contact the financial aid office for more information.
- **Is the scholarship renewable for four years?** If your child is awarded a scholarship based on scholastic achievement or talent, you need to ask these questions: Is there a minimum grade point average he has to maintain? Can he switch majors but keep the scholarship? Does he need to participate in an "honors college" program to maintain the scholarship? If he needs to change to part-time status, will the award amount be prorated, or does he need to maintain full-time status? If it is an athletic or "special talent" scholarship, will he continue to receive the award if for some reason he cannot continue with the specific program? Renewal of scholarship funds is often the biggest misunderstanding between families and colleges. Be sure you clearly understand the terms and conditions of all grants and scholarships.
- **What will the college do to your child's award if she receives outside, noninstitutional scholarships?** Will the award be used to cover unmet need or reduce her student loans? Will the college reduce her institutional grants or scholarships? Or will they reduce her work-study award? (This is a good time to compare each school's policy on this matter.) Remember, your overall aid cannot total more than the COA, and many programs cannot exceed your financial need.
- **What are the interest rates of the loans that are offered?** Did another school offer you more than one loan and why? *Do not* sign the award letter until you understand your loan obligations.

Analyzing Financial Aid Award Letters

Again, *Funding Education Beyond High School: The Guide to Federal Student Aid* can be very helpful with this part of the analysis.

- **Is the school likely to cover the same expenses every year?** In particular, ask if grant or scholarship funds are normally reduced or increased after the freshman year, even if family income and EFC remain the same. Some colleges will *increase* the self-help (loan, job) percentage every year but not necessarily the free money.
- **If work-study was awarded, how many hours a week will your child be expected to work?** If you feel working that many hours will have a negative impact on your child's academic performance, you may want to request that the awarded job funds be changed to a loan. You must ask immediately because funds are limited. Many schools are flexible with these funds early in the process.
- **What happens if (or more likely, when) tuition increases?** Check with the financial aid office to find out what its policy is for renewing an aid package. If, for example, tuition increases by 5 percent each of the next three years and your EFC remains the same, what will happen to your scholarships, grants, and loans?

You can always appeal your award letter if you feel that your needs are not being met, if your family situation has changed, or if you have received a better award from a competitive school. You have the right to ask for a reconsideration of your award. (Do not use the word *negotiate*.) When asking for reconsideration, be sure to provide the aid officer with all relevant information.

Compare Letters

After you have received and reviewed all the award letters from the schools your child is considering, the next step is to compare them and determine which schools are offering the best aid packages. Following are three sample award letters and a sample spreadsheet that shows you how to analyze and compare each school's awards.

(Note: These award letters are simply for discussion purposes. They should not be considered to be representative award letters with an EFC of $9550.)

UNIVERSITY A

FINANCIAL AID AWARD LETTER

2009–2010

Date: 4/21/09

ID#: 000000009

Dear Courtney Applicant,

We are pleased to inform you that you are eligible to receive the financial assistance indicated in the area labeled "Your Financial Aid." We estimated your budget based on the following assumptions:

In-state resident and living on campus.

	FALL	SPRING	TOTAL
Tuition and Fees	$3,849	$3,849	$ 7,698
Room & Board	3,769	3,770	7,539
Books	420	420	840
Transportation	973	974	1,947
Personal Expenses	369	369	738
Estimated Cost of Attendance	**$9,380**	**$9,382**	**$18,762**

Your Financial Aid

	FALL	SPRING	TOTAL
Federal Pell Grant	$1,950	$1,950	$ 3,900
Federal Direct Subsidized Loan	1,750	1,750	3,500
State Grant	432	432	864
Total Financial Aid	**$4,132**	**$4,132**	**$ 8,264**
Unmet Need	**$5,248**	**$5,250**	**$10,498**

What to Do Next:

- Verify that accurate assumptions have been used to determine your awards.
- Carefully review and follow the instructions on the Data Changes Form.
- To reduce or decline all or part of your loans, you must complete and return the Data Changes Form.
- We will assume you fully accept the awards above unless you submit changes to us immediately.
- Return corrections and required documents promptly.
- Retain this letter for your records.

UNIVERSITY B
FINANCIAL AID AWARD LETTER
2009–2010

Date: 4/21/09
ID#: 000000009

Dear Courtney Applicant,

We are pleased to inform you that you are eligible to receive the financial assistance indicated in the area labeled "Your Financial Aid." We estimated your budget based on the following assumptions:

Nonresident and living on campus.

	FALL	SPRING	TOTAL
Tuition and Fees	$ 9,085	$ 9,085	$18,170
Room & Board	2,835	2,835	5,670
Books	410	410	820
Transportation	875	875	1,750
Personal Expenses	378	377	755
Estimated Cost of Attendance	**$13,583**	**$13,582**	**$27,165**

Your Financial Aid

	FALL	SPRING	TOTAL
Federal Pell Grant	$ 1,950	$ 1,950	$ 3,900
Federal SEOG Grant	225	225	450
Academic Excellence Scholarship	500	500	1,000
Federal Work-Study Program	1,050	1,050	2,100
Federal Perkins Loan Program	1,250	1,250	2,500
Subsidized Federal Stafford Student Loan	1,750	1,750	3,500
University Student Loan	2,000	2,000	4,000
Total Financial Aid	**$ 8,725**	**$ 8,725**	**$17,450**
Unmet Need	**$ 4,858**	**$ 4,857**	**$ 9,715**

What to Do Next:

- Verify that accurate assumptions have been used to determine your awards.
- Carefully review and follow the instructions on the Data Changes Form.
- To reduce or decline all or part of your loans, you must complete and return the Data Changes Form.
- We will assume you fully accept the awards above unless you submit changes to us immediately.
- Return corrections and required documents promptly.
- Retain this letter for your records.

UNIVERSITY C
FINANCIAL AID AWARD LETTER
2009–2010

Date: 4/21/09
ID#: 000000009

Dear Courtney Applicant,

We are pleased to inform you that you are eligible to receive the financial assistance indicated in the area labeled "Your Financial Aid." We estimated your budget based on the following assumptions:

Living on campus.

	FALL	SPRING	TOTAL
Tuition and Fees	$14,955	$14,955	$29,910
Room & Board	4,194	4,193	8,387
Books	450	450	900
Transportation	350	350	700
Personal Expenses	1,295	1,293	2,588
Estimated Cost of Attendance	**$21,244**	**$21,241**	**$42,485**

Your Financial Aid

	FALL	SPRING	TOTAL
Institutional Grant	$10,805	$10,805	$21,610
Federal Pell Grant	1,950	1,950	3,900
Federal SEOG Grant	2,000	2,000	4,000
Federal Work-Study Program	1,713	1,712	3,425
Total Financial Aid	**$16,468**	**$16,467**	**$32,935**
Unmet Need	**$ 4,776**	**$ 4,774**	**$ 9,550**

What to Do Next:

- Verify that accurate assumptions have been used to determine your awards.
- Carefully review and follow the instructions on the Data Changes Form.
- To reduce or decline all or part of your loans, you must complete and return the Data Changes Form.
- We will assume you fully accept the awards above unless you submit changes to us immediately.
- Return corrections and required documents promptly.
- Retain this letter for your records.

Comparison Grid

	University A (State University)	University B (Nonresident State University)	University C (Private College)
Cost of Attendance	**$18,762**	**$27,165**	**$42,485**
Tuition and Fees	7,698	18,170	29,910
Room & Board	7,539	5,670	8,367
Books	840	820	900
Transportation	1,947	1,750	700
Personal Expenses	738	755	2,558
Grants and Scholarships	**4,764**	**5,350**	**29,510**
Loans	**3,500**	**10,000**	**0**
Work-Study	**0**	**2,100**	**3,425**
Expected Family Contribution	**9,550**	**9,550**	**9,550**
Balance	**$ 948**	**$ 165**	**$ 0**

Some things to notice:

- At all schools, the Federal Pell Grant remains the same.
- Even though University C (a private college) has the highest "sticker price," the net cost is less than the state schools.
- University B is a state university, but you are classified as an out-of-state resident (or nonresident). Many students in this situation find that the higher out-of-state costs combined with lower grant aid make this a costly decision.
- All schools assume that you will be residing in on-campus housing. But if you choose to commute to University A, you would save a substantial amount because you would not have the $7539 room and board cost.

Once you have entered all the information into a spreadsheet of your own and come up with the balances, here are some things to consider for each school:

- **How much is the balance?** Ideally, your balance should be $0, but look to see which school has the lowest balance amount.
- **What part of the aid package comes in the form of grants and scholarships?** It is important to note this because these awards (gift aid) do not have to be paid back.
- **Look at the loans.** Usually, the best financial deal contains more money in scholarships and less in loan dollars. Based on expected freshman-year borrowing, determine the debt burden at each school once your child graduates. You have to multiply the amount of your loan by four or five years, depending on how long it will take for your child to graduate. And remember that the loan amounts will probably increase each year. You also should take into consideration that you will have to borrow even more as the COA increases each year. To determine the best loan deal, consider:
  —What are the terms of the loans?
  —What are interest rates?
  —Do you pay the yearly interest rate during enrollment or is the interest subsidized or paid by the government?
  —Is any money due during enrollment or is it deferred until after graduation? Figuring out how much you will owe at each school at graduation will give you a clear picture of what your financial situation will be *after* graduation.

However, unless cost is your only concern, you shouldn't simply choose the school offering the lowest loan amounts.

Many other factors need to be considered, such as academic and social environment. And you should never reject a school based solely on insufficient financial aid. Consult with an aid administrator to discuss possible alternatives.

Finally, if the college that costs the most is still the one your child wants to attend, there are a number of ways to find money to cover the gap between the aid package and your actual cost, including paying more than the EFC figure, increasing student borrowing, working more hours, and taking out a PLUS loan.

Richard Woodland is the former Director of Financial Aid at Rutgers University–Camden and the current Director of Student Services and Financial Aid at the Curtis Institute of Music in Philadelphia, Pennsylvania.

Online Filing of FAFSA and CSS/Financial Aid PROFILE® Applications

Richard Woodland

Over the past few years, there have been major advancements in the way students apply both for admission to college and for financial aid. The two primary financial aid applications, the Free Application for Federal Student Aid (FAFSA) and the CSS/Financial Aid PROFILE® application from the College Scholarship Service offer direct, online applications. FAFSA on the Web and PROFILE are available in both English and Spanish.

Why File Online?

There are two reasons why it is a good idea to file online. First, the online environment prevents you from making many mistakes. For example, if there is a question that is required of all applicants, you cannot inadvertently skip it. If the application software thinks your answer may not be accurate, it will prompt you to check it before proceeding. The financial aid process can be complicated, and applying online greatly reduces the chance for error. The second reason is turnaround time. The online applications are processed in a matter of days, not weeks. Since time is an important factor when applying for financial aid, it is prudent to have your application processed as quickly as possible.

Some Common Concerns About Online Filing

Both the FASFA and PROFILE online applications have become much more user-friendly. You do not have to be a computer expert to use these programs. Both applications allow you to save your completed data and return later if you are interrupted or need to gather additional information. Both systems use secure encryption technology to protect your privacy. FASFA information is shared with other federal agencies as required as part of the application process, online or paper. FAFSA information is also sent to your state of legal residence for state aid purposes and to any college or program your child lists on the application. The information on the application is highly personal, and every precaution is taken to safeguard your privacy.

Now, let's discuss some specific issues related to each application.

The FAFSA

The FAFSA is the universal application for all federal financial aid programs. It is the primary application used for most state and college financial aid programs. Before using the FAFSA online application, you need to secure an electronic signature, or Personal Identification Number (PIN). This is similar to the access codes used at ATM machines, online banking, etc. It is easy to obtain a PIN number. Simply go to www.pin.ed.gov and apply online. You will receive a reply via e-mail in about 48 hours. If your child is under 24 years of age, he or she and one parent will need a PIN number. If there is more than one child in college, a parent only needs one PIN number. However, each college applicant will need to have his or her own PIN.

The FASFA online application is not presented in the same format as the paper FAFSA. Although all of the questions are exactly the same, the order of some of the items on the online application has been rearranged to make it easier to complete and allow for some built-in skip-logic. You can easily obtain a copy of the electronic FAFSA by logging on to www.fafsa.ed.gov. Just click on "FAFSA on the Web Worksheet." Completing this first will make the online entry that much easier. There are a number of other worksheets available that can also make the process easier. You should print them out and decide which are applicable to your situation. Everyone should review Worksheets A, B, and C. If you have not completed your federal tax return, the Income Estimator worksheets are easy to use and can reduce much of the guesswork.

After completing the online FASFA, be sure to print a copy of the pages at the end of the process so that you have a copy of your answers and the confirmation number. Although lost applications are extremely rare, having this information will give you peace of mind. You can go online as often as you wish to check the status of your application.

The CSS/Financial Aid PROFILE®

The CSS/Financial Aid PROFILE® is a more comprehensive financial aid application that is used primarily at private, higher-cost colleges and universities to award nonfederal student aid funds. Many private scholarship programs also use the PROFILE. A complete list of colleges and programs that use the PROFILE can be found at https://profileonline.collegeboard.com/index.jsp.

The PROFILE application has a $9 registration fee and an additional $16 for each school or program you select to receive your information. You must have a credit card, debit card, or checking account to use this service. (Note: A limited number of fee waivers are available for families with incomes below the poverty line. See the high school guidance officer for more information on the fee waiver program.)

Complete information on the online PROFILE application is available at www.collegeboard.com/profile. Although the customized PROFILE application is processed in about one week, you should allow for enough processing time (usually two to three weeks) to meet the earliest deadline established by the school or program.

What Happens Next?

Both the FAFSA and PROFILE processors want more applicants to use the online environment. Not only is the process easier for them, but it is faster and more accurate. Once you decide to apply online, the processors will only respond to you electronically. You will not receive any paper acknowledgments—all confirmations will be sent via e-mail. When it is time to reapply for aid in subsequent years (usually quite easy as most of the data are carried over from the previous application), all reminders will be sent to the e-mail address that is on file, so it is important to report any changes in your e-mail address.

It is easy to update the FAFSA following your initial application. For example, if you used estimated income information and now you have your federal tax return completed, you can simply return to www.fafsa.ed.gov and change your income figures. But be sure to go through the entire process and print out the updated confirmation page. In general, the PROFILE is a one-time application, filed well before tax season. Any updates are usually done directly through the schools.

Both processors offer helpful information, both in print and online. Check with your high school guidance office or local college financial aid office for additional assistance. If you need to call the FAFSA processor, the phone number is 800-4-FED-AID (toll-free). You can contact PROFILE customer service via e-mail at help@cssprofile.org or by phone at 305-829-9793 or 800-915-9990 (toll-free).

Richard Woodland is the former Director of Financial Aid at Rutgers University–Camden and the current Director of Student Services and Financial Aid at the Curtis Institute of Music in Philadelphia, Pennsylvania.

Middle-Income Families: Making the Financial Aid Process Work

Richard Woodland

A report from the U.S. Department of Education's National Center for Education Statistics took a close look at how middle-income families finance a college education. The report, *Middle Income Undergraduates: Where They Enroll and How They Pay for Their Education,* was one of the first detailed studies of these families. Even though 31 percent of middle-income families have the entire cost of attendance covered by financial aid, there is widespread angst among middle-income families that, while they earn too much to qualify for grant assistance, they are financially unable to pay the spiraling costs of higher education.

First, we have to agree on what constitutes a "middle-income" family. For the purposes of the federal study, middle income is defined as those families with incomes between $35,000 and $70,000. The good news is that 52 percent of these families received grants, while the balance received loans. Other sources of aid, including work-study, also helped close the gap.

So how do these families do it? Is there a magic key that will open the door to significant amounts of grants and scholarships?

The report found some interesting trends. One way families can make college more affordable is by choosing a less expensive college. In fact, in this income group, 29 percent choose to enroll in low- to moderate-cost schools. These include schools where the total cost is less than $8,500 per year. In this sector, we find the community colleges and lower-priced state colleges and universities. But almost half of these middle-income families choose schools in the upper-level tier, with costs ranging from $8,500 to $16,000. The remaining 23 percent enrolled at the highest-tier schools, with costs above $16,000. Clearly, while cost is a factor, middle-income families are not limiting their choices based on costs alone.

The report shows that families pay these higher costs with a combination of family assets, current income, and long-term borrowing. This is often referred to as the "past-present-future" model of financing. In fact, just by looking at the Expected Family Contributions, it is clear that there is a significant gap in what families need and what the financial aid process can provide. Families are closing this gap by making the financial sacrifices necessary to pay the price at higher-cost schools, especially if they think their child is academically strong. The report concludes that parents are more likely to pay for a higher-priced education if their child scores high on the SAT.

The best place for middle-income families to start is with the high school guidance office. This office has information on financial aid and valuable leads on local scholarships. Most guidance officers report that there are far fewer applicants for these locally based scholarships than one would expect. So read the information they send home and check on the application process. A few of those $500–$1000 scholarships can add up!

Plan to attend a financial aid awareness program. If your school does not offer one, contact your local college financial aid office and see when and where they will be speaking. You can get a lot of "inside" information on how the financial aid process works.

Next, be sure to file the correct applications for aid. Remember, each school can have a different set of requirements. For example, many higher-cost private colleges will require the CSS/Financial Aid PROFILE® application, filed in September or October of the senior year. Other schools may have their own institutional aid application. All schools will require the Free Application for Federal Student Aid (FAFSA). Watch the deadlines! It is imperative that you meet the school's published application deadline. Generally, schools are not flexible about this, so be sure to double-check the due date of all applications.

Finally, become a smart educational consumer. Peterson's has a wide range of resources available to help you understand the process. Be sure to also check your local library, bookstore, and of course, the Internet. Two great Web sites to check are www.petersons.com and www.finaid.org.

Once admitted to the various colleges and universities, you will receive an award notice outlining the aid you are eligible to receive. If you feel the offer is not sufficient, or if you have some unique financial circumstances, call the school's financial aid office to see if you can have your application reviewed again. The financial aid office is your best source for putting the pieces together and finding financial solutions.

The financial aid office will help you determine the "net price." This is the actual out-of-pocket cost that you will need to cover. Through a combination of student and parent loans, most families are able to meet these expenses with other forms of financial aid and family resources.

Many students help meet their educational expenses by working while in school. While this works for many students, research shows that too many hours spent away from your studies will negatively impact your academic success. Most experts feel that working 10 to 15 hours a week is optimal.

An overlooked source of aid is the tax credits given to middle-income families. Rather than extending eligibility for traditional sources of grant assistance to middle-income families, the federal tax system has built in a number of significant tax benefits, known as the Hope Scholarship and Lifetime Learning tax credit, for middle-income families. While it may be seven or eight months before you see the tax credit, most families in this income group can count on this benefit, usually between $1500 to $2000 per student. This is real money in your pocket. You do not need to itemize your deductions to qualify for this tax credit.

A tool to help families get a handle on the ever-rising costs of college is to assume that you can pay one third of the "net charges" from savings, another third from available (non-retirement) assets, and the rest from parent borrowing. If any one of these "thirds" is not available, shift that amount to one of the other resources. However, if it looks like you will be financing most or all of the costs from future income (borrowing), it may be wise to consider a lower-cost college.

Millions of middle-income families send their children to colleges and universities every year. Only 8 percent attend the lowest-priced schools. By using the concept of past-present-future financing, institutional assistance, federal and state aid, meaningful targeted tax relief, and student earnings, you can afford even the highest-cost schools.

Richard Woodland is the former Director of Financial Aid at Rutgers University–Camden and the current Director of Student Services and Financial Aid at the Curtis Institute of Music in Philadelphia, Pennsylvania.

Parents' and Students' Common Questions Answered

Q ***Are a student's chances of being admitted to a college reduced if the student applies for financial aid?***

A Generally no. Nearly all colleges have a policy of "need-blind" admissions, which means that a student's financial need is not taken into account in the admission decision. There are a few selective colleges, however, that do consider ability to pay before deciding whether or not to admit a student. Some colleges will mention this in their literature; others may not. The best advice is to apply for financial aid if the student needs assistance to attend college.

Q ***Are parents penalized for saving money for college?***

A No. As a matter of fact, families that have made a concerted effort to save money for college are in a much better position than those that have not. For example, a student from a family that has saved money may not have to borrow as much. Furthermore, the "taxing rate" on savings is quite low—only about 5 percent of the parents' assets are assessed and neither the home equity nor retirement savings are included. For example, a single 40-year-old parent who saved $40,000 for college expenses will have about $1900 counted as part of the parental contribution. Two parents, if the older one is 40 years old (a parent's age factors into the formulation), would have about $300 counted. (Note: The "taxing rate" for student assets is much higher—20 percent—compared to 5 percent for parents.)

Q ***How does the financial aid system work in cases of divorce or separation? How are stepparents treated?***

A In cases of divorce or separation, the financial aid application(s) should be completed by the parent with whom the student lived for the longest period of time in the past twelve months (custodial parent). If the custodial parent has remarried, the stepparent is considered a family member and must complete the application along with the biological parent. If your family has any special circumstances, you should discuss these directly with the financial aid office. (Note: Colleges that award their own aid may ask the noncustodial biological parent to complete a separate aid application and a contribution will be calculated.)

Q ***When are students considered independent of parental support in applying for financial aid?***

A The student must be at least 24 years of age in order to be considered independent. If younger than 24, the student must be married, be a graduate or professional student, have legal dependents other than a spouse, be an orphan or ward of the court, or be a veteran of the armed forces or on active military duty. However, in very unusual situations, students who can clearly document estrangement from their parents can appeal to the financial aid office for additional consideration.

Q ***What can a family do if a job loss occurs?***

A Financial aid eligibility is based on the previous year's income. So the family's 2009 income would be reported to determine eligibility for the 2009–10 academic year. In that way, the family's income can be verified with an income tax return. But the previous year's income may not accurately reflect the current financial situation, particularly if a parent lost a job or retired. In these instances, the projected income for the coming year can be used instead. Families should discuss the situation directly with the financial aid office and be prepared to provide appropriate documentation.

Q ***When my daughter first went to college, we applied for financial aid and were denied because our Expected Family Contribution was too high. Now, my***

son is a high school senior, and we will soon have two in college. Will we get the same results?

A The results will definitely be different. Both your son and your daughter should apply. As described earlier, need-based financial aid is based on your Expected Family Contribution, or EFC. When you have two children in college, this amount is divided in half for each child.

Q ***I've heard about the "middle-income squeeze" in regard to financial aid. What is it?***

A The so-called "middle-income squeeze" is the idea that low-income families qualify for aid, high-income families have adequate resources to pay for education, and those in the middle are not eligible for aid but do not have the ability to pay full college costs. There is no provision in the Federal Methodology that treats middle-income students differently than others (such as an income cutoff for eligibility). The Expected Family Contribution rises proportionately as income and assets increase. If a middle-income family does not qualify for aid, it is because the need analysis formula yields a contribution that exceeds college costs. But keep in mind that if a $65,000-income family does not qualify for grant aid at a public university with a $16,000 cost, the same family will likely be eligible for aid at a private college with a cost of $25,000 or more. Also, there are loan programs available to parents and students that are not based on need. Middle-income families should realize, however, that many of the grant programs funded by federal and state governments are directed at lower-income families. It is therefore likely that a larger share of an aid package for a middle-income student will consist of loans rather than grants.

Q ***Given our financial condition, my daughter will be receiving financial aid. We will help out as much as we can, and, in fact, we ourselves will be borrowing. But I am concerned that she will have to take on a lot of loans in order to go to the college of her choice. Does she have any options?***

A She does. If offered a loan, she can decline all or part of it. One option is for her to ask in the financial aid office to have some of the loan changed to a work-study job. If this is not possible, she can find her own part-time work. Often there is an employment office on campus that can help her locate a job. In most cases, the more she works, the less she has to borrow. It is important to remember that the education loans offered to students have very attractive terms and conditions, with flexible repayment options. Students should look upon these loans as a long-term investment that will reap significant rewards.

Q ***Is it possible to change your financial aid package?***

A Yes. Most colleges have an appeal process. A request to change a need-based loan to a work-study job is usually approved if funds are available. A request to consider special financial circumstances may also be granted. At most colleges, a request for more grant money is rarely approved unless it is based on a change in the information reported. Applicants should speak with the financial aid office if they have concerns about their financial package. Some colleges may even respond to a competitive appeal, that is, a request to match another college's offer.

Q ***My son was awarded a Federal Stafford Student Loan as part of his financial aid package. His award letter also indicated that we could take out a PLUS loan. How do we go about choosing our lender? Do we go to our local bank?***

A Read the material that came with the financial aid award letter. It is likely that the college has a "preferred lender" list for Federal Stafford Student Loans and PLUS loans. However, you can borrow from any bank that participates in the federal loan programs.

Q ***The cost of attending college seems to be going up so much faster than the Consumer Price Index. Why is that, and how can I plan for my child's four years?***

A The cost of higher education cannot be compared to the Consumer Price Index (CPI). The CPI does not take into account most of the costs faced by colleges. For example, the dollars that universities spend on grants and scholarships have risen rapidly. Many universities have increased enrollment of students from less affluent families, further increasing the need for institutional financial aid. Colleges are expected to be on the cutting edge of technology, not only in research but also in the classroom and in the library. Many colleges have deferred needed maintenance and repairs that can now no longer be put off. In addition, there is market pressure to provide many expensive lifestyle amenities that were not expected ten years ago. In general, you can expect that college costs will rise at least 2 to 3 percent faster than inflation.

Q ***I'm struggling with the idea that all students should apply to the college of their choice, regardless of cost, because financial aid will level the playing field. I feel I will be penalized because I have saved for college. My son has been required to save half of his allowance***

since age six for his college education. Will that count against him when he applies for financial aid? It's difficult to explain to him that his college choices may be limited because of the responsible choices and sacrifices we have made as a family. What can we do to make the most of our situation?

A In general, it is always better to have planned ahead for college by saving. Families that have put away sufficient funds to pay for college will quickly realize that they have made the burden easier for themselves and their children. In today's college financing world, schools assume that paying for the cost of attendance is a ten-year commitment. So by saving when your child is young, you reap significant advantages from compound interest on the assets and reduce the need to borrow as much while in school. This should reduce the number of years after college that you will be burdened with loans. Families should spend the student's assets first, since the financial aid formulas count these more heavily than parental assets. Then, after the first year, you can explain to the college how you spent these assets, and why you might now need assistance. When looking at parental information, the income of the family is by far the most important component. Contrary to popular belief, parental assets play a minor role in the calculation of need. With this strategy, you have done the right thing, and in the long run, it should prove to be a wise financial plan.

Picking the right college also involves other factors. Students should select the colleges to which they are going to apply in two ways. First, and most important, is to look at colleges that meet your son's academic and lifestyle interests. Most experts will tell him to pick a few "reach" schools (i.e., schools where he is not sure he has the grades and scores required) and at least one or two academically "safe" schools. He should also select one or two financially "safe" schools that you are sure you can afford with either moderate or little financial aid. Most students do not get into all of their first-choice schools, and not everyone can afford the schools to which they are admitted. By working closely with the guidance office in high school and the admissions and financial aid offices at the college, you can maximize your options.

Q ***My son was awarded a $2500 scholarship. This can be split and used for two years. When filling out the FAFSA, do we have to claim the full amount, or just the $1250 he plans to use the first year?***

A Congratulations to your son on the scholarship. Nowhere on the FAFSA should you report this scholarship. It is not considered income or an asset. However, once you choose a school to attend, you must notify the financial aid office for its advice on how to take the funds. But remember, do NOT report it on the FAFSA.

Q ***I will be receiving a scholarship from my local high school. How will this scholarship be treated in my financial aid award?***

A Federal student aid regulations specify that all forms of aid must be included within the defined level of need. This means that additional aid, such as outside scholarships, must be combined with any need-based aid you receive; it may not be kept separate and used to reduce your family's contribution. If the college has not filled 100 percent of your need, it will usually allow outside scholarships to close the gap. Once your total need has been met, the college must reduce other aid and replace it with the outside award. Most colleges will allow you to use some, if not all, of an outside scholarship to replace self-help aid (loans and Federal Work-Study Program awards) rather than grant aid.

Q ***I know we're supposed to apply for financial aid as soon as possible after January 1. What if I don't have my W-2s yet and my tax return isn't done?***

A The first financial aid application deadlines usually fall in early February. Most colleges use either March 1 or March 15 as their "priority filing date." Chances are you'll have your W-2 forms by then, but you won't have a completed tax return. If that is the case, complete the financial aid application using your best estimates. Then, when you receive the Student Aid Report (SAR), you can use your tax return to make corrections. Just be sure to check with each college for its deadline.

Q ***Is there enough aid available to make it worthwhile for me to consider colleges that are more expensive than I can afford?***

A Definitely. More than $100 billion in aid is awarded to undergraduates every year. With more than half of all enrolled students qualifying for some type of assistance, this totals more than $5500 per student. You should view financial aid as a large, national system of tuition discounts, some given according to a student's ability and talent, others based on what a student's family can afford to pay. If you qualify for need-based financial aid, you will essentially pay only your calculated family contribution, regardless of the cost of the college. You will not pay the "sticker price" (the cost of attendance listed in the college catalog) but a lower rate that is reduced by the amount of aid you receive. No college should be ruled out until after financial aid is considered. In addition, when deciding which college to attend, consider that the short-term cost of a college education is only one criterion. If the college meets your educational needs and you are convinced it can launch you on an exciting career, a significant up-front investment may turn out to be a bargain over the long run.

Parents' and Students' Common Questions Answered

Q ***If I don't qualify for need-based aid, what options are available?***

A You should try to put together your own aid package to help reduce your parents' share. There are three sources to look into. First, search for merit scholarships. Second, seek employment, during both the summer and the academic year. The student employment office should be able to help you find a campus job. Third, look into borrowing. Even if you don't qualify for the need-based loan programs, the unsubsidized Federal Stafford Student and Direct Loans are available to all students. The terms and conditions are the same as the subsidized loan programs except that interest accrues while you are in college.

After you have contributed what you can through scholarships, employment, and loans, your parents will be faced with their share of the college bill. Many colleges have monthly payment plans that allow families to spread their payments over the academic year. If these monthly payments turn out to be more than your parents can afford, they can take out a parent loan. By borrowing from the college itself, from a commercial agency or lender, or through PLUS, your parents can extend the payments over a ten-year period or longer. Borrowing reduces the monthly obligation to its lowest level, but the total amount paid will be the highest due to principal and interest payments. Before making a decision on where to borrow parental loan funds, be sure to first check with the financial aid office to determine what is the best source of alternative funds.

Searching for Scholarships Online

Today's students need all the help they can get when looking for ways to pay for their college education. Sky-rocketing tuition costs, state budget cuts, and diminished personal savings have combined to make financing a college education perhaps the number-one concern for parents. College sticker shock is driving many families away from college. No wonder: The "purchasing power" of all aid programs from federal, state, and institutional sources has declined over the past two decades. And it's not only lower-income families who are affected. Some fear they make *too much* money to qualify for financial aid. Regardless of their situations, most families struggle to make sense of the college financial aid process and to decide which aid package is the right one for them.

Despite the confusion, students and parents can and should research as many sources as they can to find the money they need. The Internet can be a great source of information. Many worthwhile sites are ready to help you search and apply for your fair share of awards, including Peterson's comprehensive financial aid site at www.petersons.com/finaid.

Peterson's "Pay For School"

Peterson's Pay for School financial aid Web site at www.petersons.com/finaid provides families with a wealth of information on college funding for every step of their college admission process.

Expert Advice

By logging on to www.petersons.com/finaid, you gain access to comprehensive articles that describe the ins and outs of federal and state funding, tips for filing the FAFSA and the CSS/Financial Aid PROFILE®, step-by-step advice on what you should be doing during junior and senior years of high school, and an audio clip of an interview with a real financial aid expert. Links to state programs and agencies help you connect directly to those resources. You can also access articles on specific topics, such as advice on 529 Plans, loans and payment plans, scholarship scams, the military, and international students. A section called "Financial Aid This Month" contains the latest news on government programs and other college funding topics.

Scholarship Search

Peterson's free **Scholarship Search** connects you to information on millions of scholarships, grants, and prizes totaling more than $8 billion, and lets you do an individualized search for awards that match your financial and educational needs. In just three easy steps you can register; complete a customized profile indicating your scholastic and personal background, intended major, work experience, and a host of other criteria; and access a list of scholarships that match your needs. Each scholarship is described in detail, including eligibility and application requirements and contact information, with links to the program's e-mail address and Web site. Finding money for college couldn't be easier!

Interactive Tools

When it's time to get to the nuts and bolts of your college financial planning, Peterson's has the tools to help. You can access a calculator to find your Estimated Family Contribution (EFC) and a **College Financial Planning Calculator** that lets you calculate your personal savings plan. After you have received award letters from the colleges you've applied to, you can use the **Award Analyzer**. If you click on the "Pay for School" tab and scroll down to "College-Based Awards," you will find the **Award Analyzer** under the "Have Your Award Letters?" box. The **Award Analyzer** helps you compare award letters to determine which school is prepared to give you the most aid. You simply enter the information from each award letter you receive, click on the Calculate button, and discover which school has offered you the best package.

Searching and applying for financial aid is a complicated process. The resources and tools available to you on www.petersons.com/finaid can help you get your fair share of the financial aid pie. So, what are you waiting for? Log on! Free money for college may be just a mouse click away.

How to Use This Guide

Quick-Reference Chart

The amount of aid available at colleges can vary greatly. "College Costs At-a-Glance" lists the percent of freshmen who applied for and received need-based gift aid and the percent of those whose need was fully met. Also listed are the average freshman financial aid package, the average cost after aid, and the average indebtedness upon graduation.

Profiles of College Financial Aid Programs

After the federal government, colleges provide the largest amount of financial aid to students. In addition, they control most of the money channeled to students from the federal government. The amount and makeup of your financial aid package will depend on the institution's particular circumstances and its decisions concerning your application. The main section of this book shows you the pattern and extent of each college's current awards. The profiles present detailed factual and statistical data for each school in a uniform format to enable easy, quick references and comparisons. Items that could not be collected in time for publication for specific institutions do not appear in those institutions' profiles. Colleges that supplied no data are listed by name and address only so that you do not overlook them in your search for colleges.

There is much anecdotal evidence that students and their families fail to apply for financial aid under the misconception that student aid goes only to poor families. Financial need in the context of college expenses is not the same as being needy in the broad social context. Middle-class families typically qualify for need-based financial aid; at expensive schools, even upper-middle-income families can qualify for need-based financial aid. Peterson's encourages you to apply for financial aid whether or not you think that you will qualify.

To help you understand the definition and significance of each item, the following outline of the profile format explains what is covered in each section. The term college or colleges is frequently used throughout to refer to any institution of higher education, regardless of its official definition.

The College

The name of the college is the official name as it appears on the institution's charter. The city and state listed are the official location of the school. The subhead line shows tuition and required fees, as they were charged to the majority of full-time undergraduate students in the 2008–09 academic year. Any exceptions to the 2008–09 academic year are so noted. For a public institution, the tuition and fees shown are for state residents, and this is noted. If a college's annual expenses are expressed as a comprehensive fee (including full-time tuition, mandatory fees, and college room and board), this is noted, as are any unusual definitions, such as tuition only. The average undergraduate aid package is the average total package of grant, loan, and work-study aid that was awarded to meet the officially defined financial need of full-time undergraduates enrolled in fall 2008 (or fall 2007) who applied for financial aid, were determined to have need, and then actually received financial aid. This information appears in more detail in each profile.

About the Institution

This paragraph gives the reader a brief introduction to a college. It contains the following elements:

Institutional Control

Private institutions are designated as *independent* (nonprofit), *independent/religious* (sponsored by or affiliated with a religious group or having a nondenominational or interdenominational religious orientation), or *proprietary* (profit-making). Public institutions are designated by their primary source of support, such as *federal*, *state*, *commonwealth* (Puerto Rico), *territory* (U.S. territories), *county, district* (an administrative unit of public education, often having boundaries different from those of units of local government), *state- and locally-supported* ("locally" refers to county, district, or city), *state-supported* (funded by the state), or *state-related* (funded primarily by the state but administered autonomously).

Type of Student Body

The categories are *men* (100 percent of student body), *coed-primarily men*, *women* (100 percent of student body), *coed-primarily women*, and *coed*. A few schools are designated as *undergraduate: women only, graduate: coed* or *undergraduate: men only, graduate: coed.*

Degrees Awarded
Associate, bachelor's (baccalaureate), *master's, doctoral* (doctorate), and *first professional* (in such fields as law and medicine). There are no institutions in this book that award the associate degree only. Many award the bachelor's as their highest degree.

Number of Undergraduate Majors
This shows the number of academic fields in which the institution offers associate and/or bachelor's degrees. The purpose of this is to give you an indication of the range of subjects available.

Enrollment
These figures are based on the actual number of full-time and part-time students enrolled in degree programs as of fall 2008. In most instances, they are designated as *total enrollment* (for the specific college or university) and *freshmen*. If the institution is a university and its total enrollment figure includes graduate students, a separate figure for *undergraduates* may be provided. If the profiled institution is a subunit of a university, the figures may be designated *total university enrollment* for the entire university and *total unit enrollment* for the specific subunit.

Methodology Used for Determining Need
Private colleges usually have larger financial aid programs, but public colleges usually have lower sticker prices, especially for in-state or local students. At a public college, your financial need will be less, and you will receive a smaller financial aid package. This note on whether a college uses federal (FAFSA) or institutional methodology (usually CSS/Financial Aid PROFILE®) will let you know whether you will have to complete one or two kinds of financial aid application forms. Federal Methodology is the needs-analysis formula used by the U.S. Department of Education to determine the Expected Family Contribution (EFC), which, when subtracted from the cost of attendance at an institution, determines the financial need of a student. There is no relative advantage or disadvantage to using one methodology over the other.

Undergraduate Expenses

If provided by the institution, the one-time application fee is listed. Costs are given for the 2009–10 academic year or for the 2008–09 academic year if 2009–10 figures were not yet available. (Peterson's collects information for freshmen specifically.) Annual expenses may be expressed as a comprehensive fee (including full-time tuition, mandatory fees, and college room and board) or may be given as separate figures for full-time tuition, fees, room and board, or room only. For public institutions where tuition differs according to state residence, separate figures are given for area or state residents and for nonresidents. Part-time tuition is expressed in terms of a per-unit rate (per credit, per semester hour, etc.), as specified by the institution.

The tuition structure at some institutions is complex. Freshmen and sophomores may be charged a different rate from that charged juniors and seniors, a professional or vocational division may have a different fee structure from the liberal arts division of the same institution, or part-time tuition may be prorated on a sliding scale according to the number of credit hours taken. Tuition and fees may vary according to academic program, campus/location, class time (day, evening, weekend), course/credit load, course level, degree level, reciprocity agreements, and student level. If tuition and fees differ for international students, the rate charged is listed.

Room and board charges are reported as a double occupancy and nineteen meals per week plan or the equivalent and may vary according to board plan selected, campus/location, gender, type of housing facility, or student level. If no college-owned or -operated housing facilities are offered, the phrase *college housing not available* will appear.

If a college offers a *guaranteed tuition* plan, it promises that the tuition rate of an entering student will not increase for the entire term of enrollment, from entrance to graduation. Other payment plans might include *tuition prepayment*, which allows an entering student to lock in the current tuition rate for the entire term of enrollment by paying the full amount in advance rather than year by year, and *installment* and *deferred payment* plans, which allow students to delay the payment of the full tuition.

Guaranteed tuition and tuition prepayment help you to plan the total cost of education and can save you from the financial distress sometimes caused by tuition hikes. Colleges that offer such plans may also help you to arrange financing, which in the long run can cost less than the total of four years of increasing tuition rates. Deferred payment or installment payments may better fit your personal financial situation, especially if you do not qualify for financial aid and, due to other financial commitments, find that obtaining the entire amount due is burdensome. Carefully investigate these plans, however, to see what premium you may pay at the end to allow you to defer immediate payment.

Freshman Financial Aid

Usually, these are actual figures for the 2007–08 term, beginning in fall 2007; figures may also be estimated for the 2008–09 term. The particular term for which these data apply is indicated. The figures are for degree-seeking full-time freshman students. The first figure is the number of freshmen who applied for any kind of financial aid. The next figure is the percentage of those freshmen financial aid applicants who were determined to have financial need—that is, through the formal needs-assessment process, had a calculated expected family contribution that was less than the total college cost. The next figure is the percentage of this group of eligible freshmen who received any financial aid. The next figure is the percentage of this preceding group of eligible aid recipients whose need was fully met by financial aid. The *Average percent of need met* is the average percentage of financial need met for freshmen who received any need-based aid. The *Average financial aid package* is the average dollar amount awarded (need-based or non-need-based) to freshmen who applied for aid, were deemed eligible, and received any aid; awards used to reduce the expected family contribution are excluded from this average. The final line in most profiles is the percentage of freshmen who had no financial need but who received non-need-based aid other than athletic scholarships or special-group tuition benefits.

What do these data mean to you? If financial aid is important in your comparison of colleges, the relative percentage of students who received any aid, whose need was fully met, and the average percentage of need met have the most weight. These figures reflect the relative abundance of student aid available to the average eligible applicant. The average dollar amount of the aid package has real meaning, but only in relation to the college's expense; you will be especially interested in the difference between this figure and the costs figure, which is what the average student (in any given statistical group, there actually may be no average individual) will have to pay. Of course, if the financial aid package is largely loans rather than grants, you will have to pay this amount eventually. Relative differences in the figures of the number of students who apply for aid and who are deemed eligible can hinge on any number of factors: the relative sticker price of the college, the relative level of wealth of the students' families, the proportion of only children in college and students with siblings in college (families with two or more children in college are more likely to apply for aid and be considered eligible), or the relative sophistication in financial aid matters (or quality of college counseling they may have received) of the students and their families. While these may be interesting, they will not mean too much to most students and families. If you are among the unlucky (or, perhaps, lucky) families who do not qualify for need-based financial aid, the final sentence of this paragraph in the profile will be of interest because it reveals the relative policies that the college has in distributing merit-based aid to students who cannot demonstrate need.

Undergraduate Financial Aid

This is the parallel paragraph to the Freshman Financial Aid paragraph. The same definitions apply, except that the group being considered is degree-seeking full-time undergraduate students (including freshmen).

There are cases of students who chose a particular college because they received a really generous financial aid package in their freshman year and then had to scramble to pay the tuition bill in their later years. If a financial aid package is a key factor in the decision to attend a particular college, you want to be certain that the package offered to all undergraduates is not too far from that offered to freshmen. The key figures are those for the percentage of students who received any aid, the percentage of financial aid recipients whose need was fully met, the average percentage of need met, and the dollar figure of the average financial aid package. Generally, colleges assume that after the freshman year, students develop study habits and time-management skills that will allow them to take on part-time and summer employment without hurting their academic performance. So, the proportion of self-help aid (work-study and student loans) in the financial aid package tends to increase after the freshman year. This pattern, which is true of most colleges, can be verified in the freshman-undergraduate figures in the paragraph on Gift Aid (Need-Based).

Gift Aid (Need-Based)

Total amount is the total dollar figure in 2008–09 (estimated) or 2007–08 (actual) of need-based scholarships and grant (gift) aid awarded to degree-seeking full-time and part-time students that was used to meet financial need. The percentages of this aid from federal, state, institutional (college or university), and external (e.g., foundations, civic organizations, etc.) sources are shown. *Receiving aid* shows the percentages (and number, in parentheses) of freshmen and of all undergraduates who applied for aid, were considered eligible, and received any need-based gift aid. *Average award* is the average dollar amount of awards to freshmen and all undergraduates who applied for aid, were considered eligible, and received any need-based gift aid. *Scholarships, grants, and awards* cites major categories of need-based gift aid provided by the college; these include Federal Pell Grants, Federal Supplemental Educational Opportunity Grants (FSEOG), state scholarships, private scholarships, college/university gift aid from institutional funds, United Negro College Fund aid, Federal Nursing Scholarships, and others.

Scholarships and grants are gifts awarded to students that do not need to be repaid. These are preferable to loans, which have to be repaid, or work-study wages, which may take time away from studies and personal pursuits. The total amount of need-based gift aid has to be placed into the context of the total number of undergraduate students (shown in the About the Institution paragraph) and the relative expense of the institution. Filing the FAFSA automatically puts you in line to receive any available federal grants for which you may qualify. However, if the college being considered has a higher than usual proportion of gift aid coming from state, institutional, or external sources, be sure to check with the financial aid office to find out what these sources may be and how to apply for them. For almost all colleges, the percentage of freshmen receiving need-based gift aid will be higher than the percentage of all undergraduates receiving need-based gift aid. However, if you are dependent on need-based gift aid and the particular college under consideration shows a sharper drop from the freshman to undergraduate years than other colleges of a similar type, you might want to think about how this change will affect your ability to pay for later years at this college.

Gift Aid (Non-Need-Based)

Total amount is the total dollar figure in 2008–09 (estimated) or 2007–08 (actual) of non-need-based scholarships and grant (gift) aid awarded to degree-seeking full-time and part-time students. Non-need-based aid that was used to meet financial need is not included in this total. The percentages of this aid from federal, state, institutional (college or university), and external (e.g., National Merit Scholarships, civic, religious, fraternal organizations, etc.) sources are shown. *Receiving aid* shows the percentages (and number, in parentheses) of freshmen and of all undergraduates who were determined to have need and received non-need-based gift aid. *Average award* is the average dollar amount of awards to freshmen and all undergraduates determined to have no need but received non-need-based awards. *Scholarships, grants, and awards by category* cites the major categories in which non-need-based awards are available and the number of awards made in that category (in parentheses, the total dollar value of these awards). The categories listed are *Academic interests/achievement*, *Creative arts/performance*, *Special achievements/activities*, and *Special characteristics*. *Tuition waivers* indicate special categories of students (minority students, children of alumni, college employees or children of employees, adult students, and senior citizens) who may qualify for a full or partial waiver of tuition. *ROTC* indicates Army, Naval, and Air Force ROTC programs that are offered on campus; a program offered by arrangement on another campus is indicated by the word *cooperative*.

This section covers college-administered scholarships awarded to undergraduates on the basis of merit or personal attributes without regard to need. If you do not qualify for financial aid but nevertheless lack the resources to pay for college, non-need-based awards will be of special interest to you. Some personal characteristics are completely beyond an individual's control, and talents and achievements take a number of years to develop or attain. However, certain criteria for these awards, such as religious involvement, community service, and special academic interests can be attained in a relatively brief period of time. ROTC programs offer such benefits as tuition, the cost of textbooks, and living allowances. In return, you must fulfill a service obligation after graduating from college. Because they can be a significant help in paying for college, these programs have become quite competitive. Certain subject areas, such as nursing, health care, or the technical fields, are in stronger demand than others. Among the obligations to consider about ROTC are that you must spend a regular portion of your available time in military training programs and that ROTC entails a multiyear commitment after your graduation to serve as an officer in the armed services branch sponsoring the program.

Loans

The figures here represent loans that are part of the financial aid award package. These are typically offered at rates lower than can be found in the normal loan marketplace. *Student loans* represents the total dollar amount of loans from all sources to full-time and part-time degree-seeking undergraduates or their parents. *Average need-based loan* represents the percentage of these loans that goes to meet financial need, and the percentage that goes to pay the non-need portion (the expected family contribution) are indicated. The percentage of a past graduating class who borrowed through any loan program (except parent loans) while enrolled at the college is shown, as is the average dollar figure per-borrower of cumulative undergraduate indebtedness (this does not include loans from other institutions). *Parent loans* shows the total amount borrowed through parent loan programs as well as the percentages that were applied to the need-based and non-need-based portions of financial need. *Programs* indicates the major loan programs available to undergraduates. These include Direct and Federal Stafford Student Loans (subsidized and unsubsidized and PLUS), Perkins Loans, Federal Nursing Loans, state loans, college/university loans, and other types.

Loans are forms of aid that must be repaid with interest. Most people will borrow money to pay college costs. The loans available through financial aid programs are offered at very favorable interest rates. Student loans are preferable to parent loans because the payoff is deferred. In comparing colleges, the dollar amount of total indebtedness of the last class is a factor to be considered. Typically, this amount would increase proportionate to the tuition. However, if it does not, this could mean that the college provides relatively generous grant or work-study aid rather than loans in its financial aid package.

Work-Study

The total dollar amounts, number, and average dollar amount of *Federal work-study* (FWS) jobs appear first. The total dollar figure of *State or other work-study/employment*, if available, is shown, as is the percentage of those dollars that go to meet financial need. The number of part-time jobs available on campus to undergraduates, other than work-study, is shown last.

FWS is a federally funded program that enables students with demonstrated need to earn money by working on or off campus, usually in a nonprofit organization. FWS jobs are a special category of jobs that are open to students only through the financial aid office. Other kinds of part-time jobs are routinely available at most colleges and may vary widely. In comparing colleges, you may find characteristic differences in how the "self-help" amounts (loans and work-study) are apportioned.

Athletic Awards

The total dollar amount of athletic scholarships given by the college to undergraduate students, including percentages that are need-based and non-need-based, is indicated.

Applying for Financial Aid

Required financial aid forms include the FAFSA (Free Application for Federal Student Aid), the institution's own form, CSS/Financial Aid PROFILE, a state aid form, a noncustodial (divorced/separated) parent's statement, a business/farm supplement, and others. The college's financial aid application deadline is noted as the *Financial aid deadline* and is shown in one of three ways: as a specific date if it is an absolute deadline; noted as *continuous*, which means processing goes on without a deadline or until all available aid has been awarded; or as a date with the note *(priority)*, meaning that you are encouraged to apply before that date in order to have the best chance of obtaining aid. *Notification date* is listed as either a specific date or *continuous*. The date by which a reply to the college with the decision to accept or decline its financial aid package is listed as either a specific date or as a number of weeks from the date of notification.

Be prepared to check early with the colleges as to exactly which forms will be required. All colleges require the FAFSA for students applying for federal aid. In most cases, colleges have a limited amount of funds set aside to use as financial aid. It is possible that the first eligible students will get a larger share of what is available.

Contact

The name, title, address, telephone and fax numbers, and e-mail address of the person to contact for further information (student financial aid contact) are given at the end of the profile. You should feel free to write or call for any materials you need or if you have questions.

Appendix

This section lists more than 400 state-specific grants and loans. Award amounts, number of awards, eligibility requirements, application requirements, and deadlines are given for all programs.

Indexes

Six indexes in the back of the book allow you to search for particular award programs based on the following criteria:

Non-Need Scholarships for Undergraduates

This index lists the colleges that report that they offer scholarships based on academic interests, abilities, achievements, or personal characteristics other than financial need. Specific categories appear in alphabetical order under the following broad groups:

- Academic Interests/Achievements
- Creative Arts/Performance
- Special Achievements/Activities
- Special Characteristics

See the index for specific categories in each group.

Athletic Grants for Undergraduates

This index lists the colleges that report offering scholarships on the basis of athletic abilities.

Co-op Programs

This index lists colleges that report offering cooperative education programs. These are formal arrangements with off-campus employers that are designed to allow students to combine study and work, often in a position related to the student's field of study. Salaries typically are set at regular marketplace levels, and academic credit is often given.

ROTC Programs

This index lists colleges that offer Reserve Officers' Training Corps programs. The index is arranged by the branch of service that sponsors the program.

Tuition Waivers

This index lists colleges that report offering full or partial tuition waivers for certain categories of students. A majority of colleges offer tuition waivers to employees or children of employees. Because this benefit is so common and the affected employees usually are aware of it, no separate index of schools offering this option is provided. However, this information is included in the individual college profiles.

Tuition Payment Alternatives

This index lists colleges that report offering tuition payment alternatives. These payment alternatives include deferred payment plans, guaranteed tuition plans, installment payment plans, and prepayment plans.

Data Collection Procedures

The data contained in the college chart, profiles, and indexes were collected in winter and spring 2009 through *Peterson's Annual Survey of Undergraduate Financial Aid* and *Peterson's Annual Survey of Undergraduate Institutions*. Questionnaires were sent to the more than 2,100 institutions of higher education that are accredited in the U.S. and U.S. territories and offer full four- or five-year baccalaureate degrees via full-time on-campus programs of study. Officials at the colleges—usually financial aid or admission officers but sometimes registrars or institutional research staff members—completed and returned the forms. Peterson's has every reason to believe that the data presented in this book are accurate. However, students should always confirm costs and other facts with a specific school at the time of application, since colleges can and do change policies and fees whenever necessary.

The state aid data presented in *Peterson's How to Get Money for College* was submitted by state officials (usually the director of the state scholarship commission) to Peterson's in spring 2009. Because regulations for any government-sponsored program may be changed at any time, you should request written descriptive materials from the office administering a program in which you are interested.

Criteria for Inclusion in This Book

To be included in this guide, an institution must have full accreditation or be a candidate for accreditation (preaccreditation) status by an institutional or specialized accrediting body recognized by the U.S. Department of Education or the Council for Higher Education Accreditation (CHEA). Institutional accrediting bodies, which review each institution as a whole, include the six regional associations of schools and colleges (Middle States, New England, North Central, Northwest, Southern, and Western), each of which is responsible for a specified portion of the United States and its territories. Other institutional accrediting bodies are national in scope and accredit specific kinds of institutions (e.g., Bible colleges, independent colleges, and rabbinical and Talmudic schools). Program registration by the New York State Board of Regents is considered to be the equivalent of institutional accreditation, since the board requires that all programs offered by an institution meet its standards before recognition is granted. There are recognized specialized or professional accrediting bodies in more than forty different fields, each of which is authorized to accredit institutions or specific programs in its particular field. For specialized institutions that offer programs in one field only, we designate this to be the equivalent of institutional accreditation. A full explanation of the accrediting process and complete information on recognized, institutional (regional and national) and specialized accrediting bodies can be found online at www.chea.org or at www.ed.gov/admins/finaid/accred/index.html.

Quick-Reference Chart

College Costs At-a-Glance

Michael Steidel

To help shed some light on the typical patterns of financial aid offered by colleges, we have prepared the following chart. This chart can help you to better understand financial aid practices in general, form realistic expectations about the amounts of aid that might be provided by specific colleges or universities, and prepare for meaningful discussions with the financial aid officers at colleges being considered. The data appearing in the chart have been supplied by the schools themselves and are also shown in the individual college profiles.

Tuition and fees are based on the total of full-time tuition and mandatory fees for the 2009–10 academic year or for the 2008–09 academic year if 2009–10 figures are not available. More information about these costs, as well as the costs of room and board and the year for which they are current, can be found in the individual college profiles. For institutions that have two or more tuition rates for different categories of students or types of programs, the lowest rate is used in figuring the cost.

The colleges are listed alphabetically by state. An "NR" in any individual column indicates that the applicable data element was "Not Reported."

The chart is divided into eight columns of information for each college:

1. Institutional Control
Whether the school is independent (ind.), including independent, independent–religious, and proprietary, or public (pub.), including federal, state, commonwealth, territory, county, district, city, state, local, and state-related.

2. Tuition and Fees
Based on the total of full-time tuition and mandatory fees. An asterisk indicates that the school includes room and board in their mandatory fees.

3. Room and Board
If a school has room and board costs that vary according to the type of accommodation and meal plan, either the lowest figures are represented or the figures are for the most common room arrangement and a full meal plan. If a school has only housing arrangements, a dagger appears to the right of the number. An "NA" will appear in this column if no college-owned or -operated housing facilities are offered.

4. Percent of Eligible Freshmen Receiving Need-Based Gift Awards
Calculated by dividing the number of freshman students determined to have need who received need-based gift aid by the number of full-time freshmen.

5. Percent of Freshmen Whose Need Was Fully Met
Calculated by dividing the number of freshman students whose financial need was fully met by the number of freshmen with need.

6. Average Financial Aid Package for Freshmen
The average dollar amount from all sources, including *gift aid* (scholarships and grants) and *self-help* (jobs and loans), awarded to freshmen receiving aid. Note that this aid package may exceed tuition and fees if the average aid package included coverage of room and board expenses.

7. Average Net Cost After Aid
Average aid package subtracted from published costs (tuition, fees, room, and board) to produce what the average student will have to pay.

8. Average Indebtedness Upon Graduation
Average per-student indebtedness of graduating seniors.

Because personal situations vary widely, it is very important to note that an individual's aid package can be quite different from the averages. Moreover, the data shown for each school can fluctuate widely from year to year, depending on the number of applicants, the amount of need to be met, and the financial resources and policies of the college. Peterson's intent in presenting this chart is to provide you with useful facts and figures that can serve as general guidelines in the pursuit of financial aid. We caution you to use the data only as a jumping-off point for further investigation and analysis, not as a means to rank or select colleges.

After you have narrowed down the choice of colleges based on academic and personal criteria, we recommend that you carefully study this chart. From it, you can develop a list of questions for financial aid officers at the colleges under serious consideration. Here are just a few questions you might want to ask:

- What are the specific types and sources of aid provided to freshmen at this school?

- What factors does this college consider in determining whether a financial aid applicant is qualified for its need-based aid programs?
- How does the college determine the combination of types of aid that make up an individual's package?
- How are non-need-based awards treated: as a part of the aid package or as a part of the parental/family contribution?
- Does this school "guarantee" financial aid and, if so, how is its policy implemented? Guaranteed aid means that, by policy, 100 percent of need is met for all students judged to have need. Implementation determines *how* need is met and varies widely from school to school. For example, grade point average may determine the apportioning of scholarship, loan, and work-study aid. Rules for freshmen may be different from those for upperclass students.
- To what degree is the admission process "need-blind"? Need-blind means that admission decisions are made without regard to the student's need for financial aid.
- What are the norms and practices for upperclass students? Peterson's chart presents information on *freshmen* financial aid only; however, the financial aid office should be able and willing to provide you with comparable figures for upperclass students. A college might offer a wonderful package for the freshman year, then leave students mostly on their own to fund the remaining three years. Or the school may provide a higher proportion of scholarship money for freshmen, then rebalance its aid packages to contain more self-help aid (loans and work-study) in upperclass years. There is an assumption that, all other factors being equal, students who have settled into the pattern of college time management can handle more work-study hours than freshmen. Grade point average, tuition increases, changes in parental financial circumstances, and other factors may also affect the redistribution.

Michael Steidel is Director of Admission at Carnegie Mellon University.

College Costs At-a-Glance

	Institutional Control ind.=independent; pub.=public	Tuition and Fees	Room and Board	Percent of Eligible Freshmen Receiving Need-Based Gift Awards	Percent of Freshmen Whose Need Was Fully Met	Average Financial Aid Package for Freshmen	Average Net Cost After Aid	Average Indebtedness Upon Graduation
Alabama								
Alabama Agricultural and Mechanical University	pub.	$ 3432	$ 4770	6%	3%	$ 2279	$ 5923	NR
Alabama State University	pub.	$ 5460	$ 4400	100%	23%	$ 9012	$ 848	$26,926
Amridge University	ind.	$ 7700	NA	NR	NR	NR	NR	$18,000
Athens State University	pub.	$ 3300	NA	NR	NR	NR	NR	NR
Auburn University	pub.	$ 5880	$ 8260	79%	21%	$ 8648	$ 5492	$34,398
Auburn University Montgomery	pub.	$ 5850	$ 3420†	67%	NR	NR	NR	NR
Birmingham-Southern College	ind.	$25,386	$ 9105	83%	61%	$30,480	$ 4211	$27,798
Concordia College	ind.	$ 7090	$ 3500	100%	38%	$ 4410	$ 6180	$ 5500
Faulkner University	ind.	$12,720	$ 6350	74%	9%	$ 5000	$14,070	$19,600
Heritage Christian University	ind.	$10,140	$ 3600	NR	NR	$ 1183	$12,557	$20,784
Huntingdon College	ind.	$20,020	$ 6950	54%	66%	$11,798	$15,172	$14,758
Jacksonville State University	pub.	$ 5700	$ 4215	75%	NR	$ 7862	$ 2053	NR
Judson College	ind.	$12,547	$ 7969	97%	22%	$14,507	$ 6009	$17,158
Samford University	ind.	$20,420	$ 6624	96%	29%	$14,687	$12,357	$13,996
Spring Hill College	ind.	$24,240	$ 9260	99%	26%	$24,324	$ 9176	$13,761
Stillman College	ind.	$12,712	$ 5994	89%	34%	$16,856	$ 1850	$23,000
Troy University	pub.	$ 5900	$ 5718	62%	NR	$ 3542	$ 8076	NR
Tuskegee University	ind.	$16,160	$ 7350	85%	70%	$13,824	$ 9686	$30,000
The University of Alabama	pub.	$ 6400	$ 6430	42%	20%	$10,799	$ 2031	$18,896
The University of Alabama at Birmingham	pub.	$ 4664	$ 7820	56%	21%	$ 9221	$ 3263	NR
The University of Alabama in Huntsville	pub.	$ 5952	$ 6526	85%	20%	$ 7678	$ 4800	$21,882
University of Mobile	ind.	$13,970	$ 7320	100%	NR	$11,471	$ 9819	$18,763
University of Montevallo	pub.	$ 6650	$ 4504	88%	27%	$ 8301	$ 2853	$19,674
University of North Alabama	pub.	$ 5598	$ 4658	67%	72%	$ 4989	$ 5267	$24,570
University of South Alabama	pub.	$ 5512	$ 5344	71%	74%	NR	NR	$23,622
The University of West Alabama	pub.	$ 5100	$ 3904	NR	68%	NR	NR	$18,540
Alaska								
Alaska Pacific University	ind.	$22,610	$ 8884	50%	NR	$13,302	$18,192	$10,197
University of Alaska Anchorage	pub.	$ 4580	$ 7962	76%	59%	$12,252	$ 290	NR
University of Alaska Fairbanks	pub.	$ 5398	$ 6630	73%	43%	$ 8839	$ 3189	$28,597
University of Alaska Southeast	pub.	$ 4903	$ 6260	NR	NR	NR	NR	$20,815
Arizona								
American Indian College of the Assemblies of God, Inc.	ind.	$ 5854	$ 5232	100%	9%	$ 6241	$ 4845	NR
Arizona State University	pub.	$ 6844	$ 9210	92%	26%	$10,395	$ 5659	$17,732
DeVry University (Phoenix)	ind.	$14,080	NA	86%	6%	$12,188	$ 1892	$20,667
Embry-Riddle Aeronautical University	ind.	$27,750	$ 8008	99%	NR	$18,647	$17,111	NR
Grand Canyon University	ind.	$16,030	$ 7896	NR	NR	$ 3350	$20,576	NR
Northern Arizona University	pub.	$ 5449	$ 7086	61%	21%	$ 8595	$ 3940	$14,952
Prescott College	ind.	$21,792	$ 3400†	100%	5%	$12,786	$12,406	$16,952
University of Advancing Technology	ind.	$17,800	$10,548	NR	NR	NR	NR	NR
The University of Arizona	pub.	$ 5542	$ 7812	96%	20%	$ 8138	$ 5216	$18,025

NA = not applicable; NR = not reported; * = includes room and board; † = room only; — = not available.

College Costs At-a-Glance

	Institutional Control ind.=independent; pub.=public	Tuition and Fees	Room and Board	Percent of Eligible Freshmen Receiving Need-Based Gift Awards	Percent of Freshmen Whose Need Was Fully Met	Average Financial Aid Package for Freshmen	Average Net Cost After Aid	Average Indebtedness Upon Graduation
Arkansas								
Arkansas State University	pub.	$ 6370	$ 5056	89%	27%	$ 9400	$ 2026	$ 18,750
Arkansas Tech University	pub.	$ 5430	$ 4888	84%	15%	$ 7285	$ 3033	$ 6142
Harding University	ind.	$13,130	$ 5700	95%	38%	$12,466	$ 6364	$ 31,100
Henderson State University	pub.	$ 4939	$ 4860	68%	78%	$ 4725	$ 5074	$ 17,800
Hendrix College	ind.	$26,080	$ 7950	99%	41%	$21,641	$12,389	$ 17,484
John Brown University	ind.	$18,066	$ 6580	90%	6%	$16,453	$ 8193	$ 20,704
Lyon College	ind.	$19,968	$ 7340	100%	25%	$17,086	$10,222	$ 18,428
Ouachita Baptist University	ind.	$18,940	$ 5660	99%	46%	$16,460	$ 8140	$ 16,230
Southern Arkansas University–Magnolia	pub.	$ 5646	$ 4250	83%	81%	$ 7363	$ 2533	$ 15,102
University of Arkansas	pub.	$ 6400	$ 7422	81%	24%	$ 9108	$ 4714	$ 19,439
University of the Ozarks	ind.	$18,900	$ 6050	100%	24%	$18,487	$ 6463	$ 16,852
Williams Baptist College	ind.	$10,950	$ 5000	68%	NR	$ 5008	$10,942	$ 15,878
California								
Academy of Art University	ind.	$18,050	$13,400	59%	NR	$ 6444	$25,006	$ 32,000
Alliant International University	ind.	$15,220	NR	NR	NR	NR	NR	$ 23,000
American Jewish University	ind.	$22,352	$11,216	71%	79%	$21,408	$12,160	$ 25,000
Azusa Pacific University	ind.	$26,640	$ 7742	96%	17%	$12,822	$21,560	NR
Biola University	ind.	$26,579	$ 8120	81%	100%	$32,072	$ 2627	$ 26,555
Brooks Institute	ind.	$26,760	NA	NR	NR	$ 6500	$20,260	$119,109
California Baptist University	ind.	$22,330	$ 7910	92%	67%	$ 9306	$20,934	$ 35,550
California Christian College	ind.	$ 6840	$ 3850	50%	NR	$ 8003	$ 2687	$ 23,287
California College of the Arts	ind.	$31,382	$ 6600†	97%	4%	$20,366	$17,616	$ 34,518
California Institute of Technology	ind.	$34,437	$10,146	100%	100%	$31,069	$13,514	$ 9871
California Institute of the Arts	ind.	$35,406	$ 9070	97%	5%	$26,468	$18,008	$ 40,122
California Polytechnic State University, San Luis Obispo	pub.	$ 5043	$ 9256	76%	17%	$ 8000	$ 6299	NR
California State Polytechnic University, Pomona	pub.	$ 3564	$ 9120	78%	20%	$ 8512	$ 4172	$ 12,527
California State University, Bakersfield	pub.	$ 4383	$ 7137	90%	11%	$ 8486	$ 3034	$ 5727
California State University, Chico	pub.	$ 4008	$ 8718	67%	28%	$10,120	$ 2606	$ 11,183
California State University, East Bay	pub.	$ 3810	$ 9228	87%	5%	$ 9626	$ 3412	$ 12,728
California State University, Fresno	pub.	$ 3687	$ 8590	86%	16%	$ 9447	$ 2830	$ 11,938
California State University, Fullerton	pub.	$ 3658	$ 8722	88%	2%	$ 6935	$ 5445	$ 15,338
California State University, Long Beach	pub.	$ 3698	$10,832	85%	74%	$11,300	$ 3230	$ 10,671
California State University, Los Angeles	pub.	$ 3377	$ 8406	81%	24%	$ 8893	$ 2890	NR
California State University, Northridge	pub.	$ 3702	$10,152	76%	NR	$ 7843	$ 6011	$ 14,009
California State University, Sacramento	pub.	$ 3048	$ 9428	65%	11%	$ 3067	$ 9409	$ 11,152
California State University, San Bernardino	pub.	$ 3797	$ 4311†	81%	15%	$ 8467	—	$ 17,946
California State University, San Marcos	pub.	$ 3650	$ 9000	99%	NR	$ 6034	$ 6616	$ 14,584
California State University, Stanislaus	pub.	$ 3819	$ 7832	76%	13%	$ 9177	$ 2474	$ 17,000
Chapman University	ind.	$36,764	$12,832	99%	100%	$25,481	$24,115	$ 22,905
Claremont McKenna College	ind.	$36,825	$11,930	100%	100%	$35,534	$13,221	$ 10,518
Cogswell Polytechnical College	ind.	$18,036	$ 8374†	100%	NR	NR	NR	$ 46,689
The Colburn School Conservatory of Music	ind.	$ 0	$ 0	NR	NR	NR	NR	NR

NA = not applicable; NR = not reported; * = includes room and board; † = room only; — = not available.

College Costs At-a-Glance

	Institutional Control ind.=independent; pub.=public	Tuition and Fees	Room and Board	Percent of Eligible Freshmen Receiving Need-Based Gift Awards	Percent of Freshmen Whose Need Was Fully Met	Average Financial Aid Package for Freshmen	Average Net Cost After Aid	Average Indebtedness Upon Graduation
California—*continued*								
Concordia University	ind.	$24,950	$ 7990	95%	27%	$23,014	$ 9926	$20,254
DeVry University (Fremont)	ind.	$14,720	NA	79%	NR	$12,144	$ 2576	$70,191
DeVry University (Long Beach)	ind.	$14,080	NA	68%	5%	$10,849	$ 3231	$36,961
DeVry University (Pomona)	ind.	$14,080	NA	75%	2%	$13,233	$ 847	$33,385
DeVry University (Sherman Oaks)	ind.	$14,080	NR	75%	5%	$11,844	$ 2236	$31,200
Dominican University of California	ind.	$32,390	$11,200	100%	12%	$22,554	$21,036	$19,806
Fresno Pacific University	ind.	$23,202	$ 6800	68%	15%	$20,995	$ 9007	$20,416
Golden Gate University	ind.	$12,960	NA	NR	NR	NR	NR	$17,522
Harvey Mudd College	ind.	$36,635	$11,971	99%	100%	$29,526	$19,080	$21,018
Hope International University	ind.	$22,761	$ 8230	97%	15%	$17,251	$13,740	$27,000
Humboldt State University	pub.	$ 4150	$ 8972	100%	5%	$ 8217	$ 4905	$13,368
Loyola Marymount University	ind.	$34,462	$11,810	93%	31%	$13,570	$32,702	$28,548
The Master's College and Seminary	ind.	$24,650	$ 8000	97%	23%	$17,349	$15,301	$17,800
Menlo College	ind.	$32,136	$11,330	100%	8%	$21,247	$22,219	$21,216
Mills College	ind.	$35,190	$10,550	100%	42%	$34,127	$11,613	$24,255
National University	ind.	$10,284	NA	53%	1%	$ 6733	$ 3551	$31,058
Notre Dame de Namur University	ind.	$27,200	$11,210	100%	7%	$23,430	$14,980	$23,877
Occidental College	ind.	$38,922	$10,780	96%	49%	$34,171	$15,531	$21,001
Otis College of Art and Design	ind.	$30,464	NR	100%	NR	$14,341	$16,123	$37,356
Pacific Union College	ind.	$23,979	$ 6750	100%	1%	$15,780	$14,949	$18,000
Pepperdine University (Malibu)	ind.	$36,770	$10,480	91%	42%	$33,009	$14,241	$31,546
Pitzer College	ind.	$37,870	$10,930	100%	100%	$31,755	$17,045	$21,044
Point Loma Nazarene University	ind.	$25,840	$ 8170	90%	19%	$15,894	$18,116	$21,744
Pomona College	ind.	$35,625	$12,220	100%	100%	$36,232	$11,613	$11,300
Saint Mary's College of California	ind.	$33,250	$11,680	85%	7%	$29,754	$15,176	$23,389
Samuel Merritt University	ind.	$34,148	NR	NR	NR	NR	NR	NR
San Diego Christian College	ind.	$21,095	$ 8000	71%	71%	$14,075	$15,020	$16,000
San Diego State University	pub.	$ 3754	$11,266	72%	22%	$ 8500	$ 6520	$14,700
San Francisco Conservatory of Music	ind.	$32,080	NA	93%	86%	$17,500	$14,580	$16,367
San Francisco State University	pub.	$ 3762	$10,196	68%	10%	$ 8967	$ 4991	$15,753
San Jose State University	pub.	$ 3992	$ 8663	74%	22%	$11,057	$ 1598	$12,095
Santa Clara University	ind.	$34,950	$11,070	76%	41%	$25,221	$20,799	$25,438
Scripps College	ind.	$37,950	$11,500	100%	100%	$34,781	$14,669	$13,207
Shasta Bible College	ind.	$ 7670	$ 1650†	100%	NR	$ 2582	$ 6738	NR
Simpson University	ind.	$20,400	$ 6900	100%	23%	$ 9912	$17,388	$17,940
Sonoma State University	pub.	$ 4272	$10,115	54%	27%	$ 8055	$ 6332	$14,705
Stanford University	ind.	$37,380	$11,463	98%	77%	$34,388	$14,455	$15,724
Thomas Aquinas College	ind.	$22,400	$ 7400	84%	100%	$16,164	$13,636	$14,000
University of California, Berkeley	pub.	$ 8352	$15,308	96%	50%	$18,628	$ 5032	$14,291
University of California, Davis	pub.	$ 9364	$12,361	96%	16%	$15,811	$ 5914	$15,155
University of California, Irvine	pub.	$ 8775	$10,527	93%	51%	$14,621	$ 4681	$14,323
University of California, Los Angeles	pub.	$ 8310	$12,891	96%	27%	$16,568	$ 4633	$16,733
University of California, Riverside	pub.	$ 7845	$10,850	92%	58%	$16,754	$ 1941	$15,414

NA = not applicable; NR = not reported; * = includes room and board; † = room only; — = not available.

College Costs At-a-Glance

	Institutional Control ind.=independent; pub.=public	Tuition and Fees	Room and Board	Percent of Eligible Freshmen Receiving Need-Based Gift Awards	Percent of Freshmen Whose Need Was Fully Met	Average Financial Aid Package for Freshmen	Average Net Cost After Aid	Average Indebtedness Upon Graduation
California—*continued*								
University of California, San Diego	pub.	$ 8062	$10,820	95%	19%	$16,844	$ 2038	$16,317
University of California, Santa Barbara	pub.	$ 8573	$12,485	92%	29%	$17,022	$ 4036	$17,107
University of California, Santa Cruz	pub.	$10,131	$13,641	91%	33%	$16,626	$ 7146	$15,918
University of La Verne	ind.	$28,250	$11,110	89%	1%	$23,526	$15,834	$19,467
University of Redlands	ind.	$32,294	$10,122	97%	44%	$28,662	$13,754	$17,290
University of San Diego	ind.	$36,292	$12,602	97%	24%	$27,317	$21,577	$24,920
University of San Francisco	ind.	$34,770	$11,540	83%	9%	$25,158	$21,152	$26,523
University of Southern California	ind.	$37,694	$11,298	87%	98%	$33,713	$15,279	$27,692
University of the Pacific	ind.	$30,880	$10,118	99%	26%	$25,556	$15,442	NR
Vanguard University of Southern California	ind.	$25,452	$ 7994	84%	17%	$18,797	$14,649	$24,741
Westmont College	ind.	$33,170	$10,080	100%	9%	$23,855	$19,395	$26,032
Whittier College	ind.	$32,470	$ 9050	82%	25%	$31,833	$ 9687	$40,862
William Jessup University	ind.	$20,480	$ 7470	41%	20%	$16,789	$11,161	$15,802
Woodbury University	ind.	$26,978	$ 8768	100%	4%	$19,273	$16,473	$43,854
Colorado								
Adams State College	pub.	$ 3790	$ 6780	93%	1%	$ 8314	$ 2256	$17,156
The Colorado College	ind.	$36,044	$ 9096	97%	61%	$30,402	$14,738	$16,041
Colorado School of Mines	pub.	$11,238	$ 7626	90%	82%	$16,000	$ 2864	$22,500
Colorado State University	pub.	$ 5874	$ 8134	89%	32%	$ 7710	$ 6298	$18,607
Colorado State University–Pueblo	pub.	$ 4667	$ 6300	88%	9%	$ 7980	$ 2987	$16,981
DeVry University (Westminster)	ind.	$14,080	NA	56%	16%	$ 9419	$ 4661	$11,071
Fort Lewis College	pub.	$ 6956	$ 7170	72%	23%	$ 7137	$ 6989	$17,962
Johnson & Wales University	ind.	$22,585	$ 7956	91%	10%	$16,291	$14,250	$28,354
Mesa State College	pub.	$ 4735	$ 7355	84%	17%	$ 5544	$ 6546	$19,178
Metropolitan State College of Denver	pub.	$ 3241	NA	74%	NR	$ 5902	—	$18,595
Naropa University	ind.	$22,074	$ 8478	97%	6%	$21,363	$ 9189	$19,359
Nazarene Bible College	ind.	$ 8460	NA	100%	NR	NR	NR	$27,048
Rocky Mountain College of Art + Design	ind.	$24,840	NA	25%	9%	$14,042	$10,798	$27,831
University of Colorado at Boulder	pub.	$ 7287	$ 9860	88%	74%	$12,699	$ 4448	$18,361
University of Colorado at Colorado Springs	pub.	$ 5878	$ 8750	97%	18%	$ 6868	$ 7760	$21,584
University of Colorado Denver	pub.	$ 6394	$13,524	86%	8%	$ 7145	$12,773	$17,441
University of Denver	ind.	$35,481	$ 9900	100%	28%	$26,707	$18,674	$11,218
University of Northern Colorado	pub.	$ 4680	$ 7784	80%	57%	$12,988	—	NR
Western State College of Colorado	pub.	$ 3778	$ 7516	54%	15%	$ 7500	$ 3794	$17,313
Connecticut								
Albertus Magnus College	ind.	$22,624	$ 9442	48%	4%	$11,098	$20,968	$26,404
Central Connecticut State University	pub.	$ 7042	$ 8618	86%	11%	$ 7458	$ 8202	$10,500
Connecticut College	ind.	*$49,385	NR	93%	100%	$31,583	$17,802	$21,283
Fairfield University	ind.	$36,075	$10,850	88%	26%	$27,488	$19,437	$32,857
Lyme Academy College of Fine Arts	ind.	$23,092	NA	NR	NR	NR	NR	$23,114
Post University	ind.	$23,325	$ 9000	95%	1%	$16,087	$16,238	$18,000
Quinnipiac University	ind.	$32,400	$12,380	98%	16%	$18,592	$26,188	$37,849

NA = not applicable; NR = not reported; * = includes room and board; † = room only; — = not available.

College Costs At-a-Glance

	Institutional Control ind.=independent; pub.=public	Tuition and Fees	Room and Board	Percent of Eligible Freshmen Receiving Need-Based Gift Awards	Percent of Freshmen Whose Need Was Fully Met	Average Financial Aid Package for Freshmen	Average Net Cost After Aid	Average Indebtedness Upon Graduation
Connecticut—*continued*								
Sacred Heart University	ind.	$28,990	$11,330	98%	42%	$17,717	$22,603	$27,516
Southern Connecticut State University	pub.	$ 7179	$ 8966	90%	18%	$ 8505	$ 7640	$19,007
Trinity College	ind.	$38,724	$ 9900	94%	100%	$35,967	$12,657	$17,218
University of Bridgeport	ind.	$24,470	$10,600	94%	8%	$21,309	$13,761	NR
University of Connecticut	pub.	$ 9338	$ 9300	76%	21%	$12,142	$ 6496	$21,521
University of Hartford	ind.	$28,980	$11,328	100%	50%	$17,117	$23,191	$38,852
University of New Haven	ind.	$29,682	$12,204	100%	14%	$18,781	$23,105	$33,964
Wesleyan University	ind.	$38,634	$10,636	89%	100%	$30,755	$18,515	$27,402
Western Connecticut State University	pub.	$ 7088	$ 9158	82%	93%	$10,628	$ 5618	$23,970
Yale University	ind.	$35,300	$10,700	100%	100%	$38,067	$ 7933	$12,297
Delaware								
Goldey-Beacom College	ind.	$18,840	$ 4982†	95%	22%	$13,336	$10,486	$11,000
University of Delaware	pub.	$ 8646	$ 8478	72%	52%	$10,639	$ 6485	$17,200
District of Columbia								
American University	ind.	$33,283	$12,418	44%	33%	$29,771	$15,930	$34,213
The Catholic University of America	ind.	$31,520	$11,450	99%	49%	$20,578	$22,392	NR
Gallaudet University	ind.	$10,950	$ 9340	100%	36%	$11,139	$ 9151	$14,071
Georgetown University	ind.	$38,122	$12,153	99%	100%	$35,530	$14,745	$23,333
The George Washington University	ind.	$41,655	$10,120	97%	68%	$35,311	$16,464	$30,817
Howard University	ind.	$15,270	$ 7966	65%	34%	$16,390	$ 6846	$16,473
University of the District of Columbia	pub.	$ 3140	NA	44%	27%	$ 4930	—	$16,270
Florida								
Ave Maria University	ind.	$17,745	$ 7980	100%	27%	$16,351	$ 9374	NR
The Baptist College of Florida	ind.	$ 8150	$ 3886	94%	12%	$ 6282	$ 5754	$ 5316
Clearwater Christian College	ind.	$14,040	$ 5900	100%	16%	$10,913	$ 9027	$18,000
DeVry University (Miramar)	ind.	$14,080	NA	79%	NR	$13,137	$ 943	$51,131
DeVry University (Orlando)	ind.	$14,080	NA	76%	1%	$ 9980	$ 4100	$23,511
Eckerd College	ind.	$30,590	$ 8754	99%	18%	$24,982	$14,362	$24,749
Embry-Riddle Aeronautical University	ind.	$28,114	$ 9964	100%	NR	$18,699	$19,379	NR
Embry-Riddle Aeronautical University Worldwide	ind.	$ 5304	NA	100%	NR	$ 6328	—	NR
Flagler College	ind.	$12,520	$ 6810	64%	19%	$16,711	$ 2619	$18,415
Florida Atlantic University	pub.	$ 3662	$ 8960	90%	13%	$ 7852	$ 4770	NR
Florida College	ind.	$12,060	$ 6900	100%	13%	$11,624	$ 7336	$ 7246
Florida Gulf Coast University	pub.	$ 5497	$ 7450	62%	8%	$ 6583	$ 6364	$11,747
Florida Hospital College of Health Sciences	ind.	$ 8540	NR	NR	NR	NR	NR	NR
Florida Institute of Technology	ind.	$30,440	$10,250	100%	27%	$28,520	$12,170	$35,106
Florida International University	pub.	$ 3900	$11,120	59%	12%	$ 6055	$ 8965	$10,899
Florida State University	pub.	$ 4196	$ 8178	60%	80%	$10,133	$ 2241	$16,927
Hodges University	ind.	$16,580	NA	87%	21%	$ 8000	$ 8580	$18,600
Jacksonville University	ind.	$23,900	$ 8760	99%	2%	$18,697	$13,963	NR
Johnson & Wales University	ind.	$22,585	$ 7956	95%	5%	$18,267	$12,274	$33,501
Lynn University	ind.	$29,300	$10,900	83%	13%	$19,838	$20,362	$30,175

NA = not applicable; NR = not reported; * = includes room and board; † = room only; — = not available.

College Costs At-a-Glance

	Institutional Control ind.=independent; pub.=public	Tuition and Fees	Room and Board	Percent of Eligible Freshmen Receiving Need-Based Gift Awards	Percent of Freshmen Whose Need Was Fully Met	Average Financial Aid Package for Freshmen	Average Net Cost After Aid	Average Indebtedness Upon Graduation
Florida—*continued*								
New College of Florida	pub.	$ 4127	$ 7464	100%	66%	$12,587	—	$13,162
Northwood University, Florida Campus	ind.	$18,408	$ 8562	89%	21%	$15,808	$11,162	$22,488
Nova Southeastern University	ind.	$20,350	$ 8360	63%	8%	$15,305	$13,405	$35,789
Palm Beach Atlantic University	ind.	$21,550	$ 8220	55%	8%	$16,115	$13,655	$19,420
Ringling College of Art and Design	ind.	$26,725	$10,350	89%	6%	$18,164	$18,911	$31,391
Rollins College	ind.	$34,520	$10,780	99%	22%	$32,696	$12,604	$21,904
Saint Leo University	ind.	$17,150	$ 8430	100%	32%	$18,827	$ 6753	$23,178
St. Thomas University	ind.	$20,664	$ 6206	72%	20%	NR	NR	NR
Stetson University	ind.	$31,770	$ 8934	99%	31%	$27,736	$12,968	$28,775
Trinity College of Florida	ind.	$11,200	$ 6534	100%	15%	$ 4371	$13,363	$15,233
University of Central Florida	pub.	$ 3947	$ 8492	59%	19%	$ 7235	$ 5204	$14,601
University of Florida	pub.	$ 3778	$ 7150	62%	43%	NR	NR	$15,318
University of Miami	ind.	$34,834	$10,254	98%	48%	$29,868	$15,220	$24,500
University of North Florida	pub.	$ 3775	$ 7366	62%	18%	$ 1506	$ 9635	$14,694
University of South Florida	pub.	$ 3991	$ 8080	53%	8%	$ 7889	$ 4182	$18,568
The University of Tampa	ind.	$21,712	$ 7978	96%	25%	$16,404	$13,286	$23,807
University of West Florida	pub.	$ 3655	$ 6900	NR	NR	NR	NR	NR
Webber International University	ind.	$17,000	$ 6354	100%	7%	$16,247	$ 7107	$23,902
Georgia								
Agnes Scott College	ind.	$30,105	$ 9850	100%	52%	$29,977	$ 9978	$25,577
Augusta State University	pub.	$ 3644	NR	80%	3%	$ 3289	$ 355	$ 5961
Berry College	ind.	$22,370	$ 7978	100%	25%	$18,342	$12,006	$15,808
Brenau University	ind.	$18,800	$ 9487	99%	26%	$19,235	$ 9052	$16,975
Brewton-Parker College	ind.	$14,730	$ 5620	100%	24%	$10,351	$ 9999	$24,592
Clayton State University	pub.	$ 3852	$ 3900	69%	10%	$ 8178	—	NR
Columbus State University	pub.	$ 3772	$ 6900	71%	68%	$ 3759	$ 6913	$26,905
Covenant College	ind.	$24,320	$ 6900	98%	17%	$17,837	$13,383	$18,382
Dalton State College	pub.	$ 1994	NA	54%	9%	$ 2663	—	$ 3500
DeVry University (Alpharetta)	ind.	$14,080	NA	97%	3%	$13,811	$ 269	$32,836
DeVry University (Decatur)	ind.	$14,080	NA	95%	5%	$12,824	$ 1256	$47,994
Emmanuel College	ind.	$12,880	$ 5520	98%	15%	$13,988	$ 4412	$23,880
Emory University	ind.	$36,336	$10,572	92%	100%	$29,334	$17,574	$23,181
Fort Valley State University	pub.	$ 4478	$ 7540	99%	NR	$ 2141	$ 9877	$36,700
Georgia College & State University	pub.	$ 5476	$ 7698	33%	NR	$ 6658	$ 6516	$14,312
Georgia Institute of Technology	pub.	$ 6040	$ 7694	95%	55%	$11,254	$ 2480	$20,881
Georgia Southern University	pub.	$ 4348	$ 7300	84%	16%	$ 6997	$ 4651	$18,518
Georgia Southwestern State University	pub.	$ 3816	$ 5694	59%	20%	$ 8605	$ 905	$16,920
Georgia State University	pub.	$ 6056	$ 9330	60%	24%	$10,854	$ 4532	$15,950
Kennesaw State University	pub.	$ 4144	$ 4737†	42%	83%	$11,058	—	$13,500
LaGrange College	ind.	$19,900	$ 8168	100%	32%	$15,051	$13,017	$19,224
Life University	ind.	$ 7830	$12,000	60%	NR	$ 8700	$11,130	$17,500
Medical College of Georgia	pub.	$ 5568	$ 3250†	NR	NR	NR	NR	$43,169

NA = not applicable; NR = not reported; * = includes room and board; † = room only; — = not available.

College Costs At-a-Glance

	Institutional Control ind.=independent; pub.=public	Tuition and Fees	Room and Board	Percent of Eligible Freshmen Receiving Need-Based Gift Awards	Percent of Freshmen Whose Need Was Fully Met	Average Financial Aid Package for Freshmen	Average Net Cost After Aid	Average Indebtedness Upon Graduation
Georgia—*continued*								
Mercer University	ind.	$28,700	$ 8450	100%	60%	$31,331	$ 5819	$22,835
Oglethorpe University	ind.	$25,580	$ 9500	100%	13%	$21,153	$13,927	NR
Piedmont College	ind.	$18,000	$ 6000	32%	40%	$15,963	$ 8037	$15,620
Reinhardt College	ind.	$16,070	$ 7950	61%	19%	$ 9494	$14,526	$18,328
Savannah College of Art and Design	ind.	$28,265	$11,710	24%	57%	$11,495	$28,480	NR
Shorter College	ind.	$15,770	$ 7400	100%	31%	$14,045	$ 9125	$23,455
Southern Polytechnic State University	pub.	$ 4232	$ 5870	38%	40%	$ 2472	$ 7630	$13,641
Spelman College	ind.	$20,281	$ 9734	74%	23%	$12,339	$17,676	$17,500
University of Georgia	pub.	$ 6030	$ 7528	97%	43%	$ 9422	$ 4136	$14,343
University of West Georgia	pub.	$ 4316	$ 5714	86%	20%	$ 7190	$ 2840	NR
Valdosta State University	pub.	$ 4158	$ 6230	80%	15%	$ 6923	$ 3465	$16,795
Guam								
University of Guam	pub.	$ 5285	$ 7785	93%	NR	NR	NR	NR
Hawaii								
Chaminade University of Honolulu	ind.	$16,140	$10,420	99%	13%	$11,862	$14,698	$22,263
Hawai'i Pacific University	ind.	$14,960	$11,094	48%	NR	$12,370	$13,684	$20,212
University of Hawaii at Hilo	pub.	$ 4360	$11,403	64%	13%	$ 6767	$ 8996	$16,604
University of Hawaii at Manoa	pub.	$ 7168	$ 7564	79%	23%	$ 6926	$ 7806	$14,818
Idaho								
Boise State University	pub.	$ 4632	$ 4819	78%	27%	$ 6506	$ 2945	$21,064
The College of Idaho	ind.	$20,070	$ 7478	69%	20%	$17,364	$10,184	$24,919
Idaho State University	pub.	$ 4664	$ 5270	92%	14%	$ 7264	$ 2670	$22,237
Lewis-Clark State College	pub.	$ 4296	$ 5400	62%	9%	$ 6518	$ 3178	NR
University of Idaho	pub.	$ 4632	$ 8784	63%	32%	$10,472	$ 2944	$21,702
Illinois								
Augustana College	ind.	$30,150	$ 7650	100%	39%	$22,069	$15,731	NR
Aurora University	ind.	$18,100	$ 7850	76%	32%	$18,698	$ 7252	$18,078
Benedictine University	ind.	$22,310	$ 7300	62%	NR	$16,853	$12,757	$16,802
Blessing-Rieman College of Nursing	ind.	$21,270	$ 7520	NR	NR	NR	NR	$20,000
Bradley University	ind.	$22,814	$ 7350	99%	34%	$14,032	$16,132	$18,859
Concordia University Chicago	ind.	$23,458	$ 7700	100%	19%	$22,148	$ 9010	$28,506
DePaul University	ind.	$26,067	$10,240	77%	10%	$19,014	$17,293	$19,172
DeVry University (Addison)	ind.	$14,080	NA	81%	4%	$13,167	$ 913	$31,740
DeVry University (Chicago)	ind.	$14,080	NA	89%	NR	$16,818	—	$49,157
DeVry University (Tinley Park)	ind.	$14,080	NA	75%	7%	$11,879	$ 2201	$ 4375
Dominican University	ind.	$23,800	$ 7350	100%	18%	$19,009	$12,141	$17,066
Eastern Illinois University	pub.	$ 8783	$ 7588	53%	10%	$ 8624	$ 7747	$14,233
East-West University	ind.	$13,575	NA	NR	NR	$ 9020	$ 4555	$ 2625
Elmhurst College	ind.	$27,330	$ 7874	89%	17%	$18,731	$16,473	$20,675
Eureka College	ind.	$16,255	$ 7130	100%	21%	$10,721	$12,664	$14,859
Illinois College	ind.	$20,300	$ 7600	84%	46%	$19,449	$ 8451	$20,466
Illinois Institute of Technology	ind.	$27,513	$ 9233	100%	29%	$24,230	$12,516	$15,220

NA = not applicable; NR = not reported; * = includes room and board; † = room only; — = not available.

College Costs At-a-Glance	Institutional Control ind.=independent; pub.=public	Tuition and Fees	Room and Board	Percent of Eligible Freshmen Receiving Need-Based Gift Awards	Percent of Freshmen Whose Need Was Fully Met	Average Financial Aid Package for Freshmen	Average Net Cost After Aid	Average Indebtedness Upon Graduation
Illinois—*continued*								
Illinois State University	pub.	$ 9814	$ 7458	57%	51%	$10,408	$ 6864	$18,854
Illinois Wesleyan University	ind.	$32,434	$ 7350	100%	64%	$24,788	$14,996	$26,555
Knox College	ind.	$31,911	$ 7164	100%	41%	$25,282	$13,793	$22,749
Lake Forest College	ind.	$32,520	$ 7724	100%	37%	$27,548	$12,696	$23,962
Lewis University	ind.	$21,990	$ 8750	69%	48%	$16,154	$14,586	$19,976
Lexington College	ind.	$23,800	NA	100%	11%	$13,949	$ 9851	$27,000
Lincoln Christian College	ind.	$11,790	$ 5355	46%	26%	$ 9622	$ 7523	$19,594
Loyola University Chicago	ind.	$30,656	$10,885	98%	12%	$25,452	$16,089	$32,134
MacMurray College	ind.	$17,330	$ 7290	95%	51%	$20,205	$ 4415	$25,413
McKendree University	ind.	$21,270	$ 7850	100%	27%	$20,394	$ 8726	$18,291
Millikin University	ind.	$26,345	$ 7866	95%	51%	$19,197	$15,014	$27,375
Monmouth College	ind.	$24,950	$ 7300	100%	26%	$21,722	$10,528	$23,726
National-Louis University	ind.	$18,075	NA	100%	NR	$10,185	$ 7890	$21,250
North Central College	ind.	$25,938	$ 8217	100%	29%	$19,889	$14,266	$26,395
Northeastern Illinois University	pub.	$ 8016	NA	90%	5%	$ 6848	$ 1168	$10,379
Northern Illinois University	pub.	$ 8312	$ 8230	70%	6%	$10,995	$ 5547	$19,405
North Park University	ind.	$17,600	$ 7580	97%	7%	$11,550	$13,630	NR
Northwestern University	ind.	$38,461	$11,703	95%	100%	$28,362	$21,802	$19,808
Olivet Nazarene University	ind.	$21,590	$ 6400	99%	31%	$16,155	$11,835	$25,796
Principia College	ind.	$22,650	$ 8475	100%	100%	$23,743	$ 7382	$15,784
Quincy University	ind.	$20,790	$ 7900	90%	11%	$20,257	$ 8433	$19,612
Robert Morris College	ind.	$19,200	NR	95%	2%	$12,115	$ 7085	$24,600
Rockford College	ind.	$24,250	$ 6750	99%	13%	$18,894	$12,106	$25,148
Saint Anthony College of Nursing	ind.	$18,674	NA	NR	NR	NR	NR	$21,000
Saint Francis Medical Center College of Nursing	ind.	$14,716	$ 2400†	NR	NR	NR	NR	NR
Saint Xavier University	ind.	$23,006	$ 8007	100%	20%	$20,734	$10,279	$24,920
Shimer College	ind.	$23,750	$11,200	100%	NR	$17,911	$17,039	NR
Southern Illinois University Carbondale	pub.	$ 9813	$ 7137	74%	89%	$12,176	$ 4774	$18,603
Southern Illinois University Edwardsville	pub.	$ 7819	$ 7040	47%	24%	$15,083	—	$16,656
Trinity Christian College	ind.	$20,046	$ 7420	81%	6%	$ 8896	$18,570	$42,375
Trinity International University	ind.	$21,980	$ 7430	75%	20%	$17,893	$11,517	$18,477
University of Illinois at Chicago	pub.	$11,716	$ 8744	80%	28%	$11,154	$ 9306	$16,715
University of Illinois at Springfield	pub.	$ 9069	$ 8840	92%	15%	$ 9530	$ 8379	$14,226
University of Illinois at Urbana–Champaign	pub.	$12,240	$ 8764	80%	33%	$11,233	$ 9771	$17,930
University of St. Francis	ind.	$21,860	$ 7744	87%	68%	$18,797	$10,807	$20,319
Western Illinois University	pub.	$ 8272	$ 7210	70%	38%	$ 8626	$ 6856	$17,567
Wheaton College	ind.	$25,500	$ 7618	93%	32%	$21,472	$11,646	$21,549
Indiana								
Ball State University	pub.	$ 7500	$ 7598	68%	27%	$ 9123	$ 5975	$20,326
Bethel College	ind.	$21,296	$ 5936	96%	6%	$17,108	$10,124	$16,337
Butler University	ind.	$28,266	$ 9410	99%	23%	$21,260	$16,416	$24,000
Calumet College of Saint Joseph	ind.	$12,460	NA	83%	25%	$12,474	—	$31,642

NA = not applicable; NR = not reported; * = includes room and board; † = room only; — = not available.

College Costs At-a-Glance

	Institutional Control ind.=independent; pub.=public	Tuition and Fees	Room and Board	Percent of Eligible Freshmen Receiving Need-Based Gift Awards	Percent of Freshmen Whose Need Was Fully Met	Average Financial Aid Package for Freshmen	Average Net Cost After Aid	Average Indebtedness Upon Graduation
Indiana—*continued*								
DePauw University	ind.	$31,825	$8400	100%	41%	$26,195	$14,030	$ 6863
DeVry University (Indianapolis)	ind.	$14,080	NA	NR	NR	$ 3500	$10,580	NR
Earlham College	ind.	$34,030	$6814	86%	49%	$26,889	$13,955	$20,287
Franklin College	ind.	$22,445	$6640	100%	17%	$15,347	$13,738	$42,908
Grace College	ind.	$20,376	$6648	100%	37%	$15,011	$12,013	$18,017
Hanover College	ind.	$25,220	$7500	100%	38%	$21,317	$11,403	NR
Huntington University	ind.	$20,300	$6940	97%	10%	$16,393	$10,847	$23,898
Indiana State University	pub.	$ 7148	$6672	64%	22%	$ 9579	$ 4241	$22,961
Indiana University Bloomington	pub.	$ 8231	$7138	82%	17%	$10,549	$ 4820	$22,013
Indiana University East	pub.	$ 5556	NA	86%	11%	$ 7065	—	$24,309
Indiana University Kokomo	pub.	$ 5591	NA	82%	8%	$ 6055	—	$20,492
Indiana University Northwest	pub.	$ 5669	NA	75%	6%	$ 6530	—	$22,335
Indiana University–Purdue University Fort Wayne	pub.	$ 5936	$5400†	58%	4%	$ 7584	$ 3752	$20,335
Indiana University–Purdue University Indianapolis	pub.	$ 7191	$3140†	72%	9%	$ 8619	$ 1712	$25,253
Indiana University South Bend	pub.	$ 5763	NA	84%	3%	$ 6933	—	$22,235
Indiana University Southeast	pub.	$ 5644	$3276†	82%	5%	$ 7054	$ 1866	$19,592
Manchester College	ind.	$22,720	$8100	100%	12%	$19,952	$10,868	$16,333
Marian College	ind.	$22,400	$7228	59%	29%	$22,298	$ 7330	$23,467
Oakland City University	ind.	$15,360	$6228	NR	NR	NR	NR	NR
Purdue University	pub.	$ 7750	$7930	67%	33%	$ 9716	$ 5964	$23,087
Purdue University Calumet	pub.	$ 5757	$6155	68%	1%	$ 3479	$ 8433	$19,090
Purdue University North Central	pub.	$ 6080	NA	52%	13%	$ 5857	$ 223	$19,536
Rose-Hulman Institute of Technology	ind.	$32,826	$8868	99%	15%	$31,562	$10,132	$36,818
Saint Joseph's College	ind.	$23,180	$7170	97%	35%	$22,827	$ 7523	$28,135
Saint Mary's College	ind.	$28,212	$8938	93%	28%	$22,836	$14,314	$26,684
Taylor University	ind.	$24,546	$6332	95%	24%	$16,612	$14,286	$22,942
Trine University	ind.	$24,200	$8300	65%	100%	$18,457	$14,043	$17,380
University of Evansville	ind.	$25,845	$8230	100%	31%	$23,685	$10,390	$25,390
University of Notre Dame	ind.	$36,847	$9828	95%	100%	$32,140	$14,535	$29,835
University of Southern Indiana	pub.	$ 5219	$6648	78%	22%	$10,201	$ 1666	NR
Valparaiso University	ind.	$26,950	$7620	100%	26%	$20,616	$13,954	$28,784
Wabash College	ind.	$27,950	$7400	100%	100%	$27,996	$ 7354	$21,423
Iowa								
Allen College	ind.	$14,579	$6816	88%	4%	$ 7014	$14,381	$20,612
Ashford University	ind.	$16,106	$5800	NR	NR	NR	NR	NR
Buena Vista University	ind.	$24,796	$7014	96%	64%	$28,972	$ 2838	$34,029
Central College	ind.	$23,944	$8006	100%	23%	$21,977	$ 9973	$35,103
Clarke College	ind.	$23,520	$6840	99%	32%	$20,512	$ 9848	$28,649
Coe College	ind.	$29,270	$7150	100%	37%	$24,455	$11,965	$30,385
Cornell College	ind.	$27,850	$7220	100%	58%	$26,875	$ 8195	$29,825
Dordt College	ind.	$22,080	$6010	100%	19%	$20,255	$ 7835	$19,208
Drake University	ind.	$26,622	$7800	98%	37%	$21,055	$13,367	$32,318

NA = not applicable; NR = not reported; * = includes room and board; † = room only; — = not available.

College Costs At-a-Glance	Institutional Control ind.=independent; pub.=public	Tuition and Fees	Room and Board	Percent of Eligible Freshmen Receiving Need-Based Gift Awards	Percent of Freshmen Whose Need Was Fully Met	Average Financial Aid Package for Freshmen	Average Net Cost After Aid	Average Indebtedness Upon Graduation
Iowa—*continued*								
Graceland University	ind.	$20,090	$6780	100%	32%	$20,824	$ 6046	$28,347
Grand View University	ind.	$18,614	$6164	91%	47%	$19,604	$ 5174	$27,337
Grinnell College	ind.	$35,428	$8272	99%	100%	$33,730	$ 9970	$19,526
Iowa State University of Science and Technology	pub.	$ 6651	$7277	100%	41%	$10,039	$ 3889	$31,616
Iowa Wesleyan College	ind.	$20,000	$6240	57%	31%	$16,000	$10,240	NR
Loras College	ind.	$25,348	$7026	84%	40%	$17,254	$15,120	$25,380
Luther College	ind.	$32,290	$5380	100%	36%	$25,205	$12,465	$29,770
Morningside College	ind.	$22,246	$6729	100%	46%	$18,303	$10,672	$36,937
Mount Mercy College	ind.	$21,125	$6650	100%	36%	$17,999	$ 9776	$28,430
Northwestern College	ind.	$22,950	$6580	94%	32%	$17,494	$12,036	$23,817
St. Ambrose University	ind.	$22,590	$8255	100%	31%	$15,992	$14,853	$32,675
Simpson College	ind.	$24,771	$6988	100%	29%	$24,914	$ 6845	$31,115
University of Dubuque	ind.	$20,020	$6790	98%	55%	$19,098	$ 7712	$32,500
The University of Iowa	pub.	$ 6824	NR	63%	52%	$ 7191	—	$22,856
University of Northern Iowa	pub.	$ 6636	$7082	45%	28%	$ 7867	$ 5851	$24,176
Wartburg College	ind.	$26,160	$7255	100%	36%	$20,779	$12,636	$31,063
Kansas								
Baker University	ind.	$19,880	$6370	NR	NR	$11,453	$14,797	$26,869
Benedictine College	ind.	$18,800	$6300	64%	21%	$15,880	$ 9220	$16,060
Bethany College	ind.	$18,124	$5650	85%	48%	$20,938	$ 2836	$17,161
Bethel College	ind.	$18,900	$6050	79%	46%	$20,858	$ 4092	$24,284
Central Christian College of Kansas	ind.	$17,000	$5900	55%	18%	$13,067	$ 9833	$20,000
Emporia State University	pub.	$ 4136	$5858	61%	92%	$ 6536	$ 3458	$17,680
Fort Hays State University	pub.	$ 3051	$5450	89%	19%	$ 5543	$ 2958	$15,601
Kansas State University	pub.	$ 6627	$6448	66%	20%	$ 7367	$ 5708	$18,666
Manhattan Christian College	ind.	$11,374	$6720	65%	66%	$14,589	$ 3505	$13,364
McPherson College	ind.	$17,200	$6500	94%	21%	$18,197	$ 5503	$24,024
MidAmerica Nazarene University	ind.	$18,216	$6180	100%	17%	$15,258	$ 9138	$28,859
Newman University	ind.	$19,650	$6656	62%	37%	$15,927	$10,379	$22,606
Pittsburg State University	pub.	$ 4322	$5394	87%	14%	$ 8842	$ 874	$15,643
Southwestern College	ind.	$19,630	$5750	100%	46%	$22,327	$ 3053	$25,697
Tabor College	ind.	$18,710	$6750	80%	19%	$17,661	$ 7799	$20,500
The University of Kansas	pub.	$ 7725	$6474	65%	24%	$ 7833	$ 6366	$20,902
Wichita State University	pub.	$ 5084	$5860	62%	20%	$ 7257	$ 3687	$22,116
Kentucky								
Alice Lloyd College	ind.	$ 1400	$4450	79%	19%	$ 8931	—	$ 4781
Asbury College	ind.	$22,413	$5414	98%	29%	$18,481	$ 9346	$26,150
Bellarmine University	ind.	$28,900	$8410	100%	30%	$22,285	$15,025	$19,055
Berea College	ind.	$ 866	$5768	100%	NR	$31,598	—	$ 8505
Campbellsville University	ind.	$18,810	$6540	100%	21%	$16,801	$ 8549	$15,170
Centre College	ind.	*$37,000	NR	100%	36%	$23,693	$13,307	$17,600
DeVry University	ind.	$14,080	NR	NR	NR	NR	NR	NR

NA = not applicable; NR = not reported; * = includes room and board; † = room only; — = not available.

College Costs At-a-Glance

	Institutional Control ind.=independent; pub.=public	Tuition and Fees	Room and Board	Percent of Eligible Freshmen Receiving Need-Based Gift Awards	Percent of Freshmen Whose Need Was Fully Met	Average Financial Aid Package for Freshmen	Average Net Cost After Aid	Average Indebtedness Upon Graduation
Kentucky—*continued*								
Eastern Kentucky University	pub.	$ 6080	$ 6360	60%	13%	$ 9162	$ 3278	$14,976
Georgetown College	ind.	$24,150	$ 6700	100%	51%	$24,150	$ 6700	$22,241
Kentucky Christian University	ind.	$14,088	$ 5800	73%	9%	$ 9202	$10,686	$24,703
Kentucky State University	pub.	$ 5692	$ 6392	80%	38%	$ 2796	$ 9288	$27,356
Kentucky Wesleyan College	ind.	$15,500	$ 6160	100%	16%	$13,703	$ 7957	$18,875
Lindsey Wilson College	ind.	$16,670	$ 6925	100%	47%	$13,866	$ 9729	$16,480
Mid-Continent University	ind.	$13,100	$ 6300	86%	13%	$ 8492	$10,908	$ 8805
Midway College	ind.	$17,100	$ 6600	97%	21%	$12,678	$11,022	$15,407
Morehead State University	pub.	$ 5670	$ 5852	64%	31%	$ 8023	$ 3499	$18,204
Murray State University	pub.	$ 5748	$ 6004	75%	94%	$ 4605	$ 7147	$16,305
Northern Kentucky University	pub.	$ 6528	NR	49%	22%	$ 7126	—	$22,743
Pikeville College	ind.	$14,535	$ 6000	97%	61%	$16,237	$ 4298	$14,908
Thomas More College	ind.	$22,220	$ 5870	100%	29%	$16,661	$11,429	$25,265
Transylvania University	ind.	$23,810	$ 7450	100%	30%	$19,490	$11,770	$17,885
Union College	ind.	$17,894	$ 5800	100%	31%	$17,120	$ 6574	$37,000
University of Kentucky	pub.	$ 8123	$ 9125	40%	47%	$ 8978	$ 8270	$15,891
University of Louisville	pub.	$ 7564	$ 6058	97%	18%	$10,384	$ 3238	$11,704
University of the Cumberlands	ind.	$15,658	$ 6826	100%	31%	$17,384	$ 5100	$19,339
Western Kentucky University	pub.	$ 6930	$ 5914	61%	35%	$ 9846	$ 2998	$15,042
Louisiana								
Centenary College of Louisiana	ind.	$22,000	$ 7330	100%	27%	$20,396	$ 8934	$20,640
Dillard University	ind.	$13,000	NR	98%	85%	$18,795	—	$26,000
Grambling State University	pub.	$ 3804	$ 5202	85%	4%	$ 5950	$ 3056	$29,416
Louisiana State University and Agricultural and Mechanical College	pub.	$ 5086	$ 7238	96%	18%	$ 7644	$ 4680	$16,354
Louisiana Tech University	pub.	$ 4911	$ 4740	96%	21%	$ 8921	$ 730	$12,715
Loyola University New Orleans	ind.	$29,706	$ 9826	100%	32%	$25,869	$13,663	$21,401
Nicholls State University	pub.	$ 3710	$ 5098	95%	82%	$ 7178	$ 1630	$17,229
Northwestern State University of Louisiana	pub.	$ 3598	$ 6272	60%	32%	$ 5247	$ 4623	$22,045
Our Lady of the Lake College	ind.	$ 6920	NA	84%	3%	$ 6513	$ 407	$12,019
Southeastern Louisiana University	pub.	$ 3721	$ 6220	64%	27%	$ 5857	$ 4084	$18,741
University of Louisiana at Lafayette	pub.	$ 3574	$ 4200	94%	23%	$ 6525	$ 1249	NR
University of Louisiana at Monroe	pub.	$ 3791	$ 3370	31%	30%	$ 2757	$ 4404	NR
University of New Orleans	pub.	$ 3488	$ 6130	85%	24%	$ 9196	$ 422	$14,911
Xavier University of Louisiana	ind.	$15,500	$ 6800	76%	28%	$17,348	$ 4952	$25,227
Maine								
Bates College	ind.	*$49,350	NR	95%	93%	$32,872	$16,478	$18,785
Bowdoin College	ind.	$38,190	$10,380	100%	100%	$35,544	$13,026	$17,560
Colby College	ind.	*$48,520	NR	98%	100%	$31,431	$17,089	$19,222
College of the Atlantic	ind.	$33,060	$ 8490	100%	53%	$33,029	$ 8521	$23,762
Husson University	ind.	$12,990	$ 6994	95%	8%	$10,899	$ 9085	$25,528
Maine College of Art	ind.	$27,165	$ 9400	100%	3%	$13,152	$23,413	$33,350
Maine Maritime Academy	pub.	$10,105	$ 8450	81%	13%	$ 8984	$ 9571	$35,968

NA = not applicable; NR = not reported; * = includes room and board; † = room only; — = not available.

College Costs At-a-Glance

	Institutional Control ind.=independent; pub.=public	Tuition and Fees	Room and Board	Percent of Eligible Freshmen Receiving Need-Based Gift Awards	Percent of Freshmen Whose Need Was Fully Met	Average Financial Aid Package for Freshmen	Average Net Cost After Aid	Average Indebtedness Upon Graduation
Maine—*continued*								
New England School of Communications	ind.	$10,680	$ 6725	86%	25%	$ 4441	$12,964	$34,209
Saint Joseph's College of Maine	ind.	$25,060	$ 9950	100%	33%	$19,397	$15,613	$35,451
Thomas College	ind.	$19,750	$ 8170	100%	15%	$17,077	$10,843	$38,734
Unity College	ind.	$20,750	$ 7680	100%	15%	$16,432	$11,998	NR
University of Maine	pub.	$ 9100	$ 8008	86%	32%	$11,855	$ 5253	$24,330
The University of Maine at Augusta	pub.	$ 6495	NA	91%	13%	$ 6538	—	$15,842
University of Maine at Farmington	pub.	$ 8206	$ 7158	83%	10%	$ 9208	$ 6156	$19,490
University of Maine at Fort Kent	pub.	$ 6413	$ 6940	100%	33%	$ 8404	$ 4949	NR
University of Maine at Presque Isle	pub.	$ 6475	$ 7096	92%	41%	$ 8060	$ 5511	$14,102
University of New England	ind.	$27,920	$10,870	100%	15%	$23,854	$14,936	$44,325
University of Southern Maine	pub.	$ 7467	$ 8344	84%	13%	$ 9263	$ 6548	$22,656
Maryland								
College of Notre Dame of Maryland	ind.	$27,250	$ 9100	100%	25%	$20,477	$15,873	$30,552
Coppin State University	pub.	$ 5305	$ 7138	86%	11%	$ 8390	$ 4053	$ 9904
DeVry University	ind.	$14,080	NA	NR	NR	NR	NR	NR
Frostburg State University	pub.	$ 6614	$ 7016	76%	29%	$ 8941	$ 4689	$18,408
Goucher College	ind.	$33,786	$10,006	95%	25%	$25,779	$18,013	$16,729
Hood College	ind.	$26,580	$ 8980	99%	27%	$20,894	$14,666	$19,038
The Johns Hopkins University	ind.	$37,700	$11,578	83%	97%	$30,002	$19,276	$21,984
Loyola University Maryland	ind.	$36,240	$ 7790†	74%	100%	$26,525	$17,505	$26,340
McDaniel College	ind.	$30,780	$ 6150	98%	30%	$22,446	$14,484	$25,345
Mount St. Mary's University	ind.	$29,020	$ 9878	99%	24%	$18,510	$20,388	$27,230
Peabody Conservatory of Music of The Johns Hopkins University	ind.	$34,250	$11,100	92%	33%	$16,367	$28,983	$34,442
St. Mary's College of Maryland	pub.	$12,604	$ 9225	38%	NR	$ 7500	$14,329	$17,125
Salisbury University	pub.	$ 6492	$ 7798	84%	25%	$ 7417	$ 6873	$15,939
Stevenson University	ind.	$19,200	$ 9856	97%	18%	$12,492	$16,564	NR
Towson University	pub.	$ 7314	$ 8306	65%	21%	$ 8620	$ 7000	$10,772
University of Baltimore	pub.	$ 7051	NA	77%	24%	$ 7941	—	NR
University of Maryland, Baltimore County	pub.	$ 8780	$ 8960	87%	40%	$12,980	$ 4760	$20,002
University of Maryland, College Park	pub.	$ 8005	$ 9109	69%	12%	$10,252	$ 6862	$20,091
University of Maryland Eastern Shore	pub.	$ 6042	$ 6880	95%	54%	$14,879	—	$ 8500
University of Maryland University College	pub.	$ 5760	NA	76%	NR	$ 5093	$ 667	NR
Washington Bible College	ind.	$10,200	$ 6770	93%	13%	$ 6248	$10,722	$19,723
Washington College	ind.	$34,005	$ 7180	100%	50%	$22,987	$18,198	$20,611
Massachusetts								
American International College	ind.	$24,100	$10,150	100%	12%	$20,813	$13,437	$34,753
Amherst College	ind.	$37,640	$ 9790	98%	100%	$37,077	$10,353	$12,603
Anna Maria College	ind.	$25,850	$ 9350	99%	8%	$18,507	$16,693	$35,575
The Art Institute of Boston at Lesley University	ind.	$26,590	$12,400	NR	NR	$17,174	$21,816	$17,000
Assumption College	ind.	$28,851	$ 6156	100%	23%	$18,101	$16,906	$26,691
Atlantic Union College	ind.	$16,570	$ 5000	100%	14%	$10,117	$11,453	$35,888
Babson College	ind.	$36,096	$12,020	94%	84%	$30,666	$17,450	$27,598

NA = not applicable; NR = not reported; * = includes room and board; † = room only; — = not available.

College Costs At-a-Glance

	Institutional Control ind.=independent; pub.=public	Tuition and Fees	Room and Board	Percent of Eligible Freshmen Receiving Need-Based Gift Awards	Percent of Freshmen Whose Need Was Fully Met	Average Financial Aid Package for Freshmen	Average Net Cost After Aid	Average Indebtedness Upon Graduation
Massachusetts—*continued*								
Bard College at Simon's Rock	ind.	$40,170	$10,960	74%	17%	$27,000	$24,130	$21,000
Bentley University	ind.	$34,488	$11,320	82%	45%	$26,375	$19,433	$30,577
Berklee College of Music	ind.	$30,650	$15,080	49%	8%	$12,679	$33,051	NR
Boston Architectural College	ind.	$10,620	NA	12%	2%	$11,739	—	$37,847
Boston College	ind.	$37,950	$12,395	86%	100%	$29,618	$20,727	$19,358
The Boston Conservatory	ind.	$32,200	$15,670	88%	8%	$13,972	$33,898	$34,931
Boston University	ind.	$37,050	$11,418	92%	48%	$30,935	$17,533	$26,586
Brandeis University	ind.	$37,294	$10,354	94%	23%	$29,934	$17,714	$20,095
Bridgewater State College	pub.	$ 6237	$ 6852	84%	NR	$ 7968	$ 5121	$21,399
Clark University	ind.	$35,220	$ 6750	100%	74%	$27,945	$14,025	$22,250
College of the Holy Cross	ind.	$38,722	$10,620	78%	100%	$27,569	$21,773	$17,200
Curry College	ind.	$27,720	$11,080	96%	4%	$17,478	$21,322	$35,819
Eastern Nazarene College	ind.	$22,014	$ 7913	99%	33%	$20,914	$ 9013	$42,290
Emerson College	ind.	$28,884	$11,832	84%	43%	$15,918	$24,798	$15,701
Emmanuel College	ind.	$29,200	$11,950	88%	28%	$19,725	$21,425	$24,375
Endicott College	ind.	$24,530	$11,380	72%	12%	$14,385	$21,525	$28,022
Fitchburg State College	pub.	$ 6400	$ 7148	86%	93%	$ 8467	$ 5081	$15,258
Gordon College	ind.	$27,294	$ 7424	100%	19%	$16,351	$18,367	$33,399
Hampshire College	ind.	$38,549	$10,080	100%	78%	$32,385	$16,244	$21,300
Harvard University	ind.	$36,173	$11,042	99%	100%	$40,533	$ 6682	$10,813
Hellenic College	ind.	$18,320	$11,430	100%	NR	$10,100	$19,650	$15,000
Lasell College	ind.	$25,300	$10,500	99%	22%	$16,800	$19,000	$23,600
Lesley University	ind.	$28,460	$12,400	97%	7%	$20,175	$20,685	$15,000
Massachusetts College of Art and Design	pub.	$ 7900	$12,060	55%	NR	$ 8088	$11,872	NR
Massachusetts College of Liberal Arts	pub.	$ 6425	$ 7754	87%	NR	NR	NR	$19,090
Massachusetts College of Pharmacy and Health Sciences	ind.	$23,620	$11,600	90%	61%	$16,469	$18,751	NR
Massachusetts Institute of Technology	ind.	$37,782	$11,360	97%	100%	$32,129	$17,013	$14,148
Merrimack College	ind.	$29,310	$10,190	98%	85%	$16,644	$22,856	$42,000
Mount Holyoke College	ind.	$37,646	$11,020	98%	100%	$32,913	$15,753	$23,841
Mount Ida College	ind.	$22,500	$11,100	99%	8%	$14,663	$18,937	$33,635
Newbury College	ind.	$22,000	$10,700	47%	NR	$ 2700	$30,000	$ 8400
New England Conservatory of Music	ind.	$33,325	$11,600	100%	24%	$21,002	$23,923	$30,687
Nichols College	ind.	$26,970	$ 9100	100%	10%	$20,067	$16,003	$28,091
Northeastern University	ind.	$33,721	$11,940	96%	22%	$19,820	$25,841	NR
Regis College	ind.	$27,800	$11,950	95%	13%	$23,757	$15,993	$24,178
Salem State College	pub.	$ 6460	$ 6038†	95%	27%	$ 7840	$ 4658	$12,910
Simmons College	ind.	$30,000	$11,500	99%	12%	$18,344	$23,156	$42,174
Smith College	ind.	$36,058	$12,050	92%	100%	$33,717	$14,391	$20,960
Stonehill College	ind.	$30,150	$11,830	97%	25%	$20,949	$21,031	$25,603
Suffolk University	ind.	$25,954	$13,970	82%	13%	$15,063	$24,861	NR
Tufts University	ind.	$38,840	$10,518	90%	100%	$30,298	$19,060	$23,687
University of Massachusetts Amherst	pub.	$10,232	$ 8114	85%	21%	$12,021	$ 6325	$21,614
University of Massachusetts Boston	pub.	$ 9111	NA	93%	47%	$10,774	—	$18,902

NA = not applicable; NR = not reported; * = includes room and board; † = room only; — = not available.

College Costs At-a-Glance

College Costs At-a-Glance	Institutional Control ind.=independent; pub.=public	Tuition and Fees	Room and Board	Percent of Eligible Freshmen Receiving Need-Based Gift Awards	Percent of Freshmen Whose Need Was Fully Met	Average Financial Aid Package for Freshmen	Average Net Cost After Aid	Average Indebtedness Upon Graduation
Massachusetts—*continued*								
University of Massachusetts Dartmouth	pub.	$ 8858	$ 8716	100%	61%	$11,080	$ 6494	$21,714
University of Massachusetts Lowell	pub.	$ 9181	$ 7519	92%	77%	$ 9615	$ 7085	$20,267
Wellesley College	ind.	$36,640	$11,336	96%	100%	$35,289	$12,687	$12,639
Wentworth Institute of Technology	ind.	$21,800	$10,500	34%	4%	$10,540	$21,760	$35,000
Western New England College	ind.	$27,470	$10,554	100%	14%	$19,273	$18,751	NR
Westfield State College	pub.	$ 6515	$ 7204	68%	16%	$ 7285	$ 6434	$17,059
Wheaton College	ind.	$38,860	$ 9150	91%	57%	$29,872	$18,138	$24,428
Wheelock College	ind.	$28,160	$ 1120	99%	20%	$19,739	$ 9541	$35,726
Williams College	ind.	$37,640	$ 9890	100%	100%	$39,641	$ 7889	$ 9214
Worcester Polytechnic Institute	ind.	$36,930	$10,880	98%	39%	$25,312	$22,498	$37,175
Worcester State College	pub.	$ 6170	$ 8527	87%	40%	$ 8704	$ 5993	$16,063
Michigan								
Adrian College	ind.	$24,440	$ 7460	84%	87%	$15,714	$16,186	$17,160
Albion College	ind.	$28,880	$ 8190	100%	39%	$23,987	$13,083	NR
Alma College	ind.	$24,850	$ 8120	99%	29%	$20,846	$12,124	$30,187
Andrews University	ind.	$19,930	$ 6330	68%	21%	$19,768	$ 6492	$31,510
Calvin College	ind.	$23,165	$ 7970	100%	28%	$17,309	$13,826	$27,400
Central Michigan University	pub.	$ 9720	$ 7668	90%	53%	$10,132	$ 7256	$24,236
Cleary University	ind.	$15,600	NA	77%	8%	$10,735	$ 4865	NR
College for Creative Studies	ind.	$29,985	$ 8500	NR	NR	NR	NR	$45,913
Cornerstone University	ind.	$19,530	$ 6500	100%	16%	$17,597	$ 8433	$26,710
Davenport University (Grand Rapids)	ind.	$10,640	$ 4990†	NR	NR	NR	NR	NR
DeVry University Southfield Center	ind.	$14,080	NA	NR	NR	NR	NR	NR
Eastern Michigan University	pub.	$ 8069	$ 7352	65%	12%	$ 8286	$ 7135	$20,940
Ferris State University	pub.	$ 9162	$ 7944	63%	18%	$14,581	$ 2525	$31,356
Finlandia University	ind.	$17,914	$ 5800	91%	2%	$16,000	$ 7714	$17,500
Grace Bible College	ind.	$13,320	$ 6700	98%	30%	$ 9136	$10,884	$ 8955
Grand Valley State University	pub.	$ 8196	$ 7224	93%	29%	$ 9264	$ 6156	$21,475
Hope College	ind.	$24,920	$ 7650	85%	34%	$22,146	$10,424	$25,889
Kalamazoo College	ind.	$30,723	$ 7443	95%	54%	$23,950	$14,216	NR
Kettering University	ind.	$26,936	$ 6182	84%	8%	$19,961	$13,157	$48,767
Kuyper College	ind.	$15,219	$ 5990	100%	12%	$11,291	$ 9918	$19,488
Lawrence Technological University	ind.	$21,979	$ 8071	97%	20%	$17,986	$12,064	$37,238
Madonna University	ind.	$12,430	$ 6440	97%	26%	$ 6981	$11,889	NR
Michigan State University	pub.	$10,214	$ 7026	53%	29%	$10,789	$ 6451	$17,347
Michigan Technological University	pub.	$10,761	$ 7738	81%	22%	$10,858	$ 7641	$14,184
Northern Michigan University	pub.	$ 7076	$ 7636	53%	25%	$ 7495	$ 7217	$18,498
Northwood University	ind.	$17,544	$ 7548	83%	28%	$15,694	$ 9398	$27,544
Oakland University	pub.	$ 8055	$ 7105	76%	16%	$ 9487	$ 5673	$18,428
Olivet College	ind.	$19,244	$ 6772	100%	30%	$15,631	$10,385	$24,151
Saginaw Valley State University	pub.	$ 6492	$ 6830	67%	24%	$ 7167	$ 6155	$23,561
Spring Arbor University	ind.	$19,240	$ 6650	100%	77%	$21,242	$ 4648	$22,875

NA = not applicable; NR = not reported; * = includes room and board; † = room only; — = not available.

College Costs At-a-Glance

	Institutional Control ind.=independent; pub.=public	Tuition and Fees	Room and Board	Percent of Eligible Freshmen Receiving Need-Based Gift Awards	Percent of Freshmen Whose Need Was Fully Met	Average Financial Aid Package for Freshmen	Average Net Cost After Aid	Average Indebtedness Upon Graduation
Michigan—*continued*								
University of Michigan	pub.	$11,927	$8590	49%	90%	$ 8959	$11,558	$25,586
University of Michigan–Dearborn	pub.	$ 8529	NA	72%	10%	$ 8508	$ 21	$22,644
University of Michigan–Flint	pub.	$ 7775	$6800	65%	13%	$ 7031	$ 7544	$24,090
Wayne State University	pub.	$ 8109	$6932	78%	11%	$11,827	$ 3214	$19,618
Western Michigan University	pub.	$ 7928	$7377	71%	35%	$13,000	$ 2305	$18,900
Minnesota								
Augsburg College	ind.	$27,513	NR	96%	24%	$23,065	$ 4448	$25,155
Bethany Lutheran College	ind.	$18,710	$5800	100%	34%	$14,910	$ 9600	$21,876
Bethel University	ind.	$25,860	$7620	100%	16%	$17,066	$16,414	$30,747
Carleton College	ind.	$38,046	$9993	100%	100%	$32,961	$15,078	$20,083
College of Saint Benedict	ind.	$28,668	$7959	99%	49%	$22,406	$14,221	NR
The College of St. Scholastica	ind.	$26,489	$6972	81%	16%	$21,072	$12,389	$36,075
College of Visual Arts	ind.	$23,194	NA	100%	2%	$11,474	$11,720	$46,000
Concordia College	ind.	$25,710	$6825	100%	28%	$18,678	$13,857	$29,529
Concordia University, St. Paul	ind.	$26,400	$7250	100%	21%	$19,937	$13,713	$33,775
Crossroads College	ind.	$13,210	$3900†	59%	5%	$ 4120	$12,990	$14,941
Crown College	ind.	$19,774	$7366	60%	17%	$16,158	$10,982	$31,421
DeVry University	ind.	$14,080	NR	100%	NR	$ 9410	$ 4670	NR
Gustavus Adolphus College	ind.	$29,990	$7460	100%	11%	$26,550	$10,900	$25,672
Hamline University	ind.	$28,152	$7784	100%	25%	$22,852	$13,084	$31,577
Macalester College	ind.	$38,174	$8768	99%	100%	$30,242	$16,700	$17,304
Martin Luther College	ind.	$10,660	$4140	81%	30%	$ 9388	$ 5412	$15,151
Minneapolis College of Art and Design	ind.	$28,600	$4340†	98%	13%	$14,342	$18,598	$53,646
Minnesota State University Mankato	pub.	$ 6263	$5732	61%	38%	$ 6529	$ 5466	$22,962
Minnesota State University Moorhead	pub.	$ 6144	$5936	48%	NR	$ 5810	$ 6270	$24,493
Northwestern College	ind.	$23,180	$7426	97%	9%	$15,864	$14,742	$24,224
St. Catherine University	ind.	$27,414	$7090	90%	10%	$28,247	$ 6257	$30,886
St. Cloud State University	pub.	$ 6147	$5770	78%	65%	$10,612	$ 1305	$24,484
Saint John's University	ind.	$28,628	$7248	95%	48%	$24,272	$11,604	NR
Saint Mary's University of Minnesota	ind.	$25,570	$6760	100%	19%	$19,607	$12,723	$33,639
St. Olaf College	ind.	$35,500	$8200	100%	100%	$26,626	$17,074	$25,273
Southwest Minnesota State University	pub.	$ 6696	$5984	64%	23%	$ 8262	$ 4418	$18,003
University of Minnesota, Crookston	pub.	$ 9381	$5670	97%	43%	$11,080	$ 3971	$26,565
University of Minnesota, Duluth	pub.	$10,260	$6078	96%	66%	$ 8994	$ 7344	$20,933
University of Minnesota, Morris	pub.	$10,006	$6710	NR	NR	NR	NR	NR
University of Minnesota, Twin Cities Campus	pub.	$10,273	$7280	98%	50%	$13,272	$ 4281	$23,811
University of St. Thomas	ind.	$27,822	$7614	99%	55%	$20,936	$14,500	$34,869
Winona State University	pub.	$ 7627	$6430	59%	8%	$ 5266	$ 8791	$26,236
Mississippi								
Alcorn State University	pub.	$ 4488	$5016	88%	55%	$ 9798	—	$18,123
Belhaven College	ind.	$16,780	$6120	99%	12%	$13,589	$ 9311	$23,914
Delta State University	pub.	$ 4450	$5476	NR	NR	NR	NR	$22,300

NA = not applicable; NR = not reported; * = includes room and board; † = room only; — = not available.

College Costs At-a-Glance

	Institutional Control ind.=independent; pub.=public	Tuition and Fees	Room and Board	Percent of Eligible Freshmen Receiving Need-Based Gift Awards	Percent of Freshmen Whose Need Was Fully Met	Average Financial Aid Package for Freshmen	Average Net Cost After Aid	Average Indebtedness Upon Graduation
Mississippi—*continued*								
Millsaps College	ind.	$24,754	$8800	99%	45%	$24,443	$ 9111	$ 26,576
Mississippi College	ind.	$13,290	$5800	70%	32%	$14,557	$ 4533	$ 24,508
Mississippi State University	pub.	$ 5151	$7333	99%	17%	$ 6488	$ 5996	$ 21,232
Mississippi University for Women	pub.	$ 4423	$4981	74%	89%	$ 8304	$ 1100	$ 18,506
University of Mississippi	pub.	$ 5106	$7778	89%	13%	$ 8111	$ 4773	$ 20,047
University of Southern Mississippi	pub.	$ 5096	$6032	65%	23%	$ 7573	$ 3555	$ 17,350
Wesley College	ind.	$ 8040	$2440	100%	NR	$ 5500	$ 4980	$ 8700
Missouri								
Avila University	ind.	$20,300	$6200	98%	96%	$11,847	$14,653	$ 16,508
Central Christian College of the Bible	ind.	$10,100	$5650	59%	28%	NR	NR	$ 13,540
Central Methodist University	ind.	$17,980	$6000	89%	17%	$15,778	$ 8202	$ 26,487
College of the Ozarks	ind.	$ 0	$5000	100%	27%	$14,523	—	$ 4843
Columbia College	ind.	$14,576	$5898	100%	14%	$12,841	$ 7633	$ 17,101
Culver-Stockton College	ind.	$21,750	$7200	100%	18%	$20,438	$ 8512	$ 22,996
DeVry University	ind.	$14,080	NA	79%	1%	$10,782	$ 3298	$ 8969
Drury University	ind.	$19,013	$6703	96%	100%	$ 7880	$17,836	$ 18,384
Evangel University	ind.	$15,020	$5410	92%	13%	$ 9560	$10,870	NR
Hannibal-LaGrange College	ind.	$14,506	$5270	82%	NR	$13,477	$ 6299	$ 16,689
Kansas City Art Institute	ind.	$28,580	$8710	100%	20%	$20,773	$16,517	$ 23,375
Lincoln University	pub.	$ 6175	$4660	72%	13%	$ 8287	$ 2548	$ 21,255
Lindenwood University	ind.	$13,000	$6500	67%	35%	$ 6374	$13,126	$ 11,852
Maryville University of Saint Louis	ind.	$21,145	$8300	99%	12%	$14,449	$14,996	$ 23,155
Missouri Baptist University	ind.	$16,872	$7070	NR	NR	NR	NR	NR
Missouri Southern State University	pub.	$ 4535	$5440	78%	46%	$ 9483	$ 492	$ 18,331
Missouri State University	pub.	$ 6256	NR	89%	22%	$ 6989	—	$ 18,379
Missouri University of Science and Technology	pub.	$ 8498	$7035	60%	60%	$11,611	$ 3922	$ 23,760
Missouri Valley College	ind.	$15,950	$6050	100%	38%	$13,250	$ 8750	$ 16,950
Missouri Western State University	pub.	$ 5560	$5868	97%	16%	$ 7556	$ 3872	NR
Northwest Missouri State University	pub.	$ 5529	$6876	83%	36%	$ 8680	$ 3725	$ 19,861
Park University	ind.	$ 7644	$5805	34%	43%	$ 5313	$ 8136	$ 12,800
Rockhurst University	ind.	$25,890	$7080	82%	27%	$24,588	$ 8382	NR
St. Louis Christian College	ind.	$ 9500	$3300	100%	4%	$11,202	$ 1598	$ 20,166
St. Louis College of Pharmacy	ind.	$21,925	$8154	100%	15%	$13,080	$16,999	$105,576
Saint Louis University	ind.	$30,728	$8760	97%	19%	$20,775	$18,713	$ 29,298
Saint Luke's College	ind.	$ 9520	NA	NR	NR	NR	NR	NR
Southeast Missouri State University	pub.	$ 6255	$5935	92%	20%	$ 7654	$ 4536	$ 18,893
Southwest Baptist University	ind.	$16,530	$5470	69%	36%	$15,192	$ 6808	NR
Stephens College	ind.	$23,000	$8730	100%	15%	$20,183	$11,547	$ 21,960
Truman State University	pub.	$ 6692	$6290	73%	70%	$ 7991	$ 4991	$ 16,858
University of Central Missouri	pub.	$ 7311	$6320	48%	19%	$ 7048	$ 6583	$ 18,549
University of Missouri–Columbia	pub.	$ 8467	$8100	90%	21%	$13,594	$ 2973	$ 20,889
University of Missouri–Kansas City	pub.	$ 8273	$7881	92%	14%	$10,104	$ 6050	$ 24,151

NA = not applicable; NR = not reported; * = includes room and board; † = room only; — = not available.

College Costs At-a-Glance

	Institutional Control ind.=independent; pub.=public	Tuition and Fees	Room and Board	Percent of Eligible Freshmen Receiving Need-Based Gift Awards	Percent of Freshmen Whose Need Was Fully Met	Average Financial Aid Package for Freshmen	Average Net Cost After Aid	Average Indebtedness Upon Graduation
Missouri—*continued*								
University of Missouri–St. Louis	pub.	$ 8595	$ 7782	93%	12%	$ 8309	$ 8068	$24,016
Washington University in St. Louis	ind.	$38,864	$12,465	96%	100%	$31,564	$19,765	NR
Webster University	ind.	$20,440	$ 9000	84%	NR	NR	NR	$24,224
Westminster College	ind.	$17,990	$ 7120	100%	70%	$16,862	$ 8248	$19,845
William Jewell College	ind.	$24,600	$ 6700	100%	37%	$18,443	$12,857	$24,240
Montana								
Carroll College	ind.	$22,592	$ 7118	83%	23%	$17,292	$12,418	$25,246
Montana State University	pub.	$ 5798	$ 7070	75%	8%	$ 9873	$ 2995	$21,015
Montana State University–Billings	pub.	$ 5172	$ 5134	78%	12%	$ 7713	$ 2593	$16,748
Montana Tech of The University of Montana	pub.	$ 5713	$ 6140	88%	23%	$ 7366	$ 4487	$21,000
University of Great Falls	ind.	$15,500	$ 6490	83%	1%	$13,534	$ 8456	$26,450
The University of Montana	pub.	$ 5180	$ 6258	65%	10%	$ 6975	$ 4463	$17,527
The University of Montana Western	pub.	$ 4228	$ 5350	NR	NR	$ 2659	$ 6919	$20,996
Nebraska								
College of Saint Mary	ind.	$21,260	$ 6400	100%	13%	$18,373	$ 9287	$26,244
Concordia University, Nebraska	ind.	$21,250	$ 5520	98%	27%	$15,747	$11,023	$20,393
Creighton University	ind.	$28,542	$ 8516	100%	42%	$25,421	$11,637	$32,560
Dana College	ind.	$20,120	$ 5900	76%	23%	$19,085	$ 6935	$21,170
Doane College	ind.	$20,150	$ 5600	100%	57%	$18,530	$ 7220	$16,896
Grace University	ind.	$14,290	$ 5740	100%	22%	$12,027	$ 8003	$17,820
Hastings College	ind.	$20,782	$ 5702	100%	30%	$14,972	$11,512	$16,750
Midland Lutheran College	ind.	$22,006	$ 5366	99%	56%	$18,874	$ 8498	$23,000
Nebraska Methodist College	ind.	$14,040	$ 6150†	80%	NR	$ 9699	$10,491	$33,643
Nebraska Wesleyan University	ind.	$21,392	$ 5710	100%	14%	$16,154	$10,948	$16,458
University of Nebraska at Kearney	pub.	$ 5426	$ 6330	61%	33%	$ 8903	$ 2853	$18,551
University of Nebraska at Omaha	pub.	$ 5880	$ 6980	67%	NR	$ 2079	$10,781	$19,000
University of Nebraska–Lincoln	pub.	$ 6585	$ 6882	87%	38%	$10,106	$ 3361	$18,958
York College	ind.	$14,000	$ 4500	100%	26%	$14,102	$ 4398	$22,094
Nevada								
DeVry University	ind.	$14,080	NA	100%	NR	$14,661	—	$62,400
University of Nevada, Las Vegas	pub.	$ 4808	$10,456	59%	20%	$ 8308	$ 6956	$19,700
University of Nevada, Reno	pub.	$ 4616	$10,595	83%	16%	$ 5351	$ 9860	$14,303
New Hampshire								
Dartmouth College	ind.	$38,445	$10,779	99%	100%	$34,924	$14,300	$22,126
Franklin Pierce University	ind.	$28,700	$ 9800	89%	15%	$19,282	$19,218	$38,148
Keene State College	pub.	$ 8778	$ 7796	63%	16%	$ 8141	$ 8433	$24,995
Magdalen College	ind.	$12,250	$ 6500	100%	NR	$ 4104	$14,646	$17,500
New England College	ind.	$27,450	$ 9626	99%	22%	$21,642	$15,434	$29,366
Plymouth State University	pub.	$ 8424	$ 8350	56%	21%	$ 7687	$ 9087	$26,636
Rivier College	ind.	$24,290	$ 9154	99%	12%	$17,578	$15,866	$25,959
Saint Anselm College	ind.	$29,205	$11,050	100%	23%	$21,788	$18,467	$35,025
Southern New Hampshire University	ind.	$26,442	$10,176	95%	11%	$16,704	$19,914	NR

NA = not applicable; NR = not reported; * = includes room and board; † = room only; — = not available.

College Costs At-a-Glance

	Institutional Control ind.=independent; pub.=public	Tuition and Fees	Room and Board	Percent of Eligible Freshmen Receiving Need-Based Gift Awards	Percent of Freshmen Whose Need Was Fully Met	Average Financial Aid Package for Freshmen	Average Net Cost After Aid	Average Indebtedness Upon Graduation
New Hampshire—*continued*								
Thomas More College of Liberal Arts	ind.	$13,200	$ 8800	100%	7%	$14,124	$ 7876	$16,667
University of New Hampshire	pub.	$11,738	$ 8596	60%	26%	$17,812	$ 2522	$27,516
University of New Hampshire at Manchester	pub.	$ 9901	NA	23%	16%	$ 6958	$ 2943	$18,919
New Jersey								
Bloomfield College	ind.	$20,080	$ 9500	96%	70%	$24,123	$ 5457	$23,117
Caldwell College	ind.	$23,600	$ 8846	74%	39%	$ 9053	$23,393	$21,873
Centenary College	ind.	$24,930	$ 8900	100%	23%	$19,195	$14,635	$20,649
The College of New Jersey	pub.	$12,308	$ 9612	34%	23%	$ 9900	$12,020	$22,088
DeVry University	ind.	$14,720	NA	82%	NR	$12,638	$ 2082	$24,045
Drew University	ind.	$38,017	$10,368	100%	28%	$28,828	$19,557	$16,640
Fairleigh Dickinson University, College at Florham	ind.	$30,198	$10,548	82%	NR	$18,500	$22,246	NR
Fairleigh Dickinson University, Metropolitan Campus	ind.	$28,084	$10,914	89%	NR	NR	NR	NR
Felician College	ind.	$25,050	$ 9700	70%	13%	$16,790	$17,960	$16,238
Georgian Court University	ind.	$23,360	$ 9112	100%	18%	$22,177	$10,295	$33,620
Kean University	pub.	$ 9179	$ 9677	100%	7%	$ 8744	$10,112	$17,723
Monmouth University	ind.	$24,098	$ 9221	95%	26%	$19,400	$13,919	$30,853
Montclair State University	pub.	$ 9428	$10,050	43%	24%	$ 6992	$12,486	NR
New Jersey City University	pub.	$ 8727	$ 8613	85%	4%	$ 9098	$ 8242	$11,337
New Jersey Institute of Technology	pub.	$12,482	$ 9596	58%	13%	$11,700	$10,378	$27,930
Princeton University	ind.	$34,290	$11,405	100%	100%	$32,424	$13,271	$ 5955
Ramapo College of New Jersey	pub.	$10,765	$10,830	45%	20%	$11,311	$10,284	$16,219
The Richard Stockton College of New Jersey	pub.	$10,469	$10,204	43%	33%	$15,695	$ 4978	$24,454
Rider University	ind.	$27,730	$10,280	99%	19%	$20,878	$17,132	$33,156
Rowan University	pub.	$10,908	$ 9616	35%	28%	$ 5953	$14,571	$22,746
Rutgers, The State University of New Jersey, Camden	pub.	$11,358	$ 9378	66%	53%	$12,937	$ 7799	$19,800
Rutgers, The State University of New Jersey, Newark	pub.	$11,083	$10,639	69%	49%	$12,830	$ 8892	$17,700
Rutgers, The State University of New Jersey, New Brunswick	pub.	$11,540	$10,232	57%	63%	$14,846	$ 6926	$16,300
Thomas Edison State College	pub.	$ 4555	NA	NR	NR	NR	NR	NR
William Paterson University of New Jersey	pub.	$10,492	$ 9990	54%	45%	$13,834	$ 6648	$21,459
New Mexico								
New Mexico Institute of Mining and Technology	pub.	$ 4352	$ 5320	44%	47%	$ 9072	$ 600	$ 8129
New Mexico State University	pub.	$ 4758	$ 5976	59%	1%	$ 6971	$ 3763	NR
St. John's College	ind.	$40,392	$ 9562	93%	92%	$24,650	$25,304	$24,875
University of the Southwest	ind.	$14,500	$ 7050	50%	39%	$10,248	$11,302	NR
New York								
Adelphi University	ind.	$23,925	$10,000	79%	3%	$16,400	$17,525	NR
Alfred University	ind.	$25,246	$16,174	100%	15%	$23,510	$17,910	$26,962
Bard College	ind.	$38,374	$10,866	94%	60%	$31,657	$17,583	$20,201
Barnard College	ind.	$37,538	$11,926	97%	100%	$35,625	$13,839	$15,084
Bernard M. Baruch College of the City University of New York	pub.	$ 4320	NA	73%	28%	$ 6005	—	$12,602
Buffalo State College, State University of New York	pub.	$ 5685	$ 9064	82%	57%	$ 5176	$ 9573	$18,187
Canisius College	ind.	$28,157	$10,150	100%	37%	$26,014	$12,293	$30,600

NA = not applicable; NR = not reported; * = includes room and board; † = room only; — = not available.

College Costs At-a-Glance

	Institutional Control ind.=independent; pub.=public	Tuition and Fees	Room and Board	Percent of Eligible Freshmen Receiving Need-Based Gift Awards	Percent of Freshmen Whose Need Was Fully Met	Average Financial Aid Package for Freshmen	Average Net Cost After Aid	Average Indebtedness Upon Graduation
New York—*continued*								
Cazenovia College	ind.	$22,894	$ 9502	100%	22%	$20,617	$11,779	NR
City College of the City University of New York	pub.	$ 4278	$ 8250†	98%	74%	$ 8640	$ 3888	$16,950
Clarkson University	ind.	$32,910	$11,118	83%	8%	$25,518	$18,510	$33,625
Colgate University	ind.	$39,545	$ 9625	100%	100%	$36,389	$12,781	$20,164
The College at Brockport, State University of New York	pub.	$ 5444	$ 8615	90%	20%	$ 9355	$ 4704	$24,808
The College of New Rochelle	ind.	$26,426	$ 9600	93%	7%	$24,073	$11,953	$25,055
College of Staten Island of the City University of New York	pub.	$ 4378	NA	99%	5%	$ 6167	—	NR
Columbia University, School of General Studies	ind.	$37,958	$12,045	NR	NR	NR	NR	NR
Concordia College–New York	ind.	$23,430	$ 8745	93%	16%	$22,976	$ 9199	$24,153
Cooper Union for the Advancement of Science and Art	ind.	$34,600	$13,700	100%	89%	$33,000	$15,300	$ 7500
Cornell University	ind.	$37,954	$12,110	92%	100%	$30,530	$19,534	$23,485
Daemen College	ind.	$19,870	$ 9050	93%	26%	$16,778	$12,142	$20,465
DeVry College of New York	ind.	$14,720	NA	98%	NR	$14,664	$ 56	$29,136
Dominican College	ind.	$20,300	$ 9730	100%	11%	$14,595	$15,435	$17,784
Dowling College	ind.	$20,310	$ 9200	96%	NR	$16,414	$13,096	$48,161
D'Youville College	ind.	$19,030	$ 9300	99%	20%	$15,119	$13,211	NR
Elmira College	ind.	$33,250	$10,100	100%	19%	$25,002	$18,348	$25,233
Eugene Lang College The New School for Liberal Arts	ind.	$33,060	$15,260	98%	12%	$30,199	$18,121	$21,511
Fashion Institute of Technology	pub.	$ 5008	$10,950	68%	18%	$ 9083	$ 6875	$22,857
Five Towns College	ind.	$17,800	$11,850	86%	83%	$12,000	$17,650	$17,800
Fordham University	ind.	$35,257	$12,980	98%	30%	$23,809	$24,428	$31,300
Hamilton College	ind.	$38,600	$ 9810	100%	100%	$33,665	$14,745	$18,259
Hartwick College	ind.	$31,900	$ 8685	100%	9%	$24,857	$15,728	$30,802
Hilbert College	ind.	$17,350	$ 6950	100%	18%	$11,070	$13,230	$24,444
Hobart and William Smith Colleges	ind.	$38,860	$ 9686	100%	79%	$28,492	$20,054	$26,334
Hofstra University	ind.	$28,630	$10,825	89%	19%	$17,523	$21,932	NR
Houghton College	ind.	$22,990	$ 6930	100%	16%	$21,307	$ 8613	$30,150
Hunter College of the City University of New York	pub.	$ 4349	$ 5311†	NR	NR	$ 5215	$ 4445	$ 6801
Iona College	ind.	$27,500	$11,300	77%	25%	$18,391	$20,409	$19,905
Ithaca College	ind.	$30,606	$11,162	98%	47%	$24,152	$17,616	NR
The Jewish Theological Seminary	ind.	$15,000	$ 9200†	100%	33%	$17,706	$ 6494	$18,444
John Jay College of Criminal Justice of the City University of New York	pub.	$ 4330	NA	47%	NR	$ 6672	—	$14,000
The Juilliard School	ind.	$28,640	$11,250	100%	30%	$28,400	$11,490	$26,000
Keuka College	ind.	$21,760	$ 8850	100%	23%	$17,753	$12,857	$16,119
Le Moyne College	ind.	$25,830	$ 9990	94%	23%	$19,710	$16,110	$19,123
Long Island University, Brooklyn Campus	ind.	$27,358	$10,140	98%	49%	$13,892	$23,606	$39,000
Long Island University, C.W. Post Campus	ind.	$27,400	$10,140	87%	18%	$12,500	$25,040	NR
Manhattan College	ind.	$23,385	$ 9770	90%	21%	$15,197	$17,958	$35,130
Manhattanville College	ind.	$32,760	$13,580	97%	9%	$24,581	$21,759	$23,963
Mannes College The New School for Music	ind.	$32,150	$15,260	75%	12%	$26,568	$20,842	$16,370
Marist College	ind.	$25,596	$10,730	99%	26%	$15,909	$20,417	$28,374
Marymount Manhattan College	ind.	$21,792	$12,660	98%	8%	$13,011	$21,441	$16,765

NA = not applicable; NR = not reported; * = includes room and board; † = room only; — = not available.

College Costs At-a-Glance

	Institutional Control ind.=independent; pub.=public	Tuition and Fees	Room and Board	Percent of Eligible Freshmen Receiving Need-Based Gift Awards	Percent of Freshmen Whose Need Was Fully Met	Average Financial Aid Package for Freshmen	Average Net Cost After Aid	Average Indebtedness Upon Graduation
New York—*continued*								
Medgar Evers College of the City University of New York	pub.	$ 4302	NA	98%	NR	$ 3170	$ 1132	NR
Molloy College	ind.	$19,450	NA	97%	21%	$12,351	$ 7099	$22,754
Monroe College (Bronx)	ind.	$11,212	$ 7240	81%	42%	$10,325	$ 8127	$21,825
Monroe College (New Rochelle)	ind.	$11,272	$ 7240	97%	60%	$11,256	$ 7256	$25,913
Mount Saint Mary College	ind.	$20,745	$11,030	96%	23%	$14,463	$17,312	$30,412
Nazareth College of Rochester	ind.	$24,076	$ 9916	100%	20%	$18,052	$15,940	$33,792
The New School for Jazz and Contemporary Music	ind.	$32,150	$15,260	53%	12%	$26,420	$20,990	$20,411
New York City College of Technology of the City University of New York	pub.	$ 4339	NA	100%	5%	$ 6582	—	NR
New York University	ind.	$37,372	$12,910	97%	NR	$26,823	$23,459	$34,850
Niagara University	ind.	$24,700	$10,250	97%	54%	$19,624	$15,326	$29,018
Nyack College	ind.	$18,200	$ 3900	100%	16%	$17,457	$ 4643	$23,583
Pace University	ind.	$31,357	$11,180	100%	16%	$27,024	$15,513	$29,622
Parsons The New School for Design	ind.	$34,460	$15,260	99%	10%	$28,141	$21,579	$25,582
Paul Smith's College	ind.	$20,250	$ 8350	100%	9%	$14,351	$14,249	$20,168
Polytechnic Institute of NYU	ind.	$32,644	$ 8721	89%	70%	$27,210	$14,155	$26,619
Pratt Institute	ind.	$34,880	$ 9756	82%	NR	$13,142	$31,494	$27,125
Purchase College, State University of New York	pub.	$ 6421	$ 9908	78%	7%	$ 7473	$ 8856	$20,209
Rensselaer Polytechnic Institute	ind.	$37,990	$10,730	100%	72%	$32,707	$16,013	$30,375
Roberts Wesleyan College	ind.	$23,780	$ 8520	100%	16%	$20,104	$12,196	$22,829
Rochester Institute of Technology	ind.	$28,035	$ 9381	94%	76%	$19,800	$17,616	NR
Russell Sage College	ind.	$26,540	$ 9350	72%	11%	$28,738	$ 7152	$27,500
Sage College of Albany	ind.	$19,290	$ 9350	61%	5%	$20,955	$ 7685	$19,100
St. John Fisher College	ind.	$23,390	$10,040	100%	39%	$20,822	$12,608	$29,288
St. John's University	ind.	$28,790	$12,570	91%	10%	$21,587	$19,773	$29,657
St. Lawrence University	ind.	$37,905	$ 9645	100%	55%	$36,230	$11,320	$29,941
Sarah Lawrence College	ind.	$40,350	$13,104	89%	66%	$26,990	$26,464	$15,581
Skidmore College	ind.	$38,888	$10,378	94%	86%	$31,770	$17,496	$19,163
State University of New York at Binghamton	pub.	$ 6692	$ 9774	81%	72%	$ 9651	$ 6815	$14,541
State University of New York at Fredonia	pub.	$ 6208	$ 9140	87%	13%	$ 7653	$ 7695	$23,452
State University of New York at New Paltz	pub.	$ 6039	$ 8690	41%	19%	$ 7729	$ 7000	$20,000
State University of New York at Oswego	pub.	$ 6651	NR	91%	36%	$10,253	—	$22,117
State University of New York at Plattsburgh	pub.	$ 5422	$ 8250	94%	32%	$10,409	$ 3263	$22,894
State University of New York College at Cortland	pub.	$ 6145	$ 9790	85%	18%	$10,158	$ 5777	NR
State University of New York College at Geneseo	pub.	$ 6278	$ 9070	50%	72%	$ 5260	$10,088	$18,700
State University of New York College at Old Westbury	pub.	$ 4350	$ 9032	NR	NR	$ 6880	$ 6502	$15,533
State University of New York College at Oneonta	pub.	$ 6230	$ 8680	88%	18%	$10,439	$ 4471	$19,900
State University of New York College at Potsdam	pub.	$ 5772	$ 8820	94%	90%	$13,404	$ 1188	$20,291
State University of New York College of Agriculture and Technology at Cobleskill	pub.	$ 6311	$ 9460	89%	16%	$ 5773	$ 9998	$22,475
State University of New York College of Environmental Science and Forestry	pub.	$ 4970	$11,920	100%	100%	$12,500	$ 4390	$21,160
State University of New York College of Technology at Canton	pub.	$ 5944	$ 8970	NR	NR	NR	NR	NR
State University of New York Institute of Technology	pub.	$ 5413	$ 8320	93%	13%	$ 8386	$ 5347	NR

NA = not applicable; NR = not reported; * = includes room and board; † = room only; — = not available.

College Costs At-a-Glance

	Institutional Control ind.=independent; pub.=public	Tuition and Fees	Room and Board	Percent of Eligible Freshmen Receiving Need-Based Gift Awards	Percent of Freshmen Whose Need Was Fully Met	Average Financial Aid Package for Freshmen	Average Net Cost After Aid	Average Indebtedness Upon Graduation
New York—*continued*								
State University of New York Upstate Medical University	pub.	$ 5218	$ 5768†	NR	NR	NR	NR	NR
Stony Brook University, State University of New York	pub.	$ 6430	$ 9132	93%	14%	$ 9178	$ 6384	$17,375
Syracuse University	ind.	$33,440	$11,656	90%	65%	$24,710	$20,386	$27,152
Union College	ind.	*$48,552	NR	100%	89%	$30,046	$18,506	$23,000
University at Albany, State University of New York	pub.	$ 6388	$ 9778	91%	16%	$ 8961	$ 7205	$18,189
University at Buffalo, the State University of New York	pub.	$ 6595	$ 9058	31%	3%	$ 6992	$ 8661	$52,591
University of Rochester	ind.	$37,250	$10,810	99%	100%	$31,690	$16,370	$27,121
Utica College	ind.	$26,058	$10,430	100%	14%	$21,669	$14,819	$31,899
Vassar College	ind.	$40,210	$ 9040	100%	100%	$36,413	$12,837	$19,910
Wagner College	ind.	$31,050	$ 9250	99%	27%	$19,767	$20,533	$34,326
Wells College	ind.	$29,680	$ 9000	100%	27%	$18,810	$19,870	$18,277
York College of the City University of New York	pub.	$ 4262	NA	100%	NR	$ 3586	$ 676	$ 9351
North Carolina								
Appalachian State University	pub.	$ 4275	$ 6200	84%	51%	$ 7732	$ 2743	$15,080
Barton College	ind.	$19,938	$ 6782	75%	18%	$20,567	$ 6153	$35,483
Belmont Abbey College	ind.	$20,094	$ 9866	100%	23%	$15,534	$14,426	$17,500
Brevard College	ind.	$20,040	$ 7540	100%	51%	$17,700	$ 9880	$19,500
Cabarrus College of Health Sciences	ind.	$ 9950	NA	NR	NR	NR	NR	NR
Catawba College	ind.	$23,740	$ 8200	64%	31%	$20,780	$11,160	$20,133
Chowan University	ind.	$18,120	$ 7210	100%	17%	$13,482	$11,848	$23,327
Davidson College	ind.	$33,479	$ 9471	98%	100%	$21,624	$21,326	$25,025
DeVry University	ind.	$14,080	NA	67%	NR	$14,346	—	NR
Duke University	ind.	$38,741	$11,154	96%	100%	$33,817	$16,078	$24,205
Elon University	ind.	$24,076	$ 7770	93%	NR	$15,747	$16,099	$23,392
Gardner-Webb University	ind.	$20,200	$ 6500	96%	32%	$17,575	$ 9125	NR
Greensboro College	ind.	$22,248	$ 8420	NR	NR	$19,803	$10,865	NR
Guilford College	ind.	$27,450	$ 7560	100%	1%	$20,304	$14,706	$23,680
Johnson & Wales University—Charlotte Campus	ind.	$22,585	$ 8892	94%	7%	$17,327	$14,150	$27,500
Johnson C. Smith University	ind.	$15,754	$ 6132	78%	NR	$12,856	$ 9030	$34,308
John Wesley College	ind.	$10,844	$ 2344†	78%	NR	$ 7400	$ 5788	$15,000
Lees-McRae College	ind.	$20,500	$ 7000	87%	4%	$13,950	$13,550	NR
Methodist University	ind.	$22,260	$ 8400	89%	87%	$14,447	$16,213	$26,240
Montreat College	ind.	$19,080	$ 6000	100%	25%	$13,931	$11,149	$16,379
Mount Olive College	ind.	$13,776	$ 5540	100%	15%	$ 9407	$ 9909	$13,854
North Carolina Agricultural and Technical State University	pub.	$ 3583	$ 5459	78%	4%	$ 6272	$ 2770	$17,605
North Carolina State University	pub.	$ 5274	$ 7982	99%	59%	$10,401	$ 2855	$14,996
North Carolina Wesleyan College	ind.	$20,790	$ 7380	100%	98%	$13,622	$14,548	$ 7269
Peace College	ind.	$23,958	$ 8250	100%	16%	$20,600	$11,608	$24,128
Roanoke Bible College	ind.	$10,320	$ 6790	89%	32%	$ 9822	$ 7288	$21,314
St. Andrews Presbyterian College	ind.	$20,375	$ 8425	100%	35%	$13,596	$15,204	$17,341
Salem College	ind.	$20,420	$10,705	95%	100%	$24,045	$ 7080	$19,000
The University of North Carolina at Asheville	pub.	$ 4255	$ 6620	97%	69%	$10,592	$ 283	$14,685

NA = not applicable; NR = not reported; * = includes room and board; † = room only; — = not available.

College Costs At-a-Glance

	Institutional Control ind.=independent; pub.=public	Tuition and Fees	Room and Board	Percent of Eligible Freshmen Receiving Need-Based Gift Awards	Percent of Freshmen Whose Need Was Fully Met	Average Financial Aid Package for Freshmen	Average Net Cost After Aid	Average Indebtedness Upon Graduation
North Carolina—*continued*								
The University of North Carolina at Chapel Hill	pub.	$ 5397	$ 7334	100%	97%	$11,678	$ 1053	NR
The University of North Carolina at Greensboro	pub.	$ 4276	$ 6506	45%	52%	$ 8882	$ 1900	$16,326
The University of North Carolina at Pembroke	pub.	$ 2007	$ 6250	96%	36%	$ 9656	—	NR
The University of North Carolina Wilmington	pub.	$ 4528	$ 7370	92%	47%	$ 9221	$ 2677	$15,476
Wake Forest University	ind.	$38,622	$10,410	95%	87%	$28,753	$20,279	$24,827
Warren Wilson College	ind.	$24,196	$ 7770	91%	11%	$16,460	$15,506	$17,533
Western Carolina University	pub.	$ 4325	$ 5462	99%	57%	$ 8766	$ 1021	$11,705
Wingate University	ind.	$20,140	$ 8050	79%	23%	$19,420	$ 8770	$23,279
North Dakota								
Jamestown College	ind.	$15,585	$ 5155	100%	27%	$12,497	$ 8243	$25,725
Mayville State University	pub.	$ 5654	$ 4272	87%	51%	$ 4958	$ 4968	$19,338
Medcenter One College of Nursing	ind.	$10,017	NA	NR	NR	NR	NR	NR
Minot State University	pub.	$ 5044	$ 5234	65%	27%	$ 4354	$ 5924	$15,193
North Dakota State University	pub.	$ 5264	$ 6220	67%	27%	$ 7084	$ 4400	NR
University of Mary	ind.	$12,584	$ 4940	100%	NR	$11,029	$ 6495	NR
University of North Dakota	pub.	$ 6513	$ 5472	57%	42%	$ 4787	$ 7198	$21,743
Valley City State University	pub.	$ 5781	$ 4071	79%	34%	$ 5877	$ 3975	$20,627
Ohio								
Antioch University McGregor	ind.	$15,120	NA	NR	NR	NR	NR	$20,625
Art Academy of Cincinnati	ind.	$21,880	$ 6000†	98%	17%	$11,801	$16,079	$25,030
Ashland University	ind.	$25,640	$ 7358	100%	NR	$23,910	$ 9088	$18,250
Baldwin-Wallace College	ind.	$23,524	$ 7728	100%	57%	$20,689	$10,563	$19,586
Bluffton University	ind.	$22,920	$ 7596	100%	68%	$22,348	$ 8168	$27,701
Bowling Green State University	pub.	$ 9060	$ 7220	77%	15%	$11,284	$ 4996	$26,860
Case Western Reserve University	ind.	$35,202	$10,450	100%	88%	$34,960	$10,692	$37,892
Cedarville University	ind.	$22,304	$ 5006	68%	51%	$18,217	$ 9093	$23,151
Central State University	pub.	$ 5294	$ 7402	97%	NR	NR	NR	NR
The Cleveland Institute of Art	ind.	$31,010	$ 9148	100%	15%	$22,720	$17,438	$65,000
Cleveland State University	pub.	$ 7970	$ 8700	81%	8%	$ 8047	$ 8623	NR
College of Mount St. Joseph	ind.	$22,000	$ 6900	100%	16%	$18,084	$10,816	$29,438
The College of Wooster	ind.	*$43,900	NR	100%	53%	$28,632	$15,268	$29,815
Columbus College of Art & Design	ind.	$23,564	$ 6750	100%	14%	$17,474	$12,840	$34,592
Defiance College	ind.	$22,895	$ 7750	75%	24%	$19,945	$10,700	$23,667
Denison University	ind.	$35,300	$ 8610	100%	80%	$31,371	$12,539	NR
DeVry University (Columbus)	ind.	$14,080	NA	88%	4%	$14,123	—	$40,467
Franciscan University of Steubenville	ind.	$19,650	$ 6750	93%	14%	$11,563	$14,837	$29,256
Heidelberg University	ind.	$21,330	$ 8384	100%	27%	$17,973	$11,741	$30,589
John Carroll University	ind.	$28,840	$ 8330	100%	22%	$25,347	$11,823	$19,079
Kent State University	pub.	$ 8430	$ 7200	78%	56%	$ 7959	$ 7671	$23,957
Kenyon College	ind.	$40,980	$ 7260	93%	50%	$29,202	$19,038	$19,462
Lourdes College	ind.	$14,730	NA	80%	NR	$14,003	$ 727	NR
Malone University	ind.	$21,080	$ 7100	100%	18%	$16,949	$11,231	$24,539

NA = not applicable; NR = not reported; * = includes room and board; † = room only; — = not available.

College Costs At-a-Glance

	Institutional Control ind.=independent; pub.=public	Tuition and Fees	Room and Board	Percent of Eligible Freshmen Receiving Need-Based Gift Awards	Percent of Freshmen Whose Need Was Fully Met	Average Financial Aid Package for Freshmen	Average Net Cost After Aid	Average Indebtedness Upon Graduation
Ohio—*continued*								
Marietta College	ind.	$26,080	$7764	87%	49%	$23,317	$10,527	$19,181
Mercy College of Northwest Ohio	ind.	$10,090	NR	57%	NR	$ 7195	$ 2895	$ 8562
Miami University	pub.	$11,887	$8998	84%	40%	$13,870	$ 7015	$26,798
Miami University Hamilton	pub.	$ 4350	NA	NR	NR	NR	NR	NR
Mount Union College	ind.	$23,120	$7050	100%	23%	$18,278	$11,892	$20,982
Mount Vernon Nazarene University	ind.	$20,580	$5890	96%	11%	$15,362	$11,108	$27,863
Muskingum College	ind.	$18,910	$7350	100%	20%	$17,290	$ 8970	$23,405
Notre Dame College	ind.	$22,096	$7372	100%	26%	$21,264	$ 8204	$22,178
Oberlin College	ind.	$38,280	$9870	98%	100%	$30,726	$17,424	$17,579
Ohio Christian University	ind.	$13,960	$5990	75%	25%	$11,000	$ 8950	$30,000
Ohio Northern University	ind.	$31,866	$8280	96%	20%	$26,490	$13,656	$45,753
The Ohio State University	pub.	$ 8676	$7755	91%	22%	$10,986	$ 5445	$19,978
Ohio University	pub.	$ 8907	$8946	42%	16%	$ 7891	$ 9962	$23,041
Ohio University–Chillicothe	pub.	$ 4581	NA	71%	13%	$ 7475	—	$23,041
Ohio University–Eastern	pub.	$ 4395	NA	70%	21%	$ 6195	—	$23,041
Ohio University–Lancaster	pub.	$ 4581	NA	65%	16%	$ 7014	—	$23,041
Ohio University–Southern Campus	pub.	$ 4395	NA	85%	10%	$ 8422	—	$23,041
Ohio University–Zanesville	pub.	$ 4596	NR	73%	25%	$ 7162	—	$23,041
Ohio Wesleyan University	ind.	$33,700	$8270	100%	33%	$26,591	$15,379	$26,704
Pontifical College Josephinum	ind.	$15,697	NR	NR	24%	$11,587	$ 4110	$12,417
Shawnee State University	pub.	$ 5832	$7670	91%	100%	$ 3881	$ 9621	$10,944
Tiffin University	ind.	$17,730	$7985	69%	11%	$14,085	$11,630	$26,010
The University of Akron	pub.	$ 8612	$8311	52%	9%	$ 7200	$ 9723	$18,000
University of Cincinnati	pub.	$ 9399	$9240	42%	6%	$ 8335	$10,304	$24,431
University of Dayton	ind.	$27,330	$7980	96%	44%	$20,985	$14,325	$16,738
The University of Findlay	ind.	$24,670	$8306	89%	10%	$19,022	$13,954	$32,659
Ursuline College	ind.	$22,060	$7350	100%	21%	$18,962	$10,448	$21,294
Wilmington College	ind.	$23,372	$8010	NR	NR	NR	NR	NR
Wittenberg University	ind.	$33,890	$8772	100%	44%	$27,461	$15,201	$24,699
Wright State University	pub.	$ 7278	$7180	77%	12%	$ 8663	$ 5795	$22,829
Xavier University	ind.	$28,570	$9530	97%	28%	$16,676	$21,424	$22,879
Youngstown State University	pub.	$ 6721	$7090	NR	NR	NR	NR	NR
Oklahoma								
DeVry University	ind.	$14,080	NR	25%	NR	$ 3697	$10,383	NR
Hillsdale Free Will Baptist College	ind.	$ 9260	$4700	55%	8%	$10,500	$ 3460	$12,805
Northeastern State University	pub.	$ 4155	$4544	70%	69%	$ 8478	$ 221	$18,573
Northwestern Oklahoma State University	pub.	$ 4111	$3430	88%	52%	$ 6242	$ 1299	$11,541
Oklahoma Baptist University	ind.	$16,790	$5200	96%	70%	$14,713	$ 7277	$17,859
Oklahoma Christian University	ind.	$16,266	$5940	62%	23%	$16,718	$ 5488	$24,377
Oklahoma City University	ind.	$23,400	$9200	79%	25%	$21,998	$10,602	$28,680
Oklahoma Panhandle State University	pub.	$ 4242	$3320	82%	NR	$ 7418	$ 144	NR
Oklahoma State University	pub.	$ 6202	$7402	76%	17%	$10,358	$ 3246	$18,989

NA = not applicable; NR = not reported; * = includes room and board; † = room only; — = not available.

College Costs At-a-Glance

College	Institutional Control ind.=independent; pub.=public	Tuition and Fees	Room and Board	Percent of Eligible Freshmen Receiving Need-Based Gift Awards	Percent of Freshmen Whose Need Was Fully Met	Average Financial Aid Package for Freshmen	Average Net Cost After Aid	Average Indebtedness Upon Graduation
Oklahoma—*continued*								
Oklahoma Wesleyan University	ind.	$16,585	$ 6050	100%	36%	$11,926	$10,709	$22,039
Oral Roberts University	ind.	$18,196	$ 7610	NR	NR	$15,320	$10,486	$34,555
Rogers State University	pub.	$ 4277	$ 6615	86%	1%	$ 5384	$ 5508	$12,250
Southeastern Oklahoma State University	pub.	$ 4316	$ 4290	72%	43%	$ 1049	$ 7557	$ 6852
Southern Nazarene University	ind.	$17,664	$ 6490	NR	NR	NR	NR	NR
Southwestern Christian University	ind.	$ 9800	$ 4600	100%	41%	$ 7925	$ 6475	$17,000
Southwestern Oklahoma State University	pub.	$ 4110	$ 3900	87%	16%	$ 4841	$ 3169	NR
University of Central Oklahoma	pub.	$ 4223	$ 7468	98%	8%	$ 1191	$10,500	$17,385
University of Oklahoma	pub.	$ 5245	$ 7376	9%	51%	$10,698	$ 1923	$20,341
University of Science and Arts of Oklahoma	pub.	$ 4440	$ 4710	98%	26%	$ 8408	$ 742	$15,905
University of Tulsa	ind.	$23,940	$ 7776	39%	48%	$24,118	$ 7598	$13,273
Oregon								
Concordia University	ind.	$23,400	$ 6800	92%	44%	NR	NR	$25,067
Corban College	ind.	$23,202	$ 8068	100%	18%	$15,618	$15,652	$28,347
DeVry University	ind.	$14,080	NA	67%	NR	$ 5536	$ 8544	NR
Eastern Oregon University	pub.	$ 6225	$ 8800	61%	32%	$ 7019	$ 8006	$20,745
George Fox University	ind.	$25,190	$ 8000	100%	44%	$23,459	$ 9731	$23,540
Lewis & Clark College	ind.	$33,726	$ 8820	99%	37%	$26,130	$16,416	$20,611
Linfield College	ind.	$27,414	$ 7860	86%	39%	$22,056	$13,218	$27,140
Marylhurst University	ind.	$16,200	NA	50%	NR	$ 7086	$ 9114	$20,275
Northwest Christian University	ind.	$21,900	$ 6200	100%	21%	$16,822	$11,278	$19,843
Oregon College of Art & Craft	ind.	$20,462	$ 9000	100%	NR	$ 9000	$20,462	$37,000
Oregon Health & Science University	pub.	$14,552	NA	NR	NR	NR	NR	NR
Oregon Institute of Technology	pub.	$ 6297	$ 7132	37%	37%	$ 2864	$10,565	$24,498
Oregon State University	pub.	$ 6187	$ 8208	81%	18%	$ 8812	$ 5583	$20,240
Pacific University	ind.	$28,137	$ 7516	98%	43%	$23,622	$12,031	$24,757
Portland State University	pub.	$ 6147	$ 9486	68%	19%	$ 8262	$ 7371	$19,512
Reed College	ind.	$38,190	$ 9920	94%	98%	$34,730	$13,380	$17,296
Southern Oregon University	pub.	$ 5718	$ 8250	57%	19%	$10,640	$ 3328	$26,000
University of Oregon	pub.	$ 6435	$ 8211	48%	19%	$ 8112	$ 6534	$18,805
University of Portland	ind.	$30,400	$ 8756	96%	12%	$23,432	$15,724	$21,535
Warner Pacific College	ind.	$16,630	$ 6328	89%	9%	$12,257	$10,701	$26,890
Western Oregon University	pub.	$ 5868	$ 7600	84%	20%	$ 8352	$ 5116	$22,037
Willamette University	ind.	$33,960	$ 7950	99%	25%	$27,374	$14,536	$24,465
Pennsylvania								
Albright College	ind.	$30,570	$ 8670	100%	18%	$23,472	$15,768	$31,720
Allegheny College	ind.	$32,000	$ 8000	100%	53%	$27,500	$12,500	NR
Alvernia University	ind.	$24,350	$ 9212	100%	27%	$15,184	$18,378	$28,364
Arcadia University	ind.	$29,700	$10,280	99%	54%	$22,161	$17,819	$32,120
Baptist Bible College of Pennsylvania	ind.	$16,620	$ 6200	100%	10%	$11,278	$11,542	$17,990
Bloomsburg University of Pennsylvania	pub.	$ 6848	$ 6292	46%	90%	$11,003	$ 2137	$19,645
Bryn Athyn College of the New Church	ind.	$10,620	$ 5853	100%	35%	$11,104	$ 5369	$ 8299

NA = not applicable; NR = not reported; * = includes room and board; † = room only; — = not available.

College Costs At-a-Glance

	Institutional Control ind.=independent; pub.=public	Tuition and Fees	Room and Board	Percent of Eligible Freshmen Receiving Need-Based Gift Awards	Percent of Freshmen Whose Need Was Fully Met	Average Financial Aid Package for Freshmen	Average Net Cost After Aid	Average Indebtedness Upon Graduation
Pennsylvania—*continued*								
Bryn Mawr College	ind.	$38,034	$12,000	100%	100%	$34,102	$15,932	$20,019
Bucknell University	ind.	$40,816	$ 9504	100%	97%	$26,800	$23,520	$18,500
Carnegie Mellon University	ind.	$40,920	$10,340	96%	37%	$25,376	$25,884	$29,346
Cedar Crest College	ind.	$28,135	$ 9321	100%	10%	$22,429	$15,027	$24,641
Chatham University	ind.	$27,495	$ 8286	71%	NR	$23,992	$11,789	NR
Chestnut Hill College	ind.	$27,100	$ 8800	100%	17%	$18,787	$17,113	NR
Clarion University of Pennsylvania	pub.	$ 7104	$ 6071	79%	14%	$ 7498	$ 5677	NR
The Curtis Institute of Music	ind.	$ 2290	NR	NR	NR	NR	NR	NR
Delaware Valley College	ind.	$27,292	$ 9750	100%	20%	$18,694	$18,348	$28,929
DeSales University	ind.	$25,800	$ 9330	76%	22%	$17,457	$17,673	$24,720
DeVry University (Fort Washington)	ind.	$14,720	NA	78%	NR	$12,652	$ 2068	$15,638
Dickinson College	ind.	$38,234	$ 9600	96%	87%	$31,343	$16,491	$21,924
Duquesne University	ind.	$25,480	$ 8888	99%	72%	$19,046	$15,322	$29,616
Edinboro University of Pennsylvania	pub.	$ 7042	$ 6650	90%	5%	$ 7124	$ 6568	$13,313
Elizabethtown College	ind.	$30,650	$ 7950	100%	20%	$21,986	$16,614	NR
Franklin & Marshall College	ind.	$38,630	$ 9870	96%	100%	$28,715	$19,785	$30,657
Gannon University	ind.	$22,662	$ 8710	98%	35%	$17,102	$14,270	$26,170
Geneva College	ind.	$21,400	$ 7770	100%	18%	$17,166	$12,004	$29,827
Gettysburg College	ind.	$37,600	$ 9100	96%	96%	$31,997	$14,703	$23,992
Grove City College	ind.	$12,074	$ 6440	100%	12%	$ 6345	$12,169	$24,895
Gwynedd-Mercy College	ind.	$22,790	$ 8990	99%	20%	$14,349	$17,431	$20,636
Harrisburg University of Science and Technology	ind.	$14,750	NA	NR	NR	NR	NR	NR
Haverford College	ind.	$37,525	$11,450	92%	100%	$31,769	$17,206	$17,125
Holy Family University	ind.	$22,950	$ 9900	99%	100%	$19,924	$12,926	$10,023
Immaculata University	ind.	$24,575	$10,400	78%	29%	$16,122	$18,853	NR
Indiana University of Pennsylvania	pub.	$ 6959	$ 8224	73%	8%	$10,135	$ 5048	$23,265
Juniata College	ind.	$30,280	$ 8420	100%	31%	$22,571	$16,129	$21,343
King's College	ind.	$24,680	$ 9370	100%	19%	$20,483	$13,567	$28,145
Kutztown University of Pennsylvania	pub.	$ 7126	$ 7330	71%	75%	$ 7183	$ 7273	$18,761
La Roche College	ind.	$20,330	$ 8338	84%	NR	$17,367	$11,301	$34,189
Lebanon Valley College	ind.	$29,350	$ 7760	99%	31%	$21,978	$15,132	$32,437
Lehigh University	ind.	$37,550	$ 9770	97%	52%	$31,469	$15,851	$29,756
Lincoln University	pub.	$ 7980	$ 7532	74%	8%	$ 9941	$ 5571	$29,776
Lock Haven University of Pennsylvania	pub.	$ 6917	$ 6448	66%	45%	$ 7043	$ 6322	$22,585
Lycoming College	ind.	$28,784	$ 7672	100%	21%	$22,525	$13,931	$27,179
Marywood University	ind.	$26,270	$11,498	100%	24%	$20,638	$17,130	$35,900
Mercyhurst College	ind.	$23,286	$ 8196	98%	27%	$21,207	$10,275	$19,263
Messiah College	ind.	$25,670	$ 7610	99%	25%	$18,303	$14,977	$33,820
Millersville University of Pennsylvania	pub.	$ 6866	$ 7308	76%	13%	$ 7648	$ 6526	$20,931
Misericordia University	ind.	$23,150	$ 9650	100%	15%	$16,191	$16,609	$20,345
Mount Aloysius College	ind.	$17,280	$ 7300	100%	NR	$13,162	$11,418	$24,307
Muhlenberg College	ind.	$35,375	$ 8060	97%	93%	$23,182	$20,253	$18,542
Neumann University	ind.	$20,402	$ 9258	93%	66%	$18,000	$11,660	$30,000

NA = not applicable; NR = not reported; * = includes room and board; † = room only; — = not available.

College Costs At-a-Glance	Institutional Control ind.=independent; pub.=public	Tuition and Fees	Room and Board	Percent of Eligible Freshmen Receiving Need-Based Gift Awards	Percent of Freshmen Whose Need Was Fully Met	Average Financial Aid Package for Freshmen	Average Net Cost After Aid	Average Indebtedness Upon Graduation
Pennsylvania—*continued*								
Peirce College	ind.	$14,350	NA	83%	NR	$ 6592	$ 7758	$18,724
Penn State Abington	pub.	$11,800	NA	77%	5%	$ 8669	$ 3131	$26,800
Penn State Altoona	pub.	$12,182	$ 7670	66%	4%	$ 8119	$11,733	$26,800
Penn State Berks	pub.	$12,282	$ 8390	67%	5%	$ 7495	$13,177	$26,800
Penn State Erie, The Behrend College	pub.	$12,282	$ 7670	68%	5%	$ 8449	$11,503	$26,800
Penn State Harrisburg	pub.	$12,282	$ 8780	62%	7%	$ 8069	$12,993	$26,800
Penn State University Park	pub.	$13,706	$ 7670	53%	8%	$ 8820	$12,556	$26,800
Pennsylvania College of Technology	pub.	$11,790	$ 7200	100%	NR	NR	NR	NR
Philadelphia Biblical University	ind.	$18,872	$ 7650	99%	18%	$13,971	$12,551	$26,475
Philadelphia University	ind.	$26,700	$ 8692	99%	12%	$20,533	$14,859	$30,062
Point Park University	ind.	$20,570	$ 8940	100%	19%	$17,126	$12,384	$31,149
Robert Morris University	ind.	$19,740	$ 9880	99%	23%	$17,374	$12,246	$31,049
Rosemont College	ind.	$24,810	$ 9980	100%	19%	$21,310	$13,480	$21,515
Saint Francis University	ind.	$24,840	$ 8422	100%	17%	$15,403	$17,859	$10,762
Saint Joseph's University	ind.	$32,860	$11,180	96%	23%	$18,296	$25,744	$39,116
Saint Vincent College	ind.	$26,146	$ 8184	100%	26%	$21,721	$12,609	NR
Seton Hill University	ind.	$26,002	$ 8170	100%	17%	$22,854	$11,318	$27,120
Shippensburg University of Pennsylvania	pub.	$ 7099	$ 6604	74%	18%	$ 6865	$ 6838	$20,148
Slippery Rock University of Pennsylvania	pub.	$ 6934	$ 8066	63%	51%	$ 7413	$ 7587	$22,940
Susquehanna University	ind.	$31,080	$ 8400	89%	43%	$22,907	$16,573	$17,222
Swarthmore College	ind.	$36,490	$11,314	100%	100%	$34,737	$13,067	NR
Temple University	pub.	$11,448	$ 8884	100%	34%	$14,579	$ 5753	$26,064
Thiel College	ind.	$20,998	$ 8790	100%	12%	$20,190	$ 9598	$21,712
University of Pennsylvania	ind.	$37,526	$10,621	95%	100%	$32,582	$15,565	$19,085
University of Pittsburgh	pub.	$13,642	$ 7750	78%	43%	$10,340	$11,052	NR
University of Pittsburgh at Bradford	pub.	$11,722	$ 7050	93%	46%	$12,666	$ 6106	$26,463
University of Pittsburgh at Greensburg	pub.	$11,782	$ 7530	79%	13%	$ 8953	$10,359	$21,468
University of Pittsburgh at Johnstown	pub.	$11,674	$ 6860	70%	6%	$ 9415	$ 9119	$23,295
The University of Scranton	ind.	$33,124	$11,440	98%	12%	$21,200	$23,364	$28,251
Ursinus College	ind.	$36,910	$ 8800	100%	27%	$25,675	$20,035	$21,171
Valley Forge Christian College	ind.	$13,940	$ 6990	95%	15%	$ 8055	$12,875	$36,746
Villanova University	ind.	$37,655	$10,070	91%	24%	$27,258	$20,467	$29,812
Washington & Jefferson College	ind.	$31,496	$ 8488	93%	15%	$23,554	$16,430	$20,000
Waynesburg University	ind.	$17,080	$ 7050	99%	25%	$13,435	$10,695	$21,500
West Chester University of Pennsylvania	pub.	$ 6737	$ 6874	70%	39%	$ 7084	$ 6527	$25,179
Westminster College	ind.	$26,600	$ 8110	99%	24%	$24,435	$10,275	$25,296
Widener University	ind.	$30,450	$10,840	99%	16%	$25,555	$15,735	$36,398
Wilkes University	ind.	$25,170	$10,780	82%	17%	$20,731	$15,219	$31,935
Wilson College	ind.	$25,900	$ 8630	100%	15%	$22,040	$12,490	$29,721
York College of Pennsylvania	ind.	$13,680	$ 7800	75%	28%	$10,323	$11,157	$20,625
Puerto Rico								
EDP College of Puerto Rico, Inc.	ind.	$ 4980	NA	100%	NR	$ 60	$ 4920	NR

NA = not applicable; NR = not reported; * = includes room and board; † = room only; — = not available.

College Costs At-a-Glance

	Institutional Control ind.=independent; pub.=public	Tuition and Fees	Room and Board	Percent of Eligible Freshmen Receiving Need-Based Gift Awards	Percent of Freshmen Whose Need Was Fully Met	Average Financial Aid Package for Freshmen	Average Net Cost After Aid	Average Indebtedness Upon Graduation
Puerto Rico—*continued*								
Inter American University of Puerto Rico, Arecibo Campus	ind.	$ 4212	NA	90%	NR	$ 383	$ 3829	NR
Inter American University of Puerto Rico, Guayama Campus	ind.	$ 4174	NA	69%	NR	NR	NR	NR
University of Puerto Rico, Río Piedras	pub.	$ 1272	$ 8180	100%	NR	$ 3481	$ 5971	NR
Rhode Island								
Brown University	ind.	$37,718	$10,022	94%	100%	$34,452	$13,288	$19,390
Bryant University	ind.	$32,286	$11,757	83%	65%	$21,021	$23,022	$34,268
Johnson & Wales University	ind.	$22,585	$ 8892	89%	8%	$15,862	$15,615	$28,195
Providence College	ind.	$31,394	$10,810	85%	40%	$19,380	$22,824	$33,297
Rhode Island College	pub.	$ 5771	$ 8250	85%	19%	$ 8905	$ 5116	$15,841
Roger Williams University	ind.	$27,718	$11,880	58%	4%	$17,274	$22,324	$31,874
Salve Regina University	ind.	$29,150	$10,700	94%	5%	$20,982	$18,868	$30,138
University of Rhode Island	pub.	$ 8928	$ 8826	100%	78%	$12,194	$ 5560	$22,500
South Carolina								
Charleston Southern University	ind.	$18,678	$ 7178	100%	27%	$16,210	$ 9646	$20,252
The Citadel, The Military College of South Carolina	pub.	$ 9517	$ 5750	89%	33%	$10,969	$ 4298	$20,089
Clemson University	pub.	$11,108	$ 6556	35%	31%	$13,511	$ 4153	NR
Coastal Carolina University	pub.	$ 8650	$ 7080	41%	16%	$ 8141	$ 7589	$24,856
College of Charleston	pub.	$ 8400	$ 8999	71%	37%	$11,707	$ 5692	$17,139
Columbia International University	ind.	$16,850	$ 6210	NR	NR	$ 5200	$17,860	$16,500
Converse College	ind.	$24,500	$ 7550	100%	36%	$23,775	$ 8275	$22,339
Francis Marion University	pub.	$ 7632	$ 6024	91%	NR	NR	NR	$23,487
Furman University	ind.	$34,588	$ 8966	100%	39%	$26,229	$17,325	$24,325
Limestone College	ind.	$18,300	$ 6800	100%	18%	$15,636	$ 9464	$22,416
Newberry College	ind.	$21,600	$ 7360	81%	30%	$19,918	$ 9042	$13,477
North Greenville University	ind.	$11,680	$ 6720	NR	NR	NR	NR	NR
Presbyterian College	ind.	$28,880	$ 8345	100%	58%	$27,546	$ 9679	$21,236
South Carolina State University	pub.	$ 7806	$ 8040	NR	NR	NR	NR	$26,678
University of South Carolina	pub.	$ 8838	$ 7318	42%	32%	$10,994	$ 5162	$21,315
University of South Carolina Aiken	pub.	$ 7582	$ 6620	40%	30%	$ 9342	$ 4860	$24,668
University of South Carolina Beaufort	pub.	$ 7080	$ 5600†	NR	NR	NR	NR	NR
University of South Carolina Upstate	pub.	$ 8512	$ 6150	62%	21%	$ 9744	$ 4918	$18,762
Winthrop University	pub.	$11,060	$10,040	98%	27%	$10,796	$10,304	$21,600
Wofford College	ind.	$29,465	$ 8190	86%	54%	$27,894	$ 9761	$17,831
South Dakota								
Augustana College	ind.	$22,450	$ 5920	100%	22%	$20,477	$ 7893	$25,885
Black Hills State University	pub.	$ 6590	$ 5172	NR	NR	NR	NR	$23,975
Dakota State University	pub.	$ 6498	$ 4612	48%	13%	$ 6902	$ 4208	$21,189
Dakota Wesleyan University	ind.	$19,000	$ 5650	100%	20%	$12,787	$11,863	$24,000
Mount Marty College	ind.	$18,250	$ 5210	94%	40%	$26,937	—	$27,028
Northern State University	pub.	$ 5712	$ 4664	93%	100%	$ 5335	$ 5041	$20,297
Presentation College	ind.	$14,250	$ 5500	55%	16%	$ 8457	$11,293	$27,430
South Dakota School of Mines and Technology	pub.	$ 6480	$ 4740	76%	32%	$ 8532	$ 2688	$23,898

NA = not applicable; NR = not reported; * = includes room and board; † = room only; — = not available.

College Costs At-a-Glance

	Institutional Control ind.=independent; pub.=public	Tuition and Fees	Room and Board	Percent of Eligible Freshmen Receiving Need-Based Gift Awards	Percent of Freshmen Whose Need Was Fully Met	Average Financial Aid Package for Freshmen	Average Net Cost After Aid	Average Indebtedness Upon Graduation
South Dakota—*continued*								
South Dakota State University	pub.	$ 5808	$ 5423	59%	79%	$ 7166	$ 4065	$21,044
The University of South Dakota	pub.	$ 6468	$ 5787	45%	80%	$ 4528	$ 7727	$22,781
Tennessee								
Aquinas College	ind.	$16,100	NA	81%	16%	$ 5474	$10,626	$15,410
Austin Peay State University	pub.	$ 5526	$ 5870	55%	NR	$ 8501	$ 2895	NR
Belmont University	ind.	$21,110	$10,000	60%	93%	$10,404	$20,706	$14,319
Bryan College	ind.	$17,860	$ 5354	94%	33%	$13,561	$ 9653	$15,034
Carson-Newman College	ind.	$17,800	$ 5790	99%	26%	$16,024	$ 7566	$18,552
Christian Brothers University	ind.	$22,600	$ 5880	62%	32%	$21,259	$ 7221	$27,812
Cumberland University	ind.	$16,720	$ 6070	41%	25%	$14,486	$ 8304	$21,562
DeVry University	ind.	$14,080	NR	50%	50%	$ 7055	$ 7025	NR
East Tennessee State University	pub.	$ 5201	$ 5278	87%	35%	$ 7617	$ 2862	$16,635
Fisk University	ind.	$16,240	$ 7725	96%	29%	$11,573	$12,392	$23,850
Freed-Hardeman University	ind.	$13,860	$ 6970	98%	26%	$12,396	$ 8434	$29,744
Free Will Baptist Bible College	ind.	$13,086	$ 5352	74%	NR	$ 8556	$ 9882	$18,487
Johnson Bible College	ind.	$ 8550	$ 4890	98%	NR	$ 7271	$ 6169	$18,424
King College	ind.	$20,582	$ 6900	98%	30%	$16,442	$11,040	$10,591
Lambuth University	ind.	$17,450	$ 7570	99%	52%	$16,295	$ 8725	$19,000
Lane College	ind.	$ 8000	$ 5520	92%	9%	$ 4127	$ 9393	$ 8458
Lee University	ind.	$11,164	$ 5470	91%	34%	$ 9395	$ 7239	$28,542
Lincoln Memorial University	ind.	$15,700	$ 5680	100%	22%	$18,182	$ 3198	$15,881
Lipscomb University	ind.	$18,580	$ 7400	46%	29%	$14,245	$11,735	$14,040
Maryville College	ind.	$26,947	$ 8240	75%	66%	$26,215	$ 8972	$13,929
Memphis College of Art	ind.	$21,560	$ 5760†	100%	17%	$19,102	$ 8218	$53,397
Middle Tennessee State University	pub.	$ 5700	$ 6453	53%	57%	$ 7700	$ 4453	$22,000
Milligan College	ind.	$20,560	$ 5650	100%	42%	$14,968	$11,242	$20,236
Rhodes College	ind.	$32,446	$ 7842	98%	52%	$29,647	$10,641	$26,064
Sewanee: The University of the South	ind.	$34,172	$ 9760	100%	83%	$29,827	$14,105	$15,885
Southern Adventist University	ind.	$17,112	$ 5080	100%	88%	$18,897	$ 3295	$18,846
Tennessee Technological University	pub.	$ 5244	$ 7290	53%	31%	$ 8702	$ 3832	$13,314
Trevecca Nazarene University	ind.	$16,288	$ 7134	NR	NR	NR	NR	NR
Union University	ind.	$19,610	$ 6500	75%	29%	$16,258	$ 9852	$21,543
University of Memphis	pub.	$ 6128	$ 5660	95%	9%	$ 9380	$ 2408	$21,265
The University of Tennessee	pub.	$ 6250	$ 6888	96%	39%	$ 9731	$ 3407	$24,690
The University of Tennessee at Chattanooga	pub.	$ 5310	$ 8100	89%	62%	$ 9140	$ 4270	$19,344
The University of Tennessee at Martin	pub.	$ 5255	$ 4606	58%	47%	$10,837	—	NR
Vanderbilt University	ind.	$37,005	$12,028	92%	99%	$37,890	$11,143	$19,839
Watkins College of Art, Design, & Film	ind.	$17,700	$ 6000†	70%	3%	$ 8633	$15,067	$20,000
Texas								
Abilene Christian University	ind.	$18,930	$ 7236	100%	23%	$14,019	$12,147	$33,120
Angelo State University	pub.	$ 4596	$ 6612	77%	74%	$ 4359	$ 6849	$11,400
Austin College	ind.	$27,875	$ 9090	100%	100%	$28,461	$ 8504	NR

NA = not applicable; NR = not reported; * = includes room and board; † = room only; — = not available.

College Costs At-a-Glance

	Institutional Control ind.=independent; pub.=public	Tuition and Fees	Room and Board	Percent of Eligible Freshmen Receiving Need-Based Gift Awards	Percent of Freshmen Whose Need Was Fully Met	Average Financial Aid Package for Freshmen	Average Net Cost After Aid	Average Indebtedness Upon Graduation
Texas—*continued*								
Baylor University	ind.	$27,910	$ 8569	99%	13%	$20,249	$16,230	NR
Concordia University Texas	ind.	$20,490	$ 7800	95%	23%	$17,566	$10,724	$21,427
Dallas Baptist University	ind.	$16,440	$ 5409	75%	60%	$13,740	$ 8109	$16,354
DeVry University (Houston)	ind.	$14,080	NR	81%	3%	$12,942	$ 1138	$30,068
DeVry University (Irving)	ind.	$14,080	NA	75%	2%	$12,802	$ 1278	$31,895
East Texas Baptist University	ind.	$17,180	$ 5164	87%	18%	$13,017	$ 9327	$20,492
Hardin-Simmons University	ind.	$19,790	$ 5788	74%	30%	$16,609	$ 8969	$33,745
Houston Baptist University	ind.	$20,830	$ 6975	100%	20%	$17,565	$10,240	NR
Howard Payne University	ind.	$18,650	$ 5160	99%	27%	$14,312	$ 9498	$18,960
Jarvis Christian College	ind.	$ 8208	$ 4954	96%	17%	$ 9357	$ 3805	$19,000
Lamar University	pub.	$ 6014	$ 6290	NR	17%	$10,650	$ 1654	$ 7650
LeTourneau University	ind.	$19,140	$ 7500	100%	20%	$14,182	$12,458	NR
Lubbock Christian University	ind.	$14,700	$ 5884	99%	12%	$12,284	$ 8300	$26,333
McMurry University	ind.	$17,985	$ 6657	96%	20%	$18,989	$ 5653	$25,338
Midland College	pub.	$ 1596	$ 4061	NR	NR	NR	NR	NR
Midwestern State University	pub.	$ 5571	$ 5350	88%	31%	$ 7925	$ 2996	$19,645
Northwood University, Texas Campus	ind.	$18,408	$ 7590	81%	18%	$16,727	$ 9271	$22,820
Our Lady of the Lake University of San Antonio	ind.	$20,232	$ 6238	89%	27%	$23,093	$ 3377	$18,169
Rice University	ind.	$30,479	$10,750	100%	100%	$31,863	$ 9366	$11,108
St. Edward's University	ind.	$24,440	$ 8496	90%	16%	$19,550	$13,386	$27,093
St. Mary's University	ind.	$21,300	$ 7188	98%	22%	$20,003	$ 8485	$27,416
Sam Houston State University	pub.	$ 6515	$ 6744	79%	29%	$ 7932	$ 5327	$ 5763
Schreiner University	ind.	$17,992	$ 7712	100%	20%	$12,376	$13,328	$20,486
Southern Methodist University	ind.	$35,160	$12,445	79%	44%	$27,655	$19,950	$16,756
Southwestern University	ind.	$27,940	$ 8870	100%	33%	$26,377	$10,433	$23,601
Stephen F. Austin State University	pub.	$ 6432	$ 7022	79%	69%	$ 9021	$ 4433	$15,652
Tarleton State University	pub.	$ 6975	$ 6034	NR	NR	$10,022	$ 2987	$18,223
Texas A&M University	pub.	$ 7844	$ 8000	95%	60%	$15,551	$ 293	$23,112
Texas A&M University at Galveston	pub.	$ 6454	$ 5508	62%	22%	$11,743	$ 219	$16,800
Texas A&M University–Commerce	pub.	$ 5130	$ 6650	95%	37%	$ 9963	$ 1817	$21,014
Texas A&M University–Corpus Christi	pub.	$ 5737	$ 8709	72%	5%	$ 7586	$ 6860	$19,014
Texas A&M University–Texarkana	pub.	$ 3392	NA	NR	NR	NR	NR	NR
Texas Christian University	ind.	$28,298	$ 9800	98%	35%	$19,722	$18,376	$26,503
Texas College	ind.	$ 9228	$ 6600	100%	31%	$10,871	$ 4957	$ 8263
Texas Lutheran University	ind.	$21,100	$ 6140	100%	46%	$18,107	$ 9133	$30,118
Texas State University–San Marcos	pub.	$ 6994	$ 6012	74%	10%	$12,696	$ 310	$17,994
Texas Tech University	pub.	$ 6783	$ 7310	64%	7%	$ 7492	$ 6601	$20,424
Trinity University	ind.	$27,699	$ 8822	100%	49%	$23,397	$13,124	NR
University of Dallas	ind.	$26,294	$ 8220	100%	31%	$20,907	$13,607	$25,410
University of Houston	pub.	$ 8167	$ 6935	67%	27%	$11,469	$ 3633	NR
University of Houston–Clear Lake	pub.	$ 6076	$10,308†	NR	NR	NR	NR	$19,776
University of Houston–Downtown	pub.	$ 5000	NA	91%	4%	$ 7516	—	$15,585
University of Houston–Victoria	pub.	$ 5220	NA	NR	NR	NR	NR	$17,695

NA = not applicable; NR = not reported; * = includes room and board; † = room only; — = not available.

College Costs At-a-Glance	Institutional Control ind.=independent; pub.=public	Tuition and Fees	Room and Board	Percent of Eligible Freshmen Receiving Need-Based Gift Awards	Percent of Freshmen Whose Need Was Fully Met	Average Financial Aid Package for Freshmen	Average Net Cost After Aid	Average Indebtedness Upon Graduation
Texas—*continued*								
University of Mary Hardin-Baylor	ind.	$20,650	$ 5350	NR	NR	$11,456	$14,544	$17,500
University of North Texas	pub.	$ 6767	$ 6026	87%	37%	$10,394	$ 2399	NR
University of St. Thomas	ind.	$20,190	$ 7700	100%	13%	$16,610	$11,280	$21,626
The University of Texas at Arlington	pub.	$ 7780	$ 6412	73%	14%	$ 7950	$ 6242	NR
The University of Texas at Brownsville	pub.	$ 4355	$ 2920†	91%	NR	$ 7170	$ 105	NR
The University of Texas at Dallas	pub.	$ 9850	$ 6828	66%	44%	$12,944	$ 3734	NR
The University of Texas at El Paso	pub.	$ 5925	NR	85%	40%	$11,219	—	$19,802
The University of Texas at San Antonio	pub.	$ 4800	NR	81%	26%	$ 8226	—	$20,815
The University of Texas at Tyler	pub.	$ 5742	$ 7510	87%	24%	$ 8331	$ 4921	$15,901
The University of Texas Medical Branch	pub.	$ 5502	NR	NR	NR	NR	NR	$20,116
The University of Texas of the Permian Basin	pub.	$ 4262	$ 4600	67%	19%	$ 7138	$ 1724	$16,995
The University of Texas–Pan American	pub.	$ 3898	$ 4994	97%	7%	$ 8904	—	$12,101
The University of Texas Southwestern Medical Center at Dallas	pub.	$ 4628	$11,353	NR	NR	NR	NR	NR
University of the Incarnate Word	ind.	$21,290	$ 8780	79%	33%	$15,033	$15,037	$39,985
Wayland Baptist University	ind.	$12,020	$ 3691	92%	19%	$ 7770	$ 7941	$21,575
Utah								
DeVry University	ind.	$14,080	NR	NR	NR	$ 7475	$ 6605	NR
Dixie State College of Utah	pub.	$ 2893	$ 3498	100%	11%	$ 5175	$ 1216	$12,571
Southern Utah University	pub.	$ 4028	$ 1950†	99%	13%	$ 5594	$ 384	$ 8719
University of Utah	pub.	$ 5285	$ 5972	79%	21%	$ 9295	$ 1962	$11,749
Utah State University	pub.	$ 4445	$ 4650	52%	16%	$ 7395	$ 1700	NR
Utah Valley University	pub.	$ 3752	NA	75%	4%	$ 5944	—	$13,714
Weber State University	pub.	$ 3850	NR	65%	3%	$ 4567	—	NR
Westminster College	ind.	$24,996	$ 7006	100%	54%	$17,205	$14,797	$18,548
Vermont								
Bennington College	ind.	$38,270	$10,680	98%	14%	$29,426	$19,524	$25,957
Burlington College	ind.	$19,640	$ 6750†	100%	NR	$14,598	$11,792	$28,888
Champlain College	ind.	$24,355	$11,210	87%	7%	$13,053	$22,512	NR
College of St. Joseph	ind.	$17,550	$ 8350	100%	19%	$15,125	$10,775	$32,278
Goddard College	ind.	$11,664	$ 1088	75%	12%	$ 7514	$ 5238	$21,639
Green Mountain College	ind.	$25,838	$ 9522	100%	12%	$17,509	$17,851	$32,448
Marlboro College	ind.	$33,660	$ 9220	88%	NR	$19,068	$23,812	$19,482
Middlebury College	ind.	*$49,210	NR	100%	100%	$34,849	$14,361	$19,981
Saint Michael's College	ind.	$33,215	$ 8280	97%	32%	$19,972	$21,523	$26,044
University of Vermont	pub.	$12,844	$ 8534	95%	27%	$17,576	$ 3802	$25,036
Vermont Technical College	pub.	$ 9984	$ 7510	79%	18%	$ 8400	$ 9094	$25,600
Virgin Islands								
University of the Virgin Islands	pub.	$ 4100	$ 8240	90%	3%	$ 4600	$ 7740	$ 9480
Virginia								
Averett University	ind.	$21,300	$ 7280	100%	16%	$14,140	$14,440	$30,943
Bluefield College	ind.	$15,630	$ 6584	99%	29%	$14,317	$ 7897	$16,856
Bridgewater College	ind.	$24,500	$ 9900	100%	18%	$21,286	$13,114	$29,519

NA = not applicable; NR = not reported; * = includes room and board; † = room only; — = not available.

College Costs At-a-Glance

	Institutional Control ind.=independent; pub.=public	Tuition and Fees	Room and Board	Percent of Eligible Freshmen Receiving Need-Based Gift Awards	Percent of Freshmen Whose Need Was Fully Met	Average Financial Aid Package for Freshmen	Average Net Cost After Aid	Average Indebtedness Upon Graduation
Virginia—*continued*								
Christendom College	ind.	$18,756	$ 6688	95%	100%	$12,050	$13,394	$22,000
Christopher Newport University	pub.	$10,928	$ 9100	74%	24%	$ 7428	$12,600	$17,752
The College of William and Mary	pub.	$10,246	$ 7910	75%	43%	$13,454	$ 4702	$12,859
DeVry University (Arlington)	ind.	$14,080	NA	67%	7%	$ 9908	$ 4172	$12,479
Emory & Henry College	ind.	$23,860	$ 7980	87%	27%	$23,043	$ 8797	$19,744
Ferrum College	ind.	$22,500	$ 7300	98%	NR	$20,489	$ 9311	$ 8520
George Mason University	pub.	$ 7512	$ 7360	82%	13%	$10,791	$ 4081	$18,547
Hampden-Sydney College	ind.	$29,511	$ 9228	99%	35%	$20,308	$18,431	$16,472
Hampton University	ind.	$16,392	$ 7440	99%	40%	$ 3877	$19,955	$ 9478
Hollins University	ind.	$27,055	$ 9650	100%	17%	$24,419	$12,286	$22,161
James Madison University	pub.	$ 6964	$ 7458	46%	98%	$ 9212	$ 5210	$17,395
Liberty University	ind.	$17,742	$ 5996	37%	15%	$13,952	$ 9786	$27,673
Longwood University	pub.	$ 8499	$ 6856	96%	14%	$ 7814	$ 7541	$14,935
Lynchburg College	ind.	$28,105	$ 7570	100%	23%	$19,719	$15,956	$26,915
Mary Baldwin College	ind.	$23,645	$ 6730	98%	2%	$19,455	$10,920	$23,919
Marymount University	ind.	$21,528	$ 9190	69%	17%	$16,938	$13,780	$22,993
Old Dominion University	pub.	$ 6918	$ 7092	51%	64%	$ 7571	$ 6439	$16,950
Radford University	pub.	$ 6536	$ 6716	62%	31%	$ 7885	$ 5367	$19,465
Randolph College	ind.	$28,430	$ 9715	97%	28%	$21,432	$16,713	$27,218
Randolph-Macon College	ind.	$28,355	$ 8610	100%	30%	$22,244	$14,721	$23,564
Roanoke College	ind.	$27,935	$ 9285	99%	35%	$23,541	$13,679	$25,498
Saint Paul's College	ind.	$13,210	$ 6640	71%	5%	$ 8048	$11,802	$17,541
Southern Virginia University	ind.	$16,500	$ 5100	97%	9%	$ 9422	$12,178	$15,444
Sweet Briar College	ind.	$29,135	$10,460	94%	82%	$15,051	$24,544	$20,118
University of Mary Washington	pub.	$ 6834	$ 7700	52%	14%	$11,300	$ 3234	$16,000
University of Richmond	ind.	$40,010	$ 8480	99%	97%	$35,624	$12,866	$20,915
University of Virginia	pub.	$ 9300	$ 7820	88%	100%	$17,742	—	$19,016
The University of Virginia's College at Wise	pub.	$ 6748	$ 7933	97%	95%	$ 7971	$ 6710	$10,252
Virginia Commonwealth University	pub.	$ 6779	$ 7914	82%	11%	$ 9309	$ 5384	NR
Virginia Intermont College	ind.	$24,100	$ 7430	100%	14%	$17,022	$14,508	$19,058
Virginia Military Institute	pub.	$10,556	$ 6444	75%	55%	$13,547	$ 3453	$19,114
Virginia Polytechnic Institute and State University	pub.	$ 8198	$ 5476	82%	18%	$11,609	$ 2065	$21,678
Virginia Union University	ind.	$13,662	$ 6328	68%	78%	$ 8990	$11,000	$17,415
Virginia Wesleyan College	ind.	$27,476	$ 7696	40%	16%	$18,953	$16,219	$25,740
Washington and Lee University	ind.	$37,412	$ 8428	88%	90%	$33,561	$12,279	$23,616
Washington								
Bastyr University	ind.	$19,530	$ 4100†	NR	NR	NR	NR	$32,500
Cornish College of the Arts	ind.	$25,300	NA	100%	8%	$16,102	$ 9198	$36,026
DeVry University (Federal Way)	ind.	$14,720	NA	73%	1%	$ 8750	$ 5970	$50,600
Eastern Washington University	pub.	$ 5118	$ 6894	84%	29%	$ 9782	$ 2230	$18,320
The Evergreen State College	pub.	$ 5344	$ 8052	61%	31%	$10,745	$ 2651	$15,371
Gonzaga University	ind.	$28,262	$ 7860	100%	35%	$21,350	$14,772	$24,094

NA = not applicable; NR = not reported; * = includes room and board; † = room only; — = not available.

College Costs At-a-Glance

	Institutional Control ind.=independent; pub.=public	Tuition and Fees	Room and Board	Percent of Eligible Freshmen Receiving Need-Based Gift Awards	Percent of Freshmen Whose Need Was Fully Met	Average Financial Aid Package for Freshmen	Average Net Cost After Aid	Average Indebtedness Upon Graduation
Washington—*continued*								
Northwest University	ind.	$20,790	$6578	100%	22%	$15,217	$12,151	$30,198
Pacific Lutheran University	ind.	$28,100	$8600	100%	40%	$25,805	$10,895	$22,484
Saint Martin's University	ind.	$23,810	$8040	100%	19%	$19,061	$12,789	$27,465
Seattle Pacific University	ind.	$26,817	$8454	99%	9%	$23,883	$11,388	$23,066
Seattle University	ind.	$28,260	$8340	97%	18%	$26,609	$ 9991	$16,002
Trinity Lutheran College	ind.	$19,425	$6120†	NR	NR	NR	NR	NR
University of Puget Sound	ind.	$35,635	$9190	98%	35%	$25,660	$19,165	$25,055
University of Washington	pub.	$ 6802	$7488	79%	39%	$10,587	$ 3703	$16,800
Walla Walla University	ind.	$21,936	$4320	80%	29%	$18,338	$ 7918	$28,287
Washington State University	pub.	$ 7565	$8054	58%	37%	$ 9254	$ 6365	NR
Western Washington University	pub.	$ 5535	$7712	83%	37%	$ 9925	$ 3322	$15,560
Whitman College	ind.	$35,192	$8812	100%	92%	$27,930	$16,074	$16,684
Whitworth University	ind.	$27,420	$7700	99%	22%	$23,147	$11,973	$19,305
West Virginia								
Alderson-Broaddus College	ind.	$21,020	$6798	100%	27%	$19,692	$ 8126	$21,478
Appalachian Bible College	ind.	$11,270	$5060	98%	8%	$ 7574	$ 8756	NR
Bethany College	ind.	$19,545	$8260	NR	NR	NR	NR	NR
Bluefield State College	pub.	$ 4272	NA	100%	56%	$ 6000	—	$21,500
Concord University	pub.	$ 4578	$6530	82%	41%	$ 9369	$ 1739	$13,713
Fairmont State University	pub.	$ 5224	$6652	65%	14%	$ 6866	$ 5010	NR
Glenville State College	pub.	$ 4486	$6150	84%	16%	$10,280	$ 356	$17,545
Marshall University	pub.	$ 4020	$7210	58%	38%	$ 8359	$ 2871	$16,342
Mountain State University	ind.	$ 8400	$6116	69%	100%	$ 5507	$ 9009	$31,221
Ohio Valley University	ind.	$13,510	$6140	92%	27%	$11,738	$ 7912	$13,480
Shepherd University	pub.	$ 4898	$6938	62%	28%	$ 9828	$ 2008	$18,271
University of Charleston	ind.	$23,150	$8325	50%	52%	$20,302	$11,173	$27,305
West Liberty State University	pub.	$ 4464	$6282	NR	NR	$ 5807	$ 4939	$21,097
West Virginia University	pub.	$ 5100	$7434	85%	45%	$ 6466	$ 6068	NR
West Virginia Wesleyan College	ind.	$22,880	$6800	100%	26%	$20,820	$ 8860	$19,796
Wheeling Jesuit University	ind.	$24,390	NR	77%	41%	$23,303	$ 1087	$21,383
Wisconsin								
Beloit College	ind.	$31,540	$6696	100%	96%	$25,170	$13,066	$26,014
Carroll University	ind.	$21,926	$6694	100%	58%	$17,279	$11,341	$24,097
Concordia University Wisconsin	ind.	$20,000	$7700	95%	37%	$21,950	$ 5750	$24,311
DeVry University (Milwaukee)	ind.	$14,080	NA	50%	NR	$ 8580	$ 5500	NR
Edgewood College	ind.	$20,040	$6828	98%	23%	$ 6395	$20,473	$27,885
Lawrence University	ind.	$33,264	$6975	99%	70%	$26,850	$13,389	$26,054
Maranatha Baptist Bible College	ind.	$10,560	$5800	24%	6%	$ 4993	$11,367	$15,191
Marian University	ind.	$19,940	$5380	100%	47%	$20,412	$ 4908	$22,200
Marquette University	ind.	$29,096	$6330	98%	32%	$22,008	$13,418	$30,563
Milwaukee School of Engineering	ind.	$28,665	$7164	100%	14%	$16,625	$19,204	$31,592
Mount Mary College	ind.	$21,166	$7280	100%	11%	$15,636	$12,810	$21,170

NA = not applicable; NR = not reported; * = includes room and board; † = room only; — = not available.

College Costs At-a-Glance

	Institutional Control ind.=independent; pub.=public	Tuition and Fees	Room and Board	Percent of Eligible Freshmen Receiving Need-Based Gift Awards	Percent of Freshmen Whose Need Was Fully Met	Average Financial Aid Package for Freshmen	Average Net Cost After Aid	Average Indebtedness Upon Graduation
Wisconsin—*continued*								
Northland College	ind.	$23,101	$6440	100%	28%	$19,843	$ 9698	$23,630
Ripon College	ind.	$24,245	$6770	100%	44%	$21,368	$ 9647	$24,795
St. Norbert College	ind.	$25,926	$6781	99%	30%	$18,146	$14,561	$27,207
Silver Lake College	ind.	$20,560	$6400	89%	21%	$18,735	$ 8225	$21,723
University of Wisconsin–Eau Claire	pub.	$ 6203	$5210	64%	75%	$ 7649	$ 3764	$18,548
University of Wisconsin–Green Bay	pub.	$ 6308	$5400	61%	50%	$ 9075	$ 2633	$18,587
University of Wisconsin–La Crosse	pub.	$ 6648	$5420	43%	23%	$ 5632	$ 6436	$21,250
University of Wisconsin–Madison	pub.	$ 7568	$7700	79%	24%	$ 9579	$ 5689	$21,123
University of Wisconsin–Milwaukee	pub.	$ 7309	$3840†	39%	27%	$ 6470	$ 4679	$15,772
University of Wisconsin–Oshkosh	pub.	$ 6038	$5898	62%	32%	$ 3500	$ 8436	$19,000
University of Wisconsin–Parkside	pub.	$ 6070	$5986	67%	NR	NR	NR	NR
University of Wisconsin–Stevens Point	pub.	$ 6200	$5180	47%	90%	$ 6469	$ 4911	$19,123
University of Wisconsin–Stout	pub.	$ 7584	$5170	44%	49%	$ 8292	$ 4462	$26,072
University of Wisconsin–Superior	pub.	$ 6359	$5154	48%	45%	$ 6670	$ 4843	$19,556
University of Wisconsin–Whitewater	pub.	$ 7062	$4740	43%	63%	$ 6553	$ 5249	$19,743
Wisconsin Lutheran College	ind.	$20,560	$6990	100%	20%	$17,272	$10,278	$17,596
Wyoming								
University of Wyoming	pub.	$ 3686	$8006	49%	27%	$ 7612	$ 4080	$16,307

NA = not applicable; NR = not reported; * = includes room and board; † = room only; — = not available.

Profiles of College Financial Aid Programs

ABILENE CHRISTIAN UNIVERSITY

Abilene, TX

Tuition & fees: $18,930 **Average undergraduate aid package: $13,284**

ABOUT THE INSTITUTION Independent religious, coed. ***Awards:*** associate, bachelor's, master's, doctoral, and first professional degrees and post-bachelor's and post-master's certificates. 73 undergraduate majors. ***Total enrollment:*** 4,669. Undergraduates: 3,906. Freshmen: 971. Federal methodology is used as a basis for awarding need-based institutional aid.

UNDERGRADUATE EXPENSES for 2008–09 ***Application fee:*** $50. ***Comprehensive fee:*** $26,166 includes full-time tuition ($17,880), mandatory fees ($1050), and room and board ($7236). ***College room only:*** $3150. Full-time tuition and fees vary according to course load. Room and board charges vary according to board plan and housing facility. ***Part-time tuition:*** $596 per semester hour. ***Part-time fees:*** $51.50 per semester hour; $10 per term. Part-time tuition and fees vary according to course load. ***Payment plans:*** Tuition prepayment, installment.

FRESHMAN FINANCIAL AID (Fall 2008, est.) 832 applied for aid; of those 76% were deemed to have need. 100% of freshmen with need received aid; of those 23% had need fully met. ***Average percent of need met:*** 73% (excluding resources awarded to replace EFC). ***Average financial aid package:*** $14,019 (excluding resources awarded to replace EFC). 21% of all full-time freshmen had no need and received non-need-based gift aid.

UNDERGRADUATE FINANCIAL AID (Fall 2008, est.) 2,906 applied for aid; of those 81% were deemed to have need. 100% of undergraduates with need received aid; of those 24% had need fully met. ***Average percent of need met:*** 70% (excluding resources awarded to replace EFC). ***Average financial aid package:*** $13,284 (excluding resources awarded to replace EFC). 13% of all full-time undergraduates had no need and received non-need-based gift aid.

GIFT AID (NEED-BASED) ***Total amount:*** $19,887,746 (16% federal, 22% state, 55% institutional, 7% external sources). ***Receiving aid:*** Freshmen: 65% (628); all full-time undergraduates: 63% (2,281). ***Average award:*** Freshmen: $10,654; Undergraduates: $9506. ***Scholarships, grants, and awards:*** Federal Pell, FSEOG, state, private, college/university gift aid from institutional funds, United Negro College Fund.

GIFT AID (NON-NEED-BASED) ***Total amount:*** $6,660,122 (1% state, 91% institutional, 8% external sources). ***Receiving aid:*** Freshmen: 56% (540). Undergraduates: 55% (1,996). ***Average award:*** Freshmen: $6566. Undergraduates: $6043. ***Scholarships, grants, and awards by category:*** *Academic interests/achievement:* agriculture, biological sciences, business, communication, education, English, foreign languages, general academic interests/achievements, mathematics, physical sciences, religion/biblical studies, social sciences. *Creative arts/performance:* art/fine arts, debating, journalism/publications, music, theater/drama. *Special achievements/activities:* cheerleading/drum major, leadership. *Special characteristics:* children of faculty/staff, ethnic background, first-generation college students, local/state students, members of minority groups, out-of-state students, previous college experience, relatives of clergy, religious affiliation. ***Tuition waivers:*** Full or partial for employees or children of employees.

LOANS ***Student loans:*** $26,068,675 (31% need-based, 69% non-need-based). 70% of past graduating class borrowed through all loan programs. *Average indebtedness per student:* $33,120. ***Average need-based loan:*** Freshmen: $3287. Undergraduates: $4228. ***Parent loans:*** $4,198,439 (100% non-need-based). ***Programs:*** FFEL (Subsidized and Unsubsidized Stafford, PLUS), Perkins, state, college/university.

WORK-STUDY ***Federal work-study:*** Total amount: $1,317,658; 700 jobs averaging $2315. ***State or other work-study/employment:*** Total amount: $1,092,256 (3% need-based, 97% non-need-based). Part-time jobs available.

ATHLETIC AWARDS Total amount: $2,915,894 (47% need-based, 53% non-need-based).

APPLYING FOR FINANCIAL AID ***Required financial aid forms:*** FAFSA, institution's own form. ***Financial aid deadline (priority):*** 3/1. ***Notification date:*** Continuous beginning 4/1. Students must reply within 3 weeks of notification.

CONTACT Michael Lewis, Director of Student Financial Services, Abilene Christian University, ACU Box 29007, Abilene, TX 79699-9007, 325-674-2643 or toll-free 877-APPLYUB. *E-mail:* mdl06g@acu.edu.

ACADEMY COLLEGE

Minneapolis, MN

ABOUT THE INSTITUTION Proprietary, coed. ***Awards:*** associate and bachelor's degrees. 25 undergraduate majors. ***Total enrollment:*** 150. Undergraduates: 150. Freshmen: 18.

GIFT AID (NEED-BASED) ***Scholarships, grants, and awards:*** Federal Pell, FSEOG, state, private, Institutional Scholarships.

LOANS ***Programs:*** Federal Direct (Subsidized and Unsubsidized Stafford, PLUS), state, alternative loans.

APPLYING FOR FINANCIAL AID ***Required financial aid forms:*** FAFSA, institution's own form, state aid form.

CONTACT Ms. Mary Erickson, Director of Administration, Academy College, 3050 Metro Drive #200, Minneapolis, MN 55425, 612-851-0066 or toll-free 800-292-9149. *Fax:* 612-851-0094. *E-mail:* email@academyeducation.com.

ACADEMY OF ART UNIVERSITY

San Francisco, CA

Tuition & fees: $18,050 **Average undergraduate aid package: $6549**

ABOUT THE INSTITUTION Proprietary, coed. ***Awards:*** associate, bachelor's, and master's degrees. 12 undergraduate majors. ***Total enrollment:*** 13,335. Undergraduates: 9,862. Freshmen: 2,289. Federal methodology is used as a basis for awarding need-based institutional aid.

UNDERGRADUATE EXPENSES for 2009–10 ***Application fee:*** $100. ***Comprehensive fee:*** $31,450 includes full-time tuition ($17,760), mandatory fees ($290), and room and board ($13,400). ***Part-time tuition:*** $740 per credit.

FRESHMAN FINANCIAL AID (Fall 2007) 512 applied for aid; of those 87% were deemed to have need. 99% of freshmen with need received aid; of those .5% had need fully met. ***Average percent of need met:*** 25% (excluding resources awarded to replace EFC). ***Average financial aid package:*** $6444 (excluding resources awarded to replace EFC).

UNDERGRADUATE FINANCIAL AID (Fall 2007) 2,773 applied for aid; of those 89% were deemed to have need. 98% of undergraduates with need received aid; of those 1% had need fully met. ***Average percent of need met:*** 30% (excluding resources awarded to replace EFC). ***Average financial aid package:*** $6549 (excluding resources awarded to replace EFC).

GIFT AID (NEED-BASED) ***Total amount:*** $11,370,876 (73% federal, 27% state). ***Receiving aid:*** Freshmen: 36% (261); all full-time undergraduates: 26% (1,415). ***Average award:*** Freshmen: $4275; Undergraduates: $5187. ***Scholarships, grants, and awards:*** Federal Pell, FSEOG, state, private.

GIFT AID (NON-NEED-BASED) ***Total amount:*** $401,625 (100% institutional). ***Receiving aid:*** Freshmen: 6% (43). Undergraduates: 2% (123).

LOANS ***Student loans:*** $81,434,049 (39% need-based, 61% non-need-based). 55% of past graduating class borrowed through all loan programs. *Average indebtedness per student:* $32,000. ***Average need-based loan:*** Freshmen: $2839. Undergraduates: $3523. ***Parent loans:*** $27,443,070 (100% non-need-based). ***Programs:*** Federal Direct (Subsidized and Unsubsidized Stafford, PLUS), alternative loans.

WORK-STUDY ***Federal work-study:*** Total amount: $266,967; 57 jobs averaging $3487.

APPLYING FOR FINANCIAL AID ***Required financial aid forms:*** FAFSA, institution's own form. ***Financial aid deadline (priority):*** 3/2. ***Notification date:*** Continuous. Students must reply within 3 weeks of notification.

CONTACT Mr. Joe Vollaro, Executive Vice President of Financial Aid and Compliance, Academy of Art University, 79 New Montgomery Street, San Francisco, CA 94105-3410, 415-618-6528 or toll-free 800-544-ARTS. *Fax:* 415-618-6273. *E-mail:* jvollaro@academyart.edu.

ADAMS STATE COLLEGE

Alamosa, CO

Tuition & fees (CO res): $3790 **Average undergraduate aid package: $8528**

ABOUT THE INSTITUTION State-supported, coed. ***Awards:*** associate, bachelor's, and master's degrees. 40 undergraduate majors. ***Total enrollment:*** 2,861. Undergraduates: 2,139. Freshmen: 486. Federal methodology is used as a basis for awarding need-based institutional aid.

UNDERGRADUATE EXPENSES for 2008–09 ***Application fee:*** $30. ***Tuition, state resident:*** full-time $2496; part-time $104 per credit hour. ***Tuition, nonresident:*** full-time $10,392; part-time $433 per credit hour. ***Required fees:*** full-time $1294; $54 per credit hour. Full-time tuition and fees vary according to course load and student level. Part-time tuition and fees vary according to course load. ***College room and board:*** $6780; ***Room only:*** $3460. Room and board charges vary according to board plan and housing facility. ***Payment plans:*** Installment, deferred payment.

FRESHMAN FINANCIAL AID (Fall 2007) 446 applied for aid; of those 84% were deemed to have need. 98% of freshmen with need received aid; of those 1% had need fully met. ***Average percent of need met:*** 44% (excluding resources awarded to replace EFC). ***Average financial aid package:*** $8314 (excluding resources awarded to replace EFC). 7% of all full-time freshmen had no need and received non-need-based gift aid.

UNDERGRADUATE FINANCIAL AID (Fall 2007) 1,602 applied for aid; of those 84% were deemed to have need. 98% of undergraduates with need received aid; of those 1% had need fully met. ***Average percent of need met:*** 45% (excluding resources awarded to replace EFC). ***Average financial aid package:*** $8528 (excluding resources awarded to replace EFC). 4% of all full-time undergraduates had no need and received non-need-based gift aid.

GIFT AID (NEED-BASED) ***Total amount:*** $5,818,848 (66% federal, 30% state, 2% institutional, 2% external sources). ***Receiving aid:*** Freshmen: 72% (339); all full-time undergraduates: 68% (1,178). ***Average award:*** Freshmen: $4645; Undergraduates: $4501. ***Scholarships, grants, and awards:*** Federal Pell, FSEOG, state, private, college/university gift aid from institutional funds.

GIFT AID (NON-NEED-BASED) ***Total amount:*** $2,508,397 (75% institutional, 25% external sources). ***Receiving aid:*** Freshmen: 41% (195). Undergraduates: 32% (558). ***Average award:*** Freshmen: $1942. Undergraduates: $1826. ***Tuition waivers:*** Full or partial for employees or children of employees, senior citizens.

LOANS ***Student loans:*** $6,908,863 (60% need-based, 40% non-need-based). 71% of past graduating class borrowed through all loan programs. *Average indebtedness per student:* $17,156. ***Average need-based loan:*** Freshmen: $3138. Undergraduates: $3811. ***Parent loans:*** $592,796 (100% non-need-based). ***Programs:*** FFEL (Subsidized and Unsubsidized Stafford, PLUS), Perkins, alternative loans.

WORK-STUDY ***Federal work-study:*** Total amount: $288,780; 219 jobs averaging $1313. ***State or other work-study/employment:*** Total amount: $436,099 (57% need-based, 43% non-need-based). 353 part-time jobs averaging $1234.

ATHLETIC AWARDS Total amount: $873,179 (12% need-based, 88% non-need-based).

APPLYING FOR FINANCIAL AID ***Required financial aid form:*** FAFSA. ***Financial aid deadline:*** Continuous. ***Notification date:*** Continuous.

CONTACT Phil Schroeder, Student Financial Aid Director, Adams State College, 208 Edgemont Boulevard, Alamosa, CO 81102, 719-587-7306 or toll-free 800-824-6494. *Fax:* 719-587-7366.

ADELPHI UNIVERSITY

Garden City, NY

Tuition & fees: $23,925 **Average undergraduate aid package: $16,400**

ABOUT THE INSTITUTION Independent, coed. ***Awards:*** associate, bachelor's, master's, and doctoral degrees and post-bachelor's and post-master's certificates. 46 undergraduate majors. ***Total enrollment:*** 8,177. Undergraduates: 5,139. Freshmen: 964. Federal methodology is used as a basis for awarding need-based institutional aid.

UNDERGRADUATE EXPENSES for 2008–09 ***Application fee:*** $35. ***Comprehensive fee:*** $33,925 includes full-time tuition ($22,725), mandatory fees ($1200), and room and board ($10,000). Full-time tuition and fees vary according to course level, location, and program. Room and board charges vary according to board plan and housing facility. ***Part-time tuition:*** $750 per credit. ***Part-time fees:*** $310 per term. Part-time tuition and fees vary according to course level, location, and program. ***Payment plans:*** Installment, deferred payment.

FRESHMAN FINANCIAL AID (Fall 2008, est.) 818 applied for aid; of those 79% were deemed to have need. 96% of freshmen with need received aid; of those 3% had need fully met. ***Average percent of need met:*** 56% (excluding resources awarded to replace EFC). ***Average financial aid package:*** $16,400 (excluding resources awarded to replace EFC). 27% of all full-time freshmen had no need and received non-need-based gift aid.

UNDERGRADUATE FINANCIAL AID (Fall 2008, est.) 3,353 applied for aid; of those 85% were deemed to have need. 88% of undergraduates with need received aid; of those 2% had need fully met. ***Average percent of need met:*** 52% (excluding resources awarded to replace EFC). ***Average financial aid package:*** $16,400 (excluding resources awarded to replace EFC). 32% of all full-time undergraduates had no need and received non-need-based gift aid.

GIFT AID (NEED-BASED) ***Total amount:*** $24,551,807 (16% federal, 22% state, 62% institutional). ***Receiving aid:*** Freshmen: 53% (496); all full-time undergraduates: 47% (2,003). ***Average award:*** Freshmen: $5525; Undergraduates: $6091. ***Scholarships, grants, and awards:*** Federal Pell, FSEOG, state, private, college/university gift aid from institutional funds, United Negro College Fund, endowed-donor scholarships.

GIFT AID (NON-NEED-BASED) ***Total amount:*** $10,769,908 (87% institutional, 13% external sources). ***Receiving aid:*** Freshmen: 15% (140). Undergraduates: 13% (564). ***Average award:*** Freshmen: $8410. Undergraduates: $6876. ***Scholarships, grants, and awards by category:*** *Academic interests/achievement:* 1,648 awards ($14,184,524 total): communication, foreign languages, general academic interests/achievements. *Creative arts/performance:* 313 awards ($2,713,850 total): art/fine arts, dance, music, performing arts, theater/drama. *Special achievements/activities:* 518 awards ($412,250 total): community service, general special achievements/activities, memberships. *Special characteristics:* 323 awards ($2,071,072 total): children and siblings of alumni, children of faculty/staff. ***Tuition waivers:*** Full or partial for employees or children of employees. ***ROTC:*** Army cooperative, Air Force cooperative.

LOANS ***Student loans:*** $28,489,930 (53% need-based, 47% non-need-based). ***Average need-based loan:*** Freshmen: $3897. Undergraduates: $4487. ***Parent loans:*** $15,753,940 (44% need-based, 56% non-need-based). ***Programs:*** FFEL (Subsidized and Unsubsidized Stafford, PLUS), Perkins, Federal Nursing, alternative loans.

WORK-STUDY ***Federal work-study:*** Total amount: $2,576,093; 2,709 jobs averaging $1027. ***State or other work-study/employment:*** Total amount: $1,446,716 (100% non-need-based). 720 part-time jobs averaging $2009.

ATHLETIC AWARDS Total amount: $3,109,550 (47% need-based, 53% non-need-based).

APPLYING FOR FINANCIAL AID ***Required financial aid forms:*** FAFSA, state aid form. ***Financial aid deadline (priority):*** 3/1. ***Notification date:*** Continuous.

CONTACT Ms. Sheryl Mihopulos, Director of Student Financial Services, Adelphi University, 1 South Avenue, PO Box 701, Garden City, NY 11530, 516-877-3365 or toll-free 800-ADELPHI. *Fax:* 516-877-3380. *E-mail:* mihopulos@adelphi.edu.

ADRIAN COLLEGE

Adrian, MI

Tuition & fees: $24,440 **Average undergraduate aid package: $20,945**

ABOUT THE INSTITUTION Independent religious, coed. ***Awards:*** associate and bachelor's degrees. 46 undergraduate majors. ***Total enrollment:*** 1,469. Undergraduates: 1,469. Freshmen: 500. Both federal and institutional methodology are used as a basis for awarding need-based institutional aid.

UNDERGRADUATE EXPENSES for 2009–10 ***Comprehensive fee:*** $31,900 includes full-time tuition ($24,140), mandatory fees ($300), and room and board ($7460). ***College room only:*** $3610. ***Part-time tuition:*** $685 per credit hour. ***Part-time fees:*** $75 per term.

FRESHMAN FINANCIAL AID (Fall 2008, est.) 446 applied for aid; of those 89% were deemed to have need. 100% of freshmen with need received aid; of those 87% had need fully met. ***Average percent of need met:*** 98% (excluding resources awarded to replace EFC). ***Average financial aid package:*** $15,714 (excluding resources awarded to replace EFC). 9% of all full-time freshmen had no need and received non-need-based gift aid.

UNDERGRADUATE FINANCIAL AID (Fall 2008, est.) 1,248 applied for aid; of those 92% were deemed to have need. 99% of undergraduates with need received aid; of those 89% had need fully met. ***Average percent of need met:*** 99% (excluding resources awarded to replace EFC). ***Average financial aid package:*** $20,945 (excluding resources awarded to replace EFC). 6% of all full-time undergraduates had no need and received non-need-based gift aid.

GIFT AID (NEED-BASED) ***Total amount:*** $19,832,875 (8% federal, 10% state, 80% institutional, 2% external sources). ***Receiving aid:*** Freshmen: 68% (336); all full-time undergraduates: 67% (959). ***Average award:*** Freshmen: $9594; Undergraduates: $9340. ***Scholarships, grants, and awards:*** Federal Pell, FSEOG, state, private, college/university gift aid from institutional funds.

GIFT AID (NON-NEED-BASED) ***Receiving aid:*** Freshmen: 74% (367). Undergraduates: 67% (969). ***Average award:*** Freshmen: $7426. Undergraduates: $7097. ***Scholarships, grants, and awards by category:*** *Academic interests/achievement:*

1,222 awards ($8,839,196 total): business, general academic interests/achievements. *Creative arts/performance:* 718 awards ($1,436,000 total): art/fine arts, music, theater/drama. *Special achievements/activities:* 88 awards ($132,000 total): religious involvement. *Special characteristics:* 132 awards ($330,000 total): children and siblings of alumni, children of faculty/staff, children of union members/company employees, international students, religious affiliation.

LOANS ***Student loans:*** $4,954,475 (100% need-based). 86% of past graduating class borrowed through all loan programs. *Average indebtedness per student:* $17,160. ***Average need-based loan:*** Freshmen: $4391. Undergraduates: $4802. ***Parent loans:*** $11,660,881 (100% need-based). ***Programs:*** FFEL (Subsidized and Unsubsidized Stafford, PLUS), Perkins.

WORK-STUDY ***Federal work-study:*** Total amount: $1,548,549; 874 jobs averaging $1800. ***State or other work-study/employment:*** Total amount: $90,900 (100% need-based). 584 part-time jobs averaging $1800.

APPLYING FOR FINANCIAL AID ***Required financial aid form:*** FAFSA. ***Financial aid deadline (priority):*** 3/1. ***Notification date:*** Continuous beginning 3/15. Students must reply by 5/1 or within 2 weeks of notification.

CONTACT Mr. Andrew Spohn, Director of Financial Aid, Adrian College, 110 South Madison Street, Adrian, MI 49221-2575, 517-265-5161 Ext. 4306 or toll-free 800-877-2246. *Fax:* 517-264-3153. *E-mail:* aspohn@adrian.edu.

AGNES SCOTT COLLEGE

Decatur, GA

Tuition & fees: $30,105 **Average undergraduate aid package: $29,153**

ABOUT THE INSTITUTION Independent religious, undergraduate: women only; graduate: coed. ***Awards:*** bachelor's and master's degrees and post-bachelor's certificates. 35 undergraduate majors. ***Total enrollment:*** 832. Undergraduates: 813. Freshmen: 179. Both federal and institutional methodology are used as a basis for awarding need-based institutional aid.

UNDERGRADUATE EXPENSES for 2009–10 ***Application fee:*** $35. ***Comprehensive fee:*** $39,955 includes full-time tuition ($29,890), mandatory fees ($215), and room and board ($9850). ***Part-time tuition:*** $1245 per hour.

FRESHMAN FINANCIAL AID (Fall 2008, est.) 161 applied for aid; of those 84% were deemed to have need. 100% of freshmen with need received aid; of those 52% had need fully met. ***Average percent of need met:*** 96% (excluding resources awarded to replace EFC). ***Average financial aid package:*** $29,977 (excluding resources awarded to replace EFC). 23% of all full-time freshmen had no need and received non-need-based gift aid.

UNDERGRADUATE FINANCIAL AID (Fall 2008, est.) 586 applied for aid; of those 88% were deemed to have need. 100% of undergraduates with need received aid; of those 54% had need fully met. ***Average percent of need met:*** 94% (excluding resources awarded to replace EFC). ***Average financial aid package:*** $29,153 (excluding resources awarded to replace EFC). 28% of all full-time undergraduates had no need and received non-need-based gift aid.

GIFT AID (NEED-BASED) ***Total amount:*** $11,342,210 (9% federal, 6% state, 83% institutional, 2% external sources). ***Receiving aid:*** Freshmen: 75% (135); all full-time undergraduates: 69% (512). ***Average award:*** Freshmen: $23,446; Undergraduates: $22,057. ***Scholarships, grants, and awards:*** Federal Pell, FSEOG, state, private, college/university gift aid from institutional funds.

GIFT AID (NON-NEED-BASED) ***Total amount:*** $4,125,086 (13% state, 82% institutional, 5% external sources). ***Receiving aid:*** Freshmen: 39% (69). Undergraduates: 31% (233). ***Average award:*** Freshmen: $16,655. Undergraduates: $15,635. ***Scholarships, grants, and awards by category:*** *Academic interests/achievement:* general academic interests/achievements. *Creative arts/performance:* music. *Special achievements/activities:* community service, leadership. *Special characteristics:* adult students, children of educators, children of faculty/staff, international students, religious affiliation. ***ROTC:*** Army cooperative, Air Force cooperative.

LOANS ***Student loans:*** $3,930,172 (51% need-based, 49% non-need-based). 73% of past graduating class borrowed through all loan programs. *Average indebtedness per student:* $25,577. ***Average need-based loan:*** Freshmen: $3262. Undergraduates: $4318. ***Parent loans:*** $1,312,566 (10% need-based, 90% non-need-based). ***Programs:*** FFEL (Subsidized and Unsubsidized Stafford, PLUS), college/university.

WORK-STUDY ***Federal work-study:*** Total amount: $853,677; jobs available. ***State or other work-study/employment:*** Total amount: $156,333 (1% need-based, 99% non-need-based). Part-time jobs available.

APPLYING FOR FINANCIAL AID ***Required financial aid forms:*** FAFSA, copy of previous year's tax returns. ***Financial aid deadline:*** 5/1 (priority: 2/15). ***Notification date:*** Continuous beginning 3/1. Students must reply within 2 weeks of notification.

CONTACT Lauren Cobb, Assistant Director of Financial Aid, Agnes Scott College, 141 East College Avenue, Decatur, GA 30030-3797, 404-471-6395 or toll-free 800-868-8602. *Fax:* 404-471-6159. *E-mail:* finaid@agnesscott.edu.

AIB COLLEGE OF BUSINESS

Des Moines, IA

CONTACT Connie Loven, Financial Aid Director, AIB College of Business, 2500 Fleur Drive, Des Moines, IA 50321, 515-244-4221 Ext. 4145 or toll-free 800-444-1921. *Fax:* 515-244-6773. *E-mail:* jensenc@aib.edu.

ALABAMA AGRICULTURAL AND MECHANICAL UNIVERSITY

Huntsville, AL

Tuition & fees (AL res): $3432 **Average undergraduate aid package: $2465**

ABOUT THE INSTITUTION State-supported, coed. ***Awards:*** bachelor's, master's, and doctoral degrees and post-master's certificates. 36 undergraduate majors. ***Total enrollment:*** 5,124. Undergraduates: 4,297. Freshmen: 1,046. Federal methodology is used as a basis for awarding need-based institutional aid.

UNDERGRADUATE EXPENSES for 2008–09 ***Application fee:*** $10. ***Tuition, state resident:*** full-time $3432; part-time $143 per credit hour. ***Tuition, nonresident:*** full-time $6834; part-time $286 per credit hour. ***College room and board:*** $4770; ***Room only:*** $2756. Room and board charges vary according to board plan, housing facility, and location. ***Payment plan:*** Installment.

FRESHMAN FINANCIAL AID (Fall 2008, est.) of those 3% had need fully met. ***Average percent of need met:*** 26% (excluding resources awarded to replace EFC). ***Average financial aid package:*** $2279 (excluding resources awarded to replace EFC).

UNDERGRADUATE FINANCIAL AID (Fall 2008, est.) of those 3% had need fully met. ***Average percent of need met:*** 95% (excluding resources awarded to replace EFC). ***Average financial aid package:*** $2465 (excluding resources awarded to replace EFC).

GIFT AID (NEED-BASED) ***Total amount:*** $9,775,535 (99% federal, 1% state). ***Receiving aid:*** Freshmen: 6% (61); all full-time undergraduates: 6% (223). ***Average award:*** Freshmen: $1317; Undergraduates: $1126. ***Scholarships, grants, and awards:*** Federal Pell, FSEOG, state, private, college/university gift aid from institutional funds.

GIFT AID (NON-NEED-BASED) ***Total amount:*** $6,585,645 (100% institutional). ***Scholarships, grants, and awards by category:*** *Academic interests/achievement:* general academic interests/achievements. *Creative arts/performance:* art/fine arts, music. *Special characteristics:* parents of current students. ***Tuition waivers:*** Full or partial for employees or children of employees. ***ROTC:*** Army.

LOANS ***Student loans:*** $22,521,027 (100% need-based). ***Average need-based loan:*** Freshmen: $1553. Undergraduates: $1343. ***Parent loans:*** $9,771,884 (100% need-based). ***Programs:*** FFEL (Subsidized and Unsubsidized Stafford, PLUS), Perkins.

WORK-STUDY ***Federal work-study:*** Total amount: $499,557; jobs available.

ATHLETIC AWARDS Total amount: $1,407,559 (100% non-need-based).

APPLYING FOR FINANCIAL AID ***Required financial aid form:*** FAFSA. ***Financial aid deadline (priority):*** 3/1. ***Notification date:*** Continuous beginning 4/15. Students must reply within 2 weeks of notification.

CONTACT Ms. Kai CampBell, Financial Aid Officer, Alabama Agricultural and Mechanical University, 4900 Meridian Street, Normal, AL 35762, 256-851-5400 or toll-free 800-553-0816. *Fax:* 256-851-5407.

ALABAMA STATE UNIVERSITY

Montgomery, AL

ABOUT THE INSTITUTION State-supported, coed. ***Awards:*** bachelor's, master's, doctoral, and first professional degrees and post-bachelor's and post-master's certificates. 49 undergraduate majors. ***Total enrollment:*** 5,608. Undergraduates: 4,647. Freshmen: 1,366.

GIFT AID (NEED-BASED) ***Scholarships, grants, and awards:*** Federal Pell, FSEOG, state, private, college/university gift aid from institutional funds, United Negro College Fund.

GIFT AID (NON-NEED-BASED) ***Scholarships, grants, and awards by category:*** *Academic interests/achievement:* general academic interests/achievements. *Creative arts/performance:* general creative arts/performance, music, theater/drama. *Special achievements/activities:* leadership. *Special characteristics:* general special characteristics, members of minority groups.

LOANS ***Programs:*** FFEL (Subsidized and Unsubsidized Stafford, PLUS), Perkins, state.

WORK-STUDY ***Federal work-study:*** Total amount: $1,451,113. ***State or other work-study/employment:*** Total amount: $154,360 (100% non-need-based).

APPLYING FOR FINANCIAL AID ***Required financial aid form:*** FAFSA.

CONTACT Mrs. Dorenda A. Adams, Director of Financial Aid, Alabama State University, PO Box 271, Montgomery, AL 36101-0271, 334-229-4323 or toll-free 800-253-5037. *Fax:* 334-299-4924. *E-mail:* dadams@alasu.edu.

ALASKA BIBLE COLLEGE

Glennallen, AK

Tuition & fees: N/R **Average undergraduate aid package: N/A**

ABOUT THE INSTITUTION Independent nondenominational, coed. 1 undergraduate major. Institutional methodology is used as a basis for awarding need-based institutional aid.

FRESHMAN FINANCIAL AID (Fall 2008, est.) 5 applied for aid; of those 100% were deemed to have need. 100% of freshmen with need received aid.

UNDERGRADUATE FINANCIAL AID (Fall 2008, est.) 25 applied for aid; of those 68% were deemed to have need. 100% of undergraduates with need received aid.

GIFT AID (NEED-BASED) ***Total amount:*** $10,390 (100% institutional). ***Receiving aid:*** Freshmen: 71% (5); all full-time undergraduates: 52% (17). ***Scholarships, grants, and awards:*** private, college/university gift aid from institutional funds.

GIFT AID (NON-NEED-BASED) ***Total amount:*** $500 (100% external sources). ***Scholarships, grants, and awards by category:*** *Academic interests/achievement:* 3 awards ($1150 total): general academic interests/achievements, religion/biblical studies. *Creative arts/performance:* 1 award: music. *Special achievements/activities:* 3 awards ($450 total): religious involvement. *Special characteristics:* 4 awards ($7740 total): children of faculty/staff, local/state students, religious affiliation, spouses of current students. ***Tuition waivers:*** Full or partial for employees or children of employees.

LOANS ***Student loans:*** $61,838 (100% need-based). 30% of past graduating class borrowed through all loan programs. *Average indebtedness per student:* $6184. ***Programs:*** state.

WORK-STUDY ***State or other work-study/employment:*** Total amount: $12,214 (100% need-based). 21 part-time jobs averaging $580.

APPLYING FOR FINANCIAL AID ***Required financial aid form:*** institution's own form. ***Financial aid deadline:*** 7/1 (priority: 7/1). ***Notification date:*** 8/1. Students must reply within 2 weeks of notification.

CONTACT Kevin Newman, Financial Aid Officer, Alaska Bible College, PO Box 289, Glennallen, AK 99588-0289, 907-822-3201 Ext. 253 or toll-free 800-478-7884. *Fax:* 907-822-5027. *E-mail:* knewman@akbible.edu.

ALASKA PACIFIC UNIVERSITY

Anchorage, AK

Tuition & fees: $22,610 **Average undergraduate aid package: $16,890**

ABOUT THE INSTITUTION Independent, coed. ***Awards:*** associate, bachelor's, and master's degrees and post-bachelor's certificates. 13 undergraduate majors. ***Total enrollment:*** 803. Undergraduates: 565. Freshmen: 66. Federal methodology is used as a basis for awarding need-based institutional aid.

UNDERGRADUATE EXPENSES for 2008–09 ***Application fee:*** $25. ***Comprehensive fee:*** $31,494 includes full-time tuition ($22,500), mandatory fees ($110), and room and board ($8884). Full-time tuition and fees vary according to class time, location, and program. Room and board charges vary according to board plan and housing facility. ***Part-time tuition:*** $940 per credit hour. Part-time tuition and fees vary according to class time, location, and program. ***Payment plans:*** Guaranteed tuition, installment, deferred payment.

FRESHMAN FINANCIAL AID (Fall 2008, est.) 56 applied for aid; of those 91% were deemed to have need. 94% of freshmen with need received aid. ***Average percent of need met:*** 68% (excluding resources awarded to replace EFC). ***Average financial aid package:*** $13,302 (excluding resources awarded to replace EFC). 8% of all full-time freshmen had no need and received non-need-based gift aid.

UNDERGRADUATE FINANCIAL AID (Fall 2008, est.) 271 applied for aid; of those 72% were deemed to have need. 99% of undergraduates with need received aid; of those 40% had need fully met. ***Average percent of need met:*** 81% (excluding resources awarded to replace EFC). ***Average financial aid package:*** $16,890 (excluding resources awarded to replace EFC). 16% of all full-time undergraduates had no need and received non-need-based gift aid.

GIFT AID (NEED-BASED) ***Total amount:*** $2,361,372 (21% federal, 1% state, 62% institutional, 16% external sources). ***Receiving aid:*** Freshmen: 36% (24); all full-time undergraduates: 21% (64). ***Average award:*** Freshmen: $7745; Undergraduates: $8200. ***Scholarships, grants, and awards:*** Federal Pell, FSEOG, state, private, college/university gift aid from institutional funds, Bureau of Indian Affairs Grants.

GIFT AID (NON-NEED-BASED) ***Total amount:*** $299,754 (33% institutional, 67% external sources). ***Receiving aid:*** Freshmen: 71% (47). Undergraduates: 56% (170). ***Average award:*** Freshmen: $5570. Undergraduates: $10,316. ***Scholarships, grants, and awards by category:*** *Academic interests/achievement:* 136 awards ($776,368 total): biological sciences, business, education, general academic interests/achievements, humanities, physical sciences, social sciences. *Special achievements/activities:* 89 awards ($184,626 total): community service, general special achievements/activities, leadership, religious involvement. *Special characteristics:* 58 awards ($105,300 total): children and siblings of alumni, children of faculty/staff, ethnic background, general special characteristics, international students, local/state students, members of minority groups, out-of-state students, religious affiliation. ***Tuition waivers:*** Full or partial for employees or children of employees, adult students, senior citizens. ***ROTC:*** Air Force cooperative.

LOANS ***Student loans:*** $5,467,102 (65% need-based, 35% non-need-based). 93% of past graduating class borrowed through all loan programs. *Average indebtedness per student:* $10,197. ***Average need-based loan:*** Freshmen: $3500. Undergraduates: $7250. ***Parent loans:*** $460,482 (100% non-need-based). ***Programs:*** FFEL (Subsidized and Unsubsidized Stafford, PLUS), state.

WORK-STUDY ***Federal work-study:*** Total amount: $70,978; 58 jobs averaging $1433. ***State or other work-study/employment:*** Total amount: $110,147 (100% non-need-based). Part-time jobs available.

APPLYING FOR FINANCIAL AID ***Required financial aid form:*** FAFSA. ***Financial aid deadline (priority):*** 4/15. ***Notification date:*** Continuous. Students must reply within 4 weeks of notification.

CONTACT Jo Holland, Director of Student Financial Services, Alaska Pacific University, 4101 University Drive, Anchorage, AK 99508-4672, 907-564-8341 or toll-free 800-252-7528. *Fax:* 907-564-8372. *E-mail:* sfs@alaskapacific.edu.

ALBANY COLLEGE OF PHARMACY AND HEALTH SCIENCES

Albany, NY

CONTACT Tiffany M. Gutierrez, Director of Financial Aid, Albany College of Pharmacy and Health Sciences, 106 New Scotland Avenue, Albany, NY 12208-3425, 518-445-7256 or toll-free 888-203-8010. *Fax:* 518-445-7322. *E-mail:* gutierrt@mail.acp.edu.

ALBANY STATE UNIVERSITY

Albany, GA

CONTACT Ms. Kathleen J. Caldwell, Director of Financial Aid, Albany State University, 504 College Drive, Albany, GA 31705-2717, 912-430-4650 or toll-free 800-822-RAMS (in-state). *Fax:* 912-430-3936. *E-mail:* finaid@asurams.edu.

ALBERTUS MAGNUS COLLEGE

New Haven, CT

Tuition & fees: $22,624 **Average undergraduate aid package: $9074**

ABOUT THE INSTITUTION Independent Roman Catholic, coed. ***Awards:*** associate, bachelor's, and master's degrees. 56 undergraduate majors. ***Total enrollment:*** 2,129. Undergraduates: 1,714. Freshmen: 188. Federal methodology is used as a basis for awarding need-based institutional aid.

UNDERGRADUATE EXPENSES for 2008–09 ***Application fee:*** $35. ***Comprehensive fee:*** $32,066 includes full-time tuition ($21,780), mandatory fees ($844), and room and board ($9442). Full-time tuition and fees vary according to class time and program. ***Part-time tuition:*** $2178 per course. Part-time tuition and fees vary according to class time and program. ***Payment plan:*** Installment.

FRESHMAN FINANCIAL AID (Fall 2008, est.) 316 applied for aid; of those 92% were deemed to have need. 100% of freshmen with need received aid; of those 4% had need fully met. ***Average percent of need met:*** 52% (excluding resources awarded to replace EFC). ***Average financial aid package:*** $11,098 (excluding resources awarded to replace EFC). 3% of all full-time freshmen had no need and received non-need-based gift aid.

UNDERGRADUATE FINANCIAL AID (Fall 2008, est.) 1,442 applied for aid; of those 91% were deemed to have need. 100% of undergraduates with need received aid; of those 7% had need fully met. ***Average percent of need met:*** 53% (excluding resources awarded to replace EFC). ***Average financial aid package:*** $9074 (excluding resources awarded to replace EFC). 2% of all full-time undergraduates had no need and received non-need-based gift aid.

GIFT AID (NEED-BASED) ***Total amount:*** $6,616,670 (27% federal, 36% state, 31% institutional, 6% external sources). ***Receiving aid:*** Freshmen: 37% (139); all full-time undergraduates: 21% (361). ***Average award:*** Freshmen: $6580; Undergraduates: $5739. ***Scholarships, grants, and awards:*** Federal Pell, FSEOG, state, college/university gift aid from institutional funds.

GIFT AID (NON-NEED-BASED) ***Total amount:*** $238,927 (62% institutional, 38% external sources). ***Receiving aid:*** Freshmen: 3% (11). Undergraduates: 2% (32). ***Average award:*** Freshmen: $5742. Undergraduates: $3537. ***Scholarships, grants, and awards by category:*** *Academic interests/achievement:* 257 awards: biological sciences, business, communication, computer science, education, English, foreign languages, general academic interests/achievements, humanities, international studies, mathematics, physical sciences, premedicine, religion/biblical studies, social sciences. *Creative arts/performance:* art/fine arts, performing arts, theater/drama. *Special achievements/activities:* 10 awards ($6250 total): community service, leadership. *Special characteristics:* 48 awards ($6104 total): local/state students, religious affiliation. ***Tuition waivers:*** Full or partial for employees or children of employees, senior citizens.

LOANS ***Student loans:*** $13,153,313 (41% need-based, 59% non-need-based). 85% of past graduating class borrowed through all loan programs. *Average indebtedness per student:* $26,404. ***Average need-based loan:*** Freshmen: $3530. Undergraduates: $4398. ***Parent loans:*** $727,700 (100% non-need-based). ***Programs:*** FFEL (Subsidized and Unsubsidized Stafford, PLUS), Perkins.

WORK-STUDY ***Federal work-study:*** Total amount: $171,846; 78 jobs averaging $1583. ***State or other work-study/employment:*** 34 part-time jobs averaging $3400.

APPLYING FOR FINANCIAL AID ***Required financial aid form:*** FAFSA. ***Financial aid deadline (priority):*** 3/15. ***Notification date:*** 4/15. Students must reply within 2 weeks of notification.

CONTACT Andrew Foster, Director of Financial Aid, Albertus Magnus College, 700 Prospect Street, New Haven, CT 06511-1189, 203-773-8508 or toll-free 800-578-9160. *Fax:* 203-773-8972. *E-mail:* financial_aid@albertus.edu.

ALBION COLLEGE

Albion, MI

Tuition & fees: $28,880 **Average undergraduate aid package: $23,332**

ABOUT THE INSTITUTION Independent Methodist, coed. ***Awards:*** bachelor's degrees. 37 undergraduate majors. ***Total enrollment:*** 1,860. Undergraduates: 1,860. Freshmen: 485. Federal methodology is used as a basis for awarding need-based institutional aid.

UNDERGRADUATE EXPENSES for 2008–09 ***Application fee:*** $20. ***One-time required fee:*** $160. ***Comprehensive fee:*** $37,070 includes full-time tuition ($28,380), mandatory fees ($500), and room and board ($8190). ***College room only:*** $4006. Full-time tuition and fees vary according to course load. Room and board charges vary according to housing facility. ***Part-time tuition:*** $4824 per course. ***Part-time fees:*** $250 per term; $500 per year. ***Payment plans:*** Installment, deferred payment.

FRESHMAN FINANCIAL AID (Fall 2008, est.) 384 applied for aid; of those 83% were deemed to have need. 100% of freshmen with need received aid; of those 39% had need fully met. ***Average percent of need met:*** 91% (excluding resources awarded to replace EFC). ***Average financial aid package:*** $23,987 (excluding resources awarded to replace EFC). 33% of all full-time freshmen had no need and received non-need-based gift aid.

UNDERGRADUATE FINANCIAL AID (Fall 2008, est.) 1,287 applied for aid; of those 87% were deemed to have need. 100% of undergraduates with need received aid; of those 33% had need fully met. ***Average percent of need met:*** 89% (excluding resources awarded to replace EFC). ***Average financial aid package:*** $23,332 (excluding resources awarded to replace EFC). 37% of all full-time undergraduates had no need and received non-need-based gift aid.

GIFT AID (NEED-BASED) ***Total amount:*** $20,888,730 (6% federal, 10% state, 82% institutional, 2% external sources). ***Receiving aid:*** Freshmen: 65% (318); all full-time undergraduates: 61% (1,125). ***Average award:*** Freshmen: $20,133; Undergraduates: $18,408. ***Scholarships, grants, and awards:*** Federal Pell, FSEOG, state, private, college/university gift aid from institutional funds.

GIFT AID (NON-NEED-BASED) ***Total amount:*** $9,085,813 (3% state, 96% institutional, 1% external sources). ***Receiving aid:*** Freshmen: 63% (306). Undergraduates: 56% (1,042). ***Average award:*** Freshmen: $13,448. Undergraduates: $12,788. ***Scholarships, grants, and awards by category:*** *Academic interests/achievement:* 1,631 awards ($20,057,440 total): business, communication, general academic interests/achievements, mathematics, premedicine. *Creative arts/performance:* 150 awards ($146,250 total): art/fine arts, dance, music, performing arts, theater/drama. *Special characteristics:* 252 awards ($382,838 total): children and siblings of alumni, relatives of clergy. ***Tuition waivers:*** Full or partial for employees or children of employees.

LOANS ***Student loans:*** $10,875,835 (41% need-based, 59% non-need-based). ***Average need-based loan:*** Freshmen: $3908. Undergraduates: $4965. ***Parent loans:*** $2,142,094 (100% non-need-based). ***Programs:*** Federal Direct (Subsidized and Unsubsidized Stafford, PLUS), FFEL (Subsidized and Unsubsidized Stafford, PLUS), Perkins.

WORK-STUDY ***Federal work-study:*** Total amount: $917,534; 657 jobs averaging $1397.

APPLYING FOR FINANCIAL AID ***Required financial aid form:*** FAFSA. ***Financial aid deadline (priority):*** 3/1. ***Notification date:*** Continuous beginning 3/15.

CONTACT Ms. Ann Whitmer, Director of Financial Aid, Albion College, Kellogg Center Box 4670, Albion, MI 49224-1831, 517-629-0440 or toll-free 800-858-6770. *Fax:* 517-629-0581. *E-mail:* awhitmer@albion.edu.

ALBRIGHT COLLEGE

Reading, PA

Tuition & fees: $30,570 **Average undergraduate aid package: $19,988**

ABOUT THE INSTITUTION Independent religious, coed. ***Awards:*** bachelor's and master's degrees. 45 undergraduate majors. ***Total enrollment:*** 2,305. Undergraduates: 2,245. Freshmen: 509. Federal methodology is used as a basis for awarding need-based institutional aid.

UNDERGRADUATE EXPENSES for 2008–09 ***Application fee:*** $25. ***Comprehensive fee:*** $39,240 includes full-time tuition ($29,770), mandatory fees ($800), and room and board ($8670). ***College room only:*** $4870. Full-time tuition and fees vary according to program. Room and board charges vary according to board plan and housing facility. ***Part-time tuition:*** $930 per course. Part-time tuition and fees vary according to class time. ***Payment plan:*** Installment.

FRESHMAN FINANCIAL AID (Fall 2008, est.) 435 applied for aid; of those 89% were deemed to have need. 99% of freshmen with need received aid; of those 18% had need fully met. ***Average percent of need met:*** 78% (excluding resources awarded to replace EFC). ***Average financial aid package:*** $23,472 (excluding resources awarded to replace EFC). 13% of all full-time freshmen had no need and received non-need-based gift aid.

UNDERGRADUATE FINANCIAL AID (Fall 2008, est.) 1,758 applied for aid; of those 87% were deemed to have need. 97% of undergraduates with need received aid; of those 18% had need fully met. ***Average percent of need met:*** 72% (excluding resources awarded to replace EFC). ***Average financial aid package:*** $19,988 (excluding resources awarded to replace EFC). 10% of all full-time undergraduates had no need and received non-need-based gift aid.

GIFT AID (NEED-BASED) ***Total amount:*** $22,087,158 (12% federal, 9% state, 74% institutional, 5% external sources). ***Receiving aid:*** Freshmen: 76% (385); all full-time undergraduates: 65% (1,465). ***Average award:*** Freshmen: $17,832; Undergraduates: $15,054. ***Scholarships, grants, and awards:*** Federal Pell, FSEOG, state, private, college/university gift aid from institutional funds, Academic Competitiveness Grant, National Smart Grant.

GIFT AID (NON-NEED-BASED) ***Total amount:*** $3,876,061 (1% state, 80% institutional, 19% external sources). ***Receiving aid:*** Freshmen: 9% (45). Undergraduates: 7% (147). ***Average award:*** Freshmen: $11,424. Undergraduates: $11,315. ***Scholarships, grants, and awards by category:*** *Creative arts/performance:* 99 awards ($182,750 total): art/fine arts, journalism/publications, music, theater/drama. *Special achievements/activities:* 581 awards ($1,017,231 total): general special achievements/activities, hobbies/interests, junior miss, leadership, memberships, religious involvement. *Special characteristics:* 182 awards ($355,019 total): children and siblings of alumni, ethnic background, siblings of current students. ***Tuition waivers:*** Full or partial for children of alumni, employees or children of employees, adult students, senior citizens.

LOANS ***Student loans:*** $15,982,357 (70% need-based, 30% non-need-based). 83% of past graduating class borrowed through all loan programs. *Average indebtedness per student:* $31,720. ***Average need-based loan:*** Freshmen: $4990. Undergraduates: $4879. ***Parent loans:*** $3,119,863 (34% need-based, 66% non-need-based). ***Programs:*** FFEL (Subsidized and Unsubsidized Stafford, PLUS), Perkins, private loans.

WORK-STUDY ***Federal work-study:*** Total amount: $1,540,337; 795 jobs averaging $1789. ***State or other work-study/employment:*** Total amount: $590,610 (4% need-based, 96% non-need-based). 307 part-time jobs averaging $1883.

APPLYING FOR FINANCIAL AID ***Required financial aid form:*** FAFSA. ***Financial aid deadline:*** Continuous. ***Notification date:*** Continuous beginning 2/15. Students must reply by 5/1 or within 2 weeks of notification.

CONTACT Mary Ellen Duffy, Director of Financial Aid, Albright College, PO Box 15234, Reading, PA 19612-5234, 610-921-7515 or toll-free 800-252-1856. *Fax:* 610-921-7729. *E-mail:* mduffy@alb.edu.

ALCORN STATE UNIVERSITY

Alcorn State, MS

Tuition & fees (MS res): $4488 **Average undergraduate aid package: $8670**

ABOUT THE INSTITUTION State-supported, coed. ***Awards:*** associate, bachelor's, and master's degrees and post-master's certificates. 31 undergraduate majors. ***Total enrollment:*** 3,252. Undergraduates: 2,626. Freshmen: 402. Federal methodology is used as a basis for awarding need-based institutional aid.

UNDERGRADUATE EXPENSES for 2008–09 ***Tuition, state resident:*** full-time $4488; part-time $187 per hour. ***Tuition, nonresident:*** full-time $10,088; part-time $445 per hour. ***College room and board:*** $5016.

FRESHMAN FINANCIAL AID (Fall 2008, est.) 396 applied for aid; of those 93% were deemed to have need. 100% of freshmen with need received aid; of those 55% had need fully met. ***Average percent of need met:*** 82% (excluding resources awarded to replace EFC). ***Average financial aid package:*** $9798 (excluding resources awarded to replace EFC).

UNDERGRADUATE FINANCIAL AID (Fall 2008, est.) 2,180 applied for aid; of those 100% were deemed to have need. 100% of undergraduates with need received aid; of those 87% had need fully met. ***Average percent of need met:*** 75% (excluding resources awarded to replace EFC). ***Average financial aid package:*** $8670 (excluding resources awarded to replace EFC).

GIFT AID (NEED-BASED) ***Total amount:*** $12,499,970 (71% federal, 3% state, 26% institutional). ***Receiving aid:*** Freshmen: 82% (323); all full-time undergraduates: 74% (1,760). ***Average award:*** Freshmen: $3977; Undergraduates: $3856. ***Scholarships, grants, and awards:*** Federal Pell, FSEOG, state, private, college/university gift aid from institutional funds.

GIFT AID (NON-NEED-BASED) ***Receiving aid:*** Freshmen: 42% (167). Undergraduates: 19% (460). ***Average award:*** Freshmen: $1340. Undergraduates: $1476. ***Scholarships, grants, and awards by category:*** *Academic interests/achievement:* 167 awards ($1,146,869 total): general academic interests/achievements. *Creative arts/performance:* 135 awards ($810,231 total): music. *Special characteristics:* 477 awards ($484,169 total): children of faculty/staff, local/state students, members of minority groups. ***Tuition waivers:*** Full or partial for employees or children of employees. ***ROTC:*** Army.

LOANS ***Student loans:*** $18,624,148 (54% need-based, 46% non-need-based). 69% of past graduating class borrowed through all loan programs. *Average indebtedness per student:* $18,123. ***Average need-based loan:*** Freshmen: $3352. Undergraduates: $4563. ***Parent loans:*** $796,642 (100% non-need-based). ***Programs:*** Federal Direct (Subsidized and Unsubsidized Stafford, PLUS).

WORK-STUDY ***Federal work-study:*** Total amount: $177,770; 213 jobs averaging $964.

ATHLETIC AWARDS Total amount: $1,273,022 (100% non-need-based).

APPLYING FOR FINANCIAL AID ***Required financial aid forms:*** FAFSA, institution's own form. ***Financial aid deadline (priority):*** 3/15. ***Notification date:*** Continuous beginning 4/1. Students must reply within 4 weeks of notification.

CONTACT Juanita M. Russell, Director of Financial Aid, Alcorn State University, 1000 ASU Drive #28, Alcorn State, MS 39096-7500, 601-877-6190 or toll-free 800-222-6790. *Fax:* 601-877-6110. *E-mail:* juanita@lorman.alcorn.edu.

ALDERSON-BROADDUS COLLEGE

Philippi, WV

Tuition & fees: $21,020 **Average undergraduate aid package: $19,554**

ABOUT THE INSTITUTION Independent religious, coed. ***Awards:*** bachelor's and master's degrees and post-bachelor's certificates. 32 undergraduate majors. ***Total enrollment:*** 738. Undergraduates: 609. Freshmen: 157. Federal methodology is used as a basis for awarding need-based institutional aid.

UNDERGRADUATE EXPENSES for 2008–09 ***Application fee:*** $25. ***Comprehensive fee:*** $27,818 includes full-time tuition ($20,820), mandatory fees ($200), and room and board ($6798). ***College room only:*** $3308. Full-time tuition and fees vary according to program and student level. Room and board charges vary according to housing facility. ***Part-time tuition:*** $694 per credit hour. ***Part-time fees:*** $50 per term. Part-time tuition and fees vary according to program and student level. ***Payment plan:*** Installment.

FRESHMAN FINANCIAL AID (Fall 2008, est.) 157 applied for aid; of those 91% were deemed to have need. 100% of freshmen with need received aid; of those 27% had need fully met. ***Average percent of need met:*** 85% (excluding resources awarded to replace EFC). ***Average financial aid package:*** $19,692 (excluding resources awarded to replace EFC). 8% of all full-time freshmen had no need and received non-need-based gift aid.

UNDERGRADUATE FINANCIAL AID (Fall 2008, est.) 565 applied for aid; of those 93% were deemed to have need. 100% of undergraduates with need received aid; of those 24% had need fully met. ***Average percent of need met:*** 80% (excluding resources awarded to replace EFC). ***Average financial aid package:*** $19,554 (excluding resources awarded to replace EFC). 4% of all full-time undergraduates had no need and received non-need-based gift aid.

GIFT AID (NEED-BASED) ***Total amount:*** $6,447,158 (19% federal, 16% state, 60% institutional, 5% external sources). ***Receiving aid:*** Freshmen: 91% (143); all full-time undergraduates: 92% (521). ***Average award:*** Freshmen: $15,929; Undergraduates: $14,978. ***Scholarships, grants, and awards:*** Federal Pell, FSEOG, state, private, college/university gift aid from institutional funds, Federal Nursing, National Health Service Corp., Scholarship for Disadvantaged Students.

GIFT AID (NON-NEED-BASED) ***Total amount:*** $639,154 (10% state, 86% institutional, 4% external sources). ***Receiving aid:*** Freshmen: 14% (22). Undergraduates: 13% (73). ***Average award:*** Freshmen: $8136. Undergraduates: $7615. ***Scholarships, grants, and awards by category:*** *Academic interests/achievement:* 510 awards ($3,090,807 total): biological sciences, business, communication, computer science, education, general academic interests/achievements, health fields, humanities, mathematics, physical sciences, premedicine, religion/biblical studies, social sciences. *Creative arts/performance:* 69 awards ($471,253 total): art/fine arts, creative writing, debating, journalism/publications, music, performing arts, theater/drama. *Special achievements/activities:* general special achievements/activities, leadership. *Special characteristics:* 23 awards ($344,157 total): children of faculty/staff, ethnic background, general special characteristics, international students, religious affiliation. ***Tuition waivers:*** Full or partial for employees or children of employees.

LOANS ***Student loans:*** $4,831,458 (88% need-based, 12% non-need-based). 90% of past graduating class borrowed through all loan programs. *Average indebtedness per student:* $21,478. ***Average need-based loan:*** Freshmen: $4171. Undergraduates: $4874. ***Parent loans:*** $439,545 (75% need-based, 25% non-need-based). ***Programs:*** FFEL (Subsidized and Unsubsidized Stafford, PLUS), Perkins, Federal Nursing.

WORK-STUDY ***Federal work-study:*** Total amount: $286,254; 207 jobs averaging $1400. ***State or other work-study/employment:*** Total amount: $250,724 (100% non-need-based). 135 part-time jobs averaging $1400.

ATHLETIC AWARDS Total amount: $1,866,129 (81% need-based, 19% non-need-based).

APPLYING FOR FINANCIAL AID ***Required financial aid form:*** FAFSA. ***Financial aid deadline (priority):*** 3/1. ***Notification date:*** Continuous. Students must reply within 2 weeks of notification.

CONTACT Brian Weingart, Director of Financial Aid, Alderson-Broaddus College, College Hill Road, Philippi, WV 26416, 304-457-6354 or toll-free 800-263-1549. *Fax:* 304-457-6391.

ALFRED UNIVERSITY

Alfred, NY

Tuition & fees: $25,246 **Average undergraduate aid package: $21,253**

ABOUT THE INSTITUTION Independent, coed. ***Awards:*** bachelor's, master's, and doctoral degrees and post-master's certificates. 44 undergraduate majors. ***Total enrollment:*** 2,416. Undergraduates: 1,975. Freshmen: 502. Both federal and institutional methodology are used as a basis for awarding need-based institutional aid.

UNDERGRADUATE EXPENSES for 2009–10 ***Application fee:*** $40. ***Comprehensive fee:*** $41,420 includes full-time tuition ($24,366), mandatory fees ($880), and room and board ($16,174). ***College room only:*** $5706. ***Part-time tuition:*** $790 per credit hour. ***Part-time fees:*** $72 per term.

FRESHMAN FINANCIAL AID (Fall 2008, est.) 447 applied for aid; of those 83% were deemed to have need. 100% of freshmen with need received aid; of those 15% had need fully met. ***Average percent of need met:*** 89% (excluding resources awarded to replace EFC). ***Average financial aid package:*** $23,510 (excluding resources awarded to replace EFC). 5% of all full-time freshmen had no need and received non-need-based gift aid.

UNDERGRADUATE FINANCIAL AID (Fall 2008, est.) 1,614 applied for aid; of those 86% were deemed to have need. 100% of undergraduates with need received aid; of those 22% had need fully met. ***Average percent of need met:*** 85% (excluding resources awarded to replace EFC). ***Average financial aid package:*** $21,253 (excluding resources awarded to replace EFC). 8% of all full-time undergraduates had no need and received non-need-based gift aid.

GIFT AID (NEED-BASED) ***Total amount:*** $21,429,199 (13% federal, 10% state, 77% institutional). ***Receiving aid:*** Freshmen: 74% (372); all full-time undergraduates: 73% (1,368). ***Average award:*** Freshmen: $16,817; Undergraduates: $15,062. ***Scholarships, grants, and awards:*** Federal Pell, FSEOG, state, private, college/university gift aid from institutional funds.

GIFT AID (NON-NEED-BASED) ***Total amount:*** $2,593,265 (5% federal, 2% state, 75% institutional, 18% external sources). ***Receiving aid:*** Freshmen: 36% (180). Undergraduates: 38% (708). ***Average award:*** Freshmen: $7441. Undergraduates: $8551. ***Scholarships, grants, and awards by category:*** *Academic interests/achievement:* biological sciences, business, communication, education, engineering/technologies, English, foreign languages, general academic interests/achievements, humanities, international studies, mathematics, military science, physical sciences, premedicine, social sciences. *Creative arts/performance:* art/fine arts, general creative arts/performance, performing arts. *Special achievements/activities:* leadership. *Special characteristics:* children of educators, children of faculty/staff, international students. ***ROTC:*** Army cooperative.

LOANS ***Student loans:*** $13,749,644 (51% need-based, 49% non-need-based). 79% of past graduating class borrowed through all loan programs. *Average indebtedness per student:* $26,962. ***Average need-based loan:*** Freshmen: $5037. Undergraduates: $5684. ***Parent loans:*** $6,679,410 (100% non-need-based). ***Programs:*** FFEL (Subsidized and Unsubsidized Stafford, PLUS), Perkins, college/university, alternative loans.

WORK-STUDY ***Federal work-study:*** Total amount: $1,582,332; jobs available.

APPLYING FOR FINANCIAL AID ***Required financial aid forms:*** FAFSA, institution's own form, state aid form, business/farm supplement. ***Financial aid deadline:*** 3/15. ***Notification date:*** Continuous. Students must reply by 5/1 or within 2 weeks of notification.

CONTACT Mr. Earl Pierce, Director of Student Financial Aid, Alfred University, Alumni Hall, One Saxon Drive, Alfred, NY 14802-1205, 607-871-2159 or toll-free 800-541-9229. *Fax:* 607-871-2252. *E-mail:* pierce@alfred.edu.

ALICE LLOYD COLLEGE

Pippa Passes, KY

Tuition & fees: $1400 **Average undergraduate aid package: $9125**

ABOUT THE INSTITUTION Independent, coed. ***Awards:*** bachelor's degrees. 17 undergraduate majors. ***Total enrollment:*** 609. Undergraduates: 609. Freshmen: 187. Federal methodology is used as a basis for awarding need-based institutional aid.

UNDERGRADUATE EXPENSES for 2009–10 ***One-time required fee:*** $50. includes mandatory fees ($1400) and room and board ($4450). ***College room only:*** $2070. ***Part-time tuition:*** $212 per credit hour. full-time students in the 108-county service area are granted guaranteed tuition.

FRESHMAN FINANCIAL AID (Fall 2008, est.) 176 applied for aid; of those 88% were deemed to have need. 100% of freshmen with need received aid; of those 19% had need fully met. ***Average percent of need met:*** 74% (excluding resources awarded to replace EFC). ***Average financial aid package:*** $8931 (excluding resources awarded to replace EFC). 12% of all full-time freshmen had no need and received non-need-based gift aid.

UNDERGRADUATE FINANCIAL AID (Fall 2008, est.) 531 applied for aid; of those 89% were deemed to have need. 100% of undergraduates with need received aid; of those 31% had need fully met. ***Average percent of need met:*** 76% (excluding resources awarded to replace EFC). ***Average financial aid package:*** $9125 (excluding resources awarded to replace EFC).

GIFT AID (NEED-BASED) ***Total amount:*** $3,061,696 (46% federal, 40% state, 14% institutional). ***Receiving aid:*** Freshmen: 70% (123); all full-time undergraduates: 79% (418). ***Average award:*** Freshmen: $7513; Undergraduates: $7490. ***Scholarships, grants, and awards:*** Federal Pell, FSEOG, state, private, college/university gift aid from institutional funds.

GIFT AID (NON-NEED-BASED) ***Total amount:*** $1,861,249 (33% state, 66% institutional, 1% external sources). ***Receiving aid:*** Freshmen: 12% (22). Undergraduates: 17% (91). ***Average award:*** Freshmen: $7000. Undergraduates: $8193. ***Scholarships, grants, and awards by category:*** *Special achievements/activities:* 31 awards ($226,850 total): general special achievements/activities. *Special characteristics:* 15 awards ($57,765 total): members of minority groups.

LOANS ***Student loans:*** $568,077 (49% need-based, 51% non-need-based). 34% of past graduating class borrowed through all loan programs. *Average indebtedness per student:* $4781. ***Average need-based loan:*** Freshmen: $500. Undergraduates: $3000. ***Parent loans:*** $31,173 (100% non-need-based). ***Programs:*** FFEL (Subsidized and Unsubsidized Stafford, PLUS), college/university, Bagby Loans (for freshmen).

WORK-STUDY ***Federal work-study:*** Total amount: $700,293; 402 jobs averaging $2320. ***State or other work-study/employment:*** Total amount: $462,810 (100% non-need-based). 241 part-time jobs averaging $2320.

ATHLETIC AWARDS Total amount: $261,563 (100% non-need-based).

APPLYING FOR FINANCIAL AID ***Required financial aid form:*** FAFSA. ***Financial aid deadline (priority):*** 3/15. ***Notification date:*** Continuous beginning 4/15.

CONTACT Ms. Jacqueline Stewart, Director of Financial Aid, Alice Lloyd College, 100 Purpose Road, Pippa Passes, KY 41844, 606-368-6059. *E-mail:* jacquelinestewart@alc.edu.

ALLEGHENY COLLEGE

Meadville, PA

Tuition & fees: $32,000 **Average undergraduate aid package: $25,578**

ABOUT THE INSTITUTION Independent, coed. ***Awards:*** bachelor's degrees. 48 undergraduate majors. ***Total enrollment:*** 2,125. Undergraduates: 2,125. Freshmen: 565. Federal methodology is used as a basis for awarding need-based institutional aid.

UNDERGRADUATE EXPENSES for 2008–09 ***Application fee:*** $35. ***Comprehensive fee:*** $40,000 includes full-time tuition ($31,680), mandatory fees ($320), and room and board ($8000). ***College room only:*** $4200. Room and board charges vary according to board plan and housing facility. ***Part-time tuition:*** $1320 per credit hour. ***Part-time fees:*** $160 per term. Part-time tuition and fees vary according to course load. ***Payment plans:*** Tuition prepayment, installment.

FRESHMAN FINANCIAL AID (Fall 2008, est.) 468 applied for aid; of those 83% were deemed to have need. 100% of freshmen with need received aid; of those 53% had need fully met. ***Average percent of need met:*** 95% (excluding resources awarded to replace EFC). ***Average financial aid package:*** $27,500 (excluding resources awarded to replace EFC). 29% of all full-time freshmen had no need and received non-need-based gift aid.

UNDERGRADUATE FINANCIAL AID (Fall 2008, est.) 1,625 applied for aid; of those 88% were deemed to have need. 100% of undergraduates with need received aid; of those 40% had need fully met. ***Average percent of need met:***

91% (excluding resources awarded to replace EFC). ***Average financial aid package:*** $25,578 (excluding resources awarded to replace EFC). 29% of all full-time undergraduates had no need and received non-need-based gift aid.

GIFT AID (NEED-BASED) ***Total amount:*** $26,081,059 (8% federal, 7% state, 81% institutional, 4% external sources). ***Receiving aid:*** Freshmen: 69% (389); all full-time undergraduates: 68% (1,424). ***Average award:*** Freshmen: $20,833; Undergraduates: $18,654. ***Scholarships, grants, and awards:*** Federal Pell, FSEOG, state, private, college/university gift aid from institutional funds, Academic Competitiveness Grant, National Smart Grant, Veterans Educational Benefits.

GIFT AID (NON-NEED-BASED) ***Total amount:*** $7,988,389 (94% institutional, 6% external sources). ***Receiving aid:*** Freshmen: 12% (67). Undergraduates: 10% (210). ***Average award:*** Freshmen: $10,643. Undergraduates: $10,875. ***Scholarships, grants, and awards by category:*** *Academic interests/achievement:* 1,771 awards ($20,040,103 total): general academic interests/achievements. *Special characteristics:* 58 awards: adult students, children of educators, children of faculty/staff, international students. ***Tuition waivers:*** Full or partial for employees or children of employees.

LOANS ***Student loans:*** $13,665,602 (44% need-based, 56% non-need-based). ***Average need-based loan:*** Freshmen: $4662. Undergraduates: $5093. ***Parent loans:*** $2,901,195 (100% non-need-based). ***Programs:*** Federal Direct (Subsidized and Unsubsidized Stafford, PLUS), Perkins, private loans from commercial lenders.

WORK-STUDY ***Federal work-study:*** Total amount: $2,255,651; 1,141 jobs averaging $2000. ***State or other work-study/employment:*** Total amount: $374,100 (100% non-need-based). 84 part-time jobs averaging $4500.

APPLYING FOR FINANCIAL AID ***Required financial aid form:*** FAFSA. ***Financial aid deadline (priority):*** 2/15. ***Notification date:*** Continuous beginning 3/1. Students must reply by 5/1 or within 4 weeks of notification.

CONTACT Ms. Sheryle Proper, Director of Financial Aid, Allegheny College, Box 43 520 North Main Street, Meadville, PA 16335, 800-835-7780 or toll-free 800-521-5293. *Fax:* 814-337-0431. *E-mail:* fao@allegheny.edu.

ALLEGHENY WESLEYAN COLLEGE

Salem, OH

CONTACT Financial Aid Office, Allegheny Wesleyan College, 2161 Woodsdale Road, Salem, OH 44460, 330-337-6403 or toll-free 800-292-3153.

ALLEN COLLEGE

Waterloo, IA

ABOUT THE INSTITUTION Independent, coed, primarily women. ***Awards:*** associate, bachelor's, and master's degrees (liberal arts and general education courses offered at either University of North Iowa or Wartburg College). 2 undergraduate majors. ***Total enrollment:*** 416. Undergraduates: 308. Freshmen: 4.

GIFT AID (NEED-BASED) ***Scholarships, grants, and awards:*** Federal Pell, FSEOG, state, private, college/university gift aid from institutional funds, Federal Nursing, Federal Scholarships for Disadvantaged Students.

GIFT AID (NON-NEED-BASED) ***Scholarships, grants, and awards by category:*** *Academic interests/achievement:* health fields. *Special achievements/activities:* community service, general special achievements/activities, leadership. *Special characteristics:* children of faculty/staff, general special characteristics, local/state students, members of minority groups, out-of-state students.

LOANS ***Programs:*** Federal Direct (Subsidized and Unsubsidized Stafford, PLUS), Perkins, Federal Nursing, state, college/university.

WORK-STUDY ***Federal work-study:*** Total amount: $28,532; 18 jobs averaging $2500. ***State or other work-study/employment:*** Part-time jobs available.

APPLYING FOR FINANCIAL AID ***Required financial aid forms:*** FAFSA, institution's own form.

CONTACT Kathie S. Walters, Financial Aid Director, Allen College, Barrett Forum, 1825 Logan Avenue, Waterloo, IA 50703, 319-226-2003. *Fax:* 319-226-2051. *E-mail:* walterks@ihs.org.

ALLEN UNIVERSITY

Columbia, SC

CONTACT Ms. Donna Foster, Director of Financial Aid, Allen University, 1530 Harden Street, Columbia, SC 29204-1085, 803-376-5736 or toll-free 877-625-5368 (in-state). *E-mail:* donnaf@allenuniversity.edu.

ALLIANT INTERNATIONAL UNIVERSITY

San Diego, CA

Tuition & fees: $15,220 **Average undergraduate aid package: $17,000**

ABOUT THE INSTITUTION Independent, coed. ***Awards:*** bachelor's, master's, and doctoral degrees and post-bachelor's certificates. 9 undergraduate majors. ***Total enrollment:*** 4,153. Undergraduates: 167. Federal methodology is used as a basis for awarding need-based institutional aid.

UNDERGRADUATE EXPENSES for 2009–10 ***Application fee:*** $45. ***Tuition:*** full-time $15,000; part-time $550 per unit.

UNDERGRADUATE FINANCIAL AID (Fall 2008, est.) 79 applied for aid; of those 100% were deemed to have need. 100% of undergraduates with need received aid; of those 66% had need fully met. ***Average percent of need met:*** 70% (excluding resources awarded to replace EFC). ***Average financial aid package:*** $17,000 (excluding resources awarded to replace EFC). 23% of all full-time undergraduates had no need and received non-need-based gift aid.

GIFT AID (NEED-BASED) ***Total amount:*** $549,859 (79% federal, 21% state). ***Receiving aid:*** All full-time undergraduates: 59% (79). ***Average award:*** Undergraduates: $6493. ***Scholarships, grants, and awards:*** Federal Pell, FSEOG, state, private, college/university gift aid from institutional funds.

GIFT AID (NON-NEED-BASED) ***Total amount:*** $158,870 (93% institutional, 7% external sources). ***Receiving aid:*** Undergraduates: 32% (43). ***Average award:*** Undergraduates: $1700. ***Scholarships, grants, and awards by category:*** *Academic interests/achievement:* business, communication, computer science, education, English, foreign languages, general academic interests/achievements, humanities, international studies, social sciences. *Special achievements/activities:* community service, general special achievements/activities, leadership. *Special characteristics:* children and siblings of alumni, children of current students, children of faculty/staff, ethnic background, international students, local/state students, members of minority groups, veterans. ***ROTC:*** Army cooperative.

LOANS ***Student loans:*** $723,452 (46% need-based, 54% non-need-based). 52% of past graduating class borrowed through all loan programs. *Average indebtedness per student:* $23,000. ***Average need-based loan:*** Undergraduates: $5500. ***Parent loans:*** $8500 (100% non-need-based). ***Programs:*** Federal Direct (Subsidized and Unsubsidized Stafford, PLUS), FFEL (Subsidized and Unsubsidized Stafford, PLUS), Perkins, alternative loans.

WORK-STUDY ***Federal work-study:*** Total amount: $45,238; 25 jobs averaging $1809. ***State or other work-study/employment:*** Total amount: $28,904 (100% need-based). 18 part-time jobs averaging $5300.

APPLYING FOR FINANCIAL AID ***Required financial aid form:*** FAFSA. ***Financial aid deadline (priority):*** 3/2. ***Notification date:*** Continuous beginning 3/15. Students must reply within 3 weeks of notification.

CONTACT Deborah Spindler, Director of Financial Aid, Alliant International University, 10455 Pomerado Road, San Diego, CA 92131-1799, 858-635-4559 Ext. 4700 or toll-free 866-825-5426. *Fax:* 858-635-4848.

ALMA COLLEGE

Alma, MI

Tuition & fees: $24,850 **Average undergraduate aid package: $19,768**

ABOUT THE INSTITUTION Independent Presbyterian, coed. ***Awards:*** bachelor's degrees. 69 undergraduate majors. ***Total enrollment:*** 1,384. Undergraduates: 1,384. Freshmen: 429. Federal methodology is used as a basis for awarding need-based institutional aid.

UNDERGRADUATE EXPENSES for 2008–09 ***Application fee:*** $25. ***Comprehensive fee:*** $32,970 includes full-time tuition ($24,630), mandatory fees ($220), and room and board ($8120). ***College room only:*** $4000. Room and board charges vary according to board plan and housing facility. ***Part-time tuition:*** $955 per credit. Part-time tuition and fees vary according to course load. ***Payment plans:*** Installment, deferred payment.

FRESHMAN FINANCIAL AID (Fall 2008, est.) 420 applied for aid; of those 83% were deemed to have need. 100% of freshmen with need received aid; of those 29% had need fully met. ***Average percent of need met:*** 95% (excluding resources awarded to replace EFC). ***Average financial aid package:*** $20,846 (excluding resources awarded to replace EFC). 19% of all full-time freshmen had no need and received non-need-based gift aid.

UNDERGRADUATE FINANCIAL AID (Fall 2008, est.) 1,209 applied for aid; of those 87% were deemed to have need. 100% of undergraduates with need

received aid; of those 21% had need fully met. ***Average percent of need met:*** 82% (excluding resources awarded to replace EFC). ***Average financial aid package:*** $19,768 (excluding resources awarded to replace EFC). 20% of all full-time undergraduates had no need and received non-need-based gift aid.

GIFT AID (NEED-BASED) ***Total amount:*** $16,953,299 (8% federal, 13% state, 78% institutional, 1% external sources). ***Receiving aid:*** Freshmen: 81% (346); all full-time undergraduates: 79% (1,049). ***Average award:*** Freshmen: $18,087; Undergraduates: $16,446. ***Scholarships, grants, and awards:*** Federal Pell, FSEOG, state, private, college/university gift aid from institutional funds.

GIFT AID (NON-NEED-BASED) ***Total amount:*** $4,307,004 (5% state, 91% institutional, 4% external sources). ***Receiving aid:*** Freshmen: 20% (85). Undergraduates: 13% (178). ***Average award:*** Freshmen: $12,602. Undergraduates: $12,038. ***Scholarships, grants, and awards by category:*** *Academic interests/achievement:* 1,282 awards ($12,799,067 total): general academic interests/achievements. *Creative arts/performance:* 263 awards ($323,000 total): art/fine arts, dance, music, performing arts, theater/drama. *Special achievements/activities:* 21 awards ($19,500 total): religious involvement. *Special characteristics:* 185 awards ($175,900 total): children and siblings of alumni, children of current students. ***Tuition waivers:*** Full or partial for employees or children of employees. ***ROTC:*** Army cooperative.

LOANS ***Student loans:*** $8,437,235 (68% need-based, 32% non-need-based). 85% of past graduating class borrowed through all loan programs. *Average indebtedness per student:* $30,187. ***Average need-based loan:*** Freshmen: $3767. Undergraduates: $4212. ***Parent loans:*** $3,030,677 (25% need-based, 75% non-need-based). ***Programs:*** FFEL (Subsidized and Unsubsidized Stafford, PLUS), Perkins, state, college/university, alternative loans.

WORK-STUDY ***Federal work-study:*** Total amount: $174,000; 140 jobs averaging $950. ***State or other work-study/employment:*** Total amount: $20,000 (100% need-based). 30 part-time jobs averaging $700.

APPLYING FOR FINANCIAL AID ***Required financial aid form:*** FAFSA. ***Financial aid deadline (priority):*** 3/1. ***Notification date:*** Continuous beginning 3/1. Students must reply within 3 weeks of notification.

CONTACT Mr. Christopher A. Brown, Director of Student Financial Assistance, Alma College, 614 West Superior Street, Alma, MI 48801-1599, 989-463-7347 or toll-free 800-321-ALMA. *Fax:* 989-463-7993. *E-mail:* cabrown@alma.edu.

ALVERNIA UNIVERSITY

Reading, PA

ABOUT THE INSTITUTION Independent Roman Catholic, coed. ***Awards:*** associate, bachelor's, master's, and doctoral degrees and post-bachelor's and post-master's certificates. 38 undergraduate majors. ***Total enrollment:*** 2,809. Undergraduates: 2,024. Freshmen: 383.

GIFT AID (NEED-BASED) ***Scholarships, grants, and awards:*** Federal Pell, FSEOG, state, private, college/university gift aid from institutional funds.

GIFT AID (NON-NEED-BASED) ***Scholarships, grants, and awards by category:*** *Academic interests/achievement:* general academic interests/achievements. *Special achievements/activities:* community service, memberships, religious involvement. *Special characteristics:* children of faculty/staff, general special characteristics, local/state students, siblings of current students.

LOANS ***Programs:*** FFEL (Subsidized and Unsubsidized Stafford, PLUS), Perkins.

WORK-STUDY ***Federal work-study:*** Total amount: $125,000; 233 jobs averaging $2400. ***State or other work-study/employment:*** Total amount: $175,215 (100% non-need-based). 45 part-time jobs averaging $2400.

APPLYING FOR FINANCIAL AID ***Required financial aid forms:*** FAFSA, state aid form.

CONTACT Rachel Gordon, Director of Student Financial Planning, Alvernia University, 400 St. Bernardine Street, Reading, PA 19607-1799, 610-796-8275 or toll-free 888-ALVERNIA (in-state). *Fax:* 610-796-8336. *E-mail:* rachel.gordon@alvernia.edu.

ALVERNO COLLEGE

Milwaukee, WI

CONTACT Dan Goyette, Director of Financial Aid, Alverno College, 3400 South 43rd Street, PO Box 343922, Milwaukee, WI 53234-3922, 414-382-6046 or toll-free 800-933-3401. *Fax:* 414-382-6354. *E-mail:* dan.goyette@alverno.edu.

AMERICAN ACADEMY OF ART

Chicago, IL

CONTACT Ms. Ione Fitzgerald, Director of Financial Aid, American Academy of Art, 332 South Michigan Avenue, Suite 300, Chicago, IL 60604, 312-461-0600. *Fax:* 312-294-9570.

AMERICAN BAPTIST COLLEGE OF AMERICAN BAPTIST THEOLOGICAL SEMINARY

Nashville, TN

ABOUT THE INSTITUTION Independent Baptist, coed. ***Awards:*** associate and bachelor's degrees. 1 undergraduate major. ***Total enrollment:*** 107. Undergraduates: 107. Freshmen: 20.

GIFT AID (NEED-BASED) ***Scholarships, grants, and awards:*** Federal Pell, FSEOG, state.

GIFT AID (NON-NEED-BASED) ***Scholarships, grants, and awards by category:*** *Academic interests/achievement:* religion/biblical studies. *Special characteristics:* religious affiliation.

APPLYING FOR FINANCIAL AID ***Required financial aid form:*** FAFSA.

CONTACT Marcella Lockhart, Executive Assistant for Administrator, American Baptist College of American Baptist Theological Seminary, 1800 Baptist World Center Drive, Nashville, TN 37207, 615-256-1463 Ext. 2227. *Fax:* 615-226-7855. *E-mail:* mlockhart@abcnash.edu.

AMERICAN INDIAN COLLEGE OF THE ASSEMBLIES OF GOD, INC.

Phoenix, AZ

Tuition & fees: $5854 **Average undergraduate aid package: N/A**

ABOUT THE INSTITUTION Independent religious, coed. ***Awards:*** associate and bachelor's degrees. 3 undergraduate majors. ***Total enrollment:*** 68. Undergraduates: 68. Federal methodology is used as a basis for awarding need-based institutional aid.

UNDERGRADUATE EXPENSES for 2008–09 ***Comprehensive fee:*** $11,086 includes full-time tuition ($5280), mandatory fees ($574), and room and board ($5232). Full-time tuition and fees vary according to course load. ***Part-time tuition:*** $220 per credit hour. ***Part-time fees:*** $179 per term. Part-time tuition and fees vary according to course load. ***Payment plan:*** Installment.

FRESHMAN FINANCIAL AID (Fall 2007) 12 applied for aid; of those 100% were deemed to have need. 92% of freshmen with need received aid; of those 9% had need fully met. ***Average percent of need met:*** 45% (excluding resources awarded to replace EFC). ***Average financial aid package:*** $6241 (excluding resources awarded to replace EFC).

UNDERGRADUATE FINANCIAL AID (Fall 2007) ***Average percent of need met:*** 80% (excluding resources awarded to replace EFC). 10% of all full-time undergraduates had no need and received non-need-based gift aid.

GIFT AID (NEED-BASED) ***Total amount:*** $409,712 (41% federal, 8% state, 8% institutional, 43% external sources). ***Receiving aid:*** Freshmen: 85% (11). ***Average award:*** Freshmen: $6241. ***Scholarships, grants, and awards:*** Federal Pell, FSEOG, state, private, college/university gift aid from institutional funds.

GIFT AID (NON-NEED-BASED) ***Receiving aid:*** Freshmen: 85% (11). ***Scholarships, grants, and awards by category:*** *Academic interests/achievement:* general academic interests/achievements. ***Tuition waivers:*** Full or partial for employees or children of employees.

LOANS ***Student loans:*** $14,362 (100% need-based). ***Programs:*** FFEL (Subsidized and Unsubsidized Stafford, PLUS).

WORK-STUDY Federal work-study jobs available.

APPLYING FOR FINANCIAL AID ***Required financial aid form:*** FAFSA. ***Financial aid deadline (priority):*** 4/1.

CONTACT Nadine Waldrop, Office of Student Financial Aid, American Indian College of the Assemblies of God, Inc., 10020 North Fifteenth Avenue, Phoenix, AZ 85021-2199, 602-944-3335 or toll-free 800-933-3828. *Fax:* 602-944-1952. *E-mail:* financialaid@aicag.edu.

AMERICAN INTERCONTINENTAL UNIVERSITY

Houston, TX

CONTACT Financial Aid Office, American InterContinental University, 9999 Richmond Avenue, Houston, TX 77042, 832-242-5788 or toll-free 888-607-9888.

AMERICAN INTERCONTINENTAL UNIVERSITY BUCKHEAD CAMPUS

Atlanta, GA

CONTACT Sherry Rizzi, Financial Aid Director, American InterContinental University Buckhead Campus, 3330 Peachtree Road NE, Atlanta, GA 30326, 404-965-5796 or toll-free 888-591-7888. *Fax:* 404-965-5704.

AMERICAN INTERCONTINENTAL UNIVERSITY DUNWOODY CAMPUS

Atlanta, GA

CONTACT Financial Aid Office, American InterContinental University Dunwoody Campus, 6600 Peachtree-Dunwoody Road, 500 Embassy Row, Atlanta, GA 30328, 404-965-6500 or toll-free 800-353-1744.

AMERICAN INTERCONTINENTAL UNIVERSITY ONLINE

Hoffman Estates, IL

CONTACT Financial Aid Office, American InterContinental University Online, 5550 Prairie Stone Parkway, Suite 400, Hoffman Estates, IL 60192, 847-851-5000 or toll-free 877-701-3800.

AMERICAN INTERCONTINENTAL UNIVERSITY SOUTH FLORIDA

Weston, FL

CONTACT Financial Aid Office, American InterContinental University South Florida, 2250 North Commerce Parkway, Suite 100, Weston, FL 33326, 954-446-6100 or toll-free 888-603-4888.

AMERICAN INTERNATIONAL COLLEGE

Springfield, MA

Tuition & fees: $24,100 **Average undergraduate aid package: $19,146**

ABOUT THE INSTITUTION Independent, coed. ***Awards:*** associate, bachelor's, master's, and doctoral degrees and post-master's certificates. 45 undergraduate majors. ***Total enrollment:*** 2,678. Undergraduates: 1,785. Freshmen: 391. Federal methodology is used as a basis for awarding need-based institutional aid.

UNDERGRADUATE EXPENSES for 2008–09 ***Application fee:*** $25. ***Comprehensive fee:*** $34,250 includes full-time tuition ($24,100) and room and board ($10,150). Room and board charges vary according to board plan. ***Part-time tuition:*** $497 per credit. ***Payment plans:*** Tuition prepayment, installment.

FRESHMAN FINANCIAL AID (Fall 2008, est.) 335 applied for aid; of those 94% were deemed to have need. 100% of freshmen with need received aid; of those 12% had need fully met. ***Average percent of need met:*** 74% (excluding resources awarded to replace EFC). ***Average financial aid package:*** $20,813 (excluding resources awarded to replace EFC). 16% of all full-time freshmen had no need and received non-need-based gift aid.

UNDERGRADUATE FINANCIAL AID (Fall 2008, est.) 1,361 applied for aid; of those 95% were deemed to have need. 100% of undergraduates with need received aid; of those 11% had need fully met. ***Average percent of need met:*** 68% (excluding resources awarded to replace EFC). ***Average financial aid package:*** $19,146 (excluding resources awarded to replace EFC). 11% of all full-time undergraduates had no need and received non-need-based gift aid.

GIFT AID (NEED-BASED) ***Total amount:*** $18,296,994 (15% federal, 5% state, 78% institutional, 2% external sources). ***Receiving aid:*** Freshmen: 82% (316); all full-time undergraduates: 87% (1,281). ***Average award:*** Freshmen: $16,718; Undergraduates: $14,815. ***Scholarships, grants, and awards:*** Federal Pell, FSEOG, state, private, college/university gift aid from institutional funds, Federal Nursing.

GIFT AID (NON-NEED-BASED) ***Total amount:*** $2,041,480 (1% federal, 96% institutional, 3% external sources). ***Receiving aid:*** Freshmen: 8% (32). Undergraduates: 8% (114). ***Average award:*** Freshmen: $9149. Undergraduates: $9346. ***Scholarships, grants, and awards by category:*** *Academic interests/achievement:* 749 awards ($4,046,435 total): general academic interests/achievements. *Special achievements/activities:* 10 awards ($66,000 total): general special achievements/activities. *Special characteristics:* children and siblings of alumni, children of faculty/staff, children of public servants, first-generation college students, previous college experience. ***Tuition waivers:*** Full or partial for employees or children of employees, senior citizens. ***ROTC:*** Army cooperative, Air Force cooperative.

LOANS ***Student loans:*** $14,467,070 (81% need-based, 19% non-need-based). 90% of past graduating class borrowed through all loan programs. *Average indebtedness per student:* $34,753. ***Average need-based loan:*** Freshmen: $3094. Undergraduates: $3916. ***Parent loans:*** $2,285,664 (45% need-based, 55% non-need-based). ***Programs:*** FFEL (Subsidized and Unsubsidized Stafford, PLUS), Perkins, Federal Nursing, college/university, alternative loans.

WORK-STUDY ***Federal work-study:*** Total amount: $1,038,220; 240 jobs averaging $2400.

ATHLETIC AWARDS Total amount: $3,039,399 (54% need-based, 46% non-need-based).

APPLYING FOR FINANCIAL AID ***Required financial aid forms:*** FAFSA, state aid form. ***Financial aid deadline (priority):*** 5/1. ***Notification date:*** Continuous. Students must reply within 2 weeks of notification.

CONTACT Mr. Douglas E. Fish, Associate Vice President for Financial Services, American International College, 1000 State Street, Springfield, MA 01109-3189, 413-205-3259. *Fax:* 413-205-3912. *E-mail:* douglas.fish@aic.edu.

AMERICAN JEWISH UNIVERSITY

Bel Air, CA

Tuition & fees: $22,352 **Average undergraduate aid package: $21,408**

ABOUT THE INSTITUTION Independent Jewish, coed. ***Awards:*** bachelor's and master's degrees. 8 undergraduate majors. ***Total enrollment:*** 226. Undergraduates: 96. Freshmen: 16. Both federal and institutional methodology are used as a basis for awarding need-based institutional aid.

UNDERGRADUATE EXPENSES for 2008–09 ***Application fee:*** $35. ***Comprehensive fee:*** $33,568 includes full-time tuition ($21,408), mandatory fees ($944), and room and board ($11,216). ***College room only:*** $5982. Room and board charges vary according to board plan and housing facility. ***Part-time tuition:*** $892 per unit. ***Payment plan:*** Installment.

FRESHMAN FINANCIAL AID (Fall 2008, est.) 14 applied for aid; of those 100% were deemed to have need. 100% of freshmen with need received aid; of those 79% had need fully met. ***Average percent of need met:*** 99% (excluding resources awarded to replace EFC). ***Average financial aid package:*** $21,408 (excluding resources awarded to replace EFC).

UNDERGRADUATE FINANCIAL AID (Fall 2008, est.) 94 applied for aid; of those 100% were deemed to have need. 100% of undergraduates with need received aid; of those 80% had need fully met. ***Average percent of need met:*** 100% (excluding resources awarded to replace EFC). ***Average financial aid package:*** $21,408 (excluding resources awarded to replace EFC).

GIFT AID (NEED-BASED) ***Total amount:*** $549,718 (29% federal, 15% state, 54% institutional, 2% external sources). ***Receiving aid:*** Freshmen: 71% (10); all full-time undergraduates: 43% (40). ***Average award:*** Freshmen: $8734; Undergraduates: $8971. ***Scholarships, grants, and awards:*** Federal Pell, FSEOG, state, private, college/university gift aid from institutional funds.

GIFT AID (NON-NEED-BASED) ***Total amount:*** $526,147 (100% institutional). ***Receiving aid:*** Freshmen: 57% (8). Undergraduates: 35% (33). ***Scholarships, grants, and awards by category:*** *Academic interests/achievement:* 24 awards ($230,350 total): general academic interests/achievements, premedicine. *Special achievements/activities:* 10 awards ($20,000 total): leadership. ***Tuition waivers:*** Full or partial for employees or children of employees.

LOANS ***Student loans:*** $508,549 (82% need-based, 18% non-need-based). 64% of past graduating class borrowed through all loan programs. *Average* *indebtedness per student:* $25,000. ***Average need-based loan:*** Freshmen: $3171. Undergraduates: $4165. ***Parent loans:*** $53,539 (100% need-based). ***Programs:*** FFEL (Subsidized and Unsubsidized Stafford, PLUS), alternative loans.

WORK-STUDY ***Federal work-study:*** Total amount: $36,582; 30 jobs averaging $1219.

APPLYING FOR FINANCIAL AID ***Required financial aid forms:*** FAFSA, institution's own form, parent and student income tax returns. ***Financial aid deadline (priority):*** 3/2. ***Notification date:*** Continuous beginning 3/15. Students must reply within 3 weeks of notification.

CONTACT Larisa Zadoyen, Director of Financial Aid, American Jewish University, 15600 Mulholland Drive, Bel Air, CA 90077-1599, 310-476-9777 Ext. 252 or toll-free 888-853-6763. *Fax:* 310-476-4613. *E-mail:* lzadoyen@ajula.edu.

AMERICAN MUSICAL AND DRAMATIC ACADEMY, LOS ANGELES

Los Angeles, CA

CONTACT Financial Aid Office, American Musical and Dramatic Academy, Los Angeles, 6305 Yucca Street, Los Angeles, CA 90028, 323-469-3300 or toll-free 866-374-5300.

AMERICAN SENTINEL UNIVERSITY

Englewood, CO

CONTACT Financial Aid Office, American Sentinel University, 385 Inverness Parkway, Englewood, CO 80112.

AMERICAN UNIVERSITY

Washington, DC

Tuition & fees: $33,283 **Average undergraduate aid package: $27,709**

ABOUT THE INSTITUTION Independent Methodist, coed. ***Awards:*** bachelor's, master's, doctoral, and first professional degrees and post-bachelor's certificates. 51 undergraduate majors. ***Total enrollment:*** 11,684. Undergraduates: 6,311. Freshmen: 1,577. Both federal and institutional methodology are used as a basis for awarding need-based institutional aid.

UNDERGRADUATE EXPENSES for 2008–09 ***Application fee:*** $60. ***Comprehensive fee:*** $45,701 includes full-time tuition ($32,816), mandatory fees ($467), and room and board ($12,418). ***College room only:*** $8258. Full-time tuition and fees vary according to course load. Room and board charges vary according to board plan and housing facility. ***Part-time tuition:*** $1093 per credit hour. Part-time tuition and fees vary according to course load. ***Payment plan:*** Installment.

FRESHMAN FINANCIAL AID (Fall 2008, est.) 1,076 applied for aid; of those 71% were deemed to have need. 100% of freshmen with need received aid; of those 33% had need fully met. ***Average percent of need met:*** 93% (excluding resources awarded to replace EFC). ***Average financial aid package:*** $29,771 (excluding resources awarded to replace EFC). 26% of all full-time freshmen had no need and received non-need-based gift aid.

UNDERGRADUATE FINANCIAL AID (Fall 2008, est.) 3,593 applied for aid; of those 81% were deemed to have need. 82% of undergraduates with need received aid; of those 95% had need fully met. ***Average percent of need met:*** 96% (excluding resources awarded to replace EFC). ***Average financial aid package:*** $27,709 (excluding resources awarded to replace EFC). 16% of all full-time undergraduates had no need and received non-need-based gift aid.

GIFT AID (NEED-BASED) ***Total amount:*** $26,559,515 (9% federal, 1% state, 81% institutional, 9% external sources). ***Receiving aid:*** Freshmen: 21% (333); all full-time undergraduates: 25% (1,479). ***Average award:*** Freshmen: $11,448; Undergraduates: $11,105. ***Scholarships, grants, and awards:*** Federal Pell, FSEOG, state, private, college/university gift aid from institutional funds.

GIFT AID (NON-NEED-BASED) ***Total amount:*** $31,769,265 (100% institutional). ***Receiving aid:*** Freshmen: 27% (430). Undergraduates: 20% (1,199). ***Average award:*** Freshmen: $17,630. Undergraduates: $17,846. ***Scholarships, grants, and awards by category:*** *Academic interests/achievement:* general academic interests/achievements. *Creative arts/performance:* general creative arts/performance. *Special achievements/activities:* general special achievements/activities, leadership, memberships. *Special characteristics:* adult students, children and siblings of alumni, children of faculty/staff, ethnic background, first-generation college students, local/state students, members of minority groups, previous college experience, relatives of clergy, spouses of current students. ***Tuition waivers:*** Full or partial for employees or children of employees. ***ROTC:*** Army cooperative, Air Force cooperative.

LOANS ***Student loans:*** $47,409,406 (27% need-based, 73% non-need-based). 56% of past graduating class borrowed through all loan programs. *Average indebtedness per student:* $34,213. ***Average need-based loan:*** Freshmen: $3918. Undergraduates: $5028. ***Parent loans:*** $6,698,500 (100% non-need-based). ***Programs:*** Federal Direct (Subsidized and Unsubsidized Stafford, PLUS), Perkins, college/university.

WORK-STUDY ***Federal work-study:*** Total amount: $3,246,704; jobs available.

ATHLETIC AWARDS Total amount: $3,466,447 (100% non-need-based).

APPLYING FOR FINANCIAL AID ***Required financial aid forms:*** FAFSA, institution's own form. ***Financial aid deadline:*** 2/15. ***Notification date:*** 4/1. Students must reply by 5/1 or within 4 weeks of notification.

CONTACT Brian Lee Sang, Director of Financial Aid, American University, 4400 Massachusetts Avenue, NW, Washington, DC 20016-8001, 202-885-6100. *Fax:* 202-885-1129. *E-mail:* financialaid@american.edu.

AMERICAN UNIVERSITY OF PUERTO RICO

Bayamón, PR

CONTACT Mr. Yahaira Melendez, Financial Aid Director, American University of Puerto Rico, PO Box 2037, Bayamón, PR 00960-2037, 787-620-2040 Ext. 2031. *Fax:* 787-785-7377. *E-mail:* melendezy@aupr.edu.

AMHERST COLLEGE

Amherst, MA

Tuition & fees: $37,640 **Average undergraduate aid package: $37,078**

ABOUT THE INSTITUTION Independent, coed. ***Awards:*** bachelor's degrees. 37 undergraduate majors. ***Total enrollment:*** 1,697. Undergraduates: 1,697. Freshmen: 439. Institutional methodology is used as a basis for awarding need-based institutional aid.

UNDERGRADUATE EXPENSES for 2008–09 ***Application fee:*** $60. ***Comprehensive fee:*** $47,430 includes full-time tuition ($36,970), mandatory fees ($670), and room and board ($9790). ***College room only:*** $5250. ***Payment plans:*** Installment, deferred payment.

FRESHMAN FINANCIAL AID (Fall 2008, est.) 249 applied for aid; of those 90% were deemed to have need. 100% of freshmen with need received aid; of those 100% had need fully met. ***Average percent of need met:*** 100% (excluding resources awarded to replace EFC). ***Average financial aid package:*** $37,077 (excluding resources awarded to replace EFC).

UNDERGRADUATE FINANCIAL AID (Fall 2008, est.) 1,014 applied for aid; of those 90% were deemed to have need. 100% of undergraduates with need received aid; of those 34% had need fully met. ***Average percent of need met:*** 100% (excluding resources awarded to replace EFC). ***Average financial aid package:*** $37,078 (excluding resources awarded to replace EFC).

GIFT AID (NEED-BASED) ***Total amount:*** $32,125,465 (4% federal, 94% institutional, 2% external sources). ***Receiving aid:*** Freshmen: 50% (220); all full-time undergraduates: 53% (902). ***Average award:*** Freshmen: $36,075; Undergraduates: $35,771. ***Scholarships, grants, and awards:*** Federal Pell, FSEOG, state, private, college/university gift aid from institutional funds, United Negro College Fund.

GIFT AID (NON-NEED-BASED) ***Total amount:*** $388,333 (21% federal, 79% external sources).

LOANS ***Student loans:*** $1,774,471 (28% need-based, 72% non-need-based). 46% of past graduating class borrowed through all loan programs. *Average indebtedness per student:* $12,603. ***Average need-based loan:*** Freshmen: $2375. Undergraduates: $2950. ***Parent loans:*** $2,034,350 (100% non-need-based). ***Programs:*** Federal Direct (Subsidized and Unsubsidized Stafford, PLUS), Perkins, college/university.

WORK-STUDY ***Federal work-study:*** Total amount: $820,422; 490 jobs averaging $1626. ***State or other work-study/employment:*** Total amount: $320,288 (100% need-based). 201 part-time jobs averaging $1593.

APPLYING FOR FINANCIAL AID ***Required financial aid forms:*** FAFSA, CSS Financial Aid PROFILE, income tax form(s), W-2 forms. ***Financial aid deadline (priority):*** 2/15. ***Notification date:*** 4/1. Students must reply by 5/1.

CONTACT Joe Paul Case, Dean/Director of Financial Aid, Amherst College, B-5 Converse Hall, PO Box 5000, Amherst, MA 01002-5000, 413-542-2296. *Fax:* 413-542-2628. *E-mail:* finaid@amherst.edu.

AMRIDGE UNIVERSITY

Montgomery, AL

Tuition & fees: $7700 **Average undergraduate aid package: $8500**

ABOUT THE INSTITUTION Independent religious, coed. ***Awards:*** bachelor's, master's, doctoral, and first professional degrees. 12 undergraduate majors. ***Total enrollment:*** 720. Undergraduates: 343. Freshmen: 3. Federal methodology is used as a basis for awarding need-based institutional aid.

UNDERGRADUATE EXPENSES for 2009–10 ***Application fee:*** $50. ***Tuition:*** full-time $6900; part-time $300 per semester hour. ***Required fees:*** full-time $800; $400 per term.

UNDERGRADUATE FINANCIAL AID (Fall 2008, est.) 330 applied for aid; of those 91% were deemed to have need. 100% of undergraduates with need received aid; of those 92% had need fully met. ***Average percent of need met:*** 85% (excluding resources awarded to replace EFC). ***Average financial aid package:*** $8500 (excluding resources awarded to replace EFC). 5% of all full-time undergraduates had no need and received non-need-based gift aid.

GIFT AID (NEED-BASED) ***Total amount:*** $752,000 (86% federal, 7% institutional, 7% external sources). ***Receiving aid:*** All full-time undergraduates: 73% (270). ***Average award:*** Undergraduates: $6500. ***Scholarships, grants, and awards:*** Federal Pell, FSEOG, state, private, college/university gift aid from institutional funds.

GIFT AID (NON-NEED-BASED) ***Total amount:*** $750,000 (100% institutional). ***Receiving aid:*** Undergraduates: 14% (50). ***Average award:*** Undergraduates: $4000. ***Scholarships, grants, and awards by category:*** *Special achievements/activities:* religious involvement. *Special characteristics:* children of faculty/staff, veterans.

LOANS ***Student loans:*** $6,000,000 (50% need-based, 50% non-need-based). 85% of past graduating class borrowed through all loan programs. *Average indebtedness per student:* $18,000. ***Average need-based loan:*** Undergraduates: $5500. ***Programs:*** FFEL (Subsidized and Unsubsidized Stafford, PLUS).

WORK-STUDY ***Federal work-study:*** Total amount: $5000; jobs available.

APPLYING FOR FINANCIAL AID ***Required financial aid forms:*** FAFSA, institution's own form. ***Financial aid deadline:*** Continuous. ***Notification date:*** 8/31. Students must reply within 2 weeks of notification.

CONTACT Louise Hicks, Financial Aid Director, Amridge University, 1200 Taylor Road, Montgomery, AL 36117, 334-387-3877 Ext. 7525 or toll-free 800-351-4040 Ext. 213. *Fax:* 334-387-3878. *E-mail:* financialaid@amridgeuniversity.edu.

ANDERSON UNIVERSITY

Anderson, IN

CONTACT Mr. Kenneth Nieman, Director of Student Financial Services, Anderson University, 1100 East Fifth Street, Anderson, IN 46012-3495, 765-641-4180 or toll-free 800-421-3014 (in-state), 800-428-6414 (out-of-state). *Fax:* 765-641-3831. *E-mail:* kfnieman@anderson.edu.

ANDERSON UNIVERSITY

Anderson, SC

ABOUT THE INSTITUTION Independent Baptist, coed. ***Awards:*** bachelor's and master's degrees. 32 undergraduate majors. ***Total enrollment:*** 2,064. Undergraduates: 1,977. Freshmen: 418.

GIFT AID (NEED-BASED) ***Scholarships, grants, and awards:*** Federal Pell, FSEOG, state, college/university gift aid from institutional funds.

LOANS ***Programs:*** FFEL (Subsidized and Unsubsidized Stafford, PLUS), Perkins.

APPLYING FOR FINANCIAL AID ***Required financial aid form:*** FAFSA.

CONTACT Becky Pressley, Director of Financial Aid, Anderson University, 316 Boulevard, Anderson, SC 29621-4035, 864-231-2070 or toll-free 800-542-3594. *Fax:* 864-231-2008. *E-mail:* bpressley@andersonuniversity.edu.

ANDREWS UNIVERSITY

Berrien Springs, MI

Tuition & fees: $19,930 **Average undergraduate aid package: $22,441**

ABOUT THE INSTITUTION Independent Seventh-day Adventist, coed. ***Awards:*** associate, bachelor's, master's, doctoral, and first professional degrees and post-bachelor's and post-master's certificates. 64 undergraduate majors. ***Total enrollment:*** 3,419. Undergraduates: 1,889. Freshmen: 396. Federal methodology is used as a basis for awarding need-based institutional aid.

UNDERGRADUATE EXPENSES for 2008–09 ***Application fee:*** $30. ***Comprehensive fee:*** $26,260 includes full-time tuition ($19,320), mandatory fees ($610), and room and board ($6330). ***College room only:*** $3380. ***Part-time tuition:*** $805 per credit hour.

FRESHMAN FINANCIAL AID (Fall 2007) 246 applied for aid; of those 83% were deemed to have need. 100% of freshmen with need received aid; of those 21% had need fully met. ***Average percent of need met:*** 85% (excluding resources awarded to replace EFC). ***Average financial aid package:*** $19,768 (excluding resources awarded to replace EFC). 39% of all full-time freshmen had no need and received non-need-based gift aid.

UNDERGRADUATE FINANCIAL AID (Fall 2007) 1,093 applied for aid; of those 92% were deemed to have need. 100% of undergraduates with need received aid; of those 14% had need fully met. ***Average percent of need met:*** 85% (excluding resources awarded to replace EFC). ***Average financial aid package:*** $22,441 (excluding resources awarded to replace EFC). 34% of all full-time undergraduates had no need and received non-need-based gift aid.

GIFT AID (NEED-BASED) ***Total amount:*** $15,627,474 (16% federal, 14% state, 67% institutional, 3% external sources). ***Receiving aid:*** Freshmen: 42% (139); all full-time undergraduates: 48% (759). ***Average award:*** Freshmen: $6213; Undergraduates: $7210. ***Scholarships, grants, and awards:*** Federal Pell, FSEOG, state, private, college/university gift aid from institutional funds.

GIFT AID (NON-NEED-BASED) ***Receiving aid:*** Freshmen: 61% (204). Undergraduates: 60% (950). ***Average award:*** Freshmen: $6262. Undergraduates: $5441. ***Scholarships, grants, and awards by category:*** *Academic interests/achievement:* 1,583 awards ($6,362,391 total): general academic interests/achievements. *Creative arts/performance:* 53 awards ($44,239 total): music. *Special achievements/activities:* 200 awards ($222,921 total): leadership, religious involvement. *Special characteristics:* 107 awards ($807,678 total): children of faculty/staff, general special characteristics, international students.

LOANS ***Student loans:*** $16,161,872 (28% need-based, 72% non-need-based). 71% of past graduating class borrowed through all loan programs. *Average indebtedness per student:* $31,510. ***Average need-based loan:*** Freshmen: $3457. Undergraduates: $5245. ***Parent loans:*** $2,379,277 (100% non-need-based). ***Programs:*** Federal Direct (Subsidized and Unsubsidized Stafford, PLUS), Perkins.

WORK-STUDY ***Federal work-study:*** Total amount: $629,194; 498 jobs averaging $1263. ***State or other work-study/employment:*** Total amount: $304,621 (100% need-based). 250 part-time jobs averaging $1218.

APPLYING FOR FINANCIAL AID ***Required financial aid forms:*** FAFSA, institution's own form. ***Financial aid deadline:*** Continuous.

CONTACT Cynthia Schulz, Assistant Director of Student Financial Services, Andrews University, Student Financial Services-Administration Building, Berrien Springs, MI 49104, 800-253-2874. *Fax:* 269-471-3228. *E-mail:* sfs@andrews.edu.

ANGELO STATE UNIVERSITY

San Angelo, TX

Tuition & fees (TX res): $4596 **Average undergraduate aid package: $5206**

ABOUT THE INSTITUTION State-supported, coed. ***Awards:*** associate, bachelor's, master's, and doctoral degrees. 43 undergraduate majors. ***Total enrollment:*** 6,155. Undergraduates: 5,662. Freshmen: 1,463. Federal methodology is used as a basis for awarding need-based institutional aid.

UNDERGRADUATE EXPENSES for 2008–09 ***Application fee:*** $25. ***Tuition, state resident:*** full-time $3174; part-time $132 per credit hour. ***Tuition, nonresident:*** full-time $9918; part-time $413 per credit hour. ***Required fees:*** full-time $1422; $25 per credit hour or $444 per term. Full-time tuition and fees vary according to course load. Part-time tuition and fees vary according to course load. ***College room and board:*** $6612; ***Room only:*** $4112. Room and board charges vary according to board plan and housing facility. ***Payment plan:*** Installment.

FRESHMAN FINANCIAL AID (Fall 2008, est.) 963 applied for aid; of those 67% were deemed to have need. 100% of freshmen with need received aid; of those 74% had need fully met. ***Average percent of need met:*** 72% (excluding resources awarded to replace EFC). ***Average financial aid package:*** $4359 (excluding resources awarded to replace EFC). 7% of all full-time freshmen had no need and received non-need-based gift aid.

UNDERGRADUATE FINANCIAL AID (Fall 2008, est.) 3,583 applied for aid; of those 73% were deemed to have need. 100% of undergraduates with need received aid; of those 77% had need fully met. ***Average percent of need met:*** 61% (excluding resources awarded to replace EFC). ***Average financial aid package:*** $5206 (excluding resources awarded to replace EFC). 4% of all full-time undergraduates had no need and received non-need-based gift aid.

GIFT AID (NEED-BASED) ***Total amount:*** $11,051,607 (60% federal, 34% state, 6% institutional). ***Receiving aid:*** Freshmen: 45% (498); all full-time undergraduates: 49% (2,355). ***Scholarships, grants, and awards:*** Federal Pell, FSEOG, state, private, college/university gift aid from institutional funds, Federal Nursing.

GIFT AID (NON-NEED-BASED) ***Total amount:*** $5,633,287 (83% institutional, 17% external sources). ***Receiving aid:*** Freshmen: 49% (542). Undergraduates: 31% (1,496). ***Average award:*** Freshmen: $5847. Undergraduates: $3430. ***Scholarships, grants, and awards by category:*** *Academic interests/achievement:* agriculture, biological sciences, business, communication, computer science, education, English, foreign languages, general academic interests/achievements, international studies, mathematics, military science, physical sciences, premedicine, social sciences. *Creative arts/performance:* art/fine arts, dance, journalism/publications, music, performing arts, theater/drama. *Special achievements/activities:* cheerleading/drum major, general special achievements/activities, hobbies/interests, leadership, memberships, rodeo. *Special characteristics:* first-generation college students. ***Tuition waivers:*** Full or partial for senior citizens. ***ROTC:*** Air Force.

LOANS ***Student loans:*** $18,663,886 (47% need-based, 53% non-need-based). *Average indebtedness per student:* $11,400. ***Average need-based loan:*** Freshmen: $2053. Undergraduates: $2580. ***Parent loans:*** $1,531,506 (100% non-need-based). ***Programs:*** FFEL (Subsidized and Unsubsidized Stafford, PLUS), Perkins, Federal Nursing, state, college/university, alternative loans.

WORK-STUDY ***Federal work-study:*** Total amount: $280,373; jobs available. ***State or other work-study/employment:*** Total amount: $38,269 (100% need-based). Part-time jobs available.

ATHLETIC AWARDS Total amount: $1,062,146 (100% non-need-based).

APPLYING FOR FINANCIAL AID ***Required financial aid forms:*** FAFSA, institution's own form. ***Financial aid deadline (priority):*** 4/1. ***Notification date:*** Continuous.

CONTACT Ms. Lyn Wheeler, Director of Financial Aid, Angelo State University, ASU Station #11015, San Angelo, TX 76909-1015, 325-942-2246 or toll-free 800-946-8627 (in-state). *Fax:* 325-942-2082. *E-mail:* lyn.wheeler@angelo.edu.

ANNA MARIA COLLEGE

Paxton, MA

Tuition & fees: $25,850 **Average undergraduate aid package: $17,956**

ABOUT THE INSTITUTION Independent Roman Catholic, coed. ***Awards:*** associate, bachelor's, and master's degrees and post-bachelor's and post-master's certificates. 34 undergraduate majors. ***Total enrollment:*** 1,333. Undergraduates: 1,001. Freshmen: 245. Federal methodology is used as a basis for awarding need-based institutional aid.

UNDERGRADUATE EXPENSES for 2008–09 ***Application fee:*** $40. ***Comprehensive fee:*** $35,200 includes full-time tuition ($23,500), mandatory fees ($2350), and room and board ($9350). Full-time tuition and fees vary according to program. Room and board charges vary according to board plan. ***Part-time tuition:*** $783 per credit hour. Part-time tuition and fees vary according to class time, course load, and program. ***Payment plan:*** Installment.

FRESHMAN FINANCIAL AID (Fall 2008, est.) 225 applied for aid; of those 88% were deemed to have need. 100% of freshmen with need received aid; of those 8% had need fully met. ***Average percent of need met:*** 66% (excluding resources awarded to replace EFC). ***Average financial aid package:*** $18,507 (excluding resources awarded to replace EFC). 18% of all full-time freshmen had no need and received non-need-based gift aid.

UNDERGRADUATE FINANCIAL AID (Fall 2008, est.) 692 applied for aid; of those 90% were deemed to have need. 100% of undergraduates with need received aid; of those 9% had need fully met. ***Average percent of need met:*** 66% (excluding resources awarded to replace EFC). ***Average financial aid package:*** $17,956 (excluding resources awarded to replace EFC). 16% of all full-time undergraduates had no need and received non-need-based gift aid.

GIFT AID (NEED-BASED) ***Total amount:*** $8,065,347 (13% federal, 9% state, 77% institutional, 1% external sources). ***Receiving aid:*** Freshmen: 81% (198); all full-time undergraduates: 78% (610). ***Average award:*** Freshmen: $13,617; Undergraduates: $13,214. ***Scholarships, grants, and awards:*** Federal Pell, FSEOG, state, private, college/university gift aid from institutional funds.

GIFT AID (NON-NEED-BASED) ***Total amount:*** $1,018,386 (98% institutional, 2% external sources). ***Receiving aid:*** Freshmen: 81% (198). Undergraduates: 78% (610). ***Average award:*** Freshmen: $7500. Undergraduates: $7197. ***Scholarships, grants, and awards by category:*** *Academic interests/achievement:* 502 awards ($2,833,200 total): general academic interests/achievements. *Creative arts/performance:* 8 awards ($26,900 total): music. *Special achievements/activities:* 127 awards ($177,000 total): religious involvement. *Special characteristics:* 236 awards ($797,300 total): children and siblings of alumni, children of faculty/staff, children with a deceased or disabled parent, general special characteristics, local/state students, previous college experience, siblings of current students. ***Tuition waivers:*** Full or partial for employees or children of employees, senior citizens. ***ROTC:*** Air Force cooperative.

LOANS ***Student loans:*** $8,800,744 (70% need-based, 30% non-need-based). 92% of past graduating class borrowed through all loan programs. *Average indebtedness per student:* $35,575. ***Average need-based loan:*** Freshmen: $4443. Undergraduates: $4851. ***Parent loans:*** $1,167,003 (33% need-based, 67% non-need-based). ***Programs:*** FFEL (Subsidized and Unsubsidized Stafford, PLUS), Perkins, college/university.

WORK-STUDY ***Federal work-study:*** Total amount: $220,878; 129 jobs averaging $1254.

APPLYING FOR FINANCIAL AID ***Required financial aid forms:*** FAFSA, state aid form. ***Financial aid deadline (priority):*** 3/1. ***Notification date:*** Continuous beginning 4/1. Students must reply within 4 weeks of notification.

CONTACT Colleen King, Director of Financial Aid, Anna Maria College, 50 Sunset Lane, Paxton, MA 01612-1198, 508-849-3363 or toll-free 800-344-4586 Ext. 360. *Fax:* 508-849-3229. *E-mail:* cking@annamaria.edu.

ANTIOCH UNIVERSITY McGREGOR

Yellow Springs, OH

Tuition & fees: $15,120 **Average undergraduate aid package: $6300**

ABOUT THE INSTITUTION Independent, coed. ***Awards:*** bachelor's and master's degrees and post-master's certificates. 6 undergraduate majors. ***Total enrollment:*** 630. Undergraduates: 160. Federal methodology is used as a basis for awarding need-based institutional aid.

UNDERGRADUATE EXPENSES for 2009–10 ***Application fee:*** $45. ***Tuition:*** full-time $15,120; part-time $315 per credit hour.

UNDERGRADUATE FINANCIAL AID (Fall 2007) 98 applied for aid; of those 96% were deemed to have need. 100% of undergraduates with need received aid. ***Average percent of need met:*** 22% (excluding resources awarded to replace EFC). ***Average financial aid package:*** $6300 (excluding resources awarded to replace EFC). 5% of all full-time undergraduates had no need and received non-need-based gift aid.

GIFT AID (NEED-BASED) ***Total amount:*** $190,132 (75% federal, 25% state). ***Receiving aid:*** All full-time undergraduates: 53% (56). ***Average award:*** Undergraduates: $1000. ***Scholarships, grants, and awards:*** Federal Pell, FSEOG, state.

GIFT AID (NON-NEED-BASED) ***Total amount:*** $96,093 (31% state, 68% institutional, 1% external sources).

LOANS ***Student loans:*** $1,011,412 (51% need-based, 49% non-need-based). 62% of past graduating class borrowed through all loan programs. *Average indebtedness per student:* $20,625. ***Average need-based loan:*** Undergraduates: $4000. ***Programs:*** FFEL (Subsidized and Unsubsidized Stafford, PLUS), Perkins.

WORK-STUDY ***Federal work-study:*** Total amount: $1055; jobs available.

APPLYING FOR FINANCIAL AID ***Required financial aid forms:*** FAFSA, institution's own form. ***Financial aid deadline:*** Continuous. ***Notification date:*** Continuous beginning 4/1.

CONTACT Kathy John, Director of Financial Aid, Antioch University McGregor, 900 Dayton Street, Yellow Springs, OH 45387, 937-769-1840. *Fax:* 937-769-1804. *E-mail:* kjohn@mcgregor.edu.

ANTIOCH UNIVERSITY SANTA BARBARA

Santa Barbara, CA

CONTACT Cecilia Schneider, Financial Aid Director, Antioch University Santa Barbara, 801 Garden Street, Santa Barbara, CA 93101-1580, 805-962-8179 Ext. 108. *Fax:* 805-962-4786.

ANTIOCH UNIVERSITY SEATTLE

Seattle, WA

ABOUT THE INSTITUTION Independent, coed. 1 undergraduate major.

GIFT AID (NEED-BASED) ***Scholarships, grants, and awards:*** Federal Pell, FSEOG, state, private, college/university gift aid from institutional funds, United Negro College Fund.

LOANS ***Programs:*** FFEL (Subsidized and Unsubsidized Stafford, PLUS), Perkins.

APPLYING FOR FINANCIAL AID ***Required financial aid form:*** FAFSA.

CONTACT Katy Stahl, Director of Financial Aid, Antioch University Seattle, 2326 Sixth Avenue, Seattle, WA 98121-1814, 206-268-4004. *Fax:* 206-268-4242. *E-mail:* kstahl@antiochseattle.edu.

APEX SCHOOL OF THEOLOGY

Durham, NC

CONTACT Financial Aid Office, Apex School of Theology, 5104 Revere Road, Durham, NC 27713, 919-572-1625.

APPALACHIAN BIBLE COLLEGE

Bradley, WV

Tuition & fees: $11,270 **Average undergraduate aid package: $7813**

ABOUT THE INSTITUTION Independent nondenominational, coed. ***Awards:*** associate, bachelor's, and master's degrees. 2 undergraduate majors. ***Total enrollment:*** 273. Undergraduates: 258. Freshmen: 58. Both federal and institutional methodology are used as a basis for awarding need-based institutional aid.

UNDERGRADUATE EXPENSES for 2008–09 ***Application fee:*** $20. ***Comprehensive fee:*** $16,330 includes full-time tuition ($9880), mandatory fees ($1390), and room and board ($5060). ***Part-time tuition:*** $351 per hour. ***Part-time fees:*** $550 per term. ***Payment plan:*** Installment.

FRESHMAN FINANCIAL AID (Fall 2007) 57 applied for aid; of those 93% were deemed to have need. 98% of freshmen with need received aid; of those 8% had need fully met. ***Average percent of need met:*** 57% (excluding resources awarded to replace EFC). ***Average financial aid package:*** $7574 (excluding resources awarded to replace EFC). 8% of all full-time freshmen had no need and received non-need-based gift aid.

UNDERGRADUATE FINANCIAL AID (Fall 2007) 214 applied for aid; of those 92% were deemed to have need. 97% of undergraduates with need received aid; of those 8% had need fully met. ***Average percent of need met:*** 58% (excluding resources awarded to replace EFC). ***Average financial aid package:*** $7813 (excluding resources awarded to replace EFC). 7% of all full-time undergraduates had no need and received non-need-based gift aid.

GIFT AID (NEED-BASED) ***Total amount:*** $1,091,677 (38% federal, 11% state, 39% institutional, 12% external sources). ***Receiving aid:*** Freshmen: 84% (51); all full-time undergraduates: 82% (183). ***Average award:*** Freshmen: $6458; Undergraduates: $5879. ***Scholarships, grants, and awards:*** Federal Pell, FSEOG, state, private, college/university gift aid from institutional funds.

GIFT AID (NON-NEED-BASED) ***Total amount:*** $82,958 (4% state, 76% institutional, 20% external sources). ***Receiving aid:*** Freshmen: 7% (4). Undergraduates: 4% (9). ***Average award:*** Freshmen: $2683. Undergraduates: $2740. ***Scholarships, grants, and awards by category:*** *Academic interests/achievement:* 60 awards ($83,250 total): general academic interests/achievements, religion/biblical studies. *Special achievements/activities:* 4 awards ($4000 total): general special achievements/activities, religious involvement. *Special characteristics:* 259 awards ($515,448 total): children and siblings of alumni, children of educators, children of faculty/staff, general special characteristics, international students, married students, relatives of clergy, religious affiliation, spouses of current students, veterans. ***Tuition waivers:*** Full or partial for employees or children of employees, senior citizens.

LOANS ***Student loans:*** $448,125 (91% need-based, 9% non-need-based). ***Average need-based loan:*** Freshmen: $2780. Undergraduates: $3206. ***Parent loans:*** $110,745 (57% need-based, 43% non-need-based). ***Programs:*** FFEL (Subsidized and Unsubsidized Stafford, PLUS).

WORK-STUDY ***Federal work-study:*** Total amount: $17,778; 28 jobs averaging $488. ***State or other work-study/employment:*** Total amount: $44,045 (94% need-based, 6% non-need-based). Part-time jobs available.

APPLYING FOR FINANCIAL AID ***Required financial aid forms:*** FAFSA, institution's own form. ***Financial aid deadline:*** 6/15 (priority: 3/1). ***Notification date:*** Continuous. Students must reply by 7/30 or within 4 weeks of notification.

CONTACT Cindi Turner, Director of Financial Aid, Appalachian Bible College, PO Box ABC, Sandbranch Road, Bradley, WV 25818, 304-877-6428 Ext. 3247 or toll-free 800-678-9ABC Ext. 3213. *Fax:* 304-877-5082. *E-mail:* cindi.turner@abc.edu.

APPALACHIAN STATE UNIVERSITY

Boone, NC

Tuition & fees (NC res): $4275 **Average undergraduate aid package: $7843**

ABOUT THE INSTITUTION State-supported, coed. ***Awards:*** bachelor's, master's, and doctoral degrees and post-bachelor's and post-master's certificates. 88 undergraduate majors. ***Total enrollment:*** 16,610. Undergraduates: 14,561. Freshmen: 2,781. Federal methodology is used as a basis for awarding need-based institutional aid.

UNDERGRADUATE EXPENSES for 2008–09 ***Application fee:*** $50. ***Tuition, state resident:*** full-time $2263; part-time $76.50 per semester hour. ***Tuition, nonresident:*** full-time $12,322; part-time $416.25 per semester hour. ***Required fees:*** full-time $2012; $12.25 per semester hour. Part-time tuition and fees vary according to course load. ***College room and board:*** $6200; ***Room only:*** $3600. Room and board charges vary according to board plan and housing facility. ***Payment plan:*** Installment.

FRESHMAN FINANCIAL AID (Fall 2008, est.) 1,864 applied for aid; of those 54% were deemed to have need. 95% of freshmen with need received aid; of those 51% had need fully met. ***Average percent of need met:*** 86% (excluding resources awarded to replace EFC). ***Average financial aid package:*** $7732 (excluding resources awarded to replace EFC). 4% of all full-time freshmen had no need and received non-need-based gift aid.

UNDERGRADUATE FINANCIAL AID (Fall 2008, est.) 7,989 applied for aid; of those 65% were deemed to have need. 97% of undergraduates with need received aid; of those 45% had need fully met. ***Average percent of need met:*** 85% (excluding resources awarded to replace EFC). ***Average financial aid package:*** $7843 (excluding resources awarded to replace EFC). 4% of all full-time undergraduates had no need and received non-need-based gift aid.

GIFT AID (NEED-BASED) ***Total amount:*** $28,185,883 (32% federal, 51% state, 11% institutional, 6% external sources). ***Receiving aid:*** Freshmen: 29% (801), all full-time undergraduates: 32% (4,328). ***Average award:*** Freshmen: $6422; Undergraduates: $5631. ***Scholarships, grants, and awards:*** Federal Pell, FSEOG, state, private, college/university gift aid from institutional funds.

GIFT AID (NON-NEED-BASED) ***Total amount:*** $5,475,481 (2% federal, 28% state, 22% institutional, 48% external sources). ***Receiving aid:*** Freshmen: 12% (335). Undergraduates: 8% (1,063). ***Average award:*** Freshmen: $2394. Undergraduates: $1942. ***Scholarships, grants, and awards by category:*** *Academic interests/achievement:* 3,490 awards ($3,564,490 total): general academic interests/achievements. *Creative arts/performance:* general creative arts/performance. *Special achievements/activities:* general special achievements/activities. *Special characteristics:* first-generation college students, general special characteristics, handicapped students, members of minority groups, out-of-state students, veterans, veterans' children. ***Tuition waivers:*** Full or partial for employees or children of employees, senior citizens. ***ROTC:*** Army.

LOANS ***Student loans:*** $33,968,258 (66% need-based, 34% non-need-based). 50% of past graduating class borrowed through all loan programs. *Average indebtedness per student:* $15,080. ***Average need-based loan:*** Freshmen: $2451. Undergraduates: $3328. ***Parent loans:*** $15,999,833 (45% need-based, 55% non-need-based). ***Programs:*** FFEL (Subsidized and Unsubsidized Stafford, PLUS), Perkins.

WORK-STUDY ***Federal work-study:*** Total amount: $494,668; 310 jobs averaging $1580.

ATHLETIC AWARDS Total amount: $2,093,580 (37% need-based, 63% non-need-based).

APPLYING FOR FINANCIAL AID ***Required financial aid form:*** FAFSA. ***Financial aid deadline (priority):*** 3/15. ***Notification date:*** 4/1. Students must reply within 3 weeks of notification.

CONTACT Esther Manogin, Director of Student Financial Aid, Appalachian State University, Office of Student Financial Aid, Boone, NC 28608-2059, 828-262-2190. *Fax:* 828-262-2585. *E-mail:* manoginem@appstate.edu.

AQUINAS COLLEGE

Grand Rapids, MI

CONTACT David J. Steffee, Director Financial Aid, Aquinas College, 1607 Robinson Road, Grand Rapids, MI 49506-1799, 616-459-8281 Ext. 5127 or toll-free 800-678-9593. *Fax:* 616-732-4547. *E-mail:* steffdav@aquinas.edu.

AQUINAS COLLEGE

Nashville, TN

Tuition & fees: $16,100 **Average undergraduate aid package: $5977**

ABOUT THE INSTITUTION Independent Roman Catholic, coed. ***Awards:*** associate and bachelor's degrees and post-bachelor's certificates. 6 undergraduate majors. ***Total enrollment:*** 821. Undergraduates: 821. Federal methodology is used as a basis for awarding need-based institutional aid.

UNDERGRADUATE EXPENSES for 2008–09 ***Application fee:*** $25. ***Tuition:*** full-time $15,600; part-time $520 per hour. ***Required fees:*** full-time $500; $250 per term. Full-time tuition and fees vary according to course load and program. Part-time tuition and fees vary according to course load and program. ***Payment plan:*** Installment.

FRESHMAN FINANCIAL AID (Fall 2007) 34 applied for aid; of those 94% were deemed to have need. 100% of freshmen with need received aid; of those 16% had need fully met. ***Average percent of need met:*** 82% (excluding resources awarded to replace EFC). ***Average financial aid package:*** $5474 (excluding resources awarded to replace EFC). 18% of all full-time freshmen had no need and received non-need-based gift aid.

UNDERGRADUATE FINANCIAL AID (Fall 2007) 241 applied for aid; of those 83% were deemed to have need. 74% of undergraduates with need received aid; of those 49% had need fully met. ***Average percent of need met:*** 86% (excluding resources awarded to replace EFC). ***Average financial aid package:*** $5977 (excluding resources awarded to replace EFC). 7% of all full-time undergraduates had no need and received non-need-based gift aid.

GIFT AID (NEED-BASED) ***Total amount:*** $1,284,469 (55% federal, 20% state, 25% institutional). ***Receiving aid:*** Freshmen: 65% (26); all full-time undergraduates: 23% (82). ***Average award:*** Freshmen: $3685; Undergraduates: $1838. ***Scholarships, grants, and awards:*** Federal Pell, FSEOG, state, private, college/university gift aid from institutional funds.

GIFT AID (NON-NEED-BASED) ***Total amount:*** $478,586 (34% state, 29% institutional, 37% external sources). ***Receiving aid:*** Freshmen: 22% (9). Undergraduates: 12% (44). ***Average award:*** Freshmen: $1457. Undergraduates: $1529. ***Scholarships, grants, and awards by category:*** *Academic interests/achievement:* 38 awards ($116,222 total): business, education, general academic interests/achievements, health fields. *Special achievements/activities:* 5 awards ($4500 total): leadership. *Special characteristics:* 62 awards ($155,593 total): general special characteristics. ***Tuition waivers:*** Full or partial for employees or children of employees. ***ROTC:*** Army cooperative, Air Force cooperative.

LOANS ***Student loans:*** $4,996,126 (43% need-based, 57% non-need-based). 67% of past graduating class borrowed through all loan programs. *Average indebtedness per student:* $15,410. ***Average need-based loan:*** Freshmen: $1780. Undergraduates: $2138. ***Parent loans:*** $253,025 (100% non-need-based). ***Programs:*** FFEL (Subsidized and Unsubsidized Stafford, PLUS), state, alternative loans.

WORK-STUDY ***Federal work-study:*** Total amount: $60,825; 44 jobs averaging $1382.

APPLYING FOR FINANCIAL AID ***Required financial aid form:*** FAFSA. ***Financial aid deadline (priority):*** 3/1. ***Notification date:*** Continuous beginning 3/1. Students must reply within 2 weeks of notification.

CONTACT Kylie Pruitt, Director of Financial Aid, Aquinas College, 4210 Harding Road, Nashville, TN 37205-2005, 615-297-7545 Ext. 431 or toll-free 800-649-0066. *Fax:* 615-279-0091. *E-mail:* pruittk@aquinascollege.edu.

ARCADIA UNIVERSITY

Glenside, PA

Tuition & fees: $29,700 **Average undergraduate aid package: $20,854**

ABOUT THE INSTITUTION Independent religious, coed. ***Awards:*** bachelor's, master's, and doctoral degrees. 52 undergraduate majors. ***Total enrollment:*** 3,894. Undergraduates: 2,242. Freshmen: 601. Federal methodology is used as a basis for awarding need-based institutional aid.

UNDERGRADUATE EXPENSES for 2008–09 ***Application fee:*** $30. ***One-time required fee:*** $100. ***Comprehensive fee:*** $39,980 includes full-time tuition ($29,340), mandatory fees ($360), and room and board ($10,280). ***College room only:*** $7270. Full-time tuition and fees vary according to course load, degree level, and program. Room and board charges vary according to board plan. ***Part-time tuition:*** $490 per credit. ***Payment plans:*** Installment, deferred payment.

FRESHMAN FINANCIAL AID (Fall 2008, est.) 551 applied for aid; of those 96% were deemed to have need. 99% of freshmen with need received aid; of those 54% had need fully met. ***Average percent of need met:*** 74% (excluding resources awarded to replace EFC). ***Average financial aid package:*** $22,161 (excluding resources awarded to replace EFC). 10% of all full-time freshmen had no need and received non-need-based gift aid.

UNDERGRADUATE FINANCIAL AID (Fall 2008, est.) 1,804 applied for aid; of those 99% were deemed to have need. 98% of undergraduates with need received aid; of those 59% had need fully met. ***Average percent of need met:*** 71% (excluding resources awarded to replace EFC). ***Average financial aid package:*** $20,854 (excluding resources awarded to replace EFC). 9% of all full-time undergraduates had no need and received non-need-based gift aid.

GIFT AID (NEED-BASED) ***Total amount:*** $29,886,569 (8% federal, 6% state, 82% institutional, 4% external sources). ***Receiving aid:*** Freshmen: 87% (520); all full-time undergraduates: 86% (1,742). ***Average award:*** Freshmen: $16,929; Undergraduates: $16,147. ***Scholarships, grants, and awards:*** Federal Pell, FSEOG, state, private, college/university gift aid from institutional funds, TEACH, Academic Competitiveness Grant, National Smart Grant.

GIFT AID (NON-NEED-BASED) ***Total amount:*** $1,912,172 (99% institutional, 1% external sources). ***Receiving aid:*** Freshmen: 10% (62). Undergraduates: 9% (180). ***Average award:*** Freshmen: $12,655. Undergraduates: $10,589. ***Scholarships, grants, and awards by category:*** *Academic interests/achievement:* 1,731 awards ($19,168,595 total): general academic interests/achievements. *Creative arts/performance:* 54 awards ($135,000 total): applied art and design, art/fine arts, theater/drama. *Special achievements/activities:* 443 awards ($1,019,771 total): community service, general special achievements/activities, leadership, memberships. *Special characteristics:* 21 awards ($61,500 total): children and siblings of alumni, relatives of clergy, religious affiliation. ***Tuition waivers:*** Full or partial for children of alumni, employees or children of employees.

LOANS ***Student loans:*** $20,352,086 (94% need-based, 6% non-need-based). 82% of past graduating class borrowed through all loan programs. *Average indebtedness per student:* $32,120. ***Average need-based loan:*** Freshmen: $3408. Undergraduates: $4396. ***Parent loans:*** $2,760,594 (89% need-based, 11% non-need-based). ***Programs:*** Federal Direct (Subsidized and Unsubsidized Stafford, PLUS), FFEL (Subsidized and Unsubsidized Stafford, PLUS), Perkins.

WORK-STUDY ***Federal work-study:*** Total amount: $1,511,959; jobs available. ***State or other work-study/employment:*** Total amount: $445,762 (100% non-need-based). Part-time jobs available.

APPLYING FOR FINANCIAL AID ***Required financial aid forms:*** FAFSA, institution's own form. ***Financial aid deadline (priority):*** 3/1. ***Notification date:*** Continuous. Students must reply by 5/1.

CONTACT Holly Kirkpatrick, Director of Financial Aid, Arcadia University, 450 South Easton Road, Glenside, PA 19038, 215-572-4475 or toll-free 877-ARCADIA. *Fax:* 215-572-4049. *E-mail:* kirkpath@arcadia.edu.

ARGOSY UNIVERSITY, ATLANTA

Atlanta, GA

UNDERGRADUATE EXPENSES Tuition varies by program. Students should contact Argosy University for tuition information.

CONTACT Financial Aid Office, Argosy University, Atlanta, 980 Hammond Drive, Suite 100, Atlanta, GA 30328, 770-671-1200 or toll-free 888-671-4777.

ARGOSY UNIVERSITY, CHICAGO

Chicago, IL

UNDERGRADUATE EXPENSES Tuition varies by program. Students should contact Argosy University for tuition information.

CONTACT Financial Aid Office, Argosy University, Chicago, 350 North Orleans Street, Chicago, IL 60654, 312-777-7600 or toll-free 800-626-4123.

ARGOSY UNIVERSITY, DALLAS

Dallas, TX

UNDERGRADUATE EXPENSES Tuition varies by program. Students should contact Argosy University for tuition information.

CONTACT Financial Aid Office, Argosy University, Dallas, 8080 Park Lane, Suite 400A, Dallas, TX 75231, 214-890-9900 or toll-free 866-954-9900.

ARGOSY UNIVERSITY, DENVER

Denver, CO

UNDERGRADUATE EXPENSES Tuition varies by program. Students should contact Argosy University for tuition information.

CONTACT Financial Aid Office, Argosy University, Denver, 1200 Lincoln Street, Denver, CO 80203, 303-248-2700 or toll-free 866-431-5981.

ARGOSY UNIVERSITY, HAWAI'I

Honolulu, HI

UNDERGRADUATE EXPENSES Tuition varies by program. Students should contact Argosy University for tuition information.

CONTACT Financial Aid Office, Argosy University, Hawai'i, 400 ASBTower, 1001 Bishop Street, Honolulu, HI 96813, 808-536-5555 or toll-free 888-323-2777.

ARGOSY UNIVERSITY, INLAND EMPIRE

San Bernardino, CA

UNDERGRADUATE EXPENSES Tuition varies by program. Students should contact Argosy University for tuition information.

CONTACT Financial Aid Office, Argosy University, Inland Empire, 636 East Brier Drive, Suite 235, San Bernardino, CA 92408, 909-915-3800 or toll-free 866-217-9075.

ARGOSY UNIVERSITY, NASHVILLE

Nashville, TN

UNDERGRADUATE EXPENSES Tuition varies by program. Students should contact Argosy University for tuition information.

CONTACT Financial Aid Office, Argosy University, Nashville, 100 Centerview Drive, Suite 225, Nashville, TN 37214, 615-525-2800 or toll-free 866-833-6598 (out-of-state).

ARGOSY UNIVERSITY, ORANGE COUNTY

Santa Ana, CA

UNDERGRADUATE EXPENSES Tuition varies by program. Students should contact Argosy University for tuition information.

CONTACT Financial Aid Office, Argosy University, Orange County, 3501 West Sunflower Avenue, Suite 110, Santa Ana, CA 92704, 714-338-6200 or toll-free 800-716-9598.

ARGOSY UNIVERSITY, PHOENIX

Phoenix, AZ

UNDERGRADUATE EXPENSES Tuition varies by program. Students should contact Argosy University for tuition information.

CONTACT Financial Aid Office, Argosy University, Phoenix, 2233 West Dunlap Avenue, Phoenix, AZ 85021, 602-216-2600 or toll-free 866-216-2777.

ARGOSY UNIVERSITY, SAN DIEGO

San Diego, CA

UNDERGRADUATE EXPENSES Tuition varies by program. Students should contact Argosy University for tuition information.

CONTACT Financial Aid Office, Argosy University, San Diego, 1615 Murray Canyon Road, Suite 100, San Diego, CA 92108, 619-321-3000 or toll-free 866-505-0333.

ARGOSY UNIVERSITY, SAN FRANCISCO BAY AREA

Alameda, CA

UNDERGRADUATE EXPENSES Tuition varies by program. Students should contact Argosy University for tuition information.

CONTACT Financial Aid Office, Argosy University, San Francisco Bay Area, 1005 Atlantic Avenue, Alameda, CA 94501, 510-217-4700 or toll-free 866-215-2777.

ARGOSY UNIVERSITY, SARASOTA

Sarasota, FL

UNDERGRADUATE EXPENSES Tuition varies by program. Students should contact Argosy University for tuition information.

CONTACT Financial Aid Office, Argosy University, Sarasota, 5250 17th Street, Sarasota, FL 34235, 941-379-0404 or toll-free 800-331-5995.

ARGOSY UNIVERSITY, SCHAUMBURG

Schaumburg, IL

UNDERGRADUATE EXPENSES Tuition varies by program. Students should contact Argosy University for tuition information.

CONTACT Financial Aid Office, Argosy University, Schaumburg, 999 North Plaza Drive, Suite 111, Schaumburg, IL 60173-5403, 847-969-4900 or toll-free 866-290-2777.

ARGOSY UNIVERSITY, SEATTLE

Seattle, WA

UNDERGRADUATE EXPENSES Tuition varies by program. Students should contact Argosy University for tuition information.

CONTACT Financial Aid Office, Argosy University, Seattle, 2601-A Elliott Avenue, Seattle, WA 98121, 206-283-4500 or toll-free 866-283-2777.

ARGOSY UNIVERSITY, TAMPA

Tampa, FL

UNDERGRADUATE EXPENSES Tuition varies by program. Students should contact Argosy University for tuition information.

CONTACT Financial Aid Office, Argosy University, Tampa, 4401 North Himes Avenue, Suite 150, Tampa, FL 33614, 813-393-5290 or toll-free 800-850-6488.

ARGOSY UNIVERSITY, TWIN CITIES

Eagan, MN

UNDERGRADUATE EXPENSES Tuition varies by program. Students should contact Argosy University for tuition information.

CONTACT Financial Aid Office, Argosy University, Twin Cities, 1515 Central Parkway, Eagan, MN 55121, 651-846-2882 or toll-free 888-844-2004.

ARGOSY UNIVERSITY, WASHINGTON DC

Arlington, VA

UNDERGRADUATE EXPENSES Tuition varies by program. Students should contact Argosy University for tuition information.

CONTACT Financial Aid Office, Argosy University, Washington DC, 1550 Wilson Boulevard, Suite 600, Arlington, VA 22209, 703-526-5800 or toll-free 866-703-2777.

ARIZONA STATE UNIVERSITY

Tempe, AZ

Tuition & fees (AZ res): $6844 **Average undergraduate aid package: $10,062**

ABOUT THE INSTITUTION State-supported, coed. ***Awards:*** bachelor's, master's, doctoral, and first professional degrees and post-bachelor's and post-master's certificates (profile includes data for the West, Polytechnic and Downtown Phoenix campuses). 121 undergraduate majors. ***Total enrollment:*** 67,082. Undergraduates: 53,298. Freshmen: 9,707. Federal methodology is used as a basis for awarding need-based institutional aid.

UNDERGRADUATE EXPENSES for 2009–10 ***Application fee:*** $50. ***Tuition, state resident:*** full-time $6507; part-time $464 per credit hour. ***Tuition, nonresident:*** full-time $19,292; part-time $804 per credit hour. ***Required fees:*** full-time $337; $110 per term. ***College room and board:*** $9210; ***Room only:*** $5610.

FRESHMAN FINANCIAL AID (Fall 2007) 5,188 applied for aid; of those 67% were deemed to have need. 100% of freshmen with need received aid; of those 26% had need fully met. ***Average percent of need met:*** 63% (excluding resources awarded to replace EFC). ***Average financial aid package:*** $10,395 (excluding resources awarded to replace EFC). 24% of all full-time freshmen had no need and received non-need-based gift aid.

UNDERGRADUATE FINANCIAL AID (Fall 2007) 22,315 applied for aid; of those 75% were deemed to have need. 100% of undergraduates with need received aid; of those 22% had need fully met. ***Average percent of need met:*** 60% (excluding resources awarded to replace EFC). ***Average financial aid package:*** $10,062 (excluding resources awarded to replace EFC). 16% of all full-time undergraduates had no need and received non-need-based gift aid.

GIFT AID (NEED-BASED) ***Total amount:*** $96,613,790 (38% federal, 51% institutional, 11% external sources). ***Receiving aid:*** Freshmen: 37% (3,180); all full-time undergraduates: 36% (14,731). ***Average award:*** Freshmen: $7181; Undergraduates: $5978. ***Scholarships, grants, and awards:*** Federal Pell, FSEOG, state, private, college/university gift aid from institutional funds, Federal Nursing.

GIFT AID (NON-NEED-BASED) ***Total amount:*** $61,758,907 (77% institutional, 23% external sources). ***Receiving aid:*** Freshmen: 5% (423). Undergraduates: 2% (1,008). ***Average award:*** Freshmen: $7054. Undergraduates: $6743. ***Scholarships, grants, and awards by category:*** *Academic interests/achievement:* architecture, area/ethnic studies, biological sciences, business, communication, computer science, education, engineering/technologies, English, foreign languages, general academic interests/achievements, health fields, home economics, humanities, mathematics, military science, physical sciences, premedicine, social sciences. *Creative arts/performance:* applied art and design, art/fine arts, cinema/film/broadcasting, creative writing, dance, debating, general creative arts/performance, journalism/publications, music, performing arts, theater/drama. *Special achievements/activities:* general special achievements/activities. ***ROTC:*** Army, Air Force.

LOANS ***Student loans:*** $122,165,948 (70% need-based, 30% non-need-based). 43% of past graduating class borrowed through all loan programs. *Average indebtedness per student:* $17,732. ***Average need-based loan:*** Freshmen: $3098. Undergraduates: $4012. ***Parent loans:*** $32,578,575 (34% need-based, 66% non-need-based). ***Programs:*** Federal Direct (Subsidized and Unsubsidized Stafford, PLUS), FFEL (PLUS), Perkins.

WORK-STUDY ***Federal work-study:*** Total amount: $2,582,482; 844 jobs averaging $3077. ***State or other work-study/employment:*** Total amount: $19,301,401 (25% need-based, 75% non-need-based). 6,109 part-time jobs averaging $3157.

ATHLETIC AWARDS Total amount: $6,490,831 (27% need-based, 73% non-need-based).

APPLYING FOR FINANCIAL AID ***Required financial aid form:*** FAFSA. ***Financial aid deadline (priority):*** 3/1.

CONTACT Craig Fennell, Director of Student Financial Assistance, Arizona State University, Box 870412, Tempe, AZ 85287-0412, 480-965-3355. *Fax:* 480-965-9484. *E-mail:* financialaid@asu.edu.

ARKANSAS BAPTIST COLLEGE

Little Rock, AR

CONTACT Director of Financial Aid, Arkansas Baptist College, 1600 Bishop Street, Little Rock, AR 72202-6067, 501-374-7856.

ARKANSAS STATE UNIVERSITY

Jonesboro, AR

Tuition & fees (AR res): $6370 **Average undergraduate aid package: $9900**

ABOUT THE INSTITUTION State-supported, coed. ***Awards:*** associate, bachelor's, master's, and doctoral degrees and post-bachelor's and post-master's certificates (specialist). 84 undergraduate majors. ***Total enrollment:*** 11,490. Undergraduates: 9,764. Freshmen: 1,902. Both federal and institutional methodology are used as a basis for awarding need-based institutional aid.

UNDERGRADUATE EXPENSES for 2008–09 ***Application fee:*** $15. ***Tuition, state resident:*** full-time $4890; part-time $163 per credit hour. ***Tuition, nonresident:*** full-time $12,810; part-time $427 per credit hour. ***Required fees:*** full-time $1480; $47 per credit hour or $25 per term. Full-time tuition and fees vary according to course level, course load, degree level, location, program, and reciprocity agreements. Part-time tuition and fees vary according to course level, course load, degree level, location, program, and reciprocity agreements. ***College room and board:*** $5056. Room and board charges vary according to board plan and housing facility. ***Payment plan:*** Installment.

FRESHMAN FINANCIAL AID (Fall 2008, est.) 1,576 applied for aid; of those 99% were deemed to have need. 100% of freshmen with need received aid; of those 27% had need fully met. ***Average percent of need met:*** 63% (excluding resources awarded to replace EFC). ***Average financial aid package:*** $9400 (excluding resources awarded to replace EFC). 6% of all full-time freshmen had no need and received non-need-based gift aid.

UNDERGRADUATE FINANCIAL AID (Fall 2008, est.) 7,267 applied for aid; of those 94% were deemed to have need. 100% of undergraduates with need received aid; of those 21% had need fully met. ***Average percent of need met:*** 51% (excluding resources awarded to replace EFC). ***Average financial aid package:*** $9900 (excluding resources awarded to replace EFC). 7% of all full-time undergraduates had no need and received non-need-based gift aid.

GIFT AID (NEED-BASED) ***Total amount:*** $30,300,000 (52% federal, 13% state, 31% institutional, 4% external sources). ***Receiving aid:*** Freshmen: 79% (1,385); all full-time undergraduates: 77% (5,811). ***Average award:*** Freshmen: $6800; Undergraduates: $5800. ***Scholarships, grants, and awards:*** Federal Pell, FSEOG, state, private, college/university gift aid from institutional funds.

GIFT AID (NON-NEED-BASED) ***Receiving aid:*** Freshmen: 29% (510). Undergraduates: 31% (2,352). ***Average award:*** Freshmen: $5100. Undergraduates: $5700. ***Scholarships, grants, and awards by category:*** *Academic interests/achievement:* 2,000 awards ($9,700,000 total): agriculture, area/ethnic studies, biological sciences, business, communication, computer science, education, engineering/technologies, English, general academic interests/achievements, health fields, humanities, library science, mathematics, military science, physical sciences, premedicine, social sciences. *Creative arts/performance:* 300 awards ($1,000,000 total): art/fine arts, cinema/film/broadcasting, debating, journalism/publications, music, performing arts, theater/drama. *Special achievements/activities:* 100 awards ($175,000 total): cheerleading/drum major, community service, general special achievements/activities, leadership. *Special characteristics:* 200 awards ($550,000 total): adult students, children and siblings of alumni, children of faculty/staff, ethnic background, first-generation college students, general special characteristics, handicapped students, local/state students, members of minority groups, out-of-state students, veterans, veterans' children. ***Tuition waivers:*** Full or partial for employees or children of employees, senior citizens. ***ROTC:*** Army.

LOANS ***Student loans:*** $40,600,000 (63% need-based, 37% non-need-based). 68% of past graduating class borrowed through all loan programs. *Average indebtedness per student:* $18,750. ***Average need-based loan:*** Freshmen: $3400. Undergraduates: $4500. ***Programs:*** FFEL (Subsidized and Unsubsidized Stafford, PLUS), Perkins.

WORK-STUDY ***Federal work-study:*** Total amount: $600,000; 300 jobs averaging $3500. ***State or other work-study/employment:*** Total amount: $2,200,000 (100% non-need-based). Part-time jobs available.

ATHLETIC AWARDS Total amount: $2,800,000 (79% need-based, 21% non-need-based).

APPLYING FOR FINANCIAL AID ***Required financial aid forms:*** FAFSA, institution's own form. ***Financial aid deadline:*** 7/1 (priority: 2/15). ***Notification date:*** Continuous beginning 6/1. Students must reply within 2 weeks of notification.

CONTACT Mr. Terry Finney, Director of Financial Aid, Arkansas State University, PO Box 1620, State University, AR 72467, 870-972-2310 or toll-free 800-382-3030 (in-state). *Fax:* 870-972-2794. *E-mail:* tfinney@astate.edu.

ARKANSAS TECH UNIVERSITY

Russellville, AR

Tuition & fees (AR res): $5430 **Average undergraduate aid package: $7174**

ABOUT THE INSTITUTION State-supported, coed. ***Awards:*** associate, bachelor's, and master's degrees and post-master's certificates (Educational Specialists). 53 undergraduate majors. ***Total enrollment:*** 7,492. Undergraduates: 6,960. Freshmen: 1,535. Federal methodology is used as a basis for awarding need-based institutional aid.

UNDERGRADUATE EXPENSES for 2008–09 ***Tuition, state resident:*** full-time $4830; part-time $161 per hour. ***Tuition, nonresident:*** full-time $9660; part-time $322 per hour. ***Required fees:*** full-time $600; $9 per hour or $165 per term. Full-time tuition and fees vary according to course load and location. Part-time tuition and fees vary according to course load and location. ***College room and board:*** $4888; ***Room only:*** $2824. Room and board charges vary according to board plan and housing facility. ***Payment plans:*** Installment, deferred payment.

FRESHMAN FINANCIAL AID (Fall 2007) 1,208 applied for aid; of those 70% were deemed to have need. 96% of freshmen with need received aid; of those 15% had need fully met. ***Average percent of need met:*** 68% (excluding resources awarded to replace EFC). ***Average financial aid package:*** $7285 (excluding resources awarded to replace EFC). 29% of all full-time freshmen had no need and received non-need-based gift aid.

UNDERGRADUATE FINANCIAL AID (Fall 2007) 4,075 applied for aid; of those 80% were deemed to have need. 97% of undergraduates with need received aid; of those 16% had need fully met. ***Average percent of need met:*** 70% (excluding resources awarded to replace EFC). ***Average financial aid package:*** $7174 (excluding resources awarded to replace EFC). 19% of all full-time undergraduates had no need and received non-need-based gift aid.

GIFT AID (NEED-BASED) ***Total amount:*** $10,888,550 (79% federal, 21% state). ***Receiving aid:*** Freshmen: 44% (685); all full-time undergraduates: 44% (2,484). ***Average award:*** Freshmen: $4000; Undergraduates: $3785. ***Scholarships, grants, and awards:*** Federal Pell, FSEOG, state, private.

GIFT AID (NON-NEED-BASED) ***Total amount:*** $11,710,074 (4% state, 87% institutional, 9% external sources). ***Receiving aid:*** Freshmen: 25% (381). Undergraduates: 15% (847). ***Average award:*** Freshmen: $6150. Undergraduates: $6520. ***Tuition waivers:*** Full or partial for employees or children of employees, senior citizens. ***ROTC:*** Army cooperative.

LOANS ***Student loans:*** $18,568,465 (54% need-based, 46% non-need-based). 51% of past graduating class borrowed through all loan programs. *Average indebtedness per student:* $6142. ***Average need-based loan:*** Freshmen: $2750. Undergraduates: $3691. ***Parent loans:*** $1,045,865 (100% non-need-based). ***Programs:*** FFEL (Subsidized and Unsubsidized Stafford, PLUS), Perkins.

WORK-STUDY ***Federal work-study:*** Total amount: $255,129; jobs available. ***State or other work-study/employment:*** Total amount: $924,404 (100% non-need-based). Part-time jobs available.

ATHLETIC AWARDS Total amount: $1,118,805 (100% non-need-based).

APPLYING FOR FINANCIAL AID ***Required financial aid form:*** FAFSA. ***Financial aid deadline (priority):*** 4/15. ***Notification date:*** Continuous beginning 5/1. Students must reply within 2 weeks of notification.

CONTACT Financial Aid Office, Arkansas Tech University, 1605 Coliseum Drive Suite 117, Russellville, AR 72801-2222, 479-968-0399 or toll-free 800-582-6953. *Fax:* 479-964-0857. *E-mail:* fa.help@atu.edu.

ARLINGTON BAPTIST COLLEGE

Arlington, TX

ABOUT THE INSTITUTION Independent Baptist, coed. ***Awards:*** bachelor's degrees. 10 undergraduate majors. ***Total enrollment:*** 138. Undergraduates: 138. Freshmen: 11.

GIFT AID (NEED-BASED) ***Scholarships, grants, and awards:*** Federal Pell, private, college/university gift aid from institutional funds.

GIFT AID (NON-NEED-BASED) ***Scholarships, grants, and awards by category:*** *Special characteristics:* children of faculty/staff, spouses of current students.

LOANS ***Programs:*** FFEL (Subsidized and Unsubsidized Stafford, PLUS).

APPLYING FOR FINANCIAL AID ***Required financial aid form:*** FAFSA.

CONTACT Mr. David B. Clogston Jr., Business Manager, Arlington Baptist College, 3001 West Division Street, Arlington, TX 76012-3425, 817-461-8741 Ext. 110. *Fax:* 817-274-1138.

ARMSTRONG ATLANTIC STATE UNIVERSITY

Savannah, GA

ABOUT THE INSTITUTION State-supported, coed, primarily women. ***Awards:*** associate, bachelor's, and master's degrees and post-bachelor's and post-master's certificates. 34 undergraduate majors. ***Total enrollment:*** 7,042. Undergraduates: 6,191. Freshmen: 902.

GIFT AID (NEED-BASED) ***Scholarships, grants, and awards:*** Federal Pell, FSEOG, state, private, college/university gift aid from institutional funds, Federal Nursing.

GIFT AID (NON-NEED-BASED) ***Scholarships, grants, and awards by category:*** *Academic interests/achievement:* biological sciences, computer science, education, engineering/technologies, English, foreign languages, general academic interests/achievements, health fields, humanities, international studies, mathematics, military science, physical sciences. *Creative arts/performance:* art/fine arts, music. *Special achievements/activities:* community service. *Special characteristics:* ethnic background, international students, religious affiliation.

LOANS ***Programs:*** FFEL (Subsidized and Unsubsidized Stafford, PLUS), college/university, alternative loans.

APPLYING FOR FINANCIAL AID ***Required financial aid form:*** FAFSA.

CONTACT Lee Ann Kirkland, Director of Financial Aid, Armstrong Atlantic State University, 11935 Abercorn Street, Savannah, GA 31419-1997, 912-344-2614 or toll-free 800-633-2349. *Fax:* 912-344-4338. *E-mail:* finaid@armstrong.edu.

ART ACADEMY OF CINCINNATI

Cincinnati, OH

Tuition & fees: $21,880 **Average undergraduate aid package: $13,197**

ABOUT THE INSTITUTION Independent, coed. ***Awards:*** associate, bachelor's, and master's degrees. 11 undergraduate majors. ***Total enrollment:*** 165. Undergraduates: 164. Freshmen: 47. Federal methodology is used as a basis for awarding need-based institutional aid.

UNDERGRADUATE EXPENSES for 2009–10 ***Tuition:*** full-time $21,500; part-time $900 per hour. ***Required fees:*** full-time $380; $190 per term.

FRESHMAN FINANCIAL AID (Fall 2007) 45 applied for aid; of those 93% were deemed to have need. 98% of freshmen with need received aid; of those 17% had need fully met. ***Average percent of need met:*** 60% (excluding resources awarded to replace EFC). ***Average financial aid package:*** $11,801 (excluding resources awarded to replace EFC). 10% of all full-time freshmen had no need and received non-need-based gift aid.

UNDERGRADUATE FINANCIAL AID (Fall 2007) 145 applied for aid; of those 89% were deemed to have need. 98% of undergraduates with need received aid; of those 15% had need fully met. ***Average percent of need met:*** 64% (excluding resources awarded to replace EFC). ***Average financial aid package:*** $13,197 (excluding resources awarded to replace EFC). 14% of all full-time undergraduates had no need and received non-need-based gift aid.

GIFT AID (NEED-BASED) ***Total amount:*** $1,105,262 (20% federal, 14% state, 61% institutional, 5% external sources). ***Receiving aid:*** Freshmen: 78% (40); all full-time undergraduates: 74% (122). ***Average award:*** Freshmen: $9100; Undergraduates: $8932. ***Scholarships, grants, and awards:*** Federal Pell, FSEOG, state, private, college/university gift aid from institutional funds.

GIFT AID (NON-NEED-BASED) ***Total amount:*** $303,074 (6% state, 81% institutional, 13% external sources). ***Receiving aid:*** Freshmen: 12% (6). Undergraduates: 9% (15). ***Average award:*** Freshmen: $9700. Undergraduates: $8264. ***Scholarships, grants, and awards by category:*** *Creative arts/performance:* applied art and design, art/fine arts.

LOANS ***Student loans:*** $1,222,805 (74% need-based, 26% non-need-based). *Average indebtedness per student:* $25,030. ***Average need-based loan:*** Freshmen: $3894. Undergraduates: $5640. ***Parent loans:*** $453,511 (34% need-based, 66% non-need-based). ***Programs:*** FFEL (Subsidized and Unsubsidized Stafford, PLUS), college/university, alternative loans.

WORK-STUDY ***Federal work-study:*** Total amount: $3353; jobs available. ***State or other work-study/employment:*** Part-time jobs available.

APPLYING FOR FINANCIAL AID ***Required financial aid form:*** FAFSA. ***Financial aid deadline:*** Continuous. ***Notification date:*** Continuous beginning 2/1. Students must reply within 2 weeks of notification.

CONTACT Ms. Karen Geiger, Director of Financial Aid, Art Academy of Cincinnati, 1212 Jackson Street, Cincinnati, OH 45202, 513-562-8773 or toll-free 800-323-5692 (in-state). *Fax:* 513-562-8778. *E-mail:* financialaid@artacademy.edu.

ART CENTER COLLEGE OF DESIGN

Pasadena, CA

CONTACT Clema McKenzie, Director of Financial Aid, Art Center College of Design, 1700 Lida Street, Pasadena, CA 91103-1999, 626-396-2215. *Fax:* 626-683-8684.

THE ART CENTER DESIGN COLLEGE

Tucson, AZ

CONTACT Ms. Margarita Carey, Education Finance Director, The Art Center Design College, 2525 North Country Club Road, Tucson, AZ 85716-2505, 520-325-0123 or toll-free 800-825-8753. *Fax:* 520-325-5535.

THE ART INSTITUTE OF ATLANTA

Atlanta, GA

UNDERGRADUATE EXPENSES Tuition cost varies by program. Prospective students should contact the school for current tuition costs. Other charges include a starting kit for all first-quarter students. Kits vary in price, depending on the program of study.

CONTACT Financial Aid Office, The Art Institute of Atlanta, 6600 Peachtree Dunwoody Road, 100 Embassy Row, Atlanta, GA 30328, 770-394-8300 or toll-free 800-275-4242.

THE ART INSTITUTE OF ATLANTA–DECATUR

Decatur, GA

UNDERGRADUATE EXPENSES Tuition cost varies by program. Prospective students should contact the school for current tuition costs. Other charges include a starting kit for all first-quarter students. Kits vary in price, depending on the program of study.

CONTACT Financial Aid Office, The Art Institute of Atlanta–Decatur, One West Court Square, Suite 1, Decatur, GA 30030, toll-free 866-856-6203.

THE ART INSTITUTE OF AUSTIN

Austin, TX

UNDERGRADUATE EXPENSES Tuition cost varies by program. Prospective students should contact the school for current tuition costs. Other charges include a starting kit for all first-quarter students. Kits vary in price, depending on the program of study.

CONTACT Financial Aid Office, The Art Institute of Austin, 101 W. Louis Henna Boulevard, Suite 100, Austin, TX 78728, 512-691-1707 or toll-free 866-583-7952.

THE ART INSTITUTE OF BOSTON AT LESLEY UNIVERSITY

Boston, MA

Tuition & fees: $26,590 **Average undergraduate aid package: $15,652**

ABOUT THE INSTITUTION Independent, coed. ***Awards:*** associate, bachelor's, master's, and doctoral degrees and post-bachelor's certificates. 4 undergraduate majors. ***Total enrollment:*** 6,686. Undergraduates: 1,267. Freshmen: 327. Institutional methodology is used as a basis for awarding need-based institutional aid.

UNDERGRADUATE EXPENSES for 2009–10 ***Application fee:*** $50. ***Comprehensive fee:*** $38,990 includes full-time tuition ($25,780), mandatory fees ($810), and room and board ($12,400).

FRESHMAN FINANCIAL AID (Fall 2008, est.) 309 applied for aid; of those 79% were deemed to have need. ***Average percent of need met:*** 70% (excluding resources awarded to replace EFC). ***Average financial aid package:*** $17,174 (excluding resources awarded to replace EFC). 18% of all full-time freshmen had no need and received non-need-based gift aid.

UNDERGRADUATE FINANCIAL AID (Fall 2008, est.) 1,070 applied for aid; of those 59% were deemed to have need. ***Average percent of need met:*** 70% (excluding resources awarded to replace EFC). ***Average financial aid package:*** $15,652 (excluding resources awarded to replace EFC). 20% of all full-time undergraduates had no need and received non-need-based gift aid.

GIFT AID (NEED-BASED) ***Total amount:*** $8,630,543 (13% federal, 5% state, 76% institutional, 6% external sources). ***Receiving aid:*** Freshmen: 73% (239); all full-time undergraduates: 51% (613). ***Average award:*** Freshmen: $15,024; Undergraduates: $13,218. ***Scholarships, grants, and awards:*** Federal Pell, FSEOG, state, private, college/university gift aid from institutional funds.

GIFT AID (NON-NEED-BASED) ***Total amount:*** $4,042,350 (100% institutional). ***Receiving aid:*** Freshmen: 18% (59). Undergraduates: 34% (409). ***Average award:*** Freshmen: $10,502. Undergraduates: $8439. ***Scholarships, grants, and awards by category:*** *Academic interests/achievement:* general academic interests/achievements. *Creative arts/performance:* 329 awards ($592,438 total): applied art and design, art/fine arts. *Special achievements/activities:* community service, general special achievements/activities, memberships. *Special characteristics:* 281 awards ($1,083,333 total): ethnic background, local/state students, members of minority groups.

LOANS ***Student loans:*** $10,291,202 (58% need-based, 42% non-need-based). 93% of past graduating class borrowed through all loan programs. *Average indebtedness per student:* $17,000. ***Average need-based loan:*** Freshmen: $4057. Undergraduates: $3636. ***Parent loans:*** $2,442,038 (100% non-need-based). ***Programs:*** FFEL (Subsidized and Unsubsidized Stafford, PLUS), Perkins, state.

WORK-STUDY ***Federal work-study:*** Total amount: $300,000; 225 jobs averaging $1800. ***State or other work-study/employment:*** 150 part-time jobs averaging $1500.

APPLYING FOR FINANCIAL AID ***Required financial aid forms:*** FAFSA, institution's own form, parent and student federal income tax forms. ***Financial aid deadline (priority):*** 3/12. ***Notification date:*** 4/1. Students must reply within 2 weeks of notification.

CONTACT Scott Jewell, Director of Financial Aid, The Art Institute of Boston at Lesley University, 29 Everett Street, Cambridge, MA 02138, 617-349-8714 or toll-free 800-773-0494 (in-state).

THE ART INSTITUTE OF CALIFORNIA–HOLLYWOOD

Los Angeles, CA

UNDERGRADUATE EXPENSES Tuition cost varies by program. Prospective students should contact the school for current tuition costs. Other charges include a starting kit for all first-quarter students. Kits vary in price, depending on the program of study.

CONTACT Financial Aid Office, The Art Institute of California–Hollywood, 3440 Wilshire Boulevard, Seventh Floor, Los Angeles, CA 90010, 213-251-3636 Ext. 209 or toll-free 877-468-6232. *Fax:* 213-385-3545. *E-mail:* jason@cdc.edu.

THE ART INSTITUTE OF CALIFORNIA–INLAND EMPIRE

San Bernardino, CA

UNDERGRADUATE EXPENSES Tuition cost varies by program. Prospective students should contact the school for current tuition costs. Other charges include a starting kit for all first-quarter students. Kits vary in price, depending on the program of study.

CONTACT Financial Aid Office, The Art Institute of California–Inland Empire, 630 East Brier Drive, San Bernardino, CA 92408, 909-915-2100 or toll-free 800-353-0812.

THE ART INSTITUTE OF CALIFORNIA–LOS ANGELES

Santa Monica, CA

UNDERGRADUATE EXPENSES Tuition cost varies by program. Prospective students should contact the school for current tuition costs. Other charges include a starting kit for all first-quarter students. Kits vary in price, depending on the program of study.

CONTACT Financial Aid Office, The Art Institute of California–Los Angeles, 2900 31st Street, Santa Monica, CA 90405-3035, 310-752-4700 or toll-free 888-646-4610.

THE ART INSTITUTE OF CALIFORNIA–ORANGE COUNTY

Santa Ana, CA

UNDERGRADUATE EXPENSES Tuition cost varies by program. Prospective students should contact the school for current tuition costs. Other charges include a starting kit for all first-quarter students. Kits vary in price, depending on the program of study.

CONTACT Financial Aid Office, The Art Institute of California–Orange County, 3601 West Sunflower Avenue, Santa Ana, CA 92704-9888, 714-830-0200 or toll-free 888-549-3055.

THE ART INSTITUTE OF CALIFORNIA–SACRAMENTO

Sacramento, CA

UNDERGRADUATE EXPENSES Tuition cost varies by program. Prospective students should contact the school for current tuition costs. Other charges include a starting kit for all first-quarter students. Kits vary in price, depending on the program of study.

CONTACT Financial Aid Office, The Art Institute of California–Sacramento, 2850 Gateway Oaks Drive, Suite 100, Sacramento, CA 95833, toll-free 800-477-1957.

THE ART INSTITUTE OF CALIFORNIA–SAN DIEGO

San Diego, CA

UNDERGRADUATE EXPENSES Tuition cost varies by program. Prospective students should contact the school for current tuition costs. Other charges include a starting kit for all first-quarter students. Kits vary in price, depending on the program of study.

CONTACT Financial Aid Office, The Art Institute of California–San Diego, 10025 Mesa Rim Road, San Diego, CA 92121, 619-546-0602 or toll-free 866-275-2422.

THE ART INSTITUTE OF CALIFORNIA–SAN FRANCISCO

San Francisco, CA

UNDERGRADUATE EXPENSES Tuition cost varies by program. Prospective students should contact the school for current tuition costs. Other charges include a starting kit for all first-quarter students. Kits vary in price, depending on the program of study.

CONTACT Financial Aid Office, The Art Institute of California–San Francisco, 1170 Market Street, San Francisco, CA 94102-4908, 415-865-0198 or toll-free 888-493-3261. *Fax:* 415-863-5831.

THE ART INSTITUTE OF CALIFORNIA–SUNNYVALE

Sunnyvale, CA

UNDERGRADUATE EXPENSES Tuition cost varies by program. Prospective students should contact the school for current tuition costs. Other charges include a starting kit for all first-quarter students. Kits vary in price, depending on the program of study.

CONTACT Financial Aid Office, The Art Institute of California–Sunnyvale, 1120 Kifer Road, Sunnyvale, CA 94086, 408-962-6400 or toll-free 866-583-7961.

THE ART INSTITUTE OF CHARLESTON

Charleston, SC

UNDERGRADUATE EXPENSES Tuition cost varies by program. Prospective students should contact the school for current tuition costs. Other charges include a starting kit for all first-quarter students. Kits vary in price, depending on the program of study.

CONTACT Financial Aid Office, The Art Institute of Charleston, The Carroll Building, 24 North Market Street, Charleston, SC 29401, 843-727-3500 or toll-free 866-211-0107.

THE ART INSTITUTE OF CHARLOTTE

Charlotte, NC

UNDERGRADUATE EXPENSES Tuition cost varies by program. Prospective students should contact the school for current tuition costs. Other charges include a starting kit for all first-quarter students. Kits vary in price, depending on the program of study.

CONTACT Financial Aid Office, The Art Institute of Charlotte, 2110 Water Ridge Parkway, Charlotte, NC 28217, 704-357-8020 or toll-free 800-872-4417.

THE ART INSTITUTE OF COLORADO

Denver, CO

UNDERGRADUATE EXPENSES Tuition cost varies by program. Prospective students should contact the school for current tuition costs. Other charges include a starting kit for all first-quarter students. Kits vary in price, depending on the program of study.

CONTACT Financial Aid Office, The Art Institute of Colorado, 1200 Lincoln Street, Denver, CO 80203, 303-837-0825 or toll-free 800-275-2420.

THE ART INSTITUTE OF DALLAS

Dallas, TX

UNDERGRADUATE EXPENSES Tuition cost varies by program. Prospective students should contact the school for current tuition costs. Other charges include a starting kit for all first-quarter students. Kits vary in price, depending on the program of study.

CONTACT Financial Aid Office, The Art Institute of Dallas, 8080 Park Lane, Suite 100, Dallas, TX 75231-5993, 214-692-8080 or toll-free 800-275-4243.

THE ART INSTITUTE OF FORT LAUDERDALE

Fort Lauderdale, FL

UNDERGRADUATE EXPENSES Tuition cost varies by program. Prospective students should contact the school for current tuition costs. Other charges include a starting kit for all first-quarter students. Kits vary in price, depending on the program of study.

CONTACT Financial Aid Office, The Art Institute of Fort Lauderdale, 1799 Southeast 17th Street Causeway, Fort Lauderdale, FL 33316-3000, 954-527-1799 or toll-free 800-275-7603.

THE ART INSTITUTE OF HOUSTON

Houston, TX

UNDERGRADUATE EXPENSES Tuition cost varies by program. Prospective students should contact the school for current tuition costs. Other charges include a starting kit for all first-quarter students. Kits vary in price, depending on the program of study.

CONTACT Financial Aid Office, The Art Institute of Houston, 1900 Yorktown, Houston, TX 77056, 713-623-2040 Ext. 780 or toll-free 800-275-4244. *Fax:* 713-966-2700. *E-mail:* bensons@aii.edu.

THE ART INSTITUTE OF HOUSTON—NORTH

Houston, TX

UNDERGRADUATE EXPENSES Tuition cost varies by program. Prospective students should contact the school for current tuition costs. Other charges include a starting kit for all first-quarter students. Kits vary in price, depending on the program of study.

CONTACT Financial Aid Office, The Art Institute of Houston—North, 10740 North Gessner Drive, Houston, TX 77064, toll-free 866-830-4450 (out-of-state).

THE ART INSTITUTE OF INDIANAPOLIS

Indianapolis, IN

UNDERGRADUATE EXPENSES Tuition cost varies by program. Prospective students should contact the school for current tuition costs. Other charges include a starting kit for all first-quarter students. Kits vary in price, depending on the program of study.

CONTACT Financial Aid Office, The Art Institute of Indianapolis, 3500 Depauw Boulevard, Indianapolis, IN 46268, 866-441-9031.

THE ART INSTITUTE OF JACKSONVILLE

Jacksonville, FL

UNDERGRADUATE EXPENSES Tuition cost varies by program. Prospective students should contact the school for current tuition costs. Other charges include a starting kit for all first-quarter students. Kits vary in price, depending on the program of study.

CONTACT Financial Aid Office, The Art Institute of Jacksonville, 8775 Baypine Road, Jacksonville, FL 32256, 904-732-9393 or toll-free 800-924-1589.

THE ART INSTITUTE OF LAS VEGAS

Henderson, NV

UNDERGRADUATE EXPENSES Tuition cost varies by program. Prospective students should contact the school for current tuition costs. Other charges include a starting kit for all first-quarter students. Kits vary in price, depending on the program of study.

CONTACT Financial Aid Office, The Art Institute of Las Vegas, 2350 Corporate Circle Drive, Henderson, NV 89074, 702-369-9944.

THE ART INSTITUTE OF MICHIGAN

Novi, MI

UNDERGRADUATE EXPENSES Tuition cost varies by program. Prospective students should contact the school for current tuition costs. Other charges include a starting kit for all first-quarter students. Kits vary in price, depending on the program of study.

CONTACT Financial Aid Office, The Art Institute of Michigan, 28125 Cabot Drive, Suite 120, Novi, MI 48377, 248-675-3800 or toll-free 800-479-0087.

THE ART INSTITUTE OF PHILADELPHIA

Philadelphia, PA

UNDERGRADUATE EXPENSES Tuition cost varies by program. Prospective students should contact the school for current tuition costs. Other charges include a starting kit for all first-quarter students. Kits vary in price, depending on the program of study.

CONTACT Financial Aid Office, The Art Institute of Philadelphia, 1622 Chestnut Street, Philadelphia, PA 19103-5198, 215-246-3311 or toll-free 800-275-2474. *Fax:* 215-246-3339.

THE ART INSTITUTE OF PHOENIX

Phoenix, AZ

UNDERGRADUATE EXPENSES Tuition cost varies by program. Prospective students should contact the school for current tuition costs. Other charges include a starting kit for all first-quarter students. Kits vary in price, depending on the program of study.

CONTACT Financial Aid Office, The Art Institute of Phoenix, 2233 West Dunlap Avenue, Phoenix, AZ 85021-2859, 602-331-7500 or toll-free 800-474-2479.

THE ART INSTITUTE OF PITTSBURGH

Pittsburgh, PA

UNDERGRADUATE EXPENSES Tuition cost varies by program. Prospective students should contact the school for current tuition costs. Other charges include a starting kit for all first-quarter students. Kits vary in price, depending on the program of study.

CONTACT Financial Aid Office, The Art Institute of Pittsburgh, 526 Penn Avenue, Pittsburgh, PA 15222-3269, 412-263-6600 or toll-free 800-275-2470.

THE ART INSTITUTE OF PORTLAND

Portland, OR

UNDERGRADUATE EXPENSES Tuition cost varies by program. Prospective students should contact the school for current tuition costs. Other charges include a starting kit for all first-quarter students. Kits vary in price, depending on the program of study.

CONTACT Financial Aid Office, The Art Institute of Portland, 1122 NW Davis Street, Portland, OR 97209, 503-228-6528 or toll-free 888-228-6528.

THE ART INSTITUTE OF RALEIGH-DURHAM

Durham, NC

UNDERGRADUATE EXPENSES Tuition cost varies by program. Prospective students should contact the school for current tuition costs. Other charges include a starting kit for all first-quarter students. Kits vary in price, depending on the program of study.

CONTACT Financial Aid Office, The Art Institute of Raleigh-Durham, 410 Blackwell Street, Suite 200, Durham, NC 27701, toll-free 888-245-9593.

THE ART INSTITUTE OF SALT LAKE CITY

Draper, UT

UNDERGRADUATE EXPENSES Tuition cost varies by program. Prospective students should contact the school for current tuition costs. Other charges include a starting kit for all first-quarter students. Kits vary in price, depending on the program of study.

CONTACT Financial Aid Office, The Art Institute of Salt Lake City, 121 West Election Road, Draper, UT 84020-9492, toll-free 800-978-0096.

THE ART INSTITUTE OF TAMPA

Tampa, FL

UNDERGRADUATE EXPENSES Tuition cost varies by program. Prospective students should contact the school for current tuition costs. Other charges include a starting kit for all first-quarter students. Kits vary in price, depending on the program of study.

CONTACT Financial Aid Office, The Art Institute of Tampa, 4401 North Himes Avenue, Suite 150, Tampa, FL 33614, 866-703-3277.

THE ART INSTITUTE OF TENNESSEE–NASHVILLE

Nashville, TN

UNDERGRADUATE EXPENSES Tuition cost varies by program. Prospective students should contact the school for current tuition costs. Other charges include a starting kit for all first-quarter students. Kits vary in price, depending on the program of study.

CONTACT Financial Aid Office, The Art Institute of Tennessee–Nashville, 100 CNA Drive, Nashville, TN 37214, 866-747-5770.

THE ART INSTITUTE OF TUCSON

Tucson, AZ

UNDERGRADUATE EXPENSES Tuition cost varies by program. Prospective students should contact the school for current tuition costs. Other charges include a starting kit for all first-quarter students. Kits vary in price, depending on the program of study.

CONTACT Financial Aid Office, The Art Institute of Tucson, 5099 E. Grant Road, Suite 100, Tucson, AZ 85712, 520-881-2900 or toll-free 866-690-8850.

THE ART INSTITUTE OF WASHINGTON

Arlington, VA

UNDERGRADUATE EXPENSES Tuition cost varies by program. Prospective students should contact the school for current tuition costs. Other charges include a starting kit for all first-quarter students. Kits vary in price, depending on the program of study.

CONTACT Financial Aid Office, The Art Institute of Washington, 1820 North Fort Myer Drive, Arlington, VA 22209, 703-247-6849 or toll-free 877-303-3771. *Fax:* 703-247-6829.

THE ART INSTITUTES INTERNATIONAL–KANSAS CITY

Lexena, KS

UNDERGRADUATE EXPENSES Tuition cost varies by program. Prospective students should contact the school for current tuition costs. Other charges include a starting kit for all first-quarter students. Kits vary in price, depending on the program of study.

CONTACT Financial Aid Office, The Art Institutes International–Kansas City, 8208 Melrose Drive, Lexena, KS 66214, toll-free 866-530-8508.

THE ART INSTITUTES INTERNATIONAL MINNESOTA

Minneapolis, MN

UNDERGRADUATE EXPENSES Tuition cost varies by program. Prospective students should contact the school for current tuition costs. Other charges include a starting kit for all first-quarter students. Kits vary in price, depending on the program of study.

CONTACT Financial Aid Office, The Art Institutes International Minnesota, 825 2nd Avenue South, Minneapolis, MN 55402, 612-332-3361 Ext. 110 or toll-free 800-777-3643. *Fax:* 612-332-3934. *E-mail:* robbt@aii.edu.

ASBURY COLLEGE

Wilmore, KY

Tuition & fees: $22,413 | **Average undergraduate aid package: $16,694**

ABOUT THE INSTITUTION Independent nondenominational, coed. ***Awards:*** associate, bachelor's, and master's degrees. 44 undergraduate majors. ***Total enrollment:*** 1,550. Undergraduates: 1,446. Freshmen: 313. Federal methodology is used as a basis for awarding need-based institutional aid.

UNDERGRADUATE EXPENSES for 2009–10 ***Application fee:*** $30. ***Comprehensive fee:*** $27,827 includes full-time tuition ($22,242), mandatory fees ($171), and room and board ($5414). ***College room only:*** $3206. ***Part-time tuition:*** $855 per semester hour.

FRESHMAN FINANCIAL AID (Fall 2008, est.) 285 applied for aid; of those 76% were deemed to have need. 100% of freshmen with need received aid; of those 29% had need fully met. ***Average percent of need met:*** 88% (excluding resources awarded to replace EFC). ***Average financial aid package:*** $18,481 (excluding resources awarded to replace EFC). 22% of all full-time freshmen had no need and received non-need-based gift aid.

UNDERGRADUATE FINANCIAL AID (Fall 2008, est.) 1,019 applied for aid; of those 86% were deemed to have need. 100% of undergraduates with need received aid; of those 26% had need fully met. ***Average percent of need met:*** 80% (excluding resources awarded to replace EFC). ***Average financial aid package:*** $16,694 (excluding resources awarded to replace EFC). 11% of all full-time undergraduates had no need and received non-need-based gift aid.

GIFT AID (NEED-BASED) ***Total amount:*** $11,449,669 (11% federal, 14% state, 70% institutional, 5% external sources). ***Receiving aid:*** Freshmen: 68% (213); all full-time undergraduates: 71% (852). ***Average award:*** Freshmen: $12,412; Undergraduates: $10,744. ***Scholarships, grants, and awards:*** Federal Pell, FSEOG, state, private, college/university gift aid from institutional funds.

GIFT AID (NON-NEED-BASED) ***Total amount:*** $2,297,340 (6% state, 88% institutional, 6% external sources). ***Receiving aid:*** Freshmen: 29% (90). Undergraduates: 24% (285). ***Average award:*** Freshmen: $8687. Undergraduates: $10,154. ***Scholarships, grants, and awards by category:*** *Academic interests/achievement:* general academic interests/achievements. *Creative arts/performance:* music. *Special achievements/activities:* leadership. *Special characteristics:* children and siblings of alumni, children of faculty/staff, ethnic background, international students, siblings of current students. ***ROTC:*** Army cooperative, Air Force cooperative.

LOANS ***Student loans:*** $8,222,502 (92% need-based, 8% non-need-based). 85% of past graduating class borrowed through all loan programs. *Average indebtedness per student:* $26,150. ***Average need-based loan:*** Freshmen: $3474. Undergraduates: $3999. ***Parent loans:*** $1,563,839 (79% need-based, 21% non-need-based). ***Programs:*** FFEL (Subsidized and Unsubsidized Stafford, PLUS), Perkins, college/university, private loans.

WORK-STUDY ***Federal work-study:*** Total amount: $608,968; 502 jobs averaging $1215.

ATHLETIC AWARDS Total amount: $944,850 (74% need-based, 26% non-need-based).

APPLYING FOR FINANCIAL AID ***Required financial aid forms:*** FAFSA, institution's own form. ***Financial aid deadline (priority):*** 3/1. ***Notification date:*** Continuous. Students must reply within 4 weeks of notification.

CONTACT Ronald Anderson, Director of Financial Aid, Asbury College, One Macklem Drive, Wilmore, KY 40390, 859-858-3511 Ext. 2195 or toll-free 800-888-1818. *Fax:* 859-858-3921. *E-mail:* ron.anderson@asbury.edu.

ASHFORD UNIVERSITY

Clinton, IA

ABOUT THE INSTITUTION Proprietary, coed. ***Awards:*** bachelor's and master's degrees. 32 undergraduate majors. ***Total enrollment:*** 10,568. Undergraduates: 9,866. Freshmen: 817.

GIFT AID (NEED-BASED) ***Scholarships, grants, and awards:*** Federal Pell, FSEOG, state, private, college/university gift aid from institutional funds.

LOANS ***Programs:*** FFEL (Subsidized and Unsubsidized Stafford, PLUS).

WORK-STUDY ***Federal work-study:*** Total amount: $117,680. ***State or other work-study/employment:*** Total amount: $22,303 (100% need-based).

APPLYING FOR FINANCIAL AID ***Required financial aid forms:*** FAFSA, institution's own form.

CONTACT Lisa Kramer, Director of Financial Aid, Ashford University, 400 North Bluff Boulevard, PO Box 2967, Clinton, IA 52733-2967, 563-242-4023 Ext. 1243 or toll-free 800-242-4153. *Fax:* 563-242-8684.

ASHLAND UNIVERSITY

Ashland, OH

Tuition & fees: $25,640 | **Average undergraduate aid package: $21,554**

ABOUT THE INSTITUTION Independent religious, coed. ***Awards:*** associate, bachelor's, master's, doctoral, and first professional degrees. 67 undergraduate majors. ***Total enrollment:*** 6,475. Undergraduates: 2,654. Freshmen: 576. Federal methodology is used as a basis for awarding need-based institutional aid.

UNDERGRADUATE EXPENSES for 2009–10 ***Comprehensive fee:*** $32,998 includes full-time tuition ($24,828), mandatory fees ($812), and room and board ($7358). ***College room only:*** $5028. ***Part-time tuition:*** $762 per credit.

FRESHMAN FINANCIAL AID (Fall 2008, est.) 553 applied for aid; of those 90% were deemed to have need. 100% of freshmen with need received aid. ***Average percent of need met:*** 90% (excluding resources awarded to replace EFC). ***Average financial aid package:*** $23,910 (excluding resources awarded to replace EFC). 5% of all full-time freshmen had no need and received non-need-based gift aid.

UNDERGRADUATE FINANCIAL AID (Fall 2008, est.) 1,937 applied for aid; of those 88% were deemed to have need. 100% of undergraduates with need received aid. ***Average percent of need met:*** 90% (excluding resources awarded to replace EFC). ***Average financial aid package:*** $21,554 (excluding resources awarded to replace EFC). 11% of all full-time undergraduates had no need and received non-need-based gift aid.

GIFT AID (NEED-BASED) ***Total amount:*** $20,502,469 (13% federal, 12% state, 73% institutional, 2% external sources). ***Receiving aid:*** Freshmen: 89% (499); all full-time undergraduates: 79% (1,701). ***Average award:*** Freshmen: $17,268; Undergraduates: $14,812. ***Scholarships, grants, and awards:*** Federal Pell, FSEOG, state, private, college/university gift aid from institutional funds.

GIFT AID (NON-NEED-BASED) ***Total amount:*** $2,508,293 (9% state, 89% institutional, 2% external sources). ***Receiving aid:*** Freshmen: 87% (488). Undergraduates: 79% (1,685). ***Average award:*** Freshmen: $6952. Undergraduates: $6923. ***Scholarships, grants, and awards by category:*** *Academic interests/achievement:* 1,026 awards ($6,513,429 total): general academic interests/achievements, mathematics, physical sciences, social sciences. *Creative arts/performance:* 162 awards ($373,375 total): art/fine arts, music, theater/drama. *Special achievements/activities:* 14 awards ($6750 total): cheerleading/drum major. *Special characteristics:* 343 awards ($2,623,024 total): children and siblings of alumni, children of faculty/staff, international students, relatives of clergy, religious affiliation.

LOANS ***Student loans:*** $11,422,509 (92% need-based, 8% non-need-based). 75% of past graduating class borrowed through all loan programs. *Average indebtedness per student:* $18,250. ***Average need-based loan:*** Freshmen: $4244. Undergraduates: $4653. ***Parent loans:*** $2,685,132 (89% need-based, 11% non-need-based). ***Programs:*** FFEL (Subsidized and Unsubsidized Stafford, PLUS), Perkins, college/university.

WORK-STUDY ***Federal work-study:*** Total amount: $2,397,825; 1,155 jobs averaging $1841.

ATHLETIC AWARDS Total amount: $4,132,619 (73% need-based, 27% non-need-based).

APPLYING FOR FINANCIAL AID ***Required financial aid forms:*** FAFSA, institution's own form. ***Financial aid deadline:*** Continuous. ***Notification date:*** Continuous beginning 3/15. Students must reply within 3 weeks of notification.

CONTACT Mr. Stephen C. Howell, Director of Financial Aid, Ashland University, 401 College Avenue, Ashland, OH 44805-3702, 419-289-5944 or toll-free 800-882-1548. *Fax:* 419-289-5976. *E-mail:* showell@ashland.edu.

ASHWORTH UNIVERSITY

Norcross, GA

CONTACT Financial Aid Office, Ashworth University, 430 Technology Parkway, Norcross, GA 30092, 770-729-8400 or toll-free 800-957-5412.

ASPEN UNIVERSITY

Denver, CO

Tuition & fees: N/R | **Average undergraduate aid package: N/A**

ABOUT THE INSTITUTION Independent, coed. 2 undergraduate majors. Both federal and institutional methodology are used as a basis for awarding need-based institutional aid.

GIFT AID (NEED-BASED) ***Total amount:*** $2521 (100% federal).

LOANS ***Student loans:*** $16,220 (57% need-based, 43% non-need-based).

CONTACT Jennifer Quinn, Director of Financial Aid, Aspen University, 720 South Colorado Blvd. #1150N, Denver, CO 80246, 800-441-4746 or toll-free 800-441-4746 Ext. 177 (in-state). *Fax:* 303-336-1144. *E-mail:* jquinn@aspen.edu.

ASSUMPTION COLLEGE

Worcester, MA

Tuition & fees: $28,851 | **Average undergraduate aid package: $18,341**

ABOUT THE INSTITUTION Independent Roman Catholic, coed. ***Awards:*** bachelor's and master's degrees and post-bachelor's and post-master's certificates. 42 undergraduate majors. ***Total enrollment:*** 2,626. Undergraduates: 2,169. Freshmen: 607. Federal methodology is used as a basis for awarding need-based institutional aid.

UNDERGRADUATE EXPENSES for 2008–09 ***Application fee:*** $50. ***Comprehensive fee:*** $35,007 includes full-time tuition ($28,686), mandatory fees ($165), and room and board ($6156). ***College room only:*** $3620. Full-time tuition and fees vary according to course load and reciprocity agreements. Room and board charges vary according to housing facility. ***Part-time tuition:*** $956 per credit hour. ***Part-time fees:*** $165 per year. Part-time tuition and fees vary according to course load.

FRESHMAN FINANCIAL AID (Fall 2008, est.) 542 applied for aid; of those 83% were deemed to have need. 100% of freshmen with need received aid; of those 23% had need fully met. ***Average percent of need met:*** 74% (excluding resources awarded to replace EFC). ***Average financial aid package:*** $18,101 (excluding resources awarded to replace EFC). 23% of all full-time freshmen had no need and received non-need-based gift aid.

UNDERGRADUATE FINANCIAL AID (Fall 2008, est.) 1,810 applied for aid; of those 85% were deemed to have need. 99% of undergraduates with need received aid; of those 21% had need fully met. ***Average percent of need met:*** 74% (excluding resources awarded to replace EFC). ***Average financial aid package:*** $18,341 (excluding resources awarded to replace EFC). 22% of all full-time undergraduates had no need and received non-need-based gift aid.

GIFT AID (NEED-BASED) ***Total amount:*** $21,271,009 (7% federal, 5% state, 86% institutional, 2% external sources). ***Receiving aid:*** Freshmen: 74% (450); all full-time undergraduates: 71% (1,526). ***Average award:*** Freshmen: $14,950; Undergraduates: $14,368. ***Scholarships, grants, and awards:*** Federal Pell, FSEOG, state, private, college/university gift aid from institutional funds.

GIFT AID (NON-NEED-BASED) ***Total amount:*** $4,855,329 (91% institutional, 9% external sources). ***Receiving aid:*** Freshmen: 12% (75). Undergraduates: 8% (183). ***Average award:*** Freshmen: $13,577. Undergraduates: $14,807. ***Scholarships, grants, and awards by category:*** *Academic interests/achievement:* 1,264 awards ($11,683,057 total): general academic interests/achievements. *Special characteristics:* members of minority groups. ***Tuition waivers:*** Full or partial for employees or children of employees. ***ROTC:*** Army cooperative, Air Force cooperative.

LOANS ***Student loans:*** $16,618,598 (59% need-based, 41% non-need-based). 93% of past graduating class borrowed through all loan programs. *Average indebtedness per student:* $26,691. ***Average need-based loan:*** Freshmen: $3756. Undergraduates: $4612. ***Parent loans:*** $5,918,001 (26% need-based, 74% non-need-based). ***Programs:*** Federal Direct (Subsidized and Unsubsidized Stafford, PLUS).

WORK-STUDY ***Federal work-study:*** Total amount: $310,294; jobs available.

ATHLETIC AWARDS Total amount: $955,174 (28% need-based, 72% non-need-based).

APPLYING FOR FINANCIAL AID ***Required financial aid form:*** FAFSA. ***Financial aid deadline:*** 2/1. ***Notification date:*** Continuous beginning 2/16. Students must reply by 5/1.

CONTACT Linda Mularczyk, Director of Financial Aid, Assumption College, 500 Salisbury Street, Worcester, MA 01609-1296, 508-767-7157 or toll-free 888-882-7786. *Fax:* 508-767-7376. *E-mail:* fa@assumption.edu.

ATHENS STATE UNIVERSITY

Athens, AL

Tuition & fees (AL res): $3300 | **Average undergraduate aid package: N/A**

ABOUT THE INSTITUTION State-supported, coed. ***Awards:*** bachelor's degrees. 29 undergraduate majors. ***Total enrollment:*** 3,114. Undergraduates: 3,114. Federal methodology is used as a basis for awarding need-based institutional aid.

UNDERGRADUATE EXPENSES for 2008–09 ***Application fee:*** $30. ***Tuition, state resident:*** full-time $3300. ***Tuition, nonresident:*** full-time $6600.

UNDERGRADUATE FINANCIAL AID (Fall 2008, est.) 970 applied for aid; of those 62% were deemed to have need. 1% of all full-time undergraduates had no need and received non-need-based gift aid.

GIFT AID (NEED-BASED) ***Total amount:*** $5,794,307 (98% federal, 2% state). ***Receiving aid:*** All full-time undergraduates: 13% (196). ***Scholarships, grants, and awards:*** Federal Pell, FSEOG, state, private, college/university gift aid from institutional funds.

GIFT AID (NON-NEED-BASED) ***Total amount:*** $28,417 (31% institutional, 69% external sources). ***Receiving aid:*** Undergraduates: 33% (473). ***Tuition waivers:*** Full or partial for employees or children of employees, senior citizens.

LOANS ***Student loans:*** $22,020,754 (100% non-need-based). ***Programs:*** Federal Direct (Subsidized and Unsubsidized Stafford, PLUS), college/university.

WORK-STUDY ***Federal work-study:*** Total amount: $126,574; jobs available.

APPLYING FOR FINANCIAL AID ***Required financial aid form:*** FAFSA. ***Financial aid deadline:*** Continuous. ***Notification date:*** Continuous beginning 5/1. Students must reply within 2 weeks of notification.

CONTACT Renee Stanford, Financial Aid Officer, Athens State University, 300 North Beaty Street, Athens, AL 35611, 256-233-8122 or toll-free 800-522-0272. *Fax:* 256-233-8178. *E-mail:* renee.stanford@athens.edu.

ATLANTA CHRISTIAN COLLEGE

East Point, GA

CONTACT Blair Walker, Director of Financial Aid, Atlanta Christian College, 2605 Ben Hill Road, East Point, GA 30344, 404-761-8861 or toll-free 800-776-1ACC. *Fax:* 404-669-2024. *E-mail:* blairw@acc.edu.

ATLANTIC COLLEGE

Guaynabo, PR

CONTACT Mrs. Velma Aponte, Financial Aid Coordinator, Atlantic College, Calle Colton #9, Guaynabo, PR 00970, 787-720-1092. *E-mail:* atlaneco@coqui.net.

ATLANTIC UNION COLLEGE

South Lancaster, MA

ABOUT THE INSTITUTION Independent Seventh-day Adventist, coed. ***Awards:*** associate, bachelor's, and master's degrees and post-bachelor's certificates. 21 undergraduate majors. ***Total enrollment:*** 387. Undergraduates: 385. Freshmen: 57.

GIFT AID (NEED-BASED) ***Scholarships, grants, and awards:*** Federal Pell, FSEOG, state, private, college/university gift aid from institutional funds.

GIFT AID (NON-NEED-BASED) ***Scholarships, grants, and awards by category:*** *Academic interests/achievement:* business, computer science, education, English, general academic interests/achievements, health fields, mathematics, premedicine, religion/biblical studies. *Creative arts/performance:* music. *Special achievements/activities:* leadership. *Special characteristics:* adult students, children of faculty/staff, international students, siblings of current students.

LOANS ***Programs:*** FFEL (Subsidized and Unsubsidized Stafford, PLUS), Perkins, Federal Nursing, state, college/university, TERI Loans, Signature Loans, Campus Door.

WORK-STUDY ***Federal work-study:*** Total amount: $403,032; 381 jobs averaging $2071. ***State or other work-study/employment:*** Total amount: $497,287 (27% need-based, 73% non-need-based). 75 part-time jobs averaging $2017.

APPLYING FOR FINANCIAL AID ***Required financial aid form:*** FAFSA.

CONTACT Sandra Pereira, Director of Financial Aid, Atlantic Union College, PO Box 1000, South Lancaster, MA 01561-1000, 978-368-2284 or toll-free 800-282-2030. *Fax:* 978-368-2283. *E-mail:* sandra.pereira@auc.edu.

AUBURN UNIVERSITY

Auburn University, AL

Tuition & fees (AL res): $5880 **Average undergraduate aid package: $8565**

ABOUT THE INSTITUTION State-supported, coed. ***Awards:*** bachelor's, master's, doctoral, and first professional degrees and post-master's certificates. 133 undergraduate majors. ***Total enrollment:*** 24,530. Undergraduates: 20,037. Freshmen: 3,984. Federal methodology is used as a basis for awarding need-based institutional aid.

UNDERGRADUATE EXPENSES for 2008–09 ***Application fee:*** $40. ***Tuition, state resident:*** full-time $5880; part-time $243 per credit hour. ***Tuition, nonresident:*** full-time $17,640; part-time $729 per credit hour. Full-time tuition and fees vary according to course load, program, and reciprocity agreements. Part-time tuition and fees vary according to course load, program, and reciprocity agreements. ***College room and board:*** $8260; ***Room only:*** $3772. Room and board charges vary according to board plan and housing facility. ***Payment plan:*** Tuition prepayment.

FRESHMAN FINANCIAL AID (Fall 2007) 2,133 applied for aid; of those 55% were deemed to have need. 100% of freshmen with need received aid; of those 21% had need fully met. ***Average percent of need met:*** 58% (excluding resources awarded to replace EFC). ***Average financial aid package:*** $8648 (excluding resources awarded to replace EFC). 17% of all full-time freshmen had no need and received non-need-based gift aid.

UNDERGRADUATE FINANCIAL AID (Fall 2007) 8,490 applied for aid; of those 62% were deemed to have need. 100% of undergraduates with need received aid; of those 18% had need fully met. ***Average percent of need met:*** 57% (excluding resources awarded to replace EFC). ***Average financial aid package:*** $8565 (excluding resources awarded to replace EFC). 10% of all full-time undergraduates had no need and received non-need-based gift aid.

GIFT AID (NEED-BASED) ***Total amount:*** $18,674,802 (54% federal, 7% state, 28% institutional, 11% external sources). ***Receiving aid:*** Freshmen: 22% (927); all full-time undergraduates: 20% (3,540). ***Average award:*** Freshmen: $5555; Undergraduates: $5047. ***Scholarships, grants, and awards:*** Federal Pell, FSEOG, state, private, college/university gift aid from institutional funds.

GIFT AID (NON-NEED-BASED) ***Total amount:*** $24,494,946 (9% state, 48% institutional, 43% external sources). ***Receiving aid:*** Freshmen: 4% (172). Undergraduates: 3% (501). ***Average award:*** Freshmen: $4427. Undergraduates: $4426. ***Scholarships, grants, and awards by category:*** *Academic interests/achievement:* agriculture, architecture, biological sciences, business, communication, computer science, education, engineering/technologies, English, foreign languages, general academic interests/achievements, health fields, home economics, humanities, mathematics, physical sciences, premedicine, social sciences. *Creative arts/performance:* applied art and design, art/fine arts, cinema/film/broadcasting, creative writing, journalism/publications, music, performing arts, theater/drama. *Special achievements/activities:* cheerleading/drum major, leadership, memberships. *Special characteristics:* children and siblings of alumni, children of faculty/staff, children of union members/company employees, ethnic background, local/state students, married students, out-of-state students. ***Tuition waivers:*** Full or partial for employees or children of employees. ***ROTC:*** Army, Naval, Air Force.

LOANS ***Student loans:*** $47,485,020 (66% need-based, 34% non-need-based). 39% of past graduating class borrowed through all loan programs. *Average indebtedness per student:* $34,398. ***Average need-based loan:*** Freshmen: $3872. Undergraduates: $4510. ***Parent loans:*** $16,503,394 (29% need-based, 71% non-need-based). ***Programs:*** FFEL (Subsidized and Unsubsidized Stafford, PLUS), Perkins, Federal Nursing, college/university.

WORK-STUDY ***Federal work-study:*** Total amount: $1,072,875; 380 jobs averaging $3118.

ATHLETIC AWARDS Total amount: $7,183,180 (2% need-based, 98% non-need-based).

APPLYING FOR FINANCIAL AID ***Required financial aid form:*** FAFSA. ***Financial aid deadline (priority):*** 3/1. ***Notification date:*** Continuous.

CONTACT Mr. Mike Reynolds, Director of Student Financial Services, Auburn University, 203 Mary Martin Hall, Auburn University, AL 36849, 334-844-4634 or toll-free 800-AUBURN9 (in-state). *Fax:* 334-844-6085. *E-mail:* finaid7@auburn.edu.

AUBURN UNIVERSITY MONTGOMERY

Montgomery, AL

Tuition & fees (AL res): $5850 **Average undergraduate aid package: N/A**

ABOUT THE INSTITUTION State-supported, coed. ***Awards:*** bachelor's, master's, and doctoral degrees and post-master's certificates. 24 undergraduate majors. ***Total enrollment:*** 5,284. Undergraduates: 4,457. Freshmen: 822. Federal methodology is used as a basis for awarding need-based institutional aid.

UNDERGRADUATE EXPENSES for 2008–09 ***Application fee:*** $25. ***Tuition, state resident:*** full-time $5580; part-time $177 per credit hour. ***Tuition, nonresident:*** full-time $16,200; part-time $531 per credit hour. ***Required fees:*** full-time $270; $6 per semester hour or $45 per term. Full-time tuition and fees vary according to course load. Part-time tuition and fees vary according to course load. ***College room and board: Room only:*** $3420. Room and board charges vary according to housing facility. ***Payment plan:*** Installment.

FRESHMAN FINANCIAL AID (Fall 2008, est.) 580 applied for aid; of those 69% were deemed to have need. 96% of freshmen with need received aid.

UNDERGRADUATE FINANCIAL AID (Fall 2008, est.) 2,273 applied for aid; of those 65% were deemed to have need. 96% of undergraduates with need received aid.

GIFT AID (NEED-BASED) ***Total amount:*** $7,385,654 (76% federal, 2% state, 16% institutional, 6% external sources). ***Receiving aid:*** Freshmen: 36% (256);

all full-time undergraduates: 32% (926). ***Average award:*** Freshmen: $4227; Undergraduates: $4054. ***Scholarships, grants, and awards:*** Federal Pell, FSEOG, state, private, college/university gift aid from institutional funds.

GIFT AID (NON-NEED-BASED) ***Scholarships, grants, and awards by category:*** *Academic interests/achievement:* general academic interests/achievements. ***Tuition waivers:*** Full or partial for employees or children of employees. ***ROTC:*** Army, Air Force cooperative.

LOANS ***Student loans:*** $23,344,913 (100% need-based). ***Average need-based loan:*** Freshmen: $3135. Undergraduates: $3776. ***Parent loans:*** $466,358 (100% need-based). ***Programs:*** FFEL (Subsidized and Unsubsidized Stafford, PLUS), Perkins.

WORK-STUDY ***Federal work-study:*** Total amount: $181,608; 46 jobs averaging $3418.

APPLYING FOR FINANCIAL AID ***Required financial aid form:*** FAFSA. ***Financial aid deadline (priority):*** 3/1. ***Notification date:*** 6/1. Students must reply within 3 weeks of notification.

CONTACT Anthony Richey, Senior Director of Financial Aid, Auburn University Montgomery, PO Box 244023, Montgomery, AL 36124-4023, 334-244-3571 or toll-free 800-227-2649 (in-state). *Fax:* 334-244-3913. *E-mail:* arichey@aum.edu.

AUGSBURG COLLEGE

Minneapolis, MN

Tuition & fees: $27,513 **Average undergraduate aid package: $17,449**

ABOUT THE INSTITUTION Independent Lutheran, coed. ***Awards:*** bachelor's and master's degrees and post-bachelor's and post-master's certificates. 64 undergraduate majors. ***Total enrollment:*** 3,891. Undergraduates: 3,049. Freshmen: 455. Federal methodology is used as a basis for awarding need-based institutional aid.

UNDERGRADUATE EXPENSES for 2009–10 ***Application fee:*** $25. ***Tuition:*** full-time $27,020.

FRESHMAN FINANCIAL AID (Fall 2008, est.) 442 applied for aid; of those 85% were deemed to have need. 100% of freshmen with need received aid; of those 24% had need fully met. ***Average percent of need met:*** 81% (excluding resources awarded to replace EFC). ***Average financial aid package:*** $23,065 (excluding resources awarded to replace EFC). 12% of all full-time freshmen had no need and received non-need-based gift aid.

UNDERGRADUATE FINANCIAL AID (Fall 2008, est.) 2,211 applied for aid; of those 85% were deemed to have need. 100% of undergraduates with need received aid; of those 15% had need fully met. ***Average percent of need met:*** 65% (excluding resources awarded to replace EFC). ***Average financial aid package:*** $17,449 (excluding resources awarded to replace EFC). 9% of all full-time undergraduates had no need and received non-need-based gift aid.

GIFT AID (NEED-BASED) ***Total amount:*** $21,844,435 (15% federal, 12% state, 69% institutional, 4% external sources). ***Receiving aid:*** Freshmen: 80% (361); all full-time undergraduates: 68% (1,649). ***Average award:*** Freshmen: $16,040; Undergraduates: $13,214. ***Scholarships, grants, and awards:*** Federal Pell, FSEOG, state, private, college/university gift aid from institutional funds, Federal Nursing.

GIFT AID (NON-NEED-BASED) ***Total amount:*** $5,385,338 (1% state, 76% institutional, 23% external sources). ***Receiving aid:*** Freshmen: 8% (38). Undergraduates: 9% (211). ***Average award:*** Freshmen: $6957. Undergraduates: $7698. ***Scholarships, grants, and awards by category:*** *Academic interests/achievement:* biological sciences, business, communication, computer science, education, English, foreign languages, general academic interests/achievements, health fields, international studies, mathematics, physical sciences, religion/biblical studies, social sciences. *Creative arts/performance:* art/fine arts, music, performing arts, theater/drama. *Special achievements/activities:* community service, general special achievements/activities, junior miss, leadership, religious involvement. *Special characteristics:* children and siblings of alumni, international students, members of minority groups, relatives of clergy, siblings of current students. ***ROTC:*** Army cooperative, Naval cooperative, Air Force cooperative.

LOANS ***Student loans:*** $24,199,138 (42% need-based, 58% non-need-based). 90% of past graduating class borrowed through all loan programs. *Average indebtedness per student:* $25,155. ***Average need-based loan:*** Freshmen: $5082. Undergraduates: $4554. ***Parent loans:*** $14,853,586 (8% need-based, 92% non-need-based). ***Programs:*** FFEL (Subsidized and Unsubsidized Stafford, PLUS), Perkins, Federal Nursing, state.

WORK-STUDY ***Federal work-study:*** Total amount: $1,764,208; 670 jobs averaging $2670. ***State or other work-study/employment:*** Total amount: $1,331,116 (44% need-based, 56% non-need-based). 324 part-time jobs averaging $2640.

APPLYING FOR FINANCIAL AID ***Required financial aid form:*** FAFSA. ***Financial aid deadline:*** 8/15 (priority: 5/1). ***Notification date:*** Continuous. Students must reply within 3 weeks of notification.

CONTACT Mr. Paul L. Terrio, Director of Student Financial Services, Augsburg College, 2211 Riverside Avenue, Minneapolis, MN 55454-1351, 612-330-1049 or toll-free 800-788-5678. *Fax:* 612-330-1308. *E-mail:* terriop@augsburg.edu.

AUGUSTANA COLLEGE

Rock Island, IL

Tuition & fees: $30,150 **Average undergraduate aid package: $22,510**

ABOUT THE INSTITUTION Independent religious, coed. ***Awards:*** bachelor's degrees. 68 undergraduate majors. ***Total enrollment:*** 2,546. Undergraduates: 2,546. Freshmen: 641. Federal methodology is used as a basis for awarding need-based institutional aid.

UNDERGRADUATE EXPENSES for 2008–09 ***Application fee:*** $35. ***Comprehensive fee:*** $37,800 includes full-time tuition ($30,150) and room and board ($7650). ***College room only:*** $3870. Full-time tuition and fees vary according to course load. Room and board charges vary according to board plan and housing facility. ***Part-time tuition:*** $1100 per credit hour. ***Payment plans:*** Tuition prepayment, installment.

FRESHMAN FINANCIAL AID (Fall 2007) 544 applied for aid; of those 81% were deemed to have need. 100% of freshmen with need received aid; of those 39% had need fully met. ***Average percent of need met:*** 88% (excluding resources awarded to replace EFC). ***Average financial aid package:*** $22,069 (excluding resources awarded to replace EFC). 31% of all full-time freshmen had no need and received non-need-based gift aid.

UNDERGRADUATE FINANCIAL AID (Fall 2007) 1,804 applied for aid; of those 84% were deemed to have need. 100% of undergraduates with need received aid; of those 41% had need fully met. ***Average percent of need met:*** 83% (excluding resources awarded to replace EFC). ***Average financial aid package:*** $22,510 (excluding resources awarded to replace EFC). 29% of all full-time undergraduates had no need and received non-need-based gift aid.

GIFT AID (NEED-BASED) ***Total amount:*** $20,291,779 (7% federal, 13% state, 78% institutional, 2% external sources). ***Receiving aid:*** Freshmen: 68% (442); all full-time undergraduates: 67% (1,523). ***Average award:*** Freshmen: $14,274; Undergraduates: $13,752. ***Scholarships, grants, and awards:*** Federal Pell, FSEOG, state, private, college/university gift aid from institutional funds.

GIFT AID (NON-NEED-BASED) ***Total amount:*** $8,746,823 (1% state, 96% institutional, 3% external sources). ***Receiving aid:*** Freshmen: 14% (92). Undergraduates: 10% (237). ***Average award:*** Freshmen: $11,499. Undergraduates: $10,126. ***Scholarships, grants, and awards by category:*** *Academic interests/achievement:* 1,967 awards ($17,851,542 total): biological sciences, business, communication, computer science, education, English, foreign languages, general academic interests/achievements, humanities, mathematics, physical sciences, religion/biblical studies, social sciences. *Creative arts/performance:* 384 awards ($754,338 total): art/fine arts, creative writing, debating, music, theater/drama. *Special characteristics:* 320 awards ($943,118 total): children and siblings of alumni, children of faculty/staff, international students, members of minority groups, religious affiliation, siblings of current students. ***Tuition waivers:*** Full or partial for employees or children of employees.

LOANS ***Student loans:*** $11,215,084 (65% need-based, 35% non-need-based). ***Average need-based loan:*** Freshmen: $5136. Undergraduates: $5136. ***Parent loans:*** $4,922,609 (30% need-based, 70% non-need-based). ***Programs:*** Federal Direct (Subsidized and Unsubsidized Stafford, PLUS), Perkins.

WORK-STUDY ***Federal work-study:*** Total amount: $1,359,640; 1,060 jobs averaging $1907.

APPLYING FOR FINANCIAL AID ***Required financial aid forms:*** FAFSA, institution's own form. ***Financial aid deadline (priority):*** 4/1. ***Notification date:*** Continuous. Students must reply by 5/1.

CONTACT Sue Standley, Director of Financial Aid, Augustana College, 639 38th Street, Rock Island, IL 61201-2296, 309-794-7207 or toll-free 800-798-8100. *Fax:* 309-794-7174. *E-mail:* suestandley@augustana.edu.

AUGUSTANA COLLEGE
Sioux Falls, SD

Tuition & fees: $22,450 **Average undergraduate aid package: $18,539**

ABOUT THE INSTITUTION Independent religious, coed. ***Awards:*** bachelor's and master's degrees. 55 undergraduate majors. ***Total enrollment:*** 1,754. Undergraduates: 1,733. Freshmen: 438. Federal methodology is used as a basis for awarding need-based institutional aid.

UNDERGRADUATE EXPENSES for 2008–09 ***Comprehensive fee:*** $28,370 includes full-time tuition ($22,188), mandatory fees ($262), and room and board ($5920). Full-time tuition and fees vary according to course load. Room and board charges vary according to board plan and housing facility. ***Part-time tuition:*** $336 per credit. Part-time tuition and fees vary according to course load. ***Payment plan:*** Installment.

FRESHMAN FINANCIAL AID (Fall 2008, est.) 370 applied for aid; of those 85% were deemed to have need. 100% of freshmen with need received aid; of those 22% had need fully met. ***Average percent of need met:*** 97% (excluding resources awarded to replace EFC). ***Average financial aid package:*** $20,477 (excluding resources awarded to replace EFC). 25% of all full-time freshmen had no need and received non-need-based gift aid.

UNDERGRADUATE FINANCIAL AID (Fall 2008, est.) 1,307 applied for aid; of those 85% were deemed to have need. 100% of undergraduates with need received aid; of those 18% had need fully met. ***Average percent of need met:*** 89% (excluding resources awarded to replace EFC). ***Average financial aid package:*** $18,539 (excluding resources awarded to replace EFC). 30% of all full-time undergraduates had no need and received non-need-based gift aid.

GIFT AID (NEED-BASED) ***Total amount:*** $12,760,029 (14% federal, 1% state, 80% institutional, 5% external sources). ***Receiving aid:*** Freshmen: 74% (313); all full-time undergraduates: 67% (1,104). ***Average award:*** Freshmen: $15,867; Undergraduates: $13,720. ***Scholarships, grants, and awards:*** Federal Pell, FSEOG, state, private, college/university gift aid from institutional funds, need-linked special talent scholarships, minority scholarships.

GIFT AID (NON-NEED-BASED) ***Total amount:*** $5,161,028 (1% federal, 2% state, 90% institutional, 7% external sources). ***Receiving aid:*** Freshmen: 73% (310). Undergraduates: 66% (1,083). ***Average award:*** Freshmen: $10,561. Undergraduates: $8730. ***Scholarships, grants, and awards by category:*** *Academic interests/achievement:* biological sciences, business, communication, computer science, education, English, foreign languages, general academic interests/achievements, health fields, humanities, international studies, mathematics, physical sciences, premedicine, religion/biblical studies, social sciences. *Creative arts/performance:* art/fine arts, creative writing, music, performing arts, theater/drama. *Special achievements/activities:* general special achievements/activities, leadership. *Special characteristics:* children and siblings of alumni, children of current students, children of faculty/staff, ethnic background, international students, local/state students, members of minority groups, religious affiliation, siblings of current students, spouses of current students, veterans. ***Tuition waivers:*** Full or partial for employees or children of employees, adult students, senior citizens.

LOANS ***Student loans:*** $10,621,178 (62% need-based, 38% non-need-based). 77% of past graduating class borrowed through all loan programs. *Average indebtedness per student:* $25,885. ***Average need-based loan:*** Freshmen: $5264. Undergraduates: $5421. ***Parent loans:*** $1,013,991 (16% need-based, 84% non-need-based). ***Programs:*** FFEL (Subsidized and Unsubsidized Stafford, PLUS), Perkins, Federal Nursing, college/university, Minnesota SELF Loans, alternative loans.

WORK-STUDY ***Federal work-study:*** Total amount: $620,663; 356 jobs averaging $1461. ***State or other work-study/employment:*** Total amount: $157,054 (7% need-based, 93% non-need-based). 181 part-time jobs averaging $1121.

ATHLETIC AWARDS Total amount: $2,122,149 (43% need-based, 57% non-need-based).

APPLYING FOR FINANCIAL AID ***Required financial aid form:*** FAFSA. ***Financial aid deadline (priority):*** 3/1. ***Notification date:*** Continuous beginning 4/1. Students must reply by 5/1 or within 3 weeks of notification.

CONTACT Ms. Brenda L. Murtha, Director of Financial Aid, Augustana College, 2001 South Summit Avenue, Sioux Falls, SD 57197, 605-274-5216 or toll-free 800-727-2844 Ext. 5516 (in-state), 800-727-2844 (out-of-state). *Fax:* 605-274-5295. *E-mail:* brenda.murtha@augie.edu.

AUGUSTA STATE UNIVERSITY
Augusta, GA

Tuition & fees (GA res): $3644 **Average undergraduate aid package: $3522**

ABOUT THE INSTITUTION State-supported, coed. ***Awards:*** associate, bachelor's, and master's degrees and post-master's certificates. 32 undergraduate majors. ***Total enrollment:*** 6,689. Undergraduates: 5,525. Freshmen: 941. Federal methodology is used as a basis for awarding need-based institutional aid.

UNDERGRADUATE EXPENSES for 2008–09 ***Application fee:*** $20. ***Tuition, state resident:*** full-time $3098; part-time $130 per credit hour. ***Tuition, nonresident:*** full-time $12,390; part-time $517 per credit hour. ***Required fees:*** full-time $546; $546 per year. ***Payment plan:*** Guaranteed tuition.

FRESHMAN FINANCIAL AID (Fall 2007) 545 applied for aid; of those 81% were deemed to have need. 91% of freshmen with need received aid; of those 3% had need fully met. ***Average percent of need met:*** 70% (excluding resources awarded to replace EFC). ***Average financial aid package:*** $3289 (excluding resources awarded to replace EFC). 3% of all full-time freshmen had no need and received non-need-based gift aid.

UNDERGRADUATE FINANCIAL AID (Fall 2007) 2,765 applied for aid; of those 79% were deemed to have need. 93% of undergraduates with need received aid; of those 8% had need fully met. ***Average percent of need met:*** 70% (excluding resources awarded to replace EFC). ***Average financial aid package:*** $3522 (excluding resources awarded to replace EFC). 12% of all full-time undergraduates had no need and received non-need-based gift aid.

GIFT AID (NEED-BASED) ***Total amount:*** $6,717,664 (99% federal, 1% external sources). ***Receiving aid:*** Freshmen: 36% (322); all full-time undergraduates: 37% (1,466). ***Average award:*** Freshmen: $1818; Undergraduates: $1790. ***Scholarships, grants, and awards:*** Federal Pell, FSEOG, state, private, college/university gift aid from institutional funds.

GIFT AID (NON-NEED-BASED) ***Total amount:*** $5,692,714 (81% state, 8% institutional, 11% external sources). ***Receiving aid:*** Freshmen: 12% (109). Undergraduates: 16% (622). ***Average award:*** Freshmen: $1524. Undergraduates: $1702. ***Scholarships, grants, and awards by category:*** *Academic interests/achievement:* 76 awards ($106,613 total): biological sciences, business, communication, computer science, education, English, general academic interests/achievements, health fields, mathematics, military science, physical sciences, social sciences. *Creative arts/performance:* 44 awards ($25,122 total): art/fine arts, creative writing, general creative arts/performance, music, performing arts, theater/drama. *Special achievements/activities:* 18 awards ($29,658 total): community service, general special achievements/activities, hobbies/interests, leadership. *Special characteristics:* 1,556 awards ($4,477,507 total): general special characteristics, handicapped students, local/state students. ***Tuition waivers:*** Full or partial for employees or children of employees, senior citizens. ***ROTC:*** Army.

LOANS ***Student loans:*** $23,570,384 (56% need-based, 44% non-need-based). 36% of past graduating class borrowed through all loan programs. *Average indebtedness per student:* $5961. ***Average need-based loan:*** Freshmen: $1427. Undergraduates: $1757. ***Parent loans:*** $263,800 (100% non-need-based). ***Programs:*** FFEL (Subsidized and Unsubsidized Stafford, PLUS), Perkins, state.

WORK-STUDY ***Federal work-study:*** Total amount: $211,287; 64 jobs averaging $2618. ***State or other work-study/employment:*** 263 part-time jobs averaging $1722.

ATHLETIC AWARDS Total amount: $319,748 (100% non-need-based).

APPLYING FOR FINANCIAL AID ***Required financial aid form:*** FAFSA. ***Financial aid deadline:*** 4/1. ***Notification date:*** Continuous.

CONTACT Ms. Roxanne Padgett, Assistant Director of Financial Aid, Augusta State University, 2500 Walton Way, Augusta, GA 30904-2200, 706-737-1431 or toll-free 800-341-4373. *Fax:* 706-737-1777. *E-mail:* bpadgett@aug.edu.

AURORA UNIVERSITY
Aurora, IL

ABOUT THE INSTITUTION Independent, coed. ***Awards:*** bachelor's, master's, and doctoral degrees and post-bachelor's and post-master's certificates. 28 undergraduate majors. ***Total enrollment:*** 4,291. Undergraduates: 2,202. Freshmen: 378.

GIFT AID (NEED-BASED) ***Scholarships, grants, and awards:*** Federal Pell, FSEOG, state, private, college/university gift aid from institutional funds.

GIFT AID (NON-NEED-BASED) ***Scholarships, grants, and awards by category:*** *Academic interests/achievement:* education, general academic interests/achievements, mathematics. *Creative arts/performance:* music, theater/drama. *Special achievements/activities:* general special achievements/activities. *Special characteristics:* children and siblings of alumni, children of educators, children of faculty/staff, out-of-state students, parents of current students, siblings of current students, spouses of current students.

LOANS ***Programs:*** FFEL (Subsidized and Unsubsidized Stafford, PLUS), Perkins, college/university.

WORK-STUDY ***Federal work-study:*** Total amount: $882,906; 576 jobs averaging $1761.

APPLYING FOR FINANCIAL AID ***Required financial aid form:*** FAFSA.

CONTACT Heather Gutierrez, Dean of Student Financial Services, Aurora University, 347 South Gladstone Avenue, Aurora, IL 60506-4892, 630-844-5533 or toll-free 800-742-5281. *Fax:* 630-844-5535. *E-mail:* finaid@aurora.edu.

AUSTIN COLLEGE

Sherman, TX

Tuition & fees: $27,875 **Average undergraduate aid package: $26,783**

ABOUT THE INSTITUTION Independent Presbyterian, coed. ***Awards:*** bachelor's and master's degrees. 27 undergraduate majors. ***Total enrollment:*** 1,298. Undergraduates: 1,263. Freshmen: 319. Federal methodology is used as a basis for awarding need-based institutional aid.

UNDERGRADUATE EXPENSES for 2009–10 ***Application fee:*** $35. ***One-time required fee:*** $25. ***Comprehensive fee:*** $36,965 includes full-time tuition ($27,690), mandatory fees ($185), and room and board ($9090). ***College room only:*** $4230. ***Part-time tuition:*** $4016 per course.

FRESHMAN FINANCIAL AID (Fall 2008, est.) 253 applied for aid; of those 81% were deemed to have need. 100% of freshmen with need received aid; of those 100% had need fully met. ***Average percent of need met:*** 99% (excluding resources awarded to replace EFC). ***Average financial aid package:*** $28,461 (excluding resources awarded to replace EFC). 35% of all full-time freshmen had no need and received non-need-based gift aid.

UNDERGRADUATE FINANCIAL AID (Fall 2008, est.) 900 applied for aid; of those 80% were deemed to have need. 100% of undergraduates with need received aid; of those 100% had need fully met. ***Average percent of need met:*** 99% (excluding resources awarded to replace EFC). ***Average financial aid package:*** $26,783 (excluding resources awarded to replace EFC). 40% of all full-time undergraduates had no need and received non-need-based gift aid.

GIFT AID (NEED-BASED) ***Total amount:*** $12,051,228 (10% federal, 14% state, 74% institutional, 2% external sources). ***Receiving aid:*** Freshmen: 64% (204); all full-time undergraduates: 57% (716). ***Average award:*** Freshmen: $19,197; Undergraduates: $17,212. ***Scholarships, grants, and awards:*** Federal Pell, FSEOG, state, private, college/university gift aid from institutional funds.

GIFT AID (NON-NEED-BASED) ***Total amount:*** $6,313,388 (95% institutional, 5% external sources). ***Receiving aid:*** Freshmen: 25% (81). Undergraduates: 15% (185). ***Average award:*** Freshmen: $13,653. Undergraduates: $11,669. ***Scholarships, grants, and awards by category:*** *Academic interests/achievement:* biological sciences, business, communication, education, engineering/technologies, English, foreign languages, general academic interests/achievements, health fields, humanities, international studies, physical sciences, premedicine, religion/biblical studies, social sciences. *Creative arts/performance:* art/fine arts, music, theater/drama. *Special achievements/activities:* community service, general special achievements/activities, leadership, religious involvement. *Special characteristics:* children of faculty/staff, ethnic background, first-generation college students, handicapped students, international students, local/state students, relatives of clergy.

LOANS ***Student loans:*** $10,151,694 (49% need-based, 51% non-need-based). ***Average need-based loan:*** Freshmen: $5130. Undergraduates: $5593. ***Parent loans:*** $6,988,867 (3% need-based, 97% non-need-based). ***Programs:*** FFEL (Subsidized and Unsubsidized Stafford, PLUS), Perkins, state, college/university, alternative loans through various sources.

WORK-STUDY ***Federal work-study:*** Total amount: $522,491; jobs available. ***State or other work-study/employment:*** Total amount: $285,700 (6% need-based, 94% non-need-based). Part-time jobs available.

APPLYING FOR FINANCIAL AID ***Required financial aid form:*** FAFSA. ***Financial aid deadline (priority):*** 4/1. ***Notification date:*** Continuous. Students must reply by 5/1.

CONTACT Mrs. Laurie Coulter, Executive Director of Financial Aid, Austin College, 900 North Grand Avenue, Sherman, TX 75090, 903-813-2900 or toll-free 800-442-5363. *Fax:* 903-813-3198. *E-mail:* finaid@austincollege.edu.

AUSTIN GRADUATE SCHOOL OF THEOLOGY

Austin, TX

CONTACT David Arthur, Financial Aid Officer, Austin Graduate School of Theology, 1909 University Avenue, Austin, TX 78705-5610, 512-476-2772 Ext. 204 or toll-free 866-AUS-GRAD. *Fax:* 512-476-3919. *E-mail:* darthur@austingrad.edu.

AUSTIN PEAY STATE UNIVERSITY

Clarksville, TN

Tuition & fees (TN res): $5526 **Average undergraduate aid package: $7925**

ABOUT THE INSTITUTION State-supported, coed. ***Awards:*** associate, bachelor's, and master's degrees and post-bachelor's and post-master's certificates. 35 undergraduate majors. ***Total enrollment:*** 9,401. Undergraduates: 8,573. Freshmen: 1,471. Federal methodology is used as a basis for awarding need-based institutional aid.

UNDERGRADUATE EXPENSES for 2008–09 ***Application fee:*** $15. ***Tuition, state resident:*** full-time $4302; part-time $189 per credit hour. ***Tuition, nonresident:*** full-time $15,194; part-time $662 per credit hour. ***Required fees:*** full-time $1224; $58 per credit hour or $15 per term. Full-time tuition and fees vary according to location and program. Part-time tuition and fees vary according to location and program. ***College room and board:*** $5870; ***Room only:*** $3640. Room and board charges vary according to board plan and housing facility. ***Payment plan:*** Installment.

FRESHMAN FINANCIAL AID (Fall 2007) 1,111 applied for aid; of those 78% were deemed to have need. 98% of freshmen with need received aid. ***Average financial aid package:*** $8501 (excluding resources awarded to replace EFC). 5% of all full-time freshmen had no need and received non-need-based gift aid.

UNDERGRADUATE FINANCIAL AID (Fall 2007) 5,265 applied for aid; of those 83% were deemed to have need. 98% of undergraduates with need received aid. ***Average financial aid package:*** $7925 (excluding resources awarded to replace EFC). 3% of all full-time undergraduates had no need and received non-need-based gift aid.

GIFT AID (NEED-BASED) ***Total amount:*** $13,006,164 (78% federal, 22% state). ***Receiving aid:*** Freshmen: 39% (461); all full-time undergraduates: 43% (2,621). ***Average award:*** Freshmen: $4987; Undergraduates: $4259. ***Scholarships, grants, and awards:*** Federal Pell, FSEOG, state, private, college/university gift aid from institutional funds, corporate.

GIFT AID (NON-NEED-BASED) ***Total amount:*** $12,233,574 (56% state, 15% institutional, 29% external sources). ***Receiving aid:*** Freshmen: 53% (627). Undergraduates: 29% (1,751). ***Average award:*** Freshmen: $2939. Undergraduates: $2495. ***Scholarships, grants, and awards by category:*** *Academic interests/achievement:* 396 awards ($1,001,533 total): agriculture, biological sciences, business, communication, computer science, education, English, foreign languages, general academic interests/achievements, health fields, humanities, international studies, mathematics, military science, physical sciences, social sciences. *Creative arts/performance:* 373 awards ($371,661 total): art/fine arts, creative writing, debating, journalism/publications, music, theater/drama. *Special achievements/activities:* 136 awards ($94,733 total): general special achievements/activities, leadership. *Special characteristics:* 121 awards ($248,750 total): children of educators, children of faculty/staff, ethnic background, general special characteristics, members of minority groups, veterans. ***Tuition waivers:*** Full or partial for employees or children of employees, senior citizens. ***ROTC:*** Army, Air Force cooperative.

LOANS ***Student loans:*** $27,293,410 (53% need-based, 47% non-need-based). ***Parent loans:*** $1,757,826 (100% non-need-based). ***Programs:*** FFEL (Subsidized and Unsubsidized Stafford, PLUS), Perkins.

WORK-STUDY ***Federal work-study:*** Total amount: $213,757; 158 jobs averaging $7322. ***State or other work-study/employment:*** Total amount: $695,226 (100% non-need-based). 523 part-time jobs averaging $1329.

ATHLETIC AWARDS Total amount: $1,710,985 (100% non-need-based).

APPLYING FOR FINANCIAL AID ***Required financial aid form:*** FAFSA. ***Financial aid deadline (priority):*** 4/1. ***Notification date:*** Continuous beginning 5/1.

CONTACT Donna Price, Director of Student Financial Aid, Austin Peay State University, PO Box 4546, Clarksville, TN 37044, 931-221-7907 or toll-free 800-844-2778 (out-of-state). *Fax:* 931-221-6329. *E-mail:* priced@apsu.edu.

AVE MARIA COLLEGE

Ypsilanti, MI

CONTACT Mr. Bob Hickey, Director of Financial Aid, Ave Maria College, 300 West Forest Avenue, Ypsilanti, MI 48197, 734-337-4504 or toll-free 866-866-3030. *Fax:* 734-337-4140. *E-mail:* bhickey@avemaria.edu.

AVE MARIA UNIVERSITY

Ave Maria, FL

Tuition & fees: $17,745 **Average undergraduate aid package: $17,175**

ABOUT THE INSTITUTION Independent Roman Catholic, coed. ***Awards:*** bachelor's, master's, and doctoral degrees. 13 undergraduate majors. ***Total enrollment:*** 672. Undergraduates: 532. Freshmen: 228. Federal methodology is used as a basis for awarding need-based institutional aid.

UNDERGRADUATE EXPENSES for 2009–10 ***Comprehensive fee:*** $25,725 includes full-time tuition ($17,165), mandatory fees ($580), and room and board ($7980). ***College room only:*** $4355. ***Part-time tuition:*** $536.40 per credit hour.

FRESHMAN FINANCIAL AID (Fall 2008, est.) 179 applied for aid; of those 84% were deemed to have need. 97% of freshmen with need received aid; of those 27% had need fully met. ***Average percent of need met:*** 76% (excluding resources awarded to replace EFC). ***Average financial aid package:*** $16,351 (excluding resources awarded to replace EFC). 34% of all full-time freshmen had no need and received non-need-based gift aid.

UNDERGRADUATE FINANCIAL AID (Fall 2008, est.) 396 applied for aid; of those 84% were deemed to have need. 98% of undergraduates with need received aid; of those 27% had need fully met. ***Average percent of need met:*** 79% (excluding resources awarded to replace EFC). ***Average financial aid package:*** $17,175 (excluding resources awarded to replace EFC). 33% of all full-time undergraduates had no need and received non-need-based gift aid.

GIFT AID (NEED-BASED) ***Total amount:*** $4,540,107 (12% federal, 2% state, 82% institutional, 4% external sources). ***Receiving aid:*** Freshmen: 60% (146); all full-time undergraduates: 56% (322). ***Average award:*** Freshmen: $13,922; Undergraduates: $13,748. ***Scholarships, grants, and awards:*** Federal Pell, state, private, college/university gift aid from institutional funds.

GIFT AID (NON-NEED-BASED) ***Total amount:*** $2,538,053 (4% state, 87% institutional, 9% external sources). ***Receiving aid:*** Freshmen: 12% (29). Undergraduates: 10% (59). ***Average award:*** Freshmen: $14,067. Undergraduates: $12,935. ***Scholarships, grants, and awards by category:*** *Special achievements/activities:* leadership.

LOANS ***Student loans:*** $2,005,337 (69% need-based, 31% non-need-based). ***Average need-based loan:*** Freshmen: $2937. Undergraduates: $3666. ***Parent loans:*** $815,250 (23% need-based, 77% non-need-based). ***Programs:*** college/university.

WORK-STUDY ***Federal work-study:*** Total amount: $84,493; jobs available (averaging $2000). ***State or other work-study/employment:*** Total amount: $41,455 (100% need-based). Part-time jobs available.

APPLYING FOR FINANCIAL AID ***Required financial aid forms:*** FAFSA, state aid form. ***Financial aid deadline (priority):*** 4/1. ***Notification date:*** Continuous.

CONTACT Stephanie Negip, Financial Aid Coordinator, Ave Maria University, 5050 Avenue Maria Blvd., Ave Maria, FL 34142, 239-280-1669 or toll-free 877-283-8648. *Fax:* 239-280-2566. *E-mail:* amufinancialaid@avemaria.edu.

AVERETT UNIVERSITY

Danville, VA

Tuition & fees: $21,300 **Average undergraduate aid package: $15,536**

ABOUT THE INSTITUTION Independent religious, coed. ***Awards:*** associate, bachelor's, and master's degrees. 54 undergraduate majors. ***Total enrollment:*** 842. Undergraduates: 792. Freshmen: 211. Federal methodology is used as a basis for awarding need-based institutional aid.

UNDERGRADUATE EXPENSES for 2008–09 ***Comprehensive fee:*** $28,580 includes full-time tuition ($20,300), mandatory fees ($1000), and room and board ($7280). ***College room only:*** $4890.

FRESHMAN FINANCIAL AID (Fall 2008, est.) 215 applied for aid; of those 90% were deemed to have need. 99% of freshmen with need received aid; of those 16% had need fully met. ***Average percent of need met:*** 70% (excluding resources awarded to replace EFC). ***Average financial aid package:*** $14,140 (excluding resources awarded to replace EFC). 21% of all full-time freshmen had no need and received non-need-based gift aid.

UNDERGRADUATE FINANCIAL AID (Fall 2008, est.) 694 applied for aid; of those 90% were deemed to have need. 100% of undergraduates with need received aid; of those 21% had need fully met. ***Average percent of need met:*** 75% (excluding resources awarded to replace EFC). ***Average financial aid package:*** $15,536 (excluding resources awarded to replace EFC). 20% of all full-time undergraduates had no need and received non-need-based gift aid.

GIFT AID (NEED-BASED) ***Total amount:*** $7,590,606 (18% federal, 15% state, 59% institutional, 8% external sources). ***Receiving aid:*** Freshmen: 79% (191); all full-time undergraduates: 79% (624). ***Average award:*** Freshmen: $10,559; Undergraduates: $12,073. ***Scholarships, grants, and awards:*** Federal Pell, FSEOG, state, private, college/university gift aid from institutional funds.

GIFT AID (NON-NEED-BASED) ***Total amount:*** $1,865,120 (20% state, 69% institutional, 11% external sources). ***Receiving aid:*** Freshmen: 8% (20). Undergraduates: 11% (81). ***Average award:*** Freshmen: $7444. Undergraduates: $7099. ***Scholarships, grants, and awards by category:*** *Academic interests/achievement:* 107 awards ($237,995 total): biological sciences, business, education, engineering/technologies, English, foreign languages, general academic interests/achievements, health fields, home economics, humanities, mathematics, physical sciences, premedicine, religion/biblical studies. *Creative arts/performance:* 14 awards ($14,570 total): art/fine arts, journalism/publications, music, theater/drama. *Special achievements/activities:* 7 awards ($11,628 total): general special achievements/activities, leadership, memberships, religious involvement. *Special characteristics:* 181 awards ($180,319 total): adult students, children and siblings of alumni, children of union members/company employees, first-generation college students, general special characteristics, international students, local/state students, out-of-state students, relatives of clergy, religious affiliation.

LOANS ***Student loans:*** $5,361,775 (72% need-based, 28% non-need-based). 67% of past graduating class borrowed through all loan programs. *Average indebtedness per student:* $30,943. ***Average need-based loan:*** Freshmen: $3937. Undergraduates: $4013. ***Parent loans:*** $1,546,823 (32% need-based, 68% non-need-based). ***Programs:*** FFEL (Subsidized and Unsubsidized Stafford, PLUS), Perkins, alternative loans.

WORK-STUDY ***Federal work-study:*** Total amount: $62,343; 131 jobs averaging $830.

APPLYING FOR FINANCIAL AID ***Required financial aid forms:*** FAFSA, state aid form. ***Financial aid deadline (priority):*** 4/1. ***Notification date:*** Continuous. Students must reply within 2 weeks of notification.

CONTACT Carl Bradsher, Dean of Financial Assistance, Averett University, 420 West Main Street, Danville, VA 24541-3692, 434-791-5646 or toll-free 800-AVERETT. *Fax:* 434-791-5647. *E-mail:* carl.bradsher@averett.edu.

AVILA UNIVERSITY

Kansas City, MO

Tuition & fees: $20,300 **Average undergraduate aid package: $12,976**

ABOUT THE INSTITUTION Independent Roman Catholic, coed. ***Awards:*** bachelor's and master's degrees and post-bachelor's certificates. 34 undergraduate majors. ***Total enrollment:*** 1,939. Undergraduates: 1,213. Freshmen: 183. Federal methodology is used as a basis for awarding need-based institutional aid.

UNDERGRADUATE EXPENSES for 2009–10 ***Application fee:*** $25. ***Comprehensive fee:*** $26,500 includes full-time tuition ($20,300) and room and board ($6200). ***College room only:*** $3000. ***Part-time tuition:*** $515 per credit hour. ***Part-time fees:*** $24 per credit hour.

FRESHMAN FINANCIAL AID (Fall 2008, est.) 240 applied for aid; of those 100% were deemed to have need. 100% of freshmen with need received aid; of those 96% had need fully met. ***Average percent of need met:*** 26% (excluding resources awarded to replace EFC). ***Average financial aid package:*** $11,847 (excluding resources awarded to replace EFC). 3% of all full-time freshmen had no need and received non-need-based gift aid.

UNDERGRADUATE FINANCIAL AID (Fall 2008, est.) 1,927 applied for aid; of those 96% were deemed to have need. 100% of undergraduates with need received aid; of those 100% had need fully met. ***Average percent of need met:*** 35% (excluding resources awarded to replace EFC). ***Average financial aid package:*** $12,976 (excluding resources awarded to replace EFC). 3% of all full-time undergraduates had no need and received non-need-based gift aid.

GIFT AID (NEED-BASED) ***Total amount:*** $5,759,146 (26% federal, 12% state, 60% institutional, 2% external sources). ***Receiving aid:*** Freshmen: 95% (235); all full-time undergraduates: 92% (1,822). ***Average award:*** Freshmen: $8152; Undergraduates: $7854. ***Scholarships, grants, and awards:*** Federal Pell, FSEOG, state, private, college/university gift aid from institutional funds, Federal Nursing.

GIFT AID (NON-NEED-BASED) ***Total amount:*** $2,169,597 (98% institutional, 2% external sources). ***Receiving aid:*** Freshmen: 14% (35). Undergraduates: 4% (77). ***Average award:*** Freshmen: $7057. Undergraduates: $9152. ***Scholarships, grants, and awards by category:*** *Academic interests/achievement:* 880 awards ($1,958,457 total): biological sciences, communication, general academic interests/achievements, humanities, premedicine. *Creative arts/performance:* 78 awards ($154,543 total): art/fine arts, music, performing arts, theater/drama. *Special achievements/activities:* 151 awards ($153,232 total): cheerleading/drum major, religious involvement. *Special characteristics:* 72 awards ($635,587 total): children and siblings of alumni, children of current students, children of faculty/staff, relatives of clergy, religious affiliation, siblings of current students, spouses of current students. ***ROTC:*** Army cooperative.

LOANS ***Student loans:*** $7,860,954 (75% need-based, 25% non-need-based). 96% of past graduating class borrowed through all loan programs. *Average indebtedness per student:* $16,508. ***Average need-based loan:*** Freshmen: $4025. Undergraduates: $5465. ***Parent loans:*** $784,901 (33% need-based, 67% non-need-based). ***Programs:*** FFEL (Subsidized and Unsubsidized Stafford, PLUS), Perkins.

WORK-STUDY ***Federal work-study:*** Total amount: $145,486; 161 jobs averaging $903. ***State or other work-study/employment:*** Total amount: $48,682 (100% need-based). 55 part-time jobs averaging $885.

ATHLETIC AWARDS Total amount: $1,790,418 (64% need-based, 36% non-need-based).

APPLYING FOR FINANCIAL AID ***Required financial aid forms:*** FAFSA, institution's own form. ***Financial aid deadline:*** Continuous. ***Notification date:*** Continuous beginning 2/1. Students must reply by 5/1 or within 3 weeks of notification.

CONTACT Nancy Merz, Director of Financial Aid, Avila University, 11901 Wornall Road, Kansas City, MO 64145, 816-501-3782 or toll-free 800-GO-AVILA. *Fax:* 816-501-2462. *E-mail:* nancy.merz@avila.edu.

AZUSA PACIFIC UNIVERSITY

Azusa, CA

Tuition & fees: $26,640 **Average undergraduate aid package: $11,874**

ABOUT THE INSTITUTION Independent nondenominational, coed. ***Awards:*** bachelor's, master's, doctoral, and first professional degrees. 37 undergraduate majors. ***Total enrollment:*** 8,548. Undergraduates: 4,858. Freshmen: 1,093.

UNDERGRADUATE EXPENSES for 2008–09 ***Application fee:*** $45. ***Comprehensive fee:*** $34,382 includes full-time tuition ($25,840), mandatory fees ($800), and room and board ($7742). ***College room only:*** $4520. Full-time tuition and fees vary according to course load. Room and board charges vary according to board plan, housing facility, and student level. ***Part-time tuition:*** $1075 per credit hour. Part-time tuition and fees vary according to course load. ***Payment plan:*** Installment.

FRESHMAN FINANCIAL AID (Fall 2007) 845 applied for aid; of those 64% were deemed to have need. 100% of freshmen with need received aid; of those 17% had need fully met. ***Average percent of need met:*** 56% (excluding resources awarded to replace EFC). ***Average financial aid package:*** $12,822 (excluding resources awarded to replace EFC). 29% of all full-time freshmen had no need and received non-need-based gift aid.

UNDERGRADUATE FINANCIAL AID (Fall 2007) 3,915 applied for aid; of those 63% were deemed to have need. 99% of undergraduates with need received aid; of those 13% had need fully met. ***Average percent of need met:*** 51% (excluding resources awarded to replace EFC). ***Average financial aid package:*** $11,874 (excluding resources awarded to replace EFC). 27% of all full-time undergraduates had no need and received non-need-based gift aid.

GIFT AID (NEED-BASED) ***Total amount:*** $23,146,157 (14% federal, 27% state, 54% institutional, 5% external sources). ***Receiving aid:*** Freshmen: 61% (518); all full-time undergraduates: 57% (2,219). ***Average award:*** Freshmen: $12,004; Undergraduates: $10,408. ***Scholarships, grants, and awards:*** Federal Pell, FSEOG, state, private, college/university gift aid from institutional funds, Federal Nursing.

GIFT AID (NON-NEED-BASED) ***Total amount:*** $6,060,597 (87% institutional, 13% external sources). ***Receiving aid:*** Freshmen: 6% (48). Undergraduates: 3% (128). ***Average award:*** Freshmen: $5980. Undergraduates: $5073. ***Tuition waivers:*** Full or partial for employees or children of employees. ***ROTC:*** Army cooperative.

LOANS ***Student loans:*** $9,274,475 (69% need-based, 31% non-need-based). ***Average need-based loan:*** Freshmen: $8271. Undergraduates: $10,505. ***Parent loans:*** $11,902,383 (60% need-based, 40% non-need-based). ***Programs:*** FFEL (Subsidized and Unsubsidized Stafford, PLUS), Perkins, Federal Nursing.

WORK-STUDY ***Federal work-study:*** Total amount: $903,469; jobs available.

ATHLETIC AWARDS Total amount: $2,528,459 (48% need-based, 52% non-need-based).

APPLYING FOR FINANCIAL AID ***Required financial aid forms:*** FAFSA, institution's own form. ***Financial aid deadline:*** 7/1 (priority: 3/2). ***Notification date:*** Continuous. Students must reply within 3 weeks of notification.

CONTACT Todd Ross, Interim Director, Student Financial Services, Azusa Pacific University, 901 East Alosta Avenue, PO Box 7000, Azusa, CA 91702-7000, 626-812-3009 or toll-free 800-TALK-APU. *E-mail:* tross@apu.edu.

BABSON COLLEGE

Wellesley, MA

Tuition & fees: $36,096 **Average undergraduate aid package: $30,627**

ABOUT THE INSTITUTION Independent, coed. ***Awards:*** bachelor's and master's degrees and post-master's certificates. 24 undergraduate majors. ***Total enrollment:*** 3,439. Undergraduates: 1,851. Freshmen: 469. Both federal and institutional methodology are used as a basis for awarding need-based institutional aid.

UNDERGRADUATE EXPENSES for 2008–09 ***Application fee:*** $65. ***Comprehensive fee:*** $48,116 includes full-time tuition ($36,096) and room and board ($12,020). ***College room only:*** $7756. Room and board charges vary according to board plan and housing facility. ***Payment plan:*** Installment.

FRESHMAN FINANCIAL AID (Fall 2008, est.) 253 applied for aid; of those 81% were deemed to have need. 100% of freshmen with need received aid; of those 84% had need fully met. ***Average percent of need met:*** 97% (excluding resources awarded to replace EFC). ***Average financial aid package:*** $30,666 (excluding resources awarded to replace EFC). 8% of all full-time freshmen had no need and received non-need-based gift aid.

UNDERGRADUATE FINANCIAL AID (Fall 2008, est.) 844 applied for aid; of those 93% were deemed to have need. 100% of undergraduates with need received aid; of those 84% had need fully met. ***Average percent of need met:*** 96% (excluding resources awarded to replace EFC). ***Average financial aid package:*** $30,627 (excluding resources awarded to replace EFC). 7% of all full-time undergraduates had no need and received non-need-based gift aid.

GIFT AID (NEED-BASED) ***Total amount:*** $19,833,000 (6% federal, 2% state, 92% institutional). ***Receiving aid:*** Freshmen: 41% (194); all full-time undergraduates: 40% (736). ***Average award:*** Freshmen: $26,223; Undergraduates: $25,200. ***Scholarships, grants, and awards:*** Federal Pell, FSEOG, state, college/university gift aid from institutional funds.

GIFT AID (NON-NEED-BASED) ***Total amount:*** $2,532,000 (88% institutional, 12% external sources). ***Receiving aid:*** Freshmen: 6% (26). Undergraduates: 6% (102). ***Average award:*** Freshmen: $19,023. Undergraduates: $17,400. ***Scholarships, grants, and awards by category:*** *Academic interests/achievement:* 107 awards: general academic interests/achievements. *Special achievements/activities:* 141 awards: leadership. ***Tuition waivers:*** Full or partial for employees or children of employees. ***ROTC:*** Army cooperative, Naval cooperative, Air Force cooperative.

LOANS ***Student loans:*** $7,475,000 (42% need-based, 58% non-need-based). 47% of past graduating class borrowed through all loan programs. *Average indebtedness per student:* $27,598. ***Average need-based loan:*** Freshmen: $2684. Undergraduates: $3970. ***Parent loans:*** $2,813,000 (100% non-need-based). ***Programs:*** Federal Direct (Subsidized and Unsubsidized Stafford, PLUS), Perkins, state.

WORK-STUDY ***Federal work-study:*** Total amount: $440,000; 232 jobs averaging $1428. ***State or other work-study/employment:*** Total amount: $816,000 (100% non-need-based). Part-time jobs available.

APPLYING FOR FINANCIAL AID ***Required financial aid forms:*** FAFSA, CSS Financial Aid PROFILE, noncustodial (divorced/separated) parent's statement, business/farm supplement, federal income tax form(s), W-2 forms, verification worksheet. ***Financial aid deadline:*** 2/15 (priority: 2/15). ***Notification date:*** 4/1. Students must reply by 5/1.

CONTACT Ms. Melissa Shaak, Director of Financial Aid, Babson College, Hollister Hall, 3rd Floor, Babson Park, MA 02457-0310, 781-239-4219 or toll-free 800-488-3696. *Fax:* 781-239-5510. *E-mail:* shaak@babson.edu.

BACONE COLLEGE

Muskogee, OK

CONTACT Office of Financial Aid, Bacone College, 2299 Old Bacone Road, Muskogee, OK 74403-1597, 918-683-4581 Ext. 7298 or toll-free 888-682-5514 Ext. 7340. *Fax:* 918-682-5514. *E-mail:* financialaid@bacone.edu.

BAKER UNIVERSITY

Baldwin City, KS

Tuition & fees: $19,880 **Average undergraduate aid package: $13,600**

ABOUT THE INSTITUTION Independent United Methodist, coed. ***Awards:*** bachelor's degrees. 38 undergraduate majors. ***Total enrollment:*** 998. Undergraduates: 998. Freshmen: 239. Federal methodology is used as a basis for awarding need-based institutional aid.

UNDERGRADUATE EXPENSES for 2008–09 ***One-time required fee:*** $80. ***Comprehensive fee:*** $26,250 includes full-time tuition ($19,880) and room and board ($6370). ***College room only:*** $2950. Full-time tuition and fees vary according to location and program. Room and board charges vary according to board plan and housing facility. ***Part-time tuition:*** $600 per credit hour. Part-time tuition and fees vary according to course load. ***Payment plan:*** Installment.

FRESHMAN FINANCIAL AID (Fall 2008, est.) 210 applied for aid; of those 80% were deemed to have need. ***Average percent of need met:*** 87% (excluding resources awarded to replace EFC). ***Average financial aid package:*** $11,453 (excluding resources awarded to replace EFC). 30% of all full-time freshmen had no need and received non-need-based gift aid.

UNDERGRADUATE FINANCIAL AID (Fall 2008, est.) 839 applied for aid; of those 85% were deemed to have need. ***Average percent of need met:*** 84% (excluding resources awarded to replace EFC). ***Average financial aid package:*** $13,600 (excluding resources awarded to replace EFC). 20% of all full-time undergraduates had no need and received non-need-based gift aid.

GIFT AID (NEED-BASED) ***Total amount:*** $3,170,443 (30% federal, 32% state, 38% institutional). ***Receiving aid:*** Freshmen: 75% (179); all full-time undergraduates: 94% (839). ***Average award:*** Freshmen: $6358; Undergraduates: $6787. ***Scholarships, grants, and awards:*** Federal Pell, FSEOG, state, private, college/university gift aid from institutional funds.

GIFT AID (NON-NEED-BASED) ***Total amount:*** $6,318,727 (94% institutional, 6% external sources). ***Receiving aid:*** Freshmen: 83% (199). Undergraduates: 85% (763). ***Average award:*** Freshmen: $9699. Undergraduates: $9006. ***Scholarships, grants, and awards by category:*** *Academic interests/achievement:* general academic interests/achievements. *Creative arts/performance:* art/fine arts, cinema/film/broadcasting, dance, debating, journalism/publications, music, theater/drama. *Special achievements/activities:* cheerleading/drum major, leadership, religious involvement. *Special characteristics:* children and siblings of alumni, children of faculty/staff, ethnic background, international students, members of minority groups, out-of-state students, relatives of clergy, religious affiliation. ***Tuition waivers:*** Full or partial for employees or children of employees, senior citizens. ***ROTC:*** Army cooperative, Air Force cooperative.

LOANS ***Student loans:*** $5,773,805 (49% need-based, 51% non-need-based). 81% of past graduating class borrowed through all loan programs. *Average indebtedness per student:* $26,869. ***Average need-based loan:*** Freshmen: $4136. Undergraduates: $5622. ***Parent loans:*** $670,324 (100% non-need-based). ***Programs:*** FFEL (Subsidized and Unsubsidized Stafford, PLUS), Perkins, alternative loans.

WORK-STUDY ***Federal work-study:*** Total amount: $466,974; jobs available (averaging $1000). ***State or other work-study/employment:*** Total amount: $296,541 (100% non-need-based). Part-time jobs available (averaging $1000).

ATHLETIC AWARDS Total amount: $1,611,360 (100% non-need-based).

APPLYING FOR FINANCIAL AID ***Required financial aid forms:*** FAFSA, institution's own form. ***Financial aid deadline (priority):*** 3/1. ***Notification date:*** Continuous. Students must reply by 5/1 or within 6 weeks of notification.

CONTACT Mrs. Jeanne Mott, Financial Aid Director, Baker University, Box 65, Baldwin City, KS 66006-0065, 785-594-4595 or toll-free 800-873-4282. *Fax:* 785-594-8358.

BALDWIN-WALLACE COLLEGE

Berea, OH

Tuition & fees: $23,524 **Average undergraduate aid package: $20,220**

ABOUT THE INSTITUTION Independent Methodist, coed. ***Awards:*** bachelor's and master's degrees. 57 undergraduate majors. ***Total enrollment:*** 4,382. Undergraduates: 3,681. Freshmen: 738. Federal methodology is used as a basis for awarding need-based institutional aid.

UNDERGRADUATE EXPENSES for 2008–09 ***Application fee:*** $25. ***Comprehensive fee:*** $31,252 includes full-time tuition ($23,524) and room and board ($7728). ***College room only:*** $3776. Full-time tuition and fees vary according to class time and course load. ***Part-time tuition:*** $748 per semester hour. Part-time tuition and fees vary according to class time and course load. ***Payment plans:*** Installment, deferred payment.

FRESHMAN FINANCIAL AID (Fall 2008, est.) 668 applied for aid; of those 88% were deemed to have need. 100% of freshmen with need received aid; of those 57% had need fully met. ***Average percent of need met:*** 93% (excluding resources awarded to replace EFC). ***Average financial aid package:*** $20,689 (excluding resources awarded to replace EFC). 14% of all full-time freshmen had no need and received non-need-based gift aid.

UNDERGRADUATE FINANCIAL AID (Fall 2008, est.) 2,790 applied for aid; of those 85% were deemed to have need. 100% of undergraduates with need received aid; of those 67% had need fully met. ***Average percent of need met:*** 93% (excluding resources awarded to replace EFC). ***Average financial aid package:*** $20,220 (excluding resources awarded to replace EFC).

GIFT AID (NEED-BASED) ***Total amount:*** $28,800,551 (12% federal, 12% state, 73% institutional, 3% external sources). ***Receiving aid:*** Freshmen: 79% (586); all full-time undergraduates: 76% (2,360). ***Average award:*** Freshmen: $14,522; Undergraduates: $13,341. ***Scholarships, grants, and awards:*** Federal Pell, FSEOG, state, private, college/university gift aid from institutional funds.

GIFT AID (NON-NEED-BASED) ***Total amount:*** $6,558,519 (6% state, 85% institutional, 9% external sources). ***Receiving aid:*** Freshmen: 7% (54). Undergraduates: 14% (420). ***Average award:*** Freshmen: $9340. Undergraduates: $8556. ***Scholarships, grants, and awards by category:*** *Academic interests/achievement:* 2,052 awards ($15,332,000 total): general academic interests/achievements. *Creative arts/performance:* 207 awards ($468,750 total): music. *Special achievements/activities:* 180 awards ($427,000 total): leadership. *Special characteristics:* 481 awards ($1,425,345 total): children and siblings of alumni, members of minority groups, religious affiliation, siblings of current students. ***Tuition waivers:*** Full or partial for children of alumni, employees or children of employees. ***ROTC:*** Air Force cooperative.

LOANS ***Student loans:*** $20,573,000 (58% need-based, 42% non-need-based). 82% of past graduating class borrowed through all loan programs. *Average indebtedness per student:* $19,586. ***Average need-based loan:*** Freshmen: $4389. Undergraduates: $6275. ***Parent loans:*** $8,431,000 (14% need-based, 86% non-need-based). ***Programs:*** FFEL (Subsidized and Unsubsidized Stafford, PLUS), Perkins.

WORK-STUDY ***Federal work-study:*** Total amount: $466,000; 1,033 jobs averaging $606. ***State or other work-study/employment:*** Total amount: $1,351,328 (28% need-based, 72% non-need-based). 903 part-time jobs averaging $913.

APPLYING FOR FINANCIAL AID ***Required financial aid form:*** FAFSA. ***Financial aid deadline:*** 9/1 (priority: 5/1). ***Notification date:*** Continuous.

CONTACT Dr. George L. Rolleston, Director of Financial Aid, Baldwin-Wallace College, 275 Eastland Road, Berea, OH 44017-2088, 440-826-2108 or toll-free 877-BWAPPLY (in-state). *Fax:* 440-826-8048. *E-mail:* grollest@bw.edu.

BALL STATE UNIVERSITY

Muncie, IN

Tuition & fees (IN res): $7500 **Average undergraduate aid package: $9346**

ABOUT THE INSTITUTION State-supported, coed. ***Awards:*** associate, bachelor's, master's, and doctoral degrees and post-bachelor's and post-master's certificates. 85 undergraduate majors. ***Total enrollment:*** 20,243. Undergraduates: 16,832. Freshmen: 4,039. Federal methodology is used as a basis for awarding need-based institutional aid.

UNDERGRADUATE EXPENSES for 2008–09 ***Application fee:*** $25. ***Tuition, state resident:*** full-time $7000; part-time $269 per credit hour. ***Tuition, nonresident:*** full-time $18,804; part-time $692 per credit hour. ***Required fees:*** full-time $500. Full-time tuition and fees vary according to course level and reciprocity agreements. Part-time tuition and fees vary according to course level and course load. ***College room and board:*** $7598. Room and board charges vary according to board plan and housing facility. ***Payment plan:*** Installment.

FRESHMAN FINANCIAL AID (Fall 2008, est.) 3,501 applied for aid; of those 71% were deemed to have need. 98% of freshmen with need received aid; of those 27% had need fully met. ***Average percent of need met:*** 63% (excluding resources awarded to replace EFC). ***Average financial aid package:*** $9123 (excluding resources awarded to replace EFC). 7% of all full-time freshmen had no need and received non-need-based gift aid.

UNDERGRADUATE FINANCIAL AID (Fall 2008, est.) 12,328 applied for aid; of those 75% were deemed to have need. 99% of undergraduates with need received aid; of those 26% had need fully met. ***Average percent of need met:*** 66% (excluding resources awarded to replace EFC). ***Average financial aid package:*** $9346 (excluding resources awarded to replace EFC). 7% of all full-time undergraduates had no need and received non-need-based gift aid.

GIFT AID (NEED-BASED) ***Total amount:*** $38,119,762 (38% federal, 52% state, 10% institutional). ***Receiving aid:*** Freshmen: 41% (1,649); all full-time undergraduates: 38% (6,008). ***Average award:*** Freshmen: $5692; Undergraduates: $5813. ***Scholarships, grants, and awards:*** Federal Pell, FSEOG, state, private, college/university gift aid from institutional funds.

GIFT AID (NON-NEED-BASED) ***Total amount:*** $24,984,338 (4% federal, 20% state, 57% institutional, 19% external sources). ***Receiving aid:*** Freshmen: 28% (1,115). Undergraduates: 20% (3,163). ***Average award:*** Freshmen: $5653. Undergraduates: $5727. ***Scholarships, grants, and awards by category:*** *Academic interests/achievement:* 2,349 awards ($12,571,703 total): architecture, business, communication, education, engineering/technologies, English, foreign languages, general academic interests/achievements, health fields, humanities, international studies, mathematics, military science, physical sciences, social sciences. *Creative arts/performance:* 125 awards ($149,560 total): art/fine arts, cinema/film/broadcasting, dance, debating, general creative arts/performance, journalism/publications, music, performing arts, theater/drama. *Special achievements/activities:* 160 awards ($1,031,378 total): community service, general special achievements/activities, leadership. *Special characteristics:* 705 awards ($7,017,013 total): adult students, children and siblings of alumni, children of faculty/staff, general special characteristics, international students, local/state students, members of minority groups, veterans. ***Tuition waivers:*** Full or partial for employees or children of employees. ***ROTC:*** Army.

LOANS ***Student loans:*** $82,628,785 (38% need-based, 62% non-need-based). 67% of past graduating class borrowed through all loan programs. *Average indebtedness per student:* $20,326. ***Average need-based loan:*** Freshmen: $3501. Undergraduates: $4130. ***Parent loans:*** $76,492,294 (100% non-need-based). ***Programs:*** Federal Direct (Subsidized and Unsubsidized Stafford, PLUS), Perkins.

WORK-STUDY ***Federal work-study:*** Total amount: $2,381,149; 989 jobs averaging $2140. ***State or other work-study/employment:*** Total amount: $7,049,207 (9% need-based, 91% non-need-based). Part-time jobs available.

ATHLETIC AWARDS Total amount: $4,779,088 (100% non-need-based).

APPLYING FOR FINANCIAL AID ***Required financial aid form:*** FAFSA. ***Financial aid deadline (priority):*** 3/10. ***Notification date:*** Continuous beginning 4/1.

CONTACT Robert Zellers, Director of Scholarships and Financial Aid, Ball State University, Lucina Hall, Muncie, IN 47306-1099, 765-285-8898 or toll-free 800-482-4BSU. *Fax:* 765-285-2173. *E-mail:* finaid@bsu.edu.

BALTIMORE HEBREW UNIVERSITY

Baltimore, MD

CONTACT Ms. Yelena Feldman, Financial Aid Counselor, Baltimore Hebrew University, 5800 Park Heights Avenue, Baltimore, MD 21215-3996, 410-578-0010 or toll free 800-240-7420 (out-of-state). *Fax:* 410-578-6940.

BAPTIST BIBLE COLLEGE

Springfield, MO

CONTACT Bob Kotulski, Director of Financial Aid, Baptist Bible College, 628 East Kearney, Springfield, MO 65803-3498, 417-268-6036. *Fax:* 417-268-6694.

BAPTIST BIBLE COLLEGE OF PENNSYLVANIA

Clarks Summit, PA

Tuition & fees: $16,620 **Average undergraduate aid package: $10,987**

ABOUT THE INSTITUTION Independent Baptist, coed. ***Awards:*** associate, bachelor's, master's, doctoral, and first professional degrees. 27 undergraduate majors. ***Total enrollment:*** 910. Undergraduates: 550. Freshmen: 101. Federal methodology is used as a basis for awarding need-based institutional aid.

UNDERGRADUATE EXPENSES for 2009–10 ***Application fee:*** $30. ***Comprehensive fee:*** $22,820 includes full-time tuition ($15,480), mandatory fees ($1140), and room and board ($6200). ***College room only:*** $2290. ***Part-time tuition:*** $516 per credit. ***Part-time fees:*** $38 per credit.

FRESHMAN FINANCIAL AID (Fall 2007) 170 applied for aid; of those 93% were deemed to have need. 100% of freshmen with need received aid; of those 10% had need fully met. ***Average percent of need met:*** 70% (excluding resources awarded to replace EFC). ***Average financial aid package:*** $11,278 (excluding resources awarded to replace EFC). 7% of all full-time freshmen had no need and received non-need-based gift aid.

UNDERGRADUATE FINANCIAL AID (Fall 2007) 648 applied for aid; of those 88% were deemed to have need. 89% of undergraduates with need received aid; of those 16% had need fully met. ***Average percent of need met:*** 68% (excluding resources awarded to replace EFC). ***Average financial aid package:*** $10,987 (excluding resources awarded to replace EFC). 12% of all full-time undergraduates had no need and received non-need-based gift aid.

GIFT AID (NEED-BASED) ***Total amount:*** $3,509,790 (20% federal, 14% state, 54% institutional, 12% external sources). ***Receiving aid:*** Freshmen: 93% (158); all full-time undergraduates: 74% (491). ***Average award:*** Freshmen: $7165; Undergraduates: $6918. ***Scholarships, grants, and awards:*** Federal Pell, state, private, college/university gift aid from institutional funds.

GIFT AID (NON-NEED-BASED) ***Total amount:*** $122,143 (82% institutional, 18% external sources). ***Receiving aid:*** Freshmen: 5% (8). Undergraduates: 7% (45). ***Average award:*** Freshmen: $6408. Undergraduates: $7112. ***Scholarships, grants, and awards by category:*** *Academic interests/achievement:* 392 awards ($704,537 total): education, general academic interests/achievements, religion/biblical studies. *Creative arts/performance:* 26 awards ($32,400 total): general creative arts/performance, music. *Special achievements/activities:* 94 awards ($110,550 total): general special achievements/activities, leadership, religious involvement. *Special characteristics:* 276 awards ($860,386 total): children and siblings of alumni, children of faculty/staff, general special characteristics, married students, relatives of clergy, siblings of current students. ***ROTC:*** Army cooperative.

LOANS ***Student loans:*** $3,090,421 (93% need-based, 7% non-need-based). 68% of past graduating class borrowed through all loan programs. *Average indebtedness per student:* $17,990. ***Average need-based loan:*** Freshmen: $3313. Undergraduates: $3967. ***Parent loans:*** $937,605 (100% need-based). ***Programs:*** FFEL (Subsidized and Unsubsidized Stafford, PLUS), alternative loans.

WORK-STUDY ***State or other work-study/employment:*** Total amount: $22,269 (100% need-based). 10 part-time jobs averaging $2226.

APPLYING FOR FINANCIAL AID ***Required financial aid form:*** FAFSA. ***Financial aid deadline (priority):*** 5/1. ***Notification date:*** Continuous.

CONTACT Mrs. Charis Henson, Acting Director of Student Financial Services, Baptist Bible College of Pennsylvania, 538 Venard Road, Clarks Summit, PA 18411, 570-586-2400 Ext. 9272 or toll-free 800-451-7664. *Fax:* 570-587-8045. *E-mail:* chenson@bbc.edu.

THE BAPTIST COLLEGE OF FLORIDA

Graceville, FL

Tuition & fees: $8150 **Average undergraduate aid package: $7336**

ABOUT THE INSTITUTION Independent Southern Baptist, coed. ***Awards:*** associate and bachelor's degrees. 8 undergraduate majors. ***Total enrollment:*** 588. Undergraduates: 588. Freshmen: 55. Federal methodology is used as a basis for awarding need-based institutional aid.

UNDERGRADUATE EXPENSES for 2008–09 ***Application fee:*** $20. ***Comprehensive fee:*** $12,036 includes full-time tuition ($7800), mandatory fees ($350), and room and board ($3886). Full-time tuition and fees vary according to course load and location. Room and board charges vary according to board plan and housing facility. ***Part-time tuition:*** $260 per semester hour. ***Part-time fees:*** $175 per term. Part-time tuition and fees vary according to course load and location. ***Payment plan:*** Installment.

FRESHMAN FINANCIAL AID (Fall 2008, est.) 78 applied for aid; of those 78% were deemed to have need. 85% of freshmen with need received aid; of those 12% had need fully met. ***Average percent of need met:*** 50% (excluding resources awarded to replace EFC). ***Average financial aid package:*** $6282 (excluding resources awarded to replace EFC). 6% of all full-time freshmen had no need and received non-need-based gift aid.

UNDERGRADUATE FINANCIAL AID (Fall 2008, est.) 387 applied for aid; of those 84% were deemed to have need. 90% of undergraduates with need received aid; of those 9% had need fully met. ***Average percent of need met:*** 48% (excluding resources awarded to replace EFC). ***Average financial aid package:*** $7336 (excluding resources awarded to replace EFC). 2% of all full-time undergraduates had no need and received non-need-based gift aid.

GIFT AID (NEED-BASED) ***Total amount:*** $1,592,693 (49% federal, 27% state, 2% institutional, 22% external sources). ***Receiving aid:*** Freshmen: 52% (49); all full-time undergraduates: 61% (282). ***Average award:*** Freshmen: $4892; Undergraduates: $4910. ***Scholarships, grants, and awards:*** Federal Pell, FSEOG, state, private, college/university gift aid from institutional funds.

GIFT AID (NON-NEED-BASED) ***Total amount:*** $321,348 (48% state, 5% institutional, 47% external sources). ***Receiving aid:*** Freshmen: 5% (5). Undergraduates: 5% (22). ***Average award:*** Freshmen: $1333. Undergraduates: $1545. ***Scholarships, grants, and awards by category:*** *Academic interests/achievement:* 277 awards ($208,400 total): education, religion/biblical studies. *Creative arts/performance:* 7 awards ($2489 total): music. *Special characteristics:* 287 awards ($221,785 total): children with a deceased or disabled parent, religious affiliation, spouses of current students. ***Tuition waivers:*** Full or partial for employees or children of employees.

LOANS ***Student loans:*** $1,634,229 (81% need-based, 19% non-need-based). 1% of past graduating class borrowed through all loan programs. *Average indebtedness per student:* $5316. ***Average need-based loan:*** Freshmen: $2776. Undergraduates: $3435. ***Parent loans:*** $75,962 (10% need-based, 90% non-need-based). ***Programs:*** FFEL (Subsidized and Unsubsidized Stafford, PLUS).

WORK-STUDY ***Federal work-study:*** Total amount: $45,385; 19 jobs averaging $2245.

APPLYING FOR FINANCIAL AID ***Required financial aid forms:*** FAFSA, institution's own form, state aid form, business/farm supplement, Student Authorization Form. ***Financial aid deadline:*** 4/15 (priority: 4/1). ***Notification date:*** Continuous beginning 6/15. Students must reply within 4 weeks of notification.

CONTACT Angela Rathel, Director of Financial Aid, The Baptist College of Florida, 5400 College Drive, Graceville, FL 32440-3306, 850-263-3261 Ext. 461 or toll-free 800-328-2660 Ext. 460. *Fax:* 850-263-2141. *E-mail:* finaid@baptistcollege.edu.

BAPTIST COLLEGE OF HEALTH SCIENCES

Memphis, TN

CONTACT Leanne Smith, Financial Aid Officer, Baptist College of Health Sciences, 1003 Monroe Avenue, Memphis, TN 38104, 901-227-6805 or toll-free 866-575-2247. *Fax:* 901-227-4311. *E-mail:* leanne.smith@bchs.edu.

BAPTIST MISSIONARY ASSOCIATION THEOLOGICAL SEMINARY

Jacksonville, TX

CONTACT Dr. Philip Attebery, Dean/Registrar, Baptist Missionary Association Theological Seminary, 1530 East Pine Street, Jacksonville, TX 75766-5407, 903-586-2501. *Fax:* 903-586-0378. *E-mail:* bmatsem@bmats.edu.

BAPTIST UNIVERSITY OF THE AMERICAS

San Antonio, TX

CONTACT Financial Aid Office, Baptist University of the Americas, 8019 South Pan Am Expressway, San Antonio, TX 78224-2701, 210-924-4338 or toll-free 800-721-1396.

BARCLAY COLLEGE

Haviland, KS

CONTACT Christina Foster, Financial Aid Coordinator, Barclay College, 607 North Kingman, Haviland, KS 67059, 800-862-0226. *Fax:* 620-862-5403. *E-mail:* financialaid@barclaycollege.edu.

BARD COLLEGE

Annandale-on-Hudson, NY

Tuition & fees: $38,374 **Average undergraduate aid package: $29,681**

ABOUT THE INSTITUTION Independent, coed. ***Awards:*** associate, bachelor's, master's, and doctoral degrees. 79 undergraduate majors. ***Total enrollment:*** 2,148. Undergraduates: 1,873. Freshmen: 517. Both federal and institutional methodology are used as a basis for awarding need-based institutional aid.

UNDERGRADUATE EXPENSES for 2008–09 ***Application fee:*** $50. ***One-time required fee:*** $880. ***Comprehensive fee:*** $49,240 includes full-time tuition ($37,574), mandatory fees ($800), and room and board ($10,866). ***Part-time tuition:*** $1176 per credit. ***Payment plans:*** Tuition prepayment, installment.

FRESHMAN FINANCIAL AID (Fall 2008, est.) 335 applied for aid; of those 90% were deemed to have need. 100% of freshmen with need received aid; of those 60% had need fully met. ***Average percent of need met:*** 89% (excluding resources awarded to replace EFC). ***Average financial aid package:*** $31,657 (excluding resources awarded to replace EFC). 1% of all full-time freshmen had no need and received non-need-based gift aid.

UNDERGRADUATE FINANCIAL AID (Fall 2008, est.) 1,163 applied for aid; of those 88% were deemed to have need. 100% of undergraduates with need received aid; of those 51% had need fully met. ***Average percent of need met:*** 89% (excluding resources awarded to replace EFC). ***Average financial aid package:*** $29,681 (excluding resources awarded to replace EFC). 3% of all full-time undergraduates had no need and received non-need-based gift aid.

GIFT AID (NEED-BASED) ***Total amount:*** $24,780,182 (4% federal, 3% state, 91% institutional, 2% external sources). ***Receiving aid:*** Freshmen: 55% (283); all full-time undergraduates: 53% (936). ***Average award:*** Freshmen: $29,531; Undergraduates: $27,839. ***Scholarships, grants, and awards:*** Federal Pell, FSEOG, state, private, college/university gift aid from institutional funds.

GIFT AID (NON-NEED-BASED) ***Total amount:*** $479,437 (1% state, 96% institutional, 3% external sources). ***Average award:*** Freshmen: $13,600. Undergraduates: $9976. ***Scholarships, grants, and awards by category:*** *Academic interests/achievement:* biological sciences, computer science, mathematics, physical sciences. *Special achievements/activities:* leadership. *Special characteristics:* 5 awards ($187,870 total): children of educators, children of faculty/staff. ***Tuition waivers:*** Full or partial for employees or children of employees.

LOANS ***Student loans:*** $6,193,017 (88% need-based, 12% non-need-based). 58% of past graduating class borrowed through all loan programs. *Average indebtedness per student:* $20,201. ***Average need-based loan:*** Freshmen: $3645. Undergraduates: $4134. ***Parent loans:*** $3,127,529 (76% need-based, 24% non-need-based). ***Programs:*** FFEL (Subsidized and Unsubsidized Stafford, PLUS), Perkins, college/university loans from institutional funds (for international students only).

WORK-STUDY ***Federal work-study:*** Total amount: $997,500; 633 jobs averaging $1527. ***State or other work-study/employment:*** Total amount: $166,650 (100% need-based). 100 part-time jobs averaging $1650.

APPLYING FOR FINANCIAL AID ***Required financial aid forms:*** FAFSA, CSS Financial Aid PROFILE, state aid form, noncustodial (divorced/separated) parent's statement, business/farm supplement. ***Financial aid deadline:*** 2/15 (priority: 2/1). ***Notification date:*** 4/1. Students must reply by 5/1 or within 2 weeks of notification.

CONTACT Denise Ann Ackerman, Director of Financial Aid, Bard College, Annandale Road, Annandale-on-Hudson, NY 12504, 845-758-7525. *Fax:* 845-758-7336. *E-mail:* finaid@bard.edu.

BARD COLLEGE AT SIMON'S ROCK

Great Barrington, MA

ABOUT THE INSTITUTION Independent, coed. ***Awards:*** associate and bachelor's degrees. 71 undergraduate majors. ***Total enrollment:*** 436. Undergraduates: 436.

GIFT AID (NEED-BASED) ***Scholarships, grants, and awards:*** Federal Pell, FSEOG, state, private, college/university gift aid from institutional funds.

GIFT AID (NON-NEED-BASED) ***Scholarships, grants, and awards by category:*** *Academic interests/achievement:* general academic interests/achievements. *Special characteristics:* children of faculty/staff, local/state students, members of minority groups.

LOANS ***Programs:*** FFEL (Subsidized and Unsubsidized Stafford, PLUS), Perkins, alternative loans.

WORK-STUDY ***Federal work-study:*** Total amount: $200,000; 166 jobs averaging $1200.

APPLYING FOR FINANCIAL AID ***Required financial aid forms:*** FAFSA, CSS Financial Aid PROFILE, noncustodial (divorced/separated) parent's statement, business/farm supplement, federal income tax form(s), federal verification worksheet.

CONTACT Ms. Ann Murtagh Gitto, Director of Financial Aid, Bard College at Simon's Rock, 84 Alford Road, Great Barrington, MA 01230-9702, 413-528-7297 or toll-free 800-235-7186. *Fax:* 413-528-7339. *E-mail:* agitto@simons-rock.edu.

BARNARD COLLEGE

New York, NY

Tuition & fees: $37,538 **Average undergraduate aid package: $34,527**

ABOUT THE INSTITUTION Independent, women only. ***Awards:*** bachelor's degrees. 48 undergraduate majors. ***Total enrollment:*** 2,359. Undergraduates: 2,359. Freshmen: 576. Both federal and institutional methodology are used as a basis for awarding need-based institutional aid.

UNDERGRADUATE EXPENSES for 2008–09 ***Application fee:*** $55. ***Comprehensive fee:*** $49,464 includes full-time tuition ($35,972), mandatory fees ($1566), and room and board ($11,926). ***College room only:*** $7356. Room and board charges vary according to board plan and housing facility. ***Part-time tuition:*** $1200 per credit. ***Payment plans:*** Tuition prepayment, installment, deferred payment.

FRESHMAN FINANCIAL AID (Fall 2008, est.) 326 applied for aid; of those 77% were deemed to have need. 100% of freshmen with need received aid; of those 100% had need fully met. ***Average percent of need met:*** 100% (excluding resources awarded to replace EFC). ***Average financial aid package:*** $35,625 (excluding resources awarded to replace EFC).

UNDERGRADUATE FINANCIAL AID (Fall 2008, est.) 1,185 applied for aid; of those 85% were deemed to have need. 100% of undergraduates with need received aid; of those 100% had need fully met. ***Average percent of need met:*** 100% (excluding resources awarded to replace EFC). ***Average financial aid package:*** $34,527 (excluding resources awarded to replace EFC).

GIFT AID (NEED-BASED) ***Total amount:*** $30,345,902 (8% federal, 4% state, 86% institutional, 2% external sources). ***Receiving aid:*** Freshmen: 42% (242); all full-time undergraduates: 42% (976). ***Average award:*** Freshmen: $33,907; Undergraduates: $31,197. ***Scholarships, grants, and awards:*** Federal Pell, FSEOG, state, private, college/university gift aid from institutional funds, Academic Competitiveness Grant, National Smart Grant.

GIFT AID (NON-NEED-BASED) ***Total amount:*** $494,076 (11% federal, 89% external sources). ***Tuition waivers:*** Full or partial for employees or children of employees.

LOANS ***Student loans:*** $3,795,068 (71% need-based, 29% non-need-based). 43% of past graduating class borrowed through all loan programs. *Average indebtedness per student:* $15,084. ***Average need-based loan:*** Freshmen: $2886. Undergraduates: $3849. ***Parent loans:*** $4,846,627 (100% non-need-based). ***Programs:*** FFEL (Subsidized and Unsubsidized Stafford, PLUS), Perkins, state, college/university, alternative loans.

WORK-STUDY ***Federal work-study:*** Total amount: $699,898; 435 jobs averaging $1609. ***State or other work-study/employment:*** Total amount: $967,822 (68% need-based, 32% non-need-based). 356 part-time jobs averaging $1882.

APPLYING FOR FINANCIAL AID ***Required financial aid forms:*** FAFSA, institution's own form, CSS Financial Aid PROFILE, state aid form, noncustodial (divorced/separated) parent's statement, business/farm supplement, federal income tax returns. ***Financial aid deadline:*** 2/1. ***Notification date:*** 3/31. Students must reply by 5/1.

CONTACT Director of Financial Aid, Barnard College, 3009 Broadway, New York, NY 10027-6598, 212-854-2154. *Fax:* 212-854-2902. *E-mail:* finaid@barnard.edu.

BARNES-JEWISH COLLEGE, GOLDFARB SCHOOL OF NURSING

St. Louis, MO

See Goldfarb School of Nursing at Barnes-Jewish College.

BARRY UNIVERSITY

Miami Shores, FL

ABOUT THE INSTITUTION Independent Roman Catholic, coed. ***Awards:*** bachelor's, master's, doctoral, and first professional degrees and post-bachelor's certificates. 58 undergraduate majors. ***Total enrollment:*** 8,581. Undergraduates: 5,050. Freshmen: 586.

GIFT AID (NEED-BASED) ***Scholarships, grants, and awards:*** Federal Pell, FSEOG, state, private, college/university gift aid from institutional funds, Federal Nursing.

LOANS ***Programs:*** FFEL (Subsidized and Unsubsidized Stafford, PLUS), Perkins, Federal Nursing, college/university, alternative loans.

APPLYING FOR FINANCIAL AID ***Required financial aid form:*** FAFSA.

CONTACT Mr. Dart Humeston, Assistant Dean of Enrollment Services/Director of Financial Aid, Barry University, 11300 Northeast Second Avenue, Miami Shores, FL 33161-6695, 305-899-3673 or toll-free 800-695-2279. *E-mail:* finaid@mail.barry.edu.

BARTON COLLEGE

Wilson, NC

Tuition & fees: $19,938 **Average undergraduate aid package: $18,179**

ABOUT THE INSTITUTION Independent religious, coed. ***Awards:*** bachelor's degrees. 32 undergraduate majors. ***Total enrollment:*** 1,155. Undergraduates: 1,155. Freshmen: 248. Federal methodology is used as a basis for awarding need-based institutional aid.

UNDERGRADUATE EXPENSES for 2008–09 ***Application fee:*** $25. ***Comprehensive fee:*** $26,720 includes full-time tuition ($18,460), mandatory fees ($1478), and room and board ($6782). ***College room only:*** $3178. Full-time tuition and fees vary according to class time, course load, and program. Room and board charges vary according to housing facility. ***Part-time tuition:*** $785 per credit hour. Part-time tuition and fees vary according to class time, course load, and program. ***Payment plan:*** Installment.

FRESHMAN FINANCIAL AID (Fall 2008, est.) 229 applied for aid; of those 90% were deemed to have need. 100% of freshmen with need received aid; of those 18% had need fully met. ***Average percent of need met:*** 82% (excluding resources awarded to replace EFC). ***Average financial aid package:*** $20,567 (excluding resources awarded to replace EFC). 14% of all full-time freshmen had no need and received non-need-based gift aid.

UNDERGRADUATE FINANCIAL AID (Fall 2008, est.) 757 applied for aid; of those 91% were deemed to have need. 100% of undergraduates with need received aid; of those 16% had need fully met. ***Average percent of need met:*** 72% (excluding resources awarded to replace EFC). ***Average financial aid package:*** $18,179 (excluding resources awarded to replace EFC). 19% of all full-time undergraduates had no need and received non-need-based gift aid.

GIFT AID (NEED-BASED) ***Total amount:*** $2,727,246 (55% federal, 41% state, 2% institutional, 2% external sources). ***Receiving aid:*** Freshmen: 63% (155); all full-time undergraduates: 56% (499). ***Average award:*** Freshmen: $5477; Undergraduates: $5147. ***Scholarships, grants, and awards:*** Federal Pell, FSEOG, state, private, college/university gift aid from institutional funds.

GIFT AID (NON-NEED-BASED) ***Total amount:*** $5,403,566 (30% state, 63% institutional, 7% external sources). ***Receiving aid:*** Freshmen: 83% (204). Undergraduates: 75% (672). ***Average award:*** Freshmen: $5008. Undergraduates: $5057. ***Scholarships, grants, and awards by category:*** *Academic interests/achievement:* $2,375,672 total: biological sciences, business, communication, computer science, education, English, general academic interests/achievements, health fields, humanities, international studies, mathematics, physical sciences, religion/biblical studies, social sciences. *Creative arts/performance:* 10 awards ($6100 total): art/fine arts, music, theater/drama. *Special achievements/activities:* 22 awards ($37,530 total): general special achievements/activities, leadership, religious involvement. *Special characteristics:* 149 awards ($485,650 total): adult students, children and siblings of alumni, children of faculty/staff, international students, local/state students, relatives of clergy, religious affiliation, siblings of current students, veterans. ***Tuition waivers:*** Full or partial for children of alumni, employees or children of employees, adult students, senior citizens.

LOANS ***Student loans:*** $7,255,912 (41% need-based, 59% non-need-based). 62% of past graduating class borrowed through all loan programs. *Average indebtedness per student:* $35,483. ***Average need-based loan:*** Freshmen: $4360. Undergraduates: $4975. ***Parent loans:*** $765,118 (100% non-need-based). ***Programs:*** FFEL (Subsidized and Unsubsidized Stafford, PLUS), Perkins, alternative loans.

WORK-STUDY ***Federal work-study:*** Total amount: $544,660; 429 jobs averaging $1102.

ATHLETIC AWARDS Total amount: $1,003,478 (100% non-need-based).

APPLYING FOR FINANCIAL AID ***Required financial aid form:*** FAFSA. ***Financial aid deadline (priority):*** 4/1. ***Notification date:*** Continuous. Students must reply by 5/1 or within 2 weeks of notification.

CONTACT Mrs. Shakeena White, Director of Financial Aid, Barton College, Box 5000, Wilson, NC 27893, 252-399-6371 or toll-free 800-345-4973. *Fax:* 252-399-6572. *E-mail:* aid@barton.edu.

BASTYR UNIVERSITY

Kenmore, WA

Tuition & fees: $19,530 **Average undergraduate aid package: $17,600**

ABOUT THE INSTITUTION Independent, coed. ***Awards:*** bachelor's, master's, doctoral, and first professional degrees and post-bachelor's, post-master's, and first professional certificates. 6 undergraduate majors. ***Total enrollment:*** 969. Undergraduates: 201. Federal methodology is used as a basis for awarding need-based institutional aid.

UNDERGRADUATE EXPENSES for 2008–09 ***Application fee:*** $60. ***Tuition:*** full-time $17,790; part-time $450 per credit. Full-time tuition and fees vary according to course load and program. Part-time tuition and fees vary according to course load and program. Room and board charges vary according to board plan and housing facility.

UNDERGRADUATE FINANCIAL AID (Fall 2008, est.) 189 applied for aid; of those 94% were deemed to have need. 100% of undergraduates with need received aid. ***Average percent of need met:*** 50% (excluding resources awarded to replace EFC). ***Average financial aid package:*** $17,600 (excluding resources awarded to replace EFC). 6% of all full-time undergraduates had no need and received non-need-based gift aid.

GIFT AID (NEED-BASED) ***Total amount:*** $858,070 (43% federal, 43% state, 11% institutional, 3% external sources). ***Receiving aid:*** All full-time undergraduates: 75% (157). ***Average award:*** Undergraduates: $8750. ***Scholarships, grants, and awards:*** Federal Pell, FSEOG, state, private, college/university gift aid from institutional funds.

GIFT AID (NON-NEED-BASED) ***Average award:*** Undergraduates: $500. ***Scholarships, grants, and awards by category:*** *Academic interests/achievement:* health fields. ***Tuition waivers:*** Full or partial for employees or children of employees.

LOANS ***Student loans:*** $2,521,300 (100% need-based). 90% of past graduating class borrowed through all loan programs. *Average indebtedness per student:* $32,500. ***Average need-based loan:*** Undergraduates: $5500. ***Parent loans:*** $29,400 (100% need-based). ***Programs:*** FFEL (Subsidized and Unsubsidized Stafford, PLUS), Perkins.

WORK-STUDY ***Federal work-study:*** Total amount: $67,321; 40 jobs averaging $3000. ***State or other work-study/employment:*** Total amount: $40,017 (100% need-based). 31 part-time jobs averaging $3000.

APPLYING FOR FINANCIAL AID ***Required financial aid forms:*** FAFSA, institution's own form. ***Financial aid deadline (priority):*** 5/1. ***Notification date:*** Continuous beginning 5/15. Students must reply within 3 weeks of notification.

CONTACT Sheila Arisa, Financial Aid Advisor, Bastyr University, 14500 Juanita Drive NE, Kenmore, WA 98028-4966, 425-602-3407. *Fax:* 425-602-3094. *E-mail:* finaid@bastyr.edu.

BATES COLLEGE

Lewiston, ME

Comprehensive fee: $49,350 **Average undergraduate aid package: $32,955**

ABOUT THE INSTITUTION Independent, coed. ***Awards:*** bachelor's degrees. 34 undergraduate majors. ***Total enrollment:*** 1,776. Undergraduates: 1,776. Freshmen: 521. Institutional methodology is used as a basis for awarding need-based institutional aid.

UNDERGRADUATE EXPENSES for 2008–09 ***Application fee:*** $60. ***Comprehensive fee:*** $49,350. ***Payment plans:*** Tuition prepayment, installment.

FRESHMAN FINANCIAL AID (Fall 2008, est.) 287 applied for aid; of those 83% were deemed to have need. 95% of freshmen with need received aid; of those 93% had need fully met. ***Average percent of need met:*** 100% (excluding resources awarded to replace EFC). ***Average financial aid package:*** $32,872 (excluding resources awarded to replace EFC).

UNDERGRADUATE FINANCIAL AID (Fall 2008, est.) 850 applied for aid; of those 90% were deemed to have need. 94% of undergraduates with need received aid; of those 95% had need fully met. ***Average percent of need met:*** 100% (excluding resources awarded to replace EFC). ***Average financial aid package:*** $32,955 (excluding resources awarded to replace EFC).

GIFT AID (NEED-BASED) ***Total amount:*** $20,824,836 (5% federal, 93% institutional, 2% external sources). ***Receiving aid:*** Freshmen: 41% (216); all full-time undergraduates: 39% (692). ***Average award:*** Freshmen: $31,175; Undergraduates: $30,093. ***Scholarships, grants, and awards:*** Federal Pell, FSEOG, state, private, college/university gift aid from institutional funds.

GIFT AID (NON-NEED-BASED) ***Total amount:*** $81,300 (100% external sources). ***Tuition waivers:*** Full or partial for employees or children of employees.

LOANS ***Student loans:*** $3,485,224 (53% need-based, 47% non-need-based). 40% of past graduating class borrowed through all loan programs. *Average indebtedness per student:* $18,785. ***Average need-based loan:*** Freshmen: $3786. Undergraduates: $4133. ***Parent loans:*** $2,597,465 (100% non-need-based). ***Programs:*** FFEL (Subsidized and Unsubsidized Stafford, PLUS), Perkins, state.

WORK-STUDY ***Federal work-study:*** Total amount: $907,217; 531 jobs averaging $1709. ***State or other work study/employment:*** Total amount: $197,900 (100% need-based). 113 part-time jobs averaging $1751.

APPLYING FOR FINANCIAL AID ***Required financial aid forms:*** FAFSA, CSS Financial Aid PROFILE, noncustodial (divorced/separated) parent's statement, business/farm supplement. ***Financial aid deadline:*** 2/1. ***Notification date:*** 4/1. Students must reply by 5/1.

CONTACT Wendy G. Glass, Acting Director of Student Financial Services, Bates College, 44 Mountain Avenue, Lewiston, ME 04240, 207-786-6096. *Fax:* 207-786-8350. *E-mail:* wglass@bates.edu.

BAUDER COLLEGE

Atlanta, GA

CONTACT Rhonda Staines, Director of Financial Aid, Bauder College, Phipps Plaza, 3500 Peachtree Road NE, Atlanta, GA 30326, 404-237-7573 or toll-free 800-241-3797. *Fax:* 404-261-3087. *E-mail:* finaid@bauder.edu.

BAYAMÓN CENTRAL UNIVERSITY

Bayamón, PR

CONTACT Financial Aid Director, Bayamón Central University, PO Box 1725, Bayamón, PR 00960-1725, 787-786-3030 Ext. 2115. *Fax:* 787-785-4365.

BAYLOR UNIVERSITY

Waco, TX

Tuition & fees: $27,910 **Average undergraduate aid package: $18,779**

ABOUT THE INSTITUTION Independent Baptist, coed. ***Awards:*** bachelor's, master's, doctoral, and first professional degrees and post-master's certificates. 123 undergraduate majors. ***Total enrollment:*** 14,541. Undergraduates: 12,162. Freshmen: 3,062. Federal methodology is used as a basis for awarding need-based institutional aid.

UNDERGRADUATE EXPENSES for 2009–10 ***Application fee:*** $50. ***Comprehensive fee:*** $36,479 includes full-time tuition ($25,320), mandatory fees ($2590), and room and board ($8569). ***College room only:*** $4838. ***Part-time tuition:*** $1055 per semester hour.

FRESHMAN FINANCIAL AID (Fall 2008, est.) 2,130 applied for aid; of those 78% were deemed to have need. 100% of freshmen with need received aid; of those 13% had need fully met. ***Average percent of need met:*** 69% (excluding resources awarded to replace EFC). ***Average financial aid package:*** $20,249 (excluding resources awarded to replace EFC). 37% of all full-time freshmen had no need and received non-need-based gift aid.

UNDERGRADUATE FINANCIAL AID (Fall 2008, est.) 7,042 applied for aid; of those 85% were deemed to have need. 100% of undergraduates with need received aid; of those 15% had need fully met. ***Average percent of need met:*** 64% (excluding resources awarded to replace EFC). ***Average financial aid package:*** $18,779 (excluding resources awarded to replace EFC). 33% of all full-time undergraduates had no need and received non-need-based gift aid.

GIFT AID (NEED-BASED) ***Total amount:*** $76,097,260 (11% federal, 14% state, 69% institutional, 6% external sources). ***Receiving aid:*** Freshmen: 54% (1,654); all full-time undergraduates: 48% (5,629). ***Average award:*** Freshmen: $15,395; Undergraduates: $13,550. ***Scholarships, grants, and awards:*** Federal Pell, FSEOG, state, college/university gift aid from institutional funds.

GIFT AID (NON-NEED-BASED) ***Total amount:*** $35,071,011 (93% institutional, 7% external sources). ***Receiving aid:*** Freshmen: 53% (1,616). Undergraduates: 40% (4,788). ***Average award:*** Freshmen: $7991. Undergraduates: $8282. ***Scholarships, grants, and awards by category:*** *Academic interests/achievement:* 10,738 awards ($57,371,150 total): business, communication, computer science, education, engineering/technologies, English, foreign languages, general academic interests/achievements, health fields, home economics, humanities, international studies, mathematics, military science, physical sciences, premedicine, religion/biblical studies, social sciences. *Creative arts/performance:* 571 awards ($2,368,096 total): art/fine arts, cinema/film/broadcasting, debating, journalism/publications, music, theater/drama. *Special achievements/activities:* 330 awards ($564,588 total): community service, leadership, religious involvement. *Special characteristics:* 221 awards ($3,996,451 total): children of faculty/staff. ***ROTC:*** Air Force.

LOANS ***Student loans:*** $63,083,486 (70% need-based, 30% non-need-based). ***Average need-based loan:*** Freshmen: $2636. Undergraduates: $3229. ***Parent loans:*** $12,681,358 (28% need-based, 72% non-need-based). ***Programs:*** FFEL (Subsidized and Unsubsidized Stafford, PLUS), Perkins, Federal Nursing, state, private loans—school will certify approved loan application.

WORK-STUDY ***Federal work-study:*** Total amount: $10,416,688; 3,805 jobs averaging $2737. ***State or other work-study/employment:*** Part-time jobs available.

ATHLETIC AWARDS Total amount: $7,806,484 (22% need-based, 78% non-need-based).

APPLYING FOR FINANCIAL AID ***Required financial aid forms:*** FAFSA, if Texas resident, state residency affirmation required to receive State Grant or Loan. ***Financial aid deadline (priority):*** 3/1. ***Notification date:*** Continuous beginning 3/15. Students must reply by 5/1 or within 2 weeks of notification.

CONTACT Office of Admission Services, Baylor University, PO Box 97056, Waco, TX 76798-7056, 254-710-3435 or toll-free 800-BAYLORU. *Fax:* 254-710-3436. *E-mail:* admissions@baylor.edu.

BAY PATH COLLEGE

Longmeadow, MA

CONTACT Phyllis Brand, Financial Aid Assistant, Bay Path College, 588 Longmeadow Street, Longmeadow, MA 01106-2292, 413-565-1261 or toll-free 800-782-7284 Ext. 1331. *Fax:* 413-565-1101. *E-mail:* pbrand@baypath.edu.

BEACON COLLEGE

Leesburg, FL

CONTACT Financial Aid Office, Beacon College, 105 East Main Street, Leesburg, FL 34748, 352-787-7660.

BECKER COLLEGE

Worcester, MA

ABOUT THE INSTITUTION Independent, coed. ***Awards:*** associate and bachelor's degrees (also includes Leicester, MA small town campus). 28 undergraduate majors. ***Total enrollment:*** 1,752. Undergraduates: 1,752. Freshmen: 347.

GIFT AID (NEED-BASED) ***Scholarships, grants, and awards:*** Federal Pell, FSEOG, state, private, college/university gift aid from institutional funds.

GIFT AID (NON-NEED-BASED) ***Scholarships, grants, and awards by category:*** *Academic interests/achievement:* general academic interests/achievements. *Special achievements/activities:* general special achievements/activities, leadership. *Special characteristics:* children of faculty/staff, siblings of current students, twins.

LOANS ***Programs:*** Federal Direct (Subsidized and Unsubsidized Stafford, PLUS), state, alternative loans.

APPLYING FOR FINANCIAL AID ***Required financial aid form:*** FAFSA.

CONTACT Director of Student Financial Services, Becker College, 61 Sever Street, PO Box 15071, Worcester, MA 01615-0071, 508-373-9430 or toll-free 877-5BECKER Ext. 245. *Fax:* 508-890-1511.

BEIS MEDRASH HEICHAL DOVID

Far Rockaway, NY

CONTACT Financial Aid Office, Beis Medrash Heichal Dovid, 257 Beach 17th Street, Far Rockaway, NY 11691, 718-868-2300.

BELHAVEN COLLEGE

Jackson, MS

Tuition & fees: $16,780 **Average undergraduate aid package: $13,537**

ABOUT THE INSTITUTION Independent Presbyterian, coed. ***Awards:*** associate, bachelor's, and master's degrees. 28 undergraduate majors. ***Total enrollment:*** 2,619. Undergraduates: 2,166. Freshmen: 252. Federal methodology is used as a basis for awarding need-based institutional aid.

UNDERGRADUATE EXPENSES for 2009–10 ***Application fee:*** $25. ***Comprehensive fee:*** $22,900 includes full-time tuition ($16,780) and room and board ($6120). ***Part-time tuition:*** $350 per semester hour.

FRESHMAN FINANCIAL AID (Fall 2008, est.) 165 applied for aid; of those 88% were deemed to have need. 100% of freshmen with need received aid; of those 12% had need fully met. ***Average percent of need met:*** 63% (excluding resources awarded to replace EFC). ***Average financial aid package:*** $13,589 (excluding resources awarded to replace EFC). 9% of all full-time freshmen had no need and received non-need-based gift aid.

UNDERGRADUATE FINANCIAL AID (Fall 2008, est.) 675 applied for aid; of those 89% were deemed to have need. 100% of undergraduates with need received aid; of those 15% had need fully met. ***Average percent of need met:*** 62% (excluding resources awarded to replace EFC). ***Average financial aid package:*** $13,537 (excluding resources awarded to replace EFC). 12% of all full-time undergraduates had no need and received non-need-based gift aid.

GIFT AID (NEED-BASED) ***Total amount:*** $4,669,136 (31% federal, 4% state, 60% institutional, 5% external sources). ***Receiving aid:*** Freshmen: 61% (144); all full-time undergraduates: 65% (594). ***Average award:*** Freshmen: $10,677; Undergraduates: $9754. ***Scholarships, grants, and awards:*** Federal Pell, FSEOG, state, private, college/university gift aid from institutional funds.

GIFT AID (NON-NEED-BASED) ***Total amount:*** $1,552,998 (6% state, 89% institutional, 5% external sources). ***Receiving aid:*** Freshmen: 5% (12). Undergraduates: 6% (55). ***Average award:*** Freshmen: $7061. Undergraduates: $7202. ***Scholarships, grants, and awards by category:*** *Academic interests/achievement:* 472 awards ($2,240,421 total): biological sciences, business, communication, computer science, education, English, foreign languages, general academic interests/achievements, humanities, international studies, mathematics, premedicine, religion/biblical studies, social sciences. *Creative arts/performance:* 246 awards ($1,289,078 total): applied art and design, art/fine arts, creative writing, dance, journalism/publications, music, performing arts, theater/drama. *Special achievements/activities:* 123 awards ($136,780 total): cheerleading/drum major, general special achievements/activities, junior miss, leadership. *Special characteristics:* 226 awards ($612,164 total): children of faculty/staff, general special characteristics, international students, local/state students. ***ROTC:*** Army cooperative, Air Force cooperative.

LOANS ***Student loans:*** $4,674,101 (82% need-based, 18% non-need-based). 94% of past graduating class borrowed through all loan programs. *Average indebtedness per student:* $23,914. ***Average need-based loan:*** Freshmen: $2965. Undergraduates: $4285. ***Parent loans:*** $626,815 (41% need-based, 59% non-need-based). ***Programs:*** FFEL (Subsidized and Unsubsidized Stafford, PLUS), Perkins.

WORK-STUDY ***Federal work-study:*** Total amount: $256,586; 180 jobs averaging $1432.

ATHLETIC AWARDS Total amount: $2,121,028 (79% need-based, 21% non-need-based).

APPLYING FOR FINANCIAL AID ***Required financial aid form:*** FAFSA. ***Financial aid deadline (priority):*** 3/1. ***Notification date:*** Continuous.

CONTACT Ms. Linda Phillips, Assistant Vice President for Institutional Advancement, Belhaven College, 1500 Peachtree Street, Jackson, MS 39202-1789, 601-968-5933 or toll-free 800-960-5940. *Fax:* 601-353-0701. *E-mail:* lphillips@belhaven.edu.

BELLARMINE UNIVERSITY

Louisville, KY

Tuition & fees: $28,900 **Average undergraduate aid package: $21,278**

ABOUT THE INSTITUTION Independent Roman Catholic, coed. ***Awards:*** bachelor's, master's, and doctoral degrees and post-bachelor's certificates. 31 undergraduate majors. ***Total enrollment:*** 3,040. Undergraduates: 2,344. Freshmen: 572.

UNDERGRADUATE EXPENSES for 2009–10 ***Application fee:*** $25. ***Comprehensive fee:*** $37,310 includes full-time tuition ($27,800), mandatory fees ($1100), and room and board ($8410). ***Part-time tuition:*** $660 per credit hour.

FRESHMAN FINANCIAL AID (Fall 2008, est.) 500 applied for aid; of those 86% were deemed to have need. 100% of freshmen with need received aid; of those 30% had need fully met. ***Average percent of need met:*** 74% (excluding resources awarded to replace EFC). ***Average financial aid package:*** $22,285 (excluding resources awarded to replace EFC). 24% of all full-time freshmen had no need and received non-need-based gift aid.

UNDERGRADUATE FINANCIAL AID (Fall 2008, est.) 1,532 applied for aid; of those 88% were deemed to have need. 100% of undergraduates with need received aid; of those 27% had need fully met. ***Average percent of need met:*** 71% (excluding resources awarded to replace EFC). ***Average financial aid package:*** $21,278 (excluding resources awarded to replace EFC). 29% of all full-time undergraduates had no need and received non-need-based gift aid.

GIFT AID (NEED-BASED) ***Total amount:*** $23,857,287 (6% federal, 15% state, 73% institutional, 6% external sources). ***Receiving aid:*** Freshmen: 75% (427); all full-time undergraduates: 69% (1,325). ***Average award:*** Freshmen: $19,981; Undergraduates: $18,962. ***Scholarships, grants, and awards:*** Federal Pell, FSEOG, state, private, college/university gift aid from institutional funds.

GIFT AID (NON-NEED-BASED) ***Total amount:*** $9,829,637 (7% state, 87% institutional, 6% external sources). ***Receiving aid:*** Freshmen: 30% (172). Undergraduates: 27% (518). ***Average award:*** Freshmen: $18,504. Undergraduates: $16,532. ***Scholarships, grants, and awards by category:*** *Academic interests/achievement:* biological sciences, business, education, general academic interests/achievements, health fields. *Creative arts/performance:* art/fine arts, music. *Special achievements/activities:* cheerleading/drum major, community service, general special achievements/activities, leadership, religious involvement. *Special characteristics:* adult students, children of faculty/staff, ethnic background, international students, local/state students, out-of-state students, previous college experience. ***ROTC:*** Army cooperative, Air Force cooperative.

LOANS ***Student loans:*** $10,109,274 (70% need-based, 30% non-need-based). 66% of past graduating class borrowed through all loan programs. *Average indebtedness per student:* $19,055. ***Average need-based loan:*** Freshmen: $3586. Undergraduates: $4353. ***Parent loans:*** $1,769,339 (39% need-based, 61% non-need-based). ***Programs:*** Federal Direct (Subsidized and Unsubsidized Stafford, PLUS), FFEL (Subsidized and Unsubsidized Stafford, PLUS), Perkins, state, college/university.

WORK-STUDY ***Federal work-study:*** Total amount: $403,476; jobs available. ***State or other work-study/employment:*** Total amount: $52,500 (100% non-need-based). Part-time jobs available.

ATHLETIC AWARDS Total amount: $2,141,174 (42% need-based, 58% non-need-based).

APPLYING FOR FINANCIAL AID ***Required financial aid form:*** FAFSA. ***Financial aid deadline (priority):*** 3/1. ***Notification date:*** Continuous beginning 3/15. Students must reply by 5/1.

CONTACT Ms. Heather Boutell, Director of Financial Aid, Bellarmine University, 2001 Newburg Road, Louisville, KY 40205-0671, 502-452-8124 or toll-free 800-274-4723 Ext. 8131. *Fax:* 502-452-8002. *E-mail:* hboutell@bellarmine.edu.

BELLEVUE UNIVERSITY

Bellevue, NE

CONTACT Mr. Jon Dotterer, Director of Financial Aid, Bellevue University, 1000 Galvin Road South, Bellevue, NE 68005, 402-293-3762 or toll-free 800-756-7920. *Fax:* 402-293-2062.

BELLIN COLLEGE OF NURSING

Green Bay, WI

Tuition & fees: N/R **Average undergraduate aid package: $17,711**

ABOUT THE INSTITUTION Independent, coed, primarily women. ***Awards:*** bachelor's and master's degrees. 1 undergraduate major. ***Total enrollment:*** 304. Undergraduates: 259. Federal methodology is used as a basis for awarding need-based institutional aid.

UNDERGRADUATE FINANCIAL AID (Fall 2008, est.) 98 applied for aid; of those 92% were deemed to have need. 100% of undergraduates with need received aid; of those 13% had need fully met. ***Average percent of need met:*** 81% (excluding resources awarded to replace EFC). ***Average financial aid package:*** $17,711 (excluding resources awarded to replace EFC). 2% of all full-time undergraduates had no need and received non-need-based gift aid.

GIFT AID (NEED-BASED) ***Total amount:*** $557,400 (21% federal, 19% state, 42% institutional, 18% external sources). ***Receiving aid:*** All full-time undergraduates: 44% (89). ***Average award:*** Undergraduates: $5191. ***Scholarships, grants, and awards:*** Federal Pell, FSEOG, state, private, college/university gift aid from institutional funds.

GIFT AID (NON-NEED-BASED) ***Total amount:*** $36,791 (18% institutional, 82% external sources). ***Receiving aid:*** Undergraduates: 2% (3). ***Average award:*** Undergraduates: $1000. ***Scholarships, grants, and awards by category:*** *Academic interests/achievement:* 19 awards ($45,776 total): general academic interests/achievements. ***ROTC:*** Army cooperative.

LOANS ***Student loans:*** $1,821,615 (75% need-based, 25% non-need-based). 89% of past graduating class borrowed through all loan programs. *Average indebtedness per student:* $34,137. ***Average need-based loan:*** Undergraduates: $4566. ***Parent loans:*** $246,707 (50% need-based, 50% non-need-based). ***Programs:*** FFEL (Subsidized and Unsubsidized Stafford, PLUS), state.

WORK-STUDY ***Federal work-study:*** Total amount: $2500; 2 jobs averaging $1250.

APPLYING FOR FINANCIAL AID ***Required financial aid form:*** FAFSA. ***Financial aid deadline (priority):*** 3/1. ***Notification date:*** 4/1. Students must reply within 2 weeks of notification.

CONTACT Ms. Lena C. Goodman, Director of Financial Aid, Bellin College of Nursing, 725 South Webster Avenue, Green Bay, WI 54305-3400, 920-433-5801 or toll-free 800-236-8707. *Fax:* 920-433-7416. *E-mail:* lena.goodman@bcon.edu.

BELMONT ABBEY COLLEGE

Belmont, NC

Tuition & fees: $20,094 **Average undergraduate aid package: $12,720**

ABOUT THE INSTITUTION Independent Roman Catholic, coed. ***Awards:*** bachelor's degrees. 24 undergraduate majors. ***Total enrollment:*** 1,497. Undergraduates: 1,497. Freshmen: 290. Federal methodology is used as a basis for awarding need-based institutional aid.

UNDERGRADUATE EXPENSES for 2008–09 ***Application fee:*** $35. ***One-time required fee:*** $945. ***Comprehensive fee:*** $29,960 includes full-time tuition ($19,114), mandatory fees ($980), and room and board ($9866). ***College room only:*** $5766. Full-time tuition and fees vary according to class time, course level, course load, location, program, reciprocity agreements, and student level. Room and board charges vary according to board plan, housing facility, location, and student level. ***Part-time tuition:*** $637 per credit hour. ***Part-time fees:*** $38 per credit hour. Part-time tuition and fees vary according to class time, course level, course load, location, reciprocity agreements, and student level. ***Payment plans:*** Installment, deferred payment.

FRESHMAN FINANCIAL AID (Fall 2008, est.) 249 applied for aid; of those 82% were deemed to have need. 100% of freshmen with need received aid; of those 23% had need fully met. ***Average percent of need met:*** 73% (excluding

resources awarded to replace EFC). ***Average financial aid package:*** $15,534 (excluding resources awarded to replace EFC). 17% of all full-time freshmen had no need and received non-need-based gift aid.

UNDERGRADUATE FINANCIAL AID (Fall 2008, est.) 1,233 applied for aid; of those 88% were deemed to have need. 100% of undergraduates with need received aid; of those 15% had need fully met. ***Average percent of need met:*** 60% (excluding resources awarded to replace EFC). ***Average financial aid package:*** $12,720 (excluding resources awarded to replace EFC). 11% of all full-time undergraduates had no need and received non-need-based gift aid.

GIFT AID (NEED-BASED) ***Total amount:*** $8,986,385 (23% federal, 32% state, 39% institutional, 6% external sources). ***Receiving aid:*** Freshmen: 76% (203); all full-time undergraduates: 78% (1,078). ***Average award:*** Freshmen: $12,538; Undergraduates: $8648. ***Scholarships, grants, and awards:*** Federal Pell, FSEOG, state, private, college/university gift aid from institutional funds.

GIFT AID (NON-NEED-BASED) ***Total amount:*** $3,585,255 (8% state, 78% institutional, 14% external sources). ***Receiving aid:*** Freshmen: 12% (33). Undergraduates: 7% (92). ***Average award:*** Freshmen: $9628. Undergraduates: $8568. ***Scholarships, grants, and awards by category:*** *Academic interests/achievement:* 618 awards ($4,459,144 total): general academic interests/achievements. *Creative arts/performance:* 36 awards ($68,000 total): theater/drama. *Special achievements/activities:* 19 awards ($346,567 total): religious involvement. *Special characteristics:* 23 awards ($129,574 total): children of faculty/staff. ***Tuition waivers:*** Full or partial for employees or children of employees, senior citizens. ***ROTC:*** Army cooperative, Air Force cooperative.

LOANS ***Student loans:*** $6,940,722 (59% need-based, 41% non-need-based). 78% of past graduating class borrowed through all loan programs. *Average indebtedness per student:* $17,500. ***Average need-based loan:*** Freshmen: $3209. Undergraduates: $4254. ***Parent loans:*** $2,915,959 (100% need-based). ***Programs:*** Federal Direct (Subsidized and Unsubsidized Stafford, PLUS), Perkins.

WORK-STUDY ***Federal work-study:*** Total amount: $143,016; 105 jobs averaging $1800.

ATHLETIC AWARDS Total amount: $1,288,194 (44% need-based, 56% non-need-based).

APPLYING FOR FINANCIAL AID ***Required financial aid form:*** FAFSA. ***Financial aid deadline (priority):*** 4/1. ***Notification date:*** Continuous. Students must reply within 2 weeks of notification.

CONTACT Ms. Julie Hodge, Associate Director of Financial Aid, Belmont Abbey College, 100 Belmont Mt. Holly Road, Belmont, NC 28012-1802, 704-461-6718 or toll-free 888-BAC-0110. *Fax:* 704-461-6882. *E-mail:* juliehodge@bac.edu.

BELMONT UNIVERSITY

Nashville, TN

Tuition & fees: $21,110 **Average undergraduate aid package: $9995**

ABOUT THE INSTITUTION Independent Baptist, coed. ***Awards:*** bachelor's, master's, doctoral, and first professional degrees and post-master's certificates. 67 undergraduate majors. ***Total enrollment:*** 4,991. Undergraduates: 4,174. Freshmen: 932. Federal methodology is used as a basis for awarding need-based institutional aid.

UNDERGRADUATE EXPENSES for 2008–09 ***Application fee:*** $50. ***Comprehensive fee:*** $31,110 includes full-time tuition ($20,070), mandatory fees ($1040), and room and board ($10,000). ***College room only:*** $6300. Full-time tuition and fees vary according to class time and course load. Room and board charges vary according to board plan, housing facility, and location. ***Part-time tuition:*** $770 per credit hour. ***Part-time fees:*** $350 per term. Part-time tuition and fees vary according to course load. ***Payment plans:*** Installment, deferred payment.

FRESHMAN FINANCIAL AID (Fall 2008, est.) 855 applied for aid; of those 54% were deemed to have need. 97% of freshmen with need received aid; of those 93% had need fully met. ***Average percent of need met:*** 84% (excluding resources awarded to replace EFC). ***Average financial aid package:*** $10,404 (excluding resources awarded to replace EFC). 27% of all full-time freshmen had no need and received non-need-based gift aid.

UNDERGRADUATE FINANCIAL AID (Fall 2008, est.) 3,395 applied for aid; of those 58% were deemed to have need. 97% of undergraduates with need received aid; of those 70% had need fully met. ***Average percent of need met:*** 87% (excluding resources awarded to replace EFC). ***Average financial aid package:*** $9995 (excluding resources awarded to replace EFC). 16% of all full-time undergraduates had no need and received non-need-based gift aid.

GIFT AID (NEED-BASED) ***Total amount:*** $7,464,189 (29% federal, 8% state, 63% institutional). ***Receiving aid:*** Freshmen: 29% (272); all full-time undergraduates: 31% (1,193). ***Average award:*** Freshmen: $5540; Undergraduates: $5335. ***Scholarships, grants, and awards:*** Federal Pell, FSEOG, state, private, college/university gift aid from institutional funds.

GIFT AID (NON-NEED-BASED) ***Total amount:*** $12,627,791 (32% state, 68% institutional). ***Receiving aid:*** Freshmen: 37% (343). Undergraduates: 27% (1,036). ***Average award:*** Freshmen: $5675. Undergraduates: $5395. ***Scholarships, grants, and awards by category:*** *Academic interests/achievement:* 1,486 awards ($7,216,655 total): general academic interests/achievements, religion/biblical studies. *Creative arts/performance:* 201 awards ($450,249 total): music. *Special characteristics:* 78 awards ($1,215,101 total): children of faculty/staff. ***Tuition waivers:*** Full or partial for employees or children of employees, senior citizens. ***ROTC:*** Army cooperative, Naval cooperative.

LOANS ***Student loans:*** $33,310,251 (58% need-based, 42% non-need-based). 50% of past graduating class borrowed through all loan programs. *Average indebtedness per student:* $14,319. ***Average need-based loan:*** Freshmen: $3451. Undergraduates: $4394. ***Parent loans:*** $11,027,060 (100% non-need-based). ***Programs:*** Federal Direct (PLUS), FFEL (Subsidized and Unsubsidized Stafford, PLUS), Perkins, college/university.

WORK-STUDY ***Federal work-study:*** Total amount: $258,034; 250 jobs averaging $1031.

ATHLETIC AWARDS Total amount: $3,297,537 (1% need-based, 99% non-need-based).

APPLYING FOR FINANCIAL AID ***Required financial aid form:*** FAFSA. ***Financial aid deadline (priority):*** 3/1. ***Notification date:*** Continuous beginning 3/15. Students must reply by 5/1 or within 2 weeks of notification.

CONTACT Mrs. Paula A. Gill, Director, Student Financial Services, Belmont University, 1900 Belmont Boulevard, Nashville, TN 37212-3757, 615-460-6403 or toll-free 800-56E-NROL. *E-mail:* gillp@mail.belmont.edu.

BELOIT COLLEGE

Beloit, WI

Tuition & fees: $31,540 **Average undergraduate aid package: $24,601**

ABOUT THE INSTITUTION Independent, coed. ***Awards:*** bachelor's degrees. 56 undergraduate majors. ***Total enrollment:*** 1,388. Undergraduates: 1,388. Freshmen: 339. Both federal and institutional methodology are used as a basis for awarding need-based institutional aid.

UNDERGRADUATE EXPENSES for 2008–09 ***Application fee:*** $35. ***Comprehensive fee:*** $38,236 includes full-time tuition ($31,310), mandatory fees ($230), and room and board ($6696). ***College room only:*** $3282. Room and board charges vary according to board plan. ***Part-time tuition:*** $3913 per course. ***Payment plan:*** Installment.

FRESHMAN FINANCIAL AID (Fall 2008, est.) 278 applied for aid; of those 80% were deemed to have need. 100% of freshmen with need received aid; of those 96% had need fully met. ***Average percent of need met:*** 99% (excluding resources awarded to replace EFC). ***Average financial aid package:*** $25,170 (excluding resources awarded to replace EFC). 27% of all full-time freshmen had no need and received non-need-based gift aid.

UNDERGRADUATE FINANCIAL AID (Fall 2008, est.) 993 applied for aid; of those 81% were deemed to have need. 100% of undergraduates with need received aid; of those 95% had need fully met. ***Average percent of need met:*** 100% (excluding resources awarded to replace EFC). ***Average financial aid package:*** $24,601 (excluding resources awarded to replace EFC). 27% of all full-time undergraduates had no need and received non-need-based gift aid.

GIFT AID (NEED-BASED) ***Total amount:*** $15,958,905 (6% federal, 2% state, 89% institutional, 3% external sources). ***Receiving aid:*** Freshmen: 66% (222); all full-time undergraduates: 61% (786). ***Average award:*** Freshmen: $21,253; Undergraduates: $19,831. ***Scholarships, grants, and awards:*** Federal Pell, FSEOG, state, private, college/university gift aid from institutional funds.

GIFT AID (NON-NEED-BASED) ***Total amount:*** $4,714,321 (95% institutional, 5% external sources). ***Average award:*** Freshmen: $12,565. Undergraduates: $12,417. ***Scholarships, grants, and awards by category:*** *Academic interests/achievement:* 643 awards ($6,937,863 total): general academic interests/achievements. *Creative arts/performance:* 63 awards ($252,000 total): music. *Special achievements/activities:* 25 awards ($98,000 total): community service, general special achievements/activities. *Special characteristics:* 62 awards ($717,800 total): members of minority groups, siblings of current students. ***Tuition waivers:*** Full or partial for employees or children of employees.

LOANS ***Student loans:*** $7,563,859 (86% need-based, 14% non-need-based). 68% of past graduating class borrowed through all loan programs. *Average*

indebtedness per student: $26,014. ***Average need-based loan:*** Freshmen: $3160. Undergraduates: $4279. ***Parent loans:*** $1,364,889 (65% need-based, 35% non-need-based). ***Programs:*** FFEL (Subsidized and Unsubsidized Stafford, PLUS), Perkins, college/university.

WORK-STUDY ***Federal work-study:*** Total amount: $959,763; 523 jobs averaging $1787. ***State or other work-study/employment:*** Total amount: $696,023 (50% need-based, 50% non-need-based). 523 part-time jobs averaging $1309.

APPLYING FOR FINANCIAL AID ***Required financial aid forms:*** FAFSA, institution's own form, state aid form. ***Financial aid deadline (priority):*** 3/1. ***Notification date:*** Continuous beginning 4/1. Students must reply by 5/1 or within 2 weeks of notification.

CONTACT Mr. Jon Urish, Senior Associate Director of Admissions and Financial Aid, Beloit College, 700 College Street, Beloit, WI 53511-5596, 800-356-0751 or toll-free 800-9-BELOIT. *Fax:* 608-363-2075. *E-mail:* urishj@beloit.edu.

BEMIDJI STATE UNIVERSITY

Bemidji, MN

CONTACT Financial Aid Office, Bemidji State University, 1500 Birchmont Drive, NE, Bemidji, MN 56601-2699, 218-755-2034 or toll-free 800-475-2001 (in-state), 800-652-9747 (out-of-state). *Fax:* 218-755-4361. *E-mail:* financialaid@bemidjistate.edu.

BENEDICT COLLEGE

Columbia, SC

CONTACT Assistant Director of Financial Aid, Benedict College, 1600 Harden Street, Columbia, SC 29204, 803-253-5105 or toll-free 800-868-6598 (in-state).

BENEDICTINE COLLEGE

Atchison, KS

Tuition & fees: $18,800 **Average undergraduate aid package: $15,739**

ABOUT THE INSTITUTION Independent Roman Catholic, coed. ***Awards:*** associate, bachelor's, and master's degrees. 34 undergraduate majors. ***Total enrollment:*** 2,033. Undergraduates: 1,978. Freshmen: 396. Federal methodology is used as a basis for awarding need-based institutional aid.

UNDERGRADUATE EXPENSES for 2008–09 ***Application fee:*** $25. ***Comprehensive fee:*** $25,100 includes full-time tuition ($18,800) and room and board ($6300). ***College room only:*** $3260. Full-time tuition and fees vary according to course load and degree level. Room and board charges vary according to board plan and housing facility. ***Part-time tuition:*** $530 per credit hour. Part-time tuition and fees vary according to course load and degree level. ***Payment plan:*** Installment.

FRESHMAN FINANCIAL AID (Fall 2008, est.) 360 applied for aid; of those 82% were deemed to have need. 100% of freshmen with need received aid; of those 21% had need fully met. ***Average percent of need met:*** 69% (excluding resources awarded to replace EFC). ***Average financial aid package:*** $15,880 (excluding resources awarded to replace EFC). 25% of all full-time freshmen had no need and received non-need-based gift aid.

UNDERGRADUATE FINANCIAL AID (Fall 2008, est.) 1,352 applied for aid; of those 72% were deemed to have need. 100% of undergraduates with need received aid; of those 20% had need fully met. ***Average percent of need met:*** 68% (excluding resources awarded to replace EFC). ***Average financial aid package:*** $15,739 (excluding resources awarded to replace EFC). 28% of all full-time undergraduates had no need and received non-need-based gift aid.

GIFT AID (NEED-BASED) ***Total amount:*** $7,534,620 (18% federal, 9% state, 68% institutional, 5% external sources). ***Receiving aid:*** Freshmen: 48% (189); all full-time undergraduates: 46% (617). ***Average award:*** Freshmen: $11,665; Undergraduates: $11,975. ***Scholarships, grants, and awards:*** Federal Pell, FSEOG, state, private, college/university gift aid from institutional funds.

GIFT AID (NON-NEED-BASED) ***Total amount:*** $2,222,312 (98% institutional, 2% external sources). ***Receiving aid:*** Freshmen: 74% (295). Undergraduates: 71% (961). ***Average award:*** Freshmen: $8685. Undergraduates: $7886. ***Scholarships, grants, and awards by category:*** *Academic interests/achievement:* 812 awards ($4,735,624 total): general academic interests/achievements. *Creative arts/performance:* 100 awards ($104,026 total): music, theater/drama. *Special achievements/activities:* 165 awards ($293,902 total): general special achievements/activities. *Special characteristics:* 93 awards ($252,629 total): children of educators, ethnic background, general special characteristics, international students, local/state students, members of minority groups, out-of-state students, religious affiliation, veterans' children. ***Tuition waivers:*** Full or partial for employees or children of employees, senior citizens. ***ROTC:*** Army.

LOANS ***Student loans:*** $7,874,401 (70% need-based, 30% non-need-based). 74% of past graduating class borrowed through all loan programs. *Average indebtedness per student:* $16,060. ***Average need-based loan:*** Freshmen: $3780. Undergraduates: $4426. ***Parent loans:*** $1,854,138 (41% need-based, 59% non-need-based). ***Programs:*** FFEL (Subsidized and Unsubsidized Stafford, PLUS), Perkins, alternative loans.

WORK-STUDY ***Federal work-study:*** Total amount: $863,020; 372 jobs averaging $822. ***State or other work-study/employment:*** Total amount: $97,300 (6% need-based, 94% non-need-based). 73 part-time jobs averaging $547.

ATHLETIC AWARDS Total amount: $4,595,544 (69% need-based, 31% non-need-based).

APPLYING FOR FINANCIAL AID ***Required financial aid form:*** FAFSA. ***Financial aid deadline (priority):*** 3/15. ***Notification date:*** Continuous. Students must reply within 2 weeks of notification.

CONTACT Mr. Tony Tanking, Director of Financial Aid, Benedictine College, 1020 North Second Street, Atchison, KS 66002-1499, 913-360-7484 or toll-free 800-467-5340. *Fax:* 913-367-5462. *E-mail:* ttanking@benedictine.edu.

BENEDICTINE UNIVERSITY

Lisle, IL

Tuition & fees: $22,310 **Average undergraduate aid package: $14,391**

ABOUT THE INSTITUTION Independent Roman Catholic, coed. ***Awards:*** associate, bachelor's, master's, and doctoral degrees and post-bachelor's certificates. 52 undergraduate majors. ***Total enrollment:*** 5,279. Undergraduates: 3,282. Freshmen: 435. Federal methodology is used as a basis for awarding need-based institutional aid.

UNDERGRADUATE EXPENSES for 2008–09 ***Application fee:*** $40. ***Comprehensive fee:*** $29,610 includes full-time tuition ($21,600), mandatory fees ($710), and room and board ($7300). Full-time tuition and fees vary according to class time, degree level, and location. Room and board charges vary according to board plan and housing facility. ***Part-time tuition:*** $720 per credit hour. ***Part-time fees:*** $15 per credit hour. Part-time tuition and fees vary according to class time and degree level. ***Payment plans:*** Installment, deferred payment.

FRESHMAN FINANCIAL AID (Fall 2007) 326 applied for aid; of those 84% were deemed to have need. 100% of freshmen with need received aid. ***Average financial aid package:*** $16,853 (excluding resources awarded to replace EFC). 13% of all full-time freshmen had no need and received non-need-based gift aid.

UNDERGRADUATE FINANCIAL AID (Fall 2007) 1,462 applied for aid; of those 87% were deemed to have need. 99% of undergraduates with need received aid. ***Average financial aid package:*** $14,391 (excluding resources awarded to replace EFC). 7% of all full-time undergraduates had no need and received non-need-based gift aid.

GIFT AID (NEED-BASED) ***Total amount:*** $6,700,337 (38% federal, 57% state, 5% institutional). ***Receiving aid:*** Freshmen: 43% (170); all full-time undergraduates: 42% (817). ***Average award:*** Freshmen: $7086; Undergraduates: $6583. ***Scholarships, grants, and awards:*** Federal Pell, FSEOG, state, private, college/university gift aid from institutional funds.

GIFT AID (NON-NEED-BASED) ***Total amount:*** $10,222,541 (98% institutional, 2% external sources). ***Receiving aid:*** Freshmen: 69% (271). Undergraduates: 49% (973). ***Average award:*** Freshmen: $7419. Undergraduates: $7105. ***Scholarships, grants, and awards by category:*** *Academic interests/achievement:* general academic interests/achievements. *Creative arts/performance:* music. *Special characteristics:* children and siblings of alumni, out-of-state students, previous college experience, siblings of current students. ***Tuition waivers:*** Full or partial for employees or children of employees. ***ROTC:*** Army cooperative.

LOANS ***Student loans:*** $13,720,406 (48% need-based, 52% non-need-based). 78% of past graduating class borrowed through all loan programs. *Average indebtedness per student:* $16,802. ***Average need-based loan:*** Freshmen: $3052. Undergraduates: $3920. ***Parent loans:*** $3,402,909 (100% need-based). ***Programs:*** FFEL (Subsidized and Unsubsidized Stafford, PLUS), Perkins, alternative loans.

WORK-STUDY ***Federal work-study:*** Total amount: $176,423; jobs available.

APPLYING FOR FINANCIAL AID ***Required financial aid forms:*** FAFSA, institution's own form. ***Financial aid deadline:*** Continuous. ***Notification date:*** Continuous beginning 2/15. Students must reply within 2 weeks of notification.

CONTACT Diane Battistella, Associate Dean, Financial Aid, Benedictine University, 5700 College Road, Lisle, IL 60532, 630-829-6415 or toll-free 888-829-6363 (out-of-state). *Fax:* 630-829-6456. *E-mail:* dbattistella@ben.edu.

BENNETT COLLEGE FOR WOMEN

Greensboro, NC

CONTACT Monty K. Hickman, Financial Aid Director, Bennett College For Women, 900 East Washington Street, Greensboro, NC 27401, 336-370-8677. *Fax:* 336-517-2204. *E-mail:* mhickman@bennett.edu.

BENNINGTON COLLEGE

Bennington, VT

Tuition & fees: $38,270 **Average undergraduate aid package: $30,918**

ABOUT THE INSTITUTION Independent, coed. ***Awards:*** bachelor's and master's degrees and post-bachelor's certificates. 93 undergraduate majors. ***Total enrollment:*** 759. Undergraduates: 618. Freshmen: 190. Federal methodology is used as a basis for awarding need-based institutional aid.

UNDERGRADUATE EXPENSES for 2008–09 ***Application fee:*** $60. ***Comprehensive fee:*** $48,950 includes full-time tuition ($37,280), mandatory fees ($990), and room and board ($10,680). ***College room only:*** $5720. ***Part-time tuition:*** $1165 per credit hour. ***Payment plan:*** Installment.

FRESHMAN FINANCIAL AID (Fall 2008, est.) 135 applied for aid; of those 87% were deemed to have need. 97% of freshmen with need received aid; of those 14% had need fully met. ***Average percent of need met:*** 80% (excluding resources awarded to replace EFC). ***Average financial aid package:*** $29,426 (excluding resources awarded to replace EFC). 5% of all full-time freshmen had no need and received non-need-based gift aid.

UNDERGRADUATE FINANCIAL AID (Fall 2008, est.) 443 applied for aid; of those 92% were deemed to have need. 98% of undergraduates with need received aid; of those 11% had need fully met. ***Average percent of need met:*** 81% (excluding resources awarded to replace EFC). ***Average financial aid package:*** $30,918 (excluding resources awarded to replace EFC). 6% of all full-time undergraduates had no need and received non-need-based gift aid.

GIFT AID (NEED-BASED) ***Total amount:*** $10,433,521 (6% federal, 92% institutional, 2% external sources). ***Receiving aid:*** Freshmen: 59% (113); all full-time undergraduates: 64% (395). ***Average award:*** Freshmen: $26,395; Undergraduates: $26,575. ***Scholarships, grants, and awards:*** Federal Pell, FSEOG, state, private, college/university gift aid from institutional funds.

GIFT AID (NON-NEED-BASED) ***Total amount:*** $905,524 (68% institutional, 32% external sources). ***Receiving aid:*** Freshmen: 8% (15). Undergraduates: 4% (25). ***Average award:*** Freshmen: $9750. Undergraduates: $12,182. ***Scholarships, grants, and awards by category:*** *Academic interests/achievement:* general academic interests/achievements. *Creative arts/performance:* general creative arts/performance. *Special achievements/activities:* general special achievements/activities. *Special characteristics:* children of educators, children of faculty/staff, general special characteristics. ***Tuition waivers:*** Full or partial for employees or children of employees.

LOANS ***Student loans:*** $2,517,395 (77% need-based, 23% non-need-based). 68% of past graduating class borrowed through all loan programs. *Average indebtedness per student:* $25,957. ***Average need-based loan:*** Freshmen: $2980. Undergraduates: $3938. ***Parent loans:*** $1,714,744 (29% need-based, 71% non-need-based). ***Programs:*** FFEL (Subsidized and Unsubsidized Stafford, PLUS), college/university.

WORK-STUDY ***Federal work-study:*** Total amount: $418,423; jobs available (averaging $1900). ***State or other work-study/employment:*** Total amount: $38,000 (80% need-based, 20% non-need-based). Part-time jobs available (averaging $1900).

APPLYING FOR FINANCIAL AID ***Required financial aid forms:*** FAFSA, institution's own form, CSS Financial Aid PROFILE, noncustodial (divorced/separated) parent's statement, student and parent federal tax returns and W-2s. ***Financial aid deadline (priority):*** 3/1. ***Notification date:*** 4/1. Students must reply by 5/1 or within 2 weeks of notification.

CONTACT Meg Woolmington, Director of Financial Aid, Bennington College, One College Drive, Bennington, VT 05201, 802-440-4325 or toll-free 800-833-6845. *Fax:* 802-440-4880. *E-mail:* finaid@bennington.edu.

BENTLEY UNIVERSITY

Waltham, MA

Tuition & fees: $34,488 **Average undergraduate aid package: $26,584**

ABOUT THE INSTITUTION Independent, coed. ***Awards:*** associate, bachelor's, master's, and doctoral degrees and post-bachelor's and post-master's certificates. 16 undergraduate majors. ***Total enrollment:*** 5,664. Undergraduates: 4,259. Freshmen: 974. Both federal and institutional methodology are used as a basis for awarding need-based institutional aid.

UNDERGRADUATE EXPENSES for 2008–09 ***Application fee:*** $50. ***Comprehensive fee:*** $45,808 includes full-time tuition ($33,030), mandatory fees ($1458), and room and board ($11,320). ***College room only:*** $6770. Room and board charges vary according to board plan and housing facility. ***Part-time tuition:*** $1581 per course. ***Part-time fees:*** $45 per term. Part-time tuition and fees vary according to class time. ***Payment plan:*** Installment.

FRESHMAN FINANCIAL AID (Fall 2007) 687 applied for aid; of those 65% were deemed to have need. 99% of freshmen with need received aid; of those 45% had need fully met. ***Average percent of need met:*** 95% (excluding resources awarded to replace EFC). ***Average financial aid package:*** $26,375 (excluding resources awarded to replace EFC). 17% of all full-time freshmen had no need and received non-need-based gift aid.

UNDERGRADUATE FINANCIAL AID (Fall 2007) 2,744 applied for aid; of those 73% were deemed to have need. 100% of undergraduates with need received aid; of those 37% had need fully met. ***Average percent of need met:*** 90% (excluding resources awarded to replace EFC). ***Average financial aid package:*** $26,584 (excluding resources awarded to replace EFC). 10% of all full-time undergraduates had no need and received non-need-based gift aid.

GIFT AID (NEED-BASED) ***Total amount:*** $31,439,004 (8% federal, 5% state, 87% institutional). ***Receiving aid:*** Freshmen: 39% (365); all full-time undergraduates: 41% (1,685). ***Average award:*** Freshmen: $19,436; Undergraduates: $19,733. ***Scholarships, grants, and awards:*** Federal Pell, FSEOG, state, private, college/university gift aid from institutional funds.

GIFT AID (NON-NEED-BASED) ***Total amount:*** $12,466,364 (91% institutional, 9% external sources). ***Receiving aid:*** Freshmen: 24% (227). Undergraduates: 12% (473). ***Average award:*** Freshmen: $13,825. Undergraduates: $15,538. ***Scholarships, grants, and awards by category:*** *Academic interests/achievement:* 1,037 awards ($14,799,065 total): general academic interests/achievements. *Special achievements/activities:* 17 awards ($132,500 total): community service. *Special characteristics:* 17 awards ($297,700 total): international students, members of minority groups. ***Tuition waivers:*** Full or partial for employees or children of employees. ***ROTC:*** Army cooperative, Air Force cooperative.

LOANS ***Student loans:*** $22,387,263 (46% need-based, 54% non-need-based). 65% of past graduating class borrowed through all loan programs. *Average indebtedness per student:* $30,577. ***Average need-based loan:*** Freshmen: $4402. Undergraduates: $5353. ***Parent loans:*** $10,143,368 (100% non-need-based). ***Programs:*** FFEL (Subsidized and Unsubsidized Stafford, PLUS), Perkins, state.

WORK-STUDY ***Federal work-study:*** Total amount: $1,911,239; 1,080 jobs averaging $1503. ***State or other work-study/employment:*** Total amount: $1,245,453 (100% non-need-based). 1,012 part-time jobs averaging $1694.

ATHLETIC AWARDS Total amount: $2,138,052 (43% need-based, 57% non-need-based).

APPLYING FOR FINANCIAL AID ***Required financial aid forms:*** FAFSA, CSS Financial Aid PROFILE, noncustodial (divorced/separated) parent's statement, business/farm supplement, federal tax returns, including all schedules for parents and student. ***Financial aid deadline:*** 2/1. ***Notification date:*** Continuous beginning 3/25.

CONTACT Ms. Donna Kendall, Executive Director of Financial Assistance, Bentley University, 175 Forest Street, Waltham, MA 02452-4705, 781-891-3441 or toll-free 800-523-2354. *Fax:* 781-891-2448. *E-mail:* finaid@bentley.edu.

BEREA COLLEGE

Berea, KY

Tuition & fees: $866 **Average undergraduate aid package: $30,198**

ABOUT THE INSTITUTION Independent, coed. ***Awards:*** bachelor's degrees. 38 undergraduate majors. ***Total enrollment:*** 1,549. Undergraduates: 1,549. Freshmen: 413. Federal methodology is used as a basis for awarding need-based institutional aid.

UNDERGRADUATE EXPENSES for 2008–09 includes mandatory fees ($866) and room and board ($5768). financial aid is provided to all students for tuition costs.

FRESHMAN FINANCIAL AID (Fall 2008, est.) 413 applied for aid; of those 100% were deemed to have need. 100% of freshmen with need received aid. ***Average percent of need met:*** 94% (excluding resources awarded to replace EFC). ***Average financial aid package:*** $31,598 (excluding resources awarded to replace EFC).

UNDERGRADUATE FINANCIAL AID (Fall 2008, est.) 1,488 applied for aid; of those 100% were deemed to have need. 100% of undergraduates with need received aid. ***Average percent of need met:*** 90% (excluding resources awarded to replace EFC). ***Average financial aid package:*** $30,198 (excluding resources awarded to replace EFC).

GIFT AID (NEED-BASED) ***Total amount:*** $42,429,559 (13% federal, 7% state, 80% institutional). ***Receiving aid:*** Freshmen: 100% (413); all full-time undergraduates: 100% (1,488). ***Average award:*** Freshmen: $31,200; Undergraduates: $27,903. ***Scholarships, grants, and awards:*** Federal Pell, FSEOG, state, private, college/university gift aid from institutional funds.

LOANS ***Student loans:*** $1,200,045 (43% need-based, 57% non-need-based). 78% of past graduating class borrowed through all loan programs. *Average indebtedness per student:* $8505. ***Average need-based loan:*** Freshmen: $927. Undergraduates: $1513. ***Parent loans:*** $9482 (100% need-based). ***Programs:*** FFEL (Subsidized and Unsubsidized Stafford, PLUS), Perkins.

WORK-STUDY ***Federal work-study:*** Total amount: $2,400,315; jobs available. ***State or other work-study/employment:*** Total amount: $502,000 (100% need-based). Part-time jobs available.

APPLYING FOR FINANCIAL AID ***Required financial aid form:*** FAFSA. ***Financial aid deadline (priority):*** 3/15. ***Notification date:*** 4/15.

CONTACT Bryan Erslan, Student Financial Aid Services, Berea College, CPO 2172, Berea, KY 40404, 859-985-3313 or toll-free 800-326-5948. *Fax:* 859-985-3914. *E-mail:* bryan_erslan@berea.edu.

BERKLEE COLLEGE OF MUSIC

Boston, MA

Tuition & fees: $30,650 **Average undergraduate aid package: $12,279**

ABOUT THE INSTITUTION Independent, coed. ***Awards:*** bachelor's degrees. 12 undergraduate majors. ***Total enrollment:*** 4,054. Undergraduates: 4,054. Freshmen: 634. Federal methodology is used as a basis for awarding need-based institutional aid.

UNDERGRADUATE EXPENSES for 2009–10 ***Application fee:*** $150. ***Comprehensive fee:*** $45,730 includes full-time tuition ($29,700), mandatory fees ($950), and room and board ($15,080). ***Part-time tuition:*** $1053 per credit hour. there is a one-time $2,950 charge for laptop purchase required of all entering students.

FRESHMAN FINANCIAL AID (Fall 2008, est.) 402 applied for aid; of those 85% were deemed to have need. 99% of freshmen with need received aid; of those 8% had need fully met. ***Average percent of need met:*** 26% (excluding resources awarded to replace EFC). ***Average financial aid package:*** $12,679 (excluding resources awarded to replace EFC). 14% of all full-time freshmen had no need and received non-need-based gift aid.

UNDERGRADUATE FINANCIAL AID (Fall 2008, est.) 1,764 applied for aid; of those 86% were deemed to have need. 99% of undergraduates with need received aid; of those 8% had need fully met. ***Average percent of need met:*** 27% (excluding resources awarded to replace EFC). ***Average financial aid package:*** $12,279 (excluding resources awarded to replace EFC). 24% of all full-time undergraduates had no need and received non-need-based gift aid.

GIFT AID (NEED-BASED) ***Total amount:*** $7,995,455 (44% federal, 3% state, 53% institutional). ***Receiving aid:*** Freshmen: 28% (168); all full-time undergraduates: 19% (670). ***Average award:*** Freshmen: $6826; Undergraduates: $5888. ***Scholarships, grants, and awards:*** Federal Pell, FSEOG, state, private, college/university gift aid from institutional funds, Academic Competitiveness Grant.

GIFT AID (NON-NEED-BASED) ***Total amount:*** $21,496,368 (95% institutional, 5% external sources). ***Receiving aid:*** Freshmen: 31% (187). Undergraduates: 22% (757). ***Average award:*** Freshmen: $11,638. Undergraduates: $9326. ***Scholarships, grants, and awards by category:*** *Academic interests/achievement:* education, engineering/technologies. *Creative arts/performance:* music. *Special characteristics:* children of faculty/staff.

LOANS ***Student loans:*** $35,232,874 (29% need-based, 71% non-need-based). ***Average need-based loan:*** Freshmen: $4068. Undergraduates: $4743. ***Parent loans:*** $12,056,250 (100% non-need-based). ***Programs:*** Federal Direct (Subsidized and Unsubsidized Stafford, PLUS), Perkins, state.

WORK-STUDY ***Federal work-study:*** Total amount: $400,183; jobs available. ***State or other work-study/employment:*** Total amount: $2,602,629 (100% non-need-based). Part-time jobs available.

APPLYING FOR FINANCIAL AID ***Required financial aid form:*** FAFSA. ***Financial aid deadline:*** 5/1 (priority: 5/1). ***Notification date:*** Continuous. Students must reply within 2 weeks of notification.

CONTACT Julie Poorman, Director of Financial Aid, Berklee College of Music, 1140 Boylston Street, Boston, MA 02215-3693, 617-747-2274 or toll-free 800-BERKLEE. *Fax:* 617-747-2073. *E-mail:* jpoorman@berklee.edu.

BERNARD M. BARUCH COLLEGE OF THE CITY UNIVERSITY OF NEW YORK

New York, NY

Tuition & fees (NY res): $4320 **Average undergraduate aid package: $5360**

ABOUT THE INSTITUTION State and locally supported, coed. ***Awards:*** bachelor's and master's degrees. 33 undergraduate majors. ***Total enrollment:*** 16,321. Undergraduates: 12,731. Freshmen: 1,512. Federal methodology is used as a basis for awarding need-based institutional aid.

UNDERGRADUATE EXPENSES for 2008–09 ***Application fee:*** $65. ***Tuition, state resident:*** full-time $4000; part-time $170 per credit. ***Tuition, nonresident:*** full-time $8640; part-time $360 per credit. ***Required fees:*** full-time $320; $160 per term.

FRESHMAN FINANCIAL AID (Fall 2008, est.) 1,562 applied for aid; of those 81% were deemed to have need. 86% of freshmen with need received aid; of those 28% had need fully met. ***Average percent of need met:*** 69% (excluding resources awarded to replace EFC). ***Average financial aid package:*** $6005 (excluding resources awarded to replace EFC). 2% of all full-time freshmen had no need and received non-need-based gift aid.

UNDERGRADUATE FINANCIAL AID (Fall 2008, est.) 8,201 applied for aid; of those 89% were deemed to have need. 91% of undergraduates with need received aid; of those 12% had need fully met. ***Average percent of need met:*** 61% (excluding resources awarded to replace EFC). ***Average financial aid package:*** $5360 (excluding resources awarded to replace EFC). 1% of all full-time undergraduates had no need and received non-need-based gift aid.

GIFT AID (NEED-BASED) ***Total amount:*** $32,179,093 (55% federal, 45% state). ***Receiving aid:*** Freshmen: 40% (792); all full-time undergraduates: 56% (5,714). ***Average award:*** Freshmen: $5005; Undergraduates: $4230. ***Scholarships, grants, and awards:*** Federal Pell, FSEOG, state, college/university gift aid from institutional funds.

GIFT AID (NON-NEED-BASED) ***Total amount:*** $4,499,974 (32% institutional, 68% external sources). ***Receiving aid:*** Freshmen: 53% (1,042). Undergraduates: 17% (1,697). ***Average award:*** Freshmen: $4600. Undergraduates: $4000. ***Scholarships, grants, and awards by category:*** *Academic interests/achievement:* 280 awards ($1,421,149 total): general academic interests/achievements.

LOANS ***Student loans:*** $14,519,516 (52% need-based, 48% non-need-based). 21% of past graduating class borrowed through all loan programs. *Average indebtedness per student:* $12,602. ***Average need-based loan:*** Freshmen: $2970. Undergraduates: $4760. ***Parent loans:*** $94,671 (100% non-need-based). ***Programs:*** Federal Direct (Subsidized and Unsubsidized Stafford, PLUS), Perkins.

WORK-STUDY ***Federal work-study:*** Total amount: $323,180; 550 jobs averaging $720. ***State or other work-study/employment:*** Total amount: $264,667 (100% need-based). 707 part-time jobs averaging $970.

APPLYING FOR FINANCIAL AID ***Required financial aid forms:*** FAFSA, state aid form. ***Financial aid deadline (priority):*** 3/15. ***Notification date:*** Continuous beginning 4/21. Students must reply by 6/1 or within 6 weeks of notification.

CONTACT Financial Aid Office, Bernard M. Baruch College of the City University of New York, 151 East 25th Street, Room 720, New York, NY 10010-5585, 646-312-1360. *Fax:* 646-312-1361. *E-mail:* financial_aid@baruch.cuny.edu.

BERRY COLLEGE

Mount Berry, GA

Tuition & fees: $22,370 **Average undergraduate aid package: $18,046**

ABOUT THE INSTITUTION Independent interdenominational, coed. ***Awards:*** bachelor's and master's degrees and post-master's certificates. 35 undergraduate majors. ***Total enrollment:*** 1,795. Undergraduates: 1,686. Freshmen: 448. Federal methodology is used as a basis for awarding need-based institutional aid.

UNDERGRADUATE EXPENSES for 2008–09 ***Application fee:*** $50. ***Comprehensive fee:*** $30,348 includes full-time tuition ($22,370) and room and board ($7978). ***College room only:*** $4438. Room and board charges vary according to board plan and housing facility. ***Part-time tuition:*** $739 per credit hour. ***Payment plan:*** Installment.

FRESHMAN FINANCIAL AID (Fall 2008, est.) 388 applied for aid; of those 74% were deemed to have need. 100% of freshmen with need received aid; of those 25% had need fully met. ***Average percent of need met:*** 84% (excluding resources awarded to replace EFC). ***Average financial aid package:*** $18,342 (excluding resources awarded to replace EFC). 36% of all full-time freshmen had no need and received non-need-based gift aid.

UNDERGRADUATE FINANCIAL AID (Fall 2008, est.) 1,319 applied for aid; of those 78% were deemed to have need. 100% of undergraduates with need received aid; of those 28% had need fully met. ***Average percent of need met:*** 84% (excluding resources awarded to replace EFC). ***Average financial aid package:*** $18,046 (excluding resources awarded to replace EFC). 35% of all full-time undergraduates had no need and received non-need-based gift aid.

GIFT AID (NEED-BASED) ***Total amount:*** $13,636,395 (11% federal, 19% state, 67% institutional, 3% external sources). ***Receiving aid:*** Freshmen: 64% (288); all full-time undergraduates: 62% (1,026). ***Average award:*** Freshmen: $15,088; Undergraduates: $13,854. ***Scholarships, grants, and awards:*** Federal Pell, FSEOG, state, private, college/university gift aid from institutional funds.

GIFT AID (NON-NEED-BASED) ***Total amount:*** $7,782,267 (29% state, 66% institutional, 5% external sources). ***Receiving aid:*** Freshmen: 14% (63). Undergraduates: 13% (212). ***Average award:*** Freshmen: $8874. Undergraduates: $7936. ***Scholarships, grants, and awards by category:*** *Academic interests/achievement:* agriculture, education, English, general academic interests/achievements, humanities, religion/biblical studies. *Creative arts/performance:* art/fine arts, debating, journalism/publications, music, theater/drama. *Special achievements/activities:* community service, religious involvement. *Special characteristics:* adult students, children of faculty/staff, ethnic background, local/state students, members of minority groups. ***Tuition waivers:*** Full or partial for employees or children of employees, senior citizens.

LOANS ***Student loans:*** $6,308,846 (64% need-based, 36% non-need-based). 76% of past graduating class borrowed through all loan programs. *Average indebtedness per student:* $15,808. ***Average need-based loan:*** Freshmen: $2928. Undergraduates: $3657. ***Parent loans:*** $5,324,079 (30% need-based, 70% non-need-based). ***Programs:*** FFEL (Subsidized and Unsubsidized Stafford, PLUS), Perkins, college/university.

WORK-STUDY ***Federal work-study:*** Total amount: $602,686; jobs available. ***State or other work-study/employment:*** Total amount: $5,062,179 (17% need-based, 83% non-need-based). Part-time jobs available.

ATHLETIC AWARDS Total amount: $2,109,508 (26% need-based, 74% non-need-based).

APPLYING FOR FINANCIAL AID ***Required financial aid forms:*** FAFSA, institution's own form, state aid form. ***Financial aid deadline (priority):*** 4/1. ***Notification date:*** Continuous.

CONTACT Susan Little, Director of Financial Aid, Berry College, 2277 Martha Berry Highway, NW, Mount Berry, GA 30149-5007, 706-236-1714 or toll-free 800-237-7942. *Fax:* 706-290-2160. *E-mail:* slittle@berry.edu.

BETHANY COLLEGE

Lindsborg, KS

Tuition & fees: $18,124 **Average undergraduate aid package: $20,734**

ABOUT THE INSTITUTION Independent Lutheran, coed. ***Awards:*** bachelor's degrees. 41 undergraduate majors. ***Total enrollment:*** 587. Undergraduates: 587. Freshmen: 178. Federal methodology is used as a basis for awarding need-based institutional aid.

UNDERGRADUATE EXPENSES for 2008–09 ***Application fee:*** $20. ***Comprehensive fee:*** $23,774 includes full-time tuition ($17,824), mandatory fees ($300), and room and board ($5650). ***College room only:*** $3075. ***Part-time tuition:*** $330 per credit hour. ***Payment plan:*** Installment.

FRESHMAN FINANCIAL AID (Fall 2008, est.) 175 applied for aid; of those 83% were deemed to have need. 100% of freshmen with need received aid; of those 48% had need fully met. ***Average percent of need met:*** 89% (excluding resources awarded to replace EFC). ***Average financial aid package:*** $20,938 (excluding resources awarded to replace EFC). 6% of all full-time freshmen had no need and received non-need-based gift aid.

UNDERGRADUATE FINANCIAL AID (Fall 2008, est.) 545 applied for aid; of those 83% were deemed to have need. 100% of undergraduates with need received aid; of those 46% had need fully met. ***Average percent of need met:*** 89% (excluding resources awarded to replace EFC). ***Average financial aid package:*** $20,734 (excluding resources awarded to replace EFC). 5% of all full-time undergraduates had no need and received non-need-based gift aid.

GIFT AID (NEED-BASED) ***Total amount:*** $2,621,708 (36% federal, 18% state, 46% institutional). ***Receiving aid:*** Freshmen: 70% (123); all full-time undergraduates: 68% (377). ***Average award:*** Freshmen: $7254; Undergraduates: $6941. ***Scholarships, grants, and awards:*** Federal Pell, FSEOG, state, private, college/university gift aid from institutional funds, Academic Competitiveness Grant, National Smart Grant, TEACH Grant.

GIFT AID (NON-NEED-BASED) ***Total amount:*** $988,332 (88% institutional, 12% external sources). ***Receiving aid:*** Freshmen: 33% (58). Undergraduates: 26% (143). ***Average award:*** Freshmen: $4580. Undergraduates: $6217. ***Scholarships, grants, and awards by category:*** *Academic interests/achievement:* 377 awards ($2,394,463 total): general academic interests/achievements. *Creative arts/performance:* 111 awards ($340,910 total): art/fine arts, music, theater/drama. *Special achievements/activities:* 16 awards ($39,450 total): cheerleading/drum major. *Special characteristics:* 108 awards ($214,461 total): children and siblings of alumni, international students, relatives of clergy, religious affiliation. ***Tuition waivers:*** Full or partial for employees or children of employees.

LOANS ***Student loans:*** $3,267,418 (52% need-based, 48% non-need-based). 82% of past graduating class borrowed through all loan programs. *Average indebtedness per student:* $17,161. ***Average need-based loan:*** Freshmen: $4304. Undergraduates: $5060. ***Parent loans:*** $346,091 (100% non-need-based). ***Programs:*** FFEL (Subsidized and Unsubsidized Stafford, PLUS), Perkins, college/university.

WORK-STUDY ***Federal work-study:*** Total amount: $175,000; 115 jobs averaging $1500. ***State or other work-study/employment:*** Part-time jobs available.

ATHLETIC AWARDS Total amount: $1,234,327 (35% need-based, 65% non-need-based).

APPLYING FOR FINANCIAL AID ***Required financial aid form:*** FAFSA. ***Financial aid deadline:*** Continuous. ***Notification date:*** Continuous beginning 2/1. Students must reply within 3 weeks of notification.

CONTACT Ms. Brenda L. Meagher, Director of Financial Aid, Bethany College, 335 East Swensson, Lindsborg, KS 67456-1897, 785-227-3311 Ext. 8248 or toll-free 800-826-2281. *Fax:* 785-227-2004. *E-mail:* meagherb@bethanylb.edu.

BETHANY COLLEGE

Bethany, WV

ABOUT THE INSTITUTION Independent religious, coed. ***Awards:*** bachelor's degrees. 33 undergraduate majors. ***Total enrollment:*** 825. Undergraduates: 825. Freshmen: 263.

GIFT AID (NEED-BASED) ***Scholarships, grants, and awards:*** Federal Pell, FSEOG, state, private, college/university gift aid from institutional funds.

GIFT AID (NON-NEED-BASED) ***Scholarships, grants, and awards by category:*** *Academic interests/achievement:* general academic interests/achievements. *Creative arts/performance:* music. *Special achievements/activities:* leadership. *Special characteristics:* children and siblings of alumni, children of faculty/staff, international students, relatives of clergy, religious affiliation.

LOANS ***Programs:*** FFEL (Subsidized and Unsubsidized Stafford, PLUS), Perkins, alternative loans.

WORK-STUDY ***Federal work-study:*** Total amount: $353,586; jobs available. ***State or other work-study/employment:*** Total amount: $270,000 (100% non-need-based). Part-time jobs available.

APPLYING FOR FINANCIAL AID ***Required financial aid form:*** FAFSA.

CONTACT Sandra Neel, Financial Aid Office, Bethany College, P.O. Box 488, Bethany, WV 26032, 304-829-7141 or toll-free 800-922-7611 (out-of-state). *Fax:* 304-829-7796. *E-mail:* sneel@bethanywv.edu.

BETHANY LUTHERAN COLLEGE

Mankato, MN

Tuition & fees: $18,710 **Average undergraduate aid package: $14,779**

ABOUT THE INSTITUTION Independent Lutheran, coed. ***Awards:*** bachelor's degrees. 19 undergraduate majors. ***Total enrollment:*** 615. Undergraduates: 615. Freshmen: 181. Federal methodology is used as a basis for awarding need-based institutional aid.

UNDERGRADUATE EXPENSES for 2008–09 ***One-time required fee:*** $130. ***Comprehensive fee:*** $24,510 includes full-time tuition ($18,450), mandatory fees ($260), and room and board ($5800). ***College room only:*** $2190. Room and board charges vary according to board plan and housing facility. ***Part-time tuition:*** $780 per credit hour. ***Part-time fees:*** $130 per term. ***Payment plan:*** Installment.

FRESHMAN FINANCIAL AID (Fall 2007) 160 applied for aid; of those 91% were deemed to have need. 100% of freshmen with need received aid; of those 34% had need fully met. ***Average percent of need met:*** 90% (excluding resources awarded to replace EFC). ***Average financial aid package:*** $14,910 (excluding resources awarded to replace EFC). 14% of all full-time freshmen had no need and received non-need-based gift aid.

UNDERGRADUATE FINANCIAL AID (Fall 2007) 512 applied for aid; of those 91% were deemed to have need. 100% of undergraduates with need received aid; of those 37% had need fully met. ***Average percent of need met:*** 88% (excluding resources awarded to replace EFC). ***Average financial aid package:*** $14,779 (excluding resources awarded to replace EFC). 16% of all full-time undergraduates had no need and received non-need-based gift aid.

GIFT AID (NEED-BASED) ***Total amount:*** $4,524,660 (16% federal, 17% state, 64% institutional, 3% external sources). ***Receiving aid:*** Freshmen: 83% (145); all full-time undergraduates: 81% (467). ***Average award:*** Freshmen: $11,520; Undergraduates: $10,612. ***Scholarships, grants, and awards:*** Federal Pell, FSEOG, state, private, college/university gift aid from institutional funds.

GIFT AID (NON-NEED-BASED) ***Total amount:*** $510,123 (1% state, 92% institutional, 7% external sources). ***Receiving aid:*** Freshmen: 9% (15). Undergraduates: 8% (47). ***Average award:*** Freshmen: $7057. Undergraduates: $8680. ***Scholarships, grants, and awards by category:*** *Creative arts/performance:* 73 awards ($144,000 total): art/fine arts, debating, journalism/publications, music, theater/drama. *Special characteristics:* 30 awards ($426,877 total): children of faculty/staff. ***Tuition waivers:*** Full or partial for employees or children of employees. ***ROTC:*** Army cooperative.

LOANS ***Student loans:*** $3,129,029 (65% need-based, 35% non-need-based). 87% of past graduating class borrowed through all loan programs. *Average indebtedness per student:* $21,876. ***Average need-based loan:*** Freshmen: $3619. Undergraduates: $4540. ***Parent loans:*** $541,562 (15% need-based, 85% non-need-based). ***Programs:*** Federal Direct (Subsidized and Unsubsidized Stafford, PLUS), Perkins, state, alternative loans.

WORK-STUDY ***Federal work-study:*** Total amount: $36,807; 40 jobs averaging $920. ***State or other work-study/employment:*** Total amount: $233,918 (47% need-based, 53% non-need-based). 284 part-time jobs averaging $824.

APPLYING FOR FINANCIAL AID ***Required financial aid forms:*** FAFSA, institution's own form, business/farm supplement, federal income tax form(s), W-2 forms. ***Financial aid deadline (priority):*** 4/15. ***Notification date:*** Continuous. Students must reply within 4 weeks of notification.

CONTACT Financial Aid Office, Bethany Lutheran College, 700 Luther Drive, Mankato, MN 56001-6163, 507-344-7328 or toll-free 800-944-3066 Ext. 331. *Fax:* 507-344-7376. *E-mail:* finaid@blc.edu.

BETHANY UNIVERSITY

Scotts Valley, CA

CONTACT Deborah Snow, Financial Aid Director, Bethany University, 800 Bethany Drive, Scotts Valley, CA 95066-2820, 831-438-3800 Ext. 1477 or toll-free 800-843-9410. *Fax:* 831-461-1533.

BETH BENJAMIN ACADEMY OF CONNECTICUT

Stamford, CT

CONTACT Financial Aid Office, Beth Benjamin Academy of Connecticut, 132 Prospect Street, Stamford, CT 06901-1202, 203-325-4351.

BETHEL COLLEGE

Mishawaka, IN

Tuition & fees: $21,296 **Average undergraduate aid package: $15,174**

ABOUT THE INSTITUTION Independent religious, coed. ***Awards:*** associate, bachelor's, and master's degrees and post-bachelor's certificates. 60 undergraduate majors. ***Total enrollment:*** 2,075. Undergraduates: 1,862. Freshmen: 277. Federal methodology is used as a basis for awarding need-based institutional aid.

UNDERGRADUATE EXPENSES for 2009–10 ***Application fee:*** $25. ***One-time required fee:*** $600. ***Comprehensive fee:*** $27,232 includes full-time tuition ($21,296) and room and board ($5936). ***College room only:*** $3100. ***Part-time tuition:*** $480 per credit hour.

FRESHMAN FINANCIAL AID (Fall 2008, est.) 205 applied for aid; of those 83% were deemed to have need. 82% of freshmen with need received aid; of those 6% had need fully met. ***Average percent of need met:*** 55% (excluding resources awarded to replace EFC). ***Average financial aid package:*** $17,108 (excluding resources awarded to replace EFC). 3% of all full-time freshmen had no need and received non-need-based gift aid.

UNDERGRADUATE FINANCIAL AID (Fall 2008, est.) 948 applied for aid; of those 88% were deemed to have need. 100% of undergraduates with need received aid; of those 7% had need fully met. ***Average percent of need met:*** 50% (excluding resources awarded to replace EFC). ***Average financial aid package:*** $15,174 (excluding resources awarded to replace EFC). 5% of all full-time undergraduates had no need and received non-need-based gift aid.

GIFT AID (NEED-BASED) ***Total amount:*** $6,144,515 (48% federal, 52% state). ***Receiving aid:*** Freshmen: 56% (135); all full-time undergraduates: 50% (567). ***Average award:*** Freshmen: $7597; Undergraduates: $7757. ***Scholarships, grants, and awards:*** Federal Pell, FSEOG, state, private, college/university gift aid from institutional funds, Federal Nursing.

GIFT AID (NON-NEED-BASED) ***Total amount:*** $7,323,910 (89% institutional, 11% external sources). ***Average award:*** Freshmen: $6580. Undergraduates: $7417. ***Scholarships, grants, and awards by category:*** *Academic interests/achievement:* 629 awards ($1,854,126 total): biological sciences, business, communication, computer science, education, English, general academic interests/achievements, health fields, mathematics, physical sciences, religion/biblical studies, social sciences. *Creative arts/performance:* 87 awards ($173,500 total): art/fine arts, journalism/publications, music, theater/drama. *Special achievements/activities:* 263 awards ($424,276 total): cheerleading/drum major, general special achievements/activities, leadership, religious involvement. *Special characteristics:* 536 awards ($1,963,129 total): adult students, children of faculty/staff, international students, members of minority groups, relatives of clergy, religious affiliation, siblings of current students, spouses of current students. ***ROTC:*** Army cooperative, Air Force cooperative.

LOANS ***Student loans:*** $8,766,256 (96% need-based, 4% non-need-based). 83% of past graduating class borrowed through all loan programs. *Average indebtedness per student:* $16,337. ***Average need-based loan:*** Freshmen: $3292. Undergraduates: $4149. ***Parent loans:*** $1,282,510 (100% non-need-based). ***Programs:*** FFEL (Subsidized and Unsubsidized Stafford, PLUS), Perkins, college/university, GATE Loans.

WORK-STUDY ***Federal work-study:*** Total amount: $1,108,751; 176 jobs averaging $2000. ***State or other work-study/employment:*** Total amount: $248,543 (100% non-need-based). 200 part-time jobs averaging $2000.

ATHLETIC AWARDS Total amount: $1,513,470 (100% non-need-based).

APPLYING FOR FINANCIAL AID ***Required financial aid forms:*** FAFSA, institution's own form. ***Financial aid deadline (priority):*** 3/1. ***Notification date:*** Continuous beginning 4/1.

CONTACT Mr. Guy A. Fisher, Director of Financial Aid, Bethel College, 1001 West McKinley Avenue, Mishawaka, IN 46545-5591, 574-257-3316 or toll-free 800-422-4101. *Fax:* 574-257-3326. *E-mail:* fisherg@bethelcollege.edu.

BETHEL COLLEGE

North Newton, KS

Tuition & fees: $18,900 **Average undergraduate aid package: $20,941**

ABOUT THE INSTITUTION Independent religious, coed. ***Awards:*** bachelor's degrees. 21 undergraduate majors. ***Total enrollment:*** 500. Undergraduates: 500. Freshmen: 119. Federal methodology is used as a basis for awarding need-based institutional aid.

UNDERGRADUATE EXPENSES for 2008–09 ***Application fee:*** $20. ***Comprehensive fee:*** $24,950 includes full-time tuition ($18,900) and room and board ($6050). ***College room only:*** $3050. Full-time tuition and fees vary according to course load. Room and board charges vary according to board plan and housing facility. ***Part-time tuition:*** $680 per credit hour. Part-time tuition and fees vary according to course load. ***Payment plans:*** Installment, deferred payment.

FRESHMAN FINANCIAL AID (Fall 2008, est.) 108 applied for aid; of those 88% were deemed to have need. 100% of freshmen with need received aid; of those 46% had need fully met. ***Average percent of need met:*** 95% (excluding resources awarded to replace EFC). ***Average financial aid package:*** $20,858 (excluding resources awarded to replace EFC). 19% of all full-time freshmen had no need and received non-need-based gift aid.

UNDERGRADUATE FINANCIAL AID (Fall 2008, est.) 399 applied for aid; of those 91% were deemed to have need. 100% of undergraduates with need received aid; of those 45% had need fully met. ***Average percent of need met:*** 94% (excluding resources awarded to replace EFC). ***Average financial aid package:*** $20,941 (excluding resources awarded to replace EFC). 21% of all full-time undergraduates had no need and received non-need-based gift aid.

GIFT AID (NEED-BASED) ***Total amount:*** $1,210,228 (58% federal, 41% state, 1% institutional). ***Receiving aid:*** Freshmen: 64% (75); all full-time undergraduates: 55% (263). ***Average award:*** Freshmen: $4700; Undergraduates: $4928. ***Scholarships, grants, and awards:*** Federal Pell, FSEOG, state, college/university gift aid from institutional funds.

GIFT AID (NON-NEED-BASED) ***Total amount:*** $2,783,406 (95% institutional, 5% external sources). ***Receiving aid:*** Freshmen: 79% (93). Undergraduates: 72% (343). ***Average award:*** Freshmen: $10,219. Undergraduates: $8890. ***Scholarships, grants, and awards by category:*** *Academic interests/achievement:* 320 awards ($1,674,850 total): general academic interests/achievements. *Creative arts/performance:* 163 awards ($480,788 total): art/fine arts, debating, music, theater/drama. *Special characteristics:* $1,911,278 total: children and siblings of alumni, children of current students, children of faculty/staff, ethnic background, general special characteristics, international students, local/state students, previous college experience, relatives of clergy, religious affiliation, siblings of current students, spouses of current students. ***Tuition waivers:*** Full or partial for children of alumni, employees or children of employees, senior citizens.

LOANS ***Student loans:*** $3,139,877 (60% need-based, 40% non-need-based). 77% of past graduating class borrowed through all loan programs. *Average indebtedness per student:* $24,284. ***Average need-based loan:*** Freshmen: $5079. Undergraduates: $6899. ***Parent loans:*** $442,059 (100% non-need-based). ***Programs:*** Federal Direct (Subsidized and Unsubsidized Stafford, PLUS), FFEL (Subsidized and Unsubsidized Stafford, PLUS), Perkins.

WORK-STUDY ***Federal work-study:*** Total amount: $372,853; 122 jobs averaging $1033. ***State or other work-study/employment:*** 217 part-time jobs averaging $776.

ATHLETIC AWARDS Total amount: $666,938 (100% non-need-based).

APPLYING FOR FINANCIAL AID ***Required financial aid form:*** FAFSA. ***Financial aid deadline (priority):*** 4/1. ***Notification date:*** Continuous. Students must reply by 5/1 or within 2 weeks of notification.

CONTACT Mr. Tony Graber, Financial Aid Director, Bethel College, 300 East 27th Street, North Newton, KS 67117, 316-284-5232 or toll-free 800-522-1887 Ext. 230. *Fax:* 316-284-5845. *E-mail:* tgraber@bethelks.edu.

BETHEL COLLEGE

McKenzie, TN

CONTACT Laura Bateman, Office of Financial Aid, Bethel College, 325 Cherry Avenue, McKenzie, TN 38201, 901-352-4007. *Fax:* 901-352-4069.

BETHEL UNIVERSITY

St. Paul, MN

Tuition & fees: $25,860 **Average undergraduate aid package: $16,511**

ABOUT THE INSTITUTION Independent religious, coed. ***Awards:*** associate, bachelor's, master's, and doctoral degrees and post-bachelor's and post-master's certificates. 58 undergraduate majors. ***Total enrollment:*** 4,335. Undergraduates: 3,392. Freshmen: 642. Federal methodology is used as a basis for awarding need-based institutional aid.

UNDERGRADUATE EXPENSES for 2008–09 ***Comprehensive fee:*** $33,480 includes full-time tuition ($25,750), mandatory fees ($110), and room and board ($7620). ***College room only:*** $4540. ***Part-time tuition:*** $1035 per credit hour.

FRESHMAN FINANCIAL AID (Fall 2007) 460 applied for aid; of those 84% were deemed to have need. 100% of freshmen with need received aid; of those 16% had need fully met. ***Average percent of need met:*** 75% (excluding resources awarded to replace EFC). ***Average financial aid package:*** $17,066 (excluding resources awarded to replace EFC). 27% of all full-time freshmen had no need and received non-need-based gift aid.

UNDERGRADUATE FINANCIAL AID (Fall 2007) 2,084 applied for aid; of those 86% were deemed to have need. 100% of undergraduates with need received aid; of those 18% had need fully met. ***Average percent of need met:*** 73% (excluding resources awarded to replace EFC). ***Average financial aid package:*** $16,511 (excluding resources awarded to replace EFC). 23% of all full-time undergraduates had no need and received non-need-based gift aid.

GIFT AID (NEED-BASED) ***Total amount:*** $18,591,994 (11% federal, 13% state, 72% institutional, 4% external sources). ***Receiving aid:*** Freshmen: 68% (387); all full-time undergraduates: 68% (1,780). ***Average award:*** Freshmen: $12,159; Undergraduates: $11,120. ***Scholarships, grants, and awards:*** Federal Pell, FSEOG, state, private, college/university gift aid from institutional funds.

GIFT AID (NON-NEED-BASED) ***Total amount:*** $3,542,366 (4% federal, 87% institutional, 9% external sources). ***Receiving aid:*** Freshmen: 6% (34). Undergraduates: 5% (138). ***Average award:*** Freshmen: $5119. Undergraduates: $4578. ***Scholarships, grants, and awards by category:*** *Academic interests/achievement:* 1,395 awards ($5,492,000 total): general academic interests/achievements. *Creative arts/performance:* 106 awards ($200,000 total): art/fine arts, debating, music, theater/drama. *Special achievements/activities:* 1,745 awards ($2,405,000 total): community service, junior miss, leadership, religious involvement. *Special characteristics:* 950 awards ($3,718,000 total): children and siblings of alumni, children of faculty/staff, ethnic background, international students, members of minority groups, out-of-state students, relatives of clergy, religious affiliation. ***ROTC:*** Army cooperative, Air Force cooperative.

LOANS ***Student loans:*** $16,890,916 (69% need-based, 31% non-need-based). 75% of past graduating class borrowed through all loan programs. *Average indebtedness per student:* $30,747. ***Average need-based loan:*** Freshmen: $4020. Undergraduates: $4380. ***Parent loans:*** $5,167,932 (38% need-based, 62% non-need-based). ***Programs:*** Federal Direct (Subsidized and Unsubsidized Stafford, PLUS), Perkins, state, alternative loans.

WORK-STUDY ***Federal work-study:*** Total amount: $409,315; 278 jobs averaging $2200. ***State or other work-study/employment:*** Total amount: $2,352,701 (28% need-based, 72% non-need-based). 1,500 part-time jobs averaging $2200.

APPLYING FOR FINANCIAL AID ***Required financial aid forms:*** FAFSA, institution's own form. ***Financial aid deadline (priority):*** 4/15. ***Notification date:*** Continuous. Students must reply by 5/1 or within 3 weeks of notification.

CONTACT Mr. Jeffrey D. Olson, Director of Financial Aid, Bethel University, 3900 Bethel Drive, St. Paul, MN 55112-6999, 651-638-6241 or toll-free 800-255-8706 Ext. 6242. *Fax:* 651-635-1491. *E-mail:* jeff-olson@bethel.edu.

BETHESDA CHRISTIAN UNIVERSITY

Anaheim, CA

CONTACT Myongha Prince, Financial Aid Administrator, Bethesda Christian University, 730 North Euclid Street, Anaheim, CA 92801, 714-517-1945 Ext. 130. *Fax:* 714-517-1948. *E-mail:* financialaid@bcu.edu.

BETH HAMEDRASH SHAAREI YOSHER INSTITUTE

Brooklyn, NY

CONTACT Financial Aid Office, Beth HaMedrash Shaarei Yosher Institute, 4102-10 16th Avenue, Brooklyn, NY 11204, 718-854-2290.

BETH HATALMUD RABBINICAL COLLEGE

Brooklyn, NY

CONTACT Financial Aid Office, Beth Hatalmud Rabbinical College, 2127 82nd Street, Brooklyn, NY 11204, 718-259-2525.

BETH MEDRASH GOVOHA

Lakewood, NJ

CONTACT Financial Aid Office, Beth Medrash Govoha, 617 Sixth Street, Lakewood, NJ 08701-2797, 732-367-1060.

BETHUNE-COOKMAN UNIVERSITY

Daytona Beach, FL

CONTACT Mr. Joseph Coleman, Director of Financial Aid, Bethune-Cookman University, 640 Mary McLeod Bethune Boulevard, Daytona Beach, FL 32114-3099, 386-481-2626 or toll-free 800-448-0228. *Fax:* 386-481-2621. *E-mail:* colemanj@cookman.edu.

BEULAH HEIGHTS UNIVERSITY

Atlanta, GA

ABOUT THE INSTITUTION Independent Pentecostal, coed. ***Awards:*** associate, bachelor's, and master's degrees. 2 undergraduate majors. ***Total enrollment:*** 674. Undergraduates: 577. Freshmen: 66.

GIFT AID (NEED-BASED) ***Scholarships, grants, and awards:*** Federal Pell, FSEOG, private, college/university gift aid from institutional funds.

GIFT AID (NON-NEED-BASED) ***Scholarships, grants, and awards by category:*** *Special characteristics:* children of faculty/staff, general special characteristics, international students, married students, religious affiliation, spouses of current students.

LOANS ***Programs:*** FFEL (Subsidized and Unsubsidized Stafford, PLUS).

APPLYING FOR FINANCIAL AID ***Required financial aid forms:*** FAFSA, institution's own form.

CONTACT Ms. Patricia Banks, Financial Aid Director, Beulah Heights University, 892 Berne Street, SE, Atlanta, GA 30316, 404-627-2681 or toll-free 888-777-BHBC. *Fax:* 404-627-0702. *E-mail:* pat.banks@beulah.org.

BIOLA UNIVERSITY

La Mirada, CA

Tuition & fees: $26,579 **Average undergraduate aid package: $30,431**

ABOUT THE INSTITUTION Independent interdenominational, coed. ***Awards:*** bachelor's, master's, doctoral, and first professional degrees and post-master's certificates. 32 undergraduate majors. ***Total enrollment:*** 5,893. Undergraduates: 4,002. Freshmen: 838. Federal methodology is used as a basis for awarding need-based institutional aid.

UNDERGRADUATE EXPENSES for 2008–09 ***Application fee:*** $45. ***Comprehensive fee:*** $34,699 includes full-time tuition ($26,424), mandatory fees ($155), and room and board ($8120). ***College room only:*** $4420. Room and board charges vary according to board plan and housing facility. ***Part-time tuition:*** $1101 per unit. Part-time tuition and fees vary according to course load. ***Payment plan:*** Installment.

FRESHMAN FINANCIAL AID (Fall 2008, est.) 669 applied for aid; of those 81% were deemed to have need. 100% of freshmen with need received aid; of those 100% had need fully met. ***Average percent of need met:*** 73% (excluding resources awarded to replace EFC). ***Average financial aid package:*** $32,072 (excluding resources awarded to replace EFC). 18% of all full-time freshmen had no need and received non-need-based gift aid.

UNDERGRADUATE FINANCIAL AID (Fall 2008, est.) 2,638 applied for aid; of those 86% were deemed to have need. 100% of undergraduates with need received aid; of those 100% had need fully met. ***Average percent of need met:*** 68% (excluding resources awarded to replace EFC). ***Average financial aid package:*** $30,431 (excluding resources awarded to replace EFC). 12% of all full-time undergraduates had no need and received non-need-based gift aid.

GIFT AID (NEED-BASED) ***Total amount:*** $27,637,561 (13% federal, 23% state, 64% institutional). ***Receiving aid:*** Freshmen: 55% (439); all full-time undergraduates: 53% (1,865). ***Average award:*** Freshmen: $13,425; Undergraduates: $11,980. ***Scholarships, grants, and awards:*** Federal Pell, FSEOG, state, private, college/university gift aid from institutional funds.

GIFT AID (NON-NEED-BASED) ***Total amount:*** $11,510,081 (1% state, 83% institutional, 16% external sources). ***Receiving aid:*** Freshmen: 55% (438). Undergraduates: 49% (1,712). ***Average award:*** Freshmen: $11,502. Undergraduates: $14,417. ***Scholarships, grants, and awards by category:*** *Academic interests/achievement:* 1,305 awards ($7,100,074 total): biological sciences, communication, general academic interests/achievements. *Creative arts/performance:* 243 awards ($684,132 total): art/fine arts, cinema/film/broadcasting, journalism/publications, music, theater/drama. *Special achievements/activities:* 346 awards ($897,359 total): community service, leadership. *Special characteristics:* 692 awards ($3,605,910 total): adult students, children and siblings of alumni, children of faculty/staff, ethnic background, international students, relatives of clergy. ***Tuition waivers:*** Full or partial for employees or children of employees. ***ROTC:*** Army cooperative, Air Force cooperative.

LOANS ***Student loans:*** $38,287,915 (62% need-based, 38% non-need-based). 76% of past graduating class borrowed through all loan programs. *Average indebtedness per student:* $26,555. ***Average need-based loan:*** Freshmen: $1345. Undergraduates: $628. ***Parent loans:*** $7,248,083 (100% non-need-based). ***Programs:*** FFEL (Subsidized and Unsubsidized Stafford, PLUS), Perkins, Federal Nursing, college/university, alternative loans.

WORK-STUDY ***Federal work-study:*** Total amount: $1,352,283; 490 jobs averaging $1026.

ATHLETIC AWARDS Total amount: $1,522,821 (100% non-need-based).

APPLYING FOR FINANCIAL AID ***Required financial aid forms:*** FAFSA, state aid form. ***Financial aid deadline:*** Continuous. ***Notification date:*** Continuous beginning 3/1.

CONTACT Jonathan Choy, Financial Aid Office, Biola University, 13800 Biola Avenue, La Mirada, CA 90639-0001, 562-903-4742 or toll-free 800-652-4652. *Fax:* 562-906-4541. *E-mail:* finaid@biola.edu.

BIRMINGHAM-SOUTHERN COLLEGE

Birmingham, AL

Tuition & fees: $25,586 **Average undergraduate aid package: $29,857**

ABOUT THE INSTITUTION Independent Methodist, coed. ***Awards:*** bachelor's and master's degrees. 47 undergraduate majors. ***Total enrollment:*** 1,458. Undergraduates: 1,412. Freshmen: 451. Federal methodology is used as a basis for awarding need-based institutional aid.

UNDERGRADUATE EXPENSES for 2008–09 ***Application fee:*** $40. ***Comprehensive fee:*** $34,691 includes full-time tuition ($24,780), mandatory fees ($806), and room and board ($9105). ***College room only:*** $5245. ***Part-time tuition:*** $1033 per credit hour.

FRESHMAN FINANCIAL AID (Fall 2008, est.) 299 applied for aid; of those 79% were deemed to have need. 100% of freshmen with need received aid; of those 61% had need fully met. ***Average percent of need met:*** 99% (excluding resources awarded to replace EFC). ***Average financial aid package:*** $30,480 (excluding resources awarded to replace EFC). 43% of all full-time freshmen had no need and received non-need-based gift aid.

UNDERGRADUATE FINANCIAL AID (Fall 2008, est.) 801 applied for aid; of those 84% were deemed to have need. 100% of undergraduates with need received aid; of those 52% had need fully met. ***Average percent of need met:*** 94% (excluding resources awarded to replace EFC). ***Average financial aid package:*** $29,857 (excluding resources awarded to replace EFC). 44% of all full-time undergraduates had no need and received non-need-based gift aid.

GIFT AID (NEED-BASED) ***Total amount:*** $17,456,918 (5% federal, 1% state, 94% institutional). ***Receiving aid:*** Freshmen: 44% (195); all full-time undergraduates: 38% (523). ***Average award:*** Freshmen: $4847; Undergraduates: $4814. ***Scholarships, grants, and awards:*** Federal Pell, FSEOG, state, private, college/university gift aid from institutional funds, United Negro College Fund.

GIFT AID (NON-NEED-BASED) ***Total amount:*** $2,548,135 (2% federal, 15% state, 38% institutional, 45% external sources). ***Receiving aid:*** Freshmen: 53% (234). Undergraduates: 48% (659). ***Average award:*** Freshmen: $10,302. Undergraduates: $8590. ***Scholarships, grants, and awards by category:*** *Academic interests/achievement:* area/ethnic studies, biological sciences, business, communication, computer science, education, engineering/technologies, English, foreign languages, general academic interests/achievements, health fields, humanities, international studies, mathematics, physical sciences, premedicine, religion/biblical studies, social sciences. *Creative arts/performance:* art/fine arts, dance, music, performing arts, theater/drama. *Special achievements/activities:* junior miss, memberships, religious involvement. *Special characteristics:* adult students, children and siblings of alumni, children of faculty/staff, ethnic background, first-generation college students, previous college experience, relatives of clergy, religious affiliation. ***ROTC:*** Army cooperative, Air Force cooperative.

LOANS ***Student loans:*** $4,467,679 (51% need-based, 49% non-need-based). 79% of past graduating class borrowed through all loan programs. *Average indebtedness per student:* $27,798. ***Average need-based loan:*** Freshmen: $3395. Undergraduates: $3846. ***Parent loans:*** $1,702,504 (100% non-need-based). ***Programs:*** FFEL (Subsidized and Unsubsidized Stafford, PLUS), Perkins, college/university.

WORK-STUDY ***Federal work-study:*** Total amount: $516,357; 296 jobs averaging $1665. ***State or other work-study/employment:*** Total amount: $458,895 (100% non-need-based). 346 part-time jobs averaging $1342.

ATHLETIC AWARDS Total amount: $1,348,284 (100% non-need-based).

APPLYING FOR FINANCIAL AID ***Required financial aid forms:*** FAFSA, state aid form. ***Financial aid deadline (priority):*** 3/1. ***Notification date:*** Continuous beginning 3/1.

CONTACT Financial Aid Office, Birmingham-Southern College, 900 Arkadelphia Road, Birmingham, AL 35254, 205-226-4688 or toll-free 800-523-5793. *Fax:* 205-226-3082. *E-mail:* finaid@bsc.edu.

BIRTHINGWAY COLLEGE OF MIDWIFERY

Portland, OR

CONTACT Financial Aid Office, Birthingway College of Midwifery, 12113 SE Foster Road, Portland, OR 97299, 503-760-3131.

BLACKBURN COLLEGE

Carlinville, IL

CONTACT Mrs. Jane Kelsey, Financial Aid Administrator, Blackburn College, 700 College Avenue, Carlinville, IL 62626-1498, 217-854-3231 Ext. 4227 or toll-free 800-233-3550. *Fax:* 217-854-3731.

BLACK HILLS STATE UNIVERSITY

Spearfish, SD

Tuition & fees (SD res): $6590 **Average undergraduate aid package: $4241**

ABOUT THE INSTITUTION State-supported, coed. ***Awards:*** associate, bachelor's, and master's degrees and post-bachelor's and post-master's certificates. 47 undergraduate majors. ***Total enrollment:*** 4,017. Undergraduates: 3,687. Freshmen: 583. Federal methodology is used as a basis for awarding need-based institutional aid.

UNDERGRADUATE EXPENSES for 2009–10 ***Application fee:*** $20. ***Tuition, state resident:*** full-time $2934; part-time $91.70 per credit hour. ***Tuition, nonresident:*** full-time $9320; part-time $291.25 per credit hour. ***Required fees:*** full-time $3656; $115.84 per credit hour. ***College room and board:*** $5172; ***Room only:*** $2701.

UNDERGRADUATE FINANCIAL AID (Fall 2007) ***Average financial aid package:*** $4241 (excluding resources awarded to replace EFC).

GIFT AID (NEED-BASED) ***Total amount:*** $4,116,966 (95% federal, 5% external sources). ***Scholarships, grants, and awards:*** Federal Pell, FSEOG, state, private, college/university gift aid from institutional funds, Academic Competitiveness Grant, National Smart Grant.

GIFT AID (NON-NEED-BASED) ***Total amount:*** $1,173,353 (13% state, 39% institutional, 48% external sources). ***Scholarships, grants, and awards by category:*** *Academic interests/achievement:* biological sciences, business, communication, computer science, education, English, foreign languages, general academic interests/achievements, health fields, humanities, mathematics, military science, physical sciences, social sciences. *Creative arts/performance:* art/fine arts, music, theater/drama. ***ROTC:*** Army.

LOANS ***Student loans:*** $14,113,260 (49% need-based, 51% non-need-based). 93% of past graduating class borrowed through all loan programs. *Average indebtedness per student:* $23,975. ***Parent loans:*** $771,408 (100% non-need-based). ***Programs:*** FFEL (Subsidized and Unsubsidized Stafford, PLUS), Perkins.

WORK-STUDY ***Federal work-study:*** Total amount: $359,369; 257 jobs averaging $1398. ***State or other work-study/employment:*** Total amount: $479,425 (100% non-need-based). 358 part-time jobs averaging $1339.

ATHLETIC AWARDS Total amount: $459,871 (100% non-need-based).

APPLYING FOR FINANCIAL AID ***Required financial aid form:*** FAFSA. ***Financial aid deadline (priority):*** 3/1. ***Notification date:*** Continuous beginning 5/1. Students must reply within 3 weeks of notification.

CONTACT Ms. Deb Henriksen, Director of Financial Aid, Black Hills State University, 1200 University Street, Spearfish, SD 57799-9670, 605-642-6581 or toll-free 800-255-2478. *Fax:* 605-642-6913. *E-mail:* debhenriksen@bhsu.edu.

BLESSING-RIEMAN COLLEGE OF NURSING

Quincy, IL

Tuition & fees: $21,270 **Average undergraduate aid package: N/A**

ABOUT THE INSTITUTION Independent, coed, primarily women. ***Awards:*** bachelor's and master's degrees. 1 undergraduate major. ***Total enrollment:*** 219. Undergraduates: 211. Freshmen: 20. Federal methodology is used as a basis for awarding need-based institutional aid.

UNDERGRADUATE EXPENSES for 2008–09 ***Comprehensive fee:*** $28,790 includes full-time tuition ($20,800), mandatory fees ($470), and room and board ($7520). ***College room only:*** $3720. Full-time tuition and fees vary according to course load, location, and student level. Room and board charges vary according to board plan, location, and student level. ***Part-time tuition:*** $490 per credit hour. Part-time tuition and fees vary according to course load, location, and student level. ***Payment plan:*** Installment.

UNDERGRADUATE FINANCIAL AID (Fall 2008, est.) 76 applied for aid; of those 100% were deemed to have need. 100% of undergraduates with need received aid. ***Average percent of need met:*** 75% (excluding resources awarded to replace EFC).

GIFT AID (NEED-BASED) ***Total amount:*** $865,536 (13% federal, 12% state, 63% institutional, 12% external sources). ***Receiving aid:*** All full-time undergraduates: 68% (76). ***Scholarships, grants, and awards:*** Federal Pell, state, private, college/university gift aid from institutional funds.

GIFT AID (NON-NEED-BASED) ***Tuition waivers:*** Full or partial for employees or children of employees.

LOANS ***Student loans:*** $508,301 (100% need-based). 70% of past graduating class borrowed through all loan programs. *Average indebtedness per student:* $20,000. ***Parent loans:*** $12,192 (100% need-based). ***Programs:*** FFEL (Subsidized and Unsubsidized Stafford, PLUS), Federal Nursing, college/university.

APPLYING FOR FINANCIAL AID ***Required financial aid form:*** FAFSA. ***Financial aid deadline:*** Continuous.

CONTACT Ms. Sara Brehm, Financial Aid Officer, Blessing-Rieman College of Nursing, Broadway at 11th Street, Quincy, IL 62301, 217-223-8400 Ext. 6993 or toll-free 800-877-9140 Ext. 6964. *Fax:* 217-223-1781. *E-mail:* sbrehm@brcn.edu.

BLOOMFIELD COLLEGE

Bloomfield, NJ

Tuition & fees: $20,080 **Average undergraduate aid package: $22,510**

ABOUT THE INSTITUTION Independent religious, coed. ***Awards:*** bachelor's degrees. 20 undergraduate majors. ***Total enrollment:*** 2,020. Undergraduates: 2,020. Freshmen: 424. Federal methodology is used as a basis for awarding need-based institutional aid.

UNDERGRADUATE EXPENSES for 2008–09 ***Application fee:*** $40. ***Comprehensive fee:*** $29,580 includes full-time tuition ($19,080), mandatory fees ($1000), and room and board ($9500). ***College room only:*** $4750. Room and board charges vary according to housing facility. ***Part-time tuition:*** $1950 per course. ***Part-time fees:*** $125 per term. Part-time tuition and fees vary according to course load. ***Payment plans:*** Installment, deferred payment.

FRESHMAN FINANCIAL AID (Fall 2008, est.) 395 applied for aid; of those 93% were deemed to have need. 100% of freshmen with need received aid; of those 70% had need fully met. ***Average percent of need met:*** 68% (excluding resources awarded to replace EFC). ***Average financial aid package:*** $24,123 (excluding resources awarded to replace EFC). 5% of all full-time freshmen had no need and received non-need-based gift aid.

UNDERGRADUATE FINANCIAL AID (Fall 2008, est.) 1,477 applied for aid; of those 92% were deemed to have need. 100% of undergraduates with need received aid; of those 92% had need fully met. ***Average percent of need met:*** 59% (excluding resources awarded to replace EFC). ***Average financial aid package:*** $22,510 (excluding resources awarded to replace EFC). 6% of all full-time undergraduates had no need and received non-need-based gift aid.

GIFT AID (NEED-BASED) ***Total amount:*** $16,937,854 (27% federal, 46% state, 27% institutional). ***Receiving aid:*** Freshmen: 88% (350); all full-time undergraduates: 82% (1,248). ***Average award:*** Freshmen: $15,203; Undergraduates: $12,640. ***Scholarships, grants, and awards:*** Federal Pell, FSEOG, state, private, college/university gift aid from institutional funds.

GIFT AID (NON-NEED-BASED) ***Total amount:*** $2,861,833 (2% federal, 1% state, 71% institutional, 26% external sources). ***Receiving aid:*** Freshmen: 35% (139). Undergraduates: 34% (516). ***Average award:*** Freshmen: $15,400. Undergraduates: $12,466. ***Scholarships, grants, and awards by category:*** *Academic interests/achievement:* 248 awards ($1,151,476 total): biological sciences, business, computer science, education, English, general academic interests/achievements, health fields, humanities, mathematics, physical sciences, religion/biblical studies, social sciences. *Creative arts/performance:* 1 award ($400 total): applied art and design, art/fine arts, cinema/film/broadcasting, general creative arts/performance, performing arts, theater/drama. *Special achievements/activities:* 302 awards ($2,275,211 total): community service, general special achievements/activities, leadership. *Special characteristics:* 73 awards ($107,702 total): adult students, children and siblings of alumni, general special characteristics. ***Tuition waivers:*** Full or partial for employees or children of employees, senior citizens. ***ROTC:*** Army cooperative.

LOANS ***Student loans:*** $13,257,684 (50% need-based, 50% non-need-based). 86% of past graduating class borrowed through all loan programs. *Average indebtedness per student:* $23,117. ***Average need-based loan:*** Freshmen: $6888. Undergraduates: $8350. ***Programs:*** FFEL (Subsidized and Unsubsidized Stafford, PLUS).

WORK-STUDY ***Federal work-study:*** Total amount: $968,644; 444 jobs averaging $2010. ***State or other work-study/employment:*** 16 part-time jobs averaging $2122.

ATHLETIC AWARDS Total amount: $1,403,782 (100% non-need-based).

APPLYING FOR FINANCIAL AID ***Required financial aid form:*** FAFSA. ***Financial aid deadline:*** 6/1 (priority: 3/15). ***Notification date:*** Continuous. Students must reply within 2 weeks of notification.

CONTACT Ms. Stacy Salinas, Director of Financial Aid, Bloomfield College, Bloomfield College, Bloomfield, NJ 07003-9981, 973-748-9000 Ext. 213 or toll-free 800-848-4555 Ext. 230. *Fax:* 973-748-9735. *E-mail:* stacy_salinas@bloomfield.edu.

BLOOMSBURG UNIVERSITY OF PENNSYLVANIA

Bloomsburg, PA

Tuition & fees (PA res): $6848 **Average undergraduate aid package: $11,311**

ABOUT THE INSTITUTION State-supported, coed. ***Awards:*** bachelor's, master's, and doctoral degrees and post-bachelor's certificates. 46 undergraduate majors. ***Total enrollment:*** 8,855. Undergraduates: 8,081. Freshmen: 1,811. Federal methodology is used as a basis for awarding need-based institutional aid.

UNDERGRADUATE EXPENSES for 2008–09 ***Application fee:*** $30. ***Tuition, state resident:*** full-time $5358; part-time $223 per credit. ***Tuition, nonresident:*** full-time $13,396; part-time $558 per credit. ***Required fees:*** full-time $1490; $43.25 per credit or $79 per term. Full-time tuition and fees vary according to course load. Part-time tuition and fees vary according to course load. ***College room and board:*** $6292; ***Room only:*** $3750. Room and board charges vary according to board plan and housing facility. ***Payment plan:*** Installment.

FRESHMAN FINANCIAL AID (Fall 2008, est.) 1,619 applied for aid; of those 95% were deemed to have need. 89% of freshmen with need received aid; of those 90% had need fully met. ***Average percent of need met:*** 69% (excluding resources awarded to replace EFC). ***Average financial aid package:*** $11,003 (excluding resources awarded to replace EFC). 3% of all full-time freshmen had no need and received non-need-based gift aid.

UNDERGRADUATE FINANCIAL AID (Fall 2008, est.) 6,369 applied for aid; of those 95% were deemed to have need. 97% of undergraduates with need received aid; of those 90% had need fully met. ***Average percent of need met:*** 70% (excluding resources awarded to replace EFC). ***Average financial aid package:*** $11,311 (excluding resources awarded to replace EFC). 2% of all full-time undergraduates had no need and received non-need-based gift aid.

GIFT AID (NEED-BASED) ***Total amount:*** $13,452,550 (49% federal, 46% state, 2% institutional, 3% external sources). ***Receiving aid:*** Freshmen: 35% (636); all full-time undergraduates: 35% (2,632). ***Average award:*** Freshmen: $5852; Undergraduates: $4985. ***Scholarships, grants, and awards:*** Federal Pell, FSEOG, state, private, college/university gift aid from institutional funds, Academic Competitiveness Grant, National Smart Grants.

GIFT AID (NON-NEED-BASED) ***Total amount:*** $3,640,052 (26% federal, 6% state, 32% institutional, 36% external sources). ***Receiving aid:*** Freshmen: 20% (357). Undergraduates: 15% (1,127). ***Average award:*** Freshmen: $2044. Undergraduates: $2263. ***Scholarships, grants, and awards by category:*** *Academic interests/achievement:* 437 awards ($641,817 total): biological sciences, business, communication, computer science, education, English, foreign languages, general academic interests/achievements, health fields, humanities, international studies, mathematics, physical sciences, religion/biblical studies, social sciences. *Special characteristics:* 253 awards ($911,829 total): children of faculty/staff, international students. ***Tuition waivers:*** Full or partial for minority students, employees or children of employees, senior citizens. ***ROTC:*** Army, Air Force cooperative.

LOANS ***Student loans:*** $35,521,043 (39% need-based, 61% non-need-based). 71% of past graduating class borrowed through all loan programs. *Average indebtedness per student:* $19,645. ***Average need-based loan:*** Freshmen: $3296. Undergraduates: $4132. ***Parent loans:*** $6,066,166 (100% non-need-based). ***Programs:*** FFEL (Subsidized and Unsubsidized Stafford, PLUS), Perkins, state, alternative loans.

WORK-STUDY ***Federal work-study:*** Total amount: $2,558,869; 793 jobs averaging $3227. ***State or other work-study/employment:*** Total amount: $4,018,041 (100% non-need-based). 1,028 part-time jobs averaging $3909.

ATHLETIC AWARDS Total amount: $532,547 (100% non-need-based).

APPLYING FOR FINANCIAL AID ***Required financial aid form:*** FAFSA. ***Financial aid deadline (priority):*** 3/15. ***Notification date:*** Continuous beginning 4/1.

CONTACT Mr. Thomas M. Lyons, Director of Financial Aid, Bloomsburg University of Pennsylvania, 119 Warren Student Services Center, 400 East 2nd Street, Bloomsburg, PA 17815-1301, 570-389-4279. *Fax:* 570-389-4795. *E-mail:* stfinaid@bloomu.edu.

BLUEFIELD COLLEGE

Bluefield, VA

Tuition & fees: $15,630 **Average undergraduate aid package: $11,966**

ABOUT THE INSTITUTION Independent Southern Baptist, coed. ***Awards:*** bachelor's degrees. 40 undergraduate majors. ***Total enrollment:*** 793. Undergraduates: 793. Freshmen: 90. Federal methodology is used as a basis for awarding need-based institutional aid.

UNDERGRADUATE EXPENSES for 2008–09 ***Application fee:*** $30. ***Comprehensive fee:*** $22,214 includes full-time tuition ($15,000), mandatory fees ($630), and room and board ($6584). ***Part-time tuition:*** $488 per hour. ***Part-time fees:*** $160 per term.

FRESHMAN FINANCIAL AID (Fall 2008, est.) 77 applied for aid; of those 97% were deemed to have need. 100% of freshmen with need received aid; of those 29% had need fully met. ***Average percent of need met:*** 81% (excluding resources awarded to replace EFC). ***Average financial aid package:*** $14,317 (excluding resources awarded to replace EFC).

UNDERGRADUATE FINANCIAL AID (Fall 2008, est.) 613 applied for aid; of those 89% were deemed to have need. 100% of undergraduates with need received aid; of those 19% had need fully met. ***Average percent of need met:*** 63% (excluding resources awarded to replace EFC). ***Average financial aid package:*** $11,966 (excluding resources awarded to replace EFC). 14% of all full-time undergraduates had no need and received non-need-based gift aid.

GIFT AID (NEED-BASED) ***Total amount:*** $3,627,502 (24% federal, 28% state, 31% institutional, 17% external sources). ***Receiving aid:*** Freshmen: 92% (74); all full-time undergraduates: 74% (505). ***Average award:*** Freshmen: $11,854;

Undergraduates: $8011. ***Scholarships, grants, and awards:*** Federal Pell, FSEOG, state, private, college/university gift aid from institutional funds.

GIFT AID (NON-NEED-BASED) ***Total amount:*** $815,236 (41% state, 40% institutional, 19% external sources). ***Receiving aid:*** Freshmen: 22% (18). Undergraduates: 11% (75). ***Average award:*** Freshmen: $3390. Undergraduates: $2969. ***Scholarships, grants, and awards by category:*** *Creative arts/performance:* 30 awards ($80,000 total): art/fine arts, music, performing arts, theater/drama. *Special characteristics:* children of faculty/staff, ethnic background, first-generation college students, general special characteristics, members of minority groups, religious affiliation, veterans.

LOANS ***Student loans:*** $5,617,120 (75% need-based, 25% non-need-based). 85% of past graduating class borrowed through all loan programs. *Average indebtedness per student:* $16,856. ***Average need-based loan:*** Freshmen: $3109. Undergraduates: $5098. ***Parent loans:*** $463,323 (21% need-based, 79% non-need-based). ***Programs:*** FFEL (Subsidized and Unsubsidized Stafford, PLUS), alternative loans.

WORK-STUDY ***Federal work-study:*** Total amount: $118,313; 98 jobs averaging $1500.

ATHLETIC AWARDS Total amount: $727,966 (67% need-based, 33% non-need-based).

APPLYING FOR FINANCIAL AID ***Required financial aid forms:*** FAFSA, state aid form. ***Financial aid deadline (priority):*** 3/15. ***Notification date:*** Continuous.

CONTACT Mrs. Sheila Nelson-Hensley, Director of Financial Aid, Bluefield College, 3000 College Drive, Bluefield, VA 24605, 276-326-4215 or toll-free 800-872-0175. *Fax:* 276-326-4356. *E-mail:* shensley@bluefield.edu.

BLUEFIELD STATE COLLEGE

Bluefield, WV

Tuition & fees (WV res): $4272 **Average undergraduate aid package: $6000**

ABOUT THE INSTITUTION State-supported, coed. ***Awards:*** associate and bachelor's degrees. 18 undergraduate majors. ***Total enrollment:*** 1,868. Undergraduates: 1,868. Freshmen: 205. Federal methodology is used as a basis for awarding need-based institutional aid.

UNDERGRADUATE EXPENSES for 2008–09 ***Tuition, state resident:*** full-time $4272; part-time $179 per credit hour. ***Tuition, nonresident:*** full-time $8568; part-time $357 per credit hour. ***Payment plan:*** Installment.

FRESHMAN FINANCIAL AID (Fall 2008, est.) 260 applied for aid; of those 87% were deemed to have need. 100% of freshmen with need received aid; of those 56% had need fully met. ***Average percent of need met:*** 70% (excluding resources awarded to replace EFC). ***Average financial aid package:*** $6000 (excluding resources awarded to replace EFC). 18% of all full-time freshmen had no need and received non-need-based gift aid.

UNDERGRADUATE FINANCIAL AID (Fall 2008, est.) 1,260 applied for aid; of those 84% were deemed to have need. 100% of undergraduates with need received aid; of those 41% had need fully met. ***Average percent of need met:*** 70% (excluding resources awarded to replace EFC). ***Average financial aid package:*** $6000 (excluding resources awarded to replace EFC). 28% of all full-time undergraduates had no need and received non-need-based gift aid.

GIFT AID (NEED-BASED) ***Total amount:*** $5,520,000 (76% federal, 24% state). ***Receiving aid:*** Freshmen: 75% (225); all full-time undergraduates: 72% (1,060). ***Average award:*** Freshmen: $3400; Undergraduates: $3400. ***Scholarships, grants, and awards:*** Federal Pell, FSEOG, state.

GIFT AID (NON-NEED-BASED) ***Total amount:*** $1,600,000 (32% state, 20% institutional, 48% external sources). ***Receiving aid:*** Freshmen: 26% (80). Undergraduates: 3% (40). ***Average award:*** Freshmen: $1375. Undergraduates: $1375. ***Scholarships, grants, and awards by category:*** *Academic interests/achievement:* 420 awards ($360,000 total): engineering/technologies, general academic interests/achievements. *Special achievements/activities:* 11 awards ($4500 total): cheerleading/drum major, general special achievements/activities, junior miss, leadership. *Special characteristics:* 3 awards ($1500 total): general special characteristics. ***Tuition waivers:*** Full or partial for adult students, senior citizens.

LOANS ***Student loans:*** $8,000,000 (56% need-based, 44% non-need-based). 63% of past graduating class borrowed through all loan programs. *Average indebtedness per student:* $21,500. ***Average need-based loan:*** Freshmen: $3500. Undergraduates: $3500. ***Parent loans:*** $240,000 (100% non-need-based). ***Programs:*** Federal Direct (Subsidized and Unsubsidized Stafford, PLUS), Perkins.

WORK-STUDY ***Federal work-study:*** Total amount: $170,000; 102 jobs averaging $1900. ***State or other work-study/employment:*** Total amount: $150,000 (100% non-need-based). 110 part-time jobs averaging $2600.

ATHLETIC AWARDS Total amount: $95,000 (100% non-need-based).

APPLYING FOR FINANCIAL AID ***Required financial aid forms:*** FAFSA, institution's own form. ***Financial aid deadline (priority):*** 3/1. ***Notification date:*** 6/1.

CONTACT Mr. Tom Ilse, Director of Financial Aid, Bluefield State College, 219 Rock Street, Bluefield, WV 24701-2198, 304-327-4020 or toll-free 800-344-8892 Ext. 4065 (in-state), 800-654-7798 Ext. 4065 (out-of-state). *Fax:* 304-325-7747. *E-mail:* tilse@bluefieldstate.edu.

BLUE MOUNTAIN COLLEGE

Blue Mountain, MS

CONTACT Financial Aid Assistant, Blue Mountain College, PO Box 160, Blue Mountain, MS 38610-0160, 662-685-4771 Ext. 141 or toll-free 800-235-0136. *Fax:* 662-685-4776. *E-mail:* finaid@bmc.edu.

BLUFFTON UNIVERSITY

Bluffton, OH

Tuition & fees: $22,920 **Average undergraduate aid package: $21,716**

ABOUT THE INSTITUTION Independent Mennonite, coed. ***Awards:*** bachelor's and master's degrees. 39 undergraduate majors. ***Total enrollment:*** 1,149. Undergraduates: 1,032. Freshmen: 272. Both federal and institutional methodology are used as a basis for awarding need-based institutional aid.

UNDERGRADUATE EXPENSES for 2008–09 ***Application fee:*** $20. ***Comprehensive fee:*** $30,516 includes full-time tuition ($22,470), mandatory fees ($450), and room and board ($7596). ***College room only:*** $3660. Full-time tuition and fees vary according to course load and program. Room and board charges vary according to board plan and housing facility. ***Part-time tuition:*** $936 per credit hour. Part-time tuition and fees vary according to course load and program. ***Payment plan:*** Installment.

FRESHMAN FINANCIAL AID (Fall 2008, est.) 261 applied for aid; of those 93% were deemed to have need. 100% of freshmen with need received aid; of those 68% had need fully met. ***Average percent of need met:*** 96% (excluding resources awarded to replace EFC). ***Average financial aid package:*** $22,348 (excluding resources awarded to replace EFC). 9% of all full-time freshmen had no need and received non-need-based gift aid.

UNDERGRADUATE FINANCIAL AID (Fall 2008, est.) 732 applied for aid; of those 93% were deemed to have need. 100% of undergraduates with need received aid; of those 50% had need fully met. ***Average percent of need met:*** 93% (excluding resources awarded to replace EFC). ***Average financial aid package:*** $21,716 (excluding resources awarded to replace EFC). 11% of all full-time undergraduates had no need and received non-need-based gift aid.

GIFT AID (NEED-BASED) ***Total amount:*** $9,992,740 (12% federal, 11% state, 70% institutional, 7% external sources). ***Receiving aid:*** Freshmen: 89% (242); all full-time undergraduates: 73% (681). ***Average award:*** Freshmen: $16,137; Undergraduates: $14,884. ***Scholarships, grants, and awards:*** Federal Pell, FSEOG, state, private, college/university gift aid from institutional funds.

GIFT AID (NON-NEED-BASED) ***Total amount:*** $1,655,984 (4% federal, 5% state, 72% institutional, 19% external sources). ***Receiving aid:*** Freshmen: 4% (11). Undergraduates: 4% (39). ***Average award:*** Freshmen: $8779. Undergraduates: $9990. ***Scholarships, grants, and awards by category:*** *Academic interests/achievement:* 419 awards ($3,620,746 total): general academic interests/achievements. *Creative arts/performance:* 32 awards ($32,000 total): art/fine arts, music. *Special achievements/activities:* 154 awards ($624,762 total): leadership. *Special characteristics:* 382 awards ($1,320,054 total): children of faculty/staff, international students, members of minority groups, out-of-state students, relatives of clergy, religious affiliation. ***Tuition waivers:*** Full or partial for employees or children of employees.

LOANS ***Student loans:*** $7,625,912 (95% need-based, 5% non-need-based). 86% of past graduating class borrowed through all loan programs. *Average indebtedness per student:* $27,701. ***Average need-based loan:*** Freshmen: $4682. Undergraduates: $5123. ***Parent loans:*** $1,471,942 (70% need-based, 30% non-need-based). ***Programs:*** FFEL (Subsidized and Unsubsidized Stafford, PLUS), Perkins, alternative loans.

WORK-STUDY ***Federal work-study:*** Total amount: $1,128,353; 583 jobs averaging $1935. ***State or other work-study/employment:*** Total amount: $513,600 (51% need-based, 49% non-need-based). 241 part-time jobs averaging $2124.

APPLYING FOR FINANCIAL AID ***Required financial aid form:*** FAFSA. ***Financial aid deadline:*** 10/1 (priority: 5/1). ***Notification date:*** Continuous. Students must reply within 3 weeks of notification.

CONTACT Mary Cannon, Director of Financial Aid, Bluffton University, 1 University Drive, Bluffton, OH 45817-2104, 419-358-3266 or toll-free 800-488-3257. *Fax:* 419-358-3073. *E-mail:* cannonm@bluffton.edu.

BOB JONES UNIVERSITY

Greenville, SC

CONTACT Mr. Chris Baker, Director of Financial Aid, Bob Jones University, 1700 Wade Hampton Boulevard, Greenville, SC 29614, 803-242-5100 Ext. 3037 or toll-free 800-BJANDME.

BOISE BIBLE COLLEGE

Boise, ID

CONTACT Beth Turner, Financial Aid Counselor, Boise Bible College, 8695 West Marigold Street, Boise, ID 83714-1220, 208-376-7731 Ext. 12 or toll-free 800-893-7755. *Fax:* 208-376-7743. *E-mail:* betht@boisebible.edu.

BOISE STATE UNIVERSITY

Boise, ID

Tuition & fees (ID res): $4632 **Average undergraduate aid package: $7218**

ABOUT THE INSTITUTION State-supported, coed. ***Awards:*** associate, bachelor's, master's, and doctoral degrees and post-bachelor's certificates. 93 undergraduate majors. ***Total enrollment:*** 19,667. Undergraduates: 17,574. Freshmen: 2,578. Federal methodology is used as a basis for awarding need-based institutional aid.

UNDERGRADUATE EXPENSES for 2008–09 ***Application fee:*** $40. ***One-time required fee:*** $75. ***Tuition, state resident:*** full-time $2891; part-time $157 per credit. ***Tuition, nonresident:*** full-time $11,467; part-time $157 per credit. ***Required fees:*** full-time $1741; $81 per credit. Full-time tuition and fees vary according to reciprocity agreements. Part-time tuition and fees vary according to course load. ***College room and board:*** $4819. Room and board charges vary according to board plan and housing facility. ***Payment plan:*** Installment.

FRESHMAN FINANCIAL AID (Fall 2008, est.) 1,626 applied for aid; of those 100% were deemed to have need. 100% of freshmen with need received aid; of those 27% had need fully met. ***Average percent of need met:*** 21% (excluding resources awarded to replace EFC). ***Average financial aid package:*** $6506 (excluding resources awarded to replace EFC). 19% of all full-time freshmen had no need and received non-need-based gift aid.

UNDERGRADUATE FINANCIAL AID (Fall 2008, est.) 7,205 applied for aid; of those 100% were deemed to have need. 100% of undergraduates with need received aid; of those 22% had need fully met. ***Average percent of need met:*** 24% (excluding resources awarded to replace EFC). ***Average financial aid package:*** $7218 (excluding resources awarded to replace EFC). 6% of all full-time undergraduates had no need and received non-need-based gift aid.

GIFT AID (NEED-BASED) ***Total amount:*** $21,672,309 (79% federal, 4% state, 11% institutional, 6% external sources). ***Receiving aid:*** Freshmen: 56% (1,266); all full-time undergraduates: 44% (5,056). ***Average award:*** Freshmen: $3300; Undergraduates: $3692. ***Scholarships, grants, and awards:*** Federal Pell, FSEOG, state, private, college/university gift aid from institutional funds, Leveraging Educational Assistance Program (LEAP).

GIFT AID (NON-NEED-BASED) ***Total amount:*** $1,153,915 (3% federal, 31% state, 51% institutional, 15% external sources). ***Receiving aid:*** Freshmen: 9% (207). Undergraduates: 4% (414). ***Average award:*** Freshmen: $913. Undergraduates: $1045. ***Scholarships, grants, and awards by category:*** *Academic interests/achievement:* 1,381 awards ($4,975,525 total): biological sciences, business, communication, computer science, education, engineering/technologies, English, foreign languages, general academic interests/achievements, health fields, humanities, international studies, mathematics, military science, physical sciences, premedicine, social sciences. *Creative arts/performance:* 183 awards ($152,662 total): art/fine arts, dance, debating, general creative arts/performance, journalism/publications, music, performing arts, theater/drama. *Special achievements/activities:* 68 awards ($48,225 total): cheerleading/drum major, community service, leadership, rodeo. *Special characteristics:* 2,177 awards ($2,483,974 total): ethnic background, first-generation college students, general special characteristics, handicapped students, international students, local/state students, members of minority groups, out-of-state students, previous college experience, spouses of current students, veterans, veterans' children. ***Tuition waivers:*** Full or partial for employees or children of employees, senior citizens. ***ROTC:*** Army.

LOANS ***Student loans:*** $48,681,952 (77% need-based, 23% non-need-based). 64% of past graduating class borrowed through all loan programs. *Average indebtedness per student:* $21,064. ***Average need-based loan:*** Freshmen: $4333. Undergraduates: $5864. ***Parent loans:*** $1,103,603 (24% need-based, 76% non-need-based). ***Programs:*** Federal Direct (Subsidized and Unsubsidized Stafford, PLUS), Perkins, state, college/university, Alaska Loans.

WORK-STUDY ***Federal work-study:*** Total amount: $2,523,096; 452 jobs averaging $3261. ***State or other work-study/employment:*** Total amount: $1,504,105 (100% need-based). 209 part-time jobs averaging $3337.

ATHLETIC AWARDS Total amount: $3,794,906 (71% need-based, 29% non-need-based).

APPLYING FOR FINANCIAL AID ***Required financial aid form:*** FAFSA. ***Financial aid deadline:*** 6/1 (priority: 2/15). ***Notification date:*** Continuous beginning 3/17. Students must reply by 6/1 or within 4 weeks of notification.

CONTACT Office of Financial Aid and Scholarships, Boise State University, Administration Building, Room 123, Boise, ID 83725-1315, 208-426-1664 or toll-free 800-632-6586 (in-state), 800-824-7017 (out-of-state). *Fax:* 208-426-1305. *E-mail:* faquest@boisestate.edu.

BORICUA COLLEGE

New York, NY

CONTACT Ms. Rosalia Cruz, Financial Aid Administrator, Boricua College, 3755 Broadway, New York, NY 10032-1560, 212-694-1000 Ext. 611. *Fax:* 212-694-1015. *E-mail:* rcruz@boricuacollege.edu.

BOSTON ARCHITECTURAL COLLEGE

Boston, MA

Tuition & fees: $10,620 **Average undergraduate aid package: $5766**

ABOUT THE INSTITUTION Independent, coed. ***Awards:*** bachelor's and master's degrees. 4 undergraduate majors. ***Total enrollment:*** 1,176. Undergraduates: 624. Freshmen: 61. Federal methodology is used as a basis for awarding need-based institutional aid.

UNDERGRADUATE EXPENSES for 2008–09 ***Application fee:*** $50. ***Tuition:*** full-time $10,600; part-time $883 per credit hour. ***Required fees:*** full-time $20; $10 per term. Full-time tuition and fees vary according to course load, degree level, program, and reciprocity agreements. Part-time tuition and fees vary according to course load, degree level, program, and reciprocity agreements. ***Payment plan:*** Installment.

FRESHMAN FINANCIAL AID (Fall 2008, est.) 52 applied for aid; of those 94% were deemed to have need. 98% of freshmen with need received aid; of those 2% had need fully met. ***Average percent of need met:*** 25% (excluding resources awarded to replace EFC). ***Average financial aid package:*** $11,739 (excluding resources awarded to replace EFC). 3% of all full-time freshmen had no need and received non-need-based gift aid.

UNDERGRADUATE FINANCIAL AID (Fall 2008, est.) 481 applied for aid; of those 89% were deemed to have need. 92% of undergraduates with need received aid; of those 4% had need fully met. ***Average percent of need met:*** 31% (excluding resources awarded to replace EFC). ***Average financial aid package:*** $5766 (excluding resources awarded to replace EFC).

GIFT AID (NEED-BASED) ***Total amount:*** $556,568 (85% federal, 5% state, 10% external sources). ***Receiving aid:*** Freshmen: 10% (6); all full-time undergraduates: 26% (159). ***Average award:*** Freshmen: $1879; Undergraduates: $2941. ***Scholarships, grants, and awards:*** Federal Pell, FSEOG, state, college/university gift aid from institutional funds.

GIFT AID (NON-NEED-BASED) ***Total amount:*** $86,898 (99% institutional, 1% external sources). ***Receiving aid:*** Freshmen: 3% (2). Undergraduates: 1. ***Average award:*** Freshmen: $9200. ***Scholarships, grants, and awards by category:*** *Academic interests/achievement:* 30 awards ($40,200 total): architecture. ***Tuition waivers:*** Full or partial for employees or children of employees.

LOANS ***Student loans:*** $4,115,425 (84% need-based, 16% non-need-based). 83% of past graduating class borrowed through all loan programs. *Average indebtedness per student:* $37,847. ***Average need-based loan:*** Freshmen: $2965. Undergraduates: $4479. ***Parent loans:*** $684,030 (48% need-based, 52% non-need-based). ***Programs:*** FFEL (Subsidized and Unsubsidized Stafford, PLUS), state.

WORK-STUDY ***Federal work-study:*** Total amount: $101,824; 42 jobs available.

APPLYING FOR FINANCIAL AID ***Required financial aid form:*** FAFSA. ***Financial aid deadline (priority):*** 4/15. ***Notification date:*** Continuous. Students must reply within 2 weeks of notification.

CONTACT Anne Downey, Director of Financial Aid, Boston Architectural College, 320 Newbury Street, Boston, MA 02115, 617-585-0125 or toll-free 877-585-0100. *Fax:* 617-585-0131. *E-mail:* anne.downey@the-bac.edu.

BOSTON BAPTIST COLLEGE

Boston, MA

CONTACT Curt A. Wiedenroth, Financial Aid Director, Boston Baptist College, 950 Metropolitan Avenue, Boston, MA 02136, 617-364-3510 or toll-free 888-235-2014 (out-of-state). *Fax:* 617-364-0723. *E-mail:* cw9083@aol.com.

BOSTON COLLEGE

Chestnut Hill, MA

Tuition & fees: $37,950 **Average undergraduate aid package: $29,586**

ABOUT THE INSTITUTION Independent Roman Catholic (Jesuit), coed. ***Awards:*** bachelor's, master's, doctoral, and first professional degrees and post-master's certificates (also offers continuing education program with significant enrollment not reflected in profile). 48 undergraduate majors. ***Total enrollment:*** 13,903. Undergraduates: 9,060. Freshmen: 2,167. Institutional methodology is used as a basis for awarding need-based institutional aid.

UNDERGRADUATE EXPENSES for 2008–09 ***Application fee:*** $70. ***One-time required fee:*** $425. ***Comprehensive fee:*** $50,345 includes full-time tuition ($37,410), mandatory fees ($540), and room and board ($12,395). ***College room only:*** $7945. Room and board charges vary according to housing facility. ***Payment plan:*** Installment.

FRESHMAN FINANCIAL AID (Fall 2008, est.) 1,029 applied for aid; of those 81% were deemed to have need. 100% of freshmen with need received aid; of those 100% had need fully met. ***Average percent of need met:*** 100% (excluding resources awarded to replace EFC). ***Average financial aid package:*** $29,618 (excluding resources awarded to replace EFC). 1% of all full-time freshmen had no need and received non-need-based gift aid.

UNDERGRADUATE FINANCIAL AID (Fall 2008, est.) 4,204 applied for aid; of those 87% were deemed to have need. 100% of undergraduates with need received aid; of those 100% had need fully met. ***Average percent of need met:*** 100% (excluding resources awarded to replace EFC). ***Average financial aid package:*** $29,586 (excluding resources awarded to replace EFC). 2% of all full-time undergraduates had no need and received non-need-based gift aid.

GIFT AID (NEED-BASED) ***Total amount:*** $78,938,745 (7% federal, 2% state, 88% institutional, 3% external sources). ***Receiving aid:*** Freshmen: 33% (720); all full-time undergraduates: 34% (3,090). ***Average award:*** Freshmen: $26,707; Undergraduates: $25,547. ***Scholarships, grants, and awards:*** Federal Pell, FSEOG, state, private, college/university gift aid from institutional funds.

GIFT AID (NON-NEED-BASED) ***Total amount:*** $6,269,946 (23% federal, 54% institutional, 23% external sources). ***Receiving aid:*** Freshmen: 1% (18). Undergraduates: 1% (61). ***Average award:*** Freshmen: $14,879. Undergraduates: $17,896. ***Scholarships, grants, and awards by category:*** *Academic interests/achievement:* 92 awards ($2,556,077 total): general academic interests/achievements, military science. ***Tuition waivers:*** Full or partial for employees or children of employees. ***ROTC:*** Army cooperative, Naval cooperative, Air Force cooperative.

LOANS ***Student loans:*** $18,331,429 (79% need-based, 21% non-need-based). 52% of past graduating class borrowed through all loan programs. *Average indebtedness per student:* $19,358. ***Average need-based loan:*** Freshmen: $3353. Undergraduates: $4671. ***Parent loans:*** $41,827,479 (100% non-need-based). ***Programs:*** FFEL (Subsidized and Unsubsidized Stafford, PLUS), Perkins, Federal Nursing, state.

WORK-STUDY ***Federal work-study:*** Total amount: $6,147,160; 2,879 jobs averaging $2135.

ATHLETIC AWARDS Total amount: $13,606,194 (10% need-based, 90% non-need-based).

APPLYING FOR FINANCIAL AID ***Required financial aid forms:*** FAFSA, CSS Financial Aid PROFILE, business/farm supplement, federal income tax form(s), W-2 forms. ***Financial aid deadline (priority):*** 2/1. ***Notification date:*** 4/1. Students must reply by 5/1.

CONTACT Office of Student Services, Boston College, Lyons Hall, 140 Commonwealth Avenue, Chestnut Hill, MA 02467, 617-552-3300 or toll-free 800-360-2522. *Fax:* 617-552-4889. *E-mail:* studentservices@bc.edu.

THE BOSTON CONSERVATORY

Boston, MA

Tuition & fees: $32,200 **Average undergraduate aid package: $13,967**

ABOUT THE INSTITUTION Independent, coed. ***Awards:*** bachelor's and master's degrees and post-bachelor's and post-master's certificates. 9 undergraduate majors. ***Total enrollment:*** 655. Undergraduates: 482. Freshmen: 150. Both federal and institutional methodology are used as a basis for awarding need-based institutional aid.

UNDERGRADUATE EXPENSES for 2008–09 ***Application fee:*** $105. ***Comprehensive fee:*** $47,870 includes full-time tuition ($30,400), mandatory fees ($1800), and room and board ($15,670). ***College room only:*** $10,500. Full-time tuition and fees vary according to course load, degree level, and program. Room and board charges vary according to board plan and housing facility. ***Part-time tuition:*** $1260 per credit. ***Part-time fees:*** $390 per term. Part-time tuition and fees vary according to course load, degree level, and program. ***Payment plan:*** Installment.

FRESHMAN FINANCIAL AID (Fall 2008, est.) 109 applied for aid; of those 89% were deemed to have need. 100% of freshmen with need received aid; of those 8% had need fully met. ***Average percent of need met:*** .3% (excluding resources awarded to replace EFC). ***Average financial aid package:*** $13,972 (excluding resources awarded to replace EFC). 4% of all full-time freshmen had no need and received non-need-based gift aid.

UNDERGRADUATE FINANCIAL AID (Fall 2008, est.) 335 applied for aid; of those 87% were deemed to have need. 100% of undergraduates with need received aid; of those 8% had need fully met. ***Average percent of need met:*** .3% (excluding resources awarded to replace EFC). ***Average financial aid package:*** $13,967 (excluding resources awarded to replace EFC). 4% of all full-time undergraduates had no need and received non-need-based gift aid.

GIFT AID (NEED-BASED) ***Total amount:*** $2,943,500 (12% federal, 2% state, 84% institutional, 2% external sources). ***Receiving aid:*** Freshmen: 40% (85); all full-time undergraduates: 47% (233). ***Average award:*** Freshmen: $13,775; Undergraduates: $12,772. ***Scholarships, grants, and awards:*** Federal Pell, FSEOG, state, private, college/university gift aid from institutional funds.

GIFT AID (NON-NEED-BASED) ***Total amount:*** $1,399,251 (99% institutional, 1% external sources). ***Receiving aid:*** Freshmen: 39% (82). Undergraduates: 44% (219). ***Average award:*** Freshmen: $6375. Undergraduates: $9235. ***Scholarships, grants, and awards by category:*** *Creative arts/performance:* 297 awards ($3,827,330 total): dance, music, performing arts, theater/drama. ***Tuition waivers:*** Full or partial for employees or children of employees.

LOANS ***Student loans:*** $4,134,039 (75% need-based, 25% non-need-based). 51% of past graduating class borrowed through all loan programs. *Average indebtedness per student:* $34,931. ***Average need-based loan:*** Freshmen: $3500. Undergraduates: $4257. ***Parent loans:*** $2,479,905 (80% need-based, 20% non-need-based). ***Programs:*** FFEL (Subsidized and Unsubsidized Stafford, PLUS), state, college/university.

WORK-STUDY ***Federal work-study:*** Total amount: $134,400; jobs available. ***State or other work-study/employment:*** Part-time jobs available (averaging $1335).

APPLYING FOR FINANCIAL AID ***Required financial aid form:*** FAFSA. ***Financial aid deadline (priority):*** 3/1. ***Notification date:*** Continuous beginning 4/1. Students must reply within 4 weeks of notification.

CONTACT Jessica Raine, Financial Aid Assistant, The Boston Conservatory, 8 The Fenway, Boston, MA 02215, 617-912-9147. *Fax:* 617-536-1496. *E-mail:* jraine@bostonconservatory.edu.

BOSTON UNIVERSITY

Boston, MA

Tuition & fees: $37,050 **Average undergraduate aid package: $31,650**

ABOUT THE INSTITUTION Independent, coed. ***Awards:*** bachelor's, master's, doctoral, and first professional degrees and post-bachelor's, post-master's, and first professional certificates. 121 undergraduate majors. ***Total enrollment:*** 32,053. Undergraduates: 18,733. Freshmen: 4,163. Both federal and institutional methodology are used as a basis for awarding need-based institutional aid.

UNDERGRADUATE EXPENSES for 2008–09 ***Application fee:*** $75. ***Comprehensive fee:*** $48,468 includes full-time tuition ($36,540), mandatory fees ($510), and room and board ($11,418). ***College room only:*** $7420. Full-time tuition and fees vary according to class time and degree level. Room and board charges vary according to board plan and housing facility. ***Part-time tuition:*** $1142 per credit. ***Part-time fees:*** $40 per term. Part-time tuition and fees vary according to class time, course load, and degree level. ***Payment plans:*** Tuition prepayment, installment.

FRESHMAN FINANCIAL AID (Fall 2008, est.) 2,427 applied for aid; of those 81% were deemed to have need. 100% of freshmen with need received aid; of those 48% had need fully met. ***Average percent of need met:*** 90% (excluding resources awarded to replace EFC). ***Average financial aid package:*** $30,935 (excluding resources awarded to replace EFC). 7% of all full-time freshmen had no need and received non-need-based gift aid.

UNDERGRADUATE FINANCIAL AID (Fall 2008, est.) 7,654 applied for aid; of those 89% were deemed to have need. 100% of undergraduates with need received aid; of those 49% had need fully met. ***Average percent of need met:*** 90% (excluding resources awarded to replace EFC). ***Average financial aid package:*** $31,650 (excluding resources awarded to replace EFC). 10% of all full-time undergraduates had no need and received non-need-based gift aid.

GIFT AID (NEED-BASED) ***Total amount:*** $154,441,704 (8% federal, 1% state, 86% institutional, 5% external sources). ***Receiving aid:*** Freshmen: 44% (1,802); all full-time undergraduates: 40% (6,395). ***Average award:*** Freshmen: $21,485; Undergraduates: $20,982. ***Scholarships, grants, and awards:*** Federal Pell, FSEOG, state, private, college/university gift aid from institutional funds, Academic Competitiveness Grant, National Smart Grant.

GIFT AID (NON-NEED-BASED) ***Total amount:*** $31,217,100 (13% federal, 72% institutional, 15% external sources). ***Receiving aid:*** Freshmen: 17% (702). Undergraduates: 10% (1,683). ***Average award:*** Freshmen: $18,405. Undergraduates: $18,213. ***Scholarships, grants, and awards by category:*** *Academic interests/achievement:* 2,002 awards ($28,003,570 total): education, engineering/technologies, foreign languages, general academic interests/achievements. *Creative arts/performance:* 193 awards ($1,336,054 total): art/fine arts, music, theater/drama. *Special achievements/activities:* 79 awards ($1,670,355 total): general special achievements/activities, leadership, memberships. *Special characteristics:* 752 awards ($8,530,326 total): children and siblings of alumni, local/state students, relatives of clergy, religious affiliation. ***Tuition waivers:*** Full or partial for employees or children of employees, senior citizens. ***ROTC:*** Army, Naval, Air Force.

LOANS ***Student loans:*** $73,261,896 (65% need-based, 35% non-need-based). 59% of past graduating class borrowed through all loan programs. *Average indebtedness per student:* $26,586. ***Average need-based loan:*** Freshmen: $4960. Undergraduates: $6144. ***Parent loans:*** $44,183,201 (31% need-based, 69% non-need-based). ***Programs:*** Federal Direct (Subsidized and Unsubsidized Stafford, PLUS), Perkins, state, alternative loans.

WORK-STUDY ***Federal work-study:*** Total amount: $6,679,169; 2,834 jobs averaging $2282. ***State or other work-study/employment:*** Total amount: $2,119,076 (47% need-based, 53% non-need-based). 97 part-time jobs averaging $10,698.

ATHLETIC AWARDS Total amount: $10,688,722 (17% need-based, 83% non-need-based).

APPLYING FOR FINANCIAL AID ***Required financial aid forms:*** FAFSA, CSS Financial Aid PROFILE. ***Financial aid deadline:*** 2/15. ***Notification date:*** Continuous beginning 3/15. Students must reply by 5/1 or within 2 weeks of notification.

CONTACT Christine McGuire, Director of Financial Assistance, Boston University, 881 Commonwealth Avenue, Boston, MA 02215, 617-353-4176. *Fax:* 617-353-8200. *E-mail:* finaid@bu.edu.

BOWDOIN COLLEGE

Brunswick, ME

Tuition & fees: $38,190 **Average undergraduate aid package: $33,139**

ABOUT THE INSTITUTION Independent, coed. ***Awards:*** bachelor's degrees (SAT or ACT considered if submitted. Test scores are required for home-schooled applicants). 43 undergraduate majors. ***Total enrollment:*** 1,723. Undergraduates: 1,723. Freshmen: 488. Institutional methodology is used as a basis for awarding need-based institutional aid.

UNDERGRADUATE EXPENSES for 2008–09 ***Application fee:*** $60. ***One-time required fee:*** $100. ***Comprehensive fee:*** $48,570 includes full-time tuition ($37,790), mandatory fees ($400), and room and board ($10,380). ***College room only:*** $4850. Room and board charges vary according to board plan. ***Payment plans:*** Installment, deferred payment.

FRESHMAN FINANCIAL AID (Fall 2008, est.) 273 applied for aid; of those 74% were deemed to have need. 100% of freshmen with need received aid; of those 100% had need fully met. ***Average percent of need met:*** 100% (excluding resources awarded to replace EFC). ***Average financial aid package:*** $35,544 (excluding resources awarded to replace EFC). 4% of all full-time freshmen had no need and received non-need-based gift aid.

UNDERGRADUATE FINANCIAL AID (Fall 2008, est.) 881 applied for aid; of those 84% were deemed to have need. 100% of undergraduates with need received aid; of those 100% had need fully met. ***Average percent of need met:*** 100% (excluding resources awarded to replace EFC). ***Average financial aid package:*** $33,139 (excluding resources awarded to replace EFC). 4% of all full-time undergraduates had no need and received non-need-based gift aid.

GIFT AID (NEED-BASED) ***Total amount:*** $23,444,441 (5% federal, 92% institutional, 3% external sources). ***Receiving aid:*** Freshmen: 41% (201); all full-time undergraduates: 43% (736). ***Average award:*** Freshmen: $34,289; Undergraduates: $31,791. ***Scholarships, grants, and awards:*** Federal Pell, FSEOG, state, private, college/university gift aid from institutional funds.

GIFT AID (NON-NEED-BASED) ***Total amount:*** $425,876 (20% institutional, 80% external sources). ***Average award:*** Freshmen: $1000. Undergraduates: $1000. ***Scholarships, grants, and awards by category:*** *Academic interests/achievement:* 65 awards ($65,000 total): general academic interests/achievements. *Special achievements/activities:* leadership. *Special characteristics:* children of faculty/staff. ***Tuition waivers:*** Full or partial for employees or children of employees.

LOANS ***Student loans:*** 51% of past graduating class borrowed through all loan programs. *Average indebtedness per student:* $17,560. ***Programs:*** FFEL (Subsidized and Unsubsidized Stafford, PLUS), Perkins, state.

WORK-STUDY ***Federal work-study:*** Total amount: $183,535; 111 jobs averaging $1653. ***State or other work-study/employment:*** Total amount: $808,291 (100% need-based). 488 part-time jobs averaging $1656.

APPLYING FOR FINANCIAL AID ***Required financial aid forms:*** FAFSA, CSS Financial Aid PROFILE, noncustodial (divorced/separated) parent's statement, business/farm supplement. ***Financial aid deadline:*** 2/15. ***Notification date:*** 4/5. Students must reply by 5/1 or within 1 week of notification.

CONTACT Mr. Stephen H. Joyce, Director of Student Aid, Bowdoin College, 5300 College Station, Brunswick, ME 04011-8444, 207-725-3273. *Fax:* 207-725-3864. *E-mail:* sjoyce@bowdoin.edu.

BOWIE STATE UNIVERSITY

Bowie, MD

CONTACT Deborah Riley, Interim Financial Aid Director, Bowie State University, 14000 Jericho Park Road, Bowie, MD 20715, 301-860-3543 or toll-free 877-772-6943 (out-of-state). *Fax:* 301-860-3549. *E-mail:* driley@bowiestate.edu.

BOWLING GREEN STATE UNIVERSITY

Bowling Green, OH

Tuition & fees (OH res): $9060 **Average undergraduate aid package: $12,114**

ABOUT THE INSTITUTION State-supported, coed. ***Awards:*** bachelor's, master's, and doctoral degrees and post-master's certificates. 130 undergraduate majors. ***Total enrollment:*** 17,874. Undergraduates: 14,862. Freshmen: 3,098. Federal methodology is used as a basis for awarding need-based institutional aid.

UNDERGRADUATE EXPENSES for 2008–09 ***Application fee:*** $40. ***Tuition, state resident:*** full-time $7778; part-time $380 per credit hour. ***Tuition, nonresident:***

full-time $15,086; part-time $729 per credit hour. ***Required fees:*** full-time $1282; $64 per credit hour. Full-time tuition and fees vary according to location. Part-time tuition and fees vary according to course load and location. ***College room and board:*** $7220; ***Room only:*** $4420. Room and board charges vary according to board plan and housing facility. ***Payment plan:*** Installment.

FRESHMAN FINANCIAL AID (Fall 2007) 2,717 applied for aid; of those 81% were deemed to have need. 97% of freshmen with need received aid; of those 15% had need fully met. ***Average percent of need met:*** 73% (excluding resources awarded to replace EFC). ***Average financial aid package:*** $11,284 (excluding resources awarded to replace EFC). 12% of all full-time freshmen had no need and received non-need-based gift aid.

UNDERGRADUATE FINANCIAL AID (Fall 2007) 10,389 applied for aid; of those 85% were deemed to have need. 98% of undergraduates with need received aid; of those 14% had need fully met. ***Average percent of need met:*** 74% (excluding resources awarded to replace EFC). ***Average financial aid package:*** $12,114 (excluding resources awarded to replace EFC). 13% of all full-time undergraduates had no need and received non-need-based gift aid.

GIFT AID (NEED-BASED) ***Total amount:*** $39,488,698 (34% federal, 11% state, 50% institutional, 5% external sources). ***Receiving aid:*** Freshmen: 51% (1,647); all full-time undergraduates: 42% (6,090). ***Average award:*** Freshmen: $6532; Undergraduates: $6267. ***Scholarships, grants, and awards:*** Federal Pell, FSEOG, state, private, college/university gift aid from institutional funds.

GIFT AID (NON-NEED-BASED) ***Total amount:*** $14,542,551 (1% federal, 5% state, 85% institutional, 9% external sources). ***Receiving aid:*** Freshmen: 6% (180). Undergraduates: 4% (550). ***Average award:*** Freshmen: $4462. Undergraduates: $5801. ***Scholarships, grants, and awards by category:*** *Academic interests/achievement:* biological sciences, business, communication, computer science, education, engineering/technologies, English, foreign languages, general academic interests/achievements, health fields, home economics, humanities, international studies, mathematics, military science, physical sciences, social sciences. *Creative arts/performance:* art/fine arts, cinema/film/broadcasting, creative writing, dance, debating, journalism/publications, music, performing arts, theater/drama. *Special achievements/activities:* general special achievements/activities, leadership. *Special characteristics:* children and siblings of alumni, children of faculty/staff, general special characteristics, international students, members of minority groups. ***Tuition waivers:*** Full or partial for employees or children of employees, senior citizens. ***ROTC:*** Army, Air Force.

LOANS ***Student loans:*** $90,046,838 (74% need-based, 26% non-need-based). 70% of past graduating class borrowed through all loan programs. *Average indebtedness per student:* $26,860. ***Average need-based loan:*** Freshmen: $6303. Undergraduates: $7617. ***Parent loans:*** $10,934,411 (47% need-based, 53% non-need-based). ***Programs:*** Federal Direct (Subsidized and Unsubsidized Stafford, PLUS), Perkins, Federal Nursing, state, college/university, alternative loans.

WORK-STUDY ***Federal work-study:*** Total amount: $965,129; 900 jobs averaging $1143.

ATHLETIC AWARDS Total amount: $5,282,209 (33% need-based, 67% non-need-based).

APPLYING FOR FINANCIAL AID ***Required financial aid form:*** FAFSA. ***Financial aid deadline:*** Continuous. ***Notification date:*** Continuous beginning 4/15. Students must reply within 3 weeks of notification.

CONTACT Eric Bucks, Associate Director, Office of Student Financial Aid, Bowling Green State University, 231 Administration Building, Bowling Green, OH 43403, 419-372-2651. *Fax:* 419-372-0404.

BRADLEY UNIVERSITY

Peoria, IL

Tuition & fees: $22,814 | **Average undergraduate aid package: $13,798**

ABOUT THE INSTITUTION Independent, coed. ***Awards:*** bachelor's, master's, and doctoral degrees. 89 undergraduate majors. ***Total enrollment:*** 5,872. Undergraduates: 5,074. Freshmen: 1,032. Federal methodology is used as a basis for awarding need-based institutional aid.

UNDERGRADUATE EXPENSES for 2008–09 ***Application fee:*** $35. ***Comprehensive fee:*** $30,164 includes full-time tuition ($22,600), mandatory fees ($214), and room and board ($7350). Full-time tuition and fees vary according to student level. Room and board charges vary according to board plan. Part-time tuition and fees vary according to course load. ***Payment plan:*** Installment.

FRESHMAN FINANCIAL AID (Fall 2008, est.) 876 applied for aid; of those 81% were deemed to have need. 100% of freshmen with need received aid; of those 34% had need fully met. ***Average percent of need met:*** 78% (excluding resources awarded to replace EFC). ***Average financial aid package:*** $14,032 (excluding resources awarded to replace EFC). 18% of all full-time freshmen had no need and received non-need-based gift aid.

UNDERGRADUATE FINANCIAL AID (Fall 2008, est.) 4,068 applied for aid; of those 87% were deemed to have need. 98% of undergraduates with need received aid; of those 18% had need fully met. ***Average percent of need met:*** 66% (excluding resources awarded to replace EFC). ***Average financial aid package:*** $13,798 (excluding resources awarded to replace EFC). 23% of all full-time undergraduates had no need and received non-need-based gift aid.

GIFT AID (NEED-BASED) ***Total amount:*** $40,609,998 (9% federal, 15% state, 73% institutional, 3% external sources). ***Receiving aid:*** Freshmen: 68% (699); all full-time undergraduates: 70% (3,353). ***Average award:*** Freshmen: $12,430; Undergraduates: $10,890. ***Scholarships, grants, and awards:*** Federal Pell, FSEOG, state, private, college/university gift aid from institutional funds.

GIFT AID (NON-NEED-BASED) ***Total amount:*** $8,809,884 (95% institutional, 5% external sources). ***Receiving aid:*** Freshmen: 9% (92). Undergraduates: 8% (361). ***Average award:*** Freshmen: $9476. Undergraduates: $7561. ***Scholarships, grants, and awards by category:*** *Academic interests/achievement:* 3,614 awards ($19,342,128 total): general academic interests/achievements. *Creative arts/performance:* 231 awards ($281,942 total): art/fine arts, music, theater/drama. *Special achievements/activities:* 46 awards ($41,100 total): community service, leadership. *Special characteristics:* 1,094 awards ($3,988,124 total): children and siblings of alumni, children of faculty/staff, members of minority groups. ***Tuition waivers:*** Full or partial for employees or children of employees, senior citizens. ***ROTC:*** Army cooperative.

LOANS ***Student loans:*** $28,769,032 (55% need-based, 45% non-need-based). 82% of past graduating class borrowed through all loan programs. *Average indebtedness per student:* $18,859. ***Average need-based loan:*** Freshmen: $3669. Undergraduates: $4559. ***Parent loans:*** $6,190,806 (33% need-based, 67% non-need-based). ***Programs:*** Federal Direct (Subsidized and Unsubsidized Stafford, PLUS), FFEL (PLUS), Perkins, Federal Nursing.

WORK-STUDY ***Federal work-study:*** Total amount: $525,920; 365 jobs averaging $1684.

ATHLETIC AWARDS Total amount: $1,919,890 (71% need-based, 29% non-need-based).

APPLYING FOR FINANCIAL AID ***Required financial aid form:*** FAFSA. ***Financial aid deadline (priority):*** 3/1. ***Notification date:*** Continuous. Students must reply within 3 weeks of notification.

CONTACT Mr. David L. Pardieck, Director of Financial Assistance, Bradley University, 1501 West Bradley Avenue, Peoria, IL 61625-0002, 309-677-3089 or toll-free 800-447-6460. *E-mail:* dlp@bradley.edu.

BRANDEIS UNIVERSITY

Waltham, MA

Tuition & fees: $37,294 | **Average undergraduate aid package: $29,044**

ABOUT THE INSTITUTION Independent, coed. ***Awards:*** bachelor's, master's, and doctoral degrees and post-bachelor's certificates. 41 undergraduate majors. ***Total enrollment:*** 5,327. Undergraduates: 3,196. Freshmen: 754. Institutional methodology is used as a basis for awarding need-based institutional aid.

UNDERGRADUATE EXPENSES for 2008–09 ***Application fee:*** $55. ***Comprehensive fee:*** $47,648 includes full-time tuition ($36,122), mandatory fees ($1172), and room and board ($10,354). ***College room only:*** $5808. Room and board charges vary according to board plan and housing facility. Part-time tuition and fees vary according to course load. ***Payment plan:*** Installment.

FRESHMAN FINANCIAL AID (Fall 2008, est.) 546 applied for aid; of those 74% were deemed to have need. 100% of freshmen with need received aid; of those 23% had need fully met. ***Average percent of need met:*** 86% (excluding resources awarded to replace EFC). ***Average financial aid package:*** $29,934 (excluding resources awarded to replace EFC). 19% of all full-time freshmen had no need and received non-need-based gift aid.

UNDERGRADUATE FINANCIAL AID (Fall 2008, est.) 1,815 applied for aid; of those 84% were deemed to have need. 100% of undergraduates with need received aid; of those 23% had need fully met. ***Average percent of need met:*** 84% (excluding resources awarded to replace EFC). ***Average financial aid package:*** $29,044 (excluding resources awarded to replace EFC). 20% of all full-time undergraduates had no need and received non-need-based gift aid.

GIFT AID (NEED-BASED) ***Total amount:*** $35,056,742 (7% federal, 1% state, 89% institutional, 3% external sources). ***Receiving aid:*** Freshmen: 50% (378);

all full-time undergraduates: 46% (1,459). ***Average award:*** Freshmen: $26,874; Undergraduates: $24,027. ***Scholarships, grants, and awards:*** Federal Pell, FSEOG, state, private, college/university gift aid from institutional funds.

GIFT AID (NON-NEED-BASED) ***Total amount:*** $12,702,823 (92% institutional, 8% external sources). ***Receiving aid:*** Freshmen: 6% (45). Undergraduates: 5% (147). ***Average award:*** Freshmen: $21,688. Undergraduates: $22,448. ***Scholarships, grants, and awards by category:*** *Academic interests/achievement:* general academic interests/achievements. ***Tuition waivers:*** Full or partial for employees or children of employees. ***ROTC:*** Army cooperative, Air Force cooperative.

LOANS ***Student loans:*** $12,353,823 (63% need-based, 37% non-need-based). 77% of past graduating class borrowed through all loan programs. *Average indebtedness per student:* $20,095. ***Average need-based loan:*** Freshmen: $3990. Undergraduates: $5300. ***Parent loans:*** $5,076,388 (37% need-based, 63% non-need-based). ***Programs:*** Federal Direct (Subsidized and Unsubsidized Stafford, PLUS), Perkins, state, college/university.

WORK-STUDY ***Federal work-study:*** Total amount: $1,957,378; jobs available. ***State or other work-study/employment:*** Total amount: $664,700 (26% need-based, 74% non-need-based). Part-time jobs available.

APPLYING FOR FINANCIAL AID ***Required financial aid forms:*** FAFSA, CSS Financial Aid PROFILE, noncustodial (divorced/separated) parent's statement, business/farm supplement. ***Financial aid deadline (priority):*** 2/1.

CONTACT Peter Giumette, Student Financial Services, Brandeis University, 415 South Street, Usdan Student Center, Waltham, MA 02454-9110, 781-736-3700 or toll-free 800-622-0622 (out-of-state). *Fax:* 781-736-3719. *E-mail:* sfs@brandeis.edu.

BRENAU UNIVERSITY

Gainesville, GA

Tuition & fees: $18,800 **Average undergraduate aid package: $17,881**

ABOUT THE INSTITUTION Independent, women only. ***Awards:*** bachelor's and master's degrees (also offers coed evening and weekend programs with significant enrollment not reflected in profile). 32 undergraduate majors. ***Total enrollment:*** 893. Undergraduates: 836. Freshmen: 173. Federal methodology is used as a basis for awarding need-based institutional aid.

UNDERGRADUATE EXPENSES for 2008–09 ***Application fee:*** $35. ***Comprehensive fee:*** $28,287 includes full-time tuition ($18,550), mandatory fees ($250), and room and board ($9487). Full-time tuition and fees vary according to location and program. ***Part-time tuition:*** $618 per hour. ***Part-time fees:*** $125 per term. Part-time tuition and fees vary according to course load, location, and program. ***Payment plan:*** Installment.

FRESHMAN FINANCIAL AID (Fall 2008, est.) 150 applied for aid; of those 89% were deemed to have need. 100% of freshmen with need received aid; of those 26% had need fully met. ***Average percent of need met:*** 82% (excluding resources awarded to replace EFC). ***Average financial aid package:*** $19,235 (excluding resources awarded to replace EFC). 13% of all full-time freshmen had no need and received non-need-based gift aid.

UNDERGRADUATE FINANCIAL AID (Fall 2008, est.) 624 applied for aid; of those 88% were deemed to have need. 100% of undergraduates with need received aid; of those 24% had need fully met. ***Average percent of need met:*** 77% (excluding resources awarded to replace EFC). ***Average financial aid package:*** $17,881 (excluding resources awarded to replace EFC). 19% of all full-time undergraduates had no need and received non-need-based gift aid.

GIFT AID (NEED-BASED) ***Total amount:*** $7,388,223 (18% federal, 15% state, 66% institutional, 1% external sources). ***Receiving aid:*** Freshmen: 76% (132); all full-time undergraduates: 71% (550). ***Average award:*** Freshmen: $16,404; Undergraduates: $14,426. ***Scholarships, grants, and awards:*** Federal Pell, FSEOG, state, private, college/university gift aid from institutional funds, Academic Competitiveness Grant, National Smart Grant.

GIFT AID (NON-NEED-BASED) ***Total amount:*** $2,601,583 (32% state, 68% institutional). ***Receiving aid:*** Freshmen: 14% (24). Undergraduates: 10% (78). ***Average award:*** Freshmen: $8832. Undergraduates: $9459. ***Scholarships, grants, and awards by category:*** *Academic interests/achievement:* 700 awards ($4,612,530 total): biological sciences, business, communication, education, general academic interests/achievements, health fields, humanities. *Creative arts/performance:* 109 awards ($329,286 total): applied art and design, art/fine arts, cinema/film/broadcasting, creative writing, dance, journalism/publications, music, performing arts, theater/drama. *Special achievements/activities:* 23 awards ($98,047 total): general special achievements/activities, leadership. *Special characteristics:* 19 awards ($162,413 total): children of faculty/staff, first-generation college students, general special characteristics, international students. ***Tuition waivers:*** Full or partial for employees or children of employees.

LOANS ***Student loans:*** $4,143,030 (40% need-based, 60% non-need-based). 68% of past graduating class borrowed through all loan programs. *Average indebtedness per student:* $16,975. ***Average need-based loan:*** Freshmen: $3221. Undergraduates: $4188. ***Parent loans:*** $190,465 (93% need-based, 7% non-need-based). ***Programs:*** FFEL (Subsidized and Unsubsidized Stafford, PLUS), Perkins, state.

WORK-STUDY ***Federal work-study:*** Total amount: $240,174; 157 jobs averaging $2009. ***State or other work-study/employment:*** 28 part-time jobs averaging $1024.

ATHLETIC AWARDS Total amount: $1,078,019 (43% need-based, 57% non-need-based).

APPLYING FOR FINANCIAL AID ***Required financial aid forms:*** FAFSA, state aid form. ***Financial aid deadline (priority):*** 4/1. ***Notification date:*** Continuous.

CONTACT Pam Barrett, Director of Financial Aid, Brenau University, 500 Washington Street, SE, Gainesville, GA 30501-3697, 770-534-6176 or toll-free 800-252-5119. *Fax:* 770-538-4306. *E-mail:* pbarrett@brenau.edu.

BRESCIA UNIVERSITY

Owensboro, KY

CONTACT Martie Ruxer-Boyken, Director of Financial Aid, Brescia University, 717 Frederica Street, Owensboro, KY 42301-3023, 270-686-4290 or toll-free 877-273-7242. *Fax:* 270-686-4266. *E-mail:* martieb@brescia.edu.

BREVARD COLLEGE

Brevard, NC

Tuition & fees: $20,040 **Average undergraduate aid package: $17,554**

ABOUT THE INSTITUTION Independent United Methodist, coed. ***Awards:*** bachelor's degrees. 19 undergraduate majors. ***Total enrollment:*** 650. Undergraduates: 650. Freshmen: 183. Federal methodology is used as a basis for awarding need-based institutional aid.

UNDERGRADUATE EXPENSES for 2008–09 ***Application fee:*** $30. ***Comprehensive fee:*** $27,580 includes full-time tuition ($19,990), mandatory fees ($50), and room and board ($7540). Full-time tuition and fees vary according to course load. Room and board charges vary according to board plan and housing facility. ***Part-time tuition:*** $745 per contact hour. Part-time tuition and fees vary according to course load. ***Payment plan:*** Installment.

FRESHMAN FINANCIAL AID (Fall 2008, est.) 135 applied for aid; of those 82% were deemed to have need. 100% of freshmen with need received aid; of those 51% had need fully met. ***Average percent of need met:*** 84% (excluding resources awarded to replace EFC). ***Average financial aid package:*** $17,700 (excluding resources awarded to replace EFC). 33% of all full-time freshmen had no need and received non-need-based gift aid.

UNDERGRADUATE FINANCIAL AID (Fall 2008, est.) 525 applied for aid; of those 66% were deemed to have need. 99% of undergraduates with need received aid; of those 26% had need fully met. ***Average percent of need met:*** 83% (excluding resources awarded to replace EFC). ***Average financial aid package:*** $17,554 (excluding resources awarded to replace EFC). 15% of all full-time undergraduates had no need and received non-need-based gift aid.

GIFT AID (NEED-BASED) ***Total amount:*** $4,070,500 (20% federal, 12% state, 66% institutional, 2% external sources). ***Receiving aid:*** Freshmen: 66% (111); all full-time undergraduates: 61% (343). ***Average award:*** Freshmen: $12,740; Undergraduates: $12,825. ***Scholarships, grants, and awards:*** Federal Pell, FSEOG, state, private, college/university gift aid from institutional funds.

GIFT AID (NON-NEED-BASED) ***Total amount:*** $1,566,400 (39% state, 57% institutional, 4% external sources). ***Receiving aid:*** Freshmen: 7% (12). Undergraduates: 8% (45). ***Average award:*** Freshmen: $4825. Undergraduates: $4475. ***Scholarships, grants, and awards by category:*** *Academic interests/achievement:* 375 awards ($1,133,600 total): biological sciences, business, education, English, general academic interests/achievements, health fields, mathematics, physical sciences, premedicine, religion/biblical studies, social sciences. *Creative arts/performance:* 114 awards ($162,850 total): art/fine arts, journalism/publications, music, theater/drama. *Special achievements/activities:* 172 awards ($322,400 total): cheerleading/drum major, community service, general special achievements/activities, hobbies/interests, leadership. *Special characteristics:* 562 awards ($1,509,600 total): children of faculty/staff, international students, local/state students, previous college experience, relatives of clergy, religious affiliation, siblings of current students, veterans' children. ***Tuition waivers:*** Full or partial for employees or children of employees, senior citizens.

LOANS ***Student loans:*** $2,955,100 (52% need-based, 48% non-need-based). 64% of past graduating class borrowed through all loan programs. *Average indebtedness per student:* $19,500. ***Average need-based loan:*** Freshmen: $3950. Undergraduates: $4890. ***Parent loans:*** $594,000 (40% need-based, 60% non-need-based). ***Programs:*** FFEL (Subsidized and Unsubsidized Stafford, PLUS), Perkins, state.

WORK-STUDY ***Federal work-study:*** Total amount: $46,000; 45 jobs averaging $1600. ***State or other work-study/employment:*** Total amount: $110,000 (100% non-need-based). 75 part-time jobs averaging $1650.

ATHLETIC AWARDS Total amount: $1,585,000 (55% need-based, 45% non-need-based).

APPLYING FOR FINANCIAL AID ***Required financial aid forms:*** FAFSA, state aid form. ***Financial aid deadline (priority):*** 4/15. ***Notification date:*** Continuous. Students must reply within 4 weeks of notification.

CONTACT Ms. Lisanne J. Masterson, Director of Financial Aid, Brevard College, 1 Brevard College Drive, Brevard, NC 28712, 828-884-8287 or toll-free 800-527-9090. *Fax:* 828-884-3790. *E-mail:* finaid@brevard.edu.

BREWTON-PARKER COLLEGE

Mt. Vernon, GA

Tuition & fees: $14,730 **Average undergraduate aid package: $11,809**

ABOUT THE INSTITUTION Independent Southern Baptist, coed. ***Awards:*** associate and bachelor's degrees. 31 undergraduate majors. ***Total enrollment:*** 1,017. Undergraduates: 1,017. Freshmen: 312. Federal methodology is used as a basis for awarding need-based institutional aid.

UNDERGRADUATE EXPENSES for 2008–09 ***Application fee:*** $25. ***Comprehensive fee:*** $20,350 includes full-time tuition ($13,440), mandatory fees ($1290), and room and board ($5620). ***College room only:*** $2470. Room and board charges vary according to board plan and housing facility. ***Part-time tuition:*** $420 per credit hour. ***Payment plan:*** Installment.

FRESHMAN FINANCIAL AID (Fall 2007) 145 applied for aid; of those 90% were deemed to have need. 98% of freshmen with need received aid; of those 24% had need fully met. ***Average percent of need met:*** 63% (excluding resources awarded to replace EFC). ***Average financial aid package:*** $10,351 (excluding resources awarded to replace EFC). 12% of all full-time freshmen had no need and received non-need-based gift aid.

UNDERGRADUATE FINANCIAL AID (Fall 2007) 628 applied for aid; of those 91% were deemed to have need. 98% of undergraduates with need received aid; of those 18% had need fully met. ***Average percent of need met:*** 68% (excluding resources awarded to replace EFC). ***Average financial aid package:*** $11,809 (excluding resources awarded to replace EFC). 10% of all full-time undergraduates had no need and received non-need-based gift aid.

GIFT AID (NEED-BASED) ***Total amount:*** $6,032,553 (28% federal, 21% state, 43% institutional, 8% external sources). ***Receiving aid:*** Freshmen: 81% (128); all full-time undergraduates: 85% (555). ***Average award:*** Freshmen: $8062; Undergraduates: $8785. ***Scholarships, grants, and awards:*** Federal Pell, FSEOG, state, private, college/university gift aid from institutional funds, United Negro College Fund.

GIFT AID (NON-NEED-BASED) ***Total amount:*** $941,057 (37% state, 50% institutional, 13% external sources). ***Receiving aid:*** Freshmen: 13% (21). Undergraduates: 11% (69). ***Average award:*** Freshmen: $3997. Undergraduates: $3832. ***Scholarships, grants, and awards by category:*** *Academic interests/achievement:* 262 awards ($627,748 total): general academic interests/achievements. *Creative arts/performance:* 51 awards ($124,981 total): music. *Special achievements/activities:* 76 awards ($52,521 total): cheerleading/drum major, religious involvement. *Special characteristics:* 423 awards ($287,245 total): children of faculty/staff, international students, out-of-state students, relatives of clergy, religious affiliation. ***Tuition waivers:*** Full or partial for employees or children of employees, senior citizens.

LOANS ***Student loans:*** $5,384,912 (79% need-based, 21% non-need-based). 89% of past graduating class borrowed through all loan programs. *Average indebtedness per student:* $24,592. ***Average need-based loan:*** Freshmen: $2746. Undergraduates: $3443. ***Parent loans:*** $326,247 (38% need-based, 62% non-need-based). ***Programs:*** FFEL (Subsidized and Unsubsidized Stafford, PLUS), Perkins, state, college/university.

WORK-STUDY ***Federal work-study:*** Total amount: $150,142; 161 jobs averaging $860. ***State or other work-study/employment:*** Total amount: $115,950 (25% need-based, 75% non-need-based). 88 part-time jobs averaging $1318.

ATHLETIC AWARDS Total amount: $869,783 (69% need-based, 31% non-need-based).

APPLYING FOR FINANCIAL AID ***Required financial aid forms:*** FAFSA, state aid form, individual grant forms. ***Financial aid deadline:*** 5/1. ***Notification date:*** Continuous. Students must reply within 2 weeks of notification.

CONTACT Mrs. Jackie White, Director of Financial Aid, Brewton-Parker College, PO Box 197, Mt. Vernon, GA 30445-0197, 800-342-1087 Ext. 209 or toll-free 800-342-1087 Ext. 245. *Fax:* 912-583-3598. *E-mail:* finaid@bpc.edu.

BRIARCLIFFE COLLEGE

Bethpage, NY

CONTACT Johanna Kelly, Financial Aid Director, Briarcliffe College, 1055 Stewart Avenue, Bethpage, NY 11714, 516-918-3600 or toll-free 888-333-1150 (in-state).

BRIAR CLIFF UNIVERSITY

Sioux City, IA

CONTACT Financial Aid Office, Briar Cliff University, 3303 Rebecca Street, PO Box 2100, Sioux City, IA 51104-2100, 712-279-5200 or toll-free 800-662-3303 Ext. 5200. *Fax:* 712-279-5410.

BRIDGEWATER COLLEGE

Bridgewater, VA

Tuition & fees: $24,500 **Average undergraduate aid package: $20,620**

ABOUT THE INSTITUTION Independent religious, coed. ***Awards:*** bachelor's degrees. 45 undergraduate majors. ***Total enrollment:*** 1,514. Undergraduates: 1,514. Freshmen: 488. Federal methodology is used as a basis for awarding need-based institutional aid.

UNDERGRADUATE EXPENSES for 2009–10 ***Application fee:*** $30. ***Comprehensive fee:*** $34,400 includes full-time tuition ($24,500) and room and board ($9900). ***College room only:*** $4960. ***Part-time tuition:*** $825 per credit hour. ***Part-time fees:*** $30 per term.

FRESHMAN FINANCIAL AID (Fall 2008, est.) 451 applied for aid; of those 84% were deemed to have need. 100% of freshmen with need received aid; of those 18% had need fully met. ***Average percent of need met:*** 77% (excluding resources awarded to replace EFC). ***Average financial aid package:*** $21,286 (excluding resources awarded to replace EFC). 22% of all full-time freshmen had no need and received non-need-based gift aid.

UNDERGRADUATE FINANCIAL AID (Fall 2008, est.) 1,238 applied for aid; of those 85% were deemed to have need. 100% of undergraduates with need received aid; of those 14% had need fully met. ***Average percent of need met:*** 78% (excluding resources awarded to replace EFC). ***Average financial aid package:*** $20,620 (excluding resources awarded to replace EFC). 26% of all full-time undergraduates had no need and received non-need-based gift aid.

GIFT AID (NEED-BASED) ***Total amount:*** $16,677,876 (8% federal, 16% state, 73% institutional, 3% external sources). ***Receiving aid:*** Freshmen: 77% (378); all full-time undergraduates: 71% (1,050). ***Average award:*** Freshmen: $17,739; Undergraduates: $15,877. ***Scholarships, grants, and awards:*** Federal Pell, FSEOG, state, private, college/university gift aid from institutional funds.

GIFT AID (NON-NEED-BASED) ***Total amount:*** $5,222,298 (1% federal, 20% state, 78% institutional, 1% external sources). ***Receiving aid:*** Freshmen: 76% (373). Undergraduates: 66% (976). ***Average award:*** Freshmen: $10,922. Undergraduates: $10,532. ***Scholarships, grants, and awards by category:*** *Academic interests/achievement:* 1,106 awards ($11,394,204 total): general academic interests/achievements. *Creative arts/performance:* 39 awards ($33,450 total): music. *Special characteristics:* 177 awards ($177,527 total): international students, religious affiliation, siblings of current students.

LOANS ***Student loans:*** $9,534,683 (70% need-based, 30% non-need-based). 71% of past graduating class borrowed through all loan programs. *Average indebtedness per student:* $29,519. ***Average need-based loan:*** Freshmen: $4575. Undergraduates: $5059. ***Parent loans:*** $2,227,910 (83% need-based, 17% non-need-based). ***Programs:*** FFEL (Subsidized and Unsubsidized Stafford, PLUS), Perkins.

WORK-STUDY ***Federal work-study:*** Total amount: $263,484; 226 jobs averaging $1165.

APPLYING FOR FINANCIAL AID ***Required financial aid forms:*** FAFSA, state aid form. ***Financial aid deadline (priority):*** 3/1. ***Notification date:*** Continuous beginning 3/16. Students must reply within 2 weeks of notification.

CONTACT Mr. Scott Morrison, Director of Financial Aid, Bridgewater College, College Box 27, Bridgewater, VA 22812-1599, 540-828-5376 or toll-free 800-759-8328. *Fax:* 540-828-5671. *E-mail:* smorriso@bridgewater.edu.

BRIDGEWATER STATE COLLEGE

Bridgewater, MA

Tuition & fees (MA res): $6237 **Average undergraduate aid package: $7687**

ABOUT THE INSTITUTION State-supported, coed. ***Awards:*** bachelor's and master's degrees and post-bachelor's and post-master's certificates. 75 undergraduate majors. ***Total enrollment:*** 8,497. Undergraduates: 8,497. Federal methodology is used as a basis for awarding need-based institutional aid.

UNDERGRADUATE EXPENSES for 2009–10 ***Tuition, state resident:*** full-time $910. ***Tuition, nonresident:*** full-time $7050. ***Required fees:*** full-time $5327. ***College room and board:*** $6852.

FRESHMAN FINANCIAL AID (Fall 2007) 1,369 applied for aid; of those 71% were deemed to have need. 99% of freshmen with need received aid. ***Average percent of need met:*** 75% (excluding resources awarded to replace EFC). ***Average financial aid package:*** $7968 (excluding resources awarded to replace EFC). 1% of all full-time freshmen had no need and received non-need-based gift aid.

UNDERGRADUATE FINANCIAL AID (Fall 2007) 5,187 applied for aid; of those 73% were deemed to have need. 100% of undergraduates with need received aid. ***Average percent of need met:*** 75% (excluding resources awarded to replace EFC). ***Average financial aid package:*** $7687 (excluding resources awarded to replace EFC). 1% of all full-time undergraduates had no need and received non-need-based gift aid.

GIFT AID (NEED-BASED) ***Total amount:*** $9,936,980 (46% federal, 36% state, 18% institutional). ***Receiving aid:*** Freshmen: 41% (810); all full-time undergraduates: 46% (3,109). ***Average award:*** Freshmen: $3620; Undergraduates: $3229. ***Scholarships, grants, and awards:*** Federal Pell, FSEOG, state, private, college/university gift aid from institutional funds.

GIFT AID (NON-NEED-BASED) ***Total amount:*** $365,719 (100% institutional). ***Receiving aid:*** Freshmen: 12% (231). Undergraduates: 6% (392). ***Average award:*** Freshmen: $6094. Undergraduates: $4767. ***Scholarships, grants, and awards by category:*** *Academic interests/achievement:* general academic interests/achievements. ***ROTC:*** Army cooperative, Air Force cooperative.

LOANS ***Student loans:*** $33,699,132 (42% need-based, 58% non-need-based). *Average indebtedness per student:* $21,399. ***Average need-based loan:*** Freshmen: $3400. Undergraduates: $3812. ***Parent loans:*** $2,070,335 (100% non-need-based). ***Programs:*** Federal Direct (Subsidized and Unsubsidized Stafford, PLUS), Perkins, state.

WORK-STUDY ***Federal work-study:*** Total amount: $651,784; 533 jobs averaging $1223.

APPLYING FOR FINANCIAL AID ***Required financial aid form:*** FAFSA. ***Financial aid deadline (priority):*** 3/1. ***Notification date:*** 3/20.

CONTACT Office of Financial Aid, Bridgewater State College, Tillinghast Hall, Bridgewater, MA 02325-0001, 508-531-1341. *Fax:* 508-531-1728. *E-mail:* finaid@bridgew.edu.

BRIGHAM YOUNG UNIVERSITY

Provo, UT

Tuition & fees: N/R **Average undergraduate aid package: $4719**

ABOUT THE INSTITUTION Independent religious, coed. ***Awards:*** bachelor's, master's, doctoral, and first professional degrees. 102 undergraduate majors. ***Total enrollment:*** 34,244. Undergraduates: 30,912. Freshmen: 4,665.

UNDERGRADUATE EXPENSES for 2009–10 ***Application fee:*** $30. Latter Day Saints full-time student $4,290 per year, non-LDS full-time student $8,580.

FRESHMAN FINANCIAL AID (Fall 2007) 1,975 applied for aid; of those 63% were deemed to have need. 82% of freshmen with need received aid. ***Average percent of need met:*** 24% (excluding resources awarded to replace EFC). ***Average financial aid package:*** $2816 (excluding resources awarded to replace EFC). 35% of all full-time freshmen had no need and received non-need-based gift aid.

UNDERGRADUATE FINANCIAL AID (Fall 2007) 15,910 applied for aid; of those 76% were deemed to have need. 92% of undergraduates with need received aid. ***Average percent of need met:*** 34% (excluding resources awarded to replace EFC). ***Average financial aid package:*** $4719 (excluding resources awarded to replace EFC). 29% of all full-time undergraduates had no need and received non-need-based gift aid.

GIFT AID (NEED-BASED) ***Total amount:*** $39,748,382 (90% federal, 10% institutional). ***Receiving aid:*** Freshmen: 10% (563); all full-time undergraduates: 26% (8,658). ***Average award:*** Freshmen: $1770; Undergraduates: $3042. ***Scholarships, grants, and awards:*** Federal Pell, state, private, college/university gift aid from institutional funds.

GIFT AID (NON-NEED-BASED) ***Total amount:*** $44,000,696 (83% institutional, 17% external sources). ***Receiving aid:*** Freshmen: 10% (610). Undergraduates: 16% (5,122). ***Average award:*** Freshmen: $3014. Undergraduates: $3266. ***ROTC:*** Army, Air Force.

LOANS ***Student loans:*** $27,764,701 (71% need-based, 29% non-need-based). 35% of past graduating class borrowed through all loan programs. *Average indebtedness per student:* $13,926. ***Average need-based loan:*** Freshmen: $1046. Undergraduates: $1676. ***Parent loans:*** $1,685,298 (100% non-need-based). ***Programs:*** FFEL (Subsidized and Unsubsidized Stafford, PLUS), college/university.

WORK-STUDY ***State or other work-study/employment:*** Total amount: $142,539 (100% need-based). Part-time jobs available.

ATHLETIC AWARDS Total amount: $3,831,218 (100% non-need-based).

APPLYING FOR FINANCIAL AID ***Required financial aid form:*** FAFSA. ***Financial aid deadline (priority):*** 4/15. ***Notification date:*** Continuous.

CONTACT Paul R. Conrad, Director of Financial Aid, Brigham Young University, A-41 ASB, Provo, UT 84602, 801-422-7355. *Fax:* 801-422-0234. *E-mail:* paul_conrad@byu.edu.

BRIGHAM YOUNG UNIVERSITY–HAWAII

Laie, HI

ABOUT THE INSTITUTION Independent Latter-day Saints, coed. 51 undergraduate majors.

GIFT AID (NEED-BASED) ***Scholarships, grants, and awards:*** Federal Pell, private, college/university gift aid from institutional funds.

LOANS ***Programs:*** FFEL (Subsidized and Unsubsidized Stafford, PLUS), college/university.

APPLYING FOR FINANCIAL AID ***Required financial aid forms:*** FAFSA, institution's own form.

CONTACT Mr. Wes Duke, Director of Financial Aid, Brigham Young University–Hawaii, BYUH #1980, 55-220 Kulanui Street, Laie, HI 96762, 808-293-3530. *Fax:* 808-293-3349. *E-mail:* duekw@byuh.edu.

BROOKLYN COLLEGE OF THE CITY UNIVERSITY OF NEW YORK

Brooklyn, NY

Tuition & fees: N/R **Average undergraduate aid package: $5500**

ABOUT THE INSTITUTION State and locally supported, coed. 76 undergraduate majors. Federal methodology is used as a basis for awarding need-based institutional aid.

FRESHMAN FINANCIAL AID (Fall 2008, est.) 1,168 applied for aid; of those 91% were deemed to have need. 100% of freshmen with need received aid; of those 98% had need fully met. ***Average percent of need met:*** 99% (excluding resources awarded to replace EFC). ***Average financial aid package:*** $5500 (excluding resources awarded to replace EFC). 12% of all full-time freshmen had no need and received non-need-based gift aid.

UNDERGRADUATE FINANCIAL AID (Fall 2008, est.) 7,123 applied for aid; of those 94% were deemed to have need. 100% of undergraduates with need received aid; of those 100% had need fully met. ***Average percent of need met:*** 99% (excluding resources awarded to replace EFC). ***Average financial aid package:*** $5500 (excluding resources awarded to replace EFC). 10% of all full-time undergraduates had no need and received non-need-based gift aid.

GIFT AID (NEED-BASED) ***Total amount:*** $36,598,280 (52% federal, 41% state, 7% institutional). ***Receiving aid:*** Freshmen: 74% (980); all full-time undergraduates: 66% (6,002). ***Average award:*** Freshmen: $3200; Undergraduates: $3200. ***Scholarships, grants, and awards:*** Federal Pell, FSEOG, state, private, college/university gift aid from institutional funds.

GIFT AID (NON-NEED-BASED) ***Total amount:*** $623,500 (10% federal, 74% state, 3% institutional, 13% external sources). ***Receiving aid:*** Freshmen: 24% (322). Undergraduates: 20% (1,800). ***Average award:*** Freshmen: $4000. Undergraduates: $4000. ***Scholarships, grants, and awards by category:*** *Academic interests/achievement:* 180 awards ($500,000 total): general academic interests/achievements. *Creative arts/performance:* 20 awards ($40,000 total): general creative arts/performance. *Special achievements/activities:* general special achievements/activities. *Special characteristics:* general special characteristics.

LOANS ***Student loans:*** $21,560,000 (98% need-based, 2% non-need-based). 45% of past graduating class borrowed through all loan programs. *Average indebtedness per student:* $16,600. ***Average need-based loan:*** Freshmen: $2650. Undergraduates: $2250. ***Parent loans:*** $280,000 (100% need-based). ***Programs:*** Federal Direct (Subsidized and Unsubsidized Stafford, PLUS), Perkins.

WORK-STUDY ***Federal work-study:*** Total amount: $670,000; 1,100 jobs averaging $1200.

APPLYING FOR FINANCIAL AID ***Required financial aid forms:*** FAFSA, state aid form. ***Financial aid deadline:*** 5/1 (priority: 5/1). ***Notification date:*** Continuous beginning 5/15.

CONTACT Sherwood Johnson, Director of Financial Aid, Brooklyn College of the City University of New York, 2900 Bedford Avenue, Brooklyn, NY 11210-2889, 718-951-5045. *Fax:* 718-951-4778. *E-mail:* sjohnson@brooklyn.cuny.edu.

BROOKS INSTITUTE

Santa Barbara, CA

Tuition & fees: $26,760 **Average undergraduate aid package: $7833**

ABOUT THE INSTITUTION Proprietary, coed. 3 undergraduate majors. Federal methodology is used as a basis for awarding need-based institutional aid.

UNDERGRADUATE EXPENSES for 2008–09 ***Tuition:*** full-time $26,160.

FRESHMAN FINANCIAL AID (Fall 2007) 315 applied for aid. ***Average percent of need met:*** 95% (excluding resources awarded to replace EFC). ***Average financial aid package:*** $6500 (excluding resources awarded to replace EFC).

UNDERGRADUATE FINANCIAL AID (Fall 2007) 692 applied for aid; of those 99% were deemed to have need. 100% of undergraduates with need received aid; of those 96% had need fully met. ***Average percent of need met:*** 90% (excluding resources awarded to replace EFC). ***Average financial aid package:*** $7833 (excluding resources awarded to replace EFC).

GIFT AID (NEED-BASED) ***Total amount:*** $3,695,227 (61% federal, 35% state, 2% institutional, 2% external sources). ***Receiving aid:*** Freshmen: 7% (35); all full-time undergraduates: 7% (74). ***Average award:*** Freshmen: $2300; Undergraduates: $2000. ***Scholarships, grants, and awards:*** Federal Pell, FSEOG, state, private, college/university gift aid from institutional funds.

GIFT AID (NON-NEED-BASED) ***Total amount:*** $605,333 (100% institutional). ***Receiving aid:*** Freshmen: 4% (20). Undergraduates: 4% (44). ***Scholarships, grants, and awards by category:*** *Creative arts/performance:* applied art and design.

LOANS ***Student loans:*** $43,734,711 (15% need-based, 85% non-need-based). 80% of past graduating class borrowed through all loan programs. *Average indebtedness per student:* $119,109. ***Average need-based loan:*** Freshmen: $3500. Undergraduates: $4000. ***Programs:*** FFEL (Subsidized and Unsubsidized Stafford, PLUS), alternative loans.

WORK-STUDY ***Federal work-study:*** Total amount: $341,596; 233 jobs averaging $1466.

APPLYING FOR FINANCIAL AID ***Required financial aid form:*** FAFSA. ***Financial aid deadline (priority):*** 3/2. ***Notification date:*** Continuous. Students must reply within 4 weeks of notification.

CONTACT Stacey Eymann, Acting Director of Financial Aid, Brooks Institute, 27 East Cota Street, Santa Barbara, CA 93101, 888-304-3456. *Fax:* 805-966-2909. *E-mail:* seymann@brooks.edu.

BROWN UNIVERSITY

Providence, RI

Tuition & fees: $37,718 **Average undergraduate aid package: $33,521**

ABOUT THE INSTITUTION Independent, coed. ***Awards:*** bachelor's, master's, doctoral, and first professional degrees. 76 undergraduate majors. ***Total enrollment:*** 6,095. Undergraduates: 6,095. Freshmen: 1,548. Both federal and institutional methodology are used as a basis for awarding need-based institutional aid.

UNDERGRADUATE EXPENSES for 2008–09 ***Application fee:*** $70. ***Comprehensive fee:*** $47,740 includes full-time tuition ($36,928), mandatory fees ($790), and room and board ($10,022). ***College room only:*** $6216. Room and board charges vary according to board plan. ***Part-time tuition:*** $4616 per course. ***Payment plans:*** Guaranteed tuition, tuition prepayment, installment.

FRESHMAN FINANCIAL AID (Fall 2008, est.) 918 applied for aid; of those 75% were deemed to have need. 100% of freshmen with need received aid; of those 100% had need fully met. ***Average percent of need met:*** 100% (excluding resources awarded to replace EFC). ***Average financial aid package:*** $34,452 (excluding resources awarded to replace EFC).

UNDERGRADUATE FINANCIAL AID (Fall 2008, est.) 3,007 applied for aid; of those 86% were deemed to have need. 100% of undergraduates with need received aid; of those 100% had need fully met. ***Average percent of need met:*** 100% (excluding resources awarded to replace EFC). ***Average financial aid package:*** $33,521 (excluding resources awarded to replace EFC).

GIFT AID (NEED-BASED) ***Total amount:*** $76,100,730 (6% federal, 90% institutional, 4% external sources). ***Receiving aid:*** Freshmen: 42% (645); all full-time undergraduates: 41% (2,402). ***Average award:*** Freshmen: $30,375; Undergraduates: $29,926. ***Scholarships, grants, and awards:*** Federal Pell, FSEOG, state, private, college/university gift aid from institutional funds.

GIFT AID (NON-NEED-BASED) ***Total amount:*** $3,644,193 (17% federal, 83% external sources). ***Tuition waivers:*** Full or partial for employees or children of employees. ***ROTC:*** Army cooperative.

LOANS ***Student loans:*** $13,000,771 (49% need-based, 51% non-need-based). 44% of past graduating class borrowed through all loan programs. *Average indebtedness per student:* $19,390. ***Average need-based loan:*** Freshmen: $2234. Undergraduates: $2747. ***Parent loans:*** $7,807,658 (100% non-need-based). ***Programs:*** Federal Direct (Subsidized and Unsubsidized Stafford, PLUS), Perkins, college/university.

WORK-STUDY ***Federal work-study:*** Total amount: $3,023,578; 1,441 jobs averaging $2040. ***State or other work-study/employment:*** Total amount: $753,373 (100% need-based). 329 part-time jobs averaging $2148.

APPLYING FOR FINANCIAL AID ***Required financial aid forms:*** FAFSA, CSS Financial Aid PROFILE, noncustodial (divorced/separated) parent's statement, business/farm supplement. ***Financial aid deadline:*** 2/1. ***Notification date:*** 4/1. Students must reply by 5/1.

CONTACT Office of Financial Aid, Brown University, Box 1827, Providence, RI 02912, 401-863-2721. *Fax:* 401-863-7575. *E-mail:* Financial_Aid@brown.edu.

BRYAN COLLEGE

Dayton, TN

Tuition & fees: $17,860 **Average undergraduate aid package: $10,593**

ABOUT THE INSTITUTION Independent interdenominational, coed. ***Awards:*** associate, bachelor's, and master's degrees. 28 undergraduate majors. ***Total enrollment:*** 1,079. Undergraduates: 1,036. Both federal and institutional methodology are used as a basis for awarding need-based institutional aid.

UNDERGRADUATE EXPENSES for 2009–10 ***Application fee:*** $30. ***Comprehensive fee:*** $23,214 includes full-time tuition ($17,740), mandatory fees ($120), and room and board ($5354). ***Part-time tuition:*** $760 per credit.

FRESHMAN FINANCIAL AID (Fall 2008, est.) 183 applied for aid; of those 80% were deemed to have need. 100% of freshmen with need received aid; of those 33% had need fully met. ***Average percent of need met:*** 52% (excluding resources awarded to replace EFC). ***Average financial aid package:*** $13,561 (excluding resources awarded to replace EFC). 24% of all full-time freshmen had no need and received non-need-based gift aid.

UNDERGRADUATE FINANCIAL AID (Fall 2008, est.) 859 applied for aid; of those 85% were deemed to have need. 99% of undergraduates with need received aid; of those 36% had need fully met. ***Average percent of need met:***

63% (excluding resources awarded to replace EFC). ***Average financial aid package:*** $10,593 (excluding resources awarded to replace EFC). 20% of all full-time undergraduates had no need and received non-need-based gift aid.

GIFT AID (NEED-BASED) ***Total amount:*** $4,625,052 (27% federal, 25% state, 42% institutional, 6% external sources). ***Receiving aid:*** Freshmen: 66% (137); all full-time undergraduates: 55% (568). ***Average award:*** Freshmen: $7363; Undergraduates: $6532. ***Scholarships, grants, and awards:*** Federal Pell, FSEOG, state, private, college/university gift aid from institutional funds.

GIFT AID (NON-NEED-BASED) ***Total amount:*** $711,458 (26% state, 70% institutional, 4% external sources). ***Receiving aid:*** Freshmen: 60% (126). Undergraduates: 43% (445). ***Average award:*** Freshmen: $5313. Undergraduates: $7600. ***Scholarships, grants, and awards by category:*** *Academic interests/achievement:* biological sciences, business, communication, computer science, education, English, foreign languages, general academic interests/achievements, humanities, mathematics, physical sciences, premedicine, religion/biblical studies, social sciences. *Creative arts/performance:* art/fine arts, journalism/publications, music, performing arts, theater/drama. *Special achievements/activities:* community service, general special achievements/activities, leadership, religious involvement. *Special characteristics:* children and siblings of alumni, children of current students, children of educators, children of faculty/staff, general special characteristics, handicapped students, international students, local/state students, relatives of clergy, religious affiliation, spouses of current students.

LOANS ***Student loans:*** $4,692,909 (91% need-based, 9% non-need-based). 73% of past graduating class borrowed through all loan programs. *Average indebtedness per student:* $15,034. ***Average need-based loan:*** Freshmen: $2943. Undergraduates: $3868. ***Parent loans:*** $815,525 (76% need-based, 24% non-need-based). ***Programs:*** Federal Direct (Subsidized and Unsubsidized Stafford, PLUS), FFEL (Subsidized and Unsubsidized Stafford, PLUS), Perkins.

WORK-STUDY ***Federal work-study:*** Total amount: $208,133; jobs available.

ATHLETIC AWARDS Total amount: $965,495 (83% need-based, 17% non-need-based).

APPLYING FOR FINANCIAL AID ***Required financial aid forms:*** FAFSA, institution's own form. ***Financial aid deadline (priority):*** 1/31. ***Notification date:*** Continuous. Students must reply within 2 weeks of notification.

CONTACT Rick Taphorn, Director of Financial Aid, Bryan College, PO Box 7000, Dayton, TN 37321-7000, 423-775-7339 or toll-free 800-277-9522. *Fax:* 423-775-7300. *E-mail:* finaid@bryan.edu.

BRYANT & STRATTON COLLEGE

Cleveland, OH

CONTACT Bill Davenport, Financial Aid Supervisor, Bryant & Stratton College, 1700 East 13th Street, Cleveland, OH 44114-3203, 216-771-1700. *Fax:* 216-771-7787.

BRYANT & STRATTON COLLEGE—WAUWATOSA CAMPUS

Wauwatosa, WI

CONTACT Financial Aid Office, Bryant & Stratton College—Wauwatosa Campus, 10950 W. Potter Road, Wauwatosa, WI 53226, 414-302-7000.

BRYANT UNIVERSITY

Smithfield, RI

Tuition & fees: $32,286 **Average undergraduate aid package: $20,281**

ABOUT THE INSTITUTION Independent, coed. ***Awards:*** bachelor's and master's degrees. 16 undergraduate majors. ***Total enrollment:*** 3,800. Undergraduates: 3,515. Freshmen: 911. Federal methodology is used as a basis for awarding need-based institutional aid.

UNDERGRADUATE EXPENSES for 2009–10 ***Application fee:*** $50. ***Comprehensive fee:*** $44,043 includes full-time tuition ($31,974), mandatory fees ($312), and room and board ($11,757). ***College room only:*** $7038. ***Part-time tuition:*** $1347 per credit hour.

FRESHMAN FINANCIAL AID (Fall 2008, est.) 717 applied for aid; of those 85% were deemed to have need. 100% of freshmen with need received aid; of those 65% had need fully met. ***Average percent of need met:*** 69% (excluding resources awarded to replace EFC). ***Average financial aid package:*** $21,021 (excluding resources awarded to replace EFC). 10% of all full-time freshmen had no need and received non-need-based gift aid.

UNDERGRADUATE FINANCIAL AID (Fall 2008, est.) 2,525 applied for aid; of those 88% were deemed to have need. 100% of undergraduates with need received aid; of those 69% had need fully met. ***Average percent of need met:*** 68% (excluding resources awarded to replace EFC). ***Average financial aid package:*** $20,281 (excluding resources awarded to replace EFC). 11% of all full-time undergraduates had no need and received non-need-based gift aid.

GIFT AID (NEED-BASED) ***Total amount:*** $20,705,887 (8% federal, 2% state, 87% institutional, 3% external sources). ***Receiving aid:*** Freshmen: 56% (506); all full-time undergraduates: 54% (1,794). ***Average award:*** Freshmen: $11,097; Undergraduates: $10,369. ***Scholarships, grants, and awards:*** Federal Pell, FSEOG, state, private, college/university gift aid from institutional funds.

GIFT AID (NON-NEED-BASED) ***Total amount:*** $13,578,165 (96% institutional, 4% external sources). ***Receiving aid:*** Freshmen: 42% (377). Undergraduates: 43% (1,441). ***Average award:*** Freshmen: $11,870. Undergraduates: $11,647. ***Scholarships, grants, and awards by category:*** *Academic interests/achievement:* 797 awards ($7,562,497 total): engineering/technologies, general academic interests/achievements. *Special characteristics:* 150 awards ($1,583,894 total): children and siblings of alumni, local/state students, members of minority groups, siblings of current students. ***ROTC:*** Army.

LOANS ***Student loans:*** $27,510,426 (38% need-based, 62% non-need-based). 86% of past graduating class borrowed through all loan programs. *Average indebtedness per student:* $34,268. ***Average need-based loan:*** Freshmen: $4616. Undergraduates: $4917. ***Parent loans:*** $7,618,091 (15% need-based, 85% non-need-based). ***Programs:*** Federal Direct (Subsidized and Unsubsidized Stafford, PLUS), FFEL (PLUS), Perkins, privately funded education loans.

WORK-STUDY ***Federal work-study:*** Total amount: $434,617; jobs available. ***State or other work-study/employment:*** Total amount: $827,645 (37% need-based, 63% non-need-based). Part-time jobs available.

ATHLETIC AWARDS Total amount: $2,689,882 (30% need-based, 70% non-need-based).

APPLYING FOR FINANCIAL AID ***Required financial aid form:*** FAFSA. ***Financial aid deadline (priority):*** 2/15. ***Notification date:*** 3/21. Students must reply by 5/1.

CONTACT Mr. John B. Canning, Director of Financial Aid, Bryant University, Office of Financial Aid, 1150 Douglas Pike, Smithfield, RI 02917-1284, 401-232-6020 or toll-free 800-622-7001. *Fax:* 401-232-6293. *E-mail:* jcanning@bryant.edu.

BRYN ATHYN COLLEGE OF THE NEW CHURCH

Bryn Athyn, PA

Tuition & fees: $10,620 **Average undergraduate aid package: $9987**

ABOUT THE INSTITUTION Independent religious, coed. ***Awards:*** associate, bachelor's, master's, and first professional degrees and first professional certificates. 7 undergraduate majors. ***Total enrollment:*** 164. Undergraduates: 145. Freshmen: 43. Both federal and institutional methodology are used as a basis for awarding need-based institutional aid.

UNDERGRADUATE EXPENSES for 2008–09 ***Comprehensive fee:*** $16,473 includes full-time tuition ($8676), mandatory fees ($1944), and room and board ($5853). ***Part-time tuition:*** $335 per credit. ***Part-time fees:*** $74 per credit. ***Payment plan:*** Installment.

FRESHMAN FINANCIAL AID (Fall 2008, est.) 28 applied for aid; of those 71% were deemed to have need. 100% of freshmen with need received aid; of those 35% had need fully met. ***Average percent of need met:*** 93% (excluding resources awarded to replace EFC). ***Average financial aid package:*** $11,104 (excluding resources awarded to replace EFC). 28% of all full-time freshmen had no need and received non-need-based gift aid.

UNDERGRADUATE FINANCIAL AID (Fall 2008, est.) 92 applied for aid; of those 72% were deemed to have need. 100% of undergraduates with need received aid; of those 45% had need fully met. ***Average percent of need met:*** 95% (excluding resources awarded to replace EFC). ***Average financial aid package:*** $9987 (excluding resources awarded to replace EFC). 16% of all full-time undergraduates had no need and received non-need-based gift aid.

GIFT AID (NEED-BASED) ***Total amount:*** $528,533 (14% federal, 5% state, 79% institutional, 2% external sources). ***Receiving aid:*** Freshmen: 47% (20); all full-time undergraduates: 46% (63). ***Average award:*** Freshmen: $10,011; Undergraduates: $8358. ***Scholarships, grants, and awards:*** Federal Pell, FSEOG, state, private, college/university gift aid from institutional funds.

GIFT AID (NON-NEED-BASED) ***Total amount:*** $79,747 (85% institutional, 15% external sources). ***Receiving aid:*** Freshmen: 7% (3). Undergraduates: 5% (7). ***Average award:*** Freshmen: $3115. Undergraduates: $2232. ***Scholarships, grants, and awards by category:*** *Academic interests/achievement:* 14 awards ($34,000 total): general academic interests/achievements. *Special characteristics:* 2 awards ($6374 total): general special characteristics. ***Tuition waivers:*** Full or partial for senior citizens.

LOANS ***Student loans:*** $216,895 (45% need-based, 55% non-need-based). 36% of past graduating class borrowed through all loan programs. *Average indebtedness per student:* $8299. ***Average need-based loan:*** Freshmen: $2506. Undergraduates: $3329. ***Parent loans:*** $33,423 (100% non-need-based). ***Programs:*** Federal Direct (Subsidized and Unsubsidized Stafford, PLUS), FFEL (Subsidized and Unsubsidized Stafford, PLUS), state, college/university, private/alternative loans.

WORK-STUDY ***State or other work-study/employment:*** Total amount: $62,345 (15% need-based, 85% non-need-based). Part-time jobs available.

APPLYING FOR FINANCIAL AID ***Required financial aid forms:*** FAFSA, institution's own form, income tax form(s). ***Financial aid deadline:*** 7/1 (priority: 3/1). ***Notification date:*** Continuous. Students must reply by 5/1 or within 2 weeks of notification.

CONTACT Wendy Cooper, Associate Director of Financial Aid, Bryn Athyn College of the New Church, Box 717, Bryn Athyn, PA 19009, 267-502-2630. *Fax:* 267-502-4866. *E-mail:* financialaid@brynathyn.edu.

BRYN MAWR COLLEGE

Bryn Mawr, PA

Tuition & fees: $38,034 **Average undergraduate aid package: $35,513**

ABOUT THE INSTITUTION Independent, undergraduate: women only; graduate: coed. ***Awards:*** bachelor's, master's, and doctoral degrees and post-bachelor's certificates. 33 undergraduate majors. ***Total enrollment:*** 1,745. Undergraduates: 1,287. Freshmen: 366. Both federal and institutional methodology are used as a basis for awarding need-based institutional aid.

UNDERGRADUATE EXPENSES for 2009–10 ***Application fee:*** $50. ***Comprehensive fee:*** $50,034 includes full-time tuition ($37,120), mandatory fees ($914), and room and board ($12,000). ***College room only:*** $6860. ***Part-time tuition:*** $4600 per course.

FRESHMAN FINANCIAL AID (Fall 2008, est.) 231 applied for aid; of those 76% were deemed to have need. 100% of freshmen with need received aid; of those 100% had need fully met. ***Average percent of need met:*** 100% (excluding resources awarded to replace EFC). ***Average financial aid package:*** $34,102 (excluding resources awarded to replace EFC).

UNDERGRADUATE FINANCIAL AID (Fall 2008, est.) 780 applied for aid; of those 81% were deemed to have need. 100% of undergraduates with need received aid; of those 100% had need fully met. ***Average percent of need met:*** 100% (excluding resources awarded to replace EFC). ***Average financial aid package:*** $35,513 (excluding resources awarded to replace EFC). 2% of all full-time undergraduates had no need and received non-need-based gift aid.

GIFT AID (NEED-BASED) ***Total amount:*** $17,847,698 (5% federal, 1% state, 92% institutional, 2% external sources). ***Receiving aid:*** Freshmen: 48% (175); all full-time undergraduates: 50% (633). ***Average award:*** Freshmen: $28,170; Undergraduates: $28,274. ***Scholarships, grants, and awards:*** Federal Pell, FSEOG, state, college/university gift aid from institutional funds.

GIFT AID (NON-NEED-BASED) ***Total amount:*** $571,059 (1% federal, 66% institutional, 33% external sources). ***Receiving aid:*** Freshmen: 4% (13). Undergraduates: 2% (31). ***Average award:*** Undergraduates: $10,350. ***ROTC:*** Air Force cooperative.

LOANS ***Student loans:*** $5,528,596 (66% need-based, 34% non-need-based). 54% of past graduating class borrowed through all loan programs. *Average indebtedness per student:* $20,019. ***Average need-based loan:*** Freshmen: $4496. Undergraduates: $5761. ***Parent loans:*** $2,149,703 (100% non-need-based). ***Programs:*** FFEL (Subsidized and Unsubsidized Stafford, PLUS), Perkins.

WORK-STUDY ***Federal work-study:*** Total amount: $1,074,272; 545 jobs averaging $1971. ***State or other work-study/employment:*** Total amount: $121,964 (100% need-based). Part-time jobs available.

APPLYING FOR FINANCIAL AID ***Required financial aid forms:*** FAFSA, CSS Financial Aid PROFILE, business/farm supplement. ***Financial aid deadline:*** 3/1. ***Notification date:*** 3/23. Students must reply by 5/1.

CONTACT Ethel M. Desmarais, Director of Financial Aid, Bryn Mawr College, 101 North Merion Avenue, Bryn Mawr, PA 19010-2899, 610-526-7922 or toll-free 800-BMC-1885 (out-of-state). *Fax:* 610-526-5249. *E-mail:* edesmara@brynmawr.edu.

BUCKNELL UNIVERSITY

Lewisburg, PA

Tuition & fees: $40,816 **Average undergraduate aid package: $25,400**

ABOUT THE INSTITUTION Independent, coed. ***Awards:*** bachelor's and master's degrees. 61 undergraduate majors. ***Total enrollment:*** 3,719. Undergraduates: 3,583. Freshmen: 957. Both federal and institutional methodology are used as a basis for awarding need-based institutional aid.

UNDERGRADUATE EXPENSES for 2009–10 ***Application fee:*** $60. ***One-time required fee:*** $100. ***Comprehensive fee:*** $50,320 includes full-time tuition ($40,594), mandatory fees ($222), and room and board ($9504). ***College room only:*** $5490. ***Part-time tuition:*** $1113.75 per credit.

FRESHMAN FINANCIAL AID (Fall 2008, est.) 473 applied for aid; of those 84% were deemed to have need. 100% of freshmen with need received aid; of those 97% had need fully met. ***Average percent of need met:*** 95% (excluding resources awarded to replace EFC). ***Average financial aid package:*** $26,800 (excluding resources awarded to replace EFC). 4% of all full-time freshmen had no need and received non-need-based gift aid.

UNDERGRADUATE FINANCIAL AID (Fall 2008, est.) 1,818 applied for aid; of those 87% were deemed to have need. 100% of undergraduates with need received aid; of those 95% had need fully met. ***Average percent of need met:*** 95% (excluding resources awarded to replace EFC). ***Average financial aid package:*** $25,400 (excluding resources awarded to replace EFC). 3% of all full-time undergraduates had no need and received non-need-based gift aid.

GIFT AID (NEED-BASED) ***Total amount:*** $37,472,166 (4% federal, 2% state, 91% institutional, 3% external sources). ***Receiving aid:*** Freshmen: 42% (399); all full-time undergraduates: 44% (1,579). ***Average award:*** Freshmen: $22,400; Undergraduates: $21,200. ***Scholarships, grants, and awards:*** Federal Pell, FSEOG, state, private, college/university gift aid from institutional funds, Academic Competitiveness Grant, National Smart Grant.

GIFT AID (NON-NEED-BASED) ***Total amount:*** $1,800,000 (100% institutional). ***Receiving aid:*** Freshmen: 5% (46). Undergraduates: 5% (169). ***Average award:*** Freshmen: $8388. Undergraduates: $12,616. ***Scholarships, grants, and awards by category:*** *Academic interests/achievement:* 110 awards ($2,133,103 total): business, engineering/technologies, general academic interests/achievements, mathematics, physical sciences. *Creative arts/performance:* 100 awards ($705,000 total): applied art and design, art/fine arts, creative writing, dance, music, performing arts, theater/drama. *Special achievements/activities:* 62 awards: general special achievements/activities, leadership. ***ROTC:*** Army.

LOANS ***Student loans:*** $12,500,000 (100% need-based). 61% of past graduating class borrowed through all loan programs. *Average indebtedness per student:* $18,500. ***Average need-based loan:*** Freshmen: $4500. Undergraduates: $5550. ***Parent loans:*** $8,750,000 (100% non-need-based). ***Programs:*** FFEL (Subsidized and Unsubsidized Stafford, PLUS), Perkins.

WORK-STUDY ***Federal work-study:*** Total amount: $900,000; 700 jobs averaging $1500. ***State or other work-study/employment:*** Total amount: $60,000 (100% need-based). 50 part-time jobs averaging $1500.

ATHLETIC AWARDS Total amount: $381,990 (100% non-need-based).

APPLYING FOR FINANCIAL AID ***Required financial aid forms:*** FAFSA, CSS Financial Aid PROFILE, noncustodial (divorced/separated) parent's statement. ***Financial aid deadline:*** 1/1. ***Notification date:*** 4/1. Students must reply by 5/1.

CONTACT Andrea Leithner Stauffer, Director of Financial Aid, Bucknell University, Office of Financial Aid, Lewisburg, PA 17837, 570-577-1331. *Fax:* 570-577-1481. *E-mail:* finaid@bucknell.edu.

BUENA VISTA UNIVERSITY

Storm Lake, IA

Tuition & fees: $24,796 **Average undergraduate aid package: $27,086**

ABOUT THE INSTITUTION Independent religious, coed. ***Awards:*** bachelor's and master's degrees. 59 undergraduate majors. ***Total enrollment:*** 1,070. Undergraduates: 968. Freshmen: 274. Federal methodology is used as a basis for awarding need-based institutional aid.

UNDERGRADUATE EXPENSES for 2008–09 ***Comprehensive fee:*** $31,810 includes full-time tuition ($24,796) and room and board ($7014). Room and board charges vary according to board plan. ***Part-time tuition:*** $833 per credit hour. ***Payment plan:*** Installment.

FRESHMAN FINANCIAL AID (Fall 2008, est.) 250 applied for aid; of those 93% were deemed to have need. 100% of freshmen with need received aid; of those 64% had need fully met. ***Average percent of need met:*** 62% (excluding resources awarded to replace EFC). ***Average financial aid package:*** $28,972 (excluding resources awarded to replace EFC). 8% of all full-time freshmen had no need and received non-need-based gift aid.

UNDERGRADUATE FINANCIAL AID (Fall 2008, est.) 887 applied for aid; of those 94% were deemed to have need. 100% of undergraduates with need received aid; of those 51% had need fully met. ***Average percent of need met:*** 58% (excluding resources awarded to replace EFC). ***Average financial aid package:*** $27,086 (excluding resources awarded to replace EFC). 7% of all full-time undergraduates had no need and received non-need-based gift aid.

GIFT AID (NEED-BASED) ***Total amount:*** $8,136,717 (19% federal, 26% state, 55% institutional). ***Receiving aid:*** Freshmen: 85% (224); all full-time undergraduates: 84% (789). ***Average award:*** Freshmen: $11,583; Undergraduates: $10,138. ***Scholarships, grants, and awards:*** Federal Pell, FSEOG, state, private, college/university gift aid from institutional funds.

GIFT AID (NON-NEED-BASED) ***Total amount:*** $7,439,730 (96% institutional, 4% external sources). ***Receiving aid:*** Freshmen: 78% (205). Undergraduates: 73% (690). ***Average award:*** Freshmen: $11,674. Undergraduates: $9586. ***Scholarships, grants, and awards by category:*** *Academic interests/achievement:* 933 awards ($8,268,402 total): biological sciences, business, computer science, education, general academic interests/achievements, humanities, international studies, mathematics. *Creative arts/performance:* 80 awards ($154,214 total): art/fine arts, music, theater/drama. *Special achievements/activities:* 66 awards ($275,060 total): general special achievements/activities, leadership. *Special characteristics:* 249 awards ($784,631 total): children of faculty/staff, ethnic background, international students, out-of-state students, religious affiliation, siblings of current students. ***Tuition waivers:*** Full or partial for employees or children of employees.

LOANS ***Student loans:*** $6,432,932 (57% need-based, 43% non-need-based). 96% of past graduating class borrowed through all loan programs. *Average indebtedness per student:* $34,029. ***Average need-based loan:*** Freshmen: $4511. Undergraduates: $4913. ***Programs:*** FFEL (Subsidized and Unsubsidized Stafford, PLUS), Perkins, college/university.

WORK-STUDY ***Federal work-study:*** Total amount: $543,926; 480 jobs averaging $1089. ***State or other work-study/employment:*** Total amount: $144,725 (100% non-need-based). 178 part-time jobs averaging $1944.

APPLYING FOR FINANCIAL AID ***Required financial aid form:*** FAFSA. ***Financial aid deadline (priority):*** 6/1. ***Notification date:*** Continuous.

CONTACT Mrs. Leanne Valentine, Director of Financial Assistance, Buena Vista University, 610 West Fourth Street, Storm Lake, IA 50588, 712-749-2164 or toll-free 800-383-9600. *Fax:* 712-749-1451. *E-mail:* valentinel@bvu.edu.

BUFFALO STATE COLLEGE, STATE UNIVERSITY OF NEW YORK

Buffalo, NY

Tuition & fees (NY res): $5685 **Average undergraduate aid package: $9350**

ABOUT THE INSTITUTION State-supported, coed. ***Awards:*** bachelor's and master's degrees and post-master's certificates. 80 undergraduate majors. ***Total enrollment:*** 11,224. Undergraduates: 9,361. Freshmen: 1,523. Federal methodology is used as a basis for awarding need-based institutional aid.

UNDERGRADUATE EXPENSES for 2008–09 ***Application fee:*** $40. ***Tuition, state resident:*** full-time $4660; part-time $284 per credit hour. ***Tuition, nonresident:*** full-time $11,740; part-time $489 per credit hour. ***Required fees:*** full-time $1025; $42.80 per credit hour. Part-time tuition and fees vary according to course load. ***College room and board:*** $9064; ***Room only:*** $5354. Room and board charges vary according to board plan, housing facility, and student level. ***Payment plan:*** Installment.

FRESHMAN FINANCIAL AID (Fall 2008, est.) 1,323 applied for aid; of those 99% were deemed to have need. 100% of freshmen with need received aid; of those 57% had need fully met. ***Average percent of need met:*** 70% (excluding resources awarded to replace EFC). ***Average financial aid package:*** $5176 (excluding resources awarded to replace EFC). 7% of all full-time freshmen had no need and received non-need-based gift aid.

UNDERGRADUATE FINANCIAL AID (Fall 2008, est.) 7,836 applied for aid; of those 92% were deemed to have need. 100% of undergraduates with need received aid; of those 54% had need fully met. ***Average percent of need met:*** 66% (excluding resources awarded to replace EFC). ***Average financial aid package:*** $9350 (excluding resources awarded to replace EFC). 4% of all full-time undergraduates had no need and received non-need-based gift aid.

GIFT AID (NEED-BASED) ***Total amount:*** $24,445,346 (49% federal, 47% state, 4% external sources). ***Receiving aid:*** Freshmen: 71% (1,075); all full-time undergraduates: 71% (5,867). ***Average award:*** Freshmen: $2677; Undergraduates: $4020. ***Scholarships, grants, and awards:*** Federal Pell, FSEOG, state.

GIFT AID (NON-NEED-BASED) ***Total amount:*** $547,293 (4% state, 96% institutional). ***Receiving aid:*** Freshmen: 7% (112). Undergraduates: 4% (320). ***Average award:*** Freshmen: $996. Undergraduates: $1710. ***Scholarships, grants, and awards by category:*** *Academic interests/achievement:* general academic interests/achievements. *Creative arts/performance:* general creative arts/performance. *Special achievements/activities:* general special achievements/activities. ***Tuition waivers:*** Full or partial for employees or children of employees. ***ROTC:*** Army cooperative.

LOANS ***Student loans:*** $44,855,258 (53% need-based, 47% non-need-based). 71% of past graduating class borrowed through all loan programs. *Average indebtedness per student:* $18,187. ***Average need-based loan:*** Freshmen: $1881. Undergraduates: $3902. ***Parent loans:*** $1,715,468 (100% non-need-based). ***Programs:*** FFEL (Subsidized and Unsubsidized Stafford, PLUS), Perkins.

WORK-STUDY Federal work-study jobs available. ***State or other work-study/employment:*** Total amount: $1,425,986 (100% need-based). Part-time jobs available.

APPLYING FOR FINANCIAL AID ***Required financial aid form:*** FAFSA. ***Financial aid deadline:*** 5/1 (priority: 3/15). ***Notification date:*** Continuous beginning 5/1.

CONTACT Mr. Kent McGowan, Director of Financial Aid, Buffalo State College, State University of New York, 1300 Elmwood Avenue, Buffalo, NY 14222-1095, 716-878-4902. *Fax:* 716-878-4903.

BURLINGTON COLLEGE

Burlington, VT

Tuition & fees: $19,640 **Average undergraduate aid package: $12,490**

ABOUT THE INSTITUTION Independent, coed. ***Awards:*** associate and bachelor's degrees. 12 undergraduate majors. ***Total enrollment:*** 168. Undergraduates: 168. Freshmen: 20. Federal methodology is used as a basis for awarding need-based institutional aid.

UNDERGRADUATE EXPENSES for 2008–09 ***Application fee:*** $50. ***One-time required fee:*** $200. ***Tuition:*** full-time $19,640; part-time $650 per credit hour. Full-time tuition and fees vary according to course load and program. Part-time tuition and fees vary according to course load and program. Room and board charges vary according to housing facility. ***Payment plan:*** Installment.

FRESHMAN FINANCIAL AID (Fall 2008, est.) 17 applied for aid; of those 82% were deemed to have need. 100% of freshmen with need received aid. ***Average percent of need met:*** 56% (excluding resources awarded to replace EFC). ***Average financial aid package:*** $14,598 (excluding resources awarded to replace EFC).

UNDERGRADUATE FINANCIAL AID (Fall 2008, est.) 86 applied for aid; of those 94% were deemed to have need. 99% of undergraduates with need received aid; of those 2% had need fully met. ***Average percent of need met:*** 54% (excluding resources awarded to replace EFC). ***Average financial aid package:*** $12,490 (excluding resources awarded to replace EFC). 2% of all full-time undergraduates had no need and received non-need-based gift aid.

GIFT AID (NEED-BASED) ***Total amount:*** $524,050 (46% federal, 38% state, 12% institutional, 4% external sources). ***Receiving aid:*** Freshmen: 67% (14); all full-time undergraduates: 60% (65). ***Average award:*** Freshmen: $6496; Undergraduates: $6330. ***Scholarships, grants, and awards:*** Federal Pell, FSEOG, state, private, college/university gift aid from institutional funds.

GIFT AID (NON-NEED-BASED) ***Total amount:*** $7400 (54% institutional, 46% external sources). ***Average award:*** Undergraduates: $2000. ***Scholarships, grants,***

and awards by category: *Special achievements/activities:* general special achievements/activities. ***Tuition waivers:*** Full or partial for employees or children of employees, senior citizens.

LOANS ***Student loans:*** $1,181,402 (89% need-based, 11% non-need-based). 62% of past graduating class borrowed through all loan programs. *Average indebtedness per student:* $28,888. ***Average need-based loan:*** Freshmen: $4786. Undergraduates: $5052. ***Parent loans:*** $226,090 (43% need-based, 57% non-need-based). ***Programs:*** FFEL (Subsidized and Unsubsidized Stafford, PLUS), Perkins.

WORK-STUDY ***Federal work-study:*** Total amount: $66,547; 60 jobs averaging $1211.

APPLYING FOR FINANCIAL AID ***Required financial aid form:*** FAFSA. ***Financial aid deadline:*** Continuous. ***Notification date:*** Continuous beginning 4/1. Students must reply within 4 weeks of notification.

CONTACT Ms. Lindy Walsh, Director of Financial Aid, Burlington College, 95 North Avenue, Burlington, VT 05401, 802-862-9616 or toll-free 800-862-9616. *Fax:* 802-846-3072. *E-mail:* lwalsh@burlington.edu.

BUTLER UNIVERSITY

Indianapolis, IN

Tuition & fees: $28,266 **Average undergraduate aid package: $19,880**

ABOUT THE INSTITUTION Independent, coed. ***Awards:*** associate, bachelor's, master's, and first professional degrees. 61 undergraduate majors. ***Total enrollment:*** 4,438. Undergraduates: 3,639. Freshmen: 934. Federal methodology is used as a basis for awarding need-based institutional aid.

UNDERGRADUATE EXPENSES for 2008–09 ***Application fee:*** $35. ***Comprehensive fee:*** $37,676 includes full-time tuition ($27,500), mandatory fees ($766), and room and board ($9410). ***College room only:*** $4610. Full-time tuition and fees vary according to course load, degree level, and program. Room and board charges vary according to housing facility. ***Part-time tuition:*** $1150 per credit. Part-time tuition and fees vary according to course load, degree level, and program. ***Payment plan:*** Installment.

FRESHMAN FINANCIAL AID (Fall 2008, est.) 866 applied for aid; of those 68% were deemed to have need. 100% of freshmen with need received aid; of those 23% had need fully met. ***Average financial aid package:*** $21,260 (excluding resources awarded to replace EFC).

UNDERGRADUATE FINANCIAL AID (Fall 2008, est.) 3,455 applied for aid; of those 70% were deemed to have need. 100% of undergraduates with need received aid; of those 19% had need fully met. ***Average financial aid package:*** $19,880 (excluding resources awarded to replace EFC).

GIFT AID (NEED-BASED) ***Total amount:*** $33,729,197 (5% federal, 11% state, 74% institutional, 10% external sources). ***Receiving aid:*** Freshmen: 62% (579); all full-time undergraduates: 2,297. ***Average award:*** Freshmen: $16,381; Undergraduates: $15,109. ***Scholarships, grants, and awards:*** Federal Pell, FSEOG, state, private, college/university gift aid from institutional funds.

GIFT AID (NON-NEED-BASED) ***Total amount:*** $13,129,859 (84% institutional, 16% external sources). ***Receiving aid:*** Freshmen: 15% (144). Undergraduates: 457. ***Average award:*** Freshmen: $12,476. Undergraduates: $11,401. ***Scholarships, grants, and awards by category:*** *Academic interests/achievement:* biological sciences, business, communication, computer science, education, engineering/ technologies, English, foreign languages, general academic interests/ achievements, humanities, international studies, mathematics, physical sciences, social sciences. *Creative arts/performance:* art/fine arts, cinema/film/broadcasting, dance, music, theater/drama. ***Tuition waivers:*** Full or partial for employees or children of employees. ***ROTC:*** Army, Air Force cooperative.

LOANS ***Student loans:*** $10,999,450 (100% non-need-based). 62% of past graduating class borrowed through all loan programs. *Average indebtedness per student:* $24,000. ***Average need-based loan:*** Freshmen: $4188. Undergraduates: $5286. ***Parent loans:*** $4,292,740 (20% need-based, 80% non-need-based). ***Programs:*** FFEL (Subsidized and Unsubsidized Stafford, PLUS), Perkins.

WORK-STUDY ***Federal work-study:*** Total amount: $342,000; 350 jobs averaging $1100. ***State or other work-study/employment:*** Part-time jobs available.

ATHLETIC AWARDS Total amount: $3,317,658 (30% need-based, 70% non-need-based).

APPLYING FOR FINANCIAL AID ***Required financial aid form:*** FAFSA. ***Financial aid deadline (priority):*** 3/1. ***Notification date:*** 3/15. Students must reply within 3 weeks of notification.

CONTACT Ms. Kristine Butz, Associate Director of Financial Aid, Butler University, 4600 Sunset Avenue, Indianapolis, IN 46208-3485, 317-940-8200 or toll-free 888-940-8100. *Fax:* 317-940-8250. *E-mail:* kbutz@butler.edu.

CABARRUS COLLEGE OF HEALTH SCIENCES

Concord, NC

Tuition & fees: $9950 **Average undergraduate aid package: N/A**

ABOUT THE INSTITUTION Independent, coed. ***Awards:*** associate and bachelor's degrees. 6 undergraduate majors. ***Total enrollment:*** 372. Undergraduates: 372. Freshmen: 25. Federal methodology is used as a basis for awarding need-based institutional aid.

UNDERGRADUATE EXPENSES for 2009–10 ***Application fee:*** $35. ***Tuition:*** full-time $9660; part-time $300 per semester hour.

GIFT AID (NEED-BASED) ***Total amount:*** $779,200 (30% federal, 56% state, 14% institutional). ***Scholarships, grants, and awards:*** Federal Pell, FSEOG, state, private, college/university gift aid from institutional funds.

GIFT AID (NON-NEED-BASED) ***Total amount:*** $531,238 (82% state, 5% institutional, 13% external sources). ***Scholarships, grants, and awards by category:*** *Special characteristics:* first-generation college students.

LOANS ***Student loans:*** $1,004,159 (55% need-based, 45% non-need-based). ***Parent loans:*** $23,250 (100% need-based). ***Programs:*** FFEL (Subsidized and Unsubsidized Stafford, PLUS), state.

WORK-STUDY ***Federal work-study:*** Total amount: $13,335; 18 jobs available. ***State or other work-study/employment:*** Total amount: $26,425 (100% non-need-based). Part-time jobs available.

APPLYING FOR FINANCIAL AID ***Required financial aid form:*** FAFSA. ***Financial aid deadline (priority):*** 4/15. ***Notification date:*** Continuous beginning 7/1. Students must reply within 2 weeks of notification.

CONTACT Valerie Richard, Director of Financial Aid, Cabarrus College of Health Sciences, 401 Medical Park Drive, Concord, NC 28025, 704-403-3507. *Fax:* 704-403-2077. *E-mail:* valerie.richard@carolinashealthcare.org.

CABRINI COLLEGE

Radnor, PA

CONTACT Mike Colahan, Director of Financial Aid, Cabrini College, 610 King of Prussia Road, Grace Hall, Radnor, PA 19087-3698, 610-902-8420 or toll-free 800-848-1003. *Fax:* 610-902-8426.

CALDWELL COLLEGE

Caldwell, NJ

ABOUT THE INSTITUTION Independent Roman Catholic, coed. 26 undergraduate majors.

GIFT AID (NEED-BASED) ***Scholarships, grants, and awards:*** Federal Pell, FSEOG, state, private, college/university gift aid from institutional funds.

GIFT AID (NON-NEED-BASED) ***Scholarships, grants, and awards by category:*** *Academic interests/achievement:* general academic interests/achievements.

LOANS ***Programs:*** Federal Direct (Subsidized and Unsubsidized Stafford, PLUS), FFEL (Subsidized and Unsubsidized Stafford, PLUS), state, college/university.

WORK-STUDY ***Federal work-study:*** Total amount: $79,388; 183 jobs averaging $1000.

APPLYING FOR FINANCIAL AID ***Required financial aid forms:*** FAFSA, state aid form.

CONTACT F. Shawn O'Neill, Director of Financial Aid, Caldwell College, Caldwell College, 9 Ryerson Avenue, Caldwell, NJ 07006, 973-618-3221 or toll-free 888-864-9516 (out-of-state). *E-mail:* landerson@caldwell.edu.

CALIFORNIA BAPTIST UNIVERSITY

Riverside, CA

Tuition & fees: $22,330 **Average undergraduate aid package: $8359**

ABOUT THE INSTITUTION Independent Southern Baptist, coed. ***Awards:*** bachelor's and master's degrees. 46 undergraduate majors. ***Total enrollment:*** 4,013. Undergraduates: 3,096. Freshmen: 446. Federal methodology is used as a basis for awarding need-based institutional aid.

UNDERGRADUATE EXPENSES for 2008–09 ***Application fee:*** $45. ***Comprehensive fee:*** $30,240 includes full-time tuition ($20,930), mandatory fees ($1400), and room and board ($7910). ***College room only:*** $3700. Full-time tuition and fees vary according to class time and program. Room and board charges vary according to board plan and housing facility. ***Part-time tuition:*** $805 per semester hour. ***Part-time fees:*** $175 per term. Part-time tuition and fees vary according to class time and program. ***Payment plan:*** Installment.

FRESHMAN FINANCIAL AID (Fall 2008, est.) 391 applied for aid; of those 72% were deemed to have need. 97% of freshmen with need received aid; of those 67% had need fully met. ***Average percent of need met:*** 48% (excluding resources awarded to replace EFC). ***Average financial aid package:*** $9306 (excluding resources awarded to replace EFC). 13% of all full-time freshmen had no need and received non-need-based gift aid.

UNDERGRADUATE FINANCIAL AID (Fall 2008, est.) 2,443 applied for aid; of those 74% were deemed to have need. 94% of undergraduates with need received aid; of those 64% had need fully met. ***Average percent of need met:*** 50% (excluding resources awarded to replace EFC). ***Average financial aid package:*** $8359 (excluding resources awarded to replace EFC). 9% of all full-time undergraduates had no need and received non-need-based gift aid.

GIFT AID (NEED-BASED) ***Total amount:*** $16,910,037 (21% federal, 39% state, 38% institutional, 2% external sources). ***Receiving aid:*** Freshmen: 64% (251); all full-time undergraduates: 58% (1,430). ***Average award:*** Freshmen: $5294; Undergraduates: $5246. ***Scholarships, grants, and awards:*** Federal Pell, FSEOG, state, private, college/university gift aid from institutional funds.

GIFT AID (NON-NEED-BASED) ***Total amount:*** $6,860,403 (94% institutional, 6% external sources). ***Receiving aid:*** Freshmen: 50% (195). Undergraduates: 40% (995). ***Average award:*** Freshmen: $6528. Undergraduates: $7807. ***Scholarships, grants, and awards by category:*** *Academic interests/achievement:* 845 awards ($3,727,401 total): general academic interests/achievements, religion/biblical studies. *Creative arts/performance:* 484 awards ($1,625,409 total): art/fine arts, music, theater/drama. *Special achievements/activities:* 30 awards ($112,600 total): cheerleading/drum major. *Special characteristics:* 524 awards ($2,492,266 total): adult students, children and siblings of alumni, children of faculty/staff, relatives of clergy, siblings of current students. ***Tuition waivers:*** Full or partial for employees or children of employees. ***ROTC:*** Army cooperative, Air Force cooperative.

LOANS ***Student loans:*** $40,378,557 (50% need-based, 50% non-need-based). 82% of past graduating class borrowed through all loan programs. *Average indebtedness per student:* $35,550. ***Average need-based loan:*** Freshmen: $1429. Undergraduates: $1863. ***Parent loans:*** $4,255,681 (50% need-based, 50% non-need-based). ***Programs:*** FFEL (Subsidized and Unsubsidized Stafford, PLUS), Perkins, alternative loans.

WORK-STUDY ***Federal work-study:*** Total amount: $186,894; 219 jobs averaging $866.

ATHLETIC AWARDS Total amount: $3,235,702 (50% need-based, 50% non-need-based).

APPLYING FOR FINANCIAL AID ***Required financial aid forms:*** FAFSA, state aid form. ***Financial aid deadline (priority):*** 3/2. ***Notification date:*** Continuous. Students must reply by 4/1 or within 3 weeks of notification.

CONTACT Ms. Rebecca Sanchez, Financial Aid Director, California Baptist University, 8432 Magnolia Avenue, Riverside, CA 92504-3297, 951-343-4236 or toll-free 877-228-8866. *Fax:* 951-343-4518. *E-mail:* rsanchez@calbaptist.edu.

CALIFORNIA CHRISTIAN COLLEGE

Fresno, CA

Tuition & fees: $6840 **Average undergraduate aid package: $12,030**

ABOUT THE INSTITUTION Independent religious, coed. ***Awards:*** associate and bachelor's degrees. 1 undergraduate major. ***Total enrollment:*** 28. Undergraduates: 28. Freshmen: 10. Federal methodology is used as a basis for awarding need-based institutional aid.

UNDERGRADUATE EXPENSES for 2009–10 ***Application fee:*** $40. ***Comprehensive fee:*** $10,690 includes full-time tuition ($6840) and room and board ($3850). ***Part-time tuition:*** $285 per unit.

FRESHMAN FINANCIAL AID (Fall 2008, est.) 2 applied for aid; of those 100% were deemed to have need. 100% of freshmen with need received aid. ***Average percent of need met:*** 51% (excluding resources awarded to replace EFC). ***Average financial aid package:*** $8003 (excluding resources awarded to replace EFC).

UNDERGRADUATE FINANCIAL AID (Fall 2008, est.) 22 applied for aid; of those 91% were deemed to have need. 100% of undergraduates with need received aid. ***Average percent of need met:*** 62% (excluding resources awarded to replace EFC). ***Average financial aid package:*** $12,030 (excluding resources awarded to replace EFC).

GIFT AID (NEED-BASED) ***Total amount:*** $106,263 (62% federal, 38% state). ***Receiving aid:*** Freshmen: 20% (1); all full-time undergraduates: 64% (16). ***Average award:*** Freshmen: $3181; Undergraduates: $6641. ***Scholarships, grants, and awards:*** Federal Pell, FSEOG, state, private, college/university gift aid from institutional funds.

LOANS ***Student loans:*** $156,549 (82% need-based, 18% non-need-based). 100% of past graduating class borrowed through all loan programs. *Average indebtedness per student:* $23,287. ***Average need-based loan:*** Freshmen: $3500. Undergraduates: $6797. ***Programs:*** Federal Direct (Subsidized and Unsubsidized Stafford, PLUS).

WORK-STUDY ***Federal work-study:*** Total amount: $7046; 3 jobs averaging $1500.

APPLYING FOR FINANCIAL AID ***Required financial aid forms:*** FAFSA, institution's own form, GPA verification form (for CA residents). ***Financial aid deadline (priority):*** 3/2. ***Notification date:*** 8/15.

CONTACT Mindy Scroggins, Financial Aid Coordinator, California Christian College, 4881 East University, Fresno, CA 93703, 559-251-4215. *Fax:* 559-251-4231. *E-mail:* cccfindir@sbcglobal.net.

CALIFORNIA COAST UNIVERSITY

Santa Ana, CA

CONTACT Financial Aid Office, California Coast University, 700 North Main Street, Santa Ana, CA 92701, 714-547-9625 or toll-free 888-CCU-UNIV (out-of-state).

CALIFORNIA COLLEGE OF THE ARTS

San Francisco, CA

Tuition & fees: $31,382 **Average undergraduate aid package: $19,888**

ABOUT THE INSTITUTION Independent, coed. ***Awards:*** bachelor's and master's degrees. 17 undergraduate majors. ***Total enrollment:*** 1,354. Undergraduates: 1,354. Freshmen: 248. Federal methodology is used as a basis for awarding need-based institutional aid.

UNDERGRADUATE EXPENSES for 2008–09 ***Application fee:*** $50. ***Tuition:*** full-time $31,032; part-time $1293 per unit. Full-time tuition and fees vary according to course load. Part-time tuition and fees vary according to course load. Room and board charges vary according to housing facility. ***Payment plans:*** Installment, deferred payment.

FRESHMAN FINANCIAL AID (Fall 2008, est.) 178 applied for aid; of those 90% were deemed to have need. 99% of freshmen with need received aid; of those 4% had need fully met. ***Average percent of need met:*** 58% (excluding resources awarded to replace EFC). ***Average financial aid package:*** $20,366 (excluding resources awarded to replace EFC). 21% of all full-time freshmen had no need and received non-need-based gift aid.

UNDERGRADUATE FINANCIAL AID (Fall 2008, est.) 867 applied for aid; of those 91% were deemed to have need. 99% of undergraduates with need received aid; of those 3% had need fully met. ***Average percent of need met:*** 54% (excluding resources awarded to replace EFC). ***Average financial aid package:*** $19,888 (excluding resources awarded to replace EFC). 13% of all full-time undergraduates had no need and received non-need-based gift aid.

GIFT AID (NEED-BASED) ***Total amount:*** $12,305,420 (14% federal, 10% state, 75% institutional, 1% external sources). ***Receiving aid:*** Freshmen: 64% (154); all full-time undergraduates: 64% (773). ***Average award:*** Freshmen: $17,554; Undergraduates: $15,327. ***Scholarships, grants, and awards:*** Federal Pell, FSEOG, state, private, college/university gift aid from institutional funds, Academic Competitiveness Grant.

GIFT AID (NON-NEED-BASED) ***Total amount:*** $1,214,250 (99% institutional, 1% external sources). ***Receiving aid:*** Freshmen: 49% (117). Undergraduates: 31% (367). ***Average award:*** Freshmen: $7559. Undergraduates: $6319. ***Scholarships, grants, and awards by category:*** *Academic interests/achievement:*

architecture, general academic interests/achievements. *Creative arts/performance:* applied art and design, art/fine arts, creative writing, general creative arts/performance. ***Tuition waivers:*** Full or partial for employees or children of employees.

LOANS ***Student loans:*** $7,849,490 (88% need-based, 12% non-need-based). 64% of past graduating class borrowed through all loan programs. *Average indebtedness per student:* $34,518. ***Average need-based loan:*** Freshmen: $3484. Undergraduates: $4920. ***Parent loans:*** $2,570,925 (53% need-based, 47% non-need-based). ***Programs:*** FFEL (Subsidized and Unsubsidized Stafford, PLUS), Perkins, private loans.

WORK-STUDY ***Federal work-study:*** Total amount: $461,759; 841 jobs averaging $2623. ***State or other work-study/employment:*** Total amount: $275,000 (100% non-need-based). 85 part-time jobs averaging $2223.

APPLYING FOR FINANCIAL AID ***Required financial aid form:*** FAFSA. ***Financial aid deadline (priority):*** 3/2. ***Notification date:*** Continuous beginning 4/1. Students must reply by 5/1 or within 3 weeks of notification.

CONTACT Financial Aid Office, California College of the Arts, 1111 Eighth Street, San Francisco, CA 94107, 415-703-9528 or toll-free 800-447-1ART. *Fax:* 415-551-9261. *E-mail:* finaid@cca.edu.

CALIFORNIA INSTITUTE OF INTEGRAL STUDIES

San Francisco, CA

CONTACT Financial Aid Office, California Institute of Integral Studies, 1453 Mission Street, San Francisco, CA 94103, 415-575-6122. *Fax:* 415-575-1268. *E-mail:* finaid@ciis.edu.

CALIFORNIA INSTITUTE OF TECHNOLOGY

Pasadena, CA

Tuition & fees: $34,437 **Average undergraduate aid package: $31,611**

ABOUT THE INSTITUTION Independent, coed. ***Awards:*** bachelor's, master's, and doctoral degrees and post-master's certificates. 25 undergraduate majors. ***Total enrollment:*** 2,126. Undergraduates: 921. Freshmen: 236. Federal methodology is used as a basis for awarding need-based institutional aid.

UNDERGRADUATE EXPENSES for 2008–09 ***Application fee:*** $60. ***One-time required fee:*** $500. ***Comprehensive fee:*** $44,583 includes full-time tuition ($31,437), mandatory fees ($3000), and room and board ($10,146). ***College room only:*** $5733. ***Payment plans:*** Installment, deferred payment.

FRESHMAN FINANCIAL AID (Fall 2008, est.) 166 applied for aid; of those 70% were deemed to have need. 100% of freshmen with need received aid; of those 100% had need fully met. ***Average percent of need met:*** 100% (excluding resources awarded to replace EFC). ***Average financial aid package:*** $31,069 (excluding resources awarded to replace EFC). 2% of all full-time freshmen had no need and received non-need-based gift aid.

UNDERGRADUATE FINANCIAL AID (Fall 2008, est.) 522 applied for aid; of those 83% were deemed to have need. 100% of undergraduates with need received aid; of those 100% had need fully met. ***Average percent of need met:*** 100% (excluding resources awarded to replace EFC). ***Average financial aid package:*** $31,611 (excluding resources awarded to replace EFC). 8% of all full-time undergraduates had no need and received non-need-based gift aid.

GIFT AID (NEED-BASED) ***Total amount:*** $12,958,786 (5% federal, 4% state, 87% institutional, 4% external sources). ***Receiving aid:*** Freshmen: 49% (116); all full-time undergraduates: 47% (435). ***Average award:*** Freshmen: $28,846; Undergraduates: $28,470. ***Scholarships, grants, and awards:*** Federal Pell, FSEOG, state, private, college/university gift aid from institutional funds.

GIFT AID (NON-NEED-BASED) ***Total amount:*** $2,733,078 (2% state, 83% institutional, 15% external sources). ***Receiving aid:*** Freshmen: 2% (4). Undergraduates: 4% (35). ***Average award:*** Freshmen: $30,190. Undergraduates: $28,914. ***Scholarships, grants, and awards by category:*** *Academic interests/achievement:* 78 awards ($2,255,287 total): general academic interests/achievements. ***Tuition waivers:*** Full or partial for employees or children of employees. ***ROTC:*** Army cooperative, Air Force cooperative.

LOANS ***Student loans:*** $944,261 (72% need-based, 28% non-need-based). 39% of past graduating class borrowed through all loan programs. *Average indebtedness per student:* $9871. ***Average need-based loan:*** Freshmen: $2261. Undergraduates: $1883. ***Parent loans:*** $372,909 (5% need-based, 95% non-need-based). ***Programs:*** Federal Direct (Subsidized and Unsubsidized Stafford, PLUS), Perkins, college/university.

WORK-STUDY ***Federal work-study:*** Total amount: $765,192; 358 jobs averaging $2146. ***State or other work-study/employment:*** Total amount: $62,066 (100% need-based). 41 part-time jobs averaging $1695.

APPLYING FOR FINANCIAL AID ***Required financial aid forms:*** FAFSA, institution's own form, CSS Financial Aid PROFILE, state aid form, noncustodial (divorced/separated) parent's statement, business/farm supplement. ***Financial aid deadline (priority):*** 1/15. ***Notification date:*** 4/15. Students must reply by 5/1.

CONTACT Don Crewell, Director of Financial Aid, California Institute of Technology, Financial Aid Office, Pasadena, CA 91125-8700, 626-395-6280. *Fax:* 626-564-8136. *E-mail:* dcrewell@caltech.edu.

CALIFORNIA INSTITUTE OF THE ARTS

Valencia, CA

Tuition & fees: $35,406 **Average undergraduate aid package: $29,141**

ABOUT THE INSTITUTION Independent, coed. ***Awards:*** bachelor's, master's, and doctoral degrees and post-bachelor's certificates. 23 undergraduate majors. ***Total enrollment:*** 1,374. Undergraduates: 863. Freshmen: 171. Federal methodology is used as a basis for awarding need-based institutional aid.

UNDERGRADUATE EXPENSES for 2009–10 ***Application fee:*** $70. ***Comprehensive fee:*** $44,476 includes full-time tuition ($34,830), mandatory fees ($576), and room and board ($9070). ***College room only:*** $5236.

FRESHMAN FINANCIAL AID (Fall 2008, est.) 133 applied for aid; of those 77% were deemed to have need. 99% of freshmen with need received aid; of those 5% had need fully met. ***Average percent of need met:*** 72% (excluding resources awarded to replace EFC). ***Average financial aid package:*** $26,468 (excluding resources awarded to replace EFC). 11% of all full-time freshmen had no need and received non-need-based gift aid.

UNDERGRADUATE FINANCIAL AID (Fall 2008, est.) 675 applied for aid; of those 85% were deemed to have need. 99% of undergraduates with need received aid; of those 5% had need fully met. ***Average percent of need met:*** 78% (excluding resources awarded to replace EFC). ***Average financial aid package:*** $29,141 (excluding resources awarded to replace EFC). 9% of all full-time undergraduates had no need and received non-need-based gift aid.

GIFT AID (NEED-BASED) ***Total amount:*** $7,682,960 (17% federal, 11% state, 71% institutional, 1% external sources). ***Receiving aid:*** Freshmen: 58% (99); all full-time undergraduates: 64% (550). ***Average award:*** Freshmen: $13,917; Undergraduates: $13,876. ***Scholarships, grants, and awards:*** Federal Pell, FSEOG, state, private, college/university gift aid from institutional funds.

GIFT AID (NON-NEED-BASED) ***Total amount:*** $393,450 (98% institutional, 2% external sources). ***Average award:*** Freshmen: $3826. Undergraduates: $5170. ***Scholarships, grants, and awards by category:*** *Creative arts/performance:* 83 awards ($363,162 total): applied art and design, art/fine arts, cinema/film/broadcasting, creative writing, dance, music, performing arts, theater/drama.

LOANS ***Student loans:*** $8,180,863 (92% need-based, 8% non-need-based). 68% of past graduating class borrowed through all loan programs. *Average indebtedness per student:* $40,122. ***Average need-based loan:*** Freshmen: $7535. Undergraduates: $11,537. ***Parent loans:*** $1,437,302 (77% need-based, 23% non-need-based). ***Programs:*** FFEL (Subsidized and Unsubsidized Stafford, PLUS), Perkins, college/university, private/alternative loans.

WORK-STUDY ***Federal work-study:*** Total amount: $501,879; jobs available. ***State or other work-study/employment:*** Total amount: $26,700 (100% need-based). Part-time jobs available.

APPLYING FOR FINANCIAL AID ***Required financial aid form:*** FAFSA. ***Financial aid deadline (priority):*** 3/2. ***Notification date:*** Continuous beginning 4/1. Students must reply by 5/1 or within 3 weeks of notification.

CONTACT Ms. Bobbi Heuer, Director Financial Aid, California Institute of the Arts, 24700 McBean Parkway, Valencia, CA 91355-2340, 661-253-7869 or toll-free 800-545-2787. *Fax:* 661-287-3816. *E-mail:* bheuer@calarts.edu.

CALIFORNIA LUTHERAN UNIVERSITY

Thousand Oaks, CA

ABOUT THE INSTITUTION Independent Lutheran, coed. ***Awards:*** bachelor's, master's, and doctoral degrees and post-bachelor's and post-master's certificates. 55 undergraduate majors. ***Total enrollment:*** 3,499. Undergraduates: 2,202. Freshmen: 482.

GIFT AID (NEED-BASED) ***Scholarships, grants, and awards:*** Federal Pell, FSEOG, state, private, college/university gift aid from institutional funds.

GIFT AID (NON-NEED-BASED) ***Scholarships, grants, and awards by category:*** *Academic interests/achievement:* biological sciences, business, communication, computer science, education, English, foreign languages, general academic interests/achievements, humanities, international studies, mathematics, physical sciences, religion/biblical studies, social sciences. *Creative arts/performance:* art/fine arts, creative writing, journalism/publications, music, performing arts, theater/drama. *Special achievements/activities:* community service, general special achievements/activities, leadership, religious involvement. *Special characteristics:* adult students, children and siblings of alumni, children of faculty/staff, ethnic background, first-generation college students, international students, relatives of clergy, religious affiliation.

LOANS ***Programs:*** FFEL (Subsidized and Unsubsidized Stafford, PLUS), Perkins.

APPLYING FOR FINANCIAL AID ***Required financial aid forms:*** FAFSA, institution's own form.

CONTACT Meghan Flores, Director of Financial Aid, California Lutheran University, 60 West Olsen Road, Thousand Oaks, CA 91360-2787, 805-493-3115 or toll-free 877-258-3678. *Fax:* 805-493-3114.

CALIFORNIA MARITIME ACADEMY

Vallejo, CA

CONTACT Financial Aid Manager, California Maritime Academy, 200 Maritime Academy Drive, Vallejo, CA 94590-0644, 707-654-1275 or toll-free 800-561-1945. *Fax:* 707-654-1007.

CALIFORNIA NATIONAL UNIVERSITY FOR ADVANCED STUDIES

Northridge, CA

CONTACT Office of Academic Affairs, California National University for Advanced Studies, 16909 Parthenia Street, North Hills, CA 91343, 800-782-2422 or toll-free 800-744-2822 (in-state).

CALIFORNIA POLYTECHNIC STATE UNIVERSITY, SAN LUIS OBISPO

San Luis Obispo, CA

Tuition & fees (CA res): $5043 **Average undergraduate aid package: $8347**

ABOUT THE INSTITUTION State-supported, coed. ***Awards:*** bachelor's, master's, and doctoral degrees. 60 undergraduate majors. ***Total enrollment:*** 19,471. Undergraduates: 18,516. Freshmen: 3,501. Federal methodology is used as a basis for awarding need-based institutional aid.

UNDERGRADUATE EXPENSES for 2008–09 ***Application fee:*** $55. ***Tuition, state resident:*** full-time $0. ***Tuition, nonresident:*** full-time $10,170; part-time $226 per unit. ***Required fees:*** full-time $5043; $1129 per term. Full-time tuition and fees vary according to course load, degree level, and program. Part-time tuition and fees vary according to course load, degree level, and program. ***College room and board:*** $9256; ***Room only:*** $5218. Room and board charges vary according to board plan and housing facility. ***Payment plan:*** Installment.

FRESHMAN FINANCIAL AID (Fall 2007) 2,816 applied for aid; of those 50% were deemed to have need. 88% of freshmen with need received aid; of those 17% had need fully met. ***Average percent of need met:*** 65% (excluding resources awarded to replace EFC). ***Average financial aid package:*** $8000 (excluding resources awarded to replace EFC). 4% of all full-time freshmen had no need and received non-need-based gift aid.

UNDERGRADUATE FINANCIAL AID (Fall 2007) 8,888 applied for aid; of those 65% were deemed to have need. 92% of undergraduates with need received aid; of those 13% had need fully met. ***Average percent of need met:*** 64% (excluding resources awarded to replace EFC). ***Average financial aid package:*** $8347 (excluding resources awarded to replace EFC). 3% of all full-time undergraduates had no need and received non-need-based gift aid.

GIFT AID (NEED-BASED) ***Total amount:*** $25,484,576 (40% federal, 43% state, 7% institutional, 10% external sources). ***Receiving aid:*** Freshmen: 22% (944); all full-time undergraduates: 23% (4,064). ***Average award:*** Freshmen: $1882; Undergraduates: $2138. ***Scholarships, grants, and awards:*** Federal Pell, FSEOG, state, private, college/university gift aid from institutional funds.

GIFT AID (NON-NEED-BASED) ***Total amount:*** $4,256,088 (1% federal, 34% institutional, 65% external sources). ***Receiving aid:*** Freshmen: 1% (58). Undergraduates: 1% (132). ***Average award:*** Freshmen: $2135. Undergraduates: $2312. ***Scholarships, grants, and awards by category:*** *Academic interests/achievement:* agriculture, architecture, biological sciences, business, communication, computer science, education, engineering/technologies, English, foreign languages, general academic interests/achievements, health fields, home economics, humanities, international studies, library science, mathematics, military science, physical sciences, social sciences. *Creative arts/performance:* applied art and design, art/fine arts, cinema/film/broadcasting, creative writing, dance, debating, general creative arts/performance, journalism/publications, music, performing arts, theater/drama. *Special achievements/activities:* community service, leadership, rodeo. *Special characteristics:* general special characteristics. ***Tuition waivers:*** Full or partial for employees or children of employees. ***ROTC:*** Army.

LOANS ***Student loans:*** $33,103,126 (65% need-based, 35% non-need-based). ***Average need-based loan:*** Freshmen: $3024. Undergraduates: $3610. ***Parent loans:*** $19,073,032 (20% need-based, 80% non-need-based). ***Programs:*** FFEL (Subsidized and Unsubsidized Stafford, PLUS), Perkins, college/university.

WORK-STUDY ***Federal work-study:*** Total amount: $921,573; jobs available.

ATHLETIC AWARDS Total amount: $2,837,825 (28% need-based, 72% non-need-based).

APPLYING FOR FINANCIAL AID ***Required financial aid form:*** FAFSA. ***Financial aid deadline (priority):*** 3/2. ***Notification date:*** Continuous.

CONTACT Lois Kelly, Director, Financial Aid, California Polytechnic State University, San Luis Obispo, Cal Poly State University, San Luis Obispo, CA 93407, 805-756-5993. *Fax:* 805-756-7243. *E-mail:* lkelly@calpoly.edu.

CALIFORNIA STATE POLYTECHNIC UNIVERSITY, POMONA

Pomona, CA

Tuition & fees (CA res): $3564 **Average undergraduate aid package: $9607**

ABOUT THE INSTITUTION State-supported, coed. ***Awards:*** bachelor's and master's degrees. 60 undergraduate majors. ***Total enrollment:*** 21,190. Undergraduates: 19,220. Freshmen: 2,640. Federal methodology is used as a basis for awarding need-based institutional aid.

UNDERGRADUATE EXPENSES for 2008–09 ***Application fee:*** $55. ***Tuition, state resident:*** full-time $0. ***Tuition, nonresident:*** full-time $10,170; part-time $226 per unit. ***Required fees:*** full-time $3564; $2286 per year. ***College room and board:*** $9120; ***Room only:*** $5580. Room and board charges vary according to board plan and housing facility. ***Payment plans:*** Installment, deferred payment.

FRESHMAN FINANCIAL AID (Fall 2008, est.) 1,853 applied for aid; of those 68% were deemed to have need. 95% of freshmen with need received aid; of those 20% had need fully met. ***Average percent of need met:*** 76% (excluding resources awarded to replace EFC). ***Average financial aid package:*** $8512 (excluding resources awarded to replace EFC). 1% of all full-time freshmen had no need and received non-need-based gift aid.

UNDERGRADUATE FINANCIAL AID (Fall 2008, est.) 9,657 applied for aid; of those 83% were deemed to have need. 95% of undergraduates with need received aid; of those 27% had need fully met. ***Average percent of need met:*** 79% (excluding resources awarded to replace EFC). ***Average financial aid package:*** $9607 (excluding resources awarded to replace EFC). 1% of all full-time undergraduates had no need and received non-need-based gift aid.

GIFT AID (NEED-BASED) ***Total amount:*** $57,358,736 (49% federal, 51% state). ***Receiving aid:*** Freshmen: 37% (928); all full-time undergraduates: 38% (6,126). ***Average award:*** Freshmen: $7622; Undergraduates: $7329. ***Scholarships, grants, and awards:*** Federal Pell, FSEOG, state, private, college/university gift aid from institutional funds.

GIFT AID (NON-NEED-BASED) ***Total amount:*** $2,171,892 (16% state, 29% institutional, 55% external sources). ***Receiving aid:*** Freshmen: 5% (124).

Undergraduates: 3% (489). ***Average award:*** Freshmen: $1957. Undergraduates: $1649. ***Scholarships, grants, and awards by category:*** *Academic interests/achievement:* agriculture, architecture, biological sciences, business, computer science, education, engineering/technologies, general academic interests/achievements, humanities, mathematics, physical sciences, social sciences. *Special achievements/activities:* hobbies/interests, leadership. *Special characteristics:* children and siblings of alumni, children of current students, members of minority groups. ***Tuition waivers:*** Full or partial for employees or children of employees. ***ROTC:*** Army, Air Force cooperative.

LOANS ***Student loans:*** $81,664,250 (47% need-based, 53% non-need-based). 37% of past graduating class borrowed through all loan programs. *Average indebtedness per student:* $12,527. ***Average need-based loan:*** Freshmen: $2926. Undergraduates: $4008. ***Parent loans:*** $1,929,696 (100% non-need-based). ***Programs:*** FFEL (Subsidized and Unsubsidized Stafford, PLUS), Perkins, college/university, alternative loans.

WORK-STUDY ***Federal work-study:*** Total amount: $734,088; 252 jobs averaging $2570.

ATHLETIC AWARDS Total amount: $489,319 (100% non-need-based).

APPLYING FOR FINANCIAL AID ***Required financial aid form:*** FAFSA. ***Financial aid deadline:*** Continuous. ***Notification date:*** Continuous beginning 4/1. Students must reply within 6 weeks of notification.

CONTACT Diana Minor, Director of Financial Aid & Scholarships, California State Polytechnic University, Pomona, 3801 West Temple Avenue, Pomona, CA 91768-2557, 909-869-3704. *Fax:* 909-869-4757. *E-mail:* dyminor@csupomona.edu.

CALIFORNIA STATE UNIVERSITY, BAKERSFIELD

Bakersfield, CA

Tuition & fees (CA res): $4383 **Average undergraduate aid package: $9026**

ABOUT THE INSTITUTION State-supported, coed. ***Awards:*** bachelor's and master's degrees. 30 undergraduate majors. ***Total enrollment:*** 7,684. Undergraduates: 6,171. Freshmen: 925. Federal methodology is used as a basis for awarding need-based institutional aid.

UNDERGRADUATE EXPENSES for 2008–09 ***Application fee:*** $55. ***Tuition, state resident:*** full-time $0. ***Tuition, nonresident:*** full-time $10,170; part-time $226 per unit. ***Required fees:*** full-time $4383; $933 per term. ***College room and board:*** $7137; ***Room only:*** $3195.

FRESHMAN FINANCIAL AID (Fall 2007) 751 applied for aid; of those 85% were deemed to have need. 95% of freshmen with need received aid; of those 11% had need fully met. ***Average percent of need met:*** 76% (excluding resources awarded to replace EFC). ***Average financial aid package:*** $8486 (excluding resources awarded to replace EFC). 13% of all full-time freshmen had no need and received non-need-based gift aid.

UNDERGRADUATE FINANCIAL AID (Fall 2007) 4,288 applied for aid; of those 90% were deemed to have need. 96% of undergraduates with need received aid; of those 17% had need fully met. ***Average percent of need met:*** 78% (excluding resources awarded to replace EFC). ***Average financial aid package:*** $9026 (excluding resources awarded to replace EFC). 6% of all full-time undergraduates had no need and received non-need-based gift aid.

GIFT AID (NEED-BASED) ***Total amount:*** $21,115,433 (49% federal, 51% state). ***Receiving aid:*** Freshmen: 61% (546); all full-time undergraduates: 55% (3,245). ***Average award:*** Freshmen: $7470; Undergraduates: $6199. ***Scholarships, grants, and awards:*** Federal Pell, FSEOG, state, private, college/university gift aid from institutional funds, Federal Nursing.

GIFT AID (NON-NEED-BASED) ***Total amount:*** $1,245,320 (60% institutional, 40% external sources). ***Receiving aid:*** Freshmen: 15% (134). Undergraduates: 7% (432). ***Average award:*** Freshmen: $2232. Undergraduates: $2402. ***Scholarships, grants, and awards by category:*** *Academic interests/achievement:* agriculture, architecture, biological sciences, business, communication, education, foreign languages, general academic interests/achievements, health fields, humanities, mathematics, physical sciences, premedicine, religion/biblical studies, social sciences. *Creative arts/performance:* art/fine arts, dance, music, theater/drama. *Special achievements/activities:* community service, general special achievements/activities. *Special characteristics:* children of faculty/staff, children of union members/company employees, ethnic background, first-generation college students, veterans.

LOANS ***Student loans:*** $14,013,547 (65% need-based, 35% non-need-based). 10% of past graduating class borrowed through all loan programs. *Average indebtedness per student:* $5727. ***Average need-based loan:*** Freshmen: $3165. Undergraduates: $5259. ***Parent loans:*** $579,208 (100% non-need-based). ***Programs:*** Federal Direct (Subsidized and Unsubsidized Stafford, PLUS), Perkins, Federal Nursing.

WORK-STUDY ***Federal work-study:*** Total amount: $295,603; jobs available.

APPLYING FOR FINANCIAL AID ***Required financial aid form:*** FAFSA. ***Financial aid deadline:*** Continuous. ***Notification date:*** Continuous beginning 5/1. Students must reply within 3 weeks of notification.

CONTACT Mr. Ron Radney, Interim Director of Financial Aid, California State University, Bakersfield, 9001 Stockdale Highway, Bakersfield, CA 93311-1099, 661-654-3271 or toll-free 800-788-2782 (in-state). *Fax:* 661-654-6800. *E-mail:* rradney@csub.edu.

CALIFORNIA STATE UNIVERSITY CHANNEL ISLANDS

Camarillo, CA

CONTACT Financial Aid Office, California State University Channel Islands, One University Drive, Camarillo, CA 93012, 805-437-8400.

CALIFORNIA STATE UNIVERSITY, CHICO

Chico, CA

Tuition & fees (CA res): $4008 **Average undergraduate aid package: $10,511**

ABOUT THE INSTITUTION State-supported, coed. ***Awards:*** bachelor's and master's degrees and post-bachelor's and post-master's certificates. 114 undergraduate majors. ***Total enrollment:*** 17,132. Undergraduates: 15,804. Freshmen: 2,765. Federal methodology is used as a basis for awarding need-based institutional aid.

UNDERGRADUATE EXPENSES for 2008–09 ***Application fee:*** $55. ***Tuition, state resident:*** full-time $0. ***Tuition, nonresident:*** full-time $10,170; part-time $339 per unit. ***Required fees:*** full-time $4008; $1365 per term. Part-time tuition and fees vary according to course load. ***College room and board:*** $8718; ***Room only:*** $6006. Room and board charges vary according to board plan and housing facility. ***Payment plans:*** Installment, deferred payment.

FRESHMAN FINANCIAL AID (Fall 2008, est.) 1,836 applied for aid; of those 63% were deemed to have need. 98% of freshmen with need received aid; of those 28% had need fully met. ***Average percent of need met:*** 88% (excluding resources awarded to replace EFC). ***Average financial aid package:*** $10,120 (excluding resources awarded to replace EFC). 5% of all full-time freshmen had no need and received non-need-based gift aid.

UNDERGRADUATE FINANCIAL AID (Fall 2008, est.) 8,824 applied for aid; of those 77% were deemed to have need. 98% of undergraduates with need received aid; of those 24% had need fully met. ***Average percent of need met:*** 87% (excluding resources awarded to replace EFC). ***Average financial aid package:*** $10,511 (excluding resources awarded to replace EFC). 3% of all full-time undergraduates had no need and received non-need-based gift aid.

GIFT AID (NEED-BASED) ***Total amount:*** $34,713,953 (52% federal, 48% state). ***Receiving aid:*** Freshmen: 28% (766); all full-time undergraduates: 35% (5,102). ***Average award:*** Freshmen: $7913; Undergraduates: $6700. ***Scholarships, grants, and awards:*** Federal Pell, FSEOG, state, private, college/university gift aid from institutional funds, United Negro College Fund.

GIFT AID (NON-NEED-BASED) ***Total amount:*** $2,274,808 (2% state, 48% institutional, 50% external sources). ***Receiving aid:*** Freshmen: 25% (679). Undergraduates: 12% (1,710). ***Average award:*** Freshmen: $1467. Undergraduates: $1978. ***Scholarships, grants, and awards by category:*** *Academic interests/achievement:* agriculture, area/ethnic studies, biological sciences, business, communication, computer science, education, engineering/technologies, English, foreign languages, general academic interests/achievements, health fields, humanities, international studies, mathematics, physical sciences, social sciences. *Creative arts/performance:* applied art and design, art/fine arts, cinema/film/broadcasting, creative writing, dance, debating, general creative arts/performance, journalism/publications, music, performing arts, theater/drama. *Special achievements/activities:* community service, general special achievements/activities, hobbies/interests, leadership, memberships. *Special characteristics:* adult students, children of faculty/staff, ethnic background, first-generation college students, handicapped students, international students, local/state students, married students, members of minority groups, out-of-state students. ***Tuition waivers:*** Full or partial for employees or children of employees, senior citizens.

LOANS ***Student loans:*** $40,397,615 (59% need-based, 41% non-need-based). 43% of past graduating class borrowed through all loan programs. *Average indebtedness per student:* $11,183. ***Average need-based loan:*** Freshmen: $3538. Undergraduates: $4736. ***Parent loans:*** $3,121,048 (100% non-need-based). ***Programs:*** Federal Direct (Subsidized and Unsubsidized Stafford, PLUS), Perkins, college/university.

WORK-STUDY ***Federal work-study:*** Total amount: $8,257,250; 730 jobs averaging $2300.

ATHLETIC AWARDS Total amount: $510,802 (45% need-based, 55% non-need-based).

APPLYING FOR FINANCIAL AID ***Required financial aid forms:*** FAFSA, institution's own form. ***Financial aid deadline:*** Continuous. ***Notification date:*** Continuous beginning 3/2.

CONTACT Dan Reed, Director, California State University, Chico, Financial Aid and Scholarship Office, Chico, CA 95929-0705, 530-898-6451 or toll-free 800-542-4426. *Fax:* 530-898-6883. *E-mail:* finaid@csuchico.edu.

CALIFORNIA STATE UNIVERSITY, DOMINGUEZ HILLS

Carson, CA

ABOUT THE INSTITUTION State-supported, coed. ***Awards:*** bachelor's and master's degrees and post-bachelor's and post-master's certificates. 69 undergraduate majors. ***Total enrollment:*** 12,851. Undergraduates: 9,291. Freshmen: 950.

GIFT AID (NEED-BASED) ***Scholarships, grants, and awards:*** Federal Pell, FSEOG, state, private, college/university gift aid from institutional funds.

LOANS ***Programs:*** Federal Direct (Subsidized and Unsubsidized Stafford), FFEL (PLUS), Perkins, college/university.

APPLYING FOR FINANCIAL AID ***Required financial aid form:*** FAFSA.

CONTACT Mrs. Delores S. Lee, Director of Financial Aid, California State University, Dominguez Hills, 1000 East Victoria Street, Carson, CA 90747-0001, 310-243-3691. *E-mail:* dslee@csudh.edu.

CALIFORNIA STATE UNIVERSITY, EAST BAY

Hayward, CA

Tuition & fees (CA res): $3810 **Average undergraduate aid package: $9164**

ABOUT THE INSTITUTION State-supported, coed. ***Awards:*** bachelor's and master's degrees and post-bachelor's certificates. 91 undergraduate majors. ***Total enrollment:*** 14,167. Undergraduates: 10,913. Freshmen: 1,362. Federal methodology is used as a basis for awarding need-based institutional aid.

UNDERGRADUATE EXPENSES for 2008–09 ***Application fee:*** $55. ***Tuition, state resident:*** full-time $0. ***Tuition, nonresident:*** full-time $11,940. ***Required fees:*** full-time $3810. Full-time tuition and fees vary according to reciprocity agreements. Part-time tuition and fees vary according to reciprocity agreements. ***College room and board:*** $9228; ***Room only:*** $5233. Room and board charges vary according to board plan. ***Payment plan:*** Installment.

FRESHMAN FINANCIAL AID (Fall 2008, est.) 790 applied for aid; of those 89% were deemed to have need. 97% of freshmen with need received aid; of those 5% had need fully met. ***Average percent of need met:*** 63% (excluding resources awarded to replace EFC). ***Average financial aid package:*** $9626 (excluding resources awarded to replace EFC).

UNDERGRADUATE FINANCIAL AID (Fall 2008, est.) 4,415 applied for aid; of those 94% were deemed to have need. 97% of undergraduates with need received aid; of those 5% had need fully met. ***Average percent of need met:*** 56% (excluding resources awarded to replace EFC). ***Average financial aid package:*** $9164 (excluding resources awarded to replace EFC).

GIFT AID (NEED-BASED) ***Total amount:*** $26,103,630 (47% federal, 50% state, 1% institutional, 2% external sources). ***Receiving aid:*** Freshmen: 592; all full-time undergraduates: 3,285. ***Average award:*** Freshmen: $8192; Undergraduates: $7237. ***Scholarships, grants, and awards:*** Federal Pell, FSEOG, state, private, college/university gift aid from institutional funds.

GIFT AID (NON-NEED-BASED) ***Scholarships, grants, and awards by category:*** *Academic interests/achievement:* general academic interests/achievements. *Creative arts/performance:* music.

LOANS ***Student loans:*** $22,346,562 (82% need-based, 18% non-need-based). 34% of past graduating class borrowed through all loan programs. *Average indebtedness per student:* $12,728. ***Average need-based loan:*** Freshmen: $4804. Undergraduates: $6700. ***Parent loans:*** $2,515,318 (25% need-based, 75% non-need-based). ***Programs:*** FFEL (Subsidized and Unsubsidized Stafford, PLUS), Perkins, college/university.

WORK-STUDY ***Federal work-study:*** Total amount: $446,589; jobs available.

APPLYING FOR FINANCIAL AID ***Required financial aid form:*** FAFSA. ***Financial aid deadline (priority):*** 3/2. ***Notification date:*** Continuous beginning 3/16. Students must reply within 4 weeks of notification.

CONTACT Office of Financial Aid, California State University, East Bay, 25800 Carlos Bee Boulevard, Hayward, CA 94542-3028, 510-885-2784. *Fax:* 510-885-2161. *E-mail:* finaid@csueastbay.edu.

CALIFORNIA STATE UNIVERSITY, FRESNO

Fresno, CA

Tuition & fees (CA res): $3687 **Average undergraduate aid package: $9428**

ABOUT THE INSTITUTION State-supported, coed. ***Awards:*** bachelor's, master's, and doctoral degrees. 88 undergraduate majors. ***Total enrollment:*** 21,728. Undergraduates: 19,245. Freshmen: 2,823. Federal methodology is used as a basis for awarding need-based institutional aid.

UNDERGRADUATE EXPENSES for 2009–10 ***Application fee:*** $55. ***Tuition, state resident:*** full-time $0. ***Tuition, nonresident:*** full-time $10,170. ***Required fees:*** full-time $3687. ***College room and board:*** $8590; ***Room only:*** $4100.

FRESHMAN FINANCIAL AID (Fall 2008, est.) 2,210 applied for aid; of those 82% were deemed to have need. 97% of freshmen with need received aid; of those 16% had need fully met. ***Average percent of need met:*** 73% (excluding resources awarded to replace EFC). ***Average financial aid package:*** $9447 (excluding resources awarded to replace EFC). 5% of all full-time freshmen had no need and received non-need-based gift aid.

UNDERGRADUATE FINANCIAL AID (Fall 2008, est.) 10,655 applied for aid; of those 89% were deemed to have need. 97% of undergraduates with need received aid; of those 11% had need fully met. ***Average percent of need met:*** 69% (excluding resources awarded to replace EFC). ***Average financial aid package:*** $9428 (excluding resources awarded to replace EFC). 2% of all full-time undergraduates had no need and received non-need-based gift aid.

GIFT AID (NEED-BASED) ***Total amount:*** $63,124,211 (48% federal, 52% state). ***Receiving aid:*** Freshmen: 55% (1,508); all full-time undergraduates: 49% (7,694). ***Average award:*** Freshmen: $8708; Undergraduates: $7431. ***Scholarships, grants, and awards:*** Federal Pell, FSEOG, state, private, college/university gift aid from institutional funds.

GIFT AID (NON-NEED-BASED) ***Total amount:*** $5,178,852 (49% institutional, 51% external sources). ***Receiving aid:*** Freshmen: 15% (405). Undergraduates: 11% (1,680). ***Average award:*** Freshmen: $2961. Undergraduates: $3168. ***Scholarships, grants, and awards by category:*** *Academic interests/achievement:* 1,118 awards ($2,315,843 total): agriculture, area/ethnic studies, biological sciences, business, communication, education, engineering/technologies, English, foreign languages, general academic interests/achievements, health fields, humanities, mathematics, physical sciences, social sciences. *Creative arts/performance:* 234 awards ($230,309 total): art/fine arts, journalism/publications, music, theater/drama. *Special achievements/activities:* 27 awards ($43,500 total): community service, leadership. *Special characteristics:* 5 awards ($9334 total): handicapped students, local/state students. ***ROTC:*** Army, Air Force.

LOANS ***Student loans:*** $52,080,038 (63% need-based, 37% non-need-based). 38% of past graduating class borrowed through all loan programs. *Average indebtedness per student:* $11,938. ***Average need-based loan:*** Freshmen: $2967. Undergraduates: $4127. ***Parent loans:*** $1,537,695 (100% non-need-based). ***Programs:*** FFEL (Subsidized and Unsubsidized Stafford, PLUS), Perkins, Federal Nursing, college/university, alternative loans.

WORK-STUDY ***Federal work-study:*** Total amount: $729,077; 224 jobs averaging $3254.

ATHLETIC AWARDS Total amount: $3,282,886 (100% non-need-based).

APPLYING FOR FINANCIAL AID ***Required financial aid form:*** FAFSA. ***Financial aid deadline (priority):*** 3/2. ***Notification date:*** Continuous beginning 4/1. Students must reply within 3 weeks of notification.

CONTACT Maria Hernandez, Director of Financial Aid, California State University, Fresno, 5150 North Maple Avenue, Fresno, CA 93740, 559-278-2182. *Fax:* 559-278-4833. *E-mail:* mariah@csufresno.edu.

CALIFORNIA STATE UNIVERSITY, FULLERTON

Fullerton, CA

Tuition & fees (CA res): $3658 Average undergraduate aid package: $7553

ABOUT THE INSTITUTION State-supported, coed. ***Awards:*** bachelor's, master's, and doctoral degrees and post-bachelor's and post-master's certificates. 74 undergraduate majors. ***Total enrollment:*** 36,996. Undergraduates: 31,428. Federal methodology is used as a basis for awarding need-based institutional aid.

UNDERGRADUATE EXPENSES for 2008–09 ***Application fee:*** $55. ***Tuition, state resident:*** full-time $0. ***Tuition, nonresident:*** full-time $13,828; part-time $3224 per term. ***Required fees:*** full-time $3658; $1190 per term. Full-time tuition and fees vary according to course load. Part-time tuition and fees vary according to course load. ***College room and board:*** $8722. ***Payment plans:*** Installment, deferred payment.

FRESHMAN FINANCIAL AID (Fall 2007) 2,914 applied for aid; of those 67% were deemed to have need. 81% of freshmen with need received aid; of those 2% had need fully met. ***Average percent of need met:*** 60% (excluding resources awarded to replace EFC). ***Average financial aid package:*** $6935 (excluding resources awarded to replace EFC). 9% of all full-time freshmen had no need and received non-need-based gift aid.

UNDERGRADUATE FINANCIAL AID (Fall 2007) 13,347 applied for aid; of those 74% were deemed to have need. 91% of undergraduates with need received aid; of those 2% had need fully met. ***Average percent of need met:*** 62% (excluding resources awarded to replace EFC). ***Average financial aid package:*** $7553 (excluding resources awarded to replace EFC). 8% of all full-time undergraduates had no need and received non-need-based gift aid.

GIFT AID (NEED-BASED) ***Total amount:*** $59,826,956 (43% federal, 54% state, 1% institutional, 2% external sources). ***Receiving aid:*** Freshmen: 34% (1,386); all full-time undergraduates: 33% (7,509). ***Average award:*** Freshmen: $6740; Undergraduates: $6660. ***Scholarships, grants, and awards:*** Federal Pell, FSEOG, state, private, college/university gift aid from institutional funds.

GIFT AID (NON-NEED-BASED) ***Total amount:*** $1,248,330 (15% institutional, 85% external sources). ***Average award:*** Freshmen: $4472. Undergraduates: $4834. ***Scholarships, grants, and awards by category:*** *Academic interests/achievement:* 1,748 awards ($2,914,293 total): business, communication, engineering/technologies, general academic interests/achievements, humanities, mathematics, military science, social sciences. *Creative arts/performance:* 85 awards ($52,275 total): art/fine arts, dance, music, performing arts, theater/drama. *Special achievements/activities:* 59 awards ($199,536 total): general special achievements/activities, leadership. *Special characteristics:* 43 awards ($241,568 total): general special characteristics. ***Tuition waivers:*** Full or partial for employees or children of employees, senior citizens. ***ROTC:*** Army.

LOANS ***Student loans:*** $40,616,411 (57% need-based, 43% non-need-based). 38% of past graduating class borrowed through all loan programs. *Average indebtedness per student:* $15,338. ***Average need-based loan:*** Freshmen: $3188. Undergraduates: $4224. ***Parent loans:*** $2,361,982 (100% non-need-based). ***Programs:*** FFEL (Subsidized and Unsubsidized Stafford, PLUS), Perkins, college/university.

WORK-STUDY ***Federal work-study:*** Total amount: $1,166,980; 768 jobs averaging $2185.

ATHLETIC AWARDS Total amount: $1,461,608 (17% need-based, 83% non-need-based).

APPLYING FOR FINANCIAL AID ***Required financial aid form:*** FAFSA. ***Financial aid deadline (priority):*** 3/21. ***Notification date:*** Continuous beginning 3/21. Students must reply within 4 weeks of notification.

CONTACT Ms. Jessica Schutte, Acting Director of Financial Aid, California State University, Fullerton, 800 North State College Boulevard, Fullerton, CA 92831-3599, 714-278-3128. *Fax:* 714-278-7090. *E-mail:* jschutte@fullerton.edu.

CALIFORNIA STATE UNIVERSITY, LONG BEACH

Long Beach, CA

Tuition & fees (CA res): $3698 Average undergraduate aid package: $11,950

ABOUT THE INSTITUTION State-supported, coed. ***Awards:*** bachelor's and master's degrees and post-bachelor's certificates. 149 undergraduate majors. ***Total enrollment:*** 37,891. Undergraduates: 31,564. Freshmen: 4,606. Federal methodology is used as a basis for awarding need-based institutional aid.

UNDERGRADUATE EXPENSES for 2009–10 ***Application fee:*** $55. ***Tuition, state resident:*** full-time $0. ***Tuition, nonresident:*** full-time $10,170; part-time $339 per unit. ***Required fees:*** full-time $3698. ***College room and board:*** $10,832.

FRESHMAN FINANCIAL AID (Fall 2008, est.) 3,239 applied for aid; of those 73% were deemed to have need. 91% of freshmen with need received aid; of those 74% had need fully met. ***Average percent of need met:*** 80% (excluding resources awarded to replace EFC). ***Average financial aid package:*** $11,300 (excluding resources awarded to replace EFC). 4% of all full-time freshmen had no need and received non-need-based gift aid.

UNDERGRADUATE FINANCIAL AID (Fall 2008, est.) 17,207 applied for aid; of those 91% were deemed to have need. 85% of undergraduates with need received aid; of those 50% had need fully met. ***Average percent of need met:*** 84% (excluding resources awarded to replace EFC). ***Average financial aid package:*** $11,950 (excluding resources awarded to replace EFC). 6% of all full-time undergraduates had no need and received non-need-based gift aid.

GIFT AID (NEED-BASED) ***Total amount:*** $82,980,118 (45% federal, 49% state, 3% institutional, 3% external sources). ***Receiving aid:*** Freshmen: 44% (1,838); all full-time undergraduates: 45% (10,534). ***Average award:*** Freshmen: $5450; Undergraduates: $5410. ***Scholarships, grants, and awards:*** Federal Pell, FSEOG, state, private, college/university gift aid from institutional funds.

GIFT AID (NON-NEED-BASED) ***Total amount:*** $41,477 (89% federal, 11% state). ***Receiving aid:*** Freshmen: 6% (254). Undergraduates: 9% (2,068). ***Average award:*** Freshmen: $2044. Undergraduates: $2131. ***ROTC:*** Army.

LOANS ***Student loans:*** $65,015,819 (73% need-based, 27% non-need-based). 41% of past graduating class borrowed through all loan programs. *Average indebtedness per student:* $10,671. ***Average need-based loan:*** Freshmen: $2952. Undergraduates: $3271. ***Parent loans:*** $2,710,925 (100% non-need-based). ***Programs:*** FFEL (Subsidized and Unsubsidized Stafford, PLUS), Perkins.

WORK-STUDY ***Federal work-study:*** Total amount: $1,670,000; jobs available.

ATHLETIC AWARDS Total amount: $1,511,210 (100% non-need-based).

APPLYING FOR FINANCIAL AID ***Required financial aid form:*** FAFSA. ***Financial aid deadline (priority):*** 3/2. ***Notification date:*** Continuous beginning 3/30. Students must reply within 3 weeks of notification.

CONTACT Office of Financial Aid, California State University, Long Beach, 1250 Bellflower Boulevard, Long Beach, CA 90840, 562-985-8403.

CALIFORNIA STATE UNIVERSITY, LOS ANGELES

Los Angeles, CA

Tuition & fees (CA res): $3377 Average undergraduate aid package: $9484

ABOUT THE INSTITUTION State-supported, coed. ***Awards:*** bachelor's, master's, and doctoral degrees. 63 undergraduate majors. ***Total enrollment:*** 20,743. Undergraduates: 15,588. Freshmen: 1,942. Federal methodology is used as a basis for awarding need-based institutional aid.

UNDERGRADUATE EXPENSES for 2008–09 ***Application fee:*** $55. ***Tuition, state resident:*** full-time $0. ***Tuition, nonresident:*** full-time $8136; part-time $226 per unit. ***Required fees:*** full-time $3377; $794.25 per term. Full-time tuition and fees vary according to course level and course load. Part-time tuition and fees vary according to course level and course load. ***College room and board:*** $8406. ***Payment plan:*** Installment.

FRESHMAN FINANCIAL AID (Fall 2008, est.) 1,539 applied for aid; of those 92% were deemed to have need. 94% of freshmen with need received aid; of those 24% had need fully met. ***Average percent of need met:*** 77% (excluding resources awarded to replace EFC). ***Average financial aid package:*** $8893 (excluding resources awarded to replace EFC). 1% of all full-time freshmen had no need and received non-need-based gift aid.

UNDERGRADUATE FINANCIAL AID (Fall 2008, est.) 9,412 applied for aid; of those 95% were deemed to have need. 95% of undergraduates with need received aid; of those 17% had need fully met. ***Average percent of need met:*** 66% (excluding resources awarded to replace EFC). ***Average financial aid package:*** $9484 (excluding resources awarded to replace EFC). 1% of all full-time undergraduates had no need and received non-need-based gift aid.

GIFT AID (NEED-BASED) ***Total amount:*** $57,858,204 (48% federal, 49% state, 2% institutional, 1% external sources). ***Receiving aid:*** Freshmen: 63% (1,070); all full-time undergraduates: 58% (6,785). ***Average award:*** Freshmen: $7872;

Undergraduates: $7561. ***Scholarships, grants, and awards:*** Federal Pell, FSEOG, state, private, college/university gift aid from institutional funds.

GIFT AID (NON-NEED-BASED) ***Total amount:*** $675,718 (84% institutional, 16% external sources). ***Average award:*** Freshmen: $1906. Undergraduates: $4048. ***Scholarships, grants, and awards by category:*** *Academic interests/achievement:* biological sciences, business, communication, computer science, education, engineering/technologies, English, foreign languages, general academic interests/achievements, health fields, mathematics, physical sciences, social sciences. *Creative arts/performance:* art/fine arts, general creative arts/performance, journalism/publications, music, theater/drama. *Special achievements/activities:* community service, general special achievements/activities. *Special characteristics:* general special characteristics. ***Tuition waivers:*** Full or partial for employees or children of employees. ***ROTC:*** Army cooperative, Air Force cooperative.

LOANS ***Student loans:*** $36,451,129 (99% need-based, 1% non-need-based). ***Average need-based loan:*** Freshmen: $3350. Undergraduates: $5002. ***Programs:*** Federal Direct (Subsidized and Unsubsidized Stafford, PLUS), FFEL (PLUS), Perkins, Federal Nursing.

WORK-STUDY ***Federal work-study:*** Total amount: $478,101; jobs available.

APPLYING FOR FINANCIAL AID ***Required financial aid form:*** FAFSA. ***Financial aid deadline (priority):*** 3/2. ***Notification date:*** Continuous beginning 4/1.

CONTACT Tamie L. Nguyen, Director of Financial Aid, California State University, Los Angeles, 5151 State University Drive, Los Angeles, CA 90032, 323-343-6260. *Fax:* 323-343-3166. *E-mail:* tnguyen10@cslanet.calstatela.edu.

CALIFORNIA STATE UNIVERSITY, MONTEREY BAY

Seaside, CA

CONTACT Campus Service Center, California State University, Monterey Bay, 100 Campus Center, Seaside, CA 93955-8001, 831-582-4074. *Fax:* 831-582-3782.

CALIFORNIA STATE UNIVERSITY, NORTHRIDGE

Northridge, CA

Tuition & fees (CA res): $3702 **Average undergraduate aid package: $7884**

ABOUT THE INSTITUTION State-supported, coed. ***Awards:*** bachelor's and master's degrees. 47 undergraduate majors. ***Total enrollment:*** 36,208. Undergraduates: 30,235. Freshmen: 4,625. Federal methodology is used as a basis for awarding need-based institutional aid.

UNDERGRADUATE EXPENSES for 2008–09 ***Application fee:*** $55. ***Tuition, state resident:*** full-time $0. ***Tuition, nonresident:*** full-time $10,170; part-time $339 per unit. ***Required fees:*** full-time $3702; $1093 per term. ***College room and board:*** $10,152; ***Room only:*** $5684. Room and board charges vary according to board plan and housing facility. ***Payment plan:*** Installment.

FRESHMAN FINANCIAL AID (Fall 2007) 2,897 applied for aid; of those 85% were deemed to have need. 100% of freshmen with need received aid. ***Average financial aid package:*** $7843 (excluding resources awarded to replace EFC). 2% of all full-time freshmen had no need and received non-need-based gift aid.

UNDERGRADUATE FINANCIAL AID (Fall 2007) 14,004 applied for aid; of those 93% were deemed to have need. 100% of undergraduates with need received aid. ***Average financial aid package:*** $7884 (excluding resources awarded to replace EFC). 3% of all full-time undergraduates had no need and received non-need-based gift aid.

GIFT AID (NEED-BASED) ***Total amount:*** $57,136,579 (64% federal, 36% state). ***Receiving aid:*** Freshmen: 47% (1,862); all full-time undergraduates: 43% (9,471). ***Average award:*** Freshmen: $5245; Undergraduates: $2509. ***Scholarships, grants, and awards:*** Federal Pell, FSEOG, state, private, college/university gift aid from institutional funds.

GIFT AID (NON-NEED-BASED) ***Total amount:*** $23,933,374 (91% state, 5% institutional, 4% external sources). ***Receiving aid:*** Freshmen: 43% (1,694). Undergraduates: 32% (7,039). ***Average award:*** Freshmen: $1705. Undergraduates: $1526. ***Scholarships, grants, and awards by category:*** *Academic interests/achievement:* business, communication, computer science, education, engineering/technologies, English, general academic interests/achievements, mathematics, social sciences. *Creative arts/performance:* journalism/publications, music. *Special achievements/activities:* leadership. ***Tuition waivers:*** Full or partial for employees or children of employees, senior citizens. ***ROTC:*** Army cooperative, Air Force cooperative.

LOANS ***Student loans:*** $51,441,978 (63% need-based, 37% non-need-based). 40% of past graduating class borrowed through all loan programs. *Average indebtedness per student:* $14,009. ***Average need-based loan:*** Freshmen: $3504. Undergraduates: $4196. ***Parent loans:*** $1,893,828 (100% non-need-based). ***Programs:*** FFEL (Subsidized and Unsubsidized Stafford, PLUS), Perkins.

WORK-STUDY ***Federal work-study:*** Total amount: $1,527,360; 489 jobs averaging $2951.

ATHLETIC AWARDS Total amount: $1,559,487 (100% non-need-based).

APPLYING FOR FINANCIAL AID ***Required financial aid forms:*** FAFSA, state aid form. ***Financial aid deadline (priority):*** 3/2. ***Notification date:*** Continuous beginning 4/1.

CONTACT Lili Vidal, Director of Financial Aid and Scholarships, California State University, Northridge, 18111 Nordhoff Street, Northridge, CA 91330-8307, 818-677-4085. *Fax:* 818-677-3047. *E-mail:* financial.aid@csun.edu.

CALIFORNIA STATE UNIVERSITY, SACRAMENTO

Sacramento, CA

Tuition & fees (CA res): $3048 **Average undergraduate aid package: $6606**

ABOUT THE INSTITUTION State-supported, coed. ***Awards:*** bachelor's, master's, and doctoral degrees. 56 undergraduate majors. ***Total enrollment:*** 29,011. Undergraduates: 24,034. Freshmen: 2,281. Federal methodology is used as a basis for awarding need-based institutional aid.

UNDERGRADUATE EXPENSES for 2008–09 ***Application fee:*** $55. ***Tuition, state resident:*** full-time $0. ***Tuition, nonresident:*** full-time $10,170; part-time $339 per unit. ***Required fees:*** full-time $3048; $806 per year. ***College room and board:*** $9428; ***Room only:*** $6356. Room and board charges vary according to board plan and housing facility. ***Payment plan:*** Installment.

FRESHMAN FINANCIAL AID (Fall 2007) 2,499 applied for aid; of those 87% were deemed to have need. 65% of freshmen with need received aid; of those 11% had need fully met. ***Average percent of need met:*** 47% (excluding resources awarded to replace EFC). ***Average financial aid package:*** $3067 (excluding resources awarded to replace EFC).

UNDERGRADUATE FINANCIAL AID (Fall 2007) 14,066 applied for aid; of those 91% were deemed to have need. 91% of undergraduates with need received aid; of those 11% had need fully met. ***Average percent of need met:*** 70% (excluding resources awarded to replace EFC). ***Average financial aid package:*** $6606 (excluding resources awarded to replace EFC). 1% of all full-time undergraduates had no need and received non-need-based gift aid.

GIFT AID (NEED-BASED) ***Total amount:*** $58,792,570 (45% federal, 53% state, 2% external sources). ***Receiving aid:*** Freshmen: 34% (917); all full-time undergraduates: 55% (8,442). ***Average award:*** Freshmen: $3828; Undergraduates: $6007. ***Scholarships, grants, and awards:*** Federal Pell, FSEOG, state, private, college/university gift aid from institutional funds, Federal Nursing.

GIFT AID (NON-NEED-BASED) ***Total amount:*** $1,527,496 (1% federal, 2% institutional, 97% external sources). ***Receiving aid:*** Freshmen: 6% (163). Undergraduates: 5% (759). ***Average award:*** Undergraduates: $1838. ***Tuition waivers:*** Full or partial for employees or children of employees, senior citizens. ***ROTC:*** Army cooperative, Air Force.

LOANS ***Student loans:*** $68,910,169 (58% need-based, 42% non-need-based). 35% of past graduating class borrowed through all loan programs. *Average indebtedness per student:* $11,152. ***Average need-based loan:*** Freshmen: $1584. Undergraduates: $4030. ***Parent loans:*** $5,407,974 (100% non-need-based). ***Programs:*** FFEL (Subsidized and Unsubsidized Stafford, PLUS), Perkins, Federal Nursing.

WORK-STUDY ***Federal work-study:*** Total amount: $1,060,953; jobs available. ***State or other work-study/employment:*** Total amount: $171,418 (100% need-based). Part-time jobs available.

ATHLETIC AWARDS Total amount: $2,545,948 (100% need-based).

APPLYING FOR FINANCIAL AID ***Required financial aid form:*** FAFSA. ***Notification date:*** Continuous.

CONTACT Linda Joy Clemons, Financial Aid Director, California State University, Sacramento, 6000 J Street, Sacramento, CA 95819-6044, 916-278-6554. *Fax:* 916-278-6082. *E-mail:* ljclemons@csus.edu.

CALIFORNIA STATE UNIVERSITY, SAN BERNARDINO

San Bernardino, CA

Tuition & fees (CA res): $3797 Average undergraduate aid package: $8840

ABOUT THE INSTITUTION State-supported, coed. ***Awards:*** bachelor's, master's, and doctoral degrees. 51 undergraduate majors. ***Total enrollment:*** 17,646. Undergraduates: 13,947. Freshmen: 1,968. Federal methodology is used as a basis for awarding need-based institutional aid.

UNDERGRADUATE EXPENSES for 2008–09 ***Application fee:*** $55. ***Tuition, state resident:*** full-time $0. ***Tuition, nonresident:*** full-time $8136; part-time $226 per unit. ***Required fees:*** full-time $3797; $839.50 per term. ***College room and board: Room only:*** $4311.

FRESHMAN FINANCIAL AID (Fall 2008, est.) 1,287 applied for aid; of those 84% were deemed to have need. 95% of freshmen with need received aid; of those 15% had need fully met. ***Average percent of need met:*** 72% (excluding resources awarded to replace EFC). ***Average financial aid package:*** $8467 (excluding resources awarded to replace EFC). 1% of all full-time freshmen had no need and received non-need-based gift aid.

UNDERGRADUATE FINANCIAL AID (Fall 2008, est.) 8,620 applied for aid; of those 90% were deemed to have need. 96% of undergraduates with need received aid; of those 18% had need fully met. ***Average percent of need met:*** 72% (excluding resources awarded to replace EFC). ***Average financial aid package:*** $8840 (excluding resources awarded to replace EFC). 1% of all full-time undergraduates had no need and received non-need-based gift aid.

GIFT AID (NEED-BASED) ***Total amount:*** $41,351,993 (47% federal, 48% state, 3% institutional, 2% external sources). ***Receiving aid:*** Freshmen: 51% (837); all full-time undergraduates: 55% (6,122). ***Average award:*** Freshmen: $6907; Undergraduates: $6291. ***Scholarships, grants, and awards:*** Federal Pell, FSEOG, state, private, college/university gift aid from institutional funds.

GIFT AID (NON-NEED-BASED) ***Total amount:*** $140,712 (75% institutional, 25% external sources). ***Receiving aid:*** Freshmen: 1% (20). Undergraduates: 2% (264). ***Average award:*** Freshmen: $2983. Undergraduates: $3190. ***Scholarships, grants, and awards by category:*** *Academic interests/achievement:* 361 awards ($868,828 total): biological sciences, business, computer science, education, foreign languages, general academic interests/achievements, health fields, mathematics, physical sciences, social sciences. *Creative arts/performance:* 68 awards ($79,660 total): art/fine arts, general creative arts/performance, journalism/publications, music, theater/drama. *Special achievements/activities:* 29 awards ($104,192 total): community service, general special achievements/activities, hobbies/interests, memberships. *Special characteristics:* 6 awards ($14,800 total): children of public servants, children with a deceased or disabled parent, first-generation college students, handicapped students. ***ROTC:*** Army, Air Force.

LOANS ***Student loans:*** $46,588,053 (100% need-based). 55% of past graduating class borrowed through all loan programs. *Average indebtedness per student:* $17,946. ***Average need-based loan:*** Freshmen: $3158. Undergraduates: $3928. ***Parent loans:*** $19,894,285 (100% non-need-based). ***Programs:*** Federal Direct (Subsidized and Unsubsidized Stafford, PLUS), Perkins.

WORK-STUDY ***Federal work-study:*** Total amount: $2,038,817; 350 jobs averaging $4300.

ATHLETIC AWARDS Total amount: $534,420 (100% non-need-based).

APPLYING FOR FINANCIAL AID ***Required financial aid forms:*** FAFSA, state aid form. ***Financial aid deadline (priority):*** 3/2. ***Notification date:*** Continuous beginning 4/1.

CONTACT Roseanna Ruiz, Director of Financial Aid, California State University, San Bernardino, 5500 University Parkway, San Bernardino, CA 92407-2397, 909-537-7651. *Fax:* 909-537-7024. *E-mail:* rruiz@csusb.edu.

CALIFORNIA STATE UNIVERSITY, SAN MARCOS

San Marcos, CA

ABOUT THE INSTITUTION State-supported, coed. ***Awards:*** bachelor's and master's degrees. 23 undergraduate majors. ***Total enrollment:*** 8,676. Undergraduates: 8,112. Freshmen: 1,574.

GIFT AID (NEED-BASED) ***Scholarships, grants, and awards:*** Federal Pell, FSEOG, state, private, college/university gift aid from institutional funds.

GIFT AID (NON-NEED-BASED) ***Scholarships, grants, and awards by category:*** *Academic interests/achievement:* mathematics.

LOANS ***Programs:*** Federal Direct (Subsidized and Unsubsidized Stafford, PLUS), Perkins, college/university.

WORK-STUDY ***Federal work-study:*** Total amount: $252,156; 156 jobs averaging $1962.

APPLYING FOR FINANCIAL AID ***Required financial aid form:*** FAFSA.

CONTACT Addalou Davis, Director of Financial Aid, California State University, San Marcos, 333 South Twin Oaks Valley Road, San Marcos, CA 92096-0001, 760-750-4852. *Fax:* 760-750-3047. *E-mail:* finaid@csusm.edu.

CALIFORNIA STATE UNIVERSITY, STANISLAUS

Turlock, CA

Tuition & fees (CA res): $3819 Average undergraduate aid package: $9351

ABOUT THE INSTITUTION State-supported, coed. ***Awards:*** bachelor's, master's, and doctoral degrees and post-bachelor's certificates. 36 undergraduate majors. ***Total enrollment:*** 8,601. Undergraduates: 6,907. Freshmen: 965. Federal methodology is used as a basis for awarding need-based institutional aid.

UNDERGRADUATE EXPENSES for 2008–09 ***Application fee:*** $55. ***One-time required fee:*** $55. ***Tuition, state resident:*** full-time $0. ***Tuition, nonresident:*** full-time $10,170; part-time $339 per unit. ***Required fees:*** full-time $3819; $1163 per term. Full-time tuition and fees vary according to course load, degree level, reciprocity agreements, and student level. Part-time tuition and fees vary according to course load, degree level, reciprocity agreements, and student level. ***College room and board:*** $7832; ***Room only:*** $7042. Room and board charges vary according to board plan and housing facility. ***Payment plans:*** Installment, deferred payment.

FRESHMAN FINANCIAL AID (Fall 2008, est.) 574 applied for aid; of those 78% were deemed to have need. 96% of freshmen with need received aid; of those 13% had need fully met. ***Average percent of need met:*** 68% (excluding resources awarded to replace EFC). ***Average financial aid package:*** $9177 (excluding resources awarded to replace EFC). 1% of all full-time freshmen had no need and received non-need-based gift aid.

UNDERGRADUATE FINANCIAL AID (Fall 2008, est.) 4,077 applied for aid; of those 88% were deemed to have need. 94% of undergraduates with need received aid; of those 3% had need fully met. ***Average percent of need met:*** 41% (excluding resources awarded to replace EFC). ***Average financial aid package:*** $9351 (excluding resources awarded to replace EFC). 1% of all full-time undergraduates had no need and received non-need-based gift aid.

GIFT AID (NEED-BASED) ***Total amount:*** $22,420,616 (45% federal, 54% state, 1% institutional). ***Receiving aid:*** Freshmen: 37% (328); all full-time undergraduates: 57% (2,835). ***Average award:*** Freshmen: $5190; Undergraduates: $6058. ***Scholarships, grants, and awards:*** Federal Pell, FSEOG, state, private, college/university gift aid from institutional funds.

GIFT AID (NON-NEED-BASED) ***Total amount:*** $1,053,526 (51% institutional, 49% external sources). ***Receiving aid:*** Freshmen: 3% (25). Undergraduates: 4% (202). ***Average award:*** Freshmen: $4750. Undergraduates: $4565. ***Scholarships, grants, and awards by category:*** *Academic interests/achievement:* 115 awards ($122,700 total): agriculture, area/ethnic studies, biological sciences, business, communication, computer science, education, English, foreign languages, general academic interests/achievements, health fields, humanities, international studies, mathematics, physical sciences, premedicine, social sciences. *Creative arts/performance:* 45 awards ($35,281 total): art/fine arts, music. *Special achievements/activities:* 135 awards ($304,450 total): community service, general special achievements/activities, leadership, memberships. *Special characteristics:* 41 awards ($33,430 total): children of faculty/staff, ethnic background, first-generation college students, general special characteristics, local/state students, members of minority groups. ***Tuition waivers:*** Full or partial for employees or children of employees, adult students, senior citizens.

LOANS ***Student loans:*** $19,248,177 (63% need-based, 37% non-need-based). 23% of past graduating class borrowed through all loan programs. *Average indebtedness per student:* $17,000. ***Average need-based loan:*** Freshmen: $4309. Undergraduates: $5708. ***Parent loans:*** $13,209 (100% non-need-based). ***Programs:*** FFEL (Subsidized and Unsubsidized Stafford, PLUS), Perkins, college/university.

WORK-STUDY ***Federal work-study:*** Total amount: $469,404; 147 jobs averaging $2263. ***State or other work-study/employment:*** Part-time jobs available.

ATHLETIC AWARDS Total amount: $326,762 (100% non-need-based).

APPLYING FOR FINANCIAL AID ***Required financial aid forms:*** FAFSA, state aid form. ***Financial aid deadline (priority):*** 3/2. ***Notification date:*** Continuous beginning 3/15. Students must reply within 3 weeks of notification.

CONTACT Ms. Noelia Gonzalez, Director, Financial Aid/Scholarships Department, California State University, Stanislaus, One University Circle, Turlock, CA 95382, 209-664-6583 or toll-free 800-300-7420 (in-state). *Fax:* 209-667-3337. *E-mail:* ngonzalez4@csustan.edu.

CALIFORNIA UNIVERSITY OF PENNSYLVANIA

California, PA

ABOUT THE INSTITUTION State-supported, coed. 41 undergraduate majors.

GIFT AID (NEED-BASED) ***Scholarships, grants, and awards:*** Federal Pell, FSEOG, state, private, college/university gift aid from institutional funds, Academic Competitiveness Grant, National Smart Grant.

GIFT AID (NON-NEED-BASED) ***Scholarships, grants, and awards by category:*** *Academic interests/achievement:* general academic interests/achievements. *Creative arts/performance:* general creative arts/performance. *Special achievements/activities:* general special achievements/activities. *Special characteristics:* ethnic background, international students, members of minority groups, veterans.

LOANS ***Programs:*** FFEL (Subsidized and Unsubsidized Stafford, PLUS), Perkins, college/university.

APPLYING FOR FINANCIAL AID ***Required financial aid form:*** FAFSA.

CONTACT Financial Aid Office, California University of Pennsylvania, 250 University Avenue, California, PA 15419-1394, 724-938-4415.

CALUMET COLLEGE OF SAINT JOSEPH

Whiting, IN

Tuition & fees: $12,460 **Average undergraduate aid package: $15,696**

ABOUT THE INSTITUTION Independent Roman Catholic, coed. ***Awards:*** associate, bachelor's, and master's degrees and post-bachelor's certificates. 28 undergraduate majors. ***Total enrollment:*** 1,213. Undergraduates: 1,102. Freshmen: 147. Federal methodology is used as a basis for awarding need-based institutional aid.

UNDERGRADUATE EXPENSES for 2008–09 ***Tuition:*** full-time $12,300; part-time $385 per credit hour. ***Required fees:*** full-time $160; $80 per term. ***Payment plan:*** Installment.

FRESHMAN FINANCIAL AID (Fall 2008, est.) 135 applied for aid; of those 84% were deemed to have need. 100% of freshmen with need received aid; of those 25% had need fully met. ***Average percent of need met:*** 79% (excluding resources awarded to replace EFC). ***Average financial aid package:*** $12,474 (excluding resources awarded to replace EFC). 7% of all full-time freshmen had no need and received non-need-based gift aid.

UNDERGRADUATE FINANCIAL AID (Fall 2008, est.) 508 applied for aid; of those 88% were deemed to have need. 100% of undergraduates with need received aid; of those 26% had need fully met. ***Average percent of need met:*** 74% (excluding resources awarded to replace EFC). ***Average financial aid package:*** $15,696 (excluding resources awarded to replace EFC). 4% of all full-time undergraduates had no need and received non-need-based gift aid.

GIFT AID (NEED-BASED) ***Total amount:*** $2,999,741 (45% federal, 36% state, 15% institutional, 4% external sources). ***Receiving aid:*** Freshmen: 70% (95); all full-time undergraduates: 66% (335). ***Average award:*** Freshmen: $5918; Undergraduates: $6944. ***Scholarships, grants, and awards:*** Federal Pell, FSEOG, state, private, college/university gift aid from institutional funds, United Negro College Fund.

GIFT AID (NON-NEED-BASED) ***Total amount:*** $432,469 (72% institutional, 28% external sources). ***Receiving aid:*** Freshmen: 84% (114). Undergraduates: 75% (381). ***Average award:*** Freshmen: $3082. Undergraduates: $3046. ***Scholarships, grants, and awards by category:*** *Special characteristics:* 3 awards ($8675 total): children and siblings of alumni. ***Tuition waivers:*** Full or partial for employees or children of employees, senior citizens.

LOANS ***Student loans:*** $5,068,008 (40% need-based, 60% non-need-based). 80% of past graduating class borrowed through all loan programs. *Average indebtedness per student:* $31,642. ***Average need-based loan:*** Freshmen: $3262. Undergraduates: $3990. ***Parent loans:*** $71,869 (100% non-need-based). ***Programs:*** Federal Direct (Subsidized and Unsubsidized Stafford, PLUS).

WORK-STUDY ***Federal work-study:*** Total amount: $56,203; 32 jobs averaging $1968. ***State or other work-study/employment:*** Total amount: $4480 (100% need-based). 2 part-time jobs averaging $1850.

ATHLETIC AWARDS Total amount: $999,870 (100% non-need-based).

APPLYING FOR FINANCIAL AID ***Required financial aid form:*** FAFSA. ***Financial aid deadline (priority):*** 3/1. ***Notification date:*** Continuous.

CONTACT Chuck Walz, Director of Admissions and Financial Aid, Calumet College of Saint Joseph, 2400 New York Avenue, Whiting, IN 46394, 219-473-4379 or toll-free 877-700-9100. *E-mail:* cwalz@ccsj.edu.

CALVARY BIBLE COLLEGE AND THEOLOGICAL SEMINARY

Kansas City, MO

ABOUT THE INSTITUTION Independent nondenominational, coed. ***Awards:*** associate, bachelor's, master's, and first professional degrees. 17 undergraduate majors. ***Total enrollment:*** 300. Undergraduates: 242. Freshmen: 42.

GIFT AID (NEED-BASED) ***Scholarships, grants, and awards:*** Federal Pell, FSEOG, private, college/university gift aid from institutional funds.

GIFT AID (NON-NEED-BASED) ***Scholarships, grants, and awards by category:*** *Academic interests/achievement:* general academic interests/achievements. *Special achievements/activities:* general special achievements/activities, religious involvement. *Special characteristics:* children and siblings of alumni, children of educators, children of faculty/staff, relatives of clergy, siblings of current students, spouses of current students.

LOANS ***Programs:*** FFEL (Subsidized and Unsubsidized Stafford, PLUS), alternative loans.

APPLYING FOR FINANCIAL AID ***Required financial aid forms:*** FAFSA, institution's own form.

CONTACT Jenny Olsen, Financial Aid Administrator, Calvary Bible College and Theological Seminary, 15800 Calvary Road, Kansas City, MO 64147-1341, 816-322-5152 Ext. 1323 or toll-free 800-326-3960. *Fax:* 816-331-4474. *E-mail:* finaid@calvary.edu.

CALVIN COLLEGE

Grand Rapids, MI

Tuition & fees: $23,165 **Average undergraduate aid package: $16,558**

ABOUT THE INSTITUTION Independent religious, coed. ***Awards:*** bachelor's and master's degrees and post-bachelor's certificates. 83 undergraduate majors. ***Total enrollment:*** 4,171. Undergraduates: 4,104. Freshmen: 936. Both federal and institutional methodology are used as a basis for awarding need-based institutional aid.

UNDERGRADUATE EXPENSES for 2008–09 ***Application fee:*** $35. ***Comprehensive fee:*** $31,135 includes full-time tuition ($22,940), mandatory fees ($225), and room and board ($7970). Full-time tuition and fees vary according to program. Room and board charges vary according to board plan. ***Part-time tuition:*** $550 per credit hour. Part-time tuition and fees vary according to course load. ***Payment plans:*** Tuition prepayment, installment.

FRESHMAN FINANCIAL AID (Fall 2008, est.) 773 applied for aid; of those 77% were deemed to have need. 100% of freshmen with need received aid; of those 28% had need fully met. ***Average percent of need met:*** 87% (excluding resources awarded to replace EFC). ***Average financial aid package:*** $17,309 (excluding resources awarded to replace EFC). 32% of all full-time freshmen had no need and received non-need-based gift aid.

UNDERGRADUATE FINANCIAL AID (Fall 2008, est.) 2,995 applied for aid; of those 81% were deemed to have need. 100% of undergraduates with need received aid; of those 25% had need fully met. ***Average percent of need met:*** 82% (excluding resources awarded to replace EFC). ***Average financial aid package:*** $16,558 (excluding resources awarded to replace EFC). 31% of all full-time undergraduates had no need and received non-need-based gift aid.

GIFT AID (NEED-BASED) ***Total amount:*** $26,039,994 (11% federal, 10% state, 76% institutional, 3% external sources). ***Receiving aid:*** Freshmen: 64% (596); all full-time undergraduates: 61% (2,410). ***Average award:*** Freshmen: $11,443; Undergraduates: $10,483. ***Scholarships, grants, and awards:*** Federal Pell, FSEOG, state, private, college/university gift aid from institutional funds.

GIFT AID (NON-NEED-BASED) ***Total amount:*** $7,700,797 (3% state, 93% institutional, 4% external sources). ***Receiving aid:*** Freshmen: 16% (150).

Undergraduates: 13% (520). ***Average award:*** Freshmen: $4061. Undergraduates: $4273. ***Scholarships, grants, and awards by category:*** *Academic interests/achievement:* 3,650 awards ($10,500,000 total): biological sciences, business, communication, computer science, education, engineering/technologies, English, foreign languages, general academic interests/achievements, health fields, humanities, international studies, mathematics, physical sciences, premedicine, religion/biblical studies, social sciences. *Creative arts/performance:* 80 awards ($200,000 total): art/fine arts, music, performing arts, theater/drama. *Special achievements/activities:* 50 awards ($50,000 total): community service, religious involvement. *Special characteristics:* 2,950 awards ($6,400,000 total): adult students, children and siblings of alumni, children of faculty/staff, children of union members/company employees, ethnic background, first-generation college students, handicapped students, international students, members of minority groups, religious affiliation, twins. ***Tuition waivers:*** Full or partial for employees or children of employees. ***ROTC:*** Army cooperative.

LOANS ***Student loans:*** $23,616,266 (69% need-based, 31% non-need-based). 64% of past graduating class borrowed through all loan programs. *Average indebtedness per student:* $27,400. ***Average need-based loan:*** Freshmen: $4670. Undergraduates: $6430. ***Parent loans:*** $1,197,941 (29% need-based, 71% non-need-based). ***Programs:*** Federal Direct (Subsidized and Unsubsidized Stafford, PLUS), Perkins, state, college/university, alternative loans.

WORK-STUDY ***Federal work-study:*** Total amount: $1,316,000; 929 jobs averaging $1337. ***State or other work-study/employment:*** Total amount: $1,519,000 (3% need-based, 97% non-need-based). 1,097 part-time jobs averaging $1306.

APPLYING FOR FINANCIAL AID ***Required financial aid form:*** FAFSA. ***Financial aid deadline (priority):*** 2/15. ***Notification date:*** Continuous beginning 3/15.

CONTACT Mr. Craig Heerema, Financial Aid Administrator, Calvin College, Spoelhof Center 263, Grand Rapids, MI 49546, 616-526-6134 or toll-free 800-688-0122. *Fax:* 616-526-6883. *E-mail:* cheerema@calvin.edu.

CAMBRIDGE COLLEGE

Cambridge, MA

CONTACT Dr. Gerri Major, Director of Financial Aid, Cambridge College, 1000 Massachusetts Avenue, Cambridge, MA 02138, 617-868-1000 Ext. 137 or toll-free 800-877-4723. *Fax:* 617-349-3561. *E-mail:* gmajor@idea.cambridge.edu.

CAMERON UNIVERSITY

Lawton, OK

CONTACT Caryn Pacheco, Financial Aid Director, Cameron University, 2800 West Gore Boulevard, Lawton, OK 73505-6377, 580-581-2293 or toll-free 888-454-7600. *Fax:* 580-581-2556.

CAMPBELLSVILLE UNIVERSITY

Campbellsville, KY

Tuition & fees: $18,810 **Average undergraduate aid package: $16,792**

ABOUT THE INSTITUTION Independent religious, coed. ***Awards:*** associate, bachelor's, and master's degrees and post-bachelor's certificates. 55 undergraduate majors. ***Total enrollment:*** 2,830. Undergraduates: 2,440. Freshmen: 449. Federal methodology is used as a basis for awarding need-based institutional aid.

UNDERGRADUATE EXPENSES for 2009–10 ***Application fee:*** $20. ***Comprehensive fee:*** $25,350 includes full-time tuition ($18,410), mandatory fees ($400), and room and board ($6540). ***Part-time tuition:*** $767 per credit.

FRESHMAN FINANCIAL AID (Fall 2008, est.) 319 applied for aid; of those 90% were deemed to have need. 99% of freshmen with need received aid; of those 21% had need fully met. ***Average percent of need met:*** 78% (excluding resources awarded to replace EFC). ***Average financial aid package:*** $16,801 (excluding resources awarded to replace EFC). 9% of all full-time freshmen had no need and received non-need-based gift aid.

UNDERGRADUATE FINANCIAL AID (Fall 2008, est.) 1,173 applied for aid; of those 91% were deemed to have need. 99% of undergraduates with need received aid; of those 18% had need fully met. ***Average percent of need met:*** 78% (excluding resources awarded to replace EFC). ***Average financial aid package:*** $16,792 (excluding resources awarded to replace EFC). 3% of all full-time undergraduates had no need and received non-need-based gift aid.

GIFT AID (NEED-BASED) ***Total amount:*** $13,319,318 (19% federal, 33% state, 42% institutional, 6% external sources). ***Receiving aid:*** Freshmen: 64% (283); all full-time undergraduates: 67% (1,046). ***Average award:*** Freshmen: $13,605; Undergraduates: $13,631. ***Scholarships, grants, and awards:*** Federal Pell, FSEOG, state, college/university gift aid from institutional funds.

GIFT AID (NON-NEED-BASED) ***Total amount:*** $1,605,579 (1% federal, 19% state, 71% institutional, 9% external sources). ***Receiving aid:*** Freshmen: 7% (32). Undergraduates: 7% (103). ***Average award:*** Freshmen: $5974. Undergraduates: $5954. ***Scholarships, grants, and awards by category:*** *Academic interests/achievement:* 457 awards ($2,480,591 total): biological sciences, business, communication, computer science, education, English, general academic interests/achievements, humanities, mathematics, physical sciences, premedicine, religion/biblical studies, social sciences. *Creative arts/performance:* 158 awards ($452,170 total): art/fine arts, journalism/publications, music, theater/drama. *Special achievements/activities:* 277 awards ($632,021 total): cheerleading/drum major, junior miss, leadership, religious involvement. *Special characteristics:* 131 awards ($704,890 total): adult students, children of educators, children of faculty/staff, international students, relatives of clergy, religious affiliation, veterans. ***ROTC:*** Army cooperative.

LOANS ***Student loans:*** $7,434,801 (79% need-based, 21% non-need-based). 77% of past graduating class borrowed through all loan programs. *Average indebtedness per student:* $15,170. ***Average need-based loan:*** Freshmen: $3187. Undergraduates: $3154. ***Parent loans:*** $1,204,763 (42% need-based, 58% non-need-based). ***Programs:*** FFEL (Subsidized and Unsubsidized Stafford, PLUS), Perkins, college/university.

WORK-STUDY ***Federal work-study:*** Total amount: $452,781; 312 jobs averaging $1486. ***State or other work-study/employment:*** Total amount: $121,487 (9% need-based, 91% non-need-based). 80 part-time jobs averaging $1950.

ATHLETIC AWARDS Total amount: $2,171,562 (52% need-based, 48% non-need-based).

APPLYING FOR FINANCIAL AID ***Required financial aid form:*** FAFSA. ***Financial aid deadline (priority):*** 3/1. ***Notification date:*** Continuous beginning 3/15. Students must reply within 3 weeks of notification.

CONTACT Mr. Aaron Gabehart, Financial Aid Counselor, Campbellsville University, 1 University Drive, Campbellsville, KY 42718, 270-789-5305 or toll-free 800-264-6014. *Fax:* 270-789-5060. *E-mail:* finaid@campbellsville.edu.

CAMPBELL UNIVERSITY

Buies Creek, NC

CONTACT Financial Aid Office, Campbell University, PO Box 36, Buies Creek, NC 27506, 910-893-1310 or toll-free 800-334-4111. *Fax:* 910-814-5788.

CANISIUS COLLEGE

Buffalo, NY

Tuition & fees: $28,157 **Average undergraduate aid package: $23,030**

ABOUT THE INSTITUTION Independent Roman Catholic (Jesuit), coed. ***Awards:*** associate, bachelor's, and master's degrees and post-master's certificates. 42 undergraduate majors. ***Total enrollment:*** 4,916. Undergraduates: 3,346. Freshmen: 807. Federal methodology is used as a basis for awarding need-based institutional aid.

UNDERGRADUATE EXPENSES for 2008–09 ***Application fee:*** $40. ***Comprehensive fee:*** $38,307 includes full-time tuition ($27,100), mandatory fees ($1057), and room and board ($10,150). ***College room only:*** $5990. Full-time tuition and fees vary according to course load. Room and board charges vary according to board plan and housing facility. ***Part-time tuition:*** $773 per credit hour. ***Part-time fees:*** $20.50 per credit hour; $33 per term. Part-time tuition and fees vary according to course load. ***Payment plans:*** Tuition prepayment, installment, deferred payment.

FRESHMAN FINANCIAL AID (Fall 2008, est.) 719 applied for aid; of those 90% were deemed to have need. 100% of freshmen with need received aid; of those 37% had need fully met. ***Average percent of need met:*** 88% (excluding resources awarded to replace EFC). ***Average financial aid package:*** $26,014 (excluding resources awarded to replace EFC). 17% of all full-time freshmen had no need and received non-need-based gift aid.

UNDERGRADUATE FINANCIAL AID (Fall 2008, est.) 2,579 applied for aid; of those 93% were deemed to have need. 99% of undergraduates with need received aid; of those 24% had need fully met. ***Average percent of need met:***

80% (excluding resources awarded to replace EFC). ***Average financial aid package:*** $23,030 (excluding resources awarded to replace EFC). 20% of all full-time undergraduates had no need and received non-need-based gift aid.

GIFT AID (NEED-BASED) ***Total amount:*** $38,945,576 (10% federal, 11% state, 78% institutional, 1% external sources). ***Receiving aid:*** Freshmen: 80% (644); all full-time undergraduates: 75% (2,363). ***Average award:*** Freshmen: $19,506; Undergraduates: $17,040. ***Scholarships, grants, and awards:*** Federal Pell, FSEOG, state, private, college/university gift aid from institutional funds.

GIFT AID (NON-NEED-BASED) ***Total amount:*** $3,469,852 (1% federal, 1% state, 96% institutional, 2% external sources). ***Receiving aid:*** Freshmen: 21% (169). Undergraduates: 14% (454). ***Average award:*** Freshmen: $14,649. Undergraduates: $13,104. ***Scholarships, grants, and awards by category:*** *Academic interests/achievement:* 2,575 awards ($24,265,298 total): general academic interests/achievements. *Creative arts/performance:* 59 awards ($103,000 total): art/fine arts, music. *Special achievements/activities:* 6 awards ($11,332 total): religious involvement. *Special characteristics:* 511 awards ($1,598,893 total): children and siblings of alumni, children of educators, children of faculty/staff, international students, religious affiliation. ***Tuition waivers:*** Full or partial for employees or children of employees. ***ROTC:*** Army.

LOANS ***Student loans:*** $21,294,396 (70% need-based, 30% non-need-based). 76% of past graduating class borrowed through all loan programs. *Average indebtedness per student:* $30,600. ***Average need-based loan:*** Freshmen: $3298. Undergraduates: $4273. ***Parent loans:*** $6,661,738 (20% need-based, 80% non-need-based). ***Programs:*** FFEL (Subsidized and Unsubsidized Stafford, PLUS), Perkins, college/university.

WORK-STUDY ***Federal work-study:*** Total amount: $943,253; 566 jobs averaging $1667. ***State or other work-study/employment:*** Total amount: $43,164 (57% need-based, 43% non-need-based). Part-time jobs available.

ATHLETIC AWARDS Total amount: $1,664,748 (63% need-based, 37% non-need-based).

APPLYING FOR FINANCIAL AID ***Required financial aid forms:*** FAFSA, state aid form. ***Financial aid deadline (priority):*** 2/15. ***Notification date:*** Continuous beginning 3/1. Students must reply by 5/1.

CONTACT Mr. Curtis Gaume, Director of Student Financial Aid, Canisius College, 2001 Main Street, Buffalo, NY 14208-1098, 716-888-2300 or toll-free 800-843-1517. *Fax:* 716-888-2377. *E-mail:* gaume@canisius.edu.

CAPELLA UNIVERSITY

Minneapolis, MN

CONTACT University Services, Capella University, 222 South Ninth Street, Minneapolis, MN 55402, 888-227-3552 or toll-free 888-CAPELLA.

CAPITAL UNIVERSITY

Columbus, OH

CONTACT Pamela Varda, Office of Financial Aid, Capital University, 1 College and Main Street, Columbus, OH 43209-2394, 614-236-6511 or toll-free 800-289-6289. *Fax:* 614-236-6926. *E-mail:* finaid@capital.edu.

CAPITOL COLLEGE

Laurel, MD

ABOUT THE INSTITUTION Independent, coed. ***Awards:*** associate, bachelor's, and master's degrees and post-bachelor's certificates. 13 undergraduate majors. ***Total enrollment:*** 699. Undergraduates: 309.

GIFT AID (NEED-BASED) ***Scholarships, grants, and awards:*** Federal Pell, FSEOG, state, private, college/university gift aid from institutional funds.

GIFT AID (NON-NEED-BASED) ***Scholarships, grants, and awards by category:*** *Academic interests/achievement:* general academic interests/achievements.

LOANS ***Programs:*** Federal Direct (Subsidized and Unsubsidized Stafford, PLUS), FFEL (Subsidized and Unsubsidized Stafford, PLUS), Perkins.

WORK-STUDY ***Federal work-study:*** Total amount: $68,534; 52 jobs averaging $1318.

APPLYING FOR FINANCIAL AID ***Required financial aid form:*** FAFSA.

CONTACT Suzanne Thompson, Director of Financial Aid, Capitol College, 11301 Springfield Road, Laurel, MD 20708-9759, 301-369-2800 Ext. 3037 or toll-free 800-950-1992. *Fax:* 301-369-2328. *E-mail:* sthompson@capitol-college.edu.

CARDINAL STRITCH UNIVERSITY

Milwaukee, WI

CONTACT Financial Aid Director, Cardinal Stritch University, 6801 North Yates Road, Milwaukee, WI 53217-3985, 414-410-4000 or toll-free 800-347-8822 Ext. 4040.

CARIBBEAN UNIVERSITY

Bayamón, PR

CONTACT Financial Aid Office, Caribbean University, Box 493, Bayamón, PR 00960-0493, 787-780-0070.

CARLETON COLLEGE

Northfield, MN

Tuition & fees: $38,046 **Average undergraduate aid package: $32,132**

ABOUT THE INSTITUTION Independent, coed. ***Awards:*** bachelor's degrees. 37 undergraduate majors. ***Total enrollment:*** 2,000. Undergraduates: 2,000. Freshmen: 489. Both federal and institutional methodology are used as a basis for awarding need-based institutional aid.

UNDERGRADUATE EXPENSES for 2008–09 ***Application fee:*** $30. ***Comprehensive fee:*** $48,039 includes full-time tuition ($37,845), mandatory fees ($201), and room and board ($9993). ***College room only:*** $4770.

FRESHMAN FINANCIAL AID (Fall 2007) 378 applied for aid; of those 70% were deemed to have need. 100% of freshmen with need received aid; of those 100% had need fully met. ***Average percent of need met:*** 100% (excluding resources awarded to replace EFC). ***Average financial aid package:*** $32,961 (excluding resources awarded to replace EFC). 6% of all full-time freshmen had no need and received non-need-based gift aid.

UNDERGRADUATE FINANCIAL AID (Fall 2007) 1,722 applied for aid; of those 64% were deemed to have need. 100% of undergraduates with need received aid; of those 100% had need fully met. ***Average percent of need met:*** 100% (excluding resources awarded to replace EFC). ***Average financial aid package:*** $32,132 (excluding resources awarded to replace EFC). 8% of all full-time undergraduates had no need and received non-need-based gift aid.

GIFT AID (NEED-BASED) ***Total amount:*** $26,349,565 (4% federal, 2% state, 90% institutional, 4% external sources). ***Receiving aid:*** Freshmen: 54% (264); all full-time undergraduates: 55% (1,096). ***Average award:*** Freshmen: $29,064; Undergraduates: $26,391. ***Scholarships, grants, and awards:*** Federal Pell, FSEOG, state, private, college/university gift aid from institutional funds.

GIFT AID (NON-NEED-BASED) ***Total amount:*** $1,292,272 (2% federal, 41% institutional, 57% external sources). ***Receiving aid:*** Freshmen: 10% (50). Undergraduates: 10% (204). ***Average award:*** Freshmen: $2238. Undergraduates: $3395. ***Scholarships, grants, and awards by category:*** *Academic interests/achievement:* 294 awards ($506,789 total): general academic interests/achievements. *Creative arts/performance:* 2 awards ($1190 total): music.

LOANS ***Student loans:*** $5,823,612 (95% need-based, 5% non-need-based). 52% of past graduating class borrowed through all loan programs. *Average indebtedness per student:* $20,083. ***Average need-based loan:*** Freshmen: $3896. Undergraduates: $4944. ***Parent loans:*** $1,766,111 (77% need-based, 23% non-need-based). ***Programs:*** FFEL (Subsidized and Unsubsidized Stafford, PLUS), Perkins, state, college/university.

WORK-STUDY ***Federal work-study:*** Total amount: $1,098,740; 431 jobs averaging $2565. ***State or other work-study/employment:*** Total amount: $2,782,661 (58% need-based, 42% non-need-based). 1,205 part-time jobs averaging $2306.

APPLYING FOR FINANCIAL AID ***Required financial aid forms:*** FAFSA, CSS Financial Aid PROFILE, noncustodial (divorced/separated) parent's statement, business/farm supplement. ***Financial aid deadline:*** 2/15 (priority: 2/15). ***Notification date:*** 4/1. Students must reply by 5/1 or within 2 weeks of notification.

CONTACT Mr. Rodney M. Oto, Director of Student Financial Services, Carleton College, One North College Street, Northfield, MN 55057-4001, 507-222-4138 or toll-free 800-995-2275. *Fax:* 507-222-4269.

CARLOS ALBIZU UNIVERSITY

San Juan, PR

CONTACT Financial Aid Office, Carlos Albizu University, 151 Tanca Street, San Juan, PR 00901, 787-725-6500.

CARLOS ALBIZU UNIVERSITY, MIAMI CAMPUS

Miami, FL

CONTACT Maria V. Chavez, Senior Financial Aid Officer, Carlos Albizu University, Miami Campus, 2173 Northwest 99th Avenue, Miami, FL 33172, 305-593-1223 Ext. 153 or toll-free 888-672-3246. *Fax:* 305-593-8902. *E-mail:* mchavez@albizu.edu.

CARLOW UNIVERSITY

Pittsburgh, PA

CONTACT Ms. Natalie Wilson, Director of Financial Aid, Carlow University, 3333 Fifth Avenue, Pittsburgh, PA 15213-3165, 412-578-6171 or toll-free 800-333-CARLOW.

CARNEGIE MELLON UNIVERSITY

Pittsburgh, PA

Tuition & fees: $40,920 **Average undergraduate aid package: $24,724**

ABOUT THE INSTITUTION Independent, coed. ***Awards:*** bachelor's, master's, and doctoral degrees and post-master's certificates. 71 undergraduate majors. ***Total enrollment:*** 11,064. Undergraduates: 5,998. Freshmen: 1,465. Institutional methodology is used as a basis for awarding need-based institutional aid.

UNDERGRADUATE EXPENSES for 2009–10 ***Application fee:*** $70. ***Comprehensive fee:*** $51,260 includes full-time tuition ($40,300), mandatory fees ($620), and room and board ($10,340). ***College room only:*** $6060. ***Part-time tuition:*** $560 per unit.

FRESHMAN FINANCIAL AID (Fall 2008, est.) 942 applied for aid; of those 77% were deemed to have need. 100% of freshmen with need received aid; of those 37% had need fully met. ***Average percent of need met:*** 82% (excluding resources awarded to replace EFC). ***Average financial aid package:*** $25,376 (excluding resources awarded to replace EFC). 8% of all full-time freshmen had no need and received non-need-based gift aid.

UNDERGRADUATE FINANCIAL AID (Fall 2008, est.) 3,188 applied for aid; of those 86% were deemed to have need. 99% of undergraduates with need received aid; of those 33% had need fully met. ***Average percent of need met:*** 81% (excluding resources awarded to replace EFC). ***Average financial aid package:*** $24,724 (excluding resources awarded to replace EFC). 8% of all full-time undergraduates had no need and received non-need-based gift aid.

GIFT AID (NEED-BASED) ***Total amount:*** $49,439,157 (9% federal, 2% state, 85% institutional, 4% external sources). ***Receiving aid:*** Freshmen: 49% (698); all full-time undergraduates: 46% (2,598). ***Average award:*** Freshmen: $20,072; Undergraduates: $18,745. ***Scholarships, grants, and awards:*** Federal Pell, FSEOG, state, private, college/university gift aid from institutional funds.

GIFT AID (NON-NEED-BASED) ***Total amount:*** $10,637,963 (85% institutional, 15% external sources). ***Receiving aid:*** Freshmen: 19% (262). Undergraduates: 18% (999). ***Average award:*** Freshmen: $9687. Undergraduates: $11,423. ***ROTC:*** Army, Naval, Air Force.

LOANS ***Student loans:*** $17,175,675 (93% need-based, 7% non-need-based). 50% of past graduating class borrowed through all loan programs. *Average indebtedness per student:* $29,346. ***Average need-based loan:*** Freshmen: $4442. Undergraduates: $5336. ***Parent loans:*** $9,154,585 (18% need-based, 82% non-need-based). ***Programs:*** FFEL (Subsidized and Unsubsidized Stafford, PLUS), Perkins, Gate student loan.

WORK-STUDY ***Federal work-study:*** Total amount: $4,541,831; jobs available. ***State or other work-study/employment:*** Total amount: $75,205 (100% need-based). Part-time jobs available.

APPLYING FOR FINANCIAL AID ***Required financial aid forms:*** FAFSA, institution's own form, parent and student federal tax returns and parent W-2 forms. ***Financial aid deadline:*** 5/1 (priority: 2/15). ***Notification date:*** 3/15.

CONTACT Linda M. Anderson, Director, Enrollment Services, Carnegie Mellon University, 5000 Forbes Avenue, Pittsburgh, PA 15213-3890, 412-268-8186. *Fax:* 412-268-8084. *E-mail:* thehub@andrew.cmu.edu.

CAROLINA CHRISTIAN COLLEGE

Winston-Salem, NC

CONTACT Financial Aid Office, Carolina Christian College, 4117 Northampton Drive, PO Box 777, Winston-Salem, NC 27102-0777, 336-744-0900.

CARROLL COLLEGE

Helena, MT

Tuition & fees: $22,592 **Average undergraduate aid package: $17,133**

ABOUT THE INSTITUTION Independent Roman Catholic, coed. ***Awards:*** associate and bachelor's degrees. 43 undergraduate majors. ***Total enrollment:*** 1,409. Undergraduates: 1,409. Freshmen: 345. Federal methodology is used as a basis for awarding need-based institutional aid.

UNDERGRADUATE EXPENSES for 2009–10 ***Application fee:*** $35. ***Comprehensive fee:*** $29,710 includes full-time tuition ($22,252), mandatory fees ($340), and room and board ($7118).

FRESHMAN FINANCIAL AID (Fall 2008, est.) 338 applied for aid; of those 62% were deemed to have need. 100% of freshmen with need received aid; of those 23% had need fully met. ***Average percent of need met:*** 83% (excluding resources awarded to replace EFC). ***Average financial aid package:*** $17,292 (excluding resources awarded to replace EFC). 22% of all full-time freshmen had no need and received non-need-based gift aid.

UNDERGRADUATE FINANCIAL AID (Fall 2008, est.) 1,192 applied for aid; of those 63% were deemed to have need. 100% of undergraduates with need received aid; of those 18% had need fully met. ***Average percent of need met:*** 79% (excluding resources awarded to replace EFC). ***Average financial aid package:*** $17,133 (excluding resources awarded to replace EFC). 15% of all full-time undergraduates had no need and received non-need-based gift aid.

GIFT AID (NEED-BASED) ***Total amount:*** $7,764,715 (17% federal, 1% state, 78% institutional, 4% external sources). ***Receiving aid:*** Freshmen: 50% (173); all full-time undergraduates: 55% (665). ***Average award:*** Freshmen: $13,109; Undergraduates: $11,701. ***Scholarships, grants, and awards:*** Federal Pell, FSEOG, state, private, college/university gift aid from institutional funds.

GIFT AID (NON-NEED-BASED) ***Total amount:*** $4,898,420 (5% federal, 82% institutional, 13% external sources). ***Receiving aid:*** Freshmen: 11% (39). Undergraduates: 8% (99). ***Average award:*** Freshmen: $8706. Undergraduates: $7689. ***Scholarships, grants, and awards by category:*** *Academic interests/achievement:* general academic interests/achievements. *Creative arts/performance:* debating, theater/drama. *Special achievements/activities:* general special achievements/activities, religious involvement. *Special characteristics:* children of faculty/staff, children of union members/company employees, international students, siblings of current students, spouses of current students, veterans. ***ROTC:*** Army.

LOANS ***Student loans:*** $6,731,661 (49% need-based, 51% non-need-based). 71% of past graduating class borrowed through all loan programs. *Average indebtedness per student:* $25,246. ***Average need-based loan:*** Freshmen: $4314. Undergraduates: $4907. ***Parent loans:*** $1,162,365 (10% need-based, 90% non-need-based). ***Programs:*** FFEL (Subsidized and Unsubsidized Stafford, PLUS), Perkins, private loans.

WORK-STUDY ***Federal work-study:*** Total amount: $337,136; jobs available. ***State or other work-study/employment:*** Total amount: $7712 (50% need-based, 50% non-need-based). Part-time jobs available.

ATHLETIC AWARDS Total amount: $1,523,102 (31% need-based, 69% non-need-based).

APPLYING FOR FINANCIAL AID ***Required financial aid form:*** FAFSA. ***Financial aid deadline (priority):*** 3/1. ***Notification date:*** Continuous beginning 3/1. Students must reply by 5/1 or within 2 weeks of notification.

CONTACT Ms. Janet Riis, Director of Financial Aid, Carroll College, 1601 North Benton Avenue, Helena, MT 59625-0002, 406-447-5423 or toll-free 800-992-3648. *Fax:* 406-447-4533. *E-mail:* jriis@carroll.edu.

CARROLL UNIVERSITY

Waukesha, WI

Tuition & fees: $21,926 **Average undergraduate aid package: $16,584**

ABOUT THE INSTITUTION Independent Presbyterian, coed. ***Awards:*** bachelor's, master's, and first professional degrees. 77 undergraduate majors. ***Total enroll-***

ment: 3,316. Undergraduates: 3,030. Freshmen: 690. Both federal and institutional methodology are used as a basis for awarding need-based institutional aid.

UNDERGRADUATE EXPENSES for 2008–09 ***Comprehensive fee:*** $28,620 includes full-time tuition ($21,410), mandatory fees ($516), and room and board ($6694). ***College room only:*** $3450. Full-time tuition and fees vary according to program. Room and board charges vary according to board plan and housing facility. ***Part-time tuition:*** $260 per credit. Part-time tuition and fees vary according to course load and program. ***Payment plan:*** Installment.

FRESHMAN FINANCIAL AID (Fall 2008, est.) 609 applied for aid; of those 84% were deemed to have need. 100% of freshmen with need received aid; of those 58% had need fully met. ***Average percent of need met:*** 100% (excluding resources awarded to replace EFC). ***Average financial aid package:*** $17,279 (excluding resources awarded to replace EFC). 21% of all full-time freshmen had no need and received non-need-based gift aid.

UNDERGRADUATE FINANCIAL AID (Fall 2008, est.) 2,235 applied for aid; of those 84% were deemed to have need. 100% of undergraduates with need received aid; of those 51% had need fully met. ***Average percent of need met:*** 100% (excluding resources awarded to replace EFC). ***Average financial aid package:*** $16,584 (excluding resources awarded to replace EFC). 24% of all full-time undergraduates had no need and received non-need-based gift aid.

GIFT AID (NEED-BASED) ***Total amount:*** $21,887,453 (10% federal, 10% state, 80% institutional). ***Receiving aid:*** Freshmen: 77% (513); all full-time undergraduates: 75% (1,885). ***Average award:*** Freshmen: $13,249; Undergraduates: $12,002. ***Scholarships, grants, and awards:*** Federal Pell, FSEOG, state, private, college/university gift aid from institutional funds.

GIFT AID (NON-NEED-BASED) ***Total amount:*** $6,827,905 (2% federal, 85% institutional, 13% external sources). ***Receiving aid:*** Freshmen: 69% (460). Undergraduates: 67% (1,677). ***Average award:*** Freshmen: $9737. Undergraduates: $8437. ***Scholarships, grants, and awards by category:*** *Academic interests/achievement:* 2,072 awards ($15,035,527 total): biological sciences, business, computer science, education, general academic interests/achievements, health fields, humanities, international studies, mathematics, physical sciences, premedicine, social sciences. *Creative arts/performance:* 98 awards ($155,500 total): art/fine arts, journalism/publications, music, performing arts, theater/drama. *Special achievements/activities:* 415 awards ($230,053 total): general special achievements/activities, junior miss, leadership, memberships, religious involvement. *Special characteristics:* 1,373 awards ($1,331,259 total): adult students, children and siblings of alumni, children of current students, children of faculty/staff, general special characteristics, international students, siblings of current students, spouses of current students. ***Tuition waivers:*** Full or partial for employees or children of employees. ***ROTC:*** Army cooperative, Air Force cooperative.

LOANS ***Student loans:*** $19,508,426 (39% need-based, 61% non-need-based). 73% of past graduating class borrowed through all loan programs. *Average indebtedness per student:* $24,097. ***Average need-based loan:*** Freshmen: $2459. Undergraduates: $3210. ***Parent loans:*** $2,423,765 (75% need-based, 25% non-need-based). ***Programs:*** FFEL (Subsidized and Unsubsidized Stafford, PLUS), Perkins, state, college/university.

WORK-STUDY ***Federal work-study:*** Total amount: $1,208,930; 662 jobs averaging $1826. ***State or other work-study/employment:*** Total amount: $1,329,335 (100% non-need-based). 774 part-time jobs averaging $1717.

APPLYING FOR FINANCIAL AID ***Required financial aid form:*** FAFSA. ***Financial aid deadline:*** Continuous. ***Notification date:*** Continuous beginning 2/15. Students must reply by 5/1 or within 2 weeks of notification.

CONTACT Dawn Scott, Director of Financial Aid, Carroll University, 100 North East Avenue, Waukesha, WI 53186-5593, 262-524-7297 or toll-free 800-CARROLL. *Fax:* 262-951-3037. *E-mail:* dscott@carrollu.edu.

CARSON-NEWMAN COLLEGE

Jefferson City, TN

Tuition & fees: $17,800 **Average undergraduate aid package: $15,287**

ABOUT THE INSTITUTION Independent Southern Baptist, coed. ***Awards:*** associate, bachelor's, and master's degrees. 71 undergraduate majors. ***Total enrollment:*** 2,032. Undergraduates: 1,823. Freshmen: 444. Federal methodology is used as a basis for awarding need-based institutional aid.

UNDERGRADUATE EXPENSES for 2008–09 ***Application fee:*** $25. ***Comprehensive fee:*** $23,590 includes full-time tuition ($17,000), mandatory fees ($800), and room and board ($5790). ***College room only:*** $2660. Full-time tuition and fees vary according to class time and course load. Room and board charges vary according to board plan, gender, and housing facility. ***Part-time tuition:*** $710 per semester hour. ***Part-time fees:*** $265 per term. ***Payment plans:*** Installment, deferred payment.

FRESHMAN FINANCIAL AID (Fall 2008, est.) 426 applied for aid; of those 83% were deemed to have need. 100% of freshmen with need received aid; of those 26% had need fully met. ***Average percent of need met:*** 79% (excluding resources awarded to replace EFC). ***Average financial aid package:*** $16,024 (excluding resources awarded to replace EFC). 18% of all full-time freshmen had no need and received non-need-based gift aid.

UNDERGRADUATE FINANCIAL AID (Fall 2008, est.) 1,566 applied for aid; of those 83% were deemed to have need. 100% of undergraduates with need received aid; of those 25% had need fully met. ***Average percent of need met:*** 76% (excluding resources awarded to replace EFC). ***Average financial aid package:*** $15,287 (excluding resources awarded to replace EFC). 20% of all full-time undergraduates had no need and received non-need-based gift aid.

GIFT AID (NEED-BASED) ***Total amount:*** $14,126,579 (20% federal, 26% state, 50% institutional, 4% external sources). ***Receiving aid:*** Freshmen: 79% (350); all full-time undergraduates: 74% (1,273). ***Average award:*** Freshmen: $12,838; Undergraduates: $11,007. ***Scholarships, grants, and awards:*** Federal Pell, FSEOG, state, private, college/university gift aid from institutional funds.

GIFT AID (NON-NEED-BASED) ***Total amount:*** $2,851,430 (7% federal, 24% state, 64% institutional, 5% external sources). ***Receiving aid:*** Freshmen: 77% (343). Undergraduates: 72% (1,243). ***Average award:*** Freshmen: $6960. Undergraduates: $6377. ***Scholarships, grants, and awards by category:*** *Academic interests/achievement:* biological sciences, business, education, general academic interests/achievements, home economics, mathematics, military science, religion/biblical studies. *Creative arts/performance:* art/fine arts, debating, journalism/publications, music. *Special achievements/activities:* leadership, memberships. *Special characteristics:* children and siblings of alumni, members of minority groups, relatives of clergy, siblings of current students. ***Tuition waivers:*** Full or partial for employees or children of employees, senior citizens. ***ROTC:*** Army, Air Force cooperative.

LOANS ***Student loans:*** $8,168,923 (91% need-based, 9% non-need-based). 74% of past graduating class borrowed through all loan programs. *Average indebtedness per student:* $18,552. ***Average need-based loan:*** Freshmen: $2757. Undergraduates: $3559. ***Parent loans:*** $1,306,287 (83% need-based, 17% non-need-based). ***Programs:*** FFEL (Subsidized and Unsubsidized Stafford, PLUS), Perkins, state, college/university, alternative loans.

WORK-STUDY ***Federal work-study:*** Total amount: $185,332; jobs available. ***State or other work-study/employment:*** Total amount: $130,250 (88% need-based, 12% non-need-based). Part-time jobs available.

ATHLETIC AWARDS Total amount: $1,859,940 (71% need-based, 29% non-need-based).

APPLYING FOR FINANCIAL AID ***Required financial aid forms:*** FAFSA, institution's own form. ***Financial aid deadline (priority):*** 4/1. ***Notification date:*** Continuous. Students must reply within 2 weeks of notification.

CONTACT Danette Seale, Director of Financial Aid, Carson Newman College, c/o Financial Aid, Jefferson City, TN 37760, 865-471-3247 or toll-free 800-678-9061. *Fax:* 865-471-3502. *E-mail:* dseale@cn.edu.

CARTHAGE COLLEGE

Kenosha, WI

CONTACT Robert Helgeson, Director of Student Financial Planning, Carthage College, 2001 Alford Park Drive, Kenosha, WI 53140, 262-551-6001 or toll-free 800-351-4058. *Fax:* 262-551-5762. *E-mail:* rhelgeson@carthage.edu.

CASE WESTERN RESERVE UNIVERSITY

Cleveland, OH

Tuition & fees: $35,202 **Average undergraduate aid package: $34,927**

ABOUT THE INSTITUTION Independent, coed. ***Awards:*** bachelor's, master's, doctoral, and first professional degrees and post-bachelor's certificates. 63 undergraduate majors. ***Total enrollment:*** 9,814. Undergraduates: 4,356. Freshmen: 1,026. Federal methodology is used as a basis for awarding need-based institutional aid.

UNDERGRADUATE EXPENSES for 2008–09 ***One-time required fee:*** $370. ***Comprehensive fee:*** $45,652 includes full-time tuition ($34,450), mandatory fees ($752), and room and board ($10,450). ***College room only:*** $6080.

Full-time tuition and fees vary according to student level. Room and board charges vary according to board plan, housing facility, and student level. ***Part-time tuition:*** $1436 per credit hour. Part-time tuition and fees vary according to course load and student level. ***Payment plan:*** Installment.

FRESHMAN FINANCIAL AID (Fall 2008, est.) 873 applied for aid; of those 84% were deemed to have need. 100% of freshmen with need received aid; of those 88% had need fully met. ***Average percent of need met:*** 87% (excluding resources awarded to replace EFC). ***Average financial aid package:*** $34,960 (excluding resources awarded to replace EFC). 18% of all full-time freshmen had no need and received non-need-based gift aid.

UNDERGRADUATE FINANCIAL AID (Fall 2008, est.) 3,028 applied for aid; of those 88% were deemed to have need. 100% of undergraduates with need received aid; of those 91% had need fully met. ***Average percent of need met:*** 86% (excluding resources awarded to replace EFC). ***Average financial aid package:*** $34,927 (excluding resources awarded to replace EFC). 21% of all full-time undergraduates had no need and received non-need-based gift aid.

GIFT AID (NEED-BASED) ***Total amount:*** $59,205,112 (7% federal, 5% state, 83% institutional, 5% external sources). ***Receiving aid:*** Freshmen: 71% (730); all full-time undergraduates: 63% (2,644). ***Average award:*** Freshmen: $23,372; Undergraduates: $20,966. ***Scholarships, grants, and awards:*** Federal Pell, FSEOG, state, private, college/university gift aid from institutional funds.

GIFT AID (NON-NEED-BASED) ***Total amount:*** $17,186,293 (3% state, 94% institutional, 3% external sources). ***Receiving aid:*** Freshmen: 59% (604). Undergraduates: 52% (2,205). ***Average award:*** Freshmen: $20,185. Undergraduates: $18,584. ***Scholarships, grants, and awards by category:*** *Academic interests/achievement:* 2,052 awards ($38,514,788 total): biological sciences, business, communication, computer science, education, engineering/technologies, English, foreign languages, general academic interests/achievements, health fields, humanities, international studies, mathematics, physical sciences, premedicine, religion/biblical studies, social sciences. *Creative arts/performance:* 38 awards ($455,100 total): art/fine arts, creative writing, dance, general creative arts/performance, music, performing arts, theater/drama. *Special achievements/activities:* 69 awards ($203,750 total): leadership. *Special characteristics:* 221 awards ($5,098,695 total): children of faculty/staff. ***Tuition waivers:*** Full or partial for employees or children of employees. ***ROTC:*** Army cooperative, Air Force cooperative.

LOANS ***Student loans:*** $37,223,092 (63% need-based, 37% non-need-based). 65% of past graduating class borrowed through all loan programs. *Average indebtedness per student:* $37,892. ***Average need-based loan:*** Freshmen: $6824. Undergraduates: $7327. ***Parent loans:*** $3,484,976 (84% need-based, 16% non-need-based). ***Programs:*** FFEL (Subsidized and Unsubsidized Stafford, PLUS), Perkins, Federal Nursing, state, college/university, alternative loans.

WORK-STUDY ***Federal work-study:*** Total amount: $4,581,909; 2,223 jobs averaging $2597.

APPLYING FOR FINANCIAL AID ***Required financial aid forms:*** FAFSA, institution's own form. ***Financial aid deadline (priority):*** 2/15. ***Notification date:*** Continuous beginning 3/15. Students must reply by 5/1 or within 2 weeks of notification.

CONTACT Ms. Nancy Issa, Associate Director of University Financial Aid, Case Western Reserve University, 10900 Euclid Avenue, Cleveland, OH 44106-7049, 216-368-4530. *Fax:* 216-368-5054. *E-mail:* nxi@po.cwru.edu.

CASTLETON STATE COLLEGE

Castleton, VT

ABOUT THE INSTITUTION State-supported, coed. ***Awards:*** associate, bachelor's, and master's degrees and post-master's certificates. 43 undergraduate majors. ***Total enrollment:*** 2,089. Undergraduates: 1,953. Freshmen: 463.

GIFT AID (NEED-BASED) ***Scholarships, grants, and awards:*** Federal Pell, FSEOG, state, private, college/university gift aid from institutional funds.

GIFT AID (NON-NEED-BASED) ***Scholarships, grants, and awards by category:*** *Academic interests/achievement:* foreign languages, general academic interests/achievements. *Creative arts/performance:* applied art and design, art/fine arts, music.

LOANS ***Programs:*** FFEL (Subsidized and Unsubsidized Stafford, PLUS), Perkins, Federal Nursing, state.

APPLYING FOR FINANCIAL AID ***Required financial aid forms:*** FAFSA, state aid form.

CONTACT Kathleen O'Meara, Director of Financial Aid, Castleton State College, Castleton, VT 05735, 802-468-1292 or toll-free 800-639-8521. *Fax:* 802-468-5237. *E-mail:* Kathy.omeara@castleton.edu.

CATAWBA COLLEGE

Salisbury, NC

Tuition & fees: $23,740 **Average undergraduate aid package: $17,618**

ABOUT THE INSTITUTION Independent religious, coed. ***Awards:*** bachelor's and master's degrees. 42 undergraduate majors. ***Total enrollment:*** 1,261. Undergraduates: 1,225. Freshmen: 248. Federal methodology is used as a basis for awarding need-based institutional aid.

UNDERGRADUATE EXPENSES for 2009–10 ***Application fee:*** $30. ***Comprehensive fee:*** $31,940 includes full-time tuition ($23,740) and room and board ($8200). ***Part-time tuition:*** $620 per credit hour.

FRESHMAN FINANCIAL AID (Fall 2008, est.) 207 applied for aid; of those 83% were deemed to have need. 99% of freshmen with need received aid; of those 31% had need fully met. ***Average percent of need met:*** 96% (excluding resources awarded to replace EFC). ***Average financial aid package:*** $20,780 (excluding resources awarded to replace EFC). 16% of all full-time freshmen had no need and received non-need-based gift aid.

UNDERGRADUATE FINANCIAL AID (Fall 2008, est.) 1,002 applied for aid; of those 81% were deemed to have need. 100% of undergraduates with need received aid; of those 30% had need fully met. ***Average percent of need met:*** 86% (excluding resources awarded to replace EFC). ***Average financial aid package:*** $17,618 (excluding resources awarded to replace EFC). 13% of all full-time undergraduates had no need and received non-need-based gift aid.

GIFT AID (NEED-BASED) ***Total amount:*** $3,106,883 (51% federal, 46% state, 3% institutional). ***Receiving aid:*** Freshmen: 44% (110); all full-time undergraduates: 46% (538). ***Average award:*** Freshmen: $5717; Undergraduates: $5286. ***Scholarships, grants, and awards:*** Federal Pell, FSEOG, state, private, college/university gift aid from institutional funds.

GIFT AID (NON-NEED-BASED) ***Total amount:*** $8,894,386 (19% state, 78% institutional, 3% external sources). ***Receiving aid:*** Freshmen: 69% (171). Undergraduates: 69% (805). ***Average award:*** Freshmen: $12,518. Undergraduates: $9314. ***Scholarships, grants, and awards by category:*** *Academic interests/achievement:* 940 awards ($6,398,973 total): education, general academic interests/achievements. *Creative arts/performance:* 176 awards ($274,125 total): music, theater/drama. *Special achievements/activities:* 59 awards ($40,300 total): general special achievements/activities. ***ROTC:*** Army cooperative.

LOANS ***Student loans:*** $5,628,712 (49% need-based, 51% non-need-based). 76% of past graduating class borrowed through all loan programs. *Average indebtedness per student:* $20,133. ***Average need-based loan:*** Freshmen: $4336. Undergraduates: $4522. ***Parent loans:*** $1,646,941 (100% non-need-based). ***Programs:*** FFEL (Subsidized and Unsubsidized Stafford, PLUS), Perkins, college/university, TERI Loans, Nellie Mae Loans, Advantage Loans, alternative loans, CitiAssist Loans, "Extra" loans.

WORK-STUDY ***Federal work-study:*** Total amount: $337,098; 194 jobs averaging $1648. ***State or other work-study/employment:*** Total amount: $411,760 (100% need-based). 248 part-time jobs averaging $1579.

ATHLETIC AWARDS Total amount: $2,381,158 (100% non-need-based).

APPLYING FOR FINANCIAL AID ***Required financial aid forms:*** FAFSA, state aid form. ***Financial aid deadline (priority):*** 3/15. ***Notification date:*** Continuous. Students must reply within 2 weeks of notification.

CONTACT Melanie McCulloh, Director of Scholarships and Financial Aid, Catawba College, 2300 West Innes Street, Salisbury, NC 28144-2488, 704-637-4416 or toll-free 800-CATAWBA. *Fax:* 704-637-4252. *E-mail:* mcmccull@catawba.edu.

THE CATHOLIC UNIVERSITY OF AMERICA

Washington, DC

Tuition & fees: $31,520 **Average undergraduate aid package: $19,226**

ABOUT THE INSTITUTION Independent religious, coed. ***Awards:*** associate, bachelor's, master's, doctoral, and first professional degrees. 62 undergraduate majors. ***Total enrollment:*** 6,705. Undergraduates: 3,469. Freshmen: 908. Federal methodology is used as a basis for awarding need-based institutional aid.

UNDERGRADUATE EXPENSES for 2008–09 ***Application fee:*** $55. ***One-time required fee:*** $425. ***Comprehensive fee:*** $42,970 includes full-time tuition ($30,520), mandatory fees ($1000), and room and board ($11,450). ***College room only:*** $6666. Full-time tuition and fees vary according to program. Room and board charges vary according to board plan and housing facility. ***Part-time***

tuition: $1125 per credit hour. ***Part-time fees:*** $75 per year. Part-time tuition and fees vary according to course load. ***Payment plans:*** Tuition prepayment, installment.

FRESHMAN FINANCIAL AID (Fall 2008, est.) 721 applied for aid; of those 78% were deemed to have need. 100% of freshmen with need received aid; of those 49% had need fully met. ***Average percent of need met:*** 80% (excluding resources awarded to replace EFC). ***Average financial aid package:*** $20,578 (excluding resources awarded to replace EFC). 31% of all full-time freshmen had no need and received non-need-based gift aid.

UNDERGRADUATE FINANCIAL AID (Fall 2008, est.) 2,130 applied for aid; of those 82% were deemed to have need. 100% of undergraduates with need received aid; of those 45% had need fully met. ***Average percent of need met:*** 84% (excluding resources awarded to replace EFC). ***Average financial aid package:*** $19,226 (excluding resources awarded to replace EFC). 36% of all full-time undergraduates had no need and received non-need-based gift aid.

GIFT AID (NEED-BASED) ***Total amount:*** $24,731,399 (5% federal, 93% institutional, 2% external sources). ***Receiving aid:*** Freshmen: 62% (555); all full-time undergraduates: 54% (1,714). ***Average award:*** Freshmen: $15,519; Undergraduates: $14,330. ***Scholarships, grants, and awards:*** Federal Pell, FSEOG, state, private, college/university gift aid from institutional funds, Federal Nursing.

GIFT AID (NON-NEED-BASED) ***Total amount:*** $11,492,019 (98% institutional, 2% external sources). ***Average award:*** Freshmen: $10,458. Undergraduates: $10,013. ***Scholarships, grants, and awards by category:*** *Academic interests/achievement:* general academic interests/achievements. *Creative arts/performance:* music, theater/drama. *Special achievements/activities:* general special achievements/activities. ***Tuition waivers:*** Full or partial for employees or children of employees. ***ROTC:*** Army cooperative, Naval cooperative, Air Force cooperative.

LOANS ***Student loans:*** $21,233,024 (82% need-based, 18% non-need-based). ***Average need-based loan:*** Freshmen: $4011. Undergraduates: $4832. ***Parent loans:*** $6,504,388 (81% need-based, 19% non-need-based). ***Programs:*** FFEL (Subsidized and Unsubsidized Stafford, PLUS), Perkins, Federal Nursing, college/university, commercial loans.

WORK-STUDY ***Federal work-study:*** Total amount: $2,289,831; jobs available.

APPLYING FOR FINANCIAL AID ***Required financial aid forms:*** FAFSA, institution's own form, alumni and parish scholarship application if appropriate. ***Financial aid deadline (priority):*** 2/15. ***Notification date:*** Continuous beginning 4/1. Students must reply by 5/1 or within 2 weeks of notification.

CONTACT Mr. Donald Bosse, Director of Financial Aid, The Catholic University of America, 620 Michigan Avenue, NE, Washington, DC 20064, 202-319-5307 or toll-free 800-673-2772 (out-of-state). *Fax:* 202-319-5573. *E-mail:* bosse@cua.edu.

CAZENOVIA COLLEGE

Cazenovia, NY

Tuition & fees: $22,894 **Average undergraduate aid package: $20,087**

ABOUT THE INSTITUTION Independent, coed. ***Awards:*** associate and bachelor's degrees. 21 undergraduate majors. ***Total enrollment:*** 1,062. Undergraduates: 1,062. Freshmen: 283. Federal methodology is used as a basis for awarding need-based institutional aid.

UNDERGRADUATE EXPENSES for 2008–09 ***Application fee:*** $30. ***Comprehensive fee:*** $32,396 includes full-time tuition ($22,514), mandatory fees ($380), and room and board ($9502). Full-time tuition and fees vary according to class time, course load, and program. Room and board charges vary according to board plan and housing facility. ***Part-time tuition:*** $477 per credit. ***Part-time fees:*** $115 per term. Part-time tuition and fees vary according to class time and course load. ***Payment plan:*** Installment.

FRESHMAN FINANCIAL AID (Fall 2008, est.) 259 applied for aid; of those 86% were deemed to have need. 100% of freshmen with need received aid; of those 22% had need fully met. ***Average percent of need met:*** 78% (excluding resources awarded to replace EFC). ***Average financial aid package:*** $20,617 (excluding resources awarded to replace EFC). 13% of all full-time freshmen had no need and received non-need-based gift aid.

UNDERGRADUATE FINANCIAL AID (Fall 2008, est.) 894 applied for aid; of those 91% were deemed to have need. 100% of undergraduates with need received aid; of those 17% had need fully met. ***Average percent of need met:*** 77% (excluding resources awarded to replace EFC). ***Average financial aid package:*** $20,087 (excluding resources awarded to replace EFC). 12% of all full-time undergraduates had no need and received non-need-based gift aid.

GIFT AID (NEED-BASED) ***Total amount:*** $15,775,450 (10% federal, 12% state, 77% institutional, 1% external sources). ***Receiving aid:*** Freshmen: 79% (223); all full-time undergraduates: 84% (815). ***Average award:*** Freshmen: $18,105; Undergraduates: $16,645. ***Scholarships, grants, and awards:*** Federal Pell, FSEOG, state, private, college/university gift aid from institutional funds.

GIFT AID (NON-NEED-BASED) ***Total amount:*** $2,712,737 (2% state, 96% institutional, 2% external sources). ***Receiving aid:*** Freshmen: 9% (25). Undergraduates: 8% (80). ***Average award:*** Freshmen: $12,245. Undergraduates: $11,527. ***Scholarships, grants, and awards by category:*** *Academic interests/achievement:* general academic interests/achievements. ***Tuition waivers:*** Full or partial for employees or children of employees. ***ROTC:*** Army cooperative, Air Force cooperative.

LOANS ***Student loans:*** $7,819,066 (86% need-based, 14% non-need-based). 89% of past graduating class borrowed through all loan programs. ***Average need-based loan:*** Freshmen: $3314. Undergraduates: $4272. ***Programs:*** Federal Direct (Subsidized and Unsubsidized Stafford, PLUS).

WORK-STUDY ***Federal work-study:*** Total amount: $312,000; jobs available.

APPLYING FOR FINANCIAL AID ***Required financial aid forms:*** FAFSA, state aid form. ***Financial aid deadline (priority):*** 3/15. ***Notification date:*** Continuous. Students must reply by 5/1 or within 2 weeks of notification.

CONTACT Christine L. Mandel, Director of Financial Aid, Cazenovia College, 3 Sullivan Street, Cazenovia, NY 13035, 315-655-7887 or toll-free 800-654-3210. *Fax:* 315-655-7219. *E-mail:* finaid@cazenovia.edu.

CEDAR CREST COLLEGE

Allentown, PA

Tuition & fees: $28,135 **Average undergraduate aid package: $19,946**

ABOUT THE INSTITUTION Independent religious, women only. ***Awards:*** bachelor's and master's degrees and post-bachelor's certificates. 35 undergraduate majors. ***Total enrollment:*** 1,872. Undergraduates: 1,701. Freshmen: 196. Federal methodology is used as a basis for awarding need-based institutional aid.

UNDERGRADUATE EXPENSES for 2009–10 ***Application fee:*** $30. ***Comprehensive fee:*** $37,456 includes full-time tuition ($27,735), mandatory fees ($400), and room and board ($9321). ***College room only:*** $4912. ***Part-time tuition:*** $772 per credit hour. ***Part-time fees:*** $125 per term.

FRESHMAN FINANCIAL AID (Fall 2008, est.) 189 applied for aid; of those 89% were deemed to have need. 100% of freshmen with need received aid; of those 10% had need fully met. ***Average percent of need met:*** 79% (excluding resources awarded to replace EFC). ***Average financial aid package:*** $22,429 (excluding resources awarded to replace EFC). 12% of all full-time freshmen had no need and received non-need-based gift aid.

UNDERGRADUATE FINANCIAL AID (Fall 2008, est.) 786 applied for aid; of those 90% were deemed to have need. 100% of undergraduates with need received aid; of those 13% had need fully met. ***Average percent of need met:*** 76% (excluding resources awarded to replace EFC). ***Average financial aid package:*** $19,946 (excluding resources awarded to replace EFC). 12% of all full-time undergraduates had no need and received non-need-based gift aid.

GIFT AID (NEED-BASED) ***Total amount:*** $10,582,459 (10% federal, 10% state, 74% institutional, 6% external sources). ***Receiving aid:*** Freshmen: 87% (169); all full-time undergraduates: 87% (708). ***Average award:*** Freshmen: $17,395; Undergraduates: $14,829. ***Scholarships, grants, and awards:*** Federal Pell, FSEOG, state, private, college/university gift aid from institutional funds, Federal Nursing.

GIFT AID (NON-NEED-BASED) ***Total amount:*** $1,340,213 (79% institutional, 21% external sources). ***Receiving aid:*** Freshmen: 6% (12). Undergraduates: 7% (60). ***Average award:*** Freshmen: $10,041. Undergraduates: $8979. ***Scholarships, grants, and awards by category:*** *Academic interests/achievement:* 273 awards ($3,166,800 total): general academic interests/achievements. *Creative arts/performance:* 123 awards ($184,500 total): art/fine arts, dance, performing arts, theater/drama. *Special achievements/activities:* 72 awards ($70,959 total): community service, general special achievements/activities, junior miss, leadership, memberships, religious involvement. *Special characteristics:* 56 awards ($93,797 total): adult students, children and siblings of alumni, general special characteristics, previous college experience, relatives of clergy, religious affiliation, siblings of current students. ***ROTC:*** Army cooperative.

LOANS ***Student loans:*** $7,481,908 (71% need-based, 29% non-need-based). 94% of past graduating class borrowed through all loan programs. *Average indebtedness per student:* $24,641. ***Average need-based loan:*** Freshmen: $3879. Undergraduates: $4523. ***Parent loans:*** $2,206,020 (37% need-based, 63%

non-need-based). ***Programs:*** Federal Direct (Subsidized and Unsubsidized Stafford, PLUS), Perkins, Federal Nursing, college/university.

WORK-STUDY ***Federal work-study:*** Total amount: $152,233; 104 jobs averaging $2200. ***State or other work-study/employment:*** Total amount: $912,787 (71% need-based, 29% non-need-based). 369 part-time jobs averaging $2200.

APPLYING FOR FINANCIAL AID ***Required financial aid form:*** FAFSA. ***Financial aid deadline (priority):*** 5/1. ***Notification date:*** Continuous.

CONTACT Ms. Lori Williams, Director, Student Financial Services, Cedar Crest College, 100 College Drive, Allentown, PA 18104-6196, 610-606-4602 or toll-free 800-360-1222. *Fax:* 610-606-4653. *E-mail:* finaid@cedarcrest.edu.

CEDARVILLE UNIVERSITY

Cedarville, OH

Tuition & fees: $22,304 **Average undergraduate aid package: $19,272**

ABOUT THE INSTITUTION Independent Baptist, coed. ***Awards:*** bachelor's and master's degrees. 84 undergraduate majors. ***Total enrollment:*** 3,077. Undergraduates: 2,996. Freshmen: 774. Federal methodology is used as a basis for awarding need-based institutional aid.

UNDERGRADUATE EXPENSES for 2009–10 ***Application fee:*** $30. ***One-time required fee:*** $120. ***Comprehensive fee:*** $27,310 includes full-time tuition ($22,304) and room and board ($5006). ***College room only:*** $2740. ***Part-time tuition:*** $697 per credit hour.

FRESHMAN FINANCIAL AID (Fall 2007) 701 applied for aid; of those 80% were deemed to have need. 99% of freshmen with need received aid; of those 51% had need fully met. ***Average percent of need met:*** 31% (excluding resources awarded to replace EFC). ***Average financial aid package:*** $18,217 (excluding resources awarded to replace EFC). 25% of all full-time freshmen had no need and received non-need-based gift aid.

UNDERGRADUATE FINANCIAL AID (Fall 2007) 2,081 applied for aid; of those 84% were deemed to have need. 99% of undergraduates with need received aid; of those 51% had need fully met. ***Average percent of need met:*** 39% (excluding resources awarded to replace EFC). ***Average financial aid package:*** $19,272 (excluding resources awarded to replace EFC). 19% of all full-time undergraduates had no need and received non-need-based gift aid.

GIFT AID (NEED-BASED) ***Total amount:*** $6,654,080 (29% federal, 7% state, 63% institutional, 1% external sources). ***Receiving aid:*** Freshmen: 43% (374); all full-time undergraduates: 44% (1,268). ***Average award:*** Freshmen: $2801; Undergraduates: $3575. ***Scholarships, grants, and awards:*** Federal Pell, FSEOG, state, private, college/university gift aid from institutional funds.

GIFT AID (NON-NEED-BASED) ***Total amount:*** $12,160,389 (7% state, 73% institutional, 20% external sources). ***Receiving aid:*** Freshmen: 57% (491). Undergraduates: 50% (1,422). ***Average award:*** Freshmen: $9149. Undergraduates: $10,412. ***Scholarships, grants, and awards by category:*** *Academic interests/achievement:* 1,370 awards ($3,296,277 total): general academic interests/achievements. *Creative arts/performance:* 62 awards ($140,700 total): debating, music. *Special achievements/activities:* 445 awards ($830,875 total): leadership. *Special characteristics:* 178 awards ($2,248,479 total): children and siblings of alumni, children of faculty/staff, ethnic background, general special characteristics, religious affiliation, veterans. ***ROTC:*** Army cooperative, Air Force cooperative.

LOANS ***Student loans:*** $11,245,185 (56% need-based, 44% non-need-based). 66% of past graduating class borrowed through all loan programs. *Average indebtedness per student:* $23,151. ***Average need-based loan:*** Freshmen: $3178. Undergraduates: $4406. ***Parent loans:*** $9,187,571 (100% non-need-based). ***Programs:*** FFEL (Subsidized and Unsubsidized Stafford, PLUS), Perkins, Federal Nursing, college/university.

WORK-STUDY ***Federal work-study:*** Total amount: $493,520; 261 jobs averaging $1891. ***State or other work-study/employment:*** Total amount: $1,667,604 (100% non-need-based). 1,435 part-time jobs averaging $1162.

ATHLETIC AWARDS Total amount: $674,973 (100% non-need-based).

APPLYING FOR FINANCIAL AID ***Required financial aid form:*** FAFSA. ***Financial aid deadline (priority):*** 3/1. ***Notification date:*** Continuous beginning 3/1. Students must reply within 4 weeks of notification.

CONTACT Mr. Fred Merritt, Director of Financial Aid, Cedarville University, 251 North Main Street, Cedarville, OH 45314-0601, 937-766-7866 or toll-free 800-CEDARVILLE. *E-mail:* merrittf@cedarville.edu.

CENTENARY COLLEGE

Hackettstown, NJ

Tuition & fees: $24,930 **Average undergraduate aid package: $17,867**

ABOUT THE INSTITUTION Independent religious, coed. ***Awards:*** associate, bachelor's, and master's degrees and post-bachelor's certificates. 24 undergraduate majors. ***Total enrollment:*** 3,261. Undergraduates: 2,283. Freshmen: 310. Federal methodology is used as a basis for awarding need-based institutional aid.

UNDERGRADUATE EXPENSES for 2008–09 ***Application fee:*** $30. ***Comprehensive fee:*** $33,830 includes full-time tuition ($23,900), mandatory fees ($1030), and room and board ($8900). Full-time tuition and fees vary according to course load and program. Room and board charges vary according to board plan. ***Part-time tuition:*** $465 per credit. Part-time tuition and fees vary according to course load and program. ***Payment plan:*** Installment.

FRESHMAN FINANCIAL AID (Fall 2008, est.) 263 applied for aid; of those 84% were deemed to have need. 100% of freshmen with need received aid; of those 23% had need fully met. ***Average percent of need met:*** 75% (excluding resources awarded to replace EFC). ***Average financial aid package:*** $19,195 (excluding resources awarded to replace EFC). 14% of all full-time freshmen had no need and received non-need-based gift aid.

UNDERGRADUATE FINANCIAL AID (Fall 2008, est.) 1,141 applied for aid; of those 88% were deemed to have need. 100% of undergraduates with need received aid; of those 19% had need fully met. ***Average percent of need met:*** 70% (excluding resources awarded to replace EFC). ***Average financial aid package:*** $17,867 (excluding resources awarded to replace EFC). 27% of all full-time undergraduates had no need and received non-need-based gift aid.

GIFT AID (NEED-BASED) ***Total amount:*** $8,204,601 (17% federal, 38% state, 39% institutional, 6% external sources). ***Receiving aid:*** Freshmen: 71% (220); all full-time undergraduates: 68% (981). ***Average award:*** Freshmen: $14,825; Undergraduates: $13,118. ***Scholarships, grants, and awards:*** Federal Pell, FSEOG, state, private, college/university gift aid from institutional funds.

GIFT AID (NON-NEED-BASED) ***Total amount:*** $8,794,400 (92% institutional, 8% external sources). ***Receiving aid:*** Freshmen: 8% (26). Undergraduates: 6% (84). ***Average award:*** Freshmen: $7529. Undergraduates: $7470. ***Scholarships, grants, and awards by category:*** *Academic interests/achievement:* 688 awards ($5,384,995 total): general academic interests/achievements. *Special achievements/activities:* 94 awards ($534,075 total): leadership. *Special characteristics:* 920 awards ($3,694,255 total): children and siblings of alumni, children of faculty/staff, ethnic background, general special characteristics, local/state students, out-of-state students, previous college experience, religious affiliation, siblings of current students.

LOANS ***Student loans:*** $11,549,636 (64% need-based, 36% non-need-based). 88% of past graduating class borrowed through all loan programs. *Average indebtedness per student:* $20,649. ***Average need-based loan:*** Freshmen: $3675. Undergraduates: $4493. ***Parent loans:*** $1,532,616 (42% need-based, 58% non-need-based). ***Programs:*** FFEL (Subsidized and Unsubsidized Stafford, PLUS), Perkins, state, NJ Class Loans.

WORK-STUDY ***Federal work-study:*** Total amount: $145,928; 203 jobs averaging $719. ***State or other work-study/employment:*** Total amount: $261,796 (100% non-need-based). 247 part-time jobs averaging $754.

APPLYING FOR FINANCIAL AID ***Required financial aid form:*** FAFSA. ***Financial aid deadline (priority):*** 4/1. ***Notification date:*** Continuous. Students must reply within 2 weeks of notification.

CONTACT Michael Corso, Director of Financial Aid, Centenary College, 400 Jefferson Street, Hackettstown, NJ 07840-2100, 908-852-1400 Ext. 2207 or toll-free 800-236-8679. *Fax:* 908-813-2632. *E-mail:* corsom@centenarycollege.edu.

CENTENARY COLLEGE OF LOUISIANA

Shreveport, LA

Tuition & fees: $22,000 **Average undergraduate aid package: $18,814**

ABOUT THE INSTITUTION Independent United Methodist, coed. ***Awards:*** bachelor's and master's degrees. 66 undergraduate majors. ***Total enrollment:*** 938. Undergraduates: 854. Freshmen: 198. Federal methodology is used as a basis for awarding need-based institutional aid.

UNDERGRADUATE EXPENSES for 2008–09 ***Application fee:*** $30. ***Comprehensive fee:*** $29,330 includes full-time tuition ($20,850), mandatory fees ($1150), and room and board ($7330). ***College room only:*** $3580. ***Part-time tuition:*** $665 per semester hour. ***Part-time fees:*** $60 per term.

FRESHMAN FINANCIAL AID (Fall 2008, est.) 212 applied for aid; of those 77% were deemed to have need. 100% of freshmen with need received aid; of those 27% had need fully met. ***Average percent of need met:*** 88% (excluding resources awarded to replace EFC). ***Average financial aid package:*** $20,396 (excluding resources awarded to replace EFC). 27% of all full-time freshmen had no need and received non-need-based gift aid.

UNDERGRADUATE FINANCIAL AID (Fall 2008, est.) 639 applied for aid; of those 74% were deemed to have need. 100% of undergraduates with need received aid; of those 34% had need fully met. ***Average percent of need met:*** 84% (excluding resources awarded to replace EFC). ***Average financial aid package:*** $18,814 (excluding resources awarded to replace EFC). 28% of all full-time undergraduates had no need and received non-need-based gift aid.

GIFT AID (NEED-BASED) ***Total amount:*** $6,336,678 (12% federal, 14% state, 72% institutional, 2% external sources). ***Receiving aid:*** Freshmen: 67% (164); all full-time undergraduates: 58% (473). ***Average award:*** Freshmen: $17,166; Undergraduates: $16,014. ***Scholarships, grants, and awards:*** Federal Pell, FSEOG, state, private, college/university gift aid from institutional funds.

GIFT AID (NON-NEED-BASED) ***Total amount:*** $3,779,199 (10% state, 89% institutional, 1% external sources). ***Receiving aid:*** Freshmen: 15% (36). Undergraduates: 16% (131). ***Average award:*** Freshmen: $10,662. Undergraduates: $10,076. ***Scholarships, grants, and awards by category:*** *Academic interests/achievement:* 660 awards ($521,191 total): biological sciences, business, communication, education, engineering/technologies, English, foreign languages, general academic interests/achievements, health fields, humanities, mathematics, physical sciences, premedicine, religion/biblical studies, social sciences. *Creative arts/performance:* 208 awards ($794,660 total): art/fine arts, dance, general creative arts/performance, music, performing arts, theater/drama. *Special achievements/activities:* 80 awards ($126,370 total): community service, general special achievements/activities, hobbies/interests, leadership, religious involvement. *Special characteristics:* 146 awards ($583,950 total): children of educators, children of faculty/staff, ethnic background, general special characteristics, international students, local/state students, members of minority groups, out-of-state students, relatives of clergy, religious affiliation.

LOANS ***Student loans:*** $2,244,291 (46% need-based, 54% non-need-based). 52% of past graduating class borrowed through all loan programs. *Average indebtedness per student:* $20,640. ***Average need-based loan:*** Freshmen: $3275. Undergraduates: $4073. ***Parent loans:*** $2,615,178 (100% non-need-based). ***Programs:*** FFEL (Subsidized and Unsubsidized Stafford, PLUS), Perkins.

WORK-STUDY ***Federal work-study:*** Total amount: $285,660; 161 jobs averaging $1774. ***State or other work-study/employment:*** Total amount: $87,800 (100% non-need-based). 64 part-time jobs averaging $1600.

ATHLETIC AWARDS Total amount: $2,591,272 (43% need-based, 57% non-need-based).

APPLYING FOR FINANCIAL AID ***Required financial aid form:*** FAFSA. ***Financial aid deadline (priority):*** 2/15. ***Notification date:*** 3/15. Students must reply by 5/1.

CONTACT Ms. Mary Sue Rix, Director of Financial Aid, Centenary College of Louisiana, PO Box 41188, Shreveport, LA 71134-1188, 318-869-5137 or toll-free 800-234-4448. *Fax:* 318-841-7266. *E-mail:* msrix@centenary.edu.

CENTRAL BAPTIST COLLEGE

Conway, AR

CONTACT Christi Bell, Financial Aid Director, Central Baptist College, 1501 College Avenue, Conway, AR 72032-6470, 800-205-6872 Ext. 185 or toll-free 800-205-6872. *Fax:* 501-329-2941. *E-mail:* financialaid@cbc.edu.

CENTRAL BIBLE COLLEGE

Springfield, MO

CONTACT Rick Woolverton, Director of Financial Aid, Central Bible College, 3000 North Grant, Springfield, MO 65803-1096, 417-833-2551 or toll-free 800-831-4222 Ext. 1184. *Fax:* 417-833-2168.

CENTRAL CHRISTIAN COLLEGE OF KANSAS

McPherson, KS

ABOUT THE INSTITUTION Independent Free Methodist, coed. ***Awards:*** associate and bachelor's degrees. 79 undergraduate majors. ***Total enrollment:*** 399. Undergraduates: 399. Freshmen: 125.

GIFT AID (NEED-BASED) ***Scholarships, grants, and awards:*** Federal Pell, FSEOG, state, private.

GIFT AID (NON-NEED-BASED) ***Scholarships, grants, and awards by category:*** *Academic interests/achievement:* English, general academic interests/achievements, religion/biblical studies. *Creative arts/performance:* music, theater/drama. *Special achievements/activities:* cheerleading/drum major, general special achievements/activities, junior miss, leadership, memberships, religious involvement. *Special characteristics:* children and siblings of alumni, children of faculty/staff, relatives of clergy, twins.

LOANS ***Programs:*** FFEL (Subsidized and Unsubsidized Stafford, PLUS), Perkins.

WORK-STUDY ***Federal work-study:*** Total amount: $58,725; 58 jobs averaging $1000.

APPLYING FOR FINANCIAL AID ***Required financial aid form:*** FAFSA.

CONTACT Mike Reimer, Financial Aid Director, Central Christian College of Kansas, 1200 South Main, PO Box 1403, McPherson, KS 67460, 620-241-0723 Ext. 333 or toll-free 800-835-0078 Ext. 337. *Fax:* 620-241-6032. *E-mail:* miker@centralchristian.edu.

CENTRAL CHRISTIAN COLLEGE OF THE BIBLE

Moberly, MO

Tuition & fees: $10,100 **Average undergraduate aid package: $13,186**

ABOUT THE INSTITUTION Independent religious, coed. 7 undergraduate majors. Institutional methodology is used as a basis for awarding need-based institutional aid.

UNDERGRADUATE EXPENSES for 2008–09 ***One-time required fee:*** $325. ***Comprehensive fee:*** $15,750 includes full-time tuition ($8800), mandatory fees ($1300), and room and board ($5650). Room and board charges vary according to board plan. ***Part-time tuition:*** $275 per credit hour. ***Part-time fees:*** $1300 per term. Part-time tuition and fees vary according to course load. all students receive a full tuition scholarship.

FRESHMAN FINANCIAL AID (Fall 2008, est.) 100% of freshmen with need received aid; of those 28% had need fully met.

UNDERGRADUATE FINANCIAL AID (Fall 2008, est.) 368 applied for aid; of those 100% were deemed to have need. 100% of undergraduates with need received aid; of those 2% had need fully met. ***Average percent of need met:*** 56% (excluding resources awarded to replace EFC). ***Average financial aid package:*** $13,186 (excluding resources awarded to replace EFC).

GIFT AID (NEED-BASED) ***Total amount:*** $825,220 (100% federal). ***Receiving aid:*** Freshmen: 38% (27); all full-time undergraduates: 58% (231). ***Average award:*** Freshmen: $4049; Undergraduates: $3467. ***Scholarships, grants, and awards:*** Federal Pell, FSEOG, private, college/university gift aid from institutional funds.

GIFT AID (NON-NEED-BASED) ***Total amount:*** $3,650,357 (95% institutional, 5% external sources). ***Receiving aid:*** Freshmen: 10% (7). Undergraduates: 6% (23). ***Average award:*** Freshmen: $8800. Undergraduates: $7352. ***Scholarships, grants, and awards by category:*** *Academic interests/achievement:* $3,492,628 total: religion/biblical studies. ***Tuition waivers:*** Full or partial for employees or children of employees.

LOANS ***Student loans:*** $1,606,491 (63% need-based, 37% non-need-based). 85% of past graduating class borrowed through all loan programs. *Average indebtedness per student:* $13,540. ***Average need-based loan:*** Undergraduates: $3818. ***Parent loans:*** $65,025 (100% non-need-based). ***Programs:*** FFEL (Subsidized and Unsubsidized Stafford, PLUS), alternative loans.

WORK-STUDY ***Federal work-study:*** Total amount: $25,000; 9 jobs averaging $2741.

APPLYING FOR FINANCIAL AID ***Required financial aid form:*** FAFSA. ***Financial aid deadline (priority):*** 4/1. ***Notification date:*** Continuous beginning 4/1. Students must reply by 6/15 or within 2 weeks of notification.

Central Christian College of the Bible

CONTACT Rhonda J. Dunham, Financial Aid Director, Central Christian College of the Bible, 911 East Urbandale Drive, Moberly, MO 65270-1997, 660-263-3900 Ext. 121 or toll-free 888-263-3900 (in-state). *Fax:* 660-263-3936. *E-mail:* rdunham@cccb.edu.

CENTRAL COLLEGE

Pella, IA

Tuition & fees: $23,944 **Average undergraduate aid package: $20,712**

ABOUT THE INSTITUTION Independent religious, coed. ***Awards:*** bachelor's degrees. 37 undergraduate majors. ***Total enrollment:*** 1,558. Undergraduates: 1,558. Freshmen: 405. Federal methodology is used as a basis for awarding need-based institutional aid.

UNDERGRADUATE EXPENSES for 2008–09 ***Application fee:*** $25. ***Comprehensive fee:*** $31,950 includes full-time tuition ($23,564), mandatory fees ($380), and room and board ($8006). ***College room only:*** $3926. ***Part-time tuition:*** $818 per semester hour.

FRESHMAN FINANCIAL AID (Fall 2008, est.) 384 applied for aid; of those 86% were deemed to have need. 100% of freshmen with need received aid; of those 23% had need fully met. ***Average percent of need met:*** 59% (excluding resources awarded to replace EFC). ***Average financial aid package:*** $21,977 (excluding resources awarded to replace EFC). 19% of all full-time freshmen had no need and received non-need-based gift aid.

UNDERGRADUATE FINANCIAL AID (Fall 2008, est.) 1,258 applied for aid; of those 89% were deemed to have need. 100% of undergraduates with need received aid; of those 19% had need fully met. ***Average percent of need met:*** 84% (excluding resources awarded to replace EFC). ***Average financial aid package:*** $20,712 (excluding resources awarded to replace EFC). 21% of all full-time undergraduates had no need and received non-need-based gift aid.

GIFT AID (NEED-BASED) ***Total amount:*** $16,316,082 (10% federal, 16% state, 71% institutional, 3% external sources). ***Receiving aid:*** Freshmen: 81% (330); all full-time undergraduates: 78% (1,113). ***Average award:*** Freshmen: $16,761; Undergraduates: $14,889. ***Scholarships, grants, and awards:*** Federal Pell, FSEOG, state, private, college/university gift aid from institutional funds.

GIFT AID (NON-NEED-BASED) ***Total amount:*** $3,788,509 (1% federal, 96% institutional, 3% external sources). ***Receiving aid:*** Freshmen: 13% (51). Undergraduates: 10% (148). ***Average award:*** Freshmen: $10,733. Undergraduates: $9766. ***Scholarships, grants, and awards by category:*** *Academic interests/achievement:* biological sciences, business, communication, computer science, education, foreign languages, general academic interests/achievements, health fields, humanities, international studies, mathematics, physical sciences, premedicine, religion/biblical studies, social sciences. *Creative arts/performance:* art/fine arts, creative writing, music, theater/drama. *Special achievements/activities:* religious involvement. *Special characteristics:* children and siblings of alumni, children of current students, children of faculty/staff, general special characteristics, handicapped students, international students, members of minority groups, out-of-state students, previous college experience, religious affiliation, siblings of current students, twins.

LOANS ***Student loans:*** $9,775,294 (65% need-based, 35% non-need-based). 84% of past graduating class borrowed through all loan programs. *Average indebtedness per student:* $35,103. ***Average need-based loan:*** Freshmen: $3669. Undergraduates: $4416. ***Parent loans:*** $3,047,249 (25% need-based, 75% non-need-based). ***Programs:*** Federal Direct (Subsidized and Unsubsidized Stafford, PLUS), Perkins, college/university, alternative loans.

WORK-STUDY ***Federal work-study:*** Total amount: $1,178,310; 856 jobs averaging $1369. ***State or other work-study/employment:*** Total amount: $523,478 (12% need-based, 88% non-need-based). 383 part-time jobs averaging $1365.

APPLYING FOR FINANCIAL AID ***Required financial aid form:*** FAFSA. ***Financial aid deadline (priority):*** 3/15. ***Notification date:*** Continuous beginning 3/15. Students must reply by 5/1 or within 2 weeks of notification.

CONTACT Ms. Jean Vander Wert, Director of Financial Aid, Central College, 812 University Street, Pella, IA 50219-1999, 641-628-5336 or toll-free 877-462-3687 (in-state), 877-462-3689 (out-of-state). *Fax:* 641-628-7199. *E-mail:* vanderwertj@central.edu.

CENTRAL CONNECTICUT STATE UNIVERSITY

New Britain, CT

Tuition & fees (CT res): $7042 **Average undergraduate aid package: $7329**

ABOUT THE INSTITUTION State-supported, coed. ***Awards:*** bachelor's, master's, and doctoral degrees and post-bachelor's and post-master's certificates. 50 undergraduate majors. ***Total enrollment:*** 12,233. Undergraduates: 9,906. Freshmen: 1,310. Federal methodology is used as a basis for awarding need-based institutional aid.

UNDERGRADUATE EXPENSES for 2008–09 ***Application fee:*** $50. ***Tuition, state resident:*** full-time $3514; part-time $334 per credit. ***Tuition, nonresident:*** full-time $11,373; part-time $334 per credit. ***Required fees:*** full-time $3528; $55 per term. Full-time tuition and fees vary according to course level, course load, and reciprocity agreements. Part-time tuition and fees vary according to course level and course load. ***College room and board:*** $8618; ***Room only:*** $5020. Room and board charges vary according to board plan. ***Payment plan:*** Installment.

FRESHMAN FINANCIAL AID (Fall 2008, est.) 1,056 applied for aid; of those 67% were deemed to have need. 99% of freshmen with need received aid; of those 11% had need fully met. ***Average percent of need met:*** 66% (excluding resources awarded to replace EFC). ***Average financial aid package:*** $7458 (excluding resources awarded to replace EFC). 4% of all full-time freshmen had no need and received non-need-based gift aid.

UNDERGRADUATE FINANCIAL AID (Fall 2008, est.) 5,275 applied for aid; of those 76% were deemed to have need. 99% of undergraduates with need received aid; of those 12% had need fully met. ***Average percent of need met:*** 65% (excluding resources awarded to replace EFC). ***Average financial aid package:*** $7329 (excluding resources awarded to replace EFC). 1% of all full-time undergraduates had no need and received non-need-based gift aid.

GIFT AID (NEED-BASED) ***Total amount:*** $10,605,152 (57% federal, 4% state, 39% institutional). ***Receiving aid:*** Freshmen: 46% (605); all full-time undergraduates: 44% (3,448). ***Average award:*** Freshmen: $3671; Undergraduates: $3664. ***Scholarships, grants, and awards:*** Federal Pell, FSEOG, state, private, college/university gift aid from institutional funds.

GIFT AID (NON-NEED-BASED) ***Total amount:*** $2,108,805 (61% institutional, 39% external sources). ***Receiving aid:*** Freshmen: 8% (108). Undergraduates: 3% (268). ***Average award:*** Freshmen: $2551. Undergraduates: $2368. ***Scholarships, grants, and awards by category:*** *Academic interests/achievement:* general academic interests/achievements. *Special characteristics:* members of minority groups. ***Tuition waivers:*** Full or partial for employees or children of employees, senior citizens. ***ROTC:*** Army cooperative, Air Force cooperative.

LOANS ***Student loans:*** $35,651,776 (52% need-based, 48% non-need-based). 38% of past graduating class borrowed through all loan programs. *Average indebtedness per student:* $10,500. ***Average need-based loan:*** Freshmen: $3312. Undergraduates: $4127. ***Parent loans:*** $10,157,917 (100% non-need-based). ***Programs:*** Federal Direct (Subsidized and Unsubsidized Stafford, PLUS), FFEL (Subsidized and Unsubsidized Stafford, PLUS), Perkins.

WORK-STUDY ***Federal work-study:*** Total amount: $243,422; 289 jobs averaging $1990. ***State or other work-study/employment:*** 110 part-time jobs averaging $544.

ATHLETIC AWARDS Total amount: $2,407,187 (100% non-need-based).

APPLYING FOR FINANCIAL AID ***Required financial aid forms:*** FAFSA, institution's own form. ***Financial aid deadline (priority):*** 3/1. ***Notification date:*** Continuous. Students must reply within 3 weeks of notification.

CONTACT Mr. Dennis Williams, Associate Director of Financial Aid, Central Connecticut State University, Memorial Hall, Room 103, New Britain, CT 06050-4010, 860-832-2200 or toll-free 888-733-2278 (in-state). *Fax:* 860-832-1105. *E-mail:* lupachinok@ccsu.edu.

CENTRAL METHODIST UNIVERSITY

Fayette, MO

Tuition & fees: $17,980 **Average undergraduate aid package: $14,653**

ABOUT THE INSTITUTION Independent Methodist, coed. ***Awards:*** associate, bachelor's, and master's degrees. 47 undergraduate majors. ***Total enrollment:*** 1,031. Undergraduates: 1,031. Freshmen: 300. Federal methodology is used as a basis for awarding need-based institutional aid.

UNDERGRADUATE EXPENSES for 2008–09 ***Application fee:*** $20. ***One-time required fee:*** $100. ***Comprehensive fee:*** $23,980 includes full-time tuition ($17,250), mandatory fees ($730), and room and board ($6000). ***College room only:*** $2960. Room and board charges vary according to board plan and housing facility. ***Part-time tuition:*** $180 per semester hour. ***Part-time fees:*** $31.25 per credit hour. Part-time tuition and fees vary according to course load. ***Payment plan:*** Installment.

FRESHMAN FINANCIAL AID (Fall 2008, est.) 300 applied for aid; of those 73% were deemed to have need. 100% of freshmen with need received aid; of those 17% had need fully met. ***Average percent of need met:*** 67% (excluding resources awarded to replace EFC). ***Average financial aid package:*** $15,778 (excluding resources awarded to replace EFC). 5% of all full-time freshmen had no need and received non-need-based gift aid.

UNDERGRADUATE FINANCIAL AID (Fall 2008, est.) 1,083 applied for aid; of those 68% were deemed to have need. 100% of undergraduates with need received aid; of those 11% had need fully met. ***Average percent of need met:*** 63% (excluding resources awarded to replace EFC). ***Average financial aid package:*** $14,653 (excluding resources awarded to replace EFC). 3% of all full-time undergraduates had no need and received non-need-based gift aid.

GIFT AID (NEED-BASED) ***Total amount:*** $3,269,732 (43% federal, 56% state, 1% institutional). ***Receiving aid:*** Freshmen: 65% (195); all full-time undergraduates: 56% (607). ***Average award:*** Freshmen: $5786; Undergraduates: $5317. ***Scholarships, grants, and awards:*** Federal Pell, FSEOG, state, private, college/university gift aid from institutional funds.

GIFT AID (NON-NEED-BASED) ***Total amount:*** $7,523,935 (93% institutional, 7% external sources). ***Receiving aid:*** Freshmen: 73% (218). Undergraduates: 68% (738). ***Average award:*** Freshmen: $8742. Undergraduates: $8831. ***Scholarships, grants, and awards by category:*** *Academic interests/achievement:* 661 awards ($2,401,668 total): biological sciences, business, communication, computer science, education, English, foreign languages, general academic interests/achievements, health fields, humanities, mathematics, physical sciences, premedicine, religion/biblical studies, social sciences. *Creative arts/performance:* 109 awards ($191,706 total): music, theater/drama. *Special achievements/activities:* 66 awards ($76,313 total): cheerleading/drum major, leadership, religious involvement. *Special characteristics:* 249 awards ($545,679 total): children and siblings of alumni, children of faculty/staff, general special characteristics, international students, relatives of clergy, religious affiliation, siblings of current students, spouses of current students. ***Tuition waivers:*** Full or partial for employees or children of employees. ***ROTC:*** Army cooperative, Air Force cooperative.

LOANS ***Student loans:*** $5,173,134 (47% need-based, 53% non-need-based). 82% of past graduating class borrowed through all loan programs. *Average indebtedness per student:* $26,487. ***Average need-based loan:*** Freshmen: $3181. Undergraduates: $3840. ***Parent loans:*** $936,681 (100% non-need-based). ***Programs:*** FFEL (Subsidized and Unsubsidized Stafford, PLUS), Perkins, college/university.

WORK-STUDY ***Federal work-study:*** Total amount: $124,017; 145 jobs averaging $1000. ***State or other work-study/employment:*** Total amount: $140,800 (100% non-need-based). 90 part-time jobs averaging $1619.

ATHLETIC AWARDS Total amount: $2,035,755 (100% non-need-based).

APPLYING FOR FINANCIAL AID ***Required financial aid form:*** FAFSA. ***Financial aid deadline (priority):*** 3/15. ***Notification date:*** Continuous. Students must reply within 2 weeks of notification.

CONTACT Linda Mackey, Director of Financial Assistance, Central Methodist University, 411 Central Methodist Square, Fayette, MO 65248-1198, 660-248-6244 or toll-free 888-CMU-1854 (in-state). *Fax:* 660-248-6288. *E-mail:* lmackey@centralmethodist.edu.

CENTRAL MICHIGAN UNIVERSITY

Mount Pleasant, MI

Tuition & fees (MI res): $9720 **Average undergraduate aid package: $10,048**

ABOUT THE INSTITUTION State-supported, coed. ***Awards:*** bachelor's, master's, and doctoral degrees and post-bachelor's and post-master's certificates. 131 undergraduate majors. ***Total enrollment:*** 27,225. Undergraduates: 20,540. Freshmen: 3,899. Federal methodology is used as a basis for awarding need-based institutional aid.

UNDERGRADUATE EXPENSES for 2008–09 ***Application fee:*** $35. ***Tuition, state resident:*** full-time $9720; part-time $324 per credit. ***Tuition, nonresident:*** full-time $22,590; part-time $753 per credit. Full-time tuition and fees vary according to student level. Part-time tuition and fees vary according to student level. ***College room and board:*** $7668; ***Room only:*** $3834. Room and board charges vary according to board plan, housing facility, location, and student level. ***Payment plans:*** Guaranteed tuition, installment.

FRESHMAN FINANCIAL AID (Fall 2007) 3,003 applied for aid; of those 71% were deemed to have need. 98% of freshmen with need received aid; of those 53% had need fully met. ***Average percent of need met:*** 79% (excluding resources awarded to replace EFC). ***Average financial aid package:*** $10,132 (excluding resources awarded to replace EFC). 13% of all full-time freshmen had no need and received non-need-based gift aid.

UNDERGRADUATE FINANCIAL AID (Fall 2007) 13,393 applied for aid; of those 71% were deemed to have need. 98% of undergraduates with need received aid; of those 52% had need fully met. ***Average percent of need met:*** 78% (excluding resources awarded to replace EFC). ***Average financial aid package:*** $10,048 (excluding resources awarded to replace EFC). 10% of all full-time undergraduates had no need and received non-need-based gift aid.

GIFT AID (NEED-BASED) ***Total amount:*** $31,113,625 (48% federal, 17% state, 30% institutional, 5% external sources). ***Receiving aid:*** Freshmen: 49% (1,870); all full-time undergraduates: 41% (7,228). ***Average award:*** Freshmen: $5113; Undergraduates: $4339. ***Scholarships, grants, and awards:*** Federal Pell, FSEOG, state, private, college/university gift aid from institutional funds.

GIFT AID (NON-NEED-BASED) ***Total amount:*** $12,379,162 (8% federal, 23% state, 48% institutional, 21% external sources). ***Receiving aid:*** Freshmen: 6% (212). Undergraduates: 3% (546). ***Average award:*** Freshmen: $3337. Undergraduates: $3219. ***Scholarships, grants, and awards by category:*** *Academic interests/achievement:* 3,463 awards ($8,948,029 total): biological sciences, business, communication, computer science, education, engineering/technologies, English, foreign languages, general academic interests/achievements, health fields, humanities, international studies, mathematics, military science, physical sciences, social sciences. *Creative arts/performance:* 198 awards ($276,347 total): applied art and design, art/fine arts, cinema/film/broadcasting, creative writing, dance, journalism/publications, music, performing arts, theater/drama. *Special achievements/activities:* 646 awards ($4,828,554 total): leadership. *Special characteristics:* 369 awards ($2,123,634 total): children and siblings of alumni, children of faculty/staff, children of union members/company employees, first-generation college students, international students, local/state students, members of minority groups, out-of-state students, veterans, veterans' children. ***Tuition waivers:*** Full or partial for children of alumni, employees or children of employees, senior citizens. ***ROTC:*** Army.

LOANS ***Student loans:*** $87,295,582 (60% need-based, 40% non-need-based). 70% of past graduating class borrowed through all loan programs. *Average indebtedness per student:* $24,236. ***Average need-based loan:*** Freshmen: $4747. Undergraduates: $5910. ***Parent loans:*** $17,787,463 (27% need-based, 73% non-need-based). ***Programs:*** Federal Direct (Subsidized and Unsubsidized Stafford, PLUS), Perkins, state, alternative loans.

WORK-STUDY ***Federal work-study:*** Total amount: $1,274,330; 729 jobs averaging $1748. ***State or other work-study/employment:*** Total amount: $8,818,555 (23% need-based, 77% non-need-based). 4,730 part-time jobs averaging $1999.

ATHLETIC AWARDS Total amount: $3,866,045 (31% need-based, 69% non-need-based).

APPLYING FOR FINANCIAL AID ***Required financial aid form:*** FAFSA. ***Financial aid deadline (priority):*** 3/1. ***Notification date:*** Continuous beginning 4/1.

CONTACT Mr. Michael Owens, Director of Scholarships and Financial Aid, Central Michigan University, WA 202, Mount Pleasant, MI 48859, 989-774-7428 or toll-free 888-292-5366. *Fax:* 989-774-3634. *E-mail:* owens1ma@cmich.edu.

CENTRAL PENNSYLVANIA COLLEGE

Summerdale, PA

CONTACT Kathy Shepard, Financial Aid Director, Central Pennsylvania College, College Hill and Valley Roads, Summerdale, PA 17093, 717-728-2261 or toll-free 800-759-2727 Ext. 2201. *Fax:* 717-728-2350. *E-mail:* financial-aid@centralpenn.edu.

CENTRAL STATE UNIVERSITY

Wilberforce, OH

ABOUT THE INSTITUTION State-supported, coed. ***Awards:*** bachelor's and master's degrees. 30 undergraduate majors. ***Total enrollment:*** 2,171. Undergraduates: 2,142. Freshmen: 654.

GIFT AID (NEED-BASED) ***Scholarships, grants, and awards:*** Federal Pell, FSEOG, state, private, college/university gift aid from institutional funds.

GIFT AID (NON-NEED-BASED) ***Scholarships, grants, and awards by category:*** *Academic interests/achievement:* business, computer science, education, engineering/technologies, general academic interests/achievements, physical sciences. *Creative arts/performance:* music. *Special characteristics:* children of faculty/staff, veterans, veterans' children.

LOANS ***Programs:*** FFEL (Subsidized and Unsubsidized Stafford, PLUS).

WORK-STUDY ***Federal work-study:*** Total amount: $541,518; 475 jobs averaging $1656.

APPLYING FOR FINANCIAL AID ***Required financial aid form:*** FAFSA.

CONTACT Veronica J. Leech, Director of Student Financial Aid, Central State University, PO Box 1004, Wilberforce, OH 45384, 937-376-6579 or toll-free 800-388-CSU1 (in-state).

CENTRAL WASHINGTON UNIVERSITY

Ellensburg, WA

ABOUT THE INSTITUTION State-supported, coed. ***Awards:*** bachelor's and master's degrees and post-bachelor's certificates. 73 undergraduate majors. ***Total enrollment:*** 10,662. Undergraduates: 10,181. Freshmen: 1,570.

GIFT AID (NEED-BASED) ***Scholarships, grants, and awards:*** Federal Pell, FSEOG, state, private, college/university gift aid from institutional funds.

LOANS ***Programs:*** Federal Direct (Subsidized and Unsubsidized Stafford, PLUS), Perkins, state, college/university.

APPLYING FOR FINANCIAL AID ***Required financial aid form:*** FAFSA.

CONTACT Ms. Agnes Canedo, Director of Financial Aid, Central Washington University, 400 East University Way, Ellensburg, WA 98926-7495, 509-963-3049 or toll-free 866-298-4968. *Fax:* 509-963-1788. *E-mail:* canedoa@cwu.edu.

CENTRAL YESHIVA TOMCHEI TMIMIM-LUBAVITCH

Brooklyn, NY

CONTACT Rabbi Moshe M. Gluckowsky, Director of Financial Aid, Central Yeshiva Tomchei Tmimim-Lubavitch, 841-853 Ocean Parkway, Brooklyn, NY 11230, 718-859-2277.

CENTRE COLLEGE

Danville, KY

Comprehensive fee: $37,000 **Average undergraduate aid package: $22,858**

ABOUT THE INSTITUTION Independent religious, coed. ***Awards:*** bachelor's degrees. 27 undergraduate majors. ***Total enrollment:*** 1,197. Undergraduates: 1,197. Freshmen: 336. Institutional methodology is used as a basis for awarding need-based institutional aid.

UNDERGRADUATE EXPENSES for 2008–09 ***Application fee:*** $40. ***Comprehensive fee:*** $37,000. ***Part-time tuition:*** $1096 per credit hour. ***Payment plan:*** Installment.

FRESHMAN FINANCIAL AID (Fall 2008, est.) 266 applied for aid; of those 76% were deemed to have need. 100% of freshmen with need received aid; of those 36% had need fully met. ***Average percent of need met:*** 88% (excluding resources awarded to replace EFC). ***Average financial aid package:*** $23,693 (excluding resources awarded to replace EFC). 36% of all full-time freshmen had no need and received non-need-based gift aid.

UNDERGRADUATE FINANCIAL AID (Fall 2008, est.) 819 applied for aid; of those 83% were deemed to have need. 100% of undergraduates with need received aid; of those 31% had need fully met. ***Average percent of need met:*** 86% (excluding resources awarded to replace EFC). ***Average financial aid package:*** $22,858 (excluding resources awarded to replace EFC). 38% of all full-time undergraduates had no need and received non-need-based gift aid.

GIFT AID (NEED-BASED) ***Total amount:*** $13,263,989 (6% federal, 16% state, 74% institutional, 4% external sources). ***Receiving aid:*** Freshmen: 60% (203); all full-time undergraduates: 57% (677). ***Average award:*** Freshmen: $21,160; Undergraduates: $19,592. ***Scholarships, grants, and awards:*** Federal Pell, FSEOG, state, private, college/university gift aid from institutional funds, Academic Competitiveness Grant, National Smart Grant.

GIFT AID (NON-NEED-BASED) ***Total amount:*** $5,657,261 (10% state, 86% institutional, 4% external sources). ***Average award:*** Freshmen: $13,302. Undergraduates: $12,460. ***Scholarships, grants, and awards by category:*** *Academic interests/achievement:* 854 awards ($9,226,600 total): general academic interests/achievements. *Creative arts/performance:* 92 awards ($304,750 total): music, theater/drama. *Special characteristics:* 185 awards ($1,505,791 total): children and siblings of alumni, children of faculty/staff, ethnic background, first-generation college students. ***Tuition waivers:*** Full or partial for employees or children of employees. ***ROTC:*** Army cooperative, Air Force cooperative.

LOANS ***Student loans:*** $3,560,882 (60% need-based, 40% non-need-based). 56% of past graduating class borrowed through all loan programs. *Average indebtedness per student:* $17,600. ***Average need-based loan:*** Freshmen: $3488. Undergraduates: $4732. ***Parent loans:*** $1,397,922 (100% non-need-based). ***Programs:*** FFEL (Subsidized and Unsubsidized Stafford, PLUS), Perkins, college/university.

WORK-STUDY ***Federal work-study:*** Total amount: $455,240; 296 jobs averaging $1580. ***State or other work-study/employment:*** Total amount: $16,200 (100% non-need-based). 10 part-time jobs averaging $1620.

APPLYING FOR FINANCIAL AID ***Required financial aid forms:*** FAFSA, institution's own form. ***Financial aid deadline:*** 3/1. ***Notification date:*** 4/1. Students must reply by 5/1.

CONTACT Ms. Elaine Larson, Director of Student Financial Planning, Centre College, 600 West Walnut Street, Danville, KY 40422-1394, 859-238-5365 or toll-free 800-423-6236. *Fax:* 859-238-5373. *E-mail:* finaid@centre.edu.

CHADRON STATE COLLEGE

Chadron, NE

CONTACT Ms. Sherry Douglas, Director of Financial Aid, Chadron State College, 1000 Main Street, Chadron, NE 69337, 308-432-6230 or toll-free 800-242-3766 (in-state). *Fax:* 308-432-6229. *E-mail:* finaid@csc.edu.

CHAMBERLAIN COLLEGE OF NURSING

St. Louis, MO

CONTACT Financial Aid Counselor, Chamberlain College of Nursing, 6150 Oakland Avenue, St. Louis, MO 63139-3215, 314-768-5604 or toll-free 800-942-4310.

CHAMINADE UNIVERSITY OF HONOLULU

Honolulu, HI

Tuition & fees: $16,140 **Average undergraduate aid package: $12,846**

ABOUT THE INSTITUTION Independent Roman Catholic, coed. ***Awards:*** associate, bachelor's, and master's degrees and post-bachelor's certificates. 22 undergraduate majors. ***Total enrollment:*** 2,685. Undergraduates: 2,004. Freshmen: 337. Federal methodology is used as a basis for awarding need-based institutional aid.

UNDERGRADUATE EXPENSES for 2008–09 ***Application fee:*** $50. ***Comprehensive fee:*** $26,560 includes full-time tuition ($16,000), mandatory fees ($140), and room and board ($10,420). ***College room only:*** $5300. Full-time tuition and fees vary according to course load. Room and board charges vary according to board plan and housing facility. ***Part-time tuition:*** $533 per credit. Part-time tuition and fees vary according to course load. ***Payment plan:*** Installment.

FRESHMAN FINANCIAL AID (Fall 2008, est.) 202 applied for aid; of those 83% were deemed to have need. 100% of freshmen with need received aid; of those 13% had need fully met. ***Average percent of need met:*** 65% (excluding resources awarded to replace EFC). ***Average financial aid package:*** $11,862 (excluding resources awarded to replace EFC). 14% of all full-time freshmen had no need and received non-need-based gift aid.

UNDERGRADUATE FINANCIAL AID (Fall 2008, est.) 852 applied for aid; of those 89% were deemed to have need. 100% of undergraduates with need received aid; of those 14% had need fully met. ***Average percent of need met:*** 65% (excluding resources awarded to replace EFC). ***Average financial aid package:*** $12,846 (excluding resources awarded to replace EFC). 17% of all full-time undergraduates had no need and received non-need-based gift aid.

GIFT AID (NEED-BASED) ***Total amount:*** $6,682,275 (25% federal, 60% institutional, 15% external sources). ***Receiving aid:*** Freshmen: 67% (166); all full-time undergraduates: 73% (757). ***Average award:*** Freshmen: $8258; Undergraduates: $8257. ***Scholarships, grants, and awards:*** Federal Pell, FSEOG, state, private, college/university gift aid from institutional funds.

Undergraduates: 14% (1,346). ***Average award:*** Freshmen: $2400. Undergraduates: $2630. ***Scholarships, grants, and awards by category:*** *Academic interests/achievement:* architecture, area/ethnic studies, biological sciences, communication, computer science, education, engineering/technologies, English, foreign languages, general academic interests/achievements, humanities, international studies, mathematics, premedicine, social sciences. *Creative arts/performance:* applied art and design, art/fine arts, cinema/film/broadcasting, creative writing, general creative arts/performance, music, performing arts. *Special achievements/activities:* community service, general special achievements/activities, leadership. ***Tuition waivers:*** Full or partial for senior citizens. ***ROTC:*** Army cooperative, Air Force cooperative.

LOANS ***Student loans:*** $15,299,000 (95% need-based, 5% non-need-based). 31% of past graduating class borrowed through all loan programs. *Average indebtedness per student:* $16,950. ***Average need-based loan:*** Freshmen: $1850. Undergraduates: $3774. ***Programs:*** Federal Direct (Subsidized and Unsubsidized Stafford, PLUS), Perkins.

WORK-STUDY ***Federal work-study:*** Total amount: $3,340,000; 2,155 jobs averaging $1558.

APPLYING FOR FINANCIAL AID ***Required financial aid forms:*** FAFSA, state aid form. ***Financial aid deadline (priority):*** 4/1. ***Notification date:*** Continuous.

CONTACT Thelma Mason, Director of Financial Aid, City College of the City University of New York, 160 Convent Avenue, Administration Building, Room 104, New York, NY 10031, 212-650-6656. *Fax:* 212-650-5829. *E-mail:* thelma@finance.ccny.cuny.edu.

CITY UNIVERSITY OF SEATTLE

Bellevue, WA

CONTACT Ms. Jean L. Roberts, Director of Student Financial Services, City University of Seattle, 11900 Northeast 1st Street, Bellevue, WA 98005, 425-709-5251 or toll-free 888-42-CITYU. *Fax:* 425-709-5263. *E-mail:* jroberts@cityu.edu.

CLAFLIN UNIVERSITY

Orangeburg, SC

CONTACT Ms. Yolanda Frazier, Interim Director of Financial Aid, Claflin University, Tingly Hall, Suite 12, 400 Magnolia Street, Orangeburg, SC 29115, 803-535-5720 or toll-free 800-922-1276 (in-state). *Fax:* 803-535-5383. *E-mail:* yfrazier@claflin.edu.

CLAREMONT McKENNA COLLEGE

Claremont, CA

Tuition & fees: $36,825 **Average undergraduate aid package: $32,800**

ABOUT THE INSTITUTION Independent, coed. ***Awards:*** bachelor's and master's degrees. 83 undergraduate majors. ***Total enrollment:*** 1,212. Undergraduates: 1,212. Freshmen: 320. Institutional methodology is used as a basis for awarding need-based institutional aid.

UNDERGRADUATE EXPENSES for 2008–09 ***Application fee:*** $60. ***Comprehensive fee:*** $48,755 includes full-time tuition ($36,825) and room and board ($11,930). ***College room only:*** $6110. Full-time tuition and fees vary according to reciprocity agreements. Room and board charges vary according to board plan and housing facility. ***Part-time tuition:*** $6138 per course. Part-time tuition and fees vary according to reciprocity agreements. ***Payment plans:*** Tuition prepayment, installment.

FRESHMAN FINANCIAL AID (Fall 2008, est.) 178 applied for aid; of those 81% were deemed to have need. 100% of freshmen with need received aid; of those 100% had need fully met. ***Average percent of need met:*** 100% (excluding resources awarded to replace EFC). ***Average financial aid package:*** $35,534 (excluding resources awarded to replace EFC). 7% of all full-time freshmen had no need and received non-need-based gift aid.

UNDERGRADUATE FINANCIAL AID (Fall 2008, est.) 609 applied for aid; of those 89% were deemed to have need. 100% of undergraduates with need received aid; of those 100% had need fully met. ***Average percent of need met:*** 100% (excluding resources awarded to replace EFC). ***Average financial aid package:*** $32,800 (excluding resources awarded to replace EFC). 7% of all full-time undergraduates had no need and received non-need-based gift aid.

GIFT AID (NEED-BASED) ***Total amount:*** $17,147,969 (4% federal, 6% state, 88% institutional, 2% external sources). ***Receiving aid:*** Freshmen: 45% (145); all full-time undergraduates: 44% (533). ***Average award:*** Freshmen: $34,532; Undergraduates: $32,151. ***Scholarships, grants, and awards:*** Federal Pell, FSEOG, state, college/university gift aid from institutional funds.

GIFT AID (NON-NEED-BASED) ***Total amount:*** $1,057,178 (94% institutional, 6% external sources). ***Receiving aid:*** Freshmen: 7% (22). Undergraduates: 7% (89). ***Average award:*** Freshmen: $5539. Undergraduates: $11,123. ***Scholarships, grants, and awards by category:*** *Academic interests/achievement:* general academic interests/achievements. *Special achievements/activities:* 76 awards ($700,000 total): leadership. ***Tuition waivers:*** Full or partial for employees or children of employees. ***ROTC:*** Army, Air Force cooperative.

LOANS ***Student loans:*** $422,516 (100% non-need-based). 51% of past graduating class borrowed through all loan programs. *Average indebtedness per student:* $10,518. ***Parent loans:*** $2,104,439 (100% non-need-based). ***Programs:*** FFEL (Subsidized and Unsubsidized Stafford, PLUS), Perkins, college/university.

WORK-STUDY ***Federal work-study:*** Total amount: $250,000; 280 jobs averaging $1850. ***State or other work-study/employment:*** Total amount: $890,000 (4% need-based, 96% non-need-based). Part-time jobs available.

APPLYING FOR FINANCIAL AID ***Required financial aid forms:*** FAFSA, CSS Financial Aid PROFILE, business/farm supplement. ***Notification date:*** 4/1. Students must reply by 5/1.

CONTACT Ms. Georgette R. DeVeres, Associate Vice President of Admission and Director of Financial Aid, Claremont McKenna College, 890 Columbia Avenue, Claremont, CA 91711, 909-621-8356. *Fax:* 909-621-8516. *E-mail:* gdeveres@cmc.edu.

CLARION UNIVERSITY OF PENNSYLVANIA

Clarion, PA

Tuition & fees (PA res): $7104 **Average undergraduate aid package: $8007**

ABOUT THE INSTITUTION State-supported, coed. ***Awards:*** associate, bachelor's, and master's degrees and post-master's certificates. 55 undergraduate majors. ***Total enrollment:*** 7,100. Undergraduates: 5,975. Freshmen: 1,361. Federal methodology is used as a basis for awarding need-based institutional aid.

UNDERGRADUATE EXPENSES for 2008–09 ***Application fee:*** $30. ***One-time required fee:*** $30. ***Tuition, state resident:*** full-time $5358; part-time $216 per credit hour. ***Tuition, nonresident:*** full-time $10,716; part-time $431 per credit hour. ***Required fees:*** full-time $1746; $52 per credit hour or $82 per term. Full-time tuition and fees vary according to course load and location. Part-time tuition and fees vary according to course load and location. ***College room and board:*** $6071; ***Room only:*** $4140. Room and board charges vary according to board plan. ***Payment plan:*** Installment.

FRESHMAN FINANCIAL AID (Fall 2007) 1,274 applied for aid; of those 80% were deemed to have need. 97% of freshmen with need received aid; of those 14% had need fully met. ***Average percent of need met:*** 68% (excluding resources awarded to replace EFC). ***Average financial aid package:*** $7498 (excluding resources awarded to replace EFC). 6% of all full-time freshmen had no need and received non-need-based gift aid.

UNDERGRADUATE FINANCIAL AID (Fall 2007) 4,410 applied for aid; of those 84% were deemed to have need. 97% of undergraduates with need received aid; of those 16% had need fully met. ***Average percent of need met:*** 72% (excluding resources awarded to replace EFC). ***Average financial aid package:*** $8007 (excluding resources awarded to replace EFC). 5% of all full-time undergraduates had no need and received non-need-based gift aid.

GIFT AID (NEED-BASED) ***Total amount:*** $14,871,506 (39% federal, 48% state, 5% institutional, 8% external sources). ***Receiving aid:*** Freshmen: 57% (789); all full-time undergraduates: 54% (2,763). ***Average award:*** Freshmen: $5676; Undergraduates: $5450. ***Scholarships, grants, and awards:*** Federal Pell, FSEOG, state, private, college/university gift aid from institutional funds, United Negro College Fund, Federal Nursing.

GIFT AID (NON-NEED-BASED) ***Receiving aid:*** Freshmen: 20% (272). Undergraduates: 18% (933). ***Average award:*** Freshmen: $2517. Undergraduates: $3008. ***Tuition waivers:*** Full or partial for employees or children of employees, senior citizens. ***ROTC:*** Army cooperative.

LOANS ***Student loans:*** $23,553,283 (56% need-based, 44% non-need-based). ***Average need-based loan:*** Freshmen: $3253. Undergraduates: $3953. ***Parent loans:*** $3,383,572 (100% non-need-based). ***Programs:*** Federal Direct (Subsidized and Unsubsidized Stafford, PLUS), FFEL (PLUS).

WORK-STUDY ***Federal work-study:*** Total amount: $521,861; jobs available. ***State or other work-study/employment:*** Total amount: $1,278,987 (100% non-need-based). Part-time jobs available.

ATHLETIC AWARDS Total amount: $580,213 (100% need-based).

APPLYING FOR FINANCIAL AID ***Required financial aid form:*** FAFSA. ***Financial aid deadline:*** 4/15 (priority: 4/15). ***Notification date:*** Continuous.

CONTACT Dr. Kenneth Grugel, Director of Financial Aid, Clarion University of Pennsylvania, 104 Egbert Hall, Clarion, PA 16214, 814-393-2315 or toll-free 800-672-7171. *Fax:* 814-393-2520. *E-mail:* maphillips@clarion.edu.

CLARK ATLANTA UNIVERSITY

Atlanta, GA

CONTACT Office of Financial Aid, Clark Atlanta University, 223 James P. Brawley Drive, Atlanta, GA 30314, 404-880-8992 or toll-free 800-688-3228. *Fax:* 404-880-8070. *E-mail:* studentfinancialaid@cau.edu.

CLARKE COLLEGE

Dubuque, IA

Tuition & fees: $23,520 **Average undergraduate aid package: $18,581**

ABOUT THE INSTITUTION Independent Roman Catholic, coed. ***Awards:*** associate, bachelor's, master's, and doctoral degrees. 38 undergraduate majors. ***Total enrollment:*** 1,156. Undergraduates: 956. Freshmen: 136. Federal methodology is used as a basis for awarding need-based institutional aid.

UNDERGRADUATE EXPENSES for 2009–10 ***Application fee:*** $25. ***Comprehensive fee:*** $30,360 includes full-time tuition ($22,800), mandatory fees ($720), and room and board ($6840). ***College room only:*** $3360. ***Part-time tuition:*** $578 per credit hour.

FRESHMAN FINANCIAL AID (Fall 2007) 132 applied for aid; of those 84% were deemed to have need. 100% of freshmen with need received aid; of those 32% had need fully met. ***Average percent of need met:*** 92% (excluding resources awarded to replace EFC). ***Average financial aid package:*** $20,512 (excluding resources awarded to replace EFC). 19% of all full-time freshmen had no need and received non-need-based gift aid.

UNDERGRADUATE FINANCIAL AID (Fall 2007) 756 applied for aid; of those 87% were deemed to have need. 100% of undergraduates with need received aid; of those 27% had need fully met. ***Average percent of need met:*** 92% (excluding resources awarded to replace EFC). ***Average financial aid package:*** $18,581 (excluding resources awarded to replace EFC). 13% of all full-time undergraduates had no need and received non-need-based gift aid.

GIFT AID (NEED-BASED) ***Total amount:*** $7,689,943 (14% federal, 16% state, 68% institutional, 2% external sources). ***Receiving aid:*** Freshmen: 80% (110); all full-time undergraduates: 81% (644). ***Average award:*** Freshmen: $17,066; Undergraduates: $14,362. ***Scholarships, grants, and awards:*** Federal Pell, FSEOG, state, private, college/university gift aid from institutional funds.

GIFT AID (NON-NEED-BASED) ***Total amount:*** $859,061 (97% institutional, 3% external sources). ***Receiving aid:*** Freshmen: 78% (107). Undergraduates: 74% (589). ***Average award:*** Freshmen: $19,457. Undergraduates: $15,598. ***Scholarships, grants, and awards by category:*** *Academic interests/achievement:* 552 awards ($3,156,480 total): computer science, foreign languages, general academic interests/achievements. *Creative arts/performance:* 77 awards ($153,200 total): art/fine arts, music, theater/drama. *Special achievements/activities:* 21 awards ($21,150 total): leadership. *Special characteristics:* $1,244,835 total: children and siblings of alumni, children of faculty/staff, children with a deceased or disabled parent, general special characteristics, international students, local/state students, members of minority groups, relatives of clergy, religious affiliation, siblings of current students. ***ROTC:*** Army cooperative.

LOANS ***Student loans:*** $7,049,279 (45% need-based, 55% non-need-based). 85% of past graduating class borrowed through all loan programs. *Average indebtedness per student:* $28,649. ***Average need-based loan:*** Freshmen: $3406. Undergraduates: $4534. ***Parent loans:*** $505,869 (85% need-based, 15% non-need-based). ***Programs:*** FFEL (Subsidized and Unsubsidized Stafford, PLUS), Perkins, Federal Nursing, state, college/university, private loans.

WORK-STUDY ***Federal work-study:*** Total amount: $338,754; 265 jobs averaging $1276. ***State or other work-study/employment:*** Part-time jobs available.

ATHLETIC AWARDS Total amount: $705,727 (100% non-need-based).

APPLYING FOR FINANCIAL AID ***Required financial aid form:*** FAFSA. ***Financial aid deadline (priority):*** 4/15. ***Notification date:*** Continuous. Students must reply within 2 weeks of notification.

CONTACT Sharon Willenborg, Director of Financial Aid, Clarke College, 1550 Clarke Drive, Dubuque, IA 52001-3198, 563-588-6327 or toll-free 800-383-2345. *Fax:* 563-584-8605. *E-mail:* sharon.willenborg@clarke.edu.

CLARKSON COLLEGE

Omaha, NE

CONTACT Pam Shelton, Director of Financial Aid, Clarkson College, 101 South 42nd Street, Omaha, NE 68131-2739, 402-552-2749 or toll-free 800-647-5500. *Fax:* 402-552-6165. *E-mail:* shelton@clarksoncollege.edu.

CLARKSON UNIVERSITY

Potsdam, NY

Tuition & fees: $32,910 **Average undergraduate aid package: $23,189**

ABOUT THE INSTITUTION Independent, coed. ***Awards:*** bachelor's, master's, doctoral, and first professional degrees. 63 undergraduate majors. ***Total enrollment:*** 3,045. Undergraduates: 2,593. Freshmen: 735. Federal methodology is used as a basis for awarding need-based institutional aid.

UNDERGRADUATE EXPENSES for 2009–10 ***Application fee:*** $50. ***Comprehensive fee:*** $44,028 includes full-time tuition ($32,220), mandatory fees ($690), and room and board ($11,118). ***College room only:*** $5890. ***Part-time tuition:*** $1074 per credit.

FRESHMAN FINANCIAL AID (Fall 2007) 574 applied for aid; of those 87% were deemed to have need. 100% of freshmen with need received aid; of those 8% had need fully met. ***Average percent of need met:*** 86% (excluding resources awarded to replace EFC). ***Average financial aid package:*** $25,518 (excluding resources awarded to replace EFC). 11% of all full-time freshmen had no need and received non-need-based gift aid.

UNDERGRADUATE FINANCIAL AID (Fall 2007) 2,219 applied for aid; of those 90% were deemed to have need. 93% of undergraduates with need received aid; of those 7% had need fully met. ***Average percent of need met:*** 89% (excluding resources awarded to replace EFC). ***Average financial aid package:*** $23,189 (excluding resources awarded to replace EFC). 9% of all full-time undergraduates had no need and received non-need-based gift aid.

GIFT AID (NEED-BASED) ***Total amount:*** $40,415,589 (7% federal, 6% state, 80% institutional, 7% external sources). ***Receiving aid:*** Freshmen: 61% (415); all full-time undergraduates: 64% (1,621). ***Average award:*** Freshmen: $14,270; Undergraduates: $16,218. ***Scholarships, grants, and awards:*** Federal Pell, FSEOG, state, private, college/university gift aid from institutional funds.

GIFT AID (NON-NEED-BASED) ***Total amount:*** $2,978,381 (6% state, 87% institutional, 7% external sources). ***Receiving aid:*** Freshmen: 14% (95). Undergraduates: 9% (236). ***Average award:*** Freshmen: $14,529. Undergraduates: $13,025. ***Scholarships, grants, and awards by category:*** *Academic interests/achievement:* 1,911 awards ($8,773,625 total): biological sciences, business, communication, computer science, engineering/technologies, general academic interests/achievements, humanities, mathematics, military science, physical sciences, social sciences. *Special achievements/activities:* 745 awards ($5,939,650 total): general special achievements/activities, leadership. *Special characteristics:* 422 awards ($2,240,320 total): children of faculty/staff, general special characteristics, international students, local/state students, members of minority groups. ***ROTC:*** Army, Air Force.

LOANS ***Student loans:*** $21,185,244 (95% need-based, 5% non-need-based). 84% of past graduating class borrowed through all loan programs. *Average indebtedness per student:* $33,625. ***Average need-based loan:*** Freshmen: $5100. Undergraduates: $6000. ***Parent loans:*** $4,154,829 (93% need-based, 7% non-need-based). ***Programs:*** Federal Direct (Subsidized and Unsubsidized Stafford, PLUS), FFEL (Subsidized and Unsubsidized Stafford, PLUS), Perkins, college/university, alternative loans.

WORK-STUDY ***Federal work-study:*** Total amount: $475,735; 1,312 jobs averaging $1544. ***State or other work-study/employment:*** Total amount: $421,683 (73% need-based, 27% non-need-based). 115 part-time jobs averaging $2800.

ATHLETIC AWARDS Total amount: $1,405,638 (100% non-need-based).

APPLYING FOR FINANCIAL AID ***Required financial aid forms:*** FAFSA, state aid form. ***Financial aid deadline (priority):*** 2/15. ***Notification date:*** 3/19. Students must reply by 5/1 or within 2 weeks of notification.

CONTACT Pamela Nichols, Director of Financial Aid, Clarkson University, Clarkson University, Potsdam, NY 13699-5615, 315-268-6413 or toll-free 800-527-6577. *Fax:* 315-268-6452. *E-mail:* pnichols@clarkson.edu.

CLARK UNIVERSITY
Worcester, MA

Tuition & fees: $35,220 **Average undergraduate aid package: $27,945**

ABOUT THE INSTITUTION Independent, coed. ***Awards:*** bachelor's, master's, and doctoral degrees and post-bachelor's and post-master's certificates. 49 undergraduate majors. ***Total enrollment:*** 3,330. Undergraduates: 2,380. Freshmen: 591. Institutional methodology is used as a basis for awarding need-based institutional aid.

UNDERGRADUATE EXPENSES for 2009–10 ***Application fee:*** $55. ***Comprehensive fee:*** $41,970 includes full-time tuition ($34,900), mandatory fees ($320), and room and board ($6750). ***College room only:*** $3900. ***Part-time tuition:*** $1090 per credit hour.

FRESHMAN FINANCIAL AID (Fall 2008, est.) 418 applied for aid; of those 75% were deemed to have need. 97% of freshmen with need received aid; of those 74% had need fully met. ***Average percent of need met:*** 94% (excluding resources awarded to replace EFC). ***Average financial aid package:*** $27,945 (excluding resources awarded to replace EFC). 29% of all full-time freshmen had no need and received non-need-based gift aid.

UNDERGRADUATE FINANCIAL AID (Fall 2008, est.) 1,594 applied for aid; of those 75% were deemed to have need. 97% of undergraduates with need received aid; of those 74% had need fully met. ***Average percent of need met:*** 94% (excluding resources awarded to replace EFC). ***Average financial aid package:*** $27,945 (excluding resources awarded to replace EFC). 29% of all full-time undergraduates had no need and received non-need-based gift aid.

GIFT AID (NEED-BASED) ***Total amount:*** $22,094,333 (9% federal, 2% state, 86% institutional, 3% external sources). ***Receiving aid:*** Freshmen: 51% (301); all full-time undergraduates: 51% (1,148). ***Average award:*** Freshmen: $21,932; Undergraduates: $21,932. ***Scholarships, grants, and awards:*** Federal Pell, FSEOG, state, college/university gift aid from institutional funds.

GIFT AID (NON-NEED-BASED) ***Total amount:*** $9,624,974 (100% institutional). ***Receiving aid:*** Freshmen: 30% (179). Undergraduates: 30% (683). ***Average award:*** Freshmen: $14,472. Undergraduates: $14,472. ***Scholarships, grants, and awards by category:*** *Academic interests/achievement:* general academic interests/achievements. *Special achievements/activities:* community service, general special achievements/activities. ***ROTC:*** Army cooperative, Naval cooperative, Air Force cooperative.

LOANS ***Student loans:*** $10,085,036 (61% need-based, 39% non-need-based). 90% of past graduating class borrowed through all loan programs. *Average indebtedness per student:* $22,250. ***Average need-based loan:*** Freshmen: $4731. Undergraduates: $4731. ***Parent loans:*** $2,908,187 (1% need-based, 99% non-need-based). ***Programs:*** Federal Direct (Subsidized and Unsubsidized Stafford, PLUS), Perkins, state.

WORK-STUDY ***Federal work-study:*** Total amount: $1,674,419; 900 jobs averaging $2000.

APPLYING FOR FINANCIAL AID ***Required financial aid forms:*** FAFSA, CSS Financial Aid PROFILE, noncustodial (divorced/separated) parent's statement. ***Financial aid deadline:*** 1/15 (priority: 1/15). ***Notification date:*** 3/31. Students must reply by 5/1.

CONTACT Ms. Mary Ellen Severance, Director, Office of Financial Assistance, Clark University, 950 Main Street, Worcester, MA 01610-1477, 508-793-7478 or toll-free 800-GO-CLARK. *Fax:* 508-793-8802. *E-mail:* finaid@clarku.edu.

CLAYTON STATE UNIVERSITY
Morrow, GA

Tuition & fees (GA res): $3852 **Average undergraduate aid package: $3855**

ABOUT THE INSTITUTION State-supported, coed. ***Awards:*** associate, bachelor's, and master's degrees. 93 undergraduate majors. ***Total enrollment:*** 6,074. Undergraduates: 5,921. Freshmen: 598. Federal methodology is used as a basis for awarding need-based institutional aid.

UNDERGRADUATE EXPENSES for 2008–09 ***Application fee:*** $40. ***Tuition, state resident:*** full-time $3098; part-time $130 per credit hour. ***Tuition, nonresident:*** full-time $12,390; part-time $517 per credit hour. ***Required fees:*** full-time $754; $377 per credit hour. Full-time tuition and fees vary according to course load. Part-time tuition and fees vary according to course load. ***College room and board:*** $3900; ***Room only:*** $2475. ***Payment plan:*** Guaranteed tuition.

FRESHMAN FINANCIAL AID (Fall 2007) 288 applied for aid; of those 85% were deemed to have need. 100% of freshmen with need received aid; of those 10% had need fully met. ***Average percent of need met:*** 18% (excluding resources awarded to replace EFC). ***Average financial aid package:*** $8178 (excluding resources awarded to replace EFC). 4% of all full-time freshmen had no need and received non-need-based gift aid.

UNDERGRADUATE FINANCIAL AID (Fall 2007) 2,633 applied for aid; of those 91% were deemed to have need. 98% of undergraduates with need received aid; of those 6% had need fully met. ***Average percent of need met:*** 33% (excluding resources awarded to replace EFC). ***Average financial aid package:*** $3855 (excluding resources awarded to replace EFC). 4% of all full-time undergraduates had no need and received non-need-based gift aid.

GIFT AID (NEED-BASED) ***Total amount:*** $4,884,849 (100% federal). ***Receiving aid:*** Freshmen: 54% (170); all full-time undergraduates: 49% (1,609). ***Average award:*** Freshmen: $4424; Undergraduates: $2126. ***Scholarships, grants, and awards:*** Federal Pell, FSEOG, state, college/university gift aid from institutional funds, Federal Nursing.

GIFT AID (NON-NEED-BASED) ***Total amount:*** $2,292,240 (90% state, 5% institutional, 5% external sources). ***Receiving aid:*** Freshmen: 42% (133). Undergraduates: 22% (723). ***Average award:*** Freshmen: $1067. Undergraduates: $699. ***Scholarships, grants, and awards by category:*** *Special characteristics:* general special characteristics. ***Tuition waivers:*** Full or partial for employees or children of employees, senior citizens. ***ROTC:*** Army cooperative, Naval cooperative, Air Force cooperative.

LOANS ***Student loans:*** $15,984,380 (46% need-based, 54% non-need-based). 34% of past graduating class borrowed through all loan programs. ***Average need-based loan:*** Freshmen: $3342. Undergraduates: $2133. ***Parent loans:*** $1,302,168 (100% non-need-based). ***Programs:*** FFEL (Subsidized and Unsubsidized Stafford, PLUS), Federal Nursing, state.

WORK-STUDY ***Federal work-study:*** Total amount: $102,001; jobs available. ***State or other work-study/employment:*** Total amount: $16,086,381 (46% need-based, 54% non-need-based). Part-time jobs available.

ATHLETIC AWARDS Total amount: $223,888 (100% non-need-based).

APPLYING FOR FINANCIAL AID ***Required financial aid forms:*** FAFSA, institution's own form, state aid form. ***Financial aid deadline (priority):*** 7/8. ***Notification date:*** Continuous.

CONTACT Pat Barton, Director of Financial Aid, Clayton State University, 2000 Clayton State Boulevard, Morrow, GA 30260, 678-466-4185. *Fax:* 678-466-4189. *E-mail:* financialaid@mail.clayton.edu.

CLEAR CREEK BAPTIST BIBLE COLLEGE
Pineville, KY

Tuition & fees: N/R **Average undergraduate aid package: $5873**

ABOUT THE INSTITUTION Independent Southern Baptist, coed, primarily men. ***Awards:*** bachelor's degrees. 2 undergraduate majors. ***Total enrollment:*** 166. Undergraduates: 166. Institutional methodology is used as a basis for awarding need-based institutional aid.

FRESHMAN FINANCIAL AID (Fall 2008, est.) 10 applied for aid; of those 90% were deemed to have need. 100% of freshmen with need received aid. ***Average percent of need met:*** 69% (excluding resources awarded to replace EFC). ***Average financial aid package:*** $6652 (excluding resources awarded to replace EFC). 17% of all full-time freshmen had no need and received non-need-based gift aid.

UNDERGRADUATE FINANCIAL AID (Fall 2008, est.) 116 applied for aid; of those 96% were deemed to have need. 100% of undergraduates with need received aid. ***Average percent of need met:*** 61% (excluding resources awarded to replace EFC). ***Average financial aid package:*** $5873 (excluding resources awarded to replace EFC). 9% of all full-time undergraduates had no need and received non-need-based gift aid.

GIFT AID (NEED-BASED) ***Total amount:*** $683,035 (64% federal, 2% state, 25% institutional, 9% external sources). ***Receiving aid:*** Freshmen: 75% (9); all full-time undergraduates: 88% (111). ***Average award:*** Freshmen: $6652; Undergraduates: $5873. ***Scholarships, grants, and awards:*** Federal Pell, FSEOG, state, private, college/university gift aid from institutional funds.

GIFT AID (NON-NEED-BASED) ***Total amount:*** $41,704 (75% federal, 25% institutional). ***Receiving aid:*** Freshmen: 42% (5). Undergraduates: 24% (30). ***Average award:*** Freshmen: $400. Undergraduates: $1968. ***Scholarships, grants, and awards by category:*** *Academic interests/achievement:* 8 awards ($5164 total): general academic interests/achievements. *Creative arts/performance:* 4

awards ($800 total): music. *Special characteristics:* 2 awards ($2062 total): handicapped students, international students.

LOANS ***Student loans:*** $7500 (100% non-need-based).

WORK-STUDY ***Federal work-study:*** Total amount: $28,562; 31 jobs averaging $1228. ***State or other work-study/employment:*** Total amount: $9521 (100% need-based). Part-time jobs available.

APPLYING FOR FINANCIAL AID ***Required financial aid forms:*** FAFSA, institution's own form. ***Financial aid deadline (priority):*** 6/30. ***Notification date:*** 7/1.

CONTACT Mr. Sam Risner, Director of Financial Aid, Clear Creek Baptist Bible College, 300 Clear Creek Road, Pineville, KY 40977-9754, 606-337-3196 Ext. 142. *Fax:* 606-337-1631. *E-mail:* srisner@ccbbc.edu.

CLEARWATER CHRISTIAN COLLEGE

Clearwater, FL

Tuition & fees: $14,040 **Average undergraduate aid package: $10,353**

ABOUT THE INSTITUTION Independent nondenominational, coed. ***Awards:*** associate, bachelor's, and master's degrees. 24 undergraduate majors. ***Total enrollment:*** 604. Undergraduates: 601. Freshmen: 151. Federal methodology is used as a basis for awarding need-based institutional aid.

UNDERGRADUATE EXPENSES for 2008–09 ***Application fee:*** $35. ***Comprehensive fee:*** $19,940 includes full-time tuition ($13,390), mandatory fees ($650), and room and board ($5900). ***College room only:*** $3630. ***Part-time tuition:*** $515 per hour. ***Payment plan:*** Installment.

FRESHMAN FINANCIAL AID (Fall 2008, est.) 132 applied for aid; of those 83% were deemed to have need. 99% of freshmen with need received aid; of those 16% had need fully met. ***Average percent of need met:*** 64% (excluding resources awarded to replace EFC). ***Average financial aid package:*** $10,913 (excluding resources awarded to replace EFC). 24% of all full-time freshmen had no need and received non-need-based gift aid.

UNDERGRADUATE FINANCIAL AID (Fall 2008, est.) 543 applied for aid; of those 80% were deemed to have need. 100% of undergraduates with need received aid; of those 15% had need fully met. ***Average percent of need met:*** 60% (excluding resources awarded to replace EFC). ***Average financial aid package:*** $10,353 (excluding resources awarded to replace EFC). 22% of all full-time undergraduates had no need and received non-need-based gift aid.

GIFT AID (NEED-BASED) ***Total amount:*** $3,432,692 (23% federal, 26% state, 42% institutional, 9% external sources). ***Receiving aid:*** Freshmen: 74% (108); all full-time undergraduates: 72% (427). ***Average award:*** Freshmen: $8422; Undergraduates: $7918. ***Scholarships, grants, and awards:*** Federal Pell, FSEOG, state, private, college/university gift aid from institutional funds.

GIFT AID (NON-NEED-BASED) ***Total amount:*** $860,643 (33% state, 47% institutional, 20% external sources). ***Receiving aid:*** Freshmen: 8% (11). Undergraduates: 8% (46). ***Average award:*** Freshmen: $2871. Undergraduates: $2848. ***Scholarships, grants, and awards by category:*** *Academic interests/achievement:* 134 awards ($350,000 total): business, education, general academic interests/achievements, premedicine, religion/biblical studies. *Creative arts/performance:* 45 awards ($84,000 total): music. *Special achievements/activities:* 151 awards ($75,000 total): leadership. *Special characteristics:* 145 awards ($310,000 total): children and siblings of alumni, ethnic background, religious affiliation, siblings of current students. ***Tuition waivers:*** Full or partial for employees or children of employees. ***ROTC:*** Army cooperative, Naval cooperative, Air Force cooperative.

LOANS ***Student loans:*** $2,041,141 (75% need-based, 25% non-need-based). 54% of past graduating class borrowed through all loan programs. *Average indebtedness per student:* $18,000. ***Average need-based loan:*** Freshmen: $3789. Undergraduates: $4324. ***Parent loans:*** $564,856 (39% need-based, 61% non-need-based). ***Programs:*** FFEL (Subsidized and Unsubsidized Stafford, PLUS), state, alternative loans.

WORK-STUDY ***Federal work-study:*** Total amount: $27,000; 50 jobs averaging $670. ***State or other work-study/employment:*** Total amount: $15,000 (100% need-based). 20 part-time jobs averaging $612.

APPLYING FOR FINANCIAL AID ***Required financial aid forms:*** FAFSA, institution's own form, state aid form. ***Financial aid deadline:*** Continuous. ***Notification date:*** Continuous beginning 1/1.

CONTACT Mrs. Ruth Strum, Director of Financial Aid, Clearwater Christian College, 3400 Gulf-to-Bay Boulevard, Clearwater, FL 33759-4595, 727-726-1153 Ext. 214 or toll-free 800-348-4463. *Fax:* 727-791-1347. *E-mail:* ruthstrum@clearwater.edu.

CLEARY UNIVERSITY

Ann Arbor, MI

Tuition & fees: $15,600 **Average undergraduate aid package: $10,428**

ABOUT THE INSTITUTION Independent, coed. ***Awards:*** associate, bachelor's, and master's degrees. 10 undergraduate majors. ***Total enrollment:*** 855. Undergraduates: 739. Federal methodology is used as a basis for awarding need-based institutional aid.

UNDERGRADUATE EXPENSES for 2009–10 ***Application fee:*** $25. ***Tuition:*** full-time $15,600; part-time $325 per quarter hour.

FRESHMAN FINANCIAL AID (Fall 2007) 66 applied for aid; of those 100% were deemed to have need. 100% of freshmen with need received aid; of those 8% had need fully met. ***Average percent of need met:*** 43% (excluding resources awarded to replace EFC). ***Average financial aid package:*** $10,735 (excluding resources awarded to replace EFC). 13% of all full-time freshmen had no need and received non-need-based gift aid.

UNDERGRADUATE FINANCIAL AID (Fall 2007) 369 applied for aid; of those 100% were deemed to have need. 100% of undergraduates with need received aid; of those 5% had need fully met. ***Average percent of need met:*** 39% (excluding resources awarded to replace EFC). ***Average financial aid package:*** $10,428 (excluding resources awarded to replace EFC). 11% of all full-time undergraduates had no need and received non-need-based gift aid.

GIFT AID (NEED-BASED) ***Total amount:*** $760,957 (57% federal, 42% state, 1% institutional). ***Receiving aid:*** Freshmen: 51% (51); all full-time undergraduates: 45% (259). ***Average award:*** Freshmen: $1027; Undergraduates: $1019. ***Scholarships, grants, and awards:*** Federal Pell, FSEOG, state, private, college/university gift aid from institutional funds.

GIFT AID (NON-NEED-BASED) ***Total amount:*** $27,376 (91% state, 9% institutional). ***Receiving aid:*** Freshmen: 11% (11). Undergraduates: 3% (15). ***Average award:*** Freshmen: $1917. Undergraduates: $1512. ***Scholarships, grants, and awards by category:*** *Academic interests/achievement:* 57 awards ($104,570 total): business, computer science, general academic interests/achievements. *Special characteristics:* 38 awards ($217,110 total): children of faculty/staff, veterans.

LOANS ***Student loans:*** $3,829,777 (48% need-based, 52% non-need-based). ***Average need-based loan:*** Freshmen: $1294. Undergraduates: $1405. ***Parent loans:*** $268,015 (100% non-need-based). ***Programs:*** Federal Direct (Subsidized and Unsubsidized Stafford, PLUS), FFEL (Subsidized and Unsubsidized Stafford, PLUS).

WORK-STUDY ***Federal work-study:*** Total amount: $53,889; 17 jobs averaging $2028. ***State or other work-study/employment:*** Total amount: $4485 (100% need-based). 6 part-time jobs averaging $856.

APPLYING FOR FINANCIAL AID ***Required financial aid forms:*** FAFSA, institution's own form. ***Financial aid deadline (priority):*** 3/1. ***Notification date:*** Continuous beginning 4/1. Students must reply by 7/1 or within 2 weeks of notification.

CONTACT Vesta Smith-Campbell, Director of Financial Aid, Cleary University, 3750 Cleary Drive, Howell, MI 48843, 800-589-1979 Ext. 2234 or toll-free 888-5-CLEARY Ext. 2249. *Fax:* 517-552-8022. *E-mail:* vscampbell@cleary.edu.

CLEMSON UNIVERSITY

Clemson, SC

Tuition & fees (SC res): $11,108 **Average undergraduate aid package: $12,543**

ABOUT THE INSTITUTION State-supported, coed. ***Awards:*** bachelor's, master's, and doctoral degrees and post-master's certificates. 77 undergraduate majors. ***Total enrollment:*** 18,317. Undergraduates: 14,713. Freshmen: 2,923. Federal methodology is used as a basis for awarding need-based institutional aid.

UNDERGRADUATE EXPENSES for 2008–09 ***Application fee:*** $50. ***Tuition, state resident:*** full-time $11,108. ***Tuition, nonresident:*** full-time $24,130. Full-time tuition and fees vary according to course load, location, and program. Part-time tuition and fees vary according to program. ***College room and board:*** $6556; ***Room only:*** $3914. Room and board charges vary according to board plan and housing facility. ***Payment plan:*** Installment.

FRESHMAN FINANCIAL AID (Fall 2008, est.) 1,921 applied for aid; of those 64% were deemed to have need. 97% of freshmen with need received aid; of those 31% had need fully met. ***Average percent of need met:*** 70% (excluding

resources awarded to replace EFC). ***Average financial aid package:*** $13,511 (excluding resources awarded to replace EFC). 24% of all full-time freshmen had no need and received non-need-based gift aid.

UNDERGRADUATE FINANCIAL AID (Fall 2008, est.) 7,467 applied for aid; of those 72% were deemed to have need. 97% of undergraduates with need received aid; of those 28% had need fully met. ***Average percent of need met:*** 62% (excluding resources awarded to replace EFC). ***Average financial aid package:*** $12,543 (excluding resources awarded to replace EFC). 22% of all full-time undergraduates had no need and received non-need-based gift aid.

GIFT AID (NEED-BASED) ***Total amount:*** $13,579,197 (54% federal, 15% state, 16% institutional, 15% external sources). ***Receiving aid:*** Freshmen: 14% (417); all full-time undergraduates: 16% (2,224). ***Average award:*** Freshmen: $4283; Undergraduates: $4140. ***Scholarships, grants, and awards:*** Federal Pell, FSEOG, state, private, college/university gift aid from institutional funds.

GIFT AID (NON-NEED-BASED) ***Total amount:*** $55,821,213 (70% state, 19% institutional, 11% external sources). ***Receiving aid:*** Undergraduates: 25% (3,361). ***Average award:*** Freshmen: $2653. Undergraduates: $2473. ***Scholarships, grants, and awards by category:*** *Academic interests/achievement:* agriculture, architecture, biological sciences, business, communication, computer science, education, engineering/technologies, English, foreign languages, general academic interests/achievements, health fields, humanities, international studies, mathematics, military science, physical sciences, premedicine, social sciences. *Creative arts/performance:* applied art and design, art/fine arts, performing arts, theater/drama. *Special achievements/activities:* community service, general special achievements/activities, leadership. *Special characteristics:* children of faculty/staff, ethnic background, local/state students, members of minority groups. ***Tuition waivers:*** Full or partial for senior citizens. ***ROTC:*** Army, Air Force.

LOANS ***Student loans:*** $73,150,228 (34% need-based, 66% non-need-based). ***Average need-based loan:*** Freshmen: $3660. Undergraduates: $4466. ***Parent loans:*** $10,331,845 (100% non-need-based). ***Programs:*** FFEL (Subsidized and Unsubsidized Stafford, PLUS), Perkins, state, college/university, private loans.

WORK-STUDY ***Federal work-study:*** Total amount: $1,700,592; 1,107 jobs averaging $1919. ***State or other work-study/employment:*** Total amount: $5,500,000 (100% non-need-based). 3,000 part-time jobs averaging $1700.

ATHLETIC AWARDS Total amount: $5,681,400 (100% non-need-based).

APPLYING FOR FINANCIAL AID ***Required financial aid form:*** FAFSA. ***Financial aid deadline (priority):*** 4/1. ***Notification date:*** Continuous beginning 4/15. Students must reply within 3 weeks of notification.

CONTACT Mr. Marvin G. Carmichael, Director of Financial Aid, Clemson University, G01 Sikes Hall, Clemson, SC 29634-5123, 864-656-2280. *Fax:* 864-656-1831. *E-mail:* finaid@clemson.edu.

THE CLEVELAND INSTITUTE OF ART

Cleveland, OH

Tuition & fees: $31,010 — **Average undergraduate aid package: $19,422**

ABOUT THE INSTITUTION Independent, coed. ***Awards:*** bachelor's degrees. 17 undergraduate majors. ***Total enrollment:*** 503. Undergraduates: 503. Freshmen: 103. Federal methodology is used as a basis for awarding need-based institutional aid.

UNDERGRADUATE EXPENSES for 2008–09 ***Application fee:*** $30. ***Comprehensive fee:*** $40,158 includes full-time tuition ($29,000), mandatory fees ($2010), and room and board ($9148). ***College room only:*** $4948. Full-time tuition and fees vary according to program. Room and board charges vary according to board plan. ***Part-time tuition:*** $1210 per credit hour. ***Part-time fees:*** $120 per credit hour. Part-time tuition and fees vary according to course load and program.

FRESHMAN FINANCIAL AID (Fall 2008, est.) 94 applied for aid; of those 93% were deemed to have need. 100% of freshmen with need received aid; of those 15% had need fully met. ***Average percent of need met:*** 68% (excluding resources awarded to replace EFC). ***Average financial aid package:*** $22,720 (excluding resources awarded to replace EFC). 16% of all full-time freshmen had no need and received non-need-based gift aid.

UNDERGRADUATE FINANCIAL AID (Fall 2008, est.) 452 applied for aid; of those 91% were deemed to have need. 100% of undergraduates with need received aid; of those 10% had need fully met. ***Average percent of need met:*** 57% (excluding resources awarded to replace EFC). ***Average financial aid package:*** $19,422 (excluding resources awarded to replace EFC). 17% of all full-time undergraduates had no need and received non-need-based gift aid.

GIFT AID (NEED-BASED) ***Total amount:*** $5,636,927 (12% federal, 8% state, 77% institutional, 3% external sources). ***Receiving aid:*** Freshmen: 84% (87); all full-time undergraduates: 82% (412). ***Average award:*** Freshmen: $17,067; Undergraduates: $13,672. ***Scholarships, grants, and awards:*** Federal Pell, FSEOG, state, private, college/university gift aid from institutional funds.

GIFT AID (NON-NEED-BASED) ***Total amount:*** $1,052,748 (3% state, 95% institutional, 2% external sources). ***Receiving aid:*** Freshmen: 9% (9). Undergraduates: 5% (26). ***Average award:*** Freshmen: $9282. Undergraduates: $9979. ***Scholarships, grants, and awards by category:*** *Creative arts/performance:* 499 awards ($5,313,963 total): art/fine arts. ***Tuition waivers:*** Full or partial for employees or children of employees.

LOANS ***Student loans:*** $6,187,858 (77% need-based, 23% non-need-based). 80% of past graduating class borrowed through all loan programs. *Average indebtedness per student:* $65,000. ***Average need-based loan:*** Freshmen: $4534. Undergraduates: $4819. ***Parent loans:*** $1,111,653 (61% need-based, 39% non-need-based). ***Programs:*** FFEL (Subsidized and Unsubsidized Stafford, PLUS), Perkins.

WORK-STUDY ***Federal work-study:*** Total amount: $514,749; 200 jobs averaging $2500.

APPLYING FOR FINANCIAL AID ***Required financial aid forms:*** FAFSA, institution's own form. ***Financial aid deadline (priority):*** 3/15. ***Notification date:*** Continuous. Students must reply by 5/1 or within 3 weeks of notification.

CONTACT Delores Hall, Assistant Director of Financial Aid, The Cleveland Institute of Art, 11141 East Boulevard, Cleveland, OH 44106-1700, 216-421-7425 or toll-free 800-223-4700. *Fax:* 216-754-3634. *E-mail:* financialaid@cia.edu.

CLEVELAND INSTITUTE OF MUSIC

Cleveland, OH

Tuition & fees: N/R — **Average undergraduate aid package: $21,389**

ABOUT THE INSTITUTION Independent, coed. 6 undergraduate majors. Federal methodology is used as a basis for awarding need-based institutional aid.

FRESHMAN FINANCIAL AID (Fall 2008, est.) 31 applied for aid; of those 87% were deemed to have need. 100% of freshmen with need received aid; of those 52% had need fully met. ***Average percent of need met:*** 81% (excluding resources awarded to replace EFC). ***Average financial aid package:*** $21,222 (excluding resources awarded to replace EFC). 33% of all full-time freshmen had no need and received non-need-based gift aid.

UNDERGRADUATE FINANCIAL AID (Fall 2008, est.) 164 applied for aid; of those 85% were deemed to have need. 100% of undergraduates with need received aid; of those 35% had need fully met. ***Average percent of need met:*** 77% (excluding resources awarded to replace EFC). ***Average financial aid package:*** $21,389 (excluding resources awarded to replace EFC). 35% of all full-time undergraduates had no need and received non-need-based gift aid.

GIFT AID (NEED-BASED) ***Total amount:*** $2,165,283 (7% federal, 2% state, 87% institutional, 4% external sources). ***Receiving aid:*** Freshmen: 60% (27); all full-time undergraduates: 62% (140). ***Average award:*** Freshmen: $16,870; Undergraduates: $15,427. ***Scholarships, grants, and awards:*** Federal Pell, FSEOG, state, private, college/university gift aid from institutional funds.

GIFT AID (NON-NEED-BASED) ***Total amount:*** $1,305,779 (2% state, 92% institutional, 6% external sources). ***Receiving aid:*** Freshmen: 22% (10). Undergraduates: 16% (35). ***Average award:*** Freshmen: $12,833. Undergraduates: $12,686. ***Scholarships, grants, and awards by category:*** *Creative arts/performance:* music. ***Tuition waivers:*** Full or partial for employees or children of employees.

LOANS ***Student loans:*** $1,411,780 (65% need-based, 35% non-need-based). 68% of past graduating class borrowed through all loan programs. *Average indebtedness per student:* $26,355. ***Average need-based loan:*** Freshmen: $5126. Undergraduates: $6812. ***Parent loans:*** $549,224 (29% need-based, 71% non-need-based). ***Programs:*** Federal Direct (Subsidized and Unsubsidized Stafford, PLUS), Perkins, college/university, private alternative loans.

WORK-STUDY ***Federal work-study:*** Total amount: $141,267; 76 jobs averaging $1859. ***State or other work-study/employment:*** Total amount: $45,000 (100% non-need-based). 21 part-time jobs averaging $2143.

APPLYING FOR FINANCIAL AID ***Required financial aid form:*** FAFSA. ***Financial aid deadline:*** 2/15 (priority: 2/15). ***Notification date:*** 4/1. Students must reply by 5/1.

CONTACT Ms. Kristie Gripp, Director of Financial Aid, Cleveland Institute of Music, 11021 East Boulevard, Cleveland, OH 44106-1776, 216-795-3192. *Fax:* 216-707-4519. *E-mail:* kxg26@case.edu.

CLEVELAND STATE UNIVERSITY

Cleveland, OH

Tuition & fees (OH res): $7970 **Average undergraduate aid package: $8136**

ABOUT THE INSTITUTION State-supported, coed. ***Awards:*** bachelor's, master's, doctoral, and first professional degrees and post-bachelor's, post-master's, and first professional certificates. 83 undergraduate majors. ***Total enrollment:*** 15,809. Undergraduates: 10,161. Freshmen: 1,056. Federal methodology is used as a basis for awarding need-based institutional aid.

UNDERGRADUATE EXPENSES for 2009–10 ***Application fee:*** $30. ***Tuition, state resident:*** full-time $7970; part-time $330 per credit hour. ***Tuition, nonresident:*** full-time $10,774; part-time $444.30 per credit hour. ***College room and board:*** $8700; ***Room only:*** $5410.

FRESHMAN FINANCIAL AID (Fall 2008, est.) 723 applied for aid; of those 89% were deemed to have need. 98% of freshmen with need received aid; of those 8% had need fully met. ***Average percent of need met:*** 48% (excluding resources awarded to replace EFC). ***Average financial aid package:*** $8047 (excluding resources awarded to replace EFC). 10% of all full-time freshmen had no need and received non-need-based gift aid.

UNDERGRADUATE FINANCIAL AID (Fall 2008, est.) 5,928 applied for aid; of those 91% were deemed to have need. 96% of undergraduates with need received aid; of those 8% had need fully met. ***Average percent of need met:*** 48% (excluding resources awarded to replace EFC). ***Average financial aid package:*** $8136 (excluding resources awarded to replace EFC). 12% of all full-time undergraduates had no need and received non-need-based gift aid.

GIFT AID (NEED-BASED) ***Total amount:*** $22,205,994 (64% federal, 18% state, 12% institutional, 6% external sources). ***Receiving aid:*** Freshmen: 50% (509); all full-time undergraduates: 53% (3,729). ***Average award:*** Freshmen: $5994; Undergraduates: $5831. ***Scholarships, grants, and awards:*** Federal Pell, FSEOG, state, private, college/university gift aid from institutional funds.

GIFT AID (NON-NEED-BASED) ***Total amount:*** $2,315,751 (5% state, 82% institutional, 13% external sources). ***Receiving aid:*** Freshmen: 1% (15). Undergraduates: 1% (103). ***Average award:*** Freshmen: $7954. Undergraduates: $7838. ***Scholarships, grants, and awards by category:*** *Academic interests/achievement:* business, communication, education, engineering/technologies, English, general academic interests/achievements. *Creative arts/performance:* art/fine arts, creative writing, dance, music, theater/drama. *Special achievements/activities:* cheerleading/drum major. *Special characteristics:* children and siblings of alumni, general special characteristics. ***ROTC:*** Army cooperative, Naval cooperative, Air Force cooperative.

LOANS ***Student loans:*** $48,233,176 (85% need-based, 15% non-need-based). ***Average need-based loan:*** Freshmen: $3270. Undergraduates: $4271. ***Parent loans:*** $2,878,348 (31% need-based, 69% non-need-based). ***Programs:*** FFEL (Subsidized and Unsubsidized Stafford, PLUS), Perkins, state, alternative loans.

WORK-STUDY ***Federal work-study:*** Total amount: $1,065,053; jobs available. ***State or other work-study/employment:*** Total amount: $8039 (100% non-need-based). Part-time jobs available.

ATHLETIC AWARDS Total amount: $2,250,069 (32% need-based, 68% non-need-based).

APPLYING FOR FINANCIAL AID ***Required financial aid forms:*** FAFSA, tax forms (for the base tax year), if selected for verification by Department of Education or the institution. ***Financial aid deadline (priority):*** 2/15. ***Notification date:*** Continuous beginning 4/1. Students must reply within 4 weeks of notification.

CONTACT Director of Financial Aid, Cleveland State University, 1621 Euclid Avenue, Cleveland, OH 44115, 216-687-5594 or toll-free 888-CSU-OHIO.

COASTAL CAROLINA UNIVERSITY

Conway, SC

Tuition & fees (SC res): $8650 **Average undergraduate aid package: $8094**

ABOUT THE INSTITUTION State-supported, coed. ***Awards:*** bachelor's and master's degrees and post-bachelor's certificates. 33 undergraduate majors. ***Total enrollment:*** 8,154. Undergraduates: 7,573. Freshmen: 1,655. Federal methodology is used as a basis for awarding need-based institutional aid.

UNDERGRADUATE EXPENSES for 2008–09 ***Application fee:*** $45. ***Tuition, state resident:*** full-time $8570; part-time $360 per credit hour. ***Tuition, nonresident:*** full-time $18,010; part-time $754 per credit hour. ***Required fees:*** full-time $80. Full-time tuition and fees vary according to course load. Part-time tuition and fees vary according to course load. ***College room and board:*** $7080; ***Room only:*** $4630. Room and board charges vary according to board plan and housing facility. ***Payment plan:*** Installment.

FRESHMAN FINANCIAL AID (Fall 2007) 1,382 applied for aid; of those 73% were deemed to have need. 98% of freshmen with need received aid; of those 16% had need fully met. ***Average percent of need met:*** 53% (excluding resources awarded to replace EFC). ***Average financial aid package:*** $8141 (excluding resources awarded to replace EFC). 22% of all full-time freshmen had no need and received non-need-based gift aid.

UNDERGRADUATE FINANCIAL AID (Fall 2007) 4,863 applied for aid; of those 76% were deemed to have need. 97% of undergraduates with need received aid; of those 14% had need fully met. ***Average percent of need met:*** 51% (excluding resources awarded to replace EFC). ***Average financial aid package:*** $8094 (excluding resources awarded to replace EFC). 21% of all full-time undergraduates had no need and received non-need-based gift aid.

GIFT AID (NEED-BASED) ***Total amount:*** $6,256,111 (89% federal, 11% state). ***Receiving aid:*** Freshmen: 24% (401); all full-time undergraduates: 25% (1,605). ***Average award:*** Freshmen: $4016; Undergraduates: $3767. ***Scholarships, grants, and awards:*** Federal Pell, FSEOG, state, private, college/university gift aid from institutional funds.

GIFT AID (NON-NEED-BASED) ***Total amount:*** $10,315,621 (69% state, 15% institutional, 16% external sources). ***Receiving aid:*** Freshmen: 29% (471). Undergraduates: 17% (1,072). ***Average award:*** Freshmen: $9800. Undergraduates: $10,384. ***Scholarships, grants, and awards by category:*** *Academic interests/achievement:* 1,178 awards ($2,536,039 total): biological sciences, business, education, general academic interests/achievements, humanities, mathematics. *Creative arts/performance:* 22 awards ($19,300 total): art/fine arts, music, theater/drama. *Special achievements/activities:* 26 awards ($30,000 total): cheerleading/drum major. *Special characteristics:* 983 awards ($229,696 total): general special characteristics, international students, local/state students, out-of-state students, veterans' children. ***Tuition waivers:*** Full or partial for employees or children of employees, senior citizens.

LOANS ***Student loans:*** $34,294,490 (35% need-based, 65% non-need-based). 67% of past graduating class borrowed through all loan programs. *Average indebtedness per student:* $24,856. ***Average need-based loan:*** Freshmen: $6861. Undergraduates: $7298. ***Parent loans:*** $8,498,474 (100% non-need-based). ***Programs:*** FFEL (Subsidized and Unsubsidized Stafford, PLUS), Perkins, state.

WORK-STUDY ***Federal work-study:*** Total amount: $208,783; 148 jobs averaging $1387. ***State or other work-study/employment:*** Total amount: $1,059,763 (6% need-based, 94% non-need-based). 665 part-time jobs averaging $1593.

ATHLETIC AWARDS Total amount: $2,823,676 (100% non-need-based).

APPLYING FOR FINANCIAL AID ***Required financial aid form:*** FAFSA. ***Financial aid deadline (priority):*** 3/1. ***Notification date:*** Continuous beginning 3/1. Students must reply by 5/15.

CONTACT Dawn Hitchcock, Director of Financial Aid, Coastal Carolina University, PO Box 261954, Conway, SC 29528-6054, 843-349-2190 or toll-free 800-277-7000. *Fax:* 843-349-2347. *E-mail:* dawn@coastal.edu.

COE COLLEGE

Cedar Rapids, IA

Tuition & fees: $29,270 **Average undergraduate aid package: $23,972**

ABOUT THE INSTITUTION Independent religious, coed. ***Awards:*** bachelor's and master's degrees. 64 undergraduate majors. ***Total enrollment:*** 1,326. Undergraduates: 1,310. Freshmen: 342. Federal methodology is used as a basis for awarding need-based institutional aid.

UNDERGRADUATE EXPENSES for 2009–10 ***Application fee:*** $30. ***Comprehensive fee:*** $36,420 includes full-time tuition ($28,950), mandatory fees ($320), and room and board ($7150). ***College room only:*** $3210. ***Part-time tuition:*** $3620 per course.

FRESHMAN FINANCIAL AID (Fall 2008, est.) 292 applied for aid; of those 86% were deemed to have need. 100% of freshmen with need received aid; of those 37% had need fully met. ***Average percent of need met:*** 95% (excluding resources awarded to replace EFC). ***Average financial aid package:*** $24,455 (excluding resources awarded to replace EFC). 26% of all full-time freshmen had no need and received non-need-based gift aid.

UNDERGRADUATE FINANCIAL AID (Fall 2008, est.) 1,040 applied for aid; of those 90% were deemed to have need. 100% of undergraduates with need received aid; of those 29% had need fully met. ***Average percent of need met:***

92% (excluding resources awarded to replace EFC). ***Average financial aid package:*** $23,972 (excluding resources awarded to replace EFC). 24% of all full-time undergraduates had no need and received non-need-based gift aid.

GIFT AID (NEED-BASED) ***Total amount:*** $15,364,856 (8% federal, 11% state, 78% institutional, 3% external sources). ***Receiving aid:*** Freshmen: 73% (250); all full-time undergraduates: 73% (909). ***Average award:*** Freshmen: $18,422; Undergraduates: $16,972. ***Scholarships, grants, and awards:*** Federal Pell, FSEOG, state, private, college/university gift aid from institutional funds, ROTC.

GIFT AID (NON-NEED-BASED) ***Total amount:*** $5,713,771 (2% federal, 94% institutional, 4% external sources). ***Receiving aid:*** Freshmen: 19% (66). Undergraduates: 13% (160). ***Average award:*** Freshmen: $16,478. Undergraduates: $15,180. ***Scholarships, grants, and awards by category:*** *Academic interests/achievement:* 1,131 awards ($11,737,913 total): biological sciences, business, foreign languages, general academic interests/achievements, physical sciences, premedicine. *Creative arts/performance:* 301 awards ($646,843 total): art/fine arts, creative writing, music, performing arts, theater/drama. *Special characteristics:* 342 awards ($1,719,709 total): adult students, children and siblings of alumni, children of faculty/staff, international students, members of minority groups, siblings of current students. ***ROTC:*** Army cooperative, Air Force cooperative.

LOANS ***Student loans:*** $8,179,240 (68% need-based, 32% non-need-based). 81% of past graduating class borrowed through all loan programs. *Average indebtedness per student:* $30,385. ***Average need-based loan:*** Freshmen: $5255. Undergraduates: $6715. ***Parent loans:*** $2,535,197 (21% need-based, 79% non-need-based). ***Programs:*** Federal Direct (Subsidized and Unsubsidized Stafford, PLUS), Perkins, college/university.

WORK-STUDY ***Federal work-study:*** Total amount: $565,100; 302 jobs averaging $1400. ***State or other work-study/employment:*** Total amount: $308,600 (5% need-based, 95% non-need-based). 214 part-time jobs averaging $1400.

APPLYING FOR FINANCIAL AID ***Required financial aid form:*** FAFSA. ***Financial aid deadline (priority):*** 3/1. ***Notification date:*** Continuous beginning 3/15. Students must reply by 5/1 or within 2 weeks of notification.

CONTACT Ms. Barbara Hoffman, Director of Financial Aid, Coe College, 1220 1st Avenue, NE, Cedar Rapids, IA 52402-5070, 319-399-8540 or toll-free 877-225-5263. *Fax:* 319-399-8886.

COGSWELL POLYTECHNICAL COLLEGE

Sunnyvale, CA

ABOUT THE INSTITUTION Independent, coed, primarily men. ***Awards:*** bachelor's degrees. 7 undergraduate majors. ***Total enrollment:*** 224. Undergraduates: 224. Freshmen: 14.

GIFT AID (NEED-BASED) ***Scholarships, grants, and awards:*** Federal Pell, FSEOG, state, private, college/university gift aid from institutional funds.

GIFT AID (NON-NEED-BASED) ***Scholarships, grants, and awards by category:*** *Academic interests/achievement:* computer science, engineering/technologies.

LOANS ***Programs:*** FFEL (Subsidized and Unsubsidized Stafford, PLUS).

WORK-STUDY ***Federal work-study:*** Total amount: $25,729; 15 jobs averaging $3000.

APPLYING FOR FINANCIAL AID ***Required financial aid forms:*** FAFSA, state aid form.

CONTACT Andrew Hagedorn, Financial Aid Director, Cogswell Polytechnical College, 1175 Bordeaux Drive, Sunnyvale, CA 94089, 408-541-0100 Ext. 107 or toll-free 800-264-7955. *Fax:* 408-747-0766. *E-mail:* ahagedorn@cogswell.edu.

COKER COLLEGE

Hartsville, SC

CONTACT Betty Williams, Director of Financial Aid, Coker College, 300 East College Avenue, Hartsville, SC 29550, 843-383-8055 or toll-free 800-950-1908. *Fax:* 843-383-8056. *E-mail:* bwilliams@coker.edu.

THE COLBURN SCHOOL CONSERVATORY OF MUSIC

Los Angeles, CA

CONTACT Financial Aid Office, The Colburn School Conservatory of Music, 200 South Grand Avenue, Los Angeles, CA 90012, 213-621-2200.

COLBY COLLEGE

Waterville, ME

Comprehensive fee: $48,520 **Average undergraduate aid package: $31,627**

ABOUT THE INSTITUTION Independent, coed. ***Awards:*** bachelor's degrees. 41 undergraduate majors. ***Total enrollment:*** 1,846. Undergraduates: 1,846. Freshmen: 482. Institutional methodology is used as a basis for awarding need-based institutional aid.

UNDERGRADUATE EXPENSES for 2008–09 ***Application fee:*** $65. ***Comprehensive fee:*** $48,520.

FRESHMAN FINANCIAL AID (Fall 2008, est.) 263 applied for aid; of those 73% were deemed to have need. 100% of freshmen with need received aid; of those 100% had need fully met. ***Average percent of need met:*** 100% (excluding resources awarded to replace EFC). ***Average financial aid package:*** $31,431 (excluding resources awarded to replace EFC). 1% of all full-time freshmen had no need and received non-need-based gift aid.

UNDERGRADUATE FINANCIAL AID (Fall 2008, est.) 799 applied for aid; of those 85% were deemed to have need. 100% of undergraduates with need received aid; of those 100% had need fully met. ***Average percent of need met:*** 100% (excluding resources awarded to replace EFC). ***Average financial aid package:*** $31,627 (excluding resources awarded to replace EFC). 1% of all full-time undergraduates had no need and received non-need-based gift aid.

GIFT AID (NEED-BASED) ***Total amount:*** $20,671,028 (5% federal, 93% institutional, 2% external sources). ***Receiving aid:*** Freshmen: 39% (188); all full-time undergraduates: 36% (671). ***Average award:*** Freshmen: $30,661; Undergraduates: $30,806. ***Scholarships, grants, and awards:*** Federal Pell, FSEOG, state, private, college/university gift aid from institutional funds, Academic Competitiveness Grant, National Smart Grant, Colby National Merit Scholarships.

GIFT AID (NON-NEED-BASED) ***Average award:*** Freshmen: $12,670. Undergraduates: $22,400. ***ROTC:*** Army cooperative.

LOANS ***Student loans:*** $2,241,811 (100% non-need-based). 41% of past graduating class borrowed through all loan programs. *Average indebtedness per student:* $19,222. ***Parent loans:*** $2,402,403 (100% non-need-based). ***Programs:*** Federal Direct (Subsidized and Unsubsidized Stafford, PLUS), FFEL (Subsidized and Unsubsidized Stafford, PLUS), Perkins, state, alternative loans.

WORK-STUDY ***Federal work-study:*** Total amount: $737,039; 557 jobs averaging $1557. ***State or other work-study/employment:*** Total amount: $130,000 (100% need-based). Part-time jobs available.

APPLYING FOR FINANCIAL AID ***Required financial aid forms:*** FAFSA, CSS Financial Aid PROFILE, federal tax returns for student and parents. ***Financial aid deadline:*** 2/1. ***Notification date:*** 4/1. Students must reply by 5/1.

CONTACT Ms. Lucia Whittelsey, Director of Financial Aid, Colby College, 4850 Mayflower Hill, Waterville, ME 04901-8848, 207-859-4832 or toll-free 800-723-3032. *Fax:* 207-859-4828. *E-mail:* finaid@colby.edu.

COLBY-SAWYER COLLEGE

New London, NH

CONTACT Office of Financial Aid, Colby-Sawyer College, 541 Main Street, New London, NH 03257-7835, 603-526-3717 or toll-free 800-272-1015. *Fax:* 603-526-3452. *E-mail:* cscfinaid@colby-sawyer.edu.

COLEGIO BIBLICO PENTECOSTAL

St. Just, PR

CONTACT Mr. Eric Ayala, Director of Financial Aid, Colegio Biblico Pentecostal, PO Box 901, St. Just, PR 00978-0901, 787-761-0640.

COLEGIO PENTECOSTAL MIZPA

Río Piedras, PR

CONTACT Financial Aid Office, Colegio Pentecostal Mizpa, Bo Caimito Road 199, Apartado 20966, Río Piedras, PR 00928-0966, 787-720-4476.

COLEMAN COLLEGE

San Diego, CA

CONTACT Financial Aid Office, Coleman College, 7380 Parkway Drive, La Mesa, CA 91942, 619-465-3990. *Fax:* 619-465-0162. *E-mail:* faoffice@coleman.edu.

COLGATE UNIVERSITY

Hamilton, NY

Tuition & fees: $39,545 **Average undergraduate aid package: $35,592**

ABOUT THE INSTITUTION Independent, coed. ***Awards:*** bachelor's and master's degrees. 51 undergraduate majors. ***Total enrollment:*** 2,844. Undergraduates: 2,836. Freshmen: 738. Both federal and institutional methodology are used as a basis for awarding need-based institutional aid.

UNDERGRADUATE EXPENSES for 2008–09 ***Application fee:*** $55. ***One-time required fee:*** $50. ***Comprehensive fee:*** $49,170 includes full-time tuition ($39,275), mandatory fees ($270), and room and board ($9625). ***College room only:*** $4650. Full-time tuition and fees vary according to course load. Room and board charges vary according to board plan and housing facility. ***Part-time tuition:*** $4909 per course. Part-time tuition and fees vary according to course load. ***Payment plans:*** Tuition prepayment, installment, deferred payment.

FRESHMAN FINANCIAL AID (Fall 2008, est.) 289 applied for aid; of those 81% were deemed to have need. 100% of freshmen with need received aid; of those 100% had need fully met. ***Average percent of need met:*** 100% (excluding resources awarded to replace EFC). ***Average financial aid package:*** $36,389 (excluding resources awarded to replace EFC).

UNDERGRADUATE FINANCIAL AID (Fall 2008, est.) 1,008 applied for aid; of those 93% were deemed to have need. 100% of undergraduates with need received aid; of those 100% had need fully met. ***Average percent of need met:*** 100% (excluding resources awarded to replace EFC). ***Average financial aid package:*** $35,592 (excluding resources awarded to replace EFC).

GIFT AID (NEED-BASED) ***Total amount:*** $29,653,530 (5% federal, 2% state, 92% institutional, 1% external sources). ***Receiving aid:*** Freshmen: 32% (235); all full-time undergraduates: 33% (913). ***Average award:*** Freshmen: $32,574; Undergraduates: $31,939. ***Scholarships, grants, and awards:*** Federal Pell, FSEOG, state, college/university gift aid from institutional funds.

GIFT AID (NON-NEED-BASED) ***Tuition waivers:*** Full or partial for employees or children of employees. ***ROTC:*** Army cooperative.

LOANS ***Student loans:*** $4,764,019 (47% need-based, 53% non-need-based). 34% of past graduating class borrowed through all loan programs. *Average indebtedness per student:* $20,164. ***Average need-based loan:*** Freshmen: $1769. Undergraduates: $3958. ***Parent loans:*** $4,526,062 (100% non-need-based). ***Programs:*** FFEL (Subsidized and Unsubsidized Stafford, PLUS), Perkins.

WORK-STUDY ***Federal work-study:*** Total amount: $989,774; 446 jobs averaging $2136. ***State or other work-study/employment:*** Total amount: $448,062 (100% need-based). 261 part-time jobs averaging $1868.

ATHLETIC AWARDS Total amount: $5,916,292 (100% non-need-based).

APPLYING FOR FINANCIAL AID ***Required financial aid forms:*** CSS Financial Aid PROFILE, business/farm supplement. ***Financial aid deadline:*** 1/15. ***Notification date:*** 4/1. Students must reply by 5/1 or within 2 weeks of notification.

CONTACT Financial Aid Office, Colgate University, 13 Oak Drive, Hamilton, NY 13346, 315-228-7431. *Fax:* 315-228-7050. *E-mail:* financialaid@colgate.edu.

THE COLLEGE AT BROCKPORT, STATE UNIVERSITY OF NEW YORK

Brockport, NY

Tuition & fees (NY res): $5444 **Average undergraduate aid package: $9139**

ABOUT THE INSTITUTION State-supported, coed. ***Awards:*** bachelor's and master's degrees and post-bachelor's and post-master's certificates. 107 undergraduate majors. ***Total enrollment:*** 8,275. Undergraduates: 6,970. Freshmen: 994. Federal methodology is used as a basis for awarding need-based institutional aid.

UNDERGRADUATE EXPENSES for 2008–09 ***Application fee:*** $40. ***Tuition, state resident:*** full-time $4350; part-time $181 per credit. ***Tuition, nonresident:*** full-time $10,610; part-time $442 per credit. ***Required fees:*** full-time $1094. Part-time tuition and fees vary according to course load. ***College room and board:*** $8615; ***Room only:*** $5700. Room and board charges vary according to board plan and housing facility. ***Payment plans:*** Installment, deferred payment.

FRESHMAN FINANCIAL AID (Fall 2008, est.) 847 applied for aid; of those 70% were deemed to have need. 100% of freshmen with need received aid; of those 20% had need fully met. ***Average percent of need met:*** 77% (excluding resources awarded to replace EFC). ***Average financial aid package:*** $9355 (excluding resources awarded to replace EFC). 9% of all full-time freshmen had no need and received non-need-based gift aid.

UNDERGRADUATE FINANCIAL AID (Fall 2008, est.) 4,576 applied for aid; of those 77% were deemed to have need. 100% of undergraduates with need received aid; of those 20% had need fully met. ***Average percent of need met:*** 75% (excluding resources awarded to replace EFC). ***Average financial aid package:*** $9139 (excluding resources awarded to replace EFC). 3% of all full-time undergraduates had no need and received non-need-based gift aid.

GIFT AID (NEED-BASED) ***Total amount:*** $15,398,152 (53% federal, 47% state). ***Receiving aid:*** Freshmen: 57% (534); all full-time undergraduates: 58% (3,063). ***Average award:*** Freshmen: $4701; Undergraduates: $4321. ***Scholarships, grants, and awards:*** Federal Pell, FSEOG, state, private, college/university gift aid from institutional funds.

GIFT AID (NON-NEED-BASED) ***Total amount:*** $5,370,481 (15% federal, 7% state, 69% institutional, 9% external sources). ***Receiving aid:*** Freshmen: 21% (198). Undergraduates: 12% (661). ***Average award:*** Freshmen: $3765. Undergraduates: $4686. ***Scholarships, grants, and awards by category:*** *Academic interests/achievement:* 425 awards ($1,100,000 total): biological sciences, business, communication, computer science, education, English, foreign languages, general academic interests/achievements, health fields, humanities, international studies, mathematics, military science, physical sciences, premedicine, social sciences. *Creative arts/performance:* 50 awards ($80,000 total): art/fine arts, cinema/film/broadcasting, creative writing, dance, general creative arts/performance, journalism/publications, music, performing arts, theater/drama. *Special achievements/activities:* 25 awards ($25,000 total): community service, general special achievements/activities, hobbies/interests, leadership, religious involvement. *Special characteristics:* 45 awards ($43,000 total): children and siblings of alumni, ethnic background, first-generation college students, general special characteristics, international students, local/state students, married students, members of minority groups, out-of-state students, previous college experience, religious affiliation, veterans. ***Tuition waivers:*** Full or partial for employees or children of employees, senior citizens. ***ROTC:*** Army, Naval cooperative, Air Force cooperative.

LOANS ***Student loans:*** $38,089,765 (44% need-based, 56% non-need-based). 82% of past graduating class borrowed through all loan programs. *Average indebtedness per student:* $24,808. ***Average need-based loan:*** Freshmen: $3797. Undergraduates: $4581. ***Parent loans:*** $2,827,364 (100% non-need-based). ***Programs:*** Federal Direct (Subsidized and Unsubsidized Stafford, PLUS), Perkins, Federal Nursing, alternative loans.

WORK-STUDY ***Federal work-study:*** Total amount: $1,061,923; 610 jobs averaging $1266. ***State or other work-study/employment:*** Total amount: $2,052,291 (100% non-need-based). 1,648 part-time jobs averaging $1245.

APPLYING FOR FINANCIAL AID ***Required financial aid forms:*** FAFSA, state aid form. ***Financial aid deadline (priority):*** 2/15. ***Notification date:*** Continuous beginning 3/15. Students must reply by 5/1.

CONTACT Mr. J. Scott Atkinson, Interim Assistant Vice President for Enrollment Management and Student Affairs, The College at Brockport, State University of New York, 350 New Campus Drive, Brockport, NY 14420-2937, 585-395-2501. *Fax:* 585-395-5445. *E-mail:* satkinso@brockport.edu.

COLLEGE FOR CREATIVE STUDIES

Detroit, MI

Tuition & fees: $29,985 **Average undergraduate aid package: N/A**

ABOUT THE INSTITUTION Independent, coed. ***Awards:*** bachelor's and master's degrees and post-bachelor's certificates. 10 undergraduate majors. ***Total enrollment:*** 1,369. Undergraduates: 1,365. Freshmen: 241. Federal methodology is used as a basis for awarding need-based institutional aid.

UNDERGRADUATE EXPENSES for 2009–10 ***Application fee:*** $35. ***Comprehensive fee:*** $38,485 includes full-time tuition ($28,650), mandatory fees ($1335), and room and board ($8500). ***College room only:*** $4900. ***Part-time tuition:*** $955 per credit hour.

GIFT AID (NEED-BASED) ***Total amount:*** $4,011,448 (32% federal, 29% state, 38% institutional, 1% external sources). ***Scholarships, grants, and awards:*** Federal Pell, FSEOG, state, private, college/university gift aid from institutional funds.

GIFT AID (NON-NEED-BASED) ***Total amount:*** $5,664,377 (4% state, 92% institutional, 4% external sources). ***Scholarships, grants, and awards by category:*** *Creative arts/performance:* applied art and design, art/fine arts.

LOANS ***Student loans:*** $11,638,509 (30% need-based, 70% non-need-based). 87% of past graduating class borrowed through all loan programs. *Average indebtedness per student:* $45,913. ***Parent loans:*** $2,016,735 (100% non-need-based). ***Programs:*** FFEL (Subsidized and Unsubsidized Stafford, PLUS), private/alternative loans.

WORK-STUDY ***Federal work-study:*** Total amount: $102,110; jobs available. ***State or other work-study/employment:*** Total amount: $161,530 (16% need-based, 84% non-need-based). Part-time jobs available.

APPLYING FOR FINANCIAL AID ***Required financial aid form:*** FAFSA. ***Financial aid deadline (priority):*** 7/1. ***Notification date:*** Continuous beginning 3/15. Students must reply within 3 weeks of notification.

CONTACT Financial Aid Office, College for Creative Studies, 201 East Kirby, Detroit, MI 48202-4034, 313-664-7495 or toll-free 800-872-2739. *Fax:* 313-872-1521. *E-mail:* finaid@collegeforcreativestudies.edu.

COLLEGE OF BIBLICAL STUDIES–HOUSTON

Houston, TX

CONTACT Financial Aid Office, College of Biblical Studies–Houston, 6000 Dale Carnegie Drive, Houston, TX 77036, 713-785-5995.

COLLEGE OF CHARLESTON

Charleston, SC

Tuition & fees (SC res): $8400 **Average undergraduate aid package: $12,697**

ABOUT THE INSTITUTION State-supported, coed. ***Awards:*** bachelor's and master's degrees and post-bachelor's certificates (also offers graduate degree programs through University of Charleston, South Carolina). 45 undergraduate majors. ***Total enrollment:*** 11,367. Undergraduates: 9,784. Freshmen: 1,956. Federal methodology is used as a basis for awarding need-based institutional aid.

UNDERGRADUATE EXPENSES for 2008–09 ***Application fee:*** $50. ***Tuition, state resident:*** full-time $8400; part-time $350 per semester hour. ***Tuition, nonresident:*** full-time $20,418; part-time $851 per semester hour. Full-time tuition and fees vary according to degree level. Part-time tuition and fees vary according to course load and degree level. ***College room and board:*** $8999; ***Room only:*** $6179. Room and board charges vary according to board plan and housing facility. ***Payment plan:*** Installment.

FRESHMAN FINANCIAL AID (Fall 2008, est.) 1,192 applied for aid; of those 64% were deemed to have need. 96% of freshmen with need received aid; of those 37% had need fully met. ***Average percent of need met:*** 66% (excluding resources awarded to replace EFC). ***Average financial aid package:*** $11,707 (excluding resources awarded to replace EFC). 11% of all full-time freshmen had no need and received non-need-based gift aid.

UNDERGRADUATE FINANCIAL AID (Fall 2008, est.) 4,786 applied for aid; of those 73% were deemed to have need. 96% of undergraduates with need received aid; of those 34% had need fully met. ***Average percent of need met:*** 66% (excluding resources awarded to replace EFC). ***Average financial aid package:*** $12,697 (excluding resources awarded to replace EFC). 12% of all full-time undergraduates had no need and received non-need-based gift aid.

GIFT AID (NEED-BASED) ***Total amount:*** $15,724,005 (35% federal, 39% state, 20% institutional, 6% external sources). ***Receiving aid:*** Freshmen: 27% (523); all full-time undergraduates: 24% (2,156). ***Average award:*** Freshmen: $3052; Undergraduates: $2946. ***Scholarships, grants, and awards:*** Federal Pell, FSEOG, state, private, college/university gift aid from institutional funds.

GIFT AID (NON-NEED-BASED) ***Total amount:*** $18,711,643 (59% state, 33% institutional, 8% external sources). ***Receiving aid:*** Freshmen: 30% (580). Undergraduates: 17% (1,535). ***Average award:*** Freshmen: $11,279. Undergraduates: $10,811. ***Scholarships, grants, and awards by category:*** *Academic interests/achievement:* biological sciences, business, communication, computer science, education, engineering/technologies, English, foreign languages, general academic interests/achievements, health fields, humanities, mathematics, physical sciences, premedicine, social sciences. *Creative arts/performance:* art/fine arts, music, performing arts, theater/drama. *Special characteristics:* general special characteristics. ***Tuition waivers:*** Full or partial for senior citizens. ***ROTC:*** Air Force cooperative.

LOANS ***Student loans:*** $30,328,517 (57% need-based, 43% non-need-based). 44% of past graduating class borrowed through all loan programs. *Average indebtedness per student:* $17,139. ***Average need-based loan:*** Freshmen: $3336. Undergraduates: $4123. ***Parent loans:*** $17,830,629 (48% need-based, 52% non-need-based). ***Programs:*** Federal Direct (Subsidized and Unsubsidized Stafford, PLUS), Perkins.

WORK-STUDY ***Federal work-study:*** Total amount: $527,452; jobs available. ***State or other work-study/employment:*** Total amount: $43,198 (10% need-based, 90% non-need-based). Part-time jobs available.

ATHLETIC AWARDS Total amount: $2,812,772 (26% need-based, 74% non-need-based).

APPLYING FOR FINANCIAL AID ***Required financial aid form:*** FAFSA. ***Financial aid deadline (priority):*** 4/15. ***Notification date:*** Continuous. Students must reply within 8 weeks of notification.

CONTACT Mr. Don Griggs, Financial Aid Director, College of Charleston, 66 George Street, Charleston, SC 29424, 843-953-5540 or toll-free 843-953-5670 (in-state). *Fax:* 843-953-7192.

THE COLLEGE OF IDAHO

Caldwell, ID

Tuition & fees: $20,070 **Average undergraduate aid package: $16,324**

ABOUT THE INSTITUTION Independent, coed. ***Awards:*** bachelor's and master's degrees. 26 undergraduate majors. ***Total enrollment:*** 944. Undergraduates: 928. Freshmen: 272. Federal methodology is used as a basis for awarding need-based institutional aid.

UNDERGRADUATE EXPENSES for 2009–10 ***Comprehensive fee:*** $27,548 includes full-time tuition ($19,300), mandatory fees ($770), and room and board ($7478). ***College room only:*** $3450. ***Part-time tuition:*** $810 per semester hour.

FRESHMAN FINANCIAL AID (Fall 2008, est.) 179 applied for aid; of those 100% were deemed to have need. 100% of freshmen with need received aid; of those 20% had need fully met. ***Average percent of need met:*** 88% (excluding resources awarded to replace EFC). ***Average financial aid package:*** $17,364 (excluding resources awarded to replace EFC). 34% of all full-time freshmen had no need and received non-need-based gift aid.

UNDERGRADUATE FINANCIAL AID (Fall 2008, est.) 544 applied for aid; of those 100% were deemed to have need. 99% of undergraduates with need received aid; of those 21% had need fully met. ***Average percent of need met:*** 88% (excluding resources awarded to replace EFC). ***Average financial aid package:*** $16,324 (excluding resources awarded to replace EFC). 36% of all full-time undergraduates had no need and received non-need-based gift aid.

GIFT AID (NEED-BASED) ***Total amount:*** $2,569,031 (41% federal, 41% institutional, 18% external sources). ***Receiving aid:*** Freshmen: 45% (123); all full-time undergraduates: 39% (350). ***Average award:*** Freshmen: $4888; Undergraduates: $5178. ***Scholarships, grants, and awards:*** Federal Pell, FSEOG, state, private, college/university gift aid from institutional funds.

GIFT AID (NON-NEED-BASED) ***Total amount:*** $7,662,588 (3% state, 97% institutional). ***Receiving aid:*** Freshmen: 66% (179). Undergraduates: 59% (522). ***Average award:*** Freshmen: $13,521. Undergraduates: $11,583. ***Scholarships, grants, and awards by category:*** *Academic interests/achievement:* 61 awards ($82,503 total): biological sciences, business, education, English, foreign languages, humanities, mathematics, physical sciences, premedicine, religion/biblical studies, social sciences. *Creative arts/performance:* 162 awards ($304,840 total): art/fine arts, debating, music, performing arts, theater/drama. *Special achievements/activities:* 4 awards ($15,910 total): leadership. *Special characteristics:* 142 awards ($834,915 total): children and siblings of alumni, children of educators, children of faculty/staff, first-generation college students, international students, members of minority groups. ***ROTC:*** Army cooperative.

LOANS ***Student loans:*** $3,747,865 (43% need-based, 57% non-need-based). 76% of past graduating class borrowed through all loan programs. *Average indebtedness per student:* $24,919. ***Average need-based loan:*** Freshmen: $3729. Undergraduates: $4415. ***Parent loans:*** $437,468 (100% non-need-based). ***Programs:*** FFEL (Subsidized and Unsubsidized Stafford, PLUS), Perkins, alternative private loans.

WORK-STUDY ***Federal work-study:*** Total amount: $145,010; 19 jobs averaging $830. ***State or other work-study/employment:*** Total amount: $42,830 (84% need-based, 16% non-need-based). 24 part-time jobs averaging $908.

ATHLETIC AWARDS Total amount: $1,282,381 (100% non-need-based).

APPLYING FOR FINANCIAL AID ***Required financial aid forms:*** FAFSA, institution's own form. ***Financial aid deadline (priority):*** 2/15. ***Notification date:*** Continuous. Students must reply within 3 weeks of notification.

CONTACT Merna Davis, Data Coordinator, The College of Idaho, 2112 Cleveland Boulevard, Caldwell, ID 83605-4432, 208-459-5380 or toll-free 800-244-3246. *Fax:* 208-459-5844. *E-mail:* mdavis@collegeofidaho.edu.

COLLEGE OF MOUNT ST. JOSEPH

Cincinnati, OH

Tuition & fees: $22,000 **Average undergraduate aid package: $15,984**

ABOUT THE INSTITUTION Independent Roman Catholic, coed. ***Awards:*** associate, bachelor's, master's, and doctoral degrees and post-bachelor's certificates. 33 undergraduate majors. ***Total enrollment:*** 2,133. Undergraduates: 1,831. Freshmen: 308. Federal methodology is used as a basis for awarding need-based institutional aid.

UNDERGRADUATE EXPENSES for 2008–09 ***Application fee:*** $25. ***One-time required fee:*** $150. ***Comprehensive fee:*** $28,900 includes full-time tuition ($21,200), mandatory fees ($800), and room and board ($6900). ***College room only:*** $3400. ***Part-time tuition:*** $465 per semester hour. ***Part-time fees:*** $200 per term.

FRESHMAN FINANCIAL AID (Fall 2008, est.) 282 applied for aid; of those 88% were deemed to have need. 100% of freshmen with need received aid; of those 16% had need fully met. ***Average percent of need met:*** 84% (excluding resources awarded to replace EFC). ***Average financial aid package:*** $18,084 (excluding resources awarded to replace EFC). 17% of all full-time freshmen had no need and received non-need-based gift aid.

UNDERGRADUATE FINANCIAL AID (Fall 2008, est.) 1,146 applied for aid; of those 88% were deemed to have need. 100% of undergraduates with need received aid; of those 21% had need fully met. ***Average percent of need met:*** 78% (excluding resources awarded to replace EFC). ***Average financial aid package:*** $15,984 (excluding resources awarded to replace EFC). 21% of all full-time undergraduates had no need and received non-need-based gift aid.

GIFT AID (NEED-BASED) ***Total amount:*** $12,493,452 (15% federal, 12% state, 71% institutional, 2% external sources). ***Receiving aid:*** Freshmen: 82% (247); all full-time undergraduates: 76% (1,005). ***Average award:*** Freshmen: $13,901; Undergraduates: $11,753. ***Scholarships, grants, and awards:*** Federal Pell, FSEOG, state, private, college/university gift aid from institutional funds.

GIFT AID (NON-NEED-BASED) ***Total amount:*** $1,669,124 (5% federal, 10% state, 83% institutional, 2% external sources). ***Receiving aid:*** Freshmen: 9% (26). Undergraduates: 9% (118). ***Average award:*** Freshmen: $6020. Undergraduates: $5888. ***Scholarships, grants, and awards by category:*** *Academic interests/achievement:* 744 awards ($4,999,834 total): general academic interests/achievements. *Creative arts/performance:* 50 awards ($119,230 total): art/fine arts, music. *Special achievements/activities:* 22 awards ($47,557 total): community service, leadership. *Special characteristics:* 32 awards ($567,319 total): adult students, children and siblings of alumni, children of faculty/staff. ***ROTC:*** Army cooperative, Air Force cooperative.

LOANS ***Student loans:*** $12,584,160 (89% need-based, 11% non-need-based). 81% of past graduating class borrowed through all loan programs. *Average indebtedness per student:* $29,438. ***Average need-based loan:*** Freshmen: $3908. Undergraduates: $4472. ***Parent loans:*** $1,666,515 (84% need-based, 16% non-need-based). ***Programs:*** FFEL (Subsidized and Unsubsidized Stafford, PLUS), Perkins, Federal Nursing, state.

WORK-STUDY ***Federal work-study:*** Total amount: $246,395; 168 jobs averaging $1467. ***State or other work-study/employment:*** Total amount: $182,650 (94% need-based, 6% non-need-based). 129 part-time jobs averaging $1416.

APPLYING FOR FINANCIAL AID ***Required financial aid form:*** FAFSA. ***Financial aid deadline (priority):*** 3/1. ***Notification date:*** Continuous. Students must reply by 5/1 or within 4 weeks of notification.

CONTACT Ms. Kathryn Kelly, Director of Student Administrative Services, College of Mount St. Joseph, 5701 Delhi Road, Cincinnati, OH 45233-1670, 513-244-4418 or toll-free 800-654-9314. *Fax:* 513-244-4201. *E-mail:* kathy_kelly@mail.msj.edu.

COLLEGE OF MOUNT SAINT VINCENT

Riverdale, NY

CONTACT Ms. Monica Simotas, Director of Financial Aid, College of Mount Saint Vincent, 6301 Riverdale Avenue, Riverdale, NY 10471, 718-405-3290 or toll-free 800-665-CMSV. *Fax:* 718-405-3490. *E-mail:* msimotas@mountsaintvincent.edu.

THE COLLEGE OF NEW JERSEY

Ewing, NJ

Tuition & fees (NJ res): $12,308 **Average undergraduate aid package: $10,115**

ABOUT THE INSTITUTION State-supported, coed. ***Awards:*** bachelor's and master's degrees and post-bachelor's and post-master's certificates. 54 undergraduate majors. ***Total enrollment:*** 6,949. Undergraduates: 6,244. Freshmen: 1,295. Federal methodology is used as a basis for awarding need-based institutional aid.

UNDERGRADUATE EXPENSES for 2008–09 ***Application fee:*** $70. ***Tuition, state resident:*** full-time $8718; part-time $309 per credit. ***Tuition, nonresident:*** full-time $16,825; part-time $595.50 per credit. ***Required fees:*** full-time $3590; $143.50 per credit. Part-time tuition and fees vary according to course load. ***College room and board:*** $9612; ***Room only:*** $6960. Room and board charges vary according to board plan. ***Payment plan:*** Installment.

FRESHMAN FINANCIAL AID (Fall 2008, est.) 1,124 applied for aid; of those 56% were deemed to have need. 94% of freshmen with need received aid; of those 23% had need fully met. ***Average percent of need met:*** 47% (excluding resources awarded to replace EFC). ***Average financial aid package:*** $9900 (excluding resources awarded to replace EFC). 21% of all full-time freshmen had no need and received non-need-based gift aid.

UNDERGRADUATE FINANCIAL AID (Fall 2008, est.) 4,205 applied for aid; of those 66% were deemed to have need. 94% of undergraduates with need received aid; of those 17% had need fully met. ***Average percent of need met:*** 52% (excluding resources awarded to replace EFC). ***Average financial aid package:*** $10,115 (excluding resources awarded to replace EFC). 18% of all full-time undergraduates had no need and received non-need-based gift aid.

GIFT AID (NEED-BASED) ***Total amount:*** $17,691,161 (18% federal, 39% state, 34% institutional, 9% external sources). ***Receiving aid:*** Freshmen: 16% (205); all full-time undergraduates: 16% (965). ***Average award:*** Freshmen: $14,125; Undergraduates: $10,942. ***Scholarships, grants, and awards:*** Federal Pell, FSEOG, state, private, college/university gift aid from institutional funds.

GIFT AID (NON-NEED-BASED) ***Total amount:*** $8,347,018 (1% federal, 16% state, 71% institutional, 12% external sources). ***Receiving aid:*** Freshmen: 21% (269). Undergraduates: 16% (985). ***Average award:*** Freshmen: $6111. Undergraduates: $5499. ***Scholarships, grants, and awards by category:*** *Academic interests/achievement:* engineering/technologies, general academic interests/achievements, physical sciences. *Creative arts/performance:* art/fine arts, music. *Special characteristics:* children with a deceased or disabled parent, members of minority groups. ***Tuition waivers:*** Full or partial for employees or children of employees, senior citizens. ***ROTC:*** Army cooperative, Air Force cooperative.

LOANS ***Student loans:*** $32,243,458 (71% need-based, 29% non-need-based). 58% of past graduating class borrowed through all loan programs. *Average indebtedness per student:* $22,088. ***Average need-based loan:*** Freshmen: $3285. Undergraduates: $4378. ***Parent loans:*** $4,365,189 (65% need-based, 35% non-need-based). ***Programs:*** FFEL (Subsidized and Unsubsidized Stafford, PLUS), Perkins, Federal Nursing.

WORK-STUDY ***Federal work-study:*** Total amount: $193,970; 170 jobs averaging $1320.

APPLYING FOR FINANCIAL AID ***Required financial aid form:*** FAFSA. ***Financial aid deadline:*** 10/1 (priority: 3/1). ***Notification date:*** Continuous beginning 6/1.

CONTACT Jamie Hightower, Director of Student Financial Services, The College of New Jersey, PO Box 7718, Ewing, NJ 08628, 609-771-2211 or toll-free 800-624-0967. *Fax:* 609-637-5154. *E-mail:* hightowe@tcnj.edu.

THE COLLEGE OF NEW ROCHELLE

New Rochelle, NY

Tuition & fees: $26,426 **Average undergraduate aid package: $20,308**

ABOUT THE INSTITUTION Independent, coed, primarily women. ***Awards:*** bachelor's and master's degrees and post-bachelor's and post-master's certificates (also offers a non-traditional adult program with significant enrollment not reflected in profile). 36 undergraduate majors. ***Total enrollment:*** 1,890. Undergraduates: 884. Freshmen: 139. Federal methodology is used as a basis for awarding need-based institutional aid.

UNDERGRADUATE EXPENSES for 2009–10 ***Application fee:*** $20. ***Comprehensive fee:*** $36,026 includes full-time tuition ($25,576), mandatory fees ($850), and room and board ($9600). ***Part-time tuition:*** $861 per credit. ***Part-time fees:*** $225 per term.

FRESHMAN FINANCIAL AID (Fall 2007) 91 applied for aid; of those 98% were deemed to have need. 100% of freshmen with need received aid; of those 7% had need fully met. ***Average percent of need met:*** 85% (excluding resources awarded to replace EFC). ***Average financial aid package:*** $24,073 (excluding resources awarded to replace EFC). 2% of all full-time freshmen had no need and received non-need-based gift aid.

UNDERGRADUATE FINANCIAL AID (Fall 2007) 587 applied for aid; of those 94% were deemed to have need. 100% of undergraduates with need received aid; of those 5% had need fully met. ***Average percent of need met:*** 71% (excluding resources awarded to replace EFC). ***Average financial aid package:*** $20,308 (excluding resources awarded to replace EFC). 6% of all full-time undergraduates had no need and received non-need-based gift aid.

GIFT AID (NEED-BASED) ***Total amount:*** $9,220,051 (17% federal, 13% state, 70% institutional). ***Receiving aid:*** Freshmen: 88% (83); all full-time undergraduates: 82% (508). ***Average award:*** Freshmen: $15,903; Undergraduates: $11,171. ***Scholarships, grants, and awards:*** Federal Pell, FSEOG, state, private, college/university gift aid from institutional funds.

GIFT AID (NON-NEED-BASED) ***Total amount:*** $587,289 (1% state, 98% institutional, 1% external sources). ***Receiving aid:*** Freshmen: 54% (51). Undergraduates: 57% (351). ***Average award:*** Freshmen: $14,000. Undergraduates: $12,255. ***Scholarships, grants, and awards by category:*** *Academic interests/achievement:* 300 awards ($3,225,000 total): area/ethnic studies, biological sciences, business, communication, education, English, foreign languages, general academic interests/achievements, health fields, humanities, mathematics, physical sciences, premedicine, religion/biblical studies, social sciences. *Creative arts/performance:* 69 awards ($427,500 total): applied art and design, art/fine arts, cinema/film/broadcasting, creative writing, dance, debating, general creative arts/performance, journalism/publications, music, performing arts, theater/drama. *Special achievements/activities:* 143 awards ($1,332,000 total): community service, general special achievements/activities, hobbies/interests, junior miss, leadership, memberships, religious involvement. *Special characteristics:* 85 awards ($396,803 total): children of current students, children of faculty/staff, general special characteristics, out-of-state students, parents of current students, previous college experience, siblings of current students, spouses of current students.

LOANS ***Student loans:*** $6,186,801 (53% need-based, 47% non-need-based). 85% of past graduating class borrowed through all loan programs. *Average indebtedness per student:* $25,055. ***Average need-based loan:*** Freshmen: $4258. Undergraduates: $5764. ***Parent loans:*** $432,359 (73% need-based, 27% non-need-based). ***Programs:*** Federal Direct (Subsidized and Unsubsidized Stafford, PLUS), FFEL (PLUS), Perkins, Federal Nursing.

WORK-STUDY ***Federal work-study:*** Total amount: $1,216,177; 460 jobs averaging $2644. ***State or other work-study/employment:*** Part-time jobs available.

APPLYING FOR FINANCIAL AID ***Required financial aid forms:*** FAFSA, institution's own form, federal income tax form(s). ***Financial aid deadline:*** Continuous. ***Notification date:*** Continuous beginning 1/1. Students must reply within 2 weeks of notification.

CONTACT Anne Pelak, Director of Financial Aid, The College of New Rochelle, 29 Castle Place, New Rochelle, NY 10805-2339, 914-654-5225 or toll-free 800-933-5923. *Fax:* 914-654-5420. *E-mail:* apelak@cnr.edu.

COLLEGE OF NOTRE DAME OF MARYLAND

Baltimore, MD

Tuition & fees: $27,250 **Average undergraduate aid package: $19,573**

ABOUT THE INSTITUTION Independent Roman Catholic, undergraduate: women only; graduate: coed. ***Awards:*** bachelor's, master's, and doctoral degrees and post-bachelor's certificates (offers coed undergraduate program for adult students). 38 undergraduate majors. ***Total enrollment:*** 2,935. Undergraduates: 1,338. Freshmen: 105. Federal methodology is used as a basis for awarding need-based institutional aid.

UNDERGRADUATE EXPENSES for 2009–10 ***Application fee:*** $45. ***Comprehensive fee:*** $36,350 includes full-time tuition ($26,500), mandatory fees ($750), and room and board ($9100). ***Part-time tuition:*** $410 per credit hour.

FRESHMAN FINANCIAL AID (Fall 2008, est.) 102 applied for aid; of those 90% were deemed to have need. 100% of freshmen with need received aid; of those 25% had need fully met. ***Average percent of need met:*** 79% (excluding resources awarded to replace EFC). ***Average financial aid package:*** $20,477 (excluding resources awarded to replace EFC). 10% of all full-time freshmen had no need and received non-need-based gift aid.

UNDERGRADUATE FINANCIAL AID (Fall 2008, est.) 438 applied for aid; of those 90% were deemed to have need. 100% of undergraduates with need received aid; of those 19% had need fully met. ***Average percent of need met:*** 70% (excluding resources awarded to replace EFC). ***Average financial aid package:*** $19,573 (excluding resources awarded to replace EFC). 15% of all full-time undergraduates had no need and received non-need-based gift aid.

GIFT AID (NEED-BASED) ***Total amount:*** $6,123,601 (17% federal, 14% state, 68% institutional, 1% external sources). ***Receiving aid:*** Freshmen: 88% (92); all full-time undergraduates: 77% (389). ***Average award:*** Freshmen: $16,427; Undergraduates: $15,252. ***Scholarships, grants, and awards:*** Federal Pell, FSEOG, state, private, college/university gift aid from institutional funds, Academic Competitiveness Grant, National Smart Grant, TEACH Grant.

GIFT AID (NON-NEED-BASED) ***Total amount:*** $1,334,715 (3% state, 95% institutional, 2% external sources). ***Receiving aid:*** Freshmen: 20% (21). Undergraduates: 12% (59). ***Average award:*** Freshmen: $12,773. Undergraduates: $10,688. ***Scholarships, grants, and awards by category:*** *Academic interests/achievement:* 138 awards ($1,628,154 total): general academic interests/achievements. *Creative arts/performance:* 48 awards ($216,125 total): art/fine arts, general creative arts/performance. *Special achievements/activities:* 224 awards ($1,407,250 total): community service, general special achievements/activities, leadership, memberships, religious involvement. *Special characteristics:* 3 awards ($21,617 total): international students. ***ROTC:*** Army cooperative.

LOANS ***Student loans:*** $5,950,635 (75% need-based, 25% non-need-based). 79% of past graduating class borrowed through all loan programs. *Average indebtedness per student:* $30,552. ***Average need-based loan:*** Freshmen: $3616. Undergraduates: $4456. ***Parent loans:*** $1,030,009 (58% need-based, 42% non-need-based). ***Programs:*** FFEL (Subsidized and Unsubsidized Stafford, PLUS), Perkins.

WORK-STUDY ***Federal work-study:*** Total amount: $85,440; 91 jobs averaging $939.

APPLYING FOR FINANCIAL AID ***Required financial aid form:*** FAFSA. ***Financial aid deadline (priority):*** 2/15. ***Notification date:*** Continuous beginning 3/1. Students must reply by 5/1.

CONTACT Zhanna Goltser, Director of Financial Aid, College of Notre Dame of Maryland, 4701 North Charles Street, Baltimore, MD 21210-2404, 410-532-5369 or toll-free 800-435-0200 (in-state), 800-435-0300 (out-of-state). *Fax:* 410-532-6287. *E-mail:* finaid@ndm.edu.

COLLEGE OF SAINT BENEDICT

Saint Joseph, MN

Tuition & fees: $28,668 **Average undergraduate aid package: $21,156**

ABOUT THE INSTITUTION Independent Roman Catholic, coed, primarily women. ***Awards:*** bachelor's degrees (coordinate with Saint John's University for men). 55 undergraduate majors. ***Total enrollment:*** 2,110. Undergraduates: 2,110. Freshmen: 519. Federal methodology is used as a basis for awarding need-based institutional aid.

UNDERGRADUATE EXPENSES for 2008–09 ***One-time required fee:*** $40. ***Comprehensive fee:*** $36,627 includes full-time tuition ($28,122), mandatory fees ($546), and room and board ($7959). ***College room only:*** $3832. Full-time tuition and fees vary according to student level. Room and board charges vary according to board plan and housing facility. ***Part-time tuition:*** $1171 per credit hour. Part-time tuition and fees vary according to course load. ***Payment plans:*** Tuition prepayment, installment.

FRESHMAN FINANCIAL AID (Fall 2008, est.) 419 applied for aid; of those 81% were deemed to have need. 100% of freshmen with need received aid; of those 49% had need fully met. ***Average percent of need met:*** 93% (excluding

resources awarded to replace EFC). ***Average financial aid package:*** $22,406 (excluding resources awarded to replace EFC). 31% of all full-time freshmen had no need and received non-need-based gift aid.

UNDERGRADUATE FINANCIAL AID (Fall 2008, est.) 1,540 applied for aid; of those 87% were deemed to have need. 100% of undergraduates with need received aid; of those 39% had need fully met. ***Average percent of need met:*** 88% (excluding resources awarded to replace EFC). ***Average financial aid package:*** $21,156 (excluding resources awarded to replace EFC). 32% of all full-time undergraduates had no need and received non-need-based gift aid.

GIFT AID (NEED-BASED) ***Total amount:*** $21,446,456 (8% federal, 10% state, 78% institutional, 4% external sources). ***Receiving aid:*** Freshmen: 65% (336); all full-time undergraduates: 64% (1,315). ***Average award:*** Freshmen: $17,550; Undergraduates: $15,655. ***Scholarships, grants, and awards:*** Federal Pell, FSEOG, state, private, college/university gift aid from institutional funds.

GIFT AID (NON-NEED-BASED) ***Total amount:*** $8,466,752 (93% institutional, 7% external sources). ***Receiving aid:*** Freshmen: 61% (318). Undergraduates: 61% (1,254). ***Average award:*** Freshmen: $10,685. Undergraduates: $10,158. ***Scholarships, grants, and awards by category:*** *Academic interests/achievement:* general academic interests/achievements, military science. *Creative arts/performance:* art/fine arts, music, theater/drama. *Special achievements/activities:* junior miss. *Special characteristics:* ethnic background, international students. ***Tuition waivers:*** Full or partial for employees or children of employees. ***ROTC:*** Army cooperative.

LOANS ***Student loans:*** $14,091,358 (89% need-based, 11% non-need-based). ***Average need-based loan:*** Freshmen: $4540. Undergraduates: $5259. ***Parent loans:*** $1,424,827 (76% need-based, 24% non-need-based). ***Programs:*** Federal Direct (Subsidized and Unsubsidized Stafford, PLUS), Perkins, state, private alternative loans.

WORK-STUDY ***Federal work-study:*** Total amount: $1,219,675; 600 jobs averaging $2000. ***State or other work-study/employment:*** Total amount: $1,916,130 (66% need-based, 34% non-need-based). 300 part-time jobs averaging $2000.

APPLYING FOR FINANCIAL AID ***Required financial aid forms:*** FAFSA, institution's own form. ***Financial aid deadline (priority):*** 3/15. ***Notification date:*** Continuous. Students must reply by 5/1.

CONTACT Ms. Jane Haugen, Executive Director of Financial Aid, College of Saint Benedict, 37 South College Avenue, Saint Joseph, MN 56374-2099, 320-363-5388 or toll-free 800-544-1489. *Fax:* 320-363-6099. *E-mail:* jhaugen@csbsju.edu.

COLLEGE OF ST. CATHERINE–MINNEAPOLIS

Minneapolis, MN

CONTACT Mr. Cal Mosley, Associate Dean/Director of Financial Aid, College of St. Catherine–Minneapolis, 601 25th Avenue South, Minneapolis, MN 55454, 651-690-8600 or toll-free 800-945-4599 Ext. 7800. *Fax:* 651-690-8119. *E-mail:* pajohnson@stkate.edu.

COLLEGE OF SAINT ELIZABETH

Morristown, NJ

CONTACT Vincent Tunstall, Director of Financial Aid, College of Saint Elizabeth, 2 Convent Road, Morristown, NJ 07960-6989, 973-290-4492 or toll-free 800-210-7900. *E-mail:* vtunstall@cse.edu.

COLLEGE OF ST. JOSEPH

Rutland, VT

Tuition & fees: $17,550 **Average undergraduate aid package: $14,452**

ABOUT THE INSTITUTION Independent Roman Catholic, coed. ***Awards:*** associate, bachelor's, and master's degrees and post-bachelor's certificates. 14 undergraduate majors. ***Total enrollment:*** 428. Undergraduates: 250. Freshmen: 46. Federal methodology is used as a basis for awarding need-based institutional aid.

UNDERGRADUATE EXPENSES for 2009–10 ***Application fee:*** $25. ***Comprehensive fee:*** $25,900 includes full-time tuition ($17,200), mandatory fees ($350), and room and board ($8350). ***Part-time tuition:*** $250 per credit. ***Part-time fees:*** $45 per term.

FRESHMAN FINANCIAL AID (Fall 2007) 30 applied for aid; of those 90% were deemed to have need. 100% of freshmen with need received aid; of those 19% had need fully met. ***Average percent of need met:*** 75% (excluding resources awarded to replace EFC). ***Average financial aid package:*** $15,125 (excluding resources awarded to replace EFC). 10% of all full-time freshmen had no need and received non-need-based gift aid.

UNDERGRADUATE FINANCIAL AID (Fall 2007) 146 applied for aid; of those 91% were deemed to have need. 100% of undergraduates with need received aid; of those 21% had need fully met. ***Average percent of need met:*** 73% (excluding resources awarded to replace EFC). ***Average financial aid package:*** $14,452 (excluding resources awarded to replace EFC). 8% of all full-time undergraduates had no need and received non-need-based gift aid.

GIFT AID (NEED-BASED) ***Total amount:*** $1,272,331 (29% federal, 21% state, 45% institutional, 5% external sources). ***Receiving aid:*** Freshmen: 90% (27); all full-time undergraduates: 90% (132). ***Average award:*** Freshmen: $10,766; Undergraduates: $8631. ***Scholarships, grants, and awards:*** Federal Pell, FSEOG, state, private, college/university gift aid from institutional funds.

GIFT AID (NON-NEED-BASED) ***Total amount:*** $44,319 (1% state, 99% institutional). ***Receiving aid:*** Undergraduates: 3% (4). ***Average award:*** Freshmen: $1583. Undergraduates: $3059. ***Scholarships, grants, and awards by category:*** *Academic interests/achievement:* 48 awards ($180,368 total): general academic interests/achievements. *Special achievements/activities:* 1 award ($500 total): leadership. *Special characteristics:* 47 awards ($74,500 total): general special characteristics, local/state students, previous college experience, religious affiliation.

LOANS ***Student loans:*** $1,323,101 (76% need-based, 24% non-need-based). 88% of past graduating class borrowed through all loan programs. *Average indebtedness per student:* $32,278. ***Average need-based loan:*** Freshmen: $3236. Undergraduates: $5388. ***Parent loans:*** $263,061 (49% need-based, 51% non-need-based). ***Programs:*** FFEL (Subsidized and Unsubsidized Stafford, PLUS), Perkins.

WORK-STUDY ***Federal work-study:*** Total amount: $41,022; 56 jobs averaging $926. ***State or other work-study/employment:*** Total amount: $95,715 (81% need-based, 19% non-need-based). 58 part-time jobs averaging $948.

APPLYING FOR FINANCIAL AID ***Required financial aid forms:*** FAFSA, institution's own form. ***Financial aid deadline:*** Continuous. ***Notification date:*** Continuous beginning 3/15. Students must reply within 2 weeks of notification.

CONTACT Julie Rosmus, Director of Financial Aid, College of St. Joseph, 71 Clement Road, Rutland, VT 05701-3899, 802-773-5900 Ext. 3274 or toll-free 877-270-9998 (in-state). *Fax:* 802-776-5275. *E-mail:* jrosmus@csj.edu.

COLLEGE OF SAINT MARY

Omaha, NE

Tuition & fees: $21,260 **Average undergraduate aid package: $14,958**

ABOUT THE INSTITUTION Independent Roman Catholic, women only. ***Awards:*** associate, bachelor's, master's, and doctoral degrees and post-bachelor's certificates. 28 undergraduate majors. ***Total enrollment:*** 953. Undergraduates: 748. Freshmen: 85. Federal methodology is used as a basis for awarding need-based institutional aid.

UNDERGRADUATE EXPENSES for 2008–09 ***Application fee:*** $30. ***Comprehensive fee:*** $27,660 includes full-time tuition ($20,780), mandatory fees ($480), and room and board ($6400). Full-time tuition and fees vary according to degree level and location. Room and board charges vary according to housing facility. ***Part-time tuition:*** $685 per credit. ***Part-time fees:*** $16 per credit hour. Part-time tuition and fees vary according to class time, degree level, and location. ***Payment plans:*** Installment, deferred payment.

FRESHMAN FINANCIAL AID (Fall 2008, est.) 72 applied for aid; of those 96% were deemed to have need. 100% of freshmen with need received aid; of those 13% had need fully met. ***Average percent of need met:*** 74% (excluding resources awarded to replace EFC). ***Average financial aid package:*** $18,373 (excluding resources awarded to replace EFC). 8% of all full-time freshmen had no need and received non-need-based gift aid.

UNDERGRADUATE FINANCIAL AID (Fall 2008, est.) 528 applied for aid; of those 93% were deemed to have need. 100% of undergraduates with need received aid; of those 7% had need fully met. ***Average percent of need met:*** 60% (excluding resources awarded to replace EFC). ***Average financial aid package:*** $14,958 (excluding resources awarded to replace EFC). 7% of all full-time undergraduates had no need and received non-need-based gift aid.

GIFT AID (NEED-BASED) ***Total amount:*** $4,755,153 (30% federal, 4% state, 56% institutional, 10% external sources). ***Receiving aid:*** Freshmen: 92% (69); all full-time undergraduates: 87% (467). ***Average award:*** Freshmen: $14,657; Undergraduates: $9992. ***Scholarships, grants, and awards:*** Federal Pell, FSEOG, state, college/university gift aid from institutional funds.

GIFT AID (NON-NEED-BASED) ***Total amount:*** $369,665 (1% federal, 67% institutional, 32% external sources). ***Receiving aid:*** Freshmen: 9% (7). Undergraduates: 4% (22). ***Average award:*** Freshmen: $8694. Undergraduates: $6034. ***Scholarships, grants, and awards by category:*** *Academic interests/achievement:* 450 awards ($1,948,188 total): biological sciences, education, general academic interests/achievements, mathematics. *Creative arts/performance:* 6 awards ($6000 total): art/fine arts, music. *Special achievements/activities:* 21 awards ($60,034 total): community service, general special achievements/activities, leadership. ***Tuition waivers:*** Full or partial for employees or children of employees, senior citizens. ***ROTC:*** Army cooperative, Air Force cooperative.

LOANS ***Student loans:*** $6,323,520 (82% need-based, 18% non-need-based). 69% of past graduating class borrowed through all loan programs. *Average indebtedness per student:* $26,244. ***Average need-based loan:*** Freshmen: $3618. Undergraduates: $5465. ***Parent loans:*** $953,563 (42% need-based, 58% non-need-based). ***Programs:*** Federal Direct (Subsidized and Unsubsidized Stafford, PLUS), Perkins, Federal Nursing.

WORK-STUDY ***Federal work-study:*** Total amount: $129,248; 146 jobs averaging $1200. ***State or other work-study/employment:*** Total amount: $51,200 (92% need-based, 8% non-need-based). 8 part-time jobs averaging $6400.

ATHLETIC AWARDS Total amount: $375,517 (73% need-based, 27% non-need-based).

APPLYING FOR FINANCIAL AID ***Required financial aid form:*** FAFSA. ***Financial aid deadline (priority):*** 3/15. ***Notification date:*** Continuous beginning 3/15. Students must reply within 2 weeks of notification.

CONTACT Danni Warrick, Director of Financial Aid, College of Saint Mary, 7000 Mercy Road, Omaha, NE 68106, 402-399-2415 or toll-free 800-926-5534. *Fax:* 402-399-2480. *E-mail:* dwarrick@csm.edu.

THE COLLEGE OF SAINT ROSE

Albany, NY

ABOUT THE INSTITUTION Independent, coed. ***Awards:*** bachelor's and master's degrees and post-bachelor's and post-master's certificates. 53 undergraduate majors. ***Total enrollment:*** 5,102. Undergraduates: 3,051. Freshmen: 576.

GIFT AID (NEED-BASED) ***Scholarships, grants, and awards:*** Federal Pell, FSEOG, state, private, college/university gift aid from institutional funds.

GIFT AID (NON-NEED-BASED) ***Scholarships, grants, and awards by category:*** *Academic interests/achievement:* business, education, engineering/technologies, English, foreign languages, general academic interests/achievements, mathematics, premedicine, social sciences. *Creative arts/performance:* art/fine arts, music. *Special achievements/activities:* community service. *Special characteristics:* adult students, children and siblings of alumni, children of union members/company employees, ethnic background, general special characteristics, members of minority groups, siblings of current students, twins.

LOANS ***Programs:*** FFEL (Subsidized and Unsubsidized Stafford, PLUS), Perkins.

APPLYING FOR FINANCIAL AID ***Required financial aid form:*** FAFSA.

CONTACT Steven Dwire, Director of Financial Aid, The College of Saint Rose, 432 Western Avenue, Albertus Hall, Room 206, Albany, NY 12203-1419, 518-458-4915 or toll-free 800-637-8556. *Fax:* 518-454-2802. *E-mail:* finaid@strose.edu.

THE COLLEGE OF ST. SCHOLASTICA

Duluth, MN

Tuition & fees: $26,489 **Average undergraduate aid package: $19,940**

ABOUT THE INSTITUTION Independent religious, coed. ***Awards:*** bachelor's, master's, and doctoral degrees and post-bachelor's and post-master's certificates. 37 undergraduate majors. ***Total enrollment:*** 3,593. Undergraduates: 2,769. Freshmen: 537. Federal methodology is used as a basis for awarding need-based institutional aid.

UNDERGRADUATE EXPENSES for 2008–09 ***Application fee:*** $25. ***Comprehensive fee:*** $33,461 includes full-time tuition ($26,324), mandatory fees ($165), and room and board ($6972). ***College room only:*** $3960. Full-time tuition and fees vary according to class time. Room and board charges vary according to board plan and housing facility. ***Part-time tuition:*** $819 per credit hour. Part-time tuition and fees vary according to class time and course load. ***Payment plan:*** Installment.

FRESHMAN FINANCIAL AID (Fall 2008, est.) 514 applied for aid; of those 87% were deemed to have need. 100% of freshmen with need received aid; of those 16% had need fully met. ***Average percent of need met:*** 78% (excluding resources awarded to replace EFC). ***Average financial aid package:*** $21,072 (excluding resources awarded to replace EFC). 11% of all full-time freshmen had no need and received non-need-based gift aid.

UNDERGRADUATE FINANCIAL AID (Fall 2008, est.) 1,791 applied for aid; of those 91% were deemed to have need. 99% of undergraduates with need received aid; of those 13% had need fully met. ***Average percent of need met:*** 75% (excluding resources awarded to replace EFC). ***Average financial aid package:*** $19,940 (excluding resources awarded to replace EFC). 8% of all full-time undergraduates had no need and received non-need-based gift aid.

GIFT AID (NEED-BASED) ***Total amount:*** $7,954,892 (26% federal, 33% state, 41% institutional). ***Receiving aid:*** Freshmen: 63% (363); all full-time undergraduates: 62% (1,306). ***Average award:*** Freshmen: $6458; Undergraduates: $6050. ***Scholarships, grants, and awards:*** Federal Pell, FSEOG, state, private, college/university gift aid from institutional funds.

GIFT AID (NON-NEED-BASED) ***Total amount:*** $23,287,973 (4% federal, 91% institutional, 5% external sources). ***Receiving aid:*** Freshmen: 76% (438). Undergraduates: 73% (1,541). ***Average award:*** Freshmen: $10,994. Undergraduates: $9878. ***Scholarships, grants, and awards by category:*** *Academic interests/achievement:* 2,031 awards ($16,982,246 total): general academic interests/achievements. *Creative arts/performance:* 27 awards ($31,590 total): music. *Special characteristics:* 1,229 awards ($3,522,505 total): children and siblings of alumni, children of faculty/staff, ethnic background, handicapped students, international students, members of minority groups, previous college experience, religious affiliation, siblings of current students. ***Tuition waivers:*** Full or partial for employees or children of employees, senior citizens. ***ROTC:*** Air Force cooperative.

LOANS ***Student loans:*** $17,032,514 (32% need-based, 68% non-need-based). 78% of past graduating class borrowed through all loan programs. *Average indebtedness per student:* $36,075. ***Average need-based loan:*** Freshmen: $3122. Undergraduates: $3705. ***Parent loans:*** $1,776,585 (100% non-need-based). ***Programs:*** FFEL (Subsidized and Unsubsidized Stafford, PLUS), Perkins, Federal Nursing, state, private supplemental loans.

WORK-STUDY ***Federal work-study:*** Total amount: $439,032; 288 jobs averaging $1884. ***State or other work-study/employment:*** Total amount: $1,018,695 (31% need-based, 69% non-need-based). 711 part-time jobs averaging $1414.

APPLYING FOR FINANCIAL AID ***Required financial aid form:*** FAFSA. ***Financial aid deadline (priority):*** 3/1. ***Notification date:*** Continuous beginning 3/1. Students must reply by 5/1 or within 2 weeks of notification.

CONTACT Mr. Jon P. Erickson, Director of Financial Aid, The College of St. Scholastica, 1200 Kenwood Avenue, Duluth, MN 55811-4199, 218-723-6725 or toll-free 800-249-6412. *Fax:* 218-733-2229. *E-mail:* jerickso@css.edu.

THE COLLEGE OF SAINT THOMAS MORE

Fort Worth, TX

CONTACT Mary E. Swanson, Director of Financial Aid, The College of Saint Thomas More, 3020 Lubbock Street, Fort Worth, TX 76109-2323, 325-673-1934 or toll-free 800-583-6489 (out-of-state). *Fax:* 325-673-1934. *E-mail:* corkyswanson@suddenlink.net.

COLLEGE OF SANTA FE

Santa Fe, NM

ABOUT THE INSTITUTION Independent, coed. ***Awards:*** bachelor's degrees. 29 undergraduate majors. ***Total enrollment:*** 672. Undergraduates: 672. Freshmen: 166.

GIFT AID (NEED-BASED) ***Scholarships, grants, and awards:*** Federal Pell, FSEOG, state, private, college/university gift aid from institutional funds.

GIFT AID (NON-NEED-BASED) ***Scholarships, grants, and awards by category:*** *Academic interests/achievement:* general academic interests/achievements. *Creative arts/performance:* applied art and design, art/fine arts, cinema/film/broadcasting, creative writing, dance, general creative arts/performance, journalism/publications, music, performing arts, theater/drama. *Special achievements/activities:* general special achievements/activities. *Special characteristics:* children and siblings of alumni, general special characteristics.

LOANS ***Programs:*** FFEL (Subsidized and Unsubsidized Stafford, PLUS), Perkins, state, college/university.

APPLYING FOR FINANCIAL AID ***Required financial aid form:*** FAFSA.

CONTACT Ms. Jill Robertson, Director, Student Financial Services, College of Santa Fe, 1600 St. Michael's Drive, Santa Fe, NM 87505-7634, 505-473-6454 or toll-free 800-456-2673. *Fax:* 505-473-6464. *E-mail:* sfs@csf.edu.

COLLEGE OF STATEN ISLAND OF THE CITY UNIVERSITY OF NEW YORK

Staten Island, NY

Tuition & fees (NY res): $4378 **Average undergraduate aid package: $6398**

ABOUT THE INSTITUTION State and locally supported, coed. ***Awards:*** associate, bachelor's, master's, and doctoral degrees and post-master's certificates. 35 undergraduate majors. ***Total enrollment:*** 13,092. Undergraduates: 12,183. Freshmen: 2,514. Federal methodology is used as a basis for awarding need-based institutional aid.

UNDERGRADUATE EXPENSES for 2008–09 ***Application fee:*** $65. ***Tuition, state resident:*** full-time $4000; part-time $170 per credit. ***Tuition, nonresident:*** full-time $8640; part-time $360 per credit. ***Required fees:*** full-time $378; $113 per term.

FRESHMAN FINANCIAL AID (Fall 2008, est.) 1,799 applied for aid; of those 74% were deemed to have need. 97% of freshmen with need received aid; of those 5% had need fully met. ***Average percent of need met:*** 57% (excluding resources awarded to replace EFC). ***Average financial aid package:*** $6167 (excluding resources awarded to replace EFC). 9% of all full-time freshmen had no need and received non-need-based gift aid.

UNDERGRADUATE FINANCIAL AID (Fall 2008, est.) 6,216 applied for aid; of those 76% were deemed to have need. 96% of undergraduates with need received aid; of those 5% had need fully met. ***Average percent of need met:*** 55% (excluding resources awarded to replace EFC). ***Average financial aid package:*** $6398 (excluding resources awarded to replace EFC). 5% of all full-time undergraduates had no need and received non-need-based gift aid.

GIFT AID (NEED-BASED) ***Total amount:*** $27,514,156 (55% federal, 42% state, 3% external sources). ***Receiving aid:*** Freshmen: 56% (1,272); all full-time undergraduates: 51% (4,427). ***Average award:*** Freshmen: $5725; Undergraduates: $5501. ***Scholarships, grants, and awards:*** Federal Pell, FSEOG, state, private, college/university gift aid from institutional funds, Federal Nursing.

GIFT AID (NON-NEED-BASED) ***Total amount:*** $1,561,313 (4% federal, 51% state, 45% external sources). ***Receiving aid:*** Freshmen: 14% (317). Undergraduates: 7% (613). ***Average award:*** Freshmen: $1120. Undergraduates: $1492. ***Scholarships, grants, and awards by category:*** *Academic interests/achievement:* 102 awards ($225,640 total): biological sciences, business, computer science, education, engineering/technologies, general academic interests/achievements, health fields, humanities, international studies, mathematics, physical sciences, premedicine, social sciences. *Creative arts/performance:* 2 awards ($2826 total): art/fine arts, music, theater/drama. *Special achievements/activities:* 5 awards ($5500 total): community service, general special achievements/activities. *Special characteristics:* 6 awards ($6800 total): children of public servants, children with a deceased or disabled parent, general special characteristics, handicapped students, international students, members of minority groups, public servants, spouses of deceased or disabled public servants, veterans' children.

LOANS ***Student loans:*** $6,678,512 (100% need-based). ***Average need-based loan:*** Freshmen: $2924. Undergraduates: $4119. ***Programs:*** Federal Direct (Subsidized and Unsubsidized Stafford, PLUS), Perkins.

WORK-STUDY ***Federal work-study:*** Total amount: $1,129,874; 270 jobs averaging $1500.

APPLYING FOR FINANCIAL AID ***Required financial aid forms:*** FAFSA, state aid form. ***Financial aid deadline (priority):*** 3/31. ***Notification date:*** Continuous beginning 6/1.

CONTACT Philippe Marius, Director of Financial Aid, College of Staten Island of the City University of New York, 2800 Victory Boulevard, 2A-401A, Staten Island, NY 10314-6600, 718-982-2030. *Fax:* 718-982-2037. *E-mail:* marius@mail.csi.cuny.edu.

COLLEGE OF THE ATLANTIC

Bar Harbor, ME

Tuition & fees: $33,060 **Average undergraduate aid package: $28,020**

ABOUT THE INSTITUTION Independent, coed. ***Awards:*** bachelor's and master's degrees. 37 undergraduate majors. ***Total enrollment:*** 327. Undergraduates: 324. Freshmen: 70. Both federal and institutional methodology are used as a basis for awarding need-based institutional aid.

UNDERGRADUATE EXPENSES for 2009–10 ***Application fee:*** $45. ***Comprehensive fee:*** $41,550 includes full-time tuition ($32,580), mandatory fees ($480), and room and board ($8490). ***College room only:*** $5400. ***Part-time tuition:*** $3620 per credit. ***Part-time fees:*** $160 per term.

FRESHMAN FINANCIAL AID (Fall 2008, est.) 58 applied for aid; of those 95% were deemed to have need. 100% of freshmen with need received aid; of those 53% had need fully met. ***Average percent of need met:*** 96% (excluding resources awarded to replace EFC). ***Average financial aid package:*** $33,029 (excluding resources awarded to replace EFC).

UNDERGRADUATE FINANCIAL AID (Fall 2008, est.) 252 applied for aid; of those 97% were deemed to have need. 100% of undergraduates with need received aid; of those 50% had need fully met. ***Average percent of need met:*** 96% (excluding resources awarded to replace EFC). ***Average financial aid package:*** $28,020 (excluding resources awarded to replace EFC).

GIFT AID (NEED-BASED) ***Total amount:*** $5,416,272 (6% federal, 1% state, 90% institutional, 3% external sources). ***Receiving aid:*** Freshmen: 80% (55); all full-time undergraduates: 82% (245). ***Average award:*** Freshmen: $28,949; Undergraduates: $23,537. ***Scholarships, grants, and awards:*** Federal Pell, FSEOG, state, private, college/university gift aid from institutional funds.

LOANS ***Student loans:*** $1,176,404 (68% need-based, 32% non-need-based). 56% of past graduating class borrowed through all loan programs. *Average indebtedness per student:* $23,762. ***Average need-based loan:*** Freshmen: $4031. Undergraduates: $4707. ***Parent loans:*** $583,060 (100% non-need-based). ***Programs:*** FFEL (Subsidized and Unsubsidized Stafford, PLUS), Perkins.

WORK-STUDY ***Federal work-study:*** Total amount: $461,058; 187 jobs averaging $2375. ***State or other work-study/employment:*** Total amount: $61,400 (100% need-based). 44 part-time jobs averaging $1407.

APPLYING FOR FINANCIAL AID ***Required financial aid forms:*** FAFSA, institution's own form, noncustodial (divorced/separated) parent's statement. ***Financial aid deadline (priority):*** 2/15. ***Notification date:*** 4/1. Students must reply by 5/1 or within 2 weeks of notification.

CONTACT Bruce Hazam, Director of Financial Aid, College of the Atlantic, 105 Eden Street, Bar Harbor, ME 04609-1198, 207-288-5015 Ext. 232 or toll-free 800-528-0025. *Fax:* 207-288-4126. *E-mail:* bhazam@coa.edu.

COLLEGE OF THE HOLY CROSS

Worcester, MA

Tuition & fees: $38,722 **Average undergraduate aid package: $29,166**

ABOUT THE INSTITUTION Independent Roman Catholic (Jesuit), coed. ***Awards:*** bachelor's degrees (standardized tests are optional for admission to the College of Holy Cross). 33 undergraduate majors. ***Total enrollment:*** 2,898. Undergraduates: 2,898. Freshmen: 737. Both federal and institutional methodology are used as a basis for awarding need-based institutional aid.

UNDERGRADUATE EXPENSES for 2009–10 ***Application fee:*** $60. ***Comprehensive fee:*** $49,342 includes full-time tuition ($38,180), mandatory fees ($542), and room and board ($10,620). ***College room only:*** $5440.

FRESHMAN FINANCIAL AID (Fall 2008, est.) 517 applied for aid; of those 78% were deemed to have need. 99% of freshmen with need received aid; of those 100% had need fully met. ***Average percent of need met:*** 100% (excluding resources awarded to replace EFC). ***Average financial aid package:*** $27,569 (excluding resources awarded to replace EFC). 2% of all full-time freshmen had no need and received non-need-based gift aid.

UNDERGRADUATE FINANCIAL AID (Fall 2008, est.) 1,786 applied for aid; of those 90% were deemed to have need. 99% of undergraduates with need received aid; of those 100% had need fully met. ***Average percent of need met:*** 100% (excluding resources awarded to replace EFC). ***Average financial aid package:*** $29,166 (excluding resources awarded to replace EFC). 4% of all full-time undergraduates had no need and received non-need-based gift aid.

GIFT AID (NEED-BASED) ***Total amount:*** $30,430,187 (6% federal, 1% state, 81% institutional, 12% external sources). ***Receiving aid:*** Freshmen: 42% (308); all full-time undergraduates: 45% (1,282). ***Average award:*** Freshmen: $26,693; Undergraduates: $25,624. ***Scholarships, grants, and awards:*** Federal Pell, FSEOG, state, private, college/university gift aid from institutional funds.

GIFT AID (NON-NEED-BASED) ***Total amount:*** $2,472,861 (100% institutional). ***Receiving aid:*** Freshmen: 2% (16). Undergraduates: 2% (62). ***Average award:*** Freshmen: $47,849. Undergraduates: $48,298. ***Scholarships, grants, and awards by category:*** *Academic interests/achievement:* 98 awards ($2,179,311 total): general academic interests/achievements, humanities, military science. *Creative arts/performance:* 5 awards: music. *Special characteristics:* 27 awards: children of faculty/staff. ***ROTC:*** Army cooperative, Naval, Air Force cooperative.

LOANS ***Student loans:*** $10,705,886 (74% need-based, 26% non-need-based). *Average indebtedness per student:* $17,200. ***Average need-based loan:*** Freshmen: $4673. Undergraduates: $5154. ***Parent loans:*** $9,892,074 (100% non-need-based). ***Programs:*** Federal Direct (Subsidized and Unsubsidized Stafford, PLUS), Perkins, MEFA Loans.

WORK-STUDY ***Federal work-study:*** Total amount: $1,450,545; 916 jobs averaging $1697.

ATHLETIC AWARDS Total amount: $6,286,267 (81% need-based, 19% non-need-based).

APPLYING FOR FINANCIAL AID ***Required financial aid forms:*** FAFSA, CSS Financial Aid PROFILE, noncustodial (divorced/separated) parent's statement, business/farm supplement, Parent and student federal income tax forms. ***Financial aid deadline:*** 2/1. ***Notification date:*** 4/1. Students must reply by 5/1.

CONTACT Lynne Myers, Director of Financial Aid, College of the Holy Cross, One College Street, Worcester, MA 01610-2395, 508-793-2265 or toll-free 800-442-2421. *Fax:* 508-793-2527.

COLLEGE OF THE HUMANITIES AND SCIENCES, HARRISON MIDDLETON UNIVERSITY

Tempe, AZ

CONTACT Financial Aid Office, College of the Humanities and Sciences, Harrison Middleton University, 1105 East Broadway, Tempe, AZ 85282, 480-317-5955 or toll-free 877-248-6724.

COLLEGE OF THE OZARKS

Point Lookout, MO

Tuition & fees: **Average undergraduate aid package: $15,330**

ABOUT THE INSTITUTION Independent Presbyterian, coed. ***Awards:*** bachelor's degrees. 87 undergraduate majors. ***Total enrollment:*** 1,331. Undergraduates: 1,331. Freshmen: 274. Federal methodology is used as a basis for awarding need-based institutional aid.

UNDERGRADUATE EXPENSES for 2009–10 includes room and board ($5000). the college guarantees to meet all of the tuition cost for each full-time student by using earnings from its endowment, operation of its own mandatory student work program, accepting student aid grants, gifts and other sources. In effect, each full-time student's Cost of Education (tuition) is met 100 percent by participating in the work program and a combination of private, institutional and federal/state student aid.

FRESHMAN FINANCIAL AID (Fall 2007) 372 applied for aid; of those 97% were deemed to have need. 100% of freshmen with need received aid; of those 27% had need fully met. ***Average percent of need met:*** 85% (excluding resources awarded to replace EFC). ***Average financial aid package:*** $14,523 (excluding resources awarded to replace EFC). 11% of all full-time freshmen had no need and received non-need-based gift aid.

UNDERGRADUATE FINANCIAL AID (Fall 2007) 1,429 applied for aid; of those 94% were deemed to have need. 100% of undergraduates with need received aid; of those 37% had need fully met. ***Average percent of need met:*** 85% (excluding resources awarded to replace EFC). ***Average financial aid package:*** $15,330 (excluding resources awarded to replace EFC). 9% of all full-time undergraduates had no need and received non-need-based gift aid.

GIFT AID (NEED-BASED) ***Total amount:*** $16,241,051 (14% federal, 10% state, 74% institutional, 2% external sources). ***Receiving aid:*** Freshmen: 89% (360); all full-time undergraduates: 91% (1,346). ***Average award:*** Freshmen: $10,938; Undergraduates: $12,064. ***Scholarships, grants, and awards:*** Federal Pell, FSEOG, state, private, college/university gift aid from institutional funds.

GIFT AID (NON-NEED-BASED) ***Total amount:*** $2,503,694 (1% state, 96% institutional, 3% external sources). ***Receiving aid:*** Freshmen: 12% (48). Undergraduates: 17% (258). ***Average award:*** Freshmen: $7602. Undergraduates: $10,390. ***ROTC:*** Army.

LOANS ***Student loans:*** $416,699 (81% need-based, 19% non-need-based). 10% of past graduating class borrowed through all loan programs. *Average indebtedness per student:* $4843. ***Programs:*** alternative loans.

WORK-STUDY ***Federal work-study:*** Total amount: $3,763,691; 784 jobs averaging $4802. ***State or other work-study/employment:*** Total amount: $2,318,347 (28% need-based, 72% non-need-based). 755 part-time jobs averaging $4802.

ATHLETIC AWARDS Total amount: $201,569 (48% need-based, 52% non-need-based).

APPLYING FOR FINANCIAL AID ***Required financial aid form:*** FAFSA. ***Financial aid deadline (priority):*** 2/15. ***Notification date:*** 7/1.

CONTACT Kyla R. McCarty, Director of Financial Aid, College of the Ozarks, PO Box 17, Point Lookout, MO 65726, 417-690-3290 or toll-free 800-222-0525. *Fax:* 417-690-3286.

COLLEGE OF VISUAL ARTS

St. Paul, MN

Tuition & fees: $23,194 **Average undergraduate aid package: $11,510**

ABOUT THE INSTITUTION Independent, coed. ***Awards:*** bachelor's degrees. 7 undergraduate majors. ***Total enrollment:*** 191. Undergraduates: 191. Freshmen: 49. Federal methodology is used as a basis for awarding need-based institutional aid.

UNDERGRADUATE EXPENSES for 2009–10 ***Application fee:*** $40. ***Tuition:*** full-time $22,694.

FRESHMAN FINANCIAL AID (Fall 2008, est.) 68 applied for aid; of those 90% were deemed to have need. 100% of freshmen with need received aid; of those 2% had need fully met. ***Average financial aid package:*** $11,474 (excluding resources awarded to replace EFC). 3% of all full-time freshmen had no need and received non-need-based gift aid.

UNDERGRADUATE FINANCIAL AID (Fall 2008, est.) 157 applied for aid; of those 97% were deemed to have need. 99% of undergraduates with need received aid; of those 1% had need fully met. ***Average financial aid package:*** $11,510 (excluding resources awarded to replace EFC). 10% of all full-time undergraduates had no need and received non-need-based gift aid.

GIFT AID (NEED-BASED) ***Total amount:*** $1,202,902 (17% federal, 21% state, 62% institutional). ***Receiving aid:*** Freshmen: 81% (61); all full-time undergraduates: 80% (152). ***Average award:*** Freshmen: $8468; Undergraduates: $7538. ***Scholarships, grants, and awards:*** Federal Pell, FSEOG, state, private, college/university gift aid from institutional funds, Academic Competitiveness Grant.

GIFT AID (NON-NEED-BASED) ***Total amount:*** $60,869 (60% institutional, 40% external sources). ***Receiving aid:*** Freshmen: 1% (1). Undergraduates: 1% (2). ***Average award:*** Freshmen: $200. Undergraduates: $2129. ***Scholarships, grants, and awards by category:*** *Academic interests/achievement:* 15 awards ($7500 total): general academic interests/achievements. *Creative arts/performance:* 63 awards ($135,376 total): art/fine arts. *Special characteristics:* children of faculty/staff.

LOANS ***Student loans:*** $2,171,909 (79% need-based, 21% non-need-based). 95% of past graduating class borrowed through all loan programs. *Average indebtedness per student:* $46,000. ***Average need-based loan:*** Freshmen: $3420. Undergraduates: $4222. ***Parent loans:*** $266,031 (39% need-based, 61% non-need-based). ***Programs:*** FFEL (Subsidized and Unsubsidized Stafford, PLUS), state, alternative loans.

WORK-STUDY ***Federal work-study:*** Total amount: $27,096; 14 jobs averaging $2000. ***State or other work-study/employment:*** Total amount: $75,579 (17% need-based, 83% non-need-based). 65 part-time jobs averaging $2000.

APPLYING FOR FINANCIAL AID ***Required financial aid forms:*** FAFSA, institution's own form. ***Financial aid deadline:*** 6/1 (priority: 4/1). ***Notification date:*** Continuous.

CONTACT Susan Ant, Executive Director of Enrollment Management, College of Visual Arts, 344 Summit Avenue, St. Paul, MN 55102-2124, 651-757-4020 or toll-free 800-224-1536. *Fax:* 651-224-0090. *E-mail:* financialaid@cva.edu.

THE COLLEGE OF WILLIAM AND MARY
Williamsburg, VA

Tuition & fees (VA res): $10,246 Average undergraduate aid package: $13,703

ABOUT THE INSTITUTION State-supported, coed. ***Awards:*** bachelor's, master's, doctoral, and first professional degrees and post-master's certificates. 42 undergraduate majors. ***Total enrollment:*** 7,892. Undergraduates: 5,850. Freshmen: 1,387. Federal methodology is used as a basis for awarding need-based institutional aid.

UNDERGRADUATE EXPENSES for 2008–09 ***Application fee:*** $60. ***One-time required fee:*** $144. ***Tuition, state resident:*** full-time $6090; part-time $225 per credit hour. ***Tuition, nonresident:*** full-time $24,960; part-time $840 per credit hour. ***Required fees:*** full-time $4156. Full-time tuition and fees vary according to program. Part-time tuition and fees vary according to program. ***College room and board:*** $7910; ***Room only:*** $4626. Room and board charges vary according to board plan and housing facility. ***Payment plan:*** Installment.

FRESHMAN FINANCIAL AID (Fall 2008, est.) 814 applied for aid; of those 48% were deemed to have need. 100% of freshmen with need received aid; of those 43% had need fully met. ***Average percent of need met:*** 82% (excluding resources awarded to replace EFC). ***Average financial aid package:*** $13,454 (excluding resources awarded to replace EFC). 2% of all full-time freshmen had no need and received non-need-based gift aid.

UNDERGRADUATE FINANCIAL AID (Fall 2008, est.) 2,730 applied for aid; of those 62% were deemed to have need. 100% of undergraduates with need received aid; of those 35% had need fully met. ***Average percent of need met:*** 83% (excluding resources awarded to replace EFC). ***Average financial aid package:*** $13,703 (excluding resources awarded to replace EFC). 5% of all full-time undergraduates had no need and received non-need-based gift aid.

GIFT AID (NEED-BASED) ***Total amount:*** $13,650,190 (17% federal, 19% state, 64% institutional). ***Receiving aid:*** Freshmen: 21% (295); all full-time undergraduates: 23% (1,318). ***Average award:*** Freshmen: $13,088; Undergraduates: $13,598. ***Scholarships, grants, and awards:*** Federal Pell, FSEOG, state, private, college/university gift aid from institutional funds.

GIFT AID (NON-NEED-BASED) ***Total amount:*** $5,587,312 (8% federal, 49% institutional, 43% external sources). ***Receiving aid:*** Freshmen: 13% (187). Undergraduates: 10% (566). ***Average award:*** Freshmen: $7396. Undergraduates: $6065. ***Scholarships, grants, and awards by category:*** *Academic interests/achievement:* 17 awards ($310,692 total): general academic interests/achievements. *Creative arts/performance:* 79 awards ($59,821 total): music, theater/drama. *Special characteristics:* 168 awards ($1,656,035 total): general special characteristics. ***Tuition waivers:*** Full or partial for employees or children of employees, senior citizens. ***ROTC:*** Army.

LOANS ***Student loans:*** $14,131,038 (33% need-based, 67% non-need-based). 39% of past graduating class borrowed through all loan programs. *Average indebtedness per student:* $12,859. ***Average need-based loan:*** Freshmen: $2690. Undergraduates: $3301. ***Parent loans:*** $5,159,295 (100% non-need-based). ***Programs:*** FFEL (Subsidized and Unsubsidized Stafford, PLUS), Perkins.

WORK-STUDY ***Federal work-study:*** Total amount: $213,458; 187 jobs averaging $1156.

ATHLETIC AWARDS Total amount: $5,220,582 (100% non-need-based).

APPLYING FOR FINANCIAL AID ***Required financial aid form:*** FAFSA. ***Financial aid deadline (priority):*** 2/15. ***Notification date:*** Continuous beginning 3/15. Students must reply by 5/1 or within 2 weeks of notification.

CONTACT Mr. Edward P. Irish, Director of Financial Aid, The College of William and Mary, PO Box 8795, Williamsburg, VA 23187, 757-221-2425. *Fax:* 757-221-2515. *E-mail:* epiris@wm.edu.

THE COLLEGE OF WOOSTER
Wooster, OH

Comprehensive fee: $43,900 Average undergraduate aid package: $27,950

ABOUT THE INSTITUTION Independent religious, coed. ***Awards:*** bachelor's degrees. 46 undergraduate majors. ***Total enrollment:*** 1,884. Undergraduates: 1,884. Freshmen: 519. Both federal and institutional methodology are used as a basis for awarding need-based institutional aid.

UNDERGRADUATE EXPENSES for 2009–10 ***Application fee:*** $40. ***Comprehensive fee:*** $43,900.

FRESHMAN FINANCIAL AID (Fall 2008, est.) 388 applied for aid; of those 82% were deemed to have need. 100% of freshmen with need received aid; of those 53% had need fully met. ***Average percent of need met:*** 92% (excluding resources awarded to replace EFC). ***Average financial aid package:*** $28,632 (excluding resources awarded to replace EFC). 33% of all full-time freshmen had no need and received non-need-based gift aid.

UNDERGRADUATE FINANCIAL AID (Fall 2008, est.) 1,193 applied for aid; of those 86% were deemed to have need. 100% of undergraduates with need received aid; of those 41% had need fully met. ***Average percent of need met:*** 89% (excluding resources awarded to replace EFC). ***Average financial aid package:*** $27,950 (excluding resources awarded to replace EFC). 40% of all full-time undergraduates had no need and received non-need-based gift aid.

GIFT AID (NEED-BASED) ***Total amount:*** $22,013,237 (7% federal, 3% state, 89% institutional, 1% external sources). ***Receiving aid:*** Freshmen: 62% (317); all full-time undergraduates: 55% (1,029). ***Average award:*** Freshmen: $22,343; Undergraduates: $21,393. ***Scholarships, grants, and awards:*** Federal Pell, FSEOG, state, private, college/university gift aid from institutional funds.

GIFT AID (NON-NEED-BASED) ***Total amount:*** $12,299,556 (1% state, 98% institutional, 1% external sources). ***Receiving aid:*** Freshmen: 11% (58). Undergraduates: 7% (139). ***Average award:*** Freshmen: $15,935. Undergraduates: $14,768. ***Scholarships, grants, and awards by category:*** *Academic interests/achievement:* 1,610 awards ($17,480,323 total): general academic interests/achievements. *Creative arts/performance:* 62 awards ($224,000 total): dance, music, theater/drama. *Special achievements/activities:* 89 awards ($562,626 total): community service, religious involvement. *Special characteristics:* 47 awards ($811,099 total): members of minority groups.

LOANS ***Student loans:*** $5,436,910 (78% need-based, 22% non-need-based). 63% of past graduating class borrowed through all loan programs. *Average indebtedness per student:* $29,815. ***Average need-based loan:*** Freshmen: $4495. Undergraduates: $5210. ***Parent loans:*** $5,791,519 (21% need-based, 79% non-need-based). ***Programs:*** Federal Direct (Subsidized and Unsubsidized Stafford, PLUS), Perkins, college/university.

WORK-STUDY ***Federal work-study:*** Total amount: $902,557; 672 jobs averaging $1340. ***State or other work-study/employment:*** Total amount: $175,070 (100% non-need-based). 79 part-time jobs averaging $1808.

APPLYING FOR FINANCIAL AID ***Required financial aid forms:*** FAFSA, institution's own form. ***Financial aid deadline:*** 9/1 (priority: 2/15). ***Notification date:*** 4/1. Students must reply by 5/1.

CONTACT Dr. David Miller, Director of Financial Aid, The College of Wooster, 1189 Beall Avenue, Wooster, OH 44691-2363, 800-877-3688 or toll-free 800-877-9905. *Fax:* 330-263-2634. *E-mail:* financialaid@wooster.edu.

COLLINS COLLEGE: A SCHOOL OF DESIGN AND TECHNOLOGY
Tempe, AZ

Tuition & fees: N/R Average undergraduate aid package: $5287

ABOUT THE INSTITUTION Proprietary, coed. ***Awards:*** associate and bachelor's degrees. 7 undergraduate majors. ***Total enrollment:*** 1,287. Undergraduates: 1,287. Federal methodology is used as a basis for awarding need-based institutional aid.

FRESHMAN FINANCIAL AID (Fall 2007) 586 applied for aid; of those 100% were deemed to have need. 100% of freshmen with need received aid; of those 4% had need fully met. ***Average percent of need met:*** 59% (excluding resources awarded to replace EFC). ***Average financial aid package:*** $4522 (excluding resources awarded to replace EFC). 1% of all full-time freshmen had no need and received non-need-based gift aid.

UNDERGRADUATE FINANCIAL AID (Fall 2007) 935 applied for aid; of those 100% were deemed to have need. 100% of undergraduates with need received aid; of those 3% had need fully met. ***Average percent of need met:*** 65% (excluding resources awarded to replace EFC). ***Average financial aid package:*** $5287 (excluding resources awarded to replace EFC). 1% of all full-time undergraduates had no need and received non-need-based gift aid.

GIFT AID (NEED-BASED) ***Total amount:*** $3,958,662 (96% federal, 4% state). ***Receiving aid:*** Freshmen: 55% (360); all full-time undergraduates: 56% (584). ***Average award:*** Freshmen: $3146; Undergraduates: $3014. ***Scholarships, grants, and awards:*** Federal Pell, FSEOG, state, private, college/university gift aid from institutional funds.

GIFT AID (NON-NEED-BASED) ***Total amount:*** $917,734 (79% federal, 14% institutional, 7% external sources). ***Receiving aid:*** Freshmen: 17% (113). Undergraduates: 14% (146). ***Average award:*** Freshmen: $888. Undergraduates: $750. ***Tuition waivers:*** Full or partial for employees or children of employees.

LOANS ***Student loans:*** $21,394,481 (33% need-based, 67% non-need-based). ***Average need-based loan:*** Freshmen: $2690. Undergraduates: $3513. ***Parent loans:*** $6,268,613 (100% non-need-based). ***Programs:*** Federal Direct (Subsidized and Unsubsidized Stafford, PLUS), FFEL (Subsidized and Unsubsidized Stafford, PLUS), college/university.

WORK-STUDY ***Federal work-study:*** Total amount: $234,181; 65 jobs averaging $3000.

APPLYING FOR FINANCIAL AID ***Required financial aid forms:*** FAFSA, institution's own form. ***Financial aid deadline:*** Continuous. ***Notification date:*** Continuous beginning 3/1. Students must reply within 2 weeks of notification.

CONTACT Kari Yearwood, Director of Financial Aid, Collins College: A School of Design and Technology, 4750 South 44th Place, Phoenix, AZ 85040, 800-876-7070. *Fax:* 866-553-6597. *E-mail:* fa@collinscollege.edu.

COLORADO CHRISTIAN UNIVERSITY

Lakewood, CO

CONTACT Mr. Steve Woodburn, Director of Financial Aid, Colorado Christian University, 180 South Garrison Street, Lakewood, CO 80226-7499, 303-963-3230 or toll-free 800-44-FAITH. *Fax:* 303-963-3231. *E-mail:* sfs@ccu.edu.

THE COLORADO COLLEGE

Colorado Springs, CO

Tuition & fees: $36,044 **Average undergraduate aid package: $29,412**

ABOUT THE INSTITUTION Independent, coed. ***Awards:*** bachelor's and master's degrees (master's degree in education only). 48 undergraduate majors. ***Total enrollment:*** 2,026. Undergraduates: 1,996. Freshmen: 550. Both federal and institutional methodology are used as a basis for awarding need-based institutional aid.

UNDERGRADUATE EXPENSES for 2008–09 ***Application fee:*** $50. ***One-time required fee:*** $150. ***Comprehensive fee:*** $45,140 includes full-time tuition ($35,844), mandatory fees ($200), and room and board ($9096). ***College room only:*** $5024. Room and board charges vary according to board plan and housing facility. ***Part-time tuition:*** $5974 per course. Part-time tuition and fees vary according to course load. ***Payment plan:*** Installment.

FRESHMAN FINANCIAL AID (Fall 2008, est.) 286 applied for aid; of those 83% were deemed to have need. 100% of freshmen with need received aid; of those 61% had need fully met. ***Average percent of need met:*** 95% (excluding resources awarded to replace EFC). ***Average financial aid package:*** $30,402 (excluding resources awarded to replace EFC). 9% of all full-time freshmen had no need and received non-need-based gift aid.

UNDERGRADUATE FINANCIAL AID (Fall 2008, est.) 877 applied for aid; of those 87% were deemed to have need. 100% of undergraduates with need received aid; of those 52% had need fully met. ***Average percent of need met:*** 91% (excluding resources awarded to replace EFC). ***Average financial aid package:*** $29,412 (excluding resources awarded to replace EFC). 8% of all full-time undergraduates had no need and received non-need-based gift aid.

GIFT AID (NEED-BASED) ***Total amount:*** $20,043,344 (4% federal, 1% state, 93% institutional, 2% external sources). ***Receiving aid:*** Freshmen: 42% (230); all full-time undergraduates: 37% (734). ***Average award:*** Freshmen: $29,371; Undergraduates: $27,698. ***Scholarships, grants, and awards:*** Federal Pell, FSEOG, state, private, college/university gift aid from institutional funds.

GIFT AID (NON-NEED-BASED) ***Total amount:*** $4,779,789 (1% federal, 74% institutional, 25% external sources). ***Receiving aid:*** Freshmen: 16% (88). Undergraduates: 11% (221). ***Average award:*** Freshmen: $10,098. Undergraduates: $14,386. ***Scholarships, grants, and awards by category:*** *Academic interests/achievement:* 160 awards ($1,600,000 total): biological sciences, general academic interests/achievements, mathematics, physical sciences. ***Tuition waivers:*** Full or partial for employees or children of employees. ***ROTC:*** Army cooperative.

LOANS ***Student loans:*** $3,437,715 (51% need-based, 49% non-need-based). 39% of past graduating class borrowed through all loan programs. *Average indebtedness per student:* $16,041. ***Average need-based loan:*** Freshmen: $1861. Undergraduates: $2894. ***Parent loans:*** $2,575,173 (17% need-based, 83% non-need-based). ***Programs:*** Federal Direct (Subsidized and Unsubsidized Stafford, PLUS), FFEL (Subsidized and Unsubsidized Stafford, PLUS), Perkins.

WORK-STUDY ***Federal work-study:*** Total amount: $322,722; 300 jobs averaging $1800. ***State or other work-study/employment:*** Total amount: $314,113 (74% need-based, 26% non-need-based). 150 part-time jobs averaging $1700.

ATHLETIC AWARDS Total amount: $1,409,071 (10% need-based, 90% non-need-based).

APPLYING FOR FINANCIAL AID ***Required financial aid forms:*** FAFSA, CSS Financial Aid PROFILE, noncustodial (divorced/separated) parent's statement, federal income tax form(s) for parents and student. ***Financial aid deadline:*** 2/15 (priority: 2/15). ***Notification date:*** 3/20. Students must reply by 5/1.

CONTACT Mr. James M. Swanson, Director of Financial Aid, The Colorado College, 14 East Cache La Poudre Street, Colorado Springs, CO 80903-3294, 719-389-6651 or toll-free 800-542-7214. *Fax:* 719-389-6173. *E-mail:* FinancialAid@ColoradoCollege.edu.

COLORADO SCHOOL OF MINES

Golden, CO

Tuition & fees (CO res): $11,238 **Average undergraduate aid package: $16,000**

ABOUT THE INSTITUTION State-supported, coed. ***Awards:*** bachelor's, master's, doctoral, and first professional degrees. 12 undergraduate majors. ***Total enrollment:*** 4,488. Undergraduates: 3,456. Freshmen: 851. Federal methodology is used as a basis for awarding need-based institutional aid.

UNDERGRADUATE EXPENSES for 2008–09 ***Application fee:*** $45. ***Tuition, state resident:*** full-time $9810; part-time $327 per credit hour. ***Tuition, nonresident:*** full-time $23,820; part-time $794 per credit hour. ***Required fees:*** full-time $1428. Part-time tuition and fees vary according to course load. ***College room and board:*** $7626. Room and board charges vary according to board plan and housing facility. ***Payment plan:*** Installment.

FRESHMAN FINANCIAL AID (Fall 2008, est.) 605 applied for aid; of those 91% were deemed to have need. 100% of freshmen with need received aid; of those 82% had need fully met. ***Average percent of need met:*** 93% (excluding resources awarded to replace EFC). ***Average financial aid package:*** $16,000 (excluding resources awarded to replace EFC). 11% of all full-time freshmen had no need and received non-need-based gift aid.

UNDERGRADUATE FINANCIAL AID (Fall 2008, est.) 2,550 applied for aid; of those 88% were deemed to have need. 100% of undergraduates with need received aid; of those 82% had need fully met. ***Average percent of need met:*** 93% (excluding resources awarded to replace EFC). ***Average financial aid package:*** $16,000 (excluding resources awarded to replace EFC). 9% of all full-time undergraduates had no need and received non-need-based gift aid.

GIFT AID (NEED-BASED) ***Total amount:*** $9,021,000 (22% federal, 14% state, 54% institutional, 10% external sources). ***Receiving aid:*** Freshmen: 61% (495); all full-time undergraduates: 59% (2,020). ***Average award:*** Freshmen: $8750; Undergraduates: $8750. ***Scholarships, grants, and awards:*** Federal Pell, FSEOG, state, private, college/university gift aid from institutional funds.

GIFT AID (NON-NEED-BASED) ***Total amount:*** $3,452,000 (2% state, 72% institutional, 26% external sources). ***Receiving aid:*** Freshmen: 23% (190). Undergraduates: 23% (780). ***Average award:*** Freshmen: $5500. Undergraduates: $5500. ***Scholarships, grants, and awards by category:*** *Academic interests/achievement:* 780 awards ($2,500,000 total): business, computer science, engineering/technologies, general academic interests/achievements, mathematics, military science, physical sciences. *Creative arts/performance:* 38 awards ($36,232 total): music. *Special characteristics:* 10 awards ($10,000 total): children and siblings of alumni. ***ROTC:*** Army.

LOANS ***Student loans:*** $9,200,000 (67% need-based, 33% non-need-based). 65% of past graduating class borrowed through all loan programs. *Average indebtedness per student:* $22,500. ***Average need-based loan:*** Freshmen: $5450. Undergraduates: $5450. ***Parent loans:*** $3,800,000 (100% non-need-based). ***Programs:*** FFEL (Subsidized and Unsubsidized Stafford, PLUS), Perkins, college/university.

WORK-STUDY ***Federal work-study:*** Total amount: $181,000; 138 jobs averaging $1400. ***State or other work-study/employment:*** Total amount: $710,000 (44% need-based, 56% non-need-based). 342 part-time jobs averaging $1400.

ATHLETIC AWARDS Total amount: $1,520,000 (51% need-based, 49% non-need-based).

APPLYING FOR FINANCIAL AID ***Required financial aid form:*** FAFSA. ***Financial aid deadline (priority):*** 2/15. ***Notification date:*** Continuous beginning 3/15. Students must reply by 5/1 or within 2 weeks of notification.

CONTACT Director of Financial Aid, Colorado School of Mines, 1600 Maple Street, Golden, CO 80401-1887, 303-273-3220 or toll-free 800-446-9488 Ext. 3220 (out-of-state). *Fax:* 303-384-2252. *E-mail:* finaid@mines.edu.

COLORADO STATE UNIVERSITY

Fort Collins, CO

Tuition & fees (CO res): $5874 **Average undergraduate aid package: $8776**

ABOUT THE INSTITUTION State-supported, coed. ***Awards:*** bachelor's, master's, doctoral, and first professional degrees. 127 undergraduate majors. ***Total enrollment:*** 27,800. Undergraduates: 21,783. Freshmen: 4,404. Federal methodology is used as a basis for awarding need-based institutional aid.

UNDERGRADUATE EXPENSES for 2008–09 ***Application fee:*** $50. ***Tuition, state resident:*** full-time $4424; part-time $221.20 per credit hour. ***Tuition, nonresident:*** full-time $20,140; part-time $1007 per credit hour. ***Required fees:*** full-time $1450; $24.47 per term or $122.35 per term. Full-time tuition and fees vary according to course load. Part-time tuition and fees vary according to course load. ***College room and board:*** $8134; ***Room only:*** $4114. Room and board charges vary according to board plan and housing facility. ***Payment plan:*** Installment.

FRESHMAN FINANCIAL AID (Fall 2007) 2,515 applied for aid; of those 57% were deemed to have need. 100% of freshmen with need received aid; of those 32% had need fully met. ***Average percent of need met:*** 66% (excluding resources awarded to replace EFC). ***Average financial aid package:*** $7710 (excluding resources awarded to replace EFC). 5% of all full-time freshmen had no need and received non-need-based gift aid.

UNDERGRADUATE FINANCIAL AID (Fall 2007) 11,716 applied for aid; of those 67% were deemed to have need. 100% of undergraduates with need received aid; of those 36% had need fully met. ***Average percent of need met:*** 71% (excluding resources awarded to replace EFC). ***Average financial aid package:*** $8776 (excluding resources awarded to replace EFC). 8% of all full-time undergraduates had no need and received non-need-based gift aid.

GIFT AID (NEED-BASED) ***Total amount:*** $31,837,477 (43% federal, 19% state, 29% institutional, 9% external sources). ***Receiving aid:*** Freshmen: 29% (1,280); all full-time undergraduates: 35% (6,819). ***Average award:*** Freshmen: $5422; Undergraduates: $4623. ***Scholarships, grants, and awards:*** Federal Pell, FSEOG, state, private, college/university gift aid from institutional funds.

GIFT AID (NON-NEED-BASED) ***Total amount:*** $8,976,144 (19% federal, 3% state, 54% institutional, 24% external sources). ***Average award:*** Freshmen: $2453. Undergraduates: $3201. ***Scholarships, grants, and awards by category:*** *Academic interests/achievement:* 9,907 awards ($12,668,491 total): general academic interests/achievements. *Creative arts/performance:* 129 awards ($150,000 total): art/fine arts, creative writing, dance, music, theater/drama. *Special achievements/activities:* 258 awards ($634,346 total): general special achievements/activities. *Special characteristics:* 440 awards ($959,477 total): children of faculty/staff, first-generation college students. ***Tuition waivers:*** Full or partial for employees or children of employees. ***ROTC:*** Army, Air Force.

LOANS ***Student loans:*** $55,259,451 (73% need-based, 27% non-need-based). 61% of past graduating class borrowed through all loan programs. *Average indebtedness per student:* $18,607. ***Average need-based loan:*** Freshmen: $3999. Undergraduates: $5657. ***Parent loans:*** $28,436,600 (59% need-based, 41% non-need-based). ***Programs:*** Federal Direct (Subsidized and Unsubsidized Stafford, PLUS), Perkins, alternative loans.

WORK-STUDY ***Federal work-study:*** Total amount: $662,896; 378 jobs averaging $1845. ***State or other work-study/employment:*** Total amount: $2,092,987 (73% need-based, 27% non-need-based). 1,194 part-time jobs averaging $1788.

ATHLETIC AWARDS Total amount: $4,823,567 (11% need-based, 89% non-need-based).

APPLYING FOR FINANCIAL AID ***Required financial aid form:*** FAFSA. ***Financial aid deadline (priority):*** 3/1. ***Notification date:*** Continuous beginning 3/1.

CONTACT Office of Student Financial Services, Colorado State University, Room 103, Administration Annex Building, Fort Collins, CO 80523-8024, 970-491-6321. *E-mail:* sfs@colostate.edu.

COLORADO STATE UNIVERSITY–PUEBLO

Pueblo, CO

Tuition & fees (CO res): $4667 **Average undergraduate aid package: $8278**

ABOUT THE INSTITUTION State-supported, coed. ***Awards:*** bachelor's and master's degrees. 26 undergraduate majors. ***Total enrollment:*** 6,759. Undergraduates: 5,252. Freshmen: 1,046. Federal methodology is used as a basis for awarding need-based institutional aid.

UNDERGRADUATE EXPENSES for 2008–09 ***Application fee:*** $25. ***Tuition, state resident:*** full-time $3422; part-time $142.60 per credit hour. ***Tuition, nonresident:*** full-time $13,543; part-time $564 per credit hour. ***Required fees:*** full-time $1245. ***College room and board:*** $6300; ***Room only:*** $3200.

FRESHMAN FINANCIAL AID (Fall 2008, est.) 855 applied for aid; of those 76% were deemed to have need. 100% of freshmen with need received aid; of those 9% had need fully met. ***Average percent of need met:*** 62% (excluding resources awarded to replace EFC). ***Average financial aid package:*** $7980 (excluding resources awarded to replace EFC). 10% of all full-time freshmen had no need and received non-need-based gift aid.

UNDERGRADUATE FINANCIAL AID (Fall 2008, est.) 2,136 applied for aid; of those 81% were deemed to have need. 99% of undergraduates with need received aid; of those 8% had need fully met. ***Average percent of need met:*** 59% (excluding resources awarded to replace EFC). ***Average financial aid package:*** $8278 (excluding resources awarded to replace EFC). 10% of all full-time undergraduates had no need and received non-need-based gift aid.

GIFT AID (NEED-BASED) ***Total amount:*** $11,708,825 (54% federal, 25% state, 15% institutional, 6% external sources). ***Receiving aid:*** Freshmen: 65% (577); all full-time undergraduates: 57% (1,456). ***Average award:*** Freshmen: $5612; Undergraduates: $5573. ***Scholarships, grants, and awards:*** Federal Pell, FSEOG, state, private, college/university gift aid from institutional funds, Academic Competitiveness Grant, National Smart Grant, TEACH Grant.

GIFT AID (NON-NEED-BASED) ***Total amount:*** $1,341,579 (6% state, 70% institutional, 24% external sources). ***Receiving aid:*** Freshmen: 4% (34). Undergraduates: 3% (72). ***Average award:*** Freshmen: $2042. Undergraduates: $2687. ***Scholarships, grants, and awards by category:*** *Academic interests/achievement:* 422 awards ($826,268 total): biological sciences, business, communication, computer science, education, engineering/technologies, English, foreign languages, general academic interests/achievements, health fields, mathematics, physical sciences, premedicine, social sciences. *Creative arts/performance:* 98 awards ($160,185 total): applied art and design, art/fine arts, cinema/film/broadcasting, journalism/publications, music. *Special achievements/activities:* 47 awards ($91,208 total): community service, general special achievements/activities, leadership. *Special characteristics:* 444 awards ($760,309 total): children and siblings of alumni, children of faculty/staff, ethnic background, first-generation college students, general special characteristics, handicapped students, international students, out-of-state students. ***ROTC:*** Army.

LOANS ***Student loans:*** $20,317,118 (78% need-based, 22% non-need-based). 54% of past graduating class borrowed through all loan programs. *Average indebtedness per student:* $16,981. ***Average need-based loan:*** Freshmen: $3133. Undergraduates: $3700. ***Parent loans:*** $868,003 (26% need-based, 74% non-need-based). ***Programs:*** Federal Direct (Subsidized and Unsubsidized Stafford, PLUS), FFEL (Subsidized and Unsubsidized Stafford, PLUS), Perkins.

WORK-STUDY ***Federal work-study:*** Total amount: $485,234; 225 jobs averaging $2095. ***State or other work-study/employment:*** Total amount: $916,994 (70% need-based, 30% non-need-based). 337 part-time jobs averaging $2472.

ATHLETIC AWARDS Total amount: $931,142 (51% need-based, 49% non-need-based).

APPLYING FOR FINANCIAL AID ***Required financial aid forms:*** FAFSA, institution's own form. ***Financial aid deadline (priority):*** 3/1. ***Notification date:*** Continuous beginning 3/15. Students must reply within 3 weeks of notification.

CONTACT Sean McGivney, Director of Student Financial Services, Colorado State University–Pueblo, 2200 Bonforte Boulevard, Pueblo, CO 81001-4901, 719-549-2753. *Fax:* 719-549-2088.

COLORADO TECHNICAL UNIVERSITY COLORADO SPRINGS

Colorado Springs, CO

Tuition & fees: N/R **Average undergraduate aid package: $9310**

ABOUT THE INSTITUTION Proprietary, coed. ***Awards:*** associate, bachelor's, master's, and doctoral degrees. 14 undergraduate majors. ***Total enrollment:*** 2,359. Undergraduates: 1,896. Federal methodology is used as a basis for awarding need-based institutional aid.

UNDERGRADUATE EXPENSES for 2009–10 ***Application fee:*** $50. contact campus for cost.

FRESHMAN FINANCIAL AID (Fall 2007) 55 applied for aid; of those 73% were deemed to have need. 100% of freshmen with need received aid; of those 50% had need fully met. ***Average percent of need met:*** 90% (excluding resources awarded to replace EFC). ***Average financial aid package:*** $9310 (excluding resources awarded to replace EFC). 18% of all full-time freshmen had no need and received non-need-based gift aid.

UNDERGRADUATE FINANCIAL AID (Fall 2007) 70 applied for aid; of those 79% were deemed to have need. 100% of undergraduates with need received aid; of those 55% had need fully met. ***Average percent of need met:*** 95% (excluding resources awarded to replace EFC). ***Average financial aid package:*** $9310 (excluding resources awarded to replace EFC). 31% of all full-time undergraduates had no need and received non-need-based gift aid.

GIFT AID (NEED-BASED) ***Total amount:*** $1,502,506 (81% federal, 15% state, 4% external sources). ***Receiving aid:*** Freshmen: 64% (35); all full-time undergraduates: 44% (35). ***Average award:*** Freshmen: $5000; Undergraduates: $5000. ***Scholarships, grants, and awards:*** Federal Pell, FSEOG, state, college/university gift aid from institutional funds.

GIFT AID (NON-NEED-BASED) ***Total amount:*** $333,378 (100% institutional). ***Receiving aid:*** Freshmen: 27% (15). Undergraduates: 6% (5). ***Scholarships, grants, and awards by category:*** *Academic interests/achievement:* business, computer science, engineering/technologies, general academic interests/achievements. ***ROTC:*** Army cooperative.

LOANS ***Student loans:*** $13,859,477 (40% need-based, 60% non-need-based). 55% of past graduating class borrowed through all loan programs. *Average indebtedness per student:* $7500. ***Average need-based loan:*** Freshmen: $3500. Undergraduates: $3500. ***Parent loans:*** $512,205 (100% non-need-based). ***Programs:*** FFEL (Subsidized and Unsubsidized Stafford, PLUS), Perkins.

WORK-STUDY ***Federal work-study:*** Total amount: $152,120; 35 jobs averaging $4619.

APPLYING FOR FINANCIAL AID ***Required financial aid forms:*** FAFSA, state aid form. ***Financial aid deadline:*** Continuous. ***Notification date:*** Continuous.

CONTACT Jacqueline Harris, Senior Director of Student Finance Services, Colorado Technical University Colorado Springs, 4435 North Chestnut Street, Colorado Springs, CO 80907-3896, 719-598-0200. *Fax:* 719-598-3740.

COLORADO TECHNICAL UNIVERSITY DENVER

Greenwood Village, CO

Tuition & fees: N/R — **Average undergraduate aid package: N/A**

ABOUT THE INSTITUTION Proprietary, coed. ***Awards:*** associate, bachelor's, and master's degrees. 9 undergraduate majors. ***Total enrollment:*** 733. Undergraduates: 573. Freshmen: 52. Federal methodology is used as a basis for awarding need-based institutional aid.

UNDERGRADUATE EXPENSES for 2009–10 ***Application fee:*** $50. contact campus for cost.

GIFT AID (NEED-BASED) ***Total amount:*** $59,337 (44% federal, 56% state). ***Scholarships, grants, and awards:*** Federal Pell, FSEOG, state.

GIFT AID (NON-NEED-BASED) ***Scholarships, grants, and awards by category:*** *Academic interests/achievement:* business, computer science, engineering/technologies, general academic interests/achievements.

LOANS ***Student loans:*** $454,327 (100% need-based). ***Parent loans:*** $19,665 (100% need-based). ***Programs:*** FFEL (Subsidized and Unsubsidized Stafford, PLUS), Perkins.

WORK-STUDY ***Federal work-study:*** Total amount: $7871; 2 jobs averaging $3936.

APPLYING FOR FINANCIAL AID ***Required financial aid forms:*** FAFSA, state aid form. ***Financial aid deadline:*** Continuous. ***Notification date:*** Continuous.

CONTACT Ms. Natalie Dietsch, Financial Aid Manager, Colorado Technical University Denver, 5775 Denver Tech Center Boulevard, Suite 100, Greenwood Village, CO 80111, 303-694-6600. *Fax:* 303-694-6673.

COLORADO TECHNICAL UNIVERSITY NORTH KANSAS CITY

North Kansas City, MO

CONTACT Ms. Judy Richman, Director of Financial Assistance, Colorado Technical University North Kansas City, 520 East 19th Avenue, North Kansas City, MO 64116, 816-472-7400.

COLORADO TECHNICAL UNIVERSITY SIOUX FALLS

Sioux Falls, SD

Tuition & fees: N/R — **Average undergraduate aid package: $3500**

ABOUT THE INSTITUTION Proprietary, coed. ***Awards:*** associate, bachelor's, and master's degrees. 15 undergraduate majors. ***Total enrollment:*** 912. Undergraduates: 816. Freshmen: 105.

UNDERGRADUATE EXPENSES for 2009–10 ***Application fee:*** $50. contact campus for cost.

FRESHMAN FINANCIAL AID (Fall 2007) 50 applied for aid; of those 100% were deemed to have need. 100% of freshmen with need received aid. ***Average percent of need met:*** 30% (excluding resources awarded to replace EFC). ***Average financial aid package:*** $2625 (excluding resources awarded to replace EFC).

UNDERGRADUATE FINANCIAL AID (Fall 2007) 280 applied for aid; of those 100% were deemed to have need. 100% of undergraduates with need received aid. ***Average percent of need met:*** 45% (excluding resources awarded to replace EFC). ***Average financial aid package:*** $3500 (excluding resources awarded to replace EFC).

GIFT AID (NEED-BASED) ***Total amount:*** $465,803 (100% federal). ***Receiving aid:*** Freshmen: 31% (19); all full-time undergraduates: 31% (95). ***Average award:*** Freshmen: $2475; Undergraduates: $3300. ***Scholarships, grants, and awards:*** Federal Pell, FSEOG.

GIFT AID (NON-NEED-BASED) ***ROTC:*** Army cooperative.

LOANS ***Student loans:*** $2,661,497 (100% need-based). 75% of past graduating class borrowed through all loan programs. ***Average need-based loan:*** Freshmen: $2625. Undergraduates: $4648. ***Parent loans:*** $73,660 (100% need-based). ***Programs:*** FFEL (Subsidized and Unsubsidized Stafford, PLUS), Perkins.

WORK-STUDY ***Federal work-study:*** Total amount: $40,000; jobs available.

APPLYING FOR FINANCIAL AID ***Required financial aid forms:*** FAFSA, institution's own form. ***Financial aid deadline:*** Continuous. ***Notification date:*** Continuous beginning 5/1.

CONTACT Vikki Van Hull, Financial Aid Officer, Colorado Technical University Sioux Falls, 3901 West 59th Street, Sioux Falls, SD 57108, 605-361-0200 Ext. 140. *Fax:* 605-361-5954. *E-mail:* vvanhull@sf.coloradotech.edu.

COLUMBIA COLLEGE

Columbia, MO

Tuition & fees: $14,576 — **Average undergraduate aid package: $12,510**

ABOUT THE INSTITUTION Independent religious, coed. ***Awards:*** associate, bachelor's, and master's degrees (offers continuing education program with significant enrollment not reflected in profile). 34 undergraduate majors. ***Total enrollment:*** 1,353. Undergraduates: 1,169. Freshmen: 220. Federal methodology is used as a basis for awarding need-based institutional aid.

UNDERGRADUATE EXPENSES for 2009–10 ***Application fee:*** $25. ***Comprehensive fee:*** $20,474 includes full-time tuition ($14,576) and room and board ($5898). ***College room only:*** $3670. ***Part-time tuition:*** $312 per credit hour.

FRESHMAN FINANCIAL AID (Fall 2007) 100 applied for aid; of those 90% were deemed to have need. 100% of freshmen with need received aid; of those 14% had need fully met. ***Average percent of need met:*** 69% (excluding resources awarded to replace EFC). ***Average financial aid package:*** $12,841 (excluding resources awarded to replace EFC). 26% of all full-time freshmen had no need and received non-need-based gift aid.

UNDERGRADUATE FINANCIAL AID (Fall 2007) 449 applied for aid; of those 91% were deemed to have need. 100% of undergraduates with need received aid; of those 13% had need fully met. ***Average percent of need met:*** 64%

(excluding resources awarded to replace EFC). ***Average financial aid package:*** $12,510 (excluding resources awarded to replace EFC). 15% of all full-time undergraduates had no need and received non-need-based gift aid.

GIFT AID (NEED-BASED) ***Total amount:*** $1,661,965 (50% federal, 49% state, 1% institutional). ***Receiving aid:*** Freshmen: 46% (90); all full-time undergraduates: 48% (407). ***Average award:*** Freshmen: $9264; Undergraduates: $9736. ***Scholarships, grants, and awards:*** Federal Pell, FSEOG, state, private, college/university gift aid from institutional funds, VA, vocational rehabilitation.

GIFT AID (NON-NEED-BASED) ***Total amount:*** $2,941,273 (2% state, 98% institutional). ***Receiving aid:*** Freshmen: 46% (90). Undergraduates: 45% (385). ***Average award:*** Freshmen: $7798. Undergraduates: $8019. ***Scholarships, grants, and awards by category:*** *Academic interests/achievement:* biological sciences, business, education, English, general academic interests/achievements, humanities, physical sciences, religion/biblical studies, social sciences. *Creative arts/performance:* art/fine arts, music. *Special achievements/activities:* leadership, religious involvement. *Special characteristics:* children and siblings of alumni, children of current students, children of educators, children of faculty/staff, first-generation college students, international students, local/state students, parents of current students, previous college experience, religious affiliation, siblings of current students, spouses of current students, veterans. ***ROTC:*** Army cooperative, Naval cooperative, Air Force cooperative.

LOANS ***Student loans:*** $3,707,201 (42% need-based, 58% non-need-based). 58% of past graduating class borrowed through all loan programs. *Average indebtedness per student:* $17,101. ***Average need-based loan:*** Freshmen: $3878. Undergraduates: $4486. ***Parent loans:*** $646,927 (100% non-need-based). ***Programs:*** FFEL (Subsidized and Unsubsidized Stafford, PLUS), Perkins.

WORK-STUDY ***Federal work-study:*** Total amount: $185,878; jobs available. ***State or other work-study/employment:*** Total amount: $138,420 (100% non-need-based). Part-time jobs available.

ATHLETIC AWARDS Total amount: $974,383 (100% non-need-based).

APPLYING FOR FINANCIAL AID ***Required financial aid form:*** FAFSA. ***Notification date:*** Continuous beginning 3/1.

CONTACT Sharon Abernathy, Director of Financial Aid, Columbia College, 1001 Rogers Street, Columbia, MO 65216-0002, 573-875-7390 or toll-free 800-231-2391 Ext. 7366. *Fax:* 573-875-7452. *E-mail:* saabernathy@ccis.edu.

COLUMBIA COLLEGE

Caguas, PR

CONTACT Financial Aid Officer, Columbia College, Carr 183, Km 1.7, PO Box 8517, Caguas, PR 00726, 787-743-4041 Ext. 244 or toll-free 800-981-4877 Ext. 239 (in-state).

COLUMBIA COLLEGE

Columbia, SC

CONTACT Anita Kaminer Elliott, Director of Financial Aid, Columbia College, 1301 Columbia College Drive, Columbia, SC 29203-5998, 803-786-3612 or toll-free 800-277-1301. *Fax:* 803-786-3560.

COLUMBIA COLLEGE CHICAGO

Chicago, IL

Tuition & fees: N/R **Average undergraduate aid package: $8511**

ABOUT THE INSTITUTION Independent, coed. ***Awards:*** bachelor's and master's degrees and post-bachelor's certificates. 41 undergraduate majors. ***Total enrollment:*** 11,499. Undergraduates: 11,366. Federal methodology is used as a basis for awarding need-based institutional aid.

FRESHMAN FINANCIAL AID (Fall 2007) 1,647 applied for aid; of those 87% were deemed to have need. 100% of freshmen with need received aid; of those 3% had need fully met. ***Average percent of need met:*** 48% (excluding resources awarded to replace EFC). ***Average financial aid package:*** $7799 (excluding resources awarded to replace EFC).

UNDERGRADUATE FINANCIAL AID (Fall 2007) 6,839 applied for aid; of those 90% were deemed to have need. 100% of undergraduates with need received aid; of those 4% had need fully met. ***Average percent of need met:*** 41% (excluding resources awarded to replace EFC). ***Average financial aid package:*** $8511 (excluding resources awarded to replace EFC).

GIFT AID (NEED-BASED) ***Total amount:*** $21,400,264 (43% federal, 52% state, 5% institutional). ***Receiving aid:*** Freshmen: 34% (748); all full-time undergraduates: 32% (3,249). ***Average award:*** Freshmen: $3912; Undergraduates: $4558. ***Scholarships, grants, and awards:*** Federal Pell, FSEOG, state, private, college/university gift aid from institutional funds.

GIFT AID (NON-NEED-BASED) ***Total amount:*** $6,776,652 (76% institutional, 24% external sources). ***Receiving aid:*** Freshmen: 19% (415). Undergraduates: 11% (1,089). ***Scholarships, grants, and awards by category:*** *Academic interests/achievement:* business, communication, education, general academic interests/achievements. *Creative arts/performance:* applied art and design, art/fine arts, cinema/film/broadcasting, creative writing, dance, journalism/publications, music, performing arts, theater/drama. *Special achievements/activities:* leadership. *Special characteristics:* children of faculty/staff, handicapped students.

LOANS ***Student loans:*** $91,116,464 (100% need-based). ***Average need-based loan:*** Freshmen: $3241. Undergraduates: $4305. ***Programs:*** Federal Direct (Subsidized and Unsubsidized Stafford, PLUS).

WORK-STUDY ***Federal work-study:*** Total amount: $658,747; 821 jobs averaging $2250. ***State or other work-study/employment:*** Part-time jobs available.

APPLYING FOR FINANCIAL AID ***Required financial aid forms:*** FAFSA, institution's own form. ***Financial aid deadline (priority):*** 8/15. ***Notification date:*** Continuous.

CONTACT Ms. Jennifer Waters, Executive Director of Student Financial Services, Columbia College Chicago, 600 South Michigan Avenue, Chicago, IL 60605-1996, 312-369-7831. *Fax:* 312-986-7008. *E-mail:* jwaters@colum.edu.

COLUMBIA COLLEGE HOLLYWOOD

Tarzana, CA

CONTACT Mr. Chris Freeman, Financial Aid Administrator, Columbia College Hollywood, 18618 Oxnard Street, Tarzana, CA 91356, 818-345-8414 Ext. 110 or toll-free 800-785-0585 (in-state). *Fax:* 818-345-9053. *E-mail:* finaid@columbiacollege.edu.

COLUMBIA INTERNATIONAL UNIVERSITY

Columbia, SC

Tuition & fees: $16,850 **Average undergraduate aid package: $6150**

ABOUT THE INSTITUTION Independent nondenominational, coed. ***Awards:*** associate, bachelor's, master's, doctoral, and first professional degrees and post-bachelor's certificates. 15 undergraduate majors. ***Total enrollment:*** 924. Undergraduates: 480. Freshmen: 86. Federal methodology is used as a basis for awarding need-based institutional aid.

UNDERGRADUATE EXPENSES for 2009–10 ***Application fee:*** $45. ***Comprehensive fee:*** $23,060 includes full-time tuition ($16,350), mandatory fees ($500), and room and board ($6210). ***Part-time tuition:*** $675 per credit. ***Part-time fees:*** $250 per term.

FRESHMAN FINANCIAL AID (Fall 2008, est.) 83 applied for aid; of those 86% were deemed to have need. 97% of freshmen with need received aid. ***Average percent of need met:*** 40% (excluding resources awarded to replace EFC). ***Average financial aid package:*** $5200 (excluding resources awarded to replace EFC). 16% of all full-time freshmen had no need and received non-need-based gift aid.

UNDERGRADUATE FINANCIAL AID (Fall 2008, est.) 318 applied for aid; of those 92% were deemed to have need. 93% of undergraduates with need received aid; of those .4% had need fully met. ***Average percent of need met:*** 47% (excluding resources awarded to replace EFC). ***Average financial aid package:*** $6150 (excluding resources awarded to replace EFC). 19% of all full-time undergraduates had no need and received non-need-based gift aid.

GIFT AID (NEED-BASED) ***Total amount:*** $1,301,524 (61% federal, 39% state). ***Scholarships, grants, and awards:*** Federal Pell, FSEOG, state, private, college/university gift aid from institutional funds.

GIFT AID (NON-NEED-BASED) ***Total amount:*** $3,412,709 (15% state, 79% institutional, 6% external sources). ***Receiving aid:*** Freshmen: 48% (41). Undergraduates: 38% (185). ***Average award:*** Freshmen: $3000. Undergraduates: $4000. ***Scholarships, grants, and awards by category:*** *Academic interests/achievement:* 190 awards ($400,568 total): business, communication, education, English, general academic interests/achievements, international studies, religion/biblical studies. *Creative arts/performance:* 11 awards ($8000 total): music, performing arts. *Special achievements/activities:* 183 awards ($501,235 total): general special achievements/activities, leadership. *Special characteristics:*

199 awards ($278,564 total): children and siblings of alumni, ethnic background, international students, married students, relatives of clergy, religious affiliation, spouses of current students, veterans, veterans' children.

LOANS ***Student loans:*** $2,010,831 (54% need-based, 46% non-need-based). 65% of past graduating class borrowed through all loan programs. *Average indebtedness per student:* $16,500. ***Average need-based loan:*** Freshmen: $3000. Undergraduates: $4200. ***Parent loans:*** $617,651 (100% non-need-based). ***Programs:*** FFEL (Subsidized and Unsubsidized Stafford, PLUS).

WORK-STUDY ***Federal work-study:*** Total amount: $177,500; 68 jobs averaging $2500.

APPLYING FOR FINANCIAL AID ***Required financial aid forms:*** FAFSA, institution's own form. ***Financial aid deadline:*** Continuous. ***Notification date:*** Continuous beginning 1/31. Students must reply by 6/1.

CONTACT Nicole Mathison, Office Manager, Columbia International University, 7435 Monticello Road, Columbia, SC 29203, 800-777-2227 Ext. 5036 or toll-free 800-777-2227 Ext. 3024. *Fax:* 803-223-2505. *E-mail:* nmathison@ciu.edu.

COLUMBIA UNION COLLEGE

Takoma Park, MD

CONTACT Elaine Oliver, Director, Financial Aid, Columbia Union College, 7600 Flower Avenue, Takoma Park, MD 20912, 301-891-4005 or toll-free 800-835-4212.

COLUMBIA UNIVERSITY

New York, NY

CONTACT Financial Aid Office, Columbia University, 116th Street and Broadway, New York, NY 10027, 212-854-1754.

COLUMBIA UNIVERSITY, SCHOOL OF GENERAL STUDIES

New York, NY

Tuition & fees: $37,958 **Average undergraduate aid package: N/A**

ABOUT THE INSTITUTION Independent, coed. ***Awards:*** bachelor's degrees and post-bachelor's certificates. 45 undergraduate majors. ***Total enrollment:*** 1,245. Undergraduates: 1,245. Freshmen: 63. Both federal and institutional methodology are used as a basis for awarding need-based institutional aid.

UNDERGRADUATE EXPENSES for 2008–09 ***Application fee:*** $65. ***Comprehensive fee:*** $50,003 includes full-time tuition ($36,300), mandatory fees ($1650), and room and board ($12,045). ***College room only:*** $7875. Full-time tuition and fees vary according to course load. Room and board charges vary according to board plan and housing facility. ***Part-time tuition:*** $1210 per credit. Part-time tuition and fees vary according to course load. ***Payment plans:*** Tuition prepayment, installment.

GIFT AID (NEED-BASED) ***Total amount:*** $9,609,582 (24% federal, 5% state, 68% institutional, 3% external sources). ***Scholarships, grants, and awards:*** Federal Pell, FSEOG, state, private, college/university gift aid from institutional funds.

GIFT AID (NON-NEED-BASED) ***Total amount:*** $1,723,245 (25% federal, 73% institutional, 2% external sources). ***Scholarships, grants, and awards by category:*** *Academic interests/achievement:* general academic interests/achievements. ***Tuition waivers:*** Full or partial for employees or children of employees. ***ROTC:*** Army cooperative, Air Force cooperative.

LOANS ***Student loans:*** $12,743,076 (43% need-based, 57% non-need-based). ***Parent loans:*** $2,579,941 (100% non-need-based). ***Programs:*** FFEL (Subsidized and Unsubsidized Stafford, PLUS), Perkins, college/university.

WORK-STUDY ***Federal work-study:*** Total amount: $703,622; jobs available.

APPLYING FOR FINANCIAL AID ***Required financial aid forms:*** FAFSA, institution's own form. ***Financial aid deadline:*** 6/1 (priority: 6/1). ***Notification date:*** Continuous. Students must reply within 3 weeks of notification.

CONTACT Student Financial Planning, Columbia University, School of General Studies, 208 Kent Hall, New York, NY 10027, 212-854-7040 or toll-free 800-895-1169 (out-of-state).

COLUMBUS COLLEGE OF ART & DESIGN

Columbus, OH

Tuition & fees: $23,564 **Average undergraduate aid package: $16,723**

ABOUT THE INSTITUTION Independent, coed. ***Awards:*** bachelor's degrees. 7 undergraduate majors. ***Total enrollment:*** 1,599. Undergraduates: 1,599. Freshmen: 169. Federal methodology is used as a basis for awarding need-based institutional aid.

UNDERGRADUATE EXPENSES for 2008–09 ***Application fee:*** $25. ***Comprehensive fee:*** $30,314 includes full-time tuition ($22,920), mandatory fees ($644), and room and board ($6750). ***Part-time tuition:*** $955 per credit hour. ***Part-time fees:*** $322 per term.

FRESHMAN FINANCIAL AID (Fall 2008, est.) 281 applied for aid; of those 88% were deemed to have need. 97% of freshmen with need received aid; of those 14% had need fully met. ***Average percent of need met:*** 67% (excluding resources awarded to replace EFC). ***Average financial aid package:*** $17,474 (excluding resources awarded to replace EFC). 21% of all full-time freshmen had no need and received non-need-based gift aid.

UNDERGRADUATE FINANCIAL AID (Fall 2008, est.) 1,214 applied for aid; of those 87% were deemed to have need. 99% of undergraduates with need received aid; of those 15% had need fully met. ***Average percent of need met:*** 66% (excluding resources awarded to replace EFC). ***Average financial aid package:*** $16,723 (excluding resources awarded to replace EFC). 17% of all full-time undergraduates had no need and received non-need-based gift aid.

GIFT AID (NEED-BASED) ***Total amount:*** $12,134,233 (15% federal, 12% state, 70% institutional, 3% external sources). ***Receiving aid:*** Freshmen: 76% (239); all full-time undergraduates: 80% (1,038). ***Average award:*** Freshmen: $12,814; Undergraduates: $10,846. ***Scholarships, grants, and awards:*** Federal Pell, FSEOG, state, private, college/university gift aid from institutional funds.

GIFT AID (NON-NEED-BASED) ***Total amount:*** $2,284,895 (5% state, 92% institutional, 3% external sources). ***Receiving aid:*** Freshmen: 2% (6). Undergraduates: 3% (43). ***Average award:*** Freshmen: $7787. Undergraduates: $7512. ***Scholarships, grants, and awards by category:*** *Creative arts/performance:* 1,211 awards ($8,884,637 total): art/fine arts. *Special characteristics:* 12 awards ($198,762 total): children of educators, children of faculty/staff, local/state students.

LOANS ***Student loans:*** $11,403,580 (75% need-based, 25% non-need-based). 87% of past graduating class borrowed through all loan programs. *Average indebtedness per student:* $34,592. ***Average need-based loan:*** Freshmen: $5265. Undergraduates: $6422. ***Parent loans:*** $3,230,527 (62% need-based, 38% non-need-based). ***Programs:*** FFEL (Subsidized and Unsubsidized Stafford, PLUS), Perkins, state.

WORK-STUDY ***Federal work-study:*** Total amount: $489,689; 148 jobs averaging $3250. ***State or other work-study/employment:*** 337 part-time jobs averaging $3000.

APPLYING FOR FINANCIAL AID ***Required financial aid forms:*** FAFSA, institution's own form, income tax forms, verification statement. ***Financial aid deadline (priority):*** 2/16. ***Notification date:*** 3/15. Students must reply within 2 weeks of notification.

CONTACT Mrs. Anna Schofield, Director of Financial Aid, Columbus College of Art & Design, 107 North Ninth Street, Columbus, OH 43215-1758, 614-224-9101 Ext. 3274 or toll-free 877-997-2223. *Fax:* 614-222-4034. *E-mail:* aschofield@ccad.edu.

COLUMBUS STATE UNIVERSITY

Columbus, GA

Tuition & fees (GA res): $3772 **Average undergraduate aid package: $4026**

ABOUT THE INSTITUTION State-supported, coed. ***Awards:*** associate, bachelor's, and master's degrees and post-bachelor's and post-master's certificates. 38 undergraduate majors. ***Total enrollment:*** 7,953. Undergraduates: 6,838. Freshmen: 1,244. Federal methodology is used as a basis for awarding need-based institutional aid.

UNDERGRADUATE EXPENSES for 2008–09 ***Application fee:*** $25. ***Tuition, state resident:*** full-time $3098; part-time $130 per semester hour. ***Tuition, nonresident:*** full-time $12,390; part-time $517 per semester hour. ***Required fees:*** full-time $674. Full-time tuition and fees vary according to course level. Part-time tuition and fees vary according to course level. ***College room and board:*** $6900. Room and board charges vary according to board plan and location. ***Payment plan:*** Guaranteed tuition.

FRESHMAN FINANCIAL AID (Fall 2008, est.) 927 applied for aid; of those 64% were deemed to have need. 97% of freshmen with need received aid; of those 68% had need fully met. ***Average percent of need met:*** 66% (excluding resources awarded to replace EFC). ***Average financial aid package:*** $3759 (excluding resources awarded to replace EFC). 33% of all full-time freshmen had no need and received non-need-based gift aid.

UNDERGRADUATE FINANCIAL AID (Fall 2008, est.) 3,405 applied for aid; of those 69% were deemed to have need. 98% of undergraduates with need received aid; of those 77% had need fully met. ***Average percent of need met:*** 72% (excluding resources awarded to replace EFC). ***Average financial aid package:*** $4026 (excluding resources awarded to replace EFC). 40% of all full-time undergraduates had no need and received non-need-based gift aid.

GIFT AID (NEED-BASED) ***Total amount:*** $3,769,583 (97% federal, 1% institutional, 2% external sources). ***Receiving aid:*** Freshmen: 38% (407); all full-time undergraduates: 30% (1,419). ***Average award:*** Freshmen: $3146; Undergraduates: $3873. ***Scholarships, grants, and awards:*** Federal Pell, FSEOG, state, private, college/university gift aid from institutional funds.

GIFT AID (NON-NEED-BASED) ***Total amount:*** $3,400,010 (81% state, 11% institutional, 8% external sources). ***Receiving aid:*** Freshmen: 41% (433). Undergraduates: 41% (1,943). ***Average award:*** Freshmen: $1671. Undergraduates: $1836. ***Scholarships, grants, and awards by category:*** *Academic interests/achievement:* biological sciences, business, communication, computer science, education, English, general academic interests/achievements, health fields, humanities, international studies, mathematics, military science, physical sciences. *Creative arts/performance:* art/fine arts, dance, music, performing arts, theater/drama. *Special achievements/activities:* cheerleading/drum major, community service, general special achievements/activities, leadership. ***Tuition waivers:*** Full or partial for employees or children of employees, senior citizens. ***ROTC:*** Army.

LOANS ***Student loans:*** $21,925,060 (51% need-based, 49% non-need-based). 75% of past graduating class borrowed through all loan programs. *Average indebtedness per student:* $26,905. ***Average need-based loan:*** Freshmen: $2899. Undergraduates: $3820. ***Parent loans:*** $749,143 (100% need-based). ***Programs:*** Federal Direct (Subsidized and Unsubsidized Stafford, PLUS), Perkins, state, college/university.

WORK-STUDY ***Federal work-study:*** Total amount: $130,000; 80 jobs averaging $3000.

ATHLETIC AWARDS Total amount: $398,895 (100% non-need-based).

APPLYING FOR FINANCIAL AID ***Required financial aid form:*** FAFSA. ***Financial aid deadline (priority):*** 5/1. ***Notification date:*** Continuous beginning 5/1.

CONTACT Ms. Janis Bowles, Director of Financial Aid, Columbus State University, 4225 University Avenue, Columbus, GA 31907-5645, 706-507-8800 or toll-free 866-264-2035. *Fax:* 706-568-2230. *E-mail:* bowles_janis@colstate.edu.

CONCEPTION SEMINARY COLLEGE

Conception, MO

CONTACT Br. Justin Hernandez, PhD, Financial Aid Director, Conception Seminary College, PO Box 502, Conception, MO 64433-0502, 660-944-2851. *Fax:* 660-944-2829. *E-mail:* justin@conception.edu.

CONCORDIA COLLEGE

Selma, AL

Tuition & fees: $7090 **Average undergraduate aid package: $4410**

ABOUT THE INSTITUTION Independent Lutheran, coed. ***Awards:*** associate and bachelor's degrees. 4 undergraduate majors. ***Total enrollment:*** 555. Undergraduates: 555. Both federal and institutional methodology are used as a basis for awarding need-based institutional aid.

UNDERGRADUATE EXPENSES for 2008–09 ***Application fee:*** $10. ***One-time required fee:*** $10. ***Comprehensive fee:*** $10,590 includes full-time tuition ($6826), mandatory fees ($264), and room and board ($3500). ***College room only:*** $1200. Full-time tuition and fees vary according to course load. Room and board charges vary according to housing facility. ***Part-time tuition:*** $235 per credit hour. Part-time tuition and fees vary according to course load. ***Payment plans:*** Installment, deferred payment.

FRESHMAN FINANCIAL AID (Fall 2008, est.) 298 applied for aid; of those 84% were deemed to have need. 80% of freshmen with need received aid; of those 38% had need fully met. ***Average percent of need met:*** 86% (excluding resources awarded to replace EFC). ***Average financial aid package:*** $4410 (excluding resources awarded to replace EFC). 3% of all full-time freshmen had no need and received non-need-based gift aid.

UNDERGRADUATE FINANCIAL AID (Fall 2008, est.) 800 applied for aid; of those 98% were deemed to have need. 83% of undergraduates with need received aid; of those 75% had need fully met. ***Average percent of need met:*** 92% (excluding resources awarded to replace EFC). ***Average financial aid package:*** $4410 (excluding resources awarded to replace EFC). 3% of all full-time undergraduates had no need and received non-need-based gift aid.

GIFT AID (NEED-BASED) ***Total amount:*** $2,332,483 (89% federal, 3% state, 6% institutional, 2% external sources). ***Receiving aid:*** Freshmen: 67% (200); all full-time undergraduates: 62% (511). ***Average award:*** Freshmen: $1500; Undergraduates: $1500. ***Scholarships, grants, and awards:*** Federal Pell, FSEOG, state, private, college/university gift aid from institutional funds.

GIFT AID (NON-NEED-BASED) ***Total amount:*** $131,157 (100% state). ***Receiving aid:*** Freshmen: 10% (30). Undergraduates: 11% (87). ***Average award:*** Freshmen: $500. Undergraduates: $500. ***Scholarships, grants, and awards by category:*** *Academic interests/achievement:* 300 awards: business, computer science, education, general academic interests/achievements, religion/biblical studies. *Creative arts/performance:* 75 awards: music. *Special achievements/activities:* 6 awards: cheerleading/drum major. ***Tuition waivers:*** Full or partial for employees or children of employees.

LOANS ***Student loans:*** $987,784 (99% need-based, 1% non-need-based). 56% of past graduating class borrowed through all loan programs. *Average indebtedness per student:* $5500. ***Programs:*** FFEL (Subsidized Stafford).

WORK-STUDY ***Federal work-study:*** Total amount: $60,947; 86 jobs averaging $600. ***State or other work-study/employment:*** Part-time jobs available.

ATHLETIC AWARDS Total amount: $571,774 (100% need-based).

APPLYING FOR FINANCIAL AID ***Required financial aid forms:*** FAFSA, institution's own form, state aid form. ***Financial aid deadline (priority):*** 4/15. ***Notification date:*** Continuous beginning 4/30. Students must reply within 2 weeks of notification.

CONTACT Mrs. T. H. Bridges, Financial Aid Office, Concordia College, 1804 Green Street, Selma, AL 36701, 334-874-5700. *Fax:* 334-874-3728. *E-mail:* tbridges@concordiaselma.edu.

CONCORDIA COLLEGE

Moorhead, MN

Tuition & fees: $25,710 **Average undergraduate aid package: $17,921**

ABOUT THE INSTITUTION Independent religious, coed. ***Awards:*** bachelor's and master's degrees. 72 undergraduate majors. ***Total enrollment:*** 2,823. Undergraduates: 2,810. Freshmen: 776. Federal methodology is used as a basis for awarding need-based institutional aid.

UNDERGRADUATE EXPENSES for 2009–10 ***Application fee:*** $20. ***Comprehensive fee:*** $32,535 includes full-time tuition ($25,500), mandatory fees ($210), and room and board ($6825). ***College room only:*** $2800. ***Part-time tuition:*** $4015 per course.

FRESHMAN FINANCIAL AID (Fall 2008, est.) 676 applied for aid; of those 83% were deemed to have need. 100% of freshmen with need received aid; of those 28% had need fully met. ***Average percent of need met:*** 88% (excluding resources awarded to replace EFC). ***Average financial aid package:*** $18,678 (excluding resources awarded to replace EFC). 28% of all full-time freshmen had no need and received non-need-based gift aid.

UNDERGRADUATE FINANCIAL AID (Fall 2008, est.) 2,327 applied for aid; of those 84% were deemed to have need. 100% of undergraduates with need received aid; of those 24% had need fully met. ***Average percent of need met:*** 83% (excluding resources awarded to replace EFC). ***Average financial aid package:*** $17,921 (excluding resources awarded to replace EFC). 27% of all full-time undergraduates had no need and received non-need-based gift aid.

GIFT AID (NEED-BASED) ***Total amount:*** $24,751,358 (11% federal, 11% state, 70% institutional, 8% external sources). ***Receiving aid:*** Freshmen: 70% (556); all full-time undergraduates: 69% (1,929). ***Average award:*** Freshmen: $14,204; Undergraduates: $12,779. ***Scholarships, grants, and awards:*** Federal Pell, FSEOG, state, private, college/university gift aid from institutional funds.

GIFT AID (NON-NEED-BASED) ***Total amount:*** $9,053,612 (1% federal, 80% institutional, 19% external sources). ***Receiving aid:*** Freshmen: 12% (91). Undergraduates: 9% (258). ***Average award:*** Freshmen: $9089. Undergraduates: $8510. ***Scholarships, grants, and awards by category:*** *Academic interests/achievement:* 2,400 awards ($17,255,035 total): general academic interests/achievements. *Creative arts/performance:* 239 awards ($508,136 total): debating, music, theater/drama. *Special characteristics:* 100 awards ($1,166,979 total): international students. ***ROTC:*** Army cooperative, Air Force cooperative.

LOANS ***Student loans:*** $20,185,156 (57% need-based, 43% non-need-based). 87% of past graduating class borrowed through all loan programs. *Average indebtedness per student:* $29,529. ***Average need-based loan:*** Freshmen: $3798. Undergraduates: $4483. ***Parent loans:*** $2,877,551 (17% need-based, 83% non-need-based). ***Programs:*** FFEL (Subsidized and Unsubsidized Stafford, PLUS), Perkins, state, college/university, alternative loans.

WORK-STUDY ***Federal work-study:*** Total amount: $775,285; 466 jobs averaging $1657. ***State or other work-study/employment:*** Total amount: $4,134,416 (46% need-based, 54% non-need-based). 2,289 part-time jobs averaging $1689.

APPLYING FOR FINANCIAL AID ***Required financial aid form:*** FAFSA. ***Financial aid deadline:*** Continuous. ***Notification date:*** Continuous beginning 3/1.

CONTACT Mrs. Jane Williams, Financial Aid Director, Concordia College, 901 South 8th Street, Moorhead, MN 56562, 218-299-3010 or toll-free 800-699-9897. *Fax:* 218-299-3025. *E-mail:* jwilliam@cord.edu.

CONCORDIA COLLEGE–NEW YORK

Bronxville, NY

Tuition & fees: $23,430 **Average undergraduate aid package: $22,309**

ABOUT THE INSTITUTION Independent Lutheran, coed. ***Awards:*** associate and bachelor's degrees. 21 undergraduate majors. ***Total enrollment:*** 748. Undergraduates: 748. Freshmen: 128. Federal methodology is used as a basis for awarding need-based institutional aid.

UNDERGRADUATE EXPENSES for 2008–09 ***Application fee:*** $50. ***Comprehensive fee:*** $32,175 includes full-time tuition ($22,930), mandatory fees ($500), and room and board ($8745). ***College room only:*** $4900. Room and board charges vary according to board plan. Part-time tuition and fees vary according to course load. ***Payment plan:*** Installment.

FRESHMAN FINANCIAL AID (Fall 2008, est.) 109 applied for aid; of those 79% were deemed to have need. 100% of freshmen with need received aid; of those 16% had need fully met. ***Average percent of need met:*** 65% (excluding resources awarded to replace EFC). ***Average financial aid package:*** $22,976 (excluding resources awarded to replace EFC). 23% of all full-time freshmen had no need and received non-need-based gift aid.

UNDERGRADUATE FINANCIAL AID (Fall 2008, est.) 533 applied for aid; of those 84% were deemed to have need. 100% of undergraduates with need received aid; of those 20% had need fully met. ***Average percent of need met:*** 71% (excluding resources awarded to replace EFC). ***Average financial aid package:*** $22,309 (excluding resources awarded to replace EFC). 16% of all full-time undergraduates had no need and received non-need-based gift aid.

GIFT AID (NEED-BASED) ***Total amount:*** $4,627,974 (14% federal, 15% state, 71% institutional). ***Receiving aid:*** Freshmen: 62% (80); all full-time undergraduates: 65% (417). ***Average award:*** Freshmen: $10,817; Undergraduates: $11,129. ***Scholarships, grants, and awards:*** Federal Pell, FSEOG, state, college/university gift aid from institutional funds.

GIFT AID (NON-NEED-BASED) ***Total amount:*** $855,822 (5% state, 95% institutional). ***Receiving aid:*** Freshmen: 9% (12). Undergraduates: 9% (56). ***Average award:*** Freshmen: $5963. Undergraduates: $6170. ***Scholarships, grants, and awards by category:*** *Academic interests/achievement:* education, general academic interests/achievements, religion/biblical studies, social sciences. *Creative arts/performance:* music. *Special achievements/activities:* community service. *Special characteristics:* children of faculty/staff, relatives of clergy, religious affiliation. ***Tuition waivers:*** Full or partial for employees or children of employees, senior citizens.

LOANS ***Student loans:*** $3,569,690 (40% need-based, 60% non-need-based). 74% of past graduating class borrowed through all loan programs. *Average indebtedness per student:* $24,153. ***Average need-based loan:*** Freshmen: $3144. Undergraduates: $4133. ***Parent loans:*** $1,487,162 (100% non-need-based). ***Programs:*** Federal Direct (Subsidized and Unsubsidized Stafford, PLUS), FFEL (Subsidized and Unsubsidized Stafford, PLUS).

WORK-STUDY ***Federal work-study:*** Total amount: $39,398; jobs available.

ATHLETIC AWARDS Total amount: $1,097,950 (58% need-based, 42% non-need-based).

APPLYING FOR FINANCIAL AID ***Required financial aid form:*** FAFSA. ***Financial aid deadline:*** Continuous.

CONTACT Janice Spikereit, Director of Financial Aid, Concordia College–New York, 171 White Plains Road, Bronxville, NY 10708, 914-337-9300 Ext. 2146 or toll-free 800-YES-COLLEGE. *Fax:* 914-395-4500. *E-mail:* financialaid@concordia-ny.edu.

CONCORDIA UNIVERSITY

Irvine, CA

ABOUT THE INSTITUTION Independent religious, coed. ***Awards:*** associate, bachelor's, and master's degrees (associate's degree for international students only). 23 undergraduate majors. ***Total enrollment:*** 2,453. Undergraduates: 1,375. Freshmen: 327.

GIFT AID (NEED-BASED) ***Scholarships, grants, and awards:*** Federal Pell, FSEOG, state, private, college/university gift aid from institutional funds.

GIFT AID (NON-NEED-BASED) ***Scholarships, grants, and awards by category:*** *Academic interests/achievement:* general academic interests/achievements. *Creative arts/performance:* applied art and design, debating, music, theater/drama. *Special achievements/activities:* general special achievements/activities. *Special characteristics:* children of faculty/staff, first-generation college students, religious affiliation, siblings of current students.

LOANS ***Programs:*** FFEL (Subsidized and Unsubsidized Stafford, PLUS), alternative loans.

WORK-STUDY ***Federal work-study:*** Total amount: $92,000; 49 jobs averaging $1831. ***State or other work-study/employment:*** Total amount: $281,370 (100% need-based). 171 part-time jobs averaging $1700.

APPLYING FOR FINANCIAL AID ***Required financial aid forms:*** FAFSA, institution's own form, state aid form.

CONTACT Lori McDonald, Director of Financial Aid, Concordia University, 1530 Concordia West, Irvine, CA 92612-3299, 949-854-8002 Ext. 1170 or toll-free 800-229-1200. *Fax:* 949-854-6709. *E-mail:* lori.mcdonald@cui.edu.

CONCORDIA UNIVERSITY

Ann Arbor, MI

ABOUT THE INSTITUTION Independent religious, coed. ***Awards:*** associate, bachelor's, and master's degrees and post-bachelor's certificates. 47 undergraduate majors. ***Total enrollment:*** 1,075. Undergraduates: 521. Freshmen: 94.

GIFT AID (NEED-BASED) ***Scholarships, grants, and awards:*** Federal Pell, FSEOG, state, private, college/university gift aid from institutional funds.

GIFT AID (NON-NEED-BASED) ***Scholarships, grants, and awards by category:*** *Academic interests/achievement:* general academic interests/achievements, religion/biblical studies. *Creative arts/performance:* art/fine arts, music, performing arts, theater/drama. *Special characteristics:* children and siblings of alumni, children of faculty/staff, ethnic background, religious affiliation, siblings of current students.

LOANS ***Programs:*** FFEL (Subsidized and Unsubsidized Stafford, PLUS), Perkins.

APPLYING FOR FINANCIAL AID ***Required financial aid forms:*** FAFSA, institution's own form, tax returns.

CONTACT Angela Acosta, Financial Aid Office, Concordia University, 4090 Geddes Road, Ann Arbor, MI 48105-2797, 734-995-4622 or toll-free 800-253-0680. *Fax:* 734-995-4610. *E-mail:* acosta@cuaa.edu.

CONCORDIA UNIVERSITY

Portland, OR

Tuition & fees: $23,400 **Average undergraduate aid package: $14,770**

ABOUT THE INSTITUTION Independent religious, coed. ***Awards:*** associate, bachelor's, and master's degrees and post-bachelor's certificates. 32 undergraduate majors. ***Total enrollment:*** 1,709. Undergraduates: 1,065. Freshmen: 164. Federal methodology is used as a basis for awarding need-based institutional aid.

UNDERGRADUATE EXPENSES for 2009–10 ***Application fee:*** $20. ***Comprehensive fee:*** $30,200 includes full-time tuition ($22,900), mandatory fees ($500), and room and board ($6800). ***College room only:*** $3250. ***Part-time tuition:*** $715 per credit.

FRESHMAN FINANCIAL AID (Fall 2007) 169 applied for aid; of those 82% were deemed to have need. 100% of freshmen with need received aid; of those 44% had need fully met. ***Average percent of need met:*** 85% (excluding resources awarded to replace EFC). 5% of all full-time freshmen had no need and received non-need-based gift aid.

UNDERGRADUATE FINANCIAL AID (Fall 2007) 808 applied for aid; of those 88% were deemed to have need. 99% of undergraduates with need received aid; of those 32% had need fully met. ***Average percent of need met:*** 85% (excluding resources awarded to replace EFC). ***Average financial aid package:*** $14,770 (excluding resources awarded to replace EFC). 8% of all full-time undergraduates had no need and received non-need-based gift aid.

GIFT AID (NEED-BASED) ***Total amount:*** $3,998,599 (29% federal, 9% state, 62% institutional). ***Receiving aid:*** Freshmen: 70% (128); all full-time undergraduates: 65% (602). ***Average award:*** Freshmen: $6417; Undergraduates: $5543. ***Scholarships, grants, and awards:*** Federal Pell, FSEOG, state, private, college/university gift aid from institutional funds.

GIFT AID (NON-NEED-BASED) ***Total amount:*** $4,808,718 (85% institutional, 15% external sources). ***Receiving aid:*** Freshmen: 74% (134). Undergraduates: 64% (586). ***Average award:*** Freshmen: $5545. Undergraduates: $5883. ***Scholarships, grants, and awards by category:*** *Academic interests/achievement:* general academic interests/achievements, religion/biblical studies. *Creative arts/performance:* music. *Special achievements/activities:* leadership, religious involvement. *Special characteristics:* children of faculty/staff, relatives of clergy, religious affiliation. ***ROTC:*** Air Force cooperative.

LOANS ***Student loans:*** $6,648,423 (45% need-based, 55% non-need-based). 84% of past graduating class borrowed through all loan programs. *Average indebtedness per student:* $25,067. ***Parent loans:*** $1,781,856 (100% non-need-based). ***Programs:*** FFEL (Subsidized and Unsubsidized Stafford, PLUS), Perkins, alternative loans.

WORK-STUDY ***Federal work-study:*** Total amount: $100,904; jobs available. ***State or other work-study/employment:*** Total amount: $201,998 (100% non-need-based). Part-time jobs available.

ATHLETIC AWARDS Total amount: $1,112,663 (100% non-need-based).

APPLYING FOR FINANCIAL AID ***Required financial aid form:*** FAFSA. ***Financial aid deadline:*** Continuous. ***Notification date:*** Continuous beginning 3/15. Students must reply by 5/1 or within 2 weeks of notification.

CONTACT Mr. James W. Cullen, Director of Financial Aid, Concordia University, 2811 Northeast Holman Street, Portland, OR 97211-6099, 503-493-6508 or toll-free 800-321-9371. *Fax:* 503-280-8661. *E-mail:* jcullen@cu-portland.edu.

CONCORDIA UNIVERSITY CHICAGO

River Forest, IL

Tuition & fees: $23,458 **Average undergraduate aid package: $21,018**

ABOUT THE INSTITUTION Independent religious, coed. ***Awards:*** bachelor's, master's, and doctoral degrees and post-bachelor's and post-master's certificates. 54 undergraduate majors. ***Total enrollment:*** 4,185. Undergraduates: 1,153. Freshmen: 249. Federal methodology is used as a basis for awarding need-based institutional aid.

UNDERGRADUATE EXPENSES for 2009–10 ***Comprehensive fee:*** $31,158 includes full-time tuition ($22,998), mandatory fees ($460), and room and board ($7700). ***Part-time tuition:*** $719 per semester hour.

FRESHMAN FINANCIAL AID (Fall 2008, est.) 235 applied for aid; of those 87% were deemed to have need. 100% of freshmen with need received aid; of those 19% had need fully met. ***Average percent of need met:*** 79% (excluding resources awarded to replace EFC). ***Average financial aid package:*** $22,148 (excluding resources awarded to replace EFC). 18% of all full-time freshmen had no need and received non-need-based gift aid.

UNDERGRADUATE FINANCIAL AID (Fall 2008, est.) 930 applied for aid; of those 87% were deemed to have need. 100% of undergraduates with need received aid; of those 22% had need fully met. ***Average percent of need met:*** 75% (excluding resources awarded to replace EFC). ***Average financial aid package:*** $21,018 (excluding resources awarded to replace EFC). 19% of all full-time undergraduates had no need and received non-need-based gift aid.

GIFT AID (NEED-BASED) ***Total amount:*** $9,273,109 (13% federal, 15% state, 72% institutional). ***Receiving aid:*** Freshmen: 82% (204); all full-time undergraduates: 78% (796). ***Average award:*** Freshmen: $13,755; Undergraduates: $11,589. ***Scholarships, grants, and awards:*** Federal Pell, FSEOG, state, private, college/university gift aid from institutional funds.

GIFT AID (NON-NEED-BASED) ***Total amount:*** $2,524,755 (5% state, 89% institutional, 6% external sources). ***Receiving aid:*** Freshmen: 10% (25). Undergraduates: 11% (117). ***Average award:*** Freshmen: $9634. Undergraduates: $9097. ***Scholarships, grants, and awards by category:*** *Academic interests/achievement:* biological sciences, business, communication, computer science, education, English, foreign languages, general academic interests/achievements, mathematics, religion/biblical studies. *Creative arts/performance:* art/fine arts, music. *Special characteristics:* children and siblings of alumni, children of faculty/staff, international students, religious affiliation.

LOANS ***Student loans:*** $6,885,652 (39% need-based, 61% non-need-based). 79% of past graduating class borrowed through all loan programs. *Average indebtedness per student:* $28,506. ***Average need-based loan:*** Freshmen: $3654. Undergraduates: $4200. ***Parent loans:*** $795,405 (100% non-need-based). ***Programs:*** FFEL (Subsidized and Unsubsidized Stafford, PLUS), Perkins.

WORK-STUDY ***Federal work-study:*** Total amount: $366,101; 196 jobs averaging $2375. ***State or other work-study/employment:*** Total amount: $50,000 (100% non-need-based). 200 part-time jobs averaging $2000.

APPLYING FOR FINANCIAL AID ***Required financial aid form:*** FAFSA. ***Financial aid deadline:*** 8/15 (priority: 4/1). ***Notification date:*** Continuous. Students must reply within 4 weeks of notification.

CONTACT Patricia Williamson, Director of Student Financial Planning, Concordia University Chicago, 7400 Augusta Street, River Forest, IL 60305-1499, 708-209-3261 or toll-free 800-285-2668. *Fax:* 708-209-3176. *E-mail:* patricia.williamson@cuchicago.edu.

CONCORDIA UNIVERSITY, NEBRASKA

Seward, NE

Tuition & fees: $21,250 **Average undergraduate aid package: $15,815**

ABOUT THE INSTITUTION Independent religious, coed. ***Awards:*** bachelor's and master's degrees and post-bachelor's certificates. 73 undergraduate majors. ***Total enrollment:*** 1,344. Undergraduates: 1,118. Freshmen: 273. Federal methodology is used as a basis for awarding need-based institutional aid.

UNDERGRADUATE EXPENSES for 2009–10 ***Comprehensive fee:*** $26,770 includes full-time tuition ($21,100), mandatory fees ($150), and room and board ($5520). ***College room only:*** $2340. ***Part-time tuition:*** $650 per credit.

FRESHMAN FINANCIAL AID (Fall 2008, est.) 254 applied for aid; of those 83% were deemed to have need. 100% of freshmen with need received aid; of those 27% had need fully met. ***Average percent of need met:*** 74% (excluding resources awarded to replace EFC). ***Average financial aid package:*** $15,747 (excluding resources awarded to replace EFC). 23% of all full-time freshmen had no need and received non-need-based gift aid.

UNDERGRADUATE FINANCIAL AID (Fall 2008, est.) 936 applied for aid; of those 86% were deemed to have need. 100% of undergraduates with need received aid; of those 27% had need fully met. ***Average percent of need met:*** 77% (excluding resources awarded to replace EFC). ***Average financial aid package:*** $15,815 (excluding resources awarded to replace EFC). 22% of all full-time undergraduates had no need and received non-need-based gift aid.

GIFT AID (NEED-BASED) ***Total amount:*** $8,369,368 (14% federal, 1% state, 68% institutional, 17% external sources). ***Receiving aid:*** Freshmen: 76% (207); all full-time undergraduates: 76% (786). ***Average award:*** Freshmen: $10,006; Undergraduates: $10,319. ***Scholarships, grants, and awards:*** Federal Pell, FSEOG, state, private, college/university gift aid from institutional funds.

GIFT AID (NON-NEED-BASED) ***Total amount:*** $2,214,285 (100% institutional). ***Receiving aid:*** Freshmen: 13% (36). Undergraduates: 11% (119). ***Average award:*** Freshmen: $7844. Undergraduates: $7210. ***Scholarships, grants, and awards by category:*** *Academic interests/achievement:* biological sciences, business, communication, computer science, education, English, general academic interests/achievements, health fields, humanities, mathematics, physical sciences, premedicine, religion/biblical studies, social sciences. *Creative arts/performance:* art/fine arts, dance, music, theater/drama. *Special achievements/activities:* memberships, religious involvement. *Special characteristics:* children and siblings of alumni, children of educators, children of faculty/staff, international students, local/state students, members of minority groups. ***ROTC:*** Army cooperative, Air Force cooperative.

LOANS ***Student loans:*** $5,582,883 (46% need-based, 54% non-need-based). 76% of past graduating class borrowed through all loan programs. *Average indebtedness per student:* $20,393. ***Average need-based loan:*** Freshmen: $3223. Undergraduates: $4272. ***Parent loans:*** $2,045,551 (100% non-need-based). ***Programs:*** FFEL (Subsidized and Unsubsidized Stafford, PLUS), Perkins.

WORK-STUDY ***Federal work-study:*** Total amount: $101,788; 100 jobs averaging $1018.

ATHLETIC AWARDS Total amount: $1,548,688 (74% need-based, 26% non-need-based).

APPLYING FOR FINANCIAL AID ***Required financial aid form:*** FAFSA. ***Financial aid deadline (priority):*** 3/1. ***Notification date:*** Continuous beginning 3/31. Students must reply within 4 weeks of notification.

CONTACT Mrs. Gloria F. Hennig, Director of Financial Aid, Concordia University, Nebraska, 800 North Columbia Avenue, Seward, NE 68434-1556, 800-535-5494. *Fax:* 402-643-3519. *E-mail:* finaid@cune.edu.

CONCORDIA UNIVERSITY, ST. PAUL

St. Paul, MN

Tuition & fees: $26,400 **Average undergraduate aid package: $15,674**

ABOUT THE INSTITUTION Independent religious, coed. ***Awards:*** associate, bachelor's, and master's degrees and post-bachelor's certificates. 41 undergraduate majors. ***Total enrollment:*** 2,644. Undergraduates: 1,691. Freshmen: 211. Federal methodology is used as a basis for awarding need-based institutional aid.

UNDERGRADUATE EXPENSES for 2009–10 ***Application fee:*** $30. ***Comprehensive fee:*** $33,650 includes full-time tuition ($26,400) and room and board ($7250). ***Part-time tuition:*** $550 per credit.

FRESHMAN FINANCIAL AID (Fall 2008, est.) 209 applied for aid; of those 84% were deemed to have need. 100% of freshmen with need received aid; of those 21% had need fully met. ***Average percent of need met:*** 79% (excluding resources awarded to replace EFC). ***Average financial aid package:*** $19,937 (excluding resources awarded to replace EFC). 16% of all full-time freshmen had no need and received non-need-based gift aid.

UNDERGRADUATE FINANCIAL AID (Fall 2008, est.) 1,076 applied for aid; of those 85% were deemed to have need. 100% of undergraduates with need received aid; of those 17% had need fully met. ***Average percent of need met:*** 67% (excluding resources awarded to replace EFC). ***Average financial aid package:*** $15,674 (excluding resources awarded to replace EFC). 9% of all full-time undergraduates had no need and received non-need-based gift aid.

GIFT AID (NEED-BASED) ***Total amount:*** $9,054,229 (18% federal, 16% state, 62% institutional, 4% external sources). ***Receiving aid:*** Freshmen: 83% (175); all full-time undergraduates: 60% (784). ***Average award:*** Freshmen: $15,085; Undergraduates: $12,517. ***Scholarships, grants, and awards:*** Federal Pell, FSEOG, state, private, college/university gift aid from institutional funds.

GIFT AID (NON-NEED-BASED) ***Total amount:*** $946,650 (4% federal, 1% state, 84% institutional, 11% external sources). ***Average award:*** Freshmen: $9015. Undergraduates: $6833. ***Scholarships, grants, and awards by category:*** *Academic interests/achievement:* 070 awards ($3,978,381 total): communication, English, general academic interests/achievements, mathematics, physical sciences, religion/biblical studies, social sciences. *Creative arts/performance:* 129 awards ($179,185 total): art/fine arts, music, theater/drama. *Special characteristics:* 237 awards ($344,875 total): children of faculty/staff, religious affiliation. ***ROTC:*** Army cooperative, Naval cooperative, Air Force cooperative.

LOANS ***Student loans:*** $9,536,469 (92% need-based, 8% non-need-based). 86% of past graduating class borrowed through all loan programs. *Average indebtedness per student:* $33,775. ***Average need-based loan:*** Freshmen: $4408. Undergraduates: $4950. ***Parent loans:*** $937,502 (83% need-based, 17% non-need-based). ***Programs:*** FFEL (Subsidized and Unsubsidized Stafford, PLUS), Perkins, state, private alternative loans.

WORK-STUDY ***Federal work-study:*** Total amount: $469,831; 206 jobs averaging $2281. ***State or other work-study/employment:*** Total amount: $555,376 (100% need-based). 243 part-time jobs averaging $2285.

ATHLETIC AWARDS Total amount: $1,731,088 (78% need-based, 22% non-need-based).

APPLYING FOR FINANCIAL AID ***Required financial aid form:*** FAFSA. ***Financial aid deadline (priority):*** 5/1. ***Notification date:*** Continuous.

CONTACT Carolyn Chesebrough, Financial Aid Director, Concordia University, St. Paul, 275 North Syndicate Street, St. Paul, MN 55104-5494, 651-603-6300 or toll-free 800-333-4705. *Fax:* 651-603-6298. *E-mail:* bearcenter@csp.edu.

CONCORDIA UNIVERSITY TEXAS

Austin, TX

Tuition & fees: $20,490 **Average undergraduate aid package: $17,077**

ABOUT THE INSTITUTION Independent religious, coed. ***Awards:*** associate, bachelor's, and master's degrees. 21 undergraduate majors. ***Total enrollment:*** 2,261. Undergraduates: 1,172. Freshmen: 241. Federal methodology is used as a basis for awarding need-based institutional aid.

UNDERGRADUATE EXPENSES for 2008–09 ***Application fee:*** $25. ***Comprehensive fee:*** $28,290 includes full-time tuition ($20,490) and room and board ($7800).

FRESHMAN FINANCIAL AID (Fall 2007) 82 applied for aid; of those 72% were deemed to have need. 95% of freshmen with need received aid; of those 23% had need fully met. ***Average percent of need met:*** 79% (excluding resources awarded to replace EFC). ***Average financial aid package:*** $17,566 (excluding resources awarded to replace EFC). 12% of all full-time freshmen had no need and received non-need-based gift aid.

UNDERGRADUATE FINANCIAL AID (Fall 2007) 343 applied for aid; of those 72% were deemed to have need. 98% of undergraduates with need received aid; of those 47% had need fully met. ***Average percent of need met:*** 86% (excluding resources awarded to replace EFC). ***Average financial aid package:*** $17,077 (excluding resources awarded to replace EFC). 10% of all full-time undergraduates had no need and received non-need-based gift aid.

GIFT AID (NEED-BASED) ***Total amount:*** $3,148,329 (23% federal, 34% state, 30% institutional, 13% external sources). ***Receiving aid:*** Freshmen: 38% (53); all full-time undergraduates: 32% (204). ***Average award:*** Freshmen: $10,644; Undergraduates: $9437. ***Scholarships, grants, and awards:*** Federal Pell, FSEOG, state, private, college/university gift aid from institutional funds, Federal Nursing, Academic Competitiveness Grant, National Smart Grant, TEACH Grant.

GIFT AID (NON-NEED-BASED) ***Total amount:*** $2,983,528 (100% institutional). ***Receiving aid:*** Freshmen: 15% (21). Undergraduates: 17% (108). ***Average award:*** Freshmen: $7696. Undergraduates: $6772. ***Scholarships, grants, and awards by category:*** *Academic interests/achievement:* 306 awards ($2,109,150 total): biological sciences, business, education, foreign languages, general academic interests/achievements, international studies, social sciences. *Creative arts/performance:* 7 awards ($26,700 total): music. *Special achievements/activities:* 115 awards ($626,148 total): junior miss, leadership, religious involvement. *Special characteristics:* 18 awards ($162,575 total): adult students, children and siblings of alumni, children of faculty/staff, religious affiliation, veterans, veterans' children. ***ROTC:*** Army cooperative, Air Force cooperative.

LOANS ***Student loans:*** $3,338,745 (42% need-based, 58% non-need-based). 66% of past graduating class borrowed through all loan programs. *Average indebtedness per student:* $21,427. ***Average need-based loan:*** Freshmen: $5626. Undergraduates: $7574. ***Parent loans:*** $652,186 (100% need-based). ***Programs:*** FFEL (Subsidized and Unsubsidized Stafford, PLUS), Federal Nursing, state, private loans.

WORK-STUDY ***Federal work-study:*** Total amount: $119,611; 96 jobs averaging $1246. ***State or other work-study/employment:*** Total amount: $14,014 (100% need-based). 5 part-time jobs averaging $2983.

APPLYING FOR FINANCIAL AID ***Required financial aid forms:*** FAFSA, institution's own form. ***Financial aid deadline (priority):*** 5/1. ***Notification date:*** Continuous. Students must reply within 2 weeks of notification.

CONTACT Cathy L. Schryer, Director of Student Financial Services, Concordia University Texas, 11400 Concordia University Drive, Austin, TX 78726, 512-313-4671 or toll-free 800-865-4282. *Fax:* 888-828-5120. *E-mail:* cathy.schryer@concordia.edu.

CONCORDIA UNIVERSITY WISCONSIN

Mequon, WI

Tuition & fees: $20,000 **Average undergraduate aid package: $20,534**

ABOUT THE INSTITUTION Independent religious, coed. ***Awards:*** associate, bachelor's, master's, doctoral, and first professional degrees and post-bachelor's certificates. 62 undergraduate majors. ***Total enrollment:*** 6,549. Undergraduates: 3,786. Freshmen: 405. Federal methodology is used as a basis for awarding need-based institutional aid.

UNDERGRADUATE EXPENSES for 2008–09 ***Application fee:*** $35. ***Comprehensive fee:*** $27,700 includes full-time tuition ($19,900), mandatory fees ($100), and room and board ($7700). Full-time tuition and fees vary according to program.

Room and board charges vary according to board plan. ***Part-time tuition:*** $830 per credit hour. Part-time tuition and fees vary according to program. ***Payment plans:*** Guaranteed tuition, installment, deferred payment.

FRESHMAN FINANCIAL AID (Fall 2008, est.) 410 applied for aid; of those 87% were deemed to have need. 100% of freshmen with need received aid; of those 37% had need fully met. ***Average percent of need met:*** 79% (excluding resources awarded to replace EFC). ***Average financial aid package:*** $21,950 (excluding resources awarded to replace EFC). 17% of all full-time freshmen had no need and received non-need-based gift aid.

UNDERGRADUATE FINANCIAL AID (Fall 2008, est.) 1,639 applied for aid; of those 86% were deemed to have need. 100% of undergraduates with need received aid; of those 31% had need fully met. ***Average percent of need met:*** 74% (excluding resources awarded to replace EFC). ***Average financial aid package:*** $20,534 (excluding resources awarded to replace EFC). 16% of all full-time undergraduates had no need and received non-need-based gift aid.

GIFT AID (NEED-BASED) ***Total amount:*** $14,530,219 (17% federal, 10% state, 65% institutional, 8% external sources). ***Receiving aid:*** Freshmen: 79% (339); all full-time undergraduates: 73% (1,300). ***Average award:*** Freshmen: $11,859; Undergraduates: $10,263. ***Scholarships, grants, and awards:*** Federal Pell, FSEOG, state, private, college/university gift aid from institutional funds.

GIFT AID (NON-NEED-BASED) ***Total amount:*** $4,473,532 (100% institutional). ***Receiving aid:*** Freshmen: 29% (125). Undergraduates: 23% (407). ***Average award:*** Freshmen: $9114. Undergraduates: $8005. ***Tuition waivers:*** Full or partial for employees or children of employees.

LOANS ***Student loans:*** $19,808,294 (55% need-based, 45% non-need-based). 75% of past graduating class borrowed through all loan programs. *Average indebtedness per student:* $24,311. ***Average need-based loan:*** Freshmen: $5084. Undergraduates: $6033. ***Parent loans:*** $1,911,524 (100% non-need-based). ***Programs:*** Federal Direct (Subsidized and Unsubsidized Stafford, PLUS), state.

WORK-STUDY ***Federal work-study:*** Total amount: $398,081; 217 jobs averaging $1867.

APPLYING FOR FINANCIAL AID ***Required financial aid form:*** FAFSA. ***Financial aid deadline (priority):*** 4/1. ***Notification date:*** Continuous. Students must reply within 3 weeks of notification.

CONTACT Mr. Steven P. Taylor, Director of Financial Aid, Concordia University Wisconsin, 12800 North Lake Shore Drive, Mequon, WI 53097-2402, 262-243-4392 or toll-free 888-628-9472. *Fax:* 262-243-2636. *E-mail:* steve.taylor@cuw.edu.

CONCORD UNIVERSITY

Athens, WV

Tuition & fees (WV res): $4578 **Average undergraduate aid package: $8934**

ABOUT THE INSTITUTION State-supported, coed. ***Awards:*** associate, bachelor's, and master's degrees. 36 undergraduate majors. ***Total enrollment:*** 2,837. Undergraduates: 2,816. Freshmen: 721. Federal methodology is used as a basis for awarding need-based institutional aid.

UNDERGRADUATE EXPENSES for 2008–09 ***Tuition, state resident:*** full-time $4578; part-time $191 per credit hour. ***Tuition, nonresident:*** full-time $10,170; part-time $424 per credit hour. Full-time tuition and fees vary according to course load. Part-time tuition and fees vary according to course load. ***College room and board:*** $6530; ***Room only:*** $3326. ***Payment plan:*** Installment.

FRESHMAN FINANCIAL AID (Fall 2007) 652 applied for aid; of those 78% were deemed to have need. 100% of freshmen with need received aid; of those 41% had need fully met. ***Average percent of need met:*** 100% (excluding resources awarded to replace EFC). ***Average financial aid package:*** $9369 (excluding resources awarded to replace EFC). 19% of all full-time freshmen had no need and received non-need-based gift aid.

UNDERGRADUATE FINANCIAL AID (Fall 2007) 2,089 applied for aid; of those 79% were deemed to have need. 99% of undergraduates with need received aid; of those 38% had need fully met. ***Average percent of need met:*** 99% (excluding resources awarded to replace EFC). ***Average financial aid package:*** $8934 (excluding resources awarded to replace EFC). 9% of all full-time undergraduates had no need and received non-need-based gift aid.

GIFT AID (NEED-BASED) ***Total amount:*** $5,801,063 (68% federal, 32% state). ***Receiving aid:*** Freshmen: 58% (411); all full-time undergraduates: 56% (1,331). ***Average award:*** Freshmen: $4470; Undergraduates: $4540. ***Scholarships, grants, and awards:*** Federal Pell, FSEOG, state, college/university gift aid from institutional funds.

GIFT AID (NON-NEED-BASED) ***Total amount:*** $5,069,033 (40% state, 46% institutional, 14% external sources). ***Receiving aid:*** Freshmen: 42% (294). Undergraduates: 29% (682). ***Average award:*** Freshmen: $2740. Undergraduates: $3259. ***Scholarships, grants, and awards by category:*** *Academic interests/achievement:* 680 awards ($1,442,328 total): business, communication, education, English, general academic interests/achievements, social sciences. *Creative arts/performance:* 39 awards ($93,249 total): art/fine arts, journalism/publications, music, theater/drama. *Special achievements/activities:* 348 awards ($150,300 total): community service, general special achievements/activities, leadership. ***Tuition waivers:*** Full or partial for employees or children of employees, adult students, senior citizens.

LOANS ***Student loans:*** $7,613,169 (95% need-based, 5% non-need-based). 86% of past graduating class borrowed through all loan programs. *Average indebtedness per student:* $13,713. ***Average need-based loan:*** Freshmen: $3015. Undergraduates: $3809. ***Parent loans:*** $632,363 (100% non-need-based). ***Programs:*** FFEL (Subsidized and Unsubsidized Stafford, PLUS), Perkins.

WORK-STUDY ***Federal work-study:*** Total amount: $538,868; 401 jobs averaging $1321. ***State or other work-study/employment:*** Total amount: $436,025 (100% non-need-based). 306 part-time jobs averaging $1342.

ATHLETIC AWARDS Total amount: $780,956 (100% non-need-based).

APPLYING FOR FINANCIAL AID ***Required financial aid forms:*** FAFSA, institution's own form, verification worksheet. ***Financial aid deadline (priority):*** 4/15. ***Notification date:*** Continuous. Students must reply within 2 weeks of notification.

CONTACT Patricia Harmon, Financial Aid Director, Concord University, PO Box 1000, Athens, WV 24712-1000, 304-384-6069 or toll-free 888-384-5249. *Fax:* 304-384-9044.

CONNECTICUT COLLEGE

New London, CT

Comprehensive fee: $49,385 **Average undergraduate aid package: $31,099**

ABOUT THE INSTITUTION Independent, coed. ***Awards:*** bachelor's and master's degrees. 66 undergraduate majors. ***Total enrollment:*** 1,852. Undergraduates: 1,845. Freshmen: 493. Both federal and institutional methodology are used as a basis for awarding need-based institutional aid.

UNDERGRADUATE EXPENSES for 2008–09 ***Application fee:*** $60. ***Comprehensive fee:*** $49,385. Full-time tuition and fees vary according to program. ***Part-time tuition:*** $1146 per credit hour. Part-time tuition and fees vary according to program. ***Payment plan:*** Installment.

FRESHMAN FINANCIAL AID (Fall 2008, est.) 268 applied for aid; of those 76% were deemed to have need. 100% of freshmen with need received aid; of those 100% had need fully met. ***Average percent of need met:*** 100% (excluding resources awarded to replace EFC). ***Average financial aid package:*** $31,583 (excluding resources awarded to replace EFC).

UNDERGRADUATE FINANCIAL AID (Fall 2008, est.) 910 applied for aid; of those 83% were deemed to have need. 100% of undergraduates with need received aid; of those 100% had need fully met. ***Average percent of need met:*** 100% (excluding resources awarded to replace EFC). ***Average financial aid package:*** $31,099 (excluding resources awarded to replace EFC).

GIFT AID (NEED-BASED) ***Total amount:*** $20,595,813 (4% federal, 3% state, 89% institutional, 4% external sources). ***Receiving aid:*** Freshmen: 38% (189); all full-time undergraduates: 38% (692). ***Average award:*** Freshmen: $30,699; Undergraduates: $29,247. ***Scholarships, grants, and awards:*** Federal Pell, FSEOG, state, college/university gift aid from institutional funds.

GIFT AID (NON-NEED-BASED) ***Total amount:*** $436,951 (100% external sources). ***Tuition waivers:*** Full or partial for employees or children of employees, senior citizens.

LOANS ***Student loans:*** $5,377,744 (49% need-based, 51% non-need-based). 41% of past graduating class borrowed through all loan programs. *Average indebtedness per student:* $21,283. ***Average need-based loan:*** Freshmen: $3232. Undergraduates: $4325. ***Parent loans:*** $3,726,852 (100% non-need-based). ***Programs:*** Federal Direct (Subsidized and Unsubsidized Stafford, PLUS), Perkins, college/university.

WORK-STUDY ***Federal work-study:*** Total amount: $870,045; 620 jobs averaging $1420. ***State or other work-study/employment:*** Total amount: $20,904 (100% need-based). 19 part-time jobs averaging $1079.

APPLYING FOR FINANCIAL AID ***Required financial aid forms:*** FAFSA, CSS Financial Aid PROFILE, noncustodial (divorced/separated) parent's statement, business/farm supplement. ***Financial aid deadline:*** 2/1. ***Notification date:*** 4/1. Students must reply by 5/1 or within 2 weeks of notification.

CONTACT Ms. Elaine Solinga, Director of Financial Aid Services, Connecticut College, 270 Mohegan Avenue, New London, CT 06320-4196, 860-439-2058. *Fax:* 860-439-5357. *E-mail:* finaid@conncoll.edu.

CONSERVATORY OF MUSIC OF PUERTO RICO

San Juan, PR

CONTACT Mr. Jorge Medina, Director of Financial Aid, Conservatory of Music of Puerto Rico, 350 Rafael Lamar Street at FDR Avenue, San Juan, PR 00918, 787-751-0160 Ext. 230. *Fax:* 787-758-8268. *E-mail:* jmedina@cmpr.gobierno.pr.

CONVERSE COLLEGE

Spartanburg, SC

Tuition & fees: $24,500 **Average undergraduate aid package: $21,271**

ABOUT THE INSTITUTION Independent, undergraduate: women only; graduate: coed. ***Awards:*** bachelor's and master's degrees and post-master's certificates. 40 undergraduate majors. ***Total enrollment:*** 1,881. Undergraduates: 737. Freshmen: 156. Federal methodology is used as a basis for awarding need-based institutional aid.

UNDERGRADUATE EXPENSES for 2008–09 ***Application fee:*** $40. ***Comprehensive fee:*** $32,050 includes full-time tuition ($24,500) and room and board ($7550).

FRESHMAN FINANCIAL AID (Fall 2008, est.) 145 applied for aid; of those 89% were deemed to have need. 100% of freshmen with need received aid; of those 36% had need fully met. ***Average percent of need met:*** 89% (excluding resources awarded to replace EFC). ***Average financial aid package:*** $23,775 (excluding resources awarded to replace EFC).

UNDERGRADUATE FINANCIAL AID (Fall 2008, est.) 481 applied for aid; of those 91% were deemed to have need. 100% of undergraduates with need received aid; of those 39% had need fully met. ***Average percent of need met:*** 86% (excluding resources awarded to replace EFC). ***Average financial aid package:*** $21,271 (excluding resources awarded to replace EFC).

GIFT AID (NEED-BASED) ***Total amount:*** $7,699,537 (12% federal, 22% state, 64% institutional, 2% external sources). ***Receiving aid:*** Freshmen: 80% (129); all full-time undergraduates: 74% (431). ***Average award:*** Freshmen: $20,454; Undergraduates: $17,892. ***Scholarships, grants, and awards:*** Federal Pell, FSEOG, state, private, college/university gift aid from institutional funds.

GIFT AID (NON-NEED-BASED) ***Total amount:*** $3,088,487 (27% state, 70% institutional, 3% external sources). ***Receiving aid:*** Freshmen: 24% (39). Undergraduates: 23% (134). ***Average award:*** Freshmen: $19,324. Undergraduates: $19,078. ***Scholarships, grants, and awards by category:*** *Academic interests/achievement:* 460 awards ($4,785,248 total): general academic interests/achievements. *Creative arts/performance:* 158 awards ($1,454,058 total): applied art and design, general creative arts/performance, music, theater/drama. *Special achievements/activities:* 53 awards ($363,950 total): leadership. *Special characteristics:* 52 awards ($55,394 total): children and siblings of alumni, children of faculty/staff. ***ROTC:*** Army cooperative.

LOANS ***Student loans:*** $3,843,968 (70% need-based, 30% non-need-based). 67% of past graduating class borrowed through all loan programs. *Average indebtedness per student:* $22,339. ***Average need-based loan:*** Freshmen: $4509. Undergraduates: $5208. ***Parent loans:*** $1,114,250 (14% need-based, 86% non-need-based). ***Programs:*** FFEL (Subsidized and Unsubsidized Stafford, PLUS), Perkins, state.

WORK-STUDY ***Federal work-study:*** Total amount: $186,403; 114 jobs averaging $1635. ***State or other work-study/employment:*** 60 part-time jobs averaging $1000.

ATHLETIC AWARDS Total amount: $393,050 (51% need-based, 49% non-need-based).

APPLYING FOR FINANCIAL AID ***Required financial aid form:*** FAFSA. ***Financial aid deadline (priority):*** 3/15. ***Notification date:*** Continuous beginning 3/15. Students must reply by 5/1 or within 2 weeks of notification.

CONTACT Ms. Margaret P. Collins, Director of Financial Assistance, Converse College, 580 East Main Street, Spartanburg, SC 29302-0006, 864-596-9019 or toll-free 800-766-1125. *Fax:* 864-596-9749. *E-mail:* peggy.collins@converse.edu.

COOPER UNION FOR THE ADVANCEMENT OF SCIENCE AND ART

New York, NY

Tuition & fees: $34,600 **Average undergraduate aid package: $33,000**

ABOUT THE INSTITUTION Independent, coed. ***Awards:*** bachelor's and master's degrees (also offers master's program primarily made up of currently-enrolled students). 8 undergraduate majors. ***Total enrollment:*** 969. Undergraduates: 917. Freshmen: 238.

UNDERGRADUATE EXPENSES for 2008–09 ***Application fee:*** $65. ***Comprehensive fee:*** $48,300 includes full-time tuition ($33,000), mandatory fees ($1600), and room and board ($13,700). ***College room only:*** $9700. Room and board charges vary according to board plan and housing facility. all students are awarded full-tuition scholarships. Living expenses are subsidized by college-administered financial aid.

FRESHMAN FINANCIAL AID (Fall 2008, est.) 126 applied for aid; of those 60% were deemed to have need. 100% of freshmen with need received aid; of those 89% had need fully met. ***Average percent of need met:*** 91% (excluding resources awarded to replace EFC). ***Average financial aid package:*** $33,000 (excluding resources awarded to replace EFC). 68% of all full-time freshmen had no need and received non-need-based gift aid.

UNDERGRADUATE FINANCIAL AID (Fall 2008, est.) 373 applied for aid; of those 68% were deemed to have need. 100% of undergraduates with need received aid; of those 71% had need fully met. ***Average percent of need met:*** 92% (excluding resources awarded to replace EFC). ***Average financial aid package:*** $33,000 (excluding resources awarded to replace EFC). 72% of all full-time undergraduates had no need and received non-need-based gift aid.

GIFT AID (NEED-BASED) ***Total amount:*** $1,768,018 (33% federal, 20% state, 34% institutional, 13% external sources). ***Receiving aid:*** Freshmen: 32% (75); all full-time undergraduates: 28% (255). ***Average award:*** Freshmen: $3237; Undergraduates: $3411. ***Scholarships, grants, and awards:*** Federal Pell, FSEOG, state, private, college/university gift aid from institutional funds.

GIFT AID (NON-NEED-BASED) ***Total amount:*** $28,564,515 (100% institutional). ***Receiving aid:*** Freshmen: 32% (75). Undergraduates: 28% (255). ***Average award:*** Freshmen: $33,000. Undergraduates: $33,000. ***Scholarships, grants, and awards by category:*** *Academic interests/achievement:* 626 awards: architecture, engineering/technologies. *Creative arts/performance:* 271 awards: art/fine arts.

LOANS ***Student loans:*** $840,709 (89% need-based, 11% non-need-based). 31% of past graduating class borrowed through all loan programs. *Average indebtedness per student:* $7500. ***Average need-based loan:*** Freshmen: $2259. Undergraduates: $2700. ***Parent loans:*** $106,000 (61% need-based, 39% non-need-based). ***Programs:*** FFEL (Subsidized and Unsubsidized Stafford, PLUS), Perkins, college/university.

WORK-STUDY ***Federal work-study:*** Total amount: $35,000; 35 jobs averaging $1200. ***State or other work-study/employment:*** Total amount: $542,193 (31% need-based, 69% non-need-based). 479 part-time jobs averaging $1132.

APPLYING FOR FINANCIAL AID ***Required financial aid forms:*** FAFSA, CSS Financial Aid PROFILE. ***Financial aid deadline:*** 6/1 (priority: 4/15). ***Notification date:*** 6/1. Students must reply by 6/30 or within 2 weeks of notification.

CONTACT Ms. Mary Ruokonen, Director of Financial Aid, Cooper Union for the Advancement of Science and Art, 30 Cooper Square, New York, NY 10003-7120, 212-353-4130. *Fax:* 212-353-4343. *E-mail:* ruokon@cooper.edu.

COPPIN STATE UNIVERSITY

Baltimore, MD

Tuition & fees (MD res): $5305 **Average undergraduate aid package: $8833**

ABOUT THE INSTITUTION State-supported, coed. ***Awards:*** bachelor's and master's degrees. 20 undergraduate majors. ***Total enrollment:*** 4,051. Undergraduates: 3,291. Freshmen: 610. Federal methodology is used as a basis for awarding need-based institutional aid.

UNDERGRADUATE EXPENSES for 2008–09 ***Application fee:*** $35. ***Tuition, state resident:*** full-time $3527; part-time $151 per credit hour. ***Tuition, nonresident:*** full-time $11,752; part-time $404 per credit hour. ***Required fees:*** full-time $1778; $64 per credit hour or $116 per term. ***College room and board:*** $7138; ***Room only:*** $4462.

FRESHMAN FINANCIAL AID (Fall 2008, est.) 517 applied for aid; of those 93% were deemed to have need. 92% of freshmen with need received aid; of those 11% had need fully met. ***Average percent of need met:*** 70% (excluding resources awarded to replace EFC). ***Average financial aid package:*** $8390 (excluding resources awarded to replace EFC). 1% of all full-time freshmen had no need and received non-need-based gift aid.

UNDERGRADUATE FINANCIAL AID (Fall 2008, est.) 2,232 applied for aid; of those 94% were deemed to have need. 94% of undergraduates with need received aid; of those 18% had need fully met. ***Average percent of need met:*** 76% (excluding resources awarded to replace EFC). ***Average financial aid package:*** $8833 (excluding resources awarded to replace EFC). 1% of all full-time undergraduates had no need and received non-need-based gift aid.

GIFT AID (NEED-BASED) ***Total amount:*** $9,974,649 (75% federal, 15% state, 10% institutional). ***Receiving aid:*** Freshmen: 68% (379); all full-time undergraduates: 66% (1,647). ***Average award:*** Freshmen: $5472; Undergraduates: $5398. ***Scholarships, grants, and awards:*** Federal Pell, FSEOG, state, private, college/university gift aid from institutional funds, Federal Nursing.

GIFT AID (NON-NEED-BASED) ***Total amount:*** $4,150,730 (73% state, 17% institutional, 10% external sources). ***Receiving aid:*** Freshmen: 20% (111). Undergraduates: 30% (749). ***Average award:*** Freshmen: $1109. Undergraduates: $2939. ***Scholarships, grants, and awards by category:*** *Academic interests/achievement:* general academic interests/achievements. ***ROTC:*** Army.

LOANS ***Student loans:*** $13,090,242 (66% need-based, 34% non-need-based). 99% of past graduating class borrowed through all loan programs. *Average indebtedness per student:* $9904. ***Average need-based loan:*** Freshmen: $3190. Undergraduates: $3805. ***Parent loans:*** $493,859 (100% non-need-based). ***Programs:*** Federal Direct (Subsidized and Unsubsidized Stafford, PLUS), FFEL (PLUS), Perkins, alternative loans.

WORK-STUDY ***Federal work-study:*** Total amount: $631,715; 302 jobs averaging $2100.

ATHLETIC AWARDS Total amount: $1,163,644 (100% non-need-based).

APPLYING FOR FINANCIAL AID ***Required financial aid form:*** FAFSA. ***Financial aid deadline (priority):*** 3/1. ***Notification date:*** 4/15. Students must reply within 4 weeks of notification.

CONTACT Fay Tayree, Associate Director of Financial Aid, Coppin State University, 2500 West North Avenue, Baltimore, MD 21216-3698, 410-951-3636 or toll-free 800-635-3674. *Fax:* 410-951-3637. *E-mail:* ftayree@coppin.edu.

CORBAN COLLEGE

Salem, OR

Tuition & fees: $23,202 **Average undergraduate aid package: $15,140**

ABOUT THE INSTITUTION Independent religious, coed. ***Awards:*** associate, bachelor's, and master's degrees. 46 undergraduate majors. ***Total enrollment:*** 1,031. Undergraduates: 926. Freshmen: 187. Federal methodology is used as a basis for awarding need-based institutional aid.

UNDERGRADUATE EXPENSES for 2009–10 ***Comprehensive fee:*** $31,270 includes full-time tuition ($22,932), mandatory fees ($270), and room and board ($8068). ***Part-time tuition:*** $955 per credit hour.

FRESHMAN FINANCIAL AID (Fall 2008, est.) 159 applied for aid; of those 89% were deemed to have need. 100% of freshmen with need received aid; of those 18% had need fully met. ***Average percent of need met:*** 64% (excluding resources awarded to replace EFC). ***Average financial aid package:*** $15,618 (excluding resources awarded to replace EFC). 17% of all full-time freshmen had no need and received non-need-based gift aid.

UNDERGRADUATE FINANCIAL AID (Fall 2008, est.) 625 applied for aid; of those 91% were deemed to have need. 100% of undergraduates with need received aid; of those 15% had need fully met. ***Average percent of need met:*** 63% (excluding resources awarded to replace EFC). ***Average financial aid package:*** $15,140 (excluding resources awarded to replace EFC). 15% of all full-time undergraduates had no need and received non-need-based gift aid.

GIFT AID (NEED-BASED) ***Total amount:*** $5,400,935 (15% federal, 5% state, 70% institutional, 10% external sources). ***Receiving aid:*** Freshmen: 81% (141); all full-time undergraduates: 82% (566). ***Average award:*** Freshmen: $12,878; Undergraduates: $11,563. ***Scholarships, grants, and awards:*** Federal Pell, FSEOG, state, private, college/university gift aid from institutional funds.

GIFT AID (NON-NEED-BASED) ***Total amount:*** $690,114 (2% federal, 78% institutional, 20% external sources). ***Receiving aid:*** Freshmen: 11% (20). Undergraduates: 7% (50). ***Average award:*** Freshmen: $4254. Undergraduates: $4593. ***Scholarships, grants, and awards by category:*** *Academic interests/achievement:* general academic interests/achievements. *Creative arts/performance:* music, performing arts. *Special achievements/activities:* general special achievements/activities, hobbies/interests, leadership, memberships, religious involvement. *Special characteristics:* children and siblings of alumni, children of faculty/staff, international students, relatives of clergy, siblings of current students. ***ROTC:*** Army cooperative, Air Force cooperative.

LOANS ***Student loans:*** $4,806,051 (76% need-based, 24% non-need-based). 85% of past graduating class borrowed through all loan programs. *Average indebtedness per student:* $28,347. ***Average need-based loan:*** Freshmen: $3588. Undergraduates: $4264. ***Parent loans:*** $767,475 (62% need-based, 38% non-need-based). ***Programs:*** Federal Direct (Subsidized and Unsubsidized Stafford, PLUS), Perkins, state.

WORK-STUDY ***Federal work-study:*** Total amount: $85,128; jobs available.

ATHLETIC AWARDS Total amount: $956,131 (71% need-based, 29% non-need-based).

APPLYING FOR FINANCIAL AID ***Required financial aid form:*** FAFSA. ***Financial aid deadline (priority):*** 2/15. ***Notification date:*** Continuous beginning 3/1.

CONTACT Nathan Warthan, Director of Financial Aid, Corban College, 5000 Deer Park Drive, SE, Salem, OR 97301-9392, 503-375-7006 or toll-free 800-845-3005 (out-of-state). *Fax:* 503-585-4316. *E-mail:* nwarthan@corban.edu.

CORCORAN COLLEGE OF ART AND DESIGN

Washington, DC

ABOUT THE INSTITUTION Independent, coed. ***Awards:*** associate, bachelor's, master's, and first professional degrees. 8 undergraduate majors. ***Total enrollment:*** 698. Undergraduates: 480. Freshmen: 58.

GIFT AID (NEED-BASED) ***Scholarships, grants, and awards:*** Federal Pell, FSEOG, state, college/university gift aid from institutional funds.

GIFT AID (NON-NEED-BASED) ***Scholarships, grants, and awards by category:*** *Academic interests/achievement:* general academic interests/achievements. *Creative arts/performance:* applied art and design.

LOANS ***Programs:*** FFEL (Subsidized and Unsubsidized Stafford, PLUS), Perkins.

APPLYING FOR FINANCIAL AID ***Required financial aid forms:*** FAFSA, institution's own form.

CONTACT Diane Morris, Financial Aid Director, Corcoran College of Art and Design, 500 17th Street, NW, Washington, DC 20006-4804, 202-639-1816 or toll-free 888-CORCORAN (out-of-state). *Fax:* 202-737-6921. *E-mail:* dmorris@corcoran.org.

CORNELL COLLEGE

Mount Vernon, IA

Tuition & fees: $27,850 **Average undergraduate aid package: $23,720**

ABOUT THE INSTITUTION Independent Methodist, coed. ***Awards:*** bachelor's degrees. 47 undergraduate majors. ***Total enrollment:*** 1,083. Undergraduates: 1,083. Freshmen: 316. Both federal and institutional methodology are used as a basis for awarding need-based institutional aid.

UNDERGRADUATE EXPENSES for 2008–09 ***Application fee:*** $30. ***Comprehensive fee:*** $35,070 includes full-time tuition ($27,670), mandatory fees ($180), and room and board ($7220). ***College room only:*** $3370. Room and board charges vary according to board plan and housing facility. Part-time tuition and fees vary according to course load and reciprocity agreements. ***Payment plan:*** Deferred payment.

FRESHMAN FINANCIAL AID (Fall 2008, est.) 285 applied for aid; of those 83% were deemed to have need. 100% of freshmen with need received aid; of those 58% had need fully met. ***Average percent of need met:*** 95% (excluding resources awarded to replace EFC). ***Average financial aid package:*** $26,875 (excluding resources awarded to replace EFC). 26% of all full-time freshmen had no need and received non-need-based gift aid.

UNDERGRADUATE FINANCIAL AID (Fall 2008, est.) 896 applied for aid; of those 84% were deemed to have need. 100% of undergraduates with need received aid; of those 36% had need fully met. ***Average percent of need met:*** 92% (excluding resources awarded to replace EFC). ***Average financial aid package:*** $23,720 (excluding resources awarded to replace EFC). 26% of all full-time undergraduates had no need and received non-need-based gift aid.

GIFT AID (NEED-BASED) ***Total amount:*** $15,065,912 (7% federal, 5% state, 85% institutional, 0% external sources). ***Receiving aid:*** Freshmen: 69% (236);

all full-time undergraduates: 68% (752). ***Average award:*** Freshmen: $11,895; Undergraduates: $19,420. ***Scholarships, grants, and awards:*** Federal Pell, FSEOG, state, private, college/university gift aid from institutional funds, Academic Competitiveness Grant, National Smart Grant, TEACH Grant.

GIFT AID (NON-NEED-BASED) ***Total amount:*** $3,182,776 (98% institutional, 2% external sources). ***Receiving aid:*** Freshmen: 35% (119). Undergraduates: 58% (646). ***Average award:*** Freshmen: $12,020. Undergraduates: $11,450. ***Scholarships, grants, and awards by category:*** *Academic interests/achievement:* 341 awards ($4,416,251 total): general academic interests/achievements. *Creative arts/performance:* 119 awards ($713,875 total): art/fine arts, music, performing arts, theater/drama. *Special achievements/activities:* 290 awards ($2,095,628 total): community service, leadership, religious involvement. *Special characteristics:* 212 awards ($2,366,050 total): children of educators, children of faculty/staff, ethnic background, international students, local/state students, members of minority groups, relatives of clergy, religious affiliation. ***Tuition waivers:*** Full or partial for employees or children of employees.

LOANS ***Student loans:*** $4,613,494 (55% need-based, 45% non-need-based). 73% of past graduating class borrowed through all loan programs. *Average indebtedness per student:* $29,825. ***Average need-based loan:*** Freshmen: $2715. Undergraduates: $3690. ***Parent loans:*** $763,443 (100% non-need-based). ***Programs:*** Federal Direct (Subsidized and Unsubsidized Stafford, PLUS), Perkins, state, college/university.

WORK-STUDY ***Federal work-study:*** Total amount: $664,718; 505 jobs averaging $1315. ***State or other work-study/employment:*** Total amount: $314,825 (4% need-based, 96% non-need-based). 226 part-time jobs averaging $1395.

APPLYING FOR FINANCIAL AID ***Required financial aid forms:*** FAFSA, institution's own form, noncustodial (divorced/separated) parent's statement. ***Financial aid deadline:*** 3/1 (priority: 3/1). ***Notification date:*** Continuous. Students must reply by 5/1 or within 2 weeks of notification.

CONTACT Ms. Cindi P. Reints, Director of Financial Assistance, Cornell College, Wade House, 600 1st Street West, Mount Vernon, IA 52314-1098, 319-895-4216 or toll-free 800-747-1112. *Fax:* 319-895-4106. *E-mail:* creints@cornellcollege.edu.

CORNELL UNIVERSITY

Ithaca, NY

Tuition & fees: $37,954 — **Average undergraduate aid package: $29,621**

ABOUT THE INSTITUTION Independent, coed. ***Awards:*** bachelor's, master's, doctoral, and first professional degrees. 109 undergraduate majors. ***Total enrollment:*** 20,273. Undergraduates: 13,846. Freshmen: 3,139. Institutional methodology is used as a basis for awarding need-based institutional aid.

UNDERGRADUATE EXPENSES for 2009–10 ***Application fee:*** $70. ***Comprehensive fee:*** $50,064 includes full-time tuition ($37,750), mandatory fees ($204), and room and board ($12,110). ***College room only:*** $7210.

FRESHMAN FINANCIAL AID (Fall 2008, est.) 1,414 applied for aid; of those 88% were deemed to have need. 100% of freshmen with need received aid; of those 100% had need fully met. ***Average percent of need met:*** 100% (excluding resources awarded to replace EFC). ***Average financial aid package:*** $30,530 (excluding resources awarded to replace EFC).

UNDERGRADUATE FINANCIAL AID (Fall 2008, est.) 6,165 applied for aid; of those 92% were deemed to have need. 100% of undergraduates with need received aid; of those 100% had need fully met. ***Average percent of need met:*** 100% (excluding resources awarded to replace EFC). ***Average financial aid package:*** $29,621 (excluding resources awarded to replace EFC).

GIFT AID (NEED-BASED) ***Total amount:*** $149,603,571 (7% federal, 3% state, 87% institutional, 3% external sources). ***Receiving aid:*** Freshmen: 37% (1,148); all full-time undergraduates: 38% (5,199). ***Average award:*** Freshmen: $26,649; Undergraduates: $25,272. ***Scholarships, grants, and awards:*** Federal Pell, FSEOG, state, private, college/university gift aid from institutional funds.

GIFT AID (NON-NEED-BASED) ***ROTC:*** Army, Air Force.

LOANS ***Student loans:*** $22,459,823 (100% need-based). 52% of past graduating class borrowed through all loan programs. *Average indebtedness per student:* $23,485. ***Average need-based loan:*** Freshmen: $2321. Undergraduates: $3080. ***Parent loans:*** $15,683,832 (100% need-based). ***Programs:*** Federal Direct (Subsidized and Unsubsidized Stafford, PLUS), FFEL (Subsidized and Unsubsidized Stafford, PLUS), Perkins, college/university.

WORK-STUDY ***Federal work-study:*** Total amount: $7,532,441; 4,284 jobs averaging $1760. ***State or other work-study/employment:*** Total amount: $1,085,436 (100% need-based). 732 part-time jobs averaging $1480.

APPLYING FOR FINANCIAL AID ***Required financial aid forms:*** FAFSA, institution's own form, CSS Financial Aid PROFILE, noncustodial (divorced/separated) parent's statement, business/farm supplement, prior year tax forms. ***Financial aid deadline:*** 1/5. ***Notification date:*** 4/1. Students must reply by 5/1 or within 2 weeks of notification.

CONTACT Mr. Thomas Keane, Director of Financial Aid and Student Employment, Cornell University, 410 Thurston Avenue, Ithaca, NY 14853-2488, 607-255-5147.

CORNERSTONE UNIVERSITY

Grand Rapids, MI

ABOUT THE INSTITUTION Independent nondenominational, coed. ***Awards:*** associate, bachelor's, master's, and first professional degrees. 39 undergraduate majors. ***Total enrollment:*** 2,440. Undergraduates: 1,797. Freshmen: 205.

GIFT AID (NEED-BASED) ***Scholarships, grants, and awards:*** Federal Pell, FSEOG, state, private, college/university gift aid from institutional funds.

GIFT AID (NON-NEED-BASED) ***Scholarships, grants, and awards by category:*** *Academic interests/achievement:* business, education, general academic interests/achievements, religion/biblical studies. *Creative arts/performance:* music. *Special achievements/activities:* leadership, religious involvement. *Special characteristics:* children and siblings of alumni, children of faculty/staff, children of union members/company employees, ethnic background, general special characteristics, international students, members of minority groups, out-of-state students.

LOANS ***Programs:*** FFEL (Subsidized and Unsubsidized Stafford, PLUS), Perkins, state, college/university.

WORK-STUDY ***Federal work-study:*** Total amount: $210,526; 189 jobs averaging $1069. ***State or other work-study/employment:*** Total amount: $48,550 (100% need-based). 34 part-time jobs averaging $1911.

APPLYING FOR FINANCIAL AID ***Required financial aid form:*** FAFSA.

CONTACT Director of Student Financial Services, Cornerstone University, 1001 East Beltline Avenue, NE, Grand Rapids, MI 49525-5897, 616-222-1424 or toll-free 800-787-9778. *Fax:* 616-222-1400.

CORNISH COLLEGE OF THE ARTS

Seattle, WA

Tuition & fees: $25,300 — **Average undergraduate aid package: $15,185**

ABOUT THE INSTITUTION Independent, coed. ***Awards:*** bachelor's degrees. 16 undergraduate majors. ***Total enrollment:*** 815. Undergraduates: 815. Federal methodology is used as a basis for awarding need-based institutional aid.

UNDERGRADUATE EXPENSES for 2008–09 ***Application fee:*** $35. ***Tuition:*** full-time $25,300; part-time $1070 per credit.

FRESHMAN FINANCIAL AID (Fall 2008, est.) 124 applied for aid; of those 78% were deemed to have need. 100% of freshmen with need received aid; of those 8% had need fully met. ***Average percent of need met:*** 56% (excluding resources awarded to replace EFC). ***Average financial aid package:*** $16,102 (excluding resources awarded to replace EFC). 32% of all full-time freshmen had no need and received non-need-based gift aid.

UNDERGRADUATE FINANCIAL AID (Fall 2008, est.) 578 applied for aid; of those 85% were deemed to have need. 100% of undergraduates with need received aid; of those 10% had need fully met. ***Average percent of need met:*** 56% (excluding resources awarded to replace EFC). ***Average financial aid package:*** $15,185 (excluding resources awarded to replace EFC). 18% of all full-time undergraduates had no need and received non-need-based gift aid.

GIFT AID (NEED-BASED) ***Total amount:*** $4,074,177 (22% federal, 21% state, 52% institutional, 5% external sources). ***Receiving aid:*** Freshmen: 65% (97); all full-time undergraduates: 67% (445). ***Average award:*** Freshmen: $9756; Undergraduates: $8788. ***Scholarships, grants, and awards:*** Federal Pell, FSEOG, state, private, college/university gift aid from institutional funds.

GIFT AID (NON-NEED-BASED) ***Total amount:*** $731,668 (1% state, 93% institutional, 6% external sources). ***Receiving aid:*** Freshmen: 4% (6). Undergraduates: 3% (19). ***Average award:*** Freshmen: $6023. Undergraduates: $5157. ***Scholarships, grants, and awards by category:*** *Academic interests/achievement:* general academic interests/achievements. *Creative arts/performance:* art/fine arts, dance, music, theater/drama.

LOANS ***Student loans:*** $6,165,091 (76% need-based, 24% non-need-based). 93% of past graduating class borrowed through all loan programs. *Average indebtedness per student:* $36,026. ***Average need-based loan:*** Freshmen: $3908.

Undergraduates: $4719. ***Parent loans:*** $5,365,011 (41% need-based, 59% non-need-based). ***Programs:*** Federal Direct (Subsidized and Unsubsidized Stafford, PLUS).

WORK-STUDY ***Federal work-study:*** Total amount: $1,370,094; jobs available (averaging $3000). ***State or other work-study/employment:*** Part-time jobs available (averaging $3000).

APPLYING FOR FINANCIAL AID ***Required financial aid form:*** FAFSA. ***Financial aid deadline (priority):*** 3/1. ***Notification date:*** 4/15. Students must reply by 5/1 or within 2 weeks of notification.

CONTACT Sharron Starling, Office of Admissions, Cornish College of the Arts, 1000 Lenora Street, Seattle, WA 98121, 206-726-5017 or toll-free 800-726-ARTS. *Fax:* 206-720-1011. *E-mail:* admissions@cornish.edu.

COVENANT COLLEGE

Lookout Mountain, GA

Tuition & fees: $24,320 **Average undergraduate aid package: $17,650**

ABOUT THE INSTITUTION Independent religious, coed. ***Awards:*** associate, bachelor's, and master's degrees (master's degree in education only). 27 undergraduate majors. ***Total enrollment:*** 1,073. Undergraduates: 1,006. Freshmen: 267. Federal methodology is used as a basis for awarding need-based institutional aid.

UNDERGRADUATE EXPENSES for 2008–09 ***Application fee:*** $35. ***Comprehensive fee:*** $31,220 includes full-time tuition ($23,600), mandatory fees ($720), and room and board ($6900). Full-time tuition and fees vary according to course load. ***Part-time tuition:*** $985 per credit hour. Part-time tuition and fees vary according to course load. ***Payment plan:*** Installment.

FRESHMAN FINANCIAL AID (Fall 2007) 244 applied for aid; of those 86% were deemed to have need. 100% of freshmen with need received aid; of those 17% had need fully met. ***Average percent of need met:*** 79% (excluding resources awarded to replace EFC). ***Average financial aid package:*** $17,837 (excluding resources awarded to replace EFC). 24% of all full-time freshmen had no need and received non-need-based gift aid.

UNDERGRADUATE FINANCIAL AID (Fall 2007) 766 applied for aid; of those 87% were deemed to have need. 100% of undergraduates with need received aid; of those 20% had need fully met. ***Average percent of need met:*** 77% (excluding resources awarded to replace EFC). ***Average financial aid package:*** $17,650 (excluding resources awarded to replace EFC). 26% of all full-time undergraduates had no need and received non-need-based gift aid.

GIFT AID (NEED-BASED) ***Total amount:*** $8,730,488 (10% federal, 5% state, 80% institutional, 5% external sources). ***Receiving aid:*** Freshmen: 71% (207); all full-time undergraduates: 68% (661). ***Average award:*** Freshmen: $13,388; Undergraduates: $12,563. ***Scholarships, grants, and awards:*** Federal Pell, FSEOG, state, private, college/university gift aid from institutional funds.

GIFT AID (NON-NEED-BASED) ***Total amount:*** $2,653,228 (7% state, 82% institutional, 11% external sources). ***Average award:*** Freshmen: $6022. Undergraduates: $6907. ***Scholarships, grants, and awards by category:*** *Academic interests/achievement:* 322 awards ($797,000 total): general academic interests/achievements. *Creative arts/performance:* 55 awards ($76,500 total): music. *Special achievements/activities:* 50 awards ($532,500 total): leadership. *Special characteristics:* 507 awards ($1,489,023 total): children of faculty/staff, international students, members of minority groups, religious affiliation. ***Tuition waivers:*** Full or partial for employees or children of employees, senior citizens.

LOANS ***Student loans:*** $3,164,663 (92% need-based, 8% non-need-based). 58% of past graduating class borrowed through all loan programs. *Average indebtedness per student:* $18,382. ***Average need-based loan:*** Freshmen: $4335. Undergraduates: $5113. ***Parent loans:*** $1,733,949 (83% need-based, 17% non-need-based). ***Programs:*** FFEL (Subsidized and Unsubsidized Stafford, PLUS), Perkins, state, college/university.

WORK-STUDY ***Federal work-study:*** Total amount: $231,083; 313 jobs averaging $1931. ***State or other work-study/employment:*** Total amount: $477,324 (89% need-based, 11% non-need-based). 69 part-time jobs averaging $1681.

ATHLETIC AWARDS Total amount: $3,010,887 (76% need-based, 24% non-need-based).

APPLYING FOR FINANCIAL AID ***Required financial aid forms:*** FAFSA, institution's own form, state aid form. ***Financial aid deadline:*** Continuous. ***Notification date:*** Continuous beginning 2/1. Students must reply within 3 weeks of notification.

CONTACT Mrs. Carolyn Hays, Assistant Director of Student Financial Planning, Covenant College, 14049 Scenic Highway, Lookout Mountain, GA 30750, 706-820-1560 Ext. 1150 or toll-free 888-451-2683. *Fax:* 706-820-2820. *E-mail:* hays@covenant.edu.

COX COLLEGE OF NURSING AND HEALTH SCIENCES

Springfield, MO

CONTACT Brenda Smith, Financial Aid Coordinator, Cox College of Nursing and Health Sciences, 1423 North Jefferson Avenue, Springfield, MO 65802, 417-269-3401 or toll-free 866-898-5355 (in-state). *Fax:* 417-269-3586. *E-mail:* bjsmit1@coxcollege.edu.

CREIGHTON UNIVERSITY

Omaha, NE

Tuition & fees: $28,542 **Average undergraduate aid package: $23,916**

ABOUT THE INSTITUTION Independent Roman Catholic (Jesuit), coed. ***Awards:*** associate, bachelor's, master's, doctoral, and first professional degrees and post-bachelor's certificates. 48 undergraduate majors. ***Total enrollment:*** 7,051. Undergraduates: 4,087. Freshmen: 992. Federal methodology is used as a basis for awarding need-based institutional aid.

UNDERGRADUATE EXPENSES for 2008–09 ***Application fee:*** $40. ***Comprehensive fee:*** $37,058 includes full-time tuition ($27,282), mandatory fees ($1260), and room and board ($8516). ***College room only:*** $4816. Full-time tuition and fees vary according to degree level, program, and student level. Room and board charges vary according to board plan and housing facility. ***Part-time tuition:*** $853 per semester hour. ***Part-time fees:*** $242 per year. Part-time tuition and fees vary according to degree level, program, and student level. ***Payment plan:*** Installment.

FRESHMAN FINANCIAL AID (Fall 2008, est.) 765 applied for aid; of those 77% were deemed to have need. 100% of freshmen with need received aid; of those 42% had need fully met. ***Average percent of need met:*** 92% (excluding resources awarded to replace EFC). ***Average financial aid package:*** $25,421 (excluding resources awarded to replace EFC). 35% of all full-time freshmen had no need and received non-need-based gift aid.

UNDERGRADUATE FINANCIAL AID (Fall 2008, est.) 2,428 applied for aid; of those 82% were deemed to have need. 100% of undergraduates with need received aid; of those 34% had need fully met. ***Average percent of need met:*** 89% (excluding resources awarded to replace EFC). ***Average financial aid package:*** $23,916 (excluding resources awarded to replace EFC). 35% of all full-time undergraduates had no need and received non-need-based gift aid.

GIFT AID (NEED-BASED) ***Total amount:*** $30,577,236 (10% federal, 1% state, 81% institutional, 8% external sources). ***Receiving aid:*** Freshmen: 60% (588); all full-time undergraduates: 51% (1,945). ***Average award:*** Freshmen: $19,524; Undergraduates: $17,995. ***Scholarships, grants, and awards:*** Federal Pell, FSEOG, state, private, college/university gift aid from institutional funds, Federal Nursing.

GIFT AID (NON-NEED-BASED) ***Total amount:*** $11,982,613 (93% institutional, 7% external sources). ***Receiving aid:*** Freshmen: 51% (507). Undergraduates: 44% (1,677). ***Average award:*** Freshmen: $11,988. Undergraduates: $11,568. ***Scholarships, grants, and awards by category:*** *Academic interests/achievement:* business, education, general academic interests/achievements, military science. *Creative arts/performance:* art/fine arts, creative writing, dance, debating, journalism/publications, music, performing arts, theater/drama. *Special achievements/activities:* leadership. *Special characteristics:* children of faculty/staff, first-generation college students, handicapped students, local/state students, members of minority groups, religious affiliation, siblings of current students. ***Tuition waivers:*** Full or partial for employees or children of employees, adult students. ***ROTC:*** Army, Air Force cooperative.

LOANS ***Student loans:*** $23,968,250 (51% need-based, 49% non-need-based). 61% of past graduating class borrowed through all loan programs. *Average indebtedness per student:* $32,560. ***Average need-based loan:*** Freshmen: $6066. Undergraduates: $6799. ***Parent loans:*** $4,726,616 (100% non-need-based). ***Programs:*** FFEL (Subsidized and Unsubsidized Stafford, PLUS), Perkins, Federal Nursing, college/university.

WORK-STUDY ***Federal work-study:*** Total amount: $1,656,606; 827 jobs averaging $1865.

ATHLETIC AWARDS Total amount: $3,069,857 (31% need-based, 69% non-need-based).

APPLYING FOR FINANCIAL AID ***Required financial aid forms:*** FAFSA, institution's own form. ***Financial aid deadline (priority):*** 3/1. ***Notification date:*** Continuous beginning 3/15. Students must reply by 5/1 or within 4 weeks of notification.

CONTACT Sarah Sell, Assistant Director of Financial Aid, Creighton University, 2500 California Plaza, Omaha, NE 68178, 402-280-2731 or toll-free 800-282-5835. *Fax:* 402-280-2895. *E-mail:* sarahsell@creighton.edu.

CRICHTON COLLEGE

Memphis, TN

CONTACT Mrs. Dede Pirtle, Financial Aid Director, Crichton College, 255 North Highland, Memphis, TN 38111, 901-320-9700 Ext. 1030 or toll-free 800-960-9777. *Fax:* 901-320-9709. *E-mail:* dede@crichton.edu.

THE CRISWELL COLLEGE

Dallas, TX

CONTACT Kirk Spencer, Financial Aid Director, The Criswell College, 4010 Gaston Avenue, Dallas, TX 75246, 800-899-0012. *Fax:* 214-818-1310. *E-mail:* kspencer@criswell.edu.

CROSSROADS BIBLE COLLEGE

Indianapolis, IN

CONTACT Mrs. Phyllis Dodson, Director of Financial Aid, Crossroads Bible College, 601 North Shortridge Road, Indianapolis, IN 46219, 317-352-8736 Ext. 28 or toll-free 800-273-2224 Ext. 230. *Fax:* 317-352-9145.

CROSSROADS COLLEGE

Rochester, MN

ABOUT THE INSTITUTION Independent religious, coed. ***Awards:*** associate and bachelor's degrees. 13 undergraduate majors. ***Total enrollment:*** 160. Undergraduates: 160. Freshmen: 24.

GIFT AID (NEED-BASED) ***Scholarships, grants, and awards:*** Federal Pell, FSEOG, state, private, college/university gift aid from institutional funds.

GIFT AID (NON-NEED-BASED) ***Scholarships, grants, and awards by category:*** *Academic interests/achievement:* general academic interests/achievements, religion/biblical studies. *Creative arts/performance:* music. *Special achievements/activities:* general special achievements/activities, religious involvement. *Special characteristics:* children of faculty/staff, general special characteristics, international students, parents of current students, religious affiliation, siblings of current students, spouses of current students.

LOANS ***Programs:*** FFEL (Subsidized and Unsubsidized Stafford, PLUS), state, college/university, alternative loans.

WORK-STUDY ***Federal work-study:*** Total amount: $14,701; 16 jobs averaging $1450. ***State or other work-study/employment:*** Total amount: $17,744 (66% need-based, 34% non-need-based). 9 part-time jobs averaging $3500.

APPLYING FOR FINANCIAL AID ***Required financial aid forms:*** FAFSA, institution's own form.

CONTACT Polly Kellogg-Bradley, Director of Financial Aid, Crossroads College, 920 Mayowood Road SW, Rochester, MN 55902-2275, 507-288-4563 or toll-free 800-456-7651. *Fax:* 507-288-9046. *E-mail:* pkellogbradley@crossroadscollege.edu.

CROWN COLLEGE

St. Bonifacius, MN

Tuition & fees: $19,774 | **Average undergraduate aid package: $14,632**

ABOUT THE INSTITUTION Independent religious, coed. ***Awards:*** associate, bachelor's, and master's degrees. 25 undergraduate majors. ***Total enrollment:*** 1,229. Undergraduates: 1,106. Freshmen: 168. Both federal and institutional methodology are used as a basis for awarding need-based institutional aid.

UNDERGRADUATE EXPENSES for 2009–10 ***Application fee:*** $35. ***Comprehensive fee:*** $27,140 includes full-time tuition ($19,774) and room and board ($7366). ***College room only:*** $3834. ***Part-time tuition:*** $823 per credit.

FRESHMAN FINANCIAL AID (Fall 2008, est.) 160 applied for aid; of those 81% were deemed to have need. 99% of freshmen with need received aid; of those 17% had need fully met. ***Average percent of need met:*** 67% (excluding resources awarded to replace EFC). ***Average financial aid package:*** $16,158 (excluding resources awarded to replace EFC). 11% of all full-time freshmen had no need and received non-need-based gift aid.

UNDERGRADUATE FINANCIAL AID (Fall 2008, est.) 598 applied for aid; of those 85% were deemed to have need. 100% of undergraduates with need received aid; of those 15% had need fully met. ***Average percent of need met:*** 63% (excluding resources awarded to replace EFC). ***Average financial aid package:*** $14,632 (excluding resources awarded to replace EFC). 12% of all full-time undergraduates had no need and received non-need-based gift aid.

GIFT AID (NEED-BASED) ***Total amount:*** $1,944,454 (46% federal, 34% state, 20% institutional). ***Receiving aid:*** Freshmen: 28% (77); all full-time undergraduates: 46% (329). ***Average award:*** Freshmen: $5799; Undergraduates: $5814. ***Scholarships, grants, and awards:*** Federal Pell, FSEOG, state, private, college/university gift aid from institutional funds.

GIFT AID (NON-NEED-BASED) ***Total amount:*** $3,901,377 (94% institutional, 6% external sources). ***Receiving aid:*** Freshmen: 45% (123). Undergraduates: 63% (448). ***Average award:*** Freshmen: $6904. Undergraduates: $6206. ***Scholarships, grants, and awards by category:*** *Academic interests/achievement:* 514 awards ($1,286,852 total): general academic interests/achievements. *Creative arts/performance:* 7 awards ($13,500 total): music. *Special achievements/activities:* 145 awards ($905,745 total): leadership. *Special characteristics:* 219 awards ($1,016,926 total): children and siblings of alumni, children of faculty/staff, international students, members of minority groups, relatives of clergy, siblings of current students.

LOANS ***Student loans:*** $4,851,701 (39% need-based, 61% non-need-based). 89% of past graduating class borrowed through all loan programs. *Average indebtedness per student:* $31,421. ***Average need-based loan:*** Freshmen: $3871. Undergraduates: $4545. ***Parent loans:*** $595,165 (100% non-need-based). ***Programs:*** FFEL (Subsidized and Unsubsidized Stafford, PLUS), Perkins, state, SELF Loans, CitiAssist Loans, Signature Loans, U.S. Bank No Fee Educational Loans, Wells Fargo.

WORK-STUDY ***Federal work-study:*** Total amount: $300,548; 107 jobs averaging $1348. ***State or other work-study/employment:*** Total amount: $7776 (100% need-based). 12 part-time jobs averaging $942.

APPLYING FOR FINANCIAL AID ***Required financial aid forms:*** FAFSA, institution's own form. ***Financial aid deadline:*** 8/1 (priority: 4/5). ***Notification date:*** Continuous. Students must reply within 3 weeks of notification.

CONTACT Judy Bedford, Interim Director of Financial Aid, Crown College, 8700 College View Drive, St. Bonifacius, MN 55375-9001, 952-446-4177 or toll-free 800-68-CROWN. *Fax:* 952-446-4178. *E-mail:* finaid@crown.edu.

THE CULINARY INSTITUTE OF AMERICA

Hyde Park, NY

CONTACT Patricia A. Arcuri, Director of Financial Aid, The Culinary Institute of America, 1946 Campus Drive, Hyde Park, NY 12538-1499, 845-451-1243 or toll-free 800-CULINARY. *Fax:* 845-905-4030. *E-mail:* p_arcuri@culinary.edu.

CULVER-STOCKTON COLLEGE

Canton, MO

Tuition & fees: $21,750 | **Average undergraduate aid package: $19,016**

ABOUT THE INSTITUTION Independent religious, coed. ***Awards:*** bachelor's degrees. 33 undergraduate majors. ***Total enrollment:*** 810. Undergraduates: 810. Freshmen: 227. Federal methodology is used as a basis for awarding need-based institutional aid.

UNDERGRADUATE EXPENSES for 2008–09 ***Application fee:*** $25. ***One-time required fee:*** $125. ***Comprehensive fee:*** $28,950 includes full-time tuition ($21,500), mandatory fees ($250), and room and board ($7200). ***College room only:*** $3200. Room and board charges vary according to board plan. ***Part-time tuition:*** $500 per credit hour. ***Part-time fees:*** $10.42 per credit hour. ***Payment plan:*** Installment.

FRESHMAN FINANCIAL AID (Fall 2008, est.) 207 applied for aid; of those 88% were deemed to have need. 100% of freshmen with need received aid; of those 18% had need fully met. ***Average percent of need met:*** 81% (excluding

resources awarded to replace EFC). ***Average financial aid package:*** $20,438 (excluding resources awarded to replace EFC). 19% of all full-time freshmen had no need and received non-need-based gift aid.

UNDERGRADUATE FINANCIAL AID (Fall 2008, est.) 634 applied for aid; of those 90% were deemed to have need. 100% of undergraduates with need received aid; of those 22% had need fully met. ***Average percent of need met:*** 80% (excluding resources awarded to replace EFC). ***Average financial aid package:*** $19,016 (excluding resources awarded to replace EFC). 17% of all full-time undergraduates had no need and received non-need-based gift aid.

GIFT AID (NEED-BASED) ***Total amount:*** $7,879,626 (14% federal, 11% state, 73% institutional, 2% external sources). ***Receiving aid:*** Freshmen: 81% (183); all full-time undergraduates: 83% (572). ***Average award:*** Freshmen: $16,514; Undergraduates: $14,610. ***Scholarships, grants, and awards:*** Federal Pell, FSEOG, state, private, college/university gift aid from institutional funds.

GIFT AID (NON-NEED-BASED) ***Total amount:*** $1,667,455 (2% state, 93% institutional, 5% external sources). ***Receiving aid:*** Freshmen: 12% (28). Undergraduates: 13% (87). ***Average award:*** Freshmen: $12,468. Undergraduates: $10,510. ***Scholarships, grants, and awards by category:*** *Academic interests/achievement:* 604 awards ($3,866,789 total): general academic interests/achievements, international studies. *Creative arts/performance:* 114 awards ($208,588 total): art/fine arts, debating, music, theater/drama. *Special achievements/activities:* 8 awards ($6500 total): cheerleading/drum major, general special achievements/activities. *Special characteristics:* 77 awards ($443,938 total): children and siblings of alumni, children of faculty/staff, international students, local/state students, religious affiliation. ***Tuition waivers:*** Full or partial for employees or children of employees, senior citizens.

LOANS ***Student loans:*** $5,531,291 (69% need-based, 31% non-need-based). 92% of past graduating class borrowed through all loan programs. *Average indebtedness per student:* $22,996. ***Average need-based loan:*** Freshmen: $4486. Undergraduates: $5082. ***Parent loans:*** $1,295,757 (34% need-based, 66% non-need-based). ***Programs:*** Federal Direct (Subsidized and Unsubsidized Stafford, PLUS), Perkins, Federal Nursing, state, college/university.

WORK-STUDY ***Federal work-study:*** Total amount: $53,382; 119 jobs averaging $499. ***State or other work-study/employment:*** Total amount: $290,545 (30% need-based, 70% non-need-based). 167 part-time jobs averaging $2403.

ATHLETIC AWARDS Total amount: $843,996 (72% need-based, 28% non-need-based).

APPLYING FOR FINANCIAL AID ***Required financial aid form:*** FAFSA. ***Financial aid deadline:*** 6/1 (priority: 3/1). ***Notification date:*** Continuous. Students must reply within 2 weeks of notification.

CONTACT Ms. Tina M. Wiseman, Director of Financial Aid, Culver-Stockton College, One College Hill, Canton, MO 63435, 573-288-6307 Ext. 6306 or toll-free 800-537-1883. *Fax:* 573-288-6308. *E-mail:* twiseman@culver.edu.

CUMBERLAND UNIVERSITY

Lebanon, TN

ABOUT THE INSTITUTION Independent, coed. ***Awards:*** associate, bachelor's, and master's degrees. 37 undergraduate majors. ***Total enrollment:*** 1,335. Undergraduates: 1,068. Freshmen: 212.

GIFT AID (NEED-BASED) ***Scholarships, grants, and awards:*** Federal Pell, FSEOG, state, private, college/university gift aid from institutional funds.

GIFT AID (NON-NEED-BASED) ***Scholarships, grants, and awards by category:*** *Academic interests/achievement:* general academic interests/achievements. *Creative arts/performance:* art/fine arts, music, performing arts, theater/drama. *Special achievements/activities:* leadership. *Special characteristics:* children of faculty/staff.

LOANS ***Programs:*** FFEL (Subsidized and Unsubsidized Stafford, PLUS), Perkins, alternative loans.

WORK-STUDY ***Federal work-study:*** Total amount: $79,286; 120 jobs averaging $750. ***State or other work-study/employment:*** Total amount: $11,713 (100% non-need-based). 16 part-time jobs averaging $750.

APPLYING FOR FINANCIAL AID ***Required financial aid form:*** FAFSA.

CONTACT Ms. Beatrice LaChance, Director of Student Financial Services, Cumberland University, One Cumberland Square, Lebanon, TN 37087-3554, 615-444-2562 Ext. 1244 or toll-free 800-467-0562. *Fax:* 615-443-8424. *E-mail:* lvaughan@cumberland.edu.

CURRY COLLEGE

Milton, MA

Tuition & fees: $27,720 **Average undergraduate aid package: $17,286**

ABOUT THE INSTITUTION Independent, coed. ***Awards:*** bachelor's and master's degrees. 29 undergraduate majors. ***Total enrollment:*** 3,079. Undergraduates: 2,753. Freshmen: 587. Federal methodology is used as a basis for awarding need-based institutional aid.

UNDERGRADUATE EXPENSES for 2008–09 ***Application fee:*** $40. ***Comprehensive fee:*** $38,800 includes full-time tuition ($26,700), mandatory fees ($1020), and room and board ($11,080). ***College room only:*** $6500. Room and board charges vary according to board plan and housing facility. ***Part-time tuition:*** $960 per credit hour. Part-time tuition and fees vary according to course load. ***Payment plan:*** Installment.

FRESHMAN FINANCIAL AID (Fall 2008, est.) 383 applied for aid; of those 100% were deemed to have need. 100% of freshmen with need received aid; of those 4% had need fully met. ***Average percent of need met:*** 65% (excluding resources awarded to replace EFC). ***Average financial aid package:*** $17,478 (excluding resources awarded to replace EFC). 5% of all full-time freshmen had no need and received non-need-based gift aid.

UNDERGRADUATE FINANCIAL AID (Fall 2008, est.) 1,351 applied for aid; of those 100% were deemed to have need. 100% of undergraduates with need received aid; of those 5% had need fully met. ***Average percent of need met:*** 67% (excluding resources awarded to replace EFC). ***Average financial aid package:*** $17,286 (excluding resources awarded to replace EFC). 4% of all full-time undergraduates had no need and received non-need-based gift aid.

GIFT AID (NEED-BASED) ***Total amount:*** $16,057,167 (11% federal, 6% state, 80% institutional, 3% external sources). ***Receiving aid:*** Freshmen: 64% (367); all full-time undergraduates: 60% (1,241). ***Average award:*** Freshmen: $11,948; Undergraduates: $11,429. ***Scholarships, grants, and awards:*** Federal Pell, FSEOG, state, private, college/university gift aid from institutional funds.

GIFT AID (NON-NEED-BASED) ***Total amount:*** $485,213 (90% institutional, 10% external sources). ***Receiving aid:*** Freshmen: 1% (7). Undergraduates: 1% (12). ***Average award:*** Freshmen: $4560. Undergraduates: $4894. ***Scholarships, grants, and awards by category:*** *Academic interests/achievement:* 229 awards ($1,222,500 total): general academic interests/achievements. ***Tuition waivers:*** Full or partial for employees or children of employees. ***ROTC:*** Army cooperative.

LOANS ***Student loans:*** $19,385,288 (30% need-based, 70% non-need-based). 79% of past graduating class borrowed through all loan programs. *Average indebtedness per student:* $35,819. ***Average need-based loan:*** Freshmen: $3481. Undergraduates: $4387. ***Parent loans:*** $6,337,658 (100% non-need-based). ***Programs:*** FFEL (Subsidized and Unsubsidized Stafford, PLUS), Perkins, state.

WORK-STUDY ***Federal work-study:*** Total amount: $1,141,108; 648 jobs averaging $1803.

APPLYING FOR FINANCIAL AID ***Required financial aid form:*** FAFSA. ***Financial aid deadline (priority):*** 3/1. ***Notification date:*** Continuous beginning 3/1.

CONTACT Dyan Teehan, Director of Financial Aid, Curry College, 1071 Blue Hill Avenue, Milton, MA 02186-2395, 617-333-2354 or toll-free 800-669-0686. *Fax:* 617-333-2915. *E-mail:* dteehan0107@curry.edu.

THE CURTIS INSTITUTE OF MUSIC

Philadelphia, PA

Tuition & fees: $2290 **Average undergraduate aid package: N/A**

ABOUT THE INSTITUTION Independent, coed. ***Awards:*** bachelor's and master's degrees and post-bachelor's certificates. 3 undergraduate majors. ***Total enrollment:*** 164. Undergraduates: 135. Both federal and institutional methodology are used as a basis for awarding need-based institutional aid.

UNDERGRADUATE EXPENSES for 2009–10 ***Application fee:*** $150. ***Tuition:*** The Curtis Institute of Music provides merit-based full-tuition scholarships to students.

GIFT AID (NEED-BASED) ***Scholarships, grants, and awards:*** Federal Pell, college/university gift aid from institutional funds.

LOANS ***Programs:*** FFEL (Subsidized and Unsubsidized Stafford, PLUS).

WORK-STUDY ***State or other work-study/employment:*** Part-time jobs available.

APPLYING FOR FINANCIAL AID ***Required financial aid forms:*** FAFSA, institution's own form, bank statements, tax returns. ***Financial aid deadline:*** 3/1. ***Notification date:*** 4/1. Students must reply by 5/1.

CONTACT Richard Woodland, Director of Student Financial Assistance, The Curtis Institute of Music, 1726 Locust Street, Philadelphia, PA 19103-6107, 215-717-3143. *E-mail:* richard.woodland@curtis.edu.

DAEMEN COLLEGE

Amherst, NY

Tuition & fees: $19,870 **Average undergraduate aid package: $16,176**

ABOUT THE INSTITUTION Independent, coed. ***Awards:*** bachelor's, master's, and doctoral degrees and post-master's certificates. 30 undergraduate majors. ***Total enrollment:*** 2,716. Undergraduates: 1,768. Freshmen: 406. Federal methodology is used as a basis for awarding need-based institutional aid.

UNDERGRADUATE EXPENSES for 2008–09 ***Application fee:*** $25. ***Comprehensive fee:*** $28,920 includes full-time tuition ($19,400), mandatory fees ($470), and room and board ($9050). Full-time tuition and fees vary according to course load. Room and board charges vary according to board plan and housing facility. ***Part-time tuition:*** $645 per credit. ***Part-time fees:*** $4 per credit; $70 per term. Part-time tuition and fees vary according to course load. ***Payment plans:*** Installment, deferred payment.

FRESHMAN FINANCIAL AID (Fall 2007) 349 applied for aid; of those 88% were deemed to have need. 100% of freshmen with need received aid; of those 26% had need fully met. ***Average percent of need met:*** 88% (excluding resources awarded to replace EFC). ***Average financial aid package:*** $16,778 (excluding resources awarded to replace EFC). 11% of all full-time freshmen had no need and received non-need-based gift aid.

UNDERGRADUATE FINANCIAL AID (Fall 2007) 1,360 applied for aid; of those 86% were deemed to have need. 100% of undergraduates with need received aid; of those 30% had need fully met. ***Average percent of need met:*** 88% (excluding resources awarded to replace EFC). ***Average financial aid package:*** $16,176 (excluding resources awarded to replace EFC). 13% of all full-time undergraduates had no need and received non-need-based gift aid.

GIFT AID (NEED-BASED) ***Total amount:*** $8,718,217 (22% federal, 29% state, 49% institutional). ***Receiving aid:*** Freshmen: 80% (287); all full-time undergraduates: 79% (1,074). ***Average award:*** Freshmen: $7977; Undergraduates: $7493. ***Scholarships, grants, and awards:*** Federal Pell, FSEOG, state, private, college/university gift aid from institutional funds.

GIFT AID (NON-NEED-BASED) ***Total amount:*** $8,162,044 (1% state, 92% institutional, 7% external sources). ***Receiving aid:*** Freshmen: 74% (268). Undergraduates: 73% (989). ***Average award:*** Freshmen: $7410. Undergraduates: $6834. ***Scholarships, grants, and awards by category:*** *Academic interests/achievement:* 981 awards ($4,634,702 total): general academic interests/achievements. *Creative arts/performance:* 8 awards ($4200 total): art/fine arts. *Special characteristics:* 41 awards ($453,726 total): children and siblings of alumni, children of faculty/staff, general special characteristics, siblings of current students. ***Tuition waivers:*** Full or partial for employees or children of employees, senior citizens. ***ROTC:*** Army cooperative.

LOANS ***Student loans:*** $9,045,716 (51% need-based, 49% non-need-based). 87% of past graduating class borrowed through all loan programs. *Average indebtedness per student:* $20,465. ***Average need-based loan:*** Freshmen: $3933. Undergraduates: $4529. ***Parent loans:*** $873,106 (74% need-based, 26% non-need-based). ***Programs:*** FFEL (Subsidized and Unsubsidized Stafford, PLUS), Perkins, college/university, alternative loans.

WORK-STUDY ***Federal work-study:*** Total amount: $953,199; 262 jobs averaging $1165. ***State or other work-study/employment:*** Total amount: $266,018 (89% need-based, 11% non-need-based). 45 part-time jobs averaging $1248.

ATHLETIC AWARDS Total amount: $595,608 (78% need-based, 22% non-need-based).

APPLYING FOR FINANCIAL AID ***Required financial aid forms:*** FAFSA, state aid form. ***Financial aid deadline (priority):*** 2/15. ***Notification date:*** Continuous. Students must reply within 2 weeks of notification.

CONTACT Jeffrey Pagano, Director of Financial Aid, Daemen College, 4380 Main Street, Amherst, NY 14226-3592, 716-839-8254 or toll-free 800-462-7652. *Fax:* 716-839-8378. *E-mail:* jpagano@daemen.edu.

DAKOTA STATE UNIVERSITY

Madison, SD

Tuition & fees (SD res): $6498 **Average undergraduate aid package: $7269**

ABOUT THE INSTITUTION State-supported, coed. ***Awards:*** associate, bachelor's, master's, and doctoral degrees. 30 undergraduate majors. ***Total enrollment:*** 2,675. Undergraduates: 2,296. Freshmen: 273. Federal methodology is used as a basis for awarding need-based institutional aid.

UNDERGRADUATE EXPENSES for 2008–09 ***Application fee:*** $20. ***Tuition, state resident:*** full-time $2646; part-time $88 per credit hour. ***Tuition, nonresident:*** full-time $3966; part-time $132 per credit hour. ***Required fees:*** full-time $3852; $106 per credit hour. Full-time tuition and fees vary according to location and reciprocity agreements. Part-time tuition and fees vary according to location and reciprocity agreements. ***College room and board:*** $4612; ***Room only:*** $2545. Room and board charges vary according to board plan and housing facility. ***Payment plans:*** Installment, deferred payment.

FRESHMAN FINANCIAL AID (Fall 2008, est.) 228 applied for aid; of those 74% were deemed to have need. 100% of freshmen with need received aid; of those 13% had need fully met. ***Average percent of need met:*** 80% (excluding resources awarded to replace EFC). ***Average financial aid package:*** $6902 (excluding resources awarded to replace EFC). 11% of all full-time freshmen had no need and received non-need-based gift aid.

UNDERGRADUATE FINANCIAL AID (Fall 2008, est.) 930 applied for aid; of those 76% were deemed to have need. 100% of undergraduates with need received aid; of those 18% had need fully met. ***Average percent of need met:*** 82% (excluding resources awarded to replace EFC). ***Average financial aid package:*** $7269 (excluding resources awarded to replace EFC). 9% of all full-time undergraduates had no need and received non-need-based gift aid.

GIFT AID (NEED-BASED) ***Total amount:*** $2,044,169 (70% federal, 4% state, 16% institutional, 10% external sources). ***Receiving aid:*** Freshmen: 31% (81); all full-time undergraduates: 31% (340). ***Average award:*** Freshmen: $3957; Undergraduates: $4106. ***Scholarships, grants, and awards:*** Federal Pell, FSEOG, state, private, college/university gift aid from institutional funds, Agency Assistance (Veteran Benefits/Department of Labor), National Smart Grant, ACG.

GIFT AID (NON-NEED-BASED) ***Total amount:*** $406,597 (39% federal, 9% state, 32% institutional, 20% external sources). ***Receiving aid:*** Freshmen: 43% (112). Undergraduates: 27% (300). ***Average award:*** Freshmen: $3268. Undergraduates: $3652. ***Scholarships, grants, and awards by category:*** *Academic interests/achievement:* business, communication, computer science, education, English, general academic interests/achievements, mathematics. *Creative arts/performance:* music. *Special achievements/activities:* general special achievements/activities. *Special characteristics:* children and siblings of alumni, ethnic background, local/state students, members of minority groups. ***Tuition waivers:*** Full or partial for employees or children of employees, senior citizens. ***ROTC:*** Army, Air Force cooperative.

LOANS ***Student loans:*** $7,593,841 (71% need-based, 29% non-need-based). 92% of past graduating class borrowed through all loan programs. *Average indebtedness per student:* $21,189. ***Average need-based loan:*** Freshmen: $3283. Undergraduates: $3752. ***Parent loans:*** $580,043 (71% need-based, 29% non-need-based). ***Programs:*** FFEL (Subsidized and Unsubsidized Stafford, PLUS), Perkins, alternative loans.

WORK-STUDY ***Federal work-study:*** Total amount: $261,779; jobs available. ***State or other work-study/employment:*** Total amount: $99,729 (100% non-need-based). Part-time jobs available.

ATHLETIC AWARDS Total amount: $211,467 (71% need-based, 29% non-need-based).

APPLYING FOR FINANCIAL AID ***Required financial aid forms:*** FAFSA, institution's own form. ***Financial aid deadline (priority):*** 3/1. ***Notification date:*** Continuous beginning 4/1. Students must reply within 2 weeks of notification.

CONTACT Denise Grayson, Financial Aid Director, Dakota State University, 103 Heston Hall, 820 North Washington Avenue, Madison, SD 57042-1799, 605-256-5158 or toll-free 888-DSU-9988. *Fax:* 605-256-5020. *E-mail:* fa@dsu.edu.

DAKOTA WESLEYAN UNIVERSITY

Mitchell, SD

ABOUT THE INSTITUTION Independent United Methodist, coed. ***Awards:*** associate, bachelor's, and master's degrees. 43 undergraduate majors. ***Total enrollment:*** 711. Undergraduates: 683. Freshmen: 163.

LOANS ***Programs:*** private alternative loans: Methodist loan (for members of Methodist Church).

WORK-STUDY ***Federal work-study:*** Total amount: $104,099; 178 jobs averaging $1400. ***State or other work-study/employment:*** Total amount: $17,935 (100% non-need-based). 6 part-time jobs averaging $1400.

CONTACT Emily George, Administrative Assistant for Academic Affairs, Dakota Wesleyan University, 1200 West University Avenue, Mitchell, SD 57301, 605-995-2645 or toll-free 800-333-8506. *Fax:* 605-995-2609. *E-mail:* emgeorge@dwu.edu.

DALLAS BAPTIST UNIVERSITY

Dallas, TX

Tuition & fees: $16,440 **Average undergraduate aid package: $13,024**

ABOUT THE INSTITUTION Independent religious, coed. ***Awards:*** associate, bachelor's, master's, and doctoral degrees and post-bachelor's and post-master's certificates. 45 undergraduate majors. ***Total enrollment:*** 5,297. Undergraduates: 3,575. Freshmen: 350. Federal methodology is used as a basis for awarding need-based institutional aid.

UNDERGRADUATE EXPENSES for 2008–09 ***Application fee:*** $25. ***Comprehensive fee:*** $21,849 includes full-time tuition ($16,440) and room and board ($5409). ***College room only:*** $2150. Room and board charges vary according to board plan and housing facility. ***Part-time tuition:*** $548 per credit hour. ***Payment plans:*** Installment, deferred payment.

FRESHMAN FINANCIAL AID (Fall 2008, est.) 325 applied for aid; of those 67% were deemed to have need. 100% of freshmen with need received aid; of those 60% had need fully met. ***Average percent of need met:*** 86% (excluding resources awarded to replace EFC). ***Average financial aid package:*** $13,740 (excluding resources awarded to replace EFC). 26% of all full-time freshmen had no need and received non-need-based gift aid.

UNDERGRADUATE FINANCIAL AID (Fall 2008, est.) 1,848 applied for aid; of those 70% were deemed to have need. 98% of undergraduates with need received aid; of those 45% had need fully met. ***Average percent of need met:*** 78% (excluding resources awarded to replace EFC). ***Average financial aid package:*** $13,024 (excluding resources awarded to replace EFC). 18% of all full-time undergraduates had no need and received non-need-based gift aid.

GIFT AID (NEED-BASED) ***Total amount:*** $5,048,966 (54% federal, 46% state). ***Receiving aid:*** Freshmen: 47% (163); all full-time undergraduates: 45% (1,005). ***Average award:*** Freshmen: $3046; Undergraduates: $3657. ***Scholarships, grants, and awards:*** Federal Pell, FSEOG, state, private, college/university gift aid from institutional funds.

GIFT AID (NON-NEED-BASED) ***Total amount:*** $12,209,146 (79% institutional, 21% external sources). ***Receiving aid:*** Freshmen: 59% (204). Undergraduates: 46% (1,035). ***Average award:*** Freshmen: $7617. Undergraduates: $6696. ***Scholarships, grants, and awards by category:*** *Academic interests/achievement:* 1,491 awards ($3,498,810 total): business, communication, computer science, education, general academic interests/achievements, humanities, mathematics, premedicine, religion/biblical studies. *Creative arts/performance:* 72 awards ($198,200 total): music. *Special achievements/activities:* 1,375 awards ($4,397,161 total): community service, general special achievements/activities, leadership, memberships, religious involvement. *Special characteristics:* 210 awards ($724,608 total): children of faculty/staff, general special characteristics, relatives of clergy, religious affiliation. ***Tuition waivers:*** Full or partial for employees or children of employees. ***ROTC:*** Army cooperative, Air Force cooperative.

LOANS ***Student loans:*** $16,260,354 (38% need-based, 62% non-need-based). 51% of past graduating class borrowed through all loan programs. *Average indebtedness per student:* $16,354. ***Average need-based loan:*** Freshmen: $3023. Undergraduates: $3828. ***Parent loans:*** $3,094,921 (100% non-need-based). ***Programs:*** FFEL (Subsidized and Unsubsidized Stafford, PLUS), Perkins, state, college/university.

WORK-STUDY ***Federal work-study:*** Total amount: $195,913; 185 jobs averaging $2126. ***State or other work-study/employment:*** Total amount: $36,678 (100% need-based). 63 part-time jobs averaging $627.

ATHLETIC AWARDS Total amount: $1,273,026 (100% non-need-based).

APPLYING FOR FINANCIAL AID ***Required financial aid forms:*** FAFSA, institution's own form. ***Financial aid deadline:*** Continuous. ***Notification date:*** Continuous beginning 2/1.

CONTACT Mr. Donald G. Zackary, Director of Financial Aid, Dallas Baptist University, 3000 Mountain Creek Parkway, Dallas, TX 75211-9299, 214-333-5363 or toll-free 800-460-1328. *Fax:* 214-333-5586. *E-mail:* donz@dbu.edu.

DALLAS CHRISTIAN COLLEGE

Dallas, TX

CONTACT Robin L. Walker, Director of Student Financial Aid, Dallas Christian College, 2700 Christian Parkway, Dallas, TX 75234-7299, 972-241-3371 Ext. 105. *Fax:* 972-241-8021. *E-mail:* finaid@dallas.edu.

DALTON STATE COLLEGE

Dalton, GA

Tuition & fees (GA res): $1994 **Average undergraduate aid package: $3072**

ABOUT THE INSTITUTION State-supported, coed. 64 undergraduate majors. Federal methodology is used as a basis for awarding need-based institutional aid.

UNDERGRADUATE EXPENSES for 2008–09 ***Tuition, state resident:*** full-time $1994; part-time $84 per credit hour. ***Tuition, nonresident:*** full-time $7488; part-time $340.35 per credit hour. Full-time tuition and fees vary according to student level. Part-time tuition and fees vary according to student level.

FRESHMAN FINANCIAL AID (Fall 2008, est.) 712 applied for aid; of those 69% were deemed to have need. 96% of freshmen with need received aid; of those 9% had need fully met. ***Average percent of need met:*** 76% (excluding resources awarded to replace EFC). ***Average financial aid package:*** $2663 (excluding resources awarded to replace EFC). 5% of all full-time freshmen had no need and received non-need-based gift aid.

UNDERGRADUATE FINANCIAL AID (Fall 2008, est.) 2,154 applied for aid; of those 74% were deemed to have need. 92% of undergraduates with need received aid; of those 12% had need fully met. ***Average percent of need met:*** 72% (excluding resources awarded to replace EFC). ***Average financial aid package:*** $3072 (excluding resources awarded to replace EFC). 5% of all full-time undergraduates had no need and received non-need-based gift aid.

GIFT AID (NEED-BASED) ***Total amount:*** $3,962,009 (63% federal, 34% state, 1% institutional, 2% external sources). ***Receiving aid:*** Freshmen: 29% (258); all full-time undergraduates: 42% (1,007). ***Average award:*** Freshmen: $2722; Undergraduates: $3175. ***Scholarships, grants, and awards:*** Federal Pell, FSEOG, state, private, college/university gift aid from institutional funds.

GIFT AID (NON-NEED-BASED) ***Total amount:*** $4,036,676 (58% federal, 37% state, 2% institutional, 3% external sources). ***Receiving aid:*** Freshmen: 44% (382). Undergraduates: 36% (866). ***Average award:*** Freshmen: $1309. Undergraduates: $790. ***Scholarships, grants, and awards by category:*** *Academic interests/achievement:* 14 awards ($17,225 total): biological sciences, business, computer science, education, engineering/technologies, English, health fields, humanities, social sciences. *Special achievements/activities:* 5 awards ($1900 total): community service, hobbies/interests, leadership, memberships. *Special characteristics:* 7 awards ($4400 total): adult students, children and siblings of alumni, children of faculty/staff, out-of-state students. ***Tuition waivers:*** Full or partial for senior citizens.

LOANS ***Student loans:*** $2,579,942 (68% need-based, 32% non-need-based). 25% of past graduating class borrowed through all loan programs. *Average indebtedness per student:* $3500. ***Average need-based loan:*** Freshmen: $2170. Undergraduates: $2477. ***Parent loans:*** $21,461 (100% non-need-based). ***Programs:*** FFEL (Subsidized and Unsubsidized Stafford, PLUS), state.

WORK-STUDY ***Federal work-study:*** Total amount: $104,563; 73 jobs averaging $1757. ***State or other work-study/employment:*** Total amount: $200,000 (10% need-based, 90% non-need-based). 118 part-time jobs averaging $1824.

APPLYING FOR FINANCIAL AID ***Required financial aid form:*** FAFSA. ***Financial aid deadline (priority):*** 6/1. ***Notification date:*** Continuous.

CONTACT Dianne Cox, Director of Student Financial Aid, Dalton State College, 650 College Drive, Dalton, GA 30720, 706-272-4545 or toll-free 800-829-4436. *Fax:* 706-272-2458. *E-mail:* dcox@daltonstate.edu.

DANA COLLEGE

Blair, NE

Tuition & fees: $20,120 **Average undergraduate aid package: $17,856**

ABOUT THE INSTITUTION Independent religious, coed. ***Awards:*** bachelor's degrees. 38 undergraduate majors. ***Total enrollment:*** 546. Undergraduates: 546. Freshmen: 138. Federal methodology is used as a basis for awarding need-based institutional aid.

UNDERGRADUATE EXPENSES for 2008–09 ***Comprehensive fee:*** $26,020 includes full-time tuition ($19,320), mandatory fees ($800), and room and board ($5900). ***College room only:*** $2320. Room and board charges vary according to board plan and housing facility. ***Part-time tuition:*** $550 per credit hour. ***Part-time fees:*** $45 per term. Part-time tuition and fees vary according to course load. ***Payment plans:*** Installment, deferred payment.

FRESHMAN FINANCIAL AID (Fall 2008, est.) 133 applied for aid; of those 86% were deemed to have need. 100% of freshmen with need received aid; of those 23% had need fully met. ***Average percent of need met:*** 87% (excluding resources awarded to replace EFC). ***Average financial aid package:*** $19,085 (excluding resources awarded to replace EFC). 14% of all full-time freshmen had no need and received non-need-based gift aid.

UNDERGRADUATE FINANCIAL AID (Fall 2008, est.) 491 applied for aid; of those 85% were deemed to have need. 100% of undergraduates with need received aid; of those 29% had need fully met. ***Average percent of need met:*** 89% (excluding resources awarded to replace EFC). ***Average financial aid package:*** $17,856 (excluding resources awarded to replace EFC). 13% of all full-time undergraduates had no need and received non-need-based gift aid.

GIFT AID (NEED-BASED) ***Total amount:*** $1,884,639 (36% federal, 4% state, 60% institutional). ***Receiving aid:*** Freshmen: 63% (87); all full-time undergraduates: 53% (285). ***Average award:*** Freshmen: $5799; Undergraduates: $6019. ***Scholarships, grants, and awards:*** Federal Pell, FSEOG, state, private, college/university gift aid from institutional funds.

GIFT AID (NON-NEED-BASED) ***Total amount:*** $2,687,659 (92% institutional, 8% external sources). ***Receiving aid:*** Freshmen: 59% (82). Undergraduates: 58% (309). ***Average award:*** Freshmen: $7500. Undergraduates: $4007. ***Scholarships, grants, and awards by category:*** *Academic interests/achievement:* biological sciences, business, communication, education, English, foreign languages, general academic interests/achievements, health fields, international studies, mathematics, military science, premedicine, religion/biblical studies, social sciences. *Creative arts/performance:* applied art and design, art/fine arts, music, theater/drama. *Special achievements/activities:* general special achievements/activities, leadership, religious involvement. *Special characteristics:* ethnic background, international students, local/state students, members of minority groups, out-of-state students, religious affiliation. ***Tuition waivers:*** Full or partial for children of alumni, employees or children of employees. ***ROTC:*** Army cooperative, Air Force cooperative.

LOANS ***Student loans:*** $2,478,192 (62% need-based, 38% non-need-based). 92% of past graduating class borrowed through all loan programs. *Average indebtedness per student:* $21,170. ***Average need-based loan:*** Freshmen: $4541. Undergraduates: $4631. ***Parent loans:*** $341,057 (100% non-need-based). ***Programs:*** FFEL (Subsidized and Unsubsidized Stafford, PLUS), Perkins.

WORK-STUDY ***Federal work-study:*** Total amount: $285,860; jobs available (averaging $1000). ***State or other work-study/employment:*** Part-time jobs available.

ATHLETIC AWARDS Total amount: $2,227,085 (100% non-need-based).

APPLYING FOR FINANCIAL AID ***Required financial aid forms:*** FAFSA, institution's own form. ***Financial aid deadline (priority):*** 3/15. ***Notification date:*** Continuous beginning 3/6. Students must reply within 3 weeks of notification.

CONTACT Rita McManigal, Director of Financial Aid, Dana College, 2848 College Drive, Blair, NE 68008-1099, 402-426-7227 or toll-free 800-444-3262. *Fax:* 402-426-7225. *E-mail:* rmcmanig@dana.edu.

DANIEL WEBSTER COLLEGE

Nashua, NH

CONTACT Anne-Marie Caruso, Director of Financial Assistance, Daniel Webster College, 20 University Drive, Nashua, NH 03063-1300, 603-577-6590 or toll-free 800-325-6876. *Fax:* 603-577-6593. *E-mail:* caruso@dwc.edu.

DARKEI NOAM RABBINICAL COLLEGE

Brooklyn, NY

CONTACT Ms. Rivi Horowitz, Director of Financial Aid, Darkei Noam Rabbinical College, 2822 Avenue J, Brooklyn, NY 11219, 718-338-6464.

DARTMOUTH COLLEGE

Hanover, NH

Tuition & fees: $38,445 **Average undergraduate aid package: $35,966**

ABOUT THE INSTITUTION Independent, coed. ***Awards:*** bachelor's, master's, doctoral, and first professional degrees. 60 undergraduate majors. ***Total enrollment:*** 5,848. Undergraduates: 4,147. Freshmen: 1,096. Both federal and institutional methodology are used as a basis for awarding need-based institutional aid.

UNDERGRADUATE EXPENSES for 2009–10 ***Application fee:*** $70. ***Comprehensive fee:*** $49,224 includes full-time tuition ($38,445) and room and board ($10,779). ***College room only:*** $6444.

FRESHMAN FINANCIAL AID (Fall 2008, est.) 670 applied for aid; of those 80% were deemed to have need. 100% of freshmen with need received aid; of those 100% had need fully met. ***Average percent of need met:*** 100% (excluding resources awarded to replace EFC). ***Average financial aid package:*** $34,924 (excluding resources awarded to replace EFC). 1% of all full-time freshmen had no need and received non-need-based gift aid.

UNDERGRADUATE FINANCIAL AID (Fall 2008, est.) 2,507 applied for aid; of those 86% were deemed to have need. 100% of undergraduates with need received aid; of those 100% had need fully met. ***Average percent of need met:*** 100% (excluding resources awarded to replace EFC). ***Average financial aid package:*** $35,966 (excluding resources awarded to replace EFC). 1% of all full-time undergraduates had no need and received non-need-based gift aid.

GIFT AID (NEED-BASED) ***Total amount:*** $69,387,519 (6% federal, 91% institutional, 3% external sources). ***Receiving aid:*** Freshmen: 48% (531); all full-time undergraduates: 51% (2,074). ***Average award:*** Freshmen: $34,927; Undergraduates: $33,448. ***Scholarships, grants, and awards:*** Federal Pell, FSEOG, state, private, college/university gift aid from institutional funds.

GIFT AID (NON-NEED-BASED) ***Total amount:*** $901,937 (21% federal, 79% external sources). ***Average award:*** Freshmen: $450. Undergraduates: $450. ***ROTC:*** Army cooperative.

LOANS ***Student loans:*** $8,396,963 (53% need-based, 47% non-need-based). 52% of past graduating class borrowed through all loan programs. *Average indebtedness per student:* $22,126. ***Average need-based loan:*** Freshmen: $2329. Undergraduates: $3145. ***Parent loans:*** $5,184,762 (100% non-need-based). ***Programs:*** FFEL (Subsidized and Unsubsidized Stafford, PLUS), Perkins, college/university.

WORK-STUDY ***Federal work-study:*** Total amount: $2,435,858; 1,564 jobs averaging $1787. ***State or other work-study/employment:*** Total amount: $870,365 (100% need-based). 429 part-time jobs averaging $1762.

APPLYING FOR FINANCIAL AID ***Required financial aid forms:*** FAFSA, CSS Financial Aid PROFILE, noncustodial (divorced/separated) parent's statement, business/farm supplement, W-2 forms, federal income tax form(s). ***Financial aid deadline:*** 2/1. ***Notification date:*** 3/31. Students must reply by 5/1.

CONTACT Ms. Virginia S. Hazen, Director of Financial Aid, Dartmouth College, 6024 McNutt Hall, Hanover, NH 03755, 603-646-2451. *Fax:* 603-646-1414. *E-mail:* virginia.s.hazen@dartmouth.edu.

DAVENPORT UNIVERSITY

Grand Rapids, MI

Tuition & fees: $10,640 **Average undergraduate aid package: N/A**

ABOUT THE INSTITUTION Independent, coed. ***Awards:*** associate, bachelor's, and master's degrees and post-bachelor's and post-master's certificates. 25 undergraduate majors. ***Total enrollment:*** 10,764. Undergraduates: 9,806. Freshmen: 922.

UNDERGRADUATE EXPENSES for 2008–09 ***Application fee:*** $25. ***Tuition:*** full-time $10,440; part-time $435 per credit. Full-time tuition and fees vary according to location. Part-time tuition and fees vary according to location. ***Payment plan:*** Installment.

GIFT AID (NEED-BASED) ***Total amount:*** $33,625,003 (41% federal, 25% state, 22% institutional, 12% external sources). ***Scholarships, grants, and awards:*** Federal Pell, FSEOG, state, private, college/university gift aid from institutional funds.

GIFT AID (NON-NEED-BASED) ***Total amount:*** $218,076 (100% institutional). ***Scholarships, grants, and awards by category:*** *Academic interests/achievement:* general academic interests/achievements. ***Tuition waivers:*** Full or partial for employees or children of employees.

LOANS ***Student loans:*** $88,694,557 (100% need-based). ***Parent loans:*** $1,637,128 (100% need-based). ***Programs:*** FFEL (Subsidized and Unsubsidized Stafford, PLUS), private/alternative loans.

WORK-STUDY ***Federal work-study:*** Total amount: $538,767; jobs available. ***State or other work-study/employment:*** Total amount: $167,881 (100% need-based). Part-time jobs available.

ATHLETIC AWARDS Total amount: $1,405,008 (100% need-based).

APPLYING FOR FINANCIAL AID ***Financial aid deadline (priority):*** 3/1. ***Notification date:*** 3/1.

CONTACT Mary Kay Bethune, Executive Director of Financial Aid, Davenport University, 415 East Fulton Street, Grand Rapids, MI 49503, 616-732-1132 or toll-free 800-632-9569. *Fax:* 616-732-1167. *E-mail:* david.debore@davenport.edu.

DAVIDSON COLLEGE

Davidson, NC

Tuition & fees: $33,479 • **Average undergraduate aid package: $21,506**

ABOUT THE INSTITUTION Independent Presbyterian, coed. ***Awards:*** bachelor's degrees. 21 undergraduate majors. ***Total enrollment:*** 1,668. Undergraduates: 1,668. Freshmen: 480. Both federal and institutional methodology are used as a basis for awarding need-based institutional aid.

UNDERGRADUATE EXPENSES for 2008–09 ***Application fee:*** $50. ***Comprehensive fee:*** $42,950 includes full-time tuition ($33,148), mandatory fees ($331), and room and board ($9471).

FRESHMAN FINANCIAL AID (Fall 2007) 243 applied for aid; of those 65% were deemed to have need. 97% of freshmen with need received aid; of those 100% had need fully met. ***Average percent of need met:*** 100% (excluding resources awarded to replace EFC). ***Average financial aid package:*** $21,624 (excluding resources awarded to replace EFC). 10% of all full-time freshmen had no need and received non-need-based gift aid.

UNDERGRADUATE FINANCIAL AID (Fall 2007) 779 applied for aid; of those 73% were deemed to have need. 99% of undergraduates with need received aid; of those 100% had need fully met. ***Average percent of need met:*** 100% (excluding resources awarded to replace EFC). ***Average financial aid package:*** $21,506 (excluding resources awarded to replace EFC). 13% of all full-time undergraduates had no need and received non-need-based gift aid.

GIFT AID (NEED-BASED) ***Total amount:*** $11,297,695 (5% federal, 4% state, 91% institutional). ***Receiving aid:*** Freshmen: 33% (152); all full-time undergraduates: 33% (551). ***Average award:*** Freshmen: $20,793; Undergraduates: $20,504. ***Scholarships, grants, and awards:*** Federal Pell, FSEOG, state, private, college/university gift aid from institutional funds, need-linked special talent scholarships.

GIFT AID (NON-NEED-BASED) ***Total amount:*** $10,855,991 (4% federal, 6% state, 81% institutional, 9% external sources). ***Receiving aid:*** Freshmen: 12% (54). Undergraduates: 13% (214). ***Average award:*** Freshmen: $16,610. Undergraduates: $16,597. ***Scholarships, grants, and awards by category:*** *Academic interests/achievement:* 213 awards ($258,000 total): biological sciences, education, foreign languages, general academic interests/achievements, mathematics, physical sciences, premedicine. *Creative arts/performance:* 33 awards ($258,000 total): art/fine arts, creative writing, music, theater/drama. *Special achievements/activities:* 41 awards ($666,131 total): community service, general special achievements/activities, leadership, religious involvement. *Special characteristics:* 118 awards ($1,538,700 total): general special characteristics, relatives of clergy. ***ROTC:*** Army, Air Force cooperative.

LOANS ***Student loans:*** $3,055,164 (17% need-based, 83% non-need-based). 33% of past graduating class borrowed through all loan programs. *Average indebtedness per student:* $25,025. ***Average need-based loan:*** Freshmen: $2208. Undergraduates: $3263. ***Parent loans:*** $2,232,660 (100% non-need-based). ***Programs:*** FFEL (Subsidized and Unsubsidized Stafford, PLUS), alternative loans.

WORK-STUDY ***Federal work-study:*** Total amount: $163,013; 166 jobs averaging $1742. ***State or other work-study/employment:*** Total amount: $119,320 (91% need-based, 9% non-need-based). 107 part-time jobs averaging $1798.

ATHLETIC AWARDS Total amount: $3,052,640 (1% need-based, 99% non-need-based).

APPLYING FOR FINANCIAL AID ***Required financial aid forms:*** FAFSA, CSS Financial Aid PROFILE, business/farm supplement, parent and student tax returns and W-2 forms; corporate tax returns, if applicable. ***Financial aid deadline (priority):*** 2/15. ***Notification date:*** 4/1. Students must reply by 5/1.

CONTACT Davis Gelinas, Director of Financial Aid, Davidson College, 413 North Main Street, Box 7157, Davidson, NC 28035-7157, 704-894-2232 or toll-free 800-768-0380. *Fax:* 704-894-2845. *E-mail:* dagelinas@davidson.edu.

DAVIS & ELKINS COLLEGE

Elkins, WV

ABOUT THE INSTITUTION Independent Presbyterian, coed. ***Awards:*** associate and bachelor's degrees. 46 undergraduate majors. ***Total enrollment:*** 640. Undergraduates: 640. Freshmen: 117.

GIFT AID (NEED-BASED) ***Scholarships, grants, and awards:*** Federal Pell, FSEOG, state, private, college/university gift aid from institutional funds.

GIFT AID (NON-NEED-BASED) ***Scholarships, grants, and awards by category:*** *Academic interests/achievement:* biological sciences, business, computer science, education, engineering/technologies, general academic interests/achievements, health fields, physical sciences, religion/biblical studies. *Creative arts/performance:* art/fine arts, music, performing arts, theater/drama. *Special achievements/activities:* leadership, religious involvement. *Special characteristics:* children and siblings of alumni, children of faculty/staff, first-generation college students, local/state students, relatives of clergy, religious affiliation.

LOANS ***Programs:*** FFEL (Subsidized and Unsubsidized Stafford, PLUS), Perkins, college/university.

APPLYING FOR FINANCIAL AID ***Required financial aid forms:*** FAFSA, state aid form.

CONTACT Susan M. George, Director of Financial Planning, Davis & Elkins College, 100 Campus Drive, Elkins, WV 26241-3996, 304-637-1373 or toll-free 800-624-3157 Ext. 1230. *Fax:* 304-637-1986. *E-mail:* ssw@davisandelkins.edu.

DAVIS COLLEGE

Johnson City, NY

CONTACT Mr. James P. Devine, Financial Aid Director, Davis College, PO Box 601, Bible School Park, NY 13737-0601, 607-729-1581 Ext. 401 or toll-free 800-331-4137 Ext. 406. *Fax:* 607-770-6886. *E-mail:* financialaid@practical.edu.

DEFIANCE COLLEGE

Defiance, OH

Tuition & fees: $22,895 **Average undergraduate aid package: $18,117**

ABOUT THE INSTITUTION Independent religious, coed. ***Awards:*** associate, bachelor's, and master's degrees. 33 undergraduate majors. ***Total enrollment:*** 1,001. Undergraduates: 892. Freshmen: 221. Federal methodology is used as a basis for awarding need-based institutional aid.

UNDERGRADUATE EXPENSES for 2009–10 ***Application fee:*** $25. ***One-time required fee:*** $75. ***Comprehensive fee:*** $30,645 includes full-time tuition ($22,375), mandatory fees ($520), and room and board ($7750). ***College room only:*** $4235. ***Part-time tuition:*** $360 per credit hour. ***Part-time fees:*** $70 per term.

FRESHMAN FINANCIAL AID (Fall 2008, est.) 211 applied for aid; of those 94% were deemed to have need. 100% of freshmen with need received aid; of those 24% had need fully met. ***Average percent of need met:*** 82% (excluding resources awarded to replace EFC). ***Average financial aid package:*** $19,945 (excluding resources awarded to replace EFC). 7% of all full-time freshmen had no need and received non-need-based gift aid.

UNDERGRADUATE FINANCIAL AID (Fall 2008, est.) 708 applied for aid; of those 94% were deemed to have need. 100% of undergraduates with need received aid; of those 20% had need fully met. ***Average percent of need met:*** 78% (excluding resources awarded to replace EFC). ***Average financial aid package:*** $18,117 (excluding resources awarded to replace EFC). 7% of all full-time undergraduates had no need and received non-need-based gift aid.

GIFT AID (NEED-BASED) ***Total amount:*** $7,009,942 (16% federal, 10% state, 73% institutional, 1% external sources). ***Receiving aid:*** Freshmen: 69% (150); all full-time undergraduates: 58% (416). ***Average award:*** Freshmen: $6811; Undergraduates: $6129. ***Scholarships, grants, and awards:*** Federal Pell, FSEOG, state, private, college/university gift aid from institutional funds.

GIFT AID (NON-NEED-BASED) ***Total amount:*** $2,101,310 (12% state, 85% institutional, 3% external sources). ***Receiving aid:*** Freshmen: 91% (199). Undergraduates: 92% (660). ***Average award:*** Freshmen: $9644. Undergraduates: $9734. ***Scholarships, grants, and awards by category:*** *Academic interests/achievement:* biological sciences, business, communication, computer science, education, English, general academic interests/achievements, health fields, humanities, international studies, mathematics, physical sciences, premedicine, religion/biblical studies, social sciences. *Special achievements/activities:* community service, general special achievements/activities, leadership, religious involvement. *Special characteristics:* children of faculty/staff, international students, members of minority groups, out-of-state students, previous college experience, religious affiliation.

LOANS ***Student loans:*** $7,075,548 (52% need-based, 48% non-need-based). 86% of past graduating class borrowed through all loan programs. *Average indebtedness per student:* $23,667. ***Average need-based loan:*** Freshmen: $4200. Undergraduates: $4825. ***Parent loans:*** $510,867 (24% need-based, 76% non-need-based). ***Programs:*** FFEL (Subsidized and Unsubsidized Stafford, PLUS), Perkins, alternative loans.

WORK-STUDY ***Federal work-study:*** Total amount: $818,731; 417 jobs averaging $1955. ***State or other work-study/employment:*** Total amount: $70,697 (100% non-need-based). 35 part-time jobs averaging $1963.

APPLYING FOR FINANCIAL AID ***Required financial aid form:*** FAFSA. ***Financial aid deadline (priority):*** 4/1. ***Notification date:*** Continuous. Students must reply by 5/1 or within 2 weeks of notification.

CONTACT Amy Francis, Director of Financial Aid, Defiance College, 701 North Clinton Street, Defiance, OH 43512-1610, 419-783-2376 or toll-free 800-520-4632 Ext. 2359. *Fax:* 419-783-2579. *E-mail:* afrancis@defiance.edu.

DELAWARE STATE UNIVERSITY

Dover, DE

CONTACT Associate Director of Financial Aid, Delaware State University, 1200 North DuPont Highway, Dover, DE 19901-2277, 302-857-6250 or toll-free 800-845-2544.

DELAWARE VALLEY COLLEGE

Doylestown, PA

Tuition & fees: $27,292 **Average undergraduate aid package: $20,838**

ABOUT THE INSTITUTION Independent, coed. ***Awards:*** associate, bachelor's, and master's degrees. 29 undergraduate majors. ***Total enrollment:*** 2,138. Undergraduates: 1,942. Freshmen: 430. Federal methodology is used as a basis for awarding need-based institutional aid.

UNDERGRADUATE EXPENSES for 2009–10 ***Application fee:*** $35. ***Comprehensive fee:*** $37,042 includes full-time tuition ($25,692), mandatory fees ($1600), and room and board ($9750). ***Part-time tuition:*** $681 per credit.

FRESHMAN FINANCIAL AID (Fall 2008, est.) 385 applied for aid; of those 86% were deemed to have need. 100% of freshmen with need received aid; of those 20% had need fully met. ***Average percent of need met:*** 69% (excluding resources awarded to replace EFC). ***Average financial aid package:*** $18,694 (excluding resources awarded to replace EFC). 20% of all full-time freshmen had no need and received non-need-based gift aid.

UNDERGRADUATE FINANCIAL AID (Fall 2008, est.) 1,470 applied for aid; of those 89% were deemed to have need. 97% of undergraduates with need received aid; of those 24% had need fully met. ***Average percent of need met:*** 79% (excluding resources awarded to replace EFC). ***Average financial aid package:*** $20,838 (excluding resources awarded to replace EFC). 16% of all full-time undergraduates had no need and received non-need-based gift aid.

GIFT AID (NEED-BASED) ***Total amount:*** $16,806,054 (9% federal, 8% state, 80% institutional, 3% external sources). ***Receiving aid:*** Freshmen: 77% (333); all full-time undergraduates: 77% (1,252). ***Average award:*** Freshmen: $14,578; Undergraduates: $16,034. ***Scholarships, grants, and awards:*** Federal Pell, FSEOG, state, private, college/university gift aid from institutional funds.

GIFT AID (NON-NEED-BASED) ***Total amount:*** $3,633,373 (2% state, 98% institutional). ***Receiving aid:*** Freshmen: 20% (84). Undergraduates: 16% (267). ***Average award:*** Freshmen: $10,376. Undergraduates: $9984.

LOANS ***Student loans:*** $13,132,325 (35% need-based, 65% non-need-based). 56% of past graduating class borrowed through all loan programs. *Average indebtedness per student:* $28,929. ***Average need-based loan:*** Freshmen: $3240. Undergraduates: $4703. ***Parent loans:*** $4,019,203 (21% need-based, 79% non-need-based). ***Programs:*** FFEL (Subsidized and Unsubsidized Stafford, PLUS), Perkins, alternative loans.

WORK-STUDY ***Federal work-study:*** Total amount: $223,607; jobs available.

APPLYING FOR FINANCIAL AID ***Required financial aid forms:*** FAFSA, state aid form. ***Financial aid deadline:*** 4/1 (priority: 4/1). ***Notification date:*** Continuous. Students must reply by 5/1 or within 2 weeks of notification.

CONTACT Mr. Robert Sauer, Director of Student Financial Aid, Delaware Valley College, 700 East Butler Avenue, Doylestown, PA 18901-2697, 215-489-2297 or toll-free 800-2DELVAL (in-state). *E-mail:* finaid@devalcol.edu.

DELTA STATE UNIVERSITY

Cleveland, MS

Tuition & fees (MS res): $4450 **Average undergraduate aid package: N/A**

ABOUT THE INSTITUTION State-supported, coed. ***Awards:*** bachelor's, master's, and doctoral degrees and post-master's certificates. 45 undergraduate majors. ***Total enrollment:*** 4,065. Undergraduates: 3,212. Freshmen: 397. Federal methodology is used as a basis for awarding need-based institutional aid.

UNDERGRADUATE EXPENSES for 2008–09 ***Application fee:*** $25. ***Tuition, state resident:*** full-time $4450; part-time $185 per hour. ***Tuition, nonresident:*** full-time $11,182; part-time $466 per hour. ***College room and board:*** $5476. Room and board charges vary according to board plan and housing facility. ***Payment plan:*** Installment.

GIFT AID (NEED-BASED) ***Total amount:*** $5,006,000 (92% federal, 1% state, 7% institutional). ***Scholarships, grants, and awards:*** Federal Pell, FSEOG, state, private, college/university gift aid from institutional funds.

GIFT AID (NON-NEED-BASED) ***Total amount:*** $5,685,000 (20% state, 62% institutional, 18% external sources). ***Scholarships, grants, and awards by category:*** *Academic interests/achievement:* 475 awards ($314,956 total): biological sciences, general academic interests/achievements. *Creative arts/performance:* 193 awards ($382,035 total): art/fine arts, journalism/publications, music, performing arts. *Special achievements/activities:* 413 awards ($279,099 total): cheerleading/drum major, general special achievements/activities, leadership, memberships. *Special characteristics:* $1,014,287 total: children and siblings of alumni, children of faculty/staff, general special characteristics, out-of-state students. ***Tuition waivers:*** Full or partial for children of alumni, employees or children of employees, senior citizens.

LOANS ***Student loans:*** $16,000,000 (59% need-based, 41% non-need-based). 79% of past graduating class borrowed through all loan programs. *Average indebtedness per student:* $22,300. ***Parent loans:*** $620,000 (100% non-need-based). ***Programs:*** FFEL (Subsidized and Unsubsidized Stafford, PLUS), Perkins, college/university.

WORK-STUDY ***Federal work-study:*** Total amount: $475,000; 300 jobs averaging $1850. ***State or other work-study/employment:*** Total amount: $50,000 (100% non-need-based). 50 part-time jobs averaging $1000.

ATHLETIC AWARDS Total amount: $1,490,000 (100% non-need-based).

APPLYING FOR FINANCIAL AID ***Required financial aid forms:*** FAFSA, institution's own form, state aid form. ***Financial aid deadline (priority):*** 3/1. ***Notification date:*** Continuous beginning 4/1. Students must reply within 2 weeks of notification.

CONTACT Ms. Ann Margaret Mullins, Director of Student Financial Assistance, Delta State University, PO Box 3154, Cleveland, MS 38733-0001, 662-846-4670 or toll-free 800-468-6378. *Fax:* 662-846-4683. *E-mail:* amullins@deltastate.edu.

DENISON UNIVERSITY

Granville, OH

Tuition & fees: $35,300 **Average undergraduate aid package: $30,099**

ABOUT THE INSTITUTION Independent, coed. ***Awards:*** bachelor's degrees. 39 undergraduate majors. ***Total enrollment:*** 2,200. Undergraduates: 2,200. Freshmen: 605. Federal methodology is used as a basis for awarding need-based institutional aid.

UNDERGRADUATE EXPENSES for 2008–09 ***Application fee:*** $40. ***Comprehensive fee:*** $43,910 includes full-time tuition ($34,410), mandatory fees ($890), and room and board ($8610). ***College room only:*** $4890. Room and board charges vary according to housing facility. ***Part-time tuition:*** $1080 per semester hour. Part-time tuition and fees vary according to course load. ***Payment plan:*** Installment.

FRESHMAN FINANCIAL AID (Fall 2008, est.) 373 applied for aid; of those 78% were deemed to have need. 100% of freshmen with need received aid; of those 80% had need fully met. ***Average percent of need met:*** 97% (excluding resources awarded to replace EFC). ***Average financial aid package:*** $31,371 (excluding resources awarded to replace EFC). 47% of all full-time freshmen had no need and received non-need-based gift aid.

UNDERGRADUATE FINANCIAL AID (Fall 2008, est.) 1,133 applied for aid; of those 82% were deemed to have need. 100% of undergraduates with need received aid; of those 74% had need fully met. ***Average percent of need met:*** 95% (excluding resources awarded to replace EFC). ***Average financial aid package:*** $30,099 (excluding resources awarded to replace EFC). 51% of all full-time undergraduates had no need and received non-need-based gift aid.

GIFT AID (NEED-BASED) ***Total amount:*** $21,607,791 (6% federal, 2% state, 92% institutional). ***Receiving aid:*** Freshmen: 48% (289); all full-time undergraduates: 43% (924). ***Average award:*** Freshmen: $26,212; Undergraduates: $27,317. ***Scholarships, grants, and awards:*** Federal Pell, FSEOG, state, private, college/university gift aid from institutional funds.

GIFT AID (NON-NEED-BASED) ***Total amount:*** $18,239,096 (4% state, 93% institutional, 3% external sources). ***Receiving aid:*** Freshmen: 43% (263). Undergraduates: 38% (829). ***Average award:*** Freshmen: $15,486. Undergraduates: $14,080. ***Tuition waivers:*** Full or partial for employees or children of employees. ***ROTC:*** Army cooperative.

LOANS ***Student loans:*** $4,675,510 (96% need-based, 4% non-need-based). ***Average need-based loan:*** Freshmen: $3734. Undergraduates: $4607. ***Parent loans:*** $3,037,489 (100% non-need-based). ***Programs:*** Federal Direct (Subsidized and Unsubsidized Stafford, PLUS), Perkins, college/university.

WORK-STUDY Federal work-study jobs available. ***State or other work-study/employment:*** Part-time jobs available.

APPLYING FOR FINANCIAL AID ***Required financial aid form:*** FAFSA. ***Financial aid deadline (priority):*** 2/15. ***Notification date:*** 3/30.

CONTACT Ms. Nancy Hoover, Director of Financial Aid, Denison University, PO Box M, Granville, OH 43023-0613, 740-587-6279 or toll-free 800-DENISON. *Fax:* 740-587-5706. *E-mail:* hoover@denison.edu.

DePAUL UNIVERSITY

Chicago, IL

Tuition & fees: $26,067 **Average undergraduate aid package: $17,279**

ABOUT THE INSTITUTION Independent Roman Catholic, coed. ***Awards:*** bachelor's, master's, doctoral, and first professional degrees and post-bachelor's, post-master's, and first professional certificates. 102 undergraduate majors. ***Total enrollment:*** 24,352. Undergraduates: 15,782. Freshmen: 2,555. Federal methodology is used as a basis for awarding need-based institutional aid.

UNDERGRADUATE EXPENSES for 2008–09 ***Application fee:*** $40. ***Comprehensive fee:*** $36,307 includes full-time tuition ($25,490), mandatory fees ($577), and room and board ($10,240). ***College room only:*** $7600. ***Part-time tuition:*** $460 per quarter hour.

FRESHMAN FINANCIAL AID (Fall 2008, est.) 2,195 applied for aid; of those 76% were deemed to have need. 98% of freshmen with need received aid; of those 10% had need fully met. ***Average percent of need met:*** 65% (excluding resources awarded to replace EFC). ***Average financial aid package:*** $19,014 (excluding resources awarded to replace EFC). 7% of all full-time freshmen had no need and received non-need-based gift aid.

UNDERGRADUATE FINANCIAL AID (Fall 2008, est.) 9,947 applied for aid; of those 79% were deemed to have need. 96% of undergraduates with need received aid; of those 9% had need fully met. ***Average percent of need met:*** 60% (excluding resources awarded to replace EFC). ***Average financial aid package:*** $17,279 (excluding resources awarded to replace EFC). 4% of all full-time undergraduates had no need and received non-need-based gift aid.

GIFT AID (NEED-BASED) ***Total amount:*** $78,760,000 (19% federal, 24% state, 57% institutional). ***Receiving aid:*** Freshmen: 49% (1,258); all full-time undergraduates: 46% (5,931). ***Average award:*** Freshmen: $14,229; Undergraduates: $12,907. ***Scholarships, grants, and awards:*** Federal Pell, FSEOG, state, private, college/university gift aid from institutional funds, United Negro College Fund, Academic Competitiveness Grant, National Smart Grant, Federal TEACH Grant.

GIFT AID (NON-NEED-BASED) ***Total amount:*** $23,540,000 (1% state, 92% institutional, 7% external sources). ***Receiving aid:*** Freshmen: 35% (897). Undergraduates: 21% (2,675). ***Average award:*** Freshmen: $9492. Undergraduates: $9008. ***Scholarships, grants, and awards by category:*** *Academic interests/achievement:* 3,172 awards ($26,900,000 total): general academic interests/achievements. *Creative arts/performance:* 383 awards ($2,750,000 total): art/fine arts, debating, music, performing arts, theater/drama. *Special achievements/activities:* 179 awards ($1,160,000 total): community service, leadership. *Special characteristics:* children of faculty/staff. ***ROTC:*** Army cooperative.

LOANS ***Student loans:*** $95,000,000 (72% need-based, 28% non-need-based). 66% of past graduating class borrowed through all loan programs. *Average indebtedness per student:* $19,172. ***Average need-based loan:*** Freshmen: $3739. Undergraduates: $4832. ***Parent loans:*** $38,000,000 (100% non-need-based). ***Programs:*** Federal Direct (Subsidized and Unsubsidized Stafford, PLUS), Perkins, private loans.

WORK-STUDY ***Federal work-study:*** Total amount: $1,800,000; 3,681 jobs averaging $3376. ***State or other work-study/employment:*** Total amount: $4,700,000 (34% need-based, 66% non-need-based). Part-time jobs available.

ATHLETIC AWARDS Total amount: $5,500,000 (100% non-need-based).

APPLYING FOR FINANCIAL AID ***Required financial aid form:*** FAFSA. ***Financial aid deadline (priority):*** 3/1. ***Notification date:*** Continuous beginning 3/15. Students must reply by 5/1 or within 4 weeks of notification.

CONTACT Christopher Rone, Associate Director of Financial Aid, DePaul University, 1 East Jackson Boulevard, Chicago, IL 60604-2287, 773-325-7815. *Fax:* 773-325-7746.

DePAUW UNIVERSITY

Greencastle, IN

Tuition & fees: $31,825 **Average undergraduate aid package: $25,910**

ABOUT THE INSTITUTION Independent religious, coed. ***Awards:*** bachelor's degrees. 45 undergraduate majors. ***Total enrollment:*** 2,298. Undergraduates: 2,298. Freshmen: 600. Institutional methodology is used as a basis for awarding need-based institutional aid.

UNDERGRADUATE EXPENSES for 2008–09 ***Application fee:*** $40. ***Comprehensive fee:*** $40,225 includes full-time tuition ($31,400), mandatory fees ($425), and room and board ($8400). ***College room only:*** $4400. Room and board charges vary according to board plan. ***Part-time tuition:*** $3925 per credit hour. ***Payment plans:*** Tuition prepayment, installment, deferred payment.

FRESHMAN FINANCIAL AID (Fall 2008, est.) 410 applied for aid; of those 81% were deemed to have need. 100% of freshmen with need received aid; of those 41% had need fully met. ***Average percent of need met:*** 89% (excluding resources awarded to replace EFC). ***Average financial aid package:*** $26,195 (excluding resources awarded to replace EFC). 45% of all full-time freshmen had no need and received non-need-based gift aid.

UNDERGRADUATE FINANCIAL AID (Fall 2008, est.) 1,379 applied for aid; of those 87% were deemed to have need. 100% of undergraduates with need received aid; of those 40% had need fully met. ***Average percent of need met:*** 90% (excluding resources awarded to replace EFC). ***Average financial aid package:*** $25,910 (excluding resources awarded to replace EFC). 47% of all full-time undergraduates had no need and received non-need-based gift aid.

GIFT AID (NEED-BASED) ***Total amount:*** $25,730,659 (6% federal, 6% state, 82% institutional, 6% external sources). ***Receiving aid:*** Freshmen: 55% (331); all full-time undergraduates: 53% (1,193). ***Average award:*** Freshmen: $23,106; Undergraduates: $22,425. ***Scholarships, grants, and awards:*** Federal Pell, FSEOG, state, private, college/university gift aid from institutional funds.

GIFT AID (NON-NEED-BASED) ***Total amount:*** $17,804,909 (92% institutional, 8% external sources). ***Receiving aid:*** Freshmen: 14% (83). Undergraduates: 13% (293). ***Average award:*** Freshmen: $15,303. Undergraduates: $14,002. ***Scholarships, grants, and awards by category:*** *Academic interests/achievement:* biological sciences, business, communication, computer science, English, foreign languages, general academic interests/achievements, health fields, international studies, mathematics, physical sciences. *Creative arts/performance:* art/fine arts, journalism/publications, music, performing arts. *Special achievements/activities:* community service, leadership. *Special characteristics:* children and siblings of alumni, children of faculty/staff, first-generation college students, international students, local/state students, relatives of clergy, religious affiliation. ***Tuition waivers:*** Full or partial for employees or children of employees. ***ROTC:*** Army cooperative, Air Force cooperative.

LOANS ***Student loans:*** $8,057,791 (53% need-based, 47% non-need-based). 50% of past graduating class borrowed through all loan programs. *Average indebtedness per student:* $6863. ***Average need-based loan:*** Freshmen: $3127. Undergraduates: $3602. ***Parent loans:*** $3,139,076 (19% need-based, 81% non-need-based). ***Programs:*** FFEL (Subsidized and Unsubsidized Stafford, PLUS), Perkins, college/university.

WORK-STUDY ***Federal work-study:*** Total amount: $935,253; 1,342 jobs averaging $1969. ***State or other work-study/employment:*** Total amount: $98,640 (6% need-based, 94% non-need-based). 92 part-time jobs averaging $1524.

APPLYING FOR FINANCIAL AID ***Required financial aid forms:*** FAFSA, institution's own form. ***Financial aid deadline:*** 2/15. ***Notification date:*** 3/15. Students must reply by 5/1.

CONTACT Craig Slaughter, Financial Aid Director, DePauw University, 101 East Seminary Street, Greencastle, IN 46135-0037, 765-658-4030 or toll-free 800-447-2495. *Fax:* 765-658-4177. *E-mail:* craigslaughter@depauw.edu.

DeSALES UNIVERSITY

Center Valley, PA

Tuition & fees: $25,800 **Average undergraduate aid package: $15,167**

ABOUT THE INSTITUTION Independent Roman Catholic, coed. ***Awards:*** bachelor's and master's degrees and post-bachelor's and post-master's certificates. 37 undergraduate majors. ***Total enrollment:*** 3,059. Undergraduates: 2,389. Freshmen: 402. Federal methodology is used as a basis for awarding need-based institutional aid.

UNDERGRADUATE EXPENSES for 2008–09 ***Application fee:*** $30. ***Comprehensive fee:*** $35,130 includes full-time tuition ($24,800), mandatory fees ($1000), and room and board ($9330). Room and board charges vary according to board plan and housing facility. ***Part-time tuition:*** $1035 per credit hour. ***Payment plans:*** Installment, deferred payment.

FRESHMAN FINANCIAL AID (Fall 2008, est.) 366 applied for aid; of those 85% were deemed to have need. 100% of freshmen with need received aid; of those 22% had need fully met. ***Average percent of need met:*** 65% (excluding resources awarded to replace EFC). ***Average financial aid package:*** $17,457 (excluding resources awarded to replace EFC). 22% of all full-time freshmen had no need and received non-need-based gift aid.

UNDERGRADUATE FINANCIAL AID (Fall 2008, est.) 1,516 applied for aid; of those 85% were deemed to have need. 99% of undergraduates with need received aid; of those 21% had need fully met. ***Average percent of need met:*** 61% (excluding resources awarded to replace EFC). ***Average financial aid package:*** $15,167 (excluding resources awarded to replace EFC). 22% of all full-time undergraduates had no need and received non-need-based gift aid.

GIFT AID (NEED-BASED) ***Total amount:*** $17,594,487 (6% federal, 6% state, 87% institutional, 1% external sources). ***Receiving aid:*** Freshmen: 59% (238); all full-time undergraduates: 49% (888). ***Average award:*** Freshmen: $9146; Undergraduates: $8081. ***Scholarships, grants, and awards:*** Federal Pell, FSEOG, state, private, college/university gift aid from institutional funds, Federal Nursing.

GIFT AID (NON-NEED-BASED) ***Total amount:*** $3,343,430 (3% federal, 95% institutional, 2% external sources). ***Receiving aid:*** Freshmen: 67% (268). Undergraduates: 48% (877). ***Average award:*** Freshmen: $6997. Undergraduates: $6381. ***Scholarships, grants, and awards by category:*** *Academic interests/achievement:* 347 awards ($1,678,000 total): biological sciences, business, communication, computer science, education, English, foreign languages, general academic interests/achievements, health fields, humanities, mathematics, military science, physical sciences, premedicine, religion/biblical studies, social sciences. *Creative arts/performance:* 27 awards ($57,500 total): cinema/film/broadcasting, creative writing, dance, general creative arts/performance, music, performing arts, theater/drama. *Special achievements/activities:* 153 awards ($319,824 total): general special achievements/activities, leadership. *Special characteristics:* 96 awards ($466,565 total): children of educators, children of faculty/staff, relatives of clergy, religious affiliation, siblings of current students. ***Tuition waivers:*** Full or partial for employees or children of employees, adult students, senior citizens. ***ROTC:*** Army cooperative.

LOANS ***Student loans:*** $16,102,091 (88% need-based, 12% non-need-based). 82% of past graduating class borrowed through all loan programs. *Average indebtedness per student:* $24,720. ***Average need-based loan:*** Freshmen: $3322. Undergraduates: $3855. ***Parent loans:*** $4,431,385 (84% need-based, 16% non-need-based). ***Programs:*** FFEL (Subsidized and Unsubsidized Stafford, PLUS), Perkins, Federal Nursing, alternative loans.

WORK-STUDY ***Federal work-study:*** Total amount: $981,325; 432 jobs averaging $534. ***State or other work-study/employment:*** Total amount: $802,050 (55% need-based, 45% non-need-based). 349 part-time jobs averaging $581.

APPLYING FOR FINANCIAL AID ***Required financial aid forms:*** FAFSA, institution's own form, state aid form. ***Financial aid deadline (priority):*** 2/1. ***Notification date:*** Continuous beginning 2/15. Students must reply within 2 weeks of notification.

CONTACT Mrs. Mary Birkhead, Dean of Enrollment Management, DeSales University, 2755 Station Avenue, Center Valley, PA 18034-9568, 610-282-1100 Ext. 1332 or toll-free 877-4DESALES. *Fax:* 610-282-0131. *E-mail:* mary.birkhead@desales.edu.

DESIGN INSTITUTE OF SAN DIEGO

San Diego, CA

CONTACT Financial Aid Office, Design Institute of San Diego, 8555 Commerce Avenue, San Diego, CA 92121, 858-566-1200 or toll-free 800-619-4337.

DeVRY COLLEGE OF NEW YORK

Long Island City, NY

Tuition & fees: $14,720 **Average undergraduate aid package: $15,942**

ABOUT THE INSTITUTION Proprietary, coed. ***Awards:*** associate, bachelor's, and master's degrees. 7 undergraduate majors. ***Total enrollment:*** 1,130. Undergraduates: 939. Freshmen: 238. Federal methodology is used as a basis for awarding need-based institutional aid.

UNDERGRADUATE EXPENSES for 2009–10 ***Application fee:*** $50. ***Tuition:*** full-time $14,720; part-time $575 per credit hour.

FRESHMAN FINANCIAL AID (Fall 2007) 92 applied for aid; of those 88% were deemed to have need. 99% of freshmen with need received aid. ***Average percent of need met:*** 43% (excluding resources awarded to replace EFC). ***Average financial aid package:*** $14,664 (excluding resources awarded to replace EFC). 10% of all full-time freshmen had no need and received non-need-based gift aid.

UNDERGRADUATE FINANCIAL AID (Fall 2007) 387 applied for aid; of those 96% were deemed to have need. 99% of undergraduates with need received aid; of those 2% had need fully met. ***Average percent of need met:*** 5% (excluding resources awarded to replace EFC). ***Average financial aid package:*** $15,942 (excluding resources awarded to replace EFC). 4% of all full-time undergraduates had no need and received non-need-based gift aid.

GIFT AID (NEED-BASED) ***Total amount:*** $4,934,201 (46% federal, 41% state, 11% institutional, 2% external sources). ***Receiving aid:*** Freshmen: 70% (78); all full-time undergraduates: 76% (334). ***Average award:*** Freshmen: $8390; Undergraduates: $7343. ***Scholarships, grants, and awards:*** Federal Pell, FSEOG, state, private, college/university gift aid from institutional funds.

GIFT AID (NON-NEED-BASED) ***Total amount:*** $207,388 (6% state, 78% institutional, 16% external sources). ***Receiving aid:*** Undergraduates: 1. ***Average award:*** Freshmen: $9669. Undergraduates: $11,806.

LOANS ***Student loans:*** $13,170,591 (94% need-based, 6% non-need-based). 100% of past graduating class borrowed through all loan programs. *Average indebtedness per student:* $29,136. ***Average need-based loan:*** Freshmen: $6580. Undergraduates: $8712. ***Parent loans:*** $842,604 (88% need-based, 12% non-need-based). ***Programs:*** FFEL (Subsidized and Unsubsidized Stafford, PLUS), Perkins.

WORK-STUDY ***Federal work-study:*** Total amount: $379,086; jobs available.

APPLYING FOR FINANCIAL AID ***Required financial aid form:*** FAFSA. ***Financial aid deadline:*** Continuous. ***Notification date:*** Continuous.

CONTACT Elvira Senese, Dean of Student Finance, DeVry College of New York, 30-20 Thomson Avenue, Long Island City, NY 11101, 718-472-2728. *Fax:* 718-269-4284.

DeVRY UNIVERSITY

Mesa, AZ

CONTACT Financial Aid Office, DeVry University, 1201 South Alma School Road, Mesa, AZ 85210-2011, 480-827-1511.

DeVRY UNIVERSITY
Phoenix, AZ

Tuition & fees: $14,080 **Average undergraduate aid package: $13,557**

ABOUT THE INSTITUTION Proprietary, coed. ***Awards:*** associate, bachelor's, and master's degrees. 10 undergraduate majors. ***Total enrollment:*** 1,277. Undergraduates: 1,083. Freshmen: 240. Federal methodology is used as a basis for awarding need-based institutional aid.

UNDERGRADUATE EXPENSES for 2009–10 ***Application fee:*** $50. ***Tuition:*** full-time $14,080; part-time $550 per credit hour.

FRESHMAN FINANCIAL AID (Fall 2007) 119 applied for aid; of those 94% were deemed to have need. 99% of freshmen with need received aid; of those 6% had need fully met. ***Average percent of need met:*** 40% (excluding resources awarded to replace EFC). ***Average financial aid package:*** $12,188 (excluding resources awarded to replace EFC). 9% of all full-time freshmen had no need and received non-need-based gift aid.

UNDERGRADUATE FINANCIAL AID (Fall 2007) 435 applied for aid; of those 95% were deemed to have need. 100% of undergraduates with need received aid; of those 8% had need fully met. ***Average percent of need met:*** 43% (excluding resources awarded to replace EFC). ***Average financial aid package:*** $13,557 (excluding resources awarded to replace EFC). 7% of all full-time undergraduates had no need and received non-need-based gift aid.

GIFT AID (NEED-BASED) ***Total amount:*** $3,996,978 (43% federal, 7% state, 32% institutional, 18% external sources). ***Receiving aid:*** Freshmen: 60% (95); all full-time undergraduates: 65% (329). ***Average award:*** Freshmen: $6559; Undergraduates: $6253. ***Scholarships, grants, and awards:*** Federal Pell, FSEOG, state, private, college/university gift aid from institutional funds.

GIFT AID (NON-NEED-BASED) ***Total amount:*** $395,815 (7% state, 69% institutional, 24% external sources). ***Receiving aid:*** Freshmen: 1% (2). Undergraduates: 3% (13). ***Average award:*** Freshmen: $12,201. Undergraduates: $15,538. ***ROTC:*** Air Force.

LOANS ***Student loans:*** $14,790,481 (89% need-based, 11% non-need-based). 60% of past graduating class borrowed through all loan programs. *Average indebtedness per student:* $20,667. ***Average need-based loan:*** Freshmen: $6830. Undergraduates: $8565. ***Parent loans:*** $2,096,488 (69% need-based, 31% non-need-based). ***Programs:*** FFEL (Subsidized and Unsubsidized Stafford, PLUS), Perkins.

WORK-STUDY ***Federal work-study:*** Total amount: $279,197; jobs available.

APPLYING FOR FINANCIAL AID ***Required financial aid form:*** FAFSA. ***Financial aid deadline:*** Continuous. ***Notification date:*** Continuous.

CONTACT Kathy Wyse, Dean of Student Finance, DeVry University, 2149 West Dunlap Avenue, Phoenix, AZ 85021-2995, 602-870-9222. *Fax:* 602-870-1209.

DeVRY UNIVERSITY
Elk Grove, CA

CONTACT Financial Aid Office, DeVry University, Sacramento Center, 2218 Kausen Drive, Elk Grove, CA 95758, 916-478-2847 or toll-free 866-573-3879.

DeVRY UNIVERSITY
Fremont, CA

Tuition & fees: $14,720 **Average undergraduate aid package: $12,445**

ABOUT THE INSTITUTION Proprietary, coed. ***Awards:*** associate, bachelor's, and master's degrees. 10 undergraduate majors. ***Total enrollment:*** 1,447. Undergraduates: 1,255. Freshmen: 228. Federal methodology is used as a basis for awarding need-based institutional aid.

UNDERGRADUATE EXPENSES for 2009–10 ***Application fee:*** $50. ***Tuition:*** full-time $14,720; part-time $575 per credit hour.

FRESHMAN FINANCIAL AID (Fall 2007) 154 applied for aid; of those 99% were deemed to have need. 100% of freshmen with need received aid. ***Average percent of need met:*** 39% (excluding resources awarded to replace EFC). ***Average financial aid package:*** $12,144 (excluding resources awarded to replace EFC). 2% of all full-time freshmen had no need and received non-need-based gift aid.

UNDERGRADUATE FINANCIAL AID (Fall 2007) 505 applied for aid; of those 96% were deemed to have need. 99% of undergraduates with need received aid; of those 1% had need fully met. ***Average percent of need met:*** 37% (excluding resources awarded to replace EFC). ***Average financial aid package:*** $12,445 (excluding resources awarded to replace EFC). 6% of all full-time undergraduates had no need and received non-need-based gift aid.

GIFT AID (NEED-BASED) ***Total amount:*** $5,380,458 (46% federal, 34% state, 18% institutional, 2% external sources). ***Receiving aid:*** Freshmen: 62% (120); all full-time undergraduates: 53% (317). ***Average award:*** Freshmen: $7709; Undergraduates: $7847. ***Scholarships, grants, and awards:*** Federal Pell, FSEOG, state, private, college/university gift aid from institutional funds.

GIFT AID (NON-NEED-BASED) ***Total amount:*** $340,501 (2% state, 84% institutional, 14% external sources). ***Receiving aid:*** Undergraduates: 1% (4). ***Average award:*** Freshmen: $12,525. Undergraduates: $17,920.

LOANS ***Student loans:*** $20,560,311 (88% need-based, 12% non-need-based). 50% of past graduating class borrowed through all loan programs. *Average indebtedness per student:* $70,191. ***Average need-based loan:*** Freshmen: $5826. Undergraduates: $7034. ***Parent loans:*** $1,754,709 (69% need-based, 31% non-need-based). ***Programs:*** FFEL (Subsidized and Unsubsidized Stafford, PLUS), Perkins.

WORK-STUDY ***Federal work-study:*** Total amount: $326,481; jobs available.

APPLYING FOR FINANCIAL AID ***Required financial aid form:*** FAFSA. ***Financial aid deadline:*** Continuous. ***Notification date:*** Continuous.

CONTACT Kim Kane, Director of Student Finance, DeVry University, 6600 Dumbarton Circle, Fremont, CA 94555, 510-574-1100. *Fax:* 510-742-0868.

DeVRY UNIVERSITY
Irvine, CA

CONTACT Financial Aid Office, DeVry University, 3333 Michelson Drive, Suite 420, Irvine, CA 92612-1682, 949-752-5631.

DeVRY UNIVERSITY
Long Beach, CA

Tuition & fees: $14,080 **Average undergraduate aid package: $14,244**

ABOUT THE INSTITUTION Proprietary, coed. ***Awards:*** associate, bachelor's, and master's degrees. 9 undergraduate majors. ***Total enrollment:*** 1,115. Undergraduates: 878. Freshmen: 168. Federal methodology is used as a basis for awarding need-based institutional aid.

UNDERGRADUATE EXPENSES for 2009–10 ***Application fee:*** $50. ***Tuition:*** full-time $14,080; part-time $550 per credit hour.

FRESHMAN FINANCIAL AID (Fall 2007) 45 applied for aid; of those 98% were deemed to have need. 100% of freshmen with need received aid; of those 5% had need fully met. ***Average percent of need met:*** 37% (excluding resources awarded to replace EFC). ***Average financial aid package:*** $10,849 (excluding resources awarded to replace EFC). 4% of all full-time freshmen had no need and received non-need-based gift aid.

UNDERGRADUATE FINANCIAL AID (Fall 2007) 221 applied for aid; of those 96% were deemed to have need. 100% of undergraduates with need received aid; of those 2% had need fully met. ***Average percent of need met:*** 44% (excluding resources awarded to replace EFC). ***Average financial aid package:*** $14,244 (excluding resources awarded to replace EFC). 5% of all full-time undergraduates had no need and received non-need-based gift aid.

GIFT AID (NEED-BASED) ***Total amount:*** $2,808,679 (49% federal, 38% state, 9% institutional, 4% external sources). ***Receiving aid:*** Freshmen: 37% (30); all full-time undergraduates: 46% (129). ***Average award:*** Freshmen: $6180; Undergraduates: $8196. ***Scholarships, grants, and awards:*** Federal Pell, FSEOG, state, private, college/university gift aid from institutional funds.

GIFT AID (NON-NEED-BASED) ***Total amount:*** $414,796 (78% institutional, 22% external sources). ***Average award:*** Freshmen: $12,719. Undergraduates: $16,538.

LOANS ***Student loans:*** $12,150,567 (89% need-based, 11% non-need-based). 57% of past graduating class borrowed through all loan programs. *Average indebtedness per student:* $36,961. ***Average need-based loan:*** Freshmen: $6329. Undergraduates: $8555. ***Parent loans:*** $1,132,533 (73% need-based, 27% non-need-based). ***Programs:*** FFEL (Subsidized and Unsubsidized Stafford, PLUS), Perkins.

WORK-STUDY ***Federal work-study:*** Total amount: $289,684; jobs available.

APPLYING FOR FINANCIAL AID ***Required financial aid form:*** FAFSA. ***Financial aid deadline:*** Continuous. ***Notification date:*** Continuous.

CONTACT Kathy Odom, Director of Financial Aid, DeVry University, 3880 Kilroy Airport Way, Long Beach, CA 90806, 562-427-0861. *Fax:* 562-989-1578.

DeVRY UNIVERSITY
Palmdale, CA

CONTACT Ann Logan, Dean of Student Finance, DeVry University, 22801 Roscoe Boulevard, West Hills, CA 91304, 818-932-3001 or toll-free 866-986-9388. *Fax:* 818-932-3131.

DeVRY UNIVERSITY
Pomona, CA

Tuition & fees: $14,080 | **Average undergraduate aid package: $12,689**

ABOUT THE INSTITUTION Proprietary, coed. ***Awards:*** associate, bachelor's, and master's degrees. 11 undergraduate majors. ***Total enrollment:*** 1,934. Undergraduates: 1,711. Freshmen: 247. Federal methodology is used as a basis for awarding need-based institutional aid.

UNDERGRADUATE EXPENSES for 2009–10 ***Application fee:*** $50. ***Tuition:*** full-time $14,080; part-time $550 per credit hour.

FRESHMAN FINANCIAL AID (Fall 2007) 106 applied for aid; of those 98% were deemed to have need. 98% of freshmen with need received aid; of those 2% had need fully met. ***Average percent of need met:*** 42% (excluding resources awarded to replace EFC). ***Average financial aid package:*** $13,233 (excluding resources awarded to replace EFC). 7% of all full-time freshmen had no need and received non-need-based gift aid.

UNDERGRADUATE FINANCIAL AID (Fall 2007) 414 applied for aid; of those 95% were deemed to have need. 98% of undergraduates with need received aid; of those 2% had need fully met. ***Average percent of need met:*** 36% (excluding resources awarded to replace EFC). ***Average financial aid package:*** $12,689 (excluding resources awarded to replace EFC). 9% of all full-time undergraduates had no need and received non-need-based gift aid.

GIFT AID (NEED-BASED) ***Total amount:*** $4,982,867 (50% federal, 28% state, 19% institutional, 3% external sources). ***Receiving aid:*** Freshmen: 45% (76); all full-time undergraduates: 39% (212). ***Average award:*** Freshmen: $7877; Undergraduates: $8289. ***Scholarships, grants, and awards:*** Federal Pell, FSEOG, state, private, college/university gift aid from institutional funds.

GIFT AID (NON-NEED-BASED) ***Total amount:*** $950,608 (90% institutional, 10% external sources). ***Average award:*** Freshmen: $11,699. Undergraduates: $16,971.

LOANS ***Student loans:*** $22,733,576 (87% need-based, 13% non-need-based). 67% of past graduating class borrowed through all loan programs. *Average indebtedness per student:* $33,385. ***Average need-based loan:*** Freshmen: $6985. Undergraduates: $7876. ***Parent loans:*** $1,476,301 (76% need-based, 24% non-need-based). ***Programs:*** FFEL (Subsidized and Unsubsidized Stafford, PLUS), Perkins.

WORK-STUDY ***Federal work-study:*** Total amount: $331,441; jobs available.

APPLYING FOR FINANCIAL AID ***Required financial aid form:*** FAFSA. ***Financial aid deadline:*** Continuous. ***Notification date:*** Continuous.

CONTACT Kathy Odom, Director of Financial Aid, DeVry University, 901 Corporate Center Drive, Pomona, CA 91768-2642, 909-622-8866. *Fax:* 909-623-5666.

DeVRY UNIVERSITY
San Diego, CA

CONTACT Financial Aid Office, DeVry University, 2655 Camino Del Rio North, Suite 201, San Diego, CA 92108-1633, 619-683-2446.

DeVRY UNIVERSITY
San Francisco, CA

CONTACT Financial Aid Office, DeVry University, 455 Market Street, Suite 1650, San Francisco, CA 94105-2472, 415-243-8787.

DeVRY UNIVERSITY
Sherman Oaks, CA

Tuition & fees: $14,080 | **Average undergraduate aid package: $11,834**

ABOUT THE INSTITUTION Proprietary, coed. ***Awards:*** associate, bachelor's, and master's degrees. 9 undergraduate majors. ***Total enrollment:*** 715. Undergraduates: 573. Freshmen: 89. Federal methodology is used as a basis for awarding need-based institutional aid.

UNDERGRADUATE EXPENSES for 2009–10 ***Application fee:*** $50. ***Tuition:*** full-time $14,080; part-time $550 per credit hour.

FRESHMAN FINANCIAL AID (Fall 2007) 23 applied for aid; of those 91% were deemed to have need. 95% of freshmen with need received aid; of those 5% had need fully met. ***Average percent of need met:*** 43% (excluding resources awarded to replace EFC). ***Average financial aid package:*** $11,844 (excluding resources awarded to replace EFC). 8% of all full-time freshmen had no need and received non-need-based gift aid.

UNDERGRADUATE FINANCIAL AID (Fall 2007) 120 applied for aid; of those 90% were deemed to have need. 98% of undergraduates with need received aid; of those 4% had need fully met. ***Average percent of need met:*** 39% (excluding resources awarded to replace EFC). ***Average financial aid package:*** $11,834 (excluding resources awarded to replace EFC). 12% of all full-time undergraduates had no need and received non-need-based gift aid.

GIFT AID (NEED-BASED) ***Total amount:*** $1,334,042 (54% federal, 34% state, 11% institutional, 1% external sources). ***Receiving aid:*** Freshmen: 39% (15); all full-time undergraduates: 34% (55). ***Average award:*** Freshmen: $7907; Undergraduates: $6691. ***Scholarships, grants, and awards:*** Federal Pell, FSEOG, state, private, college/university gift aid from institutional funds.

GIFT AID (NON-NEED-BASED) ***Total amount:*** $170,567 (1% state, 94% institutional, 5% external sources). ***Receiving aid:*** Undergraduates: 1% (2). ***Average award:*** Freshmen: $9203. Undergraduates: $17,847.

LOANS ***Student loans:*** $7,419,704 (87% need-based, 13% non-need-based). 100% of past graduating class borrowed through all loan programs. *Average indebtedness per student:* $31,200. ***Average need-based loan:*** Freshmen: $6337. Undergraduates: $8480. ***Parent loans:*** $961,225 (69% need-based, 31% non-need-based). ***Programs:*** FFEL (Subsidized and Unsubsidized Stafford, PLUS), Perkins.

WORK-STUDY ***Federal work-study:*** Total amount: $86,287; jobs available.

APPLYING FOR FINANCIAL AID ***Required financial aid form:*** FAFSA. ***Financial aid deadline:*** Continuous. ***Notification date:*** Continuous.

CONTACT Financial Aid Office, DeVry University, 15301 Ventura Boulevard, D-100, Sherman Oaks, CA 91403, 888-610-0800.

DeVRY UNIVERSITY
Colorado Springs, CO

CONTACT Carol Oppman, Director of Financial Aid, DeVry University, 225 South Union Boulevard, Colorado Springs, CO 80910, 719-632-3000 or toll-free 866-338-7934. *Fax:* 719-632-1909.

DeVRY UNIVERSITY
Westminster, CO

Tuition & fees: $14,080 | **Average undergraduate aid package: $11,971**

ABOUT THE INSTITUTION Proprietary, coed. ***Awards:*** associate, bachelor's, and master's degrees. 9 undergraduate majors. ***Total enrollment:*** 788. Undergraduates: 724. Freshmen: 136. Federal methodology is used as a basis for awarding need-based institutional aid.

UNDERGRADUATE EXPENSES for 2009–10 ***Application fee:*** $50. ***Tuition:*** full-time $14,080; part-time $550 per credit hour.

FRESHMAN FINANCIAL AID (Fall 2007) 29 applied for aid; of those 86% were deemed to have need. 100% of freshmen with need received aid; of those 16% had need fully met. ***Average percent of need met:*** 35% (excluding resources awarded to replace EFC). ***Average financial aid package:*** $9419 (excluding resources awarded to replace EFC). 7% of all full-time freshmen had no need and received non-need-based gift aid.

UNDERGRADUATE FINANCIAL AID (Fall 2007) 148 applied for aid; of those 92% were deemed to have need. 99% of undergraduates with need received aid; of those 4% had need fully met. ***Average percent of need met:*** 37% (excluding resources awarded to replace EFC). ***Average financial aid package:*** $11,971 (excluding resources awarded to replace EFC). 9% of all full-time undergraduates had no need and received non-need-based gift aid.

GIFT AID (NEED-BASED) ***Total amount:*** $1,804,742 (51% federal, 10% state, 33% institutional, 6% external sources). ***Receiving aid:*** Freshmen: 33% (14);

all full-time undergraduates: 40% (75). ***Average award:*** Freshmen: $5510; Undergraduates: $6094. ***Scholarships, grants, and awards:*** Federal Pell, FSEOG, state, private, college/university gift aid from institutional funds.

GIFT AID (NON-NEED-BASED) ***Total amount:*** $314,642 (93% institutional, 7% external sources). ***Receiving aid:*** Freshmen: 5% (2). Undergraduates: 2% (3). ***Average award:*** Freshmen: $5916. Undergraduates: $13,350.

LOANS ***Student loans:*** $8,544,444 (90% need-based, 10% non-need-based). 100% of past graduating class borrowed through all loan programs. *Average indebtedness per student:* $11,071. ***Average need-based loan:*** Freshmen: $6000. Undergraduates: $8024. ***Parent loans:*** $665,433 (77% need-based, 23% non-need-based). ***Programs:*** FFEL (Subsidized and Unsubsidized Stafford, PLUS), Perkins.

WORK-STUDY ***Federal work-study:*** Total amount: $205,308; jobs available.

APPLYING FOR FINANCIAL AID ***Required financial aid form:*** FAFSA. ***Financial aid deadline:*** Continuous. ***Notification date:*** Continuous.

CONTACT Office of Financial Aid, DeVry University, 1870 West 122nd Avenue, Westminster, CO 80234-2010, 303-280-7400.

DeVRY UNIVERSITY
Miami, FL

CONTACT Financial Aid Office, DeVry University, 200 South Biscayne Boulevard, Suite 500, Miami, FL 33131-5351, 786-425-1113.

DeVRY UNIVERSITY
Miramar, FL

Tuition & fees: $14,080 **Average undergraduate aid package: $12,172**

ABOUT THE INSTITUTION Proprietary, coed. ***Awards:*** associate, bachelor's, and master's degrees. 9 undergraduate majors. ***Total enrollment:*** 1,099. Undergraduates: 955. Freshmen: 154. Federal methodology is used as a basis for awarding need-based institutional aid.

UNDERGRADUATE EXPENSES for 2009–10 ***Application fee:*** $50. ***Tuition:*** full-time $14,080; part-time $550 per credit hour.

FRESHMAN FINANCIAL AID (Fall 2007) 72 applied for aid; of those 94% were deemed to have need. 99% of freshmen with need received aid. ***Average percent of need met:*** 40% (excluding resources awarded to replace EFC). ***Average financial aid package:*** $13,137 (excluding resources awarded to replace EFC). 8% of all full-time freshmen had no need and received non-need-based gift aid.

UNDERGRADUATE FINANCIAL AID (Fall 2007) 204 applied for aid; of those 97% were deemed to have need. 99% of undergraduates with need received aid; of those 1% had need fully met. ***Average percent of need met:*** 38% (excluding resources awarded to replace EFC). ***Average financial aid package:*** $12,172 (excluding resources awarded to replace EFC). 12% of all full-time undergraduates had no need and received non-need-based gift aid.

GIFT AID (NEED-BASED) ***Total amount:*** $2,656,865 (72% federal, 4% state, 22% institutional, 2% external sources). ***Receiving aid:*** Freshmen: 50% (53); all full-time undergraduates: 42% (121). ***Average award:*** Freshmen: $7349; Undergraduates: $7044. ***Scholarships, grants, and awards:*** Federal Pell, FSEOG, state, private, college/university gift aid from institutional funds.

GIFT AID (NON-NEED-BASED) ***Total amount:*** $552,075 (1% state, 61% institutional, 38% external sources). ***Receiving aid:*** Undergraduates: 1% (2). ***Average award:*** Freshmen: $14,271. Undergraduates: $12,256.

LOANS ***Student loans:*** $12,036,071 (92% need-based, 8% non-need-based). 80% of past graduating class borrowed through all loan programs. *Average indebtedness per student:* $51,131. ***Average need-based loan:*** Freshmen: $6826. Undergraduates: $7414. ***Parent loans:*** $769,849 (79% need-based, 21% non-need-based). ***Programs:*** FFEL (Subsidized and Unsubsidized Stafford, PLUS), Perkins.

WORK-STUDY ***Federal work-study:*** Total amount: $234,157; jobs available.

APPLYING FOR FINANCIAL AID ***Required financial aid form:*** FAFSA. ***Financial aid deadline:*** Continuous. ***Notification date:*** Continuous.

CONTACT Office of Financial Aid, DeVry University, 2300 Southwest 145th Avenue, Miramar, FL 33027, 954-499-9700.

DeVRY UNIVERSITY
Orlando, FL

Tuition & fees: $14,080 **Average undergraduate aid package: $10,774**

ABOUT THE INSTITUTION Proprietary, coed. ***Awards:*** associate, bachelor's, and master's degrees. 11 undergraduate majors. ***Total enrollment:*** 1,576. Undergraduates: 1,404. Freshmen: 269. Federal methodology is used as a basis for awarding need-based institutional aid.

UNDERGRADUATE EXPENSES for 2009–10 ***Application fee:*** $50. ***Tuition:*** full-time $14,080; part-time $550 per credit.

FRESHMAN FINANCIAL AID (Fall 2007) 94 applied for aid; of those 91% were deemed to have need. 100% of freshmen with need received aid; of those 1% had need fully met. ***Average percent of need met:*** 33% (excluding resources awarded to replace EFC). ***Average financial aid package:*** $9980 (excluding resources awarded to replace EFC). 7% of all full-time freshmen had no need and received non-need-based gift aid.

UNDERGRADUATE FINANCIAL AID (Fall 2007) 314 applied for aid; of those 94% were deemed to have need. 100% of undergraduates with need received aid; of those 1% had need fully met. ***Average percent of need met:*** 33% (excluding resources awarded to replace EFC). ***Average financial aid package:*** $10,774 (excluding resources awarded to replace EFC). 9% of all full-time undergraduates had no need and received non-need-based gift aid.

GIFT AID (NEED-BASED) ***Total amount:*** $3,604,518 (65% federal, 7% state, 25% institutional, 3% external sources). ***Receiving aid:*** Freshmen: 49% (65); all full-time undergraduates: 48% (191). ***Average award:*** Freshmen: $5536; Undergraduates: $5608. ***Scholarships, grants, and awards:*** Federal Pell, FSEOG, state, private, college/university gift aid from institutional funds.

GIFT AID (NON-NEED-BASED) ***Total amount:*** $569,269 (2% state, 76% institutional, 22% external sources). ***Average award:*** Freshmen: $15,280. Undergraduates: $18,240.

LOANS ***Student loans:*** $17,248,419 (91% need-based, 9% non-need-based). 100% of past graduating class borrowed through all loan programs. *Average indebtedness per student:* $23,511. ***Average need-based loan:*** Freshmen: $5768. Undergraduates: $7062. ***Parent loans:*** $1,030,011 (75% need-based, 25% non-need-based). ***Programs:*** FFEL (Subsidized and Unsubsidized Stafford, PLUS), Perkins.

WORK-STUDY ***Federal work-study:*** Total amount: $174,993; jobs available.

APPLYING FOR FINANCIAL AID ***Required financial aid form:*** FAFSA. ***Financial aid deadline:*** Continuous. ***Notification date:*** Continuous.

CONTACT Estrella Velazquez-Domenech, Director of Student Finance, DeVry University, 4000 Millenia Boulevard, Orlando, FL 32839, 407-345-2816. *Fax:* 407-355-4855.

DeVRY UNIVERSITY
Tampa, FL

CONTACT Financial Aid Office, DeVry University, 3030 North Rocky Point Drive West, Suite 100, Tampa, FL 33607-5901, 813-288-8994.

DeVRY UNIVERSITY
Alpharetta, GA

Tuition & fees: $14,080 **Average undergraduate aid package: $13,554**

ABOUT THE INSTITUTION Proprietary, coed. ***Awards:*** associate, bachelor's, and master's degrees. 9 undergraduate majors. ***Total enrollment:*** 858. Undergraduates: 711. Freshmen: 97. Federal methodology is used as a basis for awarding need-based institutional aid.

UNDERGRADUATE EXPENSES for 2009–10 ***Application fee:*** $50. ***Tuition:*** full-time $14,080; part-time $550 per credit.

FRESHMAN FINANCIAL AID (Fall 2007) 34 applied for aid; of those 85% were deemed to have need. 100% of freshmen with need received aid; of those 3% had need fully met. ***Average percent of need met:*** 44% (excluding resources awarded to replace EFC). ***Average financial aid package:*** $13,811 (excluding resources awarded to replace EFC). 12% of all full-time freshmen had no need and received non-need-based gift aid.

UNDERGRADUATE FINANCIAL AID (Fall 2007) 171 applied for aid; of those 93% were deemed to have need. 100% of undergraduates with need received aid; of those 7% had need fully met. ***Average percent of need met:*** 45% (excluding resources awarded to replace EFC). ***Average financial aid package:*** $13,554 (excluding resources awarded to replace EFC). 8% of all full-time undergraduates had no need and received non-need-based gift aid.

GIFT AID (NEED-BASED) ***Total amount:*** $2,947,928 (41% federal, 33% state, 24% institutional, 2% external sources). ***Receiving aid:*** Freshmen: 43% (28); all full-time undergraduates: 69% (149). ***Average award:*** Freshmen: $7327; Undergraduates: $5898. ***Scholarships, grants, and awards:*** Federal Pell, FSEOG, state, private, college/university gift aid from institutional funds.

GIFT AID (NON-NEED-BASED) ***Total amount:*** $710,765 (10% state, 86% institutional, 4% external sources). ***Receiving aid:*** Undergraduates: 1% (2). ***Average award:*** Freshmen: $10,948. Undergraduates: $13,569.

LOANS ***Student loans:*** $9,745,306 (87% need-based, 13% non-need-based). 100% of past graduating class borrowed through all loan programs. *Average indebtedness per student:* $32,836. ***Average need-based loan:*** Freshmen: $6761. Undergraduates: $8238. ***Parent loans:*** $402,910 (66% need-based, 34% non-need-based). ***Programs:*** FFEL (Subsidized and Unsubsidized Stafford, PLUS), Perkins.

WORK-STUDY ***Federal work-study:*** Total amount: $46,814; jobs available.

APPLYING FOR FINANCIAL AID ***Required financial aid form:*** FAFSA. ***Financial aid deadline:*** Continuous. ***Notification date:*** Continuous.

CONTACT David Pickett, Assistant Director of Financial Aid, DeVry University, 2555 Northwinds Parkway, Alpharetta, GA 30004, 770-521-4900 or toll-free 800-346-5420. *Fax:* 770-664-8024.

DeVRY UNIVERSITY

Atlanta, GA

CONTACT Financial Aid Office, DeVry University, Fifteen Piedmont Center, Plaza Level 100, Atlanta, GA 30305-1543, 404-296-7400.

DeVRY UNIVERSITY

Decatur, GA

Tuition & fees: $14,080 **Average undergraduate aid package: $14,044**

ABOUT THE INSTITUTION Proprietary, coed. ***Awards:*** associate, bachelor's, and master's degrees. 11 undergraduate majors. ***Total enrollment:*** 2,719. Undergraduates: 2,380. Freshmen: 343. Federal methodology is used as a basis for awarding need-based institutional aid.

UNDERGRADUATE EXPENSES for 2009–10 ***Application fee:*** $50. ***Tuition:*** full-time $14,080; part-time $550 per credit hour.

FRESHMAN FINANCIAL AID (Fall 2007) 84 applied for aid; of those 99% were deemed to have need. 98% of freshmen with need received aid; of those 5% had need fully met. ***Average percent of need met:*** 41% (excluding resources awarded to replace EFC). ***Average financial aid package:*** $12,824 (excluding resources awarded to replace EFC). 1% of all full-time freshmen had no need and received non-need-based gift aid.

UNDERGRADUATE FINANCIAL AID (Fall 2007) 488 applied for aid; of those 98% were deemed to have need. 99% of undergraduates with need received aid; of those 3% had need fully met. ***Average percent of need met:*** 43% (excluding resources awarded to replace EFC). ***Average financial aid package:*** $14,044 (excluding resources awarded to replace EFC). 3% of all full-time undergraduates had no need and received non-need-based gift aid.

GIFT AID (NEED-BASED) ***Total amount:*** $10,858,429 (49% federal, 28% state, 19% institutional, 4% external sources). ***Receiving aid:*** Freshmen: 69% (77); all full-time undergraduates: 83% (446). ***Average award:*** Freshmen: $6496; Undergraduates: $6480. ***Scholarships, grants, and awards:*** Federal Pell, FSEOG, state, private, college/university gift aid from institutional funds.

GIFT AID (NON-NEED-BASED) ***Total amount:*** $623,412 (1% federal, 18% state, 60% institutional, 21% external sources). ***Receiving aid:*** Freshmen: 1% (1). Undergraduates: 1% (7). ***Average award:*** Undergraduates: $15,251.

LOANS ***Student loans:*** $31,557,020 (93% need-based, 7% non-need-based). 88% of past graduating class borrowed through all loan programs. *Average indebtedness per student:* $47,994. ***Average need-based loan:*** Freshmen: $6707. Undergraduates: $8002. ***Parent loans:*** $1,024,325 (72% need-based, 28% non-need-based). ***Programs:*** FFEL (Subsidized and Unsubsidized Stafford, PLUS), Perkins.

WORK-STUDY ***Federal work-study:*** Total amount: $276,861; jobs available.

APPLYING FOR FINANCIAL AID ***Required financial aid form:*** FAFSA. ***Financial aid deadline:*** Continuous. ***Notification date:*** Continuous.

CONTACT Robin Winston, Director of Financial Aid, DeVry University, 250 North Arcadia Avenue, Decatur, GA 30030-2198, 404-292-7900. *Fax:* 404-292-2321.

DeVRY UNIVERSITY

Duluth, GA

CONTACT Financial Aid Office, DeVry University, 3505 Koger Boulevard, Suite 170, Duluth, GA 30096-7671, 678-380-9780.

DeVRY UNIVERSITY

Addison, IL

Tuition & fees: $14,080 **Average undergraduate aid package: $13,134**

ABOUT THE INSTITUTION Proprietary, coed. ***Awards:*** associate and bachelor's degrees. 9 undergraduate majors. ***Total enrollment:*** 1,403. Undergraduates: 1,403. Freshmen: 225. Federal methodology is used as a basis for awarding need-based institutional aid.

UNDERGRADUATE EXPENSES for 2009–10 ***Application fee:*** $50. ***Tuition:*** full-time $14,080; part-time $550 per credit hour.

FRESHMAN FINANCIAL AID (Fall 2007) 102 applied for aid; of those 91% were deemed to have need. 100% of freshmen with need received aid; of those 4% had need fully met. ***Average percent of need met:*** 48% (excluding resources awarded to replace EFC). ***Average financial aid package:*** $13,167 (excluding resources awarded to replace EFC). 10% of all full-time freshmen had no need and received non-need-based gift aid.

UNDERGRADUATE FINANCIAL AID (Fall 2007) 481 applied for aid; of those 93% were deemed to have need. 99% of undergraduates with need received aid; of those 4% had need fully met. ***Average percent of need met:*** 47% (excluding resources awarded to replace EFC). ***Average financial aid package:*** $13,134 (excluding resources awarded to replace EFC). 9% of all full-time undergraduates had no need and received non-need-based gift aid.

GIFT AID (NEED-BASED) ***Total amount:*** $4,099,117 (35% federal, 47% state, 16% institutional, 2% external sources). ***Receiving aid:*** Freshmen: 42% (75); all full-time undergraduates: 44% (282). ***Average award:*** Freshmen: $6606; Undergraduates: $6727. ***Scholarships, grants, and awards:*** Federal Pell, FSEOG, state, private, college/university gift aid from institutional funds.

GIFT AID (NON-NEED-BASED) ***Total amount:*** $574,781 (93% institutional, 7% external sources). ***Receiving aid:*** Undergraduates: 1. ***Average award:*** Freshmen: $13,675. Undergraduates: $15,985.

LOANS ***Student loans:*** $17,986,730 (82% need-based, 18% non-need-based). 67% of past graduating class borrowed through all loan programs. *Average indebtedness per student:* $31,740. ***Average need-based loan:*** Freshmen: $7692. Undergraduates: $8478. ***Parent loans:*** $1,161,317 (63% need-based, 37% non-need-based). ***Programs:*** FFEL (Subsidized and Unsubsidized Stafford, PLUS), Perkins.

WORK-STUDY ***Federal work-study:*** Total amount: $347,333; jobs available.

APPLYING FOR FINANCIAL AID ***Required financial aid form:*** FAFSA. ***Financial aid deadline:*** Continuous. ***Notification date:*** Continuous.

CONTACT Sejal Amin, Director of Student Finance, DeVry University, 1221 North Swift Road, Addison, IL 60101-6106, 630-953-1300 or toll-free 800-346-5420.

DeVRY UNIVERSITY

Chicago, IL

Tuition & fees: $14,080 **Average undergraduate aid package: $16,145**

ABOUT THE INSTITUTION Proprietary, coed. ***Awards:*** associate and bachelor's degrees. 10 undergraduate majors. ***Total enrollment:*** 1,890. Undergraduates: 1,890. Freshmen: 379. Federal methodology is used as a basis for awarding need-based institutional aid.

UNDERGRADUATE EXPENSES for 2009–10 ***Application fee:*** $50. ***Tuition:*** full-time $14,080; part-time $550 per credit hour.

FRESHMAN FINANCIAL AID (Fall 2007) 99 applied for aid; of those 97% were deemed to have need. 98% of freshmen with need received aid. ***Average percent of need met:*** 48% (excluding resources awarded to replace EFC).

Average financial aid package: $16,818 (excluding resources awarded to replace EFC). 3% of all full-time freshmen had no need and received non-need-based gift aid.

UNDERGRADUATE FINANCIAL AID (Fall 2007) 479 applied for aid; of those 97% were deemed to have need. 99% of undergraduates with need received aid; of those 1% had need fully met. *Average percent of need met:* 48% (excluding resources awarded to replace EFC). *Average financial aid package:* $16,145 (excluding resources awarded to replace EFC). 2% of all full-time undergraduates had no need and received non-need-based gift aid.

GIFT AID (NEED-BASED) *Total amount:* $9,605,815 (47% federal, 43% state, 9% institutional, 1% external sources). *Receiving aid:* Freshmen: 46% (84); all full-time undergraduates: 61% (386). *Average award:* Freshmen: $9892; Undergraduates: $8371. *Scholarships, grants, and awards:* Federal Pell, FSEOG, state, private, college/university gift aid from institutional funds.

GIFT AID (NON-NEED-BASED) *Total amount:* $171,535 (88% institutional, 12% external sources). *Average award:* Freshmen: $11,670. Undergraduates: $11,220.

LOANS *Student loans:* $23,175,874 (95% need-based, 5% non-need-based). 92% of past graduating class borrowed through all loan programs. *Average indebtedness per student:* $49,157. *Average need-based loan:* Freshmen: $7232. Undergraduates: $8033. *Parent loans:* $495,392 (76% need-based, 24% non-need-based). *Programs:* FFEL (Subsidized and Unsubsidized Stafford, PLUS), Perkins.

WORK-STUDY *Federal work-study:* Total amount: $1,147,124; jobs available.

APPLYING FOR FINANCIAL AID *Required financial aid form:* FAFSA. *Financial aid deadline:* Continuous. *Notification date:* Continuous.

CONTACT Milena Dobrina, Director of Financial Aid, DeVry University, 3300 North Campbell Avenue, Chicago, IL 60618-5994, 773-929-8500. *Fax:* 773-348-1780.

DeVRY UNIVERSITY
Elgin, IL

CONTACT Financial Aid Office, DeVry University, 385 Airport Road, Elgin, IL 60123-9341, 847-622-1135.

DeVRY UNIVERSITY
Gurnee, IL

CONTACT Financial Aid Office, DeVry University, 1075 Tri-State Parkway, Suite 800, Gurnee, IL 60031-9126, 847-855-2649 or toll-free 866-563-3879.

DeVRY UNIVERSITY
Naperville, IL

CONTACT Financial Aid Office, DeVry University, 2056 Westings Avenue, Suite 40, Naperville, IL 60563-2361, 630-428-9086 or toll-free 877-496-9050.

DeVRY UNIVERSITY
Oakbrook Terrace, IL

CONTACT Financial Aid Office, DeVry University, One Tower Lane, Oakbrook Terrace, IL 60181, 630-574-1960.

DeVRY UNIVERSITY
Tinley Park, IL

Tuition & fees: $14,080 **Average undergraduate aid package: $12,346**

ABOUT THE INSTITUTION Proprietary, coed. *Awards:* associate, bachelor's, and master's degrees. 9 undergraduate majors. *Total enrollment:* 1,401. Undergraduates: 1,092. Freshmen: 203. Federal methodology is used as a basis for awarding need-based institutional aid.

UNDERGRADUATE EXPENSES for 2009–10 *Application fee:* $50. *Tuition:* full-time $14,080; part-time $550 per credit hour.

FRESHMAN FINANCIAL AID (Fall 2007) 142 applied for aid; of those 97% were deemed to have need. 100% of freshmen with need received aid; of those 7% had need fully met. *Average percent of need met:* 44% (excluding resources awarded to replace EFC). *Average financial aid package:* $11,879 (excluding resources awarded to replace EFC). 5% of all full-time freshmen had no need and received non-need-based gift aid.

UNDERGRADUATE FINANCIAL AID (Fall 2007) 379 applied for aid; of those 97% were deemed to have need. 100% of undergraduates with need received aid; of those 5% had need fully met. *Average percent of need met:* 45% (excluding resources awarded to replace EFC). *Average financial aid package:* $12,346 (excluding resources awarded to replace EFC). 5% of all full-time undergraduates had no need and received non-need-based gift aid.

GIFT AID (NEED-BASED) *Total amount:* $4,502,368 (44% federal, 41% state, 12% institutional, 3% external sources). *Receiving aid:* Freshmen: 61% (103); all full-time undergraduates: 54% (240). *Average award:* Freshmen: $6680; Undergraduates: $6916. *Scholarships, grants, and awards:* Federal Pell, FSEOG, state, private, college/university gift aid from institutional funds.

GIFT AID (NON-NEED-BASED) *Total amount:* $215,147 (83% institutional, 17% external sources). *Receiving aid:* Freshmen: 2% (4). Undergraduates: 1% (4). *Average award:* Freshmen: $13,688. Undergraduates: $14,254.

LOANS *Student loans:* $15,141,423 (87% need-based, 13% non-need-based). 100% of past graduating class borrowed through all loan programs. *Average indebtedness per student:* $4375. *Average need-based loan:* Freshmen: $6617. Undergraduates: $7379. *Parent loans:* $1,521,076 (64% need-based, 36% non-need-based). *Programs:* FFEL (Subsidized and Unsubsidized Stafford, PLUS), Perkins.

WORK-STUDY *Federal work-study:* Total amount: $371,433; jobs available.

APPLYING FOR FINANCIAL AID *Required financial aid form:* FAFSA. *Financial aid deadline:* Continuous. *Notification date:* Continuous.

CONTACT Director of Student Finance, DeVry University, 18624 West Creek Drive, Tinley Park, IL 60477, 708-342-3300. *Fax:* 708-342-3120.

DeVRY UNIVERSITY
Indianapolis, IN

Tuition & fees: $14,080 **Average undergraduate aid package: $14,132**

ABOUT THE INSTITUTION Proprietary, coed. *Awards:* associate, bachelor's, and master's degrees. 6 undergraduate majors. *Total enrollment:* 302. Undergraduates: 184. Freshmen: 25. Federal methodology is used as a basis for awarding need-based institutional aid.

UNDERGRADUATE EXPENSES for 2009–10 *Application fee:* $50. *Tuition:* full-time $14,080; part-time $550 per credit hour.

FRESHMAN FINANCIAL AID (Fall 2007) 1 applied for aid; of those 100% were deemed to have need. 100% of freshmen with need received aid. *Average percent of need met:* 21% (excluding resources awarded to replace EFC). *Average financial aid package:* $3500 (excluding resources awarded to replace EFC).

UNDERGRADUATE FINANCIAL AID (Fall 2007) 19 applied for aid; of those 100% were deemed to have need. 95% of undergraduates with need received aid. *Average percent of need met:* 42% (excluding resources awarded to replace EFC). *Average financial aid package:* $14,132 (excluding resources awarded to replace EFC). 5% of all full-time undergraduates had no need and received non-need-based gift aid.

GIFT AID (NEED-BASED) *Total amount:* $507,199 (69% federal, 1% state, 17% institutional, 13% external sources). *Receiving aid:* All full-time undergraduates: 32% (7). *Average award:* Undergraduates: $6728. *Scholarships, grants, and awards:* state, college/university gift aid from institutional funds.

GIFT AID (NON-NEED-BASED) *Total amount:* $84,344 (58% institutional, 42% external sources). *Average award:* Undergraduates: $20,854.

LOANS *Student loans:* $2,927,887 (91% need-based, 9% non-need-based). *Average need-based loan:* Freshmen: $3500. Undergraduates: $10,993. *Parent loans:* $41,029 (42% need-based, 58% non-need-based).

WORK-STUDY *Federal work-study:* Total amount: $27,900; jobs available.

CONTACT Financial Aid Office, DeVry University, 9100 Keystone Crossing, Suite 350, Indianapolis, IN 46240-2158, 317-581-8854.

DeVRY UNIVERSITY
Merrillville, IN

CONTACT Financial Aid Office, DeVry University, Twin Towers, 1000 East 80th Place, Suite 222 Mall, Merrillville, IN 46410-5673, 219-736-7440.

DeVry University
Louisville, KY

Tuition & fees: $14,080 **Average undergraduate aid package: N/A**

ABOUT THE INSTITUTION Proprietary, coed. ***Awards:*** associate and bachelor's degrees. 5 undergraduate majors. ***Total enrollment:*** 34. Undergraduates: 34. Freshmen: 10. Federal methodology is used as a basis for awarding need-based institutional aid.

UNDERGRADUATE EXPENSES for 2009–10 ***Application fee:*** $50. ***Tuition:*** full-time $14,080; part-time $550 per credit hour.

GIFT AID (NEED-BASED) ***Scholarships, grants, and awards:*** Federal Pell, FSEOG, state, private, college/university gift aid from institutional funds.

LOANS ***Programs:*** FFEL (Subsidized and Unsubsidized Stafford, PLUS), Perkins.

APPLYING FOR FINANCIAL AID ***Required financial aid form:*** FAFSA. ***Financial aid deadline:*** Continuous. ***Notification date:*** Continuous.

CONTACT Financial Aid Office, DeVry University, 10172 Linn Station Road, Louisville, KY 40223, toll-free 866-906-9388.

DeVry University
Bethesda, MD

Tuition & fees: $14,080 **Average undergraduate aid package: $11,820**

ABOUT THE INSTITUTION Proprietary, coed. ***Awards:*** associate, bachelor's, and master's degrees. 3 undergraduate majors. ***Total enrollment:*** 95. Undergraduates: 44. Freshmen: 9. Federal methodology is used as a basis for awarding need-based institutional aid.

UNDERGRADUATE EXPENSES for 2009–10 ***Application fee:*** $50. ***Tuition:*** full-time $14,080; part-time $550 per credit.

UNDERGRADUATE FINANCIAL AID (Fall 2007) 5 applied for aid; of those 80% were deemed to have need. 75% of undergraduates with need received aid. ***Average percent of need met:*** 24% (excluding resources awarded to replace EFC). ***Average financial aid package:*** $11,820 (excluding resources awarded to replace EFC). 22% of all full-time undergraduates had no need and received non-need-based gift aid.

GIFT AID (NEED-BASED) ***Total amount:*** $93,547 (70% federal, 23% institutional, 7% external sources). ***Receiving aid:*** All full-time undergraduates: 11% (1). ***Average award:*** Undergraduates: $5760. ***Scholarships, grants, and awards:*** Federal Pell, FSEOG, state, private, college/university gift aid from institutional funds.

GIFT AID (NON-NEED-BASED) ***Total amount:*** $15,794 (100% institutional). ***Average award:*** Undergraduates: $22,795.

LOANS ***Student loans:*** $674,369 (83% need-based, 17% non-need-based). ***Average need-based loan:*** Undergraduates: $9900. ***Parent loans:*** $28,920 (100% need-based). ***Programs:*** FFEL (Subsidized and Unsubsidized Stafford, PLUS), Perkins.

APPLYING FOR FINANCIAL AID ***Required financial aid form:*** FAFSA. ***Financial aid deadline:*** Continuous. ***Notification date:*** Continuous.

CONTACT Financial Aid Office, DeVry University, 4550 Montgomery Avenue. Suite 100 North, Bethesda, MD 20814-3304, 301-652-8477.

DeVry University
Edina, MN

Tuition & fees: $14,080 **Average undergraduate aid package: $10,797**

ABOUT THE INSTITUTION Proprietary, coed. ***Awards:*** associate, bachelor's, and master's degrees. 8 undergraduate majors. ***Total enrollment:*** 252. Undergraduates: 190. Freshmen: 36. Federal methodology is used as a basis for awarding need-based institutional aid.

UNDERGRADUATE EXPENSES for 2009–10 ***Application fee:*** $50. ***Tuition:*** full-time $14,080; part-time $550 per credit hour.

FRESHMAN FINANCIAL AID (Fall 2007) 1 applied for aid; of those 100% were deemed to have need. 100% of freshmen with need received aid. ***Average percent of need met:*** 33% (excluding resources awarded to replace EFC). ***Average financial aid package:*** $9410 (excluding resources awarded to replace EFC). 17% of all full-time freshmen had no need and received non-need-based gift aid.

UNDERGRADUATE FINANCIAL AID (Fall 2007) 31 applied for aid; of those 94% were deemed to have need. 100% of undergraduates with need received aid. ***Average percent of need met:*** 38% (excluding resources awarded to replace EFC). ***Average financial aid package:*** $10,797 (excluding resources awarded to replace EFC). 5% of all full-time undergraduates had no need and received non-need-based gift aid.

GIFT AID (NEED-BASED) ***Total amount:*** $362,329 (60% federal, 5% state, 27% institutional, 8% external sources). ***Receiving aid:*** Freshmen: 17% (1); all full-time undergraduates: 28% (11). ***Average award:*** Freshmen: $5910; Undergraduates: $5538. ***Scholarships, grants, and awards:*** Federal Pell, FSEOG, state, private, college/university gift aid from institutional funds.

GIFT AID (NON-NEED-BASED) ***Total amount:*** $95,108 (66% institutional, 34% external sources). ***Average award:*** Undergraduates: $10,606.

LOANS ***Student loans:*** $2,228,498 (88% need-based, 12% non-need-based). ***Average need-based loan:*** Freshmen: $3500. Undergraduates: $8696. ***Parent loans:*** $3500 (24% need-based, 76% non-need-based). ***Programs:*** FFEL (Subsidized and Unsubsidized Stafford, PLUS), Perkins.

APPLYING FOR FINANCIAL AID ***Required financial aid form:*** FAFSA. ***Financial aid deadline:*** Continuous. ***Notification date:*** Continuous.

CONTACT Financial Aid Office, DeVry University, 7700 France Avenue South, Suite 575, Edina, MN 55435, 952-838-1860.

DeVry University
Kansas City, MO

Tuition & fees: $14,080 **Average undergraduate aid package: $11,948**

ABOUT THE INSTITUTION Proprietary, coed. ***Awards:*** associate, bachelor's, and master's degrees. 8 undergraduate majors. ***Total enrollment:*** 1,116. Undergraduates: 949. Freshmen: 155. Federal methodology is used as a basis for awarding need-based institutional aid.

UNDERGRADUATE EXPENSES for 2009–10 ***Application fee:*** $50. ***Tuition:*** full-time $14,080; part-time $550 per credit hour.

FRESHMAN FINANCIAL AID (Fall 2007) 77 applied for aid; of those 94% were deemed to have need. 99% of freshmen with need received aid; of those 1% had need fully met. ***Average percent of need met:*** 36% (excluding resources awarded to replace EFC). ***Average financial aid package:*** $10,782 (excluding resources awarded to replace EFC). 8% of all full-time freshmen had no need and received non-need-based gift aid.

UNDERGRADUATE FINANCIAL AID (Fall 2007) 294 applied for aid; of those 96% were deemed to have need. 99% of undergraduates with need received aid; of those 4% had need fully met. ***Average percent of need met:*** 40% (excluding resources awarded to replace EFC). ***Average financial aid package:*** $11,948 (excluding resources awarded to replace EFC). 8% of all full-time undergraduates had no need and received non-need-based gift aid.

GIFT AID (NEED-BASED) ***Total amount:*** $2,811,377 (55% federal, 37% institutional, 8% external sources). ***Receiving aid:*** Freshmen: 40% (56); all full-time undergraduates: 51% (185). ***Average award:*** Freshmen: $5193; Undergraduates: $5419. ***Scholarships, grants, and awards:*** Federal Pell, FSEOG, state, private, college/university gift aid from institutional funds.

GIFT AID (NON-NEED-BASED) ***Total amount:*** $308,838 (53% institutional, 47% external sources). ***Receiving aid:*** Undergraduates: 1% (2). ***Average award:*** Freshmen: $14,148. Undergraduates: $13,609.

LOANS ***Student loans:*** $14,499,790 (89% need-based, 11% non-need-based). 67% of past graduating class borrowed through all loan programs. *Average indebtedness per student:* $8969. ***Average need-based loan:*** Freshmen: $6771. Undergraduates: $8396. ***Parent loans:*** $663,437 (62% need-based, 38% non-need-based). ***Programs:*** FFEL (Subsidized and Unsubsidized Stafford, PLUS), Perkins.

WORK-STUDY ***Federal work-study:*** Total amount: $161,332; jobs available.

APPLYING FOR FINANCIAL AID ***Required financial aid form:*** FAFSA. ***Financial aid deadline:*** Continuous. ***Notification date:*** Continuous.

CONTACT Maureen Kelly, Senior Associate Director of Financial Aid, DeVry University, 11224 Holmes Street, Kansas City, MO 64131-3698, 816-941-0430.

DeVry University
Kansas City, MO

CONTACT Financial Aid Office, DeVry University, City Center Square, 1100 Main Street, Suite 118, Kansas City, MO 64105-2112, 816-221-1300.

DeVry University
St. Louis, MO

CONTACT Financial Aid Office, DeVry University, 1801 Park 270 Drive, Suite 260, St. Louis, MO 63146-4020, 314-542-4222.

DeVry University
Henderson, NV

Tuition & fees: $14,080 **Average undergraduate aid package: $10,877**

ABOUT THE INSTITUTION Proprietary, coed. ***Awards:*** associate, bachelor's, and master's degrees. 6 undergraduate majors. ***Total enrollment:*** 235. Undergraduates: 170. Freshmen: 25. Federal methodology is used as a basis for awarding need-based institutional aid.

UNDERGRADUATE EXPENSES for 2009–10 ***Application fee:*** $50. ***Tuition:*** full-time $14,080; part-time $550 per credit hour.

FRESHMAN FINANCIAL AID (Fall 2007) 4 applied for aid; of those 100% were deemed to have need. 100% of freshmen with need received aid. ***Average percent of need met:*** 40% (excluding resources awarded to replace EFC). ***Average financial aid package:*** $14,661 (excluding resources awarded to replace EFC).

UNDERGRADUATE FINANCIAL AID (Fall 2007) 32 applied for aid; of those 100% were deemed to have need. 100% of undergraduates with need received aid; of those 3% had need fully met. ***Average percent of need met:*** 36% (excluding resources awarded to replace EFC). ***Average financial aid package:*** $10,877 (excluding resources awarded to replace EFC).

GIFT AID (NEED-BASED) ***Total amount:*** $312,128 (63% federal, 26% institutional, 11% external sources). ***Receiving aid:*** Freshmen: 29% (4); all full-time undergraduates: 26% (11). ***Average award:*** Freshmen: $6376; Undergraduates: $5641. ***Scholarships, grants, and awards:*** Federal Pell, FSEOG, state, private, college/university gift aid from institutional funds.

GIFT AID (NON-NEED-BASED) ***Total amount:*** $20,001 (93% institutional, 7% external sources).

LOANS ***Student loans:*** $1,980,373 (91% need-based, 9% non-need-based). 100% of past graduating class borrowed through all loan programs. *Average indebtedness per student:* $62,400. ***Average need-based loan:*** Freshmen: $8282. Undergraduates: $8938. ***Parent loans:*** $250,405 (31% need-based, 69% non-need-based). ***Programs:*** FFEL (Subsidized and Unsubsidized Stafford, PLUS), Perkins.

APPLYING FOR FINANCIAL AID ***Required financial aid form:*** FAFSA. ***Financial aid deadline:*** Continuous. ***Notification date:*** Continuous.

CONTACT Financial Aid Office, DeVry University, 2490 Paseo Verde Parkway, Suite 150, Henderson, NV 89074-7120, 702-933-9700.

DeVry University
North Brunswick, NJ

Tuition & fees: $14,720 **Average undergraduate aid package: $12,399**

ABOUT THE INSTITUTION Proprietary, coed. ***Awards:*** associate and bachelor's degrees. 8 undergraduate majors. ***Total enrollment:*** 1,290. Undergraduates: 1,290. Freshmen: 287. Federal methodology is used as a basis for awarding need-based institutional aid.

UNDERGRADUATE EXPENSES for 2009–10 ***Application fee:*** $50. ***Tuition:*** full-time $14,720; part-time $575 per credit hour.

FRESHMAN FINANCIAL AID (Fall 2007) 118 applied for aid; of those 94% were deemed to have need. 98% of freshmen with need received aid. ***Average percent of need met:*** 46% (excluding resources awarded to replace EFC). ***Average financial aid package:*** $12,638 (excluding resources awarded to replace EFC). 8% of all full-time freshmen had no need and received non-need-based gift aid.

UNDERGRADUATE FINANCIAL AID (Fall 2007) 449 applied for aid; of those 96% were deemed to have need. 99% of undergraduates with need received aid; of those 2% had need fully met. ***Average percent of need met:*** 34% (excluding resources awarded to replace EFC). ***Average financial aid package:*** $12,399 (excluding resources awarded to replace EFC). 9% of all full-time undergraduates had no need and received non-need-based gift aid.

GIFT AID (NEED-BASED) ***Total amount:*** $5,111,334 (42% federal, 36% state, 19% institutional, 3% external sources). ***Receiving aid:*** Freshmen: 50% (89); all full-time undergraduates: 51% (295). ***Average award:*** Freshmen: $8698; Undergraduates: $8242. ***Scholarships, grants, and awards:*** state, college/university gift aid from institutional funds.

GIFT AID (NON-NEED-BASED) ***Total amount:*** $695,766 (84% institutional, 16% external sources). ***Average award:*** Freshmen: $10,935. Undergraduates: $11,630.

LOANS ***Student loans:*** $15,026,046 (88% need-based, 12% non-need-based). 79% of past graduating class borrowed through all loan programs. *Average indebtedness per student:* $24,045. ***Average need-based loan:*** Freshmen: $5700. Undergraduates: $6629. ***Parent loans:*** $2,086,129 (68% need-based, 32% non-need-based).

WORK-STUDY ***Federal work-study:*** Total amount: $145,290; jobs available.

CONTACT Albert Cama, Director of Financial Aid, DeVry University, 630 US Highway 1, North Brunswick, NJ 08902, 732-435-4880. *Fax:* 732-435-4867.

DeVry University
Charlotte, NC

Tuition & fees: $14,080 **Average undergraduate aid package: $12,613**

ABOUT THE INSTITUTION Proprietary, coed. ***Awards:*** associate, bachelor's, and master's degrees. 3 undergraduate majors. ***Total enrollment:*** 316. Undergraduates: 163. Freshmen: 26. Federal methodology is used as a basis for awarding need-based institutional aid.

UNDERGRADUATE EXPENSES for 2009–10 ***Application fee:*** $50. ***Tuition:*** full-time $14,080; part-time $550 per credit hour.

FRESHMAN FINANCIAL AID (Fall 2007) 5 applied for aid; of those 80% were deemed to have need. 75% of freshmen with need received aid. ***Average percent of need met:*** 37% (excluding resources awarded to replace EFC). ***Average financial aid package:*** $14,346 (excluding resources awarded to replace EFC). 9% of all full-time freshmen had no need and received non-need-based gift aid.

UNDERGRADUATE FINANCIAL AID (Fall 2007) 34 applied for aid; of those 97% were deemed to have need. 97% of undergraduates with need received aid; of those 3% had need fully met. ***Average percent of need met:*** 41% (excluding resources awarded to replace EFC). ***Average financial aid package:*** $12,613 (excluding resources awarded to replace EFC). 5% of all full-time undergraduates had no need and received non-need-based gift aid.

GIFT AID (NEED-BASED) ***Total amount:*** $383,750 (63% federal, 1% state, 34% institutional, 2% external sources). ***Receiving aid:*** Freshmen: 18% (2); all full-time undergraduates: 37% (15). ***Average award:*** Freshmen: $13,970; Undergraduates: $8335. ***Scholarships, grants, and awards:*** Federal Pell, FSEOG, state, private, college/university gift aid from institutional funds.

GIFT AID (NON-NEED-BASED) ***Total amount:*** $77,231 (76% institutional, 24% external sources). ***Average award:*** Freshmen: $10,370. Undergraduates: $7635.

LOANS ***Student loans:*** $1,983,499 (93% need-based, 7% non-need-based). ***Average need-based loan:*** Freshmen: $15,100. Undergraduates: $9286. ***Parent loans:*** $82,236 (59% need-based, 41% non-need-based). ***Programs:*** FFEL (Subsidized and Unsubsidized Stafford, PLUS), Perkins.

APPLYING FOR FINANCIAL AID ***Required financial aid form:*** FAFSA. ***Financial aid deadline:*** Continuous. ***Notification date:*** Continuous.

CONTACT Financial Aid Office, DeVry University, 4521 Sharon Road, Suite 145, Charlotte, NC 28211-3627, 704-362-2345.

DeVry University
Cleveland, OH

CONTACT Financial Aid Office, DeVry University, 200 Public Square, Suite 150, Cleveland, OH 44114-2301, 216-781-8000.

DeVry University
Columbus, OH

Tuition & fees: $14,080 **Average undergraduate aid package: $14,130**

ABOUT THE INSTITUTION Proprietary, coed. ***Awards:*** associate, bachelor's, and master's degrees. 9 undergraduate majors. ***Total enrollment:*** 2,776. Undergraduates: 2,526. Freshmen: 462. Federal methodology is used as a basis for awarding need-based institutional aid.

UNDERGRADUATE EXPENSES for 2009–10 ***Application fee:*** $50. ***Tuition:*** full-time $14,080; part-time $550 per credit hour.

FRESHMAN FINANCIAL AID (Fall 2007) 259 applied for aid; of those 96% were deemed to have need. 100% of freshmen with need received aid; of those 4% had need fully met. ***Average percent of need met:*** 47% (excluding resources awarded to replace EFC). ***Average financial aid package:*** $14,123 (excluding resources awarded to replace EFC). 5% of all full-time freshmen had no need and received non-need-based gift aid.

UNDERGRADUATE FINANCIAL AID (Fall 2007) 853 applied for aid; of those 97% were deemed to have need. 100% of undergraduates with need received aid; of those 4% had need fully met. ***Average percent of need met:*** 46% (excluding resources awarded to replace EFC). ***Average financial aid package:*** $14,130 (excluding resources awarded to replace EFC). 5% of all full-time undergraduates had no need and received non-need-based gift aid.

GIFT AID (NEED-BASED) ***Total amount:*** $10,748,220 (48% federal, 23% state, 25% institutional, 4% external sources). ***Receiving aid:*** Freshmen: 67% (218); all full-time undergraduates: 65% (631). ***Average award:*** Freshmen: $8161; Undergraduates: $7762. ***Scholarships, grants, and awards:*** Federal Pell, FSEOG, state, private, college/university gift aid from institutional funds.

GIFT AID (NON-NEED-BASED) ***Total amount:*** $1,006,246 (6% state, 81% institutional, 13% external sources). ***Receiving aid:*** Freshmen: 2% (5). Undergraduates: 1% (8). ***Average award:*** Freshmen: $9620. Undergraduates: $13,228. ***ROTC:*** Army cooperative.

LOANS ***Student loans:*** $32,756,085 (91% need-based, 9% non-need-based). 100% of past graduating class borrowed through all loan programs. *Average indebtedness per student:* $40,467. ***Average need-based loan:*** Freshmen: $6915. Undergraduates: $7868. ***Parent loans:*** $2,184,216 (72% need-based, 28% non-need-based). ***Programs:*** FFEL (Subsidized and Unsubsidized Stafford, PLUS), Perkins.

WORK-STUDY ***Federal work-study:*** Total amount: $755,288; jobs available.

APPLYING FOR FINANCIAL AID ***Required financial aid form:*** FAFSA. ***Financial aid deadline:*** Continuous. ***Notification date:*** Continuous.

CONTACT Cynthia Price, Director of Financial Aid, DeVry University, 1350 Alum Creek Drive, Columbus, OH 43209-2705, 614-253-7291. *Fax:* 614-252-4108.

DeVRY UNIVERSITY

Seven Hills, OH

ABOUT THE INSTITUTION Proprietary, coed. 2 undergraduate majors.

GIFT AID (NEED-BASED) ***Scholarships, grants, and awards:*** Federal Pell, FSEOG, state, private, college/university gift aid from institutional funds.

LOANS ***Programs:*** FFEL (Subsidized and Unsubsidized Stafford, PLUS), Perkins.

APPLYING FOR FINANCIAL AID ***Required financial aid form:*** FAFSA.

CONTACT Financial Aid Office, DeVry University, The Genesis Building, 6000 Lombardo Center, Suite 200, Seven Hills, OH 44131, 216-328-8754 or toll-free 866-453-3879.

DeVRY UNIVERSITY

Oklahoma City, OK

Tuition & fees: $14,080 **Average undergraduate aid package: $10,842**

ABOUT THE INSTITUTION Proprietary, coed. ***Awards:*** associate, bachelor's, and master's degrees. 5 undergraduate majors. ***Total enrollment:*** 81. Undergraduates: 59. Freshmen: 16. Federal methodology is used as a basis for awarding need-based institutional aid.

UNDERGRADUATE EXPENSES for 2009–10 ***Application fee:*** $50. ***Tuition:*** full-time $14,080; part-time $550 per credit hour.

FRESHMAN FINANCIAL AID (Fall 2007) 4 applied for aid; of those 100% were deemed to have need. 100% of freshmen with need received aid. ***Average percent of need met:*** 18% (excluding resources awarded to replace EFC). ***Average financial aid package:*** $3697 (excluding resources awarded to replace EFC).

UNDERGRADUATE FINANCIAL AID (Fall 2007) 16 applied for aid; of those 94% were deemed to have need. 100% of undergraduates with need received aid. ***Average percent of need met:*** 39% (excluding resources awarded to replace EFC). ***Average financial aid package:*** $10,842 (excluding resources awarded to replace EFC). 6% of all full-time undergraduates had no need and received non-need-based gift aid.

GIFT AID (NEED-BASED) ***Total amount:*** $240,485 (43% federal, 30% institutional, 27% external sources). ***Receiving aid:*** Freshmen: 17% (1); all full-time undergraduates: 50% (9). ***Average award:*** Freshmen: $5910; Undergraduates: $10,483. ***Scholarships, grants, and awards:*** Federal Pell, FSEOG, state, private, college/university gift aid from institutional funds.

GIFT AID (NON-NEED-BASED) ***Total amount:*** $29,070 (100% institutional). ***Average award:*** Undergraduates: $14,400.

LOANS ***Student loans:*** $690,294 (91% need-based, 9% non-need-based). ***Average need-based loan:*** Freshmen: $2220. Undergraduates: $4877. ***Parent loans:*** $41,050 (63% need-based, 37% non-need-based). ***Programs:*** FFEL (Subsidized and Unsubsidized Stafford, PLUS), Perkins.

APPLYING FOR FINANCIAL AID ***Required financial aid form:*** FAFSA. ***Financial aid deadline:*** Continuous. ***Notification date:*** Continuous.

CONTACT Financial Aid Office, DeVry University, Lakepointe Towers, 4013 NW Expressway Street, Suite 100, Oklahoma City, OK 73116, 405-767-9516.

DeVRY UNIVERSITY

Portland, OR

Tuition & fees: $14,080 **Average undergraduate aid package: $9247**

ABOUT THE INSTITUTION Proprietary, coed. ***Awards:*** associate, bachelor's, and master's degrees. 4 undergraduate majors. ***Total enrollment:*** 156. Undergraduates: 102. Freshmen: 12. Federal methodology is used as a basis for awarding need-based institutional aid.

UNDERGRADUATE EXPENSES for 2009–10 ***Application fee:*** $50. ***Tuition:*** full-time $14,080; part-time $550 per credit hour.

FRESHMAN FINANCIAL AID (Fall 2007) 3 applied for aid; of those 100% were deemed to have need. 100% of freshmen with need received aid. ***Average percent of need met:*** 25% (excluding resources awarded to replace EFC). ***Average financial aid package:*** $5536 (excluding resources awarded to replace EFC).

UNDERGRADUATE FINANCIAL AID (Fall 2007) 17 applied for aid; of those 100% were deemed to have need. 100% of undergraduates with need received aid. ***Average percent of need met:*** 29% (excluding resources awarded to replace EFC). ***Average financial aid package:*** $9247 (excluding resources awarded to replace EFC).

GIFT AID (NEED-BASED) ***Total amount:*** $161,578 (85% federal, 15% institutional). ***Receiving aid:*** Freshmen: 50% (2); all full-time undergraduates: 39% (9). ***Average award:*** Freshmen: $2430; Undergraduates: $4932. ***Scholarships, grants, and awards:*** Federal Pell, FSEOG, state, private, college/university gift aid from institutional funds.

LOANS ***Student loans:*** $1,045,045 (94% need-based, 6% non-need-based). ***Average need-based loan:*** Freshmen: $3916. Undergraduates: $6636. ***Parent loans:*** $53,305 (47% need-based, 53% non-need-based). ***Programs:*** FFEL (Subsidized and Unsubsidized Stafford, PLUS), Perkins.

APPLYING FOR FINANCIAL AID ***Required financial aid form:*** FAFSA. ***Financial aid deadline:*** Continuous. ***Notification date:*** Continuous.

CONTACT Financial Aid Office, DeVry University, Peterkort Center II, 9755 SW Barnes Road, Suite 150, Portland, OR 97225-6651, 503-296-7468.

DeVRY UNIVERSITY

Chesterbrook, PA

CONTACT Financial Aid Office, DeVry University, 701 Lee Road, Suite 103, Chesterbrook, PA 19087-5612, 610-889-9980.

DeVRY UNIVERSITY

Fort Washington, PA

Tuition & fees: $14,720 **Average undergraduate aid package: $12,114**

ABOUT THE INSTITUTION Proprietary, coed. ***Awards:*** associate, bachelor's, and master's degrees. 10 undergraduate majors. ***Total enrollment:*** 1,049. Undergraduates: 893. Freshmen: 198. Federal methodology is used as a basis for awarding need-based institutional aid.

UNDERGRADUATE EXPENSES for 2009–10 ***Application fee:*** $50. ***Tuition:*** full-time $14,720; part-time $575 per credit hour.

FRESHMAN FINANCIAL AID (Fall 2007) 79 applied for aid; of those 96% were deemed to have need. 97% of freshmen with need received aid. ***Average percent of need met:*** 34% (excluding resources awarded to replace EFC). ***Average financial aid package:*** $12,652 (excluding resources awarded to replace EFC). 4% of all full-time freshmen had no need and received non-need-based gift aid.

UNDERGRADUATE FINANCIAL AID (Fall 2007) 254 applied for aid; of those 96% were deemed to have need. 99% of undergraduates with need received aid; of those 1% had need fully met. ***Average percent of need met:*** 34% (excluding resources awarded to replace EFC). ***Average financial aid package:*** $12,114 (excluding resources awarded to replace EFC). 8% of all full-time undergraduates had no need and received non-need-based gift aid.

GIFT AID (NEED-BASED) ***Total amount:*** $3,023,403 (47% federal, 28% state, 21% institutional, 4% external sources). ***Receiving aid:*** Freshmen: 62% (58); all full-time undergraduates: 54% (160). ***Average award:*** Freshmen: $7020; Undergraduates: $6835. ***Scholarships, grants, and awards:*** Federal Pell, FSEOG, state, private, college/university gift aid from institutional funds.

GIFT AID (NON-NEED-BASED) ***Total amount:*** $310,795 (71% institutional, 29% external sources). ***Receiving aid:*** Undergraduates: 1. ***Average award:*** Undergraduates: $13,057.

LOANS ***Student loans:*** $13,405,409 (90% need-based, 10% non-need-based). 50% of past graduating class borrowed through all loan programs. *Average indebtedness per student:* $15,638. ***Average need-based loan:*** Freshmen: $5757. Undergraduates: $6836. ***Parent loans:*** $691,875 (75% need-based, 25% non-need-based). ***Programs:*** FFEL (Subsidized and Unsubsidized Stafford, PLUS), Perkins.

WORK-STUDY ***Federal work-study:*** Total amount: $308,552; jobs available.

APPLYING FOR FINANCIAL AID ***Required financial aid form:*** FAFSA. ***Financial aid deadline:*** Continuous. ***Notification date:*** Continuous.

CONTACT Financial Aid Office, DeVry University, 1140 Virginia Drive, Fort Washington, PA 19034, 215-591-5700.

DEVRY UNIVERSITY
Pittsburgh, PA

CONTACT Financial Aid Office, DeVry University, FreeMarkets Center, 210 Sixth Avenue, Suite 200, Pittsburgh, PA 15222-9123, 412-642-9072 or toll-free 866-77DEVRY.

DEVRY UNIVERSITY
Memphis, TN

Tuition & fees: $14,080 **Average undergraduate aid package: $11,341**

ABOUT THE INSTITUTION Proprietary, coed. ***Awards:*** associate, bachelor's, and master's degrees. 3 undergraduate majors. ***Total enrollment:*** 135. Undergraduates: 68. Freshmen: 9. Federal methodology is used as a basis for awarding need-based institutional aid.

UNDERGRADUATE EXPENSES for 2009–10 ***Application fee:*** $50. ***Tuition:*** full-time $14,080; part-time $550 per credit hour.

FRESHMAN FINANCIAL AID (Fall 2007) 2 applied for aid; of those 100% were deemed to have need. 100% of freshmen with need received aid; of those 50% had need fully met. ***Average percent of need met:*** 68% (excluding resources awarded to replace EFC). ***Average financial aid package:*** $7055 (excluding resources awarded to replace EFC).

UNDERGRADUATE FINANCIAL AID (Fall 2007) 6 applied for aid; of those 100% were deemed to have need. 100% of undergraduates with need received aid; of those 17% had need fully met. ***Average percent of need met:*** 42% (excluding resources awarded to replace EFC). ***Average financial aid package:*** $11,341 (excluding resources awarded to replace EFC).

GIFT AID (NEED-BASED) ***Total amount:*** $150,279 (87% federal, 10% institutional, 3% external sources). ***Receiving aid:*** Freshmen: 33% (1); all full-time undergraduates: 62% (5). ***Average award:*** Freshmen: $2400; Undergraduates: $4530. ***Scholarships, grants, and awards:*** Federal Pell, FSEOG, state, private, college/university gift aid from institutional funds.

LOANS ***Student loans:*** $709,657 (88% need-based, 12% non-need-based). ***Average need-based loan:*** Freshmen: $5855. Undergraduates: $7566. ***Parent loans:*** $16,000 (100% non-need-based). ***Programs:*** FFEL (Subsidized and Unsubsidized Stafford, PLUS), Perkins.

APPLYING FOR FINANCIAL AID ***Required financial aid form:*** FAFSA. ***Financial aid deadline:*** Continuous. ***Notification date:*** Continuous.

CONTACT Financial Aid Office, DeVry University, PennMarc Centre, 6401 Poplar Avenue, Suite 600, Memphis, TN 38119, 901-537-2560 or toll-free 888-563-3879.

DEVRY UNIVERSITY
Houston, TX

Tuition & fees: $14,080 **Average undergraduate aid package: $12,662**

ABOUT THE INSTITUTION Proprietary, coed. ***Awards:*** associate, bachelor's, and master's degrees. 9 undergraduate majors. ***Total enrollment:*** 1,283. Undergraduates: 1,096. Freshmen: 196. Federal methodology is used as a basis for awarding need-based institutional aid.

UNDERGRADUATE EXPENSES for 2009–10 ***Application fee:*** $50. ***Tuition:*** full-time $14,080; part-time $550 per credit hour.

FRESHMAN FINANCIAL AID (Fall 2007) 105 applied for aid; of those 95% were deemed to have need. 100% of freshmen with need received aid; of those 3% had need fully met. ***Average percent of need met:*** 42% (excluding resources awarded to replace EFC). ***Average financial aid package:*** $12,942 (excluding resources awarded to replace EFC). 7% of all full-time freshmen had no need and received non-need-based gift aid.

UNDERGRADUATE FINANCIAL AID (Fall 2007) 306 applied for aid; of those 98% were deemed to have need. 100% of undergraduates with need received aid; of those 1% had need fully met. ***Average percent of need met:*** 39% (excluding resources awarded to replace EFC). ***Average financial aid package:*** $12,662 (excluding resources awarded to replace EFC). 6% of all full-time undergraduates had no need and received non-need-based gift aid.

GIFT AID (NEED-BASED) ***Total amount:*** $3,214,359 (69% federal, 26% institutional, 5% external sources). ***Receiving aid:*** Freshmen: 59% (81); all full-time undergraduates: 56% (203). ***Average award:*** Freshmen: $5431; Undergraduates: $5374. ***Scholarships, grants, and awards:*** Federal Pell, FSEOG, state, private, college/university gift aid from institutional funds.

GIFT AID (NON-NEED-BASED) ***Total amount:*** $314,149 (76% institutional, 24% external sources). ***Receiving aid:*** Freshmen: 1% (1). Undergraduates: 1. ***Average award:*** Freshmen: $13,352. Undergraduates: $14,939.

LOANS ***Student loans:*** $13,982,259 (94% need-based, 6% non-need-based). 100% of past graduating class borrowed through all loan programs. *Average indebtedness per student:* $30,068. ***Average need-based loan:*** Freshmen: $6882. Undergraduates: $7855. ***Parent loans:*** $2,647,963 (29% need-based, 71% non-need-based). ***Programs:*** FFEL (Subsidized and Unsubsidized Stafford, PLUS), Perkins.

WORK-STUDY ***Federal work-study:*** Total amount: $892,734; jobs available.

APPLYING FOR FINANCIAL AID ***Required financial aid form:*** FAFSA. ***Financial aid deadline:*** Continuous. ***Notification date:*** Continuous.

CONTACT Financial Aid Office, DeVry University, 11125 Equity Drive, Houston, TX 77041, 713-850-0888 or toll-free 866-703-3879.

DEVRY UNIVERSITY
Irving, TX

Tuition & fees: $14,080 **Average undergraduate aid package: $12,581**

ABOUT THE INSTITUTION Proprietary, coed. ***Awards:*** associate, bachelor's, and master's degrees. 10 undergraduate majors. ***Total enrollment:*** 1,806. Undergraduates: 1,584. Freshmen: 301. Federal methodology is used as a basis for awarding need-based institutional aid.

UNDERGRADUATE EXPENSES for 2009–10 ***Application fee:*** $50. ***Tuition:*** full-time $14,080; part-time $550 per credit hour.

FRESHMAN FINANCIAL AID (Fall 2007) 130 applied for aid; of those 97% were deemed to have need. 97% of freshmen with need received aid; of those 2% had need fully met. ***Average percent of need met:*** 39% (excluding resources awarded to replace EFC). ***Average financial aid package:*** $12,802 (excluding resources awarded to replace EFC). 6% of all full-time freshmen had no need and received non-need-based gift aid.

UNDERGRADUATE FINANCIAL AID (Fall 2007) 354 applied for aid; of those 97% were deemed to have need. 98% of undergraduates with need received aid; of those 3% had need fully met. ***Average percent of need met:*** 40% (excluding resources awarded to replace EFC). ***Average financial aid package:***

$12,581 (excluding resources awarded to replace EFC). 8% of all full-time undergraduates had no need and received non-need-based gift aid.

GIFT AID (NEED-BASED) ***Total amount:*** $4,547,155 (66% federal, 22% institutional, 12% external sources). ***Receiving aid:*** Freshmen: 53% (92); all full-time undergraduates: 45% (193). ***Average award:*** Freshmen: $5371; Undergraduates: $5995. ***Scholarships, grants, and awards:*** Federal Pell, FSEOG, state, private, college/university gift aid from institutional funds.

GIFT AID (NON-NEED-BASED) ***Total amount:*** $776,719 (45% institutional, 55% external sources). ***Receiving aid:*** Freshmen: 1% (1). Undergraduates: 1. ***Average award:*** Freshmen: $11,884. Undergraduates: $17,309.

LOANS ***Student loans:*** $24,579,148 (91% need-based, 9% non-need-based). 60% of past graduating class borrowed through all loan programs. *Average indebtedness per student:* $31,895. ***Average need-based loan:*** Freshmen: $7845. Undergraduates: $8675. ***Parent loans:*** $1,650,925 (70% need-based, 30% non-need-based). ***Programs:*** FFEL (Subsidized and Unsubsidized Stafford, PLUS), Perkins.

WORK-STUDY ***Federal work-study:*** Total amount: $625,635; jobs available.

APPLYING FOR FINANCIAL AID ***Required financial aid form:*** FAFSA. ***Financial aid deadline:*** Continuous. ***Notification date:*** Continuous.

CONTACT Tommy Sims, Financial Aid Officer, DeVry University, 4800 Regent Boulevard, Irving, TX 75063-2440, 972-929-6777.

DeVRY UNIVERSITY
Richardson, TX

CONTACT Financial Aid Office, DeVry University, Richardson Center, 2201 N. Central Expressway, Richardson, TX 75080, 972-792-7450.

DeVRY UNIVERSITY
Sandy, UT

Tuition & fees: $14,080 **Average undergraduate aid package: $11,508**

ABOUT THE INSTITUTION Proprietary, coed. ***Awards:*** associate, bachelor's, and master's degrees. 5 undergraduate majors. ***Total enrollment:*** 93. Undergraduates: 52. Freshmen: 8. Federal methodology is used as a basis for awarding need-based institutional aid.

UNDERGRADUATE EXPENSES for 2009–10 ***Application fee:*** $50. ***Tuition:*** full-time $14,080; part-time $550 per credit.

FRESHMAN FINANCIAL AID (Fall 2007) 1 applied for aid; of those 100% were deemed to have need. 100% of freshmen with need received aid. ***Average percent of need met:*** 19% (excluding resources awarded to replace EFC). ***Average financial aid package:*** $7475 (excluding resources awarded to replace EFC).

UNDERGRADUATE FINANCIAL AID (Fall 2007) 9 applied for aid; of those 89% were deemed to have need. 100% of undergraduates with need received aid; of those 12% had need fully met. ***Average percent of need met:*** 34% (excluding resources awarded to replace EFC). ***Average financial aid package:*** $11,508 (excluding resources awarded to replace EFC). 8% of all full-time undergraduates had no need and received non-need-based gift aid.

GIFT AID (NEED-BASED) ***Total amount:*** $129,131 (29% federal, 71% institutional). ***Receiving aid:*** All full-time undergraduates: 31% (4). ***Average award:*** Undergraduates: $4798. ***Scholarships, grants, and awards:*** Federal Pell, FSEOG, state, private, college/university gift aid from institutional funds.

GIFT AID (NON-NEED-BASED) ***Total amount:*** $85,501 (72% institutional, 28% external sources). ***Average award:*** Undergraduates: $6900.

LOANS ***Student loans:*** $560,932 (89% need-based, 11% non-need-based). ***Average need-based loan:*** Freshmen: $7475. Undergraduates: $9109. ***Parent loans:*** $6600 (24% need-based, 76% non-need-based). ***Programs:*** FFEL (Subsidized and Unsubsidized Stafford, PLUS), Perkins.

APPLYING FOR FINANCIAL AID ***Required financial aid form:*** FAFSA. ***Financial aid deadline:*** Continuous. ***Notification date:*** Continuous.

CONTACT Financial Aid Office, DeVry University, 9350 S. 150 E., Suite 420, Sandy, UT 84070, 801-565-5110.

DeVRY UNIVERSITY
Arlington, VA

Tuition & fees: $14,080 **Average undergraduate aid package: $11,581**

ABOUT THE INSTITUTION Proprietary, coed. ***Awards:*** associate, bachelor's, and master's degrees. 8 undergraduate majors. ***Total enrollment:*** 707. Undergraduates: 593. Freshmen: 155. Federal methodology is used as a basis for awarding need-based institutional aid.

UNDERGRADUATE EXPENSES for 2009–10 ***Application fee:*** $50. ***Tuition:*** full-time $14,080; part-time $550 per credit hour.

FRESHMAN FINANCIAL AID (Fall 2007) 76 applied for aid; of those 91% were deemed to have need. 100% of freshmen with need received aid; of those 7% had need fully met. ***Average percent of need met:*** 33% (excluding resources awarded to replace EFC). ***Average financial aid package:*** $9908 (excluding resources awarded to replace EFC). 10% of all full-time freshmen had no need and received non-need-based gift aid.

UNDERGRADUATE FINANCIAL AID (Fall 2007) 175 applied for aid; of those 94% were deemed to have need. 100% of undergraduates with need received aid; of those 5% had need fully met. ***Average percent of need met:*** 38% (excluding resources awarded to replace EFC). ***Average financial aid package:*** $11,581 (excluding resources awarded to replace EFC). 10% of all full-time undergraduates had no need and received non-need-based gift aid.

GIFT AID (NEED-BASED) ***Total amount:*** $1,706,762 (52% federal, 1% state, 39% institutional, 8% external sources). ***Receiving aid:*** Freshmen: 46% (46); all full-time undergraduates: 45% (98). ***Average award:*** Freshmen: $5391; Undergraduates: $5610. ***Scholarships, grants, and awards:*** Federal Pell, FSEOG, state, private, college/university gift aid from institutional funds.

GIFT AID (NON-NEED-BASED) ***Total amount:*** $475,173 (73% institutional, 27% external sources). ***Receiving aid:*** Freshmen: 2% (2). Undergraduates: 1% (3). ***Average award:*** Freshmen: $18,085. Undergraduates: $18,172.

LOANS ***Student loans:*** $8,532,488 (85% need-based, 15% non-need-based). 100% of past graduating class borrowed through all loan programs. *Average indebtedness per student:* $12,479. ***Average need-based loan:*** Freshmen: $6508. Undergraduates: $7979. ***Parent loans:*** $1,225,121 (68% need-based, 32% non-need-based). ***Programs:*** FFEL (Subsidized and Unsubsidized Stafford, PLUS), Perkins.

WORK-STUDY ***Federal work-study:*** Total amount: $184,028; jobs available.

APPLYING FOR FINANCIAL AID ***Required financial aid form:*** FAFSA. ***Financial aid deadline:*** Continuous. ***Notification date:*** Continuous.

CONTACT Roberta McDevitt, Director of Student Finance, DeVry University, 2341 Jefferson Davis Highway, Arlington, VA 22202, 866-338-7932. *Fax:* 703-414-4040.

DeVRY UNIVERSITY
McLean, VA

CONTACT Financial Aid Office, DeVry University, 1751 Pinnacle Drive, Suite 250, McLean, VA 22102-3832, 703-556-9669.

DeVRY UNIVERSITY
Bellevue, WA

CONTACT Financial Aid Office, DeVry University, 500 108th Avenue NE, Suite 320, Bellevue, WA 98004-5519, 425-455-2242.

DeVRY UNIVERSITY
Federal Way, WA

Tuition & fees: $14,720 **Average undergraduate aid package: $10,833**

ABOUT THE INSTITUTION Proprietary, coed. ***Awards:*** associate, bachelor's, and master's degrees. 10 undergraduate majors. ***Total enrollment:*** 761. Undergraduates: 661. Freshmen: 130. Federal methodology is used as a basis for awarding need-based institutional aid.

UNDERGRADUATE EXPENSES for 2009–10 ***Application fee:*** $50. ***Tuition:*** full-time $14,720; part-time $575 per credit hour.

FRESHMAN FINANCIAL AID (Fall 2007) 76 applied for aid; of those 99% were deemed to have need. 99% of freshmen with need received aid; of those 1% had need fully met. ***Average percent of need met:*** 28% (excluding resources awarded to replace EFC). ***Average financial aid package:*** $8750 (excluding resources awarded to replace EFC).

UNDERGRADUATE FINANCIAL AID (Fall 2007) 259 applied for aid; of those 97% were deemed to have need. 100% of undergraduates with need received aid; of those 3% had need fully met. ***Average percent of need met:*** 34%

(excluding resources awarded to replace EFC). ***Average financial aid package:*** $10,833 (excluding resources awarded to replace EFC). 5% of all full-time undergraduates had no need and received non-need-based gift aid.

GIFT AID (NEED-BASED) ***Total amount:*** $2,093,602 (44% federal, 42% institutional, 14% external sources). ***Receiving aid:*** Freshmen: 66% (54); all full-time undergraduates: 59% (164). ***Average award:*** Freshmen: $4916; Undergraduates: $5975. ***Scholarships, grants, and awards:*** Federal Pell, FSEOG, state, private, college/university gift aid from institutional funds.

GIFT AID (NON-NEED-BASED) ***Total amount:*** $534,337 (71% institutional, 29% external sources). ***Receiving aid:*** Freshmen: 1% (1). Undergraduates: 1. ***Average award:*** Undergraduates: $20,202.

LOANS ***Student loans:*** $10,121,211 (88% need-based, 12% non-need-based). 88% of past graduating class borrowed through all loan programs. *Average indebtedness per student:* $50,600. ***Average need-based loan:*** Freshmen: $5061. Undergraduates: $6622. ***Parent loans:*** $1,013,854 (65% need-based, 35% non-need-based). ***Programs:*** FFEL (Subsidized and Unsubsidized Stafford, PLUS), Perkins.

WORK-STUDY ***Federal work-study:*** Total amount: $184,018; jobs available.

APPLYING FOR FINANCIAL AID ***Required financial aid form:*** FAFSA. ***Financial aid deadline:*** Continuous. ***Notification date:*** Continuous.

CONTACT Diane Rooney, Assistant Director of Student Finance, DeVry University, 3600 South 344th Way, Federal Way, WA 98001, 253-943-2800. *Fax:* 253-943-5503.

DeVRY UNIVERSITY

Milwaukee, WI

Tuition & fees: $14,080 **Average undergraduate aid package: $11,858**

ABOUT THE INSTITUTION Proprietary, coed. ***Awards:*** associate, bachelor's, and master's degrees. 3 undergraduate majors. ***Total enrollment:*** 215. Undergraduates: 119. Freshmen: 14. Federal methodology is used as a basis for awarding need-based institutional aid.

UNDERGRADUATE EXPENSES for 2009–10 ***Application fee:*** $50. ***Tuition:*** full-time $14,080; part-time $550 per credit hour.

FRESHMAN FINANCIAL AID (Fall 2007) 2 applied for aid; of those 100% were deemed to have need. 100% of freshmen with need received aid. ***Average percent of need met:*** 29% (excluding resources awarded to replace EFC). ***Average financial aid package:*** $8580 (excluding resources awarded to replace EFC).

UNDERGRADUATE FINANCIAL AID (Fall 2007) 12 applied for aid; of those 100% were deemed to have need. 100% of undergraduates with need received aid. ***Average percent of need met:*** 35% (excluding resources awarded to replace EFC). ***Average financial aid package:*** $11,858 (excluding resources awarded to replace EFC).

GIFT AID (NEED-BASED) ***Total amount:*** $378,968 (86% federal, 1% state, 10% institutional, 3% external sources). ***Receiving aid:*** Freshmen: 17% (1); all full-time undergraduates: 50% (8). ***Average award:*** Freshmen: $5910; Undergraduates: $5981. ***Scholarships, grants, and awards:*** Federal Pell, FSEOG, state, private, college/university gift aid from institutional funds.

GIFT AID (NON-NEED-BASED) ***Total amount:*** $39,730 (100% institutional).

LOANS ***Student loans:*** $1,743,117 (95% need-based, 5% non-need-based). ***Average need-based loan:*** Freshmen: $5625. Undergraduates: $7870. ***Parent loans:*** $16,000 (62% need-based, 38% non-need-based). ***Programs:*** FFEL (Subsidized and Unsubsidized Stafford, PLUS), Perkins.

APPLYING FOR FINANCIAL AID ***Required financial aid form:*** FAFSA. ***Financial aid deadline:*** Continuous. ***Notification date:*** Continuous.

CONTACT Financial Aid Office, DeVry University, 411 East Wisconsin Avenue, Suite 300, Milwaukee, WI 53202-4107, 414-278-7677.

DeVRY UNIVERSITY

Waukesha, WI

CONTACT Financial Aid Office, DeVry University, 20935 Swenson Drive, Suite 150, Waukesha, WI 53186-4047, 262-798-9889.

DeVRY UNIVERSITY ONLINE

Oakbrook Terrace, IL

ABOUT THE INSTITUTION Proprietary, coed. ***Awards:*** associate, bachelor's, and master's degrees. 8 undergraduate majors. ***Total enrollment:*** 12,276. Undergraduates: 8,729. Freshmen: 1,419.

GIFT AID (NEED-BASED) ***Scholarships, grants, and awards:*** Federal Pell, FSEOG, state, private, college/university gift aid from institutional funds.

LOANS ***Programs:*** FFEL (Subsidized and Unsubsidized Stafford, PLUS), Perkins.

APPLYING FOR FINANCIAL AID ***Required financial aid form:*** FAFSA.

CONTACT Financial Aid Office, DeVry University Online, One Tower Lane, Suite 1000, Oakbrook Terrace, IL 60181, 630-574-1960 or toll-free 866-338-7934.

DeVRY UNIVERSITY SOUTHFIELD CENTER

Southfield, MI

Tuition & fees: $14,080 **Average undergraduate aid package: $8705**

ABOUT THE INSTITUTION Proprietary, coed. ***Awards:*** associate, bachelor's, and master's degrees. 4 undergraduate majors. ***Total enrollment:*** 41. Undergraduates: 41. Freshmen: 4. Federal methodology is used as a basis for awarding need-based institutional aid.

UNDERGRADUATE EXPENSES for 2009–10 ***Application fee:*** $50. ***Tuition:*** full-time $14,080; part-time $550 per credit hour.

UNDERGRADUATE FINANCIAL AID (Fall 2007) 2 applied for aid; of those 100% were deemed to have need. 100% of undergraduates with need received aid. ***Average percent of need met:*** 38% (excluding resources awarded to replace EFC). ***Average financial aid package:*** $8705 (excluding resources awarded to replace EFC).

GIFT AID (NEED-BASED) ***Total amount:*** $9535 (100% federal). ***Receiving aid:*** All full-time undergraduates: 50% (1). ***Average award:*** Undergraduates: $5910. ***Scholarships, grants, and awards:*** Federal Pell, FSEOG, state, private, college/university gift aid from institutional funds.

LOANS ***Student loans:*** $85,452 (97% need-based, 3% non-need-based). ***Average need-based loan:*** Undergraduates: $5750. ***Parent loans:*** $12,330 (26% need-based, 74% non-need-based). ***Programs:*** FFEL (Subsidized and Unsubsidized Stafford, PLUS), Perkins.

APPLYING FOR FINANCIAL AID ***Required financial aid form:*** FAFSA. ***Financial aid deadline:*** Continuous. ***Notification date:*** Continuous.

CONTACT Mr. Stephen Haworth, Regulatory Compliance Specialist, DeVry University Southfield Center, 26999 Central Park Boulevard, Suite 125, Southfield, MI 48076-4174, 630-706-3172. *Fax:* 630-574-1991. *E-mail:* shaworth@devry.com.

DICKINSON COLLEGE

Carlisle, PA

Tuition & fees: $38,234 **Average undergraduate aid package: $31,165**

ABOUT THE INSTITUTION Independent, coed. ***Awards:*** bachelor's degrees. 41 undergraduate majors. ***Total enrollment:*** 2,388. Undergraduates: 2,388. Freshmen: 613. Both federal and institutional methodology are used as a basis for awarding need-based institutional aid.

UNDERGRADUATE EXPENSES for 2008–09 ***Application fee:*** $65. ***One-time required fee:*** $25. ***Comprehensive fee:*** $47,834 includes full-time tuition ($37,900), mandatory fees ($334), and room and board ($9600). ***College room only:*** $4950. Room and board charges vary according to housing facility. ***Part-time tuition:*** $4740 per course. ***Part-time fees:*** $42 per course. ***Payment plan:*** Installment.

FRESHMAN FINANCIAL AID (Fall 2008, est.) 392 applied for aid; of those 78% were deemed to have need. 99% of freshmen with need received aid; of those 87% had need fully met. ***Average percent of need met:*** 98% (excluding resources awarded to replace EFC). ***Average financial aid package:*** $31,343 (excluding resources awarded to replace EFC). 9% of all full-time freshmen had no need and received non-need-based gift aid.

UNDERGRADUATE FINANCIAL AID (Fall 2008, est.) 1,323 applied for aid; of those 85% were deemed to have need. 99% of undergraduates with need received aid; of those 72% had need fully met. ***Average percent of need met:*** 96% (excluding resources awarded to replace EFC). ***Average financial aid***

package: $31,165 (excluding resources awarded to replace EFC). 9% of all full-time undergraduates had no need and received non-need-based gift aid.

GIFT AID (NEED-BASED) ***Total amount:*** $27,330,232 (5% federal, 2% state, 91% institutional, 2% external sources). ***Receiving aid:*** Freshmen: 48% (293); all full-time undergraduates: 45% (1,071). ***Average award:*** Freshmen: $26,387; Undergraduates: $25,856. ***Scholarships, grants, and awards:*** Federal Pell, FSEOG, state, private, college/university gift aid from institutional funds.

GIFT AID (NON-NEED-BASED) ***Total amount:*** $4,257,729 (23% federal, 66% institutional, 11% external sources). ***Receiving aid:*** Freshmen: 7% (45). Undergraduates: 4% (99). ***Average award:*** Freshmen: $12,965. Undergraduates: $11,868. ***Scholarships, grants, and awards by category:*** *Academic interests/achievement:* 433 awards ($6,232,904 total): general academic interests/achievements, military science. *Special achievements/activities:* general special achievements/activities, leadership. *Special characteristics:* 23 awards ($463,830 total): children and siblings of alumni, children of faculty/staff, international students. ***Tuition waivers:*** Full or partial for employees or children of employees. ***ROTC:*** Army.

LOANS ***Student loans:*** $8,259,811 (62% need-based, 38% non-need-based). 53% of past graduating class borrowed through all loan programs. *Average indebtedness per student:* $21,924. ***Average need-based loan:*** Freshmen: $3887. Undergraduates: $4687. ***Parent loans:*** $4,799,011 (15% need-based, 85% non-need-based). ***Programs:*** FFEL (Subsidized and Unsubsidized Stafford, PLUS), Perkins, college/university.

WORK-STUDY ***Federal work-study:*** Total amount: $1,640,793; 796 jobs averaging $2064. ***State or other work-study/employment:*** Total amount: $577,484 (61% need-based, 39% non-need-based). 179 part-time jobs averaging $3226.

APPLYING FOR FINANCIAL AID ***Required financial aid forms:*** FAFSA, CSS Financial Aid PROFILE, state aid form, noncustodial (divorced/separated) parent's statement, business/farm supplement. ***Financial aid deadline:*** 2/1 (priority: 11/15). ***Notification date:*** 3/31. Students must reply by 5/1 or within 2 weeks of notification.

CONTACT Judith B. Carter, Director of Financial Aid, Dickinson College, PO Box 1773, Carlisle, PA 17013-2896, 717-245-1308 or toll-free 800-644-1773. *Fax:* 717-245-1972. *E-mail:* finaid@dickinson.edu.

DICKINSON STATE UNIVERSITY

Dickinson, ND

CONTACT Ms. Sandy Klein, Director of Financial Aid, Dickinson State University, 291 Campus Drive, Dickinson, ND 58601-4896, 701-483-2371 or toll-free 800-279-4295. *Fax:* 701-483-2720. *E-mail:* sandy.klein@dsu.nodak.edu.

DIGIPEN INSTITUTE OF TECHNOLOGY

Redmond, WA

CONTACT Financial Aid Office, DigiPen Institute of Technology, 5001 150th Avenue, NE, Redmond, WA 98052, 425-558-0299.

DILLARD UNIVERSITY

New Orleans, LA

Tuition & fees: $13,000 **Average undergraduate aid package: $15,241**

ABOUT THE INSTITUTION Independent interdenominational, coed. ***Awards:*** bachelor's degrees. 45 undergraduate majors. ***Total enrollment:*** 851. Undergraduates: 851. Freshmen: 173. Federal methodology is used as a basis for awarding need-based institutional aid.

UNDERGRADUATE EXPENSES for 2009–10 ***Application fee:*** $20. ***Tuition:*** full-time $13,000.

FRESHMAN FINANCIAL AID (Fall 2008, est.) 158 applied for aid; of those 95% were deemed to have need. 100% of freshmen with need received aid; of those 85% had need fully met. ***Average percent of need met:*** 80% (excluding resources awarded to replace EFC). ***Average financial aid package:*** $18,795 (excluding resources awarded to replace EFC). 5% of all full-time freshmen had no need and received non-need-based gift aid.

UNDERGRADUATE FINANCIAL AID (Fall 2008, est.) 791 applied for aid; of those 96% were deemed to have need. 100% of undergraduates with need received aid; of those 82% had need fully met. ***Average percent of need met:*** 78% (excluding resources awarded to replace EFC). ***Average financial aid package:*** $15,241 (excluding resources awarded to replace EFC). 2% of all full-time undergraduates had no need and received non-need-based gift aid.

GIFT AID (NEED-BASED) ***Total amount:*** $6,143,832 (44% federal, 5% state, 28% institutional, 23% external sources). ***Receiving aid:*** Freshmen: 85% (147); all full-time undergraduates: 52% (439). ***Average award:*** Freshmen: $4570; Undergraduates: $4426. ***Scholarships, grants, and awards:*** Federal Pell, FSEOG, state, private, college/university gift aid from institutional funds, United Negro College Fund.

GIFT AID (NON-NEED-BASED) ***Total amount:*** $238,682 (100% state). ***Receiving aid:*** Freshmen: 9% (16). Undergraduates: 9% (76). ***Scholarships, grants, and awards by category:*** *Academic interests/achievement:* 461 awards ($1,492,819 total): general academic interests/achievements. *Creative arts/performance:* 21 awards ($38,500 total): art/fine arts, music, theater/drama. *Special characteristics:* 9 awards ($85,179 total): children of faculty/staff, religious affiliation. ***ROTC:*** Army cooperative, Air Force cooperative.

LOANS ***Student loans:*** $9,844,786 (62% need-based, 38% non-need-based). 90% of past graduating class borrowed through all loan programs. *Average indebtedness per student:* $26,000. ***Average need-based loan:*** Freshmen: $3177. Undergraduates: $3980. ***Parent loans:*** $738,878 (100% non-need-based). ***Programs:*** FFEL (Subsidized and Unsubsidized Stafford, PLUS), Perkins, Federal Nursing, alternative loans.

WORK-STUDY ***Federal work-study:*** Total amount: $367,276; 209 jobs averaging $1704. ***State or other work-study/employment:*** Part-time jobs available.

ATHLETIC AWARDS Total amount: $345,364 (100% need-based).

APPLYING FOR FINANCIAL AID ***Required financial aid forms:*** FAFSA, institution's own form. ***Financial aid deadline (priority):*** 5/1. ***Notification date:*** Continuous. Students must reply within 2 weeks of notification.

CONTACT Mrs. Shannon Neal, Associate Director, Dillard University, 2601 Gentilly Boulevard, New Orleans, LA 70122-3097, 504-816-4677 or toll-free 800-716-8353 (in-state), 800-216-6637 (out-of-state). *Fax:* 504-816-5456. *E-mail:* sneal@dillard.edu.

DIXIE STATE COLLEGE OF UTAH

St. George, UT

Tuition & fees (UT res): $2893 **Average undergraduate aid package: $6046**

ABOUT THE INSTITUTION State-supported, coed. ***Awards:*** associate and bachelor's degrees. 25 undergraduate majors. ***Total enrollment:*** 6,086. Undergraduates: 6,086. Freshmen: 1,431. Federal methodology is used as a basis for awarding need-based institutional aid.

UNDERGRADUATE EXPENSES for 2008–09 ***Application fee:*** $35. ***Tuition, state resident:*** full-time $2442; part-time $102 per credit. ***Tuition, nonresident:*** full-time $9612; part-time $401 per credit. ***Required fees:*** full-time $451. Part-time tuition and fees vary according to course load. ***College room and board:*** $3498; ***Room only:*** $1500. Room and board charges vary according to board plan and housing facility. ***Payment plan:*** Installment.

FRESHMAN FINANCIAL AID (Fall 2007) 552 applied for aid; of those 76% were deemed to have need. 97% of freshmen with need received aid; of those 11% had need fully met. ***Average percent of need met:*** 44% (excluding resources awarded to replace EFC). ***Average financial aid package:*** $5175 (excluding resources awarded to replace EFC). 46% of all full-time freshmen had no need and received non-need-based gift aid.

UNDERGRADUATE FINANCIAL AID (Fall 2007) 1,753 applied for aid; of those 88% were deemed to have need. 97% of undergraduates with need received aid; of those 8% had need fully met. ***Average percent of need met:*** 46% (excluding resources awarded to replace EFC). ***Average financial aid package:*** $6046 (excluding resources awarded to replace EFC). 33% of all full-time undergraduates had no need and received non-need-based gift aid.

GIFT AID (NEED-BASED) ***Total amount:*** $6,998,876 (66% federal, 3% state, 24% institutional, 7% external sources). ***Receiving aid:*** Freshmen: 41% (406); all full-time undergraduates: 49% (1,486). ***Average award:*** Freshmen: $3994; Undergraduates: $4255. ***Scholarships, grants, and awards:*** Federal Pell, FSEOG, state, private, college/university gift aid from institutional funds.

GIFT AID (NON-NEED-BASED) ***Receiving aid:*** Freshmen: 24% (242). Undergraduates: 24% (734). ***Average award:*** Freshmen: $1738. Undergraduates: $1820. ***Tuition waivers:*** Full or partial for employees or children of employees, senior citizens.

LOANS ***Student loans:*** $7,949,533 (63% need-based, 37% non-need-based). 36% of past graduating class borrowed through all loan programs. *Average*

indebtedness per student: $12,571. ***Average need-based loan:*** Freshmen: $2838. Undergraduates: $3802. ***Parent loans:*** $220,635 (100% non-need-based). ***Programs:*** FFEL (Subsidized and Unsubsidized Stafford, PLUS), Perkins.

WORK-STUDY ***Federal work-study:*** Total amount: $203,934; jobs available. ***State or other work-study/employment:*** Total amount: $86,525 (100% need-based). Part-time jobs available.

ATHLETIC AWARDS Total amount: $738,838 (100% need-based).

APPLYING FOR FINANCIAL AID ***Required financial aid forms:*** FAFSA, institution's own form. ***Financial aid deadline:*** 5/1 (priority: 3/1). ***Notification date:*** Continuous. Students must reply within 2 weeks of notification.

CONTACT J.D. Robertson, Director, Dixie State College of Utah, 225 South 700 East, St. George, UT 84770, 435-652-7575 or toll-free 888-GO2DIXIE. *Fax:* 435-656-4087. *E-mail:* finaid@dixie.edu.

DOANE COLLEGE

Crete, NE

Tuition & fees: $20,150 **Average undergraduate aid package: $17,428**

ABOUT THE INSTITUTION Independent religious, coed. ***Awards:*** bachelor's and master's degrees (non-traditional undergraduate programs and graduate programs offered at Lincoln campus). 40 undergraduate majors. ***Total enrollment:*** 900. Undergraduates: 900. Freshmen: 248. Federal methodology is used as a basis for awarding need-based institutional aid.

UNDERGRADUATE EXPENSES for 2008–09 ***Comprehensive fee:*** $25,750 includes full-time tuition ($19,750), mandatory fees ($400), and room and board ($5600). ***College room only:*** $2000. Full-time tuition and fees vary according to location. Room and board charges vary according to board plan, housing facility, and location. ***Part-time tuition:*** $660 per credit hour. Part-time tuition and fees vary according to course load, degree level, and location. ***Payment plan:*** Installment.

FRESHMAN FINANCIAL AID (Fall 2008, est.) 212 applied for aid; of those 85% were deemed to have need. 100% of freshmen with need received aid; of those 57% had need fully met. ***Average percent of need met:*** 100% (excluding resources awarded to replace EFC). ***Average financial aid package:*** $18,530 (excluding resources awarded to replace EFC). 19% of all full-time freshmen had no need and received non-need-based gift aid.

UNDERGRADUATE FINANCIAL AID (Fall 2008, est.) 742 applied for aid; of those 87% were deemed to have need. 100% of undergraduates with need received aid; of those 46% had need fully met. ***Average percent of need met:*** 97% (excluding resources awarded to replace EFC). ***Average financial aid package:*** $17,428 (excluding resources awarded to replace EFC). 22% of all full-time undergraduates had no need and received non-need-based gift aid.

GIFT AID (NEED-BASED) ***Total amount:*** $4,664,821 (26% federal, 7% state, 53% institutional, 14% external sources). ***Receiving aid:*** Freshmen: 80% (181); all full-time undergraduates: 77% (646). ***Average award:*** Freshmen: $14,342; Undergraduates: $12,993. ***Scholarships, grants, and awards:*** Federal Pell, FSEOG, state, private, college/university gift aid from institutional funds.

GIFT AID (NON-NEED-BASED) ***Total amount:*** $2,782,591 (100% institutional). ***Receiving aid:*** Freshmen: 2% (5). Undergraduates: 3% (23). ***Average award:*** Freshmen: $12,565. Undergraduates: $10,853. ***Scholarships, grants, and awards by category:*** *Creative arts/performance:* art/fine arts, debating, music, theater/drama. *Special characteristics:* religious affiliation, siblings of current students. ***Tuition waivers:*** Full or partial for employees or children of employees, senior citizens. ***ROTC:*** Army cooperative, Air Force cooperative.

LOANS ***Student loans:*** $4,458,761 (51% need-based, 49% non-need-based). 86% of past graduating class borrowed through all loan programs. *Average indebtedness per student:* $16,896. ***Average need-based loan:*** Freshmen: $3760. Undergraduates: $4435. ***Parent loans:*** $1,470,037 (100% non-need-based). ***Programs:*** FFEL (Subsidized and Unsubsidized Stafford, PLUS), Perkins.

WORK-STUDY ***Federal work-study:*** Total amount: $457,657; jobs available. ***State or other work-study/employment:*** Total amount: $253,390 (100% non-need-based). Part-time jobs available.

ATHLETIC AWARDS Total amount: $2,956,903 (63% need-based, 37% non-need-based).

APPLYING FOR FINANCIAL AID ***Required financial aid form:*** FAFSA. ***Financial aid deadline (priority):*** 3/1. ***Notification date:*** Continuous beginning 3/1. Students must reply within 2 weeks of notification.

CONTACT Peggy Tvrdy, Director of Financial Aid, Doane College, 1014 Boswell Avenue, Crete, NE 68333-2430, 402-826-8260 or toll-free 800-333-6263. *Fax:* 402-826-8600. *E-mail:* peggy.tvrdy@doane.edu.

DOMINICAN COLLEGE

Orangeburg, NY

Tuition & fees: $20,300 **Average undergraduate aid package: $13,858**

ABOUT THE INSTITUTION Independent, coed. ***Awards:*** associate, bachelor's, master's, and doctoral degrees. 36 undergraduate majors. ***Total enrollment:*** 1,963. Undergraduates: 1,661. Freshmen: 304. Federal methodology is used as a basis for awarding need-based institutional aid.

UNDERGRADUATE EXPENSES for 2008–09 ***Application fee:*** $35. ***One-time required fee:*** $35. ***Comprehensive fee:*** $30,030 includes full-time tuition ($19,600), mandatory fees ($700), and room and board ($9730). Room and board charges vary according to board plan and housing facility. ***Part-time tuition:*** $560 per credit hour. ***Part-time fees:*** $350 per term. Part-time tuition and fees vary according to program. ***Payment plans:*** Installment, deferred payment.

FRESHMAN FINANCIAL AID (Fall 2008, est.) 293 applied for aid; of those 91% were deemed to have need. 98% of freshmen with need received aid; of those 11% had need fully met. ***Average percent of need met:*** 58% (excluding resources awarded to replace EFC). ***Average financial aid package:*** $14,595 (excluding resources awarded to replace EFC). 11% of all full-time freshmen had no need and received non-need-based gift aid.

UNDERGRADUATE FINANCIAL AID (Fall 2008, est.) 1,109 applied for aid; of those 88% were deemed to have need. 97% of undergraduates with need received aid; of those 12% had need fully met. ***Average percent of need met:*** 58% (excluding resources awarded to replace EFC). ***Average financial aid package:*** $13,858 (excluding resources awarded to replace EFC). 15% of all full-time undergraduates had no need and received non-need-based gift aid.

GIFT AID (NEED-BASED) ***Total amount:*** $8,996,163 (22% federal, 16% state, 60% institutional, 2% external sources). ***Receiving aid:*** Freshmen: 86% (261); all full-time undergraduates: 76% (922). ***Average award:*** Freshmen: $11,616; Undergraduates: $10,205. ***Scholarships, grants, and awards:*** Federal Pell, FSEOG, state, private, college/university gift aid from institutional funds.

GIFT AID (NON-NEED-BASED) ***Total amount:*** $1,457,218 (3% state, 79% institutional, 18% external sources). ***Receiving aid:*** Freshmen: 9% (26). Undergraduates: 7% (83). ***Average award:*** Freshmen: $5386. Undergraduates: $5488. ***Scholarships, grants, and awards by category:*** *Academic interests/achievement:* 183 awards ($994,840 total): education, general academic interests/achievements, health fields. *Special characteristics:* 20 awards ($196,000 total): children of faculty/staff, general special characteristics, relatives of clergy. ***Tuition waivers:*** Full or partial for employees or children of employees, senior citizens.

LOANS ***Student loans:*** $9,273,447 (87% need-based, 13% non-need-based). 100% of past graduating class borrowed through all loan programs. *Average indebtedness per student:* $17,784. ***Average need-based loan:*** Freshmen: $3323. Undergraduates: $4308. ***Parent loans:*** $2,168,189 (33% need-based, 67% non-need-based). ***Programs:*** FFEL (Subsidized and Unsubsidized Stafford, PLUS), Perkins, Federal Nursing.

WORK-STUDY ***Federal work-study:*** Total amount: $238,432; 250 jobs averaging $1200. ***State or other work-study/employment:*** Total amount: $207,185 (71% need-based, 29% non-need-based). 60 part-time jobs averaging $2900.

ATHLETIC AWARDS Total amount: $1,432,853 (57% need-based, 43% non-need-based).

APPLYING FOR FINANCIAL AID ***Financial aid deadline (priority):*** 2/15. ***Notification date:*** Continuous beginning 2/15. Students must reply within 4 weeks of notification.

CONTACT Ms. Eileen Felske, Director of Financial Aid, Dominican College, 470 Western Highway, Orangeburg, NY 10962-1210, 845-848-7818 or toll-free 866-432-4636. *Fax:* 845-359-2313. *E-mail:* eileen.felske@dc.edu.

DOMINICAN UNIVERSITY

River Forest, IL

Tuition & fees: $23,800 **Average undergraduate aid package: $17,524**

ABOUT THE INSTITUTION Independent Roman Catholic, coed. ***Awards:*** bachelor's and master's degrees and post-bachelor's and post-master's certificates. 50 undergraduate majors. ***Total enrollment:*** 3,413. Undergraduates: 1,709. Freshmen: 417. Federal methodology is used as a basis for awarding need-based institutional aid.

UNDERGRADUATE EXPENSES for 2008–09 ***Application fee:*** $25. ***One-time required fee:*** $150. ***Comprehensive fee:*** $31,150 includes full-time tuition ($23,700), mandatory fees ($100), and room and board ($7350). Full-time tuition and fees vary according to program. Room and board charges vary according to board plan and housing facility. ***Part-time tuition:*** $790 per semester hour. ***Part-time fees:*** $10 per course. Part-time tuition and fees vary according to location and program. ***Payment plan:*** Installment.

FRESHMAN FINANCIAL AID (Fall 2008, est.) 384 applied for aid; of those 92% were deemed to have need. 100% of freshmen with need received aid; of those 18% had need fully met. ***Average percent of need met:*** 83% (excluding resources awarded to replace EFC). ***Average financial aid package:*** $19,009 (excluding resources awarded to replace EFC). 10% of all full-time freshmen had no need and received non-need-based gift aid.

UNDERGRADUATE FINANCIAL AID (Fall 2008, est.) 1,481 applied for aid; of those 90% were deemed to have need. 87% of undergraduates with need received aid; of those 16% had need fully met. ***Average percent of need met:*** 66% (excluding resources awarded to replace EFC). ***Average financial aid package:*** $17,524 (excluding resources awarded to replace EFC). 11% of all full-time undergraduates had no need and received non-need-based gift aid.

GIFT AID (NEED-BASED) ***Total amount:*** $14,497,833 (15% federal, 21% state, 62% institutional, 2% external sources). ***Receiving aid:*** Freshmen: 85% (351); all full-time undergraduates: 70% (1,160). ***Average award:*** Freshmen: $14,994; Undergraduates: $13,616. ***Scholarships, grants, and awards:*** Federal Pell, FSEOG, state, private, college/university gift aid from institutional funds.

GIFT AID (NON-NEED-BASED) ***Total amount:*** $1,812,383 (96% institutional, 4% external sources). ***Receiving aid:*** Freshmen: 12% (51). Undergraduates: 8% (126). ***Average award:*** Freshmen: $10,187. Undergraduates: $10,865. ***Scholarships, grants, and awards by category:*** *Academic interests/achievement:* 922 awards ($6,976,265 total): general academic interests/achievements, physical sciences. *Special achievements/activities:* 63 awards ($101,000 total): leadership. *Special characteristics:* 247 awards ($395,540 total): children and siblings of alumni, international students, religious affiliation, siblings of current students, twins. ***Tuition waivers:*** Full or partial for children of alumni, employees or children of employees.

LOANS ***Student loans:*** $8,837,450 (70% need-based, 30% non-need-based). 91% of past graduating class borrowed through all loan programs. *Average indebtedness per student:* $17,066. ***Average need-based loan:*** Freshmen: $3246. Undergraduates: $4180. ***Parent loans:*** $1,131,055 (19% need-based, 81% non-need-based). ***Programs:*** FFEL (Subsidized and Unsubsidized Stafford, PLUS), Perkins, state.

WORK-STUDY ***Federal work-study:*** Total amount: $219,130; 184 jobs averaging $2045. ***State or other work-study/employment:*** Total amount: $336,753 (11% need-based, 89% non-need-based). 109 part-time jobs averaging $2130.

APPLYING FOR FINANCIAL AID ***Required financial aid form:*** FAFSA. ***Financial aid deadline (priority):*** 4/15. ***Notification date:*** Continuous. Students must reply within 2 weeks of notification.

CONTACT Michael Shields, Director of Financial Aid, Dominican University, 7900 West Division Street, River Forest, IL 60305-1099, 708-524-6807 or toll-free 800-828-8475. *Fax:* 708-366-6478. *E-mail:* mshields@dom.edu.

DOMINICAN UNIVERSITY OF CALIFORNIA

San Rafael, CA

Tuition & fees: $32,390 **Average undergraduate aid package: $19,992**

ABOUT THE INSTITUTION Independent religious, coed. ***Awards:*** bachelor's and master's degrees and post-bachelor's certificates. 23 undergraduate majors. ***Total enrollment:*** 2,071. Undergraduates: 1,445. Freshmen: 267. Federal methodology is used as a basis for awarding need-based institutional aid.

UNDERGRADUATE EXPENSES for 2008–09 ***Application fee:*** $40. ***Comprehensive fee:*** $43,590 includes full-time tuition ($32,090), mandatory fees ($300), and room and board ($11,200). ***College room only:*** $6420. Full-time tuition and fees vary according to course load and degree level. Room and board charges vary according to board plan. ***Part-time tuition:*** $1340 per unit. ***Part-time fees:*** $300 per term. Part-time tuition and fees vary according to degree level. ***Payment plan:*** Installment.

FRESHMAN FINANCIAL AID (Fall 2008, est.) 246 applied for aid; of those 88% were deemed to have need. 100% of freshmen with need received aid; of those 12% had need fully met. ***Average percent of need met:*** 69% (excluding resources awarded to replace EFC). ***Average financial aid package:*** $22,554 (excluding resources awarded to replace EFC). 16% of all full-time freshmen had no need and received non-need-based gift aid.

UNDERGRADUATE FINANCIAL AID (Fall 2008, est.) 929 applied for aid; of those 91% were deemed to have need. 99% of undergraduates with need received aid; of those 8% had need fully met. ***Average percent of need met:*** 59% (excluding resources awarded to replace EFC). ***Average financial aid package:*** $19,992 (excluding resources awarded to replace EFC). 18% of all full-time undergraduates had no need and received non-need-based gift aid.

GIFT AID (NEED-BASED) ***Total amount:*** $13,180,741 (11% federal, 15% state, 72% institutional, 2% external sources). ***Receiving aid:*** Freshmen: 81% (215); all full-time undergraduates: 72% (829). ***Average award:*** Freshmen: $18,826; Undergraduates: $15,682. ***Scholarships, grants, and awards:*** Federal Pell, FSEOG, state, private, college/university gift aid from institutional funds.

GIFT AID (NON-NEED-BASED) ***Total amount:*** $2,563,170 (97% institutional, 3% external sources). ***Receiving aid:*** Freshmen: 9% (24). Undergraduates: 6% (64). ***Average award:*** Freshmen: $11,697. Undergraduates: $10,067. ***Scholarships, grants, and awards by category:*** *Academic interests/achievement:* 551 awards ($5,066,936 total): general academic interests/achievements. *Creative arts/performance:* 6 awards ($10,500 total): music. *Special achievements/activities:* community service, general special achievements/activities. *Special characteristics:* 406 awards ($1,190,545 total): adult students, children and siblings of alumni, children of faculty/staff, ethnic background, first-generation college students, international students, local/state students, members of minority groups. ***Tuition waivers:*** Full or partial for employees or children of employees, senior citizens.

LOANS ***Student loans:*** $12,402,961 (75% need-based, 25% non-need-based). 93% of past graduating class borrowed through all loan programs. *Average indebtedness per student:* $19,806. ***Average need-based loan:*** Freshmen: $3913. Undergraduates: $4773. ***Parent loans:*** $2,850,313 (46% need-based, 54% non-need-based). ***Programs:*** FFEL (Subsidized and Unsubsidized Stafford, PLUS), Perkins, private loans.

WORK-STUDY ***Federal work-study:*** Total amount: $286,609; 145 jobs averaging $1977. ***State or other work-study/employment:*** Total amount: $132,620 (54% need-based, 46% non-need-based). 20 part-time jobs averaging $9638.

ATHLETIC AWARDS Total amount: $407,257 (66% need-based, 34% non-need-based).

APPLYING FOR FINANCIAL AID ***Required financial aid forms:*** FAFSA, institution's own form. ***Financial aid deadline (priority):*** 3/2. ***Notification date:*** Continuous beginning 3/15. Students must reply within 2 weeks of notification.

CONTACT Ms. Mary-Frances Causey, Director of Financial Aid, Dominican University of California, 50 Acacia Avenue, San Rafael, CA 94901-2298, 415-257-1302 or toll-free 888-323-6763. *Fax:* 415-485-3294. *E-mail:* Mary-Frances.Causey@dominican.edu.

DORDT COLLEGE

Sioux Center, IA

Tuition & fees: $22,080 **Average undergraduate aid package: $19,467**

ABOUT THE INSTITUTION Independent Christian Reformed, coed. ***Awards:*** associate, bachelor's, and master's degrees. 84 undergraduate majors. ***Total enrollment:*** 1,400. Undergraduates: 1,363. Freshmen: 396. Federal methodology is used as a basis for awarding need-based institutional aid.

UNDERGRADUATE EXPENSES for 2009–10 ***Application fee:*** $25. ***Comprehensive fee:*** $28,090 includes full-time tuition ($21,720), mandatory fees ($360), and room and board ($6010). ***College room only:*** $3170. ***Part-time tuition:*** $880 per semester hour. ***Part-time fees:*** $160 per term.

FRESHMAN FINANCIAL AID (Fall 2008, est.) 362 applied for aid; of those 84% were deemed to have need. 100% of freshmen with need received aid; of those 19% had need fully met. ***Average percent of need met:*** 91% (excluding resources awarded to replace EFC). ***Average financial aid package:*** $20,255 (excluding resources awarded to replace EFC). 20% of all full-time freshmen had no need and received non-need-based gift aid.

UNDERGRADUATE FINANCIAL AID (Fall 2008, est.) 1,106 applied for aid; of those 87% were deemed to have need. 100% of undergraduates with need received aid; of those 15% had need fully met. ***Average percent of need met:*** 90% (excluding resources awarded to replace EFC). ***Average financial aid***

package: $19,467 (excluding resources awarded to replace EFC). 20% of all full-time undergraduates had no need and received non-need-based gift aid.

GIFT AID (NEED-BASED) ***Total amount:*** $10,653,614 (11% federal, 12% state, 70% institutional, 7% external sources). ***Receiving aid:*** Freshmen: 75% (303); all full-time undergraduates: 75% (959). ***Average award:*** Freshmen: $11,295; Undergraduates: $10,060. ***Scholarships, grants, and awards:*** Federal Pell, FSEOG, state, private, college/university gift aid from institutional funds.

GIFT AID (NON-NEED-BASED) ***Total amount:*** $1,616,829 (92% institutional, 8% external sources). ***Average award:*** Freshmen: $12,925. Undergraduates: $10,526. ***Scholarships, grants, and awards by category:*** *Academic interests/achievement:* agriculture, biological sciences, business, communication, computer science, education, engineering/technologies, English, foreign languages, general academic interests/achievements, humanities, mathematics, physical sciences, premedicine, religion/biblical studies, social sciences. *Creative arts/performance:* journalism/publications, music, theater/drama. *Special achievements/activities:* general special achievements/activities, leadership. *Special characteristics:* children and siblings of alumni, children of faculty/staff, general special characteristics, handicapped students, international students, local/state students, members of minority groups, out-of-state students, religious affiliation.

LOANS ***Student loans:*** $9,111,240 (90% need-based, 10% non-need-based). 84% of past graduating class borrowed through all loan programs. *Average indebtedness per student:* $19,208. ***Average need-based loan:*** Freshmen: $5399. Undergraduates: $5600. ***Parent loans:*** $3,990,126 (89% need-based, 11% non-need-based). ***Programs:*** FFEL (Subsidized and Unsubsidized Stafford, PLUS), Perkins, state, college/university, alternative loans.

WORK-STUDY ***Federal work-study:*** Total amount: $866,600; 489 jobs averaging $1500. ***State or other work-study/employment:*** Total amount: $932,340 (71% need-based, 29% non-need-based). 602 part-time jobs averaging $1500.

ATHLETIC AWARDS Total amount: $1,094,450 (75% need-based, 25% non-need-based).

APPLYING FOR FINANCIAL AID ***Required financial aid forms:*** FAFSA, institution's own form. ***Financial aid deadline (priority):*** 4/1. ***Notification date:*** Continuous. Students must reply within 3 weeks of notification.

CONTACT Michael Epema, Director of Financial Aid, Dordt College, 498 4th Avenue NE, Sioux Center, IA 51250-1697, 712-722-6087 Ext. 6082 or toll-free 800-343-6738. *Fax:* 712-722-6035. *E-mail:* epema@dordt.edu.

DOWLING COLLEGE

Oakdale, NY

Tuition & fees: $20,310 | **Average undergraduate aid package: $15,077**

ABOUT THE INSTITUTION Independent, coed. ***Awards:*** bachelor's, master's, and doctoral degrees and post-bachelor's and post-master's certificates. 42 undergraduate majors. ***Total enrollment:*** 5,706. Undergraduates: 3,288. Freshmen: 528. Federal methodology is used as a basis for awarding need-based institutional aid.

UNDERGRADUATE EXPENSES for 2008–09 ***Application fee:*** $35. ***Comprehensive fee:*** $29,510 includes full-time tuition ($19,000), mandatory fees ($1310), and room and board ($9200). Full-time tuition and fees vary according to course load and degree level. Room and board charges vary according to housing facility and location. ***Part-time tuition:*** $636 per credit hour. ***Part-time fees:*** $265 per term. Part-time tuition and fees vary according to course load and degree level. ***Payment plans:*** Installment, deferred payment.

FRESHMAN FINANCIAL AID (Fall 2008, est.) 357 applied for aid; of those 97% were deemed to have need. 100% of freshmen with need received aid; of those .3% had need fully met. ***Average percent of need met:*** 92% (excluding resources awarded to replace EFC). ***Average financial aid package:*** $16,414 (excluding resources awarded to replace EFC). 12% of all full-time freshmen had no need and received non-need-based gift aid.

UNDERGRADUATE FINANCIAL AID (Fall 2008, est.) 1,386 applied for aid; of those 84% were deemed to have need. 100% of undergraduates with need received aid. ***Average percent of need met:*** 67% (excluding resources awarded to replace EFC). ***Average financial aid package:*** $15,077 (excluding resources awarded to replace EFC). 12% of all full-time undergraduates had no need and received non-need-based gift aid.

GIFT AID (NEED-BASED) ***Total amount:*** $7,519,146 (40% federal, 37% state, 23% institutional). ***Receiving aid:*** Freshmen: 68% (333); all full-time undergraduates: 53% (1,148). ***Average award:*** Freshmen: $3545. ***Scholarships, grants, and awards:*** Federal Pell, FSEOG, state, private, college/university gift aid from institutional funds.

GIFT AID (NON-NEED-BASED) ***Total amount:*** $7,746,543 (1% state, 98% institutional, 1% external sources). ***Receiving aid:*** Freshmen: 35% (170). Undergraduates: 22% (488). ***Average award:*** Freshmen: $5657. Undergraduates: $7077. ***Scholarships, grants, and awards by category:*** *Academic interests/achievement:* business, education, general academic interests/achievements. *Special achievements/activities:* general special achievements/activities. *Special characteristics:* children and siblings of alumni, children of educators, children of faculty/staff, children of public servants, children of union members/company employees, children of workers in trades, first-generation college students, general special characteristics, local/state students, public servants. ***Tuition waivers:*** Full or partial for minority students, children of alumni, employees or children of employees, adult students, senior citizens. ***ROTC:*** Air Force cooperative.

LOANS ***Student loans:*** $9,921,120 (58% need-based, 42% non-need-based). 89% of past graduating class borrowed through all loan programs. *Average indebtedness per student:* $48,161. ***Average need-based loan:*** Freshmen: $3632. Undergraduates: $4617. ***Parent loans:*** $3,769,365 (100% non-need-based). ***Programs:*** Federal Direct (Subsidized and Unsubsidized Stafford, PLUS), FFEL (Subsidized and Unsubsidized Stafford, PLUS), Perkins.

WORK-STUDY ***Federal work-study:*** Total amount: $1,820,147; jobs available. ***State or other work-study/employment:*** Total amount: $703,710 (100% non-need-based). Part-time jobs available.

ATHLETIC AWARDS Total amount: $2,300,101 (100% non-need-based).

APPLYING FOR FINANCIAL AID ***Required financial aid forms:*** FAFSA, state aid form. ***Financial aid deadline (priority):*** 3/1. ***Notification date:*** Continuous beginning 3/15.

CONTACT Patricia Noren, Director of Student Financial Services, Dowling College, Idle Hour Boulevard, Oakdale, NY 11769-1999, 631-244-3368 or toll-free 800-DOWLING. *E-mail:* NorenP@dowling.edu.

DRAKE UNIVERSITY

Des Moines, IA

Tuition & fees: $26,622 | **Average undergraduate aid package: $20,836**

ABOUT THE INSTITUTION Independent, coed. ***Awards:*** bachelor's, master's, doctoral, and first professional degrees and post-bachelor's, post-master's, and first professional certificates. 66 undergraduate majors. ***Total enrollment:*** 5,668. Undergraduates: 3,516. Freshmen: 902. Federal methodology is used as a basis for awarding need-based institutional aid.

UNDERGRADUATE EXPENSES for 2009–10 ***Application fee:*** $25. ***Comprehensive fee:*** $34,422 includes full-time tuition ($26,160), mandatory fees ($462), and room and board ($7800). ***College room only:*** $4100.

FRESHMAN FINANCIAL AID (Fall 2007) 725 applied for aid; of those 74% were deemed to have need. 100% of freshmen with need received aid; of those 37% had need fully met. ***Average percent of need met:*** 89% (excluding resources awarded to replace EFC). ***Average financial aid package:*** $21,055 (excluding resources awarded to replace EFC). 36% of all full-time freshmen had no need and received non-need-based gift aid.

UNDERGRADUATE FINANCIAL AID (Fall 2007) 2,320 applied for aid; of those 82% were deemed to have need. 100% of undergraduates with need received aid; of those 33% had need fully met. ***Average percent of need met:*** 84% (excluding resources awarded to replace EFC). ***Average financial aid package:*** $20,836 (excluding resources awarded to replace EFC). 35% of all full-time undergraduates had no need and received non-need-based gift aid.

GIFT AID (NEED-BASED) ***Total amount:*** $24,597,275 (11% federal, 9% state, 77% institutional, 3% external sources). ***Receiving aid:*** Freshmen: 58% (525); all full-time undergraduates: 57% (1,858). ***Average award:*** Freshmen: $14,176; Undergraduates: $13,012. ***Scholarships, grants, and awards:*** Federal Pell, FSEOG, state, private, college/university gift aid from institutional funds.

GIFT AID (NON-NEED-BASED) ***Total amount:*** $15,511,765 (2% federal, 94% institutional, 4% external sources). ***Receiving aid:*** Freshmen: 15% (138). Undergraduates: 13% (425). ***Average award:*** Freshmen: $10,898. Undergraduates: $10,718. ***Scholarships, grants, and awards by category:*** *Academic interests/achievement:* 2,472 awards ($23,142,928 total): general academic interests/achievements. *Creative arts/performance:* 266 awards ($985,986 total): art/fine arts, music, theater/drama. *Special characteristics:* 309 awards ($828,544 total): children and siblings of alumni, international students. ***ROTC:*** Army, Air Force cooperative.

LOANS ***Student loans:*** $26,934,006 (51% need-based, 49% non-need-based). 64% of past graduating class borrowed through all loan programs. *Average*

indebtedness per student: $32,318. ***Average need-based loan:*** Freshmen: $5051. Undergraduates: $5878. ***Parent loans:*** $29,480,168 (15% need-based, 85% non-need-based). ***Programs:*** FFEL (Subsidized and Unsubsidized Stafford, PLUS), Perkins, college/university.

WORK-STUDY ***Federal work-study:*** Total amount: $2,949,081; 1,541 jobs averaging $1914. ***State or other work-study/employment:*** Part-time jobs available.

ATHLETIC AWARDS Total amount: $3,094,014 (25% need-based, 75% non-need-based).

APPLYING FOR FINANCIAL AID ***Required financial aid form:*** FAFSA. ***Financial aid deadline (priority):*** 3/1. ***Notification date:*** Continuous beginning 3/1. Students must reply by 5/1 or within 3 weeks of notification.

CONTACT Office of Student Financial Planning, Drake University, 2507 University Avenue, Des Moines, IA 50311-4516, 800-44-DRAKE Ext. 2905 or toll-free 800-44DRAKE Ext. 3181. *Fax:* 515-271-4042.

DREW UNIVERSITY

Madison, NJ

Tuition & fees: $38,017 **Average undergraduate aid package: $27,675**

ABOUT THE INSTITUTION Independent religious, coed. ***Awards:*** bachelor's, master's, doctoral, and first professional degrees and post-bachelor's and post-master's certificates. 30 undergraduate majors. ***Total enrollment:*** 2,605. Undergraduates: 1,657. Freshmen: 390. Institutional methodology is used as a basis for awarding need-based institutional aid.

UNDERGRADUATE EXPENSES for 2009–10 ***Application fee:*** $50. ***Comprehensive fee:*** $48,385 includes full-time tuition ($37,310), mandatory fees ($707), and room and board ($10,368). ***College room only:*** $6702. ***Part-time tuition:*** $1554 per credit.

FRESHMAN FINANCIAL AID (Fall 2007) 311 applied for aid; of those 79% were deemed to have need. 100% of freshmen with need received aid; of those 28% had need fully met. ***Average percent of need met:*** 82% (excluding resources awarded to replace EFC). ***Average financial aid package:*** $28,828 (excluding resources awarded to replace EFC). 44% of all full-time freshmen had no need and received non-need-based gift aid.

UNDERGRADUATE FINANCIAL AID (Fall 2007) 1,029 applied for aid; of those 82% were deemed to have need. 100% of undergraduates with need received aid; of those 32% had need fully met. ***Average percent of need met:*** 81% (excluding resources awarded to replace EFC). ***Average financial aid package:*** $27,675 (excluding resources awarded to replace EFC). 35% of all full-time undergraduates had no need and received non-need-based gift aid.

GIFT AID (NEED-BASED) ***Total amount:*** $18,250,895 (8% federal, 11% state, 79% institutional, 2% external sources). ***Receiving aid:*** Freshmen: 54% (246); all full-time undergraduates: 53% (837). ***Average award:*** Freshmen: $23,778; Undergraduates: $21,805. ***Scholarships, grants, and awards:*** Federal Pell, FSEOG, state, private, college/university gift aid from institutional funds.

GIFT AID (NON-NEED-BASED) ***Total amount:*** $7,780,347 (2% state, 95% institutional, 3% external sources). ***Receiving aid:*** Freshmen: 12% (55). Undergraduates: 8% (135). ***Average award:*** Freshmen: $11,258. Undergraduates: $11,504. ***Scholarships, grants, and awards by category:*** *Academic interests/achievement:* 1,379 awards ($15,468,674 total): general academic interests/achievements. *Creative arts/performance:* 12 awards ($85,000 total): general creative arts/performance. *Special characteristics:* 48 awards ($241,443 total): ethnic background.

LOANS ***Student loans:*** $4,545,775 (75% need-based, 25% non-need-based). 61% of past graduating class borrowed through all loan programs. *Average indebtedness per student:* $16,640. ***Average need-based loan:*** Freshmen: $4347. Undergraduates: $5078. ***Parent loans:*** $7,908,073 (28% need-based, 72% non-need-based). ***Programs:*** FFEL (Subsidized and Unsubsidized Stafford, PLUS), Perkins, state.

WORK-STUDY ***Federal work-study:*** Total amount: $419,367; 294 jobs averaging $1426. ***State or other work-study/employment:*** Total amount: $330,939 (65% need-based, 35% non-need-based). 35 part-time jobs averaging $9455.

APPLYING FOR FINANCIAL AID ***Required financial aid forms:*** FAFSA, CSS Financial Aid PROFILE. ***Financial aid deadline:*** 2/15. ***Notification date:*** 3/30. Students must reply by 5/1.

CONTACT Renee Volak, Director of Financial Assistance, Drew University, 36 Madison Avenue, Madison, NJ 07940-1493, 973-408-3112. *Fax:* 973-408-3188. *E-mail:* finaid@drew.edu.

DREXEL UNIVERSITY

Philadelphia, PA

CONTACT Melissa Englund, Director of Financial Aid, Drexel University, 3141 Chestnut Street, Main Building, Room 106, Philadelphia, PA 19104-2875, 215-895-2537 or toll-free 800-2-DREXEL. *Fax:* 215-895-6903.

DRURY UNIVERSITY

Springfield, MO

Tuition & fees: $19,013 **Average undergraduate aid package: $7750**

ABOUT THE INSTITUTION Independent, coed. ***Awards:*** bachelor's and master's degrees (also offers evening program with significant enrollment not reflected in profile). 50 undergraduate majors. ***Total enrollment:*** 2,060. Undergraduates: 1,555. Freshmen: 334. Federal methodology is used as a basis for awarding need-based institutional aid.

UNDERGRADUATE EXPENSES for 2009–10 ***Application fee:*** $25. ***One-time required fee:*** $145. ***Comprehensive fee:*** $25,716 includes full-time tuition ($18,598), mandatory fees ($415), and room and board ($6703).

FRESHMAN FINANCIAL AID (Fall 2008, est.) 318 applied for aid; of those 92% were deemed to have need. 100% of freshmen with need received aid; of those 100% had need fully met. ***Average percent of need met:*** 83% (excluding resources awarded to replace EFC). ***Average financial aid package:*** $7880 (excluding resources awarded to replace EFC).

UNDERGRADUATE FINANCIAL AID (Fall 2008, est.) 1,488 applied for aid; of those 95% were deemed to have need. 100% of undergraduates with need received aid; of those 93% had need fully met. ***Average percent of need met:*** 83% (excluding resources awarded to replace EFC). ***Average financial aid package:*** $7750 (excluding resources awarded to replace EFC).

GIFT AID (NEED-BASED) ***Total amount:*** $10,052,328 (14% federal, 19% state, 60% institutional, 7% external sources). ***Receiving aid:*** Freshmen: 84% (279); all full-time undergraduates: 88% (1,371). ***Average award:*** Freshmen: $6280; Undergraduates: $7255. ***Scholarships, grants, and awards:*** Federal Pell, FSEOG, state, private, college/university gift aid from institutional funds.

GIFT AID (NON-NEED-BASED) ***Total amount:*** $3,375,597 (10% state, 83% institutional, 7% external sources). ***Receiving aid:*** Freshmen: 86% (286). Undergraduates: 88% (1,367). ***Scholarships, grants, and awards by category:*** *Academic interests/achievement:* 1,357 awards ($2,588,420 total): architecture, biological sciences, business, communication, computer science, education, English, foreign languages, general academic interests/achievements, health fields, humanities, mathematics, physical sciences, premedicine, social sciences. *Creative arts/performance:* 193 awards ($294,850 total): art/fine arts, creative writing, debating, music, theater/drama. *Special achievements/activities:* 542 awards ($197,640 total): cheerleading/drum major, leadership, religious involvement. *Special characteristics:* 105 awards ($641,565 total): children and siblings of alumni, children of faculty/staff, relatives of clergy, religious affiliation. ***ROTC:*** Army cooperative.

LOANS ***Student loans:*** $19,240,838 (95% need-based, 5% non-need-based). 61% of past graduating class borrowed through all loan programs. *Average indebtedness per student:* $18,384. ***Average need-based loan:*** Freshmen: $4950. Undergraduates: $5500. ***Parent loans:*** $1,221,330 (100% need-based). ***Programs:*** FFEL (Subsidized and Unsubsidized Stafford, PLUS), Perkins.

WORK-STUDY ***Federal work-study:*** Total amount: $374,840; 762 jobs averaging $3000. ***State or other work-study/employment:*** Total amount: $182,640 (100% non-need-based). 237 part-time jobs averaging $3000.

ATHLETIC AWARDS Total amount: $2,786,774 (29% need-based, 71% non-need-based).

APPLYING FOR FINANCIAL AID ***Required financial aid forms:*** FAFSA, institution's own form. ***Financial aid deadline (priority):*** 3/15. ***Notification date:*** Continuous beginning 3/15. Students must reply within 2 weeks of notification.

CONTACT Ms. Annette Avery, Director of Financial Aid, Drury University, 900 North Benton Avenue, Springfield, MO 65802-3791, 417-873-7312 or toll-free 800-922-2274. *Fax:* 417-873-6906. *E-mail:* aavery@drury.edu.

DUKE UNIVERSITY

Durham, NC

Tuition & fees: $38,741 **Average undergraduate aid package: $33,562**

ABOUT THE INSTITUTION Independent religious, coed. ***Awards:*** bachelor's, master's, doctoral, and first professional degrees and post-bachelor's and post-master's certificates. 45 undergraduate majors. ***Total enrollment:*** 14,060. Undergraduates: 6,496. Freshmen: 1,699. Both federal and institutional methodology are used as a basis for awarding need-based institutional aid.

UNDERGRADUATE EXPENSES for 2009–10 ***Application fee:*** $75. ***Comprehensive fee:*** $49,895 includes full-time tuition ($37,485), mandatory fees ($1256), and room and board ($11,154). ***College room only:*** $6285. ***Part-time tuition:*** $4685 per course.

FRESHMAN FINANCIAL AID (Fall 2008, est.) 846 applied for aid; of those 85% were deemed to have need. 100% of freshmen with need received aid; of those 100% had need fully met. ***Average percent of need met:*** 100% (excluding resources awarded to replace EFC). ***Average financial aid package:*** $33,817 (excluding resources awarded to replace EFC). 2% of all full-time freshmen had no need and received non-need-based gift aid.

UNDERGRADUATE FINANCIAL AID (Fall 2008, est.) 2,914 applied for aid; of those 90% were deemed to have need. 100% of undergraduates with need received aid; of those 100% had need fully met. ***Average percent of need met:*** 100% (excluding resources awarded to replace EFC). ***Average financial aid package:*** $33,562 (excluding resources awarded to replace EFC). 5% of all full-time undergraduates had no need and received non-need-based gift aid.

GIFT AID (NEED-BASED) ***Total amount:*** $75,714,165 (4% federal, 3% state, 87% institutional, 6% external sources). ***Receiving aid:*** Freshmen: 41% (691); all full-time undergraduates: 40% (2,525). ***Average award:*** Freshmen: $31,696; Undergraduates: $30,890. ***Scholarships, grants, and awards:*** Federal Pell, FSEOG, state, private, college/university gift aid from institutional funds.

GIFT AID (NON-NEED-BASED) ***Total amount:*** $11,815,188 (7% state, 68% institutional, 25% external sources). ***Receiving aid:*** Freshmen: 4% (70). Undergraduates: 5% (287). ***Average award:*** Freshmen: $46,031. Undergraduates: $27,719. ***Scholarships, grants, and awards by category:*** *Academic interests/achievement:* 96 awards ($4,456,645 total): general academic interests/achievements, mathematics. *Creative arts/performance:* creative writing. *Special achievements/activities:* 52 awards ($2,425,227 total): general special achievements/activities, leadership. *Special characteristics:* 28 awards ($1,224,625 total): children and siblings of alumni, ethnic background, local/state students. ***ROTC:*** Army, Naval, Air Force.

LOANS ***Student loans:*** $6,325,839 (96% need-based, 4% non-need-based). 41% of past graduating class borrowed through all loan programs. *Average indebtedness per student:* $24,205. ***Average need-based loan:*** Freshmen: $2528. Undergraduates: $2800. ***Parent loans:*** $33,830,418 (14% need-based, 86% non-need-based). ***Programs:*** FFEL (Subsidized and Unsubsidized Stafford, PLUS), Perkins, college/university, alternative loans from private sources.

WORK-STUDY ***Federal work-study:*** Total amount: $2,729,532; 1,547 jobs averaging $1765. ***State or other work-study/employment:*** Total amount: $988,408 (90% need-based, 10% non-need-based). 619 part-time jobs averaging $1586.

ATHLETIC AWARDS Total amount: $12,700,000 (17% need-based, 83% non-need-based).

APPLYING FOR FINANCIAL AID ***Required financial aid forms:*** FAFSA, CSS Financial Aid PROFILE, noncustodial (divorced/separated) parent's statement, business/farm supplement, complete income tax form(s), W-2 forms. ***Financial aid deadline:*** 2/1. ***Notification date:*** 4/1. Students must reply by 5/1.

CONTACT Alison Rabil, Director, Duke University, 2122 Campus Drive, Durham, NC 27708-0397, 919-684-6225. *Fax:* 919-660-9811. *E-mail:* finaid@duke.edu.

DUQUESNE UNIVERSITY

Pittsburgh, PA

Tuition & fees: $25,480 **Average undergraduate aid package: $18,949**

ABOUT THE INSTITUTION Independent Roman Catholic, coed. ***Awards:*** bachelor's, master's, doctoral, and first professional degrees and post-bachelor's and post-master's certificates. 77 undergraduate majors. ***Total enrollment:*** 10,106. Undergraduates: 5,656. Freshmen: 1,438. Federal methodology is used as a basis for awarding need-based institutional aid.

UNDERGRADUATE EXPENSES for 2008–09 ***Application fee:*** $50. ***Comprehensive fee:*** $34,368 includes full-time tuition ($23,475), mandatory fees ($2005), and room and board ($8888). ***College room only:*** $4848. Full-time tuition and fees vary according to program. Room and board charges vary according to board plan and housing facility. ***Part-time tuition:*** $765 per credit. ***Part-time fees:*** $78 per credit. Part-time tuition and fees vary according to program. ***Payment plan:*** Installment.

FRESHMAN FINANCIAL AID (Fall 2007) 1,200 applied for aid; of those 80% were deemed to have need. 100% of freshmen with need received aid; of those 72% had need fully met. ***Average percent of need met:*** 89% (excluding resources awarded to replace EFC). ***Average financial aid package:*** $19,046 (excluding resources awarded to replace EFC). 26% of all full-time freshmen had no need and received non-need-based gift aid.

UNDERGRADUATE FINANCIAL AID (Fall 2007) 4,249 applied for aid; of those 85% were deemed to have need. 100% of undergraduates with need received aid; of those 69% had need fully met. ***Average percent of need met:*** 87% (excluding resources awarded to replace EFC). ***Average financial aid package:*** $18,949 (excluding resources awarded to replace EFC). 24% of all full-time undergraduates had no need and received non-need-based gift aid.

GIFT AID (NEED-BASED) ***Total amount:*** $42,894,576 (8% federal, 17% state, 70% institutional, 5% external sources). ***Receiving aid:*** Freshmen: 71% (955); all full-time undergraduates: 67% (3,518). ***Average award:*** Freshmen: $12,428; Undergraduates: $11,443. ***Scholarships, grants, and awards:*** Federal Pell, FSEOG, state, private, college/university gift aid from institutional funds, United Negro College Fund.

GIFT AID (NON-NEED-BASED) ***Total amount:*** $9,951,147 (1% state, 93% institutional, 6% external sources). ***Receiving aid:*** Freshmen: 68% (920). Undergraduates: 59% (3,096). ***Average award:*** Freshmen: $7195. Undergraduates: $7345. ***Scholarships, grants, and awards by category:*** *Academic interests/achievement:* $25,575,204 total: general academic interests/achievements. *Creative arts/performance:* 210 awards ($1,498,802 total): dance, music. *Special characteristics:* 863 awards ($8,578,939 total): children and siblings of alumni, children of faculty/staff, general special characteristics, international students, members of minority groups, relatives of clergy, religious affiliation. ***Tuition waivers:*** Full or partial for employees or children of employees, senior citizens. ***ROTC:*** Army, Naval cooperative, Air Force cooperative.

LOANS ***Student loans:*** $41,644,119 (88% need-based, 12% non-need-based). 80% of past graduating class borrowed through all loan programs. *Average indebtedness per student:* $29,616. ***Average need-based loan:*** Freshmen: $4331. Undergraduates: $4997. ***Parent loans:*** $10,336,052 (84% need-based, 16% non-need-based). ***Programs:*** FFEL (Subsidized and Unsubsidized Stafford, PLUS), Perkins, Federal Nursing, private alternative loans.

WORK-STUDY ***Federal work-study:*** Total amount: $3,532,711; 1,195 jobs averaging $2618.

ATHLETIC AWARDS Total amount: $3,939,794 (58% need-based, 42% non-need-based).

APPLYING FOR FINANCIAL AID ***Required financial aid forms:*** FAFSA, institution's own form. ***Financial aid deadline:*** 5/1. ***Notification date:*** Continuous. Students must reply within 3 weeks of notification.

CONTACT Mr. Richard C. Esposito, Director of Financial Aid, Duquesne University, 600 Forbes Avenue, Pittsburgh, PA 15282-0299, 412-396-6607 or toll-free 800-456-0590. *Fax:* 412-396-5284. *E-mail:* esposito@duq.edu.

D'YOUVILLE COLLEGE

Buffalo, NY

Tuition & fees: $19,030 **Average undergraduate aid package: $14,988**

ABOUT THE INSTITUTION Independent, coed. ***Awards:*** bachelor's, master's, doctoral, and first professional degrees and post-bachelor's and post-master's certificates. 25 undergraduate majors. ***Total enrollment:*** 2,943. Undergraduates: 1,748. Freshmen: 221. Federal methodology is used as a basis for awarding need-based institutional aid.

UNDERGRADUATE EXPENSES for 2008–09 ***Application fee:*** $25. ***Comprehensive fee:*** $28,330 includes full-time tuition ($18,800), mandatory fees ($230), and room and board ($9300). Full-time tuition and fees vary according to course load, degree level, and program. Room and board charges vary according to board plan and housing facility. ***Part-time tuition:*** $540 per credit hour. ***Part-time fees:*** $2 per credit hour; $30 per term. Part-time tuition and fees vary according to course load, degree level, and program. ***Payment plans:*** Tuition prepayment, installment, deferred payment.

FRESHMAN FINANCIAL AID (Fall 2008, est.) 156 applied for aid; of those 86% were deemed to have need. 99% of freshmen with need received aid; of those 20% had need fully met. ***Average percent of need met:*** 79% (excluding resources awarded to replace EFC). ***Average financial aid package:*** $15,119 (excluding resources awarded to replace EFC). 14% of all full-time freshmen had no need and received non-need-based gift aid.

UNDERGRADUATE FINANCIAL AID (Fall 2008, est.) 1,102 applied for aid; of those 88% were deemed to have need. 100% of undergraduates with need received aid; of those 20% had need fully met. ***Average percent of need met:*** 71% (excluding resources awarded to replace EFC). ***Average financial aid package:*** $14,988 (excluding resources awarded to replace EFC). 11% of all full-time undergraduates had no need and received non-need-based gift aid.

GIFT AID (NEED-BASED) ***Total amount:*** $9,834,214 (23% federal, 19% state, 52% institutional, 6% external sources). ***Receiving aid:*** Freshmen: 66% (132); all full-time undergraduates: 75% (933). ***Average award:*** Freshmen: $10,555; Undergraduates: $9634. ***Scholarships, grants, and awards:*** Federal Pell, FSEOG, state, private, college/university gift aid from institutional funds.

GIFT AID (NON-NEED-BASED) ***Total amount:*** $1,143,807 (4% state, 86% institutional, 10% external sources). ***Receiving aid:*** Freshmen: 7% (13). Undergraduates: 6% (73). ***Average award:*** Freshmen: $7412. Undergraduates: $5328. ***Scholarships, grants, and awards by category:*** *Academic interests/achievement:* 920 awards ($4,215,000 total): biological sciences, business, education, English, general academic interests/achievements, health fields, humanities, international studies, premedicine, social sciences. *Special characteristics:* 48 awards ($593,747 total): children and siblings of alumni, children of faculty/staff. ***Tuition waivers:*** Full or partial for children of alumni, employees or children of employees, senior citizens. ***ROTC:*** Army cooperative.

LOANS ***Student loans:*** $14,861,528 (77% need-based, 23% non-need-based). 91% of past graduating class borrowed through all loan programs. ***Average need-based loan:*** Freshmen: $4923. Undergraduates: $6100. ***Parent loans:*** $510,457 (31% need-based, 69% non-need-based). ***Programs:*** FFEL (Subsidized and Unsubsidized Stafford, PLUS), Perkins, Federal Nursing, college/university.

WORK-STUDY ***Federal work-study:*** Total amount: $405,917; 326 jobs averaging $2000. ***State or other work-study/employment:*** Total amount: $175,000 (100% non-need-based). 116 part-time jobs averaging $2000.

APPLYING FOR FINANCIAL AID ***Required financial aid forms:*** FAFSA, state aid form. ***Financial aid deadline (priority):*** 3/1. ***Notification date:*** Continuous beginning 3/15. Students must reply within 2 weeks of notification.

CONTACT Ms. Lorraine A. Metz, Director of Financial Aid, D'Youville College, 320 Porter Avenue, Buffalo, NY 14201-1084, 716-829-7500 or toll-free 800-777-3921. *Fax:* 716-829-7779. *E-mail:* metzla@dyc.edu.

EARLHAM COLLEGE

Richmond, IN

Tuition & fees: $34,030 **Average undergraduate aid package: $24,146**

ABOUT THE INSTITUTION Independent religious, coed. ***Awards:*** bachelor's, master's, and first professional degrees. 37 undergraduate majors. ***Total enrollment:*** 1,308. Undergraduates: 1,184. Freshmen: 324. Both federal and institutional methodology are used as a basis for awarding need-based institutional aid.

UNDERGRADUATE EXPENSES for 2008–09 ***Comprehensive fee:*** $40,844 includes full-time tuition ($33,274), mandatory fees ($756), and room and board ($6814). ***College room only:*** $3124. Room and board charges vary according to board plan. ***Part-time tuition:*** $1109 per credit. ***Payment plans:*** Tuition prepayment, installment, deferred payment.

FRESHMAN FINANCIAL AID (Fall 2007) 196 applied for aid; of those 90% were deemed to have need. 99% of freshmen with need received aid; of those 49% had need fully met. ***Average percent of need met:*** 96% (excluding resources awarded to replace EFC). ***Average financial aid package:*** $26,889 (excluding resources awarded to replace EFC). 21% of all full-time freshmen had no need and received non-need-based gift aid.

UNDERGRADUATE FINANCIAL AID (Fall 2007) 725 applied for aid; of those 93% were deemed to have need. 100% of undergraduates with need received aid; of those 41% had need fully met. ***Average percent of need met:*** 88% (excluding resources awarded to replace EFC). ***Average financial aid package:*** $24,146 (excluding resources awarded to replace EFC). 32% of all full-time undergraduates had no need and received non-need-based gift aid.

GIFT AID (NEED-BASED) ***Total amount:*** $12,562,159 (9% federal, 6% state, 80% institutional, 5% external sources). ***Receiving aid:*** Freshmen: 50% (152); all full-time undergraduates: 49% (581). ***Average award:*** Freshmen: $17,016; Undergraduates: $16,118. ***Scholarships, grants, and awards:*** Federal Pell, FSEOG, state, private, college/university gift aid from institutional funds.

GIFT AID (NON-NEED-BASED) ***Total amount:*** $3,011,174 (91% institutional, 9% external sources). ***Receiving aid:*** Freshmen: 29% (89). Undergraduates: 29% (347). ***Average award:*** Freshmen: $8582. Undergraduates: $7317. ***Tuition waivers:*** Full or partial for employees or children of employees.

LOANS ***Student loans:*** $5,195,147 (69% need-based, 31% non-need-based). 64% of past graduating class borrowed through all loan programs. *Average indebtedness per student:* $20,287. ***Average need-based loan:*** Freshmen: $4594. Undergraduates: $5436. ***Parent loans:*** $1,717,429 (70% need-based, 30% non-need-based). ***Programs:*** Federal Direct (Subsidized and Unsubsidized Stafford, PLUS), Perkins, college/university.

WORK-STUDY ***Federal work-study:*** Total amount: $892,142; jobs available. ***State or other work-study/employment:*** Total amount: $346,022 (40% need-based, 60% non-need-based). Part-time jobs available.

APPLYING FOR FINANCIAL AID ***Required financial aid forms:*** FAFSA, institution's own form. ***Financial aid deadline (priority):*** 3/1. ***Notification date:*** Continuous. Students must reply by 5/1.

CONTACT Mr. Robert W. Arnold, Director of Financial Aid, Earlham College, National Road West, Richmond, IN 47374-4095, 765-983-1217 or toll-free 800-327-5426. *Fax:* 765-983-1299.

EAST CAROLINA UNIVERSITY

Greenville, NC

ABOUT THE INSTITUTION State-supported, coed. ***Awards:*** bachelor's, master's, doctoral, and first professional degrees and post-bachelor's and post-master's certificates. 86 undergraduate majors. ***Total enrollment:*** 27,677. Undergraduates: 20,974. Freshmen: 4,538.

GIFT AID (NEED-BASED) ***Scholarships, grants, and awards:*** Federal Pell, FSEOG, state, private, college/university gift aid from institutional funds.

GIFT AID (NON-NEED-BASED) ***Scholarships, grants, and awards by category:*** *Academic interests/achievement:* biological sciences, business, communication, education, engineering/technologies, English, foreign languages, general academic interests/achievements, health fields, home economics, humanities, mathematics, military science, physical sciences. *Creative arts/performance:* applied art and design, art/fine arts, music. *Special achievements/activities:* leadership. *Special characteristics:* adult students, children of faculty/staff, ethnic background, handicapped students, local/state students.

LOANS ***Programs:*** FFEL (Subsidized and Unsubsidized Stafford, PLUS), Perkins, Federal Nursing.

APPLYING FOR FINANCIAL AID ***Required financial aid form:*** FAFSA.

CONTACT Sheryl Spivey, Director, Student Financial Aid, East Carolina University, Office of Financial Aid, East 5th Street, Greenville, NC 27858-4353, 252-328-6610. *Fax:* 252-328-4347. *E-mail:* spiveys@ecu.edu.

EAST CENTRAL UNIVERSITY

Ada, OK

ABOUT THE INSTITUTION State-supported, coed. ***Awards:*** bachelor's and master's degrees. 81 undergraduate majors. ***Total enrollment:*** 4,463. Undergraduates: 3,665. Freshmen: 552.

GIFT AID (NEED-BASED) ***Scholarships, grants, and awards:*** Federal Pell, FSEOG, state, private, college/university gift aid from institutional funds.

GIFT AID (NON-NEED-BASED) ***Scholarships, grants, and awards by category:*** *Academic interests/achievement:* communication, general academic interests/achievements. *Creative arts/performance:* music, theater/drama. *Special achievements/activities:* cheerleading/drum major. *Special characteristics:* children of faculty/staff, general special characteristics, members of minority groups, out-of-state students, previous college experience, veterans, veterans' children.

LOANS ***Programs:*** FFEL (Subsidized and Unsubsidized Stafford, PLUS), Perkins, college/university.

APPLYING FOR FINANCIAL AID ***Required financial aid form:*** FAFSA.

CONTACT Marcia Carter, Director of Financial Aid, East Central University, 1100 East 14th, Ada, OK 74820-6899, 580-332-8000 Ext. 242. *Fax:* 580-436-5612.

EASTERN CONNECTICUT STATE UNIVERSITY

Willimantic, CT

ABOUT THE INSTITUTION State-supported, coed. ***Awards:*** associate, bachelor's, and master's degrees. 29 undergraduate majors. ***Total enrollment:*** 5,427. Undergraduates: 5,092. Freshmen: 1,017.

GIFT AID (NEED-BASED) ***Scholarships, grants, and awards:*** Federal Pell, FSEOG, state, private, college/university gift aid from institutional funds.

GIFT AID (NON-NEED-BASED) ***Scholarships, grants, and awards by category:*** *Academic interests/achievement:* area/ethnic studies, biological sciences, business, communication, computer science, education, English, foreign languages, general academic interests/achievements, humanities, mathematics, physical sciences, social sciences. *Special achievements/activities:* community service, general special achievements/activities, leadership, memberships. *Special characteristics:* children of faculty/staff, children of union members/company employees, general special characteristics, international students, local/state students, members of minority groups, previous college experience, veterans.

LOANS ***Programs:*** FFEL (Subsidized and Unsubsidized Stafford, PLUS), Perkins, state, college/university, alternative loans.

APPLYING FOR FINANCIAL AID ***Required financial aid form:*** FAFSA.

CONTACT Assistant to the Director of Financial Aid, Eastern Connecticut State University, 83 Windham Street, Willimantic, CT 06226-2295, 860-465-5205 or toll-free 877-353-3278. *Fax:* 860-465-2811. *E-mail:* financialaid@easternct.edu.

EASTERN ILLINOIS UNIVERSITY

Charleston, IL

Tuition & fees (IL res): $8783   Average undergraduate aid package: $8727

ABOUT THE INSTITUTION State-supported, coed. ***Awards:*** bachelor's and master's degrees and post-bachelor's and post-master's certificates. 52 undergraduate majors. ***Total enrollment:*** 12,040. Undergraduates: 10,261. Freshmen: 1,780. Federal methodology is used as a basis for awarding need-based institutional aid.

UNDERGRADUATE EXPENSES for 2008–09 ***Application fee:*** $30. ***Tuition, state resident:*** full-time $6540; part-time $218 per credit hour. ***Tuition, nonresident:*** full-time $19,620; part-time $654 per credit hour. ***Required fees:*** full-time $2243; $81 per credit hour. Full-time tuition and fees vary according to course load. Part-time tuition and fees vary according to course load. ***College room and board:*** $7588. Room and board charges vary according to board plan and housing facility. ***Payment plan:*** Installment.

FRESHMAN FINANCIAL AID (Fall 2008, est.) 1,539 applied for aid; of those 65% were deemed to have need. 98% of freshmen with need received aid; of those 10% had need fully met. ***Average percent of need met:*** 69% (excluding resources awarded to replace EFC). ***Average financial aid package:*** $8624 (excluding resources awarded to replace EFC). 5% of all full-time freshmen had no need and received non-need-based gift aid.

UNDERGRADUATE FINANCIAL AID (Fall 2008, est.) 7,407 applied for aid; of those 65% were deemed to have need. 98% of undergraduates with need received aid; of those 12% had need fully met. ***Average percent of need met:*** 73% (excluding resources awarded to replace EFC). ***Average financial aid package:*** $8727 (excluding resources awarded to replace EFC). 5% of all full-time undergraduates had no need and received non-need-based gift aid.

GIFT AID (NEED-BASED) ***Total amount:*** $25,236,760 (38% federal, 47% state, 11% institutional, 4% external sources). ***Receiving aid:*** Freshmen: 29% (516); all full-time undergraduates: 29% (2,615). ***Average award:*** Freshmen: $2625; Undergraduates: $3220. ***Scholarships, grants, and awards:*** Federal Pell, FSEOG, state, private, college/university gift aid from institutional funds.

GIFT AID (NON-NEED-BASED) ***Total amount:*** $6,025,937 (3% federal, 26% state, 60% institutional, 11% external sources). ***Receiving aid:*** Freshmen: 14% (252). Undergraduates: 12% (1,056). ***Average award:*** Freshmen: $3808. Undergraduates: $3523. ***Tuition waivers:*** Full or partial for employees or children of employees. ***ROTC:*** Army.

LOANS ***Student loans:*** $44,859,403 (80% need-based, 20% non-need-based). 59% of past graduating class borrowed through all loan programs. *Average indebtedness per student:* $14,233. ***Average need-based loan:*** Freshmen: $3188. Undergraduates: $4070. ***Parent loans:*** $6,096,475 (65% need-based, 35% non-need-based). ***Programs:*** Federal Direct (Subsidized and Unsubsidized Stafford, PLUS), Perkins, college/university.

WORK-STUDY ***Federal work-study:*** Total amount: $770,304; 466 jobs averaging $1056. ***State or other work-study/employment:*** Total amount: $6693 (7% need-based, 93% non-need-based). 2,547 part-time jobs averaging $1221.

ATHLETIC AWARDS Total amount: $2,815,647 (36% need-based, 64% non-need-based).

APPLYING FOR FINANCIAL AID ***Required financial aid form:*** FAFSA. ***Financial aid deadline (priority):*** 3/1. ***Notification date:*** Continuous beginning 3/1. Students must reply within 2 weeks of notification.

CONTACT Tracy L. Hall, Assistant Director of Financial Aid, Eastern Illinois University, 600 Lincoln Avenue, Charleston, IL 61920-3099, 217-581-7511 or toll-free 800-252-5711. *Fax:* 217-581-6422. *E-mail:* tlhall@eiu.edu.

EASTERN KENTUCKY UNIVERSITY

Richmond, KY

Tuition & fees (KY res): $6080   Average undergraduate aid package: $8688

ABOUT THE INSTITUTION State-supported, coed. ***Awards:*** associate, bachelor's, and master's degrees and post-bachelor's and post-master's certificates. 116 undergraduate majors. ***Total enrollment:*** 15,839. Undergraduates: 13,659. Freshmen: 2,493. Federal methodology is used as a basis for awarding need-based institutional aid.

UNDERGRADUATE EXPENSES for 2008–09 ***Application fee:*** $30. ***Tuition, state resident:*** full-time $6080; part-time $253.34 per credit hour. ***Tuition, nonresident:*** full-time $16,612; part-time $692.17 per credit hour. Part-time tuition and fees vary according to course load. ***College room and board:*** $6360; ***Room only:*** $2729. Room and board charges vary according to board plan and housing facility. ***Payment plan:*** Deferred payment.

FRESHMAN FINANCIAL AID (Fall 2008, est.) 2,119 applied for aid; of those 75% were deemed to have need. 99% of freshmen with need received aid; of those 13% had need fully met. ***Average percent of need met:*** 87% (excluding resources awarded to replace EFC). ***Average financial aid package:*** $9162 (excluding resources awarded to replace EFC). 14% of all full-time freshmen had no need and received non-need-based gift aid.

UNDERGRADUATE FINANCIAL AID (Fall 2008, est.) 8,472 applied for aid; of those 80% were deemed to have need. 97% of undergraduates with need received aid; of those 9% had need fully met. ***Average percent of need met:*** 85% (excluding resources awarded to replace EFC). ***Average financial aid package:*** $8688 (excluding resources awarded to replace EFC). 12% of all full-time undergraduates had no need and received non-need-based gift aid.

GIFT AID (NEED-BASED) ***Total amount:*** $33,054,815 (53% federal, 28% state, 17% institutional, 2% external sources). ***Receiving aid:*** Freshmen: 38% (942); all full-time undergraduates: 35% (3,915). ***Average award:*** Freshmen: $5704; Undergraduates: $5457. ***Scholarships, grants, and awards:*** Federal Pell, FSEOG, state, private, college/university gift aid from institutional funds, Federal Nursing.

GIFT AID (NON-NEED-BASED) ***Total amount:*** $6,276,244 (52% state, 38% institutional, 10% external sources). ***Receiving aid:*** Freshmen: 51% (1,267). Undergraduates: 31% (3,440). ***Average award:*** Freshmen: $5426. Undergraduates: $4924. ***Scholarships, grants, and awards by category:*** *Academic interests/achievement:* 1,645 awards ($7,771,990 total): general academic interests/achievements. *Creative arts/performance:* 125 awards ($305,368 total): music. *Special achievements/activities:* 24 awards ($16,100 total): cheerleading/drum major. *Special characteristics:* 479 awards ($1,202,477 total): children and siblings of alumni, children of faculty/staff, members of minority groups. ***Tuition waivers:*** Full or partial for employees or children of employees, senior citizens. ***ROTC:*** Army, Air Force cooperative.

LOANS ***Student loans:*** $71,401,517 (83% need-based, 17% non-need-based). 69% of past graduating class borrowed through all loan programs. *Average indebtedness per student:* $14,976. ***Average need-based loan:*** Freshmen: $2506. Undergraduates: $3676. ***Parent loans:*** $15,689,809 (61% need-based, 39% non-need-based). ***Programs:*** FFEL (Subsidized and Unsubsidized Stafford, PLUS), Perkins, college/university.

WORK-STUDY ***Federal work-study:*** Total amount: $3,833,155; 1,000 jobs averaging $1800. ***State or other work-study/employment:*** Total amount: $3,746,414 (100% non-need-based). 1,000 part-time jobs averaging $1800.

ATHLETIC AWARDS Total amount: $3,641,409 (38% need-based, 62% non-need-based).

APPLYING FOR FINANCIAL AID ***Required financial aid form:*** FAFSA. ***Financial aid deadline (priority):*** 3/15. ***Notification date:*** Continuous beginning 4/1.

CONTACT Financial Aid Office Staff, Eastern Kentucky University, 521 Lancaster Avenue, SSB CPO 59, Richmond, KY 40475-3102, 859-622-2361 or toll-free 800-465-9191 (in-state). *Fax:* 859-622-2019. *E-mail:* finaid@eku.edu.

EASTERN MENNONITE UNIVERSITY

Harrisonburg, VA

CONTACT Ms. Renee Leap, Assistant Director of Financial Assistance, Eastern Mennonite University, 1200 Park Road, Harrisonburg, VA 22802-2462, 540-432-4138 or toll-free 800-368-2665. *Fax:* 540-432-4081. *E-mail:* leapr@emu.edu.

EASTERN MICHIGAN UNIVERSITY

Ypsilanti, MI

Tuition & fees (MI res): $8069 **Average undergraduate aid package: $7296**

ABOUT THE INSTITUTION State-supported, coed. ***Awards:*** bachelor's, master's, and doctoral degrees and post-bachelor's and post-master's certificates. 134 undergraduate majors. ***Total enrollment:*** 21,926. Undergraduates: 17,213. Federal methodology is used as a basis for awarding need-based institutional aid.

UNDERGRADUATE EXPENSES for 2008–09 ***Application fee:*** $30. ***One-time required fee:*** $88. ***Tuition, state resident:*** full-time $6885; part-time $229.50 per credit hour. ***Tuition, nonresident:*** full-time $20,280; part-time $676 per credit hour. ***Required fees:*** full-time $1184; $36.60 per credit hour or $43 per term. Full-time tuition and fees vary according to reciprocity agreements. Part-time tuition and fees vary according to reciprocity agreements. ***College room and board:*** $7352; ***Room only:*** $3452. Room and board charges vary according to board plan, housing facility, and location. ***Payment plan:*** Installment.

FRESHMAN FINANCIAL AID (Fall 2007) 1,940 applied for aid; of those 78% were deemed to have need. 97% of freshmen with need received aid; of those 12% had need fully met. ***Average percent of need met:*** 66% (excluding resources awarded to replace EFC). ***Average financial aid package:*** $8286 (excluding resources awarded to replace EFC). 24% of all full-time freshmen had no need and received non-need-based gift aid.

UNDERGRADUATE FINANCIAL AID (Fall 2007) 8,564 applied for aid; of those 64% were deemed to have need. 98% of undergraduates with need received aid; of those 11% had need fully met. ***Average percent of need met:*** 59% (excluding resources awarded to replace EFC). ***Average financial aid package:*** $7296 (excluding resources awarded to replace EFC). 10% of all full-time undergraduates had no need and received non-need-based gift aid.

GIFT AID (NEED-BASED) ***Total amount:*** $17,745,221 (88% federal, 6% state, 6% institutional). ***Receiving aid:*** Freshmen: 40% (951); all full-time undergraduates: 27% (3,310). ***Average award:*** Freshmen: $3657; Undergraduates: $3466. ***Scholarships, grants, and awards:*** Federal Pell, FSEOG, state, private, college/university gift aid from institutional funds.

GIFT AID (NON-NEED-BASED) ***Total amount:*** $20,228,324 (7% state, 49% institutional, 44% external sources). ***Receiving aid:*** Freshmen: 50% (1,184). Undergraduates: 12% (1,546). ***Average award:*** Freshmen: $2833. Undergraduates: $3176. ***Scholarships, grants, and awards by category:*** *Academic interests/achievement:* 2,962 awards ($6,932,400 total): agriculture, architecture, biological sciences, business, communication, computer science, education, engineering/technologies, English, foreign languages, general academic interests/achievements, health fields, home economics, humanities, mathematics, physical sciences, religion/biblical studies, social sciences. *Creative arts/performance:* 146 awards ($108,685 total): applied art and design, art/fine arts, cinema/film/broadcasting, creative writing, dance, debating, general creative arts/performance, music, performing arts, theater/drama. *Special achievements/activities:* 198 awards ($198,875 total): general special achievements/activities, leadership, memberships, religious involvement. *Special characteristics:* 258 awards ($2,307,192 total): children and siblings of alumni, ethnic background, international students, members of minority groups, out-of-state students, previous college experience, religious affiliation. ***Tuition waivers:*** Full or partial for employees or children of employees. ***ROTC:*** Army, Naval cooperative, Air Force cooperative.

LOANS ***Student loans:*** $76,386,809 (42% need-based, 58% non-need-based). 62% of past graduating class borrowed through all loan programs. *Average indebtedness per student:* $20,940. ***Average need-based loan:*** Freshmen: $3824. Undergraduates: $3730. ***Parent loans:*** $9,978,208 (100% non-need-based). ***Programs:*** Federal Direct (Subsidized and Unsubsidized Stafford), FFEL (PLUS), Perkins, college/university, alternative private loans.

WORK-STUDY ***Federal work-study:*** Total amount: $914,754; 593 jobs averaging $1561. ***State or other work-study/employment:*** Total amount: $346,388 (100% need-based). 276 part-time jobs averaging $1256.

ATHLETIC AWARDS Total amount: $5,290,365 (100% non-need-based).

APPLYING FOR FINANCIAL AID ***Required financial aid form:*** FAFSA. ***Financial aid deadline:*** Continuous. ***Notification date:*** Continuous beginning 3/1.

CONTACT Cynthia Van Pelt, Director, Eastern Michigan University, 403 Pierce Hall, Ypsilanti, MI 48197, 734-487-1048 or toll-free 800-GO TO EMU. *Fax:* 734-487-0174. *E-mail:* cvanpelt@emich.edu.

EASTERN NAZARENE COLLEGE

Quincy, MA

Tuition & fees: $22,014 **Average undergraduate aid package: $20,808**

ABOUT THE INSTITUTION Independent religious, coed. ***Awards:*** associate, bachelor's, and master's degrees. 49 undergraduate majors. ***Total enrollment:*** 762. Undergraduates: 678. Freshmen: 178. Federal methodology is used as a basis for awarding need-based institutional aid.

UNDERGRADUATE EXPENSES for 2008–09 ***Application fee:*** $25. ***Comprehensive fee:*** $29,927 includes full-time tuition ($21,280), mandatory fees ($734), and room and board ($7913). ***College room only:*** $3975. ***Part-time tuition:*** $842 per credit hour.

FRESHMAN FINANCIAL AID (Fall 2008, est.) 164 applied for aid; of those 90% were deemed to have need. 100% of freshmen with need received aid; of those 33% had need fully met. ***Average percent of need met:*** 71% (excluding resources awarded to replace EFC). ***Average financial aid package:*** $20,914 (excluding resources awarded to replace EFC). 13% of all full-time freshmen had no need and received non-need-based gift aid.

UNDERGRADUATE FINANCIAL AID (Fall 2008, est.) 463 applied for aid; of those 85% were deemed to have need. 100% of undergraduates with need received aid; of those 36% had need fully met. ***Average percent of need met:*** 73% (excluding resources awarded to replace EFC). ***Average financial aid package:*** $20,808 (excluding resources awarded to replace EFC). 16% of all full-time undergraduates had no need and received non-need-based gift aid.

GIFT AID (NEED-BASED) ***Total amount:*** $4,102,570 (22% federal, 3% state, 73% institutional, 2% external sources). ***Receiving aid:*** Freshmen: 84% (145); all full-time undergraduates: 55% (349). ***Average award:*** Freshmen: $9499; Undergraduates: $7681. ***Scholarships, grants, and awards:*** Federal Pell, FSEOG, state, private, college/university gift aid from institutional funds, United Negro College Fund.

GIFT AID (NON-NEED-BASED) ***Total amount:*** $1,155,076 (94% institutional, 6% external sources). ***Receiving aid:*** Freshmen: 10% (18). Undergraduates: 3% (22). ***Average award:*** Freshmen: $9707. Undergraduates: $7618. ***ROTC:*** Army cooperative, Air Force cooperative.

LOANS ***Student loans:*** $6,417,978 (77% need-based, 23% non-need-based). 88% of past graduating class borrowed through all loan programs. *Average indebtedness per student:* $42,290. ***Average need-based loan:*** Freshmen: $8298. Undergraduates: $10,598. ***Parent loans:*** $1,036,123 (68% need-based, 32% non-need-based). ***Programs:*** FFEL (Subsidized and Unsubsidized Stafford, PLUS), Perkins, state, alternative loans.

WORK-STUDY ***Federal work-study:*** Total amount: $64,609; 228 jobs averaging $1409.

APPLYING FOR FINANCIAL AID ***Required financial aid forms:*** FAFSA, institution's own form. ***Financial aid deadline:*** Continuous. ***Notification date:*** Continuous beginning 3/15. Students must reply within 2 weeks of notification.

CONTACT Dana Parker, Director of Financial Aid, Eastern Nazarene College, 23 East Elm Avenue, Quincy, MA 02170, 617-745-3712 or toll-free 800-88-ENC88. *Fax:* 617-745-3992. *E-mail:* financialaid@enc.edu.

EASTERN NEW MEXICO UNIVERSITY

Portales, NM

CONTACT Ms. Patricia Willis, Financial Aid Specialist, Eastern New Mexico University, Station 54, Portales, NM 88130, 505-562-2194 or toll-free 800-367-3668. *Fax:* 505-562-2198. *E-mail:* pat.willis@enmu.edu.

EASTERN OREGON UNIVERSITY

La Grande, OR

ABOUT THE INSTITUTION State-supported, coed. ***Awards:*** bachelor's and master's degrees. 22 undergraduate majors. ***Total enrollment:*** 3,666. Undergraduates: 3,127. Freshmen: 350.

GIFT AID (NEED-BASED) ***Scholarships, grants, and awards:*** Federal Pell, FSEOG, state, private, college/university gift aid from institutional funds.

LOANS ***Programs:*** Federal Direct (Subsidized and Unsubsidized Stafford, PLUS), FFEL (Subsidized and Unsubsidized Stafford, PLUS), Perkins.

WORK-STUDY ***Federal work-study:*** Total amount: $402,152.

APPLYING FOR FINANCIAL AID ***Required financial aid form:*** FAFSA.

CONTACT Mr. Eric Bucks, Director of Financial Aid, Eastern Oregon University, One University Boulevard, La Grande, OR 97850-2899, 541-962-3550 or toll-free 800-452-8639 (in-state), 800-452-3393 (out-of-state). *Fax:* 541-962-3661. *E-mail:* eric.bucks@eou.edu.

EASTERN UNIVERSITY

St. Davids, PA

CONTACT Financial Aid Office, Eastern University, 1300 Eagle Road, St. Davids, PA 19087-3696, 610-341-5842 or toll-free 800-452-0996. *Fax:* 610-341-1492. *E-mail:* finaid@eastern.edu.

EASTERN WASHINGTON UNIVERSITY

Cheney, WA

Tuition & fees (WA res): $5118 Average undergraduate aid package: $10,260

ABOUT THE INSTITUTION State-supported, coed. ***Awards:*** bachelor's, master's, and doctoral degrees and post-master's certificates. 76 undergraduate majors. ***Total enrollment:*** 10,809. Undergraduates: 9,485. Freshmen: 1,509. Federal methodology is used as a basis for awarding need-based institutional aid.

UNDERGRADUATE EXPENSES for 2008–09 ***Application fee:*** $50. ***Tuition, state resident:*** full-time $4701; part-time $156.70 per credit. ***Tuition, nonresident:*** full-time $13,368; part-time $445.60 per credit. ***Required fees:*** full-time $417; $136.12 per term. Full-time tuition and fees vary according to course load and program. Part-time tuition and fees vary according to course load and program. ***College room and board:*** $6894. Room and board charges vary according to board plan and housing facility. ***Payment plan:*** Installment.

FRESHMAN FINANCIAL AID (Fall 2007) 1,015 applied for aid; of those 71% were deemed to have need. 96% of freshmen with need received aid; of those 29% had need fully met. ***Average percent of need met:*** 90% (excluding resources awarded to replace EFC). ***Average financial aid package:*** $9782 (excluding resources awarded to replace EFC). 10% of all full-time freshmen had no need and received non-need-based gift aid.

UNDERGRADUATE FINANCIAL AID (Fall 2007) 5,835 applied for aid; of those 79% were deemed to have need. 96% of undergraduates with need received aid; of those 27% had need fully met. ***Average percent of need met:*** 68% (excluding resources awarded to replace EFC). ***Average financial aid package:*** $10,260 (excluding resources awarded to replace EFC). 4% of all full-time undergraduates had no need and received non-need-based gift aid.

GIFT AID (NEED-BASED) ***Total amount:*** $22,977,028 (40% federal, 42% state, 8% institutional, 10% external sources). ***Receiving aid:*** Freshmen: 45% (584); all full-time undergraduates: 42% (3,420). ***Average award:*** Freshmen: $5199; Undergraduates: $5754. ***Scholarships, grants, and awards:*** Federal Pell, FSEOG, state, private, college/university gift aid from institutional funds.

GIFT AID (NON-NEED-BASED) ***Total amount:*** $655,516 (18% institutional, 82% external sources). ***Receiving aid:*** Freshmen: 20% (259). Undergraduates: 10% (807). ***Average award:*** Freshmen: $2942. Undergraduates: $2933. ***Scholarships, grants, and awards by category:*** *Academic interests/achievement:* 275 awards ($475,000 total): area/ethnic studies, biological sciences, business, computer science, education, engineering/technologies, English, foreign languages, general academic interests/achievements, health fields, mathematics, military science, physical sciences, social sciences. *Creative arts/performance:* 60 awards ($67,000 total): art/fine arts, cinema/film/broadcasting, creative writing, journalism/publications, music, theater/drama. *Special characteristics:* 75 awards ($72,000 total): children of union members/company employees, ethnic background, handicapped students, local/state students. ***Tuition waivers:*** Full or partial for employees or children of employees. ***ROTC:*** Army.

LOANS ***Student loans:*** $27,365,964 (82% need-based, 18% non-need-based). 65% of past graduating class borrowed through all loan programs. *Average indebtedness per student:* $18,320. ***Average need-based loan:*** Freshmen: $2180. Undergraduates: $2779. ***Parent loans:*** $6,546,635 (58% need-based, 42% non-need-based). ***Programs:*** FFEL (Subsidized and Unsubsidized Stafford, PLUS), Perkins.

WORK-STUDY ***Federal work-study:*** Total amount: $444,754; 189 jobs averaging $3120. ***State or other work-study/employment:*** Total amount: $736,196 (100% need-based). 212 part-time jobs averaging $3555.

ATHLETIC AWARDS Total amount: $1,443,764 (42% need-based, 58% non-need-based).

APPLYING FOR FINANCIAL AID ***Required financial aid form:*** FAFSA. ***Financial aid deadline (priority):*** 2/15. ***Notification date:*** Continuous beginning 4/1. Students must reply within 4 weeks of notification.

CONTACT Bruce DeFrates, Financial Aid Director, Eastern Washington University, 102 Sutton Hall, Cheney, WA 99004-2447, 509-359-2314. *Fax:* 509-359-4330. *E-mail:* finaid@ewu.edu.

EAST STROUDSBURG UNIVERSITY OF PENNSYLVANIA

East Stroudsburg, PA

CONTACT Georgia K. Prell, Director of Enrollment Services, East Stroudsburg University of Pennsylvania, 200 Prospect Street, East Stroudsburg, PA 18301-2999, 570-422-2820 or toll-free 877-230-5547. *Fax:* 570-422-2849.

EAST TENNESSEE STATE UNIVERSITY

Johnson City, TN

Tuition & fees (TN res): $5201 Average undergraduate aid package: $4675

ABOUT THE INSTITUTION State-supported, coed. ***Awards:*** bachelor's, master's, doctoral, and first professional degrees and post-bachelor's and post-master's certificates. 38 undergraduate majors. ***Total enrollment:*** 13,119. Undergraduates: 10,665. Freshmen: 1,939. Federal methodology is used as a basis for awarding need-based institutional aid.

UNDERGRADUATE EXPENSES for 2008–09 ***Application fee:*** $15. ***Tuition, state resident:*** full-time $4302. ***Tuition, nonresident:*** full-time $15,194. ***Required fees:*** full-time $899. Full-time tuition and fees vary according to course load and program. Part-time tuition and fees vary according to course load and program. ***College room and board:*** $5278; ***Room only:*** $2680. Room and board charges vary according to board plan and housing facility. ***Payment plans:*** Installment, deferred payment.

FRESHMAN FINANCIAL AID (Fall 2008, est.) 1,587 applied for aid; of those 75% were deemed to have need. 97% of freshmen with need received aid; of those 35% had need fully met. ***Average percent of need met:*** 82% (excluding resources awarded to replace EFC). ***Average financial aid package:*** $7617 (excluding resources awarded to replace EFC). 9% of all full-time freshmen had no need and received non-need-based gift aid.

UNDERGRADUATE FINANCIAL AID (Fall 2008, est.) 7,513 applied for aid; of those 73% were deemed to have need. 97% of undergraduates with need received aid; of those 47% had need fully met. ***Average percent of need met:*** 81% (excluding resources awarded to replace EFC). ***Average financial aid package:*** $4675 (excluding resources awarded to replace EFC). 12% of all full-time undergraduates had no need and received non-need-based gift aid.

GIFT AID (NEED-BASED) ***Total amount:*** $28,705,858 (39% federal, 61% state). ***Receiving aid:*** Freshmen: 54% (1,007); all full-time undergraduates: 44% (4,086). ***Average award:*** Freshmen: $4701; Undergraduates: $3207. ***Scholarships, grants, and awards:*** Federal Pell, FSEOG, state, private, college/university gift aid from institutional funds, Federal Nursing.

GIFT AID (NON-NEED-BASED) ***Total amount:*** $9,741,932 (3% federal, 9% state, 56% institutional, 32% external sources). ***Receiving aid:*** Freshmen: 20% (373). Undergraduates: 17% (1,565). ***Average award:*** Freshmen: $3492. Undergraduates: $3447. ***Scholarships, grants, and awards by category:*** *Academic interests/achievement:* biological sciences, business, computer science, education, engineering/technologies, English, general academic interests/achievements, health fields, mathematics, military science, social sciences. *Creative arts/performance:* art/fine arts, journalism/publications, music, theater/drama. *Special achievements/activities:* leadership, memberships. *Special characteristics:* children of union members/company employees, members of minority groups. ***Tuition waivers:*** Full or partial for employees or children of employees, senior citizens. ***ROTC:*** Army.

LOANS ***Student loans:*** $40,395,024 (55% need-based, 45% non-need-based). 59% of past graduating class borrowed through all loan programs. *Average indebtedness per student:* $16,635. ***Average need-based loan:*** Freshmen: $1208. Undergraduates: $3070. ***Parent loans:*** $3,830,992 (100% non-need-based). ***Programs:*** Federal Direct (Subsidized and Unsubsidized Stafford, PLUS), Perkins, Federal Nursing, college/university.

WORK-STUDY ***Federal work-study:*** Total amount: $2,279,946; 1,019 jobs averaging $1525. ***State or other work-study/employment:*** Total amount: $616,781 (100% non-need-based). 379 part-time jobs averaging $1161.

ATHLETIC AWARDS Total amount: $2,157,506 (100% non-need-based).

APPLYING FOR FINANCIAL AID ***Required financial aid form:*** FAFSA. ***Financial aid deadline (priority):*** 4/15. ***Notification date:*** Continuous beginning 5/1. Students must reply within 3 weeks of notification.

CONTACT Cindy A. Johnson, Assistant Director of Financial Aid, East Tennessee State University, PO Box 70722, Johnson City, TN 37614, 423-439-4300 or toll-free 800-462-3878.

EAST TEXAS BAPTIST UNIVERSITY

Marshall, TX

Tuition & fees: $17,180 **Average undergraduate aid package: $12,200**

ABOUT THE INSTITUTION Independent Baptist, coed. ***Awards:*** bachelor's degrees. 43 undergraduate majors. ***Total enrollment:*** 1,210. Undergraduates: 1,210. Freshmen: 295. Federal methodology is used as a basis for awarding need-based institutional aid.

UNDERGRADUATE EXPENSES for 2009–10 ***Application fee:*** $25. ***Comprehensive fee:*** $22,344 includes full-time tuition ($17,180) and room and board ($5164). ***College room only:*** $2220. ***Part-time tuition:*** $600 per credit hour.

FRESHMAN FINANCIAL AID (Fall 2007) 294 applied for aid; of those 86% were deemed to have need. 100% of freshmen with need received aid; of those 18% had need fully met. ***Average percent of need met:*** 61% (excluding resources awarded to replace EFC). ***Average financial aid package:*** $13,017 (excluding resources awarded to replace EFC). 19% of all full-time freshmen had no need and received non-need-based gift aid.

UNDERGRADUATE FINANCIAL AID (Fall 2007) 1,068 applied for aid; of those 85% were deemed to have need. 100% of undergraduates with need received aid; of those 22% had need fully met. ***Average percent of need met:*** 60% (excluding resources awarded to replace EFC). ***Average financial aid package:*** $12,200 (excluding resources awarded to replace EFC). 21% of all full-time undergraduates had no need and received non-need-based gift aid.

GIFT AID (NEED-BASED) ***Total amount:*** $3,576,789 (44% federal, 56% state). ***Receiving aid:*** Freshmen: 70% (218); all full-time undergraduates: 67% (767). ***Average award:*** Freshmen: $7156; Undergraduates: $6125. ***Scholarships, grants, and awards:*** Federal Pell, FSEOG, state, private, college/university gift aid from institutional funds, Federal Nursing.

GIFT AID (NON-NEED-BASED) ***Total amount:*** $6,302,858 (1% state, 93% institutional, 6% external sources). ***Receiving aid:*** Freshmen: 70% (217). Undergraduates: 65% (747). ***Average award:*** Freshmen: $5858. Undergraduates: $5428. ***Scholarships, grants, and awards by category:*** *Academic interests/achievement:* 210 awards ($192,362 total): biological sciences, business, communication, education, English, general academic interests/achievements, health fields, humanities, mathematics, physical sciences, religion/biblical studies, social sciences. *Creative arts/performance:* 198 awards ($226,025 total): music, theater/drama. *Special achievements/activities:* 893 awards ($886,457 total): cheerleading/drum major, general special achievements/activities, leadership, religious involvement. *Special characteristics:* 953 awards ($1,511,841 total): children and siblings of alumni, children of educators, children of faculty/staff, general special characteristics, international students, local/state students, previous college experience, religious affiliation, siblings of current students, twins.

LOANS ***Student loans:*** $5,631,462 (46% need-based, 54% non-need-based). 75% of past graduating class borrowed through all loan programs. *Average indebtedness per student:* $20,492. ***Average need-based loan:*** Freshmen: $2966. Undergraduates: $3593. ***Parent loans:*** $548,817 (100% non-need-based). ***Programs:*** FFEL (Subsidized and Unsubsidized Stafford, PLUS), Perkins, state.

WORK-STUDY ***Federal work-study:*** Total amount: $184,773; 105 jobs averaging $1120. ***State or other work-study/employment:*** Total amount: $351,300 (3% need-based, 97% non-need-based). 192 part-time jobs averaging $1220.

APPLYING FOR FINANCIAL AID ***Required financial aid forms:*** FAFSA, institution's own form. ***Financial aid deadline (priority):*** 6/1. ***Notification date:*** Continuous. Students must reply within 3 weeks of notification.

CONTACT Tommy Young, Director of Financial Aid, East Texas Baptist University, 1209 North Grove Street, Marshall, TX 75670-1498, 903-923-2137 or toll-free 800-804-ETBU. *Fax:* 903-934-8120. *E-mail:* tyoung@etbu.edu.

EAST-WEST UNIVERSITY

Chicago, IL

Tuition & fees: $13,575 **Average undergraduate aid package: $9020**

ABOUT THE INSTITUTION Independent, coed. ***Awards:*** associate and bachelor's degrees. 17 undergraduate majors. ***Total enrollment:*** 1,170. Undergraduates: 1,170. Freshmen: 358. Federal methodology is used as a basis for awarding need-based institutional aid.

UNDERGRADUATE EXPENSES for 2008–09 ***Application fee:*** $40. ***Tuition:*** full-time $12,900; part-time $430 per credit hour.

FRESHMAN FINANCIAL AID (Fall 2007) 1,257 applied for aid; of those 100% were deemed to have need. 100% of freshmen with need received aid. ***Average percent of need met:*** 90% (excluding resources awarded to replace EFC). ***Average financial aid package:*** $9020 (excluding resources awarded to replace EFC).

UNDERGRADUATE FINANCIAL AID (Fall 2007) 1,339 applied for aid; of those 100% were deemed to have need. 100% of undergraduates with need received aid. ***Average percent of need met:*** 90% (excluding resources awarded to replace EFC). ***Average financial aid package:*** $9020 (excluding resources awarded to replace EFC).

GIFT AID (NEED-BASED) ***Total amount:*** $6,077,080 (41% federal, 51% state, 8% institutional). ***Scholarships, grants, and awards:*** Federal Pell, FSEOG, state, college/university gift aid from institutional funds.

GIFT AID (NON-NEED-BASED) ***Scholarships, grants, and awards by category:*** *Academic interests/achievement:* general academic interests/achievements.

LOANS ***Student loans:*** $412,005 (100% need-based). 15% of past graduating class borrowed through all loan programs. *Average indebtedness per student:* $2625. ***Programs:*** Federal Direct (Subsidized Stafford).

WORK-STUDY ***Federal work-study:*** Total amount: $114,280; 39 jobs averaging $3200.

APPLYING FOR FINANCIAL AID ***Required financial aid form:*** FAFSA. ***Financial aid deadline (priority):*** 6/30.

CONTACT Elizabeth Guzmán, Financial Aid Office, East-West University, 816 South Michigan Avenue, Chicago, IL 60605-2103, 312-939-0111 Ext. 1809. *Fax:* 312-939-0083. *E-mail:* elizabth@eastwest.edu.

ECKERD COLLEGE

St. Petersburg, FL

ABOUT THE INSTITUTION Independent Presbyterian, coed. ***Awards:*** bachelor's degrees. 37 undergraduate majors. ***Total enrollment:*** 1,819. Undergraduates: 1,819. Freshmen: 489.

GIFT AID (NEED-BASED) ***Scholarships, grants, and awards:*** Federal Pell, FSEOG, state, private, college/university gift aid from institutional funds.

GIFT AID (NON-NEED BASED) ***Scholarships, grants, and awards by category:*** *Academic interests/achievement:* general academic interests/achievements. *Creative arts/performance:* art/fine arts, creative writing, music, theater/drama. *Special achievements/activities:* community service, leadership. *Special characteristics:* children of faculty/staff, international students, local/state students, religious affiliation.

LOANS ***Programs:*** FFEL (Subsidized and Unsubsidized Stafford, PLUS), Perkins, college/university.

WORK-STUDY ***Federal work-study:*** Total amount: $1,549,858; 661 jobs averaging $2000. ***State or other work-study/employment:*** Total amount: $132,500 (100% non-need-based). Part-time jobs available.

APPLYING FOR FINANCIAL AID ***Required financial aid form:*** FAFSA.

CONTACT Dr. Pat Watkins, Director of Financial Aid, Eckerd College, 4200 54th Avenue, South, St. Petersburg, FL 33711, 727-864-8334 or toll-free 800-456-9009. *Fax:* 727-866-2304. *E-mail:* watkinpe@eckerd.edu.

EDGEWOOD COLLEGE

Madison, WI

Tuition & fees: $20,040 **Average undergraduate aid package: $15,659**

ABOUT THE INSTITUTION Independent Roman Catholic, coed, primarily women. ***Awards:*** associate, bachelor's, master's, and doctoral degrees. 45 undergraduate majors. ***Total enrollment:*** 2,544. Undergraduates: 1,989. Freshmen: 300. Federal methodology is used as a basis for awarding need-based institutional aid.

UNDERGRADUATE EXPENSES for 2008–09 ***Application fee:*** $25. ***Comprehensive fee:*** $26,868 includes full-time tuition ($20,040) and room and board ($6828). ***College room only:*** $3468. Full-time tuition and fees vary according to degree level. Room and board charges vary according to housing facility. ***Part-time tuition:*** $630 per credit. Part-time tuition and fees vary according to course load and degree level. ***Payment plan:*** Installment.

FRESHMAN FINANCIAL AID (Fall 2008, est.) 257 applied for aid; of those 86% were deemed to have need. 100% of freshmen with need received aid; of those 23% had need fully met. ***Average percent of need met:*** 81% (excluding resources awarded to replace EFC). ***Average financial aid package:*** $6395 (excluding resources awarded to replace EFC). 22% of all full-time freshmen had no need and received non-need-based gift aid.

UNDERGRADUATE FINANCIAL AID (Fall 2008, est.) 1,171 applied for aid; of those 86% were deemed to have need. 100% of undergraduates with need received aid; of those 13% had need fully met. ***Average percent of need met:*** 73% (excluding resources awarded to replace EFC). ***Average financial aid package:*** $15,659 (excluding resources awarded to replace EFC). 19% of all full-time undergraduates had no need and received non-need-based gift aid.

GIFT AID (NEED-BASED) ***Total amount:*** $10,431,883 (17% federal, 15% state, 57% institutional, 11% external sources). ***Receiving aid:*** Freshmen: 73% (216); all full-time undergraduates: 66% (952). ***Average award:*** Freshmen: $12,395; Undergraduates: $9836. ***Scholarships, grants, and awards:*** Federal Pell, FSEOG, state, private, college/university gift aid from institutional funds.

GIFT AID (NON-NEED-BASED) ***Total amount:*** $1,773,848 (3% federal, 69% institutional, 28% external sources). ***Receiving aid:*** Freshmen: 8% (25). Undergraduates: 4% (61). ***Average award:*** Freshmen: $4701. Undergraduates: $3860. ***Scholarships, grants, and awards by category:*** *Academic interests/achievement:* foreign languages, general academic interests/achievements. *Creative arts/performance:* art/fine arts, creative writing, music, performing arts, theater/drama. *Special achievements/activities:* community service. *Special characteristics:* children of faculty/staff, local/state students. ***Tuition waivers:*** Full or partial for employees or children of employees.

LOANS ***Student loans:*** $14,382,051 (68% need-based, 32% non-need-based). 63% of past graduating class borrowed through all loan programs. *Average indebtedness per student:* $27,885. ***Average need-based loan:*** Freshmen: $3713. Undergraduates: $5344. ***Parent loans:*** $1,726,186 (36% need-based, 64% non-need-based). ***Programs:*** FFEL (Subsidized and Unsubsidized Stafford, PLUS), Perkins, state, college/university.

WORK-STUDY ***Federal work-study:*** Total amount: $550,301; jobs available. ***State or other work-study/employment:*** Total amount: $2,130,507 (46% need-based, 54% non-need-based). Part-time jobs available.

APPLYING FOR FINANCIAL AID ***Required financial aid forms:*** FAFSA, institution's own form. ***Financial aid deadline (priority):*** 3/1. ***Notification date:*** Continuous beginning 3/15. Students must reply within 2 weeks of notification.

CONTACT Kari Gribble, Director for Financial Aid, Edgewood College, 1000 Edgewood College Drive, Madison, WI 53711-1997, 608-663-2206 or toll-free 800-444-4861 Ext. 2294. *E-mail:* financialaid@edgewood.edu.

EDINBORO UNIVERSITY OF PENNSYLVANIA

Edinboro, PA

Tuition & fees (PA res): $7042 **Average undergraduate aid package: $7386**

ABOUT THE INSTITUTION State-supported, coed. ***Awards:*** associate, bachelor's, and master's degrees and post-bachelor's and post-master's certificates. 55 undergraduate majors. ***Total enrollment:*** 7,671. Undergraduates: 6,154. Freshmen: 1,247. Federal methodology is used as a basis for awarding need-based institutional aid.

UNDERGRADUATE EXPENSES for 2008–09 ***Application fee:*** $30. ***Tuition, state resident:*** full-time $5358; part-time $223 per credit hour. ***Tuition, nonresident:*** full-time $8038; part-time $335 per credit hour. ***Required fees:*** full-time $1684; $62.06 per credit. Part-time tuition and fees vary according to course load. ***College room and board:*** $6650; ***Room only:*** $4400. Room and board charges vary according to board plan. ***Payment plan:*** Installment.

FRESHMAN FINANCIAL AID (Fall 2007) 1,214 applied for aid; of those 85% were deemed to have need. 97% of freshmen with need received aid; of those 5% had need fully met. ***Average percent of need met:*** 49% (excluding resources awarded to replace EFC). ***Average financial aid package:*** $7124 (excluding resources awarded to replace EFC). 4% of all full-time freshmen had no need and received non-need-based gift aid.

UNDERGRADUATE FINANCIAL AID (Fall 2007) 5,240 applied for aid; of those 85% were deemed to have need. 98% of undergraduates with need received aid; of those 7% had need fully met. ***Average percent of need met:*** 61% (excluding resources awarded to replace EFC). ***Average financial aid package:*** $7386 (excluding resources awarded to replace EFC). 5% of all full-time undergraduates had no need and received non-need-based gift aid.

GIFT AID (NEED-BASED) ***Total amount:*** $15,647,762 (51% federal, 47% state, 1% institutional, 1% external sources). ***Receiving aid:*** Freshmen: 73% (907); all full-time undergraduates: 61% (3,964). ***Average award:*** Freshmen: $4076; Undergraduates: $3762. ***Scholarships, grants, and awards:*** Federal Pell, FSEOG, state, private, college/university gift aid from institutional funds.

GIFT AID (NON-NEED-BASED) ***Total amount:*** $3,338,760 (3% federal, 12% state, 58% institutional, 27% external sources). ***Receiving aid:*** Freshmen: 73% (909). Undergraduates: 61% (3,941). ***Average award:*** Freshmen: $2400. Undergraduates: $1905. ***Scholarships, grants, and awards by category:*** *Academic interests/achievement:* 260 awards ($286,000 total): biological sciences, business, communication, computer science, education, engineering/technologies, English, foreign languages, general academic interests/achievements, health fields, humanities, mathematics, military science, physical sciences, premedicine, religion/biblical studies, social sciences. *Creative arts/performance:* 31 awards ($14,500 total): art/fine arts, cinema/film/broadcasting, journalism/publications, music. *Special achievements/activities:* 5 awards ($3500 total): general special achievements/activities. *Special characteristics:* 856 awards ($2,422,311 total): adult students, children and siblings of alumni, children of faculty/staff, children of union members/company employees, children with a deceased or disabled parent, first-generation college students, general special characteristics, handicapped students, international students, local/state students, members of minority groups, out-of-state students, religious affiliation, veterans, veterans' children. ***Tuition waivers:*** Full or partial for minority students, employees or children of employees. ***ROTC:*** Army.

LOANS ***Student loans:*** $29,412,530 (48% need-based, 52% non-need-based). 61% of past graduating class borrowed through all loan programs. *Average indebtedness per student:* $13,313. ***Average need-based loan:*** Freshmen: $2909. Undergraduates: $3606. ***Parent loans:*** $3,945,516 (100% non-need-based). ***Programs:*** Federal Direct (Subsidized and Unsubsidized Stafford), FFEL (Subsidized and Unsubsidized Stafford, PLUS), Perkins, Federal Nursing, college/university.

WORK-STUDY ***Federal work-study:*** Total amount: $678,791; 457 jobs averaging $1485. ***State or other work-study/employment:*** Total amount: $1,096,818 (10% need-based, 90% non-need-based). 801 part-time jobs averaging $1128.

ATHLETIC AWARDS Total amount: $821,678 (100% non-need-based).

APPLYING FOR FINANCIAL AID ***Required financial aid form:*** FAFSA. ***Financial aid deadline (priority):*** 3/15. ***Notification date:*** 3/31. Students must reply within 2 weeks of notification.

CONTACT Ms. Dorothy Body, Assistant Vice President for Financial Aid, Edinboro University of Pennsylvania, Hamilton Hall, Edinboro, PA 16444, 814-732-5555 Ext. 266 or toll-free 888-846-2676 (in-state), 800-626-2203 (out-of-state). *Fax:* 814-732-2129. *E-mail:* dbody@edinboro.edu.

EDP COLLEGE OF PUERTO RICO, INC.

Hato Rey, PR

Tuition & fees: $4980 **Average undergraduate aid package: $60**

ABOUT THE INSTITUTION Proprietary, coed. ***Awards:*** associate, bachelor's, and master's degrees. 6 undergraduate majors. ***Total enrollment:*** 899. Undergraduates: 828. Freshmen: 204. Federal methodology is used as a basis for awarding need-based institutional aid.

UNDERGRADUATE EXPENSES for 2008–09 ***Application fee:*** $15. ***Tuition:*** full-time $4380; part-time $146 per credit. ***Required fees:*** full-time $600; $300 per term. ***Payment plan:*** Installment.

FRESHMAN FINANCIAL AID (Fall 2007) 170 applied for aid; of those 91% were deemed to have need. 100% of freshmen with need received aid. ***Average percent of need met:*** 53% (excluding resources awarded to replace EFC). ***Average financial aid package:*** $60 (excluding resources awarded to replace EFC).

UNDERGRADUATE FINANCIAL AID (Fall 2007) 873 applied for aid; of those 88% were deemed to have need. 100% of undergraduates with need received aid. ***Average percent of need met:*** 53% (excluding resources awarded to replace EFC). ***Average financial aid package:*** $60 (excluding resources awarded to replace EFC).

GIFT AID (NEED-BASED) ***Total amount:*** $3,448,138 (95% federal, 5% state). ***Receiving aid:*** Freshmen: 86% (154); all full-time undergraduates: 85% (772). ***Average award:*** Freshmen: $50; Undergraduates: $50. ***Scholarships, grants, and awards:*** Federal Pell, FSEOG, state.

GIFT AID (NON-NEED-BASED) ***Scholarships, grants, and awards by category:*** *Special characteristics:* veterans, veterans' children. ***Tuition waivers:*** Full or partial for employees or children of employees. ***ROTC:*** Army cooperative, Air Force cooperative.

LOANS ***Student loans:*** $720,728 (100% need-based). ***Average need-based loan:*** Freshmen: $15. Undergraduates: $20. ***Programs:*** FFEL (Subsidized and Unsubsidized Stafford, PLUS).

WORK-STUDY ***Federal work-study:*** Total amount: $120,577; 35 jobs averaging $2000.

APPLYING FOR FINANCIAL AID ***Required financial aid form:*** FAFSA. ***Financial aid deadline:*** Continuous. ***Notification date:*** Continuous beginning 8/15.

CONTACT Marie Luz Pastrana Muriel, Associate Dean of Financial Aid, EDP College of Puerto Rico, Inc., PO Box 192303, San Juan, PR 00919-2303, 787-765-3560 Ext. 249. *Fax:* 787-765-2650. *E-mail:* marieuz@edpcollege.edu.

EDWARD WATERS COLLEGE

Jacksonville, FL

CONTACT Gabriel Mbomeh, Director of Financial Aid, Edward Waters College, 1658 Kings Road, Jacksonville, FL 32209-6199, 904-366-2528 or toll-free 888-898-3191.

ELECTRONIC DATA PROCESSING COLLEGE OF PUERTO RICO–SAN SEBASTIAN

San Sebastian, PR

CONTACT Financial Aid Office, Electronic Data Processing College of Puerto Rico–San Sebastian, Avenue Betances #49, San Sebastian, PR 00685, 787-896-2137.

ELIZABETH CITY STATE UNIVERSITY

Elizabeth City, NC

CONTACT Assistant Director of Financial Aid, Elizabeth City State University, 1704 Weeksville Road, Campus Box 914, Elizabeth City, NC 27909-7806, 252-335-3285 or toll-free 800-347-3278. *Fax:* 252-335-3716.

ELIZABETHTOWN COLLEGE

Elizabethtown, PA

Tuition & fees: $30,650 **Average undergraduate aid package: $20,752**

ABOUT THE INSTITUTION Independent religious, coed. ***Awards:*** associate, bachelor's, and master's degrees and post-bachelor's certificates. 47 undergraduate majors. ***Total enrollment:*** 2,311. Undergraduates: 2,258. Freshmen: 599. Both federal and institutional methodology are used as a basis for awarding need-based institutional aid.

UNDERGRADUATE EXPENSES for 2008–09 ***Application fee:*** $30. ***Comprehensive fee:*** $38,600 includes full-time tuition ($30,650) and room and board ($7950). ***College room only:*** $3950. Full-time tuition and fees vary according to course load. Room and board charges vary according to board plan and housing facility. ***Part-time tuition:*** $740 per credit hour. Part-time tuition and fees vary according to class time and course load. ***Payment plan:*** Installment.

FRESHMAN FINANCIAL AID (Fall 2008, est.) 456 applied for aid; of those 85% were deemed to have need. 100% of freshmen with need received aid; of those 20% had need fully met. ***Average percent of need met:*** 83% (excluding resources awarded to replace EFC). ***Average financial aid package:*** $21,986 (excluding resources awarded to replace EFC). 21% of all full-time freshmen had no need and received non-need-based gift aid.

UNDERGRADUATE FINANCIAL AID (Fall 2008, est.) 1,517 applied for aid; of those 87% were deemed to have need. 100% of undergraduates with need received aid; of those 21% had need fully met. ***Average percent of need met:*** 81% (excluding resources awarded to replace EFC). ***Average financial aid package:*** $20,752 (excluding resources awarded to replace EFC). 22% of all full-time undergraduates had no need and received non-need-based gift aid.

GIFT AID (NEED-BASED) ***Total amount:*** $21,536,898 (6% federal, 8% state, 78% institutional, 8% external sources). ***Receiving aid:*** Freshmen: 74% (387); all full-time undergraduates: 71% (1,311). ***Average award:*** Freshmen: $17,932; Undergraduates: $16,151. ***Scholarships, grants, and awards:*** Federal Pell, FSEOG, state, private, college/university gift aid from institutional funds.

GIFT AID (NON-NEED-BASED) ***Total amount:*** $6,263,319 (80% institutional, 20% external sources). ***Receiving aid:*** Freshmen: 10% (52). Undergraduates: 9% (172). ***Average award:*** Freshmen: $12,503. Undergraduates: $10,973. ***Scholarships, grants, and awards by category:*** *Academic interests/achievement:* biological sciences, business, communication, computer science, education, engineering/technologies, English, foreign languages, general academic interests/achievements, health fields, humanities, international studies, mathematics, physical sciences, premedicine, religion/biblical studies, social sciences. *Creative arts/performance:* art/fine arts, music, performing arts, theater/drama. *Special achievements/activities:* religious involvement. *Special characteristics:* children of faculty/staff, international students, local/state students, members of minority groups, religious affiliation, siblings of current students. ***Tuition waivers:*** Full or partial for employees or children of employees.

LOANS ***Student loans:*** $13,491,179 (57% need-based, 43% non-need-based). ***Average need-based loan:*** Freshmen: $3557. Undergraduates: $4400. ***Parent loans:*** $5,133,840 (23% need-based, 77% non-need-based). ***Programs:*** FFEL (Subsidized and Unsubsidized Stafford, PLUS), Perkins, state, college/university.

WORK-STUDY ***Federal work-study:*** Total amount: $1,197,047; 939 jobs averaging $1372.

APPLYING FOR FINANCIAL AID ***Required financial aid forms:*** FAFSA, institution's own form, state aid form, federal income tax form(s), W-2 forms. ***Financial aid deadline (priority):*** 3/15. ***Notification date:*** Continuous beginning 3/15. Students must reply by 5/1 or within 2 weeks of notification.

CONTACT Ms. Elizabeth K. McCloud, Director of Financial Aid, Elizabethtown College, 1 Alpha Drive, Elizabethtown, PA 17022-2298, 717-361-1404. *Fax:* 717-361-1514. *E-mail:* mcclouek@etown.edu.

ELMHURST COLLEGE

Elmhurst, IL

Tuition & fees: $27,330 **Average undergraduate aid package: $19,361**

ABOUT THE INSTITUTION Independent religious, coed. ***Awards:*** bachelor's and master's degrees. 68 undergraduate majors. ***Total enrollment:*** 3,316. Undergraduates: 3,045. Freshmen: 577. Federal methodology is used as a basis for awarding need-based institutional aid.

UNDERGRADUATE EXPENSES for 2009–10 ***Comprehensive fee:*** $35,204 includes full-time tuition ($27,270), mandatory fees ($60), and room and board ($7874). ***College room only:*** $4720. ***Part-time tuition:*** $76 per semester hour.

FRESHMAN FINANCIAL AID (Fall 2008, est.) 487 applied for aid; of those 84% were deemed to have need. 100% of freshmen with need received aid; of those 17% had need fully met. ***Average percent of need met:*** 82% (excluding resources awarded to replace EFC). ***Average financial aid package:*** $18,731 (excluding resources awarded to replace EFC). 22% of all full-time freshmen had no need and received non-need-based gift aid.

UNDERGRADUATE FINANCIAL AID (Fall 2008, est.) 2,147 applied for aid; of those 89% were deemed to have need. 100% of undergraduates with need received aid; of those 14% had need fully met. ***Average percent of need met:*** 77% (excluding resources awarded to replace EFC). ***Average financial aid package:*** $19,361 (excluding resources awarded to replace EFC). 23% of all full-time undergraduates had no need and received non-need-based gift aid.

GIFT AID (NEED-BASED) ***Total amount:*** $28,298,719 (9% federal, 14% state, 76% institutional, 1% external sources). ***Receiving aid:*** Freshmen: 65% (365); all full-time undergraduates: 69% (1,880). ***Average award:*** Freshmen: $15,062; Undergraduates: $14,702. ***Scholarships, grants, and awards:*** Federal Pell, FSEOG, state, private, college/university gift aid from institutional funds.

GIFT AID (NON-NEED-BASED) ***Total amount:*** $6,349,055 (1% state, 97% institutional, 2% external sources). ***Receiving aid:*** Freshmen: 26% (146). Undergraduates: 8% (225). ***Average award:*** Freshmen: $11,491. Undergraduates: $9468. ***Scholarships, grants, and awards by category:*** *Academic interests/*

achievement: 1,789 awards ($16,698,132 total): biological sciences, business, communication, computer science, education, English, foreign languages, general academic interests/achievements, health fields, humanities, international studies, mathematics, physical sciences, premedicine, religion/biblical studies, social sciences. *Creative arts/performance:* 188 awards ($1,057,195 total): art/fine arts, music, theater/drama. *Special achievements/activities:* community service. *Special characteristics:* 583 awards ($2,156,271 total): children and siblings of alumni, children of current students, ethnic background, members of minority groups, religious affiliation, siblings of current students, spouses of current students. ***ROTC:*** Army cooperative, Air Force cooperative.

LOANS ***Student loans:*** $18,339,669 (40% need-based, 60% non-need-based). 69% of past graduating class borrowed through all loan programs. *Average indebtedness per student:* $20,675. ***Average need-based loan:*** Freshmen: $3859. Undergraduates: $4383. ***Parent loans:*** $3,816,508 (33% need-based, 67% non-need-based). ***Programs:*** Federal Direct (Subsidized and Unsubsidized Stafford, PLUS), Perkins, alternative loans.

WORK-STUDY ***Federal work-study:*** Total amount: $357,904; 354 jobs averaging $1011. ***State or other work-study/employment:*** Total amount: $397,283 (100% non-need-based). 390 part-time jobs averaging $1019.

APPLYING FOR FINANCIAL AID ***Required financial aid form:*** FAFSA. ***Financial aid deadline (priority):*** 4/15. ***Notification date:*** Continuous. Students must reply within 3 weeks of notification.

CONTACT Ruth A. Pusich, Director of Financial Aid, Elmhurst College, Goebel Hall 106A, 190 Prospect Avenue, Elmhurst, IL 60126-3296, 630-617-3080 or toll-free 800-697-1871 (out-of-state). *Fax:* 630-617-5188. *E-mail:* ruthp@elmhurst.edu.

ELMIRA COLLEGE

Elmira, NY

Tuition & fees: $33,250 **Average undergraduate aid package: $24,061**

ABOUT THE INSTITUTION Independent, coed. ***Awards:*** associate, bachelor's, and master's degrees. 61 undergraduate majors. ***Total enrollment:*** 1,551. Undergraduates: 1,387. Freshmen: 350. Federal methodology is used as a basis for awarding need-based institutional aid.

UNDERGRADUATE EXPENSES for 2008–09 ***Application fee:*** $50. ***Comprehensive fee:*** $43,350 includes full-time tuition ($32,000), mandatory fees ($1250), and room and board ($10,100). ***Payment plan:*** Tuition prepayment.

FRESHMAN FINANCIAL AID (Fall 2008, est.) 265 applied for aid; of those 93% were deemed to have need. 100% of freshmen with need received aid; of those 19% had need fully met. ***Average percent of need met:*** 80% (excluding resources awarded to replace EFC). ***Average financial aid package:*** $25,002 (excluding resources awarded to replace EFC). 21% of all full-time freshmen had no need and received non-need-based gift aid.

UNDERGRADUATE FINANCIAL AID (Fall 2008, est.) 923 applied for aid; of those 94% were deemed to have need. 99% of undergraduates with need received aid; of those 16% had need fully met. ***Average percent of need met:*** 80% (excluding resources awarded to replace EFC). ***Average financial aid package:*** $24,061 (excluding resources awarded to replace EFC). 23% of all full-time undergraduates had no need and received non-need-based gift aid.

GIFT AID (NEED-BASED) ***Total amount:*** $16,416,869 (7% federal, 5% state, 85% institutional, 3% external sources). ***Receiving aid:*** Freshmen: 78% (246); all full-time undergraduates: 74% (860). ***Average award:*** Freshmen: $21,232; Undergraduates: $19,607. ***Scholarships, grants, and awards:*** Federal Pell, FSEOG, state, private, college/university gift aid from institutional funds.

GIFT AID (NON-NEED-BASED) ***Total amount:*** $5,083,831 (1% state, 91% institutional, 8% external sources). ***Receiving aid:*** Freshmen: 10% (33). Undergraduates: 8% (91). ***Average award:*** Freshmen: $19,846. Undergraduates: $19,992. ***Scholarships, grants, and awards by category:*** *Academic interests/achievement:* 716 awards ($10,071,495 total): general academic interests/achievements. *Special achievements/activities:* 97 awards ($479,000 total): leadership. *Special characteristics:* 138 awards ($1,673,833 total): children of faculty/staff, international students, local/state students, previous college experience, siblings of current students. ***Tuition waivers:*** Full or partial for employees or children of employees. ***ROTC:*** Army, Air Force cooperative.

LOANS ***Student loans:*** $9,240,402 (69% need-based, 31% non-need-based). 81% of past graduating class borrowed through all loan programs. *Average indebtedness per student:* $25,233. ***Average need-based loan:*** Freshmen: $3818. Undergraduates: $4685. ***Parent loans:*** $2,055,771 (33% need-based, 67% non-need-based). ***Programs:*** FFEL (Subsidized and Unsubsidized Stafford, PLUS), Perkins, college/university.

WORK-STUDY ***Federal work-study:*** Total amount: $369,022; 370 jobs averaging $1000. ***State or other work-study/employment:*** Total amount: $284,200 (27% need-based, 73% non-need-based). 260 part-time jobs averaging $1100.

APPLYING FOR FINANCIAL AID ***Required financial aid forms:*** FAFSA, state aid form. ***Financial aid deadline (priority):*** 2/1. ***Notification date:*** Continuous beginning 2/1. Students must reply by 5/1 or within 3 weeks of notification.

CONTACT Kathleen L. Cohen, Dean of Financial Aid, Elmira College, Elmira College, One Park Place, Elmira, NY 14901-2099, 607-735-1728 or toll-free 800-935-6472. *Fax:* 607-735-1718. *E-mail:* kcohen@elmira.edu.

ELMS COLLEGE

Chicopee, MA

ABOUT THE INSTITUTION Independent Roman Catholic, coed, primarily women. 42 undergraduate majors.

GIFT AID (NEED-BASED) ***Scholarships, grants, and awards:*** Federal Pell, FSEOG, state, private, college/university gift aid from institutional funds.

GIFT AID (NON-NEED-BASED) ***Scholarships, grants, and awards by category:*** *Academic interests/achievement:* general academic interests/achievements. *Special characteristics:* children of faculty/staff, general special characteristics, religious affiliation, siblings of current students.

LOANS ***Programs:*** FFEL (Subsidized and Unsubsidized Stafford, PLUS), Perkins, state, alternative loans, MEFA Loans, Signature Loans.

APPLYING FOR FINANCIAL AID ***Required financial aid form:*** FAFSA.

CONTACT Ms. April Arcouette, Assistant Director of Student Financial Aid Services, Elms College, 291 Springfield Street, Chicopee, MA 01013-2839, 413-265-2249 or toll-free 800-255-ELMS. *Fax:* 413-265-2671. *E-mail:* arcouettea@elms.edu.

ELON UNIVERSITY

Elon, NC

Tuition & fees: $24,076 **Average undergraduate aid package: $15,428**

ABOUT THE INSTITUTION Independent religious, coed. ***Awards:*** bachelor's, master's, doctoral, and first professional degrees. 54 undergraduate majors. ***Total enrollment:*** 5,628. Undergraduates: 4,992. Freshmen: 1,291. Institutional methodology is used as a basis for awarding need-based institutional aid.

UNDERGRADUATE EXPENSES for 2008–09 ***Application fee:*** $50. ***Comprehensive fee:*** $31,846 includes full-time tuition ($23,746), mandatory fees ($330), and room and board ($7770). ***College room only:*** $3766. Room and board charges vary according to board plan and housing facility. ***Part-time tuition:*** $746 per hour. Part-time tuition and fees vary according to course load. ***Payment plan:*** Installment.

FRESHMAN FINANCIAL AID (Fall 2008, est.) 704 applied for aid; of those 58% were deemed to have need. 100% of freshmen with need received aid. ***Average percent of need met:*** 77% (excluding resources awarded to replace EFC). ***Average financial aid package:*** $15,747 (excluding resources awarded to replace EFC). 30% of all full-time freshmen had no need and received non-need-based gift aid.

UNDERGRADUATE FINANCIAL AID (Fall 2008, est.) 2,171 applied for aid; of those 69% were deemed to have need. 100% of undergraduates with need received aid. ***Average percent of need met:*** 71% (excluding resources awarded to replace EFC). ***Average financial aid package:*** $15,428 (excluding resources awarded to replace EFC). 23% of all full-time undergraduates had no need and received non-need-based gift aid.

GIFT AID (NEED-BASED) ***Total amount:*** $13,717,407 (10% federal, 24% state, 63% institutional, 3% external sources). ***Receiving aid:*** Freshmen: 29% (375); all full-time undergraduates: 28% (1,372). ***Average award:*** Freshmen: $10,090; Undergraduates: $9373. ***Scholarships, grants, and awards:*** Federal Pell, FSEOG, state, private, college/university gift aid from institutional funds.

GIFT AID (NON-NEED-BASED) ***Total amount:*** $6,969,795 (23% state, 73% institutional, 4% external sources). ***Receiving aid:*** Freshmen: 5% (65). Undergraduates: 4% (188). ***Average award:*** Freshmen: $5253. Undergraduates: $5420. ***Scholarships, grants, and awards by category:*** *Academic interests/achievement:* 1,793 awards ($7,218,267 total): biological sciences, business, communication, computer science, education, engineering/technologies, general academic interests/achievements, mathematics, military science, physical sciences, premedicine, religion/biblical studies, social sciences. *Creative arts/performance:* 52 awards ($116,800 total): art/fine arts, journalism/publications, music, performing arts, theater/drama. *Special achievements/activities:* 30 awards ($54,300 total): community service, general special achievements/activities, leadership, religious involvement. *Special characteristics:* 85 awards ($557,422 total): adult students, children of faculty/staff, ethnic background, first-generation college students, international students, members of minority groups, relatives of clergy. ***Tuition waivers:*** Full or partial for employees or children of employees. ***ROTC:*** Army, Air Force cooperative.

LOANS ***Student loans:*** $16,281,164 (35% need-based, 65% non-need-based). 45% of past graduating class borrowed through all loan programs. *Average indebtedness per student:* $23,392. ***Average need-based loan:*** Freshmen: $3382. Undergraduates: $4394. ***Parent loans:*** $8,219,459 (35% need-based, 65% non-need-based). ***Programs:*** FFEL (Subsidized and Unsubsidized Stafford, PLUS), Perkins, state, college/university, alternative loans.

WORK-STUDY ***Federal work-study:*** Total amount: $1,960,474; 814 jobs averaging $2333.

ATHLETIC AWARDS Total amount: $5,263,143 (45% need-based, 55% non-need-based).

APPLYING FOR FINANCIAL AID ***Required financial aid forms:*** FAFSA, institution's own form, CSS Financial Aid PROFILE. ***Financial aid deadline (priority):*** 3/15. ***Notification date:*** 3/30.

CONTACT Patrick Murphy, Director of Financial Planning, Elon University, 2725 Campus Box, Elon, NC 27244, 336-278-7640 or toll-free 800-334-8448. *Fax:* 336-278-7639. *E-mail:* finaid@elon.edu.

EMBRY-RIDDLE AERONAUTICAL UNIVERSITY

Prescott, AZ

Tuition & fees: $27,750 **Average undergraduate aid package: $18,601**

ABOUT THE INSTITUTION Independent, coed. ***Awards:*** bachelor's and master's degrees. 11 undergraduate majors. ***Total enrollment:*** 1,719. Undergraduates: 1,688. Freshmen: 418. Federal methodology is used as a basis for awarding need-based institutional aid.

UNDERGRADUATE EXPENSES for 2009–10 ***Application fee:*** $50. ***Comprehensive fee:*** $35,758 includes full-time tuition ($26,950), mandatory fees ($800), and room and board ($8008). ***College room only:*** $4524.

FRESHMAN FINANCIAL AID (Fall 2008, est.) 347 applied for aid; of those 85% were deemed to have need. 100% of freshmen with need received aid. ***Average financial aid package:*** $18,647 (excluding resources awarded to replace EFC).

UNDERGRADUATE FINANCIAL AID (Fall 2008, est.) 1,170 applied for aid; of those 87% were deemed to have need. 100% of undergraduates with need received aid. ***Average financial aid package:*** $18,601 (excluding resources awarded to replace EFC).

GIFT AID (NEED-BASED) ***Total amount:*** $18,788,826 (10% federal, 1% state, 62% institutional, 27% external sources). ***Receiving aid:*** Freshmen: 70% (291); all full-time undergraduates: 63% (970). ***Average award:*** Freshmen: $12,678; Undergraduates: $11,343. ***Scholarships, grants, and awards:*** Federal Pell, FSEOG, state, private, college/university gift aid from institutional funds.

GIFT AID (NON-NEED-BASED) ***Scholarships, grants, and awards by category:*** *Academic interests/achievement:* 685 awards ($4,981,771 total): general academic interests/achievements. *Special achievements/activities:* 20 awards ($110,612 total): leadership. *Special characteristics:* 104 awards ($918,971 total): children and siblings of alumni, children of faculty/staff. ***ROTC:*** Army, Air Force.

LOANS ***Student loans:*** $14,759,429 (100% need-based). 75% of past graduating class borrowed through all loan programs. ***Average need-based loan:*** Freshmen: $4294. Undergraduates: $5461. ***Parent loans:*** $5,557,625 (100% need-based). ***Programs:*** FFEL (Subsidized and Unsubsidized Stafford, PLUS), Perkins.

WORK-STUDY ***Federal work-study:*** Total amount: $52,091; 39 jobs averaging $1261. ***State or other work-study/employment:*** Total amount: $894,050 (100% need-based). 413 part-time jobs averaging $1352.

ATHLETIC AWARDS Total amount: $734,371 (100% need-based).

APPLYING FOR FINANCIAL AID ***Required financial aid form:*** FAFSA. ***Financial aid deadline:*** Continuous. ***Notification date:*** Continuous beginning 3/1. Students must reply within 4 weeks of notification.

CONTACT Mr. Dan Lupin, Director of Financial Aid, Embry-Riddle Aeronautical University, 3700 Willow Creek Road, Prescott, AZ 86301-3720, 928-777-3765 or toll-free 800-888-3728. *Fax:* 928-777-3893. *E-mail:* lupind@erau.edu.

EMBRY-RIDDLE AERONAUTICAL UNIVERSITY

Daytona Beach, FL

Tuition & fees: $28,114 **Average undergraduate aid package: $17,736**

ABOUT THE INSTITUTION Independent, coed. ***Awards:*** bachelor's and master's degrees. 21 undergraduate majors. ***Total enrollment:*** 5,062. Undergraduates: 4,657. Freshmen: 1,064. Federal methodology is used as a basis for awarding need-based institutional aid.

UNDERGRADUATE EXPENSES for 2009–10 ***Application fee:*** $50. ***Comprehensive fee:*** $38,078 includes full-time tuition ($26,950), mandatory fees ($1164), and room and board ($9964). ***College room only:*** $5200. ***Part-time tuition:*** $1120 per credit hour.

FRESHMAN FINANCIAL AID (Fall 2008, est.) 876 applied for aid; of those 84% were deemed to have need. 100% of freshmen with need received aid. ***Average financial aid package:*** $18,699 (excluding resources awarded to replace EFC).

UNDERGRADUATE FINANCIAL AID (Fall 2008, est.) 3,034 applied for aid; of those 86% were deemed to have need. 99% of undergraduates with need received aid. ***Average financial aid package:*** $17,736 (excluding resources awarded to replace EFC).

GIFT AID (NEED-BASED) ***Total amount:*** $42,139,875 (10% federal, 9% state, 55% institutional, 26% external sources). ***Receiving aid:*** Freshmen: 70% (738); all full-time undergraduates: 57% (2,496). ***Average award:*** Freshmen: $11,939; Undergraduates: $10,021. ***Scholarships, grants, and awards:*** Federal Pell, FSEOG, state, private, college/university gift aid from institutional funds.

GIFT AID (NON-NEED-BASED) ***Scholarships, grants, and awards by category:*** *Academic interests/achievement:* 1,742 awards ($8,547,733 total): general academic interests/achievements. *Special achievements/activities:* 74 awards ($206,060 total): leadership. *Special characteristics:* 133 awards ($1,627,722 total): children and siblings of alumni, children of faculty/staff, siblings of current students. ***ROTC:*** Army, Naval, Air Force.

LOANS ***Student loans:*** $38,266,412 (100% need-based). 68% of past graduating class borrowed through all loan programs. ***Average need-based loan:*** Freshmen: $4266. Undergraduates: $4995. ***Parent loans:*** $12,434,448 (100% need-based). ***Programs:*** FFEL (Subsidized and Unsubsidized Stafford, PLUS), Perkins.

WORK-STUDY ***Federal work-study:*** Total amount: $218,617; 121 jobs averaging $1674. ***State or other work-study/employment:*** Total amount: $3,570,747 (100% need-based). 1,335 part-time jobs averaging $1776.

ATHLETIC AWARDS Total amount: $1,810,110 (100% need-based).

APPLYING FOR FINANCIAL AID ***Required financial aid form:*** FAFSA. ***Financial aid deadline:*** Continuous. ***Notification date:*** Continuous beginning 3/1. Students must reply within 4 weeks of notification.

CONTACT Barbara Dryden, Director of Financial Aid, Embry-Riddle Aeronautical University, 600 South Clyde Morris Boulevard, Daytona Beach, FL 32114-3900, 800-943-6279 or toll-free 800-862-2416. *Fax:* 386-226-6307. *E-mail:* barbara.dryden@erau.edu.

EMBRY-RIDDLE AERONAUTICAL UNIVERSITY WORLDWIDE

Daytona Beach, FL

Tuition & fees: $5304 **Average undergraduate aid package: $6220**

ABOUT THE INSTITUTION Independent, coed. ***Awards:*** associate, bachelor's, and master's degrees (programs offered at 100 military bases worldwide). 4 undergraduate majors. ***Total enrollment:*** 16,331. Undergraduates: 12,241. Freshmen: 472. Federal methodology is used as a basis for awarding need-based institutional aid.

UNDERGRADUATE EXPENSES for 2009–10 ***Application fee:*** $50. ***Tuition:*** full-time $5304; part-time $221 per credit hour.

FRESHMAN FINANCIAL AID (Fall 2008, est.) 7 applied for aid; of those 100% were deemed to have need. 100% of freshmen with need received aid. ***Average financial aid package:*** $6328 (excluding resources awarded to replace EFC).

UNDERGRADUATE FINANCIAL AID (Fall 2008, est.) 490 applied for aid; of those 85% were deemed to have need. 97% of undergraduates with need received aid. ***Average financial aid package:*** $6220 (excluding resources awarded to replace EFC).

GIFT AID (NEED-BASED) ***Total amount:*** $3,053,677 (56% federal, 39% state, 2% institutional, 3% external sources). ***Receiving aid:*** Freshmen: 15% (7); all full-time undergraduates: 13% (252). ***Average award:*** Freshmen: $3827; Undergraduates: $3833. ***Scholarships, grants, and awards:*** Federal Pell, state, private, college/university gift aid from institutional funds.

GIFT AID (NON-NEED-BASED) ***Scholarships, grants, and awards by category:*** *Academic interests/achievement:* general academic interests/achievements. *Special achievements/activities:* 8 awards ($1904 total): leadership. *Special characteristics:* 3 awards ($13,365 total): children of faculty/staff.

LOANS ***Student loans:*** $11,508,743 (100% need-based). 15% of past graduating class borrowed through all loan programs. ***Average need-based loan:*** Freshmen: $3500. Undergraduates: $4271. ***Parent loans:*** $89,558 (100% need-based). ***Programs:*** FFEL (Subsidized and Unsubsidized Stafford, PLUS).

APPLYING FOR FINANCIAL AID ***Required financial aid form:*** FAFSA. ***Financial aid deadline:*** Continuous. ***Notification date:*** Continuous beginning 3/1. Students must reply within 4 weeks of notification.

CONTACT Barbara Dryden, Director of Financial Aid, Embry-Riddle Aeronautical University Worldwide, 600 South Clyde Morris Boulevard, Daytona Beach, FL 32114-3900, 800-943-6279 or toll-free 800-522-6787. *Fax:* 386-226-6307. *E-mail:* barbara.dryden@erau.edu.

EMERSON COLLEGE

Boston, MA

Tuition & fees: $28,884 **Average undergraduate aid package: $16,153**

ABOUT THE INSTITUTION Independent, coed. ***Awards:*** bachelor's, master's, and doctoral degrees. 29 undergraduate majors. ***Total enrollment:*** 4,536. Undergraduates: 3,644. Freshmen: 774. Both federal and institutional methodology are used as a basis for awarding need-based institutional aid.

UNDERGRADUATE EXPENSES for 2008–09 ***Application fee:*** $65. ***Comprehensive fee:*** $40,716 includes full-time tuition ($28,352), mandatory fees ($532), and room and board ($11,832). ***Payment plan:*** Installment.

FRESHMAN FINANCIAL AID (Fall 2008, est.) 637 applied for aid; of those 75% were deemed to have need. 100% of freshmen with need received aid; of those 43% had need fully met. ***Average percent of need met:*** 88% (excluding resources awarded to replace EFC). ***Average financial aid package:*** $15,918 (excluding resources awarded to replace EFC). 6% of all full-time freshmen had no need and received non-need-based gift aid.

UNDERGRADUATE FINANCIAL AID (Fall 2008, est.) 2,272 applied for aid; of those 82% were deemed to have need. 100% of undergraduates with need received aid; of those 72% had need fully met. ***Average percent of need met:*** 89% (excluding resources awarded to replace EFC). ***Average financial aid package:*** $16,153 (excluding resources awarded to replace EFC). 6% of all full-time undergraduates had no need and received non-need-based gift aid.

GIFT AID (NEED-BASED) ***Total amount:*** $18,967,424 (9% federal, 2% state, 82% institutional, 7% external sources). ***Receiving aid:*** Freshmen: 52% (403); all full-time undergraduates: 44% (1,483). ***Average award:*** Freshmen: $14,369; Undergraduates: $14,268. ***Scholarships, grants, and awards:*** Federal Pell, FSEOG, state, private, college/university gift aid from institutional funds.

GIFT AID (NON-NEED-BASED) ***Total amount:*** $1,233,086 (82% institutional, 18% external sources). ***Receiving aid:*** Freshmen: 3% (20). Undergraduates: 1% (50). ***Average award:*** Freshmen: $12,396. Undergraduates: $12,487. ***Scholarships, grants, and awards by category:*** *Academic interests/achievement:* general academic interests/achievements. *Creative arts/performance:* performing arts. *Special characteristics:* general special characteristics. ***Tuition waivers:*** Full or partial for employees or children of employees.

LOANS ***Student loans:*** $21,645,918 (64% need-based, 36% non-need-based). 65% of past graduating class borrowed through all loan programs. *Average indebtedness per student:* $15,701. ***Average need-based loan:*** Freshmen: $3875. Undergraduates: $4629. ***Parent loans:*** $10,180,739 (37% need-based, 63% non-need-based). ***Programs:*** FFEL (Subsidized and Unsubsidized Stafford, PLUS), Perkins, state.

WORK-STUDY ***Federal work-study:*** Total amount: $517,895; 545 jobs averaging $1900. ***State or other work-study/employment:*** Total amount: $477,850 (46% need-based, 54% non-need-based). 57 part-time jobs averaging $11,000.

APPLYING FOR FINANCIAL AID ***Required financial aid forms:*** FAFSA, CSS Financial Aid PROFILE, business/farm supplement, income tax returns, noncustodial statement. ***Financial aid deadline (priority):*** 3/1. ***Notification date:*** 4/1. Students must reply by 5/1 or within 3 weeks of notification.

CONTACT Michelle Smith, Director, Office of Student Financial Services, Emerson College, 120 Boylston Street, Boston, MA 02116-4624, 617-824-8655. *Fax:* 617-824-8619. *E-mail:* finaid@emerson.edu.

EMMANUEL COLLEGE

Franklin Springs, GA

Tuition & fees: $12,880 **Average undergraduate aid package: $14,160**

ABOUT THE INSTITUTION Independent religious, coed. ***Awards:*** associate and bachelor's degrees. 23 undergraduate majors. ***Total enrollment:*** 697. Undergraduates: 697. Freshmen: 129. Federal methodology is used as a basis for awarding need-based institutional aid.

UNDERGRADUATE EXPENSES for 2009–10 ***Application fee:*** $25. ***Comprehensive fee:*** $18,400 includes full-time tuition ($12,880) and room and board ($5520). ***Part-time tuition:*** $530 per hour.

FRESHMAN FINANCIAL AID (Fall 2008, est.) 120 applied for aid; of those 86% were deemed to have need. 100% of freshmen with need received aid; of those 15% had need fully met. ***Average percent of need met:*** 81% (excluding resources awarded to replace EFC). ***Average financial aid package:*** $13,988 (excluding resources awarded to replace EFC). 13% of all full-time freshmen had no need and received non-need-based gift aid.

UNDERGRADUATE FINANCIAL AID (Fall 2008, est.) 547 applied for aid; of those 89% were deemed to have need. 100% of undergraduates with need received aid; of those 18% had need fully met. ***Average percent of need met:*** 86% (excluding resources awarded to replace EFC). ***Average financial aid package:*** $14,160 (excluding resources awarded to replace EFC). 18% of all full-time undergraduates had no need and received non-need-based gift aid.

GIFT AID (NEED-BASED) ***Total amount:*** $3,272,405 (38% federal, 29% state, 29% institutional, 4% external sources). ***Receiving aid:*** Freshmen: 80% (101); all full-time undergraduates: 78% (478). ***Average award:*** Freshmen: $8481; Undergraduates: $7576. ***Scholarships, grants, and awards:*** Federal Pell, FSEOG, state, college/university gift aid from institutional funds.

GIFT AID (NON-NEED-BASED) ***Total amount:*** $626,327 (42% state, 44% institutional, 14% external sources). ***Receiving aid:*** Freshmen: 8% (10). Undergraduates: 9% (54). ***Average award:*** Freshmen: $3334. Undergraduates: $4693. ***Scholarships, grants, and awards by category:*** *Academic interests/achievement:* 207 awards ($309,120 total): business, communication, education, English, general academic interests/achievements, health fields, religion/biblical studies. *Creative arts/performance:* 77 awards ($99,535 total): applied art and design, art/fine arts, creative writing, dance, general creative arts/performance, music, performing arts, theater/drama. *Special achievements/activities:* 23 awards ($47,250 total): general special achievements/activities, leadership, memberships, religious involvement. *Special characteristics:* 398 awards ($476,374 total): adult students, children of current students, children of faculty/staff, first-generation college students, general special characteristics, international students, married students, parents of current students, relatives of clergy, religious affiliation, siblings of current students, spouses of current students, twins.

LOANS ***Student loans:*** $3,428,796 (75% need-based, 25% non-need-based). 85% of past graduating class borrowed through all loan programs. *Average indebtedness per student:* $23,880. ***Average need-based loan:*** Freshmen: $3304. Undergraduates: $4020. ***Parent loans:*** $573,813 (38% need-based, 62% non-need-based). ***Programs:*** FFEL (Subsidized and Unsubsidized Stafford, PLUS).

WORK-STUDY ***Federal work-study:*** Total amount: $430,163; 219 jobs averaging $1964. ***State or other work-study/employment:*** Total amount: $156,654 (100% non-need-based). 100 part-time jobs averaging $1567.

ATHLETIC AWARDS Total amount: $466,790 (66% need-based, 34% non-need-based).

APPLYING FOR FINANCIAL AID ***Required financial aid forms:*** FAFSA, institution's own form, state aid form. ***Financial aid deadline:*** 6/15 (priority: 5/1). ***Notification date:*** Continuous. Students must reply within 2 weeks of notification.

CONTACT Gloria Hambrick, Director of Financial Aid, Emmanuel College, PO Box 129, Franklin Springs, GA 30639-0129, 706-245-2844 or toll-free 800-860-8800 (in-state). *Fax:* 706-245-2846. *E-mail:* ghambrick@ec.edu.

EMMANUEL COLLEGE

Boston, MA

ABOUT THE INSTITUTION Independent Roman Catholic, coed. ***Awards:*** bachelor's and master's degrees and post-master's certificates. 34 undergraduate majors. ***Total enrollment:*** 1,902. Undergraduates: 1,693. Freshmen: 480.

GIFT AID (NEED-BASED) ***Scholarships, grants, and awards:*** Federal Pell, FSEOG, state, private, college/university gift aid from institutional funds.

GIFT AID (NON-NEED-BASED) ***Scholarships, grants, and awards by category:*** *Academic interests/achievement:* biological sciences, education, engineering/technologies, foreign languages, general academic interests/achievements, health fields, humanities, mathematics, physical sciences, religion/biblical studies, social sciences. *Creative arts/performance:* general creative arts/performance. *Special achievements/activities:* community service, leadership. *Special characteristics:* children and siblings of alumni, children of educators, children of faculty/staff, children of union members/company employees, ethnic background, general special characteristics, handicapped students, international students, local/state students, religious affiliation, siblings of current students.

LOANS ***Programs:*** FFEL (Subsidized and Unsubsidized Stafford, PLUS), Perkins, state, alternative loans.

WORK-STUDY ***Federal work-study:*** Total amount: $1,258,029; 698 jobs averaging $1800. ***State or other work-study/employment:*** Total amount: $345,000 (100% non-need-based). 345 part-time jobs averaging $1000.

APPLYING FOR FINANCIAL AID ***Required financial aid forms:*** FAFSA, institution's own form.

CONTACT Jennifer Porter, Associate Vice President for Student Financial Services, Emmanuel College, 400 The Fenway, Boston, MA 02115, 617-735-9938. *Fax:* 617-735-9939. *E-mail:* porterj@emmanuel.edu.

EMMAUS BIBLE COLLEGE

Dubuque, IA

CONTACT Steve Seeman, Financial Aid Director, Emmaus Bible College, 2570 Asbury Road, Dubuque, IA 52001-3097, 800-397-2425 Ext. 1309 or toll-free 800-397-2425. *Fax:* 563-588-1216. *E-mail:* financialaid@emmaus.edu.

EMORY & HENRY COLLEGE

Emory, VA

Tuition & fees: $23,860 **Average undergraduate aid package: $21,933**

ABOUT THE INSTITUTION Independent United Methodist, coed. ***Awards:*** bachelor's and master's degrees. 37 undergraduate majors. ***Total enrollment:*** 978. Undergraduates: 941. Freshmen: 241. Federal methodology is used as a basis for awarding need-based institutional aid.

UNDERGRADUATE EXPENSES for 2008–09 ***Application fee:*** $30. ***Comprehensive fee:*** $31,840 includes full-time tuition ($23,860) and room and board ($7980). ***College room only:*** $3930. Full-time tuition and fees vary according to course load and degree level. Room and board charges vary according to board plan. ***Part-time tuition:*** $995 per credit hour. Part-time tuition and fees vary according to course load and degree level. ***Payment plan:*** Installment.

FRESHMAN FINANCIAL AID (Fall 2008, est.) 226 applied for aid; of those 88% were deemed to have need. 100% of freshmen with need received aid; of those 27% had need fully met. ***Average percent of need met:*** 90% (excluding resources awarded to replace EFC). ***Average financial aid package:*** $23,043 (excluding resources awarded to replace EFC). 12% of all full-time freshmen had no need and received non-need-based gift aid.

UNDERGRADUATE FINANCIAL AID (Fall 2008, est.) 787 applied for aid; of those 88% were deemed to have need. 100% of undergraduates with need received aid; of those 27% had need fully met. ***Average percent of need met:*** 82% (excluding resources awarded to replace EFC). ***Average financial aid package:*** $21,933 (excluding resources awarded to replace EFC). 19% of all full-time undergraduates had no need and received non-need-based gift aid.

GIFT AID (NEED-BASED) ***Total amount:*** $12,044,418 (11% federal, 13% state, 74% institutional, 2% external sources). ***Receiving aid:*** Freshmen: 71% (172); all full-time undergraduates: 69% (599). ***Average award:*** Freshmen: $20,518; Undergraduates: $18,434. ***Scholarships, grants, and awards:*** Federal Pell, FSEOG, state, private, college/university gift aid from institutional funds.

GIFT AID (NON-NEED-BASED) ***Total amount:*** $2,267,735 (18% state, 80% institutional, 2% external sources). ***Receiving aid:*** Freshmen: 11% (26). Undergraduates: 8% (67). ***Average award:*** Freshmen: $12,045. Undergraduates: $11,383. ***Scholarships, grants, and awards by category:*** *Academic interests/achievement:* 843 awards ($7,939,649 total): general academic interests/achievements, premedicine, religion/biblical studies. *Creative arts/performance:* 10 awards ($20,747 total): art/fine arts, journalism/publications, music. *Special characteristics:* 149 awards ($549,131 total): children of educators, children of faculty/staff, religious affiliation. ***Tuition waivers:*** Full or partial for employees or children of employees.

LOANS ***Student loans:*** $4,151,404 (61% need-based, 39% non-need-based). 61% of past graduating class borrowed through all loan programs. *Average indebtedness per student:* $19,744. ***Average need-based loan:*** Freshmen: $3436. Undergraduates: $4180. ***Parent loans:*** $2,283,164 (42% need-based, 58% non-need-based). ***Programs:*** FFEL (Subsidized and Unsubsidized Stafford, PLUS), Perkins.

WORK-STUDY ***Federal work-study:*** Total amount: $206,213; 210 jobs averaging $1423.

APPLYING FOR FINANCIAL AID ***Required financial aid forms:*** FAFSA, state aid form. ***Financial aid deadline (priority):*** 4/15. ***Notification date:*** Continuous. Students must reply within 2 weeks of notification.

CONTACT Margaret L. Murphy, Director of Student Financial Planning, Emory & Henry College, PO Box 947, Emory, VA 24327-0010, 276-944-6115 or toll-free 800-848-5493. *Fax:* 276-944-6884. *E-mail:* mmurphy@ehc.edu.

EMORY UNIVERSITY

Atlanta, GA

Tuition & fees: $36,336 **Average undergraduate aid package: $29,627**

ABOUT THE INSTITUTION Independent Methodist, coed. ***Awards:*** bachelor's, master's, doctoral, and first professional degrees (enrollment figures include Emory University, Oxford College; application data for main campus only). 57 undergraduate majors. ***Total enrollment:*** 10,921. Undergraduates: 5,214. Freshmen: 1,278. Both federal and institutional methodology are used as a basis for awarding need-based institutional aid.

UNDERGRADUATE EXPENSES for 2008–09 ***Application fee:*** $50. ***Comprehensive fee:*** $46,908 includes full-time tuition ($35,800), mandatory fees ($536), and room and board ($10,572). ***College room only:*** $6472.

FRESHMAN FINANCIAL AID (Fall 2008, est.) 853 applied for aid; of those 80% were deemed to have need. 100% of freshmen with need received aid; of those 100% had need fully met. ***Average percent of need met:*** 100% (excluding resources awarded to replace EFC). ***Average financial aid package:*** $29,334 (excluding resources awarded to replace EFC). 13% of all full-time freshmen had no need and received non-need-based gift aid.

UNDERGRADUATE FINANCIAL AID (Fall 2008, est.) 3,079 applied for aid; of those 80% were deemed to have need. 100% of undergraduates with need received aid; of those 100% had need fully met. ***Average percent of need met:*** 100% (excluding resources awarded to replace EFC). ***Average financial aid package:*** $29,627 (excluding resources awarded to replace EFC). 16% of all full-time undergraduates had no need and received non-need-based gift aid.

GIFT AID (NEED-BASED) ***Total amount:*** $65,011,398 (8% federal, 5% state, 85% institutional, 2% external sources). ***Receiving aid:*** Freshmen: 37% (627); all full-time undergraduates: 37% (2,490). ***Average award:*** Freshmen: $27,850; Undergraduates: $26,958. ***Scholarships, grants, and awards:*** Federal Pell, FSEOG, state, private, college/university gift aid from institutional funds.

GIFT AID (NON-NEED-BASED) ***Total amount:*** $13,323,082 (19% state, 75% institutional, 6% external sources). ***Receiving aid:*** Freshmen: 2% (40). Undergraduates: 2% (152). ***Average award:*** Freshmen: $13,094. Undergraduates: $18,502. ***Scholarships, grants, and awards by category:*** *Academic interests/achievement:* general academic interests/achievements. *Creative arts/performance:* art/fine arts, music, theater/drama. *Special achievements/activities:* leadership. *Special characteristics:* religious affiliation. ***ROTC:*** Army cooperative, Naval cooperative, Air Force cooperative.

LOANS ***Student loans:*** $19,818,828 (39% need-based, 61% non-need-based). 42% of past graduating class borrowed through all loan programs. *Average indebtedness per student:* $23,181. ***Average need-based loan:*** Freshmen: $3399. Undergraduates: $4405. ***Parent loans:*** $7,606,645 (100% non-need-based). ***Programs:*** FFEL (Subsidized and Unsubsidized Stafford, PLUS), Perkins, Federal Nursing, state, college/university.

WORK-STUDY ***Federal work-study:*** Total amount: $3,555,676; 1,796 jobs available. ***State or other work-study/employment:*** Total amount: $659,380 (58% need-based, 42% non-need-based). Part-time jobs available.

APPLYING FOR FINANCIAL AID ***Required financial aid forms:*** FAFSA, CSS Financial Aid PROFILE, noncustodial (divorced/separated) parent's statement. ***Financial aid deadline:*** 3/1 (priority: 2/15). ***Notification date:*** 4/1. Students must reply by 5/1.

CONTACT Dean Bentley, Director of Financial Aid, Emory University, 200 Dowman Drive, Atlanta, GA 30322-1960, 404-727-6039 or toll-free 800-727-6036. *Fax:* 404-727-6709. *E-mail:* finaid1@emory.edu.

EMPORIA STATE UNIVERSITY

Emporia, KS

Tuition & fees (KS res): $4136 **Average undergraduate aid package: $7117**

ABOUT THE INSTITUTION State-supported, coed. ***Awards:*** bachelor's, master's, and doctoral degrees and post-bachelor's and post-master's certificates. 35 undergraduate majors. ***Total enrollment:*** 6,404. Undergraduates: 4,288. Freshmen: 681. Federal methodology is used as a basis for awarding need-based institutional aid.

UNDERGRADUATE EXPENSES for 2008–09 ***Application fee:*** $30. ***Tuition, state resident:*** full-time $3294; part-time $110 per credit hour. ***Tuition, nonresident:*** full-time $11,806; part-time $394 per credit hour. ***Required fees:*** full-time $842; $51 per credit hour. Full-time tuition and fees vary according to course level, course load, degree level, and location. Part-time tuition and fees vary according to course level, course load, degree level, and location. ***College room and board:*** $5858; ***Room only:*** $3027. Room and board charges vary according to board plan and housing facility. ***Payment plans:*** Installment, deferred payment.

FRESHMAN FINANCIAL AID (Fall 2008, est.) 642 applied for aid; of those 63% were deemed to have need. 99% of freshmen with need received aid; of those 92% had need fully met. ***Average percent of need met:*** 49% (excluding resources awarded to replace EFC). ***Average financial aid package:*** $6536 (excluding resources awarded to replace EFC). 24% of all full-time freshmen had no need and received non-need-based gift aid.

UNDERGRADUATE FINANCIAL AID (Fall 2008, est.) 3,461 applied for aid; of those 62% were deemed to have need. 99% of undergraduates with need received aid; of those 98% had need fully met. ***Average percent of need met:*** 46% (excluding resources awarded to replace EFC). ***Average financial aid package:*** $7117 (excluding resources awarded to replace EFC). 19% of all full-time undergraduates had no need and received non-need-based gift aid.

GIFT AID (NEED-BASED) ***Total amount:*** $7,305,898 (63% federal, 11% state, 16% institutional, 10% external sources). ***Receiving aid:*** Freshmen: 37% (243); all full-time undergraduates: 25% (972). ***Average award:*** Freshmen: $4367; Undergraduates: $4310. ***Scholarships, grants, and awards:*** Federal Pell, FSEOG, state, private, college/university gift aid from institutional funds, Jones Foundation Grants, grants from outside sources.

GIFT AID (NON-NEED-BASED) ***Total amount:*** $2,070,804 (6% state, 51% institutional, 43% external sources). ***Receiving aid:*** Freshmen: 26% (172). Undergraduates: 20% (760). ***Average award:*** Freshmen: $1253. Undergraduates: $1367. ***Scholarships, grants, and awards by category:*** *Academic interests/achievement:* 1,757 awards ($2,076,482 total): biological sciences, business, communication, computer science, education, engineering/technologies, English, foreign languages, general academic interests/achievements, health fields, humanities, library science, mathematics, physical sciences, premedicine, social sciences. *Creative arts/performance:* 113 awards ($87,211 total): art/fine arts, creative writing, debating, music, theater/drama. *Special achievements/activities:* 20 awards ($10,150 total): memberships. *Special characteristics:* 34 awards ($17,130 total): children and siblings of alumni, children of faculty/staff, children of union members/company employees, handicapped students, international students, members of minority groups, religious affiliation, veterans, veterans' children. ***Tuition waivers:*** Full or partial for employees or children of employees, senior citizens.

LOANS ***Student loans:*** $15,266,856 (67% need-based, 33% non-need-based). 70% of past graduating class borrowed through all loan programs. *Average indebtedness per student:* $17,680. ***Average need-based loan:*** Freshmen: $3314. Undergraduates: $4102. ***Parent loans:*** $1,489,602 (16% need-based, 84% non-need-based). ***Programs:*** FFEL (Subsidized and Unsubsidized Stafford, PLUS), Perkins, Alaska Loans, alternative loans.

WORK-STUDY ***Federal work-study:*** Total amount: $423,966; 220 jobs averaging $1905. ***State or other work-study/employment:*** Total amount: $44,311 (58% need-based, 42% non-need-based). 30 part-time jobs averaging $1477.

ATHLETIC AWARDS Total amount: $1,088,748 (47% need-based, 53% non-need-based).

APPLYING FOR FINANCIAL AID ***Required financial aid forms:*** FAFSA, state aid form. ***Financial aid deadline (priority):*** 3/15. ***Notification date:*** Continuous. Students must reply within 2 weeks of notification.

CONTACT Elaine Henrie, Director of Financial Aid, Emporia State University, 1200 Commercial Street, Emporia, KS 66801-5087, 620-341-5457 or toll-free 877-GOTOESU (in-state), 877-468-6378 (out-of-state). *Fax:* 620-341-6088. *E-mail:* ehenrie@emporia.edu.

ENDICOTT COLLEGE

Beverly, MA

Tuition & fees: $24,530 **Average undergraduate aid package: $15,615**

ABOUT THE INSTITUTION Independent, coed. ***Awards:*** associate, bachelor's, and master's degrees. 24 undergraduate majors. ***Total enrollment:*** 3,947. Undergraduates: 2,306. Freshmen: 587. Federal methodology is used as a basis for awarding need-based institutional aid.

UNDERGRADUATE EXPENSES for 2008–09 ***Application fee:*** $40. ***Comprehensive fee:*** $35,910 includes full-time tuition ($24,130), mandatory fees ($400), and room and board ($11,380). ***College room only:*** $7930. Full-time tuition and fees vary according to student level. Room and board charges vary according to board plan and housing facility. ***Part-time tuition:*** $740 per credit. ***Part-time fees:*** $150 per term. Part-time tuition and fees vary according to student level. ***Payment plan:*** Installment.

FRESHMAN FINANCIAL AID (Fall 2008, est.) 405 applied for aid; of those 70% were deemed to have need. 99% of freshmen with need received aid; of those 12% had need fully met. ***Average percent of need met:*** 58% (excluding resources awarded to replace EFC). ***Average financial aid package:*** $14,385 (excluding resources awarded to replace EFC). 16% of all full-time freshmen had no need and received non-need-based gift aid.

UNDERGRADUATE FINANCIAL AID (Fall 2008, est.) 1,689 applied for aid; of those 71% were deemed to have need. 99% of undergraduates with need received aid; of those 12% had need fully met. ***Average percent of need met:*** 60% (excluding resources awarded to replace EFC). ***Average financial aid package:*** $15,615 (excluding resources awarded to replace EFC). 19% of all full-time undergraduates had no need and received non-need-based gift aid.

GIFT AID (NEED-BASED) ***Total amount:*** $10,460,635 (10% federal, 3% state, 87% institutional). ***Receiving aid:*** Freshmen: 34% (201); all full-time undergraduates: 45% (891). ***Average award:*** Freshmen: $7651; Undergraduates: $7878. ***Scholarships, grants, and awards:*** Federal Pell, FSEOG, state, private, college/university gift aid from institutional funds.

GIFT AID (NON-NEED-BASED) ***Total amount:*** $2,767,675 (87% institutional, 13% external sources). ***Receiving aid:*** Freshmen: 29% (168). Undergraduates: 35% (694). ***Average award:*** Freshmen: $5746. Undergraduates: $6686. ***Scholarships, grants, and awards by category:*** *Academic interests/achievement:* 963 awards ($5,145,465 total): business, education, general academic interests/achievements, health fields. *Creative arts/performance:* 4 awards ($2000 total): art/fine arts. *Special achievements/activities:* 12 awards ($18,000 total): community service, general special achievements/activities, leadership, religious involvement. *Special characteristics:* 166 awards ($635,315 total): children and siblings of alumni, children of educators, general special characteristics, international students, local/state students, religious affiliation. ***Tuition waivers:*** Full or partial for employees or children of employees. ***ROTC:*** Army cooperative, Air Force cooperative.

LOANS ***Student loans:*** $15,118,771 (35% need-based, 65% non-need-based). 72% of past graduating class borrowed through all loan programs. *Average indebtedness per student:* $28,022. ***Average need-based loan:*** Freshmen: $3762. Undergraduates: $4558. ***Parent loans:*** $4,572,343 (100% non-need-based). ***Programs:*** FFEL (Subsidized and Unsubsidized Stafford, PLUS), Perkins, college/university.

WORK-STUDY ***Federal work-study:*** Total amount: $600,000; 428 jobs averaging $2000.

APPLYING FOR FINANCIAL AID ***Required financial aid forms:*** FAFSA, institution's own form. ***Financial aid deadline (priority):*** 3/15. ***Notification date:*** Continuous beginning 3/15. Students must reply within 2 weeks of notification.

CONTACT Ms. Marcia Toomey, Director of Financial Aid, Endicott College, 376 Hale Street, Beverly, MA 01915-2096, 978-232-2060 or toll-free 800-325-1114 (out-of-state). *Fax:* 978-232-2085. *E-mail:* mtoomey@endicott.edu.

ERSKINE COLLEGE

Due West, SC

CONTACT Allison Sullivan, Director of Financial Aid, Erskine College, PO Box 337, Due West, SC 29639, 864-379-8832 or toll-free 800-241-8721. *Fax:* 864-379-2172. *E-mail:* sullivan@erskine.edu.

ESCUELA DE ARTES PLASTICAS DE PUERTO RICO

San Juan, PR

Tuition & fees: N/R **Average undergraduate aid package: N/A**

ABOUT THE INSTITUTION Commonwealth-supported, coed. 7 undergraduate majors. Federal methodology is used as a basis for awarding need-based institutional aid.

FRESHMAN FINANCIAL AID (Fall 2007) 54 applied for aid; of those 100% were deemed to have need. 100% of freshmen with need received aid. ***Average percent of need met:*** 83% (excluding resources awarded to replace EFC).

UNDERGRADUATE FINANCIAL AID (Fall 2007) 276 applied for aid; of those 100% were deemed to have need. 100% of undergraduates with need received aid. ***Average percent of need met:*** 82% (excluding resources awarded to replace EFC).

GIFT AID (NEED-BASED) ***Total amount:*** $1,299,686 (93% federal, 5% state, 2% institutional). ***Scholarships, grants, and awards:*** Federal Pell, FSEOG, state, private, college/university gift aid from institutional funds.

GIFT AID (NON-NEED-BASED) ***Tuition waivers:*** Full or partial for employees or children of employees.

WORK-STUDY ***Federal work-study:*** Total amount: $18,577; 10 jobs averaging $1850.

APPLYING FOR FINANCIAL AID ***Required financial aid form:*** FAFSA. ***Financial aid deadline:*** 5/25. ***Notification date:*** 8/30.

CONTACT Mr. Alfred Diaz Melendez, Financial Aid Administrator, Escuela de Artes Plasticas de Puerto Rico, PO Box 9021112, San Juan, PR 00902-1112, 787-725-8120 Ext. 317. *Fax:* 787-725-3798. *E-mail:* adiaz@eap.edu.

EUGENE BIBLE COLLEGE

Eugene, OR

CONTACT Mrs. Rulena Mellor, Financial Aid Director, Eugene Bible College, 2155 Bailey Hill Road, Eugene, OR 97405-1194, 541-485-1780 Ext. 125 or toll-free 800-322-2638. *Fax:* 541-343-5801. *E-mail:* finaid@ebc.edu.

EUGENE LANG COLLEGE THE NEW SCHOOL FOR LIBERAL ARTS

New York, NY

Tuition & fees: $33,060 **Average undergraduate aid package: $28,432**

ABOUT THE INSTITUTION Independent, coed. ***Awards:*** bachelor's degrees. 24 undergraduate majors. ***Total enrollment:*** 1,347. Undergraduates: 1,347. Freshmen: 301. Federal methodology is used as a basis for awarding need-based institutional aid.

UNDERGRADUATE EXPENSES for 2008–09 ***Application fee:*** $50. ***Comprehensive fee:*** $48,320 includes full-time tuition ($32,350), mandatory fees ($710), and room and board ($15,260). ***College room only:*** $12,260. Room and board charges vary according to board plan and housing facility. ***Part-time tuition:*** $1100 per credit. ***Payment plan:*** Installment.

FRESHMAN FINANCIAL AID (Fall 2008, est.) 187 applied for aid; of those 91% were deemed to have need. 100% of freshmen with need received aid; of those 12% had need fully met. ***Average percent of need met:*** 80% (excluding resources awarded to replace EFC). ***Average financial aid package:*** $30,199 (excluding resources awarded to replace EFC). 17% of all full-time freshmen had no need and received non-need-based gift aid.

UNDERGRADUATE FINANCIAL AID (Fall 2008, est.) 748 applied for aid; of those 91% were deemed to have need. 100% of undergraduates with need received aid; of those 11% had need fully met. ***Average percent of need met:*** 79% (excluding resources awarded to replace EFC). ***Average financial aid package:*** $28,432 (excluding resources awarded to replace EFC). 12% of all full-time undergraduates had no need and received non-need-based gift aid.

GIFT AID (NEED-BASED) ***Total amount:*** $14,035,692 (9% federal, 3% state, 88% institutional). ***Receiving aid:*** Freshmen: 56% (167); all full-time undergraduates: 51% (666). ***Average award:*** Freshmen: $21,287; Undergraduates: $18,927. ***Scholarships, grants, and awards:*** Federal Pell, FSEOG, state, private, college/university gift aid from institutional funds.

GIFT AID (NON-NEED-BASED) ***Total amount:*** $707,322 (51% institutional, 49% external sources). ***Receiving aid:*** Freshmen: 7% (20). Undergraduates: 6% (74). ***Average award:*** Freshmen: $7010. Undergraduates: $6669. ***Scholarships, grants, and awards by category:*** *Academic interests/achievement:* general academic interests/achievements. *Special achievements/activities:* general special achievements/activities. ***Tuition waivers:*** Full or partial for employees or children of employees.

LOANS ***Student loans:*** $5,683,370 (89% need-based, 11% non-need-based). 68% of past graduating class borrowed through all loan programs. *Average indebtedness per student:* $21,511. ***Average need-based loan:*** Freshmen: $8675. Undergraduates: $9164. ***Parent loans:*** $2,201,439 (76% need-based, 24% non-need-based). ***Programs:*** FFEL (Subsidized and Unsubsidized Stafford, PLUS), Perkins, college/university.

WORK-STUDY ***Federal work-study:*** Total amount: $250,778; jobs available. ***State or other work-study/employment:*** Part-time jobs available.

APPLYING FOR FINANCIAL AID ***Required financial aid form:*** FAFSA. ***Financial aid deadline:*** Continuous. ***Notification date:*** 3/1. Students must reply within 4 weeks of notification.

CONTACT Financial Aid Counselor, Eugene Lang College The New School for Liberal Arts, 65 West 11th Street, New York, NY 10011, 212-229-5665 or toll-free 877-528-3321.

EUREKA COLLEGE

Eureka, IL

Tuition & fees: $16,255 **Average undergraduate aid package: $12,717**

ABOUT THE INSTITUTION Independent religious, coed. ***Awards:*** bachelor's degrees. 35 undergraduate majors. ***Total enrollment:*** 672. Undergraduates: 672. Both federal and institutional methodology are used as a basis for awarding need-based institutional aid.

UNDERGRADUATE EXPENSES for 2008–09 ***Comprehensive fee:*** $23,385 includes full-time tuition ($15,675), mandatory fees ($580), and room and board ($7130). ***College room only:*** $3410. ***Part-time tuition:*** $450 per semester hour.

FRESHMAN FINANCIAL AID (Fall 2008, est.) 136 applied for aid; of those 76% were deemed to have need. 100% of freshmen with need received aid; of those 21% had need fully met. ***Average percent of need met:*** 69% (excluding resources awarded to replace EFC). ***Average financial aid package:*** $10,721 (excluding resources awarded to replace EFC). 22% of all full-time freshmen had no need and received non-need-based gift aid.

UNDERGRADUATE FINANCIAL AID (Fall 2008, est.) 600 applied for aid; of those 83% were deemed to have need. 100% of undergraduates with need received aid; of those 16% had need fully met. ***Average percent of need met:*** 68% (excluding resources awarded to replace EFC). ***Average financial aid package:*** $12,717 (excluding resources awarded to replace EFC). 14% of all full-time undergraduates had no need and received non-need-based gift aid.

GIFT AID (NEED-BASED) ***Total amount:*** $4,149,840 (21% federal, 35% state, 40% institutional, 4% external sources). ***Receiving aid:*** Freshmen: 67% (103); all full-time undergraduates: 70% (500). ***Average award:*** Freshmen: $6146; Undergraduates: $8010. ***Scholarships, grants, and awards:*** Federal Pell, FSEOG, state, private, college/university gift aid from institutional funds.

GIFT AID (NON-NEED-BASED) ***Total amount:*** $788,098 (100% institutional). ***Average award:*** Freshmen: $4192. Undergraduates: $3611. ***Scholarships, grants, and awards by category:*** *Academic interests/achievement:* 500 awards ($2,453,643 total): general academic interests/achievements. *Creative arts/performance:* 81 awards ($75,273 total): art/fine arts, music, performing arts, theater/drama. *Special achievements/activities:* 18 awards ($250,824 total):

leadership. *Special characteristics:* 101 awards ($208,565 total): children and siblings of alumni, children of faculty/staff, religious affiliation, siblings of current students.

LOANS ***Student loans:*** $4,233,523 (47% need-based, 53% non-need-based). 78% of past graduating class borrowed through all loan programs. *Average indebtedness per student:* $14,859. ***Average need-based loan:*** Freshmen: $3565. Undergraduates: $4295. ***Parent loans:*** $634,321 (100% non-need-based). ***Programs:*** FFEL (Subsidized and Unsubsidized Stafford, PLUS), Perkins, college/university, alternative loans.

WORK-STUDY ***Federal work-study:*** Total amount: $73,907; 58 jobs averaging $1274. ***State or other work-study/employment:*** Total amount: $177,090 (100% non-need-based). 134 part-time jobs averaging $1321.

APPLYING FOR FINANCIAL AID ***Required financial aid form:*** FAFSA. ***Financial aid deadline (priority):*** 4/1. ***Notification date:*** 5/1. Students must reply within 2 weeks of notification.

CONTACT Ms. Ellen Rigsby, Assistant Dean and Director of Financial Aid, Eureka College, 300 East College Avenue, Eureka, IL 61530, 309-467-6311 or toll-free 888-4-EUREKA. *Fax:* 309-467-6897. *E-mail:* eraid@eureka.edu.

EVANGEL UNIVERSITY

Springfield, MO

Tuition & fees: $15,020 **Average undergraduate aid package: $9814**

ABOUT THE INSTITUTION Independent religious, coed. ***Awards:*** associate, bachelor's, and master's degrees. 49 undergraduate majors. ***Total enrollment:*** 1,911. Undergraduates: 1,726. Freshmen: 338. Federal methodology is used as a basis for awarding need-based institutional aid.

UNDERGRADUATE EXPENSES for 2008–09 ***Application fee:*** $25. ***Comprehensive fee:*** $20,430 includes full-time tuition ($14,200), mandatory fees ($820), and room and board ($5410). ***College room only:*** $2760. Full-time tuition and fees vary according to course load. Room and board charges vary according to board plan. ***Part-time tuition:*** $554 per credit hour. ***Payment plan:*** Installment.

FRESHMAN FINANCIAL AID (Fall 2007) 267 applied for aid; of those 83% were deemed to have need. 95% of freshmen with need received aid; of those 13% had need fully met. ***Average percent of need met:*** 60% (excluding resources awarded to replace EFC). ***Average financial aid package:*** $9560 (excluding resources awarded to replace EFC). 18% of all full-time freshmen had no need and received non-need-based gift aid.

UNDERGRADUATE FINANCIAL AID (Fall 2007) 1,260 applied for aid; of those 86% were deemed to have need. 95% of undergraduates with need received aid; of those 12% had need fully met. ***Average percent of need met:*** 53% (excluding resources awarded to replace EFC). ***Average financial aid package:*** $9814 (excluding resources awarded to replace EFC). 14% of all full-time undergraduates had no need and received non-need-based gift aid.

GIFT AID (NEED-BASED) ***Total amount:*** $4,127,361 (46% federal, 2% state, 34% institutional, 18% external sources). ***Receiving aid:*** Freshmen: 60% (194); all full-time undergraduates: 61% (878). ***Average award:*** Freshmen: $6569; Undergraduates: $6106. ***Scholarships, grants, and awards:*** Federal Pell, FSEOG, state, private, college/university gift aid from institutional funds.

GIFT AID (NON-NEED-BASED) ***Total amount:*** $869,640 (59% institutional, 41% external sources). ***Receiving aid:*** Freshmen: 6% (19). Undergraduates: 5% (76). ***Average award:*** Freshmen: $2500. Undergraduates: $2291. ***Scholarships, grants, and awards by category:*** *Academic interests/achievement:* 677 awards ($1,464,020 total): business, communication, computer science, education, engineering/technologies, English, foreign languages, general academic interests/achievements, humanities, mathematics, physical sciences, religion/biblical studies, social sciences. *Creative arts/performance:* 131 awards ($237,400 total): art/fine arts, music, theater/drama. *Special achievements/activities:* 224 awards ($125,000 total): cheerleading/drum major, general special achievements/activities, leadership, religious involvement. *Special characteristics:* 305 awards ($1,625,307 total): adult students, children and siblings of alumni, children of educators, children of faculty/staff, general special characteristics, relatives of clergy, religious affiliation. ***Tuition waivers:*** Full or partial for employees or children of employees. ***ROTC:*** Army.

LOANS ***Student loans:*** $10,487,278 (76% need-based, 24% non-need-based). ***Average need-based loan:*** Freshmen: $3764. Undergraduates: $4917. ***Parent loans:*** $2,500,655 (39% need-based, 61% non-need-based). ***Programs:*** FFEL (Subsidized and Unsubsidized Stafford, PLUS), Perkins, college/university.

WORK-STUDY ***Federal work-study:*** Total amount: $248,239; 562 jobs averaging $1800. ***State or other work-study/employment:*** Total amount: $102,754 (67% need-based, 33% non-need-based). 121 part-time jobs averaging $1800.

ATHLETIC AWARDS Total amount: $1,486,962 (69% need-based, 31% non-need-based).

APPLYING FOR FINANCIAL AID ***Required financial aid form:*** FAFSA. ***Financial aid deadline (priority):*** 4/1. ***Notification date:*** Continuous beginning 4/1. Students must reply within 3 weeks of notification.

CONTACT Mrs. Dorynda Carpenter, Director of Student Financial Services, Evangel University, 1111 North Glenstone Avenue, Springfield, MO 65802-2191, 417-865-2811 Ext. 7302 or toll-free 800-382-6435 (in-state). *Fax:* 417-575-5478. *E-mail:* carpenterd@evangel.edu.

EVEREST UNIVERSITY

Clearwater, FL

Tuition & fees: N/R **Average undergraduate aid package: $7500**

ABOUT THE INSTITUTION Proprietary, coed. ***Awards:*** associate, bachelor's, and master's degrees. 7 undergraduate majors. ***Total enrollment:*** 261. Undergraduates: 243. Federal methodology is used as a basis for awarding need-based institutional aid.

FRESHMAN FINANCIAL AID (Fall 2008, est.) 71 applied for aid; of those 100% were deemed to have need. 100% of freshmen with need received aid. ***Average percent of need met:*** 60% (excluding resources awarded to replace EFC). ***Average financial aid package:*** $6500 (excluding resources awarded to replace EFC).

UNDERGRADUATE FINANCIAL AID (Fall 2008, est.) 240 applied for aid; of those 100% were deemed to have need. 100% of undergraduates with need received aid. ***Average percent of need met:*** 80% (excluding resources awarded to replace EFC). ***Average financial aid package:*** $7500 (excluding resources awarded to replace EFC).

GIFT AID (NEED-BASED) ***Total amount:*** $2,155,936 (90% federal, 9% state, 1% institutional). ***Receiving aid:*** Freshmen: 82% (60); all full-time undergraduates: 90% (220). ***Average award:*** Freshmen: $3500; Undergraduates: $3500. ***Scholarships, grants, and awards:*** Federal Pell, FSEOG, state, private, college/university gift aid from institutional funds.

GIFT AID (NON-NEED-BASED) ***Receiving aid:*** Freshmen: 7% (5). Undergraduates: 4% (10). ***Scholarships, grants, and awards by category:*** *Academic interests/achievement:* business, computer science, general academic interests/achievements, health fields.

LOANS ***Student loans:*** $5,200,343 (43% need-based, 57% non-need-based). 95% of past graduating class borrowed through all loan programs. *Average indebtedness per student:* $36,000. ***Average need-based loan:*** Freshmen: $3500. Undergraduates: $5000. ***Parent loans:*** $56,631 (100% non-need-based). ***Programs:*** Federal Direct (Subsidized and Unsubsidized Stafford, PLUS), FFEL (Subsidized and Unsubsidized Stafford, PLUS), Signature Loans; career training; NLSC.

WORK-STUDY ***Federal work-study:*** Total amount: $52,395; 8 jobs averaging $6500.

APPLYING FOR FINANCIAL AID ***Required financial aid form:*** FAFSA. ***Financial aid deadline:*** Continuous. ***Notification date:*** Continuous beginning 1/8.

CONTACT Mr. Will Scott, Director of Student Finance, Everest University, 1199 East Bay Drive, Largo, FL 33770, 727-725-2688 Ext. 166 or toll-free 800-353-FMUS. *Fax:* 727-373-4408. *E-mail:* wscott@cci.edu.

EVEREST UNIVERSITY

Jacksonville, FL

CONTACT Financial Aid Office, Everest University, 8226 Phillips Highway, Jacksonville, FL 32256, 904-731-4949 or toll-free 888-741-4270.

EVEREST UNIVERSITY

Lakeland, FL

CONTACT Brian Jones, Senior Finance Officer, Everest University, Office of Financial Aid, 995 East Memorial Boulevard, Lakeland, FL 33801, 863-686-1444 Ext. 118 or toll-free 877-225-0014 (in-state). *Fax:* 863-682-1077.

EVEREST UNIVERSITY
Melbourne, FL

CONTACT Ronda Nabb-Landolfi, Director of Student Financial Aid, Everest University, 2401 North Harbor City Boulevard, Melbourne, FL 32935-6657, 321-253-2929 Ext. 19.

EVEREST UNIVERSITY
Orlando, FL

CONTACT Ms. Linda Kaisrlik, Director of Student Finance, Everest University, 5421 Diplomat Circle, Orlando, FL 32810-5674, 407-628-5870 Ext. 118 or toll-free 800-628-5870.

EVEREST UNIVERSITY
Orlando, FL

CONTACT Sherri Williams, Director of Financial Aid, Everest University, 2411 Sand Lake Road, Orlando, FL 32809, 407-851-2525 or toll-free 888-471-4270 (out-of-state).

EVEREST UNIVERSITY
Pompano Beach, FL

CONTACT Sharon Scheible, Director of Student Financial Aid, Everest University, 1040 Bayview Drive, Fort Lauderdale, FL 33304-2522, 954-568-1600 Ext. 52 or toll-free 800-468-0168. *Fax:* 954-564-5283. *E-mail:* scheible@cci.edu.

EVEREST UNIVERSITY
Tampa, FL

ABOUT THE INSTITUTION Proprietary, coed. ***Awards:*** associate, bachelor's, and master's degrees. 10 undergraduate majors. ***Total enrollment:*** 1,320. Undergraduates: 1,284.

GIFT AID (NEED-BASED) ***Scholarships, grants, and awards:*** Federal Pell, FSEOG, state, private, college/university gift aid from institutional funds.

LOANS ***Programs:*** Federal Direct (Subsidized and Unsubsidized Stafford, PLUS), FFEL (Subsidized and Unsubsidized Stafford, PLUS).

APPLYING FOR FINANCIAL AID ***Required financial aid form:*** FAFSA.

CONTACT Mr. Rod Kirkwood, Financial Aid Director, Everest University, 3319 West Hillsborough Avenue, Tampa, FL 33614, 813-879-6000 Ext. 145. *Fax:* 813-871-2483. *E-mail:* rkirkwoo@cci.edu.

EVEREST UNIVERSITY
Tampa, FL

CONTACT Ms. Ginger Waymire, Director of Financial Aid, Everest University, 3924 Coconut Palm Drive, Tampa, FL 33619, 813-621-0041 Ext. 118 or toll-free 877-338-0068. *Fax:* 813-621-6283. *E-mail:* gwaymire@cci.edu.

EVERGLADES UNIVERSITY
Altamonte Springs, FL

CONTACT Financial Aid Office, Everglades University, 887 East Altamonte Drive, Altamonte Springs, FL 32701, 407-277-0311.

EVERGLADES UNIVERSITY
Boca Raton, FL

Tuition & fees: N/R **Average undergraduate aid package: N/A**

ABOUT THE INSTITUTION Independent, coed. 6 undergraduate majors. Federal methodology is used as a basis for awarding need-based institutional aid.

GIFT AID (NEED-BASED) ***Scholarships, grants, and awards:*** Federal Pell, FSEOG, state, private, college/university gift aid from institutional funds.

LOANS ***Programs:*** Federal Direct (Subsidized and Unsubsidized Stafford, PLUS), FFEL (Subsidized and Unsubsidized Stafford, PLUS), Perkins.

WORK-STUDY Federal work-study jobs available.

APPLYING FOR FINANCIAL AID ***Required financial aid forms:*** FAFSA, institution's own form. ***Notification date:*** Continuous. Students must reply within 2 weeks of notification.

CONTACT Seeta Singh Moonilal, Financial Aid Director, Everglades University, 5002 T Rex Avenue, Suite 100, Boca Raton, FL 33431, 561-912-1211 or toll-free 888-772-6077 (out-of-state). *Fax:* 561-912-1191. *E-mail:* seetasm@evergladesuniversity.edu.

EVERGLADES UNIVERSITY
Sarasota, FL

CONTACT Financial Aid Office, Everglades University, 6151 Lake Osprey Drive, Sarasota, FL 34240, 941-907-2262 or toll-free 866-907-2262.

THE EVERGREEN STATE COLLEGE
Olympia, WA

Tuition & fees (WA res): $5344 **Average undergraduate aid package: $12,297**

ABOUT THE INSTITUTION State-supported, coed. ***Awards:*** bachelor's and master's degrees. 33 undergraduate majors. ***Total enrollment:*** 4,696. Undergraduates: 4,364. Freshmen: 665. Federal methodology is used as a basis for awarding need-based institutional aid.

UNDERGRADUATE EXPENSES for 2008–09 ***Application fee:*** $50. ***Tuition, state resident:*** full-time $4797; part-time $159.90 per credit hour. ***Tuition, nonresident:*** full-time $15,657; part-time $521.90 per credit hour. ***Required fees:*** full-time $547; $9.85 per credit hour or $50 per term. Full-time tuition and fees vary according to course load, degree level, location, and program. Part-time tuition and fees vary according to course load, degree level, location, and program. ***College room and board:*** $8052; ***Room only:*** $5454. Room and board charges vary according to board plan, housing facility, and student level. ***Payment plan:*** Installment.

FRESHMAN FINANCIAL AID (Fall 2008, est.) 449 applied for aid; of those 71% were deemed to have need. 95% of freshmen with need received aid; of those 31% had need fully met. ***Average percent of need met:*** 61% (excluding resources awarded to replace EFC). ***Average financial aid package:*** $10,745 (excluding resources awarded to replace EFC). 2% of all full-time freshmen had no need and received non-need-based gift aid.

UNDERGRADUATE FINANCIAL AID (Fall 2008, est.) 2,718 applied for aid; of those 83% were deemed to have need. 94% of undergraduates with need received aid; of those 26% had need fully met. ***Average percent of need met:*** 66% (excluding resources awarded to replace EFC). ***Average financial aid package:*** $12,297 (excluding resources awarded to replace EFC). 1% of all full-time undergraduates had no need and received non-need-based gift aid.

GIFT AID (NEED-BASED) ***Total amount:*** $11,110,883 (47% federal, 43% state, 8% institutional, 2% external sources). ***Receiving aid:*** Freshmen: 28% (184); all full-time undergraduates: 41% (1,629). ***Average award:*** Freshmen: $7387; Undergraduates: $7688. ***Scholarships, grants, and awards:*** Federal Pell, FSEOG, state, private, college/university gift aid from institutional funds.

GIFT AID (NON-NEED-BASED) ***Total amount:*** $1,447,418 (10% state, 32% institutional, 58% external sources). ***Receiving aid:*** Freshmen: 33% (218). Undergraduates: 12% (455). ***Average award:*** Freshmen: $4406. Undergraduates: $3653. ***Scholarships, grants, and awards by category:*** *Academic interests/achievement:* 601 awards ($1,022,544 total): general academic interests/achievements. *Creative arts/performance:* 3 awards ($9273 total): applied art and design, art/fine arts, creative writing. *Special achievements/activities:* 37 awards ($45,141 total): community service, general special achievements/activities. *Special characteristics:* 115 awards ($365,944 total): adult students, first-generation college students, members of minority groups, veterans, veterans' children. ***Tuition waivers:*** Full or partial for employees or children of employees.

LOANS ***Student loans:*** $11,831,067 (55% need-based, 45% non-need-based). 52% of past graduating class borrowed through all loan programs. *Average indebtedness per student:* $15,371. ***Average need-based loan:*** Freshmen: $3026. Undergraduates: $2673. ***Parent loans:*** $3,012,817 (28% need-based, 72% non-need-based). ***Programs:*** FFEL (Subsidized and Unsubsidized Stafford, PLUS), Perkins, college/university.

WORK-STUDY ***Federal work-study:*** Total amount: $327,544; 114 jobs averaging $1929. ***State or other work-study/employment:*** Total amount: $588,000 (100% need-based). 151 part-time jobs averaging $1840.

ATHLETIC AWARDS Total amount: $90,285 (71% need-based, 29% non-need-based).

APPLYING FOR FINANCIAL AID ***Required financial aid forms:*** FAFSA, institution's own form. ***Financial aid deadline (priority):*** 3/15. ***Notification date:*** Continuous beginning 3/28. Students must reply within 6 weeks of notification.

CONTACT Financial Aid Office, The Evergreen State College, 2700 Evergreen Parkway NW, Olympia, WA 98505, 360-867-6205. *Fax:* 360-866-6576. *E-mail:* financialaid@evergreen.edu.

EXCELSIOR COLLEGE

Albany, NY

Tuition & fees: N/R **Average undergraduate aid package: N/A**

ABOUT THE INSTITUTION Independent, coed. ***Awards:*** associate, bachelor's, and master's degrees and post-bachelor's and post-master's certificates (offers only external degree programs). 38 undergraduate majors. ***Total enrollment:*** 33,450. Undergraduates: 32,454. Federal methodology is used as a basis for awarding need-based institutional aid.

UNDERGRADUATE EXPENSES for 2008–09 ***Application fee:*** $75. ***Tuition:*** part-time $300 per credit hour. ***Required fees:*** $440 per year. ***Payment plan:*** Installment.

GIFT AID (NEED-BASED) ***Total amount:*** $894,805 (19% federal, 26% state, 24% institutional, 31% external sources). ***Scholarships, grants, and awards:*** Federal Pell, state, private, college/university gift aid from institutional funds.

GIFT AID (NON-NEED-BASED) ***Tuition waivers:*** Full or partial for employees or children of employees.

LOANS ***Student loans:*** $3,588,691 (100% need-based). ***Programs:*** Federal Direct (Subsidized and Unsubsidized Stafford, PLUS), private bank loans.

CONTACT Donna L. Cooper, Director of Financial Aid, Excelsior College, 7 Columbia Circle, Albany, NY 12203-5159, 518-464-8500 or toll-free 888-647-2388. *Fax:* 518-464-8777.

FAIRFIELD UNIVERSITY

Fairfield, CT

Tuition & fees: $36,075 **Average undergraduate aid package: $23,965**

ABOUT THE INSTITUTION Independent Roman Catholic (Jesuit), coed. ***Awards:*** associate, bachelor's, and master's degrees and post-master's certificates. 42 undergraduate majors. ***Total enrollment:*** 5,128. Undergraduates: 4,084. Freshmen: 899. Federal methodology is used as a basis for awarding need-based institutional aid.

UNDERGRADUATE EXPENSES for 2008–09 ***Application fee:*** $60. ***One-time required fee:*** $60. ***Comprehensive fee:*** $46,925 includes full-time tuition ($35,510), mandatory fees ($565), and room and board ($10,850). ***College room only:*** $6480. Room and board charges vary according to board plan and housing facility. ***Part-time tuition:*** $475 per credit hour. ***Part-time fees:*** $25 per term. Part-time tuition and fees vary according to course load. ***Payment plan:*** Installment.

FRESHMAN FINANCIAL AID (Fall 2008, est.) 618 applied for aid; of those 80% were deemed to have need. 100% of freshmen with need received aid; of those 26% had need fully met. ***Average percent of need met:*** 86% (excluding resources awarded to replace EFC). ***Average financial aid package:*** $27,488 (excluding resources awarded to replace EFC). 4% of all full-time freshmen had no need and received non-need-based gift aid.

UNDERGRADUATE FINANCIAL AID (Fall 2008, est.) 2,078 applied for aid; of those 84% were deemed to have need. 99% of undergraduates with need received aid; of those 22% had need fully met. ***Average percent of need met:*** 82% (excluding resources awarded to replace EFC). ***Average financial aid package:*** $23,965 (excluding resources awarded to replace EFC). 6% of all full-time undergraduates had no need and received non-need-based gift aid.

GIFT AID (NEED-BASED) ***Total amount:*** $28,217,138 (6% federal, 7% state, 87% institutional). ***Receiving aid:*** Freshmen: 48% (435); all full-time undergraduates: 45% (1,531). ***Average award:*** Freshmen: $21,344; Undergraduates: $18,140. ***Scholarships, grants, and awards:*** Federal Pell, FSEOG, state, private, college/university gift aid from institutional funds, United Negro College Fund.

GIFT AID (NON-NEED-BASED) ***Total amount:*** $7,452,853 (90% institutional, 10% external sources). ***Receiving aid:*** Freshmen: 19% (167). Undergraduates: 14% (491). ***Average award:*** Freshmen: $12,649. Undergraduates: $12,067. ***Scholarships, grants, and awards by category:*** *Academic interests/achievement:* 554 awards ($6,707,915 total): biological sciences, business, education, engineering/technologies, foreign languages, general academic interests/achievements, physical sciences. *Creative arts/performance:* 17 awards ($19,929 total): art/fine arts, music, performing arts. *Special achievements/activities:* 20 awards ($101,500 total): religious involvement. *Special characteristics:* 58 awards ($1,443,716 total): children and siblings of alumni, ethnic background, first-generation college students, members of minority groups, parents of current students, religious affiliation. ***Tuition waivers:*** Full or partial for employees or children of employees. ***ROTC:*** Army cooperative, Air Force cooperative.

LOANS ***Student loans:*** $23,572,714 (36% need-based, 64% non-need-based). 59% of past graduating class borrowed through all loan programs. *Average indebtedness per student:* $32,857. ***Average need-based loan:*** Freshmen: $3980. Undergraduates: $4574. ***Parent loans:*** $5,506,249 (100% non-need-based). ***Programs:*** FFEL (Subsidized and Unsubsidized Stafford, PLUS), Perkins, alternative loans.

WORK-STUDY ***Federal work-study:*** Total amount: $996,424; 529 jobs averaging $1517.

ATHLETIC AWARDS Total amount: $4,647,560 (100% non-need-based).

APPLYING FOR FINANCIAL AID ***Required financial aid forms:*** FAFSA, CSS Financial Aid PROFILE, noncustodial (divorced/separated) parent's statement, business/farm supplement. ***Financial aid deadline:*** 2/15 (priority: 2/15). ***Notification date:*** 4/1. Students must reply by 5/1.

CONTACT Mr. Erin Chiaro, Director of Financial Aid, Fairfield University, 1073 North Benson Road, Fairfield, CT 06824-5195, 203-254-4125. *Fax:* 203-254-4008. *E-mail:* echiaro@fairfield.edu.

FAIRLEIGH DICKINSON UNIVERSITY, COLLEGE AT FLORHAM

Madison, NJ

Tuition & fees: $30,198 **Average undergraduate aid package: $17,400**

ABOUT THE INSTITUTION Independent, coed. ***Awards:*** bachelor's and master's degrees and post-bachelor's and post-master's certificates. 33 undergraduate majors. ***Total enrollment:*** 3,465. Undergraduates: 2,454. Freshmen: 604. Federal methodology is used as a basis for awarding need-based institutional aid.

UNDERGRADUATE EXPENSES for 2008–09 ***Application fee:*** $40. ***Comprehensive fee:*** $40,746 includes full-time tuition ($29,250), mandatory fees ($948), and room and board ($10,548). ***College room only:*** $6534. Room and board charges vary according to board plan and housing facility. ***Part-time tuition:*** $821 per credit. ***Payment plans:*** Installment, deferred payment.

FRESHMAN FINANCIAL AID (Fall 2007) 421 applied for aid; of those 87% were deemed to have need. 100% of freshmen with need received aid. ***Average financial aid package:*** $18,500 (excluding resources awarded to replace EFC). 12% of all full-time freshmen had no need and received non-need-based gift aid.

UNDERGRADUATE FINANCIAL AID (Fall 2007) 1,788 applied for aid; of those 88% were deemed to have need. 99% of undergraduates with need received aid. ***Average financial aid package:*** $17,400 (excluding resources awarded to replace EFC). 9% of all full-time undergraduates had no need and received non-need-based gift aid.

GIFT AID (NEED-BASED) ***Total amount:*** $13,165,812 (13% federal, 26% state, 61% institutional). ***Receiving aid:*** Freshmen: 62% (300); all full-time undergraduates: 57% (1,292). ***Average award:*** Freshmen: $11,705; Undergraduates: $9956. ***Scholarships, grants, and awards:*** Federal Pell, FSEOG, state, private, college/university gift aid from institutional funds, Federal Nursing, FNSF Grant.

GIFT AID (NON-NEED-BASED) ***Total amount:*** $12,759,958 (100% institutional). ***Receiving aid:*** Freshmen: 56% (270). Undergraduates: 42% (968). ***Average award:*** Freshmen: $8400. Undergraduates: $6501. ***Tuition waivers:*** Full or partial for employees or children of employees. ***ROTC:*** Army cooperative, Air Force cooperative.

LOANS ***Student loans:*** $21,924,877 (32% need-based, 68% non-need-based). ***Average need-based loan:*** Freshmen: $3000. Undergraduates: $4001. ***Parent loans:*** $1,840,732 (100% non-need-based). ***Programs:*** FFEL (Subsidized and Unsubsidized Stafford, PLUS), Perkins, Federal Nursing, state.

WORK-STUDY ***Federal work-study:*** Total amount: $250,000; jobs available.

APPLYING FOR FINANCIAL AID ***Required financial aid form:*** FAFSA. ***Financial aid deadline (priority):*** 2/15. ***Notification date:*** Continuous. Students must reply by 5/1 or within 4 weeks of notification.

CONTACT Financial Aid Office, Fairleigh Dickinson University, College at Florham, 285 Madison Avenue, Madison, NJ 07940-1099, 973-443-8700 or toll-free 800-338-8803.

FAIRLEIGH DICKINSON UNIVERSITY, METROPOLITAN CAMPUS

Teaneck, NJ

Tuition & fees: $28,084 **Average undergraduate aid package: $18,283**

ABOUT THE INSTITUTION Independent, coed. ***Awards:*** associate, bachelor's, master's, and doctoral degrees and post-bachelor's and post-master's certificates. 42 undergraduate majors. ***Total enrollment:*** 8,693. Undergraduates: 5,866. Freshmen: 515. Federal methodology is used as a basis for awarding need-based institutional aid.

UNDERGRADUATE EXPENSES for 2008–09 ***Application fee:*** $40. ***Comprehensive fee:*** $38,998 includes full-time tuition ($27,136), mandatory fees ($948), and room and board ($10,914). ***College room only:*** $6900. Room and board charges vary according to board plan and housing facility. ***Part-time tuition:*** $821 per credit. ***Payment plans:*** Installment, deferred payment.

FRESHMAN FINANCIAL AID (Fall 2007) 330 applied for aid; of those 92% were deemed to have need. 100% of freshmen with need received aid. 5% of all full-time freshmen had no need and received non-need-based gift aid.

UNDERGRADUATE FINANCIAL AID (Fall 2007) 1,671 applied for aid; of those 93% were deemed to have need. 98% of undergraduates with need received aid. ***Average financial aid package:*** $18,283 (excluding resources awarded to replace EFC). 5% of all full-time undergraduates had no need and received non-need-based gift aid.

GIFT AID (NEED-BASED) ***Total amount:*** $15,476,390 (23% federal, 37% state, 40% institutional). ***Receiving aid:*** Freshmen: 67% (270); all full-time undergraduates: 59% (1,296). ***Average award:*** Freshmen: $11,250; Undergraduates: $8702. ***Scholarships, grants, and awards:*** Federal Pell, FSEOG, state, private, college/university gift aid from institutional funds, Federal Nursing, FSNF Grant.

GIFT AID (NON-NEED-BASED) ***Total amount:*** $7,375,465 (1% federal, 1% state, 95% institutional, 3% external sources). ***Receiving aid:*** Freshmen: 53% (215). Undergraduates: 36% (800). ***Average award:*** Undergraduates: $6403. ***Tuition waivers:*** Full or partial for employees or children of employees, senior citizens. ***ROTC:*** Army cooperative, Air Force cooperative.

LOANS ***Student loans:*** $17,114,114 (36% need-based, 64% non-need-based). ***Average need-based loan:*** Freshmen: $2655. Undergraduates: $3808. ***Parent loans:*** $2,000,000 (100% non-need-based). ***Programs:*** FFEL (Subsidized and Unsubsidized Stafford, PLUS), Perkins, Federal Nursing, state.

WORK-STUDY ***Federal work-study:*** Total amount: $233,000; jobs available.

ATHLETIC AWARDS Total amount: $1,800,000 (100% non-need-based).

APPLYING FOR FINANCIAL AID ***Required financial aid form:*** FAFSA. ***Financial aid deadline (priority):*** 2/15. ***Notification date:*** Continuous beginning 3/1. Students must reply by 5/1 or within 2 weeks of notification.

CONTACT Financial Aid Office, Fairleigh Dickinson University, Metropolitan Campus, 100 River Road, Teaneck, NJ 07666-1914, 201-692-2363 or toll-free 800-338-8803.

FAIRMONT STATE UNIVERSITY

Fairmont, WV

Tuition & fees (WV res): $5224 **Average undergraduate aid package: $7364**

ABOUT THE INSTITUTION State-supported, coed. ***Awards:*** associate, bachelor's, and master's degrees. 60 undergraduate majors. ***Total enrollment:*** 4,547. Undergraduates: 4,115. Freshmen: 771.

UNDERGRADUATE EXPENSES for 2008–09 ***Tuition, state resident:*** full-time $5024; part-time $210 per credit hour. ***Tuition, nonresident:*** full-time $10,590; part-time $442 per credit hour. ***Required fees:*** full-time $200. Full-time tuition and fees vary according to degree level and location. Part-time tuition and fees vary according to course load, degree level, and location. ***College room and board:*** $6652; ***Room only:*** $3280. Room and board charges vary according to board plan and housing facility. ***Payment plan:*** Installment.

FRESHMAN FINANCIAL AID (Fall 2007) 579 applied for aid; of those 72% were deemed to have need. 97% of freshmen with need received aid; of those 14% had need fully met. ***Average financial aid package:*** $6866 (excluding resources awarded to replace EFC). 12% of all full-time freshmen had no need and received non-need-based gift aid.

UNDERGRADUATE FINANCIAL AID (Fall 2007) 2,893 applied for aid; of those 81% were deemed to have need. 98% of undergraduates with need received aid; of those 10% had need fully met. ***Average financial aid package:*** $7364 (excluding resources awarded to replace EFC). 8% of all full-time undergraduates had no need and received non-need-based gift aid.

GIFT AID (NEED-BASED) ***Total amount:*** $7,032,187 (70% federal, 23% state, 3% institutional, 4% external sources). ***Receiving aid:*** Freshmen: 35% (264); all full-time undergraduates: 44% (1,556). ***Average award:*** Freshmen: $8985; Undergraduates: $10,470. ***Scholarships, grants, and awards:*** Federal Pell, FSEOG, state, private, college/university gift aid from institutional funds, Academic Competitiveness Grant, National Smart Grant.

GIFT AID (NON-NEED-BASED) ***Total amount:*** $1,161,248 (77% state, 10% institutional, 13% external sources). ***Receiving aid:*** Freshmen: 12% (93). Undergraduates: 10% (336). ***Average award:*** Freshmen: $1392. Undergraduates: $1242. ***ROTC:*** Army.

LOANS ***Student loans:*** $14,510,517 (51% need-based, 49% non-need-based). ***Average need-based loan:*** Freshmen: $2887. Undergraduates: $3842. ***Parent loans:*** $847,383 (69% need-based, 31% non-need-based). ***Programs:*** Federal Direct (Subsidized and Unsubsidized Stafford, PLUS), Perkins.

WORK-STUDY ***Federal work-study:*** Total amount: $278,748; jobs available. ***State or other work-study/employment:*** Part-time jobs available (averaging $1037).

ATHLETIC AWARDS Total amount: $746,875 (48% need-based, 52% non-need-based).

APPLYING FOR FINANCIAL AID ***Required financial aid form:*** FAFSA. ***Financial aid deadline (priority):*** 3/1. ***Notification date:*** Continuous beginning 4/1. Students must reply within 2 weeks of notification.

CONTACT Cynthia K. Hudok, Director of Financial Aid and Scholarships, Fairmont State University, 1201 Locust Avenue, Fairmont, WV 26554, 304-367-4213 or toll-free 800-641-5678. *Fax:* 304-367-4584. *E-mail:* financialaid@fairmontstate.edu.

FAITH BAPTIST BIBLE COLLEGE AND THEOLOGICAL SEMINARY

Ankeny, IA

CONTACT Mr. Breck Appell, Director of Financial Assistance, Faith Baptist Bible College and Theological Seminary, 1900 Northwest 4th Street, Ankeny, IA 50021-2152, 515-964-0601 or toll-free 888-FAITH 4U. *Fax:* 515-964-1638.

FARMINGDALE STATE COLLEGE

Farmingdale, NY

CONTACT Dionne Walker-Belgrave, Assistant Director of Financial Aid, Farmingdale State College, 2350 Broadhollow Road, Route 110, Farmingdale, NY 11735, 631-420-2328 or toll-free 877-4-FARMINGDALE. *Fax:* 631-420-3662.

FASHION INSTITUTE OF TECHNOLOGY

New York, NY

Tuition & fees (NY res): $5008 **Average undergraduate aid package: $9794**

ABOUT THE INSTITUTION State and locally supported, coed, primarily women. ***Awards:*** associate, bachelor's, and master's degrees. 21 undergraduate majors. ***Total enrollment:*** 10,065. Undergraduates: 9,854. Freshmen: 1,122. Federal methodology is used as a basis for awarding need-based institutional aid.

UNDERGRADUATE EXPENSES for 2008–09 ***Application fee:*** $40. ***Tuition, state resident:*** full-time $4568; part-time $190 per credit. ***Tuition, nonresident:*** full-time $11,140; part-time $464 per credit. ***Required fees:*** full-time $440; $70 per year. ***College room and board:*** $10,950; ***Room only:*** $9710.

FRESHMAN FINANCIAL AID (Fall 2008, est.) 852 applied for aid; of those 67% were deemed to have need. 98% of freshmen with need received aid; of those 18% had need fully met. ***Average percent of need met:*** 71% (excluding resources awarded to replace EFC). ***Average financial aid package:*** $9083 (excluding resources awarded to replace EFC). 7% of all full-time freshmen had no need and received non-need-based gift aid.

UNDERGRADUATE FINANCIAL AID (Fall 2008, est.) 4,404 applied for aid; of those 77% were deemed to have need. 98% of undergraduates with need received aid; of those 17% had need fully met. ***Average percent of need met:*** 69% (excluding resources awarded to replace EFC). ***Average financial aid package:*** $9794 (excluding resources awarded to replace EFC). 2% of all full-time undergraduates had no need and received non-need-based gift aid.

GIFT AID (NEED-BASED) ***Total amount:*** $11,910,942 (58% federal, 35% state, 7% institutional). ***Receiving aid:*** Freshmen: 33% (381); all full-time undergraduates: 32% (2,355). ***Average award:*** Freshmen: $4602; Undergraduates: $4324. ***Scholarships, grants, and awards:*** Federal Pell, FSEOG, state, private, college/university gift aid from institutional funds.

GIFT AID (NON-NEED-BASED) ***Total amount:*** $1,071,388 (7% institutional, 93% external sources). ***Receiving aid:*** Freshmen: 11% (128). Undergraduates: 4% (329). ***Average award:*** Freshmen: $1634. Undergraduates: $1697. ***Scholarships, grants, and awards by category:*** *Creative arts/performance:* 157 awards ($76,000 total): applied art and design.

LOANS ***Student loans:*** $31,343,139 (35% need-based, 65% non-need-based). 48% of past graduating class borrowed through all loan programs. *Average indebtedness per student:* $22,857. ***Average need-based loan:*** Freshmen: $3441. Undergraduates: $4147. ***Parent loans:*** $4,071,278 (100% non-need-based). ***Programs:*** FFEL (Subsidized and Unsubsidized Stafford, PLUS), Perkins, alternative loans.

WORK-STUDY ***Federal work-study:*** Total amount: $923,068; 448 jobs averaging $1625.

APPLYING FOR FINANCIAL AID ***Required financial aid forms:*** FAFSA, state aid form. ***Financial aid deadline (priority):*** 2/15. ***Notification date:*** Continuous beginning 4/15. Students must reply within 2 weeks of notification.

CONTACT Financial Aid Office, Fashion Institute of Technology, Seventh Avenue at 27th Street, New York, NY 10001-5992, 212-217-3560 or toll-free 800-GOTOFIT (out-of-state).

FAULKNER UNIVERSITY

Montgomery, AL

Tuition & fees: $12,720 **Average undergraduate aid package: $7400**

ABOUT THE INSTITUTION Independent religious, coed. ***Awards:*** associate, bachelor's, master's, and first professional degrees. 40 undergraduate majors. ***Total enrollment:*** 2,873. Undergraduates: 2,677. Freshmen: 292. Federal methodology is used as a basis for awarding need-based institutional aid.

UNDERGRADUATE EXPENSES for 2009–10 ***Application fee:*** $10. ***Comprehensive fee:*** $19,070 includes full-time tuition ($12,720) and room and board ($6350). ***College room only:*** $3150.

FRESHMAN FINANCIAL AID (Fall 2008, est.) 184 applied for aid; of those 78% were deemed to have need. 100% of freshmen with need received aid; of those 9% had need fully met. ***Average percent of need met:*** 60% (excluding resources awarded to replace EFC). ***Average financial aid package:*** $5000 (excluding resources awarded to replace EFC). 3% of all full-time freshmen had no need and received non-need-based gift aid.

UNDERGRADUATE FINANCIAL AID (Fall 2008, est.) 1,851 applied for aid; of those 78% were deemed to have need. 100% of undergraduates with need received aid; of those 9% had need fully met. ***Average percent of need met:*** 60% (excluding resources awarded to replace EFC). ***Average financial aid package:*** $7400 (excluding resources awarded to replace EFC). 3% of all full-time undergraduates had no need and received non-need-based gift aid.

GIFT AID (NEED-BASED) ***Total amount:*** $5,600,000 (100% federal). ***Receiving aid:*** Freshmen: 53% (106); all full-time undergraduates: 53% (1,066). ***Average award:*** Freshmen: $2650; Undergraduates: $4000. ***Scholarships, grants, and awards:*** Federal Pell, FSEOG, state, private, college/university gift aid from institutional funds.

GIFT AID (NON-NEED-BASED) ***Total amount:*** $3,892,000 (20% state, 74% institutional, 6% external sources). ***Receiving aid:*** Freshmen: 42% (84). Undergraduates: 42% (845). ***Average award:*** Freshmen: $2000. Undergraduates: $2800. ***Scholarships, grants, and awards by category:*** *Academic interests/achievement:* 221 awards ($1,022,568 total): general academic interests/achievements, religion/biblical studies. *Creative arts/performance:* 37 awards ($23,000 total): journalism/publications, music, theater/drama. *Special achievements/activities:* 108 awards ($193,014 total): cheerleading/drum major, leadership, religious involvement. *Special characteristics:* 450 awards ($1,354,164 total): adult students, children and siblings of alumni, children of faculty/staff, local/state students, relatives of clergy, religious affiliation, siblings of current students. ***ROTC:*** Army cooperative, Air Force cooperative.

LOANS ***Student loans:*** $16,900,000 (51% need-based, 49% non-need-based). 90% of past graduating class borrowed through all loan programs. *Average indebtedness per student:* $19,600. ***Average need-based loan:*** Freshmen: $3500. Undergraduates: $5200. ***Parent loans:*** $810,000 (100% non-need-based). ***Programs:*** FFEL (Subsidized and Unsubsidized Stafford, PLUS), Perkins.

WORK-STUDY ***Federal work-study:*** Total amount: $234,000; 141 jobs averaging $1660. ***State or other work-study/employment:*** Total amount: $1700 (100% non-need-based). 4 part-time jobs averaging $425.

ATHLETIC AWARDS Total amount: $1,660,000 (100% non-need-based).

APPLYING FOR FINANCIAL AID ***Required financial aid forms:*** FAFSA, institution's own form, state aid form. ***Financial aid deadline (priority):*** 5/1. ***Notification date:*** 4/1. Students must reply by 8/1.

CONTACT William G. Jackson II, Director of Financial Aid, Faulkner University, 5345 Atlanta Highway, Montgomery, AL 36109-3398, 334-386-7195 or toll-free 800-879-9816. *Fax:* 334-386-7201.

FAYETTEVILLE STATE UNIVERSITY

Fayetteville, NC

CONTACT Lois L. McKoy, Director of Financial Aid, Fayetteville State University, 1200 Murchison Road, Fayetteville, NC 28301-4298, 910-672-1325 or toll-free 800-222-2594. *Fax:* 910-672-1423. *E-mail:* lmckoy@uncfsu.edu.

FELICIAN COLLEGE

Lodi, NJ

Tuition & fees: $25,050 **Average undergraduate aid package: $16,790**

ABOUT THE INSTITUTION Independent Roman Catholic, coed. ***Awards:*** associate, bachelor's, and master's degrees and post-bachelor's certificates. 40 undergraduate majors. ***Total enrollment:*** 2,042. Undergraduates: 1,793. Freshmen: 252. Federal methodology is used as a basis for awarding need-based institutional aid.

UNDERGRADUATE EXPENSES for 2009–10 ***Application fee:*** $30. ***Comprehensive fee:*** $34,750 includes full-time tuition ($23,650), mandatory fees ($1400), and room and board ($9700). ***Part-time tuition:*** $780 per credit.

FRESHMAN FINANCIAL AID (Fall 2007) 210 applied for aid; of those 89% were deemed to have need. 100% of freshmen with need received aid; of those 13% had need fully met. ***Average percent of need met:*** 10% (excluding resources awarded to replace EFC). ***Average financial aid package:*** $16,790 (excluding resources awarded to replace EFC). 18% of all full-time freshmen had no need and received non-need-based gift aid.

UNDERGRADUATE FINANCIAL AID (Fall 2007) 1,166 applied for aid; of those 89% were deemed to have need. 100% of undergraduates with need received aid; of those 13% had need fully met. ***Average percent of need met:*** 10% (excluding resources awarded to replace EFC). ***Average financial aid package:*** $16,790 (excluding resources awarded to replace EFC). 18% of all full-time undergraduates had no need and received non-need-based gift aid.

GIFT AID (NEED-BASED) ***Total amount:*** $6,040,098 (33% federal, 65% state, 2% institutional). ***Receiving aid:*** Freshmen: 53% (130); all full-time undergraduates: 53% (725). ***Average award:*** Freshmen: $7700; Undergraduates: $7700. ***Scholarships, grants, and awards:*** Federal Pell, FSEOG, state, private, college/university gift aid from institutional funds.

GIFT AID (NON-NEED-BASED) ***Total amount:*** $2,327,219 (96% institutional, 4% external sources). ***Receiving aid:*** Freshmen: 15% (37). Undergraduates: 15% (207). ***Average award:*** Freshmen: $5900. Undergraduates: $5900. ***Scholarships, grants, and awards by category:*** *Academic interests/achievement:* 471 awards ($3,855,820 total): business, education, English, general academic interests/achievements, health fields, religion/biblical studies. *Special characteristics:* 10 awards ($50,000 total): children of faculty/staff, siblings of current students.

LOANS ***Student loans:*** $12,387,115 (33% need-based, 67% non-need-based). 79% of past graduating class borrowed through all loan programs. *Average indebtedness per student:* $16,238. ***Average need-based loan:*** Freshmen: $3500. Undergraduates: $4800. ***Parent loans:*** $1,481,381 (100% non-need-based). ***Programs:*** FFEL (Subsidized and Unsubsidized Stafford, PLUS), state.

WORK-STUDY ***Federal work-study:*** Total amount: $111,360; 60 jobs averaging $1841. ***State or other work-study/employment:*** Total amount: $100,000 (100% non-need-based). 116 part-time jobs averaging $1300.

ATHLETIC AWARDS Total amount: $1,528,328 (100% non-need-based).

APPLYING FOR FINANCIAL AID ***Required financial aid form:*** FAFSA. ***Financial aid deadline:*** Continuous. ***Notification date:*** Continuous beginning 4/1.

CONTACT Janet Mariano Merli, Financial Aid Director, Felician College, 262 South Main Street, Lodi, NJ 07644, 201-559-6040. *Fax:* 201-559-6025. *E-mail:* merlij@felician.edu.

FERRIS STATE UNIVERSITY

Big Rapids, MI

Tuition & fees (MI res): $9162 **Average undergraduate aid package: $14,424**

ABOUT THE INSTITUTION State-supported, coed. ***Awards:*** associate, bachelor's, master's, and first professional degrees and post-bachelor's certificates (Associate). 121 undergraduate majors. ***Total enrollment:*** 13,537. Undergraduates: 12,250. Freshmen: 2,139. Federal methodology is used as a basis for awarding need-based institutional aid.

UNDERGRADUATE EXPENSES for 2008–09 ***Application fee:*** $30. ***Tuition, state resident:*** full-time $9000; part-time $300 per credit hour. ***Tuition, nonresident:*** full-time $15,900; part-time $530 per credit hour. ***Required fees:*** full-time $162; $162 per year. Full-time tuition and fees vary according to degree level and reciprocity agreements. Part-time tuition and fees vary according to degree level. ***College room and board:*** $7944. Room and board charges vary according to board plan and housing facility. ***Payment plans:*** Installment, deferred payment.

FRESHMAN FINANCIAL AID (Fall 2007) 1,415 applied for aid; of those 76% were deemed to have need. 99% of freshmen with need received aid; of those 18% had need fully met. ***Average percent of need met:*** 86% (excluding resources awarded to replace EFC). ***Average financial aid package:*** $14,581 (excluding resources awarded to replace EFC). 14% of all full-time freshmen had no need and received non-need-based gift aid.

UNDERGRADUATE FINANCIAL AID (Fall 2007) 6,059 applied for aid; of those 76% were deemed to have need. 99% of undergraduates with need received aid; of those 16% had need fully met. ***Average percent of need met:*** 85% (excluding resources awarded to replace EFC). ***Average financial aid package:*** $14,424 (excluding resources awarded to replace EFC). 9% of all full-time undergraduates had no need and received non-need-based gift aid.

GIFT AID (NEED-BASED) ***Total amount:*** $18,041,578 (78% federal, 7% state, 15% institutional). ***Receiving aid:*** Freshmen: 43% (672); all full-time undergraduates: 41% (2,833). ***Average award:*** Freshmen: $4140; Undergraduates: $4137. ***Scholarships, grants, and awards:*** Federal Pell, FSEOG, state, private, college/university gift aid from institutional funds.

GIFT AID (NON-NEED-BASED) ***Total amount:*** $15,067,612 (37% state, 55% institutional, 8% external sources). ***Receiving aid:*** Freshmen: 48% (747). Undergraduates: 33% (2,315). ***Average award:*** Freshmen: $4401. Undergraduates: $3629. ***Scholarships, grants, and awards by category:*** *Academic interests/achievement:* 2,551 awards ($6,581,739 total): agriculture, architecture, biological sciences, business, communication, computer science, education, engineering/technologies, general academic interests/achievements, health fields, mathematics. *Creative arts/performance:* 15 awards ($10,191 total): applied art and design, art/fine arts, debating, general creative arts/performance, journalism/publications, music, theater/drama. *Special achievements/activities:* 163 awards ($66,719 total): general special achievements/activities, memberships. *Special characteristics:* 171 awards ($157,970 total): adult students, children and siblings of alumni, ethnic background, general special characteristics, international students, local/state students, members of minority groups, previous college experience, veterans. ***Tuition waivers:*** Full or partial for employees or children of employees. ***ROTC:*** Army cooperative.

LOANS ***Student loans:*** $91,423,182 (39% need-based, 61% non-need-based). 72% of past graduating class borrowed through all loan programs. *Average indebtedness per student:* $31,356. ***Average need-based loan:*** Freshmen: $3239. Undergraduates: $4203. ***Parent loans:*** $4,350,291 (100% non-need-based). ***Programs:*** Federal Direct (Subsidized and Unsubsidized Stafford, PLUS), Perkins, Federal Nursing, college/university, alternative loans.

WORK-STUDY ***Federal work-study:*** Total amount: $1,125,695; 530 jobs averaging $2167. ***State or other work-study/employment:*** Total amount: $229,083 (100% need-based). 174 part-time jobs averaging $1275.

ATHLETIC AWARDS Total amount: $1,728,081 (100% non-need-based).

APPLYING FOR FINANCIAL AID ***Required financial aid form:*** FAFSA. ***Financial aid deadline (priority):*** 3/1. ***Notification date:*** Continuous beginning 4/1. Students must reply within 3 weeks of notification.

CONTACT Sara Dew, Assistant Director of Financial Aid, Ferris State University, 1201 South State Street, Big Rapids, MI 49307-2020, 231-591-2110 or toll-free 800-433-7747. *Fax:* 231-591-2950. *E-mail:* dews@ferris.edu.

FERRUM COLLEGE

Ferrum, VA

ABOUT THE INSTITUTION Independent United Methodist, coed. ***Awards:*** bachelor's degrees. 33 undergraduate majors. ***Total enrollment:*** 1,383. Undergraduates: 1,383. Freshmen: 582.

GIFT AID (NEED-BASED) ***Scholarships, grants, and awards:*** Federal Pell, FSEOG, state, private, college/university gift aid from institutional funds.

GIFT AID (NON-NEED-BASED) ***Scholarships, grants, and awards by category:*** *Academic interests/achievement:* general academic interests/achievements. *Creative arts/performance:* art/fine arts, performing arts, theater/drama. *Special achievements/activities:* community service, general special achievements/activities, leadership, religious involvement. *Special characteristics:* adult students, children and siblings of alumni, children of educators, children of faculty/staff, international students, local/state students, out-of-state students, relatives of clergy, religious affiliation, siblings of current students.

LOANS ***Programs:*** FFEL (Subsidized and Unsubsidized Stafford, PLUS), Perkins.

WORK-STUDY ***Federal work-study:*** Total amount: $1,287,955; 504 jobs averaging $844. ***State or other work-study/employment:*** 46 part-time jobs averaging $768.

APPLYING FOR FINANCIAL AID ***Required financial aid forms:*** FAFSA, state aid form.

CONTACT Heather Hollandsworth, Director of Financial Aid, Ferrum College, PO Box 1000, Spilman-Daniel House, Ferrum, VA 24088-9001, 540-365-4282 or toll-free 800-868-9797. *Fax:* 540-365-4266.

FINLANDIA UNIVERSITY

Hancock, MI

Tuition & fees: $17,914 **Average undergraduate aid package: $16,000**

ABOUT THE INSTITUTION Independent religious, coed. ***Awards:*** associate and bachelor's degrees. 15 undergraduate majors. ***Total enrollment:*** 545. Undergraduates: 545. Freshmen: 82. Federal methodology is used as a basis for awarding need-based institutional aid.

UNDERGRADUATE EXPENSES for 2008–09 ***Application fee:*** $30. ***Comprehensive fee:*** $23,714 includes full-time tuition ($17,414), mandatory fees ($500), and room and board ($5800). Full-time tuition and fees vary according to program. Room and board charges vary according to housing facility. ***Part-time tuition:*** $580 per credit. Part-time tuition and fees vary according to course load and program. ***Payment plan:*** Installment.

FRESHMAN FINANCIAL AID (Fall 2008, est.) 70 applied for aid; of those 81% were deemed to have need. 100% of freshmen with need received aid; of those 2% had need fully met. ***Average percent of need met:*** 40% (excluding resources awarded to replace EFC). ***Average financial aid package:*** $16,000 (excluding resources awarded to replace EFC). 10% of all full-time freshmen had no need and received non-need-based gift aid.

UNDERGRADUATE FINANCIAL AID (Fall 2008, est.) 517 applied for aid; of those 89% were deemed to have need. 100% of undergraduates with need received aid; of those 1% had need fully met. ***Average percent of need met:*** 50% (excluding resources awarded to replace EFC). ***Average financial aid package:*** $16,000 (excluding resources awarded to replace EFC). 3% of all full-time undergraduates had no need and received non-need-based gift aid.

GIFT AID (NEED-BASED) ***Total amount:*** $2,193,598 (68% federal, 28% state, 4% external sources). ***Receiving aid:*** Freshmen: 66% (52); all full-time undergraduates: 82% (455). ***Average award:*** Freshmen: $5000; Undergraduates: $5000. ***Scholarships, grants, and awards:*** Federal Pell, FSEOG, state, private, college/university gift aid from institutional funds.

GIFT AID (NON-NEED-BASED) ***Total amount:*** $2,134,109 (2% state, 95% institutional, 3% external sources). ***Receiving aid:*** Undergraduates: 83% (460). ***Average award:*** Freshmen: $5000. Undergraduates: $5000. ***Scholarships, grants, and awards by category:*** *Academic interests/achievement:* 157 awards ($211,076 total): general academic interests/achievements. *Creative arts/performance:* art/

fine arts, general creative arts/performance. *Special achievements/activities:* 10 awards ($30,000 total): community service, general special achievements/activities, leadership, religious involvement. *Special characteristics:* 141 awards ($169,275 total): children of current students, children of faculty/staff, first-generation college students, international students, religious affiliation, siblings of current students, spouses of current students, twins. ***Tuition waivers:*** Full or partial for employees or children of employees. ***ROTC:*** Army cooperative, Air Force cooperative.

LOANS ***Student loans:*** $3,663,451 (53% need-based, 47% non-need-based). 90% of past graduating class borrowed through all loan programs. *Average indebtedness per student:* $17,500. ***Average need-based loan:*** Freshmen: $3500. Undergraduates: $3500. ***Parent loans:*** $216,395 (100% non-need-based). ***Programs:*** FFEL (Subsidized and Unsubsidized Stafford, PLUS), state, private loan program.

WORK-STUDY ***Federal work-study:*** Total amount: $240,000; 154 jobs averaging $1600. ***State or other work-study/employment:*** Total amount: $21,000 (100% need-based). 25 part-time jobs averaging $1200.

ATHLETIC AWARDS Total amount: $486,395 (100% non-need-based).

APPLYING FOR FINANCIAL AID ***Required financial aid forms:*** FAFSA, institution's own form. ***Financial aid deadline (priority):*** 3/1. ***Notification date:*** 3/1. Students must reply within 3 weeks of notification.

CONTACT Sandra Turnquist, Director of Financial Aid, Finlandia University, 601 Quincy Street, Hancock, MI 49930, 906-487-7240 or toll-free 877-202-5491. *Fax:* 906-487-7509. *E-mail:* sandy.turnquist@finlandia.edu.

FISK UNIVERSITY

Nashville, TN

Tuition & fees: $16,240 **Average undergraduate aid package: $13,625**

ABOUT THE INSTITUTION Independent religious, coed. ***Awards:*** bachelor's and master's degrees and post-bachelor's certificates. 22 undergraduate majors. ***Total enrollment:*** 726. Undergraduates: 683. Freshmen: 115. Both federal and institutional methodology are used as a basis for awarding need-based institutional aid.

UNDERGRADUATE EXPENSES for 2008–09 ***Application fee:*** $50. ***Comprehensive fee:*** $23,965 includes full-time tuition ($15,140), mandatory fees ($1100), and room and board ($7725). ***College room only:*** $4480. Full-time tuition and fees vary according to course load. Room and board charges vary according to board plan. ***Part-time tuition:*** $630 per credit hour. Part-time tuition and fees vary according to course load. ***Payment plan:*** Installment.

FRESHMAN FINANCIAL AID (Fall 2007) 97 applied for aid; of those 100% were deemed to have need. 95% of freshmen with need received aid; of those 29% had need fully met. ***Average percent of need met:*** 73% (excluding resources awarded to replace EFC). ***Average financial aid package:*** $11,573 (excluding resources awarded to replace EFC).

UNDERGRADUATE FINANCIAL AID (Fall 2007) 602 applied for aid; of those 100% were deemed to have need. 94% of undergraduates with need received aid; of those 34% had need fully met. ***Average percent of need met:*** 75% (excluding resources awarded to replace EFC). ***Average financial aid package:*** $13,625 (excluding resources awarded to replace EFC).

GIFT AID (NEED-BASED) ***Total amount:*** $5,684,927 (27% federal, 6% state, 62% institutional, 5% external sources). ***Receiving aid:*** Freshmen: 84% (88); all full-time undergraduates: 79% (518). ***Average award:*** Freshmen: $7918; Undergraduates: $10,847. ***Scholarships, grants, and awards:*** Federal Pell, FSEOG, state, private, college/university gift aid from institutional funds, United Negro College Fund.

GIFT AID (NON-NEED-BASED) ***Scholarships, grants, and awards by category:*** *Academic interests/achievement:* 226 awards ($2,568,919 total): general academic interests/achievements. *Special characteristics:* 15 awards ($187,300 total): children of faculty/staff. ***Tuition waivers:*** Full or partial for employees or children of employees. ***ROTC:*** Army cooperative, Naval cooperative.

LOANS ***Student loans:*** $3,188,680 (100% need-based). 90% of past graduating class borrowed through all loan programs. *Average indebtedness per student:* $23,850. ***Average need-based loan:*** Freshmen: $4030. Undergraduates: $4722. ***Parent loans:*** $2,482,097 (100% need-based). ***Programs:*** Federal Direct (Subsidized and Unsubsidized Stafford, PLUS), Perkins.

WORK-STUDY ***Federal work-study:*** Total amount: $275,844; 115 jobs averaging $2399.

APPLYING FOR FINANCIAL AID ***Required financial aid form:*** FAFSA. ***Financial aid deadline:*** 6/1 (priority: 3/1). ***Notification date:*** Continuous beginning 4/1. Students must reply within 2 weeks of notification.

CONTACT Russelle Keese, Director of Financial Aid, Fisk University, 1000 17th Avenue North, Nashville, TN 37208-3051, 615-329-8735 or toll-free 800-443-FISK. *E-mail:* finaid@fisk.edu.

FITCHBURG STATE COLLEGE

Fitchburg, MA

ABOUT THE INSTITUTION State-supported, coed. ***Awards:*** bachelor's and master's degrees and post-bachelor's and post-master's certificates. 55 undergraduate majors. ***Total enrollment:*** 6,761. Undergraduates: 4,057. Freshmen: 771.

GIFT AID (NEED-BASED) ***Scholarships, grants, and awards:*** Federal Pell, FSEOG, state, private, college/university gift aid from institutional funds.

GIFT AID (NON-NEED-BASED) ***Scholarships, grants, and awards by category:*** *Academic interests/achievement:* biological sciences, business, communication, computer science, education, English, general academic interests/achievements, health fields, mathematics, social sciences. *Creative arts/performance:* general creative arts/performance. *Special achievements/activities:* general special achievements/activities, leadership. *Special characteristics:* adult students, children and siblings of alumni.

LOANS ***Programs:*** Federal Direct (Subsidized and Unsubsidized Stafford, PLUS), Perkins, Federal Nursing, state.

WORK-STUDY ***Federal work-study:*** Total amount: $225,000; 284 jobs averaging $1740.

APPLYING FOR FINANCIAL AID ***Required financial aid form:*** FAFSA.

CONTACT Director of Financial Aid, Fitchburg State College, 160 Pearl Street, Fitchburg, MA 01420-2697, 978-665-3156 or toll-free 800-705-9692. *Fax:* 978-665-3559. *E-mail:* finaid@fsc.edu.

FIVE TOWNS COLLEGE

Dix Hills, NY

Tuition & fees: $17,800 **Average undergraduate aid package: $10,700**

ABOUT THE INSTITUTION Independent, coed. ***Awards:*** associate, bachelor's, master's, and doctoral degrees. 20 undergraduate majors. ***Total enrollment:*** 1,163. Undergraduates: 1,117. Federal methodology is used as a basis for awarding need-based institutional aid.

UNDERGRADUATE EXPENSES for 2008–09 ***Application fee:*** $35. ***Comprehensive fee:*** $29,650 includes full-time tuition ($17,400), mandatory fees ($400), and room and board ($11,850). ***Part-time tuition:*** $725 per credit.

FRESHMAN FINANCIAL AID (Fall 2008, est.) 258 applied for aid; of those 83% were deemed to have need. 100% of freshmen with need received aid; of those 83% had need fully met. ***Average percent of need met:*** 48% (excluding resources awarded to replace EFC). ***Average financial aid package:*** $12,000 (excluding resources awarded to replace EFC). 12% of all full-time freshmen had no need and received non-need-based gift aid.

UNDERGRADUATE FINANCIAL AID (Fall 2008, est.) 917 applied for aid; of those 85% were deemed to have need. 100% of undergraduates with need received aid; of those 84% had need fully met. ***Average percent of need met:*** 48% (excluding resources awarded to replace EFC). ***Average financial aid package:*** $10,700 (excluding resources awarded to replace EFC). 8% of all full-time undergraduates had no need and received non-need-based gift aid.

GIFT AID (NEED-BASED) ***Total amount:*** $3,250,000 (43% federal, 49% state, 8% institutional). ***Receiving aid:*** Freshmen: 65% (185); all full-time undergraduates: 63% (670). ***Average award:*** Freshmen: $6500; Undergraduates: $4500. ***Scholarships, grants, and awards:*** Federal Pell, FSEOG, state, private, college/university gift aid from institutional funds.

GIFT AID (NON-NEED-BASED) ***Total amount:*** $2,085,683 (3% federal, 3% state, 86% institutional, 8% external sources). ***Receiving aid:*** Freshmen: 69% (196). Undergraduates: 39% (420). ***Average award:*** Freshmen: $2500. Undergraduates: $4100. ***Scholarships, grants, and awards by category:*** *Academic interests/achievement:* 250 awards ($1,400,000 total): business, education, general academic interests/achievements. *Creative arts/performance:* 160 awards ($670,000 total): cinema/film/broadcasting, music, theater/drama.

LOANS ***Student loans:*** $6,100,000 (44% need-based, 56% non-need-based). 76% of past graduating class borrowed through all loan programs. *Average*

indebtedness per student: $17,800. ***Average need-based loan:*** Freshmen: $3500. Undergraduates: $4800. ***Parent loans:*** $3,400,000 (100% non-need-based). ***Programs:*** Federal Direct (Subsidized and Unsubsidized Stafford, PLUS).

WORK-STUDY ***Federal work-study:*** Total amount: $131,000; 100 jobs averaging $1100.

APPLYING FOR FINANCIAL AID ***Required financial aid forms:*** FAFSA, institution's own form, state aid form. ***Financial aid deadline (priority):*** 3/31. ***Notification date:*** Continuous beginning 5/1. Students must reply within 4 weeks of notification.

CONTACT Ms. Mary Venezia, Financial Aid Director, Five Towns College, 305 North Service Road, Dix Hills, NY 11746-6055, 631-656-2113. *Fax:* 631-656-2191. *E-mail:* mvenezia@ftc.edu.

FLAGLER COLLEGE

St. Augustine, FL

Tuition & fees: $12,520 **Average undergraduate aid package: $15,963**

ABOUT THE INSTITUTION Independent, coed. ***Awards:*** bachelor's degrees. 23 undergraduate majors. ***Total enrollment:*** 2,666. Undergraduates: 2,666. Freshmen: 646. Federal methodology is used as a basis for awarding need-based institutional aid.

UNDERGRADUATE EXPENSES for 2008–09 ***Application fee:*** $40. ***Comprehensive fee:*** $19,330 includes full-time tuition ($12,520) and room and board ($6810). Room and board charges vary according to board plan. ***Part-time tuition:*** $420 per credit hour.

FRESHMAN FINANCIAL AID (Fall 2008, est.) 469 applied for aid; of those 68% were deemed to have need. 99% of freshmen with need received aid; of those 19% had need fully met. ***Average percent of need met:*** 90% (excluding resources awarded to replace EFC). ***Average financial aid package:*** $16,711 (excluding resources awarded to replace EFC). 7% of all full-time freshmen had no need and received non-need-based gift aid.

UNDERGRADUATE FINANCIAL AID (Fall 2008, est.) 1,678 applied for aid; of those 74% were deemed to have need. 99% of undergraduates with need received aid; of those 14% had need fully met. ***Average percent of need met:*** 89% (excluding resources awarded to replace EFC). ***Average financial aid package:*** $15,963 (excluding resources awarded to replace EFC). 11% of all full-time undergraduates had no need and received non-need-based gift aid.

GIFT AID (NEED-BASED) ***Total amount:*** $7,141,060 (23% federal, 52% state, 22% institutional, 3% external sources). ***Receiving aid:*** Freshmen: 25% (200); all full-time undergraduates: 32% (835). ***Average award:*** Freshmen: $4494; Undergraduates: $3854. ***Scholarships, grants, and awards:*** Federal Pell, FSEOG, state, private, college/university gift aid from institutional funds.

GIFT AID (NON-NEED-BASED) ***Total amount:*** $5,122,048 (81% state, 16% institutional, 3% external sources). ***Receiving aid:*** Freshmen: 24% (195). Undergraduates: 30% (775). ***Average award:*** Freshmen: $1646. Undergraduates: $1773. ***Scholarships, grants, and awards by category:*** *Academic interests/achievement:* 52 awards ($142,009 total): business, communication, education, English, foreign languages, general academic interests/achievements, humanities, religion/biblical studies, social sciences. *Creative arts/performance:* 4 awards ($8600 total): applied art and design, art/fine arts, cinema/film/broadcasting, performing arts, theater/drama. *Special achievements/activities:* 76 awards ($143,390 total): general special achievements/activities, leadership, memberships, religious involvement. *Special characteristics:* 399 awards ($751,097 total): children of educators, children of faculty/staff, ethnic background, first-generation college students, general special characteristics, local/state students, members of minority groups, out-of-state students. ***Tuition waivers:*** Full or partial for employees or children of employees.

LOANS ***Student loans:*** $8,917,156 (69% need-based, 31% non-need-based). 61% of past graduating class borrowed through all loan programs. *Average indebtedness per student:* $18,415. ***Average need-based loan:*** Freshmen: $3586. Undergraduates: $4217. ***Parent loans:*** $1,491,878 (52% need-based, 48% non-need-based). ***Programs:*** Federal Direct (Subsidized and Unsubsidized Stafford, PLUS), Perkins.

WORK-STUDY ***Federal work-study:*** Total amount: $200,100; 190 jobs averaging $1053. ***State or other work-study/employment:*** Total amount: $68,600 (17% need-based, 83% non-need-based). 100 part-time jobs averaging $1019.

ATHLETIC AWARDS Total amount: $919,121 (37% need-based, 63% non-need-based).

APPLYING FOR FINANCIAL AID ***Required financial aid forms:*** FAFSA, institution's own form. ***Financial aid deadline (priority):*** 4/1. ***Notification date:*** Continuous. Students must reply within 2 weeks of notification.

CONTACT Ms. Sheia Pleasant, Assistant Director of Financial Aid, Flagler College, PO Box 1027, St. Augustine, FL 32085-1027, 904-819-6225 or toll-free 800-304-4208. *Fax:* 904-819-6453. *E-mail:* spleasant@flagler.edu.

FLORIDA AGRICULTURAL AND MECHANICAL UNIVERSITY

Tallahassee, FL

ABOUT THE INSTITUTION State-supported, coed. ***Awards:*** associate, bachelor's, master's, doctoral, and first professional degrees and first professional certificates. 84 undergraduate majors. ***Total enrollment:*** 11,587. Undergraduates: 9,591. Freshmen: 1,890.

GIFT AID (NEED-BASED) ***Scholarships, grants, and awards:*** Federal Pell, FSEOG, state, private, college/university gift aid from institutional funds, United Negro College Fund, Federal Nursing.

GIFT AID (NON-NEED-BASED) ***Scholarships, grants, and awards by category:*** *Academic interests/achievement:* agriculture, business, engineering/technologies, general academic interests/achievements, health fields.

LOANS ***Programs:*** FFEL (Subsidized and Unsubsidized Stafford, PLUS), Perkins.

APPLYING FOR FINANCIAL AID ***Required financial aid form:*** FAFSA.

CONTACT Dr. Marcia D. Boyd, Director of Student Financial Aid, Florida Agricultural and Mechanical University, 101 Foote-Hilyer Administration Center, Tallahassee, FL 32307, 850-599-3730. *E-mail:* marcia.boyd@famu.edu.

FLORIDA ATLANTIC UNIVERSITY

Boca Raton, FL

Tuition & fees (FL res): $3662 **Average undergraduate aid package: $7600**

ABOUT THE INSTITUTION State-supported, coed. ***Awards:*** associate, bachelor's, master's, and doctoral degrees and post-master's certificates. 66 undergraduate majors. ***Total enrollment:*** 26,897. Undergraduates: 21,713. Freshmen: 2,800. Federal methodology is used as a basis for awarding need-based institutional aid.

UNDERGRADUATE EXPENSES for 2008–09 ***Application fee:*** $30. ***Tuition, state resident:*** full-time $3662; part-time $122.06 per credit hour. ***Tuition, nonresident:*** full-time $17,389; part-time $579.62 per credit hour. Full-time tuition and fees vary according to course load. Part-time tuition and fees vary according to course load. ***College room and board:*** $8960. Room and board charges vary according to board plan and housing facility. ***Payment plans:*** Tuition prepayment, installment, deferred payment.

FRESHMAN FINANCIAL AID (Fall 2008, est.) 1,736 applied for aid; of those 68% were deemed to have need. 98% of freshmen with need received aid; of those 13% had need fully met. ***Average percent of need met:*** 85% (excluding resources awarded to replace EFC). ***Average financial aid package:*** $7852 (excluding resources awarded to replace EFC). 4% of all full-time freshmen had no need and received non-need-based gift aid.

UNDERGRADUATE FINANCIAL AID (Fall 2008, est.) 7,501 applied for aid; of those 77% were deemed to have need. 96% of undergraduates with need received aid; of those 13% had need fully met. ***Average percent of need met:*** 70% (excluding resources awarded to replace EFC). ***Average financial aid package:*** $7600 (excluding resources awarded to replace EFC). 3% of all full-time undergraduates had no need and received non-need-based gift aid.

GIFT AID (NEED-BASED) ***Total amount:*** $44,403,389 (40% federal, 40% state, 14% institutional, 6% external sources). ***Receiving aid:*** Freshmen: 40% (1,042); all full-time undergraduates: 37% (4,590). ***Average award:*** Freshmen: $6740; Undergraduates: $5948. ***Scholarships, grants, and awards:*** Federal Pell, FSEOG, state, private, college/university gift aid from institutional funds, Federal Nursing.

GIFT AID (NON-NEED-BASED) ***Average award:*** Freshmen: $1993. Undergraduates: $2443. ***Scholarships, grants, and awards by category:*** *Academic interests/achievement:* business, engineering/technologies, general academic interests/achievements, physical sciences, social sciences. *Creative arts/performance:* music, performing arts. ***Tuition waivers:*** Full or partial for employees or children of employees, senior citizens. ***ROTC:*** Army cooperative, Air Force cooperative.

LOANS ***Student loans:*** $57,276,593 (41% need-based, 59% non-need-based). ***Average need-based loan:*** Freshmen: $2929. Undergraduates: $3854. ***Parent loans:*** $1,922,583 (100% non-need-based). ***Programs:*** FFEL (Subsidized and Unsubsidized Stafford, PLUS), Perkins, college/university.

WORK-STUDY ***Federal work-study:*** Total amount: $511,454; 182 jobs averaging $2950. ***State or other work-study/employment:*** Total amount: $16,000 (100% need-based). Part-time jobs available.

ATHLETIC AWARDS Total amount: $2,667,134 (100% need-based).

APPLYING FOR FINANCIAL AID ***Required financial aid form:*** FAFSA. ***Financial aid deadline (priority):*** 3/1. ***Notification date:*** Continuous beginning 5/1. Students must reply within 3 weeks of notification.

CONTACT Carole Pfeilsticker, Director of Student Financial Aid, Florida Atlantic University, 777 Glades Road, Boca Raton, FL 33431-0991, 561-297-3528 or toll-free 800-299-4FAU. *E-mail:* pfeilsti@fau.edu.

FLORIDA CHRISTIAN COLLEGE

Kissimmee, FL

CONTACT Ms. Sandra Peppard, Director of Student Financial Aid, Florida Christian College, 1011 Bill Beck Boulevard, Kissimmee, FL 34744-5301, 407-847-8966 Ext. 365 or toll-free 888-GO-TO-FCC (in-state). *Fax:* 407-847-3925. *E-mail:* sandi.peppard@fcc.edu.

FLORIDA COLLEGE

Temple Terrace, FL

Tuition & fees: $12,060 **Average undergraduate aid package: $12,517**

ABOUT THE INSTITUTION Independent, coed. ***Awards:*** associate and bachelor's degrees. 5 undergraduate majors. ***Total enrollment:*** 506. Undergraduates: 506. Freshmen: 179.

UNDERGRADUATE EXPENSES for 2008–09 ***Application fee:*** $25. ***One-time required fee:*** $150. ***Comprehensive fee:*** $18,960 includes full-time tuition ($11,340), mandatory fees ($720), and room and board ($6900). ***College room only:*** $3200. Room and board charges vary according to board plan and housing facility. ***Part-time tuition:*** $450 per semester hour. ***Part-time fees:*** $280 per term. Part-time tuition and fees vary according to course load. ***Payment plan:*** Installment.

FRESHMAN FINANCIAL AID (Fall 2008, est.) 119 applied for aid; of those 100% were deemed to have need. 100% of freshmen with need received aid; of those 13% had need fully met. ***Average percent of need met:*** 86% (excluding resources awarded to replace EFC). ***Average financial aid package:*** $11,624 (excluding resources awarded to replace EFC). 19% of all full-time freshmen had no need and received non-need-based gift aid.

UNDERGRADUATE FINANCIAL AID (Fall 2008, est.) 255 applied for aid; of those 100% were deemed to have need. 100% of undergraduates with need received aid; of those 17% had need fully met. ***Average percent of need met:*** 88% (excluding resources awarded to replace EFC). ***Average financial aid package:*** $12,517 (excluding resources awarded to replace EFC). 18% of all full-time undergraduates had no need and received non-need-based gift aid.

GIFT AID (NEED-BASED) ***Total amount:*** $953,505 (34% federal, 3% state, 60% institutional, 3% external sources). ***Receiving aid:*** Freshmen: 52% (119); all full-time undergraduates: 52% (255). ***Average award:*** Freshmen: $3409; Undergraduates: $3418. ***Scholarships, grants, and awards:*** Federal Pell, FSEOG, state, private, college/university gift aid from institutional funds.

GIFT AID (NON-NEED-BASED) ***Total amount:*** $1,633,149 (42% state, 47% institutional, 11% external sources). ***Receiving aid:*** Freshmen: 46% (105). Undergraduates: 44% (215). ***Average award:*** Freshmen: $2085. Undergraduates: $2506. ***Scholarships, grants, and awards by category:*** *Academic interests/achievement:* general academic interests/achievements. *Creative arts/performance:* debating, journalism/publications, music, theater/drama. *Special characteristics:* children of educators, children of faculty/staff. ***Tuition waivers:*** Full or partial for employees or children of employees. ***ROTC:*** Army cooperative, Air Force cooperative.

LOANS ***Student loans:*** $1,316,238 (63% need-based, 37% non-need-based). 57% of past graduating class borrowed through all loan programs. *Average indebtedness per student:* $7246. ***Average need-based loan:*** Freshmen: $2929. Undergraduates: $3340. ***Parent loans:*** $1,165,735 (100% non-need-based). ***Programs:*** FFEL (Subsidized and Unsubsidized Stafford, PLUS), Perkins.

WORK-STUDY ***Federal work-study:*** Total amount: $17,947; jobs available. ***State or other work-study/employment:*** Total amount: $216,581 (100% non-need-based). Part-time jobs available.

ATHLETIC AWARDS Total amount: $244,205 (100% non-need-based).

APPLYING FOR FINANCIAL AID ***Required financial aid form:*** FAFSA. ***Financial aid deadline:*** 8/1 (priority: 4/1). ***Notification date:*** Continuous. Students must reply within 2 weeks of notification.

CONTACT Lisa McClister, Director of Financial Aid, Florida College, 119 North Glen Arven Avenue, Temple Terrace, FL 33617, 813-849-6720 or toll-free 800-326-7655. *Fax:* 813-899-6772. *E-mail:* mcclisterl@floridacollege.edu.

FLORIDA GULF COAST UNIVERSITY

Fort Myers, FL

Tuition & fees (FL res): $5497 **Average undergraduate aid package: $6818**

ABOUT THE INSTITUTION State-supported, coed. ***Awards:*** associate, bachelor's, and master's degrees. 47 undergraduate majors. ***Total enrollment:*** 10,214. Undergraduates: 8,848. Freshmen: 1,882.

UNDERGRADUATE EXPENSES for 2008–09 ***Application fee:*** $30. ***Tuition, state resident:*** full-time $3979. ***Tuition, nonresident:*** full-time $17,247. ***Required fees:*** full-time $1518. Full-time tuition and fees vary according to course load. Part-time tuition and fees vary according to course load. ***College room and board:*** $7450; ***Room only:*** $4312. Room and board charges vary according to board plan.

FRESHMAN FINANCIAL AID (Fall 2007) 1,491 applied for aid; of those 42% were deemed to have need. 100% of freshmen with need received aid; of those 8% had need fully met. ***Average percent of need met:*** 65% (excluding resources awarded to replace EFC). ***Average financial aid package:*** $6583 (excluding resources awarded to replace EFC). 6% of all full-time freshmen had no need and received non-need-based gift aid.

UNDERGRADUATE FINANCIAL AID (Fall 2007) 4,596 applied for aid; of those 45% were deemed to have need. 100% of undergraduates with need received aid; of those 9% had need fully met. ***Average percent of need met:*** 65% (excluding resources awarded to replace EFC). ***Average financial aid package:*** $6818 (excluding resources awarded to replace EFC). 5% of all full-time undergraduates had no need and received non-need-based gift aid.

GIFT AID (NEED-BASED) ***Total amount:*** $10,594,875 (37% federal, 36% state, 22% institutional, 5% external sources). ***Receiving aid:*** Freshmen: 22% (386); all full-time undergraduates: 22% (1,370). ***Average award:*** Freshmen: $4012; Undergraduates: $3926. ***Scholarships, grants, and awards:*** Federal Pell, FSEOG, state, private, college/university gift aid from institutional funds.

GIFT AID (NON-NEED-BASED) ***Total amount:*** $8,101,176 (68% state, 27% institutional, 5% external sources). ***Receiving aid:*** Freshmen: 28% (494). ***Average award:*** Freshmen: $5292. Undergraduates: $5404. ***Scholarships, grants, and awards by category:*** *Academic interests/achievement:* biological sciences, business, education, engineering/technologies, general academic interests/achievements, health fields, humanities, mathematics, physical sciences, religion/biblical studies, social sciences. *Creative arts/performance:* art/fine arts, music. *Special achievements/activities:* community service, leadership. *Special characteristics:* adult students, ethnic background, handicapped students, international students, local/state students, members of minority groups, out-of-state students. ***Tuition waivers:*** Full or partial for employees or children of employees, senior citizens.

LOANS ***Student loans:*** $13,347,256 (74% need-based, 26% non-need-based). 36% of past graduating class borrowed through all loan programs. *Average indebtedness per student:* $11,747. ***Average need-based loan:*** Freshmen: $3308. Undergraduates: $4556. ***Programs:*** FFEL (Subsidized and Unsubsidized Stafford, PLUS).

WORK-STUDY ***Federal work-study:*** Total amount: $159,954; jobs available. ***State or other work-study/employment:*** Total amount: $2,248,931 (100% need-based). Part-time jobs available.

ATHLETIC AWARDS Total amount: $1,280,029 (100% non-need-based).

APPLYING FOR FINANCIAL AID ***Required financial aid form:*** FAFSA. ***Financial aid deadline:*** 6/30 (priority: 3/1). ***Notification date:*** Continuous.

CONTACT Jorge Lopez-Rosado, Director, Student Financial Services, Florida Gulf Coast University, 10501 FGCU Boulevard South, Fort Myers, FL 33965, 239-590-1210 or toll-free 888-889-1095. *Fax:* 239-590-7923. *E-mail:* faso@fgcu.edu.

FLORIDA HOSPITAL COLLEGE OF HEALTH SCIENCES

Orlando, FL

Tuition & fees: $8540 **Average undergraduate aid package: N/A**

ABOUT THE INSTITUTION Independent, coed. ***Awards:*** associate and bachelor's degrees. 6 undergraduate majors. ***Total enrollment:*** 2,207. Undergraduates: 2,207. Federal methodology is used as a basis for awarding need-based institutional aid.

UNDERGRADUATE EXPENSES for 2008–09 ***Application fee:*** $20. ***Tuition:*** full-time $8250; part-time $275 per credit. ***Required fees:*** full-time $290; $145 per term. Full-time tuition and fees vary according to course load and program. Part-time tuition and fees vary according to course load and program. ***Payment plans:*** Installment, deferred payment.

GIFT AID (NEED-BASED) ***Total amount:*** $1,436,079 (82% federal, 14% state, 3% institutional, 1% external sources). ***Scholarships, grants, and awards:*** Federal Pell, FSEOG, state, private, college/university gift aid from institutional funds.

GIFT AID (NON-NEED-BASED) ***Total amount:*** $2,299,193 (72% state, 2% institutional, 26% external sources). ***Tuition waivers:*** Full or partial for employees or children of employees. ***ROTC:*** Air Force cooperative.

LOANS ***Student loans:*** $7,451,760 (38% need-based, 62% non-need-based). ***Parent loans:*** $397,314 (100% non-need-based). ***Programs:*** FFEL (Subsidized and Unsubsidized Stafford, PLUS), private alternative loans.

ATHLETIC AWARDS Total amount: $499,125 (100% non-need-based).

APPLYING FOR FINANCIAL AID ***Required financial aid forms:*** FAFSA, institution's own form. ***Financial aid deadline:*** 7/31 (priority: 4/10). ***Notification date:*** Continuous. Students must reply within 2 weeks of notification.

CONTACT Starr Bender, Financial Aid Director, Florida Hospital College of Health Sciences, 671 Winyah Drive, Orlando, FL 32803, 407-303-6963 or toll-free 800-500-7747 (out-of-state). *Fax:* 407-303-7680. *E-mail:* starr.bender@fhchs.edu.

FLORIDA INSTITUTE OF TECHNOLOGY

Melbourne, FL

Tuition & fees: $30,440 **Average undergraduate aid package: $26,768**

ABOUT THE INSTITUTION Independent, coed. ***Awards:*** associate, bachelor's, master's, and doctoral degrees and post-master's certificates. 69 undergraduate majors. ***Total enrollment:*** 6,400. Undergraduates: 3,685. Freshmen: 637. Federal methodology is used as a basis for awarding need-based institutional aid.

UNDERGRADUATE EXPENSES for 2008–09 ***Application fee:*** $50. ***Comprehensive fee:*** $40,690 includes full-time tuition ($29,940), mandatory fees ($500), and room and board ($10,250). ***College room only:*** $6000. Full-time tuition and fees vary according to course load, location, and program. Room and board charges vary according to board plan and housing facility. ***Part-time tuition:*** $898 per credit hour. Part-time tuition and fees vary according to course load, location, and program. ***Payment plan:*** Installment.

FRESHMAN FINANCIAL AID (Fall 2008, est.) 475 applied for aid; of those 83% were deemed to have need. 99% of freshmen with need received aid; of those 27% had need fully met. ***Average percent of need met:*** 84% (excluding resources awarded to replace EFC). ***Average financial aid package:*** $28,520 (excluding resources awarded to replace EFC). 34% of all full-time freshmen had no need and received non-need-based gift aid.

UNDERGRADUATE FINANCIAL AID (Fall 2008, est.) 1,652 applied for aid; of those 87% were deemed to have need. 100% of undergraduates with need received aid; of those 25% had need fully met. ***Average percent of need met:*** 80% (excluding resources awarded to replace EFC). ***Average financial aid package:*** $26,768 (excluding resources awarded to replace EFC). 28% of all full-time undergraduates had no need and received non-need-based gift aid.

GIFT AID (NEED-BASED) ***Total amount:*** $24,130,997 (15% federal, 12% state, 71% institutional, 2% external sources). ***Receiving aid:*** Freshmen: 62% (392); all full-time undergraduates: 58% (1,416). ***Average award:*** Freshmen: $20,050; Undergraduates: $17,123. ***Scholarships, grants, and awards:*** Federal Pell, FSEOG, state, private, college/university gift aid from institutional funds.

GIFT AID (NON-NEED-BASED) ***Total amount:*** $8,810,823 (17% federal, 10% state, 72% institutional, 1% external sources). ***Receiving aid:*** Freshmen: 62% (392). Undergraduates: 50% (1,234). ***Average award:*** Freshmen: $9239. Undergraduates: $9017. ***Scholarships, grants, and awards by category:*** *Academic interests/achievement:* 1,617 awards ($11,762,478 total): general academic interests/achievements, military science. *Special achievements/activities:* 49 awards ($215,500 total): cheerleading/drum major, hobbies/interests. *Special characteristics:* 636 awards ($1,089,752 total): children and siblings of alumni, children of faculty/staff, general special characteristics, previous college experience, siblings of current students. ***Tuition waivers:*** Full or partial for employees or children of employees, senior citizens. ***ROTC:*** Army.

LOANS ***Student loans:*** $16,449,803 (91% need-based, 9% non-need-based). 70% of past graduating class borrowed through all loan programs. *Average indebtedness per student:* $35,106. ***Average need-based loan:*** Freshmen: $3432. Undergraduates: $4769. ***Parent loans:*** $3,098,144 (89% need-based, 11% non-need-based). ***Programs:*** FFEL (Subsidized and Unsubsidized Stafford, PLUS), Perkins, state, college/university.

WORK-STUDY ***Federal work-study:*** Total amount: $1,177,464; 806 jobs averaging $1461. ***State or other work-study/employment:*** Total amount: $42,143 (100% need-based). 9 part-time jobs averaging $4683.

ATHLETIC AWARDS Total amount: $2,823,481 (47% need-based, 53% non-need-based).

APPLYING FOR FINANCIAL AID ***Required financial aid forms:*** FAFSA, state aid form. ***Financial aid deadline (priority):*** 3/1. ***Notification date:*** Continuous. Students must reply by 5/1 or within 4 weeks of notification.

CONTACT Melissa Todd, Financial Aid Administrative Clerk, Florida Institute of Technology, 150 West University Boulevard, Melbourne, FL 32901-6975, 321-674-8070 or toll-free 800-888-4348. *Fax:* 321-724-2778. *E-mail:* toddm@fit.edu.

FLORIDA INTERNATIONAL UNIVERSITY

Miami, FL

Tuition & fees (FL res): $3900 **Average undergraduate aid package: $6688**

ABOUT THE INSTITUTION State-supported, coed. ***Awards:*** bachelor's, master's, doctoral, and first professional degrees and post-bachelor's certificates. 91 undergraduate majors. ***Total enrollment:*** 31,589. Undergraduates: 31,589. Freshmen: 2,991. Federal methodology is used as a basis for awarding need-based institutional aid.

UNDERGRADUATE EXPENSES for 2008–09 ***Application fee:*** $30. ***Tuition, state resident:*** full-time $3582; part-time $119.40 per credit hour. ***Tuition, nonresident:*** full-time $15,981; part-time $532.70 per credit hour. ***Required fees:*** full-time $318; $318 per credit hour. Full-time tuition and fees vary according to course load. Part-time tuition and fees vary according to course load. ***College room and board:*** $11,120; ***Room only:*** $7296. Room and board charges vary according to housing facility.

FRESHMAN FINANCIAL AID (Fall 2007) 2,061 applied for aid; of those 99% were deemed to have need. 96% of freshmen with need received aid; of those 12% had need fully met. ***Average percent of need met:*** 27% (excluding resources awarded to replace EFC). ***Average financial aid package:*** $6055 (excluding resources awarded to replace EFC). 27% of all full-time freshmen had no need and received non-need-based gift aid.

UNDERGRADUATE FINANCIAL AID (Fall 2007) 10,448 applied for aid; of those 98% were deemed to have need. 97% of undergraduates with need received aid; of those 13% had need fully met. ***Average percent of need met:*** 25% (excluding resources awarded to replace EFC). ***Average financial aid package:*** $6688 (excluding resources awarded to replace EFC). 5% of all full-time undergraduates had no need and received non-need-based gift aid.

GIFT AID (NEED-BASED) ***Total amount:*** $44,221,084 (71% federal, 17% state, 12% institutional). ***Receiving aid:*** Freshmen: 38% (1,155); all full-time undergraduates: 38% (7,151). ***Average award:*** Freshmen: $4457; Undergraduates: $4342. ***Scholarships, grants, and awards:*** Federal Pell, FSEOG, state, private, college/university gift aid from institutional funds.

GIFT AID (NON-NEED-BASED) ***Total amount:*** $31,563,045 (5% federal, 64% state, 22% institutional, 9% external sources). ***Receiving aid:*** Freshmen: 53% (1,630). Undergraduates: 26% (4,764). ***Average award:*** Freshmen: $620. Undergraduates: $692. ***Scholarships, grants, and awards by category:*** *Academic interests/achievement:* biological sciences, business, communication, computer science, education, engineering/technologies, English, foreign languages, general academic interests/achievements, health fields, humanities, mathematics, physical sciences, social sciences. *Creative arts/performance:* dance, journalism/publications, music, performing arts, theater/drama. *Special characteristics:* children and siblings of alumni, members of minority groups. ***Tuition waivers:*** Full or partial for employees or children of employees, senior citizens. ***ROTC:*** Army, Air Force.

LOANS ***Student loans:*** $111,036,904 (54% need-based, 46% non-need-based). 29% of past graduating class borrowed through all loan programs. *Average indebtedness per student:* $10,899. ***Average need-based loan:*** Freshmen: $6697. Undergraduates: $7880. ***Parent loans:*** $2,104,757 (100% non-need-based). ***Programs:*** Federal Direct (Subsidized and Unsubsidized Stafford, PLUS), FFEL (Subsidized and Unsubsidized Stafford, PLUS), Perkins, college/university.

WORK-STUDY ***Federal work-study:*** Total amount: $1,640,962; jobs available. ***State or other work-study/employment:*** Total amount: $114,745 (100% need-based). Part-time jobs available.

ATHLETIC AWARDS Total amount: $4,165,448 (2% need-based, 98% non-need-based).

APPLYING FOR FINANCIAL AID ***Required financial aid form:*** FAFSA. ***Financial aid deadline:*** 5/15 (priority: 3/1). ***Notification date:*** Continuous. Students must reply within 4 weeks of notification.

CONTACT Francisco Valines, Director, Financial Aid, Florida International University, 12200 SW 8th Street, PC 125, Miami, FL 33199, 305-348-7272. *Fax:* 305-348-2346. *E-mail:* finaid@fiu.edu.

FLORIDA MEMORIAL UNIVERSITY

Miami-Dade, FL

CONTACT Brian Phillip, Director of Financial Aid, Florida Memorial University, 15800 Northwest 42nd Avenue, Miami, FL 33054, 305-626-3745 or toll-free 800-822-1362. *Fax:* 305-626-3106.

FLORIDA SOUTHERN COLLEGE

Lakeland, FL

CONTACT David M. Bodwell, Financial Aid Director, Florida Southern College, 111 Lake Hollingsworth Drive, Lakeland, FL 33801-5698, 863-680-4140 or toll-free 800-274-4131. *Fax:* 863-680-4567. *E-mail:* dbodwell@flsouthern.edu.

FLORIDA STATE UNIVERSITY

Tallahassee, FL

Tuition & fees (FL res): $4196 **Average undergraduate aid package: $10,632**

ABOUT THE INSTITUTION State-supported, coed. ***Awards:*** associate, bachelor's, master's, doctoral, and first professional degrees and post-bachelor's and post-master's certificates. 110 undergraduate majors. ***Total enrollment:*** 38,682. Undergraduates: 29,869. Freshmen: 5,012. Federal methodology is used as a basis for awarding need-based institutional aid.

UNDERGRADUATE EXPENSES for 2008–09 ***Application fee:*** $30. ***Tuition, state resident:*** full-time $3665; part-time $122.18 per credit hour. ***Tuition, nonresident:*** full-time $18,110; part-time $603.66 per credit hour. ***Required fees:*** full-time $531; $16.36 per credit hour or $20 per term. Full-time tuition and fees vary according to location. Part-time tuition and fees vary according to location. ***College room and board:*** $8178; ***Room only:*** $4780. Room and board charges vary according to board plan and housing facility. ***Payment plans:*** Tuition prepayment, installment.

FRESHMAN FINANCIAL AID (Fall 2008, est.) 3,411 applied for aid; of those 48% were deemed to have need. 100% of freshmen with need received aid; of those 80% had need fully met. ***Average percent of need met:*** 76% (excluding resources awarded to replace EFC). ***Average financial aid package:*** $10,133 (excluding resources awarded to replace EFC). 10% of all full-time freshmen had no need and received non-need-based gift aid.

UNDERGRADUATE FINANCIAL AID (Fall 2008, est.) 14,741 applied for aid; of those 55% were deemed to have need. 100% of undergraduates with need received aid; of those 79% had need fully met. ***Average percent of need met:*** 78% (excluding resources awarded to replace EFC). ***Average financial aid package:*** $10,632 (excluding resources awarded to replace EFC). 5% of all full-time undergraduates had no need and received non-need-based gift aid.

GIFT AID (NEED-BASED) ***Total amount:*** $58,790,216 (43% federal, 35% state, 19% institutional, 3% external sources). ***Receiving aid:*** Freshmen: 20% (973); all full-time undergraduates: 21% (4,838). ***Average award:*** Freshmen: $4212; Undergraduates: $4107. ***Scholarships, grants, and awards:*** Federal Pell, FSEOG, state, private, college/university gift aid from institutional funds, Academic Competitiveness Grant, National Smart Grant.

GIFT AID (NON-NEED-BASED) ***Total amount:*** $51,742,721 (79% state, 16% institutional, 5% external sources). ***Receiving aid:*** Freshmen: 32% (1,558). Undergraduates: 26% (5,882). ***Average award:*** Freshmen: $2272. Undergraduates: $2215. ***Scholarships, grants, and awards by category:*** *Academic interests/achievement:* general academic interests/achievements. *Creative arts/performance:* cinema/film/broadcasting, dance, music, theater/drama. *Special characteristics:* local/state students. ***Tuition waivers:*** Full or partial for employees or children of employees, senior citizens. ***ROTC:*** Army, Naval cooperative, Air Force.

LOANS ***Student loans:*** $87,735,409 (53% need-based, 47% non-need-based). 48% of past graduating class borrowed through all loan programs. *Average indebtedness per student:* $16,927. ***Average need-based loan:*** Freshmen: $2692. Undergraduates: $3723. ***Parent loans:*** $5,558,636 (15% need-based, 85% non-need-based). ***Programs:*** FFEL (Subsidized and Unsubsidized Stafford, PLUS), Perkins, college/university.

WORK-STUDY ***Federal work-study:*** Total amount: $2,039,412; 730 jobs averaging $1150. ***State or other work-study/employment:*** Total amount: $43,780 (100% need-based). Part-time jobs available.

ATHLETIC AWARDS Total amount: $2,373,889 (6% need-based, 94% non-need-based).

APPLYING FOR FINANCIAL AID ***Required financial aid form:*** FAFSA. ***Financial aid deadline:*** Continuous. ***Notification date:*** Continuous beginning 3/1.

CONTACT Darryl Marshall, Director of Financial Aid, Florida State University, University Center A4400, Tallahassee, FL 32306-2430, 850-644-5716. *Fax:* 850-644-6404. *E-mail:* ofacs@admin.fsu.edu.

FONTBONNE UNIVERSITY

St. Louis, MO

CONTACT Financial Aid Office, Fontbonne University, 6800 Wydown Boulevard, St. Louis, MO 63105-3098, 314-889-1414. *Fax:* 314-889-1451.

FORDHAM UNIVERSITY

New York, NY

Tuition & fees: $35,257 **Average undergraduate aid package: $23,597**

ABOUT THE INSTITUTION Independent Roman Catholic (Jesuit), coed. ***Awards:*** bachelor's, master's, doctoral, and first professional degrees and post-master's certificates (branch locations at Rose Hill and Lincoln Center). 95 undergraduate majors. ***Total enrollment:*** 14,448. Undergraduates: 7,652. Freshmen: 1,784. Both federal and institutional methodology are used as a basis for awarding need-based institutional aid.

UNDERGRADUATE EXPENSES for 2008–09 ***Application fee:*** $50. ***Comprehensive fee:*** $48,237 includes full-time tuition ($34,200), mandatory fees ($1057), and room and board ($12,980). ***College room only:*** $8560. Full-time tuition and fees vary according to student level. Room and board charges vary according to board plan and location. ***Part-time tuition:*** $739 per credit hour. Part-time tuition and fees vary according to course load. ***Payment plan:*** Installment.

FRESHMAN FINANCIAL AID (Fall 2008, est.) 1,696 applied for aid; of those 66% were deemed to have need. 100% of freshmen with need received aid; of those 30% had need fully met. ***Average percent of need met:*** 77% (excluding resources awarded to replace EFC). ***Average financial aid package:*** $23,809 (excluding resources awarded to replace EFC). 34% of all full-time freshmen had no need and received non-need-based gift aid.

UNDERGRADUATE FINANCIAL AID (Fall 2008, est.) 6,112 applied for aid; of those 76% were deemed to have need. 100% of undergraduates with need received aid; of those 26% had need fully met. ***Average percent of need met:*** 74% (excluding resources awarded to replace EFC). ***Average financial aid package:*** $23,597 (excluding resources awarded to replace EFC). 21% of all full-time undergraduates had no need and received non-need-based gift aid.

GIFT AID (NEED-BASED) ***Total amount:*** $67,398,888 (11% federal, 10% state, 75% institutional, 4% external sources). ***Receiving aid:*** Freshmen: 59% (1,095); all full-time undergraduates: 61% (4,466). ***Average award:*** Freshmen: $17,210; Undergraduates: $16,236. ***Scholarships, grants, and awards:*** Federal Pell, FSEOG, state, private, college/university gift aid from institutional funds.

GIFT AID (NON-NEED-BASED) ***Total amount:*** $19,285,338 (3% state, 86% institutional, 11% external sources). ***Receiving aid:*** Freshmen: 13% (217).

Undergraduates: 11% (793). ***Average award:*** Freshmen: $9405. Undergraduates: $9448. ***Scholarships, grants, and awards by category:*** *Academic interests/achievement:* biological sciences, business, communication, foreign languages, general academic interests/achievements. *Creative arts/performance:* dance, music. *Special achievements/activities:* general special achievements/activities. *Special characteristics:* adult students, children and siblings of alumni, children of faculty/staff, children with a deceased or disabled parent, handicapped students. ***ROTC:*** Army, Naval cooperative, Air Force cooperative.

LOANS ***Student loans:*** $47,025,736 (65% need-based, 35% non-need-based). 62% of past graduating class borrowed through all loan programs. *Average indebtedness per student:* $31,300. ***Average need-based loan:*** Freshmen: $5065. Undergraduates: $6310. ***Parent loans:*** $15,722,373 (32% need-based, 68% non-need-based). ***Programs:*** FFEL (Subsidized and Unsubsidized Stafford, PLUS), Perkins.

WORK-STUDY ***Federal work-study:*** Total amount: $3,372,322; 1,232 jobs averaging $2731. ***State or other work-study/employment:*** Total amount: $1,307,068 (52% need-based, 48% non-need-based). 114 part-time jobs averaging $11,466.

ATHLETIC AWARDS Total amount: $8,965,158 (67% need-based, 33% non-need-based).

APPLYING FOR FINANCIAL AID ***Required financial aid forms:*** FAFSA, CSS Financial Aid PROFILE, noncustodial (divorced/separated) parent's statement, business/farm supplement. ***Financial aid deadline:*** 2/1 (priority: 2/1). ***Notification date:*** Continuous beginning 4/1. Students must reply by 5/1 or within 2 weeks of notification.

CONTACT Angela Van Dekker, Associate Vice President, Student Financial Services, Fordham University, 441 East Fordham Road, Thebaud Hall, Room 211F, New York, NY 10458, 718-817-3804 or toll-free 800-FORDHAM. *Fax:* 718-817-3817. *E-mail:* avandekker@fordham.edu.

FORT HAYS STATE UNIVERSITY

Hays, KS

Tuition & fees (KS res): $3051 **Average undergraduate aid package: $5955**

ABOUT THE INSTITUTION State-supported, coed. ***Awards:*** associate, bachelor's, and master's degrees and post-master's certificates. 55 undergraduate majors. ***Total enrollment:*** 7,403. Undergraduates: 5,920. Freshmen: 904. Federal methodology is used as a basis for awarding need-based institutional aid.

UNDERGRADUATE EXPENSES for 2008–09 ***Application fee:*** $30. ***Tuition, state resident:*** full-time $3051; part-time $101.75 per credit hour. ***Tuition, nonresident:*** full-time $9575; part-time $319.17 per credit hour. Full-time tuition and fees vary according to course load and location. Part-time tuition and fees vary according to course load and location. ***College room and board:*** $5450; ***Room only:*** $2710. Room and board charges vary according to board plan, housing facility, and student level. ***Payment plan:*** Installment.

FRESHMAN FINANCIAL AID (Fall 2007) 533 applied for aid; of those 78% were deemed to have need. 99% of freshmen with need received aid; of those 19% had need fully met. ***Average percent of need met:*** 66% (excluding resources awarded to replace EFC). ***Average financial aid package:*** $5543 (excluding resources awarded to replace EFC). 40% of all full-time freshmen had no need and received non-need-based gift aid.

UNDERGRADUATE FINANCIAL AID (Fall 2007) 3,244 applied for aid; of those 82% were deemed to have need. 97% of undergraduates with need received aid; of those 19% had need fully met. ***Average percent of need met:*** 62% (excluding resources awarded to replace EFC). ***Average financial aid package:*** $5955 (excluding resources awarded to replace EFC). 29% of all full-time undergraduates had no need and received non-need-based gift aid.

GIFT AID (NEED-BASED) ***Total amount:*** $7,273,130 (69% federal, 8% state, 7% institutional, 16% external sources). ***Receiving aid:*** Freshmen: 48% (368); all full-time undergraduates: 49% (1,947). ***Average award:*** Freshmen: $3882; Undergraduates: $3390. ***Scholarships, grants, and awards:*** Federal Pell, FSEOG, state, private, college/university gift aid from institutional funds.

GIFT AID (NON-NEED-BASED) ***Total amount:*** $1,387,454 (26% institutional, 74% external sources). ***Receiving aid:*** Freshmen: 5% (40). Undergraduates: 3% (114). ***Average award:*** Freshmen: $2481. Undergraduates: $3358. ***Tuition waivers:*** Full or partial for employees or children of employees, senior citizens.

LOANS ***Student loans:*** $19,585,494 (74% need-based, 26% non-need-based). 51% of past graduating class borrowed through all loan programs. *Average indebtedness per student:* $15,601. ***Average need-based loan:*** Freshmen: $2278. Undergraduates: $3634. ***Parent loans:*** $1,214,863 (31% need-based, 69% non-need-based). ***Programs:*** FFEL (Subsidized and Unsubsidized Stafford, PLUS), Perkins, college/university.

WORK-STUDY ***Federal work-study:*** Total amount: $523,763; jobs available. ***State or other work-study/employment:*** Total amount: $168,684 (41% need-based, 59% non-need-based). Part-time jobs available.

ATHLETIC AWARDS Total amount: $1,092,289 (50% need-based, 50% non-need-based).

APPLYING FOR FINANCIAL AID ***Required financial aid forms:*** FAFSA, state aid form. ***Financial aid deadline (priority):*** 3/15. ***Notification date:*** Continuous beginning 3/15. Students must reply within 2 weeks of notification.

CONTACT Craig Karlin, Director of Financial Assistance, Fort Hays State University, Custer Hall, Room 306, 600 Park Street, Hays, KS 67601, 785-628-4408 or toll-free 800-628-FHSU. *Fax:* 785-628-4014. *E-mail:* finaid@fhsu.edu.

FORT LEWIS COLLEGE

Durango, CO

Tuition & fees (CO res): $6956 **Average undergraduate aid package: $7983**

ABOUT THE INSTITUTION State-supported, coed. ***Awards:*** bachelor's degrees. 56 undergraduate majors. ***Total enrollment:*** 3,746. Undergraduates: 3,746. Freshmen: 800. Federal methodology is used as a basis for awarding need-based institutional aid.

UNDERGRADUATE EXPENSES for 2008–09 ***Application fee:*** $30. ***One-time required fee:*** $135. ***Tuition, state resident:*** full-time $5606; part-time $142 per credit hour. ***Tuition, nonresident:*** full-time $15,162; part-time $758 per credit hour. ***Required fees:*** full-time $1350; $45 per credit hour. Full-time tuition and fees vary according to reciprocity agreements. Part-time tuition and fees vary according to course load and reciprocity agreements. ***College room and board:*** $7170; ***Room only:*** $3842. Room and board charges vary according to board plan and housing facility. ***Payment plan:*** Installment.

FRESHMAN FINANCIAL AID (Fall 2008, est.) 548 applied for aid; of those 69% were deemed to have need. 99% of freshmen with need received aid; of those 23% had need fully met. ***Average financial aid package:*** $7137 (excluding resources awarded to replace EFC). 30% of all full-time freshmen had no need and received non-need-based gift aid.

UNDERGRADUATE FINANCIAL AID (Fall 2008, est.) 2,208 applied for aid; of those 78% were deemed to have need. 98% of undergraduates with need received aid; of those 27% had need fully met. ***Average financial aid package:*** $7983 (excluding resources awarded to replace EFC). 12% of all full-time undergraduates had no need and received non-need-based gift aid.

GIFT AID (NEED-BASED) ***Total amount:*** $7,636,595 (60% federal, 15% state, 20% institutional, 5% external sources). ***Receiving aid:*** Freshmen: 34% (269); all full-time undergraduates: 41% (1,370). ***Average award:*** Freshmen: $3315; Undergraduates: $3679. ***Scholarships, grants, and awards:*** Federal Pell, FSEOG, state, private, college/university gift aid from institutional funds.

GIFT AID (NON-NEED-BASED) ***Total amount:*** $1,440,964 (1% federal, 2% state, 65% institutional, 32% external sources). ***Receiving aid:*** Freshmen: 38% (299). Undergraduates: 25% (839). ***Average award:*** Freshmen: $1036. Undergraduates: $1236. ***Scholarships, grants, and awards by category:*** *Academic interests/achievement:* 411 awards ($496,381 total): agriculture, area/ethnic studies, biological sciences, business, communication, computer science, education, English, general academic interests/achievements, humanities, mathematics, physical sciences, social sciences. *Creative arts/performance:* 56 awards ($30,841 total): art/fine arts, music, performing arts, theater/drama. *Special achievements/activities:* 58 awards ($97,547 total): general special achievements/activities, leadership. *Special characteristics:* 179 awards ($166,826 total): children and siblings of alumni, children of faculty/staff, ethnic background, first-generation college students, general special characteristics, handicapped students, international students, local/state students, out-of-state students, veterans' children. ***Tuition waivers:*** Full or partial for minority students, employees or children of employees.

LOANS ***Student loans:*** $9,234,236 (70% need-based, 30% non-need-based). *Average indebtedness per student:* $17,962. ***Average need-based loan:*** Freshmen: $3065. Undergraduates: $3791. ***Parent loans:*** $1,209,400 (24% need-based, 76% non-need-based). ***Programs:*** FFEL (Subsidized and Unsubsidized Stafford, PLUS), Perkins, college/university.

WORK-STUDY ***Federal work-study:*** Total amount: $233,802; jobs available. ***State or other work-study/employment:*** Total amount: $706,886 (70% need-based, 30% non-need-based). Part-time jobs available.

ATHLETIC AWARDS Total amount: $1,479,533 (36% need-based, 64% non-need-based).

APPLYING FOR FINANCIAL AID ***Required financial aid form:*** FAFSA. ***Financial aid deadline:*** Continuous. ***Notification date:*** Continuous. Students must reply within 2 weeks of notification.

CONTACT Ms. Elaine Redwine, Director of Financial Aid, Fort Lewis College, 1000 Rim Drive, Durango, CO 81301-3999, 970-247-7464. *Fax:* 970-247-7108. *E-mail:* redwine_e@fortlewis.edu.

FORT VALLEY STATE UNIVERSITY

Fort Valley, GA

Tuition & fees (GA res): $4478 Average undergraduate aid package: $2141

ABOUT THE INSTITUTION State-supported, coed. ***Awards:*** associate, bachelor's, master's, doctoral, and first professional degrees. 36 undergraduate majors. ***Total enrollment:*** 3,106. Undergraduates: 2,975. Freshmen: 1,043. Federal methodology is used as a basis for awarding need-based institutional aid.

UNDERGRADUATE EXPENSES for 2008–09 ***Application fee:*** $30. ***Tuition, state resident:*** full-time $3098; part-time $118 per credit. ***Tuition, nonresident:*** full-time $12,390; part-time $471 per credit. ***Required fees:*** full-time $1380; $460 per term. Full-time tuition and fees vary according to course load, degree level, and student level. Part-time tuition and fees vary according to course load, degree level, and student level. ***College room and board:*** $7540; ***Room only:*** $5000. Room and board charges vary according to board plan. ***Payment plan:*** Guaranteed tuition.

FRESHMAN FINANCIAL AID (Fall 2008, est.) 1,045 applied for aid; of those 99% were deemed to have need. 100% of freshmen with need received aid. ***Average percent of need met:*** 96% (excluding resources awarded to replace EFC). ***Average financial aid package:*** $2141 (excluding resources awarded to replace EFC).

UNDERGRADUATE FINANCIAL AID (Fall 2008, est.) 2,756 applied for aid; of those 99% were deemed to have need. 100% of undergraduates with need received aid. ***Average percent of need met:*** 96% (excluding resources awarded to replace EFC). ***Average financial aid package:*** $2141 (excluding resources awarded to replace EFC).

GIFT AID (NEED-BASED) ***Total amount:*** $22,705,089 (89% federal, 7% state, 4% institutional). ***Receiving aid:*** Freshmen: 97% (1,022); all full-time undergraduates: 98% (2,718). ***Average award:*** Freshmen: $2140; Undergraduates: $2141. ***Scholarships, grants, and awards:*** Federal Pell, FSEOG, state, private, college/university gift aid from institutional funds, United Negro College Fund, The TEACH Grant.

GIFT AID (NON-NEED-BASED) ***Total amount:*** $3,468,345 (2% federal, 50% state, 48% institutional). ***Receiving aid:*** Freshmen: 7% (72). Undergraduates: 4% (115). ***Scholarships, grants, and awards by category:*** *Academic interests/achievement:* agriculture, business, general academic interests/achievements, home economics, military science, premedicine, social sciences. *Creative arts/performance:* journalism/publications, music. *Special achievements/activities:* general special achievements/activities. *Special characteristics:* handicapped students, international students, local/state students, members of minority groups, out-of-state students. ***Tuition waivers:*** Full or partial for employees or children of employees, senior citizens. ***ROTC:*** Army.

LOANS ***Student loans:*** $12,339,936 (100% need-based). 98% of past graduating class borrowed through all loan programs. *Average indebtedness per student:* $36,700. ***Average need-based loan:*** Freshmen: $2300. Undergraduates: $3400. ***Parent loans:*** $972,995 (100% need-based). ***Programs:*** Federal Direct (Subsidized and Unsubsidized Stafford, PLUS), Perkins, state, college/university.

WORK-STUDY ***Federal work-study:*** Total amount: $359,234; jobs available.

ATHLETIC AWARDS Total amount: $720,734 (100% need-based).

APPLYING FOR FINANCIAL AID ***Required financial aid forms:*** FAFSA, state aid form. ***Financial aid deadline:*** 6/30 (priority: 4/15). ***Notification date:*** Continuous beginning 7/1.

CONTACT Financial Aid Director, Fort Valley State University, PO Box 4129, Fort Valley, GA 31030-3298, 478-825-6182 or toll-free 877-462-3878. *Fax:* 478-825-6976.

FRAMINGHAM STATE COLLEGE

Framingham, MA

CONTACT Financial Aid Office, Framingham State College, 100 State Street, PO Box 9101, Framingham, MA 01701-9101, 508-626-4534. *Fax:* 508-626-4598.

FRANCISCAN UNIVERSITY OF STEUBENVILLE

Steubenville, OH

Tuition & fees: $19,650 Average undergraduate aid package: $11,754

ABOUT THE INSTITUTION Independent Roman Catholic, coed. ***Awards:*** associate, bachelor's, and master's degrees. 32 undergraduate majors. ***Total enrollment:*** 2,449. Undergraduates: 2,049. Freshmen: 389. Federal methodology is used as a basis for awarding need-based institutional aid.

UNDERGRADUATE EXPENSES for 2009–10 ***Application fee:*** $20. ***Comprehensive fee:*** $26,400 includes full-time tuition ($19,250), mandatory fees ($400), and room and board ($6750). ***Part-time tuition:*** $645 per credit hour. ***Part-time fees:*** $15 per credit hour.

FRESHMAN FINANCIAL AID (Fall 2008, est.) 344 applied for aid; of those 75% were deemed to have need. 100% of freshmen with need received aid; of those 14% had need fully met. ***Average percent of need met:*** 62% (excluding resources awarded to replace EFC). ***Average financial aid package:*** $11,563 (excluding resources awarded to replace EFC). 9% of all full-time freshmen had no need and received non-need-based gift aid.

UNDERGRADUATE FINANCIAL AID (Fall 2008, est.) 1,487 applied for aid; of those 81% were deemed to have need. 100% of undergraduates with need received aid; of those 13% had need fully met. ***Average percent of need met:*** 60% (excluding resources awarded to replace EFC). ***Average financial aid package:*** $11,754 (excluding resources awarded to replace EFC). 14% of all full-time undergraduates had no need and received non-need-based gift aid.

GIFT AID (NEED-BASED) ***Total amount:*** $7,951,334 (22% federal, 6% state, 67% institutional, 5% external sources). ***Receiving aid:*** Freshmen: 62% (241); all full-time undergraduates: 59% (1,120). ***Average award:*** Freshmen: $8357; Undergraduates: $7492. ***Scholarships, grants, and awards:*** Federal Pell, FSEOG, state, private, college/university gift aid from institutional funds.

GIFT AID (NON-NEED-BASED) ***Total amount:*** $1,467,849 (5% state, 88% institutional, 7% external sources). ***Receiving aid:*** Freshmen: 5% (18). Undergraduates: 3% (65). ***Average award:*** Freshmen: $4488. Undergraduates: $3921. ***Scholarships, grants, and awards by category:*** *Academic interests/achievement:* 530 awards ($1,749,452 total): general academic interests/achievements. *Special achievements/activities:* 10 awards ($91,201 total): religious involvement. *Special characteristics:* 412 awards ($2,163,934 total): children of faculty/staff, international students, local/state students, siblings of current students. ***ROTC:*** Army cooperative.

LOANS ***Student loans:*** $15,161,989 (63% need-based, 37% non-need-based). 75% of past graduating class borrowed through all loan programs. *Average indebtedness per student:* $29,256. ***Average need-based loan:*** Freshmen: $3374. Undergraduates: $4328. ***Parent loans:*** $2,311,686 (33% need-based, 67% non-need-based). ***Programs:*** FFEL (Subsidized and Unsubsidized Stafford, PLUS), Perkins.

WORK-STUDY ***Federal work-study:*** Total amount: $130,590; 302 jobs averaging $540. ***State or other work-study/employment:*** Total amount: $797,288 (84% need-based, 16% non-need-based). 524 part-time jobs averaging $1044.

APPLYING FOR FINANCIAL AID ***Required financial aid form:*** FAFSA. ***Financial aid deadline (priority):*** 4/15. ***Notification date:*** Continuous.

CONTACT John Herrmann, Director of Student Financial Services, Franciscan University of Steubenville, 1235 University Boulevard, Steubenville, OH 43952-1763, 740-284-5215 or toll-free 800-783-6220. *Fax:* 740-284-5469. *E-mail:* jherrmann@franciscan.edu.

FRANCIS MARION UNIVERSITY

Florence, SC

Tuition & fees (SC res): $7632 Average undergraduate aid package: N/A

ABOUT THE INSTITUTION State-supported, coed. ***Awards:*** bachelor's and master's degrees. 31 undergraduate majors. ***Total enrollment:*** 4,019. Undergraduates: 3,468. Freshmen: 681. Federal methodology is used as a basis for awarding need-based institutional aid.

UNDERGRADUATE EXPENSES for 2008–09 ***Application fee:*** $30. ***Tuition, state resident:*** full-time $7347; part-time $367.35 per credit hour. ***Tuition, nonresident:*** full-time $14,694; part-time $743.70 per credit hour. ***Required fees:*** full-time $285; $9.75 per credit hour. Part-time tuition and fees vary according to course load. ***College room and board:*** $6024; ***Room only:*** $3424. Room and board charges vary according to board plan and housing facility. ***Payment plan:*** Installment.

FRESHMAN FINANCIAL AID (Fall 2008, est.) 582 applied for aid; of those 89% were deemed to have need. 97% of freshmen with need received aid.

UNDERGRADUATE FINANCIAL AID (Fall 2008, est.) 2,716 applied for aid; of those 84% were deemed to have need. 86% of undergraduates with need received aid.

GIFT AID (NEED-BASED) ***Total amount:*** $7,060,000 (88% federal, 12% state). ***Receiving aid:*** Freshmen: 67% (455); all full-time undergraduates: 62% (1,884). ***Scholarships, grants, and awards:*** Federal Pell, FSEOG, state, private, Academic Competitiveness Grant, National Smart Grant.

GIFT AID (NON-NEED-BASED) ***Total amount:*** $7,205,000 (82% state, 12% institutional, 6% external sources). ***Receiving aid:*** Freshmen: 39% (264). Undergraduates: 56% (1,705). ***Scholarships, grants, and awards by category:*** *Academic interests/achievement:* biological sciences, business, education, English, general academic interests/achievements, health fields, humanities, mathematics, premedicine, social sciences. *Creative arts/performance:* art/fine arts, music, theater/drama. *Special achievements/activities:* cheerleading/drum major. *Special characteristics:* adult students, children and siblings of alumni, children of faculty/staff, handicapped students, international students, out-of-state students, spouses of deceased or disabled public servants, veterans, veterans' children. ***Tuition waivers:*** Full or partial for employees or children of employees, senior citizens.

LOANS ***Student loans:*** $21,000,000 (52% need-based, 48% non-need-based). 75% of past graduating class borrowed through all loan programs. *Average indebtedness per student:* $23,487. ***Parent loans:*** $1,000,000 (100% non-need-based). ***Programs:*** FFEL (Subsidized and Unsubsidized Stafford, PLUS), Perkins, state.

WORK-STUDY ***Federal work-study:*** Total amount: $130,000; jobs available. ***State or other work-study/employment:*** Total amount: $700,000 (100% non-need-based). Part-time jobs available.

ATHLETIC AWARDS Total amount: $700,000 (100% non-need-based).

APPLYING FOR FINANCIAL AID ***Required financial aid form:*** FAFSA. ***Financial aid deadline (priority):*** 3/1. ***Notification date:*** 4/1.

CONTACT Kim Ellisor, Director of Financial Assistance, Francis Marion University, PO Box 100547, Florence, SC 29501-0547, 843-661-1190 or toll-free 800-368-7551.

FRANKLIN & MARSHALL COLLEGE

Lancaster, PA

Tuition & fees: $38,630 **Average undergraduate aid package: $27,856**

ABOUT THE INSTITUTION Independent, coed. ***Awards:*** bachelor's degrees. 38 undergraduate majors. ***Total enrollment:*** 2,164. Undergraduates: 2,164. Freshmen: 588. Both federal and institutional methodology are used as a basis for awarding need-based institutional aid.

UNDERGRADUATE EXPENSES for 2008–09 ***Application fee:*** $50. ***Comprehensive fee:*** $48,500 includes full-time tuition ($38,580), mandatory fees ($50), and room and board ($9870). ***College room only:*** $6230. Full-time tuition and fees vary according to reciprocity agreements. Room and board charges vary according to board plan, housing facility, and location. ***Part-time tuition:*** $4823 per course. ***Payment plans:*** Installment, deferred payment.

FRESHMAN FINANCIAL AID (Fall 2008, est.) 325 applied for aid; of those 67% were deemed to have need. 100% of freshmen with need received aid; of those 100% had need fully met. ***Average percent of need met:*** 100% (excluding resources awarded to replace EFC). ***Average financial aid package:*** $28,715 (excluding resources awarded to replace EFC). 12% of all full-time freshmen had no need and received non-need-based gift aid.

UNDERGRADUATE FINANCIAL AID (Fall 2008, est.) 1,132 applied for aid; of those 78% were deemed to have need. 100% of undergraduates with need received aid; of those 38% had need fully met. ***Average percent of need met:*** 90% (excluding resources awarded to replace EFC). ***Average financial aid package:*** $27,856 (excluding resources awarded to replace EFC). 15% of all full-time undergraduates had no need and received non-need-based gift aid.

GIFT AID (NEED-BASED) ***Total amount:*** $16,837,926 (6% federal, 2% state, 88% institutional, 4% external sources). ***Receiving aid:*** Freshmen: 36% (210); all full-time undergraduates: 38% (834). ***Average award:*** Freshmen: $25,230; Undergraduates: $23,356. ***Scholarships, grants, and awards:*** Federal Pell, FSEOG, state, private, college/university gift aid from institutional funds.

GIFT AID (NON-NEED-BASED) ***Total amount:*** $7,788,075 (85% institutional, 15% external sources). ***Receiving aid:*** Freshmen: 10% (56). Undergraduates: 4% (98). ***Average award:*** Freshmen: $10,654. Undergraduates: $9790. ***Scholarships, grants, and awards by category:*** *Academic interests/achievement:* general academic interests/achievements. *Creative arts/performance:* music. *Special characteristics:* children of faculty/staff, members of minority groups. ***Tuition waivers:*** Full or partial for employees or children of employees.

LOANS ***Student loans:*** $49,787,249 (91% need-based, 9% non-need-based). 54% of past graduating class borrowed through all loan programs. *Average indebtedness per student:* $30,657. ***Average need-based loan:*** Freshmen: $3246. Undergraduates: $4613. ***Parent loans:*** $4,463,215 (19% need-based, 81% non-need-based). ***Programs:*** FFEL (Subsidized and Unsubsidized Stafford, PLUS), Perkins, college/university.

WORK-STUDY ***Federal work-study:*** Total amount: $1,164,948; jobs available. ***State or other work-study/employment:*** Total amount: $294,934 (24% need-based, 76% non-need-based). Part-time jobs available.

APPLYING FOR FINANCIAL AID ***Required financial aid forms:*** FAFSA, CSS Financial Aid PROFILE, noncustodial (divorced/separated) parent's statement, business/farm supplement, federal income tax form(s), W-2 forms. ***Financial aid deadline:*** 3/1 (priority: 2/1). ***Notification date:*** 4/1. Students must reply by 5/1.

CONTACT Mr. Clarke Paine, Director of Financial Aid, Franklin & Marshall College, PO Box 3003, Lancaster, PA 17604-3003, 717-291-3991. *Fax:* 717-291-4462. *E-mail:* clarke.paine@fandm.edu.

FRANKLIN COLLEGE

Franklin, IN

Tuition & fees: $22,445 **Average undergraduate aid package: $16,564**

ABOUT THE INSTITUTION Independent religious, coed. ***Awards:*** bachelor's degrees. 32 undergraduate majors. ***Total enrollment:*** 1,153. Undergraduates: 1,099. Freshmen: 362. Federal methodology is used as a basis for awarding need-based institutional aid.

UNDERGRADUATE EXPENSES for 2008–09 ***Application fee:*** $30. ***Comprehensive fee:*** $29,085 includes full-time tuition ($22,270), mandatory fees ($175), and room and board ($6640). ***College room only:*** $3940. Room and board charges vary according to board plan and housing facility. ***Part-time tuition:*** $310 per credit hour. Part-time tuition and fees vary according to course load. ***Payment plan:*** Installment.

FRESHMAN FINANCIAL AID (Fall 2007) 360 applied for aid; of those 88% were deemed to have need. 100% of freshmen with need received aid; of those 17% had need fully met. ***Average percent of need met:*** 78% (excluding resources awarded to replace EFC). ***Average financial aid package:*** $15,347 (excluding resources awarded to replace EFC). 19% of all full-time freshmen had no need and received non-need-based gift aid.

UNDERGRADUATE FINANCIAL AID (Fall 2007) 950 applied for aid; of those 90% were deemed to have need. 100% of undergraduates with need received aid; of those 18% had need fully met. ***Average percent of need met:*** 82% (excluding resources awarded to replace EFC). ***Average financial aid package:*** $16,564 (excluding resources awarded to replace EFC). 18% of all full-time undergraduates had no need and received non-need-based gift aid.

GIFT AID (NEED-BASED) ***Total amount:*** $11,231,575 (10% federal, 29% state, 57% institutional, 4% external sources). ***Receiving aid:*** Freshmen: 80% (317); all full-time undergraduates: 81% (847). ***Average award:*** Freshmen: $12,438; Undergraduates: $13,096. ***Scholarships, grants, and awards:*** Federal Pell, FSEOG, state, private, college/university gift aid from institutional funds.

GIFT AID (NON-NEED-BASED) ***Total amount:*** $2,184,232 (2% state, 83% institutional, 15% external sources). ***Receiving aid:*** Freshmen: 13% (50). Undergraduates: 13% (133). ***Average award:*** Freshmen: $10,334. Undergraduates: $11,823. ***Scholarships, grants, and awards by category:*** *Academic interests/achievement:* 978 awards ($5,478,611 total): general academic interests/

achievements. *Creative arts/performance:* 28 awards ($194,565 total): art/fine arts, journalism/publications, music, performing arts, theater/drama. *Special characteristics:* 248 awards ($601,208 total): children and siblings of alumni, children of faculty/staff, ethnic background, members of minority groups, out-of-state students, religious affiliation, siblings of current students. ***Tuition waivers:*** Full or partial for employees or children of employees, senior citizens. ***ROTC:*** Army cooperative.

LOANS ***Student loans:*** $5,973,848 (66% need-based, 34% non-need-based). 84% of past graduating class borrowed through all loan programs. *Average indebtedness per student:* $42,908. ***Average need-based loan:*** Freshmen: $3610. Undergraduates: $4246. ***Parent loans:*** $1,789,337 (19% need-based, 81% non-need-based). ***Programs:*** FFEL (Subsidized and Unsubsidized Stafford, PLUS), Perkins, college/university.

WORK-STUDY ***Federal work-study:*** Total amount: $94,055; jobs available (averaging $1500). ***State or other work-study/employment:*** Total amount: $102,889 (67% need-based, 33% non-need-based). Part-time jobs available.

APPLYING FOR FINANCIAL AID ***Required financial aid forms:*** FAFSA, institution's own form. ***Financial aid deadline:*** 3/1. ***Notification date:*** 4/1. Students must reply by 5/1 or within 4 weeks of notification.

CONTACT Elizabeth Sappenfield, Director of Financial Aid, Franklin College, 101 Branigin Boulevard, Franklin, IN 46131-2598, 317-738-8075 or toll-free 800-852-0232. *Fax:* 317-738-8072. *E-mail:* finaid@franklincollege.edu.

FRANKLIN PIERCE UNIVERSITY

Rindge, NH

Tuition & fees: $28,700 **Average undergraduate aid package: $18,733**

ABOUT THE INSTITUTION Independent, coed. ***Awards:*** associate, bachelor's, master's, and doctoral degrees and post-master's certificates (profile does not reflect significant enrollment at 6 continuing education sites; master's degree is only offered at these sites). 50 undergraduate majors. ***Total enrollment:*** 2,601. Undergraduates: 2,102. Freshmen: 477. Federal methodology is used as a basis for awarding need-based institutional aid.

UNDERGRADUATE EXPENSES for 2009–10 ***Application fee:*** $40. ***Comprehensive fee:*** $38,500 includes full-time tuition ($27,700), mandatory fees ($1000), and room and board ($9800). ***College room only:*** $5600. ***Part-time tuition:*** $923 per credit hour.

FRESHMAN FINANCIAL AID (Fall 2008, est.) 406 applied for aid; of those 88% were deemed to have need. 99% of freshmen with need received aid; of those 15% had need fully met. ***Average percent of need met:*** 71% (excluding resources awarded to replace EFC). ***Average financial aid package:*** $19,282 (excluding resources awarded to replace EFC). 18% of all full-time freshmen had no need and received non-need-based gift aid.

UNDERGRADUATE FINANCIAL AID (Fall 2008, est.) 1,310 applied for aid; of those 89% were deemed to have need. 100% of undergraduates with need received aid; of those 17% had need fully met. ***Average percent of need met:*** 66% (excluding resources awarded to replace EFC). ***Average financial aid package:*** $18,733 (excluding resources awarded to replace EFC). 18% of all full-time undergraduates had no need and received non-need-based gift aid.

GIFT AID (NEED-BASED) ***Total amount:*** $15,527,420 (8% federal, 1% state, 85% institutional, 6% external sources). ***Receiving aid:*** Freshmen: 63% (314); all full-time undergraduates: 73% (1,146). ***Average award:*** Freshmen: $15,681; Undergraduates: $14,047. ***Scholarships, grants, and awards:*** Federal Pell, FSEOG, state, private, college/university gift aid from institutional funds.

GIFT AID (NON-NEED-BASED) ***Total amount:*** $3,681,911 (80% institutional, 20% external sources). ***Receiving aid:*** Freshmen: 8% (39). Undergraduates: 7% (105). ***Average award:*** Freshmen: $9681. Undergraduates: $8615. ***Scholarships, grants, and awards by category:*** *Academic interests/achievement:* communication, general academic interests/achievements. *Creative arts/performance:* performing arts, theater/drama. *Special achievements/activities:* general special achievements/activities, leadership. *Special characteristics:* adult students, children and siblings of alumni, children of current students, children of educators, children of faculty/staff, general special characteristics, international students, local/state students, married students, parents of current students, siblings of current students, spouses of current students. ***ROTC:*** Army cooperative, Air Force cooperative.

LOANS ***Student loans:*** $16,173,242 (63% need-based, 37% non-need-based). 83% of past graduating class borrowed through all loan programs. *Average indebtedness per student:* $38,148. ***Average need-based loan:*** Undergraduates: $4921. ***Parent loans:*** $3,510,610 (32% need-based, 68% non-need-based). ***Programs:*** FFEL (Subsidized and Unsubsidized Stafford, PLUS), Perkins.

WORK-STUDY ***Federal work-study:*** Total amount: $606,564; jobs available. ***State or other work-study/employment:*** Part-time jobs available.

ATHLETIC AWARDS Total amount: $1,594,790 (40% need-based, 60% non-need-based).

APPLYING FOR FINANCIAL AID ***Required financial aid form:*** FAFSA. ***Financial aid deadline (priority):*** 3/1. ***Notification date:*** Continuous beginning 3/1.

CONTACT Kenneth Ferreira, Executive Director of Student Financial Services, Franklin Pierce University, 20 College Road, Rindge, NH 03461-0060, 603-899-4180 or toll-free 800-437-0048. *Fax:* 603-899-4372. *E-mail:* ferreirak@fpc.edu.

FRANKLIN UNIVERSITY

Columbus, OH

CONTACT Ms. Marlowe Collier, Financial Aid Assistant, Franklin University, 201 South Grant Avenue, Columbus, OH 43215-5399, 614-797-4700 or toll-free 877-341-6300. *Fax:* 614-220-8931. *E-mail:* finaid@franklin.edu.

FREED-HARDEMAN UNIVERSITY

Henderson, TN

Tuition & fees: $13,860 **Average undergraduate aid package: $11,449**

ABOUT THE INSTITUTION Independent religious, coed. ***Awards:*** associate, bachelor's, master's, and first professional degrees and post-bachelor's and post-master's certificates. 54 undergraduate majors. ***Total enrollment:*** 2,061. Undergraduates: 1,534. Freshmen: 405. Federal methodology is used as a basis for awarding need-based institutional aid.

UNDERGRADUATE EXPENSES for 2008–09 ***Comprehensive fee:*** $20,830 includes full-time tuition ($11,700), mandatory fees ($2160), and room and board ($6970). ***College room only:*** $3980. ***Part-time tuition:*** $390 per semester hour.

FRESHMAN FINANCIAL AID (Fall 2008, est.) 384 applied for aid; of those 81% were deemed to have need. 99% of freshmen with need received aid; of those 26% had need fully met. ***Average percent of need met:*** 71% (excluding resources awarded to replace EFC). ***Average financial aid package:*** $12,396 (excluding resources awarded to replace EFC). 17% of all full-time freshmen had no need and received non-need-based gift aid.

UNDERGRADUATE FINANCIAL AID (Fall 2008, est.) 1,287 applied for aid; of those 84% were deemed to have need. 99% of undergraduates with need received aid; of those 22% had need fully met. ***Average percent of need met:*** 65% (excluding resources awarded to replace EFC). ***Average financial aid package:*** $11,449 (excluding resources awarded to replace EFC). 19% of all full-time undergraduates had no need and received non-need-based gift aid.

GIFT AID (NEED-BASED) ***Total amount:*** $7,950,624 (18% federal, 24% state, 53% institutional, 5% external sources). ***Receiving aid:*** Freshmen: 75% (304); all full-time undergraduates: 69% (984). ***Average award:*** Freshmen: $10,053; Undergraduates: $8987. ***Scholarships, grants, and awards:*** Federal Pell, FSEOG, state, private, college/university gift aid from institutional funds.

GIFT AID (NON-NEED-BASED) ***Total amount:*** $2,757,725 (24% state, 67% institutional, 9% external sources). ***Receiving aid:*** Freshmen: 16% (63). Undergraduates: 13% (182). ***Average award:*** Freshmen: $9883. Undergraduates: $11,891.

LOANS ***Student loans:*** $8,747,488 (68% need-based, 32% non-need-based). 72% of past graduating class borrowed through all loan programs. *Average indebtedness per student:* $29,744. ***Average need-based loan:*** Freshmen: $3296. Undergraduates: $3698. ***Parent loans:*** $1,152,964 (100% need-based). ***Programs:*** FFEL (Subsidized and Unsubsidized Stafford, PLUS), Perkins, alternative loans.

WORK-STUDY ***Federal work-study:*** Total amount: $430,621; jobs available.

ATHLETIC AWARDS Total amount: $1,040,790 (100% non-need-based).

APPLYING FOR FINANCIAL AID ***Required financial aid form:*** FAFSA. ***Financial aid deadline (priority):*** 8/1. ***Notification date:*** Continuous beginning 3/1. Students must reply within 4 weeks of notification.

CONTACT Larry Cyr, Director of Financial Aid, Freed-Hardeman University, 158 East Main Street, Henderson, TN 38340-2399, 731-989-6662 or toll-free 800-630-3480. *Fax:* 731-989-6775. *E-mail:* lcyr@fhu.edu.

FREE WILL BAPTIST BIBLE COLLEGE

Nashville, TN

Tuition & fees: $13,086 **Average undergraduate aid package: $11,469**

ABOUT THE INSTITUTION Independent Free Will Baptist, coed. ***Awards:*** associate and bachelor's degrees. 12 undergraduate majors. ***Total enrollment:*** 317. Undergraduates: 317. Federal methodology is used as a basis for awarding need-based institutional aid.

UNDERGRADUATE EXPENSES for 2008–09 ***Application fee:*** $35. ***Comprehensive fee:*** $18,438 includes full-time tuition ($12,270), mandatory fees ($816), and room and board ($5352). Room and board charges vary according to board plan. ***Part-time tuition:*** $409 per semester hour. ***Payment plans:*** Installment, deferred payment.

FRESHMAN FINANCIAL AID (Fall 2008, est.) 63 applied for aid; of those 100% were deemed to have need. 97% of freshmen with need received aid. ***Average percent of need met:*** 70% (excluding resources awarded to replace EFC). ***Average financial aid package:*** $8556 (excluding resources awarded to replace EFC).

UNDERGRADUATE FINANCIAL AID (Fall 2008, est.) 163 applied for aid; of those 100% were deemed to have need. 97% of undergraduates with need received aid. ***Average percent of need met:*** 70% (excluding resources awarded to replace EFC). ***Average financial aid package:*** $11,469 (excluding resources awarded to replace EFC).

GIFT AID (NEED-BASED) ***Total amount:*** $724,911 (62% federal, 7% state, 31% institutional). ***Receiving aid:*** Freshmen: 71% (45); all full-time undergraduates: 54% (119). ***Average award:*** Freshmen: $7320; Undergraduates: $4438. ***Scholarships, grants, and awards:*** Federal Pell, FSEOG, state, private, college/university gift aid from institutional funds.

GIFT AID (NON-NEED-BASED) ***Total amount:*** $890,683 (13% state, 61% institutional, 26% external sources). ***Receiving aid:*** Freshmen: 56% (35). Undergraduates: 40% (88). ***Scholarships, grants, and awards by category:*** *Special characteristics:* 47 awards ($133,022 total): children of faculty/staff, international students, married students, relatives of clergy, veterans, veterans' children. ***Tuition waivers:*** Full or partial for employees or children of employees. ***ROTC:*** Army cooperative, Air Force cooperative.

LOANS ***Student loans:*** $1,979,596 (46% need-based, 54% non-need-based). 74% of past graduating class borrowed through all loan programs. *Average indebtedness per student:* $18,487. ***Average need-based loan:*** Freshmen: $4163. Undergraduates: $5617. ***Parent loans:*** $428,325 (100% non-need-based). ***Programs:*** FFEL (Subsidized and Unsubsidized Stafford, PLUS), alternative loans.

WORK-STUDY ***Federal work-study:*** Total amount: $20,602; 6 jobs averaging $3434. ***State or other work-study/employment:*** 84 part-time jobs averaging $1414.

APPLYING FOR FINANCIAL AID ***Required financial aid forms:*** FAFSA, institution's own form. ***Financial aid deadline (priority):*** 4/15. ***Notification date:*** Continuous beginning 7/1.

CONTACT Jeff Caudill, Director of Enrollment Services, Free Will Baptist Bible College, 3606 West End Avenue, Nashville, TN 37205, 615-844-5000 or toll-free 800-763-9222. *Fax:* 615-269-6028. *E-mail:* jcaudill@fwbbc.edu.

FRESNO PACIFIC UNIVERSITY

Fresno, CA

Tuition & fees: $23,202 **Average undergraduate aid package: $14,649**

ABOUT THE INSTITUTION Independent religious, coed. ***Awards:*** associate, bachelor's, and master's degrees. 42 undergraduate majors. ***Total enrollment:*** 2,353. Undergraduates: 1,539. Freshmen: 170. Federal methodology is used as a basis for awarding need-based institutional aid.

UNDERGRADUATE EXPENSES for 2008–09 ***Application fee:*** $40. ***Comprehensive fee:*** $30,002 includes full-time tuition ($22,950), mandatory fees ($252), and room and board ($6800). ***College room only:*** $3740. Full-time tuition and fees vary according to program. Room and board charges vary according to board plan and housing facility. ***Part-time tuition:*** $820 per unit. Part-time tuition and fees vary according to program. ***Payment plan:*** Installment.

FRESHMAN FINANCIAL AID (Fall 2008, est.) 144 applied for aid; of those 86% were deemed to have need. 99% of freshmen with need received aid; of those 15% had need fully met. ***Average percent of need met:*** 75% (excluding resources awarded to replace EFC). ***Average financial aid package:*** $20,995 (excluding resources awarded to replace EFC). 1% of all full-time freshmen had no need and received non-need-based gift aid.

UNDERGRADUATE FINANCIAL AID (Fall 2008, est.) 1,245 applied for aid; of those 91% were deemed to have need. 99% of undergraduates with need received aid; of those 12% had need fully met. ***Average percent of need met:*** 61% (excluding resources awarded to replace EFC). ***Average financial aid package:*** $14,649 (excluding resources awarded to replace EFC).

GIFT AID (NEED-BASED) ***Total amount:*** $7,485,135 (33% federal, 56% state, 11% institutional). ***Receiving aid:*** Freshmen: 54% (84); all full-time undergraduates: 55% (787). ***Average award:*** Freshmen: $11,984; Undergraduates: $8213. ***Scholarships, grants, and awards:*** Federal Pell, FSEOG, state, private, college/university gift aid from institutional funds.

GIFT AID (NON-NEED-BASED) ***Total amount:*** $5,197,373 (95% institutional, 5% external sources). ***Receiving aid:*** Freshmen: 52% (81). Undergraduates: 20% (283). ***Average award:*** Freshmen: $7846. ***Scholarships, grants, and awards by category:*** *Academic interests/achievement:* business, general academic interests/achievements, humanities, social sciences. *Creative arts/performance:* music, performing arts, theater/drama. *Special characteristics:* children of faculty/staff, members of minority groups, relatives of clergy, religious affiliation, spouses of current students. ***Tuition waivers:*** Full or partial for employees or children of employees, senior citizens.

LOANS ***Student loans:*** $10,438,904 (100% need-based). 82% of past graduating class borrowed through all loan programs. *Average indebtedness per student:* $20,416. ***Average need-based loan:*** Freshmen: $5921. Undergraduates: $5163. ***Parent loans:*** $841,473 (100% need-based). ***Programs:*** FFEL (Subsidized and Unsubsidized Stafford, PLUS), Perkins.

WORK-STUDY ***Federal work-study:*** Total amount: $710,491; jobs available.

ATHLETIC AWARDS Total amount: $2,029,327 (100% non-need-based).

APPLYING FOR FINANCIAL AID ***Required financial aid forms:*** FAFSA, institution's own form. ***Financial aid deadline (priority):*** 3/2. ***Notification date:*** Continuous beginning 3/2. Students must reply by 7/30 or within 3 weeks of notification.

CONTACT April Powell, Associate Director of Financial Aid, Fresno Pacific University, 1717 South Chestnut Avenue, #2004, Fresno, CA 93702, 559-453-7137 or toll-free 800-660-6089 (in-state). *Fax:* 559-453-5595. *E-mail:* sfs@fresno.edu.

FRIENDS UNIVERSITY

Wichita, KS

CONTACT Brandon Pierce, Director of Financial Aid, Friends University, 2100 University Street, Wichita, KS 67213, 316-295-5658 or toll-free 800-577-2233. *Fax:* 316-295-5703. *E-mail:* piercb@friends.edu.

FROSTBURG STATE UNIVERSITY

Frostburg, MD

Tuition & fees (MD res): $6614 **Average undergraduate aid package: $8298**

ABOUT THE INSTITUTION State-supported, coed. ***Awards:*** bachelor's and master's degrees and post-bachelor's and post-master's certificates. 47 undergraduate majors. ***Total enrollment:*** 5,215. Undergraduates: 4,582. Freshmen: 1,031. Federal methodology is used as a basis for awarding need-based institutional aid.

UNDERGRADUATE EXPENSES for 2008–09 ***Application fee:*** $30. ***Tuition, state resident:*** full-time $5000; part-time $207 per credit hour. ***Tuition, nonresident:*** full-time $15,196; part-time $427 per credit hour. ***Required fees:*** full-time $1614; $77 per credit hour or $11 per term. Full-time tuition and fees vary according to course load and program. Part-time tuition and fees vary according to course load and program. ***College room and board:*** $7016; ***Room only:*** $3438. Room and board charges vary according to board plan. ***Payment plan:*** Deferred payment.

FRESHMAN FINANCIAL AID (Fall 2008, est.) 877 applied for aid; of those 62% were deemed to have need. 100% of freshmen with need received aid; of those 29% had need fully met. ***Average percent of need met:*** 75% (excluding resources awarded to replace EFC). ***Average financial aid package:*** $8941 (excluding resources awarded to replace EFC). 14% of all full-time freshmen had no need and received non-need-based gift aid.

UNDERGRADUATE FINANCIAL AID (Fall 2008, est.) 3,777 applied for aid; of those 60% were deemed to have need. 100% of undergraduates with need

received aid; of those 26% had need fully met. ***Average percent of need met:*** 72% (excluding resources awarded to replace EFC). ***Average financial aid package:*** $8298 (excluding resources awarded to replace EFC). 9% of all full-time undergraduates had no need and received non-need-based gift aid.

GIFT AID (NEED-BASED) ***Total amount:*** $10,654,986 (42% federal, 41% state, 12% institutional, 5% external sources). ***Receiving aid:*** Freshmen: 39% (413); all full-time undergraduates: 39% (1,753). ***Average award:*** Freshmen: $6958; Undergraduates: $5729. ***Scholarships, grants, and awards:*** Federal Pell, FSEOG, state, private, college/university gift aid from institutional funds.

GIFT AID (NON-NEED-BASED) ***Total amount:*** $3,390,060 (7% state, 82% institutional, 11% external sources). ***Receiving aid:*** Freshmen: 19% (202). Undergraduates: 14% (634). ***Average award:*** Freshmen: $2917. Undergraduates: $2909. ***Scholarships, grants, and awards by category:*** *Academic interests/achievement:* biological sciences, business, communication, computer science, education, engineering/technologies, English, foreign languages, general academic interests/achievements, health fields, humanities, international studies, mathematics, physical sciences, premedicine, social sciences. *Creative arts/performance:* art/fine arts, creative writing, journalism/publications, music, performing arts, theater/drama. *Special achievements/activities:* community service, leadership. *Special characteristics:* adult students, children of union members/company employees, international students, local/state students, out-of-state students, veterans, veterans' children. ***Tuition waivers:*** Full or partial for employees or children of employees, senior citizens.

LOANS ***Student loans:*** $19,638,886 (40% need-based, 60% non-need-based). 64% of past graduating class borrowed through all loan programs. *Average indebtedness per student:* $18,408. ***Average need-based loan:*** Freshmen: $3037. Undergraduates: $3579. ***Parent loans:*** $3,152,222 (100% non-need-based). ***Programs:*** Federal Direct (Subsidized and Unsubsidized Stafford, PLUS), FFEL (Subsidized and Unsubsidized Stafford, PLUS), Perkins.

WORK-STUDY ***Federal work-study:*** Total amount: $67,636; 131 jobs averaging $1000. ***State or other work-study/employment:*** Part-time jobs available.

APPLYING FOR FINANCIAL AID ***Required financial aid form:*** FAFSA. ***Financial aid deadline (priority):*** 3/1. ***Notification date:*** Continuous beginning 3/15. Students must reply within 3 weeks of notification.

CONTACT Mrs. Angela Hovatter, Director of Financial Aid, Frostburg State University, 114 Pullen Hall, Frostburg, MD 21532-1099, 301-687-4301. *Fax:* 301-687-7074. *E-mail:* ahovatter@frostburg.edu.

FULL SAIL UNIVERSITY

Winter Park, FL

CONTACT Ed Haddock, Chief Executive Officer, Full Sail University, 3300 University Boulevard, Winter Park, FL 32792, 407-679-6333 Ext. 4711 or toll-free 800-226-7625.

FURMAN UNIVERSITY

Greenville, SC

Tuition & fees: $34,588 | **Average undergraduate aid package: $25,638**

ABOUT THE INSTITUTION Independent, coed. ***Awards:*** bachelor's and master's degrees and post-bachelor's certificates. 48 undergraduate majors. ***Total enrollment:*** 2,977. Undergraduates: 2,801. Freshmen: 761. Both federal and institutional methodology are used as a basis for awarding need-based institutional aid.

UNDERGRADUATE EXPENSES for 2008–09 ***Application fee:*** $50. ***Comprehensive fee:*** $43,554 includes full-time tuition ($34,048), mandatory fees ($540), and room and board ($8966). ***College room only:*** $5044. Room and board charges vary according to board plan and housing facility. ***Part-time tuition:*** $1064 per credit hour. Part-time tuition and fees vary according to course load. ***Payment plan:*** Installment.

FRESHMAN FINANCIAL AID (Fall 2008, est.) 456 applied for aid; of those 69% were deemed to have need. 100% of freshmen with need received aid; of those 39% had need fully met. ***Average percent of need met:*** 85% (excluding resources awarded to replace EFC). ***Average financial aid package:*** $26,229 (excluding resources awarded to replace EFC). 29% of all full-time freshmen had no need and received non-need-based gift aid.

UNDERGRADUATE FINANCIAL AID (Fall 2008, est.) 1,357 applied for aid; of those 76% were deemed to have need. 100% of undergraduates with need received aid; of those 27% had need fully met. ***Average percent of need met:*** 83% (excluding resources awarded to replace EFC). ***Average financial aid package:*** $25,638 (excluding resources awarded to replace EFC). 29% of all full-time undergraduates had no need and received non-need-based gift aid.

GIFT AID (NEED-BASED) ***Total amount:*** $22,367,404 (12% federal, 8% state, 74% institutional, 6% external sources). ***Receiving aid:*** Freshmen: 42% (315); all full-time undergraduates: 39% (1,032). ***Average award:*** Freshmen: $23,709; Undergraduates: $21,957. ***Scholarships, grants, and awards:*** Federal Pell, FSEOG, state, private, college/university gift aid from institutional funds, National Smart Grant, Academic Competitiveness Grant.

GIFT AID (NON-NEED-BASED) ***Total amount:*** $18,380,180 (23% state, 76% institutional, 1% external sources). ***Receiving aid:*** Freshmen: 35% (264). Undergraduates: 32% (867). ***Average award:*** Freshmen: $15,360. Undergraduates: $14,732. ***Scholarships, grants, and awards by category:*** *Academic interests/achievement:* $15,994,411 total: area/ethnic studies, biological sciences, business, communication, computer science, education, engineering/technologies, English, foreign languages, general academic interests/achievements, health fields, humanities, international studies, mathematics, military science, physical sciences, premedicine, religion/biblical studies, social sciences. *Creative arts/performance:* 315 awards ($1,359,361 total): art/fine arts, creative writing, music, theater/drama. *Special achievements/activities:* 36 awards ($160,420 total): community service, leadership, religious involvement. *Special characteristics:* 1,298 awards ($8,701,219 total): children of faculty/staff, ethnic background, international students, local/state students, relatives of clergy, religious affiliation, veterans. ***Tuition waivers:*** Full or partial for employees or children of employees. ***ROTC:*** Army.

LOANS ***Student loans:*** $7,806,260 (73% need-based, 27% non-need-based). 45% of past graduating class borrowed through all loan programs. *Average indebtedness per student:* $24,325. ***Average need-based loan:*** Freshmen: $4102. Undergraduates: $5929. ***Parent loans:*** $3,210,579 (67% need-based, 33% non-need-based). ***Programs:*** FFEL (Subsidized and Unsubsidized Stafford, PLUS), Perkins, state, alternative loans.

WORK-STUDY ***Federal work-study:*** Total amount: $618,643; 420 jobs averaging $1482.

ATHLETIC AWARDS Total amount: $7,150,037 (41% need-based, 59% non-need-based).

APPLYING FOR FINANCIAL AID ***Required financial aid forms:*** FAFSA, CSS Financial Aid PROFILE, state aid form, South Carolina residents must complete required SC forms. ***Financial aid deadline:*** 1/15. ***Notification date:*** 3/15. Students must reply by 5/1.

CONTACT Forrest Stuart, Director of Financial Aid, Furman University, 3300 Poinsett Highway, Greenville, SC 29613, 864-294-2204. *Fax:* 864-294-3127. *E-mail:* forrest.stuart@furman.edu.

GALLAUDET UNIVERSITY

Washington, DC

ABOUT THE INSTITUTION Independent, coed. ***Awards:*** bachelor's, master's, and doctoral degrees and post-bachelor's certificates (undergraduate programs are open primarily to the hearing-impaired). 52 undergraduate majors. ***Total enrollment:*** 1,389. Undergraduates: 986. Freshmen: 181.

GIFT AID (NEED-BASED) ***Scholarships, grants, and awards:*** Federal Pell, FSEOG, state, private, college/university gift aid from institutional funds.

LOANS ***Programs:*** FFEL (Subsidized and Unsubsidized Stafford, PLUS), Perkins.

WORK-STUDY ***Federal work-study:*** Total amount: $43,031.

APPLYING FOR FINANCIAL AID ***Required financial aid forms:*** FAFSA, institution's own form.

CONTACT Mrs. Nancy C. Goodman, Director of Financial Aid, Gallaudet University, 800 Florida Avenue, NE, Washington, DC 20002-3695, 202-651-5290 or toll-free 800-995-0550 (out-of-state). *Fax:* 202-651-5740.

GANNON UNIVERSITY

Erie, PA

Tuition & fees: $22,662 | **Average undergraduate aid package: $18,127**

ABOUT THE INSTITUTION Independent Roman Catholic, coed. ***Awards:*** associate, bachelor's, master's, and doctoral degrees and post-bachelor's and post-master's certificates (associate). 62 undergraduate majors. ***Total enrollment:*** 4,197. Undergraduates: 2,824. Freshmen: 634. Federal methodology is used as a basis for awarding need-based institutional aid.

UNDERGRADUATE EXPENSES for 2008–09 ***Application fee:*** $25. ***Comprehensive fee:*** $31,372 includes full-time tuition ($22,160), mandatory fees ($502), and room and board ($8710). ***College room only:*** $4670. Full-time tuition and fees vary according to class time and program. Room and board charges vary according to board plan and housing facility. ***Part-time tuition:*** $685 per credit hour. ***Part-time fees:*** $16 per credit hour. Part-time tuition and fees vary according to class time and program. ***Payment plans:*** Installment, deferred payment.

FRESHMAN FINANCIAL AID (Fall 2008, est.) 601 applied for aid; of those 88% were deemed to have need. 100% of freshmen with need received aid; of those 35% had need fully met. ***Average percent of need met:*** 77% (excluding resources awarded to replace EFC). ***Average financial aid package:*** $17,102 (excluding resources awarded to replace EFC). 14% of all full-time freshmen had no need and received non-need-based gift aid.

UNDERGRADUATE FINANCIAL AID (Fall 2008, est.) 2,205 applied for aid; of those 90% were deemed to have need. 99% of undergraduates with need received aid; of those 36% had need fully met. ***Average percent of need met:*** 78% (excluding resources awarded to replace EFC). ***Average financial aid package:*** $18,127 (excluding resources awarded to replace EFC). 13% of all full-time undergraduates had no need and received non-need-based gift aid.

GIFT AID (NEED-BASED) ***Total amount:*** $24,352,665 (13% federal, 13% state, 69% institutional, 5% external sources). ***Receiving aid:*** Freshmen: 82% (513); all full-time undergraduates: 82% (1,924). ***Average award:*** Freshmen: $13,599; Undergraduates: $13,780. ***Scholarships, grants, and awards:*** Federal Pell, FSEOG, state, private, college/university gift aid from institutional funds, Federal Nursing.

GIFT AID (NON-NEED-BASED) ***Total amount:*** $2,915,020 (1% federal, 92% institutional, 7% external sources). ***Receiving aid:*** Freshmen: 17% (105). Undergraduates: 14% (326). ***Average award:*** Freshmen: $7953. Undergraduates: $7260. ***Scholarships, grants, and awards by category:*** *Academic interests/achievement:* 1,300 awards ($8,039,548 total): biological sciences, business, education, engineering/technologies, English, foreign languages, general academic interests/achievements, humanities, international studies, mathematics, premedicine, religion/biblical studies, social sciences. *Creative arts/performance:* 75 awards ($119,000 total): music, performing arts, theater/drama. *Special achievements/activities:* 1,558 awards ($2,272,750 total): community service, leadership. *Special characteristics:* 613 awards ($1,007,967 total): adult students, ethnic background, international students, members of minority groups, religious affiliation. ***Tuition waivers:*** Full or partial for employees or children of employees, senior citizens. ***ROTC:*** Army.

LOANS ***Student loans:*** $18,084,282 (71% need-based, 29% non-need-based). 91% of past graduating class borrowed through all loan programs. *Average indebtedness per student:* $26,170. ***Average need-based loan:*** Freshmen: $3347. Undergraduates: $4278. ***Parent loans:*** $3,171,306 (87% need-based, 13% non-need-based). ***Programs:*** FFEL (Subsidized and Unsubsidized Stafford, PLUS), Perkins, Federal Nursing.

WORK-STUDY ***Federal work-study:*** Total amount: $811,360; 553 jobs averaging $2300. ***State or other work-study/employment:*** Total amount: $261,340 (100% non-need-based). 156 part-time jobs averaging $1988.

ATHLETIC AWARDS Total amount: $2,904,410 (68% need-based, 32% non-need-based).

APPLYING FOR FINANCIAL AID ***Required financial aid forms:*** FAFSA, institution's own form. ***Financial aid deadline (priority):*** 3/15. ***Notification date:*** Continuous.

CONTACT Ms. Sharon Krahe, Director of Financial Aid, Gannon University, 109 University Square, Erie, PA 16541, 814-871-7670 or toll-free 800-GANNONU. *Fax:* 814-871-5826. *E-mail:* krahe001@gannon.edu.

GARDNER-WEBB UNIVERSITY

Boiling Springs, NC

Tuition & fees: $20,200 **Average undergraduate aid package: $16,481**

ABOUT THE INSTITUTION Independent Baptist, coed. ***Awards:*** associate, bachelor's, master's, doctoral, and first professional degrees. 54 undergraduate majors. ***Total enrollment:*** 3,892. Undergraduates: 2,646. Freshmen: 441. Federal methodology is used as a basis for awarding need-based institutional aid.

UNDERGRADUATE EXPENSES for 2008–09 ***Application fee:*** $40. ***One-time required fee:*** $75. ***Comprehensive fee:*** $26,700 includes full-time tuition ($19,810), mandatory fees ($390), and room and board ($6500). ***College room only:*** $3330. Full-time tuition and fees vary according to degree level and program. Room and board charges vary according to board plan and housing facility. ***Part-time tuition:*** $328 per semester hour. Part-time tuition and fees vary according to course load. ***Payment plan:*** Installment.

FRESHMAN FINANCIAL AID (Fall 2008, est.) 419 applied for aid; of those 81% were deemed to have need. 100% of freshmen with need received aid; of those 32% had need fully met. ***Average percent of need met:*** 76% (excluding resources awarded to replace EFC). ***Average financial aid package:*** $17,575 (excluding resources awarded to replace EFC).

UNDERGRADUATE FINANCIAL AID (Fall 2008, est.) 1,236 applied for aid; of those 88% were deemed to have need. 100% of undergraduates with need received aid; of those 26% had need fully met. ***Average percent of need met:*** 72% (excluding resources awarded to replace EFC). ***Average financial aid package:*** $16,481 (excluding resources awarded to replace EFC).

GIFT AID (NEED-BASED) ***Total amount:*** $10,682,844 (20% federal, 38% state, 39% institutional, 3% external sources). ***Receiving aid:*** Freshmen: 325; all full-time undergraduates: 865. ***Average award:*** Freshmen: $9624; Undergraduates: $7605. ***Scholarships, grants, and awards:*** Federal Pell, FSEOG, state, private, college/university gift aid from institutional funds.

GIFT AID (NON-NEED-BASED) ***Total amount:*** $2,444,676 (15% state, 84% institutional, 1% external sources). ***Receiving aid:*** Freshmen: 260. Undergraduates: 759. ***Average award:*** Freshmen: $7149. Undergraduates: $7002. ***Scholarships, grants, and awards by category:*** *Academic interests/achievement:* biological sciences, business, communication, computer science, education, English, foreign languages, general academic interests/achievements, health fields, humanities, mathematics, physical sciences, premedicine, religion/biblical studies, social sciences. *Creative arts/performance:* music, theater/drama. *Special achievements/activities:* cheerleading/drum major, religious involvement. *Special characteristics:* children of faculty/staff, handicapped students, local/state students, members of minority groups, out-of-state students, previous college experience, relatives of clergy. ***Tuition waivers:*** Full or partial for employees or children of employees, senior citizens. ***ROTC:*** Army.

LOANS ***Student loans:*** $7,972,085 (94% need-based, 6% non-need-based). ***Average need-based loan:*** Freshmen: $3463. Undergraduates: $4314. ***Parent loans:*** $1,713,979 (84% need-based, 16% non-need-based). ***Programs:*** FFEL (Subsidized and Unsubsidized Stafford, PLUS), Perkins, state, alternative loans.

WORK-STUDY ***Federal work-study:*** Total amount: $306,364; jobs available. ***State or other work-study/employment:*** Total amount: $221,656 (80% need-based, 20% non-need-based). Part-time jobs available.

ATHLETIC AWARDS Total amount: $4,728,339 (55% need-based, 45% non-need-based).

APPLYING FOR FINANCIAL AID ***Required financial aid forms:*** FAFSA, state aid form. ***Financial aid deadline (priority):*** 3/15. ***Notification date:*** Continuous.

CONTACT Summer Robertson, Director of Financial Planning, Gardner-Webb University, PO Box 955, Boiling Springs, NC 28017, 704-406-4243 or toll-free 800-253-6472. *Fax:* 704-406-4102.

GENEVA COLLEGE

Beaver Falls, PA

Tuition & fees: $21,400 **Average undergraduate aid package: $16,582**

ABOUT THE INSTITUTION Independent religious, coed. ***Awards:*** associate, bachelor's, and master's degrees (also offers non-traditional programs with significant enrollment not reflected in profile). 38 undergraduate majors. ***Total enrollment:*** 1,555. Undergraduates: 1,392. Freshmen: 386. Federal methodology is used as a basis for awarding need-based institutional aid.

UNDERGRADUATE EXPENSES for 2009–10 ***Application fee:*** $40. ***Comprehensive fee:*** $29,170 includes full-time tuition ($21,400) and room and board ($7770). ***Part-time tuition:*** $715 per credit.

FRESHMAN FINANCIAL AID (Fall 2008, est.) 354 applied for aid; of those 90% were deemed to have need. 100% of freshmen with need received aid; of those 18% had need fully met. ***Average percent of need met:*** 81% (excluding resources awarded to replace EFC). ***Average financial aid package:*** $17,166 (excluding resources awarded to replace EFC). 13% of all full-time freshmen had no need and received non-need-based gift aid.

UNDERGRADUATE FINANCIAL AID (Fall 2008, est.) 1,198 applied for aid; of those 91% were deemed to have need. 100% of undergraduates with need received aid; of those 18% had need fully met. ***Average percent of need met:*** 77% (excluding resources awarded to replace EFC). ***Average financial aid package:*** $16,582 (excluding resources awarded to replace EFC). 15% of all full-time undergraduates had no need and received non-need-based gift aid.

GIFT AID (NEED-BASED) ***Total amount:*** $12,874,077 (15% federal, 16% state, 65% institutional, 4% external sources). ***Receiving aid:*** Freshmen: 83% (317); all full-time undergraduates: 82% (1,087). ***Average award:*** Freshmen: $13,070; Undergraduates: $12,111. ***Scholarships, grants, and awards:*** Federal Pell, FSEOG, state, private, college/university gift aid from institutional funds.

GIFT AID (NON-NEED-BASED) ***Total amount:*** $1,719,432 (3% state, 91% institutional, 6% external sources). ***Receiving aid:*** Freshmen: 8% (30). Undergraduates: 8% (100). ***Average award:*** Freshmen: $6292. Undergraduates: $6459. ***Scholarships, grants, and awards by category:*** *Academic interests/achievement:* engineering/technologies, general academic interests/achievements, religion/biblical studies. *Creative arts/performance:* music. *Special characteristics:* children of faculty/staff, religious affiliation. ***ROTC:*** Army cooperative.

LOANS ***Student loans:*** $9,106,504 (72% need-based, 28% non-need-based). 95% of past graduating class borrowed through all loan programs. *Average indebtedness per student:* $29,827. ***Average need-based loan:*** Freshmen: $3791. Undergraduates: $4240. ***Parent loans:*** $1,258,245 (34% need-based, 66% non-need-based). ***Programs:*** FFEL (Subsidized and Unsubsidized Stafford, PLUS), Perkins.

WORK-STUDY ***Federal work-study:*** Total amount: $250,000; jobs available (averaging $2000).

ATHLETIC AWARDS Total amount: $132,325 (78% need-based, 22% non-need-based).

APPLYING FOR FINANCIAL AID ***Required financial aid form:*** FAFSA. ***Financial aid deadline (priority):*** 3/15. ***Notification date:*** Continuous. Students must reply within 4 weeks of notification.

CONTACT Mr. Steve Bell, Director of Financial Aid, Geneva College, 3200 College Avenue, Beaver Falls, PA 15010-3599, 800-847-8255. *Fax:* 724-847-6776. *E-mail:* financialaid@geneva.edu.

GEORGE FOX UNIVERSITY

Newberg, OR

Tuition & fees: $25,190 **Average undergraduate aid package: $22,872**

ABOUT THE INSTITUTION Independent Friends, coed. ***Awards:*** bachelor's, master's, doctoral, and first professional degrees and post-bachelor's and post-master's certificates. 40 undergraduate majors. ***Total enrollment:*** 3,383. Undergraduates: 1,980. Freshmen: 398. Both federal and institutional methodology are used as a basis for awarding need-based institutional aid.

UNDERGRADUATE EXPENSES for 2008–09 ***Application fee:*** $40. ***Comprehensive fee:*** $33,190 includes full-time tuition ($24,870), mandatory fees ($320), and room and board ($8000). ***College room only:*** $4500. Room and board charges vary according to board plan. ***Part-time tuition:*** $750 per hour. Part-time tuition and fees vary according to course load. ***Payment plan:*** Installment.

FRESHMAN FINANCIAL AID (Fall 2008, est.) 351 applied for aid; of those 89% were deemed to have need. 100% of freshmen with need received aid; of those 44% had need fully met. ***Average percent of need met:*** 89% (excluding resources awarded to replace EFC). ***Average financial aid package:*** $23,459 (excluding resources awarded to replace EFC). 18% of all full-time freshmen had no need and received non-need-based gift aid.

UNDERGRADUATE FINANCIAL AID (Fall 2008, est.) 1,416 applied for aid; of those 90% were deemed to have need. 100% of undergraduates with need received aid; of those 32% had need fully met. ***Average percent of need met:*** 87% (excluding resources awarded to replace EFC). ***Average financial aid package:*** $22,872 (excluding resources awarded to replace EFC). 16% of all full-time undergraduates had no need and received non-need-based gift aid.

GIFT AID (NEED-BASED) ***Total amount:*** $16,650,586 (11% federal, 7% state, 77% institutional, 5% external sources). ***Receiving aid:*** Freshmen: 81% (314); all full-time undergraduates: 77% (1,270). ***Average award:*** Freshmen: $9095; Undergraduates: $9021. ***Scholarships, grants, and awards:*** Federal Pell, FSEOG, state, private, college/university gift aid from institutional funds, Academic Competitiveness Grant, National Smart Grant.

GIFT AID (NON-NEED-BASED) ***Total amount:*** $2,863,705 (1% state, 86% institutional, 13% external sources). ***Receiving aid:*** Freshmen: 67% (261). Undergraduates: 64% (1,061). ***Average award:*** Freshmen: $786. Undergraduates: $728. ***Scholarships, grants, and awards by category:*** *Academic interests/achievement:* 1,230 awards ($5,616,521 total): biological sciences, computer science, education, engineering/technologies, general academic interests/achievements, mathematics, physical sciences, religion/biblical studies. *Creative arts/performance:* 112 awards ($147,780 total): art/fine arts, debating, music, theater/drama. *Special achievements/activities:* 137 awards ($135,000 total): leadership, religious involvement. *Special characteristics:* 830 awards ($2,584,074 total): children and siblings of alumni, children of faculty/staff, ethnic background, international students, members of minority groups, out-of-state students, relatives of clergy, religious affiliation. ***Tuition waivers:*** Full or partial for employees or children of employees, senior citizens. ***ROTC:*** Air Force cooperative.

LOANS ***Student loans:*** $11,938,755 (74% need-based, 26% non-need-based). 82% of past graduating class borrowed through all loan programs. *Average indebtedness per student:* $23,540. ***Average need-based loan:*** Freshmen: $3402. Undergraduates: $4735. ***Parent loans:*** $2,915,065 (44% need-based, 56% non-need-based). ***Programs:*** Federal Direct (Subsidized and Unsubsidized Stafford, PLUS), FFEL (Subsidized and Unsubsidized Stafford, PLUS), Perkins, alternative loans.

WORK-STUDY ***Federal work-study:*** Total amount: $329,023; 542 jobs averaging $2115. ***State or other work-study/employment:*** Total amount: $2,005,765 (100% non-need-based). Part-time jobs available.

APPLYING FOR FINANCIAL AID ***Required financial aid forms:*** FAFSA, state aid form. ***Financial aid deadline (priority):*** 2/1. ***Notification date:*** Continuous beginning 3/1. Students must reply by 5/1 or within 6 weeks of notification.

CONTACT James Oshiro, Associate Director of Financial Services, George Fox University, 414 North Meridian Street, Newberg, OR 97132-2697, 503-554-2290 or toll-free 800-765-4369. *Fax:* 503-554-3880. *E-mail:* sfs@georgefox.edu.

GEORGE MASON UNIVERSITY

Fairfax, VA

Tuition & fees (VA res): $7512 **Average undergraduate aid package: $10,140**

ABOUT THE INSTITUTION State-supported, coed. ***Awards:*** bachelor's, master's, doctoral, and first professional degrees and post-bachelor's and post-master's certificates. 56 undergraduate majors. ***Total enrollment:*** 30,714. Undergraduates: 18,809. Freshmen: 2,558. Federal methodology is used as a basis for awarding need-based institutional aid.

UNDERGRADUATE EXPENSES for 2008–09 ***Application fee:*** $70. ***Tuition, state resident:*** full-time $5526; part-time $230.25 per credit. ***Tuition, nonresident:*** full-time $20,490; part-time $853.75 per credit. ***Required fees:*** full-time $1986; $82.75 per credit. Full-time tuition and fees vary according to course load. Part-time tuition and fees vary according to course load. ***College room and board:*** $7360; ***Room only:*** $4200. Room and board charges vary according to board plan and housing facility. ***Payment plans:*** Installment, deferred payment.

FRESHMAN FINANCIAL AID (Fall 2008, est.) 1,789 applied for aid; of those 63% were deemed to have need. 96% of freshmen with need received aid; of those 13% had need fully met. ***Average percent of need met:*** 72% (excluding resources awarded to replace EFC). ***Average financial aid package:*** $10,791 (excluding resources awarded to replace EFC). 3% of all full-time freshmen had no need and received non-need-based gift aid.

UNDERGRADUATE FINANCIAL AID (Fall 2008, est.) 8,088 applied for aid; of those 73% were deemed to have need. 96% of undergraduates with need received aid; of those 12% had need fully met. ***Average percent of need met:*** 68% (excluding resources awarded to replace EFC). ***Average financial aid package:*** $10,140 (excluding resources awarded to replace EFC). 3% of all full-time undergraduates had no need and received non-need-based gift aid.

GIFT AID (NEED-BASED) ***Total amount:*** $27,737,221 (46% federal, 44% state, 10% institutional). ***Receiving aid:*** Freshmen: 35% (885); all full-time undergraduates: 30% (4,223). ***Average award:*** Freshmen: $6432; Undergraduates: $6019. ***Scholarships, grants, and awards:*** Federal Pell, FSEOG, state, private, college/university gift aid from institutional funds.

GIFT AID (NON-NEED-BASED) ***Total amount:*** $6,164,539 (67% institutional, 33% external sources). ***Receiving aid:*** Freshmen: 14% (345). Undergraduates: 7% (995). ***Average award:*** Freshmen: $7028. Undergraduates: $5668. ***Scholarships, grants, and awards by category:*** *Academic interests/achievement:* 1,061 awards ($4,139,341 total): general academic interests/achievements. *Creative arts/performance:* general creative arts/performance. *Special characteristics:* general special characteristics. ***Tuition waivers:*** Full or partial for employees or children of employees, senior citizens. ***ROTC:*** Army, Naval cooperative, Air Force cooperative.

LOANS ***Student loans:*** $54,892,665 (63% need-based, 37% non-need-based). 54% of past graduating class borrowed through all loan programs. *Average indebtedness per student:* $18,547. ***Average need-based loan:*** Freshmen: $3584.

Undergraduates: $4449. ***Parent loans:*** $8,064,860 (29% need-based, 71% non-need-based). ***Programs:*** FFEL (Subsidized and Unsubsidized Stafford, PLUS), Perkins, Federal Nursing.

WORK-STUDY ***Federal work-study:*** Total amount: $490,617; 321 jobs averaging $1527.

ATHLETIC AWARDS Total amount: $3,350,559 (100% non-need-based).

APPLYING FOR FINANCIAL AID ***Required financial aid form:*** FAFSA. ***Financial aid deadline (priority):*** 3/1. ***Notification date:*** Continuous beginning 4/1. Students must reply within 3 weeks of notification.

CONTACT Office of Student Financial Aid, George Mason University, Mail Stop 3B5, Fairfax, VA 22030-4444, 703-993-2353. *Fax:* 703-993-2350. *E-mail:* finaid@gmu.edu.

GEORGE MEANY CENTER FOR LABOR STUDIES–THE NATIONAL LABOR COLLEGE

Silver Spring, MD

CONTACT Financial Aid Office, George Meany Center for Labor Studies–The National Labor College, 10000 New Hampshire Avenue, Silver Spring, MD 20903, 301-431-6400 or toll-free 800-GMC-4CDP.

GEORGETOWN COLLEGE

Georgetown, KY

Tuition & fees: $24,150 **Average undergraduate aid package: $22,493**

ABOUT THE INSTITUTION Independent religious, coed. ***Awards:*** bachelor's and master's degrees. 32 undergraduate majors. ***Total enrollment:*** 1,856. Undergraduates: 1,338. Freshmen: 379. Federal methodology is used as a basis for awarding need-based institutional aid.

UNDERGRADUATE EXPENSES for 2008–09 ***Application fee:*** $30. ***Comprehensive fee:*** $30,850 includes full-time tuition ($24,150) and room and board ($6700). ***College room only:*** $3280. Room and board charges vary according to board plan and housing facility. ***Part-time tuition:*** $1000 per hour. ***Payment plan:*** Deferred payment.

FRESHMAN FINANCIAL AID (Fall 2008, est.) 324 applied for aid; of those 87% were deemed to have need. 100% of freshmen with need received aid; of those 51% had need fully met. ***Average percent of need met:*** 92% (excluding resources awarded to replace EFC). ***Average financial aid package:*** $24,150 (excluding resources awarded to replace EFC). 20% of all full-time freshmen had no need and received non-need-based gift aid.

UNDERGRADUATE FINANCIAL AID (Fall 2008, est.) 1,025 applied for aid; of those 89% were deemed to have need. 100% of undergraduates with need received aid; of those 47% had need fully met. ***Average percent of need met:*** 89% (excluding resources awarded to replace EFC). ***Average financial aid package:*** $22,493 (excluding resources awarded to replace EFC). 22% of all full-time undergraduates had no need and received non-need-based gift aid.

GIFT AID (NEED-BASED) ***Total amount:*** $14,524,072 (9% federal, 15% state, 74% institutional, 2% external sources). ***Receiving aid:*** Freshmen: 75% (283); all full-time undergraduates: 70% (911). ***Average award:*** Freshmen: $21,085; Undergraduates: $18,877. ***Scholarships, grants, and awards:*** Federal Pell, FSEOG, state, private, college/university gift aid from institutional funds.

GIFT AID (NON-NEED-BASED) ***Total amount:*** $6,544,490 (1% federal, 26% state, 72% institutional, 1% external sources). ***Receiving aid:*** Freshmen: 21% (79). Undergraduates: 17% (224). ***Average award:*** Freshmen: $12,027. Undergraduates: $11,140. ***Scholarships, grants, and awards by category:*** *Academic interests/achievement:* 716 awards ($6,868,604 total): general academic interests/achievements. *Creative arts/performance:* 108 awards ($228,195 total): art/fine arts, music, performing arts, theater/drama. *Special achievements/activities:* 253 awards ($478,420 total): junior miss, leadership, religious involvement. *Special characteristics:* 376 awards ($1,119,440 total): children of faculty/staff, local/state students, out-of-state students, relatives of clergy, religious affiliation. ***Tuition waivers:*** Full or partial for children of alumni, employees or children of employees. ***ROTC:*** Army cooperative, Air Force cooperative.

LOANS ***Student loans:*** $6,184,341 (44% need-based, 56% non-need-based). 66% of past graduating class borrowed through all loan programs. *Average indebtedness per student:* $22,241. ***Average need-based loan:*** Freshmen: $3686. Undergraduates: $4697. ***Parent loans:*** $1,353,362 (100% non-need-based). ***Programs:*** FFEL (Subsidized and Unsubsidized Stafford, PLUS), Perkins, college/university.

WORK-STUDY ***Federal work-study:*** Total amount: $575,474; 531 jobs averaging $1075. ***State or other work-study/employment:*** Part-time jobs available.

ATHLETIC AWARDS Total amount: $1,639,825 (58% need-based, 42% non-need-based).

APPLYING FOR FINANCIAL AID ***Required financial aid forms:*** FAFSA, institution's own form. ***Financial aid deadline (priority):*** 2/15. ***Notification date:*** Continuous beginning 3/1. Students must reply by 5/1.

CONTACT Rhyan Conyers, Director of Financial Planning, Georgetown College, 400 East College Street, Georgetown, KY 40324-1696, 502-863-8027 or toll-free 800-788-9985. *Fax:* 502-868-7733. *E-mail:* financialaid@georgetowncollege.edu.

GEORGETOWN UNIVERSITY

Washington, DC

Tuition & fees: $38,122 **Average undergraduate aid package: $34,307**

ABOUT THE INSTITUTION Independent Roman Catholic (Jesuit), coed. ***Awards:*** bachelor's, master's, doctoral, and first professional degrees. 46 undergraduate majors. ***Total enrollment:*** 15,318. Undergraduates: 7,092. Freshmen: 1,571.

UNDERGRADUATE EXPENSES for 2008–09 ***Application fee:*** $65. ***Comprehensive fee:*** $50,275 includes full-time tuition ($37,536), mandatory fees ($586), and room and board ($12,153).

FRESHMAN FINANCIAL AID (Fall 2008, est.) 850 applied for aid; of those 74% were deemed to have need. 100% of freshmen with need received aid; of those 100% had need fully met. ***Average percent of need met:*** 100% (excluding resources awarded to replace EFC). ***Average financial aid package:*** $35,530 (excluding resources awarded to replace EFC).

UNDERGRADUATE FINANCIAL AID (Fall 2008, est.) 3,123 applied for aid; of those 83% were deemed to have need. 100% of undergraduates with need received aid. ***Average percent of need met:*** 100% (excluding resources awarded to replace EFC). ***Average financial aid package:*** $34,307 (excluding resources awarded to replace EFC).

GIFT AID (NEED-BASED) ***Total amount:*** $71,910,000 (8% federal, 88% institutional, 4% external sources). ***Receiving aid:*** Freshmen: 40% (628); all full-time undergraduates: 37% (2,500). ***Average award:*** Freshmen: $28,100; Undergraduates: $28,250. ***Scholarships, grants, and awards:*** Federal Pell, FSEOG, state, private, college/university gift aid from institutional funds.

GIFT AID (NON-NEED-BASED) ***Total amount:*** $4,130,000 (49% federal, 3% institutional, 48% external sources). ***Receiving aid:*** Freshmen: 8% (125). Undergraduates: 7% (500). ***Scholarships, grants, and awards by category:*** *Special characteristics:* children of faculty/staff. ***ROTC:*** Army, Naval cooperative, Air Force cooperative.

LOANS ***Student loans:*** $21,200,000 (43% need-based, 57% non-need-based). 44% of past graduating class borrowed through all loan programs. *Average indebtedness per student:* $23,333. ***Average need-based loan:*** Freshmen: $3000. Undergraduates: $3883. ***Parent loans:*** $12,000,000 (100% non-need-based). ***Programs:*** FFEL (Subsidized and Unsubsidized Stafford, PLUS), Perkins, Federal Nursing, alternative loans.

WORK-STUDY ***Federal work-study:*** Total amount: $6,500,000; 2,000 jobs averaging $3300.

ATHLETIC AWARDS Total amount: $6,300,000 (25% need-based, 75% non-need-based).

APPLYING FOR FINANCIAL AID ***Required financial aid forms:*** FAFSA, CSS Financial Aid PROFILE, business/farm supplement. ***Financial aid deadline:*** 2/1. ***Notification date:*** 4/1. Students must reply by 5/1 or within 2 weeks of notification.

CONTACT Ms. Patricia A. McWade, Dean of Student Financial Services, Georgetown University, 37th and O Street, NW, Box 1252, Washington, DC 20057, 202-687-4547. *Fax:* 202-687-6542. *E-mail:* mcwadep@georgetown.edu.

THE GEORGE WASHINGTON UNIVERSITY

Washington, DC

Tuition & fees: $41,655 **Average undergraduate aid package: $35,780**

ABOUT THE INSTITUTION Independent, coed. ***Awards:*** associate, bachelor's, master's, doctoral, and first professional degrees and post-bachelor's and post-master's certificates. 82 undergraduate majors. ***Total enrollment:*** 25,116. Undergraduates: 10,590. Freshmen: 2,461. Federal methodology is used as a basis for awarding need-based institutional aid.

UNDERGRADUATE EXPENSES for 2009–10 ***Application fee:*** $65. ***Comprehensive fee:*** $51,775 includes full-time tuition ($41,610), mandatory fees ($45), and room and board ($10,120). ***College room only:*** $6720.

FRESHMAN FINANCIAL AID (Fall 2007) 1,028 applied for aid; of those 75% were deemed to have need. 94% of freshmen with need received aid; of those 68% had need fully met. ***Average percent of need met:*** 92% (excluding resources awarded to replace EFC). ***Average financial aid package:*** $35,311 (excluding resources awarded to replace EFC). 16% of all full-time freshmen had no need and received non-need-based gift aid.

UNDERGRADUATE FINANCIAL AID (Fall 2007) 4,688 applied for aid; of those 82% were deemed to have need. 98% of undergraduates with need received aid; of those 68% had need fully met. ***Average percent of need met:*** 92% (excluding resources awarded to replace EFC). ***Average financial aid package:*** $35,780 (excluding resources awarded to replace EFC). 24% of all full-time undergraduates had no need and received non-need-based gift aid.

GIFT AID (NEED-BASED) ***Total amount:*** $93,194,952 (6% federal, 94% institutional). ***Receiving aid:*** Freshmen: 33% (706); all full-time undergraduates: 37% (3,587). ***Average award:*** Freshmen: $22,804; Undergraduates: $22,321. ***Scholarships, grants, and awards:*** Federal Pell, FSEOG, state, college/university gift aid from institutional funds.

GIFT AID (NON-NEED-BASED) ***Total amount:*** $19,874,303 (100% institutional). ***Receiving aid:*** Freshmen: 6% (128). Undergraduates: 9% (853). ***Average award:*** Freshmen: $19,014. Undergraduates: $19,740. ***ROTC:*** Army cooperative, Naval, Air Force cooperative.

LOANS ***Student loans:*** $34,650,150 (100% need-based). 49% of past graduating class borrowed through all loan programs. *Average indebtedness per student:* $30,817. ***Average need-based loan:*** Freshmen: $5561. Undergraduates: $7589. ***Parent loans:*** $24,686,114 (100% need-based). ***Programs:*** FFEL (Subsidized and Unsubsidized Stafford, PLUS), Perkins.

WORK-STUDY ***Federal work-study:*** Total amount: $2,777,310; jobs available.

ATHLETIC AWARDS Total amount: $5,212,933 (8% need-based, 92% non-need-based).

APPLYING FOR FINANCIAL AID ***Required financial aid forms:*** FAFSA, CSS Financial Aid PROFILE. ***Financial aid deadline:*** 2/1 (priority: 2/1). ***Notification date:*** Continuous beginning 3/24. Students must reply by 5/1.

CONTACT Dan Small, Director of Student Financial Assistance, The George Washington University, 2121 Eye Street, NW, Rice Hall, 3rd Floor, Washington, DC 20052, 202-994-6620 or toll-free 800-447-3765 (in-state). *Fax:* 202-994-0906. *E-mail:* finaid@gwu.edu.

GEORGIA COLLEGE & STATE UNIVERSITY

Milledgeville, GA

Tuition & fees (GA res): $5476 **Average undergraduate aid package: $6585**

ABOUT THE INSTITUTION State-supported, coed. ***Awards:*** bachelor's and master's degrees and post-master's certificates. 36 undergraduate majors. ***Total enrollment:*** 6,506. Undergraduates: 5,490. Freshmen: 1,094. Federal methodology is used as a basis for awarding need-based institutional aid.

UNDERGRADUATE EXPENSES for 2008–09 ***Application fee:*** $40. ***Tuition, state resident:*** full-time $4546; part-time $190 per credit. ***Tuition, nonresident:*** full-time $18,178; part-time $758 per credit. ***Required fees:*** full-time $930; $465 per term. Full-time tuition and fees vary according to course load and student level. ***College room and board:*** $7698; ***Room only:*** $4308. Room and board charges vary according to board plan and housing facility. ***Payment plans:*** Guaranteed tuition, installment.

FRESHMAN FINANCIAL AID (Fall 2008, est.) 1,044 applied for aid; of those 40% were deemed to have need. 90% of freshmen with need received aid. ***Average percent of need met:*** 34% (excluding resources awarded to replace EFC). ***Average financial aid package:*** $6658 (excluding resources awarded to replace EFC). 1% of all full-time freshmen had no need and received non-need-based gift aid.

UNDERGRADUATE FINANCIAL AID (Fall 2008, est.) 4,465 applied for aid; of those 42% were deemed to have need. 97% of undergraduates with need received aid; of those .1% had need fully met. ***Average percent of need met:*** 43% (excluding resources awarded to replace EFC). ***Average financial aid package:*** $6585 (excluding resources awarded to replace EFC). 2% of all full-time undergraduates had no need and received non-need-based gift aid.

GIFT AID (NEED-BASED) ***Total amount:*** $3,066,672 (100% federal). ***Receiving aid:*** Freshmen: 11% (123); all full-time undergraduates: 15% (737). ***Average award:*** Freshmen: $3620; Undergraduates: $3537. ***Scholarships, grants, and awards:*** Federal Pell, FSEOG, state, college/university gift aid from institutional funds.

GIFT AID (NON-NEED-BASED) ***Total amount:*** $17,844,326 (93% state, 4% institutional, 3% external sources). ***Receiving aid:*** Freshmen: 34% (370). Undergraduates: 35% (1,745). ***Average award:*** Freshmen: $1047. Undergraduates: $1637. ***Scholarships, grants, and awards by category:*** *Academic interests/achievement:* business, computer science, education, English, foreign languages, general academic interests/achievements, health fields, humanities, international studies, mathematics, physical sciences, social sciences. *Creative arts/performance:* applied art and design, art/fine arts, creative writing, journalism/publications, music, performing arts, theater/drama. *Special achievements/activities:* community service, general special achievements/activities, leadership. *Special characteristics:* adult students, children of faculty/staff, children with a deceased or disabled parent, handicapped students, international students, local/state students, members of minority groups, out-of-state students, religious affiliation. ***Tuition waivers:*** Full or partial for employees or children of employees, senior citizens. ***ROTC:*** Army cooperative.

LOANS ***Student loans:*** $17,845,349 (49% need-based, 51% non-need-based). 52% of past graduating class borrowed through all loan programs. *Average indebtedness per student:* $14,312. ***Average need-based loan:*** Freshmen: $3191. Undergraduates: $4242. ***Parent loans:*** $1,754,886 (100% non-need-based). ***Programs:*** Federal Direct (PLUS), FFEL (Subsidized and Unsubsidized Stafford, PLUS), Perkins, state, college/university.

WORK-STUDY ***Federal work-study:*** Total amount: $190,000; jobs available.

ATHLETIC AWARDS Total amount: $679,476 (100% non-need-based).

APPLYING FOR FINANCIAL AID ***Required financial aid form:*** FAFSA. ***Financial aid deadline:*** Continuous. ***Notification date:*** Continuous beginning 3/1. Students must reply within 2 weeks of notification.

CONTACT Mrs. Cathy Crawley, Director of Financial Aid, Georgia College & State University, Campus Box 30, Milledgeville, GA 31061, 478-445-5149 or toll-free 800-342-0471 (in-state). *Fax:* 478-445-0729. *E-mail:* cathy.crawley@gcsu.edu.

GEORGIA INSTITUTE OF TECHNOLOGY

Atlanta, GA

Tuition & fees (GA res): $6040 **Average undergraduate aid package: $10,462**

ABOUT THE INSTITUTION State-supported, coed, primarily men. ***Awards:*** bachelor's, master's, and doctoral degrees. 35 undergraduate majors. ***Total enrollment:*** 19,413. Undergraduates: 12,973. Freshmen: 2,640. Federal methodology is used as a basis for awarding need-based institutional aid.

UNDERGRADUATE EXPENSES for 2008–09 ***Application fee:*** $50. ***Tuition, state resident:*** full-time $4856; part-time $203 per hour. ***Tuition, nonresident:*** full-time $23,998; part-time $1000 per hour. ***Required fees:*** full-time $1184; $167 per hour or $592 per term. Full-time tuition and fees vary according to course load, reciprocity agreements, and student level. Part-time tuition and fees vary according to course load, reciprocity agreements, and student level. ***College room and board:*** $7694; ***Room only:*** $4526. Room and board charges vary according to board plan and housing facility. ***Payment plan:*** Guaranteed tuition.

FRESHMAN FINANCIAL AID (Fall 2008, est.) 1,976 applied for aid; of those 41% were deemed to have need. 96% of freshmen with need received aid; of those 55% had need fully met. ***Average percent of need met:*** 87% (excluding resources awarded to replace EFC). ***Average financial aid package:*** $11,254 (excluding resources awarded to replace EFC). 47% of all full-time freshmen had no need and received non-need-based gift aid.

UNDERGRADUATE FINANCIAL AID (Fall 2008, est.) 7,220 applied for aid; of those 55% were deemed to have need. 96% of undergraduates with need received aid; of those 53% had need fully met. ***Average percent of need met:*** 80% (excluding resources awarded to replace EFC). ***Average financial aid package:*** $10,462 (excluding resources awarded to replace EFC). 32% of all full-time undergraduates had no need and received non-need-based gift aid.

GIFT AID (NEED-BASED) ***Total amount:*** $26,349,819 (27% federal, 33% state, 35% institutional, 5% external sources). ***Receiving aid:*** Freshmen: 28% (735); all full-time undergraduates: 27% (3,237). ***Average award:*** Freshmen: $8947; Undergraduates: $7846. ***Scholarships, grants, and awards:*** Federal Pell, FSEOG, state, private, college/university gift aid from institutional funds, Wayne Clough Georgia Tech Promise Scholarship, Academic Competitiveness Grant & SMART.

GIFT AID (NON-NEED-BASED) ***Total amount:*** $27,288,975 (1% federal, 74% state, 12% institutional, 13% external sources). ***Receiving aid:*** Freshmen: 1% (38). Undergraduates: 3% (307). ***Average award:*** Freshmen: $6431. Undergraduates: $5799. ***Scholarships, grants, and awards by category:*** *Academic interests/achievement:* 1,910 awards ($7,972,997 total): architecture, biological sciences, computer science, engineering/technologies, general academic interests/achievements, physical sciences. *Special achievements/activities:* 251 awards ($2,827,013 total): leadership. ***Tuition waivers:*** Full or partial for employees or children of employees. ***ROTC:*** Army, Naval, Air Force.

LOANS ***Student loans:*** $31,595,893 (67% need-based, 33% non-need-based). 48% of past graduating class borrowed through all loan programs. *Average indebtedness per student:* $20,881. ***Average need-based loan:*** Freshmen: $4666. Undergraduates: $5177. ***Parent loans:*** $14,097,059 (58% need-based, 42% non-need-based). ***Programs:*** FFEL (Subsidized and Unsubsidized Stafford, PLUS), Perkins, college/university.

WORK-STUDY ***Federal work-study:*** Total amount: $764,015; 397 jobs averaging $2107.

ATHLETIC AWARDS Total amount: $4,810,006 (32% need-based, 68% non-need-based).

APPLYING FOR FINANCIAL AID ***Required financial aid forms:*** FAFSA, institution's own form. ***Financial aid deadline:*** 3/1 (priority: 3/1). ***Notification date:*** Continuous beginning 4/1. Students must reply by 5/1.

CONTACT Ms. Marie Mons, Director of Student Financial Planning and Services, Georgia Institute of Technology, 225 North Avenue, NW, Atlanta, GA 30332-0460, 404-894-4160. *Fax:* 404-894-7412. *E-mail:* marie.mons@finaid.gatech.edu.

GEORGIAN COURT UNIVERSITY

Lakewood, NJ

Tuition & fees: $23,360 **Average undergraduate aid package: $17,598**

ABOUT THE INSTITUTION Independent Roman Catholic, undergraduate: women only; graduate: coed. ***Awards:*** bachelor's and master's degrees and post-bachelor's and post-master's certificates. 28 undergraduate majors. ***Total enrollment:*** 3,189. Undergraduates: 2,067. Freshmen: 251. Federal methodology is used as a basis for awarding need-based institutional aid.

UNDERGRADUATE EXPENSES for 2008–09 ***Application fee:*** $40. ***Comprehensive fee:*** $32,472 includes full-time tuition ($22,160), mandatory fees ($1200), and room and board ($9112). ***Part-time tuition:*** $597 per credit. ***Part-time fees:*** $300 per term. ***Payment plan:*** Installment.

FRESHMAN FINANCIAL AID (Fall 2008, est.) 234 applied for aid; of those 91% were deemed to have need. 100% of freshmen with need received aid; of those 18% had need fully met. ***Average percent of need met:*** 79% (excluding resources awarded to replace EFC). ***Average financial aid package:*** $22,177 (excluding resources awarded to replace EFC). 15% of all full-time freshmen had no need and received non-need-based gift aid.

UNDERGRADUATE FINANCIAL AID (Fall 2008, est.) 1,313 applied for aid; of those 89% were deemed to have need. 99% of undergraduates with need received aid; of those 12% had need fully met. ***Average percent of need met:*** 71% (excluding resources awarded to replace EFC). ***Average financial aid package:*** $17,598 (excluding resources awarded to replace EFC). 12% of all full-time undergraduates had no need and received non-need-based gift aid.

GIFT AID (NEED-BASED) ***Total amount:*** $14,267,853 (18% federal, 35% state, 47% institutional). ***Receiving aid:*** Freshmen: 84% (212); all full-time undergraduates: 78% (1,105). ***Average award:*** Freshmen: $18,289; Undergraduates: $13,474. ***Scholarships, grants, and awards:*** Federal Pell, FSEOG, state, private, college/university gift aid from institutional funds.

GIFT AID (NON-NEED-BASED) ***Total amount:*** $1,370,860 (1% state, 96% institutional, 3% external sources). ***Receiving aid:*** Freshmen: 9% (22). Undergraduates: 6% (83). ***Average award:*** Freshmen: $6456. Undergraduates: $6271. ***Scholarships, grants, and awards by category:*** *Academic interests/achievement:* biological sciences, business, English, foreign languages, general academic interests/achievements, mathematics, physical sciences. *Creative arts/performance:* art/fine arts, creative writing, music. *Special achievements/activities:* general special achievements/activities. *Special characteristics:* children of faculty/staff, religious affiliation, spouses of current students, veterans. ***Tuition waivers:*** Full or partial for employees or children of employees.

LOANS ***Student loans:*** $13,152,428 (70% need-based, 30% non-need-based). 81% of past graduating class borrowed through all loan programs. *Average indebtedness per student:* $33,620. ***Average need-based loan:*** Freshmen: $3785. Undergraduates: $4983. ***Parent loans:*** $555,103 (30% need-based, 70% non-need-based). ***Programs:*** Federal Direct (Subsidized and Unsubsidized Stafford, PLUS), FFEL (Subsidized and Unsubsidized Stafford, PLUS), Perkins, state.

WORK-STUDY ***Federal work-study:*** Total amount: $414,949; 184 jobs averaging $1650. ***State or other work-study/employment:*** Total amount: $155,161 (17% need-based, 83% non-need-based). 85 part-time jobs averaging $1840.

ATHLETIC AWARDS Total amount: $764,095 (75% need-based, 25% non-need-based).

APPLYING FOR FINANCIAL AID ***Required financial aid forms:*** FAFSA, institution's own form. ***Financial aid deadline:*** Continuous. ***Notification date:*** Continuous beginning 2/1. Students must reply within 2 weeks of notification.

CONTACT Larry Sharp, Director of Financial Aid, Georgian Court University, 900 Lakewood Avenue, Lakewood, NJ 08701-2697, 732-987-2258 or toll-free 800-458-8422. *Fax:* 732-987-2012. *E-mail:* financialaid@georgian.edu.

GEORGIA SOUTHERN UNIVERSITY

Statesboro, GA

Tuition & fees (GA res): $4348 **Average undergraduate aid package: $7240**

ABOUT THE INSTITUTION State-supported, coed. ***Awards:*** bachelor's, master's, and doctoral degrees and post-master's certificates. 73 undergraduate majors. ***Total enrollment:*** 17,764. Undergraduates: 15,490. Freshmen: 3,131. Federal methodology is used as a basis for awarding need-based institutional aid.

UNDERGRADUATE EXPENSES for 2008–09 ***Application fee:*** $30. ***Tuition, state resident:*** full-time $3196; part-time $134 per semester hour. ***Tuition, nonresident:*** full-time $12,778; part-time $533 per semester hour. ***Required fees:*** full-time $1152; $576 per term. Full-time tuition and fees vary according to degree level, location, and program. Part-time tuition and fees vary according to course load, degree level, location, and program. ***College room and board:*** $7300; ***Room only:*** $4630. Room and board charges vary according to board plan and housing facility. ***Payment plan:*** Guaranteed tuition.

FRESHMAN FINANCIAL AID (Fall 2007) 2,750 applied for aid; of those 56% were deemed to have need. 97% of freshmen with need received aid; of those 16% had need fully met. ***Average percent of need met:*** 60% (excluding resources awarded to replace EFC). ***Average financial aid package:*** $6997 (excluding resources awarded to replace EFC). 6% of all full-time freshmen had no need and received non-need-based gift aid.

UNDERGRADUATE FINANCIAL AID (Fall 2007) 11,237 applied for aid; of those 61% were deemed to have need. 96% of undergraduates with need received aid; of those 14% had need fully met. ***Average percent of need met:*** 58% (excluding resources awarded to replace EFC). ***Average financial aid package:*** $7240 (excluding resources awarded to replace EFC). 3% of all full-time undergraduates had no need and received non-need-based gift aid.

GIFT AID (NEED-BASED) ***Total amount:*** $25,360,078 (52% federal, 43% state, 2% institutional, 3% external sources). ***Receiving aid:*** Freshmen: 41% (1,249); all full-time undergraduates: 39% (5,191). ***Average award:*** Freshmen: $5619; Undergraduates: $4923. ***Scholarships, grants, and awards:*** Federal Pell, FSEOG, state, private, college/university gift aid from institutional funds, HOPE Scholarships, TEACH Grant, Academic Competitiveness Grant, National Smart Grant.

GIFT AID (NON-NEED-BASED) ***Total amount:*** $11,623,644 (89% state, 7% institutional, 4% external sources). ***Receiving aid:*** Freshmen: 4% (128). Undergraduates: 3% (381). ***Average award:*** Freshmen: $2121. Undergraduates: $1661. ***Scholarships, grants, and awards by category:*** *Academic interests/achievement:* 725 awards ($1,029,967 total): biological sciences, business, communication, education, engineering/technologies, English, foreign languages, general academic interests/achievements, health fields, humanities, international studies, mathematics, military science, social sciences. *Creative arts/performance:* 67 awards ($70,750 total): art/fine arts, cinema/film/broadcasting, general creative arts/performance, music, theater/drama. *Special achievements/activities:* 255 awards ($207,300 total): cheerleading/drum major, community service, junior miss, leadership, memberships, religious involvement. *Special characteristics:* 10 awards ($8200 total): children and siblings of alumni, children of public servants, first-generation college students, handicapped students, married students, members of minority groups. ***Tuition waivers:*** Full or partial for employees or children of employees, senior citizens. ***ROTC:*** Army.

LOANS ***Student loans:*** $40,575,217 (72% need-based, 28% non-need-based). 66% of past graduating class borrowed through all loan programs. *Average*

indebtedness per student: $18,518. ***Average need-based loan:*** Freshmen: $3230. Undergraduates: $4154. ***Parent loans:*** $7,778,521 (58% need-based, 42% non-need-based). ***Programs:*** Federal Direct (Subsidized and Unsubsidized Stafford, PLUS), Perkins, state, Service-Cancelable State Direct Student Loans, external alternative loans.

WORK-STUDY ***Federal work-study:*** Total amount: $380,488; 273 jobs averaging $1394.

ATHLETIC AWARDS Total amount: $1,869,848 (55% need-based, 45% non-need-based).

APPLYING FOR FINANCIAL AID ***Required financial aid form:*** FAFSA. ***Financial aid deadline (priority):*** 4/20. ***Notification date:*** Continuous beginning 4/20.

CONTACT Ms. Elise Boyett, Associate Director of Financial Aid, Georgia Southern University, Box 8065, Statesboro, GA 30460-8065, 912-478-5413. *Fax:* 912-478-0573. *E-mail:* eboyett@georgiasouthern.edu.

GEORGIA SOUTHWESTERN STATE UNIVERSITY

Americus, GA

Tuition & fees (GA res): $3816 **Average undergraduate aid package: $8514**

ABOUT THE INSTITUTION State-supported, coed. ***Awards:*** bachelor's and master's degrees and post-bachelor's and post-master's certificates. 29 undergraduate majors. ***Total enrollment:*** 2,405. Undergraduates: 2,221. Freshmen: 426. Federal methodology is used as a basis for awarding need-based institutional aid.

UNDERGRADUATE EXPENSES for 2008–09 ***Application fee:*** $25. ***Tuition, state resident:*** full-time $3098; part-time $118 per semester hour. ***Tuition, nonresident:*** full-time $12,390; part-time $471 per semester hour. ***Required fees:*** full-time $718. ***College room and board:*** $5694.

FRESHMAN FINANCIAL AID (Fall 2008, est.) 355 applied for aid; of those 77% were deemed to have need. 100% of freshmen with need received aid; of those 20% had need fully met. ***Average percent of need met:*** 64% (excluding resources awarded to replace EFC). ***Average financial aid package:*** $8605 (excluding resources awarded to replace EFC). 11% of all full-time freshmen had no need and received non-need-based gift aid.

UNDERGRADUATE FINANCIAL AID (Fall 2008, est.) 1,352 applied for aid; of those 84% were deemed to have need. 100% of undergraduates with need received aid; of those 14% had need fully met. ***Average percent of need met:*** 60% (excluding resources awarded to replace EFC). ***Average financial aid package:*** $8514 (excluding resources awarded to replace EFC). 7% of all full-time undergraduates had no need and received non-need-based gift aid.

GIFT AID (NEED-BASED) ***Total amount:*** $3,811,014 (99% federal, 1% state). ***Receiving aid:*** Freshmen: 39% (163); all full-time undergraduates: 41% (720). ***Average award:*** Freshmen: $4514; Undergraduates: $4005. ***Scholarships, grants, and awards:*** Federal Pell, FSEOG, state, private, college/university gift aid from institutional funds.

GIFT AID (NON-NEED-BASED) ***Total amount:*** $3,700,810 (80% state, 14% institutional, 6% external sources). ***Receiving aid:*** Freshmen: 40% (167). Undergraduates: 33% (573). ***Average award:*** Freshmen: $1822. Undergraduates: $1968. ***Scholarships, grants, and awards by category:*** *Academic interests/achievement:* general academic interests/achievements. *Creative arts/performance:* art/fine arts, music. *Special achievements/activities:* leadership.

LOANS ***Student loans:*** $11,568,167 (47% need-based, 53% non-need-based). 68% of past graduating class borrowed through all loan programs. *Average indebtedness per student:* $16,920. ***Average need-based loan:*** Freshmen: $3272. Undergraduates: $4036. ***Parent loans:*** $391,525 (100% non-need-based). ***Programs:*** FFEL (Subsidized and Unsubsidized Stafford, PLUS), Perkins, state, college/university.

WORK-STUDY ***Federal work-study:*** Total amount: $113,728; 64 jobs averaging $1777. ***State or other work-study/employment:*** Part-time jobs available.

ATHLETIC AWARDS Total amount: $371,020 (100% non-need-based).

APPLYING FOR FINANCIAL AID ***Required financial aid forms:*** FAFSA, institution's own form. ***Financial aid deadline (priority):*** 4/1. ***Notification date:*** Continuous beginning 5/1. Students must reply within 8 weeks of notification.

CONTACT Charlene Morgan, Interim Director of Financial Aid, Georgia Southwestern State University, 800 Georgia Southwestern State University Drive, Americus, GA 31709-4693, 229-928-1378 or toll-free 800-338-0082. *Fax:* 229-931-2061.

GEORGIA STATE UNIVERSITY

Atlanta, GA

Tuition & fees (GA res): $6056 **Average undergraduate aid package: $10,549**

ABOUT THE INSTITUTION State-supported, coed. ***Awards:*** bachelor's, master's, doctoral, and first professional degrees and post-bachelor's, post-master's, and first professional certificates. 57 undergraduate majors. ***Total enrollment:*** 28,238. Undergraduates: 20,846. Freshmen: 2,803. Federal methodology is used as a basis for awarding need-based institutional aid.

UNDERGRADUATE EXPENSES for 2008–09 ***Application fee:*** $50. ***Tuition, state resident:*** full-time $4856; part-time $203 per semester hour. ***Tuition, nonresident:*** full-time $19,424; part-time $810 per semester hour. ***Required fees:*** full-time $1200; $600 per term. Full-time tuition and fees vary according to course load. Part-time tuition and fees vary according to course load. ***College room and board:*** $9330; ***Room only:*** $6746. Room and board charges vary according to board plan and housing facility. ***Payment plan:*** Guaranteed tuition.

FRESHMAN FINANCIAL AID (Fall 2008, est.) 2,342 applied for aid; of those 76% were deemed to have need. 96% of freshmen with need received aid; of those 24% had need fully met. ***Average percent of need met:*** 27% (excluding resources awarded to replace EFC). ***Average financial aid package:*** $10,854 (excluding resources awarded to replace EFC). 23% of all full-time freshmen had no need and received non-need-based gift aid.

UNDERGRADUATE FINANCIAL AID (Fall 2008, est.) 13,103 applied for aid; of those 81% were deemed to have need. 94% of undergraduates with need received aid; of those 19% had need fully met. ***Average percent of need met:*** 30% (excluding resources awarded to replace EFC). ***Average financial aid package:*** $10,549 (excluding resources awarded to replace EFC). 16% of all full-time undergraduates had no need and received non-need-based gift aid.

GIFT AID (NEED-BASED) ***Total amount:*** $44,353,034 (56% federal, 42% state, 1% institutional, 1% external sources). ***Receiving aid:*** Freshmen: 36% (1,022); all full-time undergraduates: 33% (6,025). ***Average award:*** Freshmen: $2684; Undergraduates: $3453. ***Scholarships, grants, and awards:*** Federal Pell, FSEOG, state, private, college/university gift aid from institutional funds.

GIFT AID (NON-NEED-BASED) ***Receiving aid:*** Freshmen: 59% (1,691). Undergraduates: 51% (9,265). ***Average award:*** Freshmen: $3263. Undergraduates: $3169. ***Tuition waivers:*** Full or partial for employees or children of employees, senior citizens. ***ROTC:*** Army, Naval cooperative, Air Force cooperative.

LOANS ***Student loans:*** $53,096,521 (100% need-based). 55% of past graduating class borrowed through all loan programs. *Average indebtedness per student:* $15,950. ***Average need-based loan:*** Freshmen: $2994. Undergraduates: $3793. ***Parent loans:*** $2,642,189 (100% need-based). ***Programs:*** Federal Direct (Subsidized and Unsubsidized Stafford, PLUS), FFEL (PLUS), Perkins, state.

WORK-STUDY ***Federal work-study:*** Total amount: $185,010; jobs available.

ATHLETIC AWARDS Total amount: $160,250 (100% need-based).

APPLYING FOR FINANCIAL AID ***Required financial aid form:*** FAFSA. ***Financial aid deadline:*** 11/1 (priority: 4/1). ***Notification date:*** Continuous.

CONTACT Financial Aid Office, Georgia State University, 102 Sparks Hall, Atlanta, GA 30303, 404-651-2227.

GETTYSBURG COLLEGE

Gettysburg, PA

Tuition & fees: $37,600 **Average undergraduate aid package: $30,027**

ABOUT THE INSTITUTION Independent religious, coed. ***Awards:*** bachelor's degrees. 83 undergraduate majors. ***Total enrollment:*** 2,457. Undergraduates: 2,457. Freshmen: 714.

UNDERGRADUATE EXPENSES for 2008–09 ***Application fee:*** $55. ***Comprehensive fee:*** $46,700 includes full-time tuition ($37,600) and room and board ($9100). ***College room only:*** $4880. Full-time tuition and fees vary according to program. Room and board charges vary according to board plan and housing facility. Part-time tuition and fees vary according to program. ***Payment plans:*** Tuition prepayment, installment.

FRESHMAN FINANCIAL AID (Fall 2008, est.) 483 applied for aid; of those 80% were deemed to have need. 100% of freshmen with need received aid; of those 96% had need fully met. ***Average percent of need met:*** 100% (excluding resources awarded to replace EFC). ***Average financial aid package:*** $31,997 (excluding resources awarded to replace EFC). 15% of all full-time freshmen had no need and received non-need-based gift aid.

UNDERGRADUATE FINANCIAL AID (Fall 2008, est.) 1,670 applied for aid; of those 83% were deemed to have need. 100% of undergraduates with need received aid; of those 100% had need fully met. ***Average percent of need met:*** 100% (excluding resources awarded to replace EFC). ***Average financial aid package:*** $30,027 (excluding resources awarded to replace EFC). 15% of all full-time undergraduates had no need and received non-need-based gift aid.

GIFT AID (NEED-BASED) ***Total amount:*** $35,046,914 (3% federal, 2% state, 92% institutional, 3% external sources). ***Receiving aid:*** Freshmen: 52% (374); all full-time undergraduates: 53% (1,384). ***Average award:*** Freshmen: $25,221. ***Scholarships, grants, and awards:*** Federal Pell, FSEOG, state, private, college/university gift aid from institutional funds, Academic Competitiveness Grant, National Smart Grant.

GIFT AID (NON-NEED-BASED) ***Total amount:*** $4,392,039 (91% institutional, 9% external sources). ***Receiving aid:*** Freshmen: 25% (181). Undergraduates: 23% (609). ***Average award:*** Freshmen: $10,259. Undergraduates: $10,115. ***Scholarships, grants, and awards by category:*** *Academic interests/achievement:* 967 awards ($9,958,350 total): general academic interests/achievements. *Creative arts/performance:* 27 awards ($216,750 total): music. ***Tuition waivers:*** Full or partial for employees or children of employees. ***ROTC:*** Army cooperative.

LOANS ***Student loans:*** $9,778,026 (55% need-based, 45% non-need-based). 66% of past graduating class borrowed through all loan programs. *Average indebtedness per student:* $23,992. ***Average need-based loan:*** Freshmen: $3758. Undergraduates: $4881. ***Parent loans:*** $6,446,478 (100% non-need-based). ***Programs:*** FFEL (Subsidized and Unsubsidized Stafford, PLUS), Perkins, college/university.

WORK-STUDY ***Federal work-study:*** Total amount: $552,910; 518 jobs averaging $900. ***State or other work-study/employment:*** Total amount: $73,700 (24% need-based, 76% non-need-based). 650 part-time jobs averaging $900.

APPLYING FOR FINANCIAL AID ***Required financial aid forms:*** FAFSA, CSS Financial Aid PROFILE, business/farm supplement, income tax form(s), verification worksheet. ***Financial aid deadline:*** 2/15. ***Notification date:*** 3/27. Students must reply by 5/1.

CONTACT Christina Gormley, Director of Financial Aid, Gettysburg College, 300 North Washington Street, Gettysburg, PA 17325, 717-337-6620 or toll-free 800-431-0803. *Fax:* 717-337-8555. *E-mail:* finaid@gettysburg.edu.

GLENVILLE STATE COLLEGE

Glenville, WV

Tuition & fees (WV res): $4486 **Average undergraduate aid package: $10,496**

ABOUT THE INSTITUTION State-supported, coed. ***Awards:*** associate and bachelor's degrees. 32 undergraduate majors. ***Total enrollment:*** 1,443. Undergraduates: 1,443. Freshmen: 303. Federal methodology is used as a basis for awarding need-based institutional aid.

UNDERGRADUATE EXPENSES for 2008–09 ***Application fee:*** $10. ***Tuition, state resident:*** full-time $4486; part-time $186.92 per credit hour. ***Tuition, nonresident:*** full-time $10,730; part-time $447.42 per credit hour. Full-time tuition and fees vary according to course load and location. Part-time tuition and fees vary according to course load and location. ***College room and board:*** $6150; ***Room only:*** $3000. Room and board charges vary according to housing facility. ***Payment plan:*** Installment.

FRESHMAN FINANCIAL AID (Fall 2008, est.) 288 applied for aid; of those 88% were deemed to have need. 100% of freshmen with need received aid; of those 16% had need fully met. ***Average percent of need met:*** 72% (excluding resources awarded to replace EFC). ***Average financial aid package:*** $10,280 (excluding resources awarded to replace EFC). 9% of all full-time freshmen had no need and received non-need-based gift aid.

UNDERGRADUATE FINANCIAL AID (Fall 2008, est.) 1,017 applied for aid; of those 90% were deemed to have need. 99% of undergraduates with need received aid; of those 27% had need fully met. ***Average percent of need met:*** 77% (excluding resources awarded to replace EFC). ***Average financial aid package:*** $10,496 (excluding resources awarded to replace EFC). 6% of all full-time undergraduates had no need and received non-need-based gift aid.

GIFT AID (NEED-BASED) ***Total amount:*** $3,806,693 (65% federal, 34% state, 1% institutional). ***Receiving aid:*** Freshmen: 70% (210); all full-time undergraduates: 67% (754). ***Average award:*** Freshmen: $4859; Undergraduates: $4719. ***Scholarships, grants, and awards:*** Federal Pell, FSEOG, state, private, college/university gift aid from institutional funds.

GIFT AID (NON-NEED-BASED) ***Total amount:*** $1,148,308 (56% state, 25% institutional, 19% external sources). ***Receiving aid:*** Freshmen: 51% (155). Undergraduates: 40% (447). ***Average award:*** Freshmen: $2179. Undergraduates: $2239. ***Scholarships, grants, and awards by category:*** *Academic interests/achievement:* 179 awards ($232,450 total): biological sciences, business, education, English, general academic interests/achievements, mathematics, social sciences. *Creative arts/performance:* 19 awards ($28,900 total): journalism/publications, music. *Special characteristics:* 2 awards ($2000 total): first-generation college students, veterans' children. ***Tuition waivers:*** Full or partial for senior citizens.

LOANS ***Student loans:*** $5,694,787 (48% need-based, 52% non-need-based). 71% of past graduating class borrowed through all loan programs. *Average indebtedness per student:* $17,545. ***Average need-based loan:*** Freshmen: $3096. Undergraduates: $3636. ***Parent loans:*** $286,117 (100% non-need-based). ***Programs:*** Federal Direct (Subsidized and Unsubsidized Stafford, PLUS).

WORK-STUDY ***Federal work-study:*** Total amount: $141,328; 107 jobs averaging $1280. ***State or other work-study/employment:*** Total amount: $508,250 (100% non-need-based). 269 part-time jobs averaging $1284.

ATHLETIC AWARDS Total amount: $535,298 (100% non-need-based).

APPLYING FOR FINANCIAL AID ***Required financial aid form:*** FAFSA. ***Financial aid deadline (priority):*** 2/1. ***Notification date:*** Continuous beginning 3/1. Students must reply within 3 weeks of notification.

CONTACT Ms. Karen Lay, Director of Financial Aid, Glenville State College, 200 High Street, Glenville, WV 26351-1200, 304-462-4103 Ext. 5 or toll-free 800-924-2010 (in-state). *Fax:* 304-462-4407. *E-mail:* karen.lay@glenville.edu.

GLOBE INSTITUTE OF TECHNOLOGY

New York, NY

CONTACT Office of Admissions, Globe Institute of Technology, 291 Broadway, 2nd Floor, New York, NY 10007, 212-349-4330 or toll-free 877-394-5623. *Fax:* 212-227-5920. *E-mail:* admission@globe.edu.

GODDARD COLLEGE

Plainfield, VT

Tuition & fees: $11,664 **Average undergraduate aid package: $6356**

ABOUT THE INSTITUTION Independent, coed. ***Awards:*** bachelor's and master's degrees. 5 undergraduate majors. ***Total enrollment:*** 686. Undergraduates: 255. Freshmen: 8. Federal methodology is used as a basis for awarding need-based institutional aid.

UNDERGRADUATE EXPENSES for 2008–09 ***Application fee:*** $40. ***One-time required fee:*** $125. ***Comprehensive fee:*** $12,752 includes full-time tuition ($11,504), mandatory fees ($160), and room and board ($1088).

FRESHMAN FINANCIAL AID (Fall 2007) 9 applied for aid; of those 89% were deemed to have need. 100% of freshmen with need received aid; of those 12% had need fully met. ***Average percent of need met:*** 40% (excluding resources awarded to replace EFC). ***Average financial aid package:*** $7514 (excluding resources awarded to replace EFC).

UNDERGRADUATE FINANCIAL AID (Fall 2007) 252 applied for aid; of those 91% were deemed to have need. 99% of undergraduates with need received aid; of those 4% had need fully met. ***Average percent of need met:*** 40% (excluding resources awarded to replace EFC). ***Average financial aid package:*** $6356 (excluding resources awarded to replace EFC).

GIFT AID (NEED-BASED) ***Total amount:*** $556,116 (73% federal, 10% state, 1% institutional, 16% external sources). ***Receiving aid:*** Freshmen: 67% (6); all full-time undergraduates: 58% (146). ***Average award:*** Freshmen: $4376; Undergraduates: $3809. ***Scholarships, grants, and awards:*** Federal Pell, FSEOG, state, private, college/university gift aid from institutional funds.

GIFT AID (NON-NEED-BASED) ***Total amount:*** $41,885 (100% external sources).

LOANS ***Student loans:*** $1,704,323 (90% need-based, 10% non-need-based). 79% of past graduating class borrowed through all loan programs. *Average indebtedness per student:* $21,639. ***Average need-based loan:*** Freshmen: $4232. Undergraduates: $4133. ***Parent loans:*** $137,589 (71% need-based, 29% non-need-based). ***Programs:*** FFEL (Subsidized and Unsubsidized Stafford, PLUS), Perkins, college/university.

APPLYING FOR FINANCIAL AID ***Required financial aid form:*** FAFSA. ***Financial aid deadline:*** Continuous. ***Notification date:*** Continuous. Students must reply within 2 weeks of notification.

CONTACT Beverly Jene, Director of Financial Aid, Goddard College, 123 Pitkin Road, Plainfield, VT 05667, 802-454-8311 Ext. 324 or toll-free 800-906-8312 Ext. 243. *Fax:* 802-454-1029. *E-mail:* beverly.jene@goddard.edu.

GOD'S BIBLE SCHOOL AND COLLEGE

Cincinnati, OH

CONTACT Mrs. Lori Waggoner, Financial Aid Director, God's Bible School and College, 1810 Young Street, Cincinnati, OH 45202-6899, 513-721-7944 Ext. 205 or toll-free 800-486-4637. *Fax:* 513-721-1357. *E-mail:* lwaggoner@gbs.edu.

GOLDEN GATE UNIVERSITY

San Francisco, CA

Tuition & fees: $12,960 **Average undergraduate aid package: $2931**

ABOUT THE INSTITUTION Independent, coed. ***Awards:*** bachelor's, master's, doctoral, and first professional degrees and post-bachelor's certificates. 8 undergraduate majors. ***Total enrollment:*** 3,528. Undergraduates: 414. Federal methodology is used as a basis for awarding need-based institutional aid.

UNDERGRADUATE EXPENSES for 2008–09 ***Application fee:*** $55. ***Tuition:*** full-time $12,960; part-time $1620 per course. Full-time tuition and fees vary according to course load, degree level, and program. Part-time tuition and fees vary according to course load and program. ***Payment plans:*** Installment, deferred payment.

UNDERGRADUATE FINANCIAL AID (Fall 2008, est.) 136 applied for aid; of those 72% were deemed to have need. 100% of undergraduates with need received aid; of those 27% had need fully met. ***Average percent of need met:*** 27% (excluding resources awarded to replace EFC). ***Average financial aid package:*** $2931 (excluding resources awarded to replace EFC). 34% of all full-time undergraduates had no need and received non-need-based gift aid.

GIFT AID (NEED-BASED) ***Total amount:*** $620,780 (49% federal, 36% state, 15% institutional). ***Receiving aid:*** All full-time undergraduates: 43% (63). ***Average award:*** Undergraduates: $1000. ***Scholarships, grants, and awards:*** Federal Pell, FSEOG, state, private, college/university gift aid from institutional funds.

GIFT AID (NON-NEED-BASED) ***Total amount:*** $90,000 (64% institutional, 36% external sources). ***Receiving aid:*** Undergraduates: 34% (51). ***Average award:*** Undergraduates: $2000. ***Scholarships, grants, and awards by category:*** *Academic interests/achievement:* 42 awards ($42,000 total): business, computer science, general academic interests/achievements. *Special achievements/activities:* 7 awards ($47,330 total): leadership. *Special characteristics:* adult students, general special characteristics, members of minority groups, previous college experience. ***Tuition waivers:*** Full or partial for employees or children of employees.

LOANS ***Student loans:*** $27,608 (38% need-based, 62% non-need-based). 55% of past graduating class borrowed through all loan programs. *Average indebtedness per student:* $17,522. ***Average need-based loan:*** Undergraduates: $2931. ***Parent loans:*** $18,221 (100% non-need-based). ***Programs:*** FFEL (Subsidized and Unsubsidized Stafford, PLUS), Perkins.

WORK-STUDY ***Federal work-study:*** Total amount: $10,000; 2 jobs averaging $5000.

APPLYING FOR FINANCIAL AID ***Required financial aid forms:*** FAFSA, institution's own form. ***Financial aid deadline:*** Continuous. ***Notification date:*** Continuous beginning 4/1. Students must reply within 3 weeks of notification.

CONTACT Ken Walsh, Associate Director of Financial Services, Golden Gate University, 536 Mission Street, San Francisco, CA 94105-2968, 415-442-7262 or toll-free 800-448-3381. *Fax:* 415-442-7819. *E-mail:* kwalsh@ggu.edu.

GOLDEY-BEACOM COLLEGE

Wilmington, DE

Tuition & fees: $18,840 **Average undergraduate aid package: $12,097**

ABOUT THE INSTITUTION Independent, coed. ***Awards:*** associate, bachelor's, and master's degrees and post-bachelor's certificates. 8 undergraduate majors. ***Total enrollment:*** 1,208. Undergraduates: 874. Freshmen: 210. Federal methodology is used as a basis for awarding need-based institutional aid.

UNDERGRADUATE EXPENSES for 2008–09 ***Application fee:*** $30. ***Tuition:*** full-time $18,500; part-time $556 per credit. ***Required fees:*** full-time $340; $10 per credit. ***Payment plans:*** Installment, deferred payment.

FRESHMAN FINANCIAL AID (Fall 2008, est.) 97 applied for aid; of those 88% were deemed to have need. 95% of freshmen with need received aid; of those 22% had need fully met. ***Average percent of need met:*** 60% (excluding resources awarded to replace EFC). ***Average financial aid package:*** $13,336 (excluding resources awarded to replace EFC). 13% of all full-time freshmen had no need and received non-need-based gift aid.

UNDERGRADUATE FINANCIAL AID (Fall 2008, est.) 513 applied for aid; of those 81% were deemed to have need. 75% of undergraduates with need received aid; of those 14% had need fully met. ***Average percent of need met:*** 51% (excluding resources awarded to replace EFC). ***Average financial aid package:*** $12,097 (excluding resources awarded to replace EFC). 23% of all full-time undergraduates had no need and received non-need-based gift aid.

GIFT AID (NEED-BASED) ***Total amount:*** $3,576,355 (23% federal, 1% state, 68% institutional, 8% external sources). ***Receiving aid:*** Freshmen: 74% (77); all full-time undergraduates: 47% (304). ***Average award:*** Freshmen: $10,337; Undergraduates: $8702. ***Scholarships, grants, and awards:*** Federal Pell, FSEOG, state, private, college/university gift aid from institutional funds.

GIFT AID (NON-NEED-BASED) ***Total amount:*** $1,430,267 (84% institutional, 16% external sources). ***Receiving aid:*** Freshmen: 16% (17). Undergraduates: 6% (41). ***Average award:*** Freshmen: $7431. Undergraduates: $5131. ***Scholarships, grants, and awards by category:*** *Academic interests/achievement:* business. ***ROTC:*** Air Force cooperative.

LOANS ***Student loans:*** $2,858,877 (85% need-based, 15% non-need-based). 45% of past graduating class borrowed through all loan programs. *Average indebtedness per student:* $11,000. ***Average need-based loan:*** Freshmen: $3902. Undergraduates: $4540. ***Parent loans:*** $153,695 (54% need-based, 46% non-need-based). ***Programs:*** FFEL (Subsidized and Unsubsidized Stafford, PLUS), Perkins.

WORK-STUDY ***Federal work-study:*** Total amount: $51,030; jobs available.

ATHLETIC AWARDS Total amount: $542,515 (100% non-need-based).

APPLYING FOR FINANCIAL AID ***Required financial aid form:*** FAFSA. ***Financial aid deadline (priority):*** 4/1. ***Notification date:*** Continuous. Students must reply within 2 weeks of notification.

CONTACT Jane H. Lysle, Dean of Enrollment Management, Goldey-Beacom College, 4701 Limestone Road, Wilmington, DE 19808-1999, 302-225-6274 or toll-free 800-833-4877. *Fax:* 302-998-8631. *E-mail:* lyslej@goldey.gbc.edu.

GOLDFARB SCHOOL OF NURSING AT BARNES-JEWISH COLLEGE

St. Louis, MO

CONTACT Regina Blackshear, Chief Financial Aid Officer, Goldfarb School of Nursing at Barnes-Jewish College, 306 South Kingshighway, St. Louis, MO 63110-1091, 314-454-7770 or toll-free 800-832-9009 (in-state).

GONZAGA UNIVERSITY

Spokane, WA

Tuition & fees: $28,262 **Average undergraduate aid package: $20,630**

ABOUT THE INSTITUTION Independent Roman Catholic, coed. ***Awards:*** bachelor's, master's, doctoral, and first professional degrees and post-master's certificates. 51 undergraduate majors. ***Total enrollment:*** 7,272. Undergraduates: 4,517. Freshmen: 1,107. Federal methodology is used as a basis for awarding need-based institutional aid.

UNDERGRADUATE EXPENSES for 2008–09 ***Application fee:*** $50. ***Comprehensive fee:*** $36,122 includes full-time tuition ($27,820), mandatory fees ($442), and room and board ($7860). ***College room only:*** $3880. ***Part-time tuition:*** $810 per credit. ***Part-time fees:*** $50 per term.

FRESHMAN FINANCIAL AID (Fall 2007) 836 applied for aid; of those 68% were deemed to have need. 100% of freshmen with need received aid; of those 35% had need fully met. ***Average percent of need met:*** 88% (excluding resources awarded to replace EFC). ***Average financial aid package:*** $21,350 (excluding resources awarded to replace EFC). 26% of all full-time freshmen had no need and received non-need-based gift aid.

UNDERGRADUATE FINANCIAL AID (Fall 2007) 3,146 applied for aid; of those 76% were deemed to have need. 100% of undergraduates with need received aid; of those 37% had need fully met. ***Average percent of need met:*** 87% (excluding resources awarded to replace EFC). ***Average financial aid package:*** $20,630 (excluding resources awarded to replace EFC). 38% of all full-time undergraduates had no need and received non-need-based gift aid.

GIFT AID (NEED-BASED) ***Total amount:*** $34,398,893 (8% federal, 7% state, 78% institutional, 7% external sources). ***Receiving aid:*** Freshmen: 55% (567); all full-time undergraduates: 56% (2,289). ***Average award:*** Freshmen: $12,464; Undergraduates: $11,864. ***Scholarships, grants, and awards:*** Federal Pell, FSEOG, state, private, college/university gift aid from institutional funds, United Negro College Fund, Federal Nursing, National Smart Grant, Academic Competitiveness Grant, TEACH Grant.

GIFT AID (NON-NEED-BASED) ***Total amount:*** $13,304,311 (1% state, 86% institutional, 13% external sources). ***Receiving aid:*** Freshmen: 23% (238). Undergraduates: 21% (875). ***Average award:*** Freshmen: $7316. Undergraduates: $7176. ***Scholarships, grants, and awards by category:*** *Academic interests/achievement:* 122 awards ($289,190 total): business, engineering/technologies, military science. *Creative arts/performance:* 44 awards ($91,100 total): debating, music. *Special achievements/activities:* 104 awards ($327,100 total): leadership, memberships. *Special characteristics:* 380 awards ($2,866,452 total): children and siblings of alumni, children of faculty/staff, international students, members of minority groups, siblings of current students. ***ROTC:*** Army.

LOANS ***Student loans:*** $17,876,898 (88% need-based, 12% non-need-based). 75% of past graduating class borrowed through all loan programs. *Average indebtedness per student:* $24,094. ***Average need-based loan:*** Freshmen: $4890. Undergraduates: $5691. ***Parent loans:*** $5,203,201 (79% need-based, 21% non-need-based). ***Programs:*** FFEL (Subsidized and Unsubsidized Stafford, PLUS), Perkins, Federal Nursing, state, college/university.

WORK-STUDY ***Federal work-study:*** Total amount: $1,100,538; 418 jobs averaging $2783. ***State or other work-study/employment:*** Total amount: $1,520,469 (100% need-based). 356 part-time jobs averaging $4271.

ATHLETIC AWARDS Total amount: $3,093,762 (29% need-based, 71% non-need-based).

APPLYING FOR FINANCIAL AID ***Required financial aid form:*** FAFSA. ***Financial aid deadline (priority):*** 2/1. ***Notification date:*** Continuous beginning 3/1. Students must reply by 5/1 or within 3 weeks of notification.

CONTACT Darlene Hendrickson, Director of Operations for Financial Aid, Gonzaga University, 502 East Boone Avenue, Spokane, WA 99258-0072, 509-323-6568 or toll-free 800-322-2584 Ext. 6572. *Fax:* 509-323-5816. *E-mail:* hendrickson@gonzaga.edu.

GORDON COLLEGE

Wenham, MA

Tuition & fees: $27,294 **Average undergraduate aid package: $15,936**

ABOUT THE INSTITUTION Independent nondenominational, coed. ***Awards:*** bachelor's and master's degrees. 32 undergraduate majors. ***Total enrollment:*** 1,718. Undergraduates: 1,590. Freshmen: 421. Both federal and institutional methodology are used as a basis for awarding need-based institutional aid.

UNDERGRADUATE EXPENSES for 2008–09 ***Application fee:*** $50. ***Comprehensive fee:*** $34,718 includes full-time tuition ($26,132), mandatory fees ($1162), and room and board ($7424).

FRESHMAN FINANCIAL AID (Fall 2008, est.) 342 applied for aid; of those 81% were deemed to have need. 100% of freshmen with need received aid; of those 19% had need fully met. ***Average percent of need met:*** 70% (excluding resources awarded to replace EFC). ***Average financial aid package:*** $16,351 (excluding resources awarded to replace EFC). 31% of all full-time freshmen had no need and received non-need-based gift aid.

UNDERGRADUATE FINANCIAL AID (Fall 2008, est.) 1,187 applied for aid; of those 86% were deemed to have need. 100% of undergraduates with need received aid; of those 17% had need fully met. ***Average percent of need met:*** 67% (excluding resources awarded to replace EFC). ***Average financial aid package:*** $15,936 (excluding resources awarded to replace EFC). 25% of all full-time undergraduates had no need and received non-need-based gift aid.

GIFT AID (NEED-BASED) ***Total amount:*** $11,902,758 (9% federal, 3% state, 77% institutional, 11% external sources). ***Receiving aid:*** Freshmen: 63% (276); all full-time undergraduates: 65% (1,001). ***Average award:*** Freshmen: $12,779; Undergraduates: $11,540. ***Scholarships, grants, and awards:*** Federal Pell, FSEOG, state, private, college/university gift aid from institutional funds.

GIFT AID (NON-NEED-BASED) ***Total amount:*** $4,959,139 (78% institutional, 22% external sources). ***Receiving aid:*** Freshmen: 9% (39). Undergraduates: 7% (108). ***Average award:*** Freshmen: $9603. Undergraduates: $8770. ***Scholarships, grants, and awards by category:*** *Academic interests/achievement:* 946 awards ($6,570,092 total): general academic interests/achievements. *Creative arts/performance:* 60 awards ($155,000 total): music. *Special achievements/activities:* 33 awards ($864,308 total): leadership. *Special characteristics:* 211 awards ($136,499 total): children and siblings of alumni, relatives of clergy. ***ROTC:*** Army cooperative, Air Force cooperative.

LOANS ***Student loans:*** $12,494,743 (66% need-based, 34% non-need-based). 81% of past graduating class borrowed through all loan programs. *Average indebtedness per student:* $33,399. ***Average need-based loan:*** Freshmen: $3564. Undergraduates: $4569. ***Parent loans:*** $2,742,427 (36% need-based, 64% non-need-based). ***Programs:*** FFEL (Subsidized and Unsubsidized Stafford, PLUS), Perkins, state, college/university.

WORK-STUDY ***Federal work-study:*** Total amount: $603,748; 385 jobs averaging $1477.

APPLYING FOR FINANCIAL AID ***Required financial aid form:*** FAFSA. ***Financial aid deadline (priority):*** 3/1. ***Notification date:*** 4/15. Students must reply by 5/1 or within 2 weeks of notification.

CONTACT Daniel O'Connell, Director of Student Financial Services, Gordon College, 255 Grapevine Road, Wenham, MA 01984-1899, 978-867-4246 or toll-free 866-464-6736. *Fax:* 978-867-4657. *E-mail:* daniel.oconnell@gordon.edu.

GOSHEN COLLEGE

Goshen, IN

CONTACT Mr. Galen Graber, Director of Enrollment, Goshen College, 1700 South Main Street, Goshen, IN 46526-4794, 574-535-7525 or toll-free 800-348-7422. *Fax:* 574-535-7654.

GOUCHER COLLEGE

Baltimore, MD

Tuition & fees: $33,786 **Average undergraduate aid package: $24,213**

ABOUT THE INSTITUTION Independent, coed. ***Awards:*** bachelor's and master's degrees and post-bachelor's certificates. 29 undergraduate majors. ***Total enrollment:*** 2,319. Undergraduates: 1,447. Freshmen: 360. Both federal and institutional methodology are used as a basis for awarding need-based institutional aid.

UNDERGRADUATE EXPENSES for 2009–10 ***Application fee:*** $55. ***Comprehensive fee:*** $43,792 includes full-time tuition ($33,294), mandatory fees ($492), and room and board ($10,006). ***College room only:*** $6155. ***Part-time tuition:*** $1100 per credit.

FRESHMAN FINANCIAL AID (Fall 2008, est.) 242 applied for aid; of those 79% were deemed to have need. 99% of freshmen with need received aid; of those 25% had need fully met. ***Average percent of need met:*** 81% (excluding resources awarded to replace EFC). ***Average financial aid package:*** $25,779 (excluding resources awarded to replace EFC). 18% of all full-time freshmen had no need and received non-need-based gift aid.

UNDERGRADUATE FINANCIAL AID (Fall 2008, est.) 911 applied for aid; of those 84% were deemed to have need. 99% of undergraduates with need received aid; of those 26% had need fully met. ***Average percent of need met:*** 80% (excluding resources awarded to replace EFC). ***Average financial aid package:*** $24,213 (excluding resources awarded to replace EFC). 21% of all full-time undergraduates had no need and received non-need-based gift aid.

GIFT AID (NEED-BASED) ***Total amount:*** $14,966,996 (6% federal, 16% state, 73% institutional, 5% external sources). ***Receiving aid:*** Freshmen: 50% (181); all full-time undergraduates: 50% (730). ***Average award:*** Freshmen: $22,609; Undergraduates: $20,247. ***Scholarships, grants, and awards:*** Federal Pell, FSEOG, state, private, college/university gift aid from institutional funds.

GIFT AID (NON-NEED-BASED) ***Total amount:*** $4,886,289 (1% state, 79% institutional, 20% external sources). ***Receiving aid:*** Freshmen: 5% (17). Undergraduates: 5% (76). ***Average award:*** Freshmen: $12,670. Undergraduates: $11,927. ***Scholarships, grants, and awards by category:*** *Creative arts/performance:* 10 awards ($52,250 total): art/fine arts, dance, music, performing arts, theater/drama. ***ROTC:*** Army cooperative.

LOANS ***Student loans:*** $5,345,172 (58% need-based, 42% non-need-based). 50% of past graduating class borrowed through all loan programs. *Average indebtedness per student:* $16,729. ***Average need-based loan:*** Freshmen: $3394.

Undergraduates: $4363. ***Parent loans:*** $2,883,334 (28% need-based, 72% non-need-based). ***Programs:*** FFEL (Subsidized and Unsubsidized Stafford, PLUS), Perkins, college/university.

WORK-STUDY ***Federal work-study:*** Total amount: $614,235; 464 jobs averaging $1017. ***State or other work-study/employment:*** Total amount: $26,854 (100% non-need-based). Part-time jobs available.

APPLYING FOR FINANCIAL AID ***Required financial aid forms:*** FAFSA, CSS Financial Aid PROFILE. ***Financial aid deadline (priority):*** 2/1. ***Notification date:*** 4/1. Students must reply by 5/1 or within 2 weeks of notification.

CONTACT Sharon Hassan, Director of Student Financial Aid, Goucher College, 1021 Dulaney Valley Road, Baltimore, MD 21204-2794, 410-337-6141 or toll-free 800-468-2437. *Fax:* 410-337-6504.

GOVERNORS STATE UNIVERSITY

University Park, IL

CONTACT Financial Aid Office, Governors State University, One University Parkway, University Park, IL 60466-0975, 708-534-4480.

GRACE BIBLE COLLEGE

Grand Rapids, MI

Tuition & fees: $13,320 **Average undergraduate aid package: $9070**

ABOUT THE INSTITUTION Independent religious, coed. ***Awards:*** associate and bachelor's degrees. 20 undergraduate majors. ***Total enrollment:*** 179. Undergraduates: 179. Freshmen: 53. Federal methodology is used as a basis for awarding need-based institutional aid.

UNDERGRADUATE EXPENSES for 2008–09 ***Comprehensive fee:*** $20,020 includes full-time tuition ($12,800), mandatory fees ($520), and room and board ($6700). ***College room only:*** $3000. Room and board charges vary according to housing facility. ***Part-time tuition:*** $450 per semester hour. Part-time tuition and fees vary according to course load. ***Payment plan:*** Installment.

FRESHMAN FINANCIAL AID (Fall 2007) 46 applied for aid; of those 87% were deemed to have need. 100% of freshmen with need received aid; of those 30% had need fully met. ***Average percent of need met:*** 74% (excluding resources awarded to replace EFC). ***Average financial aid package:*** $9136 (excluding resources awarded to replace EFC). 17% of all full-time freshmen had no need and received non-need-based gift aid.

UNDERGRADUATE FINANCIAL AID (Fall 2007) 136 applied for aid; of those 94% were deemed to have need. 100% of undergraduates with need received aid; of those 17% had need fully met. ***Average percent of need met:*** 71% (excluding resources awarded to replace EFC). ***Average financial aid package:*** $9070 (excluding resources awarded to replace EFC). 12% of all full-time undergraduates had no need and received non-need-based gift aid.

GIFT AID (NEED-BASED) ***Total amount:*** $714,034 (29% federal, 28% state, 40% institutional, 3% external sources). ***Receiving aid:*** Freshmen: 75% (39); all full-time undergraduates: 79% (125). ***Average award:*** Freshmen: $6667; Undergraduates: $5524. ***Scholarships, grants, and awards:*** Federal Pell, FSEOG, state, private, college/university gift aid from institutional funds.

GIFT AID (NON-NEED-BASED) ***Total amount:*** $97,692 (5% state, 78% institutional, 17% external sources). ***Receiving aid:*** Freshmen: 8% (4). Undergraduates: 6% (9). ***Average award:*** Freshmen: $4204. Undergraduates: $3223. ***Scholarships, grants, and awards by category:*** *Academic interests/achievement:* 113 awards ($207,688 total): general academic interests/achievements. *Creative arts/performance:* 10 awards ($10,000 total): music. *Special characteristics:* 56 awards ($154,310 total): children of faculty/staff, general special characteristics, relatives of clergy. ***Tuition waivers:*** Full or partial for employees or children of employees. ***ROTC:*** Army cooperative.

LOANS ***Student loans:*** $793,328 (53% need-based, 47% non-need-based). 43% of past graduating class borrowed through all loan programs. *Average indebtedness per student:* $8955. ***Average need-based loan:*** Freshmen: $2864. Undergraduates: $3869. ***Parent loans:*** $82,700 (42% need-based, 58% non-need-based). ***Programs:*** FFEL (Subsidized and Unsubsidized Stafford, PLUS), state.

WORK-STUDY ***Federal work-study:*** Total amount: $24,581; 40 jobs averaging $755. ***State or other work-study/employment:*** Total amount: $7045 (100% need-based). 23 part-time jobs averaging $303.

APPLYING FOR FINANCIAL AID ***Required financial aid form:*** FAFSA. ***Financial aid deadline (priority):*** 2/28. ***Notification date:*** Continuous beginning 5/15. Students must reply within 2 weeks of notification.

CONTACT Mr. Daniel Wait, Director of Financial Aid, Grace Bible College, 1011 Aldon Street, SW, Grand Rapids, MI 49509-1921, 616-538-2330 or toll-free 800-968-1887. *Fax:* 616-538-0599.

GRACE COLLEGE

Winona Lake, IN

Tuition & fees: $20,376 **Average undergraduate aid package: $14,540**

ABOUT THE INSTITUTION Independent religious, coed. ***Awards:*** associate, bachelor's, master's, doctoral, and first professional degrees. 51 undergraduate majors. ***Total enrollment:*** 1,508. Undergraduates: 1,332. Freshmen: 327. Federal methodology is used as a basis for awarding need-based institutional aid.

UNDERGRADUATE EXPENSES for 2008–09 ***Application fee:*** $30. ***Comprehensive fee:*** $27,024 includes full-time tuition ($20,376) and room and board ($6648). Room and board charges vary according to board plan and housing facility. ***Part-time tuition:*** $450 per credit hour. Part-time tuition and fees vary according to course load. ***Payment plan:*** Installment.

FRESHMAN FINANCIAL AID (Fall 2007) 231 applied for aid; of those 86% were deemed to have need. 99% of freshmen with need received aid; of those 37% had need fully met. ***Average percent of need met:*** 87% (excluding resources awarded to replace EFC). ***Average financial aid package:*** $15,011 (excluding resources awarded to replace EFC). 21% of all full-time freshmen had no need and received non-need-based gift aid.

UNDERGRADUATE FINANCIAL AID (Fall 2007) 719 applied for aid; of those 87% were deemed to have need. 100% of undergraduates with need received aid; of those 33% had need fully met. ***Average percent of need met:*** 85% (excluding resources awarded to replace EFC). ***Average financial aid package:*** $14,540 (excluding resources awarded to replace EFC). 21% of all full-time undergraduates had no need and received non-need-based gift aid.

GIFT AID (NEED-BASED) ***Total amount:*** $4,955,059 (16% federal, 26% state, 51% institutional, 7% external sources). ***Receiving aid:*** Freshmen: 79% (198); all full-time undergraduates: 77% (609). ***Average award:*** Freshmen: $10,753; Undergraduates: $9121. ***Scholarships, grants, and awards:*** Federal Pell, FSEOG, state, private, college/university gift aid from institutional funds.

GIFT AID (NON-NEED-BASED) ***Total amount:*** $1,072,518 (3% state, 80% institutional, 17% external sources). ***Receiving aid:*** Freshmen: 16% (39). Undergraduates: 10% (79). ***Average award:*** Freshmen: $17,036. Undergraduates: $15,009. ***Scholarships, grants, and awards by category:*** *Academic interests/achievement:* 36 awards ($28,615 total): business. *Creative arts/performance:* 58 awards ($79,575 total): applied art and design, art/fine arts, music, theater/drama. *Special achievements/activities:* junior miss. *Special characteristics:* 209 awards ($704,788 total): children of faculty/staff, ethnic background, relatives of clergy, religious affiliation. ***Tuition waivers:*** Full or partial for employees or children of employees, senior citizens.

LOANS ***Student loans:*** $5,059,182 (73% need-based, 27% non-need-based). 72% of past graduating class borrowed through all loan programs. *Average indebtedness per student:* $18,017. ***Average need-based loan:*** Freshmen: $4689. Undergraduates: $5890. ***Parent loans:*** $4,927,631 (21% need-based, 79% non-need-based). ***Programs:*** FFEL (Subsidized and Unsubsidized Stafford, PLUS), Perkins.

WORK-STUDY ***Federal work-study:*** Total amount: $315,283; jobs available.

ATHLETIC AWARDS Total amount: $755,110 (56% need-based, 44% non-need-based).

APPLYING FOR FINANCIAL AID ***Required financial aid form:*** FAFSA. ***Financial aid deadline (priority):*** 3/10. ***Notification date:*** Continuous.

CONTACT Gretchen Bailey, Senior Financial Aid Advisor, Grace College, 200 Seminary Drive, Winona Lake, IN 46590-1294, 574-372-5100 or toll-free 800-54-GRACE Ext. 6412 (in-state), 800-54 GRACE Ext. 6412 (out-of-state). *Fax:* 574-372-5144. *E-mail:* baileyga@grace.edu.

GRACELAND UNIVERSITY

Lamoni, IA

Tuition & fees: $20,090 **Average undergraduate aid package: $17,708**

ABOUT THE INSTITUTION Independent Community of Christ, coed. ***Awards:*** bachelor's and master's degrees and post-master's certificates. 51 undergraduate majors. ***Total enrollment:*** 2,444. Undergraduates: 1,679. Freshmen: 197. Federal methodology is used as a basis for awarding need-based institutional aid.

UNDERGRADUATE EXPENSES for 2009–10 ***Application fee:*** $50. ***Comprehensive fee:*** $26,870 includes full-time tuition ($19,890), mandatory fees ($200), and room and board ($6780). ***College room only:*** $2710. ***Part-time tuition:*** $630 per semester hour.

FRESHMAN FINANCIAL AID (Fall 2008, est.) 169 applied for aid; of those 89% were deemed to have need. 97% of freshmen with need received aid; of those 32% had need fully met. ***Average percent of need met:*** 89% (excluding resources awarded to replace EFC). ***Average financial aid package:*** $20,824 (excluding resources awarded to replace EFC). 24% of all full-time freshmen had no need and received non-need-based gift aid.

UNDERGRADUATE FINANCIAL AID (Fall 2008, est.) 966 applied for aid; of those 87% were deemed to have need. 98% of undergraduates with need received aid; of those 26% had need fully met. ***Average percent of need met:*** 81% (excluding resources awarded to replace EFC). ***Average financial aid package:*** $17,708 (excluding resources awarded to replace EFC). 24% of all full-time undergraduates had no need and received non-need-based gift aid.

GIFT AID (NEED-BASED) ***Total amount:*** $8,345,911 (23% federal, 8% state, 66% institutional, 3% external sources). ***Receiving aid:*** Freshmen: 72% (147); all full-time undergraduates: 61% (761). ***Average award:*** Freshmen: $15,109; Undergraduates: $13,235. ***Scholarships, grants, and awards:*** Federal Pell, FSEOG, state, private, college/university gift aid from institutional funds.

GIFT AID (NON-NEED-BASED) ***Total amount:*** $3,338,261 (5% federal, 1% state, 87% institutional, 7% external sources). ***Receiving aid:*** Freshmen: 38% (77). Undergraduates: 30% (373). ***Average award:*** Freshmen: $10,079. Undergraduates: $10,591. ***Scholarships, grants, and awards by category:*** *Academic interests/achievement:* 880 awards ($4,402,931 total): computer science, engineering/technologies, English, general academic interests/achievements, physical sciences. *Creative arts/performance:* 179 awards ($293,087 total): applied art and design, creative writing, music, theater/drama. *Special achievements/activities:* 138 awards ($179,025 total): cheerleading/drum major, general special achievements/activities, leadership, religious involvement. *Special characteristics:* $4,328,747 total: children and siblings of alumni, children of faculty/staff, children of public servants, first-generation college students, general special characteristics, international students, local/state students, members of minority groups, religious affiliation.

LOANS ***Student loans:*** $8,334,756 (71% need-based, 29% non-need-based). 87% of past graduating class borrowed through all loan programs. *Average indebtedness per student:* $28,347. ***Average need-based loan:*** Freshmen: $5202. Undergraduates: $5346. ***Parent loans:*** $817,718 (28% need-based, 72% non-need-based). ***Programs:*** Federal Direct (Subsidized and Unsubsidized Stafford, PLUS), Perkins, state, college/university, alternative loans.

WORK-STUDY ***Federal work-study:*** Total amount: $739,680; 336 jobs averaging $2201. ***State or other work-study/employment:*** Total amount: $577,101 (2% need-based, 98% non-need-based). 370 part-time jobs averaging $1560.

ATHLETIC AWARDS Total amount: $1,645,704 (57% need-based, 43% non-need-based).

APPLYING FOR FINANCIAL AID ***Required financial aid form:*** FAFSA. ***Financial aid deadline:*** Continuous. ***Notification date:*** Continuous beginning 2/1. Students must reply within 2 weeks of notification.

CONTACT Ms. Christine McGee, Director of Financial Aid, Graceland University, 1 University Place, Lamoni, IA 50140, 641-784-5136 or toll-free 866-GRACELAND. *Fax:* 641-784-5020. *E-mail:* cmcgee@graceland.edu.

GRACELAND UNIVERSITY

Independence, MO

CONTACT Financial Aid Office, Graceland University, 1401 West Truman Road, Independence, MO 64050-3434, 816-833-0524.

GRACE UNIVERSITY

Omaha, NE

Tuition & fees: $14,290 **Average undergraduate aid package: $12,607**

ABOUT THE INSTITUTION Independent interdenominational, coed. ***Awards:*** associate, bachelor's, and master's degrees. 34 undergraduate majors. ***Total enrollment:*** 434. Undergraduates: 366. Freshmen: 97. Federal methodology is used as a basis for awarding need-based institutional aid.

UNDERGRADUATE EXPENSES for 2009–10 ***Application fee:*** $20. ***Comprehensive fee:*** $20,030 includes full-time tuition ($13,900), mandatory fees ($390), and room and board ($5740). ***College room only:*** $2550. ***Part-time tuition:*** $390 per credit hour. ***Part-time fees:*** $165 per term.

FRESHMAN FINANCIAL AID (Fall 2008, est.) 61 applied for aid; of those 84% were deemed to have need. 100% of freshmen with need received aid; of those 22% had need fully met. ***Average percent of need met:*** 74% (excluding resources awarded to replace EFC). ***Average financial aid package:*** $12,027 (excluding resources awarded to replace EFC). 24% of all full-time freshmen had no need and received non-need-based gift aid.

UNDERGRADUATE FINANCIAL AID (Fall 2008, est.) 247 applied for aid; of those 85% were deemed to have need. 100% of undergraduates with need received aid; of those 16% had need fully met. ***Average percent of need met:*** 72% (excluding resources awarded to replace EFC). ***Average financial aid package:*** $12,607 (excluding resources awarded to replace EFC). 20% of all full-time undergraduates had no need and received non-need-based gift aid.

GIFT AID (NEED-BASED) ***Total amount:*** $2,098,585 (28% federal, 3% state, 60% institutional, 9% external sources). ***Receiving aid:*** Freshmen: 67% (51); all full-time undergraduates: 73% (208). ***Average award:*** Freshmen: $9186; Undergraduates: $8841. ***Scholarships, grants, and awards:*** Federal Pell, FSEOG, state, private, college/university gift aid from institutional funds, Academic Competitiveness Grant, TEACH Grant.

GIFT AID (NON-NEED-BASED) ***Total amount:*** $565,031 (3% federal, 1% state, 78% institutional, 18% external sources). ***Receiving aid:*** Freshmen: 14% (11). Undergraduates: 9% (27). ***Average award:*** Freshmen: $6783. Undergraduates: $5924. ***Scholarships, grants, and awards by category:*** *Academic interests/achievement:* 239 awards ($1,540,898 total): business, education, general academic interests/achievements, health fields, international studies, religion/biblical studies. *Creative arts/performance:* 13 awards ($18,000 total): cinema/film/broadcasting, music. *Special achievements/activities:* 56 awards ($62,511 total): general special achievements/activities, leadership, religious involvement. *Special characteristics:* 103 awards ($224,476 total): adult students, children and siblings of alumni, children of current students, children of faculty/staff, ethnic background, general special characteristics, international students, local/state students, married students, members of minority groups, out-of-state students, relatives of clergy, siblings of current students, spouses of current students. ***ROTC:*** Army cooperative, Air Force cooperative.

LOANS ***Student loans:*** $2,331,166 (80% need-based, 20% non-need-based). 92% of past graduating class borrowed through all loan programs. *Average indebtedness per student:* $17,820. ***Average need-based loan:*** Freshmen: $3274. Undergraduates: $4089. ***Parent loans:*** $1,139,637 (34% need-based, 66% non-need-based). ***Programs:*** FFEL (Subsidized and Unsubsidized Stafford, PLUS).

WORK-STUDY ***Federal work-study:*** Total amount: $37,000; 37 jobs averaging $1103. ***State or other work-study/employment:*** Total amount: $50,200 (36% need-based, 64% non-need-based). 45 part-time jobs averaging $1101.

APPLYING FOR FINANCIAL AID ***Required financial aid forms:*** FAFSA, institution's own form. ***Financial aid deadline (priority):*** 4/1. ***Notification date:*** Continuous. Students must reply within 2 weeks of notification.

CONTACT Dale Brown, Office of Financial Aid, Grace University, 1311 South Ninth Street, Omaha, NE 68108-3629, 402-449-2810 or toll-free 800-383-1422. *Fax:* 402-449-2921. *E-mail:* gufinaid@graceu.edu.

GRAMBLING STATE UNIVERSITY

Grambling, LA

ABOUT THE INSTITUTION State-supported, coed. ***Awards:*** associate, bachelor's, master's, and doctoral degrees and post-master's certificates. 53 undergraduate majors. ***Total enrollment:*** 5,253. Undergraduates: 4,804. Freshmen: 1,215.

GIFT AID (NEED-BASED) ***Scholarships, grants, and awards:*** Federal Pell, FSEOG, state.

GIFT AID (NON-NEED-BASED) ***Scholarships, grants, and awards by category:*** *Academic interests/achievement:* biological sciences, business, communication, computer science, education, engineering/technologies, English, foreign languages, general academic interests/achievements, health fields, home economics, humanities, mathematics, military science, physical sciences, premedicine, social sciences. *Creative arts/performance:* dance, general creative arts/performance, music, performing arts, theater/drama. *Special achievements/*

activities: cheerleading/drum major, junior miss, leadership. *Special characteristics:* children and siblings of alumni, children of faculty/staff, children of public servants, ethnic background, international students, local/state students, members of minority groups, out-of-state students, public servants, veterans, veterans' children.

LOANS ***Programs:*** FFEL (Subsidized and Unsubsidized Stafford, PLUS), alternative loans.

WORK-STUDY ***Federal work-study:*** Total amount: $786,850; 1,141 jobs averaging $1310. ***State or other work-study/employment:*** Total amount: $641,044 (100% non-need-based). 431 part-time jobs averaging $1487.

APPLYING FOR FINANCIAL AID ***Required financial aid form:*** FAFSA.

CONTACT Assistant Director of Student Financial Aid and Scholarships, Grambling State University, PO Box 629, Grambling, LA 71245, 318-274-6415. *Fax:* 318-274-3358.

GRAND CANYON UNIVERSITY

Phoenix, AZ

ABOUT THE INSTITUTION Independent Southern Baptist, coed. ***Awards:*** bachelor's, master's, and doctoral degrees and post-master's certificates. 34 undergraduate majors. ***Total enrollment:*** 13,415. Undergraduates: 4,822. Freshmen: 466.

GIFT AID (NEED-BASED) ***Scholarships, grants, and awards:*** Federal Pell, FSEOG, state, private, college/university gift aid from institutional funds, Bureau of Indian Affairs Grants.

GIFT AID (NON-NEED-BASED) ***Scholarships, grants, and awards by category:*** *Academic interests/achievement:* biological sciences, business, communication, education, English, general academic interests/achievements, health fields, humanities, mathematics, military science, physical sciences, premedicine, religion/biblical studies, social sciences. *Creative arts/performance:* applied art and design, art/fine arts, music, performing arts, theater/drama. *Special achievements/activities:* leadership, memberships. *Special characteristics:* children and siblings of alumni, children of faculty/staff, ethnic background, members of minority groups, out-of-state students, relatives of clergy, religious affiliation.

LOANS ***Programs:*** FFEL (Subsidized and Unsubsidized Stafford, PLUS), Perkins, state, alternative loans.

WORK-STUDY Federal work-study jobs available.

APPLYING FOR FINANCIAL AID ***Required financial aid form:*** FAFSA.

CONTACT Director of Financial Aid, Grand Canyon University, 3300 West Camelback Road, PO Box 11097, Phoenix, AZ 85017-3030, 800-800-9776 Ext. 2885 or toll-free 800-800-9776 (in-state). *Fax:* 602-589-2044.

GRAND VALLEY STATE UNIVERSITY

Allendale, MI

Tuition & fees (MI res): $8196 **Average undergraduate aid package: $8112**

ABOUT THE INSTITUTION State-supported, coed. ***Awards:*** bachelor's, master's, and doctoral degrees and post-bachelor's and post-master's certificates. 105 undergraduate majors. ***Total enrollment:*** 23,892. Undergraduates: 20,416. Freshmen: 3,890. Federal methodology is used as a basis for awarding need-based institutional aid.

UNDERGRADUATE EXPENSES for 2008–09 ***Application fee:*** $30. ***Tuition, state resident:*** full-time $8196; part-time $356 per credit hour. ***Tuition, nonresident:*** full-time $12,510; part-time $532 per credit hour. Full-time tuition and fees vary according to degree level, program, and student level. Part-time tuition and fees vary according to course load, degree level, program, and student level. ***College room and board:*** $7224; ***Room only:*** $5174. Room and board charges vary according to board plan, housing facility, and location. ***Payment plans:*** Installment, deferred payment.

FRESHMAN FINANCIAL AID (Fall 2008, est.) 3,279 applied for aid; of those 64% were deemed to have need. 100% of freshmen with need received aid; of those 29% had need fully met. ***Average percent of need met:*** 83% (excluding resources awarded to replace EFC). ***Average financial aid package:*** $9264 (excluding resources awarded to replace EFC). 13% of all full-time freshmen had no need and received non-need-based gift aid.

UNDERGRADUATE FINANCIAL AID (Fall 2008, est.) 13,562 applied for aid; of those 72% were deemed to have need. 99% of undergraduates with need received aid; of those 25% had need fully met. ***Average percent of need met:*** 69% (excluding resources awarded to replace EFC). ***Average financial aid package:*** $8112 (excluding resources awarded to replace EFC). 10% of all full-time undergraduates had no need and received non-need-based gift aid.

GIFT AID (NEED-BASED) ***Total amount:*** $39,061,021 (46% federal, 19% state, 31% institutional, 4% external sources). ***Receiving aid:*** Freshmen: 50% (1,931); all full-time undergraduates: 42% (7,627). ***Average award:*** Freshmen: $5721; Undergraduates: $5137. ***Scholarships, grants, and awards:*** Federal Pell, FSEOG, state, private, college/university gift aid from institutional funds.

GIFT AID (NON-NEED-BASED) ***Total amount:*** $11,385,652 (27% state, 64% institutional, 9% external sources). ***Receiving aid:*** Freshmen: 4% (149). Undergraduates: 3% (510). ***Average award:*** Freshmen: $2321. Undergraduates: $3657. ***Scholarships, grants, and awards by category:*** *Academic interests/achievement:* business, communication, computer science, education, engineering/technologies, English, foreign languages, general academic interests/achievements, health fields, humanities, international studies, mathematics, physical sciences, premedicine, social sciences. *Creative arts/performance:* applied art and design, art/fine arts, cinema/film/broadcasting, dance, journalism/publications, music, theater/drama. *Special characteristics:* adult students, children and siblings of alumni, children of faculty/staff, children of union members/company employees, children of workers in trades, general special characteristics, handicapped students, international students, out-of-state students, public servants, spouses of deceased or disabled public servants, veterans, veterans' children. ***Tuition waivers:*** Full or partial for employees or children of employees.

LOANS ***Student loans:*** $95,187,246 (43% need-based, 57% non-need-based). 70% of past graduating class borrowed through all loan programs. *Average indebtedness per student:* $21,475. ***Average need-based loan:*** Freshmen: $4169. Undergraduates: $4430. ***Parent loans:*** $46,304,084 (100% non-need-based). ***Programs:*** Federal Direct (Subsidized and Unsubsidized Stafford, PLUS), Perkins, Federal Nursing.

WORK-STUDY ***Federal work-study:*** Total amount: $2,551,749; jobs available. ***State or other work-study/employment:*** Total amount: $243,456 (100% need-based). Part-time jobs available (averaging $1340).

ATHLETIC AWARDS Total amount: $2,227,992 (39% need-based, 61% non-need-based).

APPLYING FOR FINANCIAL AID ***Required financial aid form:*** FAFSA. ***Financial aid deadline (priority):*** 3/1. ***Notification date:*** 3/10. Students must reply by 5/1 or within 4 weeks of notification.

CONTACT Mr. Edward Kerestly, Director of Financial Aid, Grand Valley State University, 100 Student Services Building, Allendale, MI 49401-9403, 616-331-3234 or toll-free 800-748-0246. *Fax:* 616-331-3180. *E-mail:* kerestle@gvsu.edu.

GRAND VIEW UNIVERSITY

Des Moines, IA

Tuition & fees: $18,614 **Average undergraduate aid package: $18,489**

ABOUT THE INSTITUTION Independent religious, coed. ***Awards:*** associate, bachelor's, and master's degrees and post-bachelor's certificates. 29 undergraduate majors. ***Total enrollment:*** 1,936. Undergraduates: 1,936. Freshmen: 345. Federal methodology is used as a basis for awarding need-based institutional aid.

UNDERGRADUATE EXPENSES for 2008–09 ***Application fee:*** $35. ***Comprehensive fee:*** $24,778 includes full-time tuition ($18,234), mandatory fees ($380), and room and board ($6164). Full-time tuition and fees vary according to class time. Room and board charges vary according to board plan and housing facility. ***Part-time tuition:*** $475 per hour. Part-time tuition and fees vary according to class time. ***Payment plan:*** Installment.

FRESHMAN FINANCIAL AID (Fall 2008, est.) 331 applied for aid; of those 85% were deemed to have need. 100% of freshmen with need received aid; of those 47% had need fully met. ***Average percent of need met:*** 92% (excluding resources awarded to replace EFC). ***Average financial aid package:*** $19,604 (excluding resources awarded to replace EFC). 17% of all full-time freshmen had no need and received non-need-based gift aid.

UNDERGRADUATE FINANCIAL AID (Fall 2008, est.) 1,405 applied for aid; of those 88% were deemed to have need. 100% of undergraduates with need received aid; of those 38% had need fully met. ***Average percent of need met:*** 87% (excluding resources awarded to replace EFC). ***Average financial aid package:*** $18,489 (excluding resources awarded to replace EFC). 16% of all full-time undergraduates had no need and received non-need-based gift aid.

GIFT AID (NEED-BASED) ***Total amount:*** $11,829,150 (21% federal, 29% state, 48% institutional, 2% external sources). ***Receiving aid:*** Freshmen: 75% (256); all full-time undergraduates: 73% (1,118). ***Average award:*** Freshmen: $13,428;

Undergraduates: $10,873. ***Scholarships, grants, and awards:*** Federal Pell, FSEOG, state, private, college/university gift aid from institutional funds, Academic Competitiveness Grant, National Smart Grant.

GIFT AID (NON-NEED-BASED) ***Total amount:*** $1,896,905 (4% federal, 5% state, 83% institutional, 8% external sources). ***Receiving aid:*** Freshmen: 13% (46). Undergraduates: 9% (134). ***Average award:*** Freshmen: $6876. Undergraduates: $5478. ***Scholarships, grants, and awards by category:*** *Academic interests/achievement:* 1,489 awards ($6,166,532 total): general academic interests/achievements. *Creative arts/performance:* 72 awards ($73,025 total): art/fine arts, music, theater/drama. *Special achievements/activities:* junior miss. *Special characteristics:* 149 awards ($574,483 total): children and siblings of alumni, children of educators, children of faculty/staff. ***Tuition waivers:*** Full or partial for employees or children of employees, senior citizens. ***ROTC:*** Army cooperative, Air Force cooperative.

LOANS ***Student loans:*** $14,414,655 (62% need-based, 38% non-need-based). 83% of past graduating class borrowed through all loan programs. *Average indebtedness per student:* $27,337. ***Average need-based loan:*** Freshmen: $3554. Undergraduates: $4363. ***Parent loans:*** $768,926 (5% need-based, 95% non-need-based). ***Programs:*** FFEL (Subsidized and Unsubsidized Stafford, PLUS), Perkins, Federal Nursing.

WORK-STUDY ***Federal work-study:*** Total amount: $664,113; 488 jobs averaging $1284. ***State or other work-study/employment:*** Total amount: $3000 (100% need-based). 2 part-time jobs averaging $1500.

ATHLETIC AWARDS Total amount: $1,492,891 (58% need-based, 42% non-need-based).

APPLYING FOR FINANCIAL AID ***Required financial aid form:*** FAFSA. ***Financial aid deadline (priority):*** 3/1. ***Notification date:*** Continuous beginning 3/10. Students must reply by 5/1 or within 3 weeks of notification.

CONTACT Michele Dunne, Director of Financial Aid, Grand View University, 1200 Grandview Avenue, Des Moines, IA 50316-1599, 515-263-2820 or toll-free 800-444-6083 Ext. 2810. *Fax:* 515-263-6191. *E-mail:* mdunne@grandview.edu.

GRATZ COLLEGE

Melrose Park, PA

CONTACT Karen West, Student Financial Services Adviser, Gratz College, 7605 Old York Road, Melrose Park, PA 19027, 215-635-7300 Ext. 163 or toll-free 800-475-4635 Ext. 140 (out-of-state). *Fax:* 215-635-7320.

GREAT LAKES CHRISTIAN COLLEGE

Lansing, MI

CONTACT Financial Aid Officer, Great Lakes Christian College, 6211 West Willow Highway, Lansing, MI 48917-1299, 517-321-0242 or toll-free 800-YES-GLCC.

GREEN MOUNTAIN COLLEGE

Poultney, VT

Tuition & fees: $25,838 **Average undergraduate aid package: $20,134**

ABOUT THE INSTITUTION Independent, coed. ***Awards:*** bachelor's and master's degrees. 20 undergraduate majors. ***Total enrollment:*** 867. Undergraduates: 780. Freshmen: 219. Federal methodology is used as a basis for awarding need-based institutional aid.

UNDERGRADUATE EXPENSES for 2008–09 ***Application fee:*** $30. ***One-time required fee:*** $200. ***Comprehensive fee:*** $35,360 includes full-time tuition ($24,938), mandatory fees ($900), and room and board ($9522). ***College room only:*** $5704. Full-time tuition and fees vary according to course load. Room and board charges vary according to housing facility. ***Part-time tuition:*** $832 per credit. ***Part-time fees:*** $900 per year. Part-time tuition and fees vary according to course load. ***Payment plan:*** Installment.

FRESHMAN FINANCIAL AID (Fall 2008, est.) 176 applied for aid; of those 84% were deemed to have need. 100% of freshmen with need received aid; of those 12% had need fully met. ***Average percent of need met:*** 62% (excluding resources awarded to replace EFC). ***Average financial aid package:*** $17,509 (excluding resources awarded to replace EFC). 13% of all full-time freshmen had no need and received non-need-based gift aid.

UNDERGRADUATE FINANCIAL AID (Fall 2008, est.) 616 applied for aid; of those 91% were deemed to have need. 99% of undergraduates with need received aid; of those 17% had need fully met. ***Average percent of need met:*** 70% (excluding resources awarded to replace EFC). ***Average financial aid package:*** $20,134 (excluding resources awarded to replace EFC). 11% of all full-time undergraduates had no need and received non-need-based gift aid.

GIFT AID (NEED-BASED) ***Total amount:*** $8,087,585 (17% federal, 3% state, 77% institutional, 3% external sources). ***Receiving aid:*** Freshmen: 68% (148); all full-time undergraduates: 73% (550). ***Average award:*** Freshmen: $14,063; Undergraduates: $14,851. ***Scholarships, grants, and awards:*** Federal Pell, FSEOG, state, private, college/university gift aid from institutional funds.

GIFT AID (NON-NEED-BASED) ***Total amount:*** $1,513,671 (80% institutional, 20% external sources). ***Receiving aid:*** Freshmen: 5% (10). Undergraduates: 5% (35). ***Average award:*** Freshmen: $9365. Undergraduates: $11,953. ***Scholarships, grants, and awards by category:*** *Academic interests/achievement:* 24 awards ($52,375 total): biological sciences, business, education, English, general academic interests/achievements, social sciences. *Creative arts/performance:* 43 awards ($102,500 total): art/fine arts, music, performing arts, theater/drama. *Special achievements/activities:* 138 awards ($386,000 total): community service, leadership, religious involvement. *Special characteristics:* 59 awards ($303,679 total): children and siblings of alumni, children of current students, international students, parents of current students, relatives of clergy, religious affiliation, siblings of current students. ***Tuition waivers:*** Full or partial for employees or children of employees.

LOANS ***Student loans:*** $5,923,545 (73% need-based, 27% non-need-based). 78% of past graduating class borrowed through all loan programs. *Average indebtedness per student:* $32,448. ***Average need-based loan:*** Freshmen: $3266. Undergraduates: $5393. ***Parent loans:*** $1,724,825 (57% need-based, 43% non-need-based). ***Programs:*** FFEL (Subsidized and Unsubsidized Stafford, PLUS).

WORK-STUDY ***Federal work-study:*** Total amount: $199,696; 192 jobs averaging $1650. ***State or other work-study/employment:*** Total amount: $203,458 (63% need-based, 37% non-need-based). 118 part-time jobs averaging $1650.

APPLYING FOR FINANCIAL AID ***Required financial aid form:*** FAFSA. ***Financial aid deadline (priority):*** 3/1. ***Notification date:*** Continuous. Students must reply by 5/1 or within 4 weeks of notification.

CONTACT Wendy J. Ellis, Director of Financial Aid, Green Mountain College, One Brennan Circle, Poultney, VT 05764-1199, 800-776-6675 Ext. 8210 or toll-free 800-776-6675 (out-of-state). *Fax:* 802-287-8099. *E-mail:* ellisw@greenmtn.edu.

GREENSBORO COLLEGE

Greensboro, NC

Tuition & fees: $22,248 **Average undergraduate aid package: N/A**

ABOUT THE INSTITUTION Independent United Methodist, coed. ***Awards:*** bachelor's and master's degrees and post-bachelor's certificates. 48 undergraduate majors. ***Total enrollment:*** 1,289. Undergraduates: 1,204. Freshmen: 212. Federal methodology is used as a basis for awarding need-based institutional aid.

UNDERGRADUATE EXPENSES for 2008–09 ***Application fee:*** $35. ***Comprehensive fee:*** $30,668 includes full-time tuition ($21,978), mandatory fees ($270), and room and board ($8420). ***College room only:*** $4020. Room and board charges vary according to housing facility. ***Part-time tuition:*** $605 per credit hour. ***Payment plan:*** Installment.

FRESHMAN FINANCIAL AID (Fall 2007) ***Average financial aid package:*** $19,803 (excluding resources awarded to replace EFC).

GIFT AID (NEED-BASED) ***Total amount:*** $2,838,455 (51% federal, 34% state, 15% institutional). ***Scholarships, grants, and awards:*** Federal Pell, FSEOG, state, private, college/university gift aid from institutional funds.

GIFT AID (NON-NEED-BASED) ***Total amount:*** $8,199,347 (17% federal, 16% state, 46% institutional, 21% external sources). ***Scholarships, grants, and awards by category:*** *Academic interests/achievement:* general academic interests/achievements. *Creative arts/performance:* art/fine arts, music, theater/drama. *Special achievements/activities:* community service, leadership, religious involvement. *Special characteristics:* adult students, children and siblings of alumni, children of faculty/staff, international students, relatives of clergy, religious affiliation, siblings of current students, veterans. ***Tuition waivers:*** Full or partial for employees or children of employees. ***ROTC:*** Army cooperative, Air Force cooperative.

LOANS ***Student loans:*** $5,368,633 (33% need-based, 67% non-need-based). ***Parent loans:*** $1,381,373 (100% non-need-based). ***Programs:*** FFEL (Subsidized and Unsubsidized Stafford, PLUS), Perkins, college/university.

WORK-STUDY ***Federal work-study:*** Total amount: $131,417; jobs available. ***State or other work-study/employment:*** Part-time jobs available.

APPLYING FOR FINANCIAL AID ***Required financial aid forms:*** FAFSA, institution's own form, state aid form. ***Financial aid deadline (priority):*** 4/15. ***Notification date:*** Continuous. Students must reply within 2 weeks of notification.

CONTACT Dawn VanArsdale Young, Director of Financial Aid, Greensboro College, 815 West Market Street, Greensboro, NC 27401-1875, 336-272-7102 Ext. 408 or toll-free 800-346-8226. *Fax:* 336-271-6634. *E-mail:* dvanarsdale@reensgborocollege.edu.

GREENVILLE COLLEGE

Greenville, IL

CONTACT Mr. Karl Somerville, Director of Financial Aid, Greenville College, 315 East College Avenue, Greenville, IL 62246-0159, 618-664-7110 or toll-free 800-345-4440. *Fax:* 618-664-9841. *E-mail:* karl.somerville@greenville.edu.

GRINNELL COLLEGE

Grinnell, IA

Tuition & fees: $35,428 **Average undergraduate aid package: $30,751**

ABOUT THE INSTITUTION Independent, coed. ***Awards:*** bachelor's degrees. 24 undergraduate majors. ***Total enrollment:*** 1,678. Undergraduates: 1,678. Freshmen: 464. Both federal and institutional methodology are used as a basis for awarding need-based institutional aid.

UNDERGRADUATE EXPENSES for 2008–09 ***Application fee:*** $30. ***Comprehensive fee:*** $43,700 includes full-time tuition ($34,932), mandatory fees ($496), and room and board ($8272). ***College room only:*** $3838. Full-time tuition and fees vary according to student level. Room and board charges vary according to board plan and housing facility. ***Part-time tuition:*** $1092 per credit. Part-time tuition and fees vary according to student level. ***Payment plans:*** Tuition prepayment, installment.

FRESHMAN FINANCIAL AID (Fall 2008, est.) 388 applied for aid; of those 82% were deemed to have need. 100% of freshmen with need received aid; of those 100% had need fully met. ***Average percent of need met:*** 100% (excluding resources awarded to replace EFC). ***Average financial aid package:*** $33,730 (excluding resources awarded to replace EFC). 20% of all full-time freshmen had no need and received non-need-based gift aid.

UNDERGRADUATE FINANCIAL AID (Fall 2008, est.) 1,117 applied for aid; of those 88% were deemed to have need. 100% of undergraduates with need received aid; of those 100% had need fully met. ***Average percent of need met:*** 100% (excluding resources awarded to replace EFC). ***Average financial aid package:*** $30,751 (excluding resources awarded to replace EFC). 26% of all full-time undergraduates had no need and received non-need-based gift aid.

GIFT AID (NEED-BASED) ***Total amount:*** $25,273,067 (5% federal, 1% state, 92% institutional, 2% external sources). ***Receiving aid:*** Freshmen: 68% (314); all full-time undergraduates: 60% (975). ***Average award:*** Freshmen: $28,159; Undergraduates: $25,921. ***Scholarships, grants, and awards:*** Federal Pell, FSEOG, state, private, college/university gift aid from institutional funds.

GIFT AID (NON-NEED-BASED) ***Total amount:*** $5,764,166 (86% institutional, 14% external sources). ***Receiving aid:*** Freshmen: 10% (48). Undergraduates: 6% (101). ***Average award:*** Freshmen: $10,137. Undergraduates: $10,709. ***Scholarships, grants, and awards by category:*** *Academic interests/achievement:* general academic interests/achievements. ***Tuition waivers:*** Full or partial for employees or children of employees.

LOANS ***Student loans:*** $2,497,566 (77% need-based, 23% non-need-based). 53% of past graduating class borrowed through all loan programs. *Average indebtedness per student:* $19,526. ***Average need-based loan:*** Freshmen: $2787. Undergraduates: $2893. ***Programs:*** FFEL (Subsidized and Unsubsidized Stafford, PLUS), Perkins, college/university.

WORK-STUDY ***Federal work-study:*** Total amount: $907,520; 455 jobs averaging $1838. ***State or other work-study/employment:*** Total amount: $857,062 (37% need-based, 63% non-need-based). 376 part-time jobs averaging $1984.

APPLYING FOR FINANCIAL AID ***Required financial aid forms:*** FAFSA, institution's own form, noncustodial (divorced/separated) parent's statement. ***Financial aid deadline:*** 2/1 (priority: 2/1). ***Notification date:*** 4/1. Students must reply by 5/1.

CONTACT Mr. Arnold Woods, Director of Student Financial Aid, Grinnell College, 1103 Park Street, Grinnell, IA 50112-1690, 641-269-3250 or toll-free 800-247-0113. *Fax:* 641-269-4937. *E-mail:* woods@grinnell.edu.

GROVE CITY COLLEGE

Grove City, PA

Tuition & fees: $12,074 **Average undergraduate aid package: $6013**

ABOUT THE INSTITUTION Independent Presbyterian, coed. ***Awards:*** bachelor's degrees. 45 undergraduate majors. ***Total enrollment:*** 2,499. Undergraduates: 2,499. Freshmen: 621. Institutional methodology is used as a basis for awarding need-based institutional aid.

UNDERGRADUATE EXPENSES for 2008–09 ***Application fee:*** $50. ***Comprehensive fee:*** $18,514 includes full-time tuition ($12,074) and room and board ($6440). Full-time tuition and fees vary according to course load. Room and board charges vary according to housing facility. ***Part-time tuition:*** $380 per credit. ***Payment plan:*** Installment.

FRESHMAN FINANCIAL AID (Fall 2008, est.) 356 applied for aid; of those 70% were deemed to have need. 98% of freshmen with need received aid; of those 12% had need fully met. ***Average percent of need met:*** 60% (excluding resources awarded to replace EFC). ***Average financial aid package:*** $6345 (excluding resources awarded to replace EFC). 9% of all full-time freshmen had no need and received non-need-based gift aid.

UNDERGRADUATE FINANCIAL AID (Fall 2008, est.) 1,114 applied for aid; of those 80% were deemed to have need. 98% of undergraduates with need received aid; of those 10% had need fully met. ***Average percent of need met:*** 56% (excluding resources awarded to replace EFC). ***Average financial aid package:*** $6013 (excluding resources awarded to replace EFC). 15% of all full-time undergraduates had no need and received non-need-based gift aid.

GIFT AID (NEED-BASED) ***Total amount:*** $5,279,722 (19% state, 71% institutional, 10% external sources). ***Receiving aid:*** Freshmen: 39% (245); all full-time undergraduates: 34% (851). ***Average award:*** Freshmen: $6371; Undergraduates: $6145. ***Scholarships, grants, and awards:*** state, private, college/university gift aid from institutional funds.

GIFT AID (NON-NEED-BASED) ***Total amount:*** $1,818,952 (49% institutional, 51% external sources). ***Receiving aid:*** Freshmen: 5% (29). Undergraduates: 4% (87). ***Average award:*** Freshmen: $2583. Undergraduates: $2312. ***Scholarships, grants, and awards by category:*** *Academic interests/achievement:* 517 awards ($888,087 total): biological sciences, business, communication, education, engineering/technologies, English, foreign languages, general academic interests/achievements, physical sciences, religion/biblical studies, social sciences. *Creative arts/performance:* 6 awards ($24,911 total): creative writing, music. *Special achievements/activities:* 21 awards ($76,350 total): general special achievements/activities, leadership, memberships, religious involvement. *Special characteristics:* 12 awards ($59,100 total): ethnic background, general special characteristics, members of minority groups. ***Tuition waivers:*** Full or partial for employees or children of employees. ***ROTC:*** Army cooperative.

LOANS ***Student loans:*** $7,978,681 (30% need-based, 70% non-need-based). 43% of past graduating class borrowed through all loan programs. *Average indebtedness per student:* $24,895. ***Programs:*** alternative loans.

WORK-STUDY ***State or other work-study/employment:*** Part-time jobs available.

APPLYING FOR FINANCIAL AID ***Required financial aid forms:*** institution's own form, state aid form. ***Financial aid deadline:*** 4/15. ***Notification date:*** Continuous.

CONTACT Thomas G. Ball, Director of Financial Aid, Grove City College, 100 Campus Drive, Grove City, PA 16127-2104, 724-458-3300. *Fax:* 724-450-4040. *E-mail:* financialaid@gcc.edu.

GUILFORD COLLEGE

Greensboro, NC

Tuition & fees: $27,450 **Average undergraduate aid package: $19,867**

ABOUT THE INSTITUTION Independent religious, coed. ***Awards:*** bachelor's degrees. 37 undergraduate majors. ***Total enrollment:*** 2,641. Undergraduates: 2,641. Freshmen: 419. Federal methodology is used as a basis for awarding need-based institutional aid.

UNDERGRADUATE EXPENSES for 2009–10 ***Application fee:*** $25. ***Comprehensive fee:*** $35,010 includes full-time tuition ($27,120), mandatory fees ($330), and room and board ($7560). ***Part-time tuition:*** $840 per credit hour. ***Part-time fees:*** $285 per credit hour.

FRESHMAN FINANCIAL AID (Fall 2008, est.) 326 applied for aid; of those 88% were deemed to have need. 97% of freshmen with need received aid; of those 1% had need fully met. ***Average percent of need met:*** 86% (excluding resources

awarded to replace EFC). ***Average financial aid package:*** $20,304 (excluding resources awarded to replace EFC). 20% of all full-time freshmen had no need and received non-need-based gift aid.

UNDERGRADUATE FINANCIAL AID (Fall 2008, est.) 1,794 applied for aid; of those 83% were deemed to have need. ***Average percent of need met:*** 90% (excluding resources awarded to replace EFC). ***Average financial aid package:*** $19,867 (excluding resources awarded to replace EFC). 19% of all full-time undergraduates had no need and received non-need-based gift aid.

GIFT AID (NEED-BASED) ***Total amount:*** $15,534,238 (21% federal, 22% state, 48% institutional, 9% external sources). ***Receiving aid:*** Freshmen: 68% (278); all full-time undergraduates: 50% (1,100). ***Average award:*** Freshmen: $18,650; Undergraduates: $7137. ***Scholarships, grants, and awards:*** Federal Pell, FSEOG, state, private, college/university gift aid from institutional funds.

GIFT AID (NON-NEED-BASED) ***Total amount:*** $3,374,671 (29% state, 42% institutional, 29% external sources). ***Receiving aid:*** Freshmen: 47% (191). Undergraduates: 36% (802). ***Average award:*** Freshmen: $9000. Undergraduates: $7500. ***Scholarships, grants, and awards by category:*** *Academic interests/achievement:* 1,250 awards ($6,353,863 total): biological sciences, general academic interests/achievements. *Creative arts/performance:* 80 awards ($89,586 total): music, theater/drama. *Special achievements/activities:* 47 awards ($122,225 total): religious involvement. *Special characteristics:* 310 awards ($554,173 total): children of faculty/staff, first-generation college students, local/state students. ***ROTC:*** Army cooperative, Naval cooperative, Air Force cooperative.

LOANS ***Student loans:*** $10,374,779 (96% need-based, 4% non-need-based). 69% of past graduating class borrowed through all loan programs. *Average indebtedness per student:* $23,680. ***Average need-based loan:*** Freshmen: $3700. Undergraduates: $4124. ***Parent loans:*** $1,792,331 (93% need-based, 7% non-need-based). ***Programs:*** FFEL (Subsidized and Unsubsidized Stafford, PLUS), Perkins, college/university.

WORK-STUDY ***Federal work-study:*** Total amount: $261,291; 183 jobs averaging $1428. ***State or other work-study/employment:*** Total amount: $270,560 (76% need-based, 24% non-need-based). 171 part-time jobs averaging $1360.

APPLYING FOR FINANCIAL AID ***Required financial aid forms:*** FAFSA, noncustodial (divorced/separated) parent's statement, business/farm supplement. ***Financial aid deadline (priority):*** 3/1. ***Notification date:*** Continuous. Students must reply within 2 weeks of notification.

CONTACT Mr. Anthony E. Gurley, Director of Student Financial Services, Guilford College, 5800 West Friendly Avenue, Greensboro, NC 27410, 336-316-2142 or toll-free 800-992-7759. *Fax:* 336-316-2942. *E-mail:* agurley@guilford.edu.

GUSTAVUS ADOLPHUS COLLEGE

St. Peter, MN

Tuition & fees: $29,990 **Average undergraduate aid package: $25,531**

ABOUT THE INSTITUTION Independent religious, coed. ***Awards:*** bachelor's degrees. 67 undergraduate majors. ***Total enrollment:*** 2,578. Undergraduates: 2,578. Freshmen: 606. Both federal and institutional methodology are used as a basis for awarding need-based institutional aid.

UNDERGRADUATE EXPENSES for 2008–09 ***One-time required fee:*** $290. ***Comprehensive fee:*** $37,450 includes full-time tuition ($29,990) and room and board ($7460). ***College room only:*** $4710. ***Part-time tuition:*** $4080 per course.

FRESHMAN FINANCIAL AID (Fall 2008, est.) 541 applied for aid; of those 85% were deemed to have need. 100% of freshmen with need received aid; of those 11% had need fully met. ***Average percent of need met:*** 94% (excluding resources awarded to replace EFC). ***Average financial aid package:*** $26,550 (excluding resources awarded to replace EFC). 30% of all full-time freshmen had no need and received non-need-based gift aid.

UNDERGRADUATE FINANCIAL AID (Fall 2008, est.) 1,944 applied for aid; of those 86% were deemed to have need. 100% of undergraduates with need received aid; of those 11% had need fully met. ***Average percent of need met:*** 92% (excluding resources awarded to replace EFC). ***Average financial aid package:*** $25,531 (excluding resources awarded to replace EFC). 35% of all full-time undergraduates had no need and received non-need-based gift aid.

GIFT AID (NEED-BASED) ***Total amount:*** $27,508,821 (7% federal, 9% state, 80% institutional, 4% external sources). ***Receiving aid:*** Freshmen: 70% (461); all full-time undergraduates: 65% (1,666). ***Average award:*** Freshmen: $20,613; Undergraduates: $18,134. ***Scholarships, grants, and awards:*** Federal Pell, FSEOG, state, private, college/university gift aid from institutional funds.

GIFT AID (NON-NEED-BASED) ***Total amount:*** $8,850,311 (1% federal, 96% institutional, 3% external sources). ***Receiving aid:*** Freshmen: 8% (53). Undergraduates: 7% (186). ***Average award:*** Freshmen: $10,203. Undergraduates: $8789. ***Scholarships, grants, and awards by category:*** *Academic interests/achievement:* 415 awards ($2,275,815 total): general academic interests/achievements. *Creative arts/performance:* 75 awards ($190,000 total): art/fine arts, dance, debating, music, theater/drama. *Special achievements/activities:* junior miss. *Special characteristics:* 127 awards ($150,000 total): children and siblings of alumni, ethnic background, first-generation college students, international students, members of minority groups, out-of-state students, siblings of current students. ***ROTC:*** Army cooperative.

LOANS ***Student loans:*** $14,424,494 (41% need-based, 59% non-need-based). 69% of past graduating class borrowed through all loan programs. *Average indebtedness per student:* $25,672. ***Average need-based loan:*** Freshmen: $4254. Undergraduates: $4618. ***Parent loans:*** $2,919,969 (31% need-based, 69% non-need-based). ***Programs:*** Federal Direct (Subsidized and Unsubsidized Stafford, PLUS), Perkins, state.

WORK-STUDY ***Federal work-study:*** Total amount: $654,098; 705 jobs averaging $1705. ***State or other work-study/employment:*** Total amount: $1,353,323 (82% need-based, 18% non-need-based). 856 part-time jobs averaging $1505.

APPLYING FOR FINANCIAL AID ***Required financial aid forms:*** FAFSA, institution's own form, CSS Financial Aid PROFILE. ***Financial aid deadline:*** 4/1 (priority: 2/15). ***Notification date:*** Continuous. Students must reply by 5/1 or within 2 weeks of notification.

CONTACT Doug Minter, Director of Financial Aid, Gustavus Adolphus College, 800 West College Avenue, St. Peter, MN 56082-1498, 507-933-7527 or toll-free 800-GUSTAVU(S). *Fax:* 507-933-7727. *E-mail:* financial@gustavus.edu.

GUTENBERG COLLEGE

Eugene, OR

CONTACT Financial Aid Office, Gutenberg College, 1883 University Street, Eugene, OR 97403, 541-683-5141.

GWYNEDD-MERCY COLLEGE

Gwynedd Valley, PA

Tuition & fees: $22,790 **Average undergraduate aid package: $13,988**

ABOUT THE INSTITUTION Independent Roman Catholic, coed. ***Awards:*** associate, bachelor's, and master's degrees and post-bachelor's and post-master's certificates. 32 undergraduate majors. ***Total enrollment:*** 2,548. Undergraduates: 2,018. Freshmen: 346. Federal methodology is used as a basis for awarding need-based institutional aid.

UNDERGRADUATE EXPENSES for 2008–09 ***Application fee:*** $25. ***Comprehensive fee:*** $31,780 includes full-time tuition ($22,340), mandatory fees ($450), and room and board ($8990). Full-time tuition and fees vary according to program. Room and board charges vary according to board plan and housing facility. ***Part-time tuition:*** $495 per credit. ***Part-time fees:*** $10 per credit. Part-time tuition and fees vary according to program. ***Payment plan:*** Installment.

FRESHMAN FINANCIAL AID (Fall 2007) 264 applied for aid; of those 80% were deemed to have need. 100% of freshmen with need received aid; of those 20% had need fully met. ***Average percent of need met:*** 75% (excluding resources awarded to replace EFC). ***Average financial aid package:*** $14,349 (excluding resources awarded to replace EFC). 21% of all full-time freshmen had no need and received non-need-based gift aid.

UNDERGRADUATE FINANCIAL AID (Fall 2007) 1,081 applied for aid; of those 85% were deemed to have need. 98% of undergraduates with need received aid; of those 18% had need fully met. ***Average percent of need met:*** 72% (excluding resources awarded to replace EFC). ***Average financial aid package:*** $13,988 (excluding resources awarded to replace EFC). 20% of all full-time undergraduates had no need and received non-need-based gift aid.

GIFT AID (NEED-BASED) ***Total amount:*** $11,319,007 (10% federal, 19% state, 70% institutional, 1% external sources). ***Receiving aid:*** Freshmen: 72% (208); all full-time undergraduates: 73% (882). ***Average award:*** Freshmen: $12,370; Undergraduates: $11,561. ***Scholarships, grants, and awards:*** Federal Pell, FSEOG, state, private, college/university gift aid from institutional funds.

GIFT AID (NON-NEED-BASED) ***Total amount:*** $2,091,623 (2% federal, 2% state, 95% institutional, 1% external sources). ***Receiving aid:*** Freshmen: 60% (173). Undergraduates: 57% (694). ***Average award:*** Freshmen: $13,725.

Undergraduates: $14,595. ***Scholarships, grants, and awards by category:*** *Academic interests/achievement:* 565 awards ($4,081,930 total): general academic interests/achievements. *Special achievements/activities:* 275 awards ($1,253,000 total): general special achievements/activities. *Special characteristics:* 63 awards ($115,250 total): children and siblings of alumni, siblings of current students. ***Tuition waivers:*** Full or partial for employees or children of employees.

LOANS ***Student loans:*** $13,623,423 (43% need-based, 57% non-need-based). 83% of past graduating class borrowed through all loan programs. *Average indebtedness per student:* $20,636. ***Average need-based loan:*** Freshmen: $3225. Undergraduates: $4942. ***Parent loans:*** $1,755,501 (25% need-based, 75% non-need-based). ***Programs:*** FFEL (Subsidized and Unsubsidized Stafford, PLUS), Perkins, Federal Nursing, alternative loans.

WORK-STUDY ***Federal work-study:*** Total amount: $137,863; 156 jobs averaging $884. ***State or other work-study/employment:*** Total amount: $23,627 (100% need-based). 23 part-time jobs averaging $1031.

APPLYING FOR FINANCIAL AID ***Required financial aid forms:*** FAFSA, institution's own form. ***Financial aid deadline (priority):*** 3/1. ***Notification date:*** Continuous. Students must reply by 5/1 or within 2 weeks of notification.

CONTACT Sr. Barbara A. Kaufmann, Director of Student Financial Aid, Gwynedd-Mercy College, PO Box 901, Gwynedd Valley, PA 19437-0901, 215-641-5570 or toll-free 800-DIAL-GMC (in-state). *Fax:* 215-641-5556.

HAMILTON COLLEGE

Clinton, NY

Tuition & fees: $38,600 **Average undergraduate aid package: $33,037**

ABOUT THE INSTITUTION Independent, coed. ***Awards:*** bachelor's degrees. 46 undergraduate majors. ***Total enrollment:*** 1,872. Undergraduates: 1,872. Freshmen: 462. Both federal and institutional methodology are used as a basis for awarding need-based institutional aid.

UNDERGRADUATE EXPENSES for 2008–09 ***Application fee:*** $75. ***Comprehensive fee:*** $48,410 includes full-time tuition ($38,220), mandatory fees ($380), and room and board ($9810). ***College room only:*** $5360. Room and board charges vary according to board plan. ***Part-time tuition:*** $4778 per course. ***Payment plan:*** Installment.

FRESHMAN FINANCIAL AID (Fall 2008, est.) 241 applied for aid; of those 78% were deemed to have need. 100% of freshmen with need received aid; of those 100% had need fully met. ***Average percent of need met:*** 100% (excluding resources awarded to replace EFC). ***Average financial aid package:*** $33,665 (excluding resources awarded to replace EFC).

UNDERGRADUATE FINANCIAL AID (Fall 2008, est.) 879 applied for aid; of those 86% were deemed to have need. 100% of undergraduates with need received aid; of those 100% had need fully met. ***Average percent of need met:*** 100% (excluding resources awarded to replace EFC). ***Average financial aid package:*** $33,037 (excluding resources awarded to replace EFC). 3% of all full-time undergraduates had no need and received non-need-based gift aid.

GIFT AID (NEED-BASED) ***Total amount:*** $22,168,250 (4% federal, 2% state, 92% institutional, 2% external sources). ***Receiving aid:*** Freshmen: 41% (189); all full-time undergraduates: 41% (757). ***Average award:*** Freshmen: $28,647; Undergraduates: $27,347. ***Scholarships, grants, and awards:*** Federal Pell, FSEOG, state, private, college/university gift aid from institutional funds.

GIFT AID (NON-NEED-BASED) ***Total amount:*** $1,036,541 (15% state, 71% institutional, 14% external sources). ***Receiving aid:*** Freshmen: 2% (11). Undergraduates: 3% (63). ***Average award:*** Undergraduates: $14,451. ***Tuition waivers:*** Full or partial for employees or children of employees. ***ROTC:*** Army cooperative, Air Force cooperative.

LOANS ***Student loans:*** $2,458,514 (97% need-based, 3% non-need-based). 43% of past graduating class borrowed through all loan programs. *Average indebtedness per student:* $18,259. ***Average need-based loan:*** Freshmen: $2714. Undergraduates: $3875. ***Programs:*** FFEL (Subsidized and Unsubsidized Stafford, PLUS), Perkins, college/university.

WORK-STUDY ***Federal work-study:*** Total amount: $592,902; 429 jobs averaging $1382. ***State or other work-study/employment:*** Total amount: $91,200 (100% need-based). 59 part-time jobs averaging $1545.

APPLYING FOR FINANCIAL AID ***Required financial aid forms:*** FAFSA, institution's own form, CSS Financial Aid PROFILE, state aid form, noncustodial (divorced/separated) parent's statement, business/farm supplement. ***Financial aid deadline:*** 2/8 (priority: 2/8). ***Notification date:*** 4/1. Students must reply by 5/1.

CONTACT Colleen Seymour, Office of Financial Aid, Hamilton College, 198 College Hill Road, Clinton, NY 13323, 315-859-4413 or toll-free 800-843-2655. *Fax:* 315-859-4962. *E-mail:* finaid@hamilton.edu.

HAMILTON TECHNICAL COLLEGE

Davenport, IA

CONTACT Ms. Lisa Boyd, Executive Vice President/Director of Financial Aid, Hamilton Technical College, 1011 East 53rd Street, Davenport, IA 52807-2653, 563-386-3570 Ext. 33. *Fax:* 563-386-6756.

HAMLINE UNIVERSITY

St. Paul, MN

Tuition & fees: $28,152 **Average undergraduate aid package: $21,285**

ABOUT THE INSTITUTION Independent religious, coed. ***Awards:*** bachelor's, master's, doctoral, and first professional degrees and post-bachelor's certificates. 54 undergraduate majors. ***Total enrollment:*** 4,876. Undergraduates: 2,053. Freshmen: 452. Federal methodology is used as a basis for awarding need-based institutional aid.

UNDERGRADUATE EXPENSES for 2008–09 ***One-time required fee:*** $250. ***Comprehensive fee:*** $35,936 includes full-time tuition ($27,620), mandatory fees ($532), and room and board ($7784). ***College room only:*** $3976. Full-time tuition and fees vary according to student level. Room and board charges vary according to board plan and housing facility. ***Part-time tuition:*** $863 per credit. ***Part-time fees:*** $206 per term. Part-time tuition and fees vary according to course load and student level. ***Payment plan:*** Installment.

FRESHMAN FINANCIAL AID (Fall 2008, est.) 410 applied for aid; of those 87% were deemed to have need. 100% of freshmen with need received aid; of those 25% had need fully met. ***Average percent of need met:*** 85% (excluding resources awarded to replace EFC). ***Average financial aid package:*** $22,852 (excluding resources awarded to replace EFC). 13% of all full-time freshmen had no need and received non-need-based gift aid.

UNDERGRADUATE FINANCIAL AID (Fall 2008, est.) 1,647 applied for aid; of those 87% were deemed to have need. 100% of undergraduates with need received aid; of those 20% had need fully met. ***Average percent of need met:*** 81% (excluding resources awarded to replace EFC). ***Average financial aid package:*** $21,285 (excluding resources awarded to replace EFC). 17% of all full-time undergraduates had no need and received non-need-based gift aid.

GIFT AID (NEED-BASED) ***Total amount:*** $19,958,932 (12% federal, 12% state, 74% institutional, 2% external sources). ***Receiving aid:*** Freshmen: 79% (358); all full-time undergraduates: 75% (1,427). ***Average award:*** Freshmen: $15,448; Undergraduates: $13,947. ***Scholarships, grants, and awards:*** Federal Pell, FSEOG, state, private, college/university gift aid from institutional funds, Academic Competitiveness Grant, National Smart Grant.

GIFT AID (NON-NEED-BASED) ***Total amount:*** $5,045,628 (96% institutional, 4% external sources). ***Receiving aid:*** Freshmen: 10% (47). Undergraduates: 8% (144). ***Average award:*** Freshmen: $12,695. Undergraduates: $11,544. ***Scholarships, grants, and awards by category:*** *Academic interests/achievement:* 1,986 awards ($8,341,481 total): biological sciences, communication, English, foreign languages, general academic interests/achievements, physical sciences, premedicine. *Creative arts/performance:* 78 awards ($98,401 total): art/fine arts, creative writing, general creative arts/performance, music, theater/drama. *Special achievements/activities:* 50 awards ($43,143 total): memberships. *Special characteristics:* 268 awards ($988,012 total): ethnic background, general special characteristics, international students, local/state students, members of minority groups. ***Tuition waivers:*** Full or partial for employees or children of employees. ***ROTC:*** Air Force cooperative.

LOANS ***Student loans:*** $15,248,731 (39% need-based, 61% non-need-based). 79% of past graduating class borrowed through all loan programs. *Average indebtedness per student:* $31,577. ***Average need-based loan:*** Freshmen: $4856. Undergraduates: $5024. ***Parent loans:*** $2,951,301 (100% non-need-based). ***Programs:*** FFEL (Subsidized and Unsubsidized Stafford, PLUS), Perkins, state, non-federal alternative loans.

WORK-STUDY ***Federal work-study:*** Total amount: $626,868; 264 jobs averaging $2375. ***State or other work-study/employment:*** Total amount: $2,901,176 (69% need-based, 31% non-need-based). 1,287 part-time jobs averaging $2254.

APPLYING FOR FINANCIAL AID ***Required financial aid form:*** FAFSA. ***Financial aid deadline (priority):*** 3/1. ***Notification date:*** Continuous beginning 3/15. Students must reply by 5/1.

CONTACT Office of Financial Aid, Hamline University, 1536 Hewitt Avenue, MS C1915, St. Paul, MN 55104, 651-523-3000 or toll-free 800-753-9753. *Fax:* 651-523-2585. *E-mail:* sasmail@gw.hamline.edu.

HAMPDEN-SYDNEY COLLEGE

Hampden-Sydney, VA

ABOUT THE INSTITUTION Independent religious, men only. ***Awards:*** bachelor's degrees. 28 undergraduate majors. ***Total enrollment:*** 1,120. Undergraduates: 1,120. Freshmen: 314.

GIFT AID (NEED-BASED) ***Scholarships, grants, and awards:*** Federal Pell, FSEOG, state, private, college/university gift aid from institutional funds.

GIFT AID (NON-NEED-BASED) ***Scholarships, grants, and awards by category:*** *Academic interests/achievement:* biological sciences, education, general academic interests/achievements, health fields, international studies, premedicine, religion/biblical studies. *Creative arts/performance:* music. *Special achievements/activities:* general special achievements/activities, leadership. *Special characteristics:* children of educators, children of faculty/staff, ethnic background, international students, members of minority groups, out-of-state students, religious affiliation.

LOANS ***Programs:*** FFEL (Subsidized and Unsubsidized Stafford, PLUS), Perkins, college/university.

WORK-STUDY ***Federal work-study:*** Total amount: $317,177; 206 jobs averaging $1540.

APPLYING FOR FINANCIAL AID ***Required financial aid forms:*** FAFSA, CSS Financial Aid PROFILE, state aid form.

CONTACT Mrs. Lynn Clements, Assistant Director of Financial Aid, Hampden-Sydney College, PO Box 726, Hampden-Sydney, VA 23943-0667, 434-223-6119 or toll-free 800-755-0733. *Fax:* 434-223-6075. *E-mail:* lclements@hsc.edu.

HAMPSHIRE COLLEGE

Amherst, MA

Tuition & fees: $38,549 **Average undergraduate aid package: $32,910**

ABOUT THE INSTITUTION Independent, coed. ***Awards:*** bachelor's degrees. 135 undergraduate majors. ***Total enrollment:*** 1,428. Undergraduates: 1,428. Freshmen: 389. Institutional methodology is used as a basis for awarding need-based institutional aid.

UNDERGRADUATE EXPENSES for 2008–09 ***Application fee:*** $55. ***Comprehensive fee:*** $48,629 includes full-time tuition ($37,789), mandatory fees ($760), and room and board ($10,080). ***College room only:*** $6428. Room and board charges vary according to board plan. ***Payment plan:*** Installment.

FRESHMAN FINANCIAL AID (Fall 2008, est.) 249 applied for aid; of those 88% were deemed to have need. 100% of freshmen with need received aid; of those 78% had need fully met. ***Average percent of need met:*** 98% (excluding resources awarded to replace EFC). ***Average financial aid package:*** $32,385 (excluding resources awarded to replace EFC). 15% of all full-time freshmen had no need and received non-need-based gift aid.

UNDERGRADUATE FINANCIAL AID (Fall 2008, est.) 848 applied for aid; of those 89% were deemed to have need. 100% of undergraduates with need received aid; of those 84% had need fully met. ***Average percent of need met:*** 99% (excluding resources awarded to replace EFC). ***Average financial aid package:*** $32,910 (excluding resources awarded to replace EFC). 18% of all full-time undergraduates had no need and received non-need-based gift aid.

GIFT AID (NEED-BASED) ***Total amount:*** $19,377,950 (7% federal, 92% institutional, 1% external sources). ***Receiving aid:*** Freshmen: 55% (218); all full-time undergraduates: 54% (755). ***Average award:*** Freshmen: $26,785; Undergraduates: $25,685. ***Scholarships, grants, and awards:*** Federal Pell, FSEOG, state, private, college/university gift aid from institutional funds.

GIFT AID (NON-NEED-BASED) ***Total amount:*** $1,619,600 (1% federal, 2% state, 92% institutional, 5% external sources). ***Receiving aid:*** Freshmen: 40% (158). Undergraduates: 31% (431). ***Average award:*** Freshmen: $5760. Undergraduates: $5925. ***Scholarships, grants, and awards by category:*** *Academic interests/achievement:* 249 awards ($1,374,500 total): general academic interests/achievements, international studies, physical sciences, social sciences. *Creative arts/performance:* creative writing. *Special achievements/activities:* 3 awards ($22,500 total): community service, leadership. *Special characteristics:* 21 awards ($698,500 total): children of faculty/staff. ***Tuition waivers:*** Full or partial for employees or children of employees. ***ROTC:*** Army cooperative.

LOANS ***Student loans:*** $3,478,400 (78% need-based, 22% non-need-based). 63% of past graduating class borrowed through all loan programs. *Average indebtedness per student:* $21,300. ***Average need-based loan:*** Freshmen: $3500. Undergraduates: $4750. ***Parent loans:*** $3,490,700 (60% need-based, 40% non-need-based). ***Programs:*** Federal Direct (Subsidized and Unsubsidized Stafford, PLUS), FFEL (PLUS), Perkins.

WORK-STUDY ***Federal work-study:*** Total amount: $1,215,700; 526 jobs averaging $2475. ***State or other work-study/employment:*** Total amount: $695,900 (77% need-based, 23% non-need-based). 256 part-time jobs averaging $2475.

APPLYING FOR FINANCIAL AID ***Required financial aid forms:*** FAFSA, CSS Financial Aid PROFILE, noncustodial (divorced/separated) parent's statement. ***Financial aid deadline (priority):*** 2/1. ***Notification date:*** 4/1. Students must reply by 5/1 or within 2 weeks of notification.

CONTACT Ms. Kathleen Methot, Director of Financial Aid, Hampshire College, 893 West Street, Amherst, MA 01002, 413-559-5484 or toll-free 877-937-4267 (out-of-state). *Fax:* 413-559-5585. *E-mail:* financialaid@hampshire.edu.

HAMPTON UNIVERSITY

Hampton, VA

Tuition & fees: $16,392 **Average undergraduate aid package: $4704**

ABOUT THE INSTITUTION Independent, coed. ***Awards:*** associate, bachelor's, master's, doctoral, and first professional degrees. 82 undergraduate majors. ***Total enrollment:*** 5,427. Undergraduates: 4,700. Freshmen: 1,212. Federal methodology is used as a basis for awarding need-based institutional aid.

UNDERGRADUATE EXPENSES for 2008–09 ***Application fee:*** $35. ***Comprehensive fee:*** $23,832 includes full-time tuition ($14,728), mandatory fees ($1664), and room and board ($7440). ***College room only:*** $3870. Full-time tuition and fees vary according to course load, degree level, and program. Room and board charges vary according to board plan and housing facility. ***Part-time tuition:*** $370 per credit. ***Payment plan:*** Deferred payment.

FRESHMAN FINANCIAL AID (Fall 2008, est.) 739 applied for aid; of those 83% were deemed to have need. 88% of freshmen with need received aid; of those 40% had need fully met. ***Average percent of need met:*** 40% (excluding resources awarded to replace EFC). ***Average financial aid package:*** $3877 (excluding resources awarded to replace EFC). 10% of all full-time freshmen had no need and received non-need-based gift aid.

UNDERGRADUATE FINANCIAL AID (Fall 2008, est.) 2,159 applied for aid; of those 83% were deemed to have need. 91% of undergraduates with need received aid; of those 41% had need fully met. ***Average percent of need met:*** 41% (excluding resources awarded to replace EFC). ***Average financial aid package:*** $4704 (excluding resources awarded to replace EFC). 8% of all full-time undergraduates had no need and received non-need-based gift aid.

GIFT AID (NEED-BASED) ***Total amount:*** $11,033,598 (50% federal, 20% state, 1% institutional, 29% external sources). ***Receiving aid:*** Freshmen: 45% (533); all full-time undergraduates: 41% (1,598). ***Average award:*** Freshmen: $3339; Undergraduates: $3844. ***Scholarships, grants, and awards:*** Federal Pell, FSEOG, state, private, college/university gift aid from institutional funds, Federal Nursing.

GIFT AID (NON-NEED-BASED) ***Total amount:*** $6,972,197 (10% state, 34% institutional, 56% external sources). ***Receiving aid:*** Freshmen: 12% (137). Undergraduates: 12% (465). ***Average award:*** Freshmen: $9874. Undergraduates: $11,422. ***Scholarships, grants, and awards by category:*** *Academic interests/achievement:* general academic interests/achievements. *Creative arts/performance:* music. *Special characteristics:* international students, members of minority groups. ***Tuition waivers:*** Full or partial for employees or children of employees. ***ROTC:*** Army, Naval.

LOANS ***Student loans:*** $42,412,365 (32% need-based, 68% non-need-based). 82% of past graduating class borrowed through all loan programs. *Average indebtedness per student:* $9478. ***Average need-based loan:*** Freshmen: $3728. Undergraduates: $3500. ***Parent loans:*** $14,256,065 (100% non-need-based). ***Programs:*** FFEL (Subsidized and Unsubsidized Stafford, PLUS), Perkins, Federal Nursing, college/university.

WORK-STUDY ***Federal work-study:*** Total amount: $451,976; 331 jobs averaging $1800.

ATHLETIC AWARDS Total amount: $3,738,539 (100% non-need-based).

APPLYING FOR FINANCIAL AID ***Required financial aid form:*** FAFSA. ***Financial aid deadline:*** 3/1. ***Notification date:*** Continuous beginning 4/15. Students must reply within 2 weeks of notification.

CONTACT Martin Miles, Director, Financial Aid, Hampton University, Hampton University, Hampton, VA 23668, 757-727-5332 or toll-free 800-624-3328. *Fax:* 757-728-6567. *E-mail:* martin.miles@hamptonu.edu.

HANNIBAL-LAGRANGE COLLEGE

Hannibal, MO

ABOUT THE INSTITUTION Independent Southern Baptist, coed. ***Awards:*** associate, bachelor's, and master's degrees. 44 undergraduate majors. ***Total enrollment:*** 1,127. Undergraduates: 1,084.

GIFT AID (NEED-BASED) ***Scholarships, grants, and awards:*** Federal Pell, FSEOG, state, private.

GIFT AID (NON-NEED-BASED) ***Scholarships, grants, and awards by category:*** *Academic interests/achievement:* general academic interests/achievements, religion/biblical studies. *Creative arts/performance:* art/fine arts, journalism/publications, music, performing arts, theater/drama. *Special characteristics:* children of faculty/staff, public servants, relatives of clergy, religious affiliation.

LOANS ***Programs:*** FFEL (Subsidized and Unsubsidized Stafford, PLUS), Perkins.

WORK-STUDY ***Federal work-study:*** Total amount: $99,887; 85 jobs averaging $550.

APPLYING FOR FINANCIAL AID ***Required financial aid forms:*** FAFSA, institution's own form.

CONTACT Amy Blackwell, Director of Financial Aid, Hannibal-LaGrange College, 2800 Palmyra Road, Hannibal, MO 63401-1940, 573-221-3675 Ext. 279 or toll-free 800-HLG-1119. *Fax:* 573-221-6594.

HANOVER COLLEGE

Hanover, IN

Tuition & fees: $25,220 **Average undergraduate aid package: $20,946**

ABOUT THE INSTITUTION Independent Presbyterian, coed. ***Awards:*** bachelor's degrees. 29 undergraduate majors. ***Total enrollment:*** 926. Undergraduates: 926. Freshmen: 328. Federal methodology is used as a basis for awarding need-based institutional aid.

UNDERGRADUATE EXPENSES for 2008–09 ***Application fee:*** $40. ***One-time required fee:*** $250. ***Comprehensive fee:*** $32,720 includes full-time tuition ($24,700), mandatory fees ($520), and room and board ($7500). ***College room only:*** $3650. Full-time tuition and fees vary according to reciprocity agreements. Room and board charges vary according to housing facility and location. ***Part-time tuition:*** $2740 per unit. Part-time tuition and fees vary according to course load and reciprocity agreements. ***Payment plan:*** Installment.

FRESHMAN FINANCIAL AID (Fall 2008, est.) 326 applied for aid; of those 87% were deemed to have need. 100% of freshmen with need received aid; of those 38% had need fully met. ***Average percent of need met:*** 84% (excluding resources awarded to replace EFC). ***Average financial aid package:*** $21,317 (excluding resources awarded to replace EFC). 14% of all full-time freshmen had no need and received non-need-based gift aid.

UNDERGRADUATE FINANCIAL AID (Fall 2008, est.) 917 applied for aid; of those 74% were deemed to have need. 100% of undergraduates with need received aid; of those 38% had need fully met. ***Average percent of need met:*** 85% (excluding resources awarded to replace EFC). ***Average financial aid package:*** $20,946 (excluding resources awarded to replace EFC). 25% of all full-time undergraduates had no need and received non-need-based gift aid.

GIFT AID (NEED-BASED) ***Total amount:*** $11,692,163 (5% federal, 14% state, 71% institutional, 10% external sources). ***Receiving aid:*** Freshmen: 86% (283); all full-time undergraduates: 73% (679). ***Average award:*** Freshmen: $18,442; Undergraduates: $17,203. ***Scholarships, grants, and awards:*** Federal Pell, state, private, college/university gift aid from institutional funds.

GIFT AID (NON-NEED-BASED) ***Total amount:*** $4,172,882 (9% state, 76% institutional, 15% external sources). ***Receiving aid:*** Freshmen: 15% (48). Undergraduates: 12% (115). ***Average award:*** Freshmen: $8884. Undergraduates: $11,945. ***Scholarships, grants, and awards by category:*** *Academic interests/achievement:* general academic interests/achievements. *Creative arts/performance:* art/fine arts, music, theater/drama. *Special characteristics:* children and siblings of alumni, children of faculty/staff, international students, members of minority groups, out-of-state students, religious affiliation, siblings of current students. ***Tuition waivers:*** Full or partial for employees or children of employees, senior citizens.

LOANS ***Student loans:*** $4,516,562 (56% need-based, 44% non-need-based). ***Average need-based loan:*** Freshmen: $2697. Undergraduates: $3615. ***Parent loans:*** $1,132,772 (18% need-based, 82% non-need-based). ***Programs:*** FFEL (Subsidized and Unsubsidized Stafford, PLUS), college/university.

APPLYING FOR FINANCIAL AID ***Required financial aid form:*** FAFSA. ***Financial aid deadline (priority):*** 3/1. ***Notification date:*** Continuous beginning 3/1. Students must reply by 5/1.

CONTACT Jon Riester, Director of Admission & Financial Assistance, Hanover College, PO Box 108, Hanover, IN 47243-0108, 800-213-2178. *Fax:* 812-866-7098. *E-mail:* finaid@hanover.edu.

HARDING UNIVERSITY

Searcy, AR

Tuition & fees: $13,130 **Average undergraduate aid package: $10,757**

ABOUT THE INSTITUTION Independent religious, coed. ***Awards:*** bachelor's, master's, doctoral, and first professional degrees and post-master's certificates. 93 undergraduate majors. ***Total enrollment:*** 6,447. Undergraduates: 4,168. Freshmen: 986. Federal methodology is used as a basis for awarding need-based institutional aid.

UNDERGRADUATE EXPENSES for 2008–09 ***Application fee:*** $35. ***Comprehensive fee:*** $18,830 includes full-time tuition ($12,690), mandatory fees ($440), and room and board ($5700). ***College room only:*** $2824. Full-time tuition and fees vary according to course load. Room and board charges vary according to board plan and housing facility. ***Part-time tuition:*** $423 per semester hour. ***Part-time fees:*** $22 per semester hour. Part-time tuition and fees vary according to course load. ***Payment plans:*** Tuition prepayment, installment.

FRESHMAN FINANCIAL AID (Fall 2008, est.) 732 applied for aid; of those 70% were deemed to have need. 100% of freshmen with need received aid; of those 38% had need fully met. ***Average percent of need met:*** 83% (excluding resources awarded to replace EFC). ***Average financial aid package:*** $12,466 (excluding resources awarded to replace EFC). 20% of all full-time freshmen had no need and received non-need-based gift aid.

UNDERGRADUATE FINANCIAL AID (Fall 2008, est.) 2,746 applied for aid; of those 77% were deemed to have need. 99% of undergraduates with need received aid; of those 26% had need fully met. ***Average percent of need met:*** 70% (excluding resources awarded to replace EFC). ***Average financial aid package:*** $10,757 (excluding resources awarded to replace EFC). 12% of all full-time undergraduates had no need and received non-need-based gift aid.

GIFT AID (NEED-BASED) ***Total amount:*** $11,974,128 (33% federal, 5% state, 59% institutional, 3% external sources). ***Receiving aid:*** Freshmen: 50% (488); all full-time undergraduates: 48% (1,872). ***Average award:*** Freshmen: $8647; Undergraduates: $6723. ***Scholarships, grants, and awards:*** Federal Pell, FSEOG, state, private, college/university gift aid from institutional funds.

GIFT AID (NON-NEED-BASED) ***Total amount:*** $9,833,023 (5% state, 89% institutional, 6% external sources). ***Receiving aid:*** Freshmen: 14% (135). Undergraduates: 8% (325). ***Average award:*** Freshmen: $5933. Undergraduates: $4859. ***Scholarships, grants, and awards by category:*** *Academic interests/achievement:* 2,050 awards ($9,238,641 total): communication, computer science, engineering/technologies, English, general academic interests/achievements, health fields. *Creative arts/performance:* 261 awards ($193,901 total): art/fine arts, cinema/film/broadcasting, debating, journalism/publications, music. *Special achievements/activities:* 101 awards ($109,963 total): cheerleading/drum major, leadership, religious involvement. *Special characteristics:* 444 awards ($2,126,778 total): children of faculty/staff, children with a deceased or disabled parent, international students, relatives of clergy, siblings of current students. ***Tuition waivers:*** Full or partial for employees or children of employees, senior citizens. ***ROTC:*** Army cooperative.

LOANS ***Student loans:*** $22,030,650 (60% need-based, 40% non-need-based). 68% of past graduating class borrowed through all loan programs. *Average indebtedness per student:* $31,100. ***Average need-based loan:*** Freshmen: $4097. Undergraduates: $4598. ***Parent loans:*** $4,012,323 (21% need-based, 79% non-need-based). ***Programs:*** FFEL (Subsidized and Unsubsidized Stafford, PLUS), Perkins, Federal Nursing, state, college/university.

WORK-STUDY ***Federal work-study:*** Total amount: $325,127; 391 jobs averaging $831. ***State or other work-study/employment:*** Total amount: $1,252,884 (20% need-based, 80% non-need-based). 1,140 part-time jobs averaging $1140.

ATHLETIC AWARDS Total amount: $1,737,366 (28% need-based, 72% non-need-based).

APPLYING FOR FINANCIAL AID ***Required financial aid form:*** FAFSA. ***Financial aid deadline (priority):*** 4/15. ***Notification date:*** Continuous. Students must reply within 2 weeks of notification.

CONTACT Dr. Jonathan C. Roberts, Director of Student Financial Services, Harding University, Box 12282, Searcy, AR 72149-2282, 501-279-4257 or toll-free 800-477-4407. *Fax:* 501-279-4129. *E-mail:* jroberts@harding.edu.

HARDIN-SIMMONS UNIVERSITY

Abilene, TX

Tuition & fees: $19,790 **Average undergraduate aid package: $14,820**

ABOUT THE INSTITUTION Independent Baptist, coed. ***Awards:*** bachelor's, master's, doctoral, and first professional degrees and post-bachelor's certificates. 74 undergraduate majors. ***Total enrollment:*** 2,387. Undergraduates: 1,934. Freshmen: 471. Federal methodology is used as a basis for awarding need-based institutional aid.

UNDERGRADUATE EXPENSES for 2009–10 ***Application fee:*** $50. ***Comprehensive fee:*** $25,578 includes full-time tuition ($18,750), mandatory fees ($1040), and room and board ($5788). ***College room only:*** $2836. ***Part-time tuition:*** $625 per semester hour. ***Part-time fees:*** $150 per term.

FRESHMAN FINANCIAL AID (Fall 2008, est.) 463 applied for aid; of those 70% were deemed to have need. 100% of freshmen with need received aid; of those 30% had need fully met. ***Average percent of need met:*** 65% (excluding resources awarded to replace EFC). ***Average financial aid package:*** $16,609 (excluding resources awarded to replace EFC). 14% of all full-time freshmen had no need and received non-need-based gift aid.

UNDERGRADUATE FINANCIAL AID (Fall 2008, est.) 1,693 applied for aid; of those 70% were deemed to have need. 100% of undergraduates with need received aid; of those 80% had need fully met. ***Average percent of need met:*** 60% (excluding resources awarded to replace EFC). ***Average financial aid package:*** $14,820 (excluding resources awarded to replace EFC). 12% of all full-time undergraduates had no need and received non-need-based gift aid.

GIFT AID (NEED-BASED) ***Total amount:*** $5,067,617 (43% federal, 57% state). ***Receiving aid:*** Freshmen: 50% (237); all full-time undergraduates: 49% (861). ***Average award:*** Freshmen: $5814; Undergraduates: $5299. ***Scholarships, grants, and awards:*** Federal Pell, FSEOG, state, private, college/university gift aid from institutional funds, Academic Competitiveness Grant, National Smart Grant.

GIFT AID (NON-NEED-BASED) ***Total amount:*** $9,561,709 (92% institutional, 8% external sources). ***Receiving aid:*** Freshmen: 59% (276). Undergraduates: 56% (970). ***Average award:*** Freshmen: $4031. Undergraduates: $3895. ***Scholarships, grants, and awards by category:*** *Academic interests/achievement:* 1,860 awards ($6,492,283 total): biological sciences, business, communication, education, English, foreign languages, general academic interests/achievements, health fields, humanities, mathematics, physical sciences, premedicine, religion/biblical studies, social sciences. *Creative arts/performance:* 120 awards ($261,148 total): art/fine arts, creative writing, journalism/publications, music, theater/drama. *Special achievements/activities:* 39 awards ($43,250 total): general special achievements/activities, junior miss, leadership. *Special characteristics:* 395 awards ($1,749,991 total): children of faculty/staff, ethnic background, general special characteristics, local/state students, out-of-state students, public servants, relatives of clergy, religious affiliation, siblings of current students.

LOANS ***Student loans:*** $20,607,447 (33% need-based, 67% non-need-based). 78% of past graduating class borrowed through all loan programs. *Average indebtedness per student:* $33,745. ***Average need-based loan:*** Freshmen: $3132. Undergraduates: $4276. ***Parent loans:*** $732,456 (100% non-need-based). ***Programs:*** FFEL (Subsidized and Unsubsidized Stafford, PLUS), Perkins, state, college/university.

WORK-STUDY ***Federal work-study:*** Total amount: $104,080; 202 jobs averaging $1371. ***State or other work-study/employment:*** Total amount: $300,884 (6% need-based, 94% non-need-based). 321 part-time jobs averaging $1770.

APPLYING FOR FINANCIAL AID ***Required financial aid form:*** FAFSA. ***Financial aid deadline (priority):*** 3/15. ***Notification date:*** Continuous.

CONTACT Jim Jones, Director of Financial Aid, Hardin-Simmons University, PO Box 16050, Abilene, TX 79698-6050, 325-670-5891 or toll-free 877-464-7889. *Fax:* 325-670-5822. *E-mail:* jjones@hsutx.edu.

HARRINGTON COLLEGE OF DESIGN

Chicago, IL

CONTACT Ms. Renee Darosky, Director of Financial Aid, Harrington College of Design, 410 South Michigan Avenue, Chicago, IL 60605-1496, 312-939-4975 or toll-free 877-939-4975. *Fax:* 312-697-8058. *E-mail:* financialaid@interiordesign.edu.

HARRISBURG UNIVERSITY OF SCIENCE AND TECHNOLOGY

Harrisburg, PA

Tuition & fees: $14,750 **Average undergraduate aid package: N/A**

ABOUT THE INSTITUTION Independent, coed. ***Awards:*** bachelor's and master's degrees. 5 undergraduate majors. ***Total enrollment:*** 214. Undergraduates: 191. Federal methodology is used as a basis for awarding need-based institutional aid.

UNDERGRADUATE EXPENSES for 2008–09 ***Tuition:*** full-time $14,750; part-time $500 per semester hour. Full-time tuition and fees vary according to course load and program. Part-time tuition and fees vary according to course load and program. ***Payment plan:*** Installment.

GIFT AID (NEED-BASED) ***Total amount:*** $469,095 (56% federal, 42% state, 2% external sources). ***Scholarships, grants, and awards:*** Federal Pell, FSEOG, state, private, college/university gift aid from institutional funds.

GIFT AID (NON-NEED-BASED) ***Tuition waivers:*** Full or partial for employees or children of employees.

LOANS ***Student loans:*** $723,675 (100% need-based). ***Parent loans:*** $38,837 (100% need-based). ***Programs:*** FFEL (Subsidized and Unsubsidized Stafford, PLUS).

WORK-STUDY ***Federal work-study:*** Total amount: $2451; 8 jobs averaging $600.

APPLYING FOR FINANCIAL AID ***Required financial aid form:*** FAFSA. ***Financial aid deadline:*** Continuous. ***Notification date:*** Continuous. Students must reply within 2 weeks of notification.

CONTACT Vince Frank, Director of Financial Aid Services, Harrisburg University of Science and Technology, 326 Market Street, Harrisburg, PA 17101, 717-901-5115 or toll-free 866-HBG-UNIV. *Fax:* 717-901-6115. *E-mail:* vfrank@harrisburgu.net.

HARRIS-STOWE STATE UNIVERSITY

St. Louis, MO

CONTACT Regina Blackshear, Director of Financial Aid, Harris-Stowe State University, 3026 Laclede Avenue, St. Louis, MO 63103-2136, 314-340-3502. *Fax:* 314-340-3503.

HARTWICK COLLEGE

Oneonta, NY

Tuition & fees: $31,900 **Average undergraduate aid package: $22,955**

ABOUT THE INSTITUTION Independent, coed. ***Awards:*** bachelor's degrees. 33 undergraduate majors. ***Total enrollment:*** 1,493. Undergraduates: 1,493. Freshmen: 444. Federal methodology is used as a basis for awarding need-based institutional aid.

UNDERGRADUATE EXPENSES for 2008–09 ***Application fee:*** $35. ***One-time required fee:*** $300. ***Comprehensive fee:*** $40,585 includes full-time tuition ($31,330), mandatory fees ($570), and room and board ($8685). ***College room only:*** $4500. Full-time tuition and fees vary according to student level. Room and board charges vary according to board plan and housing facility. ***Part-time tuition:*** $990 per hour. ***Payment plan:*** Installment.

FRESHMAN FINANCIAL AID (Fall 2008, est.) 363 applied for aid; of those 90% were deemed to have need. 100% of freshmen with need received aid; of those 9% had need fully met. ***Average percent of need met:*** 81% (excluding resources awarded to replace EFC). ***Average financial aid package:*** $24,857 (excluding resources awarded to replace EFC). 24% of all full-time freshmen had no need and received non-need-based gift aid.

UNDERGRADUATE FINANCIAL AID (Fall 2008, est.) 1,150 applied for aid; of those 90% were deemed to have need. 100% of undergraduates with need received aid; of those 14% had need fully met. ***Average percent of need met:*** 78% (excluding resources awarded to replace EFC). ***Average financial aid package:*** $22,955 (excluding resources awarded to replace EFC). 25% of all full-time undergraduates had no need and received non-need-based gift aid.

GIFT AID (NEED-BASED) ***Total amount:*** $17,294,995 (9% federal, 8% state, 81% institutional, 2% external sources). ***Receiving aid:*** Freshmen: 74% (327); all full-time undergraduates: 73% (1,040). ***Average award:*** Freshmen: $18,856; Undergraduates: $17,897. ***Scholarships, grants, and awards:*** Federal Pell, FSEOG, state, private, college/university gift aid from institutional funds.

GIFT AID (NON-NEED-BASED) ***Total amount:*** $4,340,536 (2% state, 96% institutional, 2% external sources). ***Receiving aid:*** Freshmen: 8% (36). Undergraduates: 7% (97). ***Average award:*** Freshmen: $10,020. Undergraduates: $13,458. ***Scholarships, grants, and awards by category:*** *Special characteristics:* children and siblings of alumni, children of faculty/staff, international students, siblings of current students. ***Tuition waivers:*** Full or partial for employees or children of employees.

LOANS ***Student loans:*** $11,758,303 (62% need-based, 38% non-need-based). 72% of past graduating class borrowed through all loan programs. *Average indebtedness per student:* $30,802. ***Average need-based loan:*** Freshmen: $4414. Undergraduates: $4128. ***Parent loans:*** $16,553,563 (26% need-based, 74% non-need-based). ***Programs:*** FFEL (Subsidized and Unsubsidized Stafford, PLUS), Perkins, Federal Nursing, college/university, alternative loans.

WORK-STUDY ***Federal work-study:*** Total amount: $966,548; 700 jobs averaging $1550. ***State or other work-study/employment:*** Part-time jobs available.

ATHLETIC AWARDS Total amount: $606,739 (28% need-based, 72% non-need-based).

APPLYING FOR FINANCIAL AID ***Required financial aid form:*** FAFSA. ***Financial aid deadline:*** 2/15. ***Notification date:*** 3/7. Students must reply by 5/1 or within 2 weeks of notification.

CONTACT Melissa Allen, Director, Financial Aid, Hartwick College, One Hartwick Drive, Oneonta, NY 13820, 607-431-4130 or toll-free 888-HARTWICK (out-of-state). *Fax:* 607-431-4006. *E-mail:* allenm2@hartwick.edu.

HARVARD UNIVERSITY

Cambridge, MA

Tuition & fees: $36,173 **Average undergraduate aid package: $39,193**

ABOUT THE INSTITUTION Independent, coed. ***Awards:*** bachelor's, master's, doctoral, and first professional degrees and post-master's and first professional certificates. 45 undergraduate majors. ***Total enrollment:*** 19,230. Undergraduates: 6,678. Freshmen: 1,666. Institutional methodology is used as a basis for awarding need-based institutional aid.

UNDERGRADUATE EXPENSES for 2008–09 ***Application fee:*** $65. ***Comprehensive fee:*** $47,215 includes full-time tuition ($32,557), mandatory fees ($3616), and room and board ($11,042). ***College room only:*** $6060. ***Payment plans:*** Tuition prepayment, installment.

FRESHMAN FINANCIAL AID (Fall 2008, est.) 1,146 applied for aid; of those 87% were deemed to have need. 100% of freshmen with need received aid; of those 100% had need fully met. ***Average percent of need met:*** 100% (excluding resources awarded to replace EFC). ***Average financial aid package:*** $40,533 (excluding resources awarded to replace EFC).

UNDERGRADUATE FINANCIAL AID (Fall 2008, est.) 4,266 applied for aid; of those 89% were deemed to have need. 100% of undergraduates with need received aid; of those 100% had need fully met. ***Average percent of need met:*** 100% (excluding resources awarded to replace EFC). ***Average financial aid package:*** $39,193 (excluding resources awarded to replace EFC).

GIFT AID (NEED-BASED) ***Total amount:*** $142,302,000 (5% federal, 91% institutional, 4% external sources). ***Receiving aid:*** Freshmen: 60% (992); all full-time undergraduates: 57% (3,785). ***Average award:*** Freshmen: $39,164; Undergraduates: $36,850. ***Scholarships, grants, and awards:*** Federal Pell, FSEOG, state, private, college/university gift aid from institutional funds.

GIFT AID (NON-NEED-BASED) ***Total amount:*** $3,973,000 (24% federal, 76% external sources). ***ROTC:*** Army cooperative, Naval cooperative, Air Force cooperative.

LOANS ***Student loans:*** $2,950,000 (75% need-based, 25% non-need-based). 39% of past graduating class borrowed through all loan programs. *Average indebtedness per student:* $10,813. ***Average need-based loan:*** Freshmen: $2510. Undergraduates: $2699. ***Parent loans:*** $9,562,000 (100% non-need-based). ***Programs:*** Federal Direct (Subsidized and Unsubsidized Stafford, PLUS), Perkins, state, college/university.

WORK-STUDY ***Federal work-study:*** Total amount: $1,700,000; 791 jobs averaging $2248. ***State or other work-study/employment:*** Total amount: $5,650,000 (82% need-based, 18% non-need-based). 2,209 part-time jobs averaging $2380.

APPLYING FOR FINANCIAL AID ***Required financial aid forms:*** FAFSA, CSS Financial Aid PROFILE, business/farm supplement, income tax form(s). ***Financial aid deadline (priority):*** 2/1. ***Notification date:*** 4/1. Students must reply by 5/1 or within 2 weeks of notification.

CONTACT Financial Aid Office, Harvard University, 86 Brattle Street, Cambridge, MA 02138, 617-495-1581. *Fax:* 617-496-0256.

HARVEY MUDD COLLEGE

Claremont, CA

Tuition & fees: $36,635 **Average undergraduate aid package: $30,618**

ABOUT THE INSTITUTION Independent, coed. ***Awards:*** bachelor's degrees. 6 undergraduate majors. ***Total enrollment:*** 738. Undergraduates: 738. Freshmen: 202. Both federal and institutional methodology are used as a basis for awarding need-based institutional aid.

UNDERGRADUATE EXPENSES for 2008–09 ***Application fee:*** $60. ***Comprehensive fee:*** $48,606 includes full-time tuition ($36,402), mandatory fees ($233), and room and board ($11,971). ***College room only:*** $6290. Room and board charges vary according to board plan. ***Payment plan:*** Installment.

FRESHMAN FINANCIAL AID (Fall 2008, est.) 144 applied for aid; of those 78% were deemed to have need. 100% of freshmen with need received aid; of those 100% had need fully met. ***Average percent of need met:*** 100% (excluding resources awarded to replace EFC). ***Average financial aid package:*** $29,526 (excluding resources awarded to replace EFC). 27% of all full-time freshmen had no need and received non-need-based gift aid.

UNDERGRADUATE FINANCIAL AID (Fall 2008, est.) 472 applied for aid; of those 86% were deemed to have need. 100% of undergraduates with need received aid; of those 100% had need fully met. ***Average percent of need met:*** 100% (excluding resources awarded to replace EFC). ***Average financial aid package:*** $30,618 (excluding resources awarded to replace EFC). 25% of all full-time undergraduates had no need and received non-need-based gift aid.

GIFT AID (NEED-BASED) ***Total amount:*** $10,869,971 (6% federal, 5% state, 83% institutional, 6% external sources). ***Receiving aid:*** Freshmen: 55% (112); all full-time undergraduates: 54% (401). ***Average award:*** Freshmen: $27,376; Undergraduates: $26,377. ***Scholarships, grants, and awards:*** Federal Pell, FSEOG, state, private, college/university gift aid from institutional funds, Academic Competitiveness Grant, National Smart Grant.

GIFT AID (NON-NEED-BASED) ***Total amount:*** $2,259,060 (86% institutional, 14% external sources). ***Receiving aid:*** Freshmen: 29% (59). Undergraduates: 28% (205). ***Average award:*** Freshmen: $9951. Undergraduates: $10,440. ***Scholarships, grants, and awards by category:*** *Academic interests/achievement:* 348 awards ($3,925,114 total): general academic interests/achievements. *Special characteristics:* 9 awards: international students. ***Tuition waivers:*** Full or partial for employees or children of employees. ***ROTC:*** Army cooperative, Air Force.

LOANS ***Student loans:*** $2,209,124 (57% need-based, 43% non-need-based). 53% of past graduating class borrowed through all loan programs. *Average indebtedness per student:* $21,018. ***Average need-based loan:*** Freshmen: $3815. Undergraduates: $4822. ***Parent loans:*** $1,083,300 (77% need-based, 23% non-need-based). ***Programs:*** FFEL (Subsidized and Unsubsidized Stafford, PLUS), Perkins, college/university, alternative loans.

WORK-STUDY ***Federal work-study:*** Total amount: $491,907; 227 jobs averaging $2167. ***State or other work-study/employment:*** Total amount: $102,385 (59% need-based, 41% non-need-based). 7 part-time jobs averaging $2568.

APPLYING FOR FINANCIAL AID ***Required financial aid forms:*** FAFSA, CSS Financial Aid PROFILE, state aid form, noncustodial (divorced/separated) parent's statement, business/farm supplement. ***Financial aid deadline:*** 2/1. ***Notification date:*** 4/1. Students must reply by 5/1 or within 2 weeks of notification.

CONTACT Gilma Lopez, Office of Financial Aid, Harvey Mudd College, 301 Platt Boulevard, Claremont, CA 91711-5994, 909-621-8055. *Fax:* 909-607-7046. *E-mail:* financial_aid@hmc.edu.

HASKELL INDIAN NATIONS UNIVERSITY

Lawrence, KS

CONTACT Reta Beaver, Director of Financial Aid, Haskell Indian Nations University, 155 Indian Avenue, Box 5027, Lawrence, KS 66046-4800, 785-749-8468. *Fax:* 785-832-6617.

HASTINGS COLLEGE

Hastings, NE

Tuition & fees: $20,782 **Average undergraduate aid package: $14,901**

ABOUT THE INSTITUTION Independent Presbyterian, coed. ***Awards:*** bachelor's and master's degrees. 81 undergraduate majors. ***Total enrollment:*** 1,138. Undergraduates: 1,091. Freshmen: 304. Federal methodology is used as a basis for awarding need-based institutional aid.

UNDERGRADUATE EXPENSES for 2008–09 ***Application fee:*** $20. ***Comprehensive fee:*** $26,484 includes full-time tuition ($19,952), mandatory fees ($830), and room and board ($5702). ***College room only:*** $2436. Full-time tuition and fees vary according to course level and program. Room and board charges vary according to board plan and housing facility. Part-time tuition and fees vary according to course level, course load, and program. ***Payment plans:*** Installment, deferred payment.

FRESHMAN FINANCIAL AID (Fall 2008, est.) 301 applied for aid; of those 83% were deemed to have need. 98% of freshmen with need received aid; of those 30% had need fully met. ***Average percent of need met:*** 79% (excluding resources awarded to replace EFC). ***Average financial aid package:*** $14,972 (excluding resources awarded to replace EFC). 22% of all full-time freshmen had no need and received non-need-based gift aid.

UNDERGRADUATE FINANCIAL AID (Fall 2008, est.) 929 applied for aid; of those 87% were deemed to have need. 99% of undergraduates with need received aid; of those 26% had need fully met. ***Average percent of need met:*** 76% (excluding resources awarded to replace EFC). ***Average financial aid package:*** $14,901 (excluding resources awarded to replace EFC). 25% of all full-time undergraduates had no need and received non-need-based gift aid.

GIFT AID (NEED-BASED) ***Total amount:*** $6,885,076 (18% federal, 3% state, 68% institutional, 11% external sources). ***Receiving aid:*** Freshmen: 75% (246); all full-time undergraduates: 69% (784). ***Average award:*** Freshmen: $12,169; Undergraduates: $11,273. ***Scholarships, grants, and awards:*** Federal Pell, FSEOG, state, private, college/university gift aid from institutional funds.

GIFT AID (NON-NEED-BASED) ***Total amount:*** $2,697,600 (86% institutional, 14% external sources). ***Receiving aid:*** Freshmen: 15% (48). Undergraduates: 11% (125). ***Average award:*** Freshmen: $7406. Undergraduates: $7085. ***Scholarships, grants, and awards by category:*** *Academic interests/achievement:* communication, general academic interests/achievements, religion/biblical studies. *Creative arts/performance:* art/fine arts, dance, debating, journalism/publications, music, performing arts, theater/drama. *Special achievements/activities:* cheerleading/drum major, rodeo. *Special characteristics:* adult students, children of educators, children of faculty/staff, relatives of clergy, religious affiliation, siblings of current students. ***Tuition waivers:*** Full or partial for adult students.

LOANS ***Student loans:*** $5,867,521 (71% need-based, 29% non-need-based). 67% of past graduating class borrowed through all loan programs. *Average indebtedness per student:* $16,750. ***Average need-based loan:*** Freshmen: $3813. Undergraduates: $4735. ***Parent loans:*** $1,704,631 (29% need-based, 71% non-need-based). ***Programs:*** FFEL (Subsidized and Unsubsidized Stafford, PLUS), Perkins, college/university.

WORK-STUDY ***Federal work-study:*** Total amount: $55,000; jobs available (averaging $600). ***State or other work-study/employment:*** Total amount: $33,498 (35% need-based, 65% non-need-based). Part-time jobs available.

ATHLETIC AWARDS Total amount: $3,026,409 (65% need-based, 35% non-need-based).

APPLYING FOR FINANCIAL AID ***Required financial aid forms:*** FAFSA, institution's own form. ***Financial aid deadline:*** 9/1 (priority: 5/1). ***Notification date:*** Continuous. Students must reply within 2 weeks of notification.

CONTACT Mr. Ian Roberts, Associate Vice President-Administration, Hastings College, 7th and Turner, Hastings, NE 68901, 402-461-7455 or toll-free 800-532-7642. *Fax:* 402-461-7714. *E-mail:* iroberts@hastings.edu.

HAVERFORD COLLEGE

Haverford, PA

Tuition & fees: $37,525 **Average undergraduate aid package: $31,701**

ABOUT THE INSTITUTION Independent, coed. ***Awards:*** bachelor's degrees. 44 undergraduate majors. ***Total enrollment:*** 1,169. Undergraduates: 1,169. Freshmen: 327. Institutional methodology is used as a basis for awarding need-based institutional aid.

UNDERGRADUATE EXPENSES for 2008–09 ***Application fee:*** $60. ***One-time required fee:*** $180. ***Comprehensive fee:*** $48,975 includes full-time tuition ($37,175), mandatory fees ($350), and room and board ($11,450). ***Payment plan:*** Installment.

FRESHMAN FINANCIAL AID (Fall 2008, est.) 208 applied for aid; of those 81% were deemed to have need. 100% of freshmen with need received aid; of those 100% had need fully met. ***Average percent of need met:*** 100% (excluding resources awarded to replace EFC). ***Average financial aid package:*** $31,769 (excluding resources awarded to replace EFC).

UNDERGRADUATE FINANCIAL AID (Fall 2008, est.) 629 applied for aid; of those 90% were deemed to have need. 100% of undergraduates with need received aid; of those 100% had need fully met. ***Average percent of need met:*** 100% (excluding resources awarded to replace EFC). ***Average financial aid package:*** $31,701 (excluding resources awarded to replace EFC).

GIFT AID (NEED-BASED) ***Total amount:*** $16,028,509 (4% federal, 1% state, 92% institutional, 3% external sources). ***Receiving aid:*** Freshmen: 48% (156); all full-time undergraduates: 45% (521). ***Average award:*** Freshmen: $31,983; Undergraduates: $30,521. ***Scholarships, grants, and awards:*** Federal Pell, FSEOG, state, private, college/university gift aid from institutional funds.

GIFT AID (NON-NEED-BASED) ***Tuition waivers:*** Full or partial for employees or children of employees.

LOANS ***Student loans:*** $1,885,343 (57% need-based, 43% non-need-based). 41% of past graduating class borrowed through all loan programs. *Average indebtedness per student:* $17,125. ***Average need-based loan:*** Freshmen: $539. Undergraduates: $2160. ***Parent loans:*** $2,057,708 (100% non-need-based). ***Programs:*** FFEL (Subsidized and Unsubsidized Stafford, PLUS), Perkins.

WORK-STUDY ***Federal work-study:*** Total amount: $247,027; jobs available. ***State or other work-study/employment:*** Total amount: $649,007 (31% need-based, 69% non-need-based). Part-time jobs available.

APPLYING FOR FINANCIAL AID ***Required financial aid forms:*** FAFSA, CSS Financial Aid PROFILE, state aid form, business/farm supplement. ***Financial aid deadline:*** 2/1. ***Notification date:*** 4/15. Students must reply by 5/1.

CONTACT Mr. David J. Hoy, Director of Financial Aid Office, Haverford College, 370 Lancaster Avenue, Haverford, PA 19041-1392, 610-896-1350. *Fax:* 610-896-1338. *E-mail:* finaid@haverford.edu.

HAWAI'I PACIFIC UNIVERSITY

Honolulu, HI

Tuition & fees: $14,960 **Average undergraduate aid package: $13,896**

ABOUT THE INSTITUTION Independent, coed. ***Awards:*** associate, bachelor's, and master's degrees and post-bachelor's and post-master's certificates. 65 undergraduate majors. ***Total enrollment:*** 8,293. Undergraduates: 7,113. Freshmen: 622. Federal methodology is used as a basis for awarding need-based institutional aid.

UNDERGRADUATE EXPENSES for 2009–10 ***Application fee:*** $50. ***Comprehensive fee:*** $26,054 includes full-time tuition ($14,860), mandatory fees ($100), and room and board ($11,094). ***Part-time tuition:*** $300 per credit.

FRESHMAN FINANCIAL AID (Fall 2008, est.) 501 applied for aid; of those 56% were deemed to have need. 97% of freshmen with need received aid; of those .4% had need fully met. ***Average percent of need met:*** 83% (excluding resources awarded to replace EFC). ***Average financial aid package:*** $12,370 (excluding resources awarded to replace EFC). 13% of all full-time freshmen had no need and received non-need-based gift aid.

UNDERGRADUATE FINANCIAL AID (Fall 2008, est.) 2,829 applied for aid; of those 60% were deemed to have need. 98% of undergraduates with need received aid; of those 18% had need fully met. ***Average percent of need met:*** 82% (excluding resources awarded to replace EFC). ***Average financial aid package:*** $13,896 (excluding resources awarded to replace EFC). 8% of all full-time undergraduates had no need and received non-need-based gift aid.

GIFT AID (NEED-BASED) ***Total amount:*** $3,999,305 (95% federal, 5% state). ***Receiving aid:*** Freshmen: 22% (131); all full-time undergraduates: 20% (797). ***Average award:*** Freshmen: $2214; Undergraduates: $2020. ***Scholarships, grants, and awards:*** Federal Pell, FSEOG, state, private, college/university gift aid from institutional funds, Federal Nursing.

GIFT AID (NON-NEED-BASED) ***Total amount:*** $10,734,636 (79% institutional, 21% external sources). ***Receiving aid:*** Freshmen: 23% (135). Undergraduates: 13% (525). ***Average award:*** Freshmen: $2070. Undergraduates: $2803. ***Scholarships, grants, and awards by category:*** *Academic interests/achievement:* 120 awards ($580,094 total): biological sciences, business, communication, general academic interests/achievements, health fields, social sciences. *Creative arts/performance:* 124 awards ($1,322,580 total): dance, journalism/publications, music. *Special achievements/activities:* 117 awards ($1,181,146 total): cheerleading/drum major, hobbies/interests, leadership, memberships, religious involvement. *Special characteristics:* 717 awards ($5,255,528 total): ethnic background, international students, local/state students, out-of-state students, previous college experience, relatives of clergy, religious affiliation. ***ROTC:*** Army cooperative, Air Force cooperative.

LOANS ***Student loans:*** $21,649,066 (100% need-based). *Average indebtedness per student:* $20,212. ***Average need-based loan:*** Freshmen: $6003. Undergraduates: $7472. ***Parent loans:*** $6,222,787 (100% need-based). ***Programs:*** FFEL (Subsidized and Unsubsidized Stafford, PLUS), Perkins, Federal Nursing.

WORK-STUDY ***Federal work-study:*** Total amount: $327,360; 246 jobs averaging $3431.

ATHLETIC AWARDS Total amount: $1,529,021 (100% non-need-based).

APPLYING FOR FINANCIAL AID ***Required financial aid form:*** FAFSA. ***Financial aid deadline (priority):*** 3/1. ***Notification date:*** Continuous beginning 3/15. Students must reply within 3 weeks of notification.

CONTACT Adam Hatch, Director of Financial Aid, Hawai'i Pacific University, 1164 Bishop Street, Suite 201, Honolulu, HI 96813-2785, 808-544-0253 or toll-free 866-225-5478 (out-of-state). *Fax:* 808-544-0884. *E-mail:* financialaid@hpu.edu.

HEBREW COLLEGE

Newton Centre, MA

ABOUT THE INSTITUTION Independent Jewish, coed. ***Awards:*** bachelor's, master's, and doctoral degrees. 5 undergraduate majors. ***Total enrollment:*** 6. Undergraduates: 6. Freshmen: 1.

GIFT AID (NEED-BASED) ***Scholarships, grants, and awards:*** Federal Pell, state, private, college/university gift aid from institutional funds.

GIFT AID (NON-NEED-BASED) ***Scholarships, grants, and awards by category:*** *Academic interests/achievement:* education.

LOANS ***Programs:*** FFEL (Subsidized and Unsubsidized Stafford, PLUS).

APPLYING FOR FINANCIAL AID ***Required financial aid forms:*** FAFSA, institution's own form.

CONTACT Marilyn Jaye, Registrar, Hebrew College, 160 Herrick Road, Newton Centre, MA 02459, 617-559-8612 or toll-free 800-866-4814 Ext. 8619. *Fax:* 617-559-8601. *E-mail:* mjaye@hebrewcollege.edu.

HEBREW THEOLOGICAL COLLEGE

Skokie, IL

CONTACT Ms. Rhoda Morris, Financial Aid Administrator, Hebrew Theological College, 7135 Carpenter Road, Skokie, IL 60077-3263, 847-982-2500. *Fax:* 847-674-6381.

HEIDELBERG UNIVERSITY

Tiffin, OH

Tuition & fees: $21,330 **Average undergraduate aid package: $17,223**

ABOUT THE INSTITUTION Independent religious, coed. ***Awards:*** bachelor's and master's degrees. 46 undergraduate majors. ***Total enrollment:*** 1,519. Undergraduates: 1,371. Freshmen: 402. Federal methodology is used as a basis for awarding need-based institutional aid.

UNDERGRADUATE EXPENSES for 2009–10 ***Application fee:*** $25. ***Comprehensive fee:*** $29,714 includes full-time tuition ($20,826), mandatory fees ($504), and room and board ($8384). ***College room only:*** $3968. ***Part-time tuition:*** $504 per semester hour.

FRESHMAN FINANCIAL AID (Fall 2008, est.) 368 applied for aid; of those 89% were deemed to have need. 100% of freshmen with need received aid; of those 27% had need fully met. ***Average percent of need met:*** 84% (excluding resources awarded to replace EFC). ***Average financial aid package:*** $17,973 (excluding resources awarded to replace EFC). 8% of all full-time freshmen had no need and received non-need-based gift aid.

UNDERGRADUATE FINANCIAL AID (Fall 2008, est.) 1,080 applied for aid; of those 89% were deemed to have need. 100% of undergraduates with need received aid; of those 29% had need fully met. ***Average percent of need met:*** 83% (excluding resources awarded to replace EFC). ***Average financial aid package:*** $17,223 (excluding resources awarded to replace EFC). 6% of all full-time undergraduates had no need and received non-need-based gift aid.

GIFT AID (NEED-BASED) ***Total amount:*** $12,043,471 (14% federal, 12% state, 72% institutional, 2% external sources). ***Receiving aid:*** Freshmen: 84% (327); all full-time undergraduates: 81% (961). ***Average award:*** Freshmen: $13,019; Undergraduates: $12,129. ***Scholarships, grants, and awards:*** Federal Pell, FSEOG, state, private, college/university gift aid from institutional funds.

GIFT AID (NON-NEED-BASED) ***Total amount:*** $1,768,110 (7% state, 90% institutional, 3% external sources). ***Receiving aid:*** Freshmen: 10% (39). Undergraduates: 9% (110). ***Average award:*** Freshmen: $8833. Undergraduates: $7526. ***Scholarships, grants, and awards by category:*** *Academic interests/achievement:* 802 awards ($4,658,607 total): general academic interests/achievements. *Creative arts/performance:* 62 awards ($126,000 total): music. *Special characteristics:* 211 awards ($830,739 total): children of faculty/staff, out-of-state students, relatives of clergy, religious affiliation. ***ROTC:*** Army cooperative, Air Force cooperative.

LOANS ***Student loans:*** $11,138,676 (90% need-based, 10% non-need-based). 74% of past graduating class borrowed through all loan programs. *Average indebtedness per student:* $30,589. ***Average need-based loan:*** Freshmen: $4079. Undergraduates: $4626. ***Parent loans:*** $1,107,852 (77% need-based, 23% non-need-based). ***Programs:*** FFEL (Subsidized and Unsubsidized Stafford, PLUS), Perkins.

WORK-STUDY ***Federal work-study:*** Total amount: $1,078,589; 660 jobs averaging $1563. ***State or other work-study/employment:*** Total amount: $157,079 (55% need-based, 45% non-need-based). 125 part-time jobs averaging $1388.

APPLYING FOR FINANCIAL AID ***Required financial aid form:*** FAFSA. ***Financial aid deadline (priority):*** 3/1. ***Notification date:*** Continuous beginning 3/1. Students must reply within 2 weeks of notification.

CONTACT Ms. Juli L. Weininger, Director of Financial Aid, Heidelberg University, 310 East Market Street, Tiffin, OH 44883-2462, 419-448-2293 or toll-free 800-434-3352. *Fax:* 419-448-2296.

HELLENIC COLLEGE

Brookline, MA

Tuition & fees: $18,320 **Average undergraduate aid package: $9500**

ABOUT THE INSTITUTION Independent Greek Orthodox, coed. ***Awards:*** bachelor's degrees (also offers graduate degree programs through Holy Cross Greek Orthodox School of Theology). 6 undergraduate majors. ***Total enrollment:*** 187. Undergraduates: 72. Freshmen: 10. Institutional methodology is used as a basis for awarding need-based institutional aid.

UNDERGRADUATE EXPENSES for 2008–09 ***Application fee:*** $50. ***Comprehensive fee:*** $29,750 includes full-time tuition ($17,870), mandatory fees ($450), and room and board ($11,430). ***Part-time tuition:*** $744 per credit hour. ***Payment plans:*** Installment, deferred payment.

FRESHMAN FINANCIAL AID (Fall 2008, est.) 8 applied for aid; of those 100% were deemed to have need. 100% of freshmen with need received aid. ***Average percent of need met:*** 80% (excluding resources awarded to replace EFC). ***Average financial aid package:*** $10,100 (excluding resources awarded to replace EFC). 7% of all full-time freshmen had no need and received non-need-based gift aid.

UNDERGRADUATE FINANCIAL AID (Fall 2008, est.) 59 applied for aid; of those 97% were deemed to have need. 100% of undergraduates with need received aid. ***Average percent of need met:*** 80% (excluding resources awarded to replace EFC). ***Average financial aid package:*** $9500 (excluding resources awarded to replace EFC). 2% of all full-time undergraduates had no need and received non-need-based gift aid.

GIFT AID (NEED-BASED) ***Total amount:*** $2,001,835 (4% federal, 87% institutional, 9% external sources). ***Receiving aid:*** Freshmen: 57% (8); all full-time undergraduates: 88% (57). ***Average award:*** Freshmen: $10,100;

Undergraduates: $11,300. ***Scholarships, grants, and awards:*** Federal Pell, FSEOG, state, private, college/university gift aid from institutional funds.

GIFT AID (NON-NEED-BASED) ***Receiving aid:*** Freshmen: 29% (4). ***Average award:*** Freshmen: $5000. Undergraduates: $5000. ***Scholarships, grants, and awards by category:*** *Academic interests/achievement:* religion/biblical studies. *Special achievements/activities:* religious involvement. ***Tuition waivers:*** Full or partial for children of alumni, employees or children of employees.

LOANS ***Student loans:*** $129,460 (78% need-based, 22% non-need-based). 80% of past graduating class borrowed through all loan programs. *Average indebtedness per student:* $15,000. ***Average need-based loan:*** Freshmen: $4500. Undergraduates: $5500. ***Programs:*** FFEL (Subsidized and Unsubsidized Stafford, PLUS), state.

WORK-STUDY Federal work-study jobs available.

APPLYING FOR FINANCIAL AID ***Required financial aid forms:*** FAFSA, institution's own form. ***Financial aid deadline (priority):*** 4/1. ***Notification date:*** Continuous. Students must reply within 2 weeks of notification.

CONTACT Gregory Floor, Director of Admissions/Financial Aid, Hellenic College, 50 Goddard Avenue, Brookline, MA 02146-7496, 617-731-3500 Ext. 1285 or toll-free 866-424-2338. *Fax:* 617-850-1465. *E-mail:* gfloor@hchc.edu.

HENDERSON STATE UNIVERSITY

Arkadelphia, AR

Tuition & fees (AR res): $4939 **Average undergraduate aid package: $4873**

ABOUT THE INSTITUTION State-supported, coed. ***Awards:*** associate, bachelor's, and master's degrees and post-bachelor's certificates. 39 undergraduate majors. ***Total enrollment:*** 3,649. Undergraduates: 3,133. Freshmen: 734. Federal methodology is used as a basis for awarding need-based institutional aid.

UNDERGRADUATE EXPENSES for 2008–09 ***Tuition, state resident:*** full-time $3936; part-time $164 per credit hour. ***Tuition, nonresident:*** full-time $7872; part-time $328 per credit hour. ***Required fees:*** full-time $1003. ***College room and board:*** $4860.

FRESHMAN FINANCIAL AID (Fall 2008, est.) 714 applied for aid; of those 81% were deemed to have need. 99% of freshmen with need received aid; of those 78% had need fully met. ***Average percent of need met:*** 81% (excluding resources awarded to replace EFC). ***Average financial aid package:*** $4725 (excluding resources awarded to replace EFC). 16% of all full-time freshmen had no need and received non-need-based gift aid.

UNDERGRADUATE FINANCIAL AID (Fall 2008, est.) 2,362 applied for aid; of those 84% were deemed to have need. 99% of undergraduates with need received aid; of those 52% had need fully met. ***Average percent of need met:*** 86% (excluding resources awarded to replace EFC). ***Average financial aid package:*** $4873 (excluding resources awarded to replace EFC). 13% of all full-time undergraduates had no need and received non-need-based gift aid.

GIFT AID (NEED-BASED) ***Total amount:*** $5,997,709 (79% federal, 21% state). ***Receiving aid:*** Freshmen: 61% (301); all full-time undergraduates: 60% (1,368). ***Average award:*** Freshmen: $3797; Undergraduates: $3956. ***Scholarships, grants, and awards:*** Federal Pell, FSEOG, state, private, college/university gift aid from institutional funds.

GIFT AID (NON-NEED-BASED) ***Total amount:*** $8,505,502 (79% institutional, 21% external sources). ***Receiving aid:*** Freshmen: 11% (79). Undergraduates: 15% (418). ***Average award:*** Freshmen: $914. Undergraduates: $1187. ***Scholarships, grants, and awards by category:*** *Academic interests/achievement:* biological sciences, education, general academic interests/achievements, international studies, mathematics. *Creative arts/performance:* art/fine arts, cinema/film/broadcasting, dance, debating, journalism/publications, music, performing arts, theater/drama. *Special achievements/activities:* cheerleading/drum major, general special achievements/activities, leadership. *Special characteristics:* children and siblings of alumni, children of faculty/staff, international students, out-of-state students.

LOANS ***Student loans:*** $14,512,091 (56% need-based, 44% non-need-based). 37% of past graduating class borrowed through all loan programs. *Average indebtedness per student:* $17,800. ***Average need-based loan:*** Freshmen: $2048. Undergraduates: $2515. ***Parent loans:*** $663,682 (100% non-need-based). ***Programs:*** FFEL (Subsidized and Unsubsidized Stafford, PLUS), Perkins.

WORK-STUDY ***Federal work-study:*** Total amount: $238,327; jobs available. ***State or other work-study/employment:*** Total amount: $151,229 (100% non-need-based). Part-time jobs available.

ATHLETIC AWARDS Total amount: $1,271,703 (100% non-need-based).

APPLYING FOR FINANCIAL AID ***Required financial aid form:*** FAFSA. ***Financial aid deadline (priority):*** 6/1. ***Notification date:*** Continuous.

CONTACT Ms. Vicki Taylor, Director of Financial Aid, Henderson State University, 1100 Henderson Street, HSU Box 7812, Arkadelphia, AR 71999-0001, 870-230-5138 or toll-free 800-228-7333. *Fax:* 870-230-5481. *E-mail:* taylorv@hsu.edu.

HENDRIX COLLEGE

Conway, AR

Tuition & fees: $26,080 **Average undergraduate aid package: $20,890**

ABOUT THE INSTITUTION Independent United Methodist, coed. ***Awards:*** bachelor's and master's degrees. 32 undergraduate majors. ***Total enrollment:*** 1,350. Undergraduates: 1,342. Freshmen: 433. Federal methodology is used as a basis for awarding need-based institutional aid.

UNDERGRADUATE EXPENSES for 2008–09 ***Application fee:*** $40. ***Comprehensive fee:*** $34,030 includes full-time tuition ($25,780), mandatory fees ($300), and room and board ($7950). ***College room only:*** $3850. Full-time tuition and fees vary according to course load. Room and board charges vary according to board plan and housing facility. ***Part-time tuition:*** $3260 per course. Part-time tuition and fees vary according to course load. ***Payment plan:*** Installment.

FRESHMAN FINANCIAL AID (Fall 2008, est.) 365 applied for aid; of those 68% were deemed to have need. 100% of freshmen with need received aid; of those 41% had need fully met. ***Average percent of need met:*** 87% (excluding resources awarded to replace EFC). ***Average financial aid package:*** $21,641 (excluding resources awarded to replace EFC). 43% of all full-time freshmen had no need and received non-need-based gift aid.

UNDERGRADUATE FINANCIAL AID (Fall 2008, est.) 1,043 applied for aid; of those 75% were deemed to have need. 100% of undergraduates with need received aid; of those 37% had need fully met. ***Average percent of need met:*** 83% (excluding resources awarded to replace EFC). ***Average financial aid package:*** $20,890 (excluding resources awarded to replace EFC). 41% of all full-time undergraduates had no need and received non-need-based gift aid.

GIFT AID (NEED-BASED) ***Total amount:*** $12,377,056 (8% federal, 6% state, 84% institutional, 2% external sources). ***Receiving aid:*** Freshmen: 57% (248); all full-time undergraduates: 58% (776). ***Average award:*** Freshmen: $17,774; Undergraduates: $16,410. ***Scholarships, grants, and awards:*** Federal Pell, FSEOG, state, private, college/university gift aid from institutional funds.

GIFT AID (NON-NEED-BASED) ***Total amount:*** $8,949,556 (9% state, 88% institutional, 3% external sources). ***Receiving aid:*** Freshmen: 19% (81). Undergraduates: 15% (201). ***Average award:*** Freshmen: $19,277. Undergraduates: $19,243. ***Scholarships, grants, and awards by category:*** *Academic interests/achievement:* 1,260 awards ($10,083,664 total): general academic interests/achievements. *Creative arts/performance:* 125 awards ($148,500 total): art/fine arts, dance, music, theater/drama. *Special achievements/activities:* 1,337 awards ($3,717,888 total): community service, general special achievements/activities, leadership, religious involvement. *Special characteristics:* 54 awards ($1,065,280 total): children of educators, children of faculty/staff, international students, previous college experience, relatives of clergy. ***Tuition waivers:*** Full or partial for employees or children of employees. ***ROTC:*** Army cooperative.

LOANS ***Student loans:*** $5,506,034 (60% need-based, 40% non-need-based). 81% of past graduating class borrowed through all loan programs. *Average indebtedness per student:* $17,484. ***Average need-based loan:*** Freshmen: $4301. Undergraduates: $4764. ***Parent loans:*** $4,703,402 (17% need-based, 83% non-need-based). ***Programs:*** Federal Direct (Subsidized and Unsubsidized Stafford, PLUS), FFEL (Subsidized and Unsubsidized Stafford, PLUS), Perkins, United Methodist Student Loans.

WORK-STUDY ***Federal work-study:*** Total amount: $729,735; 513 jobs averaging $1386. ***State or other work-study/employment:*** Total amount: $223,859 (11% need-based, 89% non-need-based). 234 part-time jobs averaging $1100.

APPLYING FOR FINANCIAL AID ***Required financial aid forms:*** FAFSA, state aid form. ***Financial aid deadline (priority):*** 2/15. ***Notification date:*** Continuous beginning 2/15. Students must reply by 5/1.

CONTACT Mark Bandré, Director of Financial Aid, Hendrix College, 1600 Washington Avenue, Conway, AR 72032, 501-450-1368 or toll-free 800-277-9017. *Fax:* 501-450-3871. *E-mail:* bandre@hendrix.edu.

HERITAGE BIBLE COLLEGE
Dunn, NC

ABOUT THE INSTITUTION Independent Pentecostal Free Will Baptist, coed. ***Awards:*** associate and bachelor's degrees. 2 undergraduate majors. ***Total enrollment:*** 80. Undergraduates: 80.

GIFT AID (NEED-BASED) ***Scholarships, grants, and awards:*** Federal Pell, FSEOG, private, college/university gift aid from institutional funds.

GIFT AID (NON-NEED-BASED) ***Scholarships, grants, and awards by category:*** *Academic interests/achievement:* religion/biblical studies.

LOANS ***Programs:*** FFEL (Subsidized and Unsubsidized Stafford, PLUS).

APPLYING FOR FINANCIAL AID ***Required financial aid forms:*** FAFSA, institution's own form, verification documents.

CONTACT Mrs. Laurie Minard, Director of Financial Aid, Heritage Bible College, Box 1628, Dunn, NC 28335, 800-297-6351 Ext. 226 or toll-free 800-297-6351 Ext. 230. *Fax:* 910-892-1809. *E-mail:* lminard@heritagebiblecollege.edu.

HERITAGE CHRISTIAN UNIVERSITY
Florence, AL

Tuition & fees: $10,140 **Average undergraduate aid package: $2366**

ABOUT THE INSTITUTION Independent religious, coed, primarily men. ***Awards:*** associate, bachelor's, and master's degrees. 1 undergraduate major. ***Total enrollment:*** 95. Undergraduates: 81. Federal methodology is used as a basis for awarding need-based institutional aid.

UNDERGRADUATE EXPENSES for 2008–09 ***Application fee:*** $25. ***Comprehensive fee:*** $13,740 includes full-time tuition ($9660), mandatory fees ($480), and room and board ($3600). ***College room only:*** $3000. Room and board charges vary according to housing facility. ***Part-time tuition:*** $322 per hour. ***Part-time fees:*** $20 per hour. ***Payment plans:*** Installment, deferred payment.

FRESHMAN FINANCIAL AID (Fall 2007) 4 applied for aid; of those 75% were deemed to have need. 100% of freshmen with need received aid. ***Average percent of need met:*** 43% (excluding resources awarded to replace EFC). ***Average financial aid package:*** $1183 (excluding resources awarded to replace EFC). 25% of all full-time freshmen had no need and received non-need-based gift aid.

UNDERGRADUATE FINANCIAL AID (Fall 2007) 29 applied for aid; of those 97% were deemed to have need. 100% of undergraduates with need received aid. ***Average percent of need met:*** 29% (excluding resources awarded to replace EFC). ***Average financial aid package:*** $2366 (excluding resources awarded to replace EFC). 24% of all full-time undergraduates had no need and received non-need-based gift aid.

GIFT AID (NEED-BASED) ***Total amount:*** $117,109 (100% federal). ***Scholarships, grants, and awards:*** Federal Pell, FSEOG, college/university gift aid from institutional funds.

GIFT AID (NON-NEED-BASED) ***Total amount:*** $127,442 (100% institutional). ***Receiving aid:*** Freshmen: 75% (3). Undergraduates: 44% (20). ***Average award:*** Freshmen: $1000. Undergraduates: $5589. ***Scholarships, grants, and awards by category:*** *Academic interests/achievement:* general academic interests/achievements. *Special characteristics:* 6 awards ($11,744 total): children and siblings of alumni, children of educators, children of faculty/staff, spouses of current students. ***Tuition waivers:*** Full or partial for employees or children of employees.

LOANS ***Student loans:*** $287,969 (58% need-based, 42% non-need-based). 73% of past graduating class borrowed through all loan programs. *Average indebtedness per student:* $20,784. ***Parent loans:*** $2880 (100% need-based). ***Programs:*** FFEL (Subsidized and Unsubsidized Stafford, PLUS).

WORK-STUDY ***Federal work-study:*** Total amount: $5398; 10 jobs averaging $1234.

APPLYING FOR FINANCIAL AID ***Required financial aid forms:*** FAFSA, federal income tax form(s). ***Financial aid deadline (priority):*** 6/1. ***Notification date:*** Continuous beginning 7/15. Students must reply within 2 weeks of notification.

CONTACT Mechelle Thompson, Financial Aid Counselor, Heritage Christian University, PO Box HCU, Florence, AL 35630, 800-367-3565 Ext. 24 or toll-free 800-367-3565. *Fax:* 256-766-9289. *E-mail:* mthompson@hcu.edu.

HERITAGE UNIVERSITY
Toppenish, WA

CONTACT Mr. Norberto Espindola, Director of Enrollment Management Services, Heritage University, 3240 Fort Road, Toppenish, WA 98948-9599, 509-865-8500 or toll-free 888-272-6190 (in-state). *Fax:* 509-865-8659. *E-mail:* financial_aid@heritage.edu.

HIGH POINT UNIVERSITY
High Point, NC

ABOUT THE INSTITUTION Independent United Methodist, coed. ***Awards:*** bachelor's and master's degrees and post-bachelor's certificates. 49 undergraduate majors. ***Total enrollment:*** 3,384. Undergraduates: 3,056. Freshmen: 952.

GIFT AID (NEED-BASED) ***Scholarships, grants, and awards:*** Federal Pell, FSEOG, state, private, college/university gift aid from institutional funds.

GIFT AID (NON-NEED-BASED) ***Scholarships, grants, and awards by category:*** *Academic interests/achievement:* biological sciences, business, education, English, foreign languages, general academic interests/achievements, humanities, international studies, mathematics, physical sciences, premedicine, religion/biblical studies. *Creative arts/performance:* art/fine arts, music. *Special achievements/activities:* general special achievements/activities. *Special characteristics:* relatives of clergy.

LOANS ***Programs:*** Federal Direct (Subsidized and Unsubsidized Stafford, PLUS), FFEL (Subsidized and Unsubsidized Stafford, PLUS), Perkins.

APPLYING FOR FINANCIAL AID ***Required financial aid forms:*** FAFSA, state aid form.

CONTACT Julie Setzer, Director of Student Financial Planning, High Point University, Box 3232, University Station, 833 Montlieu Avenue, High Point, NC 27262, 336-841-9128 or toll-free 800-345-6993. *Fax:* 336-884-0221. *E-mail:* jsetzer@highpoint.edu.

HILBERT COLLEGE
Hamburg, NY

ABOUT THE INSTITUTION Independent, coed. ***Awards:*** associate and bachelor's degrees. 11 undergraduate majors. ***Total enrollment:*** 1,046. Undergraduates: 1,046. Freshmen: 210.

GIFT AID (NEED-BASED) ***Scholarships, grants, and awards:*** Federal Pell, FSEOG, state, private, college/university gift aid from institutional funds.

GIFT AID (NON-NEED-BASED) ***Scholarships, grants, and awards by category:*** *Academic interests/achievement:* general academic interests/achievements. *Special achievements/activities:* leadership. *Special characteristics:* children and siblings of alumni, members of minority groups, siblings of current students.

LOANS ***Programs:*** FFEL (Subsidized and Unsubsidized Stafford, PLUS), Perkins, alternative loans.

WORK-STUDY ***Federal work-study:*** Total amount: $103,648; 67 jobs averaging $1547.

APPLYING FOR FINANCIAL AID ***Required financial aid form:*** FAFSA.

CONTACT Beverly Chudy, Director of Financial Aid, Hilbert College, 5200 South Park Avenue, Hamburg, NY 14075-1597, 716-649-7900 Ext. 207. *Fax:* 716-649-1152. *E-mail:* bchudy@hilbert.edu.

HILLSDALE COLLEGE
Hillsdale, MI

CONTACT Mr. Rich Moeggengberg, Director of Student Financial Aid, Hillsdale College, 33 East College Street, Hillsdale, MI 49242-1298, 517-607-2550. *Fax:* 517-607-2298. *E-mail:* rich.moeggenbeng@hillsdale.edu.

HILLSDALE FREE WILL BAPTIST COLLEGE
Moore, OK

Tuition & fees: $9260 **Average undergraduate aid package: $12,000**

ABOUT THE INSTITUTION Independent Free Will Baptist, coed. ***Awards:*** associate, bachelor's, and master's degrees. 22 undergraduate majors. ***Total enrollment:*** 262. Undergraduates: 248. Freshmen: 84. Federal methodology is used as a basis for awarding need-based institutional aid.

UNDERGRADUATE EXPENSES for 2008–09 ***Application fee:*** $20. ***One-time required fee:*** $20. ***Comprehensive fee:*** $13,960 includes full-time tuition ($7700), mandatory fees ($1560), and room and board ($4700). ***College room only:*** $2100. Full-time tuition and fees vary according to course load. Room and board charges vary according to board plan and housing facility. ***Part-time tuition:*** $280 per credit hour. ***Part-time fees:*** $20 per credit hour; $180 per term. Part-time tuition and fees vary according to course load. ***Payment plan:*** Installment.

FRESHMAN FINANCIAL AID (Fall 2007) 73 applied for aid; of those 88% were deemed to have need. 100% of freshmen with need received aid; of those 8% had need fully met. ***Average percent of need met:*** 50% (excluding resources awarded to replace EFC). ***Average financial aid package:*** $10,500 (excluding resources awarded to replace EFC). 8% of all full-time freshmen had no need and received non-need-based gift aid.

UNDERGRADUATE FINANCIAL AID (Fall 2007) 187 applied for aid; of those 87% were deemed to have need. 100% of undergraduates with need received aid; of those 9% had need fully met. ***Average percent of need met:*** 60% (excluding resources awarded to replace EFC). ***Average financial aid package:*** $12,000 (excluding resources awarded to replace EFC). 5% of all full-time undergraduates had no need and received non-need-based gift aid.

GIFT AID (NEED-BASED) ***Total amount:*** $411,913 (82% federal, 10% state, 8% institutional). ***Receiving aid:*** Freshmen: 42% (35); all full-time undergraduates: 30% (75). ***Average award:*** Freshmen: $3600; Undergraduates: $3600. ***Scholarships, grants, and awards:*** Federal Pell, FSEOG, state, private, college/university gift aid from institutional funds, Bureau of Indian Affairs Grants.

GIFT AID (NON-NEED-BASED) ***Total amount:*** $579,420 (1% federal, 11% state, 65% institutional, 23% external sources). ***Receiving aid:*** Freshmen: 47% (39). Undergraduates: 48% (119). ***Average award:*** Freshmen: $2714. Undergraduates: $3470. ***Scholarships, grants, and awards by category:*** *Academic interests/achievement:* 24 awards ($11,054 total): business, education, English, general academic interests/achievements, mathematics, religion/biblical studies. *Creative arts/performance:* 7 awards ($3800 total): music, performing arts. *Special achievements/activities:* 24 awards ($27,000 total): community service, religious involvement. *Special characteristics:* 80 awards ($69,700 total): adult students, children and siblings of alumni, relatives of clergy, religious affiliation, siblings of current students, spouses of current students. ***Tuition waivers:*** Full or partial for children of alumni, employees or children of employees, senior citizens.

LOANS ***Student loans:*** $887,869 (93% need-based, 7% non-need-based). 89% of past graduating class borrowed through all loan programs. *Average indebtedness per student:* $12,805. ***Average need-based loan:*** Freshmen: $3500. Undergraduates: $5000. ***Parent loans:*** $58,200 (100% need-based). ***Programs:*** FFEL (Subsidized and Unsubsidized Stafford, PLUS), Perkins.

WORK-STUDY ***Federal work-study:*** Total amount: $50,867; 25 jobs averaging $1000. ***State or other work-study/employment:*** 15 part-time jobs averaging $1000.

APPLYING FOR FINANCIAL AID ***Required financial aid form:*** FAFSA. ***Financial aid deadline:*** Continuous. ***Notification date:*** Continuous beginning 6/1. Students must reply within 2 weeks of notification.

CONTACT Denise Conklin, Director of Admissions and Financial Aid, Hillsdale Free Will Baptist College, PO Box 7208, Moore, OK 73153-1208, 405-912-9006. *Fax:* 405-912-9050. *E-mail:* dconklin@hc.edu.

HIRAM COLLEGE

Hiram, OH

CONTACT Ann Marie Gruber, Associate Director of Financial Aid, Hiram College, Box 67, Hiram, OH 44234-0067, 330-569-5107 or toll-free 800-362-5280. *Fax:* 330-569-5499.

HOBART AND WILLIAM SMITH COLLEGES

Geneva, NY

Tuition & fees: $38,860 **Average undergraduate aid package: $28,021**

ABOUT THE INSTITUTION Independent, coed. ***Awards:*** bachelor's and master's degrees and post-bachelor's certificates. 54 undergraduate majors. ***Total enrollment:*** 2,009. Undergraduates: 2,001. Freshmen: 619. Both federal and institutional methodology are used as a basis for awarding need-based institutional aid.

UNDERGRADUATE EXPENSES for 2008–09 ***Application fee:*** $45. ***Comprehensive fee:*** $48,546 includes full-time tuition ($37,820), mandatory fees ($1040), and room and board ($9686). Room and board charges vary according to board plan. ***Payment plans:*** Tuition prepayment, installment.

FRESHMAN FINANCIAL AID (Fall 2008, est.) 392 applied for aid; of those 82% were deemed to have need. 100% of freshmen with need received aid; of those 79% had need fully met. ***Average percent of need met:*** 79% (excluding resources awarded to replace EFC). ***Average financial aid package:*** $28,492 (excluding resources awarded to replace EFC). 26% of all full-time freshmen had no need and received non-need-based gift aid.

UNDERGRADUATE FINANCIAL AID (Fall 2008, est.) 1,497 applied for aid; of those 83% were deemed to have need. 99% of undergraduates with need received aid; of those 60% had need fully met. ***Average percent of need met:*** 75% (excluding resources awarded to replace EFC). ***Average financial aid package:*** $28,021 (excluding resources awarded to replace EFC). 23% of all full-time undergraduates had no need and received non-need-based gift aid.

GIFT AID (NEED-BASED) ***Total amount:*** $28,848,406 (6% federal, 5% state, 84% institutional, 5% external sources). ***Receiving aid:*** Freshmen: 73% (321); all full-time undergraduates: 71% (1,224). ***Average award:*** Freshmen: $25,106; Undergraduates: $23,568. ***Scholarships, grants, and awards:*** Federal Pell, FSEOG, state, private, college/university gift aid from institutional funds, Academic Competitiveness Grant, National Smart Grant.

GIFT AID (NON-NEED-BASED) ***Total amount:*** $6,689,405 (90% institutional, 10% external sources). ***Receiving aid:*** Freshmen: 10% (44). Undergraduates: 9% (156). ***Average award:*** Freshmen: $13,046. Undergraduates: $13,108. ***Scholarships, grants, and awards by category:*** *Academic interests/achievement:* 122 awards ($1,455,250 total): general academic interests/achievements. *Creative arts/performance:* 16 awards ($163,500 total): art/fine arts, creative writing, dance, music, performing arts. *Special achievements/activities:* 47 awards ($526,800 total): leadership. ***Tuition waivers:*** Full or partial for employees or children of employees.

LOANS ***Student loans:*** $12,064,043 (63% need-based, 37% non-need-based). 68% of past graduating class borrowed through all loan programs. *Average indebtedness per student:* $26,334. ***Average need-based loan:*** Freshmen: $3032. Undergraduates: $4108. ***Parent loans:*** $3,991,729 (25% need-based, 75% non-need-based). ***Programs:*** FFEL (Subsidized and Unsubsidized Stafford, PLUS), Perkins.

WORK-STUDY ***Federal work-study:*** Total amount: $1,610,729; 922 jobs averaging $1747. ***State or other work-study/employment:*** Total amount: $1,010,346 (10% need-based, 90% non-need-based). 413 part-time jobs averaging $1891.

APPLYING FOR FINANCIAL AID ***Required financial aid forms:*** FAFSA, CSS Financial Aid PROFILE, state aid form, noncustodial (divorced/separated) parent's statement, income tax form(s). ***Financial aid deadline:*** 3/15 (priority: 2/15). ***Notification date:*** 4/1. Students must reply by 5/1.

CONTACT Beth Turner, Director of Financial Aid, Hobart and William Smith Colleges, Geneva, NY 14456-3397, 315-781-3315 or toll-free 800-245-0100. *Fax:* 315-781-3655. *E-mail:* finaid@hws.edu.

HOBE SOUND BIBLE COLLEGE

Hobe Sound, FL

CONTACT Director of Financial Aid, Hobe Sound Bible College, PO Box 1065, Hobe Sound, FL 33475-1065, 561-546-5534 or toll-free 800-881-5534. *Fax:* 561-545-1422.

HODGES UNIVERSITY

Naples, FL

Tuition & fees: $16,580 **Average undergraduate aid package: $9100**

ABOUT THE INSTITUTION Independent, coed. ***Awards:*** associate, bachelor's, and master's degrees. 8 undergraduate majors. ***Total enrollment:*** 1,906. Undergraduates: 1,675. Freshmen: 188. Federal methodology is used as a basis for awarding need-based institutional aid.

UNDERGRADUATE EXPENSES for 2008–09 ***Application fee:*** $20. ***Tuition:*** full-time $16,200; part-time $450 per semester hour. ***Payment plan:*** Installment.

FRESHMAN FINANCIAL AID (Fall 2008, est.) 161 applied for aid; of those 89% were deemed to have need. 100% of freshmen with need received aid; of those 21% had need fully met. ***Average percent of need met:*** 1% (excluding resources

awarded to replace EFC). ***Average financial aid package:*** $8000 (excluding resources awarded to replace EFC). 15% of all full-time freshmen had no need and received non-need-based gift aid.

UNDERGRADUATE FINANCIAL AID (Fall 2008, est.) 1,181 applied for aid; of those 87% were deemed to have need. 100% of undergraduates with need received aid; of those 18% had need fully met. ***Average percent of need met:*** 1% (excluding resources awarded to replace EFC). ***Average financial aid package:*** $9100 (excluding resources awarded to replace EFC). 4% of all full-time undergraduates had no need and received non-need-based gift aid.

GIFT AID (NEED-BASED) ***Total amount:*** $4,462,380 (96% federal, 4% state). ***Receiving aid:*** Freshmen: 74% (125); all full-time undergraduates: 73% (955). ***Average award:*** Freshmen: $2400; Undergraduates: $4500. ***Scholarships, grants, and awards:*** Federal Pell, FSEOG, state, private, college/university gift aid from institutional funds.

GIFT AID (NON-NEED-BASED) ***Total amount:*** $4,362,682 (78% state, 21% institutional, 1% external sources). ***Receiving aid:*** Freshmen: 34% (58). Undergraduates: 54% (706). ***Average award:*** Freshmen: $350. Undergraduates: $215. ***Scholarships, grants, and awards by category:*** *Special achievements/activities:* 305 awards ($707,517 total): general special achievements/activities. ***Tuition waivers:*** Full or partial for employees or children of employees.

LOANS ***Student loans:*** $13,600,000 (50% need-based, 50% non-need-based). 82% of past graduating class borrowed through all loan programs. *Average indebtedness per student:* $18,600. ***Average need-based loan:*** Freshmen: $2700. Undergraduates: $4225. ***Parent loans:*** $250,000 (100% need-based). ***Programs:*** FFEL (Subsidized and Unsubsidized Stafford, PLUS).

WORK-STUDY ***Federal work-study:*** Total amount: $178,380; 55 jobs averaging $3000.

APPLYING FOR FINANCIAL AID ***Required financial aid form:*** FAFSA. ***Financial aid deadline:*** Continuous. ***Notification date:*** Continuous.

CONTACT Mr. Joe Gilchrist, Vice President of Student Financial Assistance, Hodges University, 2655 Northbrooke Drive, Naples, FL 34119, 239-513-1122 Ext. 116 or toll-free 800-466-8017. *Fax:* 239-513-9579. *E-mail:* jgilchrist@internationalcollege.edu.

HOFSTRA UNIVERSITY

Hempstead, NY

Tuition & fees: $28,630 **Average undergraduate aid package: $16,505**

ABOUT THE INSTITUTION Independent, coed. ***Awards:*** bachelor's, master's, doctoral, and first professional degrees and post-bachelor's and post-master's certificates. 128 undergraduate majors. ***Total enrollment:*** 12,333. Undergraduates: 8,320. Federal methodology is used as a basis for awarding need-based institutional aid.

UNDERGRADUATE EXPENSES for 2008–09 ***Application fee:*** $70. ***Comprehensive fee:*** $39,455 includes full-time tuition ($27,600), mandatory fees ($1030), and room and board ($10,825). ***College room only:*** $7225. Full-time tuition and fees vary according to course load and program. Room and board charges vary according to board plan and housing facility. ***Part-time tuition:*** $845 per term. ***Part-time fees:*** $155 per term. Part-time tuition and fees vary according to course load and program. ***Payment plans:*** Installment, deferred payment.

FRESHMAN FINANCIAL AID (Fall 2008, est.) 1,333 applied for aid; of those 78% were deemed to have need. 99% of freshmen with need received aid; of those 19% had need fully met. ***Average percent of need met:*** 59% (excluding resources awarded to replace EFC). ***Average financial aid package:*** $17,523 (excluding resources awarded to replace EFC). 21% of all full-time freshmen had no need and received non-need-based gift aid.

UNDERGRADUATE FINANCIAL AID (Fall 2008, est.) 5,549 applied for aid; of those 81% were deemed to have need. 99% of undergraduates with need received aid; of those 18% had need fully met. ***Average percent of need met:*** 58% (excluding resources awarded to replace EFC). ***Average financial aid package:*** $16,505 (excluding resources awarded to replace EFC). 19% of all full-time undergraduates had no need and received non-need-based gift aid.

GIFT AID (NEED-BASED) ***Total amount:*** $36,350,000 (17% federal, 15% state, 66% institutional, 2% external sources). ***Receiving aid:*** Freshmen: 56% (921); all full-time undergraduates: 49% (3,727). ***Average award:*** Freshmen: $11,515; Undergraduates: $9677. ***Scholarships, grants, and awards:*** Federal Pell, FSEOG, state, private, college/university gift aid from institutional funds, Academic Competitiveness Grant, National Smart Grant.

GIFT AID (NON-NEED-BASED) ***Total amount:*** $16,300,000 (2% federal, 1% state, 93% institutional, 4% external sources). ***Receiving aid:*** Freshmen: 7% (122). Undergraduates: 5% (367). ***Average award:*** Freshmen: $11,141. Undergraduates: $8964. ***Scholarships, grants, and awards by category:*** *Academic interests/achievement:* 3,736 awards ($30,277,248 total): communication, general academic interests/achievements. *Creative arts/performance:* 172 awards ($423,733 total): art/fine arts, dance, music, theater/drama. *Special achievements/activities:* 361 awards ($8,101,777 total): general special achievements/activities, leadership. *Special characteristics:* 151 awards ($471,164 total): children and siblings of alumni, children of union members/company employees, general special characteristics, handicapped students, public servants. ***Tuition waivers:*** Full or partial for employees or children of employees, senior citizens. ***ROTC:*** Army.

LOANS ***Student loans:*** $67,400,000 (66% need-based, 34% non-need-based). 52% of past graduating class borrowed through all loan programs. ***Average need-based loan:*** Freshmen: $3410. Undergraduates: $4559. ***Parent loans:*** $35,000,000 (39% need-based, 61% non-need-based). ***Programs:*** FFEL (Subsidized and Unsubsidized Stafford, PLUS), Perkins, college/university.

WORK-STUDY ***Federal work-study:*** Total amount: $4,200,000; 1,305 jobs averaging $3147. ***State or other work-study/employment:*** Total amount: $5,000,000 (26% need-based, 74% non-need-based). 2,240 part-time jobs averaging $2214.

ATHLETIC AWARDS Total amount: $8,700,000 (52% need-based, 48% non-need-based).

APPLYING FOR FINANCIAL AID ***Required financial aid forms:*** FAFSA, state aid form. ***Financial aid deadline (priority):*** 2/15. ***Notification date:*** Continuous beginning 3/1. Students must reply by 5/1 or within 2 weeks of notification.

CONTACT Sandra Filbry, Director of Financial Aid, Hofstra University, 126 Hofstra University, Hempstead, NY 11549, 516-463-4335 or toll-free 800-HOFSTRA. *Fax:* 516-463-4936. *E-mail:* sandra.a.filbry@hofstra.edu.

HOLLINS UNIVERSITY

Roanoke, VA

Tuition & fees: $27,055 **Average undergraduate aid package: $21,407**

ABOUT THE INSTITUTION Independent, undergraduate: women only; graduate: coed. ***Awards:*** bachelor's and master's degrees and post-master's certificates. 31 undergraduate majors. ***Total enrollment:*** 1,058. Undergraduates: 797. Freshmen: 209. Federal methodology is used as a basis for awarding need-based institutional aid.

UNDERGRADUATE EXPENSES for 2008–09 ***Application fee:*** $35. ***Comprehensive fee:*** $36,705 includes full-time tuition ($26,500), mandatory fees ($555), and room and board ($9650). ***Part-time tuition:*** $830 per credit. ***Payment plan:*** Installment.

FRESHMAN FINANCIAL AID (Fall 2008, est.) 204 applied for aid; of those 79% were deemed to have need. 100% of freshmen with need received aid; of those 17% had need fully met. ***Average percent of need met:*** 80% (excluding resources awarded to replace EFC). ***Average financial aid package:*** $24,419 (excluding resources awarded to replace EFC). 22% of all full-time freshmen had no need and received non-need-based gift aid.

UNDERGRADUATE FINANCIAL AID (Fall 2008, est.) 603 applied for aid; of those 83% were deemed to have need. 100% of undergraduates with need received aid; of those 20% had need fully met. ***Average percent of need met:*** 71% (excluding resources awarded to replace EFC). ***Average financial aid package:*** $21,407 (excluding resources awarded to replace EFC). 33% of all full-time undergraduates had no need and received non-need-based gift aid.

GIFT AID (NEED-BASED) ***Total amount:*** $7,498,811 (16% federal, 10% state, 73% institutional, 1% external sources). ***Receiving aid:*** Freshmen: 78% (162); all full-time undergraduates: 66% (499). ***Average award:*** Freshmen: $17,269; Undergraduates: $16,123. ***Scholarships, grants, and awards:*** Federal Pell, FSEOG, state, private, college/university gift aid from institutional funds.

GIFT AID (NON-NEED-BASED) ***Total amount:*** $3,947,936 (10% state, 88% institutional, 2% external sources). ***Receiving aid:*** Freshmen: 58% (121). Undergraduates: 33% (253). ***Average award:*** Freshmen: $12,201. Undergraduates: $11,775. ***Scholarships, grants, and awards by category:*** *Academic interests/achievement:* 345 awards ($3,938,338 total): general academic interests/achievements. *Creative arts/performance:* 158 awards ($873,221 total): art/fine arts, creative writing, dance, music. *Special achievements/activities:* 73 awards ($413,950 total): community service, leadership. *Special characteristics:* 271 awards ($1,336,104 total): adult students, children and siblings of alumni, children of faculty/staff, international students, local/state students, out-of-state students, previous college experience, veterans. ***Tuition waivers:*** Full or partial for employees or children of employees.

LOANS ***Student loans:*** $3,902,599 (75% need-based, 25% non-need-based). 95% of past graduating class borrowed through all loan programs. *Average indebtedness per student:* $22,161. ***Average need-based loan:*** Freshmen: $5605. Undergraduates: $5218. ***Parent loans:*** $1,660,500 (27% need-based, 73% non-need-based). ***Programs:*** Federal Direct (Subsidized and Unsubsidized Stafford, PLUS), Perkins, college/university, alternative loans.

WORK-STUDY ***Federal work-study:*** Total amount: $627,350; 263 jobs averaging $2340. ***State or other work-study/employment:*** Total amount: $221,073 (41% need-based, 59% non-need-based). 105 part-time jobs averaging $2109.

APPLYING FOR FINANCIAL AID ***Required financial aid forms:*** FAFSA, state aid form. ***Financial aid deadline:*** 2/15 (priority: 2/1). ***Notification date:*** Continuous beginning 3/1. Students must reply by 5/1.

CONTACT Ms. Amy Blackstock, Acting Director of Scholarships and Financial Assistance, Hollins University, PO Box 9718, Roanoke, VA 24020-1688, 540-362-6332 or toll-free 800-456-9595. *Fax:* 540-362-6093. *E-mail:* ablackstock@hollins.edu.

HOLY FAMILY UNIVERSITY

Philadelphia, PA

Tuition & fees: $22,950 **Average undergraduate aid package: $19,203**

ABOUT THE INSTITUTION Independent Roman Catholic, coed, primarily women. ***Awards:*** associate, bachelor's, and master's degrees and post-bachelor's and post-master's certificates. 45 undergraduate majors. ***Total enrollment:*** 3,524. Undergraduates: 2,414. Freshmen: 406. Federal methodology is used as a basis for awarding need-based institutional aid.

UNDERGRADUATE EXPENSES for 2009–10 ***Application fee:*** $25. ***Comprehensive fee:*** $32,850 includes full-time tuition ($22,350), mandatory fees ($600), and room and board ($9900). ***College room only:*** $5900. ***Part-time tuition:*** $480 per credit hour.

FRESHMAN FINANCIAL AID (Fall 2008, est.) 387 applied for aid; of those 87% were deemed to have need. 100% of freshmen with need received aid; of those 100% had need fully met. ***Average percent of need met:*** 87% (excluding resources awarded to replace EFC). ***Average financial aid package:*** $19,924 (excluding resources awarded to replace EFC). 11% of all full-time freshmen had no need and received non-need-based gift aid.

UNDERGRADUATE FINANCIAL AID (Fall 2008, est.) 1,449 applied for aid; of those 89% were deemed to have need. 99% of undergraduates with need received aid; of those 100% had need fully met. ***Average percent of need met:*** 88% (excluding resources awarded to replace EFC). ***Average financial aid package:*** $19,203 (excluding resources awarded to replace EFC). 8% of all full-time undergraduates had no need and received non-need-based gift aid.

GIFT AID (NEED-BASED) ***Total amount:*** $12,283,530 (19% federal, 20% state, 61% institutional). ***Receiving aid:*** Freshmen: 83% (335); all full-time undergraduates: 79% (1,244). ***Average award:*** Freshmen: $12,570; Undergraduates: $10,609. ***Scholarships, grants, and awards:*** Federal Pell, FSEOG, state, private, college/university gift aid from institutional funds.

GIFT AID (NON-NEED-BASED) ***Total amount:*** $1,548,480 (56% institutional, 44% external sources). ***Receiving aid:*** Freshmen: 12% (47). Undergraduates: 9% (138). ***Average award:*** Freshmen: $4948. Undergraduates: $7033. ***Scholarships, grants, and awards by category:*** *Academic interests/achievement:* 183 awards ($868,764 total): general academic interests/achievements.

LOANS ***Student loans:*** $15,896,737 (33% need-based, 67% non-need-based). 70% of past graduating class borrowed through all loan programs. *Average indebtedness per student:* $10,023. ***Average need-based loan:*** Freshmen: $3727. Undergraduates: $4236. ***Parent loans:*** $1,189,808 (100% non-need-based). ***Programs:*** FFEL (Subsidized and Unsubsidized Stafford, PLUS), Perkins, Federal Nursing.

WORK-STUDY ***Federal work-study:*** Total amount: $354,950; 221 jobs averaging $1606. ***State or other work-study/employment:*** Part-time jobs available.

ATHLETIC AWARDS Total amount: $1,347,576 (100% non-need-based).

APPLYING FOR FINANCIAL AID ***Required financial aid form:*** FAFSA. ***Financial aid deadline (priority):*** 3/1. ***Notification date:*** Continuous beginning 4/1. Students must reply within 2 weeks of notification.

CONTACT Financial Aid Office, Holy Family University, 9801 Frankford Avenue, Philadelphia, PA 19114-2094, 215-637-7700 Ext. 3233 or toll-free 800-637-1191. *Fax:* 215-599-1694. *E-mail:* finaid@holyfamily.edu.

HOLY NAMES UNIVERSITY

Oakland, CA

CONTACT Christina Miller, Director of Financial Aid, Holy Names University, 3500 Mountain Boulevard, Oakland, CA 94619-1699, 510-436-1327 or toll-free 800-430-1321. *Fax:* 510-436-1199. *E-mail:* miller@hnu.edu.

HOOD COLLEGE

Frederick, MD

Tuition & fees: $26,580 **Average undergraduate aid package: $20,854**

ABOUT THE INSTITUTION Independent, coed. ***Awards:*** bachelor's and master's degrees and post-bachelor's certificates (also offers adult program with significant enrollment not reflected in profile). 28 undergraduate majors. ***Total enrollment:*** 2,533. Undergraduates: 1,449. Freshmen: 308. Federal methodology is used as a basis for awarding need-based institutional aid.

UNDERGRADUATE EXPENSES for 2008–09 ***Application fee:*** $35. ***Comprehensive fee:*** $35,560 includes full-time tuition ($26,200), mandatory fees ($380), and room and board ($8980). ***College room only:*** $4690. Full-time tuition and fees vary according to course load. Room and board charges vary according to board plan. ***Part-time tuition:*** $755 per term. ***Part-time fees:*** $120 per term. Part-time tuition and fees vary according to course load. ***Payment plans:*** Tuition prepayment, installment, deferred payment.

FRESHMAN FINANCIAL AID (Fall 2008, est.) 278 applied for aid; of those 83% were deemed to have need. 99% of freshmen with need received aid; of those 27% had need fully met. ***Average percent of need met:*** 83% (excluding resources awarded to replace EFC). ***Average financial aid package:*** $20,894 (excluding resources awarded to replace EFC). 22% of all full-time freshmen had no need and received non-need-based gift aid.

UNDERGRADUATE FINANCIAL AID (Fall 2008, est.) 1,140 applied for aid; of those 85% were deemed to have need. 99% of undergraduates with need received aid; of those 29% had need fully met. ***Average percent of need met:*** 83% (excluding resources awarded to replace EFC). ***Average financial aid package:*** $20,854 (excluding resources awarded to replace EFC). 22% of all full-time undergraduates had no need and received non-need-based gift aid.

GIFT AID (NEED-BASED) ***Total amount:*** $16,380,214 (9% federal, 11% state, 75% institutional, 5% external sources). ***Receiving aid:*** Freshmen: 73% (226); all full-time undergraduates: 76% (954). ***Average award:*** Freshmen: $18,092; Undergraduates: $17,272. ***Scholarships, grants, and awards:*** Federal Pell, FSEOG, state, private, college/university gift aid from institutional funds.

GIFT AID (NON-NEED-BASED) ***Total amount:*** $4,479,693 (1% federal, 1% state, 85% institutional, 13% external sources). ***Receiving aid:*** Freshmen: 17% (52). Undergraduates: 15% (185). ***Average award:*** Freshmen: $20,939. Undergraduates: $17,153. ***Scholarships, grants, and awards by category:*** *Academic interests/achievement:* 1,233 awards ($10,080,914 total): general academic interests/achievements. *Creative arts/performance:* 43 awards ($23,448 total): creative writing. *Special characteristics:* 185 awards ($1,388,199 total): children and siblings of alumni, children of faculty/staff, ethnic background, international students, siblings of current students. ***Tuition waivers:*** Full or partial for children of alumni, employees or children of employees, adult students. ***ROTC:*** Army cooperative.

LOANS ***Student loans:*** $6,823,713 (67% need-based, 33% non-need-based). 71% of past graduating class borrowed through all loan programs. *Average indebtedness per student:* $19,038. ***Average need-based loan:*** Freshmen: $3703. Undergraduates: $4498. ***Parent loans:*** $2,805,578 (21% need-based, 79% non-need-based). ***Programs:*** Federal Direct (Subsidized and Unsubsidized Stafford, PLUS), FFEL (Subsidized and Unsubsidized Stafford, PLUS), Perkins.

WORK-STUDY ***Federal work-study:*** Total amount: $245,248; 219 jobs averaging $1700. ***State or other work-study/employment:*** Total amount: $132,430 (13% need-based, 87% non-need-based). 89 part-time jobs averaging $1650.

APPLYING FOR FINANCIAL AID ***Required financial aid form:*** FAFSA. ***Financial aid deadline (priority):*** 2/15. ***Notification date:*** Continuous beginning 3/1. Students must reply by 5/1 or within 3 weeks of notification.

CONTACT Margherite Powell, Director of Financial Aid, Hood College, 401 Rosemont Avenue, Frederick, MD 21701-8575, 301-696-3411 or toll-free 800-922-1599. *Fax:* 301-696-3812. *E-mail:* finaid@hood.edu.

HOPE COLLEGE

Holland, MI

Tuition & fees: $24,920 **Average undergraduate aid package: $21,514**

ABOUT THE INSTITUTION Independent religious, coed. ***Awards:*** bachelor's degrees. 71 undergraduate majors. ***Total enrollment:*** 3,238. Undergraduates: 3,238. Freshmen: 808. Federal methodology is used as a basis for awarding need-based institutional aid.

UNDERGRADUATE EXPENSES for 2008–09 ***Application fee:*** $35. ***Comprehensive fee:*** $32,570 includes full-time tuition ($24,780), mandatory fees ($140), and room and board ($7650). ***College room only:*** $3490. Room and board charges vary according to board plan. Part-time tuition and fees vary according to course load. ***Payment plan:*** Installment.

FRESHMAN FINANCIAL AID (Fall 2008, est.) 650 applied for aid; of those 75% were deemed to have need. 100% of freshmen with need received aid; of those 34% had need fully met. ***Average percent of need met:*** 87% (excluding resources awarded to replace EFC). ***Average financial aid package:*** $22,146 (excluding resources awarded to replace EFC). 32% of all full-time freshmen had no need and received non-need-based gift aid.

UNDERGRADUATE FINANCIAL AID (Fall 2008, est.) 2,181 applied for aid; of those 82% were deemed to have need. 100% of undergraduates with need received aid; of those 36% had need fully met. ***Average percent of need met:*** 86% (excluding resources awarded to replace EFC). ***Average financial aid package:*** $21,514 (excluding resources awarded to replace EFC). 30% of all full-time undergraduates had no need and received non-need-based gift aid.

GIFT AID (NEED-BASED) ***Total amount:*** $21,135,274 (7% federal, 11% state, 81% institutional, 1% external sources). ***Receiving aid:*** Freshmen: 52% (414); all full-time undergraduates: 51% (1,536). ***Average award:*** Freshmen: $16,696; Undergraduates: $15,565. ***Scholarships, grants, and awards:*** Federal Pell, FSEOG, state, private, college/university gift aid from institutional funds.

GIFT AID (NON-NEED-BASED) ***Total amount:*** $8,863,657 (1% federal, 10% state, 80% institutional, 9% external sources). ***Receiving aid:*** Freshmen: 51% (410). Undergraduates: 43% (1,291). ***Average award:*** Freshmen: $6714. Undergraduates: $7207. ***Scholarships, grants, and awards by category:*** *Academic interests/achievement:* 1,923 awards ($11,992,922 total): general academic interests/achievements. *Creative arts/performance:* 139 awards ($363,250 total): art/fine arts, creative writing, dance, music, theater/drama. *Special characteristics:* 77 awards ($1,564,671 total): ethnic background. ***Tuition waivers:*** Full or partial for employees or children of employees. ***ROTC:*** Army cooperative.

LOANS ***Student loans:*** $12,169,113 (59% need-based, 41% non-need-based). 64% of past graduating class borrowed through all loan programs. *Average indebtedness per student:* $25,889. ***Average need-based loan:*** Freshmen: $4699. Undergraduates: $5251. ***Parent loans:*** $2,707,256 (100% non-need-based). ***Programs:*** Federal Direct (Subsidized and Unsubsidized Stafford, PLUS), Perkins, college/university.

WORK-STUDY ***Federal work-study:*** Total amount: $300,540; 229 jobs averaging $1377. ***State or other work-study/employment:*** Total amount: $1,050,600 (38% need-based, 62% non-need-based). 427 part-time jobs averaging $616.

APPLYING FOR FINANCIAL AID ***Required financial aid forms:*** FAFSA, institution's own form. ***Financial aid deadline (priority):*** 3/1. ***Notification date:*** Continuous beginning 3/15. Students must reply by 5/1 or within 2 weeks of notification.

CONTACT Ms. Phyllis Hooyman, Director of Financial Aid, Hope College, 141 East 12th Street, Holland, MI 49422-9000, 616-395-7765 or toll-free 800-968-7850. *Fax:* 616-395-7160. *E-mail:* hooyman@hope.edu.

HOPE INTERNATIONAL UNIVERSITY

Fullerton, CA

Tuition & fees: $22,761 **Average undergraduate aid package: $18,011**

ABOUT THE INSTITUTION Independent religious, coed. ***Awards:*** bachelor's and master's degrees and post-bachelor's and post-master's certificates. 19 undergraduate majors. ***Total enrollment:*** 1,059. Undergraduates: 794. Freshmen: 87. Federal methodology is used as a basis for awarding need-based institutional aid.

UNDERGRADUATE EXPENSES for 2009–10 ***Application fee:*** $40. ***Comprehensive fee:*** $30,991 includes full-time tuition ($21,560), mandatory fees ($1201), and room and board ($8230). ***College room only:*** $4980. ***Part-time tuition:*** $799 per unit.

FRESHMAN FINANCIAL AID (Fall 2008, est.) 81 applied for aid; of those 93% were deemed to have need. 99% of freshmen with need received aid; of those 15% had need fully met. ***Average percent of need met:*** 70% (excluding resources awarded to replace EFC). ***Average financial aid package:*** $17,251 (excluding resources awarded to replace EFC). 17% of all full-time freshmen had no need and received non-need-based gift aid.

UNDERGRADUATE FINANCIAL AID (Fall 2008, est.) 351 applied for aid; of those 92% were deemed to have need. 97% of undergraduates with need received aid; of those 18% had need fully met. ***Average percent of need met:*** 70% (excluding resources awarded to replace EFC). ***Average financial aid package:*** $18,011 (excluding resources awarded to replace EFC). 10% of all full-time undergraduates had no need and received non-need-based gift aid.

GIFT AID (NEED-BASED) ***Total amount:*** $4,727,694 (15% federal, 14% state, 68% institutional, 3% external sources). ***Receiving aid:*** Freshmen: 80% (72); all full-time undergraduates: 85% (309). ***Average award:*** Freshmen: $13,837; Undergraduates: $13,988. ***Scholarships, grants, and awards:*** Federal Pell, FSEOG, state, private, college/university gift aid from institutional funds.

GIFT AID (NON-NEED-BASED) ***Total amount:*** $1,733,386 (15% federal, 83% institutional, 2% external sources). ***Receiving aid:*** Freshmen: 8% (7). Undergraduates: 8% (29). ***Average award:*** Freshmen: $19,880. Undergraduates: $19,750. ***Scholarships, grants, and awards by category:*** *Academic interests/achievement:* area/ethnic studies, business, communication, education, English, general academic interests/achievements, humanities, international studies, religion/biblical studies, social sciences. *Creative arts/performance:* 7 awards ($27,250 total): music. *Special achievements/activities:* 48 awards ($68,200 total): leadership, religious involvement. *Special characteristics:* 56 awards ($153,993 total): children and siblings of alumni, children of faculty/staff, international students, local/state students, relatives of clergy, siblings of current students, spouses of current students, veterans, veterans' children.

LOANS ***Student loans:*** $3,392,026 (79% need-based, 21% non-need-based). 96% of past graduating class borrowed through all loan programs. *Average indebtedness per student:* $27,000. ***Average need-based loan:*** Freshmen: $3929. Undergraduates: $4755. ***Parent loans:*** $841,654 (40% need-based, 60% non-need-based). ***Programs:*** FFEL (Subsidized and Unsubsidized Stafford, PLUS), Perkins.

WORK-STUDY ***Federal work-study:*** Total amount: $126,599; 62 jobs averaging $2000. ***State or other work-study/employment:*** Total amount: $9800 (73% need-based, 27% non-need-based). Part-time jobs available.

ATHLETIC AWARDS Total amount: $1,039,041 (100% need-based).

APPLYING FOR FINANCIAL AID ***Required financial aid forms:*** FAFSA, institution's own form. ***Financial aid deadline (priority):*** 3/2. ***Notification date:*** Continuous beginning 4/1. Students must reply within 2 weeks of notification.

CONTACT Mrs. Shannon O'Shields, Director of Financial Aid, Hope International University, 2500 East Nutwood Avenue, Fullerton, CA 92831, 714-879-3901 or toll-free 800-762-1294. *Fax:* 714-681-7421. *E-mail:* soshields@hiu.edu.

HOUGHTON COLLEGE

Houghton, NY

Tuition & fees: $22,990 **Average undergraduate aid package: $18,952**

ABOUT THE INSTITUTION Independent Wesleyan, coed. ***Awards:*** associate, bachelor's, and master's degrees. 52 undergraduate majors. ***Total enrollment:*** 1,419. Undergraduates: 1,381. Freshmen: 328. Federal methodology is used as a basis for awarding need-based institutional aid.

UNDERGRADUATE EXPENSES for 2008–09 ***Application fee:*** $40. ***Comprehensive fee:*** $29,920 includes full-time tuition ($22,990) and room and board ($6930). ***College room only:*** $3710. Room and board charges vary according to board plan and housing facility. ***Part-time tuition:*** $960 per credit hour. ***Payment plan:*** Installment.

FRESHMAN FINANCIAL AID (Fall 2008, est.) 291 applied for aid; of those 90% were deemed to have need. 100% of freshmen with need received aid; of those 16% had need fully met. ***Average percent of need met:*** 82% (excluding resources awarded to replace EFC). ***Average financial aid package:*** $21,307 (excluding resources awarded to replace EFC). 19% of all full-time freshmen had no need and received non-need-based gift aid.

UNDERGRADUATE FINANCIAL AID (Fall 2008, est.) 1,106 applied for aid; of those 92% were deemed to have need. 99% of undergraduates with need received aid; of those 18% had need fully met. ***Average percent of need met:*** 79% (excluding resources awarded to replace EFC). ***Average financial aid package:*** $18,952 (excluding resources awarded to replace EFC). 18% of all full-time undergraduates had no need and received non-need-based gift aid.

GIFT AID (NEED-BASED) ***Total amount:*** $11,148,935 (15% federal, 12% state, 67% institutional, 6% external sources). ***Receiving aid:*** Freshmen: 79% (261); all full-time undergraduates: 77% (986). ***Average award:*** Freshmen: $15,718; Undergraduates: $12,692. ***Scholarships, grants, and awards:*** Federal Pell, FSEOG, state, private, college/university gift aid from institutional funds, United Negro College Fund.

GIFT AID (NON-NEED-BASED) ***Total amount:*** $2,000,010 (3% state, 83% institutional, 14% external sources). ***Receiving aid:*** Freshmen: 7% (24). Undergraduates: 7% (89). ***Average award:*** Freshmen: $12,010. Undergraduates: $11,634. ***Scholarships, grants, and awards by category:*** *Academic interests/achievement:* 647 awards ($2,927,375 total): general academic interests/achievements. *Creative arts/performance:* 99 awards ($269,950 total): art/fine arts, music. *Special achievements/activities:* 323 awards ($233,883 total): religious involvement. *Special characteristics:* 613 awards ($2,247,628 total): children and siblings of alumni, children of faculty/staff, international students, local/state students, relatives of clergy, religious affiliation, siblings of current students. ***Tuition waivers:*** Full or partial for employees or children of employees, senior citizens. ***ROTC:*** Army cooperative.

LOANS ***Student loans:*** $9,598,043 (74% need-based, 26% non-need-based). 81% of past graduating class borrowed through all loan programs. *Average indebtedness per student:* $30,150. ***Average need-based loan:*** Freshmen: $4298. Undergraduates: $5577. ***Parent loans:*** $1,405,628 (52% need-based, 48% non-need-based). ***Programs:*** FFEL (Subsidized and Unsubsidized Stafford, PLUS), Perkins, alternative loans.

WORK-STUDY ***Federal work-study:*** Total amount: $1,388,636; 714 jobs averaging $2012. ***State or other work-study/employment:*** Total amount: $36,125 (100% non-need-based). 17 part-time jobs averaging $2125.

ATHLETIC AWARDS Total amount: $578,465 (70% need-based, 30% non-need-based).

APPLYING FOR FINANCIAL AID ***Required financial aid forms:*** FAFSA, state aid form. ***Financial aid deadline (priority):*** 3/1. ***Notification date:*** Continuous beginning 3/15. Students must reply within 4 weeks of notification.

CONTACT Mr. Troy Martin, Director of Financial Aid, Houghton College, One Willard Avenue, Houghton, NY 14744, 585-567-9328 or toll-free 800-777-2556. *Fax:* 585-567-9610. *E-mail:* troy.martin@houghton.edu.

HOUSTON BAPTIST UNIVERSITY

Houston, TX

Tuition & fees: $20,830 **Average undergraduate aid package: $17,431**

ABOUT THE INSTITUTION Independent Baptist, coed. ***Awards:*** associate, bachelor's, and master's degrees and post-bachelor's and post-master's certificates. 64 undergraduate majors. ***Total enrollment:*** 2,564. Undergraduates: 2,208. Freshmen: 560. Federal methodology is used as a basis for awarding need-based institutional aid.

UNDERGRADUATE EXPENSES for 2009–10 ***Comprehensive fee:*** $27,805 includes full-time tuition ($19,990), mandatory fees ($840), and room and board ($6975).

FRESHMAN FINANCIAL AID (Fall 2008, est.) 451 applied for aid; of those 87% were deemed to have need. 100% of freshmen with need received aid; of those 20% had need fully met. ***Average percent of need met:*** 75% (excluding resources awarded to replace EFC). ***Average financial aid package:*** $17,565 (excluding resources awarded to replace EFC). 28% of all full-time freshmen had no need and received non-need-based gift aid.

UNDERGRADUATE FINANCIAL AID (Fall 2008, est.) 1,363 applied for aid; of those 90% were deemed to have need. 100% of undergraduates with need received aid; of those 18% had need fully met. ***Average percent of need met:*** 69% (excluding resources awarded to replace EFC). ***Average financial aid package:*** $17,431 (excluding resources awarded to replace EFC). 23% of all full-time undergraduates had no need and received non-need-based gift aid.

GIFT AID (NEED-BASED) ***Total amount:*** $12,495,213 (26% federal, 25% state, 46% institutional, 3% external sources). ***Receiving aid:*** Freshmen: 70% (391); all full-time undergraduates: 64% (1,204). ***Average award:*** Freshmen: $11,902; Undergraduates: $10,785. ***Scholarships, grants, and awards:*** Federal Pell, FSEOG, state, private, college/university gift aid from institutional funds.

GIFT AID (NON-NEED-BASED) ***Total amount:*** $3,650,595 (95% institutional, 5% external sources). ***Receiving aid:*** Freshmen: 67% (371). Undergraduates: 42% (795). ***Average award:*** Freshmen: $7722. Undergraduates: $7444. ***Scholarships, grants, and awards by category:*** *Academic interests/achievement:* 1,752 awards ($7,397,413 total): general academic interests/achievements, health fields, religion/biblical studies. *Creative arts/performance:* 130 awards ($329,671 total): art/fine arts, debating, music. *Special achievements/activities:* 41 awards ($87,350 total): cheerleading/drum major, community service, religious involvement. *Special characteristics:* 147 awards ($750,482 total): children and siblings of alumni, children of faculty/staff, relatives of clergy, siblings of current students. ***ROTC:*** Army cooperative.

LOANS ***Student loans:*** $9,931,852 (81% need-based, 19% non-need-based). ***Average need-based loan:*** Freshmen: $3622. Undergraduates: $3918. ***Parent loans:*** $3,747,693 (42% need-based, 58% non-need-based). ***Programs:*** Federal Direct (Subsidized and Unsubsidized Stafford, PLUS), FFEL (Subsidized and Unsubsidized Stafford, PLUS), state, alternative loans.

WORK-STUDY ***Federal work-study:*** Total amount: $1,078,795; 698 jobs available. ***State or other work-study/employment:*** Total amount: $857 (100% need-based). Part-time jobs available.

ATHLETIC AWARDS Total amount: $3,833,531 (35% need-based, 65% non-need-based).

APPLYING FOR FINANCIAL AID ***Required financial aid form:*** FAFSA. ***Financial aid deadline:*** 4/15 (priority: 3/1). ***Notification date:*** Continuous beginning 3/10.

CONTACT Sherry Byrd, Director of Student Aid Programs, Houston Baptist University, 7502 Fondren Road, Houston, TX 77074-3298, 281-649-3471 or toll-free 800-696-3210. *Fax:* 281-649-3298. *E-mail:* Financial_services@hbu.edu.

HOWARD PAYNE UNIVERSITY

Brownwood, TX

Tuition & fees: $18,650 **Average undergraduate aid package: $13,599**

ABOUT THE INSTITUTION Independent religious, coed. ***Awards:*** associate, bachelor's, and master's degrees. 77 undergraduate majors. ***Total enrollment:*** 1,388. Undergraduates: 1,371. Freshmen: 323. Federal methodology is used as a basis for awarding need-based institutional aid.

UNDERGRADUATE EXPENSES for 2009–10 ***Application fee:*** $25. ***Comprehensive fee:*** $23,810 includes full-time tuition ($17,600), mandatory fees ($1050), and room and board ($5160). ***College room only:*** $2220. ***Part-time tuition:*** $525 per credit hour.

FRESHMAN FINANCIAL AID (Fall 2008, est.) 286 applied for aid; of those 87% were deemed to have need. 100% of freshmen with need received aid; of those 27% had need fully met. ***Average percent of need met:*** 84% (excluding resources awarded to replace EFC). ***Average financial aid package:*** $14,312 (excluding resources awarded to replace EFC). 17% of all full-time freshmen had no need and received non-need-based gift aid.

UNDERGRADUATE FINANCIAL AID (Fall 2008, est.) 912 applied for aid; of those 88% were deemed to have need. 99% of undergraduates with need received aid; of those 30% had need fully met. ***Average percent of need met:*** 85% (excluding resources awarded to replace EFC). ***Average financial aid package:*** $13,599 (excluding resources awarded to replace EFC). 19% of all full-time undergraduates had no need and received non-need-based gift aid.

GIFT AID (NEED-BASED) ***Total amount:*** $6,126,997 (27% federal, 26% state, 42% institutional, 5% external sources). ***Receiving aid:*** Freshmen: 81% (246); all full-time undergraduates: 74% (774). ***Average award:*** Freshmen: $10,608; Undergraduates: $9155. ***Scholarships, grants, and awards:*** Federal Pell, FSEOG, state, private, college/university gift aid from institutional funds.

GIFT AID (NON-NEED-BASED) ***Total amount:*** $2,728,198 (91% institutional, 9% external sources). ***Receiving aid:*** Freshmen: 12% (38). Undergraduates: 9% (97). ***Average award:*** Freshmen: $6405. Undergraduates: $6065. ***Scholarships, grants, and awards by category:*** *Academic interests/achievement:* 400 awards ($1,217,159 total): biological sciences, business, communication, education, English, general academic interests/achievements, mathematics, physical sciences, premedicine, religion/biblical studies, social sciences. *Creative arts/performance:* 60 awards ($150,000 total): art/fine arts, music, theater/drama. *Special achievements/activities:* community service, leadership, religious involvement. *Special characteristics:* children and siblings of alumni, children of faculty/staff, local/state students, relatives of clergy, religious affiliation.

LOANS ***Student loans:*** $6,261,909 (56% need-based, 44% non-need-based). 69% of past graduating class borrowed through all loan programs. *Average indebtedness per student:* $18,960. ***Average need-based loan:*** Freshmen: $3212. Undergraduates: $3946. ***Parent loans:*** $918,237 (20% need-based, 80% non-need-based). ***Programs:*** FFEL (Subsidized and Unsubsidized Stafford, PLUS), Perkins, state.

WORK-STUDY ***Federal work-study:*** Total amount: $110,000; 118 jobs averaging $900. ***State or other work-study/employment:*** Total amount: $13,000 (100% need-based). 9 part-time jobs averaging $2500.

APPLYING FOR FINANCIAL AID ***Required financial aid forms:*** FAFSA, institution's own form. ***Financial aid deadline (priority):*** 3/15. ***Notification date:*** Continuous. Students must reply within 2 weeks of notification.

CONTACT Glenda Huff, Director of Financial Aid, Howard Payne University, 1000 Fisk Avenue, Brownwood, TX 76801, 325-649-8014 or toll-free 800-880-4478. *Fax:* 325-649-8901. *E-mail:* ghuff@hputx.edu.

HOWARD UNIVERSITY

Washington, DC

ABOUT THE INSTITUTION Independent, coed. ***Awards:*** bachelor's, master's, doctoral, and first professional degrees and post-master's and first professional certificates. 64 undergraduate majors. ***Total enrollment:*** 10,288. Undergraduates: 6,969.

GIFT AID (NEED-BASED) ***Scholarships, grants, and awards:*** Federal Pell, FSEOG, state, private, college/university gift aid from institutional funds, Federal Nursing.

GIFT AID (NON-NEED-BASED) ***Scholarships, grants, and awards by category:*** *Creative arts/performance:* art/fine arts, dance, music.

LOANS ***Programs:*** Federal Direct (Subsidized and Unsubsidized Stafford, PLUS), FFEL (Subsidized and Unsubsidized Stafford, PLUS), Perkins, Federal Nursing, district, college/university.

WORK-STUDY ***Federal work-study:*** Total amount: $918,544; 431 jobs averaging $3667. ***State or other work-study/employment:*** Total amount: $679,745 (100% need-based). 223 part-time jobs averaging $3590.

APPLYING FOR FINANCIAL AID ***Required financial aid forms:*** FAFSA, institution's own form.

CONTACT Marcus Decosta, Director of Financial Aid and Scholarships, Howard University, 2400 Sixth Street, NW, Washington, DC 20059-0002, 202-806-2850 or toll-free 800-HOWARD-U. *Fax:* 202-806-2818.

HUMBOLDT STATE UNIVERSITY

Arcata, CA

Tuition & fees (CA res): $4150 **Average undergraduate aid package: $9077**

ABOUT THE INSTITUTION State-supported, coed. ***Awards:*** bachelor's and master's degrees and post-bachelor's certificates. 76 undergraduate majors. ***Total enrollment:*** 7,800. Undergraduates: 6,869. Freshmen: 1,191. Federal methodology is used as a basis for awarding need-based institutional aid.

UNDERGRADUATE EXPENSES for 2008–09 ***Application fee:*** $55. ***Tuition, state resident:*** full-time $0. ***Tuition, nonresident:*** full-time $11,184; part-time $339 per unit. ***Required fees:*** full-time $4150; $222 per unit. Full-time tuition and fees vary according to degree level. Part-time tuition and fees vary according to course load and degree level. ***College room and board:*** $8972; ***Room only:*** $5660. Room and board charges vary according to board plan and housing facility. ***Payment plan:*** Installment.

FRESHMAN FINANCIAL AID (Fall 2008, est.) 909 applied for aid; of those 70% were deemed to have need. 94% of freshmen with need received aid; of those 5% had need fully met. ***Average percent of need met:*** 73% (excluding resources awarded to replace EFC). ***Average financial aid package:*** $8217 (excluding resources awarded to replace EFC). 1% of all full-time freshmen had no need and received non-need-based gift aid.

UNDERGRADUATE FINANCIAL AID (Fall 2008, est.) 4,457 applied for aid; of those 83% were deemed to have need. 96% of undergraduates with need received aid; of those 4% had need fully met. ***Average percent of need met:*** 75% (excluding resources awarded to replace EFC). ***Average financial aid package:*** $9077 (excluding resources awarded to replace EFC). 1% of all full-time undergraduates had no need and received non-need-based gift aid.

GIFT AID (NEED-BASED) ***Total amount:*** $21,607,051 (49% federal, 46% state, 2% institutional, 3% external sources). ***Receiving aid:*** Freshmen: 51% (599); all full-time undergraduates: 58% (3,560). ***Average award:*** Freshmen: $4717; Undergraduates: $4895. ***Scholarships, grants, and awards:*** Federal Pell, FSEOG, state, private, college/university gift aid from institutional funds.

GIFT AID (NON-NEED-BASED) ***Total amount:*** $461,277 (5% federal, 1% state, 13% institutional, 81% external sources). ***Average award:*** Freshmen: $1238. Undergraduates: $1229. ***Scholarships, grants, and awards by category:*** *Academic interests/achievement:* general academic interests/achievements. ***Tuition waivers:*** Full or partial for employees or children of employees.

LOANS ***Student loans:*** $20,414,817 (77% need-based, 23% non-need-based). 52% of past graduating class borrowed through all loan programs. *Average indebtedness per student:* $13,368. ***Average need-based loan:*** Freshmen: $348. Undergraduates: $663. ***Parent loans:*** $2,297,729 (20% need-based, 80% non-need-based). ***Programs:*** Federal Direct (Subsidized and Unsubsidized Stafford, PLUS), Perkins.

WORK-STUDY ***Federal work-study:*** Total amount: $432,056; 250 jobs averaging $2000.

ATHLETIC AWARDS Total amount: $572,249 (54% need-based, 46% non-need-based).

APPLYING FOR FINANCIAL AID ***Required financial aid form:*** FAFSA. ***Financial aid deadline (priority):*** 3/2. ***Notification date:*** Continuous beginning 3/7.

CONTACT Kim Coughlin-Lamphear, Director of Financial Aid, Humboldt State University, 1 Harpst Street, Arcata, CA 95521-8299, 707-826-4321. *E-mail:* coughlin@humboldt.edu.

HUMPHREYS COLLEGE

Stockton, CA

CONTACT Judi LaFeber, Director of Financial Aid, Humphreys College, 6650 Inglewood Avenue, Stockton, CA 95207-3896, 209-478-0800. *Fax:* 209-478-8721.

HUNTER COLLEGE OF THE CITY UNIVERSITY OF NEW YORK

New York, NY

Tuition & fees (NY res): $4349 **Average undergraduate aid package: $5067**

ABOUT THE INSTITUTION State and locally supported, coed. ***Awards:*** bachelor's and master's degrees and post-master's certificates. 65 undergraduate majors. ***Total enrollment:*** 21,258. Undergraduates: 15,698. Freshmen: 2,042. Federal methodology is used as a basis for awarding need-based institutional aid.

UNDERGRADUATE EXPENSES for 2008–09 ***Application fee:*** $65. ***Tuition, state resident:*** full-time $4000; part-time $170 per term. ***Tuition, nonresident:*** full-time $10,800; part-time $360 per term. ***Required fees:*** full-time $349; $133.50 per term. Full-time tuition and fees vary according to degree level and program. Part-time tuition and fees vary according to degree level and program. ***College room and board: Room only:*** $5311. ***Payment plan:*** Installment.

FRESHMAN FINANCIAL AID (Fall 2008, est.) 1,563 applied for aid; of those 72% were deemed to have need. ***Average percent of need met:*** 77% (excluding resources awarded to replace EFC). ***Average financial aid package:*** $5215 (excluding resources awarded to replace EFC). 17% of all full-time freshmen had no need and received non-need-based gift aid.

UNDERGRADUATE FINANCIAL AID (Fall 2008, est.) 7,596 applied for aid; of those 82% were deemed to have need. ***Average percent of need met:*** 78% (excluding resources awarded to replace EFC). ***Average financial aid package:*** $5067 (excluding resources awarded to replace EFC). 7% of all full-time undergraduates had no need and received non-need-based gift aid.

GIFT AID (NEED-BASED) ***Total amount:*** $33,303,251 (50% federal, 47% state, 3% institutional). ***Receiving aid:*** Freshmen: 66% (1,216); all full-time undergraduates: 59% (6,282). ***Average award:*** Freshmen: $5571; Undergraduates: $5349. ***Scholarships, grants, and awards:*** Federal Pell, FSEOG, state, private, college/university gift aid from institutional funds.

GIFT AID (NON-NEED-BASED) ***Total amount:*** $2,502,674 (55% institutional, 45% external sources). ***Receiving aid:*** Freshmen: 45% (841). Undergraduates: 21% (2,207). ***Average award:*** Freshmen: $2100. Undergraduates: $2356. ***Scholarships, grants, and awards by category:*** *Academic interests/achievement:* general academic interests/achievements.

LOANS ***Student loans:*** $4,456,225 (26% need-based, 74% non-need-based). 48% of past graduating class borrowed through all loan programs. *Average indebtedness per student:* $6801. ***Average need-based loan:*** Freshmen: $2732. Undergraduates: $3163. ***Parent loans:*** $302,291 (100% need-based). ***Programs:*** Federal Direct (Subsidized and Unsubsidized Stafford, PLUS), Perkins.

WORK-STUDY ***Federal work-study:*** Total amount: $1,370,069; jobs available.

APPLYING FOR FINANCIAL AID ***Required financial aid forms:*** FAFSA, state aid form. ***Financial aid deadline (priority):*** 4/1. ***Notification date:*** Continuous beginning 5/15.

CONTACT Aristalia Benitez, Director of Financial Aid, Hunter College of the City University of New York, 695 Park Avenue, New York, NY 10021-5085, 212-772-4400. *Fax:* 212-650-3666. *E-mail:* aristalia@hunter.cuny.edu.

HUNTINGDON COLLEGE

Montgomery, AL

Tuition & fees: $20,020 **Average undergraduate aid package: $18,278**

ABOUT THE INSTITUTION Independent United Methodist, coed. ***Awards:*** bachelor's degrees. 26 undergraduate majors. ***Total enrollment:*** 1,082. Undergraduates: 1,082. Freshmen: 253. Both federal and institutional methodology are used as a basis for awarding need-based institutional aid.

UNDERGRADUATE EXPENSES for 2008–09 *Application fee:* $20. ***Comprehensive fee:*** $26,970 includes full-time tuition ($19,320), mandatory fees ($700), and room and board ($6950). Full-time tuition and fees vary according to course load, reciprocity agreements, and student level. Room and board charges vary according to board plan. ***Part-time tuition:*** $800 per credit hour. Part-time tuition and fees vary according to course load. ***Payment plans:*** Guaranteed tuition, deferred payment.

FRESHMAN FINANCIAL AID (Fall 2008, est.) 218 applied for aid; of those 86% were deemed to have need. 100% of freshmen with need received aid; of those 66% had need fully met. ***Average percent of need met:*** 92% (excluding resources awarded to replace EFC). ***Average financial aid package:*** $11,798 (excluding resources awarded to replace EFC). 26% of all full-time freshmen had no need and received non-need-based gift aid.

UNDERGRADUATE FINANCIAL AID (Fall 2008, est.) 603 applied for aid; of those 85% were deemed to have need. 100% of undergraduates with need received aid; of those 66% had need fully met. ***Average percent of need met:*** 94% (excluding resources awarded to replace EFC). ***Average financial aid package:*** $18,278 (excluding resources awarded to replace EFC). 36% of all full-time undergraduates had no need and received non-need-based gift aid.

GIFT AID (NEED-BASED) ***Total amount:*** $1,813,478 (64% federal, 3% state, 33% institutional). ***Receiving aid:*** Freshmen: 40% (101); all full-time undergraduates: 32% (269). ***Average award:*** Freshmen: $6264; Undergraduates: $5609. ***Scholarships, grants, and awards:*** Federal Pell, FSEOG, state, private, college/university gift aid from institutional funds.

GIFT AID (NON-NEED-BASED) ***Total amount:*** $7,025,650 (4% state, 91% institutional, 5% external sources). ***Receiving aid:*** Freshmen: 74% (187). Undergraduates: 57% (486). ***Average award:*** Freshmen: $9383. Undergraduates: $8359. ***Scholarships, grants, and awards by category:*** *Academic interests/achievement:* 62 awards ($352,252 total): biological sciences, computer science, general academic interests/achievements, mathematics. *Creative arts/performance:* 3 awards ($10,160 total): music. *Special achievements/activities:* 20 awards ($158,076 total): cheerleading/drum major. *Special characteristics:* 241 awards ($1,042,503 total): children and siblings of alumni, children of faculty/staff, international students, local/state students, religious affiliation. ***Tuition waivers:*** Full or partial for children of alumni, employees or children of employees. ***ROTC:*** Army cooperative, Air Force cooperative.

LOANS ***Student loans:*** $5,037,381 (41% need-based, 59% non-need-based). 73% of past graduating class borrowed through all loan programs. *Average indebtedness per student:* $14,758. ***Average need-based loan:*** Freshmen: $3650. Undergraduates: $4181. ***Parent loans:*** $965,549 (100% non-need-based). ***Programs:*** FFEL (Subsidized and Unsubsidized Stafford, PLUS), Perkins.

WORK-STUDY ***Federal work-study:*** Total amount: $194,359; 100 jobs averaging $909.

APPLYING FOR FINANCIAL AID ***Required financial aid form:*** institution's own form. ***Financial aid deadline (priority):*** 4/14. ***Notification date:*** Continuous. Students must reply by 5/14 or within 2 weeks of notification.

CONTACT Belinda Goris Duett, Director of Student Financial Services and Financial Aid, Huntingdon College, 1500 East Fairview Avenue, Montgomery, AL 36106-2148, 334-833-4519 or toll-free 800-763-0313. *Fax:* 334-833-4235. *E-mail:* bduett@huntingdon.edu.

HUNTINGTON UNIVERSITY

Huntington, IN

Tuition & fees: $20,300 **Average undergraduate aid package: $15,322**

ABOUT THE INSTITUTION Independent religious, coed. ***Awards:*** associate, bachelor's, and master's degrees and post-bachelor's certificates. 60 undergraduate majors. ***Total enrollment:*** 1,211. Undergraduates: 978. Freshmen: 277. Federal methodology is used as a basis for awarding need-based institutional aid.

UNDERGRADUATE EXPENSES for 2008–09 *Application fee:* $20. ***Comprehensive fee:*** $27,240 includes full-time tuition ($19,840), mandatory fees ($460), and room and board ($6940). Full-time tuition and fees vary according to program. Room and board charges vary according to board plan. ***Part-time tuition:*** $590 per semester hour. ***Part-time fees:*** $160 per term. Part-time tuition and fees vary according to program. ***Payment plan:*** Installment.

FRESHMAN FINANCIAL AID (Fall 2008, est.) 250 applied for aid; of those 86% were deemed to have need. 100% of freshmen with need received aid; of those 10% had need fully met. ***Average percent of need met:*** 79% (excluding resources awarded to replace EFC). ***Average financial aid package:*** $16,393 (excluding resources awarded to replace EFC). 17% of all full-time freshmen had no need and received non-need-based gift aid.

UNDERGRADUATE FINANCIAL AID (Fall 2008, est.) 834 applied for aid; of those 86% were deemed to have need. 100% of undergraduates with need received aid; of those 9% had need fully met. ***Average percent of need met:*** 72% (excluding resources awarded to replace EFC). ***Average financial aid package:*** $15,322 (excluding resources awarded to replace EFC). 12% of all full-time undergraduates had no need and received non-need-based gift aid.

GIFT AID (NEED-BASED) ***Total amount:*** $8,045,955 (13% federal, 22% state, 60% institutional, 5% external sources). ***Receiving aid:*** Freshmen: 77% (209); all full-time undergraduates: 67% (658). ***Average award:*** Freshmen: $13,495; Undergraduates: $12,135. ***Scholarships, grants, and awards:*** Federal Pell, FSEOG, state, private, college/university gift aid from institutional funds.

GIFT AID (NON-NEED-BASED) ***Total amount:*** $826,323 (1% state, 86% institutional, 13% external sources). ***Receiving aid:*** Freshmen: 17% (47). Undergraduates: 13% (131). ***Average award:*** Freshmen: $8045. Undergraduates: $6818. ***Scholarships, grants, and awards by category:*** *Academic interests/achievement:* biological sciences, communication, computer science, general academic interests/achievements, mathematics. *Creative arts/performance:* art/fine arts, journalism/publications, music, theater/drama. *Special achievements/activities:* cheerleading/drum major, religious involvement. *Special characteristics:* children and siblings of alumni, children of current students, children of faculty/staff, international students, parents of current students, relatives of clergy, religious affiliation, siblings of current students, spouses of current students. ***Tuition waivers:*** Full or partial for employees or children of employees, senior citizens.

LOANS ***Student loans:*** $5,990,805 (70% need-based, 30% non-need-based). 73% of past graduating class borrowed through all loan programs. *Average indebtedness per student:* $23,898. ***Average need-based loan:*** Freshmen: $3950. Undergraduates: $4776. ***Parent loans:*** $992,790 (26% need-based, 74% non-need-based). ***Programs:*** FFEL (Subsidized and Unsubsidized Stafford, PLUS), Perkins.

WORK-STUDY ***Federal work-study:*** Total amount: $543,369; 277 jobs averaging $1928.

ATHLETIC AWARDS Total amount: $739,338 (69% need-based, 31% non-need-based).

APPLYING FOR FINANCIAL AID ***Required financial aid form:*** FAFSA. ***Financial aid deadline (priority):*** 3/1. ***Notification date:*** Continuous beginning 3/1. Students must reply by 5/1 or within 2 weeks of notification.

CONTACT Mrs. Cindy Kreps, Financial Aid Secretary, Huntington University, 2303 College Avenue, Huntington, IN 46750, 260-359-4015 or toll-free 800-642-6493. *Fax:* 260-358-3699. *E-mail:* ckreps@huntington.edu.

HUSSON UNIVERSITY

Bangor, ME

Tuition & fees: $12,990 **Average undergraduate aid package: $10,019**

ABOUT THE INSTITUTION Independent, coed. ***Awards:*** associate, bachelor's, master's, and doctoral degrees and post-bachelor's and post-master's certificates. 31 undergraduate majors. ***Total enrollment:*** 2,626. Undergraduates: 2,257. Freshmen: 479. Federal methodology is used as a basis for awarding need-based institutional aid.

UNDERGRADUATE EXPENSES for 2009–10 ***Application fee:*** $25. ***Comprehensive fee:*** $19,984 includes full-time tuition ($12,690), mandatory fees ($300), and room and board ($6994). ***Part-time tuition:*** $423 per credit hour.

FRESHMAN FINANCIAL AID (Fall 2008, est.) 511 applied for aid; of those 85% were deemed to have need. 98% of freshmen with need received aid; of those 8% had need fully met. ***Average percent of need met:*** 76% (excluding resources awarded to replace EFC). ***Average financial aid package:*** $10,899 (excluding resources awarded to replace EFC). 10% of all full-time freshmen had no need and received non-need-based gift aid.

UNDERGRADUATE FINANCIAL AID (Fall 2008, est.) 1,664 applied for aid; of those 86% were deemed to have need. 99% of undergraduates with need received aid; of those 11% had need fully met. ***Average percent of need met:*** 73% (excluding resources awarded to replace EFC). ***Average financial aid package:*** $10,019 (excluding resources awarded to replace EFC). 7% of all full-time undergraduates had no need and received non-need-based gift aid.

GIFT AID (NEED-BASED) ***Total amount:*** $9,128,318 (37% federal, 12% state, 45% institutional, 6% external sources). ***Receiving aid:*** Freshmen: 75% (406); all full-time undergraduates: 75% (1,266). ***Average award:*** Freshmen: $7927; Undergraduates: $6762. ***Scholarships, grants, and awards:*** Federal Pell, FSEOG, state, private, college/university gift aid from institutional funds.

GIFT AID (NON-NEED-BASED) ***Total amount:*** $609,067 (1% state, 86% institutional, 13% external sources). ***Receiving aid:*** Freshmen: 2% (13). Undergraduates: 3% (51). ***Average award:*** Freshmen: $2838. Undergraduates: $3106. ***Scholarships, grants, and awards by category:*** *Academic interests/achievement:* 152 awards ($15,897 total): business, computer science, education, general academic interests/achievements, health fields. *Special achievements/activities:* general special achievements/activities, leadership. *Special characteristics:* children of union members/company employees. ***ROTC:*** Army cooperative, Naval cooperative.

LOANS ***Student loans:*** $13,252,546 (66% need-based, 34% non-need-based). 85% of past graduating class borrowed through all loan programs. *Average indebtedness per student:* $25,528. ***Average need-based loan:*** Freshmen: $2946. Undergraduates: $3716. ***Parent loans:*** $1,347,468 (29% need-based, 71% non-need-based). ***Programs:*** FFEL (Subsidized and Unsubsidized Stafford, PLUS), Perkins, state, alternative loans.

WORK-STUDY ***Federal work-study:*** Total amount: $686,674; 696 jobs averaging $1425.

APPLYING FOR FINANCIAL AID ***Required financial aid form:*** FAFSA. ***Financial aid deadline (priority):*** 4/15. ***Notification date:*** Continuous. Students must reply by 5/1 or within 2 weeks of notification.

CONTACT Linda B. Conant, Director of Financial Aid, Husson University, One College Circle, Bangor, ME 04401, 207-941-7156 or toll-free 800-4-HUSSON. *Fax:* 207-973-1038. *E-mail:* conantl@husson.edu.

HUSTON-TILLOTSON UNIVERSITY

Austin, TX

CONTACT Anthony P. Barrientez, Director of Financial Aid, Huston-Tillotson University, 900 Chicon Street, Austin, TX 78702, 512-505-3031.

IDAHO STATE UNIVERSITY

Pocatello, ID

Tuition & fees (ID res): $4664 **Average undergraduate aid package: $10,159**

ABOUT THE INSTITUTION State-supported, coed. ***Awards:*** associate, bachelor's, master's, doctoral, and first professional degrees and post-bachelor's, post-master's, and first professional certificates. 111 undergraduate majors. ***Total enrollment:*** 12,653. Undergraduates: 10,547. Freshmen: 1,551. Federal methodology is used as a basis for awarding need-based institutional aid.

UNDERGRADUATE EXPENSES for 2008–09 ***Application fee:*** $40. ***One-time required fee:*** $40. ***Tuition, state resident:*** full-time $3114; part-time $236 per credit hour. ***Tuition, nonresident:*** full-time $12,318; part-time $364 per credit hour. ***Required fees:*** full-time $1550. Full-time tuition and fees vary according to program and reciprocity agreements. Part-time tuition and fees vary according to reciprocity agreements. ***College room and board:*** $5270; ***Room only:*** $2320. Room and board charges vary according to board plan and housing facility. ***Payment plan:*** Deferred payment.

FRESHMAN FINANCIAL AID (Fall 2007) 776 applied for aid; of those 73% were deemed to have need. 98% of freshmen with need received aid; of those 14% had need fully met. ***Average percent of need met:*** 40% (excluding resources awarded to replace EFC). ***Average financial aid package:*** $7264 (excluding resources awarded to replace EFC). 29% of all full-time freshmen had no need and received non-need-based gift aid.

UNDERGRADUATE FINANCIAL AID (Fall 2007) 5,233 applied for aid; of those 88% were deemed to have need. 98% of undergraduates with need received aid; of those 7% had need fully met. ***Average percent of need met:*** 39% (excluding resources awarded to replace EFC). ***Average financial aid package:*** $10,159 (excluding resources awarded to replace EFC). 13% of all full-time undergraduates had no need and received non-need-based gift aid.

GIFT AID (NEED-BASED) ***Total amount:*** $19,729,570 (72% federal, 5% state, 10% institutional, 13% external sources). ***Receiving aid:*** Freshmen: 52% (512); all full-time undergraduates: 56% (3,710). ***Average award:*** Freshmen: $4223; Undergraduates: $4383. ***Scholarships, grants, and awards:*** Federal Pell, FSEOG, state, private, college/university gift aid from institutional funds, Federal Nursing.

GIFT AID (NON-NEED-BASED) ***Total amount:*** $3,273,702 (2% federal, 9% state, 39% institutional, 50% external sources). ***Receiving aid:*** Freshmen: 4% (41). Undergraduates: 2% (116). ***Average award:*** Freshmen: $2590. Undergraduates: $2674. ***Scholarships, grants, and awards by category:*** *Academic interests/achievement:* 1,563 awards ($3,627,331 total): biological sciences, business, communication, computer science, education, engineering/technologies, English, foreign languages, general academic interests/achievements, health fields, home economics, humanities, international studies, mathematics, military science, physical sciences, premedicine, religion/biblical studies, social sciences. *Creative arts/performance:* 207 awards ($125,440 total): art/fine arts, dance, debating, music, performing arts, theater/drama. *Special achievements/activities:* 53 awards ($80,909 total): cheerleading/drum major, general special achievements/activities, junior miss, leadership, memberships, rodeo. *Special characteristics:* 890 awards ($437,898 total): children and siblings of alumni, children of faculty/staff, ethnic background, first-generation college students, general special characteristics, handicapped students, international students, local/state students, members of minority groups, out-of-state students, previous college experience. ***Tuition waivers:*** Full or partial for employees or children of employees, senior citizens. ***ROTC:*** Army cooperative.

LOANS ***Student loans:*** $40,401,871 (90% need-based, 10% non-need-based). 73% of past graduating class borrowed through all loan programs. *Average indebtedness per student:* $22,237. ***Average need-based loan:*** Freshmen: $3034. Undergraduates: $4462. ***Parent loans:*** $401,925 (49% need-based, 51% non-need-based). ***Programs:*** Federal Direct (Subsidized and Unsubsidized Stafford, PLUS), Perkins, Federal Nursing.

WORK-STUDY ***Federal work-study:*** Total amount: $627,340; 577 jobs averaging $1120. ***State or other work-study/employment:*** Total amount: $479,526 (100% need-based). 449 part-time jobs averaging $1092.

ATHLETIC AWARDS Total amount: $2,835,641 (41% need-based, 59% non-need-based).

APPLYING FOR FINANCIAL AID ***Required financial aid forms:*** FAFSA, University Application for admission. ***Financial aid deadline:*** 3/1. ***Notification date:*** Continuous beginning 4/1.

CONTACT Ms. Gai McCune, Interim Director of Financial Aid, Idaho State University, 921 South 8th Avenue, Stop 8077, Pocatello, ID 83209, 208-282-2981. *Fax:* 208-282-4755. *E-mail:* mccugai@isu.edu.

ILLINOIS COLLEGE

Jacksonville, IL

Tuition & fees: $20,300 **Average undergraduate aid package: $17,193**

ABOUT THE INSTITUTION Independent interdenominational, coed. ***Awards:*** bachelor's degrees. 44 undergraduate majors. ***Total enrollment:*** 898. Undergraduates: 898. Freshmen: 166. Federal methodology is used as a basis for awarding need-based institutional aid.

UNDERGRADUATE EXPENSES for 2008–09 ***Comprehensive fee:*** $27,900 includes full-time tuition ($19,900), mandatory fees ($400), and room and board ($7600). ***College room only:*** $3000. Full-time tuition and fees vary according to student level. Room and board charges vary according to board plan and housing facility. ***Payment plans:*** Installment, deferred payment.

FRESHMAN FINANCIAL AID (Fall 2008, est.) 160 applied for aid; of those 92% were deemed to have need. 100% of freshmen with need received aid; of those 46% had need fully met. ***Average percent of need met:*** 91% (excluding resources awarded to replace EFC). ***Average financial aid package:*** $19,449 (excluding resources awarded to replace EFC). 10% of all full-time freshmen had no need and received non-need-based gift aid.

UNDERGRADUATE FINANCIAL AID (Fall 2008, est.) 788 applied for aid; of those 85% were deemed to have need. 99% of undergraduates with need received aid; of those 55% had need fully met. ***Average percent of need met:*** 92% (excluding resources awarded to replace EFC). ***Average financial aid package:*** $17,193 (excluding resources awarded to replace EFC). 17% of all full-time undergraduates had no need and received non-need-based gift aid.

GIFT AID (NEED-BASED) ***Total amount:*** $7,554,277 (12% federal, 21% state, 65% institutional, 2% external sources). ***Receiving aid:*** Freshmen: 74% (123); all full-time undergraduates: 65% (564). ***Average award:*** Freshmen: $9819; Undergraduates: $8177. ***Scholarships, grants, and awards:*** Federal Pell, FSEOG, state, private, college/university gift aid from institutional funds.

GIFT AID (NON-NEED-BASED) ***Total amount:*** $1,967,256 (1% state, 92% institutional, 7% external sources). ***Receiving aid:*** Freshmen: 67% (111). Undergraduates: 56% (489). ***Average award:*** Freshmen: $7681. Undergraduates: $7181. ***Scholarships, grants, and awards by category:*** *Academic interests/achievement:* 634 awards ($3,741,063 total): general academic interests/achievements. *Creative arts/performance:* 50 awards ($64,000 total): art/fine arts, music, theater/drama. *Special achievements/activities:* 15 awards ($43,000 total): community service, leadership. *Special characteristics:* 235 awards ($1,103,390 total): children of faculty/staff, ethnic background, international students, members of minority groups, out-of-state students, previous college experience, religious affiliation. ***Tuition waivers:*** Full or partial for employees or children of employees.

LOANS ***Student loans:*** $5,342,291 (52% need-based, 48% non-need-based). 81% of past graduating class borrowed through all loan programs. *Average indebtedness per student:* $20,466. ***Average need-based loan:*** Freshmen: $4650. Undergraduates: $4910. ***Parent loans:*** $860,655 (100% non-need-based). ***Programs:*** FFEL (Subsidized and Unsubsidized Stafford, PLUS), Perkins.

WORK-STUDY ***Federal work-study:*** Total amount: $578,513; 562 jobs averaging $1491. ***State or other work-study/employment:*** Total amount: $437,380 (100% non-need-based). 297 part-time jobs averaging $634.

APPLYING FOR FINANCIAL AID ***Required financial aid form:*** FAFSA. ***Financial aid deadline (priority):*** 3/1. ***Notification date:*** Continuous beginning 3/7. Students must reply within 2 weeks of notification.

CONTACT Kate Taylor, Director of Financial Aid, Illinois College, 1101 West College Avenue, Jacksonville, IL 62650-2299, 217-245-3035 or toll-free 866-464-5265. *Fax:* 217-245-3274. *E-mail:* finaid@hilltop.ic.edu.

THE ILLINOIS INSTITUTE OF ART–CHICAGO

Chicago, IL

UNDERGRADUATE EXPENSES Tuition cost varies by program. Prospective students should contact the school for current tuition costs. Other charges include a starting kit for all first-quarter students. Kits vary in price, depending on the program of study.

CONTACT Financial Aid Office, The Illinois Institute of Art–Chicago, 350 North Orleans Street, Suite 136, Chicago, IL 60654-1593, 800-351-3450.

THE ILLINOIS INSTITUTE OF ART–SCHAUMBURG

Schaumburg, IL

UNDERGRADUATE EXPENSES Tuition cost varies by program. Prospective students should contact the school for current tuition costs. Other charges include a starting kit for all first-quarter students. Kits vary in price, depending on the program of study.

CONTACT Financial Aid Office, The Illinois Institute of Art–Schaumburg, 1000 Plaza Drive, Schaumburg, IL 60173, 847-619-3450 or toll-free 800-314-3450.

ILLINOIS INSTITUTE OF TECHNOLOGY

Chicago, IL

Tuition & fees: $27,513 **Average undergraduate aid package: $21,674**

ABOUT THE INSTITUTION Independent, coed. ***Awards:*** bachelor's, master's, doctoral, and first professional degrees. 28 undergraduate majors. ***Total enrollment:*** 7,613. Undergraduates: 2,639. Freshmen: 530. Both federal and institutional methodology are used as a basis for awarding need-based institutional aid.

UNDERGRADUATE EXPENSES for 2008–09 ***Comprehensive fee:*** $36,746 includes full-time tuition ($26,709), mandatory fees ($804), and room and board ($9233). ***College room only:*** $4921. Room and board charges vary according to board plan and housing facility. ***Part-time tuition:*** $832 per credit hour. ***Part-time fees:*** $7 per credit hour; $250 per term. Part-time tuition and fees vary according to course load. ***Payment plans:*** Installment, deferred payment.

FRESHMAN FINANCIAL AID (Fall 2008, est.) 397 applied for aid; of those 84% were deemed to have need. 100% of freshmen with need received aid; of those 29% had need fully met. ***Average percent of need met:*** 82% (excluding resources awarded to replace EFC). ***Average financial aid package:*** $24,230 (excluding resources awarded to replace EFC). 35% of all full-time freshmen had no need and received non-need-based gift aid.

UNDERGRADUATE FINANCIAL AID (Fall 2008, est.) 1,576 applied for aid; of those 90% were deemed to have need. 100% of undergraduates with need received aid; of those 23% had need fully met. ***Average percent of need met:*** 76% (excluding resources awarded to replace EFC). ***Average financial aid package:*** $21,674 (excluding resources awarded to replace EFC). 40% of all full-time undergraduates had no need and received non-need-based gift aid.

GIFT AID (NEED-BASED) ***Total amount:*** $22,152,631 (12% federal, 11% state, 76% institutional, 1% external sources). ***Receiving aid:*** Freshmen: 64% (332); all full-time undergraduates: 58% (1,403). ***Average award:*** Freshmen: $18,395; Undergraduates: $15,540. ***Scholarships, grants, and awards:*** Federal Pell, FSEOG, state, private, college/university gift aid from institutional funds.

GIFT AID (NON-NEED-BASED) ***Total amount:*** $14,415,087 (7% federal, 90% institutional, 3% external sources). ***Receiving aid:*** Freshmen: 16% (82). Undergraduates: 10% (241). ***Average award:*** Freshmen: $13,957. Undergraduates: $12,975. ***Scholarships, grants, and awards by category:*** *Academic interests/achievement:* 603 awards ($6,315,594 total): architecture, business, engineering/technologies, foreign languages, general academic interests/achievements, health fields. *Special achievements/activities:* 28 awards ($429,653 total): community service, general special achievements/activities, hobbies/interests, leadership, memberships. *Special characteristics:* 444 awards ($3,991,625 total): children and siblings of alumni, children of faculty/staff, ethnic background, general special characteristics, international students, previous college experience, veterans' children. ***Tuition waivers:*** Full or partial for minority students, employees or children of employees. ***ROTC:*** Army, Naval, Air Force.

LOANS ***Student loans:*** $10,881,687 (75% need-based, 25% non-need-based). 63% of past graduating class borrowed through all loan programs. *Average indebtedness per student:* $15,220. ***Average need-based loan:*** Freshmen: $3945. Undergraduates: $4552. ***Parent loans:*** $3,077,328 (39% need-based, 61% non-need-based). ***Programs:*** FFEL (Subsidized and Unsubsidized Stafford, PLUS), Perkins, college/university.

WORK-STUDY ***Federal work-study:*** Total amount: $976,025; jobs available.

ATHLETIC AWARDS Total amount: $944,012 (40% need-based, 60% non-need-based).

APPLYING FOR FINANCIAL AID ***Required financial aid form:*** FAFSA. ***Financial aid deadline (priority):*** 4/15. ***Notification date:*** Continuous. Students must reply by 5/1 or within 2 weeks of notification.

CONTACT Nareth Phin, Assistant Director of Financial Aid, Illinois Institute of Technology, 3300 South Federal Street, Chicago, IL 60616, 312-567-5730 or toll-free 800-448-2329 (out-of-state). *Fax:* 312-567-3982. *E-mail:* finaid@iit.edu.

ILLINOIS STATE UNIVERSITY

Normal, IL

Tuition & fees (IL res): $9814 **Average undergraduate aid package: $10,898**

ABOUT THE INSTITUTION State-supported, coed. ***Awards:*** bachelor's, master's, and doctoral degrees and post-bachelor's and post-master's certificates. 66 undergraduate majors. ***Total enrollment:*** 20,799. Undergraduates: 18,065. Freshmen: 3,394. Federal methodology is used as a basis for awarding need-based institutional aid.

UNDERGRADUATE EXPENSES for 2008–09 ***Application fee:*** $40. ***Tuition, state resident:*** full-time $7680; part-time $256 per semester hour. ***Tuition, nonresident:*** full-time $14,310; part-time $477 per semester hour. ***Required fees:*** full-time $2134; $60.40 per semester hour or $906 per term. Full-time tuition and fees vary according to course load, degree level, and student level. Part-time tuition and fees vary according to course load, degree level, and student level. ***College room and board:*** $7458; ***Room only:*** $3740. Room and board charges vary according to board plan, housing facility, and location. ***Payment plans:*** Guaranteed tuition, installment.

FRESHMAN FINANCIAL AID (Fall 2008, est.) 2,596 applied for aid; of those 69% were deemed to have need. 90% of freshmen with need received aid; of those 51% had need fully met. ***Average percent of need met:*** 81% (excluding resources awarded to replace EFC). ***Average financial aid package:*** $10,408 (excluding resources awarded to replace EFC). 2% of all full-time freshmen had no need and received non-need-based gift aid.

UNDERGRADUATE FINANCIAL AID (Fall 2008, est.) 11,305 applied for aid; of those 76% were deemed to have need. 93% of undergraduates with need received aid; of those 49% had need fully met. ***Average percent of need met:*** 82% (excluding resources awarded to replace EFC). ***Average financial aid package:*** $10,898 (excluding resources awarded to replace EFC). 2% of all full-time undergraduates had no need and received non-need-based gift aid.

GIFT AID (NEED-BASED) ***Total amount:*** $39,044,773 (34% federal, 47% state, 16% institutional, 3% external sources). ***Receiving aid:*** Freshmen: 27% (916); all full-time undergraduates: 27% (4,530). ***Average award:*** Freshmen: $8621; Undergraduates: $8618. ***Scholarships, grants, and awards:*** Federal Pell, FSEOG, state, private, college/university gift aid from institutional funds, Federal Nursing.

GIFT AID (NON-NEED-BASED) ***Total amount:*** $7,604,132 (14% federal, 57% state, 18% institutional, 11% external sources). ***Receiving aid:*** Freshmen: 20% (675). Undergraduates: 12% (2,098). ***Average award:*** Freshmen: $3219. Undergraduates: $3811. ***Scholarships, grants, and awards by category:*** *Academic interests/achievement:* 479 awards ($1,424,104 total): agriculture, biological sciences, business, communication, computer science, education, engineering/technologies, English, foreign languages, general academic interests/achievements, health fields, home economics, humanities, international studies, library science, mathematics, military science, physical sciences, premedicine, social sciences. *Creative arts/performance:* 121 awards ($237,847 total): applied art and design, art/fine arts, cinema/film/broadcasting, creative writing, debating, general creative arts/performance, music, performing arts, theater/drama. *Special achievements/activities:* 1 award ($2000 total): community service, leadership. *Special characteristics:* 379 awards ($1,604,137 total): children of faculty/staff, children of union members/company employees, children with a deceased or disabled parent, first-generation college students, general special characteristics, members of minority groups, previous college experience. ***Tuition waivers:*** Full or partial for minority students, employees or children of employees, senior citizens. ***ROTC:*** Army.

LOANS ***Student loans:*** $75,079,970 (58% need-based, 42% non-need-based). 61% of past graduating class borrowed through all loan programs. *Average indebtedness per student:* $18,854. ***Average need-based loan:*** Freshmen: $5967. Undergraduates: $6567. ***Parent loans:*** $17,717,435 (18% need-based, 82% non-need-based). ***Programs:*** Federal Direct (Subsidized and Unsubsidized Stafford, PLUS), Perkins, Federal Nursing, college/university.

WORK-STUDY ***Federal work-study:*** Total amount: $1,190,244; 401 jobs averaging $2314. ***State or other work-study/employment:*** Total amount: $117,206 (48% need-based, 52% non-need-based). 49 part-time jobs averaging $1691.

ATHLETIC AWARDS Total amount: $3,716,156 (29% need-based, 71% non-need-based).

APPLYING FOR FINANCIAL AID ***Required financial aid form:*** FAFSA. ***Financial aid deadline (priority):*** 3/1. ***Notification date:*** Continuous beginning 4/1.

CONTACT Mr. David Krueger, Assistant Director of Financial Aid, Illinois State University, Campus Box 2320, Normal, IL 61790-2320, 309-438-2231 or toll-free 800-366-2478 (in-state). *Fax:* 309-438-3755. *E-mail:* askfao@ilstu.edu.

ILLINOIS WESLEYAN UNIVERSITY

Bloomington, IL

Tuition & fees: $32,434 **Average undergraduate aid package: $25,006**

ABOUT THE INSTITUTION Independent, coed. ***Awards:*** bachelor's degrees. 49 undergraduate majors. ***Total enrollment:*** 2,125. Undergraduates: 2,125. Freshmen: 562. Both federal and institutional methodology are used as a basis for awarding need-based institutional aid.

UNDERGRADUATE EXPENSES for 2008–09 ***Comprehensive fee:*** $39,784 includes full-time tuition ($32,260), mandatory fees ($174), and room and board ($7350). ***College room only:*** $4570. Room and board charges vary according to board plan and housing facility. ***Part-time tuition:*** $4032 per course. ***Payment plan:*** Installment.

FRESHMAN FINANCIAL AID (Fall 2008, est.) 421 applied for aid; of those 86% were deemed to have need. 100% of freshmen with need received aid; of those 64% had need fully met. ***Average percent of need met:*** 95% (excluding resources awarded to replace EFC). ***Average financial aid package:*** $24,788 (excluding resources awarded to replace EFC). 33% of all full-time freshmen had no need and received non-need-based gift aid.

UNDERGRADUATE FINANCIAL AID (Fall 2008, est.) 1,301 applied for aid; of those 92% were deemed to have need. 100% of undergraduates with need received aid; of those 53% had need fully met. ***Average percent of need met:*** 95% (excluding resources awarded to replace EFC). ***Average financial aid package:*** $25,006 (excluding resources awarded to replace EFC). 36% of all full-time undergraduates had no need and received non-need-based gift aid.

GIFT AID (NEED-BASED) ***Total amount:*** $21,233,820 (5% federal, 10% state, 83% institutional, 2% external sources). ***Receiving aid:*** Freshmen: 64% (360); all full-time undergraduates: 56% (1,189). ***Average award:*** Freshmen: $18,287; Undergraduates: $17,016. ***Scholarships, grants, and awards:*** Federal Pell, FSEOG, state, private, college/university gift aid from institutional funds.

GIFT AID (NON-NEED-BASED) ***Total amount:*** $7,957,784 (99% institutional, 1% external sources). ***Receiving aid:*** Freshmen: 7% (40). Undergraduates: 4% (82). ***Average award:*** Freshmen: $12,580. Undergraduates: $10,957. ***Scholarships, grants, and awards by category:*** *Academic interests/achievement:* general academic interests/achievements. *Creative arts/performance:* general creative arts/performance, music, theater/drama. *Special characteristics:* children of faculty/staff, general special characteristics, international students, religious affiliation. ***Tuition waivers:*** Full or partial for employees or children of employees. ***ROTC:*** Army cooperative.

LOANS ***Student loans:*** $7,435,558 (71% need-based, 29% non-need-based). 62% of past graduating class borrowed through all loan programs. *Average indebtedness per student:* $26,555. ***Average need-based loan:*** Freshmen: $4627. Undergraduates: $5126. ***Parent loans:*** $2,388,465 (100% non-need-based). ***Programs:*** FFEL (Subsidized and Unsubsidized Stafford, PLUS), Perkins, Federal Nursing, college/university.

WORK-STUDY ***Federal work-study:*** Total amount: $326,790; jobs available. ***State or other work-study/employment:*** Total amount: $1,644,117 (97% need-based, 3% non-need-based). Part-time jobs available.

APPLYING FOR FINANCIAL AID ***Required financial aid forms:*** FAFSA, institution's own form, CSS Financial Aid PROFILE. ***Financial aid deadline:*** 3/1 (priority: 3/1). ***Notification date:*** Continuous. Students must reply by 5/1.

CONTACT Mr. Scott Seibring, Director of Financial Aid, Illinois Wesleyan University, 1312 North Park Street, PO Box 2900, Bloomington, IL 61702-2900, 309-556-3096 or toll-free 800-332-2498. *Fax:* 309-556-3833. *E-mail:* seibring@iwu.edu.

IMMACULATA UNIVERSITY

Immaculata, PA

ABOUT THE INSTITUTION Independent Roman Catholic, coed, primarily women. ***Awards:*** associate, bachelor's, master's, and doctoral degrees. 47 undergraduate majors. ***Total enrollment:*** 4,182. Undergraduates: 3,056. Freshmen: 555.

GIFT AID (NEED-BASED) ***Scholarships, grants, and awards:*** Federal Pell, FSEOG, state, private, college/university gift aid from institutional funds.

GIFT AID (NON-NEED-BASED) ***Scholarships, grants, and awards by category:*** *Academic interests/achievement:* general academic interests/achievements, military science. *Creative arts/performance:* general creative arts/performance, music, theater/drama. *Special achievements/activities:* leadership, religious involvement. *Special characteristics:* children and siblings of alumni, local/state students, religious affiliation.

LOANS ***Programs:*** FFEL (Subsidized and Unsubsidized Stafford, PLUS), Perkins.
WORK-STUDY ***Federal work-study:*** Total amount: $143,693. ***State or other work-study/employment:*** Total amount: $189,928 (46% need-based, 54% non-need-based).
APPLYING FOR FINANCIAL AID ***Required financial aid form:*** FAFSA.
CONTACT Mr. Peter Lysionek, Director of Student Financial Aid, Immaculata University, 1145 King Road, Box 500, Immaculata, PA 19345, 610-647-4400 Ext. 3026 or toll-free 877-428-6329. *Fax:* 610-640-0836. *E-mail:* plysionek@immaculata.edu.

INDEPENDENCE UNIVERSITY

Salt Lake City, UT

CONTACT Financial Aid Director, Independence University, 2423 Hoover Avenue, National City, CA 91950-6605, 619-477-4800 or toll-free 800-791-7353. *Fax:* 619-477-5202.

INDIANA STATE UNIVERSITY

Terre Haute, IN

Tuition & fees (IN res): $7148 **Average undergraduate aid package: $9234**

ABOUT THE INSTITUTION State-supported, coed. ***Awards:*** associate, bachelor's, master's, doctoral, and first professional degrees and post-bachelor's and post-master's certificates. 66 undergraduate majors. ***Total enrollment:*** 10,457. Undergraduates: 8,386. Freshmen: 1,940. Federal methodology is used as a basis for awarding need-based institutional aid.
UNDERGRADUATE EXPENSES for 2008–09 ***Application fee:*** $25. ***Tuition, state resident:*** full-time $6792; part-time $245 per credit hour. ***Tuition, nonresident:*** full-time $15,046; part-time $530 per credit hour. ***Required fees:*** full-time $356; $178 per term. Part-time tuition and fees vary according to course load. ***College room and board:*** $6672; ***Room only:*** $3578. Room and board charges vary according to board plan, housing facility, and student level. ***Payment plans:*** Installment, deferred payment.
FRESHMAN FINANCIAL AID (Fall 2008, est.) 1,681 applied for aid; of those 79% were deemed to have need. 98% of freshmen with need received aid; of those 22% had need fully met. ***Average percent of need met:*** 85% (excluding resources awarded to replace EFC). ***Average financial aid package:*** $9579 (excluding resources awarded to replace EFC). 14% of all full-time freshmen had no need and received non-need-based gift aid.
UNDERGRADUATE FINANCIAL AID (Fall 2008, est.) 5,798 applied for aid; of those 81% were deemed to have need. 97% of undergraduates with need received aid; of those 18% had need fully met. ***Average percent of need met:*** 83% (excluding resources awarded to replace EFC). ***Average financial aid package:*** $9234 (excluding resources awarded to replace EFC). 11% of all full-time undergraduates had no need and received non-need-based gift aid.
GIFT AID (NEED-BASED) ***Total amount:*** $18,344,130 (51% federal, 44% state, 3% institutional, 2% external sources). ***Receiving aid:*** Freshmen: 44% (836); all full-time undergraduates: 41% (2,924). ***Average award:*** Freshmen: $6772; Undergraduates: $6349. ***Scholarships, grants, and awards:*** Federal Pell, FSEOG, state, private, college/university gift aid from institutional funds.
GIFT AID (NON-NEED-BASED) ***Total amount:*** $12,010,974 (25% state, 58% institutional, 17% external sources). ***Receiving aid:*** Freshmen: 42% (804). Undergraduates: 27% (1,908). ***Average award:*** Freshmen: $3886. Undergraduates: $4545. ***Scholarships, grants, and awards by category:*** *Academic interests/achievement:* 1,604 awards ($3,561,807 total): general academic interests/achievements, premedicine. *Creative arts/performance:* 108 awards ($233,200 total): art/fine arts, performing arts. *Special characteristics:* 261 awards ($690,059 total): children and siblings of alumni, children of faculty/staff, members of minority groups, previous college experience, veterans. ***Tuition waivers:*** Full or partial for employees or children of employees, senior citizens. ***ROTC:*** Army, Air Force.
LOANS ***Student loans:*** $31,580,598 (41% need-based, 59% non-need-based). 66% of past graduating class borrowed through all loan programs. *Average indebtedness per student:* $22,961. ***Average need-based loan:*** Freshmen: $3214. Undergraduates: $3921. ***Parent loans:*** $5,312,496 (100% non-need-based). ***Programs:*** FFEL (Subsidized and Unsubsidized Stafford, PLUS), Perkins.
WORK-STUDY ***Federal work-study:*** Total amount: $2,767,189; 452 jobs averaging $1117. ***State or other work-study/employment:*** Part-time jobs available.
ATHLETIC AWARDS Total amount: $3,040,020 (100% non-need-based).
APPLYING FOR FINANCIAL AID ***Required financial aid form:*** FAFSA. ***Financial aid deadline:*** 3/1 (priority: 3/1). ***Notification date:*** Continuous beginning 4/15.
CONTACT Kim Donat, Director of Student Financial Aid, Indiana State University, 150 Tirey Hall, Terre Haute, IN 47809-1401, 812-237-2215 or toll-free 800-742-0891. *Fax:* 812-237-4330. *E-mail:* finaid@indstate.edu.

INDIANA TECH

Fort Wayne, IN

CONTACT Financial Aid Office, Indiana Tech, 1600 East Washington Boulevard, Fort Wayne, IN 46803-1297, 800-937-2448 or toll-free 888-666-TECH (out-of-state). *Fax:* 219-422-1578.

INDIANA UNIVERSITY BLOOMINGTON

Bloomington, IN

Tuition & fees (IN res): $8231 **Average undergraduate aid package: $10,206**

ABOUT THE INSTITUTION State-supported, coed. ***Awards:*** associate, bachelor's, master's, doctoral, and first professional degrees and post-bachelor's and post-master's certificates. 111 undergraduate majors. ***Total enrollment:*** 40,354. Undergraduates: 31,626. Freshmen: 7,419. Federal methodology is used as a basis for awarding need-based institutional aid.
UNDERGRADUATE EXPENSES for 2008–09 ***Application fee:*** $50. ***Tuition, state resident:*** full-time $7368; part-time $230.05 per credit hour. ***Tuition, nonresident:*** full-time $23,906; part-time $747.15 per credit hour. ***Required fees:*** full-time $863. Full-time tuition and fees vary according to location and program. Part-time tuition and fees vary according to course load, location, and program. ***College room and board:*** $7138; ***Room only:*** $4338. Room and board charges vary according to board plan and housing facility. ***Payment plan:*** Deferred payment.
FRESHMAN FINANCIAL AID (Fall 2008, est.) 5,119 applied for aid; of those 63% were deemed to have need. 97% of freshmen with need received aid; of those 17% had need fully met. ***Average percent of need met:*** 72% (excluding resources awarded to replace EFC). ***Average financial aid package:*** $10,549 (excluding resources awarded to replace EFC). 25% of all full-time freshmen had no need and received non-need-based gift aid.
UNDERGRADUATE FINANCIAL AID (Fall 2008, est.) 16,669 applied for aid; of those 70% were deemed to have need. 97% of undergraduates with need received aid; of those 12% had need fully met. ***Average percent of need met:*** 70% (excluding resources awarded to replace EFC). ***Average financial aid package:*** $10,206 (excluding resources awarded to replace EFC). 20% of all full-time undergraduates had no need and received non-need-based gift aid.
GIFT AID (NEED-BASED) ***Total amount:*** $69,414,916 (28% federal, 31% state, 35% institutional, 6% external sources). ***Receiving aid:*** Freshmen: 34% (2,564); all full-time undergraduates: 20% (6,530). ***Average award:*** Freshmen: $9060; Undergraduates: $8328. ***Scholarships, grants, and awards:*** Federal Pell, FSEOG, state, private, college/university gift aid from institutional funds.
GIFT AID (NON-NEED-BASED) ***Total amount:*** $46,750,174 (2% federal, 3% state, 80% institutional, 15% external sources). ***Receiving aid:*** Freshmen: 6% (441). Undergraduates: 4% (1,064). ***Average award:*** Freshmen: $5868. Undergraduates: $5768. ***Tuition waivers:*** Full or partial for employees or children of employees. ***ROTC:*** Army, Air Force.
LOANS ***Student loans:*** $115,299,976 (52% need-based, 48% non-need-based). 56% of past graduating class borrowed through all loan programs. *Average indebtedness per student:* $22,013. ***Average need-based loan:*** Freshmen: $3786. Undergraduates: $4487. ***Parent loans:*** $27,484,570 (25% need-based, 75% non-need-based). ***Programs:*** Federal Direct (Subsidized and Unsubsidized Stafford, PLUS), Perkins, college/university.
WORK-STUDY ***Federal work-study:*** Total amount: $910,161; jobs available. ***State or other work-study/employment:*** Total amount: $26,448 (29% need-based, 71% non-need-based). Part-time jobs available.
ATHLETIC AWARDS Total amount: $8,440,590 (28% need-based, 72% non-need-based).
APPLYING FOR FINANCIAL AID ***Required financial aid form:*** FAFSA. ***Financial aid deadline (priority):*** 3/1. ***Notification date:*** Continuous beginning 4/1.
CONTACT Susan Pugh, Director of the Office of Student Financial Assistance, Indiana University Bloomington, Franklin Hall, Bloomington, IN 47405, 812-855-0321. *Fax:* 812-855-7615. *E-mail:* rsvposfa@indiana.edu.

INDIANA UNIVERSITY EAST

Richmond, IN

Tuition & fees (IN res): $5556 **Average undergraduate aid package: $7971**

ABOUT THE INSTITUTION State-supported, coed. ***Awards:*** associate, bachelor's, and master's degrees and post-bachelor's certificates. 28 undergraduate majors. ***Total enrollment:*** 2,447. Undergraduates: 2,388. Freshmen: 326. Federal methodology is used as a basis for awarding need-based institutional aid.

UNDERGRADUATE EXPENSES for 2008–09 ***Application fee:*** $25. ***Tuition, state resident:*** full-time $5178; part-time $172.60 per credit hour. ***Tuition, nonresident:*** full-time $13,344; part-time $444.80 per credit hour. ***Required fees:*** full-time $378. Full-time tuition and fees vary according to course load, program, and reciprocity agreements. Part-time tuition and fees vary according to course load, program, and reciprocity agreements. ***Payment plan:*** Deferred payment.

FRESHMAN FINANCIAL AID (Fall 2008, est.) 271 applied for aid; of those 85% were deemed to have need. 99% of freshmen with need received aid; of those 11% had need fully met. ***Average percent of need met:*** 67% (excluding resources awarded to replace EFC). ***Average financial aid package:*** $7065 (excluding resources awarded to replace EFC). 4% of all full-time freshmen had no need and received non-need-based gift aid.

UNDERGRADUATE FINANCIAL AID (Fall 2008, est.) 1,215 applied for aid; of those 87% were deemed to have need. 98% of undergraduates with need received aid; of those 6% had need fully met. ***Average percent of need met:*** 66% (excluding resources awarded to replace EFC). ***Average financial aid package:*** $7971 (excluding resources awarded to replace EFC). 3% of all full-time undergraduates had no need and received non-need-based gift aid.

GIFT AID (NEED-BASED) ***Total amount:*** $5,760,866 (63% federal, 29% state, 4% institutional, 4% external sources). ***Receiving aid:*** Freshmen: 68% (197); all full-time undergraduates: 65% (878). ***Average award:*** Freshmen: $5602; Undergraduates: $5610. ***Scholarships, grants, and awards:*** Federal Pell, FSEOG, state, private, college/university gift aid from institutional funds.

GIFT AID (NON-NEED-BASED) ***Total amount:*** $372,395 (32% federal, 10% state, 19% institutional, 39% external sources). ***Receiving aid:*** Freshmen: 7% (19). Undergraduates: 3% (37). ***Average award:*** Freshmen: $1836. Undergraduates: $1346. ***Tuition waivers:*** Full or partial for employees or children of employees.

LOANS ***Student loans:*** $8,598,619 (81% need-based, 19% non-need-based). 78% of past graduating class borrowed through all loan programs. *Average indebtedness per student:* $24,309. ***Average need-based loan:*** Freshmen: $3016. Undergraduates: $3836. ***Parent loans:*** $95,509 (34% need-based, 66% non-need-based). ***Programs:*** Federal Direct (Subsidized and Unsubsidized Stafford, PLUS), Perkins, college/university.

WORK-STUDY ***Federal work-study:*** Total amount: $136,004; jobs available.

ATHLETIC AWARDS Total amount: $31,716 (85% need-based, 15% non-need-based).

APPLYING FOR FINANCIAL AID ***Required financial aid forms:*** FAFSA, institution's own form. ***Financial aid deadline (priority):*** 3/1. ***Notification date:*** Continuous beginning 5/1. Students must reply within 2 weeks of notification.

CONTACT William Gill, Financial Aid Director, Indiana University East, 2325 Chester Boulevard, Richmond, IN 47374-1289, 765-973-8231 or toll-free 800-959-EAST. *Fax:* 765-973-8288.

INDIANA UNIVERSITY KOKOMO

Kokomo, IN

Tuition & fees (IN res): $5591 **Average undergraduate aid package: $7271**

ABOUT THE INSTITUTION State-supported, coed. ***Awards:*** associate, bachelor's, and master's degrees and post-bachelor's certificates. 26 undergraduate majors. ***Total enrollment:*** 2,690. Undergraduates: 2,540. Freshmen: 399. Federal methodology is used as a basis for awarding need-based institutional aid.

UNDERGRADUATE EXPENSES for 2008–09 ***Application fee:*** $30. ***Tuition, state resident:*** full-time $5174; part-time $172.45 per credit hour. ***Tuition, nonresident:*** full-time $13,337; part-time $444.55 per credit hour. ***Required fees:*** full-time $417. Full-time tuition and fees vary according to course load and program. Part-time tuition and fees vary according to course load and program. ***Payment plan:*** Deferred payment.

FRESHMAN FINANCIAL AID (Fall 2008, est.) 310 applied for aid; of those 69% were deemed to have need. 91% of freshmen with need received aid; of those 8% had need fully met. ***Average percent of need met:*** 63% (excluding resources awarded to replace EFC). ***Average financial aid package:*** $6055 (excluding resources awarded to replace EFC). 6% of all full-time freshmen had no need and received non-need-based gift aid.

UNDERGRADUATE FINANCIAL AID (Fall 2008, est.) 1,081 applied for aid; of those 75% were deemed to have need. 95% of undergraduates with need received aid; of those 6% had need fully met. ***Average percent of need met:*** 65% (excluding resources awarded to replace EFC). ***Average financial aid package:*** $7271 (excluding resources awarded to replace EFC). 5% of all full-time undergraduates had no need and received non-need-based gift aid.

GIFT AID (NEED-BASED) ***Total amount:*** $4,211,628 (54% federal, 35% state, 7% institutional, 4% external sources). ***Receiving aid:*** Freshmen: 47% (160); all full-time undergraduates: 47% (616). ***Average award:*** Freshmen: $5104; Undergraduates: $5449. ***Scholarships, grants, and awards:*** Federal Pell, FSEOG, state, private, college/university gift aid from institutional funds.

GIFT AID (NON-NEED-BASED) ***Total amount:*** $750,928 (29% federal, 23% state, 16% institutional, 32% external sources). ***Receiving aid:*** Freshmen: 4% (14). Undergraduates: 3% (38). ***Average award:*** Freshmen: $1978. Undergraduates: $1572. ***Tuition waivers:*** Full or partial for employees or children of employees. ***ROTC:*** Army cooperative.

LOANS ***Student loans:*** $7,615,095 (69% need-based, 31% non-need-based). 63% of past graduating class borrowed through all loan programs. *Average indebtedness per student:* $20,492. ***Average need-based loan:*** Freshmen: $2841. Undergraduates: $3728. ***Parent loans:*** $47,208 (20% need-based, 80% non-need-based). ***Programs:*** Federal Direct (Subsidized and Unsubsidized Stafford, PLUS), Perkins, Federal Nursing, college/university.

WORK-STUDY ***Federal work-study:*** Total amount: $86,733; jobs available. ***State or other work-study/employment:*** Total amount: $517 (100% need-based). Part-time jobs available.

APPLYING FOR FINANCIAL AID ***Required financial aid forms:*** FAFSA, institution's own form. ***Financial aid deadline:*** 3/1. ***Notification date:*** Continuous beginning 5/1. Students must reply within 4 weeks of notification.

CONTACT Jolane Rohr, Director of Financial Aid, Indiana University Kokomo, 2300 South Washington Street, PO Box 9003, Kokomo, IN 46904-9003, 765-455-9216 or toll-free 888-875-4485. *Fax:* 765-455-9537.

INDIANA UNIVERSITY NORTHWEST

Gary, IN

Tuition & fees (IN res): $5669 **Average undergraduate aid package: $8070**

ABOUT THE INSTITUTION State-supported, coed. ***Awards:*** associate, bachelor's, and master's degrees and post-bachelor's certificates. 39 undergraduate majors. ***Total enrollment:*** 4,794. Undergraduates: 4,168. Freshmen: 768. Federal methodology is used as a basis for awarding need-based institutional aid.

UNDERGRADUATE EXPENSES for 2008–09 ***Application fee:*** $25. ***Tuition, state resident:*** full-time $5228; part-time $174.25 per credit hour. ***Tuition, nonresident:*** full-time $13,343; part-time $444.75 per credit hour. ***Required fees:*** full-time $441. Full-time tuition and fees vary according to course load and program. Part-time tuition and fees vary according to course load and program. ***Payment plans:*** Installment, deferred payment.

FRESHMAN FINANCIAL AID (Fall 2008, est.) 476 applied for aid; of those 78% were deemed to have need. 97% of freshmen with need received aid; of those 6% had need fully met. ***Average percent of need met:*** 57% (excluding resources awarded to replace EFC). ***Average financial aid package:*** $6530 (excluding resources awarded to replace EFC). 7% of all full-time freshmen had no need and received non-need-based gift aid.

UNDERGRADUATE FINANCIAL AID (Fall 2008, est.) 2,034 applied for aid; of those 84% were deemed to have need. 96% of undergraduates with need received aid; of those 4% had need fully met. ***Average percent of need met:*** 59% (excluding resources awarded to replace EFC). ***Average financial aid package:*** $8070 (excluding resources awarded to replace EFC). 4% of all full-time undergraduates had no need and received non-need-based gift aid.

GIFT AID (NEED-BASED) ***Total amount:*** $9,435,531 (60% federal, 34% state, 3% institutional, 3% external sources). ***Receiving aid:*** Freshmen: 45% (268); all full-time undergraduates: 49% (1,264). ***Average award:*** Freshmen: $5120; Undergraduates: $5937. ***Scholarships, grants, and awards:*** Federal Pell, FSEOG, state, private, college/university gift aid from institutional funds, Federal Nursing.

GIFT AID (NON-NEED-BASED) ***Total amount:*** $765,770 (5% federal, 5% state, 64% institutional, 26% external sources). ***Receiving aid:*** Freshmen: 2% (11).

Undergraduates: 1% (22). ***Average award:*** Freshmen: $2940. Undergraduates: $3869. ***Tuition waivers:*** Full or partial for employees or children of employees. ***ROTC:*** Army.

LOANS ***Student loans:*** $18,566,236 (77% need-based, 23% non-need-based). 69% of past graduating class borrowed through all loan programs. *Average indebtedness per student:* $22,335. ***Average need-based loan:*** Freshmen: $3268. Undergraduates: $3947. ***Parent loans:*** $174,719 (17% need-based, 83% non-need-based). ***Programs:*** Federal Direct (Subsidized and Unsubsidized Stafford, PLUS), Perkins, college/university.

WORK-STUDY ***Federal work-study:*** Total amount: $246,660; jobs available.

ATHLETIC AWARDS Total amount: $22,500 (55% need-based, 45% non-need-based).

APPLYING FOR FINANCIAL AID ***Required financial aid forms:*** FAFSA, institution's own form. ***Financial aid deadline (priority):*** 3/1. ***Notification date:*** Continuous beginning 5/1. Students must reply within 2 weeks of notification.

CONTACT Harold Burtley, Director of Scholarships and Financial Aid, Indiana University Northwest, 3400 Broadway, Gary, IN 46408-1197, 877-280-4593 or toll-free 800-968-7486. *Fax:* 219-981-5622.

INDIANA UNIVERSITY OF PENNSYLVANIA

Indiana, PA

Tuition & fees (PA res): $6959 **Average undergraduate aid package: $9002**

ABOUT THE INSTITUTION State-supported, coed. ***Awards:*** associate, bachelor's, master's, and doctoral degrees and post-bachelor's and post-master's certificates. 77 undergraduate majors. ***Total enrollment:*** 14,310. Undergraduates: 11,928. Freshmen: 3,100. Federal methodology is used as a basis for awarding need-based institutional aid.

UNDERGRADUATE EXPENSES for 2008–09 ***Application fee:*** $35. ***Tuition, state resident:*** full-time $5358; part-time $223 per credit. ***Tuition, nonresident:*** full-time $13,396; part-time $558 per credit. ***Required fees:*** full-time $1601; $22.30 per credit or $217.50 per credit. Full-time tuition and fees vary according to course load, location, and reciprocity agreements. Part-time tuition and fees vary according to course load, location, and reciprocity agreements. ***College room and board:*** $8224; ***Room only:*** $3574. Room and board charges vary according to board plan, housing facility, and location. ***Payment plans:*** Installment, deferred payment.

FRESHMAN FINANCIAL AID (Fall 2007) 2,228 applied for aid; of those 78% were deemed to have need. 99% of freshmen with need received aid; of those 8% had need fully met. ***Average percent of need met:*** 83% (excluding resources awarded to replace EFC). ***Average financial aid package:*** $10,135 (excluding resources awarded to replace EFC). 4% of all full-time freshmen had no need and received non-need-based gift aid.

UNDERGRADUATE FINANCIAL AID (Fall 2007) 8,925 applied for aid; of those 79% were deemed to have need. 99% of undergraduates with need received aid; of those 9% had need fully met. ***Average percent of need met:*** 76% (excluding resources awarded to replace EFC). ***Average financial aid package:*** $9002 (excluding resources awarded to replace EFC). 3% of all full-time undergraduates had no need and received non-need-based gift aid.

GIFT AID (NEED-BASED) ***Total amount:*** $25,859,209 (51% federal, 49% state). ***Receiving aid:*** Freshmen: 50% (1,257); all full-time undergraduates: 47% (5,100). ***Average award:*** Freshmen: $5285; Undergraduates: $4895. ***Scholarships, grants, and awards:*** Federal Pell, FSEOG, state, private, college/university gift aid from institutional funds.

GIFT AID (NON-NEED-BASED) ***Total amount:*** $6,174,072 (43% institutional, 57% external sources). ***Receiving aid:*** Freshmen: 25% (638). Undergraduates: 15% (1,647). ***Average award:*** Freshmen: $2422. Undergraduates: $2513. ***Scholarships, grants, and awards by category:*** *Academic interests/achievement:* 1,095 awards ($2,172,634 total): area/ethnic studies, biological sciences, business, communication, computer science, education, engineering/technologies, English, foreign languages, general academic interests/achievements, health fields, home economics, humanities, international studies, mathematics, physical sciences, premedicine, social sciences. *Creative arts/performance:* applied art and design, art/fine arts, dance, general creative arts/performance, journalism/publications, music, performing arts, theater/drama. *Special achievements/activities:* community service, general special achievements/activities, hobbies/interests, leadership. *Special characteristics:* 2,086 awards ($2,696,513 total): adult students, children of faculty/staff, ethnic background, international students. ***Tuition waivers:*** Full or partial for employees or children of employees. ***ROTC:*** Army.

LOANS ***Student loans:*** $51,418,127 (51% need-based, 49% non-need-based). 82% of past graduating class borrowed through all loan programs. *Average indebtedness per student:* $23,265. ***Average need-based loan:*** Freshmen: $3779. Undergraduates: $4147. ***Parent loans:*** $7,244,967 (100% non-need-based). ***Programs:*** FFEL (Subsidized and Unsubsidized Stafford, PLUS), Perkins, alternative loans, private loans.

WORK-STUDY ***Federal work-study:*** Total amount: $6,696,419; 1,171 jobs averaging $1806. ***State or other work-study/employment:*** Total amount: $554,229 (100% non-need-based). 1,684 part-time jobs averaging $2314.

ATHLETIC AWARDS Total amount: $713,185 (100% non-need-based).

APPLYING FOR FINANCIAL AID ***Required financial aid form:*** FAFSA. ***Financial aid deadline:*** 4/15. ***Notification date:*** Continuous.

CONTACT Mrs. Patricia C. McCarthy, Director of Financial Aid, Indiana University of Pennsylvania, 213 Clark Hall, Indiana, PA 15705, 724-357-2218 or toll-free 800-442-6830. *Fax:* 724-357-2094. *E-mail:* mccarthy@iup.edu.

INDIANA UNIVERSITY–PURDUE UNIVERSITY FORT WAYNE

Fort Wayne, IN

Tuition & fees (IN res): $5936 **Average undergraduate aid package: $8537**

ABOUT THE INSTITUTION State-supported, coed. ***Awards:*** associate, bachelor's, and master's degrees and post-bachelor's certificates. 101 undergraduate majors. ***Total enrollment:*** 12,338. Undergraduates: 11,578. Freshmen: 2,094. Federal methodology is used as a basis for awarding need-based institutional aid.

UNDERGRADUATE EXPENSES for 2008–09 ***Application fee:*** $30. ***Tuition, state resident:*** full-time $5181; part-time $192 per credit hour. ***Tuition, nonresident:*** full-time $13,235; part-time $490 per credit hour. ***Required fees:*** full-time $755; $28 per credit hour. Full-time tuition and fees vary according to course load and student level. Part-time tuition and fees vary according to course load and student level. ***College room and board: Room only:*** $5400. Room and board charges vary according to housing facility. ***Payment plans:*** Installment, deferred payment.

FRESHMAN FINANCIAL AID (Fall 2007) 1,554 applied for aid; of those 78% were deemed to have need. 93% of freshmen with need received aid; of those 4% had need fully met. ***Average percent of need met:*** 50% (excluding resources awarded to replace EFC). ***Average financial aid package:*** $7584 (excluding resources awarded to replace EFC). 1% of all full-time freshmen had no need and received non-need-based gift aid.

UNDERGRADUATE FINANCIAL AID (Fall 2007) 5,695 applied for aid; of those 82% were deemed to have need. 95% of undergraduates with need received aid; of those 5% had need fully met. ***Average percent of need met:*** 53% (excluding resources awarded to replace EFC). ***Average financial aid package:*** $8537 (excluding resources awarded to replace EFC). 1% of all full-time undergraduates had no need and received non-need-based gift aid.

GIFT AID (NEED-BASED) ***Total amount:*** $17,880,005 (51% federal, 42% state, 3% institutional, 4% external sources). ***Receiving aid:*** Freshmen: 35% (653); all full-time undergraduates: 38% (2,767). ***Average award:*** Freshmen: $4780; Undergraduates: $4808. ***Scholarships, grants, and awards:*** Federal Pell, FSEOG, state, private, college/university gift aid from institutional funds.

GIFT AID (NON-NEED-BASED) ***Total amount:*** $1,141,522 (29% state, 30% institutional, 41% external sources). ***Receiving aid:*** Freshmen: 22% (400). Undergraduates: 14% (1,023). ***Average award:*** Freshmen: $1396. Undergraduates: $2321. ***Tuition waivers:*** Full or partial for employees or children of employees, senior citizens.

LOANS ***Student loans:*** $34,870,820 (96% need-based, 4% non-need-based). 62% of past graduating class borrowed through all loan programs. *Average indebtedness per student:* $20,335. ***Average need-based loan:*** Freshmen: $3157. Undergraduates: $3882. ***Parent loans:*** $1,916,873 (86% need-based, 14% non-need-based). ***Programs:*** FFEL (Subsidized and Unsubsidized Stafford, PLUS), Perkins.

WORK-STUDY ***Federal work-study:*** Total amount: $271,072; jobs available.

ATHLETIC AWARDS Total amount: $1,530,612 (23% need-based, 77% non-need-based).

APPLYING FOR FINANCIAL AID ***Required financial aid form:*** FAFSA. ***Financial aid deadline (priority):*** 3/10. ***Notification date:*** Continuous beginning 5/15. Students must reply within 3 weeks of notification.

CONTACT Mr. Joel Wenger, Director of Financial Aid, Indiana University–Purdue University Fort Wayne, 2101 East Coliseum Boulevard, Fort Wayne, IN 46805-1499, 260-481-6130 or toll-free 800-324-4739 (in-state). *E-mail:* wengerj@ipfw.edu.

INDIANA UNIVERSITY–PURDUE UNIVERSITY INDIANAPOLIS

Indianapolis, IN

Tuition & fees (IN res): $7191 **Average undergraduate aid package: $8816**

ABOUT THE INSTITUTION State-supported, coed. ***Awards:*** associate, bachelor's, master's, doctoral, and first professional degrees and post-bachelor's certificates. 90 undergraduate majors. ***Total enrollment:*** 30,300. Undergraduates: 21,423. Freshmen: 2,998. Federal methodology is used as a basis for awarding need-based institutional aid.

UNDERGRADUATE EXPENSES for 2008–09 ***Application fee:*** $50. ***Tuition, state resident:*** full-time $6531; part-time $217.70 per credit hour. ***Tuition, nonresident:*** full-time $19,919; part-time $663.95 per credit hour. ***Required fees:*** full-time $660. Full-time tuition and fees vary according to course load and program. Part-time tuition and fees vary according to course load and program. ***College room and board: Room only:*** $3140. Room and board charges vary according to board plan and housing facility. ***Payment plans:*** Installment, deferred payment.

FRESHMAN FINANCIAL AID (Fall 2008, est.) 2,343 applied for aid; of those 76% were deemed to have need. 96% of freshmen with need received aid; of those 9% had need fully met. ***Average percent of need met:*** 58% (excluding resources awarded to replace EFC). ***Average financial aid package:*** $8619 (excluding resources awarded to replace EFC). 9% of all full-time freshmen had no need and received non-need-based gift aid.

UNDERGRADUATE FINANCIAL AID (Fall 2008, est.) 11,251 applied for aid; of those 83% were deemed to have need. 95% of undergraduates with need received aid; of those 5% had need fully met. ***Average percent of need met:*** 57% (excluding resources awarded to replace EFC). ***Average financial aid package:*** $8816 (excluding resources awarded to replace EFC). 7% of all full-time undergraduates had no need and received non-need-based gift aid.

GIFT AID (NEED-BASED) ***Total amount:*** $45,482,172 (44% federal, 38% state, 14% institutional, 4% external sources). ***Receiving aid:*** Freshmen: 44% (1,245); all full-time undergraduates: 42% (6,232). ***Average award:*** Freshmen: $7527; Undergraduates: $6755. ***Scholarships, grants, and awards:*** Federal Pell, FSEOG, state, private, college/university gift aid from institutional funds.

GIFT AID (NON-NEED-BASED) ***Total amount:*** $11,234,543 (6% federal, 9% state, 44% institutional, 41% external sources). ***Receiving aid:*** Freshmen: 4% (118). Undergraduates: 3% (379). ***Average award:*** Freshmen: $5365. Undergraduates: $3986. ***Tuition waivers:*** Full or partial for employees or children of employees. ***ROTC:*** Army, Naval cooperative, Air Force cooperative.

LOANS ***Student loans:*** $87,140,392 (73% need-based, 27% non-need-based). 70% of past graduating class borrowed through all loan programs. *Average indebtedness per student:* $25,253. ***Average need-based loan:*** Freshmen: $3127. Undergraduates: $4259. ***Parent loans:*** $3,549,990 (27% need-based, 73% non-need-based). ***Programs:*** FFEL (Subsidized and Unsubsidized Stafford, PLUS), Perkins, Federal Nursing, college/university.

WORK-STUDY ***Federal work-study:*** Total amount: $1,848,373; jobs available. ***State or other work-study/employment:*** Total amount: $26,729 (73% need-based, 27% non-need-based). Part-time jobs available.

ATHLETIC AWARDS Total amount: $1,472,063 (42% need-based, 58% non-need-based).

APPLYING FOR FINANCIAL AID ***Required financial aid form:*** FAFSA. ***Financial aid deadline (priority):*** 3/1. ***Notification date:*** Continuous beginning 4/1.

CONTACT Kathy Purris, Director of Financial Aid Services, Indiana University–Purdue University Indianapolis, 425 North University Boulevard, Indianapolis, IN 46202-5145, 317-274-4162. *Fax:* 317-274-5930.

INDIANA UNIVERSITY SOUTH BEND

South Bend, IN

Tuition & fees (IN res): $5763 **Average undergraduate aid package: $7495**

ABOUT THE INSTITUTION State-supported, coed. ***Awards:*** associate, bachelor's, and master's degrees and post-bachelor's certificates. 63 undergraduate majors. ***Total enrollment:*** 7,712. Undergraduates: 6,756. Freshmen: 1,130. Federal methodology is used as a basis for awarding need-based institutional aid.

UNDERGRADUATE EXPENSES for 2008–09 ***Application fee:*** $45. ***Tuition, state resident:*** full-time $5324; part-time $177.45 per credit hour. ***Tuition, nonresident:*** full-time $14,441; part-time $481.35 per credit hour. ***Required fees:*** full-time $439. Full-time tuition and fees vary according to course load and program. Part-time tuition and fees vary according to course load and program. ***Payment plan:*** Deferred payment.

FRESHMAN FINANCIAL AID (Fall 2008, est.) 770 applied for aid; of those 75% were deemed to have need. 96% of freshmen with need received aid; of those 3% had need fully met. ***Average percent of need met:*** 62% (excluding resources awarded to replace EFC). ***Average financial aid package:*** $6933 (excluding resources awarded to replace EFC). 6% of all full-time freshmen had no need and received non-need-based gift aid.

UNDERGRADUATE FINANCIAL AID (Fall 2008, est.) 3,035 applied for aid; of those 82% were deemed to have need. 95% of undergraduates with need received aid; of those 4% had need fully met. ***Average percent of need met:*** 65% (excluding resources awarded to replace EFC). ***Average financial aid package:*** $7495 (excluding resources awarded to replace EFC). 3% of all full-time undergraduates had no need and received non-need-based gift aid.

GIFT AID (NEED-BASED) ***Total amount:*** $12,604,255 (56% federal, 33% state, 8% institutional, 3% external sources). ***Receiving aid:*** Freshmen: 49% (464); all full-time undergraduates: 48% (1,874). ***Average award:*** Freshmen: $5740; Undergraduates: $5752. ***Scholarships, grants, and awards:*** Federal Pell, FSEOG, state, private, college/university gift aid from institutional funds.

GIFT AID (NON-NEED-BASED) ***Total amount:*** $1,480,043 (18% federal, 10% state, 31% institutional, 41% external sources). ***Receiving aid:*** Freshmen: 1% (13). Undergraduates: 2% (72). ***Average award:*** Freshmen: $1608. Undergraduates: $2708. ***Tuition waivers:*** Full or partial for employees or children of employees. ***ROTC:*** Army cooperative, Naval cooperative, Air Force cooperative.

LOANS ***Student loans:*** $19,406,259 (74% need-based, 26% non-need-based). 72% of past graduating class borrowed through all loan programs. *Average indebtedness per student:* $22,235. ***Average need-based loan:*** Freshmen: $3071. Undergraduates: $3739. ***Parent loans:*** $641,332 (28% need-based, 72% non-need-based). ***Programs:*** Federal Direct (Subsidized and Unsubsidized Stafford, PLUS), Perkins, college/university.

WORK-STUDY ***Federal work-study:*** Total amount: $178,344; jobs available. ***State or other work-study/employment:*** Total amount: $4275 (100% need-based). Part-time jobs available.

ATHLETIC AWARDS Total amount: $137,152 (54% need-based, 46% non-need-based).

APPLYING FOR FINANCIAL AID ***Required financial aid forms:*** FAFSA, institution's own form. ***Financial aid deadline:*** 3/1. ***Notification date:*** Continuous beginning 5/1.

CONTACT Bev Cooper, Financial Aid Director, Indiana University South Bend, 1700 Mishawaka Avenue, South Bend, IN 46634-7111, 574-520-4357 or toll-free 877-GO-2-IUSB. *Fax:* 574-520-5561. *E-mail:* beacoope@iusb.edu.

INDIANA UNIVERSITY SOUTHEAST

New Albany, IN

Tuition & fees (IN res): $5644 **Average undergraduate aid package: $7221**

ABOUT THE INSTITUTION State-supported, coed. ***Awards:*** associate, bachelor's, and master's degrees and post-bachelor's certificates. 49 undergraduate majors. ***Total enrollment:*** 6,482. Undergraduates: 5,585. Freshmen: 1,065. Federal methodology is used as a basis for awarding need-based institutional aid.

UNDERGRADUATE EXPENSES for 2008–09 ***Application fee:*** $30. ***Tuition, state resident:*** full-time $5184; part-time $172.80 per credit hour. ***Tuition, nonresident:*** full-time $13,344; part-time $444.80 per credit hour. ***Required fees:*** full-time $460. Full-time tuition and fees vary according to course load, program, and reciprocity agreements. Part-time tuition and fees vary according to course load, program, and reciprocity agreements. ***College room and board: Room only:*** $3276. Room and board charges vary according to housing facility. ***Payment plan:*** Deferred payment.

FRESHMAN FINANCIAL AID (Fall 2008, est.) 800 applied for aid; of those 71% were deemed to have need. 95% of freshmen with need received aid; of those 5% had need fully met. ***Average percent of need met:*** 62% (excluding resources awarded to replace EFC). ***Average financial aid package:*** $7054 (excluding resources awarded to replace EFC). 4% of all full-time freshmen had no need and received non-need-based gift aid.

UNDERGRADUATE FINANCIAL AID (Fall 2008, est.) 2,627 applied for aid; of those 78% were deemed to have need. 95% of undergraduates with need received aid; of those 4% had need fully met. ***Average percent of need met:*** 63% (excluding resources awarded to replace EFC). ***Average financial aid package:*** $7221 (excluding resources awarded to replace EFC). 4% of all full-time undergraduates had no need and received non-need-based gift aid.

GIFT AID (NEED-BASED) ***Total amount:*** $9,983,467 (56% federal, 32% state, 7% institutional, 5% external sources). ***Receiving aid:*** Freshmen: 46% (443); all full-time undergraduates: 42% (1,490). ***Average award:*** Freshmen: $5945; Undergraduates: $5721. ***Scholarships, grants, and awards:*** Federal Pell, FSEOG, state, private, college/university gift aid from institutional funds.

GIFT AID (NON-NEED-BASED) ***Total amount:*** $1,391,308 (12% federal, 14% state, 25% institutional, 49% external sources). ***Receiving aid:*** Freshmen: 2% (23). Undergraduates: 2% (60). ***Average award:*** Freshmen: $2296. Undergraduates: $2222. ***Tuition waivers:*** Full or partial for employees or children of employees. ***ROTC:*** Army, Naval.

LOANS ***Student loans:*** $16,245,084 (72% need-based, 28% non-need-based). 57% of past graduating class borrowed through all loan programs. *Average indebtedness per student:* $19,592. ***Average need-based loan:*** Freshmen: $3005. Undergraduates: $3713. ***Parent loans:*** $419,659 (23% need-based, 77% non-need-based). ***Programs:*** FFEL (Subsidized and Unsubsidized Stafford, PLUS), Perkins, Federal Nursing, college/university.

WORK-STUDY ***Federal work-study:*** Total amount: $314,613; jobs available. ***State or other work-study/employment:*** Total amount: $9362 (87% need-based, 13% non-need-based). Part-time jobs available.

ATHLETIC AWARDS Total amount: $81,295 (61% need-based, 39% non-need-based).

APPLYING FOR FINANCIAL AID ***Required financial aid form:*** FAFSA. ***Financial aid deadline (priority):*** 3/1. ***Notification date:*** Continuous beginning 5/1. Students must reply within 3 weeks of notification.

CONTACT Brittany Hubbard, Director of Financial Aid, Indiana University Southeast, University Center, South Room 105, New Albany, IN 47150, 812-941-2246 or toll-free 800-852-8835 (in-state). *Fax:* 812-941-2546. *E-mail:* mibarlow@ius.edu.

INDIANA WESLEYAN UNIVERSITY

Marion, IN

CONTACT Director of Financial Aid, Indiana Wesleyan University, 4201 South Washington Street, Marion, IN 46953-4999, 765-677-2116 or toll-free 800-332-6901. *Fax:* 765-677-2809.

INTER AMERICAN UNIVERSITY OF PUERTO RICO, AGUADILLA CAMPUS

Aguadilla, PR

CONTACT Mr. Juan Gonzalez, Director of Financial Aid, Inter American University of Puerto Rico, Aguadilla Campus, PO Box 20000, Aguadilla, PR 00605, 787-891-0925 Ext. 2108. *Fax:* 787-882-3020.

INTER AMERICAN UNIVERSITY OF PUERTO RICO, ARECIBO CAMPUS

Arecibo, PR

Tuition & fees: $4212 **Average undergraduate aid package: $1439**

ABOUT THE INSTITUTION Independent, coed. ***Awards:*** associate, bachelor's, and master's degrees. 22 undergraduate majors. ***Total enrollment:*** 4,729. Undergraduates: 4,454. Freshmen: 868. Federal methodology is used as a basis for awarding need-based institutional aid.

UNDERGRADUATE EXPENSES for 2008–09 ***Tuition:*** full-time $3696; part-time $154 per credit.

FRESHMAN FINANCIAL AID (Fall 2008, est.) 959 applied for aid; of those 99% were deemed to have need. 88% of freshmen with need received aid. ***Average percent of need met:*** 2% (excluding resources awarded to replace EFC). ***Average financial aid package:*** $383 (excluding resources awarded to replace EFC).

UNDERGRADUATE FINANCIAL AID (Fall 2008, est.) 2,486 applied for aid; of those 100% were deemed to have need. 88% of undergraduates with need received aid; of those 9.% had need fully met. ***Average percent of need met:*** 8% (excluding resources awarded to replace EFC). ***Average financial aid package:*** $1439 (excluding resources awarded to replace EFC).

GIFT AID (NEED-BASED) ***Total amount:*** $15,719,385 (92% federal, 3% state, 5% institutional). ***Receiving aid:*** Freshmen: 78% (754); all full-time undergraduates: 76% (1,934). ***Average award:*** Freshmen: $124; Undergraduates: $292. ***Scholarships, grants, and awards:*** Federal Pell, FSEOG, state, private, college/university gift aid from institutional funds.

GIFT AID (NON-NEED-BASED) ***Receiving aid:*** Undergraduates: 5. ***ROTC:*** Army cooperative.

LOANS ***Student loans:*** $7,604,059 (100% need-based). 50% of past graduating class borrowed through all loan programs. ***Average need-based loan:*** Freshmen: $544. Undergraduates: $2332. ***Parent loans:*** $6720 (100% need-based). ***Programs:*** Federal Direct (Subsidized and Unsubsidized Stafford, PLUS), FFEL (Subsidized and Unsubsidized Stafford, PLUS), Perkins.

WORK-STUDY ***Federal work-study:*** Total amount: $278,780; 238 jobs averaging $1600.

ATHLETIC AWARDS Total amount: $9600 (100% need-based).

APPLYING FOR FINANCIAL AID ***Required financial aid forms:*** FAFSA, institution's own form. ***Financial aid deadline (priority):*** 4/1. ***Notification date:*** Continuous beginning 6/1.

CONTACT Ramón O. de Jesús, Financial Aid Director, Inter American University of Puerto Rico, Arecibo Campus, PO Box 4050, Arecibo, PR 00614-4050, 787-878-5475 Ext. 2275. *Fax:* 787-880-1624.

INTER AMERICAN UNIVERSITY OF PUERTO RICO, BARRANQUITAS CAMPUS

Barranquitas, PR

CONTACT Mr. Eduardo Fontánez Colón, Financial Aid Officer, Inter American University of Puerto Rico, Barranquitas Campus, Box 517, Barranquitas, PR 00794, 787-857-3600 Ext. 2049. *Fax:* 787-857-2244.

INTER AMERICAN UNIVERSITY OF PUERTO RICO, BAYAMÓN CAMPUS

Bayamón, PR

CONTACT Financial Aid Office, Inter American University of Puerto Rico, Bayamón Campus, 500 Road 830, Bayamon, PR 00957, 787-279-1912 Ext. 2025.

INTER AMERICAN UNIVERSITY OF PUERTO RICO, FAJARDO CAMPUS

Fajardo, PR

CONTACT Financial Aid Director, Inter American University of Puerto Rico, Fajardo Campus, Call Box 700003, Fajardo, PR 00738-7003, 787-863-2390 Ext. 2208.

INTER AMERICAN UNIVERSITY OF PUERTO RICO, GUAYAMA CAMPUS

Guayama, PR

Tuition & fees: $4174 **Average undergraduate aid package: $1245**

ABOUT THE INSTITUTION Independent, coed. ***Awards:*** associate, bachelor's, and master's degrees. 13 undergraduate majors. ***Total enrollment:*** 2,157. Undergraduates: 2,157. Freshmen: 393. Federal methodology is used as a basis for awarding need-based institutional aid.

UNDERGRADUATE EXPENSES for 2009–10 ***Tuition:*** full-time $3696.

FRESHMAN FINANCIAL AID (Fall 2008, est.) 282 applied for aid; of those 99% were deemed to have need. 74% of freshmen with need received aid. ***Average percent of need met:*** 1% (excluding resources awarded to replace EFC).

UNDERGRADUATE FINANCIAL AID (Fall 2008, est.) 1,426 applied for aid; of those 99% were deemed to have need. 83% of undergraduates with need received aid. ***Average financial aid package:*** $1245 (excluding resources awarded to replace EFC).

GIFT AID (NEED-BASED) ***Total amount:*** $542,603 (41% federal, 44% state, 15% institutional). ***Receiving aid:*** Freshmen: 50% (142); all full-time undergraduates: 54% (773). ***Average award:*** Freshmen: $70; Undergraduates: $428. ***Scholarships, grants, and awards:*** Federal Pell, FSEOG, state, college/university gift aid from institutional funds, Federal Nursing.

GIFT AID (NON-NEED-BASED) ***Receiving aid:*** Undergraduates: 3. ***ROTC:*** Army cooperative.

LOANS ***Student loans:*** $2,364,175 (100% need-based). 80% of past graduating class borrowed through all loan programs. ***Average need-based loan:*** Freshmen: $168. Undergraduates: $1654. ***Programs:*** Federal Direct (Subsidized and Unsubsidized Stafford, PLUS), Perkins, Federal Nursing.

WORK-STUDY ***Federal work-study:*** Total amount: $44,163; jobs available. ***State or other work-study/employment:*** Part-time jobs available.

ATHLETIC AWARDS Total amount: $4800 (100% need-based).

APPLYING FOR FINANCIAL AID ***Required financial aid form:*** FAFSA. ***Financial aid deadline:*** Continuous. ***Notification date:*** Continuous beginning 7/1. Students must reply within 5 weeks of notification.

CONTACT Senor Jose A. Vechini, Director of Financial Aid Office, Inter American University of Puerto Rico, Guayama Campus, Call Box 10004, Guyama, PR 00785, 787-864-2222 Ext. 2206 or toll-free 787-864-2222 Ext. 2243 (in-state). *Fax:* 787-864-8232. *E-mail:* javechi@inter.edu.

INTER AMERICAN UNIVERSITY OF PUERTO RICO, METROPOLITAN CAMPUS

San Juan, PR

CONTACT Mrs. Luz M. Medina, Acting Director of Financial Aid, Inter American University of Puerto Rico, Metropolitan Campus, PO Box 191293, San Juan, PR 00919-1293, 787-758-2891. *Fax:* 787-250-0782.

INTER AMERICAN UNIVERSITY OF PUERTO RICO, PONCE CAMPUS

Mercedita, PR

CONTACT Financial Aid Officer, Inter American University of Puerto Rico, Ponce Campus, Street #1, Km 123.2, Mercedita, PR 00715-2201, 787-284-1912 Ext. 2015.

INTER AMERICAN UNIVERSITY OF PUERTO RICO, SAN GERMÁN CAMPUS

San Germán, PR

CONTACT Ms. María I. Lugo, Financial Aid Director, Inter American University of Puerto Rico, San Germán Campus, PO Box 5100, San Germán, PR 00683-5008, 787-264-1912 Ext. 7252. *Fax:* 787-892-6350.

INTERIOR DESIGNERS INSTITUTE

Newport Beach, CA

CONTACT Office of Financial Aid, Interior Designers Institute, 1061 Camelback Road, Newport Beach, CA 92660, 949-675-4451.

INTERNATIONAL ACADEMY OF DESIGN & TECHNOLOGY

Tampa, FL

CONTACT Financial Aid Office, International Academy of Design & Technology, 5225 Memorial Highway, Tampa, FL 33634-7350, 813-881-0007 or toll-free 800-ACADEMY. *Fax:* 813-881-3440.

INTERNATIONAL ACADEMY OF DESIGN & TECHNOLOGY

Chicago, IL

CONTACT Barbara Williams, Financial Aid Director, International Academy of Design & Technology, 1 North State Street, Suite 400, Chicago, IL 60602, 312-980-9200 or toll-free 877-ACADEMY (out-of-state). *Fax:* 312-541-3929.

INTERNATIONAL BAPTIST COLLEGE

Tempe, AZ

CONTACT Financial Aid Office, International Baptist College, 2150 East Southern Avenue, Tempe, AZ 85282, 480-838-7070 or toll-free 800-422-4858. *Fax:* 480-838-5432.

INTERNATIONAL IMPORT-EXPORT INSTITUTE

Phoenix, AZ

CONTACT Financial Aid Office, International Import-Export Institute, 2432 West Peoria Avenue, Suite 1026, Phoenix, AZ 85029, 602-648-5750 or toll-free 800-474-8013.

IONA COLLEGE

New Rochelle, NY

Tuition & fees: $27,500 **Average undergraduate aid package: $16,968**

ABOUT THE INSTITUTION Independent religious, coed. ***Awards:*** bachelor's and master's degrees and post-bachelor's and post-master's certificates. 58 undergraduate majors. ***Total enrollment:*** 4,375. Undergraduates: 3,460. Freshmen: 923. Federal methodology is used as a basis for awarding need-based institutional aid.

UNDERGRADUATE EXPENSES for 2009–10 ***Application fee:*** $50. ***Comprehensive fee:*** $38,800 includes full-time tuition ($25,600), mandatory fees ($1900), and room and board ($11,300). ***Part-time tuition:*** $850 per credit. ***Part-time fees:*** $500 per term.

FRESHMAN FINANCIAL AID (Fall 2008, est.) 912 applied for aid; of those 74% were deemed to have need. 100% of freshmen with need received aid; of those 25% had need fully met. ***Average percent of need met:*** 26% (excluding resources awarded to replace EFC). ***Average financial aid package:*** $18,391 (excluding resources awarded to replace EFC). 26% of all full-time freshmen had no need and received non-need-based gift aid.

UNDERGRADUATE FINANCIAL AID (Fall 2008, est.) 3,225 applied for aid; of those 75% were deemed to have need. 99% of undergraduates with need received aid; of those 25% had need fully met. ***Average percent of need met:*** 25% (excluding resources awarded to replace EFC). ***Average financial aid package:*** $16,968 (excluding resources awarded to replace EFC). 23% of all full-time undergraduates had no need and received non-need-based gift aid.

GIFT AID (NEED-BASED) ***Total amount:*** $9,448,774 (30% federal, 39% state, 29% institutional, 2% external sources). ***Receiving aid:*** Freshmen: 56% (517); all full-time undergraduates: 43% (1,420). ***Average award:*** Freshmen: $4391; Undergraduates: $4044. ***Scholarships, grants, and awards:*** Federal Pell, FSEOG, state, private, college/university gift aid from institutional funds.

GIFT AID (NON-NEED-BASED) ***Total amount:*** $25,158,091 (98% institutional, 2% external sources). ***Receiving aid:*** Freshmen: 72% (668). Undergraduates: 70% (2,341). ***Average award:*** Freshmen: $11,142. Undergraduates: $10,617. ***Scholarships, grants, and awards by category:*** *Academic interests/achievement:* 3,085 awards ($23,898,404 total): general academic interests/achievements. *Creative arts/performance:* 27 awards ($79,000 total): music. *Special characteristics:* 308 awards ($853,546 total): children and siblings of alumni, children of faculty/staff, religious affiliation, siblings of current students. ***ROTC:*** Army cooperative, Air Force cooperative.

LOANS ***Student loans:*** $19,708,542 (33% need-based, 67% non-need-based). 69% of past graduating class borrowed through all loan programs. *Average indebtedness per student:* $19,905. ***Average need-based loan:*** Freshmen: $2554. Undergraduates: $2712. ***Parent loans:*** $5,639,184 (100% non-need-based). ***Programs:*** FFEL (Subsidized and Unsubsidized Stafford, PLUS), Perkins, alternative loans.

WORK-STUDY ***Federal work-study:*** Total amount: $628,113; 280 jobs averaging $618. ***State or other work-study/employment:*** Total amount: $310,000 (100% non-need-based). 229 part-time jobs averaging $676.

ATHLETIC AWARDS Total amount: $2,695,633 (100% non-need-based).

APPLYING FOR FINANCIAL AID ***Required financial aid forms:*** FAFSA, institution's own form, state aid form. ***Financial aid deadline:*** 4/15 (priority: 2/15). ***Notification date:*** Continuous. Students must reply by 5/1 or within 2 weeks of notification.

CONTACT Mary Grant, Director of Financial Aid, Iona College, 715 North Avenue, New Rochelle, NY 10801-1890, 914-633-2676 or toll-free 800-231-IONA (in-state). *Fax:* 914-633-2486.

IOWA STATE UNIVERSITY OF SCIENCE AND TECHNOLOGY

Ames, IA

Tuition & fees (IA res): $6651 **Average undergraduate aid package: $10,262**

ABOUT THE INSTITUTION State-supported, coed. ***Awards:*** bachelor's, master's, doctoral, and first professional degrees and post-master's certificates. 115 undergraduate majors. ***Total enrollment:*** 26,856. Undergraduates: 21,607. Freshmen: 4,546. Federal methodology is used as a basis for awarding need-based institutional aid.

UNDERGRADUATE EXPENSES for 2009–10 ***Application fee:*** $30. ***Tuition, state resident:*** full-time $5756; part-time $240 per semester hour. ***Tuition, nonresident:*** full-time $16,976; part-time $708 per semester hour. ***Required fees:*** full-time $895. ***College room and board:*** $7277; ***Room only:*** $3750.

FRESHMAN FINANCIAL AID (Fall 2008, est.) 3,522 applied for aid; of those 67% were deemed to have need. 98% of freshmen with need received aid; of those 41% had need fully met. ***Average percent of need met:*** 80% (excluding resources awarded to replace EFC). ***Average financial aid package:*** $10,039 (excluding resources awarded to replace EFC). 33% of all full-time freshmen had no need and received non-need-based gift aid.

UNDERGRADUATE FINANCIAL AID (Fall 2008, est.) 14,712 applied for aid; of those 72% were deemed to have need. 98% of undergraduates with need received aid; of those 41% had need fully met. ***Average percent of need met:*** 80% (excluding resources awarded to replace EFC). ***Average financial aid package:*** $10,262 (excluding resources awarded to replace EFC). 31% of all full-time undergraduates had no need and received non-need-based gift aid.

GIFT AID (NEED-BASED) ***Total amount:*** $46,457,856 (33% federal, 5% state, 55% institutional, 7% external sources). ***Receiving aid:*** Freshmen: 53% (2,307); all full-time undergraduates: 53% (10,431). ***Average award:*** Freshmen: $5938; Undergraduates: $5160. ***Scholarships, grants, and awards:*** Federal Pell, FSEOG, state, college/university gift aid from institutional funds.

GIFT AID (NON-NEED-BASED) ***Total amount:*** $18,982,573 (6% federal, 2% state, 78% institutional, 14% external sources). ***Receiving aid:*** Freshmen: 25% (1,090). Undergraduates: 26% (5,047). ***Average award:*** Freshmen: $2693. Undergraduates: $2147. ***Scholarships, grants, and awards by category:*** *Academic interests/achievement:* agriculture, architecture, area/ethnic studies, biological sciences, business, communication, computer science, education, engineering/technologies, English, foreign languages, general academic interests/achievements, health fields, home economics, humanities, international studies, library science, mathematics, military science, physical sciences, premedicine, social sciences. *Creative arts/performance:* applied art and design, art/fine arts, journalism/publications, music, theater/drama. *Special achievements/activities:* community service, general special achievements/activities, leadership, rodeo. *Special characteristics:* adult students, children and siblings of alumni, ethnic background, first-generation college students, general special characteristics, international students, local/state students, members of minority groups, out-of-state students, religious affiliation. ***ROTC:*** Army, Naval, Air Force.

LOANS ***Student loans:*** $107,716,287 (58% need-based, 42% non-need-based). 71% of past graduating class borrowed through all loan programs. *Average indebtedness per student:* $31,616. ***Average need-based loan:*** Freshmen: $3698. Undergraduates: $4505. ***Parent loans:*** $16,582,068 (25% need-based, 75% non-need-based). ***Programs:*** Federal Direct (Subsidized and Unsubsidized Stafford, PLUS), Perkins, state, college/university, private alternative loans.

WORK-STUDY ***Federal work-study:*** Total amount: $2,229,158; 1,573 jobs averaging $1417. ***State or other work-study/employment:*** Total amount: $342,630 (100% need-based). 8,172 part-time jobs averaging $1826.

ATHLETIC AWARDS Total amount: $4,193,375 (48% need-based, 52% non-need-based).

APPLYING FOR FINANCIAL AID ***Required financial aid form:*** FAFSA. ***Financial aid deadline (priority):*** 3/1. ***Notification date:*** Continuous beginning 4/1. Students must reply by 5/1.

CONTACT Roberta Johnson, Director of Financial Aid, Iowa State University of Science and Technology, 0210 Beardshear Hall, Ames, IA 50011, 515-294-2223 or toll-free 800-262-3810. *Fax:* 515-294-3622. *E-mail:* rljohns@iastate.edu.

IOWA WESLEYAN COLLEGE

Mount Pleasant, IA

ABOUT THE INSTITUTION Independent United Methodist, coed. ***Awards:*** bachelor's degrees. 40 undergraduate majors. ***Total enrollment:*** 843. Undergraduates: 843. Freshmen: 150.

GIFT AID (NEED-BASED) ***Scholarships, grants, and awards:*** Federal Pell, FSEOG, state, private, college/university gift aid from institutional funds.

GIFT AID (NON-NEED-BASED) ***Scholarships, grants, and awards by category:*** *Academic interests/achievement:* general academic interests/achievements. *Creative arts/performance:* art/fine arts, music. *Special achievements/activities:* cheerleading/drum major, community service, leadership, religious involvement. *Special characteristics:* children and siblings of alumni, children of faculty/staff, international students, out-of-state students, relatives of clergy, religious affiliation.

LOANS ***Programs:*** FFEL (Subsidized and Unsubsidized Stafford, PLUS), Perkins, state, alternative loans.

WORK-STUDY ***Federal work-study:*** Total amount: $64,497; jobs available. ***State or other work-study/employment:*** Total amount: $3000 (100% non-need-based). Part-time jobs available.

APPLYING FOR FINANCIAL AID ***Required financial aid form:*** FAFSA.

CONTACT Debra Morrissey, Director of Financial Aid, Iowa Wesleyan College, 601 North Main Street, Mount Pleasant, IA 52641-1398, 319-385-6242 or toll-free 800-582-2383 Ext. 6231. *Fax:* 319-385-6203. *E-mail:* dmorrissey@iwc.edu.

ITHACA COLLEGE

Ithaca, NY

Tuition & fees: $30,606 **Average undergraduate aid package: $23,786**

ABOUT THE INSTITUTION Independent, coed. ***Awards:*** bachelor's, master's, and doctoral degrees. 106 undergraduate majors. ***Total enrollment:*** 6,448. Undergraduates: 6,031. Freshmen: 1,441. Institutional methodology is used as a basis for awarding need-based institutional aid.

UNDERGRADUATE EXPENSES for 2008–09 ***Application fee:*** $60. ***Comprehensive fee:*** $41,768 includes full-time tuition ($30,606) and room and board ($11,162). ***College room only:*** $5884. ***Part-time tuition:*** $1020 per credit hour. ***Payment plan:*** Installment.

FRESHMAN FINANCIAL AID (Fall 2008, est.) 1,479 applied for aid; of those 82% were deemed to have need. 100% of freshmen with need received aid; of those 47% had need fully met. ***Average percent of need met:*** 88% (excluding resources awarded to replace EFC). ***Average financial aid package:*** $24,152 (excluding resources awarded to replace EFC). 17% of all full-time freshmen had no need and received non-need-based gift aid.

UNDERGRADUATE FINANCIAL AID (Fall 2008, est.) 4,611 applied for aid; of those 87% were deemed to have need. 100% of undergraduates with need received aid; of those 41% had need fully met. ***Average percent of need met:*** 86% (excluding resources awarded to replace EFC). ***Average financial aid package:*** $23,786 (excluding resources awarded to replace EFC). 14% of all full-time undergraduates had no need and received non-need-based gift aid.

GIFT AID (NEED-BASED) ***Total amount:*** $62,611,372 (7% federal, 6% state, 84% institutional, 3% external sources). ***Receiving aid:*** Freshmen: 66% (1,182); all full-time undergraduates: 63% (3,868). ***Average award:*** Freshmen: $16,522; Undergraduates: $16,130. ***Scholarships, grants, and awards:*** Federal Pell, FSEOG, state, private, college/university gift aid from institutional funds.

GIFT AID (NON-NEED-BASED) ***Total amount:*** $12,323,217 (1% federal, 1% state, 87% institutional, 11% external sources). ***Receiving aid:*** Freshmen: 20% (360). Undergraduates: 15% (897). ***Average award:*** Freshmen: $7926. Undergraduates: $10,027. ***Scholarships, grants, and awards by category:*** *Academic interests/achievement:* 2,187 awards ($21,666,229 total): communication, general academic interests/achievements. *Creative arts/performance:* 41 awards ($469,376 total): cinema/film/broadcasting, dance, journalism/publications, music, performing arts, theater/drama. *Special achievements/activities:* 187 awards ($1,075,000 total): leadership. *Special characteristics:* 1,247 awards ($6,722,339 total): children and siblings of alumni, children of faculty/staff, general special characteristics, members of minority groups, siblings of current students. ***Tuition waivers:*** Full or partial for employees or children of employees. ***ROTC:*** Army cooperative, Air Force cooperative.

LOANS ***Student loans:*** $23,087,975 (81% need-based, 19% non-need-based). ***Average need-based loan:*** Freshmen: $4525. Undergraduates: $5107. ***Parent***

loans: $34,170,160 (20% need-based, 80% non-need-based). ***Programs:*** FFEL (Subsidized and Unsubsidized Stafford, PLUS), Perkins, alternative loans.

WORK-STUDY ***Federal work-study:*** Total amount: $1,500,000; 2,713 jobs averaging $2400. ***State or other work-study/employment:*** Total amount: $9,451,986 (60% need-based, 40% non-need-based). 1,739 part-time jobs averaging $2400.

APPLYING FOR FINANCIAL AID ***Required financial aid forms:*** FAFSA, CSS/Profile for Early Decision Students. ***Financial aid deadline (priority):*** 2/1. ***Notification date:*** Continuous beginning 2/15.

CONTACT Mr. Larry Chambers, Director of Financial Aid, Ithaca College, 953 Danby Road, Ithaca, NY 14850-7000, 800-429-4275 or toll-free 800-429-4274. *Fax:* 607-274-1895. *E-mail:* finaid@ithaca.edu.

ITT TECHNICAL INSTITUTE

Tempe, AZ

CONTACT Financial Aid Office, ITT Technical Institute, 5005 S. Wendler Drive, Tempe, AZ 85282, 602-437-7500 or toll-free 800-879-4881.

ITT TECHNICAL INSTITUTE

Clovis, CA

CONTACT Financial Aid Office, ITT Technical Institute, 362 N. Clovis Avenue, Clovis, CA 93612, 559-325-5400 or toll-free 800-564-9771 (in-state).

ITT TECHNICAL INSTITUTE

Concord, CA

CONTACT Financial Aid Office, ITT Technical Institute, 1140 Galaxy Way, Suite 400, Concord, CA 94520, 925-674-8200 or toll-free 800-211-7062.

ITT TECHNICAL INSTITUTE

South Bend, IN

CONTACT Financial Aid Office, ITT Technical Institute, 17390 Dugdale Drive, Suite 100, South Bend, IN 46635, 574-247-8300 or toll-free 877-474-1926.

ITT TECHNICAL INSTITUTE

Wichita, KS

CONTACT Financial Aid Office, ITT Technical Institute, One Brittany Place, Suite 100, 2024 North Woodlawn, Wichita, KS 67208, 316-681-8400 or toll-free 877-207-1047.

ITT TECHNICAL INSTITUTE

Lexington, KY

CONTACT Financial Aid Office, ITT Technical Institute, 2473 Fortune Drive, Suite 180, Lexington, KY 40509, 859-246-3300 or toll-free 800-519-8151.

ITT TECHNICAL INSTITUTE

Springfield, MO

CONTACT Financial Aid Office, ITT Technical Institute, 3216 South National Avenue, Springfield, MO 65807, 417-877-4800 or toll-free 877-219-4387.

ITT TECHNICAL INSTITUTE

Charlotte, NC

CONTACT Financial Aid Office, ITT Technical Institute, 10926 David Taylor Drive, Suite 100, Charlotte, NC 28262, 704-548-2300 or toll-free 877-243-7685.

ITT TECHNICAL INSTITUTE

Oklahoma City, OK

CONTACT Financial Aid Office, ITT Technical Institute, 50 Penn Place Office Tower, 1900 Northwest Expressway, Suite 305R, Oklahoma City, OK 73118, 405-810-4100 or toll-free 800-518-1612.

JACKSON STATE UNIVERSITY

Jackson, MS

CONTACT B. J. Moncure, Director of Financial Aid, Jackson State University, 1400 J.R. Lynch Street, PO Box 17065, Jackson, MS 39217, 601-979-2227 or toll-free 800-682-5390 (in-state), 800-848-6817 (out-of-state). *Fax:* 601-979-2237.

JACKSONVILLE STATE UNIVERSITY

Jacksonville, AL

Tuition & fees (AL res): $5700 **Average undergraduate aid package: $8829**

ABOUT THE INSTITUTION State-supported, coed. ***Awards:*** bachelor's and master's degrees and post-master's certificates. 58 undergraduate majors. ***Total enrollment:*** 9,077. Undergraduates: 7,485. Freshmen: 1,302. Federal methodology is used as a basis for awarding need-based institutional aid.

UNDERGRADUATE EXPENSES for 2008–09 ***Application fee:*** $20. ***Tuition, state resident:*** full-time $5700; part-time $190 per credit hour. ***Tuition, nonresident:*** full-time $11,400; part-time $380 per credit hour. ***College room and board:*** $4215. Room and board charges vary according to board plan and housing facility.

FRESHMAN FINANCIAL AID (Fall 2007) 1,070 applied for aid; of those 100% were deemed to have need. 100% of freshmen with need received aid. ***Average financial aid package:*** $7862 (excluding resources awarded to replace EFC).

UNDERGRADUATE FINANCIAL AID (Fall 2007) 4,690 applied for aid; of those 100% were deemed to have need. 100% of undergraduates with need received aid. ***Average financial aid package:*** $8829 (excluding resources awarded to replace EFC).

GIFT AID (NEED-BASED) ***Total amount:*** $13,822,207 (75% federal, 3% state, 22% institutional). ***Receiving aid:*** Freshmen: 65% (804); all full-time undergraduates: 55% (3,317). ***Average award:*** Freshmen: $4289; Undergraduates: $4112. ***Scholarships, grants, and awards:*** Federal Pell, FSEOG, state, private, college/university gift aid from institutional funds, Federal Nursing.

GIFT AID (NON-NEED-BASED) ***Total amount:*** $992,185 (100% external sources). ***Receiving aid:*** Freshmen: 5% (62). Undergraduates: 5% (311). ***Scholarships, grants, and awards by category:*** *Academic interests/achievement:* biological sciences, business, communication, computer science, education, English, health fields, home economics, humanities, mathematics, military science, physical sciences, social sciences. *Creative arts/performance:* art/fine arts, journalism/publications, music, theater/drama. *Special achievements/activities:* general special achievements/activities. ***Tuition waivers:*** Full or partial for employees or children of employees. ***ROTC:*** Army.

LOANS ***Student loans:*** $28,655,200 (100% need-based). ***Average need-based loan:*** Freshmen: $4212. Undergraduates: $5723. ***Parent loans:*** $1,367,615 (100% non-need-based). ***Programs:*** FFEL (Subsidized and Unsubsidized Stafford, PLUS), college/university.

WORK-STUDY ***Federal work-study:*** Total amount: $537,800; 207 jobs averaging $1302.

ATHLETIC AWARDS Total amount: $2,872,048 (100% non-need-based).

APPLYING FOR FINANCIAL AID ***Required financial aid forms:*** FAFSA, institution's own form. ***Financial aid deadline (priority):*** 3/15. ***Notification date:*** Continuous beginning 5/15. Students must reply within 2 weeks of notification.

CONTACT Mrs. Vicki Adams, Director of Financial Aid, Jacksonville State University, 700 Pelham Road North, Jacksonville, AL 36265-9982, 256-782-5006 Ext. 8399 or toll-free 800-231-5291. *Fax:* 256-782-5476. *E-mail:* finaid@jsu.edu.

JACKSONVILLE UNIVERSITY

Jacksonville, FL

Tuition & fees: $23,900 **Average undergraduate aid package: $18,698**

ABOUT THE INSTITUTION Independent, coed. ***Awards:*** bachelor's, master's, and first professional degrees and first professional certificates. 58 undergraduate majors. ***Total enrollment:*** 3,418. Undergraduates: 3,007. Freshmen: 544. Federal methodology is used as a basis for awarding need-based institutional aid.

UNDERGRADUATE EXPENSES for 2008–09 ***Application fee:*** $30. ***Comprehensive fee:*** $32,660 includes full-time tuition ($23,900) and room and board ($8760). ***College room only:*** $5000. ***Part-time tuition:*** $795 per credit hour.

FRESHMAN FINANCIAL AID (Fall 2008, est.) 420 applied for aid; of those 99% were deemed to have need. 99% of freshmen with need received aid; of those 2% had need fully met. ***Average percent of need met:*** 52% (excluding resources awarded to replace EFC). ***Average financial aid package:*** $18,697 (excluding resources awarded to replace EFC). 16% of all full-time freshmen had no need and received non-need-based gift aid.

UNDERGRADUATE FINANCIAL AID (Fall 2008, est.) 1,495 applied for aid; of those 99% were deemed to have need. 99% of undergraduates with need received aid; of those 1% had need fully met. ***Average percent of need met:*** 52% (excluding resources awarded to replace EFC). ***Average financial aid package:*** $18,698 (excluding resources awarded to replace EFC). 18% of all full-time undergraduates had no need and received non-need-based gift aid.

GIFT AID (NEED-BASED) ***Total amount:*** $20,792,375 (18% federal, 18% state, 63% institutional, 1% external sources). ***Receiving aid:*** Freshmen: 72% (410); all full-time undergraduates: 76% (1,460). ***Average award:*** Freshmen: $15,971; Undergraduates: $15,397. ***Scholarships, grants, and awards:*** Federal Pell, FSEOG, state, private, college/university gift aid from institutional funds, Academic Competitiveness Grant, National Smart Grant.

GIFT AID (NON-NEED-BASED) ***Total amount:*** $4,187,049 (23% federal, 12% state, 64% institutional, 1% external sources). ***Receiving aid:*** Freshmen: 1% (6). Undergraduates: 1% (17). ***Average award:*** Freshmen: $4261. Undergraduates: $3586. ***Scholarships, grants, and awards by category:*** *Academic interests/achievement:* business, general academic interests/achievements. *Creative arts/performance:* general creative arts/performance. *Special achievements/activities:* general special achievements/activities. *Special characteristics:* children of educators, children of faculty/staff, international students. ***ROTC:*** Naval.

LOANS ***Student loans:*** $12,260,100 (99% need-based, 1% non-need-based). ***Average need-based loan:*** Freshmen: $3906. Undergraduates: $4540. ***Parent loans:*** $1,947,710 (99% need-based, 1% non-need-based). ***Programs:*** FFEL (Subsidized and Unsubsidized Stafford, PLUS), Perkins, state, college/university.

WORK-STUDY ***Federal work-study:*** Total amount: $260,000; jobs available.

ATHLETIC AWARDS Total amount: $3,236,120 (55% need-based, 45% non-need-based).

APPLYING FOR FINANCIAL AID ***Required financial aid forms:*** FAFSA, institution's own form, state aid form. ***Financial aid deadline (priority):*** 3/15. ***Notification date:*** Continuous.

CONTACT Mrs. Catherine Huntress, Director of Student Financial Assistance, Jacksonville University, 2800 University Boulevard North, Jacksonville, FL 32211, 904-256-7060 or toll-free 800-225-2027. *Fax:* 904-256-7148. *E-mail:* chuntres@ju.edu.

JAMES MADISON UNIVERSITY

Harrisonburg, VA

Tuition & fees (VA res): $6964 **Average undergraduate aid package: $7891**

ABOUT THE INSTITUTION State-supported, coed. ***Awards:*** bachelor's, master's, and doctoral degrees and post-master's certificates (also offers specialist in education degree). 48 undergraduate majors. ***Total enrollment:*** 18,454. Undergraduates: 16,916. Freshmen: 3,957. Federal methodology is used as a basis for awarding need-based institutional aid.

UNDERGRADUATE EXPENSES for 2008–09 ***Application fee:*** $40. ***Tuition, state resident:*** full-time $3556; part-time $118 per credit hour. ***Tuition, nonresident:*** full-time $15,050; part-time $497 per credit hour. ***Required fees:*** full-time $3408. Part-time tuition and fees vary according to course load. ***College room and board:*** $7458; ***Room only:*** $3888. Room and board charges vary according to board plan and housing facility. ***Payment plan:*** Installment.

FRESHMAN FINANCIAL AID (Fall 2008, est.) 2,916 applied for aid; of those 50% were deemed to have need. 84% of freshmen with need received aid; of those 98% had need fully met. ***Average percent of need met:*** 45% (excluding resources awarded to replace EFC). ***Average financial aid package:*** $9212 (excluding resources awarded to replace EFC). 4% of all full-time freshmen had no need and received non-need-based gift aid.

UNDERGRADUATE FINANCIAL AID (Fall 2008, est.) 13,612 applied for aid; of those 40% were deemed to have need. 91% of undergraduates with need received aid; of those 77% had need fully met. ***Average percent of need met:*** 51% (excluding resources awarded to replace EFC). ***Average financial aid package:*** $7891 (excluding resources awarded to replace EFC). 2% of all full-time undergraduates had no need and received non-need-based gift aid.

GIFT AID (NEED-BASED) ***Total amount:*** $17,238,652 (33% federal, 36% state, 18% institutional, 13% external sources). ***Receiving aid:*** Freshmen: 14% (559); all full-time undergraduates: 13% (2,106). ***Average award:*** Freshmen: $7046; Undergraduates: $6784. ***Scholarships, grants, and awards:*** Federal Pell, FSEOG, state, private, college/university gift aid from institutional funds.

GIFT AID (NON-NEED-BASED) ***Total amount:*** $2,944,619 (5% state, 84% institutional, 11% external sources). ***Receiving aid:*** Freshmen: 11% (435). Undergraduates: 7% (1,085). ***Average award:*** Freshmen: $2032. Undergraduates: $2328. ***Scholarships, grants, and awards by category:*** *Academic interests/achievement:* 485 awards ($715,600 total): architecture, biological sciences, business, computer science, education, engineering/technologies, English, general academic interests/achievements, health fields, humanities, international studies, mathematics, military science, physical sciences, premedicine, religion/biblical studies, social sciences. *Creative arts/performance:* 99 awards ($127,175 total): art/fine arts, cinema/film/broadcasting, dance, journalism/publications, music, theater/drama. *Special achievements/activities:* 91 awards ($43,200 total): cheerleading/drum major, general special achievements/activities, leadership. *Special characteristics:* 86 awards ($106,300 total): children and siblings of alumni, children of faculty/staff, handicapped students, international students, out-of-state students, siblings of current students. ***Tuition waivers:*** Full or partial for employees or children of employees, senior citizens. ***ROTC:*** Army, Air Force cooperative.

LOANS ***Student loans:*** $45,592,462 (35% need-based, 65% non-need-based). 46% of past graduating class borrowed through all loan programs. *Average indebtedness per student:* $17,395. ***Average need-based loan:*** Freshmen: $3488. Undergraduates: $4087. ***Parent loans:*** $24,846,482 (100% non-need-based). ***Programs:*** FFEL (Subsidized and Unsubsidized Stafford, PLUS), Perkins.

WORK-STUDY ***Federal work-study:*** Total amount: $405,528; 263 jobs averaging $1803. ***State or other work-study/employment:*** Total amount: $4,860,000 (100% non-need-based). 2,207 part-time jobs averaging $2019.

ATHLETIC AWARDS Total amount: $4,644,407 (100% non-need-based).

APPLYING FOR FINANCIAL AID ***Required financial aid form:*** FAFSA. ***Financial aid deadline (priority):*** 3/1. ***Notification date:*** Continuous beginning 4/1. Students must reply within 4 weeks of notification.

CONTACT Lisa L. Tumer, Director of Financial Aid and Scholarships, James Madison University, 800 South Main Street, MSC 3519, Harrisonburg, VA 22807, 540-568-7820. *Fax:* 540-568-7994. *E-mail:* fin_aid@jmu.edu.

JAMESTOWN COLLEGE

Jamestown, ND

Tuition & fees: $15,585 **Average undergraduate aid package: $11,107**

ABOUT THE INSTITUTION Independent Presbyterian, coed. ***Awards:*** bachelor's degrees. 40 undergraduate majors. ***Total enrollment:*** 1,025. Undergraduates: 1,025. Freshmen: 271. Both federal and institutional methodology are used as a basis for awarding need-based institutional aid.

UNDERGRADUATE EXPENSES for 2009–10 ***Application fee:*** $20. ***Comprehensive fee:*** $20,740 includes full-time tuition ($15,585) and room and board ($5155). ***College room only:*** $2195. ***Part-time tuition:*** $350 per credit. ***Part-time fees:*** $200 per year.

FRESHMAN FINANCIAL AID (Fall 2008, est.) 232 applied for aid; of those 77% were deemed to have need. 100% of freshmen with need received aid; of those 27% had need fully met. ***Average percent of need met:*** 85% (excluding resources awarded to replace EFC). ***Average financial aid package:*** $12,497 (excluding resources awarded to replace EFC). 33% of all full-time freshmen had no need and received non-need-based gift aid.

UNDERGRADUATE FINANCIAL AID (Fall 2008, est.) 775 applied for aid; of those 77% were deemed to have need. 100% of undergraduates with need received aid; of those 24% had need fully met. ***Average percent of need met:*** 80% (excluding resources awarded to replace EFC). ***Average financial aid package:*** $11,107 (excluding resources awarded to replace EFC). 33% of all full-time undergraduates had no need and received non-need-based gift aid.

GIFT AID (NEED-BASED) ***Total amount:*** $3,844,851 (29% federal, 3% state, 60% institutional, 8% external sources). ***Receiving aid:*** Freshmen: 65% (179); all full-time undergraduates: 61% (585). ***Average award:*** Freshmen: $9416; Undergraduates: $7416. ***Scholarships, grants, and awards:*** Federal Pell, FSEOG, state, private, college/university gift aid from institutional funds, Federal Nursing, National Smart Grant, Academic Competitiveness Grant.

GIFT AID (NON-NEED-BASED) ***Total amount:*** $1,837,749 (1% state, 85% institutional, 14% external sources). ***Receiving aid:*** Freshmen: 14% (39). Undergraduates: 10% (96). ***Average award:*** Freshmen: $5472. Undergraduates: $4456. ***Scholarships, grants, and awards by category:*** *Academic interests/achievement:* 312 awards ($1,242,705 total): general academic interests/achievements, physical sciences. *Creative arts/performance:* 25 awards ($36,500 total): art/fine arts, music, theater/drama. *Special achievements/activities:* 103 awards ($73,461 total): leadership. *Special characteristics:* 23 awards ($262,590 total): children of faculty/staff, general special characteristics, international students, relatives of clergy, religious affiliation, siblings of current students, spouses of current students.

LOANS ***Student loans:*** $5,462,003 (54% need-based, 46% non-need-based). 87% of past graduating class borrowed through all loan programs. *Average indebtedness per student:* $25,725. ***Average need-based loan:*** Freshmen: $3662. Undergraduates: $4251. ***Parent loans:*** $343,997 (16% need-based, 84% non-need-based). ***Programs:*** FFEL (Subsidized and Unsubsidized Stafford, PLUS), Perkins, college/university, alternative loans.

WORK-STUDY ***Federal work-study:*** Total amount: $188,908; 251 jobs averaging $1072. ***State or other work-study/employment:*** Total amount: $55,610 (100% non-need-based). 68 part-time jobs averaging $818.

ATHLETIC AWARDS Total amount: $1,022,406 (54% need-based, 46% non-need-based).

APPLYING FOR FINANCIAL AID ***Required financial aid form:*** FAFSA. ***Financial aid deadline (priority):*** 3/15. ***Notification date:*** Continuous beginning 4/1. Students must reply within 3 weeks of notification.

CONTACT Margery Michael, Director of Financial Aid, Jamestown College, 6085 College Lane, Jamestown, ND 58405, 701-252-3467 Ext. 5568 or toll-free 800-336-2554. *Fax:* 701-253-4318. *E-mail:* mmichael@jc.edu.

JARVIS CHRISTIAN COLLEGE

Hawkins, TX

Tuition & fees: $8208 **Average undergraduate aid package: $10,263**

ABOUT THE INSTITUTION Independent religious, coed. ***Awards:*** bachelor's degrees. 17 undergraduate majors. ***Total enrollment:*** 727. Undergraduates: 727. Freshmen: 148. Federal methodology is used as a basis for awarding need-based institutional aid.

UNDERGRADUATE EXPENSES for 2009–10 ***Application fee:*** $25. ***One-time required fee:*** $25. ***Comprehensive fee:*** $13,162 includes full-time tuition ($7416), mandatory fees ($792), and room and board ($4954). ***College room only:*** $2472. ***Part-time tuition:*** $309 per semester hour.

FRESHMAN FINANCIAL AID (Fall 2008, est.) 121 applied for aid; of those 100% were deemed to have need. 100% of freshmen with need received aid; of those 17% had need fully met. ***Average percent of need met:*** 92% (excluding resources awarded to replace EFC). ***Average financial aid package:*** $9357 (excluding resources awarded to replace EFC).

UNDERGRADUATE FINANCIAL AID (Fall 2008, est.) 542 applied for aid; of those 100% were deemed to have need. 100% of undergraduates with need received aid; of those 75% had need fully met. ***Average percent of need met:*** 81% (excluding resources awarded to replace EFC). ***Average financial aid package:*** $10,263 (excluding resources awarded to replace EFC). 1% of all full-time undergraduates had no need and received non-need-based gift aid.

GIFT AID (NEED-BASED) ***Total amount:*** $2,817,589 (71% federal, 29% state). ***Receiving aid:*** Freshmen: 92% (116); all full-time undergraduates: 81% (459). ***Average award:*** Freshmen: $6956; Undergraduates: $8580. ***Scholarships, grants, and awards:*** Federal Pell, FSEOG, state, private.

GIFT AID (NON-NEED-BASED) ***Total amount:*** $795,147 (75% institutional, 25% external sources). ***Receiving aid:*** Freshmen: 17% (21). Undergraduates: 36% (206). ***Average award:*** Undergraduates: $13,078. ***Scholarships, grants, and awards by category:*** *Academic interests/achievement:* 89 awards ($619,697 total): education, general academic interests/achievements. *Special characteristics:* 8 awards ($38,999 total): religious affiliation.

LOANS ***Student loans:*** $3,163,980 (54% need-based, 46% non-need-based). 82% of past graduating class borrowed through all loan programs. *Average indebtedness per student:* $19,000. ***Average need-based loan:*** Freshmen: $3078. Undergraduates: $8926. ***Parent loans:*** $640,685 (100% non-need-based). ***Programs:*** Federal Direct (Subsidized and Unsubsidized Stafford, PLUS), FFEL (Subsidized and Unsubsidized Stafford, PLUS), Perkins.

WORK-STUDY ***Federal work-study:*** Total amount: $185,781; 129 jobs averaging $1440. ***State or other work-study/employment:*** Total amount: $5426 (100% need-based). 3 part-time jobs averaging $1809.

ATHLETIC AWARDS Total amount: $325,395 (100% non-need-based).

APPLYING FOR FINANCIAL AID ***Required financial aid form:*** FAFSA. ***Financial aid deadline (priority):*** 4/1. ***Notification date:*** Continuous beginning 5/1. Students must reply within 2 weeks of notification.

CONTACT Alice Copeland, Assistant Director of Financial Aid, Jarvis Christian College, PO Box 1470, Hawkins, TX 75765, 903-769-5733. *Fax:* 903-769-1282. *E-mail:* Alice.Copeland@jarvis.edu.

JEFFERSON COLLEGE OF HEALTH SCIENCES

Roanoke, VA

CONTACT Debra A. Johnson, Director of Financial Aid, Jefferson College of Health Sciences, 920 South Jefferson Street, PO Box 13186, Roanoke, VA 24031-3186, 540-985-8492 or toll-free 888-985-8483. *Fax:* 540-224-6916. *E-mail:* djohnson@jchs.edu.

THE JEWISH THEOLOGICAL SEMINARY

New York, NY

ABOUT THE INSTITUTION Independent Jewish, coed. ***Awards:*** bachelor's, master's, doctoral, and first professional degrees (double bachelor's degree with Barnard College, Columbia University, joint bachelor's degree with Columbia University). 12 undergraduate majors. ***Total enrollment:*** 566. Undergraduates: 190. Freshmen: 46.

GIFT AID (NEED-BASED) ***Scholarships, grants, and awards:*** Federal Pell, state, private, college/university gift aid from institutional funds.

GIFT AID (NON-NEED-BASED) ***Scholarships, grants, and awards by category:*** *Academic interests/achievement:* general academic interests/achievements.

LOANS ***Programs:*** Federal Direct (Subsidized and Unsubsidized Stafford), FFEL (Subsidized and Unsubsidized Stafford, PLUS), college/university.

APPLYING FOR FINANCIAL AID ***Required financial aid forms:*** FAFSA, institution's own form, CSS Financial Aid PROFILE, state aid form, noncustodial (divorced/separated) parent's statement.

CONTACT Linda Levine, Registrar/Director of Financial Aid, The Jewish Theological Seminary, 3080 Broadway, New York, NY 10027-4649, 212-678-8007. *Fax:* 212-678-8947. *E-mail:* financialaid@jtsa.edu.

JOHN BROWN UNIVERSITY

Siloam Springs, AR

Tuition & fees: $18,066 **Average undergraduate aid package: $13,260**

ABOUT THE INSTITUTION Independent interdenominational, coed. ***Awards:*** associate, bachelor's, and master's degrees. 57 undergraduate majors. ***Total enrollment:*** 2,017. Undergraduates: 1,709. Freshmen: 310. Federal methodology is used as a basis for awarding need-based institutional aid.

UNDERGRADUATE EXPENSES for 2008–09 ***Application fee:*** $25. ***One-time required fee:*** $25. ***Comprehensive fee:*** $24,646 includes full-time tuition ($17,256), mandatory fees ($810), and room and board ($6580). Full-time tuition and fees vary according to course load. Room and board charges vary according to board plan and housing facility. ***Part-time tuition:*** $720 per credit hour. Part-time tuition and fees vary according to course load. ***Payment plan:*** Installment.

FRESHMAN FINANCIAL AID (Fall 2008, est.) 235 applied for aid; of those 83% were deemed to have need. 100% of freshmen with need received aid; of those 6% had need fully met. ***Average percent of need met:*** 50% (excluding resources awarded to replace EFC). ***Average financial aid package:*** $16,453 (excluding resources awarded to replace EFC). 19% of all full-time freshmen had no need and received non-need-based gift aid.

UNDERGRADUATE FINANCIAL AID (Fall 2008, est.) 1,116 applied for aid; of those 88% were deemed to have need. 100% of undergraduates with need received aid; of those 3% had need fully met. ***Average percent of need met:*** 50% (excluding resources awarded to replace EFC). ***Average financial aid package:*** $13,260 (excluding resources awarded to replace EFC). 13% of all full-time undergraduates had no need and received non-need-based gift aid.

GIFT AID (NEED-BASED) ***Total amount:*** $7,794,910 (21% federal, 4% state, 67% institutional, 8% external sources). ***Receiving aid:*** Freshmen: 57% (176); all full-time undergraduates: 51% (818). ***Average award:*** Freshmen: $7462; Undergraduates: $8538. ***Scholarships, grants, and awards:*** Federal Pell, FSEOG, state, private, college/university gift aid from institutional funds.

GIFT AID (NON-NEED-BASED) ***Total amount:*** $2,202,832 (8% state, 79% institutional, 13% external sources). ***Receiving aid:*** Freshmen: 42% (131). Undergraduates: 27% (433). ***Average award:*** Freshmen: $6210. Undergraduates: $5571. ***Scholarships, grants, and awards by category:*** *Academic interests/achievement:* general academic interests/achievements. *Creative arts/performance:* journalism/publications, music. *Special achievements/activities:* cheerleading/drum major, leadership. *Special characteristics:* children and siblings of alumni, children of educators, children of faculty/staff, ethnic background, international students, members of minority groups, relatives of clergy, siblings of current students. ***Tuition waivers:*** Full or partial for minority students, children of alumni, employees or children of employees, adult students, senior citizens. ***ROTC:*** Army cooperative, Air Force cooperative.

LOANS ***Student loans:*** $7,231,150 (92% need-based, 8% non-need-based). 60% of past graduating class borrowed through all loan programs. *Average indebtedness per student:* $20,704. ***Average need-based loan:*** Freshmen: $3261. Undergraduates: $4567. ***Parent loans:*** $1,337,690 (78% need-based, 22% non-need-based). ***Programs:*** FFEL (Subsidized and Unsubsidized Stafford, PLUS), Perkins, state.

WORK-STUDY ***Federal work-study:*** Total amount: $496,070; jobs available. ***State or other work-study/employment:*** Total amount: $427,740 (66% need-based, 34% non-need-based). Part-time jobs available (averaging $1318).

ATHLETIC AWARDS Total amount: $1,252,755 (26% need-based, 74% non-need-based).

APPLYING FOR FINANCIAL AID ***Required financial aid forms:*** FAFSA, institution's own form. ***Financial aid deadline (priority):*** 3/1. ***Notification date:*** Continuous beginning 3/1. Students must reply by 6/1 or within 4 weeks of notification.

CONTACT Mr. Kim Eldridge, Director of Student Financial Aid, John Brown University, 2000 West University Street, Siloam Springs, AR 72761-2121, 479-524-7424 or toll-free 877-JBU-INFO. *Fax:* 479-524-7405. *E-mail:* keldridg@jbu.edu.

JOHN CARROLL UNIVERSITY

University Heights, OH

Tuition & fees: $28,840 **Average undergraduate aid package: $21,262**

ABOUT THE INSTITUTION Independent Roman Catholic (Jesuit), coed. ***Awards:*** bachelor's and master's degrees. 50 undergraduate majors. ***Total enrollment:*** 3,826. Undergraduates: 3,117. Freshmen: 792. Federal methodology is used as a basis for awarding need-based institutional aid.

UNDERGRADUATE EXPENSES for 2009–10 ***One-time required fee:*** $325. ***Comprehensive fee:*** $37,170 includes full-time tuition ($27,940), mandatory fees ($900), and room and board ($8330). ***College room only:*** $4420. ***Part-time tuition:*** $873 per credit hour.

FRESHMAN FINANCIAL AID (Fall 2008, est.) 695 applied for aid; of those 84% were deemed to have need. 100% of freshmen with need received aid; of those 22% had need fully met. ***Average percent of need met:*** 90% (excluding resources awarded to replace EFC). ***Average financial aid package:*** $25,347 (excluding resources awarded to replace EFC). 24% of all full-time freshmen had no need and received non-need-based gift aid.

UNDERGRADUATE FINANCIAL AID (Fall 2008, est.) 2,454 applied for aid; of those 85% were deemed to have need. 100% of undergraduates with need received aid; of those 24% had need fully met. ***Average percent of need met:*** 83% (excluding resources awarded to replace EFC). ***Average financial aid package:*** $21,262 (excluding resources awarded to replace EFC). 27% of all full-time undergraduates had no need and received non-need-based gift aid.

GIFT AID (NEED-BASED) ***Total amount:*** $21,013,877 (14% federal, 13% state, 71% institutional, 2% external sources). ***Receiving aid:*** Freshmen: 74% (584); all full-time undergraduates: 68% (2,088). ***Average award:*** Freshmen: $19,700; Undergraduates: $16,956. ***Scholarships, grants, and awards:*** Federal Pell, FSEOG, state, private, college/university gift aid from institutional funds.

GIFT AID (NON-NEED-BASED) ***Total amount:*** $21,467,667 (2% state, 95% institutional, 3% external sources). ***Receiving aid:*** Freshmen: 11% (84). Undergraduates: 9% (269). ***Average award:*** Freshmen: $9592. Undergraduates: $8650. ***Scholarships, grants, and awards by category:*** *Academic interests/achievement:* biological sciences, business, communication, computer science, education, English, foreign languages, health fields, mathematics, military science, physical sciences, premedicine, religion/biblical studies, social sciences. *Special achievements/activities:* community service, leadership, religious involvement. *Special characteristics:* children of educators, children of faculty/staff, ethnic background, first-generation college students, veterans, veterans' children. ***ROTC:*** Army.

LOANS ***Student loans:*** $13,938,243 (91% need-based, 9% non-need-based). 75% of past graduating class borrowed through all loan programs. *Average indebtedness per student:* $19,079. ***Average need-based loan:*** Freshmen: $3171. Undergraduates: $4192. ***Parent loans:*** $5,023,847 (100% need-based). ***Programs:*** FFEL (Subsidized and Unsubsidized Stafford, PLUS), Perkins.

WORK-STUDY ***Federal work-study:*** Total amount: $1,477,592; 577 jobs averaging $2007. ***State or other work-study/employment:*** 57 part-time jobs available.

APPLYING FOR FINANCIAL AID ***Required financial aid form:*** FAFSA. ***Financial aid deadline:*** 3/15 (priority: 2/15). ***Notification date:*** Students must reply by 5/1.

CONTACT Patrick Prosser, Director of Financial Aid, John Carroll University, 20700 North Park Boulevard, University Heights, OH 44118-4581, 216-397-4248. *Fax:* 216-397-3098. *E-mail:* jcuofa@jcu.edu.

JOHN F. KENNEDY UNIVERSITY

Pleasant Hill, CA

ABOUT THE INSTITUTION Independent, coed, primarily women. ***Awards:*** bachelor's, master's, doctoral, and first professional degrees and post-bachelor's certificates. 7 undergraduate majors. ***Total enrollment:*** 1,580. Undergraduates: 287.

GIFT AID (NEED-BASED) ***Scholarships, grants, and awards:*** Federal Pell, FSEOG, state, private, college/university gift aid from institutional funds.

LOANS ***Programs:*** Federal Direct (Subsidized and Unsubsidized Stafford, PLUS), FFEL (Subsidized and Unsubsidized Stafford, PLUS), Perkins, college/university.

CONTACT Mindy Bergeron, Director of Financial Aid, John F. Kennedy University, 100 Ellinwood Way, Pleasant Hill, CA 94523, 925-969-3385 or toll-free 800-696-JFKU. *Fax:* 925-969-3390. *E-mail:* bergeron@jfku.edu.

JOHN JAY COLLEGE OF CRIMINAL JUSTICE OF THE CITY UNIVERSITY OF NEW YORK

New York, NY

Tuition & fees (NY res): $4330 **Average undergraduate aid package: $6672**

ABOUT THE INSTITUTION State and locally supported, coed. ***Awards:*** associate, bachelor's, and master's degrees. 16 undergraduate majors. ***Total enrollment:*** 14,844. Undergraduates: 12,943. Freshmen: 2,442. Federal methodology is used as a basis for awarding need-based institutional aid.

UNDERGRADUATE EXPENSES for 2008–09 ***Application fee:*** $65. ***Tuition, state resident:*** full-time $4000; part-time $170 per credit. ***Tuition, nonresident:*** full-time $10,800; part-time $360 per credit. ***Required fees:*** full-time $330; $104.85 per term. Full-time tuition and fees vary according to course level and course load. Part-time tuition and fees vary according to course level and course load. ***Payment plan:*** Installment.

FRESHMAN FINANCIAL AID (Fall 2007) 93% of freshmen with need received aid. ***Average percent of need met:*** 85% (excluding resources awarded to replace EFC). ***Average financial aid package:*** $6672 (excluding resources awarded to replace EFC).

UNDERGRADUATE FINANCIAL AID (Fall 2007) 9,140 applied for aid; of those 94% were deemed to have need. 93% of undergraduates with need received aid. ***Average percent of need met:*** 85% (excluding resources awarded to replace EFC). ***Average financial aid package:*** $6672 (excluding resources awarded to replace EFC). 13% of all full-time undergraduates had no need and received non-need-based gift aid.

GIFT AID (NEED-BASED) ***Total amount:*** $40,242,968 (55% federal, 41% state, 4% external sources). ***Receiving aid:*** Freshmen: 41% (1,193). ***Average award:*** Freshmen: $2926; Undergraduates: $2926. ***Scholarships, grants, and awards:*** Federal Pell, FSEOG, state, college/university gift aid from institutional funds.

GIFT AID (NON-NEED-BASED) ***Receiving aid:*** Freshmen: 4% (112). Undergraduates: 3% (300). ***Average award:*** Freshmen: $3299. Undergraduates: $3299. ***Scholarships, grants, and awards by category:*** *Academic interests/achievement:* general academic interests/achievements. ***Tuition waivers:*** Full or partial for senior citizens. ***ROTC:*** Air Force cooperative.

LOANS ***Student loans:*** $17,665,297 (94% need-based, 6% non-need-based). 46% of past graduating class borrowed through all loan programs. *Average indebtedness per student:* $14,000. ***Average need-based loan:*** Freshmen: $2331. Undergraduates: $2331. ***Parent loans:*** $328,135 (100% need-based). ***Programs:*** Federal Direct (Subsidized and Unsubsidized Stafford, PLUS), Perkins, alternative loans.

WORK-STUDY ***Federal work-study:*** Total amount: $353,818; 442 jobs averaging $1064. ***State or other work-study/employment:*** Part-time jobs available.

APPLYING FOR FINANCIAL AID ***Required financial aid form:*** FAFSA. ***Financial aid deadline (priority):*** 6/1. ***Notification date:*** Continuous beginning 7/15. Students must reply within 2 weeks of notification.

CONTACT Sylvia Lopez-Crespo, Director of Financial Aid, John Jay College of Criminal Justice of the City University of New York, 445 West 59th Street, New York, NY 10019-1093, 212-237-8897 or toll-free 877-JOHNJAY. *Fax:* 212-237-8936. *E-mail:* slopez@jjay.cuny.edu.

THE JOHNS HOPKINS UNIVERSITY

Baltimore, MD

Tuition & fees: $37,700 **Average undergraduate aid package: $31,130**

ABOUT THE INSTITUTION Independent, coed. ***Awards:*** bachelor's, master's, doctoral, and first professional degrees and post-bachelor's and post-master's certificates. 61 undergraduate majors. ***Total enrollment:*** 6,437. Undergraduates: 4,744. Freshmen: 1,236. Institutional methodology is used as a basis for awarding need-based institutional aid.

UNDERGRADUATE EXPENSES for 2008–09 ***Application fee:*** $70. ***One-time required fee:*** $500. ***Comprehensive fee:*** $49,278 includes full-time tuition ($37,700) and room and board ($11,578). ***College room only:*** $6618. Room and board charges vary according to board plan and housing facility. ***Part-time tuition:*** $1260 per credit. ***Payment plan:*** Installment.

FRESHMAN FINANCIAL AID (Fall 2008, est.) 819 applied for aid; of those 72% were deemed to have need. 97% of freshmen with need received aid; of those 97% had need fully met. ***Average percent of need met:*** 98% (excluding resources awarded to replace EFC). ***Average financial aid package:*** $30,002 (excluding resources awarded to replace EFC). 1% of all full-time freshmen had no need and received non-need-based gift aid.

UNDERGRADUATE FINANCIAL AID (Fall 2008, est.) 2,581 applied for aid; of those 83% were deemed to have need. 99% of undergraduates with need received aid; of those 99% had need fully met. ***Average percent of need met:*** 99% (excluding resources awarded to replace EFC). ***Average financial aid package:*** $31,130 (excluding resources awarded to replace EFC). 2% of all full-time undergraduates had no need and received non-need-based gift aid.

GIFT AID (NEED-BASED) ***Total amount:*** $53,011,177 (6% federal, 2% state, 89% institutional, 3% external sources). ***Receiving aid:*** Freshmen: 39% (477); all full-time undergraduates: 39% (1,847). ***Average award:*** Freshmen: $28,182; Undergraduates: $27,352. ***Scholarships, grants, and awards:*** Federal Pell, FSEOG, state, private, college/university gift aid from institutional funds.

GIFT AID (NON-NEED-BASED) ***Total amount:*** $4,538,942 (11% federal, 5% state, 66% institutional, 18% external sources). ***Receiving aid:*** Freshmen: 6% (79). Undergraduates: 6% (289). ***Average award:*** Freshmen: $25,406. Undergraduates: $24,789. ***Scholarships, grants, and awards by category:*** *Academic interests/achievement:* 84 awards ($2,086,200 total): engineering/technologies, general academic interests/achievements. *Special characteristics:* 117 awards ($3,581,121 total): children of faculty/staff, local/state students. ***Tuition waivers:*** Full or partial for employees or children of employees. ***ROTC:*** Army, Air Force cooperative.

LOANS ***Student loans:*** $12,592,414 (63% need-based, 37% non-need-based). 50% of past graduating class borrowed through all loan programs. *Average indebtedness per student:* $21,984. ***Average need-based loan:*** Freshmen: $3377. Undergraduates: $4637. ***Parent loans:*** $9,931,065 (12% need-based, 88% non-need-based). ***Programs:*** Federal Direct (Subsidized and Unsubsidized Stafford, PLUS), Perkins, college/university.

WORK-STUDY ***Federal work-study:*** Total amount: $3,815,954; 1,623 jobs averaging $2351.

ATHLETIC AWARDS Total amount: $1,262,790 (20% need-based, 80% non-need-based).

APPLYING FOR FINANCIAL AID ***Required financial aid forms:*** FAFSA, CSS Financial Aid PROFILE, noncustodial (divorced/separated) parent's statement, business/farm supplement, current year federal income tax form(s). ***Financial aid deadline:*** 3/1 (priority: 3/1). ***Notification date:*** 4/1. Students must reply by 5/1 or within 2 weeks of notification.

CONTACT Vincent Amoroso, Director of Student Financial Services, The Johns Hopkins University, 146 Garland Hall, Baltimore, MD 21218, 410-516-8028. *Fax:* 410-516-6015. *E-mail:* vamoros1@jhu.edu.

JOHNSON & WALES UNIVERSITY

Denver, CO

Tuition & fees: $22,585 **Average undergraduate aid package: $15,707**

ABOUT THE INSTITUTION Independent, coed. ***Awards:*** associate and bachelor's degrees. 18 undergraduate majors. ***Total enrollment:*** 1,466. Undergraduates: 1,466. Freshmen: 363. Federal methodology is used as a basis for awarding need-based institutional aid.

UNDERGRADUATE EXPENSES for 2008–09 ***Comprehensive fee:*** $30,541 includes full-time tuition ($21,297), mandatory fees ($1288), and room and board ($7956). ***Part-time tuition:*** $394 per quarter hour.

FRESHMAN FINANCIAL AID (Fall 2008, est.) 377 applied for aid; of those 78% were deemed to have need. 100% of freshmen with need received aid; of those 10% had need fully met. ***Average percent of need met:*** 66% (excluding resources awarded to replace EFC). ***Average financial aid package:*** $16,291 (excluding resources awarded to replace EFC). 19% of all full-time freshmen had no need and received non-need-based gift aid.

UNDERGRADUATE FINANCIAL AID (Fall 2008, est.) 1,348 applied for aid; of those 73% were deemed to have need. 100% of undergraduates with need received aid; of those 12% had need fully met. ***Average percent of need met:*** 70% (excluding resources awarded to replace EFC). ***Average financial aid package:*** $15,707 (excluding resources awarded to replace EFC). 21% of all full-time undergraduates had no need and received non-need-based gift aid.

GIFT AID (NEED-BASED) ***Total amount:*** $5,539,181 (31% federal, 69% institutional). ***Receiving aid:*** Freshmen: 68% (268); all full-time undergraduates: 59% (830). ***Average award:*** Freshmen: $7226; Undergraduates: $6379. ***Scholarships, grants, and awards:*** Federal Pell, FSEOG, state, private, college/university gift aid from institutional funds.

GIFT AID (NON-NEED-BASED) ***Total amount:*** $6,394,159 (91% institutional, 9% external sources). ***Receiving aid:*** Freshmen: 64% (253). Undergraduates: 56% (795). ***Average award:*** Freshmen: $6025. Undergraduates: $5384. ***Scholarships, grants, and awards by category:*** *Academic interests/achievement:* general academic interests/achievements. *Special achievements/activities:* memberships. *Special characteristics:* children of faculty/staff.

LOANS ***Student loans:*** $11,147,873 (78% need-based, 22% non-need-based). 82% of past graduating class borrowed through all loan programs. *Average indebtedness per student:* $28,354. ***Average need-based loan:*** Freshmen: $3260. Undergraduates: $4876. ***Parent loans:*** $2,197,250 (100% non-need-based). ***Programs:*** FFEL (Subsidized and Unsubsidized Stafford, PLUS), Perkins, state, college/university.

WORK-STUDY ***Federal work-study:*** Total amount: $925,773; jobs available.

APPLYING FOR FINANCIAL AID ***Required financial aid form:*** FAFSA. ***Financial aid deadline:*** Continuous. ***Notification date:*** Continuous beginning 3/1.

CONTACT Ms. Lynn Robinson, Director of Financial Aid, Johnson & Wales University, 8 Abbott Park Place, Providence, RI 02903, 401-598-4648 or toll-free 877-598-3368. *Fax:* 401-598-1040. *E-mail:* fp@jwu.edu.

JOHNSON & WALES UNIVERSITY

North Miami, FL

Tuition & fees: $22,585 **Average undergraduate aid package: $17,578**

ABOUT THE INSTITUTION Independent, coed. ***Awards:*** associate and bachelor's degrees. 16 undergraduate majors. ***Total enrollment:*** 1,955. Undergraduates: 1,955. Freshmen: 539. Federal methodology is used as a basis for awarding need-based institutional aid.

UNDERGRADUATE EXPENSES for 2008–09 ***Comprehensive fee:*** $30,541 includes full-time tuition ($21,297), mandatory fees ($1288), and room and board ($7956). ***Part-time tuition:*** $394 per quarter hour.

FRESHMAN FINANCIAL AID (Fall 2008, est.) 563 applied for aid; of those 88% were deemed to have need. 100% of freshmen with need received aid; of those 5% had need fully met. ***Average percent of need met:*** 66% (excluding resources

awarded to replace EFC). ***Average financial aid package:*** $18,267 (excluding resources awarded to replace EFC). 10% of all full-time freshmen had no need and received non-need-based gift aid.

UNDERGRADUATE FINANCIAL AID (Fall 2008, est.) 1,776 applied for aid; of those 81% were deemed to have need. 100% of undergraduates with need received aid; of those 6% had need fully met. ***Average percent of need met:*** 68% (excluding resources awarded to replace EFC). ***Average financial aid package:*** $17,578 (excluding resources awarded to replace EFC). 13% of all full-time undergraduates had no need and received non-need-based gift aid.

GIFT AID (NEED-BASED) ***Total amount:*** $10,940,422 (38% federal, 5% state, 57% institutional). ***Receiving aid:*** Freshmen: 80% (465); all full-time undergraduates: 73% (1,349). ***Average award:*** Freshmen: $8864; Undergraduates: $7915. ***Scholarships, grants, and awards:*** Federal Pell, FSEOG, state, private, college/university gift aid from institutional funds.

GIFT AID (NON-NEED-BASED) ***Total amount:*** $6,599,911 (6% state, 84% institutional, 10% external sources). ***Receiving aid:*** Freshmen: 71% (410). Undergraduates: 54% (1,008). ***Average award:*** Freshmen: $5250. Undergraduates: $4710. ***Scholarships, grants, and awards by category:*** *Academic interests/achievement:* general academic interests/achievements. *Special achievements/activities:* memberships. *Special characteristics:* children of faculty/staff.

LOANS ***Student loans:*** $16,224,633 (87% need-based, 13% non-need-based). 79% of past graduating class borrowed through all loan programs. *Average indebtedness per student:* $33,501. ***Average need-based loan:*** Freshmen: $3393. Undergraduates: $5479. ***Parent loans:*** $2,479,950 (100% non-need-based). ***Programs:*** FFEL (Subsidized and Unsubsidized Stafford, PLUS), Perkins, state, college/university.

WORK-STUDY ***Federal work-study:*** Total amount: $1,538,667; jobs available. ***State or other work-study/employment:*** Part-time jobs available.

APPLYING FOR FINANCIAL AID ***Required financial aid form:*** FAFSA. ***Financial aid deadline:*** Continuous. ***Notification date:*** Continuous beginning 3/1.

CONTACT Ms. Lynn Robinson, Director of Financial Aid, Johnson & Wales University, 8 Abbott Park Place, Providence, RI 02903, 401-598-4648 or toll-free 800-232-2433. *Fax:* 401-598-1040. *E-mail:* fp@jwu.edu.

JOHNSON & WALES UNIVERSITY

Providence, RI

Tuition & fees: $22,585 **Average undergraduate aid package: $14,986**

ABOUT THE INSTITUTION Independent, coed. ***Awards:*** associate, bachelor's, master's, and doctoral degrees and post-master's certificates (branch locations in Charleston, SC; Denver, CO; North Miami, FL; Norfolk, VA; Gothenberg, Sweden). 40 undergraduate majors. ***Total enrollment:*** 10,105. Undergraduates: 9,053. Freshmen: 2,342. Federal methodology is used as a basis for awarding need-based institutional aid.

UNDERGRADUATE EXPENSES for 2008–09 ***Comprehensive fee:*** $31,477 includes full-time tuition ($21,297), mandatory fees ($1288), and room and board ($8892). ***Part-time tuition:*** $394 per quarter hour.

FRESHMAN FINANCIAL AID (Fall 2008, est.) 2,364 applied for aid; of those 76% were deemed to have need. 100% of freshmen with need received aid; of those 8% had need fully met. ***Average percent of need met:*** 66% (excluding resources awarded to replace EFC). ***Average financial aid package:*** $15,862 (excluding resources awarded to replace EFC). 20% of all full-time freshmen had no need and received non-need-based gift aid.

UNDERGRADUATE FINANCIAL AID (Fall 2008, est.) 7,900 applied for aid; of those 72% were deemed to have need. 100% of undergraduates with need received aid; of those 9% had need fully met. ***Average percent of need met:*** 68% (excluding resources awarded to replace EFC). ***Average financial aid package:*** $14,986 (excluding resources awarded to replace EFC). 17% of all full-time undergraduates had no need and received non-need-based gift aid.

GIFT AID (NEED-BASED) ***Total amount:*** $34,326,549 (28% federal, 3% state, 69% institutional). ***Receiving aid:*** Freshmen: 63% (1,575); all full-time undergraduates: 57% (4,846). ***Average award:*** Freshmen: $7848; Undergraduates: $6853. ***Scholarships, grants, and awards:*** Federal Pell, FSEOG, state, private, college/university gift aid from institutional funds.

GIFT AID (NON-NEED-BASED) ***Total amount:*** $25,601,342 (86% institutional, 14% external sources). ***Receiving aid:*** Freshmen: 56% (1,387). Undergraduates: 44% (3,760). ***Average award:*** Freshmen: $4878. Undergraduates: $4267. ***Scholarships, grants, and awards by category:*** *Academic interests/achievement:* general academic interests/achievements. *Special achievements/activities:* memberships. *Special characteristics:* children of faculty/staff.

LOANS ***Student loans:*** $69,704,936 (73% need-based, 27% non-need-based). 82% of past graduating class borrowed through all loan programs. *Average indebtedness per student:* $28,195. ***Average need-based loan:*** Freshmen: $3272. Undergraduates: $5147. ***Parent loans:*** $17,672,661 (100% non-need-based). ***Programs:*** FFEL (Subsidized and Unsubsidized Stafford, PLUS), Perkins, state, college/university.

WORK-STUDY ***Federal work-study:*** Total amount: $5,221,674; jobs available.

APPLYING FOR FINANCIAL AID ***Required financial aid form:*** FAFSA. ***Financial aid deadline:*** Continuous. ***Notification date:*** Continuous beginning 3/1.

CONTACT Ms. Lynn Robinson, Director of Financial Aid, Johnson & Wales University, 8 Abbott Park Place, Providence, RI 02903, 401-598-4648 or toll-free 800-598-1000 (in-state), 800-342-5598 (out-of-state). *Fax:* 401-598-1040.

JOHNSON & WALES UNIVERSITY—CHARLOTTE CAMPUS

Charlotte, NC

Tuition & fees: $22,585 **Average undergraduate aid package: $16,503**

ABOUT THE INSTITUTION Independent, coed. ***Awards:*** associate and bachelor's degrees. 13 undergraduate majors. ***Total enrollment:*** 2,569. Undergraduates: 2,569. Freshmen: 722. Federal methodology is used as a basis for awarding need-based institutional aid.

UNDERGRADUATE EXPENSES for 2008–09 ***Comprehensive fee:*** $31,477 includes full-time tuition ($21,297), mandatory fees ($1288), and room and board ($8892). ***Part-time tuition:*** $394 per quarter hour.

FRESHMAN FINANCIAL AID (Fall 2008, est.) 626 applied for aid; of those 83% were deemed to have need. 100% of freshmen with need received aid; of those 7% had need fully met. ***Average percent of need met:*** 66% (excluding resources awarded to replace EFC). ***Average financial aid package:*** $17,327 (excluding resources awarded to replace EFC). 15% of all full-time freshmen had no need and received non-need-based gift aid.

UNDERGRADUATE FINANCIAL AID (Fall 2008, est.) 2,306 applied for aid; of those 78% were deemed to have need. 100% of undergraduates with need received aid; of those 9% had need fully met. ***Average percent of need met:*** 70% (excluding resources awarded to replace EFC). ***Average financial aid package:*** $16,503 (excluding resources awarded to replace EFC). 16% of all full-time undergraduates had no need and received non-need-based gift aid.

GIFT AID (NEED-BASED) ***Total amount:*** $12,153,498 (30% federal, 10% state, 60% institutional). ***Receiving aid:*** Freshmen: 77% (488); all full-time undergraduates: 68% (1,627). ***Average award:*** Freshmen: $8733; Undergraduates: $7307. ***Scholarships, grants, and awards:*** Federal Pell, FSEOG, state, private, college/university gift aid from institutional funds.

GIFT AID (NON-NEED-BASED) ***Total amount:*** $9,472,225 (16% state, 78% institutional, 6% external sources). ***Receiving aid:*** Freshmen: 74% (466). Undergraduates: 63% (1,510). ***Average award:*** Freshmen: $4405. Undergraduates: $4668. ***Scholarships, grants, and awards by category:*** *Academic interests/achievement:* general academic interests/achievements. *Special achievements/activities:* memberships. *Special characteristics:* children of faculty/staff.

LOANS ***Student loans:*** $20,108,421 (81% need-based, 19% non-need-based). 85% of past graduating class borrowed through all loan programs. *Average indebtedness per student:* $27,500. ***Average need-based loan:*** Freshmen: $3314. Undergraduates: $5105. ***Parent loans:*** $4,459,574 (100% non-need-based). ***Programs:*** FFEL (Subsidized and Unsubsidized Stafford, PLUS), Perkins, state, college/university.

WORK-STUDY ***Federal work-study:*** Total amount: $1,490,117; jobs available.

APPLYING FOR FINANCIAL AID ***Required financial aid form:*** FAFSA. ***Financial aid deadline:*** Continuous. ***Notification date:*** Continuous beginning 3/1.

CONTACT Ms. Lynn Robinson, Director of Financial Aid, Johnson & Wales University—Charlotte Campus, 8 Abbott Park Place, Providence, RI 02903, 401-598-1648 or toll-free 866-598-2427. *Fax:* 401-598-4751. *E-mail:* fp@jwu.edu.

JOHNSON BIBLE COLLEGE

Knoxville, TN

Tuition & fees: $8550 **Average undergraduate aid package: $7859**

ABOUT THE INSTITUTION Independent religious, coed. ***Awards:*** associate, bachelor's, and master's degrees. 6 undergraduate majors. ***Total enrollment:***

801. Undergraduates: 685. Freshmen: 119. Institutional methodology is used as a basis for awarding need-based institutional aid.

UNDERGRADUATE EXPENSES for 2008–09 ***Application fee:*** $35. ***Comprehensive fee:*** $13,440 includes full-time tuition ($7780), mandatory fees ($770), and room and board ($4890). ***College room only:*** $2250. Room and board charges vary according to board plan and housing facility. ***Part-time tuition:*** $290 per semester hour. ***Part-time fees:*** $32 per semester hour. Part-time tuition and fees vary according to course load. ***Payment plan:*** Installment.

FRESHMAN FINANCIAL AID (Fall 2008, est.) 166 applied for aid; of those 81% were deemed to have need. 100% of freshmen with need received aid. ***Average percent of need met:*** 88% (excluding resources awarded to replace EFC). ***Average financial aid package:*** $7271 (excluding resources awarded to replace EFC).

UNDERGRADUATE FINANCIAL AID (Fall 2008, est.) 619 applied for aid; of those 84% were deemed to have need. 100% of undergraduates with need received aid. ***Average percent of need met:*** 93% (excluding resources awarded to replace EFC). ***Average financial aid package:*** $7859 (excluding resources awarded to replace EFC).

GIFT AID (NEED-BASED) ***Total amount:*** $6,362,312 (15% federal, 6% state, 79% institutional). ***Receiving aid:*** Freshmen: 70% (131); all full-time undergraduates: 73% (508). ***Average award:*** Freshmen: $3718; Undergraduates: $4042. ***Scholarships, grants, and awards:*** Federal Pell, FSEOG, state, private, college/university gift aid from institutional funds, Academic Competitiveness Grant.

GIFT AID (NON-NEED-BASED) ***Total amount:*** $657,412 (100% external sources). ***Receiving aid:*** Freshmen: 38% (70). Undergraduates: 35% (244). ***Scholarships, grants, and awards by category:*** *Academic interests/achievement:* 693 awards ($874,913 total): communication, education, general academic interests/achievements, religion/biblical studies. *Creative arts/performance:* 3 awards ($2500 total): art/fine arts, general creative arts/performance, music. *Special achievements/activities:* 148 awards ($75,550 total): community service, general special achievements/activities, leadership, religious involvement. *Special characteristics:* 268 awards ($278,258 total): children of current students, children of educators, children of faculty/staff, ethnic background, general special characteristics, international students, married students, members of minority groups, parents of current students, relatives of clergy, religious affiliation, siblings of current students, spouses of current students. ***Tuition waivers:*** Full or partial for employees or children of employees.

LOANS ***Student loans:*** $2,274,804 (49% need-based, 51% non-need-based). 74% of past graduating class borrowed through all loan programs. *Average indebtedness per student:* $18,424. ***Average need-based loan:*** Freshmen: $2618. Undergraduates: $3449. ***Parent loans:*** $366,000 (100% non-need-based). ***Programs:*** FFEL (Subsidized and Unsubsidized Stafford, PLUS), college/university, alternative loans.

WORK-STUDY ***Federal work-study:*** Total amount: $103,483; 111 jobs averaging $932.

APPLYING FOR FINANCIAL AID ***Required financial aid forms:*** FAFSA, institution's own form. ***Financial aid deadline (priority):*** 3/1. ***Notification date:*** Continuous beginning 4/15. Students must reply within 2 weeks of notification.

CONTACT Mrs. Janette Overton, Financial Aid Director, Johnson Bible College, 7900 Johnson Drive, Knoxville, TN 37998, 865-251-2303 Ext. 2292 or toll-free 800-827-2122. *Fax:* 865-251-2337. *E-mail:* joverton@jbc.edu.

JOHNSON C. SMITH UNIVERSITY

Charlotte, NC

Tuition & fees: $15,754 **Average undergraduate aid package: $14,800**

ABOUT THE INSTITUTION Independent, coed. ***Awards:*** bachelor's degrees. 28 undergraduate majors. ***Total enrollment:*** 1,571. Undergraduates: 1,571. Freshmen: 557. Federal methodology is used as a basis for awarding need-based institutional aid.

UNDERGRADUATE EXPENSES for 2008–09 ***Application fee:*** $25. ***Comprehensive fee:*** $21,886 includes full-time tuition ($13,361), mandatory fees ($2393), and room and board ($6132). ***College room only:*** $3529. Full-time tuition and fees vary according to course load. Room and board charges vary according to board plan and housing facility. ***Part-time tuition:*** $361 per credit hour. ***Part-time fees:*** $252.50 per term. Part-time tuition and fees vary according to course load. ***Payment plan:*** Installment.

FRESHMAN FINANCIAL AID (Fall 2007) 431 applied for aid; of those 94% were deemed to have need. 100% of freshmen with need received aid; of those .5% had need fully met. ***Average percent of need met:*** 59% (excluding resources awarded to replace EFC). ***Average financial aid package:*** $12,856 (excluding resources awarded to replace EFC).

UNDERGRADUATE FINANCIAL AID (Fall 2007) 1,216 applied for aid; of those 93% were deemed to have need. 100% of undergraduates with need received aid; of those 1% had need fully met. ***Average percent of need met:*** 68% (excluding resources awarded to replace EFC). ***Average financial aid package:*** $14,800 (excluding resources awarded to replace EFC). 1% of all full-time undergraduates had no need and received non-need-based gift aid.

GIFT AID (NEED-BASED) ***Total amount:*** $5,532,664 (66% federal, 12% state, 18% institutional, 4% external sources). ***Receiving aid:*** Freshmen: 63% (317); all full-time undergraduates: 58% (831). ***Average award:*** Freshmen: $4493; Undergraduates: $4700. ***Scholarships, grants, and awards:*** Federal Pell, FSEOG, state, private, college/university gift aid from institutional funds, United Negro College Fund.

GIFT AID (NON-NEED-BASED) ***Total amount:*** $1,003,514 (58% state, 42% institutional). ***Receiving aid:*** Freshmen: 50% (249). Undergraduates: 29% (408). ***Average award:*** Freshmen: $21,886. Undergraduates: $21,886. ***Scholarships, grants, and awards by category:*** *Academic interests/achievement:* computer science, general academic interests/achievements, mathematics. *Creative arts/performance:* music. *Special achievements/activities:* community service, general special achievements/activities, leadership. *Special characteristics:* children of faculty/staff, ethnic background, siblings of current students. ***Tuition waivers:*** Full or partial for employees or children of employees. ***ROTC:*** Army, Air Force cooperative.

LOANS ***Student loans:*** $10,844,669 (100% need-based). 84% of past graduating class borrowed through all loan programs. *Average indebtedness per student:* $34,308. ***Average need-based loan:*** Freshmen: $3500. Undergraduates: $5000. ***Parent loans:*** $8,904,651 (100% need-based). ***Programs:*** Federal Direct (Subsidized and Unsubsidized Stafford, PLUS), FFEL (PLUS), Perkins, alternative loans.

WORK-STUDY ***Federal work-study:*** Total amount: $443,547; jobs available. ***State or other work-study/employment:*** Total amount: $203,217 (100% non-need-based). Part-time jobs available.

ATHLETIC AWARDS Total amount: $1,355,835 (100% need-based).

APPLYING FOR FINANCIAL AID ***Required financial aid form:*** FAFSA. ***Financial aid deadline (priority):*** 3/1. ***Notification date:*** Continuous beginning 3/1. Students must reply within 2 weeks of notification.

CONTACT Ms. Keisha Ramey, Director of Financial Aid, Johnson C. Smith University, 100 Beatties Ford Road, Charlotte, NC 28216, 704-378-1207 or toll-free 800-782-7303. *Fax:* 704-378-1292. *E-mail:* kramey@jcsu.edu.

JOHNSON STATE COLLEGE

Johnson, VT

CONTACT Ms. Kimberly Goodell, Financial Aid Officer, Johnson State College, 337 College Hill, Johnson, VT 05656-9405, 802-635-2356 or toll-free 800-635-2356. *Fax:* 802-635-1463. *E-mail:* goodellk@badger.jsc.vsc.edu.

JOHN WESLEY COLLEGE

High Point, NC

ABOUT THE INSTITUTION Independent interdenominational, coed. ***Awards:*** associate and bachelor's degrees. 10 undergraduate majors. ***Total enrollment:*** 78. Undergraduates: 78. Freshmen: 8.

GIFT AID (NEED-BASED) ***Scholarships, grants, and awards:*** Federal Pell, FSEOG, private, college/university gift aid from institutional funds.

GIFT AID (NON-NEED-BASED) ***Scholarships, grants, and awards by category:*** *Academic interests/achievement:* education, general academic interests/achievements, religion/biblical studies. *Special achievements/activities:* religious involvement. *Special characteristics:* children of faculty/staff, general special characteristics, married students, spouses of current students.

LOANS ***Programs:*** FFEL (Subsidized and Unsubsidized Stafford, PLUS).

WORK-STUDY ***Federal work-study:*** Total amount: $15,100; 5 jobs averaging $3500.

APPLYING FOR FINANCIAL AID ***Required financial aid forms:*** FAFSA, institution's own form.

CONTACT Mrs. Shirley Carter, Director of Financial Aid, John Wesley College, 2314 North Centennial Street, High Point, NC 27265-3197, 336-889-2262. *Fax:* 336-889-2261. *E-mail:* scarter@johnwesley.edu.

JONES COLLEGE

Jacksonville, FL

CONTACT Mrs. Becky Davis, Director of Financial Assistance, Jones College, 5353 Arlington Expressway, Jacksonville, FL 32211-5540, 904-743-1122. *Fax:* 904-743-4446.

JONES COLLEGE

Miami, FL

CONTACT Financial Aid Office, Jones College, 11430 North Kendall Drive, Suite 200, Miami, FL 33176, 305-275-9996.

JONES INTERNATIONAL UNIVERSITY

Centennial, CO

CONTACT Steve Bidwell, Director of Financial And Accounting, Jones International University, 9697 East Mineral Avenue, Englewood, CO 80112, 303-784-8284 or toll-free 800-811-5663. *Fax:* 303-784-8524. *E-mail:* marketing@jonesknowledge.com.

JUDSON COLLEGE

Marion, AL

Tuition & fees: $12,547 **Average undergraduate aid package: $13,766**

ABOUT THE INSTITUTION Independent Baptist, women only. ***Awards:*** bachelor's degrees. 19 undergraduate majors. ***Total enrollment:*** 324. Undergraduates: 324. Freshmen: 95.

UNDERGRADUATE EXPENSES for 2009–10 ***Application fee:*** $35. ***Comprehensive fee:*** $20,516 includes full-time tuition ($12,327), mandatory fees ($220), and room and board ($7969). ***Part-time tuition:*** $410 per semester hour.

FRESHMAN FINANCIAL AID (Fall 2008, est.) 87 applied for aid; of those 84% were deemed to have need. 100% of freshmen with need received aid; of those 22% had need fully met. ***Average percent of need met:*** 79% (excluding resources awarded to replace EFC). ***Average financial aid package:*** $14,507 (excluding resources awarded to replace EFC). 16% of all full-time freshmen had no need and received non-need-based gift aid.

UNDERGRADUATE FINANCIAL AID (Fall 2008, est.) 205 applied for aid; of those 91% were deemed to have need. 100% of undergraduates with need received aid; of those 22% had need fully met. ***Average percent of need met:*** 85% (excluding resources awarded to replace EFC). ***Average financial aid package:*** $13,766 (excluding resources awarded to replace EFC). 21% of all full-time undergraduates had no need and received non-need-based gift aid.

GIFT AID (NEED-BASED) ***Total amount:*** $1,602,192 (28% federal, 8% state, 55% institutional, 9% external sources). ***Receiving aid:*** Freshmen: 76% (71); all full-time undergraduates: 77% (181). ***Average award:*** Freshmen: $10,923; Undergraduates: $9189. ***Scholarships, grants, and awards:*** Federal Pell, FSEOG, state, private, college/university gift aid from institutional funds, Academic Competitiveness Grant, National Smart Grant, TEACH Grant.

GIFT AID (NON-NEED-BASED) ***Total amount:*** $385,427 (10% state, 85% institutional, 5% external sources). ***Receiving aid:*** Freshmen: 9% (8). Undergraduates: 10% (23). ***Average award:*** Freshmen: $6910. Undergraduates: $6617. ***Scholarships, grants, and awards by category:*** *Academic interests/achievement:* 55 awards ($298,000 total): biological sciences, general academic interests/achievements, premedicine. *Creative arts/performance:* 20 awards ($19,000 total): art/fine arts, music. *Special achievements/activities:* 8 awards ($6000 total): general special achievements/activities. *Special characteristics:* 35 awards ($197,000 total): children of educators, children of faculty/staff, relatives of clergy, religious affiliation. ***ROTC:*** Army cooperative.

LOANS ***Student loans:*** $1,010,305 (51% need-based, 49% non-need-based). 74% of past graduating class borrowed through all loan programs. *Average indebtedness per student:* $17,158. ***Average need-based loan:*** Freshmen: $3440. Undergraduates: $3864. ***Parent loans:*** $212,669 (63% need-based, 37% non-need-based). ***Programs:*** FFEL (Subsidized and Unsubsidized Stafford, PLUS), Perkins, college/university.

WORK-STUDY ***Federal work-study:*** Total amount: $98,255; 63 jobs averaging $1600. ***State or other work-study/employment:*** Total amount: $57,534 (79% need-based, 21% non-need-based). 40 part-time jobs averaging $1430.

ATHLETIC AWARDS Total amount: $228,750 (69% need-based, 31% non-need-based).

APPLYING FOR FINANCIAL AID ***Required financial aid forms:*** FAFSA, institution's own form, state aid form. ***Financial aid deadline (priority):*** 3/1. ***Notification date:*** Continuous beginning 3/15. Students must reply within 2 weeks of notification.

CONTACT Mrs. Doris A. Wilson, Director of Financial Aid, Judson College, PO Box 120, Marion, AL 36756, 334-683-5157 or toll-free 800-447-9472. *Fax:* 334-683-5282. *E-mail:* dwilson@judson.edu.

JUDSON UNIVERSITY

Elgin, IL

CONTACT Michael Davis, Director of Financial Aid, Judson University, 1151 North State Street, Elgin, IL 60123-1498, 847-628-2532 or toll-free 800-879-5376. *Fax:* 847-628-2533. *E-mail:* mdavis@judsoncollege.edu.

THE JUILLIARD SCHOOL

New York, NY

Tuition & fees: $28,640 **Average undergraduate aid package: $27,900**

ABOUT THE INSTITUTION Independent, coed. ***Awards:*** bachelor's, master's, and doctoral degrees and post-bachelor's and post-master's certificates. 4 undergraduate majors. ***Total enrollment:*** 842. Undergraduates: 500. Freshmen: 118. Federal methodology is used as a basis for awarding need-based institutional aid.

UNDERGRADUATE EXPENSES for 2008–09 ***Application fee:*** $100. ***Comprehensive fee:*** $39,890 includes full-time tuition ($28,640) and room and board ($11,250). Room and board charges vary according to housing facility. ***Payment plan:*** Installment.

FRESHMAN FINANCIAL AID (Fall 2008, est.) 113 applied for aid; of those 85% were deemed to have need. 100% of freshmen with need received aid; of those 30% had need fully met. ***Average percent of need met:*** 87% (excluding resources awarded to replace EFC). ***Average financial aid package:*** $28,400 (excluding resources awarded to replace EFC). 8% of all full-time freshmen had no need and received non-need-based gift aid.

UNDERGRADUATE FINANCIAL AID (Fall 2008, est.) 470 applied for aid; of those 79% were deemed to have need. 100% of undergraduates with need received aid; of those 23% had need fully met. ***Average percent of need met:*** 83% (excluding resources awarded to replace EFC). ***Average financial aid package:*** $27,900 (excluding resources awarded to replace EFC). 9% of all full-time undergraduates had no need and received non-need-based gift aid.

GIFT AID (NEED-BASED) ***Total amount:*** $8,266,925 (6% federal, 1% state, 91% institutional, 2% external sources). ***Receiving aid:*** Freshmen: 81% (96); all full-time undergraduates: 75% (373). ***Average award:*** Freshmen: $23,776; Undergraduates: $22,030. ***Scholarships, grants, and awards:*** Federal Pell, FSEOG, state, private, college/university gift aid from institutional funds.

GIFT AID (NON-NEED-BASED) ***Total amount:*** $575,478 (96% institutional, 4% external sources). ***Average award:*** Freshmen: $15,700. Undergraduates: $12,600. ***Scholarships, grants, and awards by category:*** *Academic interests/achievement:* general academic interests/achievements. *Creative arts/performance:* dance, music, performing arts, theater/drama. ***Tuition waivers:*** Full or partial for employees or children of employees.

LOANS ***Student loans:*** $1,846,249 (88% need-based, 12% non-need-based). 71% of past graduating class borrowed through all loan programs. *Average indebtedness per student:* $26,000. ***Average need-based loan:*** Freshmen: $1980. Undergraduates: $5662. ***Parent loans:*** $762,775 (68% need-based, 32% non-need-based). ***Programs:*** Federal Direct (Subsidized and Unsubsidized Stafford, PLUS), FFEL (PLUS), Perkins.

WORK-STUDY ***Federal work-study:*** Total amount: $521,654; 211 jobs averaging $2686. ***State or other work-study/employment:*** Total amount: $783,381 (63% need-based, 37% non-need-based). 295 part-time jobs averaging $2974.

APPLYING FOR FINANCIAL AID ***Required financial aid forms:*** FAFSA, institution's own form, federal tax forms. ***Financial aid deadline:*** 3/1 (priority: 3/1). ***Notification date:*** 4/1. Students must reply by 5/1.

CONTACT Lee Cioppa, Associate Dean for Admissions, The Juilliard School, 60 Lincoln Center Plaza, New York, NY 10023, 212-799-5000 Ext. 223. *Fax:* 212-769-6420. *E-mail:* admissions@juilliard.edu.

JUNIATA COLLEGE

Huntingdon, PA

Tuition & fees: $30,280 **Average undergraduate aid package: $22,440**

ABOUT THE INSTITUTION Independent religious, coed. ***Awards:*** bachelor's degrees. 90 undergraduate majors. ***Total enrollment:*** 1,523. Undergraduates: 1,523. Freshmen: 453. Federal methodology is used as a basis for awarding need-based institutional aid.

UNDERGRADUATE EXPENSES for 2008–09 ***Application fee:*** $30. ***Comprehensive fee:*** $38,700 includes full-time tuition ($29,610), mandatory fees ($670), and room and board ($8420). ***College room only:*** $4420. ***Part-time tuition:*** $1230 per semester hour. ***Payment plan:*** Installment.

FRESHMAN FINANCIAL AID (Fall 2008, est.) 386 applied for aid; of those 85% were deemed to have need. 100% of freshmen with need received aid; of those 31% had need fully met. ***Average percent of need met:*** 87% (excluding resources awarded to replace EFC). ***Average financial aid package:*** $22,571 (excluding resources awarded to replace EFC). 28% of all full-time freshmen had no need and received non-need-based gift aid.

UNDERGRADUATE FINANCIAL AID (Fall 2008, est.) 1,182 applied for aid; of those 87% were deemed to have need. 100% of undergraduates with need received aid; of those 31% had need fully met. ***Average percent of need met:*** 84% (excluding resources awarded to replace EFC). ***Average financial aid package:*** $22,440 (excluding resources awarded to replace EFC). 29% of all full-time undergraduates had no need and received non-need-based gift aid.

GIFT AID (NEED-BASED) ***Total amount:*** $17,798,510 (7% federal, 8% state, 83% institutional, 2% external sources). ***Receiving aid:*** Freshmen: 71% (328); all full-time undergraduates: 70% (1,029). ***Average award:*** Freshmen: $18,469; Undergraduates: $17,296. ***Scholarships, grants, and awards:*** Federal Pell, FSEOG, state, private, college/university gift aid from institutional funds.

GIFT AID (NON-NEED-BASED) ***Total amount:*** $6,654,042 (1% state, 97% institutional, 2% external sources). ***Receiving aid:*** Freshmen: 14% (66). Undergraduates: 11% (168). ***Average award:*** Freshmen: $16,761. Undergraduates: $17,120. ***Scholarships, grants, and awards by category:*** *Academic interests/achievement:* biological sciences, business, communication, computer science, education, English, foreign languages, general academic interests/achievements, health fields, humanities, international studies, mathematics, physical sciences, premedicine, social sciences. *Creative arts/performance:* art/fine arts, music, performing arts. *Special achievements/activities:* community service, general special achievements/activities, leadership. *Special characteristics:* adult students, children of faculty/staff, ethnic background, international students, local/state students. ***Tuition waivers:*** Full or partial for employees or children of employees, adult students.

LOANS ***Student loans:*** $8,386,716 (60% need-based, 40% non-need-based). 85% of past graduating class borrowed through all loan programs. *Average indebtedness per student:* $21,343. ***Average need-based loan:*** Freshmen: $3822. Undergraduates: $5027. ***Parent loans:*** $3,209,952 (33% need-based, 67% non-need-based). ***Programs:*** FFEL (Subsidized and Unsubsidized Stafford, PLUS), Perkins, college/university.

WORK-STUDY ***Federal work-study:*** Total amount: $831,289; 344 jobs averaging $608. ***State or other work-study/employment:*** Total amount: $1,184,450 (16% need-based, 84% non-need-based). 360 part-time jobs averaging $1037.

APPLYING FOR FINANCIAL AID ***Required financial aid form:*** FAFSA. ***Financial aid deadline:*** 3/1 (priority: 3/1). ***Notification date:*** Continuous. Students must reply by 5/1 or within 2 weeks of notification.

CONTACT Valerie Rennell, Director of Student Financial Planning, Juniata College, 1700 Moore Street, Huntingdon, PA 16652-2119, 814-641-3141 or toll-free 877-JUNIATA. *Fax:* 814-641-5311. *E-mail:* erennelv@juniata.edu.

KALAMAZOO COLLEGE

Kalamazoo, MI

Tuition & fees: $30,723 **Average undergraduate aid package: $24,710**

ABOUT THE INSTITUTION Independent religious, coed. ***Awards:*** bachelor's degrees. 24 undergraduate majors. ***Total enrollment:*** 1,387. Undergraduates: 1,387. Freshmen: 364. Both federal and institutional methodology are used as a basis for awarding need-based institutional aid.

UNDERGRADUATE EXPENSES for 2008–09 ***Application fee:*** $35. ***One-time required fee:*** $100. ***Comprehensive fee:*** $38,166 includes full-time tuition ($30,723) and room and board ($7443). ***College room only:*** $3630.

FRESHMAN FINANCIAL AID (Fall 2008, est.) 267 applied for aid; of those 71% were deemed to have need. 100% of freshmen with need received aid; of those 54% had need fully met. ***Average financial aid package:*** $23,950 (excluding resources awarded to replace EFC). 48% of all full-time freshmen had no need and received non-need-based gift aid.

UNDERGRADUATE FINANCIAL AID (Fall 2008, est.) 864 applied for aid; of those 84% were deemed to have need. 100% of undergraduates with need received aid; of those 46% had need fully met. ***Average financial aid package:*** $24,710 (excluding resources awarded to replace EFC). 24% of all full-time undergraduates had no need and received non-need-based gift aid.

GIFT AID (NEED-BASED) ***Total amount:*** $12,326,110 (7% federal, 7% state, 86% institutional). ***Receiving aid:*** Freshmen: 50% (181); all full-time undergraduates: 52% (708). ***Average award:*** Freshmen: $18,260; Undergraduates: $16,435. ***Scholarships, grants, and awards:*** Federal Pell, FSEOG, state, private, college/university gift aid from institutional funds.

GIFT AID (NON-NEED-BASED) ***Total amount:*** $8,432,883 (5% state, 80% institutional, 15% external sources). ***Receiving aid:*** Freshmen: 50% (181). Undergraduates: 50% (683). ***Average award:*** Freshmen: $10,455. Undergraduates: $9550. ***ROTC:*** Army cooperative.

LOANS ***Student loans:*** $4,107,508 (58% need-based, 42% non-need-based). ***Average need-based loan:*** Freshmen: $4225. Undergraduates: $5778. ***Parent loans:*** $1,631,646 (100% non-need-based). ***Programs:*** Federal Direct (Subsidized and Unsubsidized Stafford, PLUS), Perkins.

WORK-STUDY ***Federal work-study:*** Total amount: $770,000; jobs available. ***State or other work-study/employment:*** Total amount: $7300 (100% need-based). Part-time jobs available.

APPLYING FOR FINANCIAL AID ***Required financial aid forms:*** FAFSA, CSS Financial Aid PROFILE. ***Financial aid deadline (priority):*** 2/15. ***Notification date:*** Continuous beginning 3/21. Students must reply by 5/1.

CONTACT Judy Clark, Associate Director of Financial Aid, Kalamazoo College, 1200 Academy Street, Kalamazoo, MI 49006-3295, 269-337-7192 or toll-free 800-253-3602. *Fax:* 269-337-7390.

KANSAS CITY ART INSTITUTE

Kansas City, MO

Tuition & fees: $28,580 **Average undergraduate aid package: $20,854**

ABOUT THE INSTITUTION Independent, coed. ***Awards:*** bachelor's degrees. 12 undergraduate majors. ***Total enrollment:*** 676. Undergraduates: 676. Freshmen: 152. Federal methodology is used as a basis for awarding need-based institutional aid.

UNDERGRADUATE EXPENSES for 2009–10 ***Application fee:*** $35. ***Comprehensive fee:*** $37,290 includes full-time tuition ($28,580) and room and board ($8710). ***Part-time tuition:*** $1190 per credit hour.

FRESHMAN FINANCIAL AID (Fall 2008, est.) 119 applied for aid; of those 93% were deemed to have need. 100% of freshmen with need received aid; of those 20% had need fully met. ***Average percent of need met:*** 70% (excluding resources awarded to replace EFC). ***Average financial aid package:*** $20,773 (excluding resources awarded to replace EFC). 7% of all full-time freshmen had no need and received non-need-based gift aid.

UNDERGRADUATE FINANCIAL AID (Fall 2008, est.) 168 applied for aid; of those 93% were deemed to have need. 100% of undergraduates with need received aid; of those 19% had need fully met. ***Average percent of need met:*** 71% (excluding resources awarded to replace EFC). ***Average financial aid package:*** $20,854 (excluding resources awarded to replace EFC). 7% of all full-time undergraduates had no need and received non-need-based gift aid.

GIFT AID (NEED-BASED) ***Total amount:*** $2,330,577 (11% federal, 6% state, 80% institutional, 3% external sources). ***Receiving aid:*** Freshmen: 93% (111); all full-time undergraduates: 93% (156). ***Average award:*** Freshmen: $15,345; Undergraduates: $14,763. ***Scholarships, grants, and awards:*** Federal Pell, FSEOG, state, private, college/university gift aid from institutional funds.

GIFT AID (NON-NEED-BASED) ***Total amount:*** $310,071 (1% state, 97% institutional, 2% external sources). ***Receiving aid:*** Freshmen: 14% (17). Undergraduates: 12% (21). ***Average award:*** Freshmen: $13,875. Undergraduates: $13,666. ***Scholarships, grants, and awards by category:*** *Creative arts/performance:* $3,254,128 total: art/fine arts.

LOANS ***Student loans:*** $1,403,278 (81% need-based, 19% non-need-based). 96% of past graduating class borrowed through all loan programs. *Average indebtedness per student:* $23,375. ***Average need-based loan:*** Freshmen: $6026. Undergraduates: $6580. ***Parent loans:*** $1,153,784 (47% need-based, 53% non-need-based). ***Programs:*** FFEL (Subsidized and Unsubsidized Stafford, PLUS), Perkins, alternative loans.

WORK-STUDY ***Federal work-study:*** Total amount: $140,768; 124 jobs averaging $997. ***State or other work-study/employment:*** Total amount: $70,967 (100% non-need-based). 30 part-time jobs averaging $1000.

APPLYING FOR FINANCIAL AID ***Required financial aid form:*** FAFSA. ***Financial aid deadline (priority):*** 3/1. ***Notification date:*** Continuous beginning 3/15. Students must reply within 2 weeks of notification.

CONTACT Ms. Kimberly Warren, Director of Financial Aid, Kansas City Art Institute, 4415 Warwick Boulevard, Kansas City, MO 64111-1874, 816-802-3448 or toll-free 800-522-5224. *Fax:* 816-802-3453. *E-mail:* kwarren@kcai.edu.

KANSAS STATE UNIVERSITY

Manhattan, KS

Tuition & fees (KS res): $6627 **Average undergraduate aid package: $6892**

ABOUT THE INSTITUTION State-supported, coed. ***Awards:*** associate, bachelor's, master's, doctoral, and first professional degrees. 81 undergraduate majors. ***Total enrollment:*** 23,520. Undergraduates: 18,491. Freshmen: 3,761. Federal methodology is used as a basis for awarding need-based institutional aid.

UNDERGRADUATE EXPENSES for 2008–09 ***Application fee:*** $30. ***Tuition, state resident:*** full-time $5954; part-time $198.47 per credit hour. ***Tuition, nonresident:*** full-time $16,259; part-time $542 per credit hour. ***Required fees:*** full-time $673. Full-time tuition and fees vary according to course load, location, program, and reciprocity agreements. Part-time tuition and fees vary according to course load, location, program, and reciprocity agreements. ***College room and board:*** $6448. Room and board charges vary according to board plan, housing facility, and location. ***Payment plans:*** Installment, deferred payment.

FRESHMAN FINANCIAL AID (Fall 2007) 2,715 applied for aid; of those 70% were deemed to have need. 98% of freshmen with need received aid; of those 20% had need fully met. ***Average percent of need met:*** 67% (excluding resources awarded to replace EFC). ***Average financial aid package:*** $7367 (excluding resources awarded to replace EFC). 15% of all full-time freshmen had no need and received non-need-based gift aid.

UNDERGRADUATE FINANCIAL AID (Fall 2007) 11,274 applied for aid; of those 76% were deemed to have need. 97% of undergraduates with need received aid; of those 17% had need fully met. ***Average percent of need met:*** 65% (excluding resources awarded to replace EFC). ***Average financial aid package:*** $6892 (excluding resources awarded to replace EFC). 7% of all full-time undergraduates had no need and received non-need-based gift aid.

GIFT AID (NEED-BASED) ***Total amount:*** $30,112,510 (44% federal, 10% state, 35% institutional, 11% external sources). ***Receiving aid:*** Freshmen: 34% (1,220); all full-time undergraduates: 31% (5,000). ***Average award:*** Freshmen: $3889; Undergraduates: $3726. ***Scholarships, grants, and awards:*** Federal Pell, FSEOG, state, private, college/university gift aid from institutional funds.

GIFT AID (NON-NEED-BASED) ***Total amount:*** $4,566,977 (2% state, 73% institutional, 25% external sources). ***Receiving aid:*** Freshmen: 34% (1,231). Undergraduates: 21% (3,429). ***Average award:*** Freshmen: $3556. Undergraduates: $2936. ***Tuition waivers:*** Full or partial for employees or children of employees. ***ROTC:*** Army, Air Force.

LOANS ***Student loans:*** $62,080,115 (71% need-based, 29% non-need-based). 57% of past graduating class borrowed through all loan programs. *Average indebtedness per student:* $18,666. ***Average need-based loan:*** Freshmen: $3297. Undergraduates: $4205. ***Parent loans:*** $20,855,888 (26% need-based, 74% non-need-based). ***Programs:*** Federal Direct (Subsidized and Unsubsidized Stafford, PLUS), FFEL (Subsidized and Unsubsidized Stafford, PLUS), Perkins, college/university.

WORK-STUDY ***Federal work-study:*** Total amount: $1,118,945; jobs available. ***State or other work-study/employment:*** Total amount: $162,015 (55% need-based, 45% non-need-based). Part-time jobs available.

ATHLETIC AWARDS Total amount: $4,220,252 (22% need-based, 78% non-need-based).

APPLYING FOR FINANCIAL AID ***Required financial aid form:*** FAFSA. ***Financial aid deadline (priority):*** 3/1. ***Notification date:*** Continuous beginning 4/1. Students must reply within 2 weeks of notification.

CONTACT Mr. Larry Moeder, Director of Admissions and Student Financial Assistance, Kansas State University, 104 Fairchild Hall, Manhattan, KS 66506, 785-532-6420 or toll-free 800-432-8270 (in-state). *E-mail:* larrym@ksu.edu.

KANSAS WESLEYAN UNIVERSITY

Salina, KS

CONTACT Mrs. Glenna Alexander, Director of Financial Assistance, Kansas Wesleyan University, 100 East Claflin, Salina, KS 67401-6196, 785-827-5541 Ext. 1130 or toll-free 800-874-1154 Ext. 1285. *Fax:* 785-827-0927. *E-mail:* kglennaa@acck.edu.

KAPLAN UNIVERSITY–DAVENPORT CAMPUS

Davenport, IA

CONTACT Matt McEnany, Coordinator of School Operations, Kaplan University–Davenport Campus, 1801 East Kimberly Road, Davenport, IA 52806, 319-355-3500 or toll-free 800-747-1035 (in-state). *Fax:* 319-355-1320.

KAPLAN UNIVERSITY–MASON CITY CAMPUS

Mason City, IA

CONTACT Financial Aid Office, Kaplan University–Mason City Campus, Plaza West, 2570 4th Street, SW, Mason City, IA 50401, 641-423-2530.

KEAN UNIVERSITY

Union, NJ

Tuition & fees (NJ res): $9179 **Average undergraduate aid package: $9013**

ABOUT THE INSTITUTION State-supported, coed. ***Awards:*** bachelor's, master's, and doctoral degrees and post-master's certificates. 50 undergraduate majors. ***Total enrollment:*** 14,203. Undergraduates: 11,240. Freshmen: 1,469. Federal methodology is used as a basis for awarding need-based institutional aid.

UNDERGRADUATE EXPENSES for 2008–09 ***Application fee:*** $50. ***Tuition, state resident:*** full-time $5988; part-time $199.60 per credit. ***Tuition, nonresident:*** full-time $10,470; part-time $349 per credit. ***Required fees:*** full-time $3191; $107.10 per credit. Part-time tuition and fees vary according to class time and course load. ***College room and board:*** $9677; ***Room only:*** $6896. Room and board charges vary according to board plan and housing facility. ***Payment plans:*** Installment, deferred payment.

FRESHMAN FINANCIAL AID (Fall 2008, est.) 1,254 applied for aid; of those 76% were deemed to have need. 93% of freshmen with need received aid; of those 7% had need fully met. ***Average percent of need met:*** 56% (excluding resources awarded to replace EFC). ***Average financial aid package:*** $8744 (excluding resources awarded to replace EFC). 4% of all full-time freshmen had no need and received non-need-based gift aid.

UNDERGRADUATE FINANCIAL AID (Fall 2008, est.) 6,396 applied for aid; of those 78% were deemed to have need. 96% of undergraduates with need received aid; of those 15% had need fully met. ***Average percent of need met:*** 52% (excluding resources awarded to replace EFC). ***Average financial aid package:*** $9013 (excluding resources awarded to replace EFC). 1% of all full-time undergraduates had no need and received non-need-based gift aid.

GIFT AID (NEED-BASED) ***Total amount:*** $23,446,158 (49% federal, 44% state, 7% institutional). ***Receiving aid:*** Freshmen: 63% (887); all full-time undergraduates: 56% (4,712). ***Average award:*** Freshmen: $7210; Undergraduates: $6888. ***Scholarships, grants, and awards:*** Federal Pell, FSEOG, state, private, college/university gift aid from institutional funds.

GIFT AID (NON-NEED-BASED) ***Total amount:*** $72,285 (100% state). ***Receiving aid:*** Freshmen: 14% (201). Undergraduates: 7% (634). ***Average award:*** Freshmen: $2905. Undergraduates: $2595. ***Scholarships, grants, and awards by category:*** *Academic interests/achievement:* 1,090 awards ($1,581,040 total): business, education, general academic interests/achievements, health fields, humanities, international studies. *Creative arts/performance:* 8 awards ($61,350 total): applied art and design, art/fine arts, music, theater/drama. *Special achievements/activities:* 19 awards ($174,382 total): community service, leadership. *Special characteristics:* 116 awards ($685,942 total): general special characteristics. ***Tuition waivers:*** Full or partial for employees or children of employees, senior citizens. ***ROTC:*** Army cooperative, Air Force cooperative.

LOANS ***Student loans:*** $48,964,397 (41% need-based, 59% non-need-based). 68% of past graduating class borrowed through all loan programs. *Average indebtedness per student:* $17,723. ***Average need-based loan:*** Freshmen: $3443. Undergraduates: $4403. ***Parent loans:*** $2,809,608 (100% non-need-based). ***Programs:*** Federal Direct (Subsidized and Unsubsidized Stafford, PLUS), Perkins.

WORK-STUDY ***Federal work-study:*** Total amount: $458,711; 166 jobs averaging $2211.

APPLYING FOR FINANCIAL AID ***Required financial aid form:*** FAFSA. ***Financial aid deadline (priority):*** 3/15. ***Notification date:*** Continuous beginning 3/15. Students must reply by 5/1.

CONTACT Sharon Audet, Associate Director, Office of Financial Aid, Kean University, 1000 Morris Avenue, Union, NJ 07083, 908-737-3190. *Fax:* 908-737-3200. *E-mail:* finaid@kean.edu.

KEENE STATE COLLEGE

Keene, NH

Tuition & fees (NH res): $8778 **Average undergraduate aid package: $8492**

ABOUT THE INSTITUTION State-supported, coed. ***Awards:*** associate, bachelor's, and master's degrees and post-bachelor's and post-master's certificates. 68 undergraduate majors. ***Total enrollment:*** 5,271. Undergraduates: 5,147. Freshmen: 1,298. Federal methodology is used as a basis for awarding need-based institutional aid.

UNDERGRADUATE EXPENSES for 2008–09 ***Application fee:*** $40. ***Tuition, state resident:*** full-time $6600; part-time $275 per credit. ***Tuition, nonresident:*** full-time $14,450; part-time $602 per credit. ***Required fees:*** full-time $2178; $86 per credit. Part-time tuition and fees vary according to course load. ***College room and board:*** $7796; ***Room only:*** $5256. Room and board charges vary according to board plan and housing facility. ***Payment plan:*** Installment.

FRESHMAN FINANCIAL AID (Fall 2007) 1,103 applied for aid; of those 65% were deemed to have need. 98% of freshmen with need received aid; of those 16% had need fully met. ***Average percent of need met:*** 66% (excluding resources awarded to replace EFC). ***Average financial aid package:*** $8141 (excluding resources awarded to replace EFC). 8% of all full-time freshmen had no need and received non-need-based gift aid.

UNDERGRADUATE FINANCIAL AID (Fall 2007) 3,322 applied for aid; of those 70% were deemed to have need. 99% of undergraduates with need received aid; of those 19% had need fully met. ***Average percent of need met:*** 68% (excluding resources awarded to replace EFC). ***Average financial aid package:*** $8492 (excluding resources awarded to replace EFC). 8% of all full-time undergraduates had no need and received non-need-based gift aid.

GIFT AID (NEED-BASED) ***Total amount:*** $7,119,193 (35% federal, 8% state, 48% institutional, 9% external sources). ***Receiving aid:*** Freshmen: 34% (439); all full-time undergraduates: 33% (1,481). ***Average award:*** Freshmen: $4960; Undergraduates: $4713. ***Scholarships, grants, and awards:*** Federal Pell, FSEOG, state, private, college/university gift aid from institutional funds.

GIFT AID (NON-NEED-BASED) ***Total amount:*** $2,727,576 (81% institutional, 19% external sources). ***Receiving aid:*** Freshmen: 11% (146). Undergraduates: 12% (524). ***Average award:*** Freshmen: $2300. Undergraduates: $2742. ***Scholarships, grants, and awards by category:*** *Academic interests/achievement:* 536 awards ($1,206,750 total): general academic interests/achievements. ***Tuition waivers:*** Full or partial for employees or children of employees, senior citizens. ***ROTC:*** Air Force cooperative.

LOANS ***Student loans:*** $25,705,382 (34% need-based, 66% non-need-based). 79% of past graduating class borrowed through all loan programs. *Average indebtedness per student:* $24,995. ***Average need-based loan:*** Freshmen: $3644. Undergraduates: $4173. ***Parent loans:*** $7,205,401 (100% non-need-based). ***Programs:*** FFEL (Subsidized and Unsubsidized Stafford, PLUS), Perkins, college/university.

WORK-STUDY ***Federal work-study:*** Total amount: $2,427,815; 655 jobs averaging $983. ***State or other work-study/employment:*** Total amount: $539,304 (100% non-need-based). 570 part-time jobs averaging $946.

APPLYING FOR FINANCIAL AID ***Required financial aid form:*** FAFSA. ***Financial aid deadline:*** 3/1. ***Notification date:*** Continuous. Students must reply within 4 weeks of notification.

CONTACT Ms. Patricia Blodgett, Director of Student Financial Management, Keene State College, 229 Main Street, Keene, NH 03435-2606, 603-358-2280 or toll-free 800-KSC-1909. *Fax:* 603-358-2794. *E-mail:* pblodget@keene.edu.

KEHILATH YAKOV RABBINICAL SEMINARY

Ossining, NY

CONTACT Financial Aid Office, Kehilath Yakov Rabbinical Seminary, 206 Wilson Street, Brooklyn, NY 11211-7207, 718-963-1212.

KEISER UNIVERSITY

Fort Lauderdale, FL

Tuition & fees: N/R **Average undergraduate aid package: N/A**

ABOUT THE INSTITUTION Proprietary, coed. ***Awards:*** associate, bachelor's, and master's degrees (profile includes data from 13 campuses located in Daytona Beach, Melbourne, Sarasota, Kendall, Tallahassee, Jacksonville, Orlando, Miami, Tampa, West Palm Beach, Port St. Lucie, Miami Lakes, Pembroke Pines, and Lakeland campuses; all programs not offered at all locations but many classes offered 100% online). 38 undergraduate majors. Federal methodology is used as a basis for awarding need-based institutional aid.

GIFT AID (NEED-BASED) ***Scholarships, grants, and awards:*** Federal Pell, FSEOG, state, private, college/university gift aid from institutional funds.

LOANS ***Programs:*** Federal Direct (Subsidized and Unsubsidized Stafford, PLUS), FFEL (Subsidized and Unsubsidized Stafford, PLUS), Perkins.

WORK-STUDY Federal work-study jobs available.

APPLYING FOR FINANCIAL AID ***Required financial aid forms:*** FAFSA, institution's own form. ***Notification date:*** Continuous. Students must reply within 2 weeks of notification.

CONTACT Judy Martin, Financial Aid Director, Keiser University, 1500 NW 49 Street, Ft. Lauderdale, FL 33309, 954-776-4456 or toll-free 888-KEISER-9 (out-of-state). *Fax:* 954-749-4456. *E-mail:* judym@keiseruniversity.edu.

KENDALL COLLEGE

Chicago, IL

Tuition & fees: N/R **Average undergraduate aid package: N/A**

ABOUT THE INSTITUTION Independent United Methodist, coed. ***Awards:*** associate and bachelor's degrees. 25 undergraduate majors. ***Total enrollment:*** 1,913. Undergraduates: 1,913. Freshmen: 173. Federal methodology is used as a basis for awarding need-based institutional aid.

UNDERGRADUATE EXPENSES for 2008–09 ***Application fee:*** $50. tuition varies by program.

GIFT AID (NEED-BASED) ***Total amount:*** $4,403,068 (51% federal, 25% state, 24% institutional). ***Scholarships, grants, and awards:*** Federal Pell, FSEOG, state, private, college/university gift aid from institutional funds.

GIFT AID (NON-NEED-BASED) ***Total amount:*** $1,090,728 (69% institutional, 31% external sources). ***Scholarships, grants, and awards by category:*** *Academic interests/achievement:* business, education, general academic interests/achievements. *Special characteristics:* children of faculty/staff, international students, members of minority groups, out-of-state students, veterans, veterans' children.

LOANS ***Student loans:*** $8,752,699 (52% need-based, 48% non-need-based). *Average indebtedness per student:* $14,125. ***Parent loans:*** $2,441,832 (100% need-based). ***Programs:*** FFEL (Subsidized and Unsubsidized Stafford, PLUS), Perkins, alternative loans.

WORK-STUDY ***Federal work-study:*** Total amount: $75,039; 30 jobs averaging $1100.

APPLYING FOR FINANCIAL AID ***Required financial aid forms:*** FAFSA, institution's own form. ***Financial aid deadline (priority):*** 4/15. ***Notification date:*** Continuous. Students must reply within 2 weeks of notification.

CONTACT Chris Miller, Director of Financial Aid, Kendall College, 900 N North Branch Street, Chicago, IL 60622, 312-752-2428 or toll-free 866-667-3344 (in-state), 877-588-8860 (out-of-state). *Fax:* 312-752-2267.

KENNESAW STATE UNIVERSITY

Kennesaw, GA

Tuition & fees (GA res): $4144 Average undergraduate aid package: $12,503

ABOUT THE INSTITUTION State-supported, coed. ***Awards:*** bachelor's, master's, and doctoral degrees. 48 undergraduate majors. ***Total enrollment:*** 21,449. Undergraduates: 19,171. Freshmen: 2,639. Federal methodology is used as a basis for awarding need-based institutional aid.

UNDERGRADUATE EXPENSES for 2008–09 ***Application fee:*** $40. ***Tuition, state resident:*** full-time $3196; part-time $134 per credit hour. ***Tuition, nonresident:*** full-time $12,778; part-time $533 per credit hour. ***Required fees:*** full-time $948. Part-time tuition and fees vary according to course load. ***College room and board: Room only:*** $4737. Room and board charges vary according to housing facility. ***Payment plan:*** Deferred payment.

FRESHMAN FINANCIAL AID (Fall 2008, est.) 1,978 applied for aid; of those 60% were deemed to have need. 98% of freshmen with need received aid; of those 83% had need fully met. ***Average percent of need met:*** 20% (excluding resources awarded to replace EFC). ***Average financial aid package:*** $11,058 (excluding resources awarded to replace EFC). 41% of all full-time freshmen had no need and received non-need-based gift aid.

UNDERGRADUATE FINANCIAL AID (Fall 2008, est.) 10,269 applied for aid; of those 64% were deemed to have need. 100% of undergraduates with need received aid; of those 63% had need fully met. ***Average percent of need met:*** 24% (excluding resources awarded to replace EFC). ***Average financial aid package:*** $12,503 (excluding resources awarded to replace EFC). 19% of all full-time undergraduates had no need and received non-need-based gift aid.

GIFT AID (NEED-BASED) ***Total amount:*** $15,575,234 (99% federal, 1% institutional). ***Receiving aid:*** Freshmen: 19% (486); all full-time undergraduates: 21% (3,086). ***Average award:*** Freshmen: $1316; Undergraduates: $1556. ***Scholarships, grants, and awards:*** Federal Pell, FSEOG, state, private, college/university gift aid from institutional funds.

GIFT AID (NON-NEED-BASED) ***Total amount:*** $34,146,505 (97% state, 1% institutional, 2% external sources). ***Receiving aid:*** Freshmen: 28% (724). Undergraduates: 18% (2,532). ***Average award:*** Freshmen: $886. Undergraduates: $989. ***Scholarships, grants, and awards by category:*** *Academic interests/achievement:* biological sciences, business, communication, computer science, education, English, foreign languages, general academic interests/achievements, health fields, humanities, international studies, mathematics, physical sciences, premedicine, social sciences. *Creative arts/performance:* music, performing arts, theater/drama. *Special achievements/activities:* community service, leadership, memberships. *Special characteristics:* children and siblings of alumni, children of union members/company employees, children of workers in trades, ethnic background, general special characteristics, handicapped students, international students, local/state students, members of minority groups, religious affiliation, veterans' children. ***Tuition waivers:*** Full or partial for employees or children of employees, senior citizens. ***ROTC:*** Army, Air Force.

LOANS ***Student loans:*** $40,708,038 (41% need-based, 59% non-need-based). 75% of past graduating class borrowed through all loan programs. *Average indebtedness per student:* $13,500. ***Average need-based loan:*** Freshmen: $1436. Undergraduates: $1776. ***Parent loans:*** $702,657 (100% non-need-based). ***Programs:*** FFEL (Subsidized and Unsubsidized Stafford, PLUS), Perkins, Federal Nursing, state.

WORK-STUDY ***Federal work-study:*** Total amount: $232,099; 1,087 jobs averaging $2433.

ATHLETIC AWARDS Total amount: $240,359 (100% non-need-based).

APPLYING FOR FINANCIAL AID ***Required financial aid form:*** FAFSA. ***Financial aid deadline (priority):*** 4/1. ***Notification date:*** Continuous beginning 4/1.

CONTACT Mr. Ron H. Day, Director of Student Financial Aid, Kennesaw State University, 1000 Chastain Road, Kennesaw, GA 30144-5591, 770-423-6021. *Fax:* 770-423-6708. *E-mail:* finaid@kennesaw.edu.

KENT STATE UNIVERSITY

Kent, OH

Tuition & fees (OH res): $8430 Average undergraduate aid package: $7895

ABOUT THE INSTITUTION State-supported, coed. ***Awards:*** bachelor's, master's, and doctoral degrees and post-bachelor's and post-master's certificates. 125 undergraduate majors. ***Total enrollment:*** 22,923. Undergraduates: 18,131. Freshmen: 3,764. Federal methodology is used as a basis for awarding need-based institutional aid.

UNDERGRADUATE EXPENSES for 2008–09 ***Application fee:*** $30. ***Tuition, state resident:*** full-time $8430; part-time $384 per credit hour. ***Tuition, nonresident:*** full-time $15,862; part-time $722 per credit hour. Full-time tuition and fees vary according to course level, course load, degree level, program, and reciprocity agreements. Part-time tuition and fees vary according to course level, course load, degree level, program, and reciprocity agreements. ***College room and board:*** $7200; ***Room only:*** $4410. Room and board charges vary according to board plan and housing facility. ***Payment plans:*** Tuition prepayment, installment, deferred payment.

FRESHMAN FINANCIAL AID (Fall 2008, est.) 3,102 applied for aid; of those 80% were deemed to have need. 100% of freshmen with need received aid; of those 56% had need fully met. ***Average percent of need met:*** 65% (excluding resources awarded to replace EFC). ***Average financial aid package:*** $7959 (excluding resources awarded to replace EFC). 18% of all full-time freshmen had no need and received non-need-based gift aid.

UNDERGRADUATE FINANCIAL AID (Fall 2008, est.) 11,121 applied for aid; of those 83% were deemed to have need. 100% of undergraduates with need received aid; of those 49% had need fully met. ***Average percent of need met:*** 60% (excluding resources awarded to replace EFC). ***Average financial aid package:*** $7895 (excluding resources awarded to replace EFC). 12% of all full-time undergraduates had no need and received non-need-based gift aid.

GIFT AID (NEED-BASED) ***Total amount:*** $40,450,063 (44% federal, 14% state, 34% institutional, 8% external sources). ***Receiving aid:*** Freshmen: 52% (1,932); all full-time undergraduates: 41% (6,406). ***Average award:*** Freshmen: $5676; Undergraduates: $6050. ***Scholarships, grants, and awards:*** Federal Pell, FSEOG, state, private, college/university gift aid from institutional funds.

GIFT AID (NON-NEED-BASED) ***Total amount:*** $8,940,091 (4% state, 86% institutional, 10% external sources). ***Receiving aid:*** Freshmen: 11% (416). Undergraduates: 5% (838). ***Average award:*** Freshmen: $3628. Undergraduates: $3926. ***Scholarships, grants, and awards by category:*** *Academic interests/achievement:* architecture, area/ethnic studies, biological sciences, business, communication, computer science, education, engineering/technologies, English, general academic interests/achievements, health fields, international studies, library science, mathematics, military science, physical sciences, social sciences. *Creative arts/performance:* art/fine arts, dance, journalism/publications, music, performing arts, theater/drama. *Special achievements/activities:* community service, general special achievements/activities, leadership. *Special characteristics:* adult students, children and siblings of alumni, children of faculty/staff, children of union members/company employees, children with a deceased or disabled parent, ethnic background, first-generation college students, handicapped students, international students, members of minority groups, out-of-state students. ***Tuition waivers:*** Full or partial for employees or children of employees, senior citizens. ***ROTC:*** Army, Air Force.

LOANS ***Student loans:*** $105,410,756 (86% need-based, 14% non-need-based). 71% of past graduating class borrowed through all loan programs. *Average indebtedness per student:* $23,957. ***Average need-based loan:*** Freshmen: $3553. Undergraduates: $4065. ***Parent loans:*** $22,362,236 (12% need-based, 88% non-need-based). ***Programs:*** Federal Direct (Subsidized and Unsubsidized Stafford, PLUS), Perkins, Federal Nursing, state, college/university, alternative loans.

WORK-STUDY ***Federal work-study:*** Total amount: $2,083,589; 740 jobs averaging $2816.

ATHLETIC AWARDS Total amount: $4,739,600 (44% need-based, 56% non-need-based).

APPLYING FOR FINANCIAL AID ***Required financial aid form:*** FAFSA. ***Financial aid deadline (priority):*** 3/1. ***Notification date:*** 3/15. Students must reply within 2 weeks of notification.

CONTACT Mark A. Evans, Director of Student Financial Aid, Kent State University, 103 Michael Schwartz Center, Kent, OH 44242-0001, 330-672-2972 or toll-free 800-988-KENT. *Fax:* 330-672-4014. *E-mail:* mevans@kent.edu.

KENT STATE UNIVERSITY, STARK CAMPUS

Canton, OH

CONTACT Ms. Mary S. Southards, Assistant Dean of Enrollment Management, Kent State University, Stark Campus, 6000 Frank Avenue N.W., Canton, OH 44720, 330-499-9600 Ext. 240. *Fax:* 330-499-0301. *E-mail:* msouthards@stark.kent.edu.

KENTUCKY CHRISTIAN UNIVERSITY
Grayson, KY

Tuition & fees: $14,088 **Average undergraduate aid package: $9798**

ABOUT THE INSTITUTION Independent religious, coed. ***Awards:*** bachelor's and master's degrees. 17 undergraduate majors. ***Total enrollment:*** 663. Undergraduates: 630. Freshmen: 191. Federal methodology is used as a basis for awarding need-based institutional aid.

UNDERGRADUATE EXPENSES for 2009–10 ***Application fee:*** $30. ***Comprehensive fee:*** $19,888 includes full-time tuition ($13,888), mandatory fees ($200), and room and board ($5800).

FRESHMAN FINANCIAL AID (Fall 2007) 158 applied for aid; of those 90% were deemed to have need. 100% of freshmen with need received aid; of those 9% had need fully met. ***Average percent of need met:*** 57% (excluding resources awarded to replace EFC). ***Average financial aid package:*** $9202 (excluding resources awarded to replace EFC). 9% of all full-time freshmen had no need and received non-need-based gift aid.

UNDERGRADUATE FINANCIAL AID (Fall 2007) 507 applied for aid; of those 90% were deemed to have need. 100% of undergraduates with need received aid; of those 12% had need fully met. ***Average percent of need met:*** 67% (excluding resources awarded to replace EFC). ***Average financial aid package:*** $9798 (excluding resources awarded to replace EFC). 9% of all full-time undergraduates had no need and received non-need-based gift aid.

GIFT AID (NEED-BASED) ***Total amount:*** $1,718,992 (48% federal, 36% state, 16% institutional). ***Receiving aid:*** Freshmen: 59% (104); all full-time undergraduates: 60% (360). ***Average award:*** Freshmen: $4125; Undergraduates: $4474. ***Scholarships, grants, and awards:*** Federal Pell, FSEOG, state, private, college/university gift aid from institutional funds, Academic Competitiveness Grant.

GIFT AID (NON-NEED-BASED) ***Total amount:*** $2,386,490 (9% state, 76% institutional, 15% external sources). ***Receiving aid:*** Freshmen: 81% (142). Undergraduates: 77% (458). ***Average award:*** Freshmen: $5516. Undergraduates: $4320. ***Scholarships, grants, and awards by category:*** *Academic interests/achievement:* 538 awards ($1,036,604 total): business, education, general academic interests/achievements, religion/biblical studies. *Creative arts/performance:* 37 awards ($104,622 total): debating, music, performing arts, theater/drama. *Special achievements/activities:* 116 awards ($144,997 total): community service, general special achievements/activities, leadership, religious involvement. *Special characteristics:* 79 awards ($531,233 total): children and siblings of alumni, children of faculty/staff, general special characteristics, international students, members of minority groups, religious affiliation.

LOANS ***Student loans:*** $2,910,764 (56% need-based, 44% non-need-based). 87% of past graduating class borrowed through all loan programs. *Average indebtedness per student:* $24,703. ***Average need-based loan:*** Freshmen: $2824. Undergraduates: $3792. ***Parent loans:*** $488,969 (100% non-need-based). ***Programs:*** FFEL (Subsidized and Unsubsidized Stafford, PLUS), Perkins.

WORK-STUDY ***Federal work-study:*** Total amount: $293,770; 241 jobs averaging $1219. ***State or other work-study/employment:*** Total amount: $78,570 (100% non-need-based). 56 part-time jobs averaging $1403.

APPLYING FOR FINANCIAL AID ***Required financial aid form:*** FAFSA. ***Financial aid deadline (priority):*** 3/1. ***Notification date:*** Continuous beginning 3/15. Students must reply within 2 weeks of notification.

CONTACT Mrs. Jennie M. Bender, Director of Financial Aid, Kentucky Christian University, 100 Academic Parkway, Grayson, KY 41143-2205, 606-474-3226 or toll-free 800-522-3181. *Fax:* 606-474-3155. *E-mail:* jbender@kcu.edu.

KENTUCKY MOUNTAIN BIBLE COLLEGE
Vancleve, KY

ABOUT THE INSTITUTION Independent interdenominational, coed. ***Awards:*** associate and bachelor's degrees. 5 undergraduate majors. ***Total enrollment:*** 64. Undergraduates: 64. Freshmen: 18.

GIFT AID (NEED-BASED) ***Scholarships, grants, and awards:*** Federal Pell, FSEOG, state, private, college/university gift aid from institutional funds.

GIFT AID (NON-NEED-BASED) ***Scholarships, grants, and awards by category:*** *Academic interests/achievement:* general academic interests/achievements. *Creative arts/performance:* music, theater/drama. *Special characteristics:* children of faculty/staff.

LOANS ***Programs:*** FFEL (Subsidized and Unsubsidized Stafford, PLUS), college/university.

APPLYING FOR FINANCIAL AID ***Required financial aid forms:*** FAFSA, institution's own form.

CONTACT Mrs. Carla Frazier, Director of Financial Aid, Kentucky Mountain Bible College, PO Box 10, Vancleve, KY 41385-0010, 800-879-KMBC Ext. 175 or toll-free 800-879-KMBC Ext. 130 (in-state), 800-879-KMBC Ext. 136 (out-of-state). *Fax:* 800-659-4324. *E-mail:* finaid@kmbc.edu.

KENTUCKY STATE UNIVERSITY
Frankfort, KY

Tuition & fees (KY res): $5692 **Average undergraduate aid package: $2814**

ABOUT THE INSTITUTION State-related, coed. ***Awards:*** associate, bachelor's, and master's degrees. 24 undergraduate majors. ***Total enrollment:*** 2,659. Undergraduates: 2,497. Freshmen: 687. Federal methodology is used as a basis for awarding need-based institutional aid.

UNDERGRADUATE EXPENSES for 2008–09 ***Application fee:*** $30. ***Tuition, state resident:*** full-time $4942; part-time $190 per hour. ***Tuition, nonresident:*** full-time $12,740; part-time $450 per hour. ***Required fees:*** full-time $750. Full-time tuition and fees vary according to course load, degree level, and reciprocity agreements. Part-time tuition and fees vary according to course load, degree level, and reciprocity agreements. ***College room and board:*** $6392; ***Room only:*** $3240. Room and board charges vary according to board plan and housing facility. ***Payment plans:*** Installment, deferred payment.

FRESHMAN FINANCIAL AID (Fall 2008, est.) 651 applied for aid; of those 90% were deemed to have need. 87% of freshmen with need received aid; of those 38% had need fully met. ***Average percent of need met:*** 25% (excluding resources awarded to replace EFC). ***Average financial aid package:*** $2796 (excluding resources awarded to replace EFC). 5% of all full-time freshmen had no need and received non-need-based gift aid.

UNDERGRADUATE FINANCIAL AID (Fall 2008, est.) 1,858 applied for aid; of those 92% were deemed to have need. 92% of undergraduates with need received aid; of those 33% had need fully met. ***Average percent of need met:*** 24% (excluding resources awarded to replace EFC). ***Average financial aid package:*** $2814 (excluding resources awarded to replace EFC). 5% of all full-time undergraduates had no need and received non-need-based gift aid.

GIFT AID (NEED-BASED) ***Total amount:*** $2,697,970 (84% federal, 12% state, 4% institutional). ***Receiving aid:*** Freshmen: 61% (407); all full-time undergraduates: 68% (1,283). ***Average award:*** Freshmen: $2746; Undergraduates: $2645. ***Scholarships, grants, and awards:*** Federal Pell, FSEOG, state, private, college/university gift aid from institutional funds, United Negro College Fund, Federal Nursing.

GIFT AID (NON-NEED-BASED) ***Total amount:*** $1,935,481 (3% federal, 19% state, 67% institutional, 11% external sources). ***Receiving aid:*** Freshmen: 41% (270). Undergraduates: 38% (723). ***Average award:*** Freshmen: $2541. Undergraduates: $2787. ***Scholarships, grants, and awards by category:*** *Academic interests/achievement:* 8 awards: general academic interests/achievements, health fields, mathematics. *Creative arts/performance:* 7 awards: art/fine arts, journalism/publications, music, performing arts. *Special achievements/activities:* 7 awards: cheerleading/drum major, general special achievements/activities. *Special characteristics:* 9 awards: children with a deceased or disabled parent, ethnic background, local/state students, public servants, veterans. ***Tuition waivers:*** Full or partial for employees or children of employees, senior citizens. ***ROTC:*** Air Force cooperative.

LOANS ***Student loans:*** $5,619,691 (48% need-based, 52% non-need-based). 90% of past graduating class borrowed through all loan programs. *Average indebtedness per student:* $27,356. ***Average need-based loan:*** Freshmen: $1781. Undergraduates: $2046. ***Parent loans:*** $834,593 (100% non-need-based). ***Programs:*** Federal Direct (Subsidized and Unsubsidized Stafford, PLUS), FFEL (Subsidized and Unsubsidized Stafford), Perkins, state.

WORK-STUDY ***Federal work-study:*** Total amount: $207,285; 331 jobs averaging $730. ***State or other work-study/employment:*** Total amount: $77,155 (100% non-need-based). 137 part-time jobs averaging $813.

ATHLETIC AWARDS Total amount: $471,737 (100% non-need-based).

APPLYING FOR FINANCIAL AID ***Required financial aid form:*** FAFSA. ***Financial aid deadline (priority):*** 4/15. ***Notification date:*** Continuous. Students must reply within 2 weeks of notification.

CONTACT Myrna C. Bryant, Assistant Director of Financial Aid, Kentucky State University, 400 East Main Street, Frankfort, KY 40601, 502-597-5960 or toll-free 800-633-9415 (in-state), 800-325-1716 (out-of-state). *Fax:* 502-597-5950. *E-mail:* myrna.bryant@kysu.edu.

KENTUCKY WESLEYAN COLLEGE

Owensboro, KY

Tuition & fees: $15,500 **Average undergraduate aid package: $13,334**

ABOUT THE INSTITUTION Independent Methodist, coed. ***Awards:*** bachelor's degrees. 41 undergraduate majors. ***Total enrollment:*** 909. Undergraduates: 909. Freshmen: 219. Federal methodology is used as a basis for awarding need-based institutional aid.

UNDERGRADUATE EXPENSES for 2008–09 ***Comprehensive fee:*** $21,660 includes full-time tuition ($15,500) and room and board ($6160). ***College room only:*** $2780. Full-time tuition and fees vary according to course load. Room and board charges vary according to board plan and housing facility. ***Part-time fees:*** $50 per term. Part-time tuition and fees vary according to course load. ***Payment plans:*** Installment, deferred payment.

FRESHMAN FINANCIAL AID (Fall 2007) 273 applied for aid; of those 90% were deemed to have need. 98% of freshmen with need received aid; of those 16% had need fully met. ***Average percent of need met:*** 70% (excluding resources awarded to replace EFC). ***Average financial aid package:*** $13,703 (excluding resources awarded to replace EFC). 11% of all full-time freshmen had no need and received non-need-based gift aid.

UNDERGRADUATE FINANCIAL AID (Fall 2007) 874 applied for aid; of those 88% were deemed to have need. 98% of undergraduates with need received aid; of those 19% had need fully met. ***Average percent of need met:*** 73% (excluding resources awarded to replace EFC). ***Average financial aid package:*** $13,334 (excluding resources awarded to replace EFC). 16% of all full-time undergraduates had no need and received non-need-based gift aid.

GIFT AID (NEED-BASED) ***Total amount:*** $8,082,030 (15% federal, 28% state, 53% institutional, 4% external sources). ***Receiving aid:*** Freshmen: 86% (242); all full-time undergraduates: 81% (748). ***Average award:*** Freshmen: $11,157; Undergraduates: $10,581. ***Scholarships, grants, and awards:*** Federal Pell, FSEOG, state, private, college/university gift aid from institutional funds.

GIFT AID (NON-NEED-BASED) ***Total amount:*** $1,823,563 (14% state, 81% institutional, 5% external sources). ***Receiving aid:*** Freshmen: 8% (23). Undergraduates: 9% (87). ***Average award:*** Freshmen: $6900. Undergraduates: $7903. ***Scholarships, grants, and awards by category:*** *Academic interests/achievement:* 669 awards ($2,881,085 total): general academic interests/achievements. *Creative arts/performance:* 47 awards ($69,273 total): general creative arts/performance. *Special achievements/activities:* 49 awards ($88,722 total): general special achievements/activities. *Special characteristics:* 275 awards ($548,014 total): general special characteristics. ***Tuition waivers:*** Full or partial for children of alumni, employees or children of employees, senior citizens. ***ROTC:*** Army cooperative.

LOANS ***Student loans:*** $3,455,188 (73% need-based, 27% non-need-based). 94% of past graduating class borrowed through all loan programs. *Average indebtedness per student:* $18,875. ***Average need-based loan:*** Freshmen: $3052. Undergraduates: $3652. ***Parent loans:*** $400,265 (39% need-based, 61% non-need-based). ***Programs:*** FFEL (Subsidized and Unsubsidized Stafford, PLUS), Perkins, alternative loans.

WORK-STUDY ***Federal work-study:*** Total amount: $120,692; 175 jobs averaging $690.

ATHLETIC AWARDS Total amount: $1,237,770 (100% non-need-based).

APPLYING FOR FINANCIAL AID ***Required financial aid form:*** FAFSA. ***Financial aid deadline:*** 3/15 (priority: 3/15). ***Notification date:*** Continuous. Students must reply within 2 weeks of notification.

CONTACT Samantha Hays, Director of Financial Aid, Kentucky Wesleyan College, 3000 Frederica Street, Owensboro, KY 42301, 270-852-3130 or toll-free 800-999-0592 (in-state), 800-990-0592 (out-of-state). *Fax:* 270-852-3133. *E-mail:* shays@kwc.edu.

KENYON COLLEGE

Gambier, OH

Tuition & fees: $40,980 **Average undergraduate aid package: $30,181**

ABOUT THE INSTITUTION Independent, coed. ***Awards:*** bachelor's degrees. 31 undergraduate majors. ***Total enrollment:*** 1,644. Undergraduates: 1,644. Freshmen: 456.

UNDERGRADUATE EXPENSES for 2009–10 ***Application fee:*** $50. ***Comprehensive fee:*** $48,240 includes full-time tuition ($39,810), mandatory fees ($1170), and room and board ($7260).

FRESHMAN FINANCIAL AID (Fall 2008, est.) 270 applied for aid; of those 70% were deemed to have need. 100% of freshmen with need received aid; of those 50% had need fully met. ***Average percent of need met:*** 98% (excluding resources awarded to replace EFC). ***Average financial aid package:*** $29,202 (excluding resources awarded to replace EFC). 28% of all full-time freshmen had no need and received non-need-based gift aid.

UNDERGRADUATE FINANCIAL AID (Fall 2008, est.) 886 applied for aid; of those 82% were deemed to have need. 100% of undergraduates with need received aid; of those 42% had need fully met. ***Average percent of need met:*** 98% (excluding resources awarded to replace EFC). ***Average financial aid package:*** $30,181 (excluding resources awarded to replace EFC). 22% of all full-time undergraduates had no need and received non-need-based gift aid.

GIFT AID (NEED-BASED) ***Total amount:*** $18,636,083 (4% federal, 2% state, 88% institutional, 6% external sources). ***Receiving aid:*** Freshmen: 39% (176); all full-time undergraduates: 40% (691). ***Average award:*** Freshmen: $28,512; Undergraduates: $26,969. ***Scholarships, grants, and awards:*** Federal Pell, FSEOG, state, private, college/university gift aid from institutional funds.

GIFT AID (NON-NEED-BASED) ***Total amount:*** $2,836,558 (4% state, 72% institutional, 24% external sources). ***Receiving aid:*** Freshmen: 10% (45). Undergraduates: 8% (139). ***Average award:*** Freshmen: $9615. Undergraduates: $11,779. ***Scholarships, grants, and awards by category:*** *Academic interests/achievement:* 309 awards ($2,813,560 total): general academic interests/achievements. *Special characteristics:* 51 awards ($683,667 total): ethnic background, first-generation college students.

LOANS ***Student loans:*** $5,622,513 (53% need-based, 47% non-need-based). 66% of past graduating class borrowed through all loan programs. *Average indebtedness per student:* $19,462. ***Average need-based loan:*** Freshmen: $3067. Undergraduates: $4497. ***Parent loans:*** $3,000,644 (14% need-based, 86% non-need-based). ***Programs:*** FFEL (Subsidized and Unsubsidized Stafford, PLUS), Perkins, college/university.

WORK-STUDY ***Federal work-study:*** Total amount: $211,788; 280 jobs averaging $639. ***State or other work-study/employment:*** Total amount: $367,205 (60% need-based, 40% non-need-based). 157 part-time jobs averaging $604.

APPLYING FOR FINANCIAL AID ***Required financial aid forms:*** FAFSA, CSS Financial Aid PROFILE, income tax form(s). ***Financial aid deadline (priority):*** 2/15. ***Notification date:*** 4/1. Students must reply by 5/1.

CONTACT Mr. Craig Daugherty, Director of Financial Aid, Kenyon College, Stephens Hall, Gambier, OH 43022-9623, 740-427-5430 or toll-free 800-848-2468. *Fax:* 740-427-5240. *E-mail:* daugherty@kenyon.edu.

KETTERING COLLEGE OF MEDICAL ARTS

Kettering, OH

CONTACT Kim Snell, Director of Student Finance, Kettering College of Medical Arts, 3737 Southern Boulevard, Kettering, OH 45429, 937-298-3399 Ext. 5617 or toll-free 800-433-5262. *Fax:* 937-296-4238. *E-mail:* kim_ snell@ketthealth.com.

KETTERING UNIVERSITY

Flint, MI

Tuition & fees: $26,936 **Average undergraduate aid package: $16,476**

ABOUT THE INSTITUTION Independent, coed, primarily men. ***Awards:*** bachelor's and master's degrees. 12 undergraduate majors. ***Total enrollment:*** 2,600. Undergraduates: 2,134. Freshmen: 441. Federal methodology is used as a basis for awarding need-based institutional aid.

UNDERGRADUATE EXPENSES for 2008–09 ***Application fee:*** $35. ***One-time required fee:*** $310. ***Comprehensive fee:*** $33,118 includes full-time tuition ($26,496), mandatory fees ($440), and room and board ($6182). ***College room only:*** $3872. ***Part-time tuition:*** $828 per credit hour. ***Payment plan:*** Installment.

FRESHMAN FINANCIAL AID (Fall 2008, est.) 413 applied for aid; of those 90% were deemed to have need. 100% of freshmen with need received aid; of those 8% had need fully met. ***Average percent of need met:*** 70% (excluding resources awarded to replace EFC). ***Average financial aid package:*** $19,961 (excluding resources awarded to replace EFC). 19% of all full-time freshmen had no need and received non-need-based gift aid.

UNDERGRADUATE FINANCIAL AID (Fall 2008, est.) 1,448 applied for aid; of those 91% were deemed to have need. 100% of undergraduates with need received aid; of those 7% had need fully met. ***Average percent of need met:*** 66% (excluding resources awarded to replace EFC). ***Average financial aid package:*** $16,476 (excluding resources awarded to replace EFC). 22% of all full-time undergraduates had no need and received non-need-based gift aid.

GIFT AID (NEED-BASED) ***Total amount:*** $14,158,521 (11% federal, 10% state, 77% institutional, 2% external sources). ***Receiving aid:*** Freshmen: 66% (312); all full-time undergraduates: 53% (1,125). ***Average award:*** Freshmen: $15,782; Undergraduates: $12,065. ***Scholarships, grants, and awards:*** Federal Pell, FSEOG, state, private, college/university gift aid from institutional funds.

GIFT AID (NON-NEED-BASED) ***Total amount:*** $6,049,100 (5% state, 92% institutional, 3% external sources). ***Receiving aid:*** Freshmen: 12% (57). Undergraduates: 7% (139). ***Average award:*** Freshmen: $13,503. Undergraduates: $10,254. ***Scholarships, grants, and awards by category:*** *Academic interests/achievement:* 1,640 awards ($10,591,918 total): business, computer science, engineering/technologies, general academic interests/achievements, mathematics, physical sciences. *Special achievements/activities:* 42 awards ($182,000 total): general special achievements/activities, memberships. *Special characteristics:* 219 awards ($908,086 total): children and siblings of alumni, children of faculty/staff, members of minority groups, siblings of current students. ***Tuition waivers:*** Full or partial for employees or children of employees.

LOANS ***Student loans:*** $18,043,045 (36% need-based, 64% non-need-based). 81% of past graduating class borrowed through all loan programs. *Average indebtedness per student:* $48,767. ***Average need-based loan:*** Freshmen: $3935. Undergraduates: $5289. ***Parent loans:*** $943,324 (21% need-based, 79% non-need-based). ***Programs:*** FFEL (Subsidized and Unsubsidized Stafford, PLUS), state, alternative loans.

WORK-STUDY ***Federal work-study:*** Total amount: $185,440; 258 jobs averaging $1204. ***State or other work-study/employment:*** Total amount: $12,142 (100% need-based). 63 part-time jobs averaging $356.

APPLYING FOR FINANCIAL AID ***Required financial aid form:*** FAFSA. ***Financial aid deadline (priority):*** 2/14. ***Notification date:*** Continuous beginning 2/15. Students must reply within 2 weeks of notification.

CONTACT Diane Bice, Director of Financial Aid, Kettering University, 1700 West Third Avenue, Flint, MI 48504-4898, 800-955-4464 Ext. 7859 or toll-free 800-955-4464 Ext. 7865 (in-state), 800-955-4464 (out-of-state). *Fax:* 810-762-9807. *E-mail:* finaid@kettering.edu.

KEUKA COLLEGE

Keuka Park, NY

Tuition & fees: $21,760 **Average undergraduate aid package: $16,344**

ABOUT THE INSTITUTION Independent religious, coed. ***Awards:*** bachelor's and master's degrees. 34 undergraduate majors. ***Total enrollment:*** 1,613. Undergraduates: 1,482. Freshmen: 272. Federal methodology is used as a basis for awarding need-based institutional aid.

UNDERGRADUATE EXPENSES for 2008–09 ***Application fee:*** $30. ***Comprehensive fee:*** $30,610 includes full-time tuition ($21,140), mandatory fees ($620), and room and board ($8850). ***College room only:*** $4200. Full-time tuition and fees vary according to program. Room and board charges vary according to board plan and housing facility. ***Part-time tuition:*** $705 per credit hour. Part-time tuition and fees vary according to program. ***Payment plan:*** Installment.

FRESHMAN FINANCIAL AID (Fall 2008, est.) 278 applied for aid; of those 94% were deemed to have need. 100% of freshmen with need received aid; of those 23% had need fully met. ***Average percent of need met:*** 74% (excluding resources awarded to replace EFC). ***Average financial aid package:*** $17,753 (excluding resources awarded to replace EFC). 7% of all full-time freshmen had no need and received non-need-based gift aid.

UNDERGRADUATE FINANCIAL AID (Fall 2008, est.) 1,117 applied for aid; of those 92% were deemed to have need. 100% of undergraduates with need received aid; of those 27% had need fully met. ***Average percent of need met:*** 76% (excluding resources awarded to replace EFC). ***Average financial aid package:*** $16,344 (excluding resources awarded to replace EFC). 9% of all full-time undergraduates had no need and received non-need-based gift aid.

GIFT AID (NEED-BASED) ***Total amount:*** $10,578,840 (15% federal, 17% state, 65% institutional, 3% external sources). ***Receiving aid:*** Freshmen: 93% (260); all full-time undergraduates: 87% (982). ***Average award:*** Freshmen: $12,805; Undergraduates: $10,756. ***Scholarships, grants, and awards:*** Federal Pell, FSEOG, state, college/university gift aid from institutional funds.

GIFT AID (NON-NEED-BASED) ***Total amount:*** $1,181,191 (1% federal, 6% state, 89% institutional, 4% external sources). ***Receiving aid:*** Freshmen: 9% (26). Undergraduates: 8% (86). ***Average award:*** Freshmen: $13,692. Undergraduates: $13,724. ***Scholarships, grants, and awards by category:*** *Academic interests/achievement:* general academic interests/achievements, international studies. *Special achievements/activities:* community service, general special achievements/activities, leadership. *Special characteristics:* children and siblings of alumni, children of faculty/staff, international students, siblings of current students. ***Tuition waivers:*** Full or partial for employees or children of employees.

LOANS ***Student loans:*** $11,555,078 (73% need-based, 27% non-need-based). 95% of past graduating class borrowed through all loan programs. *Average indebtedness per student:* $16,119. ***Average need-based loan:*** Freshmen: $5464. Undergraduates: $6541. ***Parent loans:*** $875,564 (38% need-based, 62% non-need-based). ***Programs:*** FFEL (Subsidized and Unsubsidized Stafford, PLUS), Perkins.

WORK-STUDY ***Federal work-study:*** Total amount: $306,361; 401 jobs averaging $1365. ***State or other work-study/employment:*** Total amount: $143,860 (18% need-based, 82% non-need-based). 261 part-time jobs averaging $1083.

APPLYING FOR FINANCIAL AID ***Required financial aid form:*** FAFSA. ***Financial aid deadline:*** Continuous. ***Notification date:*** Continuous beginning 3/1. Students must reply by 5/1 or within 2 weeks of notification.

CONTACT Jennifer Bates, Director of Financial Aid, Keuka College, Financial Aid Office, Keuka Park, NY 14478-0098, 315-279-5232 or toll-free 800-33-KEUKA. *Fax:* 315-536-5327. *E-mail:* jbates@keuka.edu.

KEYSTONE COLLEGE

La Plume, PA

CONTACT Dr. Sean Van Pallandt, Director of Financial Aid, Keystone College, PO Box 50, La Plume, PA 18440-0200, 717-945-5141 Ext. 6005 or toll-free 877-4COLLEGE Ext. 1. *Fax:* 717-945-6961.

KING COLLEGE

Bristol, TN

ABOUT THE INSTITUTION Independent religious, coed. ***Awards:*** bachelor's and master's degrees. 58 undergraduate majors. ***Total enrollment:*** 1,703. Undergraduates: 1,442. Freshmen: 184.

GIFT AID (NEED-BASED) ***Scholarships, grants, and awards:*** Federal Pell, FSEOG, state, private, college/university gift aid from institutional funds.

GIFT AID (NON-NEED-BASED) ***Scholarships, grants, and awards by category:*** *Academic interests/achievement:* general academic interests/achievements. *Creative arts/performance:* music, performing arts, theater/drama. *Special achievements/activities:* general special achievements/activities. *Special characteristics:* children of faculty/staff, members of minority groups, relatives of clergy.

LOANS ***Programs:*** FFEL (Subsidized and Unsubsidized Stafford, PLUS), Perkins, college/university.

WORK-STUDY ***Federal work-study:*** Total amount: $79,008; 75 jobs averaging $980. ***State or other work-study/employment:*** Part-time jobs available.

APPLYING FOR FINANCIAL AID ***Required financial aid form:*** FAFSA.

CONTACT Brenda L. Clark, Director of Financial Aid, King College, 1350 King College Road, Bristol, TN 37620-2699, 423-652-4728 or toll-free 800-362-0014. *Fax:* 423-652-6039. *E-mail:* blclark@king.edu.

THE KING'S COLLEGE

New York, NY

CONTACT Financial Aid Office, The King's College, 350 Fifth Avenue, 15th Floor Empire State Building, New York, NY 10118, 212-659-7200 or toll-free 888-969-7200 Ext. 3610.

KING'S COLLEGE

Wilkes-Barre, PA

Tuition & fees: $24,680 **Average undergraduate aid package: $19,415**

ABOUT THE INSTITUTION Independent Roman Catholic, coed. ***Awards:*** associate, bachelor's, and master's degrees and post-bachelor's certificates. 40

undergraduate majors. ***Total enrollment:*** 2,673. Undergraduates: 2,339. Freshmen: 560. Federal methodology is used as a basis for awarding need-based institutional aid.

UNDERGRADUATE EXPENSES for 2008–09 ***Application fee:*** $30. ***Comprehensive fee:*** $34,050 includes full-time tuition ($24,680) and room and board ($9370). ***College room only:*** $4360. Room and board charges vary according to board plan. ***Part-time tuition:*** $480 per credit hour. ***Payment plans:*** Installment, deferred payment.

FRESHMAN FINANCIAL AID (Fall 2008, est.) 528 applied for aid; of those 86% were deemed to have need. 100% of freshmen with need received aid; of those 19% had need fully met. ***Average percent of need met:*** 79% (excluding resources awarded to replace EFC). ***Average financial aid package:*** $20,483 (excluding resources awarded to replace EFC). 19% of all full-time freshmen had no need and received non-need-based gift aid.

UNDERGRADUATE FINANCIAL AID (Fall 2008, est.) 1,779 applied for aid; of those 88% were deemed to have need. 99% of undergraduates with need received aid; of those 17% had need fully met. ***Average percent of need met:*** 76% (excluding resources awarded to replace EFC). ***Average financial aid package:*** $19,415 (excluding resources awarded to replace EFC). 19% of all full-time undergraduates had no need and received non-need-based gift aid.

GIFT AID (NEED-BASED) ***Total amount:*** $20,155,537 (10% federal, 13% state, 76% institutional, 1% external sources). ***Receiving aid:*** Freshmen: 80% (450); all full-time undergraduates: 77% (1,537). ***Average award:*** Freshmen: $13,487; Undergraduates: $12,459. ***Scholarships, grants, and awards:*** Federal Pell, FSEOG, state, private, college/university gift aid from institutional funds.

GIFT AID (NON-NEED-BASED) ***Total amount:*** $3,858,140 (9% federal, 1% state, 88% institutional, 2% external sources). ***Receiving aid:*** Freshmen: 9% (48). Undergraduates: 7% (147). ***Average award:*** Freshmen: $9864. Undergraduates: $9503. ***Scholarships, grants, and awards by category:*** *Academic interests/achievement:* 1,609 awards ($12,508,944 total): biological sciences, business, communication, computer science, education, English, foreign languages, general academic interests/achievements, health fields, humanities, mathematics, physical sciences, premedicine, religion/biblical studies, social sciences. *Special achievements/activities:* 583 awards ($3,679,823 total): community service, general special achievements/activities, leadership. *Special characteristics:* 249 awards ($1,118,736 total): children of educators, children of faculty/staff, international students, members of minority groups, relatives of clergy, siblings of current students. ***Tuition waivers:*** Full or partial for employees or children of employees, senior citizens. ***ROTC:*** Army.

LOANS ***Student loans:*** $15,404,555 (93% need-based, 7% non-need-based). 86% of past graduating class borrowed through all loan programs. *Average indebtedness per student:* $28,145. ***Average need-based loan:*** Freshmen: $4046. Undergraduates: $4575. ***Parent loans:*** $3,868,039 (88% need-based, 12% non-need-based). ***Programs:*** FFEL (Subsidized and Unsubsidized Stafford, PLUS), Perkins, alternative loans.

WORK-STUDY ***Federal work-study:*** Total amount: $234,686; 367 jobs averaging $1081. ***State or other work-study/employment:*** Total amount: $472,314 (7% need-based, 93% non-need-based). 447 part-time jobs averaging $1251.

APPLYING FOR FINANCIAL AID ***Required financial aid forms:*** FAFSA, institution's own form. ***Financial aid deadline (priority):*** 2/15. ***Notification date:*** Continuous beginning 3/1. Students must reply by 5/1 or within 2 weeks of notification.

CONTACT Ellen E. McGuire, Director of Financial Aid, King's College, 133 North River Street, Wilkes-Barre, PA 18711-0801, 570-208-5868 or toll-free 888-KINGSPA. *Fax:* 570-208-6015. *E-mail:* finaid@kings.edu.

THE KING'S COLLEGE AND SEMINARY

Van Nuys, CA

CONTACT Financial Aid Office, The King's College and Seminary, 14800 Sherman Way, Van Nuys, CA 91405-8040, 818-779-8040 or toll-free 888-779-8040 (in-state).

KNOX COLLEGE

Galesburg, IL

Tuition & fees: $31,911 **Average undergraduate aid package: $25,060**

ABOUT THE INSTITUTION Independent, coed. ***Awards:*** bachelor's degrees. 33 undergraduate majors. ***Total enrollment:*** 1,379. Undergraduates: 1,379. Freshmen: 367. Both federal and institutional methodology are used as a basis for awarding need-based institutional aid.

UNDERGRADUATE EXPENSES for 2009–10 ***Application fee:*** $40. ***Comprehensive fee:*** $39,075 includes full-time tuition ($31,575), mandatory fees ($336), and room and board ($7164). ***College room only:*** $3603.

FRESHMAN FINANCIAL AID (Fall 2008, est.) 328 applied for aid; of those 84% were deemed to have need. 100% of freshmen with need received aid; of those 41% had need fully met. ***Average percent of need met:*** 94% (excluding resources awarded to replace EFC). ***Average financial aid package:*** $25,282 (excluding resources awarded to replace EFC). 24% of all full-time freshmen had no need and received non-need-based gift aid.

UNDERGRADUATE FINANCIAL AID (Fall 2008, est.) 1,056 applied for aid; of those 86% were deemed to have need. 100% of undergraduates with need received aid; of those 35% had need fully met. ***Average percent of need met:*** 92% (excluding resources awarded to replace EFC). ***Average financial aid package:*** $25,060 (excluding resources awarded to replace EFC). 27% of all full-time undergraduates had no need and received non-need-based gift aid.

GIFT AID (NEED-BASED) ***Total amount:*** $17,058,932 (8% federal, 7% state, 82% institutional, 3% external sources). ***Receiving aid:*** Freshmen: 75% (276); all full-time undergraduates: 67% (913). ***Average award:*** Freshmen: $19,215; Undergraduates: $18,326. ***Scholarships, grants, and awards:*** Federal Pell, FSEOG, state, private, college/university gift aid from institutional funds.

GIFT AID (NON-NEED-BASED) ***Total amount:*** $4,344,201 (90% institutional, 10% external sources). ***Receiving aid:*** Freshmen: 8% (30). Undergraduates: 6% (78). ***Average award:*** Freshmen: $10,567. Undergraduates: $10,250. ***Scholarships, grants, and awards by category:*** *Academic interests/achievement:* general academic interests/achievements, mathematics. *Creative arts/performance:* art/fine arts, creative writing, dance, music, theater/drama. *Special achievements/activities:* community service.

LOANS ***Student loans:*** $6,411,162 (60% need-based, 40% non-need-based). 70% of past graduating class borrowed through all loan programs. *Average indebtedness per student:* $22,749. ***Average need-based loan:*** Freshmen: $4729. Undergraduates: $5467. ***Parent loans:*** $2,516,991 (100% non-need-based). ***Programs:*** Federal Direct (Subsidized and Unsubsidized Stafford, PLUS), Perkins, college/university, private loans.

WORK-STUDY ***Federal work-study:*** Total amount: $1,368,060; 744 jobs averaging $1838. ***State or other work-study/employment:*** Total amount: $169,037 (100% need-based). 81 part-time jobs averaging $2086.

APPLYING FOR FINANCIAL AID ***Required financial aid forms:*** FAFSA, institution's own form, income tax form(s), W-2 forms. ***Financial aid deadline (priority):*** 2/15. ***Notification date:*** Continuous beginning 3/15. Students must reply by 5/1 or within 2 weeks of notification.

CONTACT Ms. Ann M. Brill, Director of Financial Aid, Knox College, 2 East South Street, Galesburg, IL 61401, 309-341-7130 or toll-free 800-678-KNOX. *Fax:* 309-341-7453. *E-mail:* abrill@knox.edu.

KOL YAAKOV TORAH CENTER

Monsey, NY

CONTACT Office of Financial Aid, Kol Yaakov Torah Center, 29 West Maple Avenue, Monsey, NY 10952-2954, 914-425-3863.

KUTZTOWN UNIVERSITY OF PENNSYLVANIA

Kutztown, PA

Tuition & fees (PA res): $7126 **Average undergraduate aid package: $7677**

ABOUT THE INSTITUTION State-supported, coed. ***Awards:*** bachelor's and master's degrees and post-bachelor's certificates. 54 undergraduate majors. ***Total enrollment:*** 10,393. Undergraduates: 9,404. Freshmen: 1,823. Federal methodology is used as a basis for awarding need-based institutional aid.

UNDERGRADUATE EXPENSES for 2008–09 ***Application fee:*** $35. ***Tuition, state resident:*** full-time $5358; part-time $223 per credit hour. ***Tuition, nonresident:*** full-time $13,396; part-time $558 per credit hour. ***Required fees:*** full-time $1768; $66 per credit hour or $44 per term. ***College room and board:*** $7330; ***Room only:*** $4544. Room and board charges vary according to board plan and housing facility. ***Payment plans:*** Installment, deferred payment.

FRESHMAN FINANCIAL AID (Fall 2007) 1,713 applied for aid; of those 71% were deemed to have need. 97% of freshmen with need received aid; of those 75% had need fully met. ***Average percent of need met:*** 58% (excluding resources awarded to replace EFC). ***Average financial aid package:*** $7183 (excluding resources awarded to replace EFC). 4% of all full-time freshmen had no need and received non-need-based gift aid.

UNDERGRADUATE FINANCIAL AID (Fall 2007) 7,104 applied for aid; of those 71% were deemed to have need. 96% of undergraduates with need received aid; of those 94% had need fully met. ***Average percent of need met:*** 60% (excluding resources awarded to replace EFC). ***Average financial aid package:*** $7677 (excluding resources awarded to replace EFC). 4% of all full-time undergraduates had no need and received non-need-based gift aid.

GIFT AID (NEED-BASED) ***Total amount:*** $15,910,337 (41% federal, 49% state, 5% institutional, 5% external sources). ***Receiving aid:*** Freshmen: 43% (830); all full-time undergraduates: 39% (3,369). ***Average award:*** Freshmen: $5391; Undergraduates: $4915. ***Scholarships, grants, and awards:*** Federal Pell, FSEOG, state, private, college/university gift aid from institutional funds.

GIFT AID (NON-NEED-BASED) ***Total amount:*** $1,276,818 (14% federal, 29% state, 18% institutional, 39% external sources). ***Receiving aid:*** Freshmen: 2% (40). Undergraduates: 3% (265). ***Average award:*** Freshmen: $2392. Undergraduates: $2047. ***Scholarships, grants, and awards by category:*** *Academic interests/achievement:* 507 awards ($1,189,303 total): biological sciences, business, communication, computer science, education, English, foreign languages, general academic interests/achievements, health fields, humanities, international studies, library science, mathematics, physical sciences. *Creative arts/performance:* 40 awards ($33,936 total): applied art and design, art/fine arts, dance, music. *Special achievements/activities:* 654 awards ($588,399 total): community service, general special achievements/activities, leadership, religious involvement. *Special characteristics:* 146 awards ($518,441 total): children of faculty/staff, children of union members/company employees, first-generation college students, handicapped students, local/state students. ***Tuition waivers:*** Full or partial for employees or children of employees, senior citizens. ***ROTC:*** Army cooperative.

LOANS ***Student loans:*** $38,181,099 (62% need-based, 38% non-need-based). 86% of past graduating class borrowed through all loan programs. *Average indebtedness per student:* $18,761. ***Average need-based loan:*** Freshmen: $3263. Undergraduates: $4121. ***Parent loans:*** $9,707,938 (27% need-based, 73% non-need-based). ***Programs:*** FFEL (Subsidized and Unsubsidized Stafford, PLUS), Perkins.

WORK-STUDY ***Federal work-study:*** Total amount: $350,277; 330 jobs averaging $1061.

ATHLETIC AWARDS Total amount: $531,971 (56% need-based, 44% non-need-based).

APPLYING FOR FINANCIAL AID ***Required financial aid form:*** FAFSA. ***Financial aid deadline (priority):*** 2/15. ***Notification date:*** Continuous beginning 3/30. Students must reply by 5/1 or within 4 weeks of notification.

CONTACT Mr. Bernard McCree, Director of Financial Aid, Kutztown University of Pennsylvania, 209 Stratton Administration Center, Kutztown, PA 19530-0730, 610-683-4032 or toll-free 877-628-1915. *Fax:* 610-683-1380. *E-mail:* mccree@kutztown.edu.

KUYPER COLLEGE

Grand Rapids, MI

Tuition & fees: $15,219 **Average undergraduate aid package: $11,857**

ABOUT THE INSTITUTION Independent religious, coed. ***Awards:*** associate and bachelor's degrees and post-bachelor's certificates. 26 undergraduate majors. ***Total enrollment:*** 319. Undergraduates: 315. Freshmen: 63. Federal methodology is used as a basis for awarding need-based institutional aid.

UNDERGRADUATE EXPENSES for 2009–10 ***Application fee:*** $25. ***Comprehensive fee:*** $21,209 includes full-time tuition ($14,694), mandatory fees ($525), and room and board ($5990). ***Part-time tuition:*** $705 per credit hour.

FRESHMAN FINANCIAL AID (Fall 2008, est.) 63 applied for aid; of those 89% were deemed to have need. 100% of freshmen with need received aid; of those 12% had need fully met. ***Average percent of need met:*** 78% (excluding resources awarded to replace EFC). ***Average financial aid package:*** $11,291 (excluding resources awarded to replace EFC). 11% of all full-time freshmen had no need and received non-need-based gift aid.

UNDERGRADUATE FINANCIAL AID (Fall 2008, est.) 252 applied for aid; of those 86% were deemed to have need. 100% of undergraduates with need received aid; of those 6% had need fully met. ***Average percent of need met:*** 76% (excluding resources awarded to replace EFC). ***Average financial aid package:*** $11,857 (excluding resources awarded to replace EFC). 13% of all full-time undergraduates had no need and received non-need-based gift aid.

GIFT AID (NEED-BASED) ***Total amount:*** $1,715,839 (24% federal, 22% state, 53% institutional, 1% external sources). ***Receiving aid:*** Freshmen: 88% (56); all full-time undergraduates: 82% (217). ***Average award:*** Freshmen: $7316; Undergraduates: $6178. ***Scholarships, grants, and awards:*** Federal Pell, FSEOG, state, private, college/university gift aid from institutional funds.

GIFT AID (NON-NEED-BASED) ***Total amount:*** $165,221 (11% state, 85% institutional, 4% external sources). ***Receiving aid:*** Freshmen: 11% (7). Undergraduates: 5% (14). ***Average award:*** Freshmen: $6685. Undergraduates: $3665. ***Scholarships, grants, and awards by category:*** *Academic interests/achievement:* 131 awards ($307,475 total): general academic interests/achievements. *Creative arts/performance:* 6 awards ($4000 total): general creative arts/performance. *Special achievements/activities:* 9 awards ($13,500 total): leadership, religious involvement. *Special characteristics:* 57 awards ($347,059 total): children of faculty/staff, international students, members of minority groups.

LOANS ***Student loans:*** $1,586,358 (73% need-based, 27% non-need-based). 88% of past graduating class borrowed through all loan programs. *Average indebtedness per student:* $19,488. ***Average need-based loan:*** Freshmen: $4047. Undergraduates: $5678. ***Parent loans:*** $69,011 (22% need-based, 78% non-need-based). ***Programs:*** Federal Direct (Subsidized and Unsubsidized Stafford, PLUS), FFEL (Subsidized and Unsubsidized Stafford, PLUS), alternative loans.

WORK-STUDY ***Federal work-study:*** Total amount: $23,232; 21 jobs averaging $1371. ***State or other work-study/employment:*** Total amount: $197,666 (3% need-based, 97% non-need-based). 7 part-time jobs averaging $3000.

APPLYING FOR FINANCIAL AID ***Required financial aid forms:*** FAFSA, institution's own form. ***Financial aid deadline (priority):*** 3/1. ***Notification date:*** Continuous beginning 3/20. Students must reply within 2 weeks of notification.

CONTACT Ms. Agnes Russell, Director of Financial Aid, Kuyper College, 3333 East Beltline NE, Grand Rapids, MI 49525-9749, 616-222-3000 Ext. 656 or toll-free 800-511-3749. *Fax:* 616-222-3045. *E-mail:* arussell@kuyper.edu.

LABORATORY INSTITUTE OF MERCHANDISING

New York, NY

ABOUT THE INSTITUTION Proprietary, coed, primarily women. ***Awards:*** associate, bachelor's, and master's degrees. 4 undergraduate majors. ***Total enrollment:*** 1,107. Undergraduates: 1,107. Freshmen: 286.

GIFT AID (NEED-BASED) ***Scholarships, grants, and awards:*** Federal Pell, FSEOG, state, private, college/university gift aid from institutional funds.

GIFT AID (NON-NEED-BASED) ***Scholarships, grants, and awards by category:*** *Academic interests/achievement:* general academic interests/achievements. *Special achievements/activities:* memberships. *Special characteristics:* local/state students.

LOANS ***Programs:*** Federal Direct (Subsidized and Unsubsidized Stafford, PLUS), state.

APPLYING FOR FINANCIAL AID ***Required financial aid forms:*** FAFSA, institution's own form.

CONTACT Mr. Christopher Barto, Dean of Student Financial Services, Laboratory Institute of Merchandising, 12 East 53rd Street, New York, NY 10022-5268, 212-752-1530 or toll-free 800-677-1323. *Fax:* 212-317-8602. *E-mail:* cbarto@limcollege.edu.

LA COLLEGE INTERNATIONAL

Los Angeles, CA

Tuition & fees: N/R **Average undergraduate aid package: N/A**

ABOUT THE INSTITUTION Proprietary, coed. ***Awards:*** associate and bachelor's degrees. 3 undergraduate majors. ***Total enrollment:*** 85. Undergraduates: 85. Freshmen: 70. Federal methodology is used as a basis for awarding need-based institutional aid.

GIFT AID (NEED-BASED) ***Scholarships, grants, and awards:*** Federal Pell, FSEOG, state.

GIFT AID (NON-NEED-BASED) ***Scholarships, grants, and awards by category:*** *Academic interests/achievement:* general academic interests/achievements.

LOANS ***Programs:*** FFEL (Subsidized and Unsubsidized Stafford, PLUS), college/university.

APPLYING FOR FINANCIAL AID ***Required financial aid forms:*** FAFSA, entrance exam, MPN, reference sheet, authorization forms (optional). ***Financial aid deadline:*** Continuous.

CONTACT Office of Financial Aid, LA College International, 3200 Wilshire Boulevard, Los Angeles, CA 90010, 800-218-7274 or toll-free 800-57 GO ICT (in-state). *Fax:* 866-304-7741. *E-mail:* financialaid@lac.edu.

LAFAYETTE COLLEGE

Easton, PA

CONTACT Arlinda DeNardo, Director Financial Aid, Lafayette College, 107 Markle Hall, Easton, PA 18042-1777, 610-330-5055. *Fax:* 610-330-5758. *E-mail:* denardoa@lafayette.edu.

LaGRANGE COLLEGE

LaGrange, GA

Tuition & fees: $19,900 **Average undergraduate aid package: $15,611**

ABOUT THE INSTITUTION Independent United Methodist, coed. ***Awards:*** associate, bachelor's, and master's degrees. 30 undergraduate majors. ***Total enrollment:*** 958. Undergraduates: 840. Freshmen: 157. Federal methodology is used as a basis for awarding need-based institutional aid.

UNDERGRADUATE EXPENSES for 2009–10 ***Application fee:*** $30. ***Comprehensive fee:*** $28,068 includes full-time tuition ($19,900) and room and board ($8168). ***College room only:*** $4784. ***Part-time tuition:*** $820 per hour.

FRESHMAN FINANCIAL AID (Fall 2007) 207 applied for aid; of those 83% were deemed to have need. 99% of freshmen with need received aid; of those 32% had need fully met. ***Average percent of need met:*** 86% (excluding resources awarded to replace EFC). ***Average financial aid package:*** $15,051 (excluding resources awarded to replace EFC). 18% of all full-time freshmen had no need and received non-need-based gift aid.

UNDERGRADUATE FINANCIAL AID (Fall 2007) 807 applied for aid; of those 85% were deemed to have need. 100% of undergraduates with need received aid; of those 27% had need fully met. ***Average percent of need met:*** 84% (excluding resources awarded to replace EFC). ***Average financial aid package:*** $15,611 (excluding resources awarded to replace EFC). 18% of all full-time undergraduates had no need and received non-need-based gift aid.

GIFT AID (NEED-BASED) ***Total amount:*** $6,794,467 (17% federal, 19% state, 59% institutional, 5% external sources). ***Receiving aid:*** Freshmen: 77% (170); all full-time undergraduates: 75% (685). ***Average award:*** Freshmen: $10,329; Undergraduates: $10,040. ***Scholarships, grants, and awards:*** Federal Pell, FSEOG, state, private, college/university gift aid from institutional funds.

GIFT AID (NON-NEED-BASED) ***Total amount:*** $2,233,411 (21% state, 74% institutional, 5% external sources). ***Receiving aid:*** Freshmen: 17% (38). Undergraduates: 12% (112). ***Average award:*** Freshmen: $5754. Undergraduates: $7692. ***Scholarships, grants, and awards by category:*** *Academic interests/achievement:* 644 awards ($2,932,148 total): biological sciences, education, English, general academic interests/achievements, health fields, religion/biblical studies, social sciences. *Creative arts/performance:* 56 awards ($110,447 total): music, theater/drama. *Special achievements/activities:* 2 awards ($7500 total): leadership. *Special characteristics:* 151 awards ($818,512 total): children of faculty/staff, ethnic background, first-generation college students, relatives of clergy, religious affiliation.

LOANS ***Student loans:*** $4,201,263 (79% need-based, 21% non-need-based). 76% of past graduating class borrowed through all loan programs. *Average indebtedness per student:* $19,224. ***Average need-based loan:*** Freshmen: $3231. Undergraduates: $4031. ***Parent loans:*** $1,561,916 (24% need-based, 76% non-need-based). ***Programs:*** FFEL (Subsidized and Unsubsidized Stafford, PLUS), Perkins, state.

WORK-STUDY ***Federal work-study:*** Total amount: $130,400; 90 jobs averaging $1500. ***State or other work-study/employment:*** Total amount: $428,664 (33% need-based, 67% non-need-based). Part-time jobs available.

APPLYING FOR FINANCIAL AID ***Required financial aid forms:*** FAFSA, state aid form. ***Financial aid deadline (priority):*** 3/1. ***Notification date:*** Continuous beginning 3/15. Students must reply within 3 weeks of notification.

CONTACT Michelle Reeves, Assistant Director, LaGrange College, 601 Broad Street, LaGrange, GA 30240-2999, 888-253-9918 or toll-free 800-593-2885. *Fax:* 706-880-8348. *E-mail:* mreeves@lagrange.edu.

LAGUNA COLLEGE OF ART & DESIGN

Laguna Beach, CA

CONTACT Christopher Brown, Director of Student Services, Laguna College of Art & Design, 2222 Laguna Canyon Road, Laguna Beach, CA 92651-1136, 949-376-6000 or toll-free 800-255-0762. *Fax:* 949-497-5220. *E-mail:* cbrown@lagunacollege.edu.

LAKE ERIE COLLEGE

Painesville, OH

ABOUT THE INSTITUTION Independent, coed. ***Awards:*** bachelor's and master's degrees and post-bachelor's certificates. 29 undergraduate majors. ***Total enrollment:*** 1,054. Undergraduates: 837. Freshmen: 251.

GIFT AID (NEED-BASED) ***Scholarships, grants, and awards:*** Federal Pell, FSEOG, state, private, college/university gift aid from institutional funds.

GIFT AID (NON-NEED-BASED) ***Scholarships, grants, and awards by category:*** *Academic interests/achievement:* biological sciences, business, education, English, foreign languages, general academic interests/achievements, humanities, mathematics, physical sciences, social sciences. *Creative arts/performance:* art/fine arts, dance, general creative arts/performance, music, performing arts, theater/drama. *Special achievements/activities:* community service, general special achievements/activities, hobbies/interests. *Special characteristics:* children of faculty/staff, twins.

LOANS ***Programs:*** FFEL (Subsidized and Unsubsidized Stafford, PLUS), Perkins, college/university.

APPLYING FOR FINANCIAL AID ***Required financial aid form:*** FAFSA.

CONTACT Patricia Pangonis, Director of Financial Aid, Lake Erie College, 391 West Washington Street, Painesville, OH 44077-3389, 440-375-7100 or toll-free 800-916-0904. *Fax:* 440-375-7005.

LAKE FOREST COLLEGE

Lake Forest, IL

Tuition & fees: $32,520 **Average undergraduate aid package: $26,073**

ABOUT THE INSTITUTION Independent, coed. ***Awards:*** bachelor's and master's degrees. 31 undergraduate majors. ***Total enrollment:*** 1,400. Undergraduates: 1,381. Freshmen: 379. Both federal and institutional methodology are used as a basis for awarding need-based institutional aid.

UNDERGRADUATE EXPENSES for 2008–09 ***Application fee:*** $40. ***Comprehensive fee:*** $40,244 includes full-time tuition ($32,130), mandatory fees ($390), and room and board ($7724). ***College room only:*** $3826. Full-time tuition and fees vary according to course load. Room and board charges vary according to board plan and housing facility. ***Part-time tuition:*** $4016 per course. Part-time tuition and fees vary according to course load. ***Payment plan:*** Installment.

FRESHMAN FINANCIAL AID (Fall 2008, est.) 311 applied for aid; of those 91% were deemed to have need. 100% of freshmen with need received aid; of those 37% had need fully met. ***Average percent of need met:*** 92% (excluding resources awarded to replace EFC). ***Average financial aid package:*** $27,548 (excluding resources awarded to replace EFC). 15% of all full-time freshmen had no need and received non-need-based gift aid.

UNDERGRADUATE FINANCIAL AID (Fall 2008, est.) 1,063 applied for aid; of those 92% were deemed to have need. 100% of undergraduates with need received aid; of those 37% had need fully met. ***Average percent of need met:*** 87% (excluding resources awarded to replace EFC). ***Average financial aid package:*** $26,073 (excluding resources awarded to replace EFC). 21% of all full-time undergraduates had no need and received non-need-based gift aid.

GIFT AID (NEED-BASED) ***Total amount:*** $21,711,636 (8% federal, 6% state, 82% institutional, 4% external sources). ***Receiving aid:*** Freshmen: 75% (284); all full-time undergraduates: 73% (974). ***Average award:*** Freshmen: $22,988; Undergraduates: $20,994. ***Scholarships, grants, and awards:*** Federal Pell, FSEOG, state, private, college/university gift aid from institutional funds.

GIFT AID (NON-NEED-BASED) ***Total amount:*** $1,902,793 (99% institutional, 1% external sources). ***Receiving aid:*** Freshmen: 9% (33). Undergraduates: 9% (124). ***Average award:*** Freshmen: $11,193. Undergraduates: $11,476. ***Scholar-***

ships, grants, and awards by category: *Academic interests/achievement:* 834 awards ($8,717,101 total): biological sciences, computer science, foreign languages, general academic interests/achievements, mathematics, physical sciences. *Creative arts/performance:* 159 awards ($501,300 total): art/fine arts, creative writing, music, theater/drama. *Special achievements/activities:* 105 awards ($330,875 total): leadership. *Special characteristics:* 44 awards ($499,965 total): children and siblings of alumni, previous college experience. ***Tuition waivers:*** Full or partial for employees or children of employees.

LOANS ***Student loans:*** $7,333,170 (73% need-based, 27% non-need-based). 69% of past graduating class borrowed through all loan programs. *Average indebtedness per student:* $23,962. ***Average need-based loan:*** Freshmen: $4674. Undergraduates: $4876. ***Parent loans:*** $1,632,963 (25% need-based, 75% non-need-based). ***Programs:*** FFEL (Subsidized and Unsubsidized Stafford, PLUS), Perkins, private loans.

WORK-STUDY ***Federal work-study:*** Total amount: $1,098,067; 588 jobs averaging $1800. ***State or other work-study/employment:*** Total amount: $84,000 (100% need-based). Part-time jobs available.

APPLYING FOR FINANCIAL AID ***Required financial aid forms:*** FAFSA, institution's own form, federal 1040. ***Financial aid deadline (priority):*** 3/1. ***Notification date:*** Continuous. Students must reply by 5/1 or within 3 weeks of notification.

CONTACT Mr. Jerry Cebrzynski, Director of Financial Aid, Lake Forest College, 555 North Sheridan Road, Lake Forest, IL 60045-2399, 847-735-5104 or toll-free 800-828-4751. *Fax:* 847-735-6271. *E-mail:* cebrzynski@lakeforest.edu.

LAKELAND COLLEGE

Sheboygan, WI

CONTACT Ms. Patty Taylor, Director of Financial Aid, Lakeland College, PO Box 359, Sheboygan, WI 53082-0359, 920-565-1214 or toll-free 800-242-3347 (in-state). *Fax:* 920-565-1470.

LAKE SUPERIOR STATE UNIVERSITY

Sault Sainte Marie, MI

ABOUT THE INSTITUTION State-supported, coed. ***Awards:*** associate, bachelor's, and master's degrees. 63 undergraduate majors. ***Total enrollment:*** 2,583. Undergraduates: 2,565. Freshmen: 512.

GIFT AID (NEED-BASED) ***Scholarships, grants, and awards:*** Federal Pell, FSEOG, state, private, college/university gift aid from institutional funds, Federal Nursing, third party payments.

LOANS ***Programs:*** Federal Direct (Subsidized and Unsubsidized Stafford, PLUS), Perkins, Federal Nursing, state.

APPLYING FOR FINANCIAL AID ***Required financial aid form:*** FAFSA.

CONTACT Deborah Faust, Director of Financial Aid, Lake Superior State University, 650 West Easterday Avenue, Sault Sainte Marie, MI 49783, 906-635-2678 or toll-free 888-800-LSSU Ext. 2231. *Fax:* 906-635-6669. *E-mail:* finaid@lssu.edu.

LAKEVIEW COLLEGE OF NURSING

Danville, IL

CONTACT Director of Financial Aid, Lakeview College of Nursing, 903 North Logan Avenue, Danville, IL 61832, 217-443-5238.

LAMAR UNIVERSITY

Beaumont, TX

Tuition & fees (TX res): $6014 **Average undergraduate aid package: $10,650**

ABOUT THE INSTITUTION State-supported, coed. ***Awards:*** associate, bachelor's, master's, and doctoral degrees. 102 undergraduate majors. ***Total enrollment:*** 13,465. Undergraduates: 8,993. Freshmen: 1,461. Federal methodology is used as a basis for awarding need-based institutional aid.

UNDERGRADUATE EXPENSES for 2008–09 ***Tuition, state resident:*** full-time $4350; part-time $145 per semester hour. ***Tuition, nonresident:*** full-time $12,780; part-time $426 per semester hour. ***Required fees:*** full-time $1664; $749 per term. Full-time tuition and fees vary according to course load. Part-time tuition and fees vary according to course load. ***College room and board:*** $6290. Room and board charges vary according to board plan and housing facility. ***Payment plan:*** Installment.

FRESHMAN FINANCIAL AID (Fall 2008, est.) 1,009 applied for aid; of those 63% were deemed to have need. 100% of freshmen with need received aid; of those 17% had need fully met. ***Average percent of need met:*** 51% (excluding resources awarded to replace EFC). ***Average financial aid package:*** $10,650 (excluding resources awarded to replace EFC). 38% of all full-time freshmen had no need and received non-need-based gift aid.

UNDERGRADUATE FINANCIAL AID (Fall 2008, est.) 4,573 applied for aid; of those 78% were deemed to have need. 95% of undergraduates with need received aid; of those 6% had need fully met. ***Average percent of need met:*** 48% (excluding resources awarded to replace EFC). ***Average financial aid package:*** $10,650 (excluding resources awarded to replace EFC). 16% of all full-time undergraduates had no need and received non-need-based gift aid.

GIFT AID (NEED-BASED) ***Total amount:*** $17,457,895 (66% federal, 34% state). ***Scholarships, grants, and awards:*** Federal Pell, FSEOG, state, college/university gift aid from institutional funds.

GIFT AID (NON-NEED-BASED) ***Total amount:*** $5,645,828 (76% institutional, 24% external sources). ***Receiving aid:*** Freshmen: 14% (187). Undergraduates: 8% (501). ***Average award:*** Freshmen: $908. Undergraduates: $910. ***Scholarships, grants, and awards by category:*** *Academic interests/achievement:* general academic interests/achievements. *Creative arts/performance:* general creative arts/performance. *Special achievements/activities:* general special achievements/activities. ***Tuition waivers:*** Full or partial for employees or children of employees, senior citizens.

LOANS ***Student loans:*** $22,344,711 (52% need-based, 48% non-need-based). 33% of past graduating class borrowed through all loan programs. *Average indebtedness per student:* $7650. ***Parent loans:*** $1,202,294 (100% non-need-based). ***Programs:*** FFEL (Subsidized and Unsubsidized Stafford, PLUS), Perkins, state, college/university.

WORK-STUDY ***Federal work-study:*** Total amount: $2,053,322; 261 jobs averaging $3651. ***State or other work-study/employment:*** Total amount: $180,693 (100% need-based). 49 part-time jobs averaging $3230.

ATHLETIC AWARDS Total amount: $176,697 (100% non-need-based).

APPLYING FOR FINANCIAL AID ***Required financial aid forms:*** FAFSA, institution's own form. ***Financial aid deadline (priority):*** 4/1. ***Notification date:*** Continuous beginning 5/1. Students must reply within 2 weeks of notification.

CONTACT Financial Aid Department, Lamar University, PO Box 10042, Beaumont, TX 77710, 409-880-8450. *Fax:* 409-880-8934. *E-mail:* financialaid@lamar.edu.

LAMBUTH UNIVERSITY

Jackson, TN

Tuition & fees: $17,450 **Average undergraduate aid package: $15,900**

ABOUT THE INSTITUTION Independent United Methodist, coed. ***Awards:*** bachelor's degrees. 65 undergraduate majors. ***Total enrollment:*** 815. Undergraduates: 815. Freshmen: 205. Federal methodology is used as a basis for awarding need-based institutional aid.

UNDERGRADUATE EXPENSES for 2008–09 ***Application fee:*** $25. ***Comprehensive fee:*** $25,020 includes full-time tuition ($17,000), mandatory fees ($450), and room and board ($7570). ***College room only:*** $3600. Room and board charges vary according to housing facility. ***Part-time tuition:*** $710 per credit hour. ***Part-time fees:*** $200 per term. ***Payment plan:*** Installment.

FRESHMAN FINANCIAL AID (Fall 2008, est.) 204 applied for aid; of those 81% were deemed to have need. 99% of freshmen with need received aid; of those 52% had need fully met. ***Average percent of need met:*** 77% (excluding resources awarded to replace EFC). ***Average financial aid package:*** $16,295 (excluding resources awarded to replace EFC). 15% of all full-time freshmen had no need and received non-need-based gift aid.

UNDERGRADUATE FINANCIAL AID (Fall 2008, est.) 720 applied for aid; of those 85% were deemed to have need. 99% of undergraduates with need received aid; of those 55% had need fully met. ***Average percent of need met:*** 73% (excluding resources awarded to replace EFC). ***Average financial aid package:*** $15,900 (excluding resources awarded to replace EFC). 13% of all full-time undergraduates had no need and received non-need-based gift aid.

GIFT AID (NEED-BASED) ***Total amount:*** $6,161,999 (19% federal, 28% state, 51% institutional, 2% external sources). ***Receiving aid:*** Freshmen: 80% (163); all full-time undergraduates: 80% (594). ***Average award:*** Freshmen: $13,752; Undergraduates: $13,995. ***Scholarships, grants, and awards:*** Federal Pell, FSEOG, state, private, college/university gift aid from institutional funds.

GIFT AID (NON-NEED-BASED) ***Total amount:*** $1,932,260 (15% state, 80% institutional, 5% external sources). ***Receiving aid:*** Freshmen: 19% (39). Undergraduates: 18% (136). ***Average award:*** Freshmen: $10,713. Undergraduates: $10,967. ***Scholarships, grants, and awards by category:*** *Academic interests/achievement:* 398 awards ($2,490,130 total): general academic interests/achievements. *Creative arts/performance:* 87 awards ($238,399 total): music, theater/drama. *Special achievements/activities:* 9 awards ($117,895 total): religious involvement. *Special characteristics:* 180 awards ($429,231 total): children and siblings of alumni, children of faculty/staff, relatives of clergy, religious affiliation. ***Tuition waivers:*** Full or partial for employees or children of employees.

LOANS ***Student loans:*** $2,715,076 (79% need-based, 21% non-need-based). 64% of past graduating class borrowed through all loan programs. *Average indebtedness per student:* $19,000. ***Average need-based loan:*** Freshmen: $3909. Undergraduates: $4514. ***Parent loans:*** $371,104 (34% need-based, 66% non-need-based). ***Programs:*** FFEL (Subsidized and Unsubsidized Stafford, PLUS), Perkins, United Methodist Student Loans.

WORK-STUDY ***Federal work-study:*** Total amount: $123,077; 93 jobs averaging $1348. ***State or other work-study/employment:*** Total amount: $26,522 (100% non-need-based). 20 part-time jobs averaging $1238.

ATHLETIC AWARDS Total amount: $2,679,714 (59% need-based, 41% non-need-based).

APPLYING FOR FINANCIAL AID ***Required financial aid form:*** FAFSA. ***Financial aid deadline (priority):*** 2/15. ***Notification date:*** Continuous beginning 3/1. Students must reply by 5/1 or within 2 weeks of notification.

CONTACT Ms. Karen Myers, Director of Scholarships and Financial Aid, Lambuth University, 705 Lambuth Boulevard, Jackson, TN 38301, 731-425-3332 or toll-free 800-526-2884. *Fax:* 731-425-3496. *E-mail:* myers-k@lambuth.edu.

LANCASTER BIBLE COLLEGE

Lancaster, PA

Tuition & fees: N/R **Average undergraduate aid package: $11,448**

ABOUT THE INSTITUTION Independent nondenominational, coed. 17 undergraduate majors. Federal methodology is used as a basis for awarding need-based institutional aid.

FRESHMAN FINANCIAL AID (Fall 2008, est.) 109 applied for aid; of those 85% were deemed to have need. 99% of freshmen with need received aid; of those 14% had need fully met. ***Average percent of need met:*** 44% (excluding resources awarded to replace EFC). ***Average financial aid package:*** $12,199 (excluding resources awarded to replace EFC). 19% of all full-time freshmen had no need and received non-need-based gift aid.

UNDERGRADUATE FINANCIAL AID (Fall 2008, est.) 517 applied for aid; of those 89% were deemed to have need. 100% of undergraduates with need received aid; of those 14% had need fully met. ***Average percent of need met:*** 69% (excluding resources awarded to replace EFC). ***Average financial aid package:*** $11,448 (excluding resources awarded to replace EFC). 14% of all full-time undergraduates had no need and received non-need-based gift aid.

GIFT AID (NEED-BASED) ***Total amount:*** $3,375,513 (22% federal, 18% state, 53% institutional, 7% external sources). ***Receiving aid:*** Freshmen: 77% (91); all full-time undergraduates: 74% (432). ***Average award:*** Freshmen: $8518; Undergraduates: $8088. ***Scholarships, grants, and awards:*** Federal Pell, FSEOG, state, private, college/university gift aid from institutional funds, Office of Vocational Rehabilitation, Blindness and Visual Services Awards.

GIFT AID (NON-NEED-BASED) ***Total amount:*** $511,213 (84% institutional, 16% external sources). ***Receiving aid:*** Freshmen: 75% (89). Undergraduates: 62% (362). ***Average award:*** Freshmen: $4140. Undergraduates: $5295. ***Scholarships, grants, and awards by category:*** *Academic interests/achievement:* 276 awards ($822,359 total): general academic interests/achievements. *Creative arts/performance:* 19 awards ($29,543 total): general creative arts/performance, music. *Special achievements/activities:* 264 awards ($325,590 total): general special achievements/activities, leadership, religious involvement. *Special characteristics:* 275 awards ($1,031,508 total): adult students, children and siblings of alumni, children of current students, children of faculty/staff, international students, married students, previous college experience, relatives of clergy, religious affiliation, siblings of current students, spouses of current students. ***Tuition waivers:*** Full or partial for children of alumni, employees or children of employees, senior citizens.

LOANS ***Student loans:*** $3,961,874 (79% need-based, 21% non-need-based). 27% of past graduating class borrowed through all loan programs. *Average indebtedness per student:* $19,579. ***Average need-based loan:*** Freshmen: $3288. Undergraduates: $4352. ***Parent loans:*** $641,058 (39% need-based, 61% non-need-based). ***Programs:*** FFEL (Subsidized and Unsubsidized Stafford, PLUS), Perkins, state, alternative loans.

WORK-STUDY ***Federal work-study:*** Total amount: $170,710; 92 jobs averaging $2000.

ATHLETIC AWARDS Total amount: $825,199 (38% need-based, 62% non-need-based).

APPLYING FOR FINANCIAL AID ***Required financial aid forms:*** FAFSA, state aid form. ***Financial aid deadline (priority):*** 5/1. ***Notification date:*** Continuous. Students must reply within 3 weeks of notification.

CONTACT Karen Fox, Director of Financial Aid, Lancaster Bible College, 901 Eden Road, Lancaster, PA 17601, 717-560-8254 Ext. 5352 or toll-free 866-LBC4YOU. *Fax:* 717-560-8216. *E-mail:* kfox@lbc.edu.

LANDER UNIVERSITY

Greenwood, SC

CONTACT Director of Financial Aid, Lander University, 320 Stanley Avenue, Greenwood, SC 29649, 864-388-8340 or toll-free 888-452-6337. *Fax:* 864-388-8811. *E-mail:* fhardin@lander.edu.

LANE COLLEGE

Jackson, TN

Tuition & fees: $8000 **Average undergraduate aid package: $4223**

ABOUT THE INSTITUTION Independent religious, coed. ***Awards:*** bachelor's degrees and post-bachelor's certificates. 17 undergraduate majors. ***Total enrollment:*** 1,982. Undergraduates: 1,982. Freshmen: 534. Federal methodology is used as a basis for awarding need-based institutional aid.

UNDERGRADUATE EXPENSES for 2009–10 ***Comprehensive fee:*** $13,520 includes full-time tuition ($7330), mandatory fees ($670), and room and board ($5520). ***Part-time tuition:*** $310 per hour. ***Part-time fees:*** $670 per year.

FRESHMAN FINANCIAL AID (Fall 2008, est.) 621 applied for aid; of those 99% were deemed to have need. 97% of freshmen with need received aid; of those 9% had need fully met. ***Average percent of need met:*** 27% (excluding resources awarded to replace EFC). ***Average financial aid package:*** $4127 (excluding resources awarded to replace EFC). 1% of all full-time freshmen had no need and received non-need-based gift aid.

UNDERGRADUATE FINANCIAL AID (Fall 2008, est.) 1,876 applied for aid; of those 92% were deemed to have need. 95% of undergraduates with need received aid; of those 14% had need fully met. ***Average percent of need met:*** 28% (excluding resources awarded to replace EFC). ***Average financial aid package:*** $4223 (excluding resources awarded to replace EFC). 3% of all full-time undergraduates had no need and received non-need-based gift aid.

GIFT AID (NEED-BASED) ***Total amount:*** $11,752,130 (05% federal, 25% state, 7% institutional, 3% external sources). ***Receiving aid:*** Freshmen: 87% (543); all full-time undergraduates: 84% (1,643). ***Average award:*** Freshmen: $2848; Undergraduates: $2585. ***Scholarships, grants, and awards:*** Federal Pell, FSEOG, state, private, college/university gift aid from institutional funds, United Negro College Fund.

GIFT AID (NON-NEED-BASED) ***Total amount:*** $219,506 (63% institutional, 37% external sources). ***Receiving aid:*** Freshmen: 14% (85). ***Average award:*** Freshmen: $1367. Undergraduates: $1407.

LOANS ***Student loans:*** $10,297,395 (94% need-based, 6% non-need-based). 88% of past graduating class borrowed through all loan programs. *Average indebtedness per student:* $8458. ***Average need-based loan:*** Freshmen: $1337. Undergraduates: $1407. ***Parent loans:*** $1,323,535 (85% need-based, 15% non-need-based). ***Programs:*** Federal Direct (Subsidized and Unsubsidized Stafford, PLUS).

WORK-STUDY ***Federal work-study:*** Total amount: $261,440; jobs available.

ATHLETIC AWARDS Total amount: $212,460 (85% need-based, 15% non-need-based).

APPLYING FOR FINANCIAL AID ***Required financial aid form:*** FAFSA. ***Financial aid deadline (priority):*** 4/1. ***Notification date:*** Continuous beginning 4/15. Students must reply within 2 weeks of notification.

CONTACT Mr. Tony Calhoun, Director of Financial Aid, Lane College, 545 Lane Avenue, Jackson, TN 38301, 731-426-7558 or toll-free 800-960-7533. *Fax:* 731-426-7652. *E-mail:* tcalhoun@lanecollege.edu.

LANGSTON UNIVERSITY

Langston, OK

Tuition & fees: N/R **Average undergraduate aid package: $9117**

ABOUT THE INSTITUTION State-supported, coed. 56 undergraduate majors. Federal methodology is used as a basis for awarding need-based institutional aid.

UNDERGRADUATE EXPENSES for 2008–09 contact university for tuition costs.

FRESHMAN FINANCIAL AID (Fall 2008, est.) 496 applied for aid; of those 76% were deemed to have need. 99% of freshmen with need received aid; of those 47% had need fully met. ***Average percent of need met:*** 63% (excluding resources awarded to replace EFC). ***Average financial aid package:*** $9099 (excluding resources awarded to replace EFC). 27% of all full-time freshmen had no need and received non-need-based gift aid.

UNDERGRADUATE FINANCIAL AID (Fall 2008, est.) 2,688 applied for aid; of those 70% were deemed to have need. 99% of undergraduates with need received aid; of those 50% had need fully met. ***Average percent of need met:*** 66% (excluding resources awarded to replace EFC). ***Average financial aid package:*** $9117 (excluding resources awarded to replace EFC). 35% of all full-time undergraduates had no need and received non-need-based gift aid.

GIFT AID (NEED-BASED) ***Total amount:*** $6,800,625 (91% federal, 9% state). ***Receiving aid:*** Freshmen: 61% (317); all full-time undergraduates: 54% (1,567). ***Average award:*** Freshmen: $3725; Undergraduates: $4075. ***Scholarships, grants, and awards:*** Federal Pell, FSEOG, state.

GIFT AID (NON-NEED-BASED) ***Total amount:*** $1,883,628 (16% federal, 18% state, 48% institutional, 18% external sources). ***Receiving aid:*** Freshmen: 35% (183). Undergraduates: 29% (854). ***Average award:*** Freshmen: $5436. Undergraduates: $2609. ***Scholarships, grants, and awards by category:*** *Academic interests/achievement:* 46 awards ($217,945 total): agriculture, business, education, engineering/technologies, general academic interests/achievements, health fields. *Creative arts/performance:* 68 awards ($46,750 total): music. *Special achievements/activities:* 22 awards ($66,020 total): cheerleading/drum major, leadership. *Special characteristics:* 20 awards ($13,500 total): ethnic background.

LOANS ***Student loans:*** $17,707,594 (52% need-based, 48% non-need-based). 82% of past graduating class borrowed through all loan programs. *Average indebtedness per student:* $29,021. ***Average need-based loan:*** Freshmen: $3782. Undergraduates: $5551. ***Parent loans:*** $1,662,147 (100% need-based). ***Programs:*** Federal Direct (Subsidized and Unsubsidized Stafford, PLUS), FFEL (Subsidized and Unsubsidized Stafford, PLUS).

WORK-STUDY ***Federal work-study:*** Total amount: $429,136; jobs available.

ATHLETIC AWARDS Total amount: $212,055 (100% non-need-based).

APPLYING FOR FINANCIAL AID ***Required financial aid forms:*** FAFSA, institution's own form. ***Financial aid deadline (priority):*** 3/15. ***Notification date:*** 6/30.

CONTACT Linda Morris, Associate Director of Financial Aid, Langston University, Gandy Hall, Langston, OK 73050, 405-466-3287. *Fax:* 405-466-2986. *E-mail:* lfmorris@lunet.edu.

LA ROCHE COLLEGE

Pittsburgh, PA

Tuition & fees: $20,330 **Average undergraduate aid package: $15,315**

ABOUT THE INSTITUTION Independent religious, coed. ***Awards:*** associate, bachelor's, and master's degrees and post-bachelor's certificates. 38 undergraduate majors. ***Total enrollment:*** 1,425. Undergraduates: 1,293. Freshmen: 228. Federal methodology is used as a basis for awarding need-based institutional aid.

UNDERGRADUATE EXPENSES for 2008–09 ***Application fee:*** $50. ***Comprehensive fee:*** $28,668 includes full-time tuition ($19,660), mandatory fees ($670), and room and board ($8338). ***College room only:*** $5222. Full-time tuition and fees vary according to program. Room and board charges vary according to board plan. ***Part-time tuition:*** $500 per credit. Part-time tuition and fees vary according to program. ***Payment plan:*** Installment.

FRESHMAN FINANCIAL AID (Fall 2008, est.) 172 applied for aid; of those 89% were deemed to have need. 100% of freshmen with need received aid. ***Average percent of need met:*** 92% (excluding resources awarded to replace EFC). ***Average financial aid package:*** $17,367 (excluding resources awarded to replace EFC). 8% of all full-time freshmen had no need and received non-need-based gift aid.

UNDERGRADUATE FINANCIAL AID (Fall 2008, est.) 831 applied for aid; of those 88% were deemed to have need. 100% of undergraduates with need received aid. ***Average percent of need met:*** 90% (excluding resources awarded to replace EFC). ***Average financial aid package:*** $15,315 (excluding resources awarded to replace EFC). 9% of all full-time undergraduates had no need and received non-need-based gift aid.

GIFT AID (NEED-BASED) ***Total amount:*** $3,758,730 (37% federal, 35% state, 28% institutional). ***Receiving aid:*** Freshmen: 57% (129); all full-time undergraduates: 50% (540). ***Average award:*** Freshmen: $2581; Undergraduates: $2733. ***Scholarships, grants, and awards:*** Federal Pell, FSEOG, state, private, college/university gift aid from institutional funds.

GIFT AID (NON-NEED-BASED) ***Total amount:*** $7,301,839 (93% institutional, 7% external sources). ***Receiving aid:*** Freshmen: 67% (153). Undergraduates: 69% (734). ***Average award:*** Freshmen: $7692. Undergraduates: $7638. ***Scholarships, grants, and awards by category:*** *Academic interests/achievement:* 1,081 awards ($6,079,584 total): general academic interests/achievements. ***Tuition waivers:*** Full or partial for employees or children of employees, senior citizens. ***ROTC:*** Army cooperative, Air Force cooperative.

LOANS ***Student loans:*** $9,430,466 (41% need-based, 59% non-need-based). 86% of past graduating class borrowed through all loan programs. *Average indebtedness per student:* $34,189. ***Average need-based loan:*** Freshmen: $3222. Undergraduates: $4550. ***Parent loans:*** $1,150,589 (100% non-need-based). ***Programs:*** FFEL (Subsidized and Unsubsidized Stafford, PLUS), Perkins, state.

WORK-STUDY ***Federal work-study:*** Total amount: $256,346; 160 jobs averaging $2000.

APPLYING FOR FINANCIAL AID ***Required financial aid form:*** FAFSA. ***Financial aid deadline (priority):*** 5/1. ***Notification date:*** Continuous. Students must reply within 2 weeks of notification.

CONTACT Mrs. Sharon Platt, Director of Financial Aid, La Roche College, 9000 Babcock Boulevard, Pittsburgh, PA 15237-5898, 412-536-1125 or toll-free 800-838-4LRC. *Fax:* 412-536-1072. *E-mail:* sharon.platt@laroche.edu.

LA SALLE UNIVERSITY

Philadelphia, PA

CONTACT Robert G. Voss, Dean of Admission and Financial Aid, La Salle University, 1900 West Olney Avenue, Philadelphia, PA 19141-1199, 215-951-1500 or toll-free 800-328-1910.

LASELL COLLEGE

Newton, MA

ABOUT THE INSTITUTION Independent, coed. ***Awards:*** bachelor's and master's degrees and post-bachelor's certificates. 28 undergraduate majors. ***Total enrollment:*** 1,469. Undergraduates: 1,372. Freshmen: 487.

GIFT AID (NEED-BASED) ***Scholarships, grants, and awards:*** Federal Pell, FSEOG, state, private, college/university gift aid from institutional funds.

GIFT AID (NON-NEED-BASED) ***Scholarships, grants, and awards by category:*** *Academic interests/achievement:* general academic interests/achievements. *Special achievements/activities:* community service, general special achievements/activities, leadership. *Special characteristics:* children and siblings of alumni, children of faculty/staff, siblings of current students.

LOANS ***Programs:*** FFEL (Subsidized and Unsubsidized Stafford, PLUS), Perkins, state, alternative loans.

WORK-STUDY ***Federal work-study:*** Total amount: $253,500; 632 jobs averaging $2000.

APPLYING FOR FINANCIAL AID ***Required financial aid forms:*** FAFSA, institution's own form.

CONTACT Michele R. Kosboth, Director of Student Financial Planning, Lasell College, 1844 Commonwealth Avenue, Newton, MA 02466-2709, 617-243-2227 or toll-free 888-LASELL-4. *Fax:* 617-243-2326. *E-mail:* finaid@lasell.edu.

LA SIERRA UNIVERSITY

Riverside, CA

CONTACT Financial Aid Office, La Sierra University, 4500 Riverwalk Parkway, Riverside, CA 92515, 951-785-2175 or toll-free 800-874-5587. *Fax:* 951-785-2942. *E-mail:* sfs@lasierra.edu.

LAURA AND ALVIN SIEGAL COLLEGE OF JUDAIC STUDIES

Beachwood, OH

CONTACT Ruth Kronick, Director of Student Services, Laura and Alvin Siegal College of Judaic Studies, 26500 Shaker Boulevard, Cleveland, OH 44122, 216-464-4050 Ext. 101 or toll-free 888-336-2257. *Fax:* 216-464-5278. *E-mail:* rkronick@siegalcollege.edu.

LAWRENCE TECHNOLOGICAL UNIVERSITY

Southfield, MI

Tuition & fees: $21,979 **Average undergraduate aid package: $17,201**

ABOUT THE INSTITUTION Independent, coed. ***Awards:*** associate, bachelor's, master's, and doctoral degrees and post-bachelor's certificates. 38 undergraduate majors. ***Total enrollment:*** 4,417. Undergraduates: 3,019. Freshmen: 308. Federal methodology is used as a basis for awarding need-based institutional aid.

UNDERGRADUATE EXPENSES for 2008–09 ***Application fee:*** $30. ***Comprehensive fee:*** $30,050 includes full-time tuition ($21,659), mandatory fees ($320), and room and board ($8071). ***College room only:*** $5417. Full-time tuition and fees vary according to course level, degree level, location, program, and student level. Room and board charges vary according to board plan and housing facility. ***Part-time tuition:*** $722 per credit hour. ***Part-time fees:*** $160 per term. Part-time tuition and fees vary according to course level, degree level, location, program, and student level. ***Payment plan:*** Installment.

FRESHMAN FINANCIAL AID (Fall 2007) 274 applied for aid; of those 79% were deemed to have need. 99% of freshmen with need received aid; of those 20% had need fully met. ***Average percent of need met:*** 77% (excluding resources awarded to replace EFC). ***Average financial aid package:*** $17,986 (excluding resources awarded to replace EFC). 11% of all full-time freshmen had no need and received non-need-based gift aid.

UNDERGRADUATE FINANCIAL AID (Fall 2007) 1,352 applied for aid; of those 74% were deemed to have need. 100% of undergraduates with need received aid; of those 17% had need fully met. ***Average percent of need met:*** 71% (excluding resources awarded to replace EFC). ***Average financial aid package:*** $17,201 (excluding resources awarded to replace EFC). 16% of all full-time undergraduates had no need and received non-need-based gift aid.

GIFT AID (NEED-BASED) ***Total amount:*** $8,409,648 (21% federal, 24% state, 53% institutional, 2% external sources). ***Receiving aid:*** Freshmen: 57% (209); all full-time undergraduates: 56% (919). ***Average award:*** Freshmen: $8761; Undergraduates: $7927. ***Scholarships, grants, and awards:*** Federal Pell, FSEOG, state, private, college/university gift aid from institutional funds, Michigan National Guard and ROTC.

GIFT AID (NON-NEED-BASED) ***Total amount:*** $2,266,700 (1% federal, 7% state, 90% institutional, 2% external sources). ***Receiving aid:*** Freshmen: 46% (167). Undergraduates: 36% (603). ***Average award:*** Freshmen: $6012. Undergraduates: $6646. ***Scholarships, grants, and awards by category:*** *Academic interests/achievement:* 1,416 awards ($6,479,459 total): architecture, business, computer science, education, engineering/technologies, general academic interests/achievements, humanities, international studies, mathematics, military science, physical sciences. *Special achievements/activities:* general special achievements/activities. *Special characteristics:* 35 awards ($453,044 total): children of faculty/staff, members of minority groups. ***Tuition waivers:*** Full or partial for employees or children of employees. ***ROTC:*** Army cooperative, Naval cooperative, Air Force cooperative.

LOANS ***Student loans:*** $8,144,193 (95% need-based, 5% non-need-based). 70% of past graduating class borrowed through all loan programs. *Average indebtedness per student:* $37,238. ***Average need-based loan:*** Freshmen: $3791. Undergraduates: $4802. ***Parent loans:*** $6,731,921 (83% need-based, 17% non-need-based). ***Programs:*** Federal Direct (Subsidized and Unsubsidized Stafford, PLUS), Perkins, state, college/university, alternative loans.

WORK-STUDY ***Federal work-study:*** Total amount: $1,100,253; 73 jobs averaging $2085. ***State or other work-study/employment:*** Total amount: $59,039 (100% need-based). 13 part-time jobs averaging $2323.

APPLYING FOR FINANCIAL AID ***Required financial aid form:*** FAFSA. ***Financial aid deadline (priority):*** 4/1. ***Notification date:*** Continuous beginning 4/1. Students must reply within 2 weeks of notification.

CONTACT Mr. Mark Martin, Director of Financial Aid, Lawrence Technological University, 21000 West Ten Mile Road, Southfield, MI 48075-1058, 248-204-2126 or toll-free 800-225-5588. *Fax:* 248-204-2124. *E-mail:* m_martin@ltu.edu.

LAWRENCE UNIVERSITY

Appleton, WI

Tuition & fees: $33,264 **Average undergraduate aid package: $26,800**

ABOUT THE INSTITUTION Independent, coed. ***Awards:*** bachelor's degrees. 58 undergraduate majors. ***Total enrollment:*** 1,503. Undergraduates: 1,503. Freshmen: 382. Institutional methodology is used as a basis for awarding need-based institutional aid.

UNDERGRADUATE EXPENSES for 2008–09 ***Application fee:*** $40. ***Comprehensive fee:*** $40,239 includes full-time tuition ($33,006), mandatory fees ($258), and room and board ($6975). Room and board charges vary according to board plan. ***Payment plans:*** Tuition prepayment, installment.

FRESHMAN FINANCIAL AID (Fall 2008, est.) 281 applied for aid; of those 92% were deemed to have need. 100% of freshmen with need received aid; of those 70% had need fully met. ***Average percent of need met:*** 93% (excluding resources awarded to replace EFC). ***Average financial aid package:*** $26,850 (excluding resources awarded to replace EFC). 24% of all full-time freshmen had no need and received non-need-based gift aid.

UNDERGRADUATE FINANCIAL AID (Fall 2008, est.) 1,032 applied for aid; of those 94% were deemed to have need. 100% of undergraduates with need received aid; of those 62% had need fully met. ***Average percent of need met:*** 92% (excluding resources awarded to replace EFC). ***Average financial aid package:*** $26,800 (excluding resources awarded to replace EFC). 24% of all full-time undergraduates had no need and received non-need-based gift aid.

GIFT AID (NEED-BASED) ***Total amount:*** $17,266,619 (7% federal, 4% state, 86% institutional, 3% external sources). ***Receiving aid:*** Freshmen: 67% (255); all full-time undergraduates: 66% (955). ***Average award:*** Freshmen: $19,410; Undergraduates: $18,260. ***Scholarships, grants, and awards:*** Federal Pell, FSEOG, state, private, college/university gift aid from institutional funds.

GIFT AID (NON-NEED-BASED) ***Total amount:*** $4,232,575 (1% state, 96% institutional, 3% external sources). ***Average award:*** Freshmen: $13,890. Undergraduates: $11,770. ***Scholarships, grants, and awards by category:*** *Academic interests/achievement:* 736 awards ($6,928,751 total): general academic interests/achievements. *Creative arts/performance:* 128 awards ($877,093 total): music. *Special characteristics:* 128 awards ($414,329 total): children and siblings of alumni, ethnic background. ***Tuition waivers:*** Full or partial for employees or children of employees.

LOANS ***Student loans:*** $7,516,539 (58% need-based, 42% non-need-based). 69% of past graduating class borrowed through all loan programs. *Average indebtedness per student:* $26,054. ***Average need-based loan:*** Freshmen: $5290. Undergraduates: $6040. ***Parent loans:*** $1,702,550 (100% non-need-based). ***Programs:*** Federal Direct (Subsidized and Unsubsidized Stafford, PLUS), Perkins, alternative loans.

WORK-STUDY ***Federal work-study:*** Total amount: $1,474,796; 598 jobs averaging $2350. ***State or other work-study/employment:*** Total amount: $787,172 (100% non-need-based). 309 part-time jobs averaging $2400.

APPLYING FOR FINANCIAL AID ***Required financial aid forms:*** FAFSA, institution's own form, federal tax returns and W-2 forms for parents and students, noncustodial form. ***Financial aid deadline (priority):*** 3/15. ***Notification date:*** Students must reply by 5/1.

CONTACT Mrs. Sara Beth Holman, Director of Financial Aid, Lawrence University, PO Box 599, Appleton, WI 54912-0599, 920-832-6583 or toll-free 800-227-0982. *Fax:* 920-832-6582. *E-mail:* sara.b.holman@lawrence.edu.

LEBANON VALLEY COLLEGE

Annville, PA

Tuition & fees: $29,350 **Average undergraduate aid package: $20,995**

ABOUT THE INSTITUTION Independent United Methodist, coed. ***Awards:*** associate, bachelor's, master's, and doctoral degrees and post-bachelor's certificates. 35 undergraduate majors. ***Total enrollment:*** 1,965. Undergraduates: 1,747. Freshmen: 396. Federal methodology is used as a basis for awarding need-based institutional aid.

UNDERGRADUATE EXPENSES for 2008–09 ***Application fee:*** $30. ***Comprehensive fee:*** $37,110 includes full-time tuition ($28,650), mandatory fees ($700), and room and board ($7760). ***College room only:*** $3790. Room and board charges vary according to board plan and housing facility. ***Part-time tuition:*** $480 per credit. Part-time tuition and fees vary according to class time and degree level. ***Payment plans:*** Tuition prepayment, installment.

FRESHMAN FINANCIAL AID (Fall 2008, est.) 371 applied for aid; of those 85% were deemed to have need. 100% of freshmen with need received aid; of those 31% had need fully met. ***Average percent of need met:*** 86% (excluding resources awarded to replace EFC). ***Average financial aid package:*** $21,978 (excluding resources awarded to replace EFC). 17% of all full-time freshmen had no need and received non-need-based gift aid.

UNDERGRADUATE FINANCIAL AID (Fall 2008, est.) 1,395 applied for aid; of those 89% were deemed to have need. 100% of undergraduates with need received aid; of those 32% had need fully met. ***Average percent of need met:*** 83% (excluding resources awarded to replace EFC). ***Average financial aid package:*** $20,995 (excluding resources awarded to replace EFC). 18% of all full-time undergraduates had no need and received non-need-based gift aid.

GIFT AID (NEED-BASED) ***Total amount:*** $17,830,499 (5% federal, 10% state, 85% institutional). ***Receiving aid:*** Freshmen: 79% (314); all full-time undergraduates: 77% (1,225). ***Average award:*** Freshmen: $17,604; Undergraduates: $17,495. ***Scholarships, grants, and awards:*** Federal Pell, FSEOG, state, private, college/university gift aid from institutional funds, Academic Competitiveness Grant, National Smart Grant, TEACH Grant.

GIFT AID (NON-NEED-BASED) ***Total amount:*** $5,321,825 (1% federal, 1% state, 83% institutional, 15% external sources). ***Receiving aid:*** Freshmen: 11% (43). Undergraduates: 8% (133). ***Average award:*** Freshmen: $11,781. Undergraduates: $12,207. ***Scholarships, grants, and awards by category:*** *Academic interests/achievement:* 1,299 awards ($15,262,926 total): biological sciences, general academic interests/achievements, religion/biblical studies. *Creative arts/performance:* 50 awards ($72,617 total): music. *Special achievements/activities:* 96 awards ($48,000 total): general special achievements/activities, junior miss. *Special characteristics:* 186 awards ($1,118,866 total): children and siblings of alumni, children of faculty/staff, ethnic background, international students. ***Tuition waivers:*** Full or partial for employees or children of employees, senior citizens.

LOANS ***Student loans:*** $12,871,076 (38% need-based, 62% non-need-based). 81% of past graduating class borrowed through all loan programs. *Average indebtedness per student:* $32,437. ***Average need-based loan:*** Freshmen: $4566. Undergraduates: $4635. ***Parent loans:*** $4,792,666 (100% non-need-based). ***Programs:*** FFEL (Subsidized and Unsubsidized Stafford, PLUS), Perkins.

WORK-STUDY ***Federal work-study:*** Total amount: $1,178,320; 831 jobs averaging $1410.

APPLYING FOR FINANCIAL AID ***Required financial aid forms:*** FAFSA, institution's own form. ***Financial aid deadline (priority):*** 3/1. ***Notification date:*** Continuous beginning 3/1. Students must reply by 5/1 or within 2 weeks of notification.

CONTACT Kendra M. Feigert, Director of Financial Aid, Lebanon Valley College, 101 North College Avenue, Annville, PA 17003, 866-582-4236 or toll-free 866-LVC-4ADM. *Fax:* 717-867-6027. *E-mail:* feigert@lvc.edu.

LEES-McRAE COLLEGE

Banner Elk, NC

Tuition & fees: $20,500 **Average undergraduate aid package: $14,200**

ABOUT THE INSTITUTION Independent religious, coed. ***Awards:*** bachelor's degrees. 29 undergraduate majors. ***Total enrollment:*** 882. Undergraduates: 882. Freshmen: 203. Both federal and institutional methodology are used as a basis for awarding need-based institutional aid.

UNDERGRADUATE EXPENSES for 2008–09 ***Comprehensive fee:*** $27,500 includes full-time tuition ($20,500) and room and board ($7000). ***Payment plan:*** Installment.

FRESHMAN FINANCIAL AID (Fall 2008, est.) 190 applied for aid; of those 86% were deemed to have need. 100% of freshmen with need received aid; of those 4% had need fully met. ***Average percent of need met:*** 76% (excluding resources awarded to replace EFC). ***Average financial aid package:*** $13,950 (excluding resources awarded to replace EFC). 11% of all full-time freshmen had no need and received non-need-based gift aid.

UNDERGRADUATE FINANCIAL AID (Fall 2008, est.) 789 applied for aid; of those 91% were deemed to have need. 100% of undergraduates with need received aid; of those 4% had need fully met. ***Average percent of need met:*** 74% (excluding resources awarded to replace EFC). ***Average financial aid package:*** $14,200 (excluding resources awarded to replace EFC). 8% of all full-time undergraduates had no need and received non-need-based gift aid.

GIFT AID (NEED-BASED) ***Total amount:*** $12,724,467 (11% federal, 17% state, 70% institutional, 2% external sources). ***Receiving aid:*** Freshmen: 62% (142); all full-time undergraduates: 67% (625). ***Average award:*** Freshmen: $9200; Undergraduates: $9500. ***Scholarships, grants, and awards:*** Federal Pell, FSEOG, state, private, college/university gift aid from institutional funds, Academic Competitiveness Grant, National Smart Grant.

GIFT AID (NON-NEED-BASED) ***Receiving aid:*** Freshmen: 57% (131). Undergraduates: 61% (574). ***Average award:*** Freshmen: $4500. Undergraduates: $5200. ***Scholarships, grants, and awards by category:*** *Academic interests/achievement:* biological sciences, education, general academic interests/achievements, mathematics. *Creative arts/performance:* dance, journalism/publications, performing arts, theater/drama. *Special achievements/activities:* $950,000 total: cheerleading/drum major, general special achievements/activities, leadership. *Special characteristics:* children of educators, children of faculty/staff, children with a deceased or disabled parent, international students, local/state students, previous college experience, relatives of clergy, religious affiliation, veterans. ***Tuition waivers:*** Full or partial for employees or children of employees. ***ROTC:*** Army cooperative.

LOANS ***Student loans:*** $4,373,214 (100% need-based). ***Average need-based loan:*** Freshmen: $3500. Undergraduates: $5000. ***Parent loans:*** $743,674 (100% need-based). ***Programs:*** FFEL (Subsidized and Unsubsidized Stafford, PLUS), Perkins, college/university, private alternative loans.

WORK-STUDY ***Federal work-study:*** Total amount: $217,651; jobs available. ***State or other work-study/employment:*** Total amount: $134,004 (100% need-based). Part-time jobs available.

ATHLETIC AWARDS Total amount: $1,194,904 (100% need-based).

APPLYING FOR FINANCIAL AID ***Required financial aid forms:*** FAFSA, state aid form. ***Financial aid deadline:*** Continuous. ***Notification date:*** Continuous beginning 2/15.

CONTACT Cathy Shell, Director of Financial Aid, Lees-McRae College, PO Box 128, Banner Elk, NC 28604-0128, 828-898-8740 or toll-free 800-280-4562. *Fax:* 828-898-8746. *E-mail:* shell@lmc.edu.

LEE UNIVERSITY

Cleveland, TN

Tuition & fees: $11,164 **Average undergraduate aid package: $8903**

ABOUT THE INSTITUTION Independent religious, coed. ***Awards:*** bachelor's and master's degrees and post-master's certificates. 36 undergraduate majors. ***Total enrollment:*** 4,147. Undergraduates: 3,847. Freshmen: 860. Federal methodology is used as a basis for awarding need-based institutional aid.

UNDERGRADUATE EXPENSES for 2008–09 ***Application fee:*** $25. ***Comprehensive fee:*** $16,634 includes full-time tuition ($10,824), mandatory fees ($340), and room and board ($5470). ***College room only:*** $2640. Room and board charges vary according to board plan and housing facility. ***Part-time tuition:*** $451 per credit hour. ***Payment plan:*** Deferred payment.

FRESHMAN FINANCIAL AID (Fall 2008, est.) 702 applied for aid; of those 77% were deemed to have need. 97% of freshmen with need received aid; of those 34% had need fully met. ***Average percent of need met:*** 65% (excluding resources awarded to replace EFC). ***Average financial aid package:*** $9395 (excluding resources awarded to replace EFC). 27% of all full-time freshmen had no need and received non-need-based gift aid.

UNDERGRADUATE FINANCIAL AID (Fall 2008, est.) 2,541 applied for aid; of those 82% were deemed to have need. 98% of undergraduates with need received aid; of those 18% had need fully met. ***Average percent of need met:*** 54% (excluding resources awarded to replace EFC). ***Average financial aid package:*** $8903 (excluding resources awarded to replace EFC). 24% of all full-time undergraduates had no need and received non-need-based gift aid.

GIFT AID (NEED-BASED) ***Total amount:*** $10,868,029 (35% federal, 24% state, 38% institutional, 3% external sources). ***Receiving aid:*** Freshmen: 56% (475); all full-time undergraduates: 50% (1,689). ***Average award:*** Freshmen: $7968;

Undergraduates: $6831. ***Scholarships, grants, and awards:*** Federal Pell, FSEOG, state, private, college/university gift aid from institutional funds.

GIFT AID (NON-NEED-BASED) ***Total amount:*** $5,460,670 (23% state, 71% institutional, 6% external sources). ***Receiving aid:*** Freshmen: 15% (126). Undergraduates: 7% (242). ***Average award:*** Freshmen: $10,324. Undergraduates: $8755. ***Scholarships, grants, and awards by category:*** *Academic interests/achievement:* biological sciences, business, communication, education, general academic interests/achievements, religion/biblical studies. *Creative arts/performance:* music, theater/drama. *Special achievements/activities:* cheerleading/drum major, leadership, religious involvement. *Special characteristics:* children of faculty/staff, local/state students, siblings of current students, spouses of current students. ***Tuition waivers:*** Full or partial for employees or children of employees.

LOANS ***Student loans:*** $15,359,120 (73% need-based, 27% non-need-based). 66% of past graduating class borrowed through all loan programs. *Average indebtedness per student:* $28,542. ***Average need-based loan:*** Freshmen: $3701. Undergraduates: $4244. ***Parent loans:*** $2,060,680 (34% need-based, 66% non-need-based). ***Programs:*** FFEL (Subsidized and Unsubsidized Stafford, PLUS), Perkins, college/university.

WORK-STUDY ***Federal work-study:*** Total amount: $375,258; 205 jobs averaging $1485. ***State or other work-study/employment:*** Total amount: $600,000 (100% non-need-based). 350 part-time jobs averaging $1714.

ATHLETIC AWARDS Total amount: $1,498,817 (30% need-based, 70% non-need-based).

APPLYING FOR FINANCIAL AID ***Required financial aid form:*** FAFSA. ***Financial aid deadline (priority):*** 3/15. ***Notification date:*** Continuous. Students must reply within 3 weeks of notification.

CONTACT Mr. Michael Ellis, Director of Student Financial Aid, Lee University, 1120 North Ocoee Street, Cleveland, TN 37320-3450, 423-614-8300 or toll-free 800-533-9930. *Fax:* 423-614-8308. *E-mail:* finaid@leeuniversity.edu.

LEHIGH UNIVERSITY

Bethlehem, PA

Tuition & fees: $37,550 **Average undergraduate aid package: $31,611**

ABOUT THE INSTITUTION Independent, coed. ***Awards:*** bachelor's, master's, and doctoral degrees and post-bachelor's and post-master's certificates. 79 undergraduate majors. ***Total enrollment:*** 6,994. Undergraduates: 4,876. Freshmen: 1,205. Institutional methodology is used as a basis for awarding need-based institutional aid.

UNDERGRADUATE EXPENSES for 2008–09 ***Application fee:*** $70. ***Comprehensive fee:*** $47,320 includes full-time tuition ($37,250), mandatory fees ($300), and room and board ($9770). ***College room only:*** $5660. Room and board charges vary according to board plan. ***Part-time tuition:*** $1555 per credit. ***Payment plans:*** Tuition prepayment, installment.

FRESHMAN FINANCIAL AID (Fall 2008, est.) 758 applied for aid; of those 69% were deemed to have need. 100% of freshmen with need received aid; of those 52% had need fully met. ***Average percent of need met:*** 96% (excluding resources awarded to replace EFC). ***Average financial aid package:*** $31,469 (excluding resources awarded to replace EFC). 7% of all full-time freshmen had no need and received non-need-based gift aid.

UNDERGRADUATE FINANCIAL AID (Fall 2008, est.) 2,703 applied for aid; of those 77% were deemed to have need. 100% of undergraduates with need received aid; of those 68% had need fully met. ***Average percent of need met:*** 96% (excluding resources awarded to replace EFC). ***Average financial aid package:*** $31,611 (excluding resources awarded to replace EFC). 8% of all full-time undergraduates had no need and received non-need-based gift aid.

GIFT AID (NEED-BASED) ***Total amount:*** $51,247,387 (5% federal, 2% state, 93% institutional). ***Receiving aid:*** Freshmen: 42% (506); all full-time undergraduates: 42% (2,012). ***Average award:*** Freshmen: $27,552; Undergraduates: $26,797. ***Scholarships, grants, and awards:*** Federal Pell, FSEOG, state, private, college/university gift aid from institutional funds, United Negro College Fund.

GIFT AID (NON-NEED-BASED) ***Total amount:*** $6,284,332 (62% institutional, 38% external sources). ***Receiving aid:*** Freshmen: 3% (34). Undergraduates: 5% (242). ***Average award:*** Freshmen: $11,110. Undergraduates: $10,486. ***Scholarships, grants, and awards by category:*** *Academic interests/achievement:* 480 awards ($5,238,529 total): business, communication, engineering/technologies, general academic interests/achievements, military science. *Creative arts/performance:* 30 awards ($91,060 total): general creative arts/performance, music, performing arts, theater/drama. *Special achievements/activities:* 6 awards ($34,000 total): general special achievements/activities. *Special characteristics:* 102 awards: children of faculty/staff, members of minority groups. ***Tuition waivers:*** Full or partial for employees or children of employees, senior citizens. ***ROTC:*** Army.

LOANS ***Student loans:*** $23,139,094 (36% need-based, 64% non-need-based). 58% of past graduating class borrowed through all loan programs. *Average indebtedness per student:* $29,756. ***Average need-based loan:*** Freshmen: $3420. Undergraduates: $4486. ***Parent loans:*** $5,791,068 (100% non-need-based). ***Programs:*** FFEL (Subsidized and Unsubsidized Stafford, PLUS), Perkins, college/university, private alternative loans.

WORK-STUDY ***Federal work-study:*** Total amount: $2,253,198; 1,241 jobs averaging $1816. ***State or other work-study/employment:*** Total amount: $897,408 (10% need-based, 90% non-need-based). 181 part-time jobs averaging $4477.

ATHLETIC AWARDS Total amount: $2,904,315 (37% need-based, 63% non-need-based).

APPLYING FOR FINANCIAL AID ***Required financial aid forms:*** FAFSA, CSS Financial Aid PROFILE, noncustodial (divorced/separated) parent's statement, business/farm supplement. ***Financial aid deadline:*** 2/1. ***Notification date:*** 3/30. Students must reply by 5/1 or within 3 weeks of notification.

CONTACT Linda F. Bell, Director of Financial Aid, Lehigh University, 218 West Packer Avenue, Bethlehem, PA 18015-3094, 610-758-3181. *Fax:* 610-758-6211. *E-mail:* lfn0@lehigh.edu.

LEHMAN COLLEGE OF THE CITY UNIVERSITY OF NEW YORK

Bronx, NY

ABOUT THE INSTITUTION State and locally supported, coed. ***Awards:*** bachelor's and master's degrees and post-master's certificates. 53 undergraduate majors. ***Total enrollment:*** 11,860. Undergraduates: 9,569. Freshmen: 1,001.

GIFT AID (NEED-BASED) ***Scholarships, grants, and awards:*** Federal Pell, FSEOG, state, college/university gift aid from institutional funds.

LOANS ***Programs:*** Federal Direct (Subsidized and Unsubsidized Stafford, PLUS), Perkins.

APPLYING FOR FINANCIAL AID ***Required financial aid forms:*** FAFSA, state aid form.

CONTACT David Martinez, Director of Financial Aid, Lehman College of the City University of New York, 250 Bedford Park Boulevard West, Bronx, NY 10468-1589, 718-960-8545 or toll-free 877-Lehman1 (out-of-state). *Fax:* 718-960-8328. *E-mail:* idmlc@cunyvm.cuny.edu.

LE MOYNE COLLEGE

Syracuse, NY

Tuition & fees: $25,830 **Average undergraduate aid package: $18,102**

ABOUT THE INSTITUTION Independent Roman Catholic (Jesuit), coed. ***Awards:*** bachelor's and master's degrees and post-master's certificates. 52 undergraduate majors. ***Total enrollment:*** 3,479. Undergraduates: 2,761. Freshmen: 544. Both federal and institutional methodology are used as a basis for awarding need-based institutional aid.

UNDERGRADUATE EXPENSES for 2009–10 ***Application fee:*** $35. ***Comprehensive fee:*** $35,820 includes full-time tuition ($25,110), mandatory fees ($720), and room and board ($9990). ***College room only:*** $6340. ***Part-time tuition:*** $526 per credit hour.

FRESHMAN FINANCIAL AID (Fall 2008, est.) 542 applied for aid; of those 89% were deemed to have need. 100% of freshmen with need received aid; of those 23% had need fully met. ***Average percent of need met:*** 82% (excluding resources awarded to replace EFC). ***Average financial aid package:*** $19,710 (excluding resources awarded to replace EFC). 9% of all full-time freshmen had no need and received non-need-based gift aid.

UNDERGRADUATE FINANCIAL AID (Fall 2008, est.) 2,056 applied for aid; of those 91% were deemed to have need. 99% of undergraduates with need received aid; of those 21% had need fully met. ***Average percent of need met:*** 75% (excluding resources awarded to replace EFC). ***Average financial aid package:*** $18,102 (excluding resources awarded to replace EFC). 10% of all full-time undergraduates had no need and received non-need-based gift aid.

GIFT AID (NEED-BASED) ***Total amount:*** $25,733,492 (11% federal, 13% state, 74% institutional, 2% external sources). ***Receiving aid:*** Freshmen: 78% (452);

all full-time undergraduates: 76% (1,735). ***Average award:*** Freshmen: $10,855; Undergraduates: $9748. ***Scholarships, grants, and awards:*** Federal Pell, FSEOG, state, private, college/university gift aid from institutional funds.

GIFT AID (NON-NEED-BASED) ***Total amount:*** $3,018,936 (2% state, 95% institutional, 3% external sources). ***Receiving aid:*** Freshmen: 49% (283). Undergraduates: 44% (1,012). ***Average award:*** Freshmen: $8624. Undergraduates: $9782. ***Scholarships, grants, and awards by category:*** *Academic interests/achievement:* 370 awards ($5,061,469 total): general academic interests/achievements. *Special achievements/activities:* 563 awards ($3,495,178 total): leadership. *Special characteristics:* 139 awards ($483,750 total): children and siblings of alumni, members of minority groups. ***ROTC:*** Army cooperative, Air Force cooperative.

LOANS ***Student loans:*** $16,651,693 (97% need-based, 3% non-need-based). 84% of past graduating class borrowed through all loan programs. *Average indebtedness per student:* $19,123. ***Average need-based loan:*** Freshmen: $3807. Undergraduates: $4681. ***Parent loans:*** $3,535,775 (89% need-based, 11% non-need-based). ***Programs:*** FFEL (Subsidized and Unsubsidized Stafford, PLUS), Perkins.

WORK-STUDY ***Federal work-study:*** Total amount: $330,293; 286 jobs averaging $1144. ***State or other work-study/employment:*** 569 part-time jobs averaging $944.

ATHLETIC AWARDS Total amount: $1,356,186 (60% need-based, 40% non-need-based).

APPLYING FOR FINANCIAL AID ***Required financial aid forms:*** FAFSA, institution's own form, state aid form. ***Financial aid deadline (priority):*** 2/1. ***Notification date:*** 3/15. Students must reply by 5/1 or within 2 weeks of notification.

CONTACT Mr. William Cheetham, Director of Financial Aid, Le Moyne College, Financial Aid Office, 1419 Salt Springs Road, Syracuse, NY 13214-1301, 315-445-4400 or toll-free 800-333-4733. *Fax:* 315-445-4182. *E-mail:* cheethwc@lemoyne.edu.

LeMOYNE-OWEN COLLEGE

Memphis, TN

CONTACT Phyllis Nettles Torry, Director of Student Financial Services, LeMoyne-Owen College, 807 Walker Avenue, Memphis, TN 38126-6595, 901-435-1550. *Fax:* 901-435-1574. *E-mail:* phyllis_torry@loc.edu.

LENOIR-RHYNE UNIVERSITY

Hickory, NC

ABOUT THE INSTITUTION Independent Lutheran, coed. ***Awards:*** bachelor's and master's degrees and post-bachelor's certificates. 72 undergraduate majors. ***Total enrollment:*** 1,562. Undergraduates: 1,381. Freshmen: 346.

GIFT AID (NEED-BASED) ***Scholarships, grants, and awards:*** Federal Pell, FSEOG, state, private, college/university gift aid from institutional funds, Federal Nursing.

GIFT AID (NON-NEED-BASED) ***Scholarships, grants, and awards by category:*** *Academic interests/achievement:* general academic interests/achievements. *Creative arts/performance:* music. *Special achievements/activities:* cheerleading/drum major, leadership. *Special characteristics:* children and siblings of alumni, children of faculty/staff, ethnic background, relatives of clergy, religious affiliation, siblings of current students.

LOANS ***Programs:*** FFEL (Subsidized and Unsubsidized Stafford, PLUS), Perkins, Federal Nursing, state.

APPLYING FOR FINANCIAL AID ***Required financial aid forms:*** FAFSA, state aid form.

CONTACT Eric Brandon, Director of Enrollment Services, Lenoir-Rhyne University, PO Box 7227, Hickory, NC 28603, 828-328-7300 or toll-free 800-277-5721. *Fax:* 828-328-7039. *E-mail:* admission@lrc.edu.

LESLEY UNIVERSITY

Cambridge, MA

ABOUT THE INSTITUTION Independent, coed. ***Awards:*** associate, bachelor's, master's, and doctoral degrees and post-master's certificates. 22 undergraduate majors. ***Total enrollment:*** 6,686. Undergraduates: 1,267. Freshmen: 327.

GIFT AID (NEED-BASED) ***Scholarships, grants, and awards:*** Federal Pell, FSEOG, state, private, college/university gift aid from institutional funds.

GIFT AID (NON-NEED-BASED) ***Scholarships, grants, and awards by category:*** *Academic interests/achievement:* general academic interests/achievements. *Creative arts/performance:* art/fine arts. *Special achievements/activities:* general special achievements/activities. *Special characteristics:* ethnic background, local/state students, members of minority groups.

LOANS ***Programs:*** FFEL (Subsidized and Unsubsidized Stafford, PLUS), Perkins, state.

WORK-STUDY ***Federal work-study:*** Total amount: $450,000; 261 jobs averaging $1724. ***State or other work-study/employment:*** 122 part-time jobs averaging $2000.

APPLYING FOR FINANCIAL AID ***Required financial aid forms:*** FAFSA, institution's own form.

CONTACT Scott A. Jewell, Director of Financial Aid, Lesley University, 29 Everett Street, Cambridge, MA 02138-2790, 617-349-8714 or toll-free 800-999-1959 Ext. 8800. *Fax:* 617-349-8717. *E-mail:* sjewell@lesley.edu.

LeTOURNEAU UNIVERSITY

Longview, TX

Tuition & fees: $19,140 **Average undergraduate aid package: $10,766**

ABOUT THE INSTITUTION Independent nondenominational, coed. ***Awards:*** associate, bachelor's, and master's degrees. 41 undergraduate majors. ***Total enrollment:*** 3,662. Undergraduates: 3,371. Freshmen: 341. Federal methodology is used as a basis for awarding need-based institutional aid.

UNDERGRADUATE EXPENSES for 2008–09 ***Application fee:*** $25. ***Comprehensive fee:*** $26,640 includes full-time tuition ($18,940), mandatory fees ($200), and room and board ($7500). Room and board charges vary according to board plan. ***Part-time tuition:*** $344 per hour. Part-time tuition and fees vary according to course load. ***Payment plan:*** Installment.

FRESHMAN FINANCIAL AID (Fall 2008, est.) 263 applied for aid; of those 76% were deemed to have need. 100% of freshmen with need received aid; of those 20% had need fully met. ***Average percent of need met:*** 70% (excluding resources awarded to replace EFC). ***Average financial aid package:*** $14,182 (excluding resources awarded to replace EFC). 31% of all full-time freshmen had no need and received non-need-based gift aid.

UNDERGRADUATE FINANCIAL AID (Fall 2008, est.) 1,420 applied for aid; of those 80% were deemed to have need. 99% of undergraduates with need received aid; of those 17% had need fully met. ***Average percent of need met:*** 63% (excluding resources awarded to replace EFC). ***Average financial aid package:*** $10,766 (excluding resources awarded to replace EFC). 12% of all full-time undergraduates had no need and received non-need-based gift aid.

GIFT AID (NEED-BASED) ***Total amount:*** $9,228,788 (33% federal, 10% state, 53% institutional, 4% external sources). ***Receiving aid:*** Freshmen: 60% (199); all full-time undergraduates: 41% (899). ***Average award:*** Freshmen: $10,082; Undergraduates: $8936. ***Scholarships, grants, and awards:*** Federal Pell, FSEOG, state, private, college/university gift aid from institutional funds.

GIFT AID (NON-NEED-BASED) ***Total amount:*** $1,990,376 (1% federal, 93% institutional, 6% external sources). ***Receiving aid:*** Freshmen: 50% (166). Undergraduates: 20% (430). ***Average award:*** Freshmen: $2774. Undergraduates: $5713. ***Tuition waivers:*** Full or partial for employees or children of employees.

LOANS ***Student loans:*** $12,929,534 (77% need-based, 23% non-need-based). ***Average need-based loan:*** Freshmen: $3323. Undergraduates: $4391. ***Parent loans:*** $1,778,667 (78% need-based, 22% non-need-based). ***Programs:*** FFEL (Subsidized and Unsubsidized Stafford, PLUS), Perkins, state.

WORK-STUDY ***Federal work-study:*** Total amount: $160,000; jobs available. ***State or other work-study/employment:*** Total amount: $35,000 (100% need-based). Part-time jobs available.

APPLYING FOR FINANCIAL AID ***Required financial aid form:*** FAFSA. ***Financial aid deadline (priority):*** 2/1. ***Notification date:*** Continuous beginning 3/1. Students must reply within 3 weeks of notification.

CONTACT Ms. Lindy Hall, Senior Director of Enrollment Services, LeTourneau University, 2100 South Mobberly Avenue, PO Box 7001, Longview, TX 75607, 903-233-4312 or toll-free 800-759-8811. *Fax:* 903-233-4301. *E-mail:* finaid@letu.edu.

LEWIS & CLARK COLLEGE

Portland, OR

Tuition & fees: $33,726 **Average undergraduate aid package: $26,741**

ABOUT THE INSTITUTION Independent, coed. ***Awards:*** bachelor's, master's, doctoral, and first professional degrees and post-master's certificates. 29 undergraduate majors. ***Total enrollment:*** 3,565. Undergraduates: 1,999. Freshmen: 533. Institutional methodology is used as a basis for awarding need-based institutional aid.

UNDERGRADUATE EXPENSES for 2008–09 ***Application fee:*** $50. ***Comprehensive fee:*** $42,546 includes full-time tuition ($33,490), mandatory fees ($236), and room and board ($8820). ***College room only:*** $4610. Room and board charges vary according to board plan and housing facility. ***Part-time tuition:*** $1675 per credit hour. ***Payment plan:*** Installment.

FRESHMAN FINANCIAL AID (Fall 2008, est.) 378 applied for aid; of those 73% were deemed to have need. 100% of freshmen with need received aid; of those 37% had need fully met. ***Average percent of need met:*** 88% (excluding resources awarded to replace EFC). ***Average financial aid package:*** $26,130 (excluding resources awarded to replace EFC). 19% of all full-time freshmen had no need and received non-need-based gift aid.

UNDERGRADUATE FINANCIAL AID (Fall 2008, est.) 1,294 applied for aid; of those 77% were deemed to have need. 100% of undergraduates with need received aid; of those 43% had need fully met. ***Average percent of need met:*** 90% (excluding resources awarded to replace EFC). ***Average financial aid package:*** $26,741 (excluding resources awarded to replace EFC). 17% of all full-time undergraduates had no need and received non-need-based gift aid.

GIFT AID (NEED-BASED) ***Total amount:*** $18,657,695 (7% federal, 1% state, 90% institutional, 2% external sources). ***Receiving aid:*** Freshmen: 51% (273); all full-time undergraduates: 52% (989). ***Average award:*** Freshmen: $17,363; Undergraduates: $17,724. ***Scholarships, grants, and awards:*** Federal Pell, FSEOG, state, private, college/university gift aid from institutional funds.

GIFT AID (NON-NEED-BASED) ***Total amount:*** $5,173,415 (96% institutional, 4% external sources). ***Receiving aid:*** Freshmen: 3% (18). Undergraduates: 4% (78). ***Average award:*** Freshmen: $7014. Undergraduates: $7860. ***Scholarships, grants, and awards by category:*** *Creative arts/performance:* 53 awards ($324,777 total): debating, music. *Special achievements/activities:* 94 awards ($465,000 total): community service, leadership. *Special characteristics:* 29 awards ($803,920 total): children of faculty/staff. ***Tuition waivers:*** Full or partial for employees or children of employees.

LOANS ***Student loans:*** $6,169,580 (65% need-based, 35% non-need-based). 57% of past graduating class borrowed through all loan programs. *Average indebtedness per student:* $20,611. ***Average need-based loan:*** Freshmen: $4342. Undergraduates: $5165. ***Parent loans:*** $1,936,090 (37% need-based, 63% non-need-based). ***Programs:*** FFEL (Subsidized and Unsubsidized Stafford, PLUS), Perkins.

WORK-STUDY ***Federal work-study:*** Total amount: $1,069,842; 444 jobs available. ***State or other work-study/employment:*** Total amount: $386,640 (100% non-need-based). Part-time jobs available.

APPLYING FOR FINANCIAL AID ***Required financial aid forms:*** FAFSA, CSS Financial Aid PROFILE. ***Financial aid deadline (priority):*** 2/15. ***Notification date:*** Continuous beginning 3/1. Students must reply by 5/1.

CONTACT Glendi Gaddis, Director of Student Financial Services, Lewis & Clark College, Templeton Student Center, MS 56, Portland, OR 97219-7899, 503-768-7096 or toll-free 800-444-4111. *Fax:* 503-768-7074. *E-mail:* sfs@lclark.edu.

LEWIS-CLARK STATE COLLEGE

Lewiston, ID

Tuition & fees (ID res): $4296 **Average undergraduate aid package: $7852**

ABOUT THE INSTITUTION State-supported, coed. ***Awards:*** associate and bachelor's degrees. 50 undergraduate majors. ***Total enrollment:*** 3,940. Undergraduates: 3,940. Freshmen: 649. Federal methodology is used as a basis for awarding need-based institutional aid.

UNDERGRADUATE EXPENSES for 2008–09 ***Application fee:*** $35. ***Tuition, state resident:*** full-time $4296; part-time $215 per credit. ***Tuition, nonresident:*** full-time $11,950; part-time $215 per credit. Full-time tuition and fees vary according to course load and reciprocity agreements. ***College room and board:*** $5400; ***Room only:*** $2700. Room and board charges vary according to board plan and housing facility. ***Payment plan:*** Deferred payment.

FRESHMAN FINANCIAL AID (Fall 2007) 416 applied for aid; of those 88% were deemed to have need. 95% of freshmen with need received aid; of those 9% had need fully met. ***Average percent of need met:*** 9% (excluding resources awarded to replace EFC). ***Average financial aid package:*** $6518 (excluding resources awarded to replace EFC). 12% of all full-time freshmen had no need and received non-need-based gift aid.

UNDERGRADUATE FINANCIAL AID (Fall 2007) 1,661 applied for aid; of those 91% were deemed to have need. 99% of undergraduates with need received aid; of those 10% had need fully met. ***Average percent of need met:*** 10% (excluding resources awarded to replace EFC). ***Average financial aid package:*** $7852 (excluding resources awarded to replace EFC). 7% of all full-time undergraduates had no need and received non-need-based gift aid.

GIFT AID (NEED-BASED) ***Total amount:*** $4,783,971 (80% federal, 6% state, 5% institutional, 9% external sources). ***Receiving aid:*** Freshmen: 40% (214); all full-time undergraduates: 47% (1,004). ***Average award:*** Freshmen: $3074; Undergraduates: $3587. ***Scholarships, grants, and awards:*** Federal Pell, FSEOG, state, private, college/university gift aid from institutional funds.

GIFT AID (NON-NEED-BASED) ***Total amount:*** $603,896 (42% state, 39% institutional, 19% external sources). ***Receiving aid:*** Freshmen: 35% (190). Undergraduates: 17% (363). ***Average award:*** Freshmen: $1501. Undergraduates: $2179. ***Scholarships, grants, and awards by category:*** *Academic interests/achievement:* 82 awards ($169,186 total): biological sciences, business, education, English, general academic interests/achievements, health fields, humanities, mathematics, physical sciences, social sciences. *Creative arts/performance:* 10 awards ($24,918 total): art/fine arts, creative writing, debating, music, theater/drama. *Special achievements/activities:* 182 awards ($114,861 total): community service, general special achievements/activities, junior miss, leadership, rodeo. *Special characteristics:* 349 awards ($740,131 total): children and siblings of alumni, ethnic background, first-generation college students, general special characteristics, local/state students, members of minority groups, out-of-state students, previous college experience. ***Tuition waivers:*** Full or partial for employees or children of employees, senior citizens. ***ROTC:*** Army, Air Force cooperative.

LOANS ***Student loans:*** $9,523,848 (67% need-based, 33% non-need-based). 61% of past graduating class borrowed through all loan programs. ***Average need-based loan:*** Freshmen: $2841. Undergraduates: $4051. ***Parent loans:*** $449,860 (100% non-need-based). ***Programs:*** FFEL (Subsidized and Unsubsidized Stafford, PLUS), Perkins, Federal Nursing.

WORK-STUDY ***Federal work-study:*** Total amount: $108,837; 92 jobs averaging $1183. ***State or other work-study/employment:*** Total amount: $159,894 (61% need-based, 39% non-need-based). 139 part-time jobs averaging $1150.

ATHLETIC AWARDS Total amount: $1,241,390 (100% non-need-based).

APPLYING FOR FINANCIAL AID ***Required financial aid form:*** FAFSA. ***Financial aid deadline (priority):*** 3/1. ***Notification date:*** Continuous beginning 4/15. Students must reply within 2 weeks of notification.

CONTACT Ms. Laura Hughes, Director of Financial Aid, Lewis-Clark State College, 500 8th Avenue, Lewiston, ID 83501-2698, 208-792-2224 or toll-free 800-933-5272. *Fax:* 208-792-2063. *E-mail:* lhughes@lcsc.edu.

LEWIS UNIVERSITY

Romeoville, IL

ABOUT THE INSTITUTION Independent religious, coed. ***Awards:*** associate, bachelor's, master's, and doctoral degrees and post-master's certificates. 69 undergraduate majors. ***Total enrollment:*** 5,536. Undergraduates: 3,973. Freshmen: 655.

GIFT AID (NEED-BASED) ***Scholarships, grants, and awards:*** Federal Pell, FSEOG, state, private, college/university gift aid from institutional funds, Federal Nursing.

GIFT AID (NON-NEED-BASED) ***Scholarships, grants, and awards by category:*** *Academic interests/achievement:* general academic interests/achievements. *Creative arts/performance:* art/fine arts, music, theater/drama. *Special achievements/activities:* community service, general special achievements/activities, memberships. *Special characteristics:* children and siblings of alumni, children of faculty/staff, religious affiliation.

LOANS ***Programs:*** FFEL (Subsidized and Unsubsidized Stafford, PLUS), Perkins.

WORK-STUDY ***Federal work-study:*** Total amount: $404,626; 370 jobs averaging $3000. ***State or other work-study/employment:*** Total amount: $1,087,108 (100% non-need-based). 170 part-time jobs averaging $3000.

APPLYING FOR FINANCIAL AID ***Required financial aid form:*** FAFSA.

CONTACT Ms. Janeen Decharinte, Director of Financial Aid, Lewis University, One University Parkway, Romeoville, IL 60446, 815-836-5262 or toll-free 800-897-9000. *Fax:* 815-836-5135. *E-mail:* decharja@lewisu.edu.

LEXINGTON COLLEGE

Chicago, IL

Tuition & fees: $23,800 **Average undergraduate aid package: $17,199**

ABOUT THE INSTITUTION Independent, women only. ***Awards:*** associate and bachelor's degrees. 1 undergraduate major. ***Total enrollment:*** 53. Undergraduates: 53. Freshmen: 8. Federal methodology is used as a basis for awarding need-based institutional aid.

UNDERGRADUATE EXPENSES for 2009–10 ***Application fee:*** $30. ***One-time required fee:*** $50. ***Tuition:*** full-time $22,800; part-time $760 per credit hour.

FRESHMAN FINANCIAL AID (Fall 2007) 9 applied for aid; of those 100% were deemed to have need. 100% of freshmen with need received aid; of those 11% had need fully met. ***Average percent of need met:*** 90% (excluding resources awarded to replace EFC). ***Average financial aid package:*** $13,949 (excluding resources awarded to replace EFC).

UNDERGRADUATE FINANCIAL AID (Fall 2007) 43 applied for aid; of those 72% were deemed to have need. 97% of undergraduates with need received aid. ***Average percent of need met:*** 85% (excluding resources awarded to replace EFC). ***Average financial aid package:*** $17,199 (excluding resources awarded to replace EFC).

GIFT AID (NEED-BASED) ***Total amount:*** $508,858 (20% federal, 22% state, 53% institutional, 5% external sources). ***Receiving aid:*** Freshmen: 100% (9); all full-time undergraduates: 61% (30). ***Average award:*** Freshmen: $4595; Undergraduates: $4200. ***Scholarships, grants, and awards:*** Federal Pell, FSEOG, state, private, college/university gift aid from institutional funds, Academic Competitiveness Grant.

LOANS ***Student loans:*** $266,132 (100% need-based). 45% of past graduating class borrowed through all loan programs. *Average indebtedness per student:* $27,000. ***Average need-based loan:*** Freshmen: $4165. Undergraduates: $9500. ***Parent loans:*** $72,733 (100% need-based). ***Programs:*** FFEL (Subsidized and Unsubsidized Stafford, PLUS), Sallie Mae Signature Student Loans, alternative loans.

WORK-STUDY ***Federal work-study:*** Total amount: $5425; 6 jobs averaging $5425.

APPLYING FOR FINANCIAL AID ***Required financial aid form:*** FAFSA. ***Financial aid deadline:*** 10/1 (priority: 5/15). ***Notification date:*** Continuous.

CONTACT Maria Lebron, Director of Financial Aid, Lexington College, 310 South Peoria Street, Suite 512, Chicago, IL 60607, 312-226-6294 Ext. 227. *Fax:* 312-226-6405. *E-mail:* finaid@lexingtoncollege.edu.

LIBERTY UNIVERSITY

Lynchburg, VA

Tuition & fees: $17,742 **Average undergraduate aid package: $14,124**

ABOUT THE INSTITUTION Independent nondenominational, coed. ***Awards:*** associate, bachelor's, master's, doctoral, and first professional degrees and post-master's certificates (also offers external degree program with significant enrollment not reflected in profile). 60 undergraduate majors. ***Total enrollment:*** 33,604. Undergraduates: 21,646. Freshmen: 2,978. Federal methodology is used as a basis for awarding need-based institutional aid.

UNDERGRADUATE EXPENSES for 2008–09 ***Application fee:*** $40. ***Comprehensive fee:*** $23,738 includes full-time tuition ($16,532), mandatory fees ($1210), and room and board ($5996). Full-time tuition and fees vary according to course load. Room and board charges vary according to housing facility. ***Part-time tuition:*** $515 per hour. Part-time tuition and fees vary according to course load. ***Payment plan:*** Installment.

FRESHMAN FINANCIAL AID (Fall 2008, est.) 2,218 applied for aid; of those 81% were deemed to have need. 100% of freshmen with need received aid; of those 15% had need fully met. ***Average percent of need met:*** 86% (excluding resources awarded to replace EFC). ***Average financial aid package:*** $13,952 (excluding resources awarded to replace EFC). 24% of all full-time freshmen had no need and received non-need-based gift aid.

UNDERGRADUATE FINANCIAL AID (Fall 2008, est.) 13,060 applied for aid; of those 84% were deemed to have need. 100% of undergraduates with need received aid; of those 14% had need fully met. ***Average percent of need met:*** 86% (excluding resources awarded to replace EFC). ***Average financial aid package:*** $14,124 (excluding resources awarded to replace EFC). 21% of all full-time undergraduates had no need and received non-need-based gift aid.

GIFT AID (NEED-BASED) ***Total amount:*** $23,024,396 (87% federal, 13% institutional). ***Receiving aid:*** Freshmen: 28% (664); all full-time undergraduates: 20% (2,955). ***Average award:*** Freshmen: $1415; Undergraduates: $1471. ***Scholarships, grants, and awards:*** Federal Pell, FSEOG, state, private, college/university gift aid from institutional funds, Academic Competitiveness Grant, National Smart Grant, TEACH Grant.

GIFT AID (NON-NEED-BASED) ***Total amount:*** $89,712,568 (16% federal, 12% state, 67% institutional, 5% external sources). ***Receiving aid:*** Freshmen: 75% (1,792). Undergraduates: 74% (10,803). ***Average award:*** Freshmen: $6771. Undergraduates: $6087. ***Scholarships, grants, and awards by category:*** *Academic interests/achievement:* 5,438 awards ($13,022,914 total): general academic interests/achievements. *Creative arts/performance:* 306 awards ($1,323,624 total): debating, journalism/publications, music, performing arts. *Special characteristics:* 6,704 awards ($11,284,656 total): children of faculty/staff, international students, local/state students, public servants, religious affiliation, veterans. ***Tuition waivers:*** Full or partial for employees or children of employees. ***ROTC:*** Army, Air Force cooperative.

LOANS ***Student loans:*** $106,023,191 (36% need-based, 64% non-need-based). 68% of past graduating class borrowed through all loan programs. *Average indebtedness per student:* $27,673. ***Average need-based loan:*** Freshmen: $3247. Undergraduates: $4344. ***Parent loans:*** $9,437,669 (100% non-need-based). ***Programs:*** FFEL (Subsidized and Unsubsidized Stafford, PLUS).

WORK-STUDY ***Federal work-study:*** Total amount: $638,602; 3,079 jobs averaging $1967. ***State or other work-study/employment:*** Total amount: $201,500 (100% non-need-based). 71 part-time jobs averaging $2838.

ATHLETIC AWARDS Total amount: $254,676 (100% non-need-based).

APPLYING FOR FINANCIAL AID ***Required financial aid forms:*** FAFSA, state aid form. ***Financial aid deadline:*** 3/1 (priority: 3/1). ***Notification date:*** Continuous beginning 3/15. Students must reply within 3 weeks of notification.

CONTACT Robert Ritz, Director, Financial Aid Office, Liberty University, 1971 University Boulevard, Lynchburg, VA 24502, 434-582-2270 or toll-free 800-543-5317. *Fax:* 434-582-2053. *E-mail:* financialaid@liberty.edu.

LIFE PACIFIC COLLEGE

San Dimas, CA

CONTACT Mrs. Becky Huyck, Director of Financial Aid, Life Pacific College, 1100 Covina Boulevard, San Dimas, CA 91773-3298, 909-599-5433 Ext. 319 or toll-free 877-886-5433 Ext. 314. *Fax:* 909-599-6690. *E-mail:* bhuyck@lifepacific.edu.

LIFE UNIVERSITY

Marietta, GA

Tuition & fees: $7830 **Average undergraduate aid package: $9000**

ABOUT THE INSTITUTION Independent, coed. ***Awards:*** associate, bachelor's, master's, and first professional degrees. 5 undergraduate majors. ***Total enrollment:*** 2,171. Undergraduates: 597. Freshmen: 46. Federal methodology is used as a basis for awarding need-based institutional aid.

UNDERGRADUATE EXPENSES for 2008–09 ***Application fee:*** $50. ***Comprehensive fee:*** $19,830 includes full-time tuition ($7335), mandatory fees ($495), and room and board ($12,000). ***College room only:*** $6300. Full-time tuition and fees vary according to course load and degree level. ***Part-time tuition:*** $163 per credit hour. ***Part-time fees:*** $165 per term. Part-time tuition and fees vary according to course load and degree level. ***Payment plan:*** Installment.

FRESHMAN FINANCIAL AID (Fall 2008, est.) 76 applied for aid; of those 82% were deemed to have need. 94% of freshmen with need received aid. ***Average financial aid package:*** $8700 (excluding resources awarded to replace EFC). 2% of all full-time freshmen had no need and received non-need-based gift aid.

UNDERGRADUATE FINANCIAL AID (Fall 2008, est.) 306 applied for aid; of those 90% were deemed to have need. 96% of undergraduates with need received aid; of those 3% had need fully met. ***Average percent of need met:*** 3% (excluding resources awarded to replace EFC). ***Average financial aid package:*** $9000 (excluding resources awarded to replace EFC). 1% of all full-time undergraduates had no need and received non-need-based gift aid.

GIFT AID (NEED-BASED) ***Total amount:*** $1,087,100 (99% federal, 1% institutional). ***Receiving aid:*** Freshmen: 23% (35); all full-time undergraduates: 37% (152). ***Average award:*** Freshmen: $4800; Undergraduates: $4200. ***Scholarships, grants, and awards:*** Federal Pell, FSEOG, state, private, college/university gift aid from institutional funds.

GIFT AID (NON-NEED-BASED) ***Total amount:*** $489,000 (54% state, 31% institutional, 15% external sources). ***Receiving aid:*** Freshmen: 32% (49). Undergraduates: 30% (123). ***Average award:*** Freshmen: $3900. Undergraduates: $3200. ***Scholarships, grants, and awards by category:*** *Academic interests/achievement:* 17 awards ($56,700 total): general academic interests/achievements. *Special achievements/activities:* 90 awards ($406,000 total): general special achievements/activities. *Special characteristics:* 53 awards ($422,000 total): general special characteristics, international students. ***Tuition waivers:*** Full or partial for employees or children of employees.

LOANS ***Student loans:*** $5,625,000 (47% need-based, 53% non-need-based). 36% of past graduating class borrowed through all loan programs. *Average indebtedness per student:* $17,500. ***Average need-based loan:*** Freshmen: $3800. Undergraduates: $4500. ***Parent loans:*** $180,000 (100% need-based). ***Programs:*** FFEL (Subsidized and Unsubsidized Stafford, PLUS), Perkins, college/university, alternative loans.

WORK-STUDY ***Federal work-study:*** Total amount: $214,000; 224 jobs averaging $1000.

ATHLETIC AWARDS Total amount: $256,000 (1% need-based, 99% non-need-based).

APPLYING FOR FINANCIAL AID ***Required financial aid forms:*** FAFSA, institution's own form. ***Financial aid deadline (priority):*** 3/1. ***Notification date:*** Continuous beginning 5/1.

CONTACT Michelle Nixon, Director of Financial Aid, Life University, 1269 Barclay Circle, Marietta, GA 30060, 770-426-2901 or toll-free 800-543-3202 (in-state). *Fax:* 770-426-2926. *E-mail:* finaid@life.edu.

LIMESTONE COLLEGE

Gaffney, SC

Tuition & fees: $18,300 **Average undergraduate aid package: $14,497**

ABOUT THE INSTITUTION Independent, coed. ***Awards:*** associate and bachelor's degrees. 45 undergraduate majors. ***Total enrollment:*** 742. Undergraduates: 742. Freshmen: 171. Federal methodology is used as a basis for awarding need-based institutional aid.

UNDERGRADUATE EXPENSES for 2009–10 ***Application fee:*** $25. ***Comprehensive fee:*** $25,100 includes full-time tuition ($18,300) and room and board ($6800). ***College room only:*** $3400. ***Part-time tuition:*** $762 per credit hour.

FRESHMAN FINANCIAL AID (Fall 2008, est.) 180 applied for aid; of those 88% were deemed to have need. 100% of freshmen with need received aid; of those 18% had need fully met. ***Average percent of need met:*** 68% (excluding resources awarded to replace EFC). ***Average financial aid package:*** $15,636 (excluding resources awarded to replace EFC). 25% of all full-time freshmen had no need and received non-need-based gift aid.

UNDERGRADUATE FINANCIAL AID (Fall 2008, est.) 625 applied for aid; of those 90% were deemed to have need. 100% of undergraduates with need received aid; of those 21% had need fully met. ***Average percent of need met:*** 65% (excluding resources awarded to replace EFC). ***Average financial aid package:*** $14,497 (excluding resources awarded to replace EFC). 23% of all full-time undergraduates had no need and received non-need-based gift aid.

GIFT AID (NEED-BASED) ***Total amount:*** $4,937,400 (24% federal, 27% state, 44% institutional, 5% external sources). ***Receiving aid:*** Freshmen: 74% (159); all full-time undergraduates: 76% (556). ***Average award:*** Freshmen: $12,036; Undergraduates: $10,634. ***Scholarships, grants, and awards:*** Federal Pell, FSEOG, state, private, college/university gift aid from institutional funds.

GIFT AID (NON-NEED-BASED) ***Total amount:*** $1,354,730 (14% state, 78% institutional, 8% external sources). ***Receiving aid:*** Freshmen: 13% (28). Undergraduates: 15% (108). ***Average award:*** Freshmen: $5082. Undergraduates: $5717. ***Scholarships, grants, and awards by category:*** *Academic interests/achievement:* 396 awards ($796,511 total): biological sciences, business, communication, computer science, education, English, general academic interests/achievements, humanities, mathematics, physical sciences, religion/biblical studies, social sciences. *Creative arts/performance:* 29 awards ($70,600 total): art/fine arts, music, performing arts, theater/drama. *Special achievements/activities:* 382 awards ($508,800 total): cheerleading/drum major, general special achievements/activities, leadership, religious involvement. *Special characteristics:* 715 awards ($898,211 total): children and siblings of alumni, children of faculty/staff, first-generation college students, local/state students, out-of-state students, siblings of current students. ***ROTC:*** Army cooperative.

LOANS ***Student loans:*** $4,708,709 (75% need-based, 25% non-need-based). 89% of past graduating class borrowed through all loan programs. *Average indebtedness per student:* $22,416. ***Average need-based loan:*** Freshmen: $3022. Undergraduates: $3872. ***Parent loans:*** $454,683 (37% need-based, 63% non-need-based). ***Programs:*** FFEL (Subsidized and Unsubsidized Stafford, PLUS), Perkins.

WORK-STUDY ***Federal work-study:*** Total amount: $237,567; 175 jobs averaging $2198. ***State or other work-study/employment:*** Total amount: $62,602 (16% need-based, 84% non-need-based). 51 part-time jobs averaging $927.

ATHLETIC AWARDS Total amount: $1,748,906 (52% need-based, 48% non-need-based).

APPLYING FOR FINANCIAL AID ***Required financial aid form:*** FAFSA. ***Financial aid deadline (priority):*** 2/1. ***Notification date:*** Continuous. Students must reply within 3 weeks of notification.

CONTACT Mr. Bobby Greer, Acting Director of Financial Aid, Limestone College, 1115 College Drive, Gaffney, SC 29340-3799, 864-488-4567 or toll-free 800-795-7151 Ext. 554. *Fax:* 864-487-8706. *E-mail:* bgreer@limestone.edu.

LINCOLN CHRISTIAN COLLEGE

Lincoln, IL

Tuition & fees: $11,790 **Average undergraduate aid package: $8945**

ABOUT THE INSTITUTION Independent religious, coed. 13 undergraduate majors. Federal methodology is used as a basis for awarding need-based institutional aid.

UNDERGRADUATE EXPENSES for 2008–09 ***Comprehensive fee:*** $17,145 includes full-time tuition ($11,790) and room and board ($5355). ***Part-time tuition:*** $393 per semester hour. ***Payment plans:*** Installment, deferred payment.

FRESHMAN FINANCIAL AID (Fall 2007) 118 applied for aid; of those 87% were deemed to have need. 98% of freshmen with need received aid; of those 26% had need fully met. ***Average percent of need met:*** 77% (excluding resources awarded to replace EFC). ***Average financial aid package:*** $9622 (excluding resources awarded to replace EFC). 8% of all full-time freshmen had no need and received non-need-based gift aid.

UNDERGRADUATE FINANCIAL AID (Fall 2007) 716 applied for aid; of those 85% were deemed to have need. 98% of undergraduates with need received aid; of those 18% had need fully met. ***Average percent of need met:*** 64% (excluding resources awarded to replace EFC). ***Average financial aid package:*** $8945 (excluding resources awarded to replace EFC). 7% of all full-time undergraduates had no need and received non-need-based gift aid.

GIFT AID (NEED-BASED) ***Total amount:*** $3,119,274 (27% federal, 35% state, 38% institutional). ***Receiving aid:*** Freshmen: 37% (46); all full-time undergraduates: 63% (535). ***Average award:*** Freshmen: $6458; Undergraduates: $3560. ***Scholarships, grants, and awards:*** Federal Pell, FSEOG, state, college/university gift aid from institutional funds.

GIFT AID (NON-NEED-BASED) ***Total amount:*** $755,522 (35% institutional, 65% external sources). ***Receiving aid:*** Freshmen: 70% (88). Undergraduates: 52% (439). ***Average award:*** Freshmen: $4769. Undergraduates: $4636. ***Scholarships, grants, and awards by category:*** *Academic interests/achievement:* 119 awards ($492,645 total): general academic interests/achievements. *Special achievements/activities:* 17 awards ($39,427 total): community service, leadership. *Special characteristics:* 8 awards ($26,626 total): children of faculty/staff. ***Tuition waivers:*** Full or partial for employees or children of employees.

LOANS ***Student loans:*** $3,522,544 (53% need-based, 47% non-need-based). 69% of past graduating class borrowed through all loan programs. *Average indebtedness per student:* $19,594. ***Average need-based loan:*** Freshmen: $3469. Undergraduates: $3888. ***Parent loans:*** $592,208 (100% non-need-based). ***Programs:*** FFEL (Subsidized and Unsubsidized Stafford, PLUS), Perkins, college/university.

WORK-STUDY ***Federal work-study:*** Total amount: $46,819; 47 jobs averaging $996. ***State or other work-study/employment:*** Total amount: $231,949 (100% non-need-based). 149 part-time jobs averaging $1557.

APPLYING FOR FINANCIAL AID ***Required financial aid form:*** FAFSA. ***Financial aid deadline:*** Continuous. ***Notification date:*** Continuous beginning 3/1. Students must reply within 2 weeks of notification.

CONTACT Nancy Siddens, Financial Aid Director, Lincoln Christian College, 100 Campus View Drive, Lincoln, IL 62656, 217-732-3168 Ext. 2250 or toll-free 888-522-5228. *Fax:* 217-732-5914. *E-mail:* finaid@lccs.edu.

LINCOLN COLLEGE–NORMAL

Normal, IL

CONTACT Deb Keist, Assistant Director of Financial Aid, Lincoln College–Normal, 715 West Raab Road, Normal, IL 61761, 309-452-0500 or toll-free 800-569-0558. *Fax:* 309-454-5652.

LINCOLN MEMORIAL UNIVERSITY

Harrogate, TN

Tuition & fees: $15,700 **Average undergraduate aid package: $12,884**

ABOUT THE INSTITUTION Independent, coed. ***Awards:*** associate, bachelor's, master's, and first professional degrees and post-master's certificates. 43 undergraduate majors. ***Total enrollment:*** 3,365. Undergraduates: 1,429. Freshmen: 287. Federal methodology is used as a basis for awarding need-based institutional aid.

UNDERGRADUATE EXPENSES for 2009–10 ***Application fee:*** $25. ***Comprehensive fee:*** $21,380 includes full-time tuition ($15,120), mandatory fees ($580), and room and board ($5680). ***Part-time tuition:*** $630 per credit. ***Part-time fees:*** $290 per term.

FRESHMAN FINANCIAL AID (Fall 2008, est.) 254 applied for aid; of those 85% were deemed to have need. 100% of freshmen with need received aid; of those 22% had need fully met. ***Average percent of need met:*** 82% (excluding resources awarded to replace EFC). ***Average financial aid package:*** $18,182 (excluding resources awarded to replace EFC). 7% of all full-time freshmen had no need and received non-need-based gift aid.

UNDERGRADUATE FINANCIAL AID (Fall 2008, est.) 1,122 applied for aid; of those 87% were deemed to have need. 100% of undergraduates with need received aid; of those 18% had need fully met. ***Average percent of need met:*** 84% (excluding resources awarded to replace EFC). ***Average financial aid package:*** $12,884 (excluding resources awarded to replace EFC). 3% of all full-time undergraduates had no need and received non-need-based gift aid.

GIFT AID (NEED-BASED) ***Total amount:*** $11,504,819 (23% federal, 20% state, 53% institutional, 4% external sources). ***Receiving aid:*** Freshmen: 84% (215); all full-time undergraduates: 82% (940). ***Average award:*** Freshmen: $14,156; Undergraduates: $12,424. ***Scholarships, grants, and awards:*** Federal Pell, FSEOG, state, private, college/university gift aid from institutional funds.

GIFT AID (NON-NEED-BASED) ***Total amount:*** $1,675,906 (19% state, 71% institutional, 10% external sources). ***Receiving aid:*** Freshmen: 15% (38). Undergraduates: 23% (262). ***Average award:*** Freshmen: $7604. Undergraduates: $4530. ***Scholarships, grants, and awards by category:*** *Academic interests/achievement:* 676 awards ($3,359,259 total): general academic interests/achievements. *Creative arts/performance:* 35 awards ($64,444 total): music. *Special achievements/activities:* 14 awards ($13,500 total): cheerleading/drum major. *Special characteristics:* 34 awards ($465,362 total): children of faculty/staff.

LOANS ***Student loans:*** $6,269,077 (81% need-based, 19% non-need-based). 64% of past graduating class borrowed through all loan programs. *Average indebtedness per student:* $15,881. ***Average need-based loan:*** Freshmen: $3421. Undergraduates: $3870. ***Parent loans:*** $397,596 (40% need-based, 60% non-need-based). ***Programs:*** FFEL (Subsidized and Unsubsidized Stafford, PLUS), Perkins.

WORK-STUDY ***Federal work-study:*** Total amount: $233,191; 155 jobs averaging $1437. ***State or other work-study/employment:*** Total amount: $127,492 (46% need-based, 54% non-need-based). Part-time jobs available.

ATHLETIC AWARDS Total amount: $958,527 (47% need-based, 53% non-need-based).

APPLYING FOR FINANCIAL AID ***Required financial aid form:*** FAFSA. ***Financial aid deadline (priority):*** 4/1. ***Notification date:*** Continuous. Students must reply within 3 weeks of notification.

CONTACT Bryan Erslan, Director of Financial Aid, Lincoln Memorial University, Cumberland Gap Parkway, Harrogate, TN 37752-1901, 423-869-6465 or toll-free 800-325-0900. *Fax:* 423-869-6347. *E-mail:* bryan.erslan@lmunet.edu.

LINCOLN UNIVERSITY

Jefferson City, MO

Tuition & fees (MO res): $6175 **Average undergraduate aid package: $8652**

ABOUT THE INSTITUTION State-supported, coed. ***Awards:*** associate, bachelor's, and master's degrees and post-master's certificates. 41 undergraduate majors. ***Total enrollment:*** 3,156. Undergraduates: 2,952. Freshmen: 606. Federal methodology is used as a basis for awarding need-based institutional aid.

UNDERGRADUATE EXPENSES for 2008–09 ***Application fee:*** $20. ***Tuition, state resident:*** full-time $5685; part-time $189.50 per credit hour. ***Tuition, nonresident:*** full-time $10,395; part-time $346.50 per credit hour. ***Required fees:*** full-time $490; $15 per credit hour or $20 per term. Full-time tuition and fees vary according to location and reciprocity agreements. Part-time tuition and fees vary according to location and reciprocity agreements. ***College room and board:*** $4660; ***Room only:*** $2428. Room and board charges vary according to board plan and housing facility. ***Payment plan:*** Installment.

FRESHMAN FINANCIAL AID (Fall 2008, est.) 340 applied for aid; of those 89% were deemed to have need. 100% of freshmen with need received aid; of those 13% had need fully met. ***Average percent of need met:*** 73% (excluding resources awarded to replace EFC). ***Average financial aid package:*** $8287 (excluding resources awarded to replace EFC). 1% of all full-time freshmen had no need and received non-need-based gift aid.

UNDERGRADUATE FINANCIAL AID (Fall 2008, est.) 1,295 applied for aid; of those 87% were deemed to have need. 100% of undergraduates with need received aid; of those 15% had need fully met. ***Average percent of need met:*** 74% (excluding resources awarded to replace EFC). ***Average financial aid package:*** $8652 (excluding resources awarded to replace EFC). 1% of all full-time undergraduates had no need and received non-need-based gift aid.

GIFT AID (NEED-BASED) ***Total amount:*** $7,187,800 (64% federal, 14% state, 18% institutional, 4% external sources). ***Receiving aid:*** Freshmen: 40% (216); all full-time undergraduates: 41% (799). ***Average award:*** Freshmen: $4412; Undergraduates: $4357. ***Scholarships, grants, and awards:*** Federal Pell, FSEOG, state, private, college/university gift aid from institutional funds.

GIFT AID (NON-NEED-BASED) ***Total amount:*** $285,188 (4% federal, 3% state, 93% institutional). ***Receiving aid:*** Freshmen: 2% (13). Undergraduates: 2% (38). ***Average award:*** Freshmen: $3313. Undergraduates: $3606. ***Scholarships, grants, and awards by category:*** *Academic interests/achievement:* 245 awards ($634,128 total): agriculture, education, general academic interests/achievements, military science. *Creative arts/performance:* 99 awards ($280,650 total): art/fine arts, journalism/publications, music, performing arts, theater/drama. *Special achievements/activities:* cheerleading/drum major. *Special characteristics:* 77 awards ($245,200 total): adult students, children of faculty/staff, out-of-state students. ***Tuition waivers:*** Full or partial for employees or children of employees, senior citizens. ***ROTC:*** Army, Naval cooperative, Air Force cooperative.

LOANS ***Student loans:*** $11,708,204 (49% need-based, 51% non-need-based). 47% of past graduating class borrowed through all loan programs. *Average indebtedness per student:* $21,255. ***Average need-based loan:*** Freshmen: $3288. Undergraduates: $3877. ***Parent loans:*** $894,698 (100% non-need-based). ***Programs:*** FFEL (Subsidized and Unsubsidized Stafford, PLUS).

WORK-STUDY ***Federal work-study:*** Total amount: $194,620; 156 jobs averaging $1166. ***State or other work-study/employment:*** Total amount: $575,314 (100% non-need-based). 207 part-time jobs averaging $1389.

ATHLETIC AWARDS Total amount: $935,110 (100% need-based).

APPLYING FOR FINANCIAL AID ***Required financial aid forms:*** FAFSA, institution's own form. ***Financial aid deadline (priority):*** 3/1. ***Notification date:*** Continuous beginning 3/15. Students must reply within 2 weeks of notification.

CONTACT Mr. Alfred Robinson, Director of Financial Aid, Lincoln University, 820 Chestnut Street, Jefferson City, MO 65102-0029, 573-681-6156 or toll-free 800-521-5052. *Fax:* 573-681-5871. *E-mail:* robinsona@lincolnu.edu.

LINCOLN UNIVERSITY

Lincoln University, PA

Tuition & fees (PA res): $7980 **Average undergraduate aid package: $9993**

ABOUT THE INSTITUTION State-related, coed. ***Awards:*** bachelor's and master's degrees. 46 undergraduate majors. ***Total enrollment:*** 2,524. Undergraduates: 1,973. Freshmen: 533. Federal methodology is used as a basis for awarding need-based institutional aid.

UNDERGRADUATE EXPENSES for 2008–09 ***Application fee:*** $20. ***Tuition, state resident:*** full-time $5690; part-time $238 per credit hour. ***Tuition, nonresident:*** full-time $10,296; part-time $428 per credit hour. ***Required fees:*** full-time $2290; $96 per credit hour. Part-time tuition and fees vary according to course load. ***College room and board:*** $7532; ***Room only:*** $4094. Room and board charges vary according to board plan. ***Payment plans:*** Installment, deferred payment.

FRESHMAN FINANCIAL AID (Fall 2008, est.) 521 applied for aid; of those 91% were deemed to have need. 99% of freshmen with need received aid; of those 8% had need fully met. ***Average percent of need met:*** 43% (excluding resources awarded to replace EFC). ***Average financial aid package:*** $9941 (excluding resources awarded to replace EFC). 4% of all full-time freshmen had no need and received non-need-based gift aid.

UNDERGRADUATE FINANCIAL AID (Fall 2008, est.) 1,847 applied for aid; of those 92% were deemed to have need. 100% of undergraduates with need received aid; of those 8% had need fully met. ***Average percent of need met:*** 45% (excluding resources awarded to replace EFC). ***Average financial aid package:*** $9993 (excluding resources awarded to replace EFC). 3% of all full-time undergraduates had no need and received non-need-based gift aid.

GIFT AID (NEED-BASED) ***Total amount:*** $6,851,533 (70% federal, 22% state, 4% institutional, 4% external sources). ***Receiving aid:*** Freshmen: 66% (348); all full-time undergraduates: 66% (1,272). ***Average award:*** Freshmen: $5950; Undergraduates: $5236. ***Scholarships, grants, and awards:*** Federal Pell, FSEOG, state, private, college/university gift aid from institutional funds, United Negro College Fund.

GIFT AID (NON-NEED-BASED) ***Total amount:*** $4,552,193 (5% state, 85% institutional, 10% external sources). ***Receiving aid:*** Freshmen: 36% (192). Undergraduates: 35% (668). ***Average award:*** Freshmen: $6079. Undergraduates: $5533. ***Scholarships, grants, and awards by category:*** *Academic interests/achievement:* 583 awards ($2,320,532 total): biological sciences, business, communication, computer science, education, English, general academic interests/achievements, humanities, mathematics, physical sciences, social sciences. *Creative arts/performance:* 132 awards ($236,746 total): music. *Special achievements/activities:* 134 awards ($447,257 total): general special achievements/activities. *Special characteristics:* 176 awards ($853,957 total): children and siblings of alumni, children of faculty/staff, international students. ***Tuition waivers:*** Full or partial for employees or children of employees. ***ROTC:*** Army cooperative, Air Force cooperative.

LOANS ***Student loans:*** $17,244,536 (84% need-based, 16% non-need-based). 84% of past graduating class borrowed through all loan programs. *Average indebtedness per student:* $29,776. ***Average need-based loan:*** Freshmen: $3297. Undergraduates: $3981. ***Parent loans:*** $3,486,644 (100% non-need-based). ***Programs:*** FFEL (Subsidized and Unsubsidized Stafford, PLUS), Perkins.

WORK-STUDY ***Federal work-study:*** Total amount: $352,820; 228 jobs averaging $1589.

ATHLETIC AWARDS Total amount: $433,106 (100% non-need-based).

APPLYING FOR FINANCIAL AID ***Required financial aid form:*** FAFSA. ***Financial aid deadline:*** 5/1 (priority: 5/1). ***Notification date:*** Continuous. Students must reply within 2 weeks of notification.

CONTACT Thelma Ross, Director of Financial Aid, Lincoln University, PO Box 179, Lincoln University, PA 19352, 484-365-7583 or toll-free 800-790-0191. *Fax:* 484-365-8198. *E-mail:* tross@lincoln.edu.

LINDENWOOD UNIVERSITY

St. Charles, MO

Tuition & fees: $13,000 **Average undergraduate aid package: $5490**

ABOUT THE INSTITUTION Independent Presbyterian, coed. ***Awards:*** bachelor's, master's, and doctoral degrees and post-bachelor's and post-master's certificates (education specialist). 79 undergraduate majors. ***Total enrollment:*** 10,085. Undergraduates: 6,343. Freshmen: 1,106. Federal methodology is used as a basis for awarding need-based institutional aid.

UNDERGRADUATE EXPENSES for 2008–09 ***Application fee:*** $30. ***Comprehensive fee:*** $19,500 includes full-time tuition ($12,700), mandatory fees ($300), and room and board ($6500). ***College room only:*** $3400. Full-time tuition and fees vary according to program. ***Part-time tuition:*** $360 per credit hour. Part-time tuition and fees vary according to course load. ***Payment plans:*** Installment, deferred payment.

FRESHMAN FINANCIAL AID (Fall 2008, est.) 974 applied for aid; of those 56% were deemed to have need. 100% of freshmen with need received aid; of those 35% had need fully met. ***Average percent of need met:*** 90% (excluding resources awarded to replace EFC). ***Average financial aid package:*** $6374 (excluding resources awarded to replace EFC). 13% of all full-time freshmen had no need and received non-need-based gift aid.

UNDERGRADUATE FINANCIAL AID (Fall 2008, est.) 4,876 applied for aid; of those 68% were deemed to have need. 100% of undergraduates with need received aid; of those 40% had need fully met. ***Average percent of need met:*** 91% (excluding resources awarded to replace EFC). ***Average financial aid package:*** $5490 (excluding resources awarded to replace EFC). 14% of all full-time undergraduates had no need and received non-need-based gift aid.

GIFT AID (NEED-BASED) ***Total amount:*** $24,725,988 (20% federal, 17% state, 63% institutional). ***Receiving aid:*** Freshmen: 33% (368); all full-time undergraduates: 37% (2,239). ***Average award:*** Freshmen: $2473; Undergraduates: $2928. ***Scholarships, grants, and awards:*** Federal Pell, FSEOG, state, private, college/university gift aid from institutional funds.

GIFT AID (NON-NEED-BASED) ***Total amount:*** $9,633,849 (3% state, 95% institutional, 2% external sources). ***Receiving aid:*** Freshmen: 13% (143). Undergraduates: 17% (997). ***Average award:*** Freshmen: $4609. Undergraduates: $4320. ***Scholarships, grants, and awards by category:*** *Academic interests/achievement:* biological sciences, business, communication, computer science, education, engineering/technologies, English, foreign languages, general academic interests/achievements, health fields, humanities, international studies, library science, mathematics, military science, physical sciences, premedicine, social sciences. *Creative arts/performance:* applied art and design, art/fine arts, cinema/film/broadcasting, dance, general creative arts/performance, music, performing arts, theater/drama. *Special achievements/activities:* cheerleading/drum major, community service, general special achievements/activities, junior miss, leadership. ***Tuition waivers:*** Full or partial for senior citizens. ***ROTC:*** Army, Air Force cooperative.

LOANS ***Student loans:*** $24,956,795 (69% need-based, 31% non-need-based). *Average indebtedness per student:* $11,852. ***Average need-based loan:*** Freshmen: $1668. Undergraduates: $1852. ***Parent loans:*** $2,000,000 (100% non-need-based). ***Programs:*** FFEL (Subsidized and Unsubsidized Stafford, PLUS), Perkins.

WORK-STUDY ***Federal work-study:*** Total amount: $910,000; jobs available (averaging $2400). ***State or other work-study/employment:*** Total amount: $5,705,670 (63% need-based, 37% non-need-based). Part-time jobs available.

APPLYING FOR FINANCIAL AID ***Required financial aid form:*** FAFSA. ***Financial aid deadline (priority):*** 3/15. ***Notification date:*** Continuous. Students must reply within 1 week of notification.

CONTACT Lori Bode, Director of Financial Aid, Lindenwood University, 209 South Kingshighway, St. Charles, MO 63301-1695, 636-949-4925. *Fax:* 636-949-4924. *E-mail:* lbode@lindenwood.edu.

LINDSEY WILSON COLLEGE

Columbia, KY

Tuition & fees: $16,670 **Average undergraduate aid package: $14,268**

ABOUT THE INSTITUTION Independent United Methodist, coed. ***Awards:*** associate, bachelor's, and master's degrees. 30 undergraduate majors. ***Total enrollment:*** 2,003. Undergraduates: 1,674. Freshmen: 423. Federal methodology is used as a basis for awarding need-based institutional aid.

UNDERGRADUATE EXPENSES for 2008–09 ***Comprehensive fee:*** $23,595 includes full-time tuition ($16,440), mandatory fees ($230), and room and board ($6925). ***Part-time tuition:*** $685 per credit hour. ***Payment plan:*** Installment.

FRESHMAN FINANCIAL AID (Fall 2008, est.) 420 applied for aid; of those 92% were deemed to have need. 100% of freshmen with need received aid; of those 47% had need fully met. ***Average financial aid package:*** $13,866 (excluding resources awarded to replace EFC).

UNDERGRADUATE FINANCIAL AID (Fall 2008, est.) 1,561 applied for aid; of those 93% were deemed to have need. 100% of undergraduates with need received aid; of those 41% had need fully met. ***Average financial aid package:*** $14,268 (excluding resources awarded to replace EFC).

GIFT AID (NEED-BASED) ***Total amount:*** $16,196,503 (22% federal, 30% state, 44% institutional, 4% external sources). ***Receiving aid:*** Freshmen: 92% (388); all full-time undergraduates: 91% (1,420). ***Average award:*** Freshmen: $13,618; Undergraduates: $10,928. ***Scholarships, grants, and awards:*** Federal Pell, FSEOG, state, private, college/university gift aid from institutional funds.

GIFT AID (NON-NEED-BASED) ***Scholarships, grants, and awards by category:*** *Academic interests/achievement:* biological sciences, business, education, English, general academic interests/achievements, mathematics, premedicine, religion/biblical studies. *Creative arts/performance:* applied art and design, music. *Special achievements/activities:* cheerleading/drum major, general special achievements/activities, junior miss, leadership, religious involvement. *Special characteristics:* children and siblings of alumni, children of faculty/staff, relatives of clergy, religious affiliation. ***Tuition waivers:*** Full or partial for employees or children of employees, senior citizens.

LOANS ***Student loans:*** $8,085,735 (100% need-based). 77% of past graduating class borrowed through all loan programs. *Average indebtedness per student:* $16,480. ***Average need-based loan:*** Freshmen: $2826. Undergraduates: $4437. ***Parent loans:*** $113,552 (100% need-based). ***Programs:*** FFEL (Subsidized and Unsubsidized Stafford, PLUS), Perkins, college/university.

WORK-STUDY ***Federal work-study:*** Total amount: $250,801; 186 jobs averaging $1369. ***State or other work-study/employment:*** Total amount: $7000 (100% need-based). 7 part-time jobs averaging $1000.

ATHLETIC AWARDS Total amount: $859,758 (100% need-based).

APPLYING FOR FINANCIAL AID ***Required financial aid form:*** FAFSA. ***Financial aid deadline (priority):*** 4/1. ***Notification date:*** Continuous beginning 4/15. Students must reply within 2 weeks of notification.

CONTACT Ms. Marilyn D. Radford, Director of Student Financial Services, Lindsey Wilson College, 210 Lindsey Wilson Street, Columbia, KY 42728, 270-384-8022 or toll-free 800-264-0138. *Fax:* 270-384-8591. *E-mail:* radfordm@lindsey.edu.

LINFIELD COLLEGE

McMinnville, OR

Tuition & fees: $27,414 **Average undergraduate aid package: $20,112**

ABOUT THE INSTITUTION Independent American Baptist Churches in the USA, coed. ***Awards:*** bachelor's degrees and post-bachelor's certificates. 41 undergraduate majors. ***Total enrollment:*** 1,720. Undergraduates: 1,720. Freshmen: 478. Federal methodology is used as a basis for awarding need-based institutional aid.

UNDERGRADUATE EXPENSES for 2008–09 ***Application fee:*** $40. ***Comprehensive fee:*** $35,274 includes full-time tuition ($27,150), mandatory fees ($264), and room and board ($7860). ***College room only:*** $4240. Full-time tuition and fees vary according to location. Room and board charges vary according to board plan, housing facility, and location. ***Part-time tuition:*** $845 per semester hour. Part-time tuition and fees vary according to course load and location. ***Payment plan:*** Installment.

FRESHMAN FINANCIAL AID (Fall 2008, est.) 327 applied for aid; of those 100% were deemed to have need. 100% of freshmen with need received aid; of those 39% had need fully met. ***Average percent of need met:*** 87% (excluding resources awarded to replace EFC). ***Average financial aid package:*** $22,056 (excluding resources awarded to replace EFC). 23% of all full-time freshmen had no need and received non-need-based gift aid.

UNDERGRADUATE FINANCIAL AID (Fall 2008, est.) 1,114 applied for aid; of those 100% were deemed to have need. 100% of undergraduates with need received aid; of those 27% had need fully met. ***Average percent of need met:*** 82% (excluding resources awarded to replace EFC). ***Average financial aid package:*** $20,112 (excluding resources awarded to replace EFC). 25% of all full-time undergraduates had no need and received non-need-based gift aid.

GIFT AID (NEED-BASED) ***Total amount:*** $16,623,340 (10% federal, 4% state, 80% institutional, 6% external sources). ***Receiving aid:*** Freshmen: 59% (282); all full-time undergraduates: 58% (963). ***Average award:*** Freshmen: $9536; Undergraduates: $9380. ***Scholarships, grants, and awards:*** Federal Pell, FSEOG, state, private, college/university gift aid from institutional funds.

GIFT AID (NON-NEED-BASED) ***Total amount:*** $3,579,748 (97% institutional, 3% external sources). ***Receiving aid:*** Freshmen: 41% (197). Undergraduates: 40% (663). ***Average award:*** Freshmen: $10,226. Undergraduates: $10,186. ***Scholarships, grants, and awards by category:*** *Academic interests/achievement:* 1,097 awards ($9,421,598 total): general academic interests/achievements. *Creative arts/performance:* 61 awards ($104,750 total): debating, music, theater/drama. *Special achievements/activities:* 45 awards ($67,400 total): leadership. *Special characteristics:* 36 awards ($947,026 total): children of faculty/staff. ***Tuition waivers:*** Full or partial for employees or children of employees, senior citizens. ***ROTC:*** Air Force cooperative.

LOANS ***Student loans:*** $8,855,656 (90% need-based, 10% non-need-based). 72% of past graduating class borrowed through all loan programs. *Average indebtedness per student:* $27,140. ***Average need-based loan:*** Freshmen: $3870. Undergraduates: $4798. ***Parent loans:*** $480,504 (100% non-need-based). ***Programs:*** FFEL (Subsidized and Unsubsidized Stafford, PLUS), Perkins, college/university, private loans.

WORK-STUDY ***Federal work-study:*** Total amount: $1,574,036; 726 jobs averaging $2103. ***State or other work-study/employment:*** Total amount: $1,383,792 (40% need-based, 60% non-need-based). 641 part-time jobs averaging $2139.

APPLYING FOR FINANCIAL AID ***Required financial aid form:*** FAFSA. ***Financial aid deadline (priority):*** 2/1. ***Notification date:*** 4/1. Students must reply by 5/1.

CONTACT Crisanne Werner, Director of Financial Aid, Linfield College, 900 Southeast Baker Street A484, McMinnville, OR 97128-6894, 503-883-2225 or toll-free 800-640-2287. *Fax:* 503-883-2486. *E-mail:* finaid@linfield.edu.

LIPSCOMB UNIVERSITY

Nashville, TN

Tuition & fees: $18,580 **Average undergraduate aid package: $15,817**

ABOUT THE INSTITUTION Independent religious, coed. ***Awards:*** bachelor's, master's, and first professional degrees and post-bachelor's certificates. 85 undergraduate majors. ***Total enrollment:*** 3,054. Undergraduates: 2,420. Freshmen: 658. Both federal and institutional methodology are used as a basis for awarding need-based institutional aid.

UNDERGRADUATE EXPENSES for 2008–09 ***Application fee:*** $25. ***Comprehensive fee:*** $25,980 includes full-time tuition ($17,580), mandatory fees ($1000), and room and board ($7400). ***College room only:*** $4462. Full-time tuition and fees vary according to class time, course load, and degree level. Room and board charges vary according to board plan and housing facility. ***Part-time tuition:*** $690 per hour. ***Part-time fees:*** $42 per hour. Part-time tuition and fees vary according to class time, course load, and degree level. ***Payment plans:*** Installment, deferred payment.

FRESHMAN FINANCIAL AID (Fall 2008, est.) 652 applied for aid; of those 62% were deemed to have need. 100% of freshmen with need received aid; of those 29% had need fully met. ***Average percent of need met:*** 65% (excluding resources awarded to replace EFC). ***Average financial aid package:*** $14,245 (excluding resources awarded to replace EFC). 25% of all full-time freshmen had no need and received non-need-based gift aid.

UNDERGRADUATE FINANCIAL AID (Fall 2008, est.) 2,101 applied for aid; of those 62% were deemed to have need. 100% of undergraduates with need received aid; of those 35% had need fully met. ***Average percent of need met:*** 62% (excluding resources awarded to replace EFC). ***Average financial aid package:*** $15,817 (excluding resources awarded to replace EFC). 24% of all full-time undergraduates had no need and received non-need-based gift aid.

GIFT AID (NEED-BASED) ***Total amount:*** $12,864,418 (14% federal, 25% state, 51% institutional, 10% external sources). ***Receiving aid:*** Freshmen: 28% (185); all full-time undergraduates: 26% (573). ***Average award:*** Freshmen: $5568; Undergraduates: $6446. ***Scholarships, grants, and awards:*** Federal Pell, FSEOG, state, private, college/university gift aid from institutional funds.

GIFT AID (NON-NEED-BASED) ***Total amount:*** $5,613,272 (26% state, 69% institutional, 5% external sources). ***Receiving aid:*** Freshmen: 59% (390). Undergraduates: 47% (1,042). ***Average award:*** Freshmen: $5882. Undergraduates: $8597. ***Scholarships, grants, and awards by category:*** *Academic interests/achievement:* biological sciences, business, communication, education, engineering/technologies, English, general academic interests/achievements, home economics, mathematics, premedicine, religion/biblical studies. *Creative arts/performance:* art/fine arts, journalism/publications, music, theater/drama. *Special achievements/activities:* cheerleading/drum major, community service, general special achievements/activities, leadership, religious involvement. *Special characteristics:* adult students, children and siblings of alumni, children of educators, children of faculty/staff, children with a deceased or disabled parent, international students, members of minority groups, relatives of clergy. ***Tuition waivers:*** Full or partial for employees or children of employees. ***ROTC:*** Army cooperative, Air Force cooperative.

LOANS ***Student loans:*** $9,662,702 (87% need-based, 13% non-need-based). 58% of past graduating class borrowed through all loan programs. *Average indebtedness per student:* $14,040. ***Average need-based loan:*** Freshmen: $3638. Undergraduates: $5342. ***Parent loans:*** $3,685,298 (82% need-based, 18% non-need-based). ***Programs:*** FFEL (Subsidized and Unsubsidized Stafford, PLUS), Perkins, Federal Nursing.

WORK-STUDY ***Federal work-study:*** Total amount: $216,886; jobs available.

ATHLETIC AWARDS Total amount: $2,227,319 (40% need-based, 60% non-need-based).

APPLYING FOR FINANCIAL AID ***Required financial aid form:*** FAFSA. ***Financial aid deadline (priority):*** 3/1. ***Notification date:*** Continuous.

CONTACT Mrs. Karita McCaleb Waters, Director of Financial Aid, Lipscomb University, One University Park Drive, Nashville, TN 37204-3951, 615-966-1791 or toll-free 877-582-4766. *Fax:* 615-966-7640. *E-mail:* karita.waters@lipscomb.edu.

LIVINGSTONE COLLEGE

Salisbury, NC

CONTACT Mrs. Terry Jefferies, Financial Aid Director, Livingstone College, 701 West Monroe Street, Price Building, Salisbury, NC 28144-5298, 704-216-6069 or toll-free 800-835-3435. *Fax:* 704-216-6319. *E-mail:* tjefferies@livingstone.edu.

LOCK HAVEN UNIVERSITY OF PENNSYLVANIA

Lock Haven, PA

Tuition & fees (PA res): $6917 **Average undergraduate aid package: $7043**

ABOUT THE INSTITUTION State-supported, coed. ***Awards:*** associate, bachelor's, and master's degrees. 57 undergraduate majors. ***Total enrollment:*** 5,266. Undergraduates: 4,988. Freshmen: 1,291. Federal methodology is used as a basis for awarding need-based institutional aid.

UNDERGRADUATE EXPENSES for 2008–09 ***Application fee:*** $25. ***One-time required fee:*** $25. ***Tuition, state resident:*** full-time $5358; part-time $223 per credit hour. ***Tuition, nonresident:*** full-time $11,396; part-time $475 per credit hour. ***Required fees:*** full-time $1559; $53 per credit hour or $60 per term. Full-time tuition and fees vary according to course load and location. Part-time tuition and fees vary according to course load and location. ***College room and board:*** $6448; ***Room only:*** $3520. Room and board charges vary according to board plan and housing facility. ***Payment plans:*** Installment, deferred payment.

FRESHMAN FINANCIAL AID (Fall 2008, est.) 1,246 applied for aid; of those 78% were deemed to have need. 100% of freshmen with need received aid; of those 45% had need fully met. ***Average percent of need met:*** 73% (excluding resources awarded to replace EFC). ***Average financial aid package:*** $7043 (excluding resources awarded to replace EFC). 4% of all full-time freshmen had no need and received non-need-based gift aid.

UNDERGRADUATE FINANCIAL AID (Fall 2008, est.) 4,314 applied for aid; of those 82% were deemed to have need. 100% of undergraduates with need received aid; of those 52% had need fully met. ***Average percent of need met:*** 77% (excluding resources awarded to replace EFC). ***Average financial aid package:*** $7043 (excluding resources awarded to replace EFC). 5% of all full-time undergraduates had no need and received non-need-based gift aid.

GIFT AID (NEED-BASED) ***Total amount:*** $11,253,245 (53% federal, 43% state, 1% institutional, 3% external sources). ***Receiving aid:*** Freshmen: 50% (641); all full-time undergraduates: 50% (2,271). ***Average award:*** Freshmen: $4634; Undergraduates: $4634. ***Scholarships, grants, and awards:*** Federal Pell, FSEOG, state, private, college/university gift aid from institutional funds, United Negro College Fund.

GIFT AID (NON-NEED-BASED) ***Total amount:*** $889,160 (1% state, 21% institutional, 78% external sources). ***Receiving aid:*** Freshmen: 8% (97). Undergraduates: 8% (345). ***Average award:*** Freshmen: $1245. Undergraduates: $1436. ***Scholarships, grants, and awards by category:*** *Academic interests/achievement:* 195 awards ($164,183 total): biological sciences, communication, education, English, foreign languages, general academic interests/achievements, international studies, library science, mathematics, physical sciences, social sciences. *Creative arts/performance:* 7 awards ($10,410 total): art/fine arts, journalism/publications, music. *Special achievements/activities:* 12 awards ($12,500 total): leadership, memberships. *Special characteristics:* 94 awards ($398,200 total): handicapped students, local/state students, members of minority groups, previous college experience. ***Tuition waivers:*** Full or partial for minority students, employees or children of employees, senior citizens. ***ROTC:*** Army.

LOANS ***Student loans:*** $32,253,238 (40% need-based, 60% non-need-based). 85% of past graduating class borrowed through all loan programs. *Average indebtedness per student:* $22,585. ***Average need-based loan:*** Freshmen: $3500. Undergraduates: $4500. ***Parent loans:*** $2,221,594 (100% non-need-based). ***Programs:*** FFEL (Subsidized and Unsubsidized Stafford, PLUS), Perkins, college/university.

WORK-STUDY ***Federal work-study:*** Total amount: $386,735; 253 jobs averaging $1174. ***State or other work-study/employment:*** Total amount: $1,388,332 (100% non-need-based). 951 part-time jobs averaging $711.

ATHLETIC AWARDS Total amount: $823,807 (100% non-need-based).

APPLYING FOR FINANCIAL AID ***Required financial aid form:*** FAFSA. ***Financial aid deadline:*** 3/15 (priority: 3/15). ***Notification date:*** Continuous beginning 4/1. Students must reply by 5/1 or within 2 weeks of notification.

CONTACT James Theeuwes, Director, Financial Services, Lock Haven University of Pennsylvania, Russell Hall 118, Lock Haven, PA 17745-2390, 570-484-2344 or toll-free 800-332-8900 (in-state), 800-233-8978 (out-of-state). *Fax:* 570-484-2918. *E-mail:* jtheeuwe@lhup.edu.

LOGAN UNIVERSITY–COLLEGE OF CHIROPRACTIC

Chesterfield, MO

CONTACT Linda K. Haman, Director of Financial Aid, Logan University–College of Chiropractic, 1851 Schoettler Road, PO Box 1065, Chesterfield, MO 63006-1065, 636-227-2100 Ext. 141 or toll-free 800-533-9210.

LOMA LINDA UNIVERSITY

Loma Linda, CA

CONTACT Verdell Schaefer, Director of Financial Aid, Loma Linda University, 11139 Anderson Street, Loma Linda, CA 92350, 909-558-4509. *Fax:* 909-558-4879. *E-mail:* finaid@univ.llu.edu.

LONG ISLAND UNIVERSITY, BROOKLYN CAMPUS

Brooklyn, NY

Tuition & fees: $27,358 **Average undergraduate aid package: $14,439**

ABOUT THE INSTITUTION Independent, coed. ***Awards:*** associate, bachelor's, master's, doctoral, and first professional degrees and post-bachelor's, post-master's, and first professional certificates. 65 undergraduate majors. ***Total enrollment:*** 8,051. Undergraduates: 3,945. Freshmen: 796. Federal methodology is used as a basis for awarding need-based institutional aid.

UNDERGRADUATE EXPENSES for 2008–09 ***Application fee:*** $30. ***Comprehensive fee:*** $37,498 includes full-time tuition ($26,048), mandatory fees ($1310), and room and board ($10,140). Room and board charges vary according to board plan and gender. ***Part-time tuition:*** $814 per credit. ***Part-time fees:*** $298 per term. ***Payment plans:*** Installment, deferred payment.

FRESHMAN FINANCIAL AID (Fall 2008, est.) 950 applied for aid; of those 81% were deemed to have need. 98% of freshmen with need received aid; of those 49% had need fully met. ***Average percent of need met:*** 52% (excluding resources awarded to replace EFC). ***Average financial aid package:*** $13,892 (excluding resources awarded to replace EFC). 10% of all full-time freshmen had no need and received non-need-based gift aid.

UNDERGRADUATE FINANCIAL AID (Fall 2008, est.) 4,341 applied for aid; of those 94% were deemed to have need. 97% of undergraduates with need received aid; of those 46% had need fully met. ***Average percent of need met:*** 45% (excluding resources awarded to replace EFC). ***Average financial aid package:*** $14,439 (excluding resources awarded to replace EFC). 4% of all full-time undergraduates had no need and received non-need-based gift aid.

GIFT AID (NEED-BASED) ***Total amount:*** $37,597,353 (32% federal, 24% state, 41% institutional, 3% external sources). ***Receiving aid:*** Freshmen: 74% (740); all full-time undergraduates: 81% (3,801). ***Average award:*** Freshmen: $10,779; Undergraduates: $10,627. ***Scholarships, grants, and awards:*** Federal Pell, FSEOG, state, private, college/university gift aid from institutional funds, Scholarships for Disadvantaged Students (Nursing and Pharmacy).

GIFT AID (NON-NEED-BASED) ***Total amount:*** $2,745,267 (97% institutional, 3% external sources). ***Receiving aid:*** Freshmen: 2% (24). Undergraduates: 3% (119). ***Average award:*** Freshmen: $18,208. Undergraduates: $20,878. ***Scholarships, grants, and awards by category:*** *Academic interests/achievement:* communication, education, general academic interests/achievements, health fields. *Creative arts/performance:* art/fine arts, cinema/film/broadcasting, dance, music. *Special achievements/activities:* $4,943,242 total: cheerleading/drum major, general special achievements/activities, leadership. *Special characteristics:* $4,943,242 total: children and siblings of alumni, children of faculty/staff, ethnic background, first-generation college students, general special characteristics, international students. ***Tuition waivers:*** Full or partial for employees or children of employees.

LOANS ***Student loans:*** $38,476,257 (84% need-based, 16% non-need-based). 97% of past graduating class borrowed through all loan programs. *Average indebtedness per student:* $39,000. ***Average need-based loan:*** Freshmen: $3360. Undergraduates: $4364. ***Parent loans:*** $26,162,001 (100% non-need-based). ***Programs:*** Federal Direct (Subsidized and Unsubsidized Stafford, PLUS), Perkins, Federal Health Professions Student Loans, alternative loans.

WORK-STUDY ***Federal work-study:*** Total amount: $1,008,610; 238 jobs averaging $3319. ***State or other work-study/employment:*** 53 part-time jobs averaging $4125.

ATHLETIC AWARDS Total amount: $5,082,466 (92% need-based, 8% non-need-based).

APPLYING FOR FINANCIAL AID ***Required financial aid form:*** FAFSA. ***Financial aid deadline:*** Continuous. ***Notification date:*** Continuous beginning 4/1. Students must reply within 4 weeks of notification.

CONTACT Ms. Rose Iannicelli, Dean of Financial Services, Long Island University, Brooklyn Campus, 1 University Plaza, Brooklyn, NY 11201-8423, 718-488-1037 or toll-free 800-LIU-PLAN. *Fax:* 718-488-3343.

LONG ISLAND UNIVERSITY, C.W. POST CAMPUS

Brookville, NY

Tuition & fees: $27,400 **Average undergraduate aid package: $13,700**

ABOUT THE INSTITUTION Independent, coed. ***Awards:*** bachelor's, master's, and doctoral degrees and post-bachelor's and post-master's certificates. 86 undergraduate majors. ***Total enrollment:*** 8,773. Undergraduates: 5,668. Freshmen: 952. Federal methodology is used as a basis for awarding need-based institutional aid.

UNDERGRADUATE EXPENSES for 2008–09 ***Application fee:*** $30. ***Comprehensive fee:*** $37,540 includes full-time tuition ($26,090), mandatory fees ($1310), and room and board ($10,140). Room and board charges vary according to board plan and housing facility. ***Part-time tuition:*** $814 per credit. ***Part-time fees:*** $7 per credit; $243 per term. ***Payment plans:*** Installment, deferred payment.

FRESHMAN FINANCIAL AID (Fall 2008, est.) 823 applied for aid; of those 82% were deemed to have need. 96% of freshmen with need received aid; of those 18% had need fully met. ***Average percent of need met:*** 75% (excluding resources awarded to replace EFC). ***Average financial aid package:*** $12,500 (excluding resources awarded to replace EFC). 13% of all full-time freshmen had no need and received non-need-based gift aid.

UNDERGRADUATE FINANCIAL AID (Fall 2008, est.) 3,583 applied for aid; of those 82% were deemed to have need. 97% of undergraduates with need received aid; of those 15% had need fully met. ***Average percent of need met:*** 75% (excluding resources awarded to replace EFC). ***Average financial aid package:*** $13,700 (excluding resources awarded to replace EFC). 14% of all full-time undergraduates had no need and received non-need-based gift aid.

GIFT AID (NEED-BASED) ***Total amount:*** $18,913,799 (25% federal, 30% state, 45% institutional). ***Receiving aid:*** Freshmen: 59% (564); all full-time undergraduates: 57% (2,475). ***Average award:*** Freshmen: $6000; Undergraduates: $5500. ***Scholarships, grants, and awards:*** Federal Pell, FSEOG, state, private, college/university gift aid from institutional funds.

GIFT AID (NON-NEED-BASED) ***Total amount:*** $16,526,667 (98% institutional, 2% external sources). ***Receiving aid:*** Freshmen: 47% (446). Undergraduates: 38% (1,661). ***Average award:*** Freshmen: $4030. Undergraduates: $6550. ***Scholarships, grants, and awards by category:*** *Academic interests/achievement:* biological sciences, business, computer science, education, general academic interests/achievements, health fields, mathematics. *Creative arts/performance:* art/fine arts, cinema/film/broadcasting, dance, journalism/publications, music, theater/drama. *Special characteristics:* adult students, children and siblings of alumni, children of faculty/staff, international students, siblings of current students. ***Tuition waivers:*** Full or partial for employees or children of employees. ***ROTC:*** Army cooperative, Air Force cooperative.

LOANS ***Student loans:*** $27,323,328 (40% need-based, 60% non-need-based). 65% of past graduating class borrowed through all loan programs. ***Average need-based loan:*** Freshmen: $3080. Undergraduates: $5050. ***Parent loans:*** $15,042,647 (100% non-need-based). ***Programs:*** Federal Direct (Subsidized and Unsubsidized Stafford, PLUS), Perkins, state, college/university.

WORK-STUDY ***Federal work-study:*** Total amount: $1,740,882; jobs available. ***State or other work-study/employment:*** Total amount: $41,178 (100% need-based). Part-time jobs available.

ATHLETIC AWARDS Total amount: $4,268,008 (100% non-need-based).

APPLYING FOR FINANCIAL AID ***Required financial aid forms:*** FAFSA, CSS Financial Aid PROFILE. ***Financial aid deadline:*** 3/1. ***Notification date:*** Continuous beginning 3/15. Students must reply by 5/1 or within 2 weeks of notification.

CONTACT Office of Financial Assistance, Long Island University, C.W. Post Campus, 720 Northern Boulevard, Brookville, NY 11548-1300, 516-299-2338 or toll-free 800-LIU-PLAN. *Fax:* 516-299-3833. *E-mail:* finaid@cwpost.liu.edu.

LONGWOOD UNIVERSITY

Farmville, VA

Tuition & fees (VA res): $8499 **Average undergraduate aid package: $8004**

ABOUT THE INSTITUTION State-supported, coed. ***Awards:*** bachelor's and master's degrees. 75 undergraduate majors. ***Total enrollment:*** 4,024. Undergraduates: 4,024. Freshmen: 1,049. Federal methodology is used as a basis for awarding need-based institutional aid.

UNDERGRADUATE EXPENSES for 2008–09 ***Application fee:*** $40. ***Tuition, state resident:*** full-time $4407; part-time $281 per credit hour. ***Tuition, nonresident:*** full-time $12,900; part-time $609 per credit hour. ***Required fees:*** full-time $4092. Full-time tuition and fees vary according to course load. Part-time tuition and fees vary according to course load. ***College room and board:*** $6856; ***Room only:*** $4300. Room and board charges vary according to board plan, housing facility, and location. ***Payment plan:*** Installment.

FRESHMAN FINANCIAL AID (Fall 2007) 579 applied for aid; of those 75% were deemed to have need. 100% of freshmen with need received aid; of those 14% had need fully met. ***Average percent of need met:*** 64% (excluding resources awarded to replace EFC). ***Average financial aid package:*** $7814 (excluding resources awarded to replace EFC). 2% of all full-time freshmen had no need and received non-need-based gift aid.

UNDERGRADUATE FINANCIAL AID (Fall 2007) 2,278 applied for aid; of those 74% were deemed to have need. 100% of undergraduates with need received aid; of those 9% had need fully met. ***Average percent of need met:*** 68% (excluding resources awarded to replace EFC). ***Average financial aid package:*** $8004 (excluding resources awarded to replace EFC). 2% of all full-time undergraduates had no need and received non-need-based gift aid.

GIFT AID (NEED-BASED) ***Total amount:*** $9,241,020 (26% federal, 38% state, 27% institutional, 9% external sources). ***Receiving aid:*** Freshmen: 44% (415); all full-time undergraduates: 41% (1,554). ***Average award:*** Freshmen: $5201; Undergraduates: $5037. ***Scholarships, grants, and awards:*** Federal Pell, FSEOG, state, private, college/university gift aid from institutional funds.

GIFT AID (NON-NEED-BASED) ***Total amount:*** $119,353 (2% federal, 5% state, 45% institutional, 48% external sources). ***Receiving aid:*** Freshmen: 1% (13). Undergraduates: 1% (47). ***Average award:*** Freshmen: $3729. Undergraduates: $3532. ***Scholarships, grants, and awards by category:*** *Academic interests/achievement:* 245 awards ($438,304 total): biological sciences, business, computer science, education, English, general academic interests/achievements, humanities, international studies, mathematics, military science, social sciences. *Creative arts/performance:* 35 awards ($40,758 total): art/fine arts, music, theater/drama. *Special achievements/activities:* 12 awards ($2500 total):

memberships. *Special characteristics:* 41 awards ($70,844 total): children and siblings of alumni, general special characteristics, local/state students. ***Tuition waivers:*** Full or partial for senior citizens. ***ROTC:*** Army.

LOANS ***Student loans:*** $11,504,157 (85% need-based, 15% non-need-based). 63% of past graduating class borrowed through all loan programs. *Average indebtedness per student:* $14,935. ***Average need-based loan:*** Freshmen: $3297. Undergraduates: $3785. ***Parent loans:*** $6,069,430 (59% need-based, 41% non-need-based). ***Programs:*** FFEL (Subsidized and Unsubsidized Stafford, PLUS), Perkins, college/university, private alternative loans.

WORK-STUDY ***Federal work-study:*** Total amount: $286,938; jobs available (averaging $2800). ***State or other work-study/employment:*** Part-time jobs available (averaging $2800).

ATHLETIC AWARDS Total amount: $1,652,782 (91% need-based, 9% non-need-based).

APPLYING FOR FINANCIAL AID ***Required financial aid form:*** FAFSA. ***Financial aid deadline (priority):*** 3/1. ***Notification date:*** Continuous beginning 4/1. Students must reply within 2 weeks of notification.

CONTACT Caroline Gibbs, Financial Aid Counselor, Longwood University, 201 High Street, Farmville, VA 23909, 434-395-2949 or toll-free 800-281-4677. *Fax:* 434-395-2829. *E-mail:* gibbsca@longwood.edu.

LORAS COLLEGE

Dubuque, IA

Tuition & fees: $25,348 **Average undergraduate aid package: $16,333**

ABOUT THE INSTITUTION Independent Roman Catholic, coed. ***Awards:*** associate, bachelor's, and master's degrees. 53 undergraduate majors. ***Total enrollment:*** 1,588. Undergraduates: 1,512. Freshmen: 382. Federal methodology is used as a basis for awarding need-based institutional aid.

UNDERGRADUATE EXPENSES for 2009–10 ***Application fee:*** $25. ***Comprehensive fee:*** $32,374 includes full-time tuition ($24,070), mandatory fees ($1278), and room and board ($7026). ***College room only:*** $3520. ***Part-time tuition:*** $457 per credit. ***Part-time fees:*** $25 per credit.

FRESHMAN FINANCIAL AID (Fall 2008, est.) 359 applied for aid; of those 96% were deemed to have need. 100% of freshmen with need received aid; of those 40% had need fully met. ***Average percent of need met:*** 87% (excluding resources awarded to replace EFC). ***Average financial aid package:*** $17,254 (excluding resources awarded to replace EFC).

UNDERGRADUATE FINANCIAL AID (Fall 2008, est.) 1,220 applied for aid; of those 90% were deemed to have need. 99% of undergraduates with need received aid; of those 40% had need fully met. ***Average percent of need met:*** 89% (excluding resources awarded to replace EFC). ***Average financial aid package:*** $16,333 (excluding resources awarded to replace EFC).

GIFT AID (NEED-BASED) ***Total amount:*** $13,607,850 (10% federal, 12% state, 78% institutional). ***Receiving aid:*** Freshmen: 76% (290); all full-time undergraduates: 68% (970). ***Average award:*** Freshmen: $9525; Undergraduates: $6422. ***Scholarships, grants, and awards:*** Federal Pell, FSEOG, state, college/university gift aid from institutional funds.

GIFT AID (NON-NEED-BASED) ***Total amount:*** $6,113,671 (95% institutional, 5% external sources). ***Receiving aid:*** Freshmen: 90% (345). Undergraduates: 66% (948). ***Average award:*** Freshmen: $10,750. Undergraduates: $9882. ***Scholarships, grants, and awards by category:*** *Academic interests/achievement:* 1,568 awards ($9,689,500 total): engineering/technologies, general academic interests/achievements, physical sciences. *Creative arts/performance:* 70 awards ($75,000 total): music. *Special characteristics:* 375 awards ($356,200 total): children and siblings of alumni, siblings of current students. ***ROTC:*** Army cooperative.

LOANS ***Student loans:*** $8,831,782 (49% need-based, 51% non-need-based). 64% of past graduating class borrowed through all loan programs. *Average indebtedness per student:* $25,380. ***Average need-based loan:*** Freshmen: $3174. Undergraduates: $3142. ***Parent loans:*** $1,127,827 (100% non-need-based). ***Programs:*** FFEL (Subsidized and Unsubsidized Stafford, PLUS), Perkins, college/university.

WORK-STUDY ***Federal work-study:*** Total amount: $243,368; 250 jobs averaging $2000. ***State or other work-study/employment:*** Total amount: $539,498 (3% need-based, 97% non-need-based). 290 part-time jobs averaging $2000.

APPLYING FOR FINANCIAL AID ***Required financial aid form:*** FAFSA. ***Financial aid deadline (priority):*** 4/15. ***Notification date:*** Continuous. Students must reply within 3 weeks of notification.

CONTACT Ms. Julie A. Dunn, Director of Financial Planning, Loras College, 1450 Alta Vista Street, Dubuque, IA 52004-0178, 563-588-7136 or toll-free 800-245-6727. *Fax:* 563-588-7119. *E-mail:* Julie.Dunn@loras.edu.

LOUISIANA COLLEGE

Pineville, LA

CONTACT Shelley Jinks, Financial Aid Director, Louisiana College, 1140 College Drive, Pineville, LA 71359-0001, 318-487-7386 or toll-free 800-487-1906. *Fax:* 318-487-7449. *E-mail:* jinks@lacollege.edu.

LOUISIANA STATE UNIVERSITY AND AGRICULTURAL AND MECHANICAL COLLEGE

Baton Rouge, LA

Tuition & fees (LA res): $5086 **Average undergraduate aid package: $8011**

ABOUT THE INSTITUTION State-supported, coed. ***Awards:*** bachelor's, master's, doctoral, and first professional degrees and post-master's certificates. 70 undergraduate majors. ***Total enrollment:*** 28,628. Undergraduates: 23,393. Freshmen: 4,596. Federal methodology is used as a basis for awarding need-based institutional aid.

UNDERGRADUATE EXPENSES for 2008–09 ***Application fee:*** $40. ***Tuition, state resident:*** full-time $3215. ***Tuition, nonresident:*** full-time $11,929. ***Required fees:*** full-time $1871. Part-time tuition and fees vary according to course load. ***College room and board:*** $7238; ***Room only:*** $4330. Room and board charges vary according to board plan and housing facility. ***Payment plan:*** Deferred payment.

FRESHMAN FINANCIAL AID (Fall 2007) 2,694 applied for aid; of those 63% were deemed to have need. 99% of freshmen with need received aid; of those 18% had need fully met. ***Average percent of need met:*** 62% (excluding resources awarded to replace EFC). ***Average financial aid package:*** $7644 (excluding resources awarded to replace EFC). 16% of all full-time freshmen had no need and received non-need-based gift aid.

UNDERGRADUATE FINANCIAL AID (Fall 2007) 12,618 applied for aid; of those 71% were deemed to have need. 96% of undergraduates with need received aid; of those 14% had need fully met. ***Average percent of need met:*** 58% (excluding resources awarded to replace EFC). ***Average financial aid package:*** $8011 (excluding resources awarded to replace EFC). 11% of all full-time undergraduates had no need and received non-need-based gift aid.

GIFT AID (NEED-BASED) ***Total amount:*** $37,120,682 (35% federal, 38% state, 24% institutional, 3% external sources). ***Receiving aid:*** Freshmen: 32% (1,619); all full-time undergraduates: 30% (7,281). ***Average award:*** Freshmen: $5649; Undergraduates: $5230. ***Scholarships, grants, and awards:*** Federal Pell, FSEOG, state, private, college/university gift aid from institutional funds.

GIFT AID (NON-NEED-BASED) ***Total amount:*** $46,919,923 (2% federal, 69% state, 25% institutional, 4% external sources). ***Receiving aid:*** Freshmen: 2% (76). Undergraduates: 1% (209). ***Average award:*** Freshmen: $3570. Undergraduates: $4003. ***Scholarships, grants, and awards by category:*** *Academic interests/achievement:* 1,151 awards ($2,191,000 total): agriculture, architecture, biological sciences, business, communication, computer science, education, engineering/technologies, English, foreign languages, general academic interests/achievements, home economics, humanities, mathematics, military science, physical sciences, premedicine. *Creative arts/performance:* 287 awards ($1,353,000 total): applied art and design, art/fine arts, journalism/publications, music, performing arts, theater/drama. *Special achievements/activities:* leadership. *Special characteristics:* 409 awards ($2,260,000 total): children and siblings of alumni, children with a deceased or disabled parent, general special characteristics. ***Tuition waivers:*** Full or partial for children of alumni, employees or children of employees. ***ROTC:*** Army, Naval cooperative, Air Force.

LOANS ***Student loans:*** $49,169,190 (72% need-based, 28% non-need-based). 44% of past graduating class borrowed through all loan programs. *Average indebtedness per student:* $16,354. ***Average need-based loan:*** Freshmen: $2437. Undergraduates: $3904. ***Parent loans:*** $11,323,551 (30% need-based, 70% non-need-based). ***Programs:*** FFEL (Subsidized and Unsubsidized Stafford, PLUS).

WORK-STUDY ***Federal work-study:*** Total amount: $1,483,370; 611 jobs averaging $1400. ***State or other work-study/employment:*** Total amount: $12,737,505 (25% need-based, 75% non-need-based). 4,826 part-time jobs averaging $2000.

ATHLETIC AWARDS Total amount: $6,346,235 (32% need-based, 68% non-need-based).

APPLYING FOR FINANCIAL AID ***Required financial aid forms:*** FAFSA, institution's own form. ***Financial aid deadline (priority):*** 3/1. ***Notification date:*** 3/1. Students must reply within 2 weeks of notification.

CONTACT Mary G. Parker, Executive Director of Undergraduate Admissions and Student Aid, Louisiana State University and Agricultural and Mechanical College, LSU 1104 Pleasant Hall, Baton Rouge, LA 70803-3103, 225-578-3113. *Fax:* 225-578-6300. *E-mail:* financialaid@lsu.edu.

LOUISIANA STATE UNIVERSITY HEALTH SCIENCES CENTER

New Orleans, LA

CONTACT Mr. Patrick Gorman, Director of Financial Aid, Louisiana State University Health Sciences Center, 433 Bolivar Street, New Orleans, LA 70112, 504-568-4821. *Fax:* 504-599-1390.

LOUISIANA STATE UNIVERSITY IN SHREVEPORT

Shreveport, LA

CONTACT Office of Student Financial Aid, Louisiana State University in Shreveport, One University Place, Shreveport, LA 71115-2399, 318-797-5363 or toll-free 800-229-5957 (in-state). *Fax:* 318-797-5366.

LOUISIANA TECH UNIVERSITY

Ruston, LA

Tuition & fees (LA res): $4911 **Average undergraduate aid package: $8375**

ABOUT THE INSTITUTION State-supported, coed. ***Awards:*** associate, bachelor's, master's, and doctoral degrees and first professional certificates. 79 undergraduate majors. ***Total enrollment:*** 10,564. Undergraduates: 8,356. Freshmen: 1,592. Institutional methodology is used as a basis for awarding need-based institutional aid.

UNDERGRADUATE EXPENSES for 2008–09 ***Application fee:*** $20. ***Tuition, state resident:*** full-time $4911; part-time $177 per credit hour. ***Tuition, nonresident:*** full-time $9816; part-time $177 per credit hour. Full-time tuition and fees vary according to course load, location, and program. Part-time tuition and fees vary according to course load, location, and program. ***College room and board:*** $4740; ***Room only:*** $2490. Room and board charges vary according to board plan and housing facility. ***Payment plans:*** Installment, deferred payment.

FRESHMAN FINANCIAL AID (Fall 2008, est.) 1,163 applied for aid; of those 61% were deemed to have need. 100% of freshmen with need received aid; of those 21% had need fully met. ***Average percent of need met:*** 74% (excluding resources awarded to replace EFC). ***Average financial aid package:*** $8921 (excluding resources awarded to replace EFC). 19% of all full-time freshmen had no need and received non-need-based gift aid.

UNDERGRADUATE FINANCIAL AID (Fall 2008, est.) 4,154 applied for aid; of those 64% were deemed to have need. 96% of undergraduates with need received aid; of those 18% had need fully met. ***Average percent of need met:*** 65% (excluding resources awarded to replace EFC). ***Average financial aid package:*** $8375 (excluding resources awarded to replace EFC). 15% of all full-time undergraduates had no need and received non-need-based gift aid.

GIFT AID (NEED-BASED) ***Total amount:*** $15,239,667 (44% federal, 40% state, 13% institutional, 3% external sources). ***Receiving aid:*** Freshmen: 45% (678); all full-time undergraduates: 36% (2,293). ***Average award:*** Freshmen: $7127; Undergraduates: $6270. ***Scholarships, grants, and awards:*** Federal Pell, FSEOG, state, private, college/university gift aid from institutional funds.

GIFT AID (NON-NEED-BASED) ***Total amount:*** $8,477,366 (59% state, 34% institutional, 7% external sources). ***Receiving aid:*** Freshmen: 8% (114). Undergraduates: 5% (352). ***Average award:*** Freshmen: $2430. Undergraduates: $2286. ***Scholarships, grants, and awards by category:*** *Academic interests/achievement:* agriculture, architecture, biological sciences, business, computer science, education, engineering/technologies, English, foreign languages, general academic interests/achievements, health fields, home economics, international studies, mathematics, military science, physical sciences, social sciences. *Creative arts/performance:* applied art and design, art/fine arts, creative writing, debating, general creative arts/performance, journalism/publications, music, performing arts, theater/drama. *Special achievements/activities:* cheerleading/drum major, junior miss. *Special characteristics:* children and siblings of alumni, children of faculty/staff, children of public servants, handicapped students, international students, members of minority groups, out-of-state students, veterans, veterans' children. ***Tuition waivers:*** Full or partial for children of alumni, employees or children of employees, senior citizens. ***ROTC:*** Army cooperative, Naval.

LOANS ***Student loans:*** $26,872,816 (57% need-based, 43% non-need-based). 53% of past graduating class borrowed through all loan programs. *Average indebtedness per student:* $12,715. ***Average need-based loan:*** Freshmen: $2526. Undergraduates: $3279. ***Parent loans:*** $11,972,301 (18% need-based, 82% non-need-based). ***Programs:*** FFEL (Subsidized and Unsubsidized Stafford, PLUS), Perkins.

WORK-STUDY ***Federal work-study:*** Total amount: $678,374; 262 jobs averaging $1993. ***State or other work-study/employment:*** Total amount: $1,628,545 (100% non-need-based). 1,022 part-time jobs averaging $1800.

ATHLETIC AWARDS Total amount: $2,620,155 (38% need-based, 62% non-need-based).

APPLYING FOR FINANCIAL AID ***Required financial aid forms:*** FAFSA, institution's own form. ***Financial aid deadline (priority):*** 4/15. ***Notification date:*** Continuous. Students must reply within 3 weeks of notification.

CONTACT Financial Aid Office, Louisiana Tech University, PO Box 7925, Ruston, LA 71272, 318-257-2641 or toll-free 800-528-3241. *Fax:* 318-257-2628. *E-mail:* techaid@ltfa.latech.edu.

LOURDES COLLEGE

Sylvania, OH

Tuition & fees: $14,730 **Average undergraduate aid package: $11,202**

ABOUT THE INSTITUTION Independent Roman Catholic, coed. ***Awards:*** associate, bachelor's, and master's degrees and post-bachelor's certificates. 25 undergraduate majors. ***Total enrollment:*** 2,087. Undergraduates: 1,862. Freshmen: 140. Both federal and institutional methodology are used as a basis for awarding need-based institutional aid.

UNDERGRADUATE EXPENSES for 2008–09 ***Application fee:*** $25. ***Tuition:*** full-time $12,930; part-time $431 per credit hour. ***Required fees:*** full-time $1800; $60 per credit hour. Full-time tuition and fees vary according to course load and location. Part-time tuition and fees vary according to course load and location. ***Payment plans:*** Installment, deferred payment.

FRESHMAN FINANCIAL AID (Fall 2008, est.) 97 applied for aid; of those 76% were deemed to have need. 100% of freshmen with need received aid. ***Average financial aid package:*** $14,003 (excluding resources awarded to replace EFC).

UNDERGRADUATE FINANCIAL AID (Fall 2008, est.) 888 applied for aid; of those 87% were deemed to have need. 100% of undergraduates with need received aid. ***Average financial aid package:*** $11,202 (excluding resources awarded to replace EFC).

GIFT AID (NEED-BASED) ***Total amount:*** $5,922,008 (47% federal, 32% state, 18% institutional, 3% external sources). ***Receiving aid:*** Freshmen: 52% (59); all full-time undergraduates: 56% (538). ***Average award:*** Freshmen: $7161; Undergraduates: $6765. ***Scholarships, grants, and awards:*** Federal Pell, FSEOG, state, private, college/university gift aid from institutional funds.

GIFT AID (NON-NEED-BASED) ***Receiving aid:*** Freshmen: 65% (74). Undergraduates: 80% (773). ***Scholarships, grants, and awards by category:*** *Academic interests/achievement:* 365 awards ($678,424 total): general academic interests/achievements. *Creative arts/performance:* art/fine arts, music. *Special achievements/activities:* general special achievements/activities. *Special characteristics:* adult students, ethnic background, local/state students, members of minority groups, out-of-state students, previous college experience. ***Tuition waivers:*** Full or partial for employees or children of employees, senior citizens. ***ROTC:*** Army cooperative, Air Force cooperative.

LOANS ***Student loans:*** $11,584,324 (100% need-based). ***Average need-based loan:*** Freshmen: $3387. Undergraduates: $4099. ***Parent loans:*** $457,228 (100% need-based). ***Programs:*** Federal Direct (Subsidized and Unsubsidized Stafford, PLUS), Perkins, state, college/university, alternative loans.

WORK-STUDY ***Federal work-study:*** Total amount: $189,318; 111 jobs averaging $1706. ***State or other work-study/employment:*** Total amount: $85,000 (100% need-based). 85 part-time jobs averaging $1000.

APPLYING FOR FINANCIAL AID ***Required financial aid form:*** FAFSA. ***Financial aid deadline (priority):*** 3/1. ***Notification date:*** Continuous beginning 3/1. Students must reply within 4 weeks of notification.

CONTACT Denise McClusky, Director of Financial Aid, Lourdes College, 6832 Convent Boulevard, Sylvania, OH 43560-2898, 419-824-3732 or toll-free 800-878-3210 Ext. 1299. *Fax:* 419-882-3987. *E-mail:* finaid@lourdes.edu.

LOYOLA MARYMOUNT UNIVERSITY

Los Angeles, CA

ABOUT THE INSTITUTION Independent Roman Catholic, coed. ***Awards:*** bachelor's, master's, doctoral, and first professional degrees and post-bachelor's, post-master's, and first professional certificates. 44 undergraduate majors. ***Total enrollment:*** 9,011. Undergraduates: 5,676. Freshmen: 1,261.

GIFT AID (NEED-BASED) ***Scholarships, grants, and awards:*** Federal Pell, FSEOG, state, private, college/university gift aid from institutional funds.

LOANS ***Programs:*** Federal Direct (Subsidized and Unsubsidized Stafford), FFEL (Subsidized and Unsubsidized Stafford, PLUS), college/university.

WORK-STUDY ***Federal work-study:*** Total amount: $6,085,009. ***State or other work-study/employment:*** Total amount: $1,309,189 (31% need-based, 69% non-need-based).

APPLYING FOR FINANCIAL AID ***Required financial aid forms:*** FAFSA, institution's own form, CSS Financial Aid PROFILE.

CONTACT Financial Aid Office, Loyola Marymount University, One LMU Drive, Los Angeles, CA 90045-8350, 310-338-2753 or toll-free 800-LMU-INFO. *E-mail:* finaid@lmu.edu.

LOYOLA UNIVERSITY CHICAGO

Chicago, IL

Tuition & fees: $30,656 **Average undergraduate aid package: $25,490**

ABOUT THE INSTITUTION Independent Roman Catholic (Jesuit), coed. ***Awards:*** bachelor's, master's, doctoral, and first professional degrees and post-bachelor's and post-master's certificates (also offers adult part-time program with significant enrollment not reflected in profile). 71 undergraduate majors. ***Total enrollment:*** 15,670. Undergraduates: 10,124. Freshmen: 2,176. Federal methodology is used as a basis for awarding need-based institutional aid.

UNDERGRADUATE EXPENSES for 2009–10 ***Application fee:*** $25. ***Comprehensive fee:*** $41,541 includes full-time tuition ($29,850), mandatory fees ($806), and room and board ($10,885). ***College room only:*** $7160. ***Part-time tuition:*** $605 per semester hour.

FRESHMAN FINANCIAL AID (Fall 2008, est.) 1,858 applied for aid; of those 83% were deemed to have need. 100% of freshmen with need received aid; of those 12% had need fully met. ***Average percent of need met:*** 84% (excluding resources awarded to replace EFC). ***Average financial aid package:*** $25,452 (excluding resources awarded to replace EFC). 19% of all full-time freshmen had no need and received non-need-based gift aid.

UNDERGRADUATE FINANCIAL AID (Fall 2008, est.) 7,368 applied for aid; of those 88% were deemed to have need. 99% of undergraduates with need received aid; of those 10% had need fully met. ***Average percent of need met:*** 82% (excluding resources awarded to replace EFC). ***Average financial aid package:*** $25,490 (excluding resources awarded to replace EFC). 18% of all full-time undergraduates had no need and received non-need-based gift aid.

GIFT AID (NEED-BASED) ***Total amount:*** $92,132,311 (11% federal, 12% state, 74% institutional, 3% external sources). ***Receiving aid:*** Freshmen: 69% (1,496); all full-time undergraduates: 67% (6,147). ***Average award:*** Freshmen: $16,382; Undergraduates: $15,177. ***Scholarships, grants, and awards:*** Federal Pell, FSEOG, state, private, college/university gift aid from institutional funds.

GIFT AID (NON-NEED-BASED) ***Total amount:*** $14,296,277 (90% institutional, 10% external sources). ***Receiving aid:*** Freshmen: 6% (136). Undergraduates: 4% (374). ***Average award:*** Freshmen: $8139. Undergraduates: $7260. ***Scholarships, grants, and awards by category:*** *Academic interests/achievement:* 4,035 awards ($31,161,900 total): general academic interests/achievements. *Creative arts/performance:* 90 awards ($145,750 total): art/fine arts, debating, journalism/publications, music, theater/drama. *Special achievements/activities:* 375 awards ($1,533,332 total): community service, general special achievements/activities, leadership, memberships. *Special characteristics:* 1,437 awards ($3,599,945 total): adult students, general special characteristics, religious affiliation. ***ROTC:*** Army cooperative, Naval cooperative, Air Force cooperative.

LOANS ***Student loans:*** $75,091,764 (69% need-based, 31% non-need-based). 58% of past graduating class borrowed through all loan programs. *Average indebtedness per student:* $32,134. ***Average need-based loan:*** Freshmen: $3620. Undergraduates: $4717. ***Parent loans:*** $13,361,945 (32% need-based, 68% non-need-based). ***Programs:*** FFEL (Subsidized and Unsubsidized Stafford, PLUS), Perkins, Federal Nursing.

WORK-STUDY ***Federal work-study:*** Total amount: $10,563,186; 4,766 jobs averaging $2216.

ATHLETIC AWARDS Total amount: $3,794,259 (48% need-based, 52% non-need-based).

APPLYING FOR FINANCIAL AID ***Required financial aid form:*** FAFSA. ***Financial aid deadline:*** Continuous. ***Notification date:*** Continuous beginning 2/15. Students must reply within 3 weeks of notification.

CONTACT Mr. Eric Weems, Director of Financial Aid, Loyola University Chicago, 6525 North Sheridan Road, Chicago, IL 60626, 773-508-3155 or toll-free 800-262-2373. *Fax:* 773-508-3177. *E-mail:* lufinaid@luc.edu.

LOYOLA UNIVERSITY MARYLAND

Baltimore, MD

Tuition & fees: $36,240 **Average undergraduate aid package: $25,360**

ABOUT THE INSTITUTION Independent Roman Catholic (Jesuit), coed. ***Awards:*** bachelor's, master's, and doctoral degrees and post-master's certificates. 32 undergraduate majors. ***Total enrollment:*** 6,080. Undergraduates: 3,716. Freshmen: 1,068. Institutional methodology is used as a basis for awarding need-based institutional aid.

UNDERGRADUATE EXPENSES for 2008–09 ***Application fee:*** $50. ***One-time required fee:*** $165. ***Tuition:*** full-time $35,140.

FRESHMAN FINANCIAL AID (Fall 2008, est.) 768 applied for aid; of those 75% were deemed to have need. 100% of freshmen with need received aid; of those 100% had need fully met. ***Average percent of need met:*** 100% (excluding resources awarded to replace EFC). ***Average financial aid package:*** $26,525 (excluding resources awarded to replace EFC). 10% of all full-time freshmen had no need and received non-need-based gift aid.

UNDERGRADUATE FINANCIAL AID (Fall 2008, est.) 2,164 applied for aid; of those 82% were deemed to have need. 100% of undergraduates with need received aid; of those 97% had need fully met. ***Average percent of need met:*** 97% (excluding resources awarded to replace EFC). ***Average financial aid package:*** $25,360 (excluding resources awarded to replace EFC). 10% of all full-time undergraduates had no need and received non-need-based gift aid.

GIFT AID (NEED-BASED) ***Total amount:*** $33,413,293 (6% federal, 2% state, 90% institutional, 2% external sources). ***Receiving aid:*** Freshmen: 40% (427); all full-time undergraduates: 36% (1,024). ***Average award:*** Freshmen: $19,530, Undergraduates: $17,730. ***Scholarships, grants, and awards:*** Federal Pell, FSEOG, state, private, college/university gift aid from institutional funds.

GIFT AID (NON-NEED-BASED) ***Total amount:*** $7,540,603 (12% federal, 1% state, 80% institutional, 7% external sources). ***Receiving aid:*** Freshmen: 20% (216). Undergraduates: 18% (656). ***Average award:*** Freshmen: $14,285. Undergraduates: $13,875. ***Scholarships, grants, and awards by category:*** *Academic interests/achievement:* 778 awards ($10,043,585 total): general academic interests/achievements. *Special characteristics:* 52 awards ($362,500 total): local/state students, members of minority groups. ***ROTC:*** Army, Air Force cooperative.

LOANS ***Student loans:*** $15,769,325 (46% need-based, 54% non-need-based). 71% of past graduating class borrowed through all loan programs. *Average indebtedness per student:* $26,340. ***Average need-based loan:*** Freshmen: $5235. Undergraduates: $6110. ***Parent loans:*** $12,289,952 (100% non-need-based). ***Programs:*** Federal Direct (Subsidized and Unsubsidized Stafford, PLUS), Perkins, college/university.

WORK-STUDY ***Federal work-study:*** Total amount: $1,185,575; 552 jobs averaging $2350. ***State or other work-study/employment:*** Total amount: $891,656 (49% need-based, 51% non-need-based). 60 part-time jobs averaging $10,615.

ATHLETIC AWARDS Total amount: $4,852,814 (26% need-based, 74% non-need-based).

APPLYING FOR FINANCIAL AID ***Required financial aid forms:*** FAFSA, CSS Financial Aid PROFILE, noncustodial (divorced/separated) parent's statement. ***Financial aid deadline:*** 2/15. ***Notification date:*** 4/1. Students must reply by 5/1.

CONTACT Mr. Mark Lindenmeyer, Assistant Vice President of Financial Aid, Loyola University Maryland, 4501 North Charles Street, Baltimore, MD 21210-2699, 410-617-2576 or toll-free 800-221-9107 Ext. 2252 (in-state). *Fax:* 410-617-5149. *E-mail:* lindenmeyer@loyola.edu.

LOYOLA UNIVERSITY NEW ORLEANS

New Orleans, LA

Tuition & fees: $29,706 **Average undergraduate aid package: $23,322**

ABOUT THE INSTITUTION Independent Roman Catholic (Jesuit), coed. ***Awards:*** bachelor's, master's, and first professional degrees and post-bachelor's, post-master's, and first professional certificates. 42 undergraduate majors. ***Total enrollment:*** 4,474. Undergraduates: 2,658. Freshmen: 700. Federal methodology is used as a basis for awarding need-based institutional aid.

UNDERGRADUATE EXPENSES for 2009–10 ***Application fee:*** $20. ***Comprehensive fee:*** $39,532 includes full-time tuition ($28,770), mandatory fees ($936), and room and board ($9826). ***College room only:*** $5814. ***Part-time tuition:*** $821 per credit hour.

FRESHMAN FINANCIAL AID (Fall 2008, est.) 533 applied for aid; of those 77% were deemed to have need. 100% of freshmen with need received aid; of those 32% had need fully met. ***Average percent of need met:*** 92% (excluding resources awarded to replace EFC). ***Average financial aid package:*** $25,869 (excluding resources awarded to replace EFC). 35% of all full-time freshmen had no need and received non-need-based gift aid.

UNDERGRADUATE FINANCIAL AID (Fall 2008, est.) 1,586 applied for aid; of those 81% were deemed to have need. 100% of undergraduates with need received aid; of those 27% had need fully met. ***Average percent of need met:*** 85% (excluding resources awarded to replace EFC). ***Average financial aid package:*** $23,322 (excluding resources awarded to replace EFC). 39% of all full-time undergraduates had no need and received non-need-based gift aid.

GIFT AID (NEED-BASED) ***Total amount:*** $26,335,479 (9% federal, 7% state, 80% institutional, 4% external sources). ***Receiving aid:*** Freshmen: 64% (408); all full-time undergraduates: 57% (1,260). ***Average award:*** Freshmen: $16,505; Undergraduates: $16,325. ***Scholarships, grants, and awards:*** Federal Pell, FSEOG, state, private, college/university gift aid from institutional funds.

GIFT AID (NON-NEED-BASED) ***Total amount:*** $14,829,936 (4% state, 90% institutional, 6% external sources). ***Receiving aid:*** Freshmen: 63% (404). Undergraduates: 56% (1,222). ***Average award:*** Freshmen: $18,391. Undergraduates: $14,858. ***Scholarships, grants, and awards by category:*** *Academic interests/achievement:* general academic interests/achievements. *Creative arts/performance:* general creative arts/performance. *Special characteristics:* children of faculty/staff. ***ROTC:*** Army cooperative, Naval cooperative, Air Force cooperative.

LOANS ***Student loans:*** $10,148,378 (42% need-based, 58% non-need-based). 59% of past graduating class borrowed through all loan programs. *Average indebtedness per student:* $21,401. ***Average need-based loan:*** Freshmen: $3565. Undergraduates: $4458. ***Parent loans:*** $2,070,385 (75% need-based, 25% non-need-based). ***Programs:*** FFEL (Subsidized and Unsubsidized Stafford, PLUS), Perkins.

WORK-STUDY ***Federal work-study:*** Total amount: $1,366,519; jobs available.

ATHLETIC AWARDS Total amount: $487,656 (51% need-based, 49% non-need-based).

APPLYING FOR FINANCIAL AID ***Required financial aid form:*** FAFSA. ***Financial aid deadline:*** 6/1 (priority: 2/15). ***Notification date:*** 3/1. Students must reply by 5/1 or within 2 weeks of notification.

CONTACT Catherine Simoneaux, Director of Scholarships and Financial Aid, Loyola University New Orleans, 6363 St. Charles Avenue, Box 206, New Orleans, LA 70118-6195, 504-865-3231 or toll-free 800-4-LOYOLA. *Fax:* 504-865-3233. *E-mail:* finaid@loyno.edu.

LUBBOCK CHRISTIAN UNIVERSITY

Lubbock, TX

Tuition & fees: $14,700 **Average undergraduate aid package: $12,268**

ABOUT THE INSTITUTION Independent religious, coed. ***Awards:*** associate, bachelor's, and master's degrees. 44 undergraduate majors. ***Total enrollment:*** 1,868. Undergraduates: 1,564. Freshmen: 273. Federal methodology is used as a basis for awarding need-based institutional aid.

UNDERGRADUATE EXPENSES for 2008–09 ***Application fee:*** $25. ***Comprehensive fee:*** $20,584 includes full-time tuition ($13,550), mandatory fees ($1150), and room and board ($5884). Full-time tuition and fees vary according to program. Room and board charges vary according to board plan and housing facility. ***Part-time tuition:*** $429 per semester hour. ***Part-time fees:*** $431 per term. Part-time tuition and fees vary according to course load and program. ***Payment plan:*** Installment.

FRESHMAN FINANCIAL AID (Fall 2008, est.) 200 applied for aid; of those 82% were deemed to have need. 99% of freshmen with need received aid; of those 12% had need fully met. ***Average percent of need met:*** 74% (excluding resources awarded to replace EFC). ***Average financial aid package:*** $12,284 (excluding resources awarded to replace EFC). 16% of all full-time freshmen had no need and received non-need-based gift aid.

UNDERGRADUATE FINANCIAL AID (Fall 2008, est.) 924 applied for aid; of those 85% were deemed to have need. 100% of undergraduates with need received aid; of those 9% had need fully met. ***Average percent of need met:*** 71% (excluding resources awarded to replace EFC). ***Average financial aid package:*** $12,268 (excluding resources awarded to replace EFC). 12% of all full-time undergraduates had no need and received non-need-based gift aid.

GIFT AID (NEED-BASED) ***Total amount:*** $6,234,049 (32% federal, 29% state, 32% institutional, 7% external sources). ***Receiving aid:*** Freshmen: 60% (162); all full-time undergraduates: 58% (740). ***Average award:*** Freshmen: $8789; Undergraduates: $8309. ***Scholarships, grants, and awards:*** Federal Pell, FSEOG, state, college/university gift aid from institutional funds.

GIFT AID (NON-NEED-BASED) ***Total amount:*** $974,680 (1% state, 74% institutional, 25% external sources). ***Receiving aid:*** Freshmen: 5% (14). Undergraduates: 4% (53). ***Average award:*** Freshmen: $3786. Undergraduates: $3921. ***Scholarships, grants, and awards by category:*** *Academic interests/achievement:* agriculture, business, communication, computer science, education, English, foreign languages, general academic interests/achievements, humanities, physical sciences, religion/biblical studies, social sciences. *Creative arts/performance:* art/fine arts, journalism/publications, music, performing arts, theater/drama. *Special achievements/activities:* 41 awards ($40,150 total): cheerleading/drum major, leadership. *Special characteristics:* 35 awards ($335,932 total): children of faculty/staff, general special characteristics. ***Tuition waivers:*** Full or partial for employees or children of employees. ***ROTC:*** Army cooperative, Air Force cooperative.

LOANS ***Student loans:*** $10,358,610 (73% need-based, 27% non-need-based). 76% of past graduating class borrowed through all loan programs. *Average indebtedness per student:* $26,333. ***Average need-based loan:*** Freshmen: $3252. Undergraduates: $4060. ***Parent loans:*** $3,126,454 (34% need-based, 66% non-need-based). ***Programs:*** FFEL (Subsidized and Unsubsidized Stafford, PLUS), Perkins, state.

WORK-STUDY ***Federal work-study:*** Total amount: $744,419; 716 jobs averaging $1685. ***State or other work-study/employment:*** Total amount: $23,155 (28% need-based, 72% non-need-based). 99 part-time jobs averaging $235.

ATHLETIC AWARDS Total amount: $1,309,372 (50% need-based, 50% non-need-based).

APPLYING FOR FINANCIAL AID ***Required financial aid forms:*** FAFSA, institution's own form. ***Financial aid deadline (priority):*** 6/1. ***Notification date:*** Continuous.

CONTACT Amy Hardesty, Financial Aid Director, Lubbock Christian University, 5601 19th Street, Lubbock, TX 79407, 806-720-7176 or toll-free 800-933-7601. *Fax:* 806-720-7185. *E-mail:* amy.hardesty@lcu.edu.

LUTHER COLLEGE

Decorah, IA

Tuition & fees: $32,290 **Average undergraduate aid package: $23,487**

ABOUT THE INSTITUTION Independent religious, coed. ***Awards:*** bachelor's degrees. 39 undergraduate majors. ***Total enrollment:*** 2,423. Undergraduates: 2,423. Freshmen: 630. Federal methodology is used as a basis for awarding need-based institutional aid.

UNDERGRADUATE EXPENSES for 2009–10 ***Application fee:*** $25. ***One-time required fee:*** $150. ***Comprehensive fee:*** $37,670 includes full-time tuition ($32,140), mandatory fees ($150), and room and board ($5380). ***College room only:*** $2800. ***Part-time tuition:*** $1148 per credit hour.

FRESHMAN FINANCIAL AID (Fall 2008, est.) 541 applied for aid; of those 79% were deemed to have need. 100% of freshmen with need received aid; of those 36% had need fully met. ***Average percent of need met:*** 92% (excluding

resources awarded to replace EFC). ***Average financial aid package:*** $25,205 (excluding resources awarded to replace EFC). 18% of all full-time freshmen had no need and received non-need-based gift aid.

UNDERGRADUATE FINANCIAL AID (Fall 2008, est.) 1,934 applied for aid; of those 85% were deemed to have need. 100% of undergraduates with need received aid; of those 29% had need fully met. ***Average percent of need met:*** 87% (excluding resources awarded to replace EFC). ***Average financial aid package:*** $23,487 (excluding resources awarded to replace EFC). 12% of all full-time undergraduates had no need and received non-need-based gift aid.

GIFT AID (NEED-BASED) ***Total amount:*** $27,825,885 (7% federal, 6% state, 84% institutional, 3% external sources). ***Receiving aid:*** Freshmen: 68% (427); all full-time undergraduates: 69% (1,631). ***Average award:*** Freshmen: $17,526; Undergraduates: $16,099. ***Scholarships, grants, and awards:*** Federal Pell, FSEOG, state, private, college/university gift aid from institutional funds.

GIFT AID (NON-NEED-BASED) ***Total amount:*** $2,213,477 (69% institutional, 31% external sources). ***Receiving aid:*** Freshmen: 13% (84). Undergraduates: 10% (224). ***Average award:*** Undergraduates: $9234. ***Scholarships, grants, and awards by category:*** *Academic interests/achievement:* 1,717 awards ($14,795,646 total): general academic interests/achievements. *Creative arts/performance:* 858 awards ($2,370,510 total): music. *Special characteristics:* 644 awards ($881,507 total): children and siblings of alumni, members of minority groups, religious affiliation.

LOANS ***Student loans:*** $9,629,033 (86% need-based, 14% non-need-based). 81% of past graduating class borrowed through all loan programs. *Average indebtedness per student:* $29,770. ***Average need-based loan:*** Freshmen: $5376. Undergraduates: $7244. ***Parent loans:*** $4,870,685 (27% need-based, 73% non-need-based). ***Programs:*** Federal Direct (Subsidized and Unsubsidized Stafford, PLUS), Perkins, college/university.

WORK-STUDY ***Federal work-study:*** Total amount: $1,902,484; 901 jobs averaging $2112. ***State or other work-study/employment:*** Total amount: $1,705,660 (19% need-based, 81% non-need-based). 1,096 part-time jobs averaging $2374.

APPLYING FOR FINANCIAL AID ***Required financial aid forms:*** FAFSA, institution's own form. ***Financial aid deadline (priority):*** 3/1. ***Notification date:*** Continuous beginning 3/15. Students must reply by 5/1.

CONTACT Ms. Janice Cordell, Director of Financial Aid, Luther College, 700 College Drive, Decorah, IA 52101-1045, 563-387-1018 or toll-free 800-458-8437. *Fax:* 563-387-2241. *E-mail:* cordellj@luther.edu.

LUTHER RICE UNIVERSITY

Lithonia, GA

Tuition & fees: N/R **Average undergraduate aid package: $5317**

ABOUT THE INSTITUTION Independent Baptist, coed. ***Awards:*** bachelor's, master's, and doctoral degrees. 3 undergraduate majors. ***Total enrollment:*** 1,047. Undergraduates: 375. Federal methodology is used as a basis for awarding need-based institutional aid.

UNDERGRADUATE EXPENSES for 2008–09 ***Application fee:*** $50. ***Tuition:*** part-time $199 per semester hour. ***Required fees:*** $45 per course.

FRESHMAN FINANCIAL AID (Fall 2007) 11 applied for aid; of those 100% were deemed to have need. 82% of freshmen with need received aid; of those 100% had need fully met. ***Average percent of need met:*** 100% (excluding resources awarded to replace EFC). ***Average financial aid package:*** $4836 (excluding resources awarded to replace EFC).

UNDERGRADUATE FINANCIAL AID (Fall 2007) 65 applied for aid; of those 92% were deemed to have need. 100% of undergraduates with need received aid; of those 100% had need fully met. ***Average percent of need met:*** 100% (excluding resources awarded to replace EFC). ***Average financial aid package:*** $5317 (excluding resources awarded to replace EFC).

GIFT AID (NEED-BASED) ***Total amount:*** $290,069 (100% federal). ***Receiving aid:*** Freshmen: 50% (7); all full-time undergraduates: 44% (44). ***Average award:*** Freshmen: $2877; Undergraduates: $2756. ***Scholarships, grants, and awards:*** Federal Pell, FSEOG, state, college/university gift aid from institutional funds.

LOANS ***Student loans:*** $3,380,792 (51% need-based, 49% non-need-based). 11% of past graduating class borrowed through all loan programs. *Average indebtedness per student:* $7254. ***Programs:*** FFEL (Subsidized and Unsubsidized Stafford, PLUS).

WORK-STUDY ***Federal work-study:*** Total amount: $21,645; 5 jobs averaging $4329.

APPLYING FOR FINANCIAL AID ***Required financial aid forms:*** FAFSA, Virtual Financial Aid Office Interview. ***Financial aid deadline:*** Continuous. ***Notification date:*** Continuous. Students must reply within 2 weeks of notification.

CONTACT Gary W. Cook, Director of Financial Aid, Luther Rice University, 3038 Evans Mill Road, Lithonia, GA 30038-2418, 770-484-1204 Ext. 241 or toll-free 800-442-1577. *Fax:* 678-990-5388. *E-mail:* gcook@lru.edu.

LYCOMING COLLEGE

Williamsport, PA

Tuition & fees: $28,784 **Average undergraduate aid package: $21,298**

ABOUT THE INSTITUTION Independent United Methodist, coed. ***Awards:*** bachelor's degrees. 39 undergraduate majors. ***Total enrollment:*** 1,431. Undergraduates: 1,431. Federal methodology is used as a basis for awarding need-based institutional aid.

UNDERGRADUATE EXPENSES for 2008–09 ***Application fee:*** $35. ***Comprehensive fee:*** $36,456 includes full-time tuition ($28,244), mandatory fees ($540), and room and board ($7672). ***College room only:*** $3914. Room and board charges vary according to housing facility. ***Part-time tuition:*** $882 per credit hour. Part-time tuition and fees vary according to course load. ***Payment plan:*** Installment.

FRESHMAN FINANCIAL AID (Fall 2008, est.) 325 applied for aid; of those 89% were deemed to have need. 100% of freshmen with need received aid; of those 21% had need fully met. ***Average percent of need met:*** 82% (excluding resources awarded to replace EFC). ***Average financial aid package:*** $22,525 (excluding resources awarded to replace EFC). 14% of all full-time freshmen had no need and received non-need-based gift aid.

UNDERGRADUATE FINANCIAL AID (Fall 2008, est.) 1,188 applied for aid; of those 90% were deemed to have need. 100% of undergraduates with need received aid; of those 20% had need fully met. ***Average percent of need met:*** 78% (excluding resources awarded to replace EFC). ***Average financial aid package:*** $21,298 (excluding resources awarded to replace EFC). 16% of all full-time undergraduates had no need and received non-need-based gift aid.

GIFT AID (NEED-BASED) ***Total amount:*** $17,149,938 (8% federal, 9% state, 81% institutional, 2% external sources). ***Receiving aid:*** Freshmen: 85% (289); all full-time undergraduates: 81% (1,069). ***Average award:*** Freshmen: $18,116; Undergraduates: $16,432. ***Scholarships, grants, and awards:*** Federal Pell, FSEOG, state, private, college/university gift aid from institutional funds.

GIFT AID (NON-NEED-BASED) ***Total amount:*** $2,685,996 (95% institutional, 5% external sources). ***Receiving aid:*** Freshmen: 10% (34). Undergraduates: 7% (95). ***Average award:*** Freshmen: $10,801. Undergraduates: $10,040. ***Scholarships, grants, and awards by category:*** *Academic interests/achievement:* 803 awards ($7,393,002 total): biological sciences, business, communication, computer science, education, English, foreign languages, general academic interests/achievements, health fields, humanities, international studies, mathematics, physical sciences, premedicine, religion/biblical studies, social sciences. *Creative arts/performance:* 159 awards ($292,714 total): art/fine arts, creative writing, music, theater/drama. *Special achievements/activities:* 35 awards ($207,700 total): general special achievements/activities, leadership. *Special characteristics:* 49 awards ($829,559 total): children of educators, children of faculty/staff, relatives of clergy. ***Tuition waivers:*** Full or partial for employees or children of employees. ***ROTC:*** Army cooperative.

LOANS ***Student loans:*** $10,504,587 (75% need-based, 25% non-need-based). 85% of past graduating class borrowed through all loan programs. *Average indebtedness per student:* $27,179. ***Average need-based loan:*** Freshmen: $4274. Undergraduates: $4819. ***Parent loans:*** $5,139,564 (28% need-based, 72% non-need-based). ***Programs:*** FFEL (Subsidized and Unsubsidized Stafford, PLUS), Perkins, college/university.

WORK-STUDY ***Federal work-study:*** Total amount: $297,394; 336 jobs averaging $1113.

APPLYING FOR FINANCIAL AID ***Required financial aid forms:*** FAFSA, institution's own form, state aid form. ***Financial aid deadline (priority):*** 3/1. ***Notification date:*** Continuous beginning 3/1. Students must reply by 5/1.

CONTACT James S. Lakis, Director of Financial Aid, Lycoming College, 700 College Place, Williamsport, PA 17701-5192, 570-321-4040 or toll-free 800-345-3920 Ext. 4026. *Fax:* 570-321-4993. *E-mail:* lowthert@lycoming.edu.

LYME ACADEMY COLLEGE OF FINE ARTS

Old Lyme, CT

Tuition & fees: $23,092 **Average undergraduate aid package: N/A**

ABOUT THE INSTITUTION Independent, coed. ***Awards:*** bachelor's degrees and post-bachelor's certificates. 4 undergraduate majors. ***Total enrollment:*** 128. Undergraduates: 128. Freshmen: 11. Both federal and institutional methodology are used as a basis for awarding need-based institutional aid.

UNDERGRADUATE EXPENSES for 2009–10 ***Application fee:*** $55. ***Tuition:*** full-time $21,792; part-time $908 per credit. ***Required fees:*** full-time $1300; $50 per term.

FRESHMAN FINANCIAL AID (Fall 2008, est.) 11 applied for aid; of those 100% were deemed to have need. 100% of freshmen with need received aid.

UNDERGRADUATE FINANCIAL AID (Fall 2008, est.) 70 applied for aid; of those 96% were deemed to have need. 100% of undergraduates with need received aid. 12% of all full-time undergraduates had no need and received non-need-based gift aid.

GIFT AID (NEED-BASED) ***Total amount:*** $560,409 (22% federal, 16% state, 55% institutional, 7% external sources). ***Scholarships, grants, and awards:*** Federal Pell, FSEOG, state, private, college/university gift aid from institutional funds.

GIFT AID (NON-NEED-BASED) ***Total amount:*** $86,447 (75% institutional, 25% external sources). ***Average award:*** Undergraduates: $5433. ***Scholarships, grants, and awards by category:*** *Creative arts/performance:* 80 awards ($376,800 total): art/fine arts.

LOANS ***Student loans:*** $685,039 (100% need-based). 50% of past graduating class borrowed through all loan programs. *Average indebtedness per student:* $23,114. ***Parent loans:*** $148,287 (100% need-based). ***Programs:*** FFEL (Subsidized and Unsubsidized Stafford, PLUS), Sallie Mae Private Loans, CSLF FFELP Loans, CHESLA alternative loans.

WORK-STUDY ***Federal work-study:*** Total amount: $5666; 7 jobs averaging $629. ***State or other work-study/employment:*** Total amount: $4697 (100% need-based). 2 part-time jobs averaging $1834.

APPLYING FOR FINANCIAL AID ***Required financial aid forms:*** FAFSA, CSS Financial Aid PROFILE, business/farm supplement. ***Financial aid deadline:*** Continuous. ***Notification date:*** Continuous beginning 3/1. Students must reply within 2 weeks of notification.

CONTACT Mr. James Falconer, Director of Financial Aid, Lyme Academy College of Fine Arts, 84 Lyme Street, Old Lyme, CT 06371, 860-434-3571 Ext. 114. *Fax:* 860-434-8725. *E-mail:* jfalconer@lymeacademy.edu.

LYNCHBURG COLLEGE

Lynchburg, VA

Tuition & fees: $28,105 **Average undergraduate aid package: $18,750**

ABOUT THE INSTITUTION Independent religious, coed. ***Awards:*** bachelor's and master's degrees. 33 undergraduate majors. ***Total enrollment:*** 2,572. Undergraduates: 2,183. Freshmen: 594. Federal methodology is used as a basis for awarding need-based institutional aid.

UNDERGRADUATE EXPENSES for 2008–09 ***Application fee:*** $30. ***Comprehensive fee:*** $35,675 includes full-time tuition ($27,160), mandatory fees ($945), and room and board ($7570). ***College room only:*** $3820. Room and board charges vary according to board plan and housing facility. ***Part-time tuition:*** $375 per credit hour. ***Part-time fees:*** $5.10 per credit hour. Part-time tuition and fees vary according to course load. ***Payment plans:*** Tuition prepayment, installment.

FRESHMAN FINANCIAL AID (Fall 2008, est.) 479 applied for aid; of those 80% were deemed to have need. 100% of freshmen with need received aid; of those 23% had need fully met. ***Average percent of need met:*** 82% (excluding resources awarded to replace EFC). ***Average financial aid package:*** $19,719 (excluding resources awarded to replace EFC). 29% of all full-time freshmen had no need and received non-need-based gift aid.

UNDERGRADUATE FINANCIAL AID (Fall 2008, est.) 1,489 applied for aid; of those 84% were deemed to have need. 100% of undergraduates with need received aid; of those 23% had need fully met. ***Average percent of need met:*** 77% (excluding resources awarded to replace EFC). ***Average financial aid package:*** $18,750 (excluding resources awarded to replace EFC). 29% of all full-time undergraduates had no need and received non-need-based gift aid.

GIFT AID (NEED-BASED) ***Total amount:*** $20,464,743 (9% federal, 11% state, 78% institutional, 2% external sources). ***Receiving aid:*** Freshmen: 64% (382); all full-time undergraduates: 62% (1,253). ***Average award:*** Freshmen: $16,846; Undergraduates: $15,802. ***Scholarships, grants, and awards:*** Federal Pell, FSEOG, state, private, college/university gift aid from institutional funds.

GIFT AID (NON-NEED-BASED) ***Total amount:*** $7,839,847 (18% state, 79% institutional, 3% external sources). ***Receiving aid:*** Freshmen: 11% (66). Undergraduates: 9% (186). ***Average award:*** Freshmen: $9833. Undergraduates: $9332. ***Tuition waivers:*** Full or partial for employees or children of employees, senior citizens.

LOANS ***Student loans:*** $12,485,945 (54% need-based, 46% non-need-based). 69% of past graduating class borrowed through all loan programs. *Average indebtedness per student:* $26,915. ***Average need-based loan:*** Freshmen: $2889. Undergraduates: $2987. ***Parent loans:*** $3,604,013 (48% need-based, 52% non-need-based). ***Programs:*** FFEL (Subsidized and Unsubsidized Stafford, PLUS), Perkins.

WORK-STUDY ***Federal work-study:*** Total amount: $232,384; 329 jobs averaging $943. ***State or other work-study/employment:*** Total amount: $721,956 (34% need-based, 66% non-need-based). 300 part-time jobs averaging $1373.

APPLYING FOR FINANCIAL AID ***Required financial aid forms:*** FAFSA, state aid form. ***Financial aid deadline (priority):*** 3/5. ***Notification date:*** Continuous beginning 3/5. Students must reply by 5/1 or within 2 weeks of notification.

CONTACT Mrs. Michelle Davis, Director of Financial Aid, Lynchburg College, 1501 Lakeside Drive, Lynchburg, VA 24501-3199, 434-544-8228 or toll-free 800-426-8101. *Fax:* 434-544-8653.

LYNDON STATE COLLEGE

Lyndonville, VT

CONTACT Student Services Center, Student Services Consultant, Lyndon State College, 1001 College Road, Lyndonville, VT 05851, 802-626-6396 or toll-free 800-225-1998. *Fax:* 802-626-9770. *E-mail:* financialaid@lyndonstate.edu.

LYNN UNIVERSITY

Boca Raton, FL

Tuition & fees: $29,300 **Average undergraduate aid package: $19,444**

ABOUT THE INSTITUTION Independent, coed. ***Awards:*** bachelor's, master's, and doctoral degrees and post-bachelor's and post-master's certificates. 15 undergraduate majors. ***Total enrollment:*** 2,410. Undergraduates: 2,032. Freshmen: 375. Federal methodology is used as a basis for awarding need-based institutional aid.

UNDERGRADUATE EXPENSES for 2008–09 ***Application fee:*** $35. ***Comprehensive fee:*** $40,200 includes full-time tuition ($27,800), mandatory fees ($1500), and room and board ($10,900). ***Part-time tuition:*** $800 per credit hour.

FRESHMAN FINANCIAL AID (Fall 2008, est.) 269 applied for aid; of those 49% were deemed to have need. 95% of freshmen with need received aid; of those 13% had need fully met. ***Average percent of need met:*** 58% (excluding resources awarded to replace EFC). ***Average financial aid package:*** $19,838 (excluding resources awarded to replace EFC). 33% of all full-time freshmen had no need and received non-need-based gift aid.

UNDERGRADUATE FINANCIAL AID (Fall 2008, est.) 1,140 applied for aid; of those 54% were deemed to have need. 98% of undergraduates with need received aid; of those 16% had need fully met. ***Average percent of need met:*** 61% (excluding resources awarded to replace EFC). ***Average financial aid package:*** $19,444 (excluding resources awarded to replace EFC). 25% of all full-time undergraduates had no need and received non-need-based gift aid.

GIFT AID (NEED-BASED) ***Total amount:*** $7,002,492 (17% federal, 11% state, 70% institutional, 2% external sources). ***Receiving aid:*** Freshmen: 29% (106); all full-time undergraduates: 31% (543). ***Average award:*** Freshmen: $13,022; Undergraduates: $12,243. ***Scholarships, grants, and awards:*** Federal Pell, FSEOG, state, private, college/university gift aid from institutional funds.

GIFT AID (NON-NEED-BASED) ***Total amount:*** $3,981,643 (14% state, 77% institutional, 9% external sources). ***Receiving aid:*** Freshmen: 32% (118). Undergraduates: 32% (566). ***Average award:*** Freshmen: $11,469. Undergraduates: $12,762. ***Scholarships, grants, and awards by category:*** *Academic interests/achievement:* business, communication, general academic interests/achievements. *Creative arts/performance:* music. *Special achievements/activities:*

leadership, religious involvement. *Special characteristics:* children of faculty/staff, siblings of current students. ***ROTC:*** Air Force cooperative.

LOANS ***Student loans:*** $7,527,292 (83% need-based, 17% non-need-based). 37% of past graduating class borrowed through all loan programs. *Average indebtedness per student:* $30,175. ***Average need-based loan:*** Freshmen: $4514. Undergraduates: $5510. ***Parent loans:*** $3,948,405 (73% need-based, 27% non-need-based). ***Programs:*** FFEL (Subsidized and Unsubsidized Stafford, PLUS), Perkins, state, college/university.

WORK-STUDY ***Federal work-study:*** Total amount: $308,910; jobs available. ***State or other work-study/employment:*** Total amount: $264,619 (63% need-based, 37% non-need-based). Part-time jobs available.

ATHLETIC AWARDS Total amount: $2,950,701 (53% need-based, 47% non-need-based).

APPLYING FOR FINANCIAL AID ***Required financial aid forms:*** FAFSA, institution's own form. ***Financial aid deadline (priority):*** 3/1. ***Notification date:*** Continuous. Students must reply within 2 weeks of notification.

CONTACT William Healy, Director of Student Financial Services, Lynn University, 3601 North Military Trail, Boca Raton, FL 33431-5598, 561-237-7814 or toll-free 800-888-5966. *Fax:* 561-237-7189. *E-mail:* whealy@lynn.edu.

LYON COLLEGE
Batesville, AR

Tuition & fees: $19,968 **Average undergraduate aid package: $16,456**

ABOUT THE INSTITUTION Independent Presbyterian, coed. ***Awards:*** bachelor's degrees. 18 undergraduate majors. ***Total enrollment:*** 458. Undergraduates: 458. Freshmen: 109. Federal methodology is used as a basis for awarding need-based institutional aid.

UNDERGRADUATE EXPENSES for 2009–10 ***Application fee:*** $25. ***Comprehensive fee:*** $27,308 includes full-time tuition ($19,424), mandatory fees ($544), and room and board ($7340). ***Part-time tuition:*** $730 per credit hour.

FRESHMAN FINANCIAL AID (Fall 2008, est.) 93 applied for aid; of those 85% were deemed to have need. 100% of freshmen with need received aid; of those 25% had need fully met. ***Average percent of need met:*** 82% (excluding resources awarded to replace EFC). ***Average financial aid package:*** $17,086 (excluding resources awarded to replace EFC). 28% of all full-time freshmen had no need and received non-need-based gift aid.

UNDERGRADUATE FINANCIAL AID (Fall 2008, est.) 345 applied for aid; of those 99% were deemed to have need. 100% of undergraduates with need received aid; of those 20% had need fully met. ***Average percent of need met:*** 80% (excluding resources awarded to replace EFC). ***Average financial aid package:*** $16,456 (excluding resources awarded to replace EFC).

GIFT AID (NEED-BASED) ***Total amount:*** $4,353,740 (15% federal, 7% state, 77% institutional, 1% external sources). ***Receiving aid:*** Freshmen: 72% (79); all full-time undergraduates: 79% (341). ***Average award:*** Freshmen: $13,609; Undergraduates: $13,076. ***Scholarships, grants, and awards:*** Federal Pell, FSEOG, state, private, college/university gift aid from institutional funds.

GIFT AID (NON-NEED-BASED) ***Total amount:*** $1,201,396 (18% state, 79% institutional, 3% external sources). ***Receiving aid:*** Freshmen: 71% (77). Undergraduates: 78% (339). ***Average award:*** Freshmen: $7350. ***Scholarships, grants, and awards by category:*** *Academic interests/achievement:* 461 awards ($4,302,907 total): business, general academic interests/achievements. *Creative arts/performance:* 32 awards ($52,950 total): art/fine arts, music, theater/drama. *Special achievements/activities:* 15 awards ($27,750 total): cheerleading/drum major, general special achievements/activities. *Special characteristics:* 20 awards ($206,113 total): children of faculty/staff, ethnic background, first-generation college students, local/state students, members of minority groups, religious affiliation.

LOANS ***Student loans:*** $2,053,963 (58% need-based, 42% non-need-based). 64% of past graduating class borrowed through all loan programs. *Average indebtedness per student:* $18,428. ***Average need-based loan:*** Freshmen: $3863. Undergraduates: $4904. ***Parent loans:*** $454,341 (42% need-based, 58% non-need-based). ***Programs:*** FFEL (Subsidized and Unsubsidized Stafford, PLUS), Perkins.

WORK-STUDY ***Federal work-study:*** Total amount: $105,426; 133 jobs averaging $1266. ***State or other work-study/employment:*** Total amount: $8000 (38% need-based, 62% non-need-based). Part-time jobs available.

ATHLETIC AWARDS Total amount: $948,041 (46% need-based, 54% non-need-based).

APPLYING FOR FINANCIAL AID ***Required financial aid form:*** FAFSA. ***Financial aid deadline (priority):*** 3/15. ***Notification date:*** Continuous. Students must reply by 8/15.

CONTACT Mr. Tommy Tucker, Director of Student Assistance, Lyon College, 2300 Highland Road, Batesville, AR 72501, 870-307-7257 or toll-free 800-423-2542. *Fax:* 870-307-7542. *E-mail:* financialaid@lyon.edu.

MACALESTER COLLEGE
St. Paul, MN

Tuition & fees: $38,174 **Average undergraduate aid package: $30,394**

ABOUT THE INSTITUTION Independent Presbyterian, coed. ***Awards:*** bachelor's degrees. 34 undergraduate majors. ***Total enrollment:*** 1,900. Undergraduates: 1,900. Freshmen: 479. Both federal and institutional methodology are used as a basis for awarding need-based institutional aid.

UNDERGRADUATE EXPENSES for 2009–10 ***Application fee:*** $40. ***Comprehensive fee:*** $46,942 includes full-time tuition ($37,974), mandatory fees ($200), and room and board ($8768). ***College room only:*** $4666.

FRESHMAN FINANCIAL AID (Fall 2008, est.) 359 applied for aid; of those 85% were deemed to have need. 100% of freshmen with need received aid; of those 100% had need fully met. ***Average percent of need met:*** 100% (excluding resources awarded to replace EFC). ***Average financial aid package:*** $30,242 (excluding resources awarded to replace EFC). 4% of all full-time freshmen had no need and received non-need-based gift aid.

UNDERGRADUATE FINANCIAL AID (Fall 2008, est.) 1,344 applied for aid; of those 93% were deemed to have need. 100% of undergraduates with need received aid; of those 100% had need fully met. ***Average percent of need met:*** 100% (excluding resources awarded to replace EFC). ***Average financial aid package:*** $30,394 (excluding resources awarded to replace EFC). 5% of all full-time undergraduates had no need and received non-need-based gift aid.

GIFT AID (NEED-BASED) ***Total amount:*** $31,464,318 (4% federal, 1% state, 93% institutional, 2% external sources). ***Receiving aid:*** Freshmen: 63% (301); all full-time undergraduates: 66% (1,232). ***Average award:*** Freshmen: $26,806; Undergraduates: $25,376. ***Scholarships, grants, and awards:*** Federal Pell, FSEOG, state, private, college/university gift aid from institutional funds.

GIFT AID (NON-NEED-BASED) ***Total amount:*** $609,010 (53% institutional, 47% external sources). ***Average award:*** Freshmen: $4038. Undergraduates: $5315. ***Scholarships, grants, and awards by category:*** *Academic interests/achievement:* general academic interests/achievements. *Special characteristics:* ethnic background. ***ROTC:*** Naval cooperative, Air Force cooperative.

LOANS ***Student loans:*** $5,341,101 (94% need-based, 6% non-need-based). 72% of past graduating class borrowed through all loan programs. *Average indebtedness per student:* $17,304. ***Average need-based loan:*** Freshmen: $2695. Undergraduates: $3607. ***Parent loans:*** $1,803,242 (100% non-need-based). ***Programs:*** Federal Direct (Subsidized and Unsubsidized Stafford, PLUS), Perkins, state.

WORK-STUDY ***Federal work-study:*** Total amount: $500,972; jobs available. ***State or other work-study/employment:*** Total amount: $2,118,715 (97% need-based, 3% non-need-based). Part-time jobs available.

APPLYING FOR FINANCIAL AID ***Required financial aid forms:*** FAFSA, CSS Financial Aid PROFILE, noncustodial (divorced/separated) parent's statement. ***Financial aid deadline:*** 3/1 (priority: 2/8). ***Notification date:*** 4/1. Students must reply by 5/1.

CONTACT Financial Aid Office, Macalester College, 1600 Grand Avenue, St. Paul, MN 55105, 651-696-6214 or toll-free 800-231-7974. *Fax:* 651-696-6866. *E-mail:* finaid@macalester.edu.

MACHZIKEI HADATH RABBINICAL COLLEGE
Brooklyn, NY

CONTACT Rabbi Baruch Rozmarin, Director of Financial Aid, Machzikei Hadath Rabbinical College, 5407 16th Avenue, Brooklyn, NY 11204-1805, 718-854-8777.

MACMURRAY COLLEGE
Jacksonville, IL

Tuition & fees: $17,330 **Average undergraduate aid package: $20,992**

ABOUT THE INSTITUTION Independent United Methodist, coed. ***Awards:*** associate and bachelor's degrees. 39 undergraduate majors. ***Total enrollment:*** 602. Undergraduates: 602. Freshmen: 90. Federal methodology is used as a basis for awarding need-based institutional aid.

UNDERGRADUATE EXPENSES for 2008–09 ***Comprehensive fee:*** $24,620 includes full-time tuition ($17,000), mandatory fees ($330), and room and board ($7290). ***College room only:*** $4450. Room and board charges vary according to board plan. ***Part-time tuition:*** $565 per credit hour. ***Part-time fees:*** $25 per credit. Part-time tuition and fees vary according to course load. ***Payment plan:*** Installment.

FRESHMAN FINANCIAL AID (Fall 2008, est.) 84 applied for aid; of those 94% were deemed to have need. 100% of freshmen with need received aid; of those 51% had need fully met. ***Average percent of need met:*** 92% (excluding resources awarded to replace EFC). ***Average financial aid package:*** $20,205 (excluding resources awarded to replace EFC). 6% of all full-time freshmen had no need and received non-need-based gift aid.

UNDERGRADUATE FINANCIAL AID (Fall 2008, est.) 518 applied for aid; of those 92% were deemed to have need. 100% of undergraduates with need received aid; of those 50% had need fully met. ***Average percent of need met:*** 91% (excluding resources awarded to replace EFC). ***Average financial aid package:*** $20,992 (excluding resources awarded to replace EFC). 6% of all full-time undergraduates had no need and received non-need-based gift aid.

GIFT AID (NEED-BASED) ***Total amount:*** $4,803,023 (26% federal, 28% state, 43% institutional, 3% external sources). ***Receiving aid:*** Freshmen: 88% (75); all full-time undergraduates: 80% (434). ***Average award:*** Freshmen: $5918; Undergraduates: $6103. ***Scholarships, grants, and awards:*** Federal Pell, FSEOG, state, private, college/university gift aid from institutional funds.

GIFT AID (NON-NEED-BASED) ***Total amount:*** $751,990 (92% institutional, 8% external sources). ***Receiving aid:*** Freshmen: 56% (48). Undergraduates: 60% (324). ***Average award:*** Freshmen: $6300. Undergraduates: $4800. ***Scholarships, grants, and awards by category:*** *Academic interests/achievement:* 466 awards ($2,163,614 total): biological sciences, English, foreign languages, general academic interests/achievements, religion/biblical studies. *Special characteristics:* 45 awards ($134,912 total): children and siblings of alumni, children of faculty/staff, international students, religious affiliation, siblings of current students. ***Tuition waivers:*** Full or partial for minority students, children of alumni, employees or children of employees, senior citizens.

LOANS ***Student loans:*** $3,998,637 (79% need-based, 21% non-need-based). 94% of past graduating class borrowed through all loan programs. *Average indebtedness per student:* $25,413. ***Average need-based loan:*** Freshmen: $6879. Undergraduates: $6208. ***Parent loans:*** $446,433 (60% need-based, 40% non-need-based). ***Programs:*** FFEL (Subsidized and Unsubsidized Stafford, PLUS), Perkins.

WORK-STUDY ***Federal work-study:*** Total amount: $64,516; 93 jobs averaging $845.

APPLYING FOR FINANCIAL AID ***Required financial aid form:*** FAFSA. ***Financial aid deadline (priority):*** 5/1. ***Notification date:*** 5/1. Students must reply within 2 weeks of notification.

CONTACT Charles R. Carothers, Director of Financial Aid, MacMurray College, 447 East College Avenue, Jacksonville, IL 62650, 217-479-7042 or toll-free 800-252-7485 (in-state). *Fax:* 217-291-0702. *E-mail:* charles.carothers@mac.edu.

MACON STATE COLLEGE

Macon, GA

CONTACT Office of Financial Aid, Macon State College, 100 College Station Drive, Macon, GA 31206, 478-471-2717 or toll-free 800-272-7619 Ext. 2800. *Fax:* 478-471-2790. *E-mail:* fainfo@mail.maconstate.edu.

MADONNA UNIVERSITY

Livonia, MI

ABOUT THE INSTITUTION Independent Roman Catholic, coed. ***Awards:*** associate, bachelor's, and master's degrees and post-bachelor's and post-master's certificates. 71 undergraduate majors. ***Total enrollment:*** 4,035. Undergraduates: 2,968. Freshmen: 204.

GIFT AID (NEED-BASED) ***Scholarships, grants, and awards:*** Federal Pell, FSEOG, state, private, college/university gift aid from institutional funds.

GIFT AID (NON-NEED-BASED) ***Scholarships, grants, and awards by category:*** *Academic interests/achievement:* biological sciences, business, communication, computer science, education, English, general academic interests/achievements, health fields, home economics, humanities, mathematics, physical sciences, premedicine, social sciences. *Creative arts/performance:* art/fine arts, cinema/film/broadcasting, creative writing, music, performing arts. *Special achievements/activities:* community service, leadership. *Special characteristics:* children and siblings of alumni, children of faculty/staff, previous college experience.

LOANS ***Programs:*** FFEL (Subsidized and Unsubsidized Stafford, PLUS).

WORK-STUDY ***Federal work-study:*** Total amount: $60,000; jobs available.

APPLYING FOR FINANCIAL AID ***Required financial aid form:*** FAFSA.

CONTACT Cathy Durham, Financial Aid Secretary, Madonna University, 36600 Schoolcraft Road, Livonia, MI 48150-1173, 734-432-5663 or toll-free 800-852-4951. *Fax:* 734-432-5344. *E-mail:* Finaid@madonna.edu.

MAGDALEN COLLEGE

Warner, NH

Tuition & fees: $12,250 **Average undergraduate aid package: $4534**

ABOUT THE INSTITUTION Independent Roman Catholic, coed. 1 undergraduate major. Institutional methodology is used as a basis for awarding need-based institutional aid.

UNDERGRADUATE EXPENSES for 2008–09 ***Comprehensive fee:*** $18,750 includes full-time tuition ($12,250) and room and board ($6500).

FRESHMAN FINANCIAL AID (Fall 2007) 18 applied for aid; of those 100% were deemed to have need. 100% of freshmen with need received aid. ***Average percent of need met:*** 25% (excluding resources awarded to replace EFC). ***Average financial aid package:*** $4104 (excluding resources awarded to replace EFC).

UNDERGRADUATE FINANCIAL AID (Fall 2007) 24 applied for aid; of those 100% were deemed to have need. 100% of undergraduates with need received aid. ***Average percent of need met:*** 25% (excluding resources awarded to replace EFC). ***Average financial aid package:*** $4534 (excluding resources awarded to replace EFC).

GIFT AID (NEED-BASED) ***Total amount:*** $178,875 (96% institutional, 4% external sources). ***Receiving aid:*** Freshmen: 72% (18); all full-time undergraduates: 39% (24). ***Average award:*** Freshmen: $4104; Undergraduates: $4067. ***Scholarships, grants, and awards:*** private, college/university gift aid from institutional funds.

LOANS ***Student loans:*** $303,846 (100% need-based). 50% of past graduating class borrowed through all loan programs. *Average indebtedness per student:* $17,500. ***Programs:*** alternative loans.

WORK-STUDY ***State or other work-study/employment:*** Total amount: $11,200 (100% need-based). 9 part-time jobs averaging $1244.

APPLYING FOR FINANCIAL AID ***Required financial aid form:*** institution's own form. ***Financial aid deadline:*** Continuous. ***Notification date:*** 7/1. Students must reply within 4 weeks of notification.

CONTACT Bobbie Anne Abson, Financial Aid Director, Magdalen College, 511 Kearsarge Mountain Road, Warner, NH 03278, 603-456-2656 or toll-free 877-498-1723 (out-of-state). *Fax:* 603-456-2660. *E-mail:* babson@magdalen.edu.

MAGNOLIA BIBLE COLLEGE

Kosciusko, MS

CONTACT Allen Coker, Financial Aid Director, Magnolia Bible College, PO Box 1109, Kosciusko, MS 39090-1109, 662-289-2896 or toll-free 800-748-8655 (in-state). *Fax:* 662-289-1850. *E-mail:* acoker@magnolia.edu.

MAHARISHI UNIVERSITY OF MANAGEMENT

Fairfield, IA

ABOUT THE INSTITUTION Independent, coed. ***Awards:*** bachelor's, master's, and doctoral degrees and post-bachelor's certificates. 10 undergraduate majors. ***Total enrollment:*** 948. Undergraduates: 204. Freshmen: 45.

GIFT AID (NEED-BASED) ***Scholarships, grants, and awards:*** Federal Pell, FSEOG, state, private, college/university gift aid from institutional funds.

GIFT AID (NON-NEED-BASED) ***Scholarships, grants, and awards by category:*** *Academic interests/achievement:* general academic interests/achievements. *Creative arts/performance:* creative writing, music. *Special characteristics:* children of faculty/staff, ethnic background, veterans, veterans' children.

LOANS ***Programs:*** FFEL (Subsidized and Unsubsidized Stafford, PLUS), Perkins, college/university, alternative loans.

APPLYING FOR FINANCIAL AID ***Required financial aid form:*** FAFSA.

CONTACT Mr. Bill Christensen, Director of Financial Aid, Maharishi University of Management, 1000 North 4th Street, DB 1127, Fairfield, IA 52557-1127, 641-472-1156 or toll-free 800-369-6480. *Fax:* 641-472-1133. *E-mail:* bchrist@mum.edu.

MAINE COLLEGE OF ART

Portland, ME

Tuition & fees: $27,165 **Average undergraduate aid package: $13,894**

ABOUT THE INSTITUTION Independent, coed. ***Awards:*** bachelor's and master's degrees and post-bachelor's certificates. 9 undergraduate majors. ***Total enrollment:*** 370. Undergraduates: 342. Freshmen: 103. Federal methodology is used as a basis for awarding need-based institutional aid.

UNDERGRADUATE EXPENSES for 2008–09 ***Application fee:*** $40. ***Comprehensive fee:*** $36,565 includes full-time tuition ($26,490), mandatory fees ($675), and room and board ($9400). Room and board charges vary according to board plan and housing facility. ***Part-time tuition:*** $1104 per credit hour. ***Payment plan:*** Installment.

FRESHMAN FINANCIAL AID (Fall 2008, est.) 70 applied for aid; of those 87% were deemed to have need. 100% of freshmen with need received aid; of those 3% had need fully met. ***Average percent of need met:*** 53% (excluding resources awarded to replace EFC). ***Average financial aid package:*** $13,152 (excluding resources awarded to replace EFC). 20% of all full-time freshmen had no need and received non-need-based gift aid.

UNDERGRADUATE FINANCIAL AID (Fall 2008, est.) 323 applied for aid; of those 90% were deemed to have need. 100% of undergraduates with need received aid; of those 10% had need fully met. ***Average percent of need met:*** 56% (excluding resources awarded to replace EFC). ***Average financial aid package:*** $13,894 (excluding resources awarded to replace EFC). 12% of all full-time undergraduates had no need and received non-need-based gift aid.

GIFT AID (NEED-BASED) ***Total amount:*** $3,491,648 (15% federal, 3% state, 79% institutional, 3% external sources). ***Receiving aid:*** Freshmen: 80% (61); all full-time undergraduates: 85% (290). ***Average award:*** Freshmen: $9965; Undergraduates: $10,174. ***Scholarships, grants, and awards:*** Federal Pell, FSEOG, state, private, college/university gift aid from institutional funds.

GIFT AID (NON-NEED-BASED) ***Total amount:*** $579,750 (91% institutional, 9% external sources). ***Receiving aid:*** Freshmen: 1% (1). Undergraduates: 5% (16). ***Average award:*** Freshmen: $4367. Undergraduates: $6860. ***Scholarships, grants, and awards by category:*** *Creative arts/performance:* 614 awards ($1,456,533 total): art/fine arts. *Special characteristics:* 1 award ($24,670 total): children of faculty/staff.

LOANS ***Student loans:*** $4,043,074 (78% need-based, 22% non-need-based). 80% of past graduating class borrowed through all loan programs. *Average indebtedness per student:* $33,350. ***Average need-based loan:*** Freshmen: $2860. Undergraduates: $3965. ***Parent loans:*** $1,194,978 (44% need-based, 56% non-need-based). ***Programs:*** FFEL (Subsidized and Unsubsidized Stafford, PLUS), Perkins, alternative loans.

WORK-STUDY ***Federal work-study:*** Total amount: $115,677; 54 jobs averaging $2151.

APPLYING FOR FINANCIAL AID ***Required financial aid form:*** FAFSA. ***Financial aid deadline (priority):*** 3/1. ***Notification date:*** Continuous beginning 3/15. Students must reply within 2 weeks of notification.

CONTACT Adrienne J. Amari, Director of Financial Aid, Maine College of Art, 522 Congress Street, Portland, ME 04101-3987, 207-775-3052 or toll-free 800-639-4808. *Fax:* 207-772-5069. *E-mail:* aamari@meca.edu.

MAINE MARITIME ACADEMY

Castine, ME

Tuition & fees (ME res): $10,105 **Average undergraduate aid package: $9554**

ABOUT THE INSTITUTION State-supported, coed, primarily men. ***Awards:*** associate, bachelor's, and master's degrees. 11 undergraduate majors. ***Total enrollment:*** 860. Undergraduates: 842. Freshmen: 250. Federal methodology is used as a basis for awarding need-based institutional aid.

UNDERGRADUATE EXPENSES for 2009–10 ***Application fee:*** $15. ***Tuition, state resident:*** full-time $7900; part-time $300 per credit hour. ***Tuition, nonresident:*** full-time $15,600; part-time $550 per credit hour. ***Required fees:*** full-time $2205. ***College room and board:*** $8450; ***Room only:*** $5250.

FRESHMAN FINANCIAL AID (Fall 2008, est.) 174 applied for aid; of those 75% were deemed to have need. 99% of freshmen with need received aid; of those 13% had need fully met. ***Average percent of need met:*** 51% (excluding resources awarded to replace EFC). ***Average financial aid package:*** $8984 (excluding resources awarded to replace EFC). 9% of all full-time freshmen had no need and received non-need-based gift aid.

UNDERGRADUATE FINANCIAL AID (Fall 2008, est.) 721 applied for aid; of those 81% were deemed to have need. 99% of undergraduates with need received aid; of those 15% had need fully met. ***Average percent of need met:*** 57% (excluding resources awarded to replace EFC). ***Average financial aid package:*** $9554 (excluding resources awarded to replace EFC). 5% of all full-time undergraduates had no need and received non-need-based gift aid.

GIFT AID (NEED-BASED) ***Total amount:*** $2,675,831 (44% federal, 14% state, 28% institutional, 14% external sources). ***Receiving aid:*** Freshmen: 45% (105); all full-time undergraduates: 52% (450). ***Average award:*** Freshmen: $5606; Undergraduates: $5946. ***Scholarships, grants, and awards:*** Federal Pell, FSEOG, state, private, college/university gift aid from institutional funds.

GIFT AID (NON-NEED-BASED) ***Total amount:*** $331,759 (22% federal, 5% state, 42% institutional, 31% external sources). ***Receiving aid:*** Freshmen: 2% (5). Undergraduates: 2% (21). ***Average award:*** Freshmen: $3636. Undergraduates: $3043. ***Scholarships, grants, and awards by category:*** *Academic interests/achievement:* 345 awards ($867,915 total): biological sciences, business, engineering/technologies, general academic interests/achievements. *Special characteristics:* 6 awards ($38,300 total): children of faculty/staff. ***ROTC:*** Army, Naval.

LOANS ***Student loans:*** $7,569,773 (61% need-based, 39% non-need-based). 82% of past graduating class borrowed through all loan programs. *Average indebtedness per student:* $35,968. ***Average need-based loan:*** Freshmen: $4227. Undergraduates: $4761. ***Parent loans:*** $1,373,128 (41% need-based, 59% non-need-based). ***Programs:*** FFEL (Subsidized and Unsubsidized Stafford, PLUS), Perkins, college/university, alternative loans.

WORK-STUDY ***Federal work-study:*** Total amount: $97,867; 157 jobs averaging $633.

APPLYING FOR FINANCIAL AID ***Required financial aid form:*** FAFSA. ***Financial aid deadline (priority):*** 4/15. ***Notification date:*** Continuous. Students must reply within 4 weeks of notification.

CONTACT Ms. Holly Bayle, Assistant Director of Financial Aid, Maine Maritime Academy, Pleasant Street, Castine, ME 04420, 207-326-2205 or toll-free 800-464-6565 (in-state), 800-227-8465 (out-of-state). *Fax:* 207-326-2515. *E-mail:* bbayle@mma.edu.

MALONE UNIVERSITY

Canton, OH

Tuition & fees: $21,080 **Average undergraduate aid package: $14,963**

ABOUT THE INSTITUTION Independent religious, coed. ***Awards:*** bachelor's and master's degrees and post-bachelor's certificates. 41 undergraduate majors. ***Total enrollment:*** 2,442. Undergraduates: 2,033. Freshmen: 391. Federal methodology is used as a basis for awarding need-based institutional aid.

UNDERGRADUATE EXPENSES for 2009–10 ***Application fee:*** $20. ***Comprehensive fee:*** $28,180 includes full-time tuition ($20,730), mandatory fees ($350), and room and board ($7100). ***College room only:*** $3620. ***Part-time tuition:*** $370 per credit hour. ***Part-time fees:*** $87.50 per term.

FRESHMAN FINANCIAL AID (Fall 2008, est.) 362 applied for aid; of those 91% were deemed to have need. 100% of freshmen with need received aid; of those 18% had need fully met. ***Average percent of need met:*** 77% (excluding resources awarded to replace EFC). ***Average financial aid package:*** $16,949 (excluding resources awarded to replace EFC). 10% of all full-time freshmen had no need and received non-need-based gift aid.

UNDERGRADUATE FINANCIAL AID (Fall 2008, est.) 1,444 applied for aid; of those 91% were deemed to have need. 100% of undergraduates with need received aid; of those 16% had need fully met. ***Average percent of need met:***

71% (excluding resources awarded to replace EFC). ***Average financial aid package:*** $14,963 (excluding resources awarded to replace EFC). 10% of all full-time undergraduates had no need and received non-need-based gift aid.

GIFT AID (NEED-BASED) ***Total amount:*** $11,379,102 (21% federal, 16% state, 58% institutional, 5% external sources). ***Receiving aid:*** Freshmen: 85% (329); all full-time undergraduates: 75% (1,304). ***Average award:*** Freshmen: $12,614; Undergraduates: $10,527. ***Scholarships, grants, and awards:*** Federal Pell, FSEOG, state, private, college/university gift aid from institutional funds, Academic Competitiveness Grant, National Smart Grant, TEACH Grant.

GIFT AID (NON-NEED-BASED) ***Total amount:*** $1,564,656 (12% state, 77% institutional, 11% external sources). ***Receiving aid:*** Freshmen: 82% (320). Undergraduates: 73% (1,260). ***Average award:*** Freshmen: $6522. Undergraduates: $5933. ***Scholarships, grants, and awards by category:*** *Academic interests/achievement:* 781 awards ($4,306,956 total): biological sciences, business, communication, computer science, education, English, foreign languages, general academic interests/achievements, health fields, humanities, international studies, mathematics, physical sciences, premedicine, religion/biblical studies, social sciences. *Creative arts/performance:* 93 awards ($98,050 total): debating, journalism/publications, music, theater/drama. *Special achievements/activities:* 184 awards ($275,050 total): community service, general special achievements/activities, leadership, religious involvement. *Special characteristics:* 319 awards ($1,168,916 total): children and siblings of alumni, children of faculty/staff, general special characteristics, international students, parents of current students, relatives of clergy, religious affiliation, siblings of current students, spouses of current students. ***ROTC:*** Army cooperative, Air Force cooperative.

LOANS ***Student loans:*** $11,289,484 (91% need-based, 9% non-need-based). 84% of past graduating class borrowed through all loan programs. *Average indebtedness per student:* $24,539. ***Average need-based loan:*** Freshmen: $4111. Undergraduates: $4721. ***Parent loans:*** $1,545,759 (90% need-based, 10% non-need-based). ***Programs:*** FFEL (Subsidized and Unsubsidized Stafford, PLUS), Perkins, state, college/university, alternative loans.

WORK-STUDY ***Federal work-study:*** Total amount: $584,200; 299 jobs averaging $1840. ***State or other work-study/employment:*** Total amount: $166,800 (83% need-based, 17% non-need-based). 75 part-time jobs averaging $2269.

ATHLETIC AWARDS Total amount: $1,911,428 (75% need-based, 25% non-need-based).

APPLYING FOR FINANCIAL AID ***Required financial aid forms:*** FAFSA, verification or tax information if chosen. ***Financial aid deadline:*** 7/31 (priority: 3/1). ***Notification date:*** Continuous. Students must reply within 2 weeks of notification.

CONTACT Pamela Pustay, Director of Financial Aid, Malone University, 2600 Cleveland Avenue NW, Canton, OH 44709, 330-471-8161 or toll-free 800-521-1146. *Fax:* 330-471-8652. *E-mail:* ppustay@malone.edu.

MANCHESTER COLLEGE

North Manchester, IN

Tuition & fees: $22,720 **Average undergraduate aid package: $21,380**

ABOUT THE INSTITUTION Independent religious, coed. ***Awards:*** associate and bachelor's degrees. 59 undergraduate majors. ***Total enrollment:*** 1,145. Undergraduates: 1,145. Freshmen: 397. Federal methodology is used as a basis for awarding need-based institutional aid.

UNDERGRADUATE EXPENSES for 2008–09 ***Application fee:*** $25. ***One-time required fee:*** $225. ***Comprehensive fee:*** $30,820 includes full-time tuition ($22,000), mandatory fees ($720), and room and board ($8100). ***College room only:*** $5000. Room and board charges vary according to board plan and housing facility. ***Part-time fees:*** $350 per year. Part-time tuition and fees vary according to course load. ***Payment plan:*** Installment.

FRESHMAN FINANCIAL AID (Fall 2008, est.) 380 applied for aid; of those 89% were deemed to have need. 100% of freshmen with need received aid; of those 12% had need fully met. ***Average percent of need met:*** 87% (excluding resources awarded to replace EFC). ***Average financial aid package:*** $19,952 (excluding resources awarded to replace EFC). 11% of all full-time freshmen had no need and received non-need-based gift aid.

UNDERGRADUATE FINANCIAL AID (Fall 2008, est.) 1,019 applied for aid; of those 88% were deemed to have need. 100% of undergraduates with need received aid; of those 31% had need fully met. ***Average percent of need met:*** 91% (excluding resources awarded to replace EFC). ***Average financial aid package:*** $21,380 (excluding resources awarded to replace EFC). 10% of all full-time undergraduates had no need and received non-need-based gift aid.

GIFT AID (NEED-BASED) ***Total amount:*** $14,209,622 (7% federal, 25% state, 68% institutional). ***Receiving aid:*** Freshmen: 85% (337); all full-time undergraduates: 83% (901). ***Average award:*** Freshmen: $16,557; Undergraduates: $15,755. ***Scholarships, grants, and awards:*** state, college/university gift aid from institutional funds.

GIFT AID (NON-NEED-BASED) ***Total amount:*** $2,700,686 (3% federal, 5% state, 92% institutional). ***Receiving aid:*** Freshmen: 64% (254). Undergraduates: 65% (707). ***Average award:*** Freshmen: $10,519. Undergraduates: $10,290. ***Scholarships, grants, and awards by category:*** *Academic interests/achievement:* 745 awards ($6,194,876 total): business, English, foreign languages, general academic interests/achievements, humanities. *Creative arts/performance:* 12 awards ($9000 total). *Special characteristics:* 284 awards ($1,035,803 total): children and siblings of alumni, ethnic background, international students, members of minority groups, previous college experience, religious affiliation. ***Tuition waivers:*** Full or partial for employees or children of employees.

LOANS ***Student loans:*** $4,702,658 (89% need-based, 11% non-need-based). 88% of past graduating class borrowed through all loan programs. *Average indebtedness per student:* $16,333. ***Average need-based loan:*** Freshmen: $4580. Undergraduates: $4729. ***Parent loans:*** $2,025,293 (84% need-based, 16% non-need-based).

WORK-STUDY ***Federal work-study:*** Total amount: $915,938; jobs available. ***State or other work-study/employment:*** Total amount: $405,700 (61% need-based, 39% non-need-based). Part-time jobs available.

CONTACT Mrs. Sherri Shockey, Director of Student Financial Services, Manchester College, 604 East College Avenue, North Manchester, IN 46962-1225, 260-982-5066 or toll-free 800-852-3648. *Fax:* 260-982-5043. *E-mail:* Slshockey@manchester.edu.

MANHATTAN CHRISTIAN COLLEGE

Manhattan, KS

Tuition & fees: $11,374 **Average undergraduate aid package: $10,129**

ABOUT THE INSTITUTION Independent religious, coed. ***Awards:*** associate and bachelor's degrees. 9 undergraduate majors. ***Total enrollment:*** 388. Undergraduates: 388. Federal methodology is used as a basis for awarding need-based institutional aid.

UNDERGRADUATE EXPENSES for 2008–09 ***Application fee:*** $25. ***Comprehensive fee:*** $18,094 includes full-time tuition ($10,932), mandatory fees ($442), and room and board ($6720). ***Part-time tuition:*** $449 per hour. ***Part-time fees:*** $8 per hour; $150 per term.

FRESHMAN FINANCIAL AID (Fall 2008, est.) 78 applied for aid; of those 83% were deemed to have need. 100% of freshmen with need received aid; of those 66% had need fully met. ***Average percent of need met:*** 62% (excluding resources awarded to replace EFC). ***Average financial aid package:*** $14,589 (excluding resources awarded to replace EFC). 24% of all full-time freshmen had no need and received non-need-based gift aid.

UNDERGRADUATE FINANCIAL AID (Fall 2008, est.) 290 applied for aid; of those 93% were deemed to have need. 100% of undergraduates with need received aid; of those 68% had need fully met. ***Average percent of need met:*** 60% (excluding resources awarded to replace EFC). ***Average financial aid package:*** $10,129 (excluding resources awarded to replace EFC). 12% of all full-time undergraduates had no need and received non-need-based gift aid.

GIFT AID (NEED-BASED) ***Total amount:*** $643,870 (63% federal, 37% state). ***Receiving aid:*** Freshmen: 47% (42); all full-time undergraduates: 59% (182). ***Average award:*** Freshmen: $4635; Undergraduates: $3538. ***Scholarships, grants, and awards:*** Federal Pell, FSEOG, state, private, college/university gift aid from institutional funds.

GIFT AID (NON-NEED-BASED) ***Total amount:*** $1,352,238 (3% federal, 5% state, 68% institutional, 24% external sources). ***Receiving aid:*** Freshmen: 71% (64). Undergraduates: 65% (202). ***Average award:*** Freshmen: $6198. Undergraduates: $9175. ***Scholarships, grants, and awards by category:*** *Academic interests/achievement:* 347 awards ($761,500 total): general academic interests/achievements, religion/biblical studies. *Creative arts/performance:* music. *Special achievements/activities:* 12 awards ($77,090 total): leadership. *Special characteristics:* 13 awards ($84,365 total): children of faculty/staff. ***ROTC:*** Army cooperative, Air Force cooperative.

LOANS ***Student loans:*** $1,680,588 (56% need-based, 44% non-need-based). 78% of past graduating class borrowed through all loan programs. *Average indebtedness per student:* $13,364. ***Average need-based loan:*** Freshmen: [illegible].

Undergraduates: $3983. ***Parent loans:*** $92,536 (100% non-need-based). ***Programs:*** FFEL (Subsidized and Unsubsidized Stafford, PLUS), Perkins.

WORK-STUDY ***Federal work-study:*** Total amount: $72,411; 65 jobs averaging $1114.

APPLYING FOR FINANCIAL AID ***Required financial aid forms:*** FAFSA, state aid form. ***Financial aid deadline (priority):*** 4/1. ***Notification date:*** Continuous. Students must reply within 2 weeks of notification.

CONTACT Mrs. Margaret Carlisle, Director of Financial Aid, Manhattan Christian College, 1415 Anderson Avenue, Manhattan, KS 66502-4081, 785-539-3571 or toll-free 877-246-4622. *E-mail:* carlisle@mccks.edu.

MANHATTAN COLLEGE

Riverdale, NY

Tuition & fees: $23,385 **Average undergraduate aid package: $14,828**

ABOUT THE INSTITUTION Independent religious, coed. 41 undergraduate majors. Federal methodology is used as a basis for awarding need-based institutional aid.

UNDERGRADUATE EXPENSES for 2008–09 ***Comprehensive fee:*** $33,155 includes full-time tuition ($22,940), mandatory fees ($445), and room and board ($9770). Full-time tuition and fees vary according to course load and program. Room and board charges vary according to board plan. ***Part-time tuition:*** $650 per credit hour. Part-time tuition and fees vary according to course load and program.

FRESHMAN FINANCIAL AID (Fall 2008, est.) 587 applied for aid; of those 81% were deemed to have need. 99% of freshmen with need received aid; of those 21% had need fully met. ***Average percent of need met:*** 71% (excluding resources awarded to replace EFC). ***Average financial aid package:*** $15,197 (excluding resources awarded to replace EFC). 32% of all full-time freshmen had no need and received non-need-based gift aid.

UNDERGRADUATE FINANCIAL AID (Fall 2008, est.) 1,919 applied for aid; of those 99% were deemed to have need. 99% of undergraduates with need received aid; of those 19% had need fully met. ***Average percent of need met:*** 69% (excluding resources awarded to replace EFC). ***Average financial aid package:*** $14,828 (excluding resources awarded to replace EFC). 7% of all full-time undergraduates had no need and received non-need-based gift aid.

GIFT AID (NEED-BASED) ***Total amount:*** $18,805,856 (11% federal, 14% state, 74% institutional, 1% external sources). ***Receiving aid:*** Freshmen: 61% (427); all full-time undergraduates: 59% (1,727). ***Average award:*** Freshmen: $11,011; Undergraduates: $10,265. ***Scholarships, grants, and awards:*** Federal Pell, FSEOG, state, private, college/university gift aid from institutional funds.

GIFT AID (NON-NEED-BASED) ***Total amount:*** $3,173,101 (5% state, 95% institutional). ***Receiving aid:*** Freshmen: 6% (42). Undergraduates: 5% (149). ***Average award:*** Freshmen: $8443. Undergraduates: $7859. ***Scholarships, grants, and awards by category:*** *Academic interests/achievement:* biological sciences, business, computer science, foreign languages, general academic interests/achievements, mathematics, military science. *Creative arts/performance:* music. *Special achievements/activities:* community service, leadership. *Special characteristics:* children of faculty/staff. ***Tuition waivers:*** Full or partial for employees or children of employees.

LOANS ***Student loans:*** $14,961,640 (87% need-based, 13% non-need-based). 67% of past graduating class borrowed through all loan programs. *Average indebtedness per student:* $35,130. ***Average need-based loan:*** Freshmen: $3383. Undergraduates: $4405. ***Parent loans:*** $7,045,614 (77% need-based, 23% non-need-based). ***Programs:*** Federal Direct (Subsidized and Unsubsidized Stafford, PLUS), FFEL (Subsidized and Unsubsidized Stafford, PLUS), Perkins.

WORK-STUDY ***Federal work-study:*** Total amount: $600,000; 501 jobs averaging $1118. ***State or other work-study/employment:*** Total amount: $300,000 (100% non-need-based). 224 part-time jobs averaging $893.

ATHLETIC AWARDS Total amount: $2,881,405 (53% need-based, 47% non-need-based).

APPLYING FOR FINANCIAL AID ***Required financial aid forms:*** FAFSA, institution's own form, state aid form. ***Financial aid deadline (priority):*** 3/1. ***Notification date:*** 4/1. Students must reply by 5/1.

CONTACT Mr. Edward Keough, Director of Student Financial Services, Manhattan College, 4513 Manhattan College Parkway, Riverdale, NY 10471, 718-862-7100 or toll-free 800-622-9235 (in-state). *Fax:* 718-862-8027. *E-mail:* finaid@manhattan.edu.

MANHATTAN SCHOOL OF MUSIC

New York, NY

CONTACT Ms. Amy Anderson, Assistant Dean of Admission and Financial Aid, Manhattan School of Music, 120 Claremont Avenue, New York, NY 10027-4698, 212-749-2802 Ext. 4501. *Fax:* 212-749-3025. *E-mail:* aanderson@msmnyc.edu.

MANHATTANVILLE COLLEGE

Purchase, NY

Tuition & fees: $32,760 **Average undergraduate aid package: $22,046**

ABOUT THE INSTITUTION Independent, coed. ***Awards:*** bachelor's and master's degrees and post-bachelor's certificates. 42 undergraduate majors. ***Total enrollment:*** 1,802. Undergraduates: 1,802. Federal methodology is used as a basis for awarding need-based institutional aid.

UNDERGRADUATE EXPENSES for 2009–10 ***Application fee:*** $65. ***Comprehensive fee:*** $46,340 includes full-time tuition ($31,490), mandatory fees ($1270), and room and board ($13,580). ***College room only:*** $8000. ***Part-time tuition:*** $730 per credit. ***Part-time fees:*** $50 per term.

FRESHMAN FINANCIAL AID (Fall 2008, est.) 344 applied for aid; of those 92% were deemed to have need. 100% of freshmen with need received aid; of those 9% had need fully met. ***Average percent of need met:*** 89% (excluding resources awarded to replace EFC). ***Average financial aid package:*** $24,581 (excluding resources awarded to replace EFC). 25% of all full-time freshmen had no need and received non-need-based gift aid.

UNDERGRADUATE FINANCIAL AID (Fall 2008, est.) 1,185 applied for aid; of those 91% were deemed to have need. 100% of undergraduates with need received aid; of those 9% had need fully met. ***Average percent of need met:*** 83% (excluding resources awarded to replace EFC). ***Average financial aid package:*** $22,046 (excluding resources awarded to replace EFC). 28% of all full-time undergraduates had no need and received non-need-based gift aid.

GIFT AID (NEED-BASED) ***Total amount:*** $12,018,600 (12% federal, 12% state, 76% institutional). ***Receiving aid:*** Freshmen: 66% (306); all full-time undergraduates: 60% (1,015). ***Average award:*** Freshmen: $15,744; Undergraduates: $14,226. ***Scholarships, grants, and awards:*** Federal Pell, FSEOG, state, private, college/university gift aid from institutional funds.

GIFT AID (NON-NEED-BASED) ***Total amount:*** $14,940,920 (100% institutional). ***Receiving aid:*** Freshmen: 53% (244). Undergraduates: 50% (853). ***Average award:*** Freshmen: $14,367. Undergraduates: $13,693. ***Scholarships, grants, and awards by category:*** *Academic interests/achievement:* 1,605 awards ($12,604,278 total): general academic interests/achievements, mathematics. *Creative arts/performance:* 68 awards ($660,062 total): dance, performing arts. *Special achievements/activities:* 83 awards ($158,500 total): community service, leadership. *Special characteristics:* 20 awards ($161,460 total): previous college experience.

LOANS ***Student loans:*** $11,445,527 (62% need-based, 38% non-need-based). 67% of past graduating class borrowed through all loan programs. *Average indebtedness per student:* $23,963. ***Average need-based loan:*** Freshmen: $4078. Undergraduates: $4646. ***Parent loans:*** $3,775,373 (100% non-need-based). ***Programs:*** FFEL (Subsidized and Unsubsidized Stafford, PLUS), Perkins.

WORK-STUDY ***Federal work-study:*** Total amount: $271,274; 325 jobs averaging $1750. ***State or other work-study/employment:*** Total amount: $811,643 (71% need-based, 29% non-need-based). 661 part-time jobs averaging $2200.

APPLYING FOR FINANCIAL AID ***Required financial aid forms:*** FAFSA, state aid form. ***Financial aid deadline (priority):*** 3/1. ***Notification date:*** Continuous. Students must reply by 5/1 or within 2 weeks of notification.

CONTACT Maria A. Barlaam, Director of Financial Aid, Manhattanville College, 2900 Purchase Street, Purchase, NY 10577-2132, 914-323-5357 or toll-free 800-328-4553. *Fax:* 914-323-5382. *E-mail:* barlaamm@mville.edu.

MANNES COLLEGE THE NEW SCHOOL FOR MUSIC

New York, NY

Tuition & fees: $32,150 **Average undergraduate aid package: $25,563**

ABOUT THE INSTITUTION Independent, coed. ***Awards:*** bachelor's and master's degrees and post-bachelor's and post-master's certificates. 7 undergraduate majors. ***Total enrollment:*** 411. Undergraduates: 219. Freshmen: 83. Federal methodology is used as a basis for awarding need-based institutional aid.

UNDERGRADUATE EXPENSES for 2008–09 ***Application fee:*** $100. ***Comprehensive fee:*** $47,410 includes full-time tuition ($31,440), mandatory fees ($710), and room and board ($15,260). ***College room only:*** $12,260. Room and board charges vary according to board plan. ***Part-time tuition:*** $1030 per credit.

FRESHMAN FINANCIAL AID (Fall 2008, est.) 17 applied for aid; of those 94% were deemed to have need. 100% of freshmen with need received aid; of those 12% had need fully met. ***Average percent of need met:*** 77% (excluding resources awarded to replace EFC). ***Average financial aid package:*** $26,568 (excluding resources awarded to replace EFC). 1% of all full-time freshmen had no need and received non-need-based gift aid.

UNDERGRADUATE FINANCIAL AID (Fall 2008, est.) 64 applied for aid; of those 88% were deemed to have need. 89% of undergraduates with need received aid; of those 18% had need fully met. ***Average percent of need met:*** 75% (excluding resources awarded to replace EFC). ***Average financial aid package:*** $25,563 (excluding resources awarded to replace EFC). 2% of all full-time undergraduates had no need and received non-need-based gift aid.

GIFT AID (NEED-BASED) ***Total amount:*** $306,687 (23% federal, 8% state, 48% institutional, 21% external sources). ***Receiving aid:*** Freshmen: 17% (12); all full-time undergraduates: 26% (48). ***Average award:*** Freshmen: $13,798; Undergraduates: $10,375. ***Scholarships, grants, and awards:*** Federal Pell, FSEOG, state, private, college/university gift aid from institutional funds.

GIFT AID (NON-NEED-BASED) ***Total amount:*** $174,170 (100% institutional). ***Receiving aid:*** Freshmen: 1% (1). Undergraduates: 2% (4). ***Average award:*** Freshmen: $11,790. Undergraduates: $12,220. ***Scholarships, grants, and awards by category:*** *Creative arts/performance:* 80 awards ($1,189,530 total): music, performing arts. *Special characteristics:* 32 awards ($602,976 total): international students.

LOANS ***Student loans:*** $608,722 (88% need-based, 12% non-need-based). 68% of past graduating class borrowed through all loan programs. *Average indebtedness per student:* $16,370. ***Average need-based loan:*** Freshmen: $17,537. Undergraduates: $19,004. ***Parent loans:*** $280,353 (86% need-based, 14% non-need-based). ***Programs:*** FFEL (Subsidized and Unsubsidized Stafford, PLUS), Perkins, college/university.

WORK-STUDY ***Federal work-study:*** Total amount: $12,000; 6 jobs averaging $2000.

APPLYING FOR FINANCIAL AID ***Required financial aid forms:*** FAFSA, state aid form. ***Financial aid deadline (priority):*** 3/1. ***Notification date:*** Continuous beginning 3/1. Students must reply within 4 weeks of notification.

CONTACT Michele Harris, Financial Aid Counselor, Mannes College The New School for Music, 150 West 85th Street, New York, NY 10024-4402, 212-229-8930 or toll-free 800-292-3040. *Fax:* 212-229-5919.

MANSFIELD UNIVERSITY OF PENNSYLVANIA

Mansfield, PA

CONTACT Ms. Darcie Stephens, Director of Financial Aid, Mansfield University of Pennsylvania, 109 South Hall, Mansfield, PA 16933, 570-662-4854 or toll-free 800-577-6826. *Fax:* 570-662-4136.

MAPLE SPRINGS BAPTIST BIBLE COLLEGE AND SEMINARY

Capitol Heights, MD

CONTACT Ms. Fannie G. Thompson, Director of Business Affairs, Maple Springs Baptist Bible College and Seminary, 4130 Belt Road, Capitol Heights, MD 20743, 301-736-3631. *Fax:* 301-735-6507.

MARANATHA BAPTIST BIBLE COLLEGE

Watertown, WI

Tuition & fees: $10,560 **Average undergraduate aid package: $6462**

ABOUT THE INSTITUTION Independent Baptist, coed. ***Awards:*** associate, bachelor's, and master's degrees. 34 undergraduate majors. ***Total enrollment:*** 865. Undergraduates: 817. Freshmen: 193. Federal methodology is used as a basis for awarding need-based institutional aid.

UNDERGRADUATE EXPENSES for 2008–09 ***Application fee:*** $50. ***Comprehensive fee:*** $16,360 includes full-time tuition ($9600), mandatory fees ($960), and room and board ($5800). ***Part-time tuition:*** $400 per credit hour. ***Part-time fees:*** $40 per credit hour. ***Payment plan:*** Installment.

FRESHMAN FINANCIAL AID (Fall 2008, est.) 152 applied for aid; of those 88% were deemed to have need. 95% of freshmen with need received aid; of those 6% had need fully met. ***Average percent of need met:*** 42% (excluding resources awarded to replace EFC). ***Average financial aid package:*** $4993 (excluding resources awarded to replace EFC). 4% of all full-time freshmen had no need and received non-need-based gift aid.

UNDERGRADUATE FINANCIAL AID (Fall 2008, est.) 623 applied for aid; of those 90% were deemed to have need. 97% of undergraduates with need received aid; of those 7% had need fully met. ***Average percent of need met:*** 45% (excluding resources awarded to replace EFC). ***Average financial aid package:*** $6462 (excluding resources awarded to replace EFC). 4% of all full-time undergraduates had no need and received non-need-based gift aid.

GIFT AID (NEED-BASED) ***Total amount:*** $1,816,793 (59% federal, 11% state, 16% institutional, 14% external sources). ***Receiving aid:*** Freshmen: 13% (30); all full-time undergraduates: 40% (309). ***Average award:*** Freshmen: $3856; Undergraduates: $3803. ***Scholarships, grants, and awards:*** Federal Pell, FSEOG, state, private, college/university gift aid from institutional funds.

GIFT AID (NON-NEED-BASED) ***Total amount:*** $44,810 (2% state, 63% institutional, 35% external sources). ***Receiving aid:*** Freshmen: 5% (13). Undergraduates: 8% (62). ***Average award:*** Freshmen: $1000. Undergraduates: $1006. ***Scholarships, grants, and awards by category:*** *Academic interests/achievement:* 20 awards ($18,150 total): business, general academic interests/achievements, religion/biblical studies. *Creative arts/performance:* 3 awards ($1300 total): music. *Special characteristics:* 249 awards ($725,547 total): children and siblings of alumni, children of educators, children of faculty/staff, relatives of clergy, spouses of current students. ***Tuition waivers:*** Full or partial for employees or children of employees. ***ROTC:*** Army.

LOANS ***Student loans:*** $5,329,063 (93% need-based, 7% non-need-based). 64% of past graduating class borrowed through all loan programs. *Average indebtedness per student:* $15,191. ***Average need-based loan:*** Freshmen: $3265. Undergraduates: $4265. ***Parent loans:*** $405,446 (94% need-based, 6% non-need-based). ***Programs:*** FFEL (Subsidized and Unsubsidized Stafford, PLUS), state, alternative loans.

WORK-STUDY ***State or other work-study/employment:*** Part-time jobs available.

APPLYING FOR FINANCIAL AID ***Required financial aid form:*** FAFSA. ***Financial aid deadline (priority):*** 3/1. ***Notification date:*** Continuous. Students must reply within 2 weeks of notification.

CONTACT Mr. Bruce Roth, Associate Director of Financial Aid, Maranatha Baptist Bible College, 745 West Main Street, Watertown, WI 53094, 920-206-2318 or toll-free 800-622-2947. *Fax:* 920-261-9109. *E-mail:* financialaid@mbbc.edu.

MARIAN COLLEGE

Indianapolis, IN

Tuition & fees: $22,400 **Average undergraduate aid package: $19,509**

ABOUT THE INSTITUTION Independent Roman Catholic, coed. ***Awards:*** associate, bachelor's, and master's degrees. 44 undergraduate majors. ***Total enrollment:*** 2,143. Undergraduates: 1,971. Federal methodology is used as a basis for awarding need-based institutional aid.

UNDERGRADUATE EXPENSES for 2008–09 ***Application fee:*** $20. ***Comprehensive fee:*** $29,628 includes full-time tuition ($22,400) and room and board ($7228). Full-time tuition and fees vary according to course load. Room and board charges vary according to board plan and housing facility. ***Part-time tuition:*** $940 per credit hour. Part-time tuition and fees vary according to course load. ***Payment plan:*** Installment.

FRESHMAN FINANCIAL AID (Fall 2008, est.) 309 applied for aid; of those 85% were deemed to have need. 100% of freshmen with need received aid; of those 29% had need fully met. ***Average percent of need met:*** 87% (excluding resources awarded to replace EFC). ***Average financial aid package:*** $22,298 (excluding resources awarded to replace EFC). 10% of all full-time freshmen had no need and received non-need-based gift aid.

UNDERGRADUATE FINANCIAL AID (Fall 2008, est.) 1,192 applied for aid; of those 90% were deemed to have need. 100% of undergraduates with need received aid; of those 22% had need fully met. ***Average percent of need met:*** 75% (excluding resources awarded to replace EFC). ***Average financial aid package:*** $19,509 (excluding resources awarded to replace EFC). 14% of all full-time undergraduates had no need and received non-need-based gift aid.

GIFT AID (NEED-BASED) ***Total amount:*** $11,669,087 (22% federal, 41% state, 37% institutional). ***Receiving aid:*** Freshmen: 49% (157); all full-time undergraduates: 35% (464). ***Average award:*** Freshmen: $11,257; Undergraduates: $11,188. ***Scholarships, grants, and awards:*** Federal Pell, FSEOG, state, private, college/university gift aid from institutional funds.

GIFT AID (NON-NEED-BASED) ***Total amount:*** $5,411,257 (2% federal, 93% institutional, 5% external sources). ***Receiving aid:*** Freshmen: 76% (244). Undergraduates: 62% (813). ***Average award:*** Freshmen: $12,759. Undergraduates: $12,191. ***Scholarships, grants, and awards by category:*** *Academic interests/achievement:* 549 awards ($3,535,884 total): area/ethnic studies, general academic interests/achievements, religion/biblical studies. *Creative arts/performance:* 32 awards ($173,813 total): applied art and design, art/fine arts, music, performing arts, theater/drama. *Special achievements/activities:* 171 awards ($688,606 total): community service, religious involvement. *Special characteristics:* 101 awards ($633,235 total): adult students, children and siblings of alumni, children of faculty/staff, international students, members of minority groups, religious affiliation, siblings of current students, spouses of current students. ***Tuition waivers:*** Full or partial for children of alumni, employees or children of employees, senior citizens. ***ROTC:*** Army cooperative.

LOANS ***Student loans:*** $17,097,982 (36% need-based, 64% non-need-based). 92% of past graduating class borrowed through all loan programs. *Average indebtedness per student:* $23,467. ***Average need-based loan:*** Freshmen: $3506. Undergraduates: $4478. ***Parent loans:*** $766,829 (100% non-need-based). ***Programs:*** FFEL (Subsidized and Unsubsidized Stafford, PLUS), Perkins, college/university.

WORK-STUDY ***Federal work-study:*** Total amount: $257,925; 200 jobs averaging $1500. ***State or other work-study/employment:*** Total amount: $28,500 (100% non-need-based). Part-time jobs available.

ATHLETIC AWARDS Total amount: $3,764,670 (100% non-need-based).

APPLYING FOR FINANCIAL AID ***Required financial aid forms:*** FAFSA, institution's own form. ***Financial aid deadline (priority):*** 3/1. ***Notification date:*** Continuous beginning 3/15. Students must reply within 4 weeks of notification.

CONTACT Mr. John E. Shelton, Dean of Financial Aid, Marian College, 3200 Cold Spring Road, Indianapolis, IN 46222-1997, 317-955-6040 or toll-free 800-772-7264 (in-state). *Fax:* 317-955-6424. *E-mail:* jshelton@marian.edu.

MARIAN UNIVERSITY

Fond du Lac, WI

Tuition & fees: $19,940 **Average undergraduate aid package: $20,237**

ABOUT THE INSTITUTION Independent Roman Catholic, coed. ***Awards:*** bachelor's, master's, and doctoral degrees. 45 undergraduate majors. ***Total enrollment:*** 2,891. Undergraduates: 1,996. Freshmen: 284. Federal methodology is used as a basis for awarding need-based institutional aid.

UNDERGRADUATE EXPENSES for 2008–09 ***Application fee:*** $20. ***One-time required fee:*** $100. ***Comprehensive fee:*** $25,320 includes full-time tuition ($19,590), mandatory fees ($350), and room and board ($5380). ***College room only:*** $3730. Full-time tuition and fees vary according to class time, course load, and program. Room and board charges vary according to board plan and housing facility. ***Part-time tuition:*** $300 per credit. ***Part-time fees:*** $80 per term. Part-time tuition and fees vary according to class time, course load, and program. ***Payment plan:*** Installment.

FRESHMAN FINANCIAL AID (Fall 2008, est.) 281 applied for aid; of those 91% were deemed to have need. 100% of freshmen with need received aid; of those 47% had need fully met. ***Average percent of need met:*** 92% (excluding resources awarded to replace EFC). ***Average financial aid package:*** $20,412 (excluding resources awarded to replace EFC). 8% of all full-time freshmen had no need and received non-need-based gift aid.

UNDERGRADUATE FINANCIAL AID (Fall 2008, est.) 1,316 applied for aid; of those 87% were deemed to have need. 100% of undergraduates with need received aid; of those 53% had need fully met. ***Average percent of need met:*** 93% (excluding resources awarded to replace EFC). ***Average financial aid package:*** $20,237 (excluding resources awarded to replace EFC). 12% of all full-time undergraduates had no need and received non-need-based gift aid.

GIFT AID (NEED-BASED) ***Total amount:*** $12,320,271 (17% federal, 16% state, 63% institutional, 4% external sources). ***Receiving aid:*** Freshmen: 90% (257); all full-time undergraduates: 81% (1,114). ***Average award:*** Freshmen: $11,440; Undergraduates: $10,391. ***Scholarships, grants, and awards:*** Federal Pell, FSEOG, state, private, college/university gift aid from institutional funds, endowed scholarships.

GIFT AID (NON-NEED-BASED) ***Total amount:*** $946,358 (1% state, 96% institutional, 3% external sources). ***Receiving aid:*** Freshmen: 83% (235). Undergraduates: 70% (974). ***Average award:*** Freshmen: $5986. Undergraduates: $4989. ***Scholarships, grants, and awards by category:*** *Academic interests/achievement:* 1,253 awards ($5,204,182 total): general academic interests/achievements. *Creative arts/performance:* 43 awards ($77,250 total): music. *Special characteristics:* 78 awards ($305,935 total): children of faculty/staff, children with a deceased or disabled parent, siblings of current students. ***Tuition waivers:*** Full or partial for employees or children of employees, senior citizens. ***ROTC:*** Army.

LOANS ***Student loans:*** $11,952,476 (74% need-based, 26% non-need-based). 96% of past graduating class borrowed through all loan programs. *Average indebtedness per student:* $22,200. ***Average need-based loan:*** Freshmen: $5288. Undergraduates: $6725. ***Parent loans:*** $907,139 (78% need-based, 22% non-need-based). ***Programs:*** FFEL (Subsidized and Unsubsidized Stafford, PLUS), Perkins, Federal Nursing.

WORK-STUDY ***Federal work-study:*** Total amount: $1,235,723; 682 jobs averaging $1851. ***State or other work-study/employment:*** Total amount: $418,980 (100% non-need-based). 195 part-time jobs averaging $1425.

APPLYING FOR FINANCIAL AID ***Required financial aid forms:*** FAFSA, institution's own form. ***Financial aid deadline (priority):*** 3/1. ***Notification date:*** Continuous beginning 3/1. Students must reply within 4 weeks of notification.

CONTACT Ms. Debra E. McKinney, Director of Financial Aid, Marian University, 45 South National Avenue, Fond du Lac, WI 54935-4699, 920-923-7614 or toll-free 800-2-MARIAN Ext. 7652 (in-state). *Fax:* 920-923-8767. *E-mail:* dmckinney@marianuniversity.edu.

MARIETTA COLLEGE

Marietta, OH

ABOUT THE INSTITUTION Independent, coed. ***Awards:*** associate, bachelor's, and master's degrees. 40 undergraduate majors. ***Total enrollment:*** 1,602. Undergraduates: 1,485. Freshmen: 385.

GIFT AID (NEED-BASED) ***Scholarships, grants, and awards:*** Federal Pell, FSEOG, state, private, college/university gift aid from institutional funds.

GIFT AID (NON-NEED-BASED) ***Scholarships, grants, and awards by category:*** *Academic interests/achievement:* general academic interests/achievements, physical sciences. *Creative arts/performance:* art/fine arts, music, performing arts, theater/drama. *Special achievements/activities:* general special achievements/activities. *Special characteristics:* children and siblings of alumni, ethnic background, members of minority groups, siblings of current students.

LOANS ***Programs:*** Federal Direct (Subsidized and Unsubsidized Stafford, PLUS), FFEL (Subsidized and Unsubsidized Stafford, PLUS), Perkins, college/university.

WORK-STUDY ***Federal work-study:*** Total amount: $1,748,596; 928 jobs averaging $1884.

APPLYING FOR FINANCIAL AID ***Required financial aid form:*** FAFSA.

CONTACT Mr. Kevin Lamb, Director of Financial Aid, Marietta College, 215 Fifth Street, Marietta, OH 45750-4000, 740-376-4712 or toll-free 800-331-7896. *Fax:* 740-376-4990. *E-mail:* finaid@marietta.edu.

MARIST COLLEGE

Poughkeepsie, NY

ABOUT THE INSTITUTION Independent, coed. ***Awards:*** bachelor's and master's degrees and post-bachelor's certificates. 50 undergraduate majors. ***Total enrollment:*** 5,828. Undergraduates: 5,031. Freshmen: 1,022.

GIFT AID (NEED-BASED) ***Scholarships, grants, and awards:*** Federal Pell, FSEOG, state, private, college/university gift aid from institutional funds.

GIFT AID (NON-NEED-BASED) ***Scholarships, grants, and awards by category:*** *Academic interests/achievement:* general academic interests/achievements. *Creative arts/performance:* debating, music. *Special achievements/activities:* general special achievements/activities.

LOANS ***Programs:*** FFEL (Subsidized and Unsubsidized Stafford, PLUS), Perkins, alternative loans.

WORK-STUDY ***Federal work-study:*** Total amount: $2,556,539; 649 jobs averaging $1969. ***State or other work-study/employment:*** Total amount: $818,200 (100% non-need-based). 605 part-time jobs averaging $1000.

APPLYING FOR FINANCIAL AID ***Required financial aid forms:*** FAFSA, institution's own form.

CONTACT Joseph R. Weglarz, Executive Director, Student Financial Services, Marist College, 3399 North Road, Poughkeepsie, NY 12601, 845-575-3230 or toll-free 800-436-5483. *Fax:* 845-575-3099. *E-mail:* joseph.weglarz@marist.edu.

MARLBORO COLLEGE

Marlboro, VT

Tuition & fees: $33,660 **Average undergraduate aid package: $19,062**

ABOUT THE INSTITUTION Independent, coed. ***Awards:*** bachelor's, master's, and first professional degrees. 77 undergraduate majors. ***Total enrollment:*** 330. Undergraduates: 329. Freshmen: 77. Federal methodology is used as a basis for awarding need-based institutional aid.

UNDERGRADUATE EXPENSES for 2009–10 ***Application fee:*** $50. ***Comprehensive fee:*** $42,880 includes full-time tuition ($32,550), mandatory fees ($1110), and room and board ($9220). ***College room only:*** $5080. ***Part-time tuition:*** $1038 per credit.

FRESHMAN FINANCIAL AID (Fall 2008, est.) 82 applied for aid; of those 73% were deemed to have need. 100% of freshmen with need received aid. ***Average percent of need met:*** 85% (excluding resources awarded to replace EFC). ***Average financial aid package:*** $19,068 (excluding resources awarded to replace EFC). 10% of all full-time freshmen had no need and received non-need-based gift aid.

UNDERGRADUATE FINANCIAL AID (Fall 2008, est.) 279 applied for aid; of those 89% were deemed to have need. 100% of undergraduates with need received aid. ***Average percent of need met:*** 85% (excluding resources awarded to replace EFC). ***Average financial aid package:*** $19,062 (excluding resources awarded to replace EFC). 13% of all full-time undergraduates had no need and received non-need-based gift aid.

GIFT AID (NEED-BASED) ***Total amount:*** $2,910,358 (12% federal, 3% state, 85% institutional). ***Receiving aid:*** Freshmen: 58% (53); all full-time undergraduates: 50% (161). ***Average award:*** Freshmen: $10,000; Undergraduates: $10,000. ***Scholarships, grants, and awards:*** Federal Pell, FSEOG, state, private, college/university gift aid from institutional funds.

GIFT AID (NON-NEED-BASED) ***Total amount:*** $1,491,997 (94% institutional, 6% external sources). ***Receiving aid:*** Freshmen: 31% (28). Undergraduates: 47% (151). ***Average award:*** Freshmen: $10,000. Undergraduates: $10,000. ***Scholarships, grants, and awards by category:*** *Academic interests/achievement:* 161 awards ($1,005,500 total): general academic interests/achievements.

LOANS ***Student loans:*** $1,950,275 (51% need-based, 49% non-need-based). 81% of past graduating class borrowed through all loan programs. *Average indebtedness per student:* $19,482. ***Average need-based loan:*** Freshmen: $3671. Undergraduates: $3787. ***Parent loans:*** $1,027,776 (100% non-need-based). ***Programs:*** FFEL (Subsidized and Unsubsidized Stafford, PLUS).

WORK-STUDY ***Federal work-study:*** Total amount: $401,043; 230 jobs averaging $2050. ***State or other work-study/employment:*** Part-time jobs available.

APPLYING FOR FINANCIAL AID ***Required financial aid form:*** FAFSA. ***Financial aid deadline:*** 3/1. ***Notification date:*** Continuous. Students must reply by 5/1 or within 2 weeks of notification.

CONTACT Cathy S. Fuller, Associate Director of Financial Aid, Marlboro College, PO Box A, 2582 South Road, Marlboro, VT 05344-0300, 802-258-9237 or toll-free 800-343-0049. *Fax:* 802-258-9300. *E-mail:* finaid@marlboro.edu.

MARQUETTE UNIVERSITY

Milwaukee, WI

Tuition & fees: $29,096 **Average undergraduate aid package: $20,038**

ABOUT THE INSTITUTION Independent Roman Catholic (Jesuit), coed. ***Awards:*** bachelor's, master's, doctoral, and first professional degrees and post-bachelor's, post-master's, and first professional certificates. 67 undergraduate majors. ***Total enrollment:*** 11,633. Undergraduates: 8,012. Freshmen: 1,950. Federal methodology is used as a basis for awarding need-based institutional aid.

UNDERGRADUATE EXPENSES for 2009–10 ***Application fee:*** $30. ***Comprehensive fee:*** $35,426 includes full-time tuition ($28,680), mandatory fees ($416), and room and board ($6330). ***College room only:*** $3350. ***Part-time tuition:*** $835 per credit.

FRESHMAN FINANCIAL AID (Fall 2008, est.) 1,540 applied for aid; of those 77% were deemed to have need. 100% of freshmen with need received aid; of those 32% had need fully met. ***Average percent of need met:*** 84% (excluding resources awarded to replace EFC). ***Average financial aid package:*** $22,008 (excluding resources awarded to replace EFC). 21% of all full-time freshmen had no need and received non-need-based gift aid.

UNDERGRADUATE FINANCIAL AID (Fall 2008, est.) 5,275 applied for aid; of those 83% were deemed to have need. 99% of undergraduates with need received aid; of those 29% had need fully met. ***Average percent of need met:*** 79% (excluding resources awarded to replace EFC). ***Average financial aid package:*** $20,038 (excluding resources awarded to replace EFC). 21% of all full-time undergraduates had no need and received non-need-based gift aid.

GIFT AID (NEED-BASED) ***Total amount:*** $56,961,386 (9% federal, 6% state, 77% institutional, 8% external sources). ***Receiving aid:*** Freshmen: 60% (1,161); all full-time undergraduates: 55% (4,197). ***Average award:*** Freshmen: $16,448; Undergraduates: $13,592. ***Scholarships, grants, and awards:*** Federal Pell, FSEOG, state, private, college/university gift aid from institutional funds.

GIFT AID (NON-NEED-BASED) ***Total amount:*** $19,812,840 (77% institutional, 23% external sources). ***Receiving aid:*** Freshmen: 7% (128). Undergraduates: 5% (370). ***Average award:*** Freshmen: $9227. Undergraduates: $8699. ***Scholarships, grants, and awards by category:*** *Academic interests/achievement:* 3,313 awards ($23,546,419 total): biological sciences, business, communication, engineering/technologies, foreign languages, general academic interests/achievements, health fields, mathematics. *Creative arts/performance:* theater/drama. *Special characteristics:* 176 awards ($4,717,065 total): children of faculty/staff. ***ROTC:*** Army, Naval, Air Force.

LOANS ***Student loans:*** $44,916,081 (77% need-based, 23% non-need-based). 63% of past graduating class borrowed through all loan programs. *Average indebtedness per student:* $30,563. ***Average need-based loan:*** Freshmen: $4504. Undergraduates: $5388. ***Parent loans:*** $15,663,125 (24% need-based, 76% non-need-based). ***Programs:*** Federal Direct (Subsidized and Unsubsidized Stafford, PLUS), Perkins, Federal Nursing, state, college/university.

WORK-STUDY ***Federal work-study:*** Total amount: $5,478,379; jobs available. ***State or other work-study/employment:*** Part-time jobs available.

ATHLETIC AWARDS Total amount: $3,184,910 (29% need-based, 71% non-need-based).

APPLYING FOR FINANCIAL AID ***Required financial aid form:*** FAFSA. ***Financial aid deadline:*** Continuous. ***Notification date:*** Continuous beginning 3/20. Students must reply by 5/1 or within 3 weeks of notification.

CONTACT Susan Teerink, Director of Financial Aid, Marquette University, Office of Student Financial Aid, Milwaukee, WI 53201-1881, 414-288-7390 or toll-free 800-222-6544. *Fax:* 414-288-1718. *E-mail:* financialaid@marquette.edu.

MARSHALL UNIVERSITY

Huntington, WV

ABOUT THE INSTITUTION State-supported, coed. ***Awards:*** bachelor's, master's, doctoral, and first professional degrees and post-master's certificates. 51 undergraduate majors. ***Total enrollment:*** 13,573. Undergraduates: 9,310. Freshmen: 1,686.

GIFT AID (NEED-BASED) ***Scholarships, grants, and awards:*** Federal Pell, FSEOG, state, private, college/university gift aid from institutional funds.

GIFT AID (NON-NEED-BASED) ***Scholarships, grants, and awards by category:*** *Academic interests/achievement:* general academic interests/achievements. *Special characteristics:* children of faculty/staff.

LOANS ***Programs:*** Federal Direct (Subsidized and Unsubsidized Stafford, PLUS), Perkins, state, college/university, alternative loans through outside sources.

WORK-STUDY ***Federal work-study:*** Total amount: $229,544; 359 jobs averaging $1761. ***State or other work-study/employment:*** Total amount: $339,389 (100% non-need-based). 58 part-time jobs averaging $6030.

APPLYING FOR FINANCIAL AID ***Required financial aid form:*** FAFSA.

CONTACT Ms. Nadine A. Hamrick, Interim Director of Student Financial Aid, Marshall University, One John Marshall Drive, Huntington, WV 25755, 304-696-2277 or toll-free 800-642-3499 (in-state). *Fax:* 304-696-3242. *E-mail:* hamrick@marshall.edu.

MARS HILL COLLEGE

Mars Hill, NC

CONTACT Myrtle Martin, Director of Financial Aid, Mars Hill College, PO Box 370, Mars Hill, NC 28754, 828-689-1123 or toll-free 866-MHC-4-YOU. *Fax:* 828-689-1300.

MARTIN LUTHER COLLEGE

New Ulm, MN

Tuition & fees: $10,660 **Average undergraduate aid package: $9921**

ABOUT THE INSTITUTION Independent religious, coed. ***Awards:*** bachelor's and master's degrees and post-bachelor's certificates. 6 undergraduate majors. ***Total enrollment:*** 842. Undergraduates: 780. Freshmen: 175. Federal methodology is used as a basis for awarding need-based institutional aid.

UNDERGRADUATE EXPENSES for 2009–10 ***Application fee:*** $25. ***Comprehensive fee:*** $14,800 includes full-time tuition ($10,660) and room and board ($4140).

FRESHMAN FINANCIAL AID (Fall 2007) 168 applied for aid; of those 80% were deemed to have need. 100% of freshmen with need received aid; of those 30% had need fully met. ***Average percent of need met:*** 60% (excluding resources awarded to replace EFC). ***Average financial aid package:*** $9388 (excluding resources awarded to replace EFC). 13% of all full-time freshmen had no need and received non-need-based gift aid.

UNDERGRADUATE FINANCIAL AID (Fall 2007) 631 applied for aid; of those 83% were deemed to have need. 100% of undergraduates with need received aid; of those 40% had need fully met. ***Average percent of need met:*** 64% (excluding resources awarded to replace EFC). ***Average financial aid package:*** $9921 (excluding resources awarded to replace EFC). 9% of all full-time undergraduates had no need and received non-need-based gift aid.

GIFT AID (NEED-BASED) ***Total amount:*** $3,274,164 (17% federal, 6% state, 61% institutional, 16% external sources). ***Receiving aid:*** Freshmen: 61% (109); all full-time undergraduates: 61% (421). ***Average award:*** Freshmen: $4034; Undergraduates: $3932. ***Scholarships, grants, and awards:*** Federal Pell, FSEOG, state, private, college/university gift aid from institutional funds.

GIFT AID (NON-NEED-BASED) ***Receiving aid:*** Freshmen: 46% (83). Undergraduates: 47% (325). ***Average award:*** Freshmen: $1478. Undergraduates: $1525. ***Scholarships, grants, and awards by category:*** *Academic interests/achievement:* general academic interests/achievements. *Creative arts/performance:* music. *Special achievements/activities:* general special achievements/activities. *Special characteristics:* general special characteristics.

LOANS ***Student loans:*** $1,976,528 (100% need-based). 46% of past graduating class borrowed through all loan programs. *Average indebtedness per student:* $15,151. ***Average need-based loan:*** Freshmen: $3748. Undergraduates: $3337. ***Parent loans:*** $196,409 (100% need-based). ***Programs:*** FFEL (Subsidized and Unsubsidized Stafford, PLUS), Perkins, state, college/university.

WORK-STUDY ***Federal work-study:*** Total amount: $51,397; jobs available.

APPLYING FOR FINANCIAL AID ***Required financial aid forms:*** FAFSA, institution's own form. ***Financial aid deadline:*** 4/15. ***Notification date:*** Continuous.

CONTACT Mr. Gene Slettedahl, Director of Financial Aid, Martin Luther College, 1995 Luther Court, New Ulm, MN 56073, 507-354-8221 Ext. 225. *Fax:* 507-354-8225. *E-mail:* slettega@mlc-wels.edu.

MARTIN METHODIST COLLEGE

Pulaski, TN

CONTACT Ms. Anita Beecham, Financial Aid Assistant, Martin Methodist College, 433 West Madison Street, Pulaski, TN 38478-2716, 931-363-9808 or toll-free 800-467-1273. *Fax:* 931-363-9818. *E-mail:* abeecham@martinmethodist.edu.

MARTIN UNIVERSITY

Indianapolis, IN

CONTACT Pertrina P. Briggs, Director of Financial Aid, Martin University, 2171 Avondale Place, PO Box 18567, Indianapolis, IN 46218-3867, 317-543-3670. *Fax:* 317-543-4790. *E-mail:* pbriggs@martin.edu.

MARY BALDWIN COLLEGE

Staunton, VA

Tuition & fees: $23,645 **Average undergraduate aid package: $18,057**

ABOUT THE INSTITUTION Independent, undergraduate: women only; graduate: coed. ***Awards:*** bachelor's and master's degrees. 28 undergraduate majors. ***Total enrollment:*** 1,738. Undergraduates: 1,537. Freshmen: 294. Federal methodology is used as a basis for awarding need-based institutional aid.

UNDERGRADUATE EXPENSES for 2008–09 ***Application fee:*** $35. ***One-time required fee:*** $215. ***Comprehensive fee:*** $30,375 includes full-time tuition ($23,430), mandatory fees ($215), and room and board ($6730). ***College room only:*** $4290. Full-time tuition and fees vary according to degree level. Room and board charges vary according to housing facility. ***Part-time tuition:*** $400 per semester hour. Part-time tuition and fees vary according to degree level. ***Payment plan:*** Installment.

FRESHMAN FINANCIAL AID (Fall 2007) 250 applied for aid; of those 91% were deemed to have need. 98% of freshmen with need received aid; of those 2% had need fully met. ***Average percent of need met:*** 91% (excluding resources awarded to replace EFC). ***Average financial aid package:*** $19,455 (excluding resources awarded to replace EFC). 10% of all full-time freshmen had no need and received non-need-based gift aid.

UNDERGRADUATE FINANCIAL AID (Fall 2007) 818 applied for aid; of those 86% were deemed to have need. 100% of undergraduates with need received aid; of those 2% had need fully met. ***Average percent of need met:*** 88% (excluding resources awarded to replace EFC). ***Average financial aid package:*** $18,057 (excluding resources awarded to replace EFC). 8% of all full-time undergraduates had no need and received non-need-based gift aid.

GIFT AID (NEED-BASED) ***Total amount:*** $11,680,775 (19% federal, 19% state, 60% institutional, 2% external sources). ***Receiving aid:*** Freshmen: 78% (219); all full-time undergraduates: 76% (694). ***Average award:*** Freshmen: $14,876; Undergraduates: $13,359. ***Scholarships, grants, and awards:*** Federal Pell, FSEOG, state, private, college/university gift aid from institutional funds.

GIFT AID (NON-NEED-BASED) ***Total amount:*** $849,150 (6% federal, 22% state, 70% institutional, 2% external sources). ***Receiving aid:*** Freshmen: 55% (155). Undergraduates: 55% (501). ***Average award:*** Freshmen: $8844. Undergraduates: $8369. ***Scholarships, grants, and awards by category:*** *Academic interests/achievement:* 665 awards ($4,253,380 total): general academic interests/achievements. *Special achievements/activities:* 31 awards ($67,553 total): leadership. *Special characteristics:* 11 awards ($173,199 total): children of educators, children of faculty/staff. ***Tuition waivers:*** Full or partial for employees or children of employees. ***ROTC:*** Army, Naval cooperative, Air Force cooperative.

LOANS ***Student loans:*** $7,330,643 (95% need-based, 5% non-need-based). 79% of past graduating class borrowed through all loan programs. *Average indebtedness per student:* $23,919. ***Average need-based loan:*** Freshmen: $4606. Undergraduates: $4851. ***Parent loans:*** $1,928,326 (87% need-based, 13% non-need-based). ***Programs:*** FFEL (Subsidized and Unsubsidized Stafford, PLUS), Perkins, alternative loans.

WORK-STUDY ***Federal work-study:*** Total amount: $591,567; 316 jobs averaging $1783. ***State or other work-study/employment:*** Total amount: $18,050 (8% need-based, 92% non-need-based). 57 part-time jobs averaging $1210.

APPLYING FOR FINANCIAL AID ***Required financial aid forms:*** FAFSA, state aid form (for VA residents only). ***Financial aid deadline:*** 4/15. ***Notification date:*** Continuous. Students must reply within 3 weeks of notification.

CONTACT Robin Dietrich, Director of Financial Aid, Mary Baldwin College, Office of Financial Aid and Student Campus Employment, Staunton, VA 24401, 540-887-7025 or toll-free 800-468-2262. *Fax:* 540-887-7229. *E-mail:* rdietric@mbc.edu.

MARYGROVE COLLEGE

Detroit, MI

CONTACT Mr. Donald Hurt, Director of Financial Aid, Marygrove College, 8425 West McNichols Road, Detroit, MI 48221-2599, 313-862-8000 Ext. 436 or toll-free 866-313-1297.

MARYLAND INSTITUTE COLLEGE OF ART

Baltimore, MD

CONTACT Ms. Diane Prengaman, Associate Vice President for Financial Aid, Maryland Institute College of Art, 1300 Mount Royal Avenue, Baltimore, MD 21217, 410-225-2285. *Fax:* 410-225-2337. *E-mail:* dprengam@mica.edu.

MARYLHURST UNIVERSITY

Marylhurst, OR

Tuition & fees: $16,200 **Average undergraduate aid package: $11,390**

ABOUT THE INSTITUTION Independent Roman Catholic, coed, primarily women. ***Awards:*** bachelor's and master's degrees and post-bachelor's and post-master's certificates. 22 undergraduate majors. ***Total enrollment:*** 1,802. Undergraduates: 946. Freshmen: 25. Federal methodology is used as a basis for awarding need-based institutional aid.

UNDERGRADUATE EXPENSES for 2008–09 ***Application fee:*** $20. ***Tuition:*** full-time $15,705; part-time $349 per credit. ***Required fees:*** full-time $495; $11 per credit. Full-time tuition and fees vary according to course load, degree level, and program. Part-time tuition and fees vary according to course load, degree level, and program. ***Payment plan:*** Installment.

FRESHMAN FINANCIAL AID (Fall 2008, est.) 7 applied for aid; of those 71% were deemed to have need. 80% of freshmen with need received aid. ***Average percent of need met:*** 35% (excluding resources awarded to replace EFC). ***Average financial aid package:*** $7086 (excluding resources awarded to replace EFC). 46% of all full-time freshmen had no need and received non-need-based gift aid.

UNDERGRADUATE FINANCIAL AID (Fall 2008, est.) 142 applied for aid; of those 95% were deemed to have need. 99% of undergraduates with need received aid; of those 4% had need fully met. ***Average percent of need met:*** 49% (excluding resources awarded to replace EFC). ***Average financial aid package:*** $11,390 (excluding resources awarded to replace EFC). 5% of all full-time undergraduates had no need and received non-need-based gift aid.

GIFT AID (NEED-BASED) ***Total amount:*** $2,304,545 (43% federal, 12% state, 33% institutional, 12% external sources). ***Receiving aid:*** Freshmen: 15% (2); all full-time undergraduates: 47% (109). ***Average award:*** Freshmen: $5804; Undergraduates: $8638. ***Scholarships, grants, and awards:*** Federal Pell, FSEOG, state, private, college/university gift aid from institutional funds, United Negro College Fund.

GIFT AID (NON-NEED-BASED) ***Total amount:*** $170,809 (76% institutional, 24% external sources). ***Receiving aid:*** Undergraduates: 1% (3). ***Average award:*** Freshmen: $5405. Undergraduates: $4737. ***Tuition waivers:*** Full or partial for employees or children of employees.

LOANS ***Student loans:*** $7,143,195 (80% need-based, 20% non-need-based) 80% of past graduating class borrowed through all loan programs. *Average indebtedness per student:* $20,275. ***Average need-based loan:*** Freshmen: $2896. Undergraduates: $4450. ***Parent loans:*** $128,462 (34% need-based, 66% non-need-based). ***Programs:*** FFEL (Subsidized and Unsubsidized Stafford, PLUS), Perkins.

WORK-STUDY ***Federal work-study:*** Total amount: $157,252; 62 jobs averaging $3093.

APPLYING FOR FINANCIAL AID ***Required financial aid forms:*** FAFSA, institution's own form. ***Financial aid deadline:*** Continuous. ***Notification date:*** Continuous beginning 5/1. Students must reply within 8 weeks of notification.

CONTACT Tracy Reisinger, Office of Financial Aid, Marylhurst University, 17600 Pacific Highway, PO Box 261, Marylhurst, OR 97036, 503-699-6253 or toll-free 800-634-9982. *Fax:* 503-635-6585. *E-mail:* treisinger@marylhurst.edu.

MARYMOUNT MANHATTAN COLLEGE

New York, NY

Tuition & fees: $21,792 **Average undergraduate aid package: $12,334**

ABOUT THE INSTITUTION Independent, coed. ***Awards:*** bachelor's degrees. 22 undergraduate majors. ***Total enrollment:*** 1,988. Undergraduates: 1,988. Freshmen: 562. Federal methodology is used as a basis for awarding need-based institutional aid.

UNDERGRADUATE EXPENSES for 2008–09 ***Application fee:*** $60. ***Comprehensive fee:*** $34,452 includes full-time tuition ($20,748), mandatory fees ($1044), and room and board ($12,660). ***College room only:*** $10,660. ***Part-time tuition:*** $663 per credit hour. ***Part-time fees:*** $335 per term. ***Payment plan:*** Installment.

FRESHMAN FINANCIAL AID (Fall 2008, est.) 436 applied for aid; of those 77% were deemed to have need. 100% of freshmen with need received aid; of those 8% had need fully met. ***Average percent of need met:*** 50% (excluding resources awarded to replace EFC). ***Average financial aid package:*** $13,011 (excluding resources awarded to replace EFC). 19% of all full-time freshmen had no need and received non-need-based gift aid.

UNDERGRADUATE FINANCIAL AID (Fall 2008, est.) 1,202 applied for aid; of those 80% were deemed to have need. 100% of undergraduates with need received aid; of those 7% had need fully met. ***Average percent of need met:*** 47% (excluding resources awarded to replace EFC). ***Average financial aid package:*** $12,334 (excluding resources awarded to replace EFC). 20% of all full-time undergraduates had no need and received non-need-based gift aid.

GIFT AID (NEED-BASED) ***Total amount:*** $8,434,237 (17% federal, 10% state, 70% institutional, 3% external sources). ***Receiving aid:*** Freshmen: 61% (326); all full-time undergraduates: 55% (910). ***Average award:*** Freshmen: $10,134; Undergraduates: $8630. ***Scholarships, grants, and awards:*** Federal Pell, FSEOG, state, private, college/university gift aid from institutional funds.

GIFT AID (NON-NEED-BASED) ***Total amount:*** $1,534,703 (100% institutional). ***Receiving aid:*** Freshmen: 47% (254). Undergraduates: 2% (37). ***Average award:*** Freshmen: $5712. Undergraduates: $4914. ***Scholarships, grants, and awards by category:*** *Academic interests/achievement:* general academic interests/achievements. *Creative arts/performance:* dance, performing arts, theater/drama.

LOANS ***Student loans:*** $10,437,477 (100% need-based). 41% of past graduating class borrowed through all loan programs. *Average indebtedness per student:* $16,765. ***Average need-based loan:*** Freshmen: $2860. Undergraduates: $3624. ***Parent loans:*** $14,886,726 (36% need-based, 64% non-need-based). ***Programs:*** FFEL (Subsidized and Unsubsidized Stafford, PLUS).

WORK-STUDY ***Federal work-study:*** Total amount: $76,129; jobs available. ***State or other work-study/employment:*** Part-time jobs available.

APPLYING FOR FINANCIAL AID ***Required financial aid form:*** FAFSA. ***Financial aid deadline (priority):*** 3/15. ***Notification date:*** Continuous beginning 3/15. Students must reply by 5/1 or within 3 weeks of notification.

CONTACT Maria Deinnocentiis, Director of Financial Aid, Marymount Manhattan College, Marymount Manhattan College, 221 East 71st Street, New York, NY 10021, 212-517-0500 or toll-free 800-MARYMOUNT (out-of-state). *Fax:* 212-517-0491.

MARYMOUNT UNIVERSITY

Arlington, VA

Tuition & fees: $21,528 **Average undergraduate aid package: $14,935**

ABOUT THE INSTITUTION Independent religious, coed. ***Awards:*** bachelor's, master's, and doctoral degrees and post-bachelor's and post-master's certificates (Associate). 25 undergraduate majors. ***Total enrollment:*** 3,548. Undergraduates: 2,193. Freshmen: 411. Both federal and institutional methodology are used as a basis for awarding need-based institutional aid.

UNDERGRADUATE EXPENSES for 2008–09 ***Application fee:*** $40. ***Comprehensive fee:*** $30,718 includes full-time tuition ($21,300), mandatory fees ($228), and room and board ($9190). ***Part-time tuition:*** $690 per credit hour. ***Part-time fees:*** $7 per credit hour. ***Payment plan:*** Installment.

FRESHMAN FINANCIAL AID (Fall 2008, est.) 332 applied for aid; of those 82% were deemed to have need. 100% of freshmen with need received aid; of those 17% had need fully met. ***Average percent of need met:*** 72% (excluding resources awarded to replace EFC). ***Average financial aid package:*** $16,938 (excluding resources awarded to replace EFC). 29% of all full-time freshmen had no need and received non-need-based gift aid.

UNDERGRADUATE FINANCIAL AID (Fall 2008, est.) 1,306 applied for aid; of those 85% were deemed to have need. 99% of undergraduates with need received aid; of those 19% had need fully met. ***Average percent of need met:*** 69% (excluding resources awarded to replace EFC). ***Average financial aid package:*** $14,935 (excluding resources awarded to replace EFC). 25% of all full-time undergraduates had no need and received non-need-based gift aid.

GIFT AID (NEED-BASED) ***Total amount:*** $4,635,022 (37% federal, 2% state, 61% institutional). ***Receiving aid:*** Freshmen: 46% (185); all full-time undergraduates: 39% (723). ***Average award:*** Freshmen: $5108; Undergraduates: $6186. ***Scholarships, grants, and awards:*** Federal Pell, FSEOG, state, private, college/university gift aid from institutional funds.

GIFT AID (NON-NEED-BASED) ***Total amount:*** $10,791,263 (22% state, 77% institutional, 1% external sources). ***Receiving aid:*** Freshmen: 67% (269). Undergraduates: 46% (853). ***Average award:*** Freshmen: $9765. Undergraduates: $8680. ***Scholarships, grants, and awards by category:*** *Academic interests/achievement:* 580 awards ($5,174,423 total): biological sciences, computer science, general academic interests/achievements, health fields, mathematics, social sciences. *Special achievements/activities:* 160 awards ($627,295 total): community service, general special achievements/activities, leadership, memberships. *Special characteristics:* 285 awards ($955,038 total): children and siblings of alumni, children of current students, children of faculty/staff, general special characteristics, international students, parents of current students, siblings of current students. ***Tuition waivers:*** Full or partial for children of alumni, employees or children of employees, senior citizens. ***ROTC:*** Army cooperative.

LOANS ***Student loans:*** $11,546,544 (37% need-based, 63% non-need-based). 78% of past graduating class borrowed through all loan programs. *Average indebtedness per student:* $22,993. ***Average need-based loan:*** Freshmen: $3612. Undergraduates: $4234. ***Parent loans:*** $4,365,327 (100% non-need-based). ***Programs:*** FFEL (Subsidized and Unsubsidized Stafford, PLUS), Perkins.

WORK-STUDY ***Federal work-study:*** Total amount: $1,236,384; 697 jobs averaging $1668.

APPLYING FOR FINANCIAL AID ***Required financial aid form:*** FAFSA. ***Financial aid deadline (priority):*** 3/1. ***Notification date:*** Continuous beginning 3/15. Students must reply within 2 weeks of notification.

CONTACT Ms. Debbie A. Raines, Director of Financial Aid, Marymount University, 2807 North Glebe Road, Arlington, VA 22207-4299, 703-284-1530 or toll-free 800-548-7638. *Fax:* 703-516-4771. *E-mail:* debbie.raines@marymount.edu.

MARYVILLE COLLEGE

Maryville, TN

Tuition & fees: $26,947 **Average undergraduate aid package: $28,652**

ABOUT THE INSTITUTION Independent Presbyterian, coed. ***Awards:*** bachelor's degrees. 50 undergraduate majors. ***Total enrollment:*** 1,114. Undergraduates: 1,114. Freshmen: 297. Federal methodology is used as a basis for awarding need-based institutional aid.

UNDERGRADUATE EXPENSES for 2008–09 ***Comprehensive fee:*** $35,187 includes full-time tuition ($26,272), mandatory fees ($675), and room and board ($8240). ***College room only:*** $4120. Full-time tuition and fees vary according to course load. Room and board charges vary according to board plan, housing facility, and location. ***Part-time tuition:*** $1095 per hour. Part-time tuition and fees vary according to course load. ***Payment plan:*** Installment.

FRESHMAN FINANCIAL AID (Fall 2008, est.) 259 applied for aid; of those 100% were deemed to have need. 100% of freshmen with need received aid; of those 66% had need fully met. ***Average percent of need met:*** 91% (excluding resources awarded to replace EFC). ***Average financial aid package:*** $26,215 (excluding resources awarded to replace EFC). 13% of all full-time freshmen had no need and received non-need-based gift aid.

UNDERGRADUATE FINANCIAL AID (Fall 2008, est.) 875 applied for aid; of those 100% were deemed to have need. 100% of undergraduates with need received aid; of those 82% had need fully met. ***Average percent of need met:*** 81% (excluding resources awarded to replace EFC). ***Average financial aid package:*** $28,652 (excluding resources awarded to replace EFC). 19% of all full-time undergraduates had no need and received non-need-based gift aid.

GIFT AID (NEED-BASED) ***Total amount:*** $17,128,600 (8% federal, 4% state, 72% institutional, 16% external sources). ***Receiving aid:*** Freshmen: 65% (194); all full-time undergraduates: 78% (861). ***Average award:*** Freshmen: $20,692; Undergraduates: $15,855. ***Scholarships, grants, and awards:*** Federal Pell, FSEOG, state, private, college/university gift aid from institutional funds.

GIFT AID (NON-NEED-BASED) ***Total amount:*** $3,976,778 (87% institutional, 13% external sources). ***Receiving aid:*** Freshmen: 27% (80). Undergraduates: 20% (221). ***Average award:*** Freshmen: $14,417. Undergraduates: $12,954. ***Scholarships, grants, and awards by category:*** *Academic interests/achievement:* 892 awards ($10,758,314 total): general academic interests/achievements. *Creative arts/performance:* 93 awards ($267,500 total): art/fine arts, music, theater/drama. *Special achievements/activities:* 216 awards ($1,399,548 total): community service, leadership. *Special characteristics:* 95 awards ($735,088 total): children and siblings of alumni, children of faculty/staff, members of minority groups, religious affiliation. ***Tuition waivers:*** Full or partial for employees or children of employees.

LOANS ***Student loans:*** $5,429,623 (93% need-based, 7% non-need-based). 92% of past graduating class borrowed through all loan programs. *Average indebtedness per student:* $13,929. ***Average need-based loan:*** Freshmen: $3158. Undergraduates: $4196. ***Parent loans:*** $1,270,218 (81% need-based, 19% non-need-based). ***Programs:*** Federal Direct (Subsidized and Unsubsidized Stafford, PLUS), FFEL (Subsidized and Unsubsidized Stafford, PLUS), Perkins, state, college/university.

WORK-STUDY ***Federal work-study:*** Total amount: $680,398; 450 jobs averaging $1511. ***State or other work-study/employment:*** Total amount: $98,700 (75% need-based, 25% non-need-based). 48 part-time jobs averaging $803.

APPLYING FOR FINANCIAL AID ***Required financial aid form:*** FAFSA. ***Financial aid deadline (priority):*** 3/1. ***Notification date:*** Continuous beginning 3/15. Students must reply within 4 weeks of notification.

CONTACT Mr. Richard Brand, Director of Financial Aid, Maryville College, 502 East Lamar Alexander Parkway, Maryville, TN 37804-5907, 865-981-8100 or toll-free 800-597-2687. *E-mail:* richard.brand@maryvillecollege.edu.

MARYVILLE UNIVERSITY OF SAINT LOUIS

St. Louis, MO

Tuition & fees: $21,145 **Average undergraduate aid package: $15,736**

ABOUT THE INSTITUTION Independent, coed. ***Awards:*** bachelor's, master's, and doctoral degrees. 58 undergraduate majors. ***Total enrollment:*** 3,517. Undergraduates: 2,898. Freshmen: 355. Both federal and institutional methodology are used as a basis for awarding need-based institutional aid.

UNDERGRADUATE EXPENSES for 2009–10 ***Application fee:*** $35. ***Comprehensive fee:*** $29,445 includes full-time tuition ($20,495), mandatory fees ($650), and room and board ($8300). ***Part-time tuition:*** $590 per credit hour. ***Part-time fees:*** $137.50 per term.

FRESHMAN FINANCIAL AID (Fall 2008, est.) 281 applied for aid; of those 86% were deemed to have need. 100% of freshmen with need received aid; of those 12% had need fully met. ***Average percent of need met:*** 78% (excluding resources awarded to replace EFC). ***Average financial aid package:*** $14,449 (excluding resources awarded to replace EFC). 21% of all full-time freshmen had no need and received non-need-based gift aid.

UNDERGRADUATE FINANCIAL AID (Fall 2008, est.) 1,472 applied for aid; of those 87% were deemed to have need. 100% of undergraduates with need received aid; of those 11% had need fully met. ***Average percent of need met:*** 72% (excluding resources awarded to replace EFC). ***Average financial aid package:*** $15,736 (excluding resources awarded to replace EFC). 22% of all full-time undergraduates had no need and received non-need-based gift aid.

GIFT AID (NEED-BASED) ***Total amount:*** $10,847,876 (14% federal, 18% state, 65% institutional, 3% external sources). ***Receiving aid:*** Freshmen: 75% (240); all full-time undergraduates: 71% (1,214). ***Average award:*** Freshmen: $8590; Undergraduates: $8091. ***Scholarships, grants, and awards:*** Federal Pell, FSEOG, state, private, college/university gift aid from institutional funds, Academic Competitiveness Grant, National Smart Grant.

GIFT AID (NON-NEED-BASED) ***Total amount:*** $2,366,420 (2% state, 94% institutional, 4% external sources). ***Receiving aid:*** Freshmen: 8% (24). Undergraduates: 6% (98). ***Average award:*** Freshmen: $7472. Undergraduates: $5023. ***Scholarships, grants, and awards by category:*** *Academic interests/achievement:* $7,469,713 total: biological sciences, business, education, general academic interests/achievements, health fields. *Creative arts/performance:* 40 awards ($82,000 total): art/fine arts. *Special achievements/activities:* 239 awards ($281,500 total): community service, general special achievements/activities, leadership. *Special characteristics:* 133 awards ($190,065 total): children and siblings of alumni, children of current students, children of faculty/staff, ethnic background, general special characteristics, members of minority groups, parents of current students, siblings of current students, spouses of current students, twins. ***ROTC:*** Army cooperative.

LOANS ***Student loans:*** $15,331,321 (68% need-based, 32% non-need-based). 77% of past graduating class borrowed through all loan programs. *Average indebtedness per student:* $23,155. ***Average need-based loan:*** Freshmen: $2962. Undergraduates: $3950. ***Parent loans:*** $3,315,033 (34% need-based, 66% non-need-based). ***Programs:*** Federal Direct (Subsidized and Unsubsidized Stafford, PLUS), Perkins, Sallie Mae Signature Loans, KeyBank Loans, TERI Loans, CitiAssist Loans, Wells Fargo Loans, Nelnet, Campus Door Loans.

WORK-STUDY ***Federal work-study:*** Total amount: $249,196; 184 jobs averaging $1610. ***State or other work-study/employment:*** Total amount: $365,123 (72% need-based, 28% non-need-based). 145 part-time jobs averaging $2358.

APPLYING FOR FINANCIAL AID ***Required financial aid form:*** FAFSA. ***Financial aid deadline (priority):*** 3/1. ***Notification date:*** Continuous beginning 3/15. Students must reply by 5/1 or within 2 weeks of notification.

CONTACT Ms. Martha Harbaugh, Director of Financial Aid, Maryville University of Saint Louis, 650 Maryville University Drive, St. Louis, MO 63141-7299, 800-627-9855 Ext. 9360 or toll-free 800-627-9855. *Fax:* 314-529-9199. *E-mail:* fin_aid@maryville.edu.

MARYWOOD UNIVERSITY

Scranton, PA

Tuition & fees: $26,270 **Average undergraduate aid package: $19,653**

ABOUT THE INSTITUTION Independent Roman Catholic, coed. ***Awards:*** bachelor's, master's, and doctoral degrees. 62 undergraduate majors. ***Total enrollment:*** 3,378. Undergraduates: 2,071. Freshmen: 426. Federal methodology is used as a basis for awarding need-based institutional aid.

UNDERGRADUATE EXPENSES for 2009–10 ***Application fee:*** $35. ***Comprehensive fee:*** $37,768 includes full-time tuition ($25,150), mandatory fees ($1120), and room and board ($11,498). ***College room only:*** $6566.

FRESHMAN FINANCIAL AID (Fall 2007) 394 applied for aid; of those 88% were deemed to have need. 100% of freshmen with need received aid; of those 24% had need fully met. ***Average percent of need met:*** 80% (excluding resources awarded to replace EFC). ***Average financial aid package:*** $20,638 (excluding resources awarded to replace EFC). 17% of all full-time freshmen had no need and received non-need-based gift aid.

UNDERGRADUATE FINANCIAL AID (Fall 2007) 1,737 applied for aid; of those 90% were deemed to have need. 100% of undergraduates with need received aid; of those 21% had need fully met. ***Average percent of need met:*** 75% (excluding resources awarded to replace EFC). ***Average financial aid package:*** $19,653 (excluding resources awarded to replace EFC). 18% of all full-time undergraduates had no need and received non-need-based gift aid.

GIFT AID (NEED-BASED) ***Total amount:*** $23,363,959 (10% federal, 13% state, 77% institutional). ***Receiving aid:*** Freshmen: 81% (343); all full-time undergraduates: 80% (1,546). ***Average award:*** Freshmen: $15,206; Undergraduates: $14,004. ***Scholarships, grants, and awards:*** Federal Pell, FSEOG, state, private, college/university gift aid from institutional funds, Federal Nursing, Academic Competitiveness Grant, National Smart Grant, Disadvantaged Student Scholarship.

GIFT AID (NON-NEED-BASED) ***Total amount:*** $850,646 (1% federal, 6% state, 93% external sources). ***Receiving aid:*** Freshmen: 13% (55). Undergraduates: 8% (152). ***Average award:*** Freshmen: $11,038. Undergraduates: $9761. ***Scholarships, grants, and awards by category:*** *Academic interests/achievement:* 01 awards ($1,096,025 total): business, communication, education, foreign languages, general academic interests/achievements, health fields, mathematics, religion/biblical studies. *Creative arts/performance:* 181 awards ($183,760 total): art/fine arts, cinema/film/broadcasting, journalism/publications, music, performing arts, theater/drama. *Special achievements/activities:* 48 awards ($406,069 total): community service, general special achievements/activities, leadership. *Special characteristics:* 1,800 awards ($15,970,600 total): adult students, children and siblings of alumni, children of current students, children of faculty/staff, children of workers in trades, ethnic background, general special characteristics, international students, local/state students, religious affiliation, siblings of current students, spouses of current students. ***ROTC:*** Army cooperative, Air Force cooperative.

LOANS ***Student loans:*** $13,979,811 (45% need-based, 55% non-need-based). 98% of past graduating class borrowed through all loan programs. *Average indebtedness per student:* $35,900. ***Average need-based loan:*** Freshmen: $3661. Undergraduates: $4585. ***Parent loans:*** $2,948,134 (100% non-need-based). ***Programs:*** FFEL (Subsidized and Unsubsidized Stafford, PLUS), Perkins, state.

WORK-STUDY ***Federal work-study:*** Total amount: $1,404,040; jobs available.

APPLYING FOR FINANCIAL AID ***Required financial aid form:*** FAFSA. ***Financial aid deadline (priority):*** 2/15. ***Notification date:*** Continuous. Students must reply by 5/1 or within 3 weeks of notification.

CONTACT Mr. Stanley F. Skrutski, Director of Financial Aid, Marywood University, 2300 Adams Avenue, Scranton, PA 18509-1598, 570-348-6225 or toll-free 866-279-9663. *Fax:* 570-961-4739. *E-mail:* skrutski@ac.marywood.edu.

MASSACHUSETTS COLLEGE OF ART AND DESIGN

Boston, MA

Tuition & fees (MA res): $7900 **Average undergraduate aid package: $8917**

ABOUT THE INSTITUTION State-supported, coed. ***Awards:*** bachelor's and master's degrees and post-bachelor's certificates. 17 undergraduate majors. ***Total enrollment:*** 2,349. Undergraduates: 2,199. Freshmen: 276. Federal methodology is used as a basis for awarding need-based institutional aid.

UNDERGRADUATE EXPENSES for 2008–09 ***Application fee:*** $65. ***Tuition, state resident:*** full-time $7900. ***Tuition, nonresident:*** full-time $23,000. Full-time tuition and fees vary according to course load and degree level. Part-time tuition and fees vary according to course load and degree level. ***College room and board:*** $12,060. Room and board charges vary according to housing facility. ***Payment plan:*** Installment.

FRESHMAN FINANCIAL AID (Fall 2008, est.) 227 applied for aid; of those 78% were deemed to have need. 100% of freshmen with need received aid. ***Average financial aid package:*** $8088 (excluding resources awarded to replace EFC).

UNDERGRADUATE FINANCIAL AID (Fall 2008, est.) 1,126 applied for aid; of those 79% were deemed to have need. 100% of undergraduates with need received aid. ***Average financial aid package:*** $8917 (excluding resources awarded to replace EFC).

GIFT AID (NEED-BASED) ***Total amount:*** $3,479,462 (46% federal, 28% state, 26% institutional). ***Receiving aid:*** Freshmen: 35% (96); all full-time undergraduates: 37% (563). ***Average award:*** Freshmen: $7271; Undergraduates: $5792. ***Scholarships, grants, and awards:*** Federal Pell, FSEOG, state, private, college/university gift aid from institutional funds.

GIFT AID (NON-NEED-BASED) ***Total amount:*** $596,009 (32% institutional, 68% external sources). ***Receiving aid:*** Freshmen: 17% (47). Undergraduates: 8% (118). ***Scholarships, grants, and awards by category:*** *Special characteristics:* children of faculty/staff, children of union members/company employees, veterans. ***Tuition waivers:*** Full or partial for employees or children of employees.

LOANS ***Student loans:*** $10,301,243 (38% need-based, 62% non-need-based). ***Average need-based loan:*** Freshmen: $3611. Undergraduates: $4484. ***Parent loans:*** $12,569,932 (100% non-need-based). ***Programs:*** Federal Direct (Subsidized and Unsubsidized Stafford, PLUS), FFEL (Subsidized and Unsubsidized Stafford), Perkins, state, alternative loans.

WORK-STUDY ***Federal work-study:*** Total amount: $160,000; 187 jobs averaging $860.

APPLYING FOR FINANCIAL AID ***Required financial aid form:*** FAFSA. ***Financial aid deadline (priority):*** 3/1. ***Notification date:*** Continuous beginning 3/15. Students must reply within 3 weeks of notification.

CONTACT Auelio Ramirez, Director of Student Financial Assistance, Massachusetts College of Art and Design, 621 Huntington Avenue, Boston, MA 02115-5882, 617-879-7850. *Fax:* 617-879-7880. *E-mail:* Aurelio.Ramirez@massart.edu.

MASSACHUSETTS COLLEGE OF LIBERAL ARTS

North Adams, MA

Tuition & fees (MA res): $6425 **Average undergraduate aid package: N/A**

ABOUT THE INSTITUTION State-supported, coed. ***Awards:*** bachelor's and master's degrees and post-master's certificates. 18 undergraduate majors. ***Total enrollment:*** 1,942. Undergraduates: 1,584. Freshmen: 332. Federal methodology is used as a basis for awarding need-based institutional aid.

UNDERGRADUATE EXPENSES for 2008–09 ***Application fee:*** $25. ***One-time required fee:*** $140. ***Tuition, state resident:*** full-time $1030; part-time $42.92 per credit. ***Tuition, nonresident:*** full-time $9975; part-time $415.63 per credit. ***Required fees:*** full-time $5395; $183.01 per credit. ***College room and board:*** $7754; ***Room only:*** $3278. Room and board charges vary according to board plan and housing facility.

FRESHMAN FINANCIAL AID (Fall 2008, est.) 301 applied for aid; of those 72% were deemed to have need. 100% of freshmen with need received aid. 29% of all full-time freshmen had no need and received non-need-based gift aid.

UNDERGRADUATE FINANCIAL AID (Fall 2008, est.) 1,172 applied for aid; of those 74% were deemed to have need. 99% of undergraduates with need received aid. 20% of all full-time undergraduates had no need and received non-need-based gift aid.

GIFT AID (NEED-BASED) ***Total amount:*** $3,941,731 (42% federal, 21% state, 28% institutional, 9% external sources). ***Receiving aid:*** Freshmen: 58% (187); all full-time undergraduates: 49% (665). ***Average award:*** Freshmen: $5125; Undergraduates: $4799. ***Scholarships, grants, and awards:*** Federal Pell, FSEOG, state, private, college/university gift aid from institutional funds.

GIFT AID (NON-NEED-BASED) ***Total amount:*** $82,994 (3% state, 56% institutional, 41% external sources). ***Receiving aid:*** Freshmen: 19% (63). Undergraduates: 14% (185). ***Average award:*** Freshmen: $1864. Undergraduates: $2235. ***Scholarships, grants, and awards by category:*** *Academic interests/achievement:* 175 awards ($320,074 total): biological sciences, business, communication, computer science, education, English, general academic interests/achievements, health fields, humanities, mathematics, physical sciences, social sciences. *Creative arts/performance:* 8 awards ($3830 total): applied art and design, art/fine arts, cinema/film/broadcasting, journalism/publications, music, performing arts, theater/drama. *Special achievements/activities:* 17 awards ($21,368 total): general special achievements/activities, leadership, memberships. *Special characteristics:* 12 awards ($9605 total): first-generation college students, general special characteristics, handicapped students, local/state students, members of minority groups, out-of-state students. ***Tuition waivers:*** Full or partial for employees or children of employees, senior citizens.

LOANS ***Student loans:*** $7,313,347 (98% need-based, 2% non-need-based). 37% of past graduating class borrowed through all loan programs. *Average indebtedness per student:* $19,090. ***Parent loans:*** $425,520 (100% need-based). ***Programs:*** FFEL (Subsidized and Unsubsidized Stafford, PLUS), Perkins, state.

WORK-STUDY ***Federal work-study:*** Total amount: $348,669; 222 jobs averaging $1460. ***State or other work-study/employment:*** Total amount: $666,391 (100% non-need-based). Part-time jobs available.

APPLYING FOR FINANCIAL AID ***Required financial aid forms:*** FAFSA, institution's own form. ***Financial aid deadline (priority):*** 3/1. ***Notification date:*** Continuous beginning 3/1. Students must reply by 5/1 or within 2 weeks of notification.

CONTACT Elizabeth M. Petri, Director of Financial Aid, Massachusetts College of Liberal Arts, 375 Church Street, North Adams, MA 01247, 413-662-5219 or toll-free 800-292-6632 (in-state). *Fax:* 413-662-5105. *E-mail:* e.petri@mcla.edu.

MASSACHUSETTS COLLEGE OF PHARMACY AND HEALTH SCIENCES

Boston, MA

Tuition & fees: $23,620 **Average undergraduate aid package: $12,564**

ABOUT THE INSTITUTION Independent, coed. ***Awards:*** bachelor's, master's, doctoral, and first professional degrees and post-bachelor's certificates. 13 undergraduate majors. ***Total enrollment:*** 3,909. Undergraduates: 2,746. Freshmen: 604. Federal methodology is used as a basis for awarding need-based institutional aid.

UNDERGRADUATE EXPENSES for 2008–09 ***Application fee:*** $70. ***Comprehensive fee:*** $35,220 includes full-time tuition ($22,900), mandatory fees ($720), and room and board ($11,600). Full-time tuition and fees vary according to course load, degree level, location, program, and student level. Room and board charges vary according to housing facility. ***Part-time tuition:*** $840 per credit. ***Part-time fees:*** $180 per term. ***Payment plan:*** Installment.

FRESHMAN FINANCIAL AID (Fall 2008, est.) 541 applied for aid; of those 88% were deemed to have need. 100% of freshmen with need received aid; of those 61% had need fully met. ***Average percent of need met:*** 55% (excluding resources awarded to replace EFC). ***Average financial aid package:*** $16,469 (excluding resources awarded to replace EFC). 16% of all full-time freshmen had no need and received non-need-based gift aid.

UNDERGRADUATE FINANCIAL AID (Fall 2008, est.) 1,956 applied for aid; of those 91% were deemed to have need. 100% of undergraduates with need received aid; of those 55% had need fully met. ***Average percent of need met:*** 44% (excluding resources awarded to replace EFC). ***Average financial aid package:*** $12,564 (excluding resources awarded to replace EFC). 17% of all full-time undergraduates had no need and received non-need-based gift aid.

GIFT AID (NEED-BASED) ***Total amount:*** $14,459,939 (17% federal, 5% state, 73% institutional, 5% external sources). ***Receiving aid:*** Freshmen: 76% (430); all full-time undergraduates: 65% (1,414). ***Average award:*** Freshmen: $11,000; Undergraduates: $8747. ***Scholarships, grants, and awards:*** Federal Pell, FSEOG, state, private, college/university gift aid from institutional funds.

GIFT AID (NON-NEED-BASED) ***Total amount:*** $123,640 (58% institutional, 42% external sources). ***Receiving aid:*** Undergraduates: 2% (36). ***Average award:*** Freshmen: $15,040. Undergraduates: $13,226. ***Scholarships, grants, and awards by category:*** *Academic interests/achievement:* general academic interests/achievements. *Special characteristics:* children of faculty/staff. ***Tuition waivers:*** Full or partial for employees or children of employees.

LOANS ***Student loans:*** $39,278,755 (25% need-based, 75% non-need-based). ***Average need-based loan:*** Freshmen: $6399. Undergraduates: $5739. ***Parent loans:*** $3,538,112 (100% non-need-based). ***Programs:*** Federal Direct (Subsidized and Unsubsidized Stafford, PLUS), FFEL (Subsidized and Unsubsidized Stafford, PLUS), Perkins, Health Professions Loan.

WORK-STUDY ***Federal work-study:*** Total amount: $585,450; jobs available.

APPLYING FOR FINANCIAL AID ***Required financial aid form:*** FAFSA. ***Financial aid deadline:*** 3/15. ***Notification date:*** Continuous. Students must reply by 5/1 or within 2 weeks of notification.

CONTACT Ms. Carrie Glass, Executive Director of Enrollment Services, Massachusetts College of Pharmacy and Health Sciences, 179 Longwood Avenue, Boston, MA 02115-5896, 617-732-2199 or toll-free 800-225-5506 (out-of-state). *Fax:* 617-732-2082. *E-mail:* carrie.glass@mcphs.edu.

MASSACHUSETTS INSTITUTE OF TECHNOLOGY

Cambridge, MA

Tuition & fees: $37,782 **Average undergraduate aid package: $32,437**

ABOUT THE INSTITUTION Independent, coed. ***Awards:*** bachelor's, master's, and doctoral degrees. 34 undergraduate majors. ***Total enrollment:*** 10,299. Undergraduates: 4,153. Freshmen: 1,048. Both federal and institutional methodology are used as a basis for awarding need-based institutional aid.

UNDERGRADUATE EXPENSES for 2009–10 ***Application fee:*** $75. ***Comprehensive fee:*** $49,142 includes full-time tuition ($37,510), mandatory fees ($272), and room and board ($11,360). ***College room only:*** $6850.

FRESHMAN FINANCIAL AID (Fall 2007) 853 applied for aid; of those 78% were deemed to have need. 100% of freshmen with need received aid; of those 100% had need fully met. ***Average percent of need met:*** 100% (excluding resources awarded to replace EFC). ***Average financial aid package:*** $32,129 (excluding resources awarded to replace EFC).

UNDERGRADUATE FINANCIAL AID (Fall 2007) 3,037 applied for aid; of those 84% were deemed to have need. 100% of undergraduates with need received aid; of those 100% had need fully met. ***Average percent of need met:*** 100% (excluding resources awarded to replace EFC). ***Average financial aid package:*** $32,437 (excluding resources awarded to replace EFC).

GIFT AID (NEED-BASED) ***Total amount:*** $74,880,992 (8% federal, 87% institutional, 5% external sources). ***Receiving aid:*** Freshmen: 60% (649); all full-time undergraduates: 59% (2,452). ***Average award:*** Freshmen: $30,232; Undergraduates: $30,058. ***Scholarships, grants, and awards:*** Federal Pell, FSEOG, state, private, college/university gift aid from institutional funds.

GIFT AID (NON-NEED-BASED) ***Total amount:*** $4,323,442 (25% federal, 75% external sources). ***Receiving aid:*** Freshmen: 2% (22). Undergraduates: 2% (64). ***ROTC:*** Army, Naval, Air Force.

LOANS ***Student loans:*** $9,636,253 (58% need-based, 42% non-need-based). 49% of past graduating class borrowed through all loan programs. *Average indebtedness per student:* $14,148. ***Average need-based loan:*** Freshmen: $1978. Undergraduates: $2364. ***Parent loans:*** $6,931,074 (6% need-based, 94% non-need-based). ***Programs:*** Federal Direct (Subsidized and Unsubsidized Stafford, PLUS), Perkins, college/university.

WORK-STUDY ***Federal work-study:*** Total amount: $1,841,160; 679 jobs averaging $2304. ***State or other work-study/employment:*** Total amount: $2,034,639 (13% need-based, 87% non-need-based). 1,157 part-time jobs averaging $2017.

APPLYING FOR FINANCIAL AID ***Required financial aid forms:*** FAFSA, CSS Financial Aid PROFILE, noncustodial (divorced/separated) parent's statement, business/farm supplement, parents' complete federal income returns from prior year and W-2 forms. ***Financial aid deadline:*** 2/15 (priority: 2/15). ***Notification date:*** 4/1. Students must reply by 5/1.

CONTACT Elizabeth Hicks, Interim Executive Director of Student Financial Services, Massachusetts Institute of Technology, 77 Massachusetts Avenue, Room 11-320, Cambridge, MA 02139-4307, 617-253-4971. *Fax:* 617-253-9859. *E-mail:* finaid@mit.edu.

MASSACHUSETTS MARITIME ACADEMY

Buzzards Bay, MA

CONTACT Mrs. Elizabeth Benway, Director of Financial Aid, Massachusetts Maritime Academy, 101 Academy Drive, Buzzards Bay, MA 02532, 508-830-5086 or toll-free 800-544-3411. *Fax:* 508-830-5077. *E-mail:* ebenway@maritime.edu.

THE MASTER'S COLLEGE AND SEMINARY

Santa Clarita, CA

Tuition & fees: $24,650 **Average undergraduate aid package: $18,352**

ABOUT THE INSTITUTION Independent nondenominational, coed. ***Awards:*** bachelor's, master's, doctoral, and first professional degrees and first professional certificates. 47 undergraduate majors. ***Total enrollment:*** 1,439. Undergraduates: 1,039. Freshmen: 192. Federal methodology is used as a basis for awarding need-based institutional aid.

UNDERGRADUATE EXPENSES for 2009–10 ***Application fee:*** $40. ***Comprehensive fee:*** $32,650 includes full-time tuition ($24,280), mandatory fees ($370), and room and board ($8000). ***College room only:*** $4480. ***Part-time tuition:*** $1015 per credit hour.

FRESHMAN FINANCIAL AID (Fall 2008, est.) 146 applied for aid; of those 80% were deemed to have need. 100% of freshmen with need received aid; of those 23% had need fully met. ***Average percent of need met:*** 72% (excluding resources awarded to replace EFC). ***Average financial aid package:*** $17,349 (excluding resources awarded to replace EFC). 30% of all full-time freshmen had no need and received non-need-based gift aid.

UNDERGRADUATE FINANCIAL AID (Fall 2008, est.) 686 applied for aid; of those 88% were deemed to have need. 100% of undergraduates with need received aid; of those 21% had need fully met. ***Average percent of need met:*** 74% (excluding resources awarded to replace EFC). ***Average financial aid package:*** $18,352 (excluding resources awarded to replace EFC). 21% of all full-time undergraduates had no need and received non-need-based gift aid.

GIFT AID (NEED-BASED) ***Total amount:*** $7,072,696 (13% federal, 22% state, 51% institutional, 14% external sources). ***Receiving aid:*** Freshmen: 60% (113); all full-time undergraduates: 70% (572). ***Average award:*** Freshmen: $13,041; Undergraduates: $13,159. ***Scholarships, grants, and awards:*** Federal Pell, FSEOG, state, private, college/university gift aid from institutional funds.

GIFT AID (NON-NEED-BASED) ***Total amount:*** $2,298,102 (71% institutional, 29% external sources). ***Receiving aid:*** Freshmen: 11% (21). Undergraduates: 9% (73). ***Average award:*** Freshmen: $8447. Undergraduates: $8131. ***Scholarships, grants, and awards by category:*** *Academic interests/achievement:* 490 awards ($2,923,571 total): biological sciences, business, education, general academic interests/achievements, mathematics, physical sciences, religion/biblical studies, social sciences. *Creative arts/performance:* 89 awards ($289,460 total): music. *Special achievements/activities:* 73 awards ($454,433 total): leadership. *Special characteristics:* 145 awards ($989,607 total): children and siblings of alumni, children of faculty/staff, general special characteristics, international students, relatives of clergy.

LOANS ***Student loans:*** $5,084,513 (73% need-based, 27% non-need-based). 58% of past graduating class borrowed through all loan programs. *Average indebtedness per student:* $17,800. ***Average need-based loan:*** Freshmen: $4406. Undergraduates: $5571. ***Parent loans:*** $1,422,660 (45% need-based, 55% non-need-based). ***Programs:*** FFEL (Subsidized and Unsubsidized Stafford, PLUS), Perkins, alternative loans.

WORK-STUDY ***Federal work-study:*** Total amount: $73,859; 48 jobs averaging $3113. ***State or other work-study/employment:*** Total amount: $795,875 (79% need-based, 21% non-need-based). Part-time jobs available.

ATHLETIC AWARDS Total amount: $1,306,092 (46% need-based, 54% non-need-based).

APPLYING FOR FINANCIAL AID ***Required financial aid forms:*** FAFSA, institution's own form, state aid form. ***Financial aid deadline (priority):*** 3/2. ***Notification date:*** Continuous. Students must reply by 5/1 or within 2 weeks of notification.

CONTACT Gary Edwards, Director of Financial Aid, The Master's College and Seminary, 21726 Placerita Canyon Road, Santa Clarita, CA 91321-1200, 661-259-3540 Ext. 3391 or toll-free 800-568-6248. *Fax:* 661-362-2693. *E-mail:* gedwards@masters.edu.

MAYVILLE STATE UNIVERSITY

Mayville, ND

Tuition & fees (ND res): $5654 **Average undergraduate aid package: $5679**

ABOUT THE INSTITUTION State-supported, coed. ***Awards:*** associate and bachelor's degrees. 35 undergraduate majors. ***Total enrollment:*** 789. Undergraduates: 789. Freshmen: 90. Federal methodology is used as a basis for awarding need-based institutional aid.

UNDERGRADUATE EXPENSES for 2008–09 ***Application fee:*** $35. ***Tuition, state resident:*** full-time $3985; part-time $166 per hour. ***Tuition, nonresident:*** full-time $5977; part-time $249 per hour. ***Required fees:*** full-time $1669; $70 per hour. Full-time tuition and fees vary according to course load and reciprocity agreements. Part-time tuition and fees vary according to course load and reciprocity agreements. ***College room and board:*** $4272; ***Room only:*** $1730. Room and board charges vary according to board plan and housing facility. ***Payment plan:*** Installment.

FRESHMAN FINANCIAL AID (Fall 2008, est.) 86 applied for aid; of those 92% were deemed to have need. 100% of freshmen with need received aid; of those 51% had need fully met. ***Average percent of need met:*** 100% (excluding resources awarded to replace EFC). ***Average financial aid package:*** $4958 (excluding resources awarded to replace EFC).

UNDERGRADUATE FINANCIAL AID (Fall 2008, est.) 408 applied for aid; of those 86% were deemed to have need. 100% of undergraduates with need received aid; of those 34% had need fully met. ***Average percent of need met:*** 69% (excluding resources awarded to replace EFC). ***Average financial aid package:*** $5679 (excluding resources awarded to replace EFC).

GIFT AID (NEED-BASED) ***Total amount:*** $931,847 (72% federal, 7% state, 14% institutional, 7% external sources). ***Receiving aid:*** Freshmen: 79% (69); all full-time undergraduates: 64% (268). ***Average award:*** Freshmen: $2815; Undergraduates: $2869. ***Scholarships, grants, and awards:*** Federal Pell, FSEOG, state, private, college/university gift aid from institutional funds.

GIFT AID (NON-NEED-BASED) ***Total amount:*** $71,127 (2% federal, 74% institutional, 24% external sources). ***Receiving aid:*** Freshmen: 5% (4). Undergraduates: 1% (6). ***Average award:*** Freshmen: $1005. Undergraduates: $990. ***Scholarships, grants, and awards by category:*** *Academic interests/achievement:* 260 awards ($260,000 total): biological sciences, business, computer science, education, English, general academic interests/achievements, health fields, library science, mathematics, physical sciences, premedicine, social sciences. *Creative arts/performance:* 60 awards ($22,000 total): music, theater/drama. *Special characteristics:* 116 awards ($192,000 total): international students, local/state students, members of minority groups, out-of-state students. ***Tuition waivers:*** Full or partial for minority students, senior citizens. ***ROTC:*** Army cooperative, Air Force cooperative.

LOANS ***Student loans:*** $2,878,689 (55% need-based, 45% non-need-based). 89% of past graduating class borrowed through all loan programs. *Average indebtedness per student:* $19,338. ***Average need-based loan:*** Freshmen: $2591. Undergraduates: $3468. ***Parent loans:*** $339,540 (8% need-based, 92% non-need-based). ***Programs:*** FFEL (Subsidized and Unsubsidized Stafford, PLUS), Perkins, college/university.

WORK-STUDY ***Federal work-study:*** Total amount: $54,616; 50 jobs averaging $1200.

ATHLETIC AWARDS Total amount: $140,924 (46% need-based, 54% non-need-based).

APPLYING FOR FINANCIAL AID ***Required financial aid form:*** FAFSA. ***Financial aid deadline (priority):*** 2/15. ***Notification date:*** Continuous beginning 5/1. Students must reply within 2 weeks of notification.

CONTACT Ms. Shirley Hanson, Director of Financial Aid, Mayville State University, 330 3rd Street NE, Mayville, ND 58257-1299, 701-788-4767 or toll-free 800-437-4104. *Fax:* 701-788-4818. *E-mail:* shirley.hanson@mayvillestate.edu.

McDANIEL COLLEGE

Westminster, MD

Tuition & fees: $30,780 **Average undergraduate aid package: $23,576**

ABOUT THE INSTITUTION Independent, coed. ***Awards:*** bachelor's and master's degrees and post-bachelor's certificates. 28 undergraduate majors. ***Total enrollment:*** 3,896. Undergraduates: 1,772. Freshmen: 421.

UNDERGRADUATE EXPENSES for 2008–09 ***Application fee:*** $50. ***Comprehensive fee:*** $36,930 includes full-time tuition ($30,780) and room and board ($6150). ***College room only:*** $3300. Room and board charges vary according to board plan and housing facility. ***Part-time tuition:*** $962 per credit. Part-time tuition and fees vary according to reciprocity agreements. ***Payment plans:*** Tuition prepayment, installment.

FRESHMAN FINANCIAL AID (Fall 2008, est.) 340 applied for aid; of those 84% were deemed to have need. 100% of freshmen with need received aid; of those 30% had need fully met. ***Average percent of need met:*** 93% (excluding resources awarded to replace EFC). ***Average financial aid package:*** $22,446 (excluding resources awarded to replace EFC). 32% of all full-time freshmen had no need and received non-need-based gift aid.

UNDERGRADUATE FINANCIAL AID (Fall 2008, est.) 1,274 applied for aid; of those 87% were deemed to have need. 100% of undergraduates with need received aid; of those 30% had need fully met. ***Average percent of need met:*** 93% (excluding resources awarded to replace EFC). ***Average financial aid package:*** $23,576 (excluding resources awarded to replace EFC). 34% of all full-time undergraduates had no need and received non-need-based gift aid.

GIFT AID (NEED-BASED) ***Total amount:*** $19,769,217 (8% federal, 9% state, 83% institutional). ***Receiving aid:*** Freshmen: 66% (279); all full-time undergraduates: 64% (1,075). ***Average award:*** Freshmen: $12,559; Undergraduates: $10,995. ***Scholarships, grants, and awards:*** Federal Pell, FSEOG, state, private, college/university gift aid from institutional funds.

GIFT AID (NON-NEED-BASED) ***Total amount:*** $7,211,471 (4% state, 91% institutional, 5% external sources). ***Average award:*** Freshmen: $13,368. Undergraduates: $11,778. ***Scholarships, grants, and awards by category:*** *Academic interests/achievement:* 1,101 awards ($14,589,802 total): general academic interests/achievements. *Special achievements/activities:* 5 awards ($10,000 total): junior miss, leadership. *Special characteristics:* 283 awards ($555,200 total): general special characteristics, local/state students, previous college experience, siblings of current students. ***Tuition waivers:*** Full or partial for employees or children of employees. ***ROTC:*** Army.

LOANS ***Student loans:*** $8,485,630 (46% need-based, 54% non-need-based). 65% of past graduating class borrowed through all loan programs. *Average indebtedness per student:* $25,345. ***Average need-based loan:*** Freshmen: $4680. Undergraduates: $4950. ***Parent loans:*** $2,559,731 (100% non-need-based). ***Programs:*** FFEL (Subsidized and Unsubsidized Stafford, PLUS), Perkins, college/university.

WORK-STUDY ***Federal work-study:*** Total amount: $206,429; 206 jobs averaging $814. ***State or other work-study/employment:*** Total amount: $204,961 (100% non-need-based). 261 part-time jobs averaging $821.

APPLYING FOR FINANCIAL AID ***Required financial aid forms:*** FAFSA, institution's own form, federal income tax form(s). ***Financial aid deadline (priority):*** 3/1. ***Notification date:*** Continuous beginning 3/1. Students must reply by 5/1 or within 2 weeks of notification.

CONTACT Patricia Williams, Financial Aid Office, McDaniel College, 2 College Hill, Westminster, MD 21157-4390, 410-857-2233 or toll-free 800-638-5005. *Fax:* 410-857-2729. *E-mail:* finaid@mcdaniel.edu.

McKENDREE UNIVERSITY

Lebanon, IL

Tuition & fees: $21,270 **Average undergraduate aid package: $16,988**

ABOUT THE INSTITUTION Independent religious, coed. ***Awards:*** bachelor's and master's degrees. 50 undergraduate majors. ***Total enrollment:*** 3,327. Undergraduates: 2,308. Freshmen: 308. Federal methodology is used as a basis for awarding need-based institutional aid.

UNDERGRADUATE EXPENSES for 2008–09 ***Application fee:*** $40. ***Comprehensive fee:*** $29,120 includes full-time tuition ($20,570), mandatory fees ($700), and room and board ($7850). ***College room only:*** $4180. Full-time tuition and fees vary according to course load and degree level. Room and board charges vary according to board plan and housing facility. ***Part-time tuition:*** $690 per hour. Part-time tuition and fees vary according to course load and degree level. ***Payment plan:*** Installment.

FRESHMAN FINANCIAL AID (Fall 2008, est.) 295 applied for aid; of those 91% were deemed to have need. 99% of freshmen with need received aid; of those 27% had need fully met. ***Average percent of need met:*** 87% (excluding resources awarded to replace EFC). ***Average financial aid package:*** $20,394 (excluding resources awarded to replace EFC). 14% of all full-time freshmen had no need and received non-need-based gift aid.

UNDERGRADUATE FINANCIAL AID (Fall 2008, est.) 1,380 applied for aid; of those 89% were deemed to have need. 98% of undergraduates with need received aid; of those 31% had need fully met. ***Average percent of need met:*** 80% (excluding resources awarded to replace EFC). ***Average financial aid package:*** $16,988 (excluding resources awarded to replace EFC). 15% of all full-time undergraduates had no need and received non-need-based gift aid.

GIFT AID (NEED-BASED) ***Total amount:*** $14,820,551 (15% federal, 20% state, 58% institutional, 7% external sources). ***Receiving aid:*** Freshmen: 83% (266); all full-time undergraduates: 77% (1,171). ***Average award:*** Freshmen: $16,620; Undergraduates: $13,413. ***Scholarships, grants, and awards:*** Federal Pell, FSEOG, state, private, college/university gift aid from institutional funds.

GIFT AID (NON-NEED-BASED) ***Total amount:*** $2,788,625 (1% state, 82% institutional, 17% external sources). ***Receiving aid:*** Freshmen: 11% (34). Undergraduates: 10% (150). ***Average award:*** Freshmen: $8189. Undergraduates: $8236. ***Scholarships, grants, and awards by category:*** *Academic interests/achievement:* 764 awards ($3,996,173 total): biological sciences, business, general academic interests/achievements, religion/biblical studies. *Creative arts/performance:* 142 awards ($356,220 total): music. *Special achievements/activities:* 57 awards ($97,500 total): cheerleading/drum major, community service, leadership. *Special characteristics:* 50 awards ($327,175 total): children of faculty/staff, general special characteristics, out-of-state students, religious affiliation. ***Tuition waivers:*** Full or partial for employees or children of employees. ***ROTC:*** Army cooperative, Air Force cooperative.

LOANS ***Student loans:*** $10,340,874 (59% need-based, 41% non-need-based). 72% of past graduating class borrowed through all loan programs. *Average indebtedness per student:* $18,291. ***Average need-based loan:*** Freshmen: $3502. Undergraduates: $4186. ***Parent loans:*** $2,921,622 (27% need-based, 73% non-need-based). ***Programs:*** Federal Direct (Subsidized and Unsubsidized Stafford, PLUS), Perkins.

WORK-STUDY ***Federal work-study:*** Total amount: $640,607; 492 jobs averaging $1646. ***State or other work-study/employment:*** Total amount: $166,709 (5% need-based, 95% non-need-based). 139 part-time jobs averaging $1343.

ATHLETIC AWARDS Total amount: $2,493,659 (50% need-based, 50% non-need-based).

APPLYING FOR FINANCIAL AID ***Required financial aid form:*** FAFSA. ***Financial aid deadline (priority):*** 5/31. ***Notification date:*** Continuous.

CONTACT James A. Myers, Director of Financial Aid, McKendree University, 701 College Road, Lebanon, IL 62254-1299, 618-537-6529 or toll-free 800-232-7228 Ext. 6831. *Fax:* 618-537-6530. *E-mail:* jamyers@mckendree.edu.

McMURRY UNIVERSITY

Abilene, TX

Tuition & fees: $17,985 **Average undergraduate aid package: $17,216**

ABOUT THE INSTITUTION Independent United Methodist, coed. ***Awards:*** bachelor's degrees. 42 undergraduate majors. ***Total enrollment:*** 1,515. Undergraduates: 1,515. Freshmen: 332. Federal methodology is used as a basis for awarding need-based institutional aid.

UNDERGRADUATE EXPENSES for 2008–09 ***Application fee:*** $20. ***One-time required fee:*** $150. ***Comprehensive fee:*** $24,642 includes full-time tuition ($17,225), mandatory fees ($760), and room and board ($6657). ***College room only:*** $3216. Full-time tuition and fees vary according to course load. Room and board charges vary according to board plan and housing facility. ***Part-time tuition:*** $535 per semester hour. Part-time tuition and fees vary according to course load. ***Payment plan:*** Installment.

FRESHMAN FINANCIAL AID (Fall 2008, est.) 313 applied for aid; of those 90% were deemed to have need. 100% of freshmen with need received aid; of those 20% had need fully met. ***Average percent of need met:*** 92% (excluding resources awarded to replace EFC). ***Average financial aid package:*** $18,989 (excluding resources awarded to replace EFC). 9% of all full-time freshmen had no need and received non-need-based gift aid.

UNDERGRADUATE FINANCIAL AID (Fall 2008, est.) 1,097 applied for aid; of those 91% were deemed to have need. 100% of undergraduates with need received aid; of those 20% had need fully met. ***Average percent of need met:*** 88% (excluding resources awarded to replace EFC). ***Average financial aid package:*** $17,216 (excluding resources awarded to replace EFC). 8% of all full-time undergraduates had no need and received non-need-based gift aid.

GIFT AID (NEED-BASED) ***Total amount:*** $9,849,750 (25% federal, 25% state, 46% institutional, 4% external sources). ***Receiving aid:*** Freshmen: 82% (272); all full-time undergraduates: 78% (938). ***Average award:*** Freshmen: $11,389; Undergraduates: $9441. ***Scholarships, grants, and awards:*** Federal Pell, FSEOG, state, private, college/university gift aid from institutional funds, Academic Competitiveness Grant, National Smart Grant.

GIFT AID (NON-NEED-BASED) ***Total amount:*** $3,903,925 (6% federal, 3% state, 90% institutional, 1% external sources). ***Receiving aid:*** Freshmen: 56% (185). Undergraduates: 51% (616). ***Average award:*** Freshmen: $6650. Undergraduates: $5293. ***Scholarships, grants, and awards by category:*** *Academic interests/achievement:* 93 awards ($233,369 total): biological sciences, business, communication, computer science, education, English, general academic interests/achievements, mathematics, physical sciences, premedicine, religion/biblical studies, social sciences. *Creative arts/performance:* 19 awards ($36,405 total): art/fine arts, music, theater/drama. *Special achievements/activities:* 79 awards ($112,859 total): general special achievements/activities, junior miss. *Special characteristics:* 481 awards ($2,850,394 total): children of faculty/staff, ethnic background, international students, local/state students, out-of-state students, previous college experience, relatives of clergy, religious affiliation, veterans. ***Tuition waivers:*** Full or partial for employees or children of employees. ***ROTC:*** Air Force cooperative.

LOANS ***Student loans:*** $9,253,723 (40% need-based, 60% non-need-based). 83% of past graduating class borrowed through all loan programs. *Average indebtedness per student:* $25,338. ***Average need-based loan:*** Freshmen: $3165. Undergraduates: $4296. ***Parent loans:*** $575,333 (100% non-need-based). ***Programs:*** FFEL (Subsidized and Unsubsidized Stafford, PLUS), Perkins, state, alternative loans, United Methodist Loan, Bonner Price Loan.

WORK-STUDY ***Federal work-study:*** Total amount: $797,274; 280 jobs averaging $1512. ***State or other work-study/employment:*** Total amount: $179,391 (30% need-based, 70% non-need-based). 93 part-time jobs averaging $1666.

APPLYING FOR FINANCIAL AID ***Required financial aid form:*** FAFSA. ***Financial aid deadline (priority):*** 3/15. ***Notification date:*** Continuous. Students must reply within 3 weeks of notification.

CONTACT Rachel Atkins, Director of Financial Aid, McMurry University, Box 908, Abilene, TX 79697, 325-793-4709 or toll-free 800-477-0077. *Fax:* 325-793-4718. *E-mail:* atkinsr@mcmurryadm.mcm.edu.

McNALLY SMITH COLLEGE OF MUSIC

Saint Paul, MN

CONTACT Financial Aid Office, McNally Smith College of Music, 19 Exchange Street East, Saint Paul, MN 55101, 651-291-0177 or toll-free 800-594-9500.

McNEESE STATE UNIVERSITY

Lake Charles, LA

CONTACT Ms. Taina J. Savoit, Director of Financial Aid, McNeese State University, PO Box 93260, Lake Charles, LA 70609-3260, 337-475-5065 or toll-free 800-622-3352. *Fax:* 337-475-5068. *E-mail:* tsavoit@mail.mcneese.edu.

McPHERSON COLLEGE

McPherson, KS

Tuition & fees: $17,200 **Average undergraduate aid package: $18,134**

ABOUT THE INSTITUTION Independent religious, coed. ***Awards:*** associate and bachelor's degrees. 29 undergraduate majors. ***Total enrollment:*** 544. Undergraduates: 544. Federal methodology is used as a basis for awarding need-based institutional aid.

UNDERGRADUATE EXPENSES for 2008–09 ***Application fee:*** $25. ***Comprehensive fee:*** $23,700 includes full-time tuition ($16,900), mandatory fees ($300), and room and board ($6500). ***College room only:*** $2600. Full-time tuition and fees vary according to course load and program. ***Part-time tuition:*** $260 per hour. ***Part-time fees:*** $30 per hour. ***Payment plan:*** Installment.

FRESHMAN FINANCIAL AID (Fall 2007) 124 applied for aid; of those 82% were deemed to have need. 100% of freshmen with need received aid; of those 21% had need fully met. ***Average percent of need met:*** 84% (excluding resources awarded to replace EFC). ***Average financial aid package:*** $18,197 (excluding resources awarded to replace EFC). 19% of all full-time freshmen had no need and received non-need-based gift aid.

UNDERGRADUATE FINANCIAL AID (Fall 2007) 463 applied for aid; of those 86% were deemed to have need. 100% of undergraduates with need received aid; of those 28% had need fully met. ***Average percent of need met:*** 86% (excluding resources awarded to replace EFC). ***Average financial aid package:*** $18,134 (excluding resources awarded to replace EFC). 16% of all full-time undergraduates had no need and received non-need-based gift aid.

GIFT AID (NEED-BASED) ***Total amount:*** $1,955,614 (38% federal, 19% state, 43% institutional). ***Receiving aid:*** Freshmen: 74% (96); all full-time undergraduates: 75% (364). ***Average award:*** Freshmen: $4965; Undergraduates: $5170. ***Scholarships, grants, and awards:*** Federal Pell, FSEOG, state, private, college/university gift aid from institutional funds.

GIFT AID (NON-NEED-BASED) ***Total amount:*** $2,912,816 (96% institutional, 4% external sources). ***Receiving aid:*** Freshmen: 79% (102). Undergraduates: 81% (393). ***Average award:*** Freshmen: $8138. Undergraduates: $7974. ***Scholarships, grants, and awards by category:*** *Academic interests/achievement:* 181 awards ($625,500 total): general academic interests/achievements. *Creative arts/performance:* 12 awards ($50,700 total): art/fine arts, journalism/publications, music, theater/drama. *Special achievements/activities:* cheerleading/drum major, community service, religious involvement. *Special characteristics:* 28 awards ($48,500 total): local/state students, religious affiliation. ***Tuition waivers:*** Full or partial for employees or children of employees.

LOANS ***Student loans:*** $3,348,875 (73% need-based, 27% non-need-based). 86% of past graduating class borrowed through all loan programs. *Average indebtedness per student:* $24,024. ***Average need-based loan:*** Freshmen: $5059. Undergraduates: $6287. ***Parent loans:*** $525,573 (100% non-need-based). ***Programs:*** FFEL (Subsidized and Unsubsidized Stafford, PLUS), Perkins.

WORK-STUDY ***Federal work-study:*** Total amount: $215,907; 223 jobs averaging $926.

ATHLETIC AWARDS Total amount: $819,891 (100% non-need-based).

APPLYING FOR FINANCIAL AID ***Required financial aid forms:*** FAFSA, state aid form. ***Financial aid deadline (priority):*** 3/1. ***Notification date:*** Continuous beginning 3/1. Students must reply within 3 weeks of notification.

CONTACT Mr. Steve Frick, Director of Admissions and Financial Aid, McPherson College, 1600 E. Euclid, McPherson, KS 67460-1402, 620-242-0400 Ext. 1270 or toll-free 800-365-7402. *Fax:* 620-241-8443. *E-mail:* fricks@mcpherson.edu.

MEDAILLE COLLEGE

Buffalo, NY

CONTACT Ms. Catherine Buzanski, Director of Financial Aid, Medaille College, 18 Agassiz Circle, Buffalo, NY 14214-2695, 716-880-2179 or toll-free 800-292-1582 (in-state). *Fax:* 716-884-0291. *E-mail:* cbuzanski@medaille.edu.

MEDCENTER ONE COLLEGE OF NURSING

Bismarck, ND

Tuition & fees: $10,017 **Average undergraduate aid package: $11,879**

ABOUT THE INSTITUTION Independent, coed, primarily women. ***Awards:*** bachelor's degrees. 1 undergraduate major. ***Total enrollment:*** 91. Undergraduates: 91. Both federal and institutional methodology are used as a basis for awarding need-based institutional aid.

UNDERGRADUATE EXPENSES for 2008–09 ***Application fee:*** $40. ***Tuition:*** full-time $10,017; part-time $386 per credit. ***Required fees:*** $15.01 per credit or $199.50 per term. Part-time tuition and fees vary according to course load.

UNDERGRADUATE FINANCIAL AID (Fall 2008, est.) 89 applied for aid; of those 64% were deemed to have need. 100% of undergraduates with need received aid; of those 54% had need fully met. ***Average percent of need met:*** 92% (excluding resources awarded to replace EFC). ***Average financial aid package:*** $11,879 (excluding resources awarded to replace EFC). 16% of all full-time undergraduates had no need and received non-need-based gift aid.

GIFT AID (NEED-BASED) ***Total amount:*** $146,151 (70% federal, 13% state, 14% institutional, 3% external sources). ***Receiving aid:*** All full-time undergraduates: 44% (39). ***Average award:*** Undergraduates: $2661. ***Scholarships, grants, and awards:*** Federal Pell, FSEOG, state, private, college/university gift aid from institutional funds.

GIFT AID (NON-NEED-BASED) ***Total amount:*** $22,169 (49% institutional, 51% external sources). ***Receiving aid:*** Undergraduates: 15% (13). ***Average award:*** Undergraduates: $673. ***Scholarships, grants, and awards by category:*** *Academic interests/achievement:* 13 awards ($8999 total): general academic interests/achievements, health fields. *Special achievements/activities:* 19 awards: memberships. *Special characteristics:* 27 awards ($20,324 total): children and siblings of alumni, general special characteristics, local/state students.

LOANS ***Student loans:*** $1,116,341 (20% need-based, 80% non-need-based). ***Average need-based loan:*** Undergraduates: $4275. ***Programs:*** FFEL (Subsidized and Unsubsidized Stafford, PLUS), Perkins, Federal Nursing, college/university.

WORK-STUDY ***Federal work-study:*** Total amount: $4500; 5 jobs averaging $1000.

APPLYING FOR FINANCIAL AID ***Financial aid deadline (priority):*** 3/15. ***Notification date:*** Continuous beginning 5/1. Students must reply within 2 weeks of notification.

CONTACT Ms. Janell Thomas, Financial Aid Director, Medcenter One College of Nursing, 512 North 7th Street, Bismarck, ND 58501-4494, 701-323-6270. *Fax:* 701-323-6289. *E-mail:* jthomas@mohs.org.

MEDCENTRAL COLLEGE OF NURSING

Mansfield, OH

CONTACT Financial Aid Office, MedCentral College of Nursing, 335 Glessner Avenue, Mansfield, OH 44903, 419-520-2600 or toll-free 877-656-4360.

MEDGAR EVERS COLLEGE OF THE CITY UNIVERSITY OF NEW YORK

Brooklyn, NY

Tuition & fees (NY res): $4302 Average undergraduate aid package: $3311

ABOUT THE INSTITUTION State and locally supported, coed. ***Awards:*** associate and bachelor's degrees. 13 undergraduate majors. ***Total enrollment:*** 6,037. Undergraduates: 6,037. Freshmen: 1,049. Federal methodology is used as a basis for awarding need-based institutional aid.

UNDERGRADUATE EXPENSES for 2008–09 ***Application fee:*** $65. ***Tuition, state resident:*** full-time $4000; part-time $170 per credit. ***Tuition, nonresident:*** full-time $10,800; part-time $360 per credit. ***Required fees:*** full-time $302; $202 per year. Full-time tuition and fees vary according to course load. Part-time tuition and fees vary according to course load. ***Payment plans:*** installment, deferred payment.

FRESHMAN FINANCIAL AID (Fall 2007) ***Average financial aid package:*** $3170 (excluding resources awarded to replace EFC).

UNDERGRADUATE FINANCIAL AID (Fall 2007) ***Average financial aid package:*** $3311 (excluding resources awarded to replace EFC).

GIFT AID (NEED-BASED) ***Total amount:*** $19,141,310 (53% federal, 47% state). ***Receiving aid:*** Freshmen: 79% (758); all full-time undergraduates: 77% (2,862). ***Average award:*** Freshmen: $3058; Undergraduates: $3072. ***Scholarships, grants, and awards:*** Federal Pell, FSEOG, state, private, college/university gift aid from institutional funds, Thurgood Marshall Scholarship.

GIFT AID (NON-NEED-BASED) ***Scholarships, grants, and awards by category:*** *Academic interests/achievement:* general academic interests/achievements.

LOANS ***Student loans:*** $1,700,663 (100% need-based). ***Average need-based loan:*** Freshmen: $1427. Undergraduates: $1598. ***Programs:*** Federal Direct (Subsidized and Unsubsidized Stafford, PLUS), FFEL (Subsidized and Unsubsidized Stafford, PLUS), Perkins.

WORK-STUDY ***Federal work-study:*** Total amount: $33,554; jobs available.

APPLYING FOR FINANCIAL AID ***Required financial aid forms:*** FAFSA, state aid form, University Financial Aid Information Supplemental Request (FASIR). ***Financial aid deadline (priority):*** 4/1. ***Notification date:*** Continuous beginning 9/1.

CONTACT Conley James, Director of Financial Aid (Acting), Medgar Evers College of the City University of New York, 1650 Bedford Avenue, Brooklyn, NY 11225, 718-270-6038. *Fax:* 718-270-6194. *E-mail:* conley@mec.cuny.edu.

MEDICAL COLLEGE OF GEORGIA

Augusta, GA

Tuition & fees (GA res): $5568 Average undergraduate aid package: $11,688

ABOUT THE INSTITUTION State-supported, coed. ***Awards:*** bachelor's, master's, doctoral, and first professional degrees and post-bachelor's, post-master's, and first professional certificates. 8 undergraduate majors. ***Total enrollment:*** 2,443. Undergraduates: 587. Federal methodology is used as a basis for awarding need-based institutional aid.

UNDERGRADUATE EXPENSES for 2008–09 ***Application fee:*** $30. ***Tuition, state resident:*** full-time $4856; part-time $202 per credit hour. ***Tuition, nonresident:*** full-time $19,424; part-time $723 per credit hour. ***Required fees:*** full-time $712; $356 per term. Full-time tuition and fees vary according to location. Part-time tuition and fees vary according to course load and location. ***College room and board: Room only:*** $3250. Room and board charges vary according to housing facility.

UNDERGRADUATE FINANCIAL AID (Fall 2008, est.) 481 applied for aid; of those 99% were deemed to have need. 100% of undergraduates with need received aid; of those 4% had need fully met. ***Average percent of need met:*** 66% (excluding resources awarded to replace EFC). ***Average financial aid package:*** $11,688 (excluding resources awarded to replace EFC). 1% of all full-time undergraduates had no need and received non-need-based gift aid.

GIFT AID (NEED-BASED) ***Total amount:*** $645,310 (80% federal, 16% institutional, 4% external sources). ***Receiving aid:*** All full-time undergraduates: 66% (338). ***Average award:*** Undergraduates: $3787. ***Scholarships, grants, and awards:*** Federal Pell, FSEOG, state, private, college/university gift aid from institutional funds, Federal Nursing.

GIFT AID (NON-NEED-BASED) ***Total amount:*** $1,555,672 (97% state, 3% external sources). ***Receiving aid:*** Undergraduates: 65% (335). ***Average award:*** Undergraduates: $3023. ***Scholarships, grants, and awards by category:*** *Academic interests/achievement:* $3,038,366 total: health fields. *Special characteristics:* 64 awards ($46,760 total): religious affiliation.

LOANS ***Student loans:*** $2,099,674 (54% need-based, 46% non-need-based). 71% of past graduating class borrowed through all loan programs. *Average indebtedness per student:* $43,169. ***Average need-based loan:*** Undergraduates: $7725. ***Parent loans:*** $34,954 (100% need-based). ***Programs:*** FFEL (Subsidized and Unsubsidized Stafford, PLUS), Perkins, Federal Nursing, state, college/university.

WORK-STUDY ***Federal work-study:*** Total amount: $28,578; 36 jobs averaging $774.

APPLYING FOR FINANCIAL AID ***Required financial aid forms:*** FAFSA, institution's own form, state aid form. ***Financial aid deadline:*** Continuous. ***Notification date:*** Continuous beginning 6/10. Students must reply within 2 weeks of notification.

CONTACT Dr. Beverly Boggs, Executive Director of Academic Admissions & Student Financial Aid, Medical College of Georgia, 2013 Administration Building, Augusta, GA 30912-7320, 706-721-4901 or toll-free 800-519-3388 (in-state). *Fax:* 706-721-9407. *E-mail:* osfa@mail.mcg.edu.

MEDICAL UNIVERSITY OF SOUTH CAROLINA

Charleston, SC

Tuition & fees: N/R Average undergraduate aid package: $14,637

ABOUT THE INSTITUTION State-supported, coed. ***Awards:*** bachelor's, master's, doctoral, and first professional degrees and post-bachelor's and post-master's certificates. 3 undergraduate majors. ***Total enrollment:*** 2,531. Undergraduates: 319. Federal methodology is used as a basis for awarding need-based institutional aid.

UNDERGRADUATE EXPENSES for 2008–09 ***Application fee:*** $75. tuition varies according to programs. Contact university for program costs. ***Payment plan:*** Installment.

UNDERGRADUATE FINANCIAL AID (Fall 2008, est.) 210 applied for aid; of those 90% were deemed to have need. 97% of undergraduates with need received aid; of those 14% had need fully met. ***Average percent of need met:*** 53% (excluding resources awarded to replace EFC). ***Average financial aid package:*** $14,637 (excluding resources awarded to replace EFC). 1% of all full-time undergraduates had no need and received non-need-based gift aid.

GIFT AID (NEED-BASED) ***Total amount:*** $429,532 (40% federal, 8% state, 52% institutional). ***Receiving aid:*** All full-time undergraduates: 38% (94). ***Average award:*** Undergraduates: $3471. ***Scholarships, grants, and awards:*** Federal Pell, FSEOG, state, private, college/university gift aid from institutional funds, Federal Nursing, Scholarships for Disadvantaged Students (SDS).

GIFT AID (NON-NEED-BASED) ***Total amount:*** $346,338 (14% federal, 41% state, 2% institutional, 43% external sources). ***Receiving aid:*** Undergraduates: 14% (34). ***Average award:*** Undergraduates: $2500. ***Scholarships, grants, and awards by category:*** *Academic interests/achievement:* general academic interests/achievements, health fields. *Special characteristics:* ethnic background, general special characteristics, local/state students, members of minority groups. ***Tuition waivers:*** Full or partial for employees or children of employees, senior citizens.

LOANS ***Student loans:*** $3,074,650 (34% need-based, 66% non-need-based). ***Average need-based loan:*** Undergraduates: $10,158. ***Programs:*** FFEL (Subsidized and Unsubsidized Stafford, PLUS), Perkins, Federal Nursing, state, Health Professions Loans, Loans for Disadvantaged Students program, Primary Care Loans, alternative loans.

WORK-STUDY ***Federal work-study:*** Total amount: $20,257; jobs available.

CONTACT Cecile Kamath, PhD, Director for Financial Aid, Medical University of South Carolina, 45 Courtenay Drive, Charleston, SC 29425, 843-792-2536. *Fax:* 843-792-6356. *E-mail:* finaid@musc.edu.

MEMPHIS COLLEGE OF ART

Memphis, TN

Tuition & fees: $21,560 **Average undergraduate aid package: $16,429**

ABOUT THE INSTITUTION Independent, coed. ***Awards:*** bachelor's and master's degrees. 20 undergraduate majors. ***Total enrollment:*** 403. Undergraduates: 322. Freshmen: 102. Both federal and institutional methodology are used as a basis for awarding need-based institutional aid.

UNDERGRADUATE EXPENSES for 2008–09 ***Application fee:*** $25. ***Tuition:*** full-time $21,000; part-time $2750 per course. ***Required fees:*** full-time $560; $280 per term. Full-time tuition and fees vary according to degree level and program. Part-time tuition and fees vary according to course load, degree level, and program. Room and board charges vary according to housing facility. ***Payment plan:*** Installment.

FRESHMAN FINANCIAL AID (Fall 2008, est.) 101 applied for aid; of those 87% were deemed to have need. 100% of freshmen with need received aid; of those 17% had need fully met. ***Average percent of need met:*** 73% (excluding resources awarded to replace EFC). ***Average financial aid package:*** $19,102 (excluding resources awarded to replace EFC). 13% of all full-time freshmen had no need and received non-need-based gift aid.

UNDERGRADUATE FINANCIAL AID (Fall 2008, est.) 262 applied for aid; of those 87% were deemed to have need. 100% of undergraduates with need received aid; of those 16% had need fully met. ***Average percent of need met:*** 67% (excluding resources awarded to replace EFC). ***Average financial aid package:*** $16,429 (excluding resources awarded to replace EFC). 12% of all full-time undergraduates had no need and received non-need-based gift aid.

GIFT AID (NEED-BASED) ***Total amount:*** $898,551 (57% federal, 17% state, 20% institutional, 6% external sources). ***Receiving aid:*** Freshmen: 87% (88); all full-time undergraduates: 76% (228). ***Average award:*** Freshmen: $15,573; Undergraduates: $12,328. ***Scholarships, grants, and awards:*** Federal Pell, FSEOG, state, private, college/university gift aid from institutional funds.

GIFT AID (NON-NEED-BASED) ***Total amount:*** $2,845,844 (10% state, 90% institutional). ***Receiving aid:*** Freshmen: 12% (12). Undergraduates: 9% (28). ***Average award:*** Freshmen: $12,692. Undergraduates: $10,314. ***Scholarships, grants, and awards by category:*** *Academic interests/achievement:* 323 awards ($1,568,871 total): general academic interests/achievements. *Creative arts/performance:* 41 awards ($108,700 total): applied art and design, art/fine arts. *Special characteristics:* 9 awards ($27,500 total): children of faculty/staff, previous college experience. ***Tuition waivers:*** Full or partial for employees or children of employees.

LOANS ***Student loans:*** $2,467,214 (42% need-based, 58% non-need-based). 100% of past graduating class borrowed through all loan programs. *Average indebtedness per student:* $53,397. ***Average need-based loan:*** Freshmen: $3415. Undergraduates: $3844. ***Parent loans:*** $1,046,204 (100% non-need-based). ***Programs:*** Federal Direct (Subsidized and Unsubsidized Stafford, PLUS), FFEL (Subsidized and Unsubsidized Stafford, PLUS), college/university.

WORK-STUDY ***Federal work-study:*** Total amount: $94,170; 115 jobs averaging $500. ***State or other work-study/employment:*** Total amount: $39,750 (100% non-need-based). 70 part-time jobs averaging $500.

APPLYING FOR FINANCIAL AID ***Required financial aid form:*** FAFSA. ***Financial aid deadline (priority):*** 3/1. ***Notification date:*** Continuous beginning 4/1. Students must reply within 3 weeks of notification.

CONTACT Lynn Holladay, Director of Financial Aid, Memphis College of Art, 1930 Poplar Avenue, Memphis, TN 38104-2764, 901-272-5136 or toll-free 800-727-1088. *Fax:* 901-272-5134. *E-mail:* lholladay@mca.edu.

MENLO COLLEGE

Atherton, CA

Tuition & fees: $32,136 **Average undergraduate aid package: $20,770**

ABOUT THE INSTITUTION Independent, coed. ***Awards:*** bachelor's degrees. 3 undergraduate majors. ***Total enrollment:*** 593. Undergraduates: 593. Freshmen: 161. Federal methodology is used as a basis for awarding need-based institutional aid.

UNDERGRADUATE EXPENSES for 2009–10 ***Application fee:*** $40. ***Comprehensive fee:*** $43,466 includes full-time tuition ($31,720), mandatory fees ($416), and room and board ($11,330). ***Part-time tuition:*** $1322 per credit hour. ***Part-time fees:*** $416 per term.

FRESHMAN FINANCIAL AID (Fall 2008, est.) 92 applied for aid; of those 92% were deemed to have need. 100% of freshmen with need received aid; of those 8% had need fully met. ***Average percent of need met:*** 69% (excluding resources awarded to replace EFC). ***Average financial aid package:*** $21,247 (excluding resources awarded to replace EFC). 29% of all full-time freshmen had no need and received non-need-based gift aid.

UNDERGRADUATE FINANCIAL AID (Fall 2008, est.) 325 applied for aid; of those 92% were deemed to have need. 100% of undergraduates with need received aid; of those 10% had need fully met. ***Average percent of need met:*** 70% (excluding resources awarded to replace EFC). ***Average financial aid package:*** $20,770 (excluding resources awarded to replace EFC). 27% of all full-time undergraduates had no need and received non-need-based gift aid.

GIFT AID (NEED-BASED) ***Total amount:*** $6,313,572 (10% federal, 9% state, 77% institutional, 4% external sources). ***Receiving aid:*** Freshmen: 56% (85); all full-time undergraduates: 60% (300). ***Average award:*** Freshmen: $19,045; Undergraduates: $17,738. ***Scholarships, grants, and awards:*** Federal Pell, FSEOG, state, college/university gift aid from institutional funds, Academic Competitiveness Grant.

GIFT AID (NON-NEED-BASED) ***Total amount:*** $1,719,335 (94% institutional, 6% external sources). ***Receiving aid:*** Freshmen: 5% (7). Undergraduates: 4% (20). ***Average award:*** Freshmen: $8521. Undergraduates: $8911. ***Scholarships, grants, and awards by category:*** *Academic interests/achievement:* 496 awards ($4,254,723 total): general academic interests/achievements. ***ROTC:*** Army cooperative.

LOANS ***Student loans:*** $2,805,463 (75% need-based, 25% non-need-based). 68% of past graduating class borrowed through all loan programs. *Average indebtedness per student:* $21,216. ***Average need-based loan:*** Freshmen: $2765. Undergraduates: $3744. ***Parent loans:*** $1,622,025 (47% need-based, 53% non-need-based). ***Programs:*** FFEL (Subsidized and Unsubsidized Stafford, PLUS).

WORK-STUDY ***Federal work-study:*** Total amount: $48,007; 229 jobs averaging $1000.

APPLYING FOR FINANCIAL AID ***Required financial aid forms:*** FAFSA, state aid form. ***Financial aid deadline (priority):*** 3/2. ***Notification date:*** Continuous beginning 3/15.

CONTACT Anne Heaton-Dunlap, Director of Financial Aid, Menlo College, 1000 El Camino Real, Atherton, CA 94027-4301, 650-543-3880 or toll-free 800-556-3656. *Fax:* 650-543-4103. *E-mail:* financialaid@menlo.edu.

MERCER UNIVERSITY

Macon, GA

Tuition & fees: $28,700 **Average undergraduate aid package: $29,951**

ABOUT THE INSTITUTION Independent Baptist, coed. ***Awards:*** bachelor's, master's, doctoral, and first professional degrees and post-master's certificates.

49 undergraduate majors. ***Total enrollment:*** 5,464. Undergraduates: 2,245. Freshmen: 593. Federal methodology is used as a basis for awarding need-based institutional aid.

UNDERGRADUATE EXPENSES for 2008–09 ***Application fee:*** $50. ***Comprehensive fee:*** $37,150 includes full-time tuition ($28,500), mandatory fees ($200), and room and board ($8450). ***College room only:*** $4100. Full-time tuition and fees vary according to class time, course load, and location. Room and board charges vary according to board plan, housing facility, and location. ***Part-time tuition:*** $950 per credit hour. ***Part-time fees:*** $8.50 per credit hour. Part-time tuition and fees vary according to class time, course load, and location. ***Payment plan:*** Installment.

FRESHMAN FINANCIAL AID (Fall 2008, est.) 508 applied for aid; of those 81% were deemed to have need. 100% of freshmen with need received aid; of those 60% had need fully met. ***Average percent of need met:*** 94% (excluding resources awarded to replace EFC). ***Average financial aid package:*** $31,331 (excluding resources awarded to replace EFC). 30% of all full-time freshmen had no need and received non-need-based gift aid.

UNDERGRADUATE FINANCIAL AID (Fall 2008, est.) 1,671 applied for aid; of those 83% were deemed to have need. 100% of undergraduates with need received aid; of those 53% had need fully met. ***Average percent of need met:*** 91% (excluding resources awarded to replace EFC). ***Average financial aid package:*** $29,951 (excluding resources awarded to replace EFC). 34% of all full-time undergraduates had no need and received non-need-based gift aid.

GIFT AID (NEED-BASED) ***Total amount:*** $24,841,636 (10% federal, 11% state, 75% institutional, 4% external sources). ***Receiving aid:*** Freshmen: 69% (409); all full-time undergraduates: 64% (1,391). ***Average award:*** Freshmen: $21,158; Undergraduates: $18,961. ***Scholarships, grants, and awards:*** Federal Pell, FSEOG, state, college/university gift aid from institutional funds, Federal Nursing.

GIFT AID (NON-NEED-BASED) ***Total amount:*** $15,293,866 (17% state, 76% institutional, 7% external sources). ***Receiving aid:*** Freshmen: 25% (146). Undergraduates: 19% (404). ***Average award:*** Freshmen: $21,339. Undergraduates: $19,164. ***Scholarships, grants, and awards by category:*** *Academic interests/achievement:* 2,245 awards ($13,569,443 total): biological sciences, business, education, engineering/technologies, English, foreign languages, general academic interests/achievements, international studies, military science, religion/biblical studies. *Creative arts/performance:* 128 awards ($791,835 total): art/fine arts, debating, music, theater/drama. *Special achievements/activities:* 65 awards ($453,771 total): community service, general special achievements/activities, memberships. *Special characteristics:* $17,363,587 total: adult students, children of faculty/staff, children of public servants, children of union members/company employees, general special characteristics, international students, local/state students, members of minority groups, relatives of clergy, religious affiliation, siblings of current students. ***Tuition waivers:*** Full or partial for employees or children of employees. ***ROTC:*** Army.

LOANS ***Student loans:*** $12,223,936 (62% need-based, 38% non-need-based). 66% of past graduating class borrowed through all loan programs. *Average indebtedness per student:* $22,835. ***Average need-based loan:*** Freshmen: $6897. Undergraduates: $8512. ***Parent loans:*** $2,775,017 (31% need-based, 69% non-need-based). ***Programs:*** Federal Direct (Subsidized and Unsubsidized Stafford, PLUS), Perkins, Federal Nursing, college/university.

WORK-STUDY ***Federal work-study:*** Total amount: $892,448; jobs available.

ATHLETIC AWARDS Total amount: $3,606,991 (28% need-based, 72% non-need-based).

APPLYING FOR FINANCIAL AID ***Required financial aid forms:*** FAFSA, institution's own form, state aid form (for GA residents only). ***Financial aid deadline (priority):*** 4/1. ***Notification date:*** Continuous. Students must reply within 2 weeks of notification.

CONTACT Ms. Carol Williams, Associate Vice President, Financial Planning, Mercer University, 1400 Coleman Avenue, Macon, GA 31207-0003, 478-301-2670 or toll-free 800-840-8577. *Fax:* 478-301-2671. *E-mail:* williams_ck@mercer.edu.

MERCY COLLEGE

Dobbs Ferry, NY

CONTACT Director of Financial Aid, Mercy College, 28 Wells Avenue, 5th Floor, Yonkers, NY 00701, 888-464-6737 or toll-free 800-MERCY-NY. *Fax:* 914-375-8582. *E-mail:* @mercy.edu.

MERCY COLLEGE OF HEALTH SCIENCES

Des Moines, IA

CONTACT Lisa Croat, Financial Aid Assistant Coordinator, Mercy College of Health Sciences, 928 Sixth Avenue, Des Moines, IA 50309, 515-643-6720 or toll-free 800-637-2994. *Fax:* 515-643-6702. *E-mail:* lcroat@mercydesmoines.org.

MERCY COLLEGE OF NORTHWEST OHIO

Toledo, OH

Tuition & fees: $10,090 **Average undergraduate aid package: $8076**

ABOUT THE INSTITUTION Independent religious, coed, primarily women. ***Awards:*** associate and bachelor's degrees. 6 undergraduate majors. ***Total enrollment:*** 921. Undergraduates: 921. Freshmen: 68. Federal methodology is used as a basis for awarding need-based institutional aid.

UNDERGRADUATE EXPENSES for 2009–10 ***Application fee:*** $25. ***One-time required fee:*** $15. ***Tuition:*** full-time $9440; part-time $326 per credit hour. ***Required fees:*** full-time $650; $5 per credit hour.

FRESHMAN FINANCIAL AID (Fall 2007) 47 applied for aid; of those 94% were deemed to have need. 100% of freshmen with need received aid. ***Average percent of need met:*** 37% (excluding resources awarded to replace EFC). ***Average financial aid package:*** $7195 (excluding resources awarded to replace EFC).

UNDERGRADUATE FINANCIAL AID (Fall 2007) 354 applied for aid; of those 92% were deemed to have need. 100% of undergraduates with need received aid; of those 4% had need fully met. ***Average percent of need met:*** 45% (excluding resources awarded to replace EFC). ***Average financial aid package:*** $8076 (excluding resources awarded to replace EFC). 1% of all full-time undergraduates had no need and received non-need-based gift aid.

GIFT AID (NEED-BASED) ***Total amount:*** $1,645,538 (69% federal, 31% state). ***Receiving aid:*** Freshmen: 39% (25); all full-time undergraduates: 36% (163). ***Average award:*** Freshmen: $3604; Undergraduates: $2226. ***Scholarships, grants, and awards:*** Federal Pell, FSEOG, state, private, college/university gift aid from institutional funds, Federal Nursing.

GIFT AID (NON-NEED-BASED) ***Total amount:*** $365,254 (33% state, 32% institutional, 35% external sources). ***Receiving aid:*** Freshmen: 36% (23). Undergraduates: 39% (176). ***Average award:*** Undergraduates: $4511. ***Scholarships, grants, and awards by category:*** *Academic interests/achievement:* 70 awards ($131,000 total): health fields.

LOANS ***Student loans:*** $5,789,371 (45% need-based, 55% non-need-based). 50% of past graduating class borrowed through all loan programs. *Average indebtedness per student:* $8562. ***Average need-based loan:*** Freshmen: $2969. Undergraduates: $3670. ***Parent loans:*** $119,249 (100% need-based). ***Programs:*** FFEL (Subsidized and Unsubsidized Stafford, PLUS), state, college/university.

WORK-STUDY ***Federal work-study:*** Total amount: $44,100; 21 jobs averaging $1900. ***State or other work-study/employment:*** Total amount: $25,500 (82% need-based, 18% non-need-based). Part-time jobs available.

APPLYING FOR FINANCIAL AID ***Required financial aid form:*** FAFSA. ***Financial aid deadline:*** Continuous. ***Notification date:*** Continuous beginning 3/1. Students must reply by 8/15.

CONTACT Julie Leslie, Financial Aid Director, Mercy College of Northwest Ohio, 2221 Madison Avenue, Toledo, OH 43604, 419-251-1598 or toll-free 888-80-Mercy. *Fax:* 419-251-1462. *E-mail:* julie.leslie@mercycollege.edu.

MERCYHURST COLLEGE

Erie, PA

Tuition & fees: $23,286 **Average undergraduate aid package: $17,119**

ABOUT THE INSTITUTION Independent Roman Catholic, coed. ***Awards:*** associate, bachelor's, and master's degrees and post-bachelor's certificates. 90 undergraduate majors. ***Total enrollment:*** 4,253. Undergraduates: 3,970. Freshmen: 671. Federal methodology is used as a basis for awarding need-based institutional aid.

UNDERGRADUATE EXPENSES for 2008–09 ***Application fee:*** $30. ***Comprehensive fee:*** $31,482 includes full-time tuition ($21,690), mandatory fees ($1596), and room and board ($8196). ***College room only:*** $4119. Room and board charges vary according to board plan and housing facility. ***Part-time tuition:*** $2169 per course. ***Part-time fees:*** $183 per term. Part-time tuition and fees vary according to course load and location. ***Payment plan:*** Installment.

FRESHMAN FINANCIAL AID (Fall 2008, est.) 570 applied for aid; of those 88% were deemed to have need. 100% of freshmen with need received aid; of those 27% had need fully met. ***Average percent of need met:*** 46% (excluding resources awarded to replace EFC). ***Average financial aid package:*** $21,207 (excluding resources awarded to replace EFC). 4% of all full-time freshmen had no need and received non-need-based gift aid.

UNDERGRADUATE FINANCIAL AID (Fall 2008, est.) 2,926 applied for aid; of those 90% were deemed to have need. 100% of undergraduates with need received aid; of those 22% had need fully met. ***Average percent of need met:*** 51% (excluding resources awarded to replace EFC). ***Average financial aid package:*** $17,119 (excluding resources awarded to replace EFC). 3% of all full-time undergraduates had no need and received non-need-based gift aid.

GIFT AID (NEED-BASED) ***Total amount:*** $30,254,362 (18% federal, 13% state, 68% institutional, 1% external sources). ***Receiving aid:*** Freshmen: 76% (489); all full-time undergraduates: 66% (2,246). ***Average award:*** Freshmen: $10,201; Undergraduates: $9279. ***Scholarships, grants, and awards:*** Federal Pell, FSEOG, state, private, college/university gift aid from institutional funds.

GIFT AID (NON-NEED-BASED) ***Total amount:*** $3,597,084 (7% federal, 2% state, 89% institutional, 2% external sources). ***Receiving aid:*** Freshmen: 49% (312). Undergraduates: 30% (1,027). ***Average award:*** Freshmen: $11,366. Undergraduates: $9212. ***Scholarships, grants, and awards by category:*** *Academic interests/achievement:* 944 awards ($8,754,400 total): general academic interests/achievements. *Creative arts/performance:* 131 awards ($634,814 total): applied art and design, art/fine arts, dance, music. *Special achievements/activities:* 1,662 awards ($14,353,102 total): community service, general special achievements/activities, leadership, religious involvement. *Special characteristics:* 84 awards ($687,753 total): children and siblings of alumni, children of faculty/staff. ***Tuition waivers:*** Full or partial for employees or children of employees, adult students. ***ROTC:*** Army cooperative, Air Force cooperative.

LOANS ***Student loans:*** $27,193,585 (92% need-based, 8% non-need-based). 72% of past graduating class borrowed through all loan programs. *Average indebtedness per student:* $19,263. ***Average need-based loan:*** Freshmen: $3473. Undergraduates: $4220. ***Parent loans:*** $4,497,611 (87% need-based, 13% non-need-based). ***Programs:*** Federal Direct (Subsidized and Unsubsidized Stafford, PLUS), Perkins, college/university.

WORK-STUDY ***Federal work-study:*** Total amount: $354,406; 258 jobs averaging $1250. ***State or other work-study/employment:*** Total amount: $1,037,921 (89% need-based, 11% non-need-based). 752 part-time jobs averaging $1230.

ATHLETIC AWARDS Total amount: $4,094,371 (62% need-based, 38% non-need-based).

APPLYING FOR FINANCIAL AID ***Required financial aid forms:*** FAFSA, institution's own form. ***Financial aid deadline:*** 5/1 (priority: 3/1). ***Notification date:*** Continuous.

CONTACT Ann Jelinek, Associate Director, Financial Aid, Mercyhurst College, 501 East 38th Street, Erie, PA 16546, 814-824-2288 or toll-free 800-825-1926 Ext. 2202. *Fax:* 814-824-2438. *E-mail:* ajelinek@mercyhurst.edu.

MEREDITH COLLEGE

Raleigh, NC

CONTACT Mr. Kevin Michaelsen, Director of Financial Assistance, Meredith College, 3800 Hillsborough Street, Raleigh, NC 27607-5298, 919-760-8565 or toll-free 800-MEREDITH. *Fax:* 919-760-2375. *E-mail:* michaelsen@meredith.edu.

MERRIMACK COLLEGE

North Andover, MA

Tuition & fees: $29,310 **Average undergraduate aid package: $16,035**

ABOUT THE INSTITUTION Independent Roman Catholic, coed. ***Awards:*** associate, bachelor's, and master's degrees. 35 undergraduate majors. ***Total enrollment:*** 2,147. Undergraduates: 2,087. Freshmen: 599. Federal methodology is used as a basis for awarding need-based institutional aid.

UNDERGRADUATE EXPENSES for 2009–10 ***Application fee:*** $60. ***Comprehensive fee:*** $39,500 includes full-time tuition ($29,310) and room and board ($10,190). ***College room only:*** $6040.

FRESHMAN FINANCIAL AID (Fall 2007) 485 applied for aid; of those 99% were deemed to have need. 100% of freshmen with need received aid; of those 85% had need fully met. ***Average percent of need met:*** 70% (excluding resources awarded to replace EFC). ***Average financial aid package:*** $16,644 (excluding resources awarded to replace EFC). 18% of all full-time freshmen had no need and received non-need-based gift aid.

UNDERGRADUATE FINANCIAL AID (Fall 2007) 1,392 applied for aid; of those 100% were deemed to have need. 100% of undergraduates with need received aid; of those 93% had need fully met. ***Average percent of need met:*** 70% (excluding resources awarded to replace EFC). ***Average financial aid package:*** $16,035 (excluding resources awarded to replace EFC). 16% of all full-time undergraduates had no need and received non-need-based gift aid.

GIFT AID (NEED-BASED) ***Total amount:*** $18,411,695 (6% federal, 4% state, 90% institutional). ***Receiving aid:*** Freshmen: 80% (471); all full-time undergraduates: 63% (1,198). ***Average award:*** Freshmen: $13,107; Undergraduates: $12,556. ***Scholarships, grants, and awards:*** Federal Pell, FSEOG, state, private, college/university gift aid from institutional funds.

GIFT AID (NON-NEED-BASED) ***Total amount:*** $317,548 (100% external sources). ***Receiving aid:*** Freshmen: 12% (69). Undergraduates: 19% (357). ***Average award:*** Freshmen: $9060. Undergraduates: $10,095. ***Scholarships, grants, and awards by category:*** *Academic interests/achievement:* 800 awards ($5,964,457 total): general academic interests/achievements. *Special characteristics:* 103 awards ($813,750 total): children and siblings of alumni, children of faculty/staff, international students, relatives of clergy, siblings of current students. ***ROTC:*** Air Force cooperative.

LOANS ***Student loans:*** $13,245,465 (100% need-based). 75% of past graduating class borrowed through all loan programs. *Average indebtedness per student:* $42,000. ***Average need-based loan:*** Freshmen: $3337. Undergraduates: $4302. ***Parent loans:*** $5,326,115 (100% non-need-based). ***Programs:*** FFEL (Subsidized and Unsubsidized Stafford, PLUS), Perkins, state, college/university, MEFA Loans, alternative loans.

WORK-STUDY ***Federal work-study:*** Total amount: $144,835; jobs available. ***State or other work-study/employment:*** Total amount: $572,900 (100% need-based). Part-time jobs available.

ATHLETIC AWARDS Total amount: $3,183,230 (23% need-based, 77% non-need-based).

APPLYING FOR FINANCIAL AID ***Required financial aid forms:*** FAFSA, business/farm supplement. ***Financial aid deadline:*** 2/1. ***Notification date:*** Continuous beginning 3/1. Students must reply by 5/1.

CONTACT Christine A. Mordach, Director of Student Financial Aid and Scholarships, Merrimack College, 315 Turnpike Street, North Andover, MA 01845, 978-837-5186. *Fax:* 978-837-5067. *E-mail:* christine.mordach@merrimack.edu.

MESA STATE COLLEGE

Grand Junction, CO

Tuition & fees (CO res): $4735 **Average undergraduate aid package: $5462**

ABOUT THE INSTITUTION State-supported, coed. ***Awards:*** associate, bachelor's, and master's degrees. 42 undergraduate majors. ***Total enrollment:*** 6,261. Undergraduates: 6,165. Freshmen: 1,203. Federal methodology is used as a basis for awarding need-based institutional aid.

UNDERGRADUATE EXPENSES for 2008–09 ***Application fee:*** $30. ***Tuition, state resident:*** full-time $4325; part-time $154 per hour. ***Tuition, nonresident:*** full-time $13,098; part-time $468 per hour. ***Required fees:*** full-time $410; $13.76 per hour. Part-time tuition and fees vary according to course load. ***College room and board:*** $7355; ***Room only:*** $3784. Room and board charges vary according to board plan and housing facility. ***Payment plan:*** Installment.

FRESHMAN FINANCIAL AID (Fall 2007) 917 applied for aid; of those 74% were deemed to have need. 94% of freshmen with need received aid; of those 17% had need fully met. ***Average percent of need met:*** 55% (excluding resources awarded to replace EFC). ***Average financial aid package:*** $5544 (excluding resources awarded to replace EFC). 8% of all full-time freshmen had no need and received non-need-based gift aid.

UNDERGRADUATE FINANCIAL AID (Fall 2007) 3,188 applied for aid; of those 80% were deemed to have need. 96% of undergraduates with need received aid; of those 18% had need fully met. ***Average percent of need met:*** 57% (excluding resources awarded to replace EFC). ***Average financial aid package:*** $5462 (excluding resources awarded to replace EFC). 6% of all full-time undergraduates had no need and received non-need-based gift aid.

GIFT AID (NEED-BASED) ***Total amount:*** $8,512,925 (62% federal, 35% state, 3% institutional). ***Receiving aid:*** Freshmen: 44% (528); all full-time undergraduates: 46% (2,026). ***Average award:*** Freshmen: $3689; Undergraduates: $4030. ***Scholarships, grants, and awards:*** Federal Pell, FSEOG, state, private, college/university gift aid from institutional funds.

GIFT AID (NON-NEED-BASED) ***Total amount:*** $4,555,588 (22% federal, 1% state, 31% institutional, 46% external sources). ***Receiving aid:*** Freshmen: 2% (30). Undergraduates: 2% (72). ***Average award:*** Freshmen: $1956. Undergraduates: $1800. ***Scholarships, grants, and awards by category:*** *Academic interests/achievement:* 698 awards ($828,986 total): biological sciences, business, communication, computer science, education, engineering/technologies, English, foreign languages, general academic interests/achievements, health fields, humanities, mathematics, physical sciences, social sciences. *Creative arts/performance:* 47 awards ($19,873 total): art/fine arts, creative writing, dance, journalism/publications, music, performing arts, theater/drama. *Special achievements/activities:* cheerleading/drum major, general special achievements/activities, hobbies/interests, leadership. *Special characteristics:* 112 awards ($137,866 total): first-generation college students, international students, local/state students, members of minority groups, out-of-state students. ***Tuition waivers:*** Full or partial for employees or children of employees.

LOANS ***Student loans:*** $16,298,984 (56% need-based, 44% non-need-based). 56% of past graduating class borrowed through all loan programs. *Average indebtedness per student:* $19,178. ***Average need-based loan:*** Freshmen: $3117. Undergraduates: $3734. ***Parent loans:*** $2,823,935 (100% non-need-based). ***Programs:*** Federal Direct (Subsidized and Unsubsidized Stafford, PLUS), FFEL (Subsidized and Unsubsidized Stafford, PLUS), Perkins.

WORK-STUDY ***Federal work-study:*** Total amount: $242,490; 175 jobs averaging $1506. ***State or other work-study/employment:*** Total amount: $612,927 (76% need-based, 24% non-need-based). 369 part-time jobs averaging $1696.

ATHLETIC AWARDS Total amount: $1,049,144 (100% non-need-based).

APPLYING FOR FINANCIAL AID ***Required financial aid form:*** FAFSA. ***Financial aid deadline:*** Continuous. ***Notification date:*** Continuous beginning 4/1. Students must reply within 5 weeks of notification.

CONTACT Mr. Curt Martin, Director of Financial Aid, Mesa State College, 1100 North Avenue, Grand Junction, CO 81501-3122, 970-248-1396 or toll-free 800-982-MESA. *Fax:* 970-248-1191. *E-mail:* cmartin@mesastate.edu.

MESIVTA OF EASTERN PARKWAY–YESHIVA ZICHRON MEILECH

Brooklyn, NY

CONTACT Rabbi Joseph Halberstadt, Dean, Mesivta of Eastern Parkway–Yeshiva Zichron Meilech, 510 Dahill Road, Brooklyn, NY 11218-5559, 718-438-1002.

MESIVTA TIFERETH JERUSALEM OF AMERICA

New York, NY

CONTACT Rabbi Dickstein, Director of Financial Aid, Mesivta Tifereth Jerusalem of America, 141 East Broadway, New York, NY 10002-6301, 212-964-2830.

MESIVTA TORAH VODAATH RABBINICAL SEMINARY

Brooklyn, NY

CONTACT Mrs. Kayla Goldring, Director of Financial Aid, Mesivta Torah Vodaath Rabbinical Seminary, 425 East Ninth Street, Brooklyn, NY 11218-5209, 718-941-8000.

MESSENGER COLLEGE

Joplin, MO

ABOUT THE INSTITUTION Independent Pentecostal, coed. ***Awards:*** associate and bachelor's degrees. 13 undergraduate majors. ***Total enrollment:*** 70. Undergraduates: 70. Freshmen: 9.

GIFT AID (NEED-BASED) ***Scholarships, grants, and awards:*** Federal Pell, FSEOG, private, college/university gift aid from institutional funds.

GIFT AID (NON-NEED-BASED) ***Scholarships, grants, and awards by category:*** *Academic interests/achievement:* education, general academic interests/achievements, religion/biblical studies. *Special achievements/activities:* religious involvement. *Special characteristics:* religious affiliation.

LOANS ***Programs:*** FFEL (Subsidized and Unsubsidized Stafford, PLUS).

APPLYING FOR FINANCIAL AID ***Required financial aid form:*** FAFSA.

CONTACT Susan Aleckson, Financial Aid Director, Messenger College, 300 East 50th Street, Joplin, MO 64804, 417-624-7070 Ext. 308 or toll-free 800-385-8940 (in-state). *Fax:* 417-624-5070. *E-mail:* saleckson@messengercollege.edu.

MESSIAH COLLEGE

Grantham, PA

Tuition & fees: $25,670 **Average undergraduate aid package: $16,885**

ABOUT THE INSTITUTION Independent interdenominational, coed. ***Awards:*** bachelor's degrees. 63 undergraduate majors. ***Total enrollment:*** 2,802. Undergraduates: 2,802. Freshmen: 678. Federal methodology is used as a basis for awarding need-based institutional aid.

UNDERGRADUATE EXPENSES for 2008–09 ***Application fee:*** $30. ***Comprehensive fee:*** $33,280 includes full-time tuition ($24,900), mandatory fees ($770), and room and board ($7610). ***College room only:*** $4020. Room and board charges vary according to board plan, housing facility, and location. ***Part-time tuition:*** $1040 per credit. ***Payment plan:*** Installment.

FRESHMAN FINANCIAL AID (Fall 2008, est.) 612 applied for aid; of those 83% were deemed to have need. 100% of freshmen with need received aid; of those 25% had need fully met. ***Average percent of need met:*** 75% (excluding resources awarded to replace EFC). ***Average financial aid package:*** $18,303 (excluding resources awarded to replace EFC). 28% of all full-time freshmen had no need and received non-need-based gift aid.

UNDERGRADUATE FINANCIAL AID (Fall 2008, est.) 2,185 applied for aid; of those 87% were deemed to have need. 100% of undergraduates with need received aid; of those 21% had need fully met. ***Average percent of need met:*** 70% (excluding resources awarded to replace EFC). ***Average financial aid package:*** $16,885 (excluding resources awarded to replace EFC). 29% of all full-time undergraduates had no need and received non-need-based gift aid.

GIFT AID (NEED-BASED) ***Total amount:*** $21,696,114 (8% federal, 9% state, 78% institutional, 5% external sources). ***Receiving aid:*** Freshmen: 71% (507); all full-time undergraduates: 68% (1,863). ***Average award:*** Freshmen: $13,204; Undergraduates: $11,623. ***Scholarships, grants, and awards:*** Federal Pell, FSEOG, state, private, college/university gift aid from institutional funds.

GIFT AID (NON-NEED-BASED) ***Total amount:*** $7,712,643 (94% institutional, 6% external sources). ***Receiving aid:*** Freshmen: 9% (62). Undergraduates: 6% (171). ***Average award:*** Freshmen: $9582. Undergraduates: $8027. ***Scholarships, grants, and awards by category:*** *Academic interests/achievement:* 2,137 awards ($12,102,721 total): general academic interests/achievements. *Creative arts/performance:* 36 awards ($379,862 total): art/fine arts, music, theater/drama. *Special achievements/activities:* 528 awards ($3,917,681 total): leadership. *Special characteristics:* 270 awards ($1,742,980 total): adult students, children and siblings of alumni, children of faculty/staff, relatives of clergy, religious affiliation, siblings of current students, spouses of current students. ***Tuition waivers:*** Full or partial for minority students, children of alumni, employees or children of employees, adult students, senior citizens.

LOANS ***Student loans:*** $20,117,270 (64% need-based, 36% non-need-based). 74% of past graduating class borrowed through all loan programs. *Average indebtedness per student:* $33,820. ***Average need-based loan:*** Freshmen: $3640. Undergraduates: $4625. ***Parent loans:*** $4,190,759 (33% need-based, 67% non-need-based). ***Programs:*** Federal Direct (Subsidized and Unsubsidized Stafford, PLUS), FFEL (Subsidized and Unsubsidized Stafford, PLUS), Perkins, Federal Nursing.

WORK-STUDY ***Federal work-study:*** Total amount: $1,556,147; 781 jobs averaging $2113. ***State or other work-study/employment:*** Total amount: $2,240,349 (20% need-based, 80% non-need-based). 963 part-time jobs averaging $2524.

APPLYING FOR FINANCIAL AID ***Required financial aid form:*** FAFSA. ***Financial aid deadline (priority):*** 4/1. ***Notification date:*** Continuous. Students must reply by 5/1 or within 4 weeks of notification.

CONTACT Mr. Michael Strite, Assistant Director of Financial Aid, Messiah College, PO Box 3006, Grantham, PA 17027, 717-691-6007 or toll-free 800-233-4220. *Fax:* 717-796-4791. *E-mail:* mstrite@messiah.edu.

METHODIST UNIVERSITY

Fayetteville, NC

Tuition & fees: $22,260 **Average undergraduate aid package: $12,741**

ABOUT THE INSTITUTION Independent United Methodist, coed. ***Awards:*** associate, bachelor's, and master's degrees. 56 undergraduate majors. ***Total enrollment:*** 2,190. Undergraduates: 2,032. Freshmen: 467. Federal methodology is used as a basis for awarding need-based institutional aid.

UNDERGRADUATE EXPENSES for 2009–10 ***Application fee:*** $25. ***Comprehensive fee:*** $30,660 includes full-time tuition ($22,260) and room and board ($8400). ***College room only:*** $4240.

FRESHMAN FINANCIAL AID (Fall 2007) 425 applied for aid; of those 77% were deemed to have need. 99% of freshmen with need received aid; of those 87% had need fully met. ***Average percent of need met:*** 80% (excluding resources awarded to replace EFC). ***Average financial aid package:*** $14,447 (excluding resources awarded to replace EFC). 19% of all full-time freshmen had no need and received non-need-based gift aid.

UNDERGRADUATE FINANCIAL AID (Fall 2007) 1,693 applied for aid; of those 70% were deemed to have need. 99% of undergraduates with need received aid; of those 94% had need fully met. ***Average percent of need met:*** 83% (excluding resources awarded to replace EFC). ***Average financial aid package:*** $12,741 (excluding resources awarded to replace EFC). 23% of all full-time undergraduates had no need and received non-need-based gift aid.

GIFT AID (NEED-BASED) ***Total amount:*** $9,477,607 (23% federal, 17% state, 60% institutional). ***Receiving aid:*** Freshmen: 68% (288); all full-time undergraduates: 59% (993). ***Average award:*** Freshmen: $7785; Undergraduates: $6647. ***Scholarships, grants, and awards:*** Federal Pell, FSEOG, state, private, college/university gift aid from institutional funds.

GIFT AID (NON-NEED-BASED) ***Total amount:*** $7,528,855 (16% federal, 24% state, 48% institutional, 12% external sources). ***Receiving aid:*** Freshmen: 58% (245). Undergraduates: 56% (942). ***Average award:*** Freshmen: $7677. Undergraduates: $5857. ***Scholarships, grants, and awards by category:*** *Academic interests/achievement:* 484 awards ($3,000,731 total): English, general academic interests/achievements. *Creative arts/performance:* 67 awards ($83,050 total): debating, music, theater/drama. *Special achievements/activities:* 30 awards ($11,400 total): cheerleading/drum major, leadership. *Special characteristics:* 369 awards ($768,752 total): children and siblings of alumni, children of faculty/staff, relatives of clergy, religious affiliation. ***ROTC:*** Army, Air Force cooperative.

LOANS ***Student loans:*** $9,989,029 (46% need-based, 54% non-need-based). 87% of past graduating class borrowed through all loan programs. *Average indebtedness per student:* $26,240. ***Average need-based loan:*** Freshmen: $4725. Undergraduates: $6227. ***Parent loans:*** $3,540,473 (100% non-need-based). ***Programs:*** FFEL (Subsidized and Unsubsidized Stafford, PLUS), Perkins.

WORK-STUDY ***Federal work-study:*** Total amount: $204,379; 514 jobs averaging $398. ***State or other work-study/employment:*** Total amount: $131,999 (52% need-based, 48% non-need-based). 54 part-time jobs averaging $1183.

APPLYING FOR FINANCIAL AID ***Required financial aid forms:*** FAFSA, state aid form. ***Financial aid deadline (priority):*** 8/1. ***Notification date:*** Continuous beginning 3/6. Students must reply within 2 weeks of notification.

CONTACT Bonnie Adamson, Financial Aid Office, Methodist University, 5400 Ramsey Street, Fayetteville, NC 28311-1420, 910-630-7307 or toll-free 800-488-7110 Ext. 7027. *Fax:* 910-630-7285. *E-mail:* Adamson@methodist.edu.

METROPOLITAN COLLEGE OF NEW YORK

New York, NY

CONTACT Rosibel Gomez, Financial Aid Director, Metropolitan College of New York, 75 Varick Street, New York, NY 10013-1919, 212-343-1234 Ext. 5004 or toll-free 800-33-THINK Ext. 5001 (in-state). *Fax:* 212-343-7399.

METROPOLITAN STATE COLLEGE OF DENVER

Denver, CO

Tuition & fees (CO res): $3241 **Average undergraduate aid package: $7007**

ABOUT THE INSTITUTION State-supported, coed. ***Awards:*** bachelor's degrees. 48 undergraduate majors. ***Total enrollment:*** 21,729. Undergraduates: 21,729. Freshmen: 2,504. Federal methodology is used as a basis for awarding need-based institutional aid.

UNDERGRADUATE EXPENSES for 2008–09 ***Application fee:*** $25. ***Tuition, state resident:*** full-time $2615; part-time $108.95 per credit hour. ***Tuition, nonresident:*** full-time $11,323; part-time $471.80 per credit hour. ***Required fees:*** full-time $626; $295.71 per term.

FRESHMAN FINANCIAL AID (Fall 2007) 1,355 applied for aid; of those 71% were deemed to have need. 86% of freshmen with need received aid; of those .5% had need fully met. ***Average percent of need met:*** 55% (excluding resources awarded to replace EFC). ***Average financial aid package:*** $5902 (excluding resources awarded to replace EFC). 15% of all full-time freshmen had no need and received non-need-based gift aid.

UNDERGRADUATE FINANCIAL AID (Fall 2007) 7,702 applied for aid; of those 80% were deemed to have need. 92% of undergraduates with need received aid; of those 2% had need fully met. ***Average percent of need met:*** 57% (excluding resources awarded to replace EFC). ***Average financial aid package:*** $7337 (excluding resources awarded to replace EFC). 23% of all full-time undergraduates had no need and received non-need-based gift aid.

GIFT AID (NEED-BASED) ***Total amount:*** $18,712,531 (61% federal, 28% state, 8% institutional, 3% external sources). ***Receiving aid:*** Freshmen: 29% (611); all full-time undergraduates: 34% (4,249). ***Average award:*** Freshmen: $3898; Undergraduates: $3955. ***Scholarships, grants, and awards:*** Federal Pell, FSEOG, state, private, college/university gift aid from institutional funds.

GIFT AID (NON-NEED-BASED) ***Total amount:*** $807,375 (3% federal, 3% state, 66% institutional, 28% external sources). ***Receiving aid:*** Freshmen: 5% (116). Undergraduates: 5% (654). ***Average award:*** Freshmen: $541. Undergraduates: $690. ***ROTC:*** Army cooperative, Air Force cooperative.

LOANS ***Student loans:*** $33,935,004 (84% need-based, 16% non-need-based). 51% of past graduating class borrowed through all loan programs. *Average indebtedness per student:* $18,595. ***Average need-based loan:*** Freshmen: $3368. Undergraduates: $4226. ***Parent loans:*** $2,485,284 (50% need-based, 50% non-need-based). ***Programs:*** FFEL (Subsidized and Unsubsidized Stafford, PLUS), Perkins.

WORK-STUDY ***Federal work-study:*** Total amount: $517,252; 119 jobs averaging $4347. ***State or other work-study/employment:*** Total amount: $1,711,847 (86% need-based, 14% non-need-based). 424 part-time jobs averaging $4037.

ATHLETIC AWARDS Total amount: $1,015,532 (36% need-based, 64% non-need-based).

APPLYING FOR FINANCIAL AID ***Required financial aid form:*** FAFSA. ***Financial aid deadline:*** Continuous. ***Notification date:*** Continuous beginning 4/1.

CONTACT Office of Financial Aid, Metropolitan State College of Denver, PO Box 173362, Denver, CO 80217-3362, 303-556-8593. *Fax:* 303-556-4927.

METROPOLITAN STATE UNIVERSITY

St. Paul, MN

CONTACT Mr. Michael Uran, Director of Financial Aid, Metropolitan State University, Founder's Hall, Room 105, 700 East 7th Street, St. Paul, MN 55106-5000, 651-793-1414. *E-mail:* finaid@metrostate.edu.

MIAMI INTERNATIONAL UNIVERSITY OF ART & DESIGN

Miami, FL

UNDERGRADUATE EXPENSES Tuition cost varies by program. Prospective students should contact the school for current tuition costs. Other charges include a starting kit for all first-quarter students. Kits vary in price, depending on the program of study.

CONTACT Financial Aid Office, Miami International University of Art & Design, 1737 Bayshore Drive, Miami, FL 33132, 800-225-9023 Ext. 125 or toll-free 800-225-9023. *Fax:* 305-374-7946.

MIAMI UNIVERSITY

Oxford, OH

Tuition & fees (OH res): $11,887 **Average undergraduate aid package: $10,137**

ABOUT THE INSTITUTION State-related, coed. ***Awards:*** associate, bachelor's, master's, and doctoral degrees and post-master's certificates. 113 undergraduate majors. ***Total enrollment:*** 17,191. Undergraduates: 14,785. Freshmen: 3,609. Federal methodology is used as a basis for awarding need-based institutional aid.

UNDERGRADUATE EXPENSES for 2008–09 ***Application fee:*** $45. ***Tuition, state resident:*** full-time $9721. ***Tuition, nonresident:*** full-time $23,605. ***Required fees:*** full-time $2166. ***College room and board:*** $8998; ***Room only:*** $4602. Room and board charges vary according to board plan and housing facility. ***Payment plan:*** Installment.

FRESHMAN FINANCIAL AID (Fall 2008, est.) 2,538 applied for aid; of those 59% were deemed to have need. 99% of freshmen with need received aid; of those 40% had need fully met. ***Average percent of need met:*** 77% (excluding resources awarded to replace EFC). ***Average financial aid package:*** $13,870 (excluding resources awarded to replace EFC). 20% of all full-time freshmen had no need and received non-need-based gift aid.

UNDERGRADUATE FINANCIAL AID (Fall 2008, est.) 7,989 applied for aid; of those 69% were deemed to have need. 98% of undergraduates with need received aid; of those 17% had need fully met. ***Average percent of need met:*** 59% (excluding resources awarded to replace EFC). ***Average financial aid package:*** $10,137 (excluding resources awarded to replace EFC). 18% of all full-time undergraduates had no need and received non-need-based gift aid.

GIFT AID (NEED-BASED) ***Total amount:*** $20,818,226 (38% federal, 7% state, 55% institutional). ***Receiving aid:*** Freshmen: 35% (1,258); all full-time undergraduates: 22% (3,144). ***Average award:*** Freshmen: $6716; Undergraduates: $5731. ***Scholarships, grants, and awards:*** Federal Pell, FSEOG, state, private, college/university gift aid from institutional funds.

GIFT AID (NON-NEED-BASED) ***Total amount:*** $23,527,003 (2% state, 81% institutional, 17% external sources). ***Receiving aid:*** Freshmen: 25% (876). Undergraduates: 18% (2,506). ***Average award:*** Freshmen: $3785. Undergraduates: $4322. ***Scholarships, grants, and awards by category:*** *Academic interests/achievement:* architecture, education, engineering/technologies, general academic interests/achievements. *Creative arts/performance:* art/fine arts, music, theater/drama. *Special achievements/activities:* general special achievements/activities, leadership. *Special characteristics:* children of faculty/staff, local/state students, members of minority groups, out-of-state students. ***Tuition waivers:*** Full or partial for employees or children of employees. ***ROTC:*** Army cooperative, Naval, Air Force.

LOANS ***Student loans:*** $53,614,836 (36% need-based, 64% non-need-based). 51% of past graduating class borrowed through all loan programs. *Average indebtedness per student:* $26,798. ***Average need-based loan:*** Freshmen: $5571. Undergraduates: $4835. ***Parent loans:*** $20,821,391 (100% non-need-based). ***Programs:*** Federal Direct (Subsidized and Unsubsidized Stafford, PLUS), Perkins, Federal Nursing, college/university, bank education loans.

WORK-STUDY ***Federal work-study:*** Total amount: $2,267,624; 1,042 jobs averaging $2147.

ATHLETIC AWARDS Total amount: $7,482,925 (100% non-need-based).

APPLYING FOR FINANCIAL AID ***Required financial aid form:*** FAFSA. ***Financial aid deadline (priority):*** 2/15. ***Notification date:*** Continuous beginning 3/20. Students must reply by 5/1 or within 3 weeks of notification.

CONTACT Chuck Knepfle, Office of Student Financial Aid, Miami University, Campus Avenue Building, Oxford, OH 45056-3427, 513-529-8734. *Fax:* 513-529-8713. *E-mail:* financialaid@muohio.edu.

MIAMI UNIVERSITY HAMILTON

Hamilton, OH

ABOUT THE INSTITUTION State-supported, coed. ***Awards:*** associate, bachelor's, and master's degrees (degrees awarded by Miami University main campus). 99 undergraduate majors. ***Total enrollment:*** 3,645. Undergraduates: 3,572. Freshmen: 796.

GIFT AID (NEED-BASED) ***Scholarships, grants, and awards:*** Federal Pell, FSEOG, state, private, college/university gift aid from institutional funds, Academic Competitiveness Grant, National Smart Grant, TEACH Grant.

LOANS ***Programs:*** Federal Direct (Subsidized and Unsubsidized Stafford, PLUS), Perkins.

WORK-STUDY Federal work-study jobs available.

APPLYING FOR FINANCIAL AID ***Required financial aid forms:*** FAFSA, institution's own form.

CONTACT Ken Rower, Coordinator of Financial Aid, Miami University Hamilton, 1601 Peck Boulevard, Hamilton, OH 45011, 513-785-3123. *Fax:* 513-785-3148.

MICHIGAN JEWISH INSTITUTE

Oak Park, MI

CONTACT Financial Aid Office, Michigan Jewish Institute, 25401 Coolidge Highway, Oak Park, MI 48237-1304, 248-414-6900.

MICHIGAN STATE UNIVERSITY

East Lansing, MI

Tuition & fees (MI res): $10,214 Average undergraduate aid package: $10,308

ABOUT THE INSTITUTION State-supported, coed. ***Awards:*** bachelor's, master's, doctoral, and first professional degrees and post-master's certificates. 111 undergraduate majors. ***Total enrollment:*** 46,648. Undergraduates: 36,337. Freshmen: 7,555. Federal methodology is used as a basis for awarding need-based institutional aid.

UNDERGRADUATE EXPENSES for 2008–09 ***Application fee:*** $35. ***Tuition, state resident:*** full-time $9330; part-time $311 per credit hour. ***Tuition, nonresident:*** full-time $24,788; part-time $826.25 per credit hour. ***Required fees:*** full-time $884; $312 per term. Full-time tuition and fees vary according to course load, degree level, program, and student level. Part-time tuition and fees vary according to course load, degree level, program, and student level. ***College room and board:*** $7026; ***Room only:*** $2900. Room and board charges vary according to board plan, housing facility, and student level. ***Payment plan:*** Deferred payment.

FRESHMAN FINANCIAL AID (Fall 2008, est.) 5,286 applied for aid; of those 64% were deemed to have need. 99% of freshmen with need received aid; of those 29% had need fully met. ***Average percent of need met:*** 74% (excluding resources awarded to replace EFC). ***Average financial aid package:*** $10,789 (excluding resources awarded to replace EFC). 5% of all full-time freshmen had no need and received non-need-based gift aid.

UNDERGRADUATE FINANCIAL AID (Fall 2008, est.) 19,989 applied for aid; of those 72% were deemed to have need. 99% of undergraduates with need received aid; of those 22% had need fully met. ***Average percent of need met:*** 70% (excluding resources awarded to replace EFC). ***Average financial aid package:*** $10,308 (excluding resources awarded to replace EFC). 4% of all full-time undergraduates had no need and received non-need-based gift aid.

GIFT AID (NEED-BASED) ***Total amount:*** $62,160,381 (44% federal, 56% institutional). ***Receiving aid:*** Freshmen: 24% (1,764); all full-time undergraduates: 24% (8,091). ***Average award:*** Freshmen: $8212; Undergraduates: $7147. ***Scholarships, grants, and awards:*** Federal Pell, FSEOG, state, private, college/university gift aid from institutional funds, United Negro College Fund.

GIFT AID (NON-NEED-BASED) ***Total amount:*** $80,494,836 (3% federal, 53% state, 21% institutional, 23% external sources). ***Receiving aid:*** Freshmen: 37% (2,757). Undergraduates: 25% (8,486). ***Average award:*** Freshmen: $5894. Undergraduates: $7010. ***Scholarships, grants, and awards by category:*** *Academic interests/achievement:* agriculture, architecture, biological sciences, business, communication, computer science, education, engineering/technologies, English, foreign languages, general academic interests/achievements, health fields, international studies, mathematics, military science, physical sciences, social sciences. *Creative arts/performance:* creative writing, debating, journalism/publications, music, performing arts, theater/drama. *Special achievements/activities:* community service, hobbies/interests, junior miss, leadership, memberships, rodeo. *Special characteristics:* children and siblings of alumni, children of faculty/staff, children of union members/company employees, ethnic background, first-generation college students, handicapped students, international students, local/state students, members of minority groups, out-of-state students, public servants, religious affiliation, spouses of deceased or disabled public servants, veterans, veterans' children. ***Tuition waivers:*** Full or partial for employees or children of employees. ***ROTC:*** Army, Air Force.

LOANS ***Student loans:*** $147,559,211 (40% need-based, 60% non-need-based). 41% of past graduating class borrowed through all loan programs. *Average indebtedness per student:* $17,347. ***Average need-based loan:*** Freshmen: $3392. Undergraduates: $4409. ***Parent loans:*** $50,847,976 (100% non-need-based). ***Programs:*** Federal Direct (Subsidized and Unsubsidized Stafford, PLUS), Perkins, state, college/university.

WORK-STUDY ***Federal work-study:*** Total amount: $1,878,464; 1,200 jobs averaging $1250. ***State or other work-study/employment:*** Total amount: $644,120 (100% need-based). 364 part-time jobs averaging $1582.

ATHLETIC AWARDS Total amount: $8,897,088 (41% need-based, 59% non-need-based).

APPLYING FOR FINANCIAL AID ***Required financial aid form:*** FAFSA. ***Financial aid deadline:*** Continuous. ***Notification date:*** Continuous beginning 3/15. Students must reply within 4 weeks of notification.

CONTACT Mr. Keith Williams, Associate Director, Michigan State University, 252 Student Services Building, East Lansing, MI 48824-1113, 517-353-5940. *Fax:* 517-432-1155. *E-mail:* willi398@msu.edu.

MICHIGAN TECHNOLOGICAL UNIVERSITY

Houghton, MI

Tuition & fees (MI res): $10,761 **Average undergraduate aid package: $10,020**

ABOUT THE INSTITUTION State-supported, coed. ***Awards:*** associate, bachelor's, master's, and doctoral degrees and post-bachelor's certificates. 88 undergraduate majors. ***Total enrollment:*** 7,018. Undergraduates: 6,034. Freshmen: 1,365. Federal methodology is used as a basis for awarding need-based institutional aid.

UNDERGRADUATE EXPENSES for 2008–09 ***Tuition, state resident:*** full-time $9930; part-time $331 per credit hour. ***Tuition, nonresident:*** full-time $21,690; part-time $723 per credit hour. ***Required fees:*** full-time $831; $415.74 per term. Full-time tuition and fees vary according to course load and program. Part-time tuition and fees vary according to course load and program. ***College room and board:*** $7738; ***Room only:*** $4111. Room and board charges vary according to board plan and housing facility. ***Payment plans:*** Installment, deferred payment.

FRESHMAN FINANCIAL AID (Fall 2008, est.) 1,167 applied for aid; of those 72% were deemed to have need. 100% of freshmen with need received aid; of those 22% had need fully met. ***Average percent of need met:*** 72% (excluding resources awarded to replace EFC). ***Average financial aid package:*** $10,858 (excluding resources awarded to replace EFC). 32% of all full-time freshmen had no need and received non-need-based gift aid.

UNDERGRADUATE FINANCIAL AID (Fall 2008, est.) 4,139 applied for aid; of those 77% were deemed to have need. 100% of undergraduates with need received aid; of those 21% had need fully met. ***Average percent of need met:*** 67% (excluding resources awarded to replace EFC). ***Average financial aid package:*** $10,020 (excluding resources awarded to replace EFC). 27% of all full-time undergraduates had no need and received non-need-based gift aid.

GIFT AID (NEED-BASED) ***Total amount:*** $20,078,309 (23% federal, 16% state, 50% institutional, 11% external sources). ***Receiving aid:*** Freshmen: 49% (672); all full-time undergraduates: 44% (2,467). ***Average award:*** Freshmen: $5359; Undergraduates: $4475. ***Scholarships, grants, and awards:*** Federal Pell, FSEOG, state, private, college/university gift aid from institutional funds.

GIFT AID (NON-NEED-BASED) ***Total amount:*** $8,715,376 (7% state, 59% institutional, 34% external sources). ***Receiving aid:*** Freshmen: 52% (714). Undergraduates: 38% (2,129). ***Average award:*** Freshmen: $4163. Undergraduates: $3936. ***Tuition waivers:*** Full or partial for children of alumni, employees or children of employees, senior citizens. ***ROTC:*** Army, Air Force.

LOANS ***Student loans:*** $33,162,728 (77% need-based, 23% non-need-based). 71% of past graduating class borrowed through all loan programs. *Average indebtedness per student:* $14,184. ***Average need-based loan:*** Freshmen: $3210. Undergraduates: $4391. ***Parent loans:*** $3,991,089 (70% need-based, 30% non-need-based). ***Programs:*** Federal Direct (Subsidized and Unsubsidized Stafford, PLUS), Perkins, state, college/university, External Private Loans.

WORK-STUDY ***Federal work-study:*** Total amount: $306,408; jobs available. ***State or other work-study/employment:*** Total amount: $2,249,965 (4% need-based, 96% non-need-based). Part-time jobs available.

ATHLETIC AWARDS Total amount: $2,004,838 (32% need-based, 68% non-need-based).

APPLYING FOR FINANCIAL AID ***Required financial aid form:*** FAFSA. ***Financial aid deadline (priority):*** 2/16. ***Notification date:*** 5/1.

CONTACT Mr. Richard Elenich, Office of Institutional Analysis, Michigan Technological University, 1400 Townsend Drive, Houghton, MI 49931-1295, 906-487-2700 or toll-free 888-MTU-1885. *Fax:* 906-487-3328. *E-mail:* relenic@mtu.edu.

MID-AMERICA CHRISTIAN UNIVERSITY

Oklahoma City, OK

CONTACT Mr. Todd Martin, Director of Financial Aid, Mid-America Christian University, 3500 Southwest 119th Street, Oklahoma City, OK 73170-4504, 405-691-3800. *Fax:* 405-692-3165. *E-mail:* tmartin@mabc.edu.

MIDAMERICA NAZARENE UNIVERSITY

Olathe, KS

Tuition & fees: $18,216 **Average undergraduate aid package: $13,686**

ABOUT THE INSTITUTION Independent religious, coed. ***Awards:*** associate, bachelor's, and master's degrees and post-master's certificates. 40 undergraduate majors. ***Total enrollment:*** 1,743. Undergraduates: 1,305. Freshmen: 204. Federal methodology is used as a basis for awarding need-based institutional aid.

UNDERGRADUATE EXPENSES for 2008–09 ***Application fee:*** $25. ***Comprehensive fee:*** $24,396 includes full-time tuition ($17,216), mandatory fees ($1000), and room and board ($6180). Full-time tuition and fees vary according to course load. Room and board charges vary according to board plan and housing facility. ***Part-time tuition:*** $576 per hour. ***Part-time fees:*** $365 per term. Part-time tuition and fees vary according to course load. ***Payment plan:*** Installment.

FRESHMAN FINANCIAL AID (Fall 2008, est.) 176 applied for aid; of those 81% were deemed to have need. 100% of freshmen with need received aid; of those 17% had need fully met. ***Average percent of need met:*** 71% (excluding resources awarded to replace EFC). ***Average financial aid package:*** $15,258 (excluding resources awarded to replace EFC). 28% of all full-time freshmen had no need and received non-need-based gift aid.

UNDERGRADUATE FINANCIAL AID (Fall 2008, est.) 796 applied for aid; of those 87% were deemed to have need. 100% of undergraduates with need received aid; of those 14% had need fully met. ***Average percent of need met:*** 65% (excluding resources awarded to replace EFC). ***Average financial aid package:*** $13,686 (excluding resources awarded to replace EFC). 19% of all full-time undergraduates had no need and received non-need-based gift aid.

GIFT AID (NEED-BASED) ***Total amount:*** $4,700,849 (25% federal, 8% state, 64% institutional, 3% external sources). ***Receiving aid:*** Freshmen: 70% (143); all full-time undergraduates: 69% (662). ***Average award:*** Freshmen: $10,410; Undergraduates: $8989. ***Scholarships, grants, and awards:*** Federal Pell, FSEOG, state, private, college/university gift aid from institutional funds.

GIFT AID (NON-NEED-BASED) ***Total amount:*** $1,098,986 (1% federal, 95% institutional, 4% external sources). ***Receiving aid:*** Freshmen: 13% (27). Undergraduates: 8% (74). ***Average award:*** Freshmen: $5249. Undergraduates: $4891. ***Tuition waivers:*** Full or partial for employees or children of employees, senior citizens. ***ROTC:*** Army cooperative, Air Force cooperative.

LOANS ***Student loans:*** $6,886,844 (48% need-based, 52% non-need-based). 84% of past graduating class borrowed through all loan programs. *Average indebtedness per student:* $28,859. ***Average need-based loan:*** Freshmen: $4821. Undergraduates: $5638. ***Parent loans:*** $956,951 (51% need-based, 49% non-need-based). ***Programs:*** Federal Direct (Subsidized and Unsubsidized Stafford, PLUS), Perkins, college/university.

WORK-STUDY ***Federal work-study:*** Total amount: $12,000; jobs available.

ATHLETIC AWARDS Total amount: $2,077,690 (48% need-based, 52% non-need-based).

APPLYING FOR FINANCIAL AID ***Required financial aid form:*** FAFSA. ***Financial aid deadline (priority):*** 3/1. ***Notification date:*** Continuous. Students must reply within 2 weeks of notification.

CONTACT Rhonda L. Cole, Director of Student Financial Services, MidAmerica Nazarene University, 2030 East College Way, Olathe, KS 66062-1899, 913-791-3298 or toll-free 800-800-8887. *Fax:* 913-791-3482. *E-mail:* rcole@mnu.edu.

MID-CONTINENT UNIVERSITY

Mayfield, KY

Tuition & fees: $13,100 **Average undergraduate aid package: $7675**

ABOUT THE INSTITUTION Independent Southern Baptist, coed. ***Awards:*** associate and bachelor's degrees. 13 undergraduate majors. ***Total enrollment:*** 1,541. Undergraduates: 1,541. Freshmen: 141. Federal methodology is used as a basis for awarding need-based institutional aid.

UNDERGRADUATE EXPENSES for 2008–09 ***Application fee:*** $20. ***Comprehensive fee:*** $19,400 includes full-time tuition ($11,850), mandatory fees ($1250), and room and board ($6300). Full-time tuition and fees vary according to course load and program. Room and board charges vary according to board plan and housing facility. ***Part-time tuition:*** $395 per credit hour. Part-time tuition and fees vary according to course load and program.

FRESHMAN FINANCIAL AID (Fall 2007) 110 applied for aid; of those 92% were deemed to have need. 99% of freshmen with need received aid; of those 13% had need fully met. ***Average percent of need met:*** 43% (excluding resources awarded to replace EFC). ***Average financial aid package:*** $8492 (excluding resources awarded to replace EFC).

UNDERGRADUATE FINANCIAL AID (Fall 2007) 1,156 applied for aid; of those 88% were deemed to have need. 94% of undergraduates with need received aid; of those 8% had need fully met. ***Average percent of need met:*** 41% (excluding resources awarded to replace EFC). ***Average financial aid package:*** $7675 (excluding resources awarded to replace EFC). 1% of all full-time undergraduates had no need and received non-need-based gift aid.

GIFT AID (NEED-BASED) ***Total amount:*** $5,781,073 (39% federal, 50% state, 11% external sources). ***Receiving aid:*** Freshmen: 66% (86); all full-time undergraduates: 51% (687). ***Average award:*** Freshmen: $6125; Undergraduates: $5218. ***Scholarships, grants, and awards:*** Federal Pell, FSEOG, state, private, college/university gift aid from institutional funds.

GIFT AID (NON-NEED-BASED) ***Total amount:*** $305,669 (49% state, 11% institutional, 40% external sources). ***Receiving aid:*** Freshmen: 8% (11). Undergraduates: 4% (48). ***Average award:*** Undergraduates: $16,030. ***Scholarships, grants, and awards by category:*** *Academic interests/achievement:* 16 awards ($30,419 total): education, English, general academic interests/achievements, humanities, religion/biblical studies, social sciences. *Special achievements/activities:* 8 awards ($3750 total): cheerleading/drum major. *Special characteristics:* 6 awards ($3000 total): children and siblings of alumni, children of faculty/staff, children of union members/company employees, married students, relatives of clergy. ***Tuition waivers:*** Full or partial for employees or children of employees.

LOANS ***Student loans:*** $7,313,619 (92% need-based, 8% non-need-based). 85% of past graduating class borrowed through all loan programs. *Average indebtedness per student:* $8805. ***Average need-based loan:*** Freshmen: $2540. Undergraduates: $3761. ***Parent loans:*** $120,069 (36% need-based, 64% non-need-based). ***Programs:*** Federal Direct (Subsidized and Unsubsidized Stafford, PLUS), FFEL (Subsidized and Unsubsidized Stafford, PLUS).

WORK-STUDY ***Federal work-study:*** Total amount: $451,811; 48 jobs averaging $1383. ***State or other work-study/employment:*** Total amount: $30,000 (39% need-based, 61% non-need-based). Part-time jobs available.

ATHLETIC AWARDS Total amount: $1,047,022 (46% need-based, 54% non-need-based)

APPLYING FOR FINANCIAL AID ***Required financial aid form:*** FAFSA. ***Financial aid deadline (priority):*** 3/15. ***Notification date:*** Continuous. Students must reply within 2 weeks of notification.

CONTACT Kent Youngblood, Director of Financial Aid, Mid-Continent University, 99 Powell Road East, Mayfield, KY 42066, 270-251-9400 Ext. 260. *Fax:* 270-251-9475. *E-mail:* kyoungblood@midcontinent.edu.

MIDDLEBURY COLLEGE

Middlebury, VT

Comprehensive fee: $49,210 **Average undergraduate aid package: $32,896**

ABOUT THE INSTITUTION Independent, coed. ***Awards:*** bachelor's, master's, and doctoral degrees. 44 undergraduate majors. ***Total enrollment:*** 2,455. Undergraduates: 2,455. Freshmen: 576.

UNDERGRADUATE EXPENSES for 2008–09 ***Application fee:*** $65. ***Comprehensive fee:*** $49,210. ***Payment plan:*** Tuition prepayment.

FRESHMAN FINANCIAL AID (Fall 2007) 390 applied for aid; of those 79% were deemed to have need. 100% of freshmen with need received aid; of those 100% had need fully met. ***Average percent of need met:*** 100% (excluding resources awarded to replace EFC). ***Average financial aid package:*** $34,849 (excluding resources awarded to replace EFC).

UNDERGRADUATE FINANCIAL AID (Fall 2007) 1,285 applied for aid; of those 87% were deemed to have need. 100% of undergraduates with need received aid; of those 100% had need fully met. ***Average percent of need met:*** 100% (excluding resources awarded to replace EFC). ***Average financial aid package:*** $32,896 (excluding resources awarded to replace EFC).

GIFT AID (NEED-BASED) ***Total amount:*** $30,250,329 (4% federal, 94% institutional, 2% external sources). ***Receiving aid:*** Freshmen: 48% (308); all full-time undergraduates: 45% (1,115). ***Average award:*** Freshmen: $31,446; Undergraduates: $29,308. ***Scholarships, grants, and awards:*** Federal Pell, FSEOG, state, private, college/university gift aid from institutional funds.

GIFT AID (NON-NEED-BASED) ***Tuition waivers:*** Full or partial for employees or children of employees. ***ROTC:*** Army cooperative.

LOANS ***Student loans:*** $4,149,437 (59% need-based, 41% non-need-based). 36% of past graduating class borrowed through all loan programs. *Average indebtedness per student:* $19,981. ***Average need-based loan:*** Freshmen: $3213. Undergraduates: $3870. ***Parent loans:*** $3,451,517 (100% non-need-based). ***Programs:*** FFEL (Subsidized and Unsubsidized Stafford, PLUS), Perkins, college/university.

WORK-STUDY ***Federal work-study:*** Total amount: $822,871; jobs available. ***State or other work-study/employment:*** Total amount: $2,117,624 (19% need-based, 81% non-need-based). Part-time jobs available.

APPLYING FOR FINANCIAL AID ***Required financial aid forms:*** FAFSA, CSS Financial Aid PROFILE, noncustodial (divorced/separated) parent's statement, federal income tax return. ***Financial aid deadline:*** 2/1 (priority: 11/15). ***Notification date:*** 4/1. Students must reply by 5/1.

CONTACT Marguerite Corbin, Financial Aid Assistant, Middlebury College, 2nd Floor Meeker, Middlebury, VT 05753, 802-443-5158. *E-mail:* financialaid@middlebury.edu.

MIDDLE TENNESSEE STATE UNIVERSITY

Murfreesboro, TN

ABOUT THE INSTITUTION State-supported, coed. ***Awards:*** bachelor's, master's, and doctoral degrees and post-bachelor's and post-master's certificates. 61 undergraduate majors. ***Total enrollment:*** 23,872. Undergraduates: 21,252. Freshmen: 3,456.

GIFT AID (NEED-BASED) ***Scholarships, grants, and awards:*** Federal Pell, FSEOG, state, private, college/university gift aid from institutional funds.

GIFT AID (NON-NEED-BASED) ***Scholarships, grants, and awards by category:*** *Academic interests/achievement:* agriculture, biological sciences, business, communication, computer science, education, engineering/technologies, English, foreign languages, general academic interests/achievements, health fields, home economics, humanities, international studies, mathematics, military science, physical sciences, premedicine, social sciences. *Creative arts/performance:* dance, debating, journalism/publications, music, theater/drama. *Special achievements/activities:* cheerleading/drum major, general special achievements/activities, leadership. *Special characteristics:* adult students, local/state students, members of minority groups.

LOANS ***Programs:*** FFEL (Subsidized and Unsubsidized Stafford, PLUS), Perkins, college/university.

WORK-STUDY ***Federal work-study:*** Total amount: $281,009; 256 jobs averaging $1110.

APPLYING FOR FINANCIAL AID ***Required financial aid form:*** FAFSA.

CONTACT David Hutton, Financial Aid Director, Middle Tennessee State University, 218 Cope Administration Building, Murfreesboro, TN 37132, 615-898-2830. *Fax:* 615-898-5167.

MIDLAND COLLEGE

Midland, TX

Tuition & fees (area res): $1596 **Average undergraduate aid package: N/A**

ABOUT THE INSTITUTION State and locally supported, coed. ***Awards:*** associate and bachelor's degrees. 59 undergraduate majors. ***Total enrollment:*** 5,739. Undergraduates: 5,739. Freshmen: 341. Federal methodology is used as a basis for awarding need-based institutional aid.

UNDERGRADUATE EXPENSES for 2008–09 ***Tuition, area resident:*** full-time $1204; part-time $91 per hour. ***Tuition, state resident:*** full-time $1764; part-time $111 per hour. ***Tuition, nonresident:*** full-time $2632; part-time $142 per hour. ***Required fees:*** full-time $392; $56 per hour. ***College room and board:*** $4061.

GIFT AID (NEED-BASED) ***Total amount:*** $3,625,000 (97% federal, 3% state). ***Scholarships, grants, and awards:*** Federal Pell, FSEOG, state, private, college/university gift aid from institutional funds.

GIFT AID (NON-NEED-BASED) ***Total amount:*** $730,000 (18% institutional, 82% external sources).

LOANS ***Student loans:*** $200,000 (82% need-based, 18% non-need-based). ***Parent loans:*** $10,000 (100% non-need-based). ***Programs:*** FFEL (Subsidized Stafford, PLUS).

WORK-STUDY ***Federal work-study:*** Total amount: $128,000; 75 jobs averaging $2700. ***State or other work-study/employment:*** Total amount: $45,000 (100% need-based). 5 part-time jobs averaging $2700.

ATHLETIC AWARDS Total amount: $730,000 (50% need-based, 50% non-need-based).

APPLYING FOR FINANCIAL AID ***Required financial aid form:*** FAFSA. ***Financial aid deadline (priority):*** 5/1. ***Notification date:*** Continuous.

CONTACT Latisha Williams, Director, Midland College, 3600 North Garfield, Midland, TX 79705, 432-685-4507. *Fax:* 432-685-6857. *E-mail:* lwilliams@midland.edu.

MIDLAND LUTHERAN COLLEGE

Fremont, NE

Tuition & fees: $22,006 **Average undergraduate aid package: $17,904**

ABOUT THE INSTITUTION Independent Lutheran, coed. ***Awards:*** associate and bachelor's degrees. 57 undergraduate majors. ***Total enrollment:*** 827. Undergraduates: 827. Freshmen: 215. Both federal and institutional methodology are used as a basis for awarding need-based institutional aid.

UNDERGRADUATE EXPENSES for 2008–09 ***Application fee:*** $30. ***Comprehensive fee:*** $27,372 includes full-time tuition ($22,006) and room and board ($5366). Full-time tuition and fees vary according to class time, course load, and program. Room and board charges vary according to board plan and housing facility. Part-time tuition and fees vary according to class time, course load, and program. ***Payment plan:*** Installment.

FRESHMAN FINANCIAL AID (Fall 2008, est.) 143 applied for aid; of those 92% were deemed to have need. 100% of freshmen with need received aid; of those 56% had need fully met. ***Average percent of need met:*** 87% (excluding resources awarded to replace EFC). ***Average financial aid package:*** $18,874 (excluding resources awarded to replace EFC). 3% of all full-time freshmen had no need and received non-need-based gift aid.

UNDERGRADUATE FINANCIAL AID (Fall 2008, est.) 699 applied for aid; of those 89% were deemed to have need. 100% of undergraduates with need received aid; of those 54% had need fully met. ***Average percent of need met:*** 89% (excluding resources awarded to replace EFC). ***Average financial aid package:*** $17,904 (excluding resources awarded to replace EFC). 7% of all full-time undergraduates had no need and received non-need-based gift aid.

GIFT AID (NEED-BASED) ***Total amount:*** $7,437,701 (17% federal, 3% state, 77% institutional, 3% external sources). ***Receiving aid:*** Freshmen: 86% (131); all full-time undergraduates: 78% (598). ***Average award:*** Freshmen: $12,808; Undergraduates: $11,881. ***Scholarships, grants, and awards:*** Federal Pell, FSEOG, state, private, college/university gift aid from institutional funds.

GIFT AID (NON-NEED-BASED) ***Total amount:*** $2,394,620 (89% institutional, 11% external sources). ***Receiving aid:*** Freshmen: 86% (130). Undergraduates: 80% (607). ***Average award:*** Freshmen: $18,980. Undergraduates: $12,840. ***Scholarships, grants, and awards by category:*** *Academic interests/achievement:* biological sciences, business, communication, education, English, general academic interests/achievements, health fields, humanities, physical sciences, religion/biblical studies, social sciences. *Creative arts/performance:* art/fine arts, debating, journalism/publications, music, theater/drama. *Special achievements/activities:* community service, general special achievements/activities, leadership, religious involvement. *Special characteristics:* children and siblings of alumni, children of current students, children of faculty/staff, handicapped students, international students, members of minority groups, parents of current students, previous college experience, religious affiliation, siblings of current students, spouses of current students. ***Tuition waivers:*** Full or partial for children of alumni, employees or children of employees, senior citizens.

LOANS ***Student loans:*** $5,115,410 (58% need-based, 42% non-need-based). 90% of past graduating class borrowed through all loan programs. *Average indebtedness per student:* $23,000. ***Average need-based loan:*** Freshmen: $4576. Undergraduates: $4898. ***Parent loans:*** $869,320 (14% need-based, 86% non-need-based). ***Programs:*** FFEL (Subsidized and Unsubsidized Stafford, PLUS), Perkins.

WORK-STUDY ***Federal work-study:*** Total amount: $100,000; 169 jobs averaging $1350. ***State or other work-study/employment:*** Total amount: $100,000 (50% need-based, 50% non-need-based). 121 part-time jobs averaging $1425.

ATHLETIC AWARDS Total amount: $2,283,034 (56% need-based, 44% non-need-based).

APPLYING FOR FINANCIAL AID ***Required financial aid form:*** FAFSA. ***Financial aid deadline:*** Continuous. ***Notification date:*** Continuous beginning 3/1. Students must reply within 2 weeks of notification.

CONTACT Penny James, Director of Financial Aid, Midland Lutheran College, 900 North Clarkson Street, Fremont, NE 68025-4200, 402-721-5480 Ext. 6520 or toll-free 800-642-8382 Ext. 6501. *Fax:* 402-721-0250. *E-mail:* finaid@mlc.edu.

MIDSTATE COLLEGE

Peoria, IL

CONTACT Janet Ozuna, Director of Financial Aid/Business Manager, Midstate College, 411 West Northmoor Road, Peoria, IL 61614, 309-692-4092. *Fax:* 309-692-3893.

MIDWAY COLLEGE

Midway, KY

Tuition & fees: $17,100 **Average undergraduate aid package: $12,196**

ABOUT THE INSTITUTION Independent religious, coed, primarily women. ***Awards:*** associate, bachelor's, and master's degrees. 26 undergraduate majors. ***Total enrollment:*** 1,323. Undergraduates: 1,295. Freshmen: 166. Federal methodology is used as a basis for awarding need-based institutional aid.

UNDERGRADUATE EXPENSES for 2008–09 ***Application fee:*** $25. ***Comprehensive fee:*** $23,700 includes full-time tuition ($17,100) and room and board ($6600). Full-time tuition and fees vary according to class time, location, and program. Room and board charges vary according to board plan and housing facility. ***Part-time tuition:*** $570 per semester hour. ***Part-time fees:*** $150 per year. Part-time tuition and fees vary according to class time, location, and program. ***Payment plan:*** Deferred payment.

FRESHMAN FINANCIAL AID (Fall 2007) 116 applied for aid; of those 91% were deemed to have need. 100% of freshmen with need received aid; of those 21% had need fully met. ***Average percent of need met:*** 57% (excluding resources awarded to replace EFC). ***Average financial aid package:*** $12,678 (excluding resources awarded to replace EFC). 2% of all full-time freshmen had no need and received non-need-based gift aid.

UNDERGRADUATE FINANCIAL AID (Fall 2007) 771 applied for aid; of those 91% were deemed to have need. 100% of undergraduates with need received aid; of those 26% had need fully met. ***Average percent of need met:*** 59% (excluding resources awarded to replace EFC). ***Average financial aid package:*** $12,196 (excluding resources awarded to replace EFC). 1% of all full-time undergraduates had no need and received non-need-based gift aid.

GIFT AID (NEED-BASED) ***Total amount:*** $4,689,803 (31% federal, 43% state, 14% institutional, 12% external sources). ***Receiving aid:*** Freshmen: 79% (102); all full-time undergraduates: 75% (658). ***Average award:*** Freshmen: $6530; Undergraduates: $5792. ***Scholarships, grants, and awards:*** Federal Pell, FSEOG, state, private, college/university gift aid from institutional funds.

GIFT AID (NON-NEED-BASED) ***Total amount:*** $335,271 (28% institutional, 72% external sources). ***Receiving aid:*** Freshmen: 6% (8). Undergraduates: 7% (60). ***Average award:*** Freshmen: $2417. Undergraduates: $3756. ***Scholarships, grants, and awards by category:*** *Academic interests/achievement:* agriculture, business, general academic interests/achievements, health fields, premedicine. *Special achievements/activities:* general special achievements/activities, junior miss, leadership, religious involvement. *Special characteristics:* adult students, children and siblings of alumni, children of faculty/staff, members of minority groups, previous college experience, relatives of clergy, religious affiliation, veterans. ***Tuition waivers:*** Full or partial for employees or children of employees, senior citizens. ***ROTC:*** Army cooperative.

LOANS ***Student loans:*** $5,162,351 (91% need-based, 9% non-need-based). 80% of past graduating class borrowed through all loan programs. *Average indebtedness per student:* $15,407. ***Average need-based loan:*** Freshmen: $2475. Undergraduates: $3658. ***Parent loans:*** $838,581 (87% need-based, 13% non-need-based). ***Programs:*** Federal Direct (Subsidized and Unsubsidized Stafford, PLUS), FFEL (Subsidized and Unsubsidized Stafford, PLUS), Perkins.

WORK-STUDY ***Federal work-study:*** Total amount: $158,491; 113 jobs averaging $1372. ***State or other work-study/employment:*** Part-time jobs available.

ATHLETIC AWARDS Total amount: $286,923 (97% need-based, 3% non-need-based).

APPLYING FOR FINANCIAL AID ***Required financial aid forms:*** FAFSA, institution's own form. ***Financial aid deadline (priority):*** 3/15. ***Notification date:*** Continuous. Students must reply within 4 weeks of notification.

CONTACT Katie Conrad, Director of Financial Aid, Midway College, 512 East Stephens Street, Midway, KY 40347-1120, 859-846-5410 or toll-free 800-755-0031. *Fax:* 859-846-5751. *E-mail:* kconrad@midway.edu.

MIDWESTERN STATE UNIVERSITY

Wichita Falls, TX

Tuition & fees (TX res): $5571 **Average undergraduate aid package: $7689**

ABOUT THE INSTITUTION State-supported, coed. ***Awards:*** associate, bachelor's, and master's degrees and post-bachelor's certificates. 58 undergraduate majors. ***Total enrollment:*** 6,027. Undergraduates: 5,350. Freshmen: 762. Federal methodology is used as a basis for awarding need-based institutional aid.

UNDERGRADUATE EXPENSES for 2008–09 ***Application fee:*** $25. ***Tuition, state resident:*** full-time $1500; part-time $50 per credit hour. ***Tuition, nonresident:*** full-time $2400; part-time $80 per credit hour. ***Required fees:*** full-time $4071; $123.75 per credit hour or $179 per term. ***College room and board:*** $5350; ***Room only:*** $2740.

FRESHMAN FINANCIAL AID (Fall 2008, est.) 453 applied for aid; of those 66% were deemed to have need. 100% of freshmen with need received aid; of those 31% had need fully met. ***Average percent of need met:*** 75% (excluding resources awarded to replace EFC). ***Average financial aid package:*** $7925 (excluding resources awarded to replace EFC). 13% of all full-time freshmen had no need and received non-need-based gift aid.

UNDERGRADUATE FINANCIAL AID (Fall 2008, est.) 2,480 applied for aid; of those 74% were deemed to have need. 99% of undergraduates with need received aid; of those 21% had need fully met. ***Average percent of need met:*** 70% (excluding resources awarded to replace EFC). ***Average financial aid package:*** $7689 (excluding resources awarded to replace EFC). 13% of all full-time undergraduates had no need and received non-need-based gift aid.

GIFT AID (NEED-BASED) ***Total amount:*** $8,425,822 (58% federal, 29% state, 10% institutional, 3% external sources). ***Receiving aid:*** Freshmen: 39% (265); all full-time undergraduates: 37% (1,468). ***Average award:*** Freshmen: $6175; Undergraduates: $5087. ***Scholarships, grants, and awards:*** Federal Pell, FSEOG, state, private, college/university gift aid from institutional funds, State Nursing Scholarship.

GIFT AID (NON-NEED-BASED) ***Total amount:*** $1,284,092 (1% state, 85% institutional, 14% external sources). ***Receiving aid:*** Freshmen: 1% (6). Undergraduates: 1% (21). ***Average award:*** Freshmen: $1944. Undergraduates: $1674. ***ROTC:*** Air Force cooperative.

LOANS ***Student loans:*** $17,735,710 (71% need-based, 29% non-need-based). 59% of past graduating class borrowed through all loan programs. *Average indebtedness per student:* $19,645. ***Average need-based loan:*** Freshmen: $3143. Undergraduates: $4296. ***Parent loans:*** $2,288,836 (34% need-based, 66% non-need-based). ***Programs:*** FFEL (Subsidized and Unsubsidized Stafford, PLUS), Perkins, state, college/university, alternative private loans.

WORK-STUDY ***Federal work-study:*** Total amount: $150,000; jobs available. ***State or other work-study/employment:*** Total amount: $35,000 (100% need-based). Part-time jobs available.

ATHLETIC AWARDS Total amount: $888,960 (26% need-based, 74% non-need-based).

APPLYING FOR FINANCIAL AID ***Required financial aid form:*** FAFSA. ***Financial aid deadline (priority):*** 5/1. ***Notification date:*** Continuous. Students must reply within 4 weeks of notification.

CONTACT Ms. Kathy Pennartz, Director of Financial Aid, Midwestern State University, 3410 Taft Boulevard, Wichita Falls, TX 76308-2099, 940-397-4214 or toll-free 800-842-1922. *Fax:* 940-397-4852. *E-mail:* financial-aid@mwsu.edu.

MIDWESTERN UNIVERSITY, GLENDALE CAMPUS

Glendale, AZ

CONTACT Lesa Stanford, Administrative Assistant, Office of Student Financial Services, Midwestern University, Glendale Campus, 19555 North 59th Avenue, Glendale, AZ 85308, 623-572-3321 or toll-free 888-247-9277 (in-state), 888-247-9271 (out-of-state). *Fax:* 623-572-3283. *E-mail:* az_fin_aid@arizona.midwestern.edu.

MIDWEST UNIVERSITY

Wentzville, MO

CONTACT Financial Aid Office, Midwest University, PO Box 365, 851 Parr Road, Wentzville, MO 63385, 636-327-4645.

MIDWIVES COLLEGE OF UTAH

Orem, UT

CONTACT Financial Aid Office, Midwives College of Utah, 560 South State Street, Suite B2, Orem, UT 84058, 801-764-9068 or toll-free 866-764-9068.

MILES COLLEGE

Fairfield, AL

CONTACT P. N. Lanier, Financial Aid Administrator, Miles College, PO Box 3800, Birmingham, AL 35208, 205-929-1663 or toll-free 800-445-0708. *Fax:* 205-929-1668. *E-mail:* pnlani@netscape.net.

MILLERSVILLE UNIVERSITY OF PENNSYLVANIA

Millersville, PA

Tuition & fees (PA res): $6866 **Average undergraduate aid package: $7619**

ABOUT THE INSTITUTION State-supported, coed. ***Awards:*** associate, bachelor's, and master's degrees and post-bachelor's and post-master's certificates. 42 undergraduate majors. ***Total enrollment:*** 8,319. Undergraduates: 7,216. Freshmen: 1,323. Federal methodology is used as a basis for awarding need-based institutional aid.

UNDERGRADUATE EXPENSES for 2008–09 ***Application fee:*** $50. ***Tuition, state resident:*** full-time $5358; part-time $223 per credit. ***Tuition, nonresident:*** full-time $13,396; part-time $558 per credit. ***Required fees:*** full-time $1508; $55.75 per credit or $88 per term. Full-time tuition and fees vary according to degree level. Part-time tuition and fees vary according to course load and degree level. ***College room and board:*** $7308; ***Room only:*** $4348. Room and board charges vary according to board plan and housing facility. ***Payment plan:*** Installment.

FRESHMAN FINANCIAL AID (Fall 2007) 1,152 applied for aid; of those 68% were deemed to have need. 97% of freshmen with need received aid; of those 13% had need fully met. ***Average percent of need met:*** 76% (excluding resources awarded to replace EFC). ***Average financial aid package:*** $7648 (excluding resources awarded to replace EFC). 2% of all full-time freshmen had no need and received non-need-based gift aid.

UNDERGRADUATE FINANCIAL AID (Fall 2007) 5,055 applied for aid; of those 72% were deemed to have need. 97% of undergraduates with need received aid; of those 16% had need fully met. ***Average percent of need met:*** 80% (excluding resources awarded to replace EFC). ***Average financial aid package:*** $7619 (excluding resources awarded to replace EFC). 2% of all full-time undergraduates had no need and received non-need-based gift aid.

GIFT AID (NEED-BASED) ***Total amount:*** $12,358,337 (38% federal, 53% state, 5% institutional, 4% external sources). ***Receiving aid:*** Freshmen: 43% (576); all full-time undergraduates: 38% (2,514). ***Average award:*** Freshmen: $5320; Undergraduates: $4746. ***Scholarships, grants, and awards:*** Federal Pell, FSEOG, state, private, college/university gift aid from institutional funds, Schock Scholarship.

GIFT AID (NON-NEED-BASED) ***Total amount:*** $3,032,338 (11% state, 34% institutional, 55% external sources). ***Receiving aid:*** Freshmen: 13% (170).

Undergraduates: 8% (528). ***Average award:*** Freshmen: $2262. Undergraduates: $2499. ***Scholarships, grants, and awards by category:*** *Academic interests/achievement:* 462 awards ($1,212,046 total): biological sciences, business, communication, computer science, education, English, foreign languages, general academic interests/achievements, health fields, humanities, mathematics, physical sciences, social sciences. *Creative arts/performance:* 22 awards ($17,771 total): art/fine arts, music. *Special achievements/activities:* 2 awards ($2360 total): community service. *Special characteristics:* 161 awards ($697,981 total): children of union members/company employees, international students. ***Tuition waivers:*** Full or partial for employees or children of employees, senior citizens. ***ROTC:*** Army.

LOANS ***Student loans:*** $27,110,639 (49% need-based, 51% non-need-based). 66% of past graduating class borrowed through all loan programs. *Average indebtedness per student:* $20,931. ***Average need-based loan:*** Freshmen: $3271. Undergraduates: $4072. ***Parent loans:*** $4,301,941 (100% non-need-based). ***Programs:*** FFEL (Subsidized and Unsubsidized Stafford, PLUS), Perkins, college/university.

WORK-STUDY ***Federal work-study:*** Total amount: $316,934; 287 jobs averaging $1104. ***State or other work-study/employment:*** Total amount: $2,650,649 (100% non-need-based). 1,819 part-time jobs averaging $1457.

ATHLETIC AWARDS Total amount: $318,709 (31% need-based, 69% non-need-based).

APPLYING FOR FINANCIAL AID ***Required financial aid form:*** FAFSA. ***Financial aid deadline:*** 3/15. ***Notification date:*** Continuous beginning 3/19. Students must reply within 2 weeks of notification.

CONTACT Mr. Dwight Horsey, Director of Financial Aid, Millersville University of Pennsylvania, PO Box 1002, Millersville, PA 17551-0302, 717-872-3026 or toll-free 800-MU-ADMIT (out-of-state). *Fax:* 717-871-2248. *E-mail:* dwight.horsey@millersville.edu.

MILLIGAN COLLEGE

Milligan College, TN

Tuition & fees: $20,560 **Average undergraduate aid package: $15,150**

ABOUT THE INSTITUTION Independent Christian, coed. ***Awards:*** bachelor's and master's degrees. 26 undergraduate majors. ***Total enrollment:*** 1,070. Undergraduates: 845. Freshmen: 200. Federal methodology is used as a basis for awarding need-based institutional aid.

UNDERGRADUATE EXPENSES for 2008–09 ***Application fee:*** $30. ***Comprehensive fee:*** $26,210 includes full-time tuition ($19,950), mandatory fees ($610), and room and board ($5650). ***College room only:*** $2650. Full-time tuition and fees vary according to course load. Room and board charges vary according to housing facility. ***Part-time tuition:*** $335 per credit. ***Part-time fees:*** $165 per term. Part-time tuition and fees vary according to course load. ***Payment plan:*** Installment.

FRESHMAN FINANCIAL AID (Fall 2008, est.) 165 applied for aid; of those 81% were deemed to have need. 100% of freshmen with need received aid; of those 42% had need fully met. ***Average percent of need met:*** 81% (excluding resources awarded to replace EFC). ***Average financial aid package:*** $14,968 (excluding resources awarded to replace EFC). 18% of all full-time freshmen had no need and received non-need-based gift aid.

UNDERGRADUATE FINANCIAL AID (Fall 2008, est.) 699 applied for aid; of those 82% were deemed to have need. 100% of undergraduates with need received aid; of those 32% had need fully met. ***Average percent of need met:*** 80% (excluding resources awarded to replace EFC). ***Average financial aid package:*** $15,150 (excluding resources awarded to replace EFC). 18% of all full-time undergraduates had no need and received non-need-based gift aid.

GIFT AID (NEED-BASED) ***Total amount:*** $5,340,663 (16% federal, 15% state, 53% institutional, 16% external sources). ***Receiving aid:*** Freshmen: 73% (133); all full-time undergraduates: 72% (554). ***Average award:*** Freshmen: $12,969; Undergraduates: $11,723. ***Scholarships, grants, and awards:*** Federal Pell, FSEOG, state, private, college/university gift aid from institutional funds.

GIFT AID (NON-NEED-BASED) ***Total amount:*** $1,935,111 (21% state, 60% institutional, 19% external sources). ***Receiving aid:*** Freshmen: 26% (47). Undergraduates: 16% (123). ***Average award:*** Freshmen: $8680. Undergraduates: $6896. ***Scholarships, grants, and awards by category:*** *Academic interests/achievement:* 537 awards ($3,227,155 total): general academic interests/achievements, religion/biblical studies. *Creative arts/performance:* 50 awards ($67,940 total): art/fine arts, music. *Special achievements/activities:* 93 awards ($225,755 total): cheerleading/drum major, community service. *Special characteristics:* 21 awards ($365,475 total): children of faculty/staff. ***Tuition waivers:*** Full or partial for employees or children of employees. ***ROTC:*** Army cooperative.

LOANS ***Student loans:*** $4,501,509 (66% need-based, 34% non-need-based). 90% of past graduating class borrowed through all loan programs. *Average indebtedness per student:* $20,236. ***Average need-based loan:*** Freshmen: $3124. Undergraduates: $4930. ***Parent loans:*** $639,850 (21% need-based, 79% non-need-based). ***Programs:*** FFEL (Subsidized and Unsubsidized Stafford, PLUS), Perkins, alternative loans.

WORK-STUDY ***Federal work-study:*** Total amount: $214,146; 147 jobs averaging $1460. ***State or other work-study/employment:*** Total amount: $243,061 (9% need-based, 91% non-need-based). 170 part-time jobs averaging $1425.

ATHLETIC AWARDS Total amount: $2,003,512 (54% need-based, 46% non-need-based).

APPLYING FOR FINANCIAL AID ***Required financial aid form:*** FAFSA. ***Financial aid deadline (priority):*** 3/1. ***Notification date:*** Continuous beginning 3/1. Students must reply within 2 weeks of notification.

CONTACT Diane Keasling, Coordinator of Financial Aid, Milligan College, PO Box 250, Milligan College, TN 37682, 423-461-8968 or toll-free 800-262-8337 (in-state). *Fax:* 423-929-2368. *E-mail:* dlkeasling@milligan.edu.

MILLIKIN UNIVERSITY

Decatur, IL

Tuition & fees: $26,345 **Average undergraduate aid package: $17,726**

ABOUT THE INSTITUTION Independent religious, coed. ***Awards:*** bachelor's and master's degrees. 51 undergraduate majors. ***Total enrollment:*** 2,344. Undergraduates: 2,296. Freshmen: 484. Institutional methodology is used as a basis for awarding need-based institutional aid.

UNDERGRADUATE EXPENSES for 2009–10 ***Comprehensive fee:*** $34,211 includes full-time tuition ($25,750), mandatory fees ($595), and room and board ($7866). ***College room only:*** $4306. ***Part-time tuition:*** $860 per credit hour. ***Part-time fees:*** $75 per term.

FRESHMAN FINANCIAL AID (Fall 2007) 447 applied for aid; of those 85% were deemed to have need. 100% of freshmen with need received aid; of those 51% had need fully met. ***Average percent of need met:*** 92% (excluding resources awarded to replace EFC). ***Average financial aid package:*** $19,197 (excluding resources awarded to replace EFC). 15% of all full-time freshmen had no need and received non-need-based gift aid.

UNDERGRADUATE FINANCIAL AID (Fall 2007) 1,951 applied for aid; of those 85% were deemed to have need. 100% of undergraduates with need received aid; of those 57% had need fully met. ***Average percent of need met:*** 92% (excluding resources awarded to replace EFC). ***Average financial aid package:*** $17,726 (excluding resources awarded to replace EFC). 11% of all full-time undergraduates had no need and received non-need-based gift aid.

GIFT AID (NEED-BASED) ***Total amount:*** $11,307,424 (20% federal, 35% state, 45% institutional). ***Receiving aid:*** Freshmen: 76% (360); all full-time undergraduates: 69% (1,512). ***Average award:*** Freshmen: $7714; Undergraduates: $7017. ***Scholarships, grants, and awards:*** Federal Pell, FSEOG, state, private, college/university gift aid from institutional funds.

GIFT AID (NON-NEED-BASED) ***Total amount:*** $15,157,126 (97% institutional, 3% external sources). ***Receiving aid:*** Freshmen: 80% (378). Undergraduates: 67% (1,468). ***Average award:*** Freshmen: $8510. Undergraduates: $8025. ***Scholarships, grants, and awards by category:*** *Academic interests/achievement:* 2,028 awards ($13,291,721 total): biological sciences, business, communication, education, English, foreign languages, general academic interests/achievements, health fields, humanities, international studies, mathematics, physical sciences, premedicine. *Creative arts/performance:* 526 awards ($942,863 total): art/fine arts, dance, music, theater/drama. *Special achievements/activities:* community service. *Special characteristics:* children and siblings of alumni, children of union members/company employees, children with a deceased or disabled parent, international students, parents of current students, relatives of clergy, twins.

LOANS ***Student loans:*** $14,001,424 (46% need-based, 54% non-need-based). 82% of past graduating class borrowed through all loan programs. *Average indebtedness per student:* $27,375. ***Average need-based loan:*** Freshmen: $3976. Undergraduates: $4643. ***Parent loans:*** $2,247,275 (100% non-need-based). ***Programs:*** FFEL (Subsidized and Unsubsidized Stafford, PLUS), Perkins, state.

WORK-STUDY ***Federal work-study:*** Total amount: $349,432; 430 jobs averaging $978. ***State or other work-study/employment:*** Total amount: $131,381 (100% non-need-based). Part-time jobs available.

APPLYING FOR FINANCIAL AID ***Required financial aid form:*** FAFSA. ***Financial aid deadline (priority):*** 3/15. ***Notification date:*** Continuous beginning 3/15. Students must reply by 5/1 or within 4 weeks of notification.

CONTACT Cheryl Howerton, Director of Financial Aid, Millikin University, 1184 West Main Street, Decatur, IL 62522-2084, 217-424-6317 or toll-free 800-373-7733. *Fax:* 217-424-5070. *E-mail:* studentservicecenter@millikin.edu.

MILLSAPS COLLEGE

Jackson, MS

Tuition & fees: $24,754 **Average undergraduate aid package: $22,707**

ABOUT THE INSTITUTION Independent United Methodist, coed. ***Awards:*** bachelor's and master's degrees. 32 undergraduate majors. ***Total enrollment:*** 1,118. Undergraduates: 1,013. Freshmen: 271. Federal methodology is used as a basis for awarding need-based institutional aid.

UNDERGRADUATE EXPENSES for 2008–09 ***Comprehensive fee:*** $33,554 includes full-time tuition ($23,214), mandatory fees ($1540), and room and board ($8800). ***College room only:*** $4956. ***Part-time tuition:*** $720 per credit hour. ***Part-time fees:*** $32 per credit hour.

FRESHMAN FINANCIAL AID (Fall 2008, est.) 229 applied for aid; of those 76% were deemed to have need. 100% of freshmen with need received aid; of those 45% had need fully met. ***Average percent of need met:*** 88% (excluding resources awarded to replace EFC). ***Average financial aid package:*** $24,443 (excluding resources awarded to replace EFC). 35% of all full-time freshmen had no need and received non-need-based gift aid.

UNDERGRADUATE FINANCIAL AID (Fall 2008, est.) 671 applied for aid; of those 83% were deemed to have need. 100% of undergraduates with need received aid; of those 38% had need fully met. ***Average percent of need met:*** 83% (excluding resources awarded to replace EFC). ***Average financial aid package:*** $22,707 (excluding resources awarded to replace EFC). 40% of all full-time undergraduates had no need and received non-need-based gift aid.

GIFT AID (NEED-BASED) ***Total amount:*** $9,342,753 (9% federal, 3% state, 86% institutional, 2% external sources). ***Receiving aid:*** Freshmen: 64% (174); all full-time undergraduates: 56% (553). ***Average award:*** Freshmen: $18,510; Undergraduates: $16,889. ***Scholarships, grants, and awards:*** Federal Pell, FSEOG, state, private, college/university gift aid from institutional funds.

GIFT AID (NON-NEED-BASED) ***Total amount:*** $6,964,813 (4% state, 93% institutional, 3% external sources). ***Receiving aid:*** Freshmen: 24% (64). Undergraduates: 14% (140). ***Average award:*** Freshmen: $15,141. Undergraduates: $13,826. ***Scholarships, grants, and awards by category:*** *Academic interests/achievement:* business, general academic interests/achievements. *Creative arts/performance:* art/fine arts, music, theater/drama. *Special achievements/activities:* community service, general special achievements/activities, hobbies/interests, leadership, religious involvement. *Special characteristics:* adult students, children of faculty/staff, ethnic background, first-generation college students, members of minority groups, relatives of clergy, religious affiliation. ***ROTC:*** Army cooperative.

LOANS ***Student loans:*** $4,513,586 (59% need-based, 41% non-need-based). 62% of past graduating class borrowed through all loan programs. *Average indebtedness per student:* $26,576. ***Average need-based loan:*** Freshmen: $3692. Undergraduates: $4603. ***Parent loans:*** $841,030 (11% need-based, 89% non-need-based). ***Programs:*** FFEL (Subsidized and Unsubsidized Stafford, PLUS), Perkins, college/university.

WORK-STUDY ***Federal work-study:*** Total amount: $388,205; 330 jobs averaging $1200.

APPLYING FOR FINANCIAL AID ***Required financial aid form:*** FAFSA. ***Financial aid deadline (priority):*** 3/1. ***Notification date:*** Continuous beginning 3/15. Students must reply by 5/1 or within 2 weeks of notification.

CONTACT Patrick James, Director of Financial Aid, Millsaps College, 1701 North State Street, Jackson, MS 39210-0001, 601-974-1220 or toll-free 800-352-1050. *Fax:* 601-974-1224. *E-mail:* jamespg@millsaps.edu.

MILLS COLLEGE

Oakland, CA

Tuition & fees: $35,190 **Average undergraduate aid package: $30,184**

ABOUT THE INSTITUTION Independent, undergraduate: women only; graduate: coed. ***Awards:*** bachelor's, master's, and doctoral degrees and post-bachelor's certificates. 38 undergraduate majors. ***Total enrollment:*** 1,476. Undergraduates: 969. Freshmen: 202. Federal methodology is used as a basis for awarding need-based institutional aid.

UNDERGRADUATE EXPENSES for 2008–09 ***Application fee:*** $50. ***Comprehensive fee:*** $45,740 includes full-time tuition ($34,170), mandatory fees ($1020), and room and board ($10,550). ***College room only:*** $5310. Full-time tuition and fees vary according to course load. Room and board charges vary according to board plan and housing facility. ***Part-time tuition:*** $5696 per course. ***Part-time fees:*** $1522 per term. Part-time tuition and fees vary according to course load. ***Payment plan:*** Installment.

FRESHMAN FINANCIAL AID (Fall 2008, est.) 184 applied for aid; of those 93% were deemed to have need. 100% of freshmen with need received aid; of those 42% had need fully met. ***Average percent of need met:*** 87% (excluding resources awarded to replace EFC). ***Average financial aid package:*** $34,127 (excluding resources awarded to replace EFC). 11% of all full-time freshmen had no need and received non-need-based gift aid.

UNDERGRADUATE FINANCIAL AID (Fall 2008, est.) 829 applied for aid; of those 97% were deemed to have need. 100% of undergraduates with need received aid; of those 46% had need fully met. ***Average percent of need met:*** 85% (excluding resources awarded to replace EFC). ***Average financial aid package:*** $30,184 (excluding resources awarded to replace EFC). 8% of all full-time undergraduates had no need and received non-need-based gift aid.

GIFT AID (NEED-BASED) ***Total amount:*** $18,747,002 (8% federal, 15% state, 74% institutional, 3% external sources). ***Receiving aid:*** Freshmen: 86% (171); all full-time undergraduates: 89% (801). ***Average award:*** Freshmen: $27,283; Undergraduates: $23,192. ***Scholarships, grants, and awards:*** Federal Pell, FSEOG, state, private, college/university gift aid from institutional funds.

GIFT AID (NON-NEED-BASED) ***Total amount:*** $1,118,525 (99% institutional, 1% external sources). ***Average award:*** Freshmen: $17,285. Undergraduates: $13,945. ***Scholarships, grants, and awards by category:*** *Academic interests/achievement:* biological sciences, computer science, general academic interests/achievements, mathematics, physical sciences, premedicine. *Creative arts/performance:* art/fine arts, music. *Special characteristics:* children of faculty/staff. ***Tuition waivers:*** Full or partial for employees or children of employees.

LOANS ***Student loans:*** $6,275,244 (97% need-based, 3% non-need-based). 97% of past graduating class borrowed through all loan programs. *Average indebtedness per student:* $24,255. ***Average need-based loan:*** Freshmen: $3395. Undergraduates: $4690. ***Parent loans:*** $1,090,250 (100% need-based). ***Programs:*** FFEL (Subsidized and Unsubsidized Stafford, PLUS), Perkins, college/university.

WORK-STUDY ***Federal work-study:*** Total amount: $290,183; jobs available. ***State or other work-study/employment:*** Total amount: $437,490 (97% need-based, 3% non-need-based). Part-time jobs available.

APPLYING FOR FINANCIAL AID ***Required financial aid forms:*** FAFSA, institution's own form, Noncustodial Parent Statement. ***Financial aid deadline (priority):*** 2/15. ***Notification date:*** Continuous beginning 3/1. Students must reply by 5/1 or within 2 weeks of notification.

CONTACT The M Center/Financial Aid, Mills College, 5000 MacArthur Boulevard, Oakland, CA 94613, 510-430-2000 or toll-free 800-87-MILLS. *E-mail:* mcenter-finaid@mills.edu.

MILWAUKEE INSTITUTE OF ART AND DESIGN

Milwaukee, WI

CONTACT Mr. Lloyd Mueller, Director of Financial Aid, Milwaukee Institute of Art and Design, 273 East Erie Street, Milwaukee, WI 53202-6003, 414-291-3272 or toll-free 888-749-MIAD. *Fax:* 414-291-8077. *E-mail:* llmuelle@miad.edu.

MILWAUKEE SCHOOL OF ENGINEERING

Milwaukee, WI

Tuition & fees: $28,665 **Average undergraduate aid package: $17,277**

ABOUT THE INSTITUTION Independent, coed, primarily men. ***Awards:*** bachelor's and master's degrees. 17 undergraduate majors. ***Total enrollment:*** 2,622. Undergraduates: 2,418. Freshmen: 645. Federal methodology is used as a basis for awarding need-based institutional aid.

UNDERGRADUATE EXPENSES for 2009–10 ***Application fee:*** $25. ***Comprehensive fee:*** $35,829 includes full-time tuition ($28,665) and room and board ($7164). ***College room only:*** $4599. ***Part-time tuition:*** $498 per quarter hour.

FRESHMAN FINANCIAL AID (Fall 2007) 514 applied for aid; of those 89% were deemed to have need. 100% of freshmen with need received aid; of those 14% had need fully met. ***Average percent of need met:*** 67% (excluding resources awarded to replace EFC). ***Average financial aid package:*** $16,625 (excluding resources awarded to replace EFC). 16% of all full-time freshmen had no need and received non-need-based gift aid.

UNDERGRADUATE FINANCIAL AID (Fall 2007) 1,750 applied for aid; of those 91% were deemed to have need. 100% of undergraduates with need received aid; of those 14% had need fully met. ***Average percent of need met:*** 67% (excluding resources awarded to replace EFC). ***Average financial aid package:*** $17,277 (excluding resources awarded to replace EFC). 17% of all full-time undergraduates had no need and received non-need-based gift aid.

GIFT AID (NEED-BASED) ***Total amount:*** $23,642,076 (8% federal, 8% state, 80% institutional, 4% external sources). ***Receiving aid:*** Freshmen: 82% (456); all full-time undergraduates: 76% (1,578). ***Average award:*** Freshmen: $14,511; Undergraduates: $14,271. ***Scholarships, grants, and awards:*** Federal Pell, FSEOG, state, private, college/university gift aid from institutional funds.

GIFT AID (NON-NEED-BASED) ***Total amount:*** $4,532,656 (1% state, 89% institutional, 10% external sources). ***Receiving aid:*** Freshmen: 9% (49). Undergraduates: 8% (165). ***Average award:*** Freshmen: $8935. Undergraduates: $9260. ***Scholarships, grants, and awards by category:*** *Academic interests/achievement:* 1,934 awards ($18,287,408 total): business, communication, computer science, engineering/technologies, health fields. *Special characteristics:* 31 awards ($613,836 total): children of faculty/staff. ***ROTC:*** Army cooperative, Naval cooperative, Air Force cooperative.

LOANS ***Student loans:*** $16,478,348 (67% need-based, 33% non-need-based). 89% of past graduating class borrowed through all loan programs. *Average indebtedness per student:* $31,592. ***Average need-based loan:*** Freshmen: $2304. Undergraduates: $3246. ***Parent loans:*** $4,305,415 (58% need-based, 42% non-need-based). ***Programs:*** FFEL (Subsidized and Unsubsidized Stafford, PLUS), Perkins, state, college/university.

WORK-STUDY ***Federal work-study:*** Total amount: $316,641; 360 jobs averaging $880.

APPLYING FOR FINANCIAL AID ***Required financial aid form:*** FAFSA. ***Financial aid deadline (priority):*** 3/15. ***Notification date:*** Continuous. Students must reply within 2 weeks of notification.

CONTACT Steve Midthun, Director of Financial Aid, Milwaukee School of Engineering, 1025 North Broadway Street, Milwaukee, WI 53202-3109, 414-277-7223 or toll-free 800-332-6763. *Fax:* 414-277-6952. *E-mail:* finaid@msoe.edu.

MINNEAPOLIS COLLEGE OF ART AND DESIGN

Minneapolis, MN

ABOUT THE INSTITUTION Independent, coed. ***Awards:*** bachelor's and master's degrees and post-bachelor's certificates. 11 undergraduate majors. ***Total enrollment:*** 772. Undergraduates: 709. Freshmen: 103.

GIFT AID (NEED-BASED) ***Scholarships, grants, and awards:*** Federal Pell, FSEOG, state, private, college/university gift aid from institutional funds.

GIFT AID (NON-NEED-BASED) ***Scholarships, grants, and awards by category:*** *Creative arts/performance:* applied art and design, art/fine arts, cinema/film/broadcasting, general creative arts/performance.

LOANS ***Programs:*** FFEL (Subsidized and Unsubsidized Stafford, PLUS), Perkins, state.

WORK-STUDY ***Federal work-study:*** Total amount: $65,232; 71 jobs averaging $1890. ***State or other work-study/employment:*** Total amount: $353,862 (54% need-based, 46% non-need-based). 25 part-time jobs averaging $1820.

APPLYING FOR FINANCIAL AID ***Required financial aid form:*** FAFSA.

CONTACT Ms. Laura Link, Director of Financial Aid, Minneapolis College of Art and Design, 2501 Stevens Avenue South, Minneapolis, MN 55404-4347, 612-874-3733 or toll-free 800-874-6223. *Fax:* 612-874-3701. *E-mail:* laura_link@mead.edu.

MINNESOTA SCHOOL OF BUSINESS–BLAINE

Blaine, MN

CONTACT Financial Aid Office, Minnesota School of Business–Blaine, 3680 Pheasant Ridge Drive NE, Blaine, MN 55449, 763-225-8000.

MINNESOTA SCHOOL OF BUSINESS–ROCHESTER

Rochester, MN

CONTACT Financial Aid Office, Minnesota School of Business–Rochester, 2521 Pennington Drive, NW, Rochester, MN 55901, 507-536-9500 or toll-free 888-662-8772.

MINNESOTA STATE UNIVERSITY MANKATO

Mankato, MN

Tuition & fees (MN res): $6263 **Average undergraduate aid package: $7082**

ABOUT THE INSTITUTION State-supported, coed. ***Awards:*** associate, bachelor's, master's, and doctoral degrees and post-master's certificates. 127 undergraduate majors. ***Total enrollment:*** 14,515. Undergraduates: 12,815. Freshmen: 2,360. Federal methodology is used as a basis for awarding need-based institutional aid.

UNDERGRADUATE EXPENSES for 2008–09 ***Application fee:*** $20. ***Tuition, state resident:*** full-time $5467; part-time $218.60 per credit. ***Tuition, nonresident:*** full-time $11,712; part-time $467.05 per credit. ***Required fees:*** full-time $796; $33.04 per credit. Full-time tuition and fees vary according to course load and reciprocity agreements. Part-time tuition and fees vary according to course load and reciprocity agreements. ***College room and board:*** $5732. Room and board charges vary according to board plan. ***Payment plan:*** Installment.

FRESHMAN FINANCIAL AID (Fall 2008, est.) 1,968 applied for aid; of those 61% were deemed to have need. 100% of freshmen with need received aid; of those 38% had need fully met. ***Average percent of need met:*** 80% (excluding resources awarded to replace EFC). ***Average financial aid package:*** $6529 (excluding resources awarded to replace EFC). 7% of all full-time freshmen had no need and received non-need-based gift aid.

UNDERGRADUATE FINANCIAL AID (Fall 2008, est.) 8,709 applied for aid; of those 66% were deemed to have need. 100% of undergraduates with need received aid; of those 38% had need fully met. ***Average percent of need met:*** 81% (excluding resources awarded to replace EFC). ***Average financial aid package:*** $7082 (excluding resources awarded to replace EFC). 2% of all full-time undergraduates had no need and received non-need-based gift aid.

GIFT AID (NEED-BASED) ***Total amount:*** $17,916,025 (55% federal, 34% state, 3% institutional, 8% external sources). ***Receiving aid:*** Freshmen: 31% (740); all full-time undergraduates: 33% (3,726). ***Average award:*** Freshmen: $4528; Undergraduates: $4136. ***Scholarships, grants, and awards:*** Federal Pell, FSEOG, state, private, college/university gift aid from institutional funds, Academic Competitiveness Grant, National Smart Grant.

GIFT AID (NON-NEED-BASED) ***Total amount:*** $3,605,927 (49% federal, 3% state, 16% institutional, 32% external sources). ***Receiving aid:*** Freshmen: 16% (368). Undergraduates: 10% (1,107). ***Average award:*** Freshmen: $1813. Undergraduates: $2053. ***Tuition waivers:*** Full or partial for employees or children of employees, senior citizens. ***ROTC:*** Army.

LOANS ***Student loans:*** $61,626,688 (33% need-based, 67% non-need-based). 82% of past graduating class borrowed through all loan programs. *Average indebtedness per student:* $22,962. ***Average need-based loan:*** Freshmen: $2963. Undergraduates: $3683. ***Parent loans:*** $2,329,071 (100% non-need-based). ***Programs:*** FFEL (Subsidized and Unsubsidized Stafford, PLUS), Perkins, state, alternative loans.

WORK-STUDY ***Federal work-study:*** Total amount: $748,327; 420 jobs averaging $3091. ***State or other work-study/employment:*** Total amount: $1,202,479 (100% need-based). 566 part-time jobs averaging $3137.

ATHLETIC AWARDS Total amount: $2,040,906 (27% need-based, 73% non-need-based).

APPLYING FOR FINANCIAL AID ***Required financial aid forms:*** FAFSA, SELF or Alternative Loan Application or PLUS Application. ***Financial aid deadline (priority):*** 3/15. ***Notification date:*** Continuous beginning 3/30. Students must reply within 2 weeks of notification.

CONTACT Sandra Loerts, Director of Financial Aid, Minnesota State University Mankato, Student Financial Services, Mankato, MN 56001, 507-389-1866 or toll-free 800-722-0544. *Fax:* 507-389-2227. *E-mail:* campushub@mnsu.edu.

MINNESOTA STATE UNIVERSITY MOORHEAD

Moorhead, MN

Tuition & fees (MN res): $6144   Average undergraduate aid package: $7453

ABOUT THE INSTITUTION State-supported, coed. 93 undergraduate majors. Federal methodology is used as a basis for awarding need-based institutional aid.

UNDERGRADUATE EXPENSES for 2008–09 ***Tuition, state resident:*** full-time $5236; part-time $174.54 per credit. ***Tuition, nonresident:*** full-time $10,472; part-time $349.08 per credit. ***Required fees:*** full-time $908; $25.82 per credit or $168.82 per term. Full-time tuition and fees vary according to reciprocity agreements. Part-time tuition and fees vary according to reciprocity agreements. ***College room and board:*** $5936. Room and board charges vary according to board plan and housing facility. ***Payment plan:*** Installment.

FRESHMAN FINANCIAL AID (Fall 2008, est.) 1,100 applied for aid; of those 64% were deemed to have need. 100% of freshmen with need received aid. ***Average financial aid package:*** $5810 (excluding resources awarded to replace EFC). 14% of all full-time freshmen had no need and received non-need-based gift aid.

UNDERGRADUATE FINANCIAL AID (Fall 2008, est.) 5,724 applied for aid; of those 73% were deemed to have need. 100% of undergraduates with need received aid. ***Average financial aid package:*** $7453 (excluding resources awarded to replace EFC). 12% of all full-time undergraduates had no need and received non-need-based gift aid.

GIFT AID (NEED-BASED) ***Total amount:*** $9,475,120 (63% federal, 35% state, 2% institutional). ***Receiving aid:*** Freshmen: 29% (341); all full-time undergraduates: 27% (1,931). ***Average award:*** Freshmen: $5225; Undergraduates: $4800. ***Scholarships, grants, and awards:*** Federal Pell, FSEOG, state, private, college/university gift aid from institutional funds.

GIFT AID (NON-NEED-BASED) ***Total amount:*** $3,128,505 (38% federal, 4% state, 29% institutional, 29% external sources). ***Average award:*** Freshmen: $810. Undergraduates: $930. ***Scholarships, grants, and awards by category:*** *Academic interests/achievement:* 852 awards ($795,053 total): general academic interests/achievements. *Creative arts/performance:* 80 awards ($47,297 total): art/fine arts, cinema/film/broadcasting, creative writing, music, theater/drama. *Special achievements/activities:* community service, general special achievements/activities. *Special characteristics:* 255 awards ($743,761 total): children of faculty/staff, first-generation college students, members of minority groups. ***Tuition waivers:*** Full or partial for employees or children of employees, senior citizens.

LOANS ***Student loans:*** $37,293,519 (36% need-based, 64% non-need-based). 70% of past graduating class borrowed through all loan programs. *Average indebtedness per student:* $24,493. ***Average need-based loan:*** Freshmen: $2882. Undergraduates: $3790. ***Parent loans:*** $496,657 (100% non-need-based). ***Programs:*** Federal Direct (Subsidized and Unsubsidized Stafford, PLUS), Perkins, state, alternative loans.

WORK-STUDY ***Federal work-study:*** Total amount: $544,466; 246 jobs averaging $2213. ***State or other work-study/employment:*** Total amount: $2,666,105 (13% need-based, 87% non-need-based). 1,227 part-time jobs averaging $2198.

ATHLETIC AWARDS Total amount: $450,136 (100% non-need-based).

APPLYING FOR FINANCIAL AID ***Required financial aid form:*** FAFSA. ***Financial aid deadline (priority):*** 2/15. ***Notification date:*** Continuous beginning 6/1. Students must reply within 2 weeks of notification.

CONTACT Ms. Carolyn Zehren, Director of Financial Aid, Minnesota State University Moorhead, 1104 7th Avenue South, Moorhead, MN 56563-0002, 218-477-2251 or toll-free 800-593-7246. *Fax:* 218-477-2058. *E-mail:* zehren@mnstate.edu.

MINOT STATE UNIVERSITY

Minot, ND

Tuition & fees (ND res): $5044   Average undergraduate aid package: $5415

ABOUT THE INSTITUTION State-supported, coed. ***Awards:*** associate, bachelor's, and master's degrees and post-master's certificates. 59 undergraduate majors. ***Total enrollment:*** 3,432. Undergraduates: 3,172. Freshmen: 437. Federal methodology is used as a basis for awarding need-based institutional aid.

UNDERGRADUATE EXPENSES for 2008–09 ***Application fee:*** $35. ***Tuition, state resident:*** full-time $4179; part-time $210.16 per credit. ***Tuition, nonresident:*** full-time $11,158; part-time $500.94 per credit. ***Required fees:*** full-time $865; $37 per credit. Full-time tuition and fees vary according to class time, course load, degree level, location, program, and reciprocity agreements. Part-time tuition and fees vary according to class time, degree level, location, program, and reciprocity agreements. ***College room and board:*** $5234; ***Room only:*** $2700. Room and board charges vary according to board plan and housing facility. ***Payment plan:*** Installment.

FRESHMAN FINANCIAL AID (Fall 2008, est.) 323 applied for aid; of those 100% were deemed to have need. 96% of freshmen with need received aid; of those 27% had need fully met. ***Average percent of need met:*** 81% (excluding resources awarded to replace EFC). ***Average financial aid package:*** $4354 (excluding resources awarded to replace EFC).

UNDERGRADUATE FINANCIAL AID (Fall 2008, est.) 1,677 applied for aid; of those 100% were deemed to have need. 97% of undergraduates with need received aid; of those 20% had need fully met. ***Average percent of need met:*** 62% (excluding resources awarded to replace EFC). ***Average financial aid package:*** $5415 (excluding resources awarded to replace EFC).

GIFT AID (NEED-BASED) ***Total amount:*** $4,148,231 (64% federal, 7% state, 7% institutional, 22% external sources). ***Receiving aid:*** Freshmen: 56% (202); all full-time undergraduates: 50% (973). ***Average award:*** Freshmen: $2820; Undergraduates: $3526. ***Scholarships, grants, and awards:*** Federal Pell, FSEOG, state, private, college/university gift aid from institutional funds, Federal Nursing.

GIFT AID (NON-NEED-BASED) ***Total amount:*** $1,556,166 (3% federal, 1% state, 19% institutional, 77% external sources). ***Receiving aid:*** Freshmen: 14% (50). Undergraduates: 12% (229). ***Average award:*** Freshmen: $947. Undergraduates: $903. ***Scholarships, grants, and awards by category:*** *Academic interests/achievement:* 802 awards ($537,581 total): business, communication, computer science, education, English, general academic interests/achievements, health fields, humanities, mathematics, social sciences. *Special characteristics:* 124 awards ($223,096 total): ethnic background, international students, local/state students, members of minority groups, out-of-state students, veterans, veterans' children. ***Tuition waivers:*** Full or partial for minority students, children of alumni, employees or children of employees.

LOANS ***Student loans:*** $10,199,241 (65% need-based, 35% non-need-based). 75% of past graduating class borrowed through all loan programs. *Average indebtedness per student:* $15,193. ***Average need-based loan:*** Freshmen: $3067. Undergraduates: $3988. ***Parent loans:*** $63,233 (15% need-based, 85% non-need-based). ***Programs:*** FFEL (Subsidized and Unsubsidized Stafford, PLUS), Perkins, Federal Nursing, college/university.

WORK-STUDY ***Federal work-study:*** Total amount: $161,891; 140 jobs averaging $1053.

ATHLETIC AWARDS Total amount: $224,523 (20% need-based, 80% non-need-based).

APPLYING FOR FINANCIAL AID ***Required financial aid form:*** FAFSA. ***Financial aid deadline (priority):*** 3/15. ***Notification date:*** Continuous beginning 4/1. Students must reply within 2 weeks of notification.

CONTACT Mr. Dale Gehring, Director of Financial Aid, Minot State University, 500 University Avenue, West, Minot, ND 58707-0002, 701-858-3862 or toll-free 800-777-0750 Ext. 3350. *Fax:* 701-858-4310. *E-mail:* dale.gehring@minotstateu.edu.

MIRRER YESHIVA

Brooklyn, NY

CONTACT Financial Aid Office, Mirrer Yeshiva, 1795 Ocean Parkway, Brooklyn, NY 11223-2010, 718-645-0536.

MISERICORDIA UNIVERSITY

Dallas, PA

Tuition & fees: $23,150 **Average undergraduate aid package: $15,606**

ABOUT THE INSTITUTION Independent Roman Catholic, coed, primarily women. ***Awards:*** bachelor's, master's, and doctoral degrees and post-bachelor's and post-master's certificates. 31 undergraduate majors. ***Total enrollment:*** 2,501. Undergraduates: 2,183. Freshmen: 384. Federal methodology is used as a basis for awarding need-based institutional aid.

UNDERGRADUATE EXPENSES for 2008–09 ***Application fee:*** $25. ***Comprehensive fee:*** $32,800 includes full-time tuition ($21,990), mandatory fees ($1160), and room and board ($9650). ***College room only:*** $5590. Room and board charges vary according to board plan and housing facility. ***Part-time tuition:*** $450 per credit. Part-time tuition and fees vary according to class time and location. ***Payment plans:*** Installment, deferred payment.

FRESHMAN FINANCIAL AID (Fall 2008, est.) 359 applied for aid; of those 89% were deemed to have need. 100% of freshmen with need received aid; of those 15% had need fully met. ***Average percent of need met:*** 73% (excluding resources awarded to replace EFC). ***Average financial aid package:*** $16,191 (excluding resources awarded to replace EFC). 10% of all full-time freshmen had no need and received non-need-based gift aid.

UNDERGRADUATE FINANCIAL AID (Fall 2008, est.) 1,447 applied for aid; of those 89% were deemed to have need. 99% of undergraduates with need received aid; of those 16% had need fully met. ***Average percent of need met:*** 71% (excluding resources awarded to replace EFC). ***Average financial aid package:*** $15,606 (excluding resources awarded to replace EFC). 10% of all full-time undergraduates had no need and received non-need-based gift aid.

GIFT AID (NEED-BASED) ***Total amount:*** $14,312,586 (11% federal, 15% state, 72% institutional, 2% external sources). ***Receiving aid:*** Freshmen: 84% (319); all full-time undergraduates: 81% (1,267). ***Average award:*** Freshmen: $12,295; Undergraduates: $10,895. ***Scholarships, grants, and awards:*** Federal Pell, FSEOG, state, private, college/university gift aid from institutional funds, Federal Nursing.

GIFT AID (NON-NEED-BASED) ***Total amount:*** $2,102,978 (96% institutional, 4% external sources). ***Receiving aid:*** Freshmen: 10% (38). Undergraduates: 8% (122). ***Average award:*** Freshmen: $6700. Undergraduates: $6114. ***Scholarships, grants, and awards by category:*** *Academic interests/achievement:* 1,286 awards ($5,732,880 total): business, computer science, education, general academic interests/achievements, health fields, physical sciences, social sciences. *Special achievements/activities:* 1,078 awards ($2,215,300 total): community service, general special achievements/activities, leadership. *Special characteristics:* 655 awards ($1,622,902 total): children and siblings of alumni, children of current students, children of faculty/staff, general special characteristics, members of minority groups, out-of-state students, previous college experience, relatives of clergy, religious affiliation, siblings of current students. ***Tuition waivers:*** Full or partial for employees or children of employees. ***ROTC:*** Army cooperative, Air Force cooperative.

LOANS ***Student loans:*** $13,462,858 (71% need-based, 29% non-need-based). 76% of past graduating class borrowed through all loan programs. *Average indebtedness per student:* $20,345. ***Average need-based loan:*** Freshmen: $5385. Undergraduates: $6716. ***Parent loans:*** $2,921,872 (36% need-based, 64% non-need-based). ***Programs:*** FFEL (Subsidized and Unsubsidized Stafford, PLUS), Perkins, Federal Nursing, state.

WORK-STUDY ***Federal work-study:*** Total amount: $230,162; 130 jobs averaging $1400.

APPLYING FOR FINANCIAL AID ***Required financial aid forms:*** FAFSA, institution's own form. ***Financial aid deadline (priority):*** 3/1. ***Notification date:*** 3/15. Students must reply within 2 weeks of notification.

CONTACT Jane Dessoye, Executive Director of Enrollment Management, Misericordia University, 301 Lake Street, Dallas, PA 18612-1098, 570-674-6280 or toll-free 866-262-6363. *Fax:* 570-675-2441. *E-mail:* finaid@misericordia.edu.

MISSISSIPPI COLLEGE

Clinton, MS

Tuition & fees: $13,290 **Average undergraduate aid package: $15,433**

ABOUT THE INSTITUTION Independent Southern Baptist, coed. ***Awards:*** bachelor's, master's, doctoral, and first professional degrees and post-bachelor's certificates. 62 undergraduate majors. ***Total enrollment:*** 4,741. Undergraduates: 3,039. Freshmen: 533. Federal methodology is used as a basis for awarding need-based institutional aid.

UNDERGRADUATE EXPENSES for 2008–09 ***Comprehensive fee:*** $19,090 includes full-time tuition ($12,670), mandatory fees ($620), and room and board ($5800). Full-time tuition and fees vary according to course load. Room and board charges vary according to housing facility. ***Part-time tuition:*** $397 per credit hour. ***Part-time fees:*** $155 per term. Part-time tuition and fees vary according to course load. ***Payment plans:*** Installment, deferred payment.

FRESHMAN FINANCIAL AID (Fall 2008, est.) 524 applied for aid; of those 55% were deemed to have need. 100% of freshmen with need received aid; of those 32% had need fully met. ***Average percent of need met:*** 78% (excluding resources awarded to replace EFC). ***Average financial aid package:*** $14,557 (excluding resources awarded to replace EFC). 44% of all full-time freshmen had no need and received non-need-based gift aid.

UNDERGRADUATE FINANCIAL AID (Fall 2008, est.) 2,616 applied for aid; of those 60% were deemed to have need. 100% of undergraduates with need received aid; of those 29% had need fully met. ***Average percent of need met:*** 73% (excluding resources awarded to replace EFC). ***Average financial aid package:*** $15,433 (excluding resources awarded to replace EFC). 39% of all full-time undergraduates had no need and received non-need-based gift aid.

GIFT AID (NEED-BASED) ***Total amount:*** $11,889,860 (35% federal, 6% state, 57% institutional, 2% external sources). ***Receiving aid:*** Freshmen: 38% (202); all full-time undergraduates: 45% (1,198). ***Average award:*** Freshmen: $10,952; Undergraduates: $8894. ***Scholarships, grants, and awards:*** Federal Pell, FSEOG, state, private, college/university gift aid from institutional funds, Federal Nursing.

GIFT AID (NON-NEED-BASED) ***Total amount:*** $11,349,803 (9% state, 88% institutional, 3% external sources). ***Receiving aid:*** Freshmen: 16% (86). Undergraduates: 11% (288). ***Average award:*** Freshmen: $10,252. Undergraduates: $9090. ***Scholarships, grants, and awards by category:*** *Academic interests/achievement:* 1,694 awards ($7,474,842 total): general academic interests/achievements. *Creative arts/performance:* 86 awards ($129,680 total): applied art and design, art/fine arts, music. *Special achievements/activities:* 1,276 awards ($4,842,850 total): general special achievements/activities, leadership, religious involvement. *Special characteristics:* 761 awards ($1,819,444 total): children and siblings of alumni, children of faculty/staff, general special characteristics, relatives of clergy. ***Tuition waivers:*** Full or partial for employees or children of employees. ***ROTC:*** Army cooperative.

LOANS ***Student loans:*** $14,765,430 (85% need-based, 15% non-need-based). 75% of past graduating class borrowed through all loan programs. *Average indebtedness per student:* $24,508. ***Average need-based loan:*** Freshmen: $4802. Undergraduates: $7732. ***Parent loans:*** $556,884 (100% need-based). ***Programs:*** FFEL (Subsidized and Unsubsidized Stafford, PLUS), Perkins, Federal Nursing, college/university.

WORK-STUDY ***Federal work-study:*** Total amount: $237,502; 186 jobs averaging $1231.

APPLYING FOR FINANCIAL AID ***Required financial aid forms:*** FAFSA, state aid form. ***Financial aid deadline (priority):*** 3/1. ***Notification date:*** Continuous beginning 3/1. Students must reply by 5/1.

CONTACT Karon McMillan, Director of Financial Aid, Mississippi College, PO Box 4035, Clinton, MS 39058, 601-925-3249 or toll-free 800-738-1236. *Fax:* 601-925-3950. *E-mail:* kmcmilla@mc.edu.

MISSISSIPPI STATE UNIVERSITY

Mississippi State, MS

Tuition & fees (MS res): $5151 **Average undergraduate aid package: $7568**

ABOUT THE INSTITUTION State-supported, coed. ***Awards:*** bachelor's, master's, doctoral, and first professional degrees and post-master's certificates. 70 undergraduate majors. ***Total enrollment:*** 17,824. Undergraduates: 13,991. Freshmen: 2,489. Federal methodology is used as a basis for awarding need-based institutional aid.

UNDERGRADUATE EXPENSES for 2008–09 ***Application fee:*** $35. ***Tuition, state resident:*** full-time $5151; part-time $214.75 per hour. ***Tuition, nonresident:*** full-time $12,503; part-time $521.25 per hour. Part-time tuition and fees vary according to course load. ***College room and board:*** $7333; ***Room only:*** $4098. Room and board charges vary according to board plan, housing facility, and student level. ***Payment plan:*** Installment.

FRESHMAN FINANCIAL AID (Fall 2007) 1,565 applied for aid; of those 100% were deemed to have need. 97% of freshmen with need received aid; of those 17% had need fully met. ***Average percent of need met:*** 64% (excluding resources awarded to replace EFC). ***Average financial aid package:*** $6488 (excluding resources awarded to replace EFC). 30% of all full-time freshmen had no need and received non-need-based gift aid.

UNDERGRADUATE FINANCIAL AID (Fall 2007) 7,508 applied for aid; of those 99% were deemed to have need. 97% of undergraduates with need received aid; of those 20% had need fully met. ***Average percent of need met:*** 64% (excluding resources awarded to replace EFC). ***Average financial aid package:*** $7568 (excluding resources awarded to replace EFC). 19% of all full-time undergraduates had no need and received non-need-based gift aid.

GIFT AID (NEED-BASED) ***Total amount:*** $31,278,127 (46% federal, 11% state, 19% institutional, 24% external sources). ***Receiving aid:*** Freshmen: 66% (1,506); all full-time undergraduates: 61% (7,154). ***Average award:*** Freshmen: $3708; Undergraduates: $3686. ***Scholarships, grants, and awards:*** Federal Pell, FSEOG, state, private, college/university gift aid from institutional funds, United Negro College Fund.

GIFT AID (NON-NEED-BASED) ***Total amount:*** $14,765,828 (23% state, 50% institutional, 27% external sources). ***Receiving aid:*** Freshmen: 22% (490). Undergraduates: 13% (1,466). ***Average award:*** Freshmen: $2801. Undergraduates: $2755. ***Scholarships, grants, and awards by category:*** *Academic interests/achievement:* agriculture, architecture, area/ethnic studies, biological sciences, business, communication, computer science, education, engineering/technologies, English, foreign languages, general academic interests/achievements, health fields, home economics, humanities, international studies, library science, mathematics, military science, physical sciences, premedicine, religion/biblical studies, social sciences. *Creative arts/performance:* applied art and design, art/fine arts, cinema/film/broadcasting, creative writing, dance, debating, general creative arts/performance, journalism/publications, music, performing arts, theater/drama. *Special achievements/activities:* cheerleading/drum major, general special achievements/activities, junior miss, leadership, memberships. *Special characteristics:* adult students, children and siblings of alumni, children of educators, children of faculty/staff, children of public servants, first-generation college students, handicapped students, local/state students, out-of-state students, previous college experience, spouses of deceased or disabled public servants. ***Tuition waivers:*** Full or partial for children of alumni, employees or children of employees, senior citizens. ***ROTC:*** Army, Air Force.

LOANS ***Student loans:*** $63,315,046 (82% need-based, 18% non-need-based). 40% of past graduating class borrowed through all loan programs. *Average indebtedness per student:* $21,232. ***Average need-based loan:*** Freshmen: $3542. Undergraduates: $3970. ***Parent loans:*** $3,841,211 (29% need-based, 71% non-need-based). ***Programs:*** FFEL (Subsidized and Unsubsidized Stafford, PLUS), Perkins, college/university.

WORK-STUDY ***Federal work-study:*** Total amount: $2,434,681; 970 jobs averaging $2510.

ATHLETIC AWARDS Total amount: $4,288,675 (100% non-need-based).

APPLYING FOR FINANCIAL AID ***Required financial aid forms:*** FAFSA, state grant/scholarship application. ***Financial aid deadline (priority):*** 4/1. ***Notification date:*** Continuous. Students must reply by 5/1.

CONTACT Mr. Bruce Crain, Director of Financial Aid, Mississippi State University, PO Box 6035, Mississippi State, MS 39762, 662-325-2450. *Fax:* 662-325-0702. *E-mail:* financialaid@saffairs.msstate.edu.

MISSISSIPPI UNIVERSITY FOR WOMEN

Columbus, MS

Tuition & fees (MS res): $4423 **Average undergraduate aid package: $8045**

ABOUT THE INSTITUTION State-supported, coed, primarily women. ***Awards:*** associate, bachelor's, and master's degrees and post-master's certificates. 28 undergraduate majors. ***Total enrollment:*** 2,365. Undergraduates: 2,193. Freshmen: 258. Federal methodology is used as a basis for awarding need-based institutional aid.

UNDERGRADUATE EXPENSES for 2008–09 ***Tuition, state resident:*** full-time $4423; part-time $184.25 per credit hour. ***Tuition, nonresident:*** full-time $11,688; part-time $486.95 per credit hour. Part-time tuition and fees vary according to course load. ***College room and board:*** $4981; ***Room only:*** $2924. Room and board charges vary according to housing facility. ***Payment plans:*** Installment, deferred payment.

FRESHMAN FINANCIAL AID (Fall 2008, est.) 217 applied for aid; of those 85% were deemed to have need. 100% of freshmen with need received aid; of those 89% had need fully met. ***Average percent of need met:*** 66% (excluding resources awarded to replace EFC). ***Average financial aid package:*** $8304 (excluding resources awarded to replace EFC). 21% of all full-time freshmen had no need and received non-need-based gift aid.

UNDERGRADUATE FINANCIAL AID (Fall 2008, est.) 1,368 applied for aid; of those 86% were deemed to have need. 100% of undergraduates with need received aid; of those 78% had need fully met. ***Average percent of need met:*** 66% (excluding resources awarded to replace EFC). ***Average financial aid package:*** $8045 (excluding resources awarded to replace EFC). 18% of all full-time undergraduates had no need and received non-need-based gift aid.

GIFT AID (NEED-BASED) ***Total amount:*** $4,002,467 (99% federal, 1% state). ***Receiving aid:*** Freshmen: 57% (137); all full-time undergraduates: 53% (885). ***Average award:*** Freshmen: $3907; Undergraduates: $4307. ***Scholarships, grants, and awards:*** Federal Pell, FSEOG, state, private, college/university gift aid from institutional funds.

GIFT AID (NON-NEED-BASED) ***Total amount:*** $4,820,999 (16% state, 78% institutional, 6% external sources). ***Receiving aid:*** Freshmen: 27% (64). Undergraduates: 21% (350). ***Average award:*** Freshmen: $5947. Undergraduates: $4786. ***Scholarships, grants, and awards by category:*** *Academic interests/achievement:* 785 awards ($1,884,486 total): biological sciences, business, communication, computer science, education, English, general academic interests/achievements, health fields, home economics, humanities, mathematics, physical sciences. *Creative arts/performance:* 8 awards ($20,100 total): art/fine arts, journalism/publications, music, performing arts, theater/drama. *Special achievements/activities:* 39 awards ($24,900 total): junior miss, leadership. *Special characteristics:* 227 awards ($1,113,072 total): adult students, children and siblings of alumni, children of faculty/staff, ethnic background, international students, members of minority groups, out-of-state students, parents of current students. ***Tuition waivers:*** Full or partial for employees or children of employees. ***ROTC:*** Army cooperative, Air Force cooperative.

LOANS ***Student loans:*** $9,233,633 (47% need-based, 53% non-need-based). 64% of past graduating class borrowed through all loan programs. *Average indebtedness per student:* $18,506. ***Average need-based loan:*** Freshmen: $3163. Undergraduates: $4439. ***Parent loans:*** $217,526 (100% non-need-based). ***Programs:*** FFEL (Subsidized and Unsubsidized Stafford, PLUS), Perkins.

WORK-STUDY ***Federal work-study:*** Total amount: $104,241; 67 jobs averaging $1556. ***State or other work-study/employment:*** Total amount: $256,697 (100% non-need-based). 207 part-time jobs averaging $1307.

APPLYING FOR FINANCIAL AID ***Required financial aid forms:*** FAFSA, institution's own form, state aid form. ***Financial aid deadline (priority):*** 3/1. ***Notification date:*** Continuous beginning 4/1. Students must reply within 2 weeks of notification.

CONTACT Mr. Dan Miller, Director of Financial Aid, Mississippi University for Women, 1100 College Street, MUW 1614, Columbus, MS 39701-4044, 662-329-7114 or toll-free 877-GO 2 THE W. *Fax:* 662-329-7325. *E-mail:* dmiller@finaid.muw.edu.

MISSISSIPPI VALLEY STATE UNIVERSITY

Itta Bena, MS

CONTACT Mr. Darrell G. Boyd, Director of Student Financial Aid, Mississippi Valley State University, 14000 Highway 82W #7268, Itta Bena, MS 38941-1400, 662-254-3765 or toll-free 800-844-6885 (in-state). *Fax:* 662-254-3759. *E-mail:* dboyd@mvsu.edu.

MISSOURI BAPTIST UNIVERSITY

St. Louis, MO

Tuition & fees: $16,872 **Average undergraduate aid package: $8232**

ABOUT THE INSTITUTION Independent Southern Baptist, coed. ***Awards:*** associate, bachelor's, and master's degrees and post-bachelor's and post-master's certificates. 37 undergraduate majors. ***Total enrollment:*** 4,614. Undergraduates: 3,276. Freshmen: 204. Both federal and institutional methodology are used as a basis for awarding need-based institutional aid.

UNDERGRADUATE EXPENSES for 2008–09 ***Application fee:*** $30. ***Comprehensive fee:*** $23,942 includes full-time tuition ($16,170), mandatory fees ($702), and room and board ($7070). Full-time tuition and fees vary according to course load, degree level, and location. Room and board charges vary according to housing facility. ***Part-time tuition:*** $560 per credit. ***Part-time fees:*** $13 per credit; $25 per term. Part-time tuition and fees vary according to course load, degree level, and location. ***Payment plan:*** Installment.

UNDERGRADUATE FINANCIAL AID (Fall 2008, est.) 1,412 applied for aid; of those 100% were deemed to have need. 100% of undergraduates with need received aid. ***Average percent of need met:*** 26% (excluding resources awarded to replace EFC). ***Average financial aid package:*** $8232 (excluding resources awarded to replace EFC). 12% of all full-time undergraduates had no need and received non-need-based gift aid.

GIFT AID (NEED-BASED) ***Total amount:*** $1,803,331 (64% federal, 12% state, 24% institutional). ***Receiving aid:*** All full-time undergraduates: 61% (985). ***Average award:*** Undergraduates: $5102. ***Scholarships, grants, and awards:*** Federal Pell, FSEOG, state, private, college/university gift aid from institutional funds.

GIFT AID (NON-NEED-BASED) ***Total amount:*** $2,080,387 (3% state, 71% institutional, 26% external sources). ***Receiving aid:*** Undergraduates: 13% (201). ***Average award:*** Undergraduates: $3130. ***Scholarships, grants, and awards by category:*** *Academic interests/achievement:* 133 awards ($745,130 total): general academic interests/achievements, religion/biblical studies. *Creative arts/performance:* 50 awards ($78,924 total): music, theater/drama. *Special achievements/activities:* 105 awards ($131,871 total): cheerleading/drum major, religious involvement. *Special characteristics:* 133 awards ($528,915 total): children and siblings of alumni, children of current students, children of faculty/staff, parents of current students, public servants, relatives of clergy, religious affiliation, siblings of current students. ***Tuition waivers:*** Full or partial for children of alumni, employees or children of employees, senior citizens. ***ROTC:*** Army cooperative.

LOANS ***Student loans:*** $5,663,876 (59% need-based, 41% non-need-based). ***Average need-based loan:*** Undergraduates: $4204. ***Parent loans:*** $457,350 (100% need-based). ***Programs:*** FFEL (Subsidized and Unsubsidized Stafford, PLUS).

WORK-STUDY ***Federal work-study:*** Total amount: $95,800; 63 jobs averaging $1521. ***State or other work-study/employment:*** Total amount: $24,923 (100% need-based). 5 part-time jobs averaging $4985.

ATHLETIC AWARDS Total amount: $3,631,754 (100% non-need-based).

APPLYING FOR FINANCIAL AID ***Required financial aid forms:*** FAFSA, institution's own form. ***Financial aid deadline (priority):*** 4/1. ***Notification date:*** Continuous beginning 4/15. Students must reply within 2 weeks of notification.

CONTACT Laurie Wallace, Director of Financial Services, Missouri Baptist University, One College Park Drive, St. Louis, MO 63141, 314-392-2366 or toll-free 877-434-1115 Ext. 2290. *Fax:* 314-434-7596. *E-mail:* wallace@mobap.edu.

MISSOURI SOUTHERN STATE UNIVERSITY

Joplin, MO

Tuition & fees (MO res): $4535 **Average undergraduate aid package: $10,304**

ABOUT THE INSTITUTION State-supported, coed. ***Awards:*** associate, bachelor's, and master's degrees. 38 undergraduate majors. ***Total enrollment:*** 5,264. Undergraduates: 5,219. Freshmen: 771. Federal methodology is used as a basis for awarding need-based institutional aid.

UNDERGRADUATE EXPENSES for 2008–09 ***Application fee:*** $15. ***Tuition, state resident:*** full-time $4290; part-time $143 per credit. ***Tuition, nonresident:*** full-time $8580; part-time $286 per credit. ***Required fees:*** full-time $245. Full-time tuition and fees vary according to course load. ***College room and board:*** $5440. Room and board charges vary according to board plan and housing facility.

FRESHMAN FINANCIAL AID (Fall 2008, est.) 572 applied for aid; of those 78% were deemed to have need. 99% of freshmen with need received aid; of those 46% had need fully met. ***Average percent of need met:*** 87% (excluding resources awarded to replace EFC). ***Average financial aid package:*** $9483 (excluding resources awarded to replace EFC). 14% of all full-time freshmen had no need and received non-need-based gift aid.

UNDERGRADUATE FINANCIAL AID (Fall 2008, est.) 2,974 applied for aid; of those 86% were deemed to have need. 98% of undergraduates with need received aid; of those 28% had need fully met. ***Average percent of need met:*** 79% (excluding resources awarded to replace EFC). ***Average financial aid package:*** $10,304 (excluding resources awarded to replace EFC). 19% of all full-time undergraduates had no need and received non-need-based gift aid.

GIFT AID (NEED-BASED) ***Total amount:*** $6,254,660 (100% federal). ***Receiving aid:*** Freshmen: 27% (342); all full-time undergraduates: 57% (2,166). ***Average award:*** Freshmen: $2108; Undergraduates: $2387. ***Scholarships, grants, and awards:*** Federal Pell, FSEOG, state, private, college/university gift aid from institutional funds.

GIFT AID (NON-NEED-BASED) ***Total amount:*** $6,944,424 (25% state, 63% institutional, 12% external sources). ***Receiving aid:*** Freshmen: 25% (316). Undergraduates: 32% (1,218). ***Average award:*** Freshmen: $1583. Undergraduates: $1966. ***Scholarships, grants, and awards by category:*** *Academic interests/achievement:* 585 awards ($1,467,110 total): general academic interests/achievements. *Creative arts/performance:* 190 awards ($192,811 total): art/fine arts, debating, journalism/publications, music, theater/drama. *Special achievements/activities:* 12 awards ($6000 total): general special achievements/activities, leadership. *Special characteristics:* 155 awards ($224,897 total): children and siblings of alumni, children of faculty/staff, ethnic background, local/state students. ***Tuition waivers:*** Full or partial for employees or children of employees, senior citizens.

LOANS ***Student loans:*** $15,305,792 (57% need-based, 43% non-need-based). 70% of past graduating class borrowed through all loan programs. *Average indebtedness per student:* $18,331. ***Average need-based loan:*** Freshmen: $2311. Undergraduates: $3331. ***Parent loans:*** $203,663 (100% non-need-based). ***Programs:*** Federal Direct (Subsidized and Unsubsidized Stafford, PLUS), Perkins.

WORK-STUDY ***Federal work-study:*** Total amount: $244,887; 149 jobs averaging $1575. ***State or other work-study/employment:*** 438 part-time jobs averaging $1401.

ATHLETIC AWARDS Total amount: $1,229,241 (100% non-need-based).

APPLYING FOR FINANCIAL AID ***Required financial aid form:*** FAFSA. ***Financial aid deadline (priority):*** 2/15. ***Notification date:*** Continuous beginning 3/1. Students must reply within 3 weeks of notification.

CONTACT Ms. Kathy Feith, Director of Financial Aid, Missouri Southern State University, 3950 East Newman Road, Joplin, MO 64801-1595, 417-625-9325 or toll-free 866-818-MSSU. *Fax:* 417-659-4474. *E-mail:* feith-k@mssu.edu.

MISSOURI STATE UNIVERSITY

Springfield, MO

Tuition & fees (MO res): $6256 **Average undergraduate aid package: $6906**

ABOUT THE INSTITUTION State-supported, coed. ***Awards:*** bachelor's, master's, and doctoral degrees and post-bachelor's and post-master's certificates. 95 undergraduate majors. ***Total enrollment:*** 19,348. Undergraduates: 16,255. Freshmen: 2,649. Federal methodology is used as a basis for awarding need-based institutional aid.

UNDERGRADUATE EXPENSES for 2008–09 ***Application fee:*** $35. ***Tuition, state resident:*** full-time $6256; part-time $186 per credit hour. ***Tuition, nonresident:*** full-time $11,536; part-time $362 per credit hour. Full-time tuition and fees vary according to course load, degree level, location, and program. Part-time tuition and fees vary according to course load, degree level, location, and program. Room and board charges vary according to board plan and housing facility. ***Payment plans:*** Tuition prepayment, deferred payment.

FRESHMAN FINANCIAL AID (Fall 2007) 2,032 applied for aid; of those 68% were deemed to have need. 97% of freshmen with need received aid; of those 22% had need fully met. ***Average percent of need met:*** 67% (excluding resources awarded to replace EFC). ***Average financial aid package:*** $6989 (excluding resources awarded to replace EFC). 17% of all full-time freshmen had no need and received non-need-based gift aid.

UNDERGRADUATE FINANCIAL AID (Fall 2007) 9,656 applied for aid; of those 75% were deemed to have need. 97% of undergraduates with need received aid; of those 20% had need fully met. ***Average percent of need met:*** 63% (excluding resources awarded to replace EFC). ***Average financial aid package:*** $6906 (excluding resources awarded to replace EFC). 16% of all full-time undergraduates had no need and received non-need-based gift aid.

GIFT AID (NEED-BASED) ***Total amount:*** $26,675,137 (47% federal, 21% state, 26% institutional, 6% external sources). ***Receiving aid:*** Freshmen: 48% (1,185); all full-time undergraduates: 47% (5,535). ***Average award:*** Freshmen: $5343;

Undergraduates: $4650. ***Scholarships, grants, and awards:*** Federal Pell, FSEOG, state, private, college/university gift aid from institutional funds.

GIFT AID (NON-NEED-BASED) ***Total amount:*** $12,913,697 (10% state, 75% institutional, 15% external sources). ***Receiving aid:*** Freshmen: 7% (160). Undergraduates: 4% (504). ***Average award:*** Freshmen: $4328. Undergraduates: $4678. ***Tuition waivers:*** Full or partial for children of alumni, employees or children of employees, senior citizens. ***ROTC:*** Army.

LOANS ***Student loans:*** $52,082,729 (67% need-based, 33% non-need-based). 92% of past graduating class borrowed through all loan programs. *Average indebtedness per student:* $18,379. ***Average need-based loan:*** Freshmen: $2908. Undergraduates: $3826. ***Parent loans:*** $10,896,532 (20% need-based, 80% non-need-based). ***Programs:*** FFEL (Subsidized and Unsubsidized Stafford, PLUS), Perkins, state.

WORK-STUDY ***Federal work-study:*** Total amount: $548,814; 376 jobs averaging $2000.

ATHLETIC AWARDS Total amount: $3,588,131 (26% need-based, 74% non-need-based).

APPLYING FOR FINANCIAL AID ***Required financial aid forms:*** FAFSA, state aid form. ***Financial aid deadline (priority):*** 3/31. ***Notification date:*** 4/1.

CONTACT Vicki Mattocks, Director of Financial Aid, Missouri State University, 901 South National Avenue, Springfield, MO 65804, 417-836-5262 or toll-free 800-492-7900. *E-mail:* financialaid@missouristate.edu.

MISSOURI TECH

St. Louis, MO

CONTACT Director of Financial Aid, Missouri Tech, 1167 Corporate Lake Drive, St. Louis, MO 63132-1716, 314-569-3600. *Fax:* 314-569-1167. *E-mail:* contact@motech.edu.

MISSOURI UNIVERSITY OF SCIENCE AND TECHNOLOGY

Rolla, MO

Tuition & fees (MO res): $8498 Average undergraduate aid package: $11,792

ABOUT THE INSTITUTION State-supported, coed, primarily men. ***Awards:*** bachelor's, master's, and doctoral degrees and post-bachelor's certificates. 40 undergraduate majors. ***Total enrollment:*** 6,371. Undergraduates: 4,912. Freshmen: 1,046. Federal methodology is used as a basis for awarding need-based institutional aid.

UNDERGRADUATE EXPENSES for 2008–09 ***Application fee:*** $35. ***Tuition, state resident:*** full-time $7368; part-time $246 per credit hour. ***Tuition, nonresident:*** full-time $18,459; part-time $615 per credit hour. ***Required fees:*** full-time $1130; $120.52 per credit hour. Full-time tuition and fees vary according to course load, degree level, and program. Part-time tuition and fees vary according to course load, degree level, and program. ***College room and board:*** $7035; ***Room only:*** $4350. Room and board charges vary according to board plan, housing facility, and location. ***Payment plan:*** Installment.

FRESHMAN FINANCIAL AID (Fall 2008, est.) 905 applied for aid; of those 65% were deemed to have need. 100% of freshmen with need received aid; of those 60% had need fully met. ***Average percent of need met:*** 46% (excluding resources awarded to replace EFC). ***Average financial aid package:*** $11,611 (excluding resources awarded to replace EFC). 40% of all full-time freshmen had no need and received non-need-based gift aid.

UNDERGRADUATE FINANCIAL AID (Fall 2008, est.) 4,177 applied for aid; of those 65% were deemed to have need. 100% of undergraduates with need received aid; of those 60% had need fully met. ***Average percent of need met:*** 46% (excluding resources awarded to replace EFC). ***Average financial aid package:*** $11,792 (excluding resources awarded to replace EFC). 23% of all full-time undergraduates had no need and received non-need-based gift aid.

GIFT AID (NEED-BASED) ***Total amount:*** $15,097,873 (29% federal, 12% state, 56% institutional, 3% external sources). ***Receiving aid:*** Freshmen: 35% (354); all full-time undergraduates: 35% (1,634). ***Average award:*** Freshmen: $8616; Undergraduates: $8030. ***Scholarships, grants, and awards:*** Federal Pell, FSEOG, state, private, college/university gift aid from institutional funds, ROTC-Army and Air Force.

GIFT AID (NON-NEED-BASED) ***Total amount:*** $9,348,648 (19% state, 74% institutional, 7% external sources). ***Receiving aid:*** Freshmen: 28% (287). Undergraduates: 28% (1,325). ***Scholarships, grants, and awards by category:*** *Academic interests/achievement:* 3,227 awards ($13,010,050 total): biological sciences, business, computer science, education, engineering/technologies, English, general academic interests/achievements, humanities, mathematics, military science, physical sciences, premedicine, social sciences. *Creative arts/performance:* 2 awards ($500 total): music, theater/drama. *Special characteristics:* 686 awards ($1,738,902 total): children and siblings of alumni, members of minority groups, out-of-state students. ***Tuition waivers:*** Full or partial for employees or children of employees. ***ROTC:*** Army, Naval cooperative, Air Force.

LOANS ***Student loans:*** $19,364,337 (52% need-based, 48% non-need-based). 81% of past graduating class borrowed through all loan programs. *Average indebtedness per student:* $23,760. ***Average need-based loan:*** Freshmen: $4088. Undergraduates: $5480. ***Parent loans:*** $1,448,614 (14% need-based, 86% non-need-based). ***Programs:*** Federal Direct (Subsidized and Unsubsidized Stafford), FFEL (Subsidized and Unsubsidized Stafford, PLUS), Perkins, state, college/university, alternative loans.

WORK-STUDY ***Federal work-study:*** Total amount: $289,440; 178 jobs averaging $2334. ***State or other work-study/employment:*** Total amount: $1,752,910 (57% need-based, 43% non-need-based). 1,234 part-time jobs averaging $1293.

ATHLETIC AWARDS Total amount: $1,978,667 (100% need-based).

APPLYING FOR FINANCIAL AID ***Required financial aid form:*** FAFSA. ***Financial aid deadline (priority):*** 3/1. ***Notification date:*** Continuous beginning 4/1. Students must reply within 3 weeks of notification.

CONTACT Lynn K. Stichnote, Director of Student Financial Assistance, Missouri University of Science and Technology, G1 Parker Hall, Rolla, MO 65409, 573-341-4282 or toll-free 800-522-0938. *Fax:* 573-341-4274. *E-mail:* lks@mst.edu.

MISSOURI VALLEY COLLEGE

Marshall, MO

Tuition & fees: $15,950 Average undergraduate aid package: $13,400

ABOUT THE INSTITUTION Independent religious, coed. ***Awards:*** associate and bachelor's degrees. 38 undergraduate majors. ***Total enrollment:*** 1,639. Undergraduates: 1,639. Freshmen: 444. Federal methodology is used as a basis for awarding need-based institutional aid.

UNDERGRADUATE EXPENSES for 2008–09 ***Application fee:*** $15. ***Comprehensive fee:*** $22,000 includes full-time tuition ($15,450), mandatory fees ($500), and room and board ($6050). ***College room only:*** $3100. ***Part-time tuition:*** $350 per credit hour.

FRESHMAN FINANCIAL AID (Fall 2008, est.) 366 applied for aid; of those 83% were deemed to have need. 100% of freshmen with need received aid; of those 38% had need fully met. ***Average percent of need met:*** 83% (excluding resources awarded to replace EFC). ***Average financial aid package:*** $13,250 (excluding resources awarded to replace EFC). 28% of all full-time freshmen had no need and received non-need-based gift aid.

UNDERGRADUATE FINANCIAL AID (Fall 2008, est.) 1,176 applied for aid; of those 82% were deemed to have need. 100% of undergraduates with need received aid; of those 44% had need fully met. ***Average percent of need met:*** 83% (excluding resources awarded to replace EFC). ***Average financial aid package:*** $13,400 (excluding resources awarded to replace EFC). 29% of all full-time undergraduates had no need and received non-need-based gift aid.

GIFT AID (NEED-BASED) ***Total amount:*** $8,678,956 (30% federal, 20% state, 50% institutional). ***Receiving aid:*** Freshmen: 72% (303); all full-time undergraduates: 71% (960). ***Average award:*** Freshmen: $11,440; Undergraduates: $11,080. ***Scholarships, grants, and awards:*** Federal Pell, FSEOG, state, private, college/university gift aid from institutional funds.

GIFT AID (NON-NEED-BASED) ***Total amount:*** $294,230 (100% external sources). ***Receiving aid:*** Freshmen: 72% (303). Undergraduates: 71% (960). ***Average award:*** Freshmen: $9150. Undergraduates: $8740. ***Scholarships, grants, and awards by category:*** *Academic interests/achievement:* 236 awards ($267,880 total): biological sciences, business, communication, computer science, education, English, general academic interests/achievements, humanities, mathematics, military science, physical sciences, premedicine, social sciences. *Creative arts/performance:* 29 awards ($85,800 total): applied art and design, cinema/film/broadcasting, dance, journalism/publications, music, performing arts, theater/drama. *Special achievements/activities:* 27 awards ($152,000 total): cheerleading/drum major, community service, general special achievements/activities, hobbies/interests, junior miss, leadership, rodeo. *Special characteristics:* 31 awards ($186,500 total): children and siblings of alumni, children of faculty/staff. ***ROTC:*** Army.

LOANS ***Student loans:*** $5,973,249 (50% need-based, 50% non-need-based). 79% of past graduating class borrowed through all loan programs. *Average indebtedness per student:* $16,950. ***Average need-based loan:*** Freshmen: $2818. Undergraduates: $4216. ***Parent loans:*** $448,298 (100% non-need-based). ***Programs:*** FFEL (Subsidized and Unsubsidized Stafford, PLUS), Perkins.

WORK-STUDY ***Federal work-study:*** Total amount: $185,767; 148 jobs averaging $1024. ***State or other work-study/employment:*** Total amount: $464,683 (100% non-need-based). 451 part-time jobs averaging $1008.

ATHLETIC AWARDS Total amount: $7,794,001 (100% need-based).

APPLYING FOR FINANCIAL AID ***Required financial aid form:*** FAFSA. ***Financial aid deadline:*** 9/15 (priority: 3/15). ***Notification date:*** Continuous beginning 10/1. Students must reply within 4 weeks of notification.

CONTACT Charles Mayfield, Director of Financial Aid, Missouri Valley College, 500 East College, Marshall, MO 65340-3197, 660-831-4176. *Fax:* 660-831-4003. *E-mail:* mayfieldb@moval.edu.

MISSOURI WESTERN STATE UNIVERSITY

St. Joseph, MO

Tuition & fees (MO res): $5560 **Average undergraduate aid package: $7438**

ABOUT THE INSTITUTION State-supported, coed. ***Awards:*** associate and bachelor's degrees. 45 undergraduate majors. ***Total enrollment:*** 5,276. Undergraduates: 5,276. Freshmen: 1,059. Federal methodology is used as a basis for awarding need-based institutional aid.

UNDERGRADUATE EXPENSES for 2008–09 ***Application fee:*** $15. ***Tuition, state resident:*** full-time $4992; part-time $166.40 per credit hour. ***Tuition, nonresident:*** full-time $9120; part-time $304 per credit hour. ***Required fees:*** full-time $568; $19.10 per credit hour or $30 per term. ***College room and board:*** $5868. Room and board charges vary according to board plan and housing facility. ***Payment plans:*** Installment, deferred payment.

FRESHMAN FINANCIAL AID (Fall 2008, est.) 916 applied for aid; of those 76% were deemed to have need. 99% of freshmen with need received aid; of those 16% had need fully met. ***Average percent of need met:*** 66% (excluding resources awarded to replace EFC). ***Average financial aid package:*** $7556 (excluding resources awarded to replace EFC). 13% of all full-time freshmen had no need and received non-need-based gift aid.

UNDERGRADUATE FINANCIAL AID (Fall 2008, est.) 3,449 applied for aid; of those 77% were deemed to have need. 99% of undergraduates with need received aid; of those 11% had need fully met. ***Average percent of need met:*** 64% (excluding resources awarded to replace EFC). ***Average financial aid package:*** $7438 (excluding resources awarded to replace EFC). 10% of all full-time undergraduates had no need and received non-need-based gift aid.

GIFT AID (NEED-BASED) ***Total amount:*** $12,354,986 (48% federal, 27% state, 20% institutional, 5% external sources). ***Receiving aid:*** Freshmen: 69% (665); all full-time undergraduates: 61% (2,408). ***Average award:*** Freshmen: $5648; Undergraduates: $5131. ***Scholarships, grants, and awards:*** Federal Pell, FSEOG, state, private, college/university gift aid from institutional funds.

GIFT AID (NON-NEED-BASED) ***Total amount:*** $3,211,387 (4% federal, 28% state, 53% institutional, 15% external sources). ***Receiving aid:*** Freshmen: 11% (109). Undergraduates: 7% (285). ***Average award:*** Freshmen: $3527. Undergraduates: $3623. ***Scholarships, grants, and awards by category:*** *Academic interests/achievement:* biological sciences, business, communication, computer science, education, engineering/technologies, English, general academic interests/achievements, health fields, humanities, mathematics, military science, physical sciences, social sciences. *Creative arts/performance:* art/fine arts, dance, music. *Special achievements/activities:* cheerleading/drum major, community service, general special achievements/activities, leadership. *Special characteristics:* children of faculty/staff, members of minority groups, out-of-state students. ***Tuition waivers:*** Full or partial for employees or children of employees, senior citizens. ***ROTC:*** Army.

LOANS ***Student loans:*** $6,130,506 (28% need-based, 72% non-need-based). ***Average need-based loan:*** Freshmen: $2841. Undergraduates: $3536. ***Parent loans:*** $563,200 (22% need-based, 78% non-need-based). ***Programs:*** FFEL (Subsidized and Unsubsidized Stafford, PLUS), Perkins.

WORK-STUDY ***Federal work-study:*** Total amount: $450,000; 277 jobs averaging $1447. ***State or other work-study/employment:*** 695 part-time jobs averaging $1688.

ATHLETIC AWARDS Total amount: $[illegible]41,458 (39% need-based, 61% non-need-based).

APPLYING FOR FINANCIAL AID ***Required financial aid forms:*** FAFSA, institution's own form. ***Financial aid deadline (priority):*** 3/1. ***Notification date:*** Continuous beginning 4/15. Students must reply within 3 weeks of notification.

CONTACT Angela Beam, Acting Director of Financial Aid, Missouri Western State University, 4525 Downs Drive, St. Joseph, MO 64507-2294, 816-271-5986 or toll-free 800-662-7041 Ext. 60. *Fax:* 816-271-5879. *E-mail:* lepley@missouriwestern.edu.

MITCHELL COLLEGE

New London, CT

CONTACT Jacklyn Stoltz, Director of Financial Aid, Mitchell College, 437 Pequot Avenue, New London, CT 06320-4498, 800-443-2811. *Fax:* 860-444-1209. *E-mail:* stoltz_j@mitchell.edu.

MOLLOY COLLEGE

Rockville Centre, NY

Tuition & fees: $19,450 **Average undergraduate aid package: $12,007**

ABOUT THE INSTITUTION Independent, coed. ***Awards:*** associate, bachelor's, and master's degrees and post-master's certificates. 44 undergraduate majors. ***Total enrollment:*** 3,791. Undergraduates: 2,871. Freshmen: 403. Federal methodology is used as a basis for awarding need-based institutional aid.

UNDERGRADUATE EXPENSES for 2008–09 ***Application fee:*** $30. ***Tuition:*** full-time $18,700; part-time $620 per credit. ***Payment plan:*** Installment.

FRESHMAN FINANCIAL AID (Fall 2008, est.) 371 applied for aid; of those 80% were deemed to have need. 100% of freshmen with need received aid; of those 21% had need fully met. ***Average percent of need met:*** 62% (excluding resources awarded to replace EFC). ***Average financial aid package:*** $12,351 (excluding resources awarded to replace EFC). 13% of all full-time freshmen had no need and received non-need-based gift aid.

UNDERGRADUATE FINANCIAL AID (Fall 2008, est.) 1,836 applied for aid; of those 83% were deemed to have need. 100% of undergraduates with need received aid; of those 14% had need fully met. ***Average percent of need met:*** 56% (excluding resources awarded to replace EFC). ***Average financial aid package:*** $12,007 (excluding resources awarded to replace EFC). 10% of all full-time undergraduates had no need and received non-need-based gift aid.

GIFT AID (NEED-BASED) ***Total amount:*** $11,161,094 (25% federal, 24% state, 48% institutional, 3% external sources). ***Receiving aid:*** Freshmen: 70% (287); all full-time undergraduates: 72% (1,353). ***Average award:*** Freshmen: $9410; Undergraduates: $7819. ***Scholarships, grants, and awards:*** Federal Pell, FSEOG, state, private, college/university gift aid from institutional funds, Academic Competitiveness Grant, National Smart Grant, Trio Grant, TEACH Grant.

GIFT AID (NON-NEED-BASED) ***Total amount:*** $1,759,067 (6% state, 92% institutional, 2% external sources). ***Receiving aid:*** Freshmen: 11% (45). Undergraduates: 6% (120). ***Average award:*** Freshmen: $5707. Undergraduates: $5322. ***Scholarships, grants, and awards by category:*** *Academic interests/achievement:* 165 awards ($261,025 total): biological sciences, business, communication, education, English, general academic interests/achievements, health fields, mathematics. *Creative arts/performance:* 64 awards ($133,918 total): art/fine arts, music, performing arts, theater/drama. *Special achievements/activities:* 272 awards ($463,110 total): community service, leadership, memberships, religious involvement. *Special characteristics:* 72 awards ($350,317 total): children and siblings of alumni, children of faculty/staff, ethnic background, religious affiliation, siblings of current students. ***Tuition waivers:*** Full or partial for employees or children of employees. ***ROTC:*** Army cooperative, Naval cooperative, Air Force cooperative.

LOANS ***Student loans:*** $22,504,091 (76% need-based, 24% non-need-based). 86% of past graduating class borrowed through all loan programs. *Average indebtedness per student:* $22,754. ***Average need-based loan:*** Freshmen: $4186. Undergraduates: $5718. ***Parent loans:*** $3,556,248 (42% need-based, 58% non-need-based). ***Programs:*** FFEL (Subsidized and Unsubsidized Stafford, PLUS), Perkins, Federal Nursing, alternative loans.

WORK-STUDY ***Federal work-study:*** Total amount: $409,522; 378 jobs averaging $1217.

ATHLETIC AWARDS Total amount: $1,450,118 (65% need-based, 35% non-need-based).

APPLYING FOR FINANCIAL AID ***Required financial aid forms:*** FAFSA, state aid form. ***Financial aid deadline:*** 5/1 (priority: 5/1)

CONTACT Ana C. Lockward, Director of Financial Aid, Molloy College, 1000 Hempstead Avenue, Rockville Centre, NY 11571, 516-678-5000 Ext. 6221 or toll-free 888-4MOLLOY. *Fax:* 516-256-2292. *E-mail:* alockward@molloy.edu.

MONMOUTH COLLEGE

Monmouth, IL

Tuition & fees: $24,950 **Average undergraduate aid package: $20,583**

ABOUT THE INSTITUTION Independent religious, coed. ***Awards:*** bachelor's degrees. 34 undergraduate majors. ***Total enrollment:*** 1,328. Undergraduates: 1,328. Freshmen: 383. Federal methodology is used as a basis for awarding need-based institutional aid.

UNDERGRADUATE EXPENSES for 2009–10 ***Comprehensive fee:*** $32,250 includes full-time tuition ($24,950) and room and board ($7300). ***College room only:*** $4250.

FRESHMAN FINANCIAL AID (Fall 2008, est.) 372 applied for aid; of those 83% were deemed to have need. 100% of freshmen with need received aid; of those 26% had need fully met. ***Average percent of need met:*** 91% (excluding resources awarded to replace EFC). ***Average financial aid package:*** $21,722 (excluding resources awarded to replace EFC). 19% of all full-time freshmen had no need and received non-need-based gift aid.

UNDERGRADUATE FINANCIAL AID (Fall 2008, est.) 1,205 applied for aid; of those 87% were deemed to have need. 100% of undergraduates with need received aid; of those 25% had need fully met. ***Average percent of need met:*** 88% (excluding resources awarded to replace EFC). ***Average financial aid package:*** $20,583 (excluding resources awarded to replace EFC). 20% of all full-time undergraduates had no need and received non-need-based gift aid.

GIFT AID (NEED-BASED) ***Total amount:*** $16,577,605 (10% federal, 16% state, 74% institutional). ***Receiving aid:*** Freshmen: 81% (310); all full-time undergraduates: 79% (1,046). ***Average award:*** Freshmen: $16,780; Undergraduates: $15,667. ***Scholarships, grants, and awards:*** Federal Pell, FSEOG, state, private, college/university gift aid from institutional funds.

GIFT AID (NON-NEED-BASED) ***Total amount:*** $3,262,230 (87% institutional, 13% external sources). ***Receiving aid:*** Freshmen: 14% (53). Undergraduates: 11% (147). ***Average award:*** Freshmen: $9822. Undergraduates: $9793. ***Scholarships, grants, and awards by category:*** *Academic interests/achievement:* general academic interests/achievements. *Creative arts/performance:* art/fine arts, music, theater/drama. *Special achievements/activities:* general special achievements/activities. *Special characteristics:* international students, out-of-state students, siblings of current students, veterans. ***ROTC:*** Army cooperative.

LOANS ***Student loans:*** $7,463,380 (49% need-based, 51% non-need-based). 80% of past graduating class borrowed through all loan programs. *Average indebtedness per student:* $23,726. ***Average need-based loan:*** Freshmen: $3775. Undergraduates: $4532. ***Parent loans:*** $2,282,708 (100% non-need-based). ***Programs:*** Federal Direct (Subsidized and Unsubsidized Stafford, PLUS), FFEL (Subsidized and Unsubsidized Stafford, PLUS), Perkins.

WORK-STUDY ***Federal work-study:*** Total amount: $834,169; jobs available. ***State or other work-study/employment:*** Part-time jobs available.

APPLYING FOR FINANCIAL AID ***Required financial aid forms:*** FAFSA, verification documents/tax returns if needed and requested. ***Financial aid deadline (priority):*** 3/1. ***Notification date:*** Continuous beginning 3/1. Students must reply by 8/1.

CONTACT Mrs. Jayne Schreck, Director of Financial Aid, Monmouth College, 700 East Broadway, Monmouth, IL 61462-1998, 309-457-2129 or toll-free 800-747-2687. *Fax:* 309-457-2373. *E-mail:* jayne@monm.edu.

MONMOUTH UNIVERSITY

West Long Branch, NJ

Tuition & fees: $24,098 **Average undergraduate aid package: $18,210**

ABOUT THE INSTITUTION Independent, coed. ***Awards:*** associate, bachelor's, and master's degrees and post-bachelor's and post-master's certificates. 30 undergraduate majors. ***Total enrollment:*** 6,442. Undergraduates: 4,711. Freshmen: 961. Federal methodology is used as a basis for awarding need-based institutional aid.

UNDERGRADUATE EXPENSES for 2008–09 ***Application fee:*** $50. ***One-time required fee:*** $200. ***Comprehensive fee:*** $33,319 includes full-time tuition ($23,470), mandatory fees ($628), and room and board ($9221). ***College room only:*** $5258. Room and board charges vary according to board plan and housing facility. ***Part-time tuition:*** $680 per credit hour. ***Part-time fees:*** $157 per term. ***Payment plan:*** Installment.

FRESHMAN FINANCIAL AID (Fall 2008, est.) 801 applied for aid; of those 75% were deemed to have need. 100% of freshmen with need received aid; of those 26% had need fully met. ***Average percent of need met:*** 85% (excluding resources awarded to replace EFC). ***Average financial aid package:*** $19,400 (excluding resources awarded to replace EFC). 35% of all full-time freshmen had no need and received non-need-based gift aid.

UNDERGRADUATE FINANCIAL AID (Fall 2008, est.) 3,216 applied for aid; of those 80% were deemed to have need. 100% of undergraduates with need received aid; of those 21% had need fully met. ***Average percent of need met:*** 75% (excluding resources awarded to replace EFC). ***Average financial aid package:*** $18,210 (excluding resources awarded to replace EFC). 33% of all full-time undergraduates had no need and received non-need-based gift aid.

GIFT AID (NEED-BASED) ***Total amount:*** $26,503,756 (14% federal, 25% state, 59% institutional, 2% external sources). ***Receiving aid:*** Freshmen: 60% (573); all full-time undergraduates: 56% (2,388). ***Average award:*** Freshmen: $12,433; Undergraduates: $10,876. ***Scholarships, grants, and awards:*** Federal Pell, FSEOG, state, private, college/university gift aid from institutional funds, Federal Nursing.

GIFT AID (NON-NEED-BASED) ***Total amount:*** $9,459,051 (1% state, 95% institutional, 4% external sources). ***Receiving aid:*** Freshmen: 3% (28). Undergraduates: 3% (148). ***Average award:*** Freshmen: $8101. Undergraduates: $6352. ***Scholarships, grants, and awards by category:*** *Academic interests/achievement:* 3,983 awards ($28,234,435 total): business, communication, computer science, education, general academic interests/achievements, health fields, humanities, international studies, mathematics, social sciences. *Special achievements/activities:* 35 awards ($5000 total): leadership. *Special characteristics:* 220 awards ($775,913 total): adult students, children and siblings of alumni, children of faculty/staff, children of public servants, first-generation college students, general special characteristics, international students, local/state students, members of minority groups, out-of-state students, previous college experience, veterans. ***Tuition waivers:*** Full or partial for employees or children of employees, senior citizens. ***ROTC:*** Air Force cooperative.

LOANS ***Student loans:*** $36,953,078 (28% need-based, 72% non-need-based). 75% of past graduating class borrowed through all loan programs. *Average indebtedness per student:* $30,853. ***Average need-based loan:*** Freshmen: $3696. Undergraduates: $4907. ***Parent loans:*** $5,275,345 (100% non-need-based). ***Programs:*** Federal Direct (Subsidized and Unsubsidized Stafford, PLUS), FFEL (PLUS), Perkins, state, college/university, alternative/private loans.

WORK-STUDY ***Federal work-study:*** Total amount: $919,381; 467 jobs averaging $1532.

ATHLETIC AWARDS Total amount: $3,934,593 (100% non-need-based).

APPLYING FOR FINANCIAL AID ***Required financial aid form:*** FAFSA. ***Financial aid deadline:*** Continuous. ***Notification date:*** Continuous beginning 2/1. Students must reply within 2 weeks of notification.

CONTACT Ms. Claire Alasio, Associate Vice President for Enrollment Management, Monmouth University, 400 Cedar Avenue, West Long Branch, NJ 07764-1898, 732-571-3463 or toll-free 800-543-9671. *Fax:* 732-923-4791. *E-mail:* finaid@monmouth.edu.

MONROE COLLEGE

Bronx, NY

Tuition & fees: $11,212 **Average undergraduate aid package: $10,700**

ABOUT THE INSTITUTION Proprietary, coed. ***Awards:*** associate, bachelor's, and master's degrees. 15 undergraduate majors. ***Total enrollment:*** 4,737. Undergraduates: 4,521. Freshmen: 749. Federal methodology is used as a basis for awarding need-based institutional aid.

UNDERGRADUATE EXPENSES for 2008–09 ***Application fee:*** $35. ***Comprehensive fee:*** $18,452 includes full-time tuition ($10,512), mandatory fees ($700), and room and board ($7240). Full-time tuition and fees vary according to degree level and program. Room and board charges vary according to board plan. ***Part-time tuition:*** $438 per credit hour. ***Part-time fees:*** $175 per term. Part-time tuition and fees vary according to degree level and program. ***Payment plan:*** Installment.

FRESHMAN FINANCIAL AID (Fall 2007) 737 applied for aid; of those 99% were deemed to have need. 100% of freshmen with need received aid; of those 42%

had need fully met. ***Average percent of need met:*** 89% (excluding resources awarded to replace EFC). ***Average financial aid package:*** $10,325 (excluding resources awarded to replace EFC).

UNDERGRADUATE FINANCIAL AID (Fall 2007) 4,453 applied for aid; of those 99% were deemed to have need. 100% of undergraduates with need received aid; of those 22% had need fully met. ***Average percent of need met:*** 90% (excluding resources awarded to replace EFC). ***Average financial aid package:*** $10,700 (excluding resources awarded to replace EFC).

GIFT AID (NEED-BASED) ***Total amount:*** $35,465,479 (50% federal, 44% state, 6% institutional). ***Receiving aid:*** Freshmen: 79% (589); all full-time undergraduates: 81% (3,656). ***Average award:*** Freshmen: $6900; Undergraduates: $6870. ***Scholarships, grants, and awards:*** Federal Pell, FSEOG, state, private, college/university gift aid from institutional funds.

GIFT AID (NON-NEED-BASED) ***Total amount:*** $910,782 (100% external sources). ***Receiving aid:*** Freshmen: 17% (125). Undergraduates: 18% (793). ***Tuition waivers:*** Full or partial for employees or children of employees.

LOANS ***Student loans:*** $32,801,061 (100% need-based). 95% of past graduating class borrowed through all loan programs. *Average indebtedness per student:* $21,825. ***Average need-based loan:*** Freshmen: $2100. Undergraduates: $4450. ***Parent loans:*** $371,130 (100% need-based). ***Programs:*** Federal Direct (Subsidized and Unsubsidized Stafford, PLUS), FFEL (Subsidized and Unsubsidized Stafford, PLUS), state, college/university.

WORK-STUDY ***Federal work-study:*** Total amount: $822,596; 276 jobs averaging $2980.

ATHLETIC AWARDS Total amount: $147,370 (100% non-need-based).

APPLYING FOR FINANCIAL AID ***Required financial aid forms:*** FAFSA, state aid form. ***Financial aid deadline:*** Continuous. ***Notification date:*** Continuous beginning 3/1.

CONTACT Howard Leslie, Dean of Student Financial Services, Monroe College, 434 Main Street, New Rochelle, NY 10468, 718-817-8203 or toll-free 800-55MONROE. *Fax:* 718-365-2363. *E-mail:* hleslie@monroecollege.edu.

MONROE COLLEGE

New Rochelle, NY

Tuition & fees: $11,272 **Average undergraduate aid package: $11,343**

ABOUT THE INSTITUTION Proprietary, coed. ***Awards:*** associate, bachelor's, and master's degrees. 6 undergraduate majors. ***Total enrollment:*** 2,170. Undergraduates: 1,989. Freshmen: 533. Federal methodology is used as a basis for awarding need-based institutional aid.

UNDERGRADUATE EXPENSES for 2008–09 ***Application fee:*** $35. ***Comprehensive fee:*** $18,512 includes full-time tuition ($10,572), mandatory fees ($700), and room and board ($7240). ***Part-time tuition:*** $438 per credit. ***Part-time fees:*** $175 per term.

FRESHMAN FINANCIAL AID (Fall 2007) 442 applied for aid; of those 99% were deemed to have need. 100% of freshmen with need received aid; of those 60% had need fully met. ***Average percent of need met:*** 86% (excluding resources awarded to replace EFC). ***Average financial aid package:*** $11,256 (excluding resources awarded to replace EFC).

UNDERGRADUATE FINANCIAL AID (Fall 2007) 1,838 applied for aid; of those 99% were deemed to have need. 100% of undergraduates with need received aid; of those 61% had need fully met. ***Average percent of need met:*** 89% (excluding resources awarded to replace EFC). ***Average financial aid package:*** $11,343 (excluding resources awarded to replace EFC).

GIFT AID (NEED-BASED) ***Total amount:*** $12,113,369 (43% federal, 34% state, 23% institutional). ***Receiving aid:*** Freshmen: 93% (426); all full-time undergraduates: 92% (1,783). ***Average award:*** Freshmen: $6200; Undergraduates: $6315. ***Scholarships, grants, and awards:*** Federal Pell, FSEOG, state, private, college/university gift aid from institutional funds, county scholarships.

GIFT AID (NON-NEED-BASED) ***Total amount:*** $431,226 (100% external sources). ***Receiving aid:*** Freshmen: 25% (117). Undergraduates: 39% (751).

LOANS ***Student loans:*** $12,623,992 (100% need-based). 82% of past graduating class borrowed through all loan programs. *Average indebtedness per student:* $25,913. ***Average need-based loan:*** Freshmen: $2850. Undergraduates: $4725. ***Parent loans:*** $2,024,229 (100% need-based). ***Programs:*** Federal Direct (Subsidized and Unsubsidized Stafford, PLUS), FFEL (Subsidized and Unsubsidized Stafford, PLUS), state, college/university.

WORK-STUDY ***Federal work-study:*** Total amount: $102,699; 47 jobs averaging $2206.

ATHLETIC AWARDS Total amount: $233,295 (100% non-need-based).

APPLYING FOR FINANCIAL AID ***Required financial aid forms:*** FAFSA, state aid form. ***Financial aid deadline:*** Continuous. ***Notification date:*** Continuous beginning 3/1.

CONTACT Howard Leslie, Dean of Student Financial Services, Monroe College, 2501 Jerome Avenue, Bronx, NY 10468, 718-817-8203 or toll-free 800-55MONROE. *Fax:* 718-365-2365. *E-mail:* hleslie@monroecollege.edu.

MONTANA STATE UNIVERSITY

Bozeman, MT

Tuition & fees (MT res): $5798 **Average undergraduate aid package: $9834**

ABOUT THE INSTITUTION State-supported, coed. ***Awards:*** bachelor's, master's, and doctoral degrees and post-master's certificates. 58 undergraduate majors. ***Total enrollment:*** 12,369. Undergraduates: 10,519. Freshmen: 2,070. Federal methodology is used as a basis for awarding need-based institutional aid.

UNDERGRADUATE EXPENSES for 2008–09 ***Application fee:*** $30. ***Tuition, state resident:*** full-time $5798. ***Tuition, nonresident:*** full-time $16,997. Full-time tuition and fees vary according to course load and degree level. Part-time tuition and fees vary according to course load and degree level. ***College room and board:*** $7070. Room and board charges vary according to board plan and housing facility. ***Payment plans:*** Installment, deferred payment.

FRESHMAN FINANCIAL AID (Fall 2007) 1,237 applied for aid; of those 73% were deemed to have need. 96% of freshmen with need received aid; of those 8% had need fully met. ***Average percent of need met:*** 76% (excluding resources awarded to replace EFC). ***Average financial aid package:*** $9873 (excluding resources awarded to replace EFC). 5% of all full-time freshmen had no need and received non-need-based gift aid.

UNDERGRADUATE FINANCIAL AID (Fall 2007) 5,629 applied for aid; of those 80% were deemed to have need. 97% of undergraduates with need received aid; of those 5% had need fully met. ***Average percent of need met:*** 72% (excluding resources awarded to replace EFC). ***Average financial aid package:*** $9834 (excluding resources awarded to replace EFC). 4% of all full-time undergraduates had no need and received non-need-based gift aid.

GIFT AID (NEED-BASED) ***Total amount:*** $14,407,106 (62% federal, 7% state, 11% institutional, 20% external sources). ***Receiving aid:*** Freshmen: 36% (650); all full-time undergraduates: 34% (3,007). ***Average award:*** Freshmen: $4446; Undergraduates: $4295. ***Scholarships, grants, and awards:*** Federal Pell, FSEOG, state, private, college/university gift aid from institutional funds, Federal Nursing.

GIFT AID (NON-NEED-BASED) ***Total amount:*** $4,138,970 (2% state, 24% institutional, 74% external sources). ***Receiving aid:*** Freshmen: 3% (51). Undergraduates: 1% (105). ***Average award:*** Freshmen: $1363. Undergraduates: $1813. ***Scholarships, grants, and awards by category:*** *Academic interests/achievement:* agriculture, architecture, area/ethnic studies, biological sciences, business, communication, computer science, education, engineering/technologies, English, foreign languages, general academic interests/achievements, health fields, home economics, humanities, mathematics, military science, physical sciences, social sciences. *Creative arts/performance:* art/fine arts, cinema/film/broadcasting, dance, music, theater/drama. *Special achievements/activities:* general special achievements/activities. *Special characteristics:* general special characteristics. ***Tuition waivers:*** Full or partial for minority students, employees or children of employees, senior citizens. ***ROTC:*** Army, Air Force.

LOANS ***Student loans:*** $34,528,762 (78% need-based, 22% non-need-based). 70% of past graduating class borrowed through all loan programs. *Average indebtedness per student:* $21,015. ***Average need-based loan:*** Freshmen: $3963. Undergraduates: $4640. ***Parent loans:*** $9,225,560 (31% need-based, 69% non-need-based). ***Programs:*** FFEL (Subsidized and Unsubsidized Stafford, PLUS), Perkins, Federal Nursing, college/university.

WORK-STUDY ***Federal work-study:*** Total amount: $370,174; jobs available. ***State or other work-study/employment:*** Total amount: $261,104 (100% need-based). Part-time jobs available.

ATHLETIC AWARDS Total amount: $1,238,238 (29% need-based, 71% non-need-based).

APPLYING FOR FINANCIAL AID ***Required financial aid form:*** FAFSA. ***Financial aid deadline (priority):*** 3/1. ***Notification date:*** Continuous beginning 4/1.

CONTACT Terry Dysart, Research Analyst, Montana State University, PO Box 172435, Bozeman, MT 59717-2435, 406-994-1649 or toll-free 888-MSU-CATS. *Fax:* 406-994-1893. *E-mail:* tdysart@montana.edu.

MONTANA STATE UNIVERSITY–BILLINGS

Billings, MT

Tuition & fees (MT res): $5172 **Average undergraduate aid package: $7886**

ABOUT THE INSTITUTION State-supported, coed. ***Awards:*** associate, bachelor's, and master's degrees and post-bachelor's and post-master's certificates. 74 undergraduate majors. ***Total enrollment:*** 4,912. Undergraduates: 4,425. Freshmen: 828. Federal methodology is used as a basis for awarding need-based institutional aid.

UNDERGRADUATE EXPENSES for 2008–09 ***Application fee:*** $30. ***Tuition, state resident:*** full-time $3988; part-time $144 per credit hour. ***Tuition, nonresident:*** full-time $14,085; part-time $391 per credit hour. ***Required fees:*** full-time $1184. Full-time tuition and fees vary according to course load, degree level, and location. Part-time tuition and fees vary according to course load, degree level, and location. ***College room and board:*** $5134. Room and board charges vary according to board plan and housing facility. ***Payment plan:*** Installment.

FRESHMAN FINANCIAL AID (Fall 2007) 555 applied for aid; of those 75% were deemed to have need. 98% of freshmen with need received aid; of those 12% had need fully met. ***Average percent of need met:*** 50% (excluding resources awarded to replace EFC). ***Average financial aid package:*** $7713 (excluding resources awarded to replace EFC). 7% of all full-time freshmen had no need and received non-need-based gift aid.

UNDERGRADUATE FINANCIAL AID (Fall 2007) 2,741 applied for aid; of those 87% were deemed to have need. 95% of undergraduates with need received aid; of those 19% had need fully met. ***Average percent of need met:*** 63% (excluding resources awarded to replace EFC). ***Average financial aid package:*** $7886 (excluding resources awarded to replace EFC). 5% of all full-time undergraduates had no need and received non-need-based gift aid.

GIFT AID (NEED-BASED) ***Total amount:*** $6,562,653 (76% federal, 5% state, 13% institutional, 6% external sources). ***Receiving aid:*** Freshmen: 49% (317); all full-time undergraduates: 60% (1,950). ***Average award:*** Freshmen: $3780; Undergraduates: $4409. ***Scholarships, grants, and awards:*** Federal Pell, FSEOG, state, private, college/university gift aid from institutional funds.

GIFT AID (NON-NEED-BASED) ***Total amount:*** $438,439 (78% institutional, 22% external sources). ***Receiving aid:*** Freshmen: 49% (312). Undergraduates: 17% (562). ***Average award:*** Freshmen: $4386. Undergraduates: $8843. ***Scholarships, grants, and awards by category:*** *Academic interests/achievement:* biological sciences, business, communication, computer science, education, engineering/technologies, English, general academic interests/achievements, health fields, humanities, mathematics, physical sciences, premedicine, social sciences. *Creative arts/performance:* art/fine arts, music, theater/drama. *Special achievements/activities:* cheerleading/drum major, general special achievements/activities. *Special characteristics:* adult students, children and siblings of alumni, children of faculty/staff, children of union members/company employees, ethnic background, first-generation college students, local/state students, members of minority groups, out-of-state students, veterans. ***Tuition waivers:*** Full or partial for minority students, employees or children of employees, senior citizens.

LOANS ***Student loans:*** $16,234,033 (51% need-based, 49% non-need-based). 74% of past graduating class borrowed through all loan programs. *Average indebtedness per student:* $16,748. ***Average need-based loan:*** Freshmen: $2255. Undergraduates: $3351. ***Parent loans:*** $1,108,255 (17% need-based, 83% non-need-based). ***Programs:*** FFEL (Subsidized and Unsubsidized Stafford, PLUS), Perkins, college/university.

WORK-STUDY ***Federal work-study:*** Total amount: $300,864; 214 jobs averaging $1406. ***State or other work-study/employment:*** Total amount: $95,946 (100% need-based). 67 part-time jobs averaging $1432.

ATHLETIC AWARDS Total amount: $934,497 (67% need-based, 33% non-need-based).

APPLYING FOR FINANCIAL AID ***Required financial aid form:*** FAFSA. ***Financial aid deadline (priority):*** 3/1. ***Notification date:*** Continuous beginning 4/1. Students must reply within 3 weeks of notification.

CONTACT Judy Chapman, Director of Financial Aid, Montana State University–Billings, 1500 University Drive, Billings, MT 59101, 406-657-2188 or toll-free 800-565-6782. *Fax:* 406-657-1789. *E-mail:* jchapman@msubillings.edu.

MONTANA STATE UNIVERSITY–NORTHERN

Havre, MT

CONTACT Kris Dramstad, Director of Financial Aid, Montana State University–Northern, PO Box 7751, Havre, MT 59501, 406-265-3787 or toll-free 800-662-6132 (in-state).

MONTANA TECH OF THE UNIVERSITY OF MONTANA

Butte, MT

Tuition & fees (MT res): $5713 **Average undergraduate aid package: $8418**

ABOUT THE INSTITUTION State-supported, coed. ***Awards:*** associate, bachelor's, and master's degrees and post-bachelor's certificates. 34 undergraduate majors. ***Total enrollment:*** 2,402. Undergraduates: 2,293. Freshmen: 504. Federal methodology is used as a basis for awarding need-based institutional aid.

UNDERGRADUATE EXPENSES for 2008–09 ***Application fee:*** $30. ***Tuition, state resident:*** full-time $4462; part-time $185.90 per credit hour. ***Tuition, nonresident:*** full-time $14,175; part-time $590.60 per credit hour. ***Required fees:*** full-time $1251. Full-time tuition and fees vary according to course level, course load, degree level, and location. Part-time tuition and fees vary according to course level, course load, degree level, and location. ***College room and board:*** $6140; ***Room only:*** $2656. Room and board charges vary according to board plan. ***Payment plans:*** Installment, deferred payment.

FRESHMAN FINANCIAL AID (Fall 2007) 344 applied for aid; of those 73% were deemed to have need. 100% of freshmen with need received aid; of those 23% had need fully met. ***Average percent of need met:*** 75% (excluding resources awarded to replace EFC). ***Average financial aid package:*** $7366 (excluding resources awarded to replace EFC). 11% of all full-time freshmen had no need and received non-need-based gift aid.

UNDERGRADUATE FINANCIAL AID (Fall 2007) 1,320 applied for aid; of those 77% were deemed to have need. 100% of undergraduates with need received aid; of those 15% had need fully met. ***Average percent of need met:*** 76% (excluding resources awarded to replace EFC). ***Average financial aid package:*** $8418 (excluding resources awarded to replace EFC). 12% of all full-time undergraduates had no need and received non-need-based gift aid.

GIFT AID (NEED-BASED) ***Receiving aid:*** Freshmen: 53% (222); all full-time undergraduates: 47% (876). ***Average award:*** Freshmen: $4309; Undergraduates: $4079. ***Scholarships, grants, and awards:*** Federal Pell, FSEOG, state, private, college/university gift aid from institutional funds.

GIFT AID (NON-NEED-BASED) ***Receiving aid:*** Freshmen: 9% (36). Undergraduates: 4% (69). ***Average award:*** Freshmen: $2013. Undergraduates: $2556. ***Scholarships, grants, and awards by category:*** *Academic interests/achievement:* 350 awards ($600,000 total): business, computer science, engineering/technologies, general academic interests/achievements, health fields, mathematics, physical sciences. *Special achievements/activities:* $50,000 total: general special achievements/activities. *Special characteristics:* $50,000 total: general special characteristics. ***Tuition waivers:*** Full or partial for employees or children of employees. ***ROTC:*** Army.

LOANS ***Student loans:*** 85% of past graduating class borrowed through all loan programs. *Average indebtedness per student:* $21,000. ***Average need-based loan:*** Freshmen: $2903. Undergraduates: $3801. ***Programs:*** FFEL (Subsidized and Unsubsidized Stafford, PLUS), Perkins, college/university.

WORK-STUDY ***Federal work-study:*** 64 jobs averaging $2000. ***State or other work-study/employment:*** 25 part-time jobs averaging $2000.

APPLYING FOR FINANCIAL AID ***Required financial aid forms:*** FAFSA, institution's own form. ***Financial aid deadline (priority):*** 3/1. ***Notification date:*** Continuous beginning 4/1. Students must reply within 2 weeks of notification.

CONTACT Mike Richardson, Director of Financial Aid, Montana Tech of The University of Montana, West Park Street, Butte, MT 59701-8997, 406-496-4212 or toll-free 800-445-TECH Ext. 1. *Fax:* 406-496-4710. *E-mail:* mrichardson@mtech.edu.

MONTCLAIR STATE UNIVERSITY

Montclair, NJ

Tuition & fees (NJ res): $9428 **Average undergraduate aid package: $8283**

ABOUT THE INSTITUTION State-supported, coed. ***Awards:*** bachelor's, master's, and doctoral degrees and post-bachelor's certificates. 54 undergraduate majors. ***Total enrollment:*** 17,475. Undergraduates: 13,725. Freshmen: 2,271. Federal methodology is used as a basis for awarding need-based institutional aid.

UNDERGRADUATE EXPENSES for 2008–09 ***Application fee:*** $55. ***Tuition, state resident:*** full-time $6836; part-time $227.89 per credit. ***Tuition, nonresident:*** full-time $14,616; part-time $487.07 per credit. ***Required fees:*** full-time $2592; $146.42 per credit. ***College room and board:*** $10,050; ***Room only:*** $6750. Room and board charges vary according to board plan and housing facility. ***Payment plan:*** Installment.

FRESHMAN FINANCIAL AID (Fall 2008, est.) 1,550 applied for aid; of those 75% were deemed to have need. 93% of freshmen with need received aid; of those 24% had need fully met. ***Average percent of need met:*** 66% (excluding resources awarded to replace EFC). ***Average financial aid package:*** $6992 (excluding resources awarded to replace EFC). 2% of all full-time freshmen had no need and received non-need-based gift aid.

UNDERGRADUATE FINANCIAL AID (Fall 2008, est.) 7,757 applied for aid; of those 82% were deemed to have need. 93% of undergraduates with need received aid; of those 24% had need fully met. ***Average percent of need met:*** 67% (excluding resources awarded to replace EFC). ***Average financial aid package:*** $8283 (excluding resources awarded to replace EFC). 3% of all full-time undergraduates had no need and received non-need-based gift aid.

GIFT AID (NEED-BASED) ***Total amount:*** $24,950,787 (48% federal, 52% state). ***Receiving aid:*** Freshmen: 20% (459); all full-time undergraduates: 27% (3,013). ***Average award:*** Freshmen: $7796; Undergraduates: $7699. ***Scholarships, grants, and awards:*** Federal Pell, FSEOG, state, college/university gift aid from institutional funds.

GIFT AID (NON-NEED-BASED) ***Total amount:*** $5,593,430 (16% state, 74% institutional, 10% external sources). ***Receiving aid:*** Freshmen: 8% (176). Undergraduates: 7% (807). ***Average award:*** Freshmen: $4929. Undergraduates: $5470. ***Scholarships, grants, and awards by category:*** *Academic interests/achievement:* 648 awards ($2,287,808 total): biological sciences, business, communication, education, English, foreign languages, general academic interests/achievements, home economics, humanities, international studies, mathematics, physical sciences, religion/biblical studies, social sciences. *Creative arts/performance:* 251 awards ($230,298 total): art/fine arts, cinema/film/broadcasting, dance, music, performing arts, theater/drama. *Special achievements/activities:* 6 awards ($17,500 total): community service, general special achievements/activities, leadership. *Special characteristics:* 7 awards ($44,194 total): children and siblings of alumni, international students. ***Tuition waivers:*** Full or partial for employees or children of employees, senior citizens. ***ROTC:*** Air Force cooperative.

LOANS ***Student loans:*** $69,787,066 (37% need-based, 63% non-need-based). ***Average need-based loan:*** Freshmen: $3528. Undergraduates: $4416. ***Parent loans:*** $5,509,721 (100% non-need-based). ***Programs:*** FFEL (Subsidized and Unsubsidized Stafford, PLUS), Perkins, state, private loans.

WORK-STUDY ***Federal work-study:*** Total amount: $424,955; 374 jobs averaging $1067. ***State or other work-study/employment:*** Total amount: $3,719,489 (100% non-need-based). 1,655 part-time jobs averaging $2247.

APPLYING FOR FINANCIAL AID ***Required financial aid form:*** FAFSA. ***Financial aid deadline (priority):*** 3/1. ***Notification date:*** Continuous beginning 4/1. Students must reply within 2 weeks of notification.

CONTACT Frank A. Cuozzo, Director of Financial Aid, Montclair State University, College Hall, Room 222, Montclair, NJ 07043, 973-655-7022 or toll-free 800-331-9205. *Fax:* 973-655-7712. *E-mail:* cuozzof@mail.montclair.edu.

MONTREAT COLLEGE

Montreat, NC

Tuition & fees: $19,080 **Average undergraduate aid package: $11,459**

ABOUT THE INSTITUTION Independent religious, coed. 14 undergraduate majors. Federal methodology is used as a basis for awarding need-based institutional aid.

UNDERGRADUATE EXPENSES for 2008–09 ***Comprehensive fee:*** $25,080 includes full-time tuition ($18,700), mandatory fees ($380), and room and board ($6000). Full-time tuition and fees vary according to course load, program, and reciprocity agreements. Room and board charges vary according to board plan. ***Part-time tuition:*** $480 per year. Part-time tuition and fees vary according to course load, program, and reciprocity agreements. ***Payment plan:*** Installment.

FRESHMAN FINANCIAL AID (Fall 2008, est.) 149 applied for aid; of those 86% were deemed to have need. 100% of freshmen with need received aid; of those 25% had need fully met. ***Average percent of need met:*** 69% (excluding resources awarded to replace EFC). ***Average financial aid package:*** $13,931 (excluding resources awarded to replace EFC). 9% of all full-time freshmen had no need and received non-need-based gift aid.

UNDERGRADUATE FINANCIAL AID (Fall 2008, est.) 882 applied for aid; of those 86% were deemed to have need. 100% of undergraduates with need received aid; of those 22% had need fully met. ***Average percent of need met:*** 65% (excluding resources awarded to replace EFC). ***Average financial aid package:*** $11,459 (excluding resources awarded to replace EFC). 7% of all full-time undergraduates had no need and received non-need-based gift aid.

GIFT AID (NEED-BASED) ***Total amount:*** $5,541,272 (21% federal, 29% state, 35% institutional, 15% external sources). ***Receiving aid:*** Freshmen: 73% (128); all full-time undergraduates: 78% (730). ***Average award:*** Freshmen: $11,328; Undergraduates: $8216. ***Scholarships, grants, and awards:*** Federal Pell, FSEOG, state, private, college/university gift aid from institutional funds.

GIFT AID (NON-NEED-BASED) ***Total amount:*** $1,458,065 (15% state, 22% institutional, 63% external sources). ***Receiving aid:*** Freshmen: 13% (22). Undergraduates: 11% (103). ***Average award:*** Freshmen: $5968. Undergraduates: $5276. ***Scholarships, grants, and awards by category:*** *Academic interests/achievement:* 426 awards ($2,065,343 total): general academic interests/achievements. *Creative arts/performance:* 8 awards ($8000 total): music. *Special achievements/activities:* 75 awards ($75,000 total): leadership. *Special characteristics:* 300 awards ($1,061,894 total): children of faculty/staff, first-generation college students, international students, local/state students, relatives of clergy, religious affiliation, veterans, veterans' children. ***Tuition waivers:*** Full or partial for employees or children of employees.

LOANS ***Student loans:*** $6,413,493 (67% need-based, 33% non-need-based). 75% of past graduating class borrowed through all loan programs. *Average indebtedness per student:* $16,379. ***Average need-based loan:*** Freshmen: $3275. Undergraduates: $4227. ***Parent loans:*** $337,788 (34% need-based, 66% non-need-based). ***Programs:*** FFEL (Subsidized and Unsubsidized Stafford, PLUS), Perkins.

WORK-STUDY ***Federal work-study:*** Total amount: $118,381; 87 jobs averaging $1468. ***State or other work-study/employment:*** Total amount: $35,905 (24% need-based, 76% non-need-based). 20 part-time jobs averaging $1795.

ATHLETIC AWARDS Total amount: $559,863 (79% need-based, 21% non-need-based).

APPLYING FOR FINANCIAL AID ***Required financial aid forms:*** FAFSA, state aid form. ***Financial aid deadline (priority):*** 4/1. ***Notification date:*** Continuous beginning 4/1. Students must reply within 2 weeks of notification.

CONTACT Beth Pocock, Financial Aid Office, Montreat College, PO Box 1267, Montreat, NC 28757, 828-669-8012 Ext. 3790 or toll-free 800-622-6968 (in-state). *Fax:* 828-669-0120. *E-mail:* financialaid@montreat.edu.

MONTSERRAT COLLEGE OF ART

Beverly, MA

CONTACT Creda Carney, Director of Financial Aid, Montserrat College of Art, 23 Essex Street, PO Box 26, Beverly, MA 01915, 978-922-8222 Ext. 1155 or toll-free 800-836-0487. *Fax:* 978-922-4268. *E-mail:* finaid@montserrat.edu.

MOODY BIBLE INSTITUTE

Chicago, IL

Tuition & fees: N/R **Average undergraduate aid package: N/A**

ABOUT THE INSTITUTION Independent nondenominational, coed. ***Awards:*** bachelor's, master's, and first professional degrees. 8 undergraduate majors. Institutional methodology is used as a basis for awarding need-based institutional aid.

UNDERGRADUATE FINANCIAL AID (Fall 2007) 300 applied for aid; of those 100% were deemed to have need. 100% of undergraduates with need received aid. ***Average percent of need met:*** 25% (excluding resources awarded to replace EFC).

GIFT AID (NEED-BASED) ***Total amount:*** $798,000 (81% institutional, 19% external sources). ***Receiving aid:*** All full-time undergraduates: 21% (300). ***Average award:*** Undergraduates: $750. ***Scholarships, grants, and awards:*** private, college/university gift aid from institutional funds.

GIFT AID (NON-NEED-BASED) ***Tuition waivers:*** Full or partial for employees or children of employees.

LOANS ***Student loans:*** $196,000 (100% need-based). 2% of past graduating class borrowed through all loan programs. *Average indebtedness per student:* $3000. ***Average need-based loan:*** Undergraduates: $4000. ***Programs:*** alternative loans.

APPLYING FOR FINANCIAL AID ***Required financial aid form:*** institution's own form. ***Financial aid deadline:*** Continuous.

CONTACT Esther Kim, Director of Financial Aid, Moody Bible Institute, 820 North LaSalle Boulevard, Chicago, IL 60610-3284, 312-329-4178 or toll-free 800-967-4MBI. *Fax:* 312-329-4197. *E-mail:* esther.kim@moody.edu.

MOORE COLLEGE OF ART & DESIGN

Philadelphia, PA

CONTACT Kristina Fripps, Director of Financial Aid, Moore College of Art & Design, 20th and the Parkway, Philadelphia, PA 19103-1179, 215-965-4042 or toll-free 800-523-2025. *Fax:* 215-568-1773. *E-mail:* kfripps@moore.edu.

MORAVIAN COLLEGE

Bethlehem, PA

CONTACT Mr. Stephen C. Cassel, Director of Financial Aid, Moravian College, 1200 Main Street, Bethlehem, PA 18018-6650, 610-861-1330 or toll-free 800-441-3191. *Fax:* 610-861-1346. *E-mail:* cassels@moravian.edu.

MOREHEAD STATE UNIVERSITY

Morehead, KY

ABOUT THE INSTITUTION State-supported, coed. ***Awards:*** associate, bachelor's, and master's degrees and post-bachelor's and post-master's certificates. 49 undergraduate majors. ***Total enrollment:*** 8,981. Undergraduates: 7,487. Freshmen: 1,338.

GIFT AID (NEED-BASED) ***Scholarships, grants, and awards:*** Federal Pell, FSEOG, state, private, college/university gift aid from institutional funds.

LOANS ***Programs:*** Federal Direct (Subsidized and Unsubsidized Stafford, PLUS), FFEL (Subsidized and Unsubsidized Stafford, PLUS), Perkins, college/university.

WORK-STUDY ***Federal work-study:*** Total amount: $923,259. ***State or other work-study/employment:*** Total amount: $1,474,376 (100% non-need-based).

APPLYING FOR FINANCIAL AID ***Required financial aid forms:*** FAFSA, institution's own form.

CONTACT Jill Ratliff, Director of Institutional Effectiveness, Morehead State University, 100 Admissions Center, Morehead, KY 40351, 606-783-9555 or toll-free 800-585-6781. *Fax:* 606-783-5091. *E-mail:* ji.ratliff@moreheadstate.edu.

MOREHOUSE COLLEGE

Atlanta, GA

CONTACT James A. Stotts, Director of Financial Aid, Morehouse College, 830 Westview Drive, SW, Atlanta, GA 30314, 404-681-2800 Ext. 2638 or toll-free 800-851-1254. *Fax:* 404-215-2711. *E-mail:* jstotts@morehouse.edu.

MORGAN STATE UNIVERSITY

Baltimore, MD

CONTACT Director of Financial Aid, Morgan State University, 1700 East Cold Spring Lane, Baltimore, MD 21251, 443-885-3170 or toll-free 800-332-6674.

MORNINGSIDE COLLEGE

Sioux City, IA

ABOUT THE INSTITUTION Independent religious, coed. ***Awards:*** bachelor's and master's degrees. 43 undergraduate majors. ***Total enrollment:*** 1,906. Undergraduates: 1,214. Freshmen: 302.

GIFT AID (NEED-BASED) ***Scholarships, grants, and awards:*** Federal Pell, FSEOG, state, private, college/university gift aid from institutional funds.

GIFT AID (NON-NEED-BASED) ***Scholarships, grants, and awards by category:*** *Academic interests/achievement:* computer science, general academic interests/achievements. *Creative arts/performance:* art/fine arts, cinema/film/broadcasting, creative writing, journalism/publications, music, theater/drama. *Special achievements/activities:* cheerleading/drum major, community service, leadership. *Special characteristics:* children of faculty/staff, international students, out-of-state students.

LOANS ***Programs:*** FFEL (Subsidized and Unsubsidized Stafford, PLUS), Perkins, state, college/university, private loans.

WORK-STUDY ***Federal work-study:*** Total amount: $348,577; 300 jobs averaging $1161. ***State or other work-study/employment:*** Total amount: $385,488 (18% need-based, 82% non-need-based). 1 part-time job averaging $900.

APPLYING FOR FINANCIAL AID ***Required financial aid form:*** FAFSA.

CONTACT Karen Gagnon, Director of Student Financial Planning, Morningside College, 1501 Morningside Avenue, Sioux City, IA 51106, 712-274-5272 or toll-free 800-831-0806 Ext. 5111. *Fax:* 712-274-5605. *E-mail:* gagnon@morningside.edu.

MORRIS COLLEGE

Sumter, SC

CONTACT Ms. Sandra S. Gibson, Director of Financial Aid, Morris College, 100 West College Street, Sumter, SC 29150-3599, 803-934-3238 or toll-free 866-853-1345. *Fax:* 803-773-3687.

MORRISON UNIVERSITY

Reno, NV

CONTACT Kim Droniak, Financial Aid Administrator, Morrison University, 140 Washington Street, Reno, NV 89503-5600, 775-850-0700 or toll-free 800-369-6144. *Fax:* 775-850-0711.

MOUNTAIN STATE UNIVERSITY

Beckley, WV

Tuition & fees: $8400 **Average undergraduate aid package: $6695**

ABOUT THE INSTITUTION Independent, coed. ***Awards:*** associate, bachelor's, and master's degrees and post-bachelor's and post-master's certificates. 61 undergraduate majors. ***Total enrollment:*** 5,108. Undergraduates: 4,378. Freshmen: 562. Federal methodology is used as a basis for awarding need-based institutional aid.

UNDERGRADUATE EXPENSES for 2008–09 ***Application fee:*** $25. ***Comprehensive fee:*** $14,516 includes full-time tuition ($6300), mandatory fees ($2100), and room and board ($6116). ***College room only:*** $3000. Full-time tuition and fees vary according to course load and program. Room and board charges vary according to board plan. ***Part-time tuition:*** $210 per credit hour. ***Part-time fees:*** $70 per credit hour. Part-time tuition and fees vary according to course load and program. ***Payment plan:*** Installment.

FRESHMAN FINANCIAL AID (Fall 2007) 258 applied for aid; of those 86% were deemed to have need. 100% of freshmen with need received aid; of those 100% had need fully met. ***Average percent of need met:*** 39% (excluding resources awarded to replace EFC). ***Average financial aid package:*** $5507 (excluding resources awarded to replace EFC). 1% of all full-time freshmen had no need and received non-need-based gift aid.

UNDERGRADUATE FINANCIAL AID (Fall 2007) 1,967 applied for aid; of those 91% were deemed to have need. 100% of undergraduates with need received aid; of those 100% had need fully met. ***Average percent of need met:*** 48% (excluding resources awarded to replace EFC). ***Average financial aid package:*** $6695 (excluding resources awarded to replace EFC). 1% of all full-time undergraduates had no need and received non-need-based gift aid.

GIFT AID (NEED-BASED) ***Total amount:*** $6,732,864 (81% federal, 16% state, 1% institutional, 2% external sources). ***Receiving aid:*** Freshmen: 45% (153); all full-time undergraduates: 39% (1,174). ***Average award:*** Freshmen: $3336; Undergraduates: $4026. ***Scholarships, grants, and awards:*** Federal Pell, FSEOG, state, private, college/university gift aid from institutional funds, Federal Nursing.

GIFT AID (NON-NEED-BASED) ***Total amount:*** $387,121 (63% state, 37% institutional). ***Receiving aid:*** Freshmen: 2% (8). Undergraduates: 1% (23). ***Average award:*** Freshmen: $3272. Undergraduates: $4190. ***Scholarships, grants, and awards by category:*** *Academic interests/achievement:* 33 awards ($136,870 total): general academic interests/achievements. *Special achievements/activities:* 10 awards ($10,855 total): cheerleading/drum major. ***Tuition waivers:*** Full or partial for employees or children of employees, senior citizens.

LOANS ***Student loans:*** $19,465,052 (51% need-based, 49% non-need-based). 84% of past graduating class borrowed through all loan programs. *Average indebtedness per student:* $31,221. ***Average need-based loan:*** Freshmen: $3378. Undergraduates: $4532. ***Parent loans:*** $454,031 (100% non-need-based). ***Programs:*** FFEL (Subsidized and Unsubsidized Stafford, PLUS), private loans.

WORK-STUDY ***Federal work-study:*** Total amount: $229,549; 117 jobs averaging $1947.

ATHLETIC AWARDS Total amount: $449,680 (100% non-need-based).

APPLYING FOR FINANCIAL AID ***Required financial aid form:*** FAFSA. ***Financial aid deadline:*** Continuous. ***Notification date:*** Continuous. Students must reply within 2 weeks of notification.

CONTACT Liza Zigler, Director of Financial Aid, Mountain State University, PO Box 9003, Beckley, WV 25802-9003, 304-929-1595 or toll-free 800-766-6067 Ext. 1433. *Fax:* 304-929-1390. *E-mail:* lzigler@mountainstate.edu.

MOUNT ALOYSIUS COLLEGE

Cresson, PA

Tuition & fees: $17,280 **Average undergraduate aid package: $10,500**

ABOUT THE INSTITUTION Independent Roman Catholic, coed. ***Awards:*** associate, bachelor's, and master's degrees. 34 undergraduate majors. ***Total enrollment:*** 1,644. Undergraduates: 1,594. Federal methodology is used as a basis for awarding need-based institutional aid.

UNDERGRADUATE EXPENSES for 2009–10 ***Application fee:*** $30. ***Comprehensive fee:*** $24,580 includes full-time tuition ($16,580), mandatory fees ($700), and room and board ($7300). ***College room only:*** $3750. ***Part-time tuition:*** $480 per credit. ***Part-time fees:*** $185 per term.

FRESHMAN FINANCIAL AID (Fall 2008, est.) 326 applied for aid; of those 92% were deemed to have need. 100% of freshmen with need received aid. ***Average percent of need met:*** 25% (excluding resources awarded to replace EFC). ***Average financial aid package:*** $13,162 (excluding resources awarded to replace EFC). 8% of all full-time freshmen had no need and received non-need-based gift aid.

UNDERGRADUATE FINANCIAL AID (Fall 2008, est.) 1,160 applied for aid; of those 97% were deemed to have need. 100% of undergraduates with need received aid. ***Average percent of need met:*** 28% (excluding resources awarded to replace EFC). ***Average financial aid package:*** $10,500 (excluding resources awarded to replace EFC). 3% of all full-time undergraduates had no need and received non-need-based gift aid.

GIFT AID (NEED-BASED) ***Total amount:*** $9,920,825 (30% federal, 26% state, 41% institutional, 3% external sources). ***Receiving aid:*** Freshmen: 92% (301); all full-time undergraduates: 97% (1,130). ***Average award:*** Freshmen: $2242; Undergraduates: $1800. ***Scholarships, grants, and awards:*** Federal Pell, FSEOG, state, private, college/university gift aid from institutional funds.

GIFT AID (NON-NEED-BASED) ***Receiving aid:*** Freshmen: 8% (25). Undergraduates: 3% (30). ***Average award:*** Freshmen: $2400. Undergraduates: $1800. ***Scholarships, grants, and awards by category:*** *Creative arts/performance:* 25 awards ($19,000 total): music, performing arts. *Special achievements/activities:* 52 awards ($450,000 total): leadership. *Special characteristics:* 53 awards ($51,000 total): children of current students, parents of current students, religious affiliation, siblings of current students, spouses of current students, twins.

LOANS ***Student loans:*** $8,487,887 (100% need-based). 91% of past graduating class borrowed through all loan programs. *Average indebtedness per student:* $24,307. ***Average need-based loan:*** Freshmen: $3210. Undergraduates: $3300. ***Parent loans:*** $1,690,137 (100% need-based). ***Programs:*** FFEL (Subsidized and Unsubsidized Stafford, PLUS), Perkins, Federal Nursing, alternative loans.

WORK-STUDY ***Federal work-study:*** Total amount: $140,355; 170 jobs averaging $1000.

APPLYING FOR FINANCIAL AID ***Required financial aid form:*** FAFSA. ***Financial aid deadline (priority):*** 2/15. ***Notification date:*** Continuous beginning 3/15. Students must reply within 4 weeks of notification.

CONTACT Mrs. Stacy L. Schenk, Director of Financial Aid, Mount Aloysius College, 7373 Admiral Peary Highway, Cresson, PA 16630-1900, 814-886-6357 or toll-free 888-823-2220. *Fax:* 814-886-6463. *E-mail:* sschenk@mtaloy.edu.

MOUNT ANGEL SEMINARY

Saint Benedict, OR

CONTACT Dorene Preis, Director of Student Financial Aid/Registrar, Mount Angel Seminary, 1 Abbey Drive, Saint Benedict, OR 97373, 503-845-3951. *Fax:* 503-845-3126. *E-mail:* dpreis@mtangel.edu.

MOUNT CARMEL COLLEGE OF NURSING

Columbus, OH

CONTACT Carol Graham, Director of Financial Aid, Mount Carmel College of Nursing, 127 South Davis Avenue, Columbus, OH 43222, 614-234-5800 Ext. 5177. *E-mail:* cgraham@mchs.com.

MOUNT HOLYOKE COLLEGE

South Hadley, MA

Tuition & fees: $37,646 **Average undergraduate aid package: $31,459**

ABOUT THE INSTITUTION Independent, women only. ***Awards:*** bachelor's and master's degrees and post-bachelor's certificates. 56 undergraduate majors. ***Total enrollment:*** 2,241. Undergraduates: 2,240. Freshmen: 518. Institutional methodology is used as a basis for awarding need-based institutional aid.

UNDERGRADUATE EXPENSES for 2008–09 ***Application fee:*** $60. ***Comprehensive fee:*** $48,666 includes full-time tuition ($37,460), mandatory fees ($186), and room and board ($11,020). ***College room only:*** $5400. Room and board charges vary according to board plan and housing facility. ***Part-time tuition:*** $1175 per credit hour.

FRESHMAN FINANCIAL AID (Fall 2008, est.) 387 applied for aid; of those 81% were deemed to have need. 100% of freshmen with need received aid; of those 100% had need fully met. ***Average percent of need met:*** 100% (excluding resources awarded to replace EFC). ***Average financial aid package:*** $32,913 (excluding resources awarded to replace EFC). 8% of all full-time freshmen had no need and received non-need-based gift aid.

UNDERGRADUATE FINANCIAL AID (Fall 2008, est.) 1,623 applied for aid; of those 90% were deemed to have need. 100% of undergraduates with need received aid; of those 100% had need fully met. ***Average percent of need met:*** 100% (excluding resources awarded to replace EFC). ***Average financial aid package:*** $31,459 (excluding resources awarded to replace EFC). 7% of all full-time undergraduates had no need and received non-need-based gift aid.

GIFT AID (NEED-BASED) ***Total amount:*** $37,326,501 (6% federal, 1% state, 91% institutional, 2% external sources). ***Receiving aid:*** Freshmen: 59% (308); all full-time undergraduates: 60% (1,385). ***Average award:*** Freshmen: $29,044; Undergraduates: $26,877. ***Scholarships, grants, and awards:*** Federal Pell, FSEOG, state, private, college/university gift aid from institutional funds.

GIFT AID (NON-NEED-BASED) ***Total amount:*** $3,008,210 (80% institutional, 20% external sources). ***Average award:*** Freshmen: $15,610. Undergraduates: $14,910. ***Scholarships, grants, and awards by category:*** *Academic interests/achievement:* 169 awards ($2,415,165 total): general academic interests/achievements. ***ROTC:*** Army cooperative, Air Force cooperative.

LOANS ***Student loans:*** $9,075,776 (84% need-based, 16% non-need-based). 66% of past graduating class borrowed through all loan programs. *Average indebtedness per student:* $23,841. ***Average need-based loan:*** Freshmen: $3008. Undergraduates: $4620. ***Parent loans:*** $5,643,587 (100% non-need-based). ***Programs:*** Federal Direct (Subsidized and Unsubsidized Stafford, PLUS), Perkins, college/university.

WORK-STUDY ***Federal work-study:*** Total amount: $1,535,535; 829 jobs averaging $1819. ***State or other work-study/employment:*** Total amount: $704,911 (100% need-based). 375 part-time jobs averaging $1913.

APPLYING FOR FINANCIAL AID ***Required financial aid forms:*** FAFSA, CSS Financial Aid PROFILE, noncustodial (divorced/separated) parent's statement, business/farm supplement, federal tax returns. ***Financial aid deadline:*** 3/1 (priority: 2/15). ***Notification date:*** 4/1. Students must reply by 5/1.

CONTACT Ms. Kathy Blaisdell, Director of Student Financial Services, Mount Holyoke College, 50 College Street, South Hadley, MA 01075-1492, 413-538-2291. *Fax:* 413-538-2512. *E-mail:* kblaisde@mtholyoke.edu.

MOUNT IDA COLLEGE

Newton, MA

Tuition & fees: $22,500 **Average undergraduate aid package: $14,294**

ABOUT THE INSTITUTION Independent, coed. ***Awards:*** associate and bachelor's degrees. 24 undergraduate majors. ***Total enrollment:*** 1,460. Undergraduates: 1,460. Freshmen: 411. Federal methodology is used as a basis for awarding need-based institutional aid.

UNDERGRADUATE EXPENSES for 2008–09 ***Application fee:*** $45. ***Comprehensive fee:*** $33,600 includes full-time tuition ($22,275), mandatory fees ($225), and room and board ($11,100). ***Part-time tuition:*** $600 per credit. ***Payment plan:*** Installment.

FRESHMAN FINANCIAL AID (Fall 2007) 375 applied for aid; of those 87% were deemed to have need. 100% of freshmen with need received aid; of those 8% had need fully met. ***Average percent of need met:*** 55% (excluding resources awarded to replace EFC). ***Average financial aid package:*** $14,663 (excluding resources awarded to replace EFC). 22% of all full-time freshmen had no need and received non-need-based gift aid.

UNDERGRADUATE FINANCIAL AID (Fall 2007) 1,155 applied for aid; of those 90% were deemed to have need. 100% of undergraduates with need received aid; of those 7% had need fully met. ***Average percent of need met:*** 54% (excluding resources awarded to replace EFC). ***Average financial aid package:*** $14,294 (excluding resources awarded to replace EFC). 21% of all full-time undergraduates had no need and received non-need-based gift aid.

GIFT AID (NEED-BASED) ***Total amount:*** $10,448,596 (15% federal, 6% state, 75% institutional, 4% external sources). ***Receiving aid:*** Freshmen: 74% (323); all full-time undergraduates: 75% (1,017). ***Average award:*** Freshmen: $11,015. ***Scholarships, grants, and awards:*** Federal Pell, FSEOG, state, private, college/university gift aid from institutional funds.

GIFT AID (NON-NEED-BASED) ***Total amount:*** $1,204,546 (95% institutional, 5% external sources). ***Receiving aid:*** Freshmen: 5% (21). Undergraduates: 4% (58). ***Average award:*** Freshmen: $3841. Undergraduates: $3428. ***Scholarships, grants, and awards by category:*** *Creative arts/performance:* 71 awards ($76,500 total): applied art and design, art/fine arts, general creative arts/performance. *Special achievements/activities:* 1,305 awards ($4,909,850 total): community service, general special achievements/activities, leadership. ***Tuition waivers:*** Full or partial for employees or children of employees.

LOANS ***Student loans:*** $13,391,003 (76% need-based, 24% non-need-based). 78% of past graduating class borrowed through all loan programs. *Average indebtedness per student:* $33,635. ***Average need-based loan:*** Freshmen: $3462. Undergraduates: $4260. ***Parent loans:*** $4,066,818 (45% need-based, 55% non-need-based). ***Programs:*** FFEL (Subsidized and Unsubsidized Stafford, PLUS), state, alternative loans.

WORK-STUDY ***Federal work-study:*** Total amount: $357,555; 511 jobs averaging $1006. ***State or other work-study/employment:*** Total amount: $150,000 (5% need-based, 95% non-need-based). 109 part-time jobs averaging $1495.

APPLYING FOR FINANCIAL AID ***Required financial aid form:*** FAFSA. ***Financial aid deadline (priority):*** 5/1. ***Notification date:*** Continuous.

CONTACT David L. Goldman, Director of Financial Aid, Mount Ida College, 777 Dedham Street, Newton, MA 02459-3310, 617-928-4785. *Fax:* 617-332-7869. *E-mail:* finaid@mountida.edu.

MOUNT MARTY COLLEGE

Yankton, SD

Tuition & fees: $18,250 **Average undergraduate aid package: $26,937**

ABOUT THE INSTITUTION Independent Roman Catholic, coed. ***Awards:*** associate, bachelor's, and master's degrees. 32 undergraduate majors. ***Total enrollment:*** 1,180. Undergraduates: 1,046. Freshmen: 184. Federal methodology is used as a basis for awarding need-based institutional aid.

UNDERGRADUATE EXPENSES for 2008–09 ***Application fee:*** $35. ***Comprehensive fee:*** $23,460 includes full-time tuition ($16,420), mandatory fees ($1830), and room and board ($5210). Full-time tuition and fees vary according to course load and location. ***Part-time tuition:*** $190 per credit hour. ***Part-time fees:*** $25 per credit hour. Part-time tuition and fees vary according to course load and location. ***Payment plan:*** Installment.

FRESHMAN FINANCIAL AID (Fall 2008, est.) 129 applied for aid; of those 96% were deemed to have need. 100% of freshmen with need received aid; of those 40% had need fully met. ***Average percent of need met:*** 98% (excluding resources awarded to replace EFC). ***Average financial aid package:*** $26,937 (excluding resources awarded to replace EFC). 6% of all full-time freshmen had no need and received non-need-based gift aid.

UNDERGRADUATE FINANCIAL AID (Fall 2008, est.) 549 applied for aid; of those 92% were deemed to have need. 100% of undergraduates with need received aid; of those 76% had need fully met. ***Average percent of need met:*** 98% (excluding resources awarded to replace EFC). ***Average financial aid package:*** $26,937 (excluding resources awarded to replace EFC). 7% of all full-time undergraduates had no need and received non-need-based gift aid.

GIFT AID (NEED-BASED) ***Total amount:*** $4,451,336 (30% federal, 1% state, 58% institutional, 11% external sources). ***Receiving aid:*** Freshmen: 84% (117); all full-time undergraduates: 81% (492). ***Average award:*** Freshmen: $1463; Undergraduates: $1366. ***Scholarships, grants, and awards:*** Federal Pell, FSEOG, state, private, college/university gift aid from institutional funds.

GIFT AID (NON-NEED-BASED) ***Total amount:*** $130,404 (3% federal, 2% state, 88% institutional, 7% external sources). ***Receiving aid:*** Freshmen: 6% (8). Undergraduates: 7% (45). ***Average award:*** Freshmen: $16,247. Undergraduates: $6740. ***Scholarships, grants, and awards by category:*** *Academic interests/achievement:* 467 awards ($2,626,939 total): general academic interests/achievements. *Creative arts/performance:* 65 awards ($85,069 total): music, theater/drama. *Special characteristics:* 51 awards ($179,373 total): children of current students, children of faculty/staff, international students, parents of current students, religious affiliation, siblings of current students, spouses of current students. ***ROTC:*** Army cooperative.

LOANS ***Student loans:*** $3,359,836 (98% need-based, 2% non-need-based). 85% of past graduating class borrowed through all loan programs. *Average indebtedness per student:* $27,028. ***Average need-based loan:*** Freshmen: $4835. Undergraduates: $5968. ***Parent loans:*** $454,044 (91% need-based, 9% non-need-based). ***Programs:*** Federal Direct (Subsidized and Unsubsidized Stafford, PLUS), FFEL (Subsidized and Unsubsidized Stafford, PLUS), Perkins, Federal Nursing.

WORK-STUDY ***Federal work-study:*** Total amount: $280,125; 189 jobs averaging $1500. ***State or other work-study/employment:*** Total amount: $76,500 (73% need-based, 27% non-need-based). 52 part-time jobs averaging $1500.

ATHLETIC AWARDS Total amount: $555,440 (94% need-based, 6% non-need-based).

APPLYING FOR FINANCIAL AID ***Required financial aid forms:*** FAFSA, institution's own form. ***Financial aid deadline (priority):*** 3/1. ***Notification date:*** Continuous beginning 3/15. Students must reply within 2 weeks of notification.

CONTACT Mr. Ken Kocer, Director of Financial Assistance, Mount Marty College, 1105 West 8th Street, Yankton, SD 57078-3724, 605-668-1589 or toll-free 800-658-4552. *Fax:* 605-668-1585. *E-mail:* kkocer@mtmc.edu.

MOUNT MARY COLLEGE

Milwaukee, WI

Tuition & fees: $21,166 **Average undergraduate aid package: $14,607**

ABOUT THE INSTITUTION Independent Roman Catholic, undergraduate: women only; graduate: coed. ***Awards:*** bachelor's and master's degrees and post-bachelor's certificates. 53 undergraduate majors. ***Total enrollment:*** 1,862. Undergraduates: 1,428. Freshmen: 176. Federal methodology is used as a basis for awarding need-based institutional aid.

UNDERGRADUATE EXPENSES for 2009–10 ***Application fee:*** $25. ***Comprehensive fee:*** $28,446 includes full-time tuition ($20,736), mandatory fees ($430), and room and board ($7280). ***Part-time tuition:*** $596 per credit. ***Part-time fees:*** $220 per year.

FRESHMAN FINANCIAL AID (Fall 2008, est.) 121 applied for aid; of those 92% were deemed to have need. 100% of freshmen with need received aid; of those 11% had need fully met. ***Average percent of need met:*** 70% (excluding resources awarded to replace EFC). ***Average financial aid package:*** $15,636 (excluding resources awarded to replace EFC). 9% of all full-time freshmen had no need and received non-need-based gift aid.

UNDERGRADUATE FINANCIAL AID (Fall 2008, est.) 662 applied for aid; of those 91% were deemed to have need. 100% of undergraduates with need received aid; of those 10% had need fully met. ***Average percent of need met:*** 64% (excluding resources awarded to replace EFC). ***Average financial aid package:*** $14,607 (excluding resources awarded to replace EFC). 10% of all full-time undergraduates had no need and received non-need-based gift aid.

GIFT AID (NEED-BASED) ***Total amount:*** $8,145,603 (21% federal, 18% state, 60% institutional, 1% external sources). ***Receiving aid:*** Freshmen: 64% (111); all full-time undergraduates: 68% (598). ***Average award:*** Freshmen: $11,479; Undergraduates: $9900. ***Scholarships, grants, and awards:*** Federal Pell, FSEOG, state, private, college/university gift aid from institutional funds, Metropolitan Milwaukee Association of Commerce Awards.

GIFT AID (NON-NEED-BASED) ***Total amount:*** $712,043 (1% state, 97% institutional, 2% external sources). ***Receiving aid:*** Freshmen: 4% (7). Undergraduates: 4% (33). ***Average award:*** Freshmen: $7526. Undergraduates: $5848. ***Scholarships, grants, and awards by category:*** *Academic interests/achievement:* 354 awards ($1,725,272 total): business, communication, education, English, general academic interests/achievements, health fields, home economics, humanities, mathematics, physical sciences, social sciences. *Creative arts/performance:* 29 awards ($22,032 total): applied art and design, art/fine arts, music. *Special achievements/activities:* 8 awards ($50,143 total): general special achievements/activities, leadership. *Special characteristics:* 35 awards ($207,708 total): children of faculty/staff, international students, parents of current students, siblings of current students. ***ROTC:*** Army cooperative.

LOANS ***Student loans:*** $9,053,630 (80% need-based, 20% non-need-based). 80% of past graduating class borrowed through all loan programs. *Average indebtedness per student:* $21,170. ***Average need-based loan:*** Freshmen: $3468. Undergraduates: $4469. ***Parent loans:*** $385,652 (41% need-based, 59% non-need-based). ***Programs:*** FFEL (Subsidized and Unsubsidized Stafford, PLUS), Perkins, state.

WORK-STUDY ***Federal work-study:*** Total amount: $130,778; 148 jobs averaging $1363. ***State or other work-study/employment:*** Total amount: $205,000 (100% non-need-based). 50 part-time jobs averaging $1200.

APPLYING FOR FINANCIAL AID ***Required financial aid form:*** FAFSA. ***Financial aid deadline (priority):*** 3/1. ***Notification date:*** Continuous. Students must reply within 2 weeks of notification.

CONTACT Debra Duff, Director of Financial Aid, Mount Mary College, 2900 North Menomonee River Parkway, Milwaukee, WI 53222-4597, 414-256-1258. *Fax:* 414-443-3602. *E-mail:* finaid@mtmary.edu.

MOUNT MERCY COLLEGE

Cedar Rapids, IA

Tuition & fees: $21,125 **Average undergraduate aid package: $16,977**

ABOUT THE INSTITUTION Independent Roman Catholic, coed. ***Awards:*** bachelor's and master's degrees. 45 undergraduate majors. ***Total enrollment:*** 1,555. Undergraduates: 1,474. Freshmen: 172. Federal methodology is used as a basis for awarding need-based institutional aid.

UNDERGRADUATE EXPENSES for 2008–09 ***Application fee:*** $20. ***Comprehensive fee:*** $27,775 includes full-time tuition ($21,125) and room and board ($6650). Full-time tuition and fees vary according to course load. Room and board charges vary according to board plan and housing facility. ***Part-time tuition:*** $585 per credit hour. Part-time tuition and fees vary according to course load. ***Payment plan:*** Installment.

FRESHMAN FINANCIAL AID (Fall 2008, est.) 164 applied for aid; of those 87% were deemed to have need. 97% of freshmen with need received aid; of those 36% had need fully met. ***Average percent of need met:*** 82% (excluding resources awarded to replace EFC). ***Average financial aid package:*** $17,999 (excluding resources awarded to replace EFC). 20% of all full-time freshmen had no need and received non-need-based gift aid.

UNDERGRADUATE FINANCIAL AID (Fall 2008, est.) 853 applied for aid; of those 89% were deemed to have need. 94% of undergraduates with need received aid; of those 24% had need fully met. ***Average percent of need met:*** 72% (excluding resources awarded to replace EFC). ***Average financial aid package:*** $16,977 (excluding resources awarded to replace EFC). 16% of all full-time undergraduates had no need and received non-need-based gift aid.

GIFT AID (NEED-BASED) ***Total amount:*** $9,549,733 (15% federal, 26% state, 57% institutional, 2% external sources). ***Receiving aid:*** Freshmen: 77% (138); all full-time undergraduates: 77% (706). ***Average award:*** Freshmen: $14,132; Undergraduates: $11,781. ***Scholarships, grants, and awards:*** Federal Pell, FSEOG, state, college/university gift aid from institutional funds.

GIFT AID (NON-NEED-BASED) ***Total amount:*** $1,611,254 (1% federal, 1% state, 93% institutional, 5% external sources). ***Receiving aid:*** Freshmen: 21% (37). Undergraduates: 12% (106). ***Average award:*** Freshmen: $10,772. Undergraduates: $8371. ***Scholarships, grants, and awards by category:*** *Academic interests/achievement:* 1,021 awards ($5,715,915 total): general academic interests/achievements. *Creative arts/performance:* 36 awards ($41,750 total): art/fine arts, music, theater/drama. *Special achievements/activities:* 194 awards ($213,506 total): leadership. *Special characteristics:* 19 awards ($11,729 total): previous college experience. ***Tuition waivers:*** Full or partial for employees or children of employees.

LOANS ***Student loans:*** $9,834,018 (71% need-based, 29% non-need-based). 95% of past graduating class borrowed through all loan programs. *Average indebtedness per student:* $28,430. ***Average need-based loan:*** Freshmen: $3973. Undergraduates: $5461. ***Parent loans:*** $1,205,972 (40% need-based, 60% non-need-based). ***Programs:*** Federal Direct (Subsidized and Unsubsidized Stafford, PLUS), Perkins, state, college/university.

WORK-STUDY ***Federal work-study:*** Total amount: $416,511; 326 jobs averaging $1645. ***State or other work-study/employment:*** Total amount: $409,360 (18% need-based, 82% non-need-based). 161 part-time jobs averaging $1894.

ATHLETIC AWARDS Total amount: $425,330 (57% need-based, 43% non-need-based).

APPLYING FOR FINANCIAL AID ***Required financial aid form:*** FAFSA. ***Financial aid deadline (priority):*** 3/1. ***Notification date:*** Continuous beginning 3/15. Students must reply by 5/1 or within 3 weeks of notification.

CONTACT Bethany Rinderknecht, Director of Financial Aid, Mount Mercy College, 1330 Elmhurst Drive NE, Cedar Rapids, IA 52402-4797, 319-368-6467 or toll-free 800-248-4504. *Fax:* 319-364-3546. *E-mail:* brinderknecht@mtmercy.edu.

MOUNT OLIVE COLLEGE

Mount Olive, NC

Tuition & fees: $13,776 **Average undergraduate aid package: $8223**

ABOUT THE INSTITUTION Independent Free Will Baptist, coed. ***Awards:*** associate and bachelor's degrees. 22 undergraduate majors. ***Total enrollment:*** 3,390. Undergraduates: 3,390. Freshmen: 361. Federal methodology is used as a basis for awarding need-based institutional aid.

UNDERGRADUATE EXPENSES for 2008–09 ***Application fee:*** $20. ***Comprehensive fee:*** $19,316 includes full-time tuition ($13,776) and room and board ($5540). ***College room only:*** $2300. ***Part-time tuition:*** $310 per credit hour.

FRESHMAN FINANCIAL AID (Fall 2007) 300 applied for aid. of those 15% had need fully met. ***Average percent of need met:*** 69% (excluding resources awarded to replace EFC). ***Average financial aid package:*** $9407 (excluding resources awarded to replace EFC).

UNDERGRADUATE FINANCIAL AID (Fall 2007) 2,145 applied for aid; of those 85% were deemed to have need. 98% of undergraduates with need received aid; of those 14% had need fully met. ***Average percent of need met:*** 65% (excluding resources awarded to replace EFC). ***Average financial aid package:*** $8223 (excluding resources awarded to replace EFC).

GIFT AID (NEED-BASED) ***Total amount:*** $10,111,198 (33% federal, 61% state, 6% external sources). ***Receiving aid:*** Freshmen: 87% (261); all full-time undergraduates: 80% (1,716). ***Average award:*** Freshmen: $7196; Undergraduates: $5604. ***Scholarships, grants, and awards:*** Federal Pell, FSEOG, state, private, college/university gift aid from institutional funds.

GIFT AID (NON-NEED-BASED) ***Total amount:*** $761,683 (2% federal, 59% state, 39% external sources). ***Receiving aid:*** Freshmen: 5% (16). Undergraduates: 4% (91).

LOANS ***Student loans:*** $16,539,635 (72% need-based, 28% non-need-based). 94% of past graduating class borrowed through all loan programs. *Average indebtedness per student:* $13,854. ***Average need-based loan:*** Freshmen: $2492. Undergraduates: $3137. ***Parent loans:*** $384,019 (35% need-based, 65% non-need-based). ***Programs:*** Federal Direct (Subsidized and Unsubsidized Stafford, PLUS), FFEL (Subsidized and Unsubsidized Stafford, PLUS), Perkins, state.

WORK-STUDY ***Federal work-study:*** Total amount: $107,787; 136 jobs available.

ATHLETIC AWARDS Total amount: $618,306 (75% need-based, 25% non-need-based).

APPLYING FOR FINANCIAL AID ***Required financial aid forms:*** FAFSA, state aid form. ***Financial aid deadline:*** Continuous. ***Notification date:*** Continuous beginning 2/14.

CONTACT Ms. Katrina K. Lee, Director of Financial Aid, Mount Olive College, 634 Henderson Street, Mount Olive, NC 28365, 919-658-7891 or toll-free 800-653-0854 (in-state). *Fax:* 919-658-0816. *E-mail:* klee@moc.edu.

MOUNT SAINT MARY COLLEGE

Newburgh, NY

Tuition & fees: $20,745 **Average undergraduate aid package: $13,632**

ABOUT THE INSTITUTION Independent, coed. ***Awards:*** bachelor's and master's degrees and post-bachelor's and post-master's certificates. 34 undergraduate majors. ***Total enrollment:*** 2,629. Undergraduates: 2,109. Freshmen: 439. Federal methodology is used as a basis for awarding need-based institutional aid.

UNDERGRADUATE EXPENSES for 2008–09 ***Application fee:*** $40. ***Comprehensive fee:*** $31,775 includes full-time tuition ($20,040), mandatory fees ($705), and room and board ($11,030). ***College room only:*** $6460. Full-time tuition and fees vary according to degree level. Room and board charges vary according to board plan, housing facility, and student level. ***Part-time tuition:*** $668 per credit. ***Part-time fees:*** $50 per term. Part-time tuition and fees vary according to degree level. ***Payment plan:*** Installment.

FRESHMAN FINANCIAL AID (Fall 2008, est.) 399 applied for aid; of those 82% were deemed to have need. 100% of freshmen with need received aid; of those 23% had need fully met. ***Average percent of need met:*** 68% (excluding resources awarded to replace EFC). ***Average financial aid package:*** $14,463 (excluding resources awarded to replace EFC). 20% of all full-time freshmen had no need and received non-need-based gift aid.

UNDERGRADUATE FINANCIAL AID (Fall 2008, est.) 1,545 applied for aid; of those 86% were deemed to have need. 100% of undergraduates with need received aid; of those 23% had need fully met. ***Average percent of need met:*** 64% (excluding resources awarded to replace EFC). ***Average financial aid package:*** $13,632 (excluding resources awarded to replace EFC). 17% of all full-time undergraduates had no need and received non-need-based gift aid.

GIFT AID (NEED-BASED) ***Total amount:*** $11,180,984 (20% federal, 20% state, 58% institutional, 2% external sources). ***Receiving aid:*** Freshmen: 72% (312); all full-time undergraduates: 69% (1,213). ***Average award:*** Freshmen: $10,524; Undergraduates: $9114. ***Scholarships, grants, and awards:*** Federal Pell, FSEOG, state, private, college/university gift aid from institutional funds, Federal Nursing, Academic Competitiveness Grant, National Smart Grant.

GIFT AID (NON-NEED-BASED) ***Total amount:*** $1,853,819 (1% federal, 9% state, 87% institutional, 3% external sources). ***Receiving aid:*** Freshmen: 10% (42). Undergraduates: 6% (104). ***Average award:*** Freshmen: $13,082. Undergraduates: $14,330. ***Scholarships, grants, and awards by category:*** *Academic interests/achievement:* 655 awards ($4,622,750 total): general academic interests/achievements. *Special characteristics:* 33 awards ($532,852 total): children of faculty/staff. ***Tuition waivers:*** Full or partial for employees or children of employees.

LOANS ***Student loans:*** $18,776,172 (66% need-based, 34% non-need-based). 92% of past graduating class borrowed through all loan programs. *Average indebtedness per student:* $30,412. ***Average need-based loan:*** Freshmen: $4197. Undergraduates: $5263. ***Parent loans:*** $2,880,320 (35% need-based, 65% non-need-based). ***Programs:*** FFEL (Subsidized and Unsubsidized Stafford, PLUS), Perkins, Federal Nursing.

WORK-STUDY ***Federal work-study:*** Total amount: $556,700; 348 jobs averaging $1390. ***State or other work-study/employment:*** Part-time jobs available.

APPLYING FOR FINANCIAL AID ***Required financial aid form:*** FAFSA. ***Financial aid deadline (priority):*** 2/15. ***Notification date:*** Continuous beginning 4/1. Students must reply within 2 weeks of notification.

CONTACT Michelle Taylor, Director of Financial Aid, Mount Saint Mary College, 330 Powell Avenue, Newburgh, NY 12550-3494, 845-561-0800 or toll-free 888-937-6762. *Fax:* 845-569-3302. *E-mail:* taylor@msmc.edu.

MOUNT ST. MARY'S COLLEGE

Los Angeles, CA

CONTACT La Royce Dodd, Financial Aid Director, Mount St. Mary's College, 12001 Chalon Road, Los Angeles, CA 90049, 310-954-4192 or toll-free 800-999-9893.

MOUNT ST. MARY'S UNIVERSITY

Emmitsburg, MD

Tuition & fees: $29,020 **Average undergraduate aid package: $18,074**

ABOUT THE INSTITUTION Independent Roman Catholic, coed. ***Awards:*** bachelor's, master's, and first professional degrees and post-bachelor's and post-master's certificates. 28 undergraduate majors. ***Total enrollment:*** 2,079. Undergraduates: 1,641. Freshmen: 410. Federal methodology is used as a basis for awarding need-based institutional aid.

UNDERGRADUATE EXPENSES for 2009–10 ***Application fee:*** $35. ***Comprehensive fee:*** $38,898 includes full-time tuition ($28,420), mandatory fees ($600), and room and board ($9878). ***College room only:*** $4832. ***Part-time tuition:*** $950 per credit hour.

FRESHMAN FINANCIAL AID (Fall 2008, est.) 342 applied for aid; of those 78% were deemed to have need. 99% of freshmen with need received aid; of those 24% had need fully met. ***Average percent of need met:*** 72% (excluding resources awarded to replace EFC). ***Average financial aid package:*** $18,510 (excluding resources awarded to replace EFC). 33% of all full-time freshmen had no need and received non-need-based gift aid.

UNDERGRADUATE FINANCIAL AID (Fall 2008, est.) 1,151 applied for aid; of those 83% were deemed to have need. 100% of undergraduates with need received aid; of those 28% had need fully met. ***Average percent of need met:*** 74% (excluding resources awarded to replace EFC). ***Average financial aid package:*** $18,074 (excluding resources awarded to replace EFC). 34% of all full-time undergraduates had no need and received non-need-based gift aid.

GIFT AID (NEED-BASED) ***Total amount:*** $12,192,592 (10% federal, 10% state, 78% institutional, 2% external sources). ***Receiving aid:*** Freshmen: 65% (264); all full-time undergraduates: 61% (943). ***Average award:*** Freshmen: $14,983; Undergraduates: $13,963. ***Scholarships, grants, and awards:*** Federal Pell, FSEOG, state, private, college/university gift aid from institutional funds.

GIFT AID (NON-NEED-BASED) ***Total amount:*** $6,289,310 (7% federal, 2% state, 88% institutional, 3% external sources). ***Receiving aid:*** Freshmen: 12% (49). Undergraduates: 12% (189). ***Average award:*** Freshmen: $14,008. Undergraduates: $13,739. ***Scholarships, grants, and awards by category:*** *Academic interests/achievement:* 1,256 awards ($11,488,003 total): general academic interests/achievements. *Creative arts/performance:* 31 awards ($52,100 total): art/fine arts. *Special characteristics:* 295 awards ($1,011,429 total): children of educators, children of faculty/staff, members of minority groups, siblings of current students. ***ROTC:*** Army cooperative.

LOANS ***Student loans:*** $9,427,697 (56% need-based, 44% non-need-based). 77% of past graduating class borrowed through all loan programs. *Average indebtedness per student:* $27,230. ***Average need-based loan:*** Freshmen: $3968. Undergraduates: $4777. ***Parent loans:*** $3,496,713 (27% need-based, 73% non-need-based). ***Programs:*** FFEL (Subsidized and Unsubsidized Stafford, PLUS), Perkins.

WORK-STUDY ***Federal work-study:*** Total amount: $321,300; 166 jobs averaging $1408. ***State or other work-study/employment:*** Total amount: $295,354 (80% need-based, 20% non-need-based). 332 part-time jobs averaging $959.

ATHLETIC AWARDS Total amount: $1,975,349 (44% need-based, 56% non-need-based).

APPLYING FOR FINANCIAL AID ***Required financial aid forms:*** FAFSA, institution's own form. ***Financial aid deadline:*** 3/1. ***Notification date:*** Continuous. Students must reply by 5/1.

CONTACT Mr. David C. Reeder, Director of Financial Aid, Mount St. Mary's University, 16300 Old Emmitsburg Road, Emmitsburg, MD 21727-7799, 301-447-5207 or toll-free 800-448-4347. *Fax:* 301-447-5755. *E-mail:* reeder@msmary.edu.

MT. SIERRA COLLEGE

Monrovia, CA

CONTACT Financial Aid Office, Mt. Sierra College, 101 East Huntington Drive, Monrovia, CA 91016, 888-828-8800 or toll-free 888-828-8800.

MOUNT UNION COLLEGE

Alliance, OH

Tuition & fees: $23,120 **Average undergraduate aid package: $17,712**

ABOUT THE INSTITUTION Independent United Methodist, coed. ***Awards:*** bachelor's degrees. 47 undergraduate majors. ***Total enrollment:*** 2,204. Undergraduates: 2,204. Freshmen: 663. Federal methodology is used as a basis for awarding need-based institutional aid.

UNDERGRADUATE EXPENSES for 2008–09 ***Comprehensive fee:*** $30,170 includes full-time tuition ($22,870), mandatory fees ($250), and room and board ($7050). Room and board charges vary according to board plan and housing facility. ***Part-time tuition:*** $965 per credit hour. ***Part-time fees:*** $50 per term. ***Payment plans:*** Tuition prepayment, installment.

FRESHMAN FINANCIAL AID (Fall 2007) 560 applied for aid; of those 88% were deemed to have need. 100% of freshmen with need received aid; of those 23% had need fully met. ***Average percent of need met:*** 83% (excluding resources awarded to replace EFC). ***Average financial aid package:*** $18,278 (excluding resources awarded to replace EFC). 17% of all full-time freshmen had no need and received non-need-based gift aid.

UNDERGRADUATE FINANCIAL AID (Fall 2007) 1,784 applied for aid; of those 90% were deemed to have need. 100% of undergraduates with need received aid; of those 24% had need fully met. ***Average percent of need met:*** 81% (excluding resources awarded to replace EFC). ***Average financial aid package:*** $17,712 (excluding resources awarded to replace EFC). 18% of all full-time undergraduates had no need and received non-need-based gift aid.

GIFT AID (NEED-BASED) ***Total amount:*** $19,440,295 (11% federal, 11% state, 75% institutional, 3% external sources). ***Receiving aid:*** Freshmen: 79% (490); all full-time undergraduates: 79% (1,596). ***Average award:*** Freshmen: $13,609; Undergraduates: $12,395. ***Scholarships, grants, and awards:*** Federal Pell, FSEOG, state, private, college/university gift aid from institutional funds.

GIFT AID (NON-NEED-BASED) ***Total amount:*** $3,137,728 (9% state, 84% institutional, 7% external sources). ***Receiving aid:*** Freshmen: 6% (40). Undergraduates: 6% (119). ***Average award:*** Freshmen: $6176. Undergraduates: $6441. ***Scholarships, grants, and awards by category:*** *Academic interests/achievement:* 1,159 awards ($7,239,398 total): general academic interests/achievements, physical sciences. *Creative arts/performance:* 124 awards ($352,164 total): art/fine arts, cinema/film/broadcasting, debating, journalism/publications, music, theater/drama. *Special characteristics:* 235 awards ($1,507,532 total): children and siblings of alumni, children of faculty/staff, ethnic background, international students, members of minority groups, relatives of clergy. ***Tuition waivers:*** Full or partial for children of alumni, employees or children of employees, adult students. ***ROTC:*** Army cooperative, Air Force cooperative.

LOANS ***Student loans:*** $13,796,136 (68% need-based, 32% non-need-based). 83% of past graduating class borrowed through all loan programs. *Average indebtedness per student:* $20,982. ***Average need-based loan:*** Freshmen: $5036. Undergraduates: $5606. ***Parent loans:*** $2,648,651 (36% need-based, 64% non-need-based). ***Programs:*** FFEL (Subsidized and Unsubsidized Stafford, PLUS), Perkins, alternative loans.

WORK-STUDY ***Federal work-study:*** Total amount: $251,957; 1,154 jobs averaging $348. ***State or other work-study/employment:*** Total amount: $545,486 (26% need-based, 74% non-need-based). 386 part-time jobs averaging $416.

APPLYING FOR FINANCIAL AID ***Required financial aid form:*** FAFSA. ***Financial aid deadline:*** Continuous. ***Notification date:*** Continuous beginning 3/15. Students must reply within 4 weeks of notification.

CONTACT Ms. Emily Swain, Director of Student Financial Services, Mount Union College, 1972 Clark Avenue, Alliance, OH 44601-3993, 330-823-2674 or toll-free 800-334-6682 (in-state), 800-992-6682 (out-of-state). *Fax:* 330-829-2814. *E-mail:* swainej@muc.edu.

MOUNT VERNON NAZARENE UNIVERSITY

Mount Vernon, OH

Tuition & fees: $20,580 **Average undergraduate aid package: $14,690**

ABOUT THE INSTITUTION Independent Nazarene, coed. ***Awards:*** associate, bachelor's, and master's degrees. 83 undergraduate majors. ***Total enrollment:*** 2,558. Undergraduates: 2,090. Freshmen: 368. Federal methodology is used as a basis for awarding need-based institutional aid.

UNDERGRADUATE EXPENSES for 2009–10 ***Application fee:*** $25. ***Comprehensive fee:*** $26,470 includes full-time tuition ($19,980), mandatory fees ($600), and room and board ($5890). ***College room only:*** $3290. ***Part-time tuition:*** $713 per semester hour. ***Part-time fees:*** $20 per semester hour.

FRESHMAN FINANCIAL AID (Fall 2008, est.) 368 applied for aid; of those 91% were deemed to have need. 100% of freshmen with need received aid; of those 11% had need fully met. ***Average percent of need met:*** 66% (excluding resources awarded to replace EFC). ***Average financial aid package:*** $15,362 (excluding resources awarded to replace EFC). 6% of all full-time freshmen had no need and received non-need-based gift aid.

UNDERGRADUATE FINANCIAL AID (Fall 2008, est.) 1,430 applied for aid; of those 88% were deemed to have need. 100% of undergraduates with need received aid; of those 13% had need fully met. ***Average percent of need met:*** 70% (excluding resources awarded to replace EFC). ***Average financial aid package:*** $14,690 (excluding resources awarded to replace EFC). 7% of all full-time undergraduates had no need and received non-need-based gift aid.

GIFT AID (NEED-BASED) ***Total amount:*** $11,060,043 (19% federal, 13% state, 57% institutional, 11% external sources). ***Receiving aid:*** Freshmen: 88% (322); all full-time undergraduates: 65% (1,181). ***Average award:*** Freshmen: $9570; Undergraduates: $8255. ***Scholarships, grants, and awards:*** Federal Pell, FSEOG, state, private, college/university gift aid from institutional funds.

GIFT AID (NON-NEED-BASED) ***Total amount:*** $1,836,465 (31% state, 56% institutional, 13% external sources). ***Receiving aid:*** Freshmen: 16% (60). Undergraduates: 14% (261). ***Average award:*** Freshmen: $6524. Undergraduates: $3609. ***Scholarships, grants, and awards by category:*** *Academic interests/achievement:* general academic interests/achievements. *Creative arts/performance:* music. *Special achievements/activities:* general special achievements/activities, religious involvement. *Special characteristics:* children of faculty/staff, international students, members of minority groups, relatives of clergy, religious affiliation, siblings of current students, spouses of current students.

LOANS ***Student loans:*** $13,869,844 (91% need-based, 9% non-need-based). 87% of past graduating class borrowed through all loan programs. *Average indebtedness per student:* $27,863. ***Average need-based loan:*** Freshmen: $3611. Undergraduates: $3989. ***Parent loans:*** $2,773,587 (36% need-based, 64% non-need-based). ***Programs:*** Federal Direct (Subsidized and Unsubsidized Stafford, PLUS), Perkins.

WORK-STUDY ***Federal work-study:*** Total amount: $311,556; 205 jobs averaging $1520. ***State or other work-study/employment:*** Total amount: $797,361 (38% need-based, 62% non-need-based). 515 part-time jobs averaging $1548.

ATHLETIC AWARDS Total amount: $612,486 (66% need-based, 34% non-need-based).

APPLYING FOR FINANCIAL AID ***Required financial aid forms:*** FAFSA, institution's own form. ***Financial aid deadline (priority):*** 3/15. ***Notification date:*** Continuous. Students must reply within 2 weeks of notification.

CONTACT Financial Aid Office, Mount Vernon Nazarene University, 800 Martinsburg Road, Mount Vernon, OH 43050-9500, 740-397-9000 Ext. 4520 or toll-free 866-462-6868. *Fax:* 740-393-0511. *E-mail:* finaid@mvnu.edu.

MUHLENBERG COLLEGE

Allentown, PA

Tuition & fees: $35,375 **Average undergraduate aid package: $22,294**

ABOUT THE INSTITUTION Independent religious, coed. ***Awards:*** associate and bachelor's degrees. 33 undergraduate majors. ***Total enrollment:*** 2,492. Undergraduates: 2,492. Freshmen: 597. Institutional methodology is used as a basis for awarding need-based institutional aid.

UNDERGRADUATE EXPENSES for 2008–09 ***Application fee:*** $50. ***Comprehensive fee:*** $43,435 includes full-time tuition ($35,125), mandatory fees ($250), and room and board ($8060). ***College room only:*** $4700. Room and board charges vary according to board plan, housing facility, and location. ***Part-time tuition:*** $4130 per course. ***Part-time fees:*** $275 per year. Part-time tuition and fees vary according to program. ***Payment plan:*** Installment.

FRESHMAN FINANCIAL AID (Fall 2008, est.) 390 applied for aid; of those 71% were deemed to have need. 98% of freshmen with need received aid; of those 93% had need fully met. ***Average percent of need met:*** 92% (excluding resources awarded to replace EFC). ***Average financial aid package:*** $23,182 (excluding resources awarded to replace EFC). 34% of all full-time freshmen had no need and received non-need-based gift aid.

UNDERGRADUATE FINANCIAL AID (Fall 2008, est.) 1,318 applied for aid; of those 79% were deemed to have need. 99% of undergraduates with need received aid; of those 92% had need fully met. ***Average percent of need met:*** 92% (excluding resources awarded to replace EFC). ***Average financial aid package:*** $22,294 (excluding resources awarded to replace EFC). 26% of all full-time undergraduates had no need and received non-need-based gift aid.

GIFT AID (NEED-BASED) ***Total amount:*** $18,802,427 (4% federal, 3% state, 92% institutional, 1% external sources). ***Receiving aid:*** Freshmen: 44% (264); all full-time undergraduates: 42% (983). ***Average award:*** Freshmen: $20,683; Undergraduates: $19,598. ***Scholarships, grants, and awards:*** Federal Pell, FSEOG, state, private, college/university gift aid from institutional funds.

GIFT AID (NON-NEED-BASED) ***Total amount:*** $6,584,566 (95% institutional, 5% external sources). ***Receiving aid:*** Freshmen: 12% (73). Undergraduates: 11% (261). ***Average award:*** Freshmen: $12,629. Undergraduates: $12,312. ***Tuition waivers:*** Full or partial for employees or children of employees. ***ROTC:*** Army cooperative.

LOANS ***Student loans:*** $9,295,888 (44% need-based, 56% non-need-based). 82% of past graduating class borrowed through all loan programs. *Average indebtedness per student:* $18,542. ***Average need-based loan:*** Freshmen: $3326. Undergraduates: $4238. ***Parent loans:*** $4,061,515 (11% need-based, 89% non-need-based). ***Programs:*** FFEL (Subsidized and Unsubsidized Stafford, PLUS), Perkins.

WORK-STUDY ***Federal work-study:*** Total amount: $300,000; jobs available. ***State or other work-study/employment:*** Total amount: $167,624 (11% need-based, 89% non-need-based). Part-time jobs available.

APPLYING FOR FINANCIAL AID ***Required financial aid forms:*** institution's own form, CSS Financial Aid PROFILE, state aid form. ***Financial aid deadline:*** 2/15. ***Notification date:*** 4/1.

CONTACT Mr. Greg Mitton, Director of Financial Aid, Muhlenberg College, 2400 Chew Street, Allentown, PA 18104-5586, 484-664-3175. *Fax:* 484-664-3234. *E-mail:* mitton@muhlenberg.edu.

MULTNOMAH UNIVERSITY

Portland, OR

CONTACT Mr. David Allen, Director of Financial Aid, Multnomah University, 8435 Northeast Glisan Street, Portland, OR 97220-5898, 503-251-5335 or toll-free 800-275-4672. *Fax:* 503-254-1268.

MURRAY STATE UNIVERSITY

Murray, KY

Tuition & fees (KY res): $5748 **Average undergraduate aid package: $4220**

ABOUT THE INSTITUTION State-supported, coed. ***Awards:*** bachelor's and master's degrees and post-master's certificates. 104 undergraduate majors. ***Total enrollment:*** 10,014. Undergraduates: 8,171. Freshmen: 1,478. Federal methodology is used as a basis for awarding need-based institutional aid.

UNDERGRADUATE EXPENSES for 2008–09 ***Application fee:*** $30. ***Tuition, state resident:*** full-time $4932; part-time $205 per hour. ***Tuition, nonresident:*** full-time $7426; part-time $287 per hour. ***Required fees:*** full-time $816; $34 per hour. Full-time tuition and fees vary according to reciprocity agreements. Part-time tuition and fees vary according to reciprocity agreements. ***College room and board:*** $6004; ***Room only:*** $3278. Room and board charges vary according to board plan. ***Payment plan:*** Installment.

FRESHMAN FINANCIAL AID (Fall 2008, est.) 1,058 applied for aid; of those 60% were deemed to have need. 94% of freshmen with need received aid; of those 94% had need fully met. ***Average percent of need met:*** 92% (excluding resources awarded to replace EFC). ***Average financial aid package:*** $4605 (excluding resources awarded to replace EFC). 40% of all full-time freshmen had no need and received non-need-based gift aid.

UNDERGRADUATE FINANCIAL AID (Fall 2008, est.) 6,002 applied for aid; of those 56% were deemed to have need. 92% of undergraduates with need received aid; of those 98% had need fully met. ***Average percent of need met:*** 87% (excluding resources awarded to replace EFC). ***Average financial aid package:*** $4220 (excluding resources awarded to replace EFC). 33% of all full-time undergraduates had no need and received non-need-based gift aid.

GIFT AID (NEED-BASED) ***Total amount:*** $14,021,449 (56% federal, 18% state, 17% institutional, 9% external sources). ***Receiving aid:*** Freshmen: 34% (448); all full-time undergraduates: 30% (2,103). ***Average award:*** Freshmen: $2590; Undergraduates: $2185. ***Scholarships, grants, and awards:*** Federal Pell, FSEOG, state, private, college/university gift aid from institutional funds.

GIFT AID (NON-NEED-BASED) ***Total amount:*** $13,092,794 (35% state, 48% institutional, 17% external sources). ***Receiving aid:*** Freshmen: 23% (299). Undergraduates: 21% (1,484). ***Average award:*** Freshmen: $2530. Undergraduates: $2560. ***Scholarships, grants, and awards by category:*** *Academic interests/achievement:* 4,260 awards ($4,828,800 total): agriculture, biological sciences, business, communication, computer science, education, engineering/technologies, English, foreign languages, general academic interests/achievements, health fields, humanities, international studies, library science, mathematics. *Creative arts/performance:* 184 awards ($111,500 total): applied art and design, art/fine arts, creative writing, dance, debating, general creative arts/performance, journalism/publications, music, theater/drama. *Special achievements/activities:* 820 awards ($801,550 total): cheerleading/drum major, general special achievements/activities, junior miss, leadership, rodeo. *Special characteristics:* 2,373 awards ($9,288,323 total): adult students, children and siblings of alumni, children of faculty/staff, general special characteristics, handicapped students, international students, local/state students, members of minority groups, out-of-state students. ***Tuition waivers:*** Full or partial for children of alumni, employees or children of employees, senior citizens. ***ROTC:*** Army cooperative.

LOANS ***Student loans:*** $24,340,793 (64% need-based, 36% non-need-based). 55% of past graduating class borrowed through all loan programs. *Average indebtedness per student:* $16,305. ***Average need-based loan:*** Freshmen: $1857. Undergraduates: $1963. ***Parent loans:*** $1,585,354 (100% non-need-based). ***Programs:*** FFEL (Subsidized and Unsubsidized Stafford, PLUS), Perkins, Federal Nursing, state, college/university.

WORK-STUDY ***Federal work-study:*** Total amount: $607,178; 425 jobs averaging $1271. ***State or other work-study/employment:*** Total amount: $3,880,287 (100% non-need-based). 2,099 part-time jobs averaging $1681.

ATHLETIC AWARDS Total amount: $2,920,766 (30% need-based, 70% non-need-based).

APPLYING FOR FINANCIAL AID ***Required financial aid forms:*** FAFSA, institution's own form. ***Financial aid deadline (priority):*** 4/1. ***Notification date:*** Continuous beginning 4/15.

CONTACT Lori Mitchum, Director of Student Financial Aid, Murray State University, B2 Sparks Hall, Murray, KY 42071-0009, 270-809-2546 or toll-free 800-272-4678. *Fax:* 270-809-3116. *E-mail:* lori.mitchum@murraystate.edu.

MUSICIANS INSTITUTE

Hollywood, CA

CONTACT Director of Financial Aid, Musicians Institute, 1655 North McCadden Place, Hollywood, CA 90028, 323-462-1384 or toll-free 800-255-PLAY.

MUSKINGUM COLLEGE

New Concord, OH

Tuition & fees: $18,910 **Average undergraduate aid package: $18,865**

ABOUT THE INSTITUTION Independent religious, coed. ***Awards:*** bachelor's and master's degrees. 57 undergraduate majors. ***Total enrollment:*** 2,099. Undergraduates: 1,709. Federal methodology is used as a basis for awarding need-based institutional aid.

UNDERGRADUATE EXPENSES for 2008–09 ***One-time required fee:*** $215. ***Comprehensive fee:*** $26,260 includes full-time tuition ($18,400), mandatory fees ($510), and room and board ($7350). ***College room only:*** $3750.

FRESHMAN FINANCIAL AID (Fall 2008, est.) 447 applied for aid; of those 90% were deemed to have need. 100% of freshmen with need received aid; of those 20% had need fully met. ***Average percent of need met:*** 83% (excluding resources awarded to replace EFC). ***Average financial aid package:*** $17,290 (excluding resources awarded to replace EFC). 14% of all full-time freshmen had no need and received non-need-based gift aid.

UNDERGRADUATE FINANCIAL AID (Fall 2008, est.) 1,352 applied for aid; of those 89% were deemed to have need. 100% of undergraduates with need received aid; of those 24% had need fully met. ***Average percent of need met:*** 84% (excluding resources awarded to replace EFC). ***Average financial aid package:*** $18,865 (excluding resources awarded to replace EFC). 22% of all full-time undergraduates had no need and received non-need-based gift aid.

GIFT AID (NEED-BASED) ***Total amount:*** $15,093,400 (14% federal, 14% state, 70% institutional, 2% external sources). ***Receiving aid:*** Freshmen: 83% (403); all full-time undergraduates: 78% (1,207). ***Average award:*** Freshmen: $13,678; Undergraduates: $12,634. ***Scholarships, grants, and awards:*** Federal Pell, FSEOG, state, private, college/university gift aid from institutional funds.

GIFT AID (NON-NEED-BASED) ***Total amount:*** $2,258,400 (1% federal, 12% state, 86% institutional, 1% external sources). ***Receiving aid:*** Freshmen: 68% (329). Undergraduates: 68% (1,058). ***Average award:*** Freshmen: $7516. Undergraduates: $6752. ***Scholarships, grants, and awards by category:*** *Academic interests/achievement:* 670 awards ($5,470,995 total): biological sciences, computer science, engineering/technologies, general academic interests/achievements, mathematics, physical sciences, premedicine. *Creative arts/performance:* 172 awards ($204,796 total): art/fine arts, debating, journalism/

publications, music, theater/drama. *Special achievements/activities:* 219 awards ($120,400 total): community service, leadership. *Special characteristics:* 943 awards ($1,038,105 total): children and siblings of alumni, ethnic background, local/state students, members of minority groups, relatives of clergy, religious affiliation, siblings of current students.

LOANS ***Student loans:*** $11,168,100 (60% need-based, 40% non-need-based). 80% of past graduating class borrowed through all loan programs. *Average indebtedness per student:* $23,405. ***Average need-based loan:*** Freshmen: $3945. Undergraduates: $4427. ***Parent loans:*** $1,337,000 (79% need-based, 21% non-need-based). ***Programs:*** FFEL (Subsidized and Unsubsidized Stafford, PLUS), Perkins, college/university.

WORK-STUDY ***Federal work-study:*** Total amount: $150,000; 450 jobs averaging $1000. ***State or other work-study/employment:*** Total amount: $450,000 (67% need-based, 33% non-need-based). 5 part-time jobs averaging $1000.

APPLYING FOR FINANCIAL AID ***Required financial aid form:*** FAFSA. ***Financial aid deadline (priority):*** 3/15. ***Notification date:*** Continuous. Students must reply by 5/1.

CONTACT Mr. Jeff Zellers, Vice President of Enrollment, Muskingum College, 163 Stormont Street, New Concord, OH 43762, 740-826-8139 or toll-free 800-752-6082. *Fax:* 740-826-8100. *E-mail:* jzellers@muskingum.edu.

NAROPA UNIVERSITY

Boulder, CO

Tuition & fees: $22,074 **Average undergraduate aid package: $21,612**

ABOUT THE INSTITUTION Independent, coed. ***Awards:*** bachelor's, master's, and first professional degrees. 12 undergraduate majors. ***Total enrollment:*** 1,075. Undergraduates: 456. Freshmen: 57. Federal methodology is used as a basis for awarding need-based institutional aid.

UNDERGRADUATE EXPENSES for 2008–09 ***Application fee:*** $50. ***Comprehensive fee:*** $30,552 includes full-time tuition ($21,984), mandatory fees ($90), and room and board ($8478). ***College room only:*** $6174. Full-time tuition and fees vary according to course load. Room and board charges vary according to board plan. ***Part-time tuition:*** $714 per credit hour. ***Part-time fees:*** $295 per term. Part-time tuition and fees vary according to course load. ***Payment plan:*** Installment.

FRESHMAN FINANCIAL AID (Fall 2008, est.) 38 applied for aid; of those 89% were deemed to have need. 100% of freshmen with need received aid; of those 6% had need fully met. ***Average percent of need met:*** 88% (excluding resources awarded to replace EFC). ***Average financial aid package:*** $21,363 (excluding resources awarded to replace EFC).

UNDERGRADUATE FINANCIAL AID (Fall 2008, est.) 298 applied for aid; of those 94% were deemed to have need. 100% of undergraduates with need received aid; of those .4% had need fully met. ***Average percent of need met:*** 88% (excluding resources awarded to replace EFC). ***Average financial aid package:*** $21,612 (excluding resources awarded to replace EFC).

GIFT AID (NEED-BASED) ***Total amount:*** $3,891,302 (19% federal, 77% institutional, 4% external sources). ***Receiving aid:*** Freshmen: 59% (33); all full-time undergraduates: 64% (264). ***Average award:*** Freshmen: $14,471; Undergraduates: $14,263. ***Scholarships, grants, and awards:*** Federal Pell, FSEOG, private, college/university gift aid from institutional funds.

GIFT AID (NON-NEED-BASED) ***Tuition waivers:*** Full or partial for employees or children of employees.

LOANS ***Student loans:*** $2,590,319 (89% need-based, 11% non-need-based). 68% of past graduating class borrowed through all loan programs. *Average indebtedness per student:* $19,359. ***Average need-based loan:*** Freshmen: $4344. Undergraduates: $5135. ***Parent loans:*** $2,238,043 (74% need-based, 26% non-need-based). ***Programs:*** FFEL (Subsidized and Unsubsidized Stafford, PLUS), Perkins.

WORK-STUDY ***Federal work-study:*** Total amount: $816,161; 236 jobs averaging $3458. ***State or other work-study/employment:*** Total amount: $20,000 (100% need-based). 5 part-time jobs averaging $4000.

APPLYING FOR FINANCIAL AID ***Required financial aid form:*** FAFSA. ***Financial aid deadline (priority):*** 3/1. ***Notification date:*** Continuous beginning 3/1. Students must reply within 4 weeks of notification.

CONTACT Financial Aid Office, Naropa University, 2130 Arapahoe Avenue, Boulder, CO 80302-6697, 303-546-3534 or toll-free 800-772-0410 (out of state). *Fax:* 303-546-3536. *E-mail:* finaid@naropa.edu.

NATIONAL AMERICAN UNIVERSITY

Colorado Springs, CO

CONTACT Financial Aid Coordinator, National American University, 2577 North Chelton Road, Colorado Springs, CO 80909, 719-471-4205.

NATIONAL AMERICAN UNIVERSITY

Denver, CO

CONTACT Cheryl Schunneman, Director of Financial Aid, National American University, 321 Kansas City Street, Rapid City, SD 57701, 605-394-4800.

NATIONAL AMERICAN UNIVERSITY

Roseville, MN

CONTACT Financial Aid Office, National American University, 1500 West Highway 36, Roseville, MN 55113-4035, 651-644-1265.

NATIONAL AMERICAN UNIVERSITY

Kansas City, MO

CONTACT Mary Anderson, Coordinator of Financial Aid, National American University, 4200 Blue Ridge, Kansas City, MO 64133, 816-353-4554. *Fax:* 816-353-1176.

NATIONAL AMERICAN UNIVERSITY

Albuquerque, NM

CONTACT Director of Financial Aid, National American University, 321 Kansas City Street, Rapid City, SD 57701, 605-394-4800 or toll-free 800-843-8892.

NATIONAL AMERICAN UNIVERSITY

Rapid City, SD

CONTACT Financial Aid Director, National American University, PO Box 1780, Rapid City, SD 57709-1780, 605-721-5213 or toll-free 800-843-8892.

NATIONAL AMERICAN UNIVERSITY–SIOUX FALLS BRANCH

Sioux Falls, SD

CONTACT Ms. Rhonda Kohnen, Financial Aid Coordinator, National American University–Sioux Falls Branch, 2801 South Kiwanis Avenue, Suite 100, Sioux Falls, SD 57105-4293, 605-334-5430 or toll-free 800-388-5430 (out-of-state). *Fax:* 605-334-1575. *E-mail:* rkohnen@national.edu.

THE NATIONAL HISPANIC UNIVERSITY

San Jose, CA

CONTACT Takeo Kubo, Director of Financial Aid and Scholarship, The National Hispanic University, 14271 Story Road, San Jose, CA 95127-3823, 408-273-2708. *Fax:* 408-254-1369. *E-mail:* tkubo@nhu.edu.

NATIONAL-LOUIS UNIVERSITY

Chicago, IL

ABOUT THE INSTITUTION Independent, coed. ***Awards:*** bachelor's, master's, and doctoral degrees and post-bachelor's and post-master's certificates. 26 undergraduate majors. ***Total enrollment:*** 7,056. Undergraduates: 1,749. Freshmen: 5.

GIFT AID (NEED-BASED) ***Scholarships, grants, and awards:*** Federal Pell, FSEOG, state, private, college/university gift aid from institutional funds.

GIFT AID (NON-NEED-BASED) ***Scholarships, grants, and awards by category:*** *Academic interests/achievement:* general academic interests/achievements.

LOANS ***Programs:*** FFEL (Subsidized and Unsubsidized Stafford, PLUS), Perkins.

WORK-STUDY ***Federal work-study:*** Total amount: $115,621; 45 jobs averaging $2569. ***State or other work-study/employment:*** Total amount: $147,085 (41% need-based, 59% non-need-based).

APPLYING FOR FINANCIAL AID ***Required financial aid form:*** FAFSA.

CONTACT Janet Jazwiec, Assistant Director of Student Finance, National-Louis University, 1000 Capitol Drive, Wheeling, IL 60090, 847-947-5433 or toll-free 888-NLU-TODAY (in-state), 800-443-5522 (out-of-state). *Fax:* 847-947-5433. *E-mail:* jjazwiec@nl.edu.

NATIONAL UNIVERSITY

La Jolla, CA

Tuition & fees: $10,284 **Average undergraduate aid package: $9103**

ABOUT THE INSTITUTION Independent, coed. ***Awards:*** associate, bachelor's, and master's degrees and post-bachelor's certificates. 45 undergraduate majors. ***Total enrollment:*** 26,417. Undergraduates: 7,672. Freshmen: 642. Federal methodology is used as a basis for awarding need-based institutional aid.

UNDERGRADUATE EXPENSES for 2008–09 ***Application fee:*** $60. ***Tuition:*** full-time $10,224; part-time $284 per unit. Full-time tuition and fees vary according to course load and location. Part-time tuition and fees vary according to course load and location.

FRESHMAN FINANCIAL AID (Fall 2007) 385 applied for aid; of those 97% were deemed to have need. 50% of freshmen with need received aid; of those 1% had need fully met. ***Average percent of need met:*** 89% (excluding resources awarded to replace EFC). ***Average financial aid package:*** $6733 (excluding resources awarded to replace EFC). 1% of all full-time freshmen had no need and received non-need-based gift aid.

UNDERGRADUATE FINANCIAL AID (Fall 2007) 1,840 applied for aid; of those 95% were deemed to have need. 68% of undergraduates with need received aid; of those 1% had need fully met. ***Average percent of need met:*** 87% (excluding resources awarded to replace EFC). ***Average financial aid package:*** $9103 (excluding resources awarded to replace EFC). 1% of all full-time undergraduates had no need and received non-need-based gift aid.

GIFT AID (NEED-BASED) ***Total amount:*** $5,860,660 (54% federal, 32% state, 14% institutional). ***Receiving aid:*** Freshmen: 9% (100); all full-time undergraduates: 11% (567). ***Average award:*** Freshmen: $7027; Undergraduates: $9635. ***Scholarships, grants, and awards:*** Federal Pell, FSEOG, state, college/university gift aid from institutional funds.

GIFT AID (NON-NEED-BASED) ***Total amount:*** $202,391 (100% institutional). ***Receiving aid:*** Freshmen: 16% (189). Undergraduates: 23% (1,198). ***Average award:*** Freshmen: $5598. Undergraduates: $9723. ***Scholarships, grants, and awards by category:*** *Academic interests/achievement:* general academic interests/achievements. *Special achievements/activities:* leadership. ***Tuition waivers:*** Full or partial for employees or children of employees. ***ROTC:*** Army cooperative, Air Force cooperative.

LOANS ***Student loans:*** $310,128,476 (48% need-based, 52% non-need-based). 42% of past graduating class borrowed through all loan programs. *Average indebtedness per student:* $31,058. ***Average need-based loan:*** Freshmen: $6960. Undergraduates: $10,250. ***Parent loans:*** $127,819 (100% need-based). ***Programs:*** Federal Direct (Subsidized and Unsubsidized Stafford, PLUS), FFEL (Subsidized and Unsubsidized Stafford, PLUS), Perkins, college/university.

APPLYING FOR FINANCIAL AID ***Required financial aid forms:*** FAFSA, institution's own form. ***Financial aid deadline:*** Continuous. ***Notification date:*** Continuous beginning 6/30.

CONTACT Valerie Ryan, Financial Aid Office, National University, 11255 North Torrey Pines Road, La Jolla, CA 92037-1011, 858-642-8500 or toll-free 800-NAT-UNIV. *Fax:* 858-642-8720. *E-mail:* vryan@nu.edu.

NAZARENE BIBLE COLLEGE

Colorado Springs, CO

Tuition & fees: $8460 **Average undergraduate aid package: N/A**

ABOUT THE INSTITUTION Independent religious, coed. ***Awards:*** associate and bachelor's degrees. 6 undergraduate majors. ***Total enrollment:*** 808. Undergraduates: 808. Freshmen: 21. Federal methodology is used as a basis for awarding need-based institutional aid.

UNDERGRADUATE EXPENSES for 2008–09 ***Tuition:*** full-time $8100; part-time $300 per credit hour. ***Payment plan:*** Installment.

FRESHMAN FINANCIAL AID (Fall 2007) 6 applied for aid; of those 100% were deemed to have need. 100% of freshmen with need received aid.

UNDERGRADUATE FINANCIAL AID (Fall 2007) 154 applied for aid; of those 100% were deemed to have need. 100% of undergraduates with need received aid.

GIFT AID (NEED-BASED) ***Total amount:*** $870,700 (78% federal, 18% institutional, 4% external sources). ***Receiving aid:*** Freshmen: 100% (6); all full-time undergraduates: 78% (140). ***Scholarships, grants, and awards:*** Federal Pell, FSEOG, college/university gift aid from institutional funds.

GIFT AID (NON-NEED-BASED) ***Receiving aid:*** Freshmen: 100% (6). Undergraduates: 78% (140). ***Scholarships, grants, and awards by category:*** *Academic interests/achievement:* 53 awards ($32,175 total): religion/biblical studies. ***Tuition waivers:*** Full or partial for employees or children of employees.

LOANS ***Student loans:*** $3,064,272 (58% need-based, 42% non-need-based). 87% of past graduating class borrowed through all loan programs. *Average indebtedness per student:* $27,048. ***Parent loans:*** $21,086 (100% non-need-based). ***Programs:*** FFEL (Subsidized and Unsubsidized Stafford, PLUS), Perkins, college/university.

WORK-STUDY ***Federal work-study:*** Total amount: $23,434; 8 jobs averaging $2900.

APPLYING FOR FINANCIAL AID ***Required financial aid form:*** FAFSA. ***Financial aid deadline:*** Continuous. ***Notification date:*** Continuous beginning 2/1.

CONTACT Mr. Malcolm Britton, Director of Financial Aid, Nazarene Bible College, 1111 Academy Park Loop, Colorado Springs, CO 80910-3717, 719-884-5051 or toll-free 800-873-3873. *Fax:* 719-884-5199.

NAZARETH COLLEGE OF ROCHESTER

Rochester, NY

Tuition & fees: $24,076 **Average undergraduate aid package: $17,259**

ABOUT THE INSTITUTION Independent, coed. ***Awards:*** bachelor's, master's, and doctoral degrees and post-master's certificates. 74 undergraduate majors. ***Total enrollment:*** 3,250. Undergraduates: 2,188. Freshmen: 471. Federal methodology is used as a basis for awarding need-based institutional aid.

UNDERGRADUATE EXPENSES for 2008–09 ***Application fee:*** $40. ***Comprehensive fee:*** $33,992 includes full-time tuition ($23,046), mandatory fees ($1030), and room and board ($9916). ***College room only:*** $5486. Room and board charges vary according to board plan and housing facility. ***Part-time tuition:*** $549 per credit hour. ***Payment plan:*** Deferred payment.

FRESHMAN FINANCIAL AID (Fall 2008, est.) 430 applied for aid; of those 85% were deemed to have need. 100% of freshmen with need received aid; of those 20% had need fully met. ***Average percent of need met:*** 77% (excluding resources awarded to replace EFC). ***Average financial aid package:*** $18,052 (excluding resources awarded to replace EFC). 23% of all full-time freshmen had no need and received non-need-based gift aid.

UNDERGRADUATE FINANCIAL AID (Fall 2008, est.) 1,799 applied for aid; of those 88% were deemed to have need. 100% of undergraduates with need received aid; of those 17% had need fully met. ***Average percent of need met:*** 73% (excluding resources awarded to replace EFC). ***Average financial aid package:*** $17,259 (excluding resources awarded to replace EFC). 20% of all full-time undergraduates had no need and received non-need-based gift aid.

GIFT AID (NEED-BASED) ***Total amount:*** $19,391,554 (10% federal, 14% state, 72% institutional, 4% external sources). ***Receiving aid:*** Freshmen: 77% (365); all full-time undergraduates: 78% (1,582). ***Average award:*** Freshmen: $13,635; Undergraduates: $12,102. ***Scholarships, grants, and awards:*** Federal Pell, FSEOG, state, private, college/university gift aid from institutional funds, Federal Nursing.

GIFT AID (NON-NEED-BASED) ***Total amount:*** $4,714,806 (1% federal, 1% state, 87% institutional, 11% external sources). ***Receiving aid:*** Freshmen: 35% (166). Undergraduates: 34% (698). ***Average award:*** Freshmen: $13,991. Undergraduates: $14,396. ***Scholarships, grants, and awards by category:*** *Academic interests/achievement:* 1,585 awards ($11,099,287 total): general academic interests/achievements. *Creative arts/performance:* 130 awards ($461,550 total): art/fine arts, music, theater/drama. *Special characteristics:* 225 awards ($1,616,377 total): children and siblings of alumni, children of faculty/staff, siblings of current students. ***Tuition waivers:*** Full or partial for minority students, children of alumni, employees or children of employees. ***ROTC:*** Army cooperative, Air Force cooperative.

LOANS ***Student loans:*** $18,220,680 (71% need-based, 29% non-need-based). 85% of past graduating class borrowed through all loan programs. *Average indebtedness per student:* $33,792. ***Average need-based loan:*** Freshmen: $3629. Undergraduates: $4855. ***Parent loans:*** $3,302,987 (39% need-based, 61% non-need-based). ***Programs:*** FFEL (Subsidized and Unsubsidized Stafford, PLUS), Perkins, Federal Nursing.

WORK-STUDY ***Federal work-study:*** Total amount: $1,355,814; 766 jobs averaging $1828.

APPLYING FOR FINANCIAL AID ***Required financial aid forms:*** FAFSA, state aid form. ***Financial aid deadline (priority):*** 2/15. ***Notification date:*** Continuous. Students must reply by 5/1 or within 2 weeks of notification.

CONTACT Samantha Veeder, Director of Financial Aid, Nazareth College of Rochester, 4245 East Avenue, Rochester, NY 14618-3790, 585-389-2310 or toll-free 800-462-3944 (in-state). *Fax:* 585-389-2317. *E-mail:* Sveeder0@naz.edu.

NEBRASKA CHRISTIAN COLLEGE

Papillon, NE

Tuition & fees: N/R **Average undergraduate aid package: N/A**

ABOUT THE INSTITUTION Independent religious, coed. ***Awards:*** associate and bachelor's degrees. 10 undergraduate majors. ***Total enrollment:*** 146. Undergraduates: 146. Freshmen: 48. Federal methodology is used as a basis for awarding need-based institutional aid.

UNDERGRADUATE EXPENSES for 2008–09 ***Application fee:*** $25. ***Tuition:*** part-time $275 per credit.

FRESHMAN FINANCIAL AID (Fall 2008, est.) 44 applied for aid; of those 82% were deemed to have need. 100% of freshmen with need received aid.

UNDERGRADUATE FINANCIAL AID (Fall 2008, est.) 147 applied for aid; of those 88% were deemed to have need. 100% of undergraduates with need received aid.

GIFT AID (NEED-BASED) ***Total amount:*** $684,978 (35% federal, 5% state, 25% institutional, 35% external sources). ***Receiving aid:*** Freshmen: 64% (28); all full-time undergraduates: 56% (82). ***Scholarships, grants, and awards:*** Federal Pell, FSEOG, state, private, college/university gift aid from institutional funds.

GIFT AID (NON-NEED-BASED) ***Scholarships, grants, and awards by category:*** *Academic interests/achievement:* 131 awards ($195,595 total): general academic interests/achievements. *Special characteristics:* 17 awards ($12,096 total): children of faculty/staff, international students, relatives of clergy.

LOANS ***Student loans:*** $782,152 (100% need-based). 80% of past graduating class borrowed through all loan programs. *Average indebtedness per student:* $11,593. ***Average need-based loan:*** Freshmen: $2358. Undergraduates: $2958. ***Parent loans:*** $56,209 (100% need-based). ***Programs:*** FFEL (Subsidized and Unsubsidized Stafford, PLUS).

WORK-STUDY ***Federal work-study:*** Total amount: $11,751; 13 jobs averaging $1183.

APPLYING FOR FINANCIAL AID ***Required financial aid forms:*** FAFSA, institution's own form. ***Financial aid deadline (priority):*** 6/1. ***Notification date:*** Continuous.

CONTACT Ms. Tina Larsen, Director of Financial Aid, Nebraska Christian College, 12550 South 114th St., Papillion, NE 68046, 402-935-9400. *Fax:* 402-935-9500. *E-mail:* tlarsen@nechristian.edu.

NEBRASKA METHODIST COLLEGE

Omaha, NE

Tuition & fees: $14,040 **Average undergraduate aid package: $7470**

ABOUT THE INSTITUTION Independent religious, coed, primarily women. ***Awards:*** associate, bachelor's, and master's degrees and post-master's certificates. 5 undergraduate majors. ***Total enrollment:*** 589. Undergraduates: 506. Freshmen: 56. Federal methodology is used as a basis for awarding need-based institutional aid.

UNDERGRADUATE EXPENSES for 2008–09 ***Application fee:*** $25. ***Tuition:*** full-time $13,440; part-time $428 per credit hour. ***Required fees:*** full-time $600; $20 per credit hour.

FRESHMAN FINANCIAL AID (Fall 2007) 12 applied for aid; of those 83% were deemed to have need. 100% of freshmen with need received aid. ***Average percent of need met:*** 57% (excluding resources awarded to replace EFC). ***Average financial aid package:*** $9699 (excluding resources awarded to replace EFC). 25% of all full-time freshmen had no need and received non-need-based gift aid.

UNDERGRADUATE FINANCIAL AID (Fall 2007) 168 applied for aid; of those 83% were deemed to have need. 100% of undergraduates with need received aid; of those 11% had need fully met. ***Average percent of need met:*** 54% (excluding resources awarded to replace EFC). ***Average financial aid package:*** $7470 (excluding resources awarded to replace EFC). 12% of all full-time undergraduates had no need and received non-need-based gift aid.

GIFT AID (NEED-BASED) ***Total amount:*** $1,519,258 (29% federal, 6% state, 48% institutional, 17% external sources). ***Receiving aid:*** Freshmen: 25% (8); all full-time undergraduates: 54% (109). ***Average award:*** Freshmen: $7918; Undergraduates: $4557. ***Scholarships, grants, and awards:*** Federal Pell, FSEOG, state, private, college/university gift aid from institutional funds.

GIFT AID (NON-NEED-BASED) ***Total amount:*** $294,782 (68% institutional, 32% external sources). ***Receiving aid:*** Undergraduates: 2% (5). ***Average award:*** Freshmen: $3312. Undergraduates: $3018. ***Scholarships, grants, and awards by category:*** *Academic interests/achievement:* 249 awards ($791,250 total): general academic interests/achievements. ***ROTC:*** Army cooperative, Air Force cooperative.

LOANS ***Student loans:*** $4,469,235 (63% need-based, 37% non-need-based). 95% of past graduating class borrowed through all loan programs. *Average indebtedness per student:* $33,643. ***Average need-based loan:*** Freshmen: $3472. Undergraduates: $4117. ***Parent loans:*** $341,574 (33% need-based, 67% non-need-based). ***Programs:*** FFEL (Subsidized and Unsubsidized Stafford, PLUS), Perkins, Federal Nursing, college/university, alternative loans.

WORK-STUDY ***Federal work-study:*** Total amount: $15,277; jobs available (averaging $2400).

APPLYING FOR FINANCIAL AID ***Required financial aid forms:*** FAFSA, institution's own form. ***Financial aid deadline (priority):*** 4/1. ***Notification date:*** Continuous. Students must reply within 3 weeks of notification.

CONTACT Ms. Brenda Boyd, Director of Financial Aid, Nebraska Methodist College, The Josie Harper Campus, 720 North 87th Street, Omaha, NE 68114-3426, 402-354-7225 or toll-free 800-335-5510. *Fax:* 402-354-7020. *E-mail:* brenda.boyd@methodistcollege.edu.

NEBRASKA WESLEYAN UNIVERSITY

Lincoln, NE

Tuition & fees: $21,392 **Average undergraduate aid package: $15,072**

ABOUT THE INSTITUTION Independent United Methodist, coed. ***Awards:*** bachelor's and master's degrees and post-bachelor's and post-master's certificates. 50 undergraduate majors. ***Total enrollment:*** 2,086. Undergraduates: 1,870. Freshmen: 383. Federal methodology is used as a basis for awarding need-based institutional aid.

UNDERGRADUATE EXPENSES for 2008–09 ***Application fee:*** $20. ***One-time required fee:*** $120. ***Comprehensive fee:*** $27,102 includes full-time tuition ($20,950), mandatory fees ($442), and room and board ($5710). Full-time tuition and fees vary according to class time, course load, degree level, location, and program. Room and board charges vary according to board plan. Part-time tuition and fees vary according to class time, course load, degree level, location, and program. ***Payment plans:*** Installment, deferred payment.

FRESHMAN FINANCIAL AID (Fall 2008, est.) 334 applied for aid; of those 83% were deemed to have need. 100% of freshmen with need received aid; of those 14% had need fully met. ***Average percent of need met:*** 73% (excluding resources awarded to replace EFC). ***Average financial aid package:*** $16,154 (excluding resources awarded to replace EFC). 28% of all full-time freshmen had no need and received non-need-based gift aid.

UNDERGRADUATE FINANCIAL AID (Fall 2008, est.) 1,283 applied for aid; of those 85% were deemed to have need. 100% of undergraduates with need received aid; of those 20% had need fully met. ***Average percent of need met:*** 70% (excluding resources awarded to replace EFC). ***Average financial aid package:*** $15,072 (excluding resources awarded to replace EFC). 25% of all full-time undergraduates had no need and received non-need-based gift aid.

GIFT AID (NEED-BASED) ***Total amount:*** $11,309,194 (14% federal, 3% state, 80% institutional, 3% external sources). ***Receiving aid:*** Freshmen: 72% (277); all full-time undergraduates: 66% (1,065). ***Average award:*** Freshmen: $11,847; Undergraduates: $10,595. ***Scholarships, grants, and awards:*** Federal Pell, FSEOG, state, private, college/university gift aid from institutional funds.

GIFT AID (NON-NEED-BASED) ***Total amount:*** $3,518,003 (95% institutional, 5% external sources). ***Receiving aid:*** Freshmen: 7% (28). Undergraduates: 7% (114). ***Average award:*** Freshmen: $7546. Undergraduates: $7401. ***Scholarships, grants, and awards by category:*** *Academic interests/achievement:* 1,305 awards ($8,052,447 total): general academic interests/achievements. *Creative arts/performance:* 188 awards ($234,775 total): art/fine arts. *Special characteristics:* 103 awards ($105,649 total): children and siblings of alumni, children of educators, children of faculty/staff, international students, relatives of clergy, siblings of current students. ***Tuition waivers:*** Full or partial for employees or children of employees, adult students, senior citizens. ***ROTC:*** Army cooperative, Air Force cooperative.

LOANS ***Student loans:*** $8,785,931 (70% need-based, 30% non-need-based). 82% of past graduating class borrowed through all loan programs. *Average indebtedness per student:* $16,458. ***Average need-based loan:*** Freshmen: $4421. Undergraduates: $4630. ***Parent loans:*** $2,900,104 (37% need-based, 63% non-need-based). ***Programs:*** FFEL (Subsidized and Unsubsidized Stafford, PLUS), Perkins.

WORK-STUDY ***Federal work-study:*** Total amount: $112,000; 161 jobs averaging $1051. ***State or other work-study/employment:*** Total amount: $666,789 (27% need-based, 73% non-need-based). 486 part-time jobs averaging $1205.

APPLYING FOR FINANCIAL AID ***Required financial aid form:*** FAFSA. ***Financial aid deadline:*** Continuous. ***Notification date:*** Continuous beginning 3/1. Students must reply within 4 weeks of notification.

CONTACT Mr. Thomas J. Ochsner, Director of Scholarships and Financial Aid, Nebraska Wesleyan University, 5000 Saint Paul Avenue, Lincoln, NE 68504, 402-465-2212 or toll-free 800-541-3818. *Fax:* 402-465-2194. *E-mail:* tjo@nebrwesleyan.edu.

NER ISRAEL RABBINICAL COLLEGE

Baltimore, MD

CONTACT Mr. Moshe Pelberg, Financial Aid Administrator, Ner Israel Rabbinical College, 400 Mount Wilson Lane, Baltimore, MD 21208, 410-484-7200.

NEUMANN UNIVERSITY

Aston, PA

Tuition & fees: $20,402 **Average undergraduate aid package: $18,000**

ABOUT THE INSTITUTION Independent Roman Catholic, coed. ***Awards:*** associate, bachelor's, master's, and doctoral degrees and post-bachelor's certificates. 19 undergraduate majors. ***Total enrollment:*** 3,037. Undergraduates: 2,484. Freshmen: 539. Federal methodology is used as a basis for awarding need-based institutional aid.

UNDERGRADUATE EXPENSES for 2008–09 ***Application fee:*** $35. ***Comprehensive fee:*** $29,660 includes full-time tuition ($19,742), mandatory fees ($660), and room and board ($9258). ***College room only:*** $5498. Room and board charges vary according to board plan. ***Part-time tuition:*** $451 per credit hour. ***Payment plan:*** Installment.

FRESHMAN FINANCIAL AID (Fall 2008, est.) 487 applied for aid; of those 100% were deemed to have need. 100% of freshmen with need received aid; of those 66% had need fully met. ***Average percent of need met:*** 70% (excluding resources awarded to replace EFC). ***Average financial aid package:*** $18,000 (excluding resources awarded to replace EFC).

UNDERGRADUATE FINANCIAL AID (Fall 2008, est.) 1,771 applied for aid; of those 100% were deemed to have need. 100% of undergraduates with need received aid; of those 68% had need fully met. ***Average percent of need met:*** 65% (excluding resources awarded to replace EFC). ***Average financial aid package:*** $18,000 (excluding resources awarded to replace EFC).

GIFT AID (NEED-BASED) ***Total amount:*** $17,879,400 (12% federal, 11% state, 75% institutional, 2% external sources). ***Receiving aid:*** Freshmen: 84% (451); all full-time undergraduates: 72% (1,416). ***Average award:*** Freshmen: $15,300; Undergraduates: $15,000. ***Scholarships, grants, and awards:*** Federal Pell, FSEOG, state, private, college/university gift aid from institutional funds.

GIFT AID (NON-NEED-BASED) ***Receiving aid:*** Freshmen: 19% (103). Undergraduates: 18% (354). ***Scholarships, grants, and awards by category:*** *Creative arts/performance:* 1 award ($1000 total): music. *Special characteristics:* 29 awards ($254,386 total): children of faculty/staff. ***Tuition waivers:*** Full or partial for employees or children of employees. ***ROTC:*** Army cooperative.

LOANS ***Student loans:*** $18,078,800 (100% need-based). 80% of past graduating class borrowed through all loan programs. *Average indebtedness per student:* $30,000. ***Average need-based loan:*** Freshmen: $4000. Undergraduates: $6000. ***Parent loans:*** $4,100,000 (100% need-based). ***Programs:*** Federal Direct (Subsidized and Unsubsidized Stafford, PLUS), FFEL (Subsidized and Unsubsidized Stafford, PLUS), Perkins, Federal Nursing.

WORK-STUDY ***Federal work-study:*** Total amount: $250,000; 200 jobs averaging $1600. ***State or other work-study/employment:*** Part-time jobs available.

APPLYING FOR FINANCIAL AID ***Required financial aid form:*** FAFSA. ***Financial aid deadline:*** Continuous.

CONTACT Katherine Markert, Director of Financial Aid, Neumann University, One Neumann Drive, Aston, PA 19014-1298, 610-558-5519 or toll-free 800-963-8626.

NEUMONT UNIVERSITY

South Jordan, UT

CONTACT Financial Aid Office, Neumont University, 10701 S. River Front Parkway, Suite 300, South Jordan, UT 84095, 801-438-1100 or toll-free 866-622-3448.

NEVADA STATE COLLEGE AT HENDERSON

Henderson, NV

CONTACT Financial Aid Office, Nevada State College at Henderson, 1125 Nevada State Drive, Henderson, NV 89015, 702-992-2000.

NEWBERRY COLLEGE

Newberry, SC

Tuition & fees: $21,600 **Average undergraduate aid package: $19,927**

ABOUT THE INSTITUTION Independent Evangelical Lutheran, coed. ***Awards:*** bachelor's degrees. 35 undergraduate majors. ***Total enrollment:*** 973. Undergraduates: 963. Freshmen: 297. Federal methodology is used as a basis for awarding need-based institutional aid.

UNDERGRADUATE EXPENSES for 2008–09 ***Application fee:*** $30. ***Comprehensive fee:*** $28,960 includes full-time tuition ($20,500), mandatory fees ($1100), and room and board ($7360). ***College room only:*** $3560. ***Part-time tuition:*** $500 per hour. ***Part-time fees:*** $100 per term.

FRESHMAN FINANCIAL AID (Fall 2008, est.) 284 applied for aid; of those 98% were deemed to have need. 100% of freshmen with need received aid; of those 30% had need fully met. ***Average percent of need met:*** 75% (excluding resources awarded to replace EFC). ***Average financial aid package:*** $19,918 (excluding resources awarded to replace EFC).

UNDERGRADUATE FINANCIAL AID (Fall 2008, est.) 902 applied for aid; of those 99% were deemed to have need. 100% of undergraduates with need received aid; of those 33% had need fully met. ***Average percent of need met:*** 75% (excluding resources awarded to replace EFC). ***Average financial aid package:*** $19,927 (excluding resources awarded to replace EFC).

GIFT AID (NEED-BASED) ***Total amount:*** $10,148,468 (13% federal, 26% state, 59% institutional, 2% external sources). ***Receiving aid:*** Freshmen: 74% (224); all full-time undergraduates: 74% (701). ***Average award:*** Freshmen: $4953; Undergraduates: $4957. ***Scholarships, grants, and awards:*** Federal Pell, FSEOG, state, private, college/university gift aid from institutional funds.

GIFT AID (NON-NEED-BASED) ***Total amount:*** $3,049,750 (30% state, 63% institutional, 7% external sources). ***Receiving aid:*** Freshmen: 92% (278). Undergraduates: 94% (891). ***Scholarships, grants, and awards by category:*** *Academic interests/achievement:* 3 awards ($3000 total): biological sciences, business, communication, education, foreign languages, general academic interests/achievements, humanities, mathematics, physical sciences, religion/biblical studies, social sciences. *Creative arts/performance:* 39 awards ($135,943 total): music, theater/drama. *Special achievements/activities:* 115 awards ($261,387 total): cheerleading/drum major, religious involvement. *Special characteristics:* 72 awards ($60,158 total): children and siblings of alumni, children of faculty/staff, international students, local/state students, relatives of clergy, religious affiliation, siblings of current students. ***ROTC:*** Army cooperative.

LOANS ***Student loans:*** $6,178,361 (66% need-based, 34% non-need-based). 98% of past graduating class borrowed through all loan programs. *Average indebtedness per student:* $13,477. ***Average need-based loan:*** Freshmen: $4335.

Undergraduates: $4336. ***Parent loans:*** $356,638 (35% need-based, 65% non-need-based). ***Programs:*** FFEL (Subsidized and Unsubsidized Stafford, PLUS), Perkins, state.

WORK-STUDY ***Federal work-study:*** Total amount: $40,151; 52 jobs averaging $804. ***State or other work-study/employment:*** Total amount: $23,838 (100% non-need-based). 45 part-time jobs averaging $518.

ATHLETIC AWARDS Total amount: $1,727,367 (64% need-based, 36% non-need-based).

APPLYING FOR FINANCIAL AID ***Required financial aid form:*** FAFSA. ***Financial aid deadline (priority):*** 3/15. ***Notification date:*** Continuous beginning 3/15. Students must reply within 4 weeks of notification.

CONTACT Ms. Melissa A. Lutz, Director of Financial Aid, Newberry College, 2100 College Street, Newberry, SC 29108, 803-321-5127 or toll-free 800-845-4955 Ext. 5127. *Fax:* 803-321-5627. *E-mail:* missy.lutz@newberry.edu.

NEWBURY COLLEGE

Brookline, MA

ABOUT THE INSTITUTION Independent, coed. ***Awards:*** associate and bachelor's degrees. 18 undergraduate majors. ***Total enrollment:*** 1,202. Undergraduates: 1,202. Freshmen: 320.

GIFT AID (NEED-BASED) ***Scholarships, grants, and awards:*** Federal Pell, FSEOG, state, private, college/university gift aid from institutional funds.

LOANS ***Programs:*** FFEL (Subsidized and Unsubsidized Stafford, PLUS), alternative loans, Meta Loans, Signature Loans, Nellie Mae Loans.

WORK-STUDY ***Federal work-study:*** Total amount: $119,434; 147 jobs averaging $2000.

APPLYING FOR FINANCIAL AID ***Required financial aid form:*** FAFSA.

CONTACT Office of Financial Assistance, Newbury College, 129 Fisher Avenue, Brookline, MA 02445-5796, 617-730-7100 or toll-free 800-NEWBURY. *Fax:* 617-730-7108.

NEW COLLEGE OF FLORIDA

Sarasota, FL

Tuition & fees (FL res): $4127 **Average undergraduate aid package: $12,911**

ABOUT THE INSTITUTION State-supported, coed. ***Awards:*** bachelor's degrees. 41 undergraduate majors. ***Total enrollment:*** 785. Undergraduates: 785. Freshmen: 222. Federal methodology is used as a basis for awarding need-based institutional aid.

UNDERGRADUATE EXPENSES for 2008–09 ***Application fee:*** $30. ***Tuition, state resident:*** full-time $4127. ***Tuition, nonresident:*** full-time $23,766. ***College room and board:*** $7464; ***Room only:*** $4908. Room and board charges vary according to board plan and housing facility. ***Payment plans:*** Installment, deferred payment.

FRESHMAN FINANCIAL AID (Fall 2008, est.) 155 applied for aid; of those 60% were deemed to have need. 100% of freshmen with need received aid; of those 66% had need fully met. ***Average percent of need met:*** 93% (excluding resources awarded to replace EFC). ***Average financial aid package:*** $12,587 (excluding resources awarded to replace EFC). 58% of all full-time freshmen had no need and received non-need-based gift aid.

UNDERGRADUATE FINANCIAL AID (Fall 2008, est.) 454 applied for aid; of those 68% were deemed to have need. 100% of undergraduates with need received aid; of those 72% had need fully met. ***Average percent of need met:*** 95% (excluding resources awarded to replace EFC). ***Average financial aid package:*** $12,911 (excluding resources awarded to replace EFC). 55% of all full-time undergraduates had no need and received non-need-based gift aid.

GIFT AID (NEED-BASED) ***Total amount:*** $2,302,301 (25% federal, 38% state, 36% institutional, 1% external sources). ***Receiving aid:*** Freshmen: 42% (93); all full-time undergraduates: 39% (304). ***Average award:*** Freshmen: $9010; Undergraduates: $8845. ***Scholarships, grants, and awards:*** Federal Pell, FSEOG, state, private, college/university gift aid from institutional funds, Academic Competitiveness Grant.

GIFT AID (NON-NEED-BASED) ***Total amount:*** $2,516,320 (1% federal, 58% state, 34% institutional, 7% external sources). ***Receiving aid:*** Freshmen: 11% (24). Undergraduates: 8% (65). ***Average award:*** Freshmen: $2635. Undergraduates: $3121. ***Scholarships, grants, and awards by category:*** *Academic interests/achievement:* 727 awards ($2,312,698 total): general academic interests/achievements. *Special achievements/activities:* 130 awards ($369,500 total): general special achievements/activities. *Special characteristics:* 145 awards ($1,270,557 total): out-of-state students.

LOANS ***Student loans:*** $1,156,825 (77% need-based, 23% non-need-based). 24% of past graduating class borrowed through all loan programs. *Average indebtedness per student:* $13,162. ***Average need-based loan:*** Freshmen: $2908. Undergraduates: $3494. ***Parent loans:*** $113,777 (10% need-based, 90% non-need-based). ***Programs:*** FFEL (Subsidized and Unsubsidized Stafford, PLUS), alternative loans.

WORK-STUDY ***Federal work-study:*** Total amount: $54,174; 28 jobs averaging $1393. ***State or other work-study/employment:*** Total amount: $217,458 (100% need-based). 60 part-time jobs averaging $1750.

APPLYING FOR FINANCIAL AID ***Required financial aid form:*** FAFSA. ***Financial aid deadline (priority):*** 2/15. ***Notification date:*** Continuous beginning 3/15. Students must reply by 5/1 or within 4 weeks of notification.

CONTACT Monica Baldwin, Director of Financial Aid, New College of Florida, 5800 Bay Shore Rd., Sarasota, FL 34243-2109, 941-487-5000. *Fax:* 941-487-5010. *E-mail:* ncfinaid@ncf.edu.

NEW ENGLAND COLLEGE

Henniker, NH

Tuition & fees: $27,450 **Average undergraduate aid package: $23,858**

ABOUT THE INSTITUTION Independent, coed. ***Awards:*** associate, bachelor's, and master's degrees. 40 undergraduate majors. ***Total enrollment:*** 1,752. Undergraduates: 1,061. Freshmen: 299. Both federal and institutional methodology are used as a basis for awarding need-based institutional aid.

UNDERGRADUATE EXPENSES for 2009–10 ***Application fee:*** $30. ***Comprehensive fee:*** $37,076 includes full-time tuition ($27,200), mandatory fees ($250), and room and board ($9626). ***College room only:*** $5000. ***Part-time tuition:*** $1133 per credit.

FRESHMAN FINANCIAL AID (Fall 2008, est.) 226 applied for aid; of those 88% were deemed to have need. 99% of freshmen with need received aid; of those 22% had need fully met. ***Average percent of need met:*** 80% (excluding resources awarded to replace EFC). ***Average financial aid package:*** $21,642 (excluding resources awarded to replace EFC). 30% of all full-time freshmen had no need and received non-need-based gift aid.

UNDERGRADUATE FINANCIAL AID (Fall 2008, est.) 739 applied for aid; of those 88% were deemed to have need. 100% of undergraduates with need received aid; of those 29% had need fully met. ***Average percent of need met:*** 87% (excluding resources awarded to replace EFC). ***Average financial aid package:*** $23,858 (excluding resources awarded to replace EFC). 30% of all full-time undergraduates had no need and received non-need-based gift aid.

GIFT AID (NEED-BASED) ***Total amount:*** $8,714,776 (14% federal, 1% state, 85% institutional). ***Receiving aid:*** Freshmen: 66% (197); all full-time undergraduates: 63% (636). ***Average award:*** Freshmen: $13,582; Undergraduates: $13,661. ***Scholarships, grants, and awards:*** Federal Pell, FSEOG, state, private, college/university gift aid from institutional funds.

GIFT AID (NON-NEED-BASED) ***Total amount:*** $3,268,974 (100% institutional). ***Receiving aid:*** Freshmen: 5% (15). Undergraduates: 5% (48). ***Average award:*** Freshmen: $10,777. Undergraduates: $10,723. ***Scholarships, grants, and awards by category:*** *Academic interests/achievement:* 609 awards ($5,824,136 total): biological sciences, business, communication, computer science, education, engineering/technologies, English, general academic interests/achievements, health fields, humanities, international studies, mathematics, social sciences. *Creative arts/performance:* 16 awards ($170,750 total): applied art and design, art/fine arts, creative writing, theater/drama. *Special achievements/activities:* 129 awards ($664,475 total): community service, leadership. *Special characteristics:* 51 awards ($652,782 total): children and siblings of alumni, children of educators, children of faculty/staff, ethnic background, international students, local/state students, parents of current students, siblings of current students. ***ROTC:*** Army cooperative, Air Force cooperative.

LOANS ***Student loans:*** $6,769,035 (91% need-based, 9% non-need-based). 68% of past graduating class borrowed through all loan programs. *Average indebtedness per student:* $29,366. ***Average need-based loan:*** Freshmen: $7280. Undergraduates: $8168. ***Parent loans:*** $1,690,712 (81% need-based, 19% non-need-based). ***Programs:*** FFEL (Subsidized and Unsubsidized Stafford, PLUS), Perkins, state.

WORK-STUDY ***Federal work-study:*** Total amount: $766,421; 408 jobs averaging $1878. ***State or other work-study/employment:*** Total amount: $43,743 (28% need-based, 72% non-need-based). 33 part-time jobs averaging $1339.

APPLYING FOR FINANCIAL AID ***Required financial aid forms:*** FAFSA, institution's own form. ***Financial aid deadline (priority):*** 4/1. ***Notification date:*** Continuous. Students must reply within 2 weeks of notification.

CONTACT Russell Romandini, Student Financial Services Director, New England College, 15 Main Street, Henniker, NH 03242-3293, 603-428-2226 or toll-free 800-521-7642. *Fax:* 603-428-2404. *E-mail:* rstein@nec.edu.

NEW ENGLAND CONSERVATORY OF MUSIC

Boston, MA

Tuition & fees: $33,325 **Average undergraduate aid package: $21,659**

ABOUT THE INSTITUTION Independent, coed. ***Awards:*** bachelor's, master's, and doctoral degrees and post-bachelor's certificates. 8 undergraduate majors. ***Total enrollment:*** 714. Undergraduates: 356. Freshmen: 83. Federal methodology is used as a basis for awarding need-based institutional aid.

UNDERGRADUATE EXPENSES for 2008–09 ***Application fee:*** $100. ***Comprehensive fee:*** $44,925 includes full-time tuition ($32,900), mandatory fees ($425), and room and board ($11,600). Room and board charges vary according to board plan. ***Part-time tuition:*** $1050 per credit.

FRESHMAN FINANCIAL AID (Fall 2008, est.) 44 applied for aid; of those 84% were deemed to have need. 100% of freshmen with need received aid; of those 24% had need fully met. ***Average percent of need met:*** 67% (excluding resources awarded to replace EFC). ***Average financial aid package:*** $21,002 (excluding resources awarded to replace EFC). 49% of all full-time freshmen had no need and received non-need-based gift aid.

UNDERGRADUATE FINANCIAL AID (Fall 2008, est.) 208 applied for aid; of those 87% were deemed to have need. 100% of undergraduates with need received aid; of those 21% had need fully met. ***Average percent of need met:*** 68% (excluding resources awarded to replace EFC). ***Average financial aid package:*** $21,659 (excluding resources awarded to replace EFC). 38% of all full-time undergraduates had no need and received non-need-based gift aid.

GIFT AID (NEED-BASED) ***Total amount:*** $2,782,254 (12% federal, 1% state, 77% institutional, 10% external sources). ***Receiving aid:*** Freshmen: 43% (37); all full-time undergraduates: 50% (177). ***Average award:*** Freshmen: $15,078; Undergraduates: $15,581. ***Scholarships, grants, and awards:*** Federal Pell, FSEOG, state, private, college/university gift aid from institutional funds.

GIFT AID (NON-NEED-BASED) ***Total amount:*** $2,228,901 (90% institutional, 10% external sources). ***Receiving aid:*** Freshmen: 6% (5). Undergraduates: 6% (23). ***Average award:*** Freshmen: $13,966. Undergraduates: $13,856. ***Scholarships, grants, and awards by category:*** *Creative arts/performance:* music, theater/drama. ***Tuition waivers:*** Full or partial for employees or children of employees.

LOANS ***Student loans:*** $2,203,683 (67% need-based, 33% non-need-based). 78% of past graduating class borrowed through all loan programs. *Average indebtedness per student:* $30,687. ***Average need-based loan:*** Freshmen: $5844. Undergraduates: $5830. ***Parent loans:*** $598,117 (39% need-based, 61% non-need-based). ***Programs:*** FFEL (Subsidized and Unsubsidized Stafford, PLUS), Perkins, state.

WORK-STUDY ***Federal work-study:*** Total amount: $249,682; 154 jobs averaging $1621. ***State or other work-study/employment:*** Part-time jobs available.

APPLYING FOR FINANCIAL AID ***Required financial aid forms:*** FAFSA, institution's own form. ***Financial aid deadline (priority):*** 2/1. ***Notification date:*** Continuous beginning 4/1. Students must reply by 5/1.

CONTACT Lauren G. Urbanek, Director of Financial Aid, New England Conservatory of Music, 290 Huntington Avenue, Boston, MA 02115, 617-585-1113. *Fax:* 617-585-1115. *E-mail:* lurbanek@newenglandconservatory.edu.

THE NEW ENGLAND INSTITUTE OF ART

Brookline, MA

UNDERGRADUATE EXPENSES Tuition cost varies by program. Prospective students should contact the school for current tuition costs. Other charges include a starting kit for all first-quarter students. Kits vary in price, depending on the program of study.

CONTACT Financial Aid Office, The New England Institute of Art, 142 Berkeley Street, Boston, MA 02116-5100, 617-267-7910 or toll-free 800-903-4425.

NEW ENGLAND SCHOOL OF COMMUNICATIONS

Bangor, ME

Tuition & fees: $10,680 **Average undergraduate aid package: $3927**

ABOUT THE INSTITUTION Independent, coed, primarily men. ***Awards:*** associate and bachelor's degrees. 20 undergraduate majors. ***Total enrollment:*** 393. Undergraduates: 393. Freshmen: 146. Federal methodology is used as a basis for awarding need-based institutional aid.

UNDERGRADUATE EXPENSES for 2008–09 ***Application fee:*** $15. ***Comprehensive fee:*** $17,405 includes full-time tuition ($10,400), mandatory fees ($280), and room and board ($6725). ***Part-time tuition:*** $350 per credit.

FRESHMAN FINANCIAL AID (Fall 2007) 129 applied for aid; of those 81% were deemed to have need. 96% of freshmen with need received aid; of those 25% had need fully met. ***Average percent of need met:*** 28% (excluding resources awarded to replace EFC). ***Average financial aid package:*** $4441 (excluding resources awarded to replace EFC).

UNDERGRADUATE FINANCIAL AID (Fall 2007) 309 applied for aid; of those 89% were deemed to have need. 96% of undergraduates with need received aid; of those 18% had need fully met. ***Average percent of need met:*** 23% (excluding resources awarded to replace EFC). ***Average financial aid package:*** $3927 (excluding resources awarded to replace EFC).

GIFT AID (NEED-BASED) ***Total amount:*** $974,209 (52% federal, 21% state, 4% institutional, 23% external sources). ***Receiving aid:*** Freshmen: 60% (87); all full-time undergraduates: 47% (204). ***Average award:*** Freshmen: $2668; Undergraduates: $2407. ***Scholarships, grants, and awards:*** Federal Pell, FSEOG, state, private, college/university gift aid from institutional funds.

GIFT AID (NON-NEED-BASED) ***Receiving aid:*** Freshmen: 29% (42). Undergraduates: 19% (81). ***Scholarships, grants, and awards by category:*** *Academic interests/achievement:* 48 awards ($30,000 total): communication. *Special achievements/activities:* general special achievements/activities. ***ROTC:*** Army cooperative.

LOANS ***Student loans:*** $2,437,448 (100% need-based). 80% of past graduating class borrowed through all loan programs. *Average indebtedness per student:* $34,209. ***Average need-based loan:*** Freshmen: $1909. Undergraduates: $2641. ***Parent loans:*** $742,355 (100% need-based). ***Programs:*** FFEL (Subsidized and Unsubsidized Stafford, PLUS), alternative loans.

WORK-STUDY ***Federal work-study:*** 40 jobs averaging $1000. ***State or other work-study/employment:*** 6 part-time jobs averaging $2200.

APPLYING FOR FINANCIAL AID ***Required financial aid form:*** FAFSA. ***Financial aid deadline (priority):*** 5/1. ***Notification date:*** Continuous beginning 5/1. Students must reply within 4 weeks of notification.

CONTACT Ms. Nicole Rediker, Director of Financial Aid, New England School of Communications, One College Circle, Bangor, ME 04401, 888-877-1876. *Fax:* 207-947-3987. *E-mail:* nicole@nescom.edu.

NEW HAMPSHIRE INSTITUTE OF ART

Manchester, NH

CONTACT Linda Lavallee, Director of Financial Aid, New Hampshire Institute of Art, 148 Concord Street, Manchester, NH 03104-4858, 603-623-0313 Ext. 577 or toll-free 866-241-4918 (in-state). *Fax:* 603-647-0658. *E-mail:* llavallee@nhia.edu.

NEW JERSEY CITY UNIVERSITY

Jersey City, NJ

Tuition & fees (NJ res): $8727 **Average undergraduate aid package: $8440**

ABOUT THE INSTITUTION State-supported, coed. ***Awards:*** bachelor's and master's degrees and post-bachelor's and post-master's certificates. 27 undergraduate majors. ***Total enrollment:*** 8,151. Undergraduates: 6,104.

UNDERGRADUATE EXPENSES for 2008–09 ***Application fee:*** $35. ***Tuition, state resident:*** full-time $6352; part-time $212 per credit. ***Tuition, nonresident:*** full-time $13,418; part-time $447 per credit. ***Required fees:*** full-time $2375;

$77 per credit. Full-time tuition and fees vary according to course load. Part-time tuition and fees vary according to course load. ***College room and board:*** $8613; ***Room only:*** $5513. ***Payment plan:*** Deferred payment.

FRESHMAN FINANCIAL AID (Fall 2007) 572 applied for aid; of those 90% were deemed to have need. 93% of freshmen with need received aid; of those 4% had need fully met. ***Average percent of need met:*** 58% (excluding resources awarded to replace EFC). ***Average financial aid package:*** $9098 (excluding resources awarded to replace EFC). 3% of all full-time freshmen had no need and received non-need-based gift aid.

UNDERGRADUATE FINANCIAL AID (Fall 2007) 3,611 applied for aid; of those 94% were deemed to have need. 95% of undergraduates with need received aid; of those 8% had need fully met. ***Average percent of need met:*** 59% (excluding resources awarded to replace EFC). ***Average financial aid package:*** $8440 (excluding resources awarded to replace EFC). 1% of all full-time undergraduates had no need and received non-need-based gift aid.

GIFT AID (NEED-BASED) ***Total amount:*** $16,164,928 (50% federal, 50% state). ***Receiving aid:*** Freshmen: 63% (410); all full-time undergraduates: 54% (2,395). ***Average award:*** Freshmen: $7661; Undergraduates: $6727. ***Scholarships, grants, and awards:*** Federal Pell, FSEOG, state, private, college/university gift aid from institutional funds, United Negro College Fund.

GIFT AID (NON-NEED-BASED) ***Total amount:*** $70,591 (100% state). ***Receiving aid:*** Freshmen: 10% (67). Undergraduates: 6% (283). ***Average award:*** Freshmen: $6052. Undergraduates: $4982. ***Tuition waivers:*** Full or partial for employees or children of employees, senior citizens.

LOANS ***Student loans:*** $13,177,120 (58% need-based, 42% non-need-based). 53% of past graduating class borrowed through all loan programs. *Average indebtedness per student:* $11,337. ***Average need-based loan:*** Freshmen: $3417. Undergraduates: $4280. ***Programs:*** FFEL (Subsidized and Unsubsidized Stafford, PLUS), Perkins, state.

WORK-STUDY ***Federal work-study:*** Total amount: $704,869; jobs available.

APPLYING FOR FINANCIAL AID ***Required financial aid form:*** FAFSA. ***Notification date:*** 5/15.

CONTACT Ms. Carmen Panlilio, Assistant Vice President for Admissions and Financial Aid, New Jersey City University, 2039 Kennedy Boulevard, Jersey City, NJ 07305-1597, 201-200-3173 or toll-free 888-441-NJCU.

NEW JERSEY INSTITUTE OF TECHNOLOGY

Newark, NJ

Tuition & fees (NJ res): $12,482 Average undergraduate aid package: $12,109

ABOUT THE INSTITUTION State-supported, coed. ***Awards:*** bachelor's, master's, and doctoral degrees and post-bachelor's certificates. 34 undergraduate majors. ***Total enrollment:*** 8,398. Undergraduates: 5,576. Freshmen: 907. Federal methodology is used as a basis for awarding need-based institutional aid.

UNDERGRADUATE EXPENSES for 2008–09 ***Application fee:*** $50. ***Tuition, state resident:*** full-time $10,500; part-time $400 per credit. ***Tuition, nonresident:*** full-time $19,960; part-time $853 per credit. ***Required fees:*** full-time $1982; $97 per credit or $102 per term. Full-time tuition and fees vary according to course load and degree level. Part-time tuition and fees vary according to course load and degree level. ***College room and board:*** $9596; ***Room only:*** $6680. Room and board charges vary according to board plan and housing facility. ***Payment plan:*** Installment.

FRESHMAN FINANCIAL AID (Fall 2007) 548 applied for aid; of those 82% were deemed to have need. 100% of freshmen with need received aid; of those 13% had need fully met. ***Average percent of need met:*** 65% (excluding resources awarded to replace EFC). ***Average financial aid package:*** $11,700 (excluding resources awarded to replace EFC). 20% of all full-time freshmen had no need and received non-need-based gift aid.

UNDERGRADUATE FINANCIAL AID (Fall 2007) 2,718 applied for aid; of those 89% were deemed to have need. 100% of undergraduates with need received aid; of those 9% had need fully met. ***Average percent of need met:*** 64% (excluding resources awarded to replace EFC). ***Average financial aid package:*** $12,109 (excluding resources awarded to replace EFC). 16% of all full-time undergraduates had no need and received non-need-based gift aid.

GIFT AID (NEED-BASED) ***Total amount:*** $14,631,169 (35% federal, 59% state, 6% external sources). ***Receiving aid:*** Freshmen: 36% (261); all full-time undergraduates: 42% (1,719). ***Average award:*** Freshmen: $8591; Undergraduates: $8187. ***Scholarships, grants, and awards:*** Federal Pell, FSEOG, state, private, college/university gift aid from institutional funds.

GIFT AID (NON-NEED-BASED) ***Total amount:*** $9,080,234 (5% state, 82% institutional, 13% external sources). ***Receiving aid:*** Freshmen: 49% (361). Undergraduates: 36% (1,482). ***Average award:*** Freshmen: $9164. Undergraduates: $7128. ***Scholarships, grants, and awards by category:*** *Academic interests/achievement:* architecture, biological sciences, business, communication, computer science, engineering/technologies, general academic interests/achievements, humanities, mathematics. *Special characteristics:* out-of-state students. ***Tuition waivers:*** Full or partial for employees or children of employees. ***ROTC:*** Air Force.

LOANS ***Student loans:*** $19,260,464 (41% need-based, 59% non-need-based). 1% of past graduating class borrowed through all loan programs. *Average indebtedness per student:* $27,930. ***Average need-based loan:*** Freshmen: $3529. Undergraduates: $4361. ***Parent loans:*** $1,143,256 (100% non-need-based). ***Programs:*** Federal Direct (Subsidized and Unsubsidized Stafford, PLUS), Perkins, state, college/university.

WORK-STUDY ***Federal work-study:*** Total amount: $373,829; jobs available. ***State or other work-study/employment:*** Total amount: $395,000 (100% non-need-based). Part-time jobs available.

ATHLETIC AWARDS Total amount: $2,110,429 (3% need-based, 97% non-need-based).

APPLYING FOR FINANCIAL AID ***Financial aid deadline:*** 5/5 (priority: 3/15). ***Notification date:*** Continuous. Students must reply by 5/1.

CONTACT Ivon Nunez, Assistant Director, Financial Aid Services, New Jersey Institute of Technology, Student Mall, University Heights, Newark, NJ 07102, 973-596-3476 or toll-free 800-925-NJIT. *Fax:* 973-596-6471. *E-mail:* nunez@njit.edu.

NEW LIFE THEOLOGICAL SEMINARY

Charlotte, NC

CONTACT Financial Aid Office, New Life Theological Seminary, PO Box 790106, Charlotte, NC 28206-7901, 704-334-6882.

NEWMAN UNIVERSITY

Wichita, KS

Tuition & fees: $19,650 Average undergraduate aid package: $12,624

ABOUT THE INSTITUTION Independent Roman Catholic, coed. ***Awards:*** associate, bachelor's, and master's degrees. 36 undergraduate majors. ***Total enrollment:*** 2,435. Undergraduates: 1,815. Freshmen: 117. Federal methodology is used as a basis for awarding need-based institutional aid.

UNDERGRADUATE EXPENSES for 2009–10 ***Application fee:*** $20. ***One-time required fee:*** $150. ***Comprehensive fee:*** $26,306 includes full-time tuition ($19,200), mandatory fees ($450), and room and board ($6656). ***Part-time tuition:*** $640 per credit hour. ***Part-time fees:*** $10 per credit hour.

FRESHMAN FINANCIAL AID (Fall 2008, est.) 130 applied for aid; of those 70% were deemed to have need. 100% of freshmen with need received aid; of those 37% had need fully met. ***Average percent of need met:*** 77% (excluding resources awarded to replace EFC). ***Average financial aid package:*** $15,927 (excluding resources awarded to replace EFC). 7% of all full-time freshmen had no need and received non-need-based gift aid.

UNDERGRADUATE FINANCIAL AID (Fall 2008, est.) 1,013 applied for aid; of those 80% were deemed to have need. 100% of undergraduates with need received aid; of those 15% had need fully met. ***Average percent of need met:*** 59% (excluding resources awarded to replace EFC). ***Average financial aid package:*** $12,624 (excluding resources awarded to replace EFC). 5% of all full-time undergraduates had no need and received non-need-based gift aid.

GIFT AID (NEED-BASED) ***Total amount:*** $2,124,684 (60% federal, 40% state). ***Receiving aid:*** Freshmen: 43% (56); all full-time undergraduates: 60% (614). ***Average award:*** Freshmen: $5306; Undergraduates: $4307. ***Scholarships, grants, and awards:*** Federal Pell, FSEOG, state, private, college/university gift aid from institutional funds.

GIFT AID (NON-NEED-BASED) ***Total amount:*** $5,168,437 (94% institutional, 6% external sources). ***Receiving aid:*** Freshmen: 69% (90). Undergraduates: 72% (741). ***Average award:*** Freshmen: $2938. Undergraduates: $3283. ***Scholarships, grants, and awards by category:*** *Academic interests/achievement:* 726 awards ($2,903,119 total): general academic interests/achievements. *Creative arts/performance:* 37 awards ($99,075 total): art/fine arts, journalism/publications, music, theater/drama. *Special achievements/activities:* 91 awards ($411,500 total): community service, leadership, memberships, religious involvement. *Special characteristics:* 239 awards ($880,067 total): children and siblings of alumni, children of faculty/staff, first-generation college students, international students, siblings of current students.

LOANS ***Student loans:*** $11,508,488 (40% need-based, 60% non-need-based). 77% of past graduating class borrowed through all loan programs. *Average indebtedness per student:* $22,606. ***Average need-based loan:*** Freshmen: $2943. Undergraduates: $4233. ***Parent loans:*** $721,779 (100% non-need-based). ***Programs:*** FFEL (Subsidized and Unsubsidized Stafford, PLUS), Perkins.

WORK-STUDY ***Federal work-study:*** Total amount: $69,017; 70 jobs averaging $986. ***State or other work-study/employment:*** Total amount: $134,735 (100% non-need-based). 103 part-time jobs averaging $1308.

ATHLETIC AWARDS Total amount: $989,719 (100% non-need-based).

APPLYING FOR FINANCIAL AID ***Required financial aid form:*** FAFSA. ***Financial aid deadline (priority):*** 3/1. ***Notification date:*** Continuous.

CONTACT Julie Love, Financial Aid Counselor, Newman University, 3100 McCormick Avenue, Wichita, KS 67213, 316-942-4291 Ext. 2103 or toll-free 877-NEWMANU Ext. 2144. *Fax:* 316-942-4483.

NEW MEXICO HIGHLANDS UNIVERSITY

Las Vegas, NM

CONTACT Eileen Sedillo, Director, Financial Aid & Scholarship, New Mexico Highlands University, Box 9000, Las Vegas, NM 87701, 505-454-3430 or toll-free 800-338-6648. *Fax:* 505-454-3398. *E-mail:* sedillo_e@nmhu.edu.

NEW MEXICO INSTITUTE OF MINING AND TECHNOLOGY

Socorro, NM

Tuition & fees (NM res): $4352 Average undergraduate aid package: $10,201

ABOUT THE INSTITUTION State-supported, coed. ***Awards:*** associate, bachelor's, master's, and doctoral degrees. 24 undergraduate majors. ***Total enrollment:*** 1,882. Undergraduates: 1,327. Freshmen: 240. Federal methodology is used as a basis for awarding need-based institutional aid.

UNDERGRADUATE EXPENSES for 2008–09 ***Application fee:*** $15. ***Tuition, state resident:*** full-time $4352; part-time $158 per credit hour. ***Tuition, nonresident:*** full-time $12,544; part-time $499 per credit hour. Part-time tuition and fees vary according to course load. ***College room and board:*** $5320. Room and board charges vary according to board plan and housing facility. ***Payment plan:*** Deferred payment.

FRESHMAN FINANCIAL AID (Fall 2008, est.) 280 applied for aid; of those 44% were deemed to have need. 98% of freshmen with need received aid; of those 47% had need fully met. ***Average percent of need met:*** 94% (excluding resources awarded to replace EFC). ***Average financial aid package:*** $9072 (excluding resources awarded to replace EFC). 35% of all full-time freshmen had no need and received non-need-based gift aid.

UNDERGRADUATE FINANCIAL AID (Fall 2008, est.) 963 applied for aid; of those 49% were deemed to have need. 98% of undergraduates with need received aid; of those 48% had need fully met. ***Average percent of need met:*** 94% (excluding resources awarded to replace EFC). ***Average financial aid package:*** $10,201 (excluding resources awarded to replace EFC). 37% of all full-time undergraduates had no need and received non-need-based gift aid.

GIFT AID (NEED-BASED) ***Total amount:*** $1,748,993 (81% federal, 19% state). ***Receiving aid:*** Freshmen: 15% (54); all full-time undergraduates: 22% (239). ***Average award:*** Freshmen: $4567; Undergraduates: $5334. ***Scholarships, grants, and awards:*** Federal Pell, FSEOG, state, private, college/university gift aid from institutional funds.

GIFT AID (NON-NEED-BASED) ***Total amount:*** $3,212,688 (45% state, 55% institutional). ***Receiving aid:*** Freshmen: 30% (108). Undergraduates: 29% (306). ***Average award:*** Freshmen: $4028. Undergraduates: $4777. ***Tuition waivers:*** Full or partial for employees or children of employees, senior citizens.

LOANS ***Student loans:*** $1,697,149 (100% need-based). 92% of past graduating class borrowed through all loan programs. *Average indebtedness per student:* $8129. ***Average need-based loan:*** Freshmen: $3819. Undergraduates: $4660. ***Programs:*** FFEL (Subsidized and Unsubsidized Stafford, PLUS), Perkins.

WORK-STUDY ***Federal work-study:*** Total amount: $465,245; jobs available. ***State or other work-study/employment:*** Total amount: $136,249 (46% need-based, 54% non-need-based). Part-time jobs available.

APPLYING FOR FINANCIAL AID ***Required financial aid form:*** FAFSA. ***Financial aid deadline (priority):*** 6/1. ***Notification date:*** Continuous. Students must reply within 2 weeks of notification.

CONTACT Ms. Annette Kaus, Director of Financial Aid, New Mexico Institute of Mining and Technology, Financial Aid Office, Socorro, NM 87801, 575-835-5333 or toll-free 800-428-TECH. *Fax:* 575-835-5959. *E-mail:* akaus@admin.nmt.edu.

NEW MEXICO STATE UNIVERSITY

Las Cruces, NM

Tuition & fees (NM res): $4758 Average undergraduate aid package: $7774

ABOUT THE INSTITUTION State-supported, coed. ***Awards:*** associate, bachelor's, master's, and doctoral degrees and post-bachelor's and post-master's certificates. 92 undergraduate majors. ***Total enrollment:*** 17,200. Undergraduates: 13,677. Freshmen: 2,411. Federal methodology is used as a basis for awarding need-based institutional aid.

UNDERGRADUATE EXPENSES for 2008–09 ***Application fee:*** $20. ***Tuition, state resident:*** full-time $3540; part-time $198.25 per credit. ***Tuition, nonresident:*** full-time $13,522; part-time $614.20 per credit. ***Required fees:*** full-time $1218. ***College room and board:*** $5976; ***Room only:*** $3422. Room and board charges vary according to board plan and housing facility. ***Payment plans:*** Installment, deferred payment.

FRESHMAN FINANCIAL AID (Fall 2007) 1,473 applied for aid; of those 81% were deemed to have need. 100% of freshmen with need received aid; of those 1% had need fully met. ***Average percent of need met:*** 41% (excluding resources awarded to replace EFC). ***Average financial aid package:*** $6971 (excluding resources awarded to replace EFC). 8% of all full-time freshmen had no need and received non-need-based gift aid.

UNDERGRADUATE FINANCIAL AID (Fall 2007) 7,481 applied for aid; of those 87% were deemed to have need. 100% of undergraduates with need received aid; of those 1% had need fully met. ***Average percent of need met:*** 46% (excluding resources awarded to replace EFC). ***Average financial aid package:*** $7774 (excluding resources awarded to replace EFC). 4% of all full-time undergraduates had no need and received non-need-based gift aid.

GIFT AID (NEED-BASED) ***Total amount:*** $33,390,221 (58% federal, 27% state, 14% institutional, 1% external sources). ***Receiving aid:*** Freshmen: 33% (710); all full-time undergraduates: 39% (4,458). ***Average award:*** Freshmen: $3306; Undergraduates: $3480. ***Scholarships, grants, and awards:*** Federal Pell, FSEOG, state, private, college/university gift aid from institutional funds.

GIFT AID (NON-NEED-BASED) ***Total amount:*** $10,643,027 (58% state, 40% institutional, 2% external sources). ***Receiving aid:*** Freshmen: 5. Undergraduates: 35. ***Average award:*** Freshmen: $2129. Undergraduates: $1909. ***Scholarships, grants, and awards by category:*** *Academic interests/achievement:* agriculture, biological sciences, business, communication, computer science, education, engineering/technologies, English, foreign languages, general academic interests/achievements, health fields, home economics, humanities, mathematics, military science, physical sciences, social sciences. *Creative arts/performance:* applied art and design, art/fine arts, general creative arts/performance, journalism/publications, music, performing arts, theater/drama. *Special achievements/activities:* leadership, rodeo. *Special characteristics:* adult students, children and siblings of alumni, children of faculty/staff, children of public servants, children of union members/company employees, children of workers in trades, children with a deceased or disabled parent, ethnic background, handicapped students, international students, local/state students, married students, members of minority groups, out-of-state students, previous college experience, spouses of current students, veterans, veterans' children. ***Tuition waivers:*** Full or partial for employees or children of employees, senior citizens. ***ROTC:*** Army, Air Force.

LOANS ***Student loans:*** $54,061,757 (85% need-based, 15% non-need-based). ***Average need-based loan:*** Freshmen: $3299. Undergraduates: $4345. ***Parent loans:*** $1,155,553 (63% need-based, 37% non-need-based). ***Programs:*** FFEL (Subsidized and Unsubsidized Stafford, PLUS), Perkins, state.

WORK-STUDY ***Federal work-study:*** Total amount: $578,305; 427 jobs averaging $2197. ***State or other work-study/employment:*** Total amount: $954,076 (81% need-based, 19% non-need-based). 547 part-time jobs averaging $2507.

ATHLETIC AWARDS Total amount: $1,381,878 (82% need-based, 18% non-need-based).

APPLYING FOR FINANCIAL AID ***Required financial aid forms:*** FAFSA, institution's own form. ***Financial aid deadline (priority):*** 3/1.

CONTACT Ms. Lydia Bruner, Interim Director of Financial Aid, New Mexico State University, Box 30001, Department 5100, Las Cruces, NM 88003-8001, 575-646-4105 or toll-free 800-662-6678. *Fax:* 575-646-7381.

NEW ORLEANS BAPTIST THEOLOGICAL SEMINARY

New Orleans, LA

Tuition & fees: N/R **Average undergraduate aid package: $679**

ABOUT THE INSTITUTION Independent Southern Baptist, coed, primarily men. ***Awards:*** associate, bachelor's, master's, doctoral, and first professional degrees. 4 undergraduate majors. ***Total enrollment:*** 2,036. Undergraduates: 974. Institutional methodology is used as a basis for awarding need-based institutional aid.

FRESHMAN FINANCIAL AID (Fall 2008, est.) 23 applied for aid; of those 100% were deemed to have need. 100% of freshmen with need received aid. ***Average percent of need met:*** 40% (excluding resources awarded to replace EFC). ***Average financial aid package:*** $691 (excluding resources awarded to replace EFC).

UNDERGRADUATE FINANCIAL AID (Fall 2008, est.) 134 applied for aid; of those 100% were deemed to have need. 100% of undergraduates with need received aid. ***Average percent of need met:*** 40% (excluding resources awarded to replace EFC). ***Average financial aid package:*** $679 (excluding resources awarded to replace EFC).

GIFT AID (NEED-BASED) ***Total amount:*** $106,993 (14% state, 85% institutional, 1% external sources). ***Receiving aid:*** Freshmen: 21% (23); all full-time undergraduates: 32% (134). ***Average award:*** Freshmen: $691; Undergraduates: $679. ***Scholarships, grants, and awards:*** state, private, college/university gift aid from institutional funds.

LOANS ***Student loans:*** $73,070 (100% need-based). 22% of past graduating class borrowed through all loan programs. *Average indebtedness per student:* $10,000. ***Programs:*** Signature Loans.

APPLYING FOR FINANCIAL AID ***Required financial aid form:*** institution's own form. ***Financial aid deadline:*** 6/15 (priority: 3/30). ***Notification date:*** 7/31. Students must reply within 4 weeks of notification.

CONTACT Owen Nease, Financial Aid Office, New Orleans Baptist Theological Seminary, 3939 Gentilly Boulevard, New Orleans, LA 70126-4858, 504-282-4455 Ext. 3348 or toll-free 800-662-8701. *Fax:* 504-816-8437. *E-mail:* financialaid@nobts.edu.

NEW SAINT ANDREWS COLLEGE

Moscow, ID

CONTACT Financial Aid Office, New Saint Andrews College, PO Box 9025, Moscow, ID 83843, 208-882-1566.

THE NEW SCHOOL FOR GENERAL STUDIES

New York, NY

CONTACT Financial Aid Counselor, The New School for General Studies, 65 Fifth Avenue, New York, NY 10003, 212-229-8930 or toll-free 800-862-5039 (out-of-state). *Fax:* 212-229-5919.

THE NEW SCHOOL FOR JAZZ AND CONTEMPORARY MUSIC

New York, NY

Tuition & fees: $32,150 **Average undergraduate aid package: $22,532**

ABOUT THE INSTITUTION Independent, coed. ***Awards:*** bachelor's degrees. 9 undergraduate majors. ***Total enrollment:*** 259. Undergraduates: 259. Freshmen: 43. Federal methodology is used as a basis for awarding need-based institutional aid.

UNDERGRADUATE EXPENSES for 2008–09 ***Application fee:*** $100. ***Comprehensive fee:*** $47,410 includes full-time tuition ($31,440), mandatory fees ($710), and room and board ($15,260). ***College room only:*** $12,260. ***Part-time tuition:*** $1030 per credit.

FRESHMAN FINANCIAL AID (Fall 2008, est.) 21 applied for aid; of those 81% were deemed to have need. 100% of freshmen with need received aid; of those 12% had need fully met. ***Average percent of need met:*** 82% (excluding resources awarded to replace EFC). ***Average financial aid package:*** $26,420 (excluding resources awarded to replace EFC). 7% of all full-time freshmen had no need and received non-need-based gift aid.

UNDERGRADUATE FINANCIAL AID (Fall 2008, est.) 111 applied for aid; of those 87% were deemed to have need. 100% of undergraduates with need received aid; of those 8% had need fully met. ***Average percent of need met:*** 71% (excluding resources awarded to replace EFC). ***Average financial aid package:*** $22,532 (excluding resources awarded to replace EFC). 7% of all full-time undergraduates had no need and received non-need-based gift aid.

GIFT AID (NEED-BASED) ***Total amount:*** $1,466,767 (9% federal, 4% state, 59% institutional, 28% external sources). ***Receiving aid:*** Freshmen: 21% (9); all full-time undergraduates: 32% (79). ***Average award:*** Freshmen: $15,577; Undergraduates: $10,956. ***Scholarships, grants, and awards:*** Federal Pell, FSEOG, state, private, college/university gift aid from institutional funds.

GIFT AID (NON-NEED-BASED) ***Total amount:*** $1,219,402 (98% institutional, 2% external sources). ***Receiving aid:*** Freshmen: 5% (2). Undergraduates: 3% (7). ***Average award:*** Freshmen: $10,000. Undergraduates: $10,821.

LOANS ***Student loans:*** $959,126 (75% need-based, 25% non-need-based). 70% of past graduating class borrowed through all loan programs. *Average indebtedness per student:* $20,411. ***Average need-based loan:*** Freshmen: $18,526. Undergraduates: $11,970. ***Parent loans:*** $343,761 (97% need-based, 3% non-need-based). ***Programs:*** FFEL (Subsidized and Unsubsidized Stafford, PLUS), Perkins, college/university.

WORK-STUDY ***Federal work-study:*** Total amount: $33,500; jobs available.

APPLYING FOR FINANCIAL AID ***Required financial aid form:*** FAFSA. ***Financial aid deadline:*** Continuous. ***Notification date:*** Continuous beginning 3/1. Students must reply within 4 weeks of notification.

CONTACT Financial Aid Office, The New School for Jazz and Contemporary Music, 55 West 13th Street, 5th Floor, New York, NY 10011, 212-229-5896.

NEWSCHOOL OF ARCHITECTURE & DESIGN

San Diego, CA

CONTACT Ms. Cara E. Baker, Director of Financial Aid, Newschool of Architecture & Design, 1249 F Street, San Diego, CA 92101-6634, 619-235-4100 Ext. 103. *Fax:* 619-235-4651. *E-mail:* cbaker@newschoolarch.edu.

NEW WORLD SCHOOL OF THE ARTS

Miami, FL

CONTACT Financial Aid Office, New World School of the Arts, 300 NE 2nd Avenue, Miami, FL 33132, 305-237-3135.

NEW YORK CITY COLLEGE OF TECHNOLOGY OF THE CITY UNIVERSITY OF NEW YORK

Brooklyn, NY

Tuition & fees (NY res): $4339 **Average undergraduate aid package: $6596**

ABOUT THE INSTITUTION State and locally supported, coed. ***Awards:*** associate and bachelor's degrees. 38 undergraduate majors. ***Total enrollment:*** 14,268. Undergraduates: 14,268. Freshmen: 3,158. Both federal and institutional methodology are used as a basis for awarding need-based institutional aid.

UNDERGRADUATE EXPENSES for 2008–09 ***Application fee:*** $65. ***Tuition, state resident:*** full-time $4000; part-time $170 per credit. ***Tuition, nonresident:*** full-time $10,800; part-time $360 per credit. ***Required fees:*** full-time $339; $82.50 per term. ***Payment plan:*** Deferred payment.

FRESHMAN FINANCIAL AID (Fall 2008, est.) 2,530 applied for aid; of those 89% were deemed to have need. 97% of freshmen with need received aid; of those 5% had need fully met. ***Average percent of need met:*** 59% (excluding resources awarded to replace EFC). ***Average financial aid package:*** $6582 (excluding resources awarded to replace EFC). 2% of all full-time freshmen had no need and received non-need-based gift aid.

UNDERGRADUATE FINANCIAL AID (Fall 2008, est.) 6,895 applied for aid; of those 92% were deemed to have need. 96% of undergraduates with need received aid; of those 4% had need fully met. ***Average percent of need met:*** 55% (excluding resources awarded to replace EFC). ***Average financial aid package:*** $6596 (excluding resources awarded to replace EFC). 1% of all full-time undergraduates had no need and received non-need-based gift aid.

GIFT AID (NEED-BASED) ***Total amount:*** $43,645,900 (56% federal, 43% state, 1% external sources). ***Receiving aid:*** Freshmen: 76% (2,156); all full-time undergraduates: 73% (5,993). ***Average award:*** Freshmen: $6442; Undergraduates: $6128. ***Scholarships, grants, and awards:*** Federal Pell, FSEOG, state, private, college/university gift aid from institutional funds, Federal Nursing.

GIFT AID (NON-NEED-BASED) ***Total amount:*** $107,288 (18% federal, 43% state, 39% external sources). ***Receiving aid:*** Freshmen: 12% (346). Undergraduates: 6% (474). ***Average award:*** Freshmen: $536. Undergraduates: $525. ***Scholarships, grants, and awards by category:*** *Academic interests/achievement:* general academic interests/achievements. *Creative arts/performance:* art/fine arts, music. *Special characteristics:* local/state students, members of minority groups. ***Tuition waivers:*** Full or partial for employees or children of employees. ***ROTC:*** Air Force cooperative.

LOANS ***Student loans:*** $4,543,517 (100% need-based). ***Average need-based loan:*** Freshmen: $564. Undergraduates: $1232. ***Programs:*** Federal Direct (Subsidized and Unsubsidized Stafford, PLUS), Perkins, Federal Nursing.

WORK-STUDY ***Federal work-study:*** Total amount: $2,480,437; jobs available.

APPLYING FOR FINANCIAL AID ***Required financial aid form:*** FAFSA. ***Financial aid deadline:*** 4/30 (priority: 1/1). ***Notification date:*** Continuous beginning 3/1.

CONTACT Sandra Higgins, Director of Financial Aid, New York City College of Technology of the City University of New York, 300 Jay Street, Namm Hall Room G-13, Brooklyn, NY 11201, 718-260-5700. *Fax:* 718-254-8525. *E-mail:* shiggins@citytech.cuny.edu.

NEW YORK INSTITUTE OF TECHNOLOGY

Old Westbury, NY

ABOUT THE INSTITUTION Independent, coed. ***Awards:*** associate, bachelor's, master's, doctoral, and first professional degrees and post-bachelor's and post-master's certificates. 62 undergraduate majors. ***Total enrollment:*** 11,505. Undergraduates: 7,254. Freshmen: 1,282.

GIFT AID (NEED-BASED) ***Scholarships, grants, and awards:*** Federal Pell, FSEOG, state, private, college/university gift aid from institutional funds.

GIFT AID (NON-NEED-BASED) ***Scholarships, grants, and awards by category:*** *Academic interests/achievement:* general academic interests/achievements. *Special characteristics:* children and siblings of alumni, children of educators, children of faculty/staff, children of public servants, local/state students, previous college experience, public servants, spouses of deceased or disabled public servants, veterans.

LOANS ***Programs:*** FFEL (Subsidized and Unsubsidized Stafford, PLUS), Perkins, Federal Nursing, alternative loans.

APPLYING FOR FINANCIAL AID ***Required financial aid form:*** FAFSA.

CONTACT Doreen Meyer, Director of Financial Aid Office, New York Institute of Technology, PO Box 8000, Old Westbury, NY 11568-8000, 516-686-1083 or toll-free 800-345-NYIT. *Fax:* 516-686-7997. *E-mail:* dmeyer@nyit.edu.

NEW YORK SCHOOL OF INTERIOR DESIGN

New York, NY

CONTACT Nina Bunchuk, Director of Financial Aid, New York School of Interior Design, 170 East 70th Street, New York, NY 10021-5110, 212-472-1500 Ext. 212 or toll-free 800-336-9743 Ext. 204. *Fax:* 212-472-1867. *E-mail:* nina@nysid.edu.

NEW YORK UNIVERSITY

New York, NY

Tuition & fees: $37,372 **Average undergraduate aid package: $24,507**

ABOUT THE INSTITUTION Independent, coed. ***Awards:*** associate, bachelor's, master's, doctoral, and first professional degrees and post-bachelor's, post-master's, and first professional certificates. 116 undergraduate majors. ***Total enrollment:*** 42,189. Undergraduates: 21,269. Freshmen: 4,496. Federal methodology is used as a basis for awarding need-based institutional aid.

UNDERGRADUATE EXPENSES for 2008–09 ***Application fee:*** $65. ***Comprehensive fee:*** $50,282 includes full-time tuition ($35,230), mandatory fees ($2142), and room and board ($12,910). Full-time tuition and fees vary according to course load and program. Room and board charges vary according to board plan and housing facility. ***Part-time tuition:*** $1038 per credit. ***Part-time fees:*** $58 per credit; $395 per term. Part-time tuition and fees vary according to program. ***Payment plans:*** Installment, deferred payment.

FRESHMAN FINANCIAL AID (Fall 2008, est.) 2,975 applied for aid; of those 80% were deemed to have need. 100% of freshmen with need received aid. ***Average percent of need met:*** 72% (excluding resources awarded to replace EFC). ***Average financial aid package:*** $26,823 (excluding resources awarded to replace EFC). 5% of all full-time freshmen had no need and received non-need-based gift aid.

UNDERGRADUATE FINANCIAL AID (Fall 2008, est.) 11,596 applied for aid; of those 86% were deemed to have need. 99% of undergraduates with need received aid. ***Average percent of need met:*** 66% (excluding resources awarded to replace EFC). ***Average financial aid package:*** $24,507 (excluding resources awarded to replace EFC). 8% of all full-time undergraduates had no need and received non-need-based gift aid.

GIFT AID (NEED-BASED) ***Total amount:*** $164,141,890 (12% federal, 6% state, 78% institutional, 4% external sources). ***Receiving aid:*** Freshmen: 51% (2,292); all full-time undergraduates: 48% (9,435). ***Average award:*** Freshmen: $19,391; Undergraduates: $17,404. ***Scholarships, grants, and awards:*** Federal Pell, FSEOG, state, private, college/university gift aid from institutional funds.

GIFT AID (NON-NEED-BASED) ***Total amount:*** $16,935,277 (78% institutional, 22% external sources). ***Average award:*** Freshmen: $6920. Undergraduates: $8338. ***Scholarships, grants, and awards by category:*** *Academic interests/achievement:* 1,583 awards ($13,198,740 total): general academic interests/achievements. ***Tuition waivers:*** Full or partial for employees or children of employees. ***ROTC:*** Army cooperative, Naval cooperative.

LOANS ***Student loans:*** $126,970,705 (86% need-based, 14% non-need-based). 58% of past graduating class borrowed through all loan programs. *Average indebtedness per student:* $34,850. ***Average need-based loan:*** Freshmen: $4946. Undergraduates: $5338. ***Parent loans:*** $78,423,222 (80% need-based, 20% non-need-based). ***Programs:*** Federal Direct (Subsidized and Unsubsidized Stafford, PLUS), FFEL (Subsidized and Unsubsidized Stafford, PLUS), Perkins, Federal Nursing.

WORK-STUDY ***Federal work-study:*** Total amount: $5,509,692; 2,574 jobs averaging $1609.

APPLYING FOR FINANCIAL AID ***Required financial aid forms:*** FAFSA, state aid form. ***Financial aid deadline (priority):*** 2/15. ***Notification date:*** 4/1. Students must reply by 5/1.

CONTACT Financial Aid Office, New York University, 25 West Fourth Street, New York, NY 10012-1199, 212-998-4444. *Fax:* 212-995-4661. *E-mail:* financial.aid@nyu.edu.

NIAGARA UNIVERSITY

Niagara Falls, NY

Tuition & fees: $24,700 **Average undergraduate aid package: $19,073**

ABOUT THE INSTITUTION Independent religious, coed. ***Awards:*** associate, bachelor's, and master's degrees and post-bachelor's and post-master's certificates. 59 undergraduate majors. ***Total enrollment:*** 4,255. Undergraduates: 3,326. Freshmen: 742. Federal methodology is used as a basis for awarding need-based institutional aid.

UNDERGRADUATE EXPENSES for 2009–10 ***Application fee:*** $30. ***Comprehensive fee:*** $34,950 includes full-time tuition ($23,700), mandatory fees ($1000), and room and board ($10,250). ***Part-time tuition:*** $790 per credit.

FRESHMAN FINANCIAL AID (Fall 2008, est.) 735 applied for aid; of those 96% were deemed to have need. 100% of freshmen with need received aid; of those 54% had need fully met. ***Average percent of need met:*** 79% (excluding resources awarded to replace EFC). ***Average financial aid package:*** $19,624 (excluding resources awarded to replace EFC). 5% of all full-time freshmen had no need and received non-need-based gift aid.

UNDERGRADUATE FINANCIAL AID (Fall 2008, est.) 2,688 applied for aid; of those 82% were deemed to have need. 99% of undergraduates with need received aid; of those 38% had need fully met. ***Average percent of need met:*** 77% (excluding resources awarded to replace EFC). ***Average financial aid package:*** $19,073 (excluding resources awarded to replace EFC). 19% of all full-time undergraduates had no need and received non-need-based gift aid.

GIFT AID (NEED-BASED) ***Total amount:*** $31,215,249 (12% federal, 12% state, 74% institutional, 2% external sources). ***Receiving aid:*** Freshmen: 93% (685); all full-time undergraduates: 71% (2,151). ***Average award:*** Freshmen: $15,327; Undergraduates: $14,301. ***Scholarships, grants, and awards:*** Federal Pell, FSEOG, state, private, college/university gift aid from institutional funds.

GIFT AID (NON-NEED-BASED) ***Total amount:*** $5,778,831 (5% federal, 1% state, 93% institutional, 1% external sources). ***Receiving aid:*** Freshmen: 25% (186). Undergraduates: 23% (702). ***Average award:*** Freshmen: $9179. Undergraduates: $9142. ***Scholarships, grants, and awards by category:*** *Academic interests/achievement:* 2,660 awards ($21,976,449 total): general academic interests/achievements. *Creative arts/performance:* 45 awards ($185,327 total): theater/drama. *Special achievements/activities:* 10 awards ($19,000 total): community service. *Special characteristics:* 84 awards ($1,674,103 total): children of faculty/staff, relatives of clergy. ***ROTC:*** Army.

LOANS ***Student loans:*** $24,077,586 (93% need-based, 7% non-need-based). 73% of past graduating class borrowed through all loan programs. *Average indebtedness per student:* $29,018. ***Average need-based loan:*** Freshmen: $4619. Undergraduates: $4765. ***Parent loans:*** $3,994,900 (80% need-based, 20% non-need-based). ***Programs:*** FFEL (Subsidized and Unsubsidized Stafford, PLUS), Perkins, Federal Nursing, college/university.

WORK-STUDY ***Federal work-study:*** Total amount: $1,380,129; 415 jobs averaging $2985. ***State or other work-study/employment:*** Total amount: $265,499 (100% non-need-based). 44 part-time jobs averaging $4356.

ATHLETIC AWARDS Total amount: $3,615,205 (34% need-based, 66% non-need-based).

APPLYING FOR FINANCIAL AID ***Required financial aid forms:*** FAFSA, state aid form. ***Financial aid deadline (priority):*** 2/15. ***Notification date:*** Continuous beginning 3/15. Students must reply within 3 weeks of notification.

CONTACT Mrs. Maureen E. Salfi, Director of Financial Aid, Niagara University, Financial Aid Office, Niagara University, NY 14109, 716-286-8686 or toll-free 800-462-2111. *Fax:* 716-286-8678. *E-mail:* finaid@niagara.edu.

NICHOLLS STATE UNIVERSITY

Thibodaux, LA

Tuition & fees (LA res): $3710 **Average undergraduate aid package: $6892**

ABOUT THE INSTITUTION State-supported, coed. ***Awards:*** associate, bachelor's, and master's degrees and post-master's certificates. 45 undergraduate majors. ***Total enrollment:*** 6,920. Undergraduates: 6,299. Freshmen: 1,263. Federal methodology is used as a basis for awarding need-based institutional aid.

UNDERGRADUATE EXPENSES for 2008–09 ***Application fee:*** $20. ***Tuition, state resident:*** full-time $3710. ***Tuition, nonresident:*** full-time $9158. Part-time tuition and fees vary according to course load. ***College room and board:*** $5098. Room and board charges vary according to board plan and housing facility. ***Payment plans:*** Installment, deferred payment.

FRESHMAN FINANCIAL AID (Fall 2007) 1,068 applied for aid; of those 51% were deemed to have need. 98% of freshmen with need received aid; of those 82% had need fully met. ***Average percent of need met:*** 94% (excluding resources awarded to replace EFC). ***Average financial aid package:*** $7178 (excluding resources awarded to replace EFC). 6% of all full-time freshmen had no need and received non-need-based gift aid.

UNDERGRADUATE FINANCIAL AID (Fall 2007) 4,057 applied for aid; of those 58% were deemed to have need. 98% of undergraduates with need received aid; of those 71% had need fully met. ***Average percent of need met:*** 89% (excluding resources awarded to replace EFC). ***Average financial aid package:*** $6892 (excluding resources awarded to replace EFC). 5% of all full-time undergraduates had no need and received non-need-based gift aid.

GIFT AID (NEED-BASED) ***Total amount:*** $7,909,780 (78% federal, 18% state, 3% institutional, 1% external sources). ***Receiving aid:*** Freshmen: 44% (508); all full-time undergraduates: 42% (2,037). ***Average award:*** Freshmen: $4060; Undergraduates: $3823. ***Scholarships, grants, and awards:*** Federal Pell, FSEOG, state, private, college/university gift aid from institutional funds.

GIFT AID (NON-NEED-BASED) ***Total amount:*** $5,654,955 (80% state, 11% institutional, 9% external sources). ***Receiving aid:*** Freshmen: 32% (370). Undergraduates: 16% (761). ***Average award:*** Freshmen: $1906. Undergraduates: $2065. ***Scholarships, grants, and awards by category:*** *Academic interests/achievement:* 184 awards ($527,294 total): general academic interests/achievements. *Creative arts/performance:* 165 awards ($116,695 total): dance, music. *Special achievements/activities:* 18 awards ($20,390 total): cheerleading/drum major. *Special characteristics:* 188 awards ($539,688 total): children of faculty/staff, general special characteristics, members of minority groups, out-of-state students, previous college experience, public servants, veterans. ***Tuition waivers:*** Full or partial for employees or children of employees.

LOANS ***Student loans:*** $12,847,129 (35% need-based, 65% non-need-based). 58% of past graduating class borrowed through all loan programs. *Average indebtedness per student:* $17,229. ***Average need-based loan:*** Freshmen: $2598. Undergraduates: $3572. ***Parent loans:*** $332,637 (4% need-based, 96% non-need-based). ***Programs:*** FFEL (Subsidized and Unsubsidized Stafford, PLUS), Perkins.

WORK-STUDY ***Federal work-study:*** Total amount: $204,618; 162 jobs averaging $1263. ***State or other work-study/employment:*** Total amount: $1,169,221 (3% need-based, 97% non-need-based). 628 part-time jobs averaging $1863.

ATHLETIC AWARDS Total amount: $1,132,709 (26% need-based, 74% non-need-based).

APPLYING FOR FINANCIAL AID ***Required financial aid forms:*** FAFSA, institution's own form, state aid form. ***Financial aid deadline:*** 6/30 (priority: 4/15). ***Notification date:*** Continuous. Students must reply within 2 weeks of notification.

CONTACT Casie Triche, Acting Director for the Office of Financial Aid, Nicholls State University, PO Box 2005, Thibodaux, LA 70310, 985-448-4048 or toll-free 877-NICHOLLS. *Fax:* 985-448-4124. *E-mail:* casie.triche@nicholls.edu.

NICHOLS COLLEGE

Dudley, MA

Tuition & fees: $26,970 **Average undergraduate aid package: $19,549**

ABOUT THE INSTITUTION Independent, coed. ***Awards:*** associate, bachelor's, and master's degrees. 14 undergraduate majors. ***Total enrollment:*** 1,532. Undergraduates: 1,308. Freshmen: 391. Federal methodology is used as a basis for awarding need-based institutional aid.

UNDERGRADUATE EXPENSES for 2008–09 ***Application fee:*** $25. ***Comprehensive fee:*** $36,070 includes full-time tuition ($26,670), mandatory fees ($300), and room and board ($9100). ***College room only:*** $4800. ***Part-time tuition:*** $265 per credit hour. Part-time tuition and fees vary according to class time and course load. ***Payment plan:*** Installment.

FRESHMAN FINANCIAL AID (Fall 2008, est.) 371 applied for aid; of those 99% were deemed to have need. 100% of freshmen with need received aid; of those 10% had need fully met. ***Average percent of need met:*** 76% (excluding resources awarded to replace EFC). ***Average financial aid package:*** $20,067 (excluding resources awarded to replace EFC). 6% of all full-time freshmen had no need and received non-need-based gift aid.

UNDERGRADUATE FINANCIAL AID (Fall 2008, est.) 959 applied for aid; of those 90% were deemed to have need. 100% of undergraduates with need received aid; of those 10% had need fully met. ***Average percent of need met:*** 75% (excluding resources awarded to replace EFC). ***Average financial aid package:*** $19,549 (excluding resources awarded to replace EFC). 15% of all full-time undergraduates had no need and received non-need-based gift aid.

GIFT AID (NEED-BASED) ***Total amount:*** $11,281,387 (9% federal, 4% state, 86% institutional, 1% external sources). ***Receiving aid:*** Freshmen: 94% (366); all full-time undergraduates: 69% (740). ***Average award:*** Freshmen: $14,123; Undergraduates: $13,102. ***Scholarships, grants, and awards:*** Federal Pell, FSEOG, state, private, college/university gift aid from institutional funds.

GIFT AID (NON-NEED-BASED) ***Total amount:*** $1,485,380 (100% institutional). ***Receiving aid:*** Freshmen: 9% (35). Undergraduates: 80% (857). ***Average award:*** Freshmen: $9571. Undergraduates: $9283. ***Scholarships, grants, and awards by category:*** *Academic interests/achievement:* 689 awards ($5,539,600 total): general academic interests/achievements. *Special achievements/activities:* 7 awards ($16,200 total): community service, general special achievements/activities, leadership. *Special characteristics:* 62 awards ($421,300 total): children and siblings of alumni, children of faculty/staff, siblings of current students. ***Tuition waivers:*** Full or partial for employees or children of employees, senior citizens. ***ROTC:*** Army cooperative.

LOANS ***Student loans:*** $8,867,579 (97% need-based, 3% non-need-based). 89% of past graduating class borrowed through all loan programs. *Average indebtedness per student:* $28,091. ***Average need-based loan:*** Freshmen: $3668. Undergraduates: $4171. ***Parent loans:*** $3,545,503 (100% need-based). ***Programs:*** FFEL (Subsidized and Unsubsidized Stafford, PLUS), state.

WORK-STUDY ***Federal work-study:*** Total amount: $653,078; 284 jobs averaging $1962.

APPLYING FOR FINANCIAL AID ***Required financial aid form:*** FAFSA. ***Financial aid deadline (priority):*** 3/1. ***Notification date:*** Continuous. Students must reply within 2 weeks of notification.

CONTACT Ms. Denise Brindle, Director of Financial Aid, Nichols College, PO Box 5000, Dudley, MA 01571, 508-213-2372 or toll-free 800-470-3379. *Fax:* 508-213-2118. *E-mail:* denise.brindle@nichols.edu.

NORFOLK STATE UNIVERSITY

Norfolk, VA

CONTACT Mrs. Estherine Harding, Director of Financial Aid, Norfolk State University, 700 Park Avenue, Norfolk, VA 23504-3907, 757-823-8381. *Fax:* 757-823-9059. *E-mail:* ejharding@nsu.edu.

NORTH CAROLINA AGRICULTURAL AND TECHNICAL STATE UNIVERSITY

Greensboro, NC

Tuition & fees (NC res): $3583 **Average undergraduate aid package: $6361**

ABOUT THE INSTITUTION State-supported, coed. ***Awards:*** bachelor's, master's, and doctoral degrees. 59 undergraduate majors. ***Total enrollment:*** 11,098. Undergraduates: 9,687. Freshmen: 2,094. Federal methodology is used as a basis for awarding need-based institutional aid.

UNDERGRADUATE EXPENSES for 2008–09 ***Application fee:*** $45. ***Tuition, state resident:*** full-time $1994. ***Tuition, nonresident:*** full-time $11,436. ***Required fees:*** full-time $1589. Full-time tuition and fees vary according to student level. Part-time tuition and fees vary according to student level. ***College room and board:*** $5459; ***Room only:*** $3159. Room and board charges vary according to board plan and housing facility. ***Payment plan:*** Installment.

FRESHMAN FINANCIAL AID (Fall 2007) 98% of freshmen with need received aid; of those 4% had need fully met. ***Average percent of need met:*** 52% (excluding resources awarded to replace EFC). ***Average financial aid package:*** $6272 (excluding resources awarded to replace EFC). 2% of all full-time freshmen had no need and received non-need-based gift aid.

UNDERGRADUATE FINANCIAL AID (Fall 2007) 97% of undergraduates with need received aid; of those 8% had need fully met. ***Average percent of need met:*** 52% (excluding resources awarded to replace EFC). ***Average financial aid package:*** $6361 (excluding resources awarded to replace EFC). 2% of all full-time undergraduates had no need and received non-need-based gift aid.

GIFT AID (NEED-BASED) ***Total amount:*** $8,578,705 (56% federal, 44% state). ***Receiving aid:*** Freshmen: 61% (1,771); all full-time undergraduates: 53% (5,054). ***Average award:*** Freshmen: $4805; Undergraduates: $4584. ***Scholarships, grants, and awards:*** Federal Pell, FSEOG, state, private, college/university gift aid from institutional funds, United Negro College Fund.

GIFT AID (NON-NEED-BASED) ***Total amount:*** $7,198,309 (10% federal, 6% state, 22% institutional, 62% external sources). ***Receiving aid:*** Freshmen: 53% (1,508). Undergraduates: 35% (3,297). ***Average award:*** Freshmen: $6390. Undergraduates: $4854. ***Scholarships, grants, and awards by category:*** *Academic interests/achievement:* military science. *Creative arts/performance:* music, theater/drama. *Special characteristics:* ethnic background, handicapped students, members of minority groups. ***Tuition waivers:*** Full or partial for employees or children of employees, senior citizens. ***ROTC:*** Army, Air Force.

LOANS ***Student loans:*** $8,900,684 (100% need-based). 84% of past graduating class borrowed through all loan programs. *Average indebtedness per student:* $17,605. ***Average need-based loan:*** Freshmen: $3180. Undergraduates: $5866. ***Parent loans:*** $4,281,636 (100% non-need-based). ***Programs:*** Federal Direct (Subsidized and Unsubsidized Stafford, PLUS), Perkins, state.

WORK-STUDY ***Federal work-study:*** Total amount: $268,059; jobs available. ***State or other work-study/employment:*** Part-time jobs available.

ATHLETIC AWARDS Total amount: $508,890 (100% non-need-based).

APPLYING FOR FINANCIAL AID ***Required financial aid form:*** FAFSA. ***Financial aid deadline (priority):*** 3/15. ***Notification date:*** 4/15.

CONTACT Mrs. Sherri Avent, Director of Student Financial Aid, North Carolina Agricultural and Technical State University, 1601 East Market Street, Dowdy Administration Building, Greensboro, NC 27411, 336-334-7973 or toll-free 800-443-8964 (in-state). *Fax:* 336-334-7954.

NORTH CAROLINA CENTRAL UNIVERSITY

Durham, NC

CONTACT Sharon J. Oliver, Director of Scholarships and Student Aid, North Carolina Central University, 106 Student Services Building, Durham, NC 27707-3129, 919-530-7412 or toll-free 877-667-7533.

NORTH CAROLINA SCHOOL OF THE ARTS

Winston-Salem, NC

ABOUT THE INSTITUTION State-supported, coed. ***Awards:*** bachelor's and master's degrees and post-master's certificates. 9 undergraduate majors. ***Total enrollment:*** 879. Undergraduates: 765. Freshmen: 182.

GIFT AID (NEED-BASED) ***Scholarships, grants, and awards:*** Federal Pell, FSEOG, state, private, college/university gift aid from institutional funds.

GIFT AID (NON-NEED-BASED) ***Scholarships, grants, and awards by category:*** *Creative arts/performance:* applied art and design, cinema/film/broadcasting, dance, music, performing arts, theater/drama.

LOANS ***Programs:*** Federal Direct (Subsidized and Unsubsidized Stafford, PLUS), FFEL (Subsidized and Unsubsidized Stafford, PLUS), Perkins.

APPLYING FOR FINANCIAL AID ***Required financial aid form:*** FAFSA.

CONTACT Jane C. Kamiab, Director of Financial Aid, North Carolina School of the Arts, 1533 South Main Street, Winston-Salem, NC 27127, 336-770-3297. *Fax:* 336-770-1489.

NORTH CAROLINA STATE UNIVERSITY

Raleigh, NC

Tuition & fees (NC res): $5274 **Average undergraduate aid package: $10,052**

ABOUT THE INSTITUTION State-supported, coed. ***Awards:*** associate, bachelor's, master's, doctoral, and first professional degrees and post-bachelor's and first professional certificates. 109 undergraduate majors. ***Total enrollment:*** 32,872. Undergraduates: 24,741. Freshmen: 4,804. Federal methodology is used as a basis for awarding need-based institutional aid.

UNDERGRADUATE EXPENSES for 2008–09 ***Application fee:*** $70. ***Tuition, state resident:*** full-time $3860. ***Tuition, nonresident:*** full-time $16,158. ***Required fees:*** full-time $1414. Full-time tuition and fees vary according to program. Part-time tuition and fees vary according to course load and program. ***College room and board:*** $7982; ***Room only:*** $4924. Room and board charges vary according to board plan and housing facility. ***Payment plan:*** Installment.

FRESHMAN FINANCIAL AID (Fall 2008, est.) 3,364 applied for aid; of those 61% were deemed to have need. 99% of freshmen with need received aid; of those 59% had need fully met. ***Average percent of need met:*** 90% (excluding resources awarded to replace EFC). ***Average financial aid package:*** $10,401 (excluding resources awarded to replace EFC). 4% of all full-time freshmen had no need and received non-need-based gift aid.

UNDERGRADUATE FINANCIAL AID (Fall 2008, est.) 12,405 applied for aid; of those 69% were deemed to have need. 99% of undergraduates with need received aid; of those 54% had need fully met. ***Average percent of need met:*** 86% (excluding resources awarded to replace EFC). ***Average financial aid package:*** $10,052 (excluding resources awarded to replace EFC). 5% of all full-time undergraduates had no need and received non-need-based gift aid.

GIFT AID (NEED-BASED) ***Total amount:*** $66,400,114 (24% federal, 31% state, 40% institutional, 5% external sources). ***Receiving aid:*** Freshmen: 41% (1,991); all full-time undergraduates: 39% (8,076). ***Average award:*** Freshmen: $9282; Undergraduates: $8363. ***Scholarships, grants, and awards:*** Federal Pell, FSEOG, state, private, college/university gift aid from institutional funds.

GIFT AID (NON-NEED-BASED) ***Total amount:*** $13,438,523 (12% federal, 12% state, 47% institutional, 29% external sources). ***Receiving aid:*** Freshmen: 7% (341). Undergraduates: 4% (896). ***Average award:*** Freshmen: $5946. Undergraduates: $5315. ***Scholarships, grants, and awards by category:*** *Academic interests/achievement:* agriculture, biological sciences, business, education, engineering/technologies, general academic interests/achievements, humanities, mathematics, physical sciences, social sciences. *Creative arts/performance:* music. *Special achievements/activities:* leadership. ***Tuition waivers:*** Full or partial for employees or children of employees, senior citizens. ***ROTC:*** Army, Naval, Air Force.

LOANS ***Student loans:*** $57,723,444 (36% need-based, 64% non-need-based). 49% of past graduating class borrowed through all loan programs. *Average indebtedness per student:* $14,996. ***Average need-based loan:*** Freshmen: $2427.

Undergraduates: $2871. ***Parent loans:*** $11,003,417 (6% need-based, 94% non-need-based). ***Programs:*** Federal Direct (Subsidized and Unsubsidized Stafford, PLUS), FFEL (Subsidized and Unsubsidized Stafford, PLUS), Perkins, state, college/university.

WORK-STUDY ***Federal work-study:*** Total amount: $878,257; 624 jobs averaging $1478. ***State or other work-study/employment:*** Total amount: $1,499,491 (32% need-based, 68% non-need-based). 209 part-time jobs averaging $7341.

ATHLETIC AWARDS Total amount: $4,564,492 (30% need-based, 70% non-need-based).

APPLYING FOR FINANCIAL AID ***Required financial aid forms:*** FAFSA, institution's own form. ***Financial aid deadline (priority):*** 3/1. ***Notification date:*** Continuous beginning 4/1.

CONTACT Ms. Julia Rice Mallette, Director of Scholarships and Financial Aid, North Carolina State University, 2016 Harris Hall, Box 7302, Raleigh, NC 27695-7302, 919-515-2334. *Fax:* 919-515-8422. *E-mail:* julie_mallette@ncsu.edu.

NORTH CAROLINA WESLEYAN COLLEGE

Rocky Mount, NC

Tuition & fees: $20,790 **Average undergraduate aid package: $12,524**

ABOUT THE INSTITUTION Independent religious, coed. ***Awards:*** bachelor's degrees (also offers adult part-time degree program with significant enrollment not reflected in profile). 26 undergraduate majors. ***Total enrollment:*** 1,510. Undergraduates: 1,510. Freshmen: 221. Federal methodology is used as a basis for awarding need-based institutional aid.

UNDERGRADUATE EXPENSES for 2008–09 ***Application fee:*** $25. ***Comprehensive fee:*** $28,170 includes full-time tuition ($20,790) and room and board ($7380). ***College room only:*** $3570. Full-time tuition and fees vary according to location. Room and board charges vary according to housing facility. Part-time tuition and fees vary according to location. ***Payment plan:*** Installment.

FRESHMAN FINANCIAL AID (Fall 2008, est.) 229 applied for aid; of those 86% were deemed to have need. 100% of freshmen with need received aid; of those 98% had need fully met. ***Average percent of need met:*** 75% (excluding resources awarded to replace EFC). ***Average financial aid package:*** $13,622 (excluding resources awarded to replace EFC). 8% of all full-time freshmen had no need and received non-need-based gift aid.

UNDERGRADUATE FINANCIAL AID (Fall 2008, est.) 956 applied for aid; of those 82% were deemed to have need. 100% of undergraduates with need received aid; of those 46% had need fully met. ***Average percent of need met:*** 70% (excluding resources awarded to replace EFC). ***Average financial aid package:*** $12,524 (excluding resources awarded to replace EFC). 4% of all full-time undergraduates had no need and received non-need-based gift aid.

GIFT AID (NEED-BASED) ***Total amount:*** $12,680,362 (26% federal, 28% state, 45% institutional, 1% external sources). ***Receiving aid:*** Freshmen: 79% (196); all full-time undergraduates: 74% (788). ***Average award:*** Freshmen: $10,855; Undergraduates: $6696. ***Scholarships, grants, and awards:*** Federal Pell, FSEOG, state, private, college/university gift aid from institutional funds.

GIFT AID (NON-NEED-BASED) ***Total amount:*** $465,396 (92% institutional, 8% external sources). ***Receiving aid:*** Freshmen: 39% (96). Undergraduates: 31% (329). ***Average award:*** Freshmen: $5724. Undergraduates: $7876. ***Tuition waivers:*** Full or partial for employees or children of employees.

LOANS ***Student loans:*** $9,166,643 (43% need-based, 57% non-need-based). 93% of past graduating class borrowed through all loan programs. *Average indebtedness per student:* $7269. ***Average need-based loan:*** Freshmen: $3022. Undergraduates: $3898. ***Parent loans:*** $1,314,552 (16% need-based, 84% non-need-based). ***Programs:*** FFEL (Subsidized and Unsubsidized Stafford, PLUS), Perkins, alternative loans.

WORK-STUDY ***Federal work-study:*** Total amount: $464,359; 323 jobs averaging $1438. ***State or other work-study/employment:*** Total amount: $145,337 (100% need-based). 67 part-time jobs averaging $565.

APPLYING FOR FINANCIAL AID ***Required financial aid form:*** FAFSA. ***Financial aid deadline (priority):*** 4/15. ***Notification date:*** Continuous. Students must reply within 2 weeks of notification.

CONTACT Deana M. Summerlin, Director of Financial Aid, North Carolina Wesleyan College, 3400 North Wesleyan Boulevard, Rocky Mount, NC 27804, 252-985-5200 or toll-free 800-488-6292. *Fax:* 252-985-5295. *E-mail:* finaid@ncwc.edu.

NORTH CENTRAL COLLEGE

Naperville, IL

Tuition & fees: $25,938 **Average undergraduate aid package: $18,739**

ABOUT THE INSTITUTION Independent United Methodist, coed. ***Awards:*** bachelor's and master's degrees and post-bachelor's certificates. 60 undergraduate majors. ***Total enrollment:*** 2,726. Undergraduates: 2,388. Freshmen: 528. Federal methodology is used as a basis for awarding need-based institutional aid.

UNDERGRADUATE EXPENSES for 2008–09 ***Application fee:*** $25. ***Comprehensive fee:*** $34,155 includes full-time tuition ($25,698), mandatory fees ($240), and room and board ($8217). Room and board charges vary according to housing facility. ***Part-time tuition:*** $645 per term. ***Part-time fees:*** $20 per term. Part-time tuition and fees vary according to course load. ***Payment plan:*** Installment.

FRESHMAN FINANCIAL AID (Fall 2008, est.) 461 applied for aid; of those 86% were deemed to have need. 99% of freshmen with need received aid; of those 29% had need fully met. ***Average percent of need met:*** 82% (excluding resources awarded to replace EFC). ***Average financial aid package:*** $19,889 (excluding resources awarded to replace EFC). 22% of all full-time freshmen had no need and received non-need-based gift aid.

UNDERGRADUATE FINANCIAL AID (Fall 2008, est.) 1,755 applied for aid; of those 88% were deemed to have need. 99% of undergraduates with need received aid; of those 24% had need fully met. ***Average percent of need met:*** 75% (excluding resources awarded to replace EFC). ***Average financial aid package:*** $18,739 (excluding resources awarded to replace EFC). 23% of all full-time undergraduates had no need and received non-need-based gift aid.

GIFT AID (NEED-BASED) ***Total amount:*** $21,431,346 (8% federal, 14% state, 77% institutional, 1% external sources). ***Receiving aid:*** Freshmen: 75% (393); all full-time undergraduates: 69% (1,495). ***Average award:*** Freshmen: $15,924; Undergraduates: $14,129. ***Scholarships, grants, and awards:*** Federal Pell, FSEOG, state, private, college/university gift aid from institutional funds.

GIFT AID (NON-NEED-BASED) ***Total amount:*** $6,101,087 (98% institutional, 2% external sources). ***Receiving aid:*** Freshmen: 13% (67). Undergraduates: 8% (166). ***Average award:*** Freshmen: $10,873. Undergraduates: $9894. ***Scholarships, grants, and awards by category:*** *Academic interests/achievement:* biological sciences, business, communication, computer science, education, English, foreign languages, general academic interests/achievements, humanities, international studies, mathematics, physical sciences, premedicine, religion/biblical studies, social sciences. *Creative arts/performance:* art/fine arts, cinema/film/broadcasting, debating, journalism/publications, music, theater/drama. *Special achievements/activities:* community service, religious involvement. *Special characteristics:* adult students, children of faculty/staff, general special characteristics, international students, relatives of clergy. ***Tuition waivers:*** Full or partial for employees or children of employees, senior citizens. ***ROTC:*** Army cooperative, Air Force cooperative.

LOANS ***Student loans:*** $13,458,693 (65% need-based, 35% non-need-based). 76% of past graduating class borrowed through all loan programs. *Average indebtedness per student:* $26,395. ***Average need-based loan:*** Freshmen: $3306. Undergraduates: $4384. ***Parent loans:*** $2,984,674 (20% need-based, 80% non-need-based). ***Programs:*** FFEL (Subsidized and Unsubsidized Stafford, PLUS), Perkins, state, college/university.

WORK-STUDY ***Federal work-study:*** Total amount: $203,114; 749 jobs averaging $272. ***State or other work-study/employment:*** Total amount: $335,601 (45% need-based, 55% non-need-based). Part-time jobs available.

APPLYING FOR FINANCIAL AID ***Required financial aid forms:*** FAFSA, institution's own form, federal income tax form(s). ***Financial aid deadline:*** Continuous. ***Notification date:*** Continuous beginning 3/1. Students must reply within 4 weeks of notification.

CONTACT Marty Rossman, Director of Financial Aid, North Central College, 30 North Brainard Street, Naperville, IL 60540, 630-637-5600 or toll-free 800-411-1861. *Fax:* 630-637-5608. *E-mail:* mprossman@noctrl.edu.

NORTH CENTRAL UNIVERSITY

Minneapolis, MN

CONTACT Mrs. Donna Jager, Director of Financial Aid, North Central University, 910 Elliot Avenue, Minneapolis, MN 55404-1322, 612-343-4485 or toll-free 800-289-6222. *Fax:* 612-343-8067. *E-mail:* finaid@northcentral.edu.

NORTH DAKOTA STATE UNIVERSITY

Fargo, ND

Tuition & fees (ND res): $5264 **Average undergraduate aid package: $7030**

ABOUT THE INSTITUTION State-supported, coed. ***Awards:*** bachelor's, master's, doctoral, and first professional degrees and post-bachelor's and post-master's certificates. 100 undergraduate majors. ***Total enrollment:*** 13,229. Undergraduates: 11,061. Freshmen: 2,661. Federal methodology is used as a basis for awarding need-based institutional aid.

UNDERGRADUATE EXPENSES for 2008–09 ***Application fee:*** $35. ***One-time required fee:*** $45. ***Tuition, state resident:*** full-time $5264; part-time $219.33 per credit. ***Tuition, nonresident:*** full-time $14,053; part-time $585.54 per credit. ***Required fees:*** $40.09 per credit. Full-time tuition and fees vary according to reciprocity agreements. Part-time tuition and fees vary according to course load and reciprocity agreements. ***College room and board:*** $6220; ***Room only:*** $2656. Room and board charges vary according to board plan and housing facility. ***Payment plan:*** Installment.

FRESHMAN FINANCIAL AID (Fall 2007) 2,037 applied for aid; of those 67% were deemed to have need. 98% of freshmen with need received aid; of those 27% had need fully met. ***Average percent of need met:*** 38% (excluding resources awarded to replace EFC). ***Average financial aid package:*** $7084 (excluding resources awarded to replace EFC). 25% of all full-time freshmen had no need and received non-need-based gift aid.

UNDERGRADUATE FINANCIAL AID (Fall 2007) 7,109 applied for aid; of those 69% were deemed to have need. 98% of undergraduates with need received aid; of those 20% had need fully met. ***Average percent of need met:*** 3% (excluding resources awarded to replace EFC). ***Average financial aid package:*** $7030 (excluding resources awarded to replace EFC). 21% of all full-time undergraduates had no need and received non-need-based gift aid.

GIFT AID (NEED-BASED) ***Total amount:*** $11,018,791 (61% federal, 7% state, 16% institutional, 16% external sources). ***Receiving aid:*** Freshmen: 39% (899); all full-time undergraduates: 33% (2,840). ***Average award:*** Freshmen: $3729; Undergraduates: $3419. ***Scholarships, grants, and awards:*** Federal Pell, FSEOG, state, private, college/university gift aid from institutional funds.

GIFT AID (NON-NEED-BASED) ***Total amount:*** $1,630,843 (7% state, 62% institutional, 31% external sources). ***Receiving aid:*** Freshmen: 7% (168). Undergraduates: 6% (529). ***Average award:*** Freshmen: $1692. Undergraduates: $1533. ***Scholarships, grants, and awards by category:*** *Academic interests/achievement:* agriculture, architecture, biological sciences, business, communication, computer science, education, engineering/technologies, English, general academic interests/achievements, health fields, home economics, humanities, mathematics, military science, physical sciences, premedicine, social sciences. *Creative arts/performance:* art/fine arts, debating, journalism/publications, music, theater/drama. *Special achievements/activities:* memberships, religious involvement. *Special characteristics:* children of faculty/staff, ethnic background. ***Tuition waivers:*** Full or partial for minority students, children of alumni, employees or children of employees, senior citizens. ***ROTC:*** Army, Air Force.

LOANS ***Student loans:*** $33,562,734 (73% need-based, 27% non-need-based). ***Average need-based loan:*** Freshmen: $3853. Undergraduates: $4378. ***Parent loans:*** $1,092,925 (35% need-based, 65% non-need-based). ***Programs:*** FFEL (Subsidized and Unsubsidized Stafford, PLUS), Perkins, Federal Nursing, private loans from various lending institutions.

WORK-STUDY ***Federal work-study:*** Total amount: $660,950; jobs available.

ATHLETIC AWARDS Total amount: $1,865,019 (25% need-based, 75% non-need-based).

APPLYING FOR FINANCIAL AID ***Required financial aid form:*** FAFSA. ***Financial aid deadline (priority):*** 3/15. ***Notification date:*** Continuous beginning 4/20.

CONTACT Jeanne Enebo, Director of Financial Aid, North Dakota State University, PO Box 5315, Fargo, ND 58105, 701-231-7537 or toll-free 800-488-NDSU. *Fax:* 701-231-6126. *E-mail:* j.enebo@ndsu.edu.

NORTHEASTERN ILLINOIS UNIVERSITY

Chicago, IL

ABOUT THE INSTITUTION State-supported, coed. ***Awards:*** bachelor's and master's degrees. 42 undergraduate majors. ***Total enrollment:*** 11,193. Undergraduates: 8,987. Freshmen: 1,017.

GIFT AID (NEED-BASED) ***Scholarships, grants, and awards:*** Federal Pell, FSEOG, state, private, college/university gift aid from institutional funds, Academic Competitiveness Grant, National Smart Grant.

GIFT AID (NON-NEED-BASED) ***Scholarships, grants, and awards by category:*** *Academic interests/achievement:* biological sciences, business, communication, computer science, education, English, foreign languages, general academic interests/achievements, mathematics, physical sciences, social sciences. *Creative arts/performance:* art/fine arts, creative writing, dance, journalism/publications, music, performing arts, theater/drama. *Special achievements/activities:* general special achievements/activities, leadership. *Special characteristics:* adult students, children of faculty/staff, general special characteristics.

LOANS ***Programs:*** FFEL (Subsidized and Unsubsidized Stafford, PLUS), Perkins.

WORK-STUDY ***Federal work-study:*** Total amount: $386,488; 174 jobs averaging $2221. ***State or other work-study/employment:*** Total amount: $922,843 (100% non-need-based). 458 part-time jobs averaging $1886.

APPLYING FOR FINANCIAL AID ***Required financial aid forms:*** FAFSA, institution's own form.

CONTACT Financial Aid Office, Northeastern Illinois University, 5500 North St. Louis Avenue, Chicago, IL 60625, 773-442-5000. *Fax:* 773-442-5040. *E-mail:* financial-aid@neiu.edu.

NORTHEASTERN STATE UNIVERSITY

Tahlequah, OK

Tuition & fees (OK res): $4155 **Average undergraduate aid package: $8624**

ABOUT THE INSTITUTION State-supported, coed. ***Awards:*** bachelor's, master's, and first professional degrees and post-bachelor's and post-master's certificates. 72 undergraduate majors. ***Total enrollment:*** 8,833. Undergraduates: 7,740. Freshmen: 999. Federal methodology is used as a basis for awarding need-based institutional aid.

UNDERGRADUATE EXPENSES for 2008–09 ***Tuition, state resident:*** full-time $3210; part-time $107 per credit hour. ***Tuition, nonresident:*** full-time $9300; part-time $310 per credit hour. ***Required fees:*** full-time $945; $31.50 per credit hour. Full-time tuition and fees vary according to course load and program. Part-time tuition and fees vary according to course load and program. ***College room and board:*** $4544. Room and board charges vary according to board plan and housing facility. ***Payment plan:*** Tuition prepayment.

FRESHMAN FINANCIAL AID (Fall 2008, est.) 824 applied for aid; of those 75% were deemed to have need. 95% of freshmen with need received aid; of those 69% had need fully met. ***Average percent of need met:*** 69% (excluding resources awarded to replace EFC). ***Average financial aid package:*** $8478 (excluding resources awarded to replace EFC). 30% of all full-time freshmen had no need and received non-need-based gift aid.

UNDERGRADUATE FINANCIAL AID (Fall 2008, est.) 4,355 applied for aid; of those 82% were deemed to have need. 94% of undergraduates with need received aid; of those 71% had need fully met. ***Average percent of need met:*** 70% (excluding resources awarded to replace EFC). ***Average financial aid package:*** $8624 (excluding resources awarded to replace EFC). 22% of all full-time undergraduates had no need and received non-need-based gift aid.

GIFT AID (NEED-BASED) ***Total amount:*** $18,174,432 (63% federal, 17% state, 2% institutional, 18% external sources). ***Receiving aid:*** Freshmen: 43% (409); all full-time undergraduates: 43% (2,408). ***Average award:*** Freshmen: $4710; Undergraduates: $4714. ***Scholarships, grants, and awards:*** Federal Pell, FSEOG, state, private, college/university gift aid from institutional funds.

GIFT AID (NON-NEED-BASED) ***Total amount:*** $4,425,702 (46% state, 5% institutional, 49% external sources). ***Receiving aid:*** Freshmen: 60% (574). Undergraduates: 58% (3,261). ***Average award:*** Freshmen: $1022. Undergraduates: $786. ***Scholarships, grants, and awards by category:*** *Academic interests/achievement:* 921 awards ($1,868,464 total): biological sciences, business, communication, computer science, education, English, foreign languages, general academic interests/achievements, health fields, home economics, humanities, library science, mathematics, physical sciences, premedicine, social sciences. *Creative arts/performance:* 159 awards ($180,384 total): applied art and design, art/fine arts, dance, debating, journalism/publications, music, performing arts, theater/drama. *Special achievements/activities:* 27 awards ($46,828 total): cheerleading/drum major, community service, junior miss, leadership. *Special characteristics:* 69 awards ($148,144 total): children and siblings of alumni, children of faculty/staff, children with a deceased or disabled parent, out-of-state students, spouses of deceased or disabled public servants. ***Tuition waivers:*** Full or partial for employees or children of employees, senior citizens. ***ROTC:*** Army.

LOANS ***Student loans:*** $31,236,244 (45% need-based, 55% non-need-based). 64% of past graduating class borrowed through all loan programs. *Average indebtedness per student:* $18,573. ***Average need-based loan:*** Freshmen: $2032. Undergraduates: $3666. ***Parent loans:*** $507,714 (60% need-based, 40% non-need-based). ***Programs:*** FFEL (Subsidized and Unsubsidized Stafford, PLUS), Perkins.

WORK-STUDY ***Federal work-study:*** Total amount: $462,185; 264 jobs averaging $1430. ***State or other work-study/employment:*** Total amount: $1,867,088 (100% non-need-based). 664 part-time jobs averaging $2140.

ATHLETIC AWARDS Total amount: $1,366,572 (100% non-need-based).

APPLYING FOR FINANCIAL AID ***Required financial aid forms:*** FAFSA, institution's own form. ***Financial aid deadline (priority):*** 4/1. ***Notification date:*** Continuous beginning 4/1. Students must reply within 2 weeks of notification.

CONTACT Teri Cochran, Director of Student Financial Services, Northeastern State University, 715 North Grand Avenue, Tahlequah, OK 74464-2399, 918-456-5511 Ext. 3410 or toll-free 800-722-9614 (in-state). *Fax:* 918-458-2510. *E-mail:* cochrant@nsuok.edu.

NORTHEASTERN UNIVERSITY

Boston, MA

Tuition & fees: $33,721 **Average undergraduate aid package: $17,877**

ABOUT THE INSTITUTION Independent, coed. ***Awards:*** bachelor's, master's, doctoral, and first professional degrees and post-master's certificates. 83 undergraduate majors. ***Total enrollment:*** 21,324. Undergraduates: 15,521. Freshmen: 2,923. Both federal and institutional methodology are used as a basis for awarding need-based institutional aid.

UNDERGRADUATE EXPENSES for 2008–09 ***Application fee:*** $75. ***One-time required fee:*** $250. ***Comprehensive fee:*** $45,661 includes full-time tuition ($33,320), mandatory fees ($401), and room and board ($11,940). ***College room only:*** $6340. Room and board charges vary according to board plan and housing facility. ***Payment plan:*** Installment.

FRESHMAN FINANCIAL AID (Fall 2008, est.) 2,178 applied for aid; of those 76% were deemed to have need. 100% of freshmen with need received aid; of those 22% had need fully met. ***Average percent of need met:*** 68% (excluding resources awarded to replace EFC). ***Average financial aid package:*** $19,820 (excluding resources awarded to replace EFC). 26% of all full-time freshmen had no need and received non-need-based gift aid.

UNDERGRADUATE FINANCIAL AID (Fall 2008, est.) 10,057 applied for aid; of those 83% were deemed to have need. 99% of undergraduates with need received aid; of those 17% had need fully met. ***Average percent of need met:*** 60% (excluding resources awarded to replace EFC). ***Average financial aid package:*** $17,877 (excluding resources awarded to replace EFC). 24% of all full-time undergraduates had no need and received non-need-based gift aid.

GIFT AID (NEED-BASED) ***Total amount:*** $100,561,092 (10% federal, 2% state, 84% institutional, 4% external sources). ***Receiving aid:*** Freshmen: 54% (1,591); all full-time undergraduates: 50% (7,835). ***Average award:*** Freshmen: $16,194; Undergraduates: $13,119. ***Scholarships, grants, and awards:*** Federal Pell, FSEOG, state, private, college/university gift aid from institutional funds, Federal Nursing.

GIFT AID (NON-NEED-BASED) ***Total amount:*** $39,699,555 (92% institutional, 8% external sources). ***Receiving aid:*** Freshmen: 9% (262). Undergraduates: 5% (825). ***Average award:*** Freshmen: $11,830. Undergraduates: $8875. ***Tuition waivers:*** Full or partial for employees or children of employees, senior citizens. ***ROTC:*** Army, Naval cooperative, Air Force cooperative.

LOANS ***Student loans:*** $117,081,274 (63% need-based, 37% non-need-based). ***Average need-based loan:*** Freshmen: $3931. Undergraduates: $4638. ***Parent loans:*** $21,950,466 (39% need-based, 61% non-need-based). ***Programs:*** Federal Direct (Subsidized and Unsubsidized Stafford, PLUS), Perkins, Federal Nursing, state, MEFA, TERI, CitiAssist.

WORK-STUDY ***Federal work-study:*** Total amount: $8,700,886; jobs available. ***State or other work-study/employment:*** Total amount: $2,407,460 (100% need-based). Part-time jobs available.

ATHLETIC AWARDS Total amount: $9,085,420 (30% need-based, 70% non-need-based).

APPLYING FOR FINANCIAL AID ***Required financial aid forms:*** FAFSA, CSS Financial Aid PROFILE. ***Financial aid deadline (priority):*** 2/15. ***Notification date:*** Continuous beginning 3/15. Students must reply by 5/1.

CONTACT Mr. M. Seamus Harreys, Dean of Student Financial Services, Northeastern University, 360 Huntington Avenue, Boston, MA 02115, 617-373-3190. *Fax:* 617-373-8735. *E-mail:* sfs@neu.edu.

NORTHERN ARIZONA UNIVERSITY

Flagstaff, AZ

Tuition & fees (AZ res): $5449 **Average undergraduate aid package: $8641**

ABOUT THE INSTITUTION State-supported, coed. ***Awards:*** bachelor's, master's, and doctoral degrees and post-bachelor's certificates. 109 undergraduate majors. ***Total enrollment:*** 22,507. Undergraduates: 16,787. Freshmen: 3,588. Federal methodology is used as a basis for awarding need-based institutional aid.

UNDERGRADUATE EXPENSES for 2008–09 ***Application fee:*** $25. ***Tuition, state resident:*** full-time $5145; part-time $368 per credit hour. ***Tuition, nonresident:*** full-time $16,242; part-time $677 per credit hour. ***Required fees:*** full-time $304; $3 per credit hour or $117 per term. Full-time tuition and fees vary according to location and program. Part-time tuition and fees vary according to location and program. ***College room and board:*** $7086; ***Room only:*** $3878. Room and board charges vary according to board plan and housing facility. ***Payment plans:*** Guaranteed tuition, installment.

FRESHMAN FINANCIAL AID (Fall 2008, est.) 2,609 applied for aid; of those 62% were deemed to have need. 96% of freshmen with need received aid; of those 21% had need fully met. ***Average percent of need met:*** 68% (excluding resources awarded to replace EFC). ***Average financial aid package:*** $8595 (excluding resources awarded to replace EFC). 22% of all full-time freshmen had no need and received non-need-based gift aid.

UNDERGRADUATE FINANCIAL AID (Fall 2008, est.) 9,590 applied for aid; of those 74% were deemed to have need. 97% of undergraduates with need received aid; of those 15% had need fully met. ***Average percent of need met:*** 64% (excluding resources awarded to replace EFC). ***Average financial aid package:*** $8641 (excluding resources awarded to replace EFC). 15% of all full-time undergraduates had no need and received non-need-based gift aid.

GIFT AID (NEED-BASED) ***Total amount:*** $37,735,763 (49% federal, 6% state, 35% institutional, 10% external sources). ***Receiving aid:*** Freshmen: 28% (943); all full-time undergraduates: 32% (4,492). ***Average award:*** Freshmen: $6093; Undergraduates: $5530. ***Scholarships, grants, and awards:*** Federal Pell, FSEOG, state, private, college/university gift aid from institutional funds, Federal Nursing.

GIFT AID (NON-NEED-BASED) ***Total amount:*** $8,088,022 (3% federal, 70% institutional, 27% external sources). ***Receiving aid:*** Freshmen: 25% (823). Undergraduates: 20% (2,747). ***Average award:*** Freshmen: $3565. Undergraduates: $3417. ***Scholarships, grants, and awards by category:*** *Academic interests/achievement:* 1,089 awards ($2,448,283 total): area/ethnic studies, biological sciences, business, communication, computer science, education, engineering/technologies, English, foreign languages, general academic interests/achievements, health fields, home economics, humanities, international studies, library science, mathematics, military science, physical sciences, premedicine, religion/biblical studies, social sciences. *Creative arts/performance:* 342 awards ($1,037,327 total): applied art and design, art/fine arts, cinema/film/broadcasting, creative writing, debating, general creative arts/performance, journalism/publications, music, performing arts, theater/drama. *Special characteristics:* 4,099 awards ($13,621,006 total): children and siblings of alumni, children of educators, children of faculty/staff, children of public servants, first-generation college students, general special characteristics, handicapped students, international students, local/state students, out-of-state students, spouses of deceased or disabled public servants, veterans, veterans' children. ***Tuition waivers:*** Full or partial for employees or children of employees. ***ROTC:*** Army, Air Force.

LOANS ***Student loans:*** $61,254,409 (80% need-based, 20% non-need-based). 51% of past graduating class borrowed through all loan programs. *Average indebtedness per student:* $14,952. ***Average need-based loan:*** Freshmen: $3110. Undergraduates: $3998. ***Parent loans:*** $17,554,200 (60% need-based, 40% non-need-based). ***Programs:*** Federal Direct (Subsidized and Unsubsidized Stafford, PLUS), Perkins, Federal Nursing, state, college/university.

WORK-STUDY ***Federal work-study:*** Total amount: $1,019,224; 436 jobs averaging $2360. ***State or other work-study/employment:*** Total amount: $6,846,253 (54% need-based, 46% non-need-based). 3,397 part-time jobs averaging $2016.

ATHLETIC AWARDS Total amount: $2,856,212 (38% need-based, 62% non-need-based).

APPLYING FOR FINANCIAL AID ***Required financial aid form:*** FAFSA. ***Financial aid deadline (priority):*** 2/14. ***Notification date:*** Continuous beginning 3/15.

CONTACT Michelle Castillo, Director, Financial Aid, Northern Arizona University, Box 4108, Flagstaff, AZ 86011-4108, 928-523-1383 or toll-free 888-MORE-NAU. *Fax:* 928-523-1551.

NORTHERN ILLINOIS UNIVERSITY

De Kalb, IL

Tuition & fees (IL res): $8312 **Average undergraduate aid package: $10,421**

ABOUT THE INSTITUTION State-supported, coed. ***Awards:*** bachelor's, master's, doctoral, and first professional degrees. 61 undergraduate majors. ***Total enrollment:*** 25,254. Undergraduates: 18,917. Freshmen: 3,013. Federal methodology is used as a basis for awarding need-based institutional aid.

UNDERGRADUATE EXPENSES for 2008–09 ***Tuition, state resident:*** full-time $6720; part-time $249 per credit hour. ***Tuition, nonresident:*** full-time $13,620; part-time $454 per credit hour. ***Required fees:*** full-time $1592; $66.35 per credit hour. Full-time tuition and fees vary according to course load and location. Part-time tuition and fees vary according to course load and location. ***College room and board:*** $8230. Room and board charges vary according to board plan and housing facility. ***Payment plans:*** Guaranteed tuition, installment.

FRESHMAN FINANCIAL AID (Fall 2008, est.) 2,329 applied for aid; of those 76% were deemed to have need. 99% of freshmen with need received aid; of those 6% had need fully met. ***Average percent of need met:*** 70% (excluding resources awarded to replace EFC). ***Average financial aid package:*** $10,995 (excluding resources awarded to replace EFC). 1% of all full-time freshmen had no need and received non-need-based gift aid.

UNDERGRADUATE FINANCIAL AID (Fall 2008, est.) 11,853 applied for aid; of those 79% were deemed to have need. 99% of undergraduates with need received aid; of those 8% had need fully met. ***Average percent of need met:*** 72% (excluding resources awarded to replace EFC). ***Average financial aid package:*** $10,421 (excluding resources awarded to replace EFC). 1% of all full-time undergraduates had no need and received non-need-based gift aid.

GIFT AID (NEED-BASED) ***Total amount:*** $46,783,211 (39% federal, 50% state, 7% institutional, 4% external sources). ***Receiving aid:*** Freshmen: 43% (1,219); all full-time undergraduates: 37% (6,061). ***Average award:*** Freshmen: $7979; Undergraduates: $6921. ***Scholarships, grants, and awards:*** Federal Pell, FSEOG, state, private, college/university gift aid from institutional funds, United Negro College Fund, Federal Nursing, Academic Competitiveness Grant, National Smart Grant, TEACH Grant.

GIFT AID (NON-NEED-BASED) ***Total amount:*** $19,377 (41% institutional, 59% external sources). ***Receiving aid:*** Freshmen: 3. Undergraduates: 13. ***Average award:*** Freshmen: $1000. Undergraduates: $472. ***Scholarships, grants, and awards by category:*** *Academic interests/achievement:* biological sciences, business, communication, computer science, education, engineering/technologies, English, foreign languages, general academic interests/achievements, health fields, humanities, international studies, mathematics, physical sciences, social sciences. *Creative arts/performance:* applied art and design, art/fine arts, creative writing, dance, debating, journalism/publications, music, performing arts, theater/drama. *Special achievements/activities:* leadership. *Special characteristics:* adult students, children of faculty/staff, ethnic background, international students, members of minority groups, veterans. ***Tuition waivers:*** Full or partial for minority students, employees or children of employees, senior citizens. ***ROTC:*** Army, Air Force cooperative.

LOANS ***Student loans:*** $92,234,161 (41% need-based, 59% non-need-based). 59% of past graduating class borrowed through all loan programs. *Average indebtedness per student:* $19,405. ***Average need-based loan:*** Freshmen: $3400. Undergraduates: $4286. ***Parent loans:*** $11,330,076 (100% non-need-based). ***Programs:*** Federal Direct (Subsidized and Unsubsidized Stafford, PLUS), Perkins.

WORK-STUDY ***Federal work-study:*** Total amount: $13,252,058; 4,484 jobs averaging $3016.

ATHLETIC AWARDS Total amount: $4,741,797 (100% need-based).

APPLYING FOR FINANCIAL AID ***Required financial aid form:*** FAFSA. ***Financial aid deadline (priority):*** 3/1. ***Notification date:*** Continuous beginning 3/24. Students must reply within 2 weeks of notification.

CONTACT Ms. Kathleen D. Brunson, Director of Student Financial Aid, Northern Illinois University, De Kalb, IL 60115-2854, 815-753-1395 or toll-free 800-892-3050 (in-state). *Fax:* 815-753-9475.

NORTHERN KENTUCKY UNIVERSITY

Highland Heights, KY

Tuition & fees (KY res): $6528 **Average undergraduate aid package: $7347**

ABOUT THE INSTITUTION State-supported, coed. ***Awards:*** associate, bachelor's, master's, doctoral, and first professional degrees and post-bachelor's and post-master's certificates. 58 undergraduate majors. ***Total enrollment:*** 15,082. Undergraduates: 13,003. Freshmen: 2,143. Federal methodology is used as a basis for awarding need-based institutional aid.

UNDERGRADUATE EXPENSES for 2008–09 ***Application fee:*** $40. ***Tuition, state resident:*** full-time $6528; part-time $272 per credit hour. ***Tuition, nonresident:*** full-time $11,952; part-time $498 per credit hour. Full-time tuition and fees vary according to course load, program, and reciprocity agreements. Part-time tuition and fees vary according to course load, program, and reciprocity agreements. Room and board charges vary according to board plan and housing facility. ***Payment plan:*** Installment.

FRESHMAN FINANCIAL AID (Fall 2007) 1,441 applied for aid; of those 72% were deemed to have need. 99% of freshmen with need received aid; of those 22% had need fully met. ***Average percent of need met:*** 62% (excluding resources awarded to replace EFC). ***Average financial aid package:*** $7126 (excluding resources awarded to replace EFC). 10% of all full-time freshmen had no need and received non-need-based gift aid.

UNDERGRADUATE FINANCIAL AID (Fall 2007) 6,325 applied for aid; of those 75% were deemed to have need. 97% of undergraduates with need received aid; of those 20% had need fully met. ***Average percent of need met:*** 53% (excluding resources awarded to replace EFC). ***Average financial aid package:*** $7347 (excluding resources awarded to replace EFC). 8% of all full-time undergraduates had no need and received non-need-based gift aid.

GIFT AID (NEED-BASED) ***Total amount:*** $11,624,512 (80% federal, 20% state). ***Receiving aid:*** Freshmen: 27% (500); all full-time undergraduates: 25% (2,368). ***Average award:*** Freshmen: $5134; Undergraduates: $4539. ***Scholarships, grants, and awards:*** Federal Pell, FSEOG, state, private, college/university gift aid from institutional funds.

GIFT AID (NON-NEED-BASED) ***Total amount:*** $13,845,350 (37% state, 53% institutional, 10% external sources). ***Receiving aid:*** Freshmen: 38% (707). Undergraduates: 21% (1,931). ***Average award:*** Freshmen: $3858. Undergraduates: $3907. ***Tuition waivers:*** Full or partial for employees or children of employees, senior citizens. ***ROTC:*** Army, Air Force cooperative.

LOANS ***Student loans:*** $38,563,767 (47% need-based, 53% non-need-based). 68% of past graduating class borrowed through all loan programs. *Average indebtedness per student:* $22,743. ***Average need-based loan:*** Freshmen: $2940. Undergraduates: $3858. ***Parent loans:*** $5,407,751 (100% non-need-based). ***Programs:*** FFEL (Subsidized and Unsubsidized Stafford, PLUS), Perkins, private alternative loans.

WORK-STUDY ***Federal work-study:*** Total amount: $551,689; jobs available. ***State or other work-study/employment:*** Total amount: $2,550,731 (100% non-need-based). Part-time jobs available.

ATHLETIC AWARDS Total amount: $717,177 (100% non-need-based).

APPLYING FOR FINANCIAL AID ***Required financial aid form:*** FAFSA. ***Financial aid deadline (priority):*** 3/1. ***Notification date:*** Continuous beginning 4/1.

CONTACT Leah Stewart, Director of Student Financial Assistance, Northern Kentucky University, 416 Administrative Center, Highland Heights, KY 41099, 859-572-5144 or toll-free 800-637-9948. *Fax:* 859-572-6997. *E-mail:* ofa@nku.edu.

NORTHERN MICHIGAN UNIVERSITY

Marquette, MI

Tuition & fees (MI res): $7076 **Average undergraduate aid package: $7937**

ABOUT THE INSTITUTION State-supported, coed. ***Awards:*** associate, bachelor's, and master's degrees and post-bachelor's and post-master's certificates. 133 undergraduate majors. ***Total enrollment:*** 9,111. Undergraduates: 8,488. Freshmen: 1,394. Federal methodology is used as a basis for awarding need-based institutional aid.

UNDERGRADUATE EXPENSES for 2008–09 ***Application fee:*** $30. ***One-time required fee:*** $200. ***Tuition, state resident:*** full-time $6504; part-time $271 per credit hour. ***Tuition, nonresident:*** full-time $10,656; part-time $444 per credit hour. ***Required fees:*** full-time $572; $31.13 per term. ***College room and board:***

$7636; ***Room only:*** $3842. Room and board charges vary according to board plan and housing facility. ***Payment plans:*** Installment, deferred payment.

FRESHMAN FINANCIAL AID (Fall 2007) 1,644 applied for aid; of those 67% were deemed to have need. 97% of freshmen with need received aid; of those 25% had need fully met. ***Average percent of need met:*** 65% (excluding resources awarded to replace EFC). ***Average financial aid package:*** $7495 (excluding resources awarded to replace EFC). 8% of all full-time freshmen had no need and received non-need-based gift aid.

UNDERGRADUATE FINANCIAL AID (Fall 2007) 6,567 applied for aid; of those 68% were deemed to have need. 97% of undergraduates with need received aid; of those 20% had need fully met. ***Average percent of need met:*** 66% (excluding resources awarded to replace EFC). ***Average financial aid package:*** $7937 (excluding resources awarded to replace EFC). 5% of all full-time undergraduates had no need and received non-need-based gift aid.

GIFT AID (NEED-BASED) ***Total amount:*** $12,306,920 (71% federal, 9% state, 19% institutional, 1% external sources). ***Receiving aid:*** Freshmen: 32% (572); all full-time undergraduates: 31% (2,397). ***Average award:*** Freshmen: $3940; Undergraduates: $4189. ***Scholarships, grants, and awards:*** Federal Pell, FSEOG, state, private, college/university gift aid from institutional funds, Federal Nursing.

GIFT AID (NON-NEED-BASED) ***Total amount:*** $11,721,460 (1% federal, 28% state, 51% institutional, 20% external sources). ***Receiving aid:*** Freshmen: 34% (599). Undergraduates: 23% (1,789). ***Average award:*** Freshmen: $3160. Undergraduates: $2872. ***Scholarships, grants, and awards by category:*** *Academic interests/achievement:* 414 awards ($387,280 total): biological sciences, business, communication, computer science, education, engineering/technologies, English, foreign languages, general academic interests/achievements, health fields, international studies, mathematics, military science, physical sciences, premedicine, social sciences. *Creative arts/performance:* 65 awards ($48,050 total): applied art and design, music, theater/drama. *Special achievements/activities:* 129 awards ($88,284 total): cheerleading/drum major, leadership, memberships. *Special characteristics:* 995 awards ($3,039,000 total): children of faculty/staff, children of union members/company employees, international students, members of minority groups, out-of-state students. ***Tuition waivers:*** Full or partial for employees or children of employees, senior citizens. ***ROTC:*** Army.

LOANS ***Student loans:*** $38,533,900 (48% need-based, 52% non-need-based). 61% of past graduating class borrowed through all loan programs. *Average indebtedness per student:* $18,498. ***Average need-based loan:*** Freshmen: $2931. Undergraduates: $3895. ***Parent loans:*** $2,228,698 (100% non-need-based). ***Programs:*** Federal Direct (Subsidized and Unsubsidized Stafford, PLUS), Perkins, state, alternative loans.

WORK-STUDY ***Federal work-study:*** Total amount: $930,753; 524 jobs averaging $1743. ***State or other work-study/employment:*** Total amount: $209,134 (100% need-based). 76 part-time jobs averaging $2752.

ATHLETIC AWARDS Total amount: $2,069,314 (100% non-need-based).

APPLYING FOR FINANCIAL AID ***Required financial aid form:*** FAFSA. ***Financial aid deadline (priority):*** 3/1. ***Notification date:*** Continuous beginning 4/1. Students must reply within 2 weeks of notification.

CONTACT Michael Rotundo, Director of Financial Aid, Northern Michigan University, 1401 Presque Isle Avenue, Marquette, MI 49855, 906-227-1575 or toll-free 800-682-9797. *Fax:* 906-227-2321. *E-mail:* mrotundo@nmu.edu.

NORTHERN STATE UNIVERSITY

Aberdeen, SD

Tuition & fees (SD res): $5712 **Average undergraduate aid package: $6166**

ABOUT THE INSTITUTION State-supported, coed. ***Awards:*** associate, bachelor's, and master's degrees and post-bachelor's certificates. 50 undergraduate majors. ***Total enrollment:*** 2,927. Undergraduates: 2,412. Freshmen: 400. Federal methodology is used as a basis for awarding need-based institutional aid.

UNDERGRADUATE EXPENSES for 2008–09 ***Application fee:*** $20. ***Tuition, state resident:*** full-time $2646; part-time $88.20 per credit hour. ***Tuition, nonresident:*** full-time $8404; part-time $280.15 per credit hour. ***Required fees:*** full-time $3066; $102.20 per credit hour. Full-time tuition and fees vary according to course level, course load, and reciprocity agreements. Part-time tuition and fees vary according to course level, course load, and reciprocity agreements. ***College room and board:*** $4664; ***Room only:*** $2483. Room and board charges vary according to board plan. ***Payment plan:*** Installment.

FRESHMAN FINANCIAL AID (Fall 2008, est.) 300 applied for aid; of those 78% were deemed to have need. 99% of freshmen with need received aid; of those 100% had need fully met. ***Average percent of need met:*** 100% (excluding resources awarded to replace EFC). ***Average financial aid package:*** $5335 (excluding resources awarded to replace EFC). 13% of all full-time freshmen had no need and received non-need-based gift aid.

UNDERGRADUATE FINANCIAL AID (Fall 2008, est.) 1,179 applied for aid; of those 78% were deemed to have need. 99% of undergraduates with need received aid; of those 100% had need fully met. ***Average percent of need met:*** 100% (excluding resources awarded to replace EFC). ***Average financial aid package:*** $6166 (excluding resources awarded to replace EFC). 7% of all full-time undergraduates had no need and received non-need-based gift aid.

GIFT AID (NEED-BASED) ***Total amount:*** $2,314,350 (97% federal, 3% external sources). ***Receiving aid:*** Freshmen: 54% (214); all full-time undergraduates: 43% (718). ***Average award:*** Freshmen: $2806; Undergraduates: $2576. ***Scholarships, grants, and awards:*** Federal Pell, FSEOG, state, private, college/university gift aid from institutional funds, Academic Competitiveness Grant, National Smart Grant, TEACH Grant.

GIFT AID (NON-NEED-BASED) ***Total amount:*** $1,543,450 (5% federal, 11% state, 61% institutional, 23% external sources). ***Receiving aid:*** Freshmen: 51% (201). Undergraduates: 44% (736). ***Average award:*** Freshmen: $2951. Undergraduates: $2245. ***Scholarships, grants, and awards by category:*** *Academic interests/achievement:* 216 awards ($149,627 total): biological sciences, business, communication, computer science, education, English, foreign languages, general academic interests/achievements, humanities, international studies, mathematics, physical sciences, social sciences. *Creative arts/performance:* 101 awards ($73,224 total): art/fine arts, music, theater/drama. *Special achievements/activities:* 28 awards ($14,000 total): leadership. *Special characteristics:* 24 awards ($14,812 total): adult students, ethnic background, handicapped students, international students, local/state students, members of minority groups.

LOANS ***Student loans:*** $9,666,900 (46% need-based, 54% non-need-based). 79% of past graduating class borrowed through all loan programs. *Average indebtedness per student:* $20,297. ***Average need-based loan:*** Freshmen: $3229. Undergraduates: $3698. ***Parent loans:*** $356,100 (100% non-need-based). ***Programs:*** FFEL (Subsidized and Unsubsidized Stafford, PLUS), Perkins, college/university, alternative loans.

WORK-STUDY ***Federal work-study:*** Total amount: $495,000; 328 jobs averaging $1509. ***State or other work-study/employment:*** Total amount: $525,000 (100% non-need-based). 360 part-time jobs averaging $1458.

ATHLETIC AWARDS Total amount: $649,250 (100% non-need-based).

APPLYING FOR FINANCIAL AID ***Required financial aid form:*** FAFSA. ***Financial aid deadline (priority):*** 3/1. ***Notification date:*** 4/15. Students must reply within 2 weeks of notification.

CONTACT Ms. Sharon Kienow, Director of Financial Aid, Northern State University, 1200 South Jay Street, Aberdeen, SD 57401-7198, 605-626-2640 or toll-free 800-678-5330. *Fax:* 605-626-2587. *E-mail:* kienows@northern.edu.

NORTH GEORGIA COLLEGE & STATE UNIVERSITY

Dahlonega, GA

CONTACT Jill Royner, Director, Financial Aid, North Georgia College & State University, 82 College Circle, Dahlonega, GA 30597-1001, 706-864-1688 or toll-free 800-498-9581. *Fax:* 706-864-1411. *E-mail:* jproyner@ngcsu.edu.

NORTH GREENVILLE UNIVERSITY

Tigerville, SC

Tuition & fees: $11,680 **Average undergraduate aid package: N/A**

ABOUT THE INSTITUTION Independent Southern Baptist, coed. ***Awards:*** bachelor's and master's degrees. 31 undergraduate majors. ***Total enrollment:*** 2,160. Undergraduates: 2,062. Freshmen: 508. Federal methodology is used as a basis for awarding need-based institutional aid.

UNDERGRADUATE EXPENSES for 2008–09 ***Application fee:*** $25. ***Comprehensive fee:*** $18,400 includes full-time tuition ($11,680) and room and board ($6720). ***College room only:*** $3040. Full-time tuition and fees vary according to course load. Room and board charges vary according to housing facility. ***Part-time tuition:*** $200 per hour. ***Payment plan:*** Installment.

GIFT AID (NEED-BASED) ***Total amount:*** $15,015,272 (16% federal, 22% state, 56% institutional, 6% external sources). ***Scholarships, grants, and awards:*** Federal Pell, FSEOG, state, private, college/university gift aid from institutional funds.

GIFT AID (NON-NEED-BASED) ***Total amount:*** $3,845,150 (100% state). ***Scholarships, grants, and awards by category:*** *Academic interests/achievement:* biological sciences, communication, education, general academic interests/achievements, military science, religion/biblical studies. *Creative arts/performance:* journalism/publications, music, theater/drama. *Special achievements/activities:* $4900 total. *Special characteristics:* $225,000 total: children of faculty/staff. ***Tuition waivers:*** Full or partial for employees or children of employees. ***ROTC:*** Army cooperative.

LOANS ***Student loans:*** $6,684,092 (44% need-based, 56% non-need-based). ***Parent loans:*** $780,615 (100% need-based). ***Programs:*** FFEL (Subsidized and Unsubsidized Stafford, PLUS), Perkins, state.

WORK-STUDY ***Federal work-study:*** Total amount: $150,000; 164 jobs averaging $1000. ***State or other work-study/employment:*** Total amount: $160,000 (100% need-based). 138 part-time jobs averaging $1000.

ATHLETIC AWARDS Total amount: $971,250 (100% need-based).

APPLYING FOR FINANCIAL AID ***Required financial aid form:*** FAFSA. ***Financial aid deadline:*** Continuous.

CONTACT Mike Jordan, Director of Financial Aid, North Greenville University, PO Box 1892, Tigerville, SC 29688, 864-977-7058 or toll-free 800-468-6642 Ext. 7001. *Fax:* 864-977-7177. *E-mail:* mjordan@ngu.edu.

NORTHLAND COLLEGE

Ashland, WI

Tuition & fees: $23,101 **Average undergraduate aid package: $19,551**

ABOUT THE INSTITUTION Independent religious, coed. ***Awards:*** bachelor's degrees. 29 undergraduate majors. ***Total enrollment:*** 669. Undergraduates: 669. Freshmen: 133. Federal methodology is used as a basis for awarding need-based institutional aid.

UNDERGRADUATE EXPENSES for 2008–09 ***Application fee:*** $25. ***Comprehensive fee:*** $29,541 includes full-time tuition ($22,500), mandatory fees ($601), and room and board ($6440). ***College room only:*** $2600. Full-time tuition and fees vary according to course level. Room and board charges vary according to board plan and housing facility. Part-time tuition and fees vary according to course level. ***Payment plan:*** Installment.

FRESHMAN FINANCIAL AID (Fall 2008, est.) 123 applied for aid; of those 85% were deemed to have need. 100% of freshmen with need received aid; of those 28% had need fully met. ***Average percent of need met:*** 91% (excluding resources awarded to replace EFC). ***Average financial aid package:*** $19,843 (excluding resources awarded to replace EFC). 20% of all full-time freshmen had no need and received non-need-based gift aid.

UNDERGRADUATE FINANCIAL AID (Fall 2008, est.) 539 applied for aid; of those 89% were deemed to have need. 100% of undergraduates with need received aid; of those 21% had need fully met. ***Average percent of need met:*** 82% (excluding resources awarded to replace EFC). ***Average financial aid package:*** $19,551 (excluding resources awarded to replace EFC). 20% of all full-time undergraduates had no need and received non-need-based gift aid.

GIFT AID (NEED-BASED) ***Total amount:*** $6,652,829 (12% federal, 6% state, 80% institutional, 2% external sources). ***Receiving aid:*** Freshmen: 78% (104); all full-time undergraduates: 80% (481). ***Average award:*** Freshmen: $15,341; Undergraduates: $13,577. ***Scholarships, grants, and awards:*** Federal Pell, FSEOG, state, private, college/university gift aid from institutional funds, Bureau of Indian Affairs Grants, Academic Competitiveness Grant, National Smart Grant.

GIFT AID (NON-NEED-BASED) ***Total amount:*** $920,724 (98% institutional, 2% external sources). ***Receiving aid:*** Undergraduates: 1% (4). ***Average award:*** Freshmen: $10,433. Undergraduates: $8976. ***Scholarships, grants, and awards by category:*** *Academic interests/achievement:* 347 awards ($2,829,016 total): general academic interests/achievements. *Creative arts/performance:* 24 awards ($25,925 total): art/fine arts, music. *Special achievements/activities:* 14 awards ($29,500 total): leadership. *Special characteristics:* 31 awards ($37,300 total): ethnic background. ***Tuition waivers:*** Full or partial for employees or children of employees.

LOANS ***Student loans:*** $3,492,020 (56% need-based, 44% non-need-based). 79% of past graduating class borrowed through all loan programs. *Average indebtedness per student:* $23,630. ***Average need-based loan:*** Freshmen: $3982. Undergraduates: $4759. ***Parent loans:*** $721,169 (89% need-based, 11% non-need-based). ***Programs:*** FFEL (Subsidized and Unsubsidized Stafford, PLUS), Perkins.

WORK-STUDY ***Federal work-study:*** Total amount: $491,053; 308 jobs averaging $1594. ***State or other work-study/employment:*** Total amount: $409,394 (60% need-based, 40% non-need-based). 150 part-time jobs averaging $1636.

APPLYING FOR FINANCIAL AID ***Required financial aid form:*** FAFSA. ***Financial aid deadline (priority):*** 4/15. ***Notification date:*** Continuous. Students must reply by 5/1 or within 4 weeks of notification.

CONTACT Debora L. Milanowski, Interim Director of Financial Aid, Northland College, 1411 Ellis Avenue, Ashland, WI 54806, 715-682-1255 or toll-free 800-753-1840 (in-state), 800-753-1040 (out-of-state). *Fax:* 715-682-1258. *E-mail:* dmilanow@northland.edu.

NORTH PARK UNIVERSITY

Chicago, IL

Tuition & fees: $17,600 **Average undergraduate aid package: N/A**

ABOUT THE INSTITUTION Independent religious, coed. ***Awards:*** bachelor's, master's, doctoral, and first professional degrees. 56 undergraduate majors. ***Total enrollment:*** 2,181. Undergraduates: 1,573. Freshmen: 320. Federal methodology is used as a basis for awarding need-based institutional aid.

UNDERGRADUATE EXPENSES for 2008–09 ***Application fee:*** $40. ***Comprehensive fee:*** $25,180 includes full-time tuition ($17,600) and room and board ($7580). ***College room only:*** $4180. Full-time tuition and fees vary according to program. Room and board charges vary according to board plan, housing facility, and student level. ***Part-time tuition:*** $730 per credit. Part-time tuition and fees vary according to program. ***Payment plan:*** Installment.

FRESHMAN FINANCIAL AID (Fall 2008, est.) 334 applied for aid; of those 87% were deemed to have need. 100% of freshmen with need received aid; of those 7% had need fully met. ***Average financial aid package:*** $11,550 (excluding resources awarded to replace EFC). 17% of all full-time freshmen had no need and received non-need-based gift aid.

GIFT AID (NEED-BASED) ***Total amount:*** $7,669,052 (27% federal, 26% state, 47% institutional). ***Receiving aid:*** Freshmen: 75% (280). ***Average award:*** Freshmen: $5835. ***Scholarships, grants, and awards:*** Federal Pell, FSEOG, state, private, college/university gift aid from institutional funds.

GIFT AID (NON-NEED-BASED) ***Total amount:*** $4,009,485 (89% institutional, 11% external sources). ***Receiving aid:*** Freshmen: 17% (64). ***Average award:*** Freshmen: $2559. ***Scholarships, grants, and awards by category:*** *Academic interests/achievement:* general academic interests/achievements. *Creative arts/performance:* 75 awards ($136,000 total): art/fine arts, journalism/publications, music, theater/drama. *Special achievements/activities:* 409 awards ($190,600 total): religious involvement. *Special characteristics:* 60 awards ($99,000 total): relatives of clergy. ***Tuition waivers:*** Full or partial for employees or children of employees, adult students.

LOANS ***Student loans:*** $9,530,911 (49% need-based, 51% non-need-based). 79% of past graduating class borrowed through all loan programs. ***Average need-based loan:*** Freshmen: $4280. ***Parent loans:*** $2,309,021 (100% need-based). ***Programs:*** Federal Direct (Subsidized and Unsubsidized Stafford, PLUS), Perkins, Federal Nursing.

WORK-STUDY ***Federal work-study:*** Total amount: $225,205; 158 jobs averaging $1500.

APPLYING FOR FINANCIAL AID ***Required financial aid form:*** FAFSA. ***Financial aid deadline (priority):*** 5/1. ***Notification date:*** Continuous.

CONTACT Dr. Lucy Shaker, Director of Financial Aid, North Park University, 3225 West Foster Avenue, Chicago, IL 60625-4895, 773-244-5526 or toll-free 800-888-NPC8. *Fax:* 773-244-4953.

NORTHWEST CHRISTIAN UNIVERSITY

Eugene, OR

Tuition & fees: $21,900 **Average undergraduate aid package: $18,621**

ABOUT THE INSTITUTION Independent Christian, coed. ***Awards:*** associate, bachelor's, and master's degrees and post-bachelor's certificates. 24 undergraduate majors. ***Total enrollment:*** 485. Undergraduates: 396. Freshmen: 53. Federal methodology is used as a basis for awarding need-based institutional aid.

UNDERGRADUATE EXPENSES for 2008–09 ***Comprehensive fee:*** $28,100 includes full-time tuition ($21,900) and room and board ($6200). Full-time tuition and fees vary according to course load and program. Room and board charges vary according to board plan and housing facility. ***Part-time tuition:*** $730 per credit. Part-time tuition and fees vary according to course load and program. ***Payment plans:*** Installment, deferred payment.

FRESHMAN FINANCIAL AID (Fall 2007) 75 applied for aid; of those 93% were deemed to have need. 100% of freshmen with need received aid; of those 21% had need fully met. ***Average percent of need met:*** 79% (excluding resources awarded to replace EFC). ***Average financial aid package:*** $16,822 (excluding resources awarded to replace EFC). 8% of all full-time freshmen had no need and received non-need-based gift aid.

UNDERGRADUATE FINANCIAL AID (Fall 2007) 252 applied for aid; of those 93% were deemed to have need. 100% of undergraduates with need received aid; of those 25% had need fully met. ***Average percent of need met:*** 81% (excluding resources awarded to replace EFC). ***Average financial aid package:*** $18,621 (excluding resources awarded to replace EFC). 9% of all full-time undergraduates had no need and received non-need-based gift aid.

GIFT AID (NEED-BASED) ***Total amount:*** $3,066,773 (15% federal, 5% state, 66% institutional, 14% external sources). ***Receiving aid:*** Freshmen: 91% (70); all full-time undergraduates: 89% (234). ***Average award:*** Freshmen: $13,962; Undergraduates: $14,555. ***Scholarships, grants, and awards:*** Federal Pell, FSEOG, state, private, college/university gift aid from institutional funds.

GIFT AID (NON-NEED-BASED) ***Total amount:*** $255,827 (71% institutional, 29% external sources). ***Receiving aid:*** Freshmen: 10% (8). Undergraduates: 9% (25). ***Average award:*** Freshmen: $6785. Undergraduates: $4917. ***Scholarships, grants, and awards by category:*** *Academic interests/achievement:* 128 awards ($520,000 total): general academic interests/achievements. *Creative arts/performance:* 7 awards ($7000 total): music. *Special achievements/activities:* 52 awards ($82,000 total): leadership. *Special characteristics:* 71 awards ($218,000 total): children of faculty/staff, relatives of clergy, religious affiliation, siblings of current students. ***Tuition waivers:*** Full or partial for employees or children of employees. ***ROTC:*** Army cooperative.

LOANS ***Student loans:*** $1,573,306 (67% need-based, 33% non-need-based). 90% of past graduating class borrowed through all loan programs. *Average indebtedness per student:* $19,843. ***Average need-based loan:*** Freshmen: $2385. Undergraduates: $3784. ***Parent loans:*** $562,088 (52% need-based, 48% non-need-based). ***Programs:*** FFEL (Subsidized and Unsubsidized Stafford, PLUS), Perkins.

WORK-STUDY ***Federal work-study:*** Total amount: $231,263; 88 jobs averaging $2131. ***State or other work-study/employment:*** Total amount: $24,950 (60% need-based, 40% non-need-based). Part-time jobs available.

ATHLETIC AWARDS Total amount: $372,800 (78% need-based, 22% non-need-based).

APPLYING FOR FINANCIAL AID ***Required financial aid forms:*** FAFSA, Merit Worksheet. ***Financial aid deadline (priority):*** 3/1. ***Notification date:*** Continuous beginning 3/1.

CONTACT David Haggard, Director of Financial Aid, Northwest Christian University, 828 East 11th Avenue, Eugene, OR 97401-3727, 541-684-7211 or toll-free 877-463-6622. *Fax:* 541-684-7323. *E-mail:* dhaggard@northwestchristian.edu.

NORTHWEST COLLEGE OF ART

Poulsbo, WA

CONTACT Ms. Kim Y. Perigard, Director of Financial Aid, Northwest College of Art, 16464 State Highway 305, Poulsbo, WA 98370, 360-779-9993 or toll-free 800-769-ARTS.

NORTHWESTERN COLLEGE

Orange City, IA

ABOUT THE INSTITUTION Independent religious, coed. ***Awards:*** bachelor's degrees. 40 undergraduate majors. ***Total enrollment:*** 1,315. Undergraduates: 1,315. Freshmen: 324.

GIFT AID (NEED-BASED) ***Scholarships, grants, and awards:*** Federal Pell, FSEOG, state, private, college/university gift aid from institutional funds.

GIFT AID (NON-NEED-BASED) ***Scholarships, grants, and awards by category:*** *Academic interests/achievement:* biological sciences, business, communication, computer science, education, engineering/technologies, English, foreign languages, general academic interests/achievements, health fields, humanities, mathematics, physical sciences, premedicine, religion/biblical studies, social sciences. *Creative arts/performance:* art/fine arts, journalism/publications, music, theater/drama. *Special characteristics:* adult students, children and siblings of alumni, children of faculty/staff, ethnic background, first-generation college students, handicapped students, international students, religious affiliation, siblings of current students.

LOANS ***Programs:*** FFEL (Subsidized and Unsubsidized Stafford, PLUS), Perkins, Federal Nursing, college/university, alternative loans.

WORK-STUDY ***Federal work-study:*** Total amount: $346,484; 354 jobs averaging $1120. ***State or other work-study/employment:*** Total amount: $785,151 (100% non-need-based). 412 part-time jobs averaging $1120.

APPLYING FOR FINANCIAL AID ***Required financial aid form:*** FAFSA.

CONTACT Mr. Gerry Korver, Director of Financial Aid, Northwestern College, 101 Seventh Street, SW, Orange City, IA 51041-1996, 712-707-7131 or toll-free 800-747-4757. *Fax:* 712-707-7164.

NORTHWESTERN COLLEGE

St. Paul, MN

Tuition & fees: $23,180 **Average undergraduate aid package: $15,620**

ABOUT THE INSTITUTION Independent nondenominational, coed. ***Awards:*** associate, bachelor's, and master's degrees and post-bachelor's certificates. 49 undergraduate majors. ***Total enrollment:*** 1,939. Undergraduates: 1,846. Freshmen: 437. Federal methodology is used as a basis for awarding need-based institutional aid.

UNDERGRADUATE EXPENSES for 2009–10 ***Application fee:*** $30. ***Comprehensive fee:*** $30,606 includes full-time tuition ($22,990), mandatory fees ($190), and room and board ($7426). ***College room only:*** $4266.

FRESHMAN FINANCIAL AID (Fall 2008, est.) 408 applied for aid; of those 85% were deemed to have need. 100% of freshmen with need received aid; of those 9% had need fully met. ***Average percent of need met:*** 70% (excluding resources awarded to replace EFC). ***Average financial aid package:*** $15,864 (excluding resources awarded to replace EFC). 18% of all full-time freshmen had no need and received non-need-based gift aid.

UNDERGRADUATE FINANCIAL AID (Fall 2008, est.) 1,626 applied for aid; of those 88% were deemed to have need. 100% of undergraduates with need received aid; of those 11% had need fully met. ***Average percent of need met:*** 71% (excluding resources awarded to replace EFC). ***Average financial aid package:*** $15,620 (excluding resources awarded to replace EFC). 17% of all full-time undergraduates had no need and received non-need-based gift aid.

GIFT AID (NEED-BASED) ***Total amount:*** $15,245,312 (13% federal, 14% state, 70% institutional, 3% external sources). ***Receiving aid:*** Freshmen: 78% (339); all full-time undergraduates: 78% (1,402). ***Average award:*** Freshmen: $11,949; Undergraduates: $10,758. ***Scholarships, grants, and awards:*** Federal Pell, FSEOG, state, private, college/university gift aid from institutional funds.

GIFT AID (NON-NEED-BASED) ***Total amount:*** $2,098,560 (91% institutional, 9% external sources). ***Receiving aid:*** Freshmen: 4% (17). Undergraduates: 5% (96). ***Average award:*** Freshmen: $6150. Undergraduates: $5483. ***Scholarships, grants, and awards by category:*** *Academic interests/achievement:* 806 awards ($2,863,051 total): general academic interests/achievements. *Creative arts/performance:* 164 awards ($211,725 total): music, theater/drama. *Special achievements/activities:* 158 awards ($301,187 total): leadership. *Special characteristics:* 672 awards ($3,572,327 total): children of faculty/staff, ethnic background, international students, relatives of clergy, siblings of current students. ***ROTC:*** Army cooperative, Air Force cooperative.

LOANS ***Student loans:*** $11,152,394 (74% need-based, 26% non-need-based). 83% of past graduating class borrowed through all loan programs. *Average indebtedness per student:* $24,224. ***Average need-based loan:*** Freshmen: $3830. Undergraduates: $4541. ***Parent loans:*** $5,426,520 (34% need-based, 66% non-need-based). ***Programs:*** Federal Direct (Subsidized and Unsubsidized Stafford, PLUS), Perkins, state.

WORK-STUDY ***Federal work-study:*** Total amount: $552,662; 241 jobs averaging $2305. ***State or other work-study/employment:*** Total amount: $650,770 (75% need-based, 25% non-need-based). 184 part-time jobs averaging $2126.

APPLYING FOR FINANCIAL AID ***Required financial aid forms:*** FAFSA, institution's own form. ***Financial aid deadline (priority):*** 3/1. ***Notification date:*** Continuous beginning 3/1. Students must reply within 2 weeks of notification.

CONTACT Mr. Richard L. Blatchley, Director of Financial Aid, Northwestern College, 3003 Snelling Avenue North, St. Paul, MN 55113-1598, 651-631-5321 or toll-free 800-827-6827. *Fax:* 651-628-3332. *E-mail:* rlb@nwc.edu.

NORTHWESTERN OKLAHOMA STATE UNIVERSITY

Alva, OK

Tuition & fees (OK res): $4111 Average undergraduate aid package: $6513

ABOUT THE INSTITUTION State-supported, coed. ***Awards:*** bachelor's and master's degrees and post-bachelor's and post-master's certificates. 44 undergraduate majors. ***Total enrollment:*** 2,030. Undergraduates: 1,787. Freshmen: 340. Both federal and institutional methodology are used as a basis for awarding need-based institutional aid.

UNDERGRADUATE EXPENSES for 2008–09 ***Application fee:*** $15. ***Tuition, state resident:*** full-time $3488; part-time $116.25 per credit hour. ***Tuition, nonresident:*** full-time $9518; part-time $317.25 per credit hour. ***Required fees:*** full-time $623; $20.75 per credit hour. Full-time tuition and fees vary according to course load, location, and program. Part-time tuition and fees vary according to course load, location, and program. ***College room and board:*** $3430; ***Room only:*** $1300. Room and board charges vary according to board plan. ***Payment plan:*** Installment.

FRESHMAN FINANCIAL AID (Fall 2007) 198 applied for aid; of those 74% were deemed to have need. 98% of freshmen with need received aid; of those 52% had need fully met. ***Average percent of need met:*** 69% (excluding resources awarded to replace EFC). ***Average financial aid package:*** $6242 (excluding resources awarded to replace EFC). 41% of all full-time freshmen had no need and received non-need-based gift aid.

UNDERGRADUATE FINANCIAL AID (Fall 2007) 847 applied for aid; of those 80% were deemed to have need. 97% of undergraduates with need received aid; of those 51% had need fully met. ***Average percent of need met:*** 70% (excluding resources awarded to replace EFC). ***Average financial aid package:*** $6513 (excluding resources awarded to replace EFC). 18% of all full-time undergraduates had no need and received non-need-based gift aid.

GIFT AID (NEED-BASED) ***Total amount:*** $3,462,981 (63% federal, 29% state, 8% institutional). ***Receiving aid:*** Freshmen: 42% (126); all full-time undergraduates: 44% (540). ***Average award:*** Freshmen: $5186; Undergraduates: $4761. ***Scholarships, grants, and awards:*** Federal Pell, FSEOG, state, private, college/university gift aid from institutional funds.

GIFT AID (NON-NEED-BASED) ***Total amount:*** $866,317 (7% state, 47% institutional, 46% external sources). ***Receiving aid:*** Freshmen: 9% (27). Undergraduates: 5% (60). ***Average award:*** Freshmen: $1578. Undergraduates: $1449. ***Scholarships, grants, and awards by category:*** *Academic interests/achievement:* 266 awards ($364,027 total): agriculture, biological sciences, business, communication, computer science, education, English, foreign languages, general academic interests/achievements, health fields, library science, mathematics, physical sciences, premedicine, social sciences. *Creative arts/performance:* 57 awards ($51,814 total): art/fine arts, cinema/film/broadcasting, debating, general creative arts/performance, journalism/publications, music, theater/drama. *Special achievements/activities:* 128 awards ($215,550 total): cheerleading/drum major, general special achievements/activities, leadership, memberships, rodeo. *Special characteristics:* 51 awards ($85,203 total): children of faculty/staff. ***Tuition waivers:*** Full or partial for employees or children of employees, senior citizens.

LOANS ***Student loans:*** $3,893,099 (58% need-based, 42% non-need-based). 51% of past graduating class borrowed through all loan programs. *Average indebtedness per student:* $11,541. ***Average need-based loan:*** Freshmen: $2005. Undergraduates: $3354. ***Parent loans:*** $100,817 (100% non-need-based). ***Programs:*** FFEL (Subsidized and Unsubsidized Stafford, PLUS), Perkins.

WORK-STUDY ***Federal work-study:*** Total amount: $139,207; 123 jobs averaging $1132. ***State or other work-study/employment:*** Total amount: $230,569 (100% non-need-based). 199 part-time jobs averaging $1159.

ATHLETIC AWARDS Total amount: $280,127 (74% need-based, 26% non-need-based).

APPLYING FOR FINANCIAL AID ***Required financial aid forms:*** FAFSA, institution's own form. ***Financial aid deadline:*** Continuous. ***Notification date:*** Continuous beginning 3/1. Students must reply by 8/15.

CONTACT Irala K. Magee, Director of Financial Aid, Northwestern Oklahoma State University, 709 Oklahoma Boulevard, Alva, OK 73717-2799, 580-327-1700 Ext. 8542. *Fax:* 580-327-8177. *E-mail:* ikmagee@nwosu.edu.

NORTHWESTERN STATE UNIVERSITY OF LOUISIANA

Natchitoches, LA

Tuition & fees (LA res): $3598 Average undergraduate aid package: $6090

ABOUT THE INSTITUTION State-supported, coed. ***Awards:*** associate, bachelor's, and master's degrees and post-master's certificates. 50 undergraduate majors. ***Total enrollment:*** 9,111. Undergraduates: 8,053. Freshmen: 1,233. Both federal and institutional methodology are used as a basis for awarding need-based institutional aid.

UNDERGRADUATE EXPENSES for 2008–09 ***Application fee:*** $20. ***Tuition, state resident:*** full-time $2412; part-time $385 per credit. ***Tuition, nonresident:*** full-time $8490; part-time $638 per credit. ***Required fees:*** full-time $1186. Full-time tuition and fees vary according to course load. Part-time tuition and fees vary according to course load. ***College room and board:*** $6272; ***Room only:*** $4122. Room and board charges vary according to board plan, housing facility, and location. ***Payment plan:*** Installment.

FRESHMAN FINANCIAL AID (Fall 2007) 994 applied for aid; of those 85% were deemed to have need. 96% of freshmen with need received aid; of those 32% had need fully met. ***Average percent of need met:*** 51% (excluding resources awarded to replace EFC). ***Average financial aid package:*** $5247 (excluding resources awarded to replace EFC). 21% of all full-time freshmen had no need and received non-need-based gift aid.

UNDERGRADUATE FINANCIAL AID (Fall 2007) 4,133 applied for aid; of those 88% were deemed to have need. 95% of undergraduates with need received aid; of those 25% had need fully met. ***Average percent of need met:*** 40% (excluding resources awarded to replace EFC). ***Average financial aid package:*** $6090 (excluding resources awarded to replace EFC). 22% of all full-time undergraduates had no need and received non-need-based gift aid.

GIFT AID (NEED-BASED) ***Total amount:*** $9,260,737 (99% federal, 1% state). ***Receiving aid:*** Freshmen: 38% (491); all full-time undergraduates: 40% (2,224). ***Average award:*** Freshmen: $3821; Undergraduates: $3627. ***Scholarships, grants, and awards:*** Federal Pell, FSEOG, state, private, college/university gift aid from institutional funds, United Negro College Fund, Federal Nursing, third party scholarships.

GIFT AID (NON-NEED-BASED) ***Total amount:*** $9,624,361 (59% state, 22% institutional, 19% external sources). ***Receiving aid:*** Freshmen: 42% (533). Undergraduates: 24% (1,355). ***Average award:*** Freshmen: $4403. Undergraduates: $1353. ***Scholarships, grants, and awards by category:*** *Academic interests/achievement:* 2,195 awards ($1,847,647 total): biological sciences, education, engineering/technologies, general academic interests/achievements, health fields, humanities, mathematics, physical sciences. *Creative arts/performance:* 489 awards ($578,706 total): art/fine arts, cinema/film/broadcasting, creative writing, dance, general creative arts/performance, journalism/publications, music, performing arts, theater/drama. *Special achievements/activities:* 121 awards ($126,747 total): cheerleading/drum major, general special achievements/activities, leadership, memberships. *Special characteristics:* 783 awards ($2,670,298 total): adult students, children of faculty/staff, children of public servants, general special characteristics, international students, out-of-state students, public servants, veterans, veterans' children. ***Tuition waivers:*** Full or partial for employees or children of employees, senior citizens. ***ROTC:*** Army.

LOANS ***Student loans:*** $23,356,846 (50% need-based, 50% non-need-based). 72% of past graduating class borrowed through all loan programs. *Average indebtedness per student:* $22,045. ***Average need-based loan:*** Freshmen: $4390. Undergraduates: $5953. ***Parent loans:*** $311,935 (100% non-need-based). ***Programs:*** FFEL (Subsidized and Unsubsidized Stafford, PLUS), Perkins, alternative loans.

WORK-STUDY ***Federal work-study:*** Total amount: $310,394; 300 jobs averaging $1035. ***State or other work-study/employment:*** Total amount: $871,148 (100% non-need-based). 610 part-time jobs averaging $1428.

ATHLETIC AWARDS Total amount: $2,269,511 (100% non-need-based).

APPLYING FOR FINANCIAL AID ***Required financial aid forms:*** FAFSA, institution's own form. ***Financial aid deadline (priority):*** 5/1. ***Notification date:*** Continuous beginning 5/1. Students must reply within 4 weeks of notification.

CONTACT Ms. Misti Adams, Director of Financial Aid, Northwestern State University of Louisiana, 103 Roy Hall, Northwestern State University, Natchitoches, LA 71497, 318-357-5961 or toll-free 800-327-1903. *Fax:* 318-357-5488. *E-mail:* nsufinaid@nsula.edu.

NORTHWESTERN UNIVERSITY

Evanston, IL

Tuition & fees: $38,461 **Average undergraduate aid package: $29,411**

ABOUT THE INSTITUTION Independent, coed. ***Awards:*** bachelor's, master's, doctoral, and first professional degrees and post-master's certificates. 112 undergraduate majors. ***Total enrollment:*** 18,431. Undergraduates: 8,476. Freshmen: 2,078. Both federal and institutional methodology are used as a basis for awarding need-based institutional aid.

UNDERGRADUATE EXPENSES for 2009–10 ***Application fee:*** $65. ***Comprehensive fee:*** $50,164 includes full-time tuition ($38,088), mandatory fees ($373), and room and board ($11,703). ***College room only:*** $6657.

FRESHMAN FINANCIAL AID (Fall 2008, est.) 1,095 applied for aid; of those 77% were deemed to have need. 100% of freshmen with need received aid; of those 100% had need fully met. ***Average percent of need met:*** 100% (excluding resources awarded to replace EFC). ***Average financial aid package:*** $28,362 (excluding resources awarded to replace EFC). 5% of all full-time freshmen had no need and received non-need-based gift aid.

UNDERGRADUATE FINANCIAL AID (Fall 2008, est.) 4,078 applied for aid; of those 85% were deemed to have need. 100% of undergraduates with need received aid; of those 100% had need fully met. ***Average percent of need met:*** 100% (excluding resources awarded to replace EFC). ***Average financial aid package:*** $29,411 (excluding resources awarded to replace EFC). 4% of all full-time undergraduates had no need and received non-need-based gift aid.

GIFT AID (NEED-BASED) ***Total amount:*** $87,186,481 (5% federal, 3% state, 88% institutional, 4% external sources). ***Receiving aid:*** Freshmen: 38% (796); all full-time undergraduates: 40% (3,302). ***Average award:*** Freshmen: $26,100; Undergraduates: $25,936. ***Scholarships, grants, and awards:*** Federal Pell, FSEOG, state, private, college/university gift aid from institutional funds, United Negro College Fund.

GIFT AID (NON-NEED-BASED) ***Total amount:*** $2,186,598 (38% institutional, 62% external sources). ***Average award:*** Freshmen: $2634. Undergraduates: $2243. ***Scholarships, grants, and awards by category:*** *Creative arts/performance:* 127 awards ($425,096 total): music. *Special characteristics:* 38 awards ($1,345,583 total): international students. ***ROTC:*** Army cooperative, Naval, Air Force cooperative.

LOANS ***Student loans:*** $21,901,482 (80% need-based, 20% non-need-based). 49% of past graduating class borrowed through all loan programs. *Average indebtedness per student:* $19,000. ***Average need-based loan:*** Freshmen: $3051. Undergraduates: $4560. ***Parent loans:*** $17,650,421 (100% non-need-based). ***Programs:*** FFEL (Subsidized and Unsubsidized Stafford, PLUS), Perkins, college/university.

WORK-STUDY ***Federal work-study:*** Total amount: $3,400,000; 2,301 jobs averaging $2050. ***State or other work-study/employment:*** Total amount: $1,220,486 (100% need-based). Part-time jobs available.

ATHLETIC AWARDS Total amount: $12,207,413 (100% non-need-based).

APPLYING FOR FINANCIAL AID ***Required financial aid forms:*** FAFSA, CSS Financial Aid PROFILE, noncustodial (divorced/separated) parent's statement, business/farm supplement, parent and student federal or foreign tax returns. ***Financial aid deadline:*** 2/15. ***Notification date:*** 4/15. Students must reply by 5/1 or within 2 weeks of notification.

CONTACT Office of Financial Aid, Northwestern University, PO Box 3060, Evanston, IL 60204-3060, 847-491-7400. *E-mail:* newstudentaid@northwestern.edu.

NORTHWEST MISSOURI STATE UNIVERSITY

Maryville, MO

Tuition & fees (MO res): $5529 **Average undergraduate aid package: $8497**

ABOUT THE INSTITUTION State-supported, coed. ***Awards:*** bachelor's and master's degrees and post-bachelor's and post-master's certificates. 116 undergraduate majors. ***Total enrollment:*** 6,903. Undergraduates: 5,782. Freshmen: 1,533. Federal methodology is used as a basis for awarding need-based institutional aid.

UNDERGRADUATE EXPENSES for 2009–10 ***Application fee:*** $25. ***One-time required fee:*** $100. ***Tuition, state resident:*** full-time $5145; part-time $214 per credit hour. ***Tuition, nonresident:*** full-time $8923; part-time $372 per credit hour. ***Required fees:*** full-time $384; $16 per credit hour. ***College room and board:*** $6876; ***Room only:*** $3966.

FRESHMAN FINANCIAL AID (Fall 2007) 1,348 applied for aid; of those 72% were deemed to have need. 100% of freshmen with need received aid; of those 36% had need fully met. ***Average percent of need met:*** 65% (excluding resources awarded to replace EFC). ***Average financial aid package:*** $8680 (excluding resources awarded to replace EFC). 26% of all full-time freshmen had no need and received non-need-based gift aid.

UNDERGRADUATE FINANCIAL AID (Fall 2007) 4,143 applied for aid; of those 77% were deemed to have need. 100% of undergraduates with need received aid; of those 33% had need fully met. ***Average percent of need met:*** 63% (excluding resources awarded to replace EFC). ***Average financial aid package:*** $8497 (excluding resources awarded to replace EFC). 17% of all full-time undergraduates had no need and received non-need-based gift aid.

GIFT AID (NEED-BASED) ***Total amount:*** $12,584,729 (41% federal, 19% state, 38% institutional, 2% external sources). ***Receiving aid:*** Freshmen: 52% (804); all full-time undergraduates: 43% (2,199). ***Average award:*** Freshmen: $4678; Undergraduates: $3970. ***Scholarships, grants, and awards:*** Federal Pell, FSEOG, state, private, college/university gift aid from institutional funds.

GIFT AID (NON-NEED-BASED) ***Total amount:*** $2,302,405 (10% state, 85% institutional, 5% external sources). ***Receiving aid:*** Freshmen: 54% (823). Undergraduates: 35% (1,799). ***Average award:*** Freshmen: $1554. Undergraduates: $1976. ***Scholarships, grants, and awards by category:*** *Academic interests/achievement:* agriculture, biological sciences, business, communication, computer science, education, English, foreign languages, general academic interests/achievements, health fields, home economics, humanities, mathematics, physical sciences, social sciences. *Creative arts/performance:* art/fine arts, cinema/film/broadcasting, debating, journalism/publications, music, theater/drama. *Special achievements/activities:* cheerleading/drum major, general special achievements/activities, leadership, memberships. *Special characteristics:* children and siblings of alumni, general special characteristics, members of minority groups, out-of-state students, previous college experience. ***ROTC:*** Army.

LOANS ***Student loans:*** $22,364,564 (66% need-based, 34% non-need-based). 70% of past graduating class borrowed through all loan programs. *Average indebtedness per student:* $19,861. ***Average need-based loan:*** Freshmen: $3243. Undergraduates: $3955. ***Parent loans:*** $12,503,377 (20% need-based, 80% non-need-based). ***Programs:*** Federal Direct (Subsidized and Unsubsidized Stafford, PLUS), Perkins.

WORK-STUDY ***Federal work-study:*** Total amount: $480,993; jobs available. ***State or other work-study/employment:*** Total amount: $1,552,042 (21% need-based, 79% non-need-based). Part-time jobs available.

ATHLETIC AWARDS Total amount: $1,698,400 (48% need-based, 52% non-need-based).

APPLYING FOR FINANCIAL AID ***Required financial aid form:*** FAFSA. ***Financial aid deadline:*** Continuous. ***Notification date:*** Continuous beginning 3/15. Students must reply within 3 weeks of notification.

CONTACT Mr. Del Morley, Director of Financial Assistance, Northwest Missouri State University, 800 University Drive, Maryville, MO 64468-6001, 660-562-1138 or toll-free 800-633-1175.

NORTHWEST NAZARENE UNIVERSITY

Nampa, ID

CONTACT Mr. Wes Maggard, Director of Financial Aid, Northwest Nazarene University, 623 Holly Street, Nampa, ID 83686, 208-467-8774 or toll-free 877-668-4968. *Fax:* 208-467-8375. *E-mail:* mwmaggard@nnu.edu.

NORTHWEST UNIVERSITY

Kirkland, WA

Tuition & fees: $20,790 **Average undergraduate aid package: $14,010**

ABOUT THE INSTITUTION Independent religious, coed. ***Awards:*** associate, bachelor's, and master's degrees. 43 undergraduate majors. ***Total enrollment:*** 1,290. Undergraduates: 1,114. Freshmen: 311. Federal methodology is used as a basis for awarding need-based institutional aid.

UNDERGRADUATE EXPENSES for 2008–09 ***Application fee:*** $30. ***Comprehensive fee:*** $27,368 includes full-time tuition ($20,520), mandatory fees ($270), and room and board ($6578). Full-time tuition and fees vary according to class time and program. Room and board charges vary according to board plan and housing facility. ***Part-time tuition:*** $855 per credit. ***Part-time fees:*** $135 per term. Part-time tuition and fees vary according to course load. ***Payment plan:*** Installment.

FRESHMAN FINANCIAL AID (Fall 2008, est.) 164 applied for aid; of those 83% were deemed to have need. 100% of freshmen with need received aid; of those 22% had need fully met. ***Average percent of need met:*** 75% (excluding resources awarded to replace EFC). ***Average financial aid package:*** $15,217 (excluding resources awarded to replace EFC). 17% of all full-time freshmen had no need and received non-need-based gift aid.

UNDERGRADUATE FINANCIAL AID (Fall 2008, est.) 832 applied for aid; of those 86% were deemed to have need. 99% of undergraduates with need received aid; of those 17% had need fully met. ***Average percent of need met:*** 70% (excluding resources awarded to replace EFC). ***Average financial aid package:*** $14,010 (excluding resources awarded to replace EFC). 16% of all full-time undergraduates had no need and received non-need-based gift aid.

GIFT AID (NEED-BASED) ***Total amount:*** $6,606,546 (20% federal, 15% state, 56% institutional, 9% external sources). ***Receiving aid:*** Freshmen: 74% (136); all full-time undergraduates: 73% (702). ***Average award:*** Freshmen: $12,340; Undergraduates: $10,461. ***Scholarships, grants, and awards:*** Federal Pell, FSEOG, state, private, college/university gift aid from institutional funds.

GIFT AID (NON-NEED-BASED) ***Total amount:*** $1,287,517 (83% institutional, 17% external sources). ***Receiving aid:*** Freshmen: 11% (20). Undergraduates: 7% (67). ***Average award:*** Freshmen: $5270. Undergraduates: $5614. ***Scholarships, grants, and awards by category:*** *Academic interests/achievement:* 219 awards ($717,625 total): general academic interests/achievements. *Creative arts/performance:* 102 awards ($237,101 total): debating, music, performing arts, theater/drama. *Special achievements/activities:* 25 awards ($370,031 total): leadership. *Special characteristics:* 198 awards ($1,015,098 total): children of current students, children of faculty/staff, general special characteristics, international students, married students, parents of current students, relatives of clergy, religious affiliation, siblings of current students, spouses of current students. ***Tuition waivers:*** Full or partial for employees or children of employees. ***ROTC:*** Army cooperative.

LOANS ***Student loans:*** $7,052,163 (68% need-based, 32% non-need-based). 95% of past graduating class borrowed through all loan programs. *Average indebtedness per student:* $30,198. ***Average need-based loan:*** Freshmen: $3220. Undergraduates: $4007. ***Parent loans:*** $875,141 (34% need-based, 66% non-need-based). ***Programs:*** FFEL (Subsidized and Unsubsidized Stafford, PLUS), Perkins, state, alternative loans.

WORK-STUDY ***Federal work-study:*** Total amount: $153,155; 77 jobs averaging $3500. ***State or other work-study/employment:*** Total amount: $191,069 (86% need-based, 14% non-need-based). 27 part-time jobs averaging $3500.

ATHLETIC AWARDS Total amount: $647,732 (59% need-based, 41% non-need-based).

APPLYING FOR FINANCIAL AID ***Required financial aid forms:*** FAFSA, institution's own form. ***Financial aid deadline:*** 8/1 (priority: 2/15). ***Notification date:*** Continuous beginning 3/3. Students must reply within 4 weeks of notification.

CONTACT Ms. Lana J. Walter, Director of Financial Aid, Northwest University, PO Box 579, Kirkland, WA 98083-0579, 425-889-5336 or toll-free 800-669-3781. *Fax:* 425-889-5224. *E-mail:* lana.walter@northwestu.edu.

NORTHWOOD UNIVERSITY

Midland, MI

Tuition & fees: $17,544 **Average undergraduate aid package: $14,635**

ABOUT THE INSTITUTION Independent, coed. ***Awards:*** associate, bachelor's, and master's degrees. 5 undergraduate majors. ***Total enrollment:*** 2,269. Undergraduates: 1,950. Freshmen: 442. Federal methodology is used as a basis for awarding need-based institutional aid.

UNDERGRADUATE EXPENSES for 2008–09 ***Application fee:*** $25. ***Comprehensive fee:*** $25,092 includes full-time tuition ($16,620), mandatory fees ($924), and room and board ($7548). ***College room only:*** $3900. ***Part-time tuition:*** $346 per credit hour.

FRESHMAN FINANCIAL AID (Fall 2008, est.) 372 applied for aid; of those 87% were deemed to have need. 100% of freshmen with need received aid; of those 28% had need fully met. ***Average percent of need met:*** 55% (excluding resources awarded to replace EFC). ***Average financial aid package:*** $15,694 (excluding resources awarded to replace EFC). 16% of all full-time freshmen had no need and received non-need-based gift aid.

UNDERGRADUATE FINANCIAL AID (Fall 2008, est.) 1,437 applied for aid; of those 86% were deemed to have need. 100% of undergraduates with need received aid; of those 26% had need fully met. ***Average percent of need met:*** 53% (excluding resources awarded to replace EFC). ***Average financial aid package:*** $14,635 (excluding resources awarded to replace EFC). 16% of all full-time undergraduates had no need and received non-need-based gift aid.

GIFT AID (NEED-BASED) ***Total amount:*** $10,902,605 (19% federal, 19% state, 59% institutional, 3% external sources). ***Receiving aid:*** Freshmen: 61% (271); all full-time undergraduates: 55% (1,045). ***Average award:*** Freshmen: $6457; Undergraduates: $5481. ***Scholarships, grants, and awards:*** Federal Pell, FSEOG, state, private, college/university gift aid from institutional funds.

GIFT AID (NON-NEED-BASED) ***Total amount:*** $2,992,366 (5% state, 91% institutional, 4% external sources). ***Receiving aid:*** Freshmen: 32% (140). Undergraduates: 28% (531). ***Average award:*** Freshmen: $6155. Undergraduates: $5824. ***Scholarships, grants, and awards by category:*** *Academic interests/achievement:* 1,247 awards ($7,145,823 total): business, general academic interests/achievements. *Special achievements/activities:* 258 awards ($296,574 total): cheerleading/drum major, leadership, memberships. *Special characteristics:* 151 awards ($680,202 total): children and siblings of alumni, children of faculty/staff, siblings of current students.

LOANS ***Student loans:*** $11,536,932 (70% need-based, 30% non-need-based). 71% of past graduating class borrowed through all loan programs. *Average indebtedness per student:* $27,544. ***Average need-based loan:*** Freshmen: $3196. Undergraduates: $4178. ***Parent loans:*** $1,248,396 (25% need-based, 75% non-need-based). ***Programs:*** FFEL (Subsidized and Unsubsidized Stafford, PLUS), state.

WORK-STUDY ***Federal work-study:*** Total amount: $680,919; 391 jobs averaging $1742. ***State or other work-study/employment:*** Total amount: $85,466 (100% need-based). 54 part-time jobs averaging $1583.

ATHLETIC AWARDS Total amount: $2,083,938 (53% need-based, 47% non-need-based).

APPLYING FOR FINANCIAL AID ***Required financial aid form:*** FAFSA. ***Financial aid deadline:*** Continuous. ***Notification date:*** Continuous beginning 3/1.

CONTACT Terri Mieler, Director of Financial Aid, Northwood University, 4000 Whiting Drive, Midland, MI 48640-2398, 989-837-4301 or toll-free 800-457-7878. *Fax:* 989-837-4130. *E-mail:* mieler@northwood.edu.

NORTHWOOD UNIVERSITY, FLORIDA CAMPUS

West Palm Beach, FL

Tuition & fees: $18,408 **Average undergraduate aid package: $15,875**

ABOUT THE INSTITUTION Independent, coed. ***Awards:*** associate and bachelor's degrees. 11 undergraduate majors. ***Total enrollment:*** 620. Undergraduates: 620. Freshmen: 109. Federal methodology is used as a basis for awarding need-based institutional aid.

UNDERGRADUATE EXPENSES for 2009–10 ***Application fee:*** $25. ***Comprehensive fee:*** $26,970 includes full-time tuition ($17,430), mandatory fees ($978), and room and board ($8562).

FRESHMAN FINANCIAL AID (Fall 2008, est.) 65 applied for aid; of those 86% were deemed to have need. 100% of freshmen with need received aid; of those 21% had need fully met. ***Average percent of need met:*** 60% (excluding resources awarded to replace EFC). ***Average financial aid package:*** $15,808 (excluding resources awarded to replace EFC). 13% of all full-time freshmen had no need and received non-need-based gift aid.

UNDERGRADUATE FINANCIAL AID (Fall 2008, est.) 279 applied for aid; of those 85% were deemed to have need. 99% of undergraduates with need received aid; of those 18% had need fully met. ***Average percent of need met:*** 56% (excluding resources awarded to replace EFC). ***Average financial aid***

package: $15,875 (excluding resources awarded to replace EFC). 19% of all full-time undergraduates had no need and received non-need-based gift aid.

GIFT AID (NEED-BASED) ***Total amount:*** $2,143,402 (23% federal, 9% state, 67% institutional, 1% external sources). ***Receiving aid:*** Freshmen: 46% (50); all full-time undergraduates: 33% (197). ***Average award:*** Freshmen: $7122; Undergraduates: $6943. ***Scholarships, grants, and awards:*** Federal Pell, FSEOG, state, private, college/university gift aid from institutional funds.

GIFT AID (NON-NEED-BASED) ***Total amount:*** $1,212,959 (9% state, 88% institutional, 3% external sources). ***Receiving aid:*** Freshmen: 19% (21). Undergraduates: 14% (83). ***Average award:*** Freshmen: $4739. Undergraduates: $5290. ***Scholarships, grants, and awards by category:*** *Academic interests/achievement:* 328 awards ($1,553,094 total): business, general academic interests/achievements. *Special achievements/activities:* memberships. *Special characteristics:* 23 awards ($98,910 total): children and siblings of alumni, children of faculty/staff, siblings of current students.

LOANS ***Student loans:*** $2,413,962 (69% need-based, 31% non-need-based). 61% of past graduating class borrowed through all loan programs. *Average indebtedness per student:* $22,488. ***Average need-based loan:*** Freshmen: $3309. Undergraduates: $4322. ***Parent loans:*** $555,882 (33% need-based, 67% non-need-based). ***Programs:*** FFEL (Subsidized and Unsubsidized Stafford, PLUS).

WORK-STUDY ***Federal work-study:*** Total amount: $187,379; 90 jobs averaging $2082.

ATHLETIC AWARDS Total amount: $1,310,381 (25% need-based, 75% non-need-based).

APPLYING FOR FINANCIAL AID ***Required financial aid forms:*** FAFSA, state aid form. ***Financial aid deadline:*** Continuous. ***Notification date:*** Continuous beginning 3/1.

CONTACT Ms. Teresa A. Palmer, Director of Financial Aid, Northwood University, Florida Campus, 2600 North Military Trail, West Palm Beach, FL 33409-2911, 561-478-5590 or toll-free 800-458-8325. *Fax:* 561-681-7990. *E-mail:* palmer@northwood.edu.

NORTHWOOD UNIVERSITY, TEXAS CAMPUS

Cedar Hill, TX

Tuition & fees: $18,408 **Average undergraduate aid package: $16,025**

ABOUT THE INSTITUTION Independent, coed. ***Awards:*** bachelor's degrees. 3 undergraduate majors. ***Total enrollment:*** 461. Undergraduates: 461. Freshmen: 89. Federal methodology is used as a basis for awarding need-based institutional aid.

UNDERGRADUATE EXPENSES for 2009–10 ***Application fee:*** $25. ***Comprehensive fee:*** $25,998 includes full-time tuition ($17,430), mandatory fees ($978), and room and board ($7590). ***Part-time tuition:*** $363 per quarter hour.

FRESHMAN FINANCIAL AID (Fall 2008, est.) 80 applied for aid; of those 91% were deemed to have need. 100% of freshmen with need received aid; of those 18% had need fully met. ***Average percent of need met:*** 64% (excluding resources awarded to replace EFC). ***Average financial aid package:*** $16,727 (excluding resources awarded to replace EFC). 8% of all full-time freshmen had no need and received non-need-based gift aid.

UNDERGRADUATE FINANCIAL AID (Fall 2008, est.) 334 applied for aid; of those 91% were deemed to have need. 100% of undergraduates with need received aid; of those 19% had need fully met. ***Average percent of need met:*** 60% (excluding resources awarded to replace EFC). ***Average financial aid package:*** $16,025 (excluding resources awarded to replace EFC). 12% of all full-time undergraduates had no need and received non-need-based gift aid.

GIFT AID (NEED-BASED) ***Total amount:*** $2,877,175 (23% federal, 75% institutional, 2% external sources). ***Receiving aid:*** Freshmen: 66% (59); all full-time undergraduates: 56% (246). ***Average award:*** Freshmen: $6098; Undergraduates: $5279. ***Scholarships, grants, and awards:*** Federal Pell, FSEOG, state, private, college/university gift aid from institutional funds.

GIFT AID (NON-NEED-BASED) ***Total amount:*** $732,503 (96% institutional, 4% external sources). ***Receiving aid:*** Freshmen: 21% (19). Undergraduates: 20% (89). ***Average award:*** Freshmen: $6000. Undergraduates: $5879. ***Scholarships, grants, and awards by category:*** *Academic interests/achievement:* 319 awards ($2,180,631 total): business, general academic interests/achievements. *Special achievements/activities:* general special achievements/activities, memberships. *Special characteristics:* [illegible] awards ([illegible] total): children and siblings of alumni, children of faculty/staff, siblings of current students.

LOANS ***Student loans:*** $3,007,548 (71% need-based, 29% non-need-based). 83% of past graduating class borrowed through all loan programs. *Average indebtedness per student:* $22,820. ***Average need-based loan:*** Freshmen: $3344. Undergraduates: $4432. ***Parent loans:*** $385,612 (26% need-based, 74% non-need-based). ***Programs:*** FFEL (Subsidized and Unsubsidized Stafford, PLUS).

WORK-STUDY ***Federal work-study:*** Total amount: $339,816; 36 jobs averaging $2100.

ATHLETIC AWARDS Total amount: $657,937 (44% need-based, 56% non-need-based).

APPLYING FOR FINANCIAL AID ***Required financial aid form:*** FAFSA. ***Financial aid deadline:*** Continuous. ***Notification date:*** Continuous beginning 3/1.

CONTACT Lisa Seals, Director of Financial Aid, Northwood University, Texas Campus, 1114 West FM 1382, Cedar Hill, TX 75104, 972-293-5479 or toll-free 800-927-9663. *Fax:* 972-293-7196. *E-mail:* sealsl@northwood.edu.

NORWICH UNIVERSITY

Northfield, VT

CONTACT Director of Student Financial Planning, Norwich University, 158 Harmon Drive, Northfield, VT 05663, 802-485-2015 or toll-free 800-468-6679.

NOTRE DAME COLLEGE

South Euclid, OH

ABOUT THE INSTITUTION Independent Roman Catholic, coed. 33 undergraduate majors.

GIFT AID (NEED-BASED) ***Scholarships, grants, and awards:*** Federal Pell, FSEOG, state, private, college/university gift aid from institutional funds, Academic Competitiveness Grant, National Smart Grant.

GIFT AID (NON-NEED-BASED) ***Scholarships, grants, and awards by category:*** *Academic interests/achievement:* general academic interests/achievements. *Creative arts/performance:* art/fine arts, general creative arts/performance. *Special achievements/activities:* community service, general special achievements/activities, leadership, memberships, religious involvement. *Special characteristics:* international students.

LOANS ***Programs:*** FFEL (Subsidized and Unsubsidized Stafford, PLUS), Perkins.

WORK-STUDY ***Federal work-study:*** Total amount: $56,893; 81 jobs averaging $1042.

APPLYING FOR FINANCIAL AID ***Required financial aid form:*** FAFSA.

CONTACT Zhana Goltser, Director of Financial Aid, Notre Dame College, 4701 North Charles Street, Baltimore, MD 21210-2404, 410-532-5369 or toll-free 800-632-1680. *Fax:* 410-532-6287. *E-mail:* finaid@ndm.edu.

NOTRE DAME DE NAMUR UNIVERSITY

Belmont, CA

Tuition & fees: $27,200 **Average undergraduate aid package: $21,833**

ABOUT THE INSTITUTION Independent Roman Catholic, coed. ***Awards:*** bachelor's and master's degrees and post-bachelor's certificates. 30 undergraduate majors. ***Total enrollment:*** 1,478. Undergraduates: 801. Freshmen: 147.

UNDERGRADUATE EXPENSES for 2009–10 ***Application fee:*** $50. ***Comprehensive fee:*** $38,410 includes full-time tuition ($26,830), mandatory fees ($370), and room and board ($11,210). ***College room only:*** $7350. ***Part-time tuition:*** $545 per unit. ***Part-time fees:*** $3 per unit; $35 per term.

FRESHMAN FINANCIAL AID (Fall 2007) 127 applied for aid; of those 90% were deemed to have need. 100% of freshmen with need received aid; of those 7% had need fully met. ***Average percent of need met:*** 64% (excluding resources awarded to replace EFC). ***Average financial aid package:*** $23,430 (excluding resources awarded to replace EFC).

UNDERGRADUATE FINANCIAL AID (Fall 2007) 459 applied for aid; of those 93% were deemed to have need. 99% of undergraduates with need received aid; of those 9% had need fully met. ***Average percent of need met:*** 53% (excluding resources awarded to replace EFC). ***Average financial aid package:*** $21,833 (excluding resources awarded to replace EFC).

GIFT AID (NEED-BASED) ***Total amount:*** $6,687,218 (12% federal, 11% state, 74% institutional, 3% external sources). ***Receiving aid:*** Freshmen: 78% (114); all full-time undergraduates: 80% (416). ***Average award:*** Freshmen: $17,338;

Undergraduates: $15,819. ***Scholarships, grants, and awards:*** Federal Pell, FSEOG, state, private, college/university gift aid from institutional funds.

GIFT AID (NON-NEED-BASED) ***Total amount:*** $344,200 (96% institutional, 4% external sources). ***Receiving aid:*** Freshmen: 4% (6). Undergraduates: 4% (21). ***Scholarships, grants, and awards by category:*** *Academic interests/achievement:* general academic interests/achievements. *Creative arts/performance:* music. *Special achievements/activities:* general special achievements/activities. *Special characteristics:* children and siblings of alumni, children of faculty/staff, general special characteristics.

LOANS ***Student loans:*** $4,479,373 (77% need-based, 23% non-need-based). 78% of past graduating class borrowed through all loan programs. *Average indebtedness per student:* $23,877. ***Average need-based loan:*** Freshmen: $3938. Undergraduates: $4777. ***Parent loans:*** $1,544,235 (42% need-based, 58% non-need-based). ***Programs:*** FFEL (Subsidized and Unsubsidized Stafford, PLUS), Perkins.

WORK-STUDY ***Federal work-study:*** Total amount: $167,637; jobs available. ***State or other work-study/employment:*** Total amount: $194,415 (46% need-based, 54% non-need-based). Part-time jobs available.

APPLYING FOR FINANCIAL AID ***Required financial aid form:*** FAFSA. ***Financial aid deadline (priority):*** 3/2. ***Notification date:*** Continuous. Students must reply within 2 weeks of notification.

CONTACT Susan Pace, Director of Financial Aid, Notre Dame de Namur University, 1500 Ralston Avenue, Belmont, CA 94002, 650-508-3580 or toll-free 800-263-0545. *Fax:* 650-508-3635. *E-mail:* space@ndnu.edu.

NOVA SOUTHEASTERN UNIVERSITY

Fort Lauderdale, FL

Tuition & fees: $20,350 **Average undergraduate aid package: $19,160**

ABOUT THE INSTITUTION Independent, coed. ***Awards:*** associate, bachelor's, master's, doctoral, and first professional degrees and post-master's and first professional certificates. 31 undergraduate majors. ***Total enrollment:*** 28,378. Undergraduates: 5,757. Freshmen: 476. Federal methodology is used as a basis for awarding need-based institutional aid.

UNDERGRADUATE EXPENSES for 2008–09 ***Application fee:*** $50. ***Comprehensive fee:*** $28,710 includes full-time tuition ($19,800), mandatory fees ($550), and room and board ($8360). Full-time tuition and fees vary according to class time and program. Room and board charges vary according to board plan and housing facility. ***Part-time tuition:*** $660 per credit hour. Part-time tuition and fees vary according to class time, course load, and program. ***Payment plans:*** Installment, deferred payment.

FRESHMAN FINANCIAL AID (Fall 2008, est.) 383 applied for aid; of those 79% were deemed to have need. 100% of freshmen with need received aid; of those 8% had need fully met. ***Average percent of need met:*** 62% (excluding resources awarded to replace EFC). ***Average financial aid package:*** $15,305 (excluding resources awarded to replace EFC). 22% of all full-time freshmen had no need and received non-need-based gift aid.

UNDERGRADUATE FINANCIAL AID (Fall 2008, est.) 3,115 applied for aid; of those 89% were deemed to have need. 99% of undergraduates with need received aid; of those 4% had need fully met. ***Average percent of need met:*** 54% (excluding resources awarded to replace EFC). ***Average financial aid package:*** $19,160 (excluding resources awarded to replace EFC). 13% of all full-time undergraduates had no need and received non-need-based gift aid.

GIFT AID (NEED-BASED) ***Total amount:*** $26,155,880 (29% federal, 41% state, 27% institutional, 3% external sources). ***Receiving aid:*** Freshmen: 44% (191); all full-time undergraduates: 43% (1,582). ***Average award:*** Freshmen: $5577; Undergraduates: $5027. ***Scholarships, grants, and awards:*** Federal Pell, FSEOG, state, private, college/university gift aid from institutional funds.

GIFT AID (NON-NEED-BASED) ***Total amount:*** $1,580,253 (38% state, 53% institutional, 9% external sources). ***Receiving aid:*** Freshmen: 67% (288). Undergraduates: 67% (2,464). ***Average award:*** Freshmen: $3595. Undergraduates: $4022. ***Scholarships, grants, and awards by category:*** *Academic interests/achievement:* 3,109 awards ($5,560,070 total): general academic interests/achievements. ***Tuition waivers:*** Full or partial for employees or children of employees.

LOANS ***Student loans:*** $26,257,050 (40% need-based, 60% non-need-based). 76% of past graduating class borrowed through all loan programs. *Average indebtedness per student:* $35,789. ***Average need-based loan:*** Freshmen: $8809. Undergraduates: $7131. ***Parent loans:*** $1,701,833 (84% need-based, 16% non-need-based). ***Programs:*** FFEL (Subsidized and Unsubsidized Stafford, PLUS), Perkins, college/university.

WORK-STUDY ***Federal work-study:*** Total amount: $1,002,221; 357 jobs averaging $2554. ***State or other work-study/employment:*** Total amount: $1,229,656 (100% non-need-based). 466 part-time jobs averaging $2196.

ATHLETIC AWARDS Total amount: $2,787,601 (100% non-need-based).

APPLYING FOR FINANCIAL AID ***Required financial aid forms:*** FAFSA, institution's own form, state aid form. ***Financial aid deadline (priority):*** 4/15. ***Notification date:*** Continuous. Students must reply within 4 weeks of notification.

CONTACT Stephanie G. Brown, EdD, Associate Vice President for Enrollment and Student Services, Nova Southeastern University, 3301 College Avenue, Fort Lauderdale, FL 33314, 954-262-7456 or toll-free 800-541-NOVA. *Fax:* 954-262-3967. *E-mail:* browstep@nova.edu.

NYACK COLLEGE

Nyack, NY

Tuition & fees: $18,200 **Average undergraduate aid package: $16,808**

ABOUT THE INSTITUTION Independent religious, coed. ***Awards:*** bachelor's, master's, and first professional degrees. 28 undergraduate majors. ***Total enrollment:*** 3,250. Undergraduates: 2,043. Freshmen: 512. Federal methodology is used as a basis for awarding need-based institutional aid.

UNDERGRADUATE EXPENSES for 2008–09 ***One-time required fee:*** $150. ***Comprehensive fee:*** $22,100 includes full-time tuition ($17,500), mandatory fees ($700), and room and board ($3900). ***College room only:*** $3500. Full-time tuition and fees vary according to course load, degree level, location, program, and student level. Room and board charges vary according to board plan and housing facility. ***Part-time tuition:*** $700 per credit. Part-time tuition and fees vary according to course load, degree level, location, program, and student level. ***Payment plan:*** Installment.

FRESHMAN FINANCIAL AID (Fall 2007) 282 applied for aid; of those 91% were deemed to have need. 100% of freshmen with need received aid; of those 16% had need fully met. ***Average percent of need met:*** 70% (excluding resources awarded to replace EFC). ***Average financial aid package:*** $17,457 (excluding resources awarded to replace EFC). 20% of all full-time freshmen had no need and received non-need-based gift aid.

UNDERGRADUATE FINANCIAL AID (Fall 2007) 1,175 applied for aid; of those 93% were deemed to have need. 100% of undergraduates with need received aid; of those 20% had need fully met. ***Average percent of need met:*** 69% (excluding resources awarded to replace EFC). ***Average financial aid package:*** $16,808 (excluding resources awarded to replace EFC). 15% of all full-time undergraduates had no need and received non-need-based gift aid.

GIFT AID (NEED-BASED) ***Total amount:*** $11,165,680 (25% federal, 19% state, 55% institutional, 1% external sources). ***Receiving aid:*** Freshmen: 79% (256); all full-time undergraduates: 83% (1,083). ***Average award:*** Freshmen: $12,201; Undergraduates: $10,423. ***Scholarships, grants, and awards:*** Federal Pell, FSEOG, state, private, college/university gift aid from institutional funds.

GIFT AID (NON-NEED-BASED) ***Total amount:*** $1,241,615 (4% state, 93% institutional, 3% external sources). ***Receiving aid:*** Freshmen: 4% (14). Undergraduates: 5% (71). ***Average award:*** Freshmen: $9139. Undergraduates: $8666. ***Scholarships, grants, and awards by category:*** *Academic interests/achievement:* 596 awards ($1,099,425 total): general academic interests/achievements. *Creative arts/performance:* 94 awards ($347,425 total): journalism/publications, music, performing arts, theater/drama. *Special achievements/activities:* 1,191 awards ($1,176,093 total): community service, general special achievements/activities, leadership, religious involvement. *Special characteristics:* 1,154 awards ($2,859,056 total): children and siblings of alumni, children of faculty/staff, general special characteristics, international students, local/state students, out-of-state students, relatives of clergy, religious affiliation, spouses of current students. ***Tuition waivers:*** Full or partial for children of alumni, employees or children of employees.

LOANS ***Student loans:*** $10,516,298 (84% need-based, 16% non-need-based). 86% of past graduating class borrowed through all loan programs. *Average indebtedness per student:* $23,583. ***Average need-based loan:*** Freshmen: $4259. Undergraduates: $5751. ***Parent loans:*** $1,663,506 (63% need-based, 37% non-need-based). ***Programs:*** FFEL (Subsidized and Unsubsidized Stafford, PLUS), Perkins.

WORK-STUDY ***Federal work-study:*** Total amount: $295,370; 233 jobs averaging $1268. ***State or other work-study/employment:*** Total amount: $95,488 (86% need-based, 14% non-need-based). 58 part-time jobs averaging $1646.

ATHLETIC AWARDS Total amount: $1,214,540 (68% need-based, 32% non-need-based).

APPLYING FOR FINANCIAL AID ***Required financial aid forms:*** FAFSA, state aid form. ***Financial aid deadline (priority):*** 3/1. ***Notification date:*** Continuous beginning 3/1. Students must reply by 5/1 or within 4 weeks of notification.

CONTACT Andres Valenzuela, Director of Student Financial Services, Nyack College, 1 South Boulevard, Nyack, NY 10960-3698, 845-358-1710 Ext. 4741 or toll-free 800-33-NYACK. *Fax:* 845-358-7016. *E-mail:* sfs@nyack.edu.

OAK HILLS CHRISTIAN COLLEGE

Bemidji, MN

CONTACT Daniel Hovestol, Financial Aid Director, Oak Hills Christian College, 1600 Oak Hills Road, SW, Bemidji, MN 56601-8832, 218-751-8671 Ext. 1220 or toll-free 888-751-8670 Ext. 285. *Fax:* 218-444-1311. *E-mail:* ohfinaid@oakhills.edu.

OAKLAND CITY UNIVERSITY

Oakland City, IN

ABOUT THE INSTITUTION Independent General Baptist, coed. ***Awards:*** associate, bachelor's, master's, doctoral, and first professional degrees. 54 undergraduate majors. ***Total enrollment:*** 2,007. Undergraduates: 1,744. Freshmen: 349.

GIFT AID (NEED-BASED) ***Scholarships, grants, and awards:*** Federal Pell, FSEOG, state, private, college/university gift aid from institutional funds.

GIFT AID (NON-NEED-BASED) ***Scholarships, grants, and awards by category:*** *Academic interests/achievement:* general academic interests/achievements. *Creative arts/performance:* art/fine arts, music. *Special achievements/activities:* religious involvement. *Special characteristics:* children and siblings of alumni, children of faculty/staff, ethnic background, international students, members of minority groups, religious affiliation.

LOANS ***Programs:*** FFEL (Subsidized and Unsubsidized Stafford, PLUS), Perkins, college/university.

WORK-STUDY ***Federal work-study:*** Total amount: $185,000; 150 jobs averaging $1600. ***State or other work-study/employment:*** 4 part-time jobs averaging $1500.

APPLYING FOR FINANCIAL AID ***Required financial aid form:*** FAFSA.

CONTACT Mrs. Caren K. Richeson, Director of Financial Aid, Oakland City University, 138 North Lucretia Street, Oakland City, IN 47660-1099, 812-749-1225 or toll-free 800-737-5125. *Fax:* 812-749-1438. *E-mail:* cricheson@oak.edu.

OAKLAND UNIVERSITY

Rochester, MI

Tuition & fees (MI res): $8055 **Average undergraduate aid package: $9607**

ABOUT THE INSTITUTION State-supported, coed. ***Awards:*** bachelor's, master's, and doctoral degrees and post-bachelor's and post-master's certificates. 76 undergraduate majors. ***Total enrollment:*** 18,169. Undergraduates: 14,397. Freshmen: 2,350. Federal methodology is used as a basis for awarding need-based institutional aid.

UNDERGRADUATE EXPENSES for 2008–09 ***Tuition, state resident:*** full-time $8055; part-time $268.50 per credit. ***Tuition, nonresident:*** full-time $18,802; part-time $626.75 per credit. Full-time tuition and fees vary according to program and student level. Part-time tuition and fees vary according to program and student level. ***College room and board:*** $7105. Room and board charges vary according to housing facility. ***Payment plans:*** Installment, deferred payment.

FRESHMAN FINANCIAL AID (Fall 2007) 1,533 applied for aid; of those 71% were deemed to have need. 96% of freshmen with need received aid; of those 16% had need fully met. ***Average percent of need met:*** 73% (excluding resources awarded to replace EFC). ***Average financial aid package:*** $9487 (excluding resources awarded to replace EFC). 19% of all full-time freshmen had no need and received non-need-based gift aid.

UNDERGRADUATE FINANCIAL AID (Fall 2007) 6,084 applied for aid; of those 77% were deemed to have need. 96% of undergraduates with need received aid; of those 12% had need fully met. ***Average percent of need met:*** 68% (excluding resources awarded to replace EFC). ***Average financial aid package:*** $9607 (excluding resources awarded to replace EFC). 9% of all full-time undergraduates had no need and received non-need-based gift aid.

GIFT AID (NEED-BASED) ***Total amount:*** $11,204,444 (64% federal, 7% state, 29% institutional). ***Receiving aid:*** Freshmen: 36% (802); all full-time undergraduates: 27% (2,725). ***Average award:*** Freshmen: $4487; Undergraduates: $3822. ***Scholarships, grants, and awards:*** Federal Pell, FSEOG, state, private, college/university gift aid from institutional funds.

GIFT AID (NON-NEED-BASED) ***Total amount:*** $12,255,434 (15% state, 42% institutional, 43% external sources). ***Receiving aid:*** Freshmen: 21% (467). Undergraduates: 14% (1,377). ***Average award:*** Freshmen: $2464. Undergraduates: $2774. ***Scholarships, grants, and awards by category:*** *Academic interests/achievement:* area/ethnic studies, biological sciences, business, education, engineering/technologies, English, foreign languages, general academic interests/achievements, health fields, humanities. *Creative arts/performance:* dance, music, performing arts. *Special characteristics:* adult students, ethnic background, out-of-state students. ***Tuition waivers:*** Full or partial for employees or children of employees. ***ROTC:*** Air Force cooperative.

LOANS ***Student loans:*** $32,015,444 (52% need-based, 48% non-need-based). 51% of past graduating class borrowed through all loan programs. *Average indebtedness per student:* $18,428. ***Average need-based loan:*** Freshmen: $5485. Undergraduates: $7226. ***Parent loans:*** $3,101,977 (100% need-based). ***Programs:*** Federal Direct (Subsidized and Unsubsidized Stafford, PLUS), Perkins, state, private loans.

WORK-STUDY ***Federal work-study:*** Total amount: $337,557; jobs available. ***State or other work-study/employment:*** Total amount: $111,248 (100% need-based). Part-time jobs available.

ATHLETIC AWARDS Total amount: $2,473,375 (100% non-need-based).

APPLYING FOR FINANCIAL AID ***Required financial aid form:*** FAFSA. ***Financial aid deadline (priority):*** 2/15. ***Notification date:*** Continuous beginning 3/15.

CONTACT Ms. Cindy Hermsen, Director of Financial Aid, Oakland University, 120 North Foundation Hall, Rochester, MI 48309-4481, 248-370-2550 or toll-free 800-OAK-UNIV. *E-mail:* finaid@oakland.edu.

OAKWOOD UNIVERSITY

Huntsville, AL

CONTACT Financial Aid Director, Oakwood University, 7000 Adventist Boulevard, Huntsville, AL 35896, 256-726-7210 or toll-free 800-358-3978 (in-state).

OBERLIN COLLEGE

Oberlin, OH

Tuition & fees: $38,280 **Average undergraduate aid package: $31,257**

ABOUT THE INSTITUTION Independent, coed. ***Awards:*** bachelor's and master's degrees and post-bachelor's certificates. 54 undergraduate majors. ***Total enrollment:*** 2,865. Undergraduates: 2,839. Freshmen: 766. Both federal and institutional methodology are used as a basis for awarding need-based institutional aid.

UNDERGRADUATE EXPENSES for 2008–09 ***Application fee:*** $35. ***Comprehensive fee:*** $48,150 includes full-time tuition ($38,012), mandatory fees ($268), and room and board ($9870). ***College room only:*** $5150. Full-time tuition and fees vary according to course load. Room and board charges vary according to board plan and housing facility. ***Part-time tuition:*** $1580 per credit hour. Part-time tuition and fees vary according to course load. ***Payment plan:*** Installment.

FRESHMAN FINANCIAL AID (Fall 2008, est.) 452 applied for aid; of those 88% were deemed to have need. 100% of freshmen with need received aid; of those 100% had need fully met. ***Average percent of need met:*** 100% (excluding resources awarded to replace EFC). ***Average financial aid package:*** $30,726 (excluding resources awarded to replace EFC). 32% of all full-time freshmen had no need and received non-need-based gift aid.

UNDERGRADUATE FINANCIAL AID (Fall 2008, est.) 1,717 applied for aid; of those 84% were deemed to have need. 100% of undergraduates with need received aid; of those 100% had need fully met. ***Average percent of need met:*** 100% (excluding resources awarded to replace EFC). ***Average financial aid package:*** $31,257 (excluding resources awarded to replace EFC). 15% of all full-time undergraduates had no need and received non-need-based gift aid.

GIFT AID (NEED-BASED) ***Total amount:*** $39,435,146 (3% federal, 1% state, 91% institutional, 5% external sources). ***Receiving aid:*** Freshmen: 52% (390);

all full-time undergraduates: 52% (1,440). ***Average award:*** Freshmen: $27,323; Undergraduates: $26,912. ***Scholarships, grants, and awards:*** Federal Pell, FSEOG, state, private, college/university gift aid from institutional funds.

GIFT AID (NON-NEED-BASED) ***Total amount:*** $7,580,989 (93% institutional, 7% external sources). ***Receiving aid:*** Freshmen: 29% (217). Undergraduates: 26% (722). ***Average award:*** Freshmen: $11,019. Undergraduates: $10,493. ***Scholarships, grants, and awards by category:*** *Academic interests/achievement:* 973 awards ($10,085,018 total): general academic interests/achievements, physical sciences. *Creative arts/performance:* 519 awards ($5,914,904 total): music. ***Tuition waivers:*** Full or partial for employees or children of employees.

LOANS ***Student loans:*** $7,493,039 (88% need-based, 12% non-need-based). 62% of past graduating class borrowed through all loan programs. *Average indebtedness per student:* $17,579. ***Average need-based loan:*** Freshmen: $2754. Undergraduates: $3425. ***Parent loans:*** $3,054,475 (75% need-based, 25% non-need-based). ***Programs:*** FFEL (Subsidized and Unsubsidized Stafford, PLUS), Perkins, college/university.

WORK-STUDY ***Federal work-study:*** Total amount: $2,243,067; jobs available (averaging $1750). ***State or other work-study/employment:*** Part-time jobs available (averaging $1750).

APPLYING FOR FINANCIAL AID ***Required financial aid forms:*** FAFSA, CSS Financial Aid PROFILE. ***Financial aid deadline (priority):*** 2/15. ***Notification date:*** 4/1. Students must reply by 5/1 or within 2 weeks of notification.

CONTACT Robert Reddy, Office of Financial Aid, Oberlin College, Carnegie Building 123, Oberlin, OH 44074, 800-693-3173 or toll-free 800-622-OBIE. *Fax:* 440-775-8249. *E-mail:* financial.aid@oberlin.edu.

OCCIDENTAL COLLEGE

Los Angeles, CA

Tuition & fees: $38,922 **Average undergraduate aid package: $34,431**

ABOUT THE INSTITUTION Independent, coed. ***Awards:*** bachelor's and master's degrees. 32 undergraduate majors. ***Total enrollment:*** 1,868. Undergraduates: 1,846. Freshmen: 467. Institutional methodology is used as a basis for awarding need-based institutional aid.

UNDERGRADUATE EXPENSES for 2009–10 ***Application fee:*** $50. ***Comprehensive fee:*** $49,702 includes full-time tuition ($37,970), mandatory fees ($952), and room and board ($10,780). ***College room only:*** $6130. ***Part-time tuition:*** $1585 per credit.

FRESHMAN FINANCIAL AID (Fall 2008, est.) 322 applied for aid; of those 79% were deemed to have need. 99% of freshmen with need received aid; of those 49% had need fully met. ***Average percent of need met:*** 91% (excluding resources awarded to replace EFC). ***Average financial aid package:*** $34,171 (excluding resources awarded to replace EFC). 21% of all full-time freshmen had no need and received non-need-based gift aid.

UNDERGRADUATE FINANCIAL AID (Fall 2008, est.) 1,082 applied for aid; of those 88% were deemed to have need. 100% of undergraduates with need received aid; of those 40% had need fully met. ***Average percent of need met:*** 93% (excluding resources awarded to replace EFC). ***Average financial aid package:*** $34,431 (excluding resources awarded to replace EFC). 22% of all full-time undergraduates had no need and received non-need-based gift aid.

GIFT AID (NEED-BASED) ***Total amount:*** $25,625,435 (7% federal, 9% state, 80% institutional, 4% external sources). ***Receiving aid:*** Freshmen: 50% (244); all full-time undergraduates: 52% (936). ***Average award:*** Freshmen: $28,936; Undergraduates: $27,232. ***Scholarships, grants, and awards:*** Federal Pell, FSEOG, state, private, college/university gift aid from institutional funds.

GIFT AID (NON-NEED-BASED) ***Total amount:*** $4,557,226 (82% institutional, 18% external sources). ***Receiving aid:*** Freshmen: 4% (21). Undergraduates: 3% (63). ***Average award:*** Freshmen: $8441. Undergraduates: $8553. ***Scholarships, grants, and awards by category:*** *Academic interests/achievement:* 411 awards ($3,115,528 total): general academic interests/achievements. *Creative arts/performance:* 43 awards ($28,876 total): music. *Special achievements/activities:* 16 awards ($240,000 total): general special achievements/activities, leadership. *Special characteristics:* 29 awards ($839,819 total): children of educators, children of faculty/staff. ***ROTC:*** Army cooperative, Air Force cooperative.

LOANS ***Student loans:*** $7,791,855 (75% need-based, 25% non-need-based). 73% of past graduating class borrowed through all loan programs. *Average indebtedness per student:* $21,001. ***Average need-based loan:*** Freshmen: $4827. Undergraduates: $6299. ***Parent loans:*** $4,125,791 (20% need-based, 80% non-need-based). ***Programs:*** FFEL (Subsidized and Unsubsidized Stafford, PLUS), Perkins, college/university.

WORK-STUDY ***Federal work-study:*** Total amount: $1,473,466; 685 jobs averaging $2530. ***State or other work-study/employment:*** Total amount: $539,943 (51% need-based, 49% non-need-based). 98 part-time jobs averaging $1030.

APPLYING FOR FINANCIAL AID ***Required financial aid forms:*** FAFSA, CSS Financial Aid PROFILE, state aid form, noncustodial (divorced/separated) parent's statement, business/farm supplement. ***Financial aid deadline:*** 2/1 (priority: 2/1). ***Notification date:*** 3/25. Students must reply by 5/1.

CONTACT Maureen McRae Levy, Director of Financial Aid, Occidental College, 1600 Campus Road, Los Angeles, CA 90041, 323-259-2548 or toll-free 800-825-5262. *Fax:* 323-341-4961. *E-mail:* finaid@oxy.edu.

OGLALA LAKOTA COLLEGE

Kyle, SD

CONTACT Financial Aid Director, Oglala Lakota College, 490 Piya Wiconi Road, Kyle, SD 57752-0490, 605-455-6000.

OGLETHORPE UNIVERSITY

Atlanta, GA

Tuition & fees: $25,580 **Average undergraduate aid package: $20,187**

ABOUT THE INSTITUTION Independent, coed. ***Awards:*** bachelor's and master's degrees. 32 undergraduate majors. ***Total enrollment:*** 1,053. Undergraduates: 999. Freshmen: 245. Both federal and institutional methodology are used as a basis for awarding need-based institutional aid.

UNDERGRADUATE EXPENSES for 2008–09 ***Application fee:*** $35. ***Comprehensive fee:*** $35,080 includes full-time tuition ($25,380), mandatory fees ($200), and room and board ($9500). Room and board charges vary according to board plan and housing facility. ***Part-time tuition:*** $1030 per credit hour. Part-time tuition and fees vary according to program. ***Payment plans:*** Tuition prepayment, installment.

FRESHMAN FINANCIAL AID (Fall 2008, est.) 206 applied for aid; of those 87% were deemed to have need. 100% of freshmen with need received aid; of those 13% had need fully met. ***Average percent of need met:*** 75% (excluding resources awarded to replace EFC). ***Average financial aid package:*** $21,153 (excluding resources awarded to replace EFC). 11% of all full-time freshmen had no need and received non-need-based gift aid.

UNDERGRADUATE FINANCIAL AID (Fall 2008, est.) 568 applied for aid; of those 88% were deemed to have need. 99% of undergraduates with need received aid; of those 15% had need fully met. ***Average percent of need met:*** 72% (excluding resources awarded to replace EFC). ***Average financial aid package:*** $20,187 (excluding resources awarded to replace EFC). 8% of all full-time undergraduates had no need and received non-need-based gift aid.

GIFT AID (NEED-BASED) ***Total amount:*** $9,836,002 (9% federal, 11% state, 79% institutional, 1% external sources). ***Receiving aid:*** Freshmen: 73% (179); all full-time undergraduates: 57% (486). ***Average award:*** Freshmen: $20,488; Undergraduates: $19,852. ***Scholarships, grants, and awards:*** Federal Pell, FSEOG, state, private, college/university gift aid from institutional funds.

GIFT AID (NON-NEED-BASED) ***Total amount:*** $3,924,960 (11% state, 88% institutional, 1% external sources). ***Receiving aid:*** Freshmen: 53% (131). Undergraduates: 41% (351). ***Average award:*** Freshmen: $10,204. Undergraduates: $10,043. ***Scholarships, grants, and awards by category:*** *Academic interests/achievement:* general academic interests/achievements. *Creative arts/performance:* journalism/publications, music, performing arts, theater/drama. *Special achievements/activities:* community service, religious involvement. *Special characteristics:* children of faculty/staff, siblings of current students. ***Tuition waivers:*** Full or partial for employees or children of employees.

LOANS ***Student loans:*** $3,504,460 (82% need-based, 18% non-need-based). ***Average need-based loan:*** Freshmen: $4747. Undergraduates: $5330. ***Parent loans:*** $739,858 (100% non-need-based). ***Programs:*** Federal Direct (Subsidized and Unsubsidized Stafford, PLUS), Perkins.

WORK-STUDY ***Federal work-study:*** Total amount: $213,948; jobs available.

APPLYING FOR FINANCIAL AID ***Required financial aid forms:*** FAFSA, institution's own form. ***Notification date:*** Continuous beginning 3/1. Students must reply by 5/1 or within 3 weeks of notification.

CONTACT Ms. Meg McGinnis, Director of Financial Aid, Oglethorpe University, 4484 Peachtree Road NE, Atlanta, GA 30319, 404-364-8366 or toll-free 800-428-4484. *E-mail:* mmcginnis@oglethorpe.edu.

OHIO CHRISTIAN UNIVERSITY
Circleville, OH

Tuition & fees: $13,960 **Average undergraduate aid package: $9500**

ABOUT THE INSTITUTION Independent religious, coed. ***Awards:*** associate and bachelor's degrees. 11 undergraduate majors. ***Total enrollment:*** 636. Undergraduates: 636.

UNDERGRADUATE EXPENSES for 2008–09 ***Application fee:*** $25. ***Comprehensive fee:*** $19,950 includes full-time tuition ($12,950), mandatory fees ($1010), and room and board ($5990). ***Part-time tuition:*** $550 per hour. ***Part-time fees:*** $505 per term.

FRESHMAN FINANCIAL AID (Fall 2007) 220 applied for aid; of those 91% were deemed to have need. 100% of freshmen with need received aid; of those 25% had need fully met. ***Average percent of need met:*** 50% (excluding resources awarded to replace EFC). ***Average financial aid package:*** $11,000 (excluding resources awarded to replace EFC). 11% of all full-time freshmen had no need and received non-need-based gift aid.

UNDERGRADUATE FINANCIAL AID (Fall 2007) 480 applied for aid; of those 86% were deemed to have need. 100% of undergraduates with need received aid; of those 24% had need fully met. ***Average percent of need met:*** 50% (excluding resources awarded to replace EFC). ***Average financial aid package:*** $9500 (excluding resources awarded to replace EFC). 16% of all full-time undergraduates had no need and received non-need-based gift aid.

GIFT AID (NEED-BASED) ***Total amount:*** $1,654,000 (63% federal, 37% state). ***Receiving aid:*** Freshmen: 65% (150); all full-time undergraduates: 61% (305). ***Average award:*** Freshmen: $4000; Undergraduates: $4000. ***Scholarships, grants, and awards:*** Federal Pell, FSEOG, state, private, college/university gift aid from institutional funds.

GIFT AID (NON-NEED-BASED) ***Total amount:*** $1,120,000 (29% state, 67% institutional, 4% external sources). ***Receiving aid:*** Freshmen: 85% (195). Undergraduates: 81% (405). ***Average award:*** Freshmen: $2500. Undergraduates: $1500. ***Scholarships, grants, and awards by category:*** *Academic interests/achievement:* business, education, general academic interests/achievements, health fields, religion/biblical studies. *Creative arts/performance:* music. *Special achievements/activities:* leadership. *Special characteristics:* 100 awards ($125,000 total): adult students, children of faculty/staff, international students, out-of-state students, relatives of clergy, religious affiliation, siblings of current students, veterans, veterans' children.

LOANS ***Student loans:*** $4,400,000 (43% need-based, 57% non-need-based). 90% of past graduating class borrowed through all loan programs. *Average indebtedness per student:* $30,000. ***Average need-based loan:*** Freshmen: $2500. Undergraduates: $4500. ***Parent loans:*** $98,000 (100% non-need-based). ***Programs:*** FFEL (Subsidized and Unsubsidized Stafford, PLUS), college/university, state nursing loans.

WORK-STUDY ***Federal work-study:*** Total amount: $85,000; 50 jobs averaging $1700. ***State or other work-study/employment:*** Part-time jobs available.

APPLYING FOR FINANCIAL AID ***Required financial aid form:*** FAFSA. ***Financial aid deadline (priority):*** 3/31. ***Notification date:*** 6/1. Students must reply within 2 weeks of notification.

CONTACT Michael Fracassa, Assistant Vice President of Finance, Ohio Christian University, 1476 Lancaster Pike, PO Box 458, Circleville, OH 43113-9487, 740-477-7758 or toll-free 800-701-0222. *Fax:* 740-477-5921. *E-mail:* mfracassa@ohiochristian.edu.

OHIO DOMINICAN UNIVERSITY
Columbus, OH

CONTACT Ms. Cynthia A. Hahn, Director of Financial Aid, Ohio Dominican University, 1216 Sunbury Road, Columbus, OH 43219, 614-251-4778 or toll-free 800-854-2670. *Fax:* 614-251-4456. *E-mail:* fin-aid@ohiodominican.edu.

OHIO NORTHERN UNIVERSITY
Ada, OH

Tuition & fees: $31,866 **Average undergraduate aid package: $25,084**

ABOUT THE INSTITUTION Independent religious, coed. ***Awards:*** bachelor's, master's, doctoral, and first professional degrees and post-bachelor's certificates. 108 undergraduate majors. ***Total enrollment:*** 3,721. Undergraduates: 2,744. Freshmen: 749. Federal methodology is used as a basis for awarding need-based institutional aid.

UNDERGRADUATE EXPENSES for 2009–10 ***Application fee:*** $30. ***Comprehensive fee:*** $40,146 includes full-time tuition ($31,626), mandatory fees ($240), and room and board ($8280). ***College room only:*** $4140. ***Part-time tuition:*** $880 per quarter hour.

FRESHMAN FINANCIAL AID (Fall 2008, est.) 745 applied for aid; of those 82% were deemed to have need. 100% of freshmen with need received aid; of those 20% had need fully met. ***Average percent of need met:*** 86% (excluding resources awarded to replace EFC). ***Average financial aid package:*** $26,490 (excluding resources awarded to replace EFC). 15% of all full-time freshmen had no need and received non-need-based gift aid.

UNDERGRADUATE FINANCIAL AID (Fall 2008, est.) 2,501 applied for aid; of those 78% were deemed to have need. 100% of undergraduates with need received aid; of those 18% had need fully met. ***Average percent of need met:*** 82% (excluding resources awarded to replace EFC). ***Average financial aid package:*** $25,084 (excluding resources awarded to replace EFC). 14% of all full-time undergraduates had no need and received non-need-based gift aid.

GIFT AID (NEED-BASED) ***Total amount:*** $35,582,431 (7% federal, 6% state, 84% institutional, 3% external sources). ***Receiving aid:*** Freshmen: 79% (590); all full-time undergraduates: 55% (1,418). ***Average award:*** Freshmen: $21,181; Undergraduates: $20,626. ***Scholarships, grants, and awards:*** Federal Pell, FSEOG, state, private, college/university gift aid from institutional funds.

GIFT AID (NON-NEED-BASED) ***Total amount:*** $9,416,822 (8% state, 86% institutional, 6% external sources). ***Receiving aid:*** Freshmen: 43% (322). Undergraduates: 30% (783). ***Average award:*** Freshmen: $15,930. Undergraduates: $15,248. ***Scholarships, grants, and awards by category:*** *Academic interests/achievement:* biological sciences, business, communication, computer science, education, engineering/technologies, English, foreign languages, general academic interests/achievements, health fields, humanities, international studies, mathematics, physical sciences, premedicine, religion/biblical studies, social sciences. *Creative arts/performance:* applied art and design, art/fine arts, creative writing, dance, journalism/publications, music, performing arts, theater/drama. *Special achievements/activities:* community service, general special achievements/activities, junior miss, leadership. *Special characteristics:* children of faculty/staff, international students, relatives of clergy, religious affiliation, siblings of current students. ***ROTC:*** Army cooperative, Air Force cooperative.

LOANS ***Student loans:*** $24,220,580 (32% need-based, 68% non-need-based). 83% of past graduating class borrowed through all loan programs. *Average indebtedness per student:* $45,753. ***Average need-based loan:*** Freshmen: $4979. Undergraduates: $5105. ***Parent loans:*** $3,901,860 (100% need-based). ***Programs:*** FFEL (Subsidized and Unsubsidized Stafford, PLUS), Perkins, Federal Nursing, college/university.

WORK-STUDY ***Federal work-study:*** Total amount: $1,994,168; jobs available. ***State or other work-study/employment:*** Total amount: $506,191 (37% need-based, 63% non-need-based). Part-time jobs available.

APPLYING FOR FINANCIAL AID ***Required financial aid forms:*** FAFSA, institution's own form. ***Financial aid deadline (priority):*** 4/15. ***Notification date:*** Continuous. Students must reply within 2 weeks of notification.

CONTACT Melanie Weaver, Director of Financial Aid, Ohio Northern University, 525 South Main Street, Ada, OH 45810, 419-772-2272 or toll-free 888-408-4ONU. *Fax:* 419-772-2313. *E-mail:* m-weaver.2@onu.edu.

THE OHIO STATE UNIVERSITY
Columbus, OH

Tuition & fees (OH res): $8676 **Average undergraduate aid package: $10,225**

ABOUT THE INSTITUTION State-supported, coed. ***Awards:*** associate, bachelor's, master's, doctoral, and first professional degrees and post-bachelor's and post-master's certificates. 148 undergraduate majors. ***Total enrollment:*** 53,715. Undergraduates: 40,212. Freshmen: 6,173. Federal methodology is used as a basis for awarding need-based institutional aid.

UNDERGRADUATE EXPENSES for 2008–09 ***Application fee:*** $40. ***Tuition, state resident:*** full-time $8406. ***Tuition, nonresident:*** full-time $21,015. ***Required fees:*** full-time $270. Full-time tuition and fees vary according to course load, program, reciprocity agreements, and student level. Part-time tuition and fees vary according to course load, program, reciprocity agreements, and student level. ***College room and board:*** $7755. Room and board charges vary according to board plan and housing facility. ***Payment plan:*** Installment.

FRESHMAN FINANCIAL AID (Fall 2008, est.) 4,934 applied for aid; of those 67% were deemed to have need. 100% of freshmen with need received aid; of those 22% had need fully met. ***Average percent of need met:*** 72% (excluding resources awarded to replace EFC). ***Average financial aid package:*** $10,986 (excluding resources awarded to replace EFC). 35% of all full-time freshmen had no need and received non-need-based gift aid.

UNDERGRADUATE FINANCIAL AID (Fall 2008, est.) 23,900 applied for aid; of those 79% were deemed to have need. 99% of undergraduates with need received aid; of those 19% had need fully met. ***Average percent of need met:*** 64% (excluding resources awarded to replace EFC). ***Average financial aid package:*** $10,225 (excluding resources awarded to replace EFC). 19% of all full-time undergraduates had no need and received non-need-based gift aid.

GIFT AID (NEED-BASED) ***Total amount:*** $91,957,255 (30% federal, 10% state, 55% institutional, 5% external sources). ***Receiving aid:*** Freshmen: 49% (2,995); all full-time undergraduates: 39% (13,804). ***Average award:*** Freshmen: $7123; Undergraduates: $6480. ***Scholarships, grants, and awards:*** Federal Pell, FSEOG, state, private, college/university gift aid from institutional funds.

GIFT AID (NON-NEED-BASED) ***Total amount:*** $40,434,055 (8% state, 82% institutional, 10% external sources). ***Receiving aid:*** Freshmen: 3% (209). Undergraduates: 2% (693). ***Average award:*** Freshmen: $4090. Undergraduates: $4384. ***Scholarships, grants, and awards by category:*** *Academic interests/achievement:* agriculture, architecture, area/ethnic studies, biological sciences, business, communication, computer science, education, engineering/technologies, English, foreign languages, general academic interests/achievements, health fields, home economics, humanities, international studies, mathematics, military science, physical sciences, premedicine, social sciences. *Creative arts/performance:* creative writing, dance, journalism/publications, music, performing arts, theater/drama. *Special achievements/activities:* cheerleading/drum major, hobbies/interests, leadership, memberships. *Special characteristics:* adult students, children and siblings of alumni, children of faculty/staff, children of public servants, children of union members/company employees, children of workers in trades, ethnic background, handicapped students, members of minority groups, out-of-state students, previous college experience. ***Tuition waivers:*** Full or partial for employees or children of employees, senior citizens. ***ROTC:*** Army, Naval, Air Force.

LOANS ***Student loans:*** $169,191,238 (69% need-based, 31% non-need-based). 55% of past graduating class borrowed through all loan programs. *Average indebtedness per student:* $19,978. ***Average need-based loan:*** Freshmen: $3938. Undergraduates: $4781. ***Parent loans:*** $45,418,793 (100% non-need-based). ***Programs:*** Federal Direct (Subsidized and Unsubsidized Stafford, PLUS), Perkins, Federal Nursing, college/university.

WORK-STUDY ***Federal work-study:*** Total amount: $9,374,034; 3,213 jobs averaging $2957. ***State or other work-study/employment:*** Total amount: $706,789 (61% need-based, 39% non-need-based). Part-time jobs available.

ATHLETIC AWARDS Total amount: $12,409,846 (100% non-need-based).

APPLYING FOR FINANCIAL AID ***Required financial aid form:*** FAFSA. ***Financial aid deadline (priority):*** 2/15. ***Notification date:*** 4/5. Students must reply by 5/1 or within 4 weeks of notification.

CONTACT Ms. Diane Stemper, Director of Student Financial Aid, The Ohio State University, 2400 Olentangy River Road 3rd Floor, Columbus, OH 43210, 614-292-3600. *Fax:* 614-292-9264. *E-mail:* sfa-finaid@osu.edu.

OHIO UNIVERSITY

Athens, OH

Tuition & fees (OH res): $8907 **Average undergraduate aid package: $8247**

ABOUT THE INSTITUTION State-supported, coed. ***Awards:*** associate, bachelor's, master's, doctoral, and first professional degrees. 173 undergraduate majors. ***Total enrollment:*** 20,960. Undergraduates: 17,228. Freshmen: 3,965. Federal methodology is used as a basis for awarding need-based institutional aid.

UNDERGRADUATE EXPENSES for 2008–09 ***Application fee:*** $45. ***Tuition, state resident:*** full-time $8907; part-time $283 per quarter hour. ***Tuition, nonresident:*** full-time $17,871; part-time $578 per quarter hour. ***College room and board:*** $8946; ***Room only:*** $4857. Room and board charges vary according to board plan. ***Payment plan:*** Installment.

FRESHMAN FINANCIAL AID (Fall 2008, est.) 3,513 applied for aid; of those 62% were deemed to have need. 98% of freshmen with need received aid; of those 16% had need fully met. ***Average percent of need met:*** 58% (excluding resources awarded to replace EFC). ***Average financial aid package:*** $7891 (excluding resources awarded to replace EFC). 18% of all full-time freshmen had no need and received non-need-based gift aid.

UNDERGRADUATE FINANCIAL AID (Fall 2008, est.) 11,889 applied for aid; of those 69% were deemed to have need. 99% of undergraduates with need received aid; of those 16% had need fully met. ***Average percent of need met:*** 59% (excluding resources awarded to replace EFC). ***Average financial aid package:*** $8247 (excluding resources awarded to replace EFC). 14% of all full-time undergraduates had no need and received non-need-based gift aid.

GIFT AID (NEED-BASED) ***Total amount:*** $19,371,478 (62% federal, 16% state, 22% institutional). ***Receiving aid:*** Freshmen: 23% (905); all full-time undergraduates: 23% (3,658). ***Average award:*** Freshmen: $6141; Undergraduates: $5598. ***Scholarships, grants, and awards:*** Federal Pell, FSEOG, state, college/university gift aid from institutional funds.

GIFT AID (NON-NEED-BASED) ***Total amount:*** $23,829,785 (4% state, 81% institutional, 15% external sources). ***Receiving aid:*** Freshmen: 29% (1,147). Undergraduates: 20% (3,234). ***Average award:*** Freshmen: $3916. Undergraduates: $3634. ***Scholarships, grants, and awards by category:*** *Academic interests/achievement:* area/ethnic studies, biological sciences, business, communication, computer science, education, engineering/technologies, English, foreign languages, general academic interests/achievements, health fields, home economics, humanities, international studies, mathematics, military science, physical sciences, premedicine, social sciences. *Creative arts/performance:* applied art and design, art/fine arts, cinema/film/broadcasting, dance, debating, journalism/publications, music, performing arts, theater/drama. *Special characteristics:* children of faculty/staff, members of minority groups. ***Tuition waivers:*** Full or partial for employees or children of employees. ***ROTC:*** Army, Air Force.

LOANS ***Student loans:*** $81,553,061 (37% need-based, 63% non-need-based). 66% of past graduating class borrowed through all loan programs. *Average indebtedness per student:* $23,041. ***Average need-based loan:*** Freshmen: $3423. Undergraduates: $4250. ***Parent loans:*** $18,337,281 (100% non-need-based). ***Programs:*** Federal Direct (Subsidized and Unsubsidized Stafford, PLUS), Perkins, state, college/university.

WORK-STUDY ***Federal work-study:*** Total amount: $1,659,436; 592 jobs averaging $1586. ***State or other work-study/employment:*** Total amount: $13,685,065 (100% non-need-based). Part-time jobs available.

ATHLETIC AWARDS Total amount: $5,609,078 (100% non-need-based).

APPLYING FOR FINANCIAL AID ***Required financial aid form:*** FAFSA. ***Financial aid deadline (priority):*** 3/15. ***Notification date:*** 3/15.

CONTACT Ms. Sondra Williams, Director of Financial Aid, Ohio University, 020 Chubb Hall, Athens, OH 45701-2979, 740-593-4141. *Fax:* 740-593-4140. *E-mail:* willias1@ohio.edu.

OHIO UNIVERSITY–CHILLICOTHE

Chillicothe, OH

Tuition & fees (OH res): $4581 **Average undergraduate aid package: $8265**

ABOUT THE INSTITUTION State-supported, coed. ***Awards:*** associate, bachelor's, and master's degrees (offers first 2 years of most bachelor's degree programs available at the main campus in Athens; also offers several bachelor's degree programs that can be completed at this campus and several programs exclusive to this campus; also offers some graduate programs). 15 undergraduate majors. ***Total enrollment:*** 1,836. Undergraduates: 1,836. Federal methodology is used as a basis for awarding need-based institutional aid.

UNDERGRADUATE EXPENSES for 2008–09 ***Application fee:*** $20. ***Tuition, state resident:*** full-time $4581; part-time $139 per hour. ***Tuition, nonresident:*** full-time $8904; part-time $270 per hour.

FRESHMAN FINANCIAL AID (Fall 2008, est.) 323 applied for aid; of those 81% were deemed to have need. 100% of freshmen with need received aid; of those 13% had need fully met. ***Average percent of need met:*** 64% (excluding resources awarded to replace EFC). ***Average financial aid package:*** $7475 (excluding resources awarded to replace EFC). 4% of all full-time freshmen had no need and received non-need-based gift aid.

UNDERGRADUATE FINANCIAL AID (Fall 2008, est.) 1,161 applied for aid; of those 86% were deemed to have need. 99% of undergraduates with need received aid; of those 8% had need fully met. ***Average percent of need met:*** 59% (excluding resources awarded to replace EFC). ***Average financial aid package:*** $8265 (excluding resources awarded to replace EFC). 2% of all full-time undergraduates had no need and received non-need-based gift aid.

GIFT AID (NEED-BASED) ***Total amount:*** $4,476,797 (71% federal, 25% state, 4% institutional). ***Receiving aid:*** Freshmen: 55% (187); all full-time undergraduates: 60% (764). ***Average award:*** Freshmen: $5698; Undergraduates: $5470. ***Scholarships, grants, and awards:*** Federal Pell, FSEOG, state, college/university gift aid from institutional funds.

GIFT AID (NON-NEED-BASED) ***Total amount:*** $417,836 (3% state, 49% institutional, 48% external sources). ***Receiving aid:*** Freshmen: 14% (47). Undergraduates: 8% (101). ***Average award:*** Freshmen: $2929. Undergraduates: $2589. ***Scholarships, grants, and awards by category:*** *Academic interests/achievement:* area/ethnic studies, biological sciences, business, communication, computer science, education, engineering/technologies, English, foreign languages, general academic interests/achievements, health fields, home economics, humanities, international studies, mathematics, military science, physical sciences, premedicine, social sciences. *Creative arts/performance:* applied art and design, art/fine arts, cinema/film/broadcasting, dance, debating, journalism/publications, music, performing arts, theater/drama. *Special characteristics:* children of faculty/staff, members of minority groups. ***ROTC:*** Army cooperative, Air Force cooperative.

LOANS ***Student loans:*** $9,053,982 (43% need-based, 57% non-need-based). 66% of past graduating class borrowed through all loan programs. *Average indebtedness per student:* $23,041. ***Average need-based loan:*** Freshmen: $3351. Undergraduates: $3914. ***Parent loans:*** $13,939 (100% non-need-based). ***Programs:*** Federal Direct (Subsidized and Unsubsidized Stafford, PLUS), Perkins, state, college/university.

WORK-STUDY ***Federal work-study:*** Total amount: $97,746; 8 jobs averaging $910. ***State or other work-study/employment:*** Part-time jobs available.

APPLYING FOR FINANCIAL AID ***Required financial aid form:*** FAFSA. ***Financial aid deadline (priority):*** 3/15. ***Notification date:*** 3/15.

CONTACT Ms. Sondra Williams, Director of Financial Aid, Ohio University–Chillicothe, 020 Chubb Hall, Athens, OH 45701-2979, 740-593-4141 or toll-free 877-462-6824 (in-state). *Fax:* 740-593-4140. *E-mail:* willias1@ohio.edu.

OHIO UNIVERSITY–EASTERN

St. Clairsville, OH

Tuition & fees (OH res): $4395 **Average undergraduate aid package: $6810**

ABOUT THE INSTITUTION State-supported, coed. ***Awards:*** associate, bachelor's, and master's degrees (also offers some graduate courses). 11 undergraduate majors. ***Total enrollment:*** 751. Undergraduates: 751. Federal methodology is used as a basis for awarding need-based institutional aid.

UNDERGRADUATE EXPENSES for 2008–09 ***Application fee:*** $20. ***Tuition, state resident:*** full-time $4395; part-time $134 per credit hour. ***Tuition, nonresident:*** full-time $5715; part-time $174 per credit hour. Full-time tuition and fees vary according to student level. Part-time tuition and fees vary according to student level. ***Payment plan:*** Installment.

FRESHMAN FINANCIAL AID (Fall 2008, est.) 120 applied for aid; of those 72% were deemed to have need. 95% of freshmen with need received aid; of those 21% had need fully met. ***Average percent of need met:*** 69% (excluding resources awarded to replace EFC). ***Average financial aid package:*** $6195 (excluding resources awarded to replace EFC). 14% of all full-time freshmen had no need and received non-need-based gift aid.

UNDERGRADUATE FINANCIAL AID (Fall 2008, est.) 428 applied for aid; of those 82% were deemed to have need. 97% of undergraduates with need received aid; of those 17% had need fully met. ***Average percent of need met:*** 65% (excluding resources awarded to replace EFC). ***Average financial aid package:*** $6810 (excluding resources awarded to replace EFC). 7% of all full-time undergraduates had no need and received non-need-based gift aid.

GIFT AID (NEED-BASED) ***Total amount:*** $1,107,857 (72% federal, 21% state, 7% institutional). ***Receiving aid:*** Freshmen: 47% (57); all full-time undergraduates: 53% (229). ***Average award:*** Freshmen: $4736; Undergraduates: $4659. ***Scholarships, grants, and awards:*** Federal Pell, FSEOG, state, college/university gift aid from institutional funds.

GIFT AID (NON-NEED-BASED) ***Total amount:*** $169,071 (6% state, 73% institutional, 21% external sources). ***Receiving aid:*** Freshmen: 27% (33). Undergraduates: 16% (69). ***Average award:*** Freshmen: $1378. Undergraduates: $1805. ***Scholarships, grants, and awards by category:*** *Academic interests/achievement:* area/ethnic studies, biological sciences, business, communication, computer science, education, engineering/technologies, English, foreign languages, general academic interests/achievements, health fields, home economics, humanities, international studies, mathematics, military science, physical sciences, premedicine, social sciences. *Creative arts/performance:* applied art and design, art/fine arts, cinema/film/broadcasting, dance, debating, journalism/publications, music, performing arts, theater/drama. *Special characteristics:* children of faculty/staff, members of minority groups. ***Tuition waivers:*** Full or partial for employees or children of employees, senior citizens.

LOANS ***Student loans:*** $2,449,582 (47% need-based, 53% non-need-based). 66% of past graduating class borrowed through all loan programs. *Average indebtedness per student:* $23,041. ***Average need-based loan:*** Freshmen: $3138. Undergraduates: $3972. ***Parent loans:*** $19,000 (100% non-need-based). ***Programs:*** Federal Direct (Subsidized and Unsubsidized Stafford, PLUS), Perkins, state, college/university.

WORK-STUDY ***Federal work-study:*** Total amount: $107,946; 21 jobs averaging $1529. ***State or other work-study/employment:*** Part-time jobs available.

APPLYING FOR FINANCIAL AID ***Required financial aid form:*** FAFSA. ***Financial aid deadline (priority):*** 3/15. ***Notification date:*** 3/15.

CONTACT Ms. Sondra Williams, Director of Financial Aid, Ohio University–Eastern, 020 Chubb Hall, Athens, OH 45701-2979, 740-593-4141 or toll-free 800-648-3331 (in-state). *Fax:* 740-593-4140. *E-mail:* willias1@ohio.edu.

OHIO UNIVERSITY–LANCASTER

Lancaster, OH

Tuition & fees (OH res): $4581 **Average undergraduate aid package: $7459**

ABOUT THE INSTITUTION State-supported, coed. ***Awards:*** associate, bachelor's, and master's degrees. 14 undergraduate majors. ***Total enrollment:*** 1,728. Undergraduates: 1,728. Federal methodology is used as a basis for awarding need-based institutional aid.

UNDERGRADUATE EXPENSES for 2008–09 ***Application fee:*** $20. ***Tuition, state resident:*** full-time $4581; part-time $139 per credit hour. ***Tuition, nonresident:*** full-time $8904; part-time $270 per credit hour.

FRESHMAN FINANCIAL AID (Fall 2008, est.) 346 applied for aid; of those 77% were deemed to have need. 98% of freshmen with need received aid; of those 16% had need fully met. ***Average percent of need met:*** 66% (excluding resources awarded to replace EFC). ***Average financial aid package:*** $7014 (excluding resources awarded to replace EFC). 6% of all full-time freshmen had no need and received non-need-based gift aid.

UNDERGRADUATE FINANCIAL AID (Fall 2008, est.) 1,030 applied for aid; of those 80% were deemed to have need. 99% of undergraduates with need received aid; of those 12% had need fully met. ***Average percent of need met:*** 61% (excluding resources awarded to replace EFC). ***Average financial aid package:*** $7459 (excluding resources awarded to replace EFC). 4% of all full-time undergraduates had no need and received non-need-based gift aid.

GIFT AID (NEED-BASED) ***Total amount:*** $3,219,744 (69% federal, 25% state, 6% institutional). ***Receiving aid:*** Freshmen: 46% (171); all full-time undergraduates: 55% (573). ***Average award:*** Freshmen: $5571; Undergraduates: $5304. ***Scholarships, grants, and awards:*** Federal Pell, FSEOG, state, college/university gift aid from institutional funds.

GIFT AID (NON-NEED-BASED) ***Total amount:*** $429,322 (9% state, 52% institutional, 39% external sources). ***Receiving aid:*** Freshmen: 13% (50). Undergraduates: 10% (103). ***Average award:*** Freshmen: $2340. Undergraduates: $2475. ***Scholarships, grants, and awards by category:*** *Academic interests/achievement:* area/ethnic studies, biological sciences, business, communication, computer science, education, engineering/technologies, English, foreign languages, general academic interests/achievements, health fields, home economics, humanities, international studies, mathematics, military science, physical sciences, premedicine, social sciences. *Creative arts/performance:* applied art and design, art/fine arts, cinema/film/broadcasting, dance, debating, journalism/publications, music, performing arts, theater/drama. *Special characteristics:* children of faculty/staff, members of minority groups. ***ROTC:*** Army cooperative, Air Force cooperative.

LOANS ***Student loans:*** $6,989,318 (43% need-based, 57% non-need-based). 66% of past graduating class borrowed through all loan programs. *Average indebtedness per student:* $23,041. ***Average need-based loan:*** Freshmen: $3368. Undergraduates: $3809. ***Parent loans:*** $68,120 (100% non-need-based). ***Programs:*** Federal Direct (Subsidized and Unsubsidized Stafford, PLUS), Perkins, state, college/university.

WORK-STUDY ***Federal work-study:*** Total amount: $58,834; 3 jobs averaging $1255. ***State or other work-study/employment:*** Part-time jobs available.

APPLYING FOR FINANCIAL AID ***Required financial aid form:*** FAFSA. ***Financial aid deadline (priority):*** 3/15. ***Notification date:*** 3/15.

CONTACT Ms. Sondra Williams, Director of Financial Aid, Ohio University–Lancaster, 020 Chubb Hall, Athens, OH 45701-2979, 740-593-4141 or toll-free 888-446-4468 Ext. 215. *Fax:* 740-593-4140. *E-mail:* willias1@ohio.edu.

OHIO UNIVERSITY–SOUTHERN CAMPUS

Ironton, OH

Tuition & fees (OH res): $4395 **Average undergraduate aid package: $8456**

ABOUT THE INSTITUTION State-supported, coed. ***Awards:*** associate, bachelor's, and master's degrees. 17 undergraduate majors. ***Total enrollment:*** 1,836. Undergraduates: 1,699. Federal methodology is used as a basis for awarding need-based institutional aid.

UNDERGRADUATE EXPENSES for 2008–09 ***Application fee:*** $20. ***Tuition, state resident:*** full-time $4395; part-time $134 per credit hour. ***Tuition, nonresident:*** full-time $5715; part-time $174 per credit hour.

FRESHMAN FINANCIAL AID (Fall 2008, est.) 250 applied for aid; of those 90% were deemed to have need. 100% of freshmen with need received aid; of those 10% had need fully met. ***Average percent of need met:*** 67% (excluding resources awarded to replace EFC). ***Average financial aid package:*** $8422 (excluding resources awarded to replace EFC). 3% of all full-time freshmen had no need and received non-need-based gift aid.

UNDERGRADUATE FINANCIAL AID (Fall 2008, est.) 1,065 applied for aid; of those 91% were deemed to have need. 100% of undergraduates with need received aid; of those 7% had need fully met. ***Average percent of need met:*** 60% (excluding resources awarded to replace EFC). ***Average financial aid package:*** $8456 (excluding resources awarded to replace EFC). 3% of all full-time undergraduates had no need and received non-need-based gift aid.

GIFT AID (NEED-BASED) ***Total amount:*** $4,479,052 (72% federal, 22% state, 6% institutional). ***Receiving aid:*** Freshmen: 73% (191); all full-time undergraduates: 71% (785). ***Average award:*** Freshmen: $5700; Undergraduates: $5313. ***Scholarships, grants, and awards:*** Federal Pell, FSEOG, state, college/university gift aid from institutional funds.

GIFT AID (NON-NEED-BASED) ***Total amount:*** $326,758 (11% state, 61% institutional, 28% external sources). ***Receiving aid:*** Freshmen: 14% (36). Undergraduates: 13% (144). ***Average award:*** Freshmen: $2627. Undergraduates: $2107. ***Scholarships, grants, and awards by category:*** *Academic interests/achievement:* area/ethnic studies, biological sciences, business, communication, computer science, education, engineering/technologies, English, foreign languages, general academic interests/achievements, health fields, home economics, humanities, international studies, mathematics, military science, physical sciences, premedicine, social sciences. *Creative arts/performance:* applied art and design, art/fine arts, cinema/film/broadcasting, dance, debating, journalism/publications, music, performing arts, theater/drama. *Special characteristics:* children of faculty/staff, members of minority groups.

LOANS ***Student loans:*** $8,839,065 (45% need-based, 55% non-need-based). 66% of past graduating class borrowed through all loan programs. *Average indebtedness per student:* $23,041. ***Average need-based loan:*** Freshmen: $3443. Undergraduates: $3958. ***Parent loans:*** $13,500 (100% non-need-based). ***Programs:*** Federal Direct (Subsidized and Unsubsidized Stafford, PLUS), Perkins, state, college/university.

WORK-STUDY ***Federal work-study:*** Total amount: $62,795; 20 jobs averaging $1097. ***State or other work-study/employment:*** Part-time jobs available.

APPLYING FOR FINANCIAL AID ***Required financial aid form:*** FAFSA. ***Financial aid deadline (priority):*** 3/15. ***Notification date:*** 3/15.

CONTACT Ms. Sondra Williams, Director of Financial Aid, Ohio University–Southern Campus, 020 Chubb Hall, Athens, OH 45701-2979, 740-593-4141 or toll-free 800-626-0513. *Fax:* 740-593-4140. *E-mail:* willias1@ohio.edu.

OHIO UNIVERSITY–ZANESVILLE

Zanesville, OH

Tuition & fees (OH res): $4596 **Average undergraduate aid package: $7623**

ABOUT THE INSTITUTION State-supported, coed. ***Awards:*** associate, bachelor's, and master's degrees (offers first 2 years of most bachelor's degree programs available at the main campus in Athens; also offers several bachelor's degree programs that can be completed at this campus; also offers some graduate courses). 7 undergraduate majors. ***Total enrollment:*** 1,873. Undergraduates: 1,873. Freshmen: 300. Federal methodology is used as a basis for awarding need-based institutional aid.

UNDERGRADUATE EXPENSES for 2008–09 ***Application fee:*** $20. ***Tuition, state resident:*** full-time $4515; part-time $137 per credit hour. ***Tuition, nonresident:*** full-time $8838; part-time $268 per credit hour. ***Required fees:*** full-time $81; $2 per credit hour or $5 per term.

FRESHMAN FINANCIAL AID (Fall 2008, est.) 272 applied for aid; of those 78% were deemed to have need. 98% of freshmen with need received aid; of those 25% had need fully met. ***Average percent of need met:*** 74% (excluding resources awarded to replace EFC). ***Average financial aid package:*** $7162 (excluding resources awarded to replace EFC). 11% of all full-time freshmen had no need and received non-need-based gift aid.

UNDERGRADUATE FINANCIAL AID (Fall 2008, est.) 1,012 applied for aid; of those 85% were deemed to have need. 98% of undergraduates with need received aid; of those 13% had need fully met. ***Average percent of need met:*** 63% (excluding resources awarded to replace EFC). ***Average financial aid package:*** $7623 (excluding resources awarded to replace EFC). 6% of all full-time undergraduates had no need and received non-need-based gift aid.

GIFT AID (NEED-BASED) ***Total amount:*** $3,409,111 (70% federal, 20% state, 10% institutional). ***Receiving aid:*** Freshmen: 55% (151); all full-time undergraduates: 62% (627). ***Average award:*** Freshmen: $4905; Undergraduates: $4869. ***Scholarships, grants, and awards:*** Federal Pell, FSEOG, state, college/university gift aid from institutional funds.

GIFT AID (NON-NEED-BASED) ***Total amount:*** $782,101 (5% state, 75% institutional, 20% external sources). ***Receiving aid:*** Freshmen: 32% (88). Undergraduates: 20% (199). ***Average award:*** Freshmen: $2842. Undergraduates: $2421. ***Scholarships, grants, and awards by category:*** *Academic interests/achievement:* area/ethnic studies, biological sciences, business, communication, computer science, education, engineering/technologies, English, foreign languages, general academic interests/achievements, health fields, home economics, humanities, international studies, mathematics, military science, physical sciences, premedicine, social sciences. *Creative arts/performance:* applied art and design, art/fine arts, cinema/film/broadcasting, dance, debating, journalism/publications, music, performing arts, theater/drama. *Special characteristics:* children of faculty/staff, members of minority groups.

LOANS ***Student loans:*** $7,399,545 (44% need-based, 56% non-need-based). 66% of past graduating class borrowed through all loan programs. *Average indebtedness per student:* $23,041. ***Average need-based loan:*** Freshmen: $3197. Undergraduates: $3927. ***Parent loans:*** $37,610 (100% non-need-based). ***Programs:*** Federal Direct (Subsidized and Unsubsidized Stafford, PLUS), Perkins, state, college/university.

WORK-STUDY ***Federal work-study:*** Total amount: $93,720; 18 jobs averaging $2210. ***State or other work-study/employment:*** Part-time jobs available.

APPLYING FOR FINANCIAL AID ***Required financial aid form:*** FAFSA. ***Financial aid deadline (priority):*** 3/15. ***Notification date:*** 3/15.

CONTACT Ms. Sondra Williams, Director of Financial Aid, Ohio University–Zanesville, 020 Chubb Hall, Athens, OH 45701-2979, 740-593-4141. *Fax:* 740-593-4140. *E-mail:* willias1@ohio.edu.

OHIO VALLEY UNIVERSITY

Vienna, WV

Tuition & fees: $13,510 **Average undergraduate aid package: $11,101**

ABOUT THE INSTITUTION Independent religious, coed. ***Awards:*** associate, bachelor's, and master's degrees. 16 undergraduate majors. ***Total enrollment:*** 515. Undergraduates: 488. Freshmen: 100. Federal methodology is used as a basis for awarding need-based institutional aid.

UNDERGRADUATE EXPENSES for 2008–09 ***Application fee:*** $20. ***Comprehensive fee:*** $19,650 includes full-time tuition ($11,998), mandatory fees ($1512), and room and board ($6140). ***College room only:*** $3200. Full-time tuition and fees vary according to course load. Room and board charges vary according to board plan. ***Part-time tuition:*** $500 per credit hour. ***Part-time fees:*** $63 per credit hour. Part-time tuition and fees vary according to course load. ***Payment plan:*** Installment.

FRESHMAN FINANCIAL AID (Fall 2008, est.) 104 applied for aid; of those 89% were deemed to have need. 100% of freshmen with need received aid; of those 27% had need fully met. ***Average percent of need met:*** 75% (excluding

resources awarded to replace EFC). ***Average financial aid package:*** $11,738 (excluding resources awarded to replace EFC). 15% of all full-time freshmen had no need and received non-need-based gift aid.

UNDERGRADUATE FINANCIAL AID (Fall 2008, est.) 418 applied for aid; of those 86% were deemed to have need. 97% of undergraduates with need received aid; of those 20% had need fully met. ***Average percent of need met:*** 68% (excluding resources awarded to replace EFC). ***Average financial aid package:*** $11,101 (excluding resources awarded to replace EFC). 15% of all full-time undergraduates had no need and received non-need-based gift aid.

GIFT AID (NEED-BASED) ***Total amount:*** $2,067,110 (31% federal, 11% state, 53% institutional, 5% external sources). ***Receiving aid:*** Freshmen: 74% (86); all full-time undergraduates: 66% (315). ***Average award:*** Freshmen: $9434; Undergraduates: $8290. ***Scholarships, grants, and awards:*** Federal Pell, FSEOG, state, private, college/university gift aid from institutional funds.

GIFT AID (NON-NEED-BASED) ***Total amount:*** $597,923 (11% state, 81% institutional, 8% external sources). ***Receiving aid:*** Freshmen: 21% (24). Undergraduates: 12% (59). ***Average award:*** Freshmen: $7204. Undergraduates: $5360. ***Scholarships, grants, and awards by category:*** *Academic interests/achievement:* 191 awards ($272,306 total): education, English, general academic interests/achievements, religion/biblical studies. *Creative arts/performance:* 39 awards ($84,975 total): general creative arts/performance, journalism/publications, music, performing arts, theater/drama. *Special achievements/activities:* 44 awards ($61,075 total): community service, general special achievements/activities, leadership, religious involvement. *Special characteristics:* 148 awards ($511,056 total): adult students, children of faculty/staff, ethnic background, general special characteristics, international students, local/state students, relatives of clergy, religious affiliation. ***Tuition waivers:*** Full or partial for employees or children of employees, senior citizens. ***ROTC:*** Air Force cooperative.

LOANS ***Student loans:*** $2,556,057 (75% need-based, 25% non-need-based). 81% of past graduating class borrowed through all loan programs. *Average indebtedness per student:* $13,480. ***Average need-based loan:*** Freshmen: $3296. Undergraduates: $3951. ***Parent loans:*** $1,056,150 (42% need-based, 58% non-need-based). ***Programs:*** FFEL (Subsidized and Unsubsidized Stafford, PLUS), Perkins.

WORK-STUDY ***Federal work-study:*** Total amount: $120,938; 120 jobs averaging $1000. ***State or other work-study/employment:*** Total amount: $22,750 (100% non-need-based). 78 part-time jobs averaging $1000.

ATHLETIC AWARDS Total amount: $1,104,418 (50% need-based, 50% non-need-based).

APPLYING FOR FINANCIAL AID ***Required financial aid form:*** FAFSA. ***Financial aid deadline (priority):*** 3/1. ***Notification date:*** Continuous beginning 6/30. Students must reply within 4 weeks of notification.

CONTACT Summer Cook Boggess, Assistant Director of Financial Aid, Ohio Valley University, 1 Campus View Drive, Vienna, WV 26105-8000, 304-865-6207 or toll-free 877-446-8668 Ext. 6200 (out-of-state). *Fax:* 304-865-6001. *E-mail:* summer.cook@ovc.edu.

OHIO WESLEYAN UNIVERSITY

Delaware, OH

Tuition & fees: $33,700 — **Average undergraduate aid package: $25,103**

ABOUT THE INSTITUTION Independent United Methodist, coed. ***Awards:*** bachelor's degrees. 90 undergraduate majors. ***Total enrollment:*** 1,960. Undergraduates: 1,960. Freshmen: 570. Federal methodology is used as a basis for awarding need-based institutional aid.

UNDERGRADUATE EXPENSES for 2008–09 ***Application fee:*** $35. ***Comprehensive fee:*** $41,970 includes full-time tuition ($33,240), mandatory fees ($460), and room and board ($8270). ***College room only:*** $4120. Room and board charges vary according to board plan. ***Part-time tuition:*** $3620 per course. ***Payment plan:*** Installment.

FRESHMAN FINANCIAL AID (Fall 2008, est.) 461 applied for aid; of those 79% were deemed to have need. 100% of freshmen with need received aid; of those 33% had need fully met. ***Average percent of need met:*** 88% (excluding resources awarded to replace EFC). ***Average financial aid package:*** $26,591 (excluding resources awarded to replace EFC). 34% of all full-time freshmen had no need and received non-need-based gift aid.

UNDERGRADUATE FINANCIAL AID (Fall 2008, est.) 1,255 applied for aid; of those 91% were deemed to have need. 100% of undergraduates with need received aid; of those [illegible]% had need fully met. ***Average percent of need met:*** 78% (excluding resources awarded to replace EFC). ***Average financial aid package:*** $25,103 (excluding resources awarded to replace EFC). 37% of all full-time undergraduates had no need and received non-need-based gift aid.

GIFT AID (NEED-BASED) ***Total amount:*** $20,773,345 (8% federal, 5% state, 85% institutional, 2% external sources). ***Receiving aid:*** Freshmen: 63% (362); all full-time undergraduates: 59% (1,144). ***Average award:*** Freshmen: $21,924; Undergraduates: $20,252. ***Scholarships, grants, and awards:*** Federal Pell, FSEOG, state, private, college/university gift aid from institutional funds.

GIFT AID (NON-NEED-BASED) ***Total amount:*** $12,856,781 (2% state, 97% institutional, 1% external sources). ***Receiving aid:*** Freshmen: 14% (79). Undergraduates: 8% (153). ***Average award:*** Freshmen: $15,031. Undergraduates: $14,313. ***Tuition waivers:*** Full or partial for children of alumni, employees or children of employees. ***ROTC:*** Army cooperative, Air Force cooperative.

LOANS ***Student loans:*** $7,434,473 (62% need-based, 38% non-need-based). 77% of past graduating class borrowed through all loan programs. *Average indebtedness per student:* $26,704. ***Average need-based loan:*** Freshmen: $5380. Undergraduates: $5374. ***Parent loans:*** $2,589,053 (100% non-need-based). ***Programs:*** FFEL (Subsidized and Unsubsidized Stafford, PLUS), Perkins, college/university.

WORK-STUDY ***Federal work-study:*** Total amount: $1,027,810; jobs available. ***State or other work-study/employment:*** Total amount: $398,350 (100% non-need-based). Part-time jobs available.

APPLYING FOR FINANCIAL AID ***Required financial aid form:*** FAFSA. ***Financial aid deadline:*** 5/1 (priority: 3/1). ***Notification date:*** Continuous. Students must reply by 5/1 or within 2 weeks of notification.

CONTACT Mr. Gregory W. Matthews, Director of Financial Aid, Ohio Wesleyan University, 61 South Sandusky Street, Delaware, OH 43015, 740-368-3050 or toll-free 800-922-8953. *Fax:* 740-368-3066. *E-mail:* owfinaid@owu.edu.

OHR HAMEIR THEOLOGICAL SEMINARY

Peekskill, NY

CONTACT Financial Aid Office, Ohr Hameir Theological Seminary, Furnace Woods Road, Peekskill, NY 10566, 914-736-1500.

OHR SOMAYACH/JOSEPH TANENBAUM EDUCATIONAL CENTER

Monsey, NY

CONTACT Financial Aid Office, Ohr Somayach/Joseph Tanenbaum Educational Center, PO Box 334244, Route 306, Monsey, NY 10952-0334, 914-425-1370.

OKLAHOMA BAPTIST UNIVERSITY

Shawnee, OK

Tuition & fees: $16,790 — **Average undergraduate aid package: $14,046**

ABOUT THE INSTITUTION Independent Southern Baptist, coed. ***Awards:*** bachelor's and master's degrees. 67 undergraduate majors. ***Total enrollment:*** 1,618. Undergraduates: 1,593. Federal methodology is used as a basis for awarding need-based institutional aid.

UNDERGRADUATE EXPENSES for 2008–09 ***Application fee:*** $25. ***One-time required fee:*** $25. ***Comprehensive fee:*** $21,990 includes full-time tuition ($15,468), mandatory fees ($1322), and room and board ($5200). ***Part-time tuition:*** $503 per hour. ***Part-time fees:*** $319 per term.

FRESHMAN FINANCIAL AID (Fall 2008, est.) 280 applied for aid; of those 87% were deemed to have need. 100% of freshmen with need received aid; of those 70% had need fully met. ***Average percent of need met:*** 70% (excluding resources awarded to replace EFC). ***Average financial aid package:*** $14,713 (excluding resources awarded to replace EFC). 10% of all full-time freshmen had no need and received non-need-based gift aid.

UNDERGRADUATE FINANCIAL AID (Fall 2008, est.) 960 applied for aid; of those 91% were deemed to have need. 100% of undergraduates with need received aid; of those 45% had need fully met. ***Average percent of need met:*** 69% (excluding resources awarded to replace EFC). ***Average financial aid package:*** $14,046 (excluding resources awarded to replace EFC). 11% of all full-time undergraduates had no need and received non-need-based gift aid.

GIFT AID (NEED-BASED) ***Total amount:*** $9,876,975 (16% federal, 12% state, 61% institutional, 11% external sources). ***Receiving aid:*** Freshmen: 69% (233); all full-time undergraduates: 68% (848). ***Average award:*** Freshmen: $5222;

Undergraduates: $5801. ***Scholarships, grants, and awards:*** Federal Pell, FSEOG, state, private, college/university gift aid from institutional funds, Academic Competitiveness Grant, National Smart Grant, TEACH Grant.

GIFT AID (NON-NEED-BASED) ***Total amount:*** $1,350,728 (6% federal, 4% state, 79% institutional, 11% external sources). ***Receiving aid:*** Freshmen: 69% (232). Undergraduates: 63% (790). ***Average award:*** Freshmen: $4885. Undergraduates: $4712. ***Scholarships, grants, and awards by category:*** *Academic interests/achievement:* general academic interests/achievements, religion/biblical studies. *Creative arts/performance:* applied art and design, art/fine arts, music, performing arts, theater/drama. *Special achievements/activities:* leadership, religious involvement. *Special characteristics:* children and siblings of alumni, children of faculty/staff, general special characteristics, local/state students, out-of-state students, relatives of clergy, religious affiliation. ***ROTC:*** Air Force cooperative.

LOANS ***Student loans:*** $5,593,950 (88% need-based, 12% non-need-based). 65% of past graduating class borrowed through all loan programs. *Average indebtedness per student:* $17,859. ***Average need-based loan:*** Freshmen: $2370. Undergraduates: $2766. ***Parent loans:*** $867,984 (60% need-based, 40% non-need-based). ***Programs:*** FFEL (Subsidized and Unsubsidized Stafford, PLUS), Perkins, college/university.

WORK-STUDY ***Federal work-study:*** Total amount: $147,244; 416 jobs averaging $580. ***State or other work-study/employment:*** Total amount: $2,714,239 (100% non-need-based). 338 part-time jobs averaging $2000.

ATHLETIC AWARDS Total amount: $2,247,724 (79% need-based, 21% non-need-based).

APPLYING FOR FINANCIAL AID ***Required financial aid form:*** FAFSA. ***Financial aid deadline:*** Continuous. ***Notification date:*** Continuous beginning 2/1.

CONTACT Jonna Raney, Student Financial Services, Oklahoma Baptist University, 500 West University, Shawnee, OK 74804, 405-878-2016 or toll-free 800-654-3285. *Fax:* 405-878-2167. *E-mail:* jonna.raney@okbu.edu.

OKLAHOMA CHRISTIAN UNIVERSITY

Oklahoma City, OK

Tuition & fees: $16,266 **Average undergraduate aid package: $15,445**

ABOUT THE INSTITUTION Independent religious, coed. ***Awards:*** bachelor's and master's degrees. 58 undergraduate majors. ***Total enrollment:*** 2,161. Undergraduates: 1,904. Freshmen: 436. Federal methodology is used as a basis for awarding need-based institutional aid.

UNDERGRADUATE EXPENSES for 2009–10 ***Application fee:*** $25. ***Comprehensive fee:*** $22,206 includes full-time tuition ($14,690), mandatory fees ($1576), and room and board ($5940). ***College room only:*** $2840. ***Part-time tuition:*** $612 per credit hour. ***Part-time fees:*** $788 per term; $762 per term.

FRESHMAN FINANCIAL AID (Fall 2008, est.) 429 applied for aid; of those 72% were deemed to have need. 98% of freshmen with need received aid; of those 23% had need fully met. ***Average percent of need met:*** 54% (excluding resources awarded to replace EFC). ***Average financial aid package:*** $16,718 (excluding resources awarded to replace EFC). 18% of all full-time freshmen had no need and received non-need-based gift aid.

UNDERGRADUATE FINANCIAL AID (Fall 2008, est.) 1,920 applied for aid; of those 68% were deemed to have need. 99% of undergraduates with need received aid; of those 24% had need fully met. ***Average percent of need met:*** 53% (excluding resources awarded to replace EFC). ***Average financial aid package:*** $15,445 (excluding resources awarded to replace EFC). 21% of all full-time undergraduates had no need and received non-need-based gift aid.

GIFT AID (NEED-BASED) ***Total amount:*** $11,129,016 (16% federal, 6% state, 68% institutional, 10% external sources). ***Receiving aid:*** Freshmen: 44% (189); all full-time undergraduates: 34% (673). ***Average award:*** Freshmen: $3047; Undergraduates: $2380. ***Scholarships, grants, and awards:*** Federal Pell, FSEOG, state, private, college/university gift aid from institutional funds.

GIFT AID (NON-NEED-BASED) ***Total amount:*** $3,838,737 (2% state, 91% institutional, 7% external sources). ***Receiving aid:*** Freshmen: 60% (258). Undergraduates: 54% (1,056). ***Average award:*** Freshmen: $4106. Undergraduates: $3522. ***Scholarships, grants, and awards by category:*** *Academic interests/achievement:* 989 awards ($4,954,068 total): engineering/technologies, general academic interests/achievements, religion/biblical studies. *Creative arts/performance:* 216 awards ($528,009 total): applied art and design, journalism/publications, music, theater/drama. *Special achievements/activities:* 51 awards ($41,500 total): cheerleading/drum major, leadership. *Special characteristics:* 131 awards ($1,030,457 total): children of faculty/staff, international students. ***ROTC:*** Army cooperative, Air Force cooperative.

LOANS ***Student loans:*** $10,615,159 (90% need-based, 10% non-need-based). 76% of past graduating class borrowed through all loan programs. *Average indebtedness per student:* $24,377. ***Average need-based loan:*** Freshmen: $3202. Undergraduates: $3965. ***Parent loans:*** $3,010,175 (81% need-based, 19% non-need-based). ***Programs:*** FFEL (Subsidized and Unsubsidized Stafford, PLUS), Perkins, alternative loans.

WORK-STUDY ***Federal work-study:*** Total amount: $942,362; 514 jobs averaging $2000.

ATHLETIC AWARDS Total amount: $2,100,087 (29% need-based, 71% non-need-based).

APPLYING FOR FINANCIAL AID ***Required financial aid form:*** FAFSA. ***Financial aid deadline:*** 8/31 (priority: 3/15). ***Notification date:*** Continuous. Students must reply within 4 weeks of notification.

CONTACT Clint LaRue, Director of Financial Services, Oklahoma Christian University, Box 11000, Oklahoma City, OK 73136-1100, 405-425-5190 or toll-free 800-877-5010 (in-state). *Fax:* 405-425-5197. *E-mail:* clint.larue@oc.edu.

OKLAHOMA CITY UNIVERSITY

Oklahoma City, OK

Tuition & fees: $23,400 **Average undergraduate aid package: $21,685**

ABOUT THE INSTITUTION Independent United Methodist, coed. ***Awards:*** bachelor's, master's, and first professional degrees. 74 undergraduate majors. ***Total enrollment:*** 3,897. Undergraduates: 2,190. Freshmen: 376. Federal methodology is used as a basis for awarding need-based institutional aid.

UNDERGRADUATE EXPENSES for 2008–09 ***Application fee:*** $30. ***Comprehensive fee:*** $32,600 includes full-time tuition ($21,400), mandatory fees ($2000), and room and board ($9200). ***College room only:*** $5566. Full-time tuition and fees vary according to program. Room and board charges vary according to board plan and housing facility. ***Part-time tuition:*** $730 per semester hour. ***Part-time fees:*** $60 per semester hour. Part-time tuition and fees vary according to program. ***Payment plans:*** Installment, deferred payment.

FRESHMAN FINANCIAL AID (Fall 2008, est.) 299 applied for aid; of those 80% were deemed to have need. 85% of freshmen with need received aid; of those 25% had need fully met. ***Average percent of need met:*** 78% (excluding resources awarded to replace EFC). ***Average financial aid package:*** $21,998 (excluding resources awarded to replace EFC). 15% of all full-time freshmen had no need and received non-need-based gift aid.

UNDERGRADUATE FINANCIAL AID (Fall 2008, est.) 1,323 applied for aid; of those 86% were deemed to have need. 91% of undergraduates with need received aid; of those 56% had need fully met. ***Average percent of need met:*** 81% (excluding resources awarded to replace EFC). ***Average financial aid package:*** $21,685 (excluding resources awarded to replace EFC). 8% of all full-time undergraduates had no need and received non-need-based gift aid.

GIFT AID (NEED-BASED) ***Total amount:*** $19,231,408 (8% federal, 4% state, 83% institutional, 5% external sources). ***Receiving aid:*** Freshmen: 46% (162); all full-time undergraduates: 45% (872). ***Average award:*** Freshmen: $15,115; Undergraduates: $14,224. ***Scholarships, grants, and awards:*** Federal Pell, FSEOG, state, private, college/university gift aid from institutional funds, United Negro College Fund, Federal Nursing, Native American Grants.

GIFT AID (NON-NEED-BASED) ***Total amount:*** $2,711,326 (19% state, 42% institutional, 39% external sources). ***Receiving aid:*** Freshmen: 7% (24). Undergraduates: 15% (300). ***Average award:*** Freshmen: $12,240. Undergraduates: $11,250. ***Scholarships, grants, and awards by category:*** *Academic interests/achievement:* 1,412 awards ($3,220,660 total): business, communication, education, general academic interests/achievements, health fields, religion/biblical studies. *Creative arts/performance:* 347 awards ($1,409,205 total): applied art and design, art/fine arts, dance, music, performing arts, theater/drama. *Special achievements/activities:* 289 awards ($226,337 total): cheerleading/drum major, general special achievements/activities, junior miss, leadership, religious involvement. *Special characteristics:* 169 awards ($1,487,126 total): children of faculty/staff, relatives of clergy. ***Tuition waivers:*** Full or partial for employees or children of employees. ***ROTC:*** Army cooperative, Air Force cooperative.

LOANS ***Student loans:*** $6,799,552 (46% need-based, 54% non-need-based). 45% of past graduating class borrowed through all loan programs. *Average indebtedness per student:* $28,680. ***Average need-based loan:*** Freshmen: $4064.

Undergraduates: $3753. ***Parent loans:*** $3,627,263 (100% non-need-based). ***Programs:*** FFEL (Subsidized and Unsubsidized Stafford, PLUS), Perkins, Federal Nursing.

WORK-STUDY ***Federal work-study:*** Total amount: $341,656; 190 jobs averaging $1842. ***State or other work-study/employment:*** Total amount: $468,568 (100% non-need-based). 55 part-time jobs averaging $2214.

ATHLETIC AWARDS Total amount: $3,626,723 (100% non-need-based).

APPLYING FOR FINANCIAL AID ***Required financial aid form:*** FAFSA. ***Financial aid deadline (priority):*** 3/1. ***Notification date:*** Continuous. Students must reply within 2 weeks of notification.

CONTACT Denise Flis, Senior Director Student Financial Services, Oklahoma City University, 2501 North Blackwelder, Oklahoma City, OK 73106-1493, 405-208-5848 or toll-free 800-633-7242. *Fax:* 405-208-5466. *E-mail:* dflis@okcu.edu.

OKLAHOMA PANHANDLE STATE UNIVERSITY

Goodwell, OK

Tuition & fees (OK res): $4242   Average undergraduate aid package: $7890

ABOUT THE INSTITUTION State-supported, coed. ***Awards:*** associate and bachelor's degrees. 27 undergraduate majors. ***Total enrollment:*** 1,223. Undergraduates: 1,223. Freshmen: 288.

UNDERGRADUATE EXPENSES for 2008–09 ***Tuition, state resident:*** full-time $2738. ***Tuition, nonresident:*** full-time $5340. ***Required fees:*** full-time $1504. Full-time tuition and fees vary according to course level, program, and student level. Part-time tuition and fees vary according to course level and student level. ***College room and board:*** $3320; ***Room only:*** $900. Room and board charges vary according to board plan and housing facility. ***Payment plans:*** Guaranteed tuition, installment.

FRESHMAN FINANCIAL AID (Fall 2008, est.) ***Average financial aid package:*** $7418 (excluding resources awarded to replace EFC).

UNDERGRADUATE FINANCIAL AID (Fall 2008, est.) ***Average financial aid package:*** $7890 (excluding resources awarded to replace EFC).

GIFT AID (NEED-BASED) ***Total amount:*** $2,230,127 (65% federal, 13% state, 8% institutional, 14% external sources). ***Receiving aid:*** Freshmen: 77% (220); all full-time undergraduates: 68% (650). ***Average award:*** Freshmen: $3328; Undergraduates: $3337. ***Scholarships, grants, and awards:*** Federal Pell, FSEOG, state, private, college/university gift aid from institutional funds.

GIFT AID (NON-NEED-BASED) ***Scholarships, grants, and awards by category:*** *Academic interests/achievement:* agriculture, biological sciences, business, computer science, education, English, general academic interests/achievements, health fields, mathematics, physical sciences. *Creative arts/performance:* art/fine arts, debating, music, performing arts, theater/drama. *Special achievements/activities:* cheerleading/drum major, general special achievements/activities, rodeo. *Special characteristics:* children of faculty/staff, general special characteristics, local/state students, out-of-state students, veterans, veterans' children. ***Tuition waivers:*** Full or partial for employees or children of employees, senior citizens.

LOANS ***Student loans:*** $3,085,938 (100% need-based). ***Programs:*** FFEL (Subsidized and Unsubsidized Stafford, PLUS), Perkins.

WORK-STUDY ***Federal work-study:*** Total amount: $34,936; 20 jobs averaging $1747. ***State or other work-study/employment:*** Total amount: $207,150 (100% need-based). 158 part-time jobs averaging $1311.

ATHLETIC AWARDS Total amount: $328,074 (100% need-based).

APPLYING FOR FINANCIAL AID ***Required financial aid form:*** FAFSA. ***Financial aid deadline (priority):*** 3/15. ***Notification date:*** 5/1. Students must reply by 8/1.

CONTACT Ms. Mary Ellen Riley, Director of Financial Aid, Oklahoma Panhandle State University, PO Box 430, Goodwell, OK 73939-0430, 580-349-2611 Ext. 324 or toll-free 800-664-6778. *E-mail:* mriley@opsu.edu.

OKLAHOMA STATE UNIVERSITY

Stillwater, OK

Tuition & fees (OK res): $6202   Average undergraduate aid package: $10,262

ABOUT THE INSTITUTION State-supported, coed. ***Awards:*** bachelor's, master's, doctoral, and first professional degrees and post-bachelor's and post-master's certificates. 81 undergraduate majors. ***Total enrollment:*** 22,768. Undergraduates: 17,986. Freshmen: 3,073. Federal methodology is used as a basis for awarding need-based institutional aid.

UNDERGRADUATE EXPENSES for 2008–09 ***Application fee:*** $40. ***One-time required fee:*** $95. ***Tuition, state resident:*** full-time $3941; part-time $131.35 per credit hour. ***Tuition, nonresident:*** full-time $14,295; part-time $476.50 per credit hour. ***Required fees:*** full-time $2261; $75.35 per credit hour. Full-time tuition and fees vary according to program and student level. Part-time tuition and fees vary according to program and student level. ***College room and board:*** $7402; ***Room only:*** $3402. Room and board charges vary according to board plan and housing facility. ***Payment plan:*** Installment.

FRESHMAN FINANCIAL AID (Fall 2008, est.) 2,013 applied for aid; of those 73% were deemed to have need. 97% of freshmen with need received aid; of those 17% had need fully met. ***Average percent of need met:*** 71% (excluding resources awarded to replace EFC). ***Average financial aid package:*** $10,358 (excluding resources awarded to replace EFC). 25% of all full-time freshmen had no need and received non-need-based gift aid.

UNDERGRADUATE FINANCIAL AID (Fall 2008, est.) 9,483 applied for aid; of those 80% were deemed to have need. 97% of undergraduates with need received aid; of those 16% had need fully met. ***Average percent of need met:*** 69% (excluding resources awarded to replace EFC). ***Average financial aid package:*** $10,262 (excluding resources awarded to replace EFC). 23% of all full-time undergraduates had no need and received non-need-based gift aid.

GIFT AID (NEED-BASED) ***Total amount:*** $38,958,896 (43% federal, 31% state, 15% institutional, 11% external sources). ***Receiving aid:*** Freshmen: 37% (1,086); all full-time undergraduates: 35% (5,436). ***Average award:*** Freshmen: $5823; Undergraduates: $5458. ***Scholarships, grants, and awards:*** Federal Pell, FSEOG, state, private, college/university gift aid from institutional funds.

GIFT AID (NON-NEED-BASED) ***Total amount:*** $13,564,726 (22% federal, 9% state, 36% institutional, 33% external sources). ***Receiving aid:*** Freshmen: 29% (860). Undergraduates: 20% (3,149). ***Average award:*** Freshmen: $4422. Undergraduates: $4043. ***Scholarships, grants, and awards by category:*** *Academic interests/achievement:* agriculture, architecture, area/ethnic studies, biological sciences, business, communication, computer science, education, engineering/technologies, English, foreign languages, general academic interests/achievements, home economics, humanities, international studies, mathematics, military science, physical sciences, premedicine, social sciences. *Creative arts/performance:* art/fine arts, creative writing, general creative arts/performance, journalism/publications, music, theater/drama. *Special achievements/activities:* cheerleading/drum major, community service, general special achievements/activities, leadership, memberships, rodeo. *Special characteristics:* adult students, children and siblings of alumni, ethnic background, first-generation college students, general special characteristics, handicapped students, out-of-state students, previous college experience. ***Tuition waivers:*** Full or partial for children of alumni. ***ROTC:*** Army, Air Force.

LOANS ***Student loans:*** $51,711,412 (53% need-based, 47% non-need-based). 55% of past graduating class borrowed through all loan programs. *Average indebtedness per student:* $18,989. ***Average need-based loan:*** Freshmen: $3140. Undergraduates: $4182. ***Parent loans:*** $18,870,543 (18% need-based, 82% non-need-based). ***Programs:*** Federal Direct (Subsidized and Unsubsidized Stafford, PLUS), Perkins, college/university.

WORK-STUDY ***Federal work-study:*** Total amount: $583,870; 328 jobs averaging $1796. ***State or other work-study/employment:*** Total amount: $7,694,084 (100% non-need-based). 3,746 part-time jobs averaging $2091.

ATHLETIC AWARDS Total amount: $3,754,763 (41% need-based, 59% non-need-based).

APPLYING FOR FINANCIAL AID ***Required financial aid forms:*** FAFSA, institution's own form. ***Financial aid deadline:*** Continuous. ***Notification date:*** Continuous beginning 3/1. Students must reply within 4 weeks of notification.

CONTACT Office of Scholarships and Financial Aid, Oklahoma State University, 119 Student Union, Stillwater, OK 74078-5061, 405-744-6604 or toll-free 800-233-5019 Ext. 1 (in-state), 800-852-1255 (out-of-state). *Fax:* 405-744-6438. *E-mail:* finaid@okstate.edu.

OKLAHOMA WESLEYAN UNIVERSITY

Bartlesville, OK

Tuition & fees: $16,585   Average undergraduate aid package: $12,324

ABOUT THE INSTITUTION Independent religious, coed. ***Awards:*** associate, bachelor's, and master's degrees. 36 undergraduate majors. ***Total enrollment:*** 1,159. Undergraduates: 1,001. Both federal and institutional methodology are used as a basis for awarding need-based institutional aid.

UNDERGRADUATE EXPENSES for 2008–09 ***Application fee:*** $25. ***Comprehensive fee:*** $22,635 includes full-time tuition ($15,685), mandatory fees ($900), and room and board ($6050). ***College room only:*** $3200. Full-time tuition and fees vary according to course load. Room and board charges vary according to board plan and housing facility. ***Part-time tuition:*** $650 per credit hour. ***Part-time fees:*** $55 per credit hour. ***Payment plans:*** Installment, deferred payment.

FRESHMAN FINANCIAL AID (Fall 2008, est.) 91 applied for aid; of those 99% were deemed to have need. 100% of freshmen with need received aid; of those 36% had need fully met. ***Average percent of need met:*** 40% (excluding resources awarded to replace EFC). ***Average financial aid package:*** $11,926 (excluding resources awarded to replace EFC).

UNDERGRADUATE FINANCIAL AID (Fall 2008, est.) 535 applied for aid; of those 100% were deemed to have need. 99% of undergraduates with need received aid; of those 23% had need fully met. ***Average percent of need met:*** 47% (excluding resources awarded to replace EFC). ***Average financial aid package:*** $12,324 (excluding resources awarded to replace EFC).

GIFT AID (NEED-BASED) ***Total amount:*** $4,114,604 (25% federal, 8% state, 60% institutional, 7% external sources). ***Receiving aid:*** Freshmen: 97% (90); all full-time undergraduates: 94% (526). ***Average award:*** Freshmen: $4938; Undergraduates: $5129. ***Scholarships, grants, and awards:*** Federal Pell, FSEOG, state, private, college/university gift aid from institutional funds.

GIFT AID (NON-NEED-BASED) ***Total amount:*** $1,258,915 (10% federal, 1% state, 79% institutional, 10% external sources). ***Receiving aid:*** Freshmen: 97% (90). Undergraduates: 94% (524). ***Scholarships, grants, and awards by category:*** *Academic interests/achievement:* 225 awards ($722,975 total): biological sciences, computer science, education, general academic interests/achievements, religion/biblical studies. *Creative arts/performance:* 19 awards ($22,052 total): music. *Special achievements/activities:* 138 awards ($142,450 total): religious involvement. *Special characteristics:* 257 awards ($385,838 total): children and siblings of alumni, children of educators, children of faculty/staff, international students, relatives of clergy, religious affiliation. ***Tuition waivers:*** Full or partial for employees or children of employees, senior citizens.

LOANS ***Student loans:*** $7,369,987 (67% need-based, 33% non-need-based). 97% of past graduating class borrowed through all loan programs. *Average indebtedness per student:* $22,039. ***Average need-based loan:*** Freshmen: $3329. Undergraduates: $5113. ***Parent loans:*** $1,164,013 (36% need-based, 64% non-need-based). ***Programs:*** FFEL (Subsidized and Unsubsidized Stafford, PLUS), Perkins, college/university.

WORK-STUDY ***Federal work-study:*** Total amount: $187,967; 183 jobs averaging $1521. ***State or other work-study/employment:*** Total amount: $32,340 (34% need-based, 66% non-need-based). 28 part-time jobs averaging $1499.

ATHLETIC AWARDS Total amount: $634,727 (67% need-based, 33% non-need-based).

APPLYING FOR FINANCIAL AID ***Required financial aid forms:*** FAFSA, institution's own form. ***Financial aid deadline (priority):*** 3/31. ***Notification date:*** Continuous beginning 5/1. Students must reply within 1 week of notification.

CONTACT Lee Kanakis, Director of Student Financial Services, Oklahoma Wesleyan University, 2201 Silver Lake Road, Bartlesville, OK 74006, 918-335-6282 or toll-free 866-222-8226 (in-state). *Fax:* 918-335-6811. *E-mail:* financialaid@okwu.edu.

OLD DOMINION UNIVERSITY

Norfolk, VA

Tuition & fees (VA res): $6918 **Average undergraduate aid package: $7597**

ABOUT THE INSTITUTION State-supported, coed. ***Awards:*** bachelor's, master's, and doctoral degrees and post-master's certificates. 95 undergraduate majors. ***Total enrollment:*** 23,086. Undergraduates: 17,330. Freshmen: 2,812. Federal methodology is used as a basis for awarding need-based institutional aid.

UNDERGRADUATE EXPENSES for 2008–09 ***Application fee:*** $40. ***Tuition, state resident:*** full-time $6720; part-time $224 per credit hour. ***Tuition, nonresident:*** full-time $18,390; part-time $613 per credit hour. ***Required fees:*** full-time $198; $39 per term. Full-time tuition and fees vary according to course level, course load, and location. Part-time tuition and fees vary according to course level, course load, and location. ***College room and board:*** $7092; ***Room only:*** $4234. Room and board charges vary according to board plan and housing facility. ***Payment plans:*** Installment, deferred payment.

FRESHMAN FINANCIAL AID (Fall 2008, est.) 2,105 applied for aid; of those 88% were deemed to have need. 91% of freshmen with need received aid; of those 64% had need fully met. ***Average percent of need met:*** 85% (excluding resources awarded to replace EFC). ***Average financial aid package:*** $7571 (excluding resources awarded to replace EFC). 4% of all full-time freshmen had no need and received non-need-based gift aid.

UNDERGRADUATE FINANCIAL AID (Fall 2008, est.) 9,104 applied for aid; of those 84% were deemed to have need. 94% of undergraduates with need received aid; of those 55% had need fully met. ***Average percent of need met:*** 81% (excluding resources awarded to replace EFC). ***Average financial aid package:*** $7597 (excluding resources awarded to replace EFC). 3% of all full-time undergraduates had no need and received non-need-based gift aid.

GIFT AID (NEED-BASED) ***Total amount:*** $27,957,171 (52% federal, 44% state, 3% institutional, 1% external sources). ***Receiving aid:*** Freshmen: 31% (853); all full-time undergraduates: 28% (3,691). ***Average award:*** Freshmen: $4578; Undergraduates: $4328. ***Scholarships, grants, and awards:*** Federal Pell, FSEOG, state, private, college/university gift aid from institutional funds, United Negro College Fund, Federal Nursing.

GIFT AID (NON-NEED-BASED) ***Total amount:*** $8,692,427 (5% state, 76% institutional, 19% external sources). ***Receiving aid:*** Freshmen: 24% (663). Undergraduates: 13% (1,651). ***Average award:*** Freshmen: $3422. Undergraduates: $2823. ***Scholarships, grants, and awards by category:*** *Academic interests/achievement:* 1,401 awards ($3,834,521 total): biological sciences, business, engineering/technologies, English, general academic interests/achievements, health fields, humanities, military science, physical sciences. *Creative arts/performance:* 72 awards ($84,341 total): art/fine arts, dance, music, performing arts, theater/drama. *Special achievements/activities:* 25 awards ($31,523 total): cheerleading/drum major, community service, leadership, memberships. *Special characteristics:* 37 awards ($14,382 total): children of faculty/staff, handicapped students, international students, local/state students, members of minority groups, previous college experience, veterans' children. ***Tuition waivers:*** Full or partial for employees or children of employees, senior citizens. ***ROTC:*** Army, Naval.

LOANS ***Student loans:*** $61,879,411 (45% need-based, 55% non-need-based). 80% of past graduating class borrowed through all loan programs. *Average indebtedness per student:* $16,950. ***Average need-based loan:*** Freshmen: $3370. Undergraduates: $4232. ***Parent loans:*** $7,087,225 (100% non-need-based). ***Programs:*** Federal Direct (Subsidized and Unsubsidized Stafford, PLUS), Perkins, Federal Nursing, college/university.

WORK-STUDY ***Federal work-study:*** Total amount: $1,594,648; 236 jobs averaging $1163.

ATHLETIC AWARDS Total amount: $3,206,622 (100% non-need-based).

APPLYING FOR FINANCIAL AID ***Required financial aid form:*** FAFSA. ***Financial aid deadline:*** 3/15 (priority: 2/15). ***Notification date:*** Continuous. Students must reply within 2 weeks of notification.

CONTACT Veronica Finch, Director of Student Financial Aid, Old Dominion University, 121 Rollins Hall, Norfolk, VA 23529, 757-683-3690 or toll-free 800-348-7926. *E-mail:* vfinch@odu.edu.

OLIVET COLLEGE

Olivet, MI

Tuition & fees: $19,244 **Average undergraduate aid package: $16,731**

ABOUT THE INSTITUTION Independent religious, coed. ***Awards:*** bachelor's and master's degrees. 35 undergraduate majors. ***Total enrollment:*** 1,049. Undergraduates: 1,004. Federal methodology is used as a basis for awarding need-based institutional aid.

UNDERGRADUATE EXPENSES for 2008–09 ***Application fee:*** $25. ***Comprehensive fee:*** $26,016 includes full-time tuition ($19,244) and room and board ($6772). ***College room only:*** $3472. Full-time tuition and fees vary according to reciprocity agreements. Room and board charges vary according to board plan and housing facility. Part-time tuition and fees vary according to course load and reciprocity agreements. ***Payment plan:*** Installment.

FRESHMAN FINANCIAL AID (Fall 2008, est.) 294 applied for aid; of those 96% were deemed to have need. 100% of freshmen with need received aid; of those 30% had need fully met. ***Average percent of need met:*** 77% (excluding

resources awarded to replace EFC). ***Average financial aid package:*** $15,631 (excluding resources awarded to replace EFC). 13% of all full-time freshmen had no need and received non-need-based gift aid.

UNDERGRADUATE FINANCIAL AID (Fall 2008, est.) 947 applied for aid; of those 92% were deemed to have need. 100% of undergraduates with need received aid; of those 16% had need fully met. ***Average percent of need met:*** 81% (excluding resources awarded to replace EFC). ***Average financial aid package:*** $16,731 (excluding resources awarded to replace EFC). 11% of all full-time undergraduates had no need and received non-need-based gift aid.

GIFT AID (NEED-BASED) ***Total amount:*** $12,002,803 (19% federal, 14% state, 65% institutional, 2% external sources). ***Receiving aid:*** Freshmen: 77% (282); all full-time undergraduates: 81% (862). ***Average award:*** Freshmen: $12,651; Undergraduates: $11,028. ***Scholarships, grants, and awards:*** Federal Pell, FSEOG, state, private, college/university gift aid from institutional funds.

GIFT AID (NON-NEED-BASED) ***Total amount:*** $1,427,582 (2% state, 93% institutional, 5% external sources). ***Receiving aid:*** Freshmen: 14% (50). Undergraduates: 8% (82). ***Average award:*** Freshmen: $9500. Undergraduates: $10,850. ***Scholarships, grants, and awards by category:*** *Academic interests/achievement:* 480 awards ($2,384,673 total): business, communication, education, English, foreign languages, general academic interests/achievements. *Creative arts/performance:* 46 awards ($94,320 total): art/fine arts, journalism/publications, music. *Special achievements/activities:* 117 awards ($662,557 total): community service, leadership, memberships. *Special characteristics:* 248 awards ($917,746 total): children and siblings of alumni, children of faculty/staff, international students, religious affiliation, siblings of current students. ***Tuition waivers:*** Full or partial for employees or children of employees.

LOANS ***Student loans:*** $7,359,205 (78% need-based, 22% non-need-based). 92% of past graduating class borrowed through all loan programs. *Average indebtedness per student:* $24,151. ***Average need-based loan:*** Freshmen: $2615. Undergraduates: $4280. ***Parent loans:*** $526,142 (31% need-based, 69% non-need-based). ***Programs:*** FFEL (Subsidized and Unsubsidized Stafford, PLUS), Perkins, state, Key alternative loans, CitiAssist Loans, Signature Loan.

WORK-STUDY ***Federal work-study:*** Total amount: $149,950; 130 jobs averaging $1153. ***State or other work-study/employment:*** Total amount: $465,654 (100% need-based). 401 part-time jobs averaging $1026.

APPLYING FOR FINANCIAL AID ***Required financial aid form:*** FAFSA. ***Financial aid deadline:*** Continuous. ***Notification date:*** Continuous beginning 3/1.

CONTACT Ms. Libby M. Jean, Director of Student Services, Olivet College, 320 South Main Street, Olivet, MI 49076-9701, 269-749-7655 Ext. 7655 or toll-free 800-456-7189. *Fax:* 269-749-3821. *E-mail:* ljean@olivetcollege.edu.

OLIVET NAZARENE UNIVERSITY

Bourbonnais, IL

Tuition & fees: $21,590 **Average undergraduate aid package: $15,986**

ABOUT THE INSTITUTION Independent religious, coed. ***Awards:*** associate, bachelor's, master's, and doctoral degrees. 66 undergraduate majors. ***Total enrollment:*** 4,636. Undergraduates: 3,190. Federal methodology is used as a basis for awarding need-based institutional aid.

UNDERGRADUATE EXPENSES for 2008–09 ***Application fee:*** $25. ***Comprehensive fee:*** $27,990 includes full-time tuition ($20,750), mandatory fees ($840), and room and board ($6400). Full-time tuition and fees vary according to course load. Room and board charges vary according to board plan. Part-time tuition and fees vary according to course load. ***Payment plan:*** Installment.

FRESHMAN FINANCIAL AID (Fall 2008, est.) 550 applied for aid; of those 86% were deemed to have need. 99% of freshmen with need received aid; of those 31% had need fully met. ***Average percent of need met:*** 78% (excluding resources awarded to replace EFC). ***Average financial aid package:*** $16,155 (excluding resources awarded to replace EFC). 21% of all full-time freshmen had no need and received non-need-based gift aid.

UNDERGRADUATE FINANCIAL AID (Fall 2008, est.) 2,023 applied for aid; of those 89% were deemed to have need. 100% of undergraduates with need received aid; of those 34% had need fully met. ***Average percent of need met:*** 81% (excluding resources awarded to replace EFC). ***Average financial aid package:*** $15,986 (excluding resources awarded to replace EFC). 26% of all full-time undergraduates had no need and received non-need-based gift aid.

GIFT AID (NEED-BASED) ***Total amount:*** $17,471,319 (14% federal, 15% state, 6[illegible]% institutional, [illegible]% external sources). ***Receiving aid:*** Freshmen: 77% (404); all full-time undergraduates: 72% (1,775). ***Average award:*** Freshmen: $13,068; Undergraduates: $12,312. ***Scholarships, grants, and awards:*** Federal Pell, FSEOG, state, private, college/university gift aid from institutional funds.

GIFT AID (NON-NEED-BASED) ***Total amount:*** $11,582,406 (5% federal, 1% state, 79% institutional, 15% external sources). ***Receiving aid:*** Freshmen: 76% (455). Undergraduates: 71% (1,748). ***Average award:*** Freshmen: $7762. Undergraduates: $7798. ***Scholarships, grants, and awards by category:*** *Academic interests/achievement:* 2,242 awards ($12,494,992 total): general academic interests/achievements, military science. *Creative arts/performance:* 78 awards ($292,358 total): art/fine arts, music, performing arts, theater/drama. *Special achievements/activities:* 861 awards ($657,250 total): cheerleading/drum major, religious involvement. *Special characteristics:* 703 awards ($4,229,932 total): children of faculty/staff, general special characteristics, relatives of clergy, religious affiliation. ***Tuition waivers:*** Full or partial for employees or children of employees. ***ROTC:*** Army.

LOANS ***Student loans:*** $16,871,794 (80% need-based, 20% non-need-based). 70% of past graduating class borrowed through all loan programs. *Average indebtedness per student:* $25,796. ***Average need-based loan:*** Freshmen: $4151. Undergraduates: $4517. ***Parent loans:*** $3,126,947 (74% need-based, 26% non-need-based). ***Programs:*** Federal Direct (Subsidized and Unsubsidized Stafford, PLUS), Perkins, alternative loans.

WORK-STUDY ***Federal work-study:*** Total amount: $218,789; 308 jobs averaging $741. ***State or other work-study/employment:*** Total amount: $762,889 (100% non-need-based). 752 part-time jobs averaging $506.

ATHLETIC AWARDS Total amount: $1,872,045 (33% need-based, 67% non-need-based).

APPLYING FOR FINANCIAL AID ***Financial aid deadline (priority):*** 3/1. ***Notification date:*** Continuous. Students must reply by 5/1.

CONTACT Mr. Greg Bruner, Financial Aid Director, Olivet Nazarene University, One University Avenue, Bourbonnais, IL 60914, 815-939-5249 or toll-free 800-648-1463. *Fax:* 815-939-5074. *E-mail:* gbruner@olivet.edu.

O'MORE COLLEGE OF DESIGN

Franklin, TN

CONTACT Office of Financial Aid, O'More College of Design, 423 South Margin Street, Franklin, TN 37064-2816, 615-794-4254 Ext. 30.

ORAL ROBERTS UNIVERSITY

Tulsa, OK

Tuition & fees: $18,196 **Average undergraduate aid package: $18,229**

ABOUT THE INSTITUTION Independent interdenominational, coed. ***Awards:*** bachelor's, master's, doctoral, and first professional degrees. 70 undergraduate majors. ***Total enrollment:*** 3,067. Undergraduates: 2,558. Freshmen: 358. Federal methodology is used as a basis for awarding need-based institutional aid.

UNDERGRADUATE EXPENSES for 2008–09 ***Application fee:*** $35. ***Comprehensive fee:*** $25,806 includes full-time tuition ($17,766), mandatory fees ($430), and room and board ($7610). ***College room only:*** $3710. Full-time tuition and fees vary according to course load, degree level, and program. Room and board charges vary according to board plan and housing facility. ***Part-time tuition:*** $742 per credit hour. Part-time tuition and fees vary according to course load, degree level, and program. ***Payment plan:*** Installment.

FRESHMAN FINANCIAL AID (Fall 2007) 491 applied for aid; of those 85% were deemed to have need. ***Average percent of need met:*** 86% (excluding resources awarded to replace EFC). ***Average financial aid package:*** $15,320 (excluding resources awarded to replace EFC). 25% of all full-time freshmen had no need and received non-need-based gift aid.

UNDERGRADUATE FINANCIAL AID (Fall 2007) 1,978 applied for aid; of those 88% were deemed to have need. 100% of undergraduates with need received aid; of those 37% had need fully met. ***Average percent of need met:*** 86% (excluding resources awarded to replace EFC). ***Average financial aid package:*** $18,229 (excluding resources awarded to replace EFC). 20% of all full-time undergraduates had no need and received non-need-based gift aid.

GIFT AID (NEED-BASED) ***Total amount:*** $4,670,402 (72% federal, 14% state, 14% institutional). ***Receiving aid:*** Freshmen: 69% (412); all full-time undergraduates: 67% (1,679). ***Average award:*** Freshmen: $9759; Undergraduates: $9304. ***Scholarships, grants, and awards:*** Federal Pell, FSEOG, state, private, college/university gift aid from institutional funds.

GIFT AID (NON-NEED-BASED) ***Receiving aid:*** Freshmen: 29% (173). Undergraduates: 25% (629). ***Average award:*** Freshmen: $6871. Undergraduates: $7151. ***Scholarships, grants, and awards by category:*** *Academic interests/achievement:* biological sciences, business, communication, education, engineering/technologies, general academic interests/achievements, health fields, religion/biblical studies. *Creative arts/performance:* applied art and design, art/fine arts, cinema/film/broadcasting, journalism/publications, music. *Special achievements/activities:* cheerleading/drum major, community service, general special achievements/activities, leadership, memberships, religious involvement. *Special characteristics:* children and siblings of alumni, children of faculty/staff, general special characteristics, international students, relatives of clergy, siblings of current students. ***Tuition waivers:*** Full or partial for children of alumni, employees or children of employees. ***ROTC:*** Air Force cooperative.

LOANS ***Student loans:*** $20,668,979 (100% need-based). 67% of past graduating class borrowed through all loan programs. *Average indebtedness per student:* $34,555. ***Average need-based loan:*** Freshmen: $6534. Undergraduates: $10,159. ***Parent loans:*** $5,718,217 (100% need-based). ***Programs:*** FFEL (Subsidized and Unsubsidized Stafford, PLUS), Perkins.

WORK-STUDY ***Federal work-study:*** Total amount: $490,900; jobs available. ***State or other work-study/employment:*** Total amount: $323,702 (100% non-need-based). Part-time jobs available.

ATHLETIC AWARDS Total amount: $3,610,814 (100% non-need-based).

APPLYING FOR FINANCIAL AID ***Required financial aid form:*** FAFSA. ***Financial aid deadline (priority):*** 3/15. ***Notification date:*** Students must reply by 7/15.

CONTACT Shannon Panthin, Director of Financial Aid, Oral Roberts University, PO Box 700540, Tulsa, OK 74170-0540, 918-495-6510 or toll-free 800-678-8876. *Fax:* 918-495-6803. *E-mail:* finaid@oru.edu.

OREGON COLLEGE OF ART & CRAFT

Portland, OR

Tuition & fees: $20,462 **Average undergraduate aid package: $23,217**

ABOUT THE INSTITUTION Independent, coed. 2 undergraduate majors. Both federal and institutional methodology are used as a basis for awarding need-based institutional aid.

UNDERGRADUATE EXPENSES for 2008–09 ***Comprehensive fee:*** $29,462 includes full-time tuition ($18,810), mandatory fees ($1652), and room and board ($9000). ***College room only:*** $3600. Room and board charges vary according to location. ***Part-time tuition:*** $2345 per course. ***Part-time fees:*** $50 per course. Part-time tuition and fees vary according to course load. ***Payment plan:*** Installment.

FRESHMAN FINANCIAL AID (Fall 2008, est.) 3 applied for aid; of those 100% were deemed to have need. 100% of freshmen with need received aid. ***Average percent of need met:*** 55% (excluding resources awarded to replace EFC). ***Average financial aid package:*** $9000 (excluding resources awarded to replace EFC).

UNDERGRADUATE FINANCIAL AID (Fall 2008, est.) 84 applied for aid; of those 100% were deemed to have need. 100% of undergraduates with need received aid; of those 4% had need fully met. ***Average percent of need met:*** 76% (excluding resources awarded to replace EFC). ***Average financial aid package:*** $23,217 (excluding resources awarded to replace EFC). 1% of all full-time undergraduates had no need and received non-need-based gift aid.

GIFT AID (NEED-BASED) ***Total amount:*** $791,250 (34% federal, 14% state, 39% institutional, 13% external sources). ***Receiving aid:*** Freshmen: 75% (3); all full-time undergraduates: 84% (80). ***Average award:*** Freshmen: $2500; Undergraduates: $4530. ***Scholarships, grants, and awards:*** Federal Pell, FSEOG, state, private, college/university gift aid from institutional funds.

GIFT AID (NON-NEED-BASED) ***Total amount:*** $18,000 (100% institutional). ***Receiving aid:*** Freshmen: 25% (1). Undergraduates: 3% (3). ***Average award:*** Undergraduates: $10,000. ***Scholarships, grants, and awards by category:*** *Creative arts/performance:* 5 awards ($10,000 total): art/fine arts. ***Tuition waivers:*** Full or partial for employees or children of employees.

LOANS ***Student loans:*** $1,013,336 (97% need-based, 3% non-need-based). 85% of past graduating class borrowed through all loan programs. *Average indebtedness per student:* $37,000. ***Average need-based loan:*** Freshmen: $3500. Undergraduates: $4750. ***Parent loans:*** $93,413 (75% need-based, 25% non-need-based). ***Programs:*** FFEL (Subsidized and Unsubsidized Stafford, PLUS), state, alternative loans.

WORK-STUDY ***Federal work-study:*** Total amount: $17,653; 40 jobs averaging $459. ***State or other work-study/employment:*** Total amount: $27,250 (92% need-based, 8% non-need-based). 49 part-time jobs averaging $622.

APPLYING FOR FINANCIAL AID ***Required financial aid form:*** FAFSA. ***Financial aid deadline (priority):*** 3/1. ***Notification date:*** Continuous. Students must reply by 7/1.

CONTACT Lisa Newman, Director of Financial Aid, Oregon College of Art & Craft, 8245 Southwest Barnes Road, Portland, OR 97225, 503-297-5544 Ext. 124 or toll-free 800-390-0632 Ext. 129. *Fax:* 503-297-9651. *E-mail:* lnewman@ocac.edu.

OREGON HEALTH & SCIENCE UNIVERSITY

Portland, OR

Tuition & fees (OR res): $14,552 **Average undergraduate aid package: $12,119**

ABOUT THE INSTITUTION State-related, coed. ***Awards:*** bachelor's, master's, doctoral, and first professional degrees and post-bachelor's, post-master's, and first professional certificates. 2 undergraduate majors. ***Total enrollment:*** 2,424. Undergraduates: 604. Federal methodology is used as a basis for awarding need-based institutional aid.

UNDERGRADUATE EXPENSES for 2008–09 ***Application fee:*** $125. ***Tuition, state resident:*** full-time $9216; part-time $256 per credit. ***Tuition, nonresident:*** full-time $19,188; part-time $533 per credit. ***Required fees:*** full-time $5336. Full-time tuition and fees vary according to location. Part-time tuition and fees vary according to location. ***Payment plan:*** Installment.

UNDERGRADUATE FINANCIAL AID (Fall 2008, est.) 310 applied for aid; of those 94% were deemed to have need. 98% of undergraduates with need received aid; of those 10% had need fully met. ***Average percent of need met:*** 59% (excluding resources awarded to replace EFC). ***Average financial aid package:*** $12,119 (excluding resources awarded to replace EFC). 2% of all full-time undergraduates had no need and received non-need-based gift aid.

GIFT AID (NEED-BASED) ***Total amount:*** $1,956,951 (38% federal, 15% state, 5% institutional, 42% external sources). ***Receiving aid:*** All full-time undergraduates: 58% (191). ***Average award:*** Undergraduates: $8468. ***Scholarships, grants, and awards:*** Federal Pell, FSEOG, state, private, college/university gift aid from institutional funds, Health Profession Scholarships.

GIFT AID (NON-NEED-BASED) ***Total amount:*** $37,937 (21% federal, 4% institutional, 75% external sources). ***Receiving aid:*** Undergraduates: 1% (3). ***Average award:*** Undergraduates: $3314. ***Scholarships, grants, and awards by category:*** *Academic interests/achievement:* 171 awards ($1,564,209 total): health fields. ***Tuition waivers:*** Full or partial for employees or children of employees. ***ROTC:*** Army cooperative.

LOANS ***Student loans:*** $9,655,551 (80% need-based, 20% non-need-based). ***Average need-based loan:*** Undergraduates: $5335. ***Parent loans:*** $686,197 (39% need-based, 61% non-need-based). ***Programs:*** Federal Direct (Subsidized and Unsubsidized Stafford, PLUS), Perkins, Federal Nursing, state, college/university, alternative loans.

WORK-STUDY ***Federal work-study:*** Total amount: $13,500; 9 jobs averaging $1500.

CONTACT Debbie Cox, Administrative Coordinator, Oregon Health & Science University, 3181 SW Sam Jackson Park Road, L-109, Portland, OR 97239-3089, 503-494-7800. *Fax:* 503-494-4629. *E-mail:* finaid@ohsu.edu.

OREGON INSTITUTE OF TECHNOLOGY

Klamath Falls, OR

Tuition & fees (OR res): $6297 **Average undergraduate aid package: $4984**

ABOUT THE INSTITUTION State-supported, coed. ***Awards:*** associate, bachelor's, and master's degrees. 19 undergraduate majors. ***Total enrollment:*** 3,303. Undergraduates: 3,290.

UNDERGRADUATE EXPENSES for 2008–09 ***Application fee:*** $50. ***Tuition, state resident:*** full-time $4860; part-time $108 per credit. ***Tuition, nonresident:*** full-time $15,255; part-time $108 per credit. ***Required fees:*** full-time $1437. Full-time tuition and fees vary according to course level, course load, degree level, location, program, and reciprocity agreements. Part-time tuition and fees vary according to course level, course load, degree level, location, program, and reciprocity agreements. ***College room and board:*** $7132; ***Room only:*** $4793. Room and board charges vary according to board plan and housing facility.

FRESHMAN FINANCIAL AID (Fall 2007) 210 applied for aid; of those 87% were deemed to have need. 98% of freshmen with need received aid; of those 37% had need fully met. ***Average percent of need met:*** 22% (excluding resources awarded to replace EFC). ***Average financial aid package:*** $2864 (excluding resources awarded to replace EFC).

UNDERGRADUATE FINANCIAL AID (Fall 2007) 1,725 applied for aid; of those 94% were deemed to have need. 97% of undergraduates with need received aid; of those 35% had need fully met. ***Average percent of need met:*** 22% (excluding resources awarded to replace EFC). ***Average financial aid package:*** $4984 (excluding resources awarded to replace EFC). 1% of all full-time undergraduates had no need and received non-need-based gift aid.

GIFT AID (NEED-BASED) ***Total amount:*** $5,491,021 (46% federal, 13% state, 24% institutional, 17% external sources). ***Receiving aid:*** Freshmen: 31% (66); all full-time undergraduates: 40% (744). ***Average award:*** Freshmen: $3034; Undergraduates: $4150. ***Scholarships, grants, and awards:*** Federal Pell, FSEOG, state, private, college/university gift aid from institutional funds.

GIFT AID (NON-NEED-BASED) ***Total amount:*** $123,130 (35% institutional, 65% external sources). ***Receiving aid:*** Freshmen: 7% (14). Undergraduates: 4% (67). ***Average award:*** Undergraduates: $15,563. ***Scholarships, grants, and awards by category:*** *Academic interests/achievement:* general academic interests/achievements. *Special achievements/activities:* 170 awards: general special achievements/activities. ***ROTC:*** Army cooperative.

LOANS ***Student loans:*** $10,911,259 (90% need-based, 10% non-need-based). 61% of past graduating class borrowed through all loan programs. *Average indebtedness per student:* $24,498. ***Average need-based loan:*** Freshmen: $2456. Undergraduates: $3987. ***Parent loans:*** $2,846,698 (70% need-based, 30% non-need-based). ***Programs:*** FFEL (Subsidized and Unsubsidized Stafford, PLUS), Perkins.

WORK-STUDY ***Federal work-study:*** Total amount: $180,674; jobs available.

ATHLETIC AWARDS Total amount: $288,032 (92% need-based, 8% non-need-based).

APPLYING FOR FINANCIAL AID ***Required financial aid form:*** FAFSA. ***Financial aid deadline (priority):*** 2/1. ***Notification date:*** 4/1. Students must reply within 3 weeks of notification.

CONTACT Tracey Lehman, Financial Aid Director, Oregon Institute of Technology, 3201 Campus Drive, Klamath Falls, OR 97601-8801, 541-885-1280 or toll-free 800-422-2017 (in-state), 800-343-6653 (out-of-state). *Fax:* 541-885-1024. *E-mail:* tracey.lehman@oit.edu.

OREGON STATE UNIVERSITY

Corvallis, OR

Tuition & fees (OR res): $6187 **Average undergraduate aid package: $9528**

ABOUT THE INSTITUTION State-supported, coed. ***Awards:*** bachelor's, master's, doctoral, and first professional degrees and post-bachelor's, post-master's, and first professional certificates. 106 undergraduate majors. ***Total enrollment:*** 20,320. Undergraduates: 16,673. Freshmen: 3,106. Federal methodology is used as a basis for awarding need-based institutional aid.

UNDERGRADUATE EXPENSES for 2008–09 ***Application fee:*** $50. ***Tuition, state resident:*** full-time $4608; part-time $128 per credit. ***Tuition, nonresident:*** full-time $17,244; part-time $479 per credit. ***Required fees:*** full-time $1579. Full-time tuition and fees vary according to course load. Part-time tuition and fees vary according to course load. ***College room and board:*** $8208. Room and board charges vary according to board plan and housing facility. ***Payment plan:*** Deferred payment.

FRESHMAN FINANCIAL AID (Fall 2008, est.) 2,288 applied for aid; of those 63% were deemed to have need. 97% of freshmen with need received aid; of those 18% had need fully met. ***Average percent of need met:*** 63% (excluding resources awarded to replace EFC). ***Average financial aid package:*** $8812 (excluding resources awarded to replace EFC).

UNDERGRADUATE FINANCIAL AID (Fall 2008, est.) 9,425 applied for aid; of those 74% were deemed to have need. 98% of undergraduates with need received aid; of those 18% had need fully met. ***Average percent of need met:*** 66% (excluding resources awarded to replace EFC). ***Average financial aid package:*** $9528 (excluding resources awarded to replace EFC). 1% of all full-time undergraduates had no need and received non-need-based gift aid.

GIFT AID (NEED-BASED) ***Total amount:*** $32,081,343 (49% federal, 25% state, 10% institutional, 0% external sources). ***Receiving aid:*** Freshmen: 39% (1,142); all full-time undergraduates: 37% (5,160). ***Average award:*** Freshmen: $2738; Undergraduates: $2876. ***Scholarships, grants, and awards:*** Federal Pell, FSEOG, state, private, college/university gift aid from institutional funds.

GIFT AID (NON-NEED-BASED) ***Total amount:*** $8,290,040 (1% federal, 66% institutional, 33% external sources). ***Receiving aid:*** Freshmen: 1% (43). Undergraduates: 1% (169). ***Average award:*** Undergraduates: $3556. ***Tuition waivers:*** Full or partial for employees or children of employees. ***ROTC:*** Army, Naval, Air Force.

LOANS ***Student loans:*** $62,282,112 (74% need-based, 26% non-need-based). 61% of past graduating class borrowed through all loan programs. *Average indebtedness per student:* $20,240. ***Average need-based loan:*** Freshmen: $3278. Undergraduates: $3779. ***Parent loans:*** $60,453,264 (45% need-based, 55% non-need-based). ***Programs:*** Federal Direct (Subsidized and Unsubsidized Stafford, PLUS), Perkins, college/university.

WORK-STUDY ***Federal work-study:*** Total amount: $3,801,379; 2,186 jobs averaging $1472.

ATHLETIC AWARDS Total amount: $7,208,306 (25% need-based, 75% non-need-based).

APPLYING FOR FINANCIAL AID ***Required financial aid form:*** FAFSA. ***Financial aid deadline (priority):*** 2/28. ***Notification date:*** Continuous beginning 4/1. Students must reply within 4 weeks of notification.

CONTACT Director, Financial Aid, Oregon State University, 218 Kerr Administration Building, Corvallis, OR 97331-2120, 541-737-2241 or toll-free 800-291-4192 (in-state).

OREGON STATE UNIVERSITY–CASCADES

Bend, OR

CONTACT Financial Aid Office, Oregon State University–Cascades, 2600 NW College Way, Bend, OR 97701, 541-322-3100.

OTIS COLLEGE OF ART AND DESIGN

Los Angeles, CA

Tuition & fees: $30,464 **Average undergraduate aid package: $16,750**

ABOUT THE INSTITUTION Independent, coed. ***Awards:*** bachelor's and master's degrees. 10 undergraduate majors. ***Total enrollment:*** 1,206. Undergraduates: 1,140. Freshmen: 225. Federal methodology is used as a basis for awarding need-based institutional aid.

UNDERGRADUATE EXPENSES for 2008–09 ***Application fee:*** $50. ***Tuition:*** full-time $29,764; part-time $993 per credit hour. ***Payment plan:*** Installment.

FRESHMAN FINANCIAL AID (Fall 2008, est.) 182 applied for aid; of those 79% were deemed to have need. 100% of freshmen with need received aid. ***Average percent of need met:*** 54% (excluding resources awarded to replace EFC). ***Average financial aid package:*** $14,341 (excluding resources awarded to replace EFC). 16% of all full-time freshmen had no need and received non-need-based gift aid.

UNDERGRADUATE FINANCIAL AID (Fall 2008, est.) 930 applied for aid; of those 79% were deemed to have need. 100% of undergraduates with need received aid; of those 1% had need fully met. ***Average percent of need met:*** 52% (excluding resources awarded to replace EFC). ***Average financial aid package:*** $16,750 (excluding resources awarded to replace EFC). 8% of all full-time undergraduates had no need and received non-need-based gift aid.

GIFT AID (NEED-BASED) ***Total amount:*** $10,352,102 (19% federal, 20% state, 60% institutional, 1% external sources). ***Receiving aid:*** Freshmen: 64% (143); all full-time undergraduates: 66% (737). ***Average award:*** Freshmen: $9089; Undergraduates: $8443. ***Scholarships, grants, and awards:*** Federal Pell, FSEOG, state, private, college/university gift aid from institutional funds.

GIFT AID (NON-NEED-BASED) ***Total amount:*** $1,071,885 (96% institutional, 4% external sources). ***Receiving aid:*** Freshmen: 28% (63). Undergraduates: 17% (184). ***Average award:*** Freshmen: $5613. Undergraduates: $5781. ***Scholarships, grants, and awards by category:*** *Academic interests/achievement:* 125 awards ($601,299 total): general academic interests/achievements. *Creative arts/performance:* applied art and design, art/fine arts. ***Tuition waivers:*** Full or partial for employees or children of employees.

LOANS ***Student loans:*** $8,216,371 (95% need-based, 5% non-need-based). 66% of past graduating class borrowed through all loan programs. *Average indebtedness per student:* $37,356. ***Average need-based loan:*** Freshmen: $3323.

Undergraduates: $4850. ***Parent loans:*** $2,257,918 (82% need-based, 18% non-need-based). ***Programs:*** FFEL (Subsidized and Unsubsidized Stafford, PLUS), Perkins.

WORK-STUDY ***Federal work-study:*** Total amount: $185,380; 301 jobs averaging $2073. ***State or other work-study/employment:*** Total amount: $31,000 (100% non-need-based). 20 part-time jobs averaging $1000.

APPLYING FOR FINANCIAL AID ***Required financial aid forms:*** FAFSA, institution's own form. ***Financial aid deadline (priority):*** 2/15. ***Notification date:*** 3/1. Students must reply within 2 weeks of notification.

CONTACT Nasreen Zia, Associate Director of Financial Aid, Otis College of Art and Design, 9045 Lincoln Boulevard, Los Angeles, CA 90045-9785, 310-665-6883 or toll-free 800-527-OTIS. *Fax:* 310-665-6884. *E-mail:* nzia@otis.edu.

OTTAWA UNIVERSITY

Ottawa, KS

CONTACT Financial Aid Coordinator, Ottawa University, 1001 South Cedar, Ottawa, KS 66067-3399, 785-242-5200 or toll-free 800-755-5200 Ext. 5559. *E-mail:* finaid@ottawa.edu.

OTTERBEIN COLLEGE

Westerville, OH

CONTACT Mr. Thomas V. Yarnell, Director of Financial Aid, Otterbein College, One Otterbein College, Clippinger Hall, Westerville, OH 43081-2006, 614-823-1502 or toll-free 800-488-8144. *Fax:* 614-823-1200. *E-mail:* tyarnell@otterbein.edu.

OUACHITA BAPTIST UNIVERSITY

Arkadelphia, AR

Tuition & fees: $18,940 **Average undergraduate aid package: $16,915**

ABOUT THE INSTITUTION Independent Baptist, coed. ***Awards:*** associate and bachelor's degrees. 55 undergraduate majors. ***Total enrollment:*** 1,493. Undergraduates: 1,493. Freshmen: 404. Both federal and institutional methodology are used as a basis for awarding need-based institutional aid.

UNDERGRADUATE EXPENSES for 2009–10 ***Comprehensive fee:*** $24,600 includes full-time tuition ($18,500), mandatory fees ($440), and room and board ($5660). ***Part-time tuition:*** $525 per semester hour.

FRESHMAN FINANCIAL AID (Fall 2008, est.) 333 applied for aid; of those 81% were deemed to have need. 100% of freshmen with need received aid; of those 46% had need fully met. ***Average percent of need met:*** 88% (excluding resources awarded to replace EFC). ***Average financial aid package:*** $16,460 (excluding resources awarded to replace EFC). 32% of all full-time freshmen had no need and received non-need-based gift aid.

UNDERGRADUATE FINANCIAL AID (Fall 2008, est.) 976 applied for aid; of those 81% were deemed to have need. 100% of undergraduates with need received aid; of those 49% had need fully met. ***Average percent of need met:*** 91% (excluding resources awarded to replace EFC). ***Average financial aid package:*** $16,915 (excluding resources awarded to replace EFC). 37% of all full-time undergraduates had no need and received non-need-based gift aid.

GIFT AID (NEED-BASED) ***Total amount:*** $9,876,509 (13% federal, 5% state, 76% institutional, 6% external sources). ***Receiving aid:*** Freshmen: 66% (265); all full-time undergraduates: 55% (777). ***Average award:*** Freshmen: $13,230; Undergraduates: $12,835. ***Scholarships, grants, and awards:*** Federal Pell, FSEOG, state, private, college/university gift aid from institutional funds.

GIFT AID (NON-NEED-BASED) ***Total amount:*** $5,383,668 (7% state, 79% institutional, 14% external sources). ***Receiving aid:*** Freshmen: 13% (53). Undergraduates: 12% (176). ***Average award:*** Freshmen: $7981. Undergraduates: $8019. ***Scholarships, grants, and awards by category:*** *Academic interests/achievement:* area/ethnic studies, biological sciences, business, communication, computer science, education, engineering/technologies, English, foreign languages, general academic interests/achievements, health fields, home economics, humanities, international studies, mathematics, physical sciences, premedicine, religion/biblical studies, social sciences. *Creative arts/performance:* art/fine arts, journalism/publications, music, performing arts, theater/drama. *Special achievements/activities:* cheerleading/drum major, general special achievements/activities. *Special characteristics:* children and siblings of alumni, children of faculty/staff, ethnic background, first-generation college students, general special characteristics, handicapped students, international students, local/state students, married students, members of minority groups, out-of-state students, previous college experience, relatives of clergy, religious affiliation, twins. ***ROTC:*** Army.

LOANS ***Student loans:*** $4,243,346 (61% need-based, 39% non-need-based). 61% of past graduating class borrowed through all loan programs. *Average indebtedness per student:* $16,230. ***Average need-based loan:*** Freshmen: $4456. Undergraduates: $4846. ***Parent loans:*** $1,443,790 (26% need-based, 74% non-need-based). ***Programs:*** FFEL (Subsidized and Unsubsidized Stafford, PLUS), Perkins, state, college/university, alternative private loans.

WORK-STUDY ***Federal work-study:*** Total amount: $444,522; 298 jobs available. ***State or other work-study/employment:*** Total amount: $317,021 (13% need-based, 87% non-need-based). Part-time jobs available.

ATHLETIC AWARDS Total amount: $2,024,141 (53% need-based, 47% non-need-based).

APPLYING FOR FINANCIAL AID ***Required financial aid form:*** FAFSA. ***Financial aid deadline:*** 6/1 (priority: 1/15). ***Notification date:*** Continuous. Students must reply by 5/1.

CONTACT Mr. Chris Kear, Director of Financial Aid, Ouachita Baptist University, Box 3774, Arkadelphia, AR 71998-0001, 870-245-5570 or toll-free 800-342-5628 (in-state). *Fax:* 870-245-5318. *E-mail:* kearc@obu.edu.

OUR LADY OF HOLY CROSS COLLEGE

New Orleans, LA

Tuition & fees: N/R **Average undergraduate aid package: $7550**

ABOUT THE INSTITUTION Independent Roman Catholic, coed. ***Awards:*** associate, bachelor's, and master's degrees and post-bachelor's certificates. 17 undergraduate majors. ***Total enrollment:*** 1,298. Undergraduates: 1,128. Federal methodology is used as a basis for awarding need-based institutional aid.

UNDERGRADUATE EXPENSES for 2008–09 ***Application fee:*** $15. ***Tuition:*** part-time $295 per semester hour.

FRESHMAN FINANCIAL AID (Fall 2008, est.) 105 applied for aid; of those 100% were deemed to have need. 100% of freshmen with need received aid. ***Average percent of need met:*** 15% (excluding resources awarded to replace EFC). ***Average financial aid package:*** $7550 (excluding resources awarded to replace EFC).

UNDERGRADUATE FINANCIAL AID (Fall 2008, est.) 474 applied for aid; of those 100% were deemed to have need. 100% of undergraduates with need received aid. ***Average percent of need met:*** 15% (excluding resources awarded to replace EFC). ***Average financial aid package:*** $7550 (excluding resources awarded to replace EFC).

GIFT AID (NEED-BASED) ***Total amount:*** $4,837,756 (97% federal, 3% state). ***Receiving aid:*** Freshmen: 52% (66); all full-time undergraduates: 54% (310). ***Average award:*** Freshmen: $3500; Undergraduates: $4500. ***Scholarships, grants, and awards:*** Federal Pell, FSEOG, state, private, college/university gift aid from institutional funds.

GIFT AID (NON-NEED-BASED) ***Total amount:*** $3,144,922 (84% federal, 13% state, 1% institutional, 2% external sources). ***Receiving aid:*** Freshmen: 25% (32). Undergraduates: 25% (147). ***Scholarships, grants, and awards by category:*** *Academic interests/achievement:* 202 awards ($307,566 total): general academic interests/achievements. *Special characteristics:* 23 awards ($75,646 total): children of faculty/staff, general special characteristics, relatives of clergy, religious affiliation. ***ROTC:*** Army cooperative, Air Force cooperative.

LOANS ***Student loans:*** $6,025,451 (44% need-based, 56% non-need-based). 88% of past graduating class borrowed through all loan programs. *Average indebtedness per student:* $48,000. ***Average need-based loan:*** Freshmen: $3500. Undergraduates: $4500. ***Parent loans:*** $166,028 (100% need-based). ***Programs:*** FFEL (Subsidized and Unsubsidized Stafford, PLUS).

WORK-STUDY ***Federal work-study:*** Total amount: $129,845; 28 jobs averaging $5000.

APPLYING FOR FINANCIAL AID ***Required financial aid form:*** FAFSA. ***Financial aid deadline (priority):*** 7/1. ***Notification date:*** Continuous beginning 3/15. Students must reply within 4 weeks of notification.

CONTACT Mrs. Kristine Hatfield, Vice President of Enrollment Management & Student Development, Our Lady of Holy Cross College, 4123 Woodland Drive, New Orleans, LA 70131-7399, 504-398-2185 or toll-free 800-259-7744 Ext. 175. *Fax:* 504-394-1182. *E-mail:* khatfield@olhcc.edu.

OUR LADY OF THE LAKE COLLEGE

Baton Rouge, LA

Tuition & fees: $6920 **Average undergraduate aid package: $5175**

ABOUT THE INSTITUTION Independent Roman Catholic, coed, primarily women. ***Awards:*** associate, bachelor's, and master's degrees and post-bachelor's certificates. 14 undergraduate majors. ***Total enrollment:*** 1,811. Undergraduates: 1,657. Freshmen: 89. Federal methodology is used as a basis for awarding need-based institutional aid.

UNDERGRADUATE EXPENSES for 2008–09 ***Application fee:*** $35. ***One-time required fee:*** $25. ***Tuition:*** full-time $6720; part-time $280 per credit hour.

FRESHMAN FINANCIAL AID (Fall 2007) 90 applied for aid; of those 77% were deemed to have need. 99% of freshmen with need received aid; of those 3% had need fully met. ***Average financial aid package:*** $6513 (excluding resources awarded to replace EFC).

UNDERGRADUATE FINANCIAL AID (Fall 2007) 689 applied for aid; of those 79% were deemed to have need. 96% of undergraduates with need received aid; of those 2% had need fully met. ***Average financial aid package:*** $5175 (excluding resources awarded to replace EFC).

GIFT AID (NEED-BASED) ***Total amount:*** $2,963,081 (61% federal, 28% state, 8% institutional, 3% external sources). ***Receiving aid:*** Freshmen: 60% (57); all full-time undergraduates: 56% (445). ***Average award:*** Freshmen: $4910; Undergraduates: $2486. ***Scholarships, grants, and awards:*** Federal Pell, FSEOG, state, private, college/university gift aid from institutional funds.

GIFT AID (NON-NEED-BASED) ***Receiving aid:*** Freshmen: 42% (40). Undergraduates: 17% (137). ***ROTC:*** Army cooperative, Air Force cooperative.

LOANS ***Student loans:*** $8,570,257 (100% need-based). 78% of past graduating class borrowed through all loan programs. *Average indebtedness per student:* $12,019. ***Average need-based loan:*** Freshmen: $2918. Undergraduates: $3664. ***Parent loans:*** $173,498 (100% need-based). ***Programs:*** FFEL (Subsidized and Unsubsidized Stafford, PLUS).

WORK-STUDY ***Federal work-study:*** Total amount: $58,583; 47 jobs averaging $837.

APPLYING FOR FINANCIAL AID ***Required financial aid forms:*** FAFSA, institution's own form. ***Financial aid deadline (priority):*** 3/1. ***Notification date:*** Continuous beginning 5/15.

CONTACT Tiffany D. Magee, Director of Financial Aid, Our Lady of the Lake College, 7434 Perkins Road, Baton Rouge, LA 70808, 225-768-1701 or toll-free 877-242-3509. *Fax:* 225-490-1632. *E-mail:* Tiffany.Magee@ololcollege.edu.

OUR LADY OF THE LAKE UNIVERSITY OF SAN ANTONIO

San Antonio, TX

Tuition & fees: $20,232 **Average undergraduate aid package: $21,818**

ABOUT THE INSTITUTION Independent Roman Catholic, coed. ***Awards:*** bachelor's, master's, and doctoral degrees and post-bachelor's and post-master's certificates. 31 undergraduate majors. ***Total enrollment:*** 2,642. Undergraduates: 1,563. Freshmen: 306. Federal methodology is used as a basis for awarding need-based institutional aid.

UNDERGRADUATE EXPENSES for 2008–09 ***Application fee:*** $25. ***Comprehensive fee:*** $26,470 includes full-time tuition ($19,732), mandatory fees ($500), and room and board ($6238). ***College room only:*** $3638. Full-time tuition and fees vary according to degree level and location. Room and board charges vary according to board plan. ***Part-time tuition:*** $640 per hour. ***Part-time fees:*** $12 per credit; $58 per term. Part-time tuition and fees vary according to degree level and location. ***Payment plans:*** Installment, deferred payment.

FRESHMAN FINANCIAL AID (Fall 2008, est.) 298 applied for aid; of those 96% were deemed to have need. 100% of freshmen with need received aid; of those 27% had need fully met. ***Average percent of need met:*** 82% (excluding resources awarded to replace EFC). ***Average financial aid package:*** $23,093 (excluding resources awarded to replace EFC). 3% of all full-time freshmen had no need and received non-need-based gift aid.

UNDERGRADUATE FINANCIAL AID (Fall 2008, est.) 1,084 applied for aid; of those 96% were deemed to have need. 99% of undergraduates with need received aid; of those 20% had need fully met. ***Average percent of need met:*** 80% (excluding resources awarded to replace EFC). ***Average financial aid package:*** $21,818 (excluding resources awarded to replace EFC). 3% of all full-time undergraduates had no need and received non-need-based gift aid.

GIFT AID (NEED-BASED) ***Total amount:*** $12,565,265 (31% federal, 20% state, 47% institutional, 2% external sources). ***Receiving aid:*** Freshmen: 83% (254); all full-time undergraduates: 85% (982). ***Average award:*** Freshmen: $4196; Undergraduates: $2996. ***Scholarships, grants, and awards:*** Federal Pell, FSEOG, state, private, college/university gift aid from institutional funds.

GIFT AID (NON-NEED-BASED) ***Total amount:*** $931,615 (24% federal, 1% state, 74% institutional, 1% external sources). ***Receiving aid:*** Freshmen: 85% (259). Undergraduates: 64% (736). ***Average award:*** Freshmen: $18,534. Undergraduates: $16,786. ***Scholarships, grants, and awards by category:*** *Academic interests/achievement:* general academic interests/achievements. *Creative arts/performance:* art/fine arts, music. *Special characteristics:* children of faculty/staff. ***Tuition waivers:*** Full or partial for employees or children of employees. ***ROTC:*** Army cooperative, Air Force cooperative.

LOANS ***Student loans:*** $10,081,317 (87% need-based, 13% non-need-based). 76% of past graduating class borrowed through all loan programs. *Average indebtedness per student:* $18,169. ***Average need-based loan:*** Freshmen: $2467. Undergraduates: $3200. ***Parent loans:*** $981,123 (38% need-based, 62% non-need-based). ***Programs:*** FFEL (Subsidized and Unsubsidized Stafford, PLUS), Perkins, state.

WORK-STUDY ***Federal work-study:*** Total amount: $445,457; 312 jobs averaging $1437. ***State or other work-study/employment:*** Total amount: $29,163 (100% need-based). 64 part-time jobs averaging $1508.

ATHLETIC AWARDS Total amount: $139,500 (75% need-based, 25% non-need-based).

APPLYING FOR FINANCIAL AID ***Required financial aid form:*** FAFSA. ***Financial aid deadline (priority):*** 5/1. ***Notification date:*** Continuous. Students must reply within 2 weeks of notification.

CONTACT Michael Fuller, Director of Financial Aid, Our Lady of the Lake University of San Antonio, 411 Southwest 24th Street, San Antonio, TX 78207-4689, 210-434-6711 Ext. 2299 or toll-free 800-436-6558. *Fax:* 210-431-3958. *E-mail:* mfuller@lake.ollusa.edu.

OZARK CHRISTIAN COLLEGE

Joplin, MO

CONTACT Jill Kaminsky, Application Processor, Ozark Christian College, 1111 North Main Street, Joplin, MO 64801-4804, 417-624-2518 Ext. 2017 or toll-free 800-299-4622. *Fax:* 417-624-0090. *E-mail:* finaid@occ.edu.

PACE UNIVERSITY

New York, NY

Tuition & fees: $31,357 **Average undergraduate aid package: $23,166**

ABOUT THE INSTITUTION Independent, coed. ***Awards:*** associate, bachelor's, master's, doctoral, and first professional degrees and post-bachelor's, post-master's, and first professional certificates. 72 undergraduate majors. ***Total enrollment:*** 12,704. Undergraduates: 7,807. Freshmen: 1,663. Federal methodology is used as a basis for awarding need-based institutional aid.

UNDERGRADUATE EXPENSES for 2008–09 ***Application fee:*** $45. ***Comprehensive fee:*** $42,537 includes full-time tuition ($30,632), mandatory fees ($725), and room and board ($11,180). Room and board charges vary according to board plan and housing facility. ***Part-time tuition:*** $879 per credit. Part-time tuition and fees vary according to course load. ***Payment plan:*** Installment.

FRESHMAN FINANCIAL AID (Fall 2008, est.) 1,360 applied for aid; of those 91% were deemed to have need. 100% of freshmen with need received aid; of those 16% had need fully met. ***Average percent of need met:*** 76% (excluding resources awarded to replace EFC). ***Average financial aid package:*** $27,024 (excluding resources awarded to replace EFC). 24% of all full-time freshmen had no need and received non-need-based gift aid.

UNDERGRADUATE FINANCIAL AID (Fall 2008, est.) 4,812 applied for aid; of those 91% were deemed to have need. 100% of undergraduates with need received aid; of those 15% had need fully met. ***Average percent of need met:*** 70% (excluding resources awarded to replace EFC). ***Average financial aid package:*** $23,166 (excluding resources awarded to replace EFC). 21% of all full-time undergraduates had no need and received non-need-based gift aid.

GIFT AID (NEED-BASED) ***Total amount:*** $78,311,554 (15% federal, 8% state, 74% institutional, 3% external sources). ***Receiving aid:*** Freshmen: 76% (1,227);

all full-time undergraduates: 70% (4,313). ***Average award:*** Freshmen: $21,866; Undergraduates: $18,572. ***Scholarships, grants, and awards:*** Federal Pell, FSEOG, state, private, college/university gift aid from institutional funds, Federal Nursing, endowed and restricted scholarships and grants.

GIFT AID (NON-NEED-BASED) ***Total amount:*** $14,346,521 (2% state, 88% institutional, 10% external sources). ***Receiving aid:*** Freshmen: 10% (169). Undergraduates: 8% (480). ***Average award:*** Freshmen: $7468. Undergraduates: $8106. ***Scholarships, grants, and awards by category:*** *Academic interests/achievement:* 2,021 awards ($11,258,702 total): biological sciences, business, communication, computer science, education, English, foreign languages, general academic interests/achievements, health fields, humanities, mathematics, physical sciences, social sciences. *Creative arts/performance:* creative writing, debating, performing arts, theater/drama. *Special achievements/activities:* 35 awards ($191,168 total): community service, general special achievements/activities, leadership. *Special characteristics:* 240 awards ($2,086,205 total): adult students, children of faculty/staff, children with a deceased or disabled parent, general special characteristics, international students, parents of current students, previous college experience, spouses of deceased or disabled public servants, veterans. ***Tuition waivers:*** Full or partial for employees or children of employees, senior citizens. ***ROTC:*** Army cooperative, Air Force cooperative.

LOANS ***Student loans:*** $46,586,182 (70% need-based, 30% non-need-based). 69% of past graduating class borrowed through all loan programs. *Average indebtedness per student:* $29,622. ***Average need-based loan:*** Freshmen: $3922. Undergraduates: $4553. ***Parent loans:*** $28,331,042 (43% need-based, 57% non-need-based). ***Programs:*** Federal Direct (Subsidized and Unsubsidized Stafford, PLUS), Perkins, Federal Nursing.

WORK-STUDY ***Federal work-study:*** Total amount: $1,095,357; 1,018 jobs averaging $3585.

ATHLETIC AWARDS Total amount: $1,721,997 (69% need-based, 31% non-need-based).

APPLYING FOR FINANCIAL AID ***Required financial aid forms:*** FAFSA, state aid form. ***Financial aid deadline (priority):*** 2/15. ***Notification date:*** Continuous beginning 2/25. Students must reply by 5/1 or within 2 weeks of notification.

CONTACT Mark Stephens, Pace University, 861 Bedford Road, Pleasantville, NY 10570, 212-773-3501 or toll-free 800-874-7223. *E-mail:* mstephens@pace.edu.

PACIFIC ISLANDS BIBLE COLLEGE

Mangilao, GU

CONTACT Financial Aid Office, Pacific Islands Bible College, PO Box 22619, Guam Main Facility, GU 96921-2619, 671-734-1812.

PACIFIC LUTHERAN UNIVERSITY

Tacoma, WA

Tuition & fees: $28,100 **Average undergraduate aid package: $26,063**

ABOUT THE INSTITUTION Independent religious, coed. ***Awards:*** bachelor's and master's degrees and post-bachelor's and post-master's certificates. 41 undergraduate majors. ***Total enrollment:*** 3,672. Undergraduates: 3,341. Freshmen: 736. Federal methodology is used as a basis for awarding need-based institutional aid.

UNDERGRADUATE EXPENSES for 2009–10 ***Application fee:*** $40. ***Comprehensive fee:*** $36,700 includes full-time tuition ($28,100) and room and board ($8600). ***College room only:*** $4140. ***Part-time tuition:*** $880 per credit hour.

FRESHMAN FINANCIAL AID (Fall 2008, est.) 641 applied for aid; of those 82% were deemed to have need. 99% of freshmen with need received aid; of those 40% had need fully met. ***Average percent of need met:*** 91% (excluding resources awarded to replace EFC). ***Average financial aid package:*** $25,805 (excluding resources awarded to replace EFC). 24% of all full-time freshmen had no need and received non-need-based gift aid.

UNDERGRADUATE FINANCIAL AID (Fall 2008, est.) 2,476 applied for aid; of those 86% were deemed to have need. 99% of undergraduates with need received aid; of those 28% had need fully met. ***Average percent of need met:*** 86% (excluding resources awarded to replace EFC). ***Average financial aid package:*** $26,063 (excluding resources awarded to replace EFC). 27% of all full-time undergraduates had no need and received non-need-based gift aid.

GIFT AID (NEED-BASED) ***Total amount:*** $27,266,783 (11% federal, 12% state, 73% institutional, 4% external sources). ***Receiving aid:*** Freshmen: 73% (520); all full-time undergraduates: 66% (2,075). ***Average award:*** Freshmen: $16,508; Undergraduates: $14,639. ***Scholarships, grants, and awards:*** Federal Pell, FSEOG, state, private, college/university gift aid from institutional funds, Federal Nursing.

GIFT AID (NON-NEED-BASED) ***Total amount:*** $18,770,506 (73% institutional, 27% external sources). ***Receiving aid:*** Freshmen: 57% (409). Undergraduates: 50% (1,553). ***Average award:*** Freshmen: $12,971. Undergraduates: $10,846. ***Scholarships, grants, and awards by category:*** *Academic interests/achievement:* 2,213 awards ($23,132,340 total): general academic interests/achievements. *Creative arts/performance:* 221 awards ($649,729 total): art/fine arts, dance, debating, music, theater/drama. *Special achievements/activities:* 39 awards ($65,050 total): leadership. *Special characteristics:* 870 awards ($1,845,528 total): children and siblings of alumni, first-generation college students, international students, out-of-state students, relatives of clergy, religious affiliation. ***ROTC:*** Army.

LOANS ***Student loans:*** $17,105,495 (87% need-based, 13% non-need-based). 71% of past graduating class borrowed through all loan programs. *Average indebtedness per student:* $22,484. ***Average need-based loan:*** Freshmen: $6318. Undergraduates: $8564. ***Parent loans:*** $4,930,377 (72% need-based, 28% non-need-based). ***Programs:*** FFEL (Subsidized and Unsubsidized Stafford, PLUS), Perkins, Federal Nursing, state.

WORK-STUDY ***Federal work-study:*** Total amount: $1,950,829; 636 jobs averaging $2048. ***State or other work-study/employment:*** Total amount: $3,043,896 (44% need-based, 56% non-need-based). 240 part-time jobs averaging $3793.

APPLYING FOR FINANCIAL AID ***Required financial aid form:*** FAFSA. ***Financial aid deadline (priority):*** 1/31. ***Notification date:*** Continuous beginning 3/15. Students must reply by 5/1 or within 3 weeks of notification.

CONTACT Mrs. Katherine Walker Loffer, Associate Director, Pacific Lutheran University, Financial Aid, Pacific Lutheran University, Tacoma, WA 98447, 253-535-7167 or toll-free 800-274-6758. *Fax:* 253-535-8406. *E-mail:* walkerkl@plu.edu.

PACIFIC NORTHWEST COLLEGE OF ART

Portland, OR

CONTACT Peggy Burgus, Director of Financial Aid, Pacific Northwest College of Art, 1241 Northwest Johnson Street, Portland, OR 97209, 503-821-8976. *Fax:* 503-821-8978.

PACIFIC OAKS COLLEGE

Pasadena, CA

CONTACT Rosie Tristan, Financial Aid Specialist, Pacific Oaks College, 5 Westmoreland Place, Pasadena, CA 91103, 626-397-1350 or toll-free 800-684-0900. *Fax:* 626-577-6144. *E-mail:* financial@pacificoaks.edu.

PACIFIC UNION COLLEGE

Angwin, CA

Tuition & fees: $23,979 **Average undergraduate aid package: $14,557**

ABOUT THE INSTITUTION Independent Seventh-day Adventist, coed. ***Awards:*** associate, bachelor's, and master's degrees. 68 undergraduate majors. ***Total enrollment:*** 1,278. Undergraduates: 1,276. Freshmen: 235. Federal methodology is used as a basis for awarding need-based institutional aid.

UNDERGRADUATE EXPENSES for 2009–10 ***Application fee:*** $30. ***Comprehensive fee:*** $30,729 includes full-time tuition ($23,844), mandatory fees ($135), and room and board ($6750). ***College room only:*** $3975. ***Part-time tuition:*** $656 per quarter hour.

FRESHMAN FINANCIAL AID (Fall 2008, est.) 206 applied for aid; of those 69% were deemed to have need. 100% of freshmen with need received aid; of those 1% had need fully met. ***Average percent of need met:*** 68% (excluding resources awarded to replace EFC). ***Average financial aid package:*** $15,780 (excluding resources awarded to replace EFC). 31% of all full-time freshmen had no need and received non-need-based gift aid.

UNDERGRADUATE FINANCIAL AID (Fall 2008, est.) 975 applied for aid; of those 67% were deemed to have need. 100% of undergraduates with need received aid; of those 2% had need fully met. ***Average percent of need met:*** 70% (excluding resources awarded to replace EFC). ***Average financial aid package:*** $14,557 (excluding resources awarded to replace EFC). 36% of all full-time undergraduates had no need and received non-need-based gift aid.

GIFT AID (NEED-BASED) ***Total amount:*** $14,218,283 (14% federal, 15% state, 57% institutional, 14% external sources). ***Receiving aid:*** Freshmen: 69% (143); all full-time undergraduates: 64% (657). ***Average award:*** Freshmen: $12,330; Undergraduates: $9668. ***Scholarships, grants, and awards:*** Federal Pell, FSEOG, state, private, college/university gift aid from institutional funds.

GIFT AID (NON-NEED-BASED) ***Total amount:*** $2,772,845 (52% institutional, 48% external sources). ***Receiving aid:*** Freshmen: 67% (137). Undergraduates: 59% (598). ***Average award:*** Freshmen: $912. Undergraduates: $1134. ***Scholarships, grants, and awards by category:*** *Academic interests/achievement:* education. *Special achievements/activities:* community service, general special achievements/activities, leadership, religious involvement. *Special characteristics:* $50,000 total: members of minority groups, religious affiliation, siblings of current students, spouses of current students.

LOANS ***Student loans:*** $14,299,575 (31% need-based, 69% non-need-based). 70% of past graduating class borrowed through all loan programs. *Average indebtedness per student:* $18,000. ***Average need-based loan:*** Freshmen: $3067. Undergraduates: $4477. ***Parent loans:*** $664,121 (100% need-based). ***Programs:*** FFEL (Subsidized and Unsubsidized Stafford, PLUS), Perkins, college/university.

WORK-STUDY ***Federal work-study:*** Total amount: $100,513; 91 jobs averaging $1093.

APPLYING FOR FINANCIAL AID ***Required financial aid forms:*** FAFSA, institution's own form. ***Financial aid deadline (priority):*** 3/2. ***Notification date:*** Continuous beginning 5/1. Students must reply within 3 weeks of notification.

CONTACT Laurie Wheeler, Director of Student Financial Services, Pacific Union College, One Angwin Avenue, Angwin, CA 94508, 707-965-7321 or toll-free 800-862-7080. *Fax:* 707-965-6595. *E-mail:* llwheeler@puc.edu.

PACIFIC UNIVERSITY

Forest Grove, OR

Tuition & fees: $28,137 **Average undergraduate aid package: $22,706**

ABOUT THE INSTITUTION Independent, coed. ***Awards:*** bachelor's, master's, doctoral, and first professional degrees. 50 undergraduate majors. ***Total enrollment:*** 3,167. Undergraduates: 1,481. Freshmen: 345. Federal methodology is used as a basis for awarding need-based institutional aid.

UNDERGRADUATE EXPENSES for 2008–09 ***Application fee:*** $40. ***Comprehensive fee:*** $35,653 includes full-time tuition ($27,604), mandatory fees ($533), and room and board ($7516). ***College room only:*** $3790. ***Part-time tuition:*** $1150 per credit hour.

FRESHMAN FINANCIAL AID (Fall 2008, est.) 338 applied for aid; of those 84% were deemed to have need. 100% of freshmen with need received aid; of those 43% had need fully met. ***Average percent of need met:*** 82% (excluding resources awarded to replace EFC). ***Average financial aid package:*** $23,622 (excluding resources awarded to replace EFC). 20% of all full-time freshmen had no need and received non-need-based gift aid.

UNDERGRADUATE FINANCIAL AID (Fall 2008, est.) 1,135 applied for aid; of those 88% were deemed to have need. 100% of undergraduates with need received aid; of those 33% had need fully met. ***Average percent of need met:*** 78% (excluding resources awarded to replace EFC). ***Average financial aid package:*** $22,706 (excluding resources awarded to replace EFC). 20% of all full-time undergraduates had no need and received non-need-based gift aid.

GIFT AID (NEED-BASED) ***Total amount:*** $14,796,711 (12% federal, 5% state, 78% institutional, 5% external sources). ***Receiving aid:*** Freshmen: 76% (279); all full-time undergraduates: 70% (969). ***Average award:*** Freshmen: $12,791; Undergraduates: $11,895. ***Scholarships, grants, and awards:*** Federal Pell, FSEOG, state, private, college/university gift aid from institutional funds.

GIFT AID (NON-NEED-BASED) ***Total amount:*** $3,087,603 (1% state, 95% institutional, 4% external sources). ***Receiving aid:*** Freshmen: 9% (35). Undergraduates: 5% (67). ***Average award:*** Freshmen: $11,142. Undergraduates: $9561. ***Scholarships, grants, and awards by category:*** *Academic interests/achievement:* $9,443,860 total: biological sciences, business, education, English, foreign languages, general academic interests/achievements, health fields, humanities, mathematics, physical sciences, social sciences. *Creative arts/performance:* 10 awards ($15,500 total): debating, journalism/publications, music, theater/drama. *Special achievements/activities:* 13 awards ($2500 total): community service, memberships, religious involvement. *Special characteristics:* 1,152 awards ($9,350,372 total): children and siblings of alumni, children of faculty/staff, ethnic background, first-generation college students, general special characteristics, international students, local/state students, relatives of clergy. ***ROTC:*** Army cooperative, Air Force cooperative.

LOANS ***Student loans:*** $8,433,789 (84% need-based, 16% non-need-based). 80% of past graduating class borrowed through all loan programs. *Average indebtedness per student:* $24,757. ***Average need-based loan:*** Freshmen: $6873. Undergraduates: $7885. ***Parent loans:*** $2,566,360 (66% need-based, 34% non-need-based). ***Programs:*** FFEL (Subsidized and Unsubsidized Stafford, PLUS), Perkins, private alternative loans.

WORK-STUDY ***Federal work-study:*** Total amount: $1,540,965; 789 jobs averaging $1953. ***State or other work-study/employment:*** Total amount: $104,003 (6% need-based, 94% non-need-based). 187 part-time jobs averaging $556.

APPLYING FOR FINANCIAL AID ***Required financial aid form:*** FAFSA. ***Financial aid deadline (priority):*** 3/1. ***Notification date:*** Continuous beginning 3/1.

CONTACT Financial Aid Front Desk, Pacific University, 2043 College Way, Forest Grove, OR 97116-1797, 503-352-2222 or toll-free 877-722-8648. *E-mail:* financialaid@pacificu.edu.

PAIER COLLEGE OF ART, INC.

Hamden, CT

CONTACT Mr. John DeRose, Director of Financial Aid, Paier College of Art, Inc., 20 Gorham Avenue, Hamden, CT 06514-3902, 203-287-3034. *Fax:* 203-287-3021. *E-mail:* paier.art@snet.net.

PAINE COLLEGE

Augusta, GA

CONTACT Ms. Gerri Bogan, Director of Financial Aid, Paine College, 1235 15th Street, Augusta, GA 30901, 706-821-8262 or toll-free 800-476-7703. *Fax:* 706-821-8691. *E-mail:* bogang@mail.paine.edu.

PALM BEACH ATLANTIC UNIVERSITY

West Palm Beach, FL

Tuition & fees: $21,550 **Average undergraduate aid package: $14,040**

ABOUT THE INSTITUTION Independent nondenominational, coed. ***Awards:*** associate, bachelor's, master's, and first professional degrees. 45 undergraduate majors. ***Total enrollment:*** 3,211. Undergraduates: 2,409. Freshmen: 424. Federal methodology is used as a basis for awarding need-based institutional aid.

UNDERGRADUATE EXPENSES for 2008–09 ***Application fee:*** $35. ***Comprehensive fee:*** $29,770 includes full-time tuition ($21,250), mandatory fees ($300), and room and board ($8220). ***College room only:*** $4570. Full-time tuition and fees vary according to course load, degree level, location, program, and reciprocity agreements. Room and board charges vary according to board plan and housing facility. ***Part-time tuition:*** $515 per credit hour. ***Part-time fees:*** $99 per term. Part-time tuition and fees vary according to course load, degree level, location, program, and reciprocity agreements. ***Payment plan:*** Installment.

FRESHMAN FINANCIAL AID (Fall 2008, est.) 351 applied for aid; of those 82% were deemed to have need. 100% of freshmen with need received aid; of those 8% had need fully met. ***Average percent of need met:*** 28% (excluding resources awarded to replace EFC). ***Average financial aid package:*** $16,115 (excluding resources awarded to replace EFC). 15% of all full-time freshmen had no need and received non-need-based gift aid.

UNDERGRADUATE FINANCIAL AID (Fall 2008, est.) 1,719 applied for aid; of those 86% were deemed to have need. 100% of undergraduates with need received aid; of those 24% had need fully met. ***Average percent of need met:*** 75% (excluding resources awarded to replace EFC). ***Average financial aid package:*** $14,040 (excluding resources awarded to replace EFC). 10% of all full-time undergraduates had no need and received non-need-based gift aid.

GIFT AID (NEED-BASED) ***Total amount:*** $4,482,187 (62% federal, 10% state, 28% institutional). ***Receiving aid:*** Freshmen: 38% (159); all full-time undergraduates: 43% (937). ***Average award:*** Freshmen: $2775; Undergraduates: $4323. ***Scholarships, grants, and awards:*** Federal Pell, FSEOG, state, private, college/university gift aid from institutional funds.

GIFT AID (NON-NEED-BASED) ***Total amount:*** $16,678,776 (1% federal, 32% state, 62% institutional, 5% external sources). ***Receiving aid:*** Freshmen: 65% (275). Undergraduates: 64% (1,409). ***Average award:*** Freshmen: $7267. Undergraduates: $6076. ***Scholarships, grants, and awards by category:*** *Academic interests/achievement:* 1,460 awards ($8,398,100 total): general academic interests/achievements. *Creative arts/performance:* 153 awards ($512,736 total): dance, music, theater/drama. *Special achievements/activities:*

7 awards ($6500 total): religious involvement. *Special characteristics:* 100 awards ($998,986 total): children and siblings of alumni, children of current students, children of educators, children of faculty/staff, previous college experience, siblings of current students, spouses of current students. ***Tuition waivers:*** Full or partial for employees or children of employees.

LOANS ***Student loans:*** $13,167,601 (42% need-based, 58% non-need-based). 69% of past graduating class borrowed through all loan programs. *Average indebtedness per student:* $19,420. ***Average need-based loan:*** Freshmen: $3195. Undergraduates: $4218. ***Parent loans:*** $2,665,559 (100% non-need-based). ***Programs:*** FFEL (Subsidized and Unsubsidized Stafford, PLUS), Perkins.

WORK-STUDY ***Federal work-study:*** Total amount: $519,427; 220 jobs averaging $2290. ***State or other work-study/employment:*** Total amount: $30,323 (100% need-based). 18 part-time jobs averaging $1574.

ATHLETIC AWARDS Total amount: $1,071,714 (100% non-need-based).

APPLYING FOR FINANCIAL AID ***Required financial aid form:*** FAFSA. ***Financial aid deadline:*** 8/1 (priority: 2/1). ***Notification date:*** Continuous beginning 2/15. Students must reply within 4 weeks of notification.

CONTACT Kim Vanderlaan, Assistant Director, Financial Aid, Palm Beach Atlantic University, PO Box 24708, West Palm Beach, FL 33416-4708, 561-803-2000 or toll-free 800-238-3998. *Fax:* 561-803-2130. *E-mail:* Kim_vanderlaan@pba.edu.

PALMER COLLEGE OF CHIROPRACTIC

Davenport, IA

CONTACT Sue McCabe, Financial Planning Office, Palmer College of Chiropractic, 1000 Brady Street, Davenport, IA 52803, 563-884-5888 or toll-free 800-722-3648. *Fax:* 563-884-5299. *E-mail:* sue.mccabe@palmer.edu.

PARK UNIVERSITY

Parkville, MO

ABOUT THE INSTITUTION Independent, coed. ***Awards:*** associate, bachelor's, and master's degrees and post-bachelor's certificates. 48 undergraduate majors. ***Total enrollment:*** 12,457. Undergraduates: 11,865. Freshmen: 257.

GIFT AID (NEED-BASED) ***Scholarships, grants, and awards:*** Federal Pell, FSEOG, state, private, college/university gift aid from institutional funds.

GIFT AID (NON-NEED-BASED) ***Scholarships, grants, and awards by category:*** *Academic interests/achievement:* general academic interests/achievements. *Creative arts/performance:* art/fine arts, theater/drama. *Special achievements/activities:* cheerleading/drum major. *Special characteristics:* children of faculty/staff, religious affiliation, siblings of current students.

LOANS ***Programs:*** FFEL (Subsidized and Unsubsidized Stafford, PLUS), Perkins, college/university.

WORK-STUDY ***Federal work-study:*** Total amount: $461,875; 209 jobs averaging $2875. ***State or other work-study/employment:*** Total amount: $273,797 (53% need-based, 47% non-need-based). 103 part-time jobs averaging $2675.

APPLYING FOR FINANCIAL AID ***Required financial aid forms:*** FAFSA, institution's own form.

CONTACT Carla Boren, Director of Financial Aid, Park University, 8700 NW River Park Drive, Parkville, MO 64152, 816-584-6317 or toll-free 800-745-7275. *Fax:* 816-741-9668. *E-mail:* finaid@park.edu.

PARSONS THE NEW SCHOOL FOR DESIGN

New York, NY

Tuition & fees: $34,460 **Average undergraduate aid package: $28,369**

ABOUT THE INSTITUTION Independent, coed. ***Awards:*** associate, bachelor's, and master's degrees. 12 undergraduate majors. ***Total enrollment:*** 4,241. Undergraduates: 3,815. Freshmen: 655. Federal methodology is used as a basis for awarding need-based institutional aid.

UNDERGRADUATE EXPENSES for 2008–09 ***Application fee:*** $50. ***Comprehensive fee:*** $49,720 includes full-time tuition ($33,700), mandatory fees ($760), and room and board ($15,260). ***College room only:*** $12,260. Room and board charges vary according to board plan and housing facility. ***Part-time tuition:*** $1150 per credit.

FRESHMAN FINANCIAL AID (Fall 2008, est.) 331 applied for aid; of those 88% were deemed to have need. 100% of freshmen with need received aid; of those 10% had need fully met. ***Average percent of need met:*** 76% (excluding resources awarded to replace EFC). ***Average financial aid package:*** $28,141 (excluding resources awarded to replace EFC). 4% of all full-time freshmen had no need and received non-need-based gift aid.

UNDERGRADUATE FINANCIAL AID (Fall 2008, est.) 1,389 applied for aid; of those 91% were deemed to have need. 100% of undergraduates with need received aid; of those 12% had need fully met. ***Average percent of need met:*** 74% (excluding resources awarded to replace EFC). ***Average financial aid package:*** $28,369 (excluding resources awarded to replace EFC). 2% of all full-time undergraduates had no need and received non-need-based gift aid.

GIFT AID (NEED-BASED) ***Total amount:*** $19,423,134 (13% federal, 5% state, 79% institutional, 3% external sources). ***Receiving aid:*** Freshmen: 44% (288); all full-time undergraduates: 36% (1,247). ***Average award:*** Freshmen: $16,073; Undergraduates: $13,393. ***Scholarships, grants, and awards:*** Federal Pell, FSEOG, state, private, college/university gift aid from institutional funds.

GIFT AID (NON-NEED-BASED) ***Total amount:*** $5,951,230 (89% institutional, 11% external sources). ***Receiving aid:*** Freshmen: 4% (27). Undergraduates: 4% (142). ***Average award:*** Freshmen: $4013. Undergraduates: $4204. ***Scholarships, grants, and awards by category:*** *Academic interests/achievement:* general academic interests/achievements. *Creative arts/performance:* general creative arts/performance. *Special achievements/activities:* general special achievements/activities. ***Tuition waivers:*** Full or partial for employees or children of employees.

LOANS ***Student loans:*** $17,017,469 (87% need-based, 13% non-need-based). *Average indebtedness per student:* $25,582. ***Average need-based loan:*** Freshmen: $11,991. Undergraduates: $14,806. ***Parent loans:*** $4,138,871 (87% need-based, 13% non-need-based). ***Programs:*** FFEL (Subsidized and Unsubsidized Stafford, PLUS), Perkins, college/university.

WORK-STUDY Federal work-study jobs available. ***State or other work-study/employment:*** Part-time jobs available.

APPLYING FOR FINANCIAL AID ***Required financial aid form:*** FAFSA. ***Financial aid deadline:*** Continuous. ***Notification date:*** Continuous beginning 3/1. Students must reply within 4 weeks of notification.

CONTACT Financial Aid Counselor, Parsons The New School for Design, 66 Fifth Avenue, New York, NY 10011, 212-229-8930 or toll-free 877-528-3321.

PATRICIA STEVENS COLLEGE

St. Louis, MO

ABOUT THE INSTITUTION Proprietary, coed. ***Awards:*** associate and bachelor's degrees. 4 undergraduate majors. ***Total enrollment:*** 145. Undergraduates: 145.

GIFT AID (NEED-BASED) ***Scholarships, grants, and awards:*** Federal Pell, private.

LOANS ***Programs:*** FFEL (Subsidized and Unsubsidized Stafford, PLUS).

APPLYING FOR FINANCIAL AID ***Required financial aid forms:*** FAFSA, institution's own form.

CONTACT Mr. Greg Elsenrath, Financial Aid Director, Patricia Stevens College, 1415 Olive Street, St. Louis, MO 63103, 314-421-0949 or toll-free 800-871-0949. *Fax:* 314-421-0304. *E-mail:* info@patriciastevens.com.

PATRICK HENRY COLLEGE

Purcellville, VA

CONTACT Financial Aid Office, Patrick Henry College, One Patrick Henry Circle, Purcellville, VA 20132, 540-338-1776.

PATTEN UNIVERSITY

Oakland, CA

CONTACT Mr. Robert A. Olivera, Dean of Enrollment Services, Patten University, 2433 Coolidge Avenue, Oakland, CA 94601-2699, 510-261-8500 Ext. 783. *Fax:* 510-534-8969. *E-mail:* oliverob@patten.edu.

PAUL QUINN COLLEGE

Dallas, TX

CONTACT Khaleelah Ali, Assistant Director of Financial Aid, Paul Quinn College, 3837 Simpson Stuart Road, Dallas, TX 75241, 214-302-3530 or toll-free 800-237-2648. *Fax:* 214-302-3535. *E-mail:* kali@pqc.edu.

PAUL SMITH'S COLLEGE
Paul Smiths, NY

Tuition & fees: $20,250 **Average undergraduate aid package: $15,358**

ABOUT THE INSTITUTION Independent, coed, primarily men. ***Awards:*** associate and bachelor's degrees. 12 undergraduate majors. ***Total enrollment:*** 910. Undergraduates: 910. Federal methodology is used as a basis for awarding need-based institutional aid.

UNDERGRADUATE EXPENSES for 2008–09 ***Application fee:*** $30. ***Comprehensive fee:*** $28,600 includes full-time tuition ($18,460), mandatory fees ($1790), and room and board ($8350). ***Part-time tuition:*** $520 per credit hour.

FRESHMAN FINANCIAL AID (Fall 2008, est.) 285 applied for aid; of those 92% were deemed to have need. 100% of freshmen with need received aid; of those 9% had need fully met. ***Average percent of need met:*** 69% (excluding resources awarded to replace EFC). ***Average financial aid package:*** $14,351 (excluding resources awarded to replace EFC). 12% of all full-time freshmen had no need and received non-need-based gift aid.

UNDERGRADUATE FINANCIAL AID (Fall 2008, est.) 853 applied for aid; of those 91% were deemed to have need. 100% of undergraduates with need received aid; of those 12% had need fully met. ***Average percent of need met:*** 70% (excluding resources awarded to replace EFC). ***Average financial aid package:*** $15,358 (excluding resources awarded to replace EFC). 13% of all full-time undergraduates had no need and received non-need-based gift aid.

GIFT AID (NEED-BASED) ***Total amount:*** $8,650,399 (15% federal, 13% state, 65% institutional, 7% external sources). ***Receiving aid:*** Freshmen: 86% (261); all full-time undergraduates: 85% (779). ***Average award:*** Freshmen: $10,337; Undergraduates: $10,606. ***Scholarships, grants, and awards:*** Federal Pell, FSEOG, state, private, college/university gift aid from institutional funds.

GIFT AID (NON-NEED-BASED) ***Total amount:*** $1,047,243 (85% institutional, 15% external sources). ***Receiving aid:*** Freshmen: 5% (16). Undergraduates: 6% (57). ***Average award:*** Freshmen: $5847. Undergraduates: $5844. ***Scholarships, grants, and awards by category:*** *Academic interests/achievement:* general academic interests/achievements.

LOANS ***Student loans:*** $4,676,055 (86% need-based, 14% non-need-based). 97% of past graduating class borrowed through all loan programs. *Average indebtedness per student:* $20,168. ***Average need-based loan:*** Freshmen: $2940. Undergraduates: $3813. ***Parent loans:*** $2,876,881 (100% need-based). ***Programs:*** FFEL (Subsidized and Unsubsidized Stafford, PLUS), Perkins.

WORK-STUDY ***Federal work-study:*** Total amount: $1,028,310; jobs available (averaging $2000). ***State or other work-study/employment:*** Total amount: $204,052 (2% need-based, 98% non-need-based). Part-time jobs available.

APPLYING FOR FINANCIAL AID ***Required financial aid forms:*** FAFSA, state aid form. ***Financial aid deadline (priority):*** 3/15. ***Notification date:*** Continuous. Students must reply within 4 weeks of notification.

CONTACT Mary Ellen Chamberlain, Director of Financial Aid, Paul Smith's College, Routes 86 and 30, Paul Smiths, NY 12970, 518-327-6220 or toll-free 800-421-2605. *Fax:* 518-327-6055. *E-mail:* mchamberlain@paulsmiths.edu.

PEABODY CONSERVATORY OF MUSIC OF THE JOHNS HOPKINS UNIVERSITY
Baltimore, MD

Tuition & fees: $34,250 **Average undergraduate aid package: $12,659**

ABOUT THE INSTITUTION Independent, coed. ***Awards:*** bachelor's, master's, and doctoral degrees and post-bachelor's certificates. 8 undergraduate majors. ***Total enrollment:*** 670. Undergraduates: 333. Freshmen: 83. Federal methodology is used as a basis for awarding need-based institutional aid.

UNDERGRADUATE EXPENSES for 2009–10 ***Application fee:*** $100. ***Comprehensive fee:*** $45,350 includes full-time tuition ($34,250) and room and board ($11,100). ***Part-time tuition:*** $975 per semester hour.

FRESHMAN FINANCIAL AID (Fall 2008, est.) 73 applied for aid; of those 88% were deemed to have need. 100% of freshmen with need received aid; of those 33% had need fully met. ***Average percent of need met:*** 73% (excluding resources awarded to replace EFC). ***Average financial aid package:*** $16,367 (excluding resources awarded to replace EFC). 17% of all full-time freshmen had no need and received non-need-based gift aid.

UNDERGRADUATE FINANCIAL AID (Fall 2008, est.) 214 applied for aid; of those 89% were deemed to have need. 99% of undergraduates with need received aid; of those 20% had need fully met. ***Average percent of need met:*** 68% (excluding resources awarded to replace EFC). ***Average financial aid package:*** $12,659 (excluding resources awarded to replace EFC). 27% of all full-time undergraduates had no need and received non-need-based gift aid.

GIFT AID (NEED-BASED) ***Total amount:*** $2,953,809 (11% federal, 3% state, 83% institutional, 3% external sources). ***Receiving aid:*** Freshmen: 71% (59); all full-time undergraduates: 54% (172). ***Average award:*** Freshmen: $14,130; Undergraduates: $9294. ***Scholarships, grants, and awards:*** Federal Pell, FSEOG, state, private, college/university gift aid from institutional funds.

GIFT AID (NON-NEED-BASED) ***Total amount:*** $1,268,926 (1% state, 91% institutional, 8% external sources). ***Receiving aid:*** Freshmen: 18% (15). Undergraduates: 28% (90). ***Average award:*** Freshmen: $10,338. Undergraduates: $13,629. ***Scholarships, grants, and awards by category:*** *Creative arts/performance:* 289 awards ($3,618,830 total): music.

LOANS ***Student loans:*** $2,900,329 (91% need-based, 9% non-need-based). 44% of past graduating class borrowed through all loan programs. *Average indebtedness per student:* $34,442. ***Average need-based loan:*** Freshmen: $3027. Undergraduates: $5640. ***Parent loans:*** $949,831 (100% need-based). ***Programs:*** Federal Direct (Subsidized and Unsubsidized Stafford, PLUS), Perkins, college/university.

WORK-STUDY ***Federal work-study:*** Total amount: $194,559; 104 jobs averaging $1786.

APPLYING FOR FINANCIAL AID ***Required financial aid forms:*** FAFSA, Peabody International Student Financial Aid and Scholarship Application. ***Financial aid deadline (priority):*** 2/1. ***Notification date:*** 4/1. Students must reply by 5/1.

CONTACT Tom McDermott, Director of Financial Aid, Peabody Conservatory of Music of The Johns Hopkins University, 1 East Mount Vernon Place, Baltimore, MD 21202-2397, 410-659-8100 Ext. 3023 or toll-free 800-368-2521 (out-of-state). *Fax:* 410-659-8102. *E-mail:* finaid@peabody.jhu.edu.

PEACE COLLEGE
Raleigh, NC

Tuition & fees: $23,958 **Average undergraduate aid package: $18,673**

ABOUT THE INSTITUTION Independent religious, women only. ***Awards:*** bachelor's degrees and post-bachelor's certificates. 16 undergraduate majors. ***Total enrollment:*** 713. Undergraduates: 713. Freshmen: 186. Federal methodology is used as a basis for awarding need-based institutional aid.

UNDERGRADUATE EXPENSES for 2009–10 ***Application fee:*** $25. ***Comprehensive fee:*** $32,208 includes full-time tuition ($23,958) and room and board ($8250).

FRESHMAN FINANCIAL AID (Fall 2008, est.) 165 applied for aid; of those 89% were deemed to have need. 100% of freshmen with need received aid; of those 16% had need fully met. ***Average percent of need met:*** 78% (excluding resources awarded to replace EFC). ***Average financial aid package:*** $20,600 (excluding resources awarded to replace EFC).

UNDERGRADUATE FINANCIAL AID (Fall 2008, est.) 524 applied for aid; of those 89% were deemed to have need. 100% of undergraduates with need received aid; of those 14% had need fully met. ***Average percent of need met:*** 70% (excluding resources awarded to replace EFC). ***Average financial aid package:*** $18,673 (excluding resources awarded to replace EFC). 25% of all full-time undergraduates had no need and received non-need-based gift aid.

GIFT AID (NEED-BASED) ***Total amount:*** $6,958,780 (13% federal, 26% state, 58% institutional, 3% external sources). ***Receiving aid:*** Freshmen: 79% (147); all full-time undergraduates: 74% (468). ***Average award:*** Freshmen: $17,191; Undergraduates: $14,603. ***Scholarships, grants, and awards:*** Federal Pell, FSEOG, state, private, college/university gift aid from institutional funds, Federal Nursing.

GIFT AID (NON-NEED-BASED) ***Total amount:*** $1,603,330 (19% state, 73% institutional, 8% external sources). ***Receiving aid:*** Freshmen: 7% (13). Undergraduates: 6% (40). ***Average award:*** Freshmen: $7016. Undergraduates: $7195. ***Scholarships, grants, and awards by category:*** *Academic interests/achievement:* 629 awards ($4,298,500 total): general academic interests/achievements. *Creative arts/performance:* 43 awards ($41,754 total): art/fine arts, music, theater/drama. *Special characteristics:* 16 awards ($103,678 total): children of faculty/staff, relatives of clergy, siblings of current students. ***ROTC:*** Army cooperative, Naval cooperative, Air Force cooperative.

LOANS ***Student loans:*** $4,444,774 (74% need-based, 26% non-need-based). 68% of past graduating class borrowed through all loan programs. *Average*

indebtedness per student: $24,128. ***Average need-based loan:*** Freshmen: $3076. Undergraduates: $3920. ***Parent loans:*** $1,203,900 (34% need-based, 66% non-need-based). ***Programs:*** FFEL (Subsidized and Unsubsidized Stafford, PLUS), alternative loans.

WORK-STUDY ***Federal work-study:*** Total amount: $204,922; 192 jobs averaging $2163. ***State or other work-study/employment:*** Total amount: $45,594 (44% need-based, 56% non-need-based). 20 part-time jobs averaging $1543.

APPLYING FOR FINANCIAL AID ***Required financial aid form:*** FAFSA. ***Financial aid deadline (priority):*** 3/31. ***Notification date:*** Continuous. Students must reply within 4 weeks of notification.

CONTACT Angela Kirkley, Director of Financial Aid, Peace College, 15 East Peace Street, Raleigh, NC 27604, 919-508-2249 or toll-free 800-PEACE-47. *Fax:* 919-508-2325. *E-mail:* akirkley@peace.edu.

PEIRCE COLLEGE

Philadelphia, PA

Tuition & fees: $14,350 **Average undergraduate aid package: $9081**

ABOUT THE INSTITUTION Independent, coed. ***Awards:*** associate and bachelor's degrees. 13 undergraduate majors. ***Total enrollment:*** 2,051. Undergraduates: 2,051. Freshmen: 94. Federal methodology is used as a basis for awarding need-based institutional aid.

UNDERGRADUATE EXPENSES for 2008–09 ***Application fee:*** $50. ***Tuition:*** full-time $13,350; part-time $445 per credit hour. ***Required fees:*** full-time $1000; $100 per course. Full-time tuition and fees vary according to course load. Part-time tuition and fees vary according to course load. ***Payment plan:*** Installment.

FRESHMAN FINANCIAL AID (Fall 2007) 6 applied for aid; of those 100% were deemed to have need. 100% of freshmen with need received aid. ***Average percent of need met:*** 46% (excluding resources awarded to replace EFC). ***Average financial aid package:*** $6592 (excluding resources awarded to replace EFC).

UNDERGRADUATE FINANCIAL AID (Fall 2007) 787 applied for aid; of those 92% were deemed to have need. 99% of undergraduates with need received aid; of those 4% had need fully met. ***Average percent of need met:*** 52% (excluding resources awarded to replace EFC). ***Average financial aid package:*** $9081 (excluding resources awarded to replace EFC). 5% of all full-time undergraduates had no need and received non-need-based gift aid.

GIFT AID (NEED-BASED) ***Total amount:*** $4,790,354 (59% state, 30% institutional, 11% external sources). ***Receiving aid:*** Freshmen: 56% (5); all full-time undergraduates: 74% (653). ***Average award:*** Freshmen: $4761; Undergraduates: $4497. ***Scholarships, grants, and awards:*** Federal Pell, FSEOG, state, college/university gift aid from institutional funds.

GIFT AID (NON-NEED-BASED) ***Total amount:*** $92,700 (100% external sources). ***Receiving aid:*** Undergraduates: 3% (26). ***Average award:*** Undergraduates: $1841. ***Scholarships, grants, and awards by category:*** *Academic interests/achievement:* 29 awards ($87,000 total): business. *Special achievements/activities:* 4 awards ($5000 total): leadership, memberships. *Special characteristics:* 37 awards ($54,550 total): children and siblings of alumni, children of public servants, international students. ***Tuition waivers:*** Full or partial for children of alumni, employees or children of employees.

LOANS ***Student loans:*** $9,483,628 (54% need-based, 46% non-need-based). 85% of past graduating class borrowed through all loan programs. *Average indebtedness per student:* $18,724. ***Average need-based loan:*** Freshmen: $3908. Undergraduates: $4781. ***Parent loans:*** $160,755 (100% need-based). ***Programs:*** FFEL (Subsidized and Unsubsidized Stafford, PLUS).

WORK-STUDY ***Federal work-study:*** Total amount: $173,356; 31 jobs averaging $4000.

APPLYING FOR FINANCIAL AID ***Required financial aid form:*** FAFSA. ***Financial aid deadline (priority):*** 5/1. ***Notification date:*** Continuous beginning 9/1. Students must reply within 3 weeks of notification.

CONTACT Lisa A. Gargiulo, Manager, Student Financial Services, Peirce College, 1420 Pine Street, Philadelphia, PA 19102, 215-670-9370 or toll-free 888-467-3472. *Fax:* 215-545-3671. *E-mail:* lagargiulo@peirce.edu.

PENN STATE ABINGTON

Abington, PA

Tuition & fees (PA res): $11,800 **Average undergraduate aid package: $8743**

ABOUT THE INSTITUTION State-related, coed. ***Awards:*** associate and bachelor's degrees. 118 undergraduate majors. ***Total enrollment:*** 3,394. Undergraduates: 3,376. Freshmen: 813. Federal methodology is used as a basis for awarding need-based institutional aid.

UNDERGRADUATE EXPENSES for 2008–09 ***Application fee:*** $50. ***Tuition, state resident:*** full-time $11,008; part-time $445 per credit hour. ***Tuition, nonresident:*** full-time $16,798; part-time $700 per credit hour. ***Required fees:*** full-time $792; $295 per term.

FRESHMAN FINANCIAL AID (Fall 2007) 746 applied for aid; of those 75% were deemed to have need. 97% of freshmen with need received aid; of those 5% had need fully met. ***Average percent of need met:*** 67% (excluding resources awarded to replace EFC). ***Average financial aid package:*** $8669 (excluding resources awarded to replace EFC). 6% of all full-time freshmen had no need and received non-need-based gift aid.

UNDERGRADUATE FINANCIAL AID (Fall 2007) 2,042 applied for aid; of those 80% were deemed to have need. 97% of undergraduates with need received aid; of those 6% had need fully met. ***Average percent of need met:*** 65% (excluding resources awarded to replace EFC). ***Average financial aid package:*** $8743 (excluding resources awarded to replace EFC). 3% of all full-time undergraduates had no need and received non-need-based gift aid.

GIFT AID (NEED-BASED) ***Total amount:*** $9,359,476 (40% federal, 37% state, 13% institutional, 10% external sources). ***Receiving aid:*** Freshmen: 48% (417); all full-time undergraduates: 49% (1,231). ***Average award:*** Freshmen: $6519; Undergraduates: $6323. ***Scholarships, grants, and awards:*** Federal Pell, FSEOG, state, private, college/university gift aid from institutional funds.

GIFT AID (NON-NEED-BASED) ***Total amount:*** $384,089 (1% state, 36% institutional, 63% external sources). ***Receiving aid:*** Freshmen: 34% (292). Undergraduates: 18% (444). ***Average award:*** Freshmen: $1466. Undergraduates: $1662. ***Scholarships, grants, and awards by category:*** *Academic interests/achievement:* general academic interests/achievements. *Special characteristics:* general special characteristics. ***ROTC:*** Army cooperative, Air Force cooperative.

LOANS ***Student loans:*** $10,949,140 (80% need-based, 20% non-need-based). 69% of past graduating class borrowed through all loan programs. *Average indebtedness per student:* $26,800. ***Average need-based loan:*** Freshmen: $3183. Undergraduates: $3937. ***Parent loans:*** $2,148,293 (64% need-based, 36% non-need-based). ***Programs:*** Federal Direct (Subsidized and Unsubsidized Stafford, PLUS), Perkins, college/university, private loans.

WORK-STUDY ***Federal work-study:*** Total amount: $160,680; 94 jobs averaging $1685.

APPLYING FOR FINANCIAL AID ***Required financial aid form:*** FAFSA. ***Financial aid deadline (priority):*** 2/15. ***Notification date:*** Continuous.

CONTACT Debbie Meditz, Assistant Student Aid Coordinator, Penn State Abington, 106 Sutherland Building, 1600 Woodland Road, Abington, PA 19001, 215-881-7348. *Fax:* 215-881-7655. *E-mail:* dlm175@psu.edu.

PENN STATE ALTOONA

Altoona, PA

Tuition & fees (PA res): $12,182 **Average undergraduate aid package: $9058**

ABOUT THE INSTITUTION State-related, coed. ***Awards:*** associate and bachelor's degrees. 125 undergraduate majors. ***Total enrollment:*** 4,013. Undergraduates: 4,013. Freshmen: 1,476. Federal methodology is used as a basis for awarding need-based institutional aid.

UNDERGRADUATE EXPENSES for 2008–09 ***Application fee:*** $50. ***Tuition, state resident:*** full-time $11,490; part-time $479 per credit hour. ***Tuition, nonresident:*** full-time $17,578; part-time $732 per credit hour. ***Required fees:*** full-time $692; $258 per term. ***College room and board:*** $7670; ***Room only:*** $4110.

FRESHMAN FINANCIAL AID (Fall 2007) 1,221 applied for aid; of those 77% were deemed to have need. 96% of freshmen with need received aid; of those 4% had need fully met. ***Average percent of need met:*** 59% (excluding resources awarded to replace EFC). ***Average financial aid package:*** $8119 (excluding resources awarded to replace EFC). 2% of all full-time freshmen had no need and received non-need-based gift aid.

UNDERGRADUATE FINANCIAL AID (Fall 2007) 2,959 applied for aid; of those 82% were deemed to have need. 97% of undergraduates with need received aid; of those 7% had need fully met. ***Average percent of need met:*** 62% (excluding resources awarded to replace EFC). ***Average financial aid package:*** $9058 (excluding resources awarded to replace EFC). 3% of all full-time undergraduates had no need and received non-need-based gift aid.

GIFT AID (NEED-BASED) ***Total amount:*** $11,426,908 (40% federal, 41% state, 13% institutional, 6% external sources). ***Receiving aid:*** Freshmen: 40% (594); all full-time undergraduates: 44% (1,622). ***Average award:*** Freshmen: $5676; Undergraduates: $5618. ***Scholarships, grants, and awards:*** Federal Pell, FSEOG, state, private, college/university gift aid from institutional funds.

GIFT AID (NON-NEED-BASED) ***Total amount:*** $693,551 (43% federal, 3% state, 21% institutional, 33% external sources). ***Receiving aid:*** Freshmen: 18% (272). Undergraduates: 18% (665). ***Average award:*** Freshmen: $894. Undergraduates: $1438. ***Scholarships, grants, and awards by category:*** *Academic interests/achievement:* general academic interests/achievements. *Special characteristics:* general special characteristics. ***ROTC:*** Army, Air Force.

LOANS ***Student loans:*** $19,765,884 (86% need-based, 14% non-need-based). 69% of past graduating class borrowed through all loan programs. *Average indebtedness per student:* $26,800. ***Average need-based loan:*** Freshmen: $3553. Undergraduates: $4165. ***Parent loans:*** $6,819,949 (76% need-based, 24% non-need-based). ***Programs:*** Federal Direct (Subsidized and Unsubsidized Stafford, PLUS), Perkins, college/university, private loans.

WORK-STUDY ***Federal work-study:*** Total amount: $485,874; 219 jobs averaging $2203.

APPLYING FOR FINANCIAL AID ***Required financial aid form:*** FAFSA. ***Financial aid deadline (priority):*** 2/15. ***Notification date:*** Continuous beginning 3/1.

CONTACT Mr. David Pearlman, Assistant Director of Student Affairs, Penn State Altoona, W111 Smith Building, Altoona, PA 16601-3760, 814-949-5055 or toll-free 800-848-9843. *Fax:* 814-949-5536. *E-mail:* dpp1@psu.edu.

PENN STATE BERKS
Reading, PA

Tuition & fees (PA res): $12,282   Average undergraduate aid package: $8201

ABOUT THE INSTITUTION State-related, coed. ***Awards:*** associate and bachelor's degrees. 129 undergraduate majors. ***Total enrollment:*** 2,800. Undergraduates: 2,743. Freshmen: 1,000. Federal methodology is used as a basis for awarding need-based institutional aid.

UNDERGRADUATE EXPENSES for 2008–09 ***Application fee:*** $50. ***Tuition, state resident:*** full-time $11,490; part-time $479 per credit hour. ***Tuition, nonresident:*** full-time $17,578; part-time $732 per credit hour. ***Required fees:*** full-time $792; $295 per term. ***College room and board:*** $8390; ***Room only:*** $4830.

FRESHMAN FINANCIAL AID (Fall 2007) 754 applied for aid; of those 73% were deemed to have need. 96% of freshmen with need received aid; of those 5% had need fully met. ***Average percent of need met:*** 58% (excluding resources awarded to replace EFC). ***Average financial aid package:*** $7495 (excluding resources awarded to replace EFC). 2% of all full-time freshmen had no need and received non-need-based gift aid.

UNDERGRADUATE FINANCIAL AID (Fall 2007) 1,838 applied for aid; of those 77% were deemed to have need. 97% of undergraduates with need received aid; of those 6% had need fully met. ***Average percent of need met:*** 61% (excluding resources awarded to replace EFC). ***Average financial aid package:*** $8201 (excluding resources awarded to replace EFC). 2% of all full-time undergraduates had no need and received non-need-based gift aid.

GIFT AID (NEED-BASED) ***Total amount:*** $6,200,788 (36% federal, 40% state, 17% institutional, 7% external sources). ***Receiving aid:*** Freshmen: 38% (353); all full-time undergraduates: 40% (937). ***Average award:*** Freshmen: $5493; Undergraduates: $5580. ***Scholarships, grants, and awards:*** Federal Pell, FSEOG, state, private, college/university gift aid from institutional funds.

GIFT AID (NON-NEED-BASED) ***Total amount:*** $288,835 (23% federal, 4% state, 29% institutional, 44% external sources). ***Receiving aid:*** Freshmen: 15% (136). Undergraduates: 13% (301). ***Average award:*** Freshmen: $1242. Undergraduates: $1887. ***ROTC:*** Army cooperative.

LOANS ***Student loans:*** $11,151,631 (81% need-based, 19% non-need-based). 69% of past graduating class borrowed through all loan programs. *Average indebtedness per student:* $26,800. ***Average need-based loan:*** Freshmen: $3392. Undergraduates: $4012. ***Parent loans:*** $4,773,499 (71% need-based, 29% non-need-based). ***Programs:*** Federal Direct (Subsidized and Unsubsidized Stafford, PLUS), Perkins, college/university, private loans.

WORK-STUDY ***Federal work-study:*** Total amount: $141,914; 81 jobs averaging $1747.

APPLYING FOR FINANCIAL AID ***Required financial aid form:*** FAFSA. ***Financial aid deadline (priority):*** 2/15. ***Notification date:*** Continuous beginning 3/1.

CONTACT Maryann Hubick, Financial Aid Coordinator, Penn State Berks, Perkins Student Center, Room 6, Reading, PA 19610-6009, 610-396-6071. *Fax:* 610-396-6077. *E-mail:* mxh61@psu.edu.

PENN STATE ERIE, THE BEHREND COLLEGE
Erie, PA

Tuition & fees (PA res): $12,282   Average undergraduate aid package: $9344

ABOUT THE INSTITUTION State-related, coed. ***Awards:*** associate, bachelor's, and master's degrees. 129 undergraduate majors. ***Total enrollment:*** 4,334. Undergraduates: 4,218. Freshmen: 1,085. Federal methodology is used as a basis for awarding need-based institutional aid.

UNDERGRADUATE EXPENSES for 2008–09 ***Application fee:*** $50. ***Tuition, state resident:*** full-time $11,490; part-time $479 per credit hour. ***Tuition, nonresident:*** full-time $17,578; part-time $732 per credit hour. ***Required fees:*** full-time $792; $295 per term. ***College room and board:*** $7670; ***Room only:*** $4110.

FRESHMAN FINANCIAL AID (Fall 2007) 1,026 applied for aid; of those 82% were deemed to have need. 97% of freshmen with need received aid; of those 5% had need fully met. ***Average percent of need met:*** 62% (excluding resources awarded to replace EFC). ***Average financial aid package:*** $8449 (excluding resources awarded to replace EFC). 2% of all full-time freshmen had no need and received non-need-based gift aid.

UNDERGRADUATE FINANCIAL AID (Fall 2007) 3,078 applied for aid; of those 84% were deemed to have need. 98% of undergraduates with need received aid; of those 7% had need fully met. ***Average percent of need met:*** 65% (excluding resources awarded to replace EFC). ***Average financial aid package:*** $9344 (excluding resources awarded to replace EFC). 3% of all full-time undergraduates had no need and received non-need-based gift aid.

GIFT AID (NEED-BASED) ***Total amount:*** $12,810,495 (33% federal, 43% state, 17% institutional, 7% external sources). ***Receiving aid:*** Freshmen: 48% (559); all full-time undergraduates: 48% (1,747). ***Average award:*** Freshmen: $5822; Undergraduates: $5686. ***Scholarships, grants, and awards:*** Federal Pell, FSEOG, state, private, college/university gift aid from institutional funds.

GIFT AID (NON-NEED-BASED) ***Total amount:*** $619,737 (10% federal, 6% state, 44% institutional, 40% external sources). ***Receiving aid:*** Freshmen: 22% (258). Undergraduates: 20% (743). ***Average award:*** Freshmen: $1747. Undergraduates: $2611. ***ROTC:*** Army cooperative.

LOANS ***Student loans:*** $20,924,235 (88% need-based, 12% non-need-based). 69% of past graduating class borrowed through all loan programs. *Average indebtedness per student:* $26,800. ***Average need-based loan:*** Freshmen: $3712. Undergraduates: $4480. ***Parent loans:*** $8,357,011 (83% need-based, 17% non-need-based). ***Programs:*** Federal Direct (Subsidized and Unsubsidized Stafford, PLUS), Perkins, college/university, private loans.

WORK-STUDY ***Federal work-study:*** Total amount: $392,674; 215 jobs averaging $1813.

APPLYING FOR FINANCIAL AID ***Required financial aid form:*** FAFSA. ***Financial aid deadline (priority):*** 2/15. ***Notification date:*** Continuous beginning 3/1.

CONTACT Ms. Jane Brady, Assistant Director of Admissions and Financial Aid, Penn State Erie, The Behrend College, 5091 Station Road, Erie, PA 16802, 814-898-6162 or toll-free 866-374-3378. *Fax:* 814-898-7595. *E-mail:* jub9@psu.edu.

PENN STATE HARRISBURG
Middletown, PA

Tuition & fees (PA res): $12,282   Average undergraduate aid package: $9629

ABOUT THE INSTITUTION State-related, coed. ***Awards:*** associate, bachelor's, master's, and doctoral degrees and post-bachelor's certificates. 29 undergraduate majors. ***Total enrollment:*** 3,936. Undergraduates: 2,570. Freshmen: 449. Federal methodology is used as a basis for awarding need-based institutional aid.

UNDERGRADUATE EXPENSES for 2008–09 ***Application fee:*** $50. ***Tuition, state resident:*** full-time $11,490; part-time $479 per credit hour. ***Tuition, nonresident:***

full-time $17,578; part-time $732 per credit hour. ***Required fees:*** full-time $792; $295 per term. ***College room and board:*** $8780; ***Room only:*** $5220.

FRESHMAN FINANCIAL AID (Fall 2007) 348 applied for aid; of those 71% were deemed to have need. 96% of freshmen with need received aid; of those 7% had need fully met. ***Average percent of need met:*** 55% (excluding resources awarded to replace EFC). ***Average financial aid package:*** $8069 (excluding resources awarded to replace EFC). 1% of all full-time freshmen had no need and received non-need-based gift aid.

UNDERGRADUATE FINANCIAL AID (Fall 2007) 1,538 applied for aid; of those 81% were deemed to have need. 97% of undergraduates with need received aid; of those 9% had need fully met. ***Average percent of need met:*** 61% (excluding resources awarded to replace EFC). ***Average financial aid package:*** $9629 (excluding resources awarded to replace EFC). 1% of all full-time undergraduates had no need and received non-need-based gift aid.

GIFT AID (NEED-BASED) ***Total amount:*** $6,472,827 (44% federal, 39% state, 13% institutional, 4% external sources). ***Receiving aid:*** Freshmen: 35% (147); all full-time undergraduates: 45% (864). ***Average award:*** Freshmen: $6129; Undergraduates: $5631. ***Scholarships, grants, and awards:*** Federal Pell, FSEOG, state, private, college/university gift aid from institutional funds.

GIFT AID (NON-NEED-BASED) ***Total amount:*** $448,332 (37% federal, 6% state, 10% institutional, 47% external sources). ***Receiving aid:*** Freshmen: 16% (65). Undergraduates: 16% (301). ***Average award:*** Freshmen: $2425. Undergraduates: $3054. ***Scholarships, grants, and awards by category:*** *Academic interests/achievement:* general academic interests/achievements. *Special characteristics:* general special characteristics. ***ROTC:*** Army cooperative.

LOANS ***Student loans:*** $12,511,844 (84% need-based, 16% non-need-based). 69% of past graduating class borrowed through all loan programs. *Average indebtedness per student:* $26,800. ***Average need-based loan:*** Freshmen: $3578. Undergraduates: $4667. ***Parent loans:*** $2,159,404 (72% need-based, 28% non-need-based). ***Programs:*** Federal Direct (Subsidized and Unsubsidized Stafford, PLUS), Perkins, college/university, private loans.

WORK-STUDY ***Federal work-study:*** Total amount: $93,666; 54 jobs averaging $1730.

APPLYING FOR FINANCIAL AID ***Required financial aid form:*** FAFSA. ***Financial aid deadline (priority):*** 2/15. ***Notification date:*** Continuous beginning 3/1.

CONTACT Ms. Carolyn Julian, Student Aid Adviser, Penn State Harrisburg, W112 Olmstead, 777 West Harrisburg Pike, Middletown, PA 17057-4898, 717-948-6307 or toll-free 800-222-2056. *Fax:* 717-948-6008. *E-mail:* czb3@psu.edu.

PENN STATE UNIVERSITY PARK

State College, PA

Tuition & fees (PA res): $13,706 Average undergraduate aid package: $9698

ABOUT THE INSTITUTION State-related, coed. ***Awards:*** associate, bachelor's, master's, doctoral, and first professional degrees and post-bachelor's certificates. 124 undergraduate majors. ***Total enrollment:*** 44,406. Undergraduates: 37,988. Freshmen: 7,241. Federal methodology is used as a basis for awarding need-based institutional aid.

UNDERGRADUATE EXPENSES for 2008–09 ***Application fee:*** $50. ***Tuition, state resident:*** full-time $13,014; part-time $542 per credit hour. ***Tuition, nonresident:*** full-time $24,248; part-time $1010 per credit hour. ***Required fees:*** full-time $692; $258 per term. ***College room and board:*** $7670; ***Room only:*** $4110.

FRESHMAN FINANCIAL AID (Fall 2007) 4,805 applied for aid; of those 65% were deemed to have need. 94% of freshmen with need received aid; of those 8% had need fully met. ***Average percent of need met:*** 61% (excluding resources awarded to replace EFC). ***Average financial aid package:*** $8820 (excluding resources awarded to replace EFC). 6% of all full-time freshmen had no need and received non-need-based gift aid.

UNDERGRADUATE FINANCIAL AID (Fall 2007) 23,451 applied for aid; of those 76% were deemed to have need. 97% of undergraduates with need received aid; of those 10% had need fully met. ***Average percent of need met:*** 63% (excluding resources awarded to replace EFC). ***Average financial aid package:*** $9698 (excluding resources awarded to replace EFC). 7% of all full-time undergraduates had no need and received non-need-based gift aid.

GIFT AID (NEED-BASED) ***Total amount:*** $87,015,828 (31% federal, 32% state, 29% institutional, 8% external sources). ***Receiving aid:*** Freshmen: 24% (1,540); all full-time undergraduates: 29% (10,253). ***Average award:*** Freshmen: $6266; Undergraduates: $5935. ***Scholarships, grants, and awards:*** Federal Pell, FSEOG, state, private, college/university gift aid from institutional funds.

GIFT AID (NON-NEED-BASED) ***Total amount:*** $19,300,627 (19% federal, 1% state, 39% institutional, 41% external sources). ***Receiving aid:*** Freshmen: 22% (1,396). Undergraduates: 17% (6,117). ***Average award:*** Freshmen: $3878. Undergraduates: $3098. ***ROTC:*** Army, Naval, Air Force.

LOANS ***Student loans:*** $165,579,861 (81% need-based, 19% non-need-based). 69% of past graduating class borrowed through all loan programs. *Average indebtedness per student:* $26,800. ***Average need-based loan:*** Freshmen: $3492. Undergraduates: $4619. ***Parent loans:*** $76,159,273 (76% need-based, 24% non-need-based). ***Programs:*** Federal Direct (Subsidized and Unsubsidized Stafford, PLUS), Perkins, college/university, private loans.

WORK-STUDY ***Federal work-study:*** Total amount: $2,089,826; 1,125 jobs averaging $1828.

ATHLETIC AWARDS Total amount: $10,678,300 (35% need-based, 65% non-need-based).

APPLYING FOR FINANCIAL AID ***Required financial aid form:*** FAFSA. ***Financial aid deadline (priority):*** 2/15. ***Notification date:*** Continuous.

CONTACT Ms. Anna Griswold, Assistant Vice Provost for Student Aid, Penn State University Park, 311 Shields Building, University Park, PA 16802, 814-863-0507. *Fax:* 814-863-0322. *E-mail:* amg5@psu.edu.

PENNSYLVANIA COLLEGE OF ART & DESIGN

Lancaster, PA

CONTACT J. David Hershey, Registrar/Director of Financial Aid, Pennsylvania College of Art & Design, 204 North Prince Street, PO Box 59, Lancaster, PA 17608-0059, 717-396-7833 Ext. 13. *Fax:* 717-396-1339. *E-mail:* finaid@pcad.edu.

PENNSYLVANIA COLLEGE OF TECHNOLOGY

Williamsport, PA

Tuition & fees (PA res): $11,790 Average undergraduate aid package: $12,028

ABOUT THE INSTITUTION State-related, coed. ***Awards:*** associate and bachelor's degrees. 108 undergraduate majors. ***Total enrollment:*** 6,510. Undergraduates: 6,510. Freshmen: 1,471. Federal methodology is used as a basis for awarding need-based institutional aid.

UNDERGRADUATE EXPENSES for 2008–09 ***Application fee:*** $50. ***Tuition, state resident:*** full-time $10,020; part-time $393 per credit hour. ***Tuition, nonresident:*** full-time $13,050; part-time $494 per credit hour. ***Required fees:*** full-time $1770. Full-time tuition and fees vary according to course load and program. Part-time tuition and fees vary according to course load and program. ***College room and board:*** $7200; ***Room only:*** $5125. Room and board charges vary according to board plan, housing facility, and location. ***Payment plan:*** Deferred payment.

FRESHMAN FINANCIAL AID (Fall 2007) 1,586 applied for aid; of those 77% were deemed to have need. 100% of freshmen with need received aid.

UNDERGRADUATE FINANCIAL AID (Fall 2007) 6,810 applied for aid; of those 88% were deemed to have need. 100% of undergraduates with need received aid. ***Average percent of need met:*** 77% (excluding resources awarded to replace EFC). ***Average financial aid package:*** $12,028 (excluding resources awarded to replace EFC).

GIFT AID (NEED-BASED) ***Total amount:*** $26,490,777 (29% federal, 36% state, 2% institutional, 33% external sources). ***Receiving aid:*** Freshmen: 77% (1,221); all full-time undergraduates: 88% (5,988). ***Average award:*** Undergraduates: $2864. ***Scholarships, grants, and awards:*** Federal Pell, FSEOG, state, private, college/university gift aid from institutional funds.

GIFT AID (NON-NEED-BASED) ***Tuition waivers:*** Full or partial for employees or children of employees. ***ROTC:*** Army cooperative.

LOANS ***Student loans:*** $39,235,328 (100% need-based). ***Parent loans:*** $9,893,457 (100% need-based). ***Programs:*** FFEL (Subsidized and Unsubsidized Stafford, PLUS).

WORK-STUDY ***Federal work-study:*** Total amount: $361,721; 234 jobs averaging $1546. ***State or other work-study/employment:*** Total amount: $572,814 (100% need-based). 339 part-time jobs averaging $1690.

APPLYING FOR FINANCIAL AID ***Required financial aid forms:*** FAFSA, institution's own form. ***Financial aid deadline (priority):*** 4/1. ***Notification date:*** Continuous beginning 6/1. Students must reply within 2 weeks of notification.

Pennsylvania College of Technology

CONTACT Candace Baran, Director of Financial Aid, Pennsylvania College of Technology, One College Avenue, DIF 108, Williamsport, PA 17701, 570-326-4766 or toll-free 800-367-9222 (in-state). *Fax:* 570-321-5552. *E-mail:* cbaran@pct.edu.

PEPPERDINE UNIVERSITY

Malibu, CA

Tuition & fees: $36,770 **Average undergraduate aid package: $32,760**

ABOUT THE INSTITUTION Independent religious, coed. ***Awards:*** bachelor's, master's, doctoral, and first professional degrees. 47 undergraduate majors. ***Total enrollment:*** 7,614. Undergraduates: 3,404. Freshmen: 782. Federal methodology is used as a basis for awarding need-based institutional aid.

UNDERGRADUATE EXPENSES for 2008–09 ***Application fee:*** $65. ***Comprehensive fee:*** $47,250 includes full-time tuition ($36,650), mandatory fees ($120), and room and board ($10,480). Room and board charges vary according to board plan and housing facility. ***Part-time tuition:*** $1135 per unit. ***Payment plan:*** Installment.

FRESHMAN FINANCIAL AID (Fall 2008, est.) 553 applied for aid; of those 76% were deemed to have need. 99% of freshmen with need received aid; of those 42% had need fully met. ***Average percent of need met:*** 89% (excluding resources awarded to replace EFC). ***Average financial aid package:*** $33,009 (excluding resources awarded to replace EFC). 16% of all full-time freshmen had no need and received non-need-based gift aid.

UNDERGRADUATE FINANCIAL AID (Fall 2008, est.) 1,721 applied for aid; of those 84% were deemed to have need. 98% of undergraduates with need received aid; of those 38% had need fully met. ***Average percent of need met:*** 86% (excluding resources awarded to replace EFC). ***Average financial aid package:*** $32,760 (excluding resources awarded to replace EFC). 16% of all full-time undergraduates had no need and received non-need-based gift aid.

GIFT AID (NEED-BASED) ***Total amount:*** $36,604,774 (6% federal, 6% state, 85% institutional, 3% external sources). ***Receiving aid:*** Freshmen: 48% (375); all full-time undergraduates: 38% (1,299). ***Average award:*** Freshmen: $25,665; Undergraduates: $23,074. ***Scholarships, grants, and awards:*** Federal Pell, FSEOG, state, private, college/university gift aid from institutional funds, United Negro College Fund, Academic Competitiveness Grant, National Smart Grant.

GIFT AID (NON-NEED-BASED) ***Total amount:*** $4,988,126 (97% institutional, 3% external sources). ***Receiving aid:*** Freshmen: 21% (161). Undergraduates: 14% (485). ***Average award:*** Freshmen: $20,474. Undergraduates: $16,161. ***Tuition waivers:*** Full or partial for employees or children of employees. ***ROTC:*** Army cooperative, Air Force cooperative.

LOANS ***Student loans:*** $11,204,620 (87% need-based, 13% non-need-based). 61% of past graduating class borrowed through all loan programs. *Average indebtedness per student:* $31,546. ***Average need-based loan:*** Freshmen: $3516. Undergraduates: $4962. ***Parent loans:*** $13,115,774 (70% need-based, 30% non-need-based). ***Programs:*** FFEL (Subsidized and Unsubsidized Stafford, PLUS), Perkins, college/university.

WORK-STUDY ***Federal work-study:*** Total amount: $827,500; jobs available. ***State or other work-study/employment:*** Total amount: $538,430 (71% need-based, 29% non-need-based). Part-time jobs available.

ATHLETIC AWARDS Total amount: $979,121 (60% need-based, 40% non-need-based).

APPLYING FOR FINANCIAL AID ***Required financial aid form:*** FAFSA. ***Financial aid deadline:*** 2/15 (priority: 2/15). ***Notification date:*** 4/15.

CONTACT Janet Lockhart, Director of Financial Assistance, Pepperdine University, 24255 Pacific Coast Highway, Malibu, CA 90263-4301, 310-506-4301. *Fax:* 310-506-4746. *E-mail:* finaid2@pepperdine.edu.

PERU STATE COLLEGE

Peru, NE

CONTACT Diana Lind, Director of Financial Aid, Peru State College, PO Box 10, Peru, NE 68421, 402-872-2228 or toll-free 800-742-4412 (in-state). *Fax:* 402-872-2419. *E-mail:* finaid@oakmail.peru.edu.

PFEIFFER UNIVERSITY

Misenheimer, NC

CONTACT Amy Brown, Director of Financial Aid, Pfeiffer University, PO Box 960, Misenheimer, NC 28109, 704-463-1360 Ext. 3046 or toll-free 800-338-2060. *Fax:* 704-463-1363. *E-mail:* amy.brown@pfeiffer.edu.

PHILADELPHIA BIBLICAL UNIVERSITY

Langhorne, PA

Tuition & fees: $18,872 **Average undergraduate aid package: $14,235**

ABOUT THE INSTITUTION Independent nondenominational, coed. ***Awards:*** bachelor's, master's, and first professional degrees. 11 undergraduate majors. ***Total enrollment:*** 1,373. Undergraduates: 1,061. Freshmen: 191. Federal methodology is used as a basis for awarding need-based institutional aid.

UNDERGRADUATE EXPENSES for 2009–10 ***Application fee:*** $25. ***Comprehensive fee:*** $26,522 includes full-time tuition ($18,872) and room and board ($7650). ***College room only:*** $4050. ***Part-time tuition:*** $560 per credit.

FRESHMAN FINANCIAL AID (Fall 2008, est.) 151 applied for aid; of those 91% were deemed to have need. 99% of freshmen with need received aid; of those 18% had need fully met. ***Average percent of need met:*** 71% (excluding resources awarded to replace EFC). ***Average financial aid package:*** $13,971 (excluding resources awarded to replace EFC). 8% of all full-time freshmen had no need and received non-need-based gift aid.

UNDERGRADUATE FINANCIAL AID (Fall 2008, est.) 841 applied for aid; of those 91% were deemed to have need. 99% of undergraduates with need received aid; of those 17% had need fully met. ***Average percent of need met:*** 70% (excluding resources awarded to replace EFC). ***Average financial aid package:*** $14,235 (excluding resources awarded to replace EFC). 7% of all full-time undergraduates had no need and received non-need-based gift aid.

GIFT AID (NEED-BASED) ***Total amount:*** $7,288,230 (18% federal, 10% state, 69% institutional, 3% external sources). ***Receiving aid:*** Freshmen: 73% (135); all full-time undergraduates: 73% (720). ***Average award:*** Freshmen: $10,474; Undergraduates: $10,064. ***Scholarships, grants, and awards:*** Federal Pell, FSEOG, state, private, college/university gift aid from institutional funds.

GIFT AID (NON-NEED-BASED) ***Total amount:*** $528,497 (1% federal, 96% institutional, 3% external sources). ***Receiving aid:*** Freshmen: 6% (11). Undergraduates: 4% (40). ***Average award:*** Freshmen: $9093. Undergraduates: $12,173. ***Scholarships, grants, and awards by category:*** *Academic interests/achievement:* 620 awards ($3,688,365 total): general academic interests/achievements. *Creative arts/performance:* 41 awards ($64,425 total): music. *Special achievements/activities:* 28 awards ($43,400 total): general special achievements/activities. *Special characteristics:* 145 awards ($675,000 total): children of faculty/staff, relatives of clergy. ***ROTC:*** Air Force cooperative.

LOANS ***Student loans:*** $5,774,959 (77% need-based, 23% non-need-based). 90% of past graduating class borrowed through all loan programs. *Average indebtedness per student:* $26,475. ***Average need-based loan:*** Freshmen: $4000. Undergraduates: $5197. ***Parent loans:*** $697,762 (34% need-based, 66% non-need-based). ***Programs:*** FFEL (Subsidized and Unsubsidized Stafford, PLUS), college/university.

WORK-STUDY ***Federal work-study:*** Total amount: $144,050; 121 jobs averaging $1250.

APPLYING FOR FINANCIAL AID ***Required financial aid form:*** FAFSA. ***Financial aid deadline (priority):*** 3/1. ***Notification date:*** Continuous.

CONTACT Raye Thompson, Director of Financial Aid, Philadelphia Biblical University, 200 Manor Avenue, Langhorne, PA 19047-2990, 215-702-4243 or toll-free 800-366-0049. *Fax:* 215-702-4248. *E-mail:* rthompson@pbu.edu.

PHILADELPHIA UNIVERSITY

Philadelphia, PA

Tuition & fees: $26,700 **Average undergraduate aid package: $19,368**

ABOUT THE INSTITUTION Independent, coed. ***Awards:*** associate, bachelor's, master's, and doctoral degrees and post-bachelor's and post-master's certificates. 32 undergraduate majors. ***Total enrollment:*** 3,360. Undergraduates: 2,782. Freshmen: 731. Federal methodology is used as a basis for awarding need-based institutional aid.

UNDERGRADUATE EXPENSES for 2008–09 ***Application fee:*** $35. ***Comprehensive fee:*** $35,392 includes full-time tuition ($26,630), mandatory fees ($70), and room and board ($8692). ***College room only:*** $4408. Full-time tuition and fees vary according to degree level and program. Room and board charges vary according to board plan and housing facility. ***Part-time tuition:*** $472 per credit hour. Part-time tuition and fees vary according to class time, course load, degree level, and program. ***Payment plans:*** Installment, deferred payment.

FRESHMAN FINANCIAL AID (Fall 2008, est.) 635 applied for aid; of those 86% were deemed to have need. 100% of freshmen with need received aid; of those 12% had need fully met. ***Average percent of need met:*** 73% (excluding resources awarded to replace EFC). ***Average financial aid package:*** $20,533 (excluding resources awarded to replace EFC). 24% of all full-time freshmen had no need and received non-need-based gift aid.

UNDERGRADUATE FINANCIAL AID (Fall 2008, est.) 2,084 applied for aid; of those 88% were deemed to have need. 100% of undergraduates with need received aid; of those 10% had need fully met. ***Average percent of need met:*** 69% (excluding resources awarded to replace EFC). ***Average financial aid package:*** $19,368 (excluding resources awarded to replace EFC). 26% of all full-time undergraduates had no need and received non-need-based gift aid.

GIFT AID (NEED-BASED) ***Total amount:*** $21,143,034 (10% federal, 8% state, 81% institutional, 1% external sources). ***Receiving aid:*** Freshmen: 74% (539); all full-time undergraduates: 70% (1,807). ***Average award:*** Freshmen: $14,673; Undergraduates: $12,552. ***Scholarships, grants, and awards:*** Federal Pell, FSEOG, state, private, college/university gift aid from institutional funds, gift scholarships from outside sources (non-endowed) for which university chooses recipients.

GIFT AID (NON-NEED-BASED) ***Total amount:*** $3,810,904 (98% institutional, 2% external sources). ***Receiving aid:*** Freshmen: 5% (40). Undergraduates: 4% (99). ***Average award:*** Freshmen: $6445. Undergraduates: $5293. ***Scholarships, grants, and awards by category:*** *Academic interests/achievement:* 2,364 awards ($12,766,450 total): engineering/technologies, general academic interests/achievements. ***Tuition waivers:*** Full or partial for employees or children of employees.

LOANS ***Student loans:*** $20,994,208 (75% need-based, 25% non-need-based). 75% of past graduating class borrowed through all loan programs. *Average indebtedness per student:* $30,062. ***Average need-based loan:*** Freshmen: $3853. Undergraduates: $5195. ***Parent loans:*** $6,386,957 (63% need-based, 37% non-need-based). ***Programs:*** FFEL (Subsidized and Unsubsidized Stafford, PLUS), Perkins, private loans.

WORK-STUDY ***Federal work-study:*** Total amount: $2,367,203; 1,212 jobs averaging $2000. ***State or other work-study/employment:*** Total amount: $450,683 (84% need-based, 16% non-need-based). Part-time jobs available.

ATHLETIC AWARDS Total amount: $2,140,651 (44% need-based, 56% non-need-based).

APPLYING FOR FINANCIAL AID ***Required financial aid form:*** FAFSA. ***Financial aid deadline:*** 4/15. ***Notification date:*** Continuous. Students must reply by 5/1 or within 3 weeks of notification.

CONTACT Ms. Lisa J. Cooper, Director of Financial Aid, Philadelphia University, School House Lane and Henry Avenue, Philadelphia, PA 19144-5497, 215-951-2940. *Fax:* 215-951-2907. *E-mail:* cooperl@philau.edu.

PHILANDER SMITH COLLEGE

Little Rock, AR

CONTACT Director of Financial Aid, Philander Smith College, 812 West 13th Street, Little Rock, AR 72202-3799, 501-370-5270 or toll-free 800-446-6772.

PIEDMONT BAPTIST COLLEGE AND GRADUATE SCHOOL

Winston-Salem, NC

CONTACT Ronnie Mathis, Director of Financial Aid, Piedmont Baptist College and Graduate School, 716 Franklin Street, Winston-Salem, NC 27101-5197, 336-725-8344 Ext. 2322 or toll-free 800-937-5097. *Fax:* 336-725-5522. *E-mail:* mathisr@pbc.edu.

PIEDMONT COLLEGE

Demorest, GA

Tuition & fees: $18,000 **Average undergraduate aid package: $14,475**

ABOUT THE INSTITUTION Independent religious, coed. ***Awards:*** bachelor's and master's degrees and post-master's certificates. 32 undergraduate majors. ***Total enrollment:*** 2,640. Undergraduates: 1,135. Freshmen: 214. Both federal and institutional methodology are used as a basis for awarding need-based institutional aid.

UNDERGRADUATE EXPENSES for 2009–10 ***Comprehensive fee:*** $24,000 includes full-time tuition ($18,000) and room and board ($6000). ***Part-time tuition:*** $750 per semester hour.

FRESHMAN FINANCIAL AID (Fall 2008, est.) 160 applied for aid; of those 78% were deemed to have need. 98% of freshmen with need received aid; of those 40% had need fully met. ***Average percent of need met:*** 56% (excluding resources awarded to replace EFC). ***Average financial aid package:*** $15,963 (excluding resources awarded to replace EFC). 12% of all full-time freshmen had no need and received non-need-based gift aid.

UNDERGRADUATE FINANCIAL AID (Fall 2008, est.) 785 applied for aid; of those 76% were deemed to have need. 99% of undergraduates with need received aid; of those 28% had need fully met. ***Average percent of need met:*** 59% (excluding resources awarded to replace EFC). ***Average financial aid package:*** $14,475 (excluding resources awarded to replace EFC). 7% of all full-time undergraduates had no need and received non-need-based gift aid.

GIFT AID (NEED-BASED) ***Total amount:*** $2,511,182 (65% federal, 33% institutional, 2% external sources). ***Receiving aid:*** Freshmen: 19% (39); all full-time undergraduates: 23% (224). ***Average award:*** Freshmen: $1280; Undergraduates: $2790. ***Scholarships, grants, and awards:*** Federal Pell, FSEOG, state, private, college/university gift aid from institutional funds.

GIFT AID (NON-NEED-BASED) ***Total amount:*** $6,384,234 (45% state, 51% institutional, 4% external sources). ***Receiving aid:*** Freshmen: 54% (113). Undergraduates: 57% (565). ***Average award:*** Freshmen: $8230. Undergraduates: $7985. ***Scholarships, grants, and awards by category:*** *Academic interests/achievement:* 619 awards ($1,731,230 total): biological sciences, business, education, English, foreign languages, general academic interests/achievements, health fields, humanities, mathematics, premedicine, religion/biblical studies, social sciences. *Creative arts/performance:* 66 awards ($69,840 total): art/fine arts, music, theater/drama. *Special achievements/activities:* 214 awards ($834,685 total): leadership. *Special characteristics:* 318 awards ($2,169,420 total): adult students, children of faculty/staff, international students, out-of-state students.

LOANS ***Student loans:*** $6,188,824 (49% need-based, 51% non-need-based). 69% of past graduating class borrowed through all loan programs. *Average indebtedness per student:* $15,620. ***Average need-based loan:*** Freshmen: $3190. Undergraduates: $3825. ***Parent loans:*** $1,057,958 (100% non-need-based). ***Programs:*** Federal Direct (Subsidized and Unsubsidized Stafford, PLUS), state.

WORK-STUDY ***Federal work-study:*** Total amount: $83,980; 63 jobs averaging $1590. ***State or other work-study/employment:*** Total amount: $362,490 (26% need-based, 74% non-need-based). 198 part-time jobs averaging $1626.

APPLYING FOR FINANCIAL AID ***Required financial aid forms:*** FAFSA, state aid form. ***Financial aid deadline (priority):*** 3/1. ***Notification date:*** Continuous. Students must reply within 2 weeks of notification.

CONTACT Mrs. Kim Lovell, Director of Financial Aid, Piedmont College, PO Box 10, Demorest, GA 30535-0010, 706-778-3000 Ext. 1191 or toll-free 800-277-7020. *Fax:* 706-776-2811. *E-mail:* klovell@piedmont.edu.

PIKEVILLE COLLEGE

Pikeville, KY

Tuition & fees: $14,535 **Average undergraduate aid package: $16,021**

ABOUT THE INSTITUTION Independent religious, coed. ***Awards:*** associate, bachelor's, and first professional degrees and post-bachelor's certificates. 18 undergraduate majors. ***Total enrollment:*** 1,077. Undergraduates: 771. Freshmen: 179. Federal methodology is used as a basis for awarding need-based institutional aid.

UNDERGRADUATE EXPENSES for 2009–10 ***Comprehensive fee:*** $20,535 includes full-time tuition ($14,535) and room and board ($6000). ***Part-time tuition:*** $606 per credit hour.

FRESHMAN FINANCIAL AID (Fall 2008, est.) 180 applied for aid; of those 99% were deemed to have need. 100% of freshmen with need received aid; of those 61% had need fully met. ***Average percent of need met:*** 93% (excluding resources awarded to replace EFC). ***Average financial aid package:*** $16,237 (excluding resources awarded to replace EFC).

UNDERGRADUATE FINANCIAL AID (Fall 2008, est.) 671 applied for aid; of those 100% were deemed to have need. 100% of undergraduates with need received aid; of those 65% had need fully met. ***Average percent of need met:*** 93% (excluding resources awarded to replace EFC). ***Average financial aid package:*** $16,021 (excluding resources awarded to replace EFC).

GIFT AID (NEED-BASED) ***Total amount:*** $6,226,880 (26% federal, 32% state, 40% institutional, 2% external sources). ***Receiving aid:*** Freshmen: 97% (174); all full-time undergraduates: 96% (656). ***Average award:*** Freshmen: $12,971; Undergraduates: $11,540. ***Scholarships, grants, and awards:*** Federal Pell, FSEOG, state, private, college/university gift aid from institutional funds.

LOANS ***Student loans:*** $3,431,516 (100% need-based). 71% of past graduating class borrowed through all loan programs. *Average indebtedness per student:* $14,908. ***Average need-based loan:*** Freshmen: $4573. Undergraduates: $6083. ***Parent loans:*** $90,608 (100% need-based). ***Programs:*** FFEL (Subsidized and Unsubsidized Stafford, PLUS), Perkins, college/university.

WORK-STUDY ***Federal work-study:*** Total amount: $265,050; 250 jobs averaging $1713.

ATHLETIC AWARDS Total amount: $1,457,541 (100% need-based).

APPLYING FOR FINANCIAL AID ***Required financial aid forms:*** FAFSA, institution's own form. ***Financial aid deadline (priority):*** 3/15. ***Notification date:*** Continuous. Students must reply by 5/1.

CONTACT Melinda Lynch, Assistant Dean of Student Financial Services, Pikeville College, 147 Sycamore Street, Pikeville, KY 41501, 606-218-5251 or toll-free 866-232-7700. *Fax:* 606-218-5255. *E-mail:* jbradley@pc.edu.

PINE MANOR COLLEGE

Chestnut Hill, MA

ABOUT THE INSTITUTION Independent, women only. 16 undergraduate majors.

GIFT AID (NEED-BASED) ***Scholarships, grants, and awards:*** Federal Pell, FSEOG, state, private, college/university gift aid from institutional funds.

GIFT AID (NON-NEED-BASED) ***Scholarships, grants, and awards by category:*** *Academic interests/achievement:* biological sciences, education, general academic interests/achievements. *Special achievements/activities:* general special achievements/activities, leadership. *Special characteristics:* children and siblings of alumni, members of minority groups, siblings of current students.

LOANS ***Programs:*** FFEL (Subsidized and Unsubsidized Stafford, PLUS), state.

APPLYING FOR FINANCIAL AID ***Required financial aid form:*** FAFSA.

CONTACT Adrienne Hynek, Director of Financial Aid, Pine Manor College, 400 Heath Street, Chestnut Hill, MA 02467, 617-731-7053 or toll-free 800-762-1357. *Fax:* 617-731-7102. *E-mail:* hynekadrienne@pmc.edu.

PITTSBURG STATE UNIVERSITY

Pittsburg, KS

Tuition & fees (KS res): $4322 **Average undergraduate aid package: $9390**

ABOUT THE INSTITUTION State-supported, coed. ***Awards:*** associate, bachelor's, and master's degrees (associate, specialist in education). 98 undergraduate majors. ***Total enrollment:*** 7,127. Undergraduates: 5,863. Freshmen: 909. Federal methodology is used as a basis for awarding need-based institutional aid.

UNDERGRADUATE EXPENSES for 2008–09 ***Application fee:*** $30. ***Tuition, state resident:*** full-time $3420; part-time $114 per credit hour. ***Tuition, nonresident:*** full-time $11,674; part-time $389 per credit hour. ***Required fees:*** full-time $902; $40 per credit hour. ***College room and board:*** $5394. Room and board charges vary according to board plan and housing facility. ***Payment plan:*** Installment.

FRESHMAN FINANCIAL AID (Fall 2008, est.) 807 applied for aid; of those 69% were deemed to have need. 95% of freshmen with need received aid; of those 14% had need fully met. ***Average percent of need met:*** 89% (excluding resources awarded to replace EFC). ***Average financial aid package:*** $8842 (excluding resources awarded to replace EFC). 23% of all full-time freshmen had no need and received non-need-based gift aid.

UNDERGRADUATE FINANCIAL AID (Fall 2008, est.) 3,909 applied for aid; of those 77% were deemed to have need. 97% of undergraduates with need received aid; of those 12% had need fully met. ***Average percent of need met:*** 90% (excluding resources awarded to replace EFC). ***Average financial aid package:*** $9390 (excluding resources awarded to replace EFC). 15% of all full-time undergraduates had no need and received non-need-based gift aid.

GIFT AID (NEED-BASED) ***Total amount:*** $10,597,506 (62% federal, 8% state, 14% institutional, 16% external sources). ***Receiving aid:*** Freshmen: 46% (466); all full-time undergraduates: 43% (2,335). ***Average award:*** Freshmen: $4742; Undergraduates: $4479. ***Scholarships, grants, and awards:*** Federal Pell, FSEOG, state, private, college/university gift aid from institutional funds.

GIFT AID (NON-NEED-BASED) ***Total amount:*** $2,459,249 (1% state, 57% institutional, 42% external sources). ***Receiving aid:*** Freshmen: 18% (182). Undergraduates: 4% (238). ***Average award:*** Freshmen: $2110. Undergraduates: $2011. ***Scholarships, grants, and awards by category:*** *Academic interests/achievement:* 1,910 awards ($2,035,246 total): biological sciences, business, communication, computer science, education, engineering/technologies, English, foreign languages, general academic interests/achievements, health fields, home economics, mathematics, military science, physical sciences, social sciences. *Creative arts/performance:* 230 awards ($208,652 total): music. *Special characteristics:* 117 awards ($69,581 total): children and siblings of alumni, general special characteristics. ***Tuition waivers:*** Full or partial for employees or children of employees. ***ROTC:*** Army.

LOANS ***Student loans:*** $17,525,778 (66% need-based, 34% non-need-based). 60% of past graduating class borrowed through all loan programs. *Average indebtedness per student:* $15,643. ***Average need-based loan:*** Freshmen: $3470. Undergraduates: $4191. ***Parent loans:*** $1,075,663 (1% need-based, 99% non-need-based). ***Programs:*** Federal Direct (Subsidized and Unsubsidized Stafford, PLUS), FFEL (Subsidized and Unsubsidized Stafford, PLUS), Perkins, Federal Nursing, college/university.

WORK-STUDY ***Federal work-study:*** Total amount: $430,941; 275 jobs averaging $1268. ***State or other work-study/employment:*** Total amount: $1,624,887 (29% need-based, 71% non-need-based). 1,187 part-time jobs averaging $1421.

ATHLETIC AWARDS Total amount: $1,214,517 (56% need-based, 44% non-need-based).

APPLYING FOR FINANCIAL AID ***Required financial aid form:*** FAFSA. ***Financial aid deadline (priority):*** 3/1. ***Notification date:*** Continuous beginning 3/1. Students must reply within 2 weeks of notification.

CONTACT Marilyn Haverly, Director of Student Financial Assistance, Pittsburg State University, 1701 South Broadway, Pittsburg, KS 66762-5880, 620-235-4238 or toll-free 800-854-7488 Ext. 1. *Fax:* 620-235-4078. *E-mail:* mhaverly@pittstate.edu.

PITZER COLLEGE

Claremont, CA

Tuition & fees: $37,870 **Average undergraduate aid package: $33,940**

ABOUT THE INSTITUTION Independent, coed. ***Awards:*** bachelor's degrees. 53 undergraduate majors. ***Total enrollment:*** 1,025. Undergraduates: 1,025. Freshmen: 264. Both federal and institutional methodology are used as a basis for awarding need-based institutional aid.

UNDERGRADUATE EXPENSES for 2008–09 ***Application fee:*** $50. ***Comprehensive fee:*** $48,800 includes full-time tuition ($34,500), mandatory fees ($3370), and room and board ($10,930). ***College room only:*** $6970. Full-time tuition and fees vary according to course load. Room and board charges vary according to board plan. ***Part-time tuition:*** $4702 per course. Part-time tuition and fees vary according to course load. ***Payment plans:*** Installment, deferred payment.

FRESHMAN FINANCIAL AID (Fall 2008, est.) 139 applied for aid; of those 77% were deemed to have need. 100% of freshmen with need received aid; of those 100% had need fully met. ***Average percent of need met:*** 100% (excluding resources awarded to replace EFC). ***Average financial aid package:*** $31,755 (excluding resources awarded to replace EFC). 11% of all full-time freshmen had no need and received non-need-based gift aid.

UNDERGRADUATE FINANCIAL AID (Fall 2008, est.) 432 applied for aid; of those 84% were deemed to have need. 100% of undergraduates with need received aid; of those 100% had need fully met. ***Average percent of need met:*** 100% (excluding resources awarded to replace EFC). ***Average financial aid package:*** $33,940 (excluding resources awarded to replace EFC). 7% of all full-time undergraduates had no need and received non-need-based gift aid.

GIFT AID (NEED-BASED) ***Total amount:*** $10,933,159 (7% federal, 8% state, 82% institutional, 3% external sources). ***Receiving aid:*** Freshmen: 42% (107); all full-time undergraduates: 37% (359). ***Average award:*** Freshmen: $27,064;

Undergraduates: $29,182. ***Scholarships, grants, and awards:*** Federal Pell, FSEOG, state, private, college/university gift aid from institutional funds.

GIFT AID (NON-NEED-BASED) ***Total amount:*** $498,246 (68% institutional, 32% external sources). ***Average award:*** Freshmen: $5000. Undergraduates: $4981. ***Scholarships, grants, and awards by category:*** *Academic interests/achievement:* 131 awards ($638,750 total): general academic interests/achievements. *Special achievements/activities:* community service, leadership. ***Tuition waivers:*** Full or partial for employees or children of employees. ***ROTC:*** Army cooperative, Air Force cooperative.

LOANS ***Student loans:*** $2,454,164 (52% need-based, 48% non-need-based). 37% of past graduating class borrowed through all loan programs. *Average indebtedness per student:* $21,044. ***Average need-based loan:*** Freshmen: $2613. Undergraduates: $3402. ***Parent loans:*** $1,422,070 (100% non-need-based). ***Programs:*** FFEL (Subsidized and Unsubsidized Stafford, PLUS), Perkins, college/university.

WORK-STUDY ***Federal work-study:*** Total amount: $708,730; 315 jobs averaging $2477.

APPLYING FOR FINANCIAL AID ***Required financial aid forms:*** FAFSA, CSS Financial Aid PROFILE, state aid form, business/farm supplement. ***Financial aid deadline:*** 2/1. ***Notification date:*** 4/1. Students must reply by 5/1.

CONTACT Margaret Carothers, Director of Financial Aid, Pitzer College, 1050 North Mills Avenue, Claremont, CA 91711-6101, 909-621-8208 or toll-free 800-748-9371. *Fax:* 909-607-1205. *E-mail:* margaret_carothers@pitzer.edu.

PLYMOUTH STATE UNIVERSITY

Plymouth, NH

Tuition & fees (NH res): $8424 Average undergraduate aid package: $7944

ABOUT THE INSTITUTION State-supported, coed. ***Awards:*** bachelor's and master's degrees and post-bachelor's and post-master's certificates. 43 undergraduate majors. ***Total enrollment:*** 6,562. Undergraduates: 4,300. Freshmen: 1,090. Federal methodology is used as a basis for awarding need-based institutional aid.

UNDERGRADUATE EXPENSES for 2008–09 ***Application fee:*** $40. ***Tuition, state resident:*** full-time $6600; part-time $275 per credit hour. ***Tuition, nonresident:*** full-time $14,450; part-time $602 per credit hour. ***Required fees:*** full-time $1824. Full-time tuition and fees vary according to reciprocity agreements. Part-time tuition and fees vary according to course load and reciprocity agreements. ***College room and board:*** $8350; ***Room only:*** $5850. Room and board charges vary according to board plan and housing facility. ***Payment plan:*** Installment.

FRESHMAN FINANCIAL AID (Fall 2007) 846 applied for aid; of those 74% were deemed to have need. 98% of freshmen with need received aid; of those 21% had need fully met. ***Average percent of need met:*** 61% (excluding resources awarded to replace EFC). ***Average financial aid package:*** $7687 (excluding resources awarded to replace EFC). 7% of all full-time freshmen had no need and received non-need-based gift aid.

UNDERGRADUATE FINANCIAL AID (Fall 2007) 3,158 applied for aid; of those 75% were deemed to have need. 99% of undergraduates with need received aid; of those 19% had need fully met. ***Average percent of need met:*** 61% (excluding resources awarded to replace EFC). ***Average financial aid package:*** $7944 (excluding resources awarded to replace EFC). 6% of all full-time undergraduates had no need and received non-need-based gift aid.

GIFT AID (NEED-BASED) ***Total amount:*** $6,798,052 (41% federal, 8% state, 51% institutional). ***Receiving aid:*** Freshmen: 32% (346); all full-time undergraduates: 33% (1,338). ***Average award:*** Freshmen: $5580; Undergraduates: $5028. ***Scholarships, grants, and awards:*** Federal Pell, FSEOG, state, private, college/university gift aid from institutional funds.

GIFT AID (NON-NEED-BASED) ***Total amount:*** $2,936,617 (79% institutional, 21% external sources). ***Receiving aid:*** Freshmen: 23% (255). Undergraduates: 20% (809). ***Average award:*** Freshmen: $2334. Undergraduates: $2329. ***Scholarships, grants, and awards by category:*** *Academic interests/achievement:* 505 awards ($845,233 total): business, communication, education, English, general academic interests/achievements, health fields, mathematics, physical sciences, social sciences. *Creative arts/performance:* 20 awards ($40,000 total): creative writing, dance, music, theater/drama. *Special characteristics:* 31 awards ($74,346 total): children of faculty/staff, international students. ***Tuition waivers:*** Full or partial for employees or children of employees, senior citizens. ***ROTC:*** Army cooperative, Air Force cooperative.

LOANS ***Student loans:*** $25,850,355 (37% need-based, 63% non-need-based). 80% of past graduating class borrowed through all loan programs. *Average indebtedness per student:* $26,636. ***Average need-based loan:*** Freshmen: $3450. Undergraduates: $4117. ***Parent loans:*** $6,998,607 (100% non-need-based). ***Programs:*** Federal Direct (Subsidized and Unsubsidized Stafford, PLUS), Perkins.

WORK-STUDY ***Federal work-study:*** Total amount: $2,858,864; 1,637 jobs averaging $1749.

APPLYING FOR FINANCIAL AID ***Required financial aid form:*** FAFSA. ***Financial aid deadline (priority):*** 3/1. ***Notification date:*** Continuous beginning 3/1. Students must reply by 5/1.

CONTACT June Schlabach, Director of Financial Aid, Plymouth State University, 17 High Street, Plymouth, NH 03264-1595, 603-535-2338 or toll-free 800-842-6900. *Fax:* 603-535-2627. *E-mail:* jlschlabach@plymouth.edu.

POINT LOMA NAZARENE UNIVERSITY

San Diego, CA

Tuition & fees: $25,840 Average undergraduate aid package: $17,282

ABOUT THE INSTITUTION Independent Nazarene, coed. ***Awards:*** bachelor's and master's degrees and post-master's certificates. 59 undergraduate majors. ***Total enrollment:*** 3,490. Undergraduates: 2,394. Freshmen: 538. Federal methodology is used as a basis for awarding need-based institutional aid.

UNDERGRADUATE EXPENSES for 2009–10 ***Application fee:*** $50. ***Comprehensive fee:*** $34,010 includes full-time tuition ($25,300), mandatory fees ($540), and room and board ($8170). ***College room only:*** $4640. ***Part-time tuition:*** $1055 per credit hour.

FRESHMAN FINANCIAL AID (Fall 2008, est.) 421 applied for aid; of those 73% were deemed to have need. 96% of freshmen with need received aid; of those 19% had need fully met. ***Average percent of need met:*** 59% (excluding resources awarded to replace EFC). ***Average financial aid package:*** $15,894 (excluding resources awarded to replace EFC). 18% of all full-time freshmen had no need and received non-need-based gift aid.

UNDERGRADUATE FINANCIAL AID (Fall 2008, est.) 1,634 applied for aid; of those 81% were deemed to have need. 98% of undergraduates with need received aid; of those 23% had need fully met. ***Average percent of need met:*** 65% (excluding resources awarded to replace EFC). ***Average financial aid package:*** $17,282 (excluding resources awarded to replace EFC). 22% of all full-time undergraduates had no need and received non-need-based gift aid.

GIFT AID (NEED-BASED) ***Total amount:*** $13,739,688 (13% federal, 28% state, 49% institutional, 10% external sources). ***Receiving aid:*** Freshmen: 49% (265); all full-time undergraduates: 54% (1,172). ***Average award:*** Freshmen: $12,531; Undergraduates: $12,357. ***Scholarships, grants, and awards:*** Federal Pell, FSEOG, state, private, college/university gift aid from institutional funds.

GIFT AID (NON-NEED-BASED) ***Total amount:*** $4,548,176 (1% state, 72% institutional, 27% external sources). ***Receiving aid:*** Freshmen: 5% (29). Undergraduates: 6% (121). ***Average award:*** Freshmen: $5086. Undergraduates: $6015. ***Scholarships, grants, and awards by category:*** *Academic interests/achievement:* biological sciences, business, communication, education, engineering/technologies, general academic interests/achievements, health fields, home economics, humanities, mathematics, religion/biblical studies, social sciences. *Creative arts/performance:* art/fine arts, debating, music, theater/drama. ***ROTC:*** Army cooperative, Naval cooperative, Air Force cooperative.

LOANS ***Student loans:*** $16,187,486 (68% need-based, 32% non-need-based). 88% of past graduating class borrowed through all loan programs. *Average indebtedness per student:* $21,744. ***Average need-based loan:*** Freshmen: $5160. Undergraduates: $6442. ***Parent loans:*** $5,706,277 (51% need-based, 49% non-need-based). ***Programs:*** FFEL (Subsidized and Unsubsidized Stafford, PLUS), Perkins, Federal Nursing.

WORK-STUDY ***Federal work-study:*** Total amount: $900,291; jobs available.

ATHLETIC AWARDS Total amount: $1,821,568 (39% need-based, 61% non-need-based).

APPLYING FOR FINANCIAL AID ***Required financial aid forms:*** FAFSA, institution's own form. ***Financial aid deadline (priority):*** 3/2. ***Notification date:*** Continuous.

CONTACT Student Financial Services, Point Loma Nazarene University, 3900 Lomaland Drive, San Diego, CA 92106, 619-849-2538 or toll-free 800-733-7770. *Fax:* 619-849-7017.

POINT PARK UNIVERSITY
Pittsburgh, PA

Tuition & fees: $20,570 **Average undergraduate aid package: $14,211**

ABOUT THE INSTITUTION Independent, coed. ***Awards:*** associate, bachelor's, and master's degrees and post-bachelor's and post-master's certificates. 57 undergraduate majors. ***Total enrollment:*** 3,846. Undergraduates: 3,326. Freshmen: 538. Federal methodology is used as a basis for awarding need-based institutional aid.

UNDERGRADUATE EXPENSES for 2008–09 ***Application fee:*** $40. ***Comprehensive fee:*** $29,510 includes full-time tuition ($19,980), mandatory fees ($590), and room and board ($8940). ***College room only:*** $4220. Full-time tuition and fees vary according to program. Room and board charges vary according to board plan and housing facility. ***Part-time tuition:*** $552 per credit. ***Part-time fees:*** $20 per credit. Part-time tuition and fees vary according to program. ***Payment plans:*** Installment, deferred payment.

FRESHMAN FINANCIAL AID (Fall 2008, est.) 503 applied for aid; of those 82% were deemed to have need. 99% of freshmen with need received aid; of those 19% had need fully met. ***Average percent of need met:*** 70% (excluding resources awarded to replace EFC). ***Average financial aid package:*** $17,126 (excluding resources awarded to replace EFC). 34% of all full-time freshmen had no need and received non-need-based gift aid.

UNDERGRADUATE FINANCIAL AID (Fall 2008, est.) 2,520 applied for aid; of those 84% were deemed to have need. 99% of undergraduates with need received aid; of those 13% had need fully met. ***Average percent of need met:*** 62% (excluding resources awarded to replace EFC). ***Average financial aid package:*** $14,211 (excluding resources awarded to replace EFC). 22% of all full-time undergraduates had no need and received non-need-based gift aid.

GIFT AID (NEED-BASED) ***Total amount:*** $19,125,352 (21% federal, 16% state, 52% institutional, 11% external sources). ***Receiving aid:*** Freshmen: 49% (410); all full-time undergraduates: 69% (2,060). ***Average award:*** Freshmen: $11,830; Undergraduates: $8693. ***Scholarships, grants, and awards:*** Federal Pell, FSEOG, state, private, college/university gift aid from institutional funds.

GIFT AID (NON-NEED-BASED) ***Total amount:*** $6,650,979 (6% federal, 4% state, 53% institutional, 37% external sources). ***Receiving aid:*** Freshmen: 6% (46). Undergraduates: 5% (141). ***Average award:*** Freshmen: $4766. Undergraduates: $4383. ***Scholarships, grants, and awards by category:*** *Academic interests/achievement:* 1,014 awards ($3,041,750 total): general academic interests/achievements. *Creative arts/performance:* 772 awards ($2,749,512 total): cinema/film/broadcasting, dance, journalism/publications, performing arts, theater/drama. *Special achievements/activities:* 1,299 awards ($904,500 total): community service, junior miss. *Special characteristics:* 335 awards ($977,943 total): adult students, children and siblings of alumni, children of faculty/staff, international students, members of minority groups, previous college experience, siblings of current students. ***Tuition waivers:*** Full or partial for children of alumni, employees or children of employees. ***ROTC:*** Army cooperative, Air Force cooperative.

LOANS ***Student loans:*** $27,990,112 (71% need-based, 29% non-need-based). 84% of past graduating class borrowed through all loan programs. *Average indebtedness per student:* $31,149. ***Average need-based loan:*** Freshmen: $4745. Undergraduates: $5225. ***Parent loans:*** $4,843,268 (43% need-based, 57% non-need-based). ***Programs:*** FFEL (Subsidized and Unsubsidized Stafford, PLUS), Perkins.

WORK-STUDY ***Federal work-study:*** Total amount: $288,187; 187 jobs averaging $2289. ***State or other work-study/employment:*** Total amount: $3,129,625 (61% need-based, 39% non-need-based). 304 part-time jobs averaging $2571.

ATHLETIC AWARDS Total amount: $1,146,260 (68% need-based, 32% non-need-based).

APPLYING FOR FINANCIAL AID ***Required financial aid form:*** FAFSA. ***Financial aid deadline:*** 5/1 (priority: 5/1). ***Notification date:*** Continuous. Students must reply by 8/30.

CONTACT Sandra M. Cronin, Director of Financial Aid, Point Park University, 201 Wood Street, Pittsburgh, PA 15222-1984, 412-392-3930 or toll-free 800-321-0129. *E-mail:* scronin@pointpark.edu.

POLYTECHNIC INSTITUTE OF NYU
Brooklyn, NY

Tuition & fees: $32,644 **Average undergraduate aid package: $25,997**

ABOUT THE INSTITUTION Independent, coed. ***Awards:*** bachelor's, master's, and doctoral degrees and post-bachelor's certificates. 14 undergraduate majors. ***Total enrollment:*** 3,983. Undergraduates: 1,541. Freshmen: 292. Federal methodology is used as a basis for awarding need-based institutional aid.

UNDERGRADUATE EXPENSES for 2008–09 ***Application fee:*** $50. ***Comprehensive fee:*** $41,365 includes full-time tuition ($31,538), mandatory fees ($1106), and room and board ($8721). ***College room only:*** $6721. Full-time tuition and fees vary according to course load. Room and board charges vary according to housing facility. ***Part-time tuition:*** $1003 per credit. ***Part-time fees:*** $404 per year. Part-time tuition and fees vary according to course load. ***Payment plans:*** Guaranteed tuition, installment, deferred payment.

FRESHMAN FINANCIAL AID (Fall 2008, est.) 288 applied for aid; of those 75% were deemed to have need. 100% of freshmen with need received aid; of those 70% had need fully met. ***Average percent of need met:*** 95% (excluding resources awarded to replace EFC). ***Average financial aid package:*** $27,210 (excluding resources awarded to replace EFC). 24% of all full-time freshmen had no need and received non-need-based gift aid.

UNDERGRADUATE FINANCIAL AID (Fall 2008, est.) 1,387 applied for aid; of those 73% were deemed to have need. 100% of undergraduates with need received aid; of those 60% had need fully met. ***Average percent of need met:*** 90% (excluding resources awarded to replace EFC). ***Average financial aid package:*** $25,997 (excluding resources awarded to replace EFC). 23% of all full-time undergraduates had no need and received non-need-based gift aid.

GIFT AID (NEED-BASED) ***Total amount:*** $8,999,314 (36% federal, 26% state, 38% institutional). ***Receiving aid:*** Freshmen: 66% (194); all full-time undergraduates: 60% (886). ***Average award:*** Freshmen: $12,293; Undergraduates: $9770. ***Scholarships, grants, and awards:*** Federal Pell, FSEOG, state, private, college/university gift aid from institutional funds, United Negro College Fund.

GIFT AID (NON-NEED-BASED) ***Total amount:*** $17,673,405 (1% state, 98% institutional, 1% external sources). ***Receiving aid:*** Freshmen: 57% (167). Undergraduates: 51% (757). ***Average award:*** Freshmen: $17,434. Undergraduates: $17,217. ***Scholarships, grants, and awards by category:*** *Academic interests/achievement:* computer science, engineering/technologies, general academic interests/achievements. *Special characteristics:* members of minority groups. ***Tuition waivers:*** Full or partial for employees or children of employees. ***ROTC:*** Army cooperative, Air Force cooperative.

LOANS ***Student loans:*** $9,130,917 (56% need-based, 44% non-need-based). 67% of past graduating class borrowed through all loan programs. *Average indebtedness per student:* $26,619. ***Average need-based loan:*** Freshmen: $4729. Undergraduates: $5705. ***Parent loans:*** $1,214,628 (100% non-need-based). ***Programs:*** FFEL (Subsidized and Unsubsidized Stafford, PLUS), Perkins, college/university, alternative loans.

WORK-STUDY ***Federal work-study:*** Total amount: $496,451; 221 jobs averaging $1861.

APPLYING FOR FINANCIAL AID ***Required financial aid forms:*** FAFSA, state aid form. ***Financial aid deadline:*** Continuous. ***Notification date:*** Continuous beginning 2/15. Students must reply by 5/1 or within 2 weeks of notification.

CONTACT Ms. Christine Falzerano, Director of Financial Aid, Polytechnic Institute of NYU, 6 Metrotech Center, Brooklyn, NY 11201-2990, 718-260-3333 or toll-free 800-POLYTECH. *Fax:* 718-260-3052. *E-mail:* cfalzera@poly.edu.

POLYTECHNIC UNIVERSITY OF PUERTO RICO
Hato Rey, PR

CONTACT Lidia L. Cruz, Financial Aid Administrator, Polytechnic University of Puerto Rico, 377 Ponce de Leon Avenue, Hato Rey, PR 00919, 787-754-8000 Ext. 253. *Fax:* 787-766-1163.

POMONA COLLEGE
Claremont, CA

Tuition & fees: $35,625 **Average undergraduate aid package: $35,817**

ABOUT THE INSTITUTION Independent, coed. ***Awards:*** bachelor's degrees. 54 undergraduate majors. ***Total enrollment:*** 1,532. Undergraduates: 1,532. Freshmen: 382. Both federal and institutional methodology are used as a basis for awarding need-based institutional aid.

UNDERGRADUATE EXPENSES for 2008–09 ***Application fee:*** $65. ***Comprehensive fee:*** $47,845 includes full-time tuition ($35,318), mandatory fees ($307), and room and board ($12,220). Room and board charges vary according to board plan. ***Payment plan:*** Installment.

FRESHMAN FINANCIAL AID (Fall 2008, est.) 240 applied for aid; of those 80% were deemed to have need. 100% of freshmen with need received aid; of those 100% had need fully met. ***Average percent of need met:*** 100% (excluding resources awarded to replace EFC). ***Average financial aid package:*** $36,232 (excluding resources awarded to replace EFC).

UNDERGRADUATE FINANCIAL AID (Fall 2008, est.) 1,052 applied for aid; of those 75% were deemed to have need. 100% of undergraduates with need received aid; of those 100% had need fully met. ***Average percent of need met:*** 100% (excluding resources awarded to replace EFC). ***Average financial aid package:*** $35,817 (excluding resources awarded to replace EFC).

GIFT AID (NEED-BASED) ***Total amount:*** $26,846,242 (5% federal, 2% state, 91% institutional, 2% external sources). ***Receiving aid:*** Freshmen: 51% (193); all full-time undergraduates: 52% (787). ***Average award:*** Freshmen: $34,389; Undergraduates: $34,114. ***Scholarships, grants, and awards:*** Federal Pell, FSEOG, state, private, college/university gift aid from institutional funds.

GIFT AID (NON-NEED-BASED) ***Total amount:*** $992,000 (100% external sources). ***Tuition waivers:*** Full or partial for employees or children of employees. ***ROTC:*** Army cooperative, Air Force cooperative.

LOANS ***Student loans:*** $751,000 (100% non-need-based). 53% of past graduating class borrowed through all loan programs. *Average indebtedness per student:* $11,300. ***Parent loans:*** $2,103,000 (100% non-need-based). ***Programs:*** FFEL (Subsidized and Unsubsidized Stafford, PLUS), Perkins, college/university.

WORK-STUDY ***Federal work-study:*** Total amount: $239,000; 207 jobs averaging $1154. ***State or other work-study/employment:*** Total amount: $1,261,000 (60% need-based, 40% non-need-based). 504 part-time jobs averaging $1740.

APPLYING FOR FINANCIAL AID ***Required financial aid forms:*** FAFSA, CSS Financial Aid PROFILE, state aid form, business/farm supplement. ***Financial aid deadline:*** 2/1. ***Notification date:*** 4/10. Students must reply by 5/1.

CONTACT Mary Booker, Director of Financial Aid, Pomona College, 550 North College Avenue, Claremont, CA 91711, 909-621-8205. *Fax:* 909-607-7941. *E-mail:* financial_aid@pomadm.pomona.edu.

PONTIFICAL CATHOLIC UNIVERSITY OF PUERTO RICO

Ponce, PR

CONTACT Mrs. Margaret Alustiza, Director of Financial Aid, Pontifical Catholic University of Puerto Rico, 2250 Las Americas Avenue, Suite 549, Ponce, PR 00717-0777, 787-841-2000 Ext. 1065 or toll-free 800-981-5040. *Fax:* 787-651-2041. *E-mail:* malustiza@pucpr.edu.

PONTIFICAL COLLEGE JOSEPHINUM

Columbus, OH

ABOUT THE INSTITUTION Independent Roman Catholic, men only. ***Awards:*** bachelor's, master's, and first professional degrees. 6 undergraduate majors. ***Total enrollment:*** 164. Undergraduates: 115. Freshmen: 11.

GIFT AID (NEED-BASED) ***Scholarships, grants, and awards:*** Federal Pell, FSEOG, state, private, college/university gift aid from institutional funds.

GIFT AID (NON-NEED-BASED) ***Scholarships, grants, and awards by category:*** *Special characteristics:* local/state students.

LOANS ***Programs:*** FFEL (Subsidized and Unsubsidized Stafford, PLUS), Perkins.

WORK-STUDY ***Federal work-study:*** Total amount: $4200; 6 jobs averaging $640.

APPLYING FOR FINANCIAL AID ***Required financial aid forms:*** FAFSA, institution's own form.

CONTACT Marky Leichtnam, Financial Aid Director, Pontifical College Josephinum, 7625 North High Street, Columbus, OH 43235-1498, 614-985-2212 or toll-free 888-252-5812. *Fax:* 614-885-2307. *E-mail:* mleichtnam@pcj.edu.

PORTLAND STATE UNIVERSITY

Portland, OR

Tuition & fees (OR res): $6147 **Average undergraduate aid package: $9042**

ABOUT THE INSTITUTION State-supported, coed. ***Awards:*** bachelor's, master's, and doctoral degrees and post-bachelor's certificates. 63 undergraduate majors. ***Total enrollment:*** 26,382. Undergraduates: 20,330. Freshmen: 1,766. Federal methodology is used as a basis for awarding need-based institutional aid.

UNDERGRADUATE EXPENSES for 2008–09 ***Application fee:*** $50. ***One-time required fee:*** $250. ***Tuition, state resident:*** full-time $4905; part-time $109 per credit hour. ***Tuition, nonresident:*** full-time $17,595; part-time $391 per credit hour. ***Required fees:*** full-time $1242; $16.50 per credit hour or $50 per term. Full-time tuition and fees vary according to program and reciprocity agreements. Part-time tuition and fees vary according to course level. ***College room and board:*** $9486; ***Room only:*** $6687. Room and board charges vary according to board plan and housing facility. ***Payment plan:*** Installment.

FRESHMAN FINANCIAL AID (Fall 2008, est.) 1,098 applied for aid; of those 77% were deemed to have need. 99% of freshmen with need received aid; of those 19% had need fully met. ***Average percent of need met:*** 64% (excluding resources awarded to replace EFC). ***Average financial aid package:*** $8262 (excluding resources awarded to replace EFC). 4% of all full-time freshmen had no need and received non-need-based gift aid.

UNDERGRADUATE FINANCIAL AID (Fall 2008, est.) 8,260 applied for aid; of those 86% were deemed to have need. 100% of undergraduates with need received aid; of those 14% had need fully met. ***Average percent of need met:*** 67% (excluding resources awarded to replace EFC). ***Average financial aid package:*** $9042 (excluding resources awarded to replace EFC). 2% of all full-time undergraduates had no need and received non-need-based gift aid.

GIFT AID (NEED-BASED) ***Total amount:*** $38,501,806 (61% federal, 32% state, 2% institutional, 5% external sources). ***Receiving aid:*** Freshmen: 36% (571); all full-time undergraduates: 41% (5,139). ***Average award:*** Freshmen: $5837; Undergraduates: $6050. ***Scholarships, grants, and awards:*** Federal Pell, FSEOG, state, private, college/university gift aid from institutional funds, United Negro College Fund.

GIFT AID (NON-NEED-BASED) ***Total amount:*** $2,741,733 (78% institutional, 22% external sources). ***Receiving aid:*** Freshmen: 9% (141). Undergraduates: 4% (493). ***Average award:*** Freshmen: $2603. Undergraduates: $3721. ***Scholarships, grants, and awards by category:*** *Academic interests/achievement:* architecture, area/ethnic studies, business, computer science, education, engineering/technologies, foreign languages, general academic interests/achievements, humanities, international studies, physical sciences, social sciences. *Creative arts/performance:* art/fine arts, general creative arts/performance, music, theater/drama. *Special achievements/activities:* community service, general special achievements/activities, leadership, memberships. *Special characteristics:* adult students, ethnic background, handicapped students, international students, members of minority groups, out-of-state students. ***Tuition waivers:*** Full or partial for minority students, employees or children of employees, senior citizens. ***ROTC:*** Army, Air Force cooperative.

LOANS ***Student loans:*** $76,956,989 (100% need-based). 58% of past graduating class borrowed through all loan programs. *Average indebtedness per student:* $19,512. ***Average need-based loan:*** Freshmen: $3447. Undergraduates: $4529. ***Parent loans:*** $3,994,401 (100% need-based). ***Programs:*** Federal Direct (Subsidized and Unsubsidized Stafford, PLUS), FFEL (Subsidized and Unsubsidized Stafford, PLUS), Perkins, state.

WORK-STUDY ***Federal work-study:*** Total amount: $2,128,832; 758 jobs averaging $2626.

ATHLETIC AWARDS Total amount: $2,474,691 (100% need-based).

APPLYING FOR FINANCIAL AID ***Required financial aid form:*** FAFSA. ***Financial aid deadline (priority):*** 5/28. ***Notification date:*** Continuous. Students must reply within 4 weeks of notification.

CONTACT Phillip Rodgers, Director of Financial Aid, Portland State University, PO Box 751, Portland, OR 97207-0751, 800-547-8887. *Fax:* 503-725-5965. *E-mail:* askfa@pdx.edu.

POST UNIVERSITY

Waterbury, CT

Tuition & fees: $23,325 **Average undergraduate aid package: $13,550**

ABOUT THE INSTITUTION Independent, coed. 23 undergraduate majors. Federal methodology is used as a basis for awarding need-based institutional aid.

UNDERGRADUATE EXPENSES for 2008–09 ***Comprehensive fee:*** $32,325 includes full-time tuition ($22,500), mandatory fees ($825), and room and board ($9000). ***College room only:*** $4860. Full-time tuition and fees vary according to degree level and program. Room and board charges vary according to housing facility. ***Part-time tuition:*** $747 per credit. Part-time tuition and fees vary according to class time, course load, degree level, and program. ***Payment plan:*** Installment.

FRESHMAN FINANCIAL AID (Fall 2008, est.) 251 applied for aid; of those 100% were deemed to have need. 100% of freshmen with need received aid; of those 1% had need fully met. ***Average percent of need met:*** 78% (excluding resources awarded to replace EFC). ***Average financial aid package:*** $16,087 (excluding resources awarded to replace EFC).

UNDERGRADUATE FINANCIAL AID (Fall 2008, est.) 940 applied for aid; of those 100% were deemed to have need. 100% of undergraduates with need received aid; of those 1% had need fully met. ***Average percent of need met:*** 78% (excluding resources awarded to replace EFC). ***Average financial aid package:*** $13,550 (excluding resources awarded to replace EFC).

GIFT AID (NEED-BASED) ***Total amount:*** $8,062,284 (24% federal, 11% state, 59% institutional, 6% external sources). ***Receiving aid:*** Freshmen: 93% (239); all full-time undergraduates: 75% (718). ***Average award:*** Freshmen: $12,165; Undergraduates: $10,633. ***Scholarships, grants, and awards:*** Federal Pell, FSEOG, state, private, college/university gift aid from institutional funds.

GIFT AID (NON-NEED-BASED) ***Receiving aid:*** Freshmen: 12% (31). Undergraduates: 10% (98). ***Scholarships, grants, and awards by category:*** *Academic interests/achievement:* 173 awards ($634,408 total): agriculture, biological sciences, business, communication, computer science, education, English, general academic interests/achievements, humanities, international studies, social sciences. *Special characteristics:* 492 awards ($1,274,893 total): children and siblings of alumni, local/state students, siblings of current students. ***Tuition waivers:*** Full or partial for employees or children of employees, senior citizens.

LOANS ***Student loans:*** $11,656,885 (100% need-based). 89% of past graduating class borrowed through all loan programs. *Average indebtedness per student:* $18,000. ***Average need-based loan:*** Freshmen: $3032. Undergraduates: $4391. ***Parent loans:*** $1,649,652 (100% need-based). ***Programs:*** FFEL (Subsidized and Unsubsidized Stafford, PLUS), Perkins, college/university.

WORK-STUDY ***Federal work-study:*** Total amount: $242,000; 132 jobs averaging $1833. ***State or other work-study/employment:*** Total amount: $19,000 (100% need-based). 11 part-time jobs averaging $1727.

ATHLETIC AWARDS Total amount: $783,920 (100% need-based).

APPLYING FOR FINANCIAL AID ***Required financial aid form:*** FAFSA. ***Financial aid deadline (priority):*** 3/1. ***Notification date:*** Continuous beginning 4/1. Students must reply within 2 weeks of notification.

CONTACT Regina Faulds, Director of Financial Aid, Post University, 800 Country Club Road, Waterbury, CT 06723-2540, 203-596-4528 or toll-free 800-345-2562. *Fax:* 203-596-4599. *E-mail:* rfaulds@post.edu.

POTOMAC COLLEGE

Washington, DC

CONTACT Phyllis Crews, Financial Aid Counselor, Potomac College, 4000 Chesapeake Street NW, Washington, DC 20016, 202-686-0876 or toll-free 888-686-0876. *Fax:* 202-686-0818. *E-mail:* pcrews@potomac.edu.

PRAIRIE VIEW A&M UNIVERSITY

Prairie View, TX

CONTACT Mr. A. D. James Jr., Executive Director, Student Financial Services and Scholarships, Prairie View A&M University, PO Box 2967, Prairie View, TX 77446-2967, 936-857-2423. *Fax:* 936-857-2425. *E-mail:* ad_james@pvamu.edu.

PRATT INSTITUTE

Brooklyn, NY

Tuition & fees: $34,880 **Average undergraduate aid package: $13,863**

ABOUT THE INSTITUTION Independent, coed. ***Awards:*** associate, bachelor's, and master's degrees and post-master's certificates (Associate). 26 undergraduate majors. ***Total enrollment:*** 4,763. Undergraduates: 3,109. Freshmen: 647. Federal methodology is used as a basis for awarding need-based institutional aid.

UNDERGRADUATE EXPENSES for 2009–10 ***Application fee:*** $50. ***Comprehensive fee:*** $44,636 includes full-time tuition ($33,500), mandatory fees ($1380), and room and board ($9756). ***College room only:*** $6156. ***Part-time tuition:*** $1085 per credit.

FRESHMAN FINANCIAL AID (Fall 2008, est.) 481 applied for aid; of those 85% were deemed to have need. 100% of freshmen with need received aid. ***Average percent of need met:*** 69% (excluding resources awarded to replace EFC). ***Average financial aid package:*** $13,142 (excluding resources awarded to replace EFC). 27% of all full-time freshmen had no need and received non-need-based gift aid.

UNDERGRADUATE FINANCIAL AID (Fall 2008, est.) 2,032 applied for aid; of those 90% were deemed to have need. 100% of undergraduates with need received aid. ***Average percent of need met:*** 56% (excluding resources awarded to replace EFC). ***Average financial aid package:*** $13,863 (excluding resources awarded to replace EFC). 17% of all full-time undergraduates had no need and received non-need-based gift aid.

GIFT AID (NEED-BASED) ***Total amount:*** $15,571,438 (19% federal, 6% state, 73% institutional, 2% external sources). ***Receiving aid:*** Freshmen: 53% (335); all full-time undergraduates: 60% (1,755). ***Average award:*** Freshmen: $8431; Undergraduates: $8270. ***Scholarships, grants, and awards:*** state, college/university gift aid from institutional funds.

GIFT AID (NON-NEED-BASED) ***Total amount:*** $16,449,718 (100% institutional). ***Receiving aid:*** Freshmen: 37% (238). Undergraduates: 51% (1,481). ***Average award:*** Freshmen: $7960. Undergraduates: $7750.

LOANS ***Student loans:*** $22,423,130 (60% need-based, 40% non-need-based). 65% of past graduating class borrowed through all loan programs. *Average indebtedness per student:* $27,125. ***Average need-based loan:*** Freshmen: $5663. Undergraduates: $6742. ***Parent loans:*** $12,240,826 (100% need-based).

WORK-STUDY ***Federal work-study:*** Total amount: $788,133; jobs available.

APPLYING FOR FINANCIAL AID ***Required financial aid form:*** FAFSA. ***Financial aid deadline (priority):*** 2/1.

CONTACT Karen Price-Scott, Director of Financial Aid, Pratt Institute, 200 Willoughby Avenue, Brooklyn, NY 11205-3899, 718-636-3519 or toll-free 800-331-0834. *Fax:* 718-636-3739. *E-mail:* kpricesc@pratt.edu.

PRESBYTERIAN COLLEGE

Clinton, SC

Tuition & fees: $28,880 **Average undergraduate aid package: $27,061**

ABOUT THE INSTITUTION Independent religious, coed. ***Awards:*** bachelor's degrees. 35 undergraduate majors. ***Total enrollment:*** 1,174. Undergraduates: 1,174. Freshmen: 324. Federal methodology is used as a basis for awarding need-based institutional aid.

UNDERGRADUATE EXPENSES for 2009–10 ***Application fee:*** $40. ***Comprehensive fee:*** $37,225 includes full-time tuition ($26,436), mandatory fees ($2444), and room and board ($8345). ***Part-time tuition:*** $1102 per credit hour. ***Part-time fees:*** $17 per credit hour; $22 per term.

FRESHMAN FINANCIAL AID (Fall 2008, est.) 262 applied for aid; of those 79% were deemed to have need. 100% of freshmen with need received aid; of those 58% had need fully met. ***Average percent of need met:*** 89% (excluding resources awarded to replace EFC). ***Average financial aid package:*** $27,546 (excluding resources awarded to replace EFC). 33% of all full-time freshmen had no need and received non-need-based gift aid.

UNDERGRADUATE FINANCIAL AID (Fall 2008, est.) 861 applied for aid; of those 82% were deemed to have need. 100% of undergraduates with need received aid; of those 56% had need fully met. ***Average percent of need met:*** 88% (excluding resources awarded to replace EFC). ***Average financial aid package:*** $27,061 (excluding resources awarded to replace EFC). 32% of all full-time undergraduates had no need and received non-need-based gift aid.

GIFT AID (NEED-BASED) ***Total amount:*** $11,843,320 (6% federal, 30% state, 62% institutional, 2% external sources). ***Receiving aid:*** Freshmen: 64% (207); all full-time undergraduates: 63% (704). ***Average award:*** Freshmen: $20,428; Undergraduates: $20,308. ***Scholarships, grants, and awards:*** Federal Pell, FSEOG, state, private, college/university gift aid from institutional funds.

GIFT AID (NON-NEED-BASED) ***Total amount:*** $8,943,413 (12% state, 79% institutional, 9% external sources). ***Receiving aid:*** Freshmen: 36% (115). Undergraduates: 32% (356). ***Average award:*** Freshmen: $12,124. Undergraduates: $12,004. ***Scholarships, grants, and awards by category:*** *Academic interests/achievement:* general academic interests/achievements. *Creative arts/*

performance: music. *Special achievements/activities:* leadership, religious involvement. *Special characteristics:* children of faculty/staff, relatives of clergy, religious affiliation. ***ROTC:*** Army.

LOANS ***Student loans:*** $3,511,537 (47% need-based, 53% non-need-based). 57% of past graduating class borrowed through all loan programs. *Average indebtedness per student:* $21,236. ***Average need-based loan:*** Freshmen: $3104. Undergraduates: $3794. ***Parent loans:*** $1,006,940 (20% need-based, 80% non-need-based). ***Programs:*** FFEL (Subsidized and Unsubsidized Stafford, PLUS), college/university, State and private loans.

WORK-STUDY ***Federal work-study:*** Total amount: $130,727; jobs available.

ATHLETIC AWARDS Total amount: $4,705,447 (47% need-based, 53% non-need-based).

APPLYING FOR FINANCIAL AID ***Required financial aid form:*** FAFSA. ***Financial aid deadline:*** 6/30 (priority: 3/15).

CONTACT Mr. Jeff Holliday, Director of Financial Aid, Presbyterian College, 503 South Broad Street, Clinton, SC 29325, 864-833-8287 or toll-free 800-476-7272. *Fax:* 864-833-8481. *E-mail:* jsholli@presby.edu.

PRESCOTT COLLEGE

Prescott, AZ

Tuition & fees: $21,792 **Average undergraduate aid package: $10,721**

ABOUT THE INSTITUTION Independent, coed. ***Awards:*** bachelor's, master's, and doctoral degrees and post-bachelor's and post-master's certificates. 96 undergraduate majors. ***Total enrollment:*** 1,065. Undergraduates: 754. Freshmen: 89. Federal methodology is used as a basis for awarding need-based institutional aid.

UNDERGRADUATE EXPENSES for 2008–09 ***Application fee:*** $25. ***One-time required fee:*** $1040. ***Tuition:*** full-time $21,492; part-time $597 per term. ***Required fees:*** full-time $300; $150 per term. Full-time tuition and fees vary according to course load and degree level. ***Payment plans:*** Installment, deferred payment.

FRESHMAN FINANCIAL AID (Fall 2008, est.) 50 applied for aid; of those 82% were deemed to have need. 100% of freshmen with need received aid; of those 5% had need fully met. ***Average percent of need met:*** 55% (excluding resources awarded to replace EFC). ***Average financial aid package:*** $12,786 (excluding resources awarded to replace EFC). 39% of all full-time freshmen had no need and received non-need-based gift aid.

UNDERGRADUATE FINANCIAL AID (Fall 2008, est.) 456 applied for aid; of those 92% were deemed to have need. 100% of undergraduates with need received aid; of those 4% had need fully met. ***Average percent of need met:*** 45% (excluding resources awarded to replace EFC). ***Average financial aid package:*** $10,721 (excluding resources awarded to replace EFC). 21% of all full-time undergraduates had no need and received non-need-based gift aid.

GIFT AID (NEED-BASED) ***Total amount:*** $2,782,517 (36% federal, 3% state, 55% institutional, 6% external sources). ***Receiving aid:*** Freshmen: 58% (41); all full-time undergraduates: 63% (351). ***Average award:*** Freshmen: $9589; Undergraduates: $7329. ***Scholarships, grants, and awards:*** Federal Pell, FSEOG, state, private, college/university gift aid from institutional funds.

GIFT AID (NON-NEED-BASED) ***Total amount:*** $814,680 (1% state, 81% institutional, 18% external sources). ***Receiving aid:*** Freshmen: 1% (1). Undergraduates: 1% (5). ***Average award:*** Freshmen: $6516. Undergraduates: $4559. ***Tuition waivers:*** Full or partial for employees or children of employees.

LOANS ***Student loans:*** $5,482,202 (86% need-based, 14% non-need-based). 38% of past graduating class borrowed through all loan programs. *Average indebtedness per student:* $16,952. ***Average need-based loan:*** Freshmen: $3052. Undergraduates: $4372. ***Parent loans:*** $2,617,987 (35% need-based, 65% non-need-based). ***Programs:*** Federal Direct (Subsidized and Unsubsidized Stafford, PLUS), Perkins, state.

WORK-STUDY ***Federal work-study:*** Total amount: $122,444; 176 jobs averaging $1500. ***State or other work-study/employment:*** 72 part-time jobs averaging $1121.

APPLYING FOR FINANCIAL AID ***Required financial aid form:*** FAFSA. ***Financial aid deadline (priority):*** 4/1. ***Notification date:*** Continuous beginning 4/1. Students must reply within 12 weeks of notification.

CONTACT Financial Aid Office, Prescott College, 220 Grove Avenue, Prescott, AZ 86301-2990, 928-350-1111 or toll-free 800-628-6364. *Fax:* 928-776-5225. *E-mail:* finaid@prescott.edu.

PRESENTATION COLLEGE

Aberdeen, SD

Tuition & fees: $14,250 **Average undergraduate aid package: $8737**

ABOUT THE INSTITUTION Independent Roman Catholic, coed, primarily women. ***Awards:*** associate and bachelor's degrees. 16 undergraduate majors. ***Total enrollment:*** 733. Undergraduates: 733. Freshmen: 83. Federal methodology is used as a basis for awarding need-based institutional aid.

UNDERGRADUATE EXPENSES for 2009–10 ***Application fee:*** $25. ***Comprehensive fee:*** $19,750 includes full-time tuition ($14,250) and room and board ($5500). ***College room only:*** $4100. ***Part-time tuition:*** $525 per credit.

FRESHMAN FINANCIAL AID (Fall 2007) 82 applied for aid; of those 89% were deemed to have need. 100% of freshmen with need received aid; of those 16% had need fully met. ***Average percent of need met:*** 54% (excluding resources awarded to replace EFC). ***Average financial aid package:*** $8457 (excluding resources awarded to replace EFC). 11% of all full-time freshmen had no need and received non-need-based gift aid.

UNDERGRADUATE FINANCIAL AID (Fall 2007) 494 applied for aid; of those 95% were deemed to have need. 100% of undergraduates with need received aid; of those 14% had need fully met. ***Average percent of need met:*** 43% (excluding resources awarded to replace EFC). ***Average financial aid package:*** $8737 (excluding resources awarded to replace EFC). 5% of all full-time undergraduates had no need and received non-need-based gift aid.

GIFT AID (NEED-BASED) ***Total amount:*** $1,603,459 (74% federal, 15% state, 11% institutional). ***Receiving aid:*** Freshmen: 49% (40); all full-time undergraduates: 62% (305). ***Average award:*** Freshmen: $3672; Undergraduates: $3769. ***Scholarships, grants, and awards:*** Federal Pell, FSEOG, state, private, college/university gift aid from institutional funds.

GIFT AID (NON-NEED-BASED) ***Total amount:*** $1,176,683 (53% institutional, 47% external sources). ***Receiving aid:*** Freshmen: 66% (54). Undergraduates: 58% (287). ***Average award:*** Freshmen: $2878. Undergraduates: $2814. ***Scholarships, grants, and awards by category:*** *Special achievements/activities:* 72 awards ($47,517 total): community service, general special achievements/activities, leadership, religious involvement. *Special characteristics:* children of faculty/staff.

LOANS ***Student loans:*** $4,714,439 (58% need-based, 42% non-need-based). 83% of past graduating class borrowed through all loan programs. *Average indebtedness per student:* $27,430. ***Average need-based loan:*** Freshmen: $3679. Undergraduates: $3741. ***Parent loans:*** $300,255 (100% non-need-based). ***Programs:*** FFEL (Subsidized and Unsubsidized Stafford, PLUS), Perkins, state, college/university.

WORK-STUDY ***Federal work-study:*** Total amount: $104,950; 56 jobs averaging $1874. ***State or other work-study/employment:*** Total amount: $76,050 (19% need-based, 81% non-need-based). 39 part-time jobs averaging $1950.

APPLYING FOR FINANCIAL AID ***Required financial aid forms:*** FAFSA, state aid form. ***Financial aid deadline (priority):*** 3/1. ***Notification date:*** Continuous beginning 4/1. Students must reply within 2 weeks of notification.

CONTACT Ms. Janel Wagner, Director of Financial Aid, Presentation College, 1500 North Main Street, Aberdeen, SD 57401-1299, 605-229-8427 or toll-free 800-437-6060. *Fax:* 605-229-8537. *E-mail:* janel.wagner@presentation.edu.

PRINCETON UNIVERSITY

Princeton, NJ

Tuition & fees: $34,290 **Average undergraduate aid package: $32,707**

ABOUT THE INSTITUTION Independent, coed. ***Awards:*** bachelor's, master's, and doctoral degrees. 35 undergraduate majors. ***Total enrollment:*** 7,497. Undergraduates: 4,981. Freshmen: 1,243.

UNDERGRADUATE EXPENSES for 2008–09 ***Application fee:*** $65. ***Comprehensive fee:*** $45,695 includes full-time tuition ($34,290) and room and board ($11,405). ***College room only:*** $6205. Room and board charges vary according to board plan. ***Payment plans:*** Installment, deferred payment.

FRESHMAN FINANCIAL AID (Fall 2007) 793 applied for aid; of those 85% were deemed to have need. 100% of freshmen with need received aid; of those 100% had need fully met. ***Average percent of need met:*** 100% (excluding resources awarded to replace EFC). ***Average financial aid package:*** $32,424 (excluding resources awarded to replace EFC).

UNDERGRADUATE FINANCIAL AID (Fall 2007) 2,842 applied for aid; of those 90% were deemed to have need. 100% of undergraduates with need received aid; of those 100% had need fully met. ***Average percent of need met:*** 100% (excluding resources awarded to replace EFC). ***Average financial aid package:*** $32,707 (excluding resources awarded to replace EFC).

GIFT AID (NEED-BASED) ***Total amount:*** $80,635,152 (3% federal, 1% state, 92% institutional, 4% external sources). ***Receiving aid:*** Freshmen: 54% (671); all full-time undergraduates: 53% (2,572). ***Average award:*** Freshmen: $31,187; Undergraduates: $31,351. ***Scholarships, grants, and awards:*** Federal Pell, FSEOG, state, private, college/university gift aid from institutional funds.

GIFT AID (NON-NEED-BASED) ***Tuition waivers:*** Full or partial for employees or children of employees. ***ROTC:*** Army, Air Force cooperative.

LOANS ***Student loans:*** 22% of past graduating class borrowed through all loan programs. *Average indebtedness per student:* $5955. ***Parent loans:*** $2,066,977 (100% non-need-based). ***Programs:*** FFEL (Subsidized and Unsubsidized Stafford, PLUS), Perkins, college/university.

WORK-STUDY ***Federal work-study:*** Total amount: $1,037,789; 780 jobs averaging $1330. ***State or other work-study/employment:*** Total amount: $1,211,726 (100% need-based). 959 part-time jobs averaging $1263.

APPLYING FOR FINANCIAL AID ***Required financial aid forms:*** FAFSA, institution's own form. ***Financial aid deadline (priority):*** 2/1. ***Notification date:*** 4/1. Students must reply by 5/1.

CONTACT Robin Moscato, Director of Financial Aid, Princeton University, Box 591, Princeton, NJ 08542, 609-258-3330. *Fax:* 609-258-0336. *E-mail:* moscato@princeton.edu.

PRINCIPIA COLLEGE

Elsah, IL

Tuition & fees: $22,650 **Average undergraduate aid package: $24,335**

ABOUT THE INSTITUTION Independent Christian Science, coed. 28 undergraduate majors. Institutional methodology is used as a basis for awarding need-based institutional aid.

UNDERGRADUATE EXPENSES for 2008–09 ***One-time required fee:*** $300. ***Comprehensive fee:*** $31,125 includes full-time tuition ($22,650) and room and board ($8475). ***College room only:*** $4125. Full-time tuition and fees vary according to course load. ***Payment plan:*** Installment.

FRESHMAN FINANCIAL AID (Fall 2008, est.) 110 applied for aid; of those 88% were deemed to have need. 100% of freshmen with need received aid; of those 100% had need fully met. ***Average percent of need met:*** 100% (excluding resources awarded to replace EFC). ***Average financial aid package:*** $23,743 (excluding resources awarded to replace EFC). 23% of all full-time freshmen had no need and received non-need-based gift aid.

UNDERGRADUATE FINANCIAL AID (Fall 2008, est.) 360 applied for aid; of those 88% were deemed to have need. 100% of undergraduates with need received aid; of those 100% had need fully met. ***Average percent of need met:*** 100% (excluding resources awarded to replace EFC). ***Average financial aid package:*** $24,335 (excluding resources awarded to replace EFC). 26% of all full-time undergraduates had no need and received non-need-based gift aid.

GIFT AID (NEED-BASED) ***Total amount:*** $6,917,483 (100% institutional). ***Receiving aid:*** Freshmen: 69% (97); all full-time undergraduates: 62% (316). ***Average award:*** Freshmen: $20,688; Undergraduates: $21,427. ***Scholarships, grants, and awards:*** private, college/university gift aid from institutional funds.

GIFT AID (NON-NEED-BASED) ***Total amount:*** $1,492,878 (100% institutional). ***Receiving aid:*** Freshmen: 17% (24). Undergraduates: 18% (92). ***Average award:*** Freshmen: $15,231. Undergraduates: $15,799. ***Scholarships, grants, and awards by category:*** *Academic interests/achievement:* 99 awards ($1,569,164 total): general academic interests/achievements. *Special characteristics:* 61 awards ($427,783 total): children and siblings of alumni, children of faculty/staff. ***Tuition waivers:*** Full or partial for employees or children of employees.

LOANS ***Student loans:*** $1,129,858 (100% need-based). 57% of past graduating class borrowed through all loan programs. *Average indebtedness per student:* $15,784. ***Average need-based loan:*** Freshmen: $3054. Undergraduates: $2908. ***Programs:*** college/university.

WORK-STUDY ***State or other work-study/employment:*** Total amount: $160,299 (100% need-based). 135 part-time jobs averaging $1187.

APPLYING FOR FINANCIAL AID ***Required financial aid forms:*** institution's own form, CSS Financial Aid PROFILE, income tax form(s). ***Financial aid deadline:*** 3/1. ***Notification date:*** Continuous beginning 3/15. Students must reply by 5/1 or within 4 weeks of notification.

CONTACT Tami Gavaletz, Director of Financial Aid, Principia College, 1 Maybeck Place, Elsah, IL 62028-9799, 618-374-5187 or toll-free 800-277-4648 Ext. 2802. *Fax:* 618-374-5906. *E-mail:* tami.gavaletz@principia.edu.

PROVIDENCE COLLEGE

Providence, RI

Tuition & fees: $31,394 **Average undergraduate aid package: $18,500**

ABOUT THE INSTITUTION Independent Roman Catholic, coed. ***Awards:*** associate, bachelor's, and master's degrees. 46 undergraduate majors. ***Total enrollment:*** 4,673. Undergraduates: 3,938. Freshmen: 988. Both federal and institutional methodology are used as a basis for awarding need-based institutional aid.

UNDERGRADUATE EXPENSES for 2008–09 ***Application fee:*** $55. ***Comprehensive fee:*** $42,204 includes full-time tuition ($30,800), mandatory fees ($594), and room and board ($10,810). ***College room only:*** $6160. Room and board charges vary according to board plan and housing facility. ***Part-time tuition:*** $1027 per credit. ***Payment plan:*** Installment.

FRESHMAN FINANCIAL AID (Fall 2008, est.) 730 applied for aid; of those 69% were deemed to have need. 100% of freshmen with need received aid; of those 40% had need fully met. ***Average percent of need met:*** 76% (excluding resources awarded to replace EFC). ***Average financial aid package:*** $19,380 (excluding resources awarded to replace EFC). 10% of all full-time freshmen had no need and received non-need-based gift aid.

UNDERGRADUATE FINANCIAL AID (Fall 2008, est.) 2,615 applied for aid; of those 81% were deemed to have need. 100% of undergraduates with need received aid; of those 27% had need fully met. ***Average percent of need met:*** 76% (excluding resources awarded to replace EFC). ***Average financial aid package:*** $18,500 (excluding resources awarded to replace EFC). 8% of all full-time undergraduates had no need and received non-need-based gift aid.

GIFT AID (NEED-BASED) ***Total amount:*** $29,134,604 (9% federal, 1% state, 86% institutional, 4% external sources). ***Receiving aid:*** Freshmen: 44% (428); all full-time undergraduates: 52% (2,023). ***Average award:*** Freshmen: $15,100; Undergraduates: $12,607. ***Scholarships, grants, and awards:*** Federal Pell, FSEOG, state, private, college/university gift aid from institutional funds, Academic Competitiveness Grant, National Smart Grant.

GIFT AID (NON-NEED-BASED) ***Total amount:*** $7,993,873 (92% institutional, 8% external sources). ***Receiving aid:*** Freshmen: 6% (55). Undergraduates: 6% (241). ***Average award:*** Freshmen: $21,895. Undergraduates: $20,233. ***Scholarships, grants, and awards by category:*** *Academic interests/achievement:* 400 awards ($3,750,000 total): business, general academic interests/achievements, military science, premedicine. *Creative arts/performance:* 5 awards ($15,000 total): theater/drama. *Special achievements/activities:* 20 awards ($100,000 total): community service. ***Tuition waivers:*** Full or partial for employees or children of employees, senior citizens. ***ROTC:*** Army.

LOANS ***Student loans:*** $24,840,571 (48% need-based, 52% non-need-based). 64% of past graduating class borrowed through all loan programs. *Average indebtedness per student:* $33,297. ***Average need-based loan:*** Freshmen: $4135. Undergraduates: $4909. ***Parent loans:*** $9,813,378 (70% need-based, 30% non-need-based). ***Programs:*** Federal Direct (Subsidized and Unsubsidized Stafford, PLUS), FFEL (Subsidized and Unsubsidized Stafford, PLUS), Perkins.

WORK-STUDY ***Federal work-study:*** Total amount: $1,740,726; 700 jobs averaging $1800. ***State or other work-study/employment:*** Total amount: $800,000 (100% non-need-based). 700 part-time jobs averaging $1800.

ATHLETIC AWARDS Total amount: $5,411,076 (8% need-based, 92% non-need-based).

APPLYING FOR FINANCIAL AID ***Required financial aid forms:*** FAFSA, CSS Financial Aid PROFILE, business/farm supplement. ***Financial aid deadline:*** 2/1. ***Notification date:*** 4/1. Students must reply by 5/1.

CONTACT Ms. Sandra J. Oliveira, Executive Director of Financial Aid, Providence College, 1 Cunningham Square, Providence, RI 02918, 401-865-2286 or toll-free 800-721-6444. *Fax:* 401-865-1186. *E-mail:* solivei6@providence.edu.

PURCHASE COLLEGE, STATE UNIVERSITY OF NEW YORK

Purchase, NY

Tuition & fees (NY res): $6421 **Average undergraduate aid package: $8725**

ABOUT THE INSTITUTION State-supported, coed. ***Awards:*** bachelor's and master's degrees and post-master's certificates. 43 undergraduate majors. ***Total enrollment:*** 4,251. Undergraduates: 4,106. Freshmen: 709. Federal methodology is used as a basis for awarding need-based institutional aid.

UNDERGRADUATE EXPENSES for 2009–10 ***Application fee:*** $40. ***One-time required fee:*** $200. ***Tuition, state resident:*** full-time $4970; part-time $207 per credit. ***Tuition, nonresident:*** full-time $12,870; part-time $536 per credit. ***Required fees:*** full-time $1451; $.85 per credit. ***College room and board:*** $9908; ***Room only:*** $6240.

FRESHMAN FINANCIAL AID (Fall 2008, est.) 597 applied for aid; of those 66% were deemed to have need. 100% of freshmen with need received aid; of those 7% had need fully met. ***Average percent of need met:*** 56% (excluding resources awarded to replace EFC). ***Average financial aid package:*** $7473 (excluding resources awarded to replace EFC). 5% of all full-time freshmen had no need and received non-need-based gift aid.

UNDERGRADUATE FINANCIAL AID (Fall 2008, est.) 2,555 applied for aid; of those 73% were deemed to have need. 99% of undergraduates with need received aid; of those 9% had need fully met. ***Average percent of need met:*** 61% (excluding resources awarded to replace EFC). ***Average financial aid package:*** $8725 (excluding resources awarded to replace EFC). 8% of all full-time undergraduates had no need and received non-need-based gift aid.

GIFT AID (NEED-BASED) ***Total amount:*** $7,917,734 (46% federal, 40% state, 10% institutional, 4% external sources). ***Receiving aid:*** Freshmen: 42% (308); all full-time undergraduates: 42% (1,534). ***Average award:*** Freshmen: $5218; Undergraduates: $4917. ***Scholarships, grants, and awards:*** Federal Pell, FSEOG, state, private, college/university gift aid from institutional funds.

GIFT AID (NON-NEED-BASED) ***Total amount:*** $1,067,478 (29% state, 55% institutional, 16% external sources). ***Receiving aid:*** Freshmen: 3% (23). Undergraduates: 3% (102). ***Average award:*** Freshmen: $2135. Undergraduates: $1814. ***Scholarships, grants, and awards by category:*** *Academic interests/achievement:* area/ethnic studies, biological sciences, computer science, English, general academic interests/achievements, humanities, mathematics, social sciences. *Creative arts/performance:* art/fine arts, cinema/film/broadcasting, creative writing, dance, general creative arts/performance, music, performing arts, theater/drama.

LOANS ***Student loans:*** $14,392,923 (51% need-based, 49% non-need-based). 59% of past graduating class borrowed through all loan programs. *Average indebtedness per student:* $20,209. ***Average need-based loan:*** Freshmen: $3501. Undergraduates: $4737. ***Parent loans:*** $4,754,588 (63% need-based, 37% non-need-based). ***Programs:*** FFEL (Subsidized and Unsubsidized Stafford, PLUS), Perkins.

WORK-STUDY ***Federal work-study:*** Total amount: $93,512; jobs available. ***State or other work-study/employment:*** Total amount: $746,133 (35% need-based, 65% non-need-based). Part-time jobs available.

APPLYING FOR FINANCIAL AID ***Required financial aid forms:*** FAFSA, state aid form, state aid form (for NY residents only). ***Financial aid deadline (priority):*** 3/15. ***Notification date:*** Continuous. Students must reply within 2 weeks of notification.

CONTACT Ms. Corey York, Director of Student Financial Services, Purchase College, State University of New York, 735 Anderson Hill Road, Purchase, NY 10577-1400, 914-251-6085. *Fax:* 914-251-6099. *E-mail:* corey.york@purchase.edu.

PURDUE UNIVERSITY

West Lafayette, IN

Tuition & fees (IN res): $7750 **Average undergraduate aid package: $9734**

ABOUT THE INSTITUTION State-supported, coed. ***Awards:*** associate, bachelor's, master's, doctoral, and first professional degrees. 145 undergraduate majors. ***Total enrollment:*** 40,090. Undergraduates: 31,761. Freshmen: 6,840. Federal methodology is used as a basis for awarding need-based institutional aid.

UNDERGRADUATE EXPENSES for 2008–09 ***Application fee:*** $30. ***Tuition, state resident:*** full-time $7317; part-time $278 per credit hour. ***Tuition, nonresident:*** full-time $22,791; part-time $771 per credit hour. ***Required fees:*** full-time $433. Full-time tuition and fees vary according to course load and program. Part-time tuition and fees vary according to course load. ***College room and board:*** $7930; ***Room only:*** $3410. Room and board charges vary according to board plan and housing facility. ***Payment plan:*** Installment.

FRESHMAN FINANCIAL AID (Fall 2008, est.) 5,047 applied for aid; of those 66% were deemed to have need. 100% of freshmen with need received aid; of those 33% had need fully met. ***Average percent of need met:*** 95% (excluding resources awarded to replace EFC). ***Average financial aid package:*** $9716 (excluding resources awarded to replace EFC). 11% of all full-time freshmen had no need and received non-need-based gift aid.

UNDERGRADUATE FINANCIAL AID (Fall 2008, est.) 18,646 applied for aid; of those 71% were deemed to have need. 100% of undergraduates with need received aid; of those 28% had need fully met. ***Average percent of need met:*** 94% (excluding resources awarded to replace EFC). ***Average financial aid package:*** $9734 (excluding resources awarded to replace EFC). 7% of all full-time undergraduates had no need and received non-need-based gift aid.

GIFT AID (NEED-BASED) ***Total amount:*** $66,331,435 (34% federal, 30% state, 30% institutional, 6% external sources). ***Receiving aid:*** Freshmen: 32% (2,253); all full-time undergraduates: 30% (9,077). ***Average award:*** Freshmen: $9045; Undergraduates: $8288. ***Scholarships, grants, and awards:*** Federal Pell, FSEOG, state, private, college/university gift aid from institutional funds, Academic Competitiveness Grant, National Smart Grant.

GIFT AID (NON-NEED-BASED) ***Total amount:*** $34,095,196 (27% federal, 6% state, 45% institutional, 22% external sources). ***Receiving aid:*** Freshmen: 18% (1,253). Undergraduates: 11% (3,294). ***Average award:*** Freshmen: $6975. Undergraduates: $5158. ***Scholarships, grants, and awards by category:*** *Academic interests/achievement:* agriculture, computer science, education, engineering/technologies, general academic interests/achievements, health fields, humanities, mathematics, military science, physical sciences. *Creative arts/performance:* music. *Special achievements/activities:* leadership. *Special characteristics:* children of faculty/staff. ***Tuition waivers:*** Full or partial for employees or children of employees, senior citizens. ***ROTC:*** Army, Naval, Air Force.

LOANS ***Student loans:*** $137,242,661 (55% need-based, 45% non-need-based). 52% of past graduating class borrowed through all loan programs. *Average indebtedness per student:* $23,087. ***Average need-based loan:*** Freshmen: $3392. Undergraduates: $4124. ***Parent loans:*** $145,433,323 (19% need-based, 81% non-need-based). ***Programs:*** Federal Direct (Subsidized and Unsubsidized Stafford, PLUS), Perkins, college/university.

WORK-STUDY ***Federal work-study:*** Total amount: $1,127,697; 749 jobs averaging $1506.

ATHLETIC AWARDS Total amount: $6,682,873 (18% need-based, 82% non-need-based).

APPLYING FOR FINANCIAL AID ***Required financial aid form:*** FAFSA. ***Financial aid deadline (priority):*** 3/1. ***Notification date:*** 4/15.

CONTACT Division of Financial Aid, Purdue University, Schleman Hall of Student Services, Room 305, West Lafayette, IN 47907-2050, 765-494-5056. *Fax:* 765-494-6707.

PURDUE UNIVERSITY CALUMET

Hammond, IN

Tuition & fees (IN res): $5757 **Average undergraduate aid package: $6249**

ABOUT THE INSTITUTION State-supported, coed. ***Awards:*** associate, bachelor's, and master's degrees and post-bachelor's certificates. 44 undergraduate majors. ***Total enrollment:*** 9,325. Undergraduates: 8,353. Freshmen: 1,382. Federal methodology is used as a basis for awarding need-based institutional aid.

UNDERGRADUATE EXPENSES for 2008–09 ***Tuition, state resident:*** full-time $5757; part-time $192 per credit hour. ***Tuition, nonresident:*** full-time $12,285; part-time $425 per credit hour. ***Required fees:*** $17.20 per credit hour. Full-time tuition and fees vary according to program. Part-time tuition and fees vary according to course load and program. ***College room and board:*** $6155; ***Room only:*** $4270. Room and board charges vary according to housing facility. ***Payment plan:*** Deferred payment.

FRESHMAN FINANCIAL AID (Fall 2007) 920 applied for aid; of those 78% were deemed to have need. 89% of freshmen with need received aid; of those 1% had need fully met. ***Average percent of need met:*** 18% (excluding resources awarded to replace EFC). ***Average financial aid package:*** $3479 (excluding resources awarded to replace EFC). 6% of all full-time freshmen had no need and received non-need-based gift aid.

UNDERGRADUATE FINANCIAL AID (Fall 2007) 4,447 applied for aid; of those 82% were deemed to have need. 92% of undergraduates with need received aid; of those 1% had need fully met. ***Average percent of need met:*** 20% (excluding resources awarded to replace EFC). ***Average financial aid package:*** $6249 (excluding resources awarded to replace EFC). 4% of all full-time undergraduates had no need and received non-need-based gift aid.

GIFT AID (NEED-BASED) ***Total amount:*** $12,884,275 (63% federal, 36% state, 1% institutional). ***Receiving aid:*** Freshmen: 34% (430); all full-time undergraduates: 38% (2,372). ***Average award:*** Freshmen: $2812; Undergraduates: $4612. ***Scholarships, grants, and awards:*** Federal Pell, FSEOG, state, private, college/university gift aid from institutional funds.

GIFT AID (NON-NEED-BASED) ***Total amount:*** $2,524,761 (15% state, 58% institutional, 27% external sources). ***Receiving aid:*** Freshmen: 13% (159). Undergraduates: 9% (588). ***Average award:*** Freshmen: $1338. Undergraduates: $1922. ***Scholarships, grants, and awards by category:*** *Academic interests/achievement:* 663 awards ($1,460,988 total): general academic interests/achievements. ***Tuition waivers:*** Full or partial for employees or children of employees, senior citizens.

LOANS ***Student loans:*** $22,842,053 (93% need-based, 7% non-need-based). 58% of past graduating class borrowed through all loan programs. *Average indebtedness per student:* $19,090. ***Average need-based loan:*** Freshmen: $1816. Undergraduates: $3302. ***Parent loans:*** $1,525,382 (100% need-based). ***Programs:*** Federal Direct (Subsidized and Unsubsidized Stafford, PLUS), Perkins.

WORK-STUDY ***Federal work-study:*** Total amount: $164,226; 122 jobs averaging $1518. ***State or other work-study/employment:*** Part-time jobs available.

ATHLETIC AWARDS Total amount: $22,070 (100% non-need-based).

APPLYING FOR FINANCIAL AID ***Required financial aid form:*** FAFSA. ***Financial aid deadline (priority):*** 3/10. ***Notification date:*** Continuous beginning 4/15. Students must reply within 2 weeks of notification.

CONTACT Ms. Tanika House, Assistant Director of Financial Aid, Purdue University Calumet, 2200 169th Street, Hammond, IN 46323-2094, 219-989-2301 or toll-free 800-447-8738 (in-state). *Fax:* 219-989-2141. *E-mail:* finaid@calumet.purdue.edu.

PURDUE UNIVERSITY NORTH CENTRAL

Westville, IN

Tuition & fees (IN res): $6080 **Average undergraduate aid package: $6925**

ABOUT THE INSTITUTION State-supported, coed. ***Awards:*** associate, bachelor's, and master's degrees and post-bachelor's certificates. 24 undergraduate majors. ***Total enrollment:*** 4,245. Undergraduates: 4,142. Freshmen: 856. Federal methodology is used as a basis for awarding need-based institutional aid.

UNDERGRADUATE EXPENSES for 2008–09 ***Tuition, state resident:*** full-time $5447; part-time $181.55 per credit hour. ***Tuition, nonresident:*** full-time $8125; part-time $452.40 per credit hour. ***Required fees:*** full-time $633; $21.10 per credit hour. Full-time tuition and fees vary according to course load, location, and program. Part-time tuition and fees vary according to course load, location, and program. ***Payment plan:*** Installment.

FRESHMAN FINANCIAL AID (Fall 2008, est.) 562 applied for aid; of those 79% were deemed to have need. 91% of freshmen with need received aid; of those 13% had need fully met. ***Average percent of need met:*** 36% (excluding resources awarded to replace EFC). ***Average financial aid package:*** $5857 (excluding resources awarded to replace EFC). 4% of all full-time freshmen had no need and received non-need-based gift aid.

UNDERGRADUATE FINANCIAL AID (Fall 2008, est.) 1,880 applied for aid; of those 82% were deemed to have need. 95% of undergraduates with need received aid; of those 4% had need fully met. ***Average percent of need met:*** 41% (excluding resources awarded to replace EFC). ***Average financial aid package:*** $6925 (excluding resources awarded to replace EFC). 2% of all full-time undergraduates had no need and received non-need-based gift aid.

GIFT AID (NEED-BASED) ***Total amount:*** $6,281,117 (54% federal, 45% state, 1% institutional). ***Receiving aid:*** Freshmen: 28% (212); all full-time undergraduates: 32% (809). ***Average award:*** Freshmen: $3960; Undergraduates: $4202. ***Scholarships, grants, and awards:*** Federal Pell, FSEOG, state, private, college/university gift aid from institutional funds.

GIFT AID (NON-NEED-BASED) ***Total amount:*** $380,022 (66% institutional, 34% external sources). ***Receiving aid:*** Freshmen: 29% (222). Undergraduates: 30% (756). ***Average award:*** Freshmen: $1401. Undergraduates: $1288. ***Scholarships, grants, and awards by category:*** *Academic interests/achievement:* business, education, English, general academic interests/achievements, health fields. *Special achievements/activities:* general special achievements/activities, leadership. *Special characteristics:* adult students, children of faculty/staff, veterans' children. ***Tuition waivers:*** Full or partial for employees or children of employees.

LOANS ***Student loans:*** $13,467,108 (44% need-based, 56% non-need-based). 61% of past graduating class borrowed through all loan programs. *Average indebtedness per student:* $19,536. ***Average need-based loan:*** Freshmen: $3092. Undergraduates: $3898. ***Parent loans:*** $486,700 (100% non-need-based). ***Programs:*** FFEL (Subsidized and Unsubsidized Stafford, PLUS), Perkins, alternative loans.

WORK-STUDY ***Federal work-study:*** Total amount: $62,411; jobs available. ***State or other work-study/employment:*** Part-time jobs available.

ATHLETIC AWARDS Total amount: $33,275 (100% non-need-based).

APPLYING FOR FINANCIAL AID ***Required financial aid form:*** FAFSA. ***Financial aid deadline:*** 6/30 (priority: 3/10). ***Notification date:*** Continuous beginning 4/15. Students must reply by 8/10.

CONTACT Bryant Dabney, Director of Financial Aid, Purdue University North Central, 1401 South US Highway 421, Westville, IN 46391-9528, 219-785-5749 or toll-free 800-872-1231 (in-state). *Fax:* 219-785-5538. *E-mail:* bdabney@pnc.edu.

QUEENS COLLEGE OF THE CITY UNIVERSITY OF NEW YORK

Flushing, NY

CONTACT Office of Financial Aid Services, Queens College of the City University of New York, 65-30 Kissena Boulevard, Flushing, NY 11367-1597, 718-997-5100.

QUEENS UNIVERSITY OF CHARLOTTE

Charlotte, NC

CONTACT Lauren H. Mack, Director of Financial Aid, Queens University of Charlotte, 1900 Selwyn Avenue, Charlotte, NC 28274-0002, 704-337-2230 or toll-free 800-849-0202. *Fax:* 704-337-2416. *E-mail:* mackl@queens.edu.

QUINCY UNIVERSITY

Quincy, IL

ABOUT THE INSTITUTION Independent Roman Catholic, coed. ***Awards:*** associate, bachelor's, and master's degrees. 32 undergraduate majors. ***Total enrollment:*** 1,424. Undergraduates: 1,144. Freshmen: 246.

GIFT AID (NEED-BASED) ***Scholarships, grants, and awards:*** Federal Pell, FSEOG, state, private, college/university gift aid from institutional funds.

GIFT AID (NON-NEED-BASED) ***Scholarships, grants, and awards by category:*** *Academic interests/achievement:* biological sciences, business, communication, computer science, education, English, general academic interests/achievements, health fields, international studies, mathematics, premedicine, religion/biblical studies, social sciences. *Creative arts/performance:* art/fine arts, cinema/film/broadcasting, music. *Special achievements/activities:* community service, leadership. *Special characteristics:* children of faculty/staff.

LOANS ***Programs:*** FFEL (Subsidized and Unsubsidized Stafford, PLUS), Perkins.

WORK-STUDY ***Federal work-study:*** Total amount: $374,834; 398 jobs averaging $2000. ***State or other work-study/employment:*** 35 part-time jobs averaging $3000.

APPLYING FOR FINANCIAL AID ***Required financial aid form:*** FAFSA.

CONTACT Kevin Brown, Director of Financial Aid, Quincy University, 1800 College Avenue, Quincy, IL 62301-2699, 217-228-5260 or toll-free 800-688-4295. *Fax:* 217-228-5635. *E-mail:* brownke@quincy.edu.

QUINNIPIAC UNIVERSITY

Hamden, CT

Tuition & fees: $32,400 **Average undergraduate aid package: $18,306**

ABOUT THE INSTITUTION Independent, coed. ***Awards:*** bachelor's, master's, doctoral, and first professional degrees and post-bachelor's certificates. 59 undergraduate majors. ***Total enrollment:*** 7,434. Undergraduates: 5,891. Freshmen: 1,484. Federal methodology is used as a basis for awarding need-based institutional aid.

UNDERGRADUATE EXPENSES for 2009–10 ***Application fee:*** $45. ***Comprehensive fee:*** $44,780 includes full-time tuition ($31,100), mandatory fees ($1300), and room and board ($12,380). ***Part-time tuition:*** $750 per credit. ***Part-time fees:*** $30 per credit.

FRESHMAN FINANCIAL AID (Fall 2008, est.) 1,111 applied for aid; of those 75% were deemed to have need. 100% of freshmen with need received aid; of those 16% had need fully met. ***Average percent of need met:*** 69% (excluding resources awarded to replace EFC). ***Average financial aid package:*** $18,592 (excluding resources awarded to replace EFC). 16% of all full-time freshmen had no need and received non-need-based gift aid.

UNDERGRADUATE FINANCIAL AID (Fall 2008, est.) 3,849 applied for aid; of those 82% were deemed to have need. 100% of undergraduates with need received aid; of those 14% had need fully met. ***Average percent of need met:*** 66% (excluding resources awarded to replace EFC). ***Average financial aid package:*** $18,306 (excluding resources awarded to replace EFC). 13% of all full-time undergraduates had no need and received non-need-based gift aid.

GIFT AID (NEED-BASED) ***Total amount:*** $29,968,193 (9% federal, 10% state, 77% institutional, 4% external sources). ***Receiving aid:*** Freshmen: 55% (817); all full-time undergraduates: 55% (3,056). ***Average award:*** Freshmen: $13,813; Undergraduates: $13,020. ***Scholarships, grants, and awards:*** Federal Pell, FSEOG, state, private, college/university gift aid from institutional funds.

GIFT AID (NON-NEED-BASED) ***Total amount:*** $16,711,949 (98% institutional, 2% external sources). ***Receiving aid:*** Freshmen: 28% (422). Undergraduates: 22% (1,241). ***Average award:*** Freshmen: $10,265. Undergraduates: $9065. ***Scholarships, grants, and awards by category:*** *Academic interests/achievement:* 1,678 awards ($15,675,083 total): general academic interests/achievements. *Special characteristics:* 341 awards ($2,429,002 total): children of faculty/staff, international students, siblings of current students. ***ROTC:*** Army cooperative, Air Force cooperative.

LOANS ***Student loans:*** $36,525,018 (66% need-based, 34% non-need-based). 70% of past graduating class borrowed through all loan programs. *Average indebtedness per student:* $37,849. ***Average need-based loan:*** Freshmen: $3567. Undergraduates: $4546. ***Parent loans:*** $10,526,331 (100% non-need-based). ***Programs:*** Federal Direct (Subsidized and Unsubsidized Stafford, PLUS), FFEL (Subsidized and Unsubsidized Stafford, PLUS), Perkins, Federal Nursing.

WORK-STUDY ***Federal work-study:*** Total amount: $3,011,798; 1,467 jobs averaging $2011. ***State or other work-study/employment:*** Total amount: $95,675 (100% need-based). 53 part-time jobs averaging $1814.

ATHLETIC AWARDS Total amount: $6,685,248 (100% non-need-based).

APPLYING FOR FINANCIAL AID ***Required financial aid form:*** FAFSA. ***Financial aid deadline (priority):*** 3/1. ***Notification date:*** Continuous beginning 3/1. Students must reply by 5/1 or within 2 weeks of notification.

CONTACT Mr. Dominic Yoia, Senior Director of Financial Aid, Quinnipiac University, 275 Mount Carmel Avenue, Hamden, CT 06518, 203-582-5224 or toll-free 800-462-1944 (out-of-state). *Fax:* 203-582-5238. *E-mail:* finaid@quinnipiac.edu.

RABBI JACOB JOSEPH SCHOOL

Edison, NJ

CONTACT Financial Aid Office, Rabbi Jacob Joseph School, One Plainfield Ave, Edison, NJ 08817, 908-985-6533.

RABBINICAL ACADEMY MESIVTA RABBI CHAIM BERLIN

Brooklyn, NY

CONTACT Office of Financial Aid, Rabbinical Academy Mesivta Rabbi Chaim Berlin, 1605 Coney Island Avenue, Brooklyn, NY 11230-4715, 718-377-0777.

RABBINICAL COLLEGE BETH SHRAGA

Monsey, NY

CONTACT Financial Aid Office, Rabbinical College Beth Shraga, 28 Saddle River Road, Monsey, NY 10952-3035, 914-356-1980.

RABBINICAL COLLEGE BOBOVER YESHIVA B'NEI ZION

Brooklyn, NY

CONTACT Financial Aid Office, Rabbinical College Bobover Yeshiva B'nei Zion, 1577 48th Street, Brooklyn, NY 11219, 718-438-2018.

RABBINICAL COLLEGE CH'SAN SOFER

Brooklyn, NY

CONTACT Financial Aid Office, Rabbinical College Ch'san Sofer, 1876 50th Street, Brooklyn, NY 11204, 718-236-1171.

RABBINICAL COLLEGE OF AMERICA

Morristown, NJ

CONTACT Financial Aid Office, Rabbinical College of America, 226 Sussex Avenue, Morristown, NJ 07960, 973-267-9404. *Fax:* 973-267-5208.

RABBINICAL COLLEGE OF LONG ISLAND

Long Beach, NY

CONTACT Rabbi Cone, Financial Aid Administrator, Rabbinical College of Long Island, 201 Magnolia Boulevard, Long Beach, NY 11561-3305, 516-431-7414.

RABBINICAL COLLEGE OF OHR SHIMON YISROEL

Brooklyn, NY

CONTACT Financial Aid Office, Rabbinical College of Ohr Shimon Yisroel, 215-217 Hewes Street, Brooklyn, NY 11211, 718-855-4092.

RABBINICAL COLLEGE OF TELSHE

Wickliffe, OH

CONTACT Financial Aid Office, Rabbinical College of Telshe, 28400 Euclid Avenue, Wickliffe, OH 44092-2523, 216-943-5300.

RABBINICAL SEMINARY ADAS YEREIM

Brooklyn, NY

CONTACT Mr. Israel Weingarten, Financial Aid Administrator, Rabbinical Seminary Adas Yereim, 185 Wilson Street, Brooklyn, NY 11211-7206, 718-388-1751.

RABBINICAL SEMINARY M'KOR CHAIM

Brooklyn, NY

CONTACT Financial Aid Office, Rabbinical Seminary M'kor Chaim, 1571 55th Street, Brooklyn, NY 11219, 718-851-0183.

RABBINICAL SEMINARY OF AMERICA

Flushing, NY

CONTACT Ms. Leah Eisenstein, Director of Financial Aid, Rabbinical Seminary of America, 92-15 69th Avenue, Forest Hills, NY 11375, 718-268-4700. *Fax:* 718-268-4684.

RADFORD UNIVERSITY

Radford, VA

Tuition & fees (VA res): $6536 **Average undergraduate aid package: $8529**

ABOUT THE INSTITUTION State-supported, coed. ***Awards:*** bachelor's, master's, and doctoral degrees and post-bachelor's and post-master's certificates. 37 undergraduate majors. ***Total enrollment:*** 9,157. Undergraduates: 8,155. Freshmen: 1,875. Federal methodology is used as a basis for awarding need-based institutional aid.

UNDERGRADUATE EXPENSES for 2008–09 ***Application fee:*** $50. ***Tuition, state resident:*** full-time $4187; part-time $174 per credit hour. ***Tuition, nonresident:*** full-time $13,201; part-time $550 per credit hour. ***Required fees:*** full-time $2349; $98 per credit hour. ***College room and board:*** $6716; ***Room only:*** $3556. Room and board charges vary according to board plan and housing facility. ***Payment plan:*** Installment.

FRESHMAN FINANCIAL AID (Fall 2008, est.) 1,217 applied for aid; of those 57% were deemed to have need. 94% of freshmen with need received aid; of those 31% had need fully met. ***Average percent of need met:*** 79% (excluding resources awarded to replace EFC). ***Average financial aid package:*** $7885 (excluding resources awarded to replace EFC). 2% of all full-time freshmen had no need and received non-need-based gift aid.

UNDERGRADUATE FINANCIAL AID (Fall 2008, est.) 4,340 applied for aid; of those 64% were deemed to have need. 95% of undergraduates with need received aid; of those 41% had need fully met. ***Average percent of need met:*** 82% (excluding resources awarded to replace EFC). ***Average financial aid package:*** $8529 (excluding resources awarded to replace EFC). 1% of all full-time undergraduates had no need and received non-need-based gift aid.

GIFT AID (NEED-BASED) ***Total amount:*** $13,706,709 (37% federal, 47% state, 11% institutional, 5% external sources). ***Receiving aid:*** Freshmen: 21% (400); all full-time undergraduates: 20% (1,636). ***Average award:*** Freshmen: $7635; Undergraduates: $7335. ***Scholarships, grants, and awards:*** Federal Pell, FSEOG, state, private, college/university gift aid from institutional funds.

GIFT AID (NON-NEED-BASED) ***Total amount:*** $1,767,411 (29% federal, 14% state, 28% institutional, 29% external sources). ***Receiving aid:*** Freshmen: 5% (92). Undergraduates: 6% (496). ***Average award:*** Freshmen: $4810. Undergraduates: $4211. ***Tuition waivers:*** Full or partial for employees or children of employees, senior citizens. ***ROTC:*** Army.

LOANS ***Student loans:*** $27,496,517 (42% need-based, 58% non-need-based). 88% of past graduating class borrowed through all loan programs. *Average indebtedness per student:* $19,465. ***Average need-based loan:*** Freshmen: $2733. Undergraduates: $3814. ***Parent loans:*** $3,984,649 (46% need-based, 54% non-need-based). ***Programs:*** FFEL (Subsidized and Unsubsidized Stafford, PLUS), Perkins, Federal Nursing, state, college/university.

WORK-STUDY ***Federal work-study:*** Total amount: $748,666; 361 jobs averaging $2358. ***State or other work-study/employment:*** Total amount: $1,545,207 (22% need-based, 78% non-need-based). 511 part-time jobs averaging $2358.

ATHLETIC AWARDS Total amount: $1,575,223 (38% need-based, 62% non-need-based).

APPLYING FOR FINANCIAL AID ***Required financial aid form:*** FAFSA. ***Financial aid deadline (priority):*** 3/1. ***Notification date:*** 4/15. Students must reply within 2 weeks of notification.

CONTACT Mrs. Barbara Porter, Director of Financial Aid, Radford University, PO Box 6905, Radford, VA 24142, 540-831-5408 or toll-free 800-890-4265. *Fax:* 540-831-5138. *E-mail:* bporter@radford.edu.

RAMAPO COLLEGE OF NEW JERSEY

Mahwah, NJ

Tuition & fees (NJ res): $10,765 **Average undergraduate aid package: $10,195**

ABOUT THE INSTITUTION State-supported, coed. ***Awards:*** bachelor's and master's degrees. 35 undergraduate majors. ***Total enrollment:*** 5,847. Undergraduates: 5,561. Freshmen: 880. Federal methodology is used as a basis for awarding need-based institutional aid.

UNDERGRADUATE EXPENSES for 2008–09 ***Application fee:*** $60. ***Tuition, state resident:*** full-time $7459; part-time $233.10 per credit. ***Tuition, nonresident:*** full-time $14,170; part-time $442.80 per credit. ***Required fees:*** full-time $3306; $103.30 per credit. Full-time tuition and fees vary according to reciprocity agreements. Part-time tuition and fees vary according to reciprocity agreements. ***College room and board:*** $10,830; ***Room only:*** $7860. Room and board charges vary according to board plan and housing facility. ***Payment plan:*** Installment.

FRESHMAN FINANCIAL AID (Fall 2008, est.) 698 applied for aid; of those 69% were deemed to have need. 94% of freshmen with need received aid; of those 20% had need fully met. ***Average percent of need met:*** 69% (excluding resources awarded to replace EFC). ***Average financial aid package:*** $11,311 (excluding resources awarded to replace EFC). 5% of all full-time freshmen had no need and received non-need-based gift aid.

UNDERGRADUATE FINANCIAL AID (Fall 2008, est.) 3,541 applied for aid; of those 73% were deemed to have need. 97% of undergraduates with need received aid; of those 5% had need fully met. ***Average percent of need met:*** 68% (excluding resources awarded to replace EFC). ***Average financial aid package:*** $10,195 (excluding resources awarded to replace EFC). 6% of all full-time undergraduates had no need and received non-need-based gift aid.

GIFT AID (NEED-BASED) ***Total amount:*** $8,867,046 (43% federal, 52% state, 5% institutional). ***Receiving aid:*** Freshmen: 23% (203); all full-time undergraduates: 23% (1,116). ***Average award:*** Freshmen: $11,029; Undergraduates: $7941. ***Scholarships, grants, and awards:*** Federal Pell, FSEOG, state, private, college/university gift aid from institutional funds, Federal Nursing.

GIFT AID (NON-NEED-BASED) ***Total amount:*** $6,949,722 (12% state, 77% institutional, 11% external sources). ***Receiving aid:*** Freshmen: 18% (160). Undergraduates: 17% (827). ***Average award:*** Freshmen: $13,375. Undergraduates: $11,999. ***Scholarships, grants, and awards by category:*** *Academic interests/achievement:* 222 awards ($5,931,158 total): general academic interests/achievements. *Special characteristics:* 119 awards ($1,410,361 total): children of faculty/staff, international students, out-of-state students. ***Tuition waivers:*** Full or partial for employees or children of employees, senior citizens. ***ROTC:*** Air Force cooperative.

LOANS ***Student loans:*** $27,441,837 (35% need-based, 65% non-need-based). 55% of past graduating class borrowed through all loan programs. *Average indebtedness per student:* $16,219. ***Average need-based loan:*** Freshmen: $3336. Undergraduates: $4204. ***Parent loans:*** $6,027,257 (100% non-need-based). ***Programs:*** Federal Direct (Subsidized and Unsubsidized Stafford, PLUS), Perkins, state.

WORK-STUDY ***Federal work-study:*** Total amount: $282,468; 143 jobs averaging $1975. ***State or other work-study/employment:*** Total amount: $1,553,619 (100% non-need-based). 718 part-time jobs averaging $2137.

APPLYING FOR FINANCIAL AID ***Required financial aid form:*** FAFSA. ***Financial aid deadline (priority):*** 3/1. ***Notification date:*** Continuous beginning 4/1. Students must reply by 5/1 or within 2 weeks of notification.

CONTACT Bernice Mulch, Assistant Director of Financial Aid, Ramapo College of New Jersey, 505 Ramapo Valley Road, Mahwah, NJ 07430-1680, 201-684-7252 or toll-free 800-9RAMAPO (in-state). *Fax:* 201-684-7085. *E-mail:* finaid@ramapo.edu.

RANDOLPH COLLEGE

Lynchburg, VA

Tuition & fees: $28,430 **Average undergraduate aid package: $23,600**

ABOUT THE INSTITUTION Independent Methodist, coed. ***Awards:*** bachelor's and master's degrees. 36 undergraduate majors. ***Total enrollment:*** 568. Undergraduates: 562. Freshmen: 144. Federal methodology is used as a basis for awarding need-based institutional aid.

UNDERGRADUATE EXPENSES for 2009–10 ***Application fee:*** $35. ***Comprehensive fee:*** $38,145 includes full-time tuition ($27,920), mandatory fees ($510), and room and board ($9715).

FRESHMAN FINANCIAL AID (Fall 2008, est.) 133 applied for aid; of those 83% were deemed to have need. 99% of freshmen with need received aid; of those 28% had need fully met. ***Average percent of need met:*** 85% (excluding resources awarded to replace EFC). ***Average financial aid package:*** $21,432 (excluding resources awarded to replace EFC). 23% of all full-time freshmen had no need and received non-need-based gift aid.

UNDERGRADUATE FINANCIAL AID (Fall 2008, est.) 420 applied for aid; of those 87% were deemed to have need. 99% of undergraduates with need received aid; of those 27% had need fully met. ***Average percent of need met:*** 84% (excluding resources awarded to replace EFC). ***Average financial aid package:*** $23,600 (excluding resources awarded to replace EFC). 32% of all full-time undergraduates had no need and received non-need-based gift aid.

GIFT AID (NEED-BASED) ***Total amount:*** $6,270,454 (10% federal, 8% state, 80% institutional, 2% external sources). ***Receiving aid:*** Freshmen: 74% (107); all full-time undergraduates: 66% (362). ***Average award:*** Freshmen: $16,467; Undergraduates: $17,261. ***Scholarships, grants, and awards:*** Federal Pell, FSEOG, state, private, college/university gift aid from institutional funds.

GIFT AID (NON-NEED-BASED) ***Total amount:*** $3,193,209 (7% state, 91% institutional, 2% external sources). ***Receiving aid:*** Freshmen: 22% (31). Undergraduates: 18% (99). ***Average award:*** Freshmen: $13,228. Undergraduates: $15,500. ***Scholarships, grants, and awards by category:*** *Academic interests/achievement:* 411 awards ($4,986,018 total): biological sciences, education, English, general academic interests/achievements, mathematics, physical sciences, premedicine, social sciences. *Creative arts/performance:* 10 awards

($21,000 total): art/fine arts, creative writing, music, theater/drama. *Special achievements/activities:* 90 awards ($610,875 total): community service, general special achievements/activities, leadership. *Special characteristics:* 189 awards ($1,674,050 total): adult students, children of faculty/staff, international students, local/state students, relatives of clergy, religious affiliation, twins.

LOANS ***Student loans:*** $4,208,998 (67% need-based, 33% non-need-based). 76% of past graduating class borrowed through all loan programs. *Average indebtedness per student:* $27,218. ***Average need-based loan:*** Freshmen: $4947. Undergraduates: $6659. ***Parent loans:*** $842,571 (24% need-based, 76% non-need-based). ***Programs:*** FFEL (Subsidized and Unsubsidized Stafford, PLUS), Perkins.

WORK-STUDY ***Federal work-study:*** Total amount: $260,253; 78 jobs averaging $1860. ***State or other work-study/employment:*** Total amount: $208,445 (9% need-based, 91% non-need-based). 290 part-time jobs averaging $1070.

APPLYING FOR FINANCIAL AID ***Required financial aid forms:*** FAFSA, state aid form. ***Financial aid deadline (priority):*** 3/1. ***Notification date:*** Continuous beginning 3/1. Students must reply by 5/1 or within 2 weeks of notification.

CONTACT Kay G. Mattox, Director of Student Financial Services, Randolph College, 2500 Rivermont Avenue, Lynchburg, VA 24503-1526, 434-947-8128 or toll-free 800-745-7692. *Fax:* 434-947-8996. *E-mail:* kmattox@randolphcollege.edu.

RANDOLPH-MACON COLLEGE

Ashland, VA

Tuition & fees: $28,355 **Average undergraduate aid package: $21,022**

ABOUT THE INSTITUTION Independent United Methodist, coed. ***Awards:*** bachelor's degrees. 27 undergraduate majors. ***Total enrollment:*** 1,201. Undergraduates: 1,201. Freshmen: 362. Federal methodology is used as a basis for awarding need-based institutional aid.

UNDERGRADUATE EXPENSES for 2008–09 ***Application fee:*** $30. ***Comprehensive fee:*** $36,965 includes full-time tuition ($27,570), mandatory fees ($785), and room and board ($8610). ***Part-time tuition:*** $3060 per course. ***Part-time fees:*** $785 per year.

FRESHMAN FINANCIAL AID (Fall 2008, est.) 299 applied for aid; of those 80% were deemed to have need. 100% of freshmen with need received aid; of those 30% had need fully met. ***Average percent of need met:*** 85% (excluding resources awarded to replace EFC). ***Average financial aid package:*** $22,244 (excluding resources awarded to replace EFC). 34% of all full-time freshmen had no need and received non-need-based gift aid.

UNDERGRADUATE FINANCIAL AID (Fall 2008, est.) 862 applied for aid; of those 82% were deemed to have need. 100% of undergraduates with need received aid; of those 27% had need fully met. ***Average percent of need met:*** 80% (excluding resources awarded to replace EFC). ***Average financial aid package:*** $21,022 (excluding resources awarded to replace EFC). 39% of all full-time undergraduates had no need and received non-need-based gift aid.

GIFT AID (NEED-BASED) ***Total amount:*** $11,870,937 (6% federal, 12% state, 76% institutional, 6% external sources). ***Receiving aid:*** Freshmen: 66% (240); all full-time undergraduates: 60% (706). ***Average award:*** Freshmen: $18,143; Undergraduates: $16,942. ***Scholarships, grants, and awards:*** Federal Pell, FSEOG, state, private, college/university gift aid from institutional funds.

GIFT AID (NON-NEED-BASED) ***Total amount:*** $6,332,232 (17% state, 77% institutional, 6% external sources). ***Receiving aid:*** Freshmen: 13% (48). Undergraduates: 10% (116). ***Average award:*** Freshmen: $16,319. Undergraduates: $16,255. ***Scholarships, grants, and awards by category:*** *Academic interests/achievement:* 557 awards ($6,284,467 total): general academic interests/achievements. *Special achievements/activities:* 536 awards ($2,908,631 total): general special achievements/activities. *Special characteristics:* 459 awards ($1,165,626 total): children and siblings of alumni, children of faculty/staff, ethnic background, out-of-state students, relatives of clergy, siblings of current students. ***ROTC:*** Army cooperative.

LOANS ***Student loans:*** $6,482,081 (58% need-based, 42% non-need-based). 72% of past graduating class borrowed through all loan programs. *Average indebtedness per student:* $23,564. ***Average need-based loan:*** Freshmen: $4385. Undergraduates: $4537. ***Parent loans:*** $3,406,259 (22% need-based, 78% non-need-based). ***Programs:*** FFEL (Subsidized and Unsubsidized Stafford, PLUS), Perkins, college/university.

WORK-STUDY ***Federal work-study:*** Total amount: $355,578; 220 jobs averaging $2000.

APPLYING FOR FINANCIAL AID ***Required financial aid forms:*** FAFSA, state aid form. ***Financial aid deadline (priority):*** 2/15. ***Notification date:*** 3/1. Students must reply by 5/1 or within 2 weeks of notification.

CONTACT Ms. Mary Neal, Director of Financial Aid, Randolph-Macon College, PO Box 5005, Ashland, VA 23005-5505, 804-752-7259 or toll-free 800-888-1762. *Fax:* 804-752-3719. *E-mail:* mneal@rmc.edu.

REED COLLEGE

Portland, OR

Tuition & fees: $38,190 **Average undergraduate aid package: $32,620**

ABOUT THE INSTITUTION Independent, coed. ***Awards:*** bachelor's and master's degrees. 29 undergraduate majors. ***Total enrollment:*** 1,471. Undergraduates: 1,442. Freshmen: 330. Institutional methodology is used as a basis for awarding need-based institutional aid.

UNDERGRADUATE EXPENSES for 2008–09 ***Application fee:*** $50. ***Comprehensive fee:*** $48,110 includes full-time tuition ($37,960), mandatory fees ($230), and room and board ($9920). ***College room only:*** $5180. Full-time tuition and fees vary according to course load. Room and board charges vary according to board plan and housing facility. ***Part-time tuition:*** $1625 per semester hour. Part-time tuition and fees vary according to course load. ***Payment plan:*** Installment.

FRESHMAN FINANCIAL AID (Fall 2008, est.) 213 applied for aid; of those 79% were deemed to have need. 100% of freshmen with need received aid; of those 98% had need fully met. ***Average percent of need met:*** 100% (excluding resources awarded to replace EFC). ***Average financial aid package:*** $34,730 (excluding resources awarded to replace EFC).

UNDERGRADUATE FINANCIAL AID (Fall 2008, est.) 751 applied for aid; of those 92% were deemed to have need. 100% of undergraduates with need received aid; of those 95% had need fully met. ***Average percent of need met:*** 100% (excluding resources awarded to replace EFC). ***Average financial aid package:*** $32,620 (excluding resources awarded to replace EFC).

GIFT AID (NEED-BASED) ***Total amount:*** $19,367,002 (6% federal, 1% state, 92% institutional, 1% external sources). ***Receiving aid:*** Freshmen: 48% (159); all full-time undergraduates: 45% (646). ***Average award:*** Freshmen: $31,668; Undergraduates: $29,930. ***Scholarships, grants, and awards:*** Federal Pell, FSEOG, state, private, college/university gift aid from institutional funds.

GIFT AID (NON-NEED-BASED) ***Total amount:*** $56,263 (100% external sources). ***Tuition waivers:*** Full or partial for employees or children of employees.

LOANS ***Student loans:*** $4,405,649 (58% need-based, 42% non-need-based). 53% of past graduating class borrowed through all loan programs. *Average indebtedness per student:* $17,296. ***Average need-based loan:*** Freshmen: $3043. Undergraduates: $4190. ***Parent loans:*** $1,576,391 (100% non-need-based). ***Programs:*** Federal Direct (Subsidized and Unsubsidized Stafford, PLUS), FFEL (Subsidized and Unsubsidized Stafford, PLUS), Perkins.

WORK-STUDY ***Federal work-study:*** Total amount: $613,792; 420 jobs averaging $1388. ***State or other work-study/employment:*** Total amount: $145,400 (100% need-based). 101 part-time jobs averaging $1382.

APPLYING FOR FINANCIAL AID ***Required financial aid forms:*** FAFSA, institution's own form, CSS Financial Aid PROFILE, noncustodial (divorced/separated) parent's statement, business/farm supplement. ***Financial aid deadline:*** 1/15 (priority: 1/15). ***Notification date:*** 4/1. Students must reply by 5/1 or within 2 weeks of notification.

CONTACT Leslie Limper, Financial Aid Director, Reed College, 3203 Southeast Woodstock Boulevard, Portland, OR 97202-8199, 503-777-7223 or toll-free 800-547-4750 (out-of-state). *Fax:* 503-788-6682. *E-mail:* financial.aid@reed.edu.

REGENT UNIVERSITY

Virginia Beach, VA

CONTACT Financial Aid Office, Regent University, 1000 Regent University Drive, Virginia Beach, VA 23464-9800, 757-226-4127 or toll-free 800-373-5504.

REGIS COLLEGE

Weston, MA

Tuition & fees: $27,800 **Average undergraduate aid package: $22,111**

ABOUT THE INSTITUTION Independent Roman Catholic, coed. ***Awards:*** associate, bachelor's, master's, and doctoral degrees and post-master's certificates. 27 undergraduate majors. ***Total enrollment:*** 1,590. Undergraduates: 991. Freshmen: 237.

UNDERGRADUATE EXPENSES for 2008–09 ***Application fee:*** $50. ***One-time required fee:*** $195. ***Comprehensive fee:*** $39,750 includes full-time tuition ($27,800) and room and board ($11,950). ***College room only:*** $6100. Full-time tuition and fees vary according to course load and student level. Part-time tuition and fees vary according to class time. ***Payment plan:*** Installment.

FRESHMAN FINANCIAL AID (Fall 2008, est.) 228 applied for aid; of those 93% were deemed to have need. 99% of freshmen with need received aid; of those 13% had need fully met. ***Average percent of need met:*** 62% (excluding resources awarded to replace EFC). ***Average financial aid package:*** $23,757 (excluding resources awarded to replace EFC). 7% of all full-time freshmen had no need and received non-need-based gift aid.

UNDERGRADUATE FINANCIAL AID (Fall 2008, est.) 695 applied for aid; of those 93% were deemed to have need. 100% of undergraduates with need received aid; of those 14% had need fully met. ***Average percent of need met:*** 59% (excluding resources awarded to replace EFC). ***Average financial aid package:*** $22,111 (excluding resources awarded to replace EFC). 7% of all full-time undergraduates had no need and received non-need-based gift aid.

GIFT AID (NEED-BASED) ***Total amount:*** $11,372,399 (12% federal, 5% state, 81% institutional, 2% external sources). ***Receiving aid:*** Freshmen: 84% (199); all full-time undergraduates: 67% (600). ***Average award:*** Freshmen: $14,351; Undergraduates: $12,529. ***Scholarships, grants, and awards:*** Federal Pell, FSEOG, state, private, college/university gift aid from institutional funds.

GIFT AID (NON-NEED-BASED) ***Receiving aid:*** Freshmen: 43% (103). Undergraduates: 36% (324). ***Average award:*** Freshmen: $8424. Undergraduates: $8231. ***Scholarships, grants, and awards by category:*** *Academic interests/achievement:* 210 awards ($2,041,500 total): general academic interests/achievements. *Special achievements/activities:* 155 awards ($846,096 total): community service, leadership. *Special characteristics:* 34 awards ($310,860 total): adult students, children of faculty/staff, international students, relatives of clergy, religious affiliation, siblings of current students. ***Tuition waivers:*** Full or partial for employees or children of employees.

LOANS ***Student loans:*** $5,070,628 (100% need-based). 95% of past graduating class borrowed through all loan programs. *Average indebtedness per student:* $24,178. ***Average need-based loan:*** Freshmen: $4267. Undergraduates: $4849. ***Parent loans:*** $1,749,856 (100% non-need-based). ***Programs:*** Federal Direct (Subsidized and Unsubsidized Stafford, PLUS), Perkins, state.

WORK-STUDY ***Federal work-study:*** Total amount: $907,268; 436 jobs averaging $2000. ***State or other work-study/employment:*** Total amount: $47,050 (100% non-need-based). 40 part-time jobs averaging $1500.

APPLYING FOR FINANCIAL AID ***Required financial aid forms:*** FAFSA, institution's own form. ***Financial aid deadline (priority):*** 2/15. ***Notification date:*** Continuous beginning 3/15. Students must reply by 6/1 or within 2 weeks of notification.

CONTACT Dee J. Ludwick, Director of Financial Aid, Regis College, Box 81, Weston, MA 02493, 781-768-7180 or toll-free 866-438-7344. *Fax:* 781-768-7225. *E-mail:* finaid@regiscollege.edu.

REGIS UNIVERSITY

Denver, CO

CONTACT Ellie Miller, Director of Financial Aid, Regis University, 3333 Regis Boulevard, Denver, CO 80221-1099, 303-964-5758 or toll-free 800-388-2366 Ext. 4900. *Fax:* 303-964-5449. *E-mail:* emiller@regis.edu.

REINHARDT COLLEGE

Waleska, GA

Tuition & fees: $16,070 **Average undergraduate aid package: $9845**

ABOUT THE INSTITUTION Independent religious, coed. ***Awards:*** associate, bachelor's, and master's degrees. 23 undergraduate majors. ***Total enrollment:*** 1,051. Undergraduates: 1,025. Freshmen: 274. Federal methodology is used as a basis for awarding need-based institutional aid.

UNDERGRADUATE EXPENSES for 2009–10 ***Application fee:*** $25. ***Comprehensive fee:*** $24,020 includes full-time tuition ($16,070) and room and board ($7950).

FRESHMAN FINANCIAL AID (Fall 2007) 210 applied for aid; of those 79% were deemed to have need. 100% of freshmen with need received aid; of those 19% had need fully met. ***Average percent of need met:*** 54% (excluding resources awarded to replace EFC). ***Average financial aid package:*** $9494 (excluding resources awarded to replace EFC). 12% of all full-time freshmen had no need and received non-need-based gift aid.

UNDERGRADUATE FINANCIAL AID (Fall 2007) 627 applied for aid; of those 86% were deemed to have need. 98% of undergraduates with need received aid; of those 16% had need fully met. ***Average percent of need met:*** 52% (excluding resources awarded to replace EFC). ***Average financial aid package:*** $9845 (excluding resources awarded to replace EFC). 7% of all full-time undergraduates had no need and received non-need-based gift aid.

GIFT AID (NEED-BASED) ***Total amount:*** $1,154,431 (17% federal, 23% state, 58% institutional, 2% external sources). ***Receiving aid:*** Freshmen: 38% (101); all full-time undergraduates: 51% (526). ***Average award:*** Freshmen: $7654; Undergraduates: $7340. ***Scholarships, grants, and awards:*** Federal Pell, FSEOG, state, private, college/university gift aid from institutional funds.

GIFT AID (NON-NEED-BASED) ***Total amount:*** $319,736 (47% state, 49% institutional, 4% external sources). ***Receiving aid:*** Freshmen: 12% (31). Undergraduates: 7% (76). ***Average award:*** Freshmen: $3175. Undergraduates: $3159. ***Scholarships, grants, and awards by category:*** *Academic interests/achievement:* general academic interests/achievements.

LOANS ***Student loans:*** $649,699 (65% need-based, 35% non-need-based). 84% of past graduating class borrowed through all loan programs. *Average indebtedness per student:* $18,328. ***Average need-based loan:*** Freshmen: $2725. Undergraduates: $3593. ***Parent loans:*** $547,209 (51% need-based, 49% non-need-based). ***Programs:*** FFEL (Subsidized and Unsubsidized Stafford, PLUS).

WORK-STUDY ***Federal work-study:*** Total amount: $8937; 68 jobs averaging $1138. ***State or other work-study/employment:*** 156 part-time jobs averaging $909.

ATHLETIC AWARDS Total amount: $207,940 (59% need-based, 41% non-need-based).

APPLYING FOR FINANCIAL AID ***Required financial aid forms:*** FAFSA, state aid form. ***Financial aid deadline (priority):*** 5/1. ***Notification date:*** Continuous. Students must reply by 6/1.

CONTACT Robert Gregory, Director of Financial Aid, Reinhardt College, 7300 Reinhardt College Circle, Waleska, GA 30183-2981, 770-720-5532. *Fax:* 770-720-9126.

RENSSELAER POLYTECHNIC INSTITUTE

Troy, NY

Tuition & fees: $37,990 **Average undergraduate aid package: $30,635**

ABOUT THE INSTITUTION Independent, coed. ***Awards:*** bachelor's, master's, and doctoral degrees. 51 undergraduate majors. ***Total enrollment:*** 7,521. Undergraduates: 5,394. Freshmen: 1,356. Both federal and institutional methodology are used as a basis for awarding need-based institutional aid.

UNDERGRADUATE EXPENSES for 2008–09 ***Application fee:*** $70. ***Comprehensive fee:*** $48,720 includes full-time tuition ($36,950), mandatory fees ($1040), and room and board ($10,730). ***College room only:*** $6025. Room and board charges vary according to board plan. ***Part-time tuition:*** $1155 per credit hour. ***Payment plan:*** Installment.

FRESHMAN FINANCIAL AID (Fall 2008, est.) 1,116 applied for aid; of those 80% were deemed to have need. 100% of freshmen with need received aid; of those 72% had need fully met. ***Average percent of need met:*** 82% (excluding resources awarded to replace EFC). ***Average financial aid package:*** $32,707 (excluding resources awarded to replace EFC). 32% of all full-time freshmen had no need and received non-need-based gift aid.

UNDERGRADUATE FINANCIAL AID (Fall 2008, est.) 3,934 applied for aid; of those 88% were deemed to have need. 100% of undergraduates with need received aid; of those 50% had need fully met. ***Average percent of need met:*** 75% (excluding resources awarded to replace EFC). ***Average financial aid package:*** $30,635 (excluding resources awarded to replace EFC). 29% of all full-time undergraduates had no need and received non-need-based gift aid.

GIFT AID (NEED-BASED) ***Total amount:*** $74,321,146 (10% federal, 3% state, 85% institutional, 2% external sources). ***Receiving aid:*** Freshmen: 66% (892); all full-time undergraduates: 64% (3,445). ***Average award:*** Freshmen: $23,079; Undergraduates: $21,503. ***Scholarships, grants, and awards:*** Federal Pell, FSEOG, state, private, college/university gift aid from institutional funds, Gates Millennium Scholarships, Academic Competitiveness Grant, National Smart Grant.

GIFT AID (NON-NEED-BASED) ***Total amount:*** $23,717,675 (8% federal, 1% state, 89% institutional, 2% external sources). ***Receiving aid:*** Freshmen: 17% (224). Undergraduates: 11% (599). ***Average award:*** Freshmen: $14,085. Undergraduates: $14,530. ***Scholarships, grants, and awards by category:*** *Academic interests/achievement:* general academic interests/achievements, humanities, mathematics, military science. *Creative arts/performance:* general creative arts/performance. *Special achievements/activities:* general special achievements/activities. *Special characteristics:* children and siblings of alumni, children of faculty/staff, ethnic background, general special characteristics, members of minority groups. ***Tuition waivers:*** Full or partial for employees or children of employees. ***ROTC:*** Army cooperative, Naval, Air Force.

LOANS ***Student loans:*** $38,300,000 (60% need-based, 40% non-need-based). 70% of past graduating class borrowed through all loan programs. *Average indebtedness per student:* $30,375. ***Average need-based loan:*** Freshmen: $6727. Undergraduates: $6644. ***Parent loans:*** $8,000,000 (80% need-based, 20% non-need-based). ***Programs:*** FFEL (Subsidized and Unsubsidized Stafford, PLUS), Perkins, state, college/university.

WORK-STUDY ***Federal work-study:*** Total amount: $1,800,000; 1,012 jobs averaging $2030.

ATHLETIC AWARDS Total amount: $1,330,000 (100% non-need-based).

APPLYING FOR FINANCIAL AID ***Required financial aid forms:*** FAFSA, CSS Financial Aid PROFILE. ***Financial aid deadline (priority):*** 2/15. ***Notification date:*** 3/25.

CONTACT Ms. Lynnette E. Koch, Acting Director of Financial Aid, Rensselaer Polytechnic Institute, Academy Hall, Troy, NY 12180-3590, 518-276-6813 or toll-free 800-448-6562. *Fax:* 518-276-4797. *E-mail:* financial_aid@rpi.edu.

RESEARCH COLLEGE OF NURSING

Kansas City, MO

CONTACT Ms. Stacie Withers, Financial Aid Director, Research College of Nursing, 2300 East Meyer Boulevard, Kansas City, MO 64132, 816-276-4728 or toll-free 800-842-6776. *Fax:* 816-276-3526. *E-mail:* stacie.withers@hcamidwest.com.

RHODE ISLAND COLLEGE

Providence, RI

Tuition & fees (RI res): $5771 **Average undergraduate aid package: $7817**

ABOUT THE INSTITUTION State-supported, coed. ***Awards:*** bachelor's, master's, and doctoral degrees and post-bachelor's and post-master's certificates. 72 undergraduate majors. ***Total enrollment:*** 9,085. Undergraduates: 7,601. Freshmen: 1,190. Both federal and institutional methodology are used as a basis for awarding need-based institutional aid.

UNDERGRADUATE EXPENSES for 2008–09 ***Application fee:*** $50. ***Tuition, state resident:*** full-time $4889; part-time $208 per credit. ***Tuition, nonresident:*** full-time $13,600; part-time $570 per credit. ***Required fees:*** full-time $882; $24 per credit or $68 per term. Part-time tuition and fees vary according to course load. ***College room and board:*** $8250; ***Room only:*** $4600. Room and board charges vary according to board plan and housing facility. ***Payment plan:*** Installment.

FRESHMAN FINANCIAL AID (Fall 2008, est.) 971 applied for aid; of those 70% were deemed to have need. 99% of freshmen with need received aid; of those 19% had need fully met. ***Average percent of need met:*** 27% (excluding resources awarded to replace EFC). ***Average financial aid package:*** $8905 (excluding resources awarded to replace EFC). 5% of all full-time freshmen had no need and received non-need-based gift aid.

UNDERGRADUATE FINANCIAL AID (Fall 2008, est.) 3,895 applied for aid; of those 74% were deemed to have need. 96% of undergraduates with need received aid; of those 16% had need fully met. ***Average percent of need met:*** 22% (excluding resources awarded to replace EFC). ***Average financial aid package:*** $7817 (excluding resources awarded to replace EFC). 3% of all full-time undergraduates had no need and received non-need-based gift aid.

GIFT AID (NEED-BASED) ***Total amount:*** $13,708,554 (51% federal, 16% state, 27% institutional, 6% external sources). ***Receiving aid:*** Freshmen: 50% (574); all full-time undergraduates: 43% (2,312). ***Average award:*** Freshmen: $6485; Undergraduates: $5168. ***Scholarships, grants, and awards:*** Federal Pell, FSEOG, state, private, college/university gift aid from institutional funds.

GIFT AID (NON-NEED-BASED) ***Total amount:*** $510,000 (69% institutional, 31% external sources). ***Receiving aid:*** Freshmen: 2% (26). Undergraduates: 1% (73). ***Average award:*** Freshmen: $2009. Undergraduates: $1994. ***Scholarships, grants, and awards by category:*** *Academic interests/achievement:* 410 awards ($713,778 total): general academic interests/achievements. *Creative arts/performance:* 117 awards ($107,334 total): art/fine arts, cinema/film/broadcasting, dance, journalism/publications, music, theater/drama. *Special characteristics:* 3 awards ($9000 total): children and siblings of alumni. ***Tuition waivers:*** Full or partial for employees or children of employees. ***ROTC:*** Army cooperative.

LOANS ***Student loans:*** $25,180,666 (59% need-based, 41% non-need-based). 74% of past graduating class borrowed through all loan programs. *Average indebtedness per student:* $15,841. ***Average need-based loan:*** Freshmen: $3221. Undergraduates: $3602. ***Parent loans:*** $1,592,697 (24% need-based, 76% non-need-based). ***Programs:*** FFEL (Subsidized and Unsubsidized Stafford, PLUS), Perkins, state.

WORK-STUDY ***Federal work-study:*** Total amount: $2,152,587; jobs available.

APPLYING FOR FINANCIAL AID ***Required financial aid forms:*** FAFSA, institution's own form. ***Financial aid deadline (priority):*** 3/1. ***Notification date:*** Continuous beginning 3/15. Students must reply by 5/1 or within 3 weeks of notification.

CONTACT James T. Hanbury, Office of Financial Aid, Rhode Island College, 600 Mount Pleasant Avenue, Providence, RI 02908, 401-456-8033 or toll-free 800-669-5760. *Fax:* 401-456-8686. *E-mail:* jhanbury@ric.edu.

RHODE ISLAND SCHOOL OF DESIGN

Providence, RI

CONTACT Director of Financial Aid, Rhode Island School of Design, 2 College Street, Providence, RI 02903-2784, 401-454-6661 or toll-free 800-364-7473. *Fax:* 401-454-6412.

RHODES COLLEGE

Memphis, TN

Tuition & fees: $32,446 **Average undergraduate aid package: $29,144**

ABOUT THE INSTITUTION Independent Presbyterian, coed. ***Awards:*** bachelor's and master's degrees (master's degree in accounting only). 33 undergraduate majors. ***Total enrollment:*** 1,673. Undergraduates: 1,664. Freshmen: 477. Institutional methodology is used as a basis for awarding need-based institutional aid.

UNDERGRADUATE EXPENSES for 2008–09 ***Application fee:*** $45. ***Comprehensive fee:*** $40,288 includes full-time tuition ($32,136), mandatory fees ($310), and room and board ($7842). Room and board charges vary according to board plan and housing facility. ***Part-time tuition:*** $1350 per credit. ***Payment plan:*** Installment.

FRESHMAN FINANCIAL AID (Fall 2008, est.) 99% of freshmen with need received aid; of those 52% had need fully met. ***Average percent of need met:*** 89% (excluding resources awarded to replace EFC). ***Average financial aid package:*** $29,647 (excluding resources awarded to replace EFC). 42% of all full-time freshmen had no need and received non-need-based gift aid.

UNDERGRADUATE FINANCIAL AID (Fall 2008, est.) 99% of undergraduates with need received aid; of those 42% had need fully met. ***Average percent of need met:*** 79% (excluding resources awarded to replace EFC). ***Average financial aid package:*** $29,144 (excluding resources awarded to replace EFC). 41% of all full-time undergraduates had no need and received non-need-based gift aid.

GIFT AID (NEED-BASED) ***Total amount:*** $13,186,821 (5% federal, 7% state, 85% institutional, 3% external sources). ***Receiving aid:*** Freshmen: 43% (204); all full-time undergraduates: 42% (688). ***Average award:*** Freshmen: $19,705; Undergraduates: $18,833. ***Scholarships, grants, and awards:*** Federal Pell, FSEOG, state, private, college/university gift aid from institutional funds.

GIFT AID (NON-NEED-BASED) ***Total amount:*** $10,209,765 (4% state, 90% institutional, 6% external sources). ***Receiving aid:*** Freshmen: 18% (87). Undergraduates: 14% (236). ***Average award:*** Freshmen: $13,060. Undergraduates: $12,513. ***Tuition waivers:*** Full or partial for employees or children of employees. ***ROTC:*** Army cooperative, Air Force cooperative.

LOANS ***Student loans:*** $4,445,485 (58% need-based, 42% non-need-based). 46% of past graduating class borrowed through all loan programs. *Average indebtedness per student:* $26,064. ***Average need-based loan:*** Freshmen: $2424. Undergraduates: $3670. ***Parent loans:*** $1,792,062 (20% need-based, 80%

non-need-based). ***Programs:*** Federal Direct (Subsidized and Unsubsidized Stafford, PLUS), FFEL (Subsidized and Unsubsidized Stafford, PLUS), Perkins.

WORK-STUDY ***Federal work-study:*** Total amount: $460,381; jobs available. ***State or other work-study/employment:*** Total amount: $792,217 (24% need-based, 76% non-need-based). Part-time jobs available.

APPLYING FOR FINANCIAL AID ***Required financial aid forms:*** FAFSA, CSS Financial Aid PROFILE, noncustodial (divorced/separated) parent's statement. ***Financial aid deadline:*** 3/1 (priority: 3/1). ***Notification date:*** Students must reply by 5/1.

CONTACT Art Weeden, Director of Financial Aid, Rhodes College, 2000 North Parkway, Memphis, TN 38112-1690, 901-843-3810 or toll-free 800-844-5969 (out-of-state). *Fax:* 901-843-3435. *E-mail:* weedena@rhodes.edu.

RICE UNIVERSITY

Houston, TX

Tuition & fees: $30,479 **Average undergraduate aid package: $24,981**

ABOUT THE INSTITUTION Independent, coed. ***Awards:*** bachelor's, master's, and doctoral degrees. 59 undergraduate majors. ***Total enrollment:*** 5,243. Undergraduates: 3,051. Freshmen: 742. Both federal and institutional methodology are used as a basis for awarding need-based institutional aid.

UNDERGRADUATE EXPENSES for 2008–09 ***Application fee:*** $60. ***Comprehensive fee:*** $41,229 includes full-time tuition ($29,960), mandatory fees ($519), and room and board ($10,750). ***College room only:*** $7150. ***Part-time tuition:*** $1249 per credit hour.

FRESHMAN FINANCIAL AID (Fall 2008, est.) 679 applied for aid; of those 41% were deemed to have need. 100% of freshmen with need received aid; of those 100% had need fully met. ***Average percent of need met:*** 100% (excluding resources awarded to replace EFC). ***Average financial aid package:*** $31,863 (excluding resources awarded to replace EFC). 12% of all full-time freshmen had no need and received non-need-based gift aid.

UNDERGRADUATE FINANCIAL AID (Fall 2008, est.) 1,970 applied for aid; of those 59% were deemed to have need. 100% of undergraduates with need received aid; of those 100% had need fully met. ***Average percent of need met:*** 100% (excluding resources awarded to replace EFC). ***Average financial aid package:*** $24,981 (excluding resources awarded to replace EFC). 14% of all full-time undergraduates had no need and received non-need-based gift aid.

GIFT AID (NEED-BASED) ***Total amount:*** $25,289,251 (7% federal, 7% state, 86% institutional). ***Receiving aid:*** Freshmen: 35% (275); all full-time undergraduates: 37% (1,167). ***Average award:*** Freshmen: $28,392; Undergraduates: $24,104. ***Scholarships, grants, and awards:*** Federal Pell, FSEOG, state, private, college/university gift aid from institutional funds.

GIFT AID (NON-NEED-BASED) ***Total amount:*** $11,567,023 (2% state, 73% institutional, 25% external sources). ***Receiving aid:*** Freshmen: 5% (43). Undergraduates: 9% (280). ***Average award:*** Freshmen: $9589. Undergraduates: $14,665. ***Scholarships, grants, and awards by category:*** *Academic interests/achievement:* engineering/technologies, general academic interests/achievements. *Creative arts/performance:* music. *Special achievements/activities:* general special achievements/activities, leadership. ***ROTC:*** Army cooperative, Naval, Air Force cooperative.

LOANS ***Student loans:*** $1,885,373 (94% need-based, 6% non-need-based). 42% of past graduating class borrowed through all loan programs. *Average indebtedness per student:* $11,108. ***Average need-based loan:*** Freshmen: $896. Undergraduates: $3510. ***Parent loans:*** $2,190,821 (100% non-need-based). ***Programs:*** FFEL (Subsidized and Unsubsidized Stafford, PLUS), Perkins.

WORK-STUDY ***Federal work-study:*** Total amount: $1,096,057; jobs available. ***State or other work-study/employment:*** Total amount: $10,000 (100% need-based). Part-time jobs available.

ATHLETIC AWARDS Total amount: $10,543,458 (14% need-based, 86% non-need-based).

APPLYING FOR FINANCIAL AID ***Required financial aid forms:*** FAFSA, CSS Financial Aid PROFILE, business/farm supplement, tax returns and W-2 forms. ***Financial aid deadline (priority):*** 3/1. ***Notification date:*** Continuous beginning 4/1. Students must reply by 5/1.

CONTACT Ms. Anne Walker, Director of Student Financial Services, Rice University, 116 Allen Center, MS 12, Houston, TX 77005, 713-348-4958 or toll-free 800-527-OWLS. *Fax:* 713-348-2139. *E-mail:* fina@rice.edu.

THE RICHARD STOCKTON COLLEGE OF NEW JERSEY

Pomona, NJ

Tuition & fees (NJ res): $10,469 **Average undergraduate aid package: $14,552**

ABOUT THE INSTITUTION State-supported, coed. ***Awards:*** bachelor's, master's, and doctoral degrees and post-bachelor's and post-master's certificates. 30 undergraduate majors. ***Total enrollment:*** 7,307. Undergraduates: 6,671. Freshmen: 842. Federal methodology is used as a basis for awarding need-based institutional aid.

UNDERGRADUATE EXPENSES for 2008–09 ***Application fee:*** $50. ***Tuition, state resident:*** full-time $6861; part-time $214.40 per credit. ***Tuition, nonresident:*** full-time $12,379; part-time $386.84 per credit. ***Required fees:*** full-time $3608; $112.75 per credit. ***College room and board:*** $10,204; ***Room only:*** $7295. Room and board charges vary according to board plan and housing facility. ***Payment plans:*** Installment, deferred payment.

FRESHMAN FINANCIAL AID (Fall 2008, est.) 727 applied for aid; of those 76% were deemed to have need. 97% of freshmen with need received aid; of those 33% had need fully met. ***Average percent of need met:*** 80% (excluding resources awarded to replace EFC). ***Average financial aid package:*** $15,695 (excluding resources awarded to replace EFC). 11% of all full-time freshmen had no need and received non-need-based gift aid.

UNDERGRADUATE FINANCIAL AID (Fall 2008, est.) 4,377 applied for aid; of those 82% were deemed to have need. 98% of undergraduates with need received aid; of those 23% had need fully met. ***Average percent of need met:*** 74% (excluding resources awarded to replace EFC). ***Average financial aid package:*** $14,552 (excluding resources awarded to replace EFC). 5% of all full-time undergraduates had no need and received non-need-based gift aid.

GIFT AID (NEED-BASED) ***Total amount:*** $16,900,200 (36% federal, 44% state, 18% institutional, 2% external sources). ***Receiving aid:*** Freshmen: 28% (233); all full-time undergraduates: 28% (1,637). ***Average award:*** Freshmen: $9341; Undergraduates: $7759. ***Scholarships, grants, and awards:*** Federal Pell, FSEOG, state, college/university gift aid from institutional funds.

GIFT AID (NON-NEED-BASED) ***Total amount:*** $2,171,754 (18% state, 71% institutional, 11% external sources). ***Receiving aid:*** Freshmen: 26% (220). Undergraduates: 13% (756). ***Average award:*** Freshmen: $8459. Undergraduates: $5795. ***Scholarships, grants, and awards by category:*** *Academic interests/achievement:* 129 awards ($186,675 total): area/ethnic studies, biological sciences, business, computer science, education, general academic interests/achievements, health fields, humanities, mathematics, physical sciences, social sciences. *Creative arts/performance:* 14 awards ($15,637 total): applied art and design, art/fine arts, creative writing, dance, journalism/publications, music, performing arts, theater/drama. *Special achievements/activities:* 10 awards ($13,250 total): community service, general special achievements/activities, leadership. *Special characteristics:* 29 awards ($52,820 total): adult students, children of faculty/staff, children of union members/company employees, ethnic background, first-generation college students, general special characteristics, international students, local/state students, members of minority groups, previous college experience. ***Tuition waivers:*** Full or partial for employees or children of employees, senior citizens.

LOANS ***Student loans:*** $35,332,398 (83% need-based, 17% non-need-based). 66% of past graduating class borrowed through all loan programs. *Average indebtedness per student:* $24,454. ***Average need-based loan:*** Freshmen: $3470. Undergraduates: $4564. ***Parent loans:*** $2,789,279 (60% need-based, 40% non-need-based). ***Programs:*** Federal Direct (Subsidized and Unsubsidized Stafford, PLUS), Perkins, state.

WORK-STUDY ***Federal work-study:*** Total amount: $282,233; 158 jobs averaging $1726. ***State or other work-study/employment:*** Total amount: $1,037,023 (100% non-need-based). 715 part-time jobs averaging $1450.

APPLYING FOR FINANCIAL AID ***Required financial aid form:*** FAFSA. ***Financial aid deadline (priority):*** 3/1. ***Notification date:*** Continuous beginning 4/1. Students must reply within 2 weeks of notification.

CONTACT Ms. Jeanne L. Lewis, Director of Financial Aid, The Richard Stockton College of New Jersey, Jimmie Leeds Road, Pomona, NJ 08240-9988, 609-652-4203. *Fax:* 609-626-5517. *E-mail:* jeanne.lewis@stockton.edu.

RIDER UNIVERSITY

Lawrenceville, NJ

Tuition & fees: $27,730 **Average undergraduate aid package: $20,013**

ABOUT THE INSTITUTION Independent, coed. ***Awards:*** associate, bachelor's, and master's degrees and post-master's certificates. 53 undergraduate majors. ***Total enrollment:*** 6,011. Undergraduates: 4,791. Freshmen: 880. Federal methodology is used as a basis for awarding need-based institutional aid.

UNDERGRADUATE EXPENSES for 2008–09 ***Application fee:*** $50. ***Comprehensive fee:*** $38,010 includes full-time tuition ($27,140), mandatory fees ($590), and room and board ($10,280). ***College room only:*** $6060. Full-time tuition and fees vary according to course load and program. Room and board charges vary according to board plan, housing facility, and location. ***Part-time tuition:*** $467 per credit. ***Part-time fees:*** $35 per course. Part-time tuition and fees vary according to course load and program. ***Payment plan:*** Installment.

FRESHMAN FINANCIAL AID (Fall 2008, est.) 752 applied for aid; of those 84% were deemed to have need. 100% of freshmen with need received aid; of those 19% had need fully met. ***Average percent of need met:*** 73% (excluding resources awarded to replace EFC). ***Average financial aid package:*** $20,878 (excluding resources awarded to replace EFC). 19% of all full-time freshmen had no need and received non-need-based gift aid.

UNDERGRADUATE FINANCIAL AID (Fall 2008, est.) 3,034 applied for aid; of those 86% were deemed to have need. 100% of undergraduates with need received aid; of those 19% had need fully met. ***Average percent of need met:*** 73% (excluding resources awarded to replace EFC). ***Average financial aid package:*** $20,013 (excluding resources awarded to replace EFC). 21% of all full-time undergraduates had no need and received non-need-based gift aid.

GIFT AID (NEED-BASED) ***Total amount:*** $32,874,481 (11% federal, 18% state, 69% institutional, 2% external sources). ***Receiving aid:*** Freshmen: 71% (626); all full-time undergraduates: 65% (2,575). ***Average award:*** Freshmen: $15,186; Undergraduates: $13,915. ***Scholarships, grants, and awards:*** state, college/university gift aid from institutional funds.

GIFT AID (NON-NEED-BASED) ***Total amount:*** $9,661,251 (97% institutional, 3% external sources). ***Receiving aid:*** Freshmen: 11% (94). Undergraduates: 10% (402). ***Average award:*** Freshmen: $10,649. Undergraduates: $9880. ***Scholarships, grants, and awards by category:*** *Academic interests/achievement:* 2,405 awards ($20,840,754 total): general academic interests/achievements. *Creative arts/performance:* 8 awards ($217,120 total): theater/drama. *Special characteristics:* members of minority groups. ***Tuition waivers:*** Full or partial for employees or children of employees. ***ROTC:*** Army cooperative.

LOANS ***Student loans:*** $43,122,633 (56% need-based, 44% non-need-based). 74% of past graduating class borrowed through all loan programs. *Average indebtedness per student:* $33,156. ***Average need-based loan:*** Freshmen: $3923. Undergraduates: $4438. ***Parent loans:*** $4,874,409 (30% need-based, 70% non-need-based). ***Programs:*** FFEL (Subsidized and Unsubsidized Stafford, PLUS), Perkins, state, alternative loans.

WORK-STUDY ***Federal work-study:*** Total amount: $3,976,040; 1,844 jobs averaging $2135. ***State or other work-study/employment:*** 541 part-time jobs averaging $1990.

ATHLETIC AWARDS Total amount: $2,942,089 (52% need-based, 48% non-need-based).

APPLYING FOR FINANCIAL AID ***Required financial aid form:*** FAFSA. ***Financial aid deadline (priority):*** 3/1. ***Notification date:*** Continuous beginning 3/15.

CONTACT Drew Aromando, Executive Director, Enrollment Management, Rider University, 2083 Lawrenceville Road, Lawrenceville, NJ 08648-3001, 609-896-5360 or toll-free 800-257-9026. *Fax:* 609-219-4487. *E-mail:* finaid@rider.edu.

RINGLING COLLEGE OF ART AND DESIGN

Sarasota, FL

Tuition & fees: $26,725 **Average undergraduate aid package: $18,441**

ABOUT THE INSTITUTION Independent, coed. ***Awards:*** bachelor's degrees. 12 undergraduate majors. ***Total enrollment:*** 1,229. Undergraduates: 1,229. Freshmen: 282. Federal methodology is used as a basis for awarding need-based institutional aid.

UNDERGRADUATE EXPENSES for 2008–09 ***Application fee:*** $60. ***Comprehensive fee:*** $37,075 includes full-time tuition ($26,050), mandatory fees ($675), and room and board ($10,350). ***College room only:*** $5250. Full-time tuition and fees vary according to course load, program, and student level. Room and board charges vary according to board plan and housing facility. ***Part-time tuition:*** $1230 per semester hour. Part-time tuition and fees vary according to course load, program, and student level. ***Payment plan:*** Installment.

FRESHMAN FINANCIAL AID (Fall 2008, est.) 204 applied for aid; of those 86% were deemed to have need. 100% of freshmen with need received aid; of those 6% had need fully met. ***Average percent of need met:*** 52% (excluding resources awarded to replace EFC). ***Average financial aid package:*** $18,164 (excluding resources awarded to replace EFC). 5% of all full-time freshmen had no need and received non-need-based gift aid.

UNDERGRADUATE FINANCIAL AID (Fall 2008, est.) 828 applied for aid; of those 89% were deemed to have need. 100% of undergraduates with need received aid; of those 7% had need fully met. ***Average percent of need met:*** 43% (excluding resources awarded to replace EFC). ***Average financial aid package:*** $18,441 (excluding resources awarded to replace EFC). 4% of all full-time undergraduates had no need and received non-need-based gift aid.

GIFT AID (NEED-BASED) ***Total amount:*** $5,411,862 (27% federal, 34% state, 29% institutional, 10% external sources). ***Receiving aid:*** Freshmen: 42% (156); all full-time undergraduates: 52% (635). ***Average award:*** Freshmen: $9412; Undergraduates: $7750. ***Scholarships, grants, and awards:*** Federal Pell, FSEOG, state, private, college/university gift aid from institutional funds.

GIFT AID (NON-NEED-BASED) ***Total amount:*** $699,657 (41% state, 43% institutional, 16% external sources). ***Receiving aid:*** Freshmen: 1% (3). Undergraduates: 1% (16). ***Average award:*** Freshmen: $8725. Undergraduates: $5822. ***Scholarships, grants, and awards by category:*** *Academic interests/achievement:* general academic interests/achievements. *Creative arts/performance:* applied art and design, art/fine arts. ***Tuition waivers:*** Full or partial for employees or children of employees.

LOANS ***Student loans:*** $13,891,668 (82% need-based, 18% non-need-based). 63% of past graduating class borrowed through all loan programs. *Average indebtedness per student:* $31,391. ***Average need-based loan:*** Freshmen: $10,113. Undergraduates: $12,123. ***Parent loans:*** $4,884,316 (67% need-based, 33% non-need-based). ***Programs:*** FFEL (Subsidized and Unsubsidized Stafford, PLUS), alternative loans.

WORK-STUDY ***Federal work-study:*** Total amount: $377,179; 266 jobs averaging $1920. ***State or other work-study/employment:*** Part-time jobs available.

APPLYING FOR FINANCIAL AID ***Required financial aid form:*** FAFSA. ***Financial aid deadline (priority):*** 3/1. ***Notification date:*** Continuous beginning 3/15. Students must reply within 4 weeks of notification.

CONTACT Micah Jordan, Financial Aid Assistant Director, Ringling College of Art and Design, 2700 North Tamiami Trail, Sarasota, FL 34243, 941-359-7533 or toll-free 800-255-7695. *Fax:* 941-359-6107. *E-mail:* finaid@ringling.edu.

RIPON COLLEGE

Ripon, WI

Tuition & fees: $24,245 **Average undergraduate aid package: $20,981**

ABOUT THE INSTITUTION Independent, coed. ***Awards:*** bachelor's degrees. 38 undergraduate majors. ***Total enrollment:*** 1,057. Undergraduates: 1,057. Freshmen: 283. Federal methodology is used as a basis for awarding need-based institutional aid.

UNDERGRADUATE EXPENSES for 2008–09 ***Application fee:*** $30. ***Comprehensive fee:*** $31,015 includes full-time tuition ($23,970), mandatory fees ($275), and room and board ($6770). ***College room only:*** $3490. ***Part-time tuition:*** $890 per credit. ***Payment plan:*** Installment.

FRESHMAN FINANCIAL AID (Fall 2008, est.) 257 applied for aid; of those 87% were deemed to have need. 100% of freshmen with need received aid; of those 44% had need fully met. ***Average percent of need met:*** 95% (excluding resources awarded to replace EFC). ***Average financial aid package:*** $21,368 (excluding resources awarded to replace EFC). 18% of all full-time freshmen had no need and received non-need-based gift aid.

UNDERGRADUATE FINANCIAL AID (Fall 2008, est.) 943 applied for aid; of those 90% were deemed to have need. 100% of undergraduates with need received aid; of those 33% had need fully met. ***Average percent of need met:*** 91% (excluding resources awarded to replace EFC). ***Average financial aid package:*** $20,981 (excluding resources awarded to replace EFC). 18% of all full-time undergraduates had no need and received non-need-based gift aid.

GIFT AID (NEED-BASED) ***Total amount:*** $13,587,884 (9% federal, 8% state, 65% institutional, 18% external sources). ***Receiving aid:*** Freshmen: 79% (223); all full-time undergraduates: 81% (837). ***Average award:*** Freshmen: $17,033;

Undergraduates: $16,409. ***Scholarships, grants, and awards:*** Federal Pell, FSEOG, state, private, college/university gift aid from institutional funds.

GIFT AID (NON-NEED-BASED) ***Total amount:*** $3,742,805 (58% institutional, 42% external sources). ***Receiving aid:*** Freshmen: 18% (52). Undergraduates: 15% (154). ***Average award:*** Freshmen: $9385. Undergraduates: $9497. ***Scholarships, grants, and awards by category:*** *Academic interests/achievement:* 504 awards ($4,561,346 total): biological sciences, business, computer science, education, English, foreign languages, general academic interests/achievements, humanities, mathematics, military science, physical sciences, premedicine, religion/biblical studies, social sciences. *Creative arts/performance:* 120 awards ($336,500 total): art/fine arts, debating, music, theater/drama. *Special achievements/activities:* 189 awards ($713,183 total): general special achievements/activities, leadership, memberships. *Special characteristics:* 366 awards ($1,901,529 total): children and siblings of alumni, children of faculty/staff, general special characteristics, international students, local/state students, members of minority groups, out-of-state students, previous college experience, religious affiliation, siblings of current students. ***Tuition waivers:*** Full or partial for employees or children of employees. ***ROTC:*** Army.

LOANS ***Student loans:*** $6,884,718 (58% need-based, 42% non-need-based). 96% of past graduating class borrowed through all loan programs. *Average indebtedness per student:* $24,795. ***Average need-based loan:*** Freshmen: $4551. Undergraduates: $4756. ***Parent loans:*** $949,321 (7% need-based, 93% non-need-based). ***Programs:*** FFEL (Subsidized and Unsubsidized Stafford, PLUS), Perkins, alternative loans.

WORK-STUDY ***Federal work-study:*** Total amount: $662,876; 408 jobs averaging $1488. ***State or other work-study/employment:*** Total amount: $829,662 (3% need-based, 97% non-need-based). 462 part-time jobs averaging $1609.

APPLYING FOR FINANCIAL AID ***Required financial aid form:*** FAFSA. ***Financial aid deadline (priority):*** 3/1. ***Notification date:*** Continuous. Students must reply within 2 weeks of notification.

CONTACT Steven M. Schuetz, Dean of Admission and Financial Aid, Ripon College, 300 Seward Street, Ripon, WI 54971, 920-748-8185 or toll-free 800-947-4766. *Fax:* 920-748-8335. *E-mail:* financialaid@ripon.edu.

RIVIER COLLEGE

Nashua, NH

Tuition & fees: $24,290 **Average undergraduate aid package: $16,294**

ABOUT THE INSTITUTION Independent Roman Catholic, coed. ***Awards:*** associate, bachelor's, and master's degrees and post-bachelor's and post-master's certificates. 41 undergraduate majors. ***Total enrollment:*** 2,231. Undergraduates: 1,472. Freshmen: 255. Federal methodology is used as a basis for awarding need-based institutional aid.

UNDERGRADUATE EXPENSES for 2009–10 ***Application fee:*** $25. ***One-time required fee:*** $175. ***Comprehensive fee:*** $33,444 includes full-time tuition ($23,490), mandatory fees ($800), and room and board ($9154). ***Part-time tuition:*** $793 per credit.

FRESHMAN FINANCIAL AID (Fall 2008, est.) 217 applied for aid; of those 88% were deemed to have need. 100% of freshmen with need received aid; of those 12% had need fully met. ***Average percent of need met:*** 72% (excluding resources awarded to replace EFC). ***Average financial aid package:*** $17,578 (excluding resources awarded to replace EFC). 13% of all full-time freshmen had no need and received non-need-based gift aid.

UNDERGRADUATE FINANCIAL AID (Fall 2008, est.) 763 applied for aid; of those 88% were deemed to have need. 100% of undergraduates with need received aid; of those 20% had need fully met. ***Average percent of need met:*** 73% (excluding resources awarded to replace EFC). ***Average financial aid package:*** $16,294 (excluding resources awarded to replace EFC). 16% of all full-time undergraduates had no need and received non-need-based gift aid.

GIFT AID (NEED-BASED) ***Total amount:*** $6,803,998 (16% federal, 3% state, 73% institutional, 8% external sources). ***Receiving aid:*** Freshmen: 81% (190); all full-time undergraduates: 76% (646). ***Average award:*** Freshmen: $11,639; Undergraduates: $9568. ***Scholarships, grants, and awards:*** Federal Pell, FSEOG, state, private, college/university gift aid from institutional funds.

GIFT AID (NON-NEED-BASED) ***Total amount:*** $954,575 (87% institutional, 13% external sources). ***Receiving aid:*** Freshmen: 5% (12). Undergraduates: 6% (49). ***Average award:*** Freshmen: $5416. Undergraduates: $4816. ***Scholarships, grants, and awards by category:*** *Academic interests/achievement:* biological sciences, business, communication, computer science, education, English, foreign languages, general academic interests/achievements, humanities, mathematics, premedicine, social sciences. *Creative arts/performance:* applied art and design, art/fine arts, journalism/publications. *Special achievements/activities:* general special achievements/activities. *Special characteristics:* children and siblings of alumni, children of current students, international students, siblings of current students. ***ROTC:*** Air Force cooperative.

LOANS ***Student loans:*** $12,784,478 (63% need-based, 37% non-need-based). 87% of past graduating class borrowed through all loan programs. *Average indebtedness per student:* $25,959. ***Average need-based loan:*** Freshmen: $5952. Undergraduates: $7441. ***Parent loans:*** $1,683,938 (43% need-based, 57% non-need-based). ***Programs:*** FFEL (Subsidized and Unsubsidized Stafford, PLUS), Perkins, state.

WORK-STUDY ***Federal work-study:*** Total amount: $239,184; 393 jobs averaging $1107. ***State or other work-study/employment:*** Total amount: $189,433 (3% need-based, 97% non-need-based). 153 part-time jobs averaging $1304.

APPLYING FOR FINANCIAL AID ***Required financial aid form:*** FAFSA. ***Financial aid deadline (priority):*** 3/1. ***Notification date:*** Continuous beginning 3/1. Students must reply within 3 weeks of notification.

CONTACT Valerie Patnaude, Director of Financial Aid, Rivier College, 420 Main Street, Nashua, NH 03060-5086, 603-897-8533 or toll-free 800-44RIVIER. *Fax:* 603-897-8810. *E-mail:* vpatnaude@rivier.edu.

ROANOKE BIBLE COLLEGE

Elizabeth City, NC

Tuition & fees: $10,320 **Average undergraduate aid package: $11,281**

ABOUT THE INSTITUTION Independent Christian, coed. ***Awards:*** associate and bachelor's degrees. 8 undergraduate majors. ***Total enrollment:*** 166. Undergraduates: 166. Freshmen: 41. Federal methodology is used as a basis for awarding need-based institutional aid.

UNDERGRADUATE EXPENSES for 2009–10 ***Application fee:*** $50. ***Comprehensive fee:*** $17,110 includes full-time tuition ($9920), mandatory fees ($400), and room and board ($6790). ***College room only:*** $3590. ***Part-time tuition:*** $310 per credit hour. ***Part-time fees:*** $21 per credit hour.

FRESHMAN FINANCIAL AID (Fall 2007) 31 applied for aid; of those 90% were deemed to have need. 100% of freshmen with need received aid; of those 32% had need fully met. ***Average percent of need met:*** 78% (excluding resources awarded to replace EFC). ***Average financial aid package:*** $9822 (excluding resources awarded to replace EFC). 6% of all full-time freshmen had no need and received non-need-based gift aid.

UNDERGRADUATE FINANCIAL AID (Fall 2007) 111 applied for aid; of those 92% were deemed to have need. 100% of undergraduates with need received aid; of those 24% had need fully met. ***Average percent of need met:*** 68% (excluding resources awarded to replace EFC). ***Average financial aid package:*** $11,281 (excluding resources awarded to replace EFC). 7% of all full-time undergraduates had no need and received non-need-based gift aid.

GIFT AID (NEED-BASED) ***Total amount:*** $497,693 (44% federal, 2% state, 52% institutional, 2% external sources). ***Receiving aid:*** Freshmen: 74% (25); all full-time undergraduates: 77% (93). ***Average award:*** Freshmen: $3928; Undergraduates: $4699. ***Scholarships, grants, and awards:*** Federal Pell, FSEOG, state, private, college/university gift aid from institutional funds.

GIFT AID (NON-NEED-BASED) ***Total amount:*** $56,625 (100% institutional). ***Receiving aid:*** Freshmen: 26% (9). Undergraduates: 20% (24). ***Average award:*** Undergraduates: $1879. ***Scholarships, grants, and awards by category:*** *Academic interests/achievement:* 22 awards ($73,760 total): general academic interests/achievements, religion/biblical studies. *Special achievements/activities:* 9 awards ($5767 total): general special achievements/activities, religious involvement. *Special characteristics:* 76 awards ($89,635 total): children and siblings of alumni, children of faculty/staff, general special characteristics, handicapped students, international students, married students, spouses of current students.

LOANS ***Student loans:*** $825,915 (79% need-based, 21% non-need-based). 84% of past graduating class borrowed through all loan programs. *Average indebtedness per student:* $21,314. ***Average need-based loan:*** Freshmen: $2380. Undergraduates: $3350. ***Parent loans:*** $61,340 (36% need-based, 64% non-need-based). ***Programs:*** FFEL (Subsidized and Unsubsidized Stafford, PLUS), alternative/private loans.

WORK-STUDY ***Federal work-study:*** Total amount: $13,054; 16 jobs averaging $816.

APPLYING FOR FINANCIAL AID ***Required financial aid forms:*** FAFSA, institution's own form. ***Financial aid deadline (priority):*** 2/1. ***Notification date:*** Continuous beginning 4/1. Students must reply by 5/1 or within 2 weeks of notification.

CONTACT Lisa W. Pipkin, Financial Aid Administrator, Roanoke Bible College, 715 North Poindexter Street, Elizabeth City, NC 27909, 252-334-2020 or toll-free 800-RBC-8980. *Fax:* 252-334-2064. *E-mail:* lwp@roanokebible.edu.

ROANOKE COLLEGE

Salem, VA

Tuition & fees: $27,935 **Average undergraduate aid package: $21,838**

ABOUT THE INSTITUTION Independent religious, coed. ***Awards:*** bachelor's degrees. 30 undergraduate majors. ***Total enrollment:*** 2,021. Undergraduates: 2,021. Freshmen: 529. Federal methodology is used as a basis for awarding need-based institutional aid.

UNDERGRADUATE EXPENSES for 2008–09 ***Application fee:*** $33. ***Comprehensive fee:*** $37,220 includes full-time tuition ($27,210), mandatory fees ($725), and room and board ($9285). ***College room only:*** $4340. Room and board charges vary according to housing facility. ***Part-time tuition:*** $1300 per course. Part-time tuition and fees vary according to course load. ***Payment plan:*** Installment.

FRESHMAN FINANCIAL AID (Fall 2008, est.) 411 applied for aid; of those 82% were deemed to have need. 100% of freshmen with need received aid; of those 35% had need fully met. ***Average percent of need met:*** 88% (excluding resources awarded to replace EFC). ***Average financial aid package:*** $23,541 (excluding resources awarded to replace EFC). 34% of all full-time freshmen had no need and received non-need-based gift aid.

UNDERGRADUATE FINANCIAL AID (Fall 2008, est.) 1,475 applied for aid; of those 80% were deemed to have need. 100% of undergraduates with need received aid; of those 32% had need fully met. ***Average percent of need met:*** 83% (excluding resources awarded to replace EFC). ***Average financial aid package:*** $21,838 (excluding resources awarded to replace EFC). 36% of all full-time undergraduates had no need and received non-need-based gift aid.

GIFT AID (NEED-BASED) ***Total amount:*** $21,042,482 (6% federal, 11% state, 81% institutional, 2% external sources). ***Receiving aid:*** Freshmen: 63% (331); all full-time undergraduates: 61% (1,164). ***Average award:*** Freshmen: $19,390; Undergraduates: $17,763. ***Scholarships, grants, and awards:*** Federal Pell, FSEOG, state, private, college/university gift aid from institutional funds.

GIFT AID (NON-NEED-BASED) ***Total amount:*** $7,413,921 (12% state, 86% institutional, 2% external sources). ***Receiving aid:*** Freshmen: 62% (327). Undergraduates: 61% (1,173). ***Average award:*** Freshmen: $11,010. Undergraduates: $10,077. ***Tuition waivers:*** Full or partial for employees or children of employees, senior citizens.

LOANS ***Student loans:*** $9,908,074 (90% need-based, 10% non-need-based). 68% of past graduating class borrowed through all loan programs. *Average indebtedness per student:* $25,498. ***Average need-based loan:*** Freshmen: $3958. Undergraduates: $4604. ***Parent loans:*** $1,998,771 (87% need-based, 13% non-need-based). ***Programs:*** FFEL (Subsidized and Unsubsidized Stafford, PLUS), Perkins, college/university, alternative loans.

WORK-STUDY ***Federal work-study:*** Total amount: $1,047,613; jobs available.

APPLYING FOR FINANCIAL AID ***Required financial aid forms:*** FAFSA, state aid form. ***Financial aid deadline (priority):*** 3/1. ***Notification date:*** Continuous. Students must reply within 2 weeks of notification.

CONTACT Mr. Thomas S. Blair Jr., Director of Financial Aid, Roanoke College, 221 College Lane, Salem, VA 24153-3794, 540-375-2235 or toll-free 800-388-2276. *E-mail:* finaid@roanoke.edu.

ROBERT MORRIS COLLEGE

Chicago, IL

Tuition & fees: $19,200 **Average undergraduate aid package: $12,071**

ABOUT THE INSTITUTION Independent, coed. ***Awards:*** associate, bachelor's, and master's degrees. 13 undergraduate majors. ***Total enrollment:*** 4,590. Undergraduates: 4,240. Freshmen: 995. Federal methodology is used as a basis for awarding need-based institutional aid.

UNDERGRADUATE EXPENSES for 2009–10 ***Application fee:*** $30. ***Tuition:*** full-time $19,200; part-time $2133 per term.

FRESHMAN FINANCIAL AID (Fall 2007) 1,342 applied for aid; of those 97% were deemed to have need. 97% of freshmen with need received aid; of those 2% had need fully met. ***Average percent of need met:*** 42% (excluding resources awarded to replace EFC). ***Average financial aid package:*** $12,115 (excluding resources awarded to replace EFC). 1% of all full-time freshmen had no need and received non-need-based gift aid.

UNDERGRADUATE FINANCIAL AID (Fall 2007) 5,082 applied for aid; of those 94% were deemed to have need. 97% of undergraduates with need received aid; of those 3% had need fully met. ***Average percent of need met:*** 42% (excluding resources awarded to replace EFC). ***Average financial aid package:*** $12,071 (excluding resources awarded to replace EFC). 2% of all full-time undergraduates had no need and received non-need-based gift aid.

GIFT AID (NEED-BASED) ***Total amount:*** $35,889,108 (31% federal, 34% state, 32% institutional, 3% external sources). ***Receiving aid:*** Freshmen: 84% (1,200); all full-time undergraduates: 85% (4,479). ***Average award:*** Freshmen: $8583; Undergraduates: $8264. ***Scholarships, grants, and awards:*** Federal Pell, FSEOG, state, private, college/university gift aid from institutional funds.

GIFT AID (NON-NEED-BASED) ***Total amount:*** $979,351 (95% institutional, 5% external sources). ***Receiving aid:*** Freshmen: 2% (23). Undergraduates: 2% (99). ***Average award:*** Freshmen: $6843. Undergraduates: $5319. ***Scholarships, grants, and awards by category:*** *Academic interests/achievement:* architecture, business, computer science, general academic interests/achievements, health fields. *Creative arts/performance:* applied art and design, journalism/publications. *Special achievements/activities:* community service, general special achievements/activities. *Special characteristics:* children of faculty/staff, general special characteristics, out-of-state students, veterans. ***ROTC:*** Army cooperative.

LOANS ***Student loans:*** $42,129,127 (94% need-based, 6% non-need-based). 92% of past graduating class borrowed through all loan programs. *Average indebtedness per student:* $24,600. ***Average need-based loan:*** Freshmen: $4890. Undergraduates: $5046. ***Parent loans:*** $3,950,992 (79% need-based, 21% non-need-based). ***Programs:*** Federal Direct (Subsidized and Unsubsidized Stafford, PLUS), FFEL (Subsidized and Unsubsidized Stafford, PLUS), Perkins.

WORK-STUDY ***Federal work-study:*** Total amount: $632,760; 358 jobs averaging $1878.

ATHLETIC AWARDS Total amount: $4,458,137 (85% need-based, 15% non-need-based).

APPLYING FOR FINANCIAL AID ***Required financial aid form:*** FAFSA. ***Financial aid deadline:*** Continuous. ***Notification date:*** Continuous.

CONTACT Leigh Taylor, Vice President of Financial Services, Robert Morris College, 401 South State Street, Suite 122, Chicago, IL 60605, 312-935-4408 or toll-free 800-RMC-5960. *Fax:* 312-935-4415. *E-mail:* ltaylor@robertmorris.edu.

ROBERT MORRIS COLLEGE–DuPAGE

Aurora, IL

CONTACT Financial Aid Office, Robert Morris College–DuPage, 905 Meridian Lake Drive, Aurora, IL 60504, 630-375-8000.

ROBERT MORRIS COLLEGE–ORLAND PARK

Orland Park, IL

CONTACT Financial Aid Office, Robert Morris College–Orland Park, 43 Orland Square, Orland Park, IL 60462, 708-460-8000.

ROBERT MORRIS UNIVERSITY

Moon Township, PA

Tuition & fees: $19,740 **Average undergraduate aid package: $15,882**

ABOUT THE INSTITUTION Independent, coed. ***Awards:*** bachelor's, master's, and doctoral degrees and post-bachelor's certificates. 30 undergraduate majors. ***Total enrollment:*** 4,815. Undergraduates: 3,773. Freshmen: 649. Federal methodology is used as a basis for awarding need-based institutional aid.

UNDERGRADUATE EXPENSES for 2008–09 ***Application fee:*** $30. ***Comprehensive fee:*** $29,620 includes full-time tuition ($19,190), mandatory fees ($550), and room and board ($9880). ***College room only:*** $4940. Full-time tuition and fees vary according to program. Room and board charges vary according to board plan and housing facility. ***Part-time tuition:*** $640 per credit. ***Part-time fees:*** $25 per credit. Part-time tuition and fees vary according to course load and program. ***Payment plans:*** Installment, deferred payment.

FRESHMAN FINANCIAL AID (Fall 2008, est.) 594 applied for aid; of those 87% were deemed to have need. 100% of freshmen with need received aid; of those 23% had need fully met. ***Average percent of need met:*** 77% (excluding resources awarded to replace EFC). ***Average financial aid package:*** $17,374 (excluding resources awarded to replace EFC). 19% of all full-time freshmen had no need and received non-need-based gift aid.

UNDERGRADUATE FINANCIAL AID (Fall 2008, est.) 2,615 applied for aid; of those 88% were deemed to have need. 100% of undergraduates with need received aid; of those 17% had need fully met. ***Average percent of need met:*** 72% (excluding resources awarded to replace EFC). ***Average financial aid package:*** $15,882 (excluding resources awarded to replace EFC). 19% of all full-time undergraduates had no need and received non-need-based gift aid.

GIFT AID (NEED-BASED) ***Total amount:*** $17,203,666 (20% federal, 24% state, 53% institutional, 3% external sources). ***Receiving aid:*** Freshmen: 79% (512); all full-time undergraduates: 70% (2,123). ***Average award:*** Freshmen: $11,744; Undergraduates: $8824. ***Scholarships, grants, and awards:*** Federal Pell, FSEOG, state, private, college/university gift aid from institutional funds.

GIFT AID (NON-NEED-BASED) ***Total amount:*** $3,979,835 (1% state, 95% institutional, 4% external sources). ***Receiving aid:*** Freshmen: 10% (62). Undergraduates: 5% (163). ***Average award:*** Freshmen: $13,236. Undergraduates: $12,685. ***Scholarships, grants, and awards by category:*** *Academic interests/achievement:* general academic interests/achievements. ***Tuition waivers:*** Full or partial for employees or children of employees. ***ROTC:*** Army, Air Force cooperative.

LOANS ***Student loans:*** $33,060,664 (69% need-based, 31% non-need-based). 79% of past graduating class borrowed through all loan programs. *Average indebtedness per student:* $31,049. ***Average need-based loan:*** Freshmen: $4444. Undergraduates: $6628. ***Parent loans:*** $3,907,391 (36% need-based, 64% non-need-based). ***Programs:*** FFEL (Subsidized and Unsubsidized Stafford, PLUS), Perkins, alternative private loans.

WORK-STUDY ***Federal work-study:*** Total amount: $3,823,215; jobs available. ***State or other work-study/employment:*** Part-time jobs available.

ATHLETIC AWARDS Total amount: $3,034,311 (56% need-based, 44% non-need-based).

APPLYING FOR FINANCIAL AID ***Required financial aid form:*** FAFSA. ***Financial aid deadline:*** Continuous. ***Notification date:*** Continuous beginning 3/15. Students must reply within 2 weeks of notification.

CONTACT Ms. Stephanie Hendershot, Director, Financial Aid, Robert Morris University, 6001 University Boulevard, Moon Township, PA 15108-1189, 412-397-2450 or toll-free 800-762-0097. *Fax:* 412-397-2200. *E-mail:* finaid@rmu.edu.

ROBERTS WESLEYAN COLLEGE

Rochester, NY

Tuition & fees: $23,780 **Average undergraduate aid package: $16,430**

ABOUT THE INSTITUTION Independent religious, coed. ***Awards:*** associate, bachelor's, and master's degrees. 60 undergraduate majors. ***Total enrollment:*** 1,902. Undergraduates: 1,359. Federal methodology is used as a basis for awarding need-based institutional aid.

UNDERGRADUATE EXPENSES for 2009–10 ***Application fee:*** $35. ***Comprehensive fee:*** $32,300 includes full-time tuition ($22,580), mandatory fees ($1200), and room and board ($8520). ***College room only:*** $5816. ***Part-time tuition:*** $493 per credit.

FRESHMAN FINANCIAL AID (Fall 2008, est.) 216 applied for aid; of those 95% were deemed to have need. 100% of freshmen with need received aid; of those 16% had need fully met. ***Average percent of need met:*** 80% (excluding resources awarded to replace EFC). ***Average financial aid package:*** $20,104 (excluding resources awarded to replace EFC). 9% of all full-time freshmen had no need and received non-need-based gift aid.

UNDERGRADUATE FINANCIAL AID (Fall 2008, est.) 1,171 applied for aid; of those 94% were deemed to have need. 100% of undergraduates with need received aid; of those 10% had need fully met. ***Average percent of need met:*** 69% (excluding resources awarded to replace EFC). ***Average financial aid package:*** $16,430 (excluding resources awarded to replace EFC). 8% of all full-time undergraduates had no need and received non-need-based gift aid.

GIFT AID (NEED-BASED) ***Total amount:*** $11,711,711 (16% federal, 14% state, 54% institutional, 16% external sources). ***Receiving aid:*** Freshmen: 88% (205); all full-time undergraduates: 94% (1,007). ***Average award:*** Freshmen: $14,471; Undergraduates: $10,720. ***Scholarships, grants, and awards:*** Federal Pell, FSEOG, state, private, college/university gift aid from institutional funds, Academic Competitiveness Grant, National Smart Grant.

GIFT AID (NON-NEED-BASED) ***Total amount:*** $1,332,138 (3% state, 54% institutional, 43% external sources). ***Receiving aid:*** Freshmen: 9% (22). Undergraduates: 5% (60). ***Average award:*** Freshmen: $6281. Undergraduates: $5775. ***Scholarships, grants, and awards by category:*** *Academic interests/achievement:* 589 awards ($2,176,719 total): general academic interests/achievements. *Creative arts/performance:* 171 awards ($319,500 total): art/fine arts, music. *Special achievements/activities:* 424 awards ($341,089 total): general special achievements/activities, leadership. *Special characteristics:* 576 awards ($1,468,174 total): children and siblings of alumni, children of faculty/staff, international students, out-of-state students, relatives of clergy, religious affiliation, siblings of current students. ***ROTC:*** Army cooperative, Air Force cooperative.

LOANS ***Student loans:*** $11,116,793 (82% need-based, 18% non-need-based). 95% of past graduating class borrowed through all loan programs. *Average indebtedness per student:* $22,829. ***Average need-based loan:*** Freshmen: $5127. Undergraduates: $5682. ***Parent loans:*** $1,781,609 (49% need-based, 51% non-need-based). ***Programs:*** FFEL (Subsidized and Unsubsidized Stafford, PLUS), Perkins.

WORK-STUDY ***Federal work-study:*** Total amount: $354,000; 743 jobs averaging $1711. ***State or other work-study/employment:*** Total amount: $41,500 (100% non-need-based). 26 part-time jobs averaging $1751.

ATHLETIC AWARDS Total amount: $702,598 (70% need-based, 30% non-need-based).

APPLYING FOR FINANCIAL AID ***Required financial aid forms:*** FAFSA, state aid form. ***Financial aid deadline (priority):*** 3/15. ***Notification date:*** Continuous beginning 3/15. Students must reply by 5/1 or within 2 weeks of notification.

CONTACT Financial Aid Office, Roberts Wesleyan College, 2301 Westside Drive, Rochester, NY 14624-1997, 585-594-6150 or toll-free 800-777-4RWC. *Fax:* 585-594-6036. *E-mail:* finaid@roberts.edu.

ROCHESTER COLLEGE

Rochester Hills, MI

CONTACT Burt Rutledge, Director of Financial Aid, Rochester College, 800 West Avon Road, Rochester Hills, MI 48307, 248-218-2028 or toll-free 800-521-6010. *Fax:* 248-218-2035. *E-mail:* brutledge@rc.edu.

ROCHESTER INSTITUTE OF TECHNOLOGY

Rochester, NY

Tuition & fees: $28,035 **Average undergraduate aid package: $19,200**

ABOUT THE INSTITUTION Independent, coed. ***Awards:*** associate, bachelor's, master's, and doctoral degrees and post-bachelor's and post-master's certificates. 114 undergraduate majors. ***Total enrollment:*** 16,494. Undergraduates: 13,861. Freshmen: 2,625. Both federal and institutional methodology are used as a basis for awarding need-based institutional aid.

UNDERGRADUATE EXPENSES for 2008–09 ***Application fee:*** $50. ***Comprehensive fee:*** $37,416 includes full-time tuition ($27,624), mandatory fees ($411), and room and board ($9381). ***College room only:*** $5421. Full-time tuition and fees vary according to course load. Room and board charges vary according to board plan and housing facility. ***Part-time tuition:*** $580 per credit hour. ***Part-time fees:*** $34 per term. Part-time tuition and fees vary according to class time and course load. ***Payment plans:*** Tuition prepayment, installment, deferred payment.

FRESHMAN FINANCIAL AID (Fall 2007) 2,202 applied for aid; of those 86% were deemed to have need. 100% of freshmen with need received aid; of those 76% had need fully met. ***Average percent of need met:*** 88% (excluding resources awarded to replace EFC). ***Average financial aid package:*** $19,800 (excluding resources awarded to replace EFC). 11% of all full-time freshmen had no need and received non-need-based gift aid.

UNDERGRADUATE FINANCIAL AID (Fall 2007) 8,484 applied for aid; of those 90% were deemed to have need. 100% of undergraduates with need received aid; of those 79% had need fully met. ***Average percent of need met:*** 88% (excluding resources awarded to replace EFC). ***Average financial aid package:*** $19,200 (excluding resources awarded to replace EFC). 10% of all full-time undergraduates had no need and received non-need-based gift aid.

GIFT AID (NEED-BASED) ***Total amount:*** $91,363,100 (13% federal, 9% state, 75% institutional, 3% external sources). ***Receiving aid:*** Freshmen: 71% (1,780);

all full-time undergraduates: 65% (7,146). ***Average award:*** Freshmen: $13,700; Undergraduates: $13,100. ***Scholarships, grants, and awards:*** Federal Pell, FSEOG, state, private, college/university gift aid from institutional funds, NACME, NSF.

GIFT AID (NON-NEED-BASED) ***Total amount:*** $22,471,450 (9% federal, 24% state, 54% institutional, 13% external sources). ***Receiving aid:*** Freshmen: 20% (508). Undergraduates: 20% (2,228). ***Average award:*** Freshmen: $7300. Undergraduates: $7000. ***Scholarships, grants, and awards by category:*** *Academic interests/achievement:* 3,000 awards ($21,900,000 total): biological sciences, business, communication, computer science, engineering/technologies, general academic interests/achievements, health fields, international studies, mathematics, military science, physical sciences, premedicine, social sciences. *Creative arts/performance:* 300 awards ($2,190,000 total): applied art and design, art/fine arts, cinema/film/broadcasting. *Special achievements/activities:* 200 awards ($1,460,000 total): community service, leadership. *Special characteristics:* children of faculty/staff, international students, members of minority groups, veterans. ***Tuition waivers:*** Full or partial for employees or children of employees. ***ROTC:*** Army, Naval cooperative, Air Force.

LOANS ***Student loans:*** $77,252,125 (54% need-based, 46% non-need-based). ***Average need-based loan:*** Freshmen: $5100. Undergraduates: $5500. ***Parent loans:*** $12,514,912 (40% need-based, 60% non-need-based). ***Programs:*** Federal Direct (Subsidized and Unsubsidized Stafford, PLUS), Perkins, alternative loans.

WORK-STUDY ***Federal work-study:*** Total amount: $3,247,236; 2,100 jobs averaging $2400. ***State or other work-study/employment:*** Total amount: $7,438,134 (100% non-need-based). 4,700 part-time jobs averaging $2400.

APPLYING FOR FINANCIAL AID ***Required financial aid form:*** FAFSA. ***Financial aid deadline (priority):*** 3/1. ***Notification date:*** Continuous beginning 3/15. Students must reply by 5/1.

CONTACT Mrs. Verna Hazen, Assistant Vice President, Financial Aid and Scholarships, Rochester Institute of Technology, Office of Financial Aid and Scholarships, Rochester, NY 14623-5604, 585-475-2186. *Fax:* 585-475-7270. *E-mail:* verna.hazen@rit.edu.

ROCKFORD COLLEGE

Rockford, IL

Tuition & fees: $24,250 **Average undergraduate aid package: $17,351**

ABOUT THE INSTITUTION Independent, coed. ***Awards:*** bachelor's and master's degrees. 47 undergraduate majors. ***Total enrollment:*** 1,391. Undergraduates: 874. Freshmen: 121. Federal methodology is used as a basis for awarding need-based institutional aid.

UNDERGRADUATE EXPENSES for 2009–10 ***Application fee:*** $35. ***Comprehensive fee:*** $31,000 includes full-time tuition ($24,250) and room and board ($6750). ***College room only:*** $3850. ***Part-time tuition:*** $650 per credit. ***Part-time fees:*** $30 per credit.

FRESHMAN FINANCIAL AID (Fall 2007) 104 applied for aid; of those 90% were deemed to have need. 100% of freshmen with need received aid; of those 13% had need fully met. ***Average percent of need met:*** 73% (excluding resources awarded to replace EFC). ***Average financial aid package:*** $18,894 (excluding resources awarded to replace EFC). 15% of all full-time freshmen had no need and received non-need-based gift aid.

UNDERGRADUATE FINANCIAL AID (Fall 2007) 664 applied for aid; of those 94% were deemed to have need. 100% of undergraduates with need received aid; of those 14% had need fully met. ***Average percent of need met:*** 68% (excluding resources awarded to replace EFC). ***Average financial aid package:*** $17,351 (excluding resources awarded to replace EFC). 13% of all full-time undergraduates had no need and received non-need-based gift aid.

GIFT AID (NEED-BASED) ***Total amount:*** $3,965,355 (28% federal, 45% state, 27% institutional). ***Receiving aid:*** Freshmen: 84% (93); all full-time undergraduates: 85% (611). ***Average award:*** Freshmen: $14,972; Undergraduates: $12,354. ***Scholarships, grants, and awards:*** Federal Pell, FSEOG, state, private, college/university gift aid from institutional funds.

GIFT AID (NON-NEED-BASED) ***Total amount:*** $5,352,167 (100% institutional). ***Receiving aid:*** Freshmen: 12% (13). Undergraduates: 13% (92). ***Average award:*** Freshmen: $10,964. Undergraduates: $10,820. ***Scholarships, grants, and awards by category:*** *Academic interests/achievement:* 748 awards ($4,798,641 total): biological sciences, business, computer science, education, English, foreign languages, general academic interests/achievements, mathematics, physical sciences, premedicine, social sciences. *Creative arts/performance:* 21 awards ($49,000 total): dance, music, performing arts, theater/drama. *Special achievements/activities:* 7 awards ($13,475 total): community service, leadership. *Special characteristics:* 50 awards ($555,180 total): children and siblings of alumni, children of current students, children of educators, children of faculty/staff, general special characteristics, international students, out-of-state students, parents of current students, siblings of current students. ***ROTC:*** Army cooperative.

LOANS ***Student loans:*** $7,050,808 (85% need-based, 15% non-need-based). 92% of past graduating class borrowed through all loan programs. *Average indebtedness per student:* $25,148. ***Average need-based loan:*** Freshmen: $3256. Undergraduates: $4498. ***Parent loans:*** $253,478 (100% need-based). ***Programs:*** FFEL (Subsidized and Unsubsidized Stafford, PLUS), Perkins, college/university, alternative loans.

WORK-STUDY ***Federal work-study:*** Total amount: $146,074; 136 jobs averaging $2144. ***State or other work-study/employment:*** Total amount: $162,702 (100% non-need-based). 203 part-time jobs averaging $2106.

APPLYING FOR FINANCIAL AID ***Required financial aid form:*** FAFSA. ***Financial aid deadline (priority):*** 3/1. ***Notification date:*** Continuous beginning 3/15. Students must reply within 4 weeks of notification.

CONTACT Todd M. Free, Assistant Vice President for Student Administrative Services, Rockford College, 5050 East State Street, Rockford, IL 61108, 815-226-3385 or toll-free 800-892-2984. *Fax:* 815-394-5174. *E-mail:* tfree@rockford.edu.

ROCKHURST UNIVERSITY

Kansas City, MO

Tuition & fees: $25,890 **Average undergraduate aid package: $24,533**

ABOUT THE INSTITUTION Independent Roman Catholic (Jesuit), coed. ***Awards:*** bachelor's, master's, and doctoral degrees and post-bachelor's certificates. 28 undergraduate majors. ***Total enrollment:*** 3,086. Undergraduates: 2,242. Freshmen: 350. Federal methodology is used as a basis for awarding need-based institutional aid.

UNDERGRADUATE EXPENSES for 2009–10 ***Application fee:*** $25. ***Comprehensive fee:*** $32,970 includes full-time tuition ($24,950), mandatory fees ($940), and room and board ($7080). ***College room only:*** $4180. ***Part-time tuition:*** $832 per credit hour.

FRESHMAN FINANCIAL AID (Fall 2008, est.) 356 applied for aid; of those 93% were deemed to have need. 99% of freshmen with need received aid; of those 27% had need fully met. ***Average percent of need met:*** 100% (excluding resources awarded to replace EFC). ***Average financial aid package:*** $24,588 (excluding resources awarded to replace EFC). 6% of all full-time freshmen had no need and received non-need-based gift aid.

UNDERGRADUATE FINANCIAL AID (Fall 2008, est.) 1,495 applied for aid; of those 83% were deemed to have need. 95% of undergraduates with need received aid; of those 18% had need fully met. ***Average percent of need met:*** 100% (excluding resources awarded to replace EFC). ***Average financial aid package:*** $24,533 (excluding resources awarded to replace EFC). 11% of all full-time undergraduates had no need and received non-need-based gift aid.

GIFT AID (NEED-BASED) ***Total amount:*** $10,975,087 (12% federal, 13% state, 74% institutional, 1% external sources). ***Receiving aid:*** Freshmen: 75% (268); all full-time undergraduates: 64% (993). ***Average award:*** Freshmen: $6626; Undergraduates: $7512. ***Scholarships, grants, and awards:*** Federal Pell, FSEOG, state, private, college/university gift aid from institutional funds.

GIFT AID (NON-NEED-BASED) ***Total amount:*** $9,956,031 (1% state, 97% institutional, 2% external sources). ***Receiving aid:*** Freshmen: 92% (328). Undergraduates: 76% (1,172). ***Average award:*** Freshmen: $12,415. Undergraduates: $12,167. ***Scholarships, grants, and awards by category:*** *Academic interests/achievement:* biological sciences, business, communication, English, foreign languages, general academic interests/achievements, health fields, humanities, mathematics, physical sciences, premedicine, religion/biblical studies, social sciences. *Creative arts/performance:* creative writing, music, performing arts, theater/drama. *Special achievements/activities:* community service, leadership. *Special characteristics:* children and siblings of alumni, children of faculty/staff, siblings of current students. ***ROTC:*** Army cooperative.

LOANS ***Student loans:*** $8,415,048 (51% need-based, 49% non-need-based). ***Average need-based loan:*** Freshmen: $3283. Undergraduates: $3973. ***Parent loans:*** $1,395,493 (59% need-based, 41% non-need-based). ***Programs:*** FFEL (Subsidized and Unsubsidized Stafford, PLUS), Perkins.

WORK-STUDY ***Federal work-study:*** Total amount: $220,320; jobs available.

ATHLETIC AWARDS Total amount: $2,114,857 (14% need-based, 86% non-need-based).

APPLYING FOR FINANCIAL AID ***Required financial aid form:*** FAFSA. ***Financial aid deadline (priority):*** 3/1. ***Notification date:*** Continuous beginning 3/1. Students must reply by 6/1 or within 4 weeks of notification.

CONTACT Ms. Angela Karlin, Director of Financial Aid, Rockhurst University, 1100 Rockhurst Road, Kansas City, MO 64110-2561, 816-501-4238 or toll-free 800-842-6776. *Fax:* 816-501-3139. *E-mail:* Angela.Karlin@rockhurst.edu.

ROCKY MOUNTAIN COLLEGE

Billings, MT

CONTACT Lisa Browning, Financial Aid Director, Rocky Mountain College, 1511 Poly Drive, Billings, MT 59102-1796, 406-657-1031 or toll-free 800-877-6259. *Fax:* 406-238-7351. *E-mail:* browninl@rocky.edu.

ROCKY MOUNTAIN COLLEGE OF ART + DESIGN

Lakewood, CO

Tuition & fees: $24,840 **Average undergraduate aid package: $15,072**

ABOUT THE INSTITUTION Proprietary, coed. ***Awards:*** bachelor's degrees. 8 undergraduate majors. ***Total enrollment:*** 573. Undergraduates: 573. Freshmen: 133. Federal methodology is used as a basis for awarding need-based institutional aid.

UNDERGRADUATE EXPENSES for 2009–10 ***Application fee:*** $50. ***Tuition:*** full-time $24,840; part-time $1035 per credit hour.

FRESHMAN FINANCIAL AID (Fall 2008, est.) 110 applied for aid; of those 94% were deemed to have need. 100% of freshmen with need received aid; of those 9% had need fully met. ***Average percent of need met:*** 60% (excluding resources awarded to replace EFC). ***Average financial aid package:*** $14,042 (excluding resources awarded to replace EFC). 16% of all full-time freshmen had no need and received non-need-based gift aid.

UNDERGRADUATE FINANCIAL AID (Fall 2008, est.) 392 applied for aid; of those 91% were deemed to have need. 100% of undergraduates with need received aid; of those 8% had need fully met. ***Average percent of need met:*** 67% (excluding resources awarded to replace EFC). ***Average financial aid package:*** $15,072 (excluding resources awarded to replace EFC). 14% of all full-time undergraduates had no need and received non-need-based gift aid.

GIFT AID (NEED-BASED) ***Total amount:*** $2,093,284 (21% federal, 5% state, 71% institutional, 3% external sources). ***Receiving aid:*** Freshmen: 19% (26); all full-time undergraduates: 20% (102). ***Average award:*** Freshmen: $3776; Undergraduates: $3919. ***Scholarships, grants, and awards:*** Federal Pell, FSEOG, state, college/university gift aid from institutional funds.

GIFT AID (NON-NEED-BASED) ***Total amount:*** $682,235 (98% institutional, 2% external sources). ***Receiving aid:*** Freshmen: 76% (103). Undergraduates: 64% (336). ***Average award:*** Freshmen: $5668. Undergraduates: $5507. ***Scholarships, grants, and awards by category:*** *Academic interests/achievement:* 444 awards ($1,546,043 total): general academic interests/achievements. *Creative arts/performance:* 297 awards ($486,252 total): applied art and design, art/fine arts. *Special characteristics:* 1 award ($22,992 total): children of faculty/staff.

LOANS ***Student loans:*** $4,386,888 (93% need-based, 7% non-need-based). 74% of past graduating class borrowed through all loan programs. *Average indebtedness per student:* $27,831. ***Average need-based loan:*** Freshmen: $3136. Undergraduates: $3810. ***Parent loans:*** $1,572,963 (93% need-based, 7% non-need-based). ***Programs:*** FFEL (Subsidized and Unsubsidized Stafford, PLUS), alternative loans.

WORK-STUDY ***Federal work-study:*** Total amount: $39,000; 30 jobs averaging $1399. ***State or other work-study/employment:*** Total amount: $117,000 (94% need-based, 6% non-need-based). 43 part-time jobs averaging $2721.

APPLYING FOR FINANCIAL AID ***Required financial aid form:*** FAFSA. ***Financial aid deadline (priority):*** 3/15. ***Notification date:*** Continuous beginning 4/1. Students must reply within 2 weeks of notification.

CONTACT Tammy Dybdahl, Director of Financial Aid, Rocky Mountain College of Art + Design, 1600 Pierce Street, Lakewood, CO 80214, [illegible] or toll-free 800-888-ARTS. *Fax:* 303-567-7200. *E-mail:* tdybdahl@rmcad.edu.

ROGERS STATE UNIVERSITY

Claremore, OK

ABOUT THE INSTITUTION State-supported, coed. ***Awards:*** associate and bachelor's degrees. 23 undergraduate majors. ***Total enrollment:*** 3,858. Undergraduates: 3,858. Freshmen: 750.

GIFT AID (NEED-BASED) ***Scholarships, grants, and awards:*** Federal Pell, FSEOG, state, private, college/university gift aid from institutional funds.

LOANS ***Programs:*** FFEL (Subsidized and Unsubsidized Stafford, PLUS), alternative loans.

WORK-STUDY ***Federal work-study:*** Total amount: $250,000; 73 jobs averaging $1331. ***State or other work-study/employment:*** Total amount: $591,924 (67% need-based, 33% non-need-based). 233 part-time jobs averaging $2043.

APPLYING FOR FINANCIAL AID ***Required financial aid form:*** FAFSA.

CONTACT Cynthia Hoyt, Financial Aid Office, Rogers State University, 1701 West Will Rogers Boulevard, Claremore, OK 74017-3252, 918-343-7553 or toll-free 800-256-7511. *Fax:* 918-343-7598. *E-mail:* finaid@rsu.edu.

ROGER WILLIAMS UNIVERSITY

Bristol, RI

Tuition & fees: $27,718 **Average undergraduate aid package: $17,017**

ABOUT THE INSTITUTION Independent, coed. ***Awards:*** associate, bachelor's, master's, and first professional degrees and post-bachelor's certificates. 47 undergraduate majors. ***Total enrollment:*** 5,159. Undergraduates: 4,345. Freshmen: 954. Both federal and institutional methodology are used as a basis for awarding need-based institutional aid.

UNDERGRADUATE EXPENSES for 2008–09 ***Application fee:*** $50. ***Comprehensive fee:*** $39,598 includes full-time tuition ($25,968), mandatory fees ($1750), and room and board ($11,880). ***College room only:*** $6390. Full-time tuition and fees vary according to class time, course load, and program. Room and board charges vary according to board plan and housing facility. ***Part-time tuition:*** $1082 per credit. Part-time tuition and fees vary according to class time. ***Payment plans:*** Installment, deferred payment.

FRESHMAN FINANCIAL AID (Fall 2008, est.) 724 applied for aid; of those 76% were deemed to have need. 99% of freshmen with need received aid; of those 4% had need fully met. ***Average percent of need met:*** 88% (excluding resources awarded to replace EFC). ***Average financial aid package:*** $17,274 (excluding resources awarded to replace EFC). 17% of all full-time freshmen had no need and received non-need-based gift aid.

UNDERGRADUATE FINANCIAL AID (Fall 2008, est.) 2,717 applied for aid; of those 81% were deemed to have need. 98% of undergraduates with need received aid; of those 4% had need fully met. ***Average percent of need met:*** 86% (excluding resources awarded to replace EFC). ***Average financial aid package:*** $17,017 (excluding resources awarded to replace EFC). 10% of all full-time undergraduates had no need and received non-need-based gift aid.

GIFT AID (NEED-BASED) ***Total amount:*** $27,379,790 (7% federal, 1% state, 87% institutional, 5% external sources). ***Receiving aid:*** Freshmen: 33% (314); all full-time undergraduates: 37% (1,379). ***Average award:*** Freshmen: $5769; Undergraduates: $7050. ***Scholarships, grants, and awards:*** Federal Pell, FSEOG, state, private, college/university gift aid from institutional funds.

GIFT AID (NON-NEED-BASED) ***Total amount:*** $2,662,301 (96% institutional, 4% external sources). ***Receiving aid:*** Freshmen: 43% (414). Undergraduates: 33% (1,232). ***Average award:*** Freshmen: $7315. Undergraduates: $6955. ***Scholarships, grants, and awards by category:*** *Academic interests/achievement:* 1,710 awards ($15,594,439 total): general academic interests/achievements. ***Tuition waivers:*** Full or partial for employees or children of employees. ***ROTC:*** Army cooperative.

LOANS ***Student loans:*** $26,301,360 (88% need-based, 12% non-need-based). 79% of past graduating class borrowed through all loan programs. *Average indebtedness per student:* $31,874. ***Average need-based loan:*** Freshmen: $3834. Undergraduates: $4709. ***Parent loans:*** $11,298,289 (83% need-based, 17% non-need-based). ***Programs:*** FFEL (Subsidized and Unsubsidized Stafford, PLUS), Perkins, state.

WORK-STUDY ***Federal work-study:*** Total amount: $682,292; 403 jobs averaging $1020. ***State or other work-study/employment:*** 867 part-time jobs averaging $1034.

APPLYING FOR FINANCIAL AID ***Required financial aid forms:*** FAFSA, CSS Financial Aid PROFILE. ***Financial aid deadline:*** 2/1. ***Notification date:*** Continuous beginning 3/15. Students must reply within 2 weeks of notification.

CONTACT Mr. Greg Rogers, Director of Institutional Research, Roger Williams University, 1 Old Ferry Road, Bristol, RI 02809, 401-254-3116 or toll-free 800-458-7144 (out-of-state). *Fax:* 401-254-3677. *E-mail:* grogers@rwu.edu.

ROLLINS COLLEGE

Winter Park, FL

Tuition & fees: $34,520 **Average undergraduate aid package: $31,313**

ABOUT THE INSTITUTION Independent, coed. ***Awards:*** bachelor's and master's degrees. 29 undergraduate majors. ***Total enrollment:*** 2,511. Undergraduates: 1,785. Freshmen: 464. Federal methodology is used as a basis for awarding need-based institutional aid.

UNDERGRADUATE EXPENSES for 2008–09 ***Application fee:*** $40. ***Comprehensive fee:*** $45,300 includes full-time tuition ($34,520) and room and board ($10,780). ***College room only:*** $6340. ***Payment plan:*** Installment.

FRESHMAN FINANCIAL AID (Fall 2008, est.) 242 applied for aid; of those 77% were deemed to have need. 99% of freshmen with need received aid; of those 22% had need fully met. ***Average percent of need met:*** 90% (excluding resources awarded to replace EFC). ***Average financial aid package:*** $32,696 (excluding resources awarded to replace EFC). 18% of all full-time freshmen had no need and received non-need-based gift aid.

UNDERGRADUATE FINANCIAL AID (Fall 2008, est.) 857 applied for aid; of those 87% were deemed to have need. 100% of undergraduates with need received aid; of those 21% had need fully met. ***Average percent of need met:*** 88% (excluding resources awarded to replace EFC). ***Average financial aid package:*** $31,313 (excluding resources awarded to replace EFC). 15% of all full-time undergraduates had no need and received non-need-based gift aid.

GIFT AID (NEED-BASED) ***Total amount:*** $19,293,478 (8% federal, 16% state, 75% institutional, 1% external sources). ***Receiving aid:*** Freshmen: 40% (184); all full-time undergraduates: 41% (739). ***Average award:*** Freshmen: $27,367; Undergraduates: $25,800. ***Scholarships, grants, and awards:*** Federal Pell, FSEOG, state, private, college/university gift aid from institutional funds.

GIFT AID (NON-NEED-BASED) ***Total amount:*** $7,002,856 (28% state, 70% institutional, 2% external sources). ***Receiving aid:*** Freshmen: 3% (12). Undergraduates: 4% (74). ***Average award:*** Freshmen: $14,613. Undergraduates: $15,442. ***Scholarships, grants, and awards by category:*** *Academic interests/achievement:* 543 awards ($7,351,780 total): computer science, engineering/technologies, general academic interests/achievements, mathematics, physical sciences. *Creative arts/performance:* 89 awards ($302,300 total): art/fine arts, music, theater/drama. ***Tuition waivers:*** Full or partial for employees or children of employees.

LOANS ***Student loans:*** $4,785,842 (49% need-based, 51% non-need-based). 48% of past graduating class borrowed through all loan programs. *Average indebtedness per student:* $21,904. ***Average need-based loan:*** Freshmen: $4127. Undergraduates: $4452. ***Parent loans:*** $3,059,383 (33% need-based, 67% non-need-based). ***Programs:*** Federal Direct (Subsidized and Unsubsidized Stafford, PLUS), Perkins, college/university.

WORK-STUDY ***Federal work-study:*** Total amount: $840,338; jobs available.

ATHLETIC AWARDS Total amount: $2,593,470 (16% need-based, 84% non-need-based).

APPLYING FOR FINANCIAL AID ***Required financial aid forms:*** FAFSA, institution's own form. ***Financial aid deadline:*** 3/1 (priority: 3/1). ***Notification date:*** Continuous.

CONTACT Mr. Steve Booker, Director of Student Financial Aid, Rollins College, 1000 Holt Avenue, #2721, Winter Park, FL 32789-4499, 407-646-2395. *Fax:* 407-646-2173. *E-mail:* sbooker@rollins.edu.

ROOSEVELT UNIVERSITY

Chicago, IL

CONTACT Mr. Walter J. H. O'Neill, Director of Financial Aid, Roosevelt University, 430 South Michigan Avenue, Chicago, IL 60605-1394, 312-341-2090 or toll-free 877-APPLYRU. *Fax:* 312-341-3545. *E-mail:* woneill@roosevelt.edu.

ROSE-HULMAN INSTITUTE OF TECHNOLOGY

Terre Haute, IN

Tuition & fees: $32,826 **Average undergraduate aid package: $31,456**

ABOUT THE INSTITUTION Independent, coed, primarily men. ***Awards:*** bachelor's and master's degrees. 15 undergraduate majors. ***Total enrollment:*** 1,923. Undergraduates: 1,832. Freshmen: 482. Federal methodology is used as a basis for awarding need-based institutional aid.

UNDERGRADUATE EXPENSES for 2008–09 ***Application fee:*** $40. ***Comprehensive fee:*** $41,694 includes full-time tuition ($32,286), mandatory fees ($540), and room and board ($8868). ***College room only:*** $5142. Full-time tuition and fees vary according to course load. Room and board charges vary according to board plan. ***Part-time tuition:*** $939 per credit. Part-time tuition and fees vary according to course load. ***Payment plans:*** Tuition prepayment, installment.

FRESHMAN FINANCIAL AID (Fall 2008, est.) 419 applied for aid; of those 84% were deemed to have need. 100% of freshmen with need received aid; of those 15% had need fully met. ***Average percent of need met:*** 85% (excluding resources awarded to replace EFC). ***Average financial aid package:*** $31,562 (excluding resources awarded to replace EFC). 26% of all full-time freshmen had no need and received non-need-based gift aid.

UNDERGRADUATE FINANCIAL AID (Fall 2008, est.) 1,456 applied for aid; of those 84% were deemed to have need. 100% of undergraduates with need received aid; of those 11% had need fully met. ***Average percent of need met:*** 85% (excluding resources awarded to replace EFC). ***Average financial aid package:*** $31,456 (excluding resources awarded to replace EFC). 30% of all full-time undergraduates had no need and received non-need-based gift aid.

GIFT AID (NEED-BASED) ***Total amount:*** $21,504,212 (5% federal, 8% state, 70% institutional, 17% external sources). ***Receiving aid:*** Freshmen: 72% (349); all full-time undergraduates: 67% (1,215). ***Average award:*** Freshmen: $20,042; Undergraduates: $17,686. ***Scholarships, grants, and awards:*** Federal Pell, FSEOG, state, college/university gift aid from institutional funds.

GIFT AID (NON-NEED-BASED) ***Total amount:*** $6,404,974 (74% institutional, 26% external sources). ***Average award:*** Freshmen: $10,269. Undergraduates: $8737. ***Tuition waivers:*** Full or partial for employees or children of employees. ***ROTC:*** Army, Air Force.

LOANS ***Student loans:*** $25,117,114 (83% need-based, 17% non-need-based). 78% of past graduating class borrowed through all loan programs. *Average indebtedness per student:* $36,818. ***Average need-based loan:*** Freshmen: $12,642. Undergraduates: $14,705. ***Parent loans:*** $5,668,733 (80% need-based, 20% non-need-based). ***Programs:*** Federal Direct (Subsidized and Unsubsidized Stafford, PLUS), FFEL (Subsidized Stafford).

WORK-STUDY ***Federal work-study:*** Total amount: $725,585; 434 jobs averaging $1632. ***State or other work-study/employment:*** Total amount: $1,086,927 (90% need-based, 10% non-need-based). 664 part-time jobs averaging $1636.

APPLYING FOR FINANCIAL AID ***Required financial aid form:*** FAFSA. ***Financial aid deadline (priority):*** 3/1. ***Notification date:*** 3/10.

CONTACT Melinda L. Middleton, Director of Financial Aid, Rose-Hulman Institute of Technology, 5500 Wabash Avenue, Box #5, Terre Haute, IN 47803, 812-877-8259 or toll-free 800-248-7448. *Fax:* 812-877-8746. *E-mail:* melinda.middleton@rose-hulman.edu.

ROSEMONT COLLEGE

Rosemont, PA

ABOUT THE INSTITUTION Independent Roman Catholic, coed. ***Awards:*** bachelor's and master's degrees and post-bachelor's certificates. 25 undergraduate majors. ***Total enrollment:*** 903. Undergraduates: 518. Freshmen: 126.

GIFT AID (NEED-BASED) ***Scholarships, grants, and awards:*** Federal Pell, FSEOG, state, private, college/university gift aid from institutional funds, Academic Competitiveness Grant, National Smart Grant.

GIFT AID (NON-NEED-BASED) ***Scholarships, grants, and awards by category:*** *Academic interests/achievement:* general academic interests/achievements. *Creative arts/performance:* art/fine arts. *Special achievements/activities:* community service, general special achievements/activities, leadership, religious involvement. *Special characteristics:* children and siblings of alumni, children of educators, children of faculty/staff, relatives of clergy, siblings of current students.

LOANS ***Programs:*** FFEL (Subsidized and Unsubsidized Stafford, PLUS), Perkins.

WORK-STUDY ***Federal work-study:*** Total amount: $125,694; 97 jobs averaging $1175.

APPLYING FOR FINANCIAL AID ***Required financial aid form:*** FAFSA.

CONTACT Melissa Walsh, Director of Financial Aid, Rosemont College, 1400 Montgomery Avenue, Rosemont, PA 19010, 610-527-0200 Ext. 2220 or toll-free 800-331-0708. *Fax:* 610-527-0341. *E-mail:* mwalsh@rosemont.edu.

ROWAN UNIVERSITY

Glassboro, NJ

Tuition & fees (NJ res): $10,908 Average undergraduate aid package: $6634

ABOUT THE INSTITUTION State-supported, coed. ***Awards:*** bachelor's, master's, and doctoral degrees. 47 undergraduate majors. ***Total enrollment:*** 10,271. Undergraduates: 9,037. Freshmen: 1,334. Both federal and institutional methodology are used as a basis for awarding need-based institutional aid.

UNDERGRADUATE EXPENSES for 2008–09 ***Application fee:*** $50. ***Tuition, state resident:*** full-time $7840; part-time $302 per credit hour. ***Tuition, nonresident:*** full-time $15,148; part-time $584 per credit hour. ***Required fees:*** full-time $3068; $131 per credit hour. Full-time tuition and fees vary according to degree level. Part-time tuition and fees vary according to degree level. ***College room and board:*** $9616; ***Room only:*** $6066. Room and board charges vary according to board plan and housing facility. ***Payment plan:*** Deferred payment.

FRESHMAN FINANCIAL AID (Fall 2007) 1,054 applied for aid; of those 60% were deemed to have need. 92% of freshmen with need received aid; of those 28% had need fully met. ***Average percent of need met:*** 92% (excluding resources awarded to replace EFC). ***Average financial aid package:*** $5953 (excluding resources awarded to replace EFC). 10% of all full-time freshmen had no need and received non-need-based gift aid.

UNDERGRADUATE FINANCIAL AID (Fall 2007) 5,920 applied for aid; of those 71% were deemed to have need. 96% of undergraduates with need received aid; of those 21% had need fully met. ***Average percent of need met:*** 85% (excluding resources awarded to replace EFC). ***Average financial aid package:*** $6634 (excluding resources awarded to replace EFC). 7% of all full-time undergraduates had no need and received non-need-based gift aid.

GIFT AID (NEED-BASED) ***Total amount:*** $18,728,390 (33% federal, 48% state, 15% institutional, 4% external sources). ***Receiving aid:*** Freshmen: 16% (203); all full-time undergraduates: 26% (1,964). ***Average award:*** Freshmen: $7020; Undergraduates: $7244. ***Scholarships, grants, and awards:*** Federal Pell, FSEOG, state, private, college/university gift aid from institutional funds.

GIFT AID (NON-NEED-BASED) ***Total amount:*** $2,580,611 (4% state, 82% institutional, 14% external sources). ***Receiving aid:*** Freshmen: 13% (162). Undergraduates: 8% (639). ***Average award:*** Freshmen: $5092. Undergraduates: $4443. ***Scholarships, grants, and awards by category:*** *Academic interests/achievement:* general academic interests/achievements. *Creative arts/performance:* general creative arts/performance, music. *Special characteristics:* members of minority groups. ***Tuition waivers:*** Full or partial for employees or children of employees. ***ROTC:*** Army cooperative.

LOANS ***Student loans:*** $44,276,554 (95% need-based, 5% non-need-based). 75% of past graduating class borrowed through all loan programs. *Average indebtedness per student:* $22,746. ***Average need-based loan:*** Freshmen: $3182. Undergraduates: $4236. ***Parent loans:*** $10,281,344 (68% need-based, 32% non-need-based). ***Programs:*** Federal Direct (Subsidized and Unsubsidized Stafford, PLUS), state.

WORK-STUDY ***Federal work-study:*** Total amount: $525,152; 401 jobs averaging $4369. ***State or other work-study/employment:*** Total amount: $884,094 (59% need-based, 41% non-need-based). 864 part-time jobs averaging $5050.

APPLYING FOR FINANCIAL AID ***Required financial aid form:*** FAFSA. ***Financial aid deadline (priority):*** 3/15. ***Notification date:*** Continuous beginning 3/15. Students must reply by 5/1.

CONTACT Luis Tavarez, Director of Financial Aid, Rowan University, 201 Mullica Hill Road, Glassboro, NJ 08028-1701, 856-256-4276 or toll-free 800-447-1165 (in-state). *Fax:* 856-256-4413. *E-mail:* tavarez@rowan.edu.

RUSH UNIVERSITY

Chicago, IL

ABOUT THE INSTITUTION Independent, coed. ***Awards:*** bachelor's, master's, doctoral, and first professional degrees and post-master's certificates. 3 undergraduate majors. ***Total enrollment:*** 1,566. Undergraduates: 166.

GIFT AID (NEED-BASED) ***Scholarships, grants, and awards:*** Federal Pell, FSEOG, state, private, college/university gift aid from institutional funds.

GIFT AID (NON-NEED-BASED) ***Scholarships, grants, and awards by category:*** *Academic interests/achievement:* general academic interests/achievements. *Special characteristics:* children of faculty/staff.

LOANS ***Programs:*** FFEL (Subsidized and Unsubsidized Stafford, PLUS), Perkins, Federal Nursing, college/university, credit-based loans.

APPLYING FOR FINANCIAL AID ***Required financial aid forms:*** FAFSA, institution's own form.

CONTACT David Nelson, Acting Director, Student Financial Aid, Rush University, 600 South Paulina Street, Suite 440, Chicago, IL 60612-3832, 312-942-6256. *Fax:* 312-942-2732. *E-mail:* david_j_nelson@rush.edu.

RUSSELL SAGE COLLEGE

Troy, NY

ABOUT THE INSTITUTION Independent, undergraduate: women only; graduate: coed. ***Awards:*** bachelor's degrees. 23 undergraduate majors. ***Total enrollment:*** 699. Undergraduates: 699. Freshmen: 123.

GIFT AID (NEED-BASED) ***Scholarships, grants, and awards:*** Federal Pell, FSEOG, state, private, college/university gift aid from institutional funds, Federal Nursing.

GIFT AID (NON-NEED-BASED) ***Scholarships, grants, and awards by category:*** *Academic interests/achievement:* general academic interests/achievements. *Creative arts/performance:* theater/drama. *Special achievements/activities:* community service, general special achievements/activities, leadership. *Special characteristics:* children and siblings of alumni, children of faculty/staff, siblings of current students, spouses of current students.

LOANS ***Programs:*** FFEL (Subsidized and Unsubsidized Stafford, PLUS), Perkins.

WORK-STUDY ***Federal work-study:*** Total amount: $260,725; 432 jobs averaging $1700. ***State or other work-study/employment:*** Total amount: $98,500 (100% non-need-based). 91 part-time jobs averaging $1500.

APPLYING FOR FINANCIAL AID ***Required financial aid forms:*** FAFSA, state aid form.

CONTACT James Dease, Associate Vice President for Student Services, Russell Sage College, 45 Ferry Street, Troy, NY 12180, 518-244-2062 or toll-free 888-VERY-SAGE (in-state), 888-VERY SAGE (out-of-state). *Fax:* 518-244-2460. *E-mail:* deasej@sage.edu.

RUST COLLEGE

Holly Springs, MS

CONTACT Mrs. Helen L. Street, Director of Financial Aid, Rust College, 150 Rust Avenue, Holly Springs, MS 38635, 662-252-8000 Ext. 4061 or toll-free 888-886-8492 Ext. 4065. *Fax:* 662-252-8895.

RUTGERS, THE STATE UNIVERSITY OF NEW JERSEY, CAMDEN

Camden, NJ

Tuition & fees (NJ res): $11,358 Average undergraduate aid package: $11,808

ABOUT THE INSTITUTION State-supported, coed. ***Awards:*** bachelor's, master's, doctoral, and first professional degrees. 33 undergraduate majors. ***Total enrollment:*** 5,398. Undergraduates: 3,870. Freshmen: 480. Federal methodology is used as a basis for awarding need-based institutional aid.

UNDERGRADUATE EXPENSES for 2008–09 ***Application fee:*** $65. ***Tuition, state resident:*** full-time $9268; part-time $299 per credit hour. ***Tuition, nonresident:*** full-time $19,216; part-time $623 per credit hour. ***Required fees:*** full-time $2090; $433 per term. Part-time tuition and fees vary according to course level. ***College room and board:*** $9378; ***Room only:*** $6728. Room and board charges vary according to board plan and housing facility. ***Payment plan:*** Installment.

FRESHMAN FINANCIAL AID (Fall 2008, est.) 333 applied for aid; of those 77% were deemed to have need. 99% of freshmen with need received aid; of those 53% had need fully met. ***Average percent of need met:*** 64% (excluding resources awarded to replace EFC). ***Average financial aid package:*** $12,937 (excluding resources awarded to replace EFC). 5% of all full-time freshmen had no need and received non-need-based gift aid.

UNDERGRADUATE FINANCIAL AID (Fall 2008, est.) 2,390 applied for aid; of those 82% were deemed to have need. 99% of undergraduates with need received aid; of those 52% had need fully met. ***Average percent of need met:*** 62% (excluding resources awarded to replace EFC). ***Average financial aid package:*** $11,808 (excluding resources awarded to replace EFC). 5% of all full-time undergraduates had no need and received non-need-based gift aid.

GIFT AID (NEED-BASED) ***Total amount:*** $12,908,429 (29% federal, 48% state, 23% institutional). ***Receiving aid:*** Freshmen: 19% (167); all full-time undergraduates: 38% (1,309). ***Average award:*** Freshmen: $9323; Undergraduates: $8205. ***Scholarships, grants, and awards:*** state, college/university gift aid from institutional funds.

GIFT AID (NON-NEED-BASED) ***Total amount:*** $2,082,799 (3% state, 62% institutional, 35% external sources). ***Receiving aid:*** Freshmen: 11% (97). Undergraduates: 15% (527). ***Average award:*** Freshmen: $5408. Undergraduates: $4961. ***Tuition waivers:*** Full or partial for employees or children of employees. ***ROTC:*** Army cooperative, Air Force cooperative.

LOANS ***Student loans:*** $20,479,392 (40% need-based, 60% non-need-based). 100% of past graduating class borrowed through all loan programs. *Average indebtedness per student:* $19,800. ***Average need-based loan:*** Freshmen: $3269. Undergraduates: $4108. ***Parent loans:*** $569,883 (100% non-need-based).

WORK-STUDY ***Federal work-study:*** Total amount: $355,509; jobs available. ***State or other work-study/employment:*** Total amount: $822,606 (100% non-need-based). Part-time jobs available.

ATHLETIC AWARDS Total amount: $2000 (100% non-need-based).

CONTACT Ms. Marlene Martin, Assistant Funds Manager, Rutgers, The State University of New Jersey, Camden, 620 George Street, New Brunswick, NJ 08901, 732-932-7868. *E-mail:* mgmartin@rci.rutgers.edu.

RUTGERS, THE STATE UNIVERSITY OF NEW JERSEY, NEWARK

Newark, NJ

Tuition & fees (NJ res): $11,083 Average undergraduate aid package: $12,264

ABOUT THE INSTITUTION State-supported, coed. ***Awards:*** bachelor's, master's, doctoral, and first professional degrees. 51 undergraduate majors. ***Total enrollment:*** 11,032. Undergraduates: 7,001. Freshmen: 955. Federal methodology is used as a basis for awarding need-based institutional aid.

UNDERGRADUATE EXPENSES for 2008–09 ***Application fee:*** $65. ***Tuition, state resident:*** full-time $9268; part-time $299 per credit hour. ***Tuition, nonresident:*** full-time $19,216; part-time $623 per credit hour. ***Required fees:*** full-time $1815. Part-time tuition and fees vary according to course level. ***College room and board:*** $10,639; ***Room only:*** $6649. Room and board charges vary according to board plan and housing facility. ***Payment plan:*** Installment.

FRESHMAN FINANCIAL AID (Fall 2008, est.) 775 applied for aid; of those 81% were deemed to have need. 98% of freshmen with need received aid; of those 49% had need fully met. ***Average percent of need met:*** 64% (excluding resources awarded to replace EFC). ***Average financial aid package:*** $12,830 (excluding resources awarded to replace EFC). 2% of all full-time freshmen had no need and received non-need-based gift aid.

UNDERGRADUATE FINANCIAL AID (Fall 2008, est.) 3,971 applied for aid; of those 89% were deemed to have need. 98% of undergraduates with need received aid; of those 40% had need fully met. ***Average percent of need met:*** 66% (excluding resources awarded to replace EFC). ***Average financial aid package:*** $12,264 (excluding resources awarded to replace EFC). 3% of all full-time undergraduates had no need and received non-need-based gift aid.

GIFT AID (NEED-BASED) ***Total amount:*** $27,383,045 (30% federal, 49% state, 21% institutional). ***Receiving aid:*** Freshmen: 26% (421); all full-time undergraduates: 42% (2,622). ***Average award:*** Freshmen: $9579; Undergraduates: $8995. ***Scholarships, grants, and awards:*** Federal Pell, FSEOG, state, private, college/university gift aid from institutional funds, outside scholarships.

GIFT AID (NON-NEED-BASED) ***Total amount:*** $2,434,316 (10% state, 49% institutional, 41% external sources). ***Receiving aid:*** Freshmen: 11% (182). Undergraduates: 13% (850). ***Average award:*** Freshmen: $3142. Undergraduates: $4200. ***Tuition waivers:*** Full or partial for employees or children of employees. ***ROTC:*** Army, Air Force.

LOANS ***Student loans:*** $28,034,192 (44% need-based, 56% non-need-based). 85% of past graduating class borrowed through all loan programs. *Average indebtedness per student:* $17,700. ***Average need-based loan:*** Freshmen: $3140. Undergraduates: $4026. ***Parent loans:*** $589,229 (100% non-need-based). ***Programs:*** Federal Direct (Subsidized and Unsubsidized Stafford, PLUS), Perkins, state, college/university, other educational loans.

WORK-STUDY ***Federal work-study:*** Total amount: $696,791; jobs available. ***State or other work-study/employment:*** Total amount: $1,275,829 (100% non-need-based). Part-time jobs available.

ATHLETIC AWARDS Total amount: $120,910 (100% non-need-based).

APPLYING FOR FINANCIAL AID ***Required financial aid form:*** FAFSA. ***Financial aid deadline (priority):*** 3/15. ***Notification date:*** Continuous. Students must reply within 2 weeks of notification.

CONTACT Ms. Marlene Martin, Assistant Funds Manager, Rutgers, The State University of New Jersey, Newark, 620 George Street, New Brunswick, NJ 08901, 732-932-7868. *E-mail:* mgmartin@rci.rutgers.edu.

RUTGERS, THE STATE UNIVERSITY OF NEW JERSEY, NEW BRUNSWICK

Piscataway, NJ

Tuition & fees (NJ res): $11,540 Average undergraduate aid package: $14,097

ABOUT THE INSTITUTION State-supported, coed. ***Awards:*** bachelor's, master's, doctoral, and first professional degrees and post-master's certificates. 122 undergraduate majors. ***Total enrollment:*** 36,041. Undergraduates: 28,031. Freshmen: 5,840. Federal methodology is used as a basis for awarding need-based institutional aid.

UNDERGRADUATE EXPENSES for 2008–09 ***Application fee:*** $65. ***Tuition, state resident:*** full-time $9268; part-time $299 per credit hour. ***Tuition, nonresident:*** full-time $19,216; part-time $623 per credit hour. ***Required fees:*** full-time $2272; $298 per term. Part-time tuition and fees vary according to course level. ***College room and board:*** $10,232; ***Room only:*** $6232. Room and board charges vary according to board plan and housing facility. ***Payment plan:*** Installment.

FRESHMAN FINANCIAL AID (Fall 2008, est.) 4,340 applied for aid; of those 71% were deemed to have need. 98% of freshmen with need received aid; of those 63% had need fully met. ***Average percent of need met:*** 51% (excluding resources awarded to replace EFC). ***Average financial aid package:*** $14,846 (excluding resources awarded to replace EFC). 5% of all full-time freshmen had no need and received non-need-based gift aid.

UNDERGRADUATE FINANCIAL AID (Fall 2008, est.) 16,544 applied for aid; of those 79% were deemed to have need. 98% of undergraduates with need received aid; of those 59% had need fully met. ***Average percent of need met:*** 53% (excluding resources awarded to replace EFC). ***Average financial aid package:*** $14,097 (excluding resources awarded to replace EFC). 8% of all full-time undergraduates had no need and received non-need-based gift aid.

GIFT AID (NEED-BASED) ***Total amount:*** $97,211,591 (24% federal, 39% state, 37% institutional). ***Receiving aid:*** Freshmen: 27% (1,723); all full-time undergraduates: 31% (7,872). ***Average award:*** Freshmen: $10,191; Undergraduates: $9455. ***Scholarships, grants, and awards:*** Federal Pell, FSEOG, state, private, college/university gift aid from institutional funds, outside scholarships.

GIFT AID (NON-NEED-BASED) ***Total amount:*** $20,433,594 (11% state, 67% institutional, 22% external sources). ***Receiving aid:*** Freshmen: 27% (1,755). Undergraduates: 26% (6,673). ***Average award:*** Freshmen: $6990. Undergraduates: $2397. ***Tuition waivers:*** Full or partial for employees or children of employees. ***ROTC:*** Army, Air Force.

LOANS ***Student loans:*** $132,003,590 (37% need-based, 63% non-need-based). 74% of past graduating class borrowed through all loan programs. *Average indebtedness per student:* $16,300. ***Average need-based loan:*** Freshmen: $3466. Undergraduates: $4287. ***Parent loans:*** $6,328,665 (100% non-need-based). ***Programs:*** Federal Direct (Subsidized and Unsubsidized Stafford, PLUS), Perkins, state, college/university, other educational loans.

WORK-STUDY ***Federal work-study:*** Total amount: $2,783,959; jobs available. ***State or other work-study/employment:*** Total amount: $9,805,804 (100% non-need-based). Part-time jobs available.

ATHLETIC AWARDS Total amount: $7,768,686 (100% non-need-based).

APPLYING FOR FINANCIAL AID ***Required financial aid form:*** FAFSA. ***Financial aid deadline (priority):*** 3/15. ***Notification date:*** Continuous. Students must reply within 2 weeks of notification.

CONTACT Ms. Marlene Martin, Assistant Funds Manager, Rutgers, The State University of New Jersey, New Brunswick, 620 George Street, New Brunswick, NJ 08901, 732-932-7868. *E-mail:* mgmartin@rci.rutgers.edu.

SACRED HEART MAJOR SEMINARY

Detroit, MI

ABOUT THE INSTITUTION Independent Roman Catholic, coed. ***Awards:*** associate, bachelor's, master's, and first professional degrees and post-bachelor's certificates. 3 undergraduate majors. ***Total enrollment:*** 448. Undergraduates: 244. Freshmen: 4.

GIFT AID (NEED-BASED) ***Scholarships, grants, and awards:*** Federal Pell, FSEOG, state.

GIFT AID (NON-NEED-BASED) ***Scholarships, grants, and awards by category:*** *Academic interests/achievement:* religion/biblical studies. *Special achievements/activities:* religious involvement. *Special characteristics:* local/state students, religious affiliation.

LOANS ***Programs:*** FFEL (Subsidized and Unsubsidized Stafford, PLUS), alternative loans.

WORK-STUDY ***Federal work-study:*** Total amount: $8504; jobs available. ***State or other work-study/employment:*** Total amount: $5000 (100% need-based). Part-time jobs available.

APPLYING FOR FINANCIAL AID ***Required financial aid forms:*** FAFSA, institution's own form.

CONTACT Financial Aid Office, Sacred Heart Major Seminary, 2701 Chicago Boulevard, Detroit, MI 48206-1799, 313-883-8500. *Fax:* 313-868-6440. *E-mail:* FinancialAid@shms.edu.

SACRED HEART UNIVERSITY

Fairfield, CT

Tuition & fees: $28,990 **Average undergraduate aid package: $16,757**

ABOUT THE INSTITUTION Independent Roman Catholic, coed. ***Awards:*** associate, bachelor's, master's, and doctoral degrees and post-bachelor's and post-master's certificates (also offers part-time program with significant enrollment not reflected in profile). 38 undergraduate majors. ***Total enrollment:*** 5,958. Undergraduates: 4,274. Freshmen: 980. Both federal and institutional methodology are used as a basis for awarding need-based institutional aid.

UNDERGRADUATE EXPENSES for 2008–09 ***Application fee:*** $50. ***Comprehensive fee:*** $40,320 includes full-time tuition ($28,790), mandatory fees ($200), and room and board ($11,330). ***College room only:*** $8582. Full-time tuition and fees vary according to program. Room and board charges vary according to board plan and housing facility. ***Part-time tuition:*** $425 per credit. ***Part-time fees:*** $76 per term. Part-time tuition and fees vary according to program. ***Payment plan:*** Installment.

FRESHMAN FINANCIAL AID (Fall 2008, est.) 880 applied for aid; of those 76% were deemed to have need. 100% of freshmen with need received aid; of those 42% had need fully met. ***Average percent of need met:*** 67% (excluding resources awarded to replace EFC). ***Average financial aid package:*** $17,717 (excluding resources awarded to replace EFC). 20% of all full-time freshmen had no need and received non-need-based gift aid.

UNDERGRADUATE FINANCIAL AID (Fall 2008, est.) 2,926 applied for aid; of those 79% were deemed to have need. 99% of undergraduates with need received aid; of those 24% had need fully met. ***Average percent of need met:*** 64% (excluding resources awarded to replace EFC). ***Average financial aid package:*** $16,757 (excluding resources awarded to replace EFC). 17% of all full-time undergraduates had no need and received non-need-based gift aid.

GIFT AID (NEED-BASED) ***Total amount:*** $25,968,231 (8% federal, 10% state, 73% institutional, 9% external sources). ***Receiving aid:*** Freshmen: 67% (658); all full-time undergraduates: 64% (2,249). ***Average award:*** Freshmen: $14,220; Undergraduates: $12,854. ***Scholarships, grants, and awards:*** Federal Pell, FSEOG, state, private, college/university gift aid from institutional funds.

GIFT AID (NON-NEED-BASED) ***Total amount:*** $4,355,875 (73% institutional, 27% external sources). ***Receiving aid:*** Freshmen: 6% (56). Undergraduates: 5% (172). ***Average award:*** Freshmen: $6115. Undergraduates: $4833. ***Scholarships, grants, and awards by category:*** *Academic interests/achievement:* 2,012 awards ($8,562,740 total): biological sciences, business, computer science, education, English, general academic interests/achievements, health fields, humanities, mathematics, physical sciences, premedicine. *Creative arts/performance:* 202 awards ($430,872 total): applied art and design, art/fine arts, creative writing, music. *Special achievements/activities:* 204 awards ($434,901 total): community service, general special achievements/activities, leadership, religious involvement. *Special characteristics:* 305 awards ($1,461,033 total): children of current students, children of faculty/staff, ethnic background, handicapped students, members of minority groups, religious affiliation, siblings of current students, twins. ***Tuition waivers:*** Full or partial for employees or children of employees. ***ROTC:*** Army.

LOANS ***Student loans:*** $31,263,042 (57% need-based, 43% non-need-based). 96% of past graduating class borrowed through all loan programs. *Average indebtedness per student:* $27,516. ***Average need-based loan:*** Freshmen: $3660. Undergraduates: $4438. ***Parent loans:*** $7,019,649 (35% need-based, 65% non-need-based). ***Programs:*** Federal Direct (Subsidized and Unsubsidized Stafford, PLUS), FFEL (Subsidized and Unsubsidized Stafford, PLUS), Perkins, state.

WORK-STUDY ***Federal work-study:*** Total amount: $623,800; 783 jobs averaging $1397. ***State or other work-study/employment:*** Total amount: $1,165,878 (22% need-based, 78% non-need-based). 892 part-time jobs averaging $1356.

ATHLETIC AWARDS Total amount: $7,079,885 (46% need-based, 54% non-need-based).

APPLYING FOR FINANCIAL AID ***Required financial aid forms:*** FAFSA, CSS Financial Aid PROFILE, noncustodial (divorced/separated) parent's statement. ***Financial aid deadline (priority):*** 2/15. ***Notification date:*** Continuous beginning 3/1. Students must reply within 2 weeks of notification.

CONTACT Ms. Julie B. Savino, Dean of University Financial Assistance, Sacred Heart University, 5151 Park Avenue, Fairfield, CT 06825, 203-371-7980. *Fax:* 203-365-7608. *E-mail:* savinoj@sacredheart.edu.

SAGE COLLEGE OF ALBANY

Albany, NY

ABOUT THE INSTITUTION Independent, coed. ***Awards:*** associate and bachelor's degrees. 16 undergraduate majors. ***Total enrollment:*** 879. Undergraduates: 879. Freshmen: 65.

GIFT AID (NEED-BASED) ***Scholarships, grants, and awards:*** Federal Pell, FSEOG, state, private, college/university gift aid from institutional funds.

GIFT AID (NON-NEED-BASED) ***Scholarships, grants, and awards by category:*** *Academic interests/achievement:* general academic interests/achievements. *Creative arts/performance:* art/fine arts. *Special achievements/activities:* community service. *Special characteristics:* children and siblings of alumni, children of faculty/staff.

LOANS ***Programs:*** FFEL (Subsidized and Unsubsidized Stafford, PLUS), Perkins, alternative loans.

WORK-STUDY ***Federal work-study:*** Total amount: $126,900; 210 jobs averaging $1500. ***State or other work-study/employment:*** Total amount: $29,860 (100% non-need-based). 19 part-time jobs averaging $1200.

APPLYING FOR FINANCIAL AID ***Required financial aid forms:*** FAFSA, state aid form.

CONTACT James K. Dease, Associate Vice President for Student Service, Sage College of Albany, 45 Ferry Street, Troy, NY 12180, 518-244-4525 or toll-free 888-VERY-SAGE. *Fax:* 518-244-2460. *E-mail:* deasej@sage.edu.

SAGINAW VALLEY STATE UNIVERSITY

University Center, MI

Tuition & fees (MI res): $6492 **Average undergraduate aid package: $6880**

ABOUT THE INSTITUTION State-supported, coed. ***Awards:*** bachelor's and master's degrees and post-master's certificates. 61 undergraduate majors. ***Total enrollment:*** 9,837. Undergraduates: 8,190. Freshmen: 1,661. Federal methodology is used as a basis for awarding need-based institutional aid.

UNDERGRADUATE EXPENSES for 2008–09 ***Application fee:*** $25. ***Tuition, state resident:*** full-time $6054; part-time $201.80 per credit hour. ***Tuition, nonresident:*** full-time $14,453; part-time $481.75 per credit hour. ***Required fees:*** full-time $438; $14.60 per credit hour. Full-time tuition and fees vary according to course level, course load, location, and program. Part-time tuition and fees vary according to course level, course load, location, and program. ***College room and board:*** $6830; ***Room only:*** $4100. Room and board charges vary according to board plan, housing facility, and student level. ***Payment plan:*** Installment.

FRESHMAN FINANCIAL AID (Fall 2007) 1,500 applied for aid; of those 67% were deemed to have need. 98% of freshmen with need received aid; of those 24% had need fully met. ***Average percent of need met:*** 68% (excluding resources awarded to replace EFC). ***Average financial aid package:*** $7167 (excluding resources awarded to replace EFC). 15% of all full-time freshmen had no need and received non-need-based gift aid.

UNDERGRADUATE FINANCIAL AID (Fall 2007) 5,969 applied for aid; of those 66% were deemed to have need. 97% of undergraduates with need received aid; of those 18% had need fully met. ***Average percent of need met:*** 63% (excluding resources awarded to replace EFC). ***Average financial aid package:*** $6880 (excluding resources awarded to replace EFC). 12% of all full-time undergraduates had no need and received non-need-based gift aid.

GIFT AID (NEED-BASED) ***Total amount:*** $8,377,315 (83% federal, 10% state, 7% institutional). ***Receiving aid:*** Freshmen: 43% (657); all full-time undergraduates: 39% (2,437). ***Average award:*** Freshmen: $3368; Undergraduates: $3136. ***Scholarships, grants, and awards:*** Federal Pell, FSEOG, state, private, college/university gift aid from institutional funds.

GIFT AID (NON-NEED-BASED) ***Total amount:*** $11,710,727 (1% federal, 24% state, 53% institutional, 22% external sources). ***Receiving aid:*** Freshmen: 49% (758). Undergraduates: 29% (1,811). ***Average award:*** Freshmen: $3116. Undergraduates: $3677. ***Scholarships, grants, and awards by category:*** *Academic interests/achievement:* biological sciences, business, computer science, education, engineering/technologies, general academic interests/achievements, health fields, mathematics, physical sciences. *Creative arts/performance:* art/fine arts, music, theater/drama. *Special achievements/activities:* community service, leadership. *Special characteristics:* local/state students, members of minority groups. ***Tuition waivers:*** Full or partial for employees or children of employees.

LOANS ***Student loans:*** $31,363,982 (44% need-based, 56% non-need-based). 68% of past graduating class borrowed through all loan programs. *Average indebtedness per student:* $23,561. ***Average need-based loan:*** Freshmen: $2976. Undergraduates: $3775. ***Parent loans:*** $1,711,658 (100% non-need-based). ***Programs:*** Federal Direct (Subsidized and Unsubsidized Stafford, PLUS), state, CitiAssist Loans; Signature Student Loans.

WORK-STUDY ***Federal work-study:*** Total amount: $354,508; 119 jobs averaging $1377. ***State or other work-study/employment:*** Total amount: $151,200 (100% need-based). 48 part-time jobs averaging $1288.

ATHLETIC AWARDS Total amount: $1,157,358 (100% non-need-based).

APPLYING FOR FINANCIAL AID ***Required financial aid form:*** FAFSA. ***Financial aid deadline (priority):*** 2/14. ***Notification date:*** Continuous beginning 3/20. Students must reply within 10 weeks of notification.

CONTACT Robert Lemuel, Director of Scholarships and Financial Aid, Saginaw Valley State University, 7400 Bay Road, University Center, MI 48710, 989-964-4103 or toll-free 800-968-9500. *Fax:* 989-790-0180. *E-mail:* lemuel@svsy.edu.

ST. AMBROSE UNIVERSITY

Davenport, IA

Tuition & fees: $22,590 **Average undergraduate aid package: $15,414**

ABOUT THE INSTITUTION Independent Roman Catholic, coed. ***Awards:*** bachelor's, master's, and doctoral degrees and post-bachelor's and post-master's certificates. 72 undergraduate majors. ***Total enrollment:*** 3,794. Undergraduates: 2,922. Freshmen: 574. Federal methodology is used as a basis for awarding need-based institutional aid.

UNDERGRADUATE EXPENSES for 2009–10 ***Application fee:*** $25. ***Comprehensive fee:*** $30,845 includes full-time tuition ($22,590) and room and board ($8255). ***College room only:*** $4207. ***Part-time tuition:*** $702 per credit hour.

FRESHMAN FINANCIAL AID (Fall 2008, est.) 572 applied for aid; of those 71% were deemed to have need. 100% of freshmen with need received aid; of those 31% had need fully met. ***Average percent of need met:*** 18% (excluding resources awarded to replace EFC). ***Average financial aid package:*** $15,992 (excluding resources awarded to replace EFC). 29% of all full-time freshmen had no need and received non-need-based gift aid.

UNDERGRADUATE FINANCIAL AID (Fall 2008, est.) 2,404 applied for aid; of those 72% were deemed to have need. 100% of undergraduates with need received aid; of those 26% had need fully met. ***Average percent of need met:*** 24% (excluding resources awarded to replace EFC). ***Average financial aid package:*** $15,414 (excluding resources awarded to replace EFC). 27% of all full-time undergraduates had no need and received non-need-based gift aid.

GIFT AID (NEED-BASED) ***Total amount:*** $16,613,974 (13% federal, 14% state, 70% institutional, 3% external sources). ***Receiving aid:*** Freshmen: 70% (403); all full-time undergraduates: 69% (1,683). ***Average award:*** Freshmen: $10,725; Undergraduates: $9805. ***Scholarships, grants, and awards:*** Federal Pell, FSEOG, state, private, college/university gift aid from institutional funds.

GIFT AID (NON-NEED-BASED) ***Total amount:*** $4,338,637 (98% institutional, 2% external sources). ***Receiving aid:*** Freshmen: 38% (216). Undergraduates: 26% (635). ***Average award:*** Freshmen: $6717. Undergraduates: $6373. ***Scholarships, grants, and awards by category:*** *Academic interests/achievement:* 2,268 awards ($13,423,369 total): general academic interests/achievements. *Creative arts/performance:* 118 awards ($253,582 total): art/fine arts, dance, music, theater/drama. *Special characteristics:* 147 awards ($1,163,157 total): children of faculty/staff, international students, members of minority groups.

LOANS ***Student loans:*** $20,454,721 (90% need-based, 10% non-need-based). 84% of past graduating class borrowed through all loan programs. *Average indebtedness per student:* $32,675. ***Average need-based loan:*** Freshmen: $3569. Undergraduates: $4313. ***Parent loans:*** $2,582,515 (78% need-based, 22% non-need-based). ***Programs:*** FFEL (Subsidized and Unsubsidized Stafford, PLUS), Perkins, private loans.

WORK-STUDY ***Federal work-study:*** Total amount: $767,882; 460 jobs averaging $1738. ***State or other work-study/employment:*** Total amount: $207,772 (75% need-based, 25% non-need-based). 136 part-time jobs averaging $1668.

ATHLETIC AWARDS Total amount: $2,307,341 (68% need-based, 32% non-need-based).

APPLYING FOR FINANCIAL AID ***Required financial aid form:*** FAFSA. ***Financial aid deadline (priority):*** 3/15. ***Notification date:*** Continuous. Students must reply within 2 weeks of notification.

CONTACT Ms. Julie Haack, Director of Financial Aid, St. Ambrose University, 518 West Locust Street, Davenport, IA 52803, 563-333-6314 or toll-free 800-383-2627. *Fax:* 563-333-6243. *E-mail:* haackjuliea@sau.edu.

ST. ANDREWS PRESBYTERIAN COLLEGE

Laurinburg, NC

Tuition & fees: $20,375 **Average undergraduate aid package: $14,424**

ABOUT THE INSTITUTION Independent Presbyterian, coed. ***Awards:*** bachelor's degrees. 23 undergraduate majors. ***Total enrollment:*** 623. Undergraduates: 623. Freshmen: 138. Federal methodology is used as a basis for awarding need-based institutional aid.

UNDERGRADUATE EXPENSES for 2008–09 ***Application fee:*** $30. ***One-time required fee:*** $100. ***Comprehensive fee:*** $28,800 includes full-time tuition ($20,375) and room and board ($8425). Full-time tuition and fees vary according to course load and location. Room and board charges vary according to housing facility. ***Part-time tuition:*** $450 per credit. Part-time tuition and fees vary according to location. ***Payment plan:*** Installment.

FRESHMAN FINANCIAL AID (Fall 2007) 187 applied for aid; of those 80% were deemed to have need. 100% of freshmen with need received aid; of those 35% had need fully met. ***Average percent of need met:*** 77% (excluding resources awarded to replace EFC). ***Average financial aid package:*** $13,596 (excluding resources awarded to replace EFC). 28% of all full-time freshmen had no need and received non-need-based gift aid.

UNDERGRADUATE FINANCIAL AID (Fall 2007) 536 applied for aid; of those 84% were deemed to have need. 100% of undergraduates with need received aid; of those 31% had need fully met. ***Average percent of need met:*** 77% (excluding resources awarded to replace EFC). ***Average financial aid package:*** $14,424 (excluding resources awarded to replace EFC). 30% of all full-time undergraduates had no need and received non-need-based gift aid.

GIFT AID (NEED-BASED) ***Total amount:*** $4,236,751 (14% federal, 21% state, 54% institutional, 11% external sources). ***Receiving aid:*** Freshmen: 68% (149); all full-time undergraduates: 65% (448). ***Average award:*** Freshmen: $10,974; Undergraduates: $10,695. ***Scholarships, grants, and awards:*** Federal Pell, FSEOG, state, private, college/university gift aid from institutional funds.

GIFT AID (NON-NEED-BASED) ***Total amount:*** $1,759,977 (13% state, 78% institutional, 9% external sources). ***Receiving aid:*** Freshmen: 17% (38). Undergraduates: 11% (74). ***Average award:*** Freshmen: $6034. Undergraduates: $5997. ***Scholarships, grants, and awards by category:*** *Academic interests/achievement:* 550 awards ($2,520,283 total): general academic interests/achievements. *Creative arts/performance:* 3 awards ($1750 total): general creative arts/performance, performing arts, theater/drama. *Special achievements/activities:* 26 awards ($44,633 total): general special achievements/activities, leadership. ***Tuition waivers:*** Full or partial for employees or children of employees, adult students, senior citizens.

LOANS ***Student loans:*** $3,006,985 (67% need-based, 33% non-need-based). 73% of past graduating class borrowed through all loan programs. *Average indebtedness per student:* $17,341. ***Average need-based loan:*** Freshmen: $3473. Undergraduates: $4523. ***Parent loans:*** $1,951,314 (30% need-based, 70% non-need-based). ***Programs:*** FFEL (Subsidized and Unsubsidized Stafford, PLUS).

WORK-STUDY ***Federal work-study:*** Total amount: $155,419; 166 jobs averaging $936. ***State or other work-study/employment:*** 83 part-time jobs averaging $1800.

ATHLETIC AWARDS Total amount: $980,662 (67% need-based, 33% non-need-based).

APPLYING FOR FINANCIAL AID ***Required financial aid forms:*** FAFSA, state aid form. ***Financial aid deadline:*** Continuous. ***Notification date:*** Continuous beginning 2/1. Students must reply within 2 weeks of notification.

CONTACT Kimberly Driggers, Director of Student Financial Planning, St. Andrews Presbyterian College, 1700 Dogwood Mile, Laurinburg, NC 28352, 910-277-5562 or toll-free 800-763-0198. *Fax:* 910-277-5206.

SAINT ANSELM COLLEGE

Manchester, NH

Tuition & fees: $29,205 **Average undergraduate aid package: $22,181**

ABOUT THE INSTITUTION Independent Roman Catholic, coed. 30 undergraduate majors. Both federal and institutional methodology are used as a basis for awarding need-based institutional aid.

UNDERGRADUATE EXPENSES for 2008–09 ***Comprehensive fee:*** $40,255 includes full-time tuition ($28,440), mandatory fees ($765), and room and board ($11,050). ***Part-time tuition:*** $2840 per course.

FRESHMAN FINANCIAL AID (Fall 2008, est.) 439 applied for aid; of those 82% were deemed to have need. 100% of freshmen with need received aid; of those 23% had need fully met. ***Average percent of need met:*** 84% (excluding resources awarded to replace EFC). ***Average financial aid package:*** $21,788 (excluding resources awarded to replace EFC). 16% of all full-time freshmen had no need and received non-need-based gift aid.

UNDERGRADUATE FINANCIAL AID (Fall 2008, est.) 1,513 applied for aid; of those 86% were deemed to have need. 100% of undergraduates with need received aid; of those 25% had need fully met. ***Average percent of need met:*** 84% (excluding resources awarded to replace EFC). ***Average financial aid package:*** $22,181 (excluding resources awarded to replace EFC). 19% of all full-time undergraduates had no need and received non-need-based gift aid.

GIFT AID (NEED-BASED) ***Total amount:*** $19,191,227 (5% federal, 92% institutional, 3% external sources). ***Receiving aid:*** Freshmen: 72% (359); all full-time undergraduates: 69% (1,290). ***Average award:*** Freshmen: $16,099; Undergraduates: $15,259. ***Scholarships, grants, and awards:*** Federal Pell, FSEOG, state, private, college/university gift aid from institutional funds.

GIFT AID (NON-NEED-BASED) ***Total amount:*** $2,654,771 (95% institutional, 5% external sources). ***Receiving aid:*** Freshmen: 6% (31). Undergraduates: 4% (84). ***Average award:*** Freshmen: $13,094. Undergraduates: $14,258. ***Scholarships, grants, and awards by category:*** *Academic interests/achievement:* 774 awards ($4,849,250 total): general academic interests/achievements. *Special characteristics:* 134 awards ($1,989,630 total): children of educators, children of faculty/staff, siblings of current students.

LOANS ***Student loans:*** $15,901,168 (55% need-based, 45% non-need-based). 77% of past graduating class borrowed through all loan programs. *Average indebtedness per student:* $35,025. ***Average need-based loan:*** Freshmen: $5091. Undergraduates: $6361. ***Parent loans:*** $5,308,413 (24% need-based, 76% non-need-based). ***Programs:*** FFEL (Subsidized and Unsubsidized Stafford, PLUS), Perkins.

WORK-STUDY ***Federal work-study:*** Total amount: $1,577,945; 1,067 jobs averaging $1479. ***State or other work-study/employment:*** Total amount: $18,000 (100% non-need-based). 9 part-time jobs averaging $2000.

ATHLETIC AWARDS Total amount: $820,118 (12% need-based, 88% non-need-based).

APPLYING FOR FINANCIAL AID ***Required financial aid forms:*** FAFSA, CSS Financial Aid PROFILE, noncustodial (divorced/separated) parent's statement. ***Financial aid deadline:*** 3/15 (priority: 3/15). ***Notification date:*** Continuous. Students must reply by 5/1 or within 2 weeks of notification.

CONTACT Elizabeth Keuffel, Director of Financial Aid, Saint Anselm College, 100 Saint Anselm Drive, Manchester, NH 03102-1310, 603-641-7110 or toll-free 888-4ANSELM. *Fax:* 603-656-6015. *E-mail:* financial_aid@anselm.edu.

SAINT ANTHONY COLLEGE OF NURSING

Rockford, IL

Tuition & fees: $18,674 **Average undergraduate aid package: $15,199**

ABOUT THE INSTITUTION Independent Roman Catholic, coed, primarily women. 1 undergraduate major. Federal methodology is used as a basis for awarding need-based institutional aid.

UNDERGRADUATE EXPENSES for 2008–09 ***Tuition:*** full-time $18,426; part-time $577 per credit hour. ***Required fees:*** full-time $248; $30 per term. Full-time tuition and fees vary according to course load. Part-time tuition and fees vary according to course load. ***Payment plans:*** Installment, deferred payment.

UNDERGRADUATE FINANCIAL AID (Fall 2008, est.) 181 applied for aid; of those 100% were deemed to have need. 100% of undergraduates with need received aid. ***Average financial aid package:*** $15,199 (excluding resources awarded to replace EFC).

GIFT AID (NEED-BASED) ***Total amount:*** $534,214 (32% federal, 57% state, 9% institutional, 2% external sources). ***Receiving aid:*** All full-time undergraduates: 54% (109). ***Average award:*** Undergraduates: $4901. ***Scholarships, grants, and awards:*** Federal Pell, state, private, college/university gift aid from institutional funds.

GIFT AID (NON-NEED-BASED) ***Total amount:*** $45,325 (53% state, 13% institutional, 34% external sources). ***Receiving aid:*** Undergraduates: 5% (10).

LOANS ***Student loans:*** $1,637,865 (48% need-based, 52% non-need-based). 91% of past graduating class borrowed through all loan programs. *Average indebtedness per student:* $21,000. ***Average need-based loan:*** Undergraduates: $4486. ***Parent loans:*** $103,718 (100% non-need-based). ***Programs:*** FFEL (Subsidized and Unsubsidized Stafford, PLUS), alternative loans.

APPLYING FOR FINANCIAL AID ***Financial aid deadline (priority):*** 5/1.

CONTACT Serrita Woods, Financial Aid Officer, Saint Anthony College of Nursing, 5658 East State Street, Rockford, IL 61108-2468, 815-395-5089. *Fax:* 815-395-2275. *E-mail:* serritawoods@sacn.edu.

ST. AUGUSTINE COLLEGE

Chicago, IL

CONTACT Mrs. Maria Zambonino, Director of Financial Aid, St. Augustine College, 1345 W Angyle, Chicago, IL 60640, 773-878-3813. *Fax:* 773-878-9032. *E-mail:* mzambonino@hotmail.com.

SAINT AUGUSTINE'S COLLEGE

Raleigh, NC

CONTACT Ms. Wanda C. White, Director of Financial Aid, Saint Augustine's College, 1315 Oakwood Avenue, Raleigh, NC 27610-2298, 919-516-4131 or toll-free 800-948-1126. *Fax:* 919-516-4338. *E-mail:* wwhite@es.st-aug.edu.

ST. BONAVENTURE UNIVERSITY

St. Bonaventure, NY

CONTACT Ms. Elizabeth T. Rankin, Director of Financial Aid, St. Bonaventure University, Route 417, St. Bonaventure, NY 14778-2284, 716-375-2528 or toll-free 800-462-5050. *Fax:* 716-375-2087. *E-mail:* erankin@sbu.edu.

ST. CATHERINE UNIVERSITY

St. Paul, MN

Tuition & fees: $27,414 **Average undergraduate aid package: $28,471**

ABOUT THE INSTITUTION Independent Roman Catholic, undergraduate: women only; graduate: coed. ***Awards:*** associate, bachelor's, master's, and doctoral degrees and post-bachelor's and post-master's certificates. 78 undergraduate majors. ***Total enrollment:*** 5,201. Undergraduates: 3,727. Freshmen: 449. Federal methodology is used as a basis for awarding need-based institutional aid.

UNDERGRADUATE EXPENSES for 2008–09 ***One-time required fee:*** $85. ***Comprehensive fee:*** $34,504 includes full-time tuition ($27,136), mandatory fees ($278), and room and board ($7090). ***College room only:*** $3950. Full-time tuition and fees vary according to class time and degree level. Room and board charges vary according to board plan and housing facility. ***Part-time tuition:*** $848 per credit hour. ***Part-time fees:*** $139 per term. Part-time tuition and fees vary according to class time and degree level.

FRESHMAN FINANCIAL AID (Fall 2008, est.) 340 applied for aid; of those 90% were deemed to have need. 100% of freshmen with need received aid; of those 10% had need fully met. ***Average percent of need met:*** 86% (excluding resources awarded to replace EFC). ***Average financial aid package:*** $28,247 (excluding resources awarded to replace EFC). 9% of all full-time freshmen had no need and received non-need-based gift aid.

UNDERGRADUATE FINANCIAL AID (Fall 2008, est.) 1,553 applied for aid; of those 91% were deemed to have need. 100% of undergraduates with need received aid; of those 11% had need fully met. ***Average percent of need met:*** 84% (excluding resources awarded to replace EFC). ***Average financial aid package:*** $28,471 (excluding resources awarded to replace EFC). 7% of all full-time undergraduates had no need and received non-need-based gift aid.

GIFT AID (NEED-BASED) ***Total amount:*** $12,878,000 (29% federal, 23% state, 48% institutional). ***Receiving aid:*** Freshmen: 77% (275); all full-time undergraduates: 69% (1,176). ***Average award:*** Freshmen: $12,008; Undergraduates: $9018. ***Scholarships, grants, and awards:*** Federal Pell, FSEOG, state, private, college/university gift aid from institutional funds.

GIFT AID (NON-NEED-BASED) ***Total amount:*** $12,128,000 (1% state, 89% institutional, 10% external sources). ***Receiving aid:*** Freshmen: 70% (252). Undergraduates: 61% (1,029). ***Average award:*** Freshmen: $7544. Undergraduates: $6972. ***Scholarships, grants, and awards by category:*** *Academic interests/achievement:* business, education, English, foreign languages, general academic interests/achievements, health fields, home economics, humanities, mathematics, physical sciences, premedicine, social sciences. *Creative arts/performance:* art/fine arts, music. *Special achievements/activities:* community service, general special achievements/activities, leadership, memberships. *Special characteristics:* adult students, children and siblings of alumni, children of current students, children of educators, children of faculty/staff, ethnic background, general special characteristics, international students, local/state students, out-of-state students, religious affiliation, siblings of current students, spouses of current students. ***Tuition waivers:*** Full or partial for employees or children of employees, senior citizens. ***ROTC:*** Army cooperative, Air Force cooperative.

LOANS ***Student loans:*** $51,810,000 (56% need-based, 44% non-need-based). 94% of past graduating class borrowed through all loan programs. *Average indebtedness per student:* $30,886. ***Average need-based loan:*** Freshmen: $6195. Undergraduates: $7808. ***Parent loans:*** $3,240,000 (100% non-need-based). ***Programs:*** Federal Direct (Subsidized and Unsubsidized Stafford, PLUS), Perkins, Federal Nursing, state, alternative loans.

WORK-STUDY ***Federal work-study:*** Total amount: $237,000; 500 jobs available. ***State or other work-study/employment:*** Total amount: $135,000 (100% need-based). Part-time jobs available.

APPLYING FOR FINANCIAL AID ***Required financial aid forms:*** FAFSA, institution's own form. ***Financial aid deadline (priority):*** 4/15. ***Notification date:*** Continuous. Students must reply within 2 weeks of notification.

CONTACT Beth Stevens, Director of Financial Aid, St. Catherine University, Mail #F-11, 2004 Randolph Avenue, St. Paul, MN 55105-1789, 651-690-6540 or toll-free 800-656-5283 (in-state). *Fax:* 651-690-6765. *E-mail:* finaid@stkate.edu.

ST. CHARLES BORROMEO SEMINARY, OVERBROOK

Wynnewood, PA

CONTACT Ms. Bonnie L. Behm, Coordinator of Financial Aid, St. Charles Borromeo Seminary, Overbrook, 100 East Wynnewood Road, Wynnewood, PA 19096-3099, 610-785-6582. *Fax:* 610-667-3971. *E-mail:* finaid.scs@erols.com.

ST. CLOUD STATE UNIVERSITY

St. Cloud, MN

Tuition & fees (MN res): $6147 **Average undergraduate aid package: $10,059**

ABOUT THE INSTITUTION State-supported, coed. ***Awards:*** associate, bachelor's, master's, and doctoral degrees and post-bachelor's certificates. 147 undergraduate majors. ***Total enrollment:*** 16,921. Undergraduates: 15,157. Freshmen: 2,403. Federal methodology is used as a basis for awarding need-based institutional aid.

UNDERGRADUATE EXPENSES for 2008–09 ***Application fee:*** $20. ***Tuition, state resident:*** full-time $5405; part-time $180 per credit. ***Tuition, nonresident:*** full-time $11,732; part-time $391 per credit. ***Required fees:*** full-time $742; $29.58 per credit. Full-time tuition and fees vary according to course load and reciprocity agreements. Part-time tuition and fees vary according to course load and reciprocity agreements. ***College room and board:*** $5770; ***Room only:*** $3688. Room and board charges vary according to board plan and housing facility. ***Payment plan:*** Installment.

FRESHMAN FINANCIAL AID (Fall 2008, est.) 1,790 applied for aid; of those 70% were deemed to have need. 100% of freshmen with need received aid; of those 65% had need fully met. ***Average percent of need met:*** 66% (excluding resources awarded to replace EFC). ***Average financial aid package:*** $10,612 (excluding resources awarded to replace EFC). 3% of all full-time freshmen had no need and received non-need-based gift aid.

UNDERGRADUATE FINANCIAL AID (Fall 2008, est.) 7,982 applied for aid; of those 74% were deemed to have need. 100% of undergraduates with need received aid; of those 56% had need fully met. ***Average percent of need met:*** 56% (excluding resources awarded to replace EFC). ***Average financial aid package:*** $10,059 (excluding resources awarded to replace EFC). 1% of all full-time undergraduates had no need and received non-need-based gift aid.

GIFT AID (NEED-BASED) ***Total amount:*** $22,365,623 (58% federal, 32% state, 6% institutional, 4% external sources). ***Receiving aid:*** Freshmen: 41% (976); all full-time undergraduates: 38% (4,468). ***Average award:*** Freshmen: $5094; Undergraduates: $4773. ***Scholarships, grants, and awards:*** Federal Pell, FSEOG, state, private, college/university gift aid from institutional funds.

GIFT AID (NON-NEED-BASED) ***Total amount:*** $4,300,251 (37% federal, 5% state, 34% institutional, 24% external sources). ***Receiving aid:*** Freshmen: 3% (73). Undergraduates: 2% (280). ***Average award:*** Freshmen: $1902. Undergraduates: $1928. ***Scholarships, grants, and awards by category:*** *Academic interests/achievement:* biological sciences, business, communication, computer science, education, engineering/technologies, English, general academic interests/achievements, health fields, international studies, mathematics, physical sciences, social sciences. *Creative arts/performance:* applied art and design, art/fine arts, cinema/film/broadcasting, creative writing, journalism/publications, music, performing arts, theater/drama. *Special achievements/activities:* community service, general special achievements/activities. *Special characteristics:* children of faculty/staff, children of union members/company employees, local/state students, members of minority groups, out-of-state students. ***Tuition waivers:*** Full or partial for employees or children of employees, senior citizens. ***ROTC:*** Army.

LOANS ***Student loans:*** $98,708,969 (44% need-based, 56% non-need-based). 70% of past graduating class borrowed through all loan programs. *Average indebtedness per student:* $24,484. ***Average need-based loan:*** Freshmen: $4563. Undergraduates: $4923. ***Parent loans:*** $8,284,111 (3% need-based, 97% non-need-based). ***Programs:*** FFEL (Subsidized and Unsubsidized Stafford, PLUS), Perkins, state.

WORK-STUDY ***Federal work-study:*** Total amount: $1,059,889; jobs available. ***State or other work-study/employment:*** Total amount: $946,324 (100% need-based). Part-time jobs available.

ATHLETIC AWARDS Total amount: $1,317,948 (26% need-based, 74% non-need-based).

APPLYING FOR FINANCIAL AID ***Required financial aid forms:*** FAFSA, institution's own form. ***Financial aid deadline:*** Continuous. ***Notification date:*** Continuous beginning 6/15.

CONTACT Frank P. Morrissey, Associate Director of Scholarships and Financial Aid, St. Cloud State University, St. Cloud State University, 720 4th Avenue South, AS106, St. Cloud, MN 56301-4498, 320-308-2047 or toll-free 877-654-7278. *Fax:* 320-308-5424. *E-mail:* fpmorrissey@stcloudstate.edu.

ST. EDWARD'S UNIVERSITY

Austin, TX

Tuition & fees: $24,440 **Average undergraduate aid package: $18,015**

ABOUT THE INSTITUTION Independent Roman Catholic, coed. ***Awards:*** bachelor's and master's degrees and post-bachelor's certificates. 53 undergraduate majors. ***Total enrollment:*** 5,348. Undergraduates: 4,383. Freshmen: 751. Federal methodology is used as a basis for awarding need-based institutional aid.

UNDERGRADUATE EXPENSES for 2009–10 ***Application fee:*** $45. ***Comprehensive fee:*** $32,936 includes full-time tuition ($24,040), mandatory fees ($400), and room and board ($8496). ***College room only:*** $5296. ***Part-time tuition:*** $805 per credit hour. ***Part-time fees:*** $50 per term.

FRESHMAN FINANCIAL AID (Fall 2008, est.) 586 applied for aid; of those 81% were deemed to have need. 100% of freshmen with need received aid; of those 16% had need fully met. ***Average percent of need met:*** 75% (excluding resources awarded to replace EFC). ***Average financial aid package:*** $19,550 (excluding resources awarded to replace EFC). 10% of all full-time freshmen had no need and received non-need-based gift aid.

UNDERGRADUATE FINANCIAL AID (Fall 2008, est.) 2,500 applied for aid; of those 83% were deemed to have need. 99% of undergraduates with need received aid; of those 13% had need fully met. ***Average percent of need met:*** 67% (excluding resources awarded to replace EFC). ***Average financial aid package:*** $18,015 (excluding resources awarded to replace EFC). 7% of all full-time undergraduates had no need and received non-need-based gift aid.

GIFT AID (NEED-BASED) ***Total amount:*** $21,847,968 (20% federal, 20% state, 60% institutional). ***Receiving aid:*** Freshmen: 57% (426); all full-time undergraduates: 55% (1,884). ***Average award:*** Freshmen: $12,160; Undergraduates: $10,837. ***Scholarships, grants, and awards:*** Federal Pell, FSEOG, state, private, college/university gift aid from institutional funds, endowed scholarships.

GIFT AID (NON-NEED-BASED) ***Total amount:*** $11,536,335 (1% federal, 93% institutional, 6% external sources). ***Receiving aid:*** Freshmen: 46% (345). Undergraduates: 37% (1,272). ***Average award:*** Freshmen: $7920. Undergraduates: $6725. ***Scholarships, grants, and awards by category:*** *Academic interests/achievement:* 1,768 awards ($10,654,821 total): biological sciences, business, communication, computer science, education, English, foreign languages, general academic interests/achievements, humanities, international studies, mathematics, military science, physical sciences, religion/biblical studies, social sciences. *Creative arts/performance:* 39 awards ($97,129 total): art/fine arts, theater/drama. *Special achievements/activities:* 67 awards ($133,135 total): cheerleading/drum major, community service, general special achievements/activities, leadership. *Special characteristics:* 47 awards ($682,919 total): adult students, children of faculty/staff, religious affiliation. ***ROTC:*** Army cooperative, Air Force cooperative.

LOANS ***Student loans:*** $25,222,817 (33% need-based, 67% non-need-based). 72% of past graduating class borrowed through all loan programs. *Average indebtedness per student:* $27,093. ***Average need-based loan:*** Freshmen: $3232. Undergraduates: $4399. ***Parent loans:*** $2,354,166 (100% non-need-based). ***Programs:*** Federal Direct (PLUS), FFEL (Subsidized and Unsubsidized Stafford, PLUS), Perkins, state, alternative loans.

WORK-STUDY ***Federal work-study:*** Total amount: $395,453; 235 jobs averaging $1818. ***State or other work-study/employment:*** Total amount: $29,000 (100% need-based). 8 part-time jobs averaging $1575.

ATHLETIC AWARDS Total amount: $2,013,067 (100% non-need-based).

APPLYING FOR FINANCIAL AID ***Required financial aid form:*** FAFSA. ***Financial aid deadline:*** 4/15 (priority: 3/1). ***Notification date:*** Continuous. Students must reply by 5/1 or within 2 weeks of notification.

CONTACT Office of Student Financial Services, St. Edward's University, 3001 South Congress Avenue, Austin, TX 78704, 512-448-8523 or toll-free 800-555-0164. *Fax:* 512-416-5837. *E-mail:* seu.finaid@stedwards.edu.

ST. FRANCIS COLLEGE

Brooklyn Heights, NY

CONTACT Joseph Cummings, Director of Student Financial Services, St. Francis College, 180 Remsen Street, Brooklyn Heights, NY 11201-4398, 718-489-5390. *Fax:* 718-522-1274. *E-mail:* jcummings@stfranciscollege.edu.

SAINT FRANCIS MEDICAL CENTER COLLEGE OF NURSING

Peoria, IL

Tuition & fees: $14,716 **Average undergraduate aid package: $10,956**

ABOUT THE INSTITUTION Independent Roman Catholic, coed, primarily women. ***Awards:*** bachelor's and master's degrees. 1 undergraduate major. ***Total enrollment:*** 452. Undergraduates: 333. Federal methodology is used as a basis for awarding need-based institutional aid.

UNDERGRADUATE EXPENSES for 2009–10 ***Application fee:*** $50. ***Tuition:*** full-time $14,100, part time $472 per semester hour. ***Required fees:*** full-time $550, $130 per term.

UNDERGRADUATE FINANCIAL AID (Fall 2008, est.) 227 applied for aid; of those 89% were deemed to have need. 100% of undergraduates with need received aid; of those 7% had need fully met. ***Average percent of need met:*** 56% (excluding resources awarded to replace EFC). ***Average financial aid package:*** $10,956 (excluding resources awarded to replace EFC). 17% of all full-time undergraduates had no need and received non-need-based gift aid.

GIFT AID (NEED-BASED) ***Total amount:*** $1,239,513 (27% federal, 54% state, 11% institutional, 8% external sources). ***Receiving aid:*** All full-time undergraduates: 71% (190). ***Average award:*** Undergraduates: $5775. ***Scholarships, grants, and awards:*** Federal Pell, state, private, college/university gift aid from institutional funds.

GIFT AID (NON-NEED-BASED) ***Total amount:*** $77,373 (18% state, 69% institutional, 13% external sources). ***Receiving aid:*** Undergraduates: 1% (4). ***Average award:*** Undergraduates: $1121. ***Scholarships, grants, and awards by category:*** *Academic interests/achievement:* 101 awards ($41,550 total): general academic interests/achievements, health fields.

LOANS ***Student loans:*** $2,396,717 (83% need-based, 17% non-need-based). ***Average need-based loan:*** Undergraduates: $5471. ***Parent loans:*** $96,204 (17% need-based, 83% non-need-based). ***Programs:*** FFEL (Subsidized and Unsubsidized Stafford, PLUS), college/university.

APPLYING FOR FINANCIAL AID ***Required financial aid forms:*** FAFSA, institution's own form. ***Financial aid deadline (priority):*** 3/1. ***Notification date:*** Continuous beginning 5/1.

CONTACT Ms. Nancy Perryman, Coordinator Student Finance, Financial Assistance, Saint Francis Medical Center College of Nursing, 511 Northeast Greenleaf Street, Peoria, IL 61603-3783, 309-655-4119. *E-mail:* nancy.s.perryman@osfhealthcare.org.

SAINT FRANCIS UNIVERSITY

Loretto, PA

Tuition & fees: $24,840 **Average undergraduate aid package: $17,053**

ABOUT THE INSTITUTION Independent Roman Catholic, coed. ***Awards:*** associate, bachelor's, master's, and doctoral degrees. 68 undergraduate majors. ***Total enrollment:*** 2,210. Undergraduates: 1,612. Freshmen: 408. Federal methodology is used as a basis for awarding need-based institutional aid.

UNDERGRADUATE EXPENSES for 2008–09 ***Application fee:*** $30. ***Comprehensive fee:*** $33,262 includes full-time tuition ($23,790), mandatory fees ($1050), and room and board ($8422). ***College room only:*** $4232. Full-time tuition and fees vary according to course load and program. Room and board charges vary according to board plan and housing facility. ***Part-time tuition:*** $743 per credit. ***Part-time fees:*** $351 per contact hour; $30 per term. Part-time tuition and fees vary according to class time. ***Payment plan:*** Installment.

FRESHMAN FINANCIAL AID (Fall 2007) 372 applied for aid; of those 88% were deemed to have need. 98% of freshmen with need received aid; of those 17% had need fully met. ***Average percent of need met:*** 66% (excluding resources awarded to replace EFC). ***Average financial aid package:*** $15,403 (excluding resources awarded to replace EFC). 15% of all full-time freshmen had no need and received non-need-based gift aid.

UNDERGRADUATE FINANCIAL AID (Fall 2007) 1,147 applied for aid; of those 90% were deemed to have need. 98% of undergraduates with need received aid; of those 20% had need fully met. ***Average percent of need met:*** 69% (excluding resources awarded to replace EFC). ***Average financial aid package:*** $17,053 (excluding resources awarded to replace EFC). 15% of all full-time undergraduates had no need and received non-need-based gift aid.

GIFT AID (NEED-BASED) ***Total amount:*** $14,247,945 (10% federal, 17% state, 72% institutional, 1% external sources). ***Receiving aid:*** Freshmen: 81% (318); all full-time undergraduates: 81% (1,007). ***Average award:*** Freshmen: $13,069; Undergraduates: $13,859. ***Scholarships, grants, and awards:*** Federal Pell, FSEOG, state, private, college/university gift aid from institutional funds.

GIFT AID (NON-NEED-BASED) ***Total amount:*** $2,309,638 (2% state, 96% institutional, 2% external sources). ***Receiving aid:*** Freshmen: 12% (47). Undergraduates: 12% (147). ***Average award:*** Freshmen: $12,684. Undergraduates: $13,320. ***Scholarships, grants, and awards by category:*** *Academic interests/achievement:* general academic interests/achievements, religion/biblical studies, social sciences. *Creative arts/performance:* art/fine arts, music. *Special achievements/activities:* cheerleading/drum major, religious involvement. *Special characteristics:* adult students, children of educators, children of faculty/staff, international students, previous college experience, siblings of current students. ***Tuition waivers:*** Full or partial for employees or children of employees. ***ROTC:*** Army cooperative.

LOANS ***Student loans:*** $10,877,718 (68% need-based, 32% non-need-based). 86% of past graduating class borrowed through all loan programs. *Average indebtedness per student:* $10,762. ***Average need-based loan:*** Freshmen: $2775. Undergraduates: $3739. ***Parent loans:*** $1,750,370 (93% need-based, 7% non-need-based). ***Programs:*** FFEL (Subsidized and Unsubsidized Stafford, PLUS), Perkins, private alternative loans.

WORK-STUDY ***Federal work-study:*** Total amount: $229,146; jobs available. ***State or other work-study/employment:*** Total amount: $40,631 (25% need-based, 75% non-need-based). Part-time jobs available.

ATHLETIC AWARDS Total amount: $3,589,090 (57% need-based, 43% non-need-based).

APPLYING FOR FINANCIAL AID ***Required financial aid form:*** FAFSA. ***Financial aid deadline (priority):*** 5/1. ***Notification date:*** Continuous.

CONTACT Shane Himes, Financial Aid Counselor, Saint Francis University, PO Box 600, Loretto, PA 15931, 814-472-3010 or toll-free 800-342-5732. *Fax:* 814-472-3999. *E-mail:* shimes@francis.edu.

ST. GREGORY'S UNIVERSITY

Shawnee, OK

CONTACT Matt McCoin, Director of Financial Aid, St. Gregory's University, 1900 West MacArthur Drive, Shawnee, OK 74804, 405-878-5412 or toll-free 888-STGREGS. *Fax:* 405-878-5403. *E-mail:* mdmccoin@stgregorys.edu.

ST. JOHN FISHER COLLEGE

Rochester, NY

Tuition & fees: $23,390 **Average undergraduate aid package: $19,951**

ABOUT THE INSTITUTION Independent religious, coed. ***Awards:*** bachelor's, master's, doctoral, and first professional degrees and post-bachelor's and post-master's certificates. 36 undergraduate majors. ***Total enrollment:*** 3,832. Undergraduates: 2,878. Freshmen: 569. Federal methodology is used as a basis for awarding need-based institutional aid.

UNDERGRADUATE EXPENSES for 2008–09 ***Application fee:*** $30. ***Comprehensive fee:*** $33,430 includes full-time tuition ($22,960), mandatory fees ($430), and room and board ($10,040). ***College room only:*** $6420. Room and board charges vary according to board plan. ***Part-time tuition:*** $625 per credit. ***Part-time fees:*** $25 per term. Part-time tuition and fees vary according to course load. ***Payment plans:*** Installment, deferred payment.

FRESHMAN FINANCIAL AID (Fall 2008, est.) 543 applied for aid; of those 84% were deemed to have need. 100% of freshmen with need received aid; of those 39% had need fully met. ***Average percent of need met:*** 84% (excluding resources awarded to replace EFC). ***Average financial aid package:*** $20,822 (excluding resources awarded to replace EFC). 18% of all full-time freshmen had no need and received non-need-based gift aid.

UNDERGRADUATE FINANCIAL AID (Fall 2008, est.) 2,511 applied for aid; of those 86% were deemed to have need. 100% of undergraduates with need received aid; of those 36% had need fully met. ***Average percent of need met:*** 81% (excluding resources awarded to replace EFC). ***Average financial aid package:*** $19,951 (excluding resources awarded to replace EFC). 15% of all full-time undergraduates had no need and received non-need-based gift aid.

GIFT AID (NEED-BASED) ***Total amount:*** $25,943,219 (12% federal, 14% state, 70% institutional, 4% external sources). ***Receiving aid:*** Freshmen: 80% (457); all full-time undergraduates: 81% (2,143). ***Average award:*** Freshmen: $14,893; Undergraduates: $11,473. ***Scholarships, grants, and awards:*** Federal Pell, FSEOG, state, private, college/university gift aid from institutional funds, Federal Nursing.

GIFT AID (NON-NEED-BASED) ***Total amount:*** $3,138,910 (5% federal, 2% state, 87% institutional, 6% external sources). ***Receiving aid:*** Freshmen: 53% (304). Undergraduates: 37% (996). ***Average award:*** Freshmen: $8447. Undergraduates: $6924. ***Scholarships, grants, and awards by category:*** *Academic interests/achievement:* 1,378 awards ($10,822,850 total): biological sciences, business, English, foreign languages, general academic interests/achievements, humanities, mathematics, physical sciences. *Special achievements/activities:* 101 awards ($1,004,915 total): community service. *Special characteristics:* 108 awards ($1,062,868 total): children and siblings of alumni, ethnic background, first-generation college students, local/state students, members of minority groups. ***Tuition waivers:*** Full or partial for employees or children of employees. ***ROTC:*** Army cooperative, Air Force cooperative.

LOANS ***Student loans:*** $21,190,297 (92% need-based, 8% non-need-based). 85% of past graduating class borrowed through all loan programs. *Average indebtedness per student:* $29,288. ***Average need-based loan:*** Freshmen: $4030. Undergraduates: $5218. ***Parent loans:*** $7,062,308 (81% need-based, 19% non-need-based). ***Programs:*** FFEL (Subsidized and Unsubsidized Stafford, PLUS), Perkins, beginning with the 2009-2010 academic year FFEL Stafford & PLUS loans will be replaced by Direct Student & Plus loans.

WORK-STUDY ***Federal work-study:*** Total amount: $1,540,705; 1,632 jobs averaging $1462.

APPLYING FOR FINANCIAL AID ***Required financial aid forms:*** FAFSA, state aid form. ***Financial aid deadline (priority):*** 2/15. ***Notification date:*** Continuous beginning 3/22. Students must reply by 5/1 or within 3 weeks of notification.

CONTACT Mrs. Angela Monnat, Director of Financial Aid, St. John Fisher College, 3690 East Avenue, Rochester, NY 14618-3597, 585-385-8042 or toll-free 800-444-4640. *Fax:* 585-385-8044. *E-mail:* amonnat@sjfc.edu.

ST. JOHN'S COLLEGE

Springfield, IL

CONTACT Mary M. Deatherage, Financial Aid Officer, St. John's College, 421 North Ninth Street, Springfield, IL 62702, 217-544-6464 Ext. 44705. *Fax:* 217-757-6870. *E-mail:* mdeather@st-johns.org.

ST. JOHN'S COLLEGE

Annapolis, MD

CONTACT Marybeth Sommers, Director of Financial Aid, St. John's College, PO Box 2800, Annapolis, MD 21404, 410-626-2502 or toll-free 800-727-9238. *Fax:* 410-626-2885. *E-mail:* financialaid@sjca.edu.

ST. JOHN'S COLLEGE

Santa Fe, NM

Tuition & fees: $40,392 **Average undergraduate aid package: $26,368**

ABOUT THE INSTITUTION Independent, coed. ***Awards:*** bachelor's and master's degrees. 22 undergraduate majors. ***Total enrollment:*** 511. Undergraduates: 431. Freshmen: 110. Both federal and institutional methodology are used as a basis for awarding need-based institutional aid.

UNDERGRADUATE EXPENSES for 2009–10 ***Comprehensive fee:*** $49,954 includes full-time tuition ($39,992), mandatory fees ($400), and room and board ($9562). ***College room only:*** $4781.

FRESHMAN FINANCIAL AID (Fall 2007) 88 applied for aid; of those 95% were deemed to have need. 100% of freshmen with need received aid; of those 92% had need fully met. ***Average percent of need met:*** 95% (excluding resources awarded to replace EFC). ***Average financial aid package:*** $24,650 (excluding resources awarded to replace EFC).

UNDERGRADUATE FINANCIAL AID (Fall 2007) 296 applied for aid; of those 97% were deemed to have need. 100% of undergraduates with need received aid; of those 89% had need fully met. ***Average percent of need met:*** 93% (excluding resources awarded to replace EFC). ***Average financial aid package:*** $26,368 (excluding resources awarded to replace EFC).

GIFT AID (NEED-BASED) ***Total amount:*** $5,844,239 (10% federal, 1% state, 89% institutional). ***Receiving aid:*** Freshmen: 58% (78); all full-time undergraduates: 62% (272). ***Average award:*** Freshmen: $19,460; Undergraduates: $19,209. ***Scholarships, grants, and awards:*** Federal Pell, FSEOG, state, college/university gift aid from institutional funds, Academic Competitiveness Grant, National Smart Grant.

GIFT AID (NON-NEED-BASED) ***Total amount:*** $118,019 (100% external sources). ***Scholarships, grants, and awards by category:*** *Special characteristics:* 4 awards ($127,211 total): children of faculty/staff.

LOANS ***Student loans:*** $1,957,539 (68% need-based, 32% non-need-based). 72% of past graduating class borrowed through all loan programs. *Average indebtedness per student:* $24,875. ***Average need-based loan:*** Freshmen: $3635. Undergraduates: $3975. ***Parent loans:*** $1,456,660 (100% non-need-based). ***Programs:*** FFEL (Subsidized and Unsubsidized Stafford, PLUS), Perkins, college/university.

WORK-STUDY ***Federal work-study:*** Total amount: $383,575; 147 jobs averaging $2609. ***State or other work-study/employment:*** Total amount: $47,461 (100% need-based). 19 part-time jobs averaging $2453.

APPLYING FOR FINANCIAL AID ***Required financial aid forms:*** FAFSA, CSS Financial Aid PROFILE, noncustodial (divorced/separated) parent's statement, business/farm supplement. ***Financial aid deadline:*** 2/15. ***Notification date:*** Continuous. Students must reply by 5/1 or within 2 weeks of notification.

CONTACT Michael Rodriguez, Director of Financial Aid, St. John's College, 1160 Camino Cruz Blanca, Santa Fe, NM 87505, 505-984-6058 or toll-free 800-331-5232. *Fax:* 505-984-6003. *E-mail:* mrodriguez@sjcsf.edu.

SAINT JOHN'S UNIVERSITY

Collegeville, MN

Tuition & fees: $28,628 **Average undergraduate aid package: $21,653**

ABOUT THE INSTITUTION Independent Roman Catholic, coed, primarily men. ***Awards:*** bachelor's, master's, and first professional degrees (coordinate with College of Saint Benedict for women). 49 undergraduate majors. ***Total enrollment:*** 2,063. Undergraduates: 1,938. Freshmen: 461. Federal methodology is used as a basis for awarding need-based institutional aid.

UNDERGRADUATE EXPENSES for 2008–09 ***One-time required fee:*** $40. ***Comprehensive fee:*** $35,876 includes full-time tuition ($28,122), mandatory fees ($506), and room and board ($7248). ***College room only:*** $3664. Full-time tuition and fees vary according to student level. Room and board charges vary according to board plan and housing facility. ***Part-time tuition:*** $1171 per credit hour. Part-time tuition and fees vary according to course load. ***Payment plans:*** Tuition prepayment, installment.

FRESHMAN FINANCIAL AID (Fall 2008, est.) 356 applied for aid; of those 79% were deemed to have need. 100% of freshmen with need received aid; of those 48% had need fully met. ***Average percent of need met:*** 95% (excluding resources awarded to replace EFC). ***Average financial aid package:*** $24,272 (excluding resources awarded to replace EFC). 36% of all full-time freshmen had no need and received non-need-based gift aid.

UNDERGRADUATE FINANCIAL AID (Fall 2008, est.) 1,288 applied for aid; of those 83% were deemed to have need. 100% of undergraduates with need received aid; of those 41% had need fully met. ***Average percent of need met:*** 88% (excluding resources awarded to replace EFC). ***Average financial aid package:*** $21,653 (excluding resources awarded to replace EFC). 38% of all full-time undergraduates had no need and received non-need-based gift aid.

GIFT AID (NEED-BASED) ***Total amount:*** $16,550,195 (9% federal, 9% state, 78% institutional, 4% external sources). ***Receiving aid:*** Freshmen: 58% (267); all full-time undergraduates: 54% (1,025). ***Average award:*** Freshmen: $17,934; Undergraduates: $15,572. ***Scholarships, grants, and awards:*** Federal Pell, FSEOG, state, private, college/university gift aid from institutional funds.

GIFT AID (NON-NEED-BASED) ***Total amount:*** $9,933,276 (88% institutional, 12% external sources). ***Receiving aid:*** Freshmen: 53% (244). Undergraduates: 50% (953). ***Average award:*** Freshmen: $10,713. Undergraduates: $9839. ***Scholarships, grants, and awards by category:*** *Academic interests/achievement:* 1,657 awards ($14,815,508 total): general academic interests/achievements. *Creative arts/performance:* 133 awards ($242,700 total): art/fine arts, music, theater/drama. *Special characteristics:* 119 awards ($2,399,347 total): international students. ***Tuition waivers:*** Full or partial for employees or children of employees. ***ROTC:*** Army.

LOANS ***Student loans:*** $10,848,562 (85% need-based, 15% non-need-based). ***Average need-based loan:*** Freshmen: $4635. Undergraduates: $4790. ***Parent loans:*** $1,085,732 (73% need-based, 27% non-need-based). ***Programs:*** FFEL (Subsidized and Unsubsidized Stafford, PLUS), Perkins, state, alternative loans.

WORK-STUDY ***Federal work-study:*** Total amount: $856,802; 316 jobs averaging $2500. ***State or other work-study/employment:*** Total amount: $2,205,341 (55% need-based, 45% non-need-based). 960 part-time jobs averaging $2303.

APPLYING FOR FINANCIAL AID ***Required financial aid forms:*** FAFSA, institution's own form, federal income tax form(s). ***Financial aid deadline (priority):*** 3/15. ***Notification date:*** Continuous beginning 3/15. Students must reply by 5/1 or within 3 weeks of notification.

CONTACT Ms. Mary Dehler, Associate Director of Financial Aid, Saint John's University, PO Box 5000, Collegeville, MN 56321-5000, 320-363-3664 or toll-free 800-544-1489. *Fax:* 320-363-3102. *E-mail:* mdehler@csbsju.edu.

ST. JOHN'S UNIVERSITY

Queens, NY

Tuition & fees: $28,790 **Average undergraduate aid package: $19,546**

ABOUT THE INSTITUTION Independent religious, coed. ***Awards:*** associate, bachelor's, master's, doctoral, and first professional degrees and post-bachelor's and post-master's certificates. 66 undergraduate majors. ***Total enrollment:*** 20,109. Undergraduates: 14,816. Freshmen: 3,268. Federal methodology is used as a basis for awarding need-based institutional aid.

UNDERGRADUATE EXPENSES for 2008–09 ***Application fee:*** $50. ***Comprehensive fee:*** $41,360 includes full-time tuition ($28,100), mandatory fees ($690), and room and board ($12,570). ***College room only:*** $7900. Full-time tuition and fees vary according to class time, course load, program, and student level. Room and board charges vary according to board plan, housing facility, and location. ***Part-time tuition:*** $937 per credit. ***Part-time fees:*** $247.50 per term. Part-time tuition and fees vary according to class time, course load, program, and student level. ***Payment plans:*** Guaranteed tuition, installment, deferred payment.

FRESHMAN FINANCIAL AID (Fall 2007) 2,782 applied for aid; of those 90% were deemed to have need. 99% of freshmen with need received aid; of those 10% had need fully met. ***Average percent of need met:*** 72% (excluding resources awarded to replace EFC). ***Average financial aid package:*** $21,587 (excluding resources awarded to replace EFC). 6% of all full-time freshmen had no need and received non-need-based gift aid.

UNDERGRADUATE FINANCIAL AID (Fall 2007) 9,703 applied for aid; of those 92% were deemed to have need. 99% of undergraduates with need received aid; of those 8% had need fully met. ***Average percent of need met:*** 64% (excluding resources awarded to replace EFC). ***Average financial aid package:*** $19,546 (excluding resources awarded to replace EFC). 5% of all full-time undergraduates had no need and received non-need-based gift aid.

GIFT AID (NEED-BASED) ***Total amount:*** $74,168,494 (23% federal, 23% state, 54% institutional). ***Receiving aid:*** Freshmen: 72% (2,282); all full-time undergraduates: 67% (7,871). ***Average award:*** Freshmen: $11,390; Undergraduates: $9620. ***Scholarships, grants, and awards:*** Federal Pell, FSEOG, state, private, college/university gift aid from institutional funds.

GIFT AID (NON-NEED-BASED) ***Total amount:*** $77,592,216 (1% federal, 1% state, 92% institutional, 6% external sources). ***Receiving aid:*** Freshmen: 69% (2,191). Undergraduates: 67% (7,839). ***Average award:*** Freshmen: $11,756. Undergraduates: $9757. ***Scholarships, grants, and awards by category:*** *Academic interests/achievement:* 6,533 awards ($56,682,410 total): biological sciences, business, communication, computer science, education, general academic interests/achievements, health fields, mathematics, military science. *Creative arts/performance:* 110 awards ($326,201 total): art/fine arts, cinema/film/broadcasting, dance, debating, journalism/publications, music. *Special achievements/activities:* 292 awards ($786,620 total): cheerleading/drum major, community service, general special achievements/activities, hobbies/interests, leadership, religious involvement. *Special characteristics:* 4,139 awards ($14,182,206 total): children of faculty/staff, general special characteristics, local/state students, relatives of clergy, religious affiliation. ***Tuition waivers:*** Full or partial for employees or children of employees, senior citizens. ***ROTC:*** Army.

LOANS ***Student loans:*** $72,253,358 (61% need-based, 39% non-need-based). 70% of past graduating class borrowed through all loan programs. *Average indebtedness per student:* $29,657. ***Average need-based loan:*** Freshmen: $4290. Undergraduates: $4877. ***Parent loans:*** $24,377,365 (100% non-need-based). ***Programs:*** FFEL (Subsidized and Unsubsidized Stafford, PLUS), Perkins.

WORK-STUDY ***Federal work-study:*** Total amount: $2,440,127; 914 jobs averaging $2677.

ATHLETIC AWARDS Total amount: $4,944,810 (100% non-need-based).

APPLYING FOR FINANCIAL AID ***Required financial aid form:*** FAFSA. ***Financial aid deadline (priority):*** 2/1. ***Notification date:*** Continuous beginning 3/15. Students must reply within 2 weeks of notification.

CONTACT Mr. Jorge Rodriguez, Associate Vice President for Student Financial Services, St. John's University, 8000 Utopia Parkway, Queens, NY 11439, 718-990-2000 or toll-free 888-9STJOHNS (in-state), 888-9ST JOHNS (out-of-state). *Fax:* 718-990-5945. *E-mail:* financialaid@stjohns.edu.

ST. JOHN VIANNEY COLLEGE SEMINARY

Miami, FL

CONTACT Ms. Bonnie DeAngulo, Director of Financial Aid, St. John Vianney College Seminary, 2900 Southwest 87th Avenue, Miami, FL 33165-3244, 305-223-4561 Ext. 10.

SAINT JOSEPH COLLEGE

West Hartford, CT

ABOUT THE INSTITUTION Independent Roman Catholic, undergraduate: women only; graduate: coed. ***Awards:*** bachelor's and master's degrees and post-bachelor's certificates. 31 undergraduate majors. ***Total enrollment:*** 1,926. Undergraduates: 1,062. Freshmen: 226.

GIFT AID (NEED-BASED) ***Scholarships, grants, and awards:*** Federal Pell, FSEOG, state, private, college/university gift aid from institutional funds.

LOANS ***Programs:*** FFEL (Subsidized and Unsubsidized Stafford, PLUS), Perkins, state, alternative loans.

APPLYING FOR FINANCIAL AID ***Required financial aid form:*** FAFSA.

CONTACT Patricia Del Buono, Director of Financial Aid, Saint Joseph College, 1678 Asylum Avenue, West Hartford, CT 06117, 860-231-5319 or toll-free 866-442-8752. *E-mail:* pdelbuono@sjc.edu.

SAINT JOSEPH'S COLLEGE

Rensselaer, IN

Tuition & fees: $23,180 **Average undergraduate aid package: $22,877**

ABOUT THE INSTITUTION Independent Roman Catholic, coed. ***Awards:*** associate, bachelor's, and master's degrees. 34 undergraduate majors. ***Total enrollment:*** 1,076. Undergraduates: 1,076. Freshmen: 298. Federal methodology is used as a basis for awarding need-based institutional aid.

UNDERGRADUATE EXPENSES for 2008–09 *Application fee:* $25. ***Comprehensive fee:*** $30,350 includes full-time tuition ($23,000), mandatory fees ($180), and room and board ($7170). Full-time tuition and fees vary according to reciprocity agreements. Room and board charges vary according to housing facility. ***Part-time tuition:*** $770 per credit. Part-time tuition and fees vary according to course load and reciprocity agreements. ***Payment plan:*** Installment.

FRESHMAN FINANCIAL AID (Fall 2008, est.) 272 applied for aid; of those 84% were deemed to have need. 100% of freshmen with need received aid; of those 35% had need fully met. ***Average percent of need met:*** 85% (excluding resources awarded to replace EFC). ***Average financial aid package:*** $22,827 (excluding resources awarded to replace EFC). 14% of all full-time freshmen had no need and received non-need-based gift aid.

UNDERGRADUATE FINANCIAL AID (Fall 2008, est.) 810 applied for aid; of those 83% were deemed to have need. 100% of undergraduates with need received aid; of those 40% had need fully met. ***Average percent of need met:*** 85% (excluding resources awarded to replace EFC). ***Average financial aid package:*** $22,877 (excluding resources awarded to replace EFC). 14% of all full-time undergraduates had no need and received non-need-based gift aid.

GIFT AID (NEED-BASED) ***Total amount:*** $8,400,323 (13% federal, 22% state, 61% institutional, 4% external sources). ***Receiving aid:*** Freshmen: 82% (223); all full-time undergraduates: 80% (649). ***Average award:*** Freshmen: $15,789; Undergraduates: $15,110. ***Scholarships, grants, and awards:*** Federal Pell, FSEOG, state, private, college/university gift aid from institutional funds.

GIFT AID (NON-NEED-BASED) ***Total amount:*** $1,590,507 (95% institutional, 5% external sources). ***Receiving aid:*** Freshmen: 18% (50). Undergraduates: 20% (161). ***Average award:*** Undergraduates: $11,302. ***Scholarships, grants, and awards by category:*** *Academic interests/achievement:* 459 awards ($3,769,725 total): general academic interests/achievements. *Creative arts/performance:* 137 awards ($283,397 total): cinema/film/broadcasting, music, theater/drama. *Special achievements/activities:* 13 awards ($16,500 total): cheerleading/drum major. *Special characteristics:* 134 awards ($463,607 total): children and siblings of alumni, children of faculty/staff, siblings of current students. ***Tuition waivers:*** Full or partial for minority students, children of alumni, employees or children of employees.

LOANS ***Student loans:*** $5,371,906 (81% need-based, 19% non-need-based). 77% of past graduating class borrowed through all loan programs. *Average indebtedness per student:* $28,135. ***Average need-based loan:*** Freshmen: $3757. Undergraduates: $4386. ***Parent loans:*** $959,751 (68% need-based, 32% non-need-based). ***Programs:*** FFEL (Subsidized and Unsubsidized Stafford, PLUS), Perkins.

WORK-STUDY ***Federal work-study:*** Total amount: $77,910; 71 jobs averaging $888.

ATHLETIC AWARDS Total amount: $2,187,981 (57% need-based, 43% non-need-based).

APPLYING FOR FINANCIAL AID ***Required financial aid forms:*** FAFSA, combined institutional admission/financial aid form. ***Financial aid deadline (priority):*** 3/1. ***Notification date:*** Continuous. Students must reply by 5/1 or within 2 weeks of notification.

CONTACT Debra Sizemore, Director of Student Financial Services, Saint Joseph's College, US Highway 231, Rensselaer, IN 47978, 219-866-6163 or toll-free 800-447-8781 (out-of-state). *Fax:* 219-866-6144. *E-mail:* debbie@saintjoe.edu.

ST. JOSEPH'S COLLEGE, LONG ISLAND CAMPUS

Patchogue, NY

CONTACT Joan Farley, Director of Financial Aid, St. Joseph's College, Long Island Campus, 155 West Roe Boulevard, Patchogue, NY 11772-2399, 631-447-3214 or toll-free 866-AT ST JOE (in-state). *Fax:* 631-447-1734. *E-mail:* jfarley@sjcny.edu.

ST. JOSEPH'S COLLEGE, NEW YORK

Brooklyn, NY

CONTACT Ms. Carol Sullivan, Executive Director of Financial Aid, St. Joseph's College, New York, 245 Clinton Avenue, Brooklyn, NY 11205-3688, 718-636-6808. *Fax:* 718-636-6827. *E-mail:* csullivan@sjcny.edu.

SAINT JOSEPH'S COLLEGE OF MAINE

Standish, ME

Tuition & fees: $25,060 **Average undergraduate aid package: $19,306**

ABOUT THE INSTITUTION Independent religious, coed. 47 undergraduate majors. Both federal and institutional methodology are used as a basis for awarding need-based institutional aid.

UNDERGRADUATE EXPENSES for 2008–09 ***Comprehensive fee:*** $35,010 includes full-time tuition ($24,200), mandatory fees ($860), and room and board ($9950). ***Part-time tuition:*** $430 per credit hour. Part-time tuition and fees vary according to course load. ***Payment plan:*** Installment.

FRESHMAN FINANCIAL AID (Fall 2008, est.) 315 applied for aid; of those 88% were deemed to have need. 100% of freshmen with need received aid; of those 33% had need fully met. ***Average percent of need met:*** 82% (excluding resources awarded to replace EFC). ***Average financial aid package:*** $19,397 (excluding resources awarded to replace EFC). 18% of all full-time freshmen had no need and received non-need-based gift aid.

UNDERGRADUATE FINANCIAL AID (Fall 2008, est.) 949 applied for aid; of those 90% were deemed to have need. 100% of undergraduates with need received aid; of those 34% had need fully met. ***Average percent of need met:*** 82% (excluding resources awarded to replace EFC). ***Average financial aid package:*** $19,306 (excluding resources awarded to replace EFC). 20% of all full-time undergraduates had no need and received non-need-based gift aid.

GIFT AID (NEED-BASED) ***Total amount:*** $10,484,419 (10% federal, 3% state, 80% institutional, 7% external sources). ***Receiving aid:*** Freshmen: 81% (276); all full-time undergraduates: 79% (845). ***Average award:*** Freshmen: $13,227; Undergraduates: $12,348. ***Scholarships, grants, and awards:*** Federal Pell, FSEOG, state, private, college/university gift aid from institutional funds, Federal Nursing.

GIFT AID (NON-NEED-BASED) ***Total amount:*** $2,318,350 (88% institutional, 12% external sources). ***Receiving aid:*** Freshmen: 12% (40). Undergraduates: 10% (103). ***Average award:*** Freshmen: $7898. Undergraduates: $8083. ***Scholarships, grants, and awards by category:*** *Academic interests/achievement:* 161 awards ($1,391,460 total): general academic interests/achievements. *Special characteristics:* 40 awards ($524,952 total): children of faculty/staff, siblings of current students, spouses of current students. ***Tuition waivers:*** Full or partial for employees or children of employees.

LOANS ***Student loans:*** $11,103,278 (58% need-based, 42% non-need-based). 86% of past graduating class borrowed through all loan programs. *Average indebtedness per student:* $35,451. ***Average need-based loan:*** Freshmen: $4404. Undergraduates: $4614. ***Parent loans:*** $1,964,864 (38% need-based, 62% non-need-based). ***Programs:*** FFEL (Subsidized and Unsubsidized Stafford, PLUS), Perkins, Federal Nursing, state.

WORK-STUDY ***Federal work-study:*** Total amount: $604,879; 425 jobs averaging $1400.

APPLYING FOR FINANCIAL AID ***Required financial aid forms:*** FAFSA, institution's own form. ***Financial aid deadline (priority):*** 3/1. ***Notification date:*** Continuous beginning 3/15. Students must reply by 5/1 or within 3 weeks of notification.

CONTACT Office of Financial Aid, Saint Joseph's College of Maine, 278 Whites Bridge Road, Standish, ME 04084-5263, 800-752-1266 or toll-free 800-338-7057. *Fax:* 207-893-6699. *E-mail:* finaid@sjcme.edu.

SAINT JOSEPH SEMINARY COLLEGE

Saint Benedict, LA

CONTACT George J. Binder Jr., Financial Aid Officer, Saint Joseph Seminary College, Saint Benedict, LA 70457, 985-867-2248. *Fax:* 985-867-2270. *E-mail:* gbinderregistrar@sjasc.edu.

SAINT JOSEPH'S UNIVERSITY

Philadelphia, PA

Tuition & fees: $32,860 **Average undergraduate aid package: $17,990**

ABOUT THE INSTITUTION Independent Roman Catholic (Jesuit), coed. ***Awards:*** associate, bachelor's, master's, and doctoral degrees and post-bachelor's and post-master's certificates. 52 undergraduate majors. ***Total enrollment:*** 7,900. Undergraduates: 5,331. Freshmen: 1,478. Federal methodology is used as a basis for awarding need-based institutional aid.

UNDERGRADUATE EXPENSES for 2008–09 ***Application fee:*** $60. ***One-time required fee:*** $225. ***Comprehensive fee:*** $44,040 includes full-time tuition ($32,710), mandatory fees ($150), and room and board ($11,180). ***College room only:*** $7090. Full-time tuition and fees vary according to course load and student level. Room and board charges vary according to board plan and housing facility. ***Part-time tuition:*** $1073 per credit. Part-time tuition and fees vary according to student level. evening college, continuing education student tuition: $439 per credit. ***Payment plans:*** Installment, deferred payment.

FRESHMAN FINANCIAL AID (Fall 2008, est.) 1,074 applied for aid; of those 74% were deemed to have need. 100% of freshmen with need received aid; of those 23% had need fully met. ***Average percent of need met:*** 83% (excluding resources awarded to replace EFC). ***Average financial aid package:*** $18,296 (excluding resources awarded to replace EFC). 36% of all full-time freshmen had no need and received non-need-based gift aid.

UNDERGRADUATE FINANCIAL AID (Fall 2008, est.) 2,708 applied for aid; of those 78% were deemed to have need. 100% of undergraduates with need received aid; of those 21% had need fully met. ***Average percent of need met:*** 80% (excluding resources awarded to replace EFC). ***Average financial aid package:*** $17,990 (excluding resources awarded to replace EFC). 41% of all full-time undergraduates had no need and received non-need-based gift aid.

GIFT AID (NEED-BASED) ***Total amount:*** $26,625,975 (7% federal, 4% state, 87% institutional, 2% external sources). ***Receiving aid:*** Freshmen: 52% (762); all full-time undergraduates: 44% (1,989). ***Average award:*** Freshmen: $14,746; Undergraduates: $13,868. ***Scholarships, grants, and awards:*** Federal Pell, FSEOG, state, private, college/university gift aid from institutional funds.

GIFT AID (NON-NEED-BASED) ***Total amount:*** $19,173,998 (98% institutional, 2% external sources). ***Receiving aid:*** Freshmen: 47% (690). Undergraduates: 42% (1,868). ***Average award:*** Freshmen: $10,464. Undergraduates: $10,155. ***Scholarships, grants, and awards by category:*** *Academic interests/achievement:* general academic interests/achievements. *Creative arts/performance:* general creative arts/performance, music, theater/drama. *Special achievements/activities:* general special achievements/activities, leadership. *Special characteristics:* children and siblings of alumni, members of minority groups. ***Tuition waivers:*** Full or partial for employees or children of employees. ***ROTC:*** Army cooperative, Naval cooperative, Air Force.

LOANS ***Student loans:*** $29,199,276 (81% need-based, 19% non-need-based). 60% of past graduating class borrowed through all loan programs. *Average indebtedness per student:* $39,116. ***Average need-based loan:*** Freshmen: $3685. Undergraduates: $4496. ***Parent loans:*** $17,627,168 (77% need-based, 23% non-need-based). ***Programs:*** FFEL (Subsidized and Unsubsidized Stafford, PLUS), Perkins.

WORK-STUDY ***Federal work-study:*** Total amount: $540,000; jobs available.

ATHLETIC AWARDS Total amount: $4,153,631 (47% need-based, 53% non-need-based).

APPLYING FOR FINANCIAL AID ***Required financial aid form:*** FAFSA. ***Financial aid deadline (priority):*** 2/15. ***Notification date:*** Continuous beginning 3/1. Students must reply by 5/1.

CONTACT Eileen M. Tucker, Director of Financial Assistance, Saint Joseph's University, 5600 City Avenue, Philadelphia, PA 19131-1395, 610-660-1556 or toll-free 888-BEAHAWK (in-state). *Fax:* 610-660-1342. *E-mail:* tucker@sju.edu.

ST. LAWRENCE UNIVERSITY

Canton, NY

Tuition & fees: $37,905 **Average undergraduate aid package: $35,622**

ABOUT THE INSTITUTION Independent, coed. ***Awards:*** bachelor's and master's degrees and post-master's certificates. 39 undergraduate majors. ***Total enrollment:*** 2,325. Undergraduates: 2,206. Freshmen: 616. Both federal and institutional methodology are used as a basis for awarding need-based institutional aid.

UNDERGRADUATE EXPENSES for 2008–09 ***Application fee:*** $60. ***Comprehensive fee:*** $47,550 includes full-time tuition ($37,675), mandatory fees ($230), and room and board ($9645). ***College room only:*** $5185. Room and board charges vary according to board plan. ***Payment plan:*** Installment.

FRESHMAN FINANCIAL AID (Fall 2008, est.) 447 applied for aid; of those 85% were deemed to have need. 100% of freshmen with need received aid; of those 55% had need fully met. ***Average percent of need met:*** 95% (excluding resources awarded to replace EFC). ***Average financial aid package:*** $36,230 (excluding resources awarded to replace EFC). 19% of all full-time freshmen had no need and received non-need-based gift aid.

UNDERGRADUATE FINANCIAL AID (Fall 2008, est.) 1,525 applied for aid; of those 91% were deemed to have need. 98% of undergraduates with need received aid; of those 52% had need fully met. ***Average percent of need met:*** 93% (excluding resources awarded to replace EFC). ***Average financial aid package:*** $35,622 (excluding resources awarded to replace EFC). 16% of all full-time undergraduates had no need and received non-need-based gift aid.

GIFT AID (NEED-BASED) ***Total amount:*** $34,530,885 (6% federal, 4% state, 86% institutional, 4% external sources). ***Receiving aid:*** Freshmen: 61% (376); all full-time undergraduates: 62% (1,348). ***Average award:*** Freshmen: $26,792; Undergraduates: $25,216. ***Scholarships, grants, and awards:*** Federal Pell, FSEOG, state, college/university gift aid from institutional funds.

GIFT AID (NON-NEED-BASED) ***Total amount:*** $4,728,509 (97% institutional, 3% external sources). ***Receiving aid:*** Freshmen: 17% (104). Undergraduates: 12% (253). ***Average award:*** Freshmen: $11,488. Undergraduates: $11,203. ***Scholarships, grants, and awards by category:*** *Academic interests/achievement:* general academic interests/achievements. *Special achievements/activities:* community service. *Special characteristics:* children and siblings of alumni, siblings of current students. ***Tuition waivers:*** Full or partial for employees or children of employees. ***ROTC:*** Army cooperative, Air Force cooperative.

LOANS ***Student loans:*** $11,152,404 (40% need-based, 60% non-need-based). 68% of past graduating class borrowed through all loan programs. *Average indebtedness per student:* $29,941. ***Average need-based loan:*** Freshmen: $3360. Undergraduates: $4597. ***Parent loans:*** $4,242,546 (100% non-need-based). ***Programs:*** Federal Direct (Subsidized and Unsubsidized Stafford, PLUS), Perkins, college/university.

WORK-STUDY ***Federal work-study:*** Total amount: $1,026,505; jobs available. ***State or other work-study/employment:*** Total amount: $687,426 (100% non-need-based). Part-time jobs available.

ATHLETIC AWARDS Total amount: $1,601,830 (100% non-need-based).

APPLYING FOR FINANCIAL AID ***Required financial aid forms:*** FAFSA, noncustodial (divorced/separated) parent's statement, business/farm supplement, income tax returns, W-2 forms. ***Financial aid deadline:*** 2/1. ***Notification date:*** 3/30. Students must reply by 5/1 or within 2 weeks of notification.

CONTACT Mrs. Patricia J. B. Farmer, Director of Financial Aid, St. Lawrence University, Payson Hall, Canton, NY 13617-1455, 315-229-5265 or toll-free 800-285-1856. *Fax:* 315-229-5502. *E-mail:* pfarmer@stlawu.edu.

SAINT LEO UNIVERSITY

Saint Leo, FL

Tuition & fees: $17,150 **Average undergraduate aid package: $18,226**

ABOUT THE INSTITUTION Independent Roman Catholic, coed. ***Awards:*** associate, bachelor's, and master's degrees and post-bachelor's certificates. 28 undergraduate majors. ***Total enrollment:*** 3,510. Undergraduates: 1,703. Freshmen: 500. Federal methodology is used as a basis for awarding need-based institutional aid.

UNDERGRADUATE EXPENSES for 2008–09 ***Application fee:*** $35. ***Comprehensive fee:*** $25,580 includes full-time tuition ($16,500), mandatory fees ($650), and room and board ($8430). ***College room only:*** $4450.

FRESHMAN FINANCIAL AID (Fall 2008, est.) 454 applied for aid; of those 80% were deemed to have need. 100% of freshmen with need received aid; of those 32% had need fully met. ***Average percent of need met:*** 84% (excluding resources awarded to replace EFC). ***Average financial aid package:*** $18,827 (excluding resources awarded to replace EFC).

UNDERGRADUATE FINANCIAL AID (Fall 2008, est.) 1,349 applied for aid; of those 79% were deemed to have need. 99% of undergraduates with need received aid; of those 38% had need fully met. ***Average percent of need met:*** 83% (excluding resources awarded to replace EFC). ***Average financial aid package:*** $18,226 (excluding resources awarded to replace EFC). 2% of all full-time undergraduates had no need and received non-need-based gift aid.

GIFT AID (NEED-BASED) ***Total amount:*** $12,972,339 (14% federal, 21% state, 62% institutional, 3% external sources). ***Receiving aid:*** Freshmen: 72% (361); all full-time undergraduates: 64% (1,039). ***Average award:*** Freshmen: $11,991; Undergraduates: $10,935. ***Scholarships, grants, and awards:*** Federal Pell, FSEOG, state, private, college/university gift aid from institutional funds, United Negro College Fund.

GIFT AID (NON-NEED-BASED) ***Total amount:*** $1,726,926 (57% state, 16% institutional, 27% external sources). ***Receiving aid:*** Freshmen: 7% (36). Undergraduates: 8% (124). ***Average award:*** Undergraduates: $8214. ***ROTC:*** Army cooperative, Air Force cooperative.

LOANS ***Student loans:*** $10,594,684 (62% need-based, 38% non-need-based). 69% of past graduating class borrowed through all loan programs. *Average indebtedness per student:* $23,178. ***Average need-based loan:*** Freshmen: $4143. Undergraduates: $4937. ***Parent loans:*** $1,406,227 (45% need-based, 55% non-need-based). ***Programs:*** Federal Direct (Subsidized and Unsubsidized Stafford, PLUS), Perkins.

WORK-STUDY ***Federal work-study:*** Total amount: $2,561,215; 786 jobs averaging $3263.

ATHLETIC AWARDS Total amount: $1,581,881 (57% need-based, 43% non-need-based).

APPLYING FOR FINANCIAL AID ***Required financial aid form:*** FAFSA. ***Financial aid deadline (priority):*** 3/15. ***Notification date:*** Continuous.

CONTACT Office of Student Financial Services, Saint Leo University, PO Box 6665, MC 2228, Saint Leo, FL 33574-6665, 800-240-7658 or toll-free 800-334-5532. *Fax:* 352-588-8403. *E-mail:* finaid@saintleo.edu.

ST. LOUIS CHRISTIAN COLLEGE

Florissant, MO

Tuition & fees: $9500 **Average undergraduate aid package: $13,586**

ABOUT THE INSTITUTION Independent Christian, coed. ***Awards:*** associate and bachelor's degrees. 5 undergraduate majors. ***Total enrollment:*** 321. Undergraduates: 321. Freshmen: 54. Federal methodology is used as a basis for awarding need-based institutional aid.

UNDERGRADUATE EXPENSES for 2008–09 ***Comprehensive fee:*** $12,800 includes full-time tuition ($8850), mandatory fees ($650), and room and board ($3300). Room and board charges vary according to housing facility. ***Part-time tuition:*** $295 per credit hour.

FRESHMAN FINANCIAL AID (Fall 2008, est.) 29 applied for aid; of those 83% were deemed to have need. 100% of freshmen with need received aid; of those 4% had need fully met. ***Average percent of need met:*** 70% (excluding resources awarded to replace EFC). ***Average financial aid package:*** $11,202 (excluding resources awarded to replace EFC). 15% of all full-time freshmen had no need and received non-need-based gift aid.

UNDERGRADUATE FINANCIAL AID (Fall 2008, est.) 217 applied for aid; of those 91% were deemed to have need. 100% of undergraduates with need received aid; of those 6% had need fully met. ***Average percent of need met:*** 64% (excluding resources awarded to replace EFC). ***Average financial aid package:*** $13,586 (excluding resources awarded to replace EFC). 22% of all full-time undergraduates had no need and received non-need-based gift aid.

GIFT AID (NEED-BASED) ***Total amount:*** $2,127,931 (23% federal, 73% institutional, 4% external sources). ***Receiving aid:*** Freshmen: 73% (24); all full-time undergraduates: 78% (198). ***Average award:*** Freshmen: $9633; Undergraduates: $9894. ***Scholarships, grants, and awards:*** Federal Pell, FSEOG, private, college/university gift aid from institutional funds.

GIFT AID (NON-NEED-BASED) ***Total amount:*** $174,415 (94% institutional, 6% external sources). ***Average award:*** Freshmen: $6313. Undergraduates: $7676. ***Scholarships, grants, and awards by category:*** *Special characteristics:* 2 awards ($13,500 total): children of faculty/staff, general special characteristics. ***Tuition waivers:*** Full or partial for employees or children of employees.

LOANS ***Student loans:*** $1,225,570 (90% need-based, 10% non-need-based). 75% of past graduating class borrowed through all loan programs. *Average indebtedness per student:* $20,166. ***Average need-based loan:*** Freshmen: $1508. Undergraduates: $3702. ***Parent loans:*** $54,703 (75% need-based, 25% non-need-based). ***Programs:*** FFEL (Subsidized and Unsubsidized Stafford, PLUS), private loans.

WORK-STUDY ***Federal work-study:*** Total amount: $25,333; 16 jobs averaging $1583. ***State or other work-study/employment:*** Total amount: $138,000 (100% non-need-based). 23 part-time jobs averaging $4800.

APPLYING FOR FINANCIAL AID ***Required financial aid form:*** FAFSA. ***Financial aid deadline:*** Continuous. ***Notification date:*** Continuous.

CONTACT Mrs. Catherine Wilhoit, Director of Financial Aid, St. Louis Christian College, 1360 Grandview Drive, Florissant, MO 63033-6499, 314-837-6777 Ext. 1101 or toll-free 800-887-SLCC. *Fax:* 314-837-8291.

ST. LOUIS COLLEGE OF PHARMACY

St. Louis, MO

Tuition & fees: $21,925 **Average undergraduate aid package: $12,986**

ABOUT THE INSTITUTION Independent, coed. ***Awards:*** first professional degrees. 1 undergraduate major. ***Total enrollment:*** 1,191. Undergraduates: 645. Freshmen: 237. Federal methodology is used as a basis for awarding need-based institutional aid.

UNDERGRADUATE EXPENSES for 2009–10 ***Application fee:*** $50. ***Comprehensive fee:*** $30,079 includes full-time tuition ($21,525), mandatory fees ($400), and room and board ($8154). ***College room only:*** $4600. ***Part-time tuition:*** $800 per credit hour.

FRESHMAN FINANCIAL AID (Fall 2008, est.) 226 applied for aid; of those 77% were deemed to have need. 98% of freshmen with need received aid; of those 15% had need fully met. ***Average percent of need met:*** 61% (excluding resources awarded to replace EFC). ***Average financial aid package:*** $13,080 (excluding resources awarded to replace EFC). 27% of all full-time freshmen had no need and received non-need-based gift aid.

UNDERGRADUATE FINANCIAL AID (Fall 2008, est.) 578 applied for aid; of those 83% were deemed to have need. 97% of undergraduates with need received aid; of those 12% had need fully met. ***Average percent of need met:*** 54% (excluding resources awarded to replace EFC). ***Average financial aid package:*** $12,986 (excluding resources awarded to replace EFC). 20% of all full-time undergraduates had no need and received non-need-based gift aid.

GIFT AID (NEED-BASED) ***Total amount:*** $3,682,381 (16% federal, 16% state, 56% institutional, 12% external sources). ***Receiving aid:*** Freshmen: 72% (171); all full-time undergraduates: 62% (398). ***Average award:*** Freshmen: $8873; Undergraduates: $9252. ***Scholarships, grants, and awards:*** Federal Pell, FSEOG, state, private, college/university gift aid from institutional funds.

GIFT AID (NON-NEED-BASED) ***Total amount:*** $1,007,559 (5% state, 83% institutional, 12% external sources). ***Receiving aid:*** Freshmen: 8% (20). Undergraduates: 5% (35). ***Average award:*** Freshmen: $5473. Undergraduates: $5925. ***Scholarships, grants, and awards by category:*** *Academic interests/achievement:* 495 awards ($2,895,901 total): general academic interests/achievements. *Special achievements/activities:* community service, leadership. *Special characteristics:* children of faculty/staff, local/state students. ***ROTC:*** Army cooperative, Air Force cooperative.

LOANS ***Student loans:*** $5,599,645 (73% need-based, 27% non-need-based). 94% of past graduating class borrowed through all loan programs. *Average*

indebtedness per student: $105,576. ***Average need-based loan:*** Freshmen: $4503. Undergraduates: $5276. ***Parent loans:*** $1,707,662 (41% need-based, 59% non-need-based). ***Programs:*** FFEL (Subsidized and Unsubsidized Stafford, PLUS), Perkins, Federal Health Professions Loan.

WORK-STUDY ***Federal work-study:*** Total amount: $202,888; 197 jobs averaging $1085.

APPLYING FOR FINANCIAL AID ***Required financial aid forms:*** FAFSA, institution's own form. ***Financial aid deadline (priority):*** 3/15. ***Notification date:*** Continuous. Students must reply within 2 weeks of notification.

CONTACT Mr. David Rice, Director of Financial Aid, St. Louis College of Pharmacy, 4588 Parkview Place, St. Louis, MO 63110, 314-446-8320 or toll-free 800-278-5267 (in-state). *Fax:* 314-446-8310. *E-mail:* drice@stlcop.edu.

SAINT LOUIS UNIVERSITY

St. Louis, MO

Tuition & fees: $30,728 **Average undergraduate aid package: $19,456**

ABOUT THE INSTITUTION Independent Roman Catholic (Jesuit), coed. ***Awards:*** bachelor's, master's, doctoral, and first professional degrees and post-bachelor's and post-master's certificates. 70 undergraduate majors. ***Total enrollment:*** 12,733. Undergraduates: 7,814. Freshmen: 1,645. Federal methodology is used as a basis for awarding need-based institutional aid.

UNDERGRADUATE EXPENSES for 2008–09 ***Application fee:*** $25. ***Comprehensive fee:*** $39,488 includes full-time tuition ($30,330), mandatory fees ($398), and room and board ($8760). ***College room only:*** $4900. Full-time tuition and fees vary according to location and program. Room and board charges vary according to board plan, housing facility, and location. ***Part-time tuition:*** $1060 per credit hour. ***Part-time fees:*** $120 per semester hour. Part-time tuition and fees vary according to location and program. ***Payment plan:*** Installment.

FRESHMAN FINANCIAL AID (Fall 2007) 1,241 applied for aid; of those 80% were deemed to have need. 100% of freshmen with need received aid; of those 19% had need fully met. ***Average percent of need met:*** 70% (excluding resources awarded to replace EFC). ***Average financial aid package:*** $20,775 (excluding resources awarded to replace EFC). 34% of all full-time freshmen had no need and received non-need-based gift aid.

UNDERGRADUATE FINANCIAL AID (Fall 2007) 4,525 applied for aid; of those 86% were deemed to have need. 100% of undergraduates with need received aid; of those 17% had need fully met. ***Average percent of need met:*** 65% (excluding resources awarded to replace EFC). ***Average financial aid package:*** $19,456 (excluding resources awarded to replace EFC). 30% of all full-time undergraduates had no need and received non-need-based gift aid.

GIFT AID (NEED-BASED) ***Total amount:*** $55,318,572 (11% federal, 6% state, 80% institutional, 3% external sources). ***Receiving aid:*** Freshmen: 60% (964); all full-time undergraduates: 52% (3,662). ***Average award:*** Freshmen: $16,092; Undergraduates: $14,249. ***Scholarships, grants, and awards:*** Federal Pell, FSEOG, state, private, college/university gift aid from institutional funds, Federal Nursing.

GIFT AID (NON-NEED-BASED) ***Total amount:*** $19,184,769 (2% state, 86% institutional, 12% external sources). ***Receiving aid:*** Freshmen: 6% (97). Undergraduates: 5% (320). ***Average award:*** Freshmen: $9857. Undergraduates: $9154. ***Scholarships, grants, and awards by category:*** *Academic interests/achievement:* 6,284 awards ($52,674,394 total): area/ethnic studies, biological sciences, business, communication, computer science, education, engineering/technologies, English, foreign languages, general academic interests/achievements, health fields, humanities, international studies, mathematics, military science, physical sciences, premedicine, religion/biblical studies, social sciences. *Creative arts/performance:* 109 awards ($107,140 total): art/fine arts, music, performing arts, theater/drama. *Special achievements/activities:* 427 awards ($5,075,721 total): cheerleading/drum major, community service, general special achievements/activities, leadership, memberships, religious involvement. *Special characteristics:* 1,699 awards ($19,500,697 total): children of faculty/staff, first-generation college students, general special characteristics, international students, members of minority groups, previous college experience, religious affiliation, siblings of current students. ***Tuition waivers:*** Full or partial for employees or children of employees. ***ROTC:*** Army cooperative, Air Force.

LOANS ***Student loans:*** $42,446,201 (42% need-based, 58% non-need-based). 67% of past graduating class borrowed through all loan programs. *Average indebtedness per student:* $29,298. ***Average need-based loan:*** Freshmen: $3991. Undergraduates: $5264. ***Parent loans:*** $12,323,733 (100% non-need-based). ***Programs:*** FFEL (Subsidized and Unsubsidized Stafford, PLUS), Perkins, Federal Nursing, college/university.

WORK-STUDY ***Federal work-study:*** Total amount: $1,569,804; 1,505 jobs averaging $2964. ***State or other work-study/employment:*** Total amount: $206,361 (65% need-based, 35% non-need-based). 70 part-time jobs averaging $1885.

ATHLETIC AWARDS Total amount: $3,306,708 (30% need-based, 70% non-need-based).

APPLYING FOR FINANCIAL AID ***Required financial aid form:*** FAFSA. ***Financial aid deadline (priority):*** 3/1. ***Notification date:*** Continuous beginning 3/1. Students must reply by 5/1 or within 4 weeks of notification.

CONTACT Cari Wickliffe, Assistant Vice Provost, Student Financial Services, Saint Louis University, 221 North Grand Boulevard, DuBourg Hall, Room 121, St. Louis, MO 63103-2097, 314-977-2350 or toll-free 800-758-3678 (out-of-state). *Fax:* 314-977-3437. *E-mail:* wicklics@slu.edu.

SAINT LUKE'S COLLEGE

Kansas City, MO

Tuition & fees: $9520 **Average undergraduate aid package: $7500**

ABOUT THE INSTITUTION Independent Episcopal, coed. ***Awards:*** bachelor's degrees. 1 undergraduate major. ***Total enrollment:*** 113. Undergraduates: 113. Both federal and institutional methodology are used as a basis for awarding need-based institutional aid.

UNDERGRADUATE EXPENSES for 2008–09 ***Application fee:*** $35. ***Tuition:*** full-time $8850.

UNDERGRADUATE FINANCIAL AID (Fall 2008, est.) 100 applied for aid; of those 86% were deemed to have need. 100% of undergraduates with need received aid; of those 8% had need fully met. ***Average percent of need met:*** 72% (excluding resources awarded to replace EFC). ***Average financial aid package:*** $7500 (excluding resources awarded to replace EFC). 7% of all full-time undergraduates had no need and received non-need-based gift aid.

GIFT AID (NEED-BASED) ***Total amount:*** $421,921 (24% federal, 18% state, 45% institutional, 13% external sources). ***Receiving aid:*** All full-time undergraduates: 67% (81). ***Average award:*** Undergraduates: $2000. ***Scholarships, grants, and awards:*** Federal Pell, FSEOG, state, private, college/university gift aid from institutional funds.

GIFT AID (NON-NEED-BASED) ***Total amount:*** $19,000 (100% institutional). ***Receiving aid:*** Undergraduates: 28% (34). ***Average award:*** Undergraduates: $2000. ***Scholarships, grants, and awards by category:*** *Special characteristics:* 4 awards ($8000 total): ethnic background.

LOANS ***Student loans:*** $770,120 (100% need-based). ***Average need-based loan:*** Undergraduates: $5000. ***Parent loans:*** $72,844 (35% need-based, 65% non-need-based). ***Programs:*** FFEL (Subsidized and Unsubsidized Stafford, PLUS), Perkins, Federal Nursing, college/university.

WORK-STUDY ***Federal work-study:*** Total amount: $600; jobs available.

APPLYING FOR FINANCIAL AID ***Financial aid deadline:*** Continuous.

CONTACT Marcia Shaw, Director of Financial Aid, Saint Luke's College, 8320 Ward Parkway, Suite 300, Kansas City, MO 64114, 816-932-2194. *Fax:* 816-932-9064. *E-mail:* meshaw@saint-lukes.org.

SAINT MARTIN'S UNIVERSITY

Lacey, WA

Tuition & fees: $23,810 **Average undergraduate aid package: $16,369**

ABOUT THE INSTITUTION Independent Roman Catholic, coed. ***Awards:*** bachelor's and master's degrees and post-bachelor's and post-master's certificates. 31 undergraduate majors. ***Total enrollment:*** 1,659. Undergraduates: 1,387. Freshmen: 202. Federal methodology is used as a basis for awarding need-based institutional aid.

UNDERGRADUATE EXPENSES for 2008–09 ***Application fee:*** $35. ***Comprehensive fee:*** $31,850 includes full-time tuition ($23,810) and room and board ($8040). Full-time tuition and fees vary according to location. Room and board charges vary according to board plan. ***Part-time tuition:*** $794 per credit. Part-time tuition and fees vary according to course load and location. ***Payment plan:*** Installment.

FRESHMAN FINANCIAL AID (Fall 2007) 197 applied for aid; of those 85% were deemed to have need. 100% of freshmen with need received aid; of those 19%

had need fully met. ***Average percent of need met:*** 81% (excluding resources awarded to replace EFC). ***Average financial aid package:*** $19,061 (excluding resources awarded to replace EFC). 19% of all full-time freshmen had no need and received non-need-based gift aid.

UNDERGRADUATE FINANCIAL AID (Fall 2007) 777 applied for aid; of those 90% were deemed to have need. 100% of undergraduates with need received aid; of those 16% had need fully met. ***Average percent of need met:*** 71% (excluding resources awarded to replace EFC). ***Average financial aid package:*** $16,369 (excluding resources awarded to replace EFC). 16% of all full-time undergraduates had no need and received non-need-based gift aid.

GIFT AID (NEED-BASED) ***Total amount:*** $9,436,763 (14% federal, 18% state, 49% institutional, 19% external sources). ***Receiving aid:*** Freshmen: 80% (168); all full-time undergraduates: 82% (683). ***Average award:*** Freshmen: $16,068; Undergraduates: $12,782. ***Scholarships, grants, and awards:*** Federal Pell, FSEOG, state, private, college/university gift aid from institutional funds.

GIFT AID (NON-NEED-BASED) ***Total amount:*** $1,265,604 (82% institutional, 18% external sources). ***Receiving aid:*** Freshmen: 11% (23). Undergraduates: 8% (66). ***Average award:*** Freshmen: $14,595. Undergraduates: $12,064. ***Scholarships, grants, and awards by category:*** *Academic interests/achievement:* 97 awards ($583,041 total): general academic interests/achievements. *Special characteristics:* 14 awards ($35,625 total): children and siblings of alumni, children of faculty/staff, general special characteristics, siblings of current students. ***Tuition waivers:*** Full or partial for children of alumni, employees or children of employees. ***ROTC:*** Army cooperative.

LOANS ***Student loans:*** $6,712,458 (74% need-based, 26% non-need-based). 76% of past graduating class borrowed through all loan programs. *Average indebtedness per student:* $27,465. ***Average need-based loan:*** Freshmen: $3147. Undergraduates: $4083. ***Parent loans:*** $1,832,929 (45% need-based, 55% non-need-based). ***Programs:*** FFEL (Subsidized and Unsubsidized Stafford, PLUS), Perkins, state, college/university, private alternative loans.

WORK-STUDY ***Federal work-study:*** Total amount: $164,088; 115 jobs averaging $1426. ***State or other work-study/employment:*** Total amount: $312,853 (83% need-based, 17% non-need-based). 68 part-time jobs averaging $4291.

ATHLETIC AWARDS Total amount: $1,006,067 (57% need-based, 43% non-need-based).

APPLYING FOR FINANCIAL AID ***Required financial aid form:*** FAFSA. ***Financial aid deadline (priority):*** 3/1. ***Notification date:*** Continuous.

CONTACT Rachelle Shahan-Riehl, Director of Financial Aid, Saint Martin's University, 5300 Pacific Avenue, SE, Lacey, WA 98503-1297, 360-438-4463 or toll-free 800-368-8803. *Fax:* 360-412-6190. *E-mail:* rshahanriehl@stmartin.edu.

SAINT MARY-OF-THE-WOODS COLLEGE

Saint Mary-of-the-Woods, IN

CONTACT Ms. Jan Denton, Director of Financial Aid, Saint Mary of the Woods College, 106 Guerin Hall, Saint Mary-of-the-Woods, IN 47876, 812-535-5106 or toll-free 800-926-SMWC. *Fax:* 812-535-4900. *E-mail:* jbenton@smwc.edu.

SAINT MARY'S COLLEGE

Notre Dame, IN

Tuition & fees: $28,212 **Average undergraduate aid package: $20,936**

ABOUT THE INSTITUTION Independent Roman Catholic, women only. ***Awards:*** bachelor's degrees. 36 undergraduate majors. ***Total enrollment:*** 1,628. Undergraduates: 1,628. Freshmen: 455. Both federal and institutional methodology are used as a basis for awarding need-based institutional aid.

UNDERGRADUATE EXPENSES for 2008–09 ***Application fee:*** $30. ***Comprehensive fee:*** $37,150 includes full-time tuition ($27,600), mandatory fees ($612), and room and board ($8938). ***College room only:*** $5506. Room and board charges vary according to board plan and housing facility. ***Part-time tuition:*** $1091 per credit hour. ***Part-time fees:*** $306 per term. ***Payment plan:*** Installment.

FRESHMAN FINANCIAL AID (Fall 2008, est.) 442 applied for aid; of those 65% were deemed to have need. 100% of freshmen with need received aid; of those 28% had need fully met. ***Average percent of need met:*** 84% (excluding resources awarded to replace EFC). ***Average financial aid package:*** $22,836 (excluding resources awarded to replace EFC). 31% of all full-time freshmen had no need and received non-need-based gift aid.

UNDERGRADUATE FINANCIAL AID (Fall 2008, est.) 1,192 applied for aid; of those 91% were deemed to have need. 99% of undergraduates with need received aid; of those 16% had need fully met. ***Average percent of need met:*** 71% (excluding resources awarded to replace EFC). ***Average financial aid package:*** $20,936 (excluding resources awarded to replace EFC). 24% of all full-time undergraduates had no need and received non-need-based gift aid.

GIFT AID (NEED-BASED) ***Total amount:*** $15,718,336 (7% federal, 6% state, 83% institutional, 4% external sources). ***Receiving aid:*** Freshmen: 59% (268); all full-time undergraduates: 62% (985). ***Average award:*** Freshmen: $17,804; Undergraduates: $14,577. ***Scholarships, grants, and awards:*** Federal Pell, FSEOG, state, private, college/university gift aid from institutional funds.

GIFT AID (NON-NEED-BASED) ***Total amount:*** $3,621,832 (97% institutional, 3% external sources). ***Receiving aid:*** Freshmen: 49% (223). Undergraduates: 48% (766). ***Average award:*** Freshmen: $10,498. Undergraduates: $8994. ***Tuition waivers:*** Full or partial for employees or children of employees. ***ROTC:*** Army cooperative, Naval cooperative, Air Force cooperative.

LOANS ***Student loans:*** $8,365,444 (82% need-based, 18% non-need-based). 70% of past graduating class borrowed through all loan programs. *Average indebtedness per student:* $26,684. ***Average need-based loan:*** Freshmen: $3702. Undergraduates: $4430. ***Parent loans:*** $3,198,947 (76% need-based, 24% non-need-based). ***Programs:*** FFEL (Subsidized and Unsubsidized Stafford, PLUS), Perkins.

WORK-STUDY ***Federal work-study:*** Total amount: $791,240; jobs available. ***State or other work-study/employment:*** Part-time jobs available.

APPLYING FOR FINANCIAL AID ***Required financial aid forms:*** FAFSA, CSS Financial Aid PROFILE, noncustodial (divorced/separated) parent's statement. ***Financial aid deadline (priority):*** 3/1. ***Notification date:*** Continuous beginning 3/15. Students must reply within 3 weeks of notification.

CONTACT Kathleen M. Brown, Director of Financial Aid, Saint Mary's College, 141 Le Mans Hall, Notre Dame, IN 46556, 574-284-4557 or toll-free 800-551-7621. *Fax:* 574-284-4818. *E-mail:* kbrown@saintmarys.edu.

SAINT MARY'S COLLEGE OF CALIFORNIA

Moraga, CA

Tuition & fees: $33,250 **Average undergraduate aid package: $25,897**

ABOUT THE INSTITUTION Independent Roman Catholic, coed. ***Awards:*** bachelor's, master's, and doctoral degrees. 69 undergraduate majors. ***Total enrollment:*** 3,840. Undergraduates: 2,621. Freshmen: 675. Federal methodology is used as a basis for awarding need-based institutional aid.

UNDERGRADUATE EXPENSES for 2008–09 ***Application fee:*** $55. ***Comprehensive fee:*** $44,930 includes full-time tuition ($33,100), mandatory fees ($150), and room and board ($11,680). ***College room only:*** $6570. Room and board charges vary according to board plan and housing facility. ***Part-time tuition:*** $4135 per course. ***Payment plan:*** Installment.

FRESHMAN FINANCIAL AID (Fall 2008, est.) 566 applied for aid; of those 86% were deemed to have need. 100% of freshmen with need received aid; of those 7% had need fully met. ***Average percent of need met:*** 86% (excluding resources awarded to replace EFC). ***Average financial aid package:*** $29,754 (excluding resources awarded to replace EFC). 4% of all full-time freshmen had no need and received non-need-based gift aid.

UNDERGRADUATE FINANCIAL AID (Fall 2008, est.) 1,943 applied for aid; of those 92% were deemed to have need. 98% of undergraduates with need received aid; of those 7% had need fully met. ***Average percent of need met:*** 82% (excluding resources awarded to replace EFC). ***Average financial aid package:*** $25,897 (excluding resources awarded to replace EFC). 5% of all full-time undergraduates had no need and received non-need-based gift aid.

GIFT AID (NEED-BASED) ***Total amount:*** $26,407,727 (10% federal, 18% state, 70% institutional, 2% external sources). ***Receiving aid:*** Freshmen: 62% (415); all full-time undergraduates: 57% (1,354). ***Average award:*** Freshmen: $24,277; Undergraduates: $19,359. ***Scholarships, grants, and awards:*** Federal Pell, FSEOG, state, private, college/university gift aid from institutional funds.

GIFT AID (NON-NEED-BASED) ***Total amount:*** $4,079,214 (99% institutional, 1% external sources). ***Receiving aid:*** Freshmen: 21% (143). Undergraduates: 25% (581). ***Average award:*** Freshmen: $15,564. Undergraduates: $11,180. ***Scholarships, grants, and awards by category:*** *Academic interests/achievement:* 294 awards ($3,153,223 total): general academic interests/achievements. *Special achievements/activities:* 164 awards ($1,178,340 total): leadership, memberships. *Special characteristics:* 55 awards ($1,532,707 total): children and siblings of alumni, children of educators, children of faculty/staff, general special characteristics, relatives of clergy. ***Tuition waivers:*** Full or partial for employees or children of employees. ***ROTC:*** Army cooperative, Air Force cooperative.

LOANS ***Student loans:*** $15,106,913 (88% need-based, 12% non-need-based). 71% of past graduating class borrowed through all loan programs. *Average indebtedness per student:* $23,389. ***Average need-based loan:*** Freshmen: $3979. Undergraduates: $4797. ***Parent loans:*** $6,064,332 (81% need-based, 19% non-need-based). ***Programs:*** FFEL (Subsidized and Unsubsidized Stafford, PLUS), Perkins.

WORK-STUDY ***Federal work-study:*** Total amount: $1,184,681; 418 jobs averaging $2814.

ATHLETIC AWARDS Total amount: $4,736,150 (34% need-based, 66% non-need-based).

APPLYING FOR FINANCIAL AID ***Required financial aid forms:*** FAFSA, state aid form. ***Financial aid deadline (priority):*** 2/15. ***Notification date:*** Continuous beginning 3/30. Students must reply by 5/1 or within 2 weeks of notification.

CONTACT Priscilla Muha, Director of Financial Aid, Saint Mary's College of California, PO Box 4530, Moraga, CA 94575, 925-631-4370 or toll-free 800-800-4SMC. *Fax:* 925-376-2965. *E-mail:* finaid@stmarys-ca.edu.

ST. MARY'S COLLEGE OF MARYLAND

St. Mary's City, MD

Tuition & fees (MD res): $12,604 Average undergraduate aid package: $6500

ABOUT THE INSTITUTION State-supported, coed. ***Awards:*** bachelor's and master's degrees. 23 undergraduate majors. ***Total enrollment:*** 2,065. Undergraduates: 2,035. Freshmen: 458. Federal methodology is used as a basis for awarding need-based institutional aid.

UNDERGRADUATE EXPENSES for 2008–09 ***Application fee:*** $50. ***Tuition, state resident:*** full-time $10,472; part-time $160 per credit. ***Tuition, nonresident:*** full-time $21,322; part-time $160 per credit. ***Required fees:*** full-time $2132. Part-time tuition and fees vary according to course load. ***College room and board:*** $9225; ***Room only:*** $5315. Room and board charges vary according to board plan and housing facility. ***Payment plan:*** Installment.

FRESHMAN FINANCIAL AID (Fall 2007) 345 applied for aid; of those 64% were deemed to have need. 100% of freshmen with need received aid. ***Average percent of need met:*** 59% (excluding resources awarded to replace EFC). ***Average financial aid package:*** $7500 (excluding resources awarded to replace EFC). 34% of all full-time freshmen had no need and received non-need-based gift aid.

UNDERGRADUATE FINANCIAL AID (Fall 2007) 1,174 applied for aid; of those 73% were deemed to have need. 100% of undergraduates with need received aid. ***Average percent of need met:*** 62% (excluding resources awarded to replace EFC). ***Average financial aid package:*** $6500 (excluding resources awarded to replace EFC). 24% of all full-time undergraduates had no need and received non-need-based gift aid.

GIFT AID (NEED-BASED) ***Total amount:*** $5,051,224 (13% federal, 30% state, 47% institutional, 10% external sources). ***Receiving aid:*** Freshmen: 17% (85); all full-time undergraduates: 19% (354). ***Average award:*** Freshmen: $3500; Undergraduates: $4000. ***Scholarships, grants, and awards:*** Federal Pell, FSEOG, state, private, college/university gift aid from institutional funds.

GIFT AID (NON-NEED-BASED) ***Total amount:*** $3,546,288 (9% state, 83% institutional, 8% external sources). ***Receiving aid:*** Freshmen: 17% (85). Undergraduates: 19% (354). ***Average award:*** Freshmen: $3000. Undergraduates: $4000. ***Scholarships, grants, and awards by category:*** *Academic interests/achievement:* 949 awards ($2,994,970 total): general academic interests/achievements. *Special characteristics:* 192 awards ($865,696 total): children and siblings of alumni, children of faculty/staff. ***Tuition waivers:*** Full or partial for employees or children of employees, senior citizens.

LOANS ***Student loans:*** $5,233,039 (43% need-based, 57% non-need-based). 70% of past graduating class borrowed through all loan programs. *Average indebtedness per student:* $17,125. ***Average need-based loan:*** Freshmen: $2625. Undergraduates: $5500. ***Parent loans:*** $4,807,893 (100% non-need-based). ***Programs:*** FFEL (Subsidized and Unsubsidized Stafford, PLUS), Perkins.

WORK-STUDY ***Federal work-study:*** Total amount: $54,036; 100 jobs averaging $1000. ***State or other work-study/employment:*** Part-time jobs available.

APPLYING FOR FINANCIAL AID ***Required financial aid form:*** FAFSA. ***Financial aid deadline:*** 3/1. ***Notification date:*** 4/1. Students must reply by 5/1.

CONTACT Tim Wolfe, Director of Financial Aid, St. Mary's College of Maryland, 18952 East Fisher Road, St. Mary's City, MD 20686-3001, 240-895-3000 or toll-free 800-492-7181. *Fax:* 240-895-4959. *E-mail:* tawolfe@smcm.edu.

ST. MARY'S UNIVERSITY

San Antonio, TX

Tuition & fees: $21,300 Average undergraduate aid package: $18,793

ABOUT THE INSTITUTION Independent Roman Catholic, coed. ***Awards:*** bachelor's, master's, doctoral, and first professional degrees. 39 undergraduate majors. ***Total enrollment:*** 3,889. Undergraduates: 2,372. Freshmen: 537. Federal methodology is used as a basis for awarding need-based institutional aid.

UNDERGRADUATE EXPENSES for 2008–09 ***Application fee:*** $30. ***One-time required fee:*** $1000. ***Comprehensive fee:*** $28,488 includes full-time tuition ($20,600), mandatory fees ($700), and room and board ($7188). ***College room only:*** $4222. Room and board charges vary according to board plan and housing facility. ***Part-time tuition:*** $640 per credit hour. ***Part-time fees:*** $175 per term. ***Payment plans:*** Tuition prepayment, installment.

FRESHMAN FINANCIAL AID (Fall 2008, est.) 470 applied for aid; of those 91% were deemed to have need. 100% of freshmen with need received aid; of those 22% had need fully met. ***Average percent of need met:*** 78% (excluding resources awarded to replace EFC). ***Average financial aid package:*** $20,003 (excluding resources awarded to replace EFC). 16% of all full-time freshmen had no need and received non-need-based gift aid.

UNDERGRADUATE FINANCIAL AID (Fall 2008, est.) 1,817 applied for aid; of those 93% were deemed to have need. 99% of undergraduates with need received aid; of those 20% had need fully met. ***Average percent of need met:*** 75% (excluding resources awarded to replace EFC). ***Average financial aid package:*** $18,793 (excluding resources awarded to replace EFC). 14% of all full-time undergraduates had no need and received non-need-based gift aid.

GIFT AID (NEED-BASED) ***Total amount:*** $20,651,075 (20% federal, 23% state, 56% institutional, 1% external sources). ***Receiving aid:*** Freshmen: 78% (419); all full-time undergraduates: 74% (1,640). ***Average award:*** Freshmen: $13,542; Undergraduates: $12,451. ***Scholarships, grants, and awards:*** Federal Pell, FSEOG, state, private, college/university gift aid from institutional funds.

GIFT AID (NON-NEED-BASED) ***Total amount:*** $4,356,578 (99% institutional, 1% external sources). ***Receiving aid:*** Freshmen: 66% (357). Undergraduates: 53% (1,168). ***Average award:*** Freshmen: $11,164. Undergraduates: $11,416. ***Scholarships, grants, and awards by category:*** *Academic interests/achievement:* 926 awards ($7,055,782 total): general academic interests/achievements, military science. *Creative arts/performance:* 69 awards ($197,728 total): music. *Special achievements/activities:* 24 awards ($36,590 total): cheerleading/drum major. ***Tuition waivers:*** Full or partial for employees or children of employees. ***ROTC:*** Army, Air Force cooperative.

LOANS ***Student loans:*** $16,494,832 (73% need-based, 27% non-need-based). 79% of past graduating class borrowed through all loan programs. *Average indebtedness per student:* $27,416. ***Average need-based loan:*** Freshmen: $6317. Undergraduates: $6374. ***Parent loans:*** $830,775 (42% need-based, 58% non-need-based). ***Programs:*** FFEL (Subsidized and Unsubsidized Stafford, PLUS), Perkins, state, alternative loans.

WORK-STUDY ***Federal work-study:*** Total amount: $1,712,999; 535 jobs averaging $2822. ***State or other work-study/employment:*** Total amount: $485,093 (69% need-based, 31% non-need-based). 184 part-time jobs averaging $2099.

ATHLETIC AWARDS Total amount: $1,969,859 (49% need-based, 51% non-need-based).

APPLYING FOR FINANCIAL AID ***Required financial aid form:*** FAFSA. ***Financial aid deadline:*** Continuous. ***Notification date:*** 3/15. Students must reply within 2 weeks of notification.

CONTACT Mr. David R. Krause, Director of Financial Assistance, St. Mary's University, One Camino Santa Maria, San Antonio, TX 78228-8541, 210-436-3141 or toll-free 800-FOR-STMU. *Fax:* 210-431-2221. *E-mail:* dkrause@alvin.stmarytx.edu.

SAINT MARY'S UNIVERSITY OF MINNESOTA

Winona, MN

Tuition & fees: $25,570 Average undergraduate aid package: $17,541

ABOUT THE INSTITUTION Independent Roman Catholic, coed. ***Awards:*** bachelor's, master's, and doctoral degrees and post-bachelor's and post-master's certificates. 58 undergraduate majors. ***Total enrollment:*** 5,611. Undergraduates: 2,067. Freshmen: 404. Federal methodology is used as a basis for awarding need-based institutional aid.

UNDERGRADUATE EXPENSES for 2009–10 ***Application fee:*** $25. ***Comprehensive fee:*** $32,330 includes full-time tuition ($25,090), mandatory fees ($480), and room and board ($6760). ***College room only:*** $3780. ***Part-time tuition:*** $840 per credit. ***Part-time fees:*** $480 per year.

FRESHMAN FINANCIAL AID (Fall 2008, est.) 320 applied for aid; of those 85% were deemed to have need. 99% of freshmen with need received aid; of those 19% had need fully met. ***Average percent of need met:*** 84% (excluding resources awarded to replace EFC). ***Average financial aid package:*** $19,607 (excluding resources awarded to replace EFC). 32% of all full-time freshmen had no need and received non-need-based gift aid.

UNDERGRADUATE FINANCIAL AID (Fall 2008, est.) 1,082 applied for aid; of those 86% were deemed to have need. 99% of undergraduates with need received aid; of those 20% had need fully met. ***Average percent of need met:*** 77% (excluding resources awarded to replace EFC). ***Average financial aid package:*** $17,541 (excluding resources awarded to replace EFC). 25% of all full-time undergraduates had no need and received non-need-based gift aid.

GIFT AID (NEED-BASED) ***Total amount:*** $15,284,764 (8% federal, 7% state, 83% institutional, 2% external sources). ***Receiving aid:*** Freshmen: 67% (271); all full-time undergraduates: 64% (920). ***Average award:*** Freshmen: $15,305; Undergraduates: $13,026. ***Scholarships, grants, and awards:*** Federal Pell, FSEOG, state, college/university gift aid from institutional funds.

GIFT AID (NON-NEED-BASED) ***Average award:*** Freshmen: $8707. Undergraduates: $8518. ***Scholarships, grants, and awards by category:*** *Academic interests/achievement:* 628 awards ($3,699,000 total): general academic interests/achievements. *Creative arts/performance:* 93 awards ($148,000 total): art/fine arts, music, theater/drama. *Special achievements/activities:* 241 awards ($1,008,000 total): leadership. *Special characteristics:* 244 awards ($1,556,395 total): children and siblings of alumni, children of faculty/staff, members of minority groups. ***ROTC:*** Army cooperative.

LOANS ***Student loans:*** $9,316,723 (100% need-based). 80% of past graduating class borrowed through all loan programs. *Average indebtedness per student:* $33,639. ***Average need-based loan:*** Freshmen: $4237. Undergraduates: $3692. ***Parent loans:*** $1,041,842 (100% need-based). ***Programs:*** FFEL (Subsidized and Unsubsidized Stafford, PLUS), Perkins, state.

WORK-STUDY ***Federal work-study:*** Total amount: $237,900; 169 jobs averaging $1398. ***State or other work-study/employment:*** Total amount: $824,071 (100% need-based). 397 part-time jobs averaging $1447.

APPLYING FOR FINANCIAL AID ***Required financial aid form:*** FAFSA. ***Financial aid deadline (priority):*** 3/15. ***Notification date:*** Continuous. Students must reply within 3 weeks of notification.

CONTACT Ms. Jayne P. Wobig, Director of Financial Aid, Saint Mary's University of Minnesota, 700 Terrace Heights, #5, Winona, MN 55987-1399, 507-457-1437 or toll-free 800-635-5987. *Fax:* 507-457-6698. *E-mail:* jwobig@smumn.edu.

SAINT MICHAEL'S COLLEGE

Colchester, VT

Tuition & fees: $33,215 **Average undergraduate aid package: $20,879**

ABOUT THE INSTITUTION Independent Roman Catholic, coed. ***Awards:*** bachelor's and master's degrees and post-bachelor's and post-master's certificates. 37 undergraduate majors. ***Total enrollment:*** 2,460. Undergraduates: 2,008. Freshmen: 543. Federal methodology is used as a basis for awarding need-based institutional aid.

UNDERGRADUATE EXPENSES for 2009–10 ***Application fee:*** $50. ***Comprehensive fee:*** $41,495 includes full-time tuition ($32,940), mandatory fees ($275), and room and board ($8280). ***Part-time tuition:*** $1100 per credit.

FRESHMAN FINANCIAL AID (Fall 2008, est.) 414 applied for aid; of those 77% were deemed to have need. 100% of freshmen with need received aid; of those 32% had need fully met. ***Average percent of need met:*** 76% (excluding resources awarded to replace EFC). ***Average financial aid package:*** $19,972 (excluding resources awarded to replace EFC). 32% of all full-time freshmen had no need and received non-need-based gift aid.

UNDERGRADUATE FINANCIAL AID (Fall 2008, est.) 1,412 applied for aid; of those 83% were deemed to have need. 100% of undergraduates with need received aid; of those 27% had need fully met. ***Average percent of need met:*** 76% (excluding resources awarded to replace EFC). ***Average financial aid package:*** $20,879 (excluding resources awarded to replace EFC). 27% of all full-time undergraduates had no need and received non-need-based gift aid.

GIFT AID (NEED-BASED) ***Total amount:*** $16,997,461 (7% federal, 3% state, 86% institutional, 4% external sources). ***Receiving aid:*** Freshmen: 57% (311); all full-time undergraduates: 57% (1,126). ***Average award:*** Freshmen: $14,273; Undergraduates: $15,186. ***Scholarships, grants, and awards:*** Federal Pell, FSEOG, state, private, college/university gift aid from institutional funds.

GIFT AID (NON-NEED-BASED) ***Total amount:*** $5,199,309 (96% institutional, 4% external sources). ***Receiving aid:*** Freshmen: 14% (78). Undergraduates: 8% (158). ***Average award:*** Freshmen: $7046. Undergraduates: $8104. ***Scholarships, grants, and awards by category:*** *Academic interests/achievement:* general academic interests/achievements. *Creative arts/performance:* art/fine arts. *Special characteristics:* local/state students, members of minority groups, out-of-state students, religious affiliation, siblings of current students. ***ROTC:*** Army cooperative, Air Force cooperative.

LOANS ***Student loans:*** $13,111,305 (51% need-based, 49% non-need-based). 74% of past graduating class borrowed through all loan programs. *Average indebtedness per student:* $26,044. ***Average need-based loan:*** Freshmen: $4658. Undergraduates: $5313. ***Parent loans:*** $4,833,196 (34% need-based, 66% non-need-based). ***Programs:*** FFEL (Subsidized and Unsubsidized Stafford, PLUS), Perkins.

WORK-STUDY ***Federal work-study:*** Total amount: $567,585; 450 jobs averaging $1000. ***State or other work-study/employment:*** Total amount: $337,787 (95% need-based, 5% non-need-based). 450 part-time jobs averaging $1000.

ATHLETIC AWARDS Total amount: $769,022 (6% need-based, 94% non-need-based).

APPLYING FOR FINANCIAL AID ***Required financial aid forms:*** FAFSA, federal income tax forms (student and parent). ***Financial aid deadline (priority):*** 2/15. ***Notification date:*** 4/1. Students must reply by 5/1 or within 2 weeks of notification.

CONTACT Mrs. Nelberta B. Lunde, Director of New Student Aid and Scholarships, Saint Michael's College, Winooski Park, Colchester, VT 05439, 802-654-3243 or toll-free 800-762-8000. *Fax:* 802 654 2591. *E-mail:* finaid@smcvt.edu.

ST. NORBERT COLLEGE

De Pere, WI

Tuition & fees: $25,926 **Average undergraduate aid package: $17,948**

ABOUT THE INSTITUTION Independent Roman Catholic, coed. ***Awards:*** bachelor's and master's degrees. 31 undergraduate majors. ***Total enrollment:*** 2,137. Undergraduates: 2,084. Freshmen: 532. Federal methodology is used as a basis for awarding need-based institutional aid.

UNDERGRADUATE EXPENSES for 2008–09 ***Application fee:*** $25. ***Comprehensive fee:*** $32,707 includes full-time tuition ($25,526), mandatory fees ($400), and room and board ($6781). ***College room only:*** $3552. Full-time tuition and fees vary according to course load. Room and board charges vary according to board plan, housing facility, and student level. ***Part-time tuition:*** $798 per credit. Part-time tuition and fees vary according to course load. ***Payment plans:*** Installment, deferred payment.

FRESHMAN FINANCIAL AID (Fall 2007) 439 applied for aid; of those 82% were deemed to have need. 100% of freshmen with need received aid; of those 30% had need fully met. ***Average percent of need met:*** 85% (excluding resources awarded to replace EFC). ***Average financial aid package:*** $18,146 (excluding resources awarded to replace EFC). 28% of all full-time freshmen had no need and received non-need-based gift aid.

UNDERGRADUATE FINANCIAL AID (Fall 2007) 1,533 applied for aid; of those 84% were deemed to have need. 100% of undergraduates with need received aid; of those 34% had need fully met. ***Average percent of need met:*** 85% (excluding resources awarded to replace EFC). ***Average financial aid package:*** $17,948 (excluding resources awarded to replace EFC). 31% of all full-time undergraduates had no need and received non-need-based gift aid.

GIFT AID (NEED-BASED) ***Total amount:*** $17,397,452 (8% federal, 9% state, 76% institutional, 7% external sources). ***Receiving aid:*** Freshmen: 66% (359); all full-time undergraduates: 62% (1,257). ***Average award:*** Freshmen: $14,378; Undergraduates: $13,054. ***Scholarships, grants, and awards:*** Federal Pell, FSEOG, state, private, college/university gift aid from institutional funds.

GIFT AID (NON-NEED-BASED) ***Total amount:*** $5,135,131 (1% state, 90% institutional, 9% external sources). ***Receiving aid:*** Freshmen: 2% (12). Undergraduates: 2% (41). ***Average award:*** Freshmen: $7736. Undergraduates: $7593. ***Scholarships, grants, and awards by category:*** *Academic interests/*

achievement: 1,559 awards ($10,892,433 total): general academic interests/achievements. *Creative arts/performance:* 74 awards ($100,500 total): art/fine arts, music, theater/drama. *Special characteristics:* 185 awards ($1,693,194 total): children of faculty/staff, international students. ***Tuition waivers:*** Full or partial for employees or children of employees. ***ROTC:*** Army.

LOANS ***Student loans:*** $11,592,646 (93% need-based, 7% non-need-based). 68% of past graduating class borrowed through all loan programs. *Average indebtedness per student:* $27,207. ***Average need-based loan:*** Freshmen: $3904. Undergraduates: $4941. ***Parent loans:*** $2,270,698 (74% need-based, 26% non-need-based). ***Programs:*** Federal Direct (Subsidized and Unsubsidized Stafford, PLUS), Perkins, state, college/university.

WORK-STUDY ***Federal work-study:*** Total amount: $317,654; 318 jobs averaging $1489. ***State or other work-study/employment:*** Total amount: $1,178,799 (63% need-based, 37% non-need-based). 480 part-time jobs averaging $1891.

APPLYING FOR FINANCIAL AID ***Required financial aid form:*** FAFSA. ***Financial aid deadline (priority):*** 3/1. ***Notification date:*** Continuous beginning 3/15. Students must reply within 2 weeks of notification.

CONTACT Mr. Jeffrey A. Zahn, Director of Financial Aid, St. Norbert College, 100 Grant Street, De Pere, WI 54115-2099, 920-403-3071 or toll-free 800-236-4878. *Fax:* 920-403-3062. *E-mail:* jeff.zahn@snc.edu.

ST. OLAF COLLEGE

Northfield, MN

Tuition & fees: $35,500 **Average undergraduate aid package: $27,401**

ABOUT THE INSTITUTION Independent Lutheran, coed. ***Awards:*** bachelor's degrees. 44 undergraduate majors. ***Total enrollment:*** 3,073. Undergraduates: 3,073. Freshmen: 813. Both federal and institutional methodology are used as a basis for awarding need-based institutional aid.

UNDERGRADUATE EXPENSES for 2009–10 ***Comprehensive fee:*** $43,700 includes full-time tuition ($35,500) and room and board ($8200). ***College room only:*** $3800.

FRESHMAN FINANCIAL AID (Fall 2008, est.) 690 applied for aid; of those 75% were deemed to have need. 100% of freshmen with need received aid; of those 100% had need fully met. ***Average percent of need met:*** 100% (excluding resources awarded to replace EFC). ***Average financial aid package:*** $26,626 (excluding resources awarded to replace EFC). 24% of all full-time freshmen had no need and received non-need-based gift aid.

UNDERGRADUATE FINANCIAL AID (Fall 2008, est.) 2,852 applied for aid; of those 69% were deemed to have need. 100% of undergraduates with need received aid; of those 100% had need fully met. ***Average percent of need met:*** 100% (excluding resources awarded to replace EFC). ***Average financial aid package:*** $27,401 (excluding resources awarded to replace EFC). 31% of all full-time undergraduates had no need and received non-need-based gift aid.

GIFT AID (NEED-BASED) ***Total amount:*** $37,675,264 (5% federal, 4% state, 86% institutional, 5% external sources). ***Receiving aid:*** Freshmen: 64% (519); all full-time undergraduates: 65% (1,956). ***Average award:*** Freshmen: $21,424; Undergraduates: $19,981. ***Scholarships, grants, and awards:*** Federal Pell, FSEOG, state, private, college/university gift aid from institutional funds.

GIFT AID (NON-NEED-BASED) ***Total amount:*** $7,752,174 (90% institutional, 10% external sources). ***Receiving aid:*** Freshmen: 31% (253). Undergraduates: 30% (895). ***Average award:*** Freshmen: $10,925. Undergraduates: $7963. ***Scholarships, grants, and awards by category:*** *Academic interests/achievement:* 1,286 awards ($9,449,200 total): general academic interests/achievements. *Creative arts/performance:* 248 awards ($1,117,000 total): music. *Special achievements/activities:* 299 awards ($1,113,659 total): community service, religious involvement. *Special characteristics:* 41 awards ($929,121 total): international students.

LOANS ***Student loans:*** $15,595,983 (90% need-based, 10% non-need-based). 65% of past graduating class borrowed through all loan programs. *Average indebtedness per student:* $25,273. ***Average need-based loan:*** Freshmen: $4589. Undergraduates: $5998. ***Parent loans:*** $11,202,417 (100% non-need-based). ***Programs:*** FFEL (Subsidized and Unsubsidized Stafford, PLUS), Perkins, Federal Nursing, state, college/university.

WORK-STUDY ***Federal work-study:*** Total amount: $1,851,537; 899 jobs averaging $1967. ***State or other work-study/employment:*** Total amount: $2,064,738 (83% need-based, 17% non-need-based). 859 part-time jobs averaging $1581.

APPLYING FOR FINANCIAL AID ***Required financial aid forms:*** FAFSA, CSS Financial Aid PROFILE, noncustodial (divorced/separated) parent's statement, business/farm supplement. ***Financial aid deadline:*** 4/15 (priority: 1/15). ***Notification date:*** Continuous beginning 3/1. Students must reply by 5/1.

CONTACT Ms. Katharine Ruby, Assistant Vice President of Enrollment and Dean of Student Financial Aid, St. Olaf College, 1520 Saint Olaf Avenue, Northfield, MN 55057-1098, 507-786-3019 or toll-free 800-800-3025. *Fax:* 507-786-6688. *E-mail:* ruby@stolaf.edu.

SAINT PAUL'S COLLEGE

Lawrenceville, VA

Tuition & fees: $13,210 **Average undergraduate aid package: $9452**

ABOUT THE INSTITUTION Independent Episcopal, coed. ***Awards:*** bachelor's degrees. 13 undergraduate majors. ***Total enrollment:*** 700. Undergraduates: 700. Freshmen: 252. Federal methodology is used as a basis for awarding need-based institutional aid.

UNDERGRADUATE EXPENSES for 2008–09 ***Application fee:*** $20. ***Comprehensive fee:*** $19,850 includes full-time tuition ($11,880), mandatory fees ($1330), and room and board ($6640). ***College room only:*** $3140. ***Part-time tuition:*** $495 per credit hour. ***Part-time fees:*** $29 per credit hour.

FRESHMAN FINANCIAL AID (Fall 2008, est.) 199 applied for aid; of those 98% were deemed to have need. 100% of freshmen with need received aid; of those 5% had need fully met. ***Average percent of need met:*** 80% (excluding resources awarded to replace EFC). ***Average financial aid package:*** $8048 (excluding resources awarded to replace EFC). 2% of all full-time freshmen had no need and received non-need-based gift aid.

UNDERGRADUATE FINANCIAL AID (Fall 2008, est.) 614 applied for aid; of those 97% were deemed to have need. 100% of undergraduates with need received aid; of those 6% had need fully met. ***Average percent of need met:*** 85% (excluding resources awarded to replace EFC). ***Average financial aid package:*** $9452 (excluding resources awarded to replace EFC). 4% of all full-time undergraduates had no need and received non-need-based gift aid.

GIFT AID (NEED-BASED) ***Total amount:*** $2,019,421 (93% federal, 3% state, 4% external sources). ***Receiving aid:*** Freshmen: 54% (139); all full-time undergraduates: 70% (435). ***Average award:*** Freshmen: $3998; Undergraduates: $4494. ***Scholarships, grants, and awards:*** Federal Pell, FSEOG, state, private, college/university gift aid from institutional funds, United Negro College Fund.

GIFT AID (NON-NEED-BASED) ***Total amount:*** $2,035,442 (65% state, 26% institutional, 9% external sources). ***Receiving aid:*** Freshmen: 56% (145). Undergraduates: 90% (561). ***Average award:*** Freshmen: $9734. Undergraduates: $4107. ***Scholarships, grants, and awards by category:*** *Academic interests/achievement:* 98 awards ($287,708 total): general academic interests/achievements. *Special achievements/activities:* 99 awards ($110,747 total): general special achievements/activities. *Special characteristics:* 13 awards ($47,135 total): children of faculty/staff, children of union members/company employees. ***ROTC:*** Army.

LOANS ***Student loans:*** $3,331,688 (100% need-based). 97% of past graduating class borrowed through all loan programs. *Average indebtedness per student:* $17,541. ***Average need-based loan:*** Freshmen: $3091. Undergraduates: $3860. ***Parent loans:*** $816,184 (100% need-based). ***Programs:*** Federal Direct (Subsidized and Unsubsidized Stafford, PLUS), Perkins.

WORK-STUDY ***Federal work-study:*** Total amount: $317,075; 228 jobs averaging $1384.

ATHLETIC AWARDS Total amount: $1,160,210 (100% non-need-based).

APPLYING FOR FINANCIAL AID ***Required financial aid forms:*** FAFSA, state aid form. ***Financial aid deadline (priority):*** 5/29. ***Notification date:*** Continuous. Students must reply by 7/1 or within 4 weeks of notification.

CONTACT Ms. Phenie Golatt, Office of Financial Aid, Saint Paul's College, 115 College Drive, Lawrenceville, VA 23868-1202, 434-848-6495 or toll-free 800-678-7071. *Fax:* 434-848-6498. *E-mail:* aid@saintpauls.edu.

ST. PETERSBURG THEOLOGICAL SEMINARY

St. Petersburg, FL

CONTACT Financial Aid Office, St Petersburg Theological Seminary, 10830 Navajo Drive, St. Petersburg, FL 33708, 727-399-0276.

SAINT PETER'S COLLEGE

Jersey City, NJ

CONTACT Director of Financial Aid, Saint Peter's College, 2641 Kennedy Boulevard, Jersey City, NJ 07306, 201-915-4929 or toll-free 888-SPC-9933. *Fax:* 201-434-6878.

ST. THOMAS AQUINAS COLLEGE

Sparkill, NY

CONTACT Margaret McGrail, Director of Financial Aid, St. Thomas Aquinas College, 125 Route 340, Sparkill, NY 10976, 914-398-4097 or toll-free 800-999-STAC.

ST. THOMAS UNIVERSITY

Miami Gardens, FL

Tuition & fees: $20,664 **Average undergraduate aid package: N/A**

ABOUT THE INSTITUTION Independent Roman Catholic, coed. ***Awards:*** bachelor's, master's, doctoral, and first professional degrees and post-bachelor's and post-master's certificates. 28 undergraduate majors. ***Total enrollment:*** 2,454. Undergraduates: 1,122. Freshmen: 213. Federal methodology is used as a basis for awarding need-based institutional aid.

UNDERGRADUATE EXPENSES for 2008–09 ***Application fee:*** $40. ***Comprehensive fee:*** $26,870 includes full-time tuition ($20,664) and room and board ($6206). Full-time tuition and fees vary according to program. Room and board charges vary according to board plan and housing facility. ***Part-time tuition:*** $415 per credit. ***Payment plan:*** Installment.

FRESHMAN FINANCIAL AID (Fall 2008, est.) 195 applied for aid; of those 90% were deemed to have need. 100% of freshmen with need received aid; of those 20% had need fully met. 17% of all full-time freshmen had no need and received non-need-based gift aid.

UNDERGRADUATE FINANCIAL AID (Fall 2008, est.) 915 applied for aid; of those 81% were deemed to have need. 100% of undergraduates with need received aid; of those 29% had need fully met. 16% of all full-time undergraduates had no need and received non-need-based gift aid.

GIFT AID (NEED-BASED) ***Total amount:*** $11,873,038 (18% federal, 21% state, 60% institutional, 1% external sources). ***Receiving aid:*** Freshmen: 60% (127); all full-time undergraduates: 50% (519). ***Average award:*** Freshmen: $1902; Undergraduates: $2166. ***Scholarships, grants, and awards:*** Federal Pell, FSEOG, state, private, college/university gift aid from institutional funds.

GIFT AID (NON-NEED-BASED) ***Receiving aid:*** Freshmen: 82% (171). Undergraduates: 69% (721). ***Average award:*** Freshmen: $7913. Undergraduates: $6507. ***Tuition waivers:*** Full or partial for minority students, children of alumni, employees or children of employees. ***ROTC:*** Army cooperative, Air Force cooperative.

LOANS ***Student loans:*** $5,103,304 (43% need-based, 57% non-need-based). ***Average need-based loan:*** Freshmen: $3329. Undergraduates: $4173. ***Parent loans:*** $294,198 (100% need-based). ***Programs:*** FFEL (Subsidized and Unsubsidized Stafford, PLUS), Perkins.

WORK-STUDY ***Federal work-study:*** Total amount: $410,754; jobs available.

ATHLETIC AWARDS Total amount: $1,050,922 (100% need-based).

APPLYING FOR FINANCIAL AID ***Required financial aid forms:*** FAFSA, state aid form. ***Financial aid deadline (priority):*** 4/1. ***Notification date:*** Continuous.

CONTACT Ms. Anh Do, Director of Financial Aid, St. Thomas University, 16400 Northwest 32nd Avenue, Miami, FL 33054-6459, 305-628-6547 or toll-free 800-367-9010. *Fax:* 305-628-6754. *E-mail:* ado@stu.edu.

SAINT VINCENT COLLEGE

Latrobe, PA

Tuition & fees: $26,146 **Average undergraduate aid package: $20,563**

ABOUT THE INSTITUTION Independent Roman Catholic, coed. ***Awards:*** bachelor's and master's degrees and post-bachelor's certificates. 49 undergraduate majors. ***Total enrollment:*** 2,021. Undergraduates: 1,773. Freshmen: 443. Federal methodology is used as a basis for awarding need-based institutional aid.

UNDERGRADUATE EXPENSES for 2009–10 ***Application fee:*** $25. ***Comprehensive fee:*** $34,330 includes full-time tuition ($25,350), mandatory fees ($796), and room and board ($8184). ***College room only:*** $4190. ***Part-time tuition:*** $793 per credit.

FRESHMAN FINANCIAL AID (Fall 2008, est.) 440 applied for aid; of those 82% were deemed to have need. 100% of freshmen with need received aid; of those 26% had need fully met. ***Average percent of need met:*** 87% (excluding resources awarded to replace EFC). ***Average financial aid package:*** $21,721 (excluding resources awarded to replace EFC). 19% of all full-time freshmen had no need and received non-need-based gift aid.

UNDERGRADUATE FINANCIAL AID (Fall 2008, est.) 1,642 applied for aid; of those 66% were deemed to have need. 100% of undergraduates with need received aid; of those 38% had need fully met. ***Average percent of need met:*** 79% (excluding resources awarded to replace EFC). ***Average financial aid package:*** $20,563 (excluding resources awarded to replace EFC). 23% of all full-time undergraduates had no need and received non-need-based gift aid.

GIFT AID (NEED-BASED) ***Total amount:*** $19,153,253 (9% federal, 13% state, 76% institutional, 2% external sources). ***Receiving aid:*** Freshmen: 81% (359); all full-time undergraduates: 61% (1,084). ***Average award:*** Freshmen: $15,630; Undergraduates: $14,699. ***Scholarships, grants, and awards:*** Federal Pell, FSEOG, state, private, college/university gift aid from institutional funds, United Negro College Fund.

GIFT AID (NON-NEED-BASED) ***Total amount:*** $5,704,007 (1% state, 99% institutional). ***Receiving aid:*** Freshmen: 33% (146). Undergraduates: 52% (916). ***Average award:*** Freshmen: $14,600. Undergraduates: $13,542. ***Scholarships, grants, and awards by category:*** *Academic interests/achievement:* general academic interests/achievements. *Creative arts/performance:* art/fine arts, music, theater/drama. *Special achievements/activities:* leadership. *Special characteristics:* general special characteristics, members of minority groups, religious affiliation. ***ROTC:*** Air Force cooperative.

LOANS ***Student loans:*** $9,573,202 (31% need-based, 69% non-need-based). ***Average need-based loan:*** Freshmen: $4208. Undergraduates: $4438. ***Parent loans:*** $2,419,123 (100% non-need-based). ***Programs:*** FFEL (Subsidized and Unsubsidized Stafford, PLUS), Perkins.

WORK-STUDY ***Federal work-study:*** Total amount: $423,924; jobs available. ***State or other work-study/employment:*** Total amount: $869,045 (5% need-based, 95% non-need-based). 474 part-time jobs averaging $3400.

APPLYING FOR FINANCIAL AID ***Required financial aid forms:*** FAFSA, state aid form. ***Financial aid deadline:*** 5/1 (priority: 3/1). ***Notification date:*** Continuous beginning 3/5. Students must reply within 4 weeks of notification.

CONTACT Kimberly Woodley, Director of Financial Aid, Saint Vincent College, 300 Fraser Purchase Road, Latrobe, PA 15650, 724-537-4540 or toll-free 800-782-5549. *Fax:* 724-532-5069. *E-mail:* admission@stvincent.edu.

SAINT XAVIER UNIVERSITY

Chicago, IL

Tuition & fees: $23,006 **Average undergraduate aid package: $18,960**

ABOUT THE INSTITUTION Independent Roman Catholic, coed. ***Awards:*** bachelor's and master's degrees and post-bachelor's and post-master's certificates. 39 undergraduate majors. ***Total enrollment:*** 5,337. Undergraduates: 3,169. Freshmen: 553. Federal methodology is used as a basis for awarding need-based institutional aid.

UNDERGRADUATE EXPENSES for 2008–09 ***Application fee:*** $25. ***Comprehensive fee:*** $31,013 includes full-time tuition ($22,486), mandatory fees ($520), and room and board ($8007). ***College room only:*** $4664. Full-time tuition and fees vary according to course load. Room and board charges vary according to board plan and housing facility. ***Part-time tuition:*** $753 per credit hour. ***Part-time fees:*** $350 per year. Part-time tuition and fees vary according to course load. ***Payment plan:*** Installment.

FRESHMAN FINANCIAL AID (Fall 2008, est.) 510 applied for aid; of those 92% were deemed to have need. 100% of freshmen with need received aid; of those 20% had need fully met. ***Average percent of need met:*** 82% (excluding resources awarded to replace EFC). ***Average financial aid package:*** $20,734 (excluding resources awarded to replace EFC). 11% of all full-time freshmen had no need and received non-need-based gift aid.

UNDERGRADUATE FINANCIAL AID (Fall 2008, est.) 2,328 applied for aid; of those 91% were deemed to have need. 100% of undergraduates with need received aid; of those 20% had need fully met. ***Average percent of need met:*** 76% (excluding resources awarded to replace EFC). ***Average financial aid***

package: $18,960 (excluding resources awarded to replace EFC). 13% of all full-time undergraduates had no need and received non-need-based gift aid.

GIFT AID (NEED-BASED) ***Total amount:*** $26,029,029 (20% federal, 25% state, 53% institutional, 2% external sources). ***Receiving aid:*** Freshmen: 86% (470); all full-time undergraduates: 82% (2,110). ***Average award:*** Freshmen: $14,870; Undergraduates: $12,524. ***Scholarships, grants, and awards:*** Federal Pell, FSEOG, state, private, college/university gift aid from institutional funds, United Negro College Fund, Federal Nursing.

GIFT AID (NON-NEED-BASED) ***Total amount:*** $3,570,899 (93% institutional, 7% external sources). ***Receiving aid:*** Freshmen: 13% (70). Undergraduates: 13% (326). ***Average award:*** Freshmen: $9694. Undergraduates: $6634. ***Scholarships, grants, and awards by category:*** *Academic interests/achievement:* $14,434,300 total: general academic interests/achievements. *Creative arts/performance:* 57 awards ($176,704 total): music. *Special achievements/activities:* leadership. *Special characteristics:* 107 awards ($1,349,384 total): children of faculty/staff. ***Tuition waivers:*** Full or partial for employees or children of employees, senior citizens. ***ROTC:*** Air Force cooperative.

LOANS ***Student loans:*** $24,830,922 (70% need-based, 30% non-need-based). 63% of past graduating class borrowed through all loan programs. *Average indebtedness per student:* $24,920. ***Average need-based loan:*** Freshmen: $3404. Undergraduates: $4618. ***Parent loans:*** $2,511,574 (24% need-based, 76% non-need-based). ***Programs:*** FFEL (Subsidized and Unsubsidized Stafford, PLUS), Perkins.

WORK-STUDY ***Federal work-study:*** Total amount: $3,947,970; 1,459 jobs averaging $2293. ***State or other work-study/employment:*** Total amount: $383,101 (33% need-based, 67% non-need-based). 50 part-time jobs averaging $6474.

ATHLETIC AWARDS Total amount: $1,869,892 (55% need-based, 45% non-need-based).

APPLYING FOR FINANCIAL AID ***Required financial aid form:*** FAFSA. ***Financial aid deadline (priority):*** 3/1. ***Notification date:*** Continuous. Students must reply by 5/1 or within 2 weeks of notification.

CONTACT Ms. Susan Swisher, Assistant Vice President for Student Financial Services, Saint Xavier University, 3700 West 103rd Street, Chicago, IL 60655-3105, 773-298-3070 or toll-free 800-462-9288. *Fax:* 773-779-3084. *E-mail:* swisher@sxu.edu.

SALEM COLLEGE

Winston-Salem, NC

Tuition & fees: $20,420 **Average undergraduate aid package: $18,755**

ABOUT THE INSTITUTION Independent religious, undergraduate: women only; graduate: coed. ***Awards:*** bachelor's and master's degrees (only students age 23 or over are eligible to enroll part-time). 32 undergraduate majors. ***Total enrollment:*** 966. Undergraduates: 761. Freshmen: 125. Federal methodology is used as a basis for awarding need-based institutional aid.

UNDERGRADUATE EXPENSES for 2008–09 ***Application fee:*** $30. ***Comprehensive fee:*** $31,125 includes full-time tuition ($20,075), mandatory fees ($345), and room and board ($10,705). ***Part-time tuition:*** $998 per course. ***Payment plan:*** Installment.

FRESHMAN FINANCIAL AID (Fall 2008, est.) 79 applied for aid; of those 71% were deemed to have need. 100% of freshmen with need received aid; of those 100% had need fully met. ***Average percent of need met:*** 100% (excluding resources awarded to replace EFC). ***Average financial aid package:*** $24,045 (excluding resources awarded to replace EFC). 6% of all full-time freshmen had no need and received non-need-based gift aid.

UNDERGRADUATE FINANCIAL AID (Fall 2008, est.) 476 applied for aid; of those 92% were deemed to have need. 100% of undergraduates with need received aid; of those 100% had need fully met. ***Average percent of need met:*** 100% (excluding resources awarded to replace EFC). ***Average financial aid package:*** $18,755 (excluding resources awarded to replace EFC). 6% of all full-time undergraduates had no need and received non-need-based gift aid.

GIFT AID (NEED-BASED) ***Total amount:*** $4,498,786 (29% federal, 15% state, 56% institutional). ***Receiving aid:*** Freshmen: 45% (53); all full-time undergraduates: 50% (311). ***Average award:*** Freshmen: $12,023; Undergraduates: $8440. ***Scholarships, grants, and awards:*** Federal Pell, FSEOG, state, private, college/university gift aid from institutional funds.

GIFT AID (NON-NEED-BASED) ***Total amount:*** $4,085,420 (19% state, 76% institutional, 5% external sources). ***Receiving aid:*** Freshmen: 45% (53). Undergraduates: 67% (419). ***Average award:*** Freshmen: $12,263. Undergraduates: $13,316. ***Scholarships, grants, and awards by category:*** *Academic interests/achievement:* 294 awards ($2,582,305 total): general academic interests/achievements. *Creative arts/performance:* 13 awards ($57,340 total): music. *Special achievements/activities:* 17 awards ($324,220 total): leadership. *Special characteristics:* 64 awards ($142,724 total): children of educators, children of faculty/staff, relatives of clergy. ***Tuition waivers:*** Full or partial for employees or children of employees.

LOANS ***Student loans:*** $3,493,645 (50% need-based, 50% non-need-based). 70% of past graduating class borrowed through all loan programs. *Average indebtedness per student:* $19,000. ***Average need-based loan:*** Freshmen: $2924. Undergraduates: $4406. ***Parent loans:*** $334,643 (100% non-need-based). ***Programs:*** FFEL (Subsidized and Unsubsidized Stafford, PLUS), Perkins.

WORK-STUDY ***Federal work-study:*** Total amount: $98,853; 98 jobs averaging $1009. ***State or other work-study/employment:*** Total amount: $323,688 (100% need-based). Part-time jobs available.

APPLYING FOR FINANCIAL AID ***Required financial aid forms:*** FAFSA, institution's own form. ***Financial aid deadline (priority):*** 3/1. ***Notification date:*** Continuous beginning 3/1. Students must reply by 5/1 or within 2 weeks of notification.

CONTACT Jerry Alan Donna, Director of Financial Aid, Salem College, 601 South Church Street, Winston-Salem, NC 27108, 336-721-2808 or toll-free 800-327-2536. *Fax:* 336-917-5584. *E-mail:* donna@salem.edu.

SALEM INTERNATIONAL UNIVERSITY

Salem, WV

ABOUT THE INSTITUTION Independent, coed. ***Awards:*** associate, bachelor's, and master's degrees. 15 undergraduate majors.

GIFT AID (NEED-BASED) ***Scholarships, grants, and awards:*** Federal Pell, FSEOG, state, private, college/university gift aid from institutional funds.

GIFT AID (NON-NEED-BASED) ***Scholarships, grants, and awards by category:*** *Academic interests/achievement:* business, education, general academic interests/achievements, humanities. *Special characteristics:* out-of-state students, religious affiliation.

LOANS ***Programs:*** FFEL (Subsidized and Unsubsidized Stafford, PLUS), Perkins, alternative loans.

APPLYING FOR FINANCIAL AID ***Required financial aid form:*** FAFSA.

CONTACT Pat Zinsmeister, VP Financial Aid/Compliance, Salem International University, 223 West Main Street, Salem, WV 26426-0500, 304-326-1299 or toll-free 800-283-4562. *Fax:* 304-326-1509. *E-mail:* pzinsmeister@salemu.edu.

SALEM STATE COLLEGE

Salem, MA

Tuition & fees (MA res): $6460 **Average undergraduate aid package: $8137**

ABOUT THE INSTITUTION State-supported, coed. ***Awards:*** bachelor's and master's degrees and post-master's certificates. 60 undergraduate majors. ***Total enrollment:*** 10,157. Undergraduates: 7,677. Freshmen: 1,151. Federal methodology is used as a basis for awarding need-based institutional aid.

UNDERGRADUATE EXPENSES for 2008–09 ***Application fee:*** $25. ***Tuition, state resident:*** full-time $910; part-time $37.92 per credit. ***Tuition, nonresident:*** full-time $7050; part-time $293.75 per credit. ***Required fees:*** full-time $5550; $232 per credit. Full-time tuition and fees vary according to class time and course load. Part-time tuition and fees vary according to class time and course load. ***College room and board: Room only:*** $6038. Room and board charges vary according to board plan and housing facility. ***Payment plan:*** Installment.

FRESHMAN FINANCIAL AID (Fall 2007) 863 applied for aid; of those 73% were deemed to have need. 97% of freshmen with need received aid; of those 27% had need fully met. ***Average percent of need met:*** 27% (excluding resources awarded to replace EFC). ***Average financial aid package:*** $7840 (excluding resources awarded to replace EFC). 1% of all full-time freshmen had no need and received non-need-based gift aid.

UNDERGRADUATE FINANCIAL AID (Fall 2007) 3,824 applied for aid; of those 77% were deemed to have need. 98% of undergraduates with need received aid; of those 32% had need fully met. ***Average percent of need met:*** 32% (excluding resources awarded to replace EFC). ***Average financial aid package:*** $8137 (excluding resources awarded to replace EFC). 1% of all full-time undergraduates had no need and received non-need-based gift aid.

GIFT AID (NEED-BASED) ***Total amount:*** $11,013,123 (59% federal, 33% state, 5% institutional, 3% external sources). ***Receiving aid:*** Freshmen: 55% (581); all full-time undergraduates: 48% (2,715). ***Average award:*** Freshmen: $5270;

Undergraduates: $4300. ***Scholarships, grants, and awards:*** Federal Pell, FSEOG, state, private, college/university gift aid from institutional funds, SDS Nursing Grant, MSCBA Housing Grant.

GIFT AID (NON-NEED-BASED) ***Total amount:*** $323,319 (46% state, 14% institutional, 40% external sources). ***Receiving aid:*** Freshmen: 14% (145). Undergraduates: 7% (407). ***Average award:*** Freshmen: $760. Undergraduates: $1227. ***Scholarships, grants, and awards by category:*** *Academic interests/achievement:* general academic interests/achievements. *Creative arts/performance:* applied art and design, art/fine arts, creative writing, dance, music, performing arts, theater/drama. *Special achievements/activities:* general special achievements/activities, memberships. *Special characteristics:* adult students, children and siblings of alumni, children of faculty/staff, children of public servants, children of union members/company employees, first-generation college students, general special characteristics, members of minority groups, public servants, veterans, veterans' children. ***Tuition waivers:*** Full or partial for employees or children of employees, senior citizens. ***ROTC:*** Army cooperative, Air Force cooperative.

LOANS ***Student loans:*** $12,343,526 (94% need-based, 6% non-need-based). 55% of past graduating class borrowed through all loan programs. *Average indebtedness per student:* $12,910. ***Average need-based loan:*** Freshmen: $3341. Undergraduates: $4374. ***Parent loans:*** $1,491,132 (65% need-based, 35% non-need-based). ***Programs:*** FFEL (Subsidized and Unsubsidized Stafford, PLUS), Perkins, Federal Nursing, state, MEFA Loans, CitiAssist Loans, Sallie Mae SMART Loans.

WORK-STUDY ***Federal work-study:*** Total amount: $549,102; 247 jobs averaging $2000.

APPLYING FOR FINANCIAL AID ***Required financial aid form:*** FAFSA. ***Financial aid deadline (priority):*** 4/1. ***Notification date:*** Continuous. Students must reply within 2 weeks of notification.

CONTACT Mary Benda, Director of Financial Aid, Salem State College, 352 Lafayette Street, Salem, MA 01970-5353, 978-542-6139. *Fax:* 978-542-6876.

SALISBURY UNIVERSITY

Salisbury, MD

Tuition & fees (MD res): $6492   Average undergraduate aid package: $6965

ABOUT THE INSTITUTION State-supported, coed. ***Awards:*** bachelor's and master's degrees and post-bachelor's and post-master's certificates. 39 undergraduate majors. ***Total enrollment:*** 7,868. Undergraduates: 7,281. Freshmen: 1,199. Federal methodology is used as a basis for awarding need-based institutional aid.

UNDERGRADUATE EXPENSES for 2008–09 ***Application fee:*** $45. ***Tuition, state resident:*** full-time $4814; part-time $200 per credit hour. ***Tuition, nonresident:*** full-time $13,116; part-time $545 per credit hour. ***Required fees:*** full-time $1678; $55 per credit hour. ***College room and board:*** $7798; ***Room only:*** $4000. Room and board charges vary according to board plan and housing facility. ***Payment plan:*** Installment.

FRESHMAN FINANCIAL AID (Fall 2007) 874 applied for aid; of those 57% were deemed to have need. 95% of freshmen with need received aid; of those 25% had need fully met. ***Average percent of need met:*** 61% (excluding resources awarded to replace EFC). ***Average financial aid package:*** $7417 (excluding resources awarded to replace EFC). 20% of all full-time freshmen had no need and received non-need-based gift aid.

UNDERGRADUATE FINANCIAL AID (Fall 2007) 4,055 applied for aid; of those 67% were deemed to have need. 94% of undergraduates with need received aid; of those 21% had need fully met. ***Average percent of need met:*** 58% (excluding resources awarded to replace EFC). ***Average financial aid package:*** $6965 (excluding resources awarded to replace EFC). 16% of all full-time undergraduates had no need and received non-need-based gift aid.

GIFT AID (NEED-BASED) ***Total amount:*** $10,433,777 (37% federal, 36% state, 19% institutional, 8% external sources). ***Receiving aid:*** Freshmen: 35% (396); all full-time undergraduates: 30% (1,909). ***Average award:*** Freshmen: $6467; Undergraduates: $5306. ***Scholarships, grants, and awards:*** Federal Pell, FSEOG, state, private, college/university gift aid from institutional funds.

GIFT AID (NON-NEED-BASED) ***Total amount:*** $2,235,535 (6% federal, 21% state, 49% institutional, 24% external sources). ***Average award:*** Freshmen: $3712. Undergraduates: $2649. ***Scholarships, grants, and awards by category:*** *Academic interests/achievement:* 630 awards ($1,787,099 total): biological sciences, business, communication, computer science, education, English, foreign languages, general academic interests/achievements, health fields, humanities, mathematics, physical sciences, premedicine, social sciences. *Creative arts/performance:* 4 awards ($1600 total): applied art and design, music. *Special characteristics:* 32 awards ($60,200 total): children and siblings of alumni, first-generation college students. ***Tuition waivers:*** Full or partial for employees or children of employees, senior citizens. ***ROTC:*** Army cooperative.

LOANS ***Student loans:*** $19,780,950 (67% need-based, 33% non-need-based). 53% of past graduating class borrowed through all loan programs. *Average indebtedness per student:* $15,939. ***Average need-based loan:*** Freshmen: $3034. Undergraduates: $3934. ***Parent loans:*** $11,361,732 (54% need-based, 46% non-need-based). ***Programs:*** Federal Direct (Subsidized and Unsubsidized Stafford, PLUS), Perkins.

WORK-STUDY ***Federal work-study:*** Total amount: $129,188; 63 jobs averaging $1977. ***State or other work-study/employment:*** Part-time jobs available.

APPLYING FOR FINANCIAL AID ***Required financial aid form:*** FAFSA. ***Financial aid deadline (priority):*** 3/1. ***Notification date:*** Continuous beginning 3/15. Students must reply by 5/1 or within 2 weeks of notification.

CONTACT Ms. Elizabeth B. Zimmerman, Director of Financial Aid, Salisbury University, 1101 Camden Avenue, Salisbury, MD 21801-6837, 410-543-6165 or toll-free 888-543-0148. *Fax:* 410-543-6138. *E-mail:* ebzimmerman@salisbury.edu.

SALVE REGINA UNIVERSITY

Newport, RI

Tuition & fees: $29,150   Average undergraduate aid package: $19,602

ABOUT THE INSTITUTION Independent Roman Catholic, coed. ***Awards:*** associate, bachelor's, master's, and doctoral degrees and post-bachelor's and post-master's certificates. 48 undergraduate majors. ***Total enrollment:*** 2,691. Undergraduates: 2,127. Freshmen: 556. Both federal and institutional methodology are used as a basis for awarding need-based institutional aid.

UNDERGRADUATE EXPENSES for 2008–09 ***Application fee:*** $50. ***One-time required fee:*** $2350. ***Comprehensive fee:*** $39,850 includes full-time tuition ($28,950), mandatory fees ($200), and room and board ($10,700). Room and board charges vary according to board plan and housing facility. ***Part-time tuition:*** $965 per term. ***Part-time fees:*** $40 per term. Part-time tuition and fees vary according to course load. ***Payment plan:*** Installment.

FRESHMAN FINANCIAL AID (Fall 2008, est.) 475 applied for aid; of those 84% were deemed to have need. 100% of freshmen with need received aid; of those 5% had need fully met. ***Average percent of need met:*** 70% (excluding resources awarded to replace EFC). ***Average financial aid package:*** $20,982 (excluding resources awarded to replace EFC). 17% of all full-time freshmen had no need and received non-need-based gift aid.

UNDERGRADUATE FINANCIAL AID (Fall 2008, est.) 1,621 applied for aid; of those 88% were deemed to have need. 96% of undergraduates with need received aid; of those 6% had need fully met. ***Average percent of need met:*** 67% (excluding resources awarded to replace EFC). ***Average financial aid package:*** $19,602 (excluding resources awarded to replace EFC). 15% of all full-time undergraduates had no need and received non-need-based gift aid.

GIFT AID (NEED-BASED) ***Total amount:*** $19,147,748 (6% federal, 2% state, 89% institutional, 3% external sources). ***Receiving aid:*** Freshmen: 67% (374); all full-time undergraduates: 64% (1,276). ***Average award:*** Freshmen: $17,667; Undergraduates: $15,091. ***Scholarships, grants, and awards:*** Federal Pell, FSEOG, state, private, college/university gift aid from institutional funds.

GIFT AID (NON-NEED-BASED) ***Total amount:*** $1,470,621 (87% institutional, 13% external sources). ***Receiving aid:*** Freshmen: 1% (8). Undergraduates: 2% (31). ***Average award:*** Freshmen: $4826. Undergraduates: $6120. ***Scholarships, grants, and awards by category:*** *Academic interests/achievement:* 760 awards ($4,520,290 total): general academic interests/achievements. ***Tuition waivers:*** Full or partial for employees or children of employees. ***ROTC:*** Army cooperative.

LOANS ***Student loans:*** $15,139,364 (68% need-based, 32% non-need-based). 84% of past graduating class borrowed through all loan programs. *Average indebtedness per student:* $30,138. ***Average need-based loan:*** Freshmen: $3400. Undergraduates: $4711. ***Parent loans:*** $5,625,493 (35% need-based, 65% non-need-based). ***Programs:*** FFEL (Subsidized and Unsubsidized Stafford, PLUS), Perkins, Federal Nursing, college/university, alternative loans.

WORK-STUDY ***Federal work-study:*** Total amount: $425,248; 465 jobs averaging $915. ***State or other work-study/employment:*** Total amount: $220,000 (100% non-need-based). 154 part-time jobs averaging $1429.

APPLYING FOR FINANCIAL AID ***Required financial aid forms:*** FAFSA, CSS Financial Aid PROFILE, business/farm supplement, non-custodial statement.

Financial aid deadline (priority): 3/1. ***Notification date:*** Continuous. Students must reply by 5/1 or within 2 weeks of notification.

CONTACT Aida Mirante, Director of Financial Aid, Salve Regina University, 100 Ochre Point Avenue, Newport, RI 02840-4192, 401-341-2901 or toll-free 888-GO SALVE. *Fax:* 401-341-2928. *E-mail:* financial_aid@salve.edu.

SAMFORD UNIVERSITY

Birmingham, AL

Tuition & fees: $20,420 **Average undergraduate aid package: $13,686**

ABOUT THE INSTITUTION Independent Baptist, coed. ***Awards:*** associate, bachelor's, master's, doctoral, and first professional degrees and post-master's certificates. 62 undergraduate majors. ***Total enrollment:*** 4,469. Undergraduates: 2,848. Freshmen: 708. Federal methodology is used as a basis for awarding need-based institutional aid.

UNDERGRADUATE EXPENSES for 2009–10 ***Application fee:*** $35. ***Comprehensive fee:*** $27,044 includes full-time tuition ($20,200), mandatory fees ($220), and room and board ($6624). ***College room only:*** $3240. ***Part-time tuition:*** $675 per credit. ***Part-time fees:*** $220 per year.

FRESHMAN FINANCIAL AID (Fall 2007) 427 applied for aid; of those 65% were deemed to have need. 100% of freshmen with need received aid; of those 29% had need fully met. ***Average percent of need met:*** 82% (excluding resources awarded to replace EFC). ***Average financial aid package:*** $14,687 (excluding resources awarded to replace EFC). 30% of all full-time freshmen had no need and received non-need-based gift aid.

UNDERGRADUATE FINANCIAL AID (Fall 2007) 1,358 applied for aid; of those 71% were deemed to have need. 100% of undergraduates with need received aid; of those 22% had need fully met. ***Average percent of need met:*** 76% (excluding resources awarded to replace EFC). ***Average financial aid package:*** $13,686 (excluding resources awarded to replace EFC). 29% of all full-time undergraduates had no need and received non-need-based gift aid.

GIFT AID (NEED-BASED) ***Total amount:*** $7,797,411 (19% federal, 5% state, 73% institutional, 3% external sources). ***Receiving aid:*** Freshmen: 37% (265); all full-time undergraduates: 33% (884). ***Average award:*** Freshmen: $10,669; Undergraduates: $8693. ***Scholarships, grants, and awards:*** Federal Pell, FSEOG, state, private, college/university gift aid from institutional funds.

GIFT AID (NON-NEED-BASED) ***Total amount:*** $4,443,769 (1% federal, 3% state, 94% institutional, 2% external sources). ***Receiving aid:*** Freshmen: 29% (210). Undergraduates: 29% (779). ***Average award:*** Freshmen: $5967. Undergraduates: $5749. ***Scholarships, grants, and awards by category:*** *Academic interests/achievement:* 497 awards ($3,086,174 total): general academic interests/achievements. *Creative arts/performance:* 81 awards ($179,418 total): journalism/publications, music, performing arts. *Special achievements/activities:* 11 awards ($35,500 total): leadership. *Special characteristics:* 101 awards ($1,122,473 total): children of faculty/staff, relatives of clergy. ***ROTC:*** Army cooperative, Air Force.

LOANS ***Student loans:*** $8,398,536 (82% need-based, 18% non-need-based). 36% of past graduating class borrowed through all loan programs. *Average indebtedness per student:* $13,996. ***Average need-based loan:*** Freshmen: $4068. Undergraduates: $5113. ***Parent loans:*** $5,933,115 (59% need-based, 41% non-need-based). ***Programs:*** Federal Direct (Subsidized and Unsubsidized Stafford, PLUS), FFEL (Subsidized and Unsubsidized Stafford, PLUS), Perkins, college/university.

WORK-STUDY ***Federal work-study:*** Total amount: $572,225; 409 jobs averaging $1399. ***State or other work-study/employment:*** Total amount: $406,340 (90% need-based, 10% non-need-based). 589 part-time jobs averaging $1221.

ATHLETIC AWARDS Total amount: $4,564,389 (20% need-based, 80% non-need-based).

APPLYING FOR FINANCIAL AID ***Required financial aid form:*** FAFSA. ***Financial aid deadline (priority):*** 3/1. ***Notification date:*** 4/1. Students must reply by 5/1.

CONTACT Lane Smith, Director of Financial Aid, Samford University, 800 Lakeshore Drive, Birmingham, AL 35229, 205-726-2905 or toll-free 800-888-7218. *Fax:* 205-726-2738. *E-mail:* lsmith1@samford.edu.

SAM HOUSTON STATE UNIVERSITY

Huntsville, TX

Tuition & fees (TX res): $6515 **Average undergraduate aid package: $7691**

ABOUT THE INSTITUTION State-supported, coed. ***Awards:*** bachelor's, master's, and doctoral degrees. 43 undergraduate majors. ***Total enrollment:*** 16,663. Undergraduates: 14,303. Freshmen: 2,144. Federal methodology is used as a basis for awarding need-based institutional aid.

UNDERGRADUATE EXPENSES for 2009–10 ***Application fee:*** $40. ***Tuition, state resident:*** full-time $4650; part-time $155 per hour. ***Tuition, nonresident:*** full-time $12,960; part-time $432 per hour. ***Required fees:*** full-time $1865. ***College room and board:*** $6744; ***Room only:*** $4120.

FRESHMAN FINANCIAL AID (Fall 2007) 1,494 applied for aid; of those 76% were deemed to have need. 100% of freshmen with need received aid; of those 29% had need fully met. ***Average percent of need met:*** 15% (excluding resources awarded to replace EFC). ***Average financial aid package:*** $7932 (excluding resources awarded to replace EFC). 8% of all full-time freshmen had no need and received non-need-based gift aid.

UNDERGRADUATE FINANCIAL AID (Fall 2007) 5,990 applied for aid; of those 84% were deemed to have need. 100% of undergraduates with need received aid; of those 14% had need fully met. ***Average percent of need met:*** 15% (excluding resources awarded to replace EFC). ***Average financial aid package:*** $7691 (excluding resources awarded to replace EFC). 3% of all full-time undergraduates had no need and received non-need-based gift aid.

GIFT AID (NEED-BASED) ***Total amount:*** $24,936,710 (52% federal, 47% state, 1% external sources). ***Receiving aid:*** Freshmen: 40% (900); all full-time undergraduates: 39% (3,837). ***Average award:*** Freshmen: $7063; Undergraduates: $5033. ***Scholarships, grants, and awards:*** Federal Pell, FSEOG, state, private, college/university gift aid from institutional funds.

GIFT AID (NON-NEED-BASED) ***Total amount:*** $2,972,412 (100% institutional). ***Receiving aid:*** Freshmen: 21% (484). Undergraduates: 12% (1,167). ***Average award:*** Freshmen: $2261. Undergraduates: $2382. ***Scholarships, grants, and awards by category:*** *Academic interests/achievement:* agriculture, biological sciences, business, communication, computer science, education, engineering/technologies, English, foreign languages, general academic interests/achievements, home economics, humanities, library science, mathematics, military science, physical sciences, social sciences. *Creative arts/performance:* art/fine arts, dance, music. *Special achievements/activities:* cheerleading/drum major, general special achievements/activities, leadership, rodeo. *Special characteristics:* general special characteristics, handicapped students. ***ROTC:*** Army.

LOANS ***Student loans:*** $59,521,048 (47% need-based, 53% non-need-based). 85% of past graduating class borrowed through all loan programs. *Average indebtedness per student:* $5763. ***Average need-based loan:*** Freshmen: $2926. Undergraduates: $3914. ***Parent loans:*** $3,561,013 (100% non-need-based). ***Programs:*** Federal Direct (Subsidized and Unsubsidized Stafford, PLUS), FFEL (Subsidized and Unsubsidized Stafford, PLUS), Perkins, state, college/university.

WORK-STUDY ***Federal work-study:*** Total amount: $328,968; 273 jobs averaging $1190. ***State or other work-study/employment:*** Total amount: $114,157 (86% need-based, 14% non-need-based). 123 part-time jobs averaging $795.

ATHLETIC AWARDS Total amount: $2,278,153 (100% non-need-based).

APPLYING FOR FINANCIAL AID ***Required financial aid forms:*** FAFSA, institution's own form. ***Financial aid deadline (priority):*** 5/31. ***Notification date:*** Continuous. Students must reply within 4 weeks of notification.

CONTACT Lisa Tatom, Director of Financial Aid, Sam Houston State University, Box 2328, Huntsville, TX 77341-2328, 936-294-1774 or toll-free 866-232-7528 Ext. 1828. *Fax:* 936-294-3668. *E-mail:* fao.tatom@shsu.edu.

SAMUEL MERRITT UNIVERSITY

Oakland, CA

Tuition & fees: $34,148 **Average undergraduate aid package: $13,766**

ABOUT THE INSTITUTION Independent, coed, primarily women. ***Awards:*** bachelor's, master's, doctoral, and first professional degrees (bachelor's degree offered jointly with Saint Mary's College of California). 1 undergraduate major. ***Total enrollment:*** 1,311. Undergraduates: 506. Federal methodology is used as a basis for awarding need-based institutional aid.

UNDERGRADUATE EXPENSES for 2009–10 ***Application fee:*** $50. ***One-time required fee:*** $1050. ***Tuition:*** full-time $34,148; part-time $1439 per unit.

UNDERGRADUATE FINANCIAL AID (Fall 2007) 580 applied for aid; of those 83% were deemed to have need. 100% of undergraduates with need received aid; of those 8% had need fully met. ***Average percent of need met:*** 65% (excluding resources awarded to replace EFC). ***Average financial aid package:*** $13,766 (excluding resources awarded to replace EFC).

GIFT AID (NEED-BASED) ***Total amount:*** $3,141,517 (17% federal, 17% state, 56% institutional, 10% external sources). ***Receiving aid:*** All full-time undergraduates: 33% (200). ***Average award:*** Undergraduates: $15,707. ***Scholarships, grants, and awards:*** Federal Pell, FSEOG, state, private, college/university gift aid from institutional funds, Federal Nursing.

GIFT AID (NON-NEED-BASED) ***Total amount:*** $207,349 (11% federal, 89% external sources). ***Receiving aid:*** Undergraduates: 7% (45). ***ROTC:*** Army cooperative, Air Force cooperative.

LOANS ***Student loans:*** $14,243,037 (23% need-based, 77% non-need-based). ***Average need-based loan:*** Undergraduates: $5214. ***Parent loans:*** $753,476 (53% need-based, 47% non-need-based). ***Programs:*** FFEL (Subsidized and Unsubsidized Stafford, PLUS), Perkins, Federal Nursing, college/university.

WORK-STUDY ***Federal work-study:*** Total amount: $172,628; 55 jobs averaging $3138. ***State or other work-study/employment:*** Total amount: $72,000 (100% non-need-based). 22 part-time jobs averaging $4200.

APPLYING FOR FINANCIAL AID ***Required financial aid form:*** FAFSA. ***Financial aid deadline (priority):*** 3/2. ***Notification date:*** Continuous beginning 4/15. Students must reply within 2 weeks of notification.

CONTACT Adel Mareghni, Financial Aid Counselor, Samuel Merritt University, 450 30th Street, Oakland, CA 94609, 510-869-6193 or toll-free 800-607-MERRITT. *Fax:* 510-869-1529. *E-mail:* amareghni@samuelmerritt.edu.

SAN DIEGO CHRISTIAN COLLEGE

El Cajon, CA

ABOUT THE INSTITUTION Independent nondenominational, coed. ***Awards:*** bachelor's degrees and post-bachelor's certificates. 29 undergraduate majors. ***Total enrollment:*** 385. Undergraduates: 385. Freshmen: 56.

GIFT AID (NEED-BASED) ***Scholarships, grants, and awards:*** Federal Pell, FSEOG, state, private, college/university gift aid from institutional funds.

GIFT AID (NON-NEED-BASED) ***Scholarships, grants, and awards by category:*** *Academic interests/achievement:* general academic interests/achievements. *Creative arts/performance:* music, performing arts, theater/drama. *Special achievements/activities:* leadership, religious involvement. *Special characteristics:* children of faculty/staff, international students, out-of-state students, relatives of clergy, religious affiliation, siblings of current students.

LOANS ***Programs:*** FFEL (Subsidized and Unsubsidized Stafford, PLUS), Perkins.

WORK-STUDY ***Federal work-study:*** Total amount: $24,750; 17 jobs averaging $1623. ***State or other work-study/employment:*** Total amount: $36,126 (100% need-based). 25 part-time jobs averaging $1669.

APPLYING FOR FINANCIAL AID ***Required financial aid forms:*** FAFSA, institution's own form, state aid form.

CONTACT Nancy DeMars, Director of Financial Aid, San Diego Christian College, 2100 Greenfield Drive, El Cajon, CA 92019, 619-590-1786 Ext. 3 or toll-free 800-676-2242. *Fax:* 619-590-2180. *E-mail:* ndemars@sdcc.edu.

SAN DIEGO STATE UNIVERSITY

San Diego, CA

Tuition & fees (CA res): $3754 **Average undergraduate aid package: $9000**

ABOUT THE INSTITUTION State-supported, coed. ***Awards:*** bachelor's, master's, and doctoral degrees and post-bachelor's and post-master's certificates. 105 undergraduate majors. ***Total enrollment:*** 35,832. Undergraduates: 29,481. Freshmen: 4,386. Federal methodology is used as a basis for awarding need-based institutional aid.

UNDERGRADUATE EXPENSES for 2008–09 ***Application fee:*** $55. ***Tuition, state resident:*** full-time $0. ***Tuition, nonresident:*** full-time $10,170; part-time $339 per unit. ***Required fees:*** full-time $3754; $1238 per term. Full-time tuition and fees vary according to degree level. Part-time tuition and fees vary according to course load and degree level. ***College room and board:*** $11,266. Room and board charges vary according to board plan and housing facility. ***Payment plan:*** Installment.

FRESHMAN FINANCIAL AID (Fall 2008, est.) 2,900 applied for aid; of those 66% were deemed to have need. 95% of freshmen with need received aid; of those 22% had need fully met. ***Average percent of need met:*** 67% (excluding resources awarded to replace EFC). ***Average financial aid package:*** $8500 (excluding resources awarded to replace EFC). 4% of all full-time freshmen had no need and received non-need-based gift aid.

UNDERGRADUATE FINANCIAL AID (Fall 2008, est.) 14,300 applied for aid; of those 88% were deemed to have need. 95% of undergraduates with need received aid; of those 21% had need fully met. ***Average percent of need met:*** 70% (excluding resources awarded to replace EFC). ***Average financial aid package:*** $9000 (excluding resources awarded to replace EFC). 3% of all full-time undergraduates had no need and received non-need-based gift aid.

GIFT AID (NEED-BASED) ***Total amount:*** $60,261,200 (45% federal, 28% state, 27% institutional). ***Receiving aid:*** Freshmen: 36% (1,300); all full-time undergraduates: 36% (9,000). ***Average award:*** Freshmen: $7100; Undergraduates: $6400. ***Scholarships, grants, and awards:*** Federal Pell, FSEOG, state, private, college/university gift aid from institutional funds, Federal Nursing.

GIFT AID (NON-NEED-BASED) ***Total amount:*** $6,967,800 (33% federal, 24% institutional, 43% external sources). ***Receiving aid:*** Freshmen: 18% (650). Undergraduates: 10% (2,600). ***Average award:*** Freshmen: $2400. Undergraduates: $2100. ***Scholarships, grants, and awards by category:*** *Academic interests/achievement:* area/ethnic studies, biological sciences, business, communication, computer science, education, engineering/technologies, English, foreign languages, general academic interests/achievements, health fields, international studies, mathematics, military science, physical sciences, religion/biblical studies, social sciences. *Creative arts/performance:* applied art and design, art/fine arts, cinema/film/broadcasting, creative writing, dance, journalism/publications, music, performing arts, theater/drama. *Special achievements/activities:* leadership. *Special characteristics:* adult students, children and siblings of alumni, children of faculty/staff, children of workers in trades, first-generation college students, handicapped students, local/state students, veterans. ***Tuition waivers:*** Full or partial for employees or children of employees. ***ROTC:*** Army, Naval, Air Force.

LOANS ***Student loans:*** $85,619,600 (61% need-based, 39% non-need-based). 44% of past graduating class borrowed through all loan programs. *Average indebtedness per student:* $14,700. ***Average need-based loan:*** Freshmen: $3100. Undergraduates: $4100. ***Parent loans:*** $78,258,100 (17% need-based, 83% non-need-based). ***Programs:*** Federal Direct (Subsidized and Unsubsidized Stafford, PLUS), Perkins, college/university.

WORK-STUDY ***Federal work-study:*** Total amount: $1,437,300; 5,288 jobs averaging $4000.

ATHLETIC AWARDS Total amount: $4,635,600 (100% non-need-based).

APPLYING FOR FINANCIAL AID ***Required financial aid forms:*** FAFSA, state aid form. ***Financial aid deadline:*** 3/2. ***Notification date:*** Continuous.

CONTACT Ms. Chrys Dutton, Director of Financial Aid and Scholarships, San Diego State University, 5500 Campanile Drive, SSW-3605, San Diego, CA 92182-7436, 619-594-6323.

SAN FRANCISCO ART INSTITUTE

San Francisco, CA

CONTACT Erin Zagaski, Interim Director of Financial Aid, San Francisco Art Institute, 800 Chestnut Street, San Francisco, CA 94133-2299, 415-749-4513 or toll-free 800-345-SFAI. *Fax:* 415-351-3503.

SAN FRANCISCO CONSERVATORY OF MUSIC

San Francisco, CA

Tuition & fees: $32,080 **Average undergraduate aid package: $17,500**

ABOUT THE INSTITUTION Independent, coed. ***Awards:*** bachelor's and master's degrees and post-master's certificates. 7 undergraduate majors. ***Total enrollment:*** 402. Undergraduates: 206. Freshmen: 37. Federal methodology is used as a basis for awarding need-based institutional aid.

UNDERGRADUATE EXPENSES for 2008–09 ***Application fee:*** $100. ***One-time required fee:*** $162. ***Tuition:*** full-time $31,800; part-time $1400 per credit. Part-time tuition and fees vary according to course load. ***Payment plan:*** Installment.

FRESHMAN FINANCIAL AID (Fall 2007) 30 applied for aid; of those 93% were deemed to have need. 100% of freshmen with need received aid; of those 86% had need fully met. ***Average percent of need met:*** 89% (excluding resources awarded to replace EFC). ***Average financial aid package:*** $17,500 (excluding resources awarded to replace EFC).

UNDERGRADUATE FINANCIAL AID (Fall 2007) 146 applied for aid; of those 83% were deemed to have need. 100% of undergraduates with need received aid; of those 85% had need fully met. ***Average percent of need met:*** 89% (excluding resources awarded to replace EFC). ***Average financial aid package:*** $17,500 (excluding resources awarded to replace EFC).

GIFT AID (NEED-BASED) ***Total amount:*** $4,634,215 (4% federal, 2% state, 93% institutional, 1% external sources). ***Receiving aid:*** Freshmen: 70% (26); all full-time undergraduates: 76% (119). ***Average award:*** Freshmen: $11,600; Undergraduates: $13,000. ***Scholarships, grants, and awards:*** Federal Pell, FSEOG, state, private, college/university gift aid from institutional funds.

GIFT AID (NON-NEED-BASED) ***Total amount:*** $357,981 (95% institutional, 5% external sources). ***Receiving aid:*** Freshmen: 16% (6). Undergraduates: 16% (25). ***Average award:*** Freshmen: $12,500. Undergraduates: $12,500. ***Scholarships, grants, and awards by category:*** *Creative arts/performance:* 12 awards ($98,049 total): music. ***Tuition waivers:*** Full or partial for employees or children of employees.

LOANS ***Student loans:*** $2,913,607 (65% need-based, 35% non-need-based). 52% of past graduating class borrowed through all loan programs. *Average indebtedness per student:* $16,367. ***Average need-based loan:*** Freshmen: $3500. Undergraduates: $4500. ***Parent loans:*** $1,049,656 (54% need-based, 46% non-need-based). ***Programs:*** FFEL (Subsidized and Unsubsidized Stafford, PLUS), Perkins.

WORK-STUDY ***Federal work-study:*** Total amount: $105,435; 34 jobs averaging $1500. ***State or other work-study/employment:*** Total amount: $28,500 (23% need-based, 77% non-need-based). 33 part-time jobs averaging $1500.

APPLYING FOR FINANCIAL AID ***Required financial aid forms:*** FAFSA, institution's own form. ***Financial aid deadline (priority):*** 2/17. ***Notification date:*** Continuous beginning 4/1. Students must reply by 5/1 or within 2 weeks of notification.

CONTACT Doris Howard, Director of Financial Aid, San Francisco Conservatory of Music, 50 Oak Street, San Francisco, CA 94102-6011, 415-503-6214. *Fax:* 415-503-6299. *E-mail:* dbh@sfcm.edu.

SAN FRANCISCO STATE UNIVERSITY

San Francisco, CA

Tuition & fees (CA res): $3762 **Average undergraduate aid package: $9184**

ABOUT THE INSTITUTION State-supported, coed. ***Awards:*** bachelor's, master's, and doctoral degrees and post-bachelor's certificates. 92 undergraduate majors. ***Total enrollment:*** 30,014. Undergraduates: 24,378. Freshmen: 3,603. Federal methodology is used as a basis for awarding need-based institutional aid.

UNDERGRADUATE EXPENSES for 2008–09 ***Application fee:*** $55. ***Tuition, state resident:*** full-time $0. ***Tuition, nonresident:*** full-time $10,170; part-time $339 per unit. ***Required fees:*** full-time $3762; $1242 per term. Full-time tuition and fees vary according to degree level. Part-time tuition and fees vary according to degree level. ***College room and board:*** $10,196; ***Room only:*** $6908. Room and board charges vary according to board plan and housing facility. ***Payment plan:*** Installment.

FRESHMAN FINANCIAL AID (Fall 2008, est.) 2,437 applied for aid; of those 73% were deemed to have need. 96% of freshmen with need received aid; of those 10% had need fully met. ***Average percent of need met:*** 63% (excluding resources awarded to replace EFC). ***Average financial aid package:*** $8967 (excluding resources awarded to replace EFC). 2% of all full-time freshmen had no need and received non-need-based gift aid.

UNDERGRADUATE FINANCIAL AID (Fall 2008, est.) 11,435 applied for aid; of those 85% were deemed to have need. 97% of undergraduates with need received aid; of those 8% had need fully met. ***Average percent of need met:*** 61% (excluding resources awarded to replace EFC). ***Average financial aid package:*** $9184 (excluding resources awarded to replace EFC). 1% of all full-time undergraduates had no need and received non-need-based gift aid.

GIFT AID (NEED-BASED) ***Total amount:*** $57,397,779 (47% federal, 49% state, 1% institutional, 3% external sources). ***Receiving aid:*** Freshmen: 34% (1,149); all full-time undergraduates: 37% (6,943). ***Average award:*** Freshmen: $7784; Undergraduates: $6968. ***Scholarships, grants, and awards:*** Federal Pell, FSEOG, state, private, college/university gift aid from institutional funds.

GIFT AID (NON-NEED-BASED) ***Total amount:*** $898,073 (29% institutional, 71% external sources). ***Receiving aid:*** Freshmen: 7% (231). Undergraduates: 4% (765). ***Average award:*** Freshmen: $1859. Undergraduates: $2169. ***Tuition waivers:*** Full or partial for employees or children of employees, senior citizens. ***ROTC:*** Army cooperative, Naval cooperative, Air Force cooperative.

LOANS ***Student loans:*** $53,743,314 (89% need-based, 11% non-need-based). 41% of past graduating class borrowed through all loan programs. *Average indebtedness per student:* $15,753. ***Average need-based loan:*** Freshmen: $2348. Undergraduates: $3038. ***Parent loans:*** $17,041,357 (61% need-based, 39% non-need-based). ***Programs:*** Federal Direct (Subsidized and Unsubsidized Stafford, PLUS), FFEL (PLUS), Perkins.

WORK-STUDY ***Federal work-study:*** Total amount: $799,462; jobs available.

ATHLETIC AWARDS Total amount: $332,100 (47% need-based, 53% non-need-based).

APPLYING FOR FINANCIAL AID ***Required financial aid form:*** FAFSA. ***Financial aid deadline (priority):*** 3/2. ***Notification date:*** Continuous. Students must reply within 2 weeks of notification.

CONTACT Barbara Hubler, Director of Financial Aid, San Francisco State University, 1600 Holloway Avenue, San Francisco, CA 94132-1722, 415-338-7000. *Fax:* 415-338-0949. *E-mail:* finaid@sfsu.edu.

SAN JOSE STATE UNIVERSITY

San Jose, CA

Tuition & fees (CA res): $3992 **Average undergraduate aid package: $10,884**

ABOUT THE INSTITUTION State-supported, coed. ***Awards:*** bachelor's and master's degrees. 89 undergraduate majors. ***Total enrollment:*** 32,746. Undergraduates: 25,187. Freshmen: 3,594. Federal methodology is used as a basis for awarding need-based institutional aid.

UNDERGRADUATE EXPENSES for 2009–10 ***Application fee:*** $55. ***Tuition, state resident:*** full-time $0. ***Tuition, nonresident:*** full-time $10,170; part-time $339 per unit. ***Required fees:*** full-time $3992; $1399 per term. ***College room and board:*** $8663; ***Room only:*** $4968.

FRESHMAN FINANCIAL AID (Fall 2008, est.) 3,097 applied for aid; of those 73% were deemed to have need. 92% of freshmen with need received aid; of those 22% had need fully met. ***Average percent of need met:*** 79% (excluding resources awarded to replace EFC). ***Average financial aid package:*** $11,057 (excluding resources awarded to replace EFC). 2% of all full-time freshmen had no need and received non-need-based gift aid.

UNDERGRADUATE FINANCIAL AID (Fall 2008, est.) 11,246 applied for aid; of those 89% were deemed to have need. 90% of undergraduates with need received aid; of those 20% had need fully met. ***Average percent of need met:*** 72% (excluding resources awarded to replace EFC). ***Average financial aid package:*** $10,884 (excluding resources awarded to replace EFC). 1% of all full-time undergraduates had no need and received non-need-based gift aid.

GIFT AID (NEED-BASED) ***Total amount:*** $46,711,016 (50% federal, 46% state, 2% institutional, 2% external sources). ***Receiving aid:*** Freshmen: 34% (1,544); all full-time undergraduates: 35% (6,931). ***Average award:*** Freshmen: $6667; Undergraduates: $6033. ***Scholarships, grants, and awards:*** Federal Pell, FSEOG, state, private, college/university gift aid from institutional funds, Academic Competitiveness Grant, National Smart Grant, TEACH Grant.

GIFT AID (NON-NEED-BASED) ***Total amount:*** $250,894 (48% institutional, 52% external sources). ***Receiving aid:*** Freshmen: 3. Undergraduates: 19. ***Average award:*** Freshmen: $1712. Undergraduates: $3665. ***Scholarships, grants, and awards by category:*** *Academic interests/achievement:* 135 awards ($598,996 total): general academic interests/achievements. ***ROTC:*** Army, Air Force.

LOANS ***Student loans:*** $53,536,990 (84% need-based, 16% non-need-based). 47% of past graduating class borrowed through all loan programs. *Average indebtedness per student:* $12,095. ***Average need-based loan:*** Freshmen: $3351. Undergraduates: $3928. ***Parent loans:*** $2,039,216 (38% need-based, 62% non-need-based). ***Programs:*** FFEL (Subsidized and Unsubsidized Stafford, PLUS), Perkins, college/university.

WORK-STUDY ***Federal work-study:*** Total amount: $29,996,286; 6,289 jobs averaging $4770.

ATHLETIC AWARDS Total amount: $1,763,590 (59% need-based, 41% non-need-based).

APPLYING FOR FINANCIAL AID ***Required financial aid form:*** FAFSA. ***Financial aid deadline (priority):*** 3/2. ***Notification date:*** Continuous beginning 4/1.

CONTACT Coleetta McElroy, Interim Director of Financial Aid, San Jose State University, One Washington Square, San Jose, CA 95192-0036, 408-924-6086. *E-mail:* coleeta.mcelroy@sjsu.edu.

SANTA CLARA UNIVERSITY

Santa Clara, CA

Tuition & fees: $34,950 **Average undergraduate aid package: $22,149**

ABOUT THE INSTITUTION Independent Roman Catholic (Jesuit), coed. ***Awards:*** bachelor's, master's, doctoral, and first professional degrees and post-bachelor's, post-master's, and first professional certificates. 48 undergraduate majors. ***Total enrollment:*** 8,758. Undergraduates: 5,267. Freshmen: 1,221. Both federal and institutional methodology are used as a basis for awarding need-based institutional aid.

UNDERGRADUATE EXPENSES for 2008–09 ***Application fee:*** $55. ***Comprehensive fee:*** $46,020 includes full-time tuition ($34,950) and room and board ($11,070). Room and board charges vary according to board plan, housing facility, and student level. ***Part-time tuition:*** $1165 per unit. Part-time tuition and fees vary according to course load. ***Payment plan:*** Installment.

FRESHMAN FINANCIAL AID (Fall 2008, est.) 767 applied for aid; of those 68% were deemed to have need. 98% of freshmen with need received aid; of those 41% had need fully met. ***Average percent of need met:*** 77% (excluding resources awarded to replace EFC). ***Average financial aid package:*** $25,221 (excluding resources awarded to replace EFC). 31% of all full-time freshmen had no need and received non-need-based gift aid.

UNDERGRADUATE FINANCIAL AID (Fall 2008, est.) 5,152 applied for aid; of those 71% were deemed to have need. 50% of undergraduates with need received aid; of those 36% had need fully met. ***Average percent of need met:*** 66% (excluding resources awarded to replace EFC). ***Average financial aid package:*** $22,149 (excluding resources awarded to replace EFC). 29% of all full-time undergraduates had no need and received non-need-based gift aid.

GIFT AID (NEED-BASED) ***Total amount:*** $30,521,963 (8% federal, 14% state, 78% institutional). ***Receiving aid:*** Freshmen: 32% (388); all full-time undergraduates: 28% (1,459). ***Average award:*** Freshmen: $20,490; Undergraduates: $16,470. ***Scholarships, grants, and awards:*** Federal Pell, FSEOG, state, private, college/university gift aid from institutional funds.

GIFT AID (NON-NEED-BASED) ***Total amount:*** $22,920,944 (92% institutional, 8% external sources). ***Receiving aid:*** Freshmen: 20% (240). Undergraduates: 13% (707). ***Average award:*** Freshmen: $8047. Undergraduates: $12,079. ***Scholarships, grants, and awards by category:*** *Academic interests/achievement:* 2,571 awards ($27,150,227 total): business, engineering/technologies, general academic interests/achievements, military science. *Creative arts/performance:* 66 awards ($181,985 total): dance, debating, music, theater/drama. *Special characteristics:* 95 awards: children and siblings of alumni, children of faculty/staff, children with a deceased or disabled parent, handicapped students. ***Tuition waivers:*** Full or partial for employees or children of employees. ***ROTC:*** Army, Air Force cooperative.

LOANS ***Student loans:*** $14,908,419 (38% need-based, 62% non-need-based). 44% of past graduating class borrowed through all loan programs. *Average indebtedness per student:* $25,438. ***Average need-based loan:*** Freshmen: $3270. Undergraduates: $4610. ***Parent loans:*** $14,444,029 (100% non-need-based). ***Programs:*** Federal Direct (Subsidized and Unsubsidized Stafford, PLUS), FFEL (PLUS), Perkins, alternative private loans.

WORK-STUDY ***Federal work-study:*** Total amount: $2,011,357; 643 jobs averaging $3195.

ATHLETIC AWARDS Total amount: $3,479,170 (100% non-need-based).

APPLYING FOR FINANCIAL AID ***Required financial aid forms:*** FAFSA, CSS Financial Aid PROFILE. ***Financial aid deadline (priority):*** 2/1. ***Notification date:*** 4/1. Students must reply by 5/1 or within 2 weeks of notification.

CONTACT Marta I. Murchison, Associate Director, Systems and Data, Santa Clara University, 500 El Camino Real, Santa Clara, CA 95053, 408-551-6088. *Fax:* 408-551-6085. *E-mail:* mmurchison@scu.edu.

SARAH LAWRENCE COLLEGE

Bronxville, NY

Tuition & fees: $40,350 **Average undergraduate aid package: $28,192**

ABOUT THE INSTITUTION Independent, coed. ***Awards:*** bachelor's and master's degrees. 112 undergraduate majors. ***Total enrollment:*** 1,700. Undergraduates: 1,383. Freshmen: 363. Both federal and institutional methodology are used as a basis for awarding need-based institutional aid.

UNDERGRADUATE EXPENSES for 2008–09 ***Application fee:*** $60. ***Comprehensive fee:*** $53,454 includes full-time tuition ($39,450), mandatory fees ($900), and room and board ($13,104). ***College room only:*** $8756. Full-time tuition and fees vary according to course load. Room and board charges vary according to board plan. ***Part-time tuition:*** $1315 per credit. ***Part-time fees:*** $450 per term. Part-time tuition and fees vary according to course load. ***Payment plan:*** Installment.

FRESHMAN FINANCIAL AID (Fall 2008, est.) 234 applied for aid; of those 82% were deemed to have need. 100% of freshmen with need received aid; of those 66% had need fully met. ***Average percent of need met:*** 86% (excluding resources awarded to replace EFC). ***Average financial aid package:*** $26,990 (excluding resources awarded to replace EFC). 1% of all full-time freshmen had no need and received non-need-based gift aid.

UNDERGRADUATE FINANCIAL AID (Fall 2008, est.) 861 applied for aid; of those 89% were deemed to have need. 99% of undergraduates with need received aid; of those 59% had need fully met. ***Average percent of need met:*** 85% (excluding resources awarded to replace EFC). ***Average financial aid package:*** $28,192 (excluding resources awarded to replace EFC). 1% of all full-time undergraduates had no need and received non-need-based gift aid.

GIFT AID (NEED-BASED) ***Total amount:*** $17,211,736 (5% federal, 2% state, 91% institutional, 2% external sources). ***Receiving aid:*** Freshmen: 49% (170); all full-time undergraduates: 52% (684). ***Average award:*** Freshmen: $25,164; Undergraduates: $25,165. ***Scholarships, grants, and awards:*** Federal Pell, FSEOG, state, private, college/university gift aid from institutional funds.

GIFT AID (NON-NEED-BASED) ***Total amount:*** $61,119 (1% state, 7% institutional, 92% external sources). ***Receiving aid:*** Freshmen: 1% (4). Undergraduates: 1. ***Average award:*** Freshmen: $4000. Undergraduates: $4000. ***Tuition waivers:*** Full or partial for employees or children of employees.

LOANS ***Student loans:*** $3,326,191 (92% need-based, 8% non-need-based). 61% of past graduating class borrowed through all loan programs. *Average indebtedness per student:* $15,581. ***Average need-based loan:*** Freshmen: $2618. Undergraduates: $3831. ***Parent loans:*** $3,445,284 (82% need-based, 18% non-need-based). ***Programs:*** FFEL (Subsidized and Unsubsidized Stafford, PLUS), Perkins, college/university, Signature Loans, CitiAssist Loans.

WORK-STUDY ***Federal work-study:*** Total amount: $974,634; 593 jobs averaging $1639. ***State or other work-study/employment:*** Total amount: $44,647 (88% need-based, 12% non-need-based). 27 part-time jobs averaging $1654.

APPLYING FOR FINANCIAL AID ***Required financial aid forms:*** FAFSA, CSS Financial Aid PROFILE, state aid form. ***Financial aid deadline:*** 2/1. ***Notification date:*** 4/1. Students must reply by 5/1.

CONTACT Ms. Heather McDonnell, Director of Financial Aid, Sarah Lawrence College, One Mead Way, Bronxville, NY 10708, 914-395-2570 or toll-free 800-888-2858. *Fax:* 914-395-2676. *E-mail:* hmcdonn@sarahlawrence.edu.

SAVANNAH COLLEGE OF ART AND DESIGN

Savannah, GA

Tuition & fees: $28,265 **Average undergraduate aid package: $12,550**

ABOUT THE INSTITUTION Independent, coed. ***Awards:*** bachelor's and master's degrees and post-bachelor's certificates. 31 undergraduate majors. ***Total enrollment:*** 9,332. Undergraduates: 7,855. Freshmen: 1,506. Federal methodology is used as a basis for awarding need-based institutional aid.

UNDERGRADUATE EXPENSES for 2009–10 ***Application fee:*** $50. ***Comprehensive fee:*** $39,975 includes full-time tuition ($27,765), mandatory fees ($500), and room and board ($11,710). ***Part-time tuition:*** $3085 per course. ***Part-time fees:*** $617 per credit hour.

FRESHMAN FINANCIAL AID (Fall 2008, est.) 1,004 applied for aid; of those 75% were deemed to have need. 99% of freshmen with need received aid; of those 57% had need fully met. ***Average percent of need met:*** 10% (excluding resources awarded to replace EFC). ***Average financial aid package:*** $11,495 (excluding resources awarded to replace EFC). 22% of all full-time freshmen had no need and received non-need-based gift aid.

UNDERGRADUATE FINANCIAL AID (Fall 2008, est.) 4,323 applied for aid; of those 80% were deemed to have need. 99% of undergraduates with need received aid; of those 42% had need fully met. ***Average percent of need met:*** 13% (excluding resources awarded to replace EFC). ***Average financial aid package:*** $12,550 (excluding resources awarded to replace EFC).

GIFT AID (NEED-BASED) ***Total amount:*** $5,049,864 (99% federal, 1% state). ***Receiving aid:*** Freshmen: 13% (181); all full-time undergraduates: 23% (1,006). ***Average award:*** Freshmen: $4198; Undergraduates: $4368. ***Scholarships, grants, and awards:*** Federal Pell, FSEOG, state, private, college/university gift aid from institutional funds.

GIFT AID (NON-NEED-BASED) ***Total amount:*** $8,393,770 (41% state, 59% institutional). ***Receiving aid:*** Freshmen: 39% (548). Undergraduates: 59% (2,554). ***Average award:*** Freshmen: $7234. Undergraduates: $13,734. ***Scholarships, grants, and awards by category:*** *Academic interests/achievement:* architecture, education, general academic interests/achievements, humanities.

Creative arts/performance: art/fine arts, general creative arts/performance. *Special achievements/activities:* general special achievements/activities. *Special characteristics:* general special characteristics.

LOANS ***Student loans:*** $493,189 (100% non-need-based). ***Average need-based loan:*** Freshmen: $3379. Undergraduates: $4457. ***Parent loans:*** $45,767,739 (100% non-need-based). ***Programs:*** Federal Direct (Subsidized and Unsubsidized Stafford, PLUS).

WORK-STUDY ***Federal work-study:*** Total amount: $382,045; jobs available. ***State or other work-study/employment:*** Total amount: $500,000 (100% non-need-based). Part-time jobs available.

ATHLETIC AWARDS Total amount: $3,696,266 (100% non-need-based).

APPLYING FOR FINANCIAL AID ***Required financial aid forms:*** FAFSA, institution's own form, state aid form. ***Financial aid deadline (priority):*** 2/15. ***Notification date:*** Continuous beginning 6/1. Students must reply within 4 weeks of notification.

CONTACT Brenda Clark, Director of Financial Aid, Savannah College of Art and Design, PO Box 3146, Savannah, GA 31402-3146, 912-525-6119 or toll-free 800-869-7223. *E-mail:* bclark@scad.edu.

SAVANNAH STATE UNIVERSITY

Savannah, GA

CONTACT Mark Adkins, Director of Financial Aid, Savannah State University, PO Box 20523, Savannah, GA 31404, 912-356-2253 or toll-free 800-788-0478. *Fax:* 912-353-3150. *E-mail:* finaid@savstate.edu.

SCHOOL OF THE ART INSTITUTE OF CHICAGO

Chicago, IL

Tuition & fees: N/R **Average undergraduate aid package: $27,348**

ABOUT THE INSTITUTION Independent, coed. ***Awards:*** bachelor's and master's degrees. 33 undergraduate majors. ***Total enrollment:*** 3,006. Undergraduates: 2,404. Freshmen: 452. Federal methodology is used as a basis for awarding need-based institutional aid.

FRESHMAN FINANCIAL AID (Fall 2008, est.) 281 applied for aid; of those 87% were deemed to have need. 100% of freshmen with need received aid; of those 3% had need fully met. ***Average percent of need met:*** 73% (excluding resources awarded to replace EFC). ***Average financial aid package:*** $24,480 (excluding resources awarded to replace EFC). 24% of all full-time freshmen had no need and received non-need-based gift aid.

UNDERGRADUATE FINANCIAL AID (Fall 2008, est.) 1,334 applied for aid; of those 91% were deemed to have need. 100% of undergraduates with need received aid; of those 4% had need fully met. ***Average percent of need met:*** 83% (excluding resources awarded to replace EFC). ***Average financial aid package:*** $27,348 (excluding resources awarded to replace EFC). 27% of all full-time undergraduates had no need and received non-need-based gift aid.

GIFT AID (NEED-BASED) ***Total amount:*** $15,918,005 (14% federal, 6% state, 78% institutional, 2% external sources). ***Receiving aid:*** Freshmen: 54% (243); all full-time undergraduates: 54% (1,188). ***Average award:*** Freshmen: $12,315; Undergraduates: $13,170. ***Scholarships, grants, and awards:*** Federal Pell, FSEOG, state, private, college/university gift aid from institutional funds.

GIFT AID (NON-NEED-BASED) ***Total amount:*** $3,603,380 (93% institutional, 7% external sources). ***Receiving aid:*** Freshmen: 2% (7). Undergraduates: 2% (35). ***Average award:*** Freshmen: $5450. Undergraduates: $5248. ***Scholarships, grants, and awards by category:*** *Academic interests/achievement:* general academic interests/achievements. *Creative arts/performance:* art/fine arts.

LOANS ***Student loans:*** $13,425,862 (82% need-based, 18% non-need-based). 61% of past graduating class borrowed through all loan programs. *Average indebtedness per student:* $34,578. ***Average need-based loan:*** Freshmen: $3740. Undergraduates: $4692. ***Parent loans:*** $4,054,670 (49% need-based, 51% non-need-based). ***Programs:*** FFEL (Subsidized and Unsubsidized Stafford, PLUS), Perkins.

WORK-STUDY ***Federal work-study:*** Total amount: $4,266,972; jobs available. ***State or other work-study/employment:*** Total amount: $209,652 (17% need-based, 83% non-need-based). Part-time jobs available.

APPLYING FOR FINANCIAL AID ***Required financial aid form:*** FAFSA. ***Financial aid deadline (priority):*** 3/15. ***Notification date:*** Continuous beginning 4/1.

CONTACT Student Financial Services, School of the Art Institute of Chicago, 36 South Wabash, Suite 1218, Chicago, IL 60603-3103, 312-629-6600 or toll-free 800-232-SAIC. *Fax:* 312-629-6601. *E-mail:* finaid@saic.edu.

SCHOOL OF THE MUSEUM OF FINE ARTS, BOSTON

Boston, MA

CONTACT Ms. Elizabeth Goreham, Director of Financial Aid, School of the Museum of Fine Arts, Boston, 230 The Fenway, Boston, MA 02115, 617-369-3684 or toll-free 800-643-6078 (in-state). *Fax:* 617-369-3041.

SCHOOL OF VISUAL ARTS

New York, NY

ABOUT THE INSTITUTION Proprietary, coed. ***Awards:*** bachelor's and master's degrees. 15 undergraduate majors. ***Total enrollment:*** 3,946. Undergraduates: 3,522. Freshmen: 664.

GIFT AID (NEED-BASED) ***Scholarships, grants, and awards:*** Federal Pell, FSEOG, state, private, college/university gift aid from institutional funds.

GIFT AID (NON-NEED-BASED) ***Scholarships, grants, and awards by category:*** *Creative arts/performance:* art/fine arts.

LOANS ***Programs:*** FFEL (Subsidized and Unsubsidized Stafford, PLUS), Perkins, alternative loans.

WORK-STUDY ***Federal work-study:*** Total amount: $558,958; 165 jobs averaging $2576. ***State or other work-study/employment:*** Total amount: $225,620 (68% need-based, 32% non-need-based).

APPLYING FOR FINANCIAL AID ***Required financial aid forms:*** FAFSA, state aid form.

CONTACT William Berrios, Director of Financial Aid, School of Visual Arts, 209 East 23rd Street, New York, NY 10010, 212-592-2043 or toll-free 800-436-4204. *Fax:* 212-592-2029. *E-mail:* wberrios@sva.edu.

SCHREINER UNIVERSITY

Kerrville, TX

Tuition & fees: $17,992 **Average undergraduate aid package: $12,944**

ABOUT THE INSTITUTION Independent Presbyterian, coed. ***Awards:*** bachelor's and master's degrees. 40 undergraduate majors. ***Total enrollment:*** 974. Undergraduates: 953. Freshmen: 266. Federal methodology is used as a basis for awarding need-based institutional aid.

UNDERGRADUATE EXPENSES for 2008–09 ***Application fee:*** $25. ***Comprehensive fee:*** $25,704 includes full-time tuition ($17,392), mandatory fees ($600), and room and board ($7712). ***College room only:*** $4280. Room and board charges vary according to board plan and housing facility. ***Part-time tuition:*** $742 per credit hour. ***Part-time fees:*** $75 per term. ***Payment plan:*** Installment.

FRESHMAN FINANCIAL AID (Fall 2007) 245 applied for aid; of those 82% were deemed to have need. 100% of freshmen with need received aid; of those 20% had need fully met. ***Average percent of need met:*** 71% (excluding resources awarded to replace EFC). ***Average financial aid package:*** $12,376 (excluding resources awarded to replace EFC). 24% of all full-time freshmen had no need and received non-need-based gift aid.

UNDERGRADUATE FINANCIAL AID (Fall 2007) 691 applied for aid; of those 87% were deemed to have need. 100% of undergraduates with need received aid; of those 19% had need fully met. ***Average percent of need met:*** 71% (excluding resources awarded to replace EFC). ***Average financial aid package:*** $12,944 (excluding resources awarded to replace EFC). 21% of all full-time undergraduates had no need and received non-need-based gift aid.

GIFT AID (NEED-BASED) ***Total amount:*** $6,569,097 (18% federal, 24% state, 40% institutional, 18% external sources). ***Receiving aid:*** Freshmen: 71% (202); all full-time undergraduates: 75% (600). ***Average award:*** Freshmen: $10,133; Undergraduates: $10,010. ***Scholarships, grants, and awards:*** Federal Pell, FSEOG, state, private, college/university gift aid from institutional funds.

GIFT AID (NON-NEED-BASED) ***Total amount:*** $1,806,989 (6% state, 73% institutional, 21% external sources). ***Receiving aid:*** Freshmen: 12% (34). Undergraduates: 11% (90). ***Average award:*** Freshmen: $6289. Undergraduates: $6538. ***Scholarships, grants, and awards by category:*** *Academic interests/achievement:* 765 awards ($3,734,119 total): biological sciences, business, education, English, general academic interests/achievements, mathematics, physical sciences, premedicine, religion/biblical studies, social sciences. *Creative arts/performance:* 64 awards ($63,100 total): art/fine arts, journalism/publications, music, theater/drama. *Special achievements/activities:* 25 awards ($47,890 total): community service, leadership, memberships, religious involvement. *Special characteristics:* 290 awards ($915,149 total): children of faculty/staff, general special characteristics, international students, local/state students, relatives of clergy, religious affiliation, siblings of current students. ***Tuition waivers:*** Full or partial for employees or children of employees.

LOANS ***Student loans:*** $4,800,749 (70% need-based, 30% non-need-based). 84% of past graduating class borrowed through all loan programs. *Average indebtedness per student:* $20,486. ***Average need-based loan:*** Freshmen: $2768. Undergraduates: $3489. ***Parent loans:*** $1,448,697 (23% need-based, 77% non-need-based). ***Programs:*** FFEL (Subsidized and Unsubsidized Stafford, PLUS), state, alternative loans.

WORK-STUDY ***Federal work-study:*** Total amount: $50,651; 300 jobs averaging $1500. ***State or other work-study/employment:*** Total amount: $235,302 (31% need-based, 69% non-need-based). 336 part-time jobs averaging $1500.

APPLYING FOR FINANCIAL AID ***Required financial aid forms:*** FAFSA, TASFA. ***Financial aid deadline:*** 8/1 (priority: 4/1). ***Notification date:*** Continuous. Students must reply within 2 weeks of notification.

CONTACT Toni Bryant, Director of Financial Aid, Schreiner University, 2100 Memorial Boulevard, Kerrville, TX 78028, 830-792-7217 or toll-free 800-343-4919. *Fax:* 830-792-7226. *E-mail:* finaid@schreiner.edu.

SCRIPPS COLLEGE

Claremont, CA

Tuition & fees: $37,950 **Average undergraduate aid package: $32,390**

ABOUT THE INSTITUTION Independent, women only. ***Awards:*** bachelor's degrees and post-bachelor's certificates. 60 undergraduate majors. ***Total enrollment:*** 954. Undergraduates: 954. Freshmen: 252. Both federal and institutional methodology are used as a basis for awarding need-based institutional aid.

UNDERGRADUATE EXPENSES for 2008–09 ***Application fee:*** $50. ***Comprehensive fee:*** $49,450 includes full-time tuition ($37,736), mandatory fees ($214), and room and board ($11,500). ***College room only:*** $6200. Full-time tuition and fees vary according to program. Room and board charges vary according to board plan. ***Part-time tuition:*** $4717 per course. Part-time tuition and fees vary according to program. ***Payment plan:*** Installment.

FRESHMAN FINANCIAL AID (Fall 2008, est.) 157 applied for aid; of those 71% were deemed to have need. 100% of freshmen with need received aid; of those 100% had need fully met. ***Average percent of need met:*** 100% (excluding resources awarded to replace EFC). ***Average financial aid package:*** $34,781 (excluding resources awarded to replace EFC). 6% of all full-time freshmen had no need and received non-need-based gift aid.

UNDERGRADUATE FINANCIAL AID (Fall 2008, est.) 505 applied for aid; of those 78% were deemed to have need. 100% of undergraduates with need received aid; of those 100% had need fully met. ***Average percent of need met:*** 100% (excluding resources awarded to replace EFC). ***Average financial aid package:*** $32,390 (excluding resources awarded to replace EFC). 10% of all full-time undergraduates had no need and received non-need-based gift aid.

GIFT AID (NEED-BASED) ***Total amount:*** $10,778,426 (5% federal, 5% state, 88% institutional, 2% external sources). ***Receiving aid:*** Freshmen: 44% (111); all full-time undergraduates: 42% (394). ***Average award:*** Freshmen: $31,650; Undergraduates: $28,865. ***Scholarships, grants, and awards:*** Federal Pell, FSEOG, state, private, college/university gift aid from institutional funds.

GIFT AID (NON-NEED-BASED) ***Total amount:*** $1,758,773 (1% state, 88% institutional, 11% external sources). ***Receiving aid:*** Freshmen: 15% (37). Undergraduates: 21% (198). ***Average award:*** Freshmen: $17,373. Undergraduates: $17,254. ***Scholarships, grants, and awards by category:*** *Academic interests/achievement:* 124 awards ($2,125,305 total): general academic interests/achievements. *Special achievements/activities:* leadership. ***Tuition waivers:*** Full or partial for employees or children of employees. ***ROTC:*** Army cooperative, Air Force cooperative.

LOANS ***Student loans:*** $2,227,316 (82% need-based, 18% non-need-based). 48% of past graduating class borrowed through all loan programs. *Average indebtedness per student:* $13,207. ***Average need-based loan:*** Freshmen: $2935. Undergraduates: $3507. ***Parent loans:*** $1,662,187 (52% need-based, 48% non-need-based). ***Programs:*** FFEL (Subsidized and Unsubsidized Stafford, PLUS), Perkins, college/university.

WORK-STUDY ***Federal work-study:*** Total amount: $468,295; 299 jobs averaging $1582. ***State or other work-study/employment:*** Total amount: $16,300 (89% need-based, 11% non-need-based). Part-time jobs available.

APPLYING FOR FINANCIAL AID ***Required financial aid forms:*** FAFSA, CSS Financial Aid PROFILE, noncustodial (divorced/separated) parent's statement, business/farm supplement, verification worksheet, federal income tax form(s). ***Financial aid deadline:*** 5/1 (priority: 1/15). ***Notification date:*** 4/1. Students must reply by 5/1.

CONTACT David Levy, Director of Financial Aid, Scripps College, 1030 Columbia Avenue, PMB 1293, Claremont, CA 91711-3948, 909-621-8275 or toll-free 800-770-1333. *Fax:* 909-607-7742. *E-mail:* dlevy@scrippscollege.edu.

SEATTLE PACIFIC UNIVERSITY

Seattle, WA

Tuition & fees: $26,817 **Average undergraduate aid package: $23,708**

ABOUT THE INSTITUTION Independent Free Methodist, coed. ***Awards:*** bachelor's, master's, and doctoral degrees and post-master's certificates. 56 undergraduate majors. ***Total enrollment:*** 3,891. Undergraduates: 3,007. Freshmen: 713. Federal methodology is used as a basis for awarding need-based institutional aid.

UNDERGRADUATE EXPENSES for 2008–09 ***Application fee:*** $45. ***Comprehensive fee:*** $35,271 includes full-time tuition ($26,457), mandatory fees ($360), and room and board ($8454). ***College room only:*** $4569. Room and board charges vary according to board plan and housing facility. ***Part-time tuition:*** $736 per credit. ***Part-time fees:*** $10 per credit. Part-time tuition and fees vary according to course load. ***Payment plan:*** Installment.

FRESHMAN FINANCIAL AID (Fall 2008, est.) 566 applied for aid; of those 78% were deemed to have need. 100% of freshmen with need received aid; of those 9% had need fully met. ***Average percent of need met:*** 84% (excluding resources awarded to replace EFC). ***Average financial aid package:*** $23,883 (excluding resources awarded to replace EFC). 27% of all full-time freshmen had no need and received non-need-based gift aid.

UNDERGRADUATE FINANCIAL AID (Fall 2008, est.) 1,994 applied for aid; of those 82% were deemed to have need. 100% of undergraduates with need received aid; of those 7% had need fully met. ***Average percent of need met:*** 83% (excluding resources awarded to replace EFC). ***Average financial aid package:*** $23,708 (excluding resources awarded to replace EFC). 28% of all full-time undergraduates had no need and received non-need-based gift aid.

GIFT AID (NEED-BASED) ***Total amount:*** $29,023,886 (11% federal, 8% state, 76% institutional, 5% external sources). ***Receiving aid:*** Freshmen: 64% (439); all full-time undergraduates: 60% (1,613). ***Average award:*** Freshmen: $22,030; Undergraduates: $19,480. ***Scholarships, grants, and awards:*** Federal Pell, FSEOG, state, private, college/university gift aid from institutional funds.

GIFT AID (NON-NEED-BASED) ***Total amount:*** $8,373,070 (1% state, 90% institutional, 9% external sources). ***Average award:*** Freshmen: $12,107. Undergraduates: $11,951. ***Scholarships, grants, and awards by category:*** *Academic interests/achievement:* 648 awards ($4,451,499 total): engineering/technologies, general academic interests/achievements. *Creative arts/performance:* 34 awards ($46,817 total): art/fine arts, performing arts. *Special characteristics:* 318 awards ($1,272,020 total): children and siblings of alumni, children of faculty/staff, general special characteristics, international students, relatives of clergy, religious affiliation. ***Tuition waivers:*** Full or partial for employees or children of employees, senior citizens. ***ROTC:*** Army cooperative, Naval cooperative, Air Force cooperative.

LOANS ***Student loans:*** $16,313,086 (85% need-based, 15% non-need-based). 68% of past graduating class borrowed through all loan programs. *Average indebtedness per student:* $23,066. ***Average need-based loan:*** Freshmen: $5238. Undergraduates: $5163. ***Parent loans:*** $3,953,063 (74% need-based, 26% non-need-based). ***Programs:*** FFEL (Subsidized and Unsubsidized Stafford, PLUS), Perkins, Federal Nursing, college/university.

WORK-STUDY ***Federal work-study:*** Total amount: $536,335; 361 jobs averaging $1485. ***State or other work-study/employment:*** Total amount: $769,983 (100% need-based). 313 part-time jobs averaging $2460.

ATHLETIC AWARDS Total amount: $1,503,273 (50% need-based, 50% non-need-based).

APPLYING FOR FINANCIAL AID ***Required financial aid form:*** FAFSA. ***Financial aid deadline (priority):*** 4/1. ***Notification date:*** Continuous. Students must reply by 5/1 or within 4 weeks of notification.

Seattle Pacific University

CONTACT Mr. Jordan Grant, Director of Student Financial Services, Seattle Pacific University, 3307 Third Avenue West, Seattle, WA 98119-1997, 206-281-2469 or toll-free 800-366-3344. *E-mail:* grantj@spu.edu.

SEATTLE UNIVERSITY

Seattle, WA

Tuition & fees: $28,260 **Average undergraduate aid package: $27,246**

ABOUT THE INSTITUTION Independent Roman Catholic, coed. ***Awards:*** bachelor's, master's, doctoral, and first professional degrees and post-bachelor's, post-master's, and first professional certificates. 56 undergraduate majors. ***Total enrollment:*** 7,529. Undergraduates: 4,253. Freshmen: 768. Federal methodology is used as a basis for awarding need-based institutional aid.

UNDERGRADUATE EXPENSES for 2008–09 ***Application fee:*** $45. ***Comprehensive fee:*** $36,600 includes full-time tuition ($28,260) and room and board ($8340). ***College room only:*** $5265. ***Part-time tuition:*** $628 per credit.

FRESHMAN FINANCIAL AID (Fall 2008, est.) 759 applied for aid; of those 72% were deemed to have need. 98% of freshmen with need received aid; of those 18% had need fully met. ***Average percent of need met:*** 80% (excluding resources awarded to replace EFC). ***Average financial aid package:*** $26,609 (excluding resources awarded to replace EFC). 2% of all full-time freshmen had no need and received non-need-based gift aid.

UNDERGRADUATE FINANCIAL AID (Fall 2008, est.) 3,099 applied for aid; of those 80% were deemed to have need. 98% of undergraduates with need received aid; of those 16% had need fully met. ***Average percent of need met:*** 76% (excluding resources awarded to replace EFC). ***Average financial aid package:*** $27,246 (excluding resources awarded to replace EFC). 1% of all full-time undergraduates had no need and received non-need-based gift aid.

GIFT AID (NEED-BASED) ***Total amount:*** $44,634,162 (9% federal, 8% state, 75% institutional, 8% external sources). ***Receiving aid:*** Freshmen: 59% (519); all full-time undergraduates: 59% (2,308). ***Average award:*** Freshmen: $16,421; Undergraduates: $15,275. ***Scholarships, grants, and awards:*** Federal Pell, FSEOG, state, private, college/university gift aid from institutional funds, Federal Nursing.

GIFT AID (NON-NEED-BASED) ***Total amount:*** $2,138,630 (80% federal, 13% institutional, 7% external sources). ***Receiving aid:*** Freshmen: 12% (104). Undergraduates: 61% (2,389). ***Average award:*** Freshmen: $5795. Undergraduates: $5378. ***Scholarships, grants, and awards by category:*** *Academic interests/achievement:* general academic interests/achievements. *Creative arts/performance:* art/fine arts, music, theater/drama. *Special achievements/activities:* leadership. *Special characteristics:* children and siblings of alumni, children of educators, children of faculty/staff, members of minority groups, religious affiliation. ***ROTC:*** Army, Air Force cooperative.

LOANS ***Student loans:*** $23,197,866 (62% need-based, 38% non-need-based). 81% of past graduating class borrowed through all loan programs. *Average indebtedness per student:* $16,002. ***Average need-based loan:*** Freshmen: $3903. Undergraduates: $4610. ***Parent loans:*** $4,914,303 (7% need-based, 93% non-need-based). ***Programs:*** Federal Direct (Subsidized and Unsubsidized Stafford, PLUS), Perkins, Federal Nursing.

WORK-STUDY ***Federal work-study:*** Total amount: $3,080,487; jobs available. ***State or other work-study/employment:*** Total amount: $3,859,065 (100% need-based). Part-time jobs available.

ATHLETIC AWARDS Total amount: $2,322,760 (20% need-based, 80% non-need-based).

APPLYING FOR FINANCIAL AID ***Required financial aid form:*** FAFSA. ***Financial aid deadline (priority):*** 2/1. ***Notification date:*** 3/1. Students must reply by 5/1 or within 2 weeks of notification.

CONTACT Mr. James White, Director of Student Financial Services, Seattle University, Broadway & Madison, Seattle, WA 98122-4460, 206-296-2000 or toll-free 800-542-0833 (in-state), 800-426-7123 (out-of-state). *Fax:* 206-296-5755. *E-mail:* financial-aid@seattleu.edu.

SETON HALL UNIVERSITY

South Orange, NJ

CONTACT Office of Enrollment Services, Seton Hall University, 400 South Orange Avenue, South Orange, NJ 07079, 973-761-9350 or toll-free 800-THE HALL (out-of-state). *Fax:* 973-275-2040. *E-mail:* thehall@shu.edu.

SETON HILL UNIVERSITY

Greensburg, PA

Tuition & fees: $26,002 **Average undergraduate aid package: $21,103**

ABOUT THE INSTITUTION Independent Roman Catholic, coed. ***Awards:*** bachelor's and master's degrees and post-bachelor's and post-master's certificates. 90 undergraduate majors. ***Total enrollment:*** 2,093. Undergraduates: 1,666. Freshmen: 361. Federal methodology is used as a basis for awarding need-based institutional aid.

UNDERGRADUATE EXPENSES for 2008–09 ***Application fee:*** $35. ***Comprehensive fee:*** $34,172 includes full-time tuition ($25,802), mandatory fees ($200), and room and board ($8170). Room and board charges vary according to board plan and housing facility. ***Part-time tuition:*** $690 per credit. ***Part-time fees:*** $100 per term. Part-time tuition and fees vary according to course load. ***Payment plans:*** Installment, deferred payment.

FRESHMAN FINANCIAL AID (Fall 2008, est.) 337 applied for aid; of those 89% were deemed to have need. 100% of freshmen with need received aid; of those 17% had need fully met. ***Average percent of need met:*** 80% (excluding resources awarded to replace EFC). ***Average financial aid package:*** $22,854 (excluding resources awarded to replace EFC). 15% of all full-time freshmen had no need and received non-need-based gift aid.

UNDERGRADUATE FINANCIAL AID (Fall 2008, est.) 1,201 applied for aid; of those 92% were deemed to have need. 99% of undergraduates with need received aid; of those 17% had need fully met. ***Average percent of need met:*** 77% (excluding resources awarded to replace EFC). ***Average financial aid package:*** $21,103 (excluding resources awarded to replace EFC). 13% of all full-time undergraduates had no need and received non-need-based gift aid.

GIFT AID (NEED-BASED) ***Total amount:*** $15,945,746 (13% federal, 12% state, 73% institutional, 2% external sources). ***Receiving aid:*** Freshmen: 81% (299); all full-time undergraduates: 83% (1,085). ***Average award:*** Freshmen: $17,828; Undergraduates: $15,920. ***Scholarships, grants, and awards:*** Federal Pell, FSEOG, state, private, college/university gift aid from institutional funds.

GIFT AID (NON-NEED-BASED) ***Total amount:*** $2,235,983 (1% state, 96% institutional, 3% external sources). ***Receiving aid:*** Freshmen: 9% (34). Undergraduates: 9% (123). ***Average award:*** Freshmen: $15,705. Undergraduates: $15,501. ***Scholarships, grants, and awards by category:*** *Academic interests/achievement:* 524 awards ($4,495,936 total): biological sciences, business, communication, computer science, education, English, foreign languages, general academic interests/achievements, home economics, humanities, mathematics, physical sciences, premedicine, religion/biblical studies, social sciences. *Creative arts/performance:* 50 awards ($91,100 total): applied art and design, art/fine arts, creative writing, journalism/publications, music, performing arts, theater/drama. *Special achievements/activities:* 372 awards ($687,395 total): community service, general special achievements/activities, leadership, religious involvement. *Special characteristics:* 196 awards ($862,124 total): adult students, children and siblings of alumni, children of faculty/staff, children with a deceased or disabled parent, international students, parents of current students, siblings of current students. ***Tuition waivers:*** Full or partial for employees or children of employees. ***ROTC:*** Army cooperative, Air Force cooperative.

LOANS ***Student loans:*** $10,181,355 (76% need-based, 24% non-need-based). 97% of past graduating class borrowed through all loan programs. *Average indebtedness per student:* $27,120. ***Average need-based loan:*** Freshmen: $5133. Undergraduates: $5526. ***Parent loans:*** $1,910,120 (41% need-based, 59% non-need-based). ***Programs:*** FFEL (Subsidized and Unsubsidized Stafford, PLUS), Perkins, college/university, alternative loans.

WORK-STUDY ***Federal work-study:*** Total amount: $645,560; 346 jobs averaging $1236. ***State or other work-study/employment:*** Total amount: $256,777 (7% need-based, 93% non-need-based). 211 part-time jobs averaging $1500.

ATHLETIC AWARDS Total amount: $3,103,487 (65% need-based, 35% non-need-based).

APPLYING FOR FINANCIAL AID ***Required financial aid forms:*** FAFSA, institution's own form, state aid form. ***Financial aid deadline (priority):*** 5/1. ***Notification date:*** Continuous. Students must reply within 2 weeks of notification.

CONTACT Maryann Dudas, Director of Financial Aid, Seton Hill University, Seton Hill Drive, Greensburg, PA 15601, 724-830-1000 or toll-free 800-826-6234. *Fax:* 724-830-1194. *E-mail:* dudas@setonhill.edu.

SEWANEE: THE UNIVERSITY OF THE SOUTH
Sewanee, TN

Tuition & fees: $34,172 **Average undergraduate aid package: $25,169**

ABOUT THE INSTITUTION Independent Episcopal, coed. ***Awards:*** bachelor's, master's, doctoral, and first professional degrees and post-bachelor's, post-master's, and first professional certificates. 41 undergraduate majors. ***Total enrollment:*** 1,562. Undergraduates: 1,483. Freshmen: 410. Both federal and institutional methodology are used as a basis for awarding need-based institutional aid.

UNDERGRADUATE EXPENSES for 2009–10 ***Application fee:*** $45. ***Comprehensive fee:*** $43,932 includes full-time tuition ($33,900), mandatory fees ($272), and room and board ($9760). ***College room only:*** $5080. ***Part-time tuition:*** $1230 per credit hour.

FRESHMAN FINANCIAL AID (Fall 2007) 234 applied for aid; of those 69% were deemed to have need. 99% of freshmen with need received aid; of those 83% had need fully met. ***Average percent of need met:*** 98% (excluding resources awarded to replace EFC). ***Average financial aid package:*** $29,827 (excluding resources awarded to replace EFC). 23% of all full-time freshmen had no need and received non-need-based gift aid.

UNDERGRADUATE FINANCIAL AID (Fall 2007) 749 applied for aid; of those 96% were deemed to have need. 100% of undergraduates with need received aid; of those 81% had need fully met. ***Average percent of need met:*** 97% (excluding resources awarded to replace EFC). ***Average financial aid package:*** $25,169 (excluding resources awarded to replace EFC). 23% of all full-time undergraduates had no need and received non-need-based gift aid.

GIFT AID (NEED-BASED) ***Total amount:*** $13,647,160 (6% federal, 6% state, 84% institutional, 4% external sources). ***Receiving aid:*** Freshmen: 39% (160); all full-time undergraduates: 48% (701). ***Average award:*** Freshmen: $25,676; Undergraduates: $20,536. ***Scholarships, grants, and awards:*** Federal Pell, FSEOG, state, private, college/university gift aid from institutional funds.

GIFT AID (NON-NEED-BASED) ***Total amount:*** $5,862,865 (7% state, 84% institutional, 9% external sources). ***Average award:*** Freshmen: $17,281. Undergraduates: $14,523. ***Scholarships, grants, and awards by category:*** *Academic interests/achievement:* 435 awards ($4,871,775 total): general academic interests/achievements. *Special characteristics:* 168 awards ($460,500 total): children of faculty/staff, ethnic background, members of minority groups, relatives of clergy.

LOANS ***Student loans:*** $2,457,996 (87% need-based, 13% non-need-based). 45% of past graduating class borrowed through all loan programs. *Average indebtedness per student:* $15,885. ***Average need-based loan:*** Freshmen: $3759. Undergraduates: $4177. ***Parent loans:*** $3,117,457 (43% need-based, 57% non-need-based). ***Programs:*** FFEL (Subsidized and Unsubsidized Stafford, PLUS), Perkins, state, college/university, private alternative loans.

WORK-STUDY ***Federal work-study:*** Total amount: $500,930; 350 jobs averaging $1444. ***State or other work-study/employment:*** Total amount: $132,631 (44% need-based, 56% non-need-based). 99 part-time jobs averaging $1423.

APPLYING FOR FINANCIAL AID ***Required financial aid forms:*** FAFSA, institution's own form, Student and/or Parent U.S. Income Tax Returns if applicable. ***Financial aid deadline (priority):*** 3/1. ***Notification date:*** Continuous beginning 3/1. Students must reply by 5/1.

CONTACT Beth A. Cragar, Associate Dean of Admission for Financial Aid, Sewanee: The University of the South, 735 University Avenue, Sewanee, TN 37383-1000, 931-598-1312 or toll-free 800-522-2234. *Fax:* 931-598-3273.

SHASTA BIBLE COLLEGE
Redding, CA

Tuition & fees: $7670 **Average undergraduate aid package: $2582**

ABOUT THE INSTITUTION Independent nondenominational, coed. ***Awards:*** associate, bachelor's, and master's degrees. 3 undergraduate majors. ***Total enrollment:*** 90. Undergraduates: 74. Federal methodology is used as a basis for awarding need-based institutional aid.

UNDERGRADUATE EXPENSES for 2008–09 ***Application fee:*** $35. ***Tuition:*** full-time $7200; part-time $275 per unit. ***Required fees:*** full-time $470; $540 per year. ***Payment plan:*** Installment.

FRESHMAN FINANCIAL AID (Fall 2007) 8 applied for aid; of those 100% were deemed to have need. 100% of freshmen with need received aid. ***Average percent of need met:*** 60% (excluding resources awarded to replace EFC). ***Average financial aid package:*** $2582 (excluding resources awarded to replace EFC). 8% of all full-time freshmen had no need and received non-need-based gift aid.

UNDERGRADUATE FINANCIAL AID (Fall 2007) 40 applied for aid; of those 88% were deemed to have need. 100% of undergraduates with need received aid; of those 9% had need fully met. ***Average percent of need met:*** 60% (excluding resources awarded to replace EFC). ***Average financial aid package:*** $2582 (excluding resources awarded to replace EFC). 3% of all full-time undergraduates had no need and received non-need-based gift aid.

GIFT AID (NEED-BASED) ***Total amount:*** $229,863 (54% federal, 46% state). ***Receiving aid:*** Freshmen: 67% (8); all full-time undergraduates: 38% (30). ***Average award:*** Freshmen: $4050; Undergraduates: $4050. ***Scholarships, grants, and awards:*** Federal Pell, FSEOG, state, private, college/university gift aid from institutional funds.

GIFT AID (NON-NEED-BASED) ***Total amount:*** $65,073 (85% institutional, 15% external sources). ***Receiving aid:*** Undergraduates: 4% (3). ***Average award:*** Freshmen: $1000. Undergraduates: $1000. ***Scholarships, grants, and awards by category:*** *Academic interests/achievement:* 27 awards ($20,598 total): education. *Creative arts/performance:* 10 awards ($5000 total): music. *Special achievements/activities:* general special achievements/activities. *Special characteristics:* 34 awards ($56,071 total): relatives of clergy, veterans. ***Tuition waivers:*** Full or partial for employees or children of employees, senior citizens.

WORK-STUDY ***Federal work-study:*** Total amount: $7371; 12 jobs averaging $1000. ***State or other work-study/employment:*** Total amount: $11,000 (100% non-need-based). 4 part-time jobs averaging $1000.

APPLYING FOR FINANCIAL AID ***Required financial aid forms:*** FAFSA, institution's own form, state aid form. ***Financial aid deadline:*** Continuous. ***Notification date:*** Continuous beginning 7/2. Students must reply within 3 weeks of notification.

CONTACT Connie Barton, Financial Aid Administrator, Shasta Bible College, 2951 Goodwater Avenue, Redding, CA 96002, 530-221-4275 or toll-free 800-800-45BC (in-state), 800-800-6929 (out-of-state). *Fax:* 530-221-6929. *E-mail:* finaid@shasta.edu.

SHAWNEE STATE UNIVERSITY
Portsmouth, OH

ABOUT THE INSTITUTION State-supported, coed. ***Awards:*** associate, bachelor's, and master's degrees. 66 undergraduate majors. ***Total enrollment:*** 3,976. Undergraduates: 3,935. Freshmen: 610.

GIFT AID (NEED-BASED) ***Scholarships, grants, and awards:*** Federal Pell, FSEOG, state, private, college/university gift aid from institutional funds.

GIFT AID (NON-NEED-BASED) ***Scholarships, grants, and awards by category:*** *Academic interests/achievement:* general academic interests/achievements. *Creative arts/performance:* art/fine arts, performing arts. *Special achievements/activities:* memberships. *Special characteristics:* ethnic background, first-generation college students, handicapped students, local/state students, members of minority groups, veterans.

LOANS ***Programs:*** FFEL (Subsidized and Unsubsidized Stafford, PLUS), college/university.

WORK-STUDY ***Federal work-study:*** Total amount: $209,898; 104 jobs averaging $2018.

APPLYING FOR FINANCIAL AID ***Required financial aid forms:*** FAFSA, institution's own form.

CONTACT Barbara Bradbury, Director of Financial Aid, Shawnee State University, 940 Second Street, Portsmouth, OH 45662-4344, 740-351-3245 or toll-free 800-959-2SSU. *E-mail:* bbradbury@shawnee.edu.

SHAW UNIVERSITY
Raleigh, NC

CONTACT Rochelle King, Director of Financial Aid, Shaw University, 118 East South Street, Raleigh, NC 27601-2399, 919-546-8565 or toll-free 800-214-6683. *Fax:* 919-546-8356. *E-mail:* rking@shawu.edu.

SHENANDOAH UNIVERSITY

Winchester, VA

ABOUT THE INSTITUTION Independent United Methodist, coed. ***Awards:*** associate, bachelor's, master's, doctoral, and first professional degrees and post-bachelor's and post-master's certificates. 37 undergraduate majors. ***Total enrollment:*** 3,393. Undergraduates: 1,658. Freshmen: 398.

GIFT AID (NEED-BASED) ***Scholarships, grants, and awards:*** Federal Pell, FSEOG, state, private, college/university gift aid from institutional funds, Federal Nursing.

GIFT AID (NON-NEED-BASED) ***Scholarships, grants, and awards by category:*** *Academic interests/achievement:* business, general academic interests/achievements. *Creative arts/performance:* dance, music, performing arts, theater/drama. *Special characteristics:* children of faculty/staff, local/state students, relatives of clergy, religious affiliation.

LOANS ***Programs:*** Federal Direct (Subsidized and Unsubsidized Stafford, PLUS), Perkins, Federal Nursing, college/university.

APPLYING FOR FINANCIAL AID ***Required financial aid forms:*** FAFSA, state aid form.

CONTACT Nancy Bragg, Director of Financial Aid, Shenandoah University, 1460 University Drive, Winchester, VA 22601-5195, 540-665-4538 or toll-free 800-432-2266. *Fax:* 540-665-4939. *E-mail:* nbragg@su.edu.

SHEPHERD UNIVERSITY

Shepherdstown, WV

Tuition & fees (WV res): $4898 **Average undergraduate aid package: $10,628**

ABOUT THE INSTITUTION State-supported, coed. ***Awards:*** bachelor's and master's degrees. 25 undergraduate majors. ***Total enrollment:*** 4,185. Undergraduates: 4,044. Freshmen: 707. Federal methodology is used as a basis for awarding need-based institutional aid.

UNDERGRADUATE EXPENSES for 2008–09 ***Application fee:*** $45. ***Tuition, state resident:*** full-time $4898; part-time $200 per credit hour. ***Tuition, nonresident:*** full-time $12,812; part-time $530 per credit hour. Full-time tuition and fees vary according to program and reciprocity agreements. Part-time tuition and fees vary according to program. ***College room and board:*** $6938. Room and board charges vary according to board plan and housing facility. ***Payment plan:*** Installment.

FRESHMAN FINANCIAL AID (Fall 2008, est.) 621 applied for aid; of those 59% were deemed to have need. 97% of freshmen with need received aid; of those 28% had need fully met. ***Average percent of need met:*** 91% (excluding resources awarded to replace EFC). ***Average financial aid package:*** $9828 (excluding resources awarded to replace EFC). 25% of all full-time freshmen had no need and received non-need-based gift aid.

UNDERGRADUATE FINANCIAL AID (Fall 2008, est.) 2,636 applied for aid; of those 61% were deemed to have need. 98% of undergraduates with need received aid; of those 29% had need fully met. ***Average percent of need met:*** 85% (excluding resources awarded to replace EFC). ***Average financial aid package:*** $10,628 (excluding resources awarded to replace EFC). 22% of all full-time undergraduates had no need and received non-need-based gift aid.

GIFT AID (NEED-BASED) ***Total amount:*** $4,555,806 (70% federal, 26% state, 4% institutional). ***Receiving aid:*** Freshmen: 31% (219); all full-time undergraduates: 31% (992). ***Average award:*** Freshmen: $4306; Undergraduates: $4296. ***Scholarships, grants, and awards:*** Federal Pell, FSEOG, state, private, college/university gift aid from institutional funds.

GIFT AID (NON-NEED-BASED) ***Total amount:*** $4,088,268 (39% state, 53% institutional, 8% external sources). ***Receiving aid:*** Freshmen: 20% (138). Undergraduates: 12% (379). ***Average award:*** Freshmen: $8197. Undergraduates: $8842. ***Scholarships, grants, and awards by category:*** *Academic interests/achievement:* 331 awards ($895,795 total): biological sciences, business, communication, computer science, education, engineering/technologies, English, general academic interests/achievements, health fields, home economics, humanities, mathematics, physical sciences, premedicine, social sciences. *Creative arts/performance:* 48 awards ($224,306 total): applied art and design, art/fine arts, music, performing arts, theater/drama. *Special achievements/activities:* 18 awards ($19,050 total): leadership. *Special characteristics:* 147 awards ($510,119 total): ethnic background, handicapped students, local/state students, members of minority groups, out-of-state students, previous college experience. ***Tuition waivers:*** Full or partial for minority students, senior citizens. ***ROTC:*** Air Force cooperative.

LOANS ***Student loans:*** $11,564,636 (47% need-based, 53% non-need-based). 65% of past graduating class borrowed through all loan programs. *Average indebtedness per student:* $18,271. ***Average need-based loan:*** Freshmen: $3383. Undergraduates: $4030. ***Parent loans:*** $2,182,901 (100% non-need-based). ***Programs:*** Federal Direct (Subsidized and Unsubsidized Stafford, PLUS), Perkins.

WORK-STUDY ***Federal work-study:*** Total amount: $267,755; 166 jobs averaging $1751. ***State or other work-study/employment:*** Total amount: $937,023 (100% non-need-based). 514 part-time jobs averaging $1700.

ATHLETIC AWARDS Total amount: $968,179 (100% non-need-based).

APPLYING FOR FINANCIAL AID ***Required financial aid forms:*** FAFSA, state aid form. ***Financial aid deadline (priority):*** 3/1. ***Notification date:*** Continuous beginning 3/30. Students must reply within 2 weeks of notification.

CONTACT Sandra Oerly-Bennett, Financial Aid Office, Shepherd University, PO Box 5000, Shepherdstown, WV 25443-5000, 304-876-5470 or toll-free 800-344-5231. *Fax:* 304-876-5238. *E-mail:* faoweb@shepherd.edu.

SHIMER COLLEGE

Chicago, IL

Tuition & fees: $23,750 **Average undergraduate aid package: $11,993**

ABOUT THE INSTITUTION Independent, coed. ***Awards:*** bachelor's degrees. 7 undergraduate majors. ***Total enrollment:*** 100. Undergraduates: 100. Freshmen: 27. Both federal and institutional methodology are used as a basis for awarding need-based institutional aid.

UNDERGRADUATE EXPENSES for 2008–09 ***Application fee:*** $25. ***Comprehensive fee:*** $34,950 includes full-time tuition ($23,750) and room and board ($11,200). ***College room only:*** $6900. Full-time tuition and fees vary according to class time and course load. Room and board charges vary according to housing facility. ***Part-time tuition:*** $850 per credit hour. ***Part-time fees:*** $1100 per year. Part-time tuition and fees vary according to class time and course load. ***Payment plan:*** Installment.

FRESHMAN FINANCIAL AID (Fall 2008, est.) 24 applied for aid; of those 79% were deemed to have need. 100% of freshmen with need received aid. ***Average financial aid package:*** $17,911 (excluding resources awarded to replace EFC). 19% of all full-time freshmen had no need and received non-need-based gift aid.

UNDERGRADUATE FINANCIAL AID (Fall 2008, est.) 74 applied for aid; of those 88% were deemed to have need. 100% of undergraduates with need received aid. ***Average financial aid package:*** $11,993 (excluding resources awarded to replace EFC). 9% of all full-time undergraduates had no need and received non-need-based gift aid.

GIFT AID (NEED-BASED) ***Total amount:*** $877,000 (19% federal, 12% state, 68% institutional, 1% external sources). ***Receiving aid:*** Freshmen: 73% (19); all full-time undergraduates: 83% (65). ***Average award:*** Freshmen: $8843; Undergraduates: $7971. ***Scholarships, grants, and awards:*** Federal Pell, FSEOG, state, private, college/university gift aid from institutional funds.

GIFT AID (NON-NEED-BASED) ***Average award:*** Freshmen: $3900. Undergraduates: $4000. ***Scholarships, grants, and awards by category:*** *Academic interests/achievement:* 4 awards ($72,000 total): general academic interests/achievements. *Special characteristics:* 2 awards ($2000 total): children and siblings of alumni. ***Tuition waivers:*** Full or partial for employees or children of employees, adult students, senior citizens.

LOANS ***Student loans:*** $583,233 (100% need-based). ***Average need-based loan:*** Freshmen: $3500. Undergraduates: $5159. ***Parent loans:*** $217,610 (100% need-based). ***Programs:*** FFEL (Subsidized and Unsubsidized Stafford, PLUS), Perkins.

WORK-STUDY ***Federal work-study:*** Total amount: $85,900; 25 jobs averaging $1750. ***State or other work-study/employment:*** 5 part-time jobs averaging $1750.

APPLYING FOR FINANCIAL AID ***Required financial aid forms:*** FAFSA, institution's own form. ***Financial aid deadline:*** Continuous. ***Notification date:*** Continuous beginning 4/1. Students must reply by 5/1 or within 3 weeks of notification.

CONTACT Janet Henthorn, Director of Financial Aid, Shimer College, 3424 South State Street, Chicago, IL 60616, 312-235-3507 or toll-free 800-215-7173. *Fax:* 312-235-3502. *E-mail:* j.henthorn@shimer.edu.

SHIPPENSBURG UNIVERSITY OF PENNSYLVANIA
Shippensburg, PA

Tuition & fees (PA res): $7099 **Average undergraduate aid package: $7043**

ABOUT THE INSTITUTION State-supported, coed. ***Awards:*** bachelor's and master's degrees and post-bachelor's and post-master's certificates. 33 undergraduate majors. ***Total enrollment:*** 7,942. Undergraduates: 6,733. Freshmen: 1,724. Federal methodology is used as a basis for awarding need-based institutional aid.

UNDERGRADUATE EXPENSES for 2008–09 ***Application fee:*** $30. ***Tuition, state resident:*** full-time $5358; part-time $223 per credit hour. ***Tuition, nonresident:*** full-time $13,396; part-time $558 per credit hour. ***Required fees:*** full-time $1741; $168 per course or $44 per term. ***College room and board:*** $6604; ***Room only:*** $3640. Room and board charges vary according to board plan and housing facility. ***Payment plan:*** Installment.

FRESHMAN FINANCIAL AID (Fall 2008, est.) 1,476 applied for aid; of those 65% were deemed to have need. 94% of freshmen with need received aid; of those 18% had need fully met. ***Average percent of need met:*** 68% (excluding resources awarded to replace EFC). ***Average financial aid package:*** $6865 (excluding resources awarded to replace EFC). 9% of all full-time freshmen had no need and received non-need-based gift aid.

UNDERGRADUATE FINANCIAL AID (Fall 2008, est.) 4,837 applied for aid; of those 69% were deemed to have need. 94% of undergraduates with need received aid; of those 20% had need fully met. ***Average percent of need met:*** 68% (excluding resources awarded to replace EFC). ***Average financial aid package:*** $7043 (excluding resources awarded to replace EFC). 8% of all full-time undergraduates had no need and received non-need-based gift aid.

GIFT AID (NEED-BASED) ***Total amount:*** $10,521,749 (45% federal, 43% state, 6% institutional, 6% external sources). ***Receiving aid:*** Freshmen: 39% (667); all full-time undergraduates: 35% (2,215). ***Average award:*** Freshmen: $5264; Undergraduates: $4949. ***Scholarships, grants, and awards:*** Federal Pell, FSEOG, state, private, college/university gift aid from institutional funds, Academic Competitiveness Grant, National Smart Grant.

GIFT AID (NON-NEED-BASED) ***Total amount:*** $1,005,244 (5% state, 40% institutional, 55% external sources). ***Receiving aid:*** Freshmen: 4% (61). Undergraduates: 3% (188). ***Average award:*** Freshmen: $2985. Undergraduates: $3427. ***Scholarships, grants, and awards by category:*** *Academic interests/achievement:* 376 awards ($504,989 total): biological sciences, business, communication, computer science, education, English, foreign languages, general academic interests/achievements, humanities, mathematics, military science, physical sciences, social sciences. *Creative arts/performance:* 4 awards ($3550 total): art/fine arts, music, theater/drama. *Special achievements/activities:* 297 awards ($569,694 total): community service, general special achievements/activities, leadership. *Special characteristics:* 55 awards ($140,540 total): children and siblings of alumni, general special characteristics, handicapped students, local/state students. ***Tuition waivers:*** Full or partial for employees or children of employees, senior citizens. ***ROTC:*** Army.

LOANS ***Student loans:*** $30,592,385 (53% need-based, 47% non-need-based). 72% of past graduating class borrowed through all loan programs. *Average indebtedness per student:* $20,148. ***Average need-based loan:*** Freshmen: $3244. Undergraduates: $3792. ***Parent loans:*** $3,661,798 (11% need-based, 89% non-need-based). ***Programs:*** FFEL (Subsidized and Unsubsidized Stafford, PLUS), Perkins, alternative loans.

WORK-STUDY ***Federal work-study:*** Total amount: $286,754; 184 jobs averaging $1558. ***State or other work-study/employment:*** Total amount: $438,816 (21% need-based, 79% non-need-based). 258 part-time jobs averaging $1701.

ATHLETIC AWARDS Total amount: $571,961 (45% need-based, 55% non-need-based).

APPLYING FOR FINANCIAL AID ***Required financial aid form:*** FAFSA. ***Financial aid deadline (priority):*** 3/15. ***Notification date:*** Continuous. Students must reply within 2 weeks of notification.

CONTACT Mr. Peter D'Annibale, Director of Financial Aid and Scholarships, Shippensburg University of Pennsylvania, 1871 Old Main Drive, Shippensburg, PA 17257-2299, 717-477-1131 or toll-free 800-822-8028 (in-state). *Fax:* 717-477-4028. *E-mail:* finaid@ship.edu.

SHORTER COLLEGE
Rome, GA

Tuition & fees: $15,770 **Average undergraduate aid package: $14,180**

ABOUT THE INSTITUTION Independent Baptist, coed. ***Awards:*** bachelor's and master's degrees. 39 undergraduate majors. ***Total enrollment:*** 1,136. Undergraduates: 1,136. Freshmen: 330. Federal methodology is used as a basis for awarding need-based institutional aid.

UNDERGRADUATE EXPENSES for 2008–09 ***Application fee:*** $25. ***Comprehensive fee:*** $23,170 includes full-time tuition ($15,440), mandatory fees ($330), and room and board ($7400). ***College room only:*** $4000. Full-time tuition and fees vary according to course load. Room and board charges vary according to board plan and housing facility. ***Part-time tuition:*** $420 per hour. ***Payment plan:*** Installment.

FRESHMAN FINANCIAL AID (Fall 2008, est.) 283 applied for aid; of those 83% were deemed to have need. 100% of freshmen with need received aid; of those 31% had need fully met. ***Average percent of need met:*** 75% (excluding resources awarded to replace EFC). ***Average financial aid package:*** $14,045 (excluding resources awarded to replace EFC). 14% of all full-time freshmen had no need and received non-need-based gift aid.

UNDERGRADUATE FINANCIAL AID (Fall 2008, est.) 809 applied for aid; of those 83% were deemed to have need. 100% of undergraduates with need received aid; of those 30% had need fully met. ***Average percent of need met:*** 74% (excluding resources awarded to replace EFC). ***Average financial aid package:*** $14,180 (excluding resources awarded to replace EFC). 14% of all full-time undergraduates had no need and received non-need-based gift aid.

GIFT AID (NEED-BASED) ***Total amount:*** $6,300,876 (25% federal, 26% state, 44% institutional, 5% external sources). ***Receiving aid:*** Freshmen: 71% (235); all full-time undergraduates: 61% (662). ***Average award:*** Freshmen: $11,934; Undergraduates: $11,682. ***Scholarships, grants, and awards:*** Federal Pell, FSEOG, state, private, college/university gift aid from institutional funds.

GIFT AID (NON-NEED-BASED) ***Total amount:*** $2,478,780 (53% state, 41% institutional, 6% external sources). ***Receiving aid:*** Freshmen: 19% (64). Undergraduates: 16% (171). ***Average award:*** Freshmen: $5585. Undergraduates: $5350. ***Scholarships, grants, and awards by category:*** *Academic interests/achievement:* 194 awards ($1,335,998 total): English, foreign languages, general academic interests/achievements, religion/biblical studies. *Creative arts/performance:* 150 awards ($272,410 total): art/fine arts, music, theater/drama. *Special achievements/activities:* 61 awards ($206,896 total): cheerleading/drum major, religious involvement. *Special characteristics:* 235 awards ($156,068 total): children of faculty/staff, children of union members/company employees, local/state students, out-of-state students, religious affiliation, siblings of current students. ***Tuition waivers:*** Full or partial for employees or children of employees, senior citizens.

LOANS ***Student loans:*** $4,135,650 (69% need-based, 31% non-need-based). 87% of past graduating class borrowed through all loan programs. *Average indebtedness per student:* $23,455. ***Average need-based loan:*** Freshmen: $3013. Undergraduates: $3338. ***Parent loans:*** $1,662,957 (32% need-based, 68% non-need-based). ***Programs:*** FFEL (Subsidized and Unsubsidized Stafford, PLUS), Perkins.

WORK-STUDY ***Federal work-study:*** Total amount: $218,143; 153 jobs averaging $1915. ***State or other work-study/employment:*** Total amount: $229,362 (10% need-based, 90% non-need-based). 120 part-time jobs averaging $1806.

ATHLETIC AWARDS Total amount: $3,590,852 (48% need-based, 52% non-need-based).

APPLYING FOR FINANCIAL AID ***Required financial aid forms:*** FAFSA, institution's own form, state aid form. ***Financial aid deadline (priority):*** 4/1. ***Notification date:*** Continuous beginning 4/1. Students must reply within 2 weeks of notification.

CONTACT Tara Jones, Director of Financial Aid, Shorter College, 315 Shorter Avenue, Rome, GA 30165, 706-233-7227 or toll-free 800-868-6980. *Fax:* 706-233-7314. *E-mail:* tjones@shorter.edu.

SH'OR YOSHUV RABBINICAL COLLEGE
Lawrence, NY

CONTACT Office of Financial Aid, Sh'or Yoshuv Rabbinical College, 1526 Central Avenue, Far Rockaway, NY 11691-4002, 718-327-2048.

SIENA COLLEGE

Loudonville, NY

CONTACT Mary K. Lawyer, Assistant Vice President for Financial Aid, Siena College, 515 Loudon Road, Loudonville, NY 12211-1462, 518-783-2427 or toll-free 888-AT-SIENA. *Fax:* 518-783-2410. *E-mail:* aid@siena.edu.

SIENA HEIGHTS UNIVERSITY

Adrian, MI

CONTACT Office of Financial Aid, Siena Heights University, 1247 East Siena Heights Drive, Adrian, MI 49221, 517-264-7130 or toll-free 800-521-0009.

SIERRA NEVADA COLLEGE

Incline Village, NV

CONTACT Dorothy Caruso, Director of Financial Aid, Sierra Nevada College, 999 Tahoe Boulevard, Incline Village, NV 89451, 775-831-1314 Ext. 4066. *Fax:* 775-831-1347. *E-mail:* dcaruso@sierranevada.edu.

SILICON VALLEY UNIVERSITY

San Jose, CA

CONTACT Financial Aid Office, Silicon Valley University, 2160 Lundy Avenue, Suite 110, San Jose, CA 95131, 408-435-8989.

SILVER LAKE COLLEGE

Manitowoc, WI

Tuition & fees: $20,560 **Average undergraduate aid package: $16,855**

ABOUT THE INSTITUTION Independent Roman Catholic, coed, primarily women. ***Awards:*** associate, bachelor's, and master's degrees and post-bachelor's certificates. 20 undergraduate majors. ***Total enrollment:*** 853. Undergraduates: 592. Freshmen: 33. Federal methodology is used as a basis for awarding need-based institutional aid.

UNDERGRADUATE EXPENSES for 2009–10 ***Application fee:*** $35. ***Comprehensive fee:*** $26,960 includes full-time tuition ($20,340), mandatory fees ($220), and room and board ($6400). ***College room only:*** $4900. ***Part-time tuition:*** $625 per credit. ***Part-time fees:*** $60 per term.

FRESHMAN FINANCIAL AID (Fall 2008, est.) 32 applied for aid; of those 88% were deemed to have need. 100% of freshmen with need received aid; of those 21% had need fully met. ***Average percent of need met:*** 88% (excluding resources awarded to replace EFC). ***Average financial aid package:*** $18,735 (excluding resources awarded to replace EFC). 15% of all full-time freshmen had no need and received non-need-based gift aid.

UNDERGRADUATE FINANCIAL AID (Fall 2008, est.) 157 applied for aid; of those 92% were deemed to have need. 100% of undergraduates with need received aid; of those 19% had need fully met. ***Average percent of need met:*** 76% (excluding resources awarded to replace EFC). ***Average financial aid package:*** $16,855 (excluding resources awarded to replace EFC). 10% of all full-time undergraduates had no need and received non-need-based gift aid.

GIFT AID (NEED-BASED) ***Total amount:*** $2,041,724 (32% federal, 16% state, 47% institutional, 5% external sources). ***Receiving aid:*** Freshmen: 76% (25); all full-time undergraduates: 69% (129). ***Average award:*** Freshmen: $7259; Undergraduates: $7587. ***Scholarships, grants, and awards:*** Federal Pell, FSEOG, state, private, college/university gift aid from institutional funds.

GIFT AID (NON-NEED-BASED) ***Total amount:*** $78,580 (6% federal, 88% institutional, 6% external sources). ***Receiving aid:*** Freshmen: 3% (1). Undergraduates: 6% (12). ***Average award:*** Freshmen: $4000. Undergraduates: $6223. ***Scholarships, grants, and awards by category:*** *Academic interests/achievement:* 83 awards ($296,036 total): English, general academic interests/achievements. *Creative arts/performance:* 38 awards ($43,120 total): applied art and design, art/fine arts, music. *Special achievements/activities:* 46 awards ($43,000 total): religious involvement. *Special characteristics:* 22 awards ($36,104 total): children and siblings of alumni, international students, local/state students.

LOANS ***Student loans:*** $2,416,709 (93% need-based, 7% non-need-based). 71% of past graduating class borrowed through all loan programs. *Average indebtedness per student:* $21,723. ***Average need-based loan:*** Freshmen: $3313. Undergraduates: $4216. ***Parent loans:*** $145,979 (61% need-based, 39% non-need-based). ***Programs:*** FFEL (Subsidized and Unsubsidized Stafford, PLUS), state.

WORK-STUDY ***Federal work-study:*** Total amount: $167,671; 81 jobs averaging $2015.

ATHLETIC AWARDS Total amount: $86,500 (93% need-based, 7% non-need-based).

APPLYING FOR FINANCIAL AID ***Required financial aid form:*** FAFSA. ***Financial aid deadline (priority):*** 3/15. ***Notification date:*** Continuous beginning 3/15.

CONTACT Ms. Michelle Leider, Associate Director of Financial Aid, Silver Lake College, 2406 South Alverno Road, Manitowoc, WI 54220-9319, 920-686-6122 or toll-free 800-236-4752 Ext. 175 (in-state). *Fax:* 920-684-7082. *E-mail:* financialaid@silver.sl.edu.

SIMMONS COLLEGE

Boston, MA

Tuition & fees: $30,000 **Average undergraduate aid package: $19,758**

ABOUT THE INSTITUTION Independent, undergraduate: women only; graduate: coed. ***Awards:*** bachelor's, master's, and doctoral degrees and post-bachelor's and post-master's certificates. 50 undergraduate majors. ***Total enrollment:*** 4,933. Undergraduates: 2,060. Freshmen: 391. Federal methodology is used as a basis for awarding need-based institutional aid.

UNDERGRADUATE EXPENSES for 2008–09 ***Application fee:*** $55. ***Comprehensive fee:*** $41,500 includes full-time tuition ($29,120), mandatory fees ($880), and room and board ($11,500). Full-time tuition and fees vary according to course load and program. Room and board charges vary according to board plan. ***Part-time tuition:*** $910 per credit. Part-time tuition and fees vary according to course load and program. ***Payment plan:*** Installment.

FRESHMAN FINANCIAL AID (Fall 2008, est.) 321 applied for aid; of those 86% were deemed to have need. 100% of freshmen with need received aid; of those 12% had need fully met. ***Average percent of need met:*** 63% (excluding resources awarded to replace EFC). ***Average financial aid package:*** $18,344 (excluding resources awarded to replace EFC). 22% of all full-time freshmen had no need and received non-need-based gift aid.

UNDERGRADUATE FINANCIAL AID (Fall 2008, est.) 1,375 applied for aid; of those 91% were deemed to have need. 100% of undergraduates with need received aid; of those 9% had need fully met. ***Average percent of need met:*** 64% (excluding resources awarded to replace EFC). ***Average financial aid package:*** $19,758 (excluding resources awarded to replace EFC). 20% of all full-time undergraduates had no need and received non-need-based gift aid.

GIFT AID (NEED-BASED) ***Total amount:*** $17,322,198 (10% federal, 3% state, 83% institutional, 4% external sources). ***Receiving aid:*** Freshmen: 69% (273); all full-time undergraduates: 66% (1,212). ***Average award:*** Freshmen: $13,369; Undergraduates: $13,781. ***Scholarships, grants, and awards:*** Federal Pell, FSEOG, state, private, college/university gift aid from institutional funds.

GIFT AID (NON-NEED-BASED) ***Total amount:*** $3,606,564 (99% institutional, 1% external sources). ***Receiving aid:*** Freshmen: 5% (19). Undergraduates: 3% (48). ***Average award:*** Freshmen: $8398. Undergraduates: $9289. ***Scholarships, grants, and awards by category:*** *Academic interests/achievement:* 85 awards: general academic interests/achievements. *Special achievements/activities:* 750 awards ($5,804,080 total): community service, general special achievements/activities. *Special characteristics:* 62 awards ($128,000 total): children and siblings of alumni, general special characteristics. ***Tuition waivers:*** Full or partial for employees or children of employees. ***ROTC:*** Army cooperative.

LOANS ***Student loans:*** $19,228,082 (30% need-based, 70% non-need-based). 78% of past graduating class borrowed through all loan programs. *Average indebtedness per student:* $42,174. ***Average need-based loan:*** Freshmen: $3863. Undergraduates: $4922. ***Parent loans:*** $3,623,883 (100% non-need-based). ***Programs:*** FFEL (Subsidized and Unsubsidized Stafford, PLUS), Perkins, state, college/university.

WORK-STUDY ***Federal work-study:*** Total amount: $2,632,229; 794 jobs averaging $2379.

APPLYING FOR FINANCIAL AID ***Required financial aid forms:*** FAFSA, institution's own form. ***Financial aid deadline (priority):*** 2/15. ***Notification date:*** Continuous beginning 3/15. Students must reply by 5/1 or within 4 weeks of notification.

CONTACT Diane M. Hallisey, Director of Student Financial Services, Simmons College, 300 The Fenway, Boston, MA 02115, 617-521-2001 or toll-free 800-345-8468 (out-of-state). *Fax:* 617-521-3195. *E-mail:* hallisey@simmons.edu.

SIMPSON COLLEGE

Indianola, IA

Tuition & fees: $24,771 **Average undergraduate aid package: $23,774**

ABOUT THE INSTITUTION Independent United Methodist, coed. ***Awards:*** bachelor's and master's degrees and post-bachelor's certificates. 44 undergraduate majors. ***Total enrollment:*** 2,054. Undergraduates: 2,035. Freshmen: 389. Federal methodology is used as a basis for awarding need-based institutional aid.

UNDERGRADUATE EXPENSES for 2008–09 ***One-time required fee:*** $200. ***Comprehensive fee:*** $31,759 includes full-time tuition ($24,414), mandatory fees ($357), and room and board ($6988). ***College room only:*** $3354. Room and board charges vary according to board plan and housing facility. ***Part-time tuition:*** $275 per credit hour. Part-time tuition and fees vary according to class time and course load. ***Payment plan:*** Installment.

FRESHMAN FINANCIAL AID (Fall 2008, est.) 384 applied for aid; of those 84% were deemed to have need. 100% of freshmen with need received aid; of those 29% had need fully met. ***Average percent of need met:*** 93% (excluding resources awarded to replace EFC). ***Average financial aid package:*** $24,914 (excluding resources awarded to replace EFC). 16% of all full-time freshmen had no need and received non-need-based gift aid.

UNDERGRADUATE FINANCIAL AID (Fall 2008, est.) 1,466 applied for aid; of those 85% were deemed to have need. 100% of undergraduates with need received aid; of those 27% had need fully met. ***Average percent of need met:*** 90% (excluding resources awarded to replace EFC). ***Average financial aid package:*** $23,774 (excluding resources awarded to replace EFC). 14% of all full-time undergraduates had no need and received non-need-based gift aid.

GIFT AID (NEED-BASED) ***Total amount:*** $20,232,693 (9% federal, 16% state, 72% institutional, 3% external sources). ***Receiving aid:*** Freshmen: 84% (322); all full-time undergraduates: 85% (1,249). ***Average award:*** Freshmen: $17,812; Undergraduates: $15,842. ***Scholarships, grants, and awards:*** Federal Pell, FSEOG, state, private, college/university gift aid from institutional funds.

GIFT AID (NON-NEED-BASED) ***Total amount:*** $3,297,478 (1% federal, 1% state, 92% institutional, 6% external sources). ***Receiving aid:*** Freshmen: 16% (61). Undergraduates: 13% (184). ***Average award:*** Freshmen: $11,987. Undergraduates: $11,370. ***Scholarships, grants, and awards by category:*** *Academic interests/achievement:* $7,276,163 total: general academic interests/achievements. *Creative arts/performance:* $660,574 total: art/fine arts, music, theater/drama. *Special achievements/activities:* $255,063 total: community service, leadership, religious involvement. *Special characteristics:* $2,108,206 total: adult students, children and siblings of alumni, children of educators, children of faculty/staff, ethnic background, international students, members of minority groups, relatives of clergy, religious affiliation, siblings of current students, twins. ***Tuition waivers:*** Full or partial for employees or children of employees.

LOANS ***Student loans:*** $12,946,484 (62% need-based, 38% non-need-based). 92% of past graduating class borrowed through all loan programs. *Average indebtedness per student:* $31,115. ***Average need-based loan:*** Freshmen: $3052. Undergraduates: $3745. ***Parent loans:*** $1,870,808 (22% need-based, 78% non-need-based). ***Programs:*** FFEL (Subsidized and Unsubsidized Stafford, PLUS), Perkins, state, college/university, alternative loans.

WORK-STUDY ***Federal work-study:*** Total amount: $262,467; 395 jobs averaging $761. ***State or other work-study/employment:*** Total amount: $460,769 (100% non-need-based). 777 part-time jobs averaging $886.

APPLYING FOR FINANCIAL AID ***Required financial aid form:*** FAFSA. ***Financial aid deadline:*** Continuous. ***Notification date:*** Continuous beginning 3/15. Students must reply by 5/1 or within 3 weeks of notification.

CONTACT Tracie Pavon, Assistant Vice President of Financial Aid, Simpson College, 701 North C Street, Indianola, IA 50125-1297, 515-961-1630 Ext. 1596 or toll-free 800-362-2454 (in-state), 800-362-2454 Ext. 1624 (out-of-state). *Fax:* 515-961-1300. *E-mail:* tracie.pavon@simpson.edu.

SIMPSON UNIVERSITY

Redding, CA

Tuition & fees: $20,400 **Average undergraduate aid package: $7750**

ABOUT THE INSTITUTION Independent religious, coed. ***Awards:*** associate, bachelor's, and master's degrees. 19 undergraduate majors. ***Total enrollment:*** 1,147. Undergraduates: 936. Freshmen: 164. Federal methodology is used as a basis for awarding need-based institutional aid.

UNDERGRADUATE EXPENSES for 2009–10 ***Application fee:*** $40. ***Comprehensive fee:*** $27,300 includes full-time tuition ($20,400) and room and board ($6900). ***Part-time tuition:*** $850 per unit.

FRESHMAN FINANCIAL AID (Fall 2008, est.) 143 applied for aid; of those 99% were deemed to have need. 100% of freshmen with need received aid; of those 23% had need fully met. ***Average percent of need met:*** 55% (excluding resources awarded to replace EFC). ***Average financial aid package:*** $9912 (excluding resources awarded to replace EFC). 13% of all full-time freshmen had no need and received non-need-based gift aid.

UNDERGRADUATE FINANCIAL AID (Fall 2008, est.) 814 applied for aid; of those 98% were deemed to have need. 100% of undergraduates with need received aid; of those 14% had need fully met. ***Average percent of need met:*** 45% (excluding resources awarded to replace EFC). ***Average financial aid package:*** $7750 (excluding resources awarded to replace EFC).

GIFT AID (NEED-BASED) ***Total amount:*** $4,056,275 (30% federal, 59% state, 10% institutional, 1% external sources). ***Receiving aid:*** Freshmen: 87% (141); all full-time undergraduates: 78% (651). ***Average award:*** Freshmen: $10,240; Undergraduates: $8514. ***Scholarships, grants, and awards:*** Federal Pell, FSEOG, state, private, college/university gift aid from institutional funds.

GIFT AID (NON-NEED-BASED) ***Total amount:*** $3,449,714 (97% institutional, 3% external sources). ***Receiving aid:*** Freshmen: 87% (141). Undergraduates: 79% (659). ***Average award:*** Freshmen: $4000. Undergraduates: $2000. ***Scholarships, grants, and awards by category:*** *Academic interests/achievement:* general academic interests/achievements. *Creative arts/performance:* music. *Special achievements/activities:* leadership, religious involvement. *Special characteristics:* children of faculty/staff, general special characteristics, members of minority groups, out-of-state students, relatives of clergy, religious affiliation, siblings of current students, spouses of current students.

LOANS ***Student loans:*** $5,217,413 (59% need-based, 41% non-need-based). 89% of past graduating class borrowed through all loan programs. *Average indebtedness per student:* $17,940. ***Average need-based loan:*** Freshmen: $2625. Undergraduates: $4200. ***Parent loans:*** $1,700,536 (100% non-need-based). ***Programs:*** FFEL (Subsidized and Unsubsidized Stafford, PLUS), Perkins, alternative loans.

WORK-STUDY ***Federal work-study:*** Total amount: $109,800; jobs available.

ATHLETIC AWARDS Total amount: $149,908 (100% non-need-based).

APPLYING FOR FINANCIAL AID ***Required financial aid forms:*** FAFSA, institution's own form, if selected for verification, additional forms such as income tax forms may be required. ***Financial aid deadline (priority):*** 3/2. ***Notification date:*** Continuous beginning 3/16. Students must reply within 3 weeks of notification.

CONTACT Melissa Hudson, Assistant Director of Student Financial Services, Simpson University, 2211 College View Drive, Redding, CA 96003-8606, 530-224-5600 or toll-free 800-598-2493. *Fax:* 530-226-4870. *E-mail:* financialaid@simpsonuniversity.edu.

SINTE GLESKA UNIVERSITY

Mission, SD

CONTACT Office of Financial Aid, Sinte Gleska University, PO Box 490, Rosebud, SD 57570-0490, 605-747-4258. *Fax:* 605-747-2098.

SKIDMORE COLLEGE

Saratoga Springs, NY

Tuition & fees: $38,888 **Average undergraduate aid package: $33,195**

ABOUT THE INSTITUTION Independent, coed. ***Awards:*** bachelor's and master's degrees. 43 undergraduate majors. ***Total enrollment:*** 2,777. Undergraduates: 2,717. Freshmen: 652. Both federal and institutional methodology are used as a basis for awarding need-based institutional aid.

UNDERGRADUATE EXPENSES for 2008–09 ***Application fee:*** $60. ***Comprehensive fee:*** $49,266 includes full-time tuition ($38,114), mandatory fees ($774), and room and board ($10,378). ***College room only:*** $6136. Full-time tuition and fees vary according to course load. Room and board charges vary according to board plan and housing facility. ***Part-time tuition:*** $1270 per credit hour. ***Part-time fees:*** $25 per term. Part-time tuition and fees vary according to course load. ***Payment plans:*** Tuition prepayment, installment.

FRESHMAN FINANCIAL AID (Fall 2008, est.) 350 applied for aid; of those 81% were deemed to have need. 100% of freshmen with need received aid; of those 86% had need fully met. ***Average percent of need met:*** 85% (excluding resources awarded to replace EFC). ***Average financial aid package:*** $31,770 (excluding resources awarded to replace EFC). 1% of all full-time freshmen had no need and received non-need-based gift aid.

UNDERGRADUATE FINANCIAL AID (Fall 2008, est.) 1,243 applied for aid; of those 87% were deemed to have need. 100% of undergraduates with need received aid; of those 87% had need fully met. ***Average percent of need met:*** 88% (excluding resources awarded to replace EFC). ***Average financial aid package:*** $33,195 (excluding resources awarded to replace EFC). 1% of all full-time undergraduates had no need and received non-need-based gift aid.

GIFT AID (NEED-BASED) ***Total amount:*** $29,950,000 (7% federal, 5% state, 88% institutional). ***Receiving aid:*** Freshmen: 41% (267); all full-time undergraduates: 40% (1,052). ***Average award:*** Freshmen: $29,699; Undergraduates: $29,205. ***Scholarships, grants, and awards:*** Federal Pell, FSEOG, state, college/university gift aid from institutional funds.

GIFT AID (NON-NEED-BASED) ***Total amount:*** $945,000 (9% state, 37% institutional, 54% external sources). ***Receiving aid:*** Freshmen: 17% (110). Undergraduates: 8% (201). ***Average award:*** Freshmen: $10,000. Undergraduates: $10,000. ***Scholarships, grants, and awards by category:*** *Academic interests/achievement:* 20 awards ($200,000 total): biological sciences, computer science, mathematics, physical sciences. *Creative arts/performance:* 16 awards ($160,000 total): music. *Special characteristics:* 39 awards ($1,045,000 total): children of faculty/staff. ***Tuition waivers:*** Full or partial for employees or children of employees, senior citizens. ***ROTC:*** Army cooperative, Air Force cooperative.

LOANS ***Student loans:*** $6,100,000 (75% need-based, 25% non-need-based). 46% of past graduating class borrowed through all loan programs. *Average indebtedness per student:* $19,163. ***Average need-based loan:*** Freshmen: $2574. Undergraduates: $3861. ***Parent loans:*** $5,600,000 (100% non-need-based). ***Programs:*** FFEL (Subsidized and Unsubsidized Stafford, PLUS), Perkins.

WORK-STUDY ***Federal work-study:*** Total amount: $590,000; 500 jobs averaging $1180. ***State or other work-study/employment:*** Total amount: $650,000 (100% non-need-based). 800 part-time jobs averaging $812.

APPLYING FOR FINANCIAL AID ***Required financial aid forms:*** FAFSA, CSS Financial Aid PROFILE. ***Financial aid deadline:*** 1/15. ***Notification date:*** 4/1. Students must reply by 5/1.

CONTACT Mr. Robert D. Shorb, Director of Student Aid and Family Finance, Skidmore College, 815 North Broadway, Saratoga Springs, NY 12866-1632, 518-580-5750 or toll-free 800-867-6007. *Fax:* 518-580-5752. *E-mail:* rshorb@skidmore.edu.

SLIPPERY ROCK UNIVERSITY OF PENNSYLVANIA

Slippery Rock, PA

Tuition & fees (PA res): $6934 **Average undergraduate aid package: $7842**

ABOUT THE INSTITUTION State-supported, coed. ***Awards:*** bachelor's, master's, and doctoral degrees and post-bachelor's and post-master's certificates. 69 undergraduate majors. ***Total enrollment:*** 8,458. Undergraduates: 7,691. Freshmen: 1,547. Federal methodology is used as a basis for awarding need-based institutional aid.

UNDERGRADUATE EXPENSES for 2008–09 ***Application fee:*** $30. ***Tuition, state resident:*** full-time $5358; part-time $223 per credit hour. ***Tuition, nonresident:*** full-time $8038; part-time $558 per credit hour. ***Required fees:*** full-time $1576; $74 per credit hour or $44 per term. Full-time tuition and fees vary according to course load and degree level. Part-time tuition and fees vary according to course load and degree level. ***College room and board:*** $8066; ***Room only:*** $5730. Room and board charges vary according to board plan and housing facility. ***Payment plan:*** Installment.

FRESHMAN FINANCIAL AID (Fall 2008, est.) 1,437 applied for aid; of those 71% were deemed to have need. 98% of freshmen with need received aid; of those 51% had need fully met. ***Average percent of need met:*** 64% (excluding resources awarded to replace EFC). ***Average financial aid package:*** $7413 (excluding resources awarded to replace EFC). 23% of all full-time freshmen had no need and received non-need-based gift aid.

UNDERGRADUATE FINANCIAL AID (Fall 2008, est.) 6,412 applied for aid; of those 73% were deemed to have need. 97% of undergraduates with need received aid; of those 48% had need fully met. ***Average percent of need met:*** 69% (excluding resources awarded to replace EFC). ***Average financial aid package:*** $7842 (excluding resources awarded to replace EFC). 19% of all full-time undergraduates had no need and received non-need-based gift aid.

GIFT AID (NEED-BASED) ***Total amount:*** $13,795,940 (51% federal, 49% state). ***Receiving aid:*** Freshmen: 41% (630); all full-time undergraduates: 40% (2,869). ***Average award:*** Freshmen: $3106; Undergraduates: $3068. ***Scholarships, grants, and awards:*** Federal Pell, FSEOG, state, private, college/university gift aid from institutional funds.

GIFT AID (NON-NEED-BASED) ***Total amount:*** $4,261,612 (27% institutional, 73% external sources). ***Receiving aid:*** Freshmen: 25% (384). Undergraduates: 16% (1,131). ***Average award:*** Freshmen: $6678. Undergraduates: $7345. ***Scholarships, grants, and awards by category:*** *Academic interests/achievement:* biological sciences, business, communication, computer science, education, English, general academic interests/achievements, health fields, physical sciences, social sciences. *Creative arts/performance:* applied art and design, art/fine arts, dance, music, performing arts, theater/drama. *Special achievements/activities:* community service, general special achievements/activities, leadership. *Special characteristics:* children and siblings of alumni, children of faculty/staff, children of union members/company employees, ethnic background, general special characteristics, local/state students, members of minority groups, out-of-state students, previous college experience. ***Tuition waivers:*** Full or partial for minority students, employees or children of employees, senior citizens. ***ROTC:*** Army.

LOANS ***Student loans:*** $41,851,856 (42% need-based, 58% non-need-based). 82% of past graduating class borrowed through all loan programs. *Average indebtedness per student:* $22,940. ***Average need-based loan:*** Freshmen: $3172. Undergraduates: $3794. ***Parent loans:*** $4,377,654 (100% non-need-based). ***Programs:*** FFEL (Subsidized and Unsubsidized Stafford, PLUS), Perkins.

WORK-STUDY ***Federal work-study:*** Total amount: $1,037,310; jobs available. ***State or other work-study/employment:*** Total amount: $919,220 (100% non-need-based). Part-time jobs available.

ATHLETIC AWARDS Total amount: $824,200 (100% non-need-based).

APPLYING FOR FINANCIAL AID ***Required financial aid form:*** FAFSA. ***Financial aid deadline (priority):*** 2/15. ***Notification date:*** Continuous beginning 6/1.

CONTACT Ms. Patty A. Hladio, Director of Financial Aid, Slippery Rock University of Pennsylvania, 1 Morrow Way, Slippery Rock, PA 16057, 724-738-2044 or toll-free 800-SRU-9111. *Fax:* 724-738-2922. *E-mail:* financial.aid@sru.edu.

SMITH COLLEGE

Northampton, MA

Tuition & fees: $36,058 **Average undergraduate aid package: $34,370**

ABOUT THE INSTITUTION Independent, women only. ***Awards:*** bachelor's, master's, and doctoral degrees and post-bachelor's and post-master's certificates. 51 undergraduate majors. ***Total enrollment:*** 3,065. Undergraduates: 2,596. Freshmen: 656. Institutional methodology is used as a basis for awarding need-based institutional aid.

UNDERGRADUATE EXPENSES for 2008–09 ***Application fee:*** $60. ***Comprehensive fee:*** $48,108 includes full-time tuition ($35,810), mandatory fees ($248), and room and board ($12,050). ***College room only:*** $6030. ***Part-time tuition:*** $1120 per credit hour.

FRESHMAN FINANCIAL AID (Fall 2008, est.) 475 applied for aid; of those 78% were deemed to have need. 100% of freshmen with need received aid; of those 100% had need fully met. ***Average percent of need met:*** 100% (excluding resources awarded to replace EFC). ***Average financial aid package:*** $33,717 (excluding resources awarded to replace EFC). 5% of all full-time freshmen had no need and received non-need-based gift aid.

UNDERGRADUATE FINANCIAL AID (Fall 2008, est.) 1,832 applied for aid; of those 88% were deemed to have need. 100% of undergraduates with need received aid; of those 100% had need fully met. ***Average percent of need met:*** 100% (excluding resources awarded to replace EFC). ***Average financial aid package:*** $34,370 (excluding resources awarded to replace EFC). 6% of all full-time undergraduates had no need and received non-need-based gift aid.

GIFT AID (NEED-BASED) ***Total amount:*** $45,852,194 (6% federal, 2% state, 89% institutional, 3% external sources). ***Receiving aid:*** Freshmen: 53% (340); all full-time undergraduates: 58% (1,506). ***Average award:*** Freshmen: $30,435; Undergraduates: $29,403. ***Scholarships, grants, and awards:*** Federal Pell, FSEOG, state, college/university gift aid from institutional funds.

GIFT AID (NON-NEED-BASED) ***Total amount:*** $1,611,202 (63% institutional, 37% external sources). ***Receiving aid:*** Freshmen: 1% (6). Undergraduates: 1% (15). ***Average award:*** Freshmen: $8973. Undergraduates: $6113. ***ROTC:*** Army cooperative, Air Force cooperative.

LOANS ***Student loans:*** $10,104,929 (64% need-based, 36% non-need-based). 71% of past graduating class borrowed through all loan programs. *Average indebtedness per student:* $20,960. ***Average need-based loan:*** Freshmen: $3288. Undergraduates: $4616. ***Parent loans:*** $4,496,123 (100% non-need-based). ***Programs:*** Federal Direct (Subsidized and Unsubsidized Stafford), FFEL (PLUS), Perkins, state, college/university.

WORK-STUDY ***Federal work-study:*** Total amount: $2,610,521; jobs available. ***State or other work-study/employment:*** Total amount: $948,697 (81% need-based, 19% non-need-based). Part-time jobs available.

APPLYING FOR FINANCIAL AID ***Required financial aid forms:*** FAFSA, CSS Financial Aid PROFILE, noncustodial (divorced/separated) parent's statement, business/farm supplement. ***Financial aid deadline:*** 2/15. ***Notification date:*** 4/1. Students must reply by 5/1.

CONTACT Deborah Luekens, Director of Student Financial Services, Smith College, College Hall, Northampton, MA 01063, 413-585-2530 or toll-free 800-383-3232. *Fax:* 413-585-2566. *E-mail:* sfs@smith.edu.

SOJOURNER-DOUGLASS COLLEGE

Baltimore, MD

ABOUT THE INSTITUTION Independent, coed, primarily women. ***Awards:*** bachelor's and master's degrees (offers only evening and weekend programs). 21 undergraduate majors. ***Total enrollment:*** 1,151. Undergraduates: 1,078.

GIFT AID (NEED-BASED) ***Scholarships, grants, and awards:*** Federal Pell, FSEOG, state, private, college/university gift aid from institutional funds.

LOANS ***Programs:*** FFEL (Subsidized and Unsubsidized Stafford, PLUS), college/university.

APPLYING FOR FINANCIAL AID ***Required financial aid forms:*** FAFSA, institution's own form.

CONTACT Ms. Rebecca Chalk, Financial Aid Director, Sojourner-Douglass College, 200 North Central Avenue, Baltimore, MD 21202, 410-276-0306 Ext. 258. *Fax:* 410-276-0148. *E-mail:* rchalk@host.sdc.edu.

SOKA UNIVERSITY OF AMERICA

Aliso Viejo, CA

CONTACT Financial Aid Office, Soka University of America, 1 University Drive, Aliso Viejo, CA 92656, 949-480-4000 or toll-free 888-600-SOKA (out-of-state).

SOMERSET CHRISTIAN COLLEGE

Zarephath, NJ

CONTACT Financial Aid Office, Somerset Christian College, 10 College Way, PO Box 9035, Zarephath, NJ 08890-9035, 732-356-1595 or toll-free 800-234-9305.

SONOMA STATE UNIVERSITY

Rohnert Park, CA

Tuition & fees (CA res): $4272 **Average undergraduate aid package: $8608**

ABOUT THE INSTITUTION State-supported, coed. ***Awards:*** bachelor's and master's degrees. 64 undergraduate majors. ***Total enrollment:*** 8,921. Undergraduates: 7,709. Freshmen: 1,655. Federal methodology is used as a basis for awarding need-based institutional aid.

UNDERGRADUATE EXPENSES for 2008–09 ***Application fee:*** $55. ***Tuition, state resident:*** full-time $0. ***Tuition, nonresident:*** full-time $9357; part-time $339 per term. ***Required fees:*** full-time $4272; $1296 per term. Full-time tuition and fees vary according to course load and degree level. Part-time tuition and fees vary according to course load and degree level. ***College room and board:*** $10,115. Room and board charges vary according to housing facility.

FRESHMAN FINANCIAL AID (Fall 2008, est.) 698 applied for aid; of those 58% were deemed to have need. 94% of freshmen with need received aid; of those 27% had need fully met. ***Average percent of need met:*** 64% (excluding resources awarded to replace EFC). ***Average financial aid package:*** $8055 (excluding resources awarded to replace EFC). 1% of all full-time freshmen had no need and received non-need-based gift aid.

UNDERGRADUATE FINANCIAL AID (Fall 2008, est.) 3,642 applied for aid; of those 73% were deemed to have need. 96% of undergraduates with need received aid; of those 19% had need fully met. ***Average percent of need met:*** 65% (excluding resources awarded to replace EFC). ***Average financial aid package:*** $8608 (excluding resources awarded to replace EFC). 1% of all full-time undergraduates had no need and received non-need-based gift aid.

GIFT AID (NEED-BASED) ***Total amount:*** $11,386,035 (46% federal, 54% state). ***Receiving aid:*** Freshmen: 13% (205); all full-time undergraduates: 22% (1,536). ***Average award:*** Freshmen: $8219; Undergraduates: $6868. ***Scholarships, grants, and awards:*** Federal Pell, FSEOG, state, private, college/university gift aid from institutional funds, Academic Competitiveness Grant, National Smart Grant.

GIFT AID (NON-NEED-BASED) ***Total amount:*** $758,951 (14% state, 48% institutional, 38% external sources). ***Receiving aid:*** Freshmen: 6% (96). Undergraduates: 5% (335). ***Average award:*** Freshmen: $1577. Undergraduates: $1428. ***Scholarships, grants, and awards by category:*** *Academic interests/achievement:* 167 awards ($192,083 total): area/ethnic studies, biological sciences, business, communication, computer science, education, engineering/technologies, English, foreign languages, general academic interests/achievements, health fields, humanities, mathematics, physical sciences, premedicine, social sciences. *Creative arts/performance:* 59 awards ($61,520 total): applied art and design, art/fine arts, cinema/film/broadcasting, creative writing, dance, journalism/publications, music, performing arts, theater/drama. *Special achievements/activities:* 2 awards ($1500 total): community service, leadership, memberships. *Special characteristics:* 86 awards ($105,505 total): adult students, children and siblings of alumni, children of educators, children of faculty/staff, children of public servants, children of union members/company employees, children of workers in trades, ethnic background, first-generation college students, general special characteristics, handicapped students, international students, local/state students, married students, members of minority groups, out-of-state students, previous college experience, veterans. ***Tuition waivers:*** Full or partial for employees or children of employees. ***ROTC:*** Army cooperative, Air Force cooperative.

LOANS ***Student loans:*** $20,129,796 (53% need-based, 47% non-need-based). 38% of past graduating class borrowed through all loan programs. *Average indebtedness per student:* $14,705. ***Average need-based loan:*** Freshmen: $3170. Undergraduates: $4272. ***Parent loans:*** $28,221,923 (100% non-need-based). ***Programs:*** Federal Direct (Subsidized and Unsubsidized Stafford, PLUS), Perkins.

WORK-STUDY ***Federal work-study:*** Total amount: $847,917; 218 jobs averaging $3676. ***State or other work-study/employment:*** Total amount: $1,593,766 (100% non-need-based). 620 part-time jobs averaging $2570.

ATHLETIC AWARDS Total amount: $175,573 (100% non-need-based).

APPLYING FOR FINANCIAL AID ***Required financial aid form:*** FAFSA. ***Financial aid deadline (priority):*** 1/31. ***Notification date:*** Continuous beginning 3/15. Students must reply within 2 weeks of notification.

CONTACT Susan Gutierrez, Director of Financial Aid, Sonoma State University, 1801 East Cotati Avenue, Rohnert Park, CA 94928-3609, 707-664-2287. *Fax:* 707-664-4242. *E-mail:* susan.gutierrez@sonoma.edu.

SOUTH CAROLINA STATE UNIVERSITY

Orangeburg, SC

Tuition & fees (SC res): $7806 **Average undergraduate aid package: N/A**

ABOUT THE INSTITUTION State-supported, coed. ***Awards:*** bachelor's, master's, and doctoral degrees and post-bachelor's and post-master's certificates. 42 undergraduate majors. ***Total enrollment:*** 4,888. Undergraduates: 4,153. Freshmen: 966.

UNDERGRADUATE EXPENSES for 2008–09 ***Application fee:*** $25. ***Tuition, state resident:*** full-time $7806; part-time $325 per credit hour. ***Tuition, nonresident:*** full-time $15,298; part-time $637 per credit hour. ***College room and board:*** $8040; ***Room only:*** $5460. Room and board charges vary according to housing facility. ***Payment plans:*** Installment, deferred payment.

GIFT AID (NEED-BASED) ***Total amount:*** $11,847,406 (93% federal, 7% state). ***Scholarships, grants, and awards:*** Federal Pell, FSEOG, state, private, college/university gift aid from institutional funds.

GIFT AID (NON-NEED-BASED) ***Total amount:*** $8,606,222 (37% state, 29% institutional, 34% external sources). ***Scholarships, grants, and awards by category:*** *Academic interests/achievement:* general academic interests/

achievements. *Creative arts/performance:* music. ***Tuition waivers:*** Full or partial for employees or children of employees, senior citizens. ***ROTC:*** Army, Air Force cooperative.

LOANS ***Student loans:*** $32,850,539 (50% need-based, 50% non-need-based). *Average indebtedness per student:* $26,678. ***Parent loans:*** $2,878,608 (100% non-need-based). ***Programs:*** FFEL (Subsidized and Unsubsidized Stafford, PLUS), Perkins, college/university.

WORK-STUDY ***Federal work-study:*** Total amount: $370,540; 343 jobs averaging $1048. ***State or other work-study/employment:*** Total amount: $1,094,456 (100% non-need-based). 360 part-time jobs averaging $2050.

ATHLETIC AWARDS Total amount: $3,618,763 (100% non-need-based).

APPLYING FOR FINANCIAL AID ***Required financial aid form:*** FAFSA. ***Financial aid deadline (priority):*** 5/1. ***Notification date:*** Continuous. Students must reply within 2 weeks of notification.

CONTACT Sandra S. Davis, Director of Financial Aid, South Carolina State University, 300 College Street Northeast, Orangeburg, SC 29117, 803-536-7067 or toll-free 800-260-5956. *Fax:* 803-536-8420. *E-mail:* sdavis@scsu.edu.

SOUTH DAKOTA SCHOOL OF MINES AND TECHNOLOGY

Rapid City, SD

Tuition & fees (SD res): $6480 **Average undergraduate aid package: $8260**

ABOUT THE INSTITUTION State-supported, coed. ***Awards:*** associate, bachelor's, master's, and doctoral degrees. 18 undergraduate majors. ***Total enrollment:*** 2,061. Undergraduates: 1,817. Freshmen: 317. Both federal and institutional methodology are used as a basis for awarding need-based institutional aid.

UNDERGRADUATE EXPENSES for 2008–09 ***Application fee:*** $20. ***Tuition, state resident:*** full-time $2650; part-time $88.20 per credit hour. ***Tuition, nonresident:*** full-time $3970; part-time $132.20 per credit hour. ***Required fees:*** full-time $3830; $133.54 per credit hour. Full-time tuition and fees vary according to course load, program, and reciprocity agreements. Part-time tuition and fees vary according to course load, program, and reciprocity agreements. ***College room and board:*** $4740. Room and board charges vary according to board plan and housing facility. ***Payment plan:*** Installment.

FRESHMAN FINANCIAL AID (Fall 2008, est.) 292 applied for aid; of those 56% were deemed to have need. 100% of freshmen with need received aid; of those 32% had need fully met. ***Average percent of need met:*** 74% (excluding resources awarded to replace EFC). ***Average financial aid package:*** $8532 (excluding resources awarded to replace EFC). 31% of all full-time freshmen had no need and received non-need-based gift aid.

UNDERGRADUATE FINANCIAL AID (Fall 2008, est.) 1,299 applied for aid; of those 57% were deemed to have need. 100% of undergraduates with need received aid; of those 26% had need fully met. ***Average percent of need met:*** 69% (excluding resources awarded to replace EFC). ***Average financial aid package:*** $8260 (excluding resources awarded to replace EFC). 24% of all full-time undergraduates had no need and received non-need-based gift aid.

GIFT AID (NEED-BASED) ***Total amount:*** $2,420,799 (51% federal, 28% institutional, 21% external sources). ***Receiving aid:*** Freshmen: 40% (124); all full-time undergraduates: 33% (450). ***Average award:*** Freshmen: $3789; Undergraduates: $3662. ***Scholarships, grants, and awards:*** Federal Pell, college/university gift aid from institutional funds, LEAP.

GIFT AID (NON-NEED-BASED) ***Total amount:*** $1,228,592 (57% institutional, 43% external sources). ***Receiving aid:*** Freshmen: 31% (94). Undergraduates: 18% (248). ***Average award:*** Freshmen: $3645. Undergraduates: $3131. ***Scholarships, grants, and awards by category:*** *Academic interests/achievement:* computer science, engineering/technologies, mathematics. ***Tuition waivers:*** Full or partial for senior citizens. ***ROTC:*** Army.

LOANS ***Student loans:*** $4,555,858 (100% need-based). 76% of past graduating class borrowed through all loan programs. *Average indebtedness per student:* $23,898. ***Average need-based loan:*** Freshmen: $2964. Undergraduates: $3495. ***Parent loans:*** $617,682 (57% need-based, 43% non-need-based). ***Programs:*** FFEL (Subsidized and Unsubsidized Stafford, PLUS), Perkins.

WORK-STUDY ***Federal work-study:*** Total amount: $277,865; jobs available.

ATHLETIC AWARDS Total amount: $421,954 (58% need-based, 42% non-need-based).

APPLYING FOR FINANCIAL AID ***Required financial aid forms:*** FAFSA, institution's own form. ***Financial aid deadline (priority):*** 3/15. ***Notification date:*** Continuous beginning 5/15. Students must reply within 3 weeks of notification.

CONTACT David W. Martin, Financial Aid Director, South Dakota School of Mines and Technology, 501 East Saint Joseph Street, Rapid City, SD 57701-3995, 605-394-2274 or toll-free 800-544-8162 Ext. 2414. *Fax:* 605-394-1979. *E-mail:* david.martin@sdsmt.edu.

SOUTH DAKOTA STATE UNIVERSITY

Brookings, SD

Tuition & fees (SD res): $5808 **Average undergraduate aid package: $8634**

ABOUT THE INSTITUTION State-supported, coed. ***Awards:*** associate, bachelor's, master's, doctoral, and first professional degrees and post-bachelor's and post-master's certificates. 73 undergraduate majors. ***Total enrollment:*** 11,995. Undergraduates: 10,532. Freshmen: 2,101. Federal methodology is used as a basis for awarding need-based institutional aid.

UNDERGRADUATE EXPENSES for 2008–09 ***Application fee:*** $20. ***Tuition, state resident:*** full-time $2646; part-time $88.20 per credit hour. ***Tuition, nonresident:*** full-time $3966; part-time $132.20 per credit hour. ***Required fees:*** full-time $3162; $105.40 per credit hour. Full-time tuition and fees vary according to course load, location, program, and reciprocity agreements. Part-time tuition and fees vary according to course load, location, program, and reciprocity agreements. ***College room and board:*** $5423; ***Room only:*** $2450. Room and board charges vary according to board plan and housing facility. ***Payment plans:*** Installment, deferred payment.

FRESHMAN FINANCIAL AID (Fall 2008, est.) 1,722 applied for aid; of those 82% were deemed to have need. 100% of freshmen with need received aid; of those 79% had need fully met. ***Average percent of need met:*** 89% (excluding resources awarded to replace EFC). ***Average financial aid package:*** $7166 (excluding resources awarded to replace EFC). 24% of all full-time freshmen had no need and received non-need-based gift aid.

UNDERGRADUATE FINANCIAL AID (Fall 2008, est.) 7,182 applied for aid; of those 88% were deemed to have need. 100% of undergraduates with need received aid; of those 88% had need fully met. ***Average percent of need met:*** 85% (excluding resources awarded to replace EFC). ***Average financial aid package:*** $8634 (excluding resources awarded to replace EFC). 19% of all full-time undergraduates had no need and received non-need-based gift aid.

GIFT AID (NEED-BASED) ***Total amount:*** $16,147,491 (61% federal, 7% state, 22% institutional, 10% external sources). ***Receiving aid:*** Freshmen: 42% (842); all full-time undergraduates: 47% (3,872). ***Average award:*** Freshmen: $4145; Undergraduates: $4210. ***Scholarships, grants, and awards:*** Federal Pell, FSEOG, state, private, college/university gift aid from institutional funds, United Negro College Fund, Federal Nursing, National Smart Grant, Academic Competitiveness Grant, TEACH Grant, TRiO.

GIFT AID (NON-NEED-BASED) ***Total amount:*** $4,224,013 (13% federal, 17% state, 50% institutional, 20% external sources). ***Receiving aid:*** Freshmen: 52% (1,036). Undergraduates: 68% (5,646). ***Average award:*** Freshmen: $1641. Undergraduates: $1508. ***Scholarships, grants, and awards by category:*** *Academic interests/achievement:* 3,121 awards ($3,340,144 total): agriculture, area/ethnic studies, biological sciences, business, communication, computer science, education, engineering/technologies, English, foreign languages, general academic interests/achievements, health fields, home economics, humanities, international studies, mathematics, military science, physical sciences, premedicine, social sciences. *Creative arts/performance:* 320 awards ($388,872 total): art/fine arts, debating, general creative arts/performance, journalism/publications, music, performing arts, theater/drama. *Special achievements/activities:* 165 awards ($165,140 total): community service, general special achievements/activities, hobbies/interests, junior miss, leadership, memberships, rodeo. *Special characteristics:* 169 awards ($271,956 total): adult students, children of faculty/staff, children of workers in trades, ethnic background, first-generation college students, general special characteristics, handicapped students, international students, members of minority groups, veterans, veterans' children. ***Tuition waivers:*** Full or partial for children of alumni, employees or children of employees, senior citizens. ***ROTC:*** Army, Air Force.

LOANS ***Student loans:*** $54,534,556 (63% need-based, 37% non-need-based). 79% of past graduating class borrowed through all loan programs. *Average indebtedness per student:* $21,044. ***Average need-based loan:*** Freshmen: $4432. Undergraduates: $4964. ***Parent loans:*** $1,664,588 (11% need-based, 89% non-need-based). ***Programs:*** FFEL (Subsidized and Unsubsidized Stafford, PLUS), Perkins, Federal Nursing, college/university, Health Professions Loans, private alternative loans.

WORK-STUDY ***Federal work-study:*** Total amount: $786,018; 658 jobs averaging $1276. ***State or other work-study/employment:*** Total amount: $3,598,550 (14% need-based, 86% non-need-based). 2,251 part-time jobs averaging $1582.

ATHLETIC AWARDS Total amount: $2,594,496 (51% need-based, 49% non-need-based).

APPLYING FOR FINANCIAL AID ***Required financial aid form:*** FAFSA. ***Financial aid deadline (priority):*** 3/11. ***Notification date:*** Continuous beginning 4/1. Students must reply within 3 weeks of notification.

CONTACT Mr. Jay Larsen, Director of Financial Aid, South Dakota State University, Box 2201 ADM 106, Brookings, SD 57007, 605-688-4703 or toll-free 800-952-3541. *Fax:* 605-688-5882. *E-mail:* jay.larsen@sdstate.edu.

SOUTHEASTERN BAPTIST COLLEGE

Laurel, MS

CONTACT Financial Aid Officer, Southeastern Baptist College, 4229 Highway 15 North, Laurel, MS 39440-1096, 601-426-6346.

SOUTHEASTERN BAPTIST THEOLOGICAL SEMINARY

Wake Forest, NC

CONTACT H. Allan Moseley, Vice President of Student Services/Dean of Students, Southeastern Baptist Theological Seminary, PO Box 1889, Wake Forest, NC 27588, 919-556-3101 Ext. 306 or toll-free 800-284-6317. *Fax:* 919-556-0998. *E-mail:* deanofstudents@sebts.edu.

SOUTHEASTERN BIBLE COLLEGE

Birmingham, AL

CONTACT Ms. Joanne Belin, Financial Aid Administrator, Southeastern Bible College, 2545 Valleydale Road, Birmingham, AL 35244, 205-970-9215 or toll-free 800-749-8878 (in-state). *E-mail:* jbelin@sebc.edu.

SOUTHEASTERN LOUISIANA UNIVERSITY

Hammond, LA

Tuition & fees (LA res): $3721 **Average undergraduate aid package: $6572**

ABOUT THE INSTITUTION State-supported, coed. ***Awards:*** associate, bachelor's, and master's degrees. 55 undergraduate majors. ***Total enrollment:*** 15,224. Undergraduates: 13,875. Freshmen: 2,778. Federal methodology is used as a basis for awarding need-based institutional aid.

UNDERGRADUATE EXPENSES for 2008–09 ***Application fee:*** $20. ***Tuition, state resident:*** full-time $2376; part-time $99 per credit hour. ***Tuition, nonresident:*** full-time $8376; part-time $349 per credit hour. ***Required fees:*** full-time $1345; $56 per credit hour. Full-time tuition and fees vary according to course load. Part-time tuition and fees vary according to course load. ***College room and board:*** $6220; ***Room only:*** $3900. Room and board charges vary according to board plan and housing facility. ***Payment plans:*** Installment, deferred payment.

FRESHMAN FINANCIAL AID (Fall 2007) 2,110 applied for aid; of those 61% were deemed to have need. 89% of freshmen with need received aid; of those 27% had need fully met. ***Average financial aid package:*** $5857 (excluding resources awarded to replace EFC). 7% of all full-time freshmen had no need and received non-need-based gift aid.

UNDERGRADUATE FINANCIAL AID (Fall 2007) 8,398 applied for aid; of those 71% were deemed to have need. 93% of undergraduates with need received aid; of those 28% had need fully met. ***Average financial aid package:*** $6572 (excluding resources awarded to replace EFC). 4% of all full-time undergraduates had no need and received non-need-based gift aid.

GIFT AID (NEED-BASED) ***Total amount:*** $14,430,357 (93% federal, 7% state). ***Receiving aid:*** Freshmen: 29% (734); all full-time undergraduates: 32% (3,553). ***Average award:*** Freshmen: $4307; Undergraduates: $3849. ***Scholarships, grants, and awards:*** Federal Pell, FSEOG, state, private, college/university gift aid from institutional funds, Federal Nursing.

GIFT AID (NON-NEED-BASED) ***Total amount:*** $9,277,787 (74% state, 22% institutional, 4% external sources). ***Receiving aid:*** Freshmen: 23% (591). Undergraduates: 20% (2,242). ***Average award:*** Freshmen: $1592. Undergraduates: $1625. ***Scholarships, grants, and awards by category:*** *Academic interests/achievement:* 2,933 awards ($2,115,851 total): biological sciences, business, communication, computer science, education, engineering/technologies, English, foreign languages, general academic interests/achievements, health fields, home economics, humanities, international studies, mathematics, physical sciences, social sciences. *Creative arts/performance:* 380 awards ($292,247 total): applied art and design, art/fine arts, dance, general creative arts/performance, music, performing arts, theater/drama. *Special achievements/activities:* 162 awards ($82,117 total): cheerleading/drum major, general special achievements/activities, leadership, memberships. *Special characteristics:* 1,039 awards ($23,171,117 total): children of faculty/staff, children of public servants, general special characteristics, handicapped students, international students, members of minority groups, out-of-state students, religious affiliation, veterans' children. ***Tuition waivers:*** Full or partial for employees or children of employees, senior citizens. ***ROTC:*** Army cooperative.

LOANS ***Student loans:*** $28,746,678 (57% need-based, 43% non-need-based). 57% of past graduating class borrowed through all loan programs. *Average indebtedness per student:* $18,741. ***Average need-based loan:*** Freshmen: $2698. Undergraduates: $3754. ***Parent loans:*** $732,966 (100% non-need-based). ***Programs:*** FFEL (Subsidized and Unsubsidized Stafford, PLUS), Perkins, college/university.

WORK-STUDY ***Federal work-study:*** Total amount: $589,265; 414 jobs averaging $1477. ***State or other work-study/employment:*** Total amount: $2,327,660 (100% non-need-based). 1,363 part-time jobs averaging $1708.

ATHLETIC AWARDS Total amount: $1,683,501 (100% non-need-based).

APPLYING FOR FINANCIAL AID ***Required financial aid form:*** FAFSA. ***Financial aid deadline (priority):*** 5/1. ***Notification date:*** Continuous. Students must reply within 2 weeks of notification.

CONTACT Sarah Schillage, Director of Financial Aid, Southeastern Louisiana University, SLU 10768, Hammond, LA 70402, 985-549-2244 or toll-free 800-222-7358. *Fax:* 985-549-5077. *E-mail:* finaid@selu.edu.

SOUTHEASTERN OKLAHOMA STATE UNIVERSITY

Durant, OK

Tuition & fees (OK res): $4316 **Average undergraduate aid package: $1190**

ABOUT THE INSTITUTION State-supported, coed. ***Awards:*** bachelor's and master's degrees and post-master's certificates. 44 undergraduate majors. ***Total enrollment:*** 3,889. Undergraduates: 3,481. Freshmen: 609. Federal methodology is used as a basis for awarding need-based institutional aid.

UNDERGRADUATE EXPENSES for 2008–09 ***Application fee:*** $20. ***Tuition, state resident:*** full-time $3639; part-time $121.30 per credit hour. ***Tuition, nonresident:*** full-time $10,009; part-time $333.65 per credit hour. ***Required fees:*** full-time $677; $22.55 per credit hour. Full-time tuition and fees vary according to course level. Part-time tuition and fees vary according to course level and course load. ***College room and board:*** $4290; ***Room only:*** $1850. Room and board charges vary according to board plan and housing facility.

FRESHMAN FINANCIAL AID (Fall 2007) 434 applied for aid; of those 94% were deemed to have need. 98% of freshmen with need received aid; of those 43% had need fully met. ***Average percent of need met:*** 64% (excluding resources awarded to replace EFC). ***Average financial aid package:*** $1049 (excluding resources awarded to replace EFC). 1% of all full-time freshmen had no need and received non-need-based gift aid.

UNDERGRADUATE FINANCIAL AID (Fall 2007) 1,525 applied for aid; of those 96% were deemed to have need. 97% of undergraduates with need received aid; of those 66% had need fully met. ***Average percent of need met:*** 67% (excluding resources awarded to replace EFC). ***Average financial aid package:*** $1190 (excluding resources awarded to replace EFC). 1% of all full-time undergraduates had no need and received non-need-based gift aid.

GIFT AID (NEED-BASED) ***Total amount:*** $6,615,396 (68% federal, 32% state). ***Receiving aid:*** Freshmen: 55% (288); all full-time undergraduates: 60% (1,190). ***Average award:*** Freshmen: $1055; Undergraduates: $1202. ***Scholarships, grants, and awards:*** Federal Pell, FSEOG, state, private, college/university gift aid from institutional funds.

GIFT AID (NON-NEED-BASED) ***Total amount:*** $2,024,176 (5% state, 13% institutional, 82% external sources). ***Receiving aid:*** Freshmen: 34% (178). Undergraduates: 23% (462). ***Average award:*** Freshmen: $1156. Undergraduates: $633. ***Scholarships, grants, and awards by category:*** *Academic interests/achievement:* 416 awards ($415,993 total): biological sciences, business, computer science, education, engineering/technologies, general academic interests/achievements, mathematics, physical sciences, social sciences. *Creative arts/performance:* 79 awards ($97,917 total): music, theater/drama. *Special achievements/activities:* 6 awards ($6497 total): cheerleading/drum major. *Special characteristics:* 847 awards ($2,615,460 total): children and siblings of alumni, out-of-state students. ***Tuition waivers:*** Full or partial for minority students, children of alumni, employees or children of employees, senior citizens.

LOANS ***Student loans:*** $6,865,388 (68% need-based, 32% non-need-based). 37% of past graduating class borrowed through all loan programs. *Average indebtedness per student:* $6852. ***Average need-based loan:*** Freshmen: $1199. Undergraduates: $2022. ***Parent loans:*** $309,164 (100% non-need-based). ***Programs:*** FFEL (Subsidized and Unsubsidized Stafford, PLUS), Perkins, college/university.

WORK-STUDY ***Federal work-study:*** Total amount: $175,644; 363 jobs averaging $1402. ***State or other work-study/employment:*** Total amount: $696,475 (100% non-need-based). 649 part-time jobs averaging $1821.

ATHLETIC AWARDS Total amount: $866,030 (100% non-need-based).

APPLYING FOR FINANCIAL AID ***Required financial aid forms:*** FAFSA, institution's own form. ***Financial aid deadline (priority):*** 3/1. ***Notification date:*** Continuous beginning 4/15. Students must reply within 2 weeks of notification.

CONTACT Sherry Hudson, Director of Student Financial Aid, Southeastern Oklahoma State University, 1405 North 4th Avenue, Durant, OK 74701-0609, 580-745-2186 or toll-free 800-435-1327. *Fax:* 580-745-7469. *E-mail:* shudson@se.edu.

SOUTHEASTERN UNIVERSITY

Washington, DC

CONTACT Hope Gibbs, Assistant Director of Financial Aid, Southeastern University, 501 I Street, SW, Washington, DC 20024-2788, 202-488-8162 Ext. 234. *E-mail:* hgibbs@admin.seu.edu.

SOUTHEASTERN UNIVERSITY

Lakeland, FL

CONTACT Ms. Carol B. Bradley, Financial Aid Director, Southeastern University, 1000 Longfellow Boulevard, Lakeland, FL 33801-6099, 863-667-5000 or toll-free 800-500-8760. *Fax:* 863-667-5200. *E-mail:* cbradley@seuniversity.edu.

SOUTHEAST MISSOURI STATE UNIVERSITY

Cape Girardeau, MO

Tuition & fees (MO res): $6255 **Average undergraduate aid package: $7490**

ABOUT THE INSTITUTION State-supported, coed. ***Awards:*** associate, bachelor's, and master's degrees and post-master's certificates. 68 undergraduate majors. ***Total enrollment:*** 10,814. Undergraduates: 9,381. Freshmen: 1,828. Federal methodology is used as a basis for awarding need-based institutional aid.

UNDERGRADUATE EXPENSES for 2008–09 ***Application fee:*** $25. ***Tuition, state resident:*** full-time $5544; part-time $184.80 per credit hour. ***Tuition, nonresident:*** full-time $10,179; part-time $339.30 per credit hour. ***Required fees:*** full-time $711; $23.70 per credit hour. Full-time tuition and fees vary according to course load and location. Part-time tuition and fees vary according to course load and location. ***College room and board:*** $5935; ***Room only:*** $3673. Room and board charges vary according to board plan and housing facility. ***Payment plans:*** Installment, deferred payment.

FRESHMAN FINANCIAL AID (Fall 2007) 1,317 applied for aid; of those 69% were deemed to have need. 98% of freshmen with need received aid; of those 20% had need fully met. ***Average percent of need met:*** 69% (excluding resources awarded to replace EFC). ***Average financial aid package:*** $7654 (excluding resources awarded to replace EFC). 26% of all full-time freshmen had no need and received non-need-based gift aid.

UNDERGRADUATE FINANCIAL AID (Fall 2007) 5,040 applied for aid; of those 74% were deemed to have need. 98% of undergraduates with need received aid; of those 22% had need fully met. ***Average percent of need met:*** 68% (excluding resources awarded to replace EFC). ***Average financial aid package:*** $7490 (excluding resources awarded to replace EFC). 15% of all full-time undergraduates had no need and received non-need-based gift aid.

GIFT AID (NEED-BASED) ***Total amount:*** $15,081,905 (51% federal, 20% state, 25% institutional, 4% external sources). ***Receiving aid:*** Freshmen: 51% (821); all full-time undergraduates: 45% (3,113). ***Average award:*** Freshmen: $5140; Undergraduates: $4469. ***Scholarships, grants, and awards:*** Federal Pell, FSEOG, state, private, college/university gift aid from institutional funds.

GIFT AID (NON-NEED-BASED) ***Total amount:*** $5,767,650 (6% state, 83% institutional, 11% external sources). ***Receiving aid:*** Freshmen: 6% (101). Undergraduates: 4% (268). ***Average award:*** Freshmen: $3761. Undergraduates: $4127. ***Scholarships, grants, and awards by category:*** *Academic interests/achievement:* 2,435 awards ($5,974,320 total): agriculture, biological sciences, business, communication, computer science, education, English, foreign languages, general academic interests/achievements, health fields, home economics, humanities, international studies, mathematics, military science, physical sciences, premedicine, religion/biblical studies, social sciences. *Creative arts/performance:* 283 awards ($243,204 total): music, theater/drama. *Special achievements/activities:* 495 awards ($374,639 total): cheerleading/drum major, general special achievements/activities, leadership. *Special characteristics:* 413 awards ($1,465,682 total): adult students, children of faculty/staff, first-generation college students, general special characteristics, international students, members of minority groups, out-of-state students, previous college experience. ***Tuition waivers:*** Full or partial for employees or children of employees, senior citizens. ***ROTC:*** Air Force.

LOANS ***Student loans:*** $25,259,679 (66% need-based, 34% non-need-based). 66% of past graduating class borrowed through all loan programs. *Average indebtedness per student:* $18,893. ***Average need-based loan:*** Freshmen: $3148. Undergraduates: $3889. ***Parent loans:*** $4,971,564 (18% need-based, 82% non-need-based). ***Programs:*** FFEL (Subsidized and Unsubsidized Stafford, PLUS), Perkins, state.

WORK-STUDY ***Federal work-study:*** Total amount: $227,070; 154 jobs averaging $1483. ***State or other work-study/employment:*** 1,643 part-time jobs averaging $1818.

ATHLETIC AWARDS Total amount: $2,431,861 (45% need-based, 55% non-need-based).

APPLYING FOR FINANCIAL AID ***Required financial aid form:*** FAFSA. ***Financial aid deadline (priority):*** 3/1. ***Notification date:*** Continuous beginning 4/1. Students must reply within 3 weeks of notification.

CONTACT Kerri Saylor, Lead Customer Service Representative, Southeast Missouri State University, One University Plaza, Cape Girardeau, MO 63701, 573-651-2253. *Fax:* 573-651-5006. *E-mail:* sfs@semo.edu.

SOUTHERN ADVENTIST UNIVERSITY

Collegedale, TN

Tuition & fees: $17,112 **Average undergraduate aid package: $18,851**

ABOUT THE INSTITUTION Independent Seventh-day Adventist, coed. ***Awards:*** associate, bachelor's, and master's degrees and post-master's certificates. 72 undergraduate majors. ***Total enrollment:*** 2,640. Undergraduates: 2,477. Freshmen: 535. Both federal and institutional methodology are used as a basis for awarding need-based institutional aid.

UNDERGRADUATE EXPENSES for 2009–10 ***Application fee:*** $25. ***Comprehensive fee:*** $22,192 includes full-time tuition ($16,372), mandatory fees ($740), and room and board ($5080). ***College room only:*** $3080.

FRESHMAN FINANCIAL AID (Fall 2008, est.) 407 applied for aid; of those 60% were deemed to have need. 100% of freshmen with need received aid; of those 88% had need fully met. ***Average percent of need met:*** 85% (excluding resources awarded to replace EFC). ***Average financial aid package:*** $18,897 (excluding resources awarded to replace EFC). 30% of all full-time freshmen had no need and received non-need-based gift aid.

UNDERGRADUATE FINANCIAL AID (Fall 2008, est.) 1,480 applied for aid; of those 68% were deemed to have need. 100% of undergraduates with need received aid; of those 84% had need fully met. ***Average percent of need met:*** 78% (excluding resources awarded to replace EFC). ***Average financial aid package:*** $18,851 (excluding resources awarded to replace EFC). 21% of all full-time undergraduates had no need and received non-need-based gift aid.

GIFT AID (NEED-BASED) ***Total amount:*** $6,821,138 (35% federal, 4% state, 61% institutional). ***Receiving aid:*** Freshmen: 46% (242); all full-time undergraduates: 45% (971). ***Average award:*** Freshmen: $10,115; Undergraduates: $8568. ***Scholarships, grants, and awards:*** Federal Pell, FSEOG, state, private, college/university gift aid from institutional funds.

GIFT AID (NON-NEED-BASED) ***Total amount:*** $7,444,338 (15% state, 55% institutional, 30% external sources). ***Receiving aid:*** Freshmen: 38% (202). Undergraduates: 26% (556). ***Average award:*** Freshmen: $6891. Undergraduates: $5752. ***Scholarships, grants, and awards by category:*** *Academic interests/achievement:* business, communication, education, English, general academic interests/achievements, health fields, mathematics, religion/biblical studies. *Creative arts/performance:* art/fine arts, journalism/publications, music, theater/drama. *Special achievements/activities:* community service, general special achievements/activities, leadership, religious involvement. *Special characteristics:* children and siblings of alumni, general special characteristics, international students, local/state students, members of minority groups, out-of-state students, siblings of current students, spouses of current students.

LOANS ***Student loans:*** $11,694,938 (53% need-based, 47% non-need-based). 61% of past graduating class borrowed through all loan programs. *Average indebtedness per student:* $18,846. ***Average need-based loan:*** Freshmen: $4688. Undergraduates: $5116. ***Parent loans:*** $1,371,615 (100% non-need-based). ***Programs:*** FFEL (Subsidized and Unsubsidized Stafford, PLUS), Perkins, Federal Nursing, college/university.

WORK-STUDY ***Federal work-study:*** Total amount: $1,955,407; jobs available. ***State or other work-study/employment:*** Part-time jobs available.

APPLYING FOR FINANCIAL AID ***Required financial aid form:*** FAFSA. ***Financial aid deadline (priority):*** 3/1. ***Notification date:*** Continuous. Students must reply within 2 weeks of notification.

CONTACT Mr. Marc Grundy, Director of Student Finance Office, Southern Adventist University, PO Box 370, Collegedale, TN 37315-0370, 423-236-2875 or toll-free 800-768-8437. *Fax:* 423-236-1835.

SOUTHERN ARKANSAS UNIVERSITY–MAGNOLIA

Magnolia, AR

Tuition & fees (AR res): $5646   Average undergraduate aid package: $7658

ABOUT THE INSTITUTION State-supported, coed. ***Awards:*** associate, bachelor's, and master's degrees. 45 undergraduate majors. ***Total enrollment:*** 3,117. Undergraduates: 2,674. Freshmen: 629. Federal methodology is used as a basis for awarding need-based institutional aid.

UNDERGRADUATE EXPENSES for 2008–09 ***Tuition, state resident:*** full-time $4800; part-time $160 per hour. ***Tuition, nonresident:*** full-time $7260; part-time $242 per hour. ***Required fees:*** full-time $846; $27 per hour or $18 per term. Full-time tuition and fees vary according to course load. Part-time tuition and fees vary according to course load. ***College room and board:*** $4250; ***Room only:*** $2130. Room and board charges vary according to board plan and housing facility. ***Payment plan:*** Installment.

FRESHMAN FINANCIAL AID (Fall 2008, est.) 461 applied for aid; of those 72% were deemed to have need. 78% of freshmen with need received aid; of those 81% had need fully met. ***Average percent of need met:*** 100% (excluding resources awarded to replace EFC). ***Average financial aid package:*** $7363 (excluding resources awarded to replace EFC). 8% of all full-time freshmen had no need and received non-need-based gift aid.

UNDERGRADUATE FINANCIAL AID (Fall 2008, est.) 2,204 applied for aid; of those 73% were deemed to have need. 82% of undergraduates with need received aid; of those 82% had need fully met. ***Average percent of need met:*** 100% (excluding resources awarded to replace EFC). ***Average financial aid package:*** $7658 (excluding resources awarded to replace EFC). 13% of all full-time undergraduates had no need and received non-need-based gift aid.

GIFT AID (NEED-BASED) ***Total amount:*** $5,904,637 (87% federal, 13% state). ***Receiving aid:*** Freshmen: 34% (215); all full-time undergraduates: 47% (1,054). ***Average award:*** Freshmen: $4172; Undergraduates: $4029. ***Scholarships, grants, and awards:*** Federal Pell, FSEOG, state, private, college/university gift aid from institutional funds.

GIFT AID (NON-NEED-BASED) ***Total amount:*** $5,360,515 (86% institutional, 14% external sources). ***Receiving aid:*** Freshmen: 31% (196). Undergraduates: 40% (892). ***Average award:*** Freshmen: $5922. Undergraduates: $5711. ***Scholarships, grants, and awards by category:*** *Academic interests/achievement:* 755 awards ($2,969,778 total): agriculture, business, computer science, education, English, foreign languages, general academic interests/achievements, health fields, mathematics, physical sciences, social sciences. *Creative arts/performance:* 25 awards ($73,505 total): art/fine arts, dance, music, theater/drama. *Special achievements/activities:* 57 awards ($140,450 total): cheerleading/drum major, leadership, rodeo. *Special characteristics:* 549 awards ($1,138,628 total): adult students, children and siblings of alumni, children of faculty/staff, members of minority groups, out-of-state students. ***Tuition waivers:*** Full or partial for children of alumni, employees or children of employees, senior citizens.

LOANS ***Student loans:*** $10,416,304 (55% need-based, 45% non-need-based). 67% of past graduating class borrowed through all loan programs. *Average indebtedness per student:* $15,102. ***Average need-based loan:*** Freshmen: $2758. Undergraduates: $3663. ***Parent loans:*** $165,618 (100% non-need-based). ***Programs:*** FFEL (Subsidized and Unsubsidized Stafford, PLUS), Perkins.

WORK-STUDY ***Federal work-study:*** Total amount: $2,760,180; 1,041 jobs averaging $2654. ***State or other work-study/employment:*** Total amount: $1,235,190 (100% non-need-based). 456 part-time jobs averaging $2709.

ATHLETIC AWARDS Total amount: $890,825 (100% non-need-based).

APPLYING FOR FINANCIAL AID ***Required financial aid form:*** FAFSA. ***Financial aid deadline (priority):*** 7/1. ***Notification date:*** Continuous beginning 4/1. Students must reply within 2 weeks of notification.

CONTACT Ms. Bronwyn C. Sneed, Director of Student Aid, Southern Arkansas University–Magnolia, PO Box 9344, Magnolia, AR 71754-9344, 870-235-4023 or toll-free 800-332-7286 (in-state). *Fax:* 870-235-4913. *E-mail:* bcsneed@saumag.edu.

SOUTHERN BAPTIST THEOLOGICAL SEMINARY

Louisville, KY

Tuition & fees: N/R   Average undergraduate aid package: $1120

ABOUT THE INSTITUTION Independent Southern Baptist, coed. ***Awards:*** associate, bachelor's, master's, and first professional degrees. 6 undergraduate majors. ***Total enrollment:*** 3,190. Undergraduates: 668. Freshmen: 62. Institutional methodology is used as a basis for awarding need-based institutional aid.

FRESHMAN FINANCIAL AID (Fall 2007) 9 applied for aid; of those 100% were deemed to have need. ***Average percent of need met:*** 6% (excluding resources awarded to replace EFC). ***Average financial aid package:*** $850 (excluding resources awarded to replace EFC).

UNDERGRADUATE FINANCIAL AID (Fall 2007) 80 applied for aid; of those 96% were deemed to have need. ***Average percent of need met:*** 7% (excluding resources awarded to replace EFC). ***Average financial aid package:*** $1120 (excluding resources awarded to replace EFC).

GIFT AID (NEED-BASED) ***Total amount:*** $238,828 (6% institutional, 94% external sources). ***Receiving aid:*** Freshmen: 19% (9); all full-time undergraduates: 16% (77). ***Average award:*** Freshmen: $178; Undergraduates: $182. ***Scholarships, grants, and awards:*** private, college/university gift aid from institutional funds, local church and denominational scholarships, as well as scholarships from various ministries.

GIFT AID (NON-NEED-BASED) ***Total amount:*** $92,208 (100% institutional). ***Receiving aid:*** Freshmen: 4% (2). Undergraduates: 3% (16).

LOANS ***Student loans:*** $1,226,849 (100% need-based). 35% of past graduating class borrowed through all loan programs. *Average indebtedness per student:* $6942. ***Programs:*** college/university, Non-Title IV loan programs such as Sallie Mae "Smart Option" Loans.

APPLYING FOR FINANCIAL AID ***Required financial aid form:*** institution's own form. ***Financial aid deadline:*** 8/1. ***Notification date:*** Continuous.

CONTACT Mr. David Schrock, Supervisor of Student Resources, Southern Baptist Theological Seminary, Financial Aid Office, Louisville, KY 40280, 502-897-4206. *Fax:* 502-897-4031. *E-mail:* financialaid@sbts.edu.

SOUTHERN CALIFORNIA INSTITUTE OF ARCHITECTURE

Los Angeles, CA

CONTACT Lina Johnson, Financial Aid Director, Southern California Institute of Architecture, 960 East 3rd Street, Los Angeles, CA 90013, 213-613-2200 Ext. 345 or toll-free 800-774-7242. *Fax:* 213-613-2260. *E-mail:* financialaid@sciarc.edu.

SOUTHERN CALIFORNIA SEMINARY

El Cajon, CA

CONTACT Financial Aid Office, Southern California Seminary, 2075 East Madison Avenue, El Cajon, CA 92019, 619-442-9841.

SOUTHERN CONNECTICUT STATE UNIVERSITY

New Haven, CT

Tuition & fees (CT res): $7179 Average undergraduate aid package: $8154

ABOUT THE INSTITUTION State-supported, coed. ***Awards:*** bachelor's, master's, and doctoral degrees and post-bachelor's and post-master's certificates. 43 undergraduate majors. ***Total enrollment:*** 11,769. Undergraduates: 8,496. Freshmen: 1,296. Federal methodology is used as a basis for awarding need-based institutional aid.

UNDERGRADUATE EXPENSES for 2008–09 ***Application fee:*** $50. ***Tuition, state resident:*** full-time $3514; part-time $357 per credit. ***Tuition, nonresident:*** full-time $11,373; part-time $357 per credit. ***Required fees:*** full-time $3665; $55 per term. ***College room and board:*** $8966; ***Room only:*** $4976. Room and board charges vary according to board plan and housing facility. ***Payment plans:*** Installment, deferred payment.

FRESHMAN FINANCIAL AID (Fall 2008, est.) 1,107 applied for aid; of those 62% were deemed to have need. 98% of freshmen with need received aid; of those 18% had need fully met. ***Average percent of need met:*** 87% (excluding resources awarded to replace EFC). ***Average financial aid package:*** $8505 (excluding resources awarded to replace EFC). 6% of all full-time freshmen had no need and received non-need-based gift aid.

UNDERGRADUATE FINANCIAL AID (Fall 2008, est.) 5,802 applied for aid; of those 64% were deemed to have need. 97% of undergraduates with need received aid; of those 43% had need fully met. ***Average percent of need met:*** 84% (excluding resources awarded to replace EFC). ***Average financial aid package:*** $8154 (excluding resources awarded to replace EFC). 4% of all full-time undergraduates had no need and received non-need-based gift aid.

GIFT AID (NEED-BASED) ***Total amount:*** $17,372,991 (35% federal, 29% state, 33% institutional, 3% external sources). ***Receiving aid:*** Freshmen: 47% (603); all full-time undergraduates: 41% (2,938). ***Average award:*** Freshmen: $5552; Undergraduates: $5365. ***Scholarships, grants, and awards:*** Federal Pell, FSEOG, state, college/university gift aid from institutional funds.

GIFT AID (NON-NEED-BASED) ***Total amount:*** $1,180,357 (1% state, 61% institutional, 38% external sources). ***Receiving aid:*** Freshmen: 2% (22). Undergraduates: 7% (519). ***Average award:*** Freshmen: $2621. Undergraduates: $3249. ***Scholarships, grants, and awards by category:*** *Special characteristics:* children of faculty/staff, veterans. ***Tuition waivers:*** Full or partial for employees or children of employees, senior citizens. ***ROTC:*** Army cooperative, Air Force cooperative.

LOANS ***Student loans:*** $32,560,897 (57% need-based, 43% non-need-based). 70% of past graduating class borrowed through all loan programs. *Average indebtedness per student:* $19,007. ***Average need-based loan:*** Freshmen: $3218. Undergraduates: $3648. ***Parent loans:*** $11,127,620 (14% need-based, 86% non-need-based). ***Programs:*** FFEL (Subsidized and Unsubsidized Stafford, PLUS), Perkins.

WORK-STUDY ***Federal work-study:*** Total amount: $282,769; 135 jobs averaging $3120. ***State or other work-study/employment:*** Total amount: $6 (100% need-based). Part-time jobs available.

ATHLETIC AWARDS Total amount: $1,360,330 (32% need-based, 68% non-need-based).

APPLYING FOR FINANCIAL AID ***Required financial aid form:*** FAFSA. ***Financial aid deadline:*** 3/9. ***Notification date:*** Continuous. Students must reply within 2 weeks of notification.

CONTACT Avon Dennis, Director of Financial Aid, Southern Connecticut State University, Wintergreen Building, New Haven, CT 06515-1355, 203-392-5448. *Fax:* 203-392-5229. *E-mail:* dennisa1@southernct.edu.

SOUTHERN ILLINOIS UNIVERSITY CARBONDALE

Carbondale, IL

Tuition & fees (IL res): $9813 Average undergraduate aid package: $11,682

ABOUT THE INSTITUTION State-supported, coed. ***Awards:*** associate, bachelor's, master's, doctoral, and first professional degrees and post-bachelor's and first professional certificates. 85 undergraduate majors. ***Total enrollment:*** 20,673. Undergraduates: 15,980. Freshmen: 2,686.

UNDERGRADUATE EXPENSES for 2008–09 ***Application fee:*** $30. ***Tuition, state resident:*** full-time $6975; part-time $232 per semester hour. ***Tuition, nonresident:*** full-time $17,437; part-time $581 per semester hour. ***Required fees:*** full-time $2838; $130 per semester hour. Full-time tuition and fees vary according to course load. Part-time tuition and fees vary according to course load. ***College room and board:*** $7137; ***Room only:*** $4097. Room and board charges vary according to board plan and housing facility. ***Payment plans:*** Guaranteed tuition, installment.

FRESHMAN FINANCIAL AID (Fall 2008, est.) 2,214 applied for aid; of those 80% were deemed to have need. 98% of freshmen with need received aid; of those 89% had need fully met. ***Average percent of need met:*** 96% (excluding resources awarded to replace EFC). ***Average financial aid package:*** $12,176 (excluding resources awarded to replace EFC). 6% of all full-time freshmen had no need and received non-need-based gift aid.

UNDERGRADUATE FINANCIAL AID (Fall 2008, est.) 10,271 applied for aid; of those 84% were deemed to have need. 97% of undergraduates with need received aid; of those 88% had need fully met. ***Average percent of need met:*** 97% (excluding resources awarded to replace EFC). ***Average financial aid package:*** $11,682 (excluding resources awarded to replace EFC). 7% of all full-time undergraduates had no need and received non-need-based gift aid.

GIFT AID (NEED-BASED) ***Total amount:*** $46,021,519 (43% federal, 48% state, 8% institutional, 1% external sources). ***Receiving aid:*** Freshmen: 48% (1,273); all full-time undergraduates: 43% (6,116). ***Average award:*** Freshmen: $7954; Undergraduates: $7392. ***Scholarships, grants, and awards:*** Federal Pell, FSEOG, state, private, college/university gift aid from institutional funds.

GIFT AID (NON-NEED-BASED) ***Total amount:*** $15,752,319 (29% federal, 33% state, 25% institutional, 13% external sources). ***Receiving aid:*** Freshmen: 35% (923). Undergraduates: 24% (3,470). ***Average award:*** Freshmen: $6480. Undergraduates: $6062. ***Scholarships, grants, and awards by category:*** *Academic interests/achievement:* agriculture, architecture, area/ethnic studies, biological sciences, business, communication, computer science, education, engineering/technologies, English, foreign languages, general academic interests/achievements, health fields, home economics, humanities, international studies, mathematics, military science, physical sciences, premedicine, religion/biblical studies, social sciences. *Creative arts/performance:* applied art and design, art/fine arts, cinema/film/broadcasting, creative writing, dance, debating, general creative arts/performance, journalism/publications, music, performing arts, theater/drama. *Special achievements/activities:* cheerleading/drum major, community service, general special achievements/activities, leadership. *Special characteristics:* children and siblings of alumni, children of educators, children of faculty/staff, children of public servants, children with a deceased or disabled parent, general special characteristics, handicapped students, international students, public servants, spouses of deceased or disabled public servants, veterans. ***Tuition waivers:*** Full or partial for employees or children of employees, senior citizens. ***ROTC:*** Army, Air Force.

LOANS ***Student loans:*** $68,561,771 (60% need-based, 40% non-need-based). 45% of past graduating class borrowed through all loan programs. *Average indebtedness per student:* $18,603. ***Average need-based loan:*** Freshmen: $3895. Undergraduates: $4335. ***Parent loans:*** $16,588,993 (13% need-based, 87% non-need-based). ***Programs:*** Federal Direct (Subsidized and Unsubsidized Stafford, PLUS), Perkins, college/university.

WORK-STUDY ***Federal work-study:*** Total amount: $9,115,611; jobs available. ***State or other work-study/employment:*** Total amount: $847,617 (16% need-based, 84% non-need-based). Part-time jobs available.

ATHLETIC AWARDS Total amount: $3,593,374 (28% need-based, 72% non-need-based).

APPLYING FOR FINANCIAL AID ***Required financial aid form:*** FAFSA. ***Financial aid deadline (priority):*** 4/1. ***Notification date:*** Continuous.

CONTACT Billie Jo Hamilton, Director of Financial Aid, Southern Illinois University Carbondale, Woody Hall, Third Floor, B-Wing, Carbondale, IL 62901-4702, 618-453-3102. *Fax:* 618-453-4606. *E-mail:* hamilton@siu.edu.

SOUTHERN ILLINOIS UNIVERSITY EDWARDSVILLE

Edwardsville, IL

Tuition & fees (IL res): $7819 Average undergraduate aid package: $14,527

ABOUT THE INSTITUTION State-supported, coed. ***Awards:*** bachelor's, master's, and first professional degrees and post-bachelor's, post-master's, and first professional certificates. 43 undergraduate majors. ***Total enrollment:*** 13,602. Undergraduates: 10,977. Freshmen: 1,922. Federal methodology is used as a basis for awarding need-based institutional aid.

UNDERGRADUATE EXPENSES for 2008–09 ***Application fee:*** $30. ***Tuition, state resident:*** full-time $5850; part-time $195 per semester hour. ***Tuition, nonresident:*** full-time $14,625; part-time $487.50 per semester hour. ***Required fees:*** full-time $1969. ***College room and board:*** $7040.

FRESHMAN FINANCIAL AID (Fall 2008, est.) 1,389 applied for aid; of those 87% were deemed to have need. 93% of freshmen with need received aid; of those 24% had need fully met. ***Average percent of need met:*** 44% (excluding resources awarded to replace EFC). ***Average financial aid package:*** $15,083 (excluding resources awarded to replace EFC). 2% of all full-time freshmen had no need and received non-need-based gift aid.

UNDERGRADUATE FINANCIAL AID (Fall 2008, est.) 5,343 applied for aid; of those 90% were deemed to have need. 95% of undergraduates with need received aid; of those 18% had need fully met. ***Average percent of need met:*** 44% (excluding resources awarded to replace EFC). ***Average financial aid package:*** $14,527 (excluding resources awarded to replace EFC). 4% of all full-time undergraduates had no need and received non-need-based gift aid.

GIFT AID (NEED-BASED) ***Total amount:*** $19,998,972 (45% federal, 45% state, 6% institutional, 4% external sources). ***Receiving aid:*** Freshmen: 28% (527); all full-time undergraduates: 30% (2,342). ***Average award:*** Freshmen: $9072; Undergraduates: $9024. ***Scholarships, grants, and awards:*** Federal Pell, FSEOG, state, private, college/university gift aid from institutional funds, Federal Nursing.

GIFT AID (NON-NEED-BASED) ***Total amount:*** $2,156,758 (5% federal, 48% state, 30% institutional, 17% external sources). ***Receiving aid:*** Freshmen: 2% (37). Undergraduates: 2% (129). ***Average award:*** Freshmen: $9387. Undergraduates: $7051. ***Scholarships, grants, and awards by category:*** *Academic interests/achievement:* business, education, general academic interests/achievements, health fields. *Creative arts/performance:* art/fine arts, dance, music, theater/drama. *Special characteristics:* children of faculty/staff. ***ROTC:*** Army, Air Force.

LOANS ***Student loans:*** $34,650,994 (86% need-based, 14% non-need-based). 40% of past graduating class borrowed through all loan programs. *Average indebtedness per student:* $16,656. ***Average need-based loan:*** Freshmen: $8618. Undergraduates: $9254. ***Parent loans:*** $7,737,174 (41% need-based, 59% non-need-based). ***Programs:*** Federal Direct (Subsidized and Unsubsidized Stafford, PLUS), FFEL (Subsidized and Unsubsidized Stafford, PLUS), Perkins, Federal Nursing, college/university, alternative loans.

WORK-STUDY ***Federal work-study:*** Total amount: $3,930,069; jobs available. ***State or other work-study/employment:*** Part-time jobs available.

ATHLETIC AWARDS Total amount: $419,953 (65% need-based, 35% non-need-based).

APPLYING FOR FINANCIAL AID ***Required financial aid form:*** FAFSA. ***Financial aid deadline (priority):*** 3/1. ***Notification date:*** Continuous beginning 3/15. Students must reply within 2 weeks of notification.

CONTACT Sharon Berry, Director of Financial Aid, Southern Illinois University Edwardsville, Campus Box 1060, Edwardsville, IL 62026-1060, 618-650-3834 or toll-free 800-447-SIUE. *Fax:* 618-650-3885. *E-mail:* shaberr@siue.edu.

SOUTHERN METHODIST COLLEGE

Orangeburg, SC

ABOUT THE INSTITUTION Independent religious, coed. ***Awards:*** associate and bachelor's degrees. 3 undergraduate majors. ***Total enrollment:*** 26. Undergraduates: 26.

GIFT AID (NEED-BASED) ***Scholarships, grants, and awards:*** Federal Pell, FSEOG, private, college/university gift aid from institutional funds.

GIFT AID (NON-NEED-BASED) ***Scholarships, grants, and awards by category:*** *Academic interests/achievement:* education, religion/biblical studies. *Special achievements/activities:* religious involvement. *Special characteristics:* relatives of clergy.

LOANS ***Programs:*** Federal Direct (Subsidized and Unsubsidized Stafford, PLUS).

APPLYING FOR FINANCIAL AID ***Required financial aid forms:*** FAFSA, institution's own form.

CONTACT Financial Aid Officer, Southern Methodist College, PO Box 1027, 541 Broughton Street, Orangeburg, SC 29116, 803-534-7826 Ext. 1326 or toll-free 800-360-1503. *Fax:* 803-534-7827.

SOUTHERN METHODIST UNIVERSITY

Dallas, TX

Tuition & fees: $35,160 **Average undergraduate aid package: $26,276**

ABOUT THE INSTITUTION Independent religious, coed. ***Awards:*** bachelor's, master's, doctoral, and first professional degrees and post-bachelor's certificates. 67 undergraduate majors. ***Total enrollment:*** 10,965. Undergraduates: 6,240. Freshmen: 1,398.

UNDERGRADUATE EXPENSES for 2009–10 ***Application fee:*** $60. ***Comprehensive fee:*** $47,605 includes full-time tuition ($31,200), mandatory fees ($3960), and room and board ($12,445). ***Part-time tuition:*** $1304 per credit hour. ***Part-time fees:*** $166 per credit hour.

FRESHMAN FINANCIAL AID (Fall 2007) 584 applied for aid; of those 70% were deemed to have need. 100% of freshmen with need received aid; of those 44% had need fully met. ***Average percent of need met:*** 90% (excluding resources awarded to replace EFC). ***Average financial aid package:*** $27,655 (excluding resources awarded to replace EFC). 44% of all full-time freshmen had no need and received non-need-based gift aid.

UNDERGRADUATE FINANCIAL AID (Fall 2007) 2,387 applied for aid; of those 82% were deemed to have need. 100% of undergraduates with need received aid; of those 37% had need fully met. ***Average percent of need met:*** 88% (excluding resources awarded to replace EFC). ***Average financial aid package:*** $26,276 (excluding resources awarded to replace EFC). 35% of all full-time undergraduates had no need and received non-need-based gift aid.

GIFT AID (NEED-BASED) ***Total amount:*** $36,875,321 (9% federal, 11% state, 79% institutional, 1% external sources). ***Receiving aid:*** Freshmen: 25% (322); all full-time undergraduates: 28% (1,627). ***Average award:*** Freshmen: $16,282; Undergraduates: $15,769. ***Scholarships, grants, and awards:*** Federal Pell, FSEOG, state, private, college/university gift aid from institutional funds.

GIFT AID (NON-NEED-BASED) ***Total amount:*** $17,446,296 (97% institutional, 3% external sources). ***Receiving aid:*** Freshmen: 24% (317). Undergraduates: 20% (1,150). ***Average award:*** Freshmen: $11,140. Undergraduates: $11,725. ***ROTC:*** Army, Air Force cooperative.

LOANS ***Student loans:*** $12,693,377 (66% need-based, 34% non-need-based). 33% of past graduating class borrowed through all loan programs. *Average indebtedness per student:* $16,756. ***Average need-based loan:*** Freshmen: $2609. Undergraduates: $3439. ***Parent loans:*** $12,481,813 (28% need-based, 72% non-need-based). ***Programs:*** FFEL (Subsidized and Unsubsidized Stafford, PLUS), Perkins, state, college/university.

WORK-STUDY ***Federal work-study:*** Total amount: $3,157,739; 1,780 jobs averaging $2888. ***State or other work-study/employment:*** Total amount: $192,720 (38% need-based, 62% non-need-based). 24 part-time jobs averaging $2365.

ATHLETIC AWARDS Total amount: $9,236,447 (36% need-based, 64% non-need-based).

APPLYING FOR FINANCIAL AID ***Required financial aid forms:*** FAFSA, CSS Financial Aid PROFILE, business/farm supplement. ***Financial aid deadline (priority):*** 3/1. ***Notification date:*** Continuous beginning 3/15.

CONTACT Marc Peterson, Director of Financial Aid, Southern Methodist University, PO Box 750181, Dallas, TX 75275, 214-768-3016 or toll-free 800-323-0672. *Fax:* 214-768-0202. *E-mail:* mpeterso@smu.edu.

SOUTHERN NAZARENE UNIVERSITY

Bethany, OK

Tuition & fees: $17,664 **Average undergraduate aid package: N/A**

ABOUT THE INSTITUTION Independent Nazarene, coed. ***Awards:*** associate, bachelor's, and master's degrees. 59 undergraduate majors. ***Total enrollment:*** 2,069. Undergraduates: 1,628. Freshmen: 270. Federal methodology is used as a basis for awarding need-based institutional aid.

UNDERGRADUATE EXPENSES for 2009–10 ***Application fee:*** $35. ***Comprehensive fee:*** $24,154 includes full-time tuition ($17,040), mandatory fees ($624), and room and board ($6490). ***College room only:*** $3200. ***Part-time tuition:*** $568 per credit hour. ***Part-time fees:*** $23 per credit hour.

FRESHMAN FINANCIAL AID (Fall 2007) 275 applied for aid; of those 93% were deemed to have need. 96% of freshmen with need received aid.

UNDERGRADUATE FINANCIAL AID (Fall 2007) 1,548 applied for aid; of those 94% were deemed to have need. 96% of undergraduates with need received aid.

GIFT AID (NEED-BASED) ***Total amount:*** $8,699,979 (22% federal, 8% state, 64% institutional, 6% external sources). ***Scholarships, grants, and awards:*** Federal Pell, FSEOG, state, private, college/university gift aid from institutional funds.

GIFT AID (NON-NEED-BASED) ***Scholarships, grants, and awards by category:*** *Academic interests/achievement:* biological sciences, business, communication, computer science, education, English, general academic interests/achievements, mathematics, physical sciences, religion/biblical studies. *Creative arts/performance:* art/fine arts, music, performing arts. *Special achievements/activities:* cheerleading/drum major. *Special characteristics:* children and siblings of alumni, children of faculty/staff, first-generation college students, local/state students, religious affiliation. ***ROTC:*** Army cooperative, Air Force cooperative.

LOANS ***Student loans:*** $15,414,442 (100% need-based). 75% of past graduating class borrowed through all loan programs. ***Parent loans:*** $2,448,411 (100% need-based). ***Programs:*** FFEL (Subsidized and Unsubsidized Stafford, PLUS), Perkins, alternative loans.

WORK-STUDY ***Federal work-study:*** Total amount: $202,500; 108 jobs averaging $1200. ***State or other work-study/employment:*** Total amount: $390,500 (100% need-based). 126 part-time jobs averaging $3000.

ATHLETIC AWARDS Total amount: $2,540,871 (100% need-based).

APPLYING FOR FINANCIAL AID ***Required financial aid form:*** FAFSA. ***Financial aid deadline (priority):*** 3/1. ***Notification date:*** Continuous beginning 3/15. Students must reply within 2 weeks of notification.

CONTACT Diana Lee, Director of Financial Assistance, Southern Nazarene University, 6729 Northwest 39th Expressway, Bethany, OK 73008, 405-491-6310 or toll-free 800-648-9899. *Fax:* 405-717-6271. *E-mail:* dlee@snu.edu.

SOUTHERN NEW HAMPSHIRE UNIVERSITY

Manchester, NH

Tuition & fees: $26,442 **Average undergraduate aid package: $15,514**

ABOUT THE INSTITUTION Independent, coed. ***Awards:*** associate, bachelor's, master's, and doctoral degrees and post-bachelor's certificates. 38 undergraduate majors. ***Total enrollment:*** 4,211. Undergraduates: 2,037. Freshmen: 599. Federal methodology is used as a basis for awarding need-based institutional aid.

UNDERGRADUATE EXPENSES for 2009–10 ***Application fee:*** $40. ***Comprehensive fee:*** $36,618 includes full-time tuition ($26,112), mandatory fees ($330), and room and board ($10,176). ***College room only:*** $7276. ***Part-time tuition:*** $1088 per credit.

FRESHMAN FINANCIAL AID (Fall 2007) 464 applied for aid; of those 89% were deemed to have need. 100% of freshmen with need received aid; of those 11% had need fully met. ***Average percent of need met:*** 69% (excluding resources awarded to replace EFC). ***Average financial aid package:*** $16,704 (excluding resources awarded to replace EFC). 14% of all full-time freshmen had no need and received non-need-based gift aid.

UNDERGRADUATE FINANCIAL AID (Fall 2007) 1,560 applied for aid; of those 89% were deemed to have need. 100% of undergraduates with need received aid; of those 12% had need fully met. ***Average percent of need met:*** 69% (excluding resources awarded to replace EFC). ***Average financial aid package:*** $15,514 (excluding resources awarded to replace EFC). 17% of all full-time undergraduates had no need and received non-need-based gift aid.

GIFT AID (NEED-BASED) ***Total amount:*** $13,606,766 (12% federal, 2% state, 83% institutional, 3% external sources). ***Receiving aid:*** Freshmen: 72% (392); all full-time undergraduates: 68% (1,324). ***Average award:*** Freshmen: $12,160; Undergraduates: $10,223. ***Scholarships, grants, and awards:*** Federal Pell, FSEOG, state, private, college/university gift aid from institutional funds.

GIFT AID (NON-NEED-BASED) ***Total amount:*** $1,434,770 (95% institutional, 5% external sources). ***Receiving aid:*** Freshmen: 65% (354). Undergraduates: 70% (1,344). ***Average award:*** Freshmen: $4084. Undergraduates: $3599. ***ROTC:*** Army cooperative, Air Force cooperative.

LOANS ***Student loans:*** $17,097,998 (56% need-based, 44% non-need-based). ***Average need-based loan:*** Freshmen: $4555. Undergraduates: $5174. ***Parent loans:*** $4,783,095 (5% need-based, 95% non-need-based). ***Programs:*** FFEL (Subsidized and Unsubsidized Stafford, PLUS), Perkins.

WORK-STUDY ***Federal work-study:*** Total amount: $1,535,618; jobs available.

ATHLETIC AWARDS Total amount: $1,873,095 (38% need-based, 62% non-need-based).

APPLYING FOR FINANCIAL AID ***Required financial aid form:*** FAFSA. ***Financial aid deadline (priority):*** 3/15. ***Notification date:*** Continuous. Students must reply within 3 weeks of notification.

CONTACT Financial Aid Office, Southern New Hampshire University, 2500 North River Road, Manchester, NH 03106, 603-645-9645 or toll-free 800-642-4968. *Fax:* 603-645-9639. *E-mail:* finaid@snhu.edu.

SOUTHERN OREGON UNIVERSITY

Ashland, OR

Tuition & fees (OR res): $5718 **Average undergraduate aid package: $10,892**

ABOUT THE INSTITUTION State-supported, coed. ***Awards:*** bachelor's and master's degrees and post-bachelor's certificates. 40 undergraduate majors. ***Total enrollment:*** 4,437. Undergraduates: 4,437. Federal methodology is used as a basis for awarding need-based institutional aid.

UNDERGRADUATE EXPENSES for 2008–09 ***Application fee:*** $50. ***Tuition, state resident:*** full-time $5718. ***Tuition, nonresident:*** full-time $18,264. Full-time tuition and fees vary according to course load, location, and reciprocity agreements. Part-time tuition and fees vary according to course load, location, and reciprocity agreements. ***College room and board:*** $8250. Room and board charges vary according to board plan and housing facility. ***Payment plan:*** Deferred payment.

FRESHMAN FINANCIAL AID (Fall 2008, est.) 533 applied for aid; of those 77% were deemed to have need. 89% of freshmen with need received aid; of those 19% had need fully met. ***Average percent of need met:*** 69% (excluding resources awarded to replace EFC). ***Average financial aid package:*** $10,640 (excluding resources awarded to replace EFC). 10% of all full-time freshmen had no need and received non-need-based gift aid.

UNDERGRADUATE FINANCIAL AID (Fall 2008, est.) 2,959 applied for aid; of those 86% were deemed to have need. 83% of undergraduates with need received aid; of those 15% had need fully met. ***Average percent of need met:*** 67% (excluding resources awarded to replace EFC). ***Average financial aid package:*** $10,892 (excluding resources awarded to replace EFC). 5% of all full-time undergraduates had no need and received non-need-based gift aid.

GIFT AID (NEED-BASED) ***Total amount:*** $17,852,269 (40% federal, 16% state, 35% institutional, 9% external sources). ***Receiving aid:*** Freshmen: 32% (207); all full-time undergraduates: 41% (1,341). ***Average award:*** Freshmen: $1430; Undergraduates: $1311. ***Scholarships, grants, and awards:*** Federal Pell, FSEOG, state, private, college/university gift aid from institutional funds.

GIFT AID (NON-NEED-BASED) ***Total amount:*** $1000 (100% institutional). ***Receiving aid:*** Freshmen: 50% (320). Undergraduates: 51% (1,652). ***Average award:*** Freshmen: $7964. Undergraduates: $6826. ***Scholarships, grants, and awards by category:*** *Academic interests/achievement:* 430 awards ($830,754 total): biological sciences, business, education, English, foreign languages, general academic interests/achievements, health fields, mathematics, physical sciences, social sciences. *Creative arts/performance:* 117 awards ($155,697 total): art/fine arts, creative writing, journalism/publications, music, theater/drama. *Special achievements/activities:* 25 awards ($30,125 total): community service, general special achievements/activities, hobbies/interests, leadership, memberships. *Special characteristics:* 17 awards ($375,812 total): adult students, international students, members of minority groups. ***Tuition waivers:*** Full or partial for employees or children of employees, senior citizens.

LOANS ***Student loans:*** $16,122,444 (56% need-based, 44% non-need-based). 72% of past graduating class borrowed through all loan programs. *Average indebtedness per student:* $26,000. ***Average need-based loan:*** Freshmen: $1174. Undergraduates: $1211. ***Parent loans:*** $4,807,275 (100% non-need-based). ***Programs:*** Federal Direct (Subsidized and Unsubsidized Stafford, PLUS), Perkins, state, college/university.

WORK-STUDY ***Federal work-study:*** Total amount: $696,004; jobs available.

ATHLETIC AWARDS Total amount: $329,017 (100% need-based).

APPLYING FOR FINANCIAL AID ***Required financial aid forms:*** FAFSA, institution's own form. ***Financial aid deadline (priority):*** 3/1. ***Notification date:*** Continuous beginning 3/1. Students must reply within 4 weeks of notification.

CONTACT Enrollment Services Center, Southern Oregon University, 1250 Siskiyou Boulevard, Ashland, OR 97520, 541-552-6600 or toll-free 800-482-7672 (in-state). *Fax:* 541-552-6614. *E-mail:* esc@sou.edu.

SOUTHERN POLYTECHNIC STATE UNIVERSITY

Marietta, GA

Tuition & fees (GA res): $4232 **Average undergraduate aid package: $2992**

ABOUT THE INSTITUTION State-supported, coed. ***Awards:*** associate, bachelor's, and master's degrees and post-bachelor's certificates. 27 undergraduate majors. ***Total enrollment:*** 4,818. Undergraduates: 4,251. Freshmen: 599. Federal methodology is used as a basis for awarding need-based institutional aid.

UNDERGRADUATE EXPENSES for 2008–09 ***Application fee:*** $20. ***Tuition, state resident:*** full-time $3502; part-time $146 per credit hour. ***Tuition, nonresident:*** full-time $13,998; part-time $584 per credit hour. ***Required fees:*** full-time $730; $365 per term. Full-time tuition and fees vary according to course load. Part-time tuition and fees vary according to course load. ***College room and board:*** $5870; ***Room only:*** $3400. Room and board charges vary according to board plan. ***Payment plan:*** Guaranteed tuition.

FRESHMAN FINANCIAL AID (Fall 2008, est.) 420 applied for aid; of those 100% were deemed to have need. 98% of freshmen with need received aid; of those 40% had need fully met. ***Average percent of need met:*** 79% (excluding resources awarded to replace EFC). ***Average financial aid package:*** $2472 (excluding resources awarded to replace EFC). 1% of all full-time freshmen had no need and received non-need-based gift aid.

UNDERGRADUATE FINANCIAL AID (Fall 2008, est.) 2,392 applied for aid; of those 75% were deemed to have need. 96% of undergraduates with need received aid; of those 20% had need fully met. ***Average percent of need met:*** 80% (excluding resources awarded to replace EFC). ***Average financial aid package:*** $2992 (excluding resources awarded to replace EFC). 1% of all full-time undergraduates had no need and received non-need-based gift aid.

GIFT AID (NEED-BASED) ***Total amount:*** $4,015,320 (99% federal, 1% external sources). ***Receiving aid:*** Freshmen: 30% (157); all full-time undergraduates: 26% (1,003). ***Average award:*** Freshmen: $2736; Undergraduates: $2825. ***Scholarships, grants, and awards:*** Federal Pell, FSEOG, state, private, college/university gift aid from institutional funds.

GIFT AID (NON-NEED-BASED) ***Total amount:*** $4,586,578 (90% state, 1% institutional, 9% external sources). ***Receiving aid:*** Freshmen: 55% (285). Undergraduates: 15% (573). ***Average award:*** Freshmen: $7331. Undergraduates: $6741. ***Scholarships, grants, and awards by category:*** *Academic interests/achievement:* general academic interests/achievements. *Special characteristics:* members of minority groups. ***Tuition waivers:*** Full or partial for senior citizens. ***ROTC:*** Army cooperative, Naval cooperative, Air Force cooperative.

LOANS ***Student loans:*** $13,588,584 (47% need-based, 53% non-need-based). 45% of past graduating class borrowed through all loan programs. *Average indebtedness per student:* $13,641. ***Average need-based loan:*** Freshmen: $3174. Undergraduates: $4058. ***Parent loans:*** $482,415 (100% non-need-based). ***Programs:*** FFEL (Subsidized and Unsubsidized Stafford, PLUS), state.

WORK-STUDY ***Federal work-study:*** Total amount: $75,579; jobs available (averaging $2000).

ATHLETIC AWARDS Total amount: $203,613 (100% non-need-based).

APPLYING FOR FINANCIAL AID ***Required financial aid form:*** FAFSA. ***Financial aid deadline (priority):*** 3/1. ***Notification date:*** Continuous beginning 6/1. Students must reply by 8/15.

CONTACT Mr. Gary Bush, Director of Financial Aid, Southern Polytechnic State University, 1100 South Marietta Parkway, Marietta, GA 30060-2896, 678-915-7290 or toll-free 800-635-3204. *Fax:* 678-915-4227. *E-mail:* gbush@spsu.edu.

SOUTHERN UNIVERSITY AND AGRICULTURAL AND MECHANICAL COLLEGE

Baton Rouge, LA

ABOUT THE INSTITUTION State-supported, coed. ***Awards:*** associate, bachelor's, master's, and doctoral degrees and post-master's certificates. 61 undergraduate majors. ***Total enrollment:*** 7,699. Undergraduates: 6,459. Freshmen: 1,045.

GIFT AID (NEED-BASED) ***Scholarships, grants, and awards:*** Federal Pell, FSEOG, state, private, college/university gift aid from institutional funds, LEAP, TOPS, and T.H. Harris.

GIFT AID (NON-NEED-BASED) ***Scholarships, grants, and awards by category:*** *Academic interests/achievement:* general academic interests/achievements.

LOANS ***Programs:*** Federal Direct (Subsidized and Unsubsidized Stafford, PLUS), FFEL (Subsidized and Unsubsidized Stafford, PLUS), college/university.

APPLYING FOR FINANCIAL AID ***Required financial aid forms:*** FAFSA, institution's own form.

CONTACT Mr. Phillip Rodgers Sr., Director of Financial Aid, Southern University and Agricultural and Mechanical College, PO Box 9961, Baton Rouge, LA 70813, 225-771-2790 or toll-free 800-256-1531. *Fax:* 225-771-5898. *E-mail:* phillip_rodgers@cxs.subr.edu.

SOUTHERN UNIVERSITY AT NEW ORLEANS

New Orleans, LA

CONTACT Director of Financial Aid, Southern University at New Orleans, 6400 Press Drive, New Orleans, LA 70126, 504-286-5263. *Fax:* 504-286-5213.

SOUTHERN UTAH UNIVERSITY

Cedar City, UT

Tuition & fees (UT res): $4028 **Average undergraduate aid package: $6456**

ABOUT THE INSTITUTION State-supported, coed. ***Awards:*** associate, bachelor's, and master's degrees. 49 undergraduate majors. ***Total enrollment:*** 7,516. Undergraduates: 6,784. Freshmen: 1,244. Federal methodology is used as a basis for awarding need-based institutional aid.

UNDERGRADUATE EXPENSES for 2008–09 ***Application fee:*** $40. ***Tuition, state resident:*** full-time $3502; part-time $171 per credit hour. ***Tuition, nonresident:*** full-time $12,082; part-time $565 per credit hour. ***Required fees:*** full-time $526. Part-time tuition and fees vary according to course load. ***College room and board:*** ***Room only:*** $1950. Room and board charges vary according to board plan and housing facility. ***Payment plan:*** Installment.

FRESHMAN FINANCIAL AID (Fall 2007) 743 applied for aid; of those 80% were deemed to have need. 99% of freshmen with need received aid; of those 13% had need fully met. ***Average percent of need met:*** 64% (excluding resources awarded to replace EFC). ***Average financial aid package:*** $5594 (excluding resources awarded to replace EFC). 48% of all full-time freshmen had no need and received non-need-based gift aid.

UNDERGRADUATE FINANCIAL AID (Fall 2007) 3,089 applied for aid; of those 87% were deemed to have need. 99% of undergraduates with need received aid; of those 11% had need fully met. ***Average percent of need met:*** 68% (excluding resources awarded to replace EFC). ***Average financial aid package:*** $6456 (excluding resources awarded to replace EFC). 37% of all full-time undergraduates had no need and received non-need-based gift aid.

GIFT AID (NEED-BASED) ***Total amount:*** $7,341,191 (90% federal, 4% state, 3% institutional, 3% external sources). ***Receiving aid:*** Freshmen: 50% (581); all full-time undergraduates: 58% (2,674). ***Average award:*** Freshmen: $4450; Undergraduates: $4603. ***Scholarships, grants, and awards:*** Federal Pell, FSEOG, state, private, college/university gift aid from institutional funds.

GIFT AID (NON-NEED-BASED) ***Total amount:*** $6,431,366 (87% institutional, 13% external sources). ***Receiving aid:*** Freshmen: 34% (394). Undergraduates: 18% (844). ***Average award:*** Freshmen: $5140. Undergraduates: $5672. ***Scholarships, grants, and awards by category:*** *Academic interests/achievement:* general academic interests/achievements. *Creative arts/performance:* general creative arts/performance, music, theater/drama. *Special achievements/activities:* general special achievements/activities, leadership. *Special characteristics:* children and siblings of alumni, members of minority groups. ***Tuition waivers:*** Full or partial for employees or children of employees. ***ROTC:*** Army.

LOANS ***Student loans:*** $10,172,680 (77% need-based, 23% non-need-based). 45% of past graduating class borrowed through all loan programs. *Average indebtedness per student:* $8719. ***Average need-based loan:*** Freshmen: $3141. Undergraduates: $4046. ***Parent loans:*** $435,432 (100% non-need-based). ***Programs:*** FFEL (Subsidized and Unsubsidized Stafford, PLUS), Perkins.

WORK-STUDY ***Federal work-study:*** Total amount: $284,347; jobs available. ***State or other work-study/employment:*** Total amount: $141,725 (100% need-based). Part-time jobs available.

ATHLETIC AWARDS Total amount: $1,780,818 (100% non-need-based).

APPLYING FOR FINANCIAL AID ***Required financial aid forms:*** FAFSA, institution's own form, tax forms as selected. ***Financial aid deadline:*** Continuous. ***Notification date:*** Continuous beginning 11/1. Students must reply by 5/1.

CONTACT Paul Morris, Director of Financial Aid, Southern Utah University, 351 West Center Street, Cedar City, UT 84720-2498, 435-586-7734. *Fax:* 435-586-7736. *E-mail:* morris@suu.edu.

SOUTHERN VERMONT COLLEGE

Bennington, VT

CONTACT Office of Financial Aid, Southern Vermont College, 982 Mansion Drive, Bennington, VT 05201, 802-447-6306 or toll-free 800-378-2782. *Fax:* 802-447-4695. *E-mail:* financialaid@svc.edu.

SOUTHERN VIRGINIA UNIVERSITY

Buena Vista, VA

ABOUT THE INSTITUTION Independent Latter-day Saints, coed. 13 undergraduate majors.

GIFT AID (NEED-BASED) ***Scholarships, grants, and awards:*** Federal Pell, FSEOG, state, private, college/university gift aid from institutional funds.

GIFT AID (NON-NEED-BASED) ***Scholarships, grants, and awards by category:*** *Academic interests/achievement:* general academic interests/achievements. *Creative arts/performance:* art/fine arts. *Special achievements/activities:* religious involvement. *Special characteristics:* children of faculty/staff, international students.

LOANS ***Programs:*** FFEL (Subsidized and Unsubsidized Stafford, PLUS), alternative loans.

WORK-STUDY ***Federal work-study:*** Total amount: $95,573; 164 jobs averaging $1000. ***State or other work-study/employment:*** Total amount: $41,200 (100% non-need-based). 19 part-time jobs averaging $2168.

APPLYING FOR FINANCIAL AID ***Required financial aid forms:*** FAFSA, Virginia Tuition Assistance Grant (VA residents only).

CONTACT Darin Hassell, Financial Aid Specialist, Southern Virginia University, One University Hill Drive, Buena Vista, VA 24416, 540-261-4351 or toll-free 800-229-8420. *Fax:* 540-261-8559. *E-mail:* finaid@svu.edu.

SOUTHERN WESLEYAN UNIVERSITY

Central, SC

ABOUT THE INSTITUTION Independent religious, coed. ***Awards:*** associate, bachelor's, and master's degrees. 29 undergraduate majors. ***Total enrollment:*** 2,391. Undergraduates: 1,631. Freshmen: 142.

GIFT AID (NEED-BASED) ***Scholarships, grants, and awards:*** Federal Pell, FSEOG, state, private, college/university gift aid from institutional funds.

GIFT AID (NON-NEED-BASED) ***Scholarships, grants, and awards by category:*** *Academic interests/achievement:* biological sciences, business, computer science, education, English, general academic interests/achievements, humanities, mathematics, physical sciences, premedicine, religion/biblical studies, social sciences. *Creative arts/performance:* art/fine arts, creative writing, journalism/publications, music, theater/drama. *Special achievements/activities:* community service, leadership, religious involvement. *Special characteristics:* children of faculty/staff, ethnic background, members of minority groups, relatives of clergy, religious affiliation, siblings of current students.

LOANS ***Programs:*** FFEL (Subsidized and Unsubsidized Stafford, PLUS), Perkins.

APPLYING FOR FINANCIAL AID ***Required financial aid forms:*** FAFSA, institution's own form.

CONTACT Mrs. Sherri Peters, Financial Aid Associate, Southern Wesleyan University, 907 Wesleyan Drive, Central, SC 29630-1020, 800-289-1292 Ext. 5517 or toll-free 800-289-1292 Ext. 5550. *Fax:* 864-644-5970. *E-mail:* finaid@swu.edu.

SOUTH UNIVERSITY

Montgomery, AL

UNDERGRADUATE EXPENSES Information about tuition and fees can be obtained by contacting the South University Admissions Office.

CONTACT Financial Aid Office, South University, 5355 Vaughn Road, Montgomery, AL 36116-1120, 334-395-8800 or toll-free 866-629-2962.

SOUTH UNIVERSITY

Tampa, FL

UNDERGRADUATE EXPENSES Information about tuition and fees can be obtained by contacting the South University Admissions Office.

CONTACT Financial Aid Office, South University, 4401 North Himes Avenue, Suite 175, Tampa, FL 33614, 813-393-3800 or toll-free 800-846-1472.

SOUTH UNIVERSITY

West Palm Beach, FL

UNDERGRADUATE EXPENSES Information about tuition and fees can be obtained by contacting the South University Admissions Office.

CONTACT Financial Aid Office, South University, 1760 North Congress Avenue, West Palm Beach, FL 33409, 561-697-9200 Ext. 230 or toll-free 866-629-2902. *Fax:* 561-697-9944. *E-mail:* lhartman@southcollege.edu.

SOUTH UNIVERSITY

Savannah, GA

UNDERGRADUATE EXPENSES Information about tuition and fees can be obtained by contacting the South University Admissions Office.

CONTACT Financial Aid Office, South University, 709 Mall Boulevard, Savannah, GA 31406, 912-201-8000 or toll-free 866-629-2901.

SOUTH UNIVERSITY

Columbia, SC

UNDERGRADUATE EXPENSES Information about tuition and fees can be obtained by contacting the South University Admissions Office.

CONTACT Sandra Gundlach, Financial Aid Coordinator, South University, 3810 Main Street, Columbia, SC 29203, 803-799-9082 or toll-free 866-629-3031. *Fax:* 803-799-9005.

SOUTHWEST BAPTIST UNIVERSITY

Bolivar, MO

Tuition & fees: $16,530 **Average undergraduate aid package: $13,657**

ABOUT THE INSTITUTION Independent Southern Baptist, coed. ***Awards:*** associate, bachelor's, master's, and doctoral degrees and post-master's certificates. 54 undergraduate majors. ***Total enrollment:*** 3,656. Undergraduates: 2,803. Freshmen: 516. Federal methodology is used as a basis for awarding need-based institutional aid.

UNDERGRADUATE EXPENSES for 2009–10 ***Application fee:*** $30. ***Comprehensive fee:*** $22,000 includes full-time tuition ($15,800), mandatory fees ($730), and room and board ($5470). ***College room only:*** $2820. ***Part-time fees:*** $580 per hour.

FRESHMAN FINANCIAL AID (Fall 2008, est.) 439 applied for aid; of those 79% were deemed to have need. 99% of freshmen with need received aid; of those 36% had need fully met. ***Average percent of need met:*** 86% (excluding resources awarded to replace EFC). ***Average financial aid package:*** $15,192 (excluding resources awarded to replace EFC). 23% of all full-time freshmen had no need and received non-need-based gift aid.

UNDERGRADUATE FINANCIAL AID (Fall 2008, est.) 1,581 applied for aid; of those 84% were deemed to have need. 100% of undergraduates with need received aid; of those 29% had need fully met. ***Average percent of need met:*** 77% (excluding resources awarded to replace EFC). ***Average financial aid package:*** $13,657 (excluding resources awarded to replace EFC). 21% of all full-time undergraduates had no need and received non-need-based gift aid.

GIFT AID (NEED-BASED) ***Total amount:*** $5,766,445 (53% federal, 42% state, 5% institutional). ***Receiving aid:*** Freshmen: 50% (237); all full-time undergraduates: 47% (890). ***Average award:*** Freshmen: $5852; Undergraduates: $5552. ***Scholarships, grants, and awards:*** Federal Pell, FSEOG, state, private, college/university gift aid from institutional funds.

GIFT AID (NON-NEED-BASED) ***Total amount:*** $9,085,167 (3% state, 88% institutional, 9% external sources). ***Receiving aid:*** Freshmen: 66% (313) Undergraduates: 59% (1,105). ***Average award:*** Freshmen: $7841. Undergraduates: $6675. ***Scholarships, grants, and awards by category:*** *Academic interests/*

achievement: 1,301 awards ($5,988,545 total): general academic interests/achievements. *Creative arts/performance:* 142 awards ($212,347 total): art/fine arts, debating, general creative arts/performance, music, theater/drama. *Special achievements/activities:* 201 awards ($365,000 total): religious involvement. *Special characteristics:* 759 awards ($898,702 total): general special characteristics, local/state students, relatives of clergy. ***ROTC:*** Army cooperative.

LOANS *Student loans:* $10,318,475 (47% need-based, 53% non-need-based). 74% of past graduating class borrowed through all loan programs. ***Average need-based loan:*** Freshmen: $3920. Undergraduates: $4448. ***Parent loans:*** $751,533 (100% non-need-based). ***Programs:*** FFEL (Subsidized and Unsubsidized Stafford, PLUS), Perkins, Federal Nursing, state, alternative loans.

WORK-STUDY *Federal work-study:* Total amount: $617,361; 353 jobs averaging $1809.

ATHLETIC AWARDS Total amount: $2,040,047 (100% non-need-based).

APPLYING FOR FINANCIAL AID *Required financial aid forms:* FAFSA, institution's own form. ***Financial aid deadline (priority):*** 3/15. ***Notification date:*** Continuous. Students must reply within 2 weeks of notification.

CONTACT Mr. Brad Gamble, Director of Financial Aid, Southwest Baptist University, 1600 University Avenue, Bolivar, MO 65613-2597, 417-328-1823 or toll-free 800-526-5859. *Fax:* 417-328-1514. *E-mail:* bgamble@sbuniv.edu.

SOUTHWESTERN ADVENTIST UNIVERSITY

Keene, TX

CONTACT Student Financial Services, Southwestern Adventist University, PO Box 567, Keene, TX 76059, 817-645-3921 Ext. 262 or toll-free 800-433-2240. *Fax:* 817-556-4744.

SOUTHWESTERN ASSEMBLIES OF GOD UNIVERSITY

Waxahachie, TX

CONTACT Financial Aid Office, Southwestern Assemblies of God University, 1200 Sycamore Street, Waxahachie, TX 75165-2397, 972-825-4730 or toll-free 888-937-7248. *Fax:* 972-937-4001. *E-mail:* finaid@sagu.edu.

SOUTHWESTERN CHRISTIAN COLLEGE

Terrell, TX

CONTACT Financial Aid Office, Southwestern Christian College, PO Box 10, Terrell, TX 75160, 972-524-3341. *Fax:* 972-563-7133.

SOUTHWESTERN CHRISTIAN UNIVERSITY

Bethany, OK

Tuition & fees: $9800 **Average undergraduate aid package: $9000**

ABOUT THE INSTITUTION Independent religious, coed. ***Awards:*** associate, bachelor's, and master's degrees. 11 undergraduate majors. ***Total enrollment:*** 264. Undergraduates: 180. Federal methodology is used as a basis for awarding need-based institutional aid.

UNDERGRADUATE EXPENSES for 2008–09 *Comprehensive fee:* $14,400 includes full-time tuition ($9750), mandatory fees ($50), and room and board ($4600). ***Part-time tuition:*** $345 per credit hour. ***Part-time fees:*** $25 per term.

FRESHMAN FINANCIAL AID (Fall 2008, est.) 75 applied for aid; of those 93% were deemed to have need. 100% of freshmen with need received aid; of those 41% had need fully met. ***Average percent of need met:*** 73% (excluding resources awarded to replace EFC). ***Average financial aid package:*** $7925 (excluding resources awarded to replace EFC). 7% of all full-time freshmen had no need and received non-need-based gift aid.

UNDERGRADUATE FINANCIAL AID (Fall 2008, est.) 177 applied for aid; of those 96% were deemed to have need. 99% of undergraduates with need received aid; of those 36% had need fully met. ***Average percent of need met:*** 71% (excluding resources awarded to replace EFC). ***Average financial aid package:*** $9000 (excluding resources awarded to replace EFC). 6% of all full-time undergraduates had no need and received non-need-based gift aid.

GIFT AID (NEED-BASED) *Total amount:* $750,000 (49% federal, 24% state, 20% institutional, 7% external sources). ***Receiving aid:*** Freshmen: 93% (70); all full-time undergraduates: 74% (140). ***Average award:*** Freshmen: $2750; Undergraduates: $2500. ***Scholarships, grants, and awards:*** Federal Pell, FSEOG, state, private, college/university gift aid from institutional funds.

GIFT AID (NON-NEED-BASED) *Total amount:* $175,000 (18% federal, 14% state, 57% institutional, 11% external sources). ***Receiving aid:*** Freshmen: 37% (28). Undergraduates: 35% (67). ***Average award:*** Freshmen: $1750. Undergraduates: $2000. ***Scholarships, grants, and awards by category:*** *Academic interests/achievement:* 70 awards ($90,000 total): business, education, general academic interests/achievements, religion/biblical studies. *Creative arts/performance:* 12 awards ($15,000 total): music, theater/drama. *Special achievements/activities:* cheerleading/drum major, religious involvement. *Special characteristics:* 50 awards ($50,000 total): children and siblings of alumni, children of faculty/staff, relatives of clergy, religious affiliation.

LOANS *Student loans:* $1,323,000 (92% need-based, 8% non-need-based). 74% of past graduating class borrowed through all loan programs. *Average indebtedness per student:* $17,000. ***Average need-based loan:*** Freshmen: $3000. Undergraduates: $4000. ***Parent loans:*** $23,141 (100% need-based). ***Programs:*** FFEL (Subsidized and Unsubsidized Stafford, PLUS).

WORK-STUDY *Federal work-study:* Total amount: $53,000; 60 jobs averaging $1500. ***State or other work-study/employment:*** Total amount: $15,000 (100% non-need-based). 10 part-time jobs averaging $1000.

APPLYING FOR FINANCIAL AID *Required financial aid form:* FAFSA. ***Financial aid deadline (priority):*** 8/1. ***Notification date:*** Continuous.

CONTACT Mrs. Billie Stewart, Financial Aid Director, Southwestern Christian University, PO Box 340, Bethany, OK 73008, 405-789-7661 Ext. 3456. *Fax:* 405-495-0078. *E-mail:* billie.stewart@swcu.edu.

SOUTHWESTERN COLLEGE

Phoenix, AZ

CONTACT Mr. Pete Leonard, Director of Enrollment Management, Southwestern College, 2625 East Cactus Road, Phoenix, AZ 85032-7097, 602-992-6101 Ext. 114 or toll-free 800-247-2697. *Fax:* 602-404-2159.

SOUTHWESTERN COLLEGE

Winfield, KS

Tuition & fees: $19,630 **Average undergraduate aid package: $22,382**

ABOUT THE INSTITUTION Independent United Methodist, coed. ***Awards:*** bachelor's and master's degrees. 37 undergraduate majors. ***Total enrollment:*** 1,823. Undergraduates: 1,623. Freshmen: 159. Federal methodology is used as a basis for awarding need-based institutional aid.

UNDERGRADUATE EXPENSES for 2009–10 *Application fee:* $20. ***Comprehensive fee:*** $25,380 includes full-time tuition ($19,530), mandatory fees ($100), and room and board ($5750). ***College room only:*** $2716. ***Part-time tuition:*** $814 per semester hour.

FRESHMAN FINANCIAL AID (Fall 2008, est.) 138 applied for aid; of those 83% were deemed to have need. 100% of freshmen with need received aid; of those 46% had need fully met. ***Average percent of need met:*** 90% (excluding resources awarded to replace EFC). ***Average financial aid package:*** $22,327 (excluding resources awarded to replace EFC). 15% of all full-time freshmen had no need and received non-need-based gift aid.

UNDERGRADUATE FINANCIAL AID (Fall 2008, est.) 474 applied for aid; of those 89% were deemed to have need. 100% of undergraduates with need received aid; of those 33% had need fully met. ***Average percent of need met:*** 90% (excluding resources awarded to replace EFC). ***Average financial aid package:*** $22,382 (excluding resources awarded to replace EFC). 10% of all full-time undergraduates had no need and received non-need-based gift aid.

GIFT AID (NEED-BASED) *Total amount:* $2,502,655 (72% federal, 22% state, 6% institutional). ***Receiving aid:*** Freshmen: 72% (114); all full-time undergraduates: 75% (420). ***Average award:*** Freshmen: $14,299; Undergraduates: $12,058. ***Scholarships, grants, and awards:*** Federal Pell, FSEOG, state, private, college/university gift aid from institutional funds.

GIFT AID (NON-NEED-BASED) *Total amount:* $3,994,488 (95% institutional, 5% external sources). ***Receiving aid:*** Freshmen: 34% (54). Undergraduates: 32% (180). ***Average award:*** Freshmen: $7583. Undergraduates: $6825. ***Scholarships, grants, and awards by category:*** *Academic interests/achievement:* 548 awards ($2,392,405 total): biological sciences, business, computer science, general academic interests/achievements, health fields, religion/biblical studies, social sciences. *Creative arts/performance:* 84 awards ($274,150 total): cinema/

film/broadcasting, dance, journalism/publications, music, performing arts, theater/drama. *Special achievements/activities:* 143 awards ($355,150 total): cheerleading/drum major, community service, general special achievements/activities, leadership, memberships, religious involvement. *Special characteristics:* 215 awards ($576,930 total): children of educators, children of faculty/staff, ethnic background, international students, members of minority groups, religious affiliation.

LOANS ***Student loans:*** $6,617,965 (51% need-based, 49% non-need-based). 87% of past graduating class borrowed through all loan programs. *Average indebtedness per student:* $25,697. ***Average need-based loan:*** Freshmen: $3306. Undergraduates: $4275. ***Parent loans:*** $1,471,337 (100% non-need-based). ***Programs:*** Federal Direct (Subsidized and Unsubsidized Stafford, PLUS), FFEL (Subsidized and Unsubsidized Stafford, PLUS), Perkins.

WORK-STUDY Federal work-study jobs available. ***State or other work-study/employment:*** Part-time jobs available.

ATHLETIC AWARDS Total amount: $806,450 (100% non-need-based).

APPLYING FOR FINANCIAL AID ***Required financial aid forms:*** FAFSA, institution's own form. ***Financial aid deadline:*** 8/15 (priority: 4/1). ***Notification date:*** Continuous. Students must reply within 2 weeks of notification.

CONTACT Mrs. Brenda D. Hicks, Director of Financial Aid, Southwestern College, 100 College Street, Winfield, KS 67156-2499, 620-229-6215 or toll-free 800-846-1543. *Fax:* 620-229-6363. *E-mail:* finaid@sckans.edu.

SOUTHWESTERN OKLAHOMA STATE UNIVERSITY

Weatherford, OK

Tuition & fees (OK res): $4110 **Average undergraduate aid package: $4788**

ABOUT THE INSTITUTION State-supported, coed. ***Awards:*** associate, bachelor's, master's, and first professional degrees. 53 undergraduate majors. ***Total enrollment:*** 4,869. Undergraduates: 4,196. Freshmen: 908. Institutional methodology is used as a basis for awarding need-based institutional aid.

UNDERGRADUATE EXPENSES for 2008–09 ***Application fee:*** $15. ***Tuition, state resident:*** full-time $3360; part-time $112 per credit hour. ***Tuition, nonresident:*** full-time $8700; part-time $290 per credit hour. ***Required fees:*** full-time $750; $25 per credit hour. Full-time tuition and fees vary according to program. Part-time tuition and fees vary according to program. ***College room and board:*** $3900; ***Room only:*** $1500. Room and board charges vary according to board plan. ***Payment plan:*** Installment.

FRESHMAN FINANCIAL AID (Fall 2008, est.) 679 applied for aid; of those 76% were deemed to have need. 98% of freshmen with need received aid; of those 16% had need fully met. ***Average percent of need met:*** 90% (excluding resources awarded to replace EFC). ***Average financial aid package:*** $4841 (excluding resources awarded to replace EFC). 20% of all full-time freshmen had no need and received non-need-based gift aid.

UNDERGRADUATE FINANCIAL AID (Fall 2008, est.) 2,551 applied for aid; of those 81% were deemed to have need. 97% of undergraduates with need received aid; of those 24% had need fully met. ***Average percent of need met:*** 86% (excluding resources awarded to replace EFC). ***Average financial aid package:*** $4788 (excluding resources awarded to replace EFC). 28% of all full-time undergraduates had no need and received non-need-based gift aid.

GIFT AID (NEED-BASED) ***Total amount:*** $6,473,333 (86% federal, 14% state). ***Receiving aid:*** Freshmen: 50% (439); all full-time undergraduates: 52% (1,833). ***Average award:*** Freshmen: $1155; Undergraduates: $1395. ***Scholarships, grants, and awards:*** Federal Pell, FSEOG, state, private, college/university gift aid from institutional funds.

GIFT AID (NON-NEED-BASED) ***Total amount:*** $6,434,636 (11% federal, 59% state, 13% institutional, 17% external sources). ***Receiving aid:*** Freshmen: 40% (353). Undergraduates: 30% (1,063). ***Average award:*** Freshmen: $415. Undergraduates: $458. ***Scholarships, grants, and awards by category:*** *Academic interests/achievement:* biological sciences, business, communication, computer science, education, engineering/technologies, English, foreign languages, general academic interests/achievements, health fields, mathematics, physical sciences, social sciences. *Creative arts/performance:* applied art and design, art/fine arts, music, theater/drama. *Special achievements/activities:* cheerleading/drum major, rodeo. *Special characteristics:* children and siblings of alumni, local/state students, out-of-state students. ***Tuition waivers:*** Full or partial for employees or children of employees, senior citizens.

LOANS ***Student loans:*** $15,297,309 (43% need-based, 57% non-need-based). ***Average need-based loan:*** Freshmen: $1351. Undergraduates: $1712. ***Parent loans:*** $2,664,578 (100% non-need-based). ***Programs:*** FFEL (Subsidized and Unsubsidized Stafford, PLUS).

WORK-STUDY ***Federal work-study:*** Total amount: $1,377,852; jobs available.

ATHLETIC AWARDS Total amount: $1,306,251 (100% non-need-based).

APPLYING FOR FINANCIAL AID ***Required financial aid forms:*** FAFSA, institution's own form. ***Financial aid deadline:*** 3/1 (priority: 3/1). ***Notification date:*** 3/15.

CONTACT Mr. Thomas M. Ratliff, Director of Student Financial Services, Southwestern Oklahoma State University, 100 Campus Drive, Weatherford, OK 73096-3098, 580-774-3786. *Fax:* 580-774-7066. *E-mail:* ratlift@swosu.edu.

SOUTHWESTERN UNIVERSITY

Georgetown, TX

Tuition & fees: $27,940 **Average undergraduate aid package: $25,779**

ABOUT THE INSTITUTION Independent Methodist, coed. ***Awards:*** bachelor's degrees. 43 undergraduate majors. ***Total enrollment:*** 1,270. Undergraduates: 1,270. Freshmen: 349. Both federal and institutional methodology are used as a basis for awarding need-based institutional aid.

UNDERGRADUATE EXPENSES for 2008–09 ***Application fee:*** $40. ***Comprehensive fee:*** $36,810 includes full-time tuition ($27,940) and room and board ($8870). ***College room only:*** $4630. Room and board charges vary according to board plan and housing facility. ***Part-time tuition:*** $1165 per semester hour. Part-time tuition and fees vary according to course load. ***Payment plan:*** Installment.

FRESHMAN FINANCIAL AID (Fall 2008, est.) 265 applied for aid; of those 77% were deemed to have need. 99% of freshmen with need received aid; of those 33% had need fully met. ***Average percent of need met:*** 87% (excluding resources awarded to replace EFC). ***Average financial aid package:*** $26,377 (excluding resources awarded to replace EFC). 32% of all full-time freshmen had no need and received non-need-based gift aid.

UNDERGRADUATE FINANCIAL AID (Fall 2008, est.) 810 applied for aid; of those 83% were deemed to have need. 99% of undergraduates with need received aid; of those 31% had need fully met. ***Average percent of need met:*** 83% (excluding resources awarded to replace EFC). ***Average financial aid package:*** $25,779 (excluding resources awarded to replace EFC). 32% of all full-time undergraduates had no need and received non-need-based gift aid.

GIFT AID (NEED-BASED) ***Total amount:*** $12,497,927 (8% federal, 12% state, 72% institutional, 8% external sources). ***Receiving aid:*** Freshmen: 58% (202); all full-time undergraduates: 53% (659). ***Average award:*** Freshmen: $20,783; Undergraduates: $19,015. ***Scholarships, grants, and awards:*** Federal Pell, FSEOG, state, private, college/university gift aid from institutional funds.

GIFT AID (NON-NEED-BASED) ***Total amount:*** $4,536,863 (94% institutional, 6% external sources). ***Receiving aid:*** Freshmen: 38% (134). Undergraduates: 34% (419). ***Average award:*** Freshmen: $11,733. Undergraduates: $10,341. ***Scholarships, grants, and awards by category:*** *Academic interests/achievement:* 853 awards ($7,608,052 total): business, general academic interests/achievements, humanities, international studies, mathematics, premedicine, social sciences. *Creative arts/performance:* 102 awards ($385,375 total): art/fine arts, music, theater/drama. *Special achievements/activities:* 6 awards ($6000 total): leadership. *Special characteristics:* 96 awards ($871,348 total): children of faculty/staff, general special characteristics, relatives of clergy, religious affiliation. ***Tuition waivers:*** Full or partial for employees or children of employees.

LOANS ***Student loans:*** $6,203,341 (85% need-based, 15% non-need-based). 43% of past graduating class borrowed through all loan programs. *Average indebtedness per student:* $23,601. ***Average need-based loan:*** Freshmen: $4951. Undergraduates: $5685. ***Parent loans:*** $6,389,738 (59% need-based, 41% non-need-based). ***Programs:*** FFEL (Subsidized and Unsubsidized Stafford, PLUS), Perkins, state, college/university.

WORK-STUDY ***Federal work-study:*** Total amount: $558,381; 242 jobs averaging $2124. ***State or other work-study/employment:*** Total amount: $1,312,786 (48% need-based, 52% non-need-based). 508 part-time jobs averaging $2684.

APPLYING FOR FINANCIAL AID ***Required financial aid form:*** FAFSA. ***Financial aid deadline:*** 3/1 (priority: 3/1). ***Notification date:*** Continuous. Students must reply by 5/1 or within 2 weeks of notification.

CONTACT Mr. James P. Gaeta, Director of Financial Aid, Southwestern University, PO Box 770, Georgetown, TX 78627-0770, 512-863-1259 or toll-free 800-252-3166. *Fax:* 512-863-1507. *E-mail:* gaetaj@southwestern.edu.

SOUTHWEST MINNESOTA STATE UNIVERSITY

Marshall, MN

Tuition & fees (MN res): $6696 **Average undergraduate aid package: $7810**

ABOUT THE INSTITUTION State-supported, coed. ***Awards:*** associate, bachelor's, and master's degrees. 55 undergraduate majors. ***Total enrollment:*** 6,502. Undergraduates: 6,114. Freshmen: 506. Federal methodology is used as a basis for awarding need-based institutional aid.

UNDERGRADUATE EXPENSES for 2008–09 ***Application fee:*** $20. ***Tuition, state resident:*** full-time $5780; part-time $186 per credit. ***Tuition, nonresident:*** full-time $5780; part-time $186 per credit. ***Required fees:*** full-time $916; $35.56 per credit. Full-time tuition and fees vary according to reciprocity agreements. Part-time tuition and fees vary according to class time, course load, and reciprocity agreements. ***College room and board:*** $5984; ***Room only:*** $3484. Room and board charges vary according to board plan and housing facility. ***Payment plan:*** Installment.

FRESHMAN FINANCIAL AID (Fall 2008, est.) 394 applied for aid; of those 75% were deemed to have need. 99% of freshmen with need received aid; of those 23% had need fully met. ***Average percent of need met:*** 57% (excluding resources awarded to replace EFC). ***Average financial aid package:*** $8262 (excluding resources awarded to replace EFC). 21% of all full-time freshmen had no need and received non-need-based gift aid.

UNDERGRADUATE FINANCIAL AID (Fall 2008, est.) 1,708 applied for aid; of those 78% were deemed to have need. 99% of undergraduates with need received aid; of those 30% had need fully met. ***Average percent of need met:*** 58% (excluding resources awarded to replace EFC). ***Average financial aid package:*** $7810 (excluding resources awarded to replace EFC). 16% of all full-time undergraduates had no need and received non-need-based gift aid.

GIFT AID (NEED-BASED) ***Total amount:*** $4,475,112 (62% federal, 37% state, 1% institutional). ***Receiving aid:*** Freshmen: 38% (188); all full-time undergraduates: 42% (935). ***Average award:*** Freshmen: $4995; Undergraduates: $4322. ***Scholarships, grants, and awards:*** Federal Pell, FSEOG, state, private, college/university gift aid from institutional funds.

GIFT AID (NON-NEED-BASED) ***Total amount:*** $2,565,125 (16% federal, 1% state, 58% institutional, 25% external sources). ***Receiving aid:*** Freshmen: 40% (201). Undergraduates: 30% (661). ***Average award:*** Freshmen: $2887. Undergraduates: $2652. ***Scholarships, grants, and awards by category:*** *Academic interests/achievement:* 780 awards ($1,140,136 total): agriculture, biological sciences, business, communication, computer science, education, English, general academic interests/achievements, mathematics, physical sciences, premedicine, social sciences. *Creative arts/performance:* 87 awards ($52,564 total): art/fine arts, creative writing, debating, journalism/publications, music, performing arts, theater/drama. *Special achievements/activities:* 106 awards ($56,800 total): general special achievements/activities, hobbies/interests, leadership. *Special characteristics:* 105 awards ($71,550 total): children and siblings of alumni, children of union members/company employees, ethnic background, first-generation college students, general special characteristics, handicapped students, international students, local/state students, members of minority groups, previous college experience, veterans, veterans' children. ***Tuition waivers:*** Full or partial for employees or children of employees, senior citizens.

LOANS ***Student loans:*** $14,197,023 (41% need-based, 59% non-need-based). 82% of past graduating class borrowed through all loan programs. *Average indebtedness per student:* $18,003. ***Average need-based loan:*** Freshmen: $3205. Undergraduates: $3835. ***Parent loans:*** $233,985 (100% non-need-based). ***Programs:*** Federal Direct (Subsidized and Unsubsidized Stafford), FFEL (Subsidized and Unsubsidized Stafford, PLUS), Perkins, state.

WORK-STUDY ***Federal work-study:*** Total amount: $207,416; 99 jobs averaging $2060. ***State or other work-study/employment:*** Total amount: $306,221 (100% need-based). 152 part-time jobs averaging $1987.

ATHLETIC AWARDS Total amount: $707,429 (100% non-need-based).

APPLYING FOR FINANCIAL AID ***Required financial aid forms:*** FAFSA, institution's own form. ***Financial aid deadline (priority):*** 3/1. ***Notification date:*** Continuous beginning 5/1.

CONTACT David Vikander, Director of Financial Aid, Southwest Minnesota State University, 1501 State Street, Marshall, MN 56258, 507-537-6281 or toll-free 800-642-0684. *Fax:* 507-537-6275. *E-mail:* vikander@smsu.edu.

SPALDING UNIVERSITY

Louisville, KY

CONTACT Director of Student Financial Services, Spalding University, 851 South Fourth Street, Louisville, KY 40203, 502-588-7185 or toll-free 800-896-8941 Ext. 2111. *Fax:* 502-585-7128. *E-mail:* onestop@spalding.edu.

SPELMAN COLLEGE

Atlanta, GA

Tuition & fees: $20,281 **Average undergraduate aid package: $12,691**

ABOUT THE INSTITUTION Independent, women only. ***Awards:*** bachelor's degrees. 25 undergraduate majors. ***Total enrollment:*** 2,270. Undergraduates: 2,270. Freshmen: 550. Federal methodology is used as a basis for awarding need-based institutional aid.

UNDERGRADUATE EXPENSES for 2008–09 ***Application fee:*** $35. ***Comprehensive fee:*** $30,015 includes full-time tuition ($17,266), mandatory fees ($3015), and room and board ($9734).

FRESHMAN FINANCIAL AID (Fall 2007) 549 applied for aid; of those 80% were deemed to have need. 99% of freshmen with need received aid; of those 23% had need fully met. ***Average financial aid package:*** $12,339 (excluding resources awarded to replace EFC). 1% of all full-time freshmen had no need and received non-need-based gift aid.

UNDERGRADUATE FINANCIAL AID (Fall 2007) 2,089 applied for aid; of those 77% were deemed to have need. 99% of undergraduates with need received aid; of those 24% had need fully met. ***Average financial aid package:*** $12,691 (excluding resources awarded to replace EFC). 2% of all full-time undergraduates had no need and received non-need-based gift aid.

GIFT AID (NEED-BASED) ***Total amount:*** $7,854,959 (45% federal, 17% state, 8% institutional, 30% external sources). ***Receiving aid:*** Freshmen: 58% (324); all full-time undergraduates: 57% (1,274). ***Average award:*** Freshmen: $6519; Undergraduates: $6073. ***Scholarships, grants, and awards:*** Federal Pell, FSEOG, state, private, college/university gift aid from institutional funds, United Negro College Fund.

GIFT AID (NON-NEED-BASED) ***Total amount:*** $5,216,539 (58% institutional, 42% external sources). ***Receiving aid:*** Freshmen: 54% (303). Undergraduates: 40% (900). ***Average award:*** Freshmen: $10,963. Undergraduates: $5288. ***ROTC:*** Army, Naval, Air Force cooperative.

LOANS ***Student loans:*** $15,555,140 (38% need-based, 62% non-need-based). 65% of past graduating class borrowed through all loan programs. *Average indebtedness per student:* $17,500. ***Average need-based loan:*** Freshmen: $2115. Undergraduates: $2645. ***Parent loans:*** $11,606,754 (100% non-need-based). ***Programs:*** FFEL (Subsidized and Unsubsidized Stafford, PLUS), Perkins.

WORK STUDY ***Federal work-study:*** Total amount: $211,158; jobs available.

APPLYING FOR FINANCIAL AID ***Required financial aid form:*** FAFSA. ***Financial aid deadline (priority):*** 2/15. ***Notification date:*** Continuous. Students must reply within 2 weeks of notification.

CONTACT Lenora J. Jackson, Director, Student Financial Services, Spelman College, 350 Spelman Lane, SW, PO Box 771, Atlanta, GA 30314-4399, 404-270-5212 or toll-free 800-982-2411. *Fax:* 404-270-5220. *E-mail:* lenoraj@spelman.edu.

SPRING ARBOR UNIVERSITY

Spring Arbor, MI

Tuition & fees: $19,240 **Average undergraduate aid package: $21,266**

ABOUT THE INSTITUTION Independent Free Methodist, coed. ***Awards:*** bachelor's and master's degrees and post-bachelor's certificates. 52 undergraduate majors. ***Total enrollment:*** 3,973. Undergraduates: 2,737. Freshmen: 381. Federal methodology is used as a basis for awarding need-based institutional aid.

UNDERGRADUATE EXPENSES for 2008–09 ***Application fee:*** $30. ***Comprehensive fee:*** $25,890 includes full-time tuition ($18,700), mandatory fees ($540), and room and board ($6650). ***College room only:*** $3110. Full-time tuition and fees vary according to course load, degree level, and program. Room and board charges vary according to board plan and housing facility. ***Part-time tuition:*** $470 per credit hour. ***Part-time fees:*** $225 per term. Part-time tuition and fees vary according to course load, degree level, program, and reciprocity agreements. ***Payment plan:*** Installment.

FRESHMAN FINANCIAL AID (Fall 2008, est.) 361 applied for aid; of those 86% were deemed to have need. 100% of freshmen with need received aid; of those 77% had need fully met. ***Average percent of need met:*** 97% (excluding resources awarded to replace EFC). ***Average financial aid package:*** $21,242 (excluding resources awarded to replace EFC). 1% of all full-time freshmen had no need and received non-need-based gift aid.

UNDERGRADUATE FINANCIAL AID (Fall 2008, est.) 1,314 applied for aid; of those 88% were deemed to have need. 100% of undergraduates with need received aid; of those 76% had need fully met. ***Average percent of need met:*** 96% (excluding resources awarded to replace EFC). ***Average financial aid package:*** $21,266 (excluding resources awarded to replace EFC). 1% of all full-time undergraduates had no need and received non-need-based gift aid.

GIFT AID (NEED-BASED) ***Total amount:*** $16,750,983 (20% federal, 19% state, 61% institutional). ***Receiving aid:*** Freshmen: 82% (311); all full-time undergraduates: 80% (1,146). ***Average award:*** Freshmen: $11,613; Undergraduates: $11,191. ***Scholarships, grants, and awards:*** Federal Pell, FSEOG, state, private, college/university gift aid from institutional funds.

GIFT AID (NON-NEED-BASED) ***Total amount:*** $261,631 (1% federal, 47% state, 52% external sources). ***Receiving aid:*** Freshmen: 8% (30). Undergraduates: 5% (67). ***Average award:*** Freshmen: $2456. Undergraduates: $1576. ***Scholarships, grants, and awards by category:*** *Academic interests/achievement:* 894 awards ($2,979,029 total): general academic interests/achievements. *Creative arts/performance:* 157 awards ($86,713 total): art/fine arts, music. *Special achievements/activities:* junior miss. *Special characteristics:* 399 awards ($1,432,355 total): adult students, children of faculty/staff, general special characteristics, international students, members of minority groups, relatives of clergy, religious affiliation. ***Tuition waivers:*** Full or partial for employees or children of employees. ***ROTC:*** Army, Air Force cooperative.

LOANS ***Student loans:*** $33,998,231 (38% need-based, 62% non-need-based). 84% of past graduating class borrowed through all loan programs. *Average indebtedness per student:* $22,875. ***Average need-based loan:*** Freshmen: $3822. Undergraduates: $4510. ***Parent loans:*** $13,292,900 (100% need-based). ***Programs:*** FFEL (Subsidized and Unsubsidized Stafford, PLUS), Perkins, Michigan Loan Program and alternative loans.

WORK-STUDY ***Federal work-study:*** Total amount: $307,880; 307 jobs averaging $895. ***State or other work-study/employment:*** Total amount: $51,224 (100% need-based). 87 part-time jobs averaging $632.

ATHLETIC AWARDS Total amount: $1,274,809 (100% need-based).

APPLYING FOR FINANCIAL AID ***Required financial aid form:*** FAFSA. ***Financial aid deadline (priority):*** 3/1. ***Notification date:*** Continuous beginning 4/1. Students must reply within 2 weeks of notification.

CONTACT Geoff Marsh, Director of Financial Aid, Spring Arbor University, 106 East Main Street, Spring Arbor, MI 49283-9799, 517-750-6468 or toll-free 800-968-0011. *Fax:* 517-750-6620. *E-mail:* gmarsh@arbor.edu.

SPRINGFIELD COLLEGE

Springfield, MA

CONTACT Edward J. Ciosek, Director of Financial Aid, Springfield College, 263 Alden Street, Springfield, MA 01109-3797, 413-748-3108 or toll-free 800-343-1257 (out-of-state). *Fax:* 413-748-3462. *E-mail:* finaid@spfldcol.edu.

SPRING HILL COLLEGE

Mobile, AL

Tuition & fees: $24,240 **Average undergraduate aid package: $22,571**

ABOUT THE INSTITUTION Independent Roman Catholic (Jesuit), coed. ***Awards:*** associate, bachelor's, and master's degrees and post-bachelor's certificates. 44 undergraduate majors. ***Total enrollment:*** 1,534. Undergraduates: 1,318. Freshmen: 345. Federal methodology is used as a basis for awarding need-based institutional aid.

UNDERGRADUATE EXPENSES for 2008–09 ***Application fee:*** $25. ***Comprehensive fee:*** $33,500 includes full-time tuition ($22,770), mandatory fees ($1470), and room and board ($9260). ***College room only:*** $4850. Room and board charges vary according to board plan and housing facility. ***Part-time tuition:*** $850 per semester hour. ***Part-time fees:*** $48 per semester hour. ***Payment plan:*** Installment.

FRESHMAN FINANCIAL AID (Fall 2008, est.) 298 applied for aid; of those 87% were deemed to have need. 100% of freshmen with need received aid; of those 26% had need fully met. ***Average percent of need met:*** 84% (excluding resources awarded to replace EFC). ***Average financial aid package:*** $24,324 (excluding resources awarded to replace EFC). 23% of all full-time freshmen had no need and received non-need-based gift aid.

UNDERGRADUATE FINANCIAL AID (Fall 2008, est.) 915 applied for aid; of those 87% were deemed to have need. 100% of undergraduates with need received aid; of those 24% had need fully met. ***Average percent of need met:*** 81% (excluding resources awarded to replace EFC). ***Average financial aid package:*** $22,571 (excluding resources awarded to replace EFC). 28% of all full-time undergraduates had no need and received non-need-based gift aid.

GIFT AID (NEED-BASED) ***Total amount:*** $13,702,048 (11% federal, 3% state, 85% institutional, 1% external sources). ***Receiving aid:*** Freshmen: 75% (258); all full-time undergraduates: 66% (770). ***Average award:*** Freshmen: $17,638; Undergraduates: $16,178. ***Scholarships, grants, and awards:*** Federal Pell, FSEOG, state, private, college/university gift aid from institutional funds, Academic Competitiveness Grant, National Smart Grant.

GIFT AID (NON-NEED-BASED) ***Total amount:*** $5,134,671 (1% state, 98% institutional, 1% external sources). ***Receiving aid:*** Freshmen: 51% (175). Undergraduates: 52% (599). ***Average award:*** Freshmen: $13,206. Undergraduates: $12,963. ***Scholarships, grants, and awards by category:*** *Academic interests/achievement:* 1,053 awards ($12,432,476 total): general academic interests/achievements. *Special achievements/activities:* 422 awards ($844,000 total): community service. *Special characteristics:* 14 awards ($304,549 total): children of faculty/staff, siblings of current students. ***Tuition waivers:*** Full or partial for employees or children of employees. ***ROTC:*** Army cooperative, Air Force cooperative.

LOANS ***Student loans:*** $7,385,567 (71% need-based, 29% non-need-based). 72% of past graduating class borrowed through all loan programs. *Average indebtedness per student:* $13,761. ***Average need-based loan:*** Freshmen: $4310. Undergraduates: $4660. ***Parent loans:*** $1,118,292 (23% need-based, 77% non-need-based). ***Programs:*** FFEL (Subsidized and Unsubsidized Stafford, PLUS), Perkins, alternative loans.

WORK-STUDY ***Federal work-study:*** Total amount: $267,358; 176 jobs averaging $1272. ***State or other work-study/employment:*** Total amount: $279,898 (50% need-based, 50% non-need-based). 94 part-time jobs averaging $1139.

ATHLETIC AWARDS Total amount: $794,615 (47% need-based, 53% non-need-based).

APPLYING FOR FINANCIAL AID ***Required financial aid forms:*** FAFSA, state aid form. ***Financial aid deadline (priority):*** 3/1. ***Notification date:*** Continuous. Students must reply by 5/1 or within 2 weeks of notification.

CONTACT Ms. Ellen Foster, Director of Financial Aid, Spring Hill College, 4000 Dauphin Street, Mobile, AL 36608, 251-380-3460 or toll-free 800-SHC-6704. *Fax:* 251-460-2176. *E-mail:* efoster@shc.edu.

STANFORD UNIVERSITY

Stanford, CA

Tuition & fees: $37,380 **Average undergraduate aid package: $33,538**

ABOUT THE INSTITUTION Independent, coed. ***Awards:*** bachelor's, master's, doctoral, and first professional degrees. 71 undergraduate majors. ***Total enrollment:*** 17,833. Undergraduates: 6,532. Freshmen: 1,703. Both federal and institutional methodology are used as a basis for awarding need-based institutional aid.

UNDERGRADUATE EXPENSES for 2009–10 ***Application fee:*** $75. ***Comprehensive fee:*** $48,843 includes full-time tuition ($37,380) and room and board ($11,463).

FRESHMAN FINANCIAL AID (Fall 2007) 1,020 applied for aid; of those 75% were deemed to have need. 99% of freshmen with need received aid; of those 77% had need fully met. ***Average percent of need met:*** 100% (excluding resources awarded to replace EFC). ***Average financial aid package:*** $34,388 (excluding resources awarded to replace EFC). 6% of all full-time freshmen had no need and received non-need-based gift aid.

UNDERGRADUATE FINANCIAL AID (Fall 2007) 3,470 applied for aid; of those 87% were deemed to have need. 99% of undergraduates with need received aid; of those 78% had need fully met. ***Average percent of need met:*** 100% (excluding resources awarded to replace EFC). ***Average financial aid package:*** $33,538 (excluding resources awarded to replace EFC). 13% of all full-time undergraduates had no need and received non-need-based gift aid.

GIFT AID (NEED-BASED) ***Total amount:*** $89,254,641 (6% federal, 4% state, 86% institutional, 4% external sources). ***Receiving aid:*** Freshmen: 43% (743); all full-time undergraduates: 43% (2,915). ***Average award:*** Freshmen: $31,881;

Undergraduates: $30,606. ***Scholarships, grants, and awards:*** Federal Pell, FSEOG, state, private, college/university gift aid from institutional funds.

GIFT AID (NON-NEED-BASED) ***Total amount:*** $10,975,285 (4% federal, 39% institutional, 57% external sources). ***Receiving aid:*** Freshmen: 4% (77). Undergraduates: 7% (447). ***Average award:*** Freshmen: $4019. Undergraduates: $3515. ***ROTC:*** Army cooperative, Naval cooperative, Air Force cooperative.

LOANS ***Student loans:*** $9,878,209 (38% need-based, 62% non-need-based). 40% of past graduating class borrowed through all loan programs. *Average indebtedness per student:* $15,724. ***Average need-based loan:*** Freshmen: $2406. Undergraduates: $2898. ***Parent loans:*** $9,116,198 (100% non-need-based). ***Programs:*** FFEL (Subsidized and Unsubsidized Stafford, PLUS), Perkins.

WORK-STUDY ***Federal work-study:*** Total amount: $2,163,520; 891 jobs averaging $2428. ***State or other work-study/employment:*** Total amount: $920,189 (100% need-based). 880 part-time jobs averaging $1678.

ATHLETIC AWARDS Total amount: $15,087,008 (13% need-based, 87% non-need-based).

APPLYING FOR FINANCIAL AID ***Required financial aid forms:*** FAFSA, CSS Financial Aid PROFILE, noncustodial (divorced/separated) parent's statement. ***Financial aid deadline (priority):*** 2/15. ***Notification date:*** Continuous beginning 4/3. Students must reply by 5/1.

CONTACT Financial Aid Office, Stanford University, Montag Hall, Stanford, CA 94305-3021, 650-723-3058. *Fax:* 650-725-0540. *E-mail:* financialaid@stanford.edu.

STATE UNIVERSITY OF NEW YORK AT BINGHAMTON

Binghamton, NY

Tuition & fees (NY res): $6692 **Average undergraduate aid package: $10,696**

ABOUT THE INSTITUTION State-supported, coed. ***Awards:*** bachelor's, master's, and doctoral degrees and post-master's certificates. 74 undergraduate majors. ***Total enrollment:*** 14,898. Undergraduates: 11,821. Freshmen: 2,519. Federal methodology is used as a basis for awarding need-based institutional aid.

UNDERGRADUATE EXPENSES for 2009–10 ***Application fee:*** $40. ***Tuition, state resident:*** full-time $4970; part-time $207 per credit hour. ***Tuition, nonresident:*** full-time $12,870; part-time $536 per credit hour. ***Required fees:*** full-time $1722; $63.75 per credit hour or $92 per term. ***College room and board:*** $9774; ***Room only:*** $6088.

FRESHMAN FINANCIAL AID (Fall 2008, est.) 1,947 applied for aid; of those 52% were deemed to have need. 100% of freshmen with need received aid; of those 72% had need fully met. ***Average percent of need met:*** 75% (excluding resources awarded to replace EFC). ***Average financial aid package:*** $9651 (excluding resources awarded to replace EFC). 2% of all full-time freshmen had no need and received non-need-based gift aid.

UNDERGRADUATE FINANCIAL AID (Fall 2008, est.) 7,615 applied for aid; of those 67% were deemed to have need. 99% of undergraduates with need received aid; of those 63% had need fully met. ***Average percent of need met:*** 76% (excluding resources awarded to replace EFC). ***Average financial aid package:*** $10,696 (excluding resources awarded to replace EFC). 3% of all full-time undergraduates had no need and received non-need-based gift aid.

GIFT AID (NEED-BASED) ***Total amount:*** $26,140,389 (46% federal, 46% state, 3% institutional, 5% external sources). ***Receiving aid:*** Freshmen: 34% (821); all full-time undergraduates: 38% (4,332). ***Average award:*** Freshmen: $5092; Undergraduates: $5265. ***Scholarships, grants, and awards:*** Federal Pell, FSEOG, state, private, college/university gift aid from institutional funds.

GIFT AID (NON-NEED-BASED) ***Total amount:*** $876,097 (46% state, 54% institutional). ***Receiving aid:*** Freshmen: 13% (313). Undergraduates: 12% (1,326). ***Average award:*** Freshmen: $3113. Undergraduates: $4675. ***Scholarships, grants, and awards by category:*** *Academic interests/achievement:* 225 awards ($397,036 total): area/ethnic studies, biological sciences, business, computer science, education, engineering/technologies, English, foreign languages, general academic interests/achievements, health fields, humanities, international studies, mathematics, physical sciences, premedicine. *Creative arts/performance:* 17 awards ($21,500 total): art/fine arts, cinema/film/broadcasting, creative writing, dance, general creative arts/performance, journalism/publications, music, performing arts, theater/drama. *Special achievements/activities:* 205 awards ($376,290 total): community service, general special achievements/activities, leadership. *Special characteristics:* 256 awards ($405,935 total): adult students, children of faculty/staff, ethnic background, handicapped students, local/state students, married students, members of minority groups, out-of-state students. ***ROTC:*** Air Force cooperative.

LOANS ***Student loans:*** $49,128,233 (100% need-based). 54% of past graduating class borrowed through all loan programs. *Average indebtedness per student:* $14,541. ***Average need-based loan:*** Freshmen: $3547. Undergraduates: $4630. ***Parent loans:*** $56,359,778 (100% need-based). ***Programs:*** Federal Direct (Subsidized and Unsubsidized Stafford, PLUS), Perkins, Federal Nursing, college/university.

WORK-STUDY ***Federal work-study:*** Total amount: $2,281,697; 1,572 jobs averaging $1418.

ATHLETIC AWARDS Total amount: $2,595,768 (100% non-need-based).

APPLYING FOR FINANCIAL AID ***Required financial aid forms:*** FAFSA, state aid form. ***Financial aid deadline (priority):*** 2/1. ***Notification date:*** Continuous beginning 4/1. Students must reply within 2 weeks of notification.

CONTACT Mr. Dennis Chavez, Director of Student Financial Aid Services, State University of New York at Binghamton, PO Box 6011, Binghamton, NY 13902-6011, 607-777-2428.

STATE UNIVERSITY OF NEW YORK AT FREDONIA

Fredonia, NY

Tuition & fees (NY res): $6208 **Average undergraduate aid package: $7657**

ABOUT THE INSTITUTION State-supported, coed. ***Awards:*** bachelor's and master's degrees. 74 undergraduate majors. ***Total enrollment:*** 5,573. Undergraduates: 5,163. Freshmen: 1,188. Federal methodology is used as a basis for awarding need-based institutional aid.

UNDERGRADUATE EXPENSES for 2009–10 ***Application fee:*** $40. ***Tuition, state resident:*** full-time $4970; part-time $207 per credit hour. ***Tuition, nonresident:*** full-time $12,870; part-time $442 per credit hour. ***Required fees:*** full-time $1238; $54.40 per credit hour. ***College room and board:*** $9140; ***Room only:*** $5350.

FRESHMAN FINANCIAL AID (Fall 2008, est.) 1,046 applied for aid; of those 69% were deemed to have need. 100% of freshmen with need received aid; of those 13% had need fully met. ***Average percent of need met:*** 68% (excluding resources awarded to replace EFC). ***Average financial aid package:*** $7653 (excluding resources awarded to replace EFC). 9% of all full-time freshmen had no need and received non-need-based gift aid.

UNDERGRADUATE FINANCIAL AID (Fall 2008, est.) 4,213 applied for aid; of those 75% were deemed to have need. 99% of undergraduates with need received aid; of those 1% had need fully met. ***Average percent of need met:*** 66% (excluding resources awarded to replace EFC). ***Average financial aid package:*** $7657 (excluding resources awarded to replace EFC). 6% of all full-time undergraduates had no need and received non-need-based gift aid.

GIFT AID (NEED-BASED) ***Total amount:*** $13,874,377 (45% federal, 42% state, 8% institutional, 5% external sources). ***Receiving aid:*** Freshmen: 52% (622); all full-time undergraduates: 54% (2,711). ***Average award:*** Freshmen: $3656; Undergraduates: $3384. ***Scholarships, grants, and awards:*** Federal Pell, FSEOG, state, private, college/university gift aid from institutional funds, Federal TEACH Grant, Academic Competitiveness Grant, National Smart Grant.

GIFT AID (NON-NEED-BASED) ***Receiving aid:*** Freshmen: 16% (188). Undergraduates: 10% (515). ***Average award:*** Freshmen: $1946. Undergraduates: $1770. ***Scholarships, grants, and awards by category:*** *Academic interests/achievement:* 431 awards ($518,750 total): biological sciences, business, communication, computer science, education, English, foreign languages, general academic interests/achievements, humanities, international studies, mathematics, physical sciences, social sciences. *Creative arts/performance:* 109 awards ($82,925 total): applied art and design, art/fine arts, dance, music, performing arts, theater/drama. *Special achievements/activities:* 20 awards ($56,575 total): general special achievements/activities, leadership. *Special characteristics:* 162 awards ($257,195 total): children and siblings of alumni, ethnic background, general special characteristics, international students, local/state students, members of minority groups, out-of-state students, parents of current students, previous college experience.

LOANS ***Student loans:*** $34,668,608 (42% need-based, 58% non-need-based). 62% of past graduating class borrowed through all loan programs. *Average indebtedness per student:* $23,452. ***Average need-based loan:*** Freshmen: $3613.

Undergraduates: $4268. ***Parent loans:*** $2,810,802 (100% non-need-based). ***Programs:*** FFEL (Subsidized and Unsubsidized Stafford, PLUS), Perkins.

WORK-STUDY ***Federal work-study:*** Total amount: $370,807; 260 jobs averaging $1752.

APPLYING FOR FINANCIAL AID ***Required financial aid forms:*** FAFSA, state aid form. ***Financial aid deadline:*** Continuous. ***Notification date:*** Continuous beginning 3/1. Students must reply by 5/1.

CONTACT Jeremy Corrente, Assistant Director, State University of New York at Fredonia, 215 Maytum Hall, Fredonia, NY 14063, 716-673-3253 or toll-free 800-252-1212. *Fax:* 716-673-3785. *E-mail:* corrente@fredonia.edu.

STATE UNIVERSITY OF NEW YORK AT NEW PALTZ

New Paltz, NY

Tuition & fees (NY res): $6039 **Average undergraduate aid package: $8386**

ABOUT THE INSTITUTION State-supported, coed. ***Awards:*** bachelor's and master's degrees and post-master's certificates. 58 undergraduate majors. ***Total enrollment:*** 8,205. Undergraduates: 6,707. Freshmen: 1,335. Federal methodology is used as a basis for awarding need-based institutional aid.

UNDERGRADUATE EXPENSES for 2008–09 ***Application fee:*** $40. ***Tuition, state resident:*** full-time $4970; part-time $207 per credit. ***Tuition, nonresident:*** full-time $12,870; part-time $536 per credit. ***Required fees:*** full-time $1069; $31.25 per credit or $158 per credit. ***College room and board:*** $8690; ***Room only:*** $5600. Room and board charges vary according to board plan. ***Payment plan:*** Installment.

FRESHMAN FINANCIAL AID (Fall 2008, est.) 1,084 applied for aid; of those 60% were deemed to have need. 98% of freshmen with need received aid; of those 19% had need fully met. ***Average percent of need met:*** 53% (excluding resources awarded to replace EFC). ***Average financial aid package:*** $7729 (excluding resources awarded to replace EFC). 1% of all full-time freshmen had no need and received non-need-based gift aid.

UNDERGRADUATE FINANCIAL AID (Fall 2008, est.) 4,178 applied for aid; of those 68% were deemed to have need. 99% of undergraduates with need received aid; of those 17% had need fully met. ***Average percent of need met:*** 58% (excluding resources awarded to replace EFC). ***Average financial aid package:*** $8386 (excluding resources awarded to replace EFC). 1% of all full-time undergraduates had no need and received non-need-based gift aid.

GIFT AID (NEED-BASED) ***Total amount:*** $8,289,317 (58% federal, 41% state, 1% external sources). ***Receiving aid:*** Freshmen: 20% (261); all full-time undergraduates: 24% (1,355). ***Average award:*** Freshmen: $4517; Undergraduates: $4063. ***Scholarships, grants, and awards:*** Federal Pell, FSEOG, state, private, college/university gift aid from institutional funds.

GIFT AID (NON-NEED-BASED) ***Total amount:*** $1,679,336 (21% federal, 20% state, 3% institutional, 56% external sources). ***Receiving aid:*** Freshmen: 4% (46). Undergraduates: 3% (167). ***Average award:*** Freshmen: $572. Undergraduates: $906. ***Scholarships, grants, and awards by category:*** *Academic interests/achievement:* 59 awards ($86,790 total): biological sciences, business, communication, education, health fields. *Creative arts/performance:* 22 awards ($8325 total): art/fine arts, music, performing arts. *Special characteristics:* 17 awards ($8000 total): ethnic background, first-generation college students, handicapped students, members of minority groups.

LOANS ***Student loans:*** $28,801,893 (53% need-based, 47% non-need-based). 75% of past graduating class borrowed through all loan programs. *Average indebtedness per student:* $20,000. ***Average need-based loan:*** Freshmen: $3245. Undergraduates: $4185. ***Parent loans:*** $12,888,321 (100% non-need-based). ***Programs:*** FFEL (Subsidized and Unsubsidized Stafford, PLUS), Perkins, private.

WORK-STUDY ***Federal work-study:*** Total amount: $950,492; 1,200 jobs averaging $1000. ***State or other work-study/employment:*** Total amount: $760,548 (100% non-need-based). 500 part-time jobs averaging $1250.

APPLYING FOR FINANCIAL AID ***Required financial aid forms:*** FAFSA, state aid form. ***Financial aid deadline (priority):*** 3/15. ***Notification date:*** Continuous beginning 4/1. Students must reply within 4 weeks of notification.

CONTACT Mr. Daniel Sistarenik, Director of Financial Aid, State University of New York at New Paltz, 200 Hawk Drive, New Paltz, NY 12561-2437, 845-257-3250. *Fax:* 845-257-3568. *E-mail:* sistared@newpaltz.edu.

STATE UNIVERSITY OF NEW YORK AT OSWEGO

Oswego, NY

Tuition & fees (NY res): $6651 **Average undergraduate aid package: $10,435**

ABOUT THE INSTITUTION State-supported, coed. ***Awards:*** bachelor's and master's degrees and post-master's certificates. 65 undergraduate majors. ***Total enrollment:*** 8,909. Undergraduates: 7,971. Freshmen: 1,473. Federal methodology is used as a basis for awarding need-based institutional aid.

UNDERGRADUATE EXPENSES for 2009–10 ***Application fee:*** $40. ***Tuition, state resident:*** full-time $4970; part-time $207 per credit hour. ***Tuition, nonresident:*** full-time $12,870; part-time $536 per credit hour. ***Required fees:*** full-time $1681.

FRESHMAN FINANCIAL AID (Fall 2008, est.) 1,319 applied for aid; of those 66% were deemed to have need. 97% of freshmen with need received aid; of those 36% had need fully met. ***Average percent of need met:*** 87% (excluding resources awarded to replace EFC). ***Average financial aid package:*** $10,253 (excluding resources awarded to replace EFC). 22% of all full-time freshmen had no need and received non-need-based gift aid.

UNDERGRADUATE FINANCIAL AID (Fall 2008, est.) 5,680 applied for aid; of those 74% were deemed to have need. 98% of undergraduates with need received aid; of those 32% had need fully met. ***Average percent of need met:*** 89% (excluding resources awarded to replace EFC). ***Average financial aid package:*** $10,435 (excluding resources awarded to replace EFC). 19% of all full-time undergraduates had no need and received non-need-based gift aid.

GIFT AID (NEED-BASED) ***Total amount:*** $18,708,957 (45% federal, 44% state, 10% institutional, 1% external sources). ***Receiving aid:*** Freshmen: 52% (764); all full-time undergraduates: 54% (3,634). ***Average award:*** Freshmen: $5313; Undergraduates: $4022. ***Scholarships, grants, and awards:*** Federal Pell, FSEOG, state, private, college/university gift aid from institutional funds.

GIFT AID (NON-NEED-BASED) ***Total amount:*** $2,110,928 (1% federal, 2% state, 90% institutional, 7% external sources). ***Receiving aid:*** Freshmen: 21% (313). Undergraduates: 11% (764). ***Average award:*** Freshmen: $5707. Undergraduates: $7137. ***Scholarships, grants, and awards by category:*** *Academic interests/achievement:* 1,422 awards ($3,749,928 total): area/ethnic studies, biological sciences, business, communication, computer science, education, English, foreign languages, general academic interests/achievements, humanities, international studies, mathematics, physical sciences, premedicine, social sciences. ***ROTC:*** Army cooperative.

LOANS ***Student loans:*** $39,011,579 (78% need-based, 22% non-need-based). 84% of past graduating class borrowed through all loan programs. *Average indebtedness per student:* $22,117. ***Average need-based loan:*** Freshmen: $5055. Undergraduates: $6393. ***Parent loans:*** $6,081,628 (63% need-based, 37% non-need-based). ***Programs:*** FFEL (Subsidized and Unsubsidized Stafford, PLUS), Perkins.

WORK-STUDY ***Federal work-study:*** Total amount: $537,030; 357 jobs averaging $1040. ***State or other work-study/employment:*** Total amount: $958,616 (49% need-based, 51% non-need-based). 1,414 part-time jobs averaging $1179.

APPLYING FOR FINANCIAL AID ***Required financial aid forms:*** FAFSA, state aid form. ***Financial aid deadline (priority):*** 3/1. ***Notification date:*** Continuous beginning 3/1. Students must reply by 5/1 or within 3 weeks of notification.

CONTACT Mark C. Humbert, Director of Financial Aid, State University of New York at Oswego, 206 Culkin Hall, Oswego, NY 13126, 315-312-2248. *Fax:* 315-312-3696.

STATE UNIVERSITY OF NEW YORK AT PLATTSBURGH

Plattsburgh, NY

Tuition & fees (NY res): $5422 **Average undergraduate aid package: $10,641**

ABOUT THE INSTITUTION State-supported, coed. ***Awards:*** bachelor's and master's degrees and post-master's certificates. 64 undergraduate majors. ***Total enrollment:*** 6,358. Undergraduates: 5,736. Freshmen: 1,028. Both federal and institutional methodology are used as a basis for awarding need-based institutional aid.

UNDERGRADUATE EXPENSES for 2008–09 ***Application fee:*** $40. ***Tuition, state resident:*** full-time $4350; part-time $181 per credit hour. ***Tuition, nonresident:***

full-time $10,610; part-time $442 per credit hour. ***Required fees:*** full-time $1072; $43.95 per credit hour. Part-time tuition and fees vary according to course load. ***College room and board:*** $8250; ***Room only:*** $5350. Room and board charges vary according to board plan. ***Payment plans:*** Installment, deferred payment.

FRESHMAN FINANCIAL AID (Fall 2008, est.) 891 applied for aid; of those 68% were deemed to have need. 99% of freshmen with need received aid; of those 32% had need fully met. ***Average percent of need met:*** 93% (excluding resources awarded to replace EFC). ***Average financial aid package:*** $10,409 (excluding resources awarded to replace EFC). 32% of all full-time freshmen had no need and received non-need-based gift aid.

UNDERGRADUATE FINANCIAL AID (Fall 2008, est.) 4,134 applied for aid; of those 73% were deemed to have need. 98% of undergraduates with need received aid; of those 29% had need fully met. ***Average percent of need met:*** 90% (excluding resources awarded to replace EFC). ***Average financial aid package:*** $10,641 (excluding resources awarded to replace EFC). 30% of all full-time undergraduates had no need and received non-need-based gift aid.

GIFT AID (NEED-BASED) ***Total amount:*** $13,554,158 (42% federal, 42% state, 12% institutional, 4% external sources). ***Receiving aid:*** Freshmen: 55% (566); all full-time undergraduates: 50% (2,685). ***Average award:*** Freshmen: $5823; Undergraduates: $5048. ***Scholarships, grants, and awards:*** Federal Pell, FSEOG, state, private, college/university gift aid from institutional funds.

GIFT AID (NON-NEED-BASED) ***Total amount:*** $3,650,514 (1% federal, 12% state, 83% institutional, 4% external sources). ***Receiving aid:*** Freshmen: 25% (259). Undergraduates: 21% (1,116). ***Average award:*** Freshmen: $4879. Undergraduates: $6271. ***Scholarships, grants, and awards by category:*** *Academic interests/achievement:* 2,503 awards ($4,514,071 total): area/ethnic studies, biological sciences, business, communication, computer science, education, engineering/technologies, English, general academic interests/achievements, health fields, home economics, humanities, international studies, mathematics, physical sciences, premedicine, social sciences. *Creative arts/performance:* 185 awards ($308,875 total): art/fine arts, journalism/publications, music, theater/drama. *Special achievements/activities:* 16 awards ($29,300 total): community service, general special achievements/activities, leadership. *Special characteristics:* 1,220 awards ($2,613,747 total): international students, out-of-state students. ***Tuition waivers:*** Full or partial for employees or children of employees.

LOANS ***Student loans:*** $24,089,860 (74% need-based, 26% non-need-based). 77% of past graduating class borrowed through all loan programs. *Average indebtedness per student:* $22,894. ***Average need-based loan:*** Freshmen: $5325. Undergraduates: $6833. ***Parent loans:*** $3,127,994 (62% need-based, 38% non-need-based). ***Programs:*** Federal Direct (Subsidized and Unsubsidized Stafford, PLUS), Perkins, Federal Nursing, alternative loans.

WORK-STUDY ***Federal work-study:*** Total amount: $863,976; 614 jobs averaging $2082.

APPLYING FOR FINANCIAL AID ***Required financial aid forms:*** FAFSA, state aid form. ***Financial aid deadline (priority):*** 2/15. ***Notification date:*** Continuous beginning 3/1. Students must reply within 8 weeks of notification.

CONTACT Mr. Todd Moravec, Financial Aid Director, State University of New York at Plattsburgh, 101 Broad Street, Plattsburgh, NY 12901-2681, 518-564-2072 or toll-free 888-673-0012 (in-state). *Fax:* 518-564-4079. *E-mail:* todd.moravec@plattsburgh.edu.

STATE UNIVERSITY OF NEW YORK COLLEGE AT CORTLAND

Cortland, NY

Tuition & fees (NY res): $6145 **Average undergraduate aid package: $10,786**

ABOUT THE INSTITUTION State-supported, coed. ***Awards:*** bachelor's and master's degrees and post-bachelor's and post-master's certificates. 57 undergraduate majors. ***Total enrollment:*** 7,234. Undergraduates: 6,199. Freshmen: 1,175. Federal methodology is used as a basis for awarding need-based institutional aid.

UNDERGRADUATE EXPENSES for 2008–09 ***Application fee:*** $40. ***Tuition, state resident:*** full-time $4970; part-time $207 per credit hour. ***Tuition, nonresident:*** full-time $12,870; part-time $536 per credit hour. ***Required fees:*** full-time $1175. ***College room and board:*** $9790; ***Room only:*** $5840.

FRESHMAN FINANCIAL AID (Fall 2007) 1,072 applied for aid; of those 63% were deemed to have need. 98% of freshmen with need received aid; of those 18% had need fully met. ***Average percent of need met:*** 73% (excluding resources awarded to replace EFC). ***Average financial aid package:*** $10,158 (excluding resources awarded to replace EFC). 24% of all full-time freshmen had no need and received non-need-based gift aid.

UNDERGRADUATE FINANCIAL AID (Fall 2007) 4,776 applied for aid; of those 71% were deemed to have need. 98% of undergraduates with need received aid; of those 22% had need fully met. ***Average percent of need met:*** 75% (excluding resources awarded to replace EFC). ***Average financial aid package:*** $10,786 (excluding resources awarded to replace EFC). 20% of all full-time undergraduates had no need and received non-need-based gift aid.

GIFT AID (NEED-BASED) ***Total amount:*** $9,978,567 (43% federal, 56% state, 1% institutional). ***Receiving aid:*** Freshmen: 47% (561); all full-time undergraduates: 49% (2,853). ***Average award:*** Freshmen: $3043; Undergraduates: $4133. ***Scholarships, grants, and awards:*** Federal Pell, FSEOG, state, private, college/university gift aid from institutional funds.

GIFT AID (NON-NEED-BASED) ***Total amount:*** $545,012 (46% institutional, 54% external sources). ***Receiving aid:*** Freshmen: 1% (14). Undergraduates: 4% (211). ***Average award:*** Freshmen: $7337. Undergraduates: $8218. ***Scholarships, grants, and awards by category:*** *Academic interests/achievement:* education, general academic interests/achievements, international studies, mathematics, physical sciences. *Creative arts/performance:* art/fine arts, music. *Special achievements/activities:* community service, general special achievements/activities, hobbies/interests, leadership. *Special characteristics:* adult students, children and siblings of alumni, local/state students, members of minority groups. ***ROTC:*** Army cooperative, Air Force cooperative.

LOANS ***Student loans:*** $28,890,957 (43% need-based, 57% non-need-based). ***Average need-based loan:*** Freshmen: $3747. Undergraduates: $4304. ***Parent loans:*** $5,025,550 (100% non-need-based). ***Programs:*** FFEL (Subsidized and Unsubsidized Stafford, PLUS), Perkins.

WORK-STUDY ***Federal work-study:*** Total amount: $291,236; jobs available.

APPLYING FOR FINANCIAL AID ***Required financial aid forms:*** FAFSA, state aid form. ***Financial aid deadline (priority):*** 3/1. ***Notification date:*** Continuous beginning 3/15. Students must reply by 5/1 or within 4 weeks of notification.

CONTACT Karen Gallagher, Interim Director of Financial Advisement, State University of New York College at Cortland, PO Box 2000, Cortland, NY 13045-0900, 607-753-4717. *Fax:* 607-753-5990. *E-mail:* finaid@em.cortland.edu.

STATE UNIVERSITY OF NEW YORK COLLEGE AT GENESEO

Geneseo, NY

Tuition & fees (NY res): $6278 **Average undergraduate aid package: $7379**

ABOUT THE INSTITUTION State-supported, coed. ***Awards:*** bachelor's and master's degrees. 46 undergraduate majors. ***Total enrollment:*** 5,585. Undergraduates: 5,451. Freshmen: 1,081. Federal methodology is used as a basis for awarding need-based institutional aid.

UNDERGRADUATE EXPENSES for 2009–10 ***Application fee:*** $40. ***Tuition, state resident:*** full-time $4970; part-time $207 per credit hour. ***Tuition, nonresident:*** full-time $12,870; part-time $536 per credit hour. ***Required fees:*** full-time $1308; $54.31 per credit hour. ***College room and board:*** $9070.

FRESHMAN FINANCIAL AID (Fall 2008, est.) 884 applied for aid; of those 44% were deemed to have need. 100% of freshmen with need received aid; of those 72% had need fully met. ***Average percent of need met:*** 72% (excluding resources awarded to replace EFC). ***Average financial aid package:*** $5260 (excluding resources awarded to replace EFC). 1% of all full-time freshmen had no need and received non-need-based gift aid.

UNDERGRADUATE FINANCIAL AID (Fall 2008, est.) 3,733 applied for aid; of those 59% were deemed to have need. 100% of undergraduates with need received aid; of those 75% had need fully met. ***Average percent of need met:*** 75% (excluding resources awarded to replace EFC). ***Average financial aid package:*** $7379 (excluding resources awarded to replace EFC). 4% of all full-time undergraduates had no need and received non-need-based gift aid.

GIFT AID (NEED-BASED) ***Total amount:*** $7,797,603 (46% federal, 54% state). ***Receiving aid:*** Freshmen: 18% (197); all full-time undergraduates: 41% (2,200). ***Average award:*** Freshmen: $2090; Undergraduates: $3385. ***Scholarships, grants, and awards:*** Federal Pell, FSEOG, state, private, college/university gift aid from institutional funds.

GIFT AID (NON-NEED-BASED) ***Total amount:*** $2,503,502 (1% federal, 24% state, 51% institutional, 24% external sources). ***Receiving aid:*** Freshmen: 23% (248). Undergraduates: 13% (690). ***Average award:*** Freshmen: $1780.

Undergraduates: $2605. ***Scholarships, grants, and awards by category:*** *Academic interests/achievement:* 427 awards ($403,745 total): area/ethnic studies, biological sciences, business, communication, computer science, education, English, foreign languages, general academic interests/achievements, humanities, international studies, mathematics, physical sciences, premedicine, social sciences. *Creative arts/performance:* 52 awards ($31,975 total): applied art and design, art/fine arts, creative writing, dance, general creative arts/performance, journalism/publications, music, performing arts, theater/drama. *Special achievements/activities:* 19 awards ($11,500 total): community service, leadership, memberships. *Special characteristics:* 34 awards ($26,250 total): adult students, ethnic background, local/state students, members of minority groups. ***ROTC:*** Army cooperative, Air Force cooperative.

LOANS ***Student loans:*** $20,290,330 (40% need-based, 60% non-need-based). 67% of past graduating class borrowed through all loan programs. *Average indebtedness per student:* $18,700. ***Average need-based loan:*** Freshmen: $3932. Undergraduates: $4505. ***Parent loans:*** $2,125,830 (100% non-need-based). ***Programs:*** FFEL (Subsidized and Unsubsidized Stafford, PLUS), Perkins, alternative loans.

WORK-STUDY ***Federal work-study:*** Total amount: $590,410; 404 jobs averaging $1325. ***State or other work-study/employment:*** Total amount: $590,000 (100% non-need-based). Part-time jobs available.

APPLYING FOR FINANCIAL AID ***Required financial aid forms:*** FAFSA, state aid form. ***Financial aid deadline:*** 2/15 (priority: 2/15). ***Notification date:*** Continuous beginning 3/15. Students must reply by 5/1 or within 2 weeks of notification.

CONTACT Archie Cureton, Director of Financial Aid, State University of New York College at Geneseo, 1 College Circle, Erwin Hall 104, Geneseo, NY 14454, 585-245-5731 or toll-free 866-245-5211. *Fax:* 585-245-5717. *E-mail:* cureton@geneseo.edu.

STATE UNIVERSITY OF NEW YORK COLLEGE AT OLD WESTBURY

Old Westbury, NY

Tuition & fees (NY res): $4350 **Average undergraduate aid package: $6438**

ABOUT THE INSTITUTION State-supported, coed. ***Awards:*** bachelor's and master's degrees. 42 undergraduate majors. ***Total enrollment:*** 3,505. Undergraduates: 3,457. Freshmen: 344. Both federal and institutional methodology are used as a basis for awarding need-based institutional aid.

UNDERGRADUATE EXPENSES for 2008–09 ***Application fee:*** $40. ***Tuition, state resident:*** full-time $4350; part-time $181 per credit. ***Tuition, nonresident:*** full-time $10,610; part-time $442 per credit. ***Required fees:*** $114.90 per course or $64 per term. Part-time tuition and fees vary according to course load. ***College room and board:*** $9032; ***Room only:*** $6100. Room and board charges vary according to board plan and housing facility. ***Payment plan:*** Installment.

FRESHMAN FINANCIAL AID (Fall 2007) 349 applied for aid; of those 99% were deemed to have need. ***Average percent of need met:*** 46% (excluding resources awarded to replace EFC). ***Average financial aid package:*** $6880 (excluding resources awarded to replace EFC).

UNDERGRADUATE FINANCIAL AID (Fall 2007) 2,105 applied for aid; of those 100% were deemed to have need. ***Average percent of need met:*** 45% (excluding resources awarded to replace EFC). ***Average financial aid package:*** $6438 (excluding resources awarded to replace EFC). 1% of all full-time undergraduates had no need and received non-need-based gift aid.

GIFT AID (NEED-BASED) ***Total amount:*** $9,093,483 (46% federal, 53% state, 1% institutional). ***Receiving aid:*** Freshmen: 75% (308); all full-time undergraduates: 63% (1,755). ***Average award:*** Freshmen: $5864; Undergraduates: $4791. ***Scholarships, grants, and awards:*** Federal Pell, FSEOG, state, private, college/university gift aid from institutional funds.

GIFT AID (NON-NEED-BASED) ***Total amount:*** $23,497 (100% external sources). ***Receiving aid:*** Freshmen: 5% (19). Undergraduates: 2% (56). ***Average award:*** Undergraduates: $2600. ***Scholarships, grants, and awards by category:*** *Academic interests/achievement:* biological sciences, health fields, physical sciences. ***Tuition waivers:*** Full or partial for senior citizens. ***ROTC:*** Army cooperative, Air Force cooperative.

LOANS ***Student loans:*** $5,927,860 (95% need-based, 5% non-need-based). 49% of past graduating class borrowed through all loan programs. *Average indebtedness per student:* $15,533. ***Average need-based loan:*** Freshmen: $1592. Undergraduates: $2294. ***Parent loans:*** $1,026,737 (92% need-based, 8% non-need-based). ***Programs:*** FFEL (Subsidized and Unsubsidized Stafford, PLUS), Perkins.

WORK-STUDY ***Federal work-study:*** Total amount: $184,003; 245 jobs averaging $751.

APPLYING FOR FINANCIAL AID ***Required financial aid forms:*** FAFSA, institution's own form, state aid form, income documentation. ***Financial aid deadline (priority):*** 4/12. ***Notification date:*** Continuous beginning 4/25. Students must reply within 2 weeks of notification.

CONTACT Ms. Dee Darrell, Financial Aid Assistant, State University of New York College at Old Westbury, PO Box 210, Old Westbury, NY 11568-0210, 516-876-3222. *Fax:* 516-876-3008. *E-mail:* finaid@oldwestbury.edu.

STATE UNIVERSITY OF NEW YORK COLLEGE AT ONEONTA

Oneonta, NY

Tuition & fees (NY res): $6230 **Average undergraduate aid package: $10,967**

ABOUT THE INSTITUTION State-supported, coed. ***Awards:*** bachelor's and master's degrees and post-bachelor's and post-master's certificates. 70 undergraduate majors. ***Total enrollment:*** 5,757. Undergraduates: 5,578. Freshmen: 1,018. Federal methodology is used as a basis for awarding need-based institutional aid.

UNDERGRADUATE EXPENSES for 2009–10 ***Application fee:*** $40. ***Tuition, state resident:*** full-time $4970; part-time $207 per semester hour. ***Tuition, nonresident:*** full-time $12,870; part-time $536 per semester hour. ***Required fees:*** full-time $1260; $29.85 per semester hour. ***College room and board:*** $8680; ***Room only:*** $5030.

FRESHMAN FINANCIAL AID (Fall 2008, est.) 903 applied for aid; of those 63% were deemed to have need. 97% of freshmen with need received aid; of those 18% had need fully met. ***Average percent of need met:*** 58% (excluding resources awarded to replace EFC). ***Average financial aid package:*** $10,439 (excluding resources awarded to replace EFC). 28% of all full-time freshmen had no need and received non-need-based gift aid.

UNDERGRADUATE FINANCIAL AID (Fall 2008, est.) 4,250 applied for aid; of those 71% were deemed to have need. 98% of undergraduates with need received aid; of those 19% had need fully met. ***Average percent of need met:*** 54% (excluding resources awarded to replace EFC). ***Average financial aid package:*** $10,967 (excluding resources awarded to replace EFC). 23% of all full-time undergraduates had no need and received non-need-based gift aid.

GIFT AID (NEED-BASED) ***Total amount:*** $12,911,580 (45% federal, 44% state, 7% institutional, 4% external sources). ***Receiving aid:*** Freshmen: 47% (483); all full-time undergraduates: 47% (2,524). ***Average award:*** Freshmen: $4451; Undergraduates: $4233. ***Scholarships, grants, and awards:*** Federal Pell, FSEOG, state, private, college/university gift aid from institutional funds.

GIFT AID (NON-NEED-BASED) ***Total amount:*** $1,273,423 (7% federal, 58% institutional, 35% external sources). ***Average award:*** Freshmen: $2200. Undergraduates: $2000. ***Scholarships, grants, and awards by category:*** *Academic interests/achievement:* 496 awards ($1,017,317 total): biological sciences, business, computer science, education, general academic interests/achievements, home economics, physical sciences, premedicine, social sciences. *Creative arts/performance:* 25 awards ($17,400 total): music, theater/drama. *Special achievements/activities:* 14 awards ($14,670 total): community service, general special achievements/activities, leadership. *Special characteristics:* 120 awards ($147,900 total): general special characteristics, international students, local/state students.

LOANS ***Student loans:*** $27,729,070 (41% need-based, 59% non-need-based). 75% of past graduating class borrowed through all loan programs. *Average indebtedness per student:* $19,900. ***Average need-based loan:*** Freshmen: $3494. Undergraduates: $4467. ***Parent loans:*** $5,993,615 (100% non-need-based). ***Programs:*** FFEL (Subsidized and Unsubsidized Stafford, PLUS), Perkins.

WORK-STUDY ***Federal work-study:*** Total amount: $469,940; 350 jobs averaging $1200. ***State or other work-study/employment:*** Part-time jobs available.

APPLYING FOR FINANCIAL AID ***Required financial aid forms:*** FAFSA, state aid form. ***Financial aid deadline (priority):*** 3/15. ***Notification date:*** Continuous. Students must reply by 5/1 or within 4 weeks of notification.

CONTACT Mr. Bill Goodhue, Director of Financial Aid, State University of New York College at Oneonta, Ravine Parkway, Oneonta, NY 13820, 607-436-2992 or toll-free 800-SUNY-123. *Fax:* 607-436-2659. *E-mail:* goodhucw@oneonta.edu.

STATE UNIVERSITY OF NEW YORK COLLEGE AT POTSDAM

Potsdam, NY

Tuition & fees (NY res): $5772 Average undergraduate aid package: $13,024

ABOUT THE INSTITUTION State-supported, coed. ***Awards:*** bachelor's and master's degrees. 49 undergraduate majors. ***Total enrollment:*** 4,325. Undergraduates: 3,652. Freshmen: 808. Federal methodology is used as a basis for awarding need-based institutional aid.

UNDERGRADUATE EXPENSES for 2008–09 ***Application fee:*** $40. ***Tuition, state resident:*** full-time $4660; part-time $207 per credit hour. ***Tuition, nonresident:*** full-time $11,740; part-time $536 per credit hour. ***Required fees:*** full-time $1112; $50.20 per credit hour. ***College room and board:*** $8820; ***Room only:*** $5120. Room and board charges vary according to board plan and housing facility. ***Payment plan:*** Installment.

FRESHMAN FINANCIAL AID (Fall 2008, est.) 725 applied for aid; of those 72% were deemed to have need. 99% of freshmen with need received aid; of those 90% had need fully met. ***Average percent of need met:*** 90% (excluding resources awarded to replace EFC). ***Average financial aid package:*** $13,404 (excluding resources awarded to replace EFC). 11% of all full-time freshmen had no need and received non-need-based gift aid.

UNDERGRADUATE FINANCIAL AID (Fall 2008, est.) 2,914 applied for aid; of those 76% were deemed to have need. 99% of undergraduates with need received aid; of those 85% had need fully met. ***Average percent of need met:*** 86% (excluding resources awarded to replace EFC). ***Average financial aid package:*** $13,024 (excluding resources awarded to replace EFC). 11% of all full-time undergraduates had no need and received non-need-based gift aid.

GIFT AID (NEED-BASED) ***Total amount:*** $10,963,481 (43% federal, 40% state, 14% institutional, 3% external sources). ***Receiving aid:*** Freshmen: 60% (486); all full-time undergraduates: 58% (2,027). ***Average award:*** Freshmen: $6153; Undergraduates: $5251. ***Scholarships, grants, and awards:*** Federal Pell, FSEOG, state, private, college/university gift aid from institutional funds, VESID Awards, VA Rehabilitation Awards, Bureau of Indian Affairs Grant, Native American, ACG, SMART.

GIFT AID (NON-NEED-BASED) ***Total amount:*** $3,965,781 (43% federal, 6% state, 48% institutional, 3% external sources). ***Receiving aid:*** Freshmen: 44% (356). Undergraduates: 25% (852). ***Average award:*** Freshmen: $4055. Undergraduates: $5496. ***Scholarships, grants, and awards by category:*** *Academic interests/achievement:* 246 awards ($512,742 total): biological sciences, business, communication, computer science, education, engineering/technologies, English, foreign languages, general academic interests/achievements, humanities, mathematics, physical sciences, social sciences. *Creative arts/performance:* 144 awards ($213,661 total): art/fine arts, dance, music, performing arts, theater/drama. *Special achievements/activities:* 577 awards ($1,260,374 total): community service, general special achievements/activities, leadership. *Special characteristics:* 64 awards ($76,258 total): adult students, children and siblings of alumni, children of faculty/staff, ethnic background, handicapped students, local/state students, members of minority groups, previous college experience. ***Tuition waivers:*** Full or partial for minority students, employees or children of employees. ***ROTC:*** Army cooperative, Air Force cooperative.

LOANS ***Student loans:*** $16,663,923 (47% need-based, 53% non-need-based). 85% of past graduating class borrowed through all loan programs. *Average indebtedness per student:* $20,291. ***Average need-based loan:*** Freshmen: $3584. Undergraduates: $4199. ***Parent loans:*** $5,762,377 (100% non-need-based). ***Programs:*** Federal Direct (Subsidized and Unsubsidized Stafford, PLUS), Perkins, college/university, alternative loans.

WORK-STUDY ***Federal work-study:*** Total amount: $286,083; 236 jobs averaging $1200.

APPLYING FOR FINANCIAL AID ***Required financial aid forms:*** FAFSA, state aid form. ***Financial aid deadline (priority):*** 3/1. ***Notification date:*** Continuous. Students must reply by 5/1 or within 4 weeks of notification.

CONTACT Susan C. Aldrich, Director of Financial Aid, State University of New York College at Potsdam, 44 Pierrepont Avenue, Potsdam, NY 13676, 315-267-2162 or toll-free 877-POTSDAM. *Fax:* 315-267-3067. *E-mail:* finaid@potsdam.edu.

STATE UNIVERSITY OF NEW YORK COLLEGE OF AGRICULTURE AND TECHNOLOGY AT COBLESKILL

Cobleskill, NY

Tuition & fees (NY res): $6311 Average undergraduate aid package: $5842

ABOUT THE INSTITUTION State-supported, coed. ***Awards:*** associate and bachelor's degrees. 35 undergraduate majors. ***Total enrollment:*** 2,619. Undergraduates: 2,619. Freshmen: 978. Federal methodology is used as a basis for awarding need-based institutional aid.

UNDERGRADUATE EXPENSES for 2009–10 ***Application fee:*** $40. ***Tuition, state resident:*** full-time $4970; part-time $207 per credit hour. ***Tuition, nonresident:*** full-time $12,870; part-time $536 per credit hour. ***Required fees:*** full-time $1341; $64.75 per credit hour. ***College room and board:*** $9460; ***Room only:*** $5690.

FRESHMAN FINANCIAL AID (Fall 2007) 937 applied for aid; of those 78% were deemed to have need. 97% of freshmen with need received aid; of those 16% had need fully met. ***Average percent of need met:*** 68% (excluding resources awarded to replace EFC). ***Average financial aid package:*** $5773 (excluding resources awarded to replace EFC). 17% of all full-time freshmen had no need and received non-need-based gift aid.

UNDERGRADUATE FINANCIAL AID (Fall 2007) 2,297 applied for aid; of those 78% were deemed to have need. 96% of undergraduates with need received aid; of those 14% had need fully met. ***Average percent of need met:*** 63% (excluding resources awarded to replace EFC). ***Average financial aid package:*** $5842 (excluding resources awarded to replace EFC). 13% of all full-time undergraduates had no need and received non-need-based gift aid.

GIFT AID (NEED-BASED) ***Total amount:*** $6,238,161 (44% federal, 56% state). ***Receiving aid:*** Freshmen: 62% (635); all full-time undergraduates: 54% (1,517). ***Average award:*** Freshmen: $4227; Undergraduates: $4124. ***Scholarships, grants, and awards:*** Federal Pell, FSEOG, state, private, college/university gift aid from institutional funds.

GIFT AID (NON-NEED-BASED) ***Total amount:*** $658,195 (51% institutional, 49% external sources). ***Receiving aid:*** Freshmen: 14% (142). Undergraduates: 9% (248). ***Average award:*** Freshmen: $36,975.

LOANS ***Student loans:*** $9,183,803 (45% need-based, 55% non-need-based). 75% of past graduating class borrowed through all loan programs. *Average indebtedness per student:* $22,475. ***Average need-based loan:*** Freshmen: $3337. Undergraduates: $3626. ***Parent loans:*** $3,377,593 (100% need-based). ***Programs:*** FFEL (Subsidized and Unsubsidized Stafford, PLUS), Perkins.

WORK-STUDY ***Federal work-study:*** Total amount: $190,575; 160 jobs averaging $1064. ***State or other work-study/employment:*** Part-time jobs available.

APPLYING FOR FINANCIAL AID ***Required financial aid forms:*** FAFSA, state aid form. ***Financial aid deadline:*** 3/1. ***Notification date:*** 4/1. Students must reply within 2 weeks of notification.

CONTACT Brian Smith, Director of Financial Aid, State University of New York College of Agriculture and Technology at Cobleskill, Knapp Hall, Cobleskill, NY 12043, 518-255-5623 or toll-free 800-295-8988. *Fax:* 518-255-5844. *E-mail:* finaid@cobleskill.edu.

STATE UNIVERSITY OF NEW YORK COLLEGE OF AGRICULTURE AND TECHNOLOGY AT MORRISVILLE

Morrisville, NY

ABOUT THE INSTITUTION State-supported, coed. ***Awards:*** associate and bachelor's degrees. 48 undergraduate majors. ***Total enrollment:*** 3,432. Undergraduates: 3,432. Freshmen: 1,277.

GIFT AID (NEED-BASED) ***Scholarships, grants, and awards:*** Federal Pell, FSEOG, state, college/university gift aid from institutional funds.

LOANS ***Programs:*** FFEL (Subsidized and Unsubsidized Stafford, PLUS), Perkins, Federal Nursing.

APPLYING FOR FINANCIAL AID ***Required financial aid forms:*** FAFSA, state aid form.

CONTACT Thomas David, Director of Financial Aid, State University of New York College of Agriculture and Technology at Morrisville, PO Box 901, Morrisville, NY 13408-0901, 315-684-6289 or toll-free 800-258-0111 (in-state). *Fax:* 315-684-6421. *E-mail:* davidtg@morrisville.edu.

STATE UNIVERSITY OF NEW YORK COLLEGE OF ENVIRONMENTAL SCIENCE AND FORESTRY

Syracuse, NY

Tuition & fees (NY res): $4970 **Average undergraduate aid package: $13,000**

ABOUT THE INSTITUTION State-supported, coed. ***Awards:*** associate, bachelor's, master's, and doctoral degrees and post-bachelor's certificates. 48 undergraduate majors. ***Total enrollment:*** 2,201. Undergraduates: 1,633. Freshmen: 310. Federal methodology is used as a basis for awarding need-based institutional aid.

UNDERGRADUATE EXPENSES for 2009–10 ***Application fee:*** $40. ***Tuition, state resident:*** full-time $4970; part-time $207 per credit hour. ***Tuition, nonresident:*** full-time $12,870; part-time $536 per credit hour. ***College room and board:*** $11,920.

FRESHMAN FINANCIAL AID (Fall 2008, est.) 274 applied for aid; of those 72% were deemed to have need. 100% of freshmen with need received aid; of those 100% had need fully met. ***Average percent of need met:*** 100% (excluding resources awarded to replace EFC). ***Average financial aid package:*** $12,500 (excluding resources awarded to replace EFC). 19% of all full-time freshmen had no need and received non-need-based gift aid.

UNDERGRADUATE FINANCIAL AID (Fall 2008, est.) 1,201 applied for aid; of those 73% were deemed to have need. 100% of undergraduates with need received aid; of those 93% had need fully met. ***Average percent of need met:*** 100% (excluding resources awarded to replace EFC). ***Average financial aid package:*** $13,000 (excluding resources awarded to replace EFC). 7% of all full-time undergraduates had no need and received non-need-based gift aid.

GIFT AID (NEED-BASED) ***Total amount:*** $4,485,000 (36% federal, 40% state, 20% institutional, 4% external sources). ***Receiving aid:*** Freshmen: 63% (196); all full-time undergraduates: 60% (875). ***Average award:*** Freshmen: $5000; Undergraduates: $5200. ***Scholarships, grants, and awards:*** Federal Pell, FSEOG, state, private, college/university gift aid from institutional funds.

GIFT AID (NON-NEED-BASED) ***Total amount:*** $765,000 (15% federal, 10% state, 59% institutional, 16% external sources). ***Receiving aid:*** Freshmen: 41% (127). Undergraduates: 16% (237). ***Average award:*** Freshmen: $2500. Undergraduates: $2500. ***Scholarships, grants, and awards by category:*** *Academic interests/achievement:* 210 awards ($300,000 total): agriculture, architecture, biological sciences, engineering/technologies, physical sciences, premedicine. *Special achievements/activities:* leadership. *Special characteristics:* 70 awards ($90,000 total): members of minority groups. ***ROTC:*** Army cooperative, Air Force cooperative.

LOANS ***Student loans:*** $7,210,500 (55% need-based, 45% non-need-based). 80% of past graduating class borrowed through all loan programs. *Average indebtedness per student:* $21,160. ***Average need-based loan:*** Freshmen: $5500. Undergraduates: $6750. ***Parent loans:*** $2,201,000 (45% need-based, 55% non-need-based). ***Programs:*** FFEL (Subsidized and Unsubsidized Stafford, PLUS), Perkins, college/university.

WORK-STUDY ***Federal work-study:*** Total amount: $340,000; 310 jobs averaging $1129. ***State or other work-study/employment:*** Total amount: $390,000 (46% need-based, 54% non-need-based). 120 part-time jobs averaging $1667.

APPLYING FOR FINANCIAL AID ***Required financial aid forms:*** FAFSA, state aid form. ***Financial aid deadline (priority):*** 3/1. ***Notification date:*** 4/1. Students must reply within 2 weeks of notification.

CONTACT Mr. John E. View, Director of Financial Aid, State University of New York College of Environmental Science and Forestry, One Forestry Drive, Syracuse, NY 13210-2779, 315-470-6671 or toll-free 800-777-7373. *Fax:* 315-470-4734. *E-mail:* jeview@esf.edu.

STATE UNIVERSITY OF NEW YORK COLLEGE OF TECHNOLOGY AT CANTON

Canton, NY

ABOUT THE INSTITUTION State-supported, coed. ***Awards:*** associate and bachelor's degrees. 33 undergraduate majors. ***Total enrollment:*** 2,970. Undergraduates: 2,970. Freshmen: 829.

GIFT AID (NEED-BASED) ***Scholarships, grants, and awards:*** Federal Pell, FSEOG, state, private, college/university gift aid from institutional funds, Bureau of Indian Affairs Grants.

LOANS ***Programs:*** Federal Direct (Subsidized and Unsubsidized Stafford, PLUS), Perkins, alternative loans.

WORK-STUDY ***Federal work-study:*** 232 jobs averaging $1260. ***State or other work-study/employment:*** 10 part-time jobs averaging $1000.

APPLYING FOR FINANCIAL AID ***Required financial aid forms:*** FAFSA, state aid form.

CONTACT Office of Financial Aid, State University of New York College of Technology at Canton, Student Service Center, Canton, NY 13617, 315-386-7616 or toll-free 800-388-7123. *E-mail:* finaid@canton.edu.

STATE UNIVERSITY OF NEW YORK COLLEGE OF TECHNOLOGY AT DELHI

Delhi, NY

CONTACT Dawn MacIntyre-Sohns, Director of Financial Aid, State University of New York College of Technology at Delhi, Bush Hall, Delhi, NY 13753, 607-746-4570 or toll-free 800-96-DELHI. *Fax:* 607-746-4104. *E-mail:* macintdr@snydelab.delhi.edu.

STATE UNIVERSITY OF NEW YORK DOWNSTATE MEDICAL CENTER

Brooklyn, NY

CONTACT Financial Aid Office, State University of New York Downstate Medical Center, 450 Clarkson Avenue, Brooklyn, NY 11203-2098, 718-270-2488. *Fax:* 718-270-7592. *E-mail:* finaid1@downstate.edu.

STATE UNIVERSITY OF NEW YORK INSTITUTE OF TECHNOLOGY

Utica, NY

Tuition & fees (NY res): $5413 **Average undergraduate aid package: $7988**

ABOUT THE INSTITUTION State-supported, coed. ***Awards:*** bachelor's and master's degrees and post-master's certificates. 20 undergraduate majors. ***Total enrollment:*** 2,828. Undergraduates: 2,210. Freshmen: 204. Federal methodology is used as a basis for awarding need-based institutional aid.

UNDERGRADUATE EXPENSES for 2008–09 ***Application fee:*** $40. ***Tuition, state resident:*** full-time $4350; part-time $181 per credit hour. ***Tuition, nonresident:*** full-time $10,610; part-time $442 per credit hour. ***Required fees:*** full-time $1063; $44.29 per credit hour. Full-time tuition and fees vary according to course load. Part-time tuition and fees vary according to course load. ***College room and board:*** $8320. Room and board charges vary according to board plan. ***Payment plans:*** Installment, deferred payment.

FRESHMAN FINANCIAL AID (Fall 2008, est.) 179 applied for aid; of those 75% were deemed to have need. 100% of freshmen with need received aid; of those 13% had need fully met. ***Average percent of need met:*** 78% (excluding resources awarded to replace EFC). ***Average financial aid package:*** $8386 (excluding resources awarded to replace EFC). 7% of all full-time freshmen had no need and received non-need-based gift aid.

UNDERGRADUATE FINANCIAL AID (Fall 2008, est.) 1,313 applied for aid; of those 80% were deemed to have need. 100% of undergraduates with need received aid; of those 16% had need fully met. ***Average percent of need met:*** 85% (excluding resources awarded to replace EFC). ***Average financial aid package:*** $7988 (excluding resources awarded to replace EFC). 3% of all full-time undergraduates had no need and received non-need-based gift aid.

GIFT AID (NEED-BASED) ***Total amount:*** $4,731,413 (52% federal, 41% state, 5% institutional, 2% external sources). ***Receiving aid:*** Freshmen: 60% (125); all full-time undergraduates: 63% (944). ***Average award:*** Freshmen: $5014; Undergraduates: $4829. ***Scholarships, grants, and awards:*** Federal Pell, FSEOG, state, college/university gift aid from institutional funds.

GIFT AID (NON-NEED-BASED) ***Total amount:*** $342,017 (19% federal, 34% state, 32% institutional, 15% external sources). ***Receiving aid:*** Freshmen: 13% (26). Undergraduates: 10% (145). ***Average award:*** Freshmen: $2325. Undergraduates: $1908. ***Scholarships, grants, and awards by category:*** *Academic interests/achievement:* computer science, engineering/technologies, general academic interests/achievements. *Special characteristics:* local/state students, members of minority groups, previous college experience. ***ROTC:*** Army cooperative, Air Force cooperative.

LOANS ***Student loans:*** $368,508 (100% non-need-based). ***Average need-based loan:*** Freshmen: $3567. Undergraduates: $4018. ***Parent loans:*** $1,580,624 (58% need-based, 42% non-need-based). ***Programs:*** Federal Direct (Subsidized and Unsubsidized Stafford, PLUS), Perkins, Federal Nursing.

WORK-STUDY ***Federal work-study:*** Total amount: $333,827; 117 jobs averaging $831.

APPLYING FOR FINANCIAL AID ***Required financial aid forms:*** FAFSA, state aid form. ***Financial aid deadline (priority):*** 3/15. ***Notification date:*** Continuous beginning 3/15. Students must reply within 2 weeks of notification.

CONTACT Director of Financial Aid, State University of New York Institute of Technology, PO Box 3050, Utica, NY 13504-3050, 315-792-7210 or toll-free 800-SUNYTEC. *Fax:* 315-792-7220. *E-mail:* hoskeyl@sunyit.edu.

STATE UNIVERSITY OF NEW YORK MARITIME COLLEGE

Throggs Neck, NY

CONTACT Ms. Madeline Aponte, Director of Financial Aid, State University of New York Maritime College, 6 Pennyfield Avenue, Throgs Neck, NY 10465-4198, 718-409-7267 or toll-free 800-654-1874 (in-state), 800-642-1874 (out-of-state). *Fax:* 718-409-7275. *E-mail:* finaid@sunymaritime.edu.

STATE UNIVERSITY OF NEW YORK UPSTATE MEDICAL UNIVERSITY

Syracuse, NY

Tuition & fees (NY res): $5218 **Average undergraduate aid package: $15,912**

ABOUT THE INSTITUTION State-supported, coed. ***Awards:*** bachelor's, master's, doctoral, and first professional degrees and post-master's certificates. 6 undergraduate majors. ***Total enrollment:*** 1,374. Undergraduates: 284. Federal methodology is used as a basis for awarding need-based institutional aid.

UNDERGRADUATE EXPENSES for 2009–10 ***Application fee:*** $40. ***Tuition, state resident:*** full-time $4660. ***Tuition, nonresident:*** full-time $11,740. ***Required fees:*** full-time $558. ***College room and board: Room only:*** $5768.

UNDERGRADUATE FINANCIAL AID (Fall 2007) 166 applied for aid; of those 100% were deemed to have need. 100% of undergraduates with need received aid; of those 100% had need fully met. ***Average percent of need met:*** 100% (excluding resources awarded to replace EFC). ***Average financial aid package:*** $15,912 (excluding resources awarded to replace EFC).

GIFT AID (NEED-BASED) ***Total amount:*** $496,481 (51% federal, 31% state, 8% institutional, 10% external sources). ***Receiving aid:*** All full-time undergraduates: 53% (143). ***Average award:*** Undergraduates: $3200. ***Scholarships, grants, and awards:*** Federal Pell, FSEOG, state, college/university gift aid from institutional funds.

GIFT AID (NON-NEED-BASED) ***Total amount:*** $57,340 (1% federal, 5% state, 94% institutional). ***Receiving aid:*** Undergraduates: 13% (35). ***Scholarships, grants, and awards by category:*** *Academic interests/achievement:* health fields.

LOANS ***Student loans:*** $1,454,261 (76% need-based, 24% non-need-based). ***Average need-based loan:*** Undergraduates: $11,013. ***Parent loans:*** $37,958 (100% non-need-based). ***Programs:*** FFEL (Subsidized and Unsubsidized Stafford, PLUS), Perkins.

WORK-STUDY ***Federal work-study:*** Total amount: $64,587; jobs available.

APPLYING FOR FINANCIAL AID ***Required financial aid form:*** FAFSA. ***Financial aid deadline:*** 4/1 (priority: 3/1). ***Notification date:*** Continuous beginning 5/1. Students must reply within 3 weeks of notification.

CONTACT Office of Financial Aid, State University of New York Upstate Medical University, 155 Elizabeth Blackwell Street, Syracuse, NY 13210-2375, 315-464-4329 or toll-free 800-736-2171. *E-mail:* finaid@upstate.edu.

STEPHEN F. AUSTIN STATE UNIVERSITY

Nacogdoches, TX

Tuition & fees (TX res): $6432 **Average undergraduate aid package: $8517**

ABOUT THE INSTITUTION State-supported, coed. ***Awards:*** bachelor's, master's, and doctoral degrees. 69 undergraduate majors. ***Total enrollment:*** 11,990. Undergraduates: 10,404. Freshmen: 2,354. Federal methodology is used as a basis for awarding need-based institutional aid.

UNDERGRADUATE EXPENSES for 2008–09 ***Application fee:*** $35. ***Tuition, state resident:*** full-time $4680; part-time $156 per credit hour. ***Tuition, nonresident:*** full-time $13,110; part-time $437 per credit hour. ***Required fees:*** full-time $1752; $142 per credit hour. Full-time tuition and fees vary according to course load, degree level, and location. Part-time tuition and fees vary according to course load, degree level, and location. ***College room and board:*** $7022. Room and board charges vary according to board plan and housing facility. ***Payment plan:*** Installment.

FRESHMAN FINANCIAL AID (Fall 2007) 1,570 applied for aid; of those 73% were deemed to have need. 99% of freshmen with need received aid; of those 69% had need fully met. ***Average percent of need met:*** 87% (excluding resources awarded to replace EFC). ***Average financial aid package:*** $9021 (excluding resources awarded to replace EFC). 6% of all full-time freshmen had no need and received non-need-based gift aid.

UNDERGRADUATE FINANCIAL AID (Fall 2007) 6,527 applied for aid; of those 78% were deemed to have need. 99% of undergraduates with need received aid; of those 61% had need fully met. ***Average percent of need met:*** 89% (excluding resources awarded to replace EFC). ***Average financial aid package:*** $8517 (excluding resources awarded to replace EFC). 3% of all full-time undergraduates had no need and received non-need-based gift aid.

GIFT AID (NEED-BASED) ***Total amount:*** $21,332,307 (58% federal, 20% state, 22% institutional). ***Receiving aid:*** Freshmen: 44% (899); all full-time undergraduates: 46% (4,160). ***Average award:*** Freshmen: $3186; Undergraduates: $3414. ***Scholarships, grants, and awards:*** Federal Pell, FSEOG, state, private, college/university gift aid from institutional funds.

GIFT AID (NON-NEED-BASED) ***Total amount:*** $9,484,520 (2% state, 72% institutional, 26% external sources). ***Receiving aid:*** Freshmen: 18% (365). Undergraduates: 16% (1,431). ***Average award:*** Freshmen: $3514. Undergraduates: $3023. ***Scholarships, grants, and awards by category:*** *Academic interests/achievement:* agriculture, biological sciences, business, communication, computer science, education, general academic interests/achievements, health fields, home economics, mathematics, military science, physical sciences, premedicine. *Creative arts/performance:* applied art and design, art/fine arts, journalism/publications, music, theater/drama. *Special achievements/activities:* cheerleading/drum major, general special achievements/activities, hobbies/interests, leadership, rodeo. *Special characteristics:* adult students, children of faculty/staff, children of union members/company employees, first-generation college students, general special characteristics, local/state students, previous college experience, religious affiliation. ***Tuition waivers:*** Full or partial for employees or children of employees, senior citizens. ***ROTC:*** Army.

LOANS ***Student loans:*** $55,627,149 (45% need-based, 55% non-need-based). 68% of past graduating class borrowed through all loan programs. *Average indebtedness per student:* $15,652. ***Average need-based loan:*** Freshmen: $3115. Undergraduates: $4061. ***Parent loans:*** $7,549,579 (100% non-need-based). ***Programs:*** FFEL (Subsidized and Unsubsidized Stafford, PLUS), Perkins, state, college/university, alternative loans.

WORK-STUDY ***Federal work-study:*** Total amount: $652,122; 428 jobs averaging $1524. ***State or other work-study/employment:*** Total amount: $89,242 (100% need-based). 60 part-time jobs averaging $1487.

ATHLETIC AWARDS Total amount: $2,828,186 (100% non-need-based).

APPLYING FOR FINANCIAL AID ***Required financial aid forms:*** FAFSA, institution's own form. ***Financial aid deadline (priority):*** 4/1. ***Notification date:*** Continuous beginning 4/1. Students must reply within 6 weeks of notification.

CONTACT Office of Financial Aid, Stephen F. Austin State University, PO Box 13052, Nacogdoches, TX 75962, 936-468-2403 or toll-free 800-731-2902. *Fax:* 936-468-1048. *E-mail:* finaid@sfasu.edu.

STEPHENS COLLEGE
Columbia, MO

Tuition & fees: $23,000 **Average undergraduate aid package: $20,388**

ABOUT THE INSTITUTION Independent, undergraduate: women only; graduate: coed. ***Awards:*** associate, bachelor's, and master's degrees and post-bachelor's certificates. 31 undergraduate majors. ***Total enrollment:*** 1,147. Undergraduates: 947. Freshmen: 223. Federal methodology is used as a basis for awarding need-based institutional aid.

UNDERGRADUATE EXPENSES for 2008–09 ***Application fee:*** $25. ***Comprehensive fee:*** $31,730 includes full-time tuition ($23,000) and room and board ($8730). ***College room only:*** $5080. Full-time tuition and fees vary according to program and reciprocity agreements. Room and board charges vary according to board plan and housing facility. ***Part-time tuition:*** $700 per credit. Part-time tuition and fees vary according to program. ***Payment plan:*** Installment.

FRESHMAN FINANCIAL AID (Fall 2008, est.) 197 applied for aid; of those 87% were deemed to have need. 100% of freshmen with need received aid; of those 15% had need fully met. ***Average percent of need met:*** 77% (excluding resources awarded to replace EFC). ***Average financial aid package:*** $20,183 (excluding resources awarded to replace EFC). 23% of all full-time freshmen had no need and received non-need-based gift aid.

UNDERGRADUATE FINANCIAL AID (Fall 2008, est.) 640 applied for aid; of those 90% were deemed to have need. 100% of undergraduates with need received aid; of those 17% had need fully met. ***Average percent of need met:*** 77% (excluding resources awarded to replace EFC). ***Average financial aid package:*** $20,388 (excluding resources awarded to replace EFC). 24% of all full-time undergraduates had no need and received non-need-based gift aid.

GIFT AID (NEED-BASED) ***Total amount:*** $8,374,565 (11% federal, 10% state, 77% institutional, 2% external sources). ***Receiving aid:*** Freshmen: 77% (172); all full-time undergraduates: 74% (570). ***Average award:*** Freshmen: $15,911; Undergraduates: $15,382. ***Scholarships, grants, and awards:*** Federal Pell, FSEOG, state, private, college/university gift aid from institutional funds, Academic Competitiveness Grant, National Smart Grant.

GIFT AID (NON-NEED-BASED) ***Total amount:*** $1,964,742 (97% institutional, 3% external sources). ***Receiving aid:*** Freshmen: 9% (21). Undergraduates: 8% (60). ***Average award:*** Freshmen: $10,398. Undergraduates: $9085. ***Scholarships, grants, and awards by category:*** *Academic interests/achievement:* 600 awards ($3,957,577 total): general academic interests/achievements. *Creative arts/performance:* 87 awards ($498,246 total): creative writing, dance, performing arts, theater/drama. *Special achievements/activities:* 413 awards ($928,196 total): leadership. *Special characteristics:* 587 awards ($976,645 total): children and siblings of alumni, children of faculty/staff, local/state students, out-of-state students, parents of current students, siblings of current students. ***Tuition waivers:*** Full or partial for employees or children of employees. ***ROTC:*** Army cooperative, Air Force cooperative.

LOANS ***Student loans:*** $5,320,405 (73% need-based, 27% non-need-based). 70% of past graduating class borrowed through all loan programs. *Average indebtedness per student:* $21,960. ***Average need-based loan:*** Freshmen: $2951. Undergraduates: $4361. ***Parent loans:*** $1,134,862 (31% need-based, 69% non-need-based). ***Programs:*** FFEL (Subsidized and Unsubsidized Stafford, PLUS), Perkins, alternative loans.

WORK-STUDY ***Federal work-study:*** Total amount: $73,945; 52 jobs averaging $1422. ***State or other work-study/employment:*** Total amount: $248,505 (93% need-based, 7% non-need-based). 194 part-time jobs averaging $1240.

ATHLETIC AWARDS Total amount: $283,250 (76% need-based, 24% non-need-based).

APPLYING FOR FINANCIAL AID ***Required financial aid form:*** FAFSA. ***Financial aid deadline (priority):*** 3/15. ***Notification date:*** Continuous.

CONTACT Mrs. Rachel Touchatt, Financial Aid Director, Stephens College, 1200 East Broadway, Columbia, MO 65215-0002, 800-876-7207. *Fax:* 573-876-2320. *E-mail:* finaid@stephens.edu.

STERLING COLLEGE
Sterling, KS

CONTACT Ms. Jodi Lightner, Director of Financial Aid, Sterling College, PO Box 98, Sterling, KS 67579-0098, 620-278-4207 or toll-free 800-346-1017. *Fax:* 620-278-4416. *E-mail:* jlightner@sterling.edu.

STERLING COLLEGE
Craftsbury Common, VT

CONTACT Barbara Stuart, Associate Director of Financial Aid, Sterling College, PO Box 72, Craftsbury Common, VT 05827, 800-648-3591 Ext. 2 or toll-free 800-648-3591 Ext. 100. *Fax:* 802-586-2596. *E-mail:* bstuart@sterlingcollege.edu.

STETSON UNIVERSITY
DeLand, FL

Tuition & fees: $31,770 **Average undergraduate aid package: $25,565**

ABOUT THE INSTITUTION Independent, coed. ***Awards:*** bachelor's, master's, and first professional degrees and post-master's and first professional certificates. 58 undergraduate majors. ***Total enrollment:*** 3,696. Undergraduates: 2,222. Freshmen: 588. Federal methodology is used as a basis for awarding need-based institutional aid.

UNDERGRADUATE EXPENSES for 2009–10 ***Application fee:*** $40. ***Comprehensive fee:*** $40,704 includes full-time tuition ($29,880), mandatory fees ($1890), and room and board ($8934). ***College room only:*** $5014. ***Part-time tuition:*** $914 per credit hour.

FRESHMAN FINANCIAL AID (Fall 2008, est.) 442 applied for aid; of those 84% were deemed to have need. 100% of freshmen with need received aid; of those 31% had need fully met. ***Average percent of need met:*** 88% (excluding resources awarded to replace EFC). ***Average financial aid package:*** $27,736 (excluding resources awarded to replace EFC). 31% of all full-time freshmen had no need and received non-need-based gift aid.

UNDERGRADUATE FINANCIAL AID (Fall 2008, est.) 1,433 applied for aid; of those 87% were deemed to have need. 100% of undergraduates with need received aid; of those 30% had need fully met. ***Average percent of need met:*** 83% (excluding resources awarded to replace EFC). ***Average financial aid package:*** $25,565 (excluding resources awarded to replace EFC). 31% of all full-time undergraduates had no need and received non-need-based gift aid.

GIFT AID (NEED-BASED) ***Total amount:*** $22,999,879 (11% federal, 21% state, 66% institutional, 2% external sources). ***Receiving aid:*** Freshmen: 63% (369); all full-time undergraduates: 58% (1,231). ***Average award:*** Freshmen: $21,845; Undergraduates: $19,178. ***Scholarships, grants, and awards:*** Federal Pell, FSEOG, state, private, college/university gift aid from institutional funds.

GIFT AID (NON-NEED-BASED) ***Total amount:*** $13,009,606 (27% state, 71% institutional, 2% external sources). ***Receiving aid:*** Freshmen: 13% (76). Undergraduates: 10% (209). ***Average award:*** Freshmen: $12,838. Undergraduates: $12,026. ***Scholarships, grants, and awards by category:*** *Academic interests/achievement:* area/ethnic studies, biological sciences, business, communication, computer science, education, English, foreign languages, general academic interests/achievements, humanities, mathematics, military science, physical sciences, premedicine, religion/biblical studies, social sciences. *Creative arts/performance:* applied art and design, art/fine arts, music, theater/drama. *Special achievements/activities:* cheerleading/drum major, community service, general special achievements/activities, leadership, religious involvement. *Special characteristics:* children and siblings of alumni, children of faculty/staff, ethnic background, general special characteristics, international students, local/state students, members of minority groups. ***ROTC:*** Army cooperative.

LOANS ***Student loans:*** $9,385,855 (69% need-based, 31% non-need-based). 75% of past graduating class borrowed through all loan programs. *Average indebtedness per student:* $28,775. ***Average need-based loan:*** Freshmen: $3946. Undergraduates: $4657. ***Parent loans:*** $2,451,516 (35% need-based, 65% non-need-based). ***Programs:*** FFEL (Subsidized and Unsubsidized Stafford, PLUS), Perkins, college/university.

WORK-STUDY ***Federal work-study:*** Total amount: $1,602,574; 692 jobs averaging $2316. ***State or other work-study/employment:*** Total amount: $703,977 (24% need-based, 76% non-need-based). 221 part-time jobs averaging $3185.

ATHLETIC AWARDS Total amount: $3,323,025 (34% need-based, 66% non-need-based).

APPLYING FOR FINANCIAL AID ***Required financial aid forms:*** FAFSA, institution's own form. ***Financial aid deadline (priority):*** 3/15. ***Notification date:*** Continuous. Students must reply within 2 weeks of notification.

CONTACT Martin J. Carney, Director of Financial Aid, Stetson University, 421 North Woodland Boulevard, DeLand, FL 32723, 386-822-7120 or toll-free 800-688-0101. *Fax:* 386-822-7126. *E-mail:* finaid@stetson.edu.

STEVENS-HENAGER COLLEGE

Boise, ID

CONTACT Financial Aid Office, Stevens-Henager College, 730 Americana Boulevard, Boise, ID 83702, 801-345-0700.

STEVENS INSTITUTE OF TECHNOLOGY

Hoboken, NJ

CONTACT Ms. Adrienne Hynek, Associate Director of Financial Aid, Stevens Institute of Technology, Castle Point on Hudson, Hoboken, NJ 07030, 201-216-5555 or toll-free 800-458-5323. *Fax:* 201-216-8050. *E-mail:* ahynek@stevens.edu.

STEVENSON UNIVERSITY

Stevenson, MD

Tuition & fees: $19,200 **Average undergraduate aid package: $12,730**

ABOUT THE INSTITUTION Independent, coed. ***Awards:*** bachelor's and master's degrees. 50 undergraduate majors. ***Total enrollment:*** 3,409. Undergraduates: 3,151. Freshmen: 631. Institutional methodology is used as a basis for awarding need-based institutional aid.

UNDERGRADUATE EXPENSES for 2008–09 ***Application fee:*** $40. ***Comprehensive fee:*** $29,056 includes full-time tuition ($17,976), mandatory fees ($1224), and room and board ($9856). ***College room only:*** $6460. Full-time tuition and fees vary according to degree level. Room and board charges vary according to board plan and housing facility. ***Part-time tuition:*** $455 per credit. ***Part-time fees:*** $75 per term. Part-time tuition and fees vary according to course load and degree level. ***Payment plans:*** Installment, deferred payment.

FRESHMAN FINANCIAL AID (Fall 2007) 504 applied for aid; of those 80% were deemed to have need. 100% of freshmen with need received aid; of those 18% had need fully met. ***Average percent of need met:*** 69% (excluding resources awarded to replace EFC). ***Average financial aid package:*** $12,492 (excluding resources awarded to replace EFC). 22% of all full-time freshmen had no need and received non-need-based gift aid.

UNDERGRADUATE FINANCIAL AID (Fall 2007) 1,908 applied for aid; of those 82% were deemed to have need. 100% of undergraduates with need received aid; of those 23% had need fully met. ***Average percent of need met:*** 71% (excluding resources awarded to replace EFC). ***Average financial aid package:*** $12,730 (excluding resources awarded to replace EFC). 25% of all full-time undergraduates had no need and received non-need-based gift aid.

GIFT AID (NEED-BASED) ***Total amount:*** $14,186,539 (13% federal, 22% state, 61% institutional, 4% external sources). ***Receiving aid:*** Freshmen: 64% (388); all full-time undergraduates: 58% (1,483). ***Average award:*** Freshmen: $10,005; Undergraduates: $9686. ***Scholarships, grants, and awards:*** Federal Pell, FSEOG, state, private, college/university gift aid from institutional funds.

GIFT AID (NON-NEED-BASED) ***Total amount:*** $4,969,078 (4% state, 89% institutional, 7% external sources). ***Receiving aid:*** Freshmen: 7% (43). Undergraduates: 8% (204). ***Average award:*** Freshmen: $4861. Undergraduates: $6081. ***Tuition waivers:*** Full or partial for employees or children of employees. ***ROTC:*** Army cooperative.

LOANS ***Student loans:*** $11,321,795 (62% need-based, 38% non-need-based). ***Average need-based loan:*** Freshmen: $3287. Undergraduates: $4141. ***Parent loans:*** $7,758,720 (30% need-based, 70% non-need-based). ***Programs:*** FFEL (Subsidized and Unsubsidized Stafford, PLUS), Perkins.

WORK-STUDY ***Federal work-study:*** Total amount: $233,081; jobs available.

APPLYING FOR FINANCIAL AID ***Required financial aid form:*** FAFSA. ***Financial aid deadline (priority):*** 2/15. ***Notification date:*** Continuous beginning 3/15. Students must reply by 5/1 or within 2 weeks of notification.

CONTACT Ms. Debra Bottomms, Director of Financial Aid, Stevenson University, 1525 Greenspring Valley Road, Stevenson, MD 21153, 443-334-2559 or toll-free 877-468-6852 (in-state), 877-468-3852 (out-of-state). *Fax:* 443-334-2600. *E-mail:* fa-deb1@mail.vjc.edu.

STILLMAN COLLEGE

Tuscaloosa, AL

Tuition & fees: $12,712 **Average undergraduate aid package: $17,856**

ABOUT THE INSTITUTION Independent religious, coed. ***Awards:*** bachelor's degrees. 14 undergraduate majors. ***Total enrollment:*** 1,048. Undergraduates: 493. Freshmen: 493. Federal methodology is used as a basis for awarding need-based institutional aid.

UNDERGRADUATE EXPENSES for 2008–09 ***Application fee:*** $50. ***Comprehensive fee:*** $18,706 includes full-time tuition ($11,504), mandatory fees ($1208), and room and board ($5994). Room and board charges vary according to housing facility. ***Part-time tuition:*** $476 per credit hour. ***Part-time fees:*** $86 per term. ***Payment plan:*** Deferred payment.

FRESHMAN FINANCIAL AID (Fall 2008, est.) 470 applied for aid; of those 100% were deemed to have need. 100% of freshmen with need received aid; of those 34% had need fully met. ***Average percent of need met:*** 34% (excluding resources awarded to replace EFC). ***Average financial aid package:*** $16,856 (excluding resources awarded to replace EFC). 3% of all full-time freshmen had no need and received non-need-based gift aid.

UNDERGRADUATE FINANCIAL AID (Fall 2008, est.) 972 applied for aid; of those 100% were deemed to have need. 100% of undergraduates with need received aid; of those 61% had need fully met. ***Average percent of need met:*** 61% (excluding resources awarded to replace EFC). ***Average financial aid package:*** $17,856 (excluding resources awarded to replace EFC). 5% of all full-time undergraduates had no need and received non-need-based gift aid.

GIFT AID (NEED-BASED) ***Total amount:*** $7,262,547 (53% federal, 3% state, 40% institutional, 4% external sources). ***Receiving aid:*** Freshmen: 86% (415); all full-time undergraduates: 52% (534). ***Average award:*** Freshmen: $3500; Undergraduates: $7200. ***Scholarships, grants, and awards:*** Federal Pell, FSEOG, state, private, college/university gift aid from institutional funds, United Negro College Fund.

GIFT AID (NON-NEED-BASED) ***Total amount:*** $4,292,771 (91% federal, 1% state, 1% institutional, 7% external sources). ***Average award:*** Freshmen: $3500. Undergraduates: $5654. ***Scholarships, grants, and awards by category:*** *Academic interests/achievement:* 62 awards ($643,000 total): education, general academic interests/achievements. *Creative arts/performance:* 127 awards ($511,285 total): music. *Special characteristics:* 15 awards ($41,088 total): children of faculty/staff. ***Tuition waivers:*** Full or partial for employees or children of employees. ***ROTC:*** Army cooperative.

LOANS ***Student loans:*** $10,415,555 (70% need-based, 30% non-need-based). 96% of past graduating class borrowed through all loan programs. *Average indebtedness per student:* $23,000. ***Average need-based loan:*** Freshmen: $5500. Undergraduates: $7500. ***Parent loans:*** $1,385,174 (50% need-based, 50% non-need-based). ***Programs:*** Federal Direct (Subsidized and Unsubsidized Stafford, PLUS), FFEL (Subsidized and Unsubsidized Stafford, PLUS), Perkins.

WORK-STUDY ***Federal work-study:*** Total amount: $213,000; 178 jobs averaging $1086.

ATHLETIC AWARDS Total amount: $750,000 (100% need-based).

APPLYING FOR FINANCIAL AID ***Required financial aid forms:*** FAFSA, state aid form. ***Financial aid deadline:*** 6/1 (priority: 3/1). ***Notification date:*** 6/1. Students must reply within 2 weeks of notification.

CONTACT Jacqueline S. Morris, Director of Financial Aid, Stillman College, PO Box 1430, Tuscaloosa, AL 35403, 205-366-8950 or toll-free 800-841-5722. *Fax:* 205-247-8106. *E-mail:* jmorris@stillman.edu.

STONEHILL COLLEGE

Easton, MA

Tuition & fees: $30,150 **Average undergraduate aid package: $19,987**

ABOUT THE INSTITUTION Independent Roman Catholic, coed. ***Awards:*** bachelor's degrees. 33 undergraduate majors. ***Total enrollment:*** 2,426. Undergraduates: 2,426. Freshmen: 635. Both federal and institutional methodology are used as a basis for awarding need-based institutional aid.

UNDERGRADUATE EXPENSES for 2008–09 ***Application fee:*** $60. ***Comprehensive fee:*** $41,980 includes full-time tuition ($30,150) and room and board ($11,830). Room and board charges vary according to board plan. ***Part-time tuition:*** $1005 per course. ***Part-time fees:*** $25 per term. Part-time tuition and fees vary according to course load. ***Payment plans:*** Tuition prepayment, installment.

FRESHMAN FINANCIAL AID (Fall 2008, est.) 544 applied for aid; of those 79% were deemed to have need. 100% of freshmen with need received aid; of those 25% had need fully met. ***Average percent of need met:*** 79% (excluding resources awarded to replace EFC). ***Average financial aid package:*** $20,949 (excluding resources awarded to replace EFC). 21% of all full-time freshmen had no need and received non-need-based gift aid.

UNDERGRADUATE FINANCIAL AID (Fall 2008, est.) 1,877 applied for aid; of those 82% were deemed to have need. 100% of undergraduates with need received aid; of those 20% had need fully met. ***Average percent of need met:*** 77% (excluding resources awarded to replace EFC). ***Average financial aid package:*** $19,987 (excluding resources awarded to replace EFC). 18% of all full-time undergraduates had no need and received non-need-based gift aid.

GIFT AID (NEED-BASED) ***Total amount:*** $21,765,904 (8% federal, 4% state, 85% institutional, 3% external sources). ***Receiving aid:*** Freshmen: 65% (415); all full-time undergraduates: 61% (1,450). ***Average award:*** Freshmen: $17,844; Undergraduates: $16,055. ***Scholarships, grants, and awards:*** Federal Pell, FSEOG, state, private, college/university gift aid from institutional funds.

GIFT AID (NON-NEED-BASED) ***Total amount:*** $4,949,570 (7% federal, 84% institutional, 9% external sources). ***Receiving aid:*** Freshmen: 12% (75). Undergraduates: 9% (204). ***Average award:*** Freshmen: $8493. Undergraduates: $7630. ***Scholarships, grants, and awards by category:*** *Academic interests/achievement:* 1,310 awards ($10,195,205 total): general academic interests/achievements. *Special characteristics:* 131 awards ($2,162,408 total): children of faculty/staff, children of union members/company employees, members of minority groups, relatives of clergy, siblings of current students. ***Tuition waivers:*** Full or partial for employees or children of employees. ***ROTC:*** Army.

LOANS ***Student loans:*** $15,077,130 (61% need-based, 39% non-need-based). 75% of past graduating class borrowed through all loan programs. *Average indebtedness per student:* $25,603. ***Average need-based loan:*** Freshmen: $3744. Undergraduates: $4713. ***Parent loans:*** $10,413,399 (29% need-based, 71% non-need-based). ***Programs:*** Federal Direct (Subsidized and Unsubsidized Stafford, PLUS), Perkins, state.

WORK-STUDY ***Federal work-study:*** Total amount: $969,797; 758 jobs averaging $2191. ***State or other work-study/employment:*** Total amount: $1,209,672 (19% need-based, 81% non-need-based). 381 part-time jobs averaging $1656.

ATHLETIC AWARDS Total amount: $1,863,693 (62% need-based, 38% non-need-based).

APPLYING FOR FINANCIAL AID ***Required financial aid forms:*** FAFSA, CSS Financial Aid PROFILE, noncustodial (divorced/separated) parent's statement, business/farm supplement. ***Financial aid deadline (priority):*** 2/1. ***Notification date:*** 4/1. Students must reply by 5/1.

CONTACT Rhonda Nickley, Office Manager, Stonehill College, 320 Washington Street, Easton, MA 02357, 508-565-1088. *Fax:* 508-565-1426. *E-mail:* finaid@stonehill.edu.

STONY BROOK UNIVERSITY, STATE UNIVERSITY OF NEW YORK

Stony Brook, NY

Tuition & fees (NY res): $6430 **Average undergraduate aid package: $9126**

ABOUT THE INSTITUTION State-supported, coed. ***Awards:*** bachelor's, master's, doctoral, and first professional degrees and post-bachelor's, post-master's, and first professional certificates. 59 undergraduate majors. ***Total enrollment:*** 23,994. Undergraduates: 15,924. Freshmen: 2,894. Federal methodology is used as a basis for awarding need-based institutional aid.

UNDERGRADUATE EXPENSES for 2009–10 ***Application fee:*** $40. ***Tuition, state resident:*** full-time $4970; part-time $207 per credit. ***Tuition, nonresident:*** full-time $12,870; part-time $536 per credit. ***Required fees:*** full-time $1460. ***College room and board:*** $9132.

FRESHMAN FINANCIAL AID (Fall 2008, est.) 2,318 applied for aid; of those 65% were deemed to have need. 97% of freshmen with need received aid; of those 14% had need fully met. ***Average percent of need met:*** 67% (excluding resources awarded to replace EFC). ***Average financial aid package:*** $9178 (excluding resources awarded to replace EFC). 16% of all full-time freshmen had no need and received non-need-based gift aid.

UNDERGRADUATE FINANCIAL AID (Fall 2008, est.) 10,396 applied for aid; of those 77% were deemed to have need. 97% of undergraduates with need received aid; of those 9% had need fully met. ***Average percent of need met:*** 62% (excluding resources awarded to replace EFC). ***Average financial aid package:*** $9126 (excluding resources awarded to replace EFC). 8% of all full-time undergraduates had no need and received non-need-based gift aid.

GIFT AID (NEED-BASED) ***Total amount:*** $44,648,152 (47% federal, 46% state, 5% institutional, 2% external sources). ***Receiving aid:*** Freshmen: 40% (1,307), all full-time undergraduates: 48% (7,053). ***Average award:*** Freshmen: $6464; Undergraduates: $5880. ***Scholarships, grants, and awards:*** Federal Pell, FSEOG, state, private, college/university gift aid from institutional funds.

GIFT AID (NON-NEED-BASED) ***Total amount:*** $4,944,449 (2% federal, 9% state, 77% institutional, 12% external sources). ***Receiving aid:*** Freshmen: 2% (56). Undergraduates: 1% (149). ***Average award:*** Freshmen: $3003. Undergraduates: $3134. ***Scholarships, grants, and awards by category:*** *Academic interests/achievement:* 2,091 awards ($5,852,562 total): area/ethnic studies, biological sciences, business, computer science, engineering/technologies, English, general academic interests/achievements, health fields, physical sciences, social sciences. *Creative arts/performance:* 49 awards ($116,234 total): journalism/publications, music. *Special characteristics:* 4 awards ($10,000 total): children and siblings of alumni. ***ROTC:*** Army cooperative, Air Force cooperative.

LOANS ***Student loans:*** $51,539,018 (69% need-based, 31% non-need-based). 63% of past graduating class borrowed through all loan programs. *Average indebtedness per student:* $17,375. ***Average need-based loan:*** Freshmen: $3452. Undergraduates: $4397. ***Parent loans:*** $3,451,368 (27% need-based, 73% non-need-based). ***Programs:*** Federal Direct (Subsidized and Unsubsidized Stafford, PLUS), Perkins.

WORK-STUDY ***Federal work-study:*** Total amount: $989,547; 518 jobs averaging $1910. ***State or other work-study/employment:*** Total amount: $5,033,838 (43% need-based, 57% non-need-based). 1,828 part-time jobs averaging $1960.

ATHLETIC AWARDS Total amount: $4,352,345 (32% need-based, 68% non-need-based).

APPLYING FOR FINANCIAL AID ***Required financial aid forms:*** FAFSA, institution's own form. ***Financial aid deadline (priority):*** 3/1. ***Notification date:*** Continuous beginning 3/15. Students must reply within 2 weeks of notification.

CONTACT Jacqueline Pascariello, Director of Financial Aid and Student Employment, Stony Brook University, State University of New York, 180 Administration Building, Stony Brook, NY 11794-0851, 631-632-6840 or toll-free 800-872-7869 (out-of-state). *Fax:* 631-632-9525.

STRATFORD UNIVERSITY

Falls Church, VA

CONTACT Financial Aid Office, Stratford University, 7777 Leesburg Pike, Suite 100 South, Falls Church, VA 22043, 703-821-8570 or toll-free 800-444-0804.

SUFFOLK UNIVERSITY

Boston, MA

Tuition & fees: $25,954 **Average undergraduate aid package: $15,232**

ABOUT THE INSTITUTION Independent, coed. ***Awards:*** associate, bachelor's, master's, doctoral, and first professional degrees and post-bachelor's, post-master's, and first professional certificates (doctoral degree in law). 61 undergraduate majors. ***Total enrollment:*** 9,435. Undergraduates: 5,809. Freshmen: 1,572. Both federal and institutional methodology are used as a basis for awarding need-based institutional aid.

UNDERGRADUATE EXPENSES for 2008–09 ***Application fee:*** $50. ***Comprehensive fee:*** $39,924 includes full-time tuition ($25,850), mandatory fees ($104), and room and board ($13,970). ***College room only:*** $11,630. Room and board charges vary according to board plan and housing facility. ***Part-time tuition:*** $634 per credit. ***Part-time fees:*** $10 per term. ***Payment plans:*** Installment, deferred payment.

FRESHMAN FINANCIAL AID (Fall 2008, est.) 1,121 applied for aid; of those 81% were deemed to have need. 99% of freshmen with need received aid; of those 13% had need fully met. ***Average percent of need met:*** 62% (excluding resources awarded to replace EFC). ***Average financial aid package:*** $15,063 (excluding resources awarded to replace EFC). 6% of all full-time freshmen had no need and received non-need-based gift aid.

UNDERGRADUATE FINANCIAL AID (Fall 2008, est.) 3,462 applied for aid; of those 82% were deemed to have need. 100% of undergraduates with need received aid; of those 12% had need fully met. ***Average percent of need met:*** 60% (excluding resources awarded to replace EFC). ***Average financial aid package:*** $15,232 (excluding resources awarded to replace EFC). 9% of all full-time undergraduates had no need and received non-need-based gift aid.

GIFT AID (NEED-BASED) ***Total amount:*** $21,149,422 (21% federal, 8% state, 67% institutional, 4% external sources). ***Receiving aid:*** Freshmen: 47% (740); all full-time undergraduates: 45% (2,368). ***Average award:*** Freshmen: $9755;

Undergraduates: $8974. ***Scholarships, grants, and awards:*** Federal Pell, FSEOG, state, private, college/university gift aid from institutional funds.

GIFT AID (NON-NEED-BASED) ***Total amount:*** $10,834,089 (93% institutional, 7% external sources). ***Receiving aid:*** Freshmen: 19% (293). Undergraduates: 17% (884). ***Average award:*** Freshmen: $9306. Undergraduates: $8545. ***Scholarships, grants, and awards by category:*** *Academic interests/achievement:* 1,241 awards ($9,677,036 total): general academic interests/achievements. *Special achievements/activities:* 3 awards ($10,000 total): community service. *Special characteristics:* 203 awards ($633,075 total): children and siblings of alumni, children of faculty/staff, siblings of current students. ***Tuition waivers:*** Full or partial for employees or children of employees, senior citizens. ***ROTC:*** Army cooperative.

LOANS ***Student loans:*** $40,782,909 (37% need-based, 63% non-need-based). 72% of past graduating class borrowed through all loan programs. ***Average need-based loan:*** Freshmen: $3996. Undergraduates: $4811. ***Parent loans:*** $16,034,342 (100% non-need-based). ***Programs:*** Federal Direct (Subsidized and Unsubsidized Stafford, PLUS), Perkins, state, college/university.

WORK-STUDY ***Federal work-study:*** Total amount: $2,250,600; 871 jobs averaging $2108. ***State or other work-study/employment:*** Total amount: $1,233,760 (100% non-need-based). 424 part-time jobs averaging $2993.

APPLYING FOR FINANCIAL AID ***Required financial aid forms:*** FAFSA, institution's own form. ***Financial aid deadline:*** 3/1 (priority: 3/1). ***Notification date:*** Continuous. Students must reply within 2 weeks of notification.

CONTACT Ms. Christine A. Perry, Director of Financial Aid, Suffolk University, 8 Ashburton Place, Boston, MA 02108, 617-573-8470 or toll-free 800-6-SUFFOLK. *Fax:* 617-720-3579. *E-mail:* finaid@suffolk.edu.

SULLIVAN UNIVERSITY

Louisville, KY

CONTACT Charlene Geiser, Financial Planning Office, Sullivan University, 3101 Bardstown Road, Louisville, KY 40205, 502-456-6504 Ext. 311 or toll-free 800-844-1354. *Fax:* 502-456-0040. *E-mail:* cgeiser@sullivan.edu.

SUL ROSS STATE UNIVERSITY

Alpine, TX

CONTACT Ms. Rena Gallego, Director of Financial Assistance and Recruiting, Sul Ross State University, PO Box C-113, Alpine, TX 79832, 915-837-8059 or toll-free 888-722-7778.

SUSQUEHANNA UNIVERSITY

Selinsgrove, PA

Tuition & fees: $31,080 **Average undergraduate aid package: $22,413**

ABOUT THE INSTITUTION Independent religious, coed. ***Awards:*** bachelor's degrees (also offers evening associate degree program limited to local adult students). 51 undergraduate majors. ***Total enrollment:*** 2,137. Undergraduates: 2,137. Freshmen: 616. Both federal and institutional methodology are used as a basis for awarding need-based institutional aid.

UNDERGRADUATE EXPENSES for 2008–09 ***Application fee:*** $35. ***Comprehensive fee:*** $39,480 includes full-time tuition ($30,700), mandatory fees ($380), and room and board ($8400). ***College room only:*** $4400.

FRESHMAN FINANCIAL AID (Fall 2008, est.) 508 applied for aid; of those 82% were deemed to have need. 100% of freshmen with need received aid; of those 43% had need fully met. ***Average percent of need met:*** 82% (excluding resources awarded to replace EFC). ***Average financial aid package:*** $22,907 (excluding resources awarded to replace EFC). 29% of all full-time freshmen had no need and received non-need-based gift aid.

UNDERGRADUATE FINANCIAL AID (Fall 2008, est.) 1,549 applied for aid; of those 86% were deemed to have need. 100% of undergraduates with need received aid; of those 39% had need fully met. ***Average percent of need met:*** 79% (excluding resources awarded to replace EFC). ***Average financial aid package:*** $22,413 (excluding resources awarded to replace EFC). 27% of all full-time undergraduates had no need and received non-need-based gift aid.

GIFT AID (NEED-BASED) ***Total amount:*** $23,088,020 (7% federal, 7% state, 83% institutional, 3% external sources). ***Receiving aid:*** Freshmen: 61% (373); all full-time undergraduates: 58% (1,201). ***Average award:*** Freshmen: $19,812; Undergraduates: $18,612. ***Scholarships, grants, and awards:*** Federal Pell, FSEOG, state, private, college/university gift aid from institutional funds.

GIFT AID (NON-NEED-BASED) ***Total amount:*** $6,256,634 (1% federal, 93% institutional, 6% external sources). ***Receiving aid:*** Freshmen: 9% (56). Undergraduates: 7% (138). ***Average award:*** Freshmen: $9665. Undergraduates: $9967. ***Scholarships, grants, and awards by category:*** *Academic interests/achievement:* 807 awards ($8,729,852 total): business, general academic interests/achievements. *Creative arts/performance:* 108 awards ($314,250 total): creative writing, music. *Special achievements/activities:* 737 awards ($5,350,231 total): general special achievements/activities. *Special characteristics:* 206 awards ($2,927,727 total): children and siblings of alumni, children of educators, children of faculty/staff, members of minority groups, relatives of clergy, veterans. ***ROTC:*** Army cooperative.

LOANS ***Student loans:*** $7,706,094 (63% need-based, 37% non-need-based). 83% of past graduating class borrowed through all loan programs. *Average indebtedness per student:* $17,222. ***Average need-based loan:*** Freshmen: $3711. Undergraduates: $4247. ***Parent loans:*** $4,420,662 (27% need-based, 73% non-need-based). ***Programs:*** FFEL (Subsidized and Unsubsidized Stafford, PLUS), Perkins, college/university.

WORK-STUDY ***Federal work-study:*** Total amount: $1,951,698; 1,028 jobs averaging $1856. ***State or other work-study/employment:*** Total amount: $370,200 (39% need-based, 61% non-need-based). 80 part-time jobs averaging $4632.

APPLYING FOR FINANCIAL AID ***Required financial aid forms:*** FAFSA, CSS Financial Aid PROFILE, business/farm supplement, prior year federal income tax form(s). ***Financial aid deadline (priority):*** 3/1. ***Notification date:*** 3/1. Students must reply by 5/1.

CONTACT Helen S. Nunn, Director of Financial Aid, Susquehanna University, 514 University Avenue, Selinsgrove, PA 17870, 570-372-4450 or toll-free 800-326-9672. *Fax:* 570-372-2722. *E-mail:* nunn@susqu.edu.

SWARTHMORE COLLEGE

Swarthmore, PA

Tuition & fees: $36,490 **Average undergraduate aid package: $33,193**

ABOUT THE INSTITUTION Independent, coed. ***Awards:*** bachelor's degrees. 43 undergraduate majors. ***Total enrollment:*** 1,490. Undergraduates: 1,490. Freshmen: 372. Institutional methodology is used as a basis for awarding need-based institutional aid.

UNDERGRADUATE EXPENSES for 2008–09 ***Application fee:*** $60. ***Comprehensive fee:*** $47,804 includes full-time tuition ($36,154), mandatory fees ($336), and room and board ($11,314). ***College room only:*** $5800.

FRESHMAN FINANCIAL AID (Fall 2008, est.) 242 applied for aid; of those 75% were deemed to have need. 100% of freshmen with need received aid; of those 100% had need fully met. ***Average percent of need met:*** 100% (excluding resources awarded to replace EFC). ***Average financial aid package:*** $34,737 (excluding resources awarded to replace EFC). 1% of all full-time freshmen had no need and received non-need-based gift aid.

UNDERGRADUATE FINANCIAL AID (Fall 2008, est.) 773 applied for aid; of those 91% were deemed to have need. 100% of undergraduates with need received aid; of those 100% had need fully met. ***Average percent of need met:*** 100% (excluding resources awarded to replace EFC). ***Average financial aid package:*** $33,193 (excluding resources awarded to replace EFC). 1% of all full-time undergraduates had no need and received non-need-based gift aid.

GIFT AID (NEED-BASED) ***Total amount:*** $22,061,276 (3% federal, 1% state, 94% institutional, 2% external sources). ***Receiving aid:*** Freshmen: 49% (181); all full-time undergraduates: 47% (700). ***Average award:*** Freshmen: $33,328; Undergraduates: $31,715. ***Scholarships, grants, and awards:*** Federal Pell, FSEOG, state, private, college/university gift aid from institutional funds.

GIFT AID (NON-NEED-BASED) ***Total amount:*** $986,427 (44% institutional, 56% external sources). ***Average award:*** Freshmen: $36,154. Undergraduates: $36,154. ***Scholarships, grants, and awards by category:*** *Academic interests/achievement:* 12 awards ($433,848 total): general academic interests/achievements. ***ROTC:*** Army cooperative, Air Force cooperative.

LOANS ***Student loans:*** $1,817,963 (100% non-need-based). ***Parent loans:*** $2,026,253 (100% non-need-based). ***Programs:*** FFEL (Subsidized and Unsubsidized Stafford, PLUS), Perkins, state, college/university.

WORK-STUDY ***Federal work-study:*** Total amount: $664,702; 588 jobs averaging $1625. ***State or other work-study/employment:*** Total amount: $556,759 (85% need-based, 15% non-need-based). Part-time jobs available.

APPLYING FOR FINANCIAL AID ***Required financial aid forms:*** FAFSA, institution's own form, CSS Financial Aid PROFILE, state aid form, noncustodial (divorced/separated) parent's statement, business/farm supplement, federal tax return, W-2 forms, year-end paycheck stub. ***Financial aid deadline:*** 2/15. ***Notification date:*** 4/1. Students must reply by 5/1.

CONTACT Laura Talbot, Director of Financial Aid, Swarthmore College, 500 College Avenue, Swarthmore, PA 19081-1397, 610-328-8358 or toll-free 800-667-3110. *Fax:* 610-690-5751. *E-mail:* finaid@swarthmore.edu.

SWEDISH INSTITUTE, COLLEGE OF HEALTH SCIENCES

New York, NY

CONTACT Financial Aid Office, Swedish Institute, College of Health Sciences, 226 West 26th Street, New York, NY 10001-6700, 212-924-5900.

SWEET BRIAR COLLEGE

Sweet Briar, VA

Tuition & fees: $29,135 **Average undergraduate aid package: $13,633**

ABOUT THE INSTITUTION Independent, women only. ***Awards:*** bachelor's and master's degrees. 39 undergraduate majors. ***Total enrollment:*** 828. Undergraduates: 813. Freshmen: 198. Federal methodology is used as a basis for awarding need-based institutional aid.

UNDERGRADUATE EXPENSES for 2009–10 ***Application fee:*** $40. ***One-time required fee:*** $200. ***Comprehensive fee:*** $39,595 includes full-time tuition ($28,860), mandatory fees ($275), and room and board ($10,460). ***Part-time tuition:*** $955 per credit hour.

FRESHMAN FINANCIAL AID (Fall 2008, est.) 152 applied for aid; of those 84% were deemed to have need. 100% of freshmen with need received aid; of those 82% had need fully met. ***Average percent of need met:*** 71% (excluding resources awarded to replace EFC). ***Average financial aid package:*** $15,051 (excluding resources awarded to replace EFC).

UNDERGRADUATE FINANCIAL AID (Fall 2008, est.) 422 applied for aid; of those 97% were deemed to have need. 99% of undergraduates with need received aid; of those 88% had need fully met. ***Average percent of need met:*** 70% (excluding resources awarded to replace EFC). ***Average financial aid package:*** $13,633 (excluding resources awarded to replace EFC).

GIFT AID (NEED-BASED) ***Total amount:*** $5,264,464 (11% federal, 12% state, 77% institutional). ***Receiving aid:*** Freshmen: 62% (120); all full-time undergraduates: 53% (335). ***Average award:*** Freshmen: $13,427; Undergraduates: $11,479. ***Scholarships, grants, and awards:*** Federal Pell, FSEOG, state, private, college/university gift aid from institutional funds.

GIFT AID (NON-NEED-BASED) ***Total amount:*** $3,383,875 (12% state, 83% institutional, 5% external sources). ***Receiving aid:*** Freshmen: 33% (64). Undergraduates: 40% (249). ***Scholarships, grants, and awards by category:*** *Academic interests/achievement:* 387 awards ($3,634,111 total): general academic interests/achievements, premedicine. *Creative arts/performance:* 1 award ($1000 total): art/fine arts, general creative arts/performance, music. *Special achievements/activities:* 7 awards ($7000 total): community service. *Special characteristics:* 238 awards ($1,722,180 total): adult students, general special characteristics, international students, local/state students.

LOANS ***Student loans:*** $2,727,120 (67% need-based, 33% non-need-based). 50% of past graduating class borrowed through all loan programs. *Average indebtedness per student:* $20,118. ***Average need-based loan:*** Freshmen: $4295. Undergraduates: $4585. ***Parent loans:*** $2,813,518 (74% need-based, 26% non-need-based). ***Programs:*** Federal Direct (Subsidized and Unsubsidized Stafford, PLUS), Perkins, college/university.

WORK-STUDY ***Federal work-study:*** Total amount: $95,274; 99 jobs averaging $945. ***State or other work-study/employment:*** Total amount: $115,919 (100% need-based). 115 part-time jobs averaging $949.

APPLYING FOR FINANCIAL AID ***Required financial aid forms:*** FAFSA, noncustodial (divorced/separated) parent's statement. ***Financial aid deadline (priority):*** 2/15. ***Notification date:*** Continuous beginning 3/1. Students must reply by 5/1 or within 2 weeks of notification.

CONTACT Bobbi Carpenter, Director of Financial Aid, Sweet Briar College, Box AS, Sweet Briar, VA 24595, 800-381-6156 or toll-free 800-381-6142. *Fax:* 434-381-6450. *E-mail:* bcarpenter@sbc.edu.

SYRACUSE UNIVERSITY

Syracuse, NY

ABOUT THE INSTITUTION Independent, coed. ***Awards:*** associate, bachelor's, master's, doctoral, and first professional degrees and post-bachelor's and post-master's certificates. 103 undergraduate majors. ***Total enrollment:*** 19,366. Undergraduates: 13,651. Freshmen: 3,186.

GIFT AID (NEED-BASED) ***Scholarships, grants, and awards:*** Federal Pell, FSEOG, state, private, college/university gift aid from institutional funds.

GIFT AID (NON-NEED-BASED) ***Scholarships, grants, and awards by category:*** *Academic interests/achievement:* general academic interests/achievements. *Creative arts/performance:* art/fine arts, music.

LOANS ***Programs:*** FFEL (Subsidized and Unsubsidized Stafford, PLUS), Perkins.

WORK-STUDY ***Federal work-study:*** Total amount: $3,500,000; jobs available (averaging $1300). ***State or other work-study/employment:*** Part-time jobs available.

APPLYING FOR FINANCIAL AID ***Required financial aid forms:*** FAFSA, CSS Financial Aid PROFILE, business/farm supplement.

CONTACT Kaye DeVesty, Interim Director of Financial Aid, Syracuse University, 200 Archbold Gymnasium, Syracuse, NY 13244-1140, 315-443-1513. *E-mail:* finmail@syr.edu.

TABOR COLLEGE

Hillsboro, KS

Tuition & fees: $18,710 **Average undergraduate aid package: $18,663**

ABOUT THE INSTITUTION Independent Mennonite Brethren, coed. ***Awards:*** associate, bachelor's, and master's degrees. 53 undergraduate majors. ***Total enrollment:*** 574. Undergraduates: 574. Freshmen: 120. Federal methodology is used as a basis for awarding need-based institutional aid.

UNDERGRADUATE EXPENSES for 2008–09 ***Application fee:*** $30. ***One-time required fee:*** $100. ***Comprehensive fee:*** $25,460 includes full-time tuition ($18,300), mandatory fees ($410), and room and board ($6750). ***College room only:*** $2600. ***Part-time tuition:*** $720 per credit hour. ***Part-time fees:*** $5 per credit hour.

FRESHMAN FINANCIAL AID (Fall 2008, est.) 137 applied for aid; of those 81% were deemed to have need. 100% of freshmen with need received aid; of those 19% had need fully met. ***Average percent of need met:*** 77% (excluding resources awarded to replace EFC). ***Average financial aid package:*** $17,661 (excluding resources awarded to replace EFC). 19% of all full-time freshmen had no need and received non-need-based gift aid.

UNDERGRADUATE FINANCIAL AID (Fall 2008, est.) 512 applied for aid; of those 81% were deemed to have need. 100% of undergraduates with need received aid; of those 28% had need fully met. ***Average percent of need met:*** 82% (excluding resources awarded to replace EFC). ***Average financial aid package:*** $18,663 (excluding resources awarded to replace EFC). 18% of all full-time undergraduates had no need and received non-need-based gift aid.

GIFT AID (NEED-BASED) ***Total amount:*** $1,256,138 (68% federal, 32% state). ***Receiving aid:*** Freshmen: 65% (89); all full-time undergraduates: 61% (323). ***Average award:*** Freshmen: $4156; Undergraduates: $4241. ***Scholarships, grants, and awards:*** Federal Pell, FSEOG, state, private, college/university gift aid from institutional funds.

GIFT AID (NON-NEED-BASED) ***Total amount:*** $3,197,174 (93% institutional, 7% external sources). ***Receiving aid:*** Freshmen: 81% (111). Undergraduates: 72% (381). ***Average award:*** Freshmen: $6243. Undergraduates: $6315. ***Scholarships, grants, and awards by category:*** *Academic interests/achievement:* 394 awards ($1,594,180 total): biological sciences, communication, general academic interests/achievements, humanities. *Creative arts/performance:* 112 awards ($171,990 total): journalism/publications, music, performing arts, theater/drama. *Special achievements/activities:* 352 awards ($1,030,640 total): cheerleading/drum major, general special achievements/activities, religious involvement. *Special characteristics:* 432 awards ($484,581 total): children and siblings of alumni, children of faculty/staff, general special characteristics, international students, local/state students, out-of-state students, religious affiliation.

LOANS ***Student loans:*** $3,736,699 (100% need-based). 81% of past graduating class borrowed through all loan programs. *Average indebtedness per student:* $20,500. ***Average need-based loan:*** Freshmen: $6143. Undergraduates: $8219. ***Parent loans:*** $410,864 (100% need-based). ***Programs:*** FFEL (Subsidized and Unsubsidized Stafford, PLUS), Perkins.

WORK-STUDY ***Federal work-study:*** Total amount: $72,287; 175 jobs averaging $820. ***State or other work-study/employment:*** Part-time jobs available.

ATHLETIC AWARDS Total amount: $1,001,697 (100% non-need-based).

APPLYING FOR FINANCIAL AID ***Required financial aid forms:*** FAFSA, state aid form, admissions application. ***Financial aid deadline:*** 8/15 (priority: 3/1). ***Notification date:*** Continuous beginning 3/15. Students must reply within 4 weeks of notification.

CONTACT Mr. Scott Franz, Director of Student Financial Assistance, Tabor College, 400 South Jefferson, Hillsboro, KS 67063, 620-947-3121 Ext. 1726 or toll-free 800-822-6799. *Fax:* 620-947-6276. *E-mail:* scottf@tabor.edu.

TALLADEGA COLLEGE

Talladega, AL

CONTACT K. Michael Francois, Director of Financial Aid, Talladega College, 627 West Battle Street, Talladega, AL 35160, 256-761-6341 or toll-free 800-762-2468 (in-state), 800-633-2440 (out-of-state). *Fax:* 256-761-6462.

TALMUDICAL ACADEMY OF NEW JERSEY

Adelphia, NJ

CONTACT Office of Financial Aid, Talmudical Academy of New Jersey, Route 524, Adelphia, NJ 07710, 732-431-1600.

TALMUDICAL INSTITUTE OF UPSTATE NEW YORK

Rochester, NY

CONTACT Mrs. Ella Berenstein, Financial Aid Administrator, Talmudical Institute of Upstate New York, 769 Park Avenue, Rochester, NY 14607-3046, 716-473-2810.

TALMUDICAL SEMINARY OHOLEI TORAH

Brooklyn, NY

CONTACT Financial Aid Administrator, Talmudical Seminary Oholei Torah, 667 Eastern Parkway, Brooklyn, NY 11213-3310, 718-774-5050.

TALMUDICAL YESHIVA OF PHILADELPHIA

Philadelphia, PA

CONTACT Director of Student Financial Aid/Registrar, Talmudical Yeshiva of Philadelphia, 6063 Drexel Road, Philadelphia, PA 19131-1296, 215-473-1212.

TALMUDIC COLLEGE OF FLORIDA

Miami Beach, FL

CONTACT Rabbi Ira Hill, Director of Financial Aid, Talmudic College of Florida, 1910 Alton Road, Miami Beach, FL 33139, 305-534-7050 or toll-free 888-825-6834. *Fax:* 305-534-8444.

TARLETON STATE UNIVERSITY

Stephenville, TX

Tuition & fees (TX res): $6975 **Average undergraduate aid package: $9940**

ABOUT THE INSTITUTION State-supported, coed. ***Awards:*** associate, bachelor's, master's, and doctoral degrees. 77 undergraduate majors. ***Total enrollment:*** 9,634. Undergraduates: 7,886. Freshmen: 1,252. Federal methodology is used as a basis for awarding need-based institutional aid.

UNDERGRADUATE EXPENSES for 2008–09 ***Application fee:*** $30. ***Tuition, state resident:*** full-time $5565; part-time $138.50 per credit hour. ***Tuition, nonresident:*** full-time $13,995; part-time $419.50 per credit hour. ***Required fees:*** full-time $1410. Full-time tuition and fees vary according to course load. Part-time tuition and fees vary according to course load. ***College room and board:*** $6034; ***Room only:*** $4252. Room and board charges vary according to board plan and housing facility. ***Payment plan:*** Installment.

FRESHMAN FINANCIAL AID (Fall 2007) 1,013 applied for aid; of those 62% were deemed to have need. ***Average percent of need met:*** 75% (excluding resources awarded to replace EFC). ***Average financial aid package:*** $10,022 (excluding resources awarded to replace EFC). 27% of all full-time freshmen had no need and received non-need-based gift aid.

UNDERGRADUATE FINANCIAL AID (Fall 2007) ***Average percent of need met:*** 71% (excluding resources awarded to replace EFC). ***Average financial aid package:*** $9940 (excluding resources awarded to replace EFC). 22% of all full-time undergraduates had no need and received non-need-based gift aid.

GIFT AID (NEED-BASED) ***Total amount:*** $13,492,421 (56% federal, 16% state, 9% institutional, 19% external sources). ***Receiving aid:*** Freshmen: 42% (524); all full-time undergraduates: 56% (3,273). ***Average award:*** Freshmen: $4278; Undergraduates: $3008. ***Scholarships, grants, and awards:*** Federal Pell, FSEOG, state, private, college/university gift aid from institutional funds.

GIFT AID (NON-NEED-BASED) ***Total amount:*** $3,835,893 (66% institutional, 34% external sources). ***Receiving aid:*** Freshmen: 24% (298). Undergraduates: 21% (1,250). ***Average award:*** Freshmen: $4762. Undergraduates: $1272. ***Tuition waivers:*** Full or partial for employees or children of employees, senior citizens. ***ROTC:*** Army.

LOANS ***Student loans:*** $27,618,364 (50% need-based, 50% non-need-based). 54% of past graduating class borrowed through all loan programs. *Average indebtedness per student:* $18,223. ***Average need-based loan:*** Freshmen: $2969. Undergraduates: $4032. ***Parent loans:*** $4,680,612 (100% non-need-based). ***Programs:*** FFEL (Subsidized and Unsubsidized Stafford, PLUS), state, college/university.

WORK-STUDY ***Federal work-study:*** Total amount: $113,442; jobs available. ***State or other work-study/employment:*** Total amount: $57,683 (100% need-based). Part-time jobs available.

ATHLETIC AWARDS Total amount: $1,059,312 (100% non-need-based).

APPLYING FOR FINANCIAL AID ***Financial aid deadline:*** 11/1 (priority: 4/1).

CONTACT Ms. Betty Murray, Director of Student Financial Aid, Tarleton State University, Box T-0310, Stephenville, TX 76402, 254-968-9070 or toll-free 800-687-8236 (in-state). *Fax:* 254-968-9600. *E-mail:* finaid@tarleton.edu.

TAYLOR UNIVERSITY

Upland, IN

Tuition & fees: $24,546 **Average undergraduate aid package: $16,444**

ABOUT THE INSTITUTION Independent interdenominational, coed. ***Awards:*** associate, bachelor's, and master's degrees. 55 undergraduate majors. ***Total enrollment:*** 1,871. Undergraduates: 1,871. Freshmen: 465. Federal methodology is used as a basis for awarding need-based institutional aid.

UNDERGRADUATE EXPENSES for 2008–09 ***Application fee:*** $25. ***Comprehensive fee:*** $30,898 includes full-time tuition ($24,314), mandatory fees ($232), and room and board ($6352). ***College room only:*** $3144. Full-time tuition and fees vary according to course load. Room and board charges vary according to board plan and housing facility. ***Part-time tuition:*** $870 per credit hour. ***Part-time fees:*** $36 per term. Part-time tuition and fees vary according to course load. ***Payment plan:*** Installment.

FRESHMAN FINANCIAL AID (Fall 2008, est.) 339 applied for aid; of those 78% were deemed to have need. 100% of freshmen with need received aid; of those 24% had need fully met. ***Average percent of need met:*** 76% (excluding resources awarded to replace EFC). ***Average financial aid package:*** $16,612 (excluding resources awarded to replace EFC). 30% of all full-time freshmen had no need and received non-need-based gift aid.

UNDERGRADUATE FINANCIAL AID (Fall 2008, est.) 1,266 applied for aid; of those 83% were deemed to have need. 100% of undergraduates with need received aid; of those 22% had need fully met. ***Average percent of need met:*** 74% (excluding resources awarded to replace EFC). ***Average financial aid package:*** $16,444 (excluding resources awarded to replace EFC). 26% of all full-time undergraduates had no need and received non-need-based gift aid.

GIFT AID (NEED-BASED) ***Total amount:*** $11,786,708 (12% federal, 10% state, 72% institutional, 6% external sources). ***Receiving aid:*** Freshmen: 54% (252); all full-time undergraduates: 54% (982). ***Average award:*** Freshmen: $13,352; Undergraduates: $12,976. ***Scholarships, grants, and awards:*** Federal Pell, FSEOG, state, private, college/university gift aid from institutional funds, Academic Competitiveness Grant, National Smart Grant.

GIFT AID (NON-NEED-BASED) ***Total amount:*** $3,497,866 (1% state, 81% institutional, 18% external sources). ***Receiving aid:*** Freshmen: 8% (37).

Undergraduates: 6% (108). ***Average award:*** Freshmen: $4346. Undergraduates: $4327. ***Scholarships, grants, and awards by category:*** *Academic interests/achievement:* 852 awards ($4,191,275 total): general academic interests/achievements. *Creative arts/performance:* 93 awards ($219,227 total): music, theater/drama. *Special achievements/activities:* 85 awards ($460,364 total): leadership. *Special characteristics:* 796 awards ($2,415,409 total): children and siblings of alumni, children of faculty/staff, ethnic background, international students, religious affiliation. ***Tuition waivers:*** Full or partial for employees or children of employees, senior citizens.

LOANS ***Student loans:*** $9,097,668 (68% need-based, 32% non-need-based). 54% of past graduating class borrowed through all loan programs. *Average indebtedness per student:* $22,942. ***Average need-based loan:*** Freshmen: $4421. Undergraduates: $4571. ***Parent loans:*** $14,916,668 (28% need-based, 72% non-need-based). ***Programs:*** FFEL (Subsidized and Unsubsidized Stafford, PLUS), Perkins, college/university.

WORK-STUDY ***Federal work-study:*** Total amount: $382,679; 803 jobs averaging $477.

ATHLETIC AWARDS Total amount: $1,486,290 (56% need-based, 44% non-need-based).

APPLYING FOR FINANCIAL AID ***Required financial aid form:*** FAFSA. ***Financial aid deadline:*** 3/10. ***Notification date:*** Continuous. Students must reply by 5/1.

CONTACT Mr. Timothy A. Nace, Director of Financial Aid, Taylor University, 236 West Reade Avenue, Upland, IN 46989-1001, 765-998-5358 or toll-free 800-882-3456. *Fax:* 765-998-4910. *E-mail:* tmnace@taylor.edu.

TEIKYO LORETTO HEIGHTS UNIVERSITY

Denver, CO

CONTACT Financial Aid Office, Teikyo Loretto Heights University, 3001 South Federal Boulevard, Denver, CO 80236, 303-936-4200.

TELSHE YESHIVA–CHICAGO

Chicago, IL

CONTACT Office of Financial Aid, Telshe Yeshiva–Chicago, 3535 West Foster Avenue, Chicago, IL 60625-5598, 773-463-7738.

TEMPLE BAPTIST COLLEGE

Cincinnati, OH

CONTACT Financial Aid Office, Temple Baptist College, 11965 Kenn Road, Cincinnati, OH 45240, 513-851-3800.

TEMPLE UNIVERSITY

Philadelphia, PA

Tuition & fees (PA res): $11,448   Average undergraduate aid package: $13,958

ABOUT THE INSTITUTION State-related, coed. ***Awards:*** associate, bachelor's, master's, doctoral, and first professional degrees and post-bachelor's, post-master's, and first professional certificates. 115 undergraduate majors. ***Total enrollment:*** 35,489. Undergraduates: 26,194. Freshmen: 3,769. Federal methodology is used as a basis for awarding need-based institutional aid.

UNDERGRADUATE EXPENSES for 2008–09 ***Application fee:*** $50. ***Tuition, state resident:*** full-time $10,858; part-time $420 per term. ***Tuition, nonresident:*** full-time $19,878; part-time $707 per term. ***Required fees:*** full-time $590; $220 per term. Full-time tuition and fees vary according to course load, program, and reciprocity agreements. Part-time tuition and fees vary according to course load, program, and reciprocity agreements. ***College room and board:*** $8884; ***Room only:*** $5866. Room and board charges vary according to board plan and housing facility. ***Payment plan:*** Installment.

FRESHMAN FINANCIAL AID (Fall 2007) 4,058 applied for aid; of those 73% were deemed to have need. 98% of freshmen with need received aid; of those 34% had need fully met. ***Average percent of need met:*** 87% (excluding resources awarded to replace EFC). ***Average financial aid package:*** $14,579 (excluding resources awarded to replace EFC). 17% of all full-time freshmen had no need and received non-need-based gift aid.

UNDERGRADUATE FINANCIAL AID (Fall 2007) 19,904 applied for aid; of those 76% were deemed to have need. 94% of undergraduates with need received aid; of those 34% had need fully met. ***Average percent of need met:*** 87% (excluding resources awarded to replace EFC). ***Average financial aid package:*** $13,958 (excluding resources awarded to replace EFC). 14% of all full-time undergraduates had no need and received non-need-based gift aid.

GIFT AID (NEED-BASED) ***Total amount:*** $78,337,205 (35% federal, 30% state, 35% institutional). ***Receiving aid:*** Freshmen: 72% (2,910); all full-time undergraduates: 63% (14,074). ***Average award:*** Freshmen: $5617; Undergraduates: $5248. ***Scholarships, grants, and awards:*** Federal Pell, FSEOG, state, private, college/university gift aid from institutional funds, Federal Nursing.

GIFT AID (NON-NEED-BASED) ***Total amount:*** $65,019,670 (14% institutional, 86% external sources). ***Receiving aid:*** Freshmen: 45% (1,829). Undergraduates: 32% (7,193). ***Average award:*** Freshmen: $7485. Undergraduates: $8577. ***Scholarships, grants, and awards by category:*** *Academic interests/achievement:* general academic interests/achievements. *Creative arts/performance:* art/fine arts, general creative arts/performance, music, performing arts. *Special achievements/activities:* cheerleading/drum major. *Special characteristics:* children of faculty/staff, general special characteristics. ***Tuition waivers:*** Full or partial for employees or children of employees. ***ROTC:*** Army, Naval cooperative, Air Force cooperative.

LOANS ***Student loans:*** $95,383,776 (66% need-based, 34% non-need-based). 72% of past graduating class borrowed through all loan programs. *Average indebtedness per student:* $26,064. ***Average need-based loan:*** Freshmen: $3328. Undergraduates: $4118. ***Parent loans:*** $594,017 (100% non-need-based). ***Programs:*** FFEL (Subsidized and Unsubsidized Stafford, PLUS), Perkins, Federal Nursing, state, college/university.

WORK-STUDY ***Federal work-study:*** Total amount: $1,548,813; jobs available.

ATHLETIC AWARDS Total amount: $6,811,666 (100% non-need-based).

APPLYING FOR FINANCIAL AID ***Required financial aid form:*** FAFSA. ***Financial aid deadline (priority):*** 3/1. ***Notification date:*** Continuous. Students must reply by 5/1 or within 3 weeks of notification.

CONTACT Dr. John F. Morris, Director, Student Financial Services, Temple University, Conwell Hall, Ground Floor, Philadelphia, PA 19122-6096, 215-204-8760 or toll-free 888-340-2222. *Fax:* 215-204-2016. *E-mail:* john.morris@temple.edu.

TENNESSEE STATE UNIVERSITY

Nashville, TN

ABOUT THE INSTITUTION State-supported, coed. ***Awards:*** associate, bachelor's, master's, and doctoral degrees and post-bachelor's and post-master's certificates. 59 undergraduate majors. ***Total enrollment:*** 8,254. Undergraduates: 6,431. Freshmen: 1,040.

GIFT AID (NEED-BASED) ***Scholarships, grants, and awards:*** Federal Pell, FSEOG, state, private, college/university gift aid from institutional funds.

GIFT AID (NON-NEED-BASED) ***Scholarships, grants, and awards by category:*** *Academic interests/achievement:* general academic interests/achievements. *Creative arts/performance:* music. *Special achievements/activities:* general special achievements/activities. *Special characteristics:* local/state students, members of minority groups.

LOANS ***Programs:*** FFEL (Subsidized and Unsubsidized Stafford, PLUS), Perkins, college/university.

APPLYING FOR FINANCIAL AID ***Required financial aid form:*** FAFSA.

CONTACT Mary Chambliss, Director of Financial Aid, Tennessee State University, 3500 John Merritt Boulevard, Nashville, TN 37209-1561, 615-963-5772. *Fax:* 615-963-5108. *E-mail:* mchambliss@tnstate.edu.

TENNESSEE TECHNOLOGICAL UNIVERSITY

Cookeville, TN

Tuition & fees (TN res): $5244   Average undergraduate aid package: $3305

ABOUT THE INSTITUTION State-supported, coed. ***Awards:*** bachelor's, master's, and doctoral degrees and post-bachelor's certificates. 68 undergraduate majors. ***Total enrollment:*** 10,793. Undergraduates: 8,438. Freshmen: 1,677. Federal methodology is used as a basis for awarding need-based institutional aid.

UNDERGRADUATE EXPENSES for 2008–09 ***Application fee:*** $15. ***Tuition, state resident:*** full-time $5244; part-time $189 per hour. ***Tuition, nonresident:*** full-time $16,136; part-time $662 per hour. ***Required fees:*** $63 per hour. Part-time tuition and fees vary according to course load. ***College room and board:*** $7290; ***Room only:*** $3420. Room and board charges vary according to board plan and housing facility. ***Payment plan:*** Installment.

FRESHMAN FINANCIAL AID (Fall 2008, est.) 1,502 applied for aid; of those 64% were deemed to have need. 99% of freshmen with need received aid; of those 31% had need fully met. ***Average percent of need met:*** 87% (excluding resources awarded to replace EFC). ***Average financial aid package:*** $8702 (excluding resources awarded to replace EFC). 28% of all full-time freshmen had no need and received non-need-based gift aid.

UNDERGRADUATE FINANCIAL AID (Fall 2008, est.) 6,100 applied for aid; of those 64% were deemed to have need. 98% of undergraduates with need received aid; of those 27% had need fully met. ***Average percent of need met:*** 81% (excluding resources awarded to replace EFC). ***Average financial aid package:*** $3305 (excluding resources awarded to replace EFC). 20% of all full-time undergraduates had no need and received non-need-based gift aid.

GIFT AID (NEED-BASED) ***Total amount:*** $11,013,825 (72% federal, 28% state). ***Receiving aid:*** Freshmen: 31% (506); all full-time undergraduates: 26% (2,109). ***Average award:*** Freshmen: $4409; Undergraduates: $2961. ***Scholarships, grants, and awards:*** Federal Pell, FSEOG, state, private, college/university gift aid from institutional funds, United Negro College Fund.

GIFT AID (NON-NEED-BASED) ***Total amount:*** $22,074,287 (2% federal, 67% state, 19% institutional, 12% external sources). ***Receiving aid:*** Freshmen: 50% (828). Undergraduates: 30% (2,442). ***Average award:*** Freshmen: $6171. Undergraduates: $3983. ***Scholarships, grants, and awards by category:*** *Academic interests/achievement:* 8,193 awards ($17,803,864 total): agriculture, biological sciences, business, communication, computer science, education, engineering/technologies, English, foreign languages, general academic interests/achievements, health fields, home economics, humanities, international studies, mathematics, military science, physical sciences, premedicine, social sciences. *Creative arts/performance:* art/fine arts, debating, music. *Special achievements/activities:* 874 awards ($2,758,514 total): cheerleading/drum major, general special achievements/activities. *Special characteristics:* 1,655 awards ($1,818,132 total): children and siblings of alumni, children of educators, children of faculty/staff, children of public servants, ethnic background, first-generation college students, local/state students, members of minority groups, out-of-state students, public servants. ***Tuition waivers:*** Full or partial for employees or children of employees. ***ROTC:*** Army, Air Force cooperative.

LOANS ***Student loans:*** $22,431,554 (61% need-based, 39% non-need-based). 40% of past graduating class borrowed through all loan programs. *Average indebtedness per student:* $13,314. ***Average need-based loan:*** Freshmen: $1853. Undergraduates: $3310. ***Parent loans:*** $1,374,181 (100% non-need-based). ***Programs:*** Federal Direct (Subsidized and Unsubsidized Stafford, PLUS), FFEL (PLUS), Perkins, college/university.

WORK-STUDY ***Federal work-study:*** Total amount: $707,039; 821 jobs averaging $546. ***State or other work-study/employment:*** Part-time jobs available.

ATHLETIC AWARDS Total amount: $3,255,629 (100% non-need-based).

APPLYING FOR FINANCIAL AID ***Required financial aid form:*** FAFSA. ***Financial aid deadline (priority):*** 3/15. ***Notification date:*** Continuous beginning 4/1. Students must reply within 2 weeks of notification.

CONTACT Lester McKenzie, Director of Financial Aid, Tennessee Technological University, Box 5076, 1000 North Dixie Avenue, Cookeville, TN 38501, 931-372-3073 or toll-free 800-255-8881. *Fax:* 931-372-6309. *E-mail:* lmckenzie@tntech.edu.

TENNESSEE TEMPLE UNIVERSITY

Chattanooga, TN

CONTACT Director of Financial Aid, Tennessee Temple University, 1815 Union Avenue, Chattanooga, TN 37404-3587, 423-493-4208 or toll-free 800-553-4050. *Fax:* 423-493-4497.

TENNESSEE WESLEYAN COLLEGE

Athens, TN

CONTACT Mr. Bob Perry, Director of Financial Aid, Tennessee Wesleyan College, PO Box 40, Athens, TN 37371-0040, 423-746-5209 or toll-free 800-PICK-TWC. *Fax:* 423-744-9968. *E-mail:* rkperry@twcnet.edu.

TEXAS A&M INTERNATIONAL UNIVERSITY

Laredo, TX

CONTACT Laura Elizondo, Director of Financial Aid, Texas A&M International University, 5201 University Boulevard, Laredo, TX 78041, 956-326-2225 or toll-free 888-489-2648. *Fax:* 956-326-2224. *E-mail:* laura@tamiu.edu.

TEXAS A&M UNIVERSITY

College Station, TX

Tuition & fees (TX res): $7844 **Average undergraduate aid package: $14,245**

ABOUT THE INSTITUTION State-supported, coed. ***Awards:*** bachelor's, master's, doctoral, and first professional degrees and post-bachelor's certificates. 106 undergraduate majors. ***Total enrollment:*** 48,039. Undergraduates: 38,430. Freshmen: 8,093. Federal methodology is used as a basis for awarding need-based institutional aid.

UNDERGRADUATE EXPENSES for 2008–09 ***Application fee:*** $60. ***Tuition, state resident:*** full-time $4898; part-time $163.25 per semester hour. ***Tuition, nonresident:*** full-time $19,238; part-time $641.25 per term. ***Required fees:*** full-time $2946. ***College room and board:*** $8000. Room and board charges vary according to board plan, housing facility, and location. ***Payment plan:*** Installment.

FRESHMAN FINANCIAL AID (Fall 2008, est.) 4,950 applied for aid; of those 60% were deemed to have need. 98% of freshmen with need received aid; of those 60% had need fully met. ***Average percent of need met:*** 91% (excluding resources awarded to replace EFC). ***Average financial aid package:*** $15,551 (excluding resources awarded to replace EFC). 15% of all full-time freshmen had no need and received non-need-based gift aid.

UNDERGRADUATE FINANCIAL AID (Fall 2008, est.) 18,582 applied for aid; of those 69% were deemed to have need. 97% of undergraduates with need received aid; of those 52% had need fully met. ***Average percent of need met:*** 86% (excluding resources awarded to replace EFC). ***Average financial aid package:*** $14,245 (excluding resources awarded to replace EFC). 13% of all full-time undergraduates had no need and received non-need-based gift aid.

GIFT AID (NEED-BASED) ***Total amount:*** $92,058,427 (29% federal, 23% state, 36% institutional, 12% external sources). ***Receiving aid:*** Freshmen: 37% (2,771); all full-time undergraduates: 30% (10,629). ***Average award:*** Freshmen: $10,890; Undergraduates: $8591. ***Scholarships, grants, and awards:*** Federal Pell, FSEOG, state, private, college/university gift aid from institutional funds.

GIFT AID (NON-NEED-BASED) ***Total amount:*** $35,552,271 (12% federal, 3% state, 52% institutional, 33% external sources). ***Receiving aid:*** Freshmen: 6% (470). Undergraduates: 3% (1,088). ***Average award:*** Freshmen: $4275. Undergraduates: $3723. ***Scholarships, grants, and awards by category:*** *Academic interests/achievement:* agriculture, architecture, biological sciences, business, computer science, education, engineering/technologies, general academic interests/achievements, health fields, physical sciences. *Creative arts/performance:* journalism/publications, performing arts, theater/drama. *Special achievements/activities:* general special achievements/activities, leadership, memberships, rodeo. *Special characteristics:* children of faculty/staff, first-generation college students, local/state students, veterans, veterans' children. ***ROTC:*** Army, Naval, Air Force.

LOANS ***Student loans:*** $103,709,380 (51% need-based, 49% non-need-based). 50% of past graduating class borrowed through all loan programs. *Average indebtedness per student:* $23,112. ***Average need-based loan:*** Freshmen: $4052. Undergraduates: $5931. ***Parent loans:*** $23,524,300 (9% need-based, 91% non-need-based). ***Programs:*** FFEL (Subsidized and Unsubsidized Stafford, PLUS), Perkins, state, college/university.

WORK-STUDY ***Federal work-study:*** Total amount: $1,671,167; 816 jobs averaging $2048. ***State or other work-study/employment:*** Total amount: $326,047 (100% need-based). 200 part-time jobs averaging $1630.

ATHLETIC AWARDS Total amount: $4,710,817 (32% need-based, 68% non-need-based).

APPLYING FOR FINANCIAL AID ***Required financial aid form:*** FAFSA. ***Financial aid deadline (priority):*** 3/31. ***Notification date:*** Continuous beginning 4/1. Students must reply within 4 weeks of notification.

CONTACT Financial Aid Office, Texas A&M University, Scholarships and Financial Aid, College Station, TX 77842-3016, 979-845-3236. *Fax:* 979-847-9061. *E-mail:* financialaid@tamu.edu.

TEXAS A&M UNIVERSITY AT GALVESTON

Galveston, TX

ABOUT THE INSTITUTION State-supported, coed. ***Awards:*** bachelor's and master's degrees. 12 undergraduate majors. ***Total enrollment:*** 1,612. Undergraduates: 1,566. Freshmen: 518.

GIFT AID (NEED-BASED) ***Scholarships, grants, and awards:*** Federal Pell, FSEOG, state, private, college/university gift aid from institutional funds.

GIFT AID (NON-NEED-BASED) ***Scholarships, grants, and awards by category:*** *Academic interests/achievement:* general academic interests/achievements. *Special achievements/activities:* leadership.

LOANS ***Programs:*** FFEL (Subsidized and Unsubsidized Stafford, PLUS), Perkins, college/university, alternative loans.

WORK-STUDY ***Federal work-study:*** Total amount: $5002; 6 jobs averaging $2383. ***State or other work-study/employment:*** 1 part-time job averaging $500.

APPLYING FOR FINANCIAL AID ***Required financial aid form:*** FAFSA.

CONTACT Dennis Carlton, Director for Financial Aid, Texas A&M University at Galveston, PO Box 1675, Galveston, TX 77553-1675, 409-740-4500. *Fax:* 409-740-4959. *E-mail:* carltond@tamug.tamu.edu.

TEXAS A&M UNIVERSITY–COMMERCE

Commerce, TX

Tuition & fees (TX res): $5130 **Average undergraduate aid package: $8738**

ABOUT THE INSTITUTION State-supported, coed. ***Awards:*** bachelor's, master's, doctoral, and first professional degrees. 77 undergraduate majors. ***Total enrollment:*** 8,882. Undergraduates: 5,166. Freshmen: 644. Federal methodology is used as a basis for awarding need-based institutional aid.

UNDERGRADUATE EXPENSES for 2008–09 ***Application fee:*** $25. ***Tuition, state resident:*** full-time $5130. ***Tuition, nonresident:*** full-time $13,380. Full-time tuition and fees vary according to course load. Part-time tuition and fees vary according to course load. ***College room and board:*** $6650. Room and board charges vary according to board plan and housing facility. ***Payment plan:*** Installment.

FRESHMAN FINANCIAL AID (Fall 2008, est.) 421 applied for aid; of those 74% were deemed to have need. 99% of freshmen with need received aid; of those 37% had need fully met. ***Average percent of need met:*** 81% (excluding resources awarded to replace EFC). ***Average financial aid package:*** $9963 (excluding resources awarded to replace EFC). 10% of all full-time freshmen had no need and received non-need-based gift aid.

UNDERGRADUATE FINANCIAL AID (Fall 2008, est.) 2,970 applied for aid; of those 82% were deemed to have need. 99% of undergraduates with need received aid; of those 31% had need fully met. ***Average percent of need met:*** 70% (excluding resources awarded to replace EFC). ***Average financial aid package:*** $8738 (excluding resources awarded to replace EFC). 9% of all full-time undergraduates had no need and received non-need-based gift aid.

GIFT AID (NEED-BASED) ***Total amount:*** $12,670,812 (59% federal, 19% state, 19% institutional, 3% external sources). ***Receiving aid:*** Freshmen: 60% (206); all full-time undergraduates: 6% (220). ***Average award:*** Freshmen: $8421; Undergraduates: $6005. ***Scholarships, grants, and awards:*** Federal Pell, FSEOG, state, private, college/university gift aid from institutional funds.

GIFT AID (NON-NEED-BASED) ***Total amount:*** $1,630,318 (82% institutional, 18% external sources). ***Average award:*** Freshmen: $2031. Undergraduates: $2282. ***Scholarships, grants, and awards by category:*** *Academic interests/achievement:* agriculture, general academic interests/achievements. *Creative arts/performance:* art/fine arts, journalism/publications, music, theater/drama. *Special achievements/activities:* cheerleading/drum major, general special achievements/activities, leadership. ***Tuition waivers:*** Full or partial for senior citizens.

LOANS ***Student loans:*** $19,705,718 (88% need-based, 12% non-need-based). 70% of past graduating class borrowed through all loan programs. *Average indebtedness per student:* $21,014. ***Average need-based loan:*** Freshmen: $2840. Undergraduates: $3995. ***Parent loans:*** $930,151 (49% need-based, 51% non-need-based). ***Programs:*** Federal Direct (Subsidized and Unsubsidized Stafford, PLUS), FFEL (Subsidized and Unsubsidized Stafford, PLUS), Perkins, state.

WORK-STUDY ***Federal work-study:*** Total amount: $393,698; 148 jobs averaging $2599. ***State or other work-study/employment:*** Total amount: $3000 (100% need-based). 1 part-time job averaging $3000.

ATHLETIC AWARDS Total amount: $872,920 (63% need-based, 37% non-need-based).

APPLYING FOR FINANCIAL AID ***Required financial aid form:*** FAFSA. ***Financial aid deadline (priority):*** 4/1. ***Notification date:*** Continuous beginning 5/1. Students must reply within 2 weeks of notification.

CONTACT Dalinda Lasater, Director of Financial Aid, Texas A&M University–Commerce, PO Box 3011, Commerce, TX 75429, 903-886-5091 or toll-free 800-331-3878. *Fax:* 903-886-5098. *E-mail:* dolly_lasater@tamu-commerce.edu.

TEXAS A&M UNIVERSITY–CORPUS CHRISTI

Corpus Christi, TX

ABOUT THE INSTITUTION State-supported, coed. ***Awards:*** bachelor's, master's, and doctoral degrees. 62 undergraduate majors. ***Total enrollment:*** 9,007. Undergraduates: 7,249. Freshmen: 1,230.

GIFT AID (NEED-BASED) ***Scholarships, grants, and awards:*** Federal Pell, FSEOG, state, college/university gift aid from institutional funds.

GIFT AID (NON-NEED-BASED) ***Scholarships, grants, and awards by category:*** *Academic interests/achievement:* general academic interests/achievements. *Creative arts/performance:* art/fine arts. *Special achievements/activities:* leadership. *Special characteristics:* first-generation college students, international students.

LOANS ***Programs:*** FFEL (Subsidized and Unsubsidized Stafford, PLUS), Perkins, state, college/university.

WORK-STUDY ***Federal work-study:*** Total amount: $502,008; 181 jobs averaging $2760. ***State or other work-study/employment:*** Total amount: $295,209 (100% need-based). 110 part-time jobs averaging $2684.

APPLYING FOR FINANCIAL AID ***Required financial aid form:*** FAFSA.

CONTACT Financial Aid Adviser, Texas A&M University–Corpus Christi, 6300 Ocean Drive, Corpus Christi, TX 78412-5503, 361-825-2338 or toll-free 800-482-6822. *Fax:* 361-825-6095. *E-mail:* faoweb@tamucc.edu.

TEXAS A&M UNIVERSITY–KINGSVILLE

Kingsville, TX

CONTACT Felipe Leal, Interim Director, Financial Aid, Texas A&M University–Kingsville, 700 University Boulevard, Kingsville, TX 78363, 361-593-2883 or toll-free 800-687-6000. *Fax:* 361-593-3036.

TEXAS A&M UNIVERSITY–TEXARKANA

Texarkana, TX

Tuition & fees (TX res): $3392 **Average undergraduate aid package: N/A**

ABOUT THE INSTITUTION State-supported, coed. 19 undergraduate majors. Federal methodology is used as a basis for awarding need-based institutional aid.

UNDERGRADUATE EXPENSES for 2008–09 ***Tuition, state resident:*** full-time $3392. ***Tuition, nonresident:*** full-time $10,136. Full-time tuition and fees vary according to course level, course load, and student level. Part-time tuition and fees vary according to course level, course load, and student level. ***Payment plan:*** Installment.

GIFT AID (NEED-BASED) ***Total amount:*** $2,115,000 (52% federal, 14% state, 17% institutional, 17% external sources). ***Scholarships, grants, and awards:*** Federal Pell, FSEOG, state, private, college/university gift aid from institutional funds.

GIFT AID (NON-NEED-BASED) ***Scholarships, grants, and awards by category:*** *Academic interests/achievement:* business, education, engineering/technologies, English, general academic interests/achievements, mathematics, social sciences. *Special achievements/activities:* community service, general special achievements/activities, leadership, memberships.

LOANS ***Student loans:*** $1,600,000 (75% need-based, 25% non-need-based). ***Programs:*** FFEL (Subsidized and Unsubsidized Stafford, PLUS), college/university.

WORK-STUDY ***Federal work-study:*** Total amount: $24,000; jobs available.

APPLYING FOR FINANCIAL AID ***Required financial aid forms:*** FAFSA, institution's own form, state aid form. ***Financial aid deadline (priority):*** 5/1. ***Notification date:*** Continuous beginning 6/1. Students must reply within 2 weeks of notification.

CONTACT Marilyn Raney, Director of Financial Aid and Veterans' Services, Texas A&M University–Texarkana, 2600 North Robison Road, Texarkana, TX 75505, 903-223-3060. *Fax:* 903-223-3118. *E-mail:* marilyn.raney@tamut.edu.

TEXAS CHRISTIAN UNIVERSITY

Fort Worth, TX

Tuition & fees: $28,298 **Average undergraduate aid package: $19,070**

ABOUT THE INSTITUTION Independent religious, coed. ***Awards:*** bachelor's, master's, and doctoral degrees and post-bachelor's certificates. 91 undergraduate majors. ***Total enrollment:*** 8,696. Undergraduates: 7,471. Freshmen: 1,630. Federal methodology is used as a basis for awarding need-based institutional aid.

UNDERGRADUATE EXPENSES for 2009–10 ***Application fee:*** $40. ***Comprehensive fee:*** $38,098 includes full-time tuition ($28,250), mandatory fees ($48), and room and board ($9800). ***College room only:*** $6200. ***Part-time tuition:*** $1190 per term. ***Part-time fees:*** $24 per term.

FRESHMAN FINANCIAL AID (Fall 2008, est.) 764 applied for aid; of those 73% were deemed to have need. 100% of freshmen with need received aid; of those 35% had need fully met. ***Average percent of need met:*** 75% (excluding resources awarded to replace EFC). ***Average financial aid package:*** $19,722 (excluding resources awarded to replace EFC). 25% of all full-time freshmen had no need and received non-need-based gift aid.

UNDERGRADUATE FINANCIAL AID (Fall 2008, est.) 3,468 applied for aid; of those 80% were deemed to have need. 99% of undergraduates with need received aid; of those 30% had need fully met. ***Average percent of need met:*** 71% (excluding resources awarded to replace EFC). ***Average financial aid package:*** $19,070 (excluding resources awarded to replace EFC). 25% of all full-time undergraduates had no need and received non-need-based gift aid.

GIFT AID (NEED-BASED) ***Total amount:*** $38,710,713 (10% federal, 13% state, 71% institutional, 6% external sources). ***Receiving aid:*** Freshmen: 33% (542); all full-time undergraduates: 36% (2,578). ***Average award:*** Freshmen: $16,065; Undergraduates: $15,796. ***Scholarships, grants, and awards:*** Federal Pell, FSEOG, state, private, college/university gift aid from institutional funds, United Negro College Fund.

GIFT AID (NON-NEED-BASED) ***Total amount:*** $23,175,774 (83% institutional, 17% external sources). ***Receiving aid:*** Freshmen: 6% (93). Undergraduates: 5% (349). ***Average award:*** Freshmen: $10,071. Undergraduates: $11,151. ***Scholarships, grants, and awards by category:*** *Academic interests/achievement:* 2,801 awards ($22,741,000 total): agriculture, biological sciences, business, communication, education, engineering/technologies, English, general academic interests/achievements, health fields, international studies, mathematics, military science, physical sciences, premedicine, religion/biblical studies, social sciences. *Creative arts/performance:* 405 awards ($2,525,000 total): applied art and design, art/fine arts, cinema/film/broadcasting, creative writing, dance, general creative arts/performance, journalism/publications, music, performing arts, theater/drama. *Special achievements/activities:* 615 awards ($4,443,000 total): cheerleading/drum major, general special achievements/activities, leadership, memberships, religious involvement. *Special characteristics:* 644 awards ($10,044,000 total): adult students, children of educators, children of faculty/staff, children of union members/company employees, children of workers in trades, ethnic background, general special characteristics, handicapped students, international students, local/state students, members of minority groups, out-of-state students, previous college experience, relatives of clergy, religious affiliation, veterans, veterans' children. ***ROTC:*** Army, Air Force.

LOANS ***Student loans:*** $37,553,341 (53% need-based, 47% non-need-based). 59% of past graduating class borrowed through all loan programs. *Average indebtedness per student:* $26,503. ***Average need-based loan:*** Freshmen: $3885. Undergraduates: $4392. ***Parent loans:*** $11,636,967 (22% need-based, 78% non-need-based). ***Programs:*** FFEL (Subsidized and Unsubsidized Stafford, PLUS), Perkins, Federal Nursing, state.

WORK-STUDY ***Federal work-study:*** Total amount: $2,348,137; 1,140 jobs averaging $2250. ***State or other work-study/employment:*** Total amount: $156,834 (100% need-based). 25 part-time jobs averaging $2400.

ATHLETIC AWARDS Total amount: $9,879,382 (34% need-based, 66% non-need-based).

APPLYING FOR FINANCIAL AID ***Required financial aid form:*** FAFSA. ***Financial aid deadline:*** 5/1 (priority: 5/1). ***Notification date:*** Continuous.

CONTACT Michael Scott, Director, Scholarships and Student Financial Aid, Texas Christian University, PO Box 297012, Fort Worth, TX 76129-0002, 817-257-7858 or toll-free 800-828-3764. *Fax:* 817-257-7462. *E-mail:* m.scott@tcu.edu.

TEXAS COLLEGE

Tyler, TX

Tuition & fees: $9228 **Average undergraduate aid package: $12,371**

ABOUT THE INSTITUTION Independent religious, coed. ***Awards:*** associate and bachelor's degrees and post-bachelor's certificates. 18 undergraduate majors. ***Total enrollment:*** 736. Undergraduates: 705. Freshmen: 188. Federal methodology is used as a basis for awarding need-based institutional aid.

UNDERGRADUATE EXPENSES for 2009–10 ***Application fee:*** $20. ***Comprehensive fee:*** $15,828 includes full-time tuition ($7992), mandatory fees ($1236), and room and board ($6600). ***College room only:*** $3600. ***Part-time tuition:*** $333 per credit hour. ***Part-time fees:*** $618 per term.

FRESHMAN FINANCIAL AID (Fall 2008, est.) 182 applied for aid; of those 100% were deemed to have need. 100% of freshmen with need received aid; of those 31% had need fully met. ***Average percent of need met:*** 93% (excluding resources awarded to replace EFC). ***Average financial aid package:*** $10,871 (excluding resources awarded to replace EFC).

UNDERGRADUATE FINANCIAL AID (Fall 2008, est.) 694 applied for aid; of those 99% were deemed to have need. 100% of undergraduates with need received aid; of those 42% had need fully met. ***Average percent of need met:*** 91% (excluding resources awarded to replace EFC). ***Average financial aid package:*** $12,371 (excluding resources awarded to replace EFC). 1% of all full-time undergraduates had no need and received non-need-based gift aid.

GIFT AID (NEED-BASED) ***Total amount:*** $3,997,504 (60% federal, 36% state, 4% external sources). ***Receiving aid:*** Freshmen: 100% (182); all full-time undergraduates: 99% (688). ***Average award:*** Freshmen: $2790; Undergraduates: $3750. ***Scholarships, grants, and awards:*** Federal Pell, FSEOG, state, private, college/university gift aid from institutional funds, United Negro College Fund.

GIFT AID (NON-NEED-BASED) ***Total amount:*** $948,036 (17% state, 65% institutional, 18% external sources). ***Receiving aid:*** Freshmen: 16% (29). Undergraduates: 5% (32). ***Average award:*** Undergraduates: $10,667. ***Scholarships, grants, and awards by category:*** *Academic interests/achievement:* 21 awards ($19,500 total): general academic interests/achievements. *Special achievements/activities:* 2 awards ($15,984 total): leadership.

LOANS ***Student loans:*** $3,628,250 (54% need-based, 46% non-need-based). 96% of past graduating class borrowed through all loan programs. *Average indebtedness per student:* $8263. ***Average need-based loan:*** Freshmen: $2923. Undergraduates: $3360. ***Parent loans:*** $264,638 (100% non-need-based). ***Programs:*** Federal Direct (Subsidized and Unsubsidized Stafford, PLUS), FFEL (Subsidized and Unsubsidized Stafford, PLUS), state.

WORK-STUDY ***Federal work-study:*** Total amount: $199,998; 135 jobs averaging $1481. ***State or other work-study/employment:*** Total amount: $8657 (100% need-based). 6 part-time jobs averaging $1443.

ATHLETIC AWARDS Total amount: $343,384 (100% non-need-based).

APPLYING FOR FINANCIAL AID ***Required financial aid forms:*** FAFSA, institution's own form. ***Financial aid deadline (priority):*** 6/1. ***Notification date:*** Continuous. Students must reply within 2 weeks of notification.

CONTACT Ms. Cecelia Jones, Director of Financial Aid, Texas College, 2404 North Grand Avenue, Tyler, TX 75702, 903-593-8311 Ext. 2241 or toll-free 800-306-6299 (out-of-state). *Fax:* 903-596-0001. *E-mail:* ckjones@texascollege.edu.

TEXAS LUTHERAN UNIVERSITY

Seguin, TX

Tuition & fees: $21,100 **Average undergraduate aid package: $16,882**

ABOUT THE INSTITUTION Independent religious, coed. ***Awards:*** bachelor's degrees and post-bachelor's certificates. 42 undergraduate majors. ***Total enrollment:*** 1,432. Undergraduates: 1,432. Freshmen: 396. Federal methodology is used as a basis for awarding need-based institutional aid.

UNDERGRADUATE EXPENSES for 2008–09 ***Application fee:*** $25. ***Comprehensive fee:*** $27,240 includes full-time tuition ($20,970), mandatory fees ($130), and room and board ($6140). ***College room only:*** $3000. Full-time tuition and fees vary according to course load. Room and board charges vary according to board plan, housing facility, and location. ***Part-time tuition:*** $700 per semester hour. ***Part-time fees:*** $65 per term. Part-time tuition and fees vary according to course load. ***Payment plan:*** Installment.

FRESHMAN FINANCIAL AID (Fall 2008, est.) 391 applied for aid; of those 77% were deemed to have need. 100% of freshmen with need received aid; of those 46% had need fully met. ***Average percent of need met:*** 46% (excluding resources awarded to replace EFC). ***Average financial aid package:*** $18,107 (excluding resources awarded to replace EFC). 22% of all full-time freshmen had no need and received non-need-based gift aid.

UNDERGRADUATE FINANCIAL AID (Fall 2008, est.) 1,294 applied for aid; of those 74% were deemed to have need. 100% of undergraduates with need received aid; of those 40% had need fully met. ***Average percent of need met:*** 40% (excluding resources awarded to replace EFC). ***Average financial aid package:*** $16,882 (excluding resources awarded to replace EFC). 24% of all full-time undergraduates had no need and received non-need-based gift aid.

GIFT AID (NEED-BASED) ***Total amount:*** $11,528,957 (16% federal, 19% state, 63% institutional, 2% external sources). ***Receiving aid:*** Freshmen: 76% (302); all full-time undergraduates: 71% (962). ***Average award:*** Freshmen: $13,912; Undergraduates: $12,228. ***Scholarships, grants, and awards:*** Federal Pell, FSEOG, state, private, college/university gift aid from institutional funds, Academic Competitiveness Grant, National Smart Grant, TEACH Grant.

GIFT AID (NON-NEED-BASED) ***Total amount:*** $3,298,870 (94% institutional, 6% external sources). ***Receiving aid:*** Freshmen: 13% (52). Undergraduates: 8% (102). ***Average award:*** Freshmen: $10,095. Undergraduates: $8436. ***Scholarships, grants, and awards by category:*** *Academic interests/achievement:* 1,080 awards ($6,847,421 total): biological sciences, business, education, general academic interests/achievements, mathematics, physical sciences, premedicine. *Creative arts/performance:* 196 awards ($348,850 total): journalism/publications, music, theater/drama. *Special achievements/activities:* 131 awards ($136,617 total): general special achievements/activities, junior miss, leadership, memberships, religious involvement. *Special characteristics:* 280 awards ($740,570 total): children and siblings of alumni, children of faculty/staff, first-generation college students, religious affiliation. ***Tuition waivers:*** Full or partial for children of alumni, employees or children of employees. ***ROTC:*** Army cooperative, Air Force cooperative.

LOANS ***Student loans:*** $9,010,952 (69% need-based, 31% non-need-based). 80% of past graduating class borrowed through all loan programs. *Average indebtedness per student:* $30,118. ***Average need-based loan:*** Freshmen: $4109. Undergraduates: $4836. ***Parent loans:*** $1,653,716 (24% need-based, 76% non-need-based). ***Programs:*** FFEL (Subsidized and Unsubsidized Stafford, PLUS), Perkins, state, alternative loans.

WORK-STUDY ***Federal work-study:*** Total amount: $630,064; 546 jobs averaging $1319. ***State or other work-study/employment:*** Total amount: $20,789 (100% need-based). 14 part-time jobs averaging $1523.

APPLYING FOR FINANCIAL AID ***Required financial aid form:*** FAFSA. ***Financial aid deadline (priority):*** 3/1. ***Notification date:*** Continuous beginning 3/1. Students must reply by 8/15.

CONTACT Cathleen Wright, Director of Financial Aid, Texas Lutheran University, 1000 West Court Street, Seguin, TX 78155-5999, 830-372-8075 or toll-free 800-771-8521. *Fax:* 830-372-8096. *E-mail:* cwright@tlu.edu.

TEXAS SOUTHERN UNIVERSITY

Houston, TX

CONTACT Financial Aid Office, Texas Southern University, 3100 Cleburne, Houston, TX 77004-4584, 713-313-7011. *Fax:* 713-313-1858.

TEXAS STATE UNIVERSITY–SAN MARCOS

San Marcos, TX

Tuition & fees (TX res): $6994 **Average undergraduate aid package: $12,152**

ABOUT THE INSTITUTION State-supported, coed. ***Awards:*** bachelor's, master's, doctoral, and first professional degrees and post-bachelor's certificates. 89 undergraduate majors. ***Total enrollment:*** 29,105. Undergraduates: 24,810. Freshmen: 3,256. Federal methodology is used as a basis for awarding need-based institutional aid.

UNDERGRADUATE EXPENSES for 2008–09 ***Application fee:*** $40. ***Tuition, state resident:*** full-time $5100; part-time $170 per credit hour. ***Tuition, nonresident:*** full-time $13,530; part-time $451 per credit hour. ***Required fees:*** full-time $1894; $42 per credit or $362 per term. Full-time tuition and fees vary according to course load. Part-time tuition and fees vary according to course load. ***College room and board:*** [illegible]; ***Room only:*** [illegible]. Room and board charges vary according to board plan and housing facility. ***Payment plan:*** Installment.

FRESHMAN FINANCIAL AID (Fall 2008, est.) 2,283 applied for aid; of those 69% were deemed to have need. 96% of freshmen with need received aid; of those 10% had need fully met. ***Average percent of need met:*** 73% (excluding resources awarded to replace EFC). ***Average financial aid package:*** $12,696 (excluding resources awarded to replace EFC). 5% of all full-time freshmen had no need and received non-need-based gift aid.

UNDERGRADUATE FINANCIAL AID (Fall 2008, est.) 14,474 applied for aid; of those 77% were deemed to have need. 97% of undergraduates with need received aid; of those 11% had need fully met. ***Average percent of need met:*** 66% (excluding resources awarded to replace EFC). ***Average financial aid package:*** $12,152 (excluding resources awarded to replace EFC). 2% of all full-time undergraduates had no need and received non-need-based gift aid.

GIFT AID (NEED-BASED) ***Total amount:*** $46,927,663 (51% federal, 49% state). ***Receiving aid:*** Freshmen: 34% (1,121); all full-time undergraduates: 40% (8,060). ***Average award:*** Freshmen: $6686; Undergraduates: $4894. ***Scholarships, grants, and awards:*** Federal Pell, FSEOG, state, private, college/university gift aid from institutional funds.

GIFT AID (NON-NEED-BASED) ***Total amount:*** $9,382,001 (42% institutional, 58% external sources). ***Receiving aid:*** Freshmen: 14% (464). Undergraduates: 7% (1,474). ***Average award:*** Freshmen: $2343. Undergraduates: $2720. ***Scholarships, grants, and awards by category:*** *Academic interests/achievement:* agriculture, business, education, English, general academic interests/achievements, home economics, international studies, military science. *Creative arts/performance:* applied art and design, journalism/publications, music, theater/drama. *Special characteristics:* children and siblings of alumni, first-generation college students, handicapped students. ***Tuition waivers:*** Full or partial for employees or children of employees. ***ROTC:*** Army, Air Force.

LOANS ***Student loans:*** $100,261,428 (44% need-based, 56% non-need-based). 57% of past graduating class borrowed through all loan programs. *Average indebtedness per student:* $17,994. ***Average need-based loan:*** Freshmen: $2954. Undergraduates: $3947. ***Parent loans:*** $25,835,685 (100% non-need-based). ***Programs:*** Federal Direct (Subsidized and Unsubsidized Stafford, PLUS), FFEL (Subsidized and Unsubsidized Stafford, PLUS), Perkins, state, college/university, emergency tuition loans.

WORK-STUDY ***Federal work-study:*** Total amount: $1,237,675; 880 jobs averaging $1406. ***State or other work-study/employment:*** Total amount: $218,777 (100% need-based). 146 part-time jobs averaging $1498.

ATHLETIC AWARDS Total amount: $2,000,937 (100% non-need-based).

APPLYING FOR FINANCIAL AID ***Required financial aid form:*** FAFSA. ***Financial aid deadline (priority):*** 4/1. ***Notification date:*** Continuous beginning 5/1. Students must reply within 3 weeks of notification.

CONTACT Ms. Mariko Gomez, Director of Financial Aid, Texas State University–San Marcos, 601 University Drive, San Marcos, TX 78666-4602, 512-245-2315. *Fax:* 512-245-7920. *E-mail:* mg01@txstate.edu.

TEXAS TECH UNIVERSITY

Lubbock, TX

Tuition & fees (TX res): $6783 **Average undergraduate aid package: $8467**

ABOUT THE INSTITUTION State-supported, coed. ***Awards:*** bachelor's, master's, doctoral, and first professional degrees and post-bachelor's certificates. 101 undergraduate majors. ***Total enrollment:*** 28,422. Undergraduates: 23,107. Freshmen: 4,385. Federal methodology is used as a basis for awarding need-based institutional aid.

UNDERGRADUATE EXPENSES for 2008–09 ***Application fee:*** $50. ***Tuition, state resident:*** full-time $4310; part-time $143.67 per credit hour. ***Tuition, nonresident:*** full-time $12,740; part-time $424.67 per credit hour. ***Required fees:*** full-time $2473; $69 per credit hour or $389 per term. Full-time tuition and fees vary according to course load, program, and reciprocity agreements. Part-time tuition and fees vary according to course load, program, and reciprocity agreements. ***College room and board:*** $7310; ***Room only:*** $3980. Room and board charges vary according to board plan and housing facility. ***Payment plan:*** Installment.

FRESHMAN FINANCIAL AID (Fall 2007) 3,110 applied for aid; of those 59% were deemed to have need. 96% of freshmen with need received aid; of those 7% had need fully met. ***Average percent of need met:*** 48% (excluding resources awarded to replace EFC). ***Average financial aid package:*** $7492 (excluding resources awarded to replace EFC). 6% of all full-time freshmen had no need and received non-need-based gift aid.

UNDERGRADUATE FINANCIAL AID (Fall 2007) 13,250 applied for aid; of those 65% were deemed to have need. 97% of undergraduates with need received aid; of those 5% had need fully met. ***Average percent of need met:*** 60% (excluding resources awarded to replace EFC). ***Average financial aid package:*** $8467 (excluding resources awarded to replace EFC). 3% of all full-time undergraduates had no need and received non-need-based gift aid.

GIFT AID (NEED-BASED) ***Total amount:*** $37,784,830 (43% federal, 42% state, 15% institutional). ***Receiving aid:*** Freshmen: 26% (1,137); all full-time undergraduates: 29% (6,204). ***Average award:*** Freshmen: $6717; Undergraduates: $5574. ***Scholarships, grants, and awards:*** Federal Pell, FSEOG, state, private, college/university gift aid from institutional funds.

GIFT AID (NON-NEED-BASED) ***Total amount:*** $13,094,312 (59% institutional, 41% external sources). ***Receiving aid:*** Freshmen: 18% (786). Undergraduates: 11% (2,246). ***Average award:*** Freshmen: $1947. Undergraduates: $1893. ***Scholarships, grants, and awards by category:*** *Academic interests/achievement:* agriculture, architecture, biological sciences, business, communication, computer science, education, engineering/technologies, English, foreign languages, general academic interests/achievements, home economics, humanities, international studies, mathematics, military science, physical sciences, premedicine, social sciences. *Creative arts/performance:* applied art and design, art/fine arts, dance, journalism/publications, music, performing arts, theater/drama. *Special achievements/activities:* community service, memberships, rodeo. *Special characteristics:* children of faculty/staff, first-generation college students, handicapped students, out-of-state students, veterans, veterans' children. ***Tuition waivers:*** Full or partial for employees or children of employees, senior citizens. ***ROTC:*** Army, Air Force.

LOANS ***Student loans:*** $75,179,785 (42% need-based, 58% non-need-based). 60% of past graduating class borrowed through all loan programs. *Average indebtedness per student:* $20,424. ***Average need-based loan:*** Freshmen: $3075. Undergraduates: $4061. ***Parent loans:*** $16,566,901 (100% non-need-based). ***Programs:*** FFEL (Subsidized and Unsubsidized Stafford, PLUS), Perkins, state, college/university.

WORK-STUDY ***Federal work-study:*** Total amount: $736,497; jobs available. ***State or other work-study/employment:*** Total amount: $5400 (100% need-based). Part-time jobs available.

ATHLETIC AWARDS Total amount: $4,140,161 (100% non-need-based).

APPLYING FOR FINANCIAL AID ***Required financial aid form:*** FAFSA. ***Financial aid deadline (priority):*** 4/15. ***Notification date:*** Continuous. Students must reply within 2 weeks of notification.

CONTACT Becky Wilson, Managing Director, Student Financial Aid, Texas Tech University, PO Box 45011, Lubbock, TX 79409-5011, 806-742-0454. *Fax:* 806-742-0880.

TEXAS WESLEYAN UNIVERSITY

Fort Worth, TX

CONTACT Director of Financial Aid, Texas Wesleyan University, 1201 Wesleyan Street, Fort Worth, TX 76105-1536, 817-531-4420 or toll-free 800-580-8980 (in-state). *Fax:* 817-531-4231. *E-mail:* finaid@txwes.edu.

TEXAS WOMAN'S UNIVERSITY

Denton, TX

CONTACT Mr. Governor Jackson, Director of Financial Aid, Texas Woman's University, PO Box 425408, Denton, TX 76204-5408, 940-898-3051 or toll-free 888-948-9984. *Fax:* 940-898-3068. *E-mail:* gjackson@twu.edu.

THIEL COLLEGE

Greenville, PA

Tuition & fees: $20,998 **Average undergraduate aid package: $18,708**

ABOUT THE INSTITUTION Independent religious, coed. ***Awards:*** associate and bachelor's degrees. 39 undergraduate majors. ***Total enrollment:*** 1,137. Undergraduates: 1,137. Freshmen: 317. Federal methodology is used as a basis for awarding need-based institutional aid.

UNDERGRADUATE EXPENSES for 2009–10 ***Application fee:*** $35. ***Comprehensive fee:*** $29,788 includes full-time tuition ($20,998) and room and board ($8790). ***College room only:*** $4400.

FRESHMAN FINANCIAL AID (Fall 2008, est.) 281 applied for aid; of those 95% were deemed to have need. 100% of freshmen with need received aid; of those 12% had need fully met. ***Average percent of need met:*** 77% (excluding resources awarded to replace EFC). ***Average financial aid package:*** $20,190 (excluding resources awarded to replace EFC). 10% of all full-time freshmen had no need and received non-need-based gift aid.

UNDERGRADUATE FINANCIAL AID (Fall 2008, est.) 886 applied for aid; of those 95% were deemed to have need. 100% of undergraduates with need received aid; of those 13% had need fully met. ***Average percent of need met:*** 73% (excluding resources awarded to replace EFC). ***Average financial aid package:*** $18,708 (excluding resources awarded to replace EFC). 13% of all full-time undergraduates had no need and received non-need-based gift aid.

GIFT AID (NEED-BASED) ***Total amount:*** $10,879,373 (17% federal, 12% state, 69% institutional, 2% external sources). ***Receiving aid:*** Freshmen: 84% (267); all full-time undergraduates: 78% (839). ***Average award:*** Freshmen: $14,779; Undergraduates: $13,407. ***Scholarships, grants, and awards:*** Federal Pell, FSEOG, state, private, college/university gift aid from institutional funds.

GIFT AID (NON-NEED-BASED) ***Total amount:*** $1,328,195 (96% institutional, 4% external sources). ***Receiving aid:*** Freshmen: 5% (17). Undergraduates: 5% (58). ***Average award:*** Freshmen: $11,272. Undergraduates: $11,740. ***Scholarships, grants, and awards by category:*** *Academic interests/achievement:* biological sciences, business, computer science, education, English, general academic interests/achievements, mathematics, physical sciences, religion/biblical studies. *Creative arts/performance:* 10 awards ($5750 total): music. *Special achievements/activities:* leadership. *Special characteristics:* children and siblings of alumni, children of faculty/staff, relatives of clergy, religious affiliation, siblings of current students.

LOANS ***Student loans:*** $7,494,178 (78% need-based, 22% non-need-based). 84% of past graduating class borrowed through all loan programs. *Average indebtedness per student:* $21,712. ***Average need-based loan:*** Freshmen: $5719. Undergraduates: $5524. ***Parent loans:*** $1,102,517 (43% need-based, 57% non-need-based). ***Programs:*** FFEL (Subsidized and Unsubsidized Stafford, PLUS), Perkins, college/university.

WORK-STUDY ***Federal work-study:*** Total amount: $67,581; jobs available. ***State or other work-study/employment:*** Total amount: $347,911 (66% need-based, 34% non-need-based). Part-time jobs available.

APPLYING FOR FINANCIAL AID ***Required financial aid forms:*** FAFSA, state aid form. ***Financial aid deadline (priority):*** 3/15. ***Notification date:*** Continuous. Students must reply within 2 weeks of notification.

CONTACT Ms. Cynthia H. Farrell, Director of Financial Aid, Thiel College, 75 College Avenue, Greenville, PA 16125-2181, 724-589-2178 or toll-free 800-248-4435. *Fax:* 724-589-2850. *E-mail:* cfarrell@thiel.edu.

THOMAS AQUINAS COLLEGE

Santa Paula, CA

Tuition & fees: $22,400 **Average undergraduate aid package: $16,882**

ABOUT THE INSTITUTION Independent Roman Catholic, coed. ***Awards:*** bachelor's degrees. 4 undergraduate majors. ***Total enrollment:*** 340. Undergraduates: 340. Freshmen: 102. Institutional methodology is used as a basis for awarding need-based institutional aid.

UNDERGRADUATE EXPENSES for 2009–10 ***Comprehensive fee:*** $29,800 includes full-time tuition ($22,400) and room and board ($7400).

FRESHMAN FINANCIAL AID (Fall 2008, est.) 74 applied for aid; of those 92% were deemed to have need. 100% of freshmen with need received aid; of those 100% had need fully met. ***Average percent of need met:*** 100% (excluding resources awarded to replace EFC). ***Average financial aid package:*** $16,164 (excluding resources awarded to replace EFC).

UNDERGRADUATE FINANCIAL AID (Fall 2008, est.) 254 applied for aid; of those 93% were deemed to have need. 100% of undergraduates with need received aid; of those 100% had need fully met. ***Average percent of need met:*** 100% (excluding resources awarded to replace EFC). ***Average financial aid package:*** $16,882 (excluding resources awarded to replace EFC).

GIFT AID (NEED-BASED) ***Total amount:*** $2,446,337 (8% federal, 10% state, 80% institutional, 2% external sources). ***Receiving aid:*** Freshmen: 56% (57); all full-time undergraduates: 59% (201). ***Average award:*** Freshmen: $11,916; Undergraduates: $12,180. ***Scholarships, grants, and awards:*** Federal Pell, state, private, college/university gift aid from institutional funds, Academic Competitiveness Grant.

GIFT AID (NON-NEED-BASED) ***Total amount:*** $25,800 (6% state, 94% external sources). ***Receiving aid:*** Freshmen: 2% (2). Undergraduates: 1% (4).

LOANS ***Student loans:*** $998,775 (75% need-based, 25% non-need-based). 71% of past graduating class borrowed through all loan programs. *Average indebtedness per student:* $14,000. ***Average need-based loan:*** Freshmen: $3036. Undergraduates: $3639. ***Parent loans:*** $469,409 (24% need-based, 76% non-need-based). ***Programs:*** FFEL (Subsidized and Unsubsidized Stafford, PLUS), college/university, Canada Student Loans.

WORK-STUDY ***State or other work-study/employment:*** Total amount: $779,764 (98% need-based, 2% non-need-based). 210 part-time jobs averaging $3604.

APPLYING FOR FINANCIAL AID ***Required financial aid forms:*** FAFSA, institution's own form, state aid form, income tax return; Non-custodial Parent Statement. ***Financial aid deadline:*** 3/2. ***Notification date:*** Continuous. Students must reply by 5/1 or within 2 weeks of notification.

CONTACT Mr. Gregory Becher, Director of Financial Aid, Thomas Aquinas College, 10000 North Ojai Road, Santa Paula, CA 93060-9980, 805-525-4419 Ext. 5936 or toll-free 800-634-9797. *Fax:* 805-525-9342. *E-mail:* gbecher@thomasaquinas.edu.

THOMAS COLLEGE

Waterville, ME

ABOUT THE INSTITUTION Independent, coed. ***Awards:*** associate, bachelor's, and master's degrees (associate). 16 undergraduate majors. ***Total enrollment:*** 975. Undergraduates: 765. Freshmen: 230.

GIFT AID (NEED-BASED) ***Scholarships, grants, and awards:*** Federal Pell, FSEOG, state, private, college/university gift aid from institutional funds.

LOANS ***Programs:*** Federal Direct (Subsidized and Unsubsidized Stafford, PLUS), Perkins.

WORK-STUDY ***Federal work-study:*** Total amount: $198,931.

APPLYING FOR FINANCIAL AID ***Required financial aid form:*** FAFSA.

CONTACT Jeannine Bosse, Associate Director of Student Financial Aid, Thomas College, 180 West River Road, Waterville, ME 04901-5097, 800-339-7001. *Fax:* 207-859-1114. *E-mail:* sfsassistant@thomas.edu.

THOMAS EDISON STATE COLLEGE

Trenton, NJ

Tuition & fees (NJ res): $4555 **Average undergraduate aid package: N/A**

ABOUT THE INSTITUTION State-supported, coed. ***Awards:*** associate, bachelor's, and master's degrees and post-bachelor's and post-master's certificates (offers only distance learning degree programs). [illegible] undergraduate majors. ***Total enrollment:*** 17,369. Undergraduates: 16,797. Federal methodology is used as a basis for awarding need-based institutional aid.

UNDERGRADUATE EXPENSES for 2008–09 ***Application fee:*** $75. ***Tuition, state resident:*** full-time $4555; part-time $132 per credit hour. ***Tuition, nonresident:*** full-time $6520; part-time $175 per credit hour. ***Required fees:*** $100 per year. Part-time tuition and fees vary according to student level. students may choose either the Comprehensive Tuition Plan: $4,555 per year (state residents and military personnel), $6,520 (out-of-state), which covers up to 36 credits per year for all credit-earning options, or the Enrolled Options Plan: $1,350 per year (state residents and military personnel), $2,445 (out-of-state) and $3,340 (international) for annual enrollment tuition and a technology services fee ($100); tests, portfolios, courses and other fees at additional cost. Please visit www.tesc.edu for more details.

GIFT AID (NEED-BASED) ***Total amount:*** $1,360,000 (91% federal, 9% state). ***Scholarships, grants, and awards:*** Federal Pell, state, private.

GIFT AID (NON-NEED-BASED) ***Total amount:*** $7600 (100% external sources). ***Tuition waivers:*** Full or partial for employees or children of employees.

LOANS ***Student loans:*** $6,655,611 (100% need-based). ***Programs:*** FFEL (Subsidized and Unsubsidized Stafford, PLUS), state, private loans.

APPLYING FOR FINANCIAL AID ***Required financial aid forms:*** FAFSA, institution's own form. ***Financial aid deadline:*** Continuous. ***Notification date:*** Continuous. Students must reply within 4 weeks of notification.

CONTACT Financial Aid Office, Thomas Edison State College, 101 West State Street, Trenton, NJ [illegible], [illegible] or toll-free [illegible]-442-[illegible]. *Fax:* [illegible]-633-6489. *E-mail:* finaid@tesc.edu.

THOMAS JEFFERSON UNIVERSITY

Philadelphia, PA

Tuition & fees: N/R **Average undergraduate aid package: N/A**

ABOUT THE INSTITUTION Independent, coed. 8 undergraduate majors. Institutional methodology is used as a basis for awarding need-based institutional aid.

UNDERGRADUATE EXPENSES for 2008–09 tuition varies by major. Contact institution for tuition information.

GIFT AID (NEED-BASED) ***Total amount:*** $2,375,634 (29% federal, 43% state, 18% institutional, 10% external sources). ***Scholarships, grants, and awards:*** Federal Pell, FSEOG, state, private, college/university gift aid from institutional funds, Scholarships for Disadvantaged Students (SDS).

GIFT AID (NON-NEED-BASED) ***Total amount:*** $603,310 (8% institutional, 92% external sources). ***Scholarships, grants, and awards by category:*** *Academic interests/achievement:* 45 awards ($170,000 total): general academic interests/achievements, health fields. *Special characteristics:* members of minority groups, veterans.

LOANS ***Student loans:*** $9,984,861 (90% need-based, 10% non-need-based). 75% of past graduating class borrowed through all loan programs. *Average indebtedness per student:* $36,000. ***Parent loans:*** $743,341 (100% non-need-based). ***Programs:*** FFEL (Subsidized and Unsubsidized Stafford, PLUS), Perkins, Federal Nursing, college/university.

WORK-STUDY ***Federal work-study:*** Total amount: $54,017; 100 jobs averaging $2500.

APPLYING FOR FINANCIAL AID ***Required financial aid forms:*** FAFSA, institution's own form, parent and student income tax returns. ***Financial aid deadline (priority):*** 4/1. ***Notification date:*** Continuous beginning 4/1. Students must reply within 2 weeks of notification.

CONTACT Susan McFadden, University Director of Financial Aid, Thomas Jefferson University, 1025 Walnut Street, Philadelphia, PA 19107, 215-955-2867 or toll-free 877-533-3247. *Fax:* 215-955-5186. *E-mail:* financial.aid@jefferson.edu.

THOMAS MORE COLLEGE

Crestview Hills, KY

Tuition & fees: $22,220 **Average undergraduate aid package: $10,797**

ABOUT THE INSTITUTION Independent Roman Catholic, coed. ***Awards:*** associate, bachelor's, and master's degrees. 47 undergraduate majors. ***Total enrollment:*** 1,894. Undergraduates: 1,751. Freshmen: 274. Federal methodology is used as a basis for awarding need-based institutional aid.

UNDERGRADUATE EXPENSES for 2008–09 ***Application fee:*** $25. ***Comprehensive fee:*** $28,090 includes full-time tuition ($21,500), mandatory fees ($720), and room and board ($5870). ***College room only:*** $3020. Full-time tuition and fees vary according to program and student level. Room and board charges vary according to board plan and housing facility. ***Part-time tuition:*** $515 per credit. ***Part-time fees:*** $30 per credit; $15 per term. Part-time tuition and fees vary according to course load and program. ***Payment plans:*** Installment, deferred payment.

FRESHMAN FINANCIAL AID (Fall 2008, est.) 253 applied for aid; of those 91% were deemed to have need. 100% of freshmen with need received aid; of those 29% had need fully met. ***Average percent of need met:*** 72% (excluding resources awarded to replace EFC). ***Average financial aid package:*** $16,661 (excluding resources awarded to replace EFC). 15% of all full-time freshmen had no need and received non-need-based gift aid.

UNDERGRADUATE FINANCIAL AID (Fall 2008, est.) 1,007 applied for aid; of those 86% were deemed to have need. 99% of undergraduates with need received aid; of those 27% had need fully met. ***Average percent of need met:*** 69% (excluding resources awarded to replace EFC). ***Average financial aid package:*** $10,797 (excluding resources awarded to replace EFC). 16% of all full-time undergraduates had no need and received non-need-based gift aid.

GIFT AID (NEED-BASED) ***Total amount:*** $8,627,344 (13% federal, 20% state, 62% institutional, 5% external sources). ***Receiving aid:*** Freshmen: 84% (231); all full-time undergraduates: 62% (788). ***Average award:*** Freshmen: $11,639; Undergraduates: $8189. ***Scholarships, grants, and awards:*** Federal Pell, FSEOG, state, private, college/university gift aid from institutional funds.

GIFT AID (NON-NEED-BASED) ***Total amount:*** $3,042,980 (7% state, 79% institutional, 14% external sources). ***Receiving aid:*** Freshmen: 32% (88).

Undergraduates: 26% (327). ***Average award:*** Freshmen: $11,529. Undergraduates: $9468. ***Scholarships, grants, and awards by category:*** *Academic interests/achievement:* 118 awards ($222,715 total): general academic interests/achievements, social sciences. *Creative arts/performance:* 12 awards ($17,287 total): art/fine arts, theater/drama. *Special achievements/activities:* 84 awards ($176,245 total): leadership, religious involvement. *Special characteristics:* 561 awards ($2,755,383 total): adult students, children and siblings of alumni, children of faculty/staff, members of minority groups, religious affiliation. ***Tuition waivers:*** Full or partial for children of alumni, employees or children of employees. ***ROTC:*** Army cooperative, Air Force cooperative.

LOANS ***Student loans:*** $7,839,430 (36% need-based, 64% non-need-based). 68% of past graduating class borrowed through all loan programs. *Average indebtedness per student:* $25,265. ***Average need-based loan:*** Freshmen: $3464. Undergraduates: $4034. ***Parent loans:*** $913,720 (100% non-need-based). ***Programs:*** FFEL (Subsidized and Unsubsidized Stafford, PLUS), Perkins, Federal Nursing, college/university.

WORK-STUDY ***Federal work-study:*** Total amount: $173,383; 127 jobs averaging $1365. ***State or other work-study/employment:*** Total amount: $187,221 (100% non-need-based). 166 part-time jobs averaging $1128.

APPLYING FOR FINANCIAL AID ***Required financial aid forms:*** FAFSA, institution's own form. ***Financial aid deadline (priority):*** 3/15. ***Notification date:*** Continuous. Students must reply by 5/1.

CONTACT Ms. Mary Givhan, Director of Financial Aid, Thomas More College, 333 Thomas More Parkway, Crestview Hills, KY 41017-3495, 859-344-3531 or toll-free 800-825-4557. *Fax:* 859-344-3638. *E-mail:* mary.givhan@thomasmore.edu.

THOMAS MORE COLLEGE OF LIBERAL ARTS

Merrimack, NH

Tuition & fees: $13,200 **Average undergraduate aid package: $13,898**

ABOUT THE INSTITUTION Independent religious, coed. ***Awards:*** bachelor's degrees. 4 undergraduate majors. ***Total enrollment:*** 99. Undergraduates: 99. Freshmen: 24. Federal methodology is used as a basis for awarding need-based institutional aid.

UNDERGRADUATE EXPENSES for 2008–09 ***Comprehensive fee:*** $22,000 includes full-time tuition ($13,200) and room and board ($8800). ***Part-time tuition:*** $600 per credit hour. ***Payment plan:*** Installment.

FRESHMAN FINANCIAL AID (Fall 2008, est.) 21 applied for aid; of those 71% were deemed to have need. 100% of freshmen with need received aid; of those 7% had need fully met. ***Average percent of need met:*** 81% (excluding resources awarded to replace EFC). ***Average financial aid package:*** $14,124 (excluding resources awarded to replace EFC). 31% of all full-time freshmen had no need and received non-need-based gift aid.

UNDERGRADUATE FINANCIAL AID (Fall 2008, est.) 76 applied for aid; of those 80% were deemed to have need. 95% of undergraduates with need received aid; of those 22% had need fully met. ***Average percent of need met:*** 81% (excluding resources awarded to replace EFC). ***Average financial aid package:*** $13,898 (excluding resources awarded to replace EFC). 22% of all full-time undergraduates had no need and received non-need-based gift aid.

GIFT AID (NEED-BASED) ***Total amount:*** $528,441 (20% federal, 2% state, 76% institutional, 2% external sources). ***Receiving aid:*** Freshmen: 52% (15); all full-time undergraduates: 61% (58). ***Average award:*** Freshmen: $10,516; Undergraduates: $9109. ***Scholarships, grants, and awards:*** Federal Pell, FSEOG, state, private, college/university gift aid from institutional funds.

GIFT AID (NON-NEED-BASED) ***Total amount:*** $116,525 (97% institutional, 3% external sources). ***Receiving aid:*** Freshmen: 31% (9). Undergraduates: 40% (38). ***Average award:*** Freshmen: $5550. Undergraduates: $4949. ***Scholarships, grants, and awards by category:*** *Academic interests/achievement:* 55 awards ($280,825 total): general academic interests/achievements. ***Tuition waivers:*** Full or partial for employees or children of employees.

LOANS ***Student loans:*** $351,652 (68% need-based, 32% non-need-based). 78% of past graduating class borrowed through all loan programs. *Average indebtedness per student:* $16,667. ***Average need-based loan:*** Freshmen: $3287. Undergraduates: $4446. ***Parent loans:*** $213,008 (57% need-based, 43% non-need-based). ***Programs:*** FFEL (Subsidized and Unsubsidized Stafford, PLUS).

WORK-STUDY ***State or other work-study/employment:*** Total amount: $77,923 (78% need-based, 22% non-need-based). 46 part-time jobs averaging $1329.

APPLYING FOR FINANCIAL AID ***Required financial aid form:*** FAFSA. ***Financial aid deadline:*** Continuous. ***Notification date:*** Continuous beginning 3/15. Students must reply within 2 weeks of notification.

CONTACT Clinton A. Hanson Jr., Director of Financial Aid, Thomas More College of Liberal Arts, 6 Manchester Street, Merrimack, NH 03054-4818, 603-880-8308 Ext. 23 or toll-free 800-880-8308. *Fax:* 603-880-9280. *E-mail:* chanson@thomasmorecollege.edu.

THOMAS UNIVERSITY

Thomasville, GA

CONTACT Ms. Angela Keys, Director of Financial Aid, Thomas University, 1501 Millpond Road, Thomasville, GA 31792-7499, 229-226-1621 Ext. 216 or toll-free 800-538-9784. *Fax:* 229-227-6919. *E-mail:* akeys@thomasu.edu.

TIFFIN UNIVERSITY

Tiffin, OH

Tuition & fees: $17,730 **Average undergraduate aid package: $12,141**

ABOUT THE INSTITUTION Independent, coed. ***Awards:*** associate, bachelor's, and master's degrees. 36 undergraduate majors. ***Total enrollment:*** 2,674. Undergraduates: 1,810. Freshmen: 421. Federal methodology is used as a basis for awarding need-based institutional aid.

UNDERGRADUATE EXPENSES for 2009–10 ***Application fee:*** $20. ***Comprehensive fee:*** $25,715 includes full-time tuition ($17,730) and room and board ($7985). ***College room only:*** $4145. ***Part-time tuition:*** $591 per credit hour.

FRESHMAN FINANCIAL AID (Fall 2008, est.) 405 applied for aid; of those 90% were deemed to have need. 100% of freshmen with need received aid; of those 11% had need fully met. ***Average percent of need met:*** 11% (excluding resources awarded to replace EFC). ***Average financial aid package:*** $14,085 (excluding resources awarded to replace EFC). 6% of all full-time freshmen had no need and received non-need-based gift aid.

UNDERGRADUATE FINANCIAL AID (Fall 2008, est.) 1,542 applied for aid; of those 92% were deemed to have need. 100% of undergraduates with need received aid; of those 19% had need fully met. ***Average percent of need met:*** 17% (excluding resources awarded to replace EFC). ***Average financial aid package:*** $12,141 (excluding resources awarded to replace EFC). 6% of all full-time undergraduates had no need and received non-need-based gift aid.

GIFT AID (NEED-BASED) ***Total amount:*** $11,592,199 (24% federal, 19% state, 56% institutional, 1% external sources). ***Receiving aid:*** Freshmen: 61% (250); all full-time undergraduates: 54% (840). ***Average award:*** Freshmen: $5720; Undergraduates: $5399. ***Scholarships, grants, and awards:*** Federal Pell, FSEOG, state, private, college/university gift aid from institutional funds.

GIFT AID (NON-NEED-BASED) ***Receiving aid:*** Freshmen: 76% (309). Undergraduates: 88% (1,379). ***Average award:*** Freshmen: $7231. Undergraduates: $6988. ***Scholarships, grants, and awards by category:*** *Academic interests/achievement:* 851 awards ($4,655,705 total): general academic interests/achievements. *Creative arts/performance:* 113 awards ($293,036 total): music, performing arts, theater/drama. *Special achievements/activities:* 25 awards ($26,200 total): cheerleading/drum major. *Special characteristics:* 25 awards ($252,486 total): children of faculty/staff. ***ROTC:*** Army cooperative, Air Force cooperative.

LOANS ***Student loans:*** $12,667,778 (100% need-based). 95% of past graduating class borrowed through all loan programs. *Average indebtedness per student:* $26,010. ***Average need-based loan:*** Freshmen: $3375. Undergraduates: $4312. ***Parent loans:*** $759,059 (100% need-based). ***Programs:*** Federal Direct (Subsidized and Unsubsidized Stafford, PLUS), FFEL (Subsidized and Unsubsidized Stafford, PLUS), Perkins, college/university.

WORK-STUDY ***Federal work-study:*** Total amount: $463,936; 129 jobs averaging $955.

ATHLETIC AWARDS Total amount: $2,149,171 (100% need-based).

APPLYING FOR FINANCIAL AID ***Required financial aid form:*** FAFSA. ***Financial aid deadline (priority):*** 1/1. ***Notification date:*** Continuous beginning 1/15. Students must reply within 2 weeks of notification.

CONTACT Ms. Cindy Little, Director of Financial Aid, Tiffin University, 155 Miami Street, Tiffin, OH 44883, 419-448-3415 or toll-free 800-968-6446. *Fax:* 419-443-5006. *E-mail:* clittle@tiffin.edu.

TOCCOA FALLS COLLEGE

Toccoa Falls, GA

CONTACT Vince Welch, Director of Financial Aid, Toccoa Falls College, PO Box 800900, Toccoa Falls, GA 30598, 706-886-7299 Ext. 5234. *Fax:* 706-282-6041. *E-mail:* vwelch@tfc.edu.

TORAH TEMIMAH TALMUDICAL SEMINARY

Brooklyn, NY

CONTACT Financial Aid Office, Torah Temimah Talmudical Seminary, 507 Ocean Parkway, Brooklyn, NY 11218-5913, 718-853-8500.

TOUGALOO COLLEGE

Tougaloo, MS

CONTACT Director of Financial Aid, Tougaloo College, 500 West County Line Road, Tougaloo, MS 39174, 601-977-6134 or toll-free 888-42GALOO. *Fax:* 601-977-6164.

TOURO COLLEGE

New York, NY

CONTACT Office of Financial Aid, Touro College, 27 West 23rd Street, New York, NY 10010, 212-463-0400.

TOWSON UNIVERSITY

Towson, MD

Tuition & fees (MD res): $7314 **Average undergraduate aid package: $8991**

ABOUT THE INSTITUTION State-supported, coed. ***Awards:*** bachelor's, master's, and doctoral degrees and post-bachelor's and post-master's certificates. 57 undergraduate majors. ***Total enrollment:*** 21,111. Undergraduates: 17,272. Freshmen: 2,832. Federal methodology is used as a basis for awarding need-based institutional aid.

UNDERGRADUATE EXPENSES for 2008–09 ***Application fee:*** $45. ***Tuition, state resident:*** full-time $5180; part-time $225 per credit. ***Tuition, nonresident:*** full-time $15,726; part-time $588 per credit. ***Required fees:*** full-time $2134; $85 per credit. Full-time tuition and fees vary according to course load. ***College room and board:*** $8306; ***Room only:*** $5054. Room and board charges vary according to board plan and housing facility. ***Payment plans:*** Guaranteed tuition, tuition prepayment, installment.

FRESHMAN FINANCIAL AID (Fall 2008, est.) 2,149 applied for aid; of those 62% were deemed to have need. 94% of freshmen with need received aid; of those 21% had need fully met. ***Average percent of need met:*** 69% (excluding resources awarded to replace EFC). ***Average financial aid package:*** $8620 (excluding resources awarded to replace EFC). 10% of all full-time freshmen had no need and received non-need-based gift aid.

UNDERGRADUATE FINANCIAL AID (Fall 2008, est.) 9,095 applied for aid; of those 70% were deemed to have need. 96% of undergraduates with need received aid; of those 21% had need fully met. ***Average percent of need met:*** 69% (excluding resources awarded to replace EFC). ***Average financial aid package:*** $8991 (excluding resources awarded to replace EFC). 9% of all full-time undergraduates had no need and received non-need-based gift aid.

GIFT AID (NEED-BASED) ***Total amount:*** $30,684,635 (34% federal, 28% state, 37% institutional, 1% external sources). ***Receiving aid:*** Freshmen: 29% (819); all full-time undergraduates: 28% (4,202). ***Average award:*** Freshmen: $8416; Undergraduates: $7196. ***Scholarships, grants, and awards:*** Federal Pell, FSEOG, state, private, college/university gift aid from institutional funds.

GIFT AID (NON-NEED-BASED) ***Total amount:*** $13,692,294 (1% federal, 6% state, 60% institutional, 33% external sources). ***Receiving aid:*** Freshmen: 18% (518). Undergraduates: 11% (1,707). ***Average award:*** Freshmen: $4768. Undergraduates: $4699. ***Scholarships, grants, and awards by category:*** *Academic interests/achievement:* 1,754 awards ($6,908,597 total): biological sciences, business, communication, computer science, education, English, foreign languages, general academic interests/achievements, mathematics. *Creative arts/performance:* 155 awards ($459,538 total): art/fine arts, dance, debating, music, theater/drama. *Special achievements/activities:* 41 awards ($146,100 total): memberships. *Special characteristics:* 444 awards ($1,628,718 total): adult students, children of faculty/staff, handicapped students, international students, veterans. ***Tuition waivers:*** Full or partial for employees or children of employees, senior citizens. ***ROTC:*** Army cooperative, Air Force cooperative.

LOANS ***Student loans:*** $34,813,336 (58% need-based, 42% non-need-based). 38% of past graduating class borrowed through all loan programs. *Average indebtedness per student:* $10,772. ***Average need-based loan:*** Freshmen: $3177. Undergraduates: $4039. ***Parent loans:*** $35,189,510 (2% need-based, 98% non-need-based). ***Programs:*** Federal Direct (Subsidized and Unsubsidized Stafford, PLUS), Perkins.

WORK-STUDY ***Federal work-study:*** Total amount: $874,459; 503 jobs averaging $1677.

ATHLETIC AWARDS Total amount: $4,522,611 (100% non-need-based).

APPLYING FOR FINANCIAL AID ***Required financial aid form:*** FAFSA. ***Financial aid deadline:*** 2/10 (priority: 1/31). ***Notification date:*** Continuous beginning 3/21. Students must reply within 2 weeks of notification.

CONTACT Vince Pecora, Director of Financial Aid, Towson University, 8000 York Road, Towson, MD 21252-0001, 410-704-4236 or toll-free 888-4TOWSON. *E-mail:* finaid@towson.edu.

TRANSYLVANIA UNIVERSITY

Lexington, KY

Tuition & fees: $23,810 **Average undergraduate aid package: $20,082**

ABOUT THE INSTITUTION Independent religious, coed. ***Awards:*** bachelor's degrees. 35 undergraduate majors. ***Total enrollment:*** 1,158. Undergraduates: 1,158. Freshmen: 317. Federal methodology is used as a basis for awarding need-based institutional aid.

UNDERGRADUATE EXPENSES for 2008–09 ***Application fee:*** $30. ***Comprehensive fee:*** $31,260 includes full-time tuition ($22,840), mandatory fees ($970), and room and board ($7450). ***Part-time tuition:*** $2465 per course.

FRESHMAN FINANCIAL AID (Fall 2008, est.) 272 applied for aid; of those 80% were deemed to have need. 100% of freshmen with need received aid; of those 30% had need fully met. ***Average percent of need met:*** 86% (excluding resources awarded to replace EFC). ***Average financial aid package:*** $19,490 (excluding resources awarded to replace EFC). 30% of all full-time freshmen had no need and received non-need-based gift aid.

UNDERGRADUATE FINANCIAL AID (Fall 2008, est.) 853 applied for aid; of those 86% were deemed to have need. 100% of undergraduates with need received aid; of those 28% had need fully met. ***Average percent of need met:*** 85% (excluding resources awarded to replace EFC). ***Average financial aid package:*** $20,082 (excluding resources awarded to replace EFC). 34% of all full-time undergraduates had no need and received non-need-based gift aid.

GIFT AID (NEED-BASED) ***Total amount:*** $11,491,209 (9% federal, 24% state, 64% institutional, 3% external sources). ***Receiving aid:*** Freshmen: 69% (216); all full-time undergraduates: 64% (733). ***Average award:*** Freshmen: $15,690; Undergraduates: $15,781. ***Scholarships, grants, and awards:*** Federal Pell, FSEOG, state, private, college/university gift aid from institutional funds.

GIFT AID (NON-NEED-BASED) ***Total amount:*** $4,991,021 (14% state, 83% institutional, 3% external sources). ***Receiving aid:*** Freshmen: 12% (37). Undergraduates: 8% (97). ***Average award:*** Freshmen: $14,662. Undergraduates: $13,602. ***Scholarships, grants, and awards by category:*** *Academic interests/achievement:* 1,091 awards ($8,991,843 total): computer science, general academic interests/achievements. *Creative arts/performance:* 56 awards ($129,600 total): art/fine arts, music, theater/drama. *Special achievements/activities:* 340 awards ($722,767 total): general special achievements/activities, religious involvement. *Special characteristics:* 139 awards ($955,362 total): children of faculty/staff, members of minority groups, out-of-state students, relatives of clergy, religious affiliation. ***ROTC:*** Army cooperative, Air Force cooperative.

LOANS ***Student loans:*** $5,436,376 (65% need-based, 35% non-need-based). 64% of past graduating class borrowed through all loan programs. *Average indebtedness per student:* $17,885. ***Average need-based loan:*** Freshmen: $4250. Undergraduates: $4508. ***Parent loans:*** $1,216,001 (18% need-based, 82% non-need-based). ***Programs:*** FFEL (Subsidized and Unsubsidized Stafford, PLUS), Perkins, college/university.

WORK-STUDY ***Federal work-study:*** Total amount: $484,994; 419 jobs averaging $1731. ***State or other work-study/employment:*** Total amount: $352,650 (30% need-based, 70% non-need-based). 60 part-time jobs averaging $5945.

APPLYING FOR FINANCIAL AID ***Required financial aid form:*** FAFSA. ***Financial aid deadline (priority):*** 3/1. ***Notification date:*** Continuous beginning 3/15. Students must reply within 2 weeks of notification.

CONTACT Mr. Dave Cecil, Director of Financial Aid, Transylvania University, 300 North Broadway, Lexington, KY 40508-1797, 859-233-8239 or toll-free 800-872-6798. *Fax:* 859-281-3650. *E-mail:* dcecil@transy.edu.

TREVECCA NAZARENE UNIVERSITY

Nashville, TN

Tuition & fees: $16,288 **Average undergraduate aid package: N/A**

ABOUT THE INSTITUTION Independent Nazarene, coed. ***Awards:*** associate, bachelor's, master's, and doctoral degrees and post-master's certificates. 50 undergraduate majors. ***Total enrollment:*** 2,366. Undergraduates: 1,271. Freshmen: 218. Federal methodology is used as a basis for awarding need-based institutional aid.

UNDERGRADUATE EXPENSES for 2008–09 ***Application fee:*** $25. ***Comprehensive fee:*** $23,422 includes full-time tuition ($16,288) and room and board ($7134). ***College room only:*** $3220. Full-time tuition and fees vary according to course load. Room and board charges vary according to board plan. Part-time tuition and fees vary according to course load. ***Payment plan:*** Installment.

GIFT AID (NEED-BASED) ***Total amount:*** $1,879,555 (57% federal, 16% state, 27% institutional). ***Scholarships, grants, and awards:*** Federal Pell, FSEOG, state, private, college/university gift aid from institutional funds.

GIFT AID (NON-NEED-BASED) ***Total amount:*** $5,540,974 (16% state, 77% institutional, 7% external sources). ***Scholarships, grants, and awards by category:*** *Academic interests/achievement:* biological sciences, business, communication, education, English, general academic interests/achievements, physical sciences, religion/biblical studies, social sciences. *Creative arts/performance:* cinema/film/broadcasting, music. *Special achievements/activities:* general special achievements/activities. *Special characteristics:* children of faculty/staff, general special characteristics, relatives of clergy, religious affiliation. ***Tuition waivers:*** Full or partial for employees or children of employees, senior citizens. ***ROTC:*** Army cooperative.

LOANS ***Student loans:*** $6,906,795 (50% need-based, 50% non-need-based). ***Parent loans:*** $1,567,560 (100% non-need-based). ***Programs:*** FFEL (Subsidized and Unsubsidized Stafford, PLUS), Perkins.

WORK-STUDY ***Federal work-study:*** Total amount: $99,771; jobs available.

ATHLETIC AWARDS Total amount: $995,184 (100% non-need-based).

APPLYING FOR FINANCIAL AID ***Required financial aid form:*** FAFSA. ***Financial aid deadline (priority):*** 3/1. ***Notification date:*** Continuous beginning 3/1.

CONTACT Eddie White, Assistant Director of Financial Aid, Trevecca Nazarene University, 333 Murfreesboro Road, Nashville, TN 37210-2834, 615-248-1242 or toll-free 888-210-4TNU. *Fax:* 615-248-7728. *E-mail:* ewhite@trevecca.edu.

TRINE UNIVERSITY

Angola, IN

Tuition & fees: $24,200 **Average undergraduate aid package: $17,193**

ABOUT THE INSTITUTION Independent, coed. ***Awards:*** associate, bachelor's, and master's degrees. 40 undergraduate majors. ***Total enrollment:*** 1,451. Undergraduates: 1,441. Freshmen: 435. Federal methodology is used as a basis for awarding need-based institutional aid.

UNDERGRADUATE EXPENSES for 2009–10 ***Comprehensive fee:*** $32,500 includes full-time tuition ($24,100), mandatory fees ($100), and room and board ($8300). ***Part-time tuition:*** $753 per credit hour.

FRESHMAN FINANCIAL AID (Fall 2008, est.) 420 applied for aid; of those 69% were deemed to have need. 100% of freshmen with need received aid; of those 100% had need fully met. ***Average percent of need met:*** 93% (excluding resources awarded to replace EFC). ***Average financial aid package:*** $18,457 (excluding resources awarded to replace EFC). 16% of all full-time freshmen had no need and received non-need-based gift aid.

UNDERGRADUATE FINANCIAL AID (Fall 2008, est.) 1,201 applied for aid; of those 70% were deemed to have need. 100% of undergraduates with need received aid; of those 100% had need fully met. ***Average percent of need met:*** 91% (excluding resources awarded to replace EFC). ***Average financial aid package:*** $17,193 (excluding resources awarded to replace EFC). 11% of all full-time undergraduates had no need and received non-need-based gift aid.

GIFT AID (NEED-BASED) ***Total amount:*** $6,019,691 (26% federal, 40% state, 34% institutional). ***Receiving aid:*** Freshmen: 44% (186); all full-time undergraduates: 37% (451). ***Average award:*** Freshmen: $5127; Undergraduates: $4570. ***Scholarships, grants, and awards:*** Federal Pell, FSEOG, state, private, college/university gift aid from institutional funds.

GIFT AID (NON-NEED-BASED) ***Total amount:*** $9,974,883 (95% institutional, 5% external sources). ***Receiving aid:*** Freshmen: 68% (288). Undergraduates: 68% (843). ***Average award:*** Freshmen: $9397. Undergraduates: $7779. ***Scholarships, grants, and awards by category:*** *Academic interests/achievement:* general academic interests/achievements. *Special characteristics:* children and siblings of alumni, children of faculty/staff, members of minority groups.

LOANS ***Student loans:*** $6,253,373 (57% need-based, 43% non-need-based). 79% of past graduating class borrowed through all loan programs. *Average indebtedness per student:* $17,380. ***Average need-based loan:*** Freshmen: $3350. Undergraduates: $4199. ***Parent loans:*** $3,533,996 (100% non-need-based). ***Programs:*** FFEL (Subsidized and Unsubsidized Stafford, PLUS), alternative loans.

WORK-STUDY ***Federal work-study:*** Total amount: $1,451,613; 629 jobs averaging $1794.

APPLYING FOR FINANCIAL AID ***Required financial aid form:*** FAFSA. ***Financial aid deadline (priority):*** 3/10. ***Notification date:*** Continuous. Students must reply by 5/1 or within 2 weeks of notification.

CONTACT Kim Bennett, Director of Financial Aid, Trine University, 1 University Avenue, Angola, IN 46703-1764, 260-665-4175 or toll-free 800-347-4TSU. *Fax:* 260-665-4511. *E-mail:* admit@tristate.edu.

TRINITY BAPTIST COLLEGE

Jacksonville, FL

CONTACT Mr. Donald Schaffer, Financial Aid Administrator, Trinity Baptist College, 800 Hammond Boulevard, Jacksonville, FL 32221, 904-596-2445 or toll-free 800-786-2206 (out-of-state). *Fax:* 904-596-2531. *E-mail:* financialaid@tbc.edu.

TRINITY BIBLE COLLEGE

Ellendale, ND

CONTACT Rhonda Miller, Financial Aid Associate, Trinity Bible College, 50 South 6th Avenue, Ellendale, ND 58436-7150, 888-822-2329 Ext. 2781 or toll-free 888-TBC-2DAY. *Fax:* 701-349-5786. *E-mail:* financialaid@trinitybiblecollege.edu.

TRINITY CHRISTIAN COLLEGE

Palos Heights, IL

Tuition & fees: $20,046 **Average undergraduate aid package: $6342**

ABOUT THE INSTITUTION Independent Christian Reformed, coed. ***Awards:*** bachelor's degrees and post-bachelor's certificates. 59 undergraduate majors. ***Total enrollment:*** 1,404. Undergraduates: 1,404. Freshmen: 235. Both federal and institutional methodology are used as a basis for awarding need-based institutional aid.

UNDERGRADUATE EXPENSES for 2008–09 ***Application fee:*** $20. ***Comprehensive fee:*** $27,466 includes full-time tuition ($19,936), mandatory fees ($110), and room and board ($7420). ***College room only:*** $3970. Room and board charges vary according to board plan. ***Part-time tuition:*** $664 per semester hour. Part-time tuition and fees vary according to course load. ***Payment plan:*** Installment.

FRESHMAN FINANCIAL AID (Fall 2008, est.) 205 applied for aid; of those 93% were deemed to have need. 100% of freshmen with need received aid; of those 6% had need fully met. ***Average percent of need met:*** 47% (excluding resources awarded to replace EFC). ***Average financial aid package:*** $8896 (excluding resources awarded to replace EFC). 13% of all full-time freshmen had no need and received non-need-based gift aid.

UNDERGRADUATE FINANCIAL AID (Fall 2008, est.) 1,021 applied for aid; of those 88% were deemed to have need. 100% of undergraduates with need received aid; of those 4% had need fully met. ***Average percent of need met:*** 64% (excluding resources awarded to replace EFC). ***Average financial aid package:*** $6342 (excluding resources awarded to replace EFC). 14% of all full-time undergraduates had no need and received non-need-based gift aid.

GIFT AID (NEED-BASED) ***Total amount:*** $4,465,841 (32% federal, 33% state, 35% institutional). ***Receiving aid:*** Freshmen: 66% (154); all full-time undergraduates: 65% (701). ***Average award:*** Freshmen: $6879; Undergraduates: $5918. ***Scholarships, grants, and awards:*** Federal Pell, FSEOG, state, private, college/university gift aid from institutional funds.

GIFT AID (NON-NEED-BASED) ***Total amount:*** $4,157,908 (2% state, 92% institutional, 6% external sources). ***Receiving aid:*** Freshmen: 73% (172). Undergraduates: 68% (734). ***Average award:*** Freshmen: $5718. Undergraduates: $5425. ***Scholarships, grants, and awards by category:*** *Academic interests/achievement:* business, English, general academic interests/achievements, health fields, mathematics. *Creative arts/performance:* journalism/publications, music, theater/drama. *Special achievements/activities:* general special achievements/activities, leadership. *Special characteristics:* children and siblings of alumni, children of faculty/staff, local/state students, members of minority groups, out-of-state students. ***Tuition waivers:*** Full or partial for employees or children of employees, senior citizens.

LOANS ***Student loans:*** $9,154,550 (43% need-based, 57% non-need-based). 89% of past graduating class borrowed through all loan programs. *Average indebtedness per student:* $42,375. ***Average need-based loan:*** Freshmen: $4231. Undergraduates: $4653. ***Parent loans:*** $785,358 (100% non-need-based). ***Programs:*** FFEL (Subsidized and Unsubsidized Stafford, PLUS), Perkins, Federal Nursing.

WORK-STUDY ***Federal work-study:*** Total amount: $130,500; jobs available. ***State or other work-study/employment:*** Part-time jobs available.

ATHLETIC AWARDS Total amount: $737,000 (100% non-need-based).

APPLYING FOR FINANCIAL AID ***Required financial aid forms:*** FAFSA, institution's own form. ***Financial aid deadline (priority):*** 2/15. ***Notification date:*** Continuous.

CONTACT L. Denise Coleman, Director of Financial Aid, Trinity Christian College, 6601 West College Drive, Palos Heights, IL 60463-0929, 708-239-4706 or toll-free 800-748-0085. *E-mail:* financial.aid@trnty.edu.

TRINITY COLLEGE

Hartford, CT

Tuition & fees: $38,724 | **Average undergraduate aid package: $35,002**

ABOUT THE INSTITUTION Independent, coed. ***Awards:*** bachelor's and master's degrees. 47 undergraduate majors. ***Total enrollment:*** 2,566. Undergraduates: 2,388. Freshmen: 589. Both federal and institutional methodology are used as a basis for awarding need-based institutional aid.

UNDERGRADUATE EXPENSES for 2009–10 ***Application fee:*** $60. ***One-time required fee:*** $25. ***Comprehensive fee:*** $48,624 includes full-time tuition ($36,864), mandatory fees ($1860), and room and board ($9900). ***College room only:*** $6400. ***Part-time tuition:*** $4096 per course.

FRESHMAN FINANCIAL AID (Fall 2008, est.) 302 applied for aid; of those 84% were deemed to have need. 100% of freshmen with need received aid; of those 100% had need fully met. ***Average percent of need met:*** 100% (excluding resources awarded to replace EFC). ***Average financial aid package:*** $35,967 (excluding resources awarded to replace EFC). 1% of all full-time freshmen had no need and received non-need-based gift aid.

UNDERGRADUATE FINANCIAL AID (Fall 2008, est.) 977 applied for aid; of those 90% were deemed to have need. 100% of undergraduates with need received aid; of those 100% had need fully met. ***Average percent of need met:*** 100% (excluding resources awarded to replace EFC). ***Average financial aid package:*** $35,002 (excluding resources awarded to replace EFC). 2% of all full-time undergraduates had no need and received non-need-based gift aid.

GIFT AID (NEED-BASED) ***Total amount:*** $27,292,829 (5% federal, 3% state, 90% institutional, 2% external sources). ***Receiving aid:*** Freshmen: 41% (239); all full-time undergraduates: 37% (818). ***Average award:*** Freshmen: $34,175; Undergraduates: $32,820. ***Scholarships, grants, and awards:*** Federal Pell, FSEOG, state, private, college/university gift aid from institutional funds, Academic Competitiveness Grant, National Smart Grant.

GIFT AID (NON-NEED-BASED) ***Total amount:*** $1,654,180 (97% institutional, 3% external sources). ***Receiving aid:*** Freshmen: 11% (63). Undergraduates: 7% (165). ***Average award:*** Freshmen: $35,864. Undergraduates: $25,972. ***Scholarships, grants, and awards by category:*** *Academic interests/achievement:* 3 awards ($3000 total): general academic interests/achievements. *Special achievements/activities:* 14 awards ($516,096 total): leadership. ***ROTC:*** Army cooperative.

LOANS ***Student loans:*** $5,403,978 (51% need-based, 49% non-need-based). 45% of past graduating class borrowed through all loan programs. *Average indebtedness per student:* $17,218. ***Average need-based loan:*** Freshmen: $3564. Undergraduates: $4357. ***Parent loans:*** $3,332,042 (100% non-need-based). ***Programs:*** FFEL (Subsidized and Unsubsidized Stafford, PLUS), Perkins, college/university, alternative loans.

WORK-STUDY ***Federal work-study:*** Total amount: $799,649; 694 jobs averaging $1520.

APPLYING FOR FINANCIAL AID ***Required financial aid forms:*** FAFSA, CSS Financial Aid PROFILE, noncustodial (divorced/separated) parent's statement, business/farm supplement, federal income tax form(s). ***Financial aid deadline:*** 3/1 (priority: 2/1). ***Notification date:*** 4/1. Students must reply by 5/1 or within 2 weeks of notification.

CONTACT Ms. Kelly O'Brien, Director of Financial Aid, Trinity College, 300 Summit Street, Hartford, CT 06106-3100, 860-297-2046. *Fax:* 860-987-6296.

TRINITY COLLEGE OF FLORIDA

New Port Richey, FL

Tuition & fees: $11,200 | **Average undergraduate aid package: $4855**

ABOUT THE INSTITUTION Independent nondenominational, coed. ***Awards:*** associate and bachelor's degrees. 10 undergraduate majors. ***Total enrollment:*** 183. Undergraduates: 183. Freshmen: 31. Both federal and institutional methodology are used as a basis for awarding need-based institutional aid.

UNDERGRADUATE EXPENSES for 2009–10 ***Application fee:*** $25. ***Comprehensive fee:*** $17,734 includes full-time tuition ($10,400), mandatory fees ($800), and room and board ($6534). ***Part-time tuition:*** $430 per credit hour. ***Part-time fees:*** $400 per term.

FRESHMAN FINANCIAL AID (Fall 2008, est.) 30 applied for aid; of those 87% were deemed to have need. 100% of freshmen with need received aid; of those 15% had need fully met. ***Average percent of need met:*** 78% (excluding resources awarded to replace EFC). ***Average financial aid package:*** $4371 (excluding resources awarded to replace EFC). 13% of all full-time freshmen had no need and received non-need-based gift aid.

UNDERGRADUATE FINANCIAL AID (Fall 2008, est.) 114 applied for aid; of those 89% were deemed to have need. 100% of undergraduates with need received aid; of those 27% had need fully met. ***Average percent of need met:*** 84% (excluding resources awarded to replace EFC). ***Average financial aid package:*** $4855 (excluding resources awarded to replace EFC). 10% of all full-time undergraduates had no need and received non-need-based gift aid.

GIFT AID (NEED-BASED) ***Total amount:*** $568,006 (63% federal, 10% state, 23% institutional, 4% external sources). ***Receiving aid:*** Freshmen: 87% (26); all full-time undergraduates: 74% (88). ***Average award:*** Freshmen: $3024; Undergraduates: $3191. ***Scholarships, grants, and awards:*** Federal Pell, FSEOG, state, private, college/university gift aid from institutional funds.

GIFT AID (NON-NEED-BASED) ***Total amount:*** $101,508 (59% state, 38% institutional, 3% external sources). ***Receiving aid:*** Freshmen: 47% (14). Undergraduates: 40% (48). ***Average award:*** Freshmen: $631. Undergraduates: $619. ***Scholarships, grants, and awards by category:*** *Academic interests/achievement:* religion/biblical studies. *Special achievements/activities:* community service, leadership, religious involvement. *Special characteristics:* 10 awards ($10,198 total): children of faculty/staff, relatives of clergy, spouses of current students.

LOANS ***Student loans:*** $747,558 (100% need-based). 83% of past graduating class borrowed through all loan programs. *Average indebtedness per student:* $15,233. ***Average need-based loan:*** Freshmen: $1750. Undergraduates: $2178. ***Parent loans:*** $48,385 (100% need-based). ***Programs:*** FFEL (Subsidized and Unsubsidized Stafford, PLUS).

WORK-STUDY ***Federal work-study:*** Total amount: $37,750; 22 jobs averaging $1402. ***State or other work-study/employment:*** Part-time jobs available.

APPLYING FOR FINANCIAL AID ***Required financial aid forms:*** FAFSA, institution's own form. ***Financial aid deadline (priority):*** 3/15. ***Notification date:*** Continuous. Students must reply within 6 weeks of notification.

CONTACT Sue Wayne, Financial Aid Director, Trinity College of Florida, 2430 Welbilt Boulevard, New Port Richey, FL 34655, 727-569-1413 or toll-free 800-388-0869. *Fax:* 727-376-0781. *E-mail:* swayne@trinitycollege.edu.

TRINITY COLLEGE OF NURSING AND HEALTH SCIENCES

Rock Island, IL

ABOUT THE INSTITUTION Independent, coed. 5 undergraduate majors.

GIFT AID (NEED-BASED) ***Scholarships, grants, and awards:*** Federal Pell, FSEOG, state, college/university gift aid from institutional funds.

LOANS ***Programs:*** FFEL (Subsidized and Unsubsidized Stafford, PLUS), Federal Nursing.

APPLYING FOR FINANCIAL AID ***Required financial aid forms:*** FAFSA, institution's own form.

CONTACT Kris Hodgerson, Financial Aid Specialist, Trinity College of Nursing and Health Sciences, 2122 25th Avenue, Rock Island, IL 61201, 309-779-7700. *Fax:* 309-779-7748. *E-mail:* hodgersonk@ihs.org.

TRINITY INTERNATIONAL UNIVERSITY

Deerfield, IL

Tuition & fees: $21,980 **Average undergraduate aid package: $18,908**

ABOUT THE INSTITUTION Independent religious, coed. ***Awards:*** bachelor's, master's, doctoral, and first professional degrees and post-bachelor's certificates. 39 undergraduate majors. ***Total enrollment:*** 2,671. Undergraduates: 968. Freshmen: 134. Federal methodology is used as a basis for awarding need-based institutional aid.

UNDERGRADUATE EXPENSES for 2009–10 ***Application fee:*** $25. ***Comprehensive fee:*** $29,410 includes full-time tuition ($21,980) and room and board ($7430). ***College room only:*** $4050.

FRESHMAN FINANCIAL AID (Fall 2008, est.) 114 applied for aid; of those 90% were deemed to have need. 100% of freshmen with need received aid; of those 20% had need fully met. ***Average percent of need met:*** 69% (excluding resources awarded to replace EFC). ***Average financial aid package:*** $17,893 (excluding resources awarded to replace EFC). 5% of all full-time freshmen had no need and received non-need-based gift aid.

UNDERGRADUATE FINANCIAL AID (Fall 2008, est.) 577 applied for aid; of those 89% were deemed to have need. 100% of undergraduates with need received aid; of those 23% had need fully met. ***Average percent of need met:*** 73% (excluding resources awarded to replace EFC). ***Average financial aid package:*** $18,908 (excluding resources awarded to replace EFC). 6% of all full-time undergraduates had no need and received non-need-based gift aid.

GIFT AID (NEED-BASED) ***Total amount:*** $4,052,327 (24% federal, 19% state, 57% institutional). ***Receiving aid:*** Freshmen: 58% (77); all full-time undergraduates: 59% (401). ***Average award:*** Freshmen: $7700; Undergraduates: $8623. ***Scholarships, grants, and awards:*** Federal Pell, FSEOG, state, private, college/university gift aid from institutional funds.

GIFT AID (NON-NEED-BASED) ***Total amount:*** $2,603,943 (92% institutional, 8% external sources). ***Receiving aid:*** Freshmen: 74% (98). Undergraduates: 70% (470). ***Average award:*** Freshmen: $6821. Undergraduates: $4452. ***Scholarships, grants, and awards by category:*** *Academic interests/achievement:* general academic interests/achievements. *Creative arts/performance:* music. *Special achievements/activities:* leadership, religious involvement. *Special characteristics:* children and siblings of alumni, members of minority groups, religious affiliation.

LOANS ***Student loans:*** $4,149,764 (52% need-based, 48% non-need-based). 41% of past graduating class borrowed through all loan programs. *Average indebtedness per student:* $18,477. ***Average need-based loan:*** Freshmen: $3908. Undergraduates: $5009. ***Parent loans:*** $621,884 (100% non-need-based). ***Programs:*** FFEL (Subsidized and Unsubsidized Stafford, PLUS), Perkins.

WORK-STUDY ***Federal work-study:*** Total amount: $639,487; jobs available.

ATHLETIC AWARDS Total amount: $2,059,520 (100% non-need-based).

APPLYING FOR FINANCIAL AID ***Required financial aid form:*** FAFSA. ***Financial aid deadline (priority):*** 4/1. ***Notification date:*** Continuous. Students must reply within 4 weeks of notification.

CONTACT Pat Coles, Acting Director of Financial Aid, Trinity International University, 2065 Half Day Road, Deerfield, IL 60015-1284, 847-317-8060 or toll-free 800-822-3225 (out-of-state). *Fax:* 847-317-7081. *E-mail:* finaid@tiu.edu.

TRINITY LIFE BIBLE COLLEGE

Sacramento, CA

CONTACT Financial Aid Office, Trinity Life Bible College, 5225 Hillsdale Boulevard, Sacramento, CA 95842, 916-348-4689.

TRINITY LUTHERAN COLLEGE

Issaquah, WA

Tuition & fees: $19,425 **Average undergraduate aid package: N/A**

ABOUT THE INSTITUTION Independent Lutheran, coed. ***Awards:*** associate and bachelor's degrees and post-bachelor's certificates. 8 undergraduate majors. ***Total enrollment:*** 115. Undergraduates: 115. Federal methodology is used as a basis for awarding need-based institutional aid.

UNDERGRADUATE EXPENSES for 2008–09 ***Application fee:*** $30. ***Tuition:*** full-time $18,925; part-time $790 per credit hour. ***Required fees:*** full-time $500; $150 per term. Part-time tuition and fees vary according to course load. Room and board charges vary according to board plan and housing facility. ***Payment plan:*** Installment.

GIFT AID (NEED-BASED) ***Total amount:*** $273,905 (47% federal, 53% institutional). ***Scholarships, grants, and awards:*** Federal Pell, FSEOG, college/university gift aid from institutional funds.

GIFT AID (NON-NEED-BASED) ***Total amount:*** $463,854 (100% institutional). ***Scholarships, grants, and awards by category:*** *Academic interests/achievement:* business, general academic interests/achievements, religion/biblical studies. *Creative arts/performance:* general creative arts/performance, music. *Special achievements/activities:* leadership, religious involvement. *Special characteristics:* children of faculty/staff, international students, religious affiliation. ***Tuition waivers:*** Full or partial for senior citizens.

LOANS ***Student loans:*** $493,865 (100% need-based). ***Parent loans:*** $77,750 (100% need-based). ***Programs:*** FFEL (Subsidized and Unsubsidized Stafford, PLUS), college/university.

WORK-STUDY ***Federal work-study:*** Total amount: $25,103; 45 jobs averaging $744.

APPLYING FOR FINANCIAL AID ***Required financial aid forms:*** FAFSA, institution's own form. ***Financial aid deadline (priority):*** 2/15. ***Notification date:*** Continuous. Students must reply within 4 weeks of notification.

CONTACT Ms. Susan Dalgleish, Director of Financial Aid, Trinity Lutheran College, 4221 228th Avenue SE, Issaquah, WA 98029-9299, 425-961-5514 or toll-free 800-843-5659. *Fax:* 425-392-0404. *E-mail:* susan.dalgleish@tlc.edu.

TRINITY UNIVERSITY

San Antonio, TX

Tuition & fees: $27,699 **Average undergraduate aid package: $22,529**

ABOUT THE INSTITUTION Independent religious, coed. ***Awards:*** bachelor's and master's degrees. 50 undergraduate majors. ***Total enrollment:*** 2,703. Undergraduates: 2,489. Freshmen: 656. Federal methodology is used as a basis for awarding need-based institutional aid.

UNDERGRADUATE EXPENSES for 2008–09 ***Application fee:*** $50. ***Comprehensive fee:*** $36,521 includes full-time tuition ($26,664), mandatory fees ($1035), and room and board ($8822). ***College room only:*** $5600. ***Part-time tuition:*** $1111 per hour.

FRESHMAN FINANCIAL AID (Fall 2008, est.) 394 applied for aid; of those 67% were deemed to have need. 100% of freshmen with need received aid; of those 49% had need fully met. ***Average percent of need met:*** 95% (excluding resources awarded to replace EFC). ***Average financial aid package:*** $23,397 (excluding resources awarded to replace EFC). 45% of all full-time freshmen had no need and received non-need-based gift aid.

UNDERGRADUATE FINANCIAL AID (Fall 2008, est.) 1,197 applied for aid; of those 76% were deemed to have need. 100% of undergraduates with need received aid; of those 48% had need fully met. ***Average percent of need met:*** 92% (excluding resources awarded to replace EFC). ***Average financial aid package:*** $22,529 (excluding resources awarded to replace EFC). 46% of all full-time undergraduates had no need and received non-need-based gift aid.

GIFT AID (NEED-BASED) ***Total amount:*** $13,767,705 (10% federal, 9% state, 77% institutional, 4% external sources). ***Receiving aid:*** Freshmen: 40% (263);

all full-time undergraduates: 36% (887). ***Average award:*** Freshmen: $17,299; Undergraduates: $16,215. ***Scholarships, grants, and awards:*** Federal Pell, FSEOG, state, private, college/university gift aid from institutional funds.

GIFT AID (NON-NEED-BASED) ***Total amount:*** $12,514,869 (96% institutional, 4% external sources). ***Receiving aid:*** Freshmen: 10% (64). Undergraduates: 7% (167). ***Average award:*** Freshmen: $11,999. Undergraduates: $10,122. ***Scholarships, grants, and awards by category:*** *Academic interests/achievement:* 1,568 awards ($13,804,824 total): general academic interests/achievements. *Creative arts/performance:* 91 awards ($466,300 total): art/fine arts, debating, music, theater/drama. ***ROTC:*** Air Force cooperative.

LOANS ***Student loans:*** $6,145,656 (70% need-based, 30% non-need-based). ***Average need-based loan:*** Freshmen: $4746. Undergraduates: $5819. ***Parent loans:*** $7,908,982 (9% need-based, 91% non-need-based). ***Programs:*** FFEL (Subsidized and Unsubsidized Stafford, PLUS), Perkins, state, college/university.

WORK-STUDY ***Federal work-study:*** Total amount: $909,333; jobs available (averaging $2000). ***State or other work-study/employment:*** Part-time jobs available (averaging $2000).

APPLYING FOR FINANCIAL AID ***Required financial aid form:*** FAFSA. ***Financial aid deadline (priority):*** 2/15. ***Notification date:*** 4/1. Students must reply by 5/1 or within 4 weeks of notification.

CONTACT Sean Smith, Director of Financial Aid, Trinity University, 715 Stadium Drive, San Antonio, TX 78212-7200, 210-999-8315 or toll-free 800-TRINITY. *Fax:* 210-999-8316. *E-mail:* financialaid@trinity.edu.

TRINITY (WASHINGTON) UNIVERSITY

Washington, DC

CONTACT Catherine H. Geier, Director of Student Financial Services, Trinity (Washington) University, 125 Michigan Avenue, NE, Washington, DC 20017-1094, 202-884-9530 or toll-free 800-IWANTTC. *Fax:* 202-884-9524. *E-mail:* financialaid@trinitydc.edu.

TRI-STATE BIBLE COLLEGE

South Point, OH

CONTACT Financial Aid Office, Tri-State Bible College, 506 Margaret Street, PO Box 445, South Point, OH 45680-8402, 740-377-2520.

TROY UNIVERSITY

Troy, AL

Tuition & fees (AL res): $5900 **Average undergraduate aid package: $4080**

ABOUT THE INSTITUTION State-supported, coed. ***Awards:*** associate, bachelor's, and master's degrees and post-master's certificates. 42 undergraduate majors. ***Total enrollment:*** 28,303. Undergraduates: 21,144. Freshmen: 2,908. Federal methodology is used as a basis for awarding need-based institutional aid.

UNDERGRADUATE EXPENSES for 2008–09 ***Application fee:*** $30. ***Tuition, state resident:*** full-time $5310; part-time $177 per credit hour. ***Tuition, nonresident:*** full-time $10,620; part-time $354 per credit hour. ***Required fees:*** full-time $590; $15 per credit hour or $50 per term. ***College room and board:*** $5718. Room and board charges vary according to board plan and housing facility. ***Payment plan:*** Installment.

FRESHMAN FINANCIAL AID (Fall 2008, est.) 1,209 applied for aid; of those 100% were deemed to have need. 100% of freshmen with need received aid. ***Average financial aid package:*** $3542 (excluding resources awarded to replace EFC). 3% of all full-time freshmen had no need and received non-need-based gift aid.

UNDERGRADUATE FINANCIAL AID (Fall 2008, est.) 6,437 applied for aid; of those 100% were deemed to have need. 100% of undergraduates with need received aid. ***Average financial aid package:*** $4080 (excluding resources awarded to replace EFC). 2% of all full-time undergraduates had no need and received non-need-based gift aid.

GIFT AID (NEED-BASED) ***Total amount:*** $31,526,712 (97% federal, 3% state). ***Receiving aid:*** Freshmen: 43% (745); all full-time undergraduates: 42% (4,163). ***Average award:*** Freshmen: $3760; Undergraduates: $3752. ***Scholarships, grants, and awards:*** Federal Pell, FSEOG, state, private, college/university gift aid from institutional funds.

GIFT AID (NON-NEED-BASED) ***Total amount:*** $20,707,112 (42% institutional, 58% external sources). ***Receiving aid:*** Freshmen: 24% (422). Undergraduates: 14% (1,403). ***Average award:*** Freshmen: $2699. Undergraduates: $2874. ***Scholarships, grants, and awards by category:*** *Academic interests/achievement:* general academic interests/achievements. *Creative arts/performance:* music, theater/drama. *Special achievements/activities:* leadership. *Special characteristics:* general special characteristics. ***Tuition waivers:*** Full or partial for employees or children of employees. ***ROTC:*** Army, Air Force.

LOANS ***Student loans:*** $179,470,721 (100% need-based). ***Average need-based loan:*** Freshmen: $3459. Undergraduates: $4232. ***Parent loans:*** $5,604,815 (100% need-based). ***Programs:*** FFEL (Subsidized and Unsubsidized Stafford, PLUS), Perkins.

WORK-STUDY ***Federal work-study:*** Total amount: $1,264,000; 550 jobs averaging $2000.

ATHLETIC AWARDS Total amount: $3,796,695 (100% non-need-based).

APPLYING FOR FINANCIAL AID ***Required financial aid forms:*** FAFSA, institution's own form. ***Financial aid deadline (priority):*** 3/1. ***Notification date:*** Continuous beginning 6/1. Students must reply within 2 weeks of notification.

CONTACT Ms. Carol Supri, Associate Vice-Chancellor of Financial Aid, Troy University, 131 Adams Administration Bldg., Troy, AL 36082, 334-670-3186 or toll-free 800-551-9716. *Fax:* 334-670-3702. *E-mail:* csupri@troy.edu.

TRUETT-McCONNELL COLLEGE

Cleveland, GA

CONTACT Mr. Bob Gregory, Director of Financial Aid, Truett-McConnell College, 100 Alumni Drive, Cleveland, GA 30528, 706-865-2134 Ext. 110 or toll-free 800-226-8621 (in-state). *Fax:* 706-865-7615.

TRUMAN STATE UNIVERSITY

Kirksville, MO

Tuition & fees (MO res): $6692 **Average undergraduate aid package: $7358**

ABOUT THE INSTITUTION State-supported, coed. ***Awards:*** bachelor's and master's degrees. 63 undergraduate majors. ***Total enrollment:*** 5,842. Undergraduates: 5,586. Freshmen: 1,334. Federal methodology is used as a basis for awarding need-based institutional aid.

UNDERGRADUATE EXPENSES for 2008–09 ***One-time required fee:*** $305. ***Tuition, state resident:*** full-time $6458; part-time $269 per credit. ***Tuition, nonresident:*** full-time $11,309; part-time $471 per credit. ***Required fees:*** full-time $234. Part-time tuition and fees vary according to course load. ***College room and board:*** $6290. Room and board charges vary according to housing facility. ***Payment plan:*** Installment.

FRESHMAN FINANCIAL AID (Fall 2007) 1,124 applied for aid; of those 49% were deemed to have need. 100% of freshmen with need received aid; of those 70% had need fully met. ***Average percent of need met:*** 85% (excluding resources awarded to replace EFC). ***Average financial aid package:*** $7991 (excluding resources awarded to replace EFC). 59% of all full-time freshmen had no need and received non-need-based gift aid.

UNDERGRADUATE FINANCIAL AID (Fall 2007) 3,410 applied for aid; of those 63% were deemed to have need. 100% of undergraduates with need received aid; of those 68% had need fully met. ***Average percent of need met:*** 82% (excluding resources awarded to replace EFC). ***Average financial aid package:*** $7358 (excluding resources awarded to replace EFC). 45% of all full-time undergraduates had no need and received non-need-based gift aid.

GIFT AID (NEED-BASED) ***Total amount:*** $5,075,689 (57% federal, 33% state, 10% institutional). ***Receiving aid:*** Freshmen: 29% (408); all full-time undergraduates: 28% (1,570). ***Average award:*** Freshmen: $3129; Undergraduates: $3226. ***Scholarships, grants, and awards:*** Federal Pell, FSEOG, state, private, college/university gift aid from institutional funds, Academic Competitiveness Grant, National Smart Grant, TEACH Grant.

GIFT AID (NON-NEED-BASED) ***Total amount:*** $23,458,536 (11% state, 81% institutional, 8% external sources). ***Receiving aid:*** Freshmen: 37% (517). Undergraduates: 31% (1,717). ***Average award:*** Freshmen: $4535. Undergraduates: $4817. ***Scholarships, grants, and awards by category:*** *Academic interests/achievement:* 3,853 awards ($17,831,657 total): biological sciences, business, communication, education, English, foreign languages, general academic interests/achievements, mathematics, military science, physical sciences, premedicine, social sciences. *Creative arts/performance:* 112 awards ($107,981 total): art/fine arts, debating, music, theater/drama. *Special achievements/activities:* 291 awards ($745,280 total): leadership. *Special characteristics:* 197 awards

($721,004 total): children and siblings of alumni, children of faculty/staff, international students. ***Tuition waivers:*** Full or partial for employees or children of employees, senior citizens. ***ROTC:*** Army.

LOANS ***Student loans:*** $13,811,992 (48% need-based, 52% non-need-based). 51% of past graduating class borrowed through all loan programs. *Average indebtedness per student:* $16,858. ***Average need-based loan:*** Freshmen: $3306. Undergraduates: $4366. ***Parent loans:*** $2,132,298 (100% non-need-based). ***Programs:*** FFEL (Subsidized and Unsubsidized Stafford, PLUS), Perkins, Federal Nursing, state, college/university, alternative loans.

WORK-STUDY ***Federal work-study:*** Total amount: $275,027; 255 jobs averaging $1078. ***State or other work-study/employment:*** Total amount: $1,905,628 (100% non-need-based). 1,844 part-time jobs averaging $1033.

ATHLETIC AWARDS Total amount: $1,283,851 (100% non-need-based).

APPLYING FOR FINANCIAL AID ***Required financial aid forms:*** FAFSA, institution's own form. ***Financial aid deadline (priority):*** 4/1. ***Notification date:*** Continuous beginning 4/1. Students must reply within 4 weeks of notification.

CONTACT Kathy Elsea, Director of Financial Aid, Truman State University, 103 McClain Hall, Kirksville, MO 63501-4221, 660-785-4130 or toll-free 800-892-7792 (in-state). *Fax:* 660-785-7389. *E-mail:* kelsea@truman.edu.

TUFTS UNIVERSITY

Medford, MA

Tuition & fees: $38,840 **Average undergraduate aid package: $30,363**

ABOUT THE INSTITUTION Independent, coed. ***Awards:*** bachelor's, master's, doctoral, and first professional degrees and post-master's certificates. 64 undergraduate majors. ***Total enrollment:*** 10,030. Undergraduates: 5,044. Freshmen: 1,297.

UNDERGRADUATE EXPENSES for 2008–09 ***Application fee:*** $70. ***Comprehensive fee:*** $49,358 includes full-time tuition ($37,952), mandatory fees ($888), and room and board ($10,518). ***College room only:*** $5428. Room and board charges vary according to board plan. ***Payment plans:*** Tuition prepayment, installment.

FRESHMAN FINANCIAL AID (Fall 2008, est.) 705 applied for aid; of those 74% were deemed to have need. 100% of freshmen with need received aid; of those 100% had need fully met. ***Average percent of need met:*** 100% (excluding resources awarded to replace EFC). ***Average financial aid package:*** $30,298 (excluding resources awarded to replace EFC). 1% of all full-time freshmen had no need and received non-need-based gift aid.

UNDERGRADUATE FINANCIAL AID (Fall 2008, est.) 2,375 applied for aid; of those 86% were deemed to have need. 98% of undergraduates with need received aid; of those 100% had need fully met. ***Average percent of need met:*** 100% (excluding resources awarded to replace EFC). ***Average financial aid package:*** $30,363 (excluding resources awarded to replace EFC). 1% of all full-time undergraduates had no need and received non-need-based gift aid.

GIFT AID (NEED-BASED) ***Total amount:*** $53,326,724 (7% federal, 2% state, 88% institutional, 3% external sources). ***Receiving aid:*** Freshmen: 36% (470); all full-time undergraduates: 35% (1,843). ***Average award:*** Freshmen: $28,922; Undergraduates: $27,590. ***Scholarships, grants, and awards:*** Federal Pell, FSEOG, state, private, college/university gift aid from institutional funds.

GIFT AID (NON-NEED-BASED) ***Total amount:*** $669,734 (3% federal, 7% state, 31% institutional, 59% external sources). ***Receiving aid:*** Freshmen: 1% (15). Undergraduates: 1% (47). ***Average award:*** Freshmen: $500. Undergraduates: $500. ***Scholarships, grants, and awards by category:*** *Academic interests/achievement:* 62 awards ($31,000 total): general academic interests/achievements. ***Tuition waivers:*** Full or partial for employees or children of employees. ***ROTC:*** Army cooperative, Naval cooperative, Air Force cooperative.

LOANS ***Student loans:*** $8,321,678 (83% need-based, 17% non-need-based). 40% of past graduating class borrowed through all loan programs. *Average indebtedness per student:* $23,687. ***Average need-based loan:*** Freshmen: $2311. Undergraduates: $3698. ***Parent loans:*** $12,724,406 (100% non-need-based). ***Programs:*** FFEL (Subsidized and Unsubsidized Stafford, PLUS), Perkins, college/university.

WORK-STUDY ***Federal work-study:*** Total amount: $2,801,330; 1,528 jobs averaging $1822. ***State or other work-study/employment:*** Total amount: $170,600 (100% need-based). 68 part-time jobs averaging $1895.

APPLYING FOR FINANCIAL AID ***Required financial aid forms:*** FAFSA, CSS Financial Aid PROFILE, noncustodial (divorced/separated) parent's statement, business/farm supplement, federal income tax form(s). ***Financial aid deadline:*** 2/15. ***Notification date:*** 4/5. Students must reply by 5/1.

CONTACT Patricia C. Reilly, Director of Financial Aid, Tufts University, Dowling Hall, Medford, MA 02155, 617-627-5912. *Fax:* 617-627-3987. *E-mail:* patricia.reilly@tufts.edu.

TUI UNIVERSITY

Cypress, CA

CONTACT Financial Aid Office, TUI University, 5665 Plaza Drive, 3rd Floor, Cypress, CA 90630, 714-816-0366.

TULANE UNIVERSITY

New Orleans, LA

ABOUT THE INSTITUTION Independent, coed. ***Awards:*** associate, bachelor's, master's, doctoral, and first professional degrees and post-bachelor's certificates. 82 undergraduate majors. ***Total enrollment:*** 11,157. Undergraduates: 6,749. Freshmen: 1,560.

GIFT AID (NEED-BASED) ***Scholarships, grants, and awards:*** Federal Pell, FSEOG, state, private, college/university gift aid from institutional funds, Academic Competitiveness Grant, National Smart Grant.

LOANS ***Programs:*** FFEL (Subsidized and Unsubsidized Stafford, PLUS), Perkins.

APPLYING FOR FINANCIAL AID ***Required financial aid forms:*** FAFSA, CSS Financial Aid PROFILE, noncustodial (divorced/separated) parent's statement, business/farm supplement.

CONTACT Mr. Michael T. Goodman, Director of Financial Aid, Tulane University, 6823 St. Charles Avenue, New Orleans, LA 70118-5669, 504-865-5723 or toll-free 800-873-9283. *E-mail:* finaid@tulane.edu.

TUSCULUM COLLEGE

Greeneville, TN

ABOUT THE INSTITUTION Independent Presbyterian, coed. ***Awards:*** bachelor's and master's degrees. 37 undergraduate majors. ***Total enrollment:*** 2,241. Undergraduates: 2,070. Freshmen: 354.

GIFT AID (NEED-BASED) ***Scholarships, grants, and awards:*** Federal Pell, FSEOG, state, private, college/university gift aid from institutional funds.

GIFT AID (NON-NEED-BASED) ***Scholarships, grants, and awards by category:*** *Academic interests/achievement:* general academic interests/achievements. *Creative arts/performance:* music. *Special achievements/activities:* cheerleading/drum major, community service, leadership. *Special characteristics:* adult students, children of faculty/staff, local/state students.

LOANS ***Programs:*** FFEL (Subsidized and Unsubsidized Stafford, PLUS), Perkins.

APPLYING FOR FINANCIAL AID ***Required financial aid form:*** FAFSA.

CONTACT Karon Chapman, Director of Financial Aid, Tusculum College, 5049 Tusculum Station, Greeneville, TN 37743-9997, 423-636-7377 or toll-free 800-729-0256. *Fax:* 615-250-4968. *E-mail:* kchapman@tusculum.edu.

TUSKEGEE UNIVERSITY

Tuskegee, AL

Tuition & fees: $16,160 **Average undergraduate aid package: $13,824**

ABOUT THE INSTITUTION Independent, coed. ***Awards:*** bachelor's, master's, doctoral, and first professional degrees. 43 undergraduate majors. ***Total enrollment:*** 2,994. Undergraduates: 2,541. Freshmen: 723. Federal methodology is used as a basis for awarding need-based institutional aid.

UNDERGRADUATE EXPENSES for 2009–10 ***Application fee:*** $25. ***Comprehensive fee:*** $23,510 includes full-time tuition ($15,450), mandatory fees ($710), and room and board ($7350). ***Part-time tuition:*** $500 per credit.

FRESHMAN FINANCIAL AID (Fall 2007) 635 applied for aid; of those 85% were deemed to have need. 92% of freshmen with need received aid; of those 70% had need fully met. ***Average percent of need met:*** 85% (excluding resources awarded to replace EFC). ***Average financial aid package:*** $13,824 (excluding resources awarded to replace EFC). 28% of all full-time freshmen had no need and received non-need-based gift aid.

UNDERGRADUATE FINANCIAL AID (Fall 2007) 2,519 applied for aid; of those 85% were deemed to have need. 92% of undergraduates with need received aid; of those 70% had need fully met. ***Average percent of need met:*** 85% (excluding resources awarded to replace EFC). ***Average financial aid package:***

$13,824 (excluding resources awarded to replace EFC). 22% of all full-time undergraduates had no need and received non-need-based gift aid.

GIFT AID (NEED-BASED) ***Total amount:*** $5,459,147 (98% federal, 2% institutional). ***Receiving aid:*** Freshmen: 56% (422); all full-time undergraduates: 61% (1,675). ***Average award:*** Freshmen: $8000; Undergraduates: $8000. ***Scholarships, grants, and awards:*** Federal Pell, FSEOG, state, private, college/university gift aid from institutional funds, United Negro College Fund, Federal Nursing.

GIFT AID (NON-NEED-BASED) ***Total amount:*** $3,408,097 (45% institutional, 55% external sources). ***Receiving aid:*** Freshmen: 36% (273). Undergraduates: 35% (951). ***Average award:*** Freshmen: $6000. Undergraduates: $6000. ***Scholarships, grants, and awards by category:*** *Academic interests/achievement:* 1,714 awards ($9,086,319 total): general academic interests/achievements. *Creative arts/performance:* 108 awards ($68,400 total): music. *Special characteristics:* 36 awards ($157,002 total): children of faculty/staff, local/state students. ***ROTC:*** Army, Air Force.

LOANS ***Student loans:*** $16,456,358 (53% need-based, 47% non-need-based). 91% of past graduating class borrowed through all loan programs. *Average indebtedness per student:* $30,000. ***Average need-based loan:*** Freshmen: $5625. Undergraduates: $6006. ***Parent loans:*** $3,098,631 (100% non-need-based). ***Programs:*** FFEL (Subsidized and Unsubsidized Stafford, PLUS), Perkins.

WORK-STUDY ***Federal work-study:*** Total amount: $830,097; 525 jobs averaging $1879. ***State or other work-study/employment:*** Total amount: $1,318,823 (100% non-need-based). 425 part-time jobs averaging $4739.

ATHLETIC AWARDS Total amount: $1,145,218 (100% non-need-based).

APPLYING FOR FINANCIAL AID ***Required financial aid forms:*** FAFSA, institution's own form. ***Financial aid deadline (priority):*** 3/31. ***Notification date:*** Continuous. Students must reply within 2 weeks of notification.

CONTACT Mr. A. D. James Jr., Director of Student Financial Services, Tuskegee University, Office of Student Financial Services, Tuskegee, AL 36088, 334-727-8201 or toll-free 800-622-6531. *Fax:* 334-724-4227. *E-mail:* jamesad@tuskegee.edu.

UNION COLLEGE
Barbourville, KY

Tuition & fees: $17,894 **Average undergraduate aid package: $17,397**

ABOUT THE INSTITUTION Independent United Methodist, coed. ***Awards:*** bachelor's and master's degrees and post-bachelor's certificates. 21 undergraduate majors. ***Total enrollment:*** 1,498. Undergraduates: 820. Freshmen: 243. Federal methodology is used as a basis for awarding need-based institutional aid.

UNDERGRADUATE EXPENSES for 2008–09 ***Application fee:*** $10. ***Comprehensive fee:*** $23,694 includes full-time tuition ($17,384), mandatory fees ($510), and room and board ($5800). ***College room only:*** $2500. Full-time tuition and fees vary according to course load and location. Room and board charges vary according to board plan and student level. ***Part-time tuition:*** $280 per hour. ***Part-time fees:*** $20 per term. ***Payment plan:*** Installment.

FRESHMAN FINANCIAL AID (Fall 2008, est.) 231 applied for aid; of those 93% were deemed to have need. 100% of freshmen with need received aid; of those 31% had need fully met. ***Average percent of need met:*** 82% (excluding resources awarded to replace EFC). ***Average financial aid package:*** $17,120 (excluding resources awarded to replace EFC). 7% of all full-time freshmen had no need and received non-need-based gift aid.

UNDERGRADUATE FINANCIAL AID (Fall 2008, est.) 752 applied for aid; of those 94% were deemed to have need. 100% of undergraduates with need received aid; of those 32% had need fully met. ***Average percent of need met:*** 85% (excluding resources awarded to replace EFC). ***Average financial aid package:*** $17,397 (excluding resources awarded to replace EFC). 6% of all full-time undergraduates had no need and received non-need-based gift aid.

GIFT AID (NEED-BASED) ***Total amount:*** $5,732,502 (36% federal, 30% state, 30% institutional, 4% external sources). ***Receiving aid:*** Freshmen: 93% (215); all full-time undergraduates: 92% (696). ***Average award:*** Freshmen: $11,600; Undergraduates: $11,074. ***Scholarships, grants, and awards:*** Federal Pell, FSEOG, state, college/university gift aid from institutional funds.

GIFT AID (NON-NEED-BASED) ***Total amount:*** $420,430 (100% state). ***Receiving aid:*** Freshmen: 18% (42). Undergraduates: 14% (103). ***Average award:*** Freshmen: $18,791. Undergraduates: $15,756. ***Scholarships, grants, and awards by category:*** *Academic interests/achievement:* 167 awards ($554,608 total): general academic interests/achievements. *Creative arts/performance:* 22 awards ($35,959 total): music. *Special achievements/activities:* 26 awards ($108,448 total): cheerleading/drum major. *Special characteristics:* 30 awards ($38,619 total): children and siblings of alumni, religious affiliation. ***Tuition waivers:*** Full or partial for employees or children of employees, senior citizens. ***ROTC:*** Army cooperative.

LOANS ***Student loans:*** $7,127,324 (55% need-based, 45% non-need-based). 100% of past graduating class borrowed through all loan programs. *Average indebtedness per student:* $37,000. ***Average need-based loan:*** Freshmen: $6118. Undergraduates: $6709. ***Parent loans:*** $512,346 (100% need-based). ***Programs:*** FFEL (Subsidized and Unsubsidized Stafford, PLUS), Perkins, college/university.

WORK-STUDY ***Federal work-study:*** Total amount: $166,581; 158 jobs averaging $1124. ***State or other work-study/employment:*** Part-time jobs available.

ATHLETIC AWARDS Total amount: $3,248,897 (100% need-based).

APPLYING FOR FINANCIAL AID ***Required financial aid form:*** FAFSA. ***Financial aid deadline (priority):*** 3/15. ***Notification date:*** Continuous beginning 4/1. Students must reply within 2 weeks of notification.

CONTACT Mrs. Sue Buttery, Associate Dean of Financial Aid and Admission, Union College, 310 College Street, Barbourville, KY 40906-1499, 606-546-1224 or toll-free 800-489-8646. *Fax:* 606-546-1556. *E-mail:* sbuttery@unionky.edu.

UNION COLLEGE
Lincoln, NE

CONTACT Mr. John C. Burdick, IV, Director of Financial Aid, Union College, 3800 South 48th Street, Lincoln, NE 68506-4300, 800-228-4600. *Fax:* 402-486-2895. *E-mail:* financialaid@ucollege.edu.

UNION COLLEGE
Schenectady, NY

Comprehensive fee: $48,552 **Average undergraduate aid package: $29,188**

ABOUT THE INSTITUTION Independent, coed. ***Awards:*** bachelor's degrees. 28 undergraduate majors. ***Total enrollment:*** 2,240. Undergraduates: 2,240. Freshmen: 580. Both federal and institutional methodology are used as a basis for awarding need-based institutional aid.

UNDERGRADUATE EXPENSES for 2008–09 ***Application fee:*** $50. ***Comprehensive fee:*** $48,552. ***Payment plan:*** Installment.

FRESHMAN FINANCIAL AID (Fall 2008, est.) 296 applied for aid; of those 86% were deemed to have need. 100% of freshmen with need received aid; of those 89% had need fully met. ***Average percent of need met:*** 100% (excluding resources awarded to replace EFC). ***Average financial aid package:*** $30,046 (excluding resources awarded to replace EFC). 14% of all full-time freshmen had no need and received non-need-based gift aid.

UNDERGRADUATE FINANCIAL AID (Fall 2008, est.) 1,171 applied for aid; of those 90% were deemed to have need. 100% of undergraduates with need received aid; of those 99% had need fully met. ***Average percent of need met:*** 99% (excluding resources awarded to replace EFC). ***Average financial aid package:*** $29,188 (excluding resources awarded to replace EFC). 12% of all full-time undergraduates had no need and received non-need-based gift aid.

GIFT AID (NEED-BASED) ***Total amount:*** $28,986,469 (6% federal, 4% state, 89% institutional, 1% external sources). ***Receiving aid:*** Freshmen: 44% (253); all full-time undergraduates: 47% (1,036). ***Average award:*** Freshmen: $28,957; Undergraduates: $25,278. ***Scholarships, grants, and awards:*** Federal Pell, FSEOG, state, private, college/university gift aid from institutional funds.

GIFT AID (NON-NEED-BASED) ***Total amount:*** $4,061,791 (9% federal, 4% state, 85% institutional, 2% external sources). ***Receiving aid:*** Freshmen: 5% (27). Undergraduates: 2% (49). ***Average award:*** Freshmen: $8106. Undergraduates: $10,273. ***Scholarships, grants, and awards by category:*** *Academic interests/achievement:* 341 awards ($3,388,665 total): general academic interests/achievements. *Special characteristics:* 22 awards: children of faculty/staff. ***Tuition waivers:*** Full or partial for employees or children of employees, senior citizens. ***ROTC:*** Army cooperative, Naval cooperative, Air Force cooperative.

LOANS ***Student loans:*** $8,292,831 (56% need-based, 44% non-need-based). 52% of past graduating class borrowed through all loan programs. *Average indebtedness per student:* $23,000. ***Average need-based loan:*** Freshmen: $3730. Undergraduates: $4697. ***Parent loans:*** $3,419,866 (100% non-need-based). ***Programs:*** FFEL (Subsidized and Unsubsidized Stafford, PLUS), Perkins, college/university.

WORK-STUDY ***Federal work-study:*** Total amount: $575,000; 587 jobs averaging $1609. ***State or other work-study/employment:*** Total amount: $79,000 (100% need-based). 79 part-time jobs averaging $1802.

APPLYING FOR FINANCIAL AID ***Required financial aid forms:*** FAFSA, CSS Financial Aid PROFILE, state aid form, noncustodial (divorced/separated) parent's statement, business/farm supplement. ***Financial aid deadline:*** 2/1 (priority: 2/1). ***Notification date:*** 4/1. Students must reply by 5/1.

CONTACT Ms. Linda Parker, Director of Financial Aid and Family Financing, Union College, Grant Hall, Schenectady, NY 12308-2311, 518-388-6123 or toll-free 888-843-6688 (in-state). *Fax:* 518-388-8052. *E-mail:* finaid@union.edu.

UNION INSTITUTE & UNIVERSITY

Cincinnati, OH

CONTACT Ms. Rebecca Zackerman, Director of Financial Aid, Union Institute & University, 440 East McMillan Street, Cincinnati, OH 45206-1925, 513-861-6400 or toll-free 800-486-3116. *Fax:* 513-861-0779. *E-mail:* bzackerman@tui.edu.

UNION UNIVERSITY

Jackson, TN

Tuition & fees: $19,610 **Average undergraduate aid package: $15,036**

ABOUT THE INSTITUTION Independent Southern Baptist, coed. ***Awards:*** associate, bachelor's, master's, doctoral, and first professional degrees and post-master's certificates. 66 undergraduate majors. ***Total enrollment:*** 3,700. Undergraduates: 2,574. Freshmen: 462. Federal methodology is used as a basis for awarding need-based institutional aid.

UNDERGRADUATE EXPENSES for 2008–09 ***Application fee:*** $35. ***Comprehensive fee:*** $26,110 includes full-time tuition ($18,980), mandatory fees ($630), and room and board ($6500). Full-time tuition and fees vary according to course load. Room and board charges vary according to board plan and housing facility. ***Part-time tuition:*** $655 per credit hour. ***Part-time fees:*** $200 per term. ***Payment plans:*** Installment, deferred payment.

FRESHMAN FINANCIAL AID (Fall 2008, est.) 437 applied for aid; of those 72% were deemed to have need. 100% of freshmen with need received aid; of those 29% had need fully met. ***Average percent of need met:*** 80% (excluding resources awarded to replace EFC). ***Average financial aid package:*** $16,258 (excluding resources awarded to replace EFC). 18% of all full-time freshmen had no need and received non-need-based gift aid.

UNDERGRADUATE FINANCIAL AID (Fall 2008, est.) 1,634 applied for aid; of those 67% were deemed to have need. 100% of undergraduates with need received aid; of those 25% had need fully met. ***Average percent of need met:*** 75% (excluding resources awarded to replace EFC). ***Average financial aid package:*** $15,036 (excluding resources awarded to replace EFC). 24% of all full-time undergraduates had no need and received non-need-based gift aid.

GIFT AID (NEED-BASED) ***Total amount:*** $4,341,106 (37% federal, 22% state, 41% institutional). ***Receiving aid:*** Freshmen: 47% (236); all full-time undergraduates: 47% (795). ***Average award:*** Freshmen: $5503; Undergraduates: $5085. ***Scholarships, grants, and awards:*** Federal Pell, FSEOG, state, private, college/university gift aid from institutional funds.

GIFT AID (NON-NEED-BASED) ***Total amount:*** $16,012,431 (1% federal, 18% state, 76% institutional, 5% external sources). ***Receiving aid:*** Freshmen: 62% (315). Undergraduates: 60% (1,017). ***Average award:*** Freshmen: $5433. Undergraduates: $5360. ***Scholarships, grants, and awards by category:*** *Academic interests/achievement:* 1,112 awards ($6,068,509 total): business, communication, education, engineering/technologies, general academic interests/achievements, mathematics, premedicine, religion/biblical studies. *Creative arts/performance:* 107 awards ($427,596 total): art/fine arts, cinema/film/broadcasting, journalism/publications, music, theater/drama. *Special achievements/activities:* 933 awards ($1,420,802 total): cheerleading/drum major, leadership, religious involvement. *Special characteristics:* 1,013 awards ($3,601,276 total): children and siblings of alumni, children of current students, children of educators, children of faculty/staff, ethnic background, international students, members of minority groups, relatives of clergy, religious affiliation, siblings of current students, spouses of current students, twins. ***Tuition waivers:*** Full or partial for children of alumni, employees or children of employees.

LOANS ***Student loans:*** $5,365,542 (43% need-based, 57% non-need-based). 58% of past graduating class borrowed through all loan programs. *Average indebtedness per student:* $21,543. ***Average need-based loan:*** Freshmen: $3754. Undergraduates: $4615. ***Parent loans:*** $1,132,622 (100% non-need-based). ***Programs:*** FFEL (Subsidized and Unsubsidized Stafford, PLUS), Perkins, alternative loans.

WORK-STUDY ***Federal work-study:*** Total amount: $200,025; 118 jobs averaging $1695. ***State or other work-study/employment:*** Total amount: $252,106 (100% non-need-based). 195 part-time jobs averaging $1395.

ATHLETIC AWARDS Total amount: $1,681,517 (100% non-need-based).

APPLYING FOR FINANCIAL AID ***Required financial aid forms:*** FAFSA, institution's own form. ***Financial aid deadline (priority):*** 3/1. ***Notification date:*** Continuous. Students must reply by 5/1 or within 2 weeks of notification.

CONTACT John Thomas Brandt, Director of Financial Aid, Union University, 1050 Union University Drive, Jackson, TN 38305-3697, 731-661-5015 or toll-free 800-33-UNION. *Fax:* 731-661-5570. *E-mail:* jbrandt@uu.edu.

UNITED STATES SPORTS ACADEMY

Daphne, AL

CONTACT Financial Aid Office, United States Sports Academy, One Academy Drive, Daphne, AL 36526-7055, 251-626-3303.

UNITED TALMUDICAL SEMINARY

Brooklyn, NY

CONTACT Financial Aid Office, United Talmudical Seminary, 82 Lee Avenue, Brooklyn, NY 11211-7900, 718-963-9770 Ext. 309.

UNITY COLLEGE

Unity, ME

Tuition & fees: $20,750 **Average undergraduate aid package: $16,173**

ABOUT THE INSTITUTION Independent, coed. 14 undergraduate majors. Federal methodology is used as a basis for awarding need-based institutional aid.

UNDERGRADUATE EXPENSES for 2008–09 ***Comprehensive fee:*** $28,430 includes full-time tuition ($19,650), mandatory fees ($1100), and room and board ($7680).

FRESHMAN FINANCIAL AID (Fall 2008, est.) 154 applied for aid; of those 83% were deemed to have need. 100% of freshmen with need received aid; of those 15% had need fully met. ***Average percent of need met:*** 77% (excluding resources awarded to replace EFC). ***Average financial aid package:*** $16,432 (excluding resources awarded to replace EFC). 19% of all full-time freshmen had no need and received non-need-based gift aid.

UNDERGRADUATE FINANCIAL AID (Fall 2008, est.) 489 applied for aid; of those 88% were deemed to have need. 100% of undergraduates with need received aid; of those 14% had need fully met. ***Average percent of need met:*** 77% (excluding resources awarded to replace EFC). ***Average financial aid package:*** $16,173 (excluding resources awarded to replace EFC). 14% of all full-time undergraduates had no need and received non-need-based gift aid.

GIFT AID (NEED-BASED) ***Total amount:*** $4,209,325 (20% federal, 5% state, 69% institutional, 6% external sources). ***Receiving aid:*** Freshmen: 78% (128); all full-time undergraduates: 80% (428). ***Average award:*** Freshmen: $11,049; Undergraduates: $9794. ***Scholarships, grants, and awards:*** Federal Pell, FSEOG, state, private, college/university gift aid from institutional funds.

GIFT AID (NON-NEED-BASED) ***Total amount:*** $283,567 (2% state, 82% institutional, 16% external sources). ***Receiving aid:*** Freshmen: 2% (3). Undergraduates: 2% (13). ***Average award:*** Freshmen: $3100. Undergraduates: $2876. ***Scholarships, grants, and awards by category:*** *Academic interests/achievement:* 253 awards ($995,875 total): general academic interests/achievements. *Special achievements/activities:* community service, leadership. *Special characteristics:* 67 awards ($155,850 total): children of educators, general special characteristics, local/state students, members of minority groups.

LOANS ***Student loans:*** $4,760,286 (69% need-based, 31% non-need-based). ***Average need-based loan:*** Freshmen: $5011. Undergraduates: $6118. ***Parent loans:*** $1,046,599 (33% need-based, 67% non-need-based). ***Programs:*** FFEL (Subsidized and Unsubsidized Stafford, PLUS), Perkins.

WORK-STUDY ***Federal work-study:*** Total amount: $470,403; 334 jobs averaging $1408. ***State or other work-study/employment:*** Total amount: $10,458 (100% non-need-based). 4 part-time jobs averaging $1115.

APPLYING FOR FINANCIAL AID ***Required financial aid form:*** FAFSA. ***Financial aid deadline:*** Continuous. ***Notification date:*** Continuous beginning 3/10. Students must reply within 2 weeks of notification.

CONTACT Mr. Rand E. Newell, Director of Financial Aid, Unity College, 90 Quaker Hill Road, Unity, ME 04988, 207-948-3131 Ext. 201. *Fax:* 207-948-2018. *E-mail:* rnewell@unity.edu.

UNIVERSIDAD ADVENTISTA DE LAS ANTILLAS

Mayagüez, PR

CONTACT Mr. Heriberto Juarbe, Director of Financial Aid, Universidad Adventista de las Antillas, Box 118, Mayagüez, PR 00681-0118, 787-834-9595 Ext. 2200. *Fax:* 787-834-9597.

UNIVERSIDAD DEL ESTE

Carolina, PR

CONTACT Mr. Clotilde Santiago, Director of Financial Aid, Universidad del Este, Apartado 2010, Carolina, PR 00928, 787-257-7373 Ext. 3300.

UNIVERSIDAD DEL TURABO

Gurabo, PR

CONTACT Ms. Ivette Vázquez Ríos, Directora Oficina de Asistencia Económica, Universidad del Turabo, Apartado 3030, Gurabo, PR 00778-3030, 787-743-7979 Ext. 4352. *Fax:* 787-743-7979.

UNIVERSIDAD FLET

Miami, FL

CONTACT Financial Aid Office, Universidad FLET, 14540 Southwest 136th Street, Suite 108, Miami, FL 33186, 305-232-5880 or toll-free 888-376-3538.

UNIVERSIDAD METROPOLITANA

San Juan, PR

CONTACT Economic Assistant Director, Universidad Metropolitana, Call Box 21150, Rio Piedras, PR 00928-1150, 787-766-1717 Ext. 6586 or toll-free 800-747-8362 (out-of-state).

UNIVERSITY AT ALBANY, STATE UNIVERSITY OF NEW YORK

Albany, NY

Tuition & fees (NY res): $6388 **Average undergraduate aid package: $8584**

ABOUT THE INSTITUTION State-supported, coed. ***Awards:*** bachelor's, master's, and doctoral degrees and post-bachelor's and post-master's certificates. 62 undergraduate majors. ***Total enrollment:*** 18,202. Undergraduates: 13,246. Freshmen: 2,410. Federal methodology is used as a basis for awarding need-based institutional aid.

UNDERGRADUATE EXPENSES for 2008–09 ***Application fee:*** $40. ***Tuition, state resident:*** full-time $4660; part-time $207 per credit. ***Tuition, nonresident:*** full-time $11,740; part-time $536 per credit. ***Required fees:*** full-time $1728. Part-time tuition and fees vary according to course load. ***College room and board:*** $9778; ***Room only:*** $6052. Room and board charges vary according to board plan and housing facility. ***Payment plan:*** Installment.

FRESHMAN FINANCIAL AID (Fall 2007) 2,096 applied for aid; of those 65% were deemed to have need. 98% of freshmen with need received aid; of those 16% had need fully met. ***Average percent of need met:*** 74% (excluding resources awarded to replace EFC). ***Average financial aid package:*** $8961 (excluding resources awarded to replace EFC). 9% of all full-time freshmen had no need and received non-need-based gift aid.

UNDERGRADUATE FINANCIAL AID (Fall 2007) 9,100 applied for aid; of those 73% were deemed to have need. 98% of undergraduates with need received aid; of those 10% had need fully met. ***Average percent of need met:*** 70% (excluding resources awarded to replace EFC). ***Average financial aid package:*** $8584 (excluding resources awarded to replace EFC). 6% of all full-time undergraduates had no need and received non-need-based gift aid.

GIFT AID (NEED-BASED) ***Total amount:*** $28,476,003 (46% federal, 46% state, 6% institutional, 2% external sources). ***Receiving aid:*** Freshmen: 49% (1,223); all full-time undergraduates: 50% (5,908). ***Average award:*** Freshmen: $5554; Undergraduates: $4936. ***Scholarships, grants, and awards:*** Federal Pell, FSEOG, state, private, college/university gift aid from institutional funds.

GIFT AID (NON-NEED-BASED) ***Total amount:*** $3,987,230 (5% federal, 30% state, 54% institutional, 11% external sources). ***Receiving aid:*** Freshmen: 2% (61). Undergraduates: 2% (204). ***Average award:*** Freshmen: $3332. Undergraduates: $2955. ***Scholarships, grants, and awards by category:*** *Academic interests/achievement:* 1,705 awards ($3,874,908 total): general academic interests/achievements. ***Tuition waivers:*** Full or partial for senior citizens. ***ROTC:*** Army, Air Force cooperative.

LOANS ***Student loans:*** $49,475,636 (50% need-based, 50% non-need-based). 70% of past graduating class borrowed through all loan programs. *Average indebtedness per student:* $18,189. ***Average need-based loan:*** Freshmen: $3875. Undergraduates: $4448. ***Parent loans:*** $7,595,522 (100% non-need-based). ***Programs:*** FFEL (Subsidized and Unsubsidized Stafford, PLUS), Perkins.

WORK-STUDY ***Federal work-study:*** Total amount: $1,789,347; 1,147 jobs averaging $1560. ***State or other work-study/employment:*** Total amount: $1,173,892 (59% need-based, 41% non-need-based). 218 part-time jobs averaging $5384.

ATHLETIC AWARDS Total amount: $3,235,637 (35% need-based, 65% non-need-based).

APPLYING FOR FINANCIAL AID ***Required financial aid forms:*** FAFSA, NY state residents should apply for TAP online at www.tapweb.org/totw/. ***Financial aid deadline (priority):*** 3/15. ***Notification date:*** Continuous beginning 3/15.

CONTACT Beth Post-Lundquist, Director of Financial Aid, University at Albany, State University of New York, 1400 Washington Avenue, Campus Center B52, Albany, NY 12222-0001, 518-442-3202 or toll-free 800-293-7869 (in-state). *Fax:* 518-442-5295. *E-mail:* sscweb@uamail.albany.edu.

UNIVERSITY AT BUFFALO, THE STATE UNIVERSITY OF NEW YORK

Buffalo, NY

Tuition & fees (NY res): $6595 **Average undergraduate aid package: $7166**

ABOUT THE INSTITUTION State-supported, coed. ***Awards:*** bachelor's, master's, doctoral, and first professional degrees and post-master's and first professional certificates. 71 undergraduate majors. ***Total enrollment:*** 28,192. Undergraduates: 19,022. Freshmen: 3,390. Federal methodology is used as a basis for awarding need-based institutional aid.

UNDERGRADUATE EXPENSES for 2008–09 ***Application fee:*** $40. ***Tuition, state resident:*** full-time $4660; part-time $194 per credit hour. ***Tuition, nonresident:*** full-time $11,740; part-time $489 per credit hour. ***Required fees:*** full-time $1935; $86 per credit hour. Part-time tuition and fees vary according to course load. ***College room and board:*** $9058; ***Room only:*** $5698. Room and board charges vary according to board plan and housing facility. ***Payment plan:*** Installment.

FRESHMAN FINANCIAL AID (Fall 2007) 2,572 applied for aid; of those 65% were deemed to have need. 97% of freshmen with need received aid; of those 3% had need fully met. ***Average percent of need met:*** 68% (excluding resources awarded to replace EFC). ***Average financial aid package:*** $6992 (excluding resources awarded to replace EFC). 27% of all full-time freshmen had no need and received non-need-based gift aid.

UNDERGRADUATE FINANCIAL AID (Fall 2007) 12,289 applied for aid; of those 74% were deemed to have need. 97% of undergraduates with need received aid; of those 5% had need fully met. ***Average percent of need met:*** 69% (excluding resources awarded to replace EFC). ***Average financial aid package:*** $7166 (excluding resources awarded to replace EFC). 16% of all full-time undergraduates had no need and received non-need-based gift aid.

GIFT AID (NEED-BASED) ***Total amount:*** $40,469,788 (48% federal, 46% state, 1% institutional, 5% external sources). ***Receiving aid:*** Freshmen: 15% (502); all full-time undergraduates: 45% (7,863). ***Average award:*** Freshmen: $3035; Undergraduates: $2858. ***Scholarships, grants, and awards:*** Federal Pell, FSEOG, state, private, college/university gift aid from institutional funds, Federal Nursing.

GIFT AID (NON-NEED-BASED) ***Total amount:*** $14,598,200 (100% institutional). ***Receiving aid:*** Freshmen: 3% (88). Undergraduates: 1% (181). ***Average award:***

Freshmen: $3298. Undergraduates: $2869. ***Tuition waivers:*** Full or partial for minority students. ***ROTC:*** Army cooperative.

LOANS ***Student loans:*** $36,474,704 (100% need-based). 87% of past graduating class borrowed through all loan programs. *Average indebtedness per student:* $52,591. ***Average need-based loan:*** Freshmen: $3372. Undergraduates: $4272. ***Parent loans:*** $6,807,470 (100% non-need-based). ***Programs:*** Federal Direct (Subsidized and Unsubsidized Stafford, PLUS), Perkins, Federal Nursing, college/university.

WORK-STUDY ***Federal work-study:*** Total amount: $1,275,581; 1,009 jobs averaging $1460. ***State or other work-study/employment:*** Total amount: $9,958,658 (100% non-need-based). 808 part-time jobs averaging $9111.

ATHLETIC AWARDS Total amount: $4,831,089 (100% non-need-based).

APPLYING FOR FINANCIAL AID ***Required financial aid form:*** FAFSA. ***Financial aid deadline (priority):*** 3/1. ***Notification date:*** Continuous. Students must reply by 5/1.

CONTACT Cindy L. Mack, Coordinator, Student Financial Services (SARFS), University at Buffalo, the State University of New York, 232 Capen Hall, Buffalo, NY 14260, 716-645-2450 or toll-free 888-UB-ADMIT. *Fax:* 716-645-7760. *E-mail:* src@buffalo.edu.

UNIVERSITY OF ADVANCING TECHNOLOGY

Tempe, AZ

Tuition & fees: $17,800 **Average undergraduate aid package: N/A**

ABOUT THE INSTITUTION Proprietary, coed, primarily men. ***Awards:*** associate, bachelor's, and master's degrees. 7 undergraduate majors. ***Total enrollment:*** 1,250. Undergraduates: 1,195. Freshmen: 596. Federal methodology is used as a basis for awarding need-based institutional aid.

UNDERGRADUATE EXPENSES for 2009–10 ***Comprehensive fee:*** $28,348 includes full-time tuition ($17,800) and room and board ($10,548). ***College room only:*** $6948.

GIFT AID (NEED-BASED) ***Total amount:*** $1,680,481 (100% federal). ***Scholarships, grants, and awards:*** Federal Pell, FSEOG, state, private, college/university gift aid from institutional funds.

GIFT AID (NON-NEED-BASED) ***Total amount:*** $854,264 (91% institutional, 9% external sources). ***Scholarships, grants, and awards by category:*** *Academic interests/achievement:* computer science, general academic interests/achievements. *Special characteristics:* children of faculty/staff, local/state students, veterans, veterans' children.

LOANS ***Student loans:*** $10,935,368 (33% need-based, 67% non-need-based). ***Parent loans:*** $3,075,414 (100% non-need-based). ***Programs:*** FFEL (Subsidized and Unsubsidized Stafford, PLUS).

WORK-STUDY ***Federal work-study:*** Total amount: $93,167; jobs available (averaging $3000).

APPLYING FOR FINANCIAL AID ***Required financial aid form:*** FAFSA. ***Financial aid deadline:*** Continuous.

CONTACT Financial Aid Administrator, University of Advancing Technology, 2625 West Baseline Road, Tempe, AZ 85283-1042, 602-383-8228 or toll-free 800-658-5744 (out-of-state). *Fax:* 602-383-8222. *E-mail:* fa@uat.edu.

THE UNIVERSITY OF AKRON

Akron, OH

Tuition & fees (OH res): $8612 **Average undergraduate aid package: $6961**

ABOUT THE INSTITUTION State-supported, coed. ***Awards:*** associate, bachelor's, master's, doctoral, and first professional degrees and post-bachelor's, post-master's, and first professional certificates (associate). 127 undergraduate majors. ***Total enrollment:*** 24,119. Undergraduates: 19,817. Freshmen: 4,149. Federal methodology is used as a basis for awarding need-based institutional aid.

UNDERGRADUATE EXPENSES for 2008–09 ***Application fee:*** $30. ***Tuition, state resident:*** full-time $7218; part-time $301 per credit. ***Tuition, nonresident:*** full-time $16,467; part-time $609 per credit. ***Required fees:*** full-time $1394; $49 per credit. Full-time tuition and fees vary according to course load, degree level, and location. Part-time tuition and fees vary according to course load, degree level, and location. ***College room and board:*** $8311; ***Room only:*** $5203. Room and board charges vary according to board plan and housing facility. ***Payment plan:*** Installment.

FRESHMAN FINANCIAL AID (Fall 2008, est.) 3,458 applied for aid; of those 78% were deemed to have need. 100% of freshmen with need received aid; of those 9% had need fully met. ***Average percent of need met:*** 53% (excluding resources awarded to replace EFC). ***Average financial aid package:*** $7200 (excluding resources awarded to replace EFC). 11% of all full-time freshmen had no need and received non-need-based gift aid.

UNDERGRADUATE FINANCIAL AID (Fall 2008, est.) 12,539 applied for aid; of those 78% were deemed to have need. 100% of undergraduates with need received aid; of those 8% had need fully met. ***Average percent of need met:*** 53% (excluding resources awarded to replace EFC). ***Average financial aid package:*** $6961 (excluding resources awarded to replace EFC). 8% of all full-time undergraduates had no need and received non-need-based gift aid.

GIFT AID (NEED-BASED) ***Total amount:*** $29,965,079 (79% federal, 21% state). ***Receiving aid:*** Freshmen: 36% (1,424); all full-time undergraduates: 33% (4,921). ***Average award:*** Freshmen: $5471; Undergraduates: $4976. ***Scholarships, grants, and awards:*** Federal Pell, FSEOG, state, college/university gift aid from institutional funds.

GIFT AID (NON-NEED-BASED) ***Total amount:*** $20,784,446 (7% state, 75% institutional, 18% external sources). ***Receiving aid:*** Freshmen: 38% (1,491). Undergraduates: 30% (4,550). ***Average award:*** Freshmen: $3498. Undergraduates: $3630. ***Scholarships, grants, and awards by category:*** *Academic interests/achievement:* 3,150 awards ($7,453,639 total): biological sciences, business, communication, computer science, education, engineering/technologies, English, foreign languages, general academic interests/achievements, health fields, home economics, humanities, international studies, mathematics, military science, physical sciences, premedicine, social sciences. *Creative arts/performance:* 206 awards ($237,587 total): applied art and design, art/fine arts, creative writing, dance, debating, general creative arts/performance, journalism/publications, music, performing arts, theater/drama. *Special achievements/activities:* 95 awards ($314,918 total): community service, general special achievements/activities, leadership, memberships. *Special characteristics:* 1,687 awards ($5,702,454 total): adult students, general special characteristics, handicapped students, international students, local/state students, members of minority groups, out-of-state students. ***Tuition waivers:*** Full or partial for employees or children of employees, senior citizens. ***ROTC:*** Army, Air Force cooperative.

LOANS ***Student loans:*** $105,099,370 (41% need-based, 59% non-need-based). 65% of past graduating class borrowed through all loan programs. *Average indebtedness per student:* $18,000. ***Average need-based loan:*** Freshmen: $3488. Undergraduates: $3988. ***Parent loans:*** $11,511,312 (100% non-need-based). ***Programs:*** FFEL (Subsidized and Unsubsidized Stafford, PLUS), Perkins, Federal Nursing, college/university.

WORK-STUDY ***Federal work-study:*** Total amount: $945,738; 635 jobs averaging $1489. ***State or other work-study/employment:*** Total amount: $5,269,314 (100% non-need-based). 2,934 part-time jobs averaging $1796.

ATHLETIC AWARDS Total amount: $5,278,007 (100% non-need-based).

APPLYING FOR FINANCIAL AID ***Required financial aid forms:*** FAFSA, institution's own form. ***Financial aid deadline (priority):*** 2/1. ***Notification date:*** Continuous beginning 4/1. Students must reply within 2 weeks of notification.

CONTACT Mr. Doug McNutt, Director of Financial Aid, The University of Akron, Office of Student Financial Aid, Akron, OH 44325-6211, 330-972-6334 or toll-free 800-655-4884. *Fax:* 330-972-7139. *E-mail:* mcnuttd@uakron.edu.

THE UNIVERSITY OF ALABAMA

Tuscaloosa, AL

Tuition & fees (AL res): $6400 **Average undergraduate aid package: $11,080**

ABOUT THE INSTITUTION State-supported, coed. ***Awards:*** bachelor's, master's, doctoral, and first professional degrees and post-master's certificates. 69 undergraduate majors. ***Total enrollment:*** 27,014. Undergraduates: 22,341. Freshmen: 5,116. Federal methodology is used as a basis for awarding need-based institutional aid.

UNDERGRADUATE EXPENSES for 2008–09 ***Application fee:*** $35. ***Tuition, state resident:*** full-time $6400. ***Tuition, nonresident:*** full-time $18,000. Full-time tuition and fees vary according to course load. Part-time tuition and fees vary according to course load. ***College room and board:*** $6430; ***Room only:*** $4100. Room and board charges vary according to board plan and housing facility. ***Payment plans:*** Installment, deferred payment.

FRESHMAN FINANCIAL AID (Fall 2007) 2,170 applied for aid; of those 66% were deemed to have need. 96% of freshmen with need received aid; of those 20% had need fully met. ***Average percent of need met:*** 73% (excluding

resources awarded to replace EFC). ***Average financial aid package:*** $10,799 (excluding resources awarded to replace EFC). 38% of all full-time freshmen had no need and received non-need-based gift aid.

UNDERGRADUATE FINANCIAL AID (Fall 2007) 8,986 applied for aid; of those 81% were deemed to have need. 90% of undergraduates with need received aid; of those 15% had need fully met. ***Average percent of need met:*** 70% (excluding resources awarded to replace EFC). ***Average financial aid package:*** $11,080 (excluding resources awarded to replace EFC). 29% of all full-time undergraduates had no need and received non-need-based gift aid.

GIFT AID (NEED-BASED) ***Total amount:*** $13,795,736 (92% federal, 4% state, 4% institutional). ***Receiving aid:*** Freshmen: 13% (577); all full-time undergraduates: 17% (3,358). ***Average award:*** Freshmen: $4119; Undergraduates: $3722. ***Scholarships, grants, and awards:*** Federal Pell, FSEOG, state, private, college/university gift aid from institutional funds, Federal Nursing.

GIFT AID (NON-NEED-BASED) ***Total amount:*** $29,227,164 (77% institutional, 23% external sources). ***Receiving aid:*** Freshmen: 13% (578). Undergraduates: 10% (1,866). ***Average award:*** Freshmen: $5072. Undergraduates: $4986. ***Scholarships, grants, and awards by category:*** *Academic interests/achievement:* 6,421 awards ($26,949,083 total): area/ethnic studies, biological sciences, business, communication, computer science, education, engineering/technologies, English, foreign languages, general academic interests/achievements, home economics, library science, mathematics, military science, physical sciences, premedicine, social sciences. *Creative arts/performance:* 415 awards ($836,144 total): art/fine arts, cinema/film/broadcasting, creative writing, dance, debating, journalism/publications, music, theater/drama. *Special achievements/activities:* 507 awards ($865,333 total): cheerleading/drum major, community service, general special achievements/activities, hobbies/interests, junior miss. *Special characteristics:* children of union members/company employees, general special characteristics, international students, out-of-state students, spouses of deceased or disabled public servants. ***Tuition waivers:*** Full or partial for employees or children of employees. ***ROTC:*** Army, Air Force.

LOANS ***Student loans:*** $63,024,360 (42% need-based, 58% non-need-based). 48% of past graduating class borrowed through all loan programs. *Average indebtedness per student:* $18,896. ***Average need-based loan:*** Freshmen: $3596. Undergraduates: $4319. ***Parent loans:*** $16,574,809 (100% non-need-based). ***Programs:*** Federal Direct (Subsidized and Unsubsidized Stafford, PLUS), Perkins, college/university, private student loans.

WORK-STUDY ***Federal work-study:*** Total amount: $1,459,102; 621 jobs averaging $2111.

ATHLETIC AWARDS Total amount: $7,891,875 (100% non-need-based).

APPLYING FOR FINANCIAL AID ***Required financial aid form:*** FAFSA. ***Financial aid deadline (priority):*** 3/1. ***Notification date:*** 4/1. Students must reply within 3 weeks of notification.

CONTACT Helen Leathers, Associate Director of Financial Aid, The University of Alabama, Box 870162, Tuscaloosa, AL 35487-0162, 205-348-6756 or toll-free 800-933-BAMA. *Fax:* 205-348-2989. *E-mail:* helen.leathers@ua.edu.

THE UNIVERSITY OF ALABAMA AT BIRMINGHAM

Birmingham, AL

Tuition & fees (AL res): $4664 **Average undergraduate aid package: $9049**

ABOUT THE INSTITUTION State-supported, coed. ***Awards:*** bachelor's, master's, doctoral, and first professional degrees and post-bachelor's and post-master's certificates. 49 undergraduate majors. ***Total enrollment:*** 16,149. Undergraduates: 10,369. Freshmen: 1,277. Federal methodology is used as a basis for awarding need-based institutional aid.

UNDERGRADUATE EXPENSES for 2008–09 ***Application fee:*** $35. ***Tuition, state resident:*** full-time $3792; part-time $158 per credit hour. ***Tuition, nonresident:*** full-time $9480; part-time $395 per credit hour. ***Required fees:*** full-time $872; $24 per credit hour or $124 per term. ***College room and board:*** $7820; ***Room only:*** $4170.

FRESHMAN FINANCIAL AID (Fall 2008, est.) 817 applied for aid; of those 69% were deemed to have need. 98% of freshmen with need received aid; of those 21% had need fully met. ***Average percent of need met:*** 49% (excluding resources awarded to replace EFC). ***Average financial aid package:*** $9221 (excluding resources awarded to replace EFC). 30% of all full-time freshmen had no need and received non-need-based gift aid.

UNDERGRADUATE FINANCIAL AID (Fall 2008, est.) 4,543 applied for aid; of those 80% were deemed to have need. 98% of undergraduates with need received aid; of those 16% had need fully met. ***Average percent of need met:*** 51% (excluding resources awarded to replace EFC). ***Average financial aid package:*** $9049 (excluding resources awarded to replace EFC). 17% of all full-time undergraduates had no need and received non-need-based gift aid.

GIFT AID (NEED-BASED) ***Total amount:*** $11,541,693 (94% federal, 5% state, 1% external sources). ***Receiving aid:*** Freshmen: 25% (311); all full-time undergraduates: 28% (2,102). ***Average award:*** Freshmen: $4759; Undergraduates: $4484. ***Scholarships, grants, and awards:*** Federal Pell, FSEOG, state, private, college/university gift aid from institutional funds, United Negro College Fund.

GIFT AID (NON-NEED-BASED) ***Total amount:*** $2,229,187 (1% federal, 3% state, 47% institutional, 49% external sources). ***Receiving aid:*** Freshmen: 24% (295). Undergraduates: 13% (1,006). ***Average award:*** Freshmen: $6778. Undergraduates: $6018. ***Scholarships, grants, and awards by category:*** *Academic interests/achievement:* business, communication, computer science, engineering/technologies, general academic interests/achievements, health fields, mathematics. *Creative arts/performance:* art/fine arts, music, performing arts, theater/drama. *Special achievements/activities:* cheerleading/drum major, junior miss, leadership, memberships, religious involvement. *Special characteristics:* adult students, children and siblings of alumni, children of current students, children of educators, children of faculty/staff, children of public servants, children of union members/company employees, children of workers in trades, children with a deceased or disabled parent, ethnic background, first-generation college students, general special characteristics, handicapped students, local/state students, married students, members of minority groups, out-of-state students, parents of current students, previous college experience, public servants, relatives of clergy, religious affiliation, siblings of current students, spouses of current students, spouses of deceased or disabled public servants, twins, veterans, veterans' children. ***ROTC:*** Army, Air Force cooperative.

LOANS ***Student loans:*** $36,715,067 (49% need-based, 51% non-need-based). ***Average need-based loan:*** Freshmen: $3870. Undergraduates: $4876. ***Parent loans:*** $2,258,618 (100% non-need-based). ***Programs:*** Federal Direct (Subsidized and Unsubsidized Stafford, PLUS), Perkins, state, college/university.

WORK-STUDY ***Federal work-study:*** Total amount: $1,448,788; jobs available.

ATHLETIC AWARDS Total amount: $4,514,139 (100% non-need-based).

APPLYING FOR FINANCIAL AID ***Required financial aid form:*** FAFSA. ***Financial aid deadline (priority):*** 4/1. ***Notification date:*** Continuous beginning 4/1. Students must reply within 4 weeks of notification.

CONTACT Ms. Janet B. May, Financial Aid Director, The University of Alabama at Birmingham, Hill University Center 317, 1530 3rd Avenue South, Birmingham, AL 35294-1150, 205-934-8132 or toll-free 800-421-8743.

THE UNIVERSITY OF ALABAMA IN HUNTSVILLE

Huntsville, AL

Tuition & fees (AL res): $5952 **Average undergraduate aid package: $7804**

ABOUT THE INSTITUTION State-supported, coed. ***Awards:*** bachelor's, master's, and doctoral degrees and post-bachelor's and post-master's certificates. 30 undergraduate majors. ***Total enrollment:*** 7,431. Undergraduates: 5,893. Freshmen: 796. Both federal and institutional methodology are used as a basis for awarding need-based institutional aid.

UNDERGRADUATE EXPENSES for 2008–09 ***Application fee:*** $30. ***Tuition, state resident:*** full-time $5952; part-time $206.50 per credit hour. ***Tuition, nonresident:*** full-time $13,092; part-time $458.03 per credit hour. Full-time tuition and fees vary according to course load. Part-time tuition and fees vary according to course load. ***College room and board:*** $6526; ***Room only:*** $4626. Room and board charges vary according to board plan and housing facility. ***Payment plan:*** Deferred payment.

FRESHMAN FINANCIAL AID (Fall 2008, est.) 680 applied for aid; of those 47% were deemed to have need. 100% of freshmen with need received aid; of those 20% had need fully met. ***Average percent of need met:*** 68% (excluding resources awarded to replace EFC). ***Average financial aid package:*** $7678 (excluding resources awarded to replace EFC). 35% of all full-time freshmen had no need and received non-need-based gift aid.

UNDERGRADUATE FINANCIAL AID (Fall 2008, est.) 3,522 applied for aid; of those 53% were deemed to have need. 99% of undergraduates with need

received aid; of those 16% had need fully met. ***Average percent of need met:*** 64% (excluding resources awarded to replace EFC). ***Average financial aid package:*** $7804 (excluding resources awarded to replace EFC). 20% of all full-time undergraduates had no need and received non-need-based gift aid.

GIFT AID (NEED-BASED) ***Total amount:*** $7,463,874 (75% federal, 1% state, 19% institutional, 5% external sources). ***Receiving aid:*** Freshmen: 35% (269); all full-time undergraduates: 32% (1,374). ***Average award:*** Freshmen: $5054; Undergraduates: $4875. ***Scholarships, grants, and awards:*** Federal Pell, FSEOG, state, private, college/university gift aid from institutional funds, Federal Nursing.

GIFT AID (NON-NEED-BASED) ***Total amount:*** $3,834,315 (1% state, 89% institutional, 10% external sources). ***Receiving aid:*** Freshmen: 4% (31). Undergraduates: 2% (70). ***Average award:*** Freshmen: $3788. Undergraduates: $3631. ***Scholarships, grants, and awards by category:*** *Academic interests/achievement:* 1,964 awards ($4,794,533 total): business, computer science, education, engineering/technologies, English, general academic interests/achievements, health fields, humanities, physical sciences, social sciences. *Creative arts/performance:* 70 awards ($74,800 total): art/fine arts, music. *Special achievements/activities:* 470 awards ($1,643,620 total): cheerleading/drum major, community service, general special achievements/activities, junior miss, leadership. *Special characteristics:* 41 awards ($99,850 total): general special characteristics, local/state students, members of minority groups. ***Tuition waivers:*** Full or partial for employees or children of employees. ***ROTC:*** Army cooperative.

LOANS ***Student loans:*** $20,647,317 (71% need-based, 29% non-need-based). 32% of past graduating class borrowed through all loan programs. *Average indebtedness per student:* $21,882. ***Average need-based loan:*** Freshmen: $4521. Undergraduates: $6447. ***Parent loans:*** $1,204,930 (30% need-based, 70% non-need-based). ***Programs:*** Federal Direct (Subsidized and Unsubsidized Stafford, PLUS).

WORK-STUDY ***Federal work-study:*** Total amount: $363,421; 97 jobs averaging $3744.

ATHLETIC AWARDS Total amount: $1,563,981 (16% need-based, 84% non-need-based).

APPLYING FOR FINANCIAL AID ***Required financial aid form:*** FAFSA. ***Financial aid deadline:*** 7/31 (priority: 4/1). ***Notification date:*** Continuous. Students must reply within 2 weeks of notification.

CONTACT Mr. Andrew Weaver, Director of Student Financial Services, The University of Alabama in Huntsville, Office of Financial Aid, Huntsville, AL 35899, 256-824-6241 or toll-free 800-UAH-CALL. *Fax:* 256-824-6212. *E-mail:* finaid@uah.edu.

UNIVERSITY OF ALASKA ANCHORAGE

Anchorage, AK

ABOUT THE INSTITUTION State-supported, coed. ***Awards:*** associate, bachelor's, and master's degrees and post-master's certificates. 67 undergraduate majors. ***Total enrollment:*** 17,361. Undergraduates: 16,454. Freshmen: 1,669.

GIFT AID (NEED-BASED) ***Scholarships, grants, and awards:*** Federal Pell, FSEOG, state, private, college/university gift aid from institutional funds.

GIFT AID (NON-NEED-BASED) ***Scholarships, grants, and awards by category:*** *Academic interests/achievement:* biological sciences, business, communication, computer science, education, engineering/technologies, English, general academic interests/achievements, health fields, humanities, mathematics, social sciences. *Creative arts/performance:* debating. *Special achievements/activities:* general special achievements/activities.

LOANS ***Programs:*** FFEL (Subsidized and Unsubsidized Stafford, PLUS), state.

WORK-STUDY ***Federal work-study:*** Total amount: $234,975; 129 jobs averaging $2557.

APPLYING FOR FINANCIAL AID ***Required financial aid form:*** FAFSA.

CONTACT Theodore E. Malone, Director of Student Financial Aid, University of Alaska Anchorage, PO Box 141608, Anchorage, AK 99514-1608, 907-786-1520. *Fax:* 907-786-6122.

UNIVERSITY OF ALASKA FAIRBANKS

Fairbanks, AK

Tuition & fees (AK res): $5398 **Average undergraduate aid package: $10,007**

ABOUT THE INSTITUTION State-supported, coed. ***Awards:*** associate, bachelor's, master's, and doctoral degrees. 80 undergraduate majors. ***Total enrollment:*** 8,579. Undergraduates: 7,517. Freshmen: 934. Federal methodology is used as a basis for awarding need-based institutional aid.

UNDERGRADUATE EXPENSES for 2009–10 ***Application fee:*** $50. ***Tuition, state resident:*** full-time $4500; part-time $150 per credit. ***Tuition, nonresident:*** full-time $14,130; part-time $471 per credit. ***Required fees:*** full-time $898. ***College room and board:*** $6630; ***Room only:*** $3440.

FRESHMAN FINANCIAL AID (Fall 2007) 554 applied for aid; of those 58% were deemed to have need. 95% of freshmen with need received aid; of those 43% had need fully met. ***Average percent of need met:*** 50% (excluding resources awarded to replace EFC). ***Average financial aid package:*** $8839 (excluding resources awarded to replace EFC). 32% of all full-time freshmen had no need and received non-need-based gift aid.

UNDERGRADUATE FINANCIAL AID (Fall 2007) 2,039 applied for aid; of those 70% were deemed to have need. 96% of undergraduates with need received aid; of those 41% had need fully met. ***Average percent of need met:*** 57% (excluding resources awarded to replace EFC). ***Average financial aid package:*** $10,007 (excluding resources awarded to replace EFC). 26% of all full-time undergraduates had no need and received non-need-based gift aid.

GIFT AID (NEED-BASED) ***Total amount:*** $5,172,313 (70% federal, 2% state, 23% institutional, 5% external sources). ***Receiving aid:*** Freshmen: 28% (223); all full-time undergraduates: 31% (993). ***Average award:*** Freshmen: $5309; Undergraduates: $5259. ***Scholarships, grants, and awards:*** Federal Pell, FSEOG, state, private, college/university gift aid from institutional funds, Native Non-Profit Corporations.

GIFT AID (NON-NEED-BASED) ***Total amount:*** $1,964,692 (1% federal, 83% institutional, 16% external sources). ***Receiving aid:*** Freshmen: 5% (36). Undergraduates: 4% (121). ***Average award:*** Freshmen: $6639. Undergraduates: $6689. ***Scholarships, grants, and awards by category:*** *Academic interests/achievement:* biological sciences, general academic interests/achievements, military science, physical sciences. *Creative arts/performance:* art/fine arts, creative writing, music, theater/drama. *Special achievements/activities:* community service, general special achievements/activities, leadership. *Special characteristics:* local/state students, members of minority groups. ***ROTC:*** Army.

LOANS ***Student loans:*** $16,030,416 (75% need-based, 25% non-need-based). 54% of past graduating class borrowed through all loan programs. *Average indebtedness per student:* $28,597. ***Average need-based loan:*** Freshmen: $8054. Undergraduates: $9062. ***Parent loans:*** $211,106 (52% need-based, 48% non-need-based). ***Programs:*** FFEL (Subsidized and Unsubsidized Stafford, PLUS), state.

WORK-STUDY ***Federal work-study:*** Total amount: $467,899; 221 jobs averaging $2117.

ATHLETIC AWARDS Total amount: $876,379 (17% need-based, 83% non-need-based).

APPLYING FOR FINANCIAL AID ***Required financial aid form:*** FAFSA. ***Financial aid deadline:*** 7/15 (priority: 2/15). ***Notification date:*** Continuous beginning 3/1. Students must reply within 2 weeks of notification.

CONTACT Deanna Dierenger, Director of Financial Aid, University of Alaska Fairbanks, PO Box 756360, Fairbanks, AK 99775-6360, 907-474-7256 or toll-free 800-478-1823. *Fax:* 907-474-7065. *E-mail:* financialaid@uaf.edu.

UNIVERSITY OF ALASKA SOUTHEAST

Juneau, AK

ABOUT THE INSTITUTION State-supported, coed. ***Awards:*** associate, bachelor's, and master's degrees. 17 undergraduate majors. ***Total enrollment:*** 2,954. Undergraduates: 2,640. Freshmen: 212.

GIFT AID (NEED-BASED) ***Scholarships, grants, and awards:*** Federal Pell, FSEOG, private, college/university gift aid from institutional funds.

LOANS ***Programs:*** FFEL (Subsidized and Unsubsidized Stafford, PLUS), state.

WORK-STUDY ***Federal work-study:*** Total amount: $84,774.

APPLYING FOR FINANCIAL AID ***Required financial aid form:*** FAFSA.

CONTACT Ms. Barbara Carlson Burnett, Financial Aid Director, University of Alaska Southeast, 11120 Glacier Highway, Juneau, AK 99801-8680, 907-796-6296 or toll-free 877-796-4827. *Fax:* 907-796-6250. *E-mail:* barbara.burnett@uas.alaska.edu.

THE UNIVERSITY OF ARIZONA

Tucson, AZ

Tuition & fees (AZ res): $5542 **Average undergraduate aid package: $8529**

ABOUT THE INSTITUTION State-supported, coed. ***Awards:*** bachelor's, master's, doctoral, and first professional degrees and post-bachelor's certificates. 105 undergraduate majors. ***Total enrollment:*** 38,057. Undergraduates: 29,719. Freshmen: 6,709. Federal methodology is used as a basis for awarding need-based institutional aid.

UNDERGRADUATE EXPENSES for 2008–09 ***Application fee:*** $25. ***Tuition, state resident:*** full-time $5274; part-time $276 per credit hour. ***Tuition, nonresident:*** full-time $18,408; part-time $767 per credit hour. ***Required fees:*** full-time $268; $88 per term. Full-time tuition and fees vary according to course load. Part-time tuition and fees vary according to course load. ***College room and board:*** $7812; ***Room only:*** $5044. Room and board charges vary according to board plan and housing facility.

FRESHMAN FINANCIAL AID (Fall 2007) 3,798 applied for aid; of those 63% were deemed to have need. 94% of freshmen with need received aid; of those 20% had need fully met. ***Average percent of need met:*** 66% (excluding resources awarded to replace EFC). ***Average financial aid package:*** $8138 (excluding resources awarded to replace EFC). 35% of all full-time freshmen had no need and received non-need-based gift aid.

UNDERGRADUATE FINANCIAL AID (Fall 2007) 13,477 applied for aid; of those 74% were deemed to have need. 95% of undergraduates with need received aid; of those 15% had need fully met. ***Average percent of need met:*** 63% (excluding resources awarded to replace EFC). ***Average financial aid package:*** $8529 (excluding resources awarded to replace EFC). 23% of all full-time undergraduates had no need and received non-need-based gift aid.

GIFT AID (NEED-BASED) ***Total amount:*** $68,587,019 (33% federal, 1% state, 50% institutional, 16% external sources). ***Receiving aid:*** Freshmen: 34% (2,129); all full-time undergraduates: 33% (8,451). ***Average award:*** Freshmen: $6706; Undergraduates: $6478. ***Scholarships, grants, and awards:*** Federal Pell, FSEOG, state, private, college/university gift aid from institutional funds, Federal Nursing.

GIFT AID (NON-NEED-BASED) ***Total amount:*** $43,425,791 (72% institutional, 28% external sources). ***Receiving aid:*** Freshmen: 5% (330). Undergraduates: 3% (753). ***Average award:*** Freshmen: $4662. Undergraduates: $5130. ***Scholarships, grants, and awards by category:*** *Academic interests/achievement:* agriculture, architecture, biological sciences, business, education, engineering/technologies, general academic interests/achievements, humanities, military science, physical sciences, religion/biblical studies. *Creative arts/performance:* art/fine arts, dance, music, performing arts, theater/drama. *Special achievements/activities:* leadership. *Special characteristics:* children of faculty/staff, ethnic background, international students. ***Tuition waivers:*** Full or partial for employees or children of employees. ***ROTC:*** Army, Naval, Air Force.

LOANS ***Student loans:*** $61,881,010 (82% need-based, 18% non-need-based). 44% of past graduating class borrowed through all loan programs. *Average indebtedness per student:* $18,025. ***Average need-based loan:*** Freshmen: $3515. Undergraduates: $4284. ***Parent loans:*** $23,260,009 (62% need-based, 38% non-need-based). ***Programs:*** Federal Direct (Subsidized and Unsubsidized Stafford, PLUS), FFEL (Subsidized and Unsubsidized Stafford, PLUS), Perkins, Federal Nursing, college/university.

WORK-STUDY ***Federal work-study:*** Total amount: $1,659,799; jobs available. ***State or other work-study/employment:*** Total amount: $12,645,887 (46% need-based, 54% non-need-based). Part-time jobs available.

ATHLETIC AWARDS Total amount: $4,484,825 (32% need-based, 68% non-need-based).

APPLYING FOR FINANCIAL AID ***Required financial aid form:*** FAFSA. ***Financial aid deadline:*** Continuous. ***Notification date:*** Continuous.

CONTACT John Nametz, Director, Student Financial Aid Office, The University of Arizona, PO Box 210066, Tucson, AZ 85721-0066, 520-621-1858. *Fax:* 520-621-9473. *E-mail:* askaid@arizona.edu.

UNIVERSITY OF ARKANSAS

Fayetteville, AR

Tuition & fees (AR res): $6400 **Average undergraduate aid package: $8413**

ABOUT THE INSTITUTION State-supported, coed. ***Awards:*** bachelor's, master's, doctoral, and first professional degrees and post-bachelor's and post-master's certificates. 69 undergraduate majors. ***Total enrollment:*** 19,194. Undergraduates: 15,426. Freshmen: 3,011. Federal methodology is used as a basis for awarding need-based institutional aid.

UNDERGRADUATE EXPENSES for 2008–09 ***Application fee:*** $40. ***Tuition, state resident:*** full-time $5010; part-time $167 per hour. ***Tuition, nonresident:*** full-time $13,888; part-time $463 per hour. ***Required fees:*** full-time $1390. Full-time tuition and fees vary according to course load and program. Part-time tuition and fees vary according to course load and program. ***College room and board:*** $7422. Room and board charges vary according to board plan and housing facility. ***Payment plan:*** Installment.

FRESHMAN FINANCIAL AID (Fall 2008, est.) 1,856 applied for aid; of those 65% were deemed to have need. 98% of freshmen with need received aid; of those 24% had need fully met. ***Average percent of need met:*** 68% (excluding resources awarded to replace EFC). ***Average financial aid package:*** $9108 (excluding resources awarded to replace EFC). 18% of all full-time freshmen had no need and received non-need-based gift aid.

UNDERGRADUATE FINANCIAL AID (Fall 2008, est.) 6,784 applied for aid; of those 75% were deemed to have need. 97% of undergraduates with need received aid; of those 17% had need fully met. ***Average percent of need met:*** 60% (excluding resources awarded to replace EFC). ***Average financial aid package:*** $8413 (excluding resources awarded to replace EFC). 18% of all full-time undergraduates had no need and received non-need-based gift aid.

GIFT AID (NEED-BASED) ***Total amount:*** $21,154,691 (51% federal, 18% state, 25% institutional, 6% external sources). ***Receiving aid:*** Freshmen: 32% (965); all full-time undergraduates: 28% (3,580). ***Average award:*** Freshmen: $6550; Undergraduates: $5843. ***Scholarships, grants, and awards:*** Federal Pell, FSEOG, state, private, college/university gift aid from institutional funds.

GIFT AID (NON-NEED-BASED) ***Total amount:*** $19,985,363 (22% state, 71% institutional, 7% external sources). ***Receiving aid:*** Freshmen: 6% (165). Undergraduates: 3% (382). ***Average award:*** Freshmen: $5536. Undergraduates: $5766. ***Scholarships, grants, and awards by category:*** *Academic interests/achievement:* general academic interests/achievements. *Creative arts/performance:* music, theater/drama. *Special achievements/activities:* community service, general special achievements/activities, leadership. *Special characteristics:* children and siblings of alumni, children of faculty/staff, ethnic background, international students, out-of-state students, previous college experience. ***Tuition waivers:*** Full or partial for employees or children of employees, senior citizens. ***ROTC:*** Army, Air Force.

LOANS ***Student loans:*** $45,871,894 (68% need-based, 32% non-need-based). 43% of past graduating class borrowed through all loan programs. *Average indebtedness per student:* $19,439. ***Average need-based loan:*** Freshmen: $3458. Undergraduates: $4359. ***Parent loans:*** $5,978,187 (20% need-based, 80% non-need-based). ***Programs:*** FFEL (Subsidized and Unsubsidized Stafford, PLUS), Perkins, state, college/university, alternative loans.

WORK-STUDY ***Federal work-study:*** Total amount: $2,508,035; 894 jobs averaging $2759.

ATHLETIC AWARDS Total amount: $3,619,242 (30% need-based, 70% non-need-based).

APPLYING FOR FINANCIAL AID ***Required financial aid form:*** FAFSA. ***Financial aid deadline (priority):*** 3/15. ***Notification date:*** Continuous beginning 4/1. Students must reply within 4 weeks of notification.

CONTACT Kattie Wing, Director of Financial Aid, University of Arkansas, 114 Silas H. Hunt Hall, Fayetteville, AR 72701-1201, 479-575-3806 or toll-free 800-377-5346 (in-state), 800-377-8632 (out-of-state). *E-mail:* kattie@uark.edu.

UNIVERSITY OF ARKANSAS AT FORT SMITH

Fort Smith, AR

CONTACT Tammy Malone, Interim Financial Aid Director, University of Arkansas at Fort Smith, 5210 Grand Avenue, Fort Smith, AR 72913, 479-788-7099 or toll-free 888-512-5466. *Fax:* 479-788-7095. *E-mail:* tmalone@uafortsmith.edu.

UNIVERSITY OF ARKANSAS AT LITTLE ROCK

Little Rock, AR

CONTACT Financial Aid Office, University of Arkansas at Little Rock, 2801 South University Avenue, Little Rock, AR 72204-1099, 501-569-3127 or toll-free 800-482-8892 (in-state).

UNIVERSITY OF ARKANSAS AT MONTICELLO

Monticello, AR

ABOUT THE INSTITUTION State-supported, coed. ***Awards:*** associate, bachelor's, and master's degrees and post-bachelor's certificates. 42 undergraduate majors. ***Total enrollment:*** 3,302. Undergraduates: 3,182. Freshmen: 667.

GIFT AID (NEED-BASED) ***Scholarships, grants, and awards:*** Federal Pell, FSEOG, state, private, college/university gift aid from institutional funds.

GIFT AID (NON-NEED-BASED) ***Scholarships, grants, and awards by category:*** *Academic interests/achievement:* general academic interests/achievements. *Creative arts/performance:* debating, journalism/publications, music. *Special achievements/activities:* cheerleading/drum major, general special achievements/activities, leadership, rodeo. *Special characteristics:* children of faculty/staff, out-of-state students.

LOANS ***Programs:*** FFEL (Subsidized and Unsubsidized Stafford, PLUS), Perkins.

APPLYING FOR FINANCIAL AID ***Required financial aid forms:*** FAFSA, institution's own form.

CONTACT Susan Brewer, Director of Financial Aid, University of Arkansas at Monticello, PO Box 3470, Monticello, AR 71656, 870-460-1050 or toll-free 800-844-1826 (in-state). *Fax:* 870-460-1450. *E-mail:* brewers@uamont.edu.

UNIVERSITY OF ARKANSAS AT PINE BLUFF

Pine Bluff, AR

CONTACT Mrs. Carolyn Iverson, Director of Financial Aid, University of Arkansas at Pine Bluff, 1200 North University Drive, PO Box 4985, Pine Bluff, AR 71601, 870-575-8303 or toll-free 800-264-6585. *Fax:* 870-575-4622. *E-mail:* iverson_c@uapb.edu.

UNIVERSITY OF ARKANSAS FOR MEDICAL SCIENCES

Little Rock, AR

CONTACT Mr. Paul Carter, Director of Financial Aid, University of Arkansas for Medical Sciences, 4301 West Markham Street, MS 601, Little Rock, AR 72205, 501-686-5451. *Fax:* 501-686-5661. *E-mail:* pvcarter@uams.edu.

UNIVERSITY OF ATLANTA

Atlanta, GA

CONTACT Financial Aid Office, University of Atlanta, 6685 Peachtree Industrial Boulevard, Atlanta, GA 30360, 251-471-9977 or toll-free 800-533-3378.

UNIVERSITY OF BALTIMORE

Baltimore, MD

ABOUT THE INSTITUTION State-supported, coed. ***Awards:*** bachelor's, master's, doctoral, and first professional degrees and post-bachelor's and post-master's certificates. 29 undergraduate majors. ***Total enrollment:*** 5,414. Undergraduates: 2,411.

GIFT AID (NEED-BASED) ***Scholarships, grants, and awards:*** Federal Pell, FSEOG, state, private, college/university gift aid from institutional funds.

GIFT AID (NON-NEED-BASED) ***Scholarships, grants, and awards by category:*** *Academic interests/achievement:* business, English, general academic interests/achievements. *Special achievements/activities:* community service, memberships. *Special characteristics:* handicapped students.

LOANS ***Programs:*** FFEL (Subsidized and Unsubsidized Stafford, PLUS), Perkins, college/university.

WORK-STUDY ***Federal work-study:*** Total amount: $446,538; 93 jobs averaging $4801. ***State or other work-study/employment:*** Total amount: $322,902 (100% need-based). 48 part-time jobs averaging $6727.

APPLYING FOR FINANCIAL AID ***Required financial aid form:*** FAFSA.

CONTACT Financial Aid Office, University of Baltimore, 1420 North Charles Street, CH 123, Baltimore, MD 21201-5779, 410-837-4763 or toll-free 877-APPLYUB. *Fax:* 410-837-5493. *E-mail:* Financial-aid@ubalt.edu.

UNIVERSITY OF BRIDGEPORT

Bridgeport, CT

Tuition & fees: $24,470 **Average undergraduate aid package: $20,803**

ABOUT THE INSTITUTION Independent, coed. ***Awards:*** associate, bachelor's, master's, doctoral, and first professional degrees and post-master's certificates. 31 undergraduate majors. ***Total enrollment:*** 5,323. Undergraduates: 2,028. Freshmen: 453. Federal methodology is used as a basis for awarding need-based institutional aid.

UNDERGRADUATE EXPENSES for 2008–09 ***Application fee:*** $25. ***Comprehensive fee:*** $35,070 includes full-time tuition ($22,500), mandatory fees ($1970), and room and board ($10,600). Full-time tuition and fees vary according to program. Room and board charges vary according to board plan and student level. ***Part-time tuition:*** $750 per term. ***Part-time fees:*** $75 per term. Part-time tuition and fees vary according to program. ***Payment plans:*** Installment, deferred payment.

FRESHMAN FINANCIAL AID (Fall 2007) 268 applied for aid; of those 98% were deemed to have need. 100% of freshmen with need received aid; of those 8% had need fully met. ***Average percent of need met:*** 64% (excluding resources awarded to replace EFC). ***Average financial aid package:*** $21,309 (excluding resources awarded to replace EFC). 11% of all full-time freshmen had no need and received non-need-based gift aid.

UNDERGRADUATE FINANCIAL AID (Fall 2007) 934 applied for aid; of those 98% were deemed to have need. 100% of undergraduates with need received aid; of those 9% had need fully met. ***Average percent of need met:*** 52% (excluding resources awarded to replace EFC). ***Average financial aid package:*** $20,803 (excluding resources awarded to replace EFC). 26% of all full-time undergraduates had no need and received non-need-based gift aid.

GIFT AID (NEED-BASED) ***Total amount:*** $13,621,608 (18% federal, 10% state, 70% institutional, 2% external sources). ***Receiving aid:*** Freshmen: 74% (247); all full-time undergraduates: 73% (894). ***Average award:*** Freshmen: $6725; Undergraduates: $6952. ***Scholarships, grants, and awards:*** Federal Pell, FSEOG, state, college/university gift aid from institutional funds.

GIFT AID (NON-NEED-BASED) ***Receiving aid:*** Freshmen: 75% (251). Undergraduates: 67% (823). ***Average award:*** Freshmen: $9417. Undergraduates: $8763. ***Scholarships, grants, and awards by category:*** *Academic interests/achievement:* 672 awards ($4,253,801 total): general academic interests/achievements. *Special characteristics:* children of faculty/staff, international students, local/state students, previous college experience. ***Tuition waivers:*** Full or partial for employees or children of employees, senior citizens. ***ROTC:*** Army.

LOANS ***Student loans:*** $12,386,445 (49% need-based, 51% non-need-based). ***Average need-based loan:*** Freshmen: $4915. Undergraduates: $5103. ***Parent loans:*** $2,374,135 (100% non-need-based). ***Programs:*** FFEL (Subsidized and Unsubsidized Stafford, PLUS), Perkins.

WORK-STUDY ***Federal work-study:*** Total amount: $364,919; 356 jobs averaging $2000. ***State or other work-study/employment:*** Total amount: $212,614 (100% need-based). Part-time jobs available.

ATHLETIC AWARDS Total amount: $2,191,628 (100% non-need-based).

APPLYING FOR FINANCIAL AID ***Required financial aid form:*** FAFSA. ***Financial aid deadline (priority):*** 4/1. ***Notification date:*** Continuous. Students must reply within 4 weeks of notification.

CONTACT Kathleen E. Gailor, Director of Financial Aid, University of Bridgeport, 126 Park Avenue, Bridgeport, CT 06604, 203-576-4568 or toll-free 800-EXCEL-UB (in-state), 800-243-9496 (out-of-state). *Fax:* 203-576-4570. *E-mail:* finaid@bridgeport.edu.

UNIVERSITY OF CALIFORNIA, BERKELEY

Berkeley, CA

Tuition & fees (CA res): $8352 **Average undergraduate aid package: $16,914**

ABOUT THE INSTITUTION State-supported, coed. ***Awards:*** bachelor's, master's, doctoral, and first professional degrees and post-bachelor's certificates. 93 undergraduate majors. ***Total enrollment:*** 35,409. Undergraduates: 25,151. Freshmen: 4,261. Both federal and institutional methodology are used as a basis for awarding need-based institutional aid.

UNDERGRADUATE EXPENSES for 2009–10 ***Application fee:*** $60. ***Tuition, state resident:*** full-time $0. ***Tuition, nonresident:*** full-time $21,670. ***Required fees:*** full-time $8352. ***College room and board:*** $15,308.

FRESHMAN FINANCIAL AID (Fall 2008, est.) 3,119 applied for aid; of those 63% were deemed to have need. 97% of freshmen with need received aid; of those 50% had need fully met. ***Average percent of need met:*** 88% (excluding resources awarded to replace EFC). ***Average financial aid package:*** $18,628 (excluding resources awarded to replace EFC). 8% of all full-time freshmen had no need and received non-need-based gift aid.

UNDERGRADUATE FINANCIAL AID (Fall 2008, est.) 14,872 applied for aid; of those 80% were deemed to have need. 98% of undergraduates with need received aid; of those 52% had need fully met. ***Average percent of need met:*** 88% (excluding resources awarded to replace EFC). ***Average financial aid package:*** $16,914 (excluding resources awarded to replace EFC). 7% of all full-time undergraduates had no need and received non-need-based gift aid.

GIFT AID (NEED-BASED) ***Total amount:*** $145,304,079 (23% federal, 29% state, 44% institutional, 4% external sources). ***Receiving aid:*** Freshmen: 43% (1,838); all full-time undergraduates: 46% (11,330). ***Average award:*** Freshmen: $14,154; Undergraduates: $12,496. ***Scholarships, grants, and awards:*** Federal Pell, FSEOG, state, private, college/university gift aid from institutional funds.

GIFT AID (NON-NEED-BASED) ***Total amount:*** $13,495,892 (5% federal, 4% state, 62% institutional, 29% external sources). ***Receiving aid:*** Freshmen: 1% (46). Undergraduates: 1% (138). ***Average award:*** Freshmen: $8079. Undergraduates: $7730. ***Scholarships, grants, and awards by category:*** *Academic interests/achievement:* general academic interests/achievements. ***ROTC:*** Army, Naval, Air Force.

LOANS ***Student loans:*** $52,334,928 (66% need-based, 34% non-need-based). 39% of past graduating class borrowed through all loan programs. *Average indebtedness per student:* $14,291. ***Average need-based loan:*** Freshmen: $5281. Undergraduates: $5382. ***Parent loans:*** $23,342,847 (12% need-based, 88% non-need-based). ***Programs:*** Federal Direct (Subsidized and Unsubsidized Stafford, PLUS), Perkins.

WORK-STUDY ***Federal work-study:*** Total amount: $5,610,347; jobs available. ***State or other work-study/employment:*** Total amount: $14,074,463 (100% need-based). Part-time jobs available.

ATHLETIC AWARDS Total amount: $7,395,086 (23% need-based, 77% non-need-based).

APPLYING FOR FINANCIAL AID ***Required financial aid forms:*** FAFSA, state aid form, State Cal Grants. ***Financial aid deadline:*** 3/2 (priority: 3/2). ***Notification date:*** 4/15.

CONTACT Sandy Jensen, Administrative Services Coordinator, University of California, Berkeley, 225 Sproul Hall, Berkeley, CA 94720-1960, 510-642-0649. *Fax:* 510-643-5526.

UNIVERSITY OF CALIFORNIA, DAVIS

Davis, CA

Tuition & fees (CA res): $9364 **Average undergraduate aid package: $14,275**

ABOUT THE INSTITUTION State-supported, coed. ***Awards:*** bachelor's, master's, doctoral, and first professional degrees and post-bachelor's and post-master's certificates. 83 undergraduate majors. ***Total enrollment:*** 30,568. Undergraduates: 24,209. Freshmen: 4,972. Federal methodology is used as a basis for awarding need-based institutional aid.

UNDERGRADUATE EXPENSES for 2009–10 ***Application fee:*** $60. ***Tuition, state resident:*** full-time $0. ***Tuition, nonresident:*** full-time $22,021. ***Required fees:*** full-time $9364. ***College room and board:*** $12,361.

FRESHMAN FINANCIAL AID (Fall 2008, est.) 3,896 applied for aid; of those 71% were deemed to have need. 97% of freshmen with need received aid; of those 16% had need fully met. ***Average percent of need met:*** 81% (excluding resources awarded to replace EFC). ***Average financial aid package:*** $15,811 (excluding resources awarded to replace EFC). 4% of all full-time freshmen had no need and received non-need-based gift aid.

UNDERGRADUATE FINANCIAL AID (Fall 2008, est.) 15,368 applied for aid; of those 83% were deemed to have need. 98% of undergraduates with need received aid; of those 21% had need fully met. ***Average percent of need met:*** 79% (excluding resources awarded to replace EFC). ***Average financial aid package:*** $14,275 (excluding resources awarded to replace EFC). 4% of all full-time undergraduates had no need and received non-need-based gift aid.

GIFT AID (NEED-BASED) ***Total amount:*** $136,361,472 (27% federal, 36% state, 35% institutional, 2% external sources). ***Receiving aid:*** Freshmen: 53% (2,589); all full-time undergraduates: 51% (11,857). ***Average award:*** Freshmen: $12,361; Undergraduates: $11,176. ***Scholarships, grants, and awards:*** Federal Pell, FSEOG, state, private, college/university gift aid from institutional funds, Academic Competitiveness Grant, National Smart Grant.

GIFT AID (NON-NEED-BASED) ***Total amount:*** $6,919,593 (3% federal, 1% state, 62% institutional, 34% external sources). ***Receiving aid:*** Freshmen: 1% (36). Undergraduates: 102. ***Average award:*** Freshmen: $4763. Undergraduates: $4453. ***Scholarships, grants, and awards by category:*** *Academic interests/achievement:* agriculture, area/ethnic studies, biological sciences, business, communication, computer science, engineering/technologies, English, foreign languages, general academic interests/achievements, health fields, home economics, humanities, international studies, mathematics, premedicine, religion/biblical studies, social sciences. ***ROTC:*** Army, Naval cooperative, Air Force cooperative.

LOANS ***Student loans:*** $53,003,534 (82% need-based, 18% non-need-based). 47% of past graduating class borrowed through all loan programs. *Average indebtedness per student:* $15,155. ***Average need-based loan:*** Freshmen: $5302. Undergraduates: $5152. ***Parent loans:*** $16,200,984 (9% need-based, 91% non-need-based). ***Programs:*** Federal Direct (Subsidized and Unsubsidized Stafford, PLUS), Perkins, college/university.

WORK-STUDY ***Federal work-study:*** Total amount: $2,079,663; jobs available.

ATHLETIC AWARDS Total amount: $3,900,037 (2% need-based, 98% non-need-based).

APPLYING FOR FINANCIAL AID ***Required financial aid forms:*** FAFSA, state aid form. ***Financial aid deadline (priority):*** 3/2. ***Notification date:*** Continuous beginning 3/12.

CONTACT Katy Maloney, Interim Director of Financial Aid, University of California, Davis, One Shields Avenue, Davis, CA 95616, 530-752-2396. *Fax:* 530-752-7339.

UNIVERSITY OF CALIFORNIA, IRVINE

Irvine, CA

Tuition & fees (CA res): $8775 **Average undergraduate aid package: $14,669**

ABOUT THE INSTITUTION State-supported, coed. ***Awards:*** bachelor's, master's, doctoral, and first professional degrees and post-bachelor's certificates. 76 undergraduate majors. ***Total enrollment:*** 26,984. Undergraduates: 22,122. Freshmen: 4,583. Federal methodology is used as a basis for awarding need-based institutional aid.

UNDERGRADUATE EXPENSES for 2008–09 ***Application fee:*** $60. ***Tuition, state resident:*** full-time $0. ***Tuition, nonresident:*** full-time $20,608. ***Required fees:*** full-time $8775. ***College room and board:*** $10,527. Room and board charges vary according to board plan and housing facility. ***Payment plan:*** Installment.

FRESHMAN FINANCIAL AID (Fall 2008, est.) 3,578 applied for aid; of those 66% were deemed to have need. 95% of freshmen with need received aid; of those 51% had need fully met. ***Average percent of need met:*** 84% (excluding resources awarded to replace EFC). ***Average financial aid package:*** $14,621 (excluding resources awarded to replace EFC). 3% of all full-time freshmen had no need and received non-need-based gift aid.

UNDERGRADUATE FINANCIAL AID (Fall 2008, est.) 13,826 applied for aid; of those 78% were deemed to have need. 97% of undergraduates with need received aid; of those 43% had need fully met. ***Average percent of need met:*** 82% (excluding resources awarded to replace EFC). ***Average financial aid package:*** $14,669 (excluding resources awarded to replace EFC). 4% of all full-time undergraduates had no need and received non-need-based gift aid.

GIFT AID (NEED-BASED) ***Total amount:*** $110,485,463 (23% federal, 36% state, 39% institutional, 2% external sources). ***Receiving aid:*** Freshmen: 46% (2,109); all full-time undergraduates: 45% (9,644). ***Average award:*** Freshmen: $10,946; Undergraduates: $11,353. ***Scholarships, grants, and awards:*** Federal Pell, FSEOG, state, private, college/university gift aid from institutional funds.

GIFT AID (NON-NEED-BASED) ***Total amount:*** $8,094,725 (3% federal, 1% state, 82% institutional, 14% external sources). ***Receiving aid:*** Freshmen: 1% (39). Undergraduates: 1% (114). ***Average award:*** Freshmen: $6325. Undergraduates: $7773. ***Scholarships, grants, and awards by category:*** *Academic interests/achievement:* 838 awards ($3,714,675 total): biological sciences, computer science, education, engineering/technologies, foreign languages, general academic interests/achievements, health fields, humanities, international studies, physical sciences, social sciences. *Creative arts/performance:* 56 awards ($179,650 total): art/fine arts, cinema/film/broadcasting, dance, general creative arts/performance, music, theater/drama. ***ROTC:*** Army cooperative, Air Force cooperative.

LOANS ***Student loans:*** $51,956,590 (67% need-based, 33% non-need-based). 46% of past graduating class borrowed through all loan programs. *Average indebtedness per student:* $14,323. ***Average need-based loan:*** Freshmen: $5889. Undergraduates: $6092. ***Parent loans:*** $32,993,488 (15% need-based, 85% non-need-based). ***Programs:*** Federal Direct (Subsidized and Unsubsidized Stafford, PLUS), FFEL (Subsidized and Unsubsidized Stafford, PLUS), Perkins, college/university, private loans.

WORK-STUDY ***Federal work-study:*** Total amount: $4,077,918; 3,173 jobs averaging $1885.

ATHLETIC AWARDS Total amount: $2,473,767 (24% need-based, 76% non-need-based).

APPLYING FOR FINANCIAL AID ***Required financial aid forms:*** FAFSA, state aid form. ***Financial aid deadline:*** 5/1 (priority: 3/2). ***Notification date:*** Continuous beginning 4/1.

CONTACT Penny Harrell, Associate Director of Student Services, University of California, Irvine, Office of Financial Aid and Scholarships, Irvine, CA 92697-2825, 949-824-8262. *Fax:* 949-824-4876. *E-mail:* finaid@uci.edu.

UNIVERSITY OF CALIFORNIA, LOS ANGELES

Los Angeles, CA

Tuition & fees (CA res): $8310 Average undergraduate aid package: $15,646

ABOUT THE INSTITUTION State-supported, coed. ***Awards:*** bachelor's, master's, doctoral, and first professional degrees. 100 undergraduate majors. ***Total enrollment:*** 39,650. Undergraduates: 26,536. Freshmen: 4,735. Both federal and institutional methodology are used as a basis for awarding need-based institutional aid.

UNDERGRADUATE EXPENSES for 2008–09 ***Application fee:*** $60. ***Tuition, state resident:*** full-time $0. ***Tuition, nonresident:*** full-time $20,021. ***Required fees:*** full-time $8310. ***College room and board:*** $12,891. Room and board charges vary according to board plan and housing facility.

FRESHMAN FINANCIAL AID (Fall 2008, est.) 2,924 applied for aid; of those 79% were deemed to have need. 100% of freshmen with need received aid; of those 27% had need fully met. ***Average percent of need met:*** 83% (excluding resources awarded to replace EFC). ***Average financial aid package:*** $16,568 (excluding resources awarded to replace EFC). 5% of all full-time freshmen had no need and received non-need-based gift aid.

UNDERGRADUATE FINANCIAL AID (Fall 2008, est.) 14,364 applied for aid; of those 88% were deemed to have need. 100% of undergraduates with need received aid; of those 28% had need fully met. ***Average percent of need met:*** 83% (excluding resources awarded to replace EFC). ***Average financial aid package:*** $15,646 (excluding resources awarded to replace EFC). 4% of all full-time undergraduates had no need and received non-need-based gift aid.

GIFT AID (NEED-BASED) ***Total amount:*** $153,553,943 (20% federal, 31% state, 46% institutional, 3% external sources). ***Receiving aid:*** Freshmen: 47% (2,222); all full-time undergraduates: 47% (12,013). ***Average award:*** Freshmen: $13,643; Undergraduates: $12,777. ***Scholarships, grants, and awards:*** Federal Pell, FSEOG, state, private, college/university gift aid from institutional funds, United Negro College Fund, Federal Nursing.

GIFT AID (NON-NEED-BASED) ***Total amount:*** $7,949,584 (6% federal, 1% state, 69% institutional, 24% external sources). ***Receiving aid:*** Freshmen: 1% (52). Undergraduates: 1% (153). ***Average award:*** Freshmen: $5026. Undergraduates: $4762. ***Scholarships, grants, and awards by category:*** *Academic interests/achievement:* general academic interests/achievements. *Special achievements/activities:* general special achievements/activities. ***ROTC:*** Army, Naval, Air Force.

LOANS ***Student loans:*** $58,201,401 (70% need-based, 30% non-need-based). 43% of past graduating class borrowed through all loan programs. *Average indebtedness per student:* $16,733. ***Average need-based loan:*** Freshmen: $5387. Undergraduates: $5258. ***Parent loans:*** $19,886,932 (15% need-based, 85% non-need-based). ***Programs:*** FFEL (Subsidized and Unsubsidized Stafford, PLUS), Perkins, Federal Nursing, state, college/university.

WORK-STUDY ***Federal work-study:*** Total amount: $6,101,731; 2,855 jobs averaging $1660. ***State or other work-study/employment:*** Total amount: $354,728 (100% need-based). 657 part-time jobs averaging $1079.

ATHLETIC AWARDS Total amount: $8,182,310 (27% need-based, 73% non-need-based).

APPLYING FOR FINANCIAL AID ***Required financial aid form:*** FAFSA. ***Financial aid deadline:*** Continuous. ***Notification date:*** Continuous beginning 3/15.

CONTACT Ms. Yolanda Tan, Administrative Assistant, University of California, Los Angeles, Financial Aid Office, A-129 Murphy Hall, Los Angeles, CA 90095-1435, 310-206-0404. *E-mail:* finaid@saonet.ucla.edu.

UNIVERSITY OF CALIFORNIA, MERCED

Merced, CA

CONTACT Financial Aid Office, University of California, Merced, 5200 North Lake Road, Merced, CA 95343, 209-724-4400.

UNIVERSITY OF CALIFORNIA, RIVERSIDE

Riverside, CA

Tuition & fees (CA res): $7845 Average undergraduate aid package: $15,342

ABOUT THE INSTITUTION State-supported, coed. ***Awards:*** bachelor's, master's, doctoral, and first professional degrees and post-bachelor's certificates. 81 undergraduate majors. ***Total enrollment:*** 18,079. Undergraduates: 15,708. Freshmen: 4,423. Federal methodology is used as a basis for awarding need-based institutional aid.

UNDERGRADUATE EXPENSES for 2008–09 ***Application fee:*** $60. ***Tuition, state resident:*** full-time $0. ***Tuition, nonresident:*** full-time $20,022. ***Required fees:*** full-time $7845. ***College room and board:*** $10,850. Room and board charges vary according to board plan and housing facility. ***Payment plan:*** Deferred payment.

FRESHMAN FINANCIAL AID (Fall 2008, est.) 3,729 applied for aid; of those 79% were deemed to have need. 97% of freshmen with need received aid; of those 58% had need fully met. ***Average percent of need met:*** 89% (excluding resources awarded to replace EFC). ***Average financial aid package:*** $16,754 (excluding resources awarded to replace EFC). 2% of all full-time freshmen had no need and received non-need-based gift aid.

UNDERGRADUATE FINANCIAL AID (Fall 2008, est.) 11,734 applied for aid; of those 85% were deemed to have need. 98% of undergraduates with need received aid; of those 41% had need fully met. ***Average percent of need met:*** 82% (excluding resources awarded to replace EFC). ***Average financial aid package:*** $15,342 (excluding resources awarded to replace EFC). 1% of all full-time undergraduates had no need and received non-need-based gift aid.

GIFT AID (NEED-BASED) ***Total amount:*** $103,812,668 (27% federal, 38% state, 34% institutional, 1% external sources). ***Receiving aid:*** Freshmen: 60% (2,647); all full-time undergraduates: 59% (9,044). ***Average award:*** Freshmen: $13,463; Undergraduates: $11,425. ***Scholarships, grants, and awards:*** Federal Pell, FSEOG, state, private, college/university gift aid from institutional funds.

GIFT AID (NON-NEED-BASED) ***Total amount:*** $5,432,661 (3% federal, 88% institutional, 9% external sources). ***Receiving aid:*** Freshmen: 1% (41). Undergraduates: 1% (120). ***Average award:*** Freshmen: $7012. Undergraduates: $6949. ***Scholarships, grants, and awards by category:*** *Academic interests/achievement:* agriculture, area/ethnic studies, biological sciences, business, education, engineering/technologies, English, general academic interests/achievements, humanities, mathematics, physical sciences, premedicine, social sciences. *Creative arts/performance:* art/fine arts, creative writing, dance, music, theater/drama. ***ROTC:*** Army cooperative, Air Force cooperative.

LOANS ***Student loans:*** $48,376,858 (78% need-based, 22% non-need-based). 62% of past graduating class borrowed through all loan programs. *Average indebtedness per student:* $15,414. ***Average need-based loan:*** Freshmen: $4463. Undergraduates: $6040. ***Parent loans:*** $17,123,826 (23% need-based, 77% non-need-based). ***Programs:*** Federal Direct (Subsidized and Unsubsidized Stafford, PLUS), Perkins, college/university.

WORK-STUDY ***Federal work-study:*** Total amount: $4,052,427; 3,042 jobs averaging $1656. ***State or other work-study/employment:*** Part-time jobs available.

ATHLETIC AWARDS Total amount: $2,303,166 (31% need-based, 69% non-need-based).

APPLYING FOR FINANCIAL AID ***Required financial aid forms:*** FAFSA, state aid form. ***Financial aid deadline:*** 3/2 (priority: 3/2). ***Notification date:*** Continuous. Students must reply by 5/1 or within 3 weeks of notification.

CONTACT Ms. Sheryl Hayes, Director of Financial Aid, University of California, Riverside, 2106 Student Services Bldg., Riverside, CA 92521-0209, 951-827-3878. *E-mail:* finaid@ucr.edu.

UNIVERSITY OF CALIFORNIA, SAN DIEGO

La Jolla, CA

Tuition & fees (CA res): $8062 Average undergraduate aid package: $16,249

ABOUT THE INSTITUTION State-supported, coed. ***Awards:*** bachelor's, master's, doctoral, and first professional degrees. 76 undergraduate majors. ***Total enrollment:*** 27,520. Undergraduates: 22,518. Freshmen: 4,702. Federal methodology is used as a basis for awarding need-based institutional aid.

UNDERGRADUATE EXPENSES for 2008–09 ***Application fee:*** $60. ***Tuition, state resident:*** full-time $0. ***Tuition, nonresident:*** full-time $20,021. ***Required fees:*** full-time $8062. ***College room and board:*** $10,820.

FRESHMAN FINANCIAL AID (Fall 2008, est.) 3,450 applied for aid; of those 72% were deemed to have need. 96% of freshmen with need received aid; of those 19% had need fully met. ***Average percent of need met:*** 85% (excluding resources awarded to replace EFC). ***Average financial aid package:*** $16,844 (excluding resources awarded to replace EFC). 3% of all full-time freshmen had no need and received non-need-based gift aid.

UNDERGRADUATE FINANCIAL AID (Fall 2008, est.) 14,543 applied for aid; of those 85% were deemed to have need. 97% of undergraduates with need received aid; of those 23% had need fully met. ***Average percent of need met:*** 84% (excluding resources awarded to replace EFC). ***Average financial aid package:*** $16,249 (excluding resources awarded to replace EFC). 3% of all full-time undergraduates had no need and received non-need-based gift aid.

GIFT AID (NEED-BASED) ***Total amount:*** $133,773,546 (26% federal, 38% state, 33% institutional, 3% external sources). ***Receiving aid:*** Freshmen: 53% (2,256); all full-time undergraduates: 51% (11,147). ***Average award:*** Freshmen: $12,310; Undergraduates: $11,854. ***Scholarships, grants, and awards:*** Federal Pell, FSEOG, state, private, college/university gift aid from institutional funds, Academic Competitiveness Grant, National Smart Grant.

GIFT AID (NON-NEED-BASED) ***Total amount:*** $8,747,534 (7% federal, 3% state, 74% institutional, 16% external sources). ***Receiving aid:*** Freshmen: 1% (31). Undergraduates: 76. ***Average award:*** Freshmen: $8708. Undergraduates: $8319. ***Scholarships, grants, and awards by category:*** *Academic interests/achievement:* 511 awards ($1,617,794 total): biological sciences, business, communication, computer science, engineering/technologies, general academic interests/achievements, mathematics, physical sciences, premedicine, social sciences. *Creative arts/performance:* 10 awards ($11,900 total): applied art and design, cinema/film/broadcasting, dance, journalism/publications, performing arts. *Special achievements/activities:* 283 awards ($285,116 total): community service, leadership. *Special characteristics:* 174 awards ($260,131 total): ethnic background, first-generation college students, handicapped students, members of minority groups, veterans' children. ***ROTC:*** Army cooperative.

LOANS ***Student loans:*** $63,492,745 (79% need-based, 21% non-need-based). 50% of past graduating class borrowed through all loan programs. *Average indebtedness per student:* $16,317. ***Average need-based loan:*** Freshmen: $4971. Undergraduates: $5806. ***Parent loans:*** $10,856,207 (16% need-based, 84% non-need-based). ***Programs:*** FFEL (Subsidized and Unsubsidized Stafford, PLUS), Perkins, college/university, alternative loans.

WORK-STUDY ***Federal work-study:*** Total amount: $10,433,041; jobs available (averaging $1800).

ATHLETIC AWARDS Total amount: $257,500 (30% need-based, 70% non-need-based).

APPLYING FOR FINANCIAL AID ***Required financial aid forms:*** FAFSA, state aid form. ***Financial aid deadline (priority):*** 3/2. ***Notification date:*** Continuous beginning 3/15.

CONTACT Ann Klein, Director of Financial Aid Office, University of California, San Diego, 9500 Gilman Drive-0013, La Jolla, CA 92093-0013, 858-534-3800. *Fax:* 858-534-5459. *E-mail:* aklein@ucsd.edu.

UNIVERSITY OF CALIFORNIA, SANTA BARBARA

Santa Barbara, CA

Tuition & fees (CA res): $8573 Average undergraduate aid package: $15,643

ABOUT THE INSTITUTION State-supported, coed. ***Awards:*** bachelor's, master's, and doctoral degrees and first professional certificates. 75 undergraduate majors. ***Total enrollment:*** 21,410. Undergraduates: 18,415. Freshmen: 4,335. Both federal and institutional methodology are used as a basis for awarding need-based institutional aid.

UNDERGRADUATE EXPENSES for 2008–09 ***Application fee:*** $60. ***Tuition, state resident:*** full-time $0. ***Tuition, nonresident:*** full-time $20,608. ***Required fees:*** full-time $8573. ***College room and board:*** $12,485.

FRESHMAN FINANCIAL AID (Fall 2008, est.) 3,389 applied for aid; of those 70% were deemed to have need. 93% of freshmen with need received aid; of those 29% had need fully met. ***Average percent of need met:*** 82% (excluding resources awarded to replace EFC). ***Average financial aid package:*** $17,022 (excluding resources awarded to replace EFC). 2% of all full-time freshmen had no need and received non-need-based gift aid.

UNDERGRADUATE FINANCIAL AID (Fall 2008, est.) 11,346 applied for aid; of those 78% were deemed to have need. 94% of undergraduates with need received aid; of those 27% had need fully met. ***Average percent of need met:*** 80% (excluding resources awarded to replace EFC). ***Average financial aid package:*** $15,643 (excluding resources awarded to replace EFC). 2% of all full-time undergraduates had no need and received non-need-based gift aid.

GIFT AID (NEED-BASED) ***Total amount:*** $94,482,411 (22% federal, 35% state, 41% institutional, 2% external sources). ***Receiving aid:*** Freshmen: 47% (2,033); all full-time undergraduates: 41% (7,566). ***Average award:*** Freshmen: $14,219; Undergraduates: $12,344. ***Scholarships, grants, and awards:*** Federal Pell, FSEOG, state, private, college/university gift aid from institutional funds, endowed scholarships.

GIFT AID (NON-NEED-BASED) ***Total amount:*** $3,132,100 (9% federal, 2% state, 60% institutional, 29% external sources). ***Receiving aid:*** Freshmen: 1% (26). Undergraduates: 70. ***Average award:*** Freshmen: $6105. Undergraduates: $5276. ***Scholarships, grants, and awards by category:*** *Academic interests/achievement:* general academic interests/achievements. ***ROTC:*** Army.

LOANS ***Student loans:*** $38,953,090 (76% need-based, 24% non-need-based). 47% of past graduating class borrowed through all loan programs. *Average indebtedness per student:* $17,107. ***Average need-based loan:*** Freshmen: $4935. Undergraduates: $5680. ***Parent loans:*** $25,599,170 (19% need-based, 81% non-need-based). ***Programs:*** Federal Direct (Subsidized and Unsubsidized Stafford, PLUS), Perkins.

WORK-STUDY ***Federal work-study:*** Total amount: $2,056,165; jobs available.

ATHLETIC AWARDS Total amount: $2,930,929 (15% need-based, 85% non-need-based).

APPLYING FOR FINANCIAL AID ***Required financial aid form:*** FAFSA. ***Financial aid deadline (priority):*** 3/2. ***Notification date:*** Continuous beginning 3/15. Students must reply within 2 weeks of notification.

CONTACT Office of Financial Aid, University of California, Santa Barbara, 2103 SAASB (Student Affairs/Administrative Services Building), Santa Barbara, CA 93106-3180, 805-893-2432. *Fax:* 805-893-8793.

UNIVERSITY OF CALIFORNIA, SANTA CRUZ

Santa Cruz, CA

Tuition & fees (CA res): $10,131 Average undergraduate aid package: $16,254

ABOUT THE INSTITUTION State-supported, coed. ***Awards:*** bachelor's, master's, and doctoral degrees and post-bachelor's certificates. 56 undergraduate majors. ***Total enrollment:*** 16,625. Undergraduates: 15,135. Freshmen: 3,965. Both federal and institutional methodology are used as a basis for awarding need-based institutional aid.

UNDERGRADUATE EXPENSES for 2009–10 ***Application fee:*** $60. ***Tuition, state resident:*** full-time $0. ***Tuition, nonresident:*** full-time $21,423. ***Required fees:*** full-time $10,131. ***College room and board:*** $13,641.

FRESHMAN FINANCIAL AID (Fall 2008, est.) 3,039 applied for aid; of those 67% were deemed to have need. 94% of freshmen with need received aid; of those 33% had need fully met. ***Average percent of need met:*** 84% (excluding resources awarded to replace EFC). ***Average financial aid package:*** $16,626 (excluding resources awarded to replace EFC). 2% of all full-time freshmen had no need and received non-need-based gift aid.

UNDERGRADUATE FINANCIAL AID (Fall 2008, est.) 9,500 applied for aid; of those 78% were deemed to have need. 95% of undergraduates with need received aid; of those 37% had need fully met. ***Average percent of need met:*** 86% (excluding resources awarded to replace EFC). ***Average financial aid package:*** $16,254 (excluding resources awarded to replace EFC). 2% of all full-time undergraduates had no need and received non-need-based gift aid.

GIFT AID (NEED-BASED) ***Total amount:*** $74,464,853 (22% federal, 35% state, 41% institutional, 2% external sources). ***Receiving aid:*** Freshmen: 44% (1,755); all full-time undergraduates: 44% (6,408). ***Average award:*** Freshmen: $12,009; Undergraduates: $11,448. ***Scholarships, grants, and awards:*** Federal Pell, FSEOG, state, private, college/university gift aid from institutional funds.

GIFT AID (NON-NEED-BASED) ***Total amount:*** $2,943,916 (5% federal, 2% state, 72% institutional, 21% external sources). ***Receiving aid:*** Freshmen: 19. Undergraduates: 58. ***Average award:*** Freshmen: $9745. Undergraduates: $6707. ***Scholarships, grants, and awards by category:*** *Academic interests/achievement:* 179 awards ($839,223 total): general academic interests/achievements, humanities, physical sciences, social sciences. *Creative arts/performance:* 93 awards ($87,485 total): art/fine arts, cinema/film/broadcasting, music, theater/drama. *Special achievements/activities:* 13 awards ($6832 total): general special achievements/activities, leadership. ***ROTC:*** Army cooperative, Naval cooperative, Air Force cooperative.

LOANS ***Student loans:*** $38,149,853 (72% need-based, 28% non-need-based). 53% of past graduating class borrowed through all loan programs. *Average indebtedness per student:* $15,918. ***Average need-based loan:*** Freshmen: $5033. Undergraduates: $5454. ***Parent loans:*** $24,761,969 (14% need-based, 86% non-need-based). ***Programs:*** Federal Direct (Subsidized and Unsubsidized Stafford, PLUS), Perkins.

WORK-STUDY ***Federal work-study:*** Total amount: $10,113,795; 4,992 jobs averaging $2094. ***State or other work-study/employment:*** Total amount: $2300 (100% need-based). Part-time jobs available.

APPLYING FOR FINANCIAL AID ***Required financial aid forms:*** FAFSA, state aid form. ***Financial aid deadline:*** 6/1 (priority: 3/17). ***Notification date:*** Continuous beginning 4/1. Students must reply within 4 weeks of notification.

CONTACT Ms. Ann Draper, Director of Financial Aid, University of California, Santa Cruz, 201 Hahn Student Services Building, Santa Cruz, CA 95064, 831-459-4358. *Fax:* 831-459-4631. *E-mail:* ann@ucsc.edu.

UNIVERSITY OF CENTRAL ARKANSAS

Conway, AR

ABOUT THE INSTITUTION State-supported, coed. ***Awards:*** associate, bachelor's, master's, and doctoral degrees and post-bachelor's and post-master's certificates. 60 undergraduate majors. ***Total enrollment:*** 12,974. Undergraduates: 11,048. Freshmen: 2,111.

GIFT AID (NEED-BASED) ***Scholarships, grants, and awards:*** Federal Pell, FSEOG, state, private, college/university gift aid from institutional funds, Federal Nursing.

GIFT AID (NON-NEED-BASED) ***Scholarships, grants, and awards by category:*** *Academic interests/achievement:* general academic interests/achievements.

LOANS ***Programs:*** FFEL (Subsidized and Unsubsidized Stafford, PLUS), Perkins, Federal Nursing, state, External Loans.

APPLYING FOR FINANCIAL AID ***Required financial aid form:*** FAFSA.

CONTACT Cheryl Lyons, Director of Student Aid, University of Central Arkansas, 201 Donaghey Avenue, Conway, AR 72035, 501-450-3140 or toll-free 800-243-8245 (in-state). *Fax:* 501-450-5168. *E-mail:* clyons@uca.edu.

UNIVERSITY OF CENTRAL FLORIDA

Orlando, FL

Tuition & fees (FL res): $3947 **Average undergraduate aid package: $7567**

ABOUT THE INSTITUTION State-supported, coed. ***Awards:*** associate, bachelor's, master's, and doctoral degrees and post-bachelor's certificates. 87 undergraduate majors. ***Total enrollment:*** 50,254. Undergraduates: 42,910. Freshmen: 6,344. Federal methodology is used as a basis for awarding need-based institutional aid.

UNDERGRADUATE EXPENSES for 2008–09 ***Application fee:*** $30. ***Tuition, state resident:*** full-time $3947; part-time $131.58 per credit. ***Tuition, nonresident:*** full-time $19,427; part-time $647.56 per credit. Full-time tuition and fees vary according to course load. Part-time tuition and fees vary according to course load. ***College room and board:*** $8492; ***Room only:*** $4750. Room and board charges vary according to board plan and housing facility. ***Payment plans:*** Tuition prepayment, deferred payment.

FRESHMAN FINANCIAL AID (Fall 2007) 4,429 applied for aid; of those 58% were deemed to have need. 99% of freshmen with need received aid; of those 19% had need fully met. ***Average percent of need met:*** 69% (excluding resources awarded to replace EFC). ***Average financial aid package:*** $7235 (excluding resources awarded to replace EFC). 11% of all full-time freshmen had no need and received non-need-based gift aid.

UNDERGRADUATE FINANCIAL AID (Fall 2007) 18,620 applied for aid; of those 70% were deemed to have need. 96% of undergraduates with need received aid; of those 19% had need fully met. ***Average percent of need met:*** 67% (excluding resources awarded to replace EFC). ***Average financial aid package:*** $7567 (excluding resources awarded to replace EFC). 6% of all full-time undergraduates had no need and received non-need-based gift aid.

GIFT AID (NEED-BASED) ***Total amount:*** $42,997,502 (63% federal, 19% state, 17% institutional, 1% external sources). ***Receiving aid:*** Freshmen: 23% (1,492); all full-time undergraduates: 28% (8,726). ***Average award:*** Freshmen: $4196; Undergraduates: $3974. ***Scholarships, grants, and awards:*** Federal Pell, FSEOG, state, private, college/university gift aid from institutional funds.

GIFT AID (NON-NEED-BASED) ***Total amount:*** $67,844,092 (81% state, 12% institutional, 7% external sources). ***Receiving aid:*** Freshmen: 38% (2,404). Undergraduates: 25% (7,795). ***Average award:*** Freshmen: $2177. Undergraduates: $2125. ***Scholarships, grants, and awards by category:*** *Academic interests/achievement:* general academic interests/achievements. *Creative arts/performance:* cinema/film/broadcasting, music, theater/drama. *Special achievements/activities:* general special achievements/activities, leadership. *Special characteristics:* first-generation college students. ***Tuition waivers:*** Full or partial for employees or children of employees, senior citizens. ***ROTC:*** Army, Air Force.

LOANS ***Student loans:*** $80,436,968 (55% need-based, 45% non-need-based). 44% of past graduating class borrowed through all loan programs. *Average indebtedness per student:* $14,601. ***Average need-based loan:*** Freshmen: $3265. Undergraduates: $4664. ***Parent loans:*** $6,579,506 (100% non-need-based). ***Programs:*** FFEL (Subsidized and Unsubsidized Stafford, PLUS), Perkins.

WORK-STUDY ***Federal work-study:*** Total amount: $1,490,778; jobs available. ***State or other work-study/employment:*** Part-time jobs available.

ATHLETIC AWARDS Total amount: $2,303,754 (100% non-need-based).

APPLYING FOR FINANCIAL AID ***Required financial aid form:*** FAFSA. ***Financial aid deadline:*** 6/30 (priority: 3/1). ***Notification date:*** Continuous beginning 3/15. Students must reply within 3 weeks of notification.

CONTACT Ms. Lisa Minnick, Associate Director, Student Financial Assistance, University of Central Florida, 4000 Central Florida Boulevard, Orlando, FL 32816-0113, 407-823-2827. *Fax:* 407-823-5241. *E-mail:* lminnick@mail.ucf.edu.

UNIVERSITY OF CENTRAL MISSOURI

Warrensburg, MO

Tuition & fees (MO res): $7311 **Average undergraduate aid package: $8044**

ABOUT THE INSTITUTION State-supported, coed. ***Awards:*** associate, bachelor's, and master's degrees and post-bachelor's and post-master's certificates. 69 undergraduate majors. ***Total enrollment:*** 11,063. Undergraduates: 8,980. Freshmen: 1,613. Federal methodology is used as a basis for awarding need-based institutional aid.

UNDERGRADUATE EXPENSES for 2008–09 ***Application fee:*** $30. ***Tuition, state resident:*** full-time $6585; part-time $219.50 per credit. ***Tuition, nonresident:*** full-time $12,444; part-time $414.80 per credit. ***Required fees:*** full-time $726; $24.20 per credit. Full-time tuition and fees vary according to course load and location. Part-time tuition and fees vary according to course load and location. ***College room and board:*** $6320; ***Room only:*** $4120. Room and board charges vary according to board plan and housing facility. ***Payment plans:*** Installment, deferred payment.

FRESHMAN FINANCIAL AID (Fall 2007) 1,193 applied for aid; of those 62% were deemed to have need. 100% of freshmen with need received aid; of those 19% had need fully met. ***Average percent of need met:*** 66% (excluding resources awarded to replace EFC). ***Average financial aid package:*** $7048 (excluding resources awarded to replace EFC). 27% of all full-time freshmen had no need and received non-need-based gift aid.

UNDERGRADUATE FINANCIAL AID (Fall 2007) 4,141 applied for aid; of those 69% were deemed to have need. 100% of undergraduates with need received aid; of those 10% had need fully met. ***Average percent of need met:*** 82% (excluding resources awarded to replace EFC). ***Average financial aid package:*** $8044 (excluding resources awarded to replace EFC). 20% of all full-time undergraduates had no need and received non-need-based gift aid.

GIFT AID (NEED-BASED) ***Total amount:*** $10,592,435 (97% federal, 3% institutional). ***Receiving aid:*** Freshmen: 25% (354); all full-time undergraduates: 28% (1,575). ***Average award:*** Freshmen: $2869; Undergraduates: $3101. ***Scholarships, grants, and awards:*** Federal Pell, FSEOG, state, private, college/university gift aid from institutional funds.

GIFT AID (NON-NEED-BASED) ***Total amount:*** $13,321,367 (4% federal, 28% state, 44% institutional, 24% external sources). ***Receiving aid:*** Freshmen: 50% (718). Undergraduates: 46% (2,587). ***Average award:*** Freshmen: $5374. Undergraduates: $5464. ***Scholarships, grants, and awards by category:*** *Academic interests/achievement:* 2,250 awards ($4,600,000 total): agriculture, area/ethnic studies, biological sciences, business, communication, computer science, education, engineering/technologies, English, foreign languages, general academic interests/achievements, health fields, home economics, humanities, library science, mathematics, military science, physical sciences, premedicine, religion/biblical studies, social sciences. *Creative arts/performance:* 80 awards ($31,000 total): applied art and design, art/fine arts, cinema/film/broadcasting, creative writing, debating, journalism/publications, music, performing arts, theater/drama. *Special achievements/activities:* 65 awards ($45,000 total): cheerleading/drum major, leadership. *Special characteristics:* 625 awards ($925,000 total): adult students, children and siblings of alumni, children of faculty/staff, ethnic background, members of minority groups, out-of-state students, previous college experience. ***Tuition waivers:*** Full or partial for children of alumni, employees or children of employees, senior citizens. ***ROTC:*** Army, Air Force cooperative.

LOANS ***Student loans:*** $27,370,934 (49% need-based, 51% non-need-based). 68% of past graduating class borrowed through all loan programs. *Average indebtedness per student:* $18,549. ***Average need-based loan:*** Freshmen: $3016. Undergraduates: $4185. ***Parent loans:*** $8,641,275 (100% non-need-based). ***Programs:*** Federal Direct (Subsidized and Unsubsidized Stafford, PLUS), Perkins, state.

WORK-STUDY ***Federal work-study:*** Total amount: $427,051; 310 jobs averaging $1660. ***State or other work-study/employment:*** Total amount: $1,862,973 (100% non-need-based). 1,100 part-time jobs averaging $1367.

ATHLETIC AWARDS Total amount: $1,825,880 (100% non-need-based).

APPLYING FOR FINANCIAL AID ***Required financial aid form:*** FAFSA. ***Financial aid deadline (priority):*** 4/1. ***Notification date:*** Continuous. Students must reply within 3 weeks of notification.

CONTACT Mr. Phil Shreves, Director of Student Financial Assistance, University of Central Missouri, Student Financial Assistance, WDE 1100, Warrensburg, MO 64093, 660-543-4040 or toll-free 800-729-8266 (in-state). *Fax:* 660-543-8080. *E-mail:* sfs@ucmo.edu.

UNIVERSITY OF CENTRAL OKLAHOMA

Edmond, OK

Tuition & fees (OK res): $4223 **Average undergraduate aid package: $6885**

ABOUT THE INSTITUTION State-supported, coed. ***Awards:*** bachelor's and master's degrees. 88 undergraduate majors. ***Total enrollment:*** 15,724. Undergraduates: 14,156. Freshmen: 2,131. Federal methodology is used as a basis for awarding need-based institutional aid.

UNDERGRADUATE EXPENSES for 2008–09 ***Application fee:*** $25. ***Tuition, state resident:*** full-time $3681; part-time $122.70 per credit hour. ***Tuition, nonresident:*** full-time $10,110; part-time $337 per credit hour. ***Required fees:*** full-time $542; $18.05 per credit hour. Full-time tuition and fees vary according to course load, degree level, and program. Part-time tuition and fees vary according to course load, degree level, and program. ***College room and board:*** $7468; ***Room only:*** $4588. Room and board charges vary according to board plan and housing facility. ***Payment plans:*** Guaranteed tuition, installment, deferred payment.

FRESHMAN FINANCIAL AID (Fall 2007) 1,079 applied for aid; of those 71% were deemed to have need. 90% of freshmen with need received aid; of those 8% had need fully met. ***Average percent of need met:*** 67% (excluding resources awarded to replace EFC). ***Average financial aid package:*** $1191 (excluding resources awarded to replace EFC). 12% of all full-time freshmen had no need and received non-need-based gift aid.

UNDERGRADUATE FINANCIAL AID (Fall 2007) 5,820 applied for aid; of those 81% were deemed to have need. 92% of undergraduates with need received aid; of those 10% had need fully met. ***Average percent of need met:*** 67% (excluding resources awarded to replace EFC). ***Average financial aid package:*** $6885 (excluding resources awarded to replace EFC). 9% of all full-time undergraduates had no need and received non-need-based gift aid.

GIFT AID (NEED-BASED) ***Total amount:*** $17,944,271 (63% federal, 26% state, 2% institutional, 9% external sources). ***Receiving aid:*** Freshmen: 37% (676); all full-time undergraduates: 42% (4,187). ***Average award:*** Freshmen: $7524; Undergraduates: $7022. ***Scholarships, grants, and awards:*** Federal Pell, FSEOG, state, private, college/university gift aid from institutional funds.

GIFT AID (NON-NEED-BASED) ***Total amount:*** $4,484,609 (39% state, 8% institutional, 53% external sources). ***Receiving aid:*** Freshmen: 1% (15). Undergraduates: 2% (152). ***Average award:*** Freshmen: $2767. Undergraduates: $6877. ***Scholarships, grants, and awards by category:*** *Academic interests/achievement:* biological sciences, business, computer science, education, foreign languages, general academic interests/achievements, health fields, home economics, mathematics, military science, physical sciences, social sciences. *Creative arts/performance:* applied art and design, art/fine arts, journalism/publications, music, theater/drama. *Special achievements/activities:* general special achievements/activities, leadership. *Special characteristics:* ethnic background, members of minority groups. ***Tuition waivers:*** Full or partial for employees or children of employees. ***ROTC:*** Army.

LOANS ***Student loans:*** $39,721,893 (88% need-based, 12% non-need-based). 48% of past graduating class borrowed through all loan programs. *Average indebtedness per student:* $17,385. ***Average need-based loan:*** Freshmen: $2942. Undergraduates: $4195. ***Parent loans:*** $1,569,217 (61% need-based, 39% non-need-based). ***Programs:*** Federal Direct (Subsidized and Unsubsidized Stafford, PLUS), FFEL (Subsidized Stafford), Perkins.

WORK-STUDY ***Federal work-study:*** Total amount: $435,922; 221 jobs averaging $2141.

ATHLETIC AWARDS Total amount: $663,262 (51% need-based, 49% non-need-based).

APPLYING FOR FINANCIAL AID ***Required financial aid forms:*** FAFSA, institution's own form. ***Financial aid deadline (priority):*** 5/31. ***Notification date:*** Continuous. Students must reply by 6/30 or within 4 weeks of notification.

CONTACT Ms. Becky Garrett, Assistant Director, Technical Services, University of Central Oklahoma, 100 North University Drive, Edmond, OK 73034-5209, 405-974-3334 or toll-free 800-254-4215. *Fax:* 405-340-7658. *E-mail:* bgarrett@ucok.edu.

UNIVERSITY OF CHARLESTON

Charleston, WV

ABOUT THE INSTITUTION Independent, coed. ***Awards:*** associate, bachelor's, master's, and doctoral degrees. 28 undergraduate majors. ***Total enrollment:*** 1,398. Undergraduates: 1,171. Freshmen: 328.

GIFT AID (NEED-BASED) ***Scholarships, grants, and awards:*** Federal Pell, FSEOG, state, private, college/university gift aid from institutional funds, Council of Independent Colleges Tuition Exchange grants, Tuition Exchange Inc. grants.

GIFT AID (NON-NEED-BASED) ***Scholarships, grants, and awards by category:*** *Academic interests/achievement:* general academic interests/achievements, military science. *Creative arts/performance:* music. *Special achievements/activities:* cheerleading/drum major, community service, general special achievements/activities, leadership. *Special characteristics:* children and siblings of alumni, children of educators, children of faculty/staff, international students, local/state students.

LOANS ***Programs:*** FFEL (Subsidized and Unsubsidized Stafford, PLUS), Perkins, Federal Nursing, alternative loans.

WORK-STUDY ***Federal work-study:*** Total amount: $110,000; 110 jobs averaging $975. ***State or other work-study/employment:*** 25 part-time jobs averaging $850.

APPLYING FOR FINANCIAL AID ***Required financial aid forms:*** FAFSA, institution's own form, state aid form.

CONTACT Ms. Janet M. Ruge, Director of Financial Aid, University of Charleston, 2300 MacCorkle Avenue SE, Charleston, WV 25304-1099, 304-357-4759 or toll-free 800-995-GOUC. *Fax:* 304-357-4769. *E-mail:* janetruge@ucwv.edu.

UNIVERSITY OF CHICAGO

Chicago, IL

CONTACT Office of College Aid, University of Chicago, 1116 East 59th Street, Room 203, Chicago, IL 60637, 773-702-8666. *Fax:* 773-702-5846.

UNIVERSITY OF CINCINNATI

Cincinnati, OH

Tuition & fees (OH res): $9399 **Average undergraduate aid package: $8459**

ABOUT THE INSTITUTION State-supported, coed. ***Awards:*** associate, bachelor's, master's, doctoral, and first professional degrees and post-bachelor's and post-master's certificates. 142 undergraduate majors. ***Total enrollment:*** 29,617. Undergraduates: 20,914. Freshmen: 3,738. Federal methodology is used as a basis for awarding need-based institutional aid.

UNDERGRADUATE EXPENSES for 2008–09 ***Application fee:*** $40. ***Tuition, state resident:*** full-time $7896; part-time $262 per credit hour. ***Tuition, nonresident:*** full-time $23,922; part-time $665 per credit hour. ***Required fees:*** full-time $1503; $42 per credit hour. Full-time tuition and fees vary according to course load, degree level, location, program, and reciprocity agreements. Part-time tuition and fees vary according to course load, degree level, location, program, and reciprocity agreements. ***College room and board:*** $9240; ***Room only:*** $5523. Room and board charges vary according to board plan and housing facility. ***Payment plan:*** Installment.

FRESHMAN FINANCIAL AID (Fall 2008, est.) 3,051 applied for aid; of those 73% were deemed to have need. 99% of freshmen with need received aid; of those 6% had need fully met. ***Average percent of need met:*** 59% (excluding resources awarded to replace EFC). ***Average financial aid package:*** $8335 (excluding resources awarded to replace EFC). 17% of all full-time freshmen had no need and received non-need-based gift aid.

UNDERGRADUATE FINANCIAL AID (Fall 2008, est.) 11,963 applied for aid; of those 79% were deemed to have need. 98% of undergraduates with need received aid; of those 7% had need fully met. ***Average percent of need met:*** 61% (excluding resources awarded to replace EFC). ***Average financial aid package:*** $8459 (excluding resources awarded to replace EFC). 17% of all full-time undergraduates had no need and received non-need-based gift aid.

GIFT AID (NEED-BASED) ***Total amount:*** $36,633,593 (48% federal, 12% state, 33% institutional, 7% external sources). ***Receiving aid:*** Freshmen: 25% (940); all full-time undergraduates: 23% (4,033). ***Average award:*** Freshmen: $5889; Undergraduates: $5357. ***Scholarships, grants, and awards:*** Federal Pell, FSEOG, state, private, college/university gift aid from institutional funds, United Negro College Fund, Federal Nursing, Academic Competitiveness Grant, National Smart Grant, TEACH Grant.

GIFT AID (NON-NEED-BASED) ***Total amount:*** $15,429,120 (1% state, 85% institutional, 14% external sources). ***Receiving aid:*** Freshmen: 27% (1,032). Undergraduates: 22% (3,726). ***Average award:*** Freshmen: $5237. Undergraduates: $4735. ***Tuition waivers:*** Full or partial for employees or children of employees. ***ROTC:*** Army, Air Force.

LOANS ***Student loans:*** $101,157,207 (58% need-based, 42% non-need-based). 65% of past graduating class borrowed through all loan programs. *Average indebtedness per student:* $24,431. ***Average need-based loan:*** Freshmen: $3266. Undergraduates: $3645. ***Parent loans:*** $94,867,127 (11% need-based, 89% non-need-based). ***Programs:*** FFEL (Subsidized and Unsubsidized Stafford, PLUS), Perkins, Federal Nursing, state, college/university.

WORK-STUDY ***Federal work-study:*** Total amount: $4,623,901; jobs available.

ATHLETIC AWARDS Total amount: $5,785,803 (33% need-based, 67% non-need-based).

APPLYING FOR FINANCIAL AID ***Required financial aid form:*** FAFSA. ***Financial aid deadline:*** Continuous. ***Notification date:*** Continuous beginning 3/10. Students must reply within 2 weeks of notification.

CONTACT Mrs. Dana Pawlowicz, Associate Director, University of Cincinnati, PO Box 210125, Cincinnati, OH 45221-0125, 513-556-2441. *Fax:* 513-556-9171. *E-mail:* dana.pawlowicz@uc.edu.

UNIVERSITY OF COLORADO AT BOULDER

Boulder, CO

Tuition & fees (CO res): $7287 **Average undergraduate aid package: $13,605**

ABOUT THE INSTITUTION State-supported, coed. ***Awards:*** bachelor's, master's, doctoral, and first professional degrees and post-master's certificates. 63 undergraduate majors. ***Total enrollment:*** 32,191. Undergraduates: 26,725. Freshmen: 5,863. Federal methodology is used as a basis for awarding need-based institutional aid.

UNDERGRADUATE EXPENSES for 2008–09 ***Application fee:*** $50. ***One-time required fee:*** $112. ***Tuition, state resident:*** full-time $5922. ***Tuition, nonresident:*** full-time $25,400. ***Required fees:*** full-time $1365. Full-time tuition and fees vary according to program. Part-time tuition and fees vary according to course load and program. ***College room and board:*** $9860. Room and board charges vary according to board plan, housing facility, and location. ***Payment plan:*** Deferred payment.

FRESHMAN FINANCIAL AID (Fall 2008, est.) 4,170 applied for aid; of those 46% were deemed to have need. 100% of freshmen with need received aid; of those 74% had need fully met. ***Average percent of need met:*** 93% (excluding resources awarded to replace EFC). ***Average financial aid package:*** $12,699 (excluding resources awarded to replace EFC). 30% of all full-time freshmen had no need and received non-need-based gift aid.

UNDERGRADUATE FINANCIAL AID (Fall 2008, est.) 15,495 applied for aid; of those 49% were deemed to have need. 100% of undergraduates with need received aid; of those 68% had need fully met. ***Average percent of need met:*** 91% (excluding resources awarded to replace EFC). ***Average financial aid package:*** $13,605 (excluding resources awarded to replace EFC). 23% of all full-time undergraduates had no need and received non-need-based gift aid.

GIFT AID (NEED-BASED) ***Total amount:*** $51,199,415 (29% federal, 12% state, 49% institutional, 10% external sources). ***Receiving aid:*** Freshmen: 29% (1,687); all full-time undergraduates: 28% (6,813). ***Average award:*** Freshmen: $7460; Undergraduates: $6729. ***Scholarships, grants, and awards:*** Federal Pell, FSEOG, state, private, college/university gift aid from institutional funds.

GIFT AID (NON-NEED-BASED) ***Total amount:*** $16,873,852 (17% federal, 1% state, 58% institutional, 24% external sources). ***Receiving aid:*** Freshmen: 1% (75). Undergraduates: 1% (178). ***Average award:*** Freshmen: $6355. Undergraduates: $7122. ***Scholarships, grants, and awards by category:*** *Academic interests/achievement:* architecture, area/ethnic studies, biological sciences, business, communication, computer science, education, engineering/technologies, English, foreign languages, general academic interests/achievements, health fields, humanities, international studies, mathematics, military science, physical sciences, premedicine, social sciences. *Creative arts/performance:* art/fine arts, cinema/film/broadcasting, creative writing, dance, journalism/publications, music, performing arts, theater/drama. *Special achievements/activities:* community service, general special achievements/activities, leadership. *Special characteristics:* first-generation college students, general special characteristics, local/state students. ***Tuition waivers:*** Full or partial for senior citizens. ***ROTC:*** Army, Naval, Air Force.

LOANS ***Student loans:*** $79,743,486 (58% need-based, 42% non-need-based). 42% of past graduating class borrowed through all loan programs. *Average indebtedness per student:* $18,361. ***Average need-based loan:*** Freshmen: $5000. Undergraduates: $6281. ***Parent loans:*** $132,240,006 (22% need-based, 78% non-need-based). ***Programs:*** Federal Direct (Subsidized and Unsubsidized Stafford, PLUS), Perkins, college/university, private lenders.

WORK-STUDY ***Federal work-study:*** Total amount: $1,769,700; 1,222 jobs averaging $1776. ***State or other work-study/employment:*** Total amount: $2,618,441 (78% need-based, 22% non-need-based). 792 part-time jobs averaging $2211.

ATHLETIC AWARDS Total amount: $5,350,220 (29% need-based, 71% non-need-based).

APPLYING FOR FINANCIAL AID ***Required financial aid forms:*** FAFSA, tax return required. ***Financial aid deadline (priority):*** 4/1. ***Notification date:*** Continuous. Students must reply within 3 weeks of notification.

CONTACT Gwen E. Pomper, Director of Financial Aid, University of Colorado at Boulder, University Campus Box 77, Boulder, CO 80309, 303-492-8223. *Fax:* 303-492-0838. *E-mail:* finaid@colorado.edu.

UNIVERSITY OF COLORADO AT COLORADO SPRINGS

Colorado Springs, CO

Tuition & fees (CO res): $5878 **Average undergraduate aid package: $7789**

ABOUT THE INSTITUTION State-supported, coed. ***Awards:*** bachelor's, master's, and doctoral degrees and post-bachelor's certificates. 34 undergraduate majors. ***Total enrollment:*** 8,912. Undergraduates: 6,810. Freshmen: 1,159. Federal methodology is used as a basis for awarding need-based institutional aid.

UNDERGRADUATE EXPENSES for 2008–09 ***Application fee:*** $50. ***Tuition, state resident:*** full-time $4916; part-time $278 per credit hour. ***Tuition, nonresident:*** full-time $15,600; part-time $765 per credit hour. ***Required fees:*** full-time $962. Full-time tuition and fees vary according to course level, course load, program, and student level. Part-time tuition and fees vary according to course level, course load, program, and student level. ***College room and board:*** $8750; ***Room only:*** $7650. Room and board charges vary according to board plan and housing facility. ***Payment plan:*** Installment.

FRESHMAN FINANCIAL AID (Fall 2008, est.) 713 applied for aid; of those 54% were deemed to have need. 97% of freshmen with need received aid; of those

18% had need fully met. ***Average percent of need met:*** 56% (excluding resources awarded to replace EFC). ***Average financial aid package:*** $6868 (excluding resources awarded to replace EFC). 15% of all full-time freshmen had no need and received non-need-based gift aid.

UNDERGRADUATE FINANCIAL AID (Fall 2008, est.) 4,212 applied for aid; of those 64% were deemed to have need. 97% of undergraduates with need received aid; of those 17% had need fully met. ***Average percent of need met:*** 57% (excluding resources awarded to replace EFC). ***Average financial aid package:*** $7789 (excluding resources awarded to replace EFC). 6% of all full-time undergraduates had no need and received non-need-based gift aid.

GIFT AID (NEED-BASED) ***Total amount:*** $14,560,068 (38% federal, 21% state, 32% institutional, 9% external sources). ***Receiving aid:*** Freshmen: 44% (363); all full-time undergraduates: 47% (2,437). ***Average award:*** Freshmen: $4713; Undergraduates: $4880. ***Scholarships, grants, and awards:*** Federal Pell, FSEOG, state, private, college/university gift aid from institutional funds.

GIFT AID (NON-NEED-BASED) ***Total amount:*** $133,827 (100% institutional). ***Receiving aid:*** Freshmen: 4. Undergraduates: 1% (33). ***Average award:*** Freshmen: $1284. Undergraduates: $1639. ***Scholarships, grants, and awards by category:*** *Academic interests/achievement:* biological sciences, business, computer science, education, engineering/technologies, English, general academic interests/achievements, health fields, mathematics, military science, physical sciences, premedicine. *Special achievements/activities:* community service, leadership. *Special characteristics:* children and siblings of alumni, first-generation college students, general special characteristics, handicapped students, local/state students, out-of-state students. ***ROTC:*** Army.

LOANS ***Student loans:*** $19,573,330 (100% need-based). 64% of past graduating class borrowed through all loan programs. *Average indebtedness per student:* $21,584. ***Average need-based loan:*** Freshmen: $3136. Undergraduates: $3854. ***Parent loans:*** $3,408,671 (100% need-based). ***Programs:*** FFEL (Subsidized and Unsubsidized Stafford, PLUS), Perkins, college/university.

WORK-STUDY ***Federal work-study:*** Total amount: $603,557; 164 jobs averaging $3680. ***State or other work-study/employment:*** Total amount: $722,174 (80% need-based, 20% non-need-based). 205 part-time jobs averaging $3735.

ATHLETIC AWARDS Total amount: $536,009 (100% need-based).

APPLYING FOR FINANCIAL AID ***Required financial aid form:*** FAFSA. ***Financial aid deadline (priority):*** 4/1. ***Notification date:*** Continuous beginning 4/15.

CONTACT Ms. Lee Ingalls-Noble, Director of Financial Aid, University of Colorado at Colorado Springs, 1420 Austin Bluffs Parkway, Colorado Springs, CO 80918, 719-255-3466 or toll-free 800-990-8227 Ext. 3383. *Fax:* 719-255-3650. *E-mail:* Lnoble@uccs.edu.

UNIVERSITY OF COLORADO DENVER

Denver, CO

Tuition & fees (CO res): $6394 **Average undergraduate aid package: $8294**

ABOUT THE INSTITUTION State-supported, coed. ***Awards:*** bachelor's, master's, doctoral, and first professional degrees and post-master's certificates. 33 undergraduate majors. ***Total enrollment:*** 21,903. Undergraduates: 12,087. Freshmen: 1,125. Federal methodology is used as a basis for awarding need-based institutional aid.

UNDERGRADUATE EXPENSES for 2009–10 ***Application fee:*** $50. ***Tuition, state resident:*** full-time $5484; part-time $234 per credit hour. ***Tuition, nonresident:*** full-time $18,456; part-time $769 per credit hour. ***Required fees:*** full-time $910. ***College room and board:*** $13,524; ***Room only:*** $8889.

FRESHMAN FINANCIAL AID (Fall 2007) 448 applied for aid; of those 78% were deemed to have need. 96% of freshmen with need received aid; of those 8% had need fully met. ***Average percent of need met:*** 52% (excluding resources awarded to replace EFC). ***Average financial aid package:*** $7145 (excluding resources awarded to replace EFC). 12% of all full-time freshmen had no need and received non-need-based gift aid.

UNDERGRADUATE FINANCIAL AID (Fall 2007) 2,947 applied for aid; of those 85% were deemed to have need. 92% of undergraduates with need received aid; of those 6% had need fully met. ***Average percent of need met:*** 52% (excluding resources awarded to replace EFC). ***Average financial aid package:*** $8294 (excluding resources awarded to replace EFC). 9% of all full-time undergraduates had no need and received non-need-based gift aid.

GIFT AID (NEED-BASED) ***Total amount:*** $10,912,772 (40% federal, 26% state, 25% institutional, 9% external sources). ***Receiving aid:*** Freshmen: 33% (286); all full-time undergraduates: 34% (2,034). ***Average award:*** Freshmen: $4334; Undergraduates: $4090. ***Scholarships, grants, and awards:*** Federal Pell, FSEOG, state, private, college/university gift aid from institutional funds, Federal Nursing.

GIFT AID (NON-NEED-BASED) ***Total amount:*** $452,670 (59% institutional, 41% external sources). ***Receiving aid:*** Freshmen: 15% (128). Undergraduates: 7% (392). ***Average award:*** Freshmen: $6683. Undergraduates: $6984. ***ROTC:*** Army, Air Force cooperative.

LOANS ***Student loans:*** $22,011,178 (77% need-based, 23% non-need-based). 46% of past graduating class borrowed through all loan programs. *Average indebtedness per student:* $17,441. ***Average need-based loan:*** Freshmen: $2628. Undergraduates: $4688. ***Parent loans:*** $2,384,835 (21% need-based, 79% non-need-based). ***Programs:*** FFEL (Subsidized and Unsubsidized Stafford, PLUS), Perkins, Federal Nursing, college/university.

WORK-STUDY ***Federal work-study:*** Total amount: $497,347; jobs available. ***State or other work-study/employment:*** Total amount: $725,358 (92% need-based, 8% non-need-based). Part-time jobs available.

APPLYING FOR FINANCIAL AID ***Required financial aid forms:*** FAFSA, institution's own form. ***Financial aid deadline (priority):*** 4/1. ***Notification date:*** Continuous beginning 5/1.

CONTACT Patrick McTee, Director of Financial Aid, University of Colorado Denver, PO Box 173364, Denver, CO 80217-3364, 303-556-2886. *Fax:* 303-556-2325. *E-mail:* patrick.mctee@ucdenver.edu.

UNIVERSITY OF CONNECTICUT

Storrs, CT

Tuition & fees (CT res): $9338 **Average undergraduate aid package: $11,048**

ABOUT THE INSTITUTION State-supported, coed. ***Awards:*** associate, bachelor's, master's, doctoral, and first professional degrees and post-bachelor's and post-master's certificates. 96 undergraduate majors. ***Total enrollment:*** 24,273. Undergraduates: 16,765. Freshmen: 3,604. Federal methodology is used as a basis for awarding need-based institutional aid.

UNDERGRADUATE EXPENSES for 2008–09 ***Application fee:*** $70. ***Tuition, state resident:*** full-time $7200; part-time $300 per credit. ***Tuition, nonresident:*** full-time $21,912; part-time $913 per credit. ***Required fees:*** full-time $2138. Part-time tuition and fees vary according to course load. ***College room and board:*** $9300; ***Room only:*** $5090. Room and board charges vary according to board plan and housing facility. ***Payment plans:*** Installment, deferred payment.

FRESHMAN FINANCIAL AID (Fall 2008, est.) 2,866 applied for aid; of those 63% were deemed to have need. 97% of freshmen with need received aid; of those 21% had need fully met. ***Average percent of need met:*** 72% (excluding resources awarded to replace EFC). ***Average financial aid package:*** $12,142 (excluding resources awarded to replace EFC). 11% of all full-time freshmen had no need and received non-need-based gift aid.

UNDERGRADUATE FINANCIAL AID (Fall 2008, est.) 10,944 applied for aid; of those 72% were deemed to have need. 97% of undergraduates with need received aid; of those 20% had need fully met. ***Average percent of need met:*** 67% (excluding resources awarded to replace EFC). ***Average financial aid package:*** $11,048 (excluding resources awarded to replace EFC). 8% of all full-time undergraduates had no need and received non-need-based gift aid.

GIFT AID (NEED-BASED) ***Total amount:*** $53,094,089 (20% federal, 24% state, 51% institutional, 5% external sources). ***Receiving aid:*** Freshmen: 37% (1,341); all full-time undergraduates: 34% (5,513). ***Average award:*** Freshmen: $7389; Undergraduates: $6649. ***Scholarships, grants, and awards:*** Federal Pell, FSEOG, state, private, college/university gift aid from institutional funds.

GIFT AID (NON-NEED-BASED) ***Total amount:*** $8,561,478 (70% institutional, 30% external sources). ***Receiving aid:*** Freshmen: 37% (1,332). Undergraduates: 24% (3,795). ***Average award:*** Freshmen: $6609. Undergraduates: $6080. ***Scholarships, grants, and awards by category:*** *Academic interests/achievement:* 5,189 awards ($16,699,367 total): agriculture, biological sciences, business, computer science, education, engineering/technologies, English, foreign languages, general academic interests/achievements, health fields, humanities, international studies, mathematics, physical sciences, premedicine, religion/biblical studies, social sciences. *Creative arts/performance:* 120 awards ($200,000 total): art/fine arts, music, theater/drama. *Special achievements/activities:* 443 awards ($5,581,969 total): community service, leadership. *Special characteristics:* 4,502 awards ($12,636,124 total): adult students, children of faculty/staff, children of union members/company employees, local/state students, out-of-state students, spouses of deceased or disabled public servants, veterans. ***Tuition waivers:*** Full or partial for employees or children of employees, senior citizens. ***ROTC:*** Army, Air Force.

LOANS ***Student loans:*** $70,135,192 (78% need-based, 22% non-need-based). 61% of past graduating class borrowed through all loan programs. *Average indebtedness per student:* $21,521. ***Average need-based loan:*** Freshmen: $3835. Undergraduates: $4305. ***Parent loans:*** $30,875,849 (30% need-based, 70% non-need-based). ***Programs:*** FFEL (Subsidized and Unsubsidized Stafford, PLUS), Perkins, state.

WORK-STUDY ***Federal work-study:*** Total amount: $2,709,320; 1,603 jobs averaging $1747. ***State or other work-study/employment:*** Total amount: $13,240,000 (26% need-based, 74% non-need-based). 5,423 part-time jobs averaging $2189.

ATHLETIC AWARDS Total amount: $8,524,164 (28% need-based, 72% non-need-based).

APPLYING FOR FINANCIAL AID ***Required financial aid form:*** FAFSA. ***Financial aid deadline (priority):*** 3/1. ***Notification date:*** Continuous beginning 3/1. Students must reply within 4 weeks of notification.

CONTACT Client Service Staff, University of Connecticut, 233 Glenbrook Road, Unit 4116, Storrs, CT 06269-4116, 860-486-2819. *Fax:* 860-486-5098. *E-mail:* financialaid@uconn.edu.

UNIVERSITY OF DALLAS

Irving, TX

Tuition & fees: $26,294 **Average undergraduate aid package: $20,520**

ABOUT THE INSTITUTION Independent Roman Catholic, coed. ***Awards:*** bachelor's, master's, and doctoral degrees and post-bachelor's and post-master's certificates. 32 undergraduate majors. ***Total enrollment:*** 2,977. Undergraduates: 1,299. Freshmen: 342. Federal methodology is used as a basis for awarding need-based institutional aid.

UNDERGRADUATE EXPENSES for 2009–10 ***Application fee:*** $40. ***Comprehensive fee:*** $34,514 includes full-time tuition ($24,646), mandatory fees ($1648), and room and board ($8220). ***College room only:*** $4570. ***Part-time tuition:*** $1034 per credit hour. ***Part-time fees:*** $1648 per year.

FRESHMAN FINANCIAL AID (Fall 2008, est.) 256 applied for aid; of those 81% were deemed to have need. 100% of freshmen with need received aid; of those 31% had need fully met. ***Average percent of need met:*** 79% (excluding resources awarded to replace EFC). ***Average financial aid package:*** $20,907 (excluding resources awarded to replace EFC). 35% of all full-time freshmen had no need and received non-need-based gift aid.

UNDERGRADUATE FINANCIAL AID (Fall 2008, est.) 891 applied for aid; of those 88% were deemed to have need. 100% of undergraduates with need received aid; of those 24% had need fully met. ***Average percent of need met:*** 76% (excluding resources awarded to replace EFC). ***Average financial aid package:*** $20,520 (excluding resources awarded to replace EFC). 33% of all full-time undergraduates had no need and received non-need-based gift aid.

GIFT AID (NEED-BASED) ***Total amount:*** $12,249,302 (9% federal, 6% state, 82% institutional, 3% external sources). ***Receiving aid:*** Freshmen: 61% (208); all full-time undergraduates: 62% (778). ***Average award:*** Freshmen: $15,880; Undergraduates: $15,531. ***Scholarships, grants, and awards:*** Federal Pell, FSEOG, state, private, college/university gift aid from institutional funds.

GIFT AID (NON-NEED-BASED) ***Total amount:*** $4,966,494 (1% federal, 99% institutional). ***Receiving aid:*** Freshmen: 7% (24). Undergraduates: 6% (70). ***Average award:*** Freshmen: $11,487. Undergraduates: $11,084. ***Scholarships, grants, and awards by category:*** *Academic interests/achievement:* 1,200 awards ($8,527,150 total): business, education, foreign languages, general academic interests/achievements, mathematics, physical sciences, premedicine, religion/biblical studies. *Creative arts/performance:* 40 awards ($83,200 total): art/fine arts, music, theater/drama. *Special achievements/activities:* 31 awards ($67,000 total): leadership. *Special characteristics:* 140 awards ($557,700 total): children of faculty/staff, religious affiliation, siblings of current students. ***ROTC:*** Army cooperative, Air Force cooperative.

LOANS ***Student loans:*** $6,349,888 (47% need-based, 53% non-need-based). 71% of past graduating class borrowed through all loan programs. *Average indebtedness per student:* $25,410. ***Average need-based loan:*** Freshmen: $3894. Undergraduates: $4525. ***Parent loans:*** $1,008,767 (100% non-need-based). ***Programs:*** FFEL (Subsidized and Unsubsidized Stafford, PLUS), Perkins, state.

WORK-STUDY ***Federal work-study:*** Total amount: $365,624; 296 jobs averaging $1655. ***State or other work-study/employment:*** Total amount: $5506 (100% need-based). 9 part-time jobs averaging $1200.

APPLYING FOR FINANCIAL AID ***Required financial aid form:*** FAFSA. ***Financial aid deadline (priority):*** 3/1. ***Notification date:*** Continuous. Students must reply by 5/1 or within 2 weeks of notification.

CONTACT Laurie Rosenkrantz, Assistant Dean of Enrollment Management, University of Dallas, 1845 East Northgate Drive, Irving, TX 75062, 972-721-5266 or toll-free 800-628-6999. *Fax:* 972-721-5017. *E-mail:* ugadmis@udallas.edu.

UNIVERSITY OF DAYTON

Dayton, OH

Tuition & fees: $27,330 **Average undergraduate aid package: $19,563**

ABOUT THE INSTITUTION Independent Roman Catholic, coed. ***Awards:*** bachelor's, master's, doctoral, and first professional degrees and post-master's certificates. 74 undergraduate majors. ***Total enrollment:*** 10,920. Undergraduates: 7,731. Freshmen: 1,984. Federal methodology is used as a basis for awarding need-based institutional aid.

UNDERGRADUATE EXPENSES for 2008–09 ***Application fee:*** $50. ***Comprehensive fee:*** $35,310 includes full-time tuition ($26,200), mandatory fees ($1130), and room and board ($7980). ***College room only:*** $4780. Full-time tuition and fees vary according to program. Room and board charges vary according to board plan, housing facility, and student level. ***Part-time tuition:*** $873 per credit hour. ***Part-time fees:*** $25 per term. Part-time tuition and fees vary according to course load and program. ***Payment plan:*** Deferred payment.

FRESHMAN FINANCIAL AID (Fall 2007) 1,380 applied for aid; of those 75% were deemed to have need. 100% of freshmen with need received aid; of those 44% had need fully met. ***Average percent of need met:*** 95% (excluding resources awarded to replace EFC). ***Average financial aid package:*** $20,985 (excluding resources awarded to replace EFC).

UNDERGRADUATE FINANCIAL AID (Fall 2007) 4,907 applied for aid; of those 80% were deemed to have need. 97% of undergraduates with need received aid; of those 50% had need fully met. ***Average percent of need met:*** 92% (excluding resources awarded to replace EFC). ***Average financial aid package:*** $19,563 (excluding resources awarded to replace EFC). 40% of all full-time undergraduates had no need and received non-need-based gift aid.

GIFT AID (NEED-BASED) ***Total amount:*** $39,612,416 (9% federal, 7% state, 80% institutional, 4% external sources). ***Receiving aid:*** Freshmen: 56% (992); all full-time undergraduates: 52% (3,582). ***Average award:*** Freshmen: $12,448; Undergraduates: $9966. ***Scholarships, grants, and awards:*** Federal Pell, FSEOG, state, private, college/university gift aid from institutional funds.

GIFT AID (NON-NEED-BASED) ***Total amount:*** $21,938,362 (4% federal, 5% state, 88% institutional, 3% external sources). ***Receiving aid:*** Freshmen: 50% (882). Undergraduates: 50% (3,394). ***Average award:*** Freshmen: $6832. Undergraduates: $7181. ***Scholarships, grants, and awards by category:*** *Academic interests/achievement:* 5,679 awards ($39,224,035 total): business, education, engineering/technologies, general academic interests/achievements, humanities. *Creative arts/performance:* 108 awards ($374,778 total): art/fine arts, music. *Special achievements/activities:* general special achievements/activities. *Special characteristics:* 437 awards ($8,596,123 total): children of faculty/staff, religious affiliation. ***Tuition waivers:*** Full or partial for employees or children of employees, senior citizens. ***ROTC:*** Army, Air Force cooperative.

LOANS ***Student loans:*** $37,651,566 (82% need-based, 18% non-need-based). 59% of past graduating class borrowed through all loan programs. *Average indebtedness per student:* $16,738. ***Average need-based loan:*** Freshmen: $6877. Undergraduates: $7817. ***Parent loans:*** $7,638,611 (74% need-based, 26% non-need-based). ***Programs:*** FFEL (Subsidized and Unsubsidized Stafford, PLUS), Perkins, state, college/university.

WORK-STUDY ***Federal work-study:*** Total amount: $1,260,000; 865 jobs averaging $1456. ***State or other work-study/employment:*** Total amount: $4,144,138 (100% non-need-based). 2,768 part-time jobs averaging $1497.

ATHLETIC AWARDS Total amount: $2,919,443 (44% need-based, 56% non-need-based).

APPLYING FOR FINANCIAL AID ***Required financial aid form:*** FAFSA. ***Financial aid deadline (priority):*** 3/31. ***Notification date:*** Continuous. Students must reply within 3 weeks of notification.

CONTACT Kathy Harmon, Director of Scholarships and Financial Aid, University of Dayton, 300 College Park Drive, Dayton, OH 45469-1305, 937-229-4311 or toll-free 800-837-7433. *Fax:* 937-229-4338. *E-mail:* kharmon@udayton.edu.

UNIVERSITY OF DELAWARE

Newark, DE

Tuition & fees (DE res): $8646 **Average undergraduate aid package: $11,257**

ABOUT THE INSTITUTION State-related, coed. ***Awards:*** associate, bachelor's, master's, and doctoral degrees. 117 undergraduate majors. ***Total enrollment:*** 19,832. Undergraduates: 16,384. Freshmen: 3,422. Federal methodology is used as a basis for awarding need-based institutional aid.

UNDERGRADUATE EXPENSES for 2008–09 ***Application fee:*** $70. ***Tuition, state resident:*** full-time $7780; part-time $325 per credit. ***Tuition, nonresident:*** full-time $20,260; part-time $845 per credit. ***Required fees:*** full-time $866. ***College room and board:*** $8478; ***Room only:*** $5128. Room and board charges vary according to housing facility. ***Payment plan:*** Installment.

FRESHMAN FINANCIAL AID (Fall 2008, est.) 2,901 applied for aid; of those 51% were deemed to have need. 97% of freshmen with need received aid; of those 52% had need fully met. ***Average percent of need met:*** 73% (excluding resources awarded to replace EFC). ***Average financial aid package:*** $10,639 (excluding resources awarded to replace EFC). 17% of all full-time freshmen had no need and received non-need-based gift aid.

UNDERGRADUATE FINANCIAL AID (Fall 2008, est.) 9,169 applied for aid; of those 61% were deemed to have need. 98% of undergraduates with need received aid; of those 53% had need fully met. ***Average percent of need met:*** 77% (excluding resources awarded to replace EFC). ***Average financial aid package:*** $11,257 (excluding resources awarded to replace EFC). 16% of all full-time undergraduates had no need and received non-need-based gift aid.

GIFT AID (NEED-BASED) ***Total amount:*** $23,890,246 (23% federal, 29% state, 38% institutional, 10% external sources). ***Receiving aid:*** Freshmen: 27% (1,045); all full-time undergraduates: 25% (3,866). ***Average award:*** Freshmen: $5892; Undergraduates: $6025. ***Scholarships, grants, and awards:*** Federal Pell, FSEOG, state, private, college/university gift aid from institutional funds.

GIFT AID (NON-NEED-BASED) ***Total amount:*** $17,435,535 (8% state, 79% institutional, 13% external sources). ***Receiving aid:*** Freshmen: 22% (848). Undergraduates: 12% (1,840). ***Average award:*** Freshmen: $6073. Undergraduates: $5758. ***Scholarships, grants, and awards by category:*** *Academic interests/achievement:* agriculture, biological sciences, business, communication, computer science, education, engineering/technologies, English, foreign languages, general academic interests/achievements, health fields, humanities, international studies, mathematics, military science, physical sciences, premedicine, religion/biblical studies, social sciences. *Creative arts/performance:* applied art and design, art/fine arts, music, theater/drama. *Special achievements/activities:* cheerleading/drum major, community service, general special achievements/activities, leadership. *Special characteristics:* children and siblings of alumni, children of faculty/staff, children of public servants, ethnic background, first-generation college students, general special characteristics, local/state students, members of minority groups. ***Tuition waivers:*** Full or partial for employees or children of employees, senior citizens. ***ROTC:*** Army, Air Force.

LOANS ***Student loans:*** $63,088,633 (49% need-based, 51% non-need-based). 44% of past graduating class borrowed through all loan programs. *Average indebtedness per student:* $17,200. ***Average need-based loan:*** Freshmen: $5634. Undergraduates: $6604. ***Parent loans:*** $19,503,169 (27% need-based, 73% non-need-based). ***Programs:*** Federal Direct (Subsidized and Unsubsidized Stafford, PLUS), Perkins, Federal Nursing.

WORK-STUDY ***Federal work-study:*** Total amount: $1,079,847; jobs available. ***State or other work-study/employment:*** Total amount: $189,368 (64% need-based, 36% non-need-based). Part-time jobs available.

ATHLETIC AWARDS Total amount: $6,721,630 (20% need-based, 80% non-need-based).

APPLYING FOR FINANCIAL AID ***Required financial aid form:*** FAFSA. ***Financial aid deadline:*** 3/15 (priority: 2/1). ***Notification date:*** Continuous beginning 3/15. Students must reply by 5/1 or within 3 weeks of notification.

CONTACT Mr. Johnie A. Burton, Director of Scholarships and Financial Aid, University of Delaware, 224 Hullihen Hall, Newark, DE 19716, 302-831-8081. *E-mail:* jburton@udel.edu.

UNIVERSITY OF DENVER

Denver, CO

Tuition & fees: $35,481 **Average undergraduate aid package: $26,599**

ABOUT THE INSTITUTION Independent, coed. ***Awards:*** bachelor's, master's, doctoral, and first professional degrees and post-bachelor's and post-master's certificates. 73 undergraduate majors. ***Total enrollment:*** 11,328. Undergraduates: 5,324. Freshmen: 1,134. Federal methodology is used as a basis for awarding need-based institutional aid.

UNDERGRADUATE EXPENSES for 2009–10 ***Application fee:*** $50. ***Comprehensive fee:*** $45,381 includes full-time tuition ($34,596), mandatory fees ($885), and room and board ($9900). ***College room only:*** $5955. ***Part-time tuition:*** $961 per quarter hour.

FRESHMAN FINANCIAL AID (Fall 2007) 646 applied for aid; of those 76% were deemed to have need. 100% of freshmen with need received aid; of those 28% had need fully met. ***Average percent of need met:*** 77% (excluding resources awarded to replace EFC). ***Average financial aid package:*** $26,707 (excluding resources awarded to replace EFC). 34% of all full-time freshmen had no need and received non-need-based gift aid.

UNDERGRADUATE FINANCIAL AID (Fall 2007) 2,372 applied for aid; of those 82% were deemed to have need. 99% of undergraduates with need received aid; of those 23% had need fully met. ***Average percent of need met:*** 75% (excluding resources awarded to replace EFC). ***Average financial aid package:*** $26,599 (excluding resources awarded to replace EFC). 38% of all full-time undergraduates had no need and received non-need-based gift aid.

GIFT AID (NEED-BASED) ***Total amount:*** $36,574,943 (9% federal, 4% state, 78% institutional, 9% external sources). ***Receiving aid:*** Freshmen: 43% (486); all full-time undergraduates: 42% (1,897). ***Average award:*** Freshmen: $18,908; Undergraduates: $19,412. ***Scholarships, grants, and awards:*** Federal Pell, FSEOG, state, private, college/university gift aid from institutional funds.

GIFT AID (NON-NEED-BASED) ***Total amount:*** $16,286,353 (1% state, 91% institutional, 8% external sources). ***Receiving aid:*** Freshmen: 5% (61). Undergraduates: 4% (176). ***Average award:*** Freshmen: $10,376. Undergraduates: $9639. ***Scholarships, grants, and awards by category:*** *Academic interests/achievement:* business. *Creative arts/performance:* art/fine arts, debating, music, theater/drama. *Special achievements/activities:* community service, leadership. *Special characteristics:* children of faculty/staff, local/state students. ***ROTC:*** Army cooperative, Air Force cooperative.

LOANS ***Student loans:*** $10,765,693 (85% need-based, 15% non-need-based). 34% of past graduating class borrowed through all loan programs. *Average indebtedness per student:* $11,218. ***Average need-based loan:*** Freshmen: $3252. Undergraduates: $4182. ***Parent loans:*** $7,080,288 (31% need-based, 69% non-need-based). ***Programs:*** Federal Direct (Subsidized and Unsubsidized Stafford, PLUS), FFEL (Subsidized and Unsubsidized Stafford, PLUS), Perkins, college/university.

WORK-STUDY ***Federal work-study:*** Total amount: $741,161; 360 jobs averaging $2089. ***State or other work-study/employment:*** Total amount: $428,475 (99% need-based, 1% non-need-based). 212 part-time jobs averaging $2021.

ATHLETIC AWARDS Total amount: $6,979,267 (13% need-based, 87% non-need-based).

APPLYING FOR FINANCIAL AID ***Required financial aid forms:*** FAFSA, CSS Financial Aid PROFILE, noncustodial (divorced/separated) parent's statement. ***Financial aid deadline (priority):*** 3/1. ***Notification date:*** 4/1. Students must reply by 5/1.

CONTACT Ms. Barbara McFall, Director of Financial Aid, University of Denver, Office of Financial Aid, Denver, CO 80208, 303-871-2342 or toll-free 800-525-9495 (out-of-state). *Fax:* 303-871-2341. *E-mail:* bmcfall@du.edu.

UNIVERSITY OF DETROIT MERCY

Detroit, MI

CONTACT Sandy Ross, Director of Financial Aid and Scholarships, University of Detroit Mercy, 4001 West McNichols Road, Detroit, MI 48221-3038, 313-993-3350 or toll-free 800-635-5020 (out-of-state). *Fax:* 313-993-3347.

UNIVERSITY OF DUBUQUE

Dubuque, IA

ABOUT THE INSTITUTION Independent Presbyterian, coed. 32 undergraduate majors.

GIFT AID (NEED-BASED) ***Scholarships, grants, and awards:*** Federal Pell, FSEOG, state, private, college/university gift aid from institutional funds.

GIFT AID (NON-NEED-BASED) ***Scholarships, grants, and awards by category:*** *Academic interests/achievement:* general academic interests/achievements. *Special* *characteristics:* children and siblings of alumni, children of educators, children of faculty/staff, ethnic background, members of minority groups, out-of-state students, relatives of clergy, religious affiliation, siblings of current students.

LOANS ***Programs:*** FFEL (Subsidized and Unsubsidized Stafford, PLUS), Perkins, state, college/university.

WORK-STUDY ***Federal work-study:*** Total amount: $166,894; 175 jobs averaging $1500. ***State or other work-study/employment:*** Total amount: $143,439 (100% need-based). 150 part-time jobs averaging $1500.

APPLYING FOR FINANCIAL AID ***Required financial aid form:*** FAFSA.

CONTACT Mr. Timothy Kremer, Director of Financial Aid, University of Dubuque, 2000 University Avenue, Dubuque, IA 52001-5050, 563-589-3170 or toll-free 800-722-5583 (in-state). *Fax:* 563-589-3690.

UNIVERSITY OF EVANSVILLE

Evansville, IN

Tuition & fees: $25,845 **Average undergraduate aid package: $21,693**

ABOUT THE INSTITUTION Independent religious, coed. ***Awards:*** associate, bachelor's, master's, and doctoral degrees. 84 undergraduate majors. ***Total enrollment:*** 2,789. Undergraduates: 2,632. Freshmen: 619. Federal methodology is used as a basis for awarding need-based institutional aid.

UNDERGRADUATE EXPENSES for 2008–09 ***Application fee:*** $35. ***Comprehensive fee:*** $34,075 includes full-time tuition ($25,130), mandatory fees ($715), and room and board ($8230). ***College room only:*** $4250. Room and board charges vary according to board plan and housing facility. ***Part-time tuition:*** $690 per hour. ***Part-time fees:*** $45 per term. Part-time tuition and fees vary according to course load. ***Payment plan:*** Installment.

FRESHMAN FINANCIAL AID (Fall 2008, est.) 520 applied for aid; of those 87% were deemed to have need. 100% of freshmen with need received aid; of those 31% had need fully met. ***Average percent of need met:*** 92% (excluding resources awarded to replace EFC). ***Average financial aid package:*** $23,685 (excluding resources awarded to replace EFC). 23% of all full-time freshmen had no need and received non-need-based gift aid.

UNDERGRADUATE FINANCIAL AID (Fall 2008, est.) 1,952 applied for aid; of those 82% were deemed to have need. 100% of undergraduates with need received aid; of those 29% had need fully met. ***Average percent of need met:*** 86% (excluding resources awarded to replace EFC). ***Average financial aid package:*** $21,693 (excluding resources awarded to replace EFC). 23% of all full-time undergraduates had no need and received non-need-based gift aid.

GIFT AID (NEED-BASED) ***Total amount:*** $28,319,305 (10% federal, 18% state, 67% institutional, 5% external sources). ***Receiving aid:*** Freshmen: 73% (451); all full-time undergraduates: 67% (1,579). ***Average award:*** Freshmen: $20,695; Undergraduates: $18,442. ***Scholarships, grants, and awards:*** Federal Pell, FSEOG, state, private, college/university gift aid from institutional funds.

GIFT AID (NON-NEED-BASED) ***Total amount:*** $6,933,716 (91% institutional, 9% external sources). ***Receiving aid:*** Freshmen: 65% (401). Undergraduates: 57% (1,349). ***Average award:*** Freshmen: $13,011. Undergraduates: $12,103. ***Scholarships, grants, and awards by category:*** *Academic interests/achievement:* 1,268 awards ($12,776,473 total): biological sciences, business, communication, computer science, education, engineering/technologies, English, foreign languages, general academic interests/achievements, health fields, humanities, international studies, mathematics, physical sciences, premedicine, religion/biblical studies, social sciences. *Creative arts/performance:* 220 awards ($2,077,268 total): art/fine arts, music, theater/drama. *Special achievements/activities:* 75 awards ($352,884 total): leadership. *Special characteristics:* 277 awards ($2,988,848 total): children and siblings of alumni, children of faculty/staff, international students, members of minority groups, religious affiliation, siblings of current students. ***Tuition waivers:*** Full or partial for minority students, children of alumni, employees or children of employees, senior citizens.

LOANS ***Student loans:*** $8,992,132 (94% need-based, 6% non-need-based). 70% of past graduating class borrowed through all loan programs. *Average indebtedness per student:* $25,390. ***Average need-based loan:*** Freshmen: $4040. Undergraduates: $4908. ***Parent loans:*** $4,497,401 (82% need-based, 18% non-need-based). ***Programs:*** FFEL (Subsidized and Unsubsidized Stafford, PLUS), Perkins, Federal Nursing.

WORK-STUDY ***Federal work-study:*** Total amount: $462,337; 401 jobs averaging $1190. ***State or other work-study/employment:*** Total amount: $62,400 (100% non-need-based). 50 part-time jobs averaging $1248.

ATHLETIC AWARDS Total amount: $3,770,290 (38% need-based, 62% non-need-based).

APPLYING FOR FINANCIAL AID ***Required financial aid form:*** FAFSA. ***Financial aid deadline (priority):*** 3/10. ***Notification date:*** Continuous beginning 3/25. Students must reply by 5/1.

CONTACT Ms. JoAnn E. Laugel, Director of Financial Aid, University of Evansville, 1800 Lincoln Avenue, Evansville, IN 47722, 812-488-2364 or toll-free 800-423-8633 Ext. 2468. *Fax:* 812-488-2028. *E-mail:* jl25@evansville.edu.

THE UNIVERSITY OF FINDLAY

Findlay, OH

Tuition & fees: $24,670 **Average undergraduate aid package: $17,345**

ABOUT THE INSTITUTION Independent religious, coed. ***Awards:*** associate, bachelor's, master's, and first professional degrees. 58 undergraduate majors. ***Total enrollment:*** 5,761. Undergraduates: 4,210. Freshmen: 622. Federal methodology is used as a basis for awarding need-based institutional aid.

UNDERGRADUATE EXPENSES for 2008–09 ***Comprehensive fee:*** $32,976 includes full-time tuition ($23,938), mandatory fees ($732), and room and board ($8306). ***College room only:*** $4144. Full-time tuition and fees vary according to course load and program. ***Part-time tuition:*** $528 per semester hour. ***Part-time fees:*** $632 per term. Part-time tuition and fees vary according to course load and program. ***Payment plan:*** Installment.

FRESHMAN FINANCIAL AID (Fall 2008, est.) 585 applied for aid; of those 79% were deemed to have need. 100% of freshmen with need received aid; of those 10% had need fully met. ***Average percent of need met:*** 71% (excluding resources awarded to replace EFC). ***Average financial aid package:*** $19,022 (excluding resources awarded to replace EFC). 15% of all full-time freshmen had no need and received non-need-based gift aid.

UNDERGRADUATE FINANCIAL AID (Fall 2008, est.) 2,428 applied for aid; of those 79% were deemed to have need. 100% of undergraduates with need received aid; of those 10% had need fully met. ***Average percent of need met:*** 68% (excluding resources awarded to replace EFC). ***Average financial aid package:*** $17,345 (excluding resources awarded to replace EFC). 15% of all full-time undergraduates had no need and received non-need-based gift aid.

GIFT AID (NEED-BASED) ***Total amount:*** $23,888,000 (10% federal, 6% state, 81% institutional, 3% external sources). ***Receiving aid:*** Freshmen: 63% (409); all full-time undergraduates: 63% (1,695). ***Average award:*** Freshmen: $12,203; Undergraduates: $10,362. ***Scholarships, grants, and awards:*** Federal Pell, FSEOG, state, college/university gift aid from institutional funds.

GIFT AID (NON-NEED-BASED) ***Total amount:*** $3,775,000 (7% state, 90% institutional, 3% external sources). ***Receiving aid:*** Freshmen: 72% (462). Undergraduates: 71% (1,915). ***Average award:*** Freshmen: $11,464. Undergraduates: $10,110. ***Scholarships, grants, and awards by category:*** *Academic interests/achievement:* 2,214 awards ($18,980,000 total): general academic interests/achievements. *Creative arts/performance:* 151 awards ($150,000 total): music, theater/drama. *Special characteristics:* 145 awards ($1,455,000 total): children of faculty/staff. ***Tuition waivers:*** Full or partial for children of alumni, employees or children of employees, senior citizens. ***ROTC:*** Army cooperative, Air Force cooperative.

LOANS ***Student loans:*** $25,450,000 (73% need-based, 27% non-need-based). 89% of past graduating class borrowed through all loan programs. *Average indebtedness per student:* $32,659. ***Average need-based loan:*** Freshmen: $2828. Undergraduates: $4950. ***Parent loans:*** $2,105,000 (65% need-based, 35% non-need-based). ***Programs:*** FFEL (Subsidized and Unsubsidized Stafford, PLUS), Perkins, college/university.

WORK-STUDY ***Federal work-study:*** Total amount: $500,000; 420 jobs averaging $830. ***State or other work-study/employment:*** Total amount: $800,000 (100% non-need-based). 300 part-time jobs averaging $850.

ATHLETIC AWARDS Total amount: $2,668,000 (85% need-based, 15% non-need-based).

APPLYING FOR FINANCIAL AID ***Required financial aid form:*** FAFSA. ***Financial aid deadline:*** Continuous. ***Notification date:*** Continuous beginning 3/1. Students must reply within 2 weeks of notification.

CONTACT Mr. Arman Habegger, Director of Financial Aid, The University of Findlay, 1000 North Main Street, Findlay, OH 45840-3695, 419-434-4791 or toll-free 800-548-0932. *Fax:* 419-434-4344. *E-mail:* finaid@findlay.edu.

UNIVERSITY OF FLORIDA
Gainesville, FL

Tuition & fees (FL res): $3778 **Average undergraduate aid package: N/A**

ABOUT THE INSTITUTION State-supported, coed. ***Awards:*** bachelor's, master's, doctoral, and first professional degrees. 105 undergraduate majors. ***Total enrollment:*** 51,474. Undergraduates: 34,654. Freshmen: 6,384. Federal methodology is used as a basis for awarding need-based institutional aid.

UNDERGRADUATE EXPENSES for 2008–09 ***Application fee:*** $30. ***Tuition, state resident:*** full-time $2670; part-time $88.99 per credit hour. ***Tuition, nonresident:*** full-time $18,713; part-time $623.75 per credit hour. ***Required fees:*** full-time $1108; $36.92 per credit hour. ***College room and board:*** $7150; ***Room only:*** $4630. Room and board charges vary according to board plan. an additional financial aid fee of $26.73 per credit hour or $801.90 for a full academic year is paid by out-of-state students. ***Payment plans:*** Tuition prepayment, deferred payment.

FRESHMAN FINANCIAL AID (Fall 2007) 4,155 applied for aid; of those 64% were deemed to have need. 100% of freshmen with need received aid; of those 43% had need fully met. ***Average percent of need met:*** 86% (excluding resources awarded to replace EFC). 56% of all full-time freshmen had no need and received non-need-based gift aid.

UNDERGRADUATE FINANCIAL AID (Fall 2007) 16,180 applied for aid; of those 78% were deemed to have need. 99% of undergraduates with need received aid; of those 37% had need fully met. ***Average percent of need met:*** 84% (excluding resources awarded to replace EFC). 50% of all full-time undergraduates had no need and received non-need-based gift aid.

GIFT AID (NEED-BASED) ***Total amount:*** $44,041,931 (62% federal, 15% state, 23% institutional). ***Receiving aid:*** Freshmen: 26% (1,651); all full-time undergraduates: 23% (8,057). ***Average award:*** Freshmen: $6149; Undergraduates: $5991. ***Scholarships, grants, and awards:*** Federal Pell, FSEOG, state, private, college/university gift aid from institutional funds.

GIFT AID (NON-NEED-BASED) ***Total amount:*** $137,296,129 (1% federal, 57% state, 13% institutional, 29% external sources). ***Receiving aid:*** Freshmen: 39% (2,537). Undergraduates: 29% (9,845). ***Average award:*** Freshmen: $5811. Undergraduates: $5093. ***Scholarships, grants, and awards by category:*** *Academic interests/achievement:* agriculture, architecture, business, communication, computer science, education, engineering/technologies, general academic interests/achievements, health fields, military science. *Creative arts/performance:* art/fine arts, dance, general creative arts/performance, journalism/publications, music, performing arts, theater/drama. *Special achievements/activities:* community service, general special achievements/activities, leadership. *Special characteristics:* children of faculty/staff, members of minority groups, out-of-state students. ***Tuition waivers:*** Full or partial for employees or children of employees, senior citizens. ***ROTC:*** Army, Air Force.

LOANS ***Student loans:*** $51,384,989 (53% need-based, 47% non-need-based). 41% of past graduating class borrowed through all loan programs. *Average indebtedness per student:* $15,318. ***Average need-based loan:*** Freshmen: $3465. Undergraduates: $4453. ***Parent loans:*** $5,622,136 (100% non-need-based). ***Programs:*** Federal Direct (Subsidized and Unsubsidized Stafford, PLUS), Perkins, college/university.

WORK-STUDY ***Federal work-study:*** Total amount: $1,575,930; 998 jobs averaging $1599. ***State or other work-study/employment:*** Total amount: $7,487,299 (100% non-need-based). 4,263 part-time jobs averaging $1756.

ATHLETIC AWARDS Total amount: $5,633,718 (100% non-need-based).

APPLYING FOR FINANCIAL AID ***Required financial aid form:*** FAFSA. ***Financial aid deadline (priority):*** 3/15. ***Notification date:*** Continuous beginning 3/20.

CONTACT Ms. Karen L. Fooks, Director of Student Financial Affairs, University of Florida, S-107 Criser Hall, Gainesville, FL 32611-4025, 352-392-1271. *Fax:* 352-392-2861. *E-mail:* kfooks@ufl.edu.

UNIVERSITY OF GEORGIA
Athens, GA

Tuition & fees (GA res): $6030 **Average undergraduate aid package: $8498**

ABOUT THE INSTITUTION State-supported, coed. ***Awards:*** bachelor's, master's, doctoral, and first professional degrees and post-bachelor's, post-master's, and first professional certificates. 126 undergraduate majors. ***Total enrollment:*** 34,180. Undergraduates: 25,467. Freshmen: 4,791. Federal methodology is used as a basis for awarding need-based institutional aid.

UNDERGRADUATE EXPENSES for 2008–09 ***Application fee:*** $50. ***Tuition, state resident:*** full-time $4856; part-time $203 per credit. ***Tuition, nonresident:*** full-time $21,168; part-time $882 per credit. ***Required fees:*** full-time $1174; $587 per term. Full-time tuition and fees vary according to course load, location, program, and student level. Part-time tuition and fees vary according to course load, location, program, and student level. ***College room and board:*** $7528; ***Room only:*** $4238. Room and board charges vary according to board plan and housing facility. ***Payment plan:*** Guaranteed tuition.

FRESHMAN FINANCIAL AID (Fall 2008, est.) 3,074 applied for aid; of those 47% were deemed to have need. 100% of freshmen with need received aid; of those 43% had need fully met. ***Average percent of need met:*** 80% (excluding resources awarded to replace EFC). ***Average financial aid package:*** $9422 (excluding resources awarded to replace EFC). 8% of all full-time freshmen had no need and received non-need-based gift aid.

UNDERGRADUATE FINANCIAL AID (Fall 2008, est.) 11,747 applied for aid; of those 58% were deemed to have need. 99% of undergraduates with need received aid; of those 36% had need fully met. ***Average percent of need met:*** 75% (excluding resources awarded to replace EFC). ***Average financial aid package:*** $8498 (excluding resources awarded to replace EFC). 7% of all full-time undergraduates had no need and received non-need-based gift aid.

GIFT AID (NEED-BASED) ***Total amount:*** $39,625,462 (36% federal, 58% state, 2% institutional, 4% external sources). ***Receiving aid:*** Freshmen: 29% (1,391); all full-time undergraduates: 25% (5,868). ***Average award:*** Freshmen: $8192; Undergraduates: $6918. ***Scholarships, grants, and awards:*** Federal Pell, FSEOG, state, private, college/university gift aid from institutional funds.

GIFT AID (NON-NEED-BASED) ***Total amount:*** $72,587,126 (1% federal, 91% state, 4% institutional, 4% external sources). ***Receiving aid:*** Freshmen: 9% (425). Undergraduates: 5% (1,187). ***Average award:*** Freshmen: $1749. Undergraduates: $1906. ***Scholarships, grants, and awards by category:*** *Academic interests/achievement:* 21,741 awards ($96,927,487 total): agriculture, business, education, general academic interests/achievements. *Creative arts/performance:* 116 awards ($110,805 total): music. *Special characteristics:* 246 awards ($419,916 total): local/state students. ***Tuition waivers:*** Full or partial for senior citizens. ***ROTC:*** Army, Air Force.

LOANS ***Student loans:*** $55,932,489 (44% need-based, 56% non-need-based). 39% of past graduating class borrowed through all loan programs. *Average indebtedness per student:* $14,343. ***Average need-based loan:*** Freshmen: $2905. Undergraduates: $3790. ***Parent loans:*** $9,352,679 (22% need-based, 78% non-need-based). ***Programs:*** Federal Direct (Subsidized and Unsubsidized Stafford, PLUS), Perkins, state, college/university.

WORK-STUDY ***Federal work-study:*** Total amount: $985,588; 380 jobs averaging $2594.

ATHLETIC AWARDS Total amount: $5,927,302 (22% need-based, 78% non-need-based).

APPLYING FOR FINANCIAL AID ***Required financial aid form:*** FAFSA. ***Financial aid deadline (priority):*** 3/1. ***Notification date:*** Continuous beginning 4/1. Students must reply within 2 weeks of notification.

CONTACT Mrs. Bonnie C. Joerschke, Financial Aid Director, University of Georgia, 220 Holmes/Hunter Academic Building, Athens, GA 30602-6114, 706-542-8208. *Fax:* 706-542-8217. *E-mail:* bonniej@uga.edu.

UNIVERSITY OF GREAT FALLS
Great Falls, MT

ABOUT THE INSTITUTION Independent Roman Catholic, coed. ***Awards:*** associate, bachelor's, and master's degrees. 76 undergraduate majors. ***Total enrollment:*** 723. Undergraduates: 640. Freshmen: 137.

GIFT AID (NEED-BASED) ***Scholarships, grants, and awards:*** Federal Pell, FSEOG, state, private, college/university gift aid from institutional funds.

GIFT AID (NON-NEED-BASED) ***Scholarships, grants, and awards by category:*** *Academic interests/achievement:* biological sciences, business, computer science, education, general academic interests/achievements, humanities, mathematics, physical sciences, premedicine, religion/biblical studies, social sciences. *Creative arts/performance:* art/fine arts, dance, music. *Special achievements/activities:* cheerleading/drum major, religious involvement. *Special characteristics:* children of current students, children of faculty/staff, ethnic background, first-generation college students, international students, parents of current students, religious affiliation, siblings of current students, spouses of current students.

LOANS ***Programs:*** FFEL (Subsidized and Unsubsidized Stafford, PLUS), Perkins.

WORK-STUDY ***Federal work-study:*** Total amount: $140,000; 52 jobs averaging $1992. ***State or other work-study/employment:*** Total amount: $9000 (100% non-need-based). Part-time jobs available.

APPLYING FOR FINANCIAL AID ***Required financial aid form:*** FAFSA.

CONTACT Sandra Bauman, Director of Financial Aid, University of Great Falls, 1301 20th Street South, Great Falls, MT 59405, 406-791-5237 or toll-free 800-856-9544. *Fax:* 406-791-5242. *E-mail:* sbauman01@ugf.edu.

UNIVERSITY OF GUAM

Mangilao, GU

Tuition & fees (GU res): $5285 **Average undergraduate aid package: N/A**

ABOUT THE INSTITUTION Territory-supported, coed. ***Awards:*** bachelor's and master's degrees. 36 undergraduate majors. ***Total enrollment:*** 3,282. Undergraduates: 3,020. Freshmen: 572. Federal methodology is used as a basis for awarding need-based institutional aid.

UNDERGRADUATE EXPENSES for 2008–09 ***Application fee:*** $49. ***Tuition, state resident:*** full-time $4835; part-time $173 per credit. ***Tuition, nonresident:*** full-time $14,414; part-time $515 per credit. ***Required fees:*** full-time $450; $225 per term. ***College room and board:*** $7785; ***Room only:*** $3668.

FRESHMAN FINANCIAL AID (Fall 2008, est.) 318 applied for aid; of those 84% were deemed to have need. 100% of freshmen with need received aid.

GIFT AID (NEED-BASED) ***Total amount:*** $8,541,371 (54% federal, 33% state, 1% institutional, 12% external sources). ***Receiving aid:*** Freshmen: 76% (250). ***Scholarships, grants, and awards:*** Federal Pell, FSEOG, state, private, college/university gift aid from institutional funds.

GIFT AID (NON-NEED-BASED) ***Receiving aid:*** Freshmen: 5% (18). ***Scholarships, grants, and awards by category:*** *Academic interests/achievement:* agriculture, business, communication, computer science, education, general academic interests/achievements, health fields. *Creative arts/performance:* art/fine arts, general creative arts/performance, journalism/publications, music, performing arts. *Special characteristics:* children and siblings of alumni, children of faculty/staff, children of union members/company employees, international students. ***ROTC:*** Army.

LOANS ***Student loans:*** $3,876,226 (100% need-based). ***Parent loans:*** $39,176 (100% non-need-based). ***Programs:*** Federal Direct (Subsidized and Unsubsidized Stafford, PLUS), FFEL (Subsidized and Unsubsidized Stafford, PLUS), territory.

WORK-STUDY ***Federal work-study:*** Total amount: $361,380; jobs available.

APPLYING FOR FINANCIAL AID ***Required financial aid form:*** FAFSA. ***Financial aid deadline (priority):*** 4/30.

CONTACT Office of Financial Aid, University of Guam, UOG Station, Mangilao, GU 96923, 671-735-2288. *Fax:* 071-734-2907.

UNIVERSITY OF HARTFORD

West Hartford, CT

Tuition & fees: $28,980 **Average undergraduate aid package: $17,441**

ABOUT THE INSTITUTION Independent, coed. ***Awards:*** associate, bachelor's, master's, and doctoral degrees and post-bachelor's and post-master's certificates. 90 undergraduate majors. ***Total enrollment:*** 7,366. Undergraduates: 5,695. Freshmen: 1,469. Federal methodology is used as a basis for awarding need-based institutional aid.

UNDERGRADUATE EXPENSES for 2009–10 ***Application fee:*** $35. ***Comprehensive fee:*** $40,308 includes full-time tuition ($27,750), mandatory fees ($1230), and room and board ($11,328). ***Part-time tuition:*** $410 per credit.

FRESHMAN FINANCIAL AID (Fall 2008, est.) 1,072 applied for aid; of those 100% were deemed to have need. 100% of freshmen with need received aid; of those 50% had need fully met. ***Average percent of need met:*** 79% (excluding resources awarded to replace EFC). ***Average financial aid package:*** $17,117 (excluding resources awarded to replace EFC).

UNDERGRADUATE FINANCIAL AID (Fall 2008, est.) 3,403 applied for aid; of those 96% were deemed to have need. 95% of undergraduates with need received aid; of those 56% had need fully met. ***Average percent of need met:*** 80% (excluding resources awarded to replace EFC). ***Average financial aid package:*** $17,441 (excluding resources awarded to replace EFC). 28% of all full-time undergraduates had no need and received non-need-based gift aid.

GIFT AID (NEED-BASED) ***Total amount:*** $47,060,621 (9% federal, 7% state, 79% institutional, 5% external sources). ***Receiving aid:*** Freshmen: 74% (1,072); all full-time undergraduates: 64% (3,083). ***Average award:*** Freshmen: $14,465; Undergraduates: $14,427. ***Scholarships, grants, and awards:*** Federal Pell, FSEOG, state, private, college/university gift aid from institutional funds.

GIFT AID (NON-NEED-BASED) ***Total amount:*** $10,261,683 (96% institutional, 4% external sources). ***Receiving aid:*** Freshmen: 20% (297). Undergraduates: 17% (831). ***Average award:*** Freshmen: $7291. Undergraduates: $7782. ***Scholarships, grants, and awards by category:*** *Academic interests/achievement:* 4,118 awards ($31,071,524 total): engineering/technologies, general academic interests/achievements, health fields, premedicine. *Creative arts/performance:* 626 awards ($6,613,181 total): art/fine arts, dance, music, performing arts, theater/drama. *Special achievements/activities:* community service. *Special characteristics:* adult students, children of current students, children of faculty/staff, children of union members/company employees, children with a deceased or disabled parent, ethnic background, first-generation college students, handicapped students, international students, local/state students, members of minority groups, parents of current students, previous college experience, religious affiliation, siblings of current students, twins. ***ROTC:*** Army cooperative, Air Force cooperative.

LOANS ***Student loans:*** $31,041,352 (97% need-based, 3% non-need-based). 78% of past graduating class borrowed through all loan programs. *Average indebtedness per student:* $38,852. ***Average need-based loan:*** Freshmen: $6561. Undergraduates: $6892. ***Parent loans:*** $11,205,228 (91% need-based, 9% non-need-based). ***Programs:*** FFEL (Subsidized and Unsubsidized Stafford, PLUS), Perkins.

WORK-STUDY ***Federal work-study:*** Total amount: $633,173; 435 jobs averaging $1431. ***State or other work-study/employment:*** Total amount: $1,184,356 (85% need-based, 15% non-need-based). 146 part-time jobs averaging $3874.

ATHLETIC AWARDS Total amount: $4,231,913 (43% need-based, 57% non-need-based).

APPLYING FOR FINANCIAL AID ***Required financial aid form:*** FAFSA. ***Financial aid deadline (priority):*** 2/1. ***Notification date:*** Continuous beginning 3/1. Students must reply by 5/1.

CONTACT Financial Aid Office, University of Hartford, 200 Bloomfield Avenue, West Hartford, CT 06117-1599, 860-768-4296 or toll-free 800-947-4303. *Fax:* 860-768-4961. *E-mail:* finaid@hartford.edu.

UNIVERSITY OF HAWAII AT HILO

Hilo, HI

Tuition & fees (HI res): $4360 **Average undergraduate aid package: $7763**

ABOUT THE INSTITUTION State-supported, coed. ***Awards:*** bachelor's, master's, and first professional degrees and post-bachelor's certificates. 29 undergraduate majors. ***Total enrollment:*** 3,573. Undergraduates: 3,205. Freshmen: 511. Federal methodology is used as a basis for awarding need-based institutional aid.

UNDERGRADUATE EXPENSES for 2008–09 ***Application fee:*** $50. ***Tuition, state resident:*** full-time $4056; part-time $169 per credit hour. ***Tuition, nonresident:*** full-time $12,576; part-time $524 per credit hour. ***Required fees:*** full-time $304. Full-time tuition and fees vary according to reciprocity agreements. Part-time tuition and fees vary according to course load. ***College room and board:*** $11,403; ***Room only:*** $7780. Room and board charges vary according to board plan and housing facility.

FRESHMAN FINANCIAL AID (Fall 2008, est.) 273 applied for aid; of those 100% were deemed to have need. 100% of freshmen with need received aid; of those 13% had need fully met. ***Average percent of need met:*** 54% (excluding resources awarded to replace EFC). ***Average financial aid package:*** $6767 (excluding resources awarded to replace EFC).

UNDERGRADUATE FINANCIAL AID (Fall 2008, est.) 1,332 applied for aid; of those 100% were deemed to have need. 100% of undergraduates with need received aid; of those 11% had need fully met. ***Average percent of need met:*** 66% (excluding resources awarded to replace EFC). ***Average financial aid package:*** $7763 (excluding resources awarded to replace EFC). 1% of all full-time undergraduates had no need and received non-need-based gift aid.

GIFT AID (NEED-BASED) ***Total amount:*** $4,875,270 (89% federal, 6% state, 5% institutional). ***Receiving aid:*** Freshmen: 40% (173); all full-time undergraduates: 50% (942). ***Average award:*** Freshmen: $4583; Undergraduates: $4385. ***Scholarships, grants, and awards:*** Federal Pell, FSEOG, state, private, college/university gift aid from institutional funds.

GIFT AID (NON-NEED-BASED) ***Total amount:*** $3,086,984 (7% institutional, 93% external sources). ***Receiving aid:*** Freshmen: 15% (66). Undergraduates: 12% (228). ***Average award:*** Undergraduates: $929. ***Scholarships, grants, and awards by category:*** *Academic interests/achievement:* 49 awards ($70,015 total): business, computer science, English, general academic interests/ achievements, health fields, social sciences. *Creative arts/performance:* 10 awards ($3100 total): art/fine arts, music, performing arts, theater/drama. *Special achievements/activities:* 22 awards ($20,860 total): community service, general special achievements/activities, leadership. *Special characteristics:* 20 awards ($75,915 total): general special characteristics, local/state students.

LOANS ***Student loans:*** $12,212,663 (49% need-based, 51% non-need-based). 47% of past graduating class borrowed through all loan programs. *Average indebtedness per student:* $16,604. ***Average need-based loan:*** Freshmen: $3170. Undergraduates: $4257. ***Parent loans:*** $311,159 (100% non-need-based). ***Programs:*** FFEL (Subsidized and Unsubsidized Stafford, PLUS), Perkins, state.

WORK-STUDY ***Federal work-study:*** Total amount: $278,892; 200 jobs averaging $1394. ***State or other work-study/employment:*** Total amount: $1,255,953 (100% non-need-based). 524 part-time jobs averaging $2397.

ATHLETIC AWARDS Total amount: $375,482 (100% non-need-based).

APPLYING FOR FINANCIAL AID ***Required financial aid form:*** FAFSA. ***Financial aid deadline (priority):*** 3/1. ***Notification date:*** Continuous beginning 3/1. Students must reply within 3 weeks of notification.

CONTACT Financial Aid Director, University of Hawaii at Hilo, 200 West Kawili Street, Hilo, HI 96720-4091, 808-974-7324 or toll-free 800-897-4456 (out-of-state). *Fax:* 808-933-0861. *E-mail:* uhhfao@hawaii.edu.

UNIVERSITY OF HAWAII AT MANOA

Honolulu, HI

Tuition & fees (HI res): $7168 Average undergraduate aid package: $7687

ABOUT THE INSTITUTION State-supported, coed. ***Awards:*** bachelor's, master's, doctoral, and first professional degrees and post-bachelor's certificates. 82 undergraduate majors. ***Total enrollment:*** 20,169. Undergraduates: 13,810. Freshmen: 1,866. Federal methodology is used as a basis for awarding need-based institutional aid.

UNDERGRADUATE EXPENSES for 2009–10 ***Application fee:*** $50. ***Tuition, state resident:*** full-time $6768; part-time $282 per credit hour. ***Tuition, nonresident:*** full-time $18,816; part-time $784 per credit hour. ***Required fees:*** full-time $400; $194.70 per term. ***College room and board:*** $7564; ***Room only:*** $4917.

FRESHMAN FINANCIAL AID (Fall 2007) 1,220 applied for aid; of those 48% were deemed to have need. 87% of freshmen with need received aid; of those 23% had need fully met. ***Average percent of need met:*** 59% (excluding resources awarded to replace EFC). ***Average financial aid package:*** $6926 (excluding resources awarded to replace EFC). 21% of all full-time freshmen had no need and received non-need-based gift aid.

UNDERGRADUATE FINANCIAL AID (Fall 2007) 6,777 applied for aid; of those 60% were deemed to have need. 91% of undergraduates with need received aid; of those 21% had need fully met. ***Average percent of need met:*** 60% (excluding resources awarded to replace EFC). ***Average financial aid package:*** $7687 (excluding resources awarded to replace EFC). 18% of all full-time undergraduates had no need and received non-need-based gift aid.

GIFT AID (NEED-BASED) ***Total amount:*** $11,745,806 (80% federal, 4% state, 8% institutional, 8% external sources). ***Receiving aid:*** Freshmen: 25% (407); all full-time undergraduates: 25% (2,896). ***Average award:*** Freshmen: $5119; Undergraduates: $5072. ***Scholarships, grants, and awards:*** Federal Pell, FSEOG, state, private, college/university gift aid from institutional funds, Federal Nursing.

GIFT AID (NON-NEED-BASED) ***Total amount:*** $3,104,568 (13% institutional, 87% external sources). ***Receiving aid:*** Freshmen: 7% (109). Undergraduates: 5% (617). ***Average award:*** Freshmen: $5632. Undergraduates: $5576. ***ROTC:*** Army, Air Force.

LOANS ***Student loans:*** $21,212,807 (61% need-based, 39% non-need-based). 34% of past graduating class borrowed through all loan programs. *Average indebtedness per student:* $14,818. ***Average need-based loan:*** Freshmen: $3088. Undergraduates: $4280. ***Parent loans:*** $7,515,362 (100% non-need-based). ***Programs:*** FFEL (Subsidized and Unsubsidized Stafford, PLUS), Perkins, Federal Nursing, state.

WORK-STUDY ***Federal work-study:*** Total amount: $417,961; jobs available.

ATHLETIC AWARDS Total amount: $2,210,004 (15% need-based, 85% non-need-based).

APPLYING FOR FINANCIAL AID ***Required financial aid form:*** FAFSA. ***Financial aid deadline (priority):*** 3/1. ***Notification date:*** Continuous beginning 4/1.

CONTACT Linda Clemons, Director of Financial Aid Services, University of Hawaii at Manoa, 2600 Campus Road, Suite 112, Honolulu, HI 96822, 808-956-3989 or toll-free 800-823-9771. *Fax:* 808-956-3985. *E-mail:* finaid@hawaii.edu.

UNIVERSITY OF HAWAII–WEST OAHU

Pearl City, HI

ABOUT THE INSTITUTION State-supported, coed. ***Awards:*** bachelor's degrees. 21 undergraduate majors. ***Total enrollment:*** 1,140. Undergraduates: 1,140. Freshmen: 74.

GIFT AID (NEED-BASED) ***Scholarships, grants, and awards:*** Federal Pell, FSEOG, state, private, college/university gift aid from institutional funds.

GIFT AID (NON-NEED-BASED) ***Scholarships, grants, and awards by category:*** *Academic interests/achievement:* general academic interests/achievements. *Special achievements/activities:* general special achievements/activities.

LOANS ***Programs:*** FFEL (Subsidized and Unsubsidized Stafford, PLUS).

APPLYING FOR FINANCIAL AID ***Required financial aid form:*** FAFSA.

CONTACT Student Services Office, University of Hawaii–West Oahu, 96-129 Ala Ike, Pearl City, HI 96782-3366, 808-454-4700. *Fax:* 808-453-6075. *E-mail:* finaid@uhwo.hawaii.edu.

UNIVERSITY OF HOUSTON

Houston, TX

Tuition & fees (TX res): $8167 Average undergraduate aid package: $11,660

ABOUT THE INSTITUTION State-supported, coed. ***Awards:*** bachelor's, master's, doctoral, and first professional degrees. 98 undergraduate majors. ***Total enrollment:*** 37,104. Undergraduates: 29,800. Freshmen: 3,797. Federal methodology is used as a basis for awarding need-based institutional aid.

UNDERGRADUATE EXPENSES for 2008–09 ***Application fee:*** $50. ***Tuition, state resident:*** full-time $5213; part-time $174 per hour. ***Tuition, nonresident:*** full-time $13,643; part-time $455 per hour. ***Required fees:*** full-time $2954. Full-time tuition and fees vary according to course level, course load, degree level, location, program, reciprocity agreements, and student level. Part-time tuition and fees vary according to course level, course load, degree level, location, program, reciprocity agreements, and student level. ***College room and board:*** $6935; ***Room only:*** $4062. Room and board charges vary according to board plan and housing facility. ***Payment plan:*** Installment.

FRESHMAN FINANCIAL AID (Fall 2008, est.) 2,546 applied for aid; of those 82% were deemed to have need. 96% of freshmen with need received aid; of those 27% had need fully met. ***Average percent of need met:*** 74% (excluding resources awarded to replace EFC). ***Average financial aid package:*** $11,469 (excluding resources awarded to replace EFC). 5% of all full-time freshmen had no need and received non-need-based gift aid.

UNDERGRADUATE FINANCIAL AID (Fall 2008, est.) 12,903 applied for aid; of those 88% were deemed to have need. 95% of undergraduates with need received aid; of those 26% had need fully met. ***Average percent of need met:*** 73% (excluding resources awarded to replace EFC). ***Average financial aid package:*** $11,660 (excluding resources awarded to replace EFC). 2% of all full-time undergraduates had no need and received non-need-based gift aid.

GIFT AID (NEED-BASED) ***Total amount:*** $65,552,989 (45% federal, 17% state, 32% institutional, 6% external sources). ***Receiving aid:*** Freshmen: 38% (1,340); all full-time undergraduates: 35% (7,081). ***Average award:*** Freshmen: $7481; Undergraduates: $5635. ***Scholarships, grants, and awards:*** Federal Pell, FSEOG, state, private, college/university gift aid from institutional funds, United Negro College Fund.

GIFT AID (NON-NEED-BASED) ***Total amount:*** $3,730,606 (82% institutional, 18% external sources). ***Receiving aid:*** Freshmen: 7% (236). Undergraduates: 4% (855). ***Average award:*** Freshmen: $4603. Undergraduates: $3871. ***ROTC:*** Army, Naval cooperative.

LOANS ***Student loans:*** $99,581,807 (97% need-based, 3% non-need-based). ***Average need-based loan:*** Freshmen: $5031. Undergraduates: $7149. ***Parent loans:*** $3,493,397 (25% need-based, 75% non-need-based). ***Programs:*** FFEL (Subsidized and Unsubsidized Stafford, PLUS), Perkins, state.

WORK-STUDY ***Federal work-study:*** Total amount: $5,546,410; jobs available. ***State or other work-study/employment:*** Total amount: $177,681 (100% need-based). Part-time jobs available.

ATHLETIC AWARDS Total amount: $3,293,765 (88% need-based, 12% non-need-based).

APPLYING FOR FINANCIAL AID ***Required financial aid form:*** FAFSA. ***Financial aid deadline (priority):*** 4/1. ***Notification date:*** Continuous beginning 5/1. Students must reply within 4 weeks of notification.

CONTACT Financial Aid Office, University of Houston, 4800 Calhoun Road, Houston, TX 77204-2160, 713-743-1010. *Fax:* 713-743-9098.

UNIVERSITY OF HOUSTON–CLEAR LAKE

Houston, TX

Tuition & fees (TX res): $6076 Average undergraduate aid package: $6686

ABOUT THE INSTITUTION State-supported, coed. ***Awards:*** bachelor's, master's, and doctoral degrees. 35 undergraduate majors. ***Total enrollment:*** 7,659. Undergraduates: 4,052. Federal methodology is used as a basis for awarding need-based institutional aid.

UNDERGRADUATE EXPENSES for 2008–09 ***Application fee:*** $35. ***Tuition, state resident:*** full-time $4984; part-time $285 per credit hour. ***Tuition, nonresident:*** full-time $13,894; part-time $582 per credit hour. ***Required fees:*** full-time $1092; $420 per term. Full-time tuition and fees vary according to course load and program. Part-time tuition and fees vary according to course load and program. ***College room and board:*** ***Room only:*** $10,308. Room and board charges vary according to housing facility. ***Payment plans:*** Installment, deferred payment.

UNDERGRADUATE FINANCIAL AID (Fall 2008, est.) 1,202 applied for aid; of those 88% were deemed to have need. 95% of undergraduates with need received aid; of those 26% had need fully met. ***Average percent of need met:*** 41% (excluding resources awarded to replace EFC). ***Average financial aid package:*** $6686 (excluding resources awarded to replace EFC). 2% of all full-time undergraduates had no need and received non-need-based gift aid.

GIFT AID (NEED-BASED) ***Total amount:*** $6,533,428 (56% federal, 34% state, 1% institutional, 9% external sources). ***Receiving aid:*** All full-time undergraduates: 38% (653). ***Average award:*** Undergraduates: $2237. ***Scholarships, grants, and awards:*** Federal Pell, FSEOG, state, college/university gift aid from institutional funds.

GIFT AID (NON-NEED-BASED) ***Total amount:*** $593,879 (86% institutional, 14% external sources). ***Receiving aid:*** Undergraduates: 20% (340). ***Average award:*** Undergraduates: $899. ***Scholarships, grants, and awards by category:*** *Academic interests/achievement:* biological sciences, business, computer science, education, humanities, mathematics, social sciences. *Special achievements/activities:* community service, general special achievements/activities, leadership. *Special characteristics:* children and siblings of alumni. ***Tuition waivers:*** Full or partial for senior citizens.

LOANS ***Student loans:*** $15,481,019 (48% need-based, 52% non-need-based). 68% of past graduating class borrowed through all loan programs. *Average indebtedness per student:* $19,776. ***Average need-based loan:*** Undergraduates: $4789. ***Parent loans:*** $38,564 (100% non-need-based). ***Programs:*** Federal Direct (Subsidized and Unsubsidized Stafford, PLUS), Perkins, state.

WORK-STUDY ***Federal work-study:*** Total amount: $79,423; 58 jobs available. ***State or other work-study/employment:*** 5 part-time jobs available.

CONTACT Lynda McKendree, Executive Director of Student Financial Aid, University of Houston–Clear Lake, 2700 Bay Area Boulevard, Houston, TX 77058-1098, 281-283-2485. *Fax:* 281-283-2502. *E-mail:* mckendree@cl.uh.edu.

UNIVERSITY OF HOUSTON–DOWNTOWN

Houston, TX

Tuition & fees (TX res): $5000 Average undergraduate aid package: $6555

ABOUT THE INSTITUTION State-supported, coed. ***Awards:*** bachelor's and master's degrees. 38 undergraduate majors. ***Total enrollment:*** 12,283. Undergraduates: 12,134. Freshmen: 990. Federal methodology is used as a basis for awarding need-based institutional aid.

UNDERGRADUATE EXPENSES for 2008–09 ***Application fee:*** $35. ***One-time required fee:*** $10. ***Tuition, state resident:*** full-time $4050; part-time $135 per credit hour. ***Tuition, nonresident:*** full-time $12,480; part-time $416 per credit hour. ***Required fees:*** full-time $950. Full-time tuition and fees vary according to course load and reciprocity agreements. Part-time tuition and fees vary according to course load and reciprocity agreements. international students must also pay an international student service fee of $45 per year. ***Payment plan:*** Installment.

FRESHMAN FINANCIAL AID (Fall 2008, est.) 643 applied for aid; of those 92% were deemed to have need. 90% of freshmen with need received aid; of those 4% had need fully met. ***Average percent of need met:*** 48% (excluding resources awarded to replace EFC). ***Average financial aid package:*** $7516 (excluding resources awarded to replace EFC).

UNDERGRADUATE FINANCIAL AID (Fall 2008, est.) 5,058 applied for aid; of those 93% were deemed to have need. 88% of undergraduates with need received aid; of those 4% had need fully met. ***Average percent of need met:*** 40% (excluding resources awarded to replace EFC). ***Average financial aid package:*** $6555 (excluding resources awarded to replace EFC). 3% of all full-time undergraduates had no need and received non-need-based gift aid.

GIFT AID (NEED-BASED) ***Total amount:*** $23,830,943 (64% federal, 15% state, 18% institutional, 3% external sources). ***Receiving aid:*** Freshmen: 69% (484); all full-time undergraduates: 56% (3,301). ***Average award:*** Freshmen: $6485; Undergraduates: $4577. ***Scholarships, grants, and awards:*** Federal Pell, FSEOG, state, private, college/university gift aid from institutional funds.

GIFT AID (NON-NEED-BASED) ***Total amount:*** $1,288,934 (5% state, 33% institutional, 62% external sources). ***Receiving aid:*** Freshmen: 3. Undergraduates: 14. ***Average award:*** Freshmen: $1922. Undergraduates: $2106. ***Scholarships, grants, and awards by category:*** *Academic interests/achievement:* general academic interests/achievements. *Special achievements/activities:* community service, general special achievements/activities, leadership. *Special characteristics:* general special characteristics. ***Tuition waivers:*** Full or partial for senior citizens. ***ROTC:*** Army cooperative.

LOANS ***Student loans:*** $39,011,945 (88% need-based, 12% non-need-based). 75% of past graduating class borrowed through all loan programs. *Average indebtedness per student:* $15,585. ***Average need-based loan:*** Freshmen: $2607. Undergraduates: $3665. ***Parent loans:*** $246,080 (34% need-based, 66% non-need-based). ***Programs:*** FFEL (Subsidized and Unsubsidized Stafford, PLUS), state.

WORK-STUDY ***Federal work-study:*** Total amount: $169,563; 116 jobs averaging $3200. ***State or other work-study/employment:*** Total amount: $41,715 (100% need-based). 32 part-time jobs averaging $3200.

APPLYING FOR FINANCIAL AID ***Required financial aid form:*** FAFSA. ***Financial aid deadline (priority):*** 4/1. ***Notification date:*** Continuous beginning 4/15. Students must reply within 4 weeks of notification.

CONTACT Office of Scholarships and Financial Aid, University of Houston–Downtown, One Main Street, Houston, TX 77002-1001, 713-221-8041. *Fax:* 713-221-8648. *E-mail:* uhd.finaid@dt.uh.edu.

UNIVERSITY OF HOUSTON–VICTORIA

Victoria, TX

Tuition & fees (TX res): $5220 Average undergraduate aid package: $5311

ABOUT THE INSTITUTION State-supported, coed. ***Awards:*** bachelor's and master's degrees and post-bachelor's and post-master's certificates. 13 undergraduate majors. ***Total enrollment:*** 3,174. Undergraduates: 1,569. Entering class: 329. Federal methodology is used as a basis for awarding need-based institutional aid.

UNDERGRADUATE EXPENSES for 2008–09 ***Tuition, state resident:*** full-time $4110; part-time $137 per semester hour. ***Tuition, nonresident:*** full-time $12,540; part-time $418 per semester hour. ***Required fees:*** full-time $1110; $52 per semester hour. Full-time tuition and fees vary according to course load. Part-time tuition and fees vary according to course load. ***Payment plan:*** Installment.

UNDERGRADUATE FINANCIAL AID (Fall 2007) 201 applied for aid; of those 84% were deemed to have need. 96% of undergraduates with need received aid; of those 20% had need fully met. ***Average percent of need met:*** 41% (excluding resources awarded to replace EFC). ***Average financial aid package:*** $5311 (excluding resources awarded to replace EFC). 1% of all full-time undergraduates had no need and received non-need-based gift aid.

GIFT AID (NEED-BASED) ***Total amount:*** $1,936,217 (75% federal, 3% state, 22% institutional). ***Receiving aid:*** All full-time undergraduates: 48% (139). ***Average award:*** Undergraduates: $1376. ***Scholarships, grants, and awards:*** Federal Pell, FSEOG, state, private, college/university gift aid from institutional funds.

GIFT AID (NON-NEED-BASED) ***Total amount:*** $366,221 (2% state, 82% institutional, 16% external sources). ***Receiving aid:*** Undergraduates: 21% (62).

Average award: Undergraduates: $818. ***Scholarships, grants, and awards by category:*** *Academic interests/achievement:* 162 awards ($46,423 total): biological sciences, business, communication, computer science, education, general academic interests/achievements, humanities, mathematics, social sciences. *Special achievements/activities:* 2 awards ($1300 total): community service, leadership, memberships. ***Tuition waivers:*** Full or partial for employees or children of employees, senior citizens.

LOANS ***Student loans:*** $4,109,341 (46% need-based, 54% non-need-based). 27% of past graduating class borrowed through all loan programs. *Average indebtedness per student:* $17,695. ***Average need-based loan:*** Undergraduates: $3676. ***Parent loans:*** $19,500 (100% non-need-based). ***Programs:*** FFEL (Subsidized and Unsubsidized Stafford, PLUS), state, college/university.

WORK-STUDY ***Federal work-study:*** Total amount: $43,696; 17 jobs averaging $2755. ***State or other work-study/employment:*** Total amount: $8542 (100% need-based). 7 part-time jobs averaging $1272.

ATHLETIC AWARDS Total amount: $46,750 (100% non-need-based).

APPLYING FOR FINANCIAL AID ***Required financial aid form:*** FAFSA. ***Financial aid deadline (priority):*** 4/15. ***Notification date:*** Continuous beginning 5/20. Students must reply within 3 weeks of notification.

CONTACT Carolyn Mallory, Financial Aid Director, University of Houston–Victoria, 3007 North Ben Wilson, Victoria, TX 77901-5731, 361-570-4131 or toll-free 877-970-4848 Ext. 110. *Fax:* 361-580-5555. *E-mail:* malloryc@uhv.edu.

UNIVERSITY OF IDAHO

Moscow, ID

Tuition & fees (ID res): $4632 **Average undergraduate aid package: $10,609**

ABOUT THE INSTITUTION State-supported, coed. ***Awards:*** bachelor's, master's, doctoral, and first professional degrees and post-master's certificates. 113 undergraduate majors. ***Total enrollment:*** 11,791. Undergraduates: 9,241. Freshmen: 1,718. Federal methodology is used as a basis for awarding need-based institutional aid.

UNDERGRADUATE EXPENSES for 2008–09 ***Application fee:*** $40. ***Tuition, state resident:*** full-time $0. ***Tuition, nonresident:*** full-time $10,080; part-time $336 per credit. ***Required fees:*** full-time $4632; $238 per credit. Full-time tuition and fees vary according to degree level and program. Part-time tuition and fees vary according to course load, degree level, and program. ***College room and board:*** $8784. Room and board charges vary according to board plan and housing facility. ***Payment plans:*** Installment, deferred payment.

FRESHMAN FINANCIAL AID (Fall 2007) 1,300 applied for aid; of those 73% were deemed to have need. 98% of freshmen with need received aid; of those 32% had need fully met. ***Average percent of need met:*** 78% (excluding resources awarded to replace EFC). ***Average financial aid package:*** $10,472 (excluding resources awarded to replace EFC). 30% of all full-time freshmen had no need and received non-need-based gift aid.

UNDERGRADUATE FINANCIAL AID (Fall 2007) 6,132 applied for aid; of those 81% were deemed to have need. 97% of undergraduates with need received aid; of those 26% had need fully met. ***Average percent of need met:*** 74% (excluding resources awarded to replace EFC). ***Average financial aid package:*** $10,609 (excluding resources awarded to replace EFC). 22% of all full-time undergraduates had no need and received non-need-based gift aid.

GIFT AID (NEED-BASED) ***Total amount:*** $12,140,975 (83% federal, 17% institutional). ***Receiving aid:*** Freshmen: 35% (589); all full-time undergraduates: 37% (3,120). ***Average award:*** Freshmen: $3469; Undergraduates: $3404. ***Scholarships, grants, and awards:*** Federal Pell, FSEOG, state, private, college/university gift aid from institutional funds.

GIFT AID (NON-NEED-BASED) ***Total amount:*** $8,974,273 (1% state, 70% institutional, 29% external sources). ***Receiving aid:*** Freshmen: 44% (735). Undergraduates: 39% (3,271). ***Average award:*** Freshmen: $3892. Undergraduates: $4188. ***Scholarships, grants, and awards by category:*** *Academic interests/achievement:* 7,750 awards ($18,000,000 total): agriculture, architecture, biological sciences, business, communication, computer science, education, engineering/technologies, English, foreign languages, general academic interests/achievements, home economics, humanities, library science, mathematics, military science, physical sciences, premedicine, social sciences. *Creative arts/performance:* 300 awards ($600,000 total): applied art and design, art/fine arts, creative writing, dance, general creative arts/performance, journalism/publications, music, performing arts, theater/drama. *Special achievements/activities:* 70 awards ($100,000 total): cheerleading/drum major, general special achievements/activities, junior miss, leadership, rodeo. *Special characteristics:* 400 awards ($300,000 total): children and siblings of alumni, children of faculty/staff, ethnic background, first-generation college students, general special characteristics, handicapped students, international students, local/state students, members of minority groups, out-of-state students. ***Tuition waivers:*** Full or partial for minority students, children of alumni, employees or children of employees, senior citizens. ***ROTC:*** Army, Naval, Air Force cooperative.

LOANS ***Student loans:*** $32,494,164 (57% need-based, 43% non-need-based). 66% of past graduating class borrowed through all loan programs. *Average indebtedness per student:* $21,702. ***Average need-based loan:*** Freshmen: $4066. Undergraduates: $6001. ***Parent loans:*** $5,998,826 (100% non-need-based). ***Programs:*** Federal Direct (Subsidized and Unsubsidized Stafford, PLUS), Perkins, college/university.

WORK-STUDY ***Federal work-study:*** Total amount: $762,029; 383 jobs averaging $2000. ***State or other work-study/employment:*** Total amount: $387,740 (100% need-based). 174 part-time jobs averaging $2000.

ATHLETIC AWARDS Total amount: $4,007,900 (100% non-need-based).

APPLYING FOR FINANCIAL AID ***Required financial aid form:*** FAFSA. ***Financial aid deadline (priority):*** 2/15. ***Notification date:*** Continuous beginning 3/30. Students must reply within 4 weeks of notification.

CONTACT Mr. Dan Davenport, Director of Admissions and Financial Aid, University of Idaho, Financial Aid Office, P.O. Box 444291, Moscow, ID 83844-4291, 208-885-6312 or toll-free 888-884-3246. *Fax:* 208-885-5592. *E-mail:* dand@uidaho.edu.

UNIVERSITY OF ILLINOIS AT CHICAGO

Chicago, IL

Tuition & fees (IL res): $11,716 **Average undergraduate aid package: $11,136**

ABOUT THE INSTITUTION State-supported, coed. ***Awards:*** bachelor's, master's, doctoral, and first professional degrees and post-bachelor's, post-master's, and first professional certificates. 78 undergraduate majors. ***Total enrollment:*** 25,835. Undergraduates: 15,665. Freshmen: 2,964. Federal methodology is used as a basis for awarding need-based institutional aid.

UNDERGRADUATE EXPENSES for 2008–09 ***Application fee:*** $40. ***Tuition, state resident:*** full-time $8130. ***Tuition, nonresident:*** full-time $20,250. ***Required fees:*** full-time $3586. Full-time tuition and fees vary according to program. Part-time tuition and fees vary according to program. ***College room and board:*** $8744; ***Room only:*** $6144. Room and board charges vary according to board plan and housing facility. ***Payment plans:*** Guaranteed tuition, installment.

FRESHMAN FINANCIAL AID (Fall 2007) 2,577 applied for aid; of those 82% were deemed to have need. 94% of freshmen with need received aid; of those 28% had need fully met. ***Average percent of need met:*** 75% (excluding resources awarded to replace EFC). ***Average financial aid package:*** $11,154 (excluding resources awarded to replace EFC). 7% of all full-time freshmen had no need and received non-need-based gift aid.

UNDERGRADUATE FINANCIAL AID (Fall 2007) 10,435 applied for aid; of those 83% were deemed to have need. 96% of undergraduates with need received aid; of those 25% had need fully met. ***Average percent of need met:*** 74% (excluding resources awarded to replace EFC). ***Average financial aid package:*** $11,136 (excluding resources awarded to replace EFC). 5% of all full-time undergraduates had no need and received non-need-based gift aid.

GIFT AID (NEED-BASED) ***Total amount:*** $64,530,692 (29% federal, 39% state, 30% institutional, 2% external sources). ***Receiving aid:*** Freshmen: 49% (1,588); all full-time undergraduates: 48% (6,814). ***Average award:*** Freshmen: $10,580; Undergraduates: $9587. ***Scholarships, grants, and awards:*** Federal Pell, FSEOG, state, private, college/university gift aid from institutional funds.

GIFT AID (NON-NEED-BASED) ***Total amount:*** $2,641,389 (52% state, 29% institutional, 19% external sources). ***Receiving aid:*** Freshmen: 4% (125). Undergraduates: 2% (340). ***Average award:*** Freshmen: $2233. Undergraduates: $3173. ***Scholarships, grants, and awards by category:*** *Academic interests/achievement:* 1,205 awards ($1,839,252 total): architecture, business, general academic interests/achievements. *Creative arts/performance:* 166 awards ($482,349 total): applied art and design, art/fine arts, music, performing arts, theater/drama. ***Tuition waivers:*** Full or partial for employees or children of employees, senior citizens. ***ROTC:*** Army, Naval cooperative, Air Force cooperative.

LOANS ***Student loans:*** $40,786,670 (83% need-based, 17% non-need-based). 57% of past graduating class borrowed through all loan programs. *Average indebtedness per student:* $16,715. ***Average need-based loan:*** Freshmen: $3941. Undergraduates: $4396. ***Parent loans:*** $15,349,779 (68% need-based, 32%

non-need-based). ***Programs:*** Federal Direct (Subsidized and Unsubsidized Stafford, PLUS), Perkins, Federal Nursing, college/university, private alternative loans.

WORK-STUDY ***Federal work-study:*** Total amount: $1,615,887; 951 jobs averaging $1708. ***State or other work-study/employment:*** Total amount: $6,011,517 (100% non-need-based). 2,924 part-time jobs averaging $2632.

ATHLETIC AWARDS Total amount: $3,119,383 (27% need-based, 73% non-need-based).

APPLYING FOR FINANCIAL AID ***Required financial aid form:*** FAFSA. ***Financial aid deadline (priority):*** 3/1. ***Notification date:*** Continuous beginning 3/15. Students must reply by 5/1.

CONTACT Deidre Rush, Associate Director of Financial Aid, University of Illinois at Chicago, 1200 West Harrison, M/C 334, Chicago, IL 60607-7128, 312-996-5563. *Fax:* 312-996-3385. *E-mail:* deidreb@uic.edu.

UNIVERSITY OF ILLINOIS AT SPRINGFIELD

Springfield, IL

Tuition & fees (IL res): $9069 **Average undergraduate aid package: $9582**

ABOUT THE INSTITUTION State-supported, coed. ***Awards:*** bachelor's, master's, and doctoral degrees and post-bachelor's and post-master's certificates. 22 undergraduate majors. ***Total enrollment:*** 4,711. Undergraduates: 2,889. Freshmen: 309. Federal methodology is used as a basis for awarding need-based institutional aid.

UNDERGRADUATE EXPENSES for 2008–09 ***Application fee:*** $40. ***Tuition, state resident:*** full-time $7215; part-time $240.50 per credit hour. ***Tuition, nonresident:*** full-time $16,365; part-time $545.50 per credit hour. ***Required fees:*** full-time $1854; $670 per term. ***College room and board:*** $8840; ***Room only:*** $6140. Room and board charges vary according to board plan and housing facility. ***Payment plans:*** Guaranteed tuition, installment.

FRESHMAN FINANCIAL AID (Fall 2007) 215 applied for aid; of those 74% were deemed to have need. 98% of freshmen with need received aid; of those 15% had need fully met. ***Average percent of need met:*** 74% (excluding resources awarded to replace EFC). ***Average financial aid package:*** $9530 (excluding resources awarded to replace EFC). 25% of all full-time freshmen had no need and received non-need-based gift aid.

UNDERGRADUATE FINANCIAL AID (Fall 2007) 1,284 applied for aid; of those 79% were deemed to have need. 97% of undergraduates with need received aid; of those 10% had need fully met. ***Average percent of need met:*** 69% (excluding resources awarded to replace EFC). ***Average financial aid package:*** $9582 (excluding resources awarded to replace EFC). 15% of all full-time undergraduates had no need and received non-need-based gift aid.

GIFT AID (NEED-BASED) ***Total amount:*** $5,896,048 (36% federal, 50% state, 11% institutional, 3% external sources). ***Receiving aid:*** Freshmen: 56% (144); all full-time undergraduates: 48% (812). ***Average award:*** Freshmen: $7722; Undergraduates: $6831. ***Scholarships, grants, and awards:*** Federal Pell, FSEOG, state, private, college/university gift aid from institutional funds.

GIFT AID (NON-NEED-BASED) ***Total amount:*** $1,202,506 (2% federal, 47% state, 27% institutional, 24% external sources). ***Receiving aid:*** Freshmen: 16% (42). Undergraduates: 8% (141). ***Average award:*** Freshmen: $2726. Undergraduates: $3379. ***Tuition waivers:*** Full or partial for employees or children of employees, senior citizens.

LOANS ***Student loans:*** $7,578,718 (84% need-based, 16% non-need-based). 76% of past graduating class borrowed through all loan programs. *Average indebtedness per student:* $14,226. ***Average need-based loan:*** Freshmen: $2943. Undergraduates: $4120. ***Parent loans:*** $1,275,135 (59% need-based, 41% non-need-based). ***Programs:*** FFEL (Subsidized and Unsubsidized Stafford, PLUS), Perkins, college/university.

WORK-STUDY ***Federal work-study:*** Total amount: $190,073; jobs available. ***State or other work-study/employment:*** Total amount: $898,069 (61% need-based, 39% non-need-based). Part-time jobs available.

ATHLETIC AWARDS Total amount: $459,591 (52% need-based, 48% non-need-based).

APPLYING FOR FINANCIAL AID ***Required financial aid form:*** FAFSA. ***Financial aid deadline:*** 11/15 (priority: 4/1). ***Notification date:*** Continuous. Students must reply within 3 weeks of notification.

CONTACT Mr. Gerard Joseph, Director of Financial Aid, University of Illinois at Springfield, One University Plaza, MS UHB 1015, Springfield, IL 62703-5407, 217-206-6724 or toll-free 888-977-4847. *Fax:* 217-206-7376. *E-mail:* finaid@uis.edu.

UNIVERSITY OF ILLINOIS AT URBANA–CHAMPAIGN

Champaign, IL

Tuition & fees (IL res): $12,240 **Average undergraduate aid package: $11,029**

ABOUT THE INSTITUTION State-supported, coed. ***Awards:*** bachelor's, master's, doctoral, and first professional degrees and post-master's certificates. 219 undergraduate majors. ***Total enrollment:*** 42,326. Undergraduates: 30,895. Freshmen: 6,940. Federal methodology is used as a basis for awarding need-based institutional aid.

UNDERGRADUATE EXPENSES for 2008–09 ***Application fee:*** $40. ***Tuition, state resident:*** full-time $9242. ***Tuition, nonresident:*** full-time $23,026. ***Required fees:*** full-time $2998. Full-time tuition and fees vary according to course load, program, and student level. ***College room and board:*** $8764. Room and board charges vary according to board plan and housing facility. ***Payment plan:*** Guaranteed tuition.

FRESHMAN FINANCIAL AID (Fall 2008, est.) 4,921 applied for aid; of those 66% were deemed to have need. 95% of freshmen with need received aid; of those 33% had need fully met. ***Average percent of need met:*** 70% (excluding resources awarded to replace EFC). ***Average financial aid package:*** $11,233 (excluding resources awarded to replace EFC). 15% of all full-time freshmen had no need and received non-need-based gift aid.

UNDERGRADUATE FINANCIAL AID (Fall 2008, est.) 17,237 applied for aid; of those 74% were deemed to have need. 97% of undergraduates with need received aid; of those 28% had need fully met. ***Average percent of need met:*** 70% (excluding resources awarded to replace EFC). ***Average financial aid package:*** $11,029 (excluding resources awarded to replace EFC). 13% of all full-time undergraduates had no need and received non-need-based gift aid.

GIFT AID (NEED-BASED) ***Total amount:*** $76,775,836 (24% federal, 36% state, 34% institutional, 6% external sources). ***Receiving aid:*** Freshmen: 35% (2,460); all full-time undergraduates: 32% (9,651). ***Average award:*** Freshmen: $10,050; Undergraduates: $9153. ***Scholarships, grants, and awards:*** Federal Pell, FSEOG, state, private, college/university gift aid from institutional funds, United Negro College Fund.

GIFT AID (NON-NEED-BASED) ***Total amount:*** $15,039,933 (9% federal, 7% state, 45% institutional, 39% external sources). ***Receiving aid:*** Freshmen: 9% (669). Undergraduates: 5% (1,569). ***Average award:*** Freshmen: $3982. Undergraduates: $3885. ***Scholarships, grants, and awards by category:*** *Academic interests/achievement:* agriculture, architecture, area/ethnic studies, biological sciences, business, communication, computer science, education, engineering/technologies, English, foreign languages, general academic interests/achievements, health fields, home economics, humanities, international studies, library science, mathematics, military science, physical sciences, premedicine, religion/biblical studies, social sciences. *Creative arts/performance:* applied art and design, art/fine arts, dance, general creative arts/performance, journalism/publications, music, performing arts, theater/drama. *Special achievements/activities:* general special achievements/activities, leadership. *Special characteristics:* children and siblings of alumni, children of faculty/staff, first-generation college students, general special characteristics, local/state students, veterans. ***Tuition waivers:*** Full or partial for employees or children of employees, senior citizens. ***ROTC:*** Army, Naval, Air Force.

LOANS ***Student loans:*** $75,801,296 (80% need-based, 20% non-need-based). 51% of past graduating class borrowed through all loan programs. *Average indebtedness per student:* $17,930. ***Average need-based loan:*** Freshmen: $3824. Undergraduates: $4349. ***Parent loans:*** $45,755,624 (66% need-based, 34% non-need-based). ***Programs:*** Federal Direct (Subsidized and Unsubsidized Stafford, PLUS), Perkins, college/university.

WORK-STUDY ***Federal work-study:*** Total amount: $2,336,588; jobs available. ***State or other work-study/employment:*** Total amount: $15,779,308 (49% need-based, 51% non-need-based). Part-time jobs available (averaging $1732).

ATHLETIC AWARDS Total amount: $5,803,442 (37% need-based, 63% non-need-based).

APPLYING FOR FINANCIAL AID ***Required financial aid form:*** FAFSA. ***Financial aid deadline (priority):*** 3/15. ***Notification date:*** 3/15.

University of Illinois at Urbana–Champaign

CONTACT Daniel Mann, Director of Student Financial Aid, University of Illinois at Urbana–Champaign, Student Services Arcade Building, 620 East John Street, Champaign, IL 61820-5711, 217-333-0100.

UNIVERSITY OF INDIANAPOLIS

Indianapolis, IN

CONTACT Ms. Linda B. Handy, Director of Financial Aid, University of Indianapolis, 1400 East Hanna Avenue, Indianapolis, IN 46227-3697, 317-788-3217 or toll-free 800-232-8634 Ext. 3216. *Fax:* 317-788-6136. *E-mail:* handy@uindy.edu.

THE UNIVERSITY OF IOWA

Iowa City, IA

Tuition & fees (IA res): $6824 **Average undergraduate aid package: $7512**

ABOUT THE INSTITUTION State-supported, coed. ***Awards:*** bachelor's, master's, doctoral, and first professional degrees and post-master's and first professional certificates. 119 undergraduate majors. ***Total enrollment:*** 29,747. Undergraduates: 20,823. Freshmen: 4,246. Federal methodology is used as a basis for awarding need-based institutional aid.

UNDERGRADUATE EXPENSES for 2009–10 ***Application fee:*** $40. ***Tuition, state resident:*** full-time $5782; part-time $241 per semester hour. ***Tuition, nonresident:*** full-time $21,156; part-time $882 per semester hour. ***Required fees:*** full-time $1042; $69 per semester hour.

FRESHMAN FINANCIAL AID (Fall 2008, est.) 3,420 applied for aid; of those 67% were deemed to have need. 91% of freshmen with need received aid; of those 52% had need fully met. ***Average percent of need met:*** 52% (excluding resources awarded to replace EFC). ***Average financial aid package:*** $7191 (excluding resources awarded to replace EFC). 22% of all full-time freshmen had no need and received non-need-based gift aid.

UNDERGRADUATE FINANCIAL AID (Fall 2008, est.) 13,742 applied for aid; of those 74% were deemed to have need. 93% of undergraduates with need received aid; of those 62% had need fully met. ***Average percent of need met:*** 62% (excluding resources awarded to replace EFC). ***Average financial aid package:*** $7512 (excluding resources awarded to replace EFC). 14% of all full-time undergraduates had no need and received non-need-based gift aid.

GIFT AID (NEED-BASED) ***Total amount:*** $22,572,128 (49% federal, 6% state, 45% institutional). ***Receiving aid:*** Freshmen: 32% (1,320); all full-time undergraduates: 30% (5,706). ***Average award:*** Freshmen: $4179; Undergraduates: $4282. ***Scholarships, grants, and awards:*** Federal Pell, FSEOG, state, college/university gift aid from institutional funds.

GIFT AID (NON-NEED-BASED) ***Total amount:*** $30,619,795 (5% federal, 3% state, 71% institutional, 21% external sources). ***Receiving aid:*** Freshmen: 26% (1,105). Undergraduates: 17% (3,143). ***Average award:*** Freshmen: $2313. Undergraduates: $2398. ***Scholarships, grants, and awards by category:*** *Academic interests/achievement:* business, engineering/technologies, general academic interests/achievements, military science. *Creative arts/performance:* general creative arts/performance, music. *Special achievements/activities:* general special achievements/activities. ***ROTC:*** Army, Air Force.

LOANS ***Student loans:*** $81,958,035 (37% need-based, 63% non-need-based). 61% of past graduating class borrowed through all loan programs. *Average indebtedness per student:* $22,856. ***Average need-based loan:*** Freshmen: $2904. Undergraduates: $3826. ***Parent loans:*** $28,060,171 (100% non-need-based). ***Programs:*** Federal Direct (Subsidized and Unsubsidized Stafford, PLUS), Perkins, Federal Nursing.

WORK-STUDY ***Federal work-study:*** Total amount: $2,339,266; jobs available. ***State or other work-study/employment:*** Total amount: $58,824 (100% need-based). Part-time jobs available.

ATHLETIC AWARDS Total amount: $6,953,441 (100% non-need-based).

APPLYING FOR FINANCIAL AID ***Required financial aid forms:*** FAFSA, institution's own form. ***Financial aid deadline:*** Continuous. ***Notification date:*** Continuous beginning 3/1.

CONTACT Mark Warner, Director of Student Financial Aid, The University of Iowa, 208 Calvin Hall, Iowa City, IA 52242, 319-335-0127 or toll-free 800-553-4692.

THE UNIVERSITY OF KANSAS

Lawrence, KS

Tuition & fees (KS res): $7725 **Average undergraduate aid package: $9358**

ABOUT THE INSTITUTION State-supported, coed. ***Awards:*** bachelor's, master's, doctoral, and first professional degrees and post-master's certificates (University of Kansas is a single institution with academic programs and facilities at two primary locations: Lawrence and Kansas City.). 109 undergraduate majors. ***Total enrollment:*** 29,365. Undergraduates: 21,332. Freshmen: 4,483. Federal methodology is used as a basis for awarding need-based institutional aid.

UNDERGRADUATE EXPENSES for 2008–09 ***Application fee:*** $30. ***Tuition, state resident:*** full-time $6878; part-time $229.25 per credit hour. ***Tuition, nonresident:*** full-time $18,062; part-time $602.05 per credit hour. ***Required fees:*** full-time $847; $70.56 per credit hour. Full-time tuition and fees vary according to program, reciprocity agreements, and student level. Part-time tuition and fees vary according to program, reciprocity agreements, and student level. ***College room and board:*** $6474; ***Room only:*** $3386. Room and board charges vary according to board plan and housing facility. ***Payment plans:*** Guaranteed tuition, installment.

FRESHMAN FINANCIAL AID (Fall 2007) 3,173 applied for aid; of those 50% were deemed to have need. 95% of freshmen with need received aid; of those 24% had need fully met. ***Average percent of need met:*** 58% (excluding resources awarded to replace EFC). ***Average financial aid package:*** $7833 (excluding resources awarded to replace EFC). 22% of all full-time freshmen had no need and received non-need-based gift aid.

UNDERGRADUATE FINANCIAL AID (Fall 2007) 13,949 applied for aid; of those 53% were deemed to have need. 96% of undergraduates with need received aid; of those 30% had need fully met. ***Average percent of need met:*** 65% (excluding resources awarded to replace EFC). ***Average financial aid package:*** $9358 (excluding resources awarded to replace EFC). 11% of all full-time undergraduates had no need and received non-need-based gift aid.

GIFT AID (NEED-BASED) ***Total amount:*** $21,732,796 (50% federal, 10% state, 40% institutional). ***Receiving aid:*** Freshmen: 24% (987); all full-time undergraduates: 26% (4,691). ***Average award:*** Freshmen: $4550; Undergraduates: $4860. ***Scholarships, grants, and awards:*** Federal Pell, FSEOG, state, private, college/university gift aid from institutional funds.

GIFT AID (NON-NEED-BASED) ***Total amount:*** $13,829,752 (78% institutional, 22% external sources). ***Receiving aid:*** Freshmen: 15% (615). Undergraduates: 11% (1,940). ***Average award:*** Freshmen: $3282. Undergraduates: $3379. ***Scholarships, grants, and awards by category:*** *Academic interests/achievement:* architecture, area/ethnic studies, biological sciences, business, communication, computer science, education, engineering/technologies, English, foreign languages, general academic interests/achievements, health fields, humanities, international studies, mathematics, physical sciences, premedicine, religion/biblical studies, social sciences. *Creative arts/performance:* applied art and design, art/fine arts, cinema/film/broadcasting, creative writing, dance, debating, general creative arts/performance, journalism/publications, music, performing arts, theater/drama. *Special achievements/activities:* community service, general special achievements/activities, leadership. *Special characteristics:* adult students, children of faculty/staff, ethnic background, first-generation college students, general special characteristics, international students, local/state students, married students, members of minority groups, out-of-state students, previous college experience. ***Tuition waivers:*** Full or partial for employees or children of employees. ***ROTC:*** Army, Naval, Air Force.

LOANS ***Student loans:*** $63,064,428 (45% need-based, 55% non-need-based). 46% of past graduating class borrowed through all loan programs. *Average indebtedness per student:* $20,902. ***Average need-based loan:*** Freshmen: $2873. Undergraduates: $3472. ***Parent loans:*** $29,931,416 (100% non-need-based). ***Programs:*** Federal Direct (Subsidized and Unsubsidized Stafford, PLUS), FFEL (Subsidized and Unsubsidized Stafford, PLUS), Perkins, college/university.

WORK-STUDY ***Federal work-study:*** Total amount: $1,642,142; 512 jobs averaging $3725. ***State or other work-study/employment:*** Total amount: $335,972 (100% non-need-based). 59 part-time jobs averaging $3790.

ATHLETIC AWARDS Total amount: $6,933,881 (100% non-need-based).

APPLYING FOR FINANCIAL AID ***Required financial aid form:*** FAFSA. ***Financial aid deadline (priority):*** 3/1. ***Notification date:*** Continuous beginning 4/1. Students must reply within 4 weeks of notification.

CONTACT Ms. Brenda Maigaard, Director of Student Financial Aid, The University of Kansas, Office of Student Financial Aid, 50 Strong Hall, Lawrence, KS 66045-7535, 785-864-4700 or toll-free 888-686-7323 (in-state). *Fax:* 785-864-5469. *E-mail:* financialaid@ku.edu.

UNIVERSITY OF KENTUCKY

Lexington, KY

Tuition & fees (KY res): $8123 **Average undergraduate aid package: $8794**

ABOUT THE INSTITUTION State-supported, coed. ***Awards:*** bachelor's, master's, doctoral, and first professional degrees and post-master's certificates. 80 undergraduate majors. ***Total enrollment:*** 26,054. Undergraduates: 18,942. Freshmen: 4,110. Federal methodology is used as a basis for awarding need-based institutional aid.

UNDERGRADUATE EXPENSES for 2009–10 ***Application fee:*** $50. ***Tuition, state resident:*** full-time $7214; part-time $301 per credit hour. ***Tuition, nonresident:*** full-time $15,769; part-time $658 per credit hour. ***Required fees:*** full-time $909; $21.50 per credit hour. ***College room and board:*** $9125; ***Room only:*** $3975.

FRESHMAN FINANCIAL AID (Fall 2008, est.) 2,809 applied for aid; of those 67% were deemed to have need. 100% of freshmen with need received aid; of those 47% had need fully met. ***Average percent of need met:*** 81% (excluding resources awarded to replace EFC). ***Average financial aid package:*** $8978 (excluding resources awarded to replace EFC). 22% of all full-time freshmen had no need and received non-need-based gift aid.

UNDERGRADUATE FINANCIAL AID (Fall 2008, est.) 9,670 applied for aid; of those 74% were deemed to have need. 98% of undergraduates with need received aid; of those 47% had need fully met. ***Average percent of need met:*** 82% (excluding resources awarded to replace EFC). ***Average financial aid package:*** $8794 (excluding resources awarded to replace EFC). 19% of all full-time undergraduates had no need and received non-need-based gift aid.

GIFT AID (NEED-BASED) ***Total amount:*** $69,716,528 (18% federal, 29% state, 47% institutional, 6% external sources). ***Receiving aid:*** Freshmen: 18% (744); all full-time undergraduates: 18% (3,070). ***Average award:*** Freshmen: $5348; Undergraduates: $5118. ***Scholarships, grants, and awards:*** Federal Pell, FSEOG, state, private, college/university gift aid from institutional funds.

GIFT AID (NON-NEED-BASED) ***Receiving aid:*** Freshmen: 41% (1,656). Undergraduates: 27% (4,734). ***Average award:*** Freshmen: $8712. Undergraduates: $5493. ***Scholarships, grants, and awards by category:*** *Academic interests/achievement:* agriculture, architecture, area/ethnic studies, biological sciences, business, communication, computer science, education, engineering/technologies, English, foreign languages, general academic interests/achievements, health fields, home economics, international studies, mathematics, military science, physical sciences. *Creative arts/performance:* applied art and design, art/fine arts, cinema/film/broadcasting, creative writing, dance, debating, general creative arts/performance, journalism/publications, music, performing arts, theater/drama. *Special achievements/activities:* cheerleading/drum major, general special achievements/activities, leadership. *Special characteristics:* adult students, children and siblings of alumni, children of educators, children of faculty/staff, children of public servants, children of union members/company employees, children of workers in trades, children with a deceased or disabled parent, ethnic background, first-generation college students, general special characteristics, handicapped students, international students, members of minority groups, public servants, spouses of deceased or disabled public servants, veterans, veterans' children. ***ROTC:*** Army, Air Force.

LOANS ***Student loans:*** $56,328,873 (100% need-based). 33% of past graduating class borrowed through all loan programs. *Average indebtedness per student:* $15,891. ***Average need-based loan:*** Freshmen: $3278. Undergraduates: $4062. ***Parent loans:*** $11,679,176 (100% need-based). ***Programs:*** Federal Direct (Subsidized and Unsubsidized Stafford, PLUS), FFEL (Subsidized and Unsubsidized Stafford, PLUS), Perkins, college/university.

WORK-STUDY ***Federal work-study:*** Total amount: $576,000; jobs available. ***State or other work-study/employment:*** Total amount: $258,951 (100% need-based). Part-time jobs available.

ATHLETIC AWARDS Total amount: $7,023,008 (100% need-based).

APPLYING FOR FINANCIAL AID ***Required financial aid form:*** FAFSA. ***Financial aid deadline (priority):*** 2/15. ***Notification date:*** Continuous beginning 4/1. Students must reply within 3 weeks of notification.

CONTACT Ms. Lynda S. George, Director of Financial Aid, University of Kentucky, 128 Funkhouser Building, Lexington, KY 40506-0054, 859-257-3172 Ext. 241 or toll-free 800-432-0967 (in-state). *Fax:* 859-257-4398. *E-mail:* lgeorge@email.uky.edu.

UNIVERSITY OF LA VERNE

La Verne, CA

Tuition & fees: $28,250 **Average undergraduate aid package: $22,535**

ABOUT THE INSTITUTION Independent, coed. ***Awards:*** associate, bachelor's, master's, doctoral, and first professional degrees and post-bachelor's and post-master's certificates (also offers continuing education program with significant enrollment not reflected in profile). 46 undergraduate majors. ***Total enrollment:*** 3,923. Undergraduates: 1,548. Freshmen: 302. Federal methodology is used as a basis for awarding need-based institutional aid.

UNDERGRADUATE EXPENSES for 2009–10 ***Application fee:*** $50. ***Comprehensive fee:*** $39,360 includes full-time tuition ($28,250) and room and board ($11,110). ***College room only:*** $5620. ***Part-time tuition:*** $800 per unit.

FRESHMAN FINANCIAL AID (Fall 2008, est.) 258 applied for aid; of those 93% were deemed to have need. 100% of freshmen with need received aid; of those 1% had need fully met. ***Average percent of need met:*** 50% (excluding resources awarded to replace EFC). ***Average financial aid package:*** $23,526 (excluding resources awarded to replace EFC). 10% of all full-time freshmen had no need and received non-need-based gift aid.

UNDERGRADUATE FINANCIAL AID (Fall 2008, est.) 1,240 applied for aid; of those 94% were deemed to have need. 99% of undergraduates with need received aid; of those 1% had need fully met. ***Average percent of need met:*** 50% (excluding resources awarded to replace EFC). ***Average financial aid package:*** $22,535 (excluding resources awarded to replace EFC). 13% of all full-time undergraduates had no need and received non-need-based gift aid.

GIFT AID (NEED-BASED) ***Total amount:*** $18,220,125 (12% federal, 23% state, 64% institutional, 1% external sources). ***Receiving aid:*** Freshmen: 72% (213); all full-time undergraduates: 73% (1,061). ***Average award:*** Freshmen: $12,209; Undergraduates: $11,268. ***Scholarships, grants, and awards:*** Federal Pell, FSEOG, state, private, college/university gift aid from institutional funds.

GIFT AID (NON-NEED-BASED) ***Total amount:*** $3,584,065 (100% institutional). ***Receiving aid:*** Freshmen: 62% (185). Undergraduates: 67% (975). ***Average award:*** Freshmen: $11,333. Undergraduates: $8489. ***Scholarships, grants, and awards by category:*** *Academic interests/achievement:* general academic interests/achievements. *Creative arts/performance:* art/fine arts, debating, journalism/publications, music, theater/drama. *Special achievements/activities:* community service, leadership. *Special characteristics:* children and siblings of alumni, children of faculty/staff, ethnic background, first-generation college students, general special characteristics, international students, religious affiliation. ***ROTC:*** Army cooperative.

LOANS ***Student loans:*** $10,321,818 (92% need-based, 8% non-need-based). 81% of past graduating class borrowed through all loan programs. *Average indebtedness per student:* $19,467. ***Average need-based loan:*** Freshmen: $4798. Undergraduates: $5428. ***Parent loans:*** $1,431,055 (86% need-based, 14% non-need-based). ***Programs:*** FFEL (Subsidized and Unsubsidized Stafford, PLUS), Perkins, college/university, alternative loans.

WORK-STUDY ***Federal work-study:*** Total amount: $451,977; jobs available. ***State or other work-study/employment:*** Part-time jobs available.

APPLYING FOR FINANCIAL AID ***Required financial aid forms:*** FAFSA, state aid form. ***Financial aid deadline (priority):*** 3/2. ***Notification date:*** Continuous beginning 3/17. Students must reply within 2 weeks of notification.

CONTACT Leatha Webster, Director of Financial Aid, University of La Verne, 1950 3rd Street, La Verne, CA 91750-4443, 909-593-3511 Ext. 4180 or toll-free 800-876-4858. *Fax:* 909-392-2751. *E-mail:* websterl@ulv.edu.

UNIVERSITY OF LOUISIANA AT LAFAYETTE

Lafayette, LA

Tuition & fees (LA res): $3574 **Average undergraduate aid package: $6123**

ABOUT THE INSTITUTION State-supported, coed. ***Awards:*** bachelor's, master's, and doctoral degrees and post-master's certificates. 89 undergraduate majors. ***Total enrollment:*** 16,345. Undergraduates: 14,931. Freshmen: 2,763. Federal methodology is used as a basis for awarding need-based institutional aid.

UNDERGRADUATE EXPENSES for 2008–09 ***Application fee:*** $25. ***Tuition, state resident:*** full-time $3574; part-time $100 per credit hour. ***Tuition, nonresident:*** full-time $9754; part-time $357.70 per credit hour. Full-time tuition and fees vary according to course load. Part-time tuition and fees vary according to course load. ***College room and board:*** $4200. Room and board charges vary according to housing facility. ***Payment plan:*** Deferred payment.

FRESHMAN FINANCIAL AID (Fall 2007) 2,393 applied for aid; of those 58% were deemed to have need. 97% of freshmen with need received aid; of those 23% had need fully met. ***Average percent of need met:*** 68% (excluding resources awarded to replace EFC). ***Average financial aid package:*** $6525 (excluding resources awarded to replace EFC). 12% of all full-time freshmen had no need and received non-need-based gift aid.

UNDERGRADUATE FINANCIAL AID (Fall 2007) 9,324 applied for aid; of those 66% were deemed to have need. 97% of undergraduates with need received aid; of those 14% had need fully met. ***Average percent of need met:*** 55% (excluding resources awarded to replace EFC). ***Average financial aid package:*** $6123 (excluding resources awarded to replace EFC). 7% of all full-time undergraduates had no need and received non-need-based gift aid.

GIFT AID (NEED-BASED) ***Total amount:*** $14,862,289 (90% federal, 10% state). ***Receiving aid:*** Freshmen: 46% (1,259); all full-time undergraduates: 41% (5,108). ***Average award:*** Freshmen: $5285; Undergraduates: $4307. ***Scholarships, grants, and awards:*** Federal Pell, FSEOG, state, college/university gift aid from institutional funds.

GIFT AID (NON-NEED-BASED) ***Total amount:*** $16,573,715 (75% state, 22% institutional, 3% external sources). ***Receiving aid:*** Freshmen: 9% (239). Undergraduates: 4% (524). ***Average award:*** Freshmen: $1558. Undergraduates: $1592. ***Scholarships, grants, and awards by category:*** *Academic interests/achievement:* 2,023 awards ($3,654,756 total): general academic interests/achievements. *Creative arts/performance:* general creative arts/performance. *Special achievements/activities:* general special achievements/activities. ***Tuition waivers:*** Full or partial for children of alumni, employees or children of employees, senior citizens. ***ROTC:*** Army.

LOANS ***Student loans:*** $23,996,487 (63% need-based, 37% non-need-based). ***Average need-based loan:*** Freshmen: $3081. Undergraduates: $3721. ***Parent loans:*** $1,285,381 (100% non-need-based). ***Programs:*** FFEL (Subsidized and Unsubsidized Stafford, PLUS), Perkins, Federal Nursing.

WORK-STUDY ***Federal work-study:*** Total amount: $680,584; 481 jobs averaging $1415. ***State or other work-study/employment:*** Total amount: $345,663 (100% non-need-based). 240 part-time jobs averaging $1440.

ATHLETIC AWARDS Total amount: $1,832,285 (100% non-need-based).

APPLYING FOR FINANCIAL AID ***Required financial aid form:*** FAFSA. ***Financial aid deadline (priority):*** 5/1. ***Notification date:*** Continuous. Students must reply within 2 weeks of notification.

CONTACT Cindy S. Perez, Director of Financial Aid, University of Louisiana at Lafayette, PO Box 41206, Lafayette, LA 70504-1206, 337-482-6497 or toll-free 800-752-6553 (in-state). *Fax:* 337-482-6502. *E-mail:* cperez@louisiana.edu.

UNIVERSITY OF LOUISIANA AT MONROE

Monroe, LA

Tuition & fees (LA res): $3791 **Average undergraduate aid package: $2956**

ABOUT THE INSTITUTION State-supported, coed. ***Awards:*** associate, bachelor's, master's, doctoral, and first professional degrees and post-bachelor's and post-master's certificates. 57 undergraduate majors. ***Total enrollment:*** 8,772. Undergraduates: 7,519. Freshmen: 1,227. Federal methodology is used as a basis for awarding need-based institutional aid.

UNDERGRADUATE EXPENSES for 2008–09 ***Application fee:*** $20. ***Tuition, state resident:*** full-time $2400. ***Tuition, nonresident:*** full-time $8734. ***Required fees:*** full-time $1391. Full-time tuition and fees vary according to course load and program. Part-time tuition and fees vary according to course load and program. ***College room and board:*** $3370; ***Room only:*** $2150. Room and board charges vary according to board plan and housing facility. ***Payment plan:*** Deferred payment.

FRESHMAN FINANCIAL AID (Fall 2007) 1,266 applied for aid; of those 98% were deemed to have need. 98% of freshmen with need received aid; of those 30% had need fully met. ***Average financial aid package:*** $2757 (excluding resources awarded to replace EFC). 7% of all full-time freshmen had no need and received non-need-based gift aid.

UNDERGRADUATE FINANCIAL AID (Fall 2007) 4,011 applied for aid; of those 95% were deemed to have need. 98% of undergraduates with need received aid; of those 42% had need fully met. ***Average financial aid package:*** $2956 (excluding resources awarded to replace EFC). 4% of all full-time undergraduates had no need and received non-need-based gift aid.

GIFT AID (NEED-BASED) ***Total amount:*** $10,072,411 (95% federal, 5% state). ***Receiving aid:*** Freshmen: 27% (378); all full-time undergraduates: 32% (1,868). ***Average award:*** Freshmen: $3501; Undergraduates: $3055. ***Scholarships, grants, and awards:*** Federal Pell, FSEOG, state, private, college/university gift aid from institutional funds, Leveraging Educational Assistance Partnership Program (LEAP).

GIFT AID (NON-NEED-BASED) ***Total amount:*** $11,005,788 (50% state, 47% institutional, 3% external sources). ***Receiving aid:*** Freshmen: 57% (792). Undergraduates: 39% (2,312). ***Average award:*** Freshmen: $2028. Undergraduates: $2019. ***Scholarships, grants, and awards by category:*** *Academic interests/achievement:* agriculture, biological sciences, business, communication, computer science, education, English, foreign languages, general academic interests/achievements, health fields, home economics, library science, mathematics, military science, physical sciences, social sciences. *Creative arts/performance:* art/fine arts, creative writing, debating, journalism/publications, music, performing arts, theater/drama. *Special achievements/activities:* cheerleading/drum major, community service, leadership. *Special characteristics:* children of faculty/staff, children with a deceased or disabled parent, international students, out-of-state students. ***Tuition waivers:*** Full or partial for children of alumni, employees or children of employees. ***ROTC:*** Army.

LOANS ***Student loans:*** $27,532,058 (53% need-based, 47% non-need-based). 46% of past graduating class borrowed through all loan programs. ***Average need-based loan:*** Freshmen: $2491. Undergraduates: $2626. ***Parent loans:*** $800,735 (100% non-need-based). ***Programs:*** FFEL (Subsidized and Unsubsidized Stafford, PLUS), Perkins, college/university, Federal Health Professions Student Loans.

WORK-STUDY ***Federal work-study:*** Total amount: $663,991; 1,184 jobs averaging $1478. ***State or other work-study/employment:*** Total amount: $596,666 (100% non-need-based). 165 part-time jobs averaging $1337.

ATHLETIC AWARDS Total amount: $1,949,857 (100% non-need-based).

APPLYING FOR FINANCIAL AID ***Required financial aid forms:*** FAFSA, institution's own form. ***Financial aid deadline (priority):*** 4/1. ***Notification date:*** Continuous beginning 6/15. Students must reply within 2 weeks of notification.

CONTACT Roslynn Pogue, Assistant Director, Financial Aid, University of Louisiana at Monroe, 700 University Avenue, Monroe, LA 71209, 318-342-5320 or toll-free 800-372-5272 (in-state), 800-372-5127 (out-of-state). *Fax:* 318-342-3539. *E-mail:* sspogue@ulm.edu.

UNIVERSITY OF LOUISVILLE

Louisville, KY

Tuition & fees (KY res): $7564 **Average undergraduate aid package: $9981**

ABOUT THE INSTITUTION State-supported, coed. ***Awards:*** associate, bachelor's, master's, doctoral, and first professional degrees and post-bachelor's and post-master's certificates. 51 undergraduate majors. ***Total enrollment:*** 20,834. Undergraduates: 15,352. Freshmen: 2,609. Federal methodology is used as a basis for awarding need-based institutional aid.

UNDERGRADUATE EXPENSES for 2008–09 ***Application fee:*** $40. ***Tuition, state resident:*** full-time $7564; part-time $361 per hour. ***Tuition, nonresident:*** full-time $18,354; part-time $765 per hour. ***College room and board:*** $6058; ***Room only:*** $4068.

FRESHMAN FINANCIAL AID (Fall 2008, est.) 1,939 applied for aid; of those 80% were deemed to have need. 99% of freshmen with need received aid; of those 18% had need fully met. ***Average percent of need met:*** 58% (excluding resources awarded to replace EFC). ***Average financial aid package:*** $10,384 (excluding resources awarded to replace EFC). 15% of all full-time freshmen had no need and received non-need-based gift aid.

UNDERGRADUATE FINANCIAL AID (Fall 2008, est.) 7,752 applied for aid; of those 85% were deemed to have need. 98% of undergraduates with need received aid; of those 15% had need fully met. ***Average percent of need met:*** 55% (excluding resources awarded to replace EFC). ***Average financial aid package:*** $9981 (excluding resources awarded to replace EFC). 13% of all full-time undergraduates had no need and received non-need-based gift aid.

GIFT AID (NEED-BASED) ***Total amount:*** $42,475,778 (29% federal, 21% state, 32% institutional, 18% external sources). ***Receiving aid:*** Freshmen: 58% (1,482); all full-time undergraduates: 49% (5,704). ***Average award:*** Freshmen: $8093;

Undergraduates: $7456. ***Scholarships, grants, and awards:*** Federal Pell, FSEOG, state, private, college/university gift aid from institutional funds.

GIFT AID (NON-NEED-BASED) ***Total amount:*** $24,128,755 (25% state, 54% institutional, 21% external sources). ***Receiving aid:*** Freshmen: 7% (191). Undergraduates: 5% (568). ***Average award:*** Freshmen: $6803. Undergraduates: $6916. ***Scholarships, grants, and awards by category:*** *Academic interests/achievement:* general academic interests/achievements. *Creative arts/performance:* general creative arts/performance. *Special achievements/activities:* general special achievements/activities, memberships. *Special characteristics:* general special characteristics. ***ROTC:*** Army, Air Force.

LOANS ***Student loans:*** $41,971,107 (79% need-based, 21% non-need-based). 63% of past graduating class borrowed through all loan programs. *Average indebtedness per student:* $11,704. ***Average need-based loan:*** Freshmen: $3217. Undergraduates: $4178. ***Parent loans:*** $2,378,842 (35% need-based, 65% non-need-based). ***Programs:*** FFEL (Subsidized and Unsubsidized Stafford, PLUS), Perkins, Federal Nursing, college/university.

WORK-STUDY ***Federal work-study:*** Total amount: $1,322,992; 941 jobs averaging $1431.

ATHLETIC AWARDS Total amount: $7,286,834 (37% need-based, 63% non-need-based).

APPLYING FOR FINANCIAL AID ***Required financial aid form:*** FAFSA. ***Financial aid deadline (priority):*** 3/15. ***Notification date:*** Continuous beginning 4/1. Students must reply by 5/1.

CONTACT Ms. Patricia O. Arauz, Director of Financial Aid, University of Louisville, 2301 South Third Street, Louisville, KY 40292-0001, 502-852-6145 or toll-free 800-334-8635 (out-of-state). *Fax:* 502-852-0182. *E-mail:* finaid@louisville.edu.

UNIVERSITY OF MAINE

Orono, ME

Tuition & fees (ME res): $9100 **Average undergraduate aid package: $11,369**

ABOUT THE INSTITUTION State-supported, coed. ***Awards:*** bachelor's, master's, and doctoral degrees and post-master's certificates. 108 undergraduate majors. ***Total enrollment:*** 11,818. Undergraduates: 9,667. Freshmen: 2,062. Federal methodology is used as a basis for awarding need-based institutional aid.

UNDERGRADUATE EXPENSES for 2008–09 ***Application fee:*** $40. ***Tuition, state resident:*** full-time $7170; part-time $239 per credit hour. ***Tuition, nonresident:*** full-time $20,580; part-time $686 per credit hour. ***Required fees:*** full-time $1930. Full-time tuition and fees vary according to reciprocity agreements. Part-time tuition and fees vary according to reciprocity agreements. ***College room and board:*** $8008. Room and board charges vary according to board plan and housing facility. ***Payment plan:*** Installment.

FRESHMAN FINANCIAL AID (Fall 2008, est.) 2,054 applied for aid; of those 80% were deemed to have need. 98% of freshmen with need received aid; of those 32% had need fully met. ***Average percent of need met:*** 76% (excluding resources awarded to replace EFC). ***Average financial aid package:*** $11,855 (excluding resources awarded to replace EFC). 21% of all full-time freshmen had no need and received non-need-based gift aid.

UNDERGRADUATE FINANCIAL AID (Fall 2008, est.) 6,766 applied for aid; of those 81% were deemed to have need. 98% of undergraduates with need received aid; of those 36% had need fully met. ***Average percent of need met:*** 78% (excluding resources awarded to replace EFC). ***Average financial aid package:*** $11,369 (excluding resources awarded to replace EFC). 17% of all full-time undergraduates had no need and received non-need-based gift aid.

GIFT AID (NEED-BASED) ***Total amount:*** $26,398,047 (41% federal, 12% state, 38% institutional, 9% external sources). ***Receiving aid:*** Freshmen: 67% (1,387); all full-time undergraduates: 46% (4,021). ***Average award:*** Freshmen: $6608; Undergraduates: $6427. ***Scholarships, grants, and awards:*** Federal Pell, FSEOG, state, private, college/university gift aid from institutional funds, Academic Competitiveness Grant, National Smart Grant.

GIFT AID (NON-NEED-BASED) ***Total amount:*** $8,643,049 (5% federal, 12% institutional, 83% external sources). ***Receiving aid:*** Freshmen: 5% (106). Undergraduates: 4% (331). ***Average award:*** Freshmen: $9896. Undergraduates: $11,399. ***Tuition waivers:*** Full or partial for employees or children of employees. ***ROTC:*** Army, Naval.

LOANS ***Student loans:*** $61,841,592 (48% need-based, 52% non-need-based). 73% of past graduating class borrowed through all loan programs. *Average indebtedness per student:* $24,330. ***Average need-based loan:*** Freshmen: $4312. Undergraduates: $5061. ***Parent loans:*** $6,588,327 (100% non-need-based). ***Programs:*** FFEL (Subsidized and Unsubsidized Stafford, PLUS), Perkins, state, college/university.

WORK-STUDY ***Federal work-study:*** Total amount: $2,386,598; 1,081 jobs averaging $2222.

ATHLETIC AWARDS Total amount: $4,649,057 (23% need-based, 77% non-need-based).

APPLYING FOR FINANCIAL AID ***Required financial aid form:*** FAFSA. ***Financial aid deadline:*** 5/1 (priority: 3/1). ***Notification date:*** Continuous beginning 3/15. Students must reply by 5/1 or within 2 weeks of notification.

CONTACT Ms. Peggy L. Crawford, Director of Student Aid, University of Maine, 5781 Wingate Hall, Orono, ME 04469, 207-581-1324 or toll-free 877-486-2364. *Fax:* 207-581-3261. *E-mail:* pcrawf@maine.edu.

THE UNIVERSITY OF MAINE AT AUGUSTA

Augusta, ME

Tuition & fees (ME res): $6495 **Average undergraduate aid package: $8467**

ABOUT THE INSTITUTION State-supported, coed. ***Awards:*** associate and bachelor's degrees and post-bachelor's certificates (also offers some graduate courses and continuing education programs with significant enrollment not reflected in profile). 26 undergraduate majors. ***Total enrollment:*** 5,202. Undergraduates: 5,202. Freshmen: 575. Federal methodology is used as a basis for awarding need-based institutional aid.

UNDERGRADUATE EXPENSES for 2008–09 ***Application fee:*** $40. ***Tuition, state resident:*** full-time $5700; part-time $190 per credit hour. ***Tuition, nonresident:*** full-time $13,800; part-time $460 per credit hour. ***Required fees:*** full-time $795; $26.50 per credit hour. Full-time tuition and fees vary according to reciprocity agreements. Part-time tuition and fees vary according to reciprocity agreements. ***Payment plan:*** Installment.

FRESHMAN FINANCIAL AID (Fall 2008, est.) 288 applied for aid; of those 88% were deemed to have need. 97% of freshmen with need received aid; of those 13% had need fully met. ***Average percent of need met:*** 63% (excluding resources awarded to replace EFC). ***Average financial aid package:*** $6538 (excluding resources awarded to replace EFC). 6% of all full-time freshmen had no need and received non-need-based gift aid.

UNDERGRADUATE FINANCIAL AID (Fall 2008, est.) 1,604 applied for aid; of those 89% were deemed to have need. 98% of undergraduates with need received aid; of those 18% had need fully met. ***Average percent of need met:*** 70% (excluding resources awarded to replace EFC). ***Average financial aid package:*** $8467 (excluding resources awarded to replace EFC). 8% of all full-time undergraduates had no need and received non-need-based gift aid.

GIFT AID (NEED-BASED) ***Total amount:*** $9,364,390 (72% federal, 18% state, 9% institutional, 1% external sources). ***Receiving aid:*** Freshmen: 65% (223); all full-time undergraduates: 75% (1,245). ***Average award:*** Freshmen: $4497; Undergraduates: $4828. ***Scholarships, grants, and awards:*** Federal Pell, FSEOG, state, private, college/university gift aid from institutional funds.

GIFT AID (NON-NEED-BASED) ***Total amount:*** $428,684 (25% institutional, 75% external sources). ***Receiving aid:*** Freshmen: 2% (6). Undergraduates: 1% (21). ***Average award:*** Freshmen: $3978. Undergraduates: $4862. ***Scholarships, grants, and awards by category:*** *Academic interests/achievement:* 28 awards ($70,000 total): biological sciences, business, general academic interests/achievements, mathematics. *Creative arts/performance:* 14 awards ($35,000 total): music. *Special achievements/activities:* 31 awards ($77,500 total): general special achievements/activities, leadership. *Special characteristics:* 127 awards ($304,800 total): children of faculty/staff, ethnic background, international students, local/state students, veterans' children. ***Tuition waivers:*** Full or partial for employees or children of employees, senior citizens. ***ROTC:*** Army cooperative, Naval cooperative, Air Force cooperative.

LOANS ***Student loans:*** $13,083,429 (69% need-based, 31% non-need-based). 68% of past graduating class borrowed through all loan programs. *Average indebtedness per student:* $15,842. ***Average need-based loan:*** Freshmen: $2941. Undergraduates: $4063. ***Parent loans:*** $86,149 (100% non-need-based). ***Programs:*** Federal Direct (Subsidized and Unsubsidized Stafford, PLUS), FFEL (Subsidized and Unsubsidized Stafford, PLUS), Perkins, Federal Nursing.

WORK-STUDY ***Federal work-study:*** Total amount: $390,674; 220 jobs averaging $1500.

ATHLETIC AWARDS Total amount: $33,960 (100% non-need-based).

APPLYING FOR FINANCIAL AID ***Required financial aid form:*** FAFSA. ***Financial aid deadline (priority):*** 3/1. ***Notification date:*** Continuous beginning 3/15. Students must reply by 5/1 or within 2 weeks of notification.

CONTACT Sherry McCollett, Director of Financial Aid, The University of Maine at Augusta, 46 University Drive, Augusta, ME 04330-9410, 207-621-3455 or toll-free 877-862-1234 Ext. 3185 (in-state). *Fax:* 207-621-3116. *E-mail:* umafa@maine.edu.

UNIVERSITY OF MAINE AT FARMINGTON

Farmington, ME

ABOUT THE INSTITUTION State-supported, coed. ***Awards:*** bachelor's and master's degrees. 41 undergraduate majors. ***Total enrollment:*** 2,229. Undergraduates: 2,194. Freshmen: 516.

GIFT AID (NEED-BASED) ***Scholarships, grants, and awards:*** Federal Pell, FSEOG, state, private, college/university gift aid from institutional funds.

GIFT AID (NON-NEED-BASED) ***Scholarships, grants, and awards by category:*** *Academic interests/achievement:* general academic interests/achievements. *Special characteristics:* children of faculty/staff, members of minority groups, out-of-state students, veterans' children.

LOANS ***Programs:*** FFEL (Subsidized and Unsubsidized Stafford, PLUS), Perkins, state, college/university, Educators For Maine Loans.

WORK-STUDY ***Federal work-study:*** Total amount: $751,946; 519 jobs averaging $1448. ***State or other work-study/employment:*** Total amount: $708,311 (100% non-need-based). 406 part-time jobs averaging $1719.

APPLYING FOR FINANCIAL AID ***Required financial aid form:*** FAFSA.

CONTACT Mr. Ronald P. Milliken, Director of Financial Aid, University of Maine at Farmington, 224 Main Street, Farmington, ME 04938-1990, 207-778-7105. *Fax:* 207-778-8178. *E-mail:* milliken@maine.edu.

UNIVERSITY OF MAINE AT FORT KENT

Fort Kent, ME

Tuition & fees (ME res): $6413 **Average undergraduate aid package: $8825**

ABOUT THE INSTITUTION State-supported, coed. ***Awards:*** associate and bachelor's degrees. 25 undergraduate majors. ***Total enrollment:*** 1,102. Undergraduates: 1,102. Freshmen: 119. Federal methodology is used as a basis for awarding need-based institutional aid.

UNDERGRADUATE EXPENSES for 2008–09 ***Application fee:*** $40. ***Tuition, state resident:*** full-time $5700; part-time $190 per credit hour. ***Tuition, nonresident:*** full-time $14,310; part-time $477 per credit hour. ***Required fees:*** full-time $713; $23.75 per credit hour. Full-time tuition and fees vary according to course load. Part-time tuition and fees vary according to course load. ***College room and board:*** $6040; ***Room only:*** $4000. Room and board charges vary according to board plan and housing facility. ***Payment plan:*** Installment.

FRESHMAN FINANCIAL AID (Fall 2008, est.) 118 applied for aid; of those 88% were deemed to have need. 100% of freshmen with need received aid; of those 33% had need fully met. ***Average percent of need met:*** 78% (excluding resources awarded to replace EFC). ***Average financial aid package:*** $8404 (excluding resources awarded to replace EFC). 2% of all full-time freshmen had no need and received non-need-based gift aid.

UNDERGRADUATE FINANCIAL AID (Fall 2008, est.) 468 applied for aid; of those 88% were deemed to have need. 98% of undergraduates with need received aid; of those 38% had need fully met. ***Average percent of need met:*** 77% (excluding resources awarded to replace EFC). ***Average financial aid package:*** $8825 (excluding resources awarded to replace EFC). 5% of all full-time undergraduates had no need and received non-need-based gift aid.

GIFT AID (NEED-BASED) ***Total amount:*** $2,440,776 (63% federal, 8% state, 16% institutional, 13% external sources). ***Receiving aid:*** Freshmen: 80% (104); all full-time undergraduates: 66% (401). ***Average award:*** Freshmen: $5698; Undergraduates: $4818. ***Scholarships, grants, and awards:*** Federal Pell, FSEOG, state, private, college/university gift aid from institutional funds.

GIFT AID (NON-NEED-BASED) ***Total amount:*** $32,118 (1% institutional, 99% external sources). ***Receiving aid:*** Undergraduates: 3. ***Average award:*** Freshmen: $7417. Undergraduates: $7195. ***Scholarships, grants, and awards by category:*** *Academic interests/achievement:* biological sciences, business, communication, computer science, education, English, foreign languages, general academic interests/achievements, health fields, humanities, mathematics, social sciences. *Creative arts/performance:* general creative arts/performance, performing arts. *Special achievements/activities:* general special achievements/activities. *Special characteristics:* adult students, children of faculty/staff, general special characteristics, international students, members of minority groups. ***Tuition waivers:*** Full or partial for minority students, employees or children of employees, senior citizens.

LOANS ***Student loans:*** $2,062,676 (53% need-based, 47% non-need-based). ***Average need-based loan:*** Freshmen: $2659. Undergraduates: $4041. ***Parent loans:*** $137,943 (100% non-need-based). ***Programs:*** Federal Direct (Subsidized and Unsubsidized Stafford, PLUS), FFEL (Subsidized and Unsubsidized Stafford, PLUS), Perkins, state.

WORK-STUDY ***Federal work-study:*** Total amount: $181,253; 90 jobs averaging $1800. ***State or other work-study/employment:*** Part-time jobs available.

APPLYING FOR FINANCIAL AID ***Required financial aid form:*** FAFSA. ***Financial aid deadline (priority):*** 3/1. ***Notification date:*** Continuous beginning 3/1.

CONTACT Ellen Cost, Director of Financial Aid, University of Maine at Fort Kent, 23 University Drive, Fort Kent, ME 04743-1292, 207-834-7606 or toll-free 888-TRY-UMFK. *Fax:* 207-834-7841. *E-mail:* ecost@maine.edu.

UNIVERSITY OF MAINE AT MACHIAS

Machias, ME

CONTACT Ms. Stephanie Larrabee, Director of Financial Aid, University of Maine at Machias, 9 O'Brien Avenue, Machias, ME 04654, 207-255-1203 or toll-free 888-GOTOUMM (in-state), 888-468-6866 (out-of-state). *Fax:* 207-255-4864.

UNIVERSITY OF MAINE AT PRESQUE ISLE

Presque Isle, ME

Tuition & fees (ME res): $6475 **Average undergraduate aid package: $8770**

ABOUT THE INSTITUTION State-supported, coed. ***Awards:*** associate and bachelor's degrees. 28 undergraduate majors. ***Total enrollment:*** 1,460. Undergraduates: 1,460. Freshmen: 200. Federal methodology is used as a basis for awarding need-based institutional aid.

UNDERGRADUATE EXPENSES for 2008–09 ***Application fee:*** $40. ***Tuition, state resident:*** full-time $5700; part-time $190 per credit hour. ***Tuition, nonresident:*** full-time $14,310; part-time $477 per credit hour. ***Required fees:*** full-time $775; $16 per credit hour. Full-time tuition and fees vary according to course load and reciprocity agreements. Part-time tuition and fees vary according to course load and reciprocity agreements. ***College room and board:*** $7096; ***Room only:*** $3540. Room and board charges vary according to board plan and housing facility. ***Payment plans:*** Installment, deferred payment.

FRESHMAN FINANCIAL AID (Fall 2007) 200 applied for aid; of those 90% were deemed to have need. 86% of freshmen with need received aid; of those 41% had need fully met. ***Average percent of need met:*** 90% (excluding resources awarded to replace EFC). ***Average financial aid package:*** $8060 (excluding resources awarded to replace EFC). 8% of all full-time freshmen had no need and received non-need-based gift aid.

UNDERGRADUATE FINANCIAL AID (Fall 2007) 705 applied for aid; of those 90% were deemed to have need. 89% of undergraduates with need received aid; of those 38% had need fully met. ***Average percent of need met:*** 90% (excluding resources awarded to replace EFC). ***Average financial aid package:*** $8770 (excluding resources awarded to replace EFC). 5% of all full-time undergraduates had no need and received non-need-based gift aid.

GIFT AID (NEED-BASED) ***Total amount:*** $3,109,578 (65% federal, 13% state, 9% institutional, 13% external sources). ***Receiving aid:*** Freshmen: 71% (142); all full-time undergraduates: 48% (528). ***Average award:*** Freshmen: $5686; Undergraduates: $5363. ***Scholarships, grants, and awards:*** Federal Pell, FSEOG, state, private, college/university gift aid from institutional funds.

GIFT AID (NON-NEED-BASED) ***Total amount:*** $173,364 (23% institutional, 77% external sources). ***Receiving aid:*** Freshmen: 6% (11). Undergraduates: 2% (25). ***Average award:*** Freshmen: $6164. Undergraduates: $5753. ***Scholarships, grants, and awards by category:*** *Academic interests/achievement:* general academic interests/achievements. *Creative arts/performance:* art/fine arts. *Special achievements/activities:* community service. *Special characteristics:* children of faculty/staff, ethnic background, international students, veterans' children. ***Tuition waivers:*** Full or partial for minority students, employees or children of employees, senior citizens.

LOANS ***Student loans:*** $2,682,364 (60% need-based, 40% non-need-based). 32% of past graduating class borrowed through all loan programs. *Average*

indebtedness per student: $14,102. ***Average need-based loan:*** Freshmen: $3121. Undergraduates: $3812. ***Parent loans:*** $45,557 (100% non-need-based). ***Programs:*** Federal Direct (Subsidized and Unsubsidized Stafford, PLUS), Perkins, state, college/university.

WORK-STUDY ***Federal work-study:*** Total amount: $576,682; 283 jobs averaging $1318.

APPLYING FOR FINANCIAL AID ***Required financial aid form:*** FAFSA. ***Financial aid deadline (priority):*** 4/1. ***Notification date:*** Continuous. Students must reply within 2 weeks of notification.

CONTACT Christopher A. R. Bell, Acting Director of Financial Aid, University of Maine at Presque Isle, 181 Main Street, Presque Isle, ME 04769-2888, 207-768-9511. *Fax:* 207-768-9608. *E-mail:* chris@maine.edu.

UNIVERSITY OF MANAGEMENT AND TECHNOLOGY

Arlington, VA

CONTACT Financial Aid Office, University of Management and Technology, 1901 North Fort Myer Drive, Arlington, VA 22209, 703-516-0035 or toll-free 800-924-4885 (in-state). *E-mail:* info@umtweb.edu.

UNIVERSITY OF MARY

Bismarck, ND

Tuition & fees: $12,584 **Average undergraduate aid package: $10,801**

ABOUT THE INSTITUTION Independent Roman Catholic, coed. ***Awards:*** associate, bachelor's, master's, and doctoral degrees. 45 undergraduate majors. ***Total enrollment:*** 2,863. Undergraduates: 2,092. Freshmen: 374. Federal methodology is used as a basis for awarding need-based institutional aid.

UNDERGRADUATE EXPENSES for 2009–10 ***Application fee:*** $25. ***Comprehensive fee:*** $17,524 includes full-time tuition ($12,360), mandatory fees ($224), and room and board ($4940). ***College room only:*** $2300. ***Part-time tuition:*** $390 per credit. ***Part-time fees:*** $7 per credit.

FRESHMAN FINANCIAL AID (Fall 2008, est.) 308 applied for aid; of those 80% were deemed to have need. 100% of freshmen with need received aid. ***Average financial aid package:*** $11,029 (excluding resources awarded to replace EFC). 16% of all full-time freshmen had no need and received non-need-based gift aid.

UNDERGRADUATE FINANCIAL AID (Fall 2008, est.) 1,227 applied for aid; of those 80% were deemed to have need. 100% of undergraduates with need received aid. ***Average financial aid package:*** $10,801 (excluding resources awarded to replace EFC). 14% of all full-time undergraduates had no need and received non-need-based gift aid.

GIFT AID (NEED-BASED) ***Total amount:*** $8,686,430 (27% federal, 6% state, 58% institutional, 9% external sources). ***Receiving aid:*** Freshmen: 66% (246); all full-time undergraduates: 59% (968). ***Average award:*** Freshmen: $8115; Undergraduates: $7058. ***Scholarships, grants, and awards:*** Federal Pell, FSEOG, state, private, college/university gift aid from institutional funds, Academic Competitiveness Grant, National Smart Grant, TEACH Grant.

GIFT AID (NON-NEED-BASED) ***Average award:*** Freshmen: $4534. Undergraduates: $4176. ***Scholarships, grants, and awards by category:*** *Academic interests/achievement:* 1,231 awards ($4,033,265 total): general academic interests/achievements. *Creative arts/performance:* 36 awards ($132,300 total): debating, music, theater/drama. *Special achievements/activities:* 369 awards ($248,388 total): cheerleading/drum major, general special achievements/activities, leadership, memberships. *Special characteristics:* 204 awards ($488,441 total): children of faculty/staff, international students, local/state students, siblings of current students, veterans.

LOANS ***Student loans:*** $13,558,362 (38% need-based, 62% non-need-based). ***Average need-based loan:*** Freshmen: $3275. Undergraduates: $4119. ***Parent loans:*** $1,010,936 (100% non-need-based). ***Programs:*** FFEL (Subsidized and Unsubsidized Stafford, PLUS), Perkins, Federal Nursing, alternative private loans.

WORK-STUDY ***Federal work-study:*** Total amount: $267,492; 311 jobs averaging $860. ***State or other work-study/employment:*** Total amount: $100,503 (100% non-need-based). 61 part-time jobs averaging $1648.

ATHLETIC AWARDS Total amount: $862,901 (100% need-based).

APPLYING FOR FINANCIAL AID ***Required financial aid form:*** FAFSA. ***Financial aid deadline:*** Continuous. ***Notification date:*** Continuous beginning 2/15. Students must reply within 2 weeks of notification.

CONTACT Brenda Zastoupil, Financial Assistance Director, University of Mary, 7500 University Drive, Bismarck, ND 58504-9652, 701-255-7500 Ext. 8244 or toll-free 800-288-6279. *Fax:* 701-255-7687. *E-mail:* brendaz@umary.edu.

UNIVERSITY OF MARY HARDIN-BAYLOR

Belton, TX

Tuition & fees: $20,650 **Average undergraduate aid package: $11,206**

ABOUT THE INSTITUTION Independent Southern Baptist, coed. ***Awards:*** bachelor's, master's, and doctoral degrees. 54 undergraduate majors. ***Total enrollment:*** 2,696. Undergraduates: 2,497. Freshmen: 479. Federal methodology is used as a basis for awarding need-based institutional aid.

UNDERGRADUATE EXPENSES for 2009–10 ***Application fee:*** $35. ***Comprehensive fee:*** $26,000 includes full-time tuition ($18,300), mandatory fees ($2350), and room and board ($5350). ***Part-time tuition:*** $610 per credit hour.

FRESHMAN FINANCIAL AID (Fall 2007) 425 applied for aid; of those 88% were deemed to have need. ***Average percent of need met:*** 67% (excluding resources awarded to replace EFC). ***Average financial aid package:*** $11,456 (excluding resources awarded to replace EFC). 21% of all full-time freshmen had no need and received non-need-based gift aid.

UNDERGRADUATE FINANCIAL AID (Fall 2007) 2,217 applied for aid; of those 92% were deemed to have need. 100% of undergraduates with need received aid; of those 22% had need fully met. ***Average percent of need met:*** 71% (excluding resources awarded to replace EFC). ***Average financial aid package:*** $11,206 (excluding resources awarded to replace EFC). 16% of all full-time undergraduates had no need and received non-need-based gift aid.

GIFT AID (NEED-BASED) ***Total amount:*** $12,451,503 (24% federal, 39% state, 37% institutional). ***Receiving aid:*** Freshmen: 69% (329); all full-time undergraduates: 68% (1,658). ***Average award:*** Freshmen: $7314; Undergraduates: $5947. ***Scholarships, grants, and awards:*** Federal Pell, FSEOG, state, private, college/university gift aid from institutional funds.

GIFT AID (NON-NEED-BASED) ***Total amount:*** $3,089,912 (1% federal, 61% institutional, 38% external sources). ***Receiving aid:*** Freshmen: 63% (299). Undergraduates: 62% (1,503). ***Average award:*** Freshmen: $3402. Undergraduates: $3402. ***Scholarships, grants, and awards by category:*** *Academic interests/achievement:* 160 awards ($391,856 total): biological sciences, business, communication, computer science, education, English, foreign languages, general academic interests/achievements, health fields, humanities, international studies, mathematics, physical sciences, premedicine, religion/biblical studies, social sciences. *Creative arts/performance:* 156 awards ($215,605 total): art/fine arts, music. *Special achievements/activities:* 98 awards ($382,260 total): cheerleading/drum major, community service, leadership, religious involvement. *Special characteristics:* 234 awards ($1,045,348 total): children and siblings of alumni, children of faculty/staff, ethnic background, handicapped students, international students, local/state students, members of minority groups, out-of-state students, relatives of clergy, religious affiliation. ***ROTC:*** Air Force cooperative.

LOANS ***Student loans:*** $15,013,273 (47% need-based, 53% non-need-based). 80% of past graduating class borrowed through all loan programs. *Average indebtedness per student:* $17,500. ***Average need-based loan:*** Freshmen: $2583. Undergraduates: $3488. ***Parent loans:*** $3,040,485 (100% non-need-based). ***Programs:*** FFEL (Subsidized and Unsubsidized Stafford, PLUS), Perkins, state.

WORK-STUDY ***Federal work-study:*** Total amount: $385,656; 263 jobs averaging $1486. ***State or other work-study/employment:*** Total amount: $350,759 (34% need-based, 66% non-need-based). 259 part-time jobs averaging $1379.

APPLYING FOR FINANCIAL AID ***Required financial aid form:*** FAFSA. ***Financial aid deadline (priority):*** 3/1. ***Notification date:*** Continuous. Students must reply within 2 weeks of notification.

CONTACT Mr. David Orsag, Associate Director of Financial Aid, University of Mary Hardin-Baylor, Box 8080, Belton, TX 76513, 254-295-4517 or toll-free 800-727-8642. *Fax:* 254-295-5049. *E-mail:* dorsag@umhb.edu.

UNIVERSITY OF MARYLAND, BALTIMORE COUNTY

Baltimore, MD

Tuition & fees (MD res): $8780 **Average undergraduate aid package: $11,479**

ABOUT THE INSTITUTION State-supported, coed. ***Awards:*** bachelor's, master's, and doctoral degrees and post-bachelor's certificates. 43 undergraduate majors. ***Total enrollment:*** 12,268. Undergraduates: 9,612. Freshmen: 1,569. Federal methodology is used as a basis for awarding need-based institutional aid.

UNDERGRADUATE EXPENSES for 2008–09 ***Application fee:*** $50. ***One-time required fee:*** $100. ***Tuition, state resident:*** full-time $6484; part-time $270 per credit hour. ***Tuition, nonresident:*** full-time $15,216; part-time $633 per credit hour. ***Required fees:*** full-time $2296; $102 per credit hour. Full-time tuition and fees vary according to location and program. Part-time tuition and fees vary according to location and program. ***College room and board:*** $8960; ***Room only:*** $5500. Room and board charges vary according to board plan and housing facility. ***Payment plan:*** Installment.

FRESHMAN FINANCIAL AID (Fall 2007) 981 applied for aid; of those 67% were deemed to have need. 100% of freshmen with need received aid; of those 40% had need fully met. ***Average percent of need met:*** 99% (excluding resources awarded to replace EFC). ***Average financial aid package:*** $12,980 (excluding resources awarded to replace EFC). 28% of all full-time freshmen had no need and received non-need-based gift aid.

UNDERGRADUATE FINANCIAL AID (Fall 2007) 4,752 applied for aid; of those 77% were deemed to have need. 100% of undergraduates with need received aid; of those 4% had need fully met. ***Average percent of need met:*** 77% (excluding resources awarded to replace EFC). ***Average financial aid package:*** $11,479 (excluding resources awarded to replace EFC). 11% of all full-time undergraduates had no need and received non-need-based gift aid.

GIFT AID (NEED-BASED) ***Total amount:*** $20,384,295 (31% federal, 36% state, 29% institutional, 4% external sources). ***Receiving aid:*** Freshmen: 40% (571); all full-time undergraduates: 39% (3,135). ***Average award:*** Freshmen: $10,287; Undergraduates: $7604. ***Scholarships, grants, and awards:*** Federal Pell, FSEOG, state, private, college/university gift aid from institutional funds.

GIFT AID (NON-NEED-BASED) ***Total amount:*** $11,100,205 (6% state, 90% institutional, 4% external sources). ***Receiving aid:*** Freshmen: 10% (143). Undergraduates: 5% (372). ***Average award:*** Freshmen: $3619. Undergraduates: $3601. ***Scholarships, grants, and awards by category:*** *Academic interests/achievement:* 1,464 awards ($10,572,956 total): biological sciences, computer science, education, engineering/technologies, English, foreign languages, general academic interests/achievements, humanities, mathematics, physical sciences, social sciences. *Creative arts/performance:* 32 awards ($47,800 total): art/fine arts, cinema/film/broadcasting, creative writing, dance, music, performing arts, theater/drama. ***Tuition waivers:*** Full or partial for employees or children of employees, senior citizens. ***ROTC:*** Army cooperative.

LOANS ***Student loans:*** $24,342,118 (45% need-based, 55% non-need-based). 49% of past graduating class borrowed through all loan programs. *Average indebtedness per student:* $20,002. ***Average need-based loan:*** Freshmen: $3622. Undergraduates: $4621. ***Parent loans:*** $7,097,995 (100% non-need-based). ***Programs:*** FFEL (Subsidized and Unsubsidized Stafford, PLUS), Perkins.

WORK-STUDY ***Federal work-study:*** Total amount: $270,175; 106 jobs averaging $2456. ***State or other work-study/employment:*** Total amount: $557,221 (76% need-based, 24% non-need-based). Part-time jobs available.

ATHLETIC AWARDS Total amount: $1,981,009 (26% need-based, 74% non-need-based).

APPLYING FOR FINANCIAL AID ***Required financial aid form:*** FAFSA. ***Financial aid deadline (priority):*** 2/14. ***Notification date:*** Continuous beginning 3/15.

CONTACT Stephanie Johnson, Director, University of Maryland, Baltimore County, 1000 Hilltop Circle, Baltimore, MD 21250, 410-455-2387 or toll-free 800-UMBC-4U2 (in-state), 800-862-2402 (out-of-state). *Fax:* 410-455-1288. *E-mail:* finaid@umbc.edu.

UNIVERSITY OF MARYLAND, COLLEGE PARK

College Park, MD

Tuition & fees (MD res): $8005 **Average undergraduate aid package: $9219**

ABOUT THE INSTITUTION State-supported, coed. ***Awards:*** bachelor's, master's, doctoral, and first professional degrees and post-bachelor's and post-master's certificates. 94 undergraduate majors. ***Total enrollment:*** 36,956. Undergraduates: 26,431. Freshmen: 3,912. Federal methodology is used as a basis for awarding need-based institutional aid.

UNDERGRADUATE EXPENSES for 2008–09 ***Application fee:*** $55. ***Tuition, state resident:*** full-time $6566; part-time $273 per credit hour. ***Tuition, nonresident:*** full-time $21,637; part-time $902 per credit hour. ***Required fees:*** full-time $1439; $328.15 per term. Part-time tuition and fees vary according to course load. ***College room and board:*** $9109; ***Room only:*** $5402. Room and board charges vary according to board plan. ***Payment plans:*** Installment, deferred payment.

FRESHMAN FINANCIAL AID (Fall 2007) 3,036 applied for aid; of those 55% were deemed to have need. 92% of freshmen with need received aid; of those 12% had need fully met. ***Average percent of need met:*** 65% (excluding resources awarded to replace EFC). ***Average financial aid package:*** $10,252 (excluding resources awarded to replace EFC). 18% of all full-time freshmen had no need and received non-need-based gift aid.

UNDERGRADUATE FINANCIAL AID (Fall 2007) 12,917 applied for aid; of those 72% were deemed to have need. 93% of undergraduates with need received aid; of those 12% had need fully met. ***Average percent of need met:*** 61% (excluding resources awarded to replace EFC). ***Average financial aid package:*** $9219 (excluding resources awarded to replace EFC). 11% of all full-time undergraduates had no need and received non-need-based gift aid.

GIFT AID (NEED-BASED) ***Total amount:*** $35,541,508 (36% federal, 35% state, 29% institutional). ***Receiving aid:*** Freshmen: 25% (1,068); all full-time undergraduates: 26% (6,195). ***Average award:*** Freshmen: $6233; Undergraduates: $5623. ***Scholarships, grants, and awards:*** Federal Pell, FSEOG, state, private, college/university gift aid from institutional funds.

GIFT AID (NON-NEED-BASED) ***Total amount:*** $37,266,911 (11% state, 63% institutional, 26% external sources). ***Receiving aid:*** Freshmen: 21% (891). Undergraduates: 14% (3,390). ***Average award:*** Freshmen: $5842. Undergraduates: $6179. ***Scholarships, grants, and awards by category:*** *Academic interests/achievement:* 4,912 awards ($18,789,040 total): agriculture, architecture, biological sciences, business, communication, computer science, education, engineering/technologies, English, foreign languages, general academic interests/achievements, health fields, humanities, international studies, library science, mathematics, military science, physical sciences, premedicine, social sciences. *Creative arts/performance:* 59 awards ($493,630 total): applied art and design, art/fine arts, dance, music, performing arts, theater/drama. *Special achievements/activities:* 71 awards ($347,974 total): cheerleading/drum major. *Special characteristics:* 1,708 awards ($7,189,330 total): adult students, out-of-state students. ***Tuition waivers:*** Full or partial for employees or children of employees. ***ROTC:*** Army, Naval cooperative, Air Force.

LOANS ***Student loans:*** $65,874,302 (42% need-based, 58% non-need-based). 44% of past graduating class borrowed through all loan programs. *Average indebtedness per student:* $20,091. ***Average need-based loan:*** Freshmen: $3778. Undergraduates: $4444. ***Parent loans:*** $21,484,030 (38% need-based, 62% non-need-based). ***Programs:*** FFEL (Subsidized and Unsubsidized Stafford, PLUS), Perkins.

WORK-STUDY ***Federal work-study:*** Total amount: $1,110,932; 720 jobs averaging $1526.

ATHLETIC AWARDS Total amount: $11,115,537 (100% non-need-based).

APPLYING FOR FINANCIAL AID ***Required financial aid form:*** FAFSA. ***Financial aid deadline (priority):*** 2/15. ***Notification date:*** Continuous beginning 4/1.

CONTACT Sarah Bauder, Director of Financial Aid, University of Maryland, College Park, 0102 Lee Building, College Park, MD 20742, 301-314-8279 or toll-free 800-422-5867. *Fax:* 301-314-9587. *E-mail:* sbauder@umd.edu.

UNIVERSITY OF MARYLAND EASTERN SHORE

Princess Anne, MD

Tuition & fees (MD res): $6042 **Average undergraduate aid package: $13,352**

ABOUT THE INSTITUTION State-supported, coed. ***Awards:*** bachelor's, master's, and doctoral degrees. 53 undergraduate majors. ***Total enrollment:*** 3,762. Undergraduates: 3,326. Freshmen: 846. Federal methodology is used as a basis for awarding need-based institutional aid.

UNDERGRADUATE EXPENSES for 2008–09 ***Application fee:*** $25. ***Tuition, state resident:*** full-time $4112; part-time $171 per credit hour. ***Tuition, nonresident:*** full-time $10,900; part-time $401 per credit hour. ***Required fees:*** full-time $1930; $41 per term. Full-time tuition and fees vary according to course load. Part-time tuition and fees vary according to course load. ***College room and board:*** $6880; ***Room only:*** $3780. Room and board charges vary according to board plan and housing facility. ***Payment plans:*** Installment, deferred payment.

FRESHMAN FINANCIAL AID (Fall 2008, est.) 935 applied for aid; of those 90% were deemed to have need. 100% of freshmen with need received aid; of those 54% had need fully met. ***Average percent of need met:*** 84% (excluding resources awarded to replace EFC). ***Average financial aid package:*** $14,879 (excluding resources awarded to replace EFC). 8% of all full-time freshmen had no need and received non-need-based gift aid.

UNDERGRADUATE FINANCIAL AID (Fall 2008, est.) 3,162 applied for aid; of those 90% were deemed to have need. 100% of undergraduates with need received aid; of those 55% had need fully met. ***Average percent of need met:*** 84% (excluding resources awarded to replace EFC). ***Average financial aid package:*** $13,352 (excluding resources awarded to replace EFC). 10% of all full-time undergraduates had no need and received non-need-based gift aid.

GIFT AID (NEED-BASED) ***Total amount:*** $14,393,916 (50% federal, 37% state, 13% institutional). ***Receiving aid:*** Freshmen: 77% (798); all full-time undergraduates: 77% (2,703). ***Average award:*** Freshmen: $7250; Undergraduates: $7125. ***Scholarships, grants, and awards:*** Federal Pell, FSEOG, state, college/university gift aid from institutional funds.

GIFT AID (NON-NEED-BASED) ***Total amount:*** $4,164,856 (81% institutional, 19% external sources). ***Receiving aid:*** Freshmen: 5% (53). Undergraduates: 12% (420). ***Average award:*** Freshmen: $2579. Undergraduates: $2839. ***Scholarships, grants, and awards by category:*** *Academic interests/achievement:* 75 awards ($68,000 total): agriculture, business, computer science, education, engineering/technologies, English, general academic interests/achievements, health fields, home economics, mathematics, physical sciences, social sciences. *Creative arts/performance:* 25 awards ($25,000 total): art/fine arts, music, performing arts, theater/drama. *Special characteristics:* 175 awards ($225,000 total): adult students, children of faculty/staff, first-generation college students, veterans. ***Tuition waivers:*** Full or partial for employees or children of employees, senior citizens.

LOANS ***Student loans:*** $20,733,695 (46% need-based, 54% non-need-based). 89% of past graduating class borrowed through all loan programs. *Average indebtedness per student:* $8500. ***Average need-based loan:*** Freshmen: $2779. Undergraduates: $4875. ***Parent loans:*** $8,832,463 (100% non-need-based). ***Programs:*** Federal Direct (Subsidized and Unsubsidized Stafford, PLUS), Perkins.

WORK-STUDY ***Federal work-study:*** Total amount: $274,138; 156 jobs averaging $1757. ***State or other work-study/employment:*** Total amount: $1,500,000 (100% non-need-based). Part-time jobs available.

ATHLETIC AWARDS Total amount: $1,435,356 (100% non-need-based).

APPLYING FOR FINANCIAL AID ***Required financial aid form:*** FAFSA. ***Financial aid deadline (priority):*** 3/1. ***Notification date:*** Continuous beginning 4/15.

CONTACT Mr. James W. Kellam, Director of Financial Aid, University of Maryland Eastern Shore, Backbone Road, Princess Anne, MD 21853-1299, 410-651-6172. *Fax:* 410-651-7670. *E-mail:* jwkellam@umes.edu.

UNIVERSITY OF MARYLAND UNIVERSITY COLLEGE

Adelphi, MD

Tuition & fees (MD res): $5760 **Average undergraduate aid package: $6520**

ABOUT THE INSTITUTION State-supported, coed. ***Awards:*** associate, bachelor's, master's, and doctoral degrees and post-bachelor's certificates (offers primarily part-time evening and weekend degree programs at more than 30 off-campus locations in Maryland and the Washington, DC area, and more than 180 military communities in Europe and Asia with military enrollment not reflected in this profile; associate of arts program available to military students only). 19 undergraduate majors. ***Total enrollment:*** 34,172. Undergraduates: 22,308. Freshmen: 862. Federal methodology is used as a basis for awarding need-based institutional aid.

UNDERGRADUATE EXPENSES for 2009–10 ***Application fee:*** $50. ***Tuition, state resident:*** full-time $5520; part-time $230 per credit hour. ***Tuition, nonresident:*** full-time $11,976; part-time $499 per credit hour. ***Required fees:*** full-time $240; $10 per credit hour.

FRESHMAN FINANCIAL AID (Fall 2008, est.) 72 applied for aid; of those 97% were deemed to have need. 77% of freshmen with need received aid. ***Average percent of need met:*** 18% (excluding resources awarded to replace EFC). ***Average financial aid package:*** $5093 (excluding resources awarded to replace EFC).

UNDERGRADUATE FINANCIAL AID (Fall 2008, est.) 1,810 applied for aid; of those 96% were deemed to have need. 89% of undergraduates with need received aid; of those 1% had need fully met. ***Average percent of need met:*** 24% (excluding resources awarded to replace EFC). ***Average financial aid package:*** $6520 (excluding resources awarded to replace EFC).

GIFT AID (NEED-BASED) ***Total amount:*** $9,763,310 (67% federal, 11% state, 21% institutional, 1% external sources). ***Receiving aid:*** Freshmen: 38% (41); all full-time undergraduates: 29% (847). ***Average award:*** Freshmen: $3624; Undergraduates: $3654. ***Scholarships, grants, and awards:*** Federal Pell, FSEOG, state, private, college/university gift aid from institutional funds.

GIFT AID (NON-NEED-BASED) ***Total amount:*** $1,658,238 (7% state, 82% institutional, 11% external sources). ***Receiving aid:*** Freshmen: 1% (1). Undergraduates: 10% (280). ***Scholarships, grants, and awards by category:*** *Academic interests/achievement:* general academic interests/achievements. *Special achievements/activities:* general special achievements/activities.

LOANS ***Student loans:*** $52,990,510 (47% need-based, 53% non-need-based). ***Average need-based loan:*** Freshmen: $2799. Undergraduates: $4128. ***Parent loans:*** $136,125 (100% non-need-based). ***Programs:*** Federal Direct (Subsidized and Unsubsidized Stafford, PLUS), FFEL (Subsidized and Unsubsidized Stafford, PLUS), Perkins.

WORK-STUDY ***Federal work-study:*** Total amount: $594,701; jobs available. ***State or other work-study/employment:*** Total amount: $273,299 (100% non-need-based). Part-time jobs available.

APPLYING FOR FINANCIAL AID ***Required financial aid form:*** FAFSA. ***Financial aid deadline (priority):*** 6/1. ***Notification date:*** Continuous. Students must reply within 2 weeks of notification.

CONTACT Cheryl Storie, Associate Vice President of Financial Aid, University of Maryland University College, 3501 University Boulevard East, Adelphi, MD 20783, 301-985-7847 or toll-free 800-888-8682 (in-state). *Fax:* 301-985-7462. *E-mail:* finaid@umuc.edu.

UNIVERSITY OF MARY WASHINGTON

Fredericksburg, VA

Tuition & fees (VA res): $6834 **Average undergraduate aid package: $11,500**

ABOUT THE INSTITUTION State-supported, coed. ***Awards:*** bachelor's and master's degrees and post-bachelor's certificates. 32 undergraduate majors. ***Total enrollment:*** 5,084. Undergraduates: 4,231. Freshmen: 877. Federal methodology is used as a basis for awarding need-based institutional aid.

UNDERGRADUATE EXPENSES for 2008–09 ***Application fee:*** $50. ***Tuition, state resident:*** full-time $3386; part-time $141 per credit hour. ***Tuition, nonresident:*** full-time $14,554; part-time $606 per credit hour. ***Required fees:*** full-time $3448; $96 per credit hour. Part-time tuition and fees vary according to location. ***College room and board:*** $7700; ***Room only:*** $4580. Room and board charges vary according to board plan and housing facility. ***Payment plan:*** Installment.

FRESHMAN FINANCIAL AID (Fall 2008, est.) 259 applied for aid; of those 97% were deemed to have need. 88% of freshmen with need received aid; of those 14% had need fully met. ***Average percent of need met:*** 50% (excluding resources awarded to replace EFC). ***Average financial aid package:*** $11,300 (excluding resources awarded to replace EFC). 9% of all full-time freshmen had no need and received non-need-based gift aid.

UNDERGRADUATE FINANCIAL AID (Fall 2008, est.) 1,760 applied for aid; of those 55% were deemed to have need. 93% of undergraduates with need received aid; of those 18% had need fully met. ***Average percent of need met:*** 56% (excluding resources awarded to replace EFC). ***Average financial aid package:*** $11,500 (excluding resources awarded to replace EFC). 6% of all full-time undergraduates had no need and received non-need-based gift aid.

GIFT AID (NEED-BASED) ***Total amount:*** $3,550,000 (40% federal, 39% state, 12% institutional, 9% external sources). ***Receiving aid:*** Freshmen: 14% (115); all full-time undergraduates: 12% (430). ***Average award:*** Freshmen: $5600; Undergraduates: $5000. ***Scholarships, grants, and awards:*** Federal Pell, FSEOG, state, private, college/university gift aid from institutional funds.

GIFT AID (NON-NEED-BASED) ***Total amount:*** $1,190,000 (1% federal, 2% state, 63% institutional, 34% external sources). ***Receiving aid:*** Freshmen: 12%

(100). Undergraduates: 6% (210). ***Average award:*** Freshmen: $1450. Undergraduates: $1370. ***Scholarships, grants, and awards by category:*** *Academic interests/achievement:* 750 awards ($905,000 total): business, computer science, education, English, foreign languages, general academic interests/achievements, humanities, mathematics, physical sciences, religion/biblical studies, social sciences. *Creative arts/performance:* 65 awards ($120,000 total): art/fine arts, dance, journalism/publications, music, theater/drama. *Special achievements/activities:* 2 awards ($13,500 total): leadership. *Special characteristics:* 15 awards ($36,000 total): adult students, children and siblings of alumni, children of faculty/staff, local/state students. ***Tuition waivers:*** Full or partial for senior citizens.

LOANS ***Student loans:*** $13,800,000 (34% need-based, 66% non-need-based). 57% of past graduating class borrowed through all loan programs. *Average indebtedness per student:* $16,000. ***Average need-based loan:*** Freshmen: $2600. Undergraduates: $3900. ***Parent loans:*** $3,600,000 (100% non-need-based). ***Programs:*** FFEL (Subsidized and Unsubsidized Stafford, PLUS), Perkins.

WORK-STUDY ***Federal work-study:*** Total amount: $46,000; 32 jobs averaging $1400. ***State or other work-study/employment:*** Total amount: $1,200,000 (100% non-need-based). 733 part-time jobs averaging $1610.

APPLYING FOR FINANCIAL AID ***Required financial aid forms:*** FAFSA, UMW Scholarship Information Form. ***Financial aid deadline:*** 5/15 (priority: 3/1). ***Notification date:*** 4/15. Students must reply by 5/1 or within 2 weeks of notification.

CONTACT Ms. Debra J. Harber, Associate Dean for Financial Aid, University of Mary Washington, 1301 College Avenue, Fredericksburg, VA 22401-5358, 540-654-2468 or toll-free 800-468-5614. *Fax:* 540-654-1858. *E-mail:* dharber@umw.edu.

UNIVERSITY OF MASSACHUSETTS AMHERST

Amherst, MA

Tuition & fees (MA res): $10,232 Average undergraduate aid package: $12,593

ABOUT THE INSTITUTION State-supported, coed. ***Awards:*** associate, bachelor's, master's, and doctoral degrees and post-bachelor's and post-master's certificates. 84 undergraduate majors. ***Total enrollment:*** 26,359. Undergraduates: 20,539. Freshmen: 4,270. Federal methodology is used as a basis for awarding need-based institutional aid.

UNDERGRADUATE EXPENSES for 2008–09 ***Application fee:*** $70. ***One-time required fee:*** $185. ***Tuition, state resident:*** full-time $1714; part-time $71.50 per credit. ***Tuition, nonresident:*** full-time $9937; part-time $414.50 per credit. ***Required fees:*** full-time $8518. Full-time tuition and fees vary according to course load, degree level, reciprocity agreements, and student level. Part-time tuition and fees vary according to course load, degree level, reciprocity agreements, and student level. ***College room and board:*** $8114; ***Room only:*** $4524. Room and board charges vary according to board plan and housing facility. ***Payment plan:*** Installment.

FRESHMAN FINANCIAL AID (Fall 2007) 3,701 applied for aid; of those 61% were deemed to have need. 97% of freshmen with need received aid; of those 21% had need fully met. ***Average percent of need met:*** 83% (excluding resources awarded to replace EFC). ***Average financial aid package:*** $12,021 (excluding resources awarded to replace EFC). 10% of all full-time freshmen had no need and received non-need-based gift aid.

UNDERGRADUATE FINANCIAL AID (Fall 2007) 13,605 applied for aid; of those 71% were deemed to have need. 98% of undergraduates with need received aid; of those 24% had need fully met. ***Average percent of need met:*** 86% (excluding resources awarded to replace EFC). ***Average financial aid package:*** $12,593 (excluding resources awarded to replace EFC). 5% of all full-time undergraduates had no need and received non-need-based gift aid.

GIFT AID (NEED-BASED) ***Total amount:*** $54,747,889 (29% federal, 13% state, 51% institutional, 7% external sources). ***Receiving aid:*** Freshmen: 44% (1,885); all full-time undergraduates: 38% (7,437). ***Average award:*** Freshmen: $7865; Undergraduates: $8182. ***Scholarships, grants, and awards:*** Federal Pell, FSEOG, state, private, college/university gift aid from institutional funds.

GIFT AID (NON-NEED-BASED) ***Total amount:*** $7,378,959 (4% state, 52% institutional, 44% external sources). ***Receiving aid:*** Freshmen: 4% (161). Undergraduates: 2% (467). ***Average award:*** Freshmen: $2265. Undergraduates: $3079. ***Scholarships, grants, and awards by category:*** *Academic interests/achievement:* agriculture, architecture, biological sciences, business, communication, computer science, education, engineering/technologies, English, health fields, humanities, mathematics, military science, physical sciences, premedicine, social sciences. *Creative arts/performance:* art/fine arts, dance, journalism/publications, music, theater/drama. *Special achievements/activities:* cheerleading/drum major, general special achievements/activities, leadership. *Special characteristics:* children and siblings of alumni, children of faculty/staff, handicapped students, veterans. ***Tuition waivers:*** Full or partial for employees or children of employees, senior citizens. ***ROTC:*** Army, Air Force.

LOANS ***Student loans:*** $81,448,673 (57% need-based, 43% non-need-based). 66% of past graduating class borrowed through all loan programs. *Average indebtedness per student:* $21,614. ***Average need-based loan:*** Freshmen: $3577. Undergraduates: $4327. ***Parent loans:*** $26,868,168 (20% need-based, 80% non-need-based). ***Programs:*** Federal Direct (Subsidized and Unsubsidized Stafford, PLUS), Perkins, state.

WORK-STUDY ***Federal work-study:*** Total amount: $8,637,086; 5,131 jobs averaging $1710.

ATHLETIC AWARDS Total amount: $6,840,571 (25% need-based, 75% non-need-based).

APPLYING FOR FINANCIAL AID ***Required financial aid form:*** FAFSA. ***Financial aid deadline (priority):*** 2/14. ***Notification date:*** Continuous beginning 3/1.

CONTACT Office of Financial Aid Services, University of Massachusetts Amherst, 255 Whitmore Administration Building, Amherst, MA 01003, 413-545-0801. *Fax:* 413-545-1700.

UNIVERSITY OF MASSACHUSETTS BOSTON

Boston, MA

Tuition & fees (MA res): $9111 Average undergraduate aid package: $11,852

ABOUT THE INSTITUTION State-supported, coed. ***Awards:*** bachelor's, master's, and doctoral degrees and post-bachelor's and post-master's certificates. 45 undergraduate majors. ***Total enrollment:*** 14,117. Undergraduates: 10,478. Freshmen: 1,020. Federal methodology is used as a basis for awarding need-based institutional aid.

UNDERGRADUATE EXPENSES for 2008–09 ***Application fee:*** $40. ***Tuition, state resident:*** full-time $1714; part-time $71.50 per credit hour. ***Tuition, nonresident:*** full-time $9758; part-time $406.50 per credit hour. ***Required fees:*** full-time $7397; $308 per credit hour. Full-time tuition and fees vary according to class time, course load, program, reciprocity agreements, and student level. Part-time tuition and fees vary according to class time, course load, program, reciprocity agreements, and student level. ***Payment plan:*** Installment.

FRESHMAN FINANCIAL AID (Fall 2007) 737 applied for aid; of those 84% were deemed to have need. 100% of freshmen with need received aid; of those 47% had need fully met. ***Average percent of need met:*** 90% (excluding resources awarded to replace EFC). ***Average financial aid package:*** $10,774 (excluding resources awarded to replace EFC). 8% of all full-time freshmen had no need and received non-need-based gift aid.

UNDERGRADUATE FINANCIAL AID (Fall 2007) 4,546 applied for aid; of those 88% were deemed to have need. 100% of undergraduates with need received aid; of those 67% had need fully met. ***Average percent of need met:*** 94% (excluding resources awarded to replace EFC). ***Average financial aid package:*** $11,852 (excluding resources awarded to replace EFC). 3% of all full-time undergraduates had no need and received non-need-based gift aid.

GIFT AID (NEED-BASED) ***Total amount:*** $22,109,318 (46% federal, 19% state, 31% institutional, 4% external sources). ***Receiving aid:*** Freshmen: 60% (570); all full-time undergraduates: 54% (3,442). ***Average award:*** Freshmen: $6757; Undergraduates: $6323. ***Scholarships, grants, and awards:*** Federal Pell, FSEOG, state, private, college/university gift aid from institutional funds, Academic Competitiveness Grant, Smart Grant, TEACH Grant, Scholarship-Disadvantaged Nursing Students.

GIFT AID (NON-NEED-BASED) ***Total amount:*** $2,446,249 (3% federal, 3% state, 79% institutional, 15% external sources). ***Receiving aid:*** Freshmen: 4% (37). Undergraduates: 1% (88). ***Average award:*** Freshmen: $3618. Undergraduates: $3493. ***Scholarships, grants, and awards by category:*** *Academic interests/achievement:* general academic interests/achievements, health fields. *Special achievements/activities:* 870 awards ($1,210,050 total): general special achievements/activities, leadership. *Special characteristics:* 913 awards ($780,842 total): adult students, children of faculty/staff, children of union members/company employees, first-generation college students, veterans. ***Tuition waivers:*** Full or partial for employees or children of employees, senior citizens.

LOANS *Student loans:* $35,044,825 (65% need-based, 35% non-need-based). 60% of past graduating class borrowed through all loan programs. *Average indebtedness per student:* $18,902. ***Average need-based loan:*** Freshmen: $3730. Undergraduates: $5620. ***Parent loans:*** $3,156,846 (22% need-based, 78% non-need-based). ***Programs:*** Federal Direct (Subsidized and Unsubsidized Stafford, PLUS), Perkins.

WORK-STUDY *Federal work-study:* Total amount: $1,988,292; jobs available. ***State or other work-study/employment:*** 591 part-time jobs averaging $3500.

APPLYING FOR FINANCIAL AID *Required financial aid form:* FAFSA. ***Financial aid deadline (priority):*** 3/1. ***Notification date:*** Continuous beginning 3/26.

CONTACT Judy L. Keyes, Director of Financial Aid Services, University of Massachusetts Boston, 100 Morrissey Boulevard, Boston, MA 02125-3393, 617-287-6300. *Fax:* 617-287-6323. *E-mail:* judy.keyes@umb.edu.

UNIVERSITY OF MASSACHUSETTS DARTMOUTH

North Dartmouth, MA

Tuition & fees (MA res): $8858 Average undergraduate aid package: $11,562

ABOUT THE INSTITUTION State-supported, coed. ***Awards:*** bachelor's, master's, and doctoral degrees and post-bachelor's and post-master's certificates. 50 undergraduate majors. ***Total enrollment:*** 9,155. Undergraduates: 7,982. Freshmen: 1,786. Federal methodology is used as a basis for awarding need-based institutional aid.

UNDERGRADUATE EXPENSES for 2008–09 *Application fee:* $40. ***Tuition, state resident:*** full-time $1417; part-time $59.04 per credit. ***Tuition, nonresident:*** full-time $8099; part-time $337.46 per credit. ***Required fees:*** full-time $7441; $310.04 per credit. Full-time tuition and fees vary according to program and reciprocity agreements. Part-time tuition and fees vary according to course load, program, and reciprocity agreements. ***College room and board:*** $8716; ***Room only:*** $5954. Room and board charges vary according to board plan and housing facility. ***Payment plan:*** Installment.

FRESHMAN FINANCIAL AID (Fall 2007) 1,560 applied for aid; of those 74% were deemed to have need. 100% of freshmen with need received aid; of those 61% had need fully met. ***Average percent of need met:*** 91% (excluding resources awarded to replace EFC). ***Average financial aid package:*** $11,080 (excluding resources awarded to replace EFC). 10% of all full-time freshmen had no need and received non-need-based gift aid.

UNDERGRADUATE FINANCIAL AID (Fall 2007) 4,758 applied for aid; of those 77% were deemed to have need. 100% of undergraduates with need received aid; of those 56% had need fully met. ***Average percent of need met:*** 91% (excluding resources awarded to replace EFC). ***Average financial aid package:*** $11,562 (excluding resources awarded to replace EFC). 6% of all full-time undergraduates had no need and received non-need-based gift aid.

GIFT AID (NEED-BASED) *Total amount:* $16,744,453 (34% federal, 15% state, 47% institutional, 4% external sources). ***Receiving aid:*** Freshmen: 60% (1,155); all full-time undergraduates: 53% (3,642). ***Average award:*** Freshmen: $6433; Undergraduates: $6473. ***Scholarships, grants, and awards:*** Federal Pell, FSEOG, state, private, college/university gift aid from institutional funds.

GIFT AID (NON-NEED-BASED) *Total amount:* $2,304,692 (1% federal, 2% state, 88% institutional, 9% external sources). ***Receiving aid:*** Freshmen: 2% (31). Undergraduates: 1% (88). ***Average award:*** Freshmen: $2310. Undergraduates: $2641. ***Scholarships, grants, and awards by category:*** *Academic interests/achievement:* 625 awards ($1,443,389 total): general academic interests/achievements. *Special achievements/activities:* 132 awards ($61,003 total): community service. *Special characteristics:* 261 awards ($150,874 total): adult students, children of faculty/staff, children with a deceased or disabled parent, first-generation college students, members of minority groups, veterans. ***Tuition waivers:*** Full or partial for employees or children of employees, senior citizens. ***ROTC:*** Army cooperative.

LOANS *Student loans:* $41,434,738 (50% need-based, 50% non-need-based). 68% of past graduating class borrowed through all loan programs. *Average indebtedness per student:* $21,714. ***Average need-based loan:*** Freshmen: $4841. Undergraduates: $5825. ***Parent loans:*** $2,416,357 (26% need-based, 74% non-need-based). ***Programs:*** Federal Direct (Subsidized and Unsubsidized Stafford, PLUS), Perkins, Federal Nursing, state.

WORK-STUDY *Federal work-study:* Total amount: $1,395,807; 943 jobs averaging $1504. ***State or other work-study/employment:*** Total amount: $4,300,000 (74% need-based, 26% non-need-based). 1,807 part-time jobs averaging $2511.

APPLYING FOR FINANCIAL AID *Required financial aid form:* FAFSA. ***Financial aid deadline (priority):*** 3/1. ***Notification date:*** Continuous beginning 3/25.

CONTACT Bruce Palmer, Director of Financial Aid, University of Massachusetts Dartmouth, 285 Old Westport Road, North Dartmouth, MA 02747-2300, 508-999-8643. *Fax:* 508-999-8935. *E-mail:* financialaid@umassd.edu.

UNIVERSITY OF MASSACHUSETTS LOWELL

Lowell, MA

Tuition & fees (MA res): $9181 Average undergraduate aid package: $9609

ABOUT THE INSTITUTION State-supported, coed. ***Awards:*** associate, bachelor's, master's, and doctoral degrees and post-master's certificates. 39 undergraduate majors. ***Total enrollment:*** 10,075. Undergraduates: 7,316. Freshmen: 1,528. Federal methodology is used as a basis for awarding need-based institutional aid.

UNDERGRADUATE EXPENSES for 2008–09 *Application fee:* $40. ***Tuition, state resident:*** full-time $1454; part-time $60.58 per credit. ***Tuition, nonresident:*** full-time $8567; part-time $356.96 per credit. ***Required fees:*** full-time $7727; $328.17 per credit. Part-time tuition and fees vary according to course load. ***College room and board:*** $7519; ***Room only:*** $4902. Room and board charges vary according to board plan and housing facility. ***Payment plan:*** Installment.

FRESHMAN FINANCIAL AID (Fall 2007) 977 applied for aid; of those 66% were deemed to have need. 100% of freshmen with need received aid; of those 77% had need fully met. ***Average percent of need met:*** 94% (excluding resources awarded to replace EFC). ***Average financial aid package:*** $9615 (excluding resources awarded to replace EFC). 17% of all full-time freshmen had no need and received non-need-based gift aid.

UNDERGRADUATE FINANCIAL AID (Fall 2007) 4,151 applied for aid; of those 71% were deemed to have need. 100% of undergraduates with need received aid; of those 75% had need fully met. ***Average percent of need met:*** 94% (excluding resources awarded to replace EFC). ***Average financial aid package:*** $9609 (excluding resources awarded to replace EFC). 8% of all full-time undergraduates had no need and received non-need-based gift aid.

GIFT AID (NEED-BASED) *Total amount:* $11,061,414 (46% federal, 21% state, 29% institutional, 4% external sources). ***Receiving aid:*** Freshmen: 48% (591); all full-time undergraduates: 41% (2,465). ***Average award:*** Freshmen: $5843; Undergraduates: $5221. ***Scholarships, grants, and awards:*** Federal Pell, FSEOG, state, private, college/university gift aid from institutional funds.

GIFT AID (NON-NEED-BASED) *Total amount:* $2,658,427 (2% federal, 1% state, 87% institutional, 10% external sources). ***Receiving aid:*** Freshmen: 3% (38). Undergraduates: 2% (116). ***Average award:*** Freshmen: $2791. Undergraduates: $2926. ***Scholarships, grants, and awards by category:*** *Academic interests/achievement:* computer science, engineering/technologies, general academic interests/achievements, health fields, humanities. *Creative arts/performance:* music. *Special achievements/activities:* community service, general special achievements/activities. *Special characteristics:* general special characteristics. ***Tuition waivers:*** Full or partial for employees or children of employees, senior citizens. ***ROTC:*** Air Force.

LOANS *Student loans:* $27,866,796 (48% need-based, 52% non-need-based). 65% of past graduating class borrowed through all loan programs. *Average indebtedness per student:* $20,267. ***Average need-based loan:*** Freshmen: $3766. Undergraduates: $4988. ***Parent loans:*** $4,309,346 (10% need-based, 90% non-need-based). ***Programs:*** Federal Direct (Subsidized and Unsubsidized Stafford, PLUS), Perkins.

WORK-STUDY *Federal work-study:* Total amount: $313,906; 108 jobs averaging $2500. ***State or other work-study/employment:*** Total amount: $1,920,236 (100% need-based). 630 part-time jobs averaging $2900.

ATHLETIC AWARDS Total amount: $1,084,877 (25% need-based, 75% non-need-based).

APPLYING FOR FINANCIAL AID *Required financial aid form:* FAFSA. ***Financial aid deadline (priority):*** 3/1. ***Notification date:*** Continuous beginning 3/20.

CONTACT Joyce McLaughlin, Director of Financial Aid, University of Massachusetts Lowell, 883 Broadway Street, Room 102, Lowell, MA 01854, 978-934-4237 or toll-free 800-410-4607. *Fax:* 978-934-3009. *E-mail:* joyce_mclaughlin@uml.edu.

UNIVERSITY OF MEMPHIS

Memphis, TN

Tuition & fees (TN res): $6128 **Average undergraduate aid package: $7699**

ABOUT THE INSTITUTION State-supported, coed. ***Awards:*** bachelor's, master's, doctoral, and first professional degrees and post-bachelor's and post-master's certificates. 59 undergraduate majors. ***Total enrollment:*** 20,214. Undergraduates: 15,813. Freshmen: 1,989. Federal methodology is used as a basis for awarding need-based institutional aid.

UNDERGRADUATE EXPENSES for 2008–09 ***Application fee:*** $25. ***Tuition, state resident:*** full-time $4978; part-time $210 per credit. ***Tuition, nonresident:*** full-time $16,564; part-time $695 per credit. ***Required fees:*** full-time $1150; $78 per credit. Full-time tuition and fees vary according to program and reciprocity agreements. Part-time tuition and fees vary according to course load and program. ***College room and board:*** $5660; ***Room only:*** $3480. Room and board charges vary according to housing facility. ***Payment plan:*** Installment.

FRESHMAN FINANCIAL AID (Fall 2008, est.) 1,849 applied for aid; of those 73% were deemed to have need. 84% of freshmen with need received aid; of those 9% had need fully met. ***Average percent of need met:*** 79% (excluding resources awarded to replace EFC). ***Average financial aid package:*** $9380 (excluding resources awarded to replace EFC). 26% of all full-time freshmen had no need and received non-need-based gift aid.

UNDERGRADUATE FINANCIAL AID (Fall 2008, est.) 10,162 applied for aid; of those 78% were deemed to have need. 88% of undergraduates with need received aid; of those 8% had need fully met. ***Average percent of need met:*** 77% (excluding resources awarded to replace EFC). ***Average financial aid package:*** $7699 (excluding resources awarded to replace EFC). 14% of all full-time undergraduates had no need and received non-need-based gift aid.

GIFT AID (NEED-BASED) ***Total amount:*** $32,059,648 (78% federal, 20% state, 2% institutional). ***Receiving aid:*** Freshmen: 56% (1,080); all full-time undergraduates: 45% (5,286). ***Average award:*** Freshmen: $5759; Undergraduates: $4821. ***Scholarships, grants, and awards:*** Federal Pell, FSEOG, state, private, college/university gift aid from institutional funds.

GIFT AID (NON-NEED-BASED) ***Total amount:*** $25,074,816 (61% state, 36% institutional, 3% external sources). ***Receiving aid:*** Freshmen: 32% (613). Undergraduates: 38% (4,460). ***Average award:*** Freshmen: $5841. Undergraduates: $5770. ***Scholarships, grants, and awards by category:*** *Academic interests/achievement:* biological sciences, business, communication, education, engineering/technologies, English, general academic interests/achievements, health fields, humanities, international studies, mathematics, military science, physical sciences, premedicine, social sciences. *Creative arts/performance:* art/fine arts, cinema/film/broadcasting, dance, journalism/publications, music. *Special achievements/activities:* cheerleading/drum major, general special achievements/activities, leadership. *Special characteristics:* adult students, children of educators, children of faculty/staff, children of public servants, handicapped students, members of minority groups, public servants. ***Tuition waivers:*** Full or partial for employees or children of employees, senior citizens. ***ROTC:*** Army, Naval, Air Force.

LOANS ***Student loans:*** $65,221,819 (46% need-based, 54% non-need-based). 22% of past graduating class borrowed through all loan programs. *Average indebtedness per student:* $21,265. ***Average need-based loan:*** Freshmen: $1667. Undergraduates: $3970. ***Parent loans:*** $2,118,407 (100% non-need-based). ***Programs:*** Federal Direct (Subsidized and Unsubsidized Stafford, PLUS), Perkins, college/university.

WORK-STUDY ***Federal work-study:*** Total amount: $548,688; 231 jobs averaging $1726. ***State or other work-study/employment:*** Total amount: $2,900,427 (100% non-need-based). Part-time jobs available.

ATHLETIC AWARDS Total amount: $3,417,986 (100% non-need-based).

APPLYING FOR FINANCIAL AID ***Required financial aid form:*** FAFSA. ***Financial aid deadline (priority):*** 3/1. ***Notification date:*** Continuous beginning 4/1. Students must reply by 8/1.

CONTACT Richard Ritzman, Director of Student Financial Aid, University of Memphis, Wilder Tower 103, Memphis, TN 38152, 901-678-2832 or toll-free 800-669-2678 (out-of-state). *Fax:* 901-678-3590. *E-mail:* rritzman@memphis.edu.

UNIVERSITY OF MIAMI

Coral Gables, FL

Tuition & fees: $34,834 **Average undergraduate aid package: $29,170**

ABOUT THE INSTITUTION Independent, coed. ***Awards:*** bachelor's, master's, doctoral, and first professional degrees and post-bachelor's and post-master's certificates. 83 undergraduate majors. ***Total enrollment:*** 15,323. Undergraduates: 10,422. Freshmen: 2,010. Both federal and institutional methodology are used as a basis for awarding need-based institutional aid.

UNDERGRADUATE EXPENSES for 2008–09 ***Application fee:*** $65. ***Comprehensive fee:*** $45,088 includes full-time tuition ($34,206), mandatory fees ($628), and room and board ($10,254). ***College room only:*** $6050. Full-time tuition and fees vary according to course load, location, and program. Room and board charges vary according to board plan and housing facility. ***Part-time tuition:*** $1424 per credit. Part-time tuition and fees vary according to course load, location, and program. ***Payment plans:*** Tuition prepayment, installment, deferred payment.

FRESHMAN FINANCIAL AID (Fall 2008, est.) 1,234 applied for aid; of those 74% were deemed to have need. 100% of freshmen with need received aid; of those 48% had need fully met. ***Average percent of need met:*** 88% (excluding resources awarded to replace EFC). ***Average financial aid package:*** $29,868 (excluding resources awarded to replace EFC). 23% of all full-time freshmen had no need and received non-need-based gift aid.

UNDERGRADUATE FINANCIAL AID (Fall 2008, est.) 5,284 applied for aid; of those 83% were deemed to have need. 100% of undergraduates with need received aid; of those 41% had need fully met. ***Average percent of need met:*** 84% (excluding resources awarded to replace EFC). ***Average financial aid package:*** $29,170 (excluding resources awarded to replace EFC). 23% of all full-time undergraduates had no need and received non-need-based gift aid.

GIFT AID (NEED-BASED) ***Total amount:*** $86,305,198 (11% federal, 14% state, 73% institutional, 2% external sources). ***Receiving aid:*** Freshmen: 45% (893); all full-time undergraduates: 45% (4,267). ***Average award:*** Freshmen: $22,661; Undergraduates: $21,767. ***Scholarships, grants, and awards:*** Federal Pell, FSEOG, state, private, college/university gift aid from institutional funds, Federal Nursing, Academic Competitiveness Grant, National Smart Grant.

GIFT AID (NON-NEED-BASED) ***Total amount:*** $55,832,966 (1% federal, 22% state, 74% institutional, 3% external sources). ***Receiving aid:*** Freshmen: 15% (297). Undergraduates: 13% (1,208). ***Average award:*** Freshmen: $18,963. Undergraduates: $17,701. ***Scholarships, grants, and awards by category:*** *Academic interests/achievement:* 4,077 awards ($71,685,685 total): architecture, area/ethnic studies, biological sciences, business, communication, computer science, education, engineering/technologies, English, foreign languages, general academic interests/achievements, health fields, humanities, international studies, mathematics, physical sciences, premedicine, religion/biblical studies, social sciences. *Creative arts/performance:* 353 awards ($5,023,935 total): art/fine arts, cinema/film/broadcasting, debating, journalism/publications, music, performing arts, theater/drama. *Special characteristics:* 856 awards ($21,219,499 total): children of faculty/staff, international students. ***Tuition waivers:*** Full or partial for employees or children of employees. ***ROTC:*** Army, Air Force.

LOANS ***Student loans:*** $56,230,338 (60% need-based, 40% non-need-based). 56% of past graduating class borrowed through all loan programs. *Average indebtedness per student:* $24,500. ***Average need-based loan:*** Freshmen: $4554. Undergraduates: $5407. ***Parent loans:*** $11,138,268 (20% need-based, 80% non-need-based). ***Programs:*** FFEL (Subsidized and Unsubsidized Stafford, PLUS), Perkins, Federal Nursing, college/university, private alternative loans.

WORK-STUDY ***Federal work-study:*** Total amount: $6,030,464; 2,112 jobs averaging $2855. ***State or other work-study/employment:*** Total amount: $1,371,263 (17% need-based, 83% non-need-based). 234 part-time jobs averaging $5860.

ATHLETIC AWARDS Total amount: $10,209,832 (37% need-based, 63% non-need-based).

APPLYING FOR FINANCIAL AID ***Required financial aid form:*** FAFSA. ***Financial aid deadline (priority):*** 2/1. ***Notification date:*** Continuous beginning 3/1.

CONTACT Mr. James M. Bauer, Director of Financial Assistance, University of Miami, Rhodes House, Building 37R, Coral Gables, FL 33124-5240, 305-284-2270. *Fax:* 305-284-8641. *E-mail:* jbauer@miami.edu.

UNIVERSITY OF MICHIGAN

Ann Arbor, MI

Tuition & fees (MI res): $11,927 Average undergraduate aid package: $11,408

ABOUT THE INSTITUTION State-supported, coed. ***Awards:*** bachelor's, master's, doctoral, and first professional degrees and post-bachelor's and post-master's certificates. 117 undergraduate majors. ***Total enrollment:*** 41,028. Undergraduates: 25,994. Freshmen: 5,783. Federal methodology is used as a basis for awarding need-based institutional aid.

UNDERGRADUATE EXPENSES for 2008–09 ***Application fee:*** $40. ***Tuition, state resident:*** full-time $11,738; part-time $423 per credit hour. ***Tuition, nonresident:*** full-time $34,230; part-time $1341 per credit hour. ***Required fees:*** full-time $189; $95 per term. Full-time tuition and fees vary according to program and student level. Part-time tuition and fees vary according to course load, program, and student level. ***College room and board:*** $8590. Room and board charges vary according to board plan and housing facility. ***Payment plan:*** Installment.

FRESHMAN FINANCIAL AID (Fall 2007) 3,514 applied for aid; of those 81% were deemed to have need. 100% of freshmen with need received aid; of those 90% had need fully met. ***Average percent of need met:*** 90% (excluding resources awarded to replace EFC). ***Average financial aid package:*** $8959 (excluding resources awarded to replace EFC). 46% of all full-time freshmen had no need and received non-need-based gift aid.

UNDERGRADUATE FINANCIAL AID (Fall 2007) 14,056 applied for aid; of those 82% were deemed to have need. 100% of undergraduates with need received aid; of those 90% had need fully met. ***Average percent of need met:*** 90% (excluding resources awarded to replace EFC). ***Average financial aid package:*** $11,408 (excluding resources awarded to replace EFC). 30% of all full-time undergraduates had no need and received non-need-based gift aid.

GIFT AID (NEED-BASED) ***Total amount:*** $59,479,410 (22% federal, 78% institutional). ***Receiving aid:*** Freshmen: 24% (1,393); all full-time undergraduates: 25% (6,356). ***Average award:*** Freshmen: $7737; Undergraduates: $9358. ***Scholarships, grants, and awards:*** Federal Pell, FSEOG, state, private, college/university gift aid from institutional funds, Academic Competitiveness Grant, National Smart Grant.

GIFT AID (NON-NEED-BASED) ***Total amount:*** $85,601,951 (6% federal, 19% state, 57% institutional, 18% external sources). ***Receiving aid:*** Freshmen: 42% (2,421). Undergraduates: 29% (7,362). ***Average award:*** Freshmen: $6681. Undergraduates: $6488. ***Scholarships, grants, and awards by category:*** *Academic interests/achievement:* architecture, area/ethnic studies, biological sciences, business, communication, computer science, education, engineering/technologies, English, foreign languages, general academic interests/achievements, health fields, humanities, international studies, library science, mathematics, military science, physical sciences, premedicine, social sciences. *Creative arts/performance:* journalism/publications, music, theater/drama. *Special achievements/activities:* community service, general special achievements/activities, leadership. *Special characteristics:* children of faculty/staff, children of workers in trades, handicapped students, international students, local/state students, members of minority groups, out-of-state students. ***Tuition waivers:*** Full or partial for senior citizens. ***ROTC:*** Army, Air Force.

LOANS ***Student loans:*** $91,032,588 (58% need-based, 42% non-need-based). 46% of past graduating class borrowed through all loan programs. *Average indebtedness per student:* $25,586. ***Average need-based loan:*** Freshmen: $6623. Undergraduates: $4611. ***Parent loans:*** $18,807,359 (100% non-need-based). ***Programs:*** Federal Direct (Subsidized and Unsubsidized Stafford, PLUS), Perkins, Federal Nursing, college/university, Health Professions Student Loans (HPSL).

WORK-STUDY ***Federal work-study:*** Total amount: $11,320,878; 4,508 jobs averaging $2511. ***State or other work-study/employment:*** Total amount: $1,313,898 (100% need-based). 594 part-time jobs averaging $2212.

ATHLETIC AWARDS Total amount: $13,504,952 (100% non-need-based).

APPLYING FOR FINANCIAL AID ***Required financial aid forms:*** FAFSA, CSS Financial Aid PROFILE, federal income tax form(s). ***Financial aid deadline:*** 5/30 (priority: 4/30). ***Notification date:*** Continuous.

CONTACT Financial Aid Counseling and Advising Office, University of Michigan, 2500 Student Activities Building, 515 East Jefferson Street, Ann Arbor, MI 48109-1316, 734-763-6600. *Fax:* 734-647-3081. *E-mail:* financial.aid@umich.edu.

UNIVERSITY OF MICHIGAN–DEARBORN

Dearborn, MI

Tuition & fees (MI res): $8529 Average undergraduate aid package: $10,056

ABOUT THE INSTITUTION State-supported, coed. ***Awards:*** bachelor's and master's degrees and post-bachelor's certificates. 53 undergraduate majors. ***Total enrollment:*** 8,311. Undergraduates: 6,588. Freshmen: 953. Federal methodology is used as a basis for awarding need-based institutional aid.

UNDERGRADUATE EXPENSES for 2008–09 ***Application fee:*** $30. ***Tuition, state resident:*** full-time $8035; part-time $317.95 per credit hour. ***Tuition, nonresident:*** full-time $18,141; part-time $722 per credit hour. ***Required fees:*** full-time $494; $153 per term. Full-time tuition and fees vary according to course level, course load, program, and student level. Part-time tuition and fees vary according to course level, course load, program, and student level. ***Payment plan:*** Installment.

FRESHMAN FINANCIAL AID (Fall 2008, est.) 896 applied for aid; of those 48% were deemed to have need. 96% of freshmen with need received aid; of those 10% had need fully met. ***Average percent of need met:*** 51% (excluding resources awarded to replace EFC). ***Average financial aid package:*** $8508 (excluding resources awarded to replace EFC). 44% of all full-time freshmen had no need and received non-need-based gift aid.

UNDERGRADUATE FINANCIAL AID (Fall 2008, est.) 3,991 applied for aid; of those 56% were deemed to have need. 100% of undergraduates with need received aid; of those 24% had need fully met. ***Average percent of need met:*** 22% (excluding resources awarded to replace EFC). ***Average financial aid package:*** $10,056 (excluding resources awarded to replace EFC). 30% of all full-time undergraduates had no need and received non-need-based gift aid.

GIFT AID (NEED-BASED) ***Total amount:*** $9,112,054 (79% federal, 6% state, 15% institutional). ***Receiving aid:*** Freshmen: 32% (295); all full-time undergraduates: 35% (1,525). ***Average award:*** Freshmen: $4203; Undergraduates: $4420. ***Scholarships, grants, and awards:*** Federal Pell, FSEOG, state, private, college/university gift aid from institutional funds, United Negro College Fund.

GIFT AID (NON-NEED-BASED) ***Total amount:*** $6,023,393 (20% state, 71% institutional, 9% external sources). ***Receiving aid:*** Freshmen: 41% (375). Undergraduates: 23% (1,002). ***Average award:*** Freshmen: $4227. Undergraduates: $5226. ***Scholarships, grants, and awards by category:*** *Academic interests/achievement:* 573 awards ($2,218,548 total): biological sciences, business, communication, computer science, education, engineering/technologies, foreign languages, general academic interests/achievements, international studies, mathematics, physical sciences, social sciences. *Creative arts/performance:* 59 awards ($59,465 total): art/fine arts, cinema/film/broadcasting, creative writing, debating, general creative arts/performance, journalism/publications. *Special achievements/activities:* 175 awards ($1,325,027 total): community service, general special achievements/activities, leadership, memberships. *Special characteristics:* 354 awards ($1,432,077 total): children and siblings of alumni, children of current students, children of faculty/staff, children of workers in trades, ethnic background, general special characteristics, handicapped students, international students, members of minority groups, out-of-state students, previous college experience, veterans, veterans' children. ***Tuition waivers:*** Full or partial for employees or children of employees, senior citizens. ***ROTC:*** Army cooperative, Naval cooperative, Air Force cooperative.

LOANS ***Student loans:*** $23,695,944 (47% need-based, 53% non-need-based). 35% of past graduating class borrowed through all loan programs. *Average indebtedness per student:* $22,644. ***Average need-based loan:*** Freshmen: $3177. Undergraduates: $4981. ***Parent loans:*** $1,160,964 (100% non-need-based). ***Programs:*** Federal Direct (Subsidized and Unsubsidized Stafford, PLUS), Perkins, college/university, alternative loans.

WORK-STUDY ***Federal work-study:*** Total amount: $168,155; 201 jobs averaging $1585. ***State or other work-study/employment:*** Total amount: $90,571 (100% need-based). 75 part-time jobs averaging $1235.

ATHLETIC AWARDS Total amount: $133,905 (100% non-need-based).

APPLYING FOR FINANCIAL AID ***Required financial aid form:*** FAFSA. ***Financial aid deadline (priority):*** 2/14. ***Notification date:*** Continuous beginning 3/10. Students must reply within 5 weeks of notification.

CONTACT Judy Benfield Tatum, Director, University of Michigan–Dearborn, 4901 Evergreen Road, 1183 UC, Dearborn, MI 48128-1491, 313-593-5300. *Fax:* 313-593-5313. *E-mail:* ask-ofa@umd.umich.edu.

UNIVERSITY OF MICHIGAN–FLINT

Flint, MI

Tuition & fees (MI res): $7775 **Average undergraduate aid package: $7656**

ABOUT THE INSTITUTION State-supported, coed. ***Awards:*** bachelor's, master's, and doctoral degrees. 83 undergraduate majors. ***Total enrollment:*** 7,260. Undergraduates: 6,155. Freshmen: 909. Federal methodology is used as a basis for awarding need-based institutional aid.

UNDERGRADUATE EXPENSES for 2008–09 ***Application fee:*** $30. ***One-time required fee:*** $30. ***Tuition, state resident:*** full-time $7407; part-time $292 per credit hour. ***Tuition, nonresident:*** full-time $14,454; part-time $584 per credit hour. ***Required fees:*** full-time $368; $141 per term. Full-time tuition and fees vary according to course level, course load, degree level, program, reciprocity agreements, and student level. Part-time tuition and fees vary according to course level, course load, degree level, program, reciprocity agreements, and student level. ***College room and board:*** $6800; ***Room only:*** $4200. Room and board charges vary according to board plan. ***Payment plan:*** Installment.

FRESHMAN FINANCIAL AID (Fall 2007) 460 applied for aid; of those 68% were deemed to have need. 97% of freshmen with need received aid; of those 13% had need fully met. ***Average percent of need met:*** 68% (excluding resources awarded to replace EFC). ***Average financial aid package:*** $7031 (excluding resources awarded to replace EFC). 7% of all full-time freshmen had no need and received non-need-based gift aid.

UNDERGRADUATE FINANCIAL AID (Fall 2007) 2,721 applied for aid; of those 82% were deemed to have need. 98% of undergraduates with need received aid; of those 8% had need fully met. ***Average percent of need met:*** 60% (excluding resources awarded to replace EFC). ***Average financial aid package:*** $7656 (excluding resources awarded to replace EFC). 2% of all full-time undergraduates had no need and received non-need-based gift aid.

GIFT AID (NEED-BASED) ***Total amount:*** $9,879,830 (59% federal, 4% state, 37% institutional). ***Receiving aid:*** Freshmen: 33% (196); all full-time undergraduates: 39% (1,400). ***Average award:*** Freshmen: $4365; Undergraduates: $4600. ***Scholarships, grants, and awards:*** Federal Pell, FSEOG, state, private, college/university gift aid from institutional funds.

GIFT AID (NON-NEED-BASED) ***Total amount:*** $1,347,171 (76% state, 24% external sources). ***Receiving aid:*** Freshmen: 34% (201). Undergraduates: 33% (1,172). ***Average award:*** Freshmen: $3229. Undergraduates: $3608. ***Scholarships, grants, and awards by category:*** *Academic interests/achievement:* biological sciences, business, communication, computer science, education, engineering/technologies, English, foreign languages, general academic interests/achievements, health fields, humanities, international studies, mathematics, physical sciences, premedicine, social sciences. *Creative arts/performance:* art/fine arts, music, theater/drama. *Special achievements/activities:* community service, general special achievements/activities, hobbies/interests, leadership. *Special characteristics:* adult students, children and siblings of alumni, children of union members/company employees, first-generation college students, general special characteristics, handicapped students, international students, local/state students, members of minority groups. ***Tuition waivers:*** Full or partial for minority students, employees or children of employees, senior citizens.

LOANS ***Student loans:*** $22,542,796 (91% need-based, 9% non-need-based). 22% of past graduating class borrowed through all loan programs. *Average indebtedness per student:* $24,090. ***Average need-based loan:*** Freshmen: $3161. Undergraduates: $4208. ***Parent loans:*** $487,714 (100% non-need-based). ***Programs:*** Federal Direct (Subsidized and Unsubsidized Stafford, PLUS), Perkins, alternative loans.

WORK-STUDY ***Federal work-study:*** Total amount: $512,443; 343 jobs averaging $1755. ***State or other work-study/employment:*** Total amount: $147,770 (100% need-based). 85 part-time jobs averaging $1847.

APPLYING FOR FINANCIAL AID ***Required financial aid form:*** FAFSA. ***Financial aid deadline (priority):*** 3/1. ***Notification date:*** Continuous beginning 3/15.

CONTACT Lori Vedder, Financial Aid Office, University of Michigan–Flint, Room 277 UPAV, Flint, MI 48502-1950, 810-762-3444 or toll-free 800-942-5636 (in-state). *Fax:* 810-766-6757. *E-mail:* financial_aid@list.flint.umich.edu.

UNIVERSITY OF MINNESOTA, CROOKSTON

Crookston, MN

Tuition & fees (MN res): $9381 **Average undergraduate aid package: $11,043**

ABOUT THE INSTITUTION State-supported, coed. ***Awards:*** bachelor's degrees. 28 undergraduate majors. ***Total enrollment:*** 2,199. Undergraduates: 2,199. Freshmen: 276. Federal methodology is used as a basis for awarding need-based institutional aid.

UNDERGRADUATE EXPENSES for 2008–09 ***Application fee:*** $30. ***Tuition, state resident:*** full-time $6888. ***Tuition, nonresident:*** full-time $6888. ***Required fees:*** full-time $2493. Full-time tuition and fees vary according to course load. Part-time tuition and fees vary according to course load and reciprocity agreements. ***College room and board:*** $5670; ***Room only:*** $2820. Room and board charges vary according to board plan and housing facility. The U of M, Crookston has restructured the tuition policy in favor of a flat-rate tuition strategy which makes all credits above 13 per semester tuition-free. Students taking 13 or more credits will pay a flat tuition rate of $3,444 per semester. Students taking 1 to 12 credits will be assessed $264.92 per credit. ***Payment plans:*** Guaranteed tuition, installment.

FRESHMAN FINANCIAL AID (Fall 2008, est.) 230 applied for aid; of those 77% were deemed to have need. 100% of freshmen with need received aid; of those 43% had need fully met. ***Average percent of need met:*** 79% (excluding resources awarded to replace EFC). ***Average financial aid package:*** $11,080 (excluding resources awarded to replace EFC). 19% of all full-time freshmen had no need and received non-need-based gift aid.

UNDERGRADUATE FINANCIAL AID (Fall 2008, est.) 781 applied for aid; of those 83% were deemed to have need. 100% of undergraduates with need received aid; of those 36% had need fully met. ***Average percent of need met:*** 78% (excluding resources awarded to replace EFC). ***Average financial aid package:*** $11,043 (excluding resources awarded to replace EFC). 12% of all full-time undergraduates had no need and received non-need-based gift aid.

GIFT AID (NEED-BASED) ***Total amount:*** $4,150,532 (33% federal, 29% state, 34% institutional, 4% external sources). ***Receiving aid:*** Freshmen: 64% (171); all full-time undergraduates: 60% (611). ***Average award:*** Freshmen: $7248; Undergraduates: $6668. ***Scholarships, grants, and awards:*** Federal Pell, FSEOG, state, college/university gift aid from institutional funds, Academic Competitiveness Grant, National Smart Grant.

GIFT AID (NON-NEED-BASED) ***Total amount:*** $319,982 (65% institutional, 35% external sources). ***Receiving aid:*** Freshmen: 21% (55). Undergraduates: 13% (134). ***Average award:*** Freshmen: $2393. Undergraduates: $1692. ***Tuition waivers:*** Full or partial for senior citizens. ***ROTC:*** Air Force cooperative.

LOANS ***Student loans:*** $5,233,483 (80% need-based, 20% non-need-based). 84% of past graduating class borrowed through all loan programs. *Average indebtedness per student:* $26,565. ***Average need-based loan:*** Freshmen: $4929. Undergraduates: $5227. ***Parent loans:*** $304,782 (100% non-need-based). ***Programs:*** Federal Direct (Subsidized and Unsubsidized Stafford, PLUS), Perkins, state, private loans.

WORK-STUDY ***Federal work-study:*** Total amount: $199,560; jobs available. ***State or other work-study/employment:*** Total amount: $146,985 (100% need-based). Part-time jobs available.

ATHLETIC AWARDS Total amount: $606,931 (100% non-need-based).

APPLYING FOR FINANCIAL AID ***Required financial aid form:*** FAFSA. ***Financial aid deadline (priority):*** 3/1. ***Notification date:*** 3/1. Students must reply within 8 weeks of notification.

CONTACT Melissa Dingmann, Director of Financial Aid, University of Minnesota, Crookston, 170 Owen Hall, Crookston, MN 56716-5001, 218-281-8563 or toll-free 800-862-6466. *Fax:* 218-281-8575. *E-mail:* dingmann@umn.edu.

UNIVERSITY OF MINNESOTA, DULUTH

Duluth, MN

Tuition & fees (MN res): $10,260 **Average undergraduate aid package: $9265**

ABOUT THE INSTITUTION State-supported, coed. ***Awards:*** bachelor's, master's, doctoral, and first professional degrees and post-bachelor's certificates. 67 undergraduate majors. ***Total enrollment:*** 11,365. Undergraduates: 10,243. Federal methodology is used as a basis for awarding need-based institutional aid.

UNDERGRADUATE EXPENSES for 2008–09 ***Application fee:*** $35. ***Tuition, state resident:*** full-time $8230; part-time $316.54 per credit. ***Tuition, nonresident:*** full-time $10,230; part-time $393.47 per credit. ***Required fees:*** full-time $2030; $55 per credit. Full-time tuition and fees vary according to course load, degree level, program, and reciprocity agreements. Part-time tuition and fees vary according to course load, degree level, program, and reciprocity agreements. ***College room and board:*** $6078. ***Payment plan:*** Installment.

FRESHMAN FINANCIAL AID (Fall 2008, est.) 1,810 applied for aid; of those 67% were deemed to have need. 99% of freshmen with need received aid; of those 66% had need fully met. ***Average percent of need met:*** 65% (excluding resources awarded to replace EFC). ***Average financial aid package:*** $8994 (excluding resources awarded to replace EFC). 31% of all full-time freshmen had no need and received non-need-based gift aid.

UNDERGRADUATE FINANCIAL AID (Fall 2008, est.) 6,657 applied for aid; of those 71% were deemed to have need. 99% of undergraduates with need received aid; of those 70% had need fully met. ***Average percent of need met:*** 65% (excluding resources awarded to replace EFC). ***Average financial aid package:*** $9265 (excluding resources awarded to replace EFC). 22% of all full-time undergraduates had no need and received non-need-based gift aid.

GIFT AID (NEED-BASED) ***Total amount:*** $25,588,046 (26% federal, 29% state, 35% institutional, 10% external sources). ***Receiving aid:*** Freshmen: 51% (1,152); all full-time undergraduates: 49% (4,405). ***Average award:*** Freshmen: $7212; Undergraduates: $6922. ***Scholarships, grants, and awards:*** Federal Pell, FSEOG, state, private, college/university gift aid from institutional funds, Founders Opportunity Grant.

GIFT AID (NON-NEED-BASED) ***Total amount:*** $2,388,569 (1% state, 67% institutional, 32% external sources). ***Receiving aid:*** Freshmen: 4% (80). Undergraduates: 3% (224). ***Average award:*** Freshmen: $2000. Undergraduates: $1914. ***Tuition waivers:*** Full or partial for children of alumni. ***ROTC:*** Air Force.

LOANS ***Student loans:*** $66,405,713 (94% need-based, 6% non-need-based). 73% of past graduating class borrowed through all loan programs. *Average indebtedness per student:* $20,933. ***Average need-based loan:*** Freshmen: $3050. Undergraduates: $3638. ***Parent loans:*** $6,048,680 (100% non-need-based). ***Programs:*** Federal Direct (Subsidized and Unsubsidized Stafford, PLUS), Perkins, state, college/university, Primary Care Loans.

WORK-STUDY ***Federal work-study:*** Total amount: $474,276; 293 jobs averaging $2206. ***State or other work-study/employment:*** Total amount: $687,335 (100% need-based). 301 part-time jobs averaging $2316.

ATHLETIC AWARDS Total amount: $1,807,002 (24% need-based, 76% non-need-based).

APPLYING FOR FINANCIAL AID ***Required financial aid form:*** FAFSA. ***Financial aid deadline (priority):*** 3/1. ***Notification date:*** Continuous beginning 3/1. Students must reply within 2 weeks of notification.

CONTACT Ms. Brenda Herzig, Director of Financial Aid, University of Minnesota, Duluth, 10 University Drive, 184 Darland Administration Building, Duluth, MN 55812-2496, 218-726-8000 or toll-free 800-232-1339. *Fax:* 218-726-8219.

UNIVERSITY OF MINNESOTA, MORRIS

Morris, MN

Tuition & fees (MN res): $10,006 Average undergraduate aid package: $10,923

ABOUT THE INSTITUTION State-supported, coed. ***Awards:*** bachelor's degrees. 42 undergraduate majors. ***Total enrollment:*** 1,607. Undergraduates: 1,607. Freshmen: 492. Federal methodology is used as a basis for awarding need-based institutional aid.

UNDERGRADUATE EXPENSES for 2008–09 ***Application fee:*** $35. ***Tuition, state resident:*** full-time $8230. ***Tuition, nonresident:*** full-time $8230. ***Required fees:*** full-time $1776. Full-time tuition and fees vary according to reciprocity agreements. Part-time tuition and fees vary according to course load and reciprocity agreements. ***College room and board:*** $6710; ***Room only:*** $3130. Room and board charges vary according to board plan and housing facility. ***Payment plan:*** Installment.

UNDERGRADUATE FINANCIAL AID (Fall 2007) 1,234 applied for aid; of those 81% were deemed to have need. 100% of undergraduates with need received aid. ***Average financial aid package:*** $10,923 (excluding resources awarded to replace EFC).

GIFT AID (NEED-BASED) ***Total amount:*** $4,084,392 (49% federal, 41% state, 10% institutional). ***Receiving aid:*** All full-time undergraduates: 26% (441). ***Scholarships, grants, and awards:*** Federal Pell, FSEOG, state, private, college/university gift aid from institutional funds.

GIFT AID (NON-NEED-BASED) ***Total amount:*** $2,957,972 (74% institutional, 26% external sources). ***Scholarships, grants, and awards by category:*** *Academic interests/achievement:* 1,250 awards ($1,932,870 total): general academic interests/achievements. *Creative arts/performance:* 5 awards ($3500 total): music. *Special achievements/activities:* 65 awards ($108,575 total): general special achievements/activities. *Special characteristics:* 104 awards ($237,137 total): ethnic background, international students, members of minority groups, veterans, veterans' children. ***Tuition waivers:*** Full or partial for minority students, senior citizens.

LOANS ***Student loans:*** $6,825,585 (46% need-based, 54% non-need-based). ***Parent loans:*** $353,207 (100% non-need-based). ***Programs:*** Federal Direct (Subsidized and Unsubsidized Stafford, PLUS), Perkins, state.

WORK-STUDY ***Federal work-study:*** Total amount: $409,063; 334 jobs averaging $1224. ***State or other work-study/employment:*** Total amount: $374,024 (33% need-based, 67% non-need-based). 420 part-time jobs averaging $890.

APPLYING FOR FINANCIAL AID ***Required financial aid form:*** FAFSA. ***Financial aid deadline (priority):*** 3/1. ***Notification date:*** Continuous. Students must reply within 3 weeks of notification.

CONTACT Ms. Jill Beauregard, Director of Financial Aid, University of Minnesota, Morris, 600 East 4th Street, Morris, MN 56267, 320-589-6035 or toll-free 800-992-8863. *Fax:* 320-589-1673. *E-mail:* morrisfa@morris.umn.edu.

UNIVERSITY OF MINNESOTA, TWIN CITIES CAMPUS

Minneapolis, MN

Tuition & fees (MN res): $10,273 Average undergraduate aid package: $12,823

ABOUT THE INSTITUTION State-supported, coed. ***Awards:*** bachelor's, master's, doctoral, and first professional degrees and post-bachelor's, post-master's, and first professional certificates. 132 undergraduate majors. ***Total enrollment:*** 51,140. Undergraduates: 32,557. Freshmen: 5,106. Both federal and institutional methodology are used as a basis for awarding need-based institutional aid.

UNDERGRADUATE EXPENSES for 2008–09 ***Application fee:*** $45. ***Tuition, state resident:*** full-time $8500; part-time $326.92 per credit. ***Tuition, nonresident:*** full-time $20,130; part-time $774.23 per credit. ***Required fees:*** full-time $1773. Full-time tuition and fees vary according to program and reciprocity agreements. Part-time tuition and fees vary according to course load, program, and reciprocity agreements. ***College room and board:*** $7280; ***Room only:*** $4294. Room and board charges vary according to board plan, housing facility, and location. ***Payment plan:*** Installment.

FRESHMAN FINANCIAL AID (Fall 2008, est.) 3,970 applied for aid; of those 65% were deemed to have need. 99% of freshmen with need received aid; of those 50% had need fully met. ***Average percent of need met:*** 86% (excluding resources awarded to replace EFC). ***Average financial aid package:*** $13,272 (excluding resources awarded to replace EFC). 29% of all full-time freshmen had no need and received non-need-based gift aid.

UNDERGRADUATE FINANCIAL AID (Fall 2008, est.) 18,156 applied for aid; of those 70% were deemed to have need. 99% of undergraduates with need received aid; of those 45% had need fully met. ***Average percent of need met:*** 83% (excluding resources awarded to replace EFC). ***Average financial aid package:*** $12,823 (excluding resources awarded to replace EFC). 19% of all full-time undergraduates had no need and received non-need-based gift aid.

GIFT AID (NEED-BASED) ***Total amount:*** $95,796,422 (24% federal, 29% state, 42% institutional, 5% external sources). ***Receiving aid:*** Freshmen: 50% (2,540); all full-time undergraduates: 46% (11,969). ***Average award:*** Freshmen: $7809; Undergraduates: $7304. ***Scholarships, grants, and awards:*** Federal Pell, FSEOG, state, private, college/university gift aid from institutional funds, Federal Nursing.

GIFT AID (NON-NEED-BASED) ***Total amount:*** $19,582,310 (88% institutional, 12% external sources). ***Receiving aid:*** Freshmen: 17% (882). Undergraduates: 13% (3,318). ***Average award:*** Freshmen: $2913. Undergraduates: $3581. ***Scholarships, grants, and awards by category:*** *Academic interests/achievement:* agriculture, architecture, area/ethnic studies, biological sciences, business, communication, computer science, education, engineering/technologies, English, foreign languages, general academic interests/achievements, health fields, home economics, humanities, international studies, library science, mathematics, military science, physical sciences, premedicine, religion/biblical studies, social sciences. *Creative arts/performance:* general creative arts/performance. *Special achievements/activities:* hobbies/interests, leadership. *Special characteristics:* general special characteristics. ***Tuition waivers:*** Full or partial for senior citizens. ***ROTC:*** Army, Naval, Air Force.

LOANS ***Student loans:*** $135,902,839 (72% need-based, 28% non-need-based). 64% of past graduating class borrowed through all loan programs. *Average indebtedness per student:* $23,811. ***Average need-based loan:*** Freshmen: $6273.

Undergraduates: $6624. ***Parent loans:*** $14,104,063 (100% non-need-based). ***Programs:*** Federal Direct (Subsidized and Unsubsidized Stafford, PLUS), Perkins, Federal Nursing, state, college/university.

WORK-STUDY ***Federal work-study:*** Total amount: $5,380,740; jobs available. ***State or other work-study/employment:*** Total amount: $10,675,515 (100% need-based). Part-time jobs available.

APPLYING FOR FINANCIAL AID ***Required financial aid forms:*** FAFSA, institution's own form. ***Financial aid deadline:*** Continuous. ***Notification date:*** Continuous.

CONTACT Judy Swanson, Associate Director, Office of Student Finance Admissions, University of Minnesota, Twin Cities Campus, 200 Fraser Hall, Minneapolis, MN 55455, 612-624-1111 or toll-free 800-752-1000. *Fax:* 612-624-9584. *E-mail:* helpingu@umn.edu.

UNIVERSITY OF MISSISSIPPI

Oxford, MS

Tuition & fees (MS res): $5106 **Average undergraduate aid package: $6890**

ABOUT THE INSTITUTION State-supported, coed. ***Awards:*** bachelor's, master's, doctoral, and first professional degrees and post-master's certificates. 61 undergraduate majors. ***Total enrollment:*** 15,289. Undergraduates: 12,762. Freshmen: 2,377. Federal methodology is used as a basis for awarding need-based institutional aid.

UNDERGRADUATE EXPENSES for 2008–09 ***Application fee:*** $50. ***Tuition, state resident:*** full-time $5106; part-time $212.75 per semester hour. ***Tuition, nonresident:*** full-time $12,468; part-time $519.50 per semester hour. ***College room and board:*** $7778; ***Room only:*** $4200. Room and board charges vary according to board plan and housing facility. ***Payment plan:*** Tuition prepayment.

FRESHMAN FINANCIAL AID (Fall 2007) 1,483 applied for aid; of those 64% were deemed to have need. 96% of freshmen with need received aid; of those 13% had need fully met. ***Average percent of need met:*** 76% (excluding resources awarded to replace EFC). ***Average financial aid package:*** $8111 (excluding resources awarded to replace EFC). 23% of all full-time freshmen had no need and received non-need-based gift aid.

UNDERGRADUATE FINANCIAL AID (Fall 2007) 6,562 applied for aid; of those 74% were deemed to have need. 97% of undergraduates with need received aid; of those 13% had need fully met. ***Average percent of need met:*** 76% (excluding resources awarded to replace EFC). ***Average financial aid package:*** $6890 (excluding resources awarded to replace EFC). 18% of all full-time undergraduates had no need and received non-need-based gift aid.

GIFT AID (NEED-BASED) ***Total amount:*** $20,687,698 (46% federal, 11% state, 35% institutional, 8% external sources). ***Receiving aid:*** Freshmen: 34% (818); all full-time undergraduates: 35% (4,073). ***Average award:*** Freshmen: $6299; Undergraduates: $5612. ***Scholarships, grants, and awards:*** Federal Pell, FSEOG, state, private, college/university gift aid from institutional funds.

GIFT AID (NON-NEED-BASED) ***Total amount:*** $12,972,012 (1% federal, 21% state, 63% institutional, 15% external sources). ***Receiving aid:*** Freshmen: 6% (151). Undergraduates: 4% (451). ***Average award:*** Freshmen: $3765. Undergraduates: $3963. ***Scholarships, grants, and awards by category:*** *Academic interests/achievement:* 5,445 awards ($11,558,881 total): biological sciences, business, communication, computer science, education, engineering/technologies, English, foreign languages, general academic interests/achievements, health fields, humanities, international studies, mathematics, military science, physical sciences, premedicine, religion/biblical studies, social sciences. *Creative arts/performance:* 739 awards ($1,008,768 total): art/fine arts, cinema/film/broadcasting, creative writing, debating, journalism/publications, music, performing arts, theater/drama. *Special achievements/activities:* 3,614 awards ($6,020,551 total): cheerleading/drum major, community service, general special achievements/activities, junior miss, leadership, memberships. *Special characteristics:* 4,144 awards ($7,407,131 total): adult students, children and siblings of alumni, children of faculty/staff, ethnic background, first-generation college students, general special characteristics, handicapped students, international students, local/state students, members of minority groups, out-of-state students, previous college experience, spouses of current students. ***Tuition waivers:*** Full or partial for children of alumni, employees or children of employees, senior citizens. ***ROTC:*** Army, Naval, Air Force.

LOANS ***Student loans:*** $35,547,809 (73% need-based, 27% non-need-based). 39% of past graduating class borrowed through all loan programs. *Average indebtedness per student:* $20,047. ***Average need-based loan:*** Freshmen: $3809. Undergraduates: $5046. ***Parent loans:*** $10,518,201 (27% need-based, 73% non-need-based). ***Programs:*** FFEL (Subsidized and Unsubsidized Stafford, PLUS), Perkins, college/university.

WORK-STUDY ***Federal work-study:*** Total amount: $597,462; 404 jobs averaging $1463.

ATHLETIC AWARDS Total amount: $4,540,851 (46% need-based, 54% non-need-based).

APPLYING FOR FINANCIAL AID ***Required financial aid form:*** FAFSA. ***Financial aid deadline (priority):*** 3/15. ***Notification date:*** Continuous beginning 4/1. Students must reply within 3 weeks of notification.

CONTACT Ms. Laura Diven-Brown, Director of Financial Aid, University of Mississippi, 257 Martindale Center, University, MS 38677, 662-915-5788 or toll-free 800-653-6477 (in-state). *Fax:* 662-915-1164. *E-mail:* ldivenbr@olemiss.edu.

UNIVERSITY OF MISSISSIPPI MEDICAL CENTER

Jackson, MS

CONTACT Minetta Veazey, Administrative Secretary, University of Mississippi Medical Center, 2500 North State Street, Jackson, MS 39216, 601-984-1117. *Fax:* 601-984-6984. *E-mail:* mveazey@registrar.umsmed.edu.

UNIVERSITY OF MISSOURI–COLUMBIA

Columbia, MO

Tuition & fees (MO res): $8467 **Average undergraduate aid package: $12,757**

ABOUT THE INSTITUTION State-supported, coed. ***Awards:*** bachelor's, master's, doctoral, and first professional degrees and post-master's and first professional certificates. 116 undergraduate majors. ***Total enrollment:*** 30,200. Undergraduates: 23,042. Freshmen: 5,782. Federal methodology is used as a basis for awarding need-based institutional aid.

UNDERGRADUATE EXPENSES for 2008–09 ***Application fee:*** $45. ***Tuition, state resident:*** full-time $7368; part-time $245.60 per credit hour. ***Tuition, nonresident:*** full-time $18,459; part-time $615.30 per credit hour. ***Required fees:*** full-time $1099. Full-time tuition and fees vary according to course load, program, and reciprocity agreements. Part-time tuition and fees vary according to course load, program, and reciprocity agreements. ***College room and board:*** $8100. Room and board charges vary according to board plan and housing facility. ***Payment plan:*** Installment.

FRESHMAN FINANCIAL AID (Fall 2008, est.) 4,201 applied for aid; of those 65% were deemed to have need. 98% of freshmen with need received aid; of those 21% had need fully met. ***Average percent of need met:*** 87% (excluding resources awarded to replace EFC). ***Average financial aid package:*** $13,594 (excluding resources awarded to replace EFC). 23% of all full-time freshmen had no need and received non-need-based gift aid.

UNDERGRADUATE FINANCIAL AID (Fall 2008, est.) 13,764 applied for aid; of those 70% were deemed to have need. 98% of undergraduates with need received aid; of those 22% had need fully met. ***Average percent of need met:*** 85% (excluding resources awarded to replace EFC). ***Average financial aid package:*** $12,757 (excluding resources awarded to replace EFC). 19% of all full-time undergraduates had no need and received non-need-based gift aid.

GIFT AID (NEED-BASED) ***Total amount:*** $51,806,028 (30% federal, 19% state, 44% institutional, 7% external sources). ***Receiving aid:*** Freshmen: 42% (2,386); all full-time undergraduates: 37% (7,940). ***Average award:*** Freshmen: $7660; Undergraduates: $7259. ***Scholarships, grants, and awards:*** Federal Pell, FSEOG, state, private, college/university gift aid from institutional funds.

GIFT AID (NON-NEED-BASED) ***Total amount:*** $23,212,686 (6% federal, 12% state, 62% institutional, 20% external sources). ***Receiving aid:*** Freshmen: 3% (174). Undergraduates: 2% (398). ***Average award:*** Freshmen: $3617. Undergraduates: $3450. ***Scholarships, grants, and awards by category:*** *Academic interests/achievement:* agriculture, biological sciences, business, communication, computer science, education, engineering/technologies, English, foreign languages, general academic interests/achievements, health fields, home economics, mathematics, premedicine, religion/biblical studies, social sciences. *Creative arts/performance:* journalism/publications, music, theater/drama. *Special achievements/activities:* general special achievements/activities. *Special characteristics:* children and siblings of alumni, international students, members of minority groups, out-of-state students. ***Tuition waivers:*** Full or partial for employees or children of employees, senior citizens. ***ROTC:*** Army, Naval, Air Force.

LOANS ***Student loans:*** $76,219,701 (62% need-based, 38% non-need-based). 60% of past graduating class borrowed through all loan programs. *Average indebtedness per student:* $20,889. ***Average need-based loan:*** Freshmen: $3515. Undergraduates: $4230. ***Parent loans:*** $35,134,737 (39% need-based, 61% non-need-based). ***Programs:*** Federal Direct (Subsidized and Unsubsidized Stafford, PLUS), FFEL (PLUS), Perkins, Federal Nursing, state, college/university, outside loans.

WORK-STUDY ***Federal work-study:*** Total amount: $2,339,570; jobs available.

ATHLETIC AWARDS Total amount: $5,705,305 (37% need-based, 63% non-need-based).

APPLYING FOR FINANCIAL AID ***Required financial aid form:*** FAFSA. ***Financial aid deadline (priority):*** 3/1. ***Notification date:*** Continuous beginning 4/1. Students must reply within 4 weeks of notification.

CONTACT James Brooks, Director, Student Financial Aid, University of Missouri–Columbia, 11 Jesse Hall, Columbia, MO 65211, 573-882-7506 or toll-free 800-225-6075 (in-state). *Fax:* 573-884-5335. *E-mail:* finaldinfo@missouri.edu.

UNIVERSITY OF MISSOURI–KANSAS CITY

Kansas City, MO

Tuition & fees (MO res): $8273 Average undergraduate aid package: $9596

ABOUT THE INSTITUTION State-supported, coed. ***Awards:*** bachelor's, master's, doctoral, and first professional degrees and post-master's and first professional certificates. 50 undergraduate majors. ***Total enrollment:*** 14,499. Undergraduates: 9,274. Freshmen: 1,007. Federal methodology is used as a basis for awarding need-based institutional aid.

UNDERGRADUATE EXPENSES for 2008–09 ***Application fee:*** $45. ***Tuition, state resident:*** full-time $7368; part-time $245.60 per credit hour. ***Tuition, nonresident:*** full-time $18,459; part-time $615.30 per credit hour. ***Required fees:*** full-time $905; $30.15 per credit hour or $30 per term. Full-time tuition and fees vary according to course load and program. Part-time tuition and fees vary according to course load and program. ***College room and board:*** $7881; ***Room only:*** $5269. Room and board charges vary according to board plan and housing facility. ***Payment plan:*** Installment.

FRESHMAN FINANCIAL AID (Fall 2008, est.) 787 applied for aid; of those 79% were deemed to have need. 98% of freshmen with need received aid; of those 14% had need fully met. ***Average percent of need met:*** 59% (excluding resources awarded to replace EFC). ***Average financial aid package:*** $10,104 (excluding resources awarded to replace EFC). 25% of all full-time freshmen had no need and received non-need-based gift aid.

UNDERGRADUATE FINANCIAL AID (Fall 2008, est.) 4,334 applied for aid; of those 86% were deemed to have need. 97% of undergraduates with need received aid; of those 10% had need fully met. ***Average percent of need met:*** 54% (excluding resources awarded to replace EFC). ***Average financial aid package:*** $9596 (excluding resources awarded to replace EFC). 15% of all full-time undergraduates had no need and received non-need-based gift aid.

GIFT AID (NEED-BASED) ***Total amount:*** $19,612,877 (41% federal, 14% state, 40% institutional, 5% external sources). ***Receiving aid:*** Freshmen: 58% (565); all full-time undergraduates: 49% (2,862). ***Average award:*** Freshmen: $7411; Undergraduates: $6623. ***Scholarships, grants, and awards:*** Federal Pell, FSEOG, state, private, college/university gift aid from institutional funds, United Negro College Fund.

GIFT AID (NON-NEED-BASED) ***Total amount:*** $5,466,544 (5% state, 85% institutional, 10% external sources). ***Receiving aid:*** Freshmen: 2% (18). Undergraduates: 1% (62). ***Average award:*** Freshmen: $4438. Undergraduates: $5027. ***Scholarships, grants, and awards by category:*** *Academic interests/achievement:* general academic interests/achievements. *Creative arts/performance:* debating, general creative arts/performance, music, performing arts. *Special achievements/activities:* general special achievements/activities. *Special characteristics:* ethnic background, members of minority groups, out-of-state students. ***Tuition waivers:*** Full or partial for employees or children of employees. ***ROTC:*** Army, Air Force cooperative.

LOANS ***Student loans:*** $38,213,068 (82% need-based, 18% non-need-based). 65% of past graduating class borrowed through all loan programs. *Average indebtedness per student:* $24,151. ***Average need-based loan:*** Freshmen: $6710. Undergraduates: $8877. ***Parent loans:*** $3,146,085 (53% need-based, 47% non-need-based). ***Programs:*** Federal Direct (Subsidized and Unsubsidized Stafford, PLUS), Perkins, Federal Nursing, state, college/university.

WORK-STUDY ***Federal work-study:*** Total amount: $1,732,274; jobs available.

ATHLETIC AWARDS Total amount: $1,901,859 (34% need-based, 66% non-need-based).

APPLYING FOR FINANCIAL AID ***Required financial aid form:*** FAFSA. ***Financial aid deadline (priority):*** 3/1. ***Notification date:*** Continuous beginning 4/15. Students must reply within 2 weeks of notification.

CONTACT Jan Brandow, Director of Financial Aid and Scholarships, University of Missouri–Kansas City, 5100 Rockhill Road, Kansas City, MO 64110-2499, 816-235-1154 or toll-free 800-775-8652 (out-of-state). *Fax:* 816-235-5511. *E-mail:* brandowj@umkc.edu.

UNIVERSITY OF MISSOURI–ST. LOUIS

St. Louis, MO

Tuition & fees (MO res): $8595 Average undergraduate aid package: $7838

ABOUT THE INSTITUTION State-supported, coed. ***Awards:*** bachelor's, master's, doctoral, and first professional degrees and post-bachelor's certificates. 71 undergraduate majors. ***Total enrollment:*** 15,617. Undergraduates: 12,245. Freshmen: 469. Federal methodology is used as a basis for awarding need-based institutional aid.

UNDERGRADUATE EXPENSES for 2008–09 ***Application fee:*** $35. ***Tuition, state resident:*** full-time $7368; part-time $245.60 per credit hour. ***Tuition, nonresident:*** full-time $18,459; part-time $615.30 per credit hour. ***Required fees:*** full-time $1227; $47.09 per credit hour. Full-time tuition and fees vary according to course load, program, and reciprocity agreements. Part-time tuition and fees vary according to course load, program, and reciprocity agreements. ***College room and board:*** $7782; ***Room only:*** $5610. Room and board charges vary according to board plan and housing facility. ***Payment plan:*** Installment.

FRESHMAN FINANCIAL AID (Fall 2008, est.) 347 applied for aid; of those 84% were deemed to have need. 98% of freshmen with need received aid; of those 12% had need fully met. ***Average percent of need met:*** 52% (excluding resources awarded to replace EFC). ***Average financial aid package:*** $8309 (excluding resources awarded to replace EFC). 20% of all full-time freshmen had no need and received non-need-based gift aid.

UNDERGRADUATE FINANCIAL AID (Fall 2008, est.) 4,184 applied for aid; of those 88% were deemed to have need. 97% of undergraduates with need received aid; of those 8% had need fully met. ***Average percent of need met:*** 48% (excluding resources awarded to replace EFC). ***Average financial aid package:*** $7838 (excluding resources awarded to replace EFC). 9% of all full-time undergraduates had no need and received non-need-based gift aid.

GIFT AID (NEED-BASED) ***Total amount:*** $16,989,860 (51% federal, 16% state, 27% institutional, 6% external sources). ***Receiving aid:*** Freshmen: 61% (266); all full-time undergraduates: 49% (2,752). ***Average award:*** Freshmen: $6466; Undergraduates: $5140. ***Scholarships, grants, and awards:*** Federal Pell, FSEOG, state, private, college/university gift aid from institutional funds, Federal Nursing, Academic Competitiveness Grant, National Smart Grant.

GIFT AID (NON-NEED-BASED) ***Total amount:*** $3,706,715 (8% state, 70% institutional, 22% external sources). ***Receiving aid:*** Freshmen: 6% (25). Undergraduates: 2% (100). ***Average award:*** Freshmen: $4620. Undergraduates: $3934. ***Scholarships, grants, and awards by category:*** *Academic interests/achievement:* biological sciences, business, communication, computer science, education, engineering/technologies, English, foreign languages, general academic interests/achievements, health fields, humanities, international studies, mathematics. *Creative arts/performance:* art/fine arts, music. *Special achievements/activities:* memberships. *Special characteristics:* ethnic background, general special characteristics, local/state students, members of minority groups. ***Tuition waivers:*** Full or partial for employees or children of employees, senior citizens. ***ROTC:*** Army cooperative, Air Force cooperative.

LOANS ***Student loans:*** $42,689,071 (86% need-based, 14% non-need-based). 78% of past graduating class borrowed through all loan programs. *Average indebtedness per student:* $24,016. ***Average need-based loan:*** Freshmen: $3157. Undergraduates: $4431. ***Parent loans:*** $3,123,350 (38% need-based, 62% non-need-based). ***Programs:*** FFEL (Subsidized and Unsubsidized Stafford, PLUS), Perkins, Federal Nursing.

WORK-STUDY ***Federal work-study:*** Total amount: $208,248; 58 jobs averaging $2732.

ATHLETIC AWARDS Total amount: $1,440,220 (37% need-based, 63% non-need-based).

APPLYING FOR FINANCIAL AID ***Required financial aid form:*** FAFSA. ***Financial aid deadline (priority):*** 4/1. ***Notification date:*** Continuous beginning 4/1. Students must reply within 2 weeks of notification.

CONTACT Samantha Ruffini, Associate Director, Student Financial Aid, University of Missouri–St. Louis, One University Boulevard, 327 Millennium Student Center, St. Louis, MO 63121-4400, 314-516-6893 or toll-free 888-GO2-UMSL (in-state). *Fax:* 314-516-5408. *E-mail:* ruffinis@umsl.edu.

UNIVERSITY OF MOBILE

Mobile, AL

Tuition & fees: $13,970 **Average undergraduate aid package: $11,189**

ABOUT THE INSTITUTION Independent Southern Baptist, coed. ***Awards:*** associate, bachelor's, and master's degrees. 29 undergraduate majors. ***Total enrollment:*** 1,597. Undergraduates: 1,422. Freshmen: 251. Federal methodology is used as a basis for awarding need-based institutional aid.

UNDERGRADUATE EXPENSES for 2008–09 ***Application fee:*** $50. ***Comprehensive fee:*** $21,290 includes full-time tuition ($13,500), mandatory fees ($470), and room and board ($7320). ***College room only:*** $4370. Full-time tuition and fees vary according to course load and program. Room and board charges vary according to housing facility. ***Part-time tuition:*** $480 per credit hour. ***Part-time fees:*** $120.50 per degree program. Part-time tuition and fees vary according to course load. ***Payment plan:*** Installment.

FRESHMAN FINANCIAL AID (Fall 2008, est.) 194 applied for aid; of those 100% were deemed to have need. 99% of freshmen with need received aid. ***Average percent of need met:*** 70% (excluding resources awarded to replace EFC). ***Average financial aid package:*** $11,471 (excluding resources awarded to replace EFC). 4% of all full-time freshmen had no need and received non-need-based gift aid.

UNDERGRADUATE FINANCIAL AID (Fall 2008, est.) 856 applied for aid; of those 100% were deemed to have need. 99% of undergraduates with need received aid. ***Average percent of need met:*** 75% (excluding resources awarded to replace EFC). ***Average financial aid package:*** $11,189 (excluding resources awarded to replace EFC). 10% of all full-time undergraduates had no need and received non-need-based gift aid.

GIFT AID (NEED-BASED) ***Total amount:*** $8,666,711 (22% federal, 6% state, 57% institutional, 15% external sources). ***Receiving aid:*** Freshmen: 78% (193); all full-time undergraduates: 72% (796). ***Average award:*** Freshmen: $8469; Undergraduates: $7424. ***Scholarships, grants, and awards:*** Federal Pell, FSEOG, state, college/university gift aid from institutional funds, Federal Nursing.

GIFT AID (NON-NEED-BASED) ***Receiving aid:*** Freshmen: 16% (39). Undergraduates: 12% (132). ***Average award:*** Freshmen: $5210. Undergraduates: $6336. ***Tuition waivers:*** Full or partial for employees or children of employees. ***ROTC:*** Army cooperative, Air Force cooperative.

LOANS ***Student loans:*** $6,840,436 (53% need-based, 47% non-need-based). 63% of past graduating class borrowed through all loan programs. *Average indebtedness per student:* $18,763. ***Average need-based loan:*** Freshmen: $3302. Undergraduates: $4483. ***Parent loans:*** $630,936 (100% non-need-based). ***Programs:*** FFEL (Subsidized and Unsubsidized Stafford, PLUS), Perkins.

WORK-STUDY ***Federal work-study:*** Total amount: $100,000; 67 jobs averaging $1965.

ATHLETIC AWARDS Total amount: $1,897,993 (100% non-need-based).

APPLYING FOR FINANCIAL AID ***Required financial aid forms:*** FAFSA, institution's own form, state aid form. ***Financial aid deadline (priority):*** 2/15. ***Notification date:*** Continuous beginning 2/15. Students must reply within 2 weeks of notification.

CONTACT Marie Thomas Baston, Associate Vice President for Enrollment Services, University of Mobile, 5735 College Parkway, Mobile, AL 36613, 251-442-2370 or toll-free 800-946-7267. *Fax:* 251-442-2498. *E-mail:* mariet@umobile.edu.

THE UNIVERSITY OF MONTANA

Missoula, MT

Tuition & fees (MT res): $5180 **Average undergraduate aid package: $7458**

ABOUT THE INSTITUTION State-supported, coed. ***Awards:*** associate, bachelor's, master's, doctoral, and first professional degrees and post-master's certificates. 119 undergraduate majors. ***Total enrollment:*** 14,207. Undergraduates: 12,196. Freshmen: 2,430. Federal methodology is used as a basis for awarding need-based institutional aid.

UNDERGRADUATE EXPENSES for 2008–09 ***Application fee:*** $30. ***Tuition, state resident:*** full-time $3739; part-time $156 per credit. ***Tuition, nonresident:*** full-time $15,014; part-time $669 per credit. ***Required fees:*** full-time $1441; $87 per credit. Full-time tuition and fees vary according to degree level, location, program, reciprocity agreements, and student level. Part-time tuition and fees vary according to course load, degree level, location, and student level. ***College room and board:*** $6258; ***Room only:*** $2808. Room and board charges vary according to board plan and housing facility. ***Payment plans:*** Installment, deferred payment.

FRESHMAN FINANCIAL AID (Fall 2008, est.) 2,237 applied for aid; of those 65% were deemed to have need. 98% of freshmen with need received aid; of those 10% had need fully met. ***Average percent of need met:*** 61% (excluding resources awarded to replace EFC). ***Average financial aid package:*** $6975 (excluding resources awarded to replace EFC). 29% of all full-time freshmen had no need and received non-need-based gift aid.

UNDERGRADUATE FINANCIAL AID (Fall 2008, est.) 8,344 applied for aid; of those 69% were deemed to have need. 99% of undergraduates with need received aid; of those 11% had need fully met. ***Average percent of need met:*** 63% (excluding resources awarded to replace EFC). ***Average financial aid package:*** $7458 (excluding resources awarded to replace EFC). 23% of all full-time undergraduates had no need and received non-need-based gift aid.

GIFT AID (NEED-BASED) ***Total amount:*** $19,530,470 (84% federal, 4% state, 12% institutional). ***Receiving aid:*** Freshmen: 35% (933); all full-time undergraduates: 36% (3,868). ***Average award:*** Freshmen: $4310; Undergraduates: $5094. ***Scholarships, grants, and awards:*** Federal Pell, FSEOG, state, private, college/university gift aid from institutional funds.

GIFT AID (NON-NEED-BASED) ***Total amount:*** $10,163,421 (56% institutional, 44% external sources). ***Receiving aid:*** Freshmen: 2% (45). Undergraduates: 1% (94). ***Average award:*** Freshmen: $5785. Undergraduates: $5879. ***Scholarships, grants, and awards by category:*** *Academic interests/achievement:* biological sciences, business, computer science, education, English, foreign languages, general academic interests/achievements, health fields, humanities, international studies, mathematics, military science, physical sciences, premedicine, social sciences. *Creative arts/performance:* art/fine arts, creative writing, dance, journalism/publications, music, performing arts, theater/drama. *Special achievements/activities:* cheerleading/drum major, leadership, rodeo. *Special characteristics:* children and siblings of alumni, children with a deceased or disabled parent, general special characteristics, international students, members of minority groups, out-of-state students, veterans. ***Tuition waivers:*** Full or partial for minority students, employees or children of employees, senior citizens. ***ROTC:*** Army.

LOANS ***Student loans:*** $48,839,623 (100% need-based). 67% of past graduating class borrowed through all loan programs. *Average indebtedness per student:* $17,527. ***Average need-based loan:*** Freshmen: $3175. Undergraduates: $3923. ***Parent loans:*** $10,362,970 (100% non-need-based). ***Programs:*** FFEL (Subsidized and Unsubsidized Stafford, PLUS), Perkins.

WORK-STUDY ***Federal work-study:*** Total amount: $4,439,334; jobs available. ***State or other work-study/employment:*** Total amount: $468,130 (100% need-based). Part-time jobs available.

ATHLETIC AWARDS Total amount: $1,329,228 (100% non-need-based).

APPLYING FOR FINANCIAL AID ***Required financial aid forms:*** FAFSA, UM Supplemental Information Sheet. ***Financial aid deadline (priority):*** 2/15. ***Notification date:*** Continuous beginning 4/1. Students must reply within 4 weeks of notification.

CONTACT Mick Hanson, Director of Financial Aid, The University of Montana, Enrollment Services, Missoula, MT 59812-0002, 406-243-5373 or toll-free 800-462-8636. *Fax:* 406-243-4930. *E-mail:* faid@mso.umt.edu.

THE UNIVERSITY OF MONTANA WESTERN

Dillon, MT

Tuition & fees (MT res): $4228 **Average undergraduate aid package: $2961**

ABOUT THE INSTITUTION State-supported, coed. ***Awards:*** associate and bachelor's degrees. 35 undergraduate majors. ***Total enrollment:*** 1,190. Undergraduates: 1,190. Freshmen: 227. Federal methodology is used as a basis for awarding need-based institutional aid.

UNDERGRADUATE EXPENSES for 2008–09 ***Application fee:*** $30. ***Tuition, state resident:*** full-time $3355; part-time $162.80 per credit. ***Tuition, nonresident:*** full-time $11,795; part-time $498.80 per credit. ***Required fees:*** full-time $873; $14 per credit or $71 per term. Full-time tuition and fees vary according to course load and student level. Part-time tuition and fees vary according to course load and student level. ***College room and board:*** $5350; ***Room only:*** $2120. Room and board charges vary according to housing facility. ***Payment plan:*** Deferred payment.

FRESHMAN FINANCIAL AID (Fall 2007) 192 applied for aid; of those 81% were deemed to have need. ***Average percent of need met:*** 16% (excluding resources awarded to replace EFC). ***Average financial aid package:*** $2659 (excluding resources awarded to replace EFC).

UNDERGRADUATE FINANCIAL AID (Fall 2007) 950 applied for aid; of those 82% were deemed to have need. ***Average percent of need met:*** 18% (excluding resources awarded to replace EFC). ***Average financial aid package:*** $2961 (excluding resources awarded to replace EFC). 1% of all full-time undergraduates had no need and received non-need-based gift aid.

GIFT AID (NEED-BASED) ***Total amount:*** $2,556,829 (61% federal, 6% state, 8% institutional, 25% external sources). ***Receiving aid:*** Freshmen: 56% (121); all full-time undergraduates: 63% (629). ***Average award:*** Freshmen: $2516; Undergraduates: $2635. ***Scholarships, grants, and awards:*** Federal Pell, FSEOG, state, private, college/university gift aid from institutional funds, Academic Competitiveness Grant, National Smart Grant, institutional grants and scholarships.

GIFT AID (NON-NEED-BASED) ***Total amount:*** $450,279 (15% institutional, 85% external sources). ***Receiving aid:*** Freshmen: 5% (10). Undergraduates: 4% (35). ***Average award:*** Undergraduates: $1376. ***Scholarships, grants, and awards by category:*** *Academic interests/achievement:* 189 awards ($199,379 total): biological sciences, business, education, English, general academic interests/achievements, humanities, mathematics, physical sciences, premedicine, social sciences. *Creative arts/performance:* 18 awards ($43,300 total): art/fine arts. *Special achievements/activities:* 45 awards ($55,284 total): rodeo. *Special characteristics:* 35 awards ($31,780 total): children of faculty/staff, first-generation college students, international students, members of minority groups, veterans. ***Tuition waivers:*** Full or partial for senior citizens.

LOANS ***Student loans:*** $4,056,184 (63% need-based, 37% non-need-based). 83% of past graduating class borrowed through all loan programs. *Average indebtedness per student:* $20,996. ***Average need-based loan:*** Freshmen: $3181. Undergraduates: $3781. ***Parent loans:*** $453,697 (60% need-based, 40% non-need-based). ***Programs:*** FFEL (Subsidized and Unsubsidized Stafford, PLUS), Perkins, Federal TEACH Grant/Loan.

WORK-STUDY ***Federal work-study:*** Total amount: $247,405; 137 jobs averaging $1589. ***State or other work-study/employment:*** Total amount: $348,817 (15% need-based, 85% non-need-based). 246 part-time jobs averaging $1682.

ATHLETIC AWARDS Total amount: $629,497 (48% need-based, 52% non-need-based).

APPLYING FOR FINANCIAL AID ***Required financial aid forms:*** FAFSA, Student Data Form, and if applicable, Verification materials. ***Financial aid deadline (priority):*** 3/1. ***Notification date:*** Continuous beginning 4/15. Students must reply within 2 weeks of notification.

CONTACT Erica L. Jones, Director of Financial Aid, The University of Montana Western, 710 South Atlantic Street, Dillon, MT 59725, 406-683-7511 or toll-free 866-869-6668 (in-state), 877-683-7493 (out-of-state). *Fax:* 406-683-7510. *E-mail:* e_jones@umwestern.edu.

UNIVERSITY OF MONTEVALLO

Montevallo, AL

Tuition & fees (AL res): $6650 **Average undergraduate aid package: $7926**

ABOUT THE INSTITUTION State-supported, coed. ***Awards:*** bachelor's and master's degrees and post-master's certificates. 26 undergraduate majors. ***Total enrollment:*** 3,025. Undergraduates: 2,572. Freshmen: 518. Federal methodology is used as a basis for awarding need-based institutional aid.

UNDERGRADUATE EXPENSES for 2008–09 ***Application fee:*** $25. ***Tuition, state resident:*** full-time $6150; part-time $205 per credit hour. ***Tuition, nonresident:*** full-time $12,300; part-time $410 per credit hour. ***Required fees:*** full-time $500. Full-time tuition and fees vary according to course load. Part-time tuition and fees vary according to course load. ***College room and board:*** $4504. Room and board charges vary according to housing facility. ***Payment plan:*** Installment.

FRESHMAN FINANCIAL AID (Fall 2008, est.) 349 applied for aid; of those 71% were deemed to have need. 98% of freshmen with need received aid; of those 27% had need fully met. ***Average percent of need met:*** 71% (excluding resources awarded to replace EFC). ***Average financial aid package:*** $8301 (excluding resources awarded to replace EFC). 24% of all full-time freshmen had no need and received non-need-based gift aid.

UNDERGRADUATE FINANCIAL AID (Fall 2008, est.) 1,457 applied for aid; of those 75% were deemed to have need. 98% of undergraduates with need received aid; of those 30% had need fully met. ***Average percent of need met:*** 67% (excluding resources awarded to replace EFC). ***Average financial aid package:*** $7926 (excluding resources awarded to replace EFC). 18% of all full-time undergraduates had no need and received non-need-based gift aid.

GIFT AID (NEED-BASED) ***Total amount:*** $4,756,960 (59% federal, 1% state, 29% institutional, 11% external sources). ***Receiving aid:*** Freshmen: 42% (213); all full-time undergraduates: 37% (856). ***Average award:*** Freshmen: $5941; Undergraduates: $5300. ***Scholarships, grants, and awards:*** Federal Pell, FSEOG, state, private, college/university gift aid from institutional funds.

GIFT AID (NON-NEED-BASED) ***Total amount:*** $2,437,256 (82% institutional, 18% external sources). ***Average award:*** Freshmen: $4891. Undergraduates: $4658. ***Scholarships, grants, and awards by category:*** *Academic interests/achievement:* biological sciences, education, general academic interests/achievements, physical sciences. *Creative arts/performance:* art/fine arts, music. *Special achievements/activities:* junior miss. *Special characteristics:* international students, out-of-state students, veterans, veterans' children. ***Tuition waivers:*** Full or partial for employees or children of employees. ***ROTC:*** Army cooperative, Air Force cooperative.

LOANS ***Student loans:*** $8,510,831 (80% need-based, 20% non-need-based). 57% of past graduating class borrowed through all loan programs. *Average indebtedness per student:* $19,674. ***Average need-based loan:*** Freshmen: $3479. Undergraduates: $4014. ***Parent loans:*** $340,260 (48% need-based, 52% non-need-based). ***Programs:*** FFEL (Subsidized and Unsubsidized Stafford, PLUS), Perkins.

WORK-STUDY ***Federal work-study:*** Total amount: $166,486; 136 jobs averaging $1410. ***State or other work-study/employment:*** Part-time jobs available.

ATHLETIC AWARDS Total amount: $946,762 (25% need-based, 75% non-need-based).

APPLYING FOR FINANCIAL AID ***Required financial aid form:*** FAFSA. ***Financial aid deadline (priority):*** 4/1. ***Notification date:*** Continuous beginning 4/15. Students must reply within 2 weeks of notification.

CONTACT Ms. Maria Parker, Director of Student Financial Aid, University of Montevallo, Station 6050, Montevallo, AL 35115, 205-665-6050 or toll-free 800-292-4349. *Fax:* 205-665-6047. *E-mail:* finaid@montevallo.edu.

UNIVERSITY OF NEBRASKA AT KEARNEY

Kearney, NE

Tuition & fees (NE res): $5426 **Average undergraduate aid package: $8494**

ABOUT THE INSTITUTION State-supported, coed. ***Awards:*** bachelor's and master's degrees and post-master's certificates. 41 undergraduate majors. ***Total enrollment:*** 6,543. Undergraduates: 5,104. Freshmen: 1,045. Federal methodology is used as a basis for awarding need-based institutional aid.

UNDERGRADUATE EXPENSES for 2008–09 ***Application fee:*** $45. ***Tuition, state resident:*** full-time $4365; part-time $145.50 per hour. ***Tuition, nonresident:*** full-time $8940; part-time $298 per hour. ***Required fees:*** full-time $1061; $21.25 per hour or $73.50 per term. Full-time tuition and fees vary according to course level, course load, degree level, and location. Part-time tuition and fees vary according to course level, course load, degree level, and location. ***College room and board:*** $6330; ***Room only:*** $3270. Room and board charges vary according to board plan and housing facility. ***Payment plan:*** Installment.

FRESHMAN FINANCIAL AID (Fall 2008, est.) 828 applied for aid; of those 77% were deemed to have need. 99% of freshmen with need received aid; of those 35% had need fully met. ***Average percent of need met:*** 80% (excluding resources awarded to replace EFC). ***Average financial aid package:*** $8903 (excluding resources awarded to replace EFC). 4% of all full-time freshmen had no need and received non-need-based gift aid.

UNDERGRADUATE FINANCIAL AID (Fall 2008, est.) 3,527 applied for aid; of those 74% were deemed to have need. 98% of undergraduates with need received aid; of those 33% had need fully met. ***Average percent of need met:*** 79% (excluding resources awarded to replace EFC). ***Average financial aid package:*** $8494 (excluding resources awarded to replace EFC). 13% of all full-time undergraduates had no need and received non-need-based gift aid.

GIFT AID (NEED-BASED) ***Total amount:*** $110,876,984 (4% federal, 1% state, 94% institutional, 1% external sources). ***Receiving aid:*** Freshmen: 37% (380); all full-time undergraduates: 35% (1,554). ***Average award:*** Freshmen: $4439; Undergraduates: $3858. ***Scholarships, grants, and awards:*** Federal Pell, FSEOG, state, private, college/university gift aid from institutional funds.

GIFT AID (NON-NEED-BASED) ***Total amount:*** $3,931,248 (1% federal, 56% institutional, 43% external sources). ***Receiving aid:*** Freshmen: 39% (403). Undergraduates: 22% (985). ***Average award:*** Freshmen: $1842. Undergraduates: $2338. ***Scholarships, grants, and awards by category:*** *Academic interests/achievement:* communication. *Creative arts/performance:* applied art and design, art/fine arts, debating, journalism/publications, music. *Special achievements/activities:* cheerleading/drum major. *Special characteristics:* children of faculty/staff, ethnic background, first-generation college students, international students, out-of-state students, veterans, veterans' children. ***Tuition waivers:*** Full or partial for employees or children of employees.

LOANS ***Student loans:*** $20,461,246 (44% need-based, 56% non-need-based). 70% of past graduating class borrowed through all loan programs. *Average indebtedness per student:* $18,551. ***Average need-based loan:*** Freshmen: $2542. Undergraduates: $3454. ***Parent loans:*** $990,108 (100% non-need-based). ***Programs:*** FFEL (Subsidized Stafford, PLUS), Perkins, college/university.

WORK-STUDY ***Federal work-study:*** Total amount: $1,080,889; jobs available.

ATHLETIC AWARDS Total amount: $519,561 (100% non-need-based).

APPLYING FOR FINANCIAL AID ***Required financial aid forms:*** FAFSA, institution's own form. ***Financial aid deadline (priority):*** 4/1. ***Notification date:*** Continuous.

CONTACT Financial Aid Office, University of Nebraska at Kearney, Memorial Student Affairs Building, 905 West 25th Street, Kearney, NE 68849-0001, 308-865-8520 or toll-free 800-532-7639. *Fax:* 308-865-8096.

UNIVERSITY OF NEBRASKA AT OMAHA

Omaha, NE

Tuition & fees (NE res): $5880 Average undergraduate aid package: $2445

ABOUT THE INSTITUTION State-supported, coed. ***Awards:*** bachelor's, master's, and doctoral degrees and post-bachelor's and post-master's certificates. 66 undergraduate majors. ***Total enrollment:*** 14,213. Undergraduates: 11,327. Freshmen: 1,816. Federal methodology is used as a basis for awarding need-based institutional aid.

UNDERGRADUATE EXPENSES for 2008–09 ***Application fee:*** $45. ***Tuition, state resident:*** full-time $4920; part-time $164 per credit hour. ***Tuition, nonresident:*** full-time $14,498; part-time $483.25 per credit hour. ***Required fees:*** full-time $960. Full-time tuition and fees vary according to course load and reciprocity agreements. Part-time tuition and fees vary according to course load and reciprocity agreements. ***College room and board:*** $6980. Room and board charges vary according to board plan. ***Payment plans:*** Installment, deferred payment.

FRESHMAN FINANCIAL AID (Fall 2008, est.) 1,093 applied for aid; of those 67% were deemed to have need. 96% of freshmen with need received aid. ***Average financial aid package:*** $2079 (excluding resources awarded to replace EFC). 10% of all full-time freshmen had no need and received non-need-based gift aid.

UNDERGRADUATE FINANCIAL AID (Fall 2008, est.) 5,445 applied for aid; of those 72% were deemed to have need. 96% of undergraduates with need received aid. ***Average financial aid package:*** $2445 (excluding resources awarded to replace EFC). 5% of all full-time undergraduates had no need and received non-need-based gift aid.

GIFT AID (NEED-BASED) ***Total amount:*** $17,447,000 (45% federal, 9% state, 30% institutional, 16% external sources). ***Receiving aid:*** Freshmen: 30% (470); all full-time undergraduates: 30% (2,584). ***Average award:*** Freshmen: $1758; Undergraduates: $2023. ***Scholarships, grants, and awards:*** Federal Pell, FSEOG, state, private, college/university gift aid from institutional funds.

GIFT AID (NON-NEED-BASED) ***Receiving aid:*** Freshmen: 33% (519). Undergraduates: 21% (1,781). ***Average award:*** Freshmen: $2285. Undergraduates: $2250. ***Scholarships, grants, and awards by category:*** *Academic interests/achievement:* biological sciences, business, communication, computer science, education, engineering/technologies, English, foreign languages, general academic interests/achievements, home economics, mathematics, physical sciences, premedicine, social sciences. *Creative arts/performance:* art/fine arts, creative writing, debating, journalism/publications, music, performing arts, theater/drama. *Special achievements/activities:* general special achievements/activities, leadership, memberships. *Special characteristics:* adult students, children and siblings of alumni, children of faculty/staff, ethnic background, first-generation college students, handicapped students, international students, members of minority groups, out-of-state students, veterans' children. ***Tuition waivers:*** Full or partial for children of alumni, employees or children of employees. ***ROTC:*** Army cooperative, Air Force.

LOANS ***Student loans:*** $43,566,000 (47% need-based, 53% non-need-based). 48% of past graduating class borrowed through all loan programs. *Average indebtedness per student:* $19,000. ***Average need-based loan:*** Freshmen: $2659. Undergraduates: $3201. ***Parent loans:*** $1,749,000 (100% non-need-based). ***Programs:*** FFEL (Subsidized and Unsubsidized Stafford, PLUS), Perkins, college/university.

WORK-STUDY ***Federal work-study:*** Total amount: $574,000; 400 jobs averaging $1500.

ATHLETIC AWARDS Total amount: $766,000 (100% need-based).

APPLYING FOR FINANCIAL AID ***Required financial aid form:*** FAFSA. ***Financial aid deadline (priority):*** 3/1. ***Notification date:*** Continuous beginning 4/1. Students must reply within 2 weeks of notification.

CONTACT Office of Financial Aid, University of Nebraska at Omaha, 103 Eppley Administration Building, Omaha, NE 68182-0187, 402-554-2327 or toll-free 800-858-8648 (in-state). *Fax:* 402-554-3472. *E-mail:* finaid@unomaha.edu.

UNIVERSITY OF NEBRASKA–LINCOLN

Lincoln, NE

Tuition & fees (NE res): $6585 Average undergraduate aid package: $9521

ABOUT THE INSTITUTION State-supported, coed. ***Awards:*** associate, bachelor's, master's, doctoral, and first professional degrees and post-bachelor's and post-master's certificates. 131 undergraduate majors. ***Total enrollment:*** 23,537. Undergraduates: 18,490. Freshmen: 4,164. Both federal and institutional methodology are used as a basis for awarding need-based institutional aid.

UNDERGRADUATE EXPENSES for 2008–09 ***Application fee:*** $45. ***Tuition, state resident:*** full-time $5393; part-time $179.75 per semester hour. ***Tuition, nonresident:*** full-time $16,013; part-time $533.75 per semester hour. ***Required fees:*** full-time $1192; $242 per term. Full-time tuition and fees vary according to course load, program, and reciprocity agreements. Part-time tuition and fees vary according to course load, program, and reciprocity agreements. ***College room and board:*** $6882; ***Room only:*** $3629. Room and board charges vary according to board plan and housing facility. ***Payment plan:*** Installment.

FRESHMAN FINANCIAL AID (Fall 2007) 2,895 applied for aid; of those 67% were deemed to have need. 98% of freshmen with need received aid; of those 38% had need fully met. ***Average percent of need met:*** 75% (excluding resources awarded to replace EFC). ***Average financial aid package:*** $10,106 (excluding resources awarded to replace EFC). 14% of all full-time freshmen had no need and received non-need-based gift aid.

UNDERGRADUATE FINANCIAL AID (Fall 2007) 10,653 applied for aid; of those 72% were deemed to have need. 97% of undergraduates with need received aid; of those 32% had need fully met. ***Average percent of need met:*** 73% (excluding resources awarded to replace EFC). ***Average financial aid package:*** $9521 (excluding resources awarded to replace EFC). 8% of all full-time undergraduates had no need and received non-need-based gift aid.

GIFT AID (NEED-BASED) ***Total amount:*** $35,119,861 (32% federal, 6% state, 49% institutional, 13% external sources). ***Receiving aid:*** Freshmen: 39% (1,661); all full-time undergraduates: 34% (5,667). ***Average award:*** Freshmen: $7219; Undergraduates: $6459. ***Scholarships, grants, and awards:*** Federal Pell, FSEOG, state, private, college/university gift aid from institutional funds.

GIFT AID (NON-NEED-BASED) ***Total amount:*** $21,571,198 (5% federal, 82% institutional, 13% external sources). ***Receiving aid:*** Freshmen: 6% (243). Undergraduates: 4% (651). ***Average award:*** Freshmen: $5049. Undergraduates: $5262. ***Scholarships, grants, and awards by category:*** *Academic interests/achievement:* agriculture, architecture, biological sciences, business, computer science, education, engineering/technologies, English, foreign languages, general academic interests/achievements, health fields, home economics, humanities, international studies, mathematics, physical sciences, premedicine, social sciences. *Creative arts/performance:* art/fine arts, cinema/film/broadcasting, dance, journalism/publications, music, performing arts, theater/drama. *Special achievements/activities:* cheerleading/drum major, community service, leadership. *Special characteristics:* children and siblings of alumni, ethnic background, handicapped students, international students, members of minority groups, out-of-state students, veterans' children. ***Tuition waivers:*** Full or partial for employees or children of employees. ***ROTC:*** Army, Naval, Air Force.

LOANS ***Student loans:*** $48,036,276 (66% need-based, 34% non-need-based). 61% of past graduating class borrowed through all loan programs. *Average indebtedness per student:* $18,958. ***Average need-based loan:*** Freshmen: $3266. Undergraduates: $4085. ***Parent loans:*** $24,452,090 (44% need-based, 56% non-need-based). ***Programs:*** Federal Direct (Subsidized and Unsubsidized Stafford, PLUS), Perkins, college/university.

WORK-STUDY ***Federal work-study:*** Total amount: $2,662,982; 1,166 jobs averaging $2284.

ATHLETIC AWARDS Total amount: $6,256,294 (100% non-need-based).

APPLYING FOR FINANCIAL AID ***Required financial aid form:*** FAFSA. ***Financial aid deadline (priority):*** 4/8. ***Notification date:*** Continuous.

CONTACT Ms. Jo Tederman, Assistant Director of Scholarships and Financial Aid, University of Nebraska–Lincoln, 17 Canfield Administration Building, Lincoln, NE 68588-0411, 402-472-2030 or toll-free 800-742-8800. *Fax:* 402-472-9826.

UNIVERSITY OF NEBRASKA MEDICAL CENTER

Omaha, NE

ABOUT THE INSTITUTION State-supported, coed. ***Awards:*** bachelor's, master's, doctoral, and first professional degrees and post-bachelor's, post-master's, and first professional certificates. 7 undergraduate majors. ***Total enrollment:*** 3,194. Undergraduates: 806.

GIFT AID (NEED-BASED) ***Scholarships, grants, and awards:*** Federal Pell, FSEOG, state, private, college/university gift aid from institutional funds.

LOANS ***Programs:*** FFEL (Subsidized and Unsubsidized Stafford, PLUS), Perkins, Federal Nursing, state, college/university.

APPLYING FOR FINANCIAL AID ***Required financial aid forms:*** FAFSA, institution's own form.

CONTACT Judi Walker, Director of Financial Aid, University of Nebraska Medical Center, 984265 Nebraska Medical Center, Omaha, NE 68198-4265, 402-559-6409 or toll-free 800-626-8431 Ext. 6468. *Fax:* 402-559-6796. *E-mail:* jdwalker@unmc.edu.

UNIVERSITY OF NEVADA, LAS VEGAS

Las Vegas, NV

Tuition & fees (NV res): $4808 **Average undergraduate aid package: $7910**

ABOUT THE INSTITUTION State-supported, coed. ***Awards:*** bachelor's, master's, doctoral, and first professional degrees and post-bachelor's, post-master's, and first professional certificates. 92 undergraduate majors. ***Total enrollment:*** 28,617. Undergraduates: 22,149. Freshmen: 3,255. Federal methodology is used as a basis for awarding need-based institutional aid.

UNDERGRADUATE EXPENSES for 2009–10 ***Application fee:*** $60. ***Tuition, state resident:*** full-time $4200; part-time $136 per credit hour. ***Tuition, nonresident:*** full-time $16,540; part-time $285.50 per credit hour. ***Required fees:*** full-time $608. ***College room and board:*** $10,456; ***Room only:*** $6546.

FRESHMAN FINANCIAL AID (Fall 2008, est.) 1,988 applied for aid; of those 72% were deemed to have need. 97% of freshmen with need received aid; of those 20% had need fully met. ***Average percent of need met:*** 66% (excluding resources awarded to replace EFC). ***Average financial aid package:*** $8308 (excluding resources awarded to replace EFC). 2% of all full-time freshmen had no need and received non-need-based gift aid.

UNDERGRADUATE FINANCIAL AID (Fall 2008, est.) 8,005 applied for aid; of those 80% were deemed to have need. 96% of undergraduates with need received aid; of those 15% had need fully met. ***Average percent of need met:*** 62% (excluding resources awarded to replace EFC). ***Average financial aid package:*** $7910 (excluding resources awarded to replace EFC). 3% of all full-time undergraduates had no need and received non-need-based gift aid.

GIFT AID (NEED-BASED) ***Total amount:*** $22,748,790 (62% federal, 19% state, 15% institutional, 4% external sources). ***Receiving aid:*** Freshmen: 25% (815); all full-time undergraduates: 24% (3,740). ***Average award:*** Freshmen: $4341; Undergraduates: $4305. ***Scholarships, grants, and awards:*** Federal Pell, FSEOG, state, private, college/university gift aid from institutional funds.

GIFT AID (NON-NEED-BASED) ***Total amount:*** $13,490,543 (18% federal, 61% state, 14% institutional, 7% external sources). ***Receiving aid:*** Freshmen: 29% (954). Undergraduates: 18% (2,889). ***Average award:*** Freshmen: $950. Undergraduates: $1063. ***Scholarships, grants, and awards by category:*** *Academic interests/achievement:* architecture, biological sciences, business, communication, computer science, education, engineering/technologies, English, foreign languages, general academic interests/achievements, health fields, humanities, international studies, mathematics, physical sciences, premedicine, social sciences. *Creative arts/performance:* applied art and design, art/fine arts, cinema/film/broadcasting, creative writing, dance, debating, general creative arts/performance, journalism/publications, music, performing arts, theater/drama. *Special achievements/activities:* cheerleading/drum major, community service, general special achievements/activities, leadership, rodeo. *Special characteristics:* adult students, children and siblings of alumni, children of faculty/staff, children of public servants, children of union members/company employees, children with a deceased or disabled parent, ethnic background, first-generation college students, general special characteristics, handicapped students, international students, local/state students, members of minority groups, out-of-state students, previous college experience, veterans, veterans' children.

LOANS ***Student loans:*** $39,600,903 (71% need-based, 29% non-need-based). 42% of past graduating class borrowed through all loan programs. *Average indebtedness per student:* $19,700. ***Average need-based loan:*** Freshmen: $2495. Undergraduates: $3893. ***Parent loans:*** $13,567,479 (41% need-based, 59% non-need-based). ***Programs:*** Federal Direct (Subsidized and Unsubsidized Stafford, PLUS), Perkins, Federal Nursing, state, college/university.

WORK-STUDY ***Federal work-study:*** Total amount: $1,169,635; 482 jobs averaging $2736. ***State or other work-study/employment:*** Total amount: $1,426,671 (95% need-based, 5% non-need-based). 629 part-time jobs averaging $2556.

ATHLETIC AWARDS Total amount: $5,302,941 (23% need-based, 77% non-need-based).

APPLYING FOR FINANCIAL AID ***Required financial aid forms:*** FAFSA, institution's own form. ***Financial aid deadline (priority):*** 2/1. ***Notification date:*** Continuous beginning 3/20. Students must reply within 2 weeks of notification.

CONTACT Financial Aid & Scholarships, University of Nevada, Las Vegas, 4505 Maryland Parkway, Las Vegas, NV 89154-2016, 702-895-3424. *Fax:* 702-895-1353. *E-mail:* financialaid@unlv.edu.

UNIVERSITY OF NEVADA, RENO

Reno, NV

Tuition & fees (NV res): $4616 **Average undergraduate aid package: $6943**

ABOUT THE INSTITUTION State-supported, coed. ***Awards:*** bachelor's, master's, doctoral, and first professional degrees and post-bachelor's and post-master's certificates. 97 undergraduate majors. ***Total enrollment:*** 16,867. Undergraduates: 13,367. Freshmen: 2,296. Federal methodology is used as a basis for awarding need-based institutional aid.

UNDERGRADUATE EXPENSES for 2009–10 ***Application fee:*** $60. ***One-time required fee:*** $106. ***Tuition, state resident:*** full-time $4200; part-time $140 per credit. ***Tuition, nonresident:*** full-time $16,540; part-time $289.50 per credit. ***Required fees:*** full-time $416. ***College room and board:*** $10,595; ***Room only:*** $6100.

FRESHMAN FINANCIAL AID (Fall 2007) 1,267 applied for aid; of those 62% were deemed to have need. 100% of freshmen with need received aid; of those 16% had need fully met. ***Average percent of need met:*** 54% (excluding resources awarded to replace EFC). ***Average financial aid package:*** $5351 (excluding resources awarded to replace EFC). 54% of all full-time freshmen had no need and received non-need-based gift aid.

UNDERGRADUATE FINANCIAL AID (Fall 2007) 4,699 applied for aid; of those 74% were deemed to have need. 96% of undergraduates with need received aid; of those 17% had need fully met. ***Average percent of need met:*** 59% (excluding resources awarded to replace EFC). ***Average financial aid package:*** $6943 (excluding resources awarded to replace EFC). 46% of all full-time undergraduates had no need and received non-need-based gift aid.

GIFT AID (NEED-BASED) ***Total amount:*** $15,611,600 (35% federal, 29% state, 29% institutional, 7% external sources). ***Receiving aid:*** Freshmen: 29% (647); all full-time undergraduates: 28% (2,856). ***Average award:*** Freshmen: $5324; Undergraduates: $5499. ***Scholarships, grants, and awards:*** Federal Pell, FSEOG, state, private, college/university gift aid from institutional funds.

GIFT AID (NON-NEED-BASED) ***Total amount:*** $13,629,462 (2% federal, 54% state, 34% institutional, 10% external sources). ***Receiving aid:*** Freshmen: 31% (681). Undergraduates: 25% (2,536). ***Average award:*** Freshmen: $2495. Undergraduates: $2471. ***Scholarships, grants, and awards by category:*** *Academic interests/achievement:* general academic interests/achievements. *Creative arts/performance:* general creative arts/performance, music, theater/

drama. *Special characteristics:* adult students, children and siblings of alumni, ethnic background, first-generation college students, local/state students, married students, members of minority groups. ***ROTC:*** Army.

LOANS ***Student loans:*** $17,730,170 (76% need-based, 24% non-need-based). 36% of past graduating class borrowed through all loan programs. *Average indebtedness per student:* $14,303. ***Average need-based loan:*** Freshmen: $3044. Undergraduates: $4324. ***Parent loans:*** $2,322,112 (42% need-based, 58% non-need-based). ***Programs:*** FFEL (Subsidized and Unsubsidized Stafford), Perkins, Federal Nursing, college/university.

WORK-STUDY ***Federal work-study:*** Total amount: $410,998; jobs available. ***State or other work-study/employment:*** Total amount: $32,980 (43% need-based, 57% non-need-based). Part-time jobs available.

ATHLETIC AWARDS Total amount: $5,219,322 (15% need-based, 85% non-need-based).

APPLYING FOR FINANCIAL AID ***Required financial aid form:*** FAFSA. ***Financial aid deadline (priority):*** 2/15. ***Notification date:*** Continuous beginning 4/1. Students must reply within 2 weeks of notification.

CONTACT Ms. Sandy Guidry, Interim Director of Student Financial Aid, University of Nevada, Reno, Student Services Building, Room 316, Reno, NV 89557, 775-784-4666 or toll-free 866-263-8232. *Fax:* 775-784-1025. *E-mail:* sguidry@unr.nevada.edu.

UNIVERSITY OF NEW ENGLAND

Biddeford, ME

Tuition & fees: $27,920 **Average undergraduate aid package: $23,956**

ABOUT THE INSTITUTION Independent, coed. ***Awards:*** associate, bachelor's, master's, and first professional degrees and post-bachelor's and post-master's certificates. 38 undergraduate majors. ***Total enrollment:*** 4,267. Undergraduates: 2,140. Federal methodology is used as a basis for awarding need-based institutional aid.

UNDERGRADUATE EXPENSES for 2009–10 ***Application fee:*** $40. ***Comprehensive fee:*** $38,790 includes full-time tuition ($26,940), mandatory fees ($980), and room and board ($10,870). ***Part-time tuition:*** $970 per credit hour.

FRESHMAN FINANCIAL AID (Fall 2008, est.) 523 applied for aid; of those 92% were deemed to have need. 100% of freshmen with need received aid; of those 15% had need fully met. ***Average percent of need met:*** 81% (excluding resources awarded to replace EFC). ***Average financial aid package:*** $23,854 (excluding resources awarded to replace EFC). 14% of all full-time freshmen had no need and received non-need-based gift aid.

UNDERGRADUATE FINANCIAL AID (Fall 2008, est.) 1,777 applied for aid; of those 93% were deemed to have need. 100% of undergraduates with need received aid; of those 19% had need fully met. ***Average percent of need met:*** 83% (excluding resources awarded to replace EFC). ***Average financial aid package:*** $23,956 (excluding resources awarded to replace EFC). 17% of all full-time undergraduates had no need and received non-need-based gift aid.

GIFT AID (NEED-BASED) ***Total amount:*** $20,923,861 (9% federal, 3% state, 84% institutional, 4% external sources). ***Receiving aid:*** Freshmen: 86% (480); all full-time undergraduates: 82% (1,637). ***Average award:*** Freshmen: $13,787; Undergraduates: $12,857. ***Scholarships, grants, and awards:*** Federal Pell, FSEOG, state, private, college/university gift aid from institutional funds.

GIFT AID (NON-NEED-BASED) ***Total amount:*** $3,482,270 (95% institutional, 5% external sources). ***Receiving aid:*** Freshmen: 5% (27). Undergraduates: 5% (101). ***Average award:*** Freshmen: $8965. Undergraduates: $8424. ***Scholarships, grants, and awards by category:*** *Academic interests/achievement:* 1,840 awards ($13,181,283 total): biological sciences, business, communication, education, English, general academic interests/achievements, health fields, humanities, international studies, mathematics, physical sciences, premedicine, social sciences. *Special achievements/activities:* 456 awards ($302,040 total): community service, general special achievements/activities, leadership. *Special characteristics:* 99 awards ($339,569 total): children and siblings of alumni, ethnic background, members of minority groups, siblings of current students. ***ROTC:*** Army cooperative.

LOANS ***Student loans:*** $24,048,043 (73% need-based, 27% non-need-based). 95% of past graduating class borrowed through all loan programs. *Average indebtedness per student:* $44,325. ***Average need-based loan:*** Freshmen: $8540. Undergraduates: $10,836. ***Parent loans:*** $4,592,181 (42% need-based, 58% non-need-based). ***Programs:*** FFEL (Subsidized and Unsubsidized Stafford, PLUS), Perkins, Federal Nursing, state, college/university.

WORK-STUDY ***Federal work-study:*** Total amount: $2,412,992; 850 jobs averaging $1946. ***State or other work-study/employment:*** Part-time jobs available.

APPLYING FOR FINANCIAL AID ***Required financial aid form:*** FAFSA. ***Financial aid deadline (priority):*** 5/1. ***Notification date:*** Continuous.

CONTACT John R. Bowie, Director of Financial Aid, University of New England, 11 Hills Beach Road, Biddeford, ME 04005, 207-602-2342 or toll-free 800-477-4UNE. *Fax:* 207-602-5946. *E-mail:* finaid@une.edu.

UNIVERSITY OF NEW HAMPSHIRE

Durham, NH

Tuition & fees (NH res): $11,738 **Average undergraduate aid package: $17,910**

ABOUT THE INSTITUTION State-supported, coed. ***Awards:*** associate, bachelor's, master's, and doctoral degrees and post-bachelor's and post-master's certificates. 86 undergraduate majors. ***Total enrollment:*** 14,964. Undergraduates: 12,218. Freshmen: 2,692. Federal methodology is used as a basis for awarding need-based institutional aid.

UNDERGRADUATE EXPENSES for 2008–09 ***Application fee:*** $50. ***Tuition, state resident:*** full-time $9402; part-time $393 per credit hour. ***Tuition, nonresident:*** full-time $22,900; part-time $954 per credit hour. ***Required fees:*** full-time $2336; $584 per term. Part-time tuition and fees vary according to course load. ***College room and board:*** $8596; ***Room only:*** $5306. Room and board charges vary according to board plan and housing facility. ***Payment plan:*** Installment.

FRESHMAN FINANCIAL AID (Fall 2007) 2,030 applied for aid; of those 75% were deemed to have need. 98% of freshmen with need received aid; of those 26% had need fully met. ***Average percent of need met:*** 84% (excluding resources awarded to replace EFC). ***Average financial aid package:*** $17,812 (excluding resources awarded to replace EFC). 22% of all full-time freshmen had no need and received non-need-based gift aid.

UNDERGRADUATE FINANCIAL AID (Fall 2007) 8,082 applied for aid; of those 80% were deemed to have need. 99% of undergraduates with need received aid; of those 22% had need fully met. ***Average percent of need met:*** 81% (excluding resources awarded to replace EFC). ***Average financial aid package:*** $17,910 (excluding resources awarded to replace EFC). 22% of all full-time undergraduates had no need and received non-need-based gift aid.

GIFT AID (NEED-BASED) ***Total amount:*** $36,887,800 (22% federal, 3% state, 57% institutional, 18% external sources). ***Receiving aid:*** Freshmen: 36% (889); all full-time undergraduates: 39% (4,230). ***Average award:*** Freshmen: $4122; Undergraduates: $3025. ***Scholarships, grants, and awards:*** Federal Pell, FSEOG, state, private, college/university gift aid from institutional funds.

GIFT AID (NON-NEED-BASED) ***Total amount:*** $14,682,959 (100% institutional). ***Receiving aid:*** Undergraduates: 3% (341). ***Average award:*** Freshmen: $6345. Undergraduates: $7552. ***Scholarships, grants, and awards by category:*** *Academic interests/achievement:* agriculture, business, education, engineering/technologies, English, general academic interests/achievements, health fields, humanities, mathematics, military science. *Creative arts/performance:* art/fine arts, dance, music, theater/drama. *Special achievements/activities:* community service. *Special characteristics:* children and siblings of alumni, children of faculty/staff, handicapped students, international students, local/state students. ***Tuition waivers:*** Full or partial for employees or children of employees. ***ROTC:*** Army, Air Force.

LOANS ***Student loans:*** $79,893,915 (43% need-based, 57% non-need-based). 75% of past graduating class borrowed through all loan programs. *Average indebtedness per student:* $27,516. ***Average need-based loan:*** Freshmen: $2841. Undergraduates: $3848. ***Parent loans:*** $18,948,717 (100% non-need-based). ***Programs:*** FFEL (Subsidized and Unsubsidized Stafford, PLUS), Perkins, state, college/university.

WORK-STUDY ***Federal work-study:*** Total amount: $9,416,757; 3,786 jobs averaging $2192. ***State or other work-study/employment:*** Total amount: $5,920,328 (100% non-need-based). 2,782 part-time jobs averaging $1657.

ATHLETIC AWARDS Total amount: $6,779,490 (100% non-need-based).

APPLYING FOR FINANCIAL AID ***Required financial aid form:*** FAFSA. ***Financial aid deadline (priority):*** 3/1. ***Notification date:*** Continuous beginning 3/1.

CONTACT Susan K. Allen, Director of Financial Aid, University of New Hampshire, 11 Garrison Avenue, Durham, NH 03824, 603-862-3600. *Fax:* 603-862-1947. *E-mail:* financial.aid@unh.edu.

UNIVERSITY OF NEW HAMPSHIRE AT MANCHESTER

Manchester, NH

Tuition & fees (NH res): $9901 **Average undergraduate aid package: $9326**

ABOUT THE INSTITUTION State-supported, coed. ***Awards:*** associate, bachelor's, and master's degrees. 13 undergraduate majors. ***Total enrollment:*** 792. Undergraduates: 792. Freshmen: 109. Federal methodology is used as a basis for awarding need-based institutional aid.

UNDERGRADUATE EXPENSES for 2008–09 ***Application fee:*** $45. ***Tuition, state resident:*** full-time $8980; part-time $374 per credit. ***Tuition, nonresident:*** full-time $22,740; part-time $948 per credit. ***Required fees:*** full-time $921. Full-time tuition and fees vary according to course load and program. Part-time tuition and fees vary according to course load and program.

FRESHMAN FINANCIAL AID (Fall 2007) 88 applied for aid; of those 70% were deemed to have need. 92% of freshmen with need received aid; of those 16% had need fully met. ***Average percent of need met:*** 60% (excluding resources awarded to replace EFC). ***Average financial aid package:*** $6958 (excluding resources awarded to replace EFC).

UNDERGRADUATE FINANCIAL AID (Fall 2007) 468 applied for aid; of those 80% were deemed to have need. 97% of undergraduates with need received aid; of those 14% had need fully met. ***Average percent of need met:*** 60% (excluding resources awarded to replace EFC). ***Average financial aid package:*** $9326 (excluding resources awarded to replace EFC). 1% of all full-time undergraduates had no need and received non-need-based gift aid.

GIFT AID (NEED-BASED) ***Total amount:*** $601,447 (52% federal, 8% state, 20% institutional, 20% external sources). ***Receiving aid:*** Freshmen: 11% (13); all full-time undergraduates: 16% (127). ***Average award:*** Freshmen: $1119; Undergraduates: $1097. ***Scholarships, grants, and awards:*** Federal Pell, FSEOG, state, private, college/university gift aid from institutional funds.

GIFT AID (NON-NEED-BASED) ***Total amount:*** $67,832 (100% institutional). ***Receiving aid:*** Undergraduates: 1% (10). ***Average award:*** Undergraduates: $750. ***Scholarships, grants, and awards by category:*** *Academic interests/achievement:* general academic interests/achievements. *Special characteristics:* children of faculty/staff. ***Tuition waivers:*** Full or partial for employees or children of employees, senior citizens. ***ROTC:*** Army cooperative, Air Force cooperative.

LOANS ***Student loans:*** $3,225,164 (47% need-based, 53% non-need-based). 69% of past graduating class borrowed through all loan programs. *Average indebtedness per student:* $18,919. ***Average need-based loan:*** Freshmen: $2366. Undergraduates: $3340. ***Parent loans:*** $125,122 (100% non-need-based). ***Programs:*** FFEL (Subsidized and Unsubsidized Stafford, PLUS), Perkins, state, college/university.

WORK-STUDY ***Federal work-study:*** Total amount: $228,608; 106 jobs averaging $2138.

APPLYING FOR FINANCIAL AID ***Required financial aid form:*** FAFSA. ***Financial aid deadline (priority):*** 3/1. ***Notification date:*** Continuous beginning 4/1.

CONTACT Jodi Abad, Assistant Director of Financial Aid, University of New Hampshire at Manchester, French Hall, Manchester, NH 03101-1113, 603-641-4146. *Fax:* 603-641-4125.

UNIVERSITY OF NEW HAVEN

West Haven, CT

Tuition & fees: $29,682 **Average undergraduate aid package: $17,762**

ABOUT THE INSTITUTION Independent, coed. ***Awards:*** associate, bachelor's, and master's degrees and post-bachelor's and post-master's certificates. 48 undergraduate majors. ***Total enrollment:*** 5,233. Undergraduates: 3,552. Freshmen: 1,148. Federal methodology is used as a basis for awarding need-based institutional aid.

UNDERGRADUATE EXPENSES for 2009–10 ***Application fee:*** $75. ***Comprehensive fee:*** $41,886 includes full-time tuition ($28,250), mandatory fees ($1432), and room and board ($12,204). ***College room only:*** $7600. ***Part-time tuition:*** $471 per credit hour. ***Part-time fees:*** $63 per credit hour.

FRESHMAN FINANCIAL AID (Fall 2008, est.) 1,038 applied for aid; of those 90% were deemed to have need. 100% of freshmen with need received aid; of those 14% had need fully met. ***Average percent of need met:*** 68% (excluding resources awarded to replace EFC). ***Average financial aid package:*** $18,781 (excluding resources awarded to replace EFC). 15% of all full-time freshmen had no need and received non-need-based gift aid.

UNDERGRADUATE FINANCIAL AID (Fall 2008, est.) 2,698 applied for aid; of those 89% were deemed to have need. 100% of undergraduates with need received aid; of those 14% had need fully met. ***Average percent of need met:*** 65% (excluding resources awarded to replace EFC). ***Average financial aid package:*** $17,762 (excluding resources awarded to replace EFC). 10% of all full-time undergraduates had no need and received non-need-based gift aid.

GIFT AID (NEED-BASED) ***Total amount:*** $32,358,250 (10% federal, 10% state, 77% institutional, 3% external sources). ***Receiving aid:*** Freshmen: 83% (932); all full-time undergraduates: 78% (2,391). ***Average award:*** Freshmen: $15,807; Undergraduates: $14,208. ***Scholarships, grants, and awards:*** Federal Pell, FSEOG, state, private, college/university gift aid from institutional funds.

GIFT AID (NON-NEED-BASED) ***Total amount:*** $3,405,413 (100% institutional). ***Receiving aid:*** Freshmen: 9% (99). Undergraduates: 8% (240). ***Average award:*** Freshmen: $9007. Undergraduates: $7922.

LOANS ***Student loans:*** $35,283,776 (26% need-based, 74% non-need-based). 82% of past graduating class borrowed through all loan programs. *Average indebtedness per student:* $33,964. ***Average need-based loan:*** Freshmen: $3502. Undergraduates: $4467. ***Parent loans:*** $5,239,270 (100% non-need-based). ***Programs:*** FFEL (Subsidized and Unsubsidized Stafford, PLUS), Perkins.

WORK-STUDY ***Federal work-study:*** Total amount: $210,000; 160 jobs averaging $1050.

ATHLETIC AWARDS Total amount: $1,795,129 (84% need-based, 16% non-need-based).

APPLYING FOR FINANCIAL AID ***Required financial aid forms:*** FAFSA, federal tax returns. ***Financial aid deadline:*** 3/1 (priority: 3/1). ***Notification date:*** Continuous beginning 3/15. Students must reply by 5/1 or within 2 weeks of notification.

CONTACT Mrs. Karen Flynn, Director of Financial Aid, University of New Haven, 300 Boston Post Road, West Haven, CT 06516-1916, 203-932-7315 or toll-free 800-DIAL-UNH. *Fax:* 203-931-6050. *E-mail:* financialaid@newhaven.edu.

UNIVERSITY OF NEW MEXICO

Albuquerque, NM

CONTACT Office of Student Financial Aid, University of New Mexico, Mesa Vista Hall North, Albuquerque, NM 87131, 505-277-2041 or toll-free 800-CALLUNM (in-state). *Fax:* 505-277-6326. *E-mail:* finaid@unm.edu.

UNIVERSITY OF NEW ORLEANS

New Orleans, LA

Tuition & fees (LA res): $3488 **Average undergraduate aid package: $9312**

ABOUT THE INSTITUTION State-supported, coed. ***Awards:*** bachelor's, master's, and doctoral degrees and post-bachelor's certificates. 50 undergraduate majors. ***Total enrollment:*** 11,428. Undergraduates: 8,628. Freshmen: 1,267. Federal methodology is used as a basis for awarding need-based institutional aid.

UNDERGRADUATE EXPENSES for 2008–09 ***Application fee:*** $40. ***Tuition, state resident:*** full-time $3488; part-time $116.27 per credit hour. ***Tuition, nonresident:*** full-time $10,884; part-time $362.80 per credit hour. Full-time tuition and fees vary according to course load. Part-time tuition and fees vary according to course load. ***College room and board:*** $6130. Room and board charges vary according to board plan and housing facility. ***Payment plans:*** Installment, deferred payment.

FRESHMAN FINANCIAL AID (Fall 2008, est.) 838 applied for aid; of those 89% were deemed to have need. 90% of freshmen with need received aid; of those 24% had need fully met. ***Average percent of need met:*** 74% (excluding resources awarded to replace EFC). ***Average financial aid package:*** $9196 (excluding resources awarded to replace EFC). 28% of all full-time freshmen had no need and received non-need-based gift aid.

UNDERGRADUATE FINANCIAL AID (Fall 2008, est.) 3,826 applied for aid; of those 97% were deemed to have need. 93% of undergraduates with need received aid; of those 27% had need fully met. ***Average percent of need met:*** 70% (excluding resources awarded to replace EFC). ***Average financial aid package:*** $9312 (excluding resources awarded to replace EFC). 12% of all full-time undergraduates had no need and received non-need-based gift aid.

GIFT AID (NEED-BASED) ***Total amount:*** $15,684,617 (55% federal, 8% state, 37% institutional). ***Receiving aid:*** Freshmen: 47% (572); all full-time undergraduates: 41% (2,686). ***Average award:*** Freshmen: $6690; Undergraduates: $5283. ***Scholarships, grants, and awards:*** Federal Pell, FSEOG, state, private, college/university gift aid from institutional funds.

GIFT AID (NON-NEED-BASED) ***Total amount:*** $7,045,162 (75% state, 21% institutional, 4% external sources). ***Receiving aid:*** Freshmen: 28% (344). Undergraduates: 17% (1,135). ***Average award:*** Freshmen: $1510. Undergraduates: $1511. ***Scholarships, grants, and awards by category:*** *Academic interests/achievement:* 2,659 awards ($11,063,805 total): communication, computer science, education, foreign languages, general academic interests/achievements, international studies, mathematics, military science, physical sciences. *Creative arts/performance:* 63 awards ($166,122 total): general creative arts/performance, music, theater/drama. *Special achievements/activities:* 122 awards ($704,874 total): general special achievements/activities, leadership. *Special characteristics:* 1,927 awards ($5,742,206 total): adult students, children and siblings of alumni, children of public servants, children with a deceased or disabled parent, international students, local/state students, members of minority groups, out-of-state students, previous college experience, public servants, veterans' children. ***Tuition waivers:*** Full or partial for employees or children of employees, senior citizens. ***ROTC:*** Army cooperative, Naval cooperative, Air Force cooperative.

LOANS ***Student loans:*** $21,462,239 (48% need-based, 52% non-need-based). 9% of past graduating class borrowed through all loan programs. *Average indebtedness per student:* $14,911. ***Average need-based loan:*** Freshmen: $3212. Undergraduates: $4101. ***Parent loans:*** $372,847 (100% non-need-based). ***Programs:*** Federal Direct (Subsidized and Unsubsidized Stafford, PLUS), FFEL (Subsidized and Unsubsidized Stafford, PLUS), Perkins, college/university.

WORK-STUDY ***Federal work-study:*** Total amount: $319,419; 134 jobs averaging $2384. ***State or other work-study/employment:*** Total amount: $803,971 (100% non-need-based). 1,352 part-time jobs averaging $595.

ATHLETIC AWARDS Total amount: $1,272,059 (38% need-based, 62% non-need-based).

APPLYING FOR FINANCIAL AID ***Required financial aid form:*** FAFSA. ***Financial aid deadline (priority):*** 5/15. ***Notification date:*** Continuous. Students must reply within 4 weeks of notification.

CONTACT Ms. Emily London-Jones, Director of Student Financial Aid, University of New Orleans, Administration Building, Room 1005, New Orleans, LA 70148, 504-280-6687 or toll-free 800-256-5866 (out-of-state). *Fax:* 504-280-3973. *E-mail:* elondon@uno.edu.

UNIVERSITY OF NORTH ALABAMA

Florence, AL

Tuition & fees (AL res): $5598 **Average undergraduate aid package: $5393**

ABOUT THE INSTITUTION State-supported, coed. ***Awards:*** bachelor's and master's degrees and post-master's certificates. 38 undergraduate majors. ***Total enrollment:*** 7,203. Undergraduates: 5,917. Freshmen: 1,033. Federal methodology is used as a basis for awarding need-based institutional aid.

UNDERGRADUATE EXPENSES for 2008–09 ***Application fee:*** $25. ***Tuition, state resident:*** full-time $4590; part-time $153 per credit hour. ***Tuition, nonresident:*** full-time $9180; part-time $306 per credit hour. ***Required fees:*** full-time $1008. Full-time tuition and fees vary according to course load and program. Part-time tuition and fees vary according to course load and program. ***College room and board:*** $4658. Room and board charges vary according to board plan and housing facility. ***Payment plan:*** Installment.

FRESHMAN FINANCIAL AID (Fall 2008, est.) 686 applied for aid; of those 76% were deemed to have need. 95% of freshmen with need received aid; of those 72% had need fully met. ***Average percent of need met:*** 61% (excluding resources awarded to replace EFC). ***Average financial aid package:*** $4989 (excluding resources awarded to replace EFC). 28% of all full-time freshmen had no need and received non-need-based gift aid.

UNDERGRADUATE FINANCIAL AID (Fall 2008, est.) 3,628 applied for aid; of those 61% were deemed to have need. 97% of undergraduates with need received aid; of those 62% had need fully met. ***Average percent of need met:*** 65% (excluding resources awarded to replace EFC). ***Average financial aid package:*** $5393 (excluding resources awarded to replace EFC). 23% of all full-time undergraduates had no need and received non-need-based gift aid.

GIFT AID (NEED-BASED) ***Total amount:*** $6,194,433 (96% federal, 4% state). ***Receiving aid:*** Freshmen: 32% (330); all full-time undergraduates: 30% (1,451). ***Average award:*** Freshmen: $4063; Undergraduates: $3795. ***Scholarships, grants, and awards:*** Federal Pell, FSEOG, state, private, college/university gift aid from institutional funds.

GIFT AID (NON-NEED-BASED) ***Total amount:*** $4,493,455 (82% institutional, 18% external sources). ***Receiving aid:*** Freshmen: 46% (474). Undergraduates: 39% (1,876). ***Average award:*** Freshmen: $2751. Undergraduates: $2588. ***Scholarships, grants, and awards by category:*** *Academic interests/achievement:* 333 awards ($577,344 total): general academic interests/achievements. *Creative arts/performance:* 248 awards ($317,068 total): art/fine arts, journalism/publications, music. *Special achievements/activities:* 840 awards ($1,461,126 total): cheerleading/drum major, general special achievements/activities, leadership. *Special characteristics:* 462 awards ($556,873 total): children of faculty/staff, first-generation college students, general special characteristics, out-of-state students. ***Tuition waivers:*** Full or partial for employees or children of employees, senior citizens. ***ROTC:*** Army.

LOANS ***Student loans:*** $18,465,311 (45% need-based, 55% non-need-based). 64% of past graduating class borrowed through all loan programs. *Average indebtedness per student:* $24,570. ***Average need-based loan:*** Freshmen: $2188. Undergraduates: $2780. ***Parent loans:*** $439,997 (100% non-need-based). ***Programs:*** FFEL (Subsidized and Unsubsidized Stafford, PLUS), Perkins.

WORK-STUDY ***Federal work-study:*** Total amount: $280,869; 214 jobs averaging $1240. ***State or other work-study/employment:*** Total amount: $405,978 (100% non-need-based). Part-time jobs available.

ATHLETIC AWARDS Total amount: $1,452,620 (100% non-need-based).

APPLYING FOR FINANCIAL AID ***Required financial aid form:*** FAFSA. ***Financial aid deadline (priority):*** 4/1. ***Notification date:*** 5/31. Students must reply within 2 weeks of notification.

CONTACT Mr. Ben Baker, Director of Student Financial Services, University of North Alabama, UNA Box 5014, Florence, AL 35632-0001, 256-765-4278 or toll-free 800-TALKUNA. *Fax:* 256-765-4920. *E-mail:* bjbaker@una.edu.

THE UNIVERSITY OF NORTH CAROLINA AT ASHEVILLE

Asheville, NC

Tuition & fees (NC res): $4255 **Average undergraduate aid package: $10,467**

ABOUT THE INSTITUTION State-supported, coed. ***Awards:*** bachelor's and master's degrees and post-bachelor's certificates. 32 undergraduate majors. ***Total enrollment:*** 3,629. Undergraduates: 3,589. Freshmen: 586. Federal methodology is used as a basis for awarding need-based institutional aid.

UNDERGRADUATE EXPENSES for 2008–09 ***Application fee:*** $50. ***Tuition, state resident:*** full-time $2339. ***Tuition, nonresident:*** full-time $13,669. ***Required fees:*** full-time $1916. Full-time tuition and fees vary according to course load. Part-time tuition and fees vary according to course load. ***College room and board:*** $6620; ***Room only:*** $3760. Room and board charges vary according to housing facility.

FRESHMAN FINANCIAL AID (Fall 2008, est.) 457 applied for aid; of those 58% were deemed to have need. 99% of freshmen with need received aid; of those 69% had need fully met. ***Average percent of need met:*** 91% (excluding resources awarded to replace EFC). ***Average financial aid package:*** $10,592 (excluding resources awarded to replace EFC). 7% of all full-time freshmen had no need and received non-need-based gift aid.

UNDERGRADUATE FINANCIAL AID (Fall 2008, est.) 1,915 applied for aid; of those 64% were deemed to have need. 99% of undergraduates with need received aid; of those 57% had need fully met. ***Average percent of need met:*** 87% (excluding resources awarded to replace EFC). ***Average financial aid package:*** $10,467 (excluding resources awarded to replace EFC). 6% of all full-time undergraduates had no need and received non-need-based gift aid.

GIFT AID (NEED-BASED) ***Total amount:*** $6,892,123 (39% federal, 43% state, 18% institutional). ***Receiving aid:*** Freshmen: 44% (255); all full-time undergraduates: 42% (1,191). ***Average award:*** Freshmen: $6339; Undergraduates: $5679. ***Scholarships, grants, and awards:*** Federal Pell, FSEOG, state, private, college/university gift aid from institutional funds.

GIFT AID (NON-NEED-BASED) ***Total amount:*** $1,316,918 (2% federal, 61% state, 37% institutional). ***Receiving aid:*** Freshmen: 8% (49). Undergraduates: 6% (174). ***Average award:*** Freshmen: $2405. Undergraduates: $3277. ***Scholarships, grants, and awards by category:*** *Academic interests/achievement:* biological sciences, business, communication, computer science, education, engineering/technologies, English, general academic interests/achievements, health fields, mathematics, physical sciences, premedicine, social sciences. *Creative arts/performance:* art/fine arts, general creative arts/performance, music, theater/drama. *Special achievements/activities:* community service, general special achievements/activities, junior miss, leadership. *Special characteristics:* adult students, children and siblings of alumni, children of faculty/staff, ethnic background, first-generation college students, general special characteristics, handicapped students, international students, local/state students, members of minority groups, veterans, veterans' children. ***Tuition waivers:*** Full or partial for employees or children of employees, senior citizens.

LOANS ***Student loans:*** $8,524,413 (53% need-based, 47% non-need-based). 50% of past graduating class borrowed through all loan programs. *Average indebtedness per student:* $14,685. ***Average need-based loan:*** Freshmen: $4957. Undergraduates: $4250. ***Parent loans:*** $697,527 (9% need-based, 91% non-need-based). ***Programs:*** Federal Direct (Subsidized and Unsubsidized Stafford, PLUS), Perkins, state, college/university.

WORK-STUDY ***Federal work-study:*** Total amount: $160,697; 76 jobs averaging $2114.

ATHLETIC AWARDS Total amount: $898,398 (22% need-based, 78% non-need-based).

APPLYING FOR FINANCIAL AID ***Required financial aid form:*** FAFSA. ***Financial aid deadline (priority):*** 3/1. ***Notification date:*** Continuous beginning 3/15. Students must reply within 2 weeks of notification.

CONTACT Ms. Elizabeth D. Bartlett, Associate Director of Financial Aid, The University of North Carolina at Asheville, 1 University Heights, Asheville, NC 28804-8510, 828-232-6535 or toll-free 800-531-9842. *Fax:* 828-251-2294. *E-mail:* bbartlett@unca.edu.

THE UNIVERSITY OF NORTH CAROLINA AT CHAPEL HILL

Chapel Hill, NC

Tuition & fees (NC res): $5397 **Average undergraduate aid package: $11,881**

ABOUT THE INSTITUTION State-supported, coed. ***Awards:*** bachelor's, master's, doctoral, and first professional degrees and post-bachelor's, post-master's, and first professional certificates. 62 undergraduate majors. ***Total enrollment:*** 28,567. Undergraduates: 17,895. Freshmen: 3,865. Both federal and institutional methodology are used as a basis for awarding need-based institutional aid.

UNDERGRADUATE EXPENSES for 2008–09 ***Application fee:*** $70. ***Tuition, state resident:*** full-time $3705. ***Tuition, nonresident:*** full-time $20,603. ***Required fees:*** full-time $1692. Full-time tuition and fees vary according to program. Part-time tuition and fees vary according to course load and program. ***College room and board:*** $7334; ***Room only:*** $3960. Room and board charges vary according to board plan, housing facility, and location. ***Payment plans:*** Installment, deferred payment.

FRESHMAN FINANCIAL AID (Fall 2007) 2,934 applied for aid; of those 43% were deemed to have need. 99% of freshmen with need received aid; of those 97% had need fully met. ***Average percent of need met:*** 100% (excluding resources awarded to replace EFC). ***Average financial aid package:*** $11,678 (excluding resources awarded to replace EFC). 23% of all full-time freshmen had no need and received non-need-based gift aid.

UNDERGRADUATE FINANCIAL AID (Fall 2007) 10,625 applied for aid; of those 52% were deemed to have need. 99% of undergraduates with need received aid; of those 97% had need fully met. ***Average percent of need met:*** 100% (excluding resources awarded to replace EFC). ***Average financial aid package:*** $11,881 (excluding resources awarded to replace EFC). 14% of all full-time undergraduates had no need and received non-need-based gift aid.

GIFT AID (NEED-BASED) ***Total amount:*** $52,020,355 (18% federal, 21% state, 53% institutional, 8% external sources). ***Receiving aid:*** Freshmen: 32% (1,254); all full-time undergraduates: 32% (5,425). ***Average award:*** Freshmen: $9795; Undergraduates: $9384. ***Scholarships, grants, and awards:*** Federal Pell, FSEOG, state, private, college/university gift aid from institutional funds, state grants.

GIFT AID (NON-NEED-BASED) ***Total amount:*** $13,843,364 (6% federal, 9% state, 38% institutional, 47% external sources). ***Receiving aid:*** Freshmen: 16% (634). Undergraduates: 10% (1,713). ***Average award:*** Freshmen: $4271. Undergraduates: $4924. ***Scholarships, grants, and awards by category:*** *Academic interests/achievement:* business, communication, education, English, general academic interests/achievements, health fields, mathematics. *Creative arts/performance:* applied art and design, art/fine arts, journalism/publications, music, theater/drama. *Special achievements/activities:* community service, general special achievements/activities, leadership. *Special characteristics:* children of faculty/staff, international students, out-of-state students, relatives of clergy, religious affiliation. ***Tuition waivers:*** Full or partial for employees or children of employees, senior citizens. ***ROTC:*** Army, Naval, Air Force.

LOANS ***Student loans:*** $27,871,371 (64% need-based, 36% non-need-based). ***Average need-based loan:*** Freshmen: $3053. Undergraduates: $4001. ***Parent loans:*** $7,990,696 (37% need-based, 63% non-need-based). ***Programs:*** FFEL (Subsidized and Unsubsidized Stafford, PLUS), Perkins, state, college/university, alternative loans.

WORK-STUDY ***Federal work-study:*** Total amount: $2,082,274; 1,291 jobs averaging $1624.

ATHLETIC AWARDS Total amount: $6,390,960 (30% need-based, 70% non-need-based).

APPLYING FOR FINANCIAL AID ***Required financial aid forms:*** FAFSA, CSS Financial Aid PROFILE. ***Financial aid deadline (priority):*** 3/1. ***Notification date:*** Continuous beginning 3/15. Students must reply by 5/1.

CONTACT Ms. Shirley A. Ort, Associate Provost and Director, Office of Scholarships and Student Aid, The University of North Carolina at Chapel Hill, CB # 2300, Chapel Hill, NC 27514, 919-962-2315. *Fax:* 919-962-2716. *E-mail:* aidinfo@unc.edu.

THE UNIVERSITY OF NORTH CAROLINA AT CHARLOTTE

Charlotte, NC

ABOUT THE INSTITUTION State-supported, coed. ***Awards:*** bachelor's, master's, and doctoral degrees and post-master's certificates. 71 undergraduate majors. ***Total enrollment:*** 23,300. Undergraduates: 18,329. Freshmen: 3,090.

GIFT AID (NEED-BASED) ***Scholarships, grants, and awards:*** Federal Pell, FSEOG, state, private, college/university gift aid from institutional funds.

GIFT AID (NON-NEED-BASED) ***Scholarships, grants, and awards by category:*** *Academic interests/achievement:* architecture, business, computer science, education, engineering/technologies, general academic interests/achievements, health fields, humanities, mathematics, military science. *Creative arts/performance:* music, performing arts. *Special characteristics:* adult students.

LOANS ***Programs:*** FFEL (Subsidized and Unsubsidized Stafford, PLUS), Perkins, state, college/university.

APPLYING FOR FINANCIAL AID ***Required financial aid form:*** FAFSA.

CONTACT Anthony D. Carter, Director of Financial Aid, The University of North Carolina at Charlotte, 9201 University City Boulevard, Charlotte, NC 28223-0001, 704-687-2426. *Fax:* 704-687-3132. *E-mail:* acarte1@uncc.edu.

THE UNIVERSITY OF NORTH CAROLINA AT GREENSBORO

Greensboro, NC

Tuition & fees (NC res): $4276 **Average undergraduate aid package: $8664**

ABOUT THE INSTITUTION State-supported, coed. ***Awards:*** bachelor's, master's, and doctoral degrees and post-bachelor's and post-master's certificates. 70 undergraduate majors. ***Total enrollment:*** 17,407. Undergraduates: 13,678. Freshmen: 2,492. Federal methodology is used as a basis for awarding need-based institutional aid.

UNDERGRADUATE EXPENSES for 2009–10 ***Application fee:*** $45. ***Tuition, state resident:*** full-time $2632; part-time $329 per course. ***Tuition, nonresident:*** full-time $14,351; part-time $1794 per course. ***Required fees:*** full-time $1644; $59.09 per credit hour. ***College room and board:*** $6506; ***Room only:*** $3706.

FRESHMAN FINANCIAL AID (Fall 2008, est.) 1,997 applied for aid; of those 92% were deemed to have need. 100% of freshmen with need received aid; of those 52% had need fully met. ***Average percent of need met:*** 64% (excluding resources awarded to replace EFC). ***Average financial aid package:*** $8882 (excluding resources awarded to replace EFC). 6% of all full-time freshmen had no need and received non-need-based gift aid.

UNDERGRADUATE FINANCIAL AID (Fall 2008, est.) 8,599 applied for aid; of those 98% were deemed to have need. 100% of undergraduates with need received aid; of those 38% had need fully met. ***Average percent of need met:*** 57% (excluding resources awarded to replace EFC). ***Average financial aid package:*** $8664 (excluding resources awarded to replace EFC). 5% of all full-time undergraduates had no need and received non-need-based gift aid.

GIFT AID (NEED-BASED) ***Total amount:*** $24,342,946 (66% federal, 14% state, 20% institutional). ***Receiving aid:*** Freshmen: 33% (823); all full-time undergraduates: 33% (3,973). ***Average award:*** Freshmen: $8512; Undergraduates: $5823. ***Scholarships, grants, and awards:*** Federal Pell, FSEOG, state, private, college/university gift aid from institutional funds.

GIFT AID (NON-NEED-BASED) ***Total amount:*** $18,774,893 (77% state, 22% institutional, 1% external sources). ***Receiving aid:*** Freshmen: 53% (1,307). Undergraduates: 49% (5,829). ***Average award:*** Freshmen: $2447. Undergraduates: $2426. ***Scholarships, grants, and awards by category:*** *Academic interests/achievement:* biological sciences, business, communication, education, English, foreign languages, general academic interests/achievements, health fields, home economics, humanities, library science, mathematics, physical sciences, premedicine, religion/biblical studies, social sciences. *Creative arts/performance:* art/fine arts, cinema/film/broadcasting, dance, music, performing arts, theater/drama. *Special achievements/activities:* community service, general special achievements/activities, junior miss, leadership, religious involvement. *Special characteristics:* adult students, children of faculty/staff, ethnic background, general special characteristics, handicapped students, international students, members of minority groups, out-of-state students, religious affiliation, veterans, veterans' children. ***ROTC:*** Army cooperative, Air Force cooperative.

LOANS ***Student loans:*** $47,795,035 (41% need-based, 59% non-need-based). 65% of past graduating class borrowed through all loan programs. *Average indebtedness per student:* $16,326. ***Average need-based loan:*** Freshmen: $2586. Undergraduates: $3959. ***Parent loans:*** $8,900,042 (100% non-need-based). ***Programs:*** FFEL (Subsidized and Unsubsidized Stafford, PLUS), Perkins, college/university.

WORK-STUDY ***Federal work-study:*** Total amount: $561,378; 298 jobs averaging $1884.

ATHLETIC AWARDS Total amount: $1,686,073 (100% non-need-based).

APPLYING FOR FINANCIAL AID ***Required financial aid form:*** FAFSA. ***Financial aid deadline (priority):*** 3/1. ***Notification date:*** Continuous beginning 3/15. Students must reply within 3 weeks of notification.

CONTACT Mr. Bruce Cabiness, Associate Director of Financial Aid, The University of North Carolina at Greensboro, PO Box 26170, Greensboro, NC 27402-6170, 336-334-5702. *Fax:* 336-334-3010. *E-mail:* bruce_cabiness@uncg.edu.

THE UNIVERSITY OF NORTH CAROLINA AT PEMBROKE

Pembroke, NC

Tuition & fees (NC res): $2007 **Average undergraduate aid package: $8761**

ABOUT THE INSTITUTION State-supported, coed. ***Awards:*** bachelor's and master's degrees. 51 undergraduate majors. ***Total enrollment:*** 6,303. Undergraduates: 5,578. Freshmen: 1,073. Federal methodology is used as a basis for awarding need-based institutional aid.

UNDERGRADUATE EXPENSES for 2008–09 ***Application fee:*** $40. ***Tuition, state resident:*** full-time $2007; part-time $255.81 per credit hour. ***Tuition, nonresident:*** full-time $11,267; part-time $1471.19 per credit hour. ***Required fees:*** $66.21 per credit hour. Full-time tuition and fees vary according to course load and location. Part-time tuition and fees vary according to course load and location. ***College room and board:*** $6250. Room and board charges vary according to board plan and housing facility. ***Payment plan:*** Installment.

FRESHMAN FINANCIAL AID (Fall 2008, est.) 857 applied for aid; of those 78% were deemed to have need. 99% of freshmen with need received aid; of those 36% had need fully met. ***Average percent of need met:*** 84% (excluding resources awarded to replace EFC). ***Average financial aid package:*** $9656 (excluding resources awarded to replace EFC). 1% of all full-time freshmen had no need and received non-need-based gift aid.

UNDERGRADUATE FINANCIAL AID (Fall 2008, est.) 3,696 applied for aid; of those 84% were deemed to have need. 98% of undergraduates with need received aid; of those 24% had need fully met. ***Average percent of need met:*** 77% (excluding resources awarded to replace EFC). ***Average financial aid package:*** $8761 (excluding resources awarded to replace EFC). 1% of all full-time undergraduates had no need and received non-need-based gift aid.

GIFT AID (NEED-BASED) ***Total amount:*** $18,759,667 (47% federal, 47% state, 4% institutional, 2% external sources). ***Receiving aid:*** Freshmen: 67% (639); all full-time undergraduates: 65% (2,820). ***Average award:*** Freshmen: $7929; Undergraduates: $6110. ***Scholarships, grants, and awards:*** Federal Pell, FSEOG, state, private, college/university gift aid from institutional funds.

GIFT AID (NON-NEED-BASED) ***Total amount:*** $391,337 (75% federal, 4% institutional, 21% external sources). ***Receiving aid:*** Freshmen: 9% (89). Undergraduates: 5% (234). ***Average award:*** Freshmen: $2000. Undergraduates: $885. ***Scholarships, grants, and awards by category:*** *Academic interests/achievement:* 272 awards ($409,638 total): business, communication, education, English, general academic interests/achievements, health fields, physical sciences. *Creative arts/performance:* 3 awards ($2465 total): journalism/publications, music. *Special characteristics:* 6 awards ($16,500 total): children and siblings of alumni, general special characteristics. ***Tuition waivers:*** Full or partial for senior citizens. ***ROTC:*** Army, Air Force.

LOANS ***Student loans:*** $19,202,280 (84% need-based, 16% non-need-based). ***Average need-based loan:*** Freshmen: $2712. Undergraduates: $3710. ***Parent loans:*** $1,121,002 (54% need-based, 46% non-need-based). ***Programs:*** FFEL (Subsidized and Unsubsidized Stafford, PLUS), Perkins, college/university.

WORK-STUDY ***Federal work-study:*** Total amount: $321,991; 252 jobs averaging $1278. ***State or other work-study/employment:*** Total amount: $16,000 (100% non-need-based). 8 part-time jobs averaging $2000.

ATHLETIC AWARDS Total amount: $148,000 (100% need-based).

APPLYING FOR FINANCIAL AID ***Required financial aid form:*** FAFSA. ***Financial aid deadline:*** Continuous. ***Notification date:*** 4/15.

CONTACT Mildred Weber, Associate Director of Financial Aid, The University of North Carolina at Pembroke, PO Box 1510, Pembroke, NC 28372, 910-521-6612 or toll-free 800-949-UNCP. *Fax:* 910-775-4159. *E-mail:* mildred.weber@uncp.edu.

THE UNIVERSITY OF NORTH CAROLINA WILMINGTON

Wilmington, NC

Tuition & fees (NC res): $4528 **Average undergraduate aid package: $8664**

ABOUT THE INSTITUTION State-supported, coed. ***Awards:*** bachelor's, master's, and doctoral degrees and post-bachelor's and post-master's certificates. 62 undergraduate majors. ***Total enrollment:*** 12,195. Undergraduates: 10,989. Freshmen: 2,073. Federal methodology is used as a basis for awarding need-based institutional aid.

UNDERGRADUATE EXPENSES for 2008–09 ***Application fee:*** $60. ***Tuition, state resident:*** full-time $2459. ***Tuition, nonresident:*** full-time $12,626. ***Required fees:*** full-time $2069. Full-time tuition and fees vary according to course load. Part-time tuition and fees vary according to course load. ***College room and board:*** $7370. Room and board charges vary according to board plan and housing facility. ***Payment plan:*** Installment.

FRESHMAN FINANCIAL AID (Fall 2008, est.) 1,413 applied for aid; of those 54% were deemed to have need. 98% of freshmen with need received aid; of those 47% had need fully met. ***Average percent of need met:*** 87% (excluding resources awarded to replace EFC). ***Average financial aid package:*** $9221 (excluding resources awarded to replace EFC). 3% of all full-time freshmen had no need and received non-need-based gift aid.

UNDERGRADUATE FINANCIAL AID (Fall 2008, est.) 6,060 applied for aid; of those 65% were deemed to have need. 98% of undergraduates with need received aid; of those 40% had need fully met. ***Average percent of need met:*** 86% (excluding resources awarded to replace EFC). ***Average financial aid package:*** $8664 (excluding resources awarded to replace EFC). 4% of all full-time undergraduates had no need and received non-need-based gift aid.

GIFT AID (NEED-BASED) ***Total amount:*** $21,088,542 (36% federal, 42% state, 18% institutional, 4% external sources). ***Receiving aid:*** Freshmen: 34% (690); all full-time undergraduates: 34% (3,433). ***Average award:*** Freshmen: $6236; Undergraduates: $5484. ***Scholarships, grants, and awards:*** Federal Pell, FSEOG, state, private, college/university gift aid from institutional funds, Academic Competitiveness Grant, National Smart Grant, TEACH Grant.

GIFT AID (NON-NEED-BASED) ***Total amount:*** $3,678,468 (20% state, 25% institutional, 55% external sources). ***Receiving aid:*** Freshmen: 5% (93). Undergraduates: 5% (467). ***Average award:*** Freshmen: $1714. Undergraduates: $2377. ***Scholarships, grants, and awards by category:*** *Academic interests/achievement:* 136 awards ($276,235 total): biological sciences, business, communication, computer science, education, engineering/technologies, English, foreign languages, general academic interests/achievements, health fields, humanities, international studies, mathematics, physical sciences, premedicine, social sciences. *Creative arts/performance:* 21 awards ($14,500 total): art/fine arts, cinema/film/broadcasting, creative writing, music, theater/drama. *Special* *achievements/activities:* 63 awards ($14,430 total): cheerleading/drum major, general special achievements/activities, leadership. *Special characteristics:* 5 awards ($5000 total): children of faculty/staff, local/state students, married students, previous college experience. ***Tuition waivers:*** Full or partial for employees or children of employees, senior citizens.

LOANS ***Student loans:*** $35,421,223 (41% need-based, 59% non-need-based). 54% of past graduating class borrowed through all loan programs. *Average indebtedness per student:* $15,476. ***Average need-based loan:*** Freshmen: $2608. Undergraduates: $3775. ***Parent loans:*** $9,926,070 (100% non-need-based). ***Programs:*** Federal Direct (Subsidized and Unsubsidized Stafford, PLUS), FFEL (Subsidized and Unsubsidized Stafford, PLUS), Perkins, state, college/university.

WORK-STUDY ***Federal work-study:*** Total amount: $350,000; 259 jobs averaging $2500.

ATHLETIC AWARDS Total amount: $1,666,217 (22% need-based, 78% non-need-based).

APPLYING FOR FINANCIAL AID ***Required financial aid form:*** FAFSA. ***Financial aid deadline:*** Continuous. ***Notification date:*** Continuous beginning 3/15. Students must reply within 3 weeks of notification.

CONTACT Emily Bliss, Director of Financial Aid and Veterans' Services Office, The University of North Carolina Wilmington, 601 South College Road, Wilmington, NC 28403-5951, 910-962-3177 or toll-free 800-228-5571 (out-of-state). *Fax:* 910-962-3851. *E-mail:* finaid@uncw.edu.

UNIVERSITY OF NORTH DAKOTA

Grand Forks, ND

Tuition & fees (ND res): $6513 **Average undergraduate aid package: $5492**

ABOUT THE INSTITUTION State-supported, coed. ***Awards:*** bachelor's, master's, doctoral, and first professional degrees and post-master's certificates. 84 undergraduate majors. ***Total enrollment:*** 12,748. Undergraduates: 10,129. Freshmen: 1,942. Federal methodology is used as a basis for awarding need-based institutional aid.

UNDERGRADUATE EXPENSES for 2008–09 ***Application fee:*** $35. ***Tuition, state resident:*** full-time $5276. ***Tuition, nonresident:*** full-time $14,088. ***Required fees:*** full-time $1237. Full-time tuition and fees vary according to degree level, program, and reciprocity agreements. Part-time tuition and fees vary according to course load, degree level, program, and reciprocity agreements. ***College room and board:*** $5472; ***Room only:*** $2222. Room and board charges vary according to board plan and housing facility. ***Payment plan:*** Deferred payment.

FRESHMAN FINANCIAL AID (Fall 2007) 1,662 applied for aid; of those 100% were deemed to have need. 99% of freshmen with need received aid; of those 42% had need fully met. ***Average percent of need met:*** 55% (excluding resources awarded to replace EFC). ***Average financial aid package:*** $4787 (excluding resources awarded to replace EFC).

UNDERGRADUATE FINANCIAL AID (Fall 2007) 6,729 applied for aid; of those 100% were deemed to have need. 98% of undergraduates with need received aid; of those 28% had need fully met. ***Average percent of need met:*** 38% (excluding resources awarded to replace EFC). ***Average financial aid package:*** $5492 (excluding resources awarded to replace EFC).

GIFT AID (NEED-BASED) ***Total amount:*** $10,172,743 (65% federal, 7% state, 15% institutional, 13% external sources). ***Receiving aid:*** Freshmen: 50% (939); all full-time undergraduates: 39% (3,170). ***Average award:*** Freshmen: $2315; Undergraduates: $2809. ***Scholarships, grants, and awards:*** Federal Pell, FSEOG, state, private, college/university gift aid from institutional funds, Federal Nursing.

GIFT AID (NON-NEED-BASED) ***Total amount:*** $3,181,562 (2% federal, 9% state, 59% institutional, 30% external sources). ***Receiving aid:*** Freshmen: 10% (183). Undergraduates: 8% (653). ***Average award:*** Freshmen: $1279. Undergraduates: $1303. ***Scholarships, grants, and awards by category:*** *Academic interests/achievement:* biological sciences, business, communication, computer science, education, engineering/technologies, English, foreign languages, general academic interests/achievements, health fields, humanities, international studies, mathematics, military science, physical sciences, premedicine, social sciences. *Creative arts/performance:* art/fine arts, debating, music, theater/drama. *Special achievements/activities:* general special achievements/activities, leadership, memberships. *Special characteristics:* children of faculty/staff, ethnic background, general special characteristics, handicapped students, international students, members of minority groups, veterans' children. ***Tuition waivers:*** Full or partial for minority students, employees or children of employees, adult students, senior citizens. ***ROTC:*** Army, Air Force.

LOANS ***Student loans:*** $56,346,593 (54% need-based, 46% non-need-based). 65% of past graduating class borrowed through all loan programs. *Average indebtedness per student:* $21,743. ***Average need-based loan:*** Freshmen: $3155. Undergraduates: $4038. ***Parent loans:*** $2,533,770 (23% need-based, 77% non-need-based). ***Programs:*** FFEL (Subsidized and Unsubsidized Stafford, PLUS), Perkins, Federal Nursing, alternative commercial loans.

WORK-STUDY ***Federal work-study:*** Total amount: $3,582,945; 1,902 jobs available.

ATHLETIC AWARDS Total amount: $2,433,895 (15% need-based, 85% non-need-based).

APPLYING FOR FINANCIAL AID ***Required financial aid form:*** FAFSA. ***Financial aid deadline (priority):*** 3/15. ***Notification date:*** Continuous beginning 5/15. Students must reply within 4 weeks of notification.

CONTACT Ms. Robin Holden, Director of Student Financial Aid Office, University of North Dakota, 264 Centennial Drive Stop 8371, Grand Forks, ND 58202, 701-777-3121 or toll-free 800-CALL UND. *Fax:* 701-777-2040. *E-mail:* robinholden@mail.und.nodak.edu.

UNIVERSITY OF NORTHERN COLORADO

Greeley, CO

Tuition & fees (CO res): $4680 **Average undergraduate aid package: $13,101**

ABOUT THE INSTITUTION State-supported, coed. ***Awards:*** bachelor's, master's, and doctoral degrees and post-master's certificates (specialist). 43 undergraduate majors. ***Total enrollment:*** 11,925. Undergraduates: 9,851. Freshmen: 2,114. Federal methodology is used as a basis for awarding need-based institutional aid.

UNDERGRADUATE EXPENSES for 2008–09 ***Application fee:*** $45. ***Tuition, state resident:*** full-time $3942; part-time $164.25 per credit hour. ***Tuition, nonresident:*** full-time $13,344; part-time $556 per credit hour. ***Required fees:*** full-time $738; $36.90 per credit hour. Full-time tuition and fees vary according to program. Part-time tuition and fees vary according to program. ***College room and board:*** $7784; ***Room only:*** $3664. Room and board charges vary according to board plan and housing facility. ***Payment plan:*** Deferred payment.

FRESHMAN FINANCIAL AID (Fall 2007) 1,684 applied for aid; of those 59% were deemed to have need. 94% of freshmen with need received aid; of those 57% had need fully met. ***Average percent of need met:*** 100% (excluding resources awarded to replace EFC). ***Average financial aid package:*** $12,988 (excluding resources awarded to replace EFC). 18% of all full-time freshmen had no need and received non-need-based gift aid.

UNDERGRADUATE FINANCIAL AID (Fall 2007) 6,626 applied for aid; of those 60% were deemed to have need. 96% of undergraduates with need received aid; of those 56% had need fully met. ***Average percent of need met:*** 100% (excluding resources awarded to replace EFC). ***Average financial aid package:*** $13,101 (excluding resources awarded to replace EFC). 12% of all full-time undergraduates had no need and received non-need-based gift aid.

GIFT AID (NEED-BASED) ***Total amount:*** $14,859,873 (47% federal, 41% state, 10% institutional, 2% external sources). ***Receiving aid:*** Freshmen: 35% (749); all full-time undergraduates: 34% (3,064). ***Average award:*** Freshmen: $4405; Undergraduates: $4268. ***Scholarships, grants, and awards:*** Federal Pell, FSEOG, state, private, college/university gift aid from institutional funds.

GIFT AID (NON-NEED-BASED) ***Total amount:*** $9,187,419 (3% federal, 4% state, 53% institutional, 40% external sources). ***Receiving aid:*** Freshmen: 23% (493). Undergraduates: 15% (1,389). ***Average award:*** Freshmen: $2198. Undergraduates: $2536. ***Scholarships, grants, and awards by category:*** *Academic interests/achievement:* 728 awards ($764,238 total): biological sciences, business, communication, education, English, general academic interests/achievements, health fields, home economics, mathematics, military science, physical sciences, social sciences. *Creative arts/performance:* 167 awards ($137,132 total): dance, music, performing arts, theater/drama. *Special characteristics:* 3,527 awards ($7,485,525 total): adult students, children and siblings of alumni, children of faculty/staff, children of union members/company employees, ethnic background, general special characteristics, handicapped students, international students, local/state students, members of minority groups, out-of-state students, veterans. ***ROTC:*** Army, Air Force.

LOANS ***Student loans:*** $32,696,663 (48% need-based, 52% non-need-based). ***Average need-based loan:*** Freshmen: $3788. Undergraduates: $4622. ***Parent loans:*** $18,105,399 (100% non-need-based). ***Programs:*** FFEL (Subsidized and Unsubsidized Stafford, PLUS), Perkins, college/university.

WORK-STUDY ***Federal work-study:*** Total amount: $568,137; 150 jobs averaging $1798. ***State or other work-study/employment:*** Total amount: $2,324,396 (52% need-based, 48% non-need-based). 1,518 part-time jobs averaging $1134.

ATHLETIC AWARDS Total amount: $2,398,627 (100% non-need-based).

APPLYING FOR FINANCIAL AID ***Required financial aid form:*** FAFSA. ***Financial aid deadline (priority):*** 3/1. ***Notification date:*** Continuous beginning 3/19. Students must reply within 4 weeks of notification.

CONTACT Donni Clark, Director of Student Financial Resources, University of Northern Colorado, Carter Hall 1005, Greeley, CO 80639, 970-351-2502 or toll-free 888-700-4UNC (in-state). *Fax:* 970-351-3737. *E-mail:* sfr@unco.edu.

UNIVERSITY OF NORTHERN IOWA

Cedar Falls, IA

Tuition & fees (IA res): $6636 **Average undergraduate aid package: $7597**

ABOUT THE INSTITUTION State-supported, coed. ***Awards:*** bachelor's, master's, and doctoral degrees. 110 undergraduate majors. ***Total enrollment:*** 12,998. Undergraduates: 11,086. Freshmen: 2,015. Federal methodology is used as a basis for awarding need-based institutional aid.

UNDERGRADUATE EXPENSES for 2009–10 ***Application fee:*** $40. ***Tuition, state resident:*** full-time $5756; part-time $240 per hour. ***Tuition, nonresident:*** full-time $14,020; part-time $584 per hour. ***Required fees:*** full-time $880. ***College room and board:*** $7082; ***Room only:*** $3380.

FRESHMAN FINANCIAL AID (Fall 2008, est.) 1,693 applied for aid; of those 67% were deemed to have need. 98% of freshmen with need received aid; of those 28% had need fully met. ***Average percent of need met:*** 73% (excluding resources awarded to replace EFC). ***Average financial aid package:*** $7867 (excluding resources awarded to replace EFC). 26% of all full-time freshmen had no need and received non-need-based gift aid.

UNDERGRADUATE FINANCIAL AID (Fall 2008, est.) 7,939 applied for aid; of those 74% were deemed to have need. 97% of undergraduates with need received aid; of those 22% had need fully met. ***Average percent of need met:*** 65% (excluding resources awarded to replace EFC). ***Average financial aid package:*** $7597 (excluding resources awarded to replace EFC). 13% of all full-time undergraduates had no need and received non-need-based gift aid.

GIFT AID (NEED-BASED) ***Total amount:*** $12,951,139 (71% federal, 11% state, 18% institutional). ***Receiving aid:*** Freshmen: 25% (503); all full-time undergraduates: 29% (2,929). ***Average award:*** Freshmen: $3825; Undergraduates: $3670. ***Scholarships, grants, and awards:*** Federal Pell, FSEOG, state, private, college/university gift aid from institutional funds.

GIFT AID (NON-NEED-BASED) ***Total amount:*** $9,703,822 (5% state, 69% institutional, 26% external sources). ***Receiving aid:*** Freshmen: 40% (789). Undergraduates: 21% (2,060). ***Average award:*** Freshmen: $2590. Undergraduates: $2860. ***Scholarships, grants, and awards by category:*** *Academic interests/achievement:* biological sciences, business, education, general academic interests/achievements, mathematics, physical sciences, social sciences. *Creative arts/performance:* applied art and design, art/fine arts, music, theater/drama. *Special achievements/activities:* leadership. *Special characteristics:* general special characteristics, members of minority groups. ***ROTC:*** Army.

LOANS ***Student loans:*** $52,050,373 (44% need-based, 56% non-need-based). 78% of past graduating class borrowed through all loan programs. *Average indebtedness per student:* $24,176. ***Average need-based loan:*** Freshmen: $3213. Undergraduates: $4226. ***Parent loans:*** $11,104,903 (100% non-need-based). ***Programs:*** Federal Direct (Subsidized and Unsubsidized Stafford, PLUS), Perkins, state, private alternative loans.

WORK-STUDY ***Federal work-study:*** Total amount: $1,065,311; 486 jobs averaging $1831. ***State or other work-study/employment:*** Total amount: $416,699 (79% need-based, 21% non-need-based). 216 part-time jobs averaging $1865.

ATHLETIC AWARDS Total amount: $3,251,982 (100% non-need-based).

APPLYING FOR FINANCIAL AID ***Required financial aid form:*** FAFSA. ***Financial aid deadline:*** Continuous. ***Notification date:*** Continuous beginning 3/1.

CONTACT Heather Soesbe, Assistant Director, Office of Student Financial Aid, University of Northern Iowa, 105 Gilchrist Hall, Cedar Falls, IA 50614-0024, 319-273-2700 or toll-free 800-772-2037. *Fax:* 319-273-6950. *E-mail:* heather.soesbe@uni.edu.

UNIVERSITY OF NORTH FLORIDA

Jacksonville, FL

Tuition & fees (FL res): $3775 **Average undergraduate aid package: $1570**

ABOUT THE INSTITUTION State-supported, coed. ***Awards:*** associate, bachelor's, master's, and doctoral degrees and post-bachelor's and post-master's certificates (doctoral degree in education only). 54 undergraduate majors. ***Total enrollment:*** 15,280. Undergraduates: 13,387. Freshmen: 1,851. Federal methodology is used as a basis for awarding need-based institutional aid.

UNDERGRADUATE EXPENSES for 2008–09 ***Application fee:*** $30. ***Tuition, state resident:*** full-time $3775; part-time $125.83 per credit hour. ***Tuition, nonresident:*** full-time $15,417; part-time $513.90 per credit hour. ***College room and board:*** $7366; ***Room only:*** $4273. Room and board charges vary according to board plan and housing facility. ***Payment plan:*** Deferred payment.

FRESHMAN FINANCIAL AID (Fall 2008, est.) 1,063 applied for aid; of those 59% were deemed to have need. 99% of freshmen with need received aid; of those 18% had need fully met. ***Average percent of need met:*** 90% (excluding resources awarded to replace EFC). ***Average financial aid package:*** $1506 (excluding resources awarded to replace EFC). 10% of all full-time freshmen had no need and received non-need-based gift aid.

UNDERGRADUATE FINANCIAL AID (Fall 2008, est.) 5,137 applied for aid; of those 73% were deemed to have need. 97% of undergraduates with need received aid; of those 10% had need fully met. ***Average percent of need met:*** 89% (excluding resources awarded to replace EFC). ***Average financial aid package:*** $1570 (excluding resources awarded to replace EFC). 13% of all full-time undergraduates had no need and received non-need-based gift aid.

GIFT AID (NEED-BASED) ***Total amount:*** $21,319,305 (46% federal, 35% state, 17% institutional, 2% external sources). ***Receiving aid:*** Freshmen: 24% (381); all full-time undergraduates: 23% (2,234). ***Average award:*** Freshmen: $975; Undergraduates: $1217. ***Scholarships, grants, and awards:*** Federal Pell, FSEOG, state, private, college/university gift aid from institutional funds, 2+2 Scholarships (jointly sponsored with Florida Community College at Jacksonville).

GIFT AID (NON-NEED-BASED) ***Total amount:*** $13,427,313 (79% state, 19% institutional, 2% external sources). ***Receiving aid:*** Freshmen: 34% (540). Undergraduates: 20% (1,881). ***Average award:*** Freshmen: $1084. Undergraduates: $1236. ***Scholarships, grants, and awards by category:*** *Academic interests/achievement:* 855 awards ($2,752,223 total): business, computer science, education, engineering/technologies, general academic interests/achievements, health fields, international studies. *Creative arts/performance:* 46 awards ($74,685 total): art/fine arts, music. *Special achievements/activities:* 73 awards ($95,078 total): community service, general special achievements/activities, leadership. *Special characteristics:* 21 awards ($49,125 total): first-generation college students, general special characteristics, international students, members of minority groups, out-of-state students. ***Tuition waivers:*** Full or partial for employees or children of employees, senior citizens. ***ROTC:*** Naval cooperative.

LOANS ***Student loans:*** $26,241,065 (81% need-based, 19% non-need-based). 41% of past graduating class borrowed through all loan programs. *Average indebtedness per student:* $14,694. ***Average need-based loan:*** Freshmen: $1717. Undergraduates: $1820. ***Parent loans:*** $907,084 (42% need-based, 58% non-need-based). ***Programs:*** FFEL (Subsidized and Unsubsidized Stafford, PLUS).

WORK-STUDY ***Federal work-study:*** Total amount: $338,240; 116 jobs averaging $3208.

ATHLETIC AWARDS Total amount: $908,183 (23% need-based, 77% non-need-based).

APPLYING FOR FINANCIAL AID ***Required financial aid forms:*** FAFSA, financial aid transcript (for transfers). ***Financial aid deadline (priority):*** 4/1. ***Notification date:*** Continuous. Students must reply within 2 weeks of notification.

CONTACT Mrs. Anissa Agne, Director of Financial Aid, University of North Florida, 1 UNF Drive, Jacksonville, FL 32224-7699, 904-620-2604. *E-mail:* anissa.agne@unf.edu.

UNIVERSITY OF NORTH TEXAS

Denton, TX

Tuition & fees (TX res): $6767 **Average undergraduate aid package: $9518**

ABOUT THE INSTITUTION State-supported, coed. ***Awards:*** bachelor's, master's, doctoral, and first professional degrees and post-bachelor's certificates. 82

undergraduate majors. ***Total enrollment:*** 34,698. Undergraduates: 27,779. Freshmen: 3,606. Federal methodology is used as a basis for awarding need-based institutional aid.

UNDERGRADUATE EXPENSES for 2008–09 ***Application fee:*** $40. ***Tuition, state resident:*** full-time $4828; part-time $161 per credit hour. ***Tuition, nonresident:*** full-time $13,168; part-time $439 per credit hour. ***Required fees:*** full-time $1939; $517.35 per term. Full-time tuition and fees vary according to course load. Part-time tuition and fees vary according to course load. ***College room and board:*** $6026. Room and board charges vary according to board plan and housing facility. ***Payment plan:*** Installment.

FRESHMAN FINANCIAL AID (Fall 2008, est.) 2,436 applied for aid; of those 65% were deemed to have need. 98% of freshmen with need received aid; of those 37% had need fully met. ***Average percent of need met:*** 82% (excluding resources awarded to replace EFC). ***Average financial aid package:*** $10,394 (excluding resources awarded to replace EFC). 12% of all full-time freshmen had no need and received non-need-based gift aid.

UNDERGRADUATE FINANCIAL AID (Fall 2008, est.) 13,708 applied for aid; of those 76% were deemed to have need. 97% of undergraduates with need received aid; of those 25% had need fully met. ***Average percent of need met:*** 68% (excluding resources awarded to replace EFC). ***Average financial aid package:*** $9518 (excluding resources awarded to replace EFC). 9% of all full-time undergraduates had no need and received non-need-based gift aid.

GIFT AID (NEED-BASED) ***Total amount:*** $61,855,651 (37% federal, 28% state, 26% institutional, 9% external sources). ***Receiving aid:*** Freshmen: 40% (1,358); all full-time undergraduates: 38% (8,286). ***Average award:*** Freshmen: $6553; Undergraduates: $4993. ***Scholarships, grants, and awards:*** Federal Pell, FSEOG, state, college/university gift aid from institutional funds.

GIFT AID (NON-NEED-BASED) ***Total amount:*** $6,149,950 (1% state, 27% institutional, 72% external sources). ***Receiving aid:*** Freshmen: 16% (562). Undergraduates: 11% (2,309). ***Average award:*** Freshmen: $3893. Undergraduates: $3937. ***Tuition waivers:*** Full or partial for employees or children of employees, senior citizens. ***ROTC:*** Army cooperative, Air Force.

LOANS ***Student loans:*** $108,739,070 (81% need-based, 19% non-need-based). ***Average need-based loan:*** Freshmen: $2687. Undergraduates: $4280. ***Parent loans:*** $47,025,012 (56% need-based, 44% non-need-based). ***Programs:*** FFEL (Subsidized and Unsubsidized Stafford, PLUS), Perkins, Federal Nursing, state, college/university.

WORK-STUDY ***Federal work-study:*** Total amount: $4,789,454; jobs available. ***State or other work-study/employment:*** Total amount: $1,163,990 (100% need-based). Part-time jobs available.

ATHLETIC AWARDS Total amount: $2,730,107 (39% need-based, 61% non-need-based).

APPLYING FOR FINANCIAL AID ***Required financial aid form:*** FAFSA. ***Financial aid deadline (priority):*** 4/15. ***Notification date:*** Continuous.

CONTACT Mrs. Carolyn Cunningham, Director of Financial Aid, University of North Texas, PO Box 311370, Denton, TX 76203-1370, 940-565-2302 or toll-free 800-868-8211 (in-state). *Fax:* 940-565-2738. *E-mail:* carolyn.cunningham@unt.edu.

UNIVERSITY OF NOTRE DAME

Notre Dame, IN

Tuition & fees: $36,847 **Average undergraduate aid package: $32,113**

ABOUT THE INSTITUTION Independent Roman Catholic, coed. ***Awards:*** bachelor's, master's, doctoral, and first professional degrees. 55 undergraduate majors. ***Total enrollment:*** 11,731. Undergraduates: 8,363. Freshmen: 2,000. Both federal and institutional methodology are used as a basis for awarding need-based institutional aid.

UNDERGRADUATE EXPENSES for 2008–09 ***Application fee:*** $65. ***Comprehensive fee:*** $46,675 includes full-time tuition ($36,340), mandatory fees ($507), and room and board ($9828). ***Part-time tuition:*** $1514 per credit. ***Payment plan:*** Installment.

FRESHMAN FINANCIAL AID (Fall 2008, est.) 1,393 applied for aid; of those 67% were deemed to have need. 100% of freshmen with need received aid; of those 100% had need fully met. ***Average percent of need met:*** 100% (excluding resources awarded to replace EFC). ***Average financial aid package:*** $32,140 (excluding resources awarded to replace EFC). 2% of all full-time freshmen had no need and received non-need-based gift aid.

UNDERGRADUATE FINANCIAL AID (Fall 2008, est.) 4,945 applied for aid; of those 78% were deemed to have need. 100% of undergraduates with need received aid; of those 99% had need fully met. ***Average percent of need met:*** 100% (excluding resources awarded to replace EFC). ***Average financial aid package:*** $32,113 (excluding resources awarded to replace EFC). 3% of all full-time undergraduates had no need and received non-need-based gift aid.

GIFT AID (NEED-BASED) ***Total amount:*** $83,719,313 (7% federal, 1% state, 88% institutional, 4% external sources). ***Receiving aid:*** Freshmen: 45% (891); all full-time undergraduates: 44% (3,654). ***Average award:*** Freshmen: $25,757; Undergraduates: $24,137. ***Scholarships, grants, and awards:*** Federal Pell, state, private, college/university gift aid from institutional funds, Academic Competitiveness Grant, National Smart Grant.

GIFT AID (NON-NEED-BASED) ***Total amount:*** $15,234,983 (34% federal, 1% state, 32% institutional, 33% external sources). ***Receiving aid:*** Freshmen: 30% (604). Undergraduates: 28% (2,347). ***Average award:*** Freshmen: $5806. Undergraduates: $6106. ***Scholarships, grants, and awards by category:*** *Special characteristics:* 239 awards ($7,934,829 total): children of faculty/staff. ***Tuition waivers:*** Full or partial for employees or children of employees. ***ROTC:*** Army, Naval, Air Force.

LOANS ***Student loans:*** $39,792,395 (48% need-based, 52% non-need-based). 57% of past graduating class borrowed through all loan programs. *Average indebtedness per student:* $29,835. ***Average need-based loan:*** Freshmen: $3547. Undergraduates: $5142. ***Parent loans:*** $10,437,490 (2% need-based, 98% non-need-based). ***Programs:*** FFEL (Subsidized and Unsubsidized Stafford, PLUS), Perkins, Federal Nursing, Notre Dame Undergraduate Loan.

WORK-STUDY ***Federal work-study:*** Total amount: $3,189,938; 1,523 jobs averaging $2273. ***State or other work-study/employment:*** Total amount: $9,027,157 (9% need-based, 91% non-need-based). 3,281 part-time jobs averaging $2751.

ATHLETIC AWARDS Total amount: $14,201,957 (14% need-based, 86% non-need-based).

APPLYING FOR FINANCIAL AID ***Required financial aid forms:*** FAFSA, CSS Financial Aid PROFILE, business/farm supplement, income tax form(s), W-2 forms. ***Financial aid deadline:*** 2/15. ***Notification date:*** 4/1. Students must reply by 5/1.

CONTACT Mr. Joseph A. Russo, Director, Student Financial Strategies, University of Notre Dame, 115 Main Building, Notre Dame, IN 46556, 574-631-6436. *Fax:* 574-631-6899. *E-mail:* finaid.1@nd.edu.

UNIVERSITY OF OKLAHOMA

Norman, OK

Tuition & fees (OK res): $5245 **Average undergraduate aid package: $10,468**

ABOUT THE INSTITUTION State-supported, coed. ***Awards:*** bachelor's, master's, doctoral, and first professional degrees and post-bachelor's and post-master's certificates. 93 undergraduate majors. ***Total enrollment:*** 26,185. Undergraduates: 19,592. Freshmen: 3,803. Federal methodology is used as a basis for awarding need-based institutional aid.

UNDERGRADUATE EXPENSES for 2008–09 ***Application fee:*** $40. ***Tuition, state resident:*** full-time $2830; part-time $117.90 per credit hour. ***Tuition, nonresident:*** full-time $10,814; part-time $450.60 per credit hour. ***Required fees:*** full-time $2415; $90.10 per credit hour or $126.50 per term. Full-time tuition and fees vary according to course load, location, program, and reciprocity agreements. Part-time tuition and fees vary according to course load, location, program, and reciprocity agreements. ***College room and board:*** $7376; ***Room only:*** $4038. Room and board charges vary according to board plan and housing facility. ***Payment plans:*** Guaranteed tuition, installment.

FRESHMAN FINANCIAL AID (Fall 2007) 2,405 applied for aid; of those 96% were deemed to have need. 100% of freshmen with need received aid; of those 51% had need fully met. ***Average percent of need met:*** 93% (excluding resources awarded to replace EFC). ***Average financial aid package:*** $10,698 (excluding resources awarded to replace EFC). 11% of all full-time freshmen had no need and received non-need-based gift aid.

UNDERGRADUATE FINANCIAL AID (Fall 2007) 8,999 applied for aid; of those 95% were deemed to have need. 100% of undergraduates with need received aid; of those 51% had need fully met. ***Average percent of need met:*** 93% (excluding resources awarded to replace EFC). ***Average financial aid package:*** $10,468 (excluding resources awarded to replace EFC). 9% of all full-time undergraduates had no need and received non-need-based gift aid.

GIFT AID (NEED-BASED) ***Total amount:*** $32,166,833 (46% federal, 28% state, 16% institutional, 10% external sources). ***Receiving aid:*** Freshmen: 5% (207);

all full-time undergraduates: 11% (1,779). ***Average award:*** Freshmen: $5004; Undergraduates: $4077. ***Scholarships, grants, and awards:*** Federal Pell, FSEOG, state, private, college/university gift aid from institutional funds, United Negro College Fund.

GIFT AID (NON-NEED-BASED) ***Total amount:*** $8,835,098 (13% federal, 42% state, 29% institutional, 16% external sources). ***Receiving aid:*** Freshmen: 48% (1,855). Undergraduates: 32% (5,414). ***Average award:*** Freshmen: $1124. Undergraduates: $1397. ***Scholarships, grants, and awards by category:*** *Academic interests/achievement:* 8,776 awards ($20,197,823 total): architecture, area/ethnic studies, biological sciences, business, communication, computer science, education, engineering/technologies, foreign languages, general academic interests/achievements, humanities, international studies, mathematics, physical sciences, social sciences. *Creative arts/performance:* 110 awards ($1,661,106 total): art/fine arts, dance, journalism/publications, music, performing arts, theater/drama. *Special achievements/activities:* 52 awards ($111,087 total): leadership. *Special characteristics:* 430 awards ($1,038,367 total): children and siblings of alumni, members of minority groups, previous college experience. ***Tuition waivers:*** Full or partial for children of alumni, employees or children of employees, senior citizens. ***ROTC:*** Army, Naval, Air Force.

LOANS ***Student loans:*** $47,344,681 (97% need-based, 3% non-need-based). 53% of past graduating class borrowed through all loan programs. *Average indebtedness per student:* $20,341. ***Average need-based loan:*** Freshmen: $3732. Undergraduates: $4548. ***Parent loans:*** $13,812,493 (97% need-based, 3% non-need-based). ***Programs:*** FFEL (Subsidized and Unsubsidized Stafford, PLUS), Perkins, college/university, alternative loans.

WORK-STUDY ***Federal work-study:*** Total amount: $1,401,891; 665 jobs averaging $2108.

ATHLETIC AWARDS Total amount: $5,167,689 (40% need-based, 60% non-need-based).

APPLYING FOR FINANCIAL AID ***Required financial aid form:*** FAFSA. ***Financial aid deadline:*** Continuous. ***Notification date:*** Continuous beginning 3/15. Students must reply within 6 weeks of notification.

CONTACT Financial Aid Assistant, University of Oklahoma, 1000 Asp Avenue, Room 216, Norman, OK 73019-4078, 405-325-4521 or toll-free 800-234-6868. *Fax:* 405-325-0819. *E-mail:* financialaid@ou.edu.

UNIVERSITY OF OKLAHOMA—TULSA

Tulsa, OK

CONTACT Financial Aid Office, University of Oklahoma—Tulsa, Schusterman Center, 4502 East 41st Street, Tulsa, OK 74135-2512, 918-660-3000.

UNIVERSITY OF OREGON

Eugene, OR

Tuition & fees (OR res): $6435 **Average undergraduate aid package: $8735**

ABOUT THE INSTITUTION State-supported, coed. ***Awards:*** bachelor's, master's, doctoral, and first professional degrees and post-bachelor's certificates. 82 undergraduate majors. ***Total enrollment:*** 21,452. Undergraduates: 17,619. Freshmen: 4,260. Federal methodology is used as a basis for awarding need-based institutional aid.

UNDERGRADUATE EXPENSES for 2008–09 ***Application fee:*** $50. ***One-time required fee:*** $250. ***Tuition, state resident:*** full-time $5202; part-time $124 per credit hour. ***Tuition, nonresident:*** full-time $18,759; part-time $469 per credit hour. ***Required fees:*** full-time $1233. Full-time tuition and fees vary according to class time, course load, degree level, and program. Part-time tuition and fees vary according to class time, course load, degree level, and program. ***College room and board:*** $8211. Room and board charges vary according to board plan and housing facility. ***Payment plan:*** Installment.

FRESHMAN FINANCIAL AID (Fall 2008, est.) 2,687 applied for aid; of those 58% were deemed to have need. 92% of freshmen with need received aid; of those 19% had need fully met. ***Average percent of need met:*** 55% (excluding resources awarded to replace EFC). ***Average financial aid package:*** $8112 (excluding resources awarded to replace EFC). 12% of all full-time freshmen had no need and received non-need-based gift aid.

UNDERGRADUATE FINANCIAL AID (Fall 2008, est.) 9,197 applied for aid; of those 69% were deemed to have need. 95% of undergraduates with need received aid; of those 21% had need fully met. ***Average percent of need met:*** 72% (excluding resources awarded to replace EFC). ***Average financial aid package:*** $8735 (excluding resources awarded to replace EFC). 6% of all full-time undergraduates had no need and received non-need-based gift aid.

GIFT AID (NEED-BASED) ***Total amount:*** $21,341,001 (64% federal, 33% state, 3% institutional). ***Receiving aid:*** Freshmen: 16% (683); all full-time undergraduates: 21% (3,420). ***Average award:*** Freshmen: $6114; Undergraduates: $5753. ***Scholarships, grants, and awards:*** Federal Pell, FSEOG, state, private, college/university gift aid from institutional funds.

GIFT AID (NON-NEED-BASED) ***Total amount:*** $11,972,784 (96% institutional, 4% external sources). ***Receiving aid:*** Freshmen: 18% (759). Undergraduates: 11% (1,850). ***Average award:*** Freshmen: $2457. Undergraduates: $2264. ***Scholarships, grants, and awards by category:*** *Academic interests/achievement:* architecture, biological sciences, business, education, foreign languages, general academic interests/achievements, physical sciences, social sciences. *Creative arts/performance:* art/fine arts, dance, journalism/publications, music, performing arts, theater/drama. *Special achievements/activities:* general special achievements/activities. *Special characteristics:* general special characteristics, international students, local/state students. ***Tuition waivers:*** Full or partial for employees or children of employees. ***ROTC:*** Army, Air Force cooperative.

LOANS ***Student loans:*** $51,808,304 (46% need-based, 54% non-need-based). 55% of past graduating class borrowed through all loan programs. *Average indebtedness per student:* $18,805. ***Average need-based loan:*** Freshmen: $3755. Undergraduates: $4590. ***Parent loans:*** $27,078,322 (24% need-based, 76% non-need-based). ***Programs:*** Federal Direct (Subsidized and Unsubsidized Stafford, PLUS), Perkins, college/university.

WORK-STUDY ***Federal work-study:*** Total amount: $2,649,446; 1,740 jobs averaging $1456. ***State or other work-study/employment:*** Total amount: $247,597 (100% need-based). 130 part-time jobs averaging $1905.

ATHLETIC AWARDS Total amount: $6,634,799 (100% non-need-based).

APPLYING FOR FINANCIAL AID ***Required financial aid form:*** FAFSA. ***Financial aid deadline (priority):*** 3/1. ***Notification date:*** Continuous beginning 4/1. Students must reply within 4 weeks of notification.

CONTACT Elizabeth Bickford, Director of Financial Aid and Scholarships, University of Oregon, 1278 University of Oregon, Eugene, OR 97403-1278, 541-346-3221 or toll-free 800-232-3825 (in-state). *Fax:* 541-346-1175. *E-mail:* ebick@uoregon.edu.

UNIVERSITY OF PENNSYLVANIA

Philadelphia, PA

Tuition & fees: $37,526 **Average undergraduate aid package: $31,508**

ABOUT THE INSTITUTION Independent, coed. ***Awards:*** associate, bachelor's, master's, doctoral, and first professional degrees and post-bachelor's, post-master's, and first professional certificates (also offers evening program with significant enrollment not reflected in profile). 97 undergraduate majors. ***Total enrollment:*** 19,018. Undergraduates: 9,756. Freshmen: 2,400. Both federal and institutional methodology are used as a basis for awarding need-based institutional aid.

UNDERGRADUATE EXPENSES for 2008–09 ***Application fee:*** $75. ***Comprehensive fee:*** $48,147 includes full-time tuition ($33,608), mandatory fees ($3918), and room and board ($10,621). ***College room only:*** $6640. Room and board charges vary according to board plan and housing facility. ***Part-time tuition:*** $4292 per course. ***Part-time fees:*** $459 per course. Part-time tuition and fees vary according to course load. ***Payment plans:*** Tuition prepayment, installment.

FRESHMAN FINANCIAL AID (Fall 2007) 1,243 applied for aid; of those 74% were deemed to have need. 100% of freshmen with need received aid; of those 100% had need fully met. ***Average percent of need met:*** 100% (excluding resources awarded to replace EFC). ***Average financial aid package:*** $32,582 (excluding resources awarded to replace EFC).

UNDERGRADUATE FINANCIAL AID (Fall 2007) 4,603 applied for aid; of those 85% were deemed to have need. 100% of undergraduates with need received aid; of those 100% had need fully met. ***Average percent of need met:*** 100% (excluding resources awarded to replace EFC). ***Average financial aid package:*** $31,508 (excluding resources awarded to replace EFC).

GIFT AID (NEED-BASED) ***Total amount:*** $105,608,518 (5% federal, 2% state, 89% institutional, 4% external sources). ***Receiving aid:*** Freshmen: 36% (876); all full-time undergraduates: 39% (3,714). ***Average award:*** Freshmen: $29,284; Undergraduates: $27,111. ***Scholarships, grants, and awards:*** Federal Pell, FSEOG, state, private, college/university gift aid from institutional funds.

GIFT AID (NON-NEED-BASED) ***Total amount:*** $6,889,823 (1% federal, 1% state, 98% external sources). ***Tuition waivers:*** Full or partial for employees or children of employees. ***ROTC:*** Army cooperative, Naval, Air Force cooperative.

LOANS ***Student loans:*** $29,147,614 (37% need-based, 63% non-need-based). 41% of past graduating class borrowed through all loan programs. *Average indebtedness per student:* $19,085. ***Average need-based loan:*** Freshmen: $1912. Undergraduates: $2879. ***Parent loans:*** $11,962,894 (60% need-based, 40% non-need-based). ***Programs:*** FFEL (Subsidized and Unsubsidized Stafford, PLUS), Perkins, Federal Nursing, college/university, supplemental third-party loans (guaranteed by institution).

WORK-STUDY ***Federal work-study:*** Total amount: $8,234,200; 2,855 jobs averaging $2884. ***State or other work-study/employment:*** Total amount: $1,394,484 (100% need-based). 480 part-time jobs averaging $2905.

APPLYING FOR FINANCIAL AID ***Required financial aid forms:*** FAFSA, institution's own form, CSS Financial Aid PROFILE, noncustodial (divorced/separated) parent's statement, business/farm supplement, student most recently completed income tax. ***Financial aid deadline (priority):*** 2/15. ***Notification date:*** 4/1. Students must reply by 5/1.

CONTACT Mr. William Schilling, Director of Financial Aid, University of Pennsylvania, 212 Franklin Building, Philadelphia, PA 19104-6270, 215-898-6784. *Fax:* 215-573-2208. *E-mail:* schilling@sfs.upenn.edu.

UNIVERSITY OF PHOENIX

Phoenix, AZ

CONTACT ACS/AFS, University of Phoenix, 875 West Elliot Road, Suite 116, Tempe, AZ 85284, 480-735-3000 or toll-free 800-776-4867 (in-state), 800-228-7240 (out-of-state). *Fax:* 480-940-2060.

UNIVERSITY OF PHOENIX–ATLANTA CAMPUS

Sandy Springs, GA

CONTACT ACS/AFS, University of Phoenix–Atlanta Campus, 875 West Elliot Road, Suite 116, Tempe, AZ 85284, 480-735-3000 or toll-free 800-776-4867 (in-state), 800-228-7240 (out-of-state). *Fax:* 480-940-2060.

UNIVERSITY OF PHOENIX–BAY AREA CAMPUS

Pleasanton, CA

CONTACT ACS/AFS, University of Phoenix–Bay Area Campus, 875 West Elliot Road, Suite 116, Tempe, AZ 85284, 480-735-3000 or toll-free 877-4-STUDENT. *Fax:* 480-940-2060.

UNIVERSITY OF PHOENIX–BOSTON CAMPUS

Braintree, MA

CONTACT ACS/AFS, University of Phoenix–Boston Campus, 875 West Elliot Road, Suite 116, Tempe, AZ 85284, 480-735-3000 or toll-free 800-228-7240. *Fax:* 480-940-2060.

UNIVERSITY OF PHOENIX–CENTRAL FLORIDA CAMPUS

Maitland, FL

CONTACT ACS/AFS, University of Phoenix–Central Florida Campus, 875 West Elliot Road, Suite 116, Tempe, AZ 85284, 480-735-3000 or toll-free 800-776-4867 (in-state), 800-228-7240 (out-of-state). *Fax:* 480-940-2060.

UNIVERSITY OF PHOENIX–CENTRAL MASSACHUSETTS CAMPUS

Westborough, MA

CONTACT ACS/AFS, University of Phoenix–Central Massachusetts Campus, 875 West Elliot Road, Suite 116, Tempe, AZ 85284, 480-735-3000 or toll-free 800-776-4867 (in-state), 800-228-7240 (out-of-state). *Fax:* 480-940-2060.

UNIVERSITY OF PHOENIX–CENTRAL VALLEY CAMPUS

Fresno, CA

CONTACT ACS/AFS, University of Phoenix–Central Valley Campus, 875 West Elliot Road, Suite 116, Tempe, AZ 85284, 480-735-3000 or toll-free 888-776-4867 (in-state), 888-228-7240 (out-of-state). *Fax:* 480-940-2060.

UNIVERSITY OF PHOENIX–CHARLOTTE CAMPUS

Charlotte, NC

CONTACT ACS/AFS, University of Phoenix–Charlotte Campus, 875 West Elliot Road, Suite 116, Tempe, AZ 85284, 480-735-3000 or toll-free 800-776-4867 (in-state), 800-228-7240 (out-of-state). *Fax:* 480-940-2060.

UNIVERSITY OF PHOENIX–CHICAGO CAMPUS

Schaumburg, IL

CONTACT ACS/AFS, University of Phoenix–Chicago Campus, 875 West Elliot Road, Suite 116, Tempe, AZ 85284, 480-735-3000 or toll-free 800-776-4867 (in-state), 800-228-7240 (out-of-state). *Fax:* 480-940-2060.

UNIVERSITY OF PHOENIX–CINCINNATI CAMPUS

West Chester, OH

CONTACT ACS/AFS, University of Phoenix–Cincinnati Campus, 875 West Elliot Road, Suite 116, Tempe, AZ 85284, 480-735-3000 or toll-free 800-776-4867 (in-state), 800-228-7240 (out-of-state). *Fax:* 480-940-2060.

UNIVERSITY OF PHOENIX–CLEVELAND CAMPUS

Independence, OH

CONTACT ACS/AFS, University of Phoenix–Cleveland Campus, 875 West Elliot Road, Suite 116, Tempe, AZ 85284, 480-735-3000 or toll-free 800-776-4867 (in-state), 800-228-7240 (out-of-state). *Fax:* 480-940-2060.

UNIVERSITY OF PHOENIX–COLUMBUS GEORGIA CAMPUS

Columbus, GA

CONTACT ACS/AFS, University of Phoenix–Columbus Georgia Campus, 875 West Elliot Road, Suite 116, Tempe, AZ 85284, 480-735-3000 or toll-free 800-776-4867 (in-state), 800-228-7240 (out-of-state). *Fax:* 480-940-2060.

UNIVERSITY OF PHOENIX–COLUMBUS OHIO CAMPUS

Columbus, OH

CONTACT ACS/AFS, University of Phoenix–Columbus Ohio Campus, 875 West Elliot Road, Suite 116, Tempe, AZ 85284, 480-735-3000 or toll-free 800-776-4867 (in-state), 800-228-7240 (out-of-state). *Fax:* 480-940-2060.

UNIVERSITY OF PHOENIX–DALLAS CAMPUS

Dallas, TX

CONTACT ACS/AFS, University of Phoenix–Dallas Campus, 875 West Elliot Road, Suite 116, Tempe, AZ 85284, 480-735-3000 or toll-free 800-776-4867 (in-state), 800-228-7240 (out-of-state). *Fax:* 480-940-2060.

UNIVERSITY OF PHOENIX–DENVER CAMPUS

Lone Tree, CO

CONTACT ACS/AFS, University of Phoenix–Denver Campus, 875 West Elliot Road, Suite 116, Tempe, AZ 85284, 480-735-3000 or toll-free 800-776-4867 (in-state), 800-228-7240 (out-of-state). *Fax:* 480-940-2060.

UNIVERSITY OF PHOENIX–EASTERN WASHINGTON CAMPUS

Spokane Valley, WA

CONTACT ACS/AFS, University of Phoenix–Eastern Washington Campus, 875 West Elliot Road, Suite 116, Tempe, AZ 85284, 480-735-3000 or toll-free 800-697-8223 (in-state), 800-228-7240 (out-of-state). *Fax:* 480-940-2060.

UNIVERSITY OF PHOENIX–HAWAII CAMPUS

Honolulu, HI

CONTACT ACS/AFS, University of Phoenix–Hawaii Campus, 875 West Elliot Road, Suite 116, Tempe, AZ 85284, 480-735-3000 or toll-free 800-776-4867 (in-state), 800-228-7240 (out-of-state). *Fax:* 480-940-2060.

UNIVERSITY OF PHOENIX–HOUSTON CAMPUS

Houston, TX

CONTACT ACS/AFS, University of Phoenix–Houston Campus, 875 West Elliot Road, Suite 116, Tempe, AZ 85284, 480-735-3000 or toll-free 800-776-4867 (in-state), 800-228-7240 (out-of-state). *Fax:* 480-940-2060.

UNIVERSITY OF PHOENIX–IDAHO CAMPUS

Meridian, ID

CONTACT ACS/AFS, University of Phoenix–Idaho Campus, 875 West Elliot Road, Suite 116, Tempe, AZ 85284, 480-735-3000 or toll-free 800-776-4867 (in-state), 800-228-7240 (out-of-state). *Fax:* 480-940-2060.

UNIVERSITY OF PHOENIX–INDIANAPOLIS CAMPUS

Indianapolis, IN

CONTACT ACS/AFS, University of Phoenix–Indianapolis Campus, 875 West Elliot Road, Suite 116, Tempe, AZ 85284, 480-735-3000 or toll-free 800-776-4867 (in-state), 800-228-7240 (out-of-state). *Fax:* 480-940-2060.

UNIVERSITY OF PHOENIX–KANSAS CITY CAMPUS

Kansas City, MO

CONTACT ACS/AFS, University of Phoenix–Kansas City Campus, 875 West Elliot Road, Suite 116, Tempe, AZ 85284, 480-735-3000 or toll-free 800-776-4867 (in-state), 800-228-7240 (out-of-state). *Fax:* 480-940-2060.

UNIVERSITY OF PHOENIX–LAS VEGAS CAMPUS

Las Vegas, NV

CONTACT ACS/AFS, University of Phoenix–Las Vegas Campus, 875 West Elliot Road, Suite 116, Tempe, AZ 85284, 480-735-3000 or toll-free 800-776-4867 (in-state), 800-228-7240 (out-of-state). *Fax:* 480-940-2060.

UNIVERSITY OF PHOENIX–LITTLE ROCK CAMPUS

Little Rock, AR

CONTACT ACS/AFS, University of Phoenix–Little Rock Campus, 875 West Elliot Road, Suite 116, Tempe, AZ 85284, 480-735-3000 or toll-free 800-776-4867 (in-state), 800-228-7240 (out-of-state). *Fax:* 480-940-2060.

UNIVERSITY OF PHOENIX–LOUISIANA CAMPUS

Metairie, LA

CONTACT ACS/AFS, University of Phoenix–Louisiana Campus, 875 West Elliot Road, Suite 116, Tempe, AZ 85284, 480-735-3000 or toll-free 800-776-4867 (in-state), 800-228-7240 (out-of-state). *Fax:* 480-940-2060.

UNIVERSITY OF PHOENIX–MARYLAND CAMPUS

Columbia, MD

CONTACT ACS/AFS, University of Phoenix–Maryland Campus, 875 West Elliot Road, Suite 116, Tempe, AZ 85284, 480-735-3000 or toll-free 800-776-4867 (in-state), 800-228-7240 (out-of-state). *Fax:* 480-940-2060.

UNIVERSITY OF PHOENIX–METRO DETROIT CAMPUS

Troy, MI

CONTACT ACS/AFS, University of Phoenix–Metro Detroit Campus, 875 West Elliot Road, Suite 116, Tempe, AZ 85284, 480-735-3000 or toll-free 800-776-4867 (in-state), 800-228-7240 (out-of-state). *Fax:* 480-940-2060.

UNIVERSITY OF PHOENIX–NASHVILLE CAMPUS

Nashville, TN

CONTACT ACS/AFS, University of Phoenix–Nashville Campus, 875 West Elliot Road, Suite 116, Tempe, AZ 85284, 480-735-3000 or toll-free 800-776-4867 (in-state), 800-228-7240 (out-of-state). *Fax:* 480-940-2060.

UNIVERSITY OF PHOENIX–NEW MEXICO CAMPUS

Albuquerque, NM

CONTACT ACS/AFS, University of Phoenix–New Mexico Campus, 875 West Elliot Road, Suite 116, Tempe, AZ 85284, 480-735-3000 or toll-free 800-776-4867 (in-state), 800-228-7240 (out-of-state). *Fax:* 480-940-2060.

UNIVERSITY OF PHOENIX–NORTHERN VIRGINIA CAMPUS

Reston, VA

CONTACT ACS/AFS, University of Phoenix–Northern Virginia Campus, 875 W. Elliott Road, Suite 116, Tempe, AZ 85284, 480-735-3000 or toll-free 800-776-4867 (in-state), 800-228-7240 (out-of-state). *Fax:* 480-940-2060.

UNIVERSITY OF PHOENIX–NORTH FLORIDA CAMPUS

Jacksonville, FL

CONTACT ACS/AFS, University of Phoenix–North Florida Campus, 875 West Elliot Road, Suite 116, Tempe, AZ 85284, 480-735-3000 or toll-free 800-776-4867 (in-state), 800-894-1758 (out-of-state). *Fax:* 480-940-2060.

UNIVERSITY OF PHOENIX–OKLAHOMA CITY CAMPUS

Oklahoma City, OK

CONTACT ACS/AFS, University of Phoenix–Oklahoma City Campus, 875 West Elliot Road, Suite 116, Tempe, AZ 85284, 480-735-3000 or toll-free 800-776-4867 (in-state), 800-228-7240 (out-of-state). *Fax:* 480-940-2060.

UNIVERSITY OF PHOENIX–OREGON CAMPUS

Tigard, OR

CONTACT ACS/AFS, University of Phoenix–Oregon Campus, 875 West Elliot Road, Suite 116, Tempe, AZ 85284, 480-735-3000 or toll-free 800-776-4867 (in-state), 800-228-7240 (out-of-state). *Fax:* 480-940-2060.

UNIVERSITY OF PHOENIX–PHILADELPHIA CAMPUS

Wayne, PA

CONTACT ACS/AFS, University of Phoenix–Philadelphia Campus, 875 West Elliot Road, Suite 116, Tempe, AZ 85284, 480-735-3000 or toll-free 800-776-4867 (in-state), 800-228-7240 (out-of-state). *Fax:* 480-940-2060.

UNIVERSITY OF PHOENIX–PHOENIX CAMPUS

Phoenix, AZ

CONTACT ACS/AFS, University of Phoenix–Phoenix Campus, 875 West Elliot Road, Suite 116, Tempe, AZ 85284, 480-735-3000 or toll-free 800-776-4867 (in-state), 800-228-7240 (out-of-state). *Fax:* 480-940-2060.

UNIVERSITY OF PHOENIX–PITTSBURGH CAMPUS

Pittsburgh, PA

CONTACT ACS/AFS, University of Phoenix–Pittsburgh Campus, 875 West Elliot Road, Suite 116, Tempe, AZ 85284, 480-735-3000 or toll-free 800-776-4867 (in-state), 800-228-7240 (out-of-state). *Fax:* 480-940-2060.

UNIVERSITY OF PHOENIX–PUERTO RICO CAMPUS

Guaynabo, PR

CONTACT ACS/AFS, University of Phoenix–Puerto Rico Campus, 875 West Elliot Road, Suite 116, Tempe, AZ 85284, 480-735-3000 or toll-free 800-776-4867 (in-state), 800-228-7240 (out-of-state). *Fax:* 480-940-2060.

UNIVERSITY OF PHOENIX–RALEIGH CAMPUS

Raleigh, NC

CONTACT ACS/AFS, University of Phoenix–Raleigh Campus, 875 West Elliot Road, Suite 116, Tempe, AZ 85284, 480-735-3000 or toll-free 800-776-4867 (in-state), 800-228-7240 (out-of-state). *Fax:* 480-940-2060.

UNIVERSITY OF PHOENIX–RICHMOND CAMPUS

Richmond, VA

CONTACT ACS/AFS, University of Phoenix–Richmond Campus, 875 West Elliot Road, Suite 116, Tempe, AZ 85284, 480-735-3000 or toll-free 800-776-4867 (in-state), 800-228-7240 (out-of-state). *Fax:* 480-940-2060.

UNIVERSITY OF PHOENIX–SACRAMENTO VALLEY CAMPUS

Sacramento, CA

CONTACT ACS/AFS, University of Phoenix–Sacramento Valley Campus, 875 West Elliot Road, Suite 116, Tempe, AZ 85284, 480-735-3000 or toll-free 800-776-4867 (in-state), 800-228-7240 (out-of-state). *Fax:* 480-940-2060.

UNIVERSITY OF PHOENIX–ST. LOUIS CAMPUS

St. Louis, MO

CONTACT ACS/AFS, University of Phoenix–St. Louis Campus, 875 West Elliot Road, Suite 116, Tempe, AZ 85284, 480-735-3000 or toll-free 800-776-4867 (in-state), 800-228-7240 (out-of-state). *Fax:* 480-940-2060.

UNIVERSITY OF PHOENIX–SAN DIEGO CAMPUS

San Diego, CA

CONTACT ACS/AFS, University of Phoenix–San Diego Campus, 875 West Elliot Road, Suite 116, Tempe, AZ 85284, 480-735-3000 or toll-free 888-776-4867 (in-state), 888-228-7240 (out-of-state). *Fax:* 480-940-2060.

UNIVERSITY OF PHOENIX–SOUTHERN ARIZONA CAMPUS

Tucson, AZ

CONTACT ACS/AFS, University of Phoenix–Southern Arizona Campus, 875 West Elliot Road, Suite 116, Tempe, AZ 85284, 480-735-3000 or toll-free 800-776-4867 (in-state), 800-228-7240 (out-of-state). *Fax:* 480-940-2060.

UNIVERSITY OF PHOENIX–SOUTHERN CALIFORNIA CAMPUS

Costa Mesa, CA

CONTACT ACS/AFS, University of Phoenix–Southern California Campus, 875 West Elliot Road, Suite 116, Tempe, AZ 85284, 480-735-3000 or toll-free 800-776-4867 (in-state), 800-228-7240 (out-of-state). *Fax:* 480-940-2060.

UNIVERSITY OF PHOENIX–SOUTHERN COLORADO CAMPUS

Colorado Springs, CO

CONTACT ACS/AFS, University of Phoenix–Southern Colorado Campus, 875 West Elliot Road, Suite 116, Tempe, AZ 85284, 480-735-3000 or toll-free 800-776-4867 (in-state), 800-228-7240 (out-of-state). *Fax:* 480-940-2060.

UNIVERSITY OF PHOENIX–SOUTH FLORIDA CAMPUS

Fort Lauderdale, FL

CONTACT ACS/AFS, University of Phoenix–South Florida Campus, 875 West Elliot Road, Suite 116, Tempe, AZ 85284, 480-735-3000 or toll-free 800-228-7240. *Fax:* 480-940-2060.

UNIVERSITY OF PHOENIX–SPRINGFIELD CAMPUS

Springfield, MO

CONTACT ACS/AFS, University of Phoenix–Springfield Campus, 875 West Elliot Road, Suite 116, Tempe, AZ 85284, 480-735-3000 or toll-free 800-776-4867 (in-state), 800-228-7240 (out-of-state). *Fax:* 480-940-2060.

UNIVERSITY OF PHOENIX–TULSA CAMPUS

Tulsa, OK

CONTACT ACS/AFS, University of Phoenix–Tulsa Campus, 875 West Elliot Road, Suite 116, Tempe, AZ 85284, 480-735-3000 or toll-free 800-776-4867 (in-state), 800-228-7240 (out-of-state). *Fax:* 480-940-2060.

UNIVERSITY OF PHOENIX–UTAH CAMPUS

Salt Lake City, UT

CONTACT ACS/AFS, University of Phoenix–Utah Campus, 875 West Elliot Road, Suite 116, Tempe, AZ 85284, 480-735-3000 or toll-free 800-776-4867 (in-state), 800-228-7240 (out-of-state). *Fax:* 480-940-2060.

UNIVERSITY OF PHOENIX–WASHINGTON CAMPUS

Seattle, WA

CONTACT ACS/AFS, University of Phoenix–Washington Campus, 875 West Elliot Road, Suite 116, Tempe, AZ 85284, 480-735-3000 or toll-free 800-776-4867 (in-state), 800-228-7240 (out-of-state). *Fax:* 480-940-2060.

UNIVERSITY OF PHOENIX–WASHINGTON D.C. CAMPUS

Washington, DC

CONTACT Financial Aid Office, University of Phoenix–Washington D.C. Campus, 25 Massachusetts Avenue NW, Suite 150, Washington, DC 20001.

UNIVERSITY OF PHOENIX–WEST FLORIDA CAMPUS

Temple Terrace, FL

CONTACT ACS/AFS, University of Phoenix–West Florida Campus, 875 West Elliot Road, Suite 116, Tempe, AZ 85284, 480-735-3000 or toll-free 800-776-4867 (in-state), 800-228-7240 (out-of-state). *Fax:* 480-940-2060.

UNIVERSITY OF PHOENIX–WEST MICHIGAN CAMPUS

Walker, MI

CONTACT ACS/AFS, University of Phoenix–West Michigan Campus, 875 West Elliot Road, Suite 116, Tempe, AZ 85284, 480-735-3000 or toll-free 800-776-4867 (in-state), 800-228-7240 (out-of-state). *Fax:* 480-940-2060.

UNIVERSITY OF PHOENIX–WICHITA CAMPUS

Wichita, KS

CONTACT ACS/AFS, University of Phoenix–Wichita Campus, 875 West Elliot Road, Suite 116, Tempe, AZ 85284, 480-735-3000 or toll-free 800-776-4867 (in-state), 800-228-7240 (out-of-state). *Fax:* 480-940-2060.

UNIVERSITY OF PHOENIX–WISCONSIN CAMPUS

Brookfield, WI

CONTACT ACS/AFS, University of Phoenix–Wisconsin Campus, 875 West Elliot Road, Suite 116, Tempe, AZ 85284, 480-735-3000 or toll-free 800-776-4867 (in-state), 800-228-7240 (out-of-state). *Fax:* 480-940-2060.

UNIVERSITY OF PITTSBURGH

Pittsburgh, PA

Tuition & fees (PA res): $13,642 Average undergraduate aid package: $9696

ABOUT THE INSTITUTION State-related, coed. ***Awards:*** bachelor's, master's, doctoral, and first professional degrees and post-bachelor's and post-master's certificates. 85 undergraduate majors. ***Total enrollment:*** 27,562. Undergraduates: 17,427. Freshmen: 3,524. Federal methodology is used as a basis for awarding need-based institutional aid.

UNDERGRADUATE EXPENSES for 2008–09 ***Application fee:*** $45. ***Tuition, state resident:*** full-time $12,832; part-time $534 per credit. ***Tuition, nonresident:*** full-time $22,480; part-time $936 per credit. ***Required fees:*** full-time $810; $189 per term. Full-time tuition and fees vary according to degree level and program. Part-time tuition and fees vary according to degree level and program. ***College room and board:*** $7750; ***Room only:*** $4940. Room and board charges vary according to board plan and housing facility. ***Payment plans:*** Installment, deferred payment.

FRESHMAN FINANCIAL AID (Fall 2008, est.) 2,792 applied for aid; of those 68% were deemed to have need. 98% of freshmen with need received aid; of those 43% had need fully met. ***Average percent of need met:*** 82% (excluding resources awarded to replace EFC). ***Average financial aid package:*** $10,340 (excluding resources awarded to replace EFC). 8% of all full-time freshmen had no need and received non-need-based gift aid.

UNDERGRADUATE FINANCIAL AID (Fall 2008, est.) 11,135 applied for aid; of those 78% were deemed to have need. 97% of undergraduates with need received aid; of those 40% had need fully met. ***Average percent of need met:*** 81% (excluding resources awarded to replace EFC). ***Average financial aid package:*** $9696 (excluding resources awarded to replace EFC). 7% of all full-time undergraduates had no need and received non-need-based gift aid.

GIFT AID (NEED-BASED) ***Total amount:*** $44,500,450 (25% federal, 22% state, 40% institutional, 13% external sources). ***Receiving aid:*** Freshmen: 41% (1,456); all full-time undergraduates: 37% (5,950). ***Average award:*** Freshmen: $9170; Undergraduates: $7762. ***Scholarships, grants, and awards:*** Federal Pell, FSEOG, state, private, college/university gift aid from institutional funds, Federal Nursing.

GIFT AID (NON-NEED-BASED) ***Total amount:*** $21,259,946 (2% state, 72% institutional, 26% external sources). ***Receiving aid:*** Freshmen: 25% (884). Undergraduates: 17% (2,657). ***Average award:*** Freshmen: $13,504. Undergraduates: $14,630. ***Scholarships, grants, and awards by category:*** *Academic interests/achievement:* 1,118 awards ($16,356,340 total): general academic interests/achievements. ***Tuition waivers:*** Full or partial for employees or children of employees. ***ROTC:*** Army, Naval cooperative, Air Force.

LOANS ***Student loans:*** $90,902,522 (39% need-based, 61% non-need-based). ***Average need-based loan:*** Freshmen: $4356. Undergraduates: $4899. ***Parent loans:*** $16,729,044 (73% need-based, 27% non-need-based). ***Programs:*** FFEL (Subsidized and Unsubsidized Stafford, PLUS), Perkins, Federal Nursing, college/university.

WORK-STUDY ***Federal work-study:*** Total amount: $2,500,000; 1,487 jobs averaging $1796.

ATHLETIC AWARDS Total amount: $7,182,245 (39% need-based, 61% non-need-based).

APPLYING FOR FINANCIAL AID ***Required financial aid form:*** FAFSA. ***Financial aid deadline (priority):*** 3/1. ***Notification date:*** Continuous beginning 3/15. Students must reply by 5/1 or within 3 weeks of notification.

CONTACT Dr. Betsy A. Porter, Director, Office of Admissions and Financial Aid, University of Pittsburgh, 4227 Fifth Avenue, First Floor, Pittsburgh, PA 15260, 412-624-7488. *Fax:* 412-648-8815. *E-mail:* oafa@pitt.edu.

UNIVERSITY OF PITTSBURGH AT BRADFORD

Bradford, PA

Tuition & fees (PA res): $11,722 Average undergraduate aid package: $12,093

ABOUT THE INSTITUTION State-related, coed. ***Awards:*** associate and bachelor's degrees. 33 undergraduate majors. ***Total enrollment:*** 1,504. Undergraduates: 1,504. Freshmen: 379. Federal methodology is used as a basis for awarding need-based institutional aid.

UNDERGRADUATE EXPENSES for 2008–09 ***Application fee:*** $45. ***Tuition, state resident:*** full-time $11,012; part-time $458 per credit. ***Tuition, nonresident:***

full-time $20,572; part-time $857 per credit. ***Required fees:*** full-time $710; $105 per term. Full-time tuition and fees vary according to course load and program. Part-time tuition and fees vary according to course load and program. ***College room and board:*** $7050; ***Room only:*** $4240. Room and board charges vary according to board plan and housing facility. ***Payment plan:*** Installment.

FRESHMAN FINANCIAL AID (Fall 2008, est.) 355 applied for aid; of those 86% were deemed to have need. 100% of freshmen with need received aid; of those 46% had need fully met. ***Average percent of need met:*** 89% (excluding resources awarded to replace EFC). ***Average financial aid package:*** $12,666 (excluding resources awarded to replace EFC). 3% of all full-time freshmen had no need and received non-need-based gift aid.

UNDERGRADUATE FINANCIAL AID (Fall 2008, est.) 1,227 applied for aid; of those 89% were deemed to have need. 100% of undergraduates with need received aid; of those 44% had need fully met. ***Average percent of need met:*** 84% (excluding resources awarded to replace EFC). ***Average financial aid package:*** $12,093 (excluding resources awarded to replace EFC). 2% of all full-time undergraduates had no need and received non-need-based gift aid.

GIFT AID (NEED-BASED) ***Total amount:*** $8,680,788 (23% federal, 23% state, 48% institutional, 6% external sources). ***Receiving aid:*** Freshmen: 75% (283); all full-time undergraduates: 73% (964). ***Average award:*** Freshmen: $8722; Undergraduates: $4088. ***Scholarships, grants, and awards:*** Federal Pell, FSEOG, state, private, college/university gift aid from institutional funds, Academic Competitiveness Grant, National Smart Grant.

GIFT AID (NON-NEED-BASED) ***Average award:*** Freshmen: $7125. Undergraduates: $5352. ***Scholarships, grants, and awards by category:*** *Academic interests/achievement:* biological sciences, business, communication, computer science, education, engineering/technologies, English, general academic interests/achievements, health fields, humanities, mathematics, physical sciences, premedicine, social sciences. ***Tuition waivers:*** Full or partial for employees or children of employees. ***ROTC:*** Army cooperative.

LOANS ***Student loans:*** $9,839,461 (39% need-based, 61% non-need-based). 92% of past graduating class borrowed through all loan programs. *Average indebtedness per student:* $26,463. ***Average need-based loan:*** Freshmen: $3245. Undergraduates: $4044. ***Parent loans:*** $1,189,030 (100% non-need-based). ***Programs:*** FFEL (Subsidized and Unsubsidized Stafford, PLUS), Perkins.

WORK-STUDY ***Federal work-study:*** Total amount: $1,188,238; 156 jobs averaging $1725. ***State or other work-study/employment:*** Total amount: $6960 (100% non-need-based). 29 part-time jobs averaging $1315.

APPLYING FOR FINANCIAL AID ***Required financial aid form:*** FAFSA. ***Financial aid deadline (priority):*** 3/1. ***Notification date:*** Continuous beginning 4/1. Students must reply within 2 weeks of notification.

CONTACT Melissa Ibanez, Director of Financial Aid, University of Pittsburgh at Bradford, 300 Campus Drive, Bradford, PA 16701-2812, 814-362-7550 or toll-free 800-872-1787. *Fax:* 814-362-7578. *E-mail:* ibanez@pitt.edu.

UNIVERSITY OF PITTSBURGH AT GREENSBURG

Greensburg, PA

Tuition & fees (PA res): $11,782 Average undergraduate aid package: $8901

ABOUT THE INSTITUTION State-related, coed. ***Awards:*** bachelor's degrees. 22 undergraduate majors. ***Total enrollment:*** 1,826. Undergraduates: 1,826. Freshmen: 462. Federal methodology is used as a basis for awarding need-based institutional aid.

UNDERGRADUATE EXPENSES for 2008–09 ***Application fee:*** $45. ***Tuition, state resident:*** full-time $11,012; part-time $458 per credit. ***Tuition, nonresident:*** full-time $20,572; part-time $857 per credit. ***Required fees:*** full-time $770. ***College room and board:*** $7530.

FRESHMAN FINANCIAL AID (Fall 2008, est.) 406 applied for aid; of those 84% were deemed to have need. 99% of freshmen with need received aid; of those 13% had need fully met. ***Average percent of need met:*** 53% (excluding resources awarded to replace EFC). ***Average financial aid package:*** $8953 (excluding resources awarded to replace EFC). 8% of all full-time freshmen had no need and received non-need-based gift aid.

UNDERGRADUATE FINANCIAL AID (Fall 2008, est.) 1,363 applied for aid; of those 83% were deemed to have need. 98% of undergraduates with need received aid; of those 17% had need fully met. ***Average percent of need met:*** 54% (excluding resources awarded to replace EFC). ***Average financial aid package:*** $8901 (excluding resources awarded to replace EFC). 5% of all full-time undergraduates had no need and received non-need-based gift aid.

GIFT AID (NEED-BASED) ***Total amount:*** $5,743,963 (30% federal, 53% state, 10% institutional, 7% external sources). ***Receiving aid:*** Freshmen: 59% (270); all full-time undergraduates: 47% (796). ***Average award:*** Freshmen: $6177; Undergraduates: $5563. ***Scholarships, grants, and awards:*** Federal Pell, FSEOG, state, private, college/university gift aid from institutional funds, United Negro College Fund.

GIFT AID (NON-NEED-BASED) ***Total amount:*** $572,468 (10% state, 46% institutional, 44% external sources). ***Receiving aid:*** Freshmen: 16% (75). Undergraduates: 13% (211). ***Average award:*** Freshmen: $1526. Undergraduates: $3572. ***Scholarships, grants, and awards by category:*** *Special achievements/activities:* leadership. ***ROTC:*** Army cooperative, Air Force cooperative.

LOANS ***Student loans:*** $10,589,070 (83% need-based, 17% non-need-based). 80% of past graduating class borrowed through all loan programs. *Average indebtedness per student:* $21,468. ***Average need-based loan:*** Freshmen: $3592. Undergraduates: $4316. ***Parent loans:*** $1,418,908 (68% need-based, 32% non-need-based). ***Programs:*** FFEL (Subsidized and Unsubsidized Stafford, PLUS), Perkins, college/university.

WORK-STUDY ***Federal work-study:*** Total amount: $311,959; jobs available.

APPLYING FOR FINANCIAL AID ***Required financial aid forms:*** FAFSA, state aid form. ***Financial aid deadline (priority):*** 2/15. ***Notification date:*** Continuous beginning 3/15. Students must reply within 3 weeks of notification.

CONTACT Ms. Brandi S. Darr, Director of Financial Aid, University of Pittsburgh at Greensburg, 150 Finoli Drive, Greensburg, PA 15601-5860, 724-836-7167. *E-mail:* bsd@pitt.edu.

UNIVERSITY OF PITTSBURGH AT JOHNSTOWN

Johnstown, PA

Tuition & fees (PA res): $11,674 Average undergraduate aid package: $9678

ABOUT THE INSTITUTION State-related, coed. ***Awards:*** associate and bachelor's degrees. 50 undergraduate majors. ***Total enrollment:*** 3,032. Undergraduates: 3,032. Freshmen: 850. Federal methodology is used as a basis for awarding need-based institutional aid.

UNDERGRADUATE EXPENSES for 2008–09 ***Application fee:*** $45. ***Tuition, state resident:*** full-time $11,012; part-time $458 per credit. ***Tuition, nonresident:*** full-time $20,572; part-time $857 per credit. ***Required fees:*** full-time $662; $87 per term. ***College room and board:*** $6860; ***Room only:*** $4200.

FRESHMAN FINANCIAL AID (Fall 2008, est.) 715 applied for aid; of those 83% were deemed to have need. 99% of freshmen with need received aid; of those 6% had need fully met. ***Average percent of need met:*** 62% (excluding resources awarded to replace EFC). ***Average financial aid package:*** $9415 (excluding resources awarded to replace EFC). 4% of all full-time freshmen had no need and received non-need-based gift aid.

UNDERGRADUATE FINANCIAL AID (Fall 2008, est.) 2,607 applied for aid; of those 85% were deemed to have need. 95% of undergraduates with need received aid; of those 11% had need fully met. ***Average percent of need met:*** 56% (excluding resources awarded to replace EFC). ***Average financial aid package:*** $9678 (excluding resources awarded to replace EFC). 3% of all full-time undergraduates had no need and received non-need-based gift aid.

GIFT AID (NEED-BASED) ***Total amount:*** $7,792,346 (37% federal, 50% state, 9% institutional, 4% external sources). ***Receiving aid:*** Freshmen: 51% (407); all full-time undergraduates: 51% (1,482). ***Average award:*** Freshmen: $5040; Undergraduates: $4903. ***Scholarships, grants, and awards:*** Federal Pell, FSEOG, state, private, college/university gift aid from institutional funds.

GIFT AID (NON-NEED-BASED) ***Total amount:*** $2,176,034 (12% state, 73% institutional, 15% external sources). ***Receiving aid:*** Freshmen: 21% (169). Undergraduates: 20% (580). ***Average award:*** Freshmen: $2494. Undergraduates: $3421. ***Scholarships, grants, and awards by category:*** *Academic interests/achievement:* 489 awards ($1,580,430 total): biological sciences, business, communication, computer science, education, engineering/technologies, English, general academic interests/achievements, humanities, mathematics, physical sciences, premedicine, social sciences. *Creative arts/performance:* 5 awards ($23,580 total): journalism/publications, theater/drama. *Special achievements/activities:* 181 awards ($198,370 total): leadership. *Special characteristics:* 172 awards ($1,809,466 total): children of faculty/staff.

LOANS ***Student loans:*** $19,769,028 (40% need-based, 60% non-need-based). 86% of past graduating class borrowed through all loan programs. *Average indebtedness per student:* $23,295. ***Average need-based loan:*** Freshmen: $3421. Undergraduates: $4261. ***Parent loans:*** $3,020,087 (100% non-need-based). ***Programs:*** FFEL (Subsidized and Unsubsidized Stafford, PLUS), Perkins.

WORK-STUDY ***Federal work-study:*** Total amount: $539,736; 183 jobs averaging $1699. ***State or other work-study/employment:*** Total amount: $530,265 (6% need-based, 94% non-need-based). 273 part-time jobs averaging $2874.

ATHLETIC AWARDS Total amount: $537,732 (100% non-need-based).

APPLYING FOR FINANCIAL AID ***Required financial aid form:*** FAFSA. ***Financial aid deadline (priority):*** 4/1. ***Notification date:*** Continuous beginning 4/1. Students must reply within 2 weeks of notification.

CONTACT Ms. Jeanine M. Lawn, Director of Student Financial Aid, University of Pittsburgh at Johnstown, 125 Biddle Hall, Johnstown, PA 15904-2990, 814-269-7045 or toll-free 800-765-4875. *Fax:* 814-269-7061. *E-mail:* lawn@pitt.edu.

UNIVERSITY OF PORTLAND

Portland, OR

Tuition & fees: $30,400 **Average undergraduate aid package: $23,045**

ABOUT THE INSTITUTION Independent Roman Catholic, coed. ***Awards:*** bachelor's, master's, and doctoral degrees and post-master's certificates. 42 undergraduate majors. ***Total enrollment:*** 3,661. Undergraduates: 3,041. Freshmen: 794. Federal methodology is used as a basis for awarding need-based institutional aid.

UNDERGRADUATE EXPENSES for 2008–09 ***Application fee:*** $50. ***Comprehensive fee:*** $39,156 includes full-time tuition ($29,400), mandatory fees ($1000), and room and board ($8756). ***College room only:*** $4273. Room and board charges vary according to board plan and housing facility. ***Part-time tuition:*** $925 per credit hour.

FRESHMAN FINANCIAL AID (Fall 2008, est.) 675 applied for aid; of those 77% were deemed to have need. 100% of freshmen with need received aid; of those 12% had need fully met. ***Average percent of need met:*** 90% (excluding resources awarded to replace EFC). ***Average financial aid package:*** $23,432 (excluding resources awarded to replace EFC). 24% of all full-time freshmen had no need and received non-need-based gift aid.

UNDERGRADUATE FINANCIAL AID (Fall 2008, est.) 2,219 applied for aid; of those 81% were deemed to have need. 100% of undergraduates with need received aid; of those 9% had need fully met. ***Average percent of need met:*** 88% (excluding resources awarded to replace EFC). ***Average financial aid package:*** $23,045 (excluding resources awarded to replace EFC). 29% of all full-time undergraduates had no need and received non-need-based gift aid.

GIFT AID (NEED-BASED) ***Total amount:*** $29,059,850 (7% federal, 2% state, 85% institutional, 6% external sources). ***Receiving aid:*** Freshmen: 63% (501); all full-time undergraduates: 57% (1,716). ***Average award:*** Freshmen: $16,643; Undergraduates: $15,319. ***Scholarships, grants, and awards:*** Federal Pell, FSEOG, state, private, college/university gift aid from institutional funds.

GIFT AID (NON-NEED-BASED) ***Total amount:*** $9,354,417 (98% institutional, 2% external sources). ***Receiving aid:*** Freshmen: 26% (206). Undergraduates: 20% (614). ***Average award:*** Freshmen: $11,189. Undergraduates: $10,552. ***Scholarships, grants, and awards by category:*** *Academic interests/achievement:* 85 awards: biological sciences, business, communication, computer science, education, engineering/technologies, English, foreign languages, general academic interests/achievements, health fields, humanities, mathematics, military science, physical sciences, premedicine, religion/biblical studies, social sciences. *Creative arts/performance:* 71 awards ($2282 total): music, performing arts, theater/drama. *Special characteristics:* 68 awards ($27,424 total): children of faculty/staff, relatives of clergy. ***ROTC:*** Army, Air Force.

LOANS ***Student loans:*** $16,753,495 (88% need-based, 12% non-need-based). 63% of past graduating class borrowed through all loan programs. *Average indebtedness per student:* $21,535. ***Average need-based loan:*** Freshmen: $3425. Undergraduates: $4613. ***Parent loans:*** $7,053,506 (80% need-based, 20% non-need-based). ***Programs:*** FFEL (Subsidized and Unsubsidized Stafford, PLUS), Perkins, Federal Nursing, college/university.

WORK-STUDY ***Federal work-study:*** Total amount: $2,691,697; 858 jobs averaging $2639.

ATHLETIC AWARDS Total amount: $3,816,094 (25% need-based, 75% non-need-based).

APPLYING FOR FINANCIAL AID ***Required financial aid form:*** FAFSA. ***Financial aid deadline (priority):*** 3/1. ***Notification date:*** Continuous beginning 3/15. Students must reply within 3 weeks of notification.

CONTACT Ms. Janet Turner, Director of Financial Aid, University of Portland, 5000 North Willamette Boulevard, Portland, OR 97203-5798, 503-943-7311 or toll-free 888-627-5601 (out-of-state). *Fax:* 503-943-7508. *E-mail:* finaid@up.edu.

UNIVERSITY OF PUERTO RICO, AGUADILLA UNIVERSITY COLLEGE

Aguadilla, PR

CONTACT Director of Financial Aid, University of Puerto Rico, Aguadilla University College, PO Box 250-160, Aguadilla, PR 00604-0160, 787-890-2681 Ext. 273.

UNIVERSITY OF PUERTO RICO AT ARECIBO

Arecibo, PR

CONTACT Mr. Luis Rodriguez, Director of Financial Aid, University of Puerto Rico at Arecibo, PO Box 4010, Arecibo, PR 00613, 787-878-2830 Ext. 2008.

UNIVERSITY OF PUERTO RICO AT BAYAMÓN

Bayamón, PR

CONTACT Financial Aid Director, University of Puerto Rico at Bayamón, 170 Carr 174 Parque Indust Minillas, Bayamon, PR 00959-1919, 787-786-2885 Ext. 2434.

UNIVERSITY OF PUERTO RICO AT HUMACAO

Humacao, PR

CONTACT Larry Cruz, Director of Financial Aid, University of Puerto Rico at Humacao, HUC Station, Humacao, PR 00791-4300, 787-850-9342.

UNIVERSITY OF PUERTO RICO AT PONCE

Ponce, PR

CONTACT Carmelo Vega Montes, Director of Financial Aid, University of Puerto Rico at Ponce, Box 7186, Ponce, PR 00732-7186, 787-844-8181. *Fax:* 787-840-8108.

UNIVERSITY OF PUERTO RICO AT UTUADO

Utuado, PR

ABOUT THE INSTITUTION Commonwealth-supported, coed. ***Awards:*** associate and bachelor's degrees. 41 undergraduate majors. ***Total enrollment:*** 1,682. Undergraduates: 1,682. Freshmen: 612.

GIFT AID (NEED-BASED) ***Scholarships, grants, and awards:*** Federal Pell, FSEOG, state, private, college/university gift aid from institutional funds.

LOANS ***Programs:*** Federal Direct (Subsidized Stafford).

APPLYING FOR FINANCIAL AID ***Required financial aid forms:*** FAFSA, institution's own form.

CONTACT Edgar Salvá, Director of Financial Assistance, University of Puerto Rico at Utuado, PO Box 2500, Utuado, PR 00641, 787-894-2828 Ext. 2603. *Fax:* 787-894-3810. *E-mail:* esalva@uprutuado.edu.

UNIVERSITY OF PUERTO RICO, CAYEY UNIVERSITY COLLEGE

Cayey, PR

CONTACT Mr. Hector Maldonado Otero, Director of Financial Aid, University of Puerto Rico, Cayey University College, Antonio Barcelo, Cayey, PR 00736, 787-738-2161. *Fax:* 787-263-0676.

UNIVERSITY OF PUERTO RICO, MAYAGÜEZ CAMPUS

Mayagüez, PR

Tuition & fees: N/R **Average undergraduate aid package: $4293**

ABOUT THE INSTITUTION Commonwealth-supported, coed. 54 undergraduate majors. Federal methodology is used as a basis for awarding need-based institutional aid.

FRESHMAN FINANCIAL AID (Fall 2008, est.) 1,821 applied for aid; of those 82% were deemed to have need. 100% of freshmen with need received aid. ***Average percent of need met:*** 38% (excluding resources awarded to replace EFC). ***Average financial aid package:*** $4293 (excluding resources awarded to replace EFC).

UNDERGRADUATE FINANCIAL AID (Fall 2008, est.) 7,756 applied for aid; of those 85% were deemed to have need. 100% of undergraduates with need received aid. ***Average percent of need met:*** 38% (excluding resources awarded to replace EFC). ***Average financial aid package:*** $4293 (excluding resources awarded to replace EFC).

GIFT AID (NEED-BASED) ***Total amount:*** $25,110,458 (86% federal, 12% state, 2% external sources). ***Receiving aid:*** Freshmen: 65% (1,494); all full-time undergraduates: 54% (6,629). ***Average award:*** Freshmen: $4293; Undergraduates: $4293. ***Scholarships, grants, and awards:*** Federal Pell, FSEOG, state, private, college/university gift aid from institutional funds.

GIFT AID (NON-NEED-BASED) ***Total amount:*** $117,000 (100% external sources). ***Receiving aid:*** Freshmen: 2% (45). Undergraduates: 2% (249). ***Scholarships, grants, and awards by category:*** *Academic interests/achievement:* military science. *Creative arts/performance:* 251 awards ($341,360 total): dance, music. *Special achievements/activities:* 295 awards ($26,220 total): cheerleading/drum major. *Special characteristics:* 3,552 awards ($1257 total): children of faculty/staff, veterans' children. ***Tuition waivers:*** Full or partial for employees or children of employees.

LOANS ***Student loans:*** $6,703,437 (94% need-based, 6% non-need-based). 52% of past graduating class borrowed through all loan programs. *Average indebtedness per student:* $6400. ***Average need-based loan:*** Freshmen: $2625. Undergraduates: $3875. ***Programs:*** FFEL (Subsidized and Unsubsidized Stafford), college/university.

WORK-STUDY ***Federal work-study:*** Total amount: $730,280; 810 jobs averaging $982.

ATHLETIC AWARDS Total amount: $382,500 (100% non-need-based).

APPLYING FOR FINANCIAL AID ***Required financial aid forms:*** FAFSA, institution's own form, business/farm supplement. ***Financial aid deadline:*** Continuous. ***Notification date:*** Continuous beginning 5/1. Students must reply within 2 weeks of notification.

CONTACT Ms. Ana I. Rodríguez, Director of Financial Aid, University of Puerto Rico, Mayagüez Campus, PO Box 9000, Mayagüez, PR 00681-9000, 787-265-3863. *Fax:* 787-265-1920. *E-mail:* a_rodriguez@rumad.uprm.edu.

UNIVERSITY OF PUERTO RICO, MEDICAL SCIENCES CAMPUS

San Juan, PR

ABOUT THE INSTITUTION Commonwealth-supported, coed, primarily women. 12 undergraduate majors.

GIFT AID (NEED-BASED) ***Scholarships, grants, and awards:*** Federal Pell, FSEOG, state, college/university gift aid from institutional funds, Department of Health and Human Services Scholarships.

GIFT AID (NON-NEED-BASED) ***Scholarships, grants, and awards by category:*** *Academic interests/achievement:* general academic interests/achievements. *Special achievements/activities:* general special achievements/activities. *Special characteristics:* children of faculty/staff, general special characteristics, veterans.

LOANS ***Programs:*** FFEL (Subsidized and Unsubsidized Stafford), Perkins, alternative loans.

APPLYING FOR FINANCIAL AID ***Required financial aid forms:*** FAFSA, institution's own form.

CONTACT Mrs. Zoraida Figueroa, Financial Aid Director, University of Puerto Rico, Medical Sciences Campus, Terreno Centro Médico-Edificio Decanato Farmacia y Estudiantes, PO Box 365067, San Juan, PR 00936-5067, 787-763-2525. *Fax:* 787-282-7117. *E-mail:* zfigueroa@rcm.upr.edu.

UNIVERSITY OF PUERTO RICO, RÍO PIEDRAS

San Juan, PR

Tuition & fees (PR res): $1272 **Average undergraduate aid package: $3218**

ABOUT THE INSTITUTION Commonwealth-supported, coed. ***Awards:*** bachelor's, master's, doctoral, and first professional degrees and post-bachelor's, post-master's, and first professional certificates. 59 undergraduate majors. ***Total enrollment:*** 20,892. Undergraduates: 15,186.

UNDERGRADUATE EXPENSES for 2008–09 ***Application fee:*** $20. ***Tuition, state resident:*** full-time $1128; part-time $47 per credit. ***Tuition, nonresident:*** full-time $3744; part-time $156 per credit. ***Required fees:*** full-time $144; $72 per term. ***College room and board:*** $8180. ***Payment plan:*** Deferred payment.

FRESHMAN FINANCIAL AID (Fall 2007) ***Average financial aid package:*** $3481 (excluding resources awarded to replace EFC).

UNDERGRADUATE FINANCIAL AID (Fall 2007) ***Average financial aid package:*** $3218 (excluding resources awarded to replace EFC).

GIFT AID (NEED-BASED) ***Total amount:*** $36,442,553 (91% federal, 8% state, 1% external sources). ***Receiving aid:*** Freshmen: 57% (1,531); all full-time undergraduates: 67% (8,616). ***Scholarships, grants, and awards:*** Federal Pell, FSEOG, state, private.

GIFT AID (NON-NEED-BASED) ***Tuition waivers:*** Full or partial for employees or children of employees. ***ROTC:*** Army, Air Force.

LOANS ***Average need-based loan:*** Freshmen: $3082. Undergraduates: $4061. ***Programs:*** Federal Direct (Subsidized and Unsubsidized Stafford, PLUS), Perkins, college/university, law access loans.

WORK-STUDY ***Federal work-study:*** 637 jobs available.

APPLYING FOR FINANCIAL AID ***Required financial aid forms:*** FAFSA, institution's own form. ***Financial aid deadline:*** 4/25 (priority: 2/25). ***Notification date:*** 7/26.

CONTACT Mr. Efraim Williams, EDP Manager, University of Puerto Rico, Río Piedras, PO Box 23300, San Juan, PR 00931-3300, 787-764-0000 Ext. 5573.

UNIVERSITY OF PUGET SOUND

Tacoma, WA

Tuition & fees: $35,635 **Average undergraduate aid package: $26,047**

ABOUT THE INSTITUTION Independent, coed. ***Awards:*** bachelor's, master's, and first professional degrees and post-master's certificates. 40 undergraduate majors. ***Total enrollment:*** 2,858. Undergraduates: 2,577. Freshmen: 676. Federal methodology is used as a basis for awarding need-based institutional aid.

UNDERGRADUATE EXPENSES for 2009–10 ***Application fee:*** $50. ***Comprehensive fee:*** $44,825 includes full-time tuition ($35,440), mandatory fees ($195), and room and board ($9190). ***College room only:*** $5130. ***Part-time tuition:*** $4470 per unit.

FRESHMAN FINANCIAL AID (Fall 2008, est.) 461 applied for aid; of those 80% were deemed to have need. 100% of freshmen with need received aid; of those 35% had need fully met. ***Average percent of need met:*** 84% (excluding resources awarded to replace EFC). ***Average financial aid package:*** $25,660 (excluding resources awarded to replace EFC). 26% of all full-time freshmen had no need and received non-need-based gift aid.

UNDERGRADUATE FINANCIAL AID (Fall 2008, est.) 1,730 applied for aid; of those 88% were deemed to have need. 100% of undergraduates with need received aid; of those 28% had need fully met. ***Average percent of need met:*** 83% (excluding resources awarded to replace EFC). ***Average financial aid package:*** $26,047 (excluding resources awarded to replace EFC). 25% of all full-time undergraduates had no need and received non-need-based gift aid.

GIFT AID (NEED-BASED) ***Total amount:*** $30,195,815 (7% federal, 3% state, 86% institutional, 4% external sources). ***Receiving aid:*** Freshmen: 53% (361); all full-time undergraduates: 59% (1,497). ***Average award:*** Freshmen: $21,649; Undergraduates: $20,688. ***Scholarships, grants, and awards:*** Federal Pell, FSEOG, state, private, college/university gift aid from institutional funds.

GIFT AID (NON-NEED-BASED) ***Total amount:*** $5,124,601 (1% state, 95% institutional, 4% external sources). ***Receiving aid:*** Freshmen: 5% (34). Undergraduates: 4% (103). ***Average award:*** Freshmen: $9537. Undergraduates: $7620. ***Scholarships, grants, and awards by category:*** *Academic interests/achievement:* 727 awards ($4,250,108 total): biological sciences, business, communication, computer science, English, foreign languages, general academic interests/achievements, humanities, international studies, mathematics, physical sciences, premedicine, social sciences. *Creative arts/performance:* 68 awards ($221,297 total): art/fine arts, debating, music, theater/drama. *Special achievements/activities:* 5 awards ($16,000 total): leadership, religious involvement. *Special characteristics:* 25 awards ($719,663 total): children of faculty/staff, international students. ***ROTC:*** Army cooperative.

LOANS ***Student loans:*** $13,234,652 (89% need-based, 11% non-need-based). 64% of past graduating class borrowed through all loan programs. *Average indebtedness per student:* $25,055. ***Average need-based loan:*** Freshmen: $4701. Undergraduates: $5741. ***Parent loans:*** $3,512,522 (78% need-based, 22% non-need-based). ***Programs:*** FFEL (Subsidized and Unsubsidized Stafford, PLUS), Perkins, Alaska Loans.

WORK-STUDY ***Federal work-study:*** Total amount: $1,343,000; 483 jobs averaging $2780. ***State or other work-study/employment:*** Total amount: $2,505,687 (100% need-based). 987 part-time jobs averaging $2540.

APPLYING FOR FINANCIAL AID ***Required financial aid form:*** FAFSA. ***Financial aid deadline (priority):*** 2/1. ***Notification date:*** Continuous beginning 3/15. Students must reply by 5/1.

CONTACT Maggie A. Mittuch, Associate Vice President for Student Financial Services, University of Puget Sound, 1500 North Warner Street #1039, Tacoma, WA 98416-1039, 253-879-3214 or toll-free 800-396-7191. *Fax:* 253-879-8508. *E-mail:* mmittuch@pugetsound.edu.

UNIVERSITY OF REDLANDS

Redlands, CA

Tuition & fees: $32,294 **Average undergraduate aid package: $28,690**

ABOUT THE INSTITUTION Independent, coed. ***Awards:*** bachelor's, master's, and doctoral degrees and post-bachelor's and post-master's certificates. 42 undergraduate majors. ***Total enrollment:*** 4,317. Undergraduates: 2,820. Freshmen: 574. Federal methodology is used as a basis for awarding need-based institutional aid.

UNDERGRADUATE EXPENSES for 2008–09 ***Application fee:*** $30. ***Comprehensive fee:*** $42,416 includes full-time tuition ($31,994), mandatory fees ($300), and room and board ($10,122). ***College room only:*** $5644. Room and board charges vary according to board plan and housing facility. ***Part-time tuition:*** $1000 per credit. ***Part-time fees:*** $150 per term. Part-time tuition and fees vary according to course load. ***Payment plan:*** Installment.

FRESHMAN FINANCIAL AID (Fall 2008, est.) 467 applied for aid; of those 76% were deemed to have need. 100% of freshmen with need received aid; of those 44% had need fully met. ***Average percent of need met:*** 81% (excluding resources awarded to replace EFC). ***Average financial aid package:*** $20,002 (excluding resources awarded to replace EFC). 11% of all full-time freshmen had no need and received non-need-based gift aid.

UNDERGRADUATE FINANCIAL AID (Fall 2008, est.) 1,847 applied for aid; of those 81% were deemed to have need. 100% of undergraduates with need received aid; of those 40% had need fully met. ***Average percent of need met:*** 81% (excluding resources awarded to replace EFC). ***Average financial aid package:*** $28,690 (excluding resources awarded to replace EFC). 7% of all full-time undergraduates had no need and received non-need-based gift aid.

GIFT AID (NEED-BASED) ***Total amount:*** $34,761,595 (6% federal, 12% state, 82% institutional). ***Receiving aid:*** Freshmen: 60% (343); all full-time undergraduates: 63% (1,466). ***Average award:*** Freshmen: $21,661; Undergraduates: $20,790. ***Scholarships, grants, and awards:*** Federal Pell, FSEOG, state, private, college/university gift aid from institutional funds.

GIFT AID (NON-NEED-BASED) ***Total amount:*** $3,823,516 (79% institutional, 21% external sources). ***Receiving aid:*** Freshmen: 8% (47). Undergraduates: 7% (158). ***Average award:*** Freshmen: $11,672. Undergraduates: $11,515. ***Scholarships, grants, and awards by category:*** *Academic interests/achievement:* general academic interests/achievements. *Creative arts/performance:* art/fine arts, creative writing, debating, music. *Special achievements/activities:* general special achievements/activities. *Special characteristics:* international students. ***Tuition waivers:*** Full or partial for employees or children of employees. ***ROTC:*** Army cooperative, Air Force cooperative.

LOANS ***Student loans:*** $12,404,593 (56% need-based, 44% non-need-based). 60% of past graduating class borrowed through all loan programs. *Average indebtedness per student:* $17,290. ***Average need-based loan:*** Freshmen: $5313. Undergraduates: $6344. ***Parent loans:*** $3,784,593 (100% non-need-based). ***Programs:*** FFEL (Subsidized and Unsubsidized Stafford, PLUS), Perkins, college/university.

WORK-STUDY ***Federal work-study:*** Total amount: $3,432,675; jobs available. ***State or other work-study/employment:*** Part-time jobs available.

APPLYING FOR FINANCIAL AID ***Required financial aid forms:*** FAFSA, state aid form. ***Financial aid deadline (priority):*** 2/15. ***Notification date:*** Continuous beginning 2/28. Students must reply by 5/1.

CONTACT Director of Financial Aid, University of Redlands, PO Box 3080, Redlands, CA 92373-0999, 909-748-8261 or toll-free 800-455-5064. *Fax:* 909-335-4089. *E-mail:* financialaid@redlands.edu.

UNIVERSITY OF RHODE ISLAND

Kingston, RI

Tuition & fees (RI res): $8928 **Average undergraduate aid package: $12,654**

ABOUT THE INSTITUTION State-supported, coed. ***Awards:*** bachelor's, master's, doctoral, and first professional degrees and post-bachelor's certificates. 75 undergraduate majors. ***Total enrollment:*** 15,904. Undergraduates: 12,793. Freshmen: 3,042. Federal methodology is used as a basis for awarding need-based institutional aid.

UNDERGRADUATE EXPENSES for 2008–09 ***Application fee:*** $65. ***Tuition, state resident:*** full-time $7454; part-time $311 per credit hour. ***Tuition, nonresident:*** full-time $23,552; part-time $981 per credit hour. ***Required fees:*** full-time $1474; $27 per credit hour or $49 per credit hour. Full-time tuition and fees vary according to course load, location, and reciprocity agreements. Part-time tuition and fees vary according to course load, location, and reciprocity agreements. ***College room and board:*** $8826; ***Room only:*** $5316. Room and board charges vary according to board plan and housing facility. ***Payment plan:*** Installment.

FRESHMAN FINANCIAL AID (Fall 2008, est.) 2,485 applied for aid; of those 79% were deemed to have need. 81% of freshmen with need received aid; of those 78% had need fully met. ***Average percent of need met:*** 57% (excluding resources awarded to replace EFC). ***Average financial aid package:*** $12,194 (excluding resources awarded to replace EFC). 5% of all full-time freshmen had no need and received non-need-based gift aid.

UNDERGRADUATE FINANCIAL AID (Fall 2008, est.) 9,561 applied for aid; of those 83% were deemed to have need. 77% of undergraduates with need received aid; of those 70% had need fully met. ***Average percent of need met:*** 57% (excluding resources awarded to replace EFC). ***Average financial aid package:*** $12,654 (excluding resources awarded to replace EFC). 4% of all full-time undergraduates had no need and received non-need-based gift aid.

GIFT AID (NEED-BASED) ***Total amount:*** $48,086,517 (21% federal, 6% state, 69% institutional, 4% external sources). ***Receiving aid:*** Freshmen: 53% (1,591); all full-time undergraduates: 52% (5,818). ***Average award:*** Freshmen: $6563; Undergraduates: $7236. ***Scholarships, grants, and awards:*** Federal Pell, FSEOG, state, private, college/university gift aid from institutional funds.

GIFT AID (NON-NEED-BASED) ***Total amount:*** $2,554,388 (92% institutional, 8% external sources). ***Receiving aid:*** Freshmen: 5% (157). Undergraduates: 5% (509). ***Average award:*** Freshmen: $3931. Undergraduates: $5468. ***Tuition waivers:*** Full or partial for minority students, employees or children of employees, senior citizens. ***ROTC:*** Army.

LOANS ***Student loans:*** $61,106,984 (79% need-based, 21% non-need-based). 71% of past graduating class borrowed through all loan programs. *Average indebtedness per student:* $22,500. ***Average need-based loan:*** Freshmen: $5905. Undergraduates: $6557. ***Parent loans:*** $25,085,891 (68% need-based, 32% non-need-based). ***Programs:*** Federal Direct (Subsidized and Unsubsidized Stafford, PLUS), Perkins, Federal Nursing, state, college/university.

WORK-STUDY ***Federal work-study:*** Total amount: $740,160; jobs available.

ATHLETIC AWARDS Total amount: $5,152,442 (99% need-based, 1% non-need-based).

APPLYING FOR FINANCIAL AID ***Required financial aid form:*** FAFSA. ***Financial aid deadline (priority):*** 3/1. ***Notification date:*** Continuous beginning 3/31. Students must reply by 5/1.

CONTACT Mr. Horace J. Amaral Jr., Director of Enrollment Services, University of Rhode Island, Green Hall, Kingston, RI 02881, 401-874-9500.

UNIVERSITY OF RICHMOND

Richmond, VA

Tuition & fees: $40,010 **Average undergraduate aid package: $34,423**

ABOUT THE INSTITUTION Independent, coed. ***Awards:*** associate, bachelor's, master's, and first professional degrees and post-bachelor's certificates. 49 undergraduate majors. ***Total enrollment:*** 3,445. Undergraduates: 2,795. Freshmen: 738. Federal methodology is used as a basis for awarding need-based institutional aid.

UNDERGRADUATE EXPENSES for 2009–10 ***Application fee:*** $50. ***Comprehensive fee:*** $48,490 includes full-time tuition ($40,010) and room and board ($8480). ***College room only:*** $3780. ***Part-time tuition:*** $7000 per unit.

FRESHMAN FINANCIAL AID (Fall 2008, est.) 412 applied for aid; of those 75% were deemed to have need. 100% of freshmen with need received aid; of those 97% had need fully met. ***Average percent of need met:*** 100% (excluding resources awarded to replace EFC). ***Average financial aid package:*** $35,624 (excluding resources awarded to replace EFC). 7% of all full-time freshmen had no need and received non-need-based gift aid.

UNDERGRADUATE FINANCIAL AID (Fall 2008, est.) 1,422 applied for aid; of those 83% were deemed to have need. 100% of undergraduates with need received aid; of those 95% had need fully met. ***Average percent of need met:*** 100% (excluding resources awarded to replace EFC). ***Average financial aid package:*** $34,423 (excluding resources awarded to replace EFC). 15% of all full-time undergraduates had no need and received non-need-based gift aid.

GIFT AID (NEED-BASED) ***Total amount:*** $34,377,419 (4% federal, 3% state, 92% institutional, 1% external sources). ***Receiving aid:*** Freshmen: 42% (306); all full-time undergraduates: 40% (1,165). ***Average award:*** Freshmen: $31,626; Undergraduates: $31,055. ***Scholarships, grants, and awards:*** Federal Pell, FSEOG, state, private, college/university gift aid from institutional funds.

GIFT AID (NON-NEED-BASED) ***Total amount:*** $10,834,616 (7% federal, 6% state, 83% institutional, 4% external sources). ***Receiving aid:*** Freshmen: 5% (38). Undergraduates: 4% (115). ***Average award:*** Freshmen: $32,724. Undergraduates: $19,210. ***Scholarships, grants, and awards by category:*** *Academic interests/achievement:* 196 awards: biological sciences, computer science, general academic interests/achievements, mathematics, physical sciences. *Creative arts/performance:* 25 awards ($632,750 total): art/fine arts, dance, music, performing arts, theater/drama. *Special achievements/activities:* 93 awards ($232,500 total): community service. ***ROTC:*** Army.

LOANS ***Student loans:*** $9,235,310 (24% need-based, 76% non-need-based). 43% of past graduating class borrowed through all loan programs. *Average indebtedness per student:* $20,915. ***Average need-based loan:*** Freshmen: $2961. Undergraduates: $2833. ***Parent loans:*** $3,849,056 (2% need-based, 98% non-need-based). ***Programs:*** Federal Direct (Subsidized and Unsubsidized Stafford, PLUS), Perkins.

WORK-STUDY ***Federal work-study:*** Total amount: $578,772; 486 jobs averaging $1190.

ATHLETIC AWARDS Total amount: $7,844,999 (16% need-based, 84% non-need-based).

APPLYING FOR FINANCIAL AID ***Required financial aid forms:*** FAFSA, institution's own form. ***Financial aid deadline:*** 2/15. ***Notification date:*** 4/1. Students must reply within 4 weeks of notification.

CONTACT Financial Aid Office, University of Richmond, Sarah Brunet Hall, University of Richmond, VA 23173, 804-289-8438 or toll-free 800-700-1662. *Fax:* 804-484-1650. *E-mail:* finaid@richmond.edu.

UNIVERSITY OF RIO GRANDE

Rio Grande, OH

CONTACT Dr. John Hill, Director of Financial Aid, University of Rio Grande, 218 North College Avenue, Rio Grande, OH 45674, 740-245-7218 or toll-free 800-282-7201 (in-state). *Fax:* 740-245-7102.

UNIVERSITY OF ROCHESTER

Rochester, NY

Tuition & fees: $37,250 **Average undergraduate aid package: $30,123**

ABOUT THE INSTITUTION Independent, coed. ***Awards:*** bachelor's, master's, doctoral, and first professional degrees and post-bachelor's, post-master's, and first professional certificates. 57 undergraduate majors. ***Total enrollment:*** 9,712. Undergraduates: 5,355. Freshmen: 1,282. Institutional methodology is used as a basis for awarding need-based institutional aid.

UNDERGRADUATE EXPENSES for 2008–09 ***Application fee:*** $60. ***Comprehensive fee:*** $48,060 includes full-time tuition ($36,410), mandatory fees ($840), and room and board ($10,810). ***College room only:*** $6490. Room and board charges vary according to board plan. ***Part-time tuition:*** $1138 per credit hour. Part-time tuition and fees vary according to course load. ***Payment plan:*** Installment.

FRESHMAN FINANCIAL AID (Fall 2008, est.) 784 applied for aid; of those 83% were deemed to have need. 100% of freshmen with need received aid; of those 100% had need fully met. ***Average percent of need met:*** 100% (excluding resources awarded to replace EFC). ***Average financial aid package:*** $31,690 (excluding resources awarded to replace EFC). 36% of all full-time freshmen had no need and received non-need-based gift aid.

UNDERGRADUATE FINANCIAL AID (Fall 2008, est.) 2,856 applied for aid; of those 88% were deemed to have need. 100% of undergraduates with need received aid; of those 75% had need fully met. ***Average percent of need met:*** 95% (excluding resources awarded to replace EFC). ***Average financial aid package:*** $30,123 (excluding resources awarded to replace EFC). 32% of all full-time undergraduates had no need and received non-need-based gift aid.

GIFT AID (NEED-BASED) ***Total amount:*** $58,320,477 (7% federal, 6% state, 84% institutional, 3% external sources). ***Receiving aid:*** Freshmen: 56% (643); all full-time undergraduates: 55% (2,457). ***Average award:*** Freshmen: $27,021; Undergraduates: $24,662. ***Scholarships, grants, and awards:*** Federal Pell, FSEOG, state, college/university gift aid from institutional funds.

GIFT AID (NON-NEED-BASED) ***Total amount:*** $14,734,181 (1% state, 85% institutional, 14% external sources). ***Receiving aid:*** Freshmen: 5% (57). Undergraduates: 4% (187). ***Average award:*** Freshmen: $8610. Undergraduates: $8276. ***Scholarships, grants, and awards by category:*** *Academic interests/achievement:* engineering/technologies, general academic interests/achievements, military science. *Creative arts/performance:* general creative arts/performance. *Special achievements/activities:* general special achievements/activities. *Special characteristics:* children and siblings of alumni, children of faculty/staff, general special characteristics, international students, veterans. ***Tuition waivers:*** Full or partial for employees or children of employees. ***ROTC:*** Army cooperative, Naval, Air Force cooperative.

LOANS ***Student loans:*** $21,189,593 (74% need-based, 26% non-need-based). 55% of past graduating class borrowed through all loan programs. *Average indebtedness per student:* $27,121. ***Average need-based loan:*** Freshmen: $4154. Undergraduates: $4963. ***Parent loans:*** $7,990,791 (32% need-based, 68% non-need-based). ***Programs:*** Federal Direct (Subsidized and Unsubsidized Stafford, PLUS), Perkins, Federal Nursing, college/university, alternative loans.

WORK-STUDY ***Federal work-study:*** Total amount: $3,743,682; 1,603 jobs averaging $2283. ***State or other work-study/employment:*** Total amount: $935,045 (47% need-based, 53% non-need-based). Part-time jobs available.

APPLYING FOR FINANCIAL AID ***Required financial aid forms:*** FAFSA, CSS Financial Aid PROFILE, state aid form, noncustodial (divorced/separated) parent's statement, business/farm supplement. ***Financial aid deadline (priority):*** 2/1. ***Notification date:*** 4/1. Students must reply by 5/1.

CONTACT Charles W. Puls, Director of Financial Aid, University of Rochester, Financial Aid Office, 124 Wallis Hall, Rochester, NY 14627-0250, 585-275-3226 or toll-free 888-822-2256. *Fax:* 585-756-7664.

UNIVERSITY OF ST. FRANCIS

Joliet, IL

ABOUT THE INSTITUTION Independent Roman Catholic, coed. ***Awards:*** bachelor's and master's degrees and post-master's certificates. 43 undergraduate majors. ***Total enrollment:*** 2,146. Undergraduates: 1,273. Freshmen: 203.

GIFT AID (NEED-BASED) ***Scholarships, grants, and awards:*** Federal Pell, FSEOG, state, private, college/university gift aid from institutional funds.

GIFT AID (NON-NEED-BASED) ***Scholarships, grants, and awards by category:*** *Academic interests/achievement:* biological sciences, communication, education, general academic interests/achievements, health fields, social sciences. *Creative arts/performance:* applied art and design, art/fine arts, music. *Special achievements/activities:* community service, general special achievements/activities, leadership, religious involvement. *Special characteristics:* children and siblings of alumni, children of educators, ethnic background, first-generation college students, religious affiliation, siblings of current students.

LOANS ***Programs:*** Federal Direct (Subsidized and Unsubsidized Stafford, PLUS), Perkins, alternative loans.

WORK-STUDY ***Federal work-study:*** Total amount: $432,815; 200 jobs averaging $2164. ***State or other work-study/employment:*** Total amount: $322,899 (100% non-need-based). 182 part-time jobs averaging $1774.

APPLYING FOR FINANCIAL AID ***Required financial aid forms:*** FAFSA, institution's own form.

CONTACT Mrs. Mary V. Shaw, Director of Financial Aid Services, University of St. Francis, 500 North Wilcox Street, Joliet, IL 60435-6188, 815-740-3403 or toll-free 800-735-3500 (in-state), 800-735-7500 (out-of-state). *Fax:* 815-740-3822. *E-mail:* mshaw@stfrancis.edu.

UNIVERSITY OF SAINT FRANCIS

Fort Wayne, IN

Tuition & fees: N/R **Average undergraduate aid package: $16,101**

ABOUT THE INSTITUTION Independent Roman Catholic, coed. ***Awards:*** associate, bachelor's, and master's degrees and post-bachelor's certificates. 50 undergraduate majors. ***Total enrollment:*** 2,112. Undergraduates: 1,800. Freshmen: 322. Federal methodology is used as a basis for awarding need-based institutional aid.

FRESHMAN FINANCIAL AID (Fall 2008, est.) 299 applied for aid; of those 86% were deemed to have need. 100% of freshmen with need received aid; of those 33% had need fully met. ***Average percent of need met:*** 82% (excluding resources awarded to replace EFC). ***Average financial aid package:*** $16,699 (excluding resources awarded to replace EFC). 13% of all full-time freshmen had no need and received non-need-based gift aid.

UNDERGRADUATE FINANCIAL AID (Fall 2008, est.) 1,380 applied for aid; of those 87% were deemed to have need. 100% of undergraduates with need received aid; of those 25% had need fully met. ***Average percent of need met:*** 78% (excluding resources awarded to replace EFC). ***Average financial aid package:*** $16,101 (excluding resources awarded to replace EFC). 11% of all full-time undergraduates had no need and received non-need-based gift aid.

GIFT AID (NEED-BASED) ***Total amount:*** $13,022,804 (17% federal, 36% state, 34% institutional, 13% external sources). ***Receiving aid:*** Freshmen: 84% (256); all full-time undergraduates: 85% (1,195). ***Average award:*** Freshmen: $13,167; Undergraduates: $12,024. ***Scholarships, grants, and awards:*** Federal Pell, FSEOG, state, private, college/university gift aid from institutional funds.

GIFT AID (NON-NEED-BASED) ***Total amount:*** $2,052,557 (4% state, 57% institutional, 39% external sources). ***Receiving aid:*** Freshmen: 15% (46). Undergraduates: 12% (166). ***Average award:*** Freshmen: $6436. Undergraduates: $6019. ***Scholarships, grants, and awards by category:*** *Academic interests/achievement:* 737 awards ($3,037,601 total): general academic interests/achievements, health fields. *Creative arts/performance:* 237 awards ($832,577 total): art/fine arts, dance, music. *Special achievements/activities:* 38 awards ($66,576 total): cheerleading/drum major, religious involvement. *Special characteristics:* 30 awards ($452,809 total): children of faculty/staff. ***Tuition waivers:*** Full or partial for children of alumni, employees or children of employees, senior citizens.

LOANS ***Student loans:*** $14,349,006 (65% need-based, 35% non-need-based). 98% of past graduating class borrowed through all loan programs. *Average indebtedness per student:* $27,131. ***Average need-based loan:*** Freshmen: $3303. Undergraduates: $3853. ***Parent loans:*** $1,057,627 (40% need-based, 60% non-need-based). ***Programs:*** FFEL (Subsidized and Unsubsidized Stafford, PLUS), Perkins.

WORK-STUDY ***Federal work-study:*** Total amount: $1,192,468; 759 jobs averaging $1644. ***State or other work-study/employment:*** Part-time jobs available.

ATHLETIC AWARDS Total amount: $3,583,735 (71% need-based, 29% non-need-based).

APPLYING FOR FINANCIAL AID ***Required financial aid form:*** FAFSA. ***Financial aid deadline:*** 6/30 (priority: 3/10). ***Notification date:*** Continuous. Students must reply within 2 weeks of notification.

CONTACT Jamie McGrath, Director of Financial Aid, University of Saint Francis, 2701 Spring Street, Fort Wayne, IN [illegible], [illegible] or toll-free 800-729-4732. *Fax:* 260-434-7526.

UNIVERSITY OF SAINT MARY

Leavenworth, KS

CONTACT Mrs. Judy Wiedower, Financial Aid Director, University of Saint Mary, 4100 South Fourth Street, Leavenworth, KS 66048, 913-758-6314 or toll-free 800-752-7043 (out-of-state). *Fax:* 913-758-6146. *E-mail:* wiedower@hub.smcks.edu.

UNIVERSITY OF ST. THOMAS

St. Paul, MN

Tuition & fees: $27,822 **Average undergraduate aid package: $20,886**

ABOUT THE INSTITUTION Independent Roman Catholic, coed. ***Awards:*** bachelor's, master's, doctoral, and first professional degrees and post-bachelor's and post-master's certificates. 83 undergraduate majors. ***Total enrollment:*** 10,984. Undergraduates: 6,076. Freshmen: 1,315. Federal methodology is used as a basis for awarding need-based institutional aid.

UNDERGRADUATE EXPENSES for 2008–09 ***Comprehensive fee:*** $35,436 includes full-time tuition ($27,328), mandatory fees ($494), and room and board ($7614). ***College room only:*** $4872. ***Part-time tuition:*** $854 per credit hour.

FRESHMAN FINANCIAL AID (Fall 2008, est.) 1,004 applied for aid; of those 75% were deemed to have need. 100% of freshmen with need received aid; of those 55% had need fully met. ***Average percent of need met:*** 87% (excluding resources awarded to replace EFC). ***Average financial aid package:*** $20,936 (excluding resources awarded to replace EFC). 42% of all full-time freshmen had no need and received non-need-based gift aid.

UNDERGRADUATE FINANCIAL AID (Fall 2008, est.) 4,010 applied for aid; of those 80% were deemed to have need. 100% of undergraduates with need received aid; of those 42% had need fully met. ***Average percent of need met:*** 83% (excluding resources awarded to replace EFC). ***Average financial aid package:*** $20,886 (excluding resources awarded to replace EFC). 35% of all full-time undergraduates had no need and received non-need-based gift aid.

GIFT AID (NEED-BASED) ***Total amount:*** $41,332,466 (9% federal, 10% state, 77% institutional, 4% external sources). ***Receiving aid:*** Freshmen: 56% (744); all full-time undergraduates: 54% (3,100). ***Average award:*** Freshmen: $14,344; Undergraduates: $13,189. ***Scholarships, grants, and awards:*** Federal Pell, FSEOG, state, private, college/university gift aid from institutional funds.

GIFT AID (NON-NEED-BASED) ***Total amount:*** $8,667,431 (94% institutional, 6% external sources). ***Receiving aid:*** Freshmen: 11% (139). Undergraduates: 7% (379). ***Average award:*** Freshmen: $10,504. Undergraduates: $9573. ***Scholarships, grants, and awards by category:*** *Academic interests/achievement:* 2,800 awards ($18,862,152 total): biological sciences, business, education, English, general academic interests/achievements, humanities, international studies, mathematics, physical sciences, religion/biblical studies, social sciences. *Creative arts/performance:* 24 awards ($53,040 total): journalism/publications, music. *Special characteristics:* 164 awards ($2,307,094 total): children of educators, children of faculty/staff, general special characteristics. ***ROTC:*** Army cooperative, Naval cooperative, Air Force.

LOANS ***Student loans:*** $29,534,449 (66% need-based, 34% non-need-based). 68% of past graduating class borrowed through all loan programs. *Average indebtedness per student:* $34,869. ***Average need-based loan:*** Freshmen: $6555. Undergraduates: $7340. ***Parent loans:*** $8,378,142 (25% need-based, 75% non-need-based). ***Programs:*** Federal Direct (Subsidized and Unsubsidized Stafford, PLUS), Perkins, state, alternative loans.

WORK-STUDY ***Federal work-study:*** Total amount: $1,754,181; 649 jobs averaging $2703. ***State or other work-study/employment:*** Total amount: $2,999,085 (80% need-based, 20% non-need-based). 1,101 part-time jobs averaging $2724.

APPLYING FOR FINANCIAL AID ***Required financial aid form:*** FAFSA. ***Financial aid deadline:*** Continuous. ***Notification date:*** Continuous beginning 3/1. Students must reply within 3 weeks of notification.

CONTACT Ms. Ginny Reese, Associate Director, Student Financial Services, University of St. Thomas, 2115 Summit Avenue, AQU 328, St. Paul, MN 55105-1096, 651-962-6557 or toll-free 800-328-6819 Ext. 26150. *Fax:* 651-962-6599. *E-mail:* ginny.reese@stthomas.edu.

UNIVERSITY OF ST. THOMAS

Houston, TX

Tuition & fees: $20,190 **Average undergraduate aid package: $15,315**

ABOUT THE INSTITUTION Independent Roman Catholic, coed. ***Awards:*** bachelor's, master's, doctoral, and first professional degrees. 37 undergraduate majors. ***Total enrollment:*** 3,246. Undergraduates: 1,750. Freshmen: 298. Federal methodology is used as a basis for awarding need-based institutional aid.

UNDERGRADUATE EXPENSES for 2008–09 ***Application fee:*** $25. ***Comprehensive fee:*** $27,890 includes full-time tuition ($20,190) and room and board ($7700). Full-time tuition and fees vary according to course load. Room and board charges vary according to board plan and housing facility. ***Part-time tuition:*** $675 per credit. Part-time tuition and fees vary according to course load. ***Payment plans:*** Installment, deferred payment.

FRESHMAN FINANCIAL AID (Fall 2008, est.) 205 applied for aid; of those 79% were deemed to have need. 99% of freshmen with need received aid; of those 13% had need fully met. ***Average percent of need met:*** 78% (excluding resources awarded to replace EFC). ***Average financial aid package:*** $16,610 (excluding resources awarded to replace EFC). 31% of all full-time freshmen had no need and received non-need-based gift aid.

UNDERGRADUATE FINANCIAL AID (Fall 2008, est.) 820 applied for aid; of those 88% were deemed to have need. 99% of undergraduates with need received aid; of those 10% had need fully met. ***Average percent of need met:*** 68% (excluding resources awarded to replace EFC). ***Average financial aid package:*** $15,315 (excluding resources awarded to replace EFC). 1% of all full-time undergraduates had no need and received non-need-based gift aid.

GIFT AID (NEED-BASED) ***Total amount:*** $7,883,252 (23% federal, 25% state, 52% institutional). ***Receiving aid:*** Freshmen: 55% (160); all full-time undergraduates: 54% (690). ***Average award:*** Freshmen: $13,251; Undergraduates: $11,049. ***Scholarships, grants, and awards:*** Federal Pell, FSEOG, state, private, college/university gift aid from institutional funds, Academic Competitiveness Grant, National Smart Grant.

GIFT AID (NON-NEED-BASED) ***Total amount:*** $3,039,734 (1% federal, 88% institutional, 11% external sources). ***Receiving aid:*** Freshmen: 24% (69). Undergraduates: 13% (164). ***Average award:*** Freshmen: $9277. ***Tuition waivers:*** Full or partial for employees or children of employees, senior citizens. ***ROTC:*** Army cooperative.

LOANS ***Student loans:*** $5,759,150 (46% need-based, 54% non-need-based). 69% of past graduating class borrowed through all loan programs. *Average indebtedness per student:* $21,626. ***Average need-based loan:*** Freshmen: $3521. Undergraduates: $4848. ***Parent loans:*** $990,179 (100% non-need-based). ***Programs:*** FFEL (Subsidized and Unsubsidized Stafford, PLUS), Perkins, private loans.

WORK-STUDY ***Federal work-study:*** Total amount: $111,700; 32 jobs averaging $3491. ***State or other work-study/employment:*** Total amount: $16,000 (100% need-based). 4 part-time jobs averaging $4000.

ATHLETIC AWARDS Total amount: $132,000 (100% non-need-based).

APPLYING FOR FINANCIAL AID ***Required financial aid form:*** FAFSA. ***Financial aid deadline:*** Continuous. ***Notification date:*** Continuous beginning 3/1. Students must reply within 2 weeks of notification.

CONTACT Scott Moore, Dean of Scholarships and Financial Aid, University of St. Thomas, 3800 Montrose Boulevard, Houston, TX 77006-4696, 713-942-3465 or toll-free 800-856-8565. *Fax:* 713-525-2142. *E-mail:* finaid@stthom.edu.

UNIVERSITY OF SAN DIEGO

San Diego, CA

Tuition & fees: $36,292 **Average undergraduate aid package: $25,224**

ABOUT THE INSTITUTION Independent Roman Catholic, coed. ***Awards:*** bachelor's, master's, doctoral, and first professional degrees and post-bachelor's, post-master's, and first professional certificates. 36 undergraduate majors. ***Total enrollment:*** 7,882. Undergraduates: 5,119. Freshmen: 1,260. Federal methodology is used as a basis for awarding need-based institutional aid.

UNDERGRADUATE EXPENSES for 2009–10 ***Application fee:*** $55. ***Comprehensive fee:*** $48,894 includes full-time tuition ($35,870), mandatory fees ($422), and room and board ($12,602). ***Part-time tuition:*** $1240 per unit. ***Part-time fees:*** $151 per term.

FRESHMAN FINANCIAL AID (Fall 2008, est.) 813 applied for aid; of those 73% were deemed to have need. 100% of freshmen with need received aid; of those 24% had need fully met. ***Average percent of need met:*** 76% (excluding resources awarded to replace EFC). ***Average financial aid package:*** $27,317 (excluding resources awarded to replace EFC). 18% of all full-time freshmen had no need and received non-need-based gift aid.

UNDERGRADUATE FINANCIAL AID (Fall 2008, est.) 2,634 applied for aid; of those 83% were deemed to have need. 100% of undergraduates with need received aid; of those 19% had need fully met. ***Average percent of need met:*** 72% (excluding resources awarded to replace EFC). ***Average financial aid package:*** $25,224 (excluding resources awarded to replace EFC). 16% of all full-time undergraduates had no need and received non-need-based gift aid.

GIFT AID (NEED-BASED) ***Total amount:*** $35,374,301 (9% federal, 12% state, 77% institutional, 2% external sources). ***Receiving aid:*** Freshmen: 45% (572); all full-time undergraduates: 42% (2,049). ***Average award:*** Freshmen: $21,026; Undergraduates: $17,886. ***Scholarships, grants, and awards:*** Federal Pell, FSEOG, state, private, college/university gift aid from institutional funds, Federal Nursing.

GIFT AID (NON-NEED-BASED) ***Total amount:*** $13,162,725 (18% federal, 79% institutional, 3% external sources). ***Receiving aid:*** Freshmen: 9% (116). Undergraduates: 6% (283). ***Average award:*** Freshmen: $13,663. Undergraduates: $11,814. ***Scholarships, grants, and awards by category:*** *Academic interests/achievement:* general academic interests/achievements. *Creative arts/performance:* music. *Special characteristics:* children of faculty/staff. ***ROTC:*** Army cooperative, Naval, Air Force cooperative.

LOANS ***Student loans:*** $22,608,975 (85% need-based, 15% non-need-based). 57% of past graduating class borrowed through all loan programs. *Average indebtedness per student:* $24,920. ***Average need-based loan:*** Freshmen: $5426. Undergraduates: $7305. ***Parent loans:*** $34,777,746 (28% need-based, 72% non-need-based). ***Programs:*** FFEL (Subsidized and Unsubsidized Stafford, PLUS), Perkins, college/university.

WORK-STUDY ***Federal work-study:*** Total amount: $1,842,159; jobs available. ***State or other work-study/employment:*** Total amount: $2,382,381 (14% need-based, 86% non-need-based). Part-time jobs available.

ATHLETIC AWARDS Total amount: $4,792,139 (18% need-based, 82% non-need-based).

APPLYING FOR FINANCIAL AID ***Required financial aid form:*** FAFSA. ***Financial aid deadline (priority):*** 3/2. ***Notification date:*** Continuous. Students must reply by 5/1 or within 3 weeks of notification.

CONTACT Judith Lewis Logue, Director of Financial Aid Services, University of San Diego, 5998 Alcala Park, San Diego, CA 92110-2492, 619-260-4514 or toll-free 800-248-4873.

UNIVERSITY OF SAN FRANCISCO

San Francisco, CA

CONTACT Ms. Susan Murphy, Director of Financial Aid, University of San Francisco, 2130 Fulton Street, San Francisco, CA 94117-1080, 415-422-2620 or toll-free 800-CALLUSF (out-of-state). *Fax:* 415-422-6084. *E-mail:* murphy@usfca.edu.

UNIVERSITY OF SCIENCE AND ARTS OF OKLAHOMA

Chickasha, OK

Tuition & fees (OK res): $4440 **Average undergraduate aid package: $8334**

ABOUT THE INSTITUTION State-supported, coed. ***Awards:*** bachelor's degrees. 25 undergraduate majors. ***Total enrollment:*** 1,158. Undergraduates: 1,158. Freshmen: 225. Federal methodology is used as a basis for awarding need-based institutional aid.

UNDERGRADUATE EXPENSES for 2008–09 ***Application fee:*** $15. ***Tuition, state resident:*** full-time $3270; part-time $109 per hour. ***Tuition, nonresident:*** full-time $9390; part-time $313 per hour. ***Required fees:*** full-time $1170; $39 per hour. ***College room and board:*** $4710; ***Room only:*** $2460. Room and board charges vary according to board plan and housing facility. ***Payment plan:*** Installment.

FRESHMAN FINANCIAL AID (Fall 2008, est.) 165 applied for aid; of those 77% were deemed to have need. 100% of freshmen with need received aid; of those 26% had need fully met. ***Average percent of need met:*** 74% (excluding

resources awarded to replace EFC). ***Average financial aid package:*** $8408 (excluding resources awarded to replace EFC). 24% of all full-time freshmen had no need and received non-need-based gift aid.

UNDERGRADUATE FINANCIAL AID (Fall 2008, est.) 679 applied for aid; of those 83% were deemed to have need. 97% of undergraduates with need received aid; of those 20% had need fully met. ***Average percent of need met:*** 70% (excluding resources awarded to replace EFC). ***Average financial aid package:*** $8334 (excluding resources awarded to replace EFC). 22% of all full-time undergraduates had no need and received non-need-based gift aid.

GIFT AID (NEED-BASED) ***Total amount:*** $2,738,549 (56% federal, 24% state, 9% institutional, 11% external sources). ***Receiving aid:*** Freshmen: 57% (125); all full-time undergraduates: 54% (504). ***Average award:*** Freshmen: $6861; Undergraduates: $6352. ***Scholarships, grants, and awards:*** Federal Pell, FSEOG, state, private, college/university gift aid from institutional funds, USAO Foundation Grants.

GIFT AID (NON-NEED-BASED) ***Total amount:*** $677,507 (48% state, 36% institutional, 16% external sources). ***Receiving aid:*** Freshmen: 9% (20). Undergraduates: 5% (51). ***Average award:*** Freshmen: $4867. Undergraduates: $4584. ***Scholarships, grants, and awards by category:*** *Academic interests/achievement:* 148 awards ($236,333 total): general academic interests/achievements. *Creative arts/performance:* 17 awards ($22,300 total): art/fine arts, music, theater/drama. *Special achievements/activities:* 18 awards ($12,625 total): cheerleading/drum major. *Special characteristics:* 83 awards ($236,767 total): children of faculty/staff, international students, out-of-state students, previous college experience. ***Tuition waivers:*** Full or partial for employees or children of employees, senior citizens.

LOANS ***Student loans:*** $2,154,711 (71% need-based, 29% non-need-based). 59% of past graduating class borrowed through all loan programs. *Average indebtedness per student:* $15,905. ***Average need-based loan:*** Freshmen: $2671. Undergraduates: $3090. ***Parent loans:*** $91,224 (6% need-based, 94% non-need-based). ***Programs:*** FFEL (Subsidized and Unsubsidized Stafford, PLUS), Perkins, college/university.

WORK-STUDY ***Federal work-study:*** Total amount: $248,980; 144 jobs averaging $1587.

ATHLETIC AWARDS Total amount: $992,146 (29% need-based, 71% non-need-based).

APPLYING FOR FINANCIAL AID ***Required financial aid forms:*** FAFSA, institution's own form. ***Financial aid deadline (priority):*** 3/15. ***Notification date:*** Continuous beginning 3/15. Students must reply within 4 weeks of notification.

CONTACT Nancy Moats, Director of Financial Aid, University of Science and Arts of Oklahoma, 1727 West Alabama, Chickasha, OK 73018-5322, 405-574-1251 or toll-free 800-933-8726 Ext. 1212. *Fax:* 405-574-1220. *E-mail:* nmoats@usao.edu.

THE UNIVERSITY OF SCRANTON

Scranton, PA

Tuition & fees: $33,124 **Average undergraduate aid package: $19,228**

ABOUT THE INSTITUTION Independent Roman Catholic (Jesuit), coed. ***Awards:*** associate, bachelor's, master's, and doctoral degrees and post-bachelor's and post-master's certificates. 55 undergraduate majors. ***Total enrollment:*** 5,651. Undergraduates: 4,132. Freshmen: 968. Federal methodology is used as a basis for awarding need-based institutional aid.

UNDERGRADUATE EXPENSES for 2009–10 ***Comprehensive fee:*** $44,564 includes full-time tuition ($32,824), mandatory fees ($300), and room and board ($11,440). ***Part-time tuition:*** $846 per credit.

FRESHMAN FINANCIAL AID (Fall 2008, est.) 813 applied for aid; of those 83% were deemed to have need. 99% of freshmen with need received aid; of those 12% had need fully met. ***Average percent of need met:*** 74% (excluding resources awarded to replace EFC). ***Average financial aid package:*** $21,200 (excluding resources awarded to replace EFC). 16% of all full-time freshmen had no need and received non-need-based gift aid.

UNDERGRADUATE FINANCIAL AID (Fall 2008, est.) 3,026 applied for aid; of those 86% were deemed to have need. 98% of undergraduates with need received aid; of those 12% had need fully met. ***Average percent of need met:*** 72% (excluding resources awarded to replace EFC). ***Average financial aid package:*** $19,228 (excluding resources awarded to replace EFC). 17% of all full-time undergraduates had no need and received non-need-based gift aid.

GIFT AID (NEED-BASED) ***Total amount:*** $42,068,839 (6% federal, 6% state, 83% institutional, 5% external sources). ***Receiving aid:*** Freshmen: 68% (653); all full-time undergraduates: 63% (2,447). ***Average award:*** Freshmen: $16,043; Undergraduates: $14,467. ***Scholarships, grants, and awards:*** Federal Pell, FSEOG, state, private, college/university gift aid from institutional funds, Federal TEACH Grant.

GIFT AID (NON-NEED-BASED) ***Total amount:*** $3,187,164 (90% institutional, 10% external sources). ***Receiving aid:*** Freshmen: 7% (71). Undergraduates: 5% (200). ***Average award:*** Freshmen: $9614. Undergraduates: $9281. ***Scholarships, grants, and awards by category:*** *Academic interests/achievement:* 2,022 awards ($16,392,630 total): general academic interests/achievements, military science. *Special characteristics:* children of educators, children of faculty/staff, members of minority groups, siblings of current students. ***ROTC:*** Army, Air Force cooperative.

LOANS ***Student loans:*** $27,137,252 (65% need-based, 35% non-need-based). 77% of past graduating class borrowed through all loan programs. *Average indebtedness per student:* $28,251. ***Average need-based loan:*** Freshmen: $3561. Undergraduates: $4589. ***Parent loans:*** $11,212,414 (48% need-based, 52% non-need-based). ***Programs:*** Federal Direct (Subsidized and Unsubsidized Stafford, PLUS), FFEL (Subsidized and Unsubsidized Stafford, PLUS), Perkins, Federal Nursing.

WORK-STUDY ***Federal work-study:*** Total amount: $1,641,869; 800 jobs averaging $1800. ***State or other work-study/employment:*** Total amount: $715,365 (37% need-based, 63% non-need-based). 480 part-time jobs averaging $1800.

APPLYING FOR FINANCIAL AID ***Required financial aid form:*** FAFSA. ***Financial aid deadline (priority):*** 2/15. ***Notification date:*** Continuous beginning 3/15. Students must reply by 5/1.

CONTACT Mr. William R. Burke, Director of Financial Aid, The University of Scranton, St. Thomas Hall 401, Scranton, PA 18510, 570-941-7887 or toll-free 888-SCRANTON. *Fax:* 570-941-4370. *E-mail:* finaid@scranton.edu.

UNIVERSITY OF SIOUX FALLS

Sioux Falls, SD

CONTACT Rachel Gunn, Financial Aid Counselor, University of Sioux Falls, 1101 West 22nd Street, Sioux Falls, SD 57105-1699, 605-331-6623 or toll-free 800-888-1047. *Fax:* 605-331-6615. *E-mail:* rachel.gunn@usiouxfalls.edu.

UNIVERSITY OF SOUTH ALABAMA

Mobile, AL

Tuition & fees (AL res): $5512 **Average undergraduate aid package: N/A**

ABOUT THE INSTITUTION State-supported, coed. ***Awards:*** bachelor's, master's, doctoral, and first professional degrees and post-bachelor's and post-master's certificates. 47 undergraduate majors. ***Total enrollment:*** 14,064. Undergraduates: 11,048. Freshmen: 1,617. Federal methodology is used as a basis for awarding need-based institutional aid.

UNDERGRADUATE EXPENSES for 2008–09 ***Application fee:*** $35. ***Tuition, state resident:*** full-time $4410; part-time $147 per credit hour. ***Tuition, nonresident:*** full-time $8820; part-time $294 per credit hour. ***Required fees:*** full-time $1102; $363 per term. ***College room and board:*** $5344; ***Room only:*** $2744. Room and board charges vary according to board plan, housing facility, and location. ***Payment plan:*** Installment.

FRESHMAN FINANCIAL AID (Fall 2008, est.) 641 applied for aid; of those 100% were deemed to have need. 100% of freshmen with need received aid; of those 74% had need fully met. ***Average percent of need met:*** 24% (excluding resources awarded to replace EFC).

UNDERGRADUATE FINANCIAL AID (Fall 2008, est.) 3,175 applied for aid; of those 100% were deemed to have need. 100% of undergraduates with need received aid; of those 87% had need fully met. ***Average percent of need met:*** 26% (excluding resources awarded to replace EFC).

GIFT AID (NEED-BASED) ***Total amount:*** $10,641,876 (96% federal, 4% state). ***Receiving aid:*** Freshmen: 31% (456); all full-time undergraduates: 27% (2,080). ***Scholarships, grants, and awards:*** Federal Pell, FSEOG, state, college/university gift aid from institutional funds.

GIFT AID (NON-NEED-BASED) ***Total amount:*** $7,620,836 (88% institutional, 12% external sources). ***Receiving aid:*** Freshmen: 38% (568). Undergraduates: 37% (2,865). ***Scholarships, grants, and awards by category:*** *Academic interests/achievement:* business, computer science, general academic interests/achievements, humanities, international studies, military science. *Creative arts/performance:* art/fine arts, journalism/publications, music, theater/drama. *Special* *achievements/activities:* general special achievements/activities, hobbies/interests, junior miss, leadership. *Special characteristics:* children and siblings of alumni, children of faculty/staff, members of minority groups. ***Tuition waivers:*** Full or partial for employees or children of employees. ***ROTC:*** Army, Air Force.

LOANS ***Student loans:*** $71,864,261 (35% need-based, 65% non-need-based). 73% of past graduating class borrowed through all loan programs. *Average indebtedness per student:* $23,622. ***Parent loans:*** $1,973,164 (100% non-need-based). ***Programs:*** FFEL (Subsidized and Unsubsidized Stafford, PLUS), Perkins.

WORK-STUDY ***Federal work-study:*** Total amount: $325,714; jobs available (averaging $2600). ***State or other work-study/employment:*** Part-time jobs available.

ATHLETIC AWARDS Total amount: $2,813,186 (100% non-need-based).

APPLYING FOR FINANCIAL AID ***Required financial aid forms:*** FAFSA, institution's own form. ***Financial aid deadline:*** Continuous. ***Notification date:*** Continuous beginning 5/1. Students must reply within 5 weeks of notification.

CONTACT Financial Aid Office, University of South Alabama, Meisler Hall Suite 1200, Mobile, AL 36688-0002, 251-460-6231 or toll-free 800-872-5247. *Fax:* 251-460-6079. *E-mail:* finaid@usouthal.edu.

UNIVERSITY OF SOUTH CAROLINA

Columbia, SC

Tuition & fees (SC res): $8838 **Average undergraduate aid package: $11,283**

ABOUT THE INSTITUTION State-supported, coed. ***Awards:*** bachelor's, master's, doctoral, and first professional degrees and post-bachelor's and post-master's certificates. 68 undergraduate majors. ***Total enrollment:*** 27,488. Undergraduates: 19,765. Freshmen: 3,859. Federal methodology is used as a basis for awarding need-based institutional aid.

UNDERGRADUATE EXPENSES for 2008–09 ***Application fee:*** $50. ***Tuition, state resident:*** full-time $8438; part-time $395 per credit hour. ***Tuition, nonresident:*** full-time $22,508; part-time $1029 per credit hour. ***Required fees:*** full-time $400; $17 per credit hour. Full-time tuition and fees vary according to course load, program, and reciprocity agreements. ***College room and board:*** $7318; ***Room only:*** $4526. Room and board charges vary according to board plan, housing facility, and location. ***Payment plans:*** Installment, deferred payment.

FRESHMAN FINANCIAL AID (Fall 2007) 2,541 applied for aid; of those 60% were deemed to have need. 100% of freshmen with need received aid; of those 32% had need fully met. ***Average percent of need met:*** 75% (excluding resources awarded to replace EFC). ***Average financial aid package:*** $10,994 (excluding resources awarded to replace EFC). 47% of all full-time freshmen had no need and received non-need-based gift aid.

UNDERGRADUATE FINANCIAL AID (Fall 2007) 10,668 applied for aid; of those 74% were deemed to have need. 99% of undergraduates with need received aid; of those 20% had need fully met. ***Average percent of need met:*** 71% (excluding resources awarded to replace EFC). ***Average financial aid package:*** $11,283 (excluding resources awarded to replace EFC). 36% of all full-time undergraduates had no need and received non-need-based gift aid.

GIFT AID (NEED-BASED) ***Total amount:*** $40,309,967 (32% federal, 49% state, 11% institutional, 8% external sources). ***Receiving aid:*** Freshmen: 17% (639); all full-time undergraduates: 23% (3,839). ***Average award:*** Freshmen: $4368; Undergraduates: $4069. ***Scholarships, grants, and awards:*** Federal Pell, FSEOG, state, private, college/university gift aid from institutional funds, United Negro College Fund, Federal Nursing.

GIFT AID (NON-NEED-BASED) ***Total amount:*** $41,924,211 (57% state, 26% institutional, 17% external sources). ***Receiving aid:*** Freshmen: 37% (1,367). Undergraduates: 28% (4,681). ***Average award:*** Freshmen: $6382. Undergraduates: $6576. ***Scholarships, grants, and awards by category:*** *Academic interests/achievement:* 7,874 awards ($19,836,472 total): area/ethnic studies, biological sciences, business, communication, computer science, education, engineering/technologies, English, foreign languages, general academic interests/achievements, health fields, humanities, international studies, library science, mathematics, military science, physical sciences, premedicine, religion/biblical studies, social sciences. *Creative arts/performance:* 206 awards ($891,945 total): art/fine arts, dance, debating, journalism/publications, music, theater/drama. *Special achievements/activities:* 236 awards ($360,685 total): cheerleading/drum major, community service, general special achievements/activities, leadership, memberships, religious involvement. *Special characteristics:* 5,435 awards ($12,379,062 total): adult students, children and siblings of alumni, children of faculty/staff, children of union members/company employees, children of workers in trades, children with a deceased or disabled parent, ethnic background, first-generation college students, general special characteristics, handicapped students, international students, local/state students, members of minority groups, out-of-state students, relatives of clergy, religious affiliation, spouses of deceased or disabled public servants. ***Tuition waivers:*** Full or partial for employees or children of employees, senior citizens. ***ROTC:*** Army, Naval, Air Force.

LOANS ***Student loans:*** $63,422,858 (54% need-based, 46% non-need-based). 45% of past graduating class borrowed through all loan programs. *Average indebtedness per student:* $21,315. ***Average need-based loan:*** Freshmen: $2401. Undergraduates: $3781. ***Parent loans:*** $12,045,210 (14% need-based, 86% non-need-based). ***Programs:*** FFEL (Subsidized and Unsubsidized Stafford, PLUS), Perkins, Federal Nursing.

WORK-STUDY ***Federal work-study:*** Total amount: $1,687,897; 798 jobs averaging $1648. ***State or other work-study/employment:*** Total amount: $5,034,156 (100% non-need-based). 2,617 part-time jobs averaging $1583.

ATHLETIC AWARDS Total amount: $6,000,268 (32% need-based, 68% non-need-based).

APPLYING FOR FINANCIAL AID ***Required financial aid form:*** FAFSA. ***Financial aid deadline (priority):*** 4/1. ***Notification date:*** Continuous beginning 4/1.

CONTACT Dr. Ed Miller, Financial Aid Director, University of South Carolina, 1714 College Street, Columbia, SC 29208, 803-777-8134 or toll-free 800-868-5872 (in-state). *Fax:* 803-777-0941. *E-mail:* ewmiller@mailbox.sc.edu.

UNIVERSITY OF SOUTH CAROLINA AIKEN

Aiken, SC

Tuition & fees (SC res): $7582 **Average undergraduate aid package: $9468**

ABOUT THE INSTITUTION State-supported, coed. ***Awards:*** bachelor's and master's degrees. 20 undergraduate majors. ***Total enrollment:*** 3,232. Undergraduates: 3,078. Freshmen: 594. Federal methodology is used as a basis for awarding need-based institutional aid.

UNDERGRADUATE EXPENSES for 2008–09 ***Application fee:*** $45. ***Tuition, state resident:*** full-time $7332; part-time $318 per credit hour. ***Tuition, nonresident:*** full-time $14,696; part-time $631 per credit hour. ***Required fees:*** full-time $250; $8 per credit hour. Full-time tuition and fees vary according to reciprocity agreements. Part-time tuition and fees vary according to course load and reciprocity agreements. ***College room and board:*** $6620; ***Room only:*** $4870. Room and board charges vary according to board plan and housing facility. ***Payment plan:*** Deferred payment.

FRESHMAN FINANCIAL AID (Fall 2007) 520 applied for aid; of those 54% were deemed to have need. 84% of freshmen with need received aid; of those 30% had need fully met. ***Average percent of need met:*** 61% (excluding resources awarded to replace EFC). ***Average financial aid package:*** $9342 (excluding resources awarded to replace EFC). 4% of all full-time freshmen had no need and received non-need-based gift aid.

UNDERGRADUATE FINANCIAL AID (Fall 2007) 2,121 applied for aid; of those 57% were deemed to have need. 85% of undergraduates with need received aid; of those 23% had need fully met. ***Average percent of need met:*** 65% (excluding resources awarded to replace EFC). ***Average financial aid package:*** $9468 (excluding resources awarded to replace EFC). 2% of all full-time undergraduates had no need and received non-need-based gift aid.

GIFT AID (NEED-BASED) ***Total amount:*** $9,683,818 (30% federal, 61% state, 6% institutional, 3% external sources). ***Receiving aid:*** Freshmen: 16% (94); all full-time undergraduates: 13% (314). ***Average award:*** Freshmen: $1310; Undergraduates: $1375. ***Scholarships, grants, and awards:*** Federal Pell, FSEOG, state, college/university gift aid from institutional funds.

GIFT AID (NON-NEED-BASED) ***Receiving aid:*** Freshmen: 12% (71). Undergraduates: 19% (451). ***Average award:*** Freshmen: $1550. Undergraduates: $1720. ***Scholarships, grants, and awards by category:*** *Academic interests/achievement:* biological sciences, business, communication, computer science, education, engineering/technologies, English, general academic interests/achievements, humanities, mathematics, physical sciences, social sciences. *Creative arts/performance:* art/fine arts, creative writing, journalism/publications, music. *Special achievements/activities:* cheerleading/drum major. ***Tuition waivers:*** Full or partial for employees or children of employees, senior citizens.

LOANS ***Student loans:*** $16,457,883 (100% need-based). 47% of past graduating class borrowed through all loan programs. *Average indebtedness per student:* $24,668. ***Average need-based loan:*** Freshmen: $3330. Undergraduates: $4510. ***Parent loans:*** $838,902 (100% need-based). ***Programs:*** FFEL (Subsidized and Unsubsidized Stafford, PLUS), Perkins.

WORK-STUDY ***Federal work-study:*** Total amount: $732,456; jobs available. ***State or other work-study/employment:*** Total amount: $465,880 (100% need-based). Part-time jobs available.

ATHLETIC AWARDS Total amount: $589,257 (100% need-based).

APPLYING FOR FINANCIAL AID ***Required financial aid form:*** FAFSA. ***Financial aid deadline (priority):*** 3/15. ***Notification date:*** Continuous beginning 5/1. Students must reply within 4 weeks of notification.

CONTACT Mr. Glenn Shumpert, Director of Financial Aid, University of South Carolina Aiken, 471 University Parkway, Aiken, SC 29801, 803-641-3476 or toll-free 888-WOW-USCA. *Fax:* 803-641-6840. *E-mail:* glens@usca.edu.

UNIVERSITY OF SOUTH CAROLINA BEAUFORT

Beaufort, SC

Tuition & fees (SC res): $7080 **Average undergraduate aid package: N/A**

ABOUT THE INSTITUTION State-supported, coed. ***Awards:*** associate and bachelor's degrees. 10 undergraduate majors. ***Total enrollment:*** 1,461. Undergraduates: 1,461. Freshmen: 288. Federal methodology is used as a basis for awarding need-based institutional aid.

UNDERGRADUATE EXPENSES for 2008–09 ***Application fee:*** $40. ***Tuition, state resident:*** full-time $6664; part-time $278 per credit hour. ***Tuition, nonresident:*** full-time $14,240; part-time $593 per credit hour. ***Required fees:*** full-time $416; $14 per credit hour or $40 per term. Full-time tuition and fees vary according to reciprocity agreements. Part-time tuition and fees vary according to reciprocity agreements. ***College room and board: Room only:*** $5600.

GIFT AID (NEED-BASED) ***Total amount:*** $1,527,392 (82% federal, 11% state, 7% institutional). ***Scholarships, grants, and awards:*** Federal Pell, FSEOG, state, private, college/university gift aid from institutional funds.

GIFT AID (NON-NEED-BASED) ***Total amount:*** $1,637,993 (69% state, 6% institutional, 25% external sources). ***Tuition waivers:*** Full or partial for employees or children of employees, senior citizens.

LOANS ***Student loans:*** $5,294,047 (39% need-based, 61% non-need-based). ***Parent loans:*** $419,270 (100% non-need-based). ***Programs:*** FFEL (Subsidized and Unsubsidized Stafford, PLUS).

WORK-STUDY ***Federal work-study:*** Total amount: $43,128; 30 jobs averaging $2800.

ATHLETIC AWARDS Total amount: $80,000 (100% non-need-based).

APPLYING FOR FINANCIAL AID ***Required financial aid form:*** FAFSA. ***Financial aid deadline (priority):*** 4/16. ***Notification date:*** Continuous. Students must reply within 2 weeks of notification.

CONTACT Tina Wells, Financial Aid Administrative Assistant, University of South Carolina Beaufort, 801 Carteret Street, Beaufort, SC 29902, 843-521-3104. *Fax:* 843-521-3194. *E-mail:* uscbfina@uscb.edu.

UNIVERSITY OF SOUTH CAROLINA UPSTATE

Spartanburg, SC

Tuition & fees (SC res): $8512 **Average undergraduate aid package: $8944**

ABOUT THE INSTITUTION State-supported, coed. ***Awards:*** bachelor's and master's degrees and post-bachelor's certificates. 27 undergraduate majors. ***Total enrollment:*** 5,063. Undergraduates: 4,997. Freshmen: 721. Federal methodology is used as a basis for awarding need-based institutional aid.

UNDERGRADUATE EXPENSES for 2008–09 ***Application fee:*** $40. ***Tuition, state resident:*** full-time $8062; part-time $345 per semester hour. ***Tuition, nonresident:*** full-time $16,404; part-time $699 per semester hour. ***Required fees:*** full-time $450. Full-time tuition and fees vary according to course load and program. Part-time tuition and fees vary according to course load and program. ***College room and board:*** $6150; ***Room only:*** $3500. Room and board charges vary according to board plan and housing facility. ***Payment plan:*** Deferred payment.

FRESHMAN FINANCIAL AID (Fall 2008, est.) 598 applied for aid; of those 78% were deemed to have need. 99% of freshmen with need received aid; of those 21% had need fully met. ***Average percent of need met:*** 62% (excluding resources awarded to replace EFC). ***Average financial aid package:*** $9744 (excluding resources awarded to replace EFC). 2% of all full-time freshmen had no need and received non-need-based gift aid.

UNDERGRADUATE FINANCIAL AID (Fall 2008, est.) 3,328 applied for aid; of those 84% were deemed to have need. 99% of undergraduates with need received aid; of those 15% had need fully met. ***Average percent of need met:*** 53% (excluding resources awarded to replace EFC). ***Average financial aid package:*** $8944 (excluding resources awarded to replace EFC). 2% of all full-time undergraduates had no need and received non-need-based gift aid.

GIFT AID (NEED-BASED) ***Total amount:*** $7,407,874 (84% federal, 16% state). ***Receiving aid:*** Freshmen: 41% (289); all full-time undergraduates: 40% (1,658). ***Average award:*** Freshmen: $4527; Undergraduates: $4214. ***Scholarships, grants, and awards:*** Federal Pell, FSEOG, state, private, college/university gift aid from institutional funds.

GIFT AID (NON-NEED-BASED) ***Total amount:*** $8,364,957 (87% state, 6% institutional, 7% external sources). ***Receiving aid:*** Freshmen: 57% (403). Undergraduates: 26% (1,065). ***Average award:*** Freshmen: $2346. Undergraduates: $2048. ***Scholarships, grants, and awards by category:*** *Academic interests/achievement:* 239 awards ($457,585 total): general academic interests/achievements. *Special characteristics:* 48 awards ($28,655 total): first-generation college students. ***Tuition waivers:*** Full or partial for senior citizens. ***ROTC:*** Army cooperative.

LOANS ***Student loans:*** $22,378,071 (44% need-based, 56% non-need-based). 71% of past graduating class borrowed through all loan programs. *Average indebtedness per student:* $18,762. ***Average need-based loan:*** Freshmen: $3094. Undergraduates: $4011. ***Parent loans:*** $702,057 (100% non-need-based). ***Programs:*** FFEL (Subsidized and Unsubsidized Stafford, PLUS), Perkins, state, private loans.

WORK-STUDY ***Federal work-study:*** Total amount: $167,849; 97 jobs averaging $1730. ***State or other work-study/employment:*** Total amount: $546,246 (100% non-need-based). 439 part-time jobs averaging $1244.

ATHLETIC AWARDS Total amount: $1,274,671 (100% non-need-based).

APPLYING FOR FINANCIAL AID ***Required financial aid form:*** FAFSA. ***Financial aid deadline (priority):*** 3/1. ***Notification date:*** Continuous beginning 4/1. Students must reply within 2 weeks of notification.

CONTACT Kim Jenerette, Director of Financial Aid, University of South Carolina Upstate, 800 University Way, Spartanburg, SC 29303, 864-503-5340 or toll-free 800-277-8727. *Fax:* 864-503-5974. *E-mail:* kjenerette@uscupstate.edu.

THE UNIVERSITY OF SOUTH DAKOTA

Vermillion, SD

Tuition & fees (SD res): $6468 **Average undergraduate aid package: $5660**

ABOUT THE INSTITUTION State-supported, coed. ***Awards:*** associate, bachelor's, master's, doctoral, and first professional degrees and post-bachelor's and post-master's certificates. 60 undergraduate majors. ***Total enrollment:*** 9,291. Undergraduates: 6,958. Freshmen: 1,162. Federal methodology is used as a basis for awarding need-based institutional aid.

UNDERGRADUATE EXPENSES for 2009–10 ***Application fee:*** $20. ***Tuition, state resident:*** full-time $2751; part-time $91.70 per credit hour. ***Tuition, nonresident:*** full-time $8405; part-time $291.25 per credit hour. ***Required fees:*** full-time $3717; $123.90 per credit hour. ***College room and board:*** $5787; ***Room only:*** $2859.

FRESHMAN FINANCIAL AID (Fall 2007) 886 applied for aid; of those 68% were deemed to have need. 90% of freshmen with need received aid; of those 80% had need fully met. ***Average percent of need met:*** 72% (excluding resources awarded to replace EFC). ***Average financial aid package:*** $4528 (excluding resources awarded to replace EFC). 26% of all full-time freshmen had no need and received non-need-based gift aid.

UNDERGRADUATE FINANCIAL AID (Fall 2007) 3,796 applied for aid; of those 75% were deemed to have need. 93% of undergraduates with need received aid; of those 74% had need fully met. ***Average percent of need met:*** 71% (excluding resources awarded to replace EFC). ***Average financial aid package:*** $5660 (excluding resources awarded to replace EFC). 17% of all full-time undergraduates had no need and received non-need-based gift aid.

GIFT AID (NEED-BASED) ***Total amount:*** $5,396,154 (100% federal). ***Receiving aid:*** Freshmen: 24% (246); all full-time undergraduates: 27% (1,279). ***Average award:*** Freshmen: $3700; Undergraduates: $3381. ***Scholarships, grants, and awards:*** Federal Pell, FSEOG, private, college/university gift aid from institutional funds, Federal Nursing.

GIFT AID (NON-NEED-BASED) ***Total amount:*** $6,716,548 (19% federal, 7% state, 55% institutional, 19% external sources). ***Receiving aid:*** Freshmen: 25% (259). Undergraduates: 18% (860). ***Average award:*** Freshmen: $3224.

Undergraduates: $3248. ***Scholarships, grants, and awards by category:*** *Academic interests/achievement:* biological sciences, business, communication, computer science, education, English, foreign languages, general academic interests/achievements, humanities, mathematics, military science, premedicine, social sciences. *Creative arts/performance:* art/fine arts, creative writing, debating, music, theater/drama. ***ROTC:*** Army.

LOANS ***Student loans:*** $21,963,062 (55% need-based, 45% non-need-based). 88% of past graduating class borrowed through all loan programs. *Average indebtedness per student:* $22,781. ***Average need-based loan:*** Freshmen: $2785. Undergraduates: $3864. ***Parent loans:*** $3,363,351 (100% non-need-based). ***Programs:*** FFEL (Subsidized and Unsubsidized Stafford, PLUS), Perkins, Federal Nursing, college/university, alternative loans.

WORK-STUDY ***Federal work-study:*** Total amount: $908,154; 517 jobs averaging $1777. ***State or other work-study/employment:*** Total amount: $255,822 (95% need-based, 5% non-need-based). 674 part-time jobs averaging $1116.

ATHLETIC AWARDS Total amount: $1,151,783 (100% non-need-based).

APPLYING FOR FINANCIAL AID ***Required financial aid form:*** FAFSA. ***Financial aid deadline (priority):*** 3/15. ***Notification date:*** Continuous.

CONTACT Julie Pier, Director of Student Financial Aid, The University of South Dakota, Belbas Center, Vermillion, SD 57069-2390, 605-677-5446 or toll-free 877-269-6837. *Fax:* 605-677-5238.

UNIVERSITY OF SOUTHERN CALIFORNIA

Los Angeles, CA

Tuition & fees: $37,694 **Average undergraduate aid package: $33,025**

ABOUT THE INSTITUTION Independent, coed. ***Awards:*** bachelor's, master's, doctoral, and first professional degrees and post-bachelor's, post-master's, and first professional certificates. 79 undergraduate majors. ***Total enrollment:*** 33,747. Undergraduates: 16,608. Freshmen: 2,766.

UNDERGRADUATE EXPENSES for 2008–09 ***Application fee:*** $65. ***Comprehensive fee:*** $48,992 includes full-time tuition ($37,096), mandatory fees ($598), and room and board ($11,298). ***College room only:*** $6256. Full-time tuition and fees vary according to program. Room and board charges vary according to board plan and housing facility. ***Part-time tuition:*** $1249 per credit hour. Part-time tuition and fees vary according to course load and program. ***Payment plans:*** Tuition prepayment, installment, deferred payment.

FRESHMAN FINANCIAL AID (Fall 2007) 1,849 applied for aid; of those 65% were deemed to have need. 100% of freshmen with need received aid; of those 98% had need fully met. ***Average percent of need met:*** 100% (excluding resources awarded to replace EFC). ***Average financial aid package:*** $33,713 (excluding resources awarded to replace EFC). 26% of all full-time freshmen had no need and received non-need-based gift aid.

UNDERGRADUATE FINANCIAL AID (Fall 2007) 8,121 applied for aid; of those 78% were deemed to have need. 100% of undergraduates with need received aid; of those 96% had need fully met. ***Average percent of need met:*** 100% (excluding resources awarded to replace EFC). ***Average financial aid package:*** $33,025 (excluding resources awarded to replace EFC). 21% of all full-time undergraduates had no need and received non-need-based gift aid.

GIFT AID (NEED-BASED) ***Total amount:*** $154,946,098 (8% federal, 9% state, 80% institutional, 3% external sources). ***Receiving aid:*** Freshmen: 35% (1,040); all full-time undergraduates: 36% (5,705). ***Average award:*** Freshmen: $23,131; Undergraduates: $22,366. ***Scholarships, grants, and awards:*** Federal Pell, FSEOG, state, private, college/university gift aid from institutional funds.

GIFT AID (NON-NEED-BASED) ***Total amount:*** $45,119,689 (81% institutional, 19% external sources). ***Receiving aid:*** Freshmen: 25% (739). Undergraduates: 18% (2,811). ***Average award:*** Freshmen: $14,721. Undergraduates: $13,906. ***Scholarships, grants, and awards by category:*** *Academic interests/achievement:* 5,299 awards ($72,350,009 total): general academic interests/achievements. *Creative arts/performance:* 15 awards ($369,160 total): debating. *Special achievements/activities:* 6 awards ($60,000 total): leadership. *Special characteristics:* 837 awards ($16,978,641 total): children and siblings of alumni, children of faculty/staff, international students, members of minority groups. ***Tuition waivers:*** Full or partial for employees or children of employees. ***ROTC:*** Army, Naval, Air Force.

LOANS ***Student loans:*** $48,447,387 (72% need-based, 28% non-need-based). 51% of past graduating class borrowed through all loan programs. *Average indebtedness per student:* $27,692. ***Average need-based loan:*** Freshmen: $4016. Undergraduates: $6478. ***Parent loans:*** $62,666,840 (100% non-need-based). ***Programs:*** FFEL (Subsidized and Unsubsidized Stafford, PLUS), Perkins, 'Credit Ready' and credit-based loans.

WORK-STUDY ***Federal work-study:*** Total amount: $12,204,373; 4,384 jobs averaging $2764.

ATHLETIC AWARDS Total amount: $13,579,192 (23% need-based, 77% non-need-based).

APPLYING FOR FINANCIAL AID ***Required financial aid forms:*** FAFSA, CSS Financial Aid PROFILE, 2s, USC non-filing forms. ***Financial aid deadline (priority):*** 2/2. ***Notification date:*** Continuous beginning 3/15. Students must reply by 5/1.

CONTACT Susan Grogan Ikerd, Associate Dean and Director of Financial Aid, University of Southern California, University of Southern California, Los Angeles, CA 90089-0914, 213-740-5445. *Fax:* 213-740-0680. *E-mail:* fao@usc.edu.

UNIVERSITY OF SOUTHERN INDIANA

Evansville, IN

Tuition & fees (IN res): $5219 **Average undergraduate aid package: $10,574**

ABOUT THE INSTITUTION State-supported, coed. ***Awards:*** associate, bachelor's, master's, and doctoral degrees and post-bachelor's certificates. 54 undergraduate majors. ***Total enrollment:*** 10,126. Undergraduates: 9,320. Freshmen: 2,104. Federal methodology is used as a basis for awarding need-based institutional aid.

UNDERGRADUATE EXPENSES for 2009–10 ***Application fee:*** $25. ***Tuition, state resident:*** full-time $5019; part-time $167.30 per credit hour. ***Tuition, nonresident:*** full-time $11,954; part-time $398.45 per credit hour. ***Required fees:*** full-time $200; $22.75 per term. ***College room and board:*** $6648; ***Room only:*** $3350.

FRESHMAN FINANCIAL AID (Fall 2008, est.) 1,715 applied for aid; of those 68% were deemed to have need. 98% of freshmen with need received aid; of those 22% had need fully met. ***Average percent of need met:*** 83% (excluding resources awarded to replace EFC). ***Average financial aid package:*** $10,201 (excluding resources awarded to replace EFC). 12% of all full-time freshmen had no need and received non-need-based gift aid.

UNDERGRADUATE FINANCIAL AID (Fall 2008, est.) 5,749 applied for aid; of those 73% were deemed to have need. 97% of undergraduates with need received aid; of those 21% had need fully met. ***Average percent of need met:*** 81% (excluding resources awarded to replace EFC). ***Average financial aid package:*** $10,574 (excluding resources awarded to replace EFC). 10% of all full-time undergraduates had no need and received non-need-based gift aid.

GIFT AID (NEED-BASED) ***Total amount:*** $16,853,682 (47% federal, 38% state, 12% institutional, 3% external sources). ***Receiving aid:*** Freshmen: 43% (892); all full-time undergraduates: 38% (2,942). ***Average award:*** Freshmen: $5593; Undergraduates: $5442. ***Scholarships, grants, and awards:*** Federal Pell, FSEOG, state, private, college/university gift aid from institutional funds, Federal Nursing.

GIFT AID (NON-NEED-BASED) ***Total amount:*** $4,144,229 (58% institutional, 42% external sources). ***Receiving aid:*** Freshmen: 8% (167). Undergraduates: 6% (423). ***Average award:*** Freshmen: $3672. Undergraduates: $2549. ***Scholarships, grants, and awards by category:*** *Academic interests/achievement:* 1,915 awards ($1,126,637 total): biological sciences, business, education, engineering/technologies, general academic interests/achievements, health fields, humanities, mathematics, premedicine, social sciences. *Creative arts/performance:* 33 awards ($15,899 total): art/fine arts, creative writing, theater/drama. *Special achievements/activities:* leadership. *Special characteristics:* 309 awards ($501,935 total): children of faculty/staff, members of minority groups, out-of-state students, spouses of current students, veterans' children. ***ROTC:*** Army.

LOANS ***Student loans:*** $36,025,001 (63% need-based, 37% non-need-based). ***Average need-based loan:*** Freshmen: $2136. Undergraduates: $2860. ***Parent loans:*** $3,117,503 (20% need-based, 80% non-need-based). ***Programs:*** Federal Direct (Subsidized and Unsubsidized Stafford, PLUS).

WORK-STUDY ***Federal work-study:*** Total amount: $119,783; 81 jobs averaging $1479.

ATHLETIC AWARDS Total amount: $817,438 (40% need-based, 60% non-need-based).

APPLYING FOR FINANCIAL AID ***Required financial aid forms:*** FAFSA, institution's own form. ***Financial aid deadline:*** 3/1. ***Notification date:*** Continuous beginning 4/15.

CONTACT Financial Aid Counselor, University of Southern Indiana, 8600 University Boulevard, Evansville, IN 47712-3590, 812-464-1767 or toll-free 800-467-1965. *Fax:* 812-465-7154. *E-mail:* finaid@usi.edu.

UNIVERSITY OF SOUTHERN MAINE

Portland, ME

Tuition & fees (ME res): $7467 Average undergraduate aid package: $10,677

ABOUT THE INSTITUTION State-supported, coed. ***Awards:*** associate, bachelor's, master's, doctoral, and first professional degrees and post-master's certificates. 46 undergraduate majors. ***Total enrollment:*** 7,879. Undergraduates: 7,879. Freshmen: 1,027. Federal methodology is used as a basis for awarding need-based institutional aid.

UNDERGRADUATE EXPENSES for 2008–09 ***Application fee:*** $40. ***Tuition, state resident:*** full-time $6540; part-time $218 per credit hour. ***Tuition, nonresident:*** full-time $18,060; part-time $602 per credit hour. ***Required fees:*** full-time $927. Full-time tuition and fees vary according to course load, degree level, and reciprocity agreements. Part-time tuition and fees vary according to course load, degree level, and reciprocity agreements. ***College room and board:*** $8344; ***Room only:*** $4472. Room and board charges vary according to board plan, housing facility, and location. ***Payment plan:*** Installment.

FRESHMAN FINANCIAL AID (Fall 2008, est.) 885 applied for aid; of those 82% were deemed to have need. 97% of freshmen with need received aid; of those 13% had need fully met. ***Average percent of need met:*** 62% (excluding resources awarded to replace EFC). ***Average financial aid package:*** $9263 (excluding resources awarded to replace EFC). 14% of all full-time freshmen had no need and received non-need-based gift aid.

UNDERGRADUATE FINANCIAL AID (Fall 2008, est.) 3,980 applied for aid; of those 86% were deemed to have need. 97% of undergraduates with need received aid; of those 16% had need fully met. ***Average percent of need met:*** 67% (excluding resources awarded to replace EFC). ***Average financial aid package:*** $10,677 (excluding resources awarded to replace EFC). 10% of all full-time undergraduates had no need and received non-need-based gift aid.

GIFT AID (NEED-BASED) ***Total amount:*** $14,966,517 (55% federal, 13% state, 15% institutional, 17% external sources). ***Receiving aid:*** Freshmen: 60% (588); all full-time undergraduates: 55% (2,576). ***Average award:*** Freshmen: $4923; Undergraduates: $4877. ***Scholarships, grants, and awards:*** Federal Pell, FSEOG, state, college/university gift aid from institutional funds.

GIFT AID (NON-NEED-BASED) ***Total amount:*** $3,715,053 (20% institutional, 80% external sources). ***Receiving aid:*** Freshmen: 4% (36). Undergraduates: 2% (100). ***Average award:*** Freshmen: $4936. Undergraduates: $5558. ***Scholarships, grants, and awards by category:*** *Academic interests/achievement:* general academic interests/achievements. *Creative arts/performance:* music, theater/drama. *Special achievements/activities:* community service. *Special characteristics:* children of faculty/staff, general special characteristics, local/state students, out-of-state students. ***Tuition waivers:*** Full or partial for minority students, employees or children of employees. ***ROTC:*** Army cooperative, Air Force cooperative.

LOANS ***Student loans:*** $30,877,410 (60% need-based, 40% non-need-based). 53% of past graduating class borrowed through all loan programs. *Average indebtedness per student:* $22,656. ***Average need-based loan:*** Freshmen: $3556. Undergraduates: $4772. ***Parent loans:*** $4,582,903 (100% non-need-based). ***Programs:*** FFEL (Subsidized and Unsubsidized Stafford, PLUS), Perkins, Federal Nursing, college/university.

WORK-STUDY ***Federal work-study:*** Total amount: $4,046,418; jobs available.

APPLYING FOR FINANCIAL AID ***Required financial aid form:*** FAFSA. ***Financial aid deadline (priority):*** 2/15. ***Notification date:*** Continuous beginning 3/15. Students must reply within 2 weeks of notification.

CONTACT Mr. Keith P. Dubois, Director of Student Financial Aid, University of Southern Maine, 96 Falmouth Street, PO Box 9300, Portland, ME 04104-9300, 207-780-5122 or toll-free 800-800-4USM Ext. 5670. *Fax:* 207-780-5143. *E-mail:* dubois@maine.edu.

UNIVERSITY OF SOUTHERN MISSISSIPPI

Hattiesburg, MS

Tuition & fees (MS res): $5096 Average undergraduate aid package: $7931

ABOUT THE INSTITUTION State-supported, coed. ***Awards:*** bachelor's, master's, and doctoral degrees and post-master's certificates. 68 undergraduate majors. ***Total enrollment:*** 14,793. Undergraduates: 12,062. Freshmen: 1,527. Federal methodology is used as a basis for awarding need-based institutional aid.

UNDERGRADUATE EXPENSES for 2008–09 ***Application fee:*** $25. ***Tuition, state resident:*** full-time $5096; part-time $213 per credit. ***Tuition, nonresident:*** full-time $12,746; part-time $532 per credit. Part-time tuition and fees vary according to course load and degree level. ***College room and board:*** $6032; ***Room only:*** $3732. Room and board charges vary according to board plan and housing facility. ***Payment plan:*** Installment.

FRESHMAN FINANCIAL AID (Fall 2007) 1,227 applied for aid; of those 77% were deemed to have need. 97% of freshmen with need received aid; of those 23% had need fully met. ***Average percent of need met:*** 79% (excluding resources awarded to replace EFC). ***Average financial aid package:*** $7573 (excluding resources awarded to replace EFC). 15% of all full-time freshmen had no need and received non-need-based gift aid.

UNDERGRADUATE FINANCIAL AID (Fall 2007) 7,645 applied for aid; of those 84% were deemed to have need. 97% of undergraduates with need received aid; of those 23% had need fully met. ***Average percent of need met:*** 81% (excluding resources awarded to replace EFC). ***Average financial aid package:*** $7931 (excluding resources awarded to replace EFC). 9% of all full-time undergraduates had no need and received non-need-based gift aid.

GIFT AID (NEED-BASED) ***Total amount:*** $20,424,285 (78% federal, 6% state, 11% institutional, 5% external sources). ***Receiving aid:*** Freshmen: 39% (600); all full-time undergraduates: 42% (4,303). ***Average award:*** Freshmen: $3698; Undergraduates: $3467. ***Scholarships, grants, and awards:*** Federal Pell, FSEOG, state, private, college/university gift aid from institutional funds.

GIFT AID (NON-NEED-BASED) ***Total amount:*** $12,154,129 (7% federal, 23% state, 56% institutional, 14% external sources). ***Receiving aid:*** Freshmen: 36% (565). Undergraduates: 27% (2,740). ***Average award:*** Freshmen: $3831. Undergraduates: $3297. ***Scholarships, grants, and awards by category:*** *Academic interests/achievement:* 2,795 awards ($4,956,009 total): general academic interests/achievements. *Creative arts/performance:* 450 awards ($477,145 total): art/fine arts, dance, music, theater/drama. *Special achievements/activities:* 122 awards ($139,080 total): cheerleading/drum major, leadership. *Special characteristics:* 7,817 awards ($14,953,030 total): children and siblings of alumni, children of faculty/staff, ethnic background, local/state students, out-of-state students, veterans. ***Tuition waivers:*** Full or partial for children of alumni, employees or children of employees, senior citizens. ***ROTC:*** Army, Air Force.

LOANS ***Student loans:*** $53,775,095 (55% need-based, 45% non-need-based). 66% of past graduating class borrowed through all loan programs. *Average indebtedness per student:* $17,350. ***Average need-based loan:*** Freshmen: $3657. Undergraduates: $4717. ***Parent loans:*** $4,092,841 (4% need-based, 96% non-need-based). ***Programs:*** FFEL (Subsidized and Unsubsidized Stafford, PLUS), Perkins, Federal Nursing.

WORK-STUDY ***Federal work-study:*** Total amount: $205,518; 119 jobs averaging $1741.

ATHLETIC AWARDS Total amount: $3,190,724 (40% need-based, 60% non-need-based).

APPLYING FOR FINANCIAL AID ***Required financial aid forms:*** FAFSA, institution's own form, state aid form. ***Financial aid deadline (priority):*** 3/15. ***Notification date:*** Continuous. Students must reply within 2 weeks of notification.

CONTACT Mr. David Williamson, Assistant Director of Financial Aid, University of Southern Mississippi, 118 College Drive #5101, Hattiesburg, MS 39406-0001, 601-266-4774. *E-mail:* david.williamson@usm.edu.

UNIVERSITY OF SOUTH FLORIDA

Tampa, FL

Tuition & fees (FL res): $3991 Average undergraduate aid package: $9666

ABOUT THE INSTITUTION State-supported, coed. ***Awards:*** associate, bachelor's, master's, doctoral, and first professional degrees and post-bachelor's certificates. 84 undergraduate majors. ***Total enrollment:*** 46,189. Undergraduates: 35,918. Freshmen: 4,417. Federal methodology is used as a basis for awarding need-based institutional aid.

UNDERGRADUATE EXPENSES for 2008–09 ***Application fee:*** $30. ***One-time required fee:*** $74. ***Tuition, state resident:*** full-time $3917; part-time $130.55 per credit hour. ***Tuition, nonresident:*** full-time $16,634; part-time $554.45 per credit hour. ***Required fees:*** full-time $74; $37 per term. Full-time tuition and fees vary according to course level, course load, and location. Part-time tuition and fees vary according to course level, course load, and location. ***College room and board:*** $8080; ***Room only:*** $4060. Room and board charges vary according to board plan, housing facility, and location. ***Payment plan:*** Installment.

FRESHMAN FINANCIAL AID (Fall 2007) 2,515 applied for aid; of those 71% were deemed to have need. 99% of freshmen with need received aid; of those 8% had need fully met. ***Average percent of need met:*** 32% (excluding resources awarded to replace EFC). ***Average financial aid package:*** $7889 (excluding resources awarded to replace EFC). 16% of all full-time freshmen had no need and received non-need-based gift aid.

UNDERGRADUATE FINANCIAL AID (Fall 2007) 15,172 applied for aid; of those 83% were deemed to have need. 97% of undergraduates with need received aid; of those 5% had need fully met. ***Average percent of need met:*** 38% (excluding resources awarded to replace EFC). ***Average financial aid package:*** $9666 (excluding resources awarded to replace EFC). 7% of all full-time undergraduates had no need and received non-need-based gift aid.

GIFT AID (NEED-BASED) ***Total amount:*** $42,902,179 (66% federal, 18% state, 16% institutional). ***Receiving aid:*** Freshmen: 22% (935); all full-time undergraduates: 29% (7,302). ***Average award:*** Freshmen: $4785; Undergraduates: $4786. ***Scholarships, grants, and awards:*** Federal Pell, FSEOG, state, private, college/university gift aid from institutional funds.

GIFT AID (NON-NEED-BASED) ***Total amount:*** $48,434,078 (72% state, 21% institutional, 7% external sources). ***Receiving aid:*** Freshmen: 21% (914). Undergraduates: 18% (4,511). ***Average award:*** Freshmen: $3992. Undergraduates: $1997. ***Scholarships, grants, and awards by category:*** *Academic interests/achievement:* 4,291 awards ($7,808,919 total): architecture, biological sciences, business, communication, computer science, education, engineering/technologies, English, foreign languages, general academic interests/achievements, health fields, humanities, international studies, library science, mathematics, military science, physical sciences, premedicine, religion/biblical studies, social sciences. *Creative arts/performance:* applied art and design, art/fine arts, cinema/film/broadcasting, creative writing, dance, debating, journalism/publications, music, performing arts, theater/drama. *Special achievements/activities:* general special achievements/activities. *Special characteristics:* general special characteristics. ***Tuition waivers:*** Full or partial for senior citizens. ***ROTC:*** Army, Naval, Air Force.

LOANS ***Student loans:*** $94,120,213 (51% need-based, 49% non-need-based). 50% of past graduating class borrowed through all loan programs. *Average indebtedness per student:* $18,568. ***Average need-based loan:*** Freshmen: $2617. Undergraduates: $4633. ***Parent loans:*** $4,384,479 (100% non-need-based). ***Programs:*** FFEL (Subsidized and Unsubsidized Stafford, PLUS), Perkins, college/university.

WORK-STUDY ***Federal work-study:*** Total amount: $2,747,771; 924 jobs averaging $3600.

ATHLETIC AWARDS Total amount: $2,057,385 (100% non-need-based).

APPLYING FOR FINANCIAL AID ***Required financial aid form:*** FAFSA. ***Financial aid deadline (priority):*** 3/1. ***Notification date:*** Continuous beginning 3/1. Students must reply within 4 weeks of notification.

CONTACT Ms. Billie Jo Hamilton, Director of Student Financial Aid, University of South Florida, 4202 East Fowler Avenue, SVC 1102, Tampa, FL 33620-6960, 813-974-4700. *Fax:* 813-974-5144. *E-mail:* bjhamilton@admin.usf.edu.

THE UNIVERSITY OF TAMPA

Tampa, FL

Tuition & fees: $21,712 **Average undergraduate aid package: $16,193**

ABOUT THE INSTITUTION Independent, coed. ***Awards:*** associate, bachelor's, and master's degrees and post-master's certificates. 64 undergraduate majors. ***Total enrollment:*** 5,800. Undergraduates: 5,128. Freshmen: 1,237. Federal methodology is used as a basis for awarding need-based institutional aid.

UNDERGRADUATE EXPENSES for 2008–09 ***Application fee:*** $40. ***Comprehensive fee:*** $29,690 includes full-time tuition ($20,690), mandatory fees ($1022), and room and board ($7978). ***College room only:*** $4260. Full-time tuition and fees vary according to class time. Room and board charges vary according to board plan and housing facility. ***Part-time tuition:*** $440 per credit hour. ***Part-time fees:*** $35 per term. Part-time tuition and fees vary according to class time. ***Payment plan:*** Installment.

FRESHMAN FINANCIAL AID (Fall 2008, est.) 845 applied for aid; of those 74% were deemed to have need. 100% of freshmen with need received aid; of those 25% had need fully met. ***Average percent of need met:*** 77% (excluding resources awarded to replace EFC). ***Average financial aid package:*** $16,404 (excluding resources awarded to replace EFC). 16% of all full-time freshmen had no need and received non-need-based gift aid.

UNDERGRADUATE FINANCIAL AID (Fall 2008, est.) 2,916 applied for aid; of those 80% were deemed to have need. 100% of undergraduates with need received aid; of those 22% had need fully met. ***Average percent of need met:*** 74% (excluding resources awarded to replace EFC). ***Average financial aid package:*** $16,193 (excluding resources awarded to replace EFC). 11% of all full-time undergraduates had no need and received non-need-based gift aid.

GIFT AID (NEED-BASED) ***Total amount:*** $27,500,563 (14% federal, 16% state, 64% institutional, 6% external sources). ***Receiving aid:*** Freshmen: 49% (605); all full-time undergraduates: 47% (2,228). ***Average award:*** Freshmen: $7031; Undergraduates: $6922. ***Scholarships, grants, and awards:*** Federal Pell, FSEOG, state, private, college/university gift aid from institutional funds.

GIFT AID (NON-NEED-BASED) ***Total amount:*** $15,750,184 (19% state, 70% institutional, 11% external sources). ***Receiving aid:*** Freshmen: 47% (581). Undergraduates: 38% (1,803). ***Average award:*** Freshmen: $6385. Undergraduates: $6381. ***Scholarships, grants, and awards by category:*** *Academic interests/achievement:* biological sciences, business, communication, education, general academic interests/achievements, health fields, military science, social sciences. *Creative arts/performance:* art/fine arts, creative writing, journalism/publications, music, performing arts. *Special achievements/activities:* general special achievements/activities, leadership. *Special characteristics:* children and siblings of alumni, children of faculty/staff, international students. ***Tuition waivers:*** Full or partial for employees or children of employees. ***ROTC:*** Army, Air Force cooperative.

LOANS ***Student loans:*** $25,100,601 (52% need-based, 48% non-need-based). 59% of past graduating class borrowed through all loan programs. *Average indebtedness per student:* $23,807. ***Average need-based loan:*** Freshmen: $4230. Undergraduates: $4978. ***Parent loans:*** $8,048,488 (65% need-based, 35% non-need-based). ***Programs:*** FFEL (Subsidized and Unsubsidized Stafford, PLUS), Perkins, state, college/university.

WORK-STUDY ***Federal work-study:*** Total amount: $417,504; jobs available (averaging $2000).

ATHLETIC AWARDS Total amount: $1,307,754 (37% need-based, 63% non-need-based).

APPLYING FOR FINANCIAL AID ***Required financial aid forms:*** FAFSA, state aid form. ***Financial aid deadline:*** Continuous. ***Notification date:*** Continuous beginning 2/1. Students must reply within 3 weeks of notification.

CONTACT John C. Marsh, Financial Aid Office, The University of Tampa, 401 West Kennedy Boulevard, Tampa, FL 33606-1490, 813-253-6219 or toll-free 888-646-2438 (in-state), 888-MINARET (out-of-state). *Fax:* 813-258-7439. *E-mail:* finaid@ut.edu.

THE UNIVERSITY OF TENNESSEE

Knoxville, TN

Tuition & fees (TN res): $6250 **Average undergraduate aid package: $9611**

ABOUT THE INSTITUTION State-supported, coed. ***Awards:*** bachelor's, master's, doctoral, and first professional degrees and post-bachelor's, post-master's, and first professional certificates. 92 undergraduate majors. ***Total enrollment:*** 30,410. Undergraduates: 21,717. Freshmen: 4,215. Federal methodology is used as a basis for awarding need-based institutional aid.

UNDERGRADUATE EXPENSES for 2008–09 ***Application fee:*** $30. ***Tuition, state resident:*** full-time $5428; part-time $263 per hour. ***Tuition, nonresident:*** full-time $18,086; part-time $807 per hour. ***Required fees:*** full-time $822; $36 per hour. Full-time tuition and fees vary according to location and program. Part-time tuition and fees vary according to course load, location, and program. ***College room and board:*** $6888; ***Room only:*** $3728. Room and board charges vary according to board plan and housing facility. ***Payment plan:*** Installment.

FRESHMAN FINANCIAL AID (Fall 2008, est.) 3,966 applied for aid; of those 50% were deemed to have need. 99% of freshmen with need received aid; of those 39% had need fully met. ***Average percent of need met:*** 79% (excluding resources awarded to replace EFC). ***Average financial aid package:*** $9731 (excluding resources awarded to replace EFC). 19% of all full-time freshmen had no need and received non-need-based gift aid.

UNDERGRADUATE FINANCIAL AID (Fall 2008, est.) 16,852 applied for aid; of those 55% were deemed to have need. 97% of undergraduates with need received aid; of those 31% had need fully met. ***Average percent of need met:*** 72% (excluding resources awarded to replace EFC). ***Average financial aid***

package: $9611 (excluding resources awarded to replace EFC). 12% of all full-time undergraduates had no need and received non-need-based gift aid.

GIFT AID (NEED-BASED) ***Total amount:*** $91,819,948 (17% federal, 56% state, 23% institutional, 4% external sources). ***Receiving aid:*** Freshmen: 45% (1,897); all full-time undergraduates: 38% (7,725). ***Average award:*** Freshmen: $2746; Undergraduates: $2955. ***Scholarships, grants, and awards:*** Federal Pell, FSEOG, state, private, college/university gift aid from institutional funds, Federal Nursing.

GIFT AID (NON-NEED-BASED) ***Average award:*** Freshmen: $2631. Undergraduates: $2805. ***Scholarships, grants, and awards by category:*** *Academic interests/achievement:* 3,261 awards ($8,403,914 total): agriculture, architecture, business, communication, computer science, education, engineering/technologies, general academic interests/achievements, health fields, humanities, international studies, library science, military science, social sciences. *Creative arts/performance:* art/fine arts. *Special characteristics:* children and siblings of alumni. ***Tuition waivers:*** Full or partial for employees or children of employees, senior citizens. ***ROTC:*** Army, Air Force.

LOANS ***Student loans:*** $50,738,462 (86% need-based, 14% non-need-based). 51% of past graduating class borrowed through all loan programs. *Average indebtedness per student:* $24,690. ***Average need-based loan:*** Freshmen: $3708. Undergraduates: $4409. ***Parent loans:*** $7,755,019 (100% need-based). ***Programs:*** FFEL (Subsidized and Unsubsidized Stafford, PLUS), Perkins, college/university.

WORK-STUDY ***Federal work-study:*** Total amount: $874,924; 378 jobs averaging $2315.

ATHLETIC AWARDS Total amount: $6,280,368 (100% need-based).

APPLYING FOR FINANCIAL AID ***Required financial aid form:*** FAFSA. ***Financial aid deadline (priority):*** 3/1. ***Notification date:*** Continuous beginning 3/15. Students must reply within 3 weeks of notification.

CONTACT Office of Financial Aid and Scholarships, The University of Tennessee, 115 Student Services Building, Knoxville, TN 37996-0210, 865-974-3131 or toll-free 800-221-8657 (in-state). *Fax:* 865-974-2175. *E-mail:* finaid@utk.edu.

THE UNIVERSITY OF TENNESSEE AT CHATTANOOGA

Chattanooga, TN

Tuition & fees (TN res): $5310 **Average undergraduate aid package: $9544**

ABOUT THE INSTITUTION State-supported, coed. ***Awards:*** bachelor's, master's, doctoral, and first professional degrees and post-bachelor's and post-master's certificates. 43 undergraduate majors. ***Total enrollment:*** 9,807. Undergraduates: 8,405. Freshmen: 2,083. Both federal and institutional methodology are used as a basis for awarding need-based institutional aid.

UNDERGRADUATE EXPENSES for 2008–09 ***Application fee:*** $30. ***Tuition, state resident:*** full-time $4210; part-time $176 per credit hour. ***Tuition, nonresident:*** full-time $10,560; part-time $440 per credit hour. ***Required fees:*** full-time $1100; $128 per credit hour. ***College room and board:*** $8100; ***Room only:*** $5100. Room and board charges vary according to board plan and housing facility. ***Payment plan:*** Deferred payment.

FRESHMAN FINANCIAL AID (Fall 2008, est.) 1,974 applied for aid; of those 60% were deemed to have need. 99% of freshmen with need received aid; of those 62% had need fully met. ***Average percent of need met:*** 86% (excluding resources awarded to replace EFC). ***Average financial aid package:*** $9140 (excluding resources awarded to replace EFC). 19% of all full-time freshmen had no need and received non-need-based gift aid.

UNDERGRADUATE FINANCIAL AID (Fall 2008, est.) 6,203 applied for aid; of those 65% were deemed to have need. 98% of undergraduates with need received aid; of those 73% had need fully met. ***Average percent of need met:*** 82% (excluding resources awarded to replace EFC). ***Average financial aid package:*** $9544 (excluding resources awarded to replace EFC). 13% of all full-time undergraduates had no need and received non-need-based gift aid.

GIFT AID (NEED-BASED) ***Total amount:*** $11,176,476 (75% federal, 25% state). ***Receiving aid:*** Freshmen: 51% (1,041); all full-time undergraduates: 46% (3,277). ***Average award:*** Freshmen: $4270; Undergraduates: $4274. ***Scholarships, grants, and awards:*** Federal Pell, FSEOG, state, private, college/university gift aid from institutional funds, United Negro College Fund, Federal Nursing.

GIFT AID (NON-NEED-BASED) ***Total amount:*** $10,054,172 (69% state, 26% institutional, 5% external sources). ***Receiving aid:*** Freshmen: 43% (877). Undergraduates: 36% (2,585). ***Average award:*** Freshmen: $3001. Undergraduates: $2640. ***Tuition waivers:*** Full or partial for employees or children of employees, senior citizens.

LOANS ***Student loans:*** $28,898,138 (43% need-based, 57% non-need-based). 64% of past graduating class borrowed through all loan programs. *Average indebtedness per student:* $19,344. ***Average need-based loan:*** Freshmen: $3803. Undergraduates: $4227. ***Parent loans:*** $1,127,433 (100% non-need-based). ***Programs:*** FFEL (Subsidized and Unsubsidized Stafford, PLUS), Perkins, college/university.

WORK-STUDY ***Federal work-study:*** Total amount: $456,116; jobs available. ***State or other work-study/employment:*** Total amount: $401,668 (100% non-need-based). Part-time jobs available.

ATHLETIC AWARDS Total amount: $3,132,737 (100% non-need-based).

APPLYING FOR FINANCIAL AID ***Required financial aid forms:*** FAFSA, institution's own form. ***Financial aid deadline (priority):*** 4/1. ***Notification date:*** Continuous. Students must reply within 6 weeks of notification.

CONTACT Rexann Bumpus, Financial Aid Director, The University of Tennessee at Chattanooga, 615 McCallie Avenue, Chattanooga, TN 37403-2598, 423-425-4677 or toll-free 800-UTC-MOCS (in-state). *Fax:* 423-425-2292. *E-mail:* rexann-bumpus@utc.edu.

THE UNIVERSITY OF TENNESSEE AT MARTIN

Martin, TN

Tuition & fees (TN res): $5255 **Average undergraduate aid package: $10,393**

ABOUT THE INSTITUTION State-supported, coed. ***Awards:*** bachelor's and master's degrees. 86 undergraduate majors. ***Total enrollment:*** 7,578. Undergraduates: 7,127. Freshmen: 1,392. Federal methodology is used as a basis for awarding need-based institutional aid.

UNDERGRADUATE EXPENSES for 2008–09 ***Application fee:*** $30. ***Tuition, state resident:*** full-time $4400; part-time $184 per credit hour. ***Tuition, nonresident:*** full-time $15,042; part-time $628 per credit hour. ***Required fees:*** full-time $855; $37 per credit hour. Part-time tuition and fees vary according to course load. ***College room and board:*** $4606; ***Room only:*** $2220. Room and board charges vary according to board plan and housing facility. ***Payment plan:*** Deferred payment.

FRESHMAN FINANCIAL AID (Fall 2008, est.) 1,320 applied for aid; of those 69% were deemed to have need. 99% of freshmen with need received aid; of those 47% had need fully met. ***Average percent of need met:*** 83% (excluding resources awarded to replace EFC). ***Average financial aid package:*** $10,837 (excluding resources awarded to replace EFC).

UNDERGRADUATE FINANCIAL AID (Fall 2008, est.) 5,115 applied for aid; of those 70% were deemed to have need. 97% of undergraduates with need received aid; of those 38% had need fully met. ***Average percent of need met:*** 77% (excluding resources awarded to replace EFC). ***Average financial aid package:*** $10,393 (excluding resources awarded to replace EFC).

GIFT AID (NEED-BASED) ***Total amount:*** $13,537,692 (68% federal, 28% state, 4% institutional). ***Receiving aid:*** Freshmen: 38% (522); all full-time undergraduates: 40% (2,173). ***Average award:*** Freshmen: $5774; Undergraduates: $5550. ***Scholarships, grants, and awards:*** Federal Pell, FSEOG, state, private, college/university gift aid from institutional funds.

GIFT AID (NON-NEED-BASED) ***Total amount:*** $13,967,067 (75% state, 21% institutional, 4% external sources). ***Receiving aid:*** Freshmen: 57% (771). Undergraduates: 37% (2,005). ***Scholarships, grants, and awards by category:*** *Academic interests/achievement:* agriculture, biological sciences, business, communication, computer science, education, engineering/technologies, English, general academic interests/achievements, health fields, home economics, humanities, mathematics, military science, physical sciences, premedicine, social sciences. *Creative arts/performance:* art/fine arts, journalism/publications, music, theater/drama. *Special achievements/activities:* cheerleading/drum major, general special achievements/activities, leadership, rodeo. *Special characteristics:* adult students, children of educators, children of faculty/staff, ethnic background, handicapped students, members of minority groups, out-of-state students. ***Tuition waivers:*** Full or partial for employees or children of employees, senior citizens. ***ROTC:*** Army.

LOANS ***Student loans:*** $18,053,532 (50% need-based, 50% non-need-based). ***Average need-based loan:*** Freshmen: $2693. Undergraduates: $3928. ***Parent loans:*** $897,065 (100% non-need-based). ***Programs:*** FFEL (Subsidized and Unsubsidized Stafford, PLUS), Perkins.

WORK-STUDY ***Federal work-study:*** Total amount: $451,500; jobs available.

ATHLETIC AWARDS Total amount: $2,618,835 (100% non-need-based).

APPLYING FOR FINANCIAL AID ***Required financial aid form:*** FAFSA. ***Financial aid deadline (priority):*** 3/1. ***Notification date:*** Continuous beginning 4/1. Students must reply within 2 weeks of notification.

CONTACT Sandra J. Neel, Director of Student Financial Assistance, The University of Tennessee at Martin, 205 Administration Building, Martin, TN 38238-1000, 731-881-7040 or toll-free 800-829-8861. *Fax:* 731-881-7036. *E-mail:* sneel@utm.edu.

THE UNIVERSITY OF TEXAS AT ARLINGTON

Arlington, TX

Tuition & fees (TX res): $7780 **Average undergraduate aid package: $8427**

ABOUT THE INSTITUTION State-supported, coed. ***Awards:*** bachelor's, master's, and doctoral degrees and post-bachelor's and post-master's certificates. 59 undergraduate majors. ***Total enrollment:*** 25,084. Undergraduates: 18,985. Freshmen: 2,068. Federal methodology is used as a basis for awarding need-based institutional aid.

UNDERGRADUATE EXPENSES for 2008–09 ***Application fee:*** $35. ***Tuition, state resident:*** full-time $7780. ***Tuition, nonresident:*** full-time $16,210. Full-time tuition and fees vary according to course level, course load, and program. Part-time tuition and fees vary according to course level, course load, and program. ***College room and board:*** $6412; ***Room only:*** $3398. Room and board charges vary according to board plan and housing facility. ***Payment plan:*** Installment.

FRESHMAN FINANCIAL AID (Fall 2008, est.) 1,575 applied for aid; of those 80% were deemed to have need. 100% of freshmen with need received aid; of those 14% had need fully met. ***Average percent of need met:*** 70% (excluding resources awarded to replace EFC). ***Average financial aid package:*** $7950 (excluding resources awarded to replace EFC). 7% of all full-time freshmen had no need and received non-need-based gift aid.

UNDERGRADUATE FINANCIAL AID (Fall 2008, est.) 8,979 applied for aid; of those 86% were deemed to have need. 100% of undergraduates with need received aid; of those 11% had need fully met. ***Average percent of need met:*** 69% (excluding resources awarded to replace EFC). ***Average financial aid package:*** $8427 (excluding resources awarded to replace EFC). 3% of all full-time undergraduates had no need and received non-need-based gift aid.

GIFT AID (NEED-BASED) ***Total amount:*** $47,262,321 (43% federal, 18% state, 35% institutional, 4% external sources). ***Receiving aid:*** Freshmen: 42% (929); all full-time undergraduates: 42% (5,600). ***Average award:*** Freshmen: $6565; Undergraduates: $5657. ***Scholarships, grants, and awards:*** Federal Pell, FSEOG, state, private, college/university gift aid from institutional funds, United Negro College Fund.

GIFT AID (NON-NEED-BASED) ***Total amount:*** $2,849,063 (7% state, 69% institutional, 24% external sources). ***Receiving aid:*** Freshmen: 26% (586). Undergraduates: 15% (2,047). ***Average award:*** Freshmen: $2691. Undergraduates: $2417. ***Scholarships, grants, and awards by category:*** *Academic interests/achievement:* 2,689 awards ($7,270,587 total): architecture, biological sciences, business, communication, computer science, education, engineering/technologies, English, foreign languages, general academic interests/achievements, health fields, humanities, international studies, mathematics, military science, physical sciences, social sciences. *Creative arts/performance:* journalism/publications, music, theater/drama. *Special achievements/activities:* cheerleading/drum major, community service, general special achievements/activities, leadership. *Special characteristics:* children with a deceased or disabled parent, first-generation college students, general special characteristics, handicapped students, public servants. ***Tuition waivers:*** Full or partial for employees or children of employees. ***ROTC:*** Army, Air Force cooperative.

LOANS ***Student loans:*** $69,406,390 (76% need-based, 24% non-need-based). ***Average need-based loan:*** Freshmen: $3037. Undergraduates: $4207. ***Parent loans:*** $2,098,827 (37% need-based, 63% non-need-based). ***Programs:*** FFEL (Subsidized and Unsubsidized Stafford, PLUS), Perkins, state.

WORK-STUDY ***Federal work-study:*** Total amount: $4,922,785; 679 jobs averaging $1618. ***State or other work-study/employment:*** Total amount: $175,279 (100% need-based). 184 part-time jobs averaging $952.

ATHLETIC AWARDS Total amount: $1,677,224 (87% need-based, 13% non-need-based).

APPLYING FOR FINANCIAL AID ***Required financial aid form:*** FAFSA. ***Financial aid deadline (priority):*** 5/15. ***Notification date:*** Continuous. Students must reply within 3 weeks of notification.

CONTACT Karen Krause, Director of Financial Aid, The University of Texas at Arlington, PO Box 19199, Arlington, TX 76019, 817-272-3568. *Fax:* 817-272-3555. *E-mail:* kkrause@uta.edu.

THE UNIVERSITY OF TEXAS AT AUSTIN

Austin, TX

ABOUT THE INSTITUTION State-supported, coed. ***Awards:*** bachelor's, master's, doctoral, and first professional degrees. 107 undergraduate majors. ***Total enrollment:*** 49,984. Undergraduates: 37,389. Freshmen: 6,718.

GIFT AID (NEED-BASED) ***Scholarships, grants, and awards:*** Federal Pell, FSEOG, state, private, college/university gift aid from institutional funds.

LOANS ***Programs:*** FFEL (Subsidized and Unsubsidized Stafford, PLUS), Perkins, state.

APPLYING FOR FINANCIAL AID ***Required financial aid form:*** FAFSA.

CONTACT Associate Director of Student Financial Services, The University of Texas at Austin, PO Box 7758, UT Station, Austin, TX 78713-7758, 512-475-6282. *Fax:* 512-475-6296.

THE UNIVERSITY OF TEXAS AT BROWNSVILLE

Brownsville, TX

Tuition & fees (TX res): $4355 **Average undergraduate aid package: $7830**

ABOUT THE INSTITUTION State-supported, coed. ***Awards:*** associate, bachelor's, master's, and doctoral degrees. 37 undergraduate majors. ***Total enrollment:*** 17,189. Undergraduates: 16,340. Freshmen: 1,797. Federal methodology is used as a basis for awarding need-based institutional aid.

UNDERGRADUATE EXPENSES for 2008–09 ***Tuition, state resident:*** full-time $3060; part-time $127.50 per semester hour. ***Tuition, nonresident:*** full-time $9804; part-time $408.50 per semester hour. ***Required fees:*** full-time $1295; $35 per semester hour or $249.30 per term. Full-time tuition and fees vary according to class time and course load. Part-time tuition and fees vary according to class time and course load. ***College room and board: Room only:*** $2920. ***Payment plan:*** Installment.

FRESHMAN FINANCIAL AID (Fall 2008, est.) 1,191 applied for aid; of those 94% were deemed to have need. 100% of freshmen with need received aid. ***Average percent of need met:*** 64% (excluding resources awarded to replace EFC). ***Average financial aid package:*** $7170 (excluding resources awarded to replace EFC). 3% of all full-time freshmen had no need and received non-need-based gift aid.

UNDERGRADUATE FINANCIAL AID (Fall 2008, est.) 3,704 applied for aid; of those 95% were deemed to have need. 100% of undergraduates with need received aid. ***Average percent of need met:*** 56% (excluding resources awarded to replace EFC). ***Average financial aid package:*** $7830 (excluding resources awarded to replace EFC). 2% of all full-time undergraduates had no need and received non-need-based gift aid.

GIFT AID (NEED-BASED) ***Total amount:*** $27,462,930 (77% federal, 23% state). ***Receiving aid:*** Freshmen: 74% (1,020); all full-time undergraduates: 70% (3,126). ***Average award:*** Freshmen: $6259; Undergraduates: $6024. ***Scholarships, grants, and awards:*** Federal Pell, FSEOG, state, private, college/university gift aid from institutional funds.

GIFT AID (NON-NEED-BASED) ***Total amount:*** $4,722,524 (6% state, 81% institutional, 13% external sources). ***Receiving aid:*** Freshmen: 75% (1,038). Undergraduates: 70% (3,119). ***Average award:*** Freshmen: $4106. Undergraduates: $3415. ***Scholarships, grants, and awards by category:*** *Academic interests/achievement:* biological sciences, education, engineering/technologies, general academic interests/achievements, health fields, mathematics. *Creative arts/performance:* art/fine arts, music. *Special characteristics:* general special characteristics. ***Tuition waivers:*** Full or partial for senior citizens.

LOANS ***Student loans:*** $23,166,283 (69% need-based, 31% non-need-based). ***Average need-based loan:*** Freshmen: $2991. Undergraduates: $3876. ***Parent loans:*** $32,256 (100% non-need-based). ***Programs:*** FFEL (Subsidized and Unsubsidized Stafford, PLUS), state, college/university.

WORK-STUDY ***Federal work-study:*** Total amount: $546,793; jobs available. ***State or other work-study/employment:*** Total amount: $98,476 (100% need-based). Part-time jobs available.

ATHLETIC AWARDS Total amount: $265,419 (100% non-need-based).

APPLYING FOR FINANCIAL AID ***Required financial aid form:*** FAFSA. ***Financial aid deadline (priority):*** 4/1. ***Notification date:*** 5/1. Students must reply by 7/1 or within 12 weeks of notification.

CONTACT Ms. Georgiana M. Velarde, Assistant Director of Financial Aid, The University of Texas at Brownsville, 80 Fort Brown, Brownsville, TX 78520-4991, 956-882-8830 or toll-free 800-850-0160 (in-state). *Fax:* 956-882-8229. *E-mail:* georgiana.velarde@utb.edu.

THE UNIVERSITY OF TEXAS AT DALLAS

Richardson, TX

Tuition & fees (TX res): $9850 **Average undergraduate aid package: $10,317**

ABOUT THE INSTITUTION State-supported, coed. ***Awards:*** bachelor's, master's, doctoral, and first professional degrees and post-bachelor's certificates. 36 undergraduate majors. ***Total enrollment:*** 14,944. Undergraduates: 9,393. Freshmen: 1,118. Both federal and institutional methodology are used as a basis for awarding need-based institutional aid.

UNDERGRADUATE EXPENSES for 2008–09 ***Application fee:*** $50. ***Tuition, state resident:*** full-time $9850; part-time $328.33 per credit hour. ***Tuition, nonresident:*** full-time $21,000; part-time $700 per credit hour. Full-time tuition and fees vary according to course load and degree level. Part-time tuition and fees vary according to course load and degree level. ***College room and board:*** $6828. Room and board charges vary according to board plan and housing facility. ***Payment plans:*** Guaranteed tuition, installment.

FRESHMAN FINANCIAL AID (Fall 2008, est.) 947 applied for aid; of those 52% were deemed to have need. 100% of freshmen with need received aid; of those 44% had need fully met. ***Average percent of need met:*** 81% (excluding resources awarded to replace EFC). ***Average financial aid package:*** $12,944 (excluding resources awarded to replace EFC). 32% of all full-time freshmen had no need and received non-need-based gift aid.

UNDERGRADUATE FINANCIAL AID (Fall 2008, est.) 3,845 applied for aid; of those 82% were deemed to have need. 100% of undergraduates with need received aid; of those 29% had need fully met. ***Average percent of need met:*** 73% (excluding resources awarded to replace EFC). ***Average financial aid package:*** $10,317 (excluding resources awarded to replace EFC). 22% of all full-time undergraduates had no need and received non-need-based gift aid.

GIFT AID (NEED-BASED) ***Total amount:*** $13,547,377 (57% federal, 27% state, 11% institutional, 5% external sources). ***Receiving aid:*** Freshmen: 30% (326); all full-time undergraduates: 35% (2,372). ***Average award:*** Freshmen: $7336; Undergraduates: $5197. ***Scholarships, grants, and awards:*** Federal Pell, FSEOG, state, private, college/university gift aid from institutional funds.

GIFT AID (NON-NEED-BASED) ***Total amount:*** $19,100,314 (97% institutional, 3% external sources). ***Receiving aid:*** Freshmen: 26% (280). Undergraduates: 15% (1,027). ***Average award:*** Freshmen: $9926. Undergraduates: $8063. ***Scholarships, grants, and awards by category:*** *Academic interests/achievement:* biological sciences, business, computer science, engineering/technologies, general academic interests/achievements, mathematics, physical sciences. *Special achievements/activities:* general special achievements/activities, leadership. *Special characteristics:* adult students, children of public servants, general special characteristics, handicapped students, international students, local/state students, members of minority groups, out-of-state students, public servants, veterans, veterans' children. ***Tuition waivers:*** Full or partial for senior citizens. ***ROTC:*** Army cooperative, Air Force cooperative.

LOANS ***Student loans:*** $41,075,103 (59% need-based, 41% non-need-based). ***Average need-based loan:*** Freshmen: $3228. Undergraduates: $4667. ***Parent loans:*** $23,417,077 (1% need-based, 99% non-need-based). ***Programs:*** FFEL (Subsidized and Unsubsidized Stafford, PLUS), Perkins, state, college/university.

WORK-STUDY ***Federal work-study:*** Total amount: $1,564,577; jobs available. ***State or other work-study/employment:*** Total amount: $7087 (100% need-based). Part-time jobs available.

APPLYING FOR FINANCIAL AID ***Required financial aid form:*** FAFSA. ***Financial aid deadline (priority):*** 8/01. ***Notification date:*** Continuous. Students must reply within 2 weeks of notification.

CONTACT Karen M. Jarrell, Assistant Vice President Financial Aid & Academic Records, The University of Texas at Dallas, 800 West Campbell Road, MC12, Richardson, TX 75083-3021, 972-883-2941 or toll-free 800-889-2443. *Fax:* 972-883-2947. *E-mail:* karenl@utdallas.edu.

THE UNIVERSITY OF TEXAS AT EL PASO

El Paso, TX

Tuition & fees (TX res): $5925 **Average undergraduate aid package: $11,905**

ABOUT THE INSTITUTION State-supported, coed. ***Awards:*** bachelor's, master's, and doctoral degrees. 61 undergraduate majors. ***Total enrollment:*** 20,458. Undergraduates: 16,976. Freshmen: 2,565. Federal methodology is used as a basis for awarding need-based institutional aid.

UNDERGRADUATE EXPENSES for 2008–09 ***Tuition, state resident:*** full-time $4551; part-time $196 per credit hour. ***Tuition, nonresident:*** full-time $12,981; part-time $477 per credit hour. ***Required fees:*** full-time $1374. Full-time tuition and fees vary according to course load and degree level. Part-time tuition and fees vary according to course load and degree level. Room and board charges vary according to housing facility. ***Payment plans:*** Guaranteed tuition, installment.

FRESHMAN FINANCIAL AID (Fall 2007) 1,509 applied for aid; of those 81% were deemed to have need. 99% of freshmen with need received aid; of those 40% had need fully met. ***Average percent of need met:*** 84% (excluding resources awarded to replace EFC). ***Average financial aid package:*** $11,219 (excluding resources awarded to replace EFC). 10% of all full-time freshmen had no need and received non-need-based gift aid.

UNDERGRADUATE FINANCIAL AID (Fall 2007) 7,872 applied for aid; of those 80% were deemed to have need. 98% of undergraduates with need received aid; of those 40% had need fully met. ***Average percent of need met:*** 84% (excluding resources awarded to replace EFC). ***Average financial aid package:*** $11,905 (excluding resources awarded to replace EFC). 8% of all full-time undergraduates had no need and received non-need-based gift aid.

GIFT AID (NEED-BASED) ***Total amount:*** $47,455,145 (65% federal, 24% state, 11% institutional). ***Receiving aid:*** Freshmen: 48% (1,024); all full-time undergraduates: 48% (5,295). ***Average award:*** Freshmen: $7828; Undergraduates: $5931. ***Scholarships, grants, and awards:*** Federal Pell, FSEOG, state, private, college/university gift aid from institutional funds, United Negro College Fund, Federal Nursing.

GIFT AID (NON-NEED-BASED) ***Total amount:*** $5,511,874 (9% state, 68% institutional, 23% external sources). ***Receiving aid:*** Freshmen: 6% (133). Undergraduates: 6% (629). ***Average award:*** Freshmen: $1478. Undergraduates: $2299. ***Scholarships, grants, and awards by category:*** *Academic interests/achievement:* biological sciences, business, communication, computer science, education, engineering/technologies, English, general academic interests/achievements, health fields, humanities, international studies, mathematics, military science, physical sciences. *Creative arts/performance:* applied art and design, art/fine arts, journalism/publications, music, performing arts, theater/drama. *Special achievements/activities:* cheerleading/drum major, leadership. *Special characteristics:* ethnic background, international students, local/state students, members of minority groups, out-of-state students. ***Tuition waivers:*** Full or partial for employees or children of employees. ***ROTC:*** Army, Air Force.

LOANS ***Student loans:*** $61,893,158 (100% need-based). 60% of past graduating class borrowed through all loan programs. *Average indebtedness per student:* $19,802. ***Average need-based loan:*** Freshmen: $3460. Undergraduates: $5757. ***Parent loans:*** $257,303,346 (100% non-need-based). ***Programs:*** FFEL (Subsidized and Unsubsidized Stafford, PLUS), Perkins, Federal Nursing, state, college/university.

WORK-STUDY ***Federal work-study:*** Total amount: $1,822,321; jobs available. ***State or other work-study/employment:*** Total amount: $169,363 (100% need-based). Part-time jobs available.

ATHLETIC AWARDS Total amount: $3,581,589 (100% non-need-based).

APPLYING FOR FINANCIAL AID ***Required financial aid forms:*** FAFSA, institution's own form. ***Financial aid deadline (priority):*** 3/15. ***Notification date:*** 6/30. Students must reply within 2 weeks of notification.

CONTACT Mr. Raul Lerma, Director of Financial Aid, The University of Texas at El Paso, 500 West University Avenue, El Paso, TX 79968-0001, 915-747-5204 or toll-free 877-746-4636. *Fax:* 915-747-5631. *E-mail:* rlerma@utep.edu.

THE UNIVERSITY OF TEXAS AT SAN ANTONIO

San Antonio, TX

Tuition & fees (TX res): $4800 **Average undergraduate aid package: $7855**

ABOUT THE INSTITUTION State-supported, coed. ***Awards:*** bachelor's, master's, and doctoral degrees. 56 undergraduate majors. ***Total enrollment:*** 28,413. Undergraduates: 24,648. Freshmen: 4,843. Federal methodology is used as a basis for awarding need-based institutional aid.

UNDERGRADUATE EXPENSES for 2008–09 ***Application fee:*** $40. ***Tuition, state resident:*** full-time $4800; part-time $160 per hour. ***Tuition, nonresident:*** full-time $13,230; part-time $441 per hour. ***Required fees:*** $83.40 per credit hour. Room and board charges vary according to board plan and housing facility. ***Payment plans:*** Installment, deferred payment.

FRESHMAN FINANCIAL AID (Fall 2007) 3,639 applied for aid; of those 69% were deemed to have need. 95% of freshmen with need received aid; of those 26% had need fully met. ***Average percent of need met:*** 60% (excluding resources awarded to replace EFC). ***Average financial aid package:*** $8226 (excluding resources awarded to replace EFC). 7% of all full-time freshmen had no need and received non-need-based gift aid.

UNDERGRADUATE FINANCIAL AID (Fall 2007) 14,395 applied for aid; of those 75% were deemed to have need. 96% of undergraduates with need received aid; of those 23% had need fully met. ***Average percent of need met:*** 56% (excluding resources awarded to replace EFC). ***Average financial aid package:*** $7855 (excluding resources awarded to replace EFC). 4% of all full-time undergraduates had no need and received non-need-based gift aid.

GIFT AID (NEED-BASED) ***Total amount:*** $45,529,893 (61% federal, 19% state, 20% institutional). ***Receiving aid:*** Freshmen: 40% (1,941); all full-time undergraduates: 45% (8,533). ***Average award:*** Freshmen: $6317; Undergraduates: $4736. ***Scholarships, grants, and awards:*** Federal Pell, FSEOG, state, private, college/university gift aid from institutional funds.

GIFT AID (NON-NEED-BASED) ***Total amount:*** $7,144,552 (1% state, 45% institutional, 54% external sources). ***Receiving aid:*** Freshmen: 14% (701). Undergraduates: 10% (1,868). ***Average award:*** Freshmen: $1504. Undergraduates: $1976. ***Scholarships, grants, and awards by category:*** *Academic interests/achievement:* agriculture, architecture, area/ethnic studies, biological sciences, business, communication, computer science, education, engineering/technologies, English, foreign languages, general academic interests/achievements, humanities, international studies, mathematics, physical sciences, social sciences. *Creative arts/performance:* art/fine arts, creative writing, debating, music. *Special achievements/activities:* cheerleading/drum major, general special achievements/activities. *Special characteristics:* ethnic background, first-generation college students, general special characteristics, handicapped students, local/state students, members of minority groups, out-of-state students. ***Tuition waivers:*** Full or partial for employees or children of employees. ***ROTC:*** Army, Air Force.

LOANS ***Student loans:*** $80,819,997 (53% need-based, 47% non-need-based). 69% of past graduating class borrowed through all loan programs. *Average indebtedness per student:* $20,815. ***Average need-based loan:*** Freshmen: $3176. Undergraduates: $4076. ***Parent loans:*** $11,547,001 (100% non-need-based). ***Programs:*** FFEL (Subsidized and Unsubsidized Stafford, PLUS), Perkins, state, college/university.

WORK-STUDY ***Federal work-study:*** Total amount: $1,310,728; 482 jobs averaging $2727. ***State or other work-study/employment:*** Total amount: $635,505 (100% need-based). 145 part-time jobs averaging $1322.

ATHLETIC AWARDS Total amount: $1,973,837 (100% non-need-based).

APPLYING FOR FINANCIAL AID ***Required financial aid forms:*** FAFSA, institution's own form. ***Financial aid deadline (priority):*** 3/31. ***Notification date:*** Continuous beginning 4/1. Students must reply within 4 weeks of notification.

CONTACT Kim Canady, Assistant Director of Student Financial Aid, The University of Texas at San Antonio, One UTSA Cirlce, San Antonio, TX 78249, 210-458-8000 or toll-free 800-669-0919. *Fax:* 210-458-4638. *E-mail:* financialaid@utsa.edu.

THE UNIVERSITY OF TEXAS AT TYLER

Tyler, TX

Tuition & fees (TX res): $5742 **Average undergraduate aid package: $8427**

ABOUT THE INSTITUTION State-supported, coed. ***Awards:*** bachelor's and master's degrees and post-bachelor's certificates. 38 undergraduate majors. ***Total enrollment:*** 6,117. Undergraduates: 4,977. Freshmen: 585. Federal methodology is used as a basis for awarding need-based institutional aid.

UNDERGRADUATE EXPENSES for 2008–09 ***Application fee:*** $25. ***Tuition, state resident:*** full-time $4350; part-time $20 per semester hour. ***Tuition, nonresident:*** full-time $12,780; part-time $325 per semester hour. ***Required fees:*** full-time $1392. Full-time tuition and fees vary according to course level, course load, and degree level. ***College room and board:*** $7510; ***Room only:*** $4784. Room and board charges vary according to board plan and housing facility. ***Payment plan:*** Installment.

FRESHMAN FINANCIAL AID (Fall 2008, est.) 401 applied for aid; of those 72% were deemed to have need. 98% of freshmen with need received aid; of those 24% had need fully met. ***Average percent of need met:*** 58% (excluding resources awarded to replace EFC). ***Average financial aid package:*** $8331 (excluding resources awarded to replace EFC). 19% of all full-time freshmen had no need and received non-need-based gift aid.

UNDERGRADUATE FINANCIAL AID (Fall 2008, est.) 2,456 applied for aid; of those 82% were deemed to have need. 99% of undergraduates with need received aid; of those 12% had need fully met. ***Average percent of need met:*** 58% (excluding resources awarded to replace EFC). ***Average financial aid package:*** $8427 (excluding resources awarded to replace EFC). 9% of all full-time undergraduates had no need and received non-need-based gift aid.

GIFT AID (NEED-BASED) ***Total amount:*** $10,650,141 (56% federal, 19% state, 18% institutional, 7% external sources). ***Receiving aid:*** Freshmen: 42% (244); all full-time undergraduates: 42% (1,589). ***Average award:*** Freshmen: $7485; Undergraduates: $5858. ***Scholarships, grants, and awards:*** Federal Pell, FSEOG, state, private, college/university gift aid from institutional funds, Texas Grant, Institutional Grants (Education Affordability Prog).

GIFT AID (NON-NEED-BASED) ***Total amount:*** $2,918,664 (2% state, 55% institutional, 43% external sources). ***Receiving aid:*** Freshmen: 5% (32). Undergraduates: 2% (93). ***Average award:*** Freshmen: $3223. Undergraduates: $2493. ***Scholarships, grants, and awards by category:*** *Academic interests/achievement:* 889 awards ($2,140,900 total): communication, engineering/technologies, general academic interests/achievements, health fields. *Creative arts/performance:* 53 awards ($39,375 total): art/fine arts, music. *Special characteristics:* 23 awards ($173,802 total): children of faculty/staff. ***Tuition waivers:*** Full or partial for employees or children of employees, senior citizens.

LOANS ***Student loans:*** $19,840,594 (72% need-based, 28% non-need-based). 49% of past graduating class borrowed through all loan programs. *Average indebtedness per student:* $15,901. ***Average need-based loan:*** Freshmen: $2292. Undergraduates: $4077. ***Parent loans:*** $5,310,939 (18% need-based, 82% non-need-based). ***Programs:*** FFEL (Subsidized and Unsubsidized Stafford, PLUS), state.

WORK-STUDY ***Federal work-study:*** Total amount: $357,839; 105 jobs averaging $3408. ***State or other work-study/employment:*** Total amount: $187,610 (36% need-based, 64% non-need-based). 14 part-time jobs averaging $4444.

APPLYING FOR FINANCIAL AID ***Required financial aid forms:*** FAFSA, institution's own form. ***Financial aid deadline (priority):*** 4/1. ***Notification date:*** Continuous beginning 4/15. Students must reply within 2 weeks of notification.

CONTACT Candice A. Lindsey, Associate Dean for Enrollment Management, The University of Texas at Tyler, 3900 University Boulevard Adm 224A, Tyler, TX 75799-0001, 903-566-7221 or toll-free 800-UTTYLER (in-state). *Fax:* 903-566-7183. *E-mail:* clindsey@uttyler.edu.

THE UNIVERSITY OF TEXAS HEALTH SCIENCE CENTER AT HOUSTON

Houston, TX

Tuition & fees: N/R **Average undergraduate aid package: $11,590**

ABOUT THE INSTITUTION State-supported, coed. 2 undergraduate majors. Federal methodology is used as a basis for awarding need-based institutional aid.

UNDERGRADUATE FINANCIAL AID (Fall 2007) 245 applied for aid; of those 91% were deemed to have need. 100% of undergraduates with need received aid; of those 14% had need fully met. ***Average percent of need met:*** 53% (excluding resources awarded to replace EFC). ***Average financial aid package:*** $11,590 (excluding resources awarded to replace EFC). 2% of all full-time undergraduates had no need and received non-need-based gift aid.

GIFT AID (NEED-BASED) ***Total amount:*** $912,682 (36% federal, 4% state, 50% institutional, 10% external sources). ***Receiving aid:*** All full-time undergraduates: 39% (146). ***Average award:*** Undergraduates: $5674. ***Scholarships, grants, and awards:*** Federal Pell, FSEOG, state, private, college/university gift aid from institutional funds.

GIFT AID (NON-NEED-BASED) ***Average award:*** Undergraduates: $5008. ***Scholarships, grants, and awards by category:*** *Academic interests/achievement:* 10 awards ($42,062 total): health fields.

LOANS ***Student loans:*** $3,445,879 (100% need-based). ***Average need-based loan:*** Undergraduates: $8019. ***Parent loans:*** $757,230 (100% need-based). ***Programs:*** FFEL (Subsidized and Unsubsidized Stafford, PLUS), Perkins, Federal Nursing, state, college/university, alternative loans.

APPLYING FOR FINANCIAL AID ***Required financial aid forms:*** FAFSA, Institutional Supplemental. ***Financial aid deadline:*** Continuous. ***Notification date:*** Continuous.

CONTACT Ms. Wanda Williams, Director, The University of Texas Health Science Center at Houston, PO Box 20036, Houston, TX 77225, 713-500-3860. *Fax:* 713-500-3863. *E-mail:* wanda.k.williams@uth.tmc.edu.

THE UNIVERSITY OF TEXAS HEALTH SCIENCE CENTER AT SAN ANTONIO

San Antonio, TX

CONTACT Robert T. Lawson, Financial Aid Administrator, The University of Texas Health Science Center at San Antonio, 7703 Floyd Curl Drive, MSC 7708, San Antonio, TX 78284, 210-567-0025. *Fax:* 210-567-6643.

THE UNIVERSITY OF TEXAS MEDICAL BRANCH

Galveston, TX

ABOUT THE INSTITUTION State-supported, coed. ***Awards:*** bachelor's, master's, doctoral, and first professional degrees and post-master's certificates. 3 undergraduate majors. ***Total enrollment:*** 2,338. Undergraduates: 470.

GIFT AID (NEED-BASED) ***Scholarships, grants, and awards:*** Federal Pell, FSEOG, state, private, college/university gift aid from institutional funds.

GIFT AID (NON-NEED-BASED) ***Scholarships, grants, and awards by category:*** *Academic interests/achievement:* health fields.

LOANS ***Programs:*** Federal Direct (Subsidized and Unsubsidized Stafford, PLUS), Perkins, Federal Nursing, state, college/university.

WORK-STUDY ***Federal work-study:*** Total amount: $42,415; 24 jobs averaging $1767.

CONTACT Mr. Carl Gordon, University Financial Aid Officer, The University of Texas Medical Branch, 301 University Boulevard, Galveston, TX 77555-1305, 409-772-1215. *Fax:* 409-772-4466. *E-mail:* enrollment.services@utmb.edu.

THE UNIVERSITY OF TEXAS OF THE PERMIAN BASIN

Odessa, TX

Tuition & fees (TX res): $4262 **Average undergraduate aid package: $6888**

ABOUT THE INSTITUTION State-supported, coed. ***Awards:*** bachelor's and master's degrees. 28 undergraduate majors. ***Total enrollment:*** 3,496. Undergraduates: 2,584. Freshmen: 323. Institutional methodology is used as a basis for awarding need-based institutional aid.

UNDERGRADUATE EXPENSES for 2008–09 ***Tuition, state resident:*** full-time $3264; part-time $136 per semester hour. ***Tuition, nonresident:*** full-time $10,008; part-time $417 per semester hour. ***Required fees:*** full-time $998. ***College room and board:*** $4600.

FRESHMAN FINANCIAL AID (Fall 2008, est.) 240 applied for aid; of those 71% were deemed to have need. 100% of freshmen with need received aid; of those 19% had need fully met. ***Average percent of need met:*** 38% (excluding resources awarded to replace EFC). ***Average financial aid package:*** $7138 (excluding resources awarded to replace EFC). 24% of all full-time freshmen had no need and received non-need-based gift aid.

UNDERGRADUATE FINANCIAL AID (Fall 2008, est.) 1,391 applied for aid; of those 81% were deemed to have need. 100% of undergraduates with need received aid; of those 18% had need fully met. ***Average percent of need met:*** 38% (excluding resources awarded to replace EFC). ***Average financial aid package:*** $6888 (excluding resources awarded to replace EFC). 26% of all full-time undergraduates had no need and received non-need-based gift aid.

GIFT AID (NEED-BASED) ***Total amount:*** $4,013,584 (77% federal, 22% state, 1% institutional). ***Receiving aid:*** Freshmen: 35% (114); all full-time undergraduates: 42% (786). ***Average award:*** Freshmen: $6155; Undergraduates: $4500. ***Scholarships, grants, and awards:*** Federal Pell, FSEOG, state, private, college/university gift aid from institutional funds.

GIFT AID (NON-NEED-BASED) ***Total amount:*** $3,085,790 (5% state, 69% institutional, 26% external sources). ***Receiving aid:*** Freshmen: 44% (143). Undergraduates: 38% (709). ***Average award:*** Freshmen: $1905. Undergraduates: $1872. ***Scholarships, grants, and awards by category:*** *Academic interests/achievement:* 1,139 awards ($2,046,515 total): general academic interests/achievements. *Creative arts/performance:* 16 awards ($32,000 total): art/fine arts, dance, general creative arts/performance, music.

LOANS ***Student loans:*** $5,442,227 (52% need-based, 48% non-need-based). 55% of past graduating class borrowed through all loan programs. *Average indebtedness per student:* $16,995. ***Average need-based loan:*** Freshmen: $1798. Undergraduates: $3370. ***Parent loans:*** $117,652 (100% non-need-based). ***Programs:*** FFEL (Subsidized and Unsubsidized Stafford, PLUS), state.

WORK-STUDY ***Federal work-study:*** Total amount: $172,523; 64 jobs averaging $2440. ***State or other work-study/employment:*** Total amount: $10,152 (100% need-based). 9 part-time jobs averaging $1128.

ATHLETIC AWARDS Total amount: $351,588 (100% non-need-based).

APPLYING FOR FINANCIAL AID ***Required financial aid form:*** FAFSA. ***Financial aid deadline (priority):*** 5/1. ***Notification date:*** Continuous beginning 5/1. Students must reply within 2 weeks of notification.

CONTACT Mr. Robert L. Vasquez, Director, Office of Student Financial Aid, The University of Texas of the Permian Basin, 4901 East University Blvd., Odessa, TX 79762, 432-552-2620 or toll-free 866-552-UTPB. *Fax:* 432-552-2621. *E-mail:* finaid@utpb.edu.

THE UNIVERSITY OF TEXAS–PAN AMERICAN

Edinburg, TX

Tuition & fees (TX res): $3898 **Average undergraduate aid package: $9149**

ABOUT THE INSTITUTION State-supported, coed. ***Awards:*** bachelor's, master's, and doctoral degrees. 50 undergraduate majors. ***Total enrollment:*** 17,534. Undergraduates: 15,336. Freshmen: 2,663. Federal methodology is used as a basis for awarding need-based institutional aid.

UNDERGRADUATE EXPENSES for 2008–09 ***Tuition, state resident:*** full-time $3100; part-time $137.70 per credit hour. ***Tuition, nonresident:*** full-time $9772; part-time $418.70 per credit hour. ***Required fees:*** full-time $798. Full-time tuition and fees vary according to course load and location. Part-time tuition and fees vary according to course load and location. ***College room and board:*** $4994; ***Room only:*** $3000. Room and board charges vary according to board plan and housing facility. ***Payment plan:*** Installment.

FRESHMAN FINANCIAL AID (Fall 2007) 1,862 applied for aid; of those 96% were deemed to have need. 97% of freshmen with need received aid; of those 7% had need fully met. ***Average percent of need met:*** 69% (excluding resources awarded to replace EFC). ***Average financial aid package:*** $8904 (excluding resources awarded to replace EFC). 4% of all full-time freshmen had no need and received non-need-based gift aid.

UNDERGRADUATE FINANCIAL AID (Fall 2007) 9,147 applied for aid; of those 96% were deemed to have need. 96% of undergraduates with need received aid; of those 8% had need fully met. ***Average percent of need met:*** 71% (excluding resources awarded to replace EFC). ***Average financial aid package:*** $9149 (excluding resources awarded to replace EFC). 5% of all full-time undergraduates had no need and received non-need-based gift aid.

GIFT AID (NEED-BASED) ***Total amount:*** $61,241,655 (51% federal, 33% state, 14% institutional, 2% external sources). ***Receiving aid:*** Freshmen: 64% (1,677); all full-time undergraduates: 71% (8,020). ***Average award:*** Freshmen: $9037; Undergraduates: $9313. ***Scholarships, grants, and awards:*** Federal Pell, FSEOG, state, private, college/university gift aid from institutional funds.

GIFT AID (NON-NEED-BASED) ***Total amount:*** $2,703,225 (17% federal, 1% state, 69% institutional, 13% external sources). ***Receiving aid:*** Freshmen: 1% (33). Undergraduates: 2% (190). ***Average award:*** Freshmen: $5393. Undergraduates: $5905. ***Scholarships, grants, and awards by category:*** *Academic interests/*

achievement: 1,537 awards ($4,369,159 total): biological sciences; business, communication, computer science, education, engineering/technologies, English, general academic interests/achievements, health fields, mathematics, military science, premedicine, social sciences. *Creative arts/performance:* 136 awards ($89,968 total): art/fine arts, dance, journalism/publications, music, theater/drama. *Special achievements/activities:* 107 awards ($136,724 total): cheerleading/drum major, community service, general special achievements/activities, leadership, memberships. *Special characteristics:* 122 awards ($81,837 total): ethnic background, general special characteristics, international students, local/state students, out-of-state students, veterans. ***Tuition waivers:*** Full or partial for senior citizens. ***ROTC:*** Army.

LOANS ***Student loans:*** $31,976,675 (100% need-based). 68% of past graduating class borrowed through all loan programs. *Average indebtedness per student:* $12,101. ***Average need-based loan:*** Freshmen: $1844. Undergraduates: $4321. ***Parent loans:*** $216,478 (29% need-based, 71% non-need-based). ***Programs:*** FFEL (Subsidized and Unsubsidized Stafford, PLUS), Perkins, college/university.

WORK-STUDY ***Federal work-study:*** Total amount: $1,699,832; 834 jobs averaging $2038. ***State or other work-study/employment:*** Total amount: $404,541 (100% need-based). 213 part-time jobs averaging $1899.

ATHLETIC AWARDS Total amount: $582,993 (43% need-based, 57% non-need-based).

APPLYING FOR FINANCIAL AID ***Required financial aid form:*** FAFSA. ***Financial aid deadline (priority):*** 4/1. ***Notification date:*** Continuous beginning 4/1. Students must reply within 2 weeks of notification.

CONTACT Mrs. Elaine Rivera, Executive Director of Student Financial Services, The University of Texas–Pan American, 1201 West University Drive, Edinburg, TX 78541, 956-381-5372. *Fax:* 956-381-2396. *E-mail:* eriverall@utpa.edu.

THE UNIVERSITY OF TEXAS SOUTHWESTERN MEDICAL CENTER AT DALLAS

Dallas, TX

Tuition & fees (TX res): $4628 **Average undergraduate aid package: N/A**

ABOUT THE INSTITUTION State-supported, coed. ***Awards:*** bachelor's, master's, doctoral, and first professional degrees and post-bachelor's certificates. 3 undergraduate majors. ***Total enrollment:*** 2,461. Undergraduates: 103. Federal methodology is used as a basis for awarding need-based institutional aid.

UNDERGRADUATE EXPENSES for 2008–09 ***Application fee:*** $10. ***Tuition, state resident:*** full-time $3503; part-time $113 per credit hour. ***Tuition, nonresident:*** full-time $12,121; part-time $391 per credit hour. ***Required fees:*** full-time $1125. Full-time tuition and fees vary according to course load and program. Part-time tuition and fees vary according to course load and program. ***College room and board:*** $11,353. ***Payment plan:*** Installment.

UNDERGRADUATE FINANCIAL AID (Fall 2008, est.) 89 applied for aid; of those 100% were deemed to have need. 100% of undergraduates with need received aid.

GIFT AID (NEED-BASED) ***Total amount:*** $736,967 (15% federal, 85% institutional). ***Scholarships, grants, and awards:*** Federal Pell, FSEOG, state, private, college/university gift aid from institutional funds.

GIFT AID (NON-NEED-BASED) ***Total amount:*** $10,669 (20% state, 80% institutional). ***Scholarships, grants, and awards by category:*** *Special achievements/activities:* community service.

LOANS ***Student loans:*** $8,060,380 (100% need-based). ***Parent loans:*** $30,500 (100% non-need-based). ***Programs:*** FFEL (Subsidized and Unsubsidized Stafford, PLUS), Perkins, state, college/university, alternative loans.

WORK-STUDY ***Federal work-study:*** Total amount: $69,376; 10 jobs averaging $1933.

APPLYING FOR FINANCIAL AID ***Required financial aid forms:*** FAFSA, we do not enroll freshmen. ***Financial aid deadline (priority):*** 3/15. ***Notification date:*** 4/15. Students must reply within 2 weeks of notification.

CONTACT Ms. Lisa J. McGaha, Associate Director of Student Financial Aid, The University of Texas Southwestern Medical Center at Dallas, 5323 Harry Hines Boulevard, Dallas, TX 75390-9064, 214-648-3611. *Fax:* 214-648-3289. *E-mail:* lisa.mcgaha@utsouthwestern.edu.

THE UNIVERSITY OF THE ARTS

Philadelphia, PA

CONTACT Office of Financial Aid, The University of the Arts, 320 South Broad Street, Philadelphia, PA 19102-4944, 800-616-ARTS Ext. 6170 or toll-free 800-616-ARTS. *E-mail:* finaid@uarts.edu.

UNIVERSITY OF THE CUMBERLANDS

Williamsburg, KY

Tuition & fees: $15,658 **Average undergraduate aid package: $16,421**

ABOUT THE INSTITUTION Independent Kentucky Baptist, coed. ***Awards:*** associate, bachelor's, and master's degrees. 34 undergraduate majors. ***Total enrollment:*** 2,553. Undergraduates: 1,754. Freshmen: 432. Federal methodology is used as a basis for awarding need-based institutional aid.

UNDERGRADUATE EXPENSES for 2009–10 ***Application fee:*** $30. ***Comprehensive fee:*** $22,484 includes full-time tuition ($15,298), mandatory fees ($360), and room and board ($6826). ***Part-time tuition:*** $460 per hour. ***Part-time fees:*** $90 per term.

FRESHMAN FINANCIAL AID (Fall 2008, est.) 420 applied for aid; of those 92% were deemed to have need. 100% of freshmen with need received aid; of those 31% had need fully met. ***Average percent of need met:*** 86% (excluding resources awarded to replace EFC). ***Average financial aid package:*** $17,384 (excluding resources awarded to replace EFC). 9% of all full-time freshmen had no need and received non-need-based gift aid.

UNDERGRADUATE FINANCIAL AID (Fall 2008, est.) 1,256 applied for aid; of those 93% were deemed to have need. 100% of undergraduates with need received aid; of those 31% had need fully met. ***Average percent of need met:*** 85% (excluding resources awarded to replace EFC). ***Average financial aid package:*** $16,421 (excluding resources awarded to replace EFC). 14% of all full-time undergraduates had no need and received non-need-based gift aid.

GIFT AID (NEED-BASED) ***Total amount:*** $12,134,154 (24% federal, 27% state, 47% institutional, 2% external sources). ***Receiving aid:*** Freshmen: 89% (386); all full-time undergraduates: 81% (1,163). ***Average award:*** Freshmen: $11,734; Undergraduates: $9050. ***Scholarships, grants, and awards:*** Federal Pell, FSEOG, state, private, college/university gift aid from institutional funds.

GIFT AID (NON-NEED-BASED) ***Total amount:*** $2,262,581 (12% state, 84% institutional, 4% external sources). ***Receiving aid:*** Freshmen: 89% (386). Undergraduates: 81% (1,163). ***Average award:*** Freshmen: $5656. Undergraduates: $7235. ***Scholarships, grants, and awards by category:*** *Academic interests/achievement:* 977 awards ($3,842,500 total): general academic interests/achievements. *Creative arts/performance:* 100 awards ($227,177 total): art/fine arts, debating, journalism/publications, music, theater/drama. *Special achievements/activities:* 237 awards ($269,211 total): cheerleading/drum major, community service, leadership, religious involvement. *Special characteristics:* 334 awards ($706,979 total): children and siblings of alumni, children of faculty/staff, relatives of clergy, religious affiliation, siblings of current students. ***ROTC:*** Army.

LOANS ***Student loans:*** $5,744,885 (68% need-based, 32% non-need-based). 78% of past graduating class borrowed through all loan programs. *Average indebtedness per student:* $19,339. ***Average need-based loan:*** Freshmen: $3478. Undergraduates: $3725. ***Parent loans:*** $444,125 (26% need-based, 74% non-need-based). ***Programs:*** FFEL (Subsidized and Unsubsidized Stafford, PLUS), Perkins, college/university.

WORK-STUDY ***Federal work-study:*** Total amount: $960,090; 491 jobs averaging $1947. ***State or other work-study/employment:*** Total amount: $396,033 (75% need-based, 25% non-need-based). 210 part-time jobs averaging $1567.

ATHLETIC AWARDS Total amount: $2,836,039 (75% need-based, 25% non-need-based).

APPLYING FOR FINANCIAL AID ***Required financial aid form:*** FAFSA. ***Financial aid deadline (priority):*** 3/1. ***Notification date:*** Continuous beginning 4/1. Students must reply within 2 weeks of notification.

CONTACT Mr. Steve Allen, Vice President of Student Financial Planning, University of the Cumberlands, 6190 College Station Drive, Williamsburg, KY 40769-1372, 606-549-2200 or toll-free 800-343-1609. *Fax:* 606-539-4515. *E-mail:* finplan@ucumberlands.edu.

UNIVERSITY OF THE DISTRICT OF COLUMBIA

Washington, DC

ABOUT THE INSTITUTION District-supported, coed. ***Awards:*** associate, bachelor's, and master's degrees. 83 undergraduate majors. ***Total enrollment:*** 5,339. Undergraduates: 5,121. Freshmen: 1,015.

GIFT AID (NEED-BASED) ***Scholarships, grants, and awards:*** Federal Pell, FSEOG, state, college/university gift aid from institutional funds.

GIFT AID (NON-NEED-BASED) ***Scholarships, grants, and awards by category:*** *Academic interests/achievement:* general academic interests/achievements. *Creative arts/performance:* music. *Special characteristics:* children of faculty/staff.

LOANS ***Programs:*** FFEL (Subsidized and Unsubsidized Stafford, PLUS), Perkins, college/university.

WORK-STUDY ***Federal work-study:*** Total amount: $239,796; 110 jobs averaging $3000. ***State or other work-study/employment:*** Total amount: $116,978 (100% non-need-based). Part-time jobs available.

APPLYING FOR FINANCIAL AID ***Required financial aid forms:*** FAFSA, institution's own form, district aid form.

CONTACT Henry Anderson, Director, Officer of Financial Aid, University of the District of Columbia, 4200 Connecticut Avenue NW, Washington, DC 20008-1175, 202-274-6053. *E-mail:* handerson@udc.edu.

UNIVERSITY OF THE INCARNATE WORD

San Antonio, TX

Tuition & fees: $21,290 **Average undergraduate aid package: $14,840**

ABOUT THE INSTITUTION Independent Roman Catholic, coed. ***Awards:*** associate, bachelor's, master's, doctoral, and first professional degrees and post-bachelor's certificates. 39 undergraduate majors. ***Total enrollment:*** 6,361. Undergraduates: 5,110. Freshmen: 888. Federal methodology is used as a basis for awarding need-based institutional aid.

UNDERGRADUATE EXPENSES for 2009–10 ***Application fee:*** $20. ***Comprehensive fee:*** $30,070 includes full-time tuition ($20,400), mandatory fees ($890), and room and board ($8780). ***College room only:*** $4390. ***Part-time tuition:*** $675 per semester hour.

FRESHMAN FINANCIAL AID (Fall 2008, est.) 868 applied for aid; of those 79% were deemed to have need. 100% of freshmen with need received aid; of those 33% had need fully met. ***Average percent of need met:*** 65% (excluding resources awarded to replace EFC). ***Average financial aid package:*** $15,033 (excluding resources awarded to replace EFC). 20% of all full-time freshmen had no need and received non-need-based gift aid.

UNDERGRADUATE FINANCIAL AID (Fall 2008, est.) 2,960 applied for aid; of those 79% were deemed to have need. 100% of undergraduates with need received aid; of those 27% had need fully met. ***Average percent of need met:*** 62% (excluding resources awarded to replace EFC). ***Average financial aid package:*** $14,840 (excluding resources awarded to replace EFC). 17% of all full-time undergraduates had no need and received non-need-based gift aid.

GIFT AID (NEED-BASED) ***Total amount:*** $20,150,512 (34% federal, 20% state, 42% institutional, 4% external sources). ***Receiving aid:*** Freshmen: 61% (542); all full-time undergraduates: 61% (2,010). ***Average award:*** Freshmen: $7132; Undergraduates: $7066. ***Scholarships, grants, and awards:*** Federal Pell, FSEOG, state, private, college/university gift aid from institutional funds, United Negro College Fund, Federal Nursing.

GIFT AID (NON-NEED-BASED) ***Total amount:*** $3,086,987 (96% institutional, 4% external sources). ***Receiving aid:*** Freshmen: 76% (673). Undergraduates: 53% (1,736). ***Average award:*** Freshmen: $6391. Undergraduates: $5784. ***Scholarships, grants, and awards by category:*** *Academic interests/achievement:* 2,295 awards ($10,158,340 total): general academic interests/achievements. *Creative arts/performance:* 72 awards ($155,250 total): art/fine arts. *Special achievements/activities:* 26 awards ($51,000 total): religious involvement. *Special characteristics:* 397 awards ($2,035,002 total): children and siblings of alumni, children of faculty/staff, parents of current students. ***ROTC:*** Army cooperative, Air Force cooperative.

LOANS ***Student loans:*** $25,616,088 (71% need-based, 29% non-need-based). 86% of past graduating class borrowed through all loan programs. *Average indebtedness per student:* $39,985. ***Average need-based loan:*** Freshmen: $3550. Undergraduates: $4860. ***Parent loans:*** $2,796,867 (76% need-based, 24% non-need-based). ***Programs:*** FFEL (Subsidized and Unsubsidized Stafford, PLUS), Perkins, Federal Nursing, state, alternative loans.

WORK-STUDY ***Federal work-study:*** Total amount: $674,330; 465 jobs averaging $1807. ***State or other work-study/employment:*** Total amount: $36,943 (100% need-based). 19 part-time jobs averaging $2011.

ATHLETIC AWARDS Total amount: $3,164,580 (77% need-based, 23% non-need-based).

APPLYING FOR FINANCIAL AID ***Required financial aid form:*** FAFSA. ***Financial aid deadline (priority):*** 4/1. ***Notification date:*** Continuous. Students must reply within 2 weeks of notification.

CONTACT Ms. Amy Carcanagues, Director of Financial Assistance, University of the Incarnate Word, 4301 Broadway, San Antonio, TX 78209, 210-829-6008 or toll-free 800-749-WORD. *Fax:* 210-283-5053. *E-mail:* amyc@uiwtx.edu.

UNIVERSITY OF THE OZARKS

Clarksville, AR

Tuition & fees: $18,900 **Average undergraduate aid package: $17,554**

ABOUT THE INSTITUTION Independent Presbyterian, coed. ***Awards:*** bachelor's degrees. 32 undergraduate majors. ***Total enrollment:*** 675. Undergraduates: 675. Freshmen: 195. Federal methodology is used as a basis for awarding need-based institutional aid.

UNDERGRADUATE EXPENSES for 2009–10 ***Application fee:*** $30. ***Comprehensive fee:*** $24,950 includes full-time tuition ($18,300), mandatory fees ($600), and room and board ($6050). ***College room only:*** $2750. ***Part-time tuition:*** $700 per credit hour.

FRESHMAN FINANCIAL AID (Fall 2008, est.) 155 applied for aid; of those 92% were deemed to have need. 100% of freshmen with need received aid; of those 24% had need fully met. ***Average percent of need met:*** 87% (excluding resources awarded to replace EFC). ***Average financial aid package:*** $18,487 (excluding resources awarded to replace EFC). 23% of all full-time freshmen had no need and received non-need-based gift aid.

UNDERGRADUATE FINANCIAL AID (Fall 2008, est.) 395 applied for aid; of those 93% were deemed to have need. 100% of undergraduates with need received aid; of those 23% had need fully met. ***Average percent of need met:*** 86% (excluding resources awarded to replace EFC). ***Average financial aid package:*** $17,554 (excluding resources awarded to replace EFC). 33% of all full-time undergraduates had no need and received non-need-based gift aid.

GIFT AID (NEED-BASED) ***Total amount:*** $4,834,243 (19% federal, 9% state, 69% institutional, 3% external sources). ***Receiving aid:*** Freshmen: 73% (143); all full-time undergraduates: 58% (365). ***Average award:*** Freshmen: $15,183; Undergraduates: $13,125. ***Scholarships, grants, and awards:*** Federal Pell, FSEOG, state, private, college/university gift aid from institutional funds, United Negro College Fund, Federal Nursing.

GIFT AID (NON-NEED-BASED) ***Total amount:*** $3,040,523 (99% institutional, 1% external sources). ***Average award:*** Freshmen: $15,077. Undergraduates: $14,658. ***Scholarships, grants, and awards by category:*** *Academic interests/achievement:* 297 awards ($1,988,525 total): biological sciences, business, communication, education, English, general academic interests/achievements, humanities, mathematics, premedicine, religion/biblical studies, social sciences. *Creative arts/performance:* 46 awards ($142,266 total): art/fine arts, music, theater/drama. *Special achievements/activities:* 210 awards ($566,147 total): leadership. *Special characteristics:* 219 awards ($953,554 total): children and siblings of alumni, children of faculty/staff, ethnic background, general special characteristics, international students, members of minority groups, relatives of clergy, religious affiliation, siblings of current students.

LOANS ***Student loans:*** $2,325,726 (95% need-based, 5% non-need-based). 44% of past graduating class borrowed through all loan programs. *Average indebtedness per student:* $16,852. ***Average need-based loan:*** Freshmen: $6476. Undergraduates: $9041. ***Parent loans:*** $294,756 (84% need-based, 16% non-need-based). ***Programs:*** FFEL (Subsidized and Unsubsidized Stafford, PLUS), Perkins, college/university.

WORK-STUDY ***Federal work-study:*** Total amount: $270,286; 164 jobs averaging $1648. ***State or other work-study/employment:*** Total amount: $114,058 (54% need-based, 46% non-need-based). 23 part-time jobs averaging $4959.

APPLYING FOR FINANCIAL AID ***Required financial aid form:*** FAFSA. ***Financial aid deadline (priority):*** 3/15. ***Notification date:*** Continuous beginning 3/1. Students must reply within 2 weeks of notification.

CONTACT Ms. Jana D. Hart, Director of Financial Aid, University of the Ozarks, 415 North College Avenue, Clarksville, AR 72830-2880, 479-979-1221 or toll-free 800-264-8636. *Fax:* 479-979-1417. *E-mail:* jhart@ozarks.edu.

UNIVERSITY OF THE PACIFIC

Stockton, CA

Tuition & fees: $30,880 **Average undergraduate aid package: $27,263**

ABOUT THE INSTITUTION Independent, coed. ***Awards:*** bachelor's, master's, doctoral, and first professional degrees. 54 undergraduate majors. ***Total enrollment:*** 6,251. Undergraduates: 3,457. Freshmen: 882. Federal methodology is used as a basis for awarding need-based institutional aid.

UNDERGRADUATE EXPENSES for 2008–09 ***Application fee:*** $60. ***Comprehensive fee:*** $40,998 includes full-time tuition ($30,380), mandatory fees ($500), and room and board ($10,118). Room and board charges vary according to board plan and housing facility. ***Part-time tuition:*** $1048 per unit. Part-time tuition and fees vary according to course load. ***Payment plan:*** Deferred payment.

FRESHMAN FINANCIAL AID (Fall 2008, est.) 716 applied for aid; of those 84% were deemed to have need. 100% of freshmen with need received aid; of those 26% had need fully met. ***Average financial aid package:*** $25,556 (excluding resources awarded to replace EFC). 18% of all full-time freshmen had no need and received non-need-based gift aid.

UNDERGRADUATE FINANCIAL AID (Fall 2008, est.) 2,509 applied for aid; of those 90% were deemed to have need. 100% of undergraduates with need received aid; of those 22% had need fully met. ***Average financial aid package:*** $27,263 (excluding resources awarded to replace EFC). 13% of all full-time undergraduates had no need and received non-need-based gift aid.

GIFT AID (NEED-BASED) ***Total amount:*** $42,631,648 (12% federal, 21% state, 67% institutional). ***Receiving aid:*** Freshmen: 68% (597); all full-time undergraduates: 65% (2,186). ***Average award:*** Freshmen: $20,548; Undergraduates: $19,418. ***Scholarships, grants, and awards:*** Federal Pell, FSEOG, state, private, college/university gift aid from institutional funds.

GIFT AID (NON-NEED-BASED) ***Total amount:*** $3,901,323 (100% institutional). ***Average award:*** Freshmen: $9164. Undergraduates: $8620. ***Scholarships, grants, and awards by category:*** *Academic interests/achievement:* 1,361 awards ($11,500,000 total): general academic interests/achievements. *Creative arts/performance:* 121 awards ($833,000 total): debating, music. *Special achievements/activities:* 17 awards ($42,500 total): religious involvement. ***Tuition waivers:*** Full or partial for employees or children of employees. ***ROTC:*** Air Force cooperative.

LOANS ***Student loans:*** $14,845,785 (89% need-based, 11% non-need-based). ***Average need-based loan:*** Freshmen: $3764. Undergraduates: $5702. ***Parent loans:*** $6,965,662 (82% need-based, 18% non-need-based). ***Programs:*** Federal Direct (Subsidized and Unsubsidized Stafford, PLUS), FFEL (Subsidized and Unsubsidized Stafford, PLUS), Perkins, state.

WORK-STUDY ***Federal work-study:*** Total amount: $4,035,695; jobs available (averaging $2330).

ATHLETIC AWARDS Total amount: $4,637,565 (40% need-based, 60% non-need-based).

APPLYING FOR FINANCIAL AID ***Required financial aid form:*** FAFSA. ***Financial aid deadline (priority):*** 2/15. ***Notification date:*** Continuous beginning 3/15.

CONTACT Lynn Fox, Director of Financial Aid, University of the Pacific, 3601 Pacific Avenue, Stockton, CA 95211-0197, 209-946-2421 or toll-free 800-959-2867.

UNIVERSITY OF THE SACRED HEART

San Juan, PR

CONTACT Ms. Maria Torres, Director of Financial Aid, University of the Sacred Heart, PO Box 12383, San Juan, PR 00914-0383, 787-728-1515 Ext. 3605.

UNIVERSITY OF THE SCIENCES IN PHILADELPHIA

Philadelphia, PA

ABOUT THE INSTITUTION Independent, coed. ***Awards:*** bachelor's, master's, doctoral, and first professional degrees and post-bachelor's certificates. 20 undergraduate majors. ***Total enrollment:*** 3,000. Undergraduates: 2,076. Freshmen: 534.

GIFT AID (NEED-BASED) ***Scholarships, grants, and awards:*** Federal Pell, FSEOG, state, college/university gift aid from institutional funds.

GIFT AID (NON-NEED-BASED) ***Scholarships, grants, and awards by category:*** *Academic interests/achievement:* general academic interests/achievements.

LOANS ***Programs:*** FFEL (Subsidized and Unsubsidized Stafford, PLUS), Perkins.

APPLYING FOR FINANCIAL AID ***Required financial aid form:*** FAFSA.

CONTACT Ms. Paula Lehrberger, Director of Financial Aid, University of the Sciences in Philadelphia, 600 South 43rd Street, Philadelphia, PA 19104-4495, 215-596-8894 or toll-free 888-996-8747 (in-state). *Fax:* 215-596-8554.

UNIVERSITY OF THE SOUTHWEST

Hobbs, NM

Tuition & fees: $14,500 **Average undergraduate aid package: $5856**

ABOUT THE INSTITUTION Independent, coed. ***Awards:*** bachelor's and master's degrees. 18 undergraduate majors. ***Total enrollment:*** 588. Undergraduates: 397. Freshmen: 79. Both federal and institutional methodology are used as a basis for awarding need-based institutional aid.

UNDERGRADUATE EXPENSES for 2009–10 ***Application fee:*** $25. ***Comprehensive fee:*** $21,550 includes full-time tuition ($14,500) and room and board ($7050). ***College room only:*** $4200. ***Part-time tuition:*** $463 per semester hour.

FRESHMAN FINANCIAL AID (Fall 2008, est.) 87 applied for aid; of those 64% were deemed to have need. 100% of freshmen with need received aid; of those 39% had need fully met. ***Average percent of need met:*** 64% (excluding resources awarded to replace EFC). ***Average financial aid package:*** $10,248 (excluding resources awarded to replace EFC). 33% of all full-time freshmen had no need and received non-need-based gift aid.

UNDERGRADUATE FINANCIAL AID (Fall 2008, est.) 317 applied for aid; of those 63% were deemed to have need. 100% of undergraduates with need received aid; of those 40% had need fully met. ***Average percent of need met:*** 64% (excluding resources awarded to replace EFC). ***Average financial aid package:*** $5856 (excluding resources awarded to replace EFC). 31% of all full-time undergraduates had no need and received non-need-based gift aid.

GIFT AID (NEED-BASED) ***Total amount:*** $1,038,492 (67% federal, 31% state, 2% institutional). ***Receiving aid:*** Freshmen: 32% (28); all full-time undergraduates: 36% (118). ***Average award:*** Freshmen: $4112; Undergraduates: $3132. ***Scholarships, grants, and awards:*** Federal Pell, FSEOG, state, private, college/university gift aid from institutional funds.

GIFT AID (NON-NEED-BASED) ***Total amount:*** $683,240 (86% institutional, 14% external sources). ***Receiving aid:*** Freshmen: 64% (56). Undergraduates: 61% (200). ***Average award:*** Freshmen: $1950. Undergraduates: $1840. ***Scholarships, grants, and awards by category:*** *Academic interests/achievement:* 205 awards ($385,504 total): biological sciences, business, education, English, general academic interests/achievements, humanities, mathematics, premedicine, religion/biblical studies, social sciences. *Creative arts/performance:* 11 awards ($16,500 total): debating, music. *Special achievements/activities:* 12 awards ($15,500 total): general special achievements/activities, leadership. *Special characteristics:* 19 awards ($38,717 total): children of faculty/staff.

LOANS ***Student loans:*** $3,838,190 (46% need-based, 54% non-need-based). ***Average need-based loan:*** Freshmen: $2882. Undergraduates: $3603. ***Parent loans:*** $82,644 (100% non-need-based). ***Programs:*** FFEL (Subsidized and Unsubsidized Stafford, PLUS).

WORK-STUDY ***Federal work-study:*** Total amount: $32,000; 27 jobs averaging $1581. ***State or other work-study/employment:*** Total amount: $87,571 (68% need-based, 32% non-need-based). 43 part-time jobs averaging $1420.

ATHLETIC AWARDS Total amount: $692,603 (100% non-need-based).

APPLYING FOR FINANCIAL AID ***Required financial aid forms:*** FAFSA, institution's own form. ***Financial aid deadline:*** 8/1 (priority: 4/1). ***Notification date:*** Continuous. Students must reply within 2 weeks of notification.

CONTACT Kerrie Mitchell, Director of Financial Aid, University of the Southwest, 6610 Lovington Highway, Hobbs, NM 88240-9129, 575-392-6561 Ext. 1075 or toll-free 800-530-4400. *Fax:* 575-392-6006. *E-mail:* kmitchell@usw.edu.

UNIVERSITY OF THE VIRGIN ISLANDS

Saint Thomas, VI

Tuition & fees (VI res): $4100 **Average undergraduate aid package: $4450**

ABOUT THE INSTITUTION Territory-supported, coed. ***Awards:*** associate, bachelor's, and master's degrees. 21 undergraduate majors. ***Total enrollment:*** 2,393. Undergraduates: 2,212. Freshmen: 555. Federal methodology is used as a basis for awarding need-based institutional aid.

UNDERGRADUATE EXPENSES for 2009–10 ***Application fee:*** $30. ***Tuition, state resident:*** full-time $3600. ***Tuition, nonresident:*** full-time $10,800. ***Required fees:*** full-time $500. ***College room and board:*** $8240; ***Room only:*** $2890.

FRESHMAN FINANCIAL AID (Fall 2007) 304 applied for aid; of those 94% were deemed to have need. 95% of freshmen with need received aid; of those 3% had need fully met. ***Average financial aid package:*** $4600 (excluding resources awarded to replace EFC). 1% of all full-time freshmen had no need and received non-need-based gift aid.

UNDERGRADUATE FINANCIAL AID (Fall 2007) 1,202 applied for aid; of those 93% were deemed to have need. 94% of undergraduates with need received aid; of those 1% had need fully met. ***Average financial aid package:*** $4450 (excluding resources awarded to replace EFC). 1% of all full-time undergraduates had no need and received non-need-based gift aid.

GIFT AID (NEED-BASED) ***Total amount:*** $3,583,743 (83% federal, 17% institutional). ***Receiving aid:*** Freshmen: 70% (244); all full-time undergraduates: 74% (943). ***Average award:*** Freshmen: $3870; Undergraduates: $3440. ***Scholarships, grants, and awards:*** Federal Pell, FSEOG, state, college/university gift aid from institutional funds, Federal Nursing.

GIFT AID (NON-NEED-BASED) ***Total amount:*** $301,577 (14% federal, 86% institutional). ***Receiving aid:*** Freshmen: 9% (31). Undergraduates: 5% (63). ***Average award:*** Freshmen: $9500. Undergraduates: $8500. ***Scholarships, grants, and awards by category:*** *Special characteristics:* 53 awards ($123,620 total): children of faculty/staff, veterans. ***ROTC:*** Army.

LOANS ***Student loans:*** $1,848,542 (73% need-based, 27% non-need-based). 53% of past graduating class borrowed through all loan programs. *Average indebtedness per student:* $9480. ***Average need-based loan:*** Freshmen: $2875. Undergraduates: $3240. ***Parent loans:*** $133,730 (100% need-based). ***Programs:*** Federal Direct (Subsidized and Unsubsidized Stafford, PLUS), Perkins, college/university.

WORK-STUDY ***Federal work-study:*** Total amount: $83,005; 39 jobs averaging $2130. ***State or other work-study/employment:*** Total amount: $52,354 (100% need-based). 28 part-time jobs averaging $1900.

ATHLETIC AWARDS Total amount: $17,975 (100% need-based).

APPLYING FOR FINANCIAL AID ***Required financial aid form:*** FAFSA. ***Financial aid deadline (priority):*** 3/1. ***Notification date:*** Continuous beginning 4/1. Students must reply within 2 weeks of notification.

CONTACT Mavis M. Gilchrist, Director of Financial Aid, University of the Virgin Islands, RR #2, Box 10,000, Kingshill, St. Thomas, VI 00850, 340-692-4186. *Fax:* 340-692-4145. *E-mail:* mgilchr@uvi.edu.

UNIVERSITY OF THE WEST

Rosemead, CA

CONTACT Dr. Teresa Ku, Director of Student Services, University of the West, 1409 Walnut Grove Avenue, Rosemead, CA 91770, 626-571-8811 Ext. 355. *Fax:* 626-571-1413. *E-mail:* naikuangk@hlu.edu.

THE UNIVERSITY OF TOLEDO

Toledo, OH

CONTACT Lisa Hasselschwert, Interim Director, The University of Toledo, 2801 West Bancroft Street, 1200 Rocket Hall, MS-314, Toledo, OH 43606, 419-530-8700 or toll-free 800-5TOLEDO (in-state). *Fax:* 419-530-5835. *E-mail:* lhassel@utnet.utoledo.edu.

UNIVERSITY OF TULSA

Tulsa, OK

Tuition & fees: $23,940 **Average undergraduate aid package: $23,285**

ABOUT THE INSTITUTION Independent religious, coed. ***Awards:*** bachelor's, master's, doctoral, and first professional degrees and post-bachelor's and first professional certificates. 63 undergraduate majors. ***Total enrollment:*** 4,192. Undergraduates: 3,049. Freshmen: 695. Federal methodology is used as a basis for awarding need-based institutional aid.

UNDERGRADUATE EXPENSES for 2008–09 ***Application fee:*** $35. ***One-time required fee:*** $425. ***Comprehensive fee:*** $31,716 includes full-time tuition ($23,860), mandatory fees ($80), and room and board ($7776). ***College room only:*** $4294. Room and board charges vary according to board plan and housing facility. ***Part-time tuition:*** $856 per credit hour. ***Payment plans:*** Tuition prepayment, installment.

FRESHMAN FINANCIAL AID (Fall 2007) 591 applied for aid; of those 49% were deemed to have need. 100% of freshmen with need received aid; of those 48% had need fully met. ***Average percent of need met:*** 88% (excluding resources awarded to replace EFC). ***Average financial aid package:*** $24,118 (excluding resources awarded to replace EFC). 39% of all full-time freshmen had no need and received non-need-based gift aid.

UNDERGRADUATE FINANCIAL AID (Fall 2007) 2,460 applied for aid; of those 47% were deemed to have need. 100% of undergraduates with need received aid; of those 45% had need fully met. ***Average percent of need met:*** 86% (excluding resources awarded to replace EFC). ***Average financial aid package:*** $23,285 (excluding resources awarded to replace EFC). 38% of all full-time undergraduates had no need and received non-need-based gift aid.

GIFT AID (NEED-BASED) ***Total amount:*** $2,795,930 (66% federal, 22% state, 12% institutional). ***Receiving aid:*** Freshmen: 17% (113); all full-time undergraduates: 20% (549). ***Average award:*** Freshmen: $5332; Undergraduates: $5002. ***Scholarships, grants, and awards:*** Federal Pell, FSEOG, state, private, college/university gift aid from institutional funds.

GIFT AID (NON-NEED-BASED) ***Total amount:*** $21,645,627 (10% state, 85% institutional, 5% external sources). ***Receiving aid:*** Freshmen: 43% (281). Undergraduates: 38% (1,059). ***Average award:*** Freshmen: $11,224. Undergraduates: $11,727. ***Scholarships, grants, and awards by category:*** *Academic interests/achievement:* 1,771 awards ($17,199,836 total): biological sciences, business, communication, computer science, education, engineering/technologies, English, foreign languages, general academic interests/achievements, health fields, international studies, mathematics, physical sciences, premedicine, religion/biblical studies, social sciences. *Creative arts/performance:* 218 awards ($1,357,653 total): art/fine arts, music, performing arts, theater/drama. *Special achievements/activities:* 84 awards ($221,450 total): cheerleading/drum major, community service, leadership. *Special characteristics:* 443 awards ($3,577,785 total): children and siblings of alumni, children of faculty/staff, relatives of clergy, religious affiliation, siblings of current students. ***Tuition waivers:*** Full or partial for employees or children of employees. ***ROTC:*** Air Force cooperative.

LOANS ***Student loans:*** $9,017,929 (51% need-based, 49% non-need-based). 56% of past graduating class borrowed through all loan programs. *Average indebtedness per student:* $13,273. ***Average need-based loan:*** Freshmen: $5486. Undergraduates: $6201. ***Parent loans:*** $2,927,060 (100% non-need-based). ***Programs:*** FFEL (Subsidized and Unsubsidized Stafford, PLUS), Perkins.

WORK-STUDY ***Federal work-study:*** Total amount: $1,462,602; 559 jobs averaging $2730. ***State or other work-study/employment:*** Total amount: $18,815 (100% non-need-based). 5 part-time jobs averaging $1379.

ATHLETIC AWARDS Total amount: $684,748 (100% non-need-based).

APPLYING FOR FINANCIAL AID ***Required financial aid forms:*** FAFSA, institution's own form. ***Financial aid deadline (priority):*** 4/1. ***Notification date:*** Continuous. Students must reply by 5/1 or within 2 weeks of notification.

CONTACT Ms. Vicki Hendrickson, Director of Student Financial Services, University of Tulsa, 600 South College, Tulsa, OK 74104, 918-631-2526 or toll-free 800-331-3050. *Fax:* 918-631-5105. *E-mail:* vicki-hendrickson@utulsa.edu.

UNIVERSITY OF UTAH

Salt Lake City, UT

Tuition & fees (UT res): $5285 **Average undergraduate aid package: $9146**

ABOUT THE INSTITUTION State-supported, coed. ***Awards:*** bachelor's, master's, doctoral, and first professional degrees and post-bachelor's and post-master's certificates. 83 undergraduate majors. ***Total enrollment:*** 28,211. Undergraduates: 21,526. Freshmen: 2,642. Federal methodology is used as a basis for awarding need-based institutional aid.

UNDERGRADUATE EXPENSES for 2008–09 ***Application fee:*** $35. ***Tuition, state resident:*** full-time $4526; part-time $127 per credit hour. ***Tuition, nonresident:*** full-time $15,841; part-time $437 per credit hour. ***Required fees:*** full-time $759. Full-time tuition and fees vary according to course level, course load, degree level, program, reciprocity agreements, and student level. Part-time tuition and fees vary according to course level, course load, degree level, program, reciprocity agreements, and student level. ***College room and board:*** $5972; ***Room only:*** $2977. Room and board charges vary according to board plan and housing facility. ***Payment plan:*** Installment.

FRESHMAN FINANCIAL AID (Fall 2008, est.) 1,033 applied for aid; of those 69% were deemed to have need. 99% of freshmen with need received aid; of those 21% had need fully met. ***Average percent of need met:*** 57% (excluding resources awarded to replace EFC). ***Average financial aid package:*** $9295 (excluding resources awarded to replace EFC). 9% of all full-time freshmen had no need and received non-need-based gift aid.

UNDERGRADUATE FINANCIAL AID (Fall 2008, est.) 6,129 applied for aid; of those 87% were deemed to have need. 99% of undergraduates with need received aid; of those 13% had need fully met. ***Average percent of need met:*** 58% (excluding resources awarded to replace EFC). ***Average financial aid package:*** $9146 (excluding resources awarded to replace EFC). 5% of all full-time undergraduates had no need and received non-need-based gift aid.

GIFT AID (NEED-BASED) ***Total amount:*** $21,471,000 (71% federal, 7% state, 6% institutional, 16% external sources). ***Receiving aid:*** Freshmen: 24% (561); all full-time undergraduates: 26% (3,786). ***Average award:*** Freshmen: $5896; Undergraduates: $4803. ***Scholarships, grants, and awards:*** Federal Pell, FSEOG, state, private, college/university gift aid from institutional funds, Federal Nursing.

GIFT AID (NON-NEED-BASED) ***Total amount:*** $3,994,000 (7% institutional, 93% external sources). ***Receiving aid:*** Freshmen: 2% (56). Undergraduates: 1% (102). ***Average award:*** Freshmen: $5347. Undergraduates: $4619. ***Scholarships, grants, and awards by category:*** *Academic interests/achievement:* architecture, area/ethnic studies, biological sciences, business, communication, computer science, education, engineering/technologies, English, foreign languages, general academic interests/achievements, health fields, humanities, international studies, mathematics, military science, physical sciences, social sciences. *Creative arts/performance:* art/fine arts, cinema/film/broadcasting, creative writing, dance, journalism/publications, music, performing arts, theater/drama. *Special achievements/activities:* cheerleading/drum major, general special achievements/activities, leadership. *Special characteristics:* children of faculty/staff, children of public servants, children with a deceased or disabled parent, ethnic background, first-generation college students, handicapped students, out-of-state students, spouses of deceased or disabled public servants. ***Tuition waivers:*** Full or partial for employees or children of employees, senior citizens. ***ROTC:*** Army, Naval, Air Force.

LOANS ***Student loans:*** $43,124,000 (85% need-based, 15% non-need-based). 40% of past graduating class borrowed through all loan programs. *Average indebtedness per student:* $11,749. ***Average need-based loan:*** Freshmen: $4050. Undergraduates: $4797. ***Parent loans:*** $1,703,000 (27% need-based, 73% non-need-based). ***Programs:*** FFEL (Subsidized and Unsubsidized Stafford, PLUS), Perkins, Federal Nursing, college/university.

WORK-STUDY ***Federal work-study:*** Total amount: $1,434,000; jobs available.

ATHLETIC AWARDS Total amount: $5,736,000 (16% need-based, 84% non-need-based).

APPLYING FOR FINANCIAL AID ***Required financial aid forms:*** FAFSA, institution's own form. ***Financial aid deadline (priority):*** 3/15. ***Notification date:*** Continuous beginning 4/15. Students must reply within 6 weeks of notification.

CONTACT Amy Capps, Assistant Director, University of Utah, 201 South 1460 East, Room 105, Salt Lake City, UT 84112-9055, 801-581-6211 or toll-free 800-444-8638. *Fax:* 801-585-6350. *E-mail:* fawin1@saff.utah.edu.

UNIVERSITY OF VERMONT

Burlington, VT

Tuition & fees (VT res): $12,844　Average undergraduate aid package: $16,809

ABOUT THE INSTITUTION State-supported, coed. ***Awards:*** bachelor's, master's, doctoral, and first professional degrees and post-bachelor's and post-master's certificates. 100 undergraduate majors. ***Total enrollment:*** 12,800. Undergraduates: 10,937. Freshmen: 2,468. Federal methodology is used as a basis for awarding need-based institutional aid.

UNDERGRADUATE EXPENSES for 2008–09 ***Application fee:*** $55. ***Tuition, state resident:*** full-time $11,048; part-time $460 per credit. ***Tuition, nonresident:*** full-time $27,886; part-time $1162 per credit. ***Required fees:*** full-time $1796. Part-time tuition and fees vary according to course load. ***College room and board:*** $8534; ***Room only:*** $5752. Room and board charges vary according to board plan and housing facility. ***Payment plans:*** Installment, deferred payment.

FRESHMAN FINANCIAL AID (Fall 2007) 1,753 applied for aid; of those 74% were deemed to have need. 100% of freshmen with need received aid; of those 27% had need fully met. ***Average percent of need met:*** 81% (excluding resources awarded to replace EFC). ***Average financial aid package:*** $17,576 (excluding resources awarded to replace EFC). 31% of all full-time freshmen had no need and received non-need-based gift aid.

UNDERGRADUATE FINANCIAL AID (Fall 2007) 6,052 applied for aid; of those 81% were deemed to have need. 100% of undergraduates with need received aid; of those 24% had need fully met. ***Average percent of need met:*** 76% (excluding resources awarded to replace EFC). ***Average financial aid package:*** $16,809 (excluding resources awarded to replace EFC). 19% of all full-time undergraduates had no need and received non-need-based gift aid.

GIFT AID (NEED-BASED) ***Total amount:*** $54,790,440 (13% federal, 11% state, 72% institutional, 4% external sources). ***Receiving aid:*** Freshmen: 50% (1,227); all full-time undergraduates: 48% (4,390). ***Average award:*** Freshmen: $12,311; Undergraduates: $11,733. ***Scholarships, grants, and awards:*** Federal Pell, FSEOG, state, private, college/university gift aid from institutional funds, Federal Nursing.

GIFT AID (NON-NEED-BASED) ***Total amount:*** $5,945,089 (70% institutional, 30% external sources). ***Receiving aid:*** Freshmen: 3% (67). Undergraduates: 2% (222). ***Average award:*** Freshmen: $1920. Undergraduates: $2180. ***Scholarships, grants, and awards by category:*** *Academic interests/achievement:* 4,790 awards ($10,481,367 total): agriculture, area/ethnic studies, business, computer science, education, engineering/technologies, English, foreign languages, general academic interests/achievements, health fields, home economics, humanities, international studies, mathematics, military science, physical sciences, premedicine, social sciences. *Creative arts/performance:* 32 awards ($32,794 total): debating, music, theater/drama. *Special achievements/activities:* 59 awards ($172,734 total): community service, leadership, memberships. *Special characteristics:* 149 awards ($576,623 total): adult students, ethnic background, first-generation college students. ***Tuition waivers:*** Full or partial for employees or children of employees, senior citizens. ***ROTC:*** Army.

LOANS ***Student loans:*** $36,744,569 (60% need-based, 40% non-need-based). 60% of past graduating class borrowed through all loan programs. *Average indebtedness per student:* $25,036. ***Average need-based loan:*** Freshmen: $5670. Undergraduates: $6013. ***Parent loans:*** $31,775,556 (100% non-need-based). ***Programs:*** FFEL (Subsidized and Unsubsidized Stafford, PLUS), Perkins, Federal Nursing, state, college/university.

WORK-STUDY ***Federal work-study:*** Total amount: $1,675,005; 1,886 jobs averaging $1100.

ATHLETIC AWARDS Total amount: $4,089,581 (30% need-based, 70% non-need-based).

APPLYING FOR FINANCIAL AID ***Required financial aid form:*** FAFSA. ***Financial aid deadline (priority):*** 2/10. ***Notification date:*** Continuous beginning 3/15. Students must reply within 4 weeks of notification.

CONTACT Student Financial Services, University of Vermont, 221 Waterman Building, Burlington, VT 05405-0160, 802-656-5700. *Fax:* 802-656-4076. *E-mail:* financialaid@uvm.edu.

UNIVERSITY OF VIRGINIA

Charlottesville, VA

Tuition & fees (VA res): $9300　Average undergraduate aid package: $18,532

ABOUT THE INSTITUTION State-supported, coed. ***Awards:*** bachelor's, master's, doctoral, and first professional degrees and post-master's certificates. 48 undergraduate majors. ***Total enrollment:*** 24,541. Undergraduates: 15,208. Freshmen: 3,256. Federal methodology is used as a basis for awarding need-based institutional aid.

UNDERGRADUATE EXPENSES for 2008–09 ***Application fee:*** $60. ***Tuition, state resident:*** full-time $7121. ***Tuition, nonresident:*** full-time $27,203. ***Required fees:*** full-time $2179. ***College room and board:*** $7820; ***Room only:*** $4230. Room and board charges vary according to board plan and housing facility. ***Payment plan:*** Installment.

FRESHMAN FINANCIAL AID (Fall 2008, est.) 1,993 applied for aid; of those 44% were deemed to have need. 100% of freshmen with need received aid; of those 100% had need fully met. ***Average percent of need met:*** 100% (excluding resources awarded to replace EFC). ***Average financial aid package:*** $17,742 (excluding resources awarded to replace EFC). 14% of all full-time freshmen had no need and received non-need-based gift aid.

UNDERGRADUATE FINANCIAL AID (Fall 2008, est.) 6,240 applied for aid; of those 61% were deemed to have need. 100% of undergraduates with need received aid; of those 100% had need fully met. ***Average percent of need met:***

100% (excluding resources awarded to replace EFC). ***Average financial aid package:*** $18,532 (excluding resources awarded to replace EFC). 14% of all full-time undergraduates had no need and received non-need-based gift aid.

GIFT AID (NEED-BASED) ***Total amount:*** $44,152,691 (12% federal, 11% state, 71% institutional, 6% external sources). ***Receiving aid:*** Freshmen: 24% (780); all full-time undergraduates: 23% (3,098). ***Average award:*** Freshmen: $13,381; Undergraduates: $14,497. ***Scholarships, grants, and awards:*** Federal Pell, FSEOG, state, private, college/university gift aid from institutional funds, Federal Nursing.

GIFT AID (NON-NEED-BASED) ***Total amount:*** $7,529,676 (1% federal, 6% state, 31% institutional, 62% external sources). ***Receiving aid:*** Freshmen: 4% (118). Undergraduates: 2% (315). ***Average award:*** Freshmen: $9815. Undergraduates: $9917. ***Scholarships, grants, and awards by category:*** *Academic interests/achievement:* general academic interests/achievements. *Creative arts/performance:* music. ***Tuition waivers:*** Full or partial for employees or children of employees, senior citizens. ***ROTC:*** Army, Naval, Air Force.

LOANS ***Student loans:*** $28,938,347 (36% need-based, 64% non-need-based). 33% of past graduating class borrowed through all loan programs. *Average indebtedness per student:* $19,016. ***Average need-based loan:*** Freshmen: $4304. Undergraduates: $4549. ***Parent loans:*** $8,131,094 (2% need-based, 98% non-need-based). ***Programs:*** FFEL (Subsidized and Unsubsidized Stafford, PLUS), Perkins, Federal Nursing, college/university, alternative private loans.

WORK-STUDY ***Federal work-study:*** Total amount: $1,793,501; 689 jobs averaging $2594.

ATHLETIC AWARDS Total amount: $3,270,013 (79% need-based, 21% non-need-based).

APPLYING FOR FINANCIAL AID ***Required financial aid forms:*** FAFSA, institution's own form. ***Financial aid deadline (priority):*** 3/1. ***Notification date:*** 4/5. Students must reply by 5/1.

CONTACT Ms. Yvonne B. Hubbard, Director, Student Financial Services, University of Virginia, PO Box 400207, Charlottesville, VA 22904-4207, 434-982-6000. *E-mail:* faid@virginia.edu.

THE UNIVERSITY OF VIRGINIA'S COLLEGE AT WISE

Wise, VA

Tuition & fees (VA res): $6748 **Average undergraduate aid package: $7815**

ABOUT THE INSTITUTION State-supported, coed. ***Awards:*** bachelor's degrees and post-bachelor's certificates. 24 undergraduate majors. ***Total enrollment:*** 1,964. Undergraduates: 1,964. Freshmen: 427. Federal methodology is used as a basis for awarding need-based institutional aid.

UNDERGRADUATE EXPENSES for 2009–10 ***Application fee:*** $25. ***Tuition, state resident:*** full-time $3586; part-time $153 per semester hour. ***Tuition, nonresident:*** full-time $16,114; part-time $666 per semester hour. ***Required fees:*** full-time $3162. ***College room and board:*** $7933; ***Room only:*** $4604.

FRESHMAN FINANCIAL AID (Fall 2008, est.) 349 applied for aid; of those 78% were deemed to have need. 100% of freshmen with need received aid; of those 95% had need fully met. ***Average percent of need met:*** 94% (excluding resources awarded to replace EFC). ***Average financial aid package:*** $7971 (excluding resources awarded to replace EFC). 30% of all full-time freshmen had no need and received non-need-based gift aid.

UNDERGRADUATE FINANCIAL AID (Fall 2008, est.) 1,190 applied for aid; of those 78% were deemed to have need. 100% of undergraduates with need received aid; of those 95% had need fully met. ***Average percent of need met:*** 94% (excluding resources awarded to replace EFC). ***Average financial aid package:*** $7815 (excluding resources awarded to replace EFC). 25% of all full-time undergraduates had no need and received non-need-based gift aid.

GIFT AID (NEED-BASED) ***Total amount:*** $4,448,314 (50% federal, 41% state, 6% institutional, 3% external sources). ***Receiving aid:*** Freshmen: 62% (265); all full-time undergraduates: 63% (917). ***Average award:*** Freshmen: $5837; Undergraduates: $5307. ***Scholarships, grants, and awards:*** Federal Pell, FSEOG, state, private, college/university gift aid from institutional funds.

GIFT AID (NON-NEED-BASED) ***Total amount:*** $1,384,082 (63% institutional, 37% external sources). ***Receiving aid:*** Freshmen: 52% (220). Undergraduates: 37% (537). ***Average award:*** Freshmen: $2505. Undergraduates: $2217. ***Scholarships, grants, and awards by category:*** *Academic interests/achievement:* agriculture, biological sciences, business, computer science, education, English, general academic interests/achievements, health fields, humanities, mathematics, physical sciences, premedicine, social sciences. *Creative arts/performance:* creative writing, general creative arts/performance, journalism/publications, music, performing arts, theater/drama. *Special achievements/activities:* community service, religious involvement. *Special characteristics:* children with a deceased or disabled parent, ethnic background, local/state students, veterans, veterans' children.

LOANS ***Student loans:*** $4,379,927 (48% need-based, 52% non-need-based). 59% of past graduating class borrowed through all loan programs. *Average indebtedness per student:* $10,252. ***Average need-based loan:*** Freshmen: $2180. Undergraduates: $3207. ***Parent loans:*** $838,552 (100% non-need-based). ***Programs:*** FFEL (Subsidized and Unsubsidized Stafford, PLUS), Perkins, state, college/university.

WORK-STUDY ***Federal work-study:*** Total amount: $288,712; 195 jobs averaging $1072.

ATHLETIC AWARDS Total amount: $274,306 (100% non-need-based).

APPLYING FOR FINANCIAL AID ***Required financial aid form:*** FAFSA. ***Financial aid deadline (priority):*** 4/1. ***Notification date:*** Continuous. Students must reply within 4 weeks of notification.

CONTACT Bill Wendle, Director of Financial Aid, The University of Virginia's College at Wise, 1 College Avenue, Wise, VA 24293, 276-328-0103 or toll-free 888-282-9324. *Fax:* 276-328-0251. *E-mail:* wdw8m@uvawise.edu.

UNIVERSITY OF WASHINGTON

Seattle, WA

Tuition & fees (WA res): $6802 **Average undergraduate aid package: $11,552**

ABOUT THE INSTITUTION State-supported, coed. ***Awards:*** bachelor's, master's, doctoral, and first professional degrees and first professional certificates. 155 undergraduate majors. ***Total enrollment:*** 40,218. Undergraduates: 28,570. Freshmen: 5,325. Federal methodology is used as a basis for awarding need-based institutional aid.

UNDERGRADUATE EXPENSES for 2008–09 ***Application fee:*** $50. ***Tuition, state resident:*** full-time $6250. ***Tuition, nonresident:*** full-time $22,667. ***Required fees:*** full-time $552. Full-time tuition and fees vary according to course load. Part-time tuition and fees vary according to course load. ***College room and board:*** $7488. Room and board charges vary according to board plan and housing facility.

FRESHMAN FINANCIAL AID (Fall 2008, est.) 3,741 applied for aid; of those 59% were deemed to have need. 92% of freshmen with need received aid; of those 39% had need fully met. ***Average percent of need met:*** 80% (excluding resources awarded to replace EFC). ***Average financial aid package:*** $10,587 (excluding resources awarded to replace EFC). 1% of all full-time freshmen had no need and received non-need-based gift aid.

UNDERGRADUATE FINANCIAL AID (Fall 2008, est.) 13,572 applied for aid; of those 72% were deemed to have need. 94% of undergraduates with need received aid; of those 35% had need fully met. ***Average percent of need met:*** 79% (excluding resources awarded to replace EFC). ***Average financial aid package:*** $11,552 (excluding resources awarded to replace EFC). 3% of all full-time undergraduates had no need and received non-need-based gift aid.

GIFT AID (NEED-BASED) ***Total amount:*** $72,063,000 (32% federal, 45% state, 18% institutional, 5% external sources). ***Receiving aid:*** Freshmen: 29% (1,608); all full-time undergraduates: 29% (7,138). ***Average award:*** Freshmen: $7583; Undergraduates: $8722. ***Scholarships, grants, and awards:*** Federal Pell, FSEOG, state, private, college/university gift aid from institutional funds.

GIFT AID (NON-NEED-BASED) ***Total amount:*** $9,952,000 (2% federal, 5% state, 55% institutional, 38% external sources). ***Receiving aid:*** Freshmen: 7% (385). Undergraduates: 4% (973). ***Average award:*** Freshmen: $4790. Undergraduates: $4430. ***Scholarships, grants, and awards by category:*** *Academic interests/achievement:* architecture, business, computer science, education, engineering/technologies, general academic interests/achievements, health fields. *Creative arts/performance:* art/fine arts, general creative arts/performance, music, performing arts. *Special achievements/activities:* general special achievements/activities, leadership, memberships. ***Tuition waivers:*** Full or partial for senior citizens. ***ROTC:*** Army, Naval, Air Force.

LOANS ***Student loans:*** $61,925,000 (75% need-based, 25% non-need-based). 50% of past graduating class borrowed through all loan programs. *Average indebtedness per student:* $16,800. ***Average need-based loan:*** Freshmen: $1963. Undergraduates: $2855. ***Parent loans:*** $23,946,000 (28% need-based, 72% non-need-based). ***Programs:*** Federal Direct (Subsidized and Unsubsidized Stafford, PLUS), Perkins, Federal Nursing, college/university.

WORK-STUDY ***Federal work-study:*** Total amount: $2,596,000; 478 jobs averaging $2800. ***State or other work-study/employment:*** Total amount: $525,000 (100% need-based). 327 part-time jobs averaging $3160.

ATHLETIC AWARDS Total amount: $3,954,000 (54% need-based, 46% non-need-based).

APPLYING FOR FINANCIAL AID ***Required financial aid form:*** FAFSA. ***Financial aid deadline (priority):*** 2/28. ***Notification date:*** 3/31.

CONTACT Office of Student Financial Aid, University of Washington, Box 355880, Seattle, WA 98195-5880, 206-543-6101. *E-mail:* osfa@u.washington.edu.

UNIVERSITY OF WASHINGTON, BOTHELL

Bothell, WA

CONTACT Financial Aid Office, University of Washington, Bothell, 18115 Campus Way NE, Bothell, WA 98011-8246, 425-352-5000.

UNIVERSITY OF WASHINGTON, TACOMA

Tacoma, WA

CONTACT Financial Aid Office, University of Washington, Tacoma, 1900 Commerce Street, Tacoma, WA 98402-3100, 253-692-4000 or toll-free 800-736-7750 (out-of-state).

THE UNIVERSITY OF WEST ALABAMA

Livingston, AL

Tuition & fees (AL res): $5100 **Average undergraduate aid package: N/A**

ABOUT THE INSTITUTION State-supported, coed. ***Awards:*** associate, bachelor's, and master's degrees. 19 undergraduate majors. ***Total enrollment:*** 4,011. Undergraduates: 1,827. Freshmen: 366. Federal methodology is used as a basis for awarding need-based institutional aid.

UNDERGRADUATE EXPENSES for 2008–09 ***Application fee:*** $20. ***Tuition, state resident:*** full-time $4600; part-time $195 per semester hour. ***Tuition, nonresident:*** full-time $9200; part-time $390 per semester hour. ***Required fees:*** full-time $500. Part-time tuition and fees vary according to course level. ***College room and board:*** $3904; ***Room only:*** $1840. Room and board charges vary according to board plan and housing facility. ***Payment plan:*** Deferred payment.

FRESHMAN FINANCIAL AID (Fall 2008, est.) 196 applied for aid; of those 100% were deemed to have need. 81% of freshmen with need received aid; of those 68% had need fully met. ***Average percent of need met:*** 68% (excluding resources awarded to replace EFC). 12% of all full-time freshmen had no need and received non-need-based gift aid.

UNDERGRADUATE FINANCIAL AID (Fall 2008, est.) 935 applied for aid; of those 100% were deemed to have need. 90% of undergraduates with need received aid; of those 56% had need fully met. ***Average percent of need met:*** 55% (excluding resources awarded to replace EFC). 9% of all full-time undergraduates had no need and received non-need-based gift aid.

GIFT AID (NEED-BASED) ***Total amount:*** $4,049,645 (98% federal, 2% state). ***Receiving aid:*** All full-time undergraduates: 47% (783). ***Average award:*** Freshmen: $3102; Undergraduates: $3647. ***Scholarships, grants, and awards:*** Federal Pell, FSEOG, state, private, college/university gift aid from institutional funds.

GIFT AID (NON-NEED-BASED) ***Total amount:*** $1,181,732 (5% federal, 93% institutional, 2% external sources). ***Receiving aid:*** Freshmen: 35% (108). Undergraduates: 16% (261). ***Average award:*** Freshmen: $2555. Undergraduates: $2795. ***Scholarships, grants, and awards by category:*** *Academic interests/achievement:* business, computer science, education, English, general academic interests/achievements. *Creative arts/performance:* creative writing, dance, journalism/publications, music. *Special achievements/activities:* cheerleading/drum major, rodeo. *Special characteristics:* children of faculty/staff, first-generation college students. ***Tuition waivers:*** Full or partial for employees or children of employees. ***ROTC:*** Army cooperative, Air Force cooperative.

LOANS ***Student loans:*** $5,118,008 (42% need-based, 58% non-need-based). 76% of past graduating class borrowed through all loan programs. *Average indebtedness per student:* $18,540. ***Average need-based loan:*** Freshmen: $3116. Undergraduates: $3708. ***Parent loans:*** $162,333 (100% non-need-based). ***Programs:*** FFEL (Subsidized and Unsubsidized Stafford, PLUS), Perkins, Stafford Federal Loan Teacher Loan Forgiveness.

WORK-STUDY ***Federal work-study:*** Total amount: $199,970; 49 jobs averaging $2865.

ATHLETIC AWARDS Total amount: $684,185 (100% non-need-based).

APPLYING FOR FINANCIAL AID ***Required financial aid form:*** FAFSA. ***Financial aid deadline (priority):*** 4/1. ***Notification date:*** Continuous beginning 5/1. Students must reply within 2 weeks of notification.

CONTACT Mr. Don Rainer, Director of Financial Aid, The University of West Alabama, Station 3, Livingston, AL 35470, 205-652-3576 or toll-free 800-621-7742 (in-state), 800-621-8044 (out-of-state). *Fax:* 205-652-3847. *E-mail:* drainer@uwa.edu.

UNIVERSITY OF WEST FLORIDA

Pensacola, FL

Tuition & fees (FL res): $3655 **Average undergraduate aid package: N/A**

ABOUT THE INSTITUTION State-supported, coed. ***Awards:*** associate, bachelor's, master's, and doctoral degrees (specialists). 49 undergraduate majors. ***Total enrollment:*** 10,491. Undergraduates: 8,718. Freshmen: 1,082. Federal methodology is used as a basis for awarding need-based institutional aid.

UNDERGRADUATE EXPENSES for 2009–10 ***Application fee:*** $30. ***Tuition, state resident:*** full-time $2461; part-time $121.84 per semester hour. ***Tuition, nonresident:*** full-time $14,729; part-time $551.22 per semester hour. ***Required fees:*** full-time $1194. ***College room and board:*** $6900.

GIFT AID (NEED-BASED) ***Total amount:*** $10,532,130 (68% federal, 22% state, 10% institutional). ***Scholarships, grants, and awards:*** Federal Pell, FSEOG, state, private, college/university gift aid from institutional funds.

GIFT AID (NON-NEED-BASED) ***Total amount:*** $10,104,504 (1% federal, 74% state, 17% institutional, 8% external sources). ***Scholarships, grants, and awards by category:*** *Academic interests/achievement:* 1,050 awards ($1,056,806 total): biological sciences, business, general academic interests/achievements, military science. *Creative arts/performance:* 100 awards ($74,750 total): applied art and design, art/fine arts, music, theater/drama. *Special characteristics:* 70 awards ($73,900 total): children and siblings of alumni, first-generation college students, handicapped students, members of minority groups. ***ROTC:*** Army, Air Force.

LOANS ***Student loans:*** $23,035,018 (58% need-based, 42% non-need-based). ***Programs:*** Federal Direct (Subsidized and Unsubsidized Stafford, PLUS), Perkins, college/university.

WORK-STUDY ***Federal work-study:*** Total amount: $449,611; jobs available. ***State or other work-study/employment:*** Part-time jobs available.

ATHLETIC AWARDS Total amount: $1,157,771 (100% non-need-based).

APPLYING FOR FINANCIAL AID ***Required financial aid forms:*** FAFSA, institution's own form. ***Financial aid deadline:*** Continuous. ***Notification date:*** Continuous beginning 2/1.

CONTACT Ms. Georganne E. Major, Coordinator, University of West Florida, 11000 University Parkway, Pensacola, FL 32514-5750, 850-474-2397 or toll-free 800-263-1074. *E-mail:* gmajor@uwf.edu.

UNIVERSITY OF WEST GEORGIA

Carrollton, GA

Tuition & fees (GA res): $4316 **Average undergraduate aid package: $7125**

ABOUT THE INSTITUTION State-supported, coed. ***Awards:*** bachelor's, master's, and doctoral degrees and post-bachelor's and post-master's certificates. 55 undergraduate majors. ***Total enrollment:*** 11,252. Undergraduates: 9,230. Freshmen: 2,097. Federal methodology is used as a basis for awarding need-based institutional aid.

UNDERGRADUATE EXPENSES for 2008–09 ***Application fee:*** $30. ***Tuition, state resident:*** full-time $3196; part-time $134 per semester hour. ***Tuition, nonresident:*** full-time $12,778; part-time $533 per semester hour. ***Required fees:*** full-time $1120; $41.56 per semester hour or $186 per term. Full-time tuition and fees vary according to course load. Part-time tuition and fees vary according to course load. ***College room and board:*** $5714; ***Room only:*** $2882. Room and board charges vary according to board plan and housing facility. ***Payment plan:*** Guaranteed tuition.

FRESHMAN FINANCIAL AID (Fall 2008, est.) 1,689 applied for aid; of those 69% were deemed to have need. 98% of freshmen with need received aid; of those 20% had need fully met. ***Average percent of need met:*** 66% (excluding resources awarded to replace EFC). ***Average financial aid package:*** $7190 (excluding resources awarded to replace EFC). 2% of all full-time freshmen had no need and received non-need-based gift aid.

UNDERGRADUATE FINANCIAL AID (Fall 2008, est.) 5,999 applied for aid; of those 70% were deemed to have need. 98% of undergraduates with need received aid; of those 20% had need fully met. ***Average percent of need met:*** 63% (excluding resources awarded to replace EFC). ***Average financial aid package:*** $7125 (excluding resources awarded to replace EFC). 2% of all full-time undergraduates had no need and received non-need-based gift aid.

GIFT AID (NEED-BASED) ***Total amount:*** $18,261,406 (66% federal, 32% state, 1% institutional, 1% external sources). ***Receiving aid:*** Freshmen: 49% (988); all full-time undergraduates: 42% (3,298). ***Average award:*** Freshmen: $5540; Undergraduates: $4967. ***Scholarships, grants, and awards:*** Federal Pell, FSEOG, state, private, college/university gift aid from institutional funds, Academic Competitiveness Grant, National Smart Grant, LEAP.

GIFT AID (NON-NEED-BASED) ***Total amount:*** $6,307,269 (89% state, 6% institutional, 5% external sources). ***Receiving aid:*** Freshmen: 19% (392). Undergraduates: 13% (1,002). ***Average award:*** Freshmen: $2091. Undergraduates: $1972. ***Scholarships, grants, and awards by category:*** *Academic interests/achievement:* biological sciences, business, communication, computer science, education, English, foreign languages, general academic interests/achievements, health fields, humanities, mathematics, physical sciences, premedicine, social sciences. *Creative arts/performance:* applied art and design, art/fine arts, debating, general creative arts/performance, journalism/publications, music, performing arts, theater/drama. *Special achievements/activities:* community service, leadership, memberships, religious involvement. *Special characteristics:* adult students, children and siblings of alumni, general special characteristics, handicapped students, international students, local/state students, members of minority groups. ***Tuition waivers:*** Full or partial for senior citizens. ***ROTC:*** Army.

LOANS ***Student loans:*** $15,147,276 (66% need-based, 34% non-need-based). ***Average need-based loan:*** Freshmen: $3185. Undergraduates: $3915. ***Programs:*** Federal Direct (Subsidized and Unsubsidized Stafford, PLUS), Perkins, state.

WORK-STUDY ***Federal work-study:*** Total amount: $425,000; 861 jobs averaging $1619. ***State or other work-study/employment:*** Part-time jobs available.

ATHLETIC AWARDS Total amount: $1,023,505 (40% need-based, 60% non-need-based).

APPLYING FOR FINANCIAL AID ***Required financial aid form:*** FAFSA. ***Financial aid deadline:*** 7/1 (priority: 4/1). ***Notification date:*** Continuous beginning 5/15.

CONTACT Kimberly Jordan, Director of Financial Aid, University of West Georgia, 1601 Maple Street, Aycock Hall, Carrollton, GA 30118, 678-839-6421. *Fax:* 678-839-6422. *E-mail:* kjordan@westga.edu.

UNIVERSITY OF WISCONSIN–EAU CLAIRE

Eau Claire, WI

Tuition & fees (WI res): $6203   Average undergraduate aid package: $8056

ABOUT THE INSTITUTION State-supported, coed. ***Awards:*** associate, bachelor's, and master's degrees and post-bachelor's and post-master's certificates. 48 undergraduate majors. ***Total enrollment:*** 10,889. Undergraduates: 10,346. Freshmen: 2,058. Federal methodology is used as a basis for awarding need-based institutional aid.

UNDERGRADUATE EXPENSES for 2008–09 ***Application fee:*** $35. ***Tuition, state resident:*** full-time $5240; part-time $258 per credit. ***Tuition, nonresident:*** full-time $12,814; part-time $574 per credit. ***Required fees:*** full-time $963; $40 per credit or $2 per term. Full-time tuition and fees vary according to reciprocity agreements. Part-time tuition and fees vary according to reciprocity agreements. ***College room and board:*** $5210; ***Room only:*** $2730. Room and board charges vary according to board plan and housing facility. ***Payment plan:*** Installment.

FRESHMAN FINANCIAL AID (Fall 2007) 1,555 applied for aid; of those 56% were deemed to have need. 99% of freshmen with need received aid; of those 75% had need fully met. ***Average percent of need met:*** 94% (excluding resources awarded to replace EFC). ***Average financial aid package:*** $7649 (excluding resources awarded to replace EFC). 17% of all full-time freshmen had no need and received non-need-based gift aid.

UNDERGRADUATE FINANCIAL AID (Fall 2007) 6,424 applied for aid; of those 64% were deemed to have need. 99% of undergraduates with need received aid; of those 73% had need fully met. ***Average percent of need met:*** 93% (excluding resources awarded to replace EFC). ***Average financial aid package:*** $8056 (excluding resources awarded to replace EFC). 9% of all full-time undergraduates had no need and received non-need-based gift aid.

GIFT AID (NEED-BASED) ***Total amount:*** $12,263,193 (59% federal, 29% state, 4% institutional, 8% external sources). ***Receiving aid:*** Freshmen: 27% (555); all full-time undergraduates: 25% (2,311). ***Average award:*** Freshmen: $4764; Undergraduates: $5161. ***Scholarships, grants, and awards:*** Federal Pell, FSEOG, state, private, college/university gift aid from institutional funds, Federal Nursing, Academic Competitiveness Grant, National Smart Grant, BIA Excellence in Math/Comp. Science/EMAC.

GIFT AID (NON-NEED-BASED) ***Total amount:*** $1,569,592 (6% federal, 1% state, 36% institutional, 57% external sources). ***Average award:*** Freshmen: $1781. Undergraduates: $1744. ***Scholarships, grants, and awards by category:*** *Academic interests/achievement:* biological sciences, business, communication, computer science, education, English, foreign languages, general academic interests/achievements, health fields, international studies, mathematics, physical sciences, premedicine, social sciences. *Creative arts/performance:* debating, music, theater/drama. *Special achievements/activities:* community service, general special achievements/activities, hobbies/interests, leadership, memberships. *Special characteristics:* adult students, ethnic background, first-generation college students, general special characteristics, international students, local/state students, members of minority groups, previous college experience. ***Tuition waivers:*** Full or partial for minority students.

LOANS ***Student loans:*** $29,200,243 (61% need-based, 39% non-need-based). 68% of past graduating class borrowed through all loan programs. *Average indebtedness per student:* $18,548. ***Average need-based loan:*** Freshmen: $4264. Undergraduates: $4707. ***Parent loans:*** $1,660,779 (1% need-based, 99% non-need-based). ***Programs:*** Federal Direct (Subsidized and Unsubsidized Stafford, PLUS), Perkins, state, college/university, alternative loans.

WORK-STUDY ***Federal work-study:*** Total amount: $3,358,522; 2,143 jobs averaging $1690. ***State or other work-study/employment:*** Total amount: $2,388,620 (49% need-based, 51% non-need-based). 2,119 part-time jobs averaging $1628.

APPLYING FOR FINANCIAL AID ***Required financial aid form:*** FAFSA. ***Financial aid deadline (priority):*** 4/15. ***Notification date:*** Continuous beginning 4/15. Students must reply within 3 weeks of notification.

CONTACT Ms. Kathleen Sahlhoff, Director of Financial Aid, University of Wisconsin–Eau Claire, 115 Schofield Hall, Eau Claire, WI 54701, 715-836-3373. *Fax:* 715-836-3846. *E-mail:* sahlhoka@uwec.edu.

UNIVERSITY OF WISCONSIN–GREEN BAY

Green Bay, WI

Tuition & fees (WI res): $6308   Average undergraduate aid package: $9610

ABOUT THE INSTITUTION State-supported, coed. ***Awards:*** associate, bachelor's, and master's degrees and post-bachelor's certificates. 37 undergraduate majors. ***Total enrollment:*** 6,275. Undergraduates: 6,059. Freshmen: 1,017. Federal methodology is used as a basis for awarding need-based institutional aid.

UNDERGRADUATE EXPENSES for 2008–09 ***Application fee:*** $44. ***One-time required fee:*** $200. ***Tuition, state resident:*** full-time $5084; part-time $212 per credit. ***Tuition, nonresident:*** full-time $12,667; part-time $527 per credit. ***Required fees:*** full-time $1224; $52 per credit. Full-time tuition and fees vary according to reciprocity agreements. ***College room and board:*** $5400; ***Room only:*** $3100. Room and board charges vary according to housing facility. ***Payment plan:*** Installment.

FRESHMAN FINANCIAL AID (Fall 2008, est.) 869 applied for aid; of those 67% were deemed to have need. 96% of freshmen with need received aid; of those 50% had need fully met. ***Average percent of need met:*** 86% (excluding resources awarded to replace EFC). ***Average financial aid package:*** $9075 (excluding resources awarded to replace EFC). 2% of all full-time freshmen had no need and received non-need-based gift aid.

UNDERGRADUATE FINANCIAL AID (Fall 2008, est.) 3,729 applied for aid; of those 74% were deemed to have need. 96% of undergraduates with need received aid; of those 57% had need fully met. ***Average percent of need met:*** 88% (excluding resources awarded to replace EFC). ***Average financial aid package:*** $9610 (excluding resources awarded to replace EFC). 1% of all full-time undergraduates had no need and received non-need-based gift aid.

GIFT AID (NEED-BASED) ***Total amount:*** $8,965,855 (54% federal, 35% state, 1% institutional, 10% external sources). ***Receiving aid:*** Freshmen: 34% (343); all full-time undergraduates: 31% (1,472). ***Average award:*** Freshmen: $5278; Undergraduates: $5640. ***Scholarships, grants, and awards:*** Federal Pell, FSEOG, state, private, college/university gift aid from institutional funds.

GIFT AID (NON-NEED-BASED) ***Total amount:*** $757,296 (9% state, 19% institutional, 72% external sources). ***Receiving aid:*** Freshmen: 23% (227). Undergraduates: 25% (1,169). ***Average award:*** Freshmen: $1294. Undergraduates: $3806. ***Scholarships, grants, and awards by category:*** *Academic interests/*

achievement: 51 awards ($312,150 total): area/ethnic studies, biological sciences, business, communication, education, engineering/technologies, general academic interests/achievements, health fields, humanities, physical sciences, premedicine, social sciences. *Creative arts/performance:* 19 awards ($24,628 total): art/fine arts, dance, journalism/publications, music, theater/drama. *Special achievements/activities:* 3 awards ($14,885 total): community service, general special achievements/activities, leadership. *Special characteristics:* 16 awards ($190,397 total): adult students, children and siblings of alumni, children of public servants, ethnic background, handicapped students, local/state students, members of minority groups, veterans. ***Tuition waivers:*** Full or partial for senior citizens. ***ROTC:*** Army cooperative.

LOANS ***Student loans:*** $21,478,038 (48% need-based, 52% non-need-based). 72% of past graduating class borrowed through all loan programs. *Average indebtedness per student:* $18,587. ***Average need-based loan:*** Freshmen: $3876. Undergraduates: $4447. ***Parent loans:*** $1,017,305 (100% non-need-based). ***Programs:*** FFEL (Subsidized and Unsubsidized Stafford, PLUS), Perkins.

WORK-STUDY ***Federal work-study:*** Total amount: $479,767; 221 jobs averaging $1869. ***State or other work-study/employment:*** Part-time jobs available.

ATHLETIC AWARDS Total amount: $1,876,511 (65% need-based, 35% non-need-based).

APPLYING FOR FINANCIAL AID ***Required financial aid form:*** FAFSA. ***Financial aid deadline (priority):*** 4/15. ***Notification date:*** Continuous. Students must reply within 3 weeks of notification.

CONTACT Mr. Ron Ronnenberg, Director of Financial Aid, University of Wisconsin–Green Bay, 2420 Nicolet Drive, Green Bay, WI 54311-7001, 920-465-2073 or toll-free 888-367-8942 (out-of-state). *E-mail:* ronnenbr@uwgb.edu.

UNIVERSITY OF WISCONSIN–LA CROSSE

La Crosse, WI

Tuition & fees (WI res): $6648 **Average undergraduate aid package: $6092**

ABOUT THE INSTITUTION State-supported, coed. ***Awards:*** associate, bachelor's, master's, and first professional degrees and post-bachelor's certificates. 45 undergraduate majors. ***Total enrollment:*** 9,900. Undergraduates: 8,634. Freshmen: 1,784. Federal methodology is used as a basis for awarding need-based institutional aid.

UNDERGRADUATE EXPENSES for 2008–09 ***Application fee:*** $44. ***Tuition, state resident:*** full-time $5643; part-time $235.13 per credit hour. ***Tuition, nonresident:*** full-time $13,216; part-time $550.68 per credit hour. ***Required fees:*** full-time $1005. Full-time tuition and fees vary according to degree level, program, and reciprocity agreements. Part-time tuition and fees vary according to course load, degree level, program, and reciprocity agreements. ***College room and board:*** $5420; ***Room only:*** $3130. Room and board charges vary according to board plan and housing facility. ***Payment plan:*** Installment.

FRESHMAN FINANCIAL AID (Fall 2007) 1,228 applied for aid; of those 54% were deemed to have need. 91% of freshmen with need received aid; of those 23% had need fully met. ***Average percent of need met:*** 79% (excluding resources awarded to replace EFC). ***Average financial aid package:*** $5632 (excluding resources awarded to replace EFC). 3% of all full-time freshmen had no need and received non-need-based gift aid.

UNDERGRADUATE FINANCIAL AID (Fall 2007) 5,149 applied for aid; of those 63% were deemed to have need. 94% of undergraduates with need received aid; of those 27% had need fully met. ***Average percent of need met:*** 80% (excluding resources awarded to replace EFC). ***Average financial aid package:*** $6092 (excluding resources awarded to replace EFC). 2% of all full-time undergraduates had no need and received non-need-based gift aid.

GIFT AID (NEED-BASED) ***Total amount:*** $8,817,989 (57% federal, 33% state, 6% institutional, 4% external sources). ***Receiving aid:*** Freshmen: 15% (264); all full-time undergraduates: 17% (1,355). ***Average award:*** Freshmen: $5493; Undergraduates: $5182. ***Scholarships, grants, and awards:*** Federal Pell, FSEOG, state, private, college/university gift aid from institutional funds.

GIFT AID (NON-NEED-BASED) ***Total amount:*** $2,053,057 (20% state, 7% institutional, 73% external sources). ***Receiving aid:*** Freshmen: 5% (77). Undergraduates: 3% (234). ***Average award:*** Freshmen: $1187. Undergraduates: $1159. ***Scholarships, grants, and awards by category:*** *Academic interests/achievement:* area/ethnic studies, biological sciences, business, communication, computer science, education, English, foreign languages, general academic interests/achievements, health fields, mathematics, military science, physical sciences, social sciences. *Creative arts/performance:* art/fine arts, music, theater/drama. *Special achievements/activities:* community service, leadership, memberships. *Special characteristics:* adult students, children and siblings of alumni, children of union members/company employees, ethnic background, first-generation college students, general special characteristics, international students, local/state students, members of minority groups, out-of-state students, veterans' children. ***Tuition waivers:*** Full or partial for minority students. ***ROTC:*** Army.

LOANS ***Student loans:*** $34,502,802 (47% need-based, 53% non-need-based). 63% of past graduating class borrowed through all loan programs. *Average indebtedness per student:* $21,250. ***Average need-based loan:*** Freshmen: $3087. Undergraduates: $3829. ***Parent loans:*** $2,607,345 (100% non-need-based). ***Programs:*** FFEL (Subsidized and Unsubsidized Stafford, PLUS), Perkins.

WORK-STUDY ***Federal work-study:*** Total amount: $453,738; jobs available. ***State or other work-study/employment:*** Total amount: $2,814,329 (100% non-need-based). Part-time jobs available.

APPLYING FOR FINANCIAL AID ***Required financial aid forms:*** FAFSA, institution's own form. ***Financial aid deadline (priority):*** 3/15. ***Notification date:*** Continuous beginning 4/1.

CONTACT Louise Larson Janke, Director of Financial Aid, University of Wisconsin–La Crosse, 1725 State Street, La Crosse, WI 54601-3742, 608-785-8604. *Fax:* 608-785-8843. *E-mail:* finaid@uwlax.edu.

UNIVERSITY OF WISCONSIN–MADISON

Madison, WI

Tuition & fees (WI res): $7568 **Average undergraduate aid package: $9948**

ABOUT THE INSTITUTION State-supported, coed. ***Awards:*** bachelor's, master's, doctoral, and first professional degrees and post-master's and first professional certificates. 117 undergraduate majors. ***Total enrollment:*** 42,030. Undergraduates: 30,750. Freshmen: 5,774. Federal methodology is used as a basis for awarding need-based institutional aid.

UNDERGRADUATE EXPENSES for 2008–09 ***Application fee:*** $44. ***Tuition, state resident:*** full-time $6678; part-time $278.27 per credit hour. ***Tuition, nonresident:*** full-time $20,920; part-time $872.01 per credit hour. ***Required fees:*** full-time $890; $38.92 per credit hour. Full-time tuition and fees vary according to degree level, program, and reciprocity agreements. Part-time tuition and fees vary according to course load, degree level, program, and reciprocity agreements. ***College room and board:*** $7700. Room and board charges vary according to board plan, housing facility, and location.

FRESHMAN FINANCIAL AID (Fall 2007) 3,498 applied for aid; of those 55% were deemed to have need. 100% of freshmen with need received aid; of those 24% had need fully met. ***Average percent of need met:*** 78% (excluding resources awarded to replace EFC). ***Average financial aid package:*** $9579 (excluding resources awarded to replace EFC). 30% of all full-time freshmen had no need and received non-need-based gift aid.

UNDERGRADUATE FINANCIAL AID (Fall 2007) 13,752 applied for aid; of those 67% were deemed to have need. 99% of undergraduates with need received aid; of those 23% had need fully met. ***Average percent of need met:*** 79% (excluding resources awarded to replace EFC). ***Average financial aid package:*** $9948 (excluding resources awarded to replace EFC). 17% of all full-time undergraduates had no need and received non-need-based gift aid.

GIFT AID (NEED-BASED) ***Total amount:*** $27,324,110 (50% federal, 26% state, 24% institutional). ***Receiving aid:*** Freshmen: 25% (1,511); all full-time undergraduates: 26% (7,308). ***Average award:*** Freshmen: $3287; Undergraduates: $3597. ***Scholarships, grants, and awards:*** Federal Pell, FSEOG, state, private, college/university gift aid from institutional funds.

GIFT AID (NON-NEED-BASED) ***Total amount:*** $29,647,894 (10% federal, 17% state, 46% institutional, 27% external sources). ***Receiving aid:*** Freshmen: 18% (1,092). Undergraduates: 13% (3,535). ***Average award:*** Freshmen: $1544. Undergraduates: $1665. ***Scholarships, grants, and awards by category:*** *Academic interests/achievement:* general academic interests/achievements. *Creative arts/performance:* general creative arts/performance. *Special achievements/activities:* general special achievements/activities. *Special characteristics:* general special characteristics. ***ROTC:*** Army, Naval, Air Force.

LOANS ***Student loans:*** $76,883,863 (50% need-based, 50% non-need-based). 52% of past graduating class borrowed through all loan programs. *Average indebtedness per student:* $21,123. ***Average need-based loan:*** Freshmen: $4385. Undergraduates: $5062. ***Parent loans:*** $14,687,146 (100% non-need-based). ***Programs:*** FFEL (Subsidized and Unsubsidized Stafford, PLUS), Perkins, Federal Nursing, state.

WORK-STUDY ***Federal work-study:*** Total amount: $8,541,097; jobs available.

ATHLETIC AWARDS Total amount: $8,062,698 (100% non-need-based).

APPLYING FOR FINANCIAL AID ***Required financial aid forms:*** FAFSA, institution's own form. ***Financial aid deadline:*** Continuous. ***Notification date:*** Continuous beginning 4/1. Students must reply within 3 weeks of notification.

CONTACT Office of Student Financial Aid, University of Wisconsin–Madison, 333 East Campus Mall #9701, Madison, WI 53715-1382, 608-262-3060. *Fax:* 608-262-9068. *E-mail:* finaid@finaid.wisc.edu.

UNIVERSITY OF WISCONSIN–MILWAUKEE

Milwaukee, WI

Tuition & fees (WI res): $7309 Average undergraduate aid package: $7311

ABOUT THE INSTITUTION State-supported, coed. ***Awards:*** bachelor's, master's, and doctoral degrees and post-bachelor's and post-master's certificates. 105 undergraduate majors. ***Total enrollment:*** 29,215. Undergraduates: 24,299. Freshmen: 4,118. Federal methodology is used as a basis for awarding need-based institutional aid.

UNDERGRADUATE EXPENSES for 2008–09 ***Application fee:*** $44. ***Tuition, state resident:*** full-time $6531; part-time $272.13 per credit. ***Tuition, nonresident:*** full-time $16,260; part-time $677.48 per credit. ***Required fees:*** full-time $778. Full-time tuition and fees vary according to location, program, and reciprocity agreements. Part-time tuition and fees vary according to course load, location, program, and reciprocity agreements. ***College room and board: Room only:*** $3840. Room and board charges vary according to board plan and housing facility. ***Payment plan:*** Installment.

FRESHMAN FINANCIAL AID (Fall 2008, est.) 3,131 applied for aid; of those 76% were deemed to have need. 94% of freshmen with need received aid; of those 27% had need fully met. ***Average percent of need met:*** 53% (excluding resources awarded to replace EFC). ***Average financial aid package:*** $6470 (excluding resources awarded to replace EFC). 1% of all full-time freshmen had no need and received non-need-based gift aid.

UNDERGRADUATE FINANCIAL AID (Fall 2008, est.) 16,237 applied for aid; of those 83% were deemed to have need. 82% of undergraduates with need received aid; of those 31% had need fully met. ***Average percent of need met:*** 57% (excluding resources awarded to replace EFC). ***Average financial aid package:*** $7311 (excluding resources awarded to replace EFC). 1% of all full-time undergraduates had no need and received non-need-based gift aid.

GIFT AID (NEED-BASED) ***Total amount:*** $31,709,657 (60% federal, 40% state). ***Receiving aid:*** Freshmen: 22% (879); all full-time undergraduates: 24% (4,708). ***Average award:*** Freshmen: $6190; Undergraduates: $5996. ***Scholarships, grants, and awards:*** Federal Pell, FSEOG, state, private, college/university gift aid from institutional funds, Federal Nursing.

GIFT AID (NON-NEED-BASED) ***Total amount:*** $10,441,652 (44% federal, 9% state, 26% institutional, 21% external sources). ***Receiving aid:*** Freshmen: 12% (463). Undergraduates: 8% (1,664). ***Average award:*** Freshmen: $1953. Undergraduates: $2606. ***Scholarships, grants, and awards by category:*** *Academic interests/achievement:* general academic interests/achievements. *Creative arts/performance:* general creative arts/performance. *Special achievements/activities:* general special achievements/activities. *Special characteristics:* general special characteristics. ***Tuition waivers:*** Full or partial for senior citizens. ***ROTC:*** Army cooperative, Air Force cooperative.

LOANS ***Student loans:*** $102,359,124 (44% need-based, 56% non-need-based). 58% of past graduating class borrowed through all loan programs. *Average indebtedness per student:* $15,772. ***Average need-based loan:*** Freshmen: $3704. Undergraduates: $4499. ***Parent loans:*** $4,715,945 (100% non-need-based). ***Programs:*** FFEL (Subsidized and Unsubsidized Stafford, PLUS), Perkins, Federal Nursing, state, alternative loans.

WORK-STUDY ***Federal work-study:*** Total amount: $1,539,315; jobs available.

ATHLETIC AWARDS Total amount: $387,844 (100% non-need-based).

APPLYING FOR FINANCIAL AID ***Required financial aid form:*** FAFSA. ***Financial aid deadline (priority):*** 3/1. ***Notification date:*** Continuous beginning 3/10. Students must reply within 2 weeks of notification.

CONTACT Ms. Jane Hojan-Clark, Director of Financial Aid and Student Employment Services, University of Wisconsin Milwaukee, Mellencamp Hall 102, Milwaukee, WI 53201, 414-229-6300. *E-mail:* jhojan@uwm.edu.

UNIVERSITY OF WISCONSIN–OSHKOSH

Oshkosh, WI

Tuition & fees (WI res): $6038 Average undergraduate aid package: $4500

ABOUT THE INSTITUTION State-supported, coed. ***Awards:*** associate, bachelor's, and master's degrees and post-bachelor's certificates. 56 undergraduate majors. ***Total enrollment:*** 12,669. Undergraduates: 11,355. Freshmen: 1,842. Federal methodology is used as a basis for awarding need-based institutional aid.

UNDERGRADUATE EXPENSES for 2008–09 ***Application fee:*** $35. ***Tuition, state resident:*** full-time $6038; part-time $252 per credit hour. ***Tuition, nonresident:*** full-time $13,610; part-time $567 per credit hour. ***College room and board:*** $5898; ***Room only:*** $3378. ***Payment plan:*** Installment.

FRESHMAN FINANCIAL AID (Fall 2008, est.) 1,240 applied for aid; of those 45% were deemed to have need. 100% of freshmen with need received aid; of those 32% had need fully met. ***Average percent of need met:*** 32% (excluding resources awarded to replace EFC). ***Average financial aid package:*** $3500 (excluding resources awarded to replace EFC). 27% of all full-time freshmen had no need and received non-need-based gift aid.

UNDERGRADUATE FINANCIAL AID (Fall 2008, est.) 6,020 applied for aid; of those 68% were deemed to have need. 100% of undergraduates with need received aid; of those 17% had need fully met. ***Average percent of need met:*** 35% (excluding resources awarded to replace EFC). ***Average financial aid package:*** $4500 (excluding resources awarded to replace EFC). 17% of all full-time undergraduates had no need and received non-need-based gift aid.

GIFT AID (NEED-BASED) ***Total amount:*** $11,923,846 (59% federal, 38% state, 3% institutional). ***Receiving aid:*** Freshmen: 19% (345); all full-time undergraduates: 32% (2,800). ***Average award:*** Freshmen: $1000; Undergraduates: $1000. ***Scholarships, grants, and awards:*** Federal Pell, FSEOG, state, private, college/university gift aid from institutional funds, Federal Nursing.

GIFT AID (NON-NEED-BASED) ***Total amount:*** $2,294,687 (7% federal, 8% state, 51% institutional, 34% external sources). ***Receiving aid:*** Freshmen: 19% (345). Undergraduates: 22% (1,960). ***Average award:*** Freshmen: $800. Undergraduates: $800. ***ROTC:*** Army.

LOANS ***Student loans:*** $40,702,231 (51% need-based, 49% non-need-based). 68% of past graduating class borrowed through all loan programs. *Average indebtedness per student:* $19,000. ***Average need-based loan:*** Freshmen: $3500. Undergraduates: $4000. ***Parent loans:*** $4,563,514 (100% non-need-based). ***Programs:*** FFEL (Subsidized and Unsubsidized Stafford, PLUS), Perkins, Federal Nursing, state, college/university.

WORK-STUDY ***Federal work-study:*** Total amount: $664,391; jobs available. ***State or other work-study/employment:*** Total amount: $3,000,000 (100% non-need-based). Part-time jobs available.

APPLYING FOR FINANCIAL AID ***Required financial aid form:*** FAFSA. ***Financial aid deadline (priority).*** 3/15. ***Notification date:*** 4/15. Students must reply within 2 weeks of notification.

CONTACT Ms. Sheila Denney, Financial Aid Counselor, University of Wisconsin–Oshkosh, 800 Algoma Boulevard, Oshkosh, WI 54901, 920-424-3377. *E-mail:* denney@uwosh.edu.

UNIVERSITY OF WISCONSIN–PARKSIDE

Kenosha, WI

Tuition & fees (WI res): $6070 Average undergraduate aid package: N/A

ABOUT THE INSTITUTION State-supported, coed. ***Awards:*** bachelor's and master's degrees. 37 undergraduate majors. ***Total enrollment:*** 5,167. Undergraduates: 5,045. Freshmen: 928. Federal methodology is used as a basis for awarding need-based institutional aid.

UNDERGRADUATE EXPENSES for 2008–09 ***Application fee:*** $44. ***Tuition, state resident:*** full-time $5084; part-time $212 per credit hour. ***Tuition, nonresident:*** full-time $12,922; part-time $538 per credit hour. ***Required fees:*** full-time $986. Full-time tuition and fees vary according to course load and reciprocity agreements. Part-time tuition and fees vary according to course load. ***College room and board:*** $5986; ***Room only:*** $3792. Room and board charges vary according to board plan and housing facility. ***Payment plan:*** Installment.

FRESHMAN FINANCIAL AID (Fall 2007) 665 applied for aid; of those 80% were deemed to have need. 96% of freshmen with need received aid.

UNDERGRADUATE FINANCIAL AID (Fall 2007) 2,594 applied for aid; of those 80% were deemed to have need. 94% of undergraduates with need received aid.

GIFT AID (NEED-BASED) ***Total amount:*** $8,730,874 (58% federal, 42% state). ***Receiving aid:*** Freshmen: 41% (343); all full-time undergraduates: 34% (1,221). ***Average award:*** Freshmen: $5725; Undergraduates: $4631. ***Scholarships, grants, and awards:*** Federal Pell, FSEOG, state, private, college/university gift aid from institutional funds, Federal Nursing.

GIFT AID (NON-NEED-BASED) ***Total amount:*** $1,882,359 (36% federal, 6% state, 34% institutional, 24% external sources). ***Receiving aid:*** Freshmen: 16% (131). Undergraduates: 12% (435). ***Scholarships, grants, and awards by category:*** *Academic interests/achievement:* biological sciences, business, communication, education, engineering/technologies, English, foreign languages, general academic interests/achievements, health fields, mathematics, physical sciences, premedicine. *Creative arts/performance:* applied art and design, art/fine arts, music, theater/drama. *Special achievements/activities:* community service, leadership. *Special characteristics:* adult students, children of union members/company employees, children of workers in trades, ethnic background, general special characteristics, international students, local/state students, members of minority groups. ***Tuition waivers:*** Full or partial for senior citizens. ***ROTC:*** Army cooperative.

LOANS ***Student loans:*** $14,913,157 (52% need-based, 48% non-need-based). ***Parent loans:*** $973,673 (100% non-need-based). ***Programs:*** FFEL (Subsidized and Unsubsidized Stafford, PLUS), Perkins, Federal Nursing, state.

WORK-STUDY ***Federal work-study:*** Total amount: $76,482; jobs available. ***State or other work-study/employment:*** Total amount: $25,494 (100% non-need-based). Part-time jobs available.

ATHLETIC AWARDS Total amount: $990,033 (100% non-need-based).

APPLYING FOR FINANCIAL AID ***Required financial aid form:*** FAFSA. ***Financial aid deadline (priority):*** 11/15. ***Notification date:*** Continuous beginning 4/1. Students must reply within 2 weeks of notification.

CONTACT Dr. Randall McCready, Director of Financial Aid and Scholarships, University of Wisconsin–Parkside, 900 Wood Road, Kenosha, WI 53141-2000, 262-595-2574. *Fax:* 262-595-2216. *E-mail:* randall.mccready@uwp.edu.

UNIVERSITY OF WISCONSIN–PLATTEVILLE

Platteville, WI

CONTACT Elizabeth Tucker, Director of Financial Aid, University of Wisconsin–Platteville, 1 University Plaza, Platteville, WI 53818-3099, 608-342-1836 or toll-free 800-362-5515. *Fax:* 608-342-1281. *E-mail:* tucker@uwplatt.edu.

UNIVERSITY OF WISCONSIN–RIVER FALLS

River Falls, WI

CONTACT Mr. David Woodward, Director of Financial Aid, University of Wisconsin–River Falls, 410 South Third Street, River Falls, WI 54022-5001, 715-425-3272. *Fax:* 715-425-0708.

UNIVERSITY OF WISCONSIN–STEVENS POINT

Stevens Point, WI

Tuition & fees (WI res): $6200 **Average undergraduate aid package: $7585**

ABOUT THE INSTITUTION State-supported, coed. ***Awards:*** associate, bachelor's, master's, and doctoral degrees. 55 undergraduate majors. ***Total enrollment:*** 9,155. Undergraduates: 8,710. Freshmen: 1,618. Federal methodology is used as a basis for awarding need-based institutional aid.

UNDERGRADUATE EXPENSES for 2008–09 ***Application fee:*** $44. ***Tuition, state resident:*** full-time $5084; part-time $212 per credit. ***Tuition, nonresident:*** full-time $12,657; part-time $527 per credit. ***Required fees:*** full-time $1116; $98 per credit. Full-time tuition and fees vary according to course load and reciprocity agreements. Part-time tuition and fees vary according to course load and reciprocity agreements. ***College room and board:*** $5180; ***Room only:*** $3148. ***Payment plan:*** Installment.

FRESHMAN FINANCIAL AID (Fall 2007) 1,272 applied for aid; of those 64% were deemed to have need. 93% of freshmen with need received aid; of those 90% had need fully met. ***Average percent of need met:*** 82% (excluding resources awarded to replace EFC). ***Average financial aid package:*** $6469 (excluding resources awarded to replace EFC). 7% of all full-time freshmen had no need and received non-need-based gift aid.

UNDERGRADUATE FINANCIAL AID (Fall 2007) 6,051 applied for aid; of those 71% were deemed to have need. 97% of undergraduates with need received aid; of those 74% had need fully met. ***Average percent of need met:*** 76% (excluding resources awarded to replace EFC). ***Average financial aid package:*** $7585 (excluding resources awarded to replace EFC). 7% of all full-time undergraduates had no need and received non-need-based gift aid.

GIFT AID (NEED-BASED) ***Total amount:*** $12,278,279 (61% federal, 33% state, 3% institutional, 3% external sources). ***Receiving aid:*** Freshmen: 22% (355); all full-time undergraduates: 25% (2,106). ***Average award:*** Freshmen: $5761; Undergraduates: $5459. ***Scholarships, grants, and awards:*** Federal Pell, FSEOG, state, college/university gift aid from institutional funds.

GIFT AID (NON-NEED-BASED) ***Total amount:*** $2,191,375 (4% state, 34% institutional, 62% external sources). ***Receiving aid:*** Freshmen: 5% (83). Undergraduates: 5% (457). ***Average award:*** Freshmen: $2178. Undergraduates: $2393. ***Scholarships, grants, and awards by category:*** *Academic interests/achievement:* 485 awards ($265,495 total): agriculture, architecture, biological sciences, business, communication, computer science, education, engineering/technologies, English, foreign languages, general academic interests/achievements, health fields, home economics, humanities, international studies, mathematics, military science, physical sciences, premedicine, social sciences. *Creative arts/performance:* 52 awards ($13,205 total): applied art and design, creative writing, dance, music, performing arts, theater/drama. *Special achievements/activities:* 8 awards ($8100 total): general special achievements/activities, leadership. *Special characteristics:* 2 awards ($7074 total): adult students, ethnic background, general special characteristics, international students, members of minority groups, out-of-state students, veterans. ***Tuition waivers:*** Full or partial for children of alumni, senior citizens. ***ROTC:*** Army.

LOANS ***Student loans:*** $29,643,261 (64% need-based, 36% non-need-based). 70% of past graduating class borrowed through all loan programs. *Average indebtedness per student:* $19,123. ***Average need-based loan:*** Freshmen: $3661. Undergraduates: $4715. ***Parent loans:*** $2,524,032 (7% need-based, 93% non-need-based). ***Programs:*** FFEL (Subsidized and Unsubsidized Stafford, PLUS); Perkins.

WORK-STUDY ***Federal work-study:*** Total amount: $2,258,148; 935 jobs averaging $1351. ***State or other work-study/employment:*** 1,761 part-time jobs averaging $1970.

APPLYING FOR FINANCIAL AID ***Required financial aid form:*** FAFSA. ***Financial aid deadline (priority):*** 5/15. ***Notification date:*** Continuous. Students must reply within 4 weeks of notification.

CONTACT Mr. Paul Watson, Director of Financial Aid, University of Wisconsin–Stevens Point, 105 Student Services Center, Stevens Point, WI 54481-3897, 715-346-4771. *Fax:* 715-346-3526. *E-mail:* pwatson@uwsp.edu.

UNIVERSITY OF WISCONSIN–STOUT

Menomonie, WI

Tuition & fees (WI res): $7584 **Average undergraduate aid package: $8710**

ABOUT THE INSTITUTION State-supported, coed. ***Awards:*** bachelor's and master's degrees and post-master's certificates. 34 undergraduate majors. ***Total enrollment:*** 8,811. Undergraduates: 7,766. Freshmen: 1,631. Federal methodology is used as a basis for awarding need-based institutional aid.

UNDERGRADUATE EXPENSES for 2008–09 ***Application fee:*** $44. ***Tuition, state resident:*** full-time $5662; part-time $189 per credit. ***Tuition, nonresident:*** full-time $13,408; part-time $447 per credit. ***Required fees:*** full-time $1922; $64 per credit. Full-time tuition and fees vary according to reciprocity agreements. Part-time tuition and fees vary according to reciprocity agreements. ***College room and board:*** $5170; ***Room only:*** $3200. Room and board charges vary according to board plan and housing facility. ***Payment plan:*** Installment.

FRESHMAN FINANCIAL AID (Fall 2008, est.) 1,310 applied for aid; of those 62% were deemed to have need. 100% of freshmen with need received aid; of those 49% had need fully met. ***Average percent of need met:*** 87% (excluding resources awarded to replace EFC). ***Average financial aid package:*** $8292 (excluding resources awarded to replace EFC). 2% of all full-time freshmen had no need and received non-need-based gift aid.

UNDERGRADUATE FINANCIAL AID (Fall 2008, est.) 5,110 applied for aid; of those 68% were deemed to have need. 100% of undergraduates with need received aid; of those 59% had need fully met. ***Average percent of need met:***

89% (excluding resources awarded to replace EFC). ***Average financial aid package:*** $8710 (excluding resources awarded to replace EFC). 2% of all full-time undergraduates had no need and received non-need-based gift aid.

GIFT AID (NEED-BASED) ***Total amount:*** $9,629,220 (64% federal, 33% state, 3% external sources). ***Receiving aid:*** Freshmen: 22% (356); all full-time undergraduates: 24% (1,605). ***Average award:*** Freshmen: $5933; Undergraduates: $5608. ***Scholarships, grants, and awards:*** Federal Pell, FSEOG, state, private, college/university gift aid from institutional funds, Bureau of Indian Affairs Grants, GEAR UP grants, Academic Competitiveness Grant, SMART grant.

GIFT AID (NON-NEED-BASED) ***Total amount:*** $2,834,695 (8% federal, 2% state, 19% institutional, 71% external sources). ***Receiving aid:*** Freshmen: 22% (352). Undergraduates: 12% (835). ***Average award:*** Freshmen: $1217. Undergraduates: $1330. ***Scholarships, grants, and awards by category:*** *Academic interests/achievement:* 268 awards ($285,300 total): business, computer science, education, engineering/technologies, general academic interests/achievements, home economics, international studies, mathematics, physical sciences. *Creative arts/performance:* 16 awards ($19,000 total): applied art and design, art/fine arts, music. *Special achievements/activities:* 29 awards ($28,675 total): community service, general special achievements/activities, leadership, memberships, religious involvement. *Special characteristics:* 53 awards ($67,350 total): adult students, first-generation college students, handicapped students, international students, local/state students, members of minority groups, out-of-state students, previous college experience, veterans, veterans' children.

LOANS ***Student loans:*** $35,754,882 (40% need-based, 60% non-need-based). 75% of past graduating class borrowed through all loan programs. *Average indebtedness per student:* $26,072. ***Average need-based loan:*** Freshmen: $3491. Undergraduates: $4235. ***Parent loans:*** $2,115,485 (100% non-need-based). ***Programs:*** FFEL (Subsidized and Unsubsidized Stafford, PLUS), Perkins, alternative loans.

WORK-STUDY ***Federal work-study:*** Total amount: $2,376,853; 1,256 jobs averaging $1659.

APPLYING FOR FINANCIAL AID ***Required financial aid form:*** FAFSA. ***Financial aid deadline (priority):*** 3/15. ***Notification date:*** Continuous beginning 4/1. Students must reply within 4 weeks of notification.

CONTACT Beth M. Boisen, Director of Financial Aid, University of Wisconsin–Stout, 210 Bowman Hall, Menomonie, WI 54751, 715-232-1363 or toll-free 800-HI-STOUT (in-state). *Fax:* 715-232-5246. *E-mail:* boisenb@uwstout.edu.

UNIVERSITY OF WISCONSIN–SUPERIOR

Superior, WI

Tuition & fees (WI res): $6359 **Average undergraduate aid package: $7621**

ABOUT THE INSTITUTION State-supported, coed. ***Awards:*** bachelor's and master's degrees (associate, educational specialist). 65 undergraduate majors. ***Total enrollment:*** 2,688. Undergraduates: 2,439. Federal methodology is used as a basis for awarding need-based institutional aid.

UNDERGRADUATE EXPENSES for 2008–09 ***Application fee:*** $44. ***Tuition, state resident:*** full-time $5293; part-time $386 per semester hour. ***Tuition, nonresident:*** full-time $12,866; part-time $702 per semester hour. ***Required fees:*** full-time $1066. Full-time tuition and fees vary according to reciprocity agreements. Part-time tuition and fees vary according to reciprocity agreements. ***College room and board:*** $5154; ***Room only:*** $2874. Room and board charges vary according to board plan and housing facility. ***Payment plan:*** Installment.

FRESHMAN FINANCIAL AID (Fall 2008, est.) 216 applied for aid; of those 76% were deemed to have need. 99% of freshmen with need received aid; of those 45% had need fully met. ***Average financial aid package:*** $6670 (excluding resources awarded to replace EFC). 4% of all full-time freshmen had no need and received non-need-based gift aid.

UNDERGRADUATE FINANCIAL AID (Fall 2008, est.) 1,400 applied for aid; of those 82% were deemed to have need. 99% of undergraduates with need received aid; of those 33% had need fully met. ***Average financial aid package:*** $7621 (excluding resources awarded to replace EFC). 3% of all full-time undergraduates had no need and received non-need-based gift aid.

GIFT AID (NEED-BASED) ***Total amount:*** $3,627,690 (70% federal, 28% state, 2% external sources). ***Receiving aid:*** Freshmen: 26% (78); all full-time undergraduates: 32% (615). ***Average award:*** Freshmen: $5786; Undergraduates: $5345. ***Scholarships, grants, and awards:*** Federal Pell, FSEOG, state, private, college/university gift aid from institutional funds.

GIFT AID (NON-NEED-BASED) ***Total amount:*** $1,293,980 (11% federal, 6% state, 55% institutional, 28% external sources). ***Receiving aid:*** Freshmen: 24% (72). Undergraduates: 15% (301). ***Average award:*** Freshmen: $2256. Undergraduates: $2558. ***Scholarships, grants, and awards by category:*** *Academic interests/achievement:* biological sciences, business, communication, computer science, education, English, general academic interests/achievements, health fields, humanities, mathematics, physical sciences, social sciences. *Special characteristics:* general special characteristics. ***ROTC:*** Air Force cooperative.

LOANS ***Student loans:*** $9,842,521 (44% need-based, 56% non-need-based). 73% of past graduating class borrowed through all loan programs. *Average indebtedness per student:* $19,556. ***Average need-based loan:*** Freshmen: $2892. Undergraduates: $3899. ***Parent loans:*** $320,113 (100% non-need-based). ***Programs:*** Federal Direct (Subsidized and Unsubsidized Stafford, PLUS), Perkins, state, college/university, alternative loans.

WORK-STUDY ***Federal work-study:*** Total amount: $338,000; 536 jobs averaging $1430. ***State or other work-study/employment:*** Part-time jobs available.

APPLYING FOR FINANCIAL AID ***Required financial aid form:*** FAFSA. ***Financial aid deadline (priority):*** 4/1. ***Notification date:*** Continuous.

CONTACT Tammi Reijo, Financial Aid Office, University of Wisconsin–Superior, Belknap and Catlin, Superior, WI 54880-4500, 715-394-8200. *Fax:* 715-394-8027. *E-mail:* treijo@uwsuper.edu.

UNIVERSITY OF WISCONSIN–WHITEWATER

Whitewater, WI

Tuition & fees (WI res): $7062 **Average undergraduate aid package: $7280**

ABOUT THE INSTITUTION State-supported, coed. ***Awards:*** associate, bachelor's, and master's degrees. 56 undergraduate majors. ***Total enrollment:*** 10,962. Undergraduates: 9,621. Freshmen: 2,154. Federal methodology is used as a basis for awarding need-based institutional aid.

UNDERGRADUATE EXPENSES for 2008–09 ***Application fee:*** $44. ***Tuition, state resident:*** full-time $6162; part-time $219.26 per credit. ***Tuition, nonresident:*** full-time $13,736; part-time $534.80 per credit. ***Required fees:*** full-time $900. Full-time tuition and fees vary according to degree level and reciprocity agreements. ***College room and board:*** $4740. Room and board charges vary according to board plan. ***Payment plan:*** Installment.

FRESHMAN FINANCIAL AID (Fall 2008, est.) 1,825 applied for aid; of those 63% were deemed to have need. 95% of freshmen with need received aid; of those 63% had need fully met. ***Average percent of need met:*** 68% (excluding resources awarded to replace EFC). ***Average financial aid package:*** $6553 (excluding resources awarded to replace EFC). 5% of all full-time freshmen had no need and received non-need-based gift aid.

UNDERGRADUATE FINANCIAL AID (Fall 2008, est.) 6,127 applied for aid; of those 66% were deemed to have need. 97% of undergraduates with need received aid; of those 66% had need fully met. ***Average percent of need met:*** 74% (excluding resources awarded to replace EFC). ***Average financial aid package:*** $7280 (excluding resources awarded to replace EFC). 5% of all full-time undergraduates had no need and received non-need-based gift aid.

GIFT AID (NEED-BASED) ***Total amount:*** $11,716,000 (59% federal, 39% state, 2% external sources). ***Receiving aid:*** Freshmen: 22% (466); all full-time undergraduates: 21% (1,836). ***Average award:*** Freshmen: $6236; Undergraduates: $5708. ***Scholarships, grants, and awards:*** Federal Pell, FSEOG, state, private, college/university gift aid from institutional funds.

GIFT AID (NON-NEED-BASED) ***Total amount:*** $3,739,000 (1% federal, 11% state, 29% institutional, 59% external sources). ***Receiving aid:*** Freshmen: 14% (307). Undergraduates: 8% (694). ***Average award:*** Freshmen: $1600. Undergraduates: $1853. ***Scholarships, grants, and awards by category:*** *Academic interests/achievement:* biological sciences, business, communication, computer science, education, English, foreign languages, general academic interests/achievements, humanities, mathematics, physical sciences, premedicine, social sciences. *Creative arts/performance:* art/fine arts, cinema/film/broadcasting, creative writing, journalism/publications, music, theater/drama. *Special achievements/activities:* leadership. *Special characteristics:* adult students, ethnic background, handicapped students, international students, local/state students, members of minority groups, out-of-state students. ***Tuition waivers:*** Full or partial for children of alumni, senior citizens. ***ROTC:*** Army, Air Force.

LOANS ***Student loans:*** $44,100,000 (39% need-based, 61% non-need-based). 60% of past graduating class borrowed through all loan programs. *Average indebtedness per student:* $19,743. ***Average need-based loan:*** Freshmen: $3320.

Undergraduates: $3960. ***Parent loans:*** $6,200,000 (100% non-need-based). ***Programs:*** Federal Direct (Subsidized and Unsubsidized Stafford, PLUS), Perkins.

WORK-STUDY ***Federal work-study:*** Total amount: $656,000; 593 jobs averaging $1106. ***State or other work-study/employment:*** Total amount: $3,300,000 (100% non-need-based). 1,507 part-time jobs averaging $1900.

APPLYING FOR FINANCIAL AID ***Required financial aid form:*** FAFSA. ***Financial aid deadline (priority):*** 3/15. ***Notification date:*** Continuous beginning 4/1. Students must reply within 3 weeks of notification.

CONTACT Ms. Carol Miller, Director of Financial Aid, University of Wisconsin–Whitewater, 800 West Main Street, Whitewater, WI 53190-1790, 262-472-1130. *Fax:* 262-472-5655.

UNIVERSITY OF WYOMING

Laramie, WY

Tuition & fees (WY res): $3686 **Average undergraduate aid package: $8050**

ABOUT THE INSTITUTION State-supported, coed. ***Awards:*** bachelor's, master's, doctoral, and first professional degrees and post-bachelor's and post-master's certificates. 80 undergraduate majors. ***Total enrollment:*** 12,067. Undergraduates: 9,544. Freshmen: 1,693. Federal methodology is used as a basis for awarding need-based institutional aid.

UNDERGRADUATE EXPENSES for 2009–10 ***Application fee:*** $40. ***One-time required fee:*** $100. ***Tuition, state resident:*** full-time $2820; part-time $94 per credit hour. ***Tuition, nonresident:*** full-time $10,740; part-time $358 per credit hour. ***Required fees:*** full-time $866; $210.23 per term. ***College room and board:*** $8006; ***Room only:*** $3466.

FRESHMAN FINANCIAL AID (Fall 2007) 1,205 applied for aid; of those 59% were deemed to have need. 97% of freshmen with need received aid; of those 27% had need fully met. ***Average percent of need met:*** 35% (excluding resources awarded to replace EFC). ***Average financial aid package:*** $7612 (excluding resources awarded to replace EFC). 10% of all full-time freshmen had no need and received non-need-based gift aid.

UNDERGRADUATE FINANCIAL AID (Fall 2007) 5,098 applied for aid; of those 71% were deemed to have need. 98% of undergraduates with need received aid; of those 19% had need fully met. ***Average percent of need met:*** 43% (excluding resources awarded to replace EFC). ***Average financial aid package:*** $8050 (excluding resources awarded to replace EFC). 16% of all full-time undergraduates had no need and received non-need-based gift aid.

GIFT AID (NEED-BASED) ***Total amount:*** $7,858,476 (81% federal, 7% state, 3% institutional, 9% external sources). ***Receiving aid:*** Freshmen: 21% (343); all full-time undergraduates: 23% (1,870). ***Average award:*** Freshmen: $3085; Undergraduates: $3474. ***Scholarships, grants, and awards:*** Federal Pell, FSEOG, state, private, college/university gift aid from institutional funds.

GIFT AID (NON-NEED-BASED) ***Total amount:*** $23,158,243 (55% state, 37% institutional, 8% external sources). ***Receiving aid:*** Freshmen: 33% (544). Undergraduates: 28% (2,273). ***Average award:*** Freshmen: $3475. Undergraduates: $3684. ***Scholarships, grants, and awards by category:*** *Academic interests/achievement:* 5,638 awards ($10,700,514 total): agriculture, business, communication, computer science, education, engineering/technologies, English, foreign languages, general academic interests/achievements, health fields, home economics, international studies, mathematics, military science, physical sciences, social sciences. *Creative arts/performance:* 562 awards ($685,836 total): dance, debating, music, theater/drama. *Special achievements/activities:* 179 awards ($292,941 total): cheerleading/drum major, junior miss, leadership, rodeo. *Special characteristics:* 1,828 awards ($5,128,270 total): adult students, children and siblings of alumni, ethnic background, first-generation college students, handicapped students, international students, local/state students, out-of-state students, veterans. ***ROTC:*** Army, Air Force.

LOANS ***Student loans:*** $24,179,129 (46% need-based, 54% non-need-based). 48% of past graduating class borrowed through all loan programs. *Average indebtedness per student:* $16,307. ***Average need-based loan:*** Freshmen: $2816. Undergraduates: $4193. ***Parent loans:*** $2,340,612 (100% non-need-based). ***Programs:*** FFEL (Subsidized and Unsubsidized Stafford, PLUS), Perkins, alternative loans.

WORK-STUDY ***Federal work-study:*** Total amount: $485,187; 285 jobs averaging $1694.

ATHLETIC AWARDS Total amount: $3,579,616 (100% non-need-based).

APPLYING FOR FINANCIAL AID ***Required financial aid form:*** FAFSA. ***Financial aid deadline (priority):*** 2/1. ***Notification date:*** Continuous beginning 3/15. Students must reply within 3 weeks of notification.

CONTACT Mr. David Gruen, Director of Student Financial Aid, University of Wyoming, Department 3335, Laramie, WY 82071, 307-766-2116 or toll-free 800-342-5996. *Fax:* 307-766-3800. *E-mail:* finaid@uwyo.edu.

UPPER IOWA UNIVERSITY

Fayette, IA

CONTACT Jobyna Johnston, Director of Financial Aid, Upper Iowa University, Parker Fox Hall, Box 1859, Fayette, IA 52142-1859, 563-425-5393 or toll-free 800-553-4150 Ext. 2. *Fax:* 563-425-5277. *E-mail:* jobyna@uiu.edu.

URBANA UNIVERSITY

Urbana, OH

ABOUT THE INSTITUTION Independent, coed. 28 undergraduate majors.

GIFT AID (NEED-BASED) ***Scholarships, grants, and awards:*** Federal Pell, FSEOG, state, private, college/university gift aid from institutional funds.

GIFT AID (NON-NEED-BASED) ***Scholarships, grants, and awards by category:*** *Academic interests/achievement:* general academic interests/achievements. *Creative arts/performance:* music, performing arts, theater/drama. *Special achievements/activities:* community service, leadership, religious involvement. *Special characteristics:* children and siblings of alumni, children of faculty/staff, religious affiliation, spouses of current students.

LOANS ***Programs:*** FFEL (Subsidized and Unsubsidized Stafford, PLUS), Perkins.

APPLYING FOR FINANCIAL AID ***Required financial aid forms:*** FAFSA, institution's own form.

CONTACT Mrs. Amy M. Barnhart, Director of Financial Aid, Urbana University, 579 College Way, Urbana, OH 43078-2091, 937-484-1359 or toll-free 800-7-URBANA. *Fax:* 937-652-6870. *E-mail:* abarnhart@urbana.edu.

URSINUS COLLEGE

Collegeville, PA

Tuition & fees: $36,910 **Average undergraduate aid package: $25,921**

ABOUT THE INSTITUTION Independent, coed. ***Awards:*** bachelor's degrees. 35 undergraduate majors. ***Total enrollment:*** 1,680. Undergraduates: 1,680. Freshmen: 543. Institutional methodology is used as a basis for awarding need-based institutional aid.

UNDERGRADUATE EXPENSES for 2008–09 ***Application fee:*** $50. ***Comprehensive fee:*** $45,710 includes full-time tuition ($36,750), mandatory fees ($160), and room and board ($8800). ***College room only:*** $4400. Full-time tuition and fees vary according to course load. ***Part-time tuition:*** $1148 per credit hour. ***Part-time fees:*** $160 per year. Part-time tuition and fees vary according to course load. ***Payment plan:*** Installment.

FRESHMAN FINANCIAL AID (Fall 2008, est.) 454 applied for aid; of those 77% were deemed to have need. 100% of freshmen with need received aid; of those 27% had need fully met. ***Average percent of need met:*** 84% (excluding resources awarded to replace EFC). ***Average financial aid package:*** $25,675 (excluding resources awarded to replace EFC). 27% of all full-time freshmen had no need and received non-need-based gift aid.

UNDERGRADUATE FINANCIAL AID (Fall 2008, est.) 1,347 applied for aid; of those 81% were deemed to have need. 100% of undergraduates with need received aid; of those 24% had need fully met. ***Average percent of need met:*** 80% (excluding resources awarded to replace EFC). ***Average financial aid package:*** $25,921 (excluding resources awarded to replace EFC). 26% of all full-time undergraduates had no need and received non-need-based gift aid.

GIFT AID (NEED-BASED) ***Total amount:*** $18,226,146 (6% federal, 7% state, 87% institutional). ***Receiving aid:*** Freshmen: 64% (347); all full-time undergraduates: 66% (1,091). ***Average award:*** Freshmen: $22,007; Undergraduates: $21,203. ***Scholarships, grants, and awards:*** Federal Pell, FSEOG, state, private, college/university gift aid from institutional funds.

GIFT AID (NON-NEED-BASED) ***Total amount:*** $8,993,769 (2% federal, 90% institutional, 8% external sources). ***Receiving aid:*** Freshmen: 14% (74). Undergraduates: 10% (172). ***Average award:*** Freshmen: $13,562. Undergraduates: $12,524. ***Scholarships, grants, and awards by category:*** *Academic interests/achievement:* 471 awards ($7,822,900 total): general academic interests/achievements. *Creative arts/performance:* 3 awards ($75,000 total): creative writing. *Special achievements/activities:* 406 awards ($4,379,250 total): leadership. *Special characteristics:* 176 awards ($1,021,074 total): children and siblings of alumni, children of faculty/staff, international students, siblings of current students. ***Tuition waivers:*** Full or partial for employees or children of employees, senior citizens.

LOANS ***Student loans:*** $11,141,042 (100% need-based). 75% of past graduating class borrowed through all loan programs. *Average indebtedness per student:* $21,171. ***Average need-based loan:*** Freshmen: $3832. Undergraduates: $4829. ***Parent loans:*** $2,519,759 (100% need-based). ***Programs:*** FFEL (Subsidized and Unsubsidized Stafford, PLUS), Perkins.

WORK-STUDY ***Federal work-study:*** Total amount: $1,218,800; 722 jobs averaging $1761.

APPLYING FOR FINANCIAL AID ***Required financial aid forms:*** FAFSA, institution's own form, CSS Financial Aid PROFILE. ***Financial aid deadline:*** 2/15 (priority: 2/15). ***Notification date:*** 4/1. Students must reply by 5/1.

CONTACT Ms. Suzanne B. Sparrow, Director of Student Financial Services, Ursinus College, PO Box 1000, Collegeville, PA 19426-1000, 610-409-3600 Ext. 2242. *Fax:* 610-409-3662. *E-mail:* ssparrow@ursinus.edu.

URSULINE COLLEGE

Pepper Pike, OH

Tuition & fees: $22,060 **Average undergraduate aid package: $15,758**

ABOUT THE INSTITUTION Independent Roman Catholic, undergraduate: women only; graduate: coed. ***Awards:*** bachelor's and master's degrees and post-bachelor's and post-master's certificates (applications from men are also accepted). 45 undergraduate majors. ***Total enrollment:*** 1,426. Undergraduates: 1,103. Freshmen: 113. Federal methodology is used as a basis for awarding need-based institutional aid.

UNDERGRADUATE EXPENSES for 2008–09 ***Application fee:*** $25. ***Comprehensive fee:*** $29,410 includes full-time tuition ($21,840), mandatory fees ($220), and room and board ($7350). ***College room only:*** $3756. Full-time tuition and fees vary according to location. Room and board charges vary according to board plan and housing facility. ***Part-time tuition:*** $728 per credit. ***Part-time fees:*** $140 per term. Part-time tuition and fees vary according to location. ***Payment plan:*** Installment.

FRESHMAN FINANCIAL AID (Fall 2007) 96 applied for aid; of those 90% were deemed to have need. 100% of freshmen with need received aid; of those 21% had need fully met. ***Average percent of need met:*** 87% (excluding resources awarded to replace EFC). ***Average financial aid package:*** $18,962 (excluding resources awarded to replace EFC). 21% of all full-time freshmen had no need and received non-need-based gift aid.

UNDERGRADUATE FINANCIAL AID (Fall 2007) 612 applied for aid; of those 93% were deemed to have need. 100% of undergraduates with need received aid; of those 22% had need fully met. ***Average percent of need met:*** 73% (excluding resources awarded to replace EFC). ***Average financial aid package:*** $15,758 (excluding resources awarded to replace EFC). 15% of all full-time undergraduates had no need and received non-need-based gift aid.

GIFT AID (NEED-BASED) ***Total amount:*** $6,602,902 (24% federal, 18% state, 53% institutional, 5% external sources). ***Receiving aid:*** Freshmen: 78% (86); all full-time undergraduates: 82% (549). ***Average award:*** Freshmen: $13,674; Undergraduates: $10,168. ***Scholarships, grants, and awards:*** Federal Pell, FSEOG, state, private, college/university gift aid from institutional funds, United Negro College Fund.

GIFT AID (NON-NEED-BASED) ***Total amount:*** $518,513 (14% state, 79% institutional, 7% external sources). ***Average award:*** Freshmen: $8343. Undergraduates: $8159. ***Scholarships, grants, and awards by category:*** *Academic interests/achievement:* general academic interests/achievements. *Special achievements/activities:* community service, leadership. *Special characteristics:* children and siblings of alumni, children of faculty/staff, relatives of clergy, religious affiliation, siblings of current students. ***Tuition waivers:*** Full or partial for employees or children of employees. ***ROTC:*** Army cooperative.

LOANS ***Student loans:*** $9,451,864 (78% need-based, 22% non-need-based). 28% of past graduating class borrowed through all loan programs. *Average indebtedness per student:* $21,294. ***Average need-based loan:*** Freshmen: $4615. Undergraduates: $5684. ***Parent loans:*** $352,415 (51% need-based, 49% non-need-based). ***Programs:*** FFEL (Subsidized and Unsubsidized Stafford, PLUS), Perkins, college/university.

WORK-STUDY ***Federal work-study:*** Total amount: $285,220; jobs available.

ATHLETIC AWARDS Total amount: $361,867 (81% need-based, 19% non-need-based).

APPLYING FOR FINANCIAL AID ***Required financial aid forms:*** FAFSA, institution's own form. ***Financial aid deadline (priority):*** 3/1. ***Notification date:*** Continuous beginning 4/1. Students must reply within 4 weeks of notification.

CONTACT Ms. Mary Lynn Perri, Director of Financial Aid and Enrollment Services, Ursuline College, 2550 Lander Road, Pepper Pike, OH 44124-4398, 440-646-8330 or toll-free 888-URSULINE. *Fax:* 440-684-6114. *E-mail:* mperri@ursuline.edu.

UTAH STATE UNIVERSITY

Logan, UT

Tuition & fees (UT res): $4445 **Average undergraduate aid package: $7077**

ABOUT THE INSTITUTION State-supported, coed. ***Awards:*** associate, bachelor's, master's, and doctoral degrees and post-bachelor's and post-master's certificates. 118 undergraduate majors. ***Total enrollment:*** 15,099. Undergraduates: 13,394. Freshmen: 2,762. Federal methodology is used as a basis for awarding need-based institutional aid.

UNDERGRADUATE EXPENSES for 2008–09 ***Application fee:*** $40. ***Tuition, state resident:*** full-time $3832. ***Tuition, nonresident:*** full-time $12,338. ***Required fees:*** full-time $613. Full-time tuition and fees vary according to course load, program, and student level. Part-time tuition and fees vary according to course load, program, and student level. ***College room and board:*** $4650; ***Room only:*** $1650. Room and board charges vary according to board plan and housing facility. ***Payment plan:*** Deferred payment.

FRESHMAN FINANCIAL AID (Fall 2008, est.) 1,247 applied for aid; of those 72% were deemed to have need. 97% of freshmen with need received aid; of those 16% had need fully met. ***Average percent of need met:*** 61% (excluding resources awarded to replace EFC). ***Average financial aid package:*** $7395 (excluding resources awarded to replace EFC). 27% of all full-time freshmen had no need and received non-need-based gift aid.

UNDERGRADUATE FINANCIAL AID (Fall 2008, est.) 6,286 applied for aid; of those 85% were deemed to have need. 96% of undergraduates with need received aid; of those 10% had need fully met. ***Average percent of need met:*** 56% (excluding resources awarded to replace EFC). ***Average financial aid package:*** $7077 (excluding resources awarded to replace EFC). 18% of all full-time undergraduates had no need and received non-need-based gift aid.

GIFT AID (NEED-BASED) ***Total amount:*** $16,233,491 (98% federal, 2% state). ***Receiving aid:*** Freshmen: 18% (453); all full-time undergraduates: 32% (3,562). ***Average award:*** Freshmen: $3800; Undergraduates: $4004. ***Scholarships, grants, and awards:*** Federal Pell, FSEOG, state, private, college/university gift aid from institutional funds.

GIFT AID (NON-NEED-BASED) ***Total amount:*** $15,473,307 (69% institutional, 31% external sources). ***Receiving aid:*** Freshmen: 19% (472). Undergraduates: 10% (1,010). ***Average award:*** Freshmen: $2322. Undergraduates: $2642. ***Scholarships, grants, and awards by category:*** *Academic interests/achievement:* agriculture, architecture, biological sciences, business, communication, computer science, education, engineering/technologies, English, foreign languages, general academic interests/achievements, health fields, home economics, humanities, international studies, library science, mathematics, physical sciences, premedicine, social sciences. *Creative arts/performance:* applied art and design, art/fine arts, general creative arts/performance, journalism/publications, music, performing arts, theater/drama. *Special characteristics:* children and siblings of alumni, children of faculty/staff, international students. ***Tuition waivers:*** Full or partial for minority students, children of alumni, employees or children of employees, adult students, senior citizens. ***ROTC:*** Army, Air Force.

LOANS ***Student loans:*** $21,307,702 (65% need-based, 35% non-need-based). ***Average need-based loan:*** Freshmen: $3240. Undergraduates: $4175. ***Parent loans:*** $393,746 (100% non-need-based). ***Programs:*** FFEL (Subsidized and Unsubsidized Stafford, PLUS), Perkins, college/university.

WORK-STUDY ***Federal work-study:*** Total amount: $600,000; 427 jobs averaging $3300. ***State or other work-study/employment:*** Total amount: $621,400 (100% need-based). 272 part-time jobs averaging $3300.

ATHLETIC AWARDS Total amount: $1,406,425 (100% non-need-based).

APPLYING FOR FINANCIAL AID ***Required financial aid form:*** FAFSA. ***Financial aid deadline:*** Continuous. ***Notification date:*** Continuous beginning 4/1. Students must reply within 4 weeks of notification.

CONTACT Tamara Allen, Associate Director of Financial Aid, Utah State University, Old Main Hill, Logan, UT 84322, 435-797-3369 or toll-free 800-488-8108. *Fax:* 435-797-0654. *E-mail:* tamara.allen@usu.edu.

UTAH VALLEY UNIVERSITY

Orem, UT

Tuition & fees (UT res): $3752 **Average undergraduate aid package: $7090**

ABOUT THE INSTITUTION State-supported, coed. ***Awards:*** associate, bachelor's, and master's degrees. 91 undergraduate majors. ***Total enrollment:*** 26,696. Undergraduates: 26,676. Freshmen: 3,697. Both federal and institutional methodology are used as a basis for awarding need-based institutional aid.

UNDERGRADUATE EXPENSES for 2008–09 ***Application fee:*** $35. ***Tuition, state resident:*** full-time $3188; part-time $133 per credit. ***Tuition, nonresident:*** full-time $10,950; part-time $456 per credit. ***Required fees:*** full-time $564; $564 per year. Full-time tuition and fees vary according to course load. Part-time tuition and fees vary according to course load. Room and board charges vary according to housing facility. ***Payment plans:*** Installment, deferred payment.

FRESHMAN FINANCIAL AID (Fall 2008, est.) 1,161 applied for aid; of those 86% were deemed to have need. 89% of freshmen with need received aid; of those 4% had need fully met. ***Average percent of need met:*** 64% (excluding resources awarded to replace EFC). ***Average financial aid package:*** $5944 (excluding resources awarded to replace EFC). 1% of all full-time freshmen had no need and received non-need-based gift aid.

UNDERGRADUATE FINANCIAL AID (Fall 2008, est.) 7,219 applied for aid; of those 92% were deemed to have need. 92% of undergraduates with need received aid; of those 5% had need fully met. ***Average percent of need met:*** 86% (excluding resources awarded to replace EFC). ***Average financial aid package:*** $7090 (excluding resources awarded to replace EFC). 1% of all full-time undergraduates had no need and received non-need-based gift aid.

GIFT AID (NEED-BASED) ***Total amount:*** $22,264,347 (97% federal, 1% state, 2% external sources). ***Receiving aid:*** Freshmen: 28% (669); all full-time undergraduates: 36% (4,538). ***Average award:*** Freshmen: $4104; Undergraduates: $4177. ***Scholarships, grants, and awards:*** Federal Pell, FSEOG, state, private, college/university gift aid from institutional funds.

GIFT AID (NON-NEED-BASED) ***Total amount:*** $535,060 (7% federal, 17% state, 17% institutional, 59% external sources). ***Average award:*** Freshmen: $3709. Undergraduates: $3692. ***Tuition waivers:*** Full or partial for employees or children of employees. ***ROTC:*** Army, Air Force cooperative.

LOANS ***Student loans:*** $50,509,624 (92% need-based, 8% non-need-based). 66% of past graduating class borrowed through all loan programs. *Average indebtedness per student:* $13,714. ***Average need-based loan:*** Freshmen: $3397. Undergraduates: $4354. ***Parent loans:*** $407,616 (67% need-based, 33% non-need-based). ***Programs:*** FFEL (Subsidized and Unsubsidized Stafford, PLUS), Perkins, state, college/university.

WORK-STUDY ***Federal work-study:*** Total amount: $829,820; jobs available. ***State or other work-study/employment:*** Total amount: $983,627 (95% need-based, 5% non-need-based). Part-time jobs available.

ATHLETIC AWARDS Total amount: $815,926 (32% need-based, 68% non-need-based).

APPLYING FOR FINANCIAL AID ***Required financial aid forms:*** FAFSA, institution's own form. ***Financial aid deadline (priority):*** 5/1. ***Notification date:*** Continuous beginning 5/15. Students must reply by 6/15.

CONTACT Mr. Michael H. Johnson, Director of Financial Aid, Utah Valley University, Mail Code—164, 800 West 1200 South Street, Orem, UT 84058-0001, 801-222-8442. *Fax:* 801-222-8448.

U.T.A. MESIVTA OF KIRYAS JOEL

Monroe, NY

CONTACT Financial Aid Office, U.T.A. Mesivta of Kiryas Joel, 9 Nickelsburg Road Unit 312, Monroe, NY 10950, 845-873-9901.

UTICA COLLEGE

Utica, NY

Tuition & fees: $26,058 **Average undergraduate aid package: $19,490**

ABOUT THE INSTITUTION Independent, coed. ***Awards:*** bachelor's, master's, and first professional degrees and post-bachelor's certificates. 46 undergraduate majors. ***Total enrollment:*** 3,101. Undergraduates: 2,502. Freshmen: 574. Federal methodology is used as a basis for awarding need-based institutional aid.

UNDERGRADUATE EXPENSES for 2008–09 ***Application fee:*** $40. ***Comprehensive fee:*** $36,488 includes full-time tuition ($25,538), mandatory fees ($520), and room and board ($10,430). Full-time tuition and fees vary according to class time and course load. Room and board charges vary according to board plan and housing facility. ***Part-time tuition:*** $862 per hour. Part-time tuition and fees vary according to class time and course load. ***Payment plans:*** Installment, deferred payment.

FRESHMAN FINANCIAL AID (Fall 2008, est.) 528 applied for aid; of those 94% were deemed to have need. 100% of freshmen with need received aid; of those 14% had need fully met. ***Average percent of need met:*** 74% (excluding resources awarded to replace EFC). ***Average financial aid package:*** $21,669 (excluding resources awarded to replace EFC). 7% of all full-time freshmen had no need and received non-need-based gift aid.

UNDERGRADUATE FINANCIAL AID (Fall 2008, est.) 1,896 applied for aid; of those 94% were deemed to have need. 99% of undergraduates with need received aid; of those 13% had need fully met. ***Average percent of need met:*** 69% (excluding resources awarded to replace EFC). ***Average financial aid package:*** $19,490 (excluding resources awarded to replace EFC). 7% of all full-time undergraduates had no need and received non-need-based gift aid.

GIFT AID (NEED-BASED) ***Total amount:*** $25,653,774 (13% federal, 13% state, 72% institutional, 2% external sources). ***Receiving aid:*** Freshmen: 91% (492); all full-time undergraduates: 89% (1,757). ***Average award:*** Freshmen: $10,042; Undergraduates: $8400. ***Scholarships, grants, and awards:*** Federal Pell, FSEOG, state, private, college/university gift aid from institutional funds, Federal Nursing.

GIFT AID (NON-NEED-BASED) ***Total amount:*** $2,009,228 (95% institutional, 5% external sources). ***Receiving aid:*** Freshmen: 6% (31). Undergraduates: 6% (110). ***Average award:*** Freshmen: $11,913. Undergraduates: $9466. ***Scholarships, grants, and awards by category:*** *Academic interests/achievement:* general academic interests/achievements. ***Tuition waivers:*** Full or partial for employees or children of employees, senior citizens. ***ROTC:*** Army, Air Force cooperative.

LOANS ***Student loans:*** $13,708,425 (92% need-based, 8% non-need-based). 86% of past graduating class borrowed through all loan programs. *Average indebtedness per student:* $31,899. ***Average need-based loan:*** Freshmen: $3404. Undergraduates: $4308. ***Parent loans:*** $4,074,863 (96% need-based, 4% non-need-based). ***Programs:*** Federal Direct (Subsidized and Unsubsidized Stafford, PLUS), Perkins.

WORK-STUDY ***Federal work-study:*** Total amount: $731,916; jobs available. ***State or other work-study/employment:*** Part-time jobs available.

APPLYING FOR FINANCIAL AID ***Required financial aid form:*** FAFSA. ***Financial aid deadline (priority):*** 2/15. ***Notification date:*** Continuous. Students must reply by 5/1 or within 4 weeks of notification.

CONTACT Laura Bedford, Director of Student Financial Services, Utica College, 1600 Burrstone Road, Utica, NY 13502-4892, 315-792-3179 or toll-free 800-782-8884. *Fax:* 315-792-3368. *E-mail:* lbedford@utica.edu.

VALDOSTA STATE UNIVERSITY

Valdosta, GA

Tuition & fees (GA res): $4158 **Average undergraduate aid package: $8213**

ABOUT THE INSTITUTION State-supported, coed. ***Awards:*** associate, bachelor's, master's, and doctoral degrees and post-master's certificates. 50 undergraduate majors. ***Total enrollment:*** 11,490. Undergraduates: 9,708. Freshmen: 2,143. Federal methodology is used as a basis for awarding need-based institutional aid.

UNDERGRADUATE EXPENSES for 2008–09 ***Application fee:*** $40. ***Tuition, state resident:*** full-time $2898; part-time $121 per hour. ***Tuition, nonresident:*** full-time $11,590; part-time $483 per hour. ***Required fees:*** full-time $1260. ***College room and board:*** $6230; ***Room only:*** $3100.

FRESHMAN FINANCIAL AID (Fall 2008, est.) 1,766 applied for aid; of those 74% were deemed to have need. 97% of freshmen with need received aid; of those 15% had need fully met. ***Average percent of need met:*** 55% (excluding resources awarded to replace EFC). ***Average financial aid package:*** $6923 (excluding resources awarded to replace EFC). 1% of all full-time freshmen had no need and received non-need-based gift aid.

UNDERGRADUATE FINANCIAL AID (Fall 2008, est.) 6,247 applied for aid; of those 77% were deemed to have need. 100% of undergraduates with need received aid; of those 15% had need fully met. ***Average percent of need met:*** 61% (excluding resources awarded to replace EFC). ***Average financial aid package:*** $8213 (excluding resources awarded to replace EFC). 1% of all full-time undergraduates had no need and received non-need-based gift aid.

GIFT AID (NEED-BASED) ***Total amount:*** $19,163,339 (55% federal, 41% state, 1% institutional, 3% external sources). ***Receiving aid:*** Freshmen: 48% (1,005); all full-time undergraduates: 44% (3,627). ***Average award:*** Freshmen: $5969; Undergraduates: $5252. ***Scholarships, grants, and awards:*** Federal Pell, FSEOG, state, private, college/university gift aid from institutional funds.

GIFT AID (NON-NEED-BASED) ***Total amount:*** $3,462,897 (90% state, 3% institutional, 7% external sources). ***Receiving aid:*** Freshmen: 1% (23). Undergraduates: 3% (233). ***Average award:*** Freshmen: $1376. Undergraduates: $1471. ***Scholarships, grants, and awards by category:*** *Academic interests/achievement:* 354 awards ($165,500 total): biological sciences, business, communication, computer science, education, engineering/technologies, English, foreign languages, general academic interests/achievements, health fields, humanities, library science, mathematics, military science, physical sciences, premedicine, social sciences. *Creative arts/performance:* 65 awards ($50,000 total): art/fine arts, music, theater/drama. *Special achievements/activities:* 80 awards ($65,000 total): community service, general special achievements/activities, hobbies/interests. *Special characteristics:* 36 awards ($32,200 total): children of public servants, general special characteristics, international students, members of minority groups. ***ROTC:*** Air Force.

LOANS ***Student loans:*** $42,631,862 (70% need-based, 30% non-need-based). 62% of past graduating class borrowed through all loan programs. *Average indebtedness per student:* $16,795. ***Average need-based loan:*** Freshmen: $3247. Undergraduates: $3855. ***Parent loans:*** $33,602,887 (28% need-based, 72% non-need-based). ***Programs:*** Federal Direct (Subsidized and Unsubsidized Stafford, PLUS), college/university.

WORK-STUDY ***Federal work-study:*** Total amount: $436,802; 267 jobs averaging $2210.

ATHLETIC AWARDS Total amount: $561,318 (84% need-based, 16% non-need-based).

APPLYING FOR FINANCIAL AID ***Required financial aid form:*** FAFSA. ***Financial aid deadline (priority):*** 5/1. ***Notification date:*** Continuous beginning 5/15.

CONTACT Mr. Douglas R. Tanner, Director of Financial Aid, Valdosta State University, 1500 North Patterson Street, Valdosta, GA 31698, 229-333-5935 or toll-free 800-618-1878 Ext. 1. *Fax:* 229-333-5430.

VALLEY CITY STATE UNIVERSITY

Valley City, ND

Tuition & fees (ND res): $5781 **Average undergraduate aid package: $5831**

ABOUT THE INSTITUTION State-supported, coed. ***Awards:*** bachelor's and master's degrees. 40 undergraduate majors. ***Total enrollment:*** 1,019. Undergraduates: 900. Freshmen: 159. Federal methodology is used as a basis for awarding need-based institutional aid.

UNDERGRADUATE EXPENSES for 2008–09 ***Application fee:*** $35. ***Tuition, state resident:*** full-time $4138; part-time $137.93 per semester hour. ***Tuition, nonresident:*** full-time $11,048; part-time $368.27 per semester hour. ***Required fees:*** full-time $1643; $68.44 per semester hour. Full-time tuition and fees vary according to course load, location, program, and reciprocity agreements. Part-time tuition and fees vary according to course load, location, program, and reciprocity agreements. ***College room and board:*** $4071; ***Room only:*** $1592. Room and board charges vary according to board plan and housing facility.

FRESHMAN FINANCIAL AID (Fall 2008, est.) 160 applied for aid; of those 100% were deemed to have need. 100% of freshmen with need received aid; of those 34% had need fully met. ***Average percent of need met:*** 88% (excluding resources awarded to replace EFC). ***Average financial aid package:*** $5877 (excluding resources awarded to replace EFC).

UNDERGRADUATE FINANCIAL AID (Fall 2008, est.) 593 applied for aid; of those 100% were deemed to have need. 99% of undergraduates with need received aid; of those 27% had need fully met. ***Average percent of need met:*** 66% (excluding resources awarded to replace EFC). ***Average financial aid package:*** $5831 (excluding resources awarded to replace EFC).

GIFT AID (NEED-BASED) ***Total amount:*** $1,361,356 (62% federal, 6% state, 21% institutional, 11% external sources). ***Receiving aid:*** Freshmen: 77% (127); all full-time undergraduates: 61% (394). ***Average award:*** Freshmen: $3297; Undergraduates: $3169. ***Scholarships, grants, and awards:*** Federal Pell, FSEOG, state, private, college/university gift aid from institutional funds.

GIFT AID (NON-NEED-BASED) ***Total amount:*** $320,636 (2% federal, 1% state, 68% institutional, 29% external sources). ***Receiving aid:*** Freshmen: 15% (25). Undergraduates: 10% (64). ***Scholarships, grants, and awards by category:*** *Academic interests/achievement:* biological sciences, business, communication, computer science, education, English, general academic interests/achievements, humanities, library science, mathematics, physical sciences, social sciences. *Creative arts/performance:* applied art and design, art/fine arts, journalism/publications, music, theater/drama. *Special achievements/activities:* general special achievements/activities. *Special characteristics:* children of faculty/staff, ethnic background, general special characteristics, international students, members of minority groups. ***Tuition waivers:*** Full or partial for children of alumni, employees or children of employees.

LOANS ***Student loans:*** $3,572,027 (54% need-based, 46% non-need-based). 83% of past graduating class borrowed through all loan programs. *Average indebtedness per student:* $20,627. ***Average need-based loan:*** Freshmen: $2477. Undergraduates: $3375. ***Parent loans:*** $40,833 (1% need-based, 99% non-need-based). ***Programs:*** FFEL (Subsidized and Unsubsidized Stafford, PLUS), Perkins, college/university.

WORK-STUDY ***Federal work-study:*** Total amount: $84,748; 52 jobs averaging $1653. ***State or other work-study/employment:*** Part-time jobs available.

ATHLETIC AWARDS Total amount: $149,107 (31% need-based, 69% non-need-based).

APPLYING FOR FINANCIAL AID ***Required financial aid form:*** FAFSA. ***Financial aid deadline (priority):*** 3/15. ***Notification date:*** Continuous. Students must reply within 4 weeks of notification.

CONTACT Betty Kuss Schumacher, Director of Student Financial Aid, Valley City State University, 101 College Street SW, Valley City, ND 58072, 701-845-7412 or toll-free 800-532-8641 Ext. 37101. *Fax:* 701-845-7410. *E-mail:* betty.schumacher@vcsu.edu.

VALLEY FORGE CHRISTIAN COLLEGE

Phoenixville, PA

Tuition & fees: $13,940 **Average undergraduate aid package: $8934**

ABOUT THE INSTITUTION Independent Assemblies of God, coed. 6 undergraduate majors. Federal methodology is used as a basis for awarding need-based institutional aid.

UNDERGRADUATE EXPENSES for 2008–09 ***One-time required fee:*** $55. ***Comprehensive fee:*** $20,930 includes full-time tuition ($12,040), mandatory fees ($1900), and room and board ($6990). ***College room only:*** $3420. Full-time tuition and fees vary according to course load and location. Room and board charges vary according to board plan and housing facility. ***Part-time tuition:*** $464 per credit. ***Part-time fees:*** $1450 per term. Part-time tuition and fees vary according to course load and location. ***Payment plan:*** Installment.

FRESHMAN FINANCIAL AID (Fall 2008, est.) 179 applied for aid; of those 87% were deemed to have need. 99% of freshmen with need received aid; of those 15% had need fully met. ***Average percent of need met:*** 51% (excluding resources awarded to replace EFC). ***Average financial aid package:*** $8055 (excluding resources awarded to replace EFC). 50% of all full-time freshmen had no need and received non-need-based gift aid.

UNDERGRADUATE FINANCIAL AID (Fall 2008, est.) 782 applied for aid; of those 91% were deemed to have need. 99% of undergraduates with need received aid; of those 12% had need fully met. ***Average percent of need met:*** 54% (excluding resources awarded to replace EFC). ***Average financial aid package:*** $8934 (excluding resources awarded to replace EFC). 23% of all full-time undergraduates had no need and received non-need-based gift aid.

GIFT AID (NEED-BASED) ***Total amount:*** $3,899,720 (33% federal, 16% state, 41% institutional, 10% external sources). ***Receiving aid:*** Freshmen: 45% (148); all full-time undergraduates: 69% (657). ***Average award:*** Freshmen: $5444; Undergraduates: $5648. ***Scholarships, grants, and awards:*** Federal Pell, FSEOG, state, private, college/university gift aid from institutional funds.

GIFT AID (NON-NEED-BASED) ***Total amount:*** $663,068 (85% institutional, 15% external sources). ***Receiving aid:*** Freshmen: 5% (16). Undergraduates: 4% (37). ***Average award:*** Freshmen: $1897. Undergraduates: $2389. ***Scholarships, grants, and awards by category:*** *Academic interests/achievement:* 234 awards ($492,877 total): general academic interests/achievements, social sciences. *Creative arts/performance:* 370 awards ($693,911 total): art/fine arts, music. *Special achievements/activities:* 375 awards ($347,986 total): community service, general special achievements/activities, leadership, religious involvement. *Special characteristics:* 260 awards ($380,675 total): children of current students, children of faculty/staff, general special characteristics, local/state students, married students, relatives of clergy, siblings of current students, spouses of current students. ***Tuition waivers:*** Full or partial for employees or children of employees.

LOANS ***Student loans:*** $7,827,851 (75% need-based, 25% non-need-based). 96% of past graduating class borrowed through all loan programs. *Average indebtedness per student:* $36,746. ***Average need-based loan:*** Freshmen: $3157. Undergraduates: $3953. ***Parent loans:*** $1,926,701 (49% need-based, 51% non-need-based). ***Programs:*** FFEL (Subsidized and Unsubsidized Stafford, PLUS), Perkins.

WORK-STUDY ***Federal work-study:*** Total amount: $66,425; 51 jobs averaging $1302.

APPLYING FOR FINANCIAL AID ***Required financial aid form:*** FAFSA. ***Financial aid deadline (priority):*** 5/1. ***Notification date:*** Continuous. Students must reply within 3 weeks of notification.

CONTACT Mrs. Linda Stein, Director of Financial Aid, Valley Forge Christian College, 1401 Charlestown Road, Phoenixville, PA 19460-2399, 610-917-1416 or toll-free 800-432-8322. *Fax:* 610-917-2069. *E-mail:* listein@vfcc.edu.

VALLEY FORGE CHRISTIAN COLLEGE–WOODBRIDGE CAMPUS

Woodbridge, VA

CONTACT Financial Aid Office, Valley Forge Christian College–Woodbridge Campus, 13909 Smoketown Road, Woodbridge, VA 22192, 703-580-4810.

VALPARAISO UNIVERSITY

Valparaiso, IN

Tuition & fees: $26,950 **Average undergraduate aid package: $24,061**

ABOUT THE INSTITUTION Independent religious, coed. ***Awards:*** associate, bachelor's, master's, doctoral, and first professional degrees and post-bachelor's and post-master's certificates. 88 undergraduate majors. ***Total enrollment:*** 3,976. Undergraduates: 2,881. Freshmen: 657. Federal methodology is used as a basis for awarding need-based institutional aid.

UNDERGRADUATE EXPENSES for 2008–09 ***Application fee:*** $30. ***Comprehensive fee:*** $34,570 includes full-time tuition ($26,070), mandatory fees ($880), and room and board ($7620). ***College room only:*** $4680. Room and board charges vary according to housing facility and student level. ***Part-time tuition:*** $1205 per credit hour. ***Part-time fees:*** $25 per credit hour. Part-time tuition and fees vary according to course load. ***Payment plans:*** Installment, deferred payment.

FRESHMAN FINANCIAL AID (Fall 2007) 657 applied for aid; of those 83% were deemed to have need. 100% of freshmen with need received aid; of those 26% had need fully met. ***Average percent of need met:*** 86% (excluding resources awarded to replace EFC). ***Average financial aid package:*** $20,616 (excluding resources awarded to replace EFC). 19% of all full-time freshmen had no need and received non-need-based gift aid.

UNDERGRADUATE FINANCIAL AID (Fall 2007) 2,273 applied for aid; of those 85% were deemed to have need. 100% of undergraduates with need received aid; of those 25% had need fully met. ***Average percent of need met:*** 82% (excluding resources awarded to replace EFC). ***Average financial aid package:*** $24,061 (excluding resources awarded to replace EFC). 23% of all full-time undergraduates had no need and received non-need-based gift aid.

GIFT AID (NEED-BASED) ***Total amount:*** $26,171,675 (10% federal, 11% state, 74% institutional, 5% external sources). ***Receiving aid:*** Freshmen: 76% (543); all full-time undergraduates: 69% (1,890). ***Average award:*** Freshmen: $16,375; Undergraduates: $14,101. ***Scholarships, grants, and awards:*** Federal Pell, FSEOG, state, private, college/university gift aid from institutional funds.

GIFT AID (NON-NEED-BASED) ***Total amount:*** $7,190,898 (1% federal, 88% institutional, 11% external sources). ***Receiving aid:*** Freshmen: 12% (88). Undergraduates: 9% (247). ***Average award:*** Freshmen: $9145. Undergraduates: $8586. ***Scholarships, grants, and awards by category:*** *Academic interests/achievement:* 1,900 awards ($14,000,000 total): business, engineering/technologies, foreign languages, general academic interests/achievements, health fields, physical sciences, religion/biblical studies. *Creative arts/performance:* 200 awards ($210,000 total): art/fine arts, music, performing arts, theater/drama. *Special achievements/activities:* 400 awards ($1,155,000 total): general special achievements/activities, religious involvement. *Special characteristics:* 1,910 awards ($4,935,000 total): children and siblings of alumni, children of faculty/staff, international students, relatives of clergy, religious affiliation. ***Tuition waivers:*** Full or partial for employees or children of employees. ***ROTC:*** Air Force cooperative.

LOANS ***Student loans:*** $16,233,681 (67% need-based, 33% non-need-based). 73% of past graduating class borrowed through all loan programs. *Average indebtedness per student:* $28,784. ***Average need-based loan:*** Freshmen: $5243. Undergraduates: $5379. ***Parent loans:*** $3,160,956 (26% need-based, 74% non-need-based). ***Programs:*** Federal Direct (Subsidized and Unsubsidized Stafford, PLUS), Perkins, college/university.

WORK-STUDY ***Federal work-study:*** Total amount: $563,830; 550 jobs averaging $2000. ***State or other work-study/employment:*** Total amount: $895,987 (10% need-based, 90% non-need-based). 650 part-time jobs averaging $2000.

ATHLETIC AWARDS Total amount: $2,579,385 (27% need-based, 73% non-need-based).

APPLYING FOR FINANCIAL AID ***Required financial aid form:*** FAFSA. ***Financial aid deadline (priority):*** 3/1. ***Notification date:*** Continuous beginning 3/1. Students must reply by 5/1.

CONTACT Mr. Robert Helgeson, Director of Financial Aid, Valparaiso University, 1700 Chapel Drive, Valparaiso, IN 46383-6493, 219-464-5015 or toll-free 888-GO-VALPO. *Fax:* 219-464-5012. *E-mail:* Robert.helgeson@valpo.edu.

VANDERBILT UNIVERSITY

Nashville, TN

Tuition & fees: $37,005 **Average undergraduate aid package: $37,553**

ABOUT THE INSTITUTION Independent, coed. ***Awards:*** bachelor's, master's, doctoral, and first professional degrees. 56 undergraduate majors. ***Total enrollment:*** 12,093. Undergraduates: 6,637. Freshmen: 1,569. Both federal and institutional methodology are used as a basis for awarding need-based institutional aid.

UNDERGRADUATE EXPENSES for 2008–09 ***Application fee:*** $50. ***Comprehensive fee:*** $49,033 includes full-time tuition ($36,100), mandatory fees ($905), and room and board ($12,028). ***College room only:*** $7828. Room and board charges vary according to board plan. ***Part-time tuition:*** $1504 per hour. ***Payment plans:*** Tuition prepayment, installment.

FRESHMAN FINANCIAL AID (Fall 2008, est.) 788 applied for aid; of those 84% were deemed to have need. 100% of freshmen with need received aid; of those 99% had need fully met. ***Average percent of need met:*** 100% (excluding resources awarded to replace EFC). ***Average financial aid package:*** $37,890 (excluding resources awarded to replace EFC). 13% of all full-time freshmen had no need and received non-need-based gift aid.

UNDERGRADUATE FINANCIAL AID (Fall 2008, est.) 2,868 applied for aid; of those 91% were deemed to have need. 100% of undergraduates with need received aid; of those 96% had need fully met. ***Average percent of need met:*** 99% (excluding resources awarded to replace EFC). ***Average financial aid package:*** $37,553 (excluding resources awarded to replace EFC). 13% of all full-time undergraduates had no need and received non-need-based gift aid.

GIFT AID (NEED-BASED) ***Total amount:*** $93,989,947 (4% federal, 3% state, 91% institutional, 2% external sources). ***Receiving aid:*** Freshmen: 38% (603); all full-time undergraduates: 37% (2,451). ***Average award:*** Freshmen: $31,711; Undergraduates: $30,416. ***Scholarships, grants, and awards:*** Federal Pell, FSEOG, state, private, college/university gift aid from institutional funds.

GIFT AID (NON-NEED-BASED) ***Total amount:*** $16,554,271 (6% state, 87% institutional, 7% external sources). ***Receiving aid:*** Freshmen: 25% (394). Undergraduates: 19% (1,274). ***Average award:*** Freshmen: $12,359. Undergraduates: $18,244. ***Scholarships, grants, and awards by category:*** *Academic interests/achievement:* 934 awards ($13,992,893 total): general academic interests/achievements. *Creative arts/performance:* 89 awards ($1,009,199 total): general creative arts/performance. *Special achievements/activities:* 278 awards ($6,983,416 total): general special achievements/activities. *Special characteristics:* 106 awards ($2,844,745 total): general special characteristics. ***Tuition waivers:*** Full or partial for employees or children of employees. ***ROTC:*** Army, Naval, Air Force cooperative.

LOANS ***Student loans:*** $14,868,196 (84% need-based, 16% non-need-based). 38% of past graduating class borrowed through all loan programs. *Average indebtedness per student:* $19,839. ***Average need-based loan:*** Freshmen: $2899. Undergraduates: $3294. ***Parent loans:*** $6,098,480 (50% need-based, 50% non-need-based). ***Programs:*** FFEL (Subsidized and Unsubsidized Stafford, PLUS), Perkins, Federal Nursing, college/university.

WORK-STUDY ***Federal work-study:*** Total amount: $1,920,711; 1,032 jobs averaging $3432.

ATHLETIC AWARDS Total amount: $9,309,092 (30% need-based, 70% non-need-based).

APPLYING FOR FINANCIAL AID ***Required financial aid forms:*** FAFSA, CSS Financial Aid PROFILE. ***Financial aid deadline (priority):*** 2/1. ***Notification date:*** 4/1. Students must reply by 5/1.

CONTACT David Mohning, Director of Financial Aid, Vanderbilt University, 2309 West End Avenue, Nashville, TN 37235, 615-322-3591 or toll-free 800-288-0432. *Fax:* 615-343-8512. *E-mail:* finaid@vanderbilt.edu.

VANDERCOOK COLLEGE OF MUSIC

Chicago, IL

CONTACT Ms. D. Denny, Director of Financial Aid, VanderCook College of Music, 3140 South Federal Street, Chicago, IL 60616-3731, 312-225-6288 Ext. 233 or toll-free 800-448-2655. *Fax:* 312-225-5211. *E-mail:* ddenny@vandercook.edu.

VANGUARD UNIVERSITY OF SOUTHERN CALIFORNIA

Costa Mesa, CA

Tuition & fees: $25,452 **Average undergraduate aid package: $16,810**

ABOUT THE INSTITUTION Independent religious, coed. ***Awards:*** bachelor's and master's degrees. 46 undergraduate majors. ***Total enrollment:*** 2,149. Undergraduates: 1,859. Freshmen: 302. Federal methodology is used as a basis for awarding need-based institutional aid.

UNDERGRADUATE EXPENSES for 2009–10 ***Application fee:*** $45. ***Comprehensive fee:*** $33,446 includes full-time tuition ($25,452) and room and board ($7994). ***College room only:*** $3936. ***Part-time tuition:*** $1039 per unit.

FRESHMAN FINANCIAL AID (Fall 2008, est.) 248 applied for aid; of those 83% were deemed to have need. 100% of freshmen with need received aid; of those 17% had need fully met. ***Average percent of need met:*** 73% (excluding resources awarded to replace EFC). ***Average financial aid package:*** $18,797 (excluding resources awarded to replace EFC). 21% of all full-time freshmen had no need and received non-need-based gift aid.

UNDERGRADUATE FINANCIAL AID (Fall 2008, est.) 1,130 applied for aid; of those 86% were deemed to have need. 100% of undergraduates with need received aid; of those 15% had need fully met. ***Average percent of need met:*** 66% (excluding resources awarded to replace EFC). ***Average financial aid package:*** $16,810 (excluding resources awarded to replace EFC). 21% of all full-time undergraduates had no need and received non-need-based gift aid.

GIFT AID (NEED-BASED) ***Total amount:*** $11,862,886 (12% federal, 20% state, 66% institutional, 2% external sources). ***Receiving aid:*** Freshmen: 63% (174); all full-time undergraduates: 62% (771). ***Average award:*** Freshmen: $9424; Undergraduates: $8998. ***Scholarships, grants, and awards:*** Federal Pell, FSEOG, state, private, college/university gift aid from institutional funds.

GIFT AID (NON-NEED-BASED) ***Total amount:*** $2,251,453 (89% institutional, 11% external sources). ***Receiving aid:*** Freshmen: 68% (188). Undergraduates: 61% (759). ***Average award:*** Freshmen: $8069. Undergraduates: $7208. ***Scholarships, grants, and awards by category:*** *Academic interests/achievement:* 860 awards ($5,397,829 total): general academic interests/achievements. *Creative arts/performance:* 281 awards ($716,744 total): debating, music, theater/drama. *Special characteristics:* 30 awards ($457,330 total): children of faculty/staff. ***ROTC:*** Air Force cooperative.

LOANS ***Student loans:*** $10,178,432 (67% need-based, 33% non-need-based). 70% of past graduating class borrowed through all loan programs. *Average indebtedness per student:* $24,741. ***Average need-based loan:*** Freshmen: $3864. Undergraduates: $4342. ***Parent loans:*** $2,277,592 (30% need-based, 70% non-need-based). ***Programs:*** FFEL (Subsidized and Unsubsidized Stafford, PLUS), Perkins.

WORK-STUDY ***Federal work-study:*** Total amount: $331,156; 130 jobs averaging $2547.

ATHLETIC AWARDS Total amount: $1,693,669 (33% need-based, 67% non-need-based).

APPLYING FOR FINANCIAL AID ***Required financial aid forms:*** FAFSA, state aid form. ***Financial aid deadline (priority):*** 3/2. ***Notification date:*** Continuous beginning 3/15. Students must reply within 3 weeks of notification.

CONTACT Undergraduate Admissions Office, Vanguard University of Southern California, 55 Fair Drive, Costa Mesa, CA 92626-6597, 800-722-6279. *Fax:* 714-966-5471. *E-mail:* admissions@vanguard.edu.

VASSAR COLLEGE

Poughkeepsie, NY

Tuition & fees: $40,210 **Average undergraduate aid package: $34,790**

ABOUT THE INSTITUTION Independent, coed. ***Awards:*** bachelor's degrees. 52 undergraduate majors. ***Total enrollment:*** 2,389. Undergraduates: 2,389. Freshmen: 638.

UNDERGRADUATE EXPENSES for 2008–09 ***Application fee:*** $60. ***Comprehensive fee:*** $49,250 includes full-time tuition ($39,635), mandatory fees ($575), and room and board ($9040). ***College room only:*** $4820. Room and board charges vary according to board plan and housing facility. ***Part-time tuition:*** $4674 per course. Part-time tuition and fees vary according to course load. ***Payment plan:*** Installment.

FRESHMAN FINANCIAL AID (Fall 2008, est.) 438 applied for aid; of those 84% were deemed to have need. 100% of freshmen with need received aid; of those 100% had need fully met. ***Average percent of need met:*** 100% (excluding resources awarded to replace EFC). ***Average financial aid package:*** $36,413 (excluding resources awarded to replace EFC).

UNDERGRADUATE FINANCIAL AID (Fall 2008, est.) 1,498 applied for aid; of those 87% were deemed to have need. 100% of undergraduates with need received aid; of those 100% had need fully met. ***Average percent of need met:*** 100% (excluding resources awarded to replace EFC). ***Average financial aid package:*** $34,790 (excluding resources awarded to replace EFC).

GIFT AID (NEED-BASED) ***Total amount:*** $38,815,525 (4% federal, 2% state, 92% institutional, 2% external sources). ***Receiving aid:*** Freshmen: 57% (365); all full-time undergraduates: 55% (1,288). ***Average award:*** Freshmen: $33,145; Undergraduates: $30,699. ***Scholarships, grants, and awards:*** Federal Pell, FSEOG, state, private, college/university gift aid from institutional funds.

GIFT AID (NON-NEED-BASED) ***Total amount:*** $198,311 (30% federal, 15% state, 55% external sources). ***Tuition waivers:*** Full or partial for employees or children of employees.

LOANS ***Student loans:*** $5,666,073 (50% need-based, 50% non-need-based). 50% of past graduating class borrowed through all loan programs. *Average indebtedness per student:* $19,910. ***Average need-based loan:*** Freshmen: $1698. Undergraduates: $2549. ***Parent loans:*** $3,001,364 (100% non-need-based). ***Programs:*** FFEL (Subsidized and Unsubsidized Stafford, PLUS), Perkins, college/university.

WORK-STUDY ***Federal work-study:*** Total amount: $1,472,782; 787 jobs averaging $1848. ***State or other work-study/employment:*** Total amount: $890,130 (100% need-based). 490 part-time jobs averaging $1853.

APPLYING FOR FINANCIAL AID ***Required financial aid forms:*** FAFSA, institution's own form, CSS Financial Aid PROFILE, state aid form, business/farm supplement. ***Financial aid deadline:*** 2/1. ***Notification date:*** 3/29. Students must reply by 5/1.

CONTACT Mr. Michael Fraher, Director of Financial Aid, Vassar College, 124 Raymond Avenue, Poughkeepsie, NY 12604, 845-437-5320 or toll-free 800-827-7270. *Fax:* 845-437-5325. *E-mail:* mafraher@vassar.edu.

VAUGHN COLLEGE OF AERONAUTICS AND TECHNOLOGY

Flushing, NY

CONTACT Sinu Jacob, Acting Director of Financial Aid, Vaughn College of Aeronautics and Technology, 8601 23rd Avenue, Flushing, NY 11369-1037, 718-429-6600 Ext. 187 or toll-free 800-776-2376 Ext. 145 (in-state).

VERMONT TECHNICAL COLLEGE

Randolph Center, VT

Tuition & fees (area res): $9984 **Average undergraduate aid package: $9900**

ABOUT THE INSTITUTION State-supported, coed. ***Awards:*** associate and bachelor's degrees. 25 undergraduate majors. ***Total enrollment:*** 1,651. Undergraduates: 1,651. Freshmen: 293. Federal methodology is used as a basis for awarding need-based institutional aid.

UNDERGRADUATE EXPENSES for 2008–09 ***Application fee:*** $37. ***One-time required fee:*** $200. ***Tuition, area resident:*** full-time $9288; part-time $387 per credit. ***Tuition, state resident:*** full-time $13,920; part-time $580 per credit.

Tuition, nonresident: full-time $17,712; part-time $738 per credit. ***Required fees:*** full-time $696; $29 per credit. ***College room and board:*** $7510.

FRESHMAN FINANCIAL AID (Fall 2008, est.) 260 applied for aid; of those 87% were deemed to have need. 100% of freshmen with need received aid; of those 18% had need fully met. ***Average percent of need met:*** 72% (excluding resources awarded to replace EFC). ***Average financial aid package:*** $8400 (excluding resources awarded to replace EFC). 1% of all full-time freshmen had no need and received non-need-based gift aid.

UNDERGRADUATE FINANCIAL AID (Fall 2008, est.) 924 applied for aid; of those 87% were deemed to have need. 99% of undergraduates with need received aid; of those 18% had need fully met. ***Average percent of need met:*** 72% (excluding resources awarded to replace EFC). ***Average financial aid package:*** $9900 (excluding resources awarded to replace EFC). 1% of all full-time undergraduates had no need and received non-need-based gift aid.

GIFT AID (NEED-BASED) ***Total amount:*** $3,555,660 (40% federal, 30% state, 12% institutional, 18% external sources). ***Receiving aid:*** Freshmen: 62% (177); all full-time undergraduates: 55% (635). ***Average award:*** Freshmen: $5305; Undergraduates: $5580. ***Scholarships, grants, and awards:*** Federal Pell, FSEOG, state, private, college/university gift aid from institutional funds.

GIFT AID (NON-NEED-BASED) ***Total amount:*** $717,611 (46% institutional, 54% external sources). ***Receiving aid:*** Freshmen: 3% (9). Undergraduates: 2% (24). ***Average award:*** Undergraduates: $6540. ***Scholarships, grants, and awards by category:*** *Academic interests/achievement:* 38 awards ($267,792 total): agriculture, general academic interests/achievements. ***ROTC:*** Army cooperative.

LOANS ***Student loans:*** $6,859,727 (70% need-based, 30% non-need-based). 80% of past graduating class borrowed through all loan programs. *Average indebtedness per student:* $25,600. ***Average need-based loan:*** Freshmen: $2840. Undergraduates: $3756. ***Parent loans:*** $2,211,305 (62% need-based, 38% non-need-based). ***Programs:*** FFEL (Subsidized and Unsubsidized Stafford, PLUS), Perkins.

WORK-STUDY ***Federal work-study:*** Total amount: $161,665; 170 jobs averaging $1200.

APPLYING FOR FINANCIAL AID ***Required financial aid forms:*** FAFSA, state aid form. ***Financial aid deadline (priority):*** 3/1. ***Notification date:*** Continuous beginning 3/19.

CONTACT Catherine R. McCullough, Director of Financial Aid, Vermont Technical College, PO Box 500, Randolph Center, VT 05061-0500, 802-728-1248 or toll-free 800-442-VTC1. *Fax:* 802-728-1390.

VILLANOVA UNIVERSITY

Villanova, PA

Tuition & fees: $37,655 **Average undergraduate aid package: $25,258**

ABOUT THE INSTITUTION Independent Roman Catholic, coed. ***Awards:*** associate, bachelor's, master's, doctoral, and first professional degrees. 45 undergraduate majors. ***Total enrollment:*** 10,275. Undergraduates: 7,161. Freshmen: 1,604. Federal methodology is used as a basis for awarding need-based institutional aid.

UNDERGRADUATE EXPENSES for 2009–10 ***Application fee:*** $75. ***Comprehensive fee:*** $47,725 includes full-time tuition ($36,950), mandatory fees ($705), and room and board ($10,070). ***College room only:*** $5330. ***Part-time tuition:*** $1540 per credit.

FRESHMAN FINANCIAL AID (Fall 2008, est.) 1,045 applied for aid; of those 72% were deemed to have need. 99% of freshmen with need received aid; of those 24% had need fully met. ***Average percent of need met:*** 84% (excluding resources awarded to replace EFC). ***Average financial aid package:*** $27,258 (excluding resources awarded to replace EFC). 6% of all full-time freshmen had no need and received non-need-based gift aid.

UNDERGRADUATE FINANCIAL AID (Fall 2008, est.) 3,662 applied for aid; of those 80% were deemed to have need. 99% of undergraduates with need received aid; of those 18% had need fully met. ***Average percent of need met:*** 81% (excluding resources awarded to replace EFC). ***Average financial aid package:*** $25,258 (excluding resources awarded to replace EFC). 6% of all full-time undergraduates had no need and received non-need-based gift aid.

GIFT AID (NEED-BASED) ***Total amount:*** $54,018,217 (8% federal, 3% state, 86% institutional, 3% external sources). ***Receiving aid:*** Freshmen: 42% (677); all full-time undergraduates: 39% (2,557). ***Average award:*** Freshmen: $23,198; Undergraduates: $20,529. ***Scholarships, grants, and awards:*** Federal Pell, FSEOG, state, private, college/university gift aid from institutional funds, endowed and restricted grants.

GIFT AID (NON-NEED-BASED) ***Total amount:*** $8,155,962 (31% federal, 59% institutional, 10% external sources). ***Receiving aid:*** Freshmen: 11% (175). Undergraduates: 11% (723). ***Average award:*** Freshmen: $9274. Undergraduates: $11,061. ***Scholarships, grants, and awards by category:*** *Academic interests/achievement:* 735 awards ($5,405,147 total): general academic interests/achievements, international studies, military science. *Special achievements/activities:* 22 awards ($21,500 total): general special achievements/activities. *Special characteristics:* 289 awards ($8,077,873 total): children of educators, children of faculty/staff, general special characteristics, members of minority groups, religious affiliation. ***ROTC:*** Army cooperative, Naval, Air Force cooperative.

LOANS ***Student loans:*** $34,265,585 (81% need-based, 19% non-need-based). 56% of past graduating class borrowed through all loan programs. *Average indebtedness per student:* $29,812. ***Average need-based loan:*** Freshmen: $3692. Undergraduates: $5014. ***Parent loans:*** $12,687,802 (70% need-based, 30% non-need-based). ***Programs:*** FFEL (Subsidized and Unsubsidized Stafford, PLUS), Perkins, Federal Nursing, Villanova Loan.

WORK-STUDY ***Federal work-study:*** Total amount: $5,572,650; 2,339 jobs averaging $2326. ***State or other work-study/employment:*** 51 part-time jobs averaging $2575.

ATHLETIC AWARDS Total amount: $8,548,056 (26% need-based, 74% non-need-based).

APPLYING FOR FINANCIAL AID ***Required financial aid forms:*** FAFSA, institution's own form, CSS Financial Aid PROFILE, W-2 forms, federal income tax forms. ***Financial aid deadline (priority):*** 2/7. ***Notification date:*** 4/1. Students must reply by 5/1.

CONTACT Bonnie Lee Behm, Director of Financial Assistance, Villanova University, 800 Lancaster Avenue, Villanova, PA 19085-1699, 610-519-4010. *Fax:* 610-519-7599.

VIRGINIA COLLEGE AT BIRMINGHAM

Birmingham, AL

CONTACT Vice President, Campus Administration, Virginia College at Birmingham, 65 Bagby Drive, Birmingham, AL 35209, 205-802-1200. *Fax:* 205-271-8273.

VIRGINIA COMMONWEALTH UNIVERSITY

Richmond, VA

Tuition & fees (VA res): $6779 **Average undergraduate aid package: $8717**

ABOUT THE INSTITUTION State-supported, coed. ***Awards:*** bachelor's, master's, doctoral, and first professional degrees and post-bachelor's, post-master's, and first professional certificates. 62 undergraduate majors. ***Total enrollment:*** 32,284. Undergraduates: 22,792. Freshmen: 3,724. Federal methodology is used as a basis for awarding need-based institutional aid.

UNDERGRADUATE EXPENSES for 2008–09 ***Application fee:*** $50. ***Tuition, state resident:*** full-time $4992; part-time $208.55 per credit. ***Tuition, nonresident:*** full-time $17,769; part-time $740.95 per credit. ***Required fees:*** full-time $1787; $73.55 per credit. ***College room and board:*** $7914; ***Room only:*** $4734. Room and board charges vary according to board plan. ***Payment plan:*** Installment.

FRESHMAN FINANCIAL AID (Fall 2007) 2,526 applied for aid; of those 68% were deemed to have need. 100% of freshmen with need received aid; of those 11% had need fully met. ***Average percent of need met:*** 69% (excluding resources awarded to replace EFC). ***Average financial aid package:*** $9309 (excluding resources awarded to replace EFC). 6% of all full-time freshmen had no need and received non-need-based gift aid.

UNDERGRADUATE FINANCIAL AID (Fall 2007) 10,440 applied for aid; of those 69% were deemed to have need. 100% of undergraduates with need received aid; of those 14% had need fully met. ***Average percent of need met:*** 67% (excluding resources awarded to replace EFC). ***Average financial aid package:*** $8717 (excluding resources awarded to replace EFC). 3% of all full-time undergraduates had no need and received non-need-based gift aid.

GIFT AID (NEED-BASED) ***Total amount:*** $35,959,488 (41% federal, 41% state, 9% institutional, 9% external sources). ***Receiving aid:*** Freshmen: 38% (1,409); all full-time undergraduates: 32% (5,816). ***Average award:*** Freshmen: $5166; Undergraduates: $4602. ***Scholarships, grants, and awards:*** Federal Pell, FSEOG, state, private, college/university gift aid from institutional funds, United Negro College Fund.

GIFT AID (NON-NEED-BASED) ***Total amount:*** $7,920,647 (9% federal, 2% state, 25% institutional, 64% external sources). ***Receiving aid:*** Freshmen: 22%

(815). Undergraduates: 10% (1,846). ***Average award:*** Freshmen: $4000. Undergraduates: $6386. ***Scholarships, grants, and awards by category:*** *Academic interests/achievement:* 2,678 awards ($6,849,144 total): biological sciences, business, computer science, education, engineering/technologies, foreign languages, general academic interests/achievements, health fields, humanities, mathematics, military science, physical sciences. *Creative arts/performance:* 437 awards ($369,607 total): art/fine arts, dance, music, performing arts, theater/drama. *Special characteristics:* 63 awards ($533,560 total): veterans' children. ***Tuition waivers:*** Full or partial for employees or children of employees, senior citizens. ***ROTC:*** Army cooperative.

LOANS ***Student loans:*** $69,090,614 (75% need-based, 25% non-need-based). 60% of past graduating class borrowed through all loan programs. ***Average need-based loan:*** Freshmen: $3965. Undergraduates: $4308. ***Parent loans:*** $9,183,558 (100% non-need-based). ***Programs:*** Federal Direct (Subsidized and Unsubsidized Stafford, PLUS), Perkins, Federal Nursing, college/university.

WORK-STUDY ***Federal work-study:*** Total amount: $561,619; 344 jobs averaging $1633. ***State or other work-study/employment:*** Total amount: $966 (100% non-need-based). Part-time jobs available.

ATHLETIC AWARDS Total amount: $3,348,532 (46% need-based, 54% non-need-based).

APPLYING FOR FINANCIAL AID ***Required financial aid form:*** FAFSA. ***Financial aid deadline (priority):*** 3/1. ***Notification date:*** Continuous beginning 4/1. Students must reply within 2 weeks of notification.

CONTACT Financial Aid Office, Virginia Commonwealth University, 901 West Franklin Street, Richmond, VA 23284-3026, 804-828-6669 or toll-free 800-841-3638. *Fax:* 804-827-0060. *E-mail:* faidmail@vcu.edu.

VIRGINIA INTERMONT COLLEGE

Bristol, VA

Tuition & fees: $24,100 **Average undergraduate aid package: $15,034**

ABOUT THE INSTITUTION Independent religious, coed. ***Awards:*** associate and bachelor's degrees. 39 undergraduate majors. ***Total enrollment:*** 549. Undergraduates: 549. Federal methodology is used as a basis for awarding need-based institutional aid.

UNDERGRADUATE EXPENSES for 2009–10 ***Application fee:*** $25. ***Comprehensive fee:*** $31,530 includes full-time tuition ($24,100) and room and board ($7430). ***Part-time tuition:*** $240 per credit.

FRESHMAN FINANCIAL AID (Fall 2008, est.) 82 applied for aid; of those 90% were deemed to have need. 100% of freshmen with need received aid; of those 14% had need fully met. ***Average percent of need met:*** 69% (excluding resources awarded to replace EFC). ***Average financial aid package:*** $17,022 (excluding resources awarded to replace EFC). 17% of all full-time freshmen had no need and received non-need-based gift aid.

UNDERGRADUATE FINANCIAL AID (Fall 2008, est.) 405 applied for aid; of those 91% were deemed to have need. 100% of undergraduates with need received aid; of those 12% had need fully met. ***Average percent of need met:*** 62% (excluding resources awarded to replace EFC). ***Average financial aid package:*** $15,034 (excluding resources awarded to replace EFC). 14% of all full-time undergraduates had no need and received non-need-based gift aid.

GIFT AID (NEED-BASED) ***Total amount:*** $3,006,489 (26% federal, 21% state, 44% institutional, 9% external sources). ***Receiving aid:*** Freshmen: 76% (74); all full-time undergraduates: 81% (352). ***Average award:*** Freshmen: $12,798; Undergraduates: $10,096. ***Scholarships, grants, and awards:*** Federal Pell, FSEOG, state, private, college/university gift aid from institutional funds.

GIFT AID (NON-NEED-BASED) ***Total amount:*** $642,932 (14% state, 85% institutional, 1% external sources). ***Receiving aid:*** Freshmen: 6% (6). Undergraduates: 4% (19). ***Average award:*** Freshmen: $7630. Undergraduates: $7736. ***Scholarships, grants, and awards by category:*** *Academic interests/achievement:* 247 awards ($1,469,894 total): general academic interests/achievements. *Creative arts/performance:* 128 awards ($169,490 total): applied art and design, art/fine arts, dance, general creative arts/performance, music, performing arts, theater/drama. *Special achievements/activities:* 8 awards ($4000 total): cheerleading/drum major. *Special characteristics:* 23 awards ($232,790 total): children of faculty/staff, first-generation college students, members of minority groups, religious affiliation.

LOANS ***Student loans:*** $3,363,335 (86% need-based, 14% non-need-based). 68% of past graduating class borrowed through all loan programs. *Average indebtedness per student:* $19,058. ***Average need-based loan:*** Freshmen: $3853. Undergraduates: $5353. ***Parent loans:*** $928,430 (41% need-based, 59% non-need-based). ***Programs:*** FFEL (Subsidized and Unsubsidized Stafford, PLUS), Perkins, alternative loans.

WORK-STUDY ***Federal work-study:*** Total amount: $160,714; 85 jobs averaging $2000. ***State or other work-study/employment:*** Total amount: $17,000 (21% need-based, 79% non-need-based). Part-time jobs available.

ATHLETIC AWARDS Total amount: $617,286 (88% need-based, 12% non-need-based).

APPLYING FOR FINANCIAL AID ***Required financial aid forms:*** FAFSA, state aid form. ***Financial aid deadline:*** 6/1 (priority: 3/1). ***Notification date:*** Continuous. Students must reply within 3 weeks of notification.

CONTACT Ms. Denise Posey, Director of Financial Aid, Virginia Intermont College, 1013 Moore Street, Bristol, VA 24201-4298, 276-466-7872 or toll-free 800-451-1842. *Fax:* 276-669-5763.

VIRGINIA INTERNATIONAL UNIVERSITY

Fairfax, VA

CONTACT Financial Aid Office, Virginia International University, 11200 Waples Mill Road, Fairfax, VA 22030, 703-591-7042 or toll-free 800-514 6848.

VIRGINIA MILITARY INSTITUTE

Lexington, VA

Tuition & fees (VA res): $10,556 **Average undergraduate aid package: $16,165**

ABOUT THE INSTITUTION State-supported, coed, primarily men. ***Awards:*** bachelor's degrees. 14 undergraduate majors. ***Total enrollment:*** 1,428. Undergraduates: 1,428. Freshmen: 392. Federal methodology is used as a basis for awarding need-based institutional aid.

UNDERGRADUATE EXPENSES for 2008–09 ***Application fee:*** $35. ***One-time required fee:*** $2155. ***Tuition, state resident:*** full-time $5262; part-time $164 per credit hour. ***Tuition, nonresident:*** full-time $22,160; part-time $551 per credit hour. ***Required fees:*** full-time $5294. ***College room and board:*** $6444. ***Payment plan:*** Installment.

FRESHMAN FINANCIAL AID (Fall 2007) 283 applied for aid; of those 69% were deemed to have need. 100% of freshmen with need received aid; of those 55% had need fully met. ***Average percent of need met:*** 91% (excluding resources awarded to replace EFC). ***Average financial aid package:*** $13,547 (excluding resources awarded to replace EFC). 14% of all full-time freshmen had no need and received non-need-based gift aid.

UNDERGRADUATE FINANCIAL AID (Fall 2007) 796 applied for aid; of those 75% were deemed to have need. 99% of undergraduates with need received aid; of those 51% had need fully met. ***Average percent of need met:*** 90% (excluding resources awarded to replace EFC). ***Average financial aid package:*** $16,165 (excluding resources awarded to replace EFC). 14% of all full-time undergraduates had no need and received non-need-based gift aid.

GIFT AID (NEED-BASED) ***Total amount:*** $4,542,268 (15% federal, 16% state, 64% institutional, 5% external sources). ***Receiving aid:*** Freshmen: 34% (147); all full-time undergraduates: 32% (452). ***Average award:*** Freshmen: $8398; Undergraduates: $10,667. ***Scholarships, grants, and awards:*** Federal Pell, FSEOG, state, private, college/university gift aid from institutional funds.

GIFT AID (NON-NEED-BASED) ***Total amount:*** $7,662,706 (82% federal, 16% institutional, 2% external sources). ***Receiving aid:*** Freshmen: 12% (53). Undergraduates: 12% (167). ***Average award:*** Freshmen: $6185. Undergraduates: $5983. ***Scholarships, grants, and awards by category:*** *Academic interests/achievement:* 100 awards ($850,000 total): biological sciences, business, computer science, engineering/technologies, English, general academic interests/achievements, international studies, mathematics, military science, premedicine. *Creative arts/performance:* 12 awards ($7500 total): music. *Special achievements/activities:* 20 awards ($75,000 total): general special achievements/activities, leadership. *Special characteristics:* 300 awards ($1,000,000 total): children and siblings of alumni, children of faculty/staff, general special characteristics, local/state students, out-of-state students. ***ROTC:*** Army, Naval, Air Force.

LOANS ***Student loans:*** $2,971,097 (38% need-based, 62% non-need-based). 52% of past graduating class borrowed through all loan programs. *Average indebtedness per student:* $19,114. ***Average need-based loan:*** Freshmen: $3358. Undergraduates: $3895. ***Parent loans:*** $1,505,488 (100% non-need-based). ***Programs:*** Federal Direct (Subsidized and Unsubsidized Stafford, PLUS), Perkins.

WORK-STUDY ***Federal work-study:*** Total amount: $5118; 32 jobs averaging $573.

ATHLETIC AWARDS Total amount: $2,440,892 (28% need-based, 72% non-need-based).

APPLYING FOR FINANCIAL AID ***Required financial aid forms:*** FAFSA, institution's own form. ***Financial aid deadline (priority):*** 3/1. ***Notification date:*** Continuous beginning 3/15. Students must reply by 5/1.

CONTACT Col. Timothy P. Golden, Director of Financial Aid, Virginia Military Institute, 306 Carroll Hall, Lexington, VA 24450, 540-464-7208 or toll-free 800-767-4207. *Fax:* 540-464-7629. *E-mail:* goldentp@vmi.edu.

VIRGINIA POLYTECHNIC INSTITUTE AND STATE UNIVERSITY

Blacksburg, VA

Tuition & fees (VA res): $8198 **Average undergraduate aid package: $10,813**

ABOUT THE INSTITUTION State-supported, coed. ***Awards:*** associate, bachelor's, master's, doctoral, and first professional degrees. 66 undergraduate majors. ***Total enrollment:*** 30,739. Undergraduates: 23,567. Freshmen: 5,460. Federal methodology is used as a basis for awarding need-based institutional aid.

UNDERGRADUATE EXPENSES for 2008–09 ***Application fee:*** $50. ***Tuition, state resident:*** full-time $6332; part-time $264 per credit hour. ***Tuition, nonresident:*** full-time $18,789; part-time $783 per credit hour. ***Required fees:*** full-time $1866. Full-time tuition and fees vary according to program. Part-time tuition and fees vary according to program. ***College room and board:*** $5476. Room and board charges vary according to board plan and location. ***Payment plan:*** Installment.

FRESHMAN FINANCIAL AID (Fall 2007) 3,687 applied for aid; of those 60% were deemed to have need. 82% of freshmen with need received aid; of those 18% had need fully met. ***Average percent of need met:*** 64% (excluding resources awarded to replace EFC). ***Average financial aid package:*** $11,609 (excluding resources awarded to replace EFC). 12% of all full-time freshmen had no need and received non-need-based gift aid.

UNDERGRADUATE FINANCIAL AID (Fall 2007) 13,597 applied for aid; of those 62% were deemed to have need. 92% of undergraduates with need received aid; of those 23% had need fully met. ***Average percent of need met:*** 72% (excluding resources awarded to replace EFC). ***Average financial aid package:*** $10,813 (excluding resources awarded to replace EFC). 9% of all full-time undergraduates had no need and received non-need-based gift aid.

GIFT AID (NEED-BASED) ***Total amount:*** $31,918,252 (30% federal, 39% state, 11% institutional, 20% external sources). ***Receiving aid:*** Freshmen: 29% (1,499); all full-time undergraduates: 29% (6,403). ***Average award:*** Freshmen: $6924; Undergraduates: $5803. ***Scholarships, grants, and awards:*** state, college/university gift aid from institutional funds.

GIFT AID (NON-NEED-BASED) ***Total amount:*** $27,176,333 (26% institutional, 74% external sources). ***Receiving aid:*** Freshmen: 8% (431). Undergraduates: 6% (1,337). ***Average award:*** Freshmen: $2562. Undergraduates: $2480. ***Scholarships, grants, and awards by category:*** *Academic interests/achievement:* library science. *Creative arts/performance:* applied art and design, art/fine arts, cinema/film/broadcasting, creative writing, journalism/publications, music, performing arts, theater/drama. *Special achievements/activities:* cheerleading/drum major, community service, general special achievements/activities, leadership, memberships, religious involvement. *Special characteristics:* children of faculty/staff, first-generation college students, local/state students, members of minority groups, out-of-state students, twins, veterans' children. ***Tuition waivers:*** Full or partial for senior citizens. ***ROTC:*** Army, Naval, Air Force.

LOANS ***Student loans:*** $61,612,408 (42% need-based, 58% non-need-based). 52% of past graduating class borrowed through all loan programs. *Average indebtedness per student:* $21,678. ***Average need-based loan:*** Freshmen: $3917. Undergraduates: $4139. ***Parent loans:*** $15,612,661 (100% non-need-based).

WORK-STUDY ***Federal work-study:*** Total amount: $877,038; 812 jobs averaging $1178. ***State or other work-study/employment:*** Total amount: $6,975,076 (100% non-need-based). 4,305 part-time jobs averaging $1685.

ATHLETIC AWARDS Total amount: $6,063,289 (39% need-based, 61% non-need-based).

APPLYING FOR FINANCIAL AID ***Required financial aid form:*** FAFSA. ***Financial aid deadline (priority):*** 3/11. ***Notification date:*** Continuous beginning 3/30. Students must reply by 5/1 or within 4 weeks of notification.

CONTACT Dr. Barry Simmons, Director, Virginia Polytechnic Institute and State University, 300 Student Service Building, Virginia Tech, Blacksburg, VA 24061, 540-231-5179. *Fax:* 540-231-9139. *E-mail:* simmonsb@vt.edu.

VIRGINIA STATE UNIVERSITY

Petersburg, VA

CONTACT Henry DeBose, Director, Virginia State University, PO Box 9031, Petersburg, VA 23806-2096, 804-524-5992 or toll-free 800-871-7611. *Fax:* 804-524-6818. *E-mail:* hedebose@vsu.edu.

VIRGINIA UNION UNIVERSITY

Richmond, VA

ABOUT THE INSTITUTION Independent Baptist, coed. 22 undergraduate majors.

GIFT AID (NEED-BASED) ***Scholarships, grants, and awards:*** Federal Pell, FSEOG, state, private, college/university gift aid from institutional funds.

GIFT AID (NON-NEED-BASED) ***Scholarships, grants, and awards by category:*** *Academic interests/achievement:* general academic interests/achievements.

LOANS ***Programs:*** Federal Direct (Subsidized and Unsubsidized Stafford), FFEL (PLUS), Perkins.

WORK-STUDY ***Federal work-study:*** Total amount: $364,736; 177 jobs averaging $1958.

APPLYING FOR FINANCIAL AID ***Required financial aid forms:*** FAFSA, state aid form.

CONTACT Mrs. Donna Mack-Tatum, Director of Financial Aid, Virginia Union University, 1500 North Lombardy Street, Richmond, VA 23220-1170, 804-257-5882 or toll-free 800-368-3227 (out-of-state). *E-mail:* dtatum@vuu.edu.

VIRGINIA UNIVERSITY OF LYNCHBURG

Lynchburg, VA

CONTACT Financial Aid Office, Virginia University of Lynchburg, 2058 Garfield Avenue, Lynchburg, VA 24501-6417, 804-528-5276.

VIRGINIA WESLEYAN COLLEGE

Norfolk, VA

Tuition & fees: $27,476 **Average undergraduate aid package: $16,935**

ABOUT THE INSTITUTION Independent United Methodist, coed. ***Awards:*** bachelor's degrees. 45 undergraduate majors. ***Total enrollment:*** 1,381. Undergraduates: 1,381. Freshmen: 359. Federal methodology is used as a basis for awarding need-based institutional aid.

UNDERGRADUATE EXPENSES for 2009–10 ***Application fee:*** $40. ***Comprehensive fee:*** $35,172 includes full-time tuition ($26,976), mandatory fees ($500), and room and board ($7696).

FRESHMAN FINANCIAL AID (Fall 2007) 327 applied for aid; of those 87% were deemed to have need. 100% of freshmen with need received aid; of those 16% had need fully met. ***Average percent of need met:*** 77% (excluding resources awarded to replace EFC). ***Average financial aid package:*** $18,953 (excluding resources awarded to replace EFC). 20% of all full-time freshmen had no need and received non-need-based gift aid.

UNDERGRADUATE FINANCIAL AID (Fall 2007) 1,033 applied for aid; of those 87% were deemed to have need. 100% of undergraduates with need received aid; of those 14% had need fully met. ***Average percent of need met:*** 71% (excluding resources awarded to replace EFC). ***Average financial aid package:*** $16,935 (excluding resources awarded to replace EFC). 24% of all full-time undergraduates had no need and received non-need-based gift aid.

GIFT AID (NEED-BASED) ***Total amount:*** $1,434,848 (89% federal, 4% state, 7% institutional). ***Receiving aid:*** Freshmen: 31% (113); all full-time undergraduates: 30% (361). ***Average award:*** Freshmen: $4005; Undergraduates: $3568. ***Scholarships, grants, and awards:*** Federal Pell, FSEOG, state, private, college/university gift aid from institutional funds, United Negro College Fund.

GIFT AID (NON-NEED-BASED) ***Total amount:*** $12,588,907 (20% state, 78% institutional, 2% external sources). ***Receiving aid:*** Freshmen: 79% (286). Undergraduates: 74% (894). ***Average award:*** Freshmen: $8059. Undergraduates: $7502. ***Scholarships, grants, and awards by category:*** *Academic interests/achievement:* general academic interests/achievements. *Creative arts/performance:*

art/fine arts, music, theater/drama. *Special achievements/activities:* community service, leadership, religious involvement. *Special characteristics:* children of faculty/staff, relatives of clergy, religious affiliation. ***ROTC:*** Army cooperative.

LOANS ***Student loans:*** $7,493,448 (46% need-based, 54% non-need-based). 71% of past graduating class borrowed through all loan programs. *Average indebtedness per student:* $25,740. ***Average need-based loan:*** Freshmen: $3950. Undergraduates: $4504. ***Parent loans:*** $3,284,159 (100% non-need-based). ***Programs:*** FFEL (Subsidized and Unsubsidized Stafford, PLUS), Perkins, alternative loans.

WORK-STUDY ***Federal work-study:*** Total amount: $144,725; 164 jobs averaging $150.

APPLYING FOR FINANCIAL AID ***Required financial aid forms:*** FAFSA, state aid form. ***Financial aid deadline (priority):*** 3/1. ***Notification date:*** Continuous. Students must reply by 5/1 or within 2 weeks of notification.

CONTACT Mrs. Angie T. Hawkins, Director of Financial Aid, Virginia Wesleyan College, 1584 Wesleyan Drive, Norfolk, VA 23502-5599, 757-455-3345 or toll-free 800-737-8684. *Fax:* 757-455-6779. *E-mail:* finaid@vwc.edu.

VITERBO UNIVERSITY

La Crosse, WI

CONTACT Ms. Terry Norman, Director of Financial Aid, Viterbo University, 900 Viterbo Drive, La Crosse, WI 54601-4797, 608-796-3900 or toll-free 800-VITERBO Ext. 3010. *Fax:* 608-796-3050. *E-mail:* twnorman@viterbo.edu.

VOORHEES COLLEGE

Denmark, SC

CONTACT Augusta L. Kitchen, Director of Financial Aid, Voorhees College, PO Box 678, Denmark, SC 29042, 803-703-7109 Ext. 7106 or toll-free 866-685-9904. *Fax:* 803-793-0831. *E-mail:* akitchen@voorhees.edu.

WABASH COLLEGE

Crawfordsville, IN

Tuition & fees: $27,950 **Average undergraduate aid package: $25,732**

ABOUT THE INSTITUTION Independent, men only. ***Awards:*** bachelor's degrees. 24 undergraduate majors. ***Total enrollment:*** 917. Undergraduates: 917. Freshmen: 253. Both federal and institutional methodology are used as a basis for awarding need-based institutional aid.

UNDERGRADUATE EXPENSES for 2008–09 ***Application fee:*** $40. ***Comprehensive fee:*** $35,350 includes full-time tuition ($27,500), mandatory fees ($450), and room and board ($7400). ***College room only:*** $3300. Full-time tuition and fees vary according to reciprocity agreements. Room and board charges vary according to board plan and housing facility. ***Part-time tuition:*** $4583 per course. Part-time tuition and fees vary according to course load and reciprocity agreements. ***Payment plans:*** Tuition prepayment, installment.

FRESHMAN FINANCIAL AID (Fall 2008, est.) 239 applied for aid; of those 93% were deemed to have need. 100% of freshmen with need received aid; of those 100% had need fully met. ***Average percent of need met:*** 100% (excluding resources awarded to replace EFC). ***Average financial aid package:*** $27,996 (excluding resources awarded to replace EFC). 11% of all full-time freshmen had no need and received non-need-based gift aid.

UNDERGRADUATE FINANCIAL AID (Fall 2008, est.) 747 applied for aid; of those 91% were deemed to have need. 100% of undergraduates with need received aid; of those 100% had need fully met. ***Average percent of need met:*** 100% (excluding resources awarded to replace EFC). ***Average financial aid package:*** $25,732 (excluding resources awarded to replace EFC). 22% of all full-time undergraduates had no need and received non-need-based gift aid.

GIFT AID (NEED-BASED) ***Total amount:*** $11,644,728 (5% federal, 14% state, 78% institutional, 3% external sources). ***Receiving aid:*** Freshmen: 87% (221); all full-time undergraduates: 72% (654). ***Average award:*** Freshmen: $19,159; Undergraduates: $17,784. ***Scholarships, grants, and awards:*** Federal Pell, state, private, college/university gift aid from institutional funds.

GIFT AID (NON-NEED-BASED) ***Total amount:*** $4,188,274 (91% institutional, 9% external sources). ***Receiving aid:*** Freshmen: 33% (83). Undergraduates: 14% (125). ***Average award:*** Freshmen: $16,356. Undergraduates: $15,604. ***Scholarships, grants, and awards by category:*** *Academic interests/achievement:* 1,076 awards ($7,947,165 total): general academic interests/achievements. *Creative arts/performance:* 58 awards ($138,500 total): art/fine arts, creative writing, journalism/publications, music, theater/drama. *Special achievements/activities:* 29 awards ($629,549 total): community service, leadership. *Special characteristics:* 8 awards ($200,576 total): children of faculty/staff, international students. ***Tuition waivers:*** Full or partial for employees or children of employees.

LOANS ***Student loans:*** $4,624,826 (55% need-based, 45% non-need-based). 90% of past graduating class borrowed through all loan programs. *Average indebtedness per student:* $21,423. ***Average need-based loan:*** Freshmen: $4597. Undergraduates: $4994. ***Parent loans:*** $1,102,672 (100% non-need-based). ***Programs:*** FFEL (Subsidized and Unsubsidized Stafford, PLUS), college/university.

WORK-STUDY ***State or other work-study/employment:*** Total amount: $2,459,004 (83% need-based, 17% non-need-based). 769 part-time jobs averaging $2509.

APPLYING FOR FINANCIAL AID ***Required financial aid forms:*** FAFSA, CSS Financial Aid PROFILE, federal income tax form(s), W-2 forms. ***Financial aid deadline:*** 3/1 (priority: 2/15). ***Notification date:*** 4/1. Students must reply by 5/1 or within 2 weeks of notification.

CONTACT Mr. Clint Gasaway, Financial Aid Director, Wabash College, PO Box 352, Crawfordsville, IN 47933-0352, 800-718-9746 or toll-free 800-345-5385. *Fax:* 765-361-6166. *E-mail:* financialaid@wabash.edu.

WAGNER COLLEGE

Staten Island, NY

Tuition & fees: $31,050 **Average undergraduate aid package: $18,894**

ABOUT THE INSTITUTION Independent, coed. ***Awards:*** bachelor's and master's degrees and post-bachelor's certificates. 36 undergraduate majors. ***Total enrollment:*** 2,294. Undergraduates: 1,924. Freshmen: 481. Federal methodology is used as a basis for awarding need-based institutional aid.

UNDERGRADUATE EXPENSES for 2008–09 ***Application fee:*** $50. ***Comprehensive fee:*** $40,300 includes full-time tuition ($30,900), mandatory fees ($150), and room and board ($9250). ***Part-time tuition:*** $3862 per unit.

FRESHMAN FINANCIAL AID (Fall 2008, est.) 384 applied for aid; of those 79% were deemed to have need. 100% of freshmen with need received aid; of those 27% had need fully met. ***Average percent of need met:*** 74% (excluding resources awarded to replace EFC). ***Average financial aid package:*** $19,767 (excluding resources awarded to replace EFC). 33% of all full-time freshmen had no need and received non-need-based gift aid.

UNDERGRADUATE FINANCIAL AID (Fall 2008, est.) 1,271 applied for aid; of those 82% were deemed to have need. 100% of undergraduates with need received aid; of those 28% had need fully met. ***Average percent of need met:*** 72% (excluding resources awarded to replace EFC). ***Average financial aid package:*** $18,894 (excluding resources awarded to replace EFC). 30% of all full-time undergraduates had no need and received non-need-based gift aid.

GIFT AID (NEED-BASED) ***Total amount:*** $11,230,200 (7% federal, 6% state, 84% institutional, 3% external sources). ***Receiving aid:*** Freshmen: 62% (300); all full-time undergraduates: 55% (1,026). ***Average award:*** Freshmen: $11,797; Undergraduates: $14,824. ***Scholarships, grants, and awards:*** Federal Pell, FSEOG, state, private, college/university gift aid from institutional funds.

GIFT AID (NON-NEED-BASED) ***Total amount:*** $6,648,219 (1% state, 98% institutional, 1% external sources). ***Average award:*** Freshmen: $10,528. Undergraduates: $10,479. ***Scholarships, grants, and awards by category:*** *Academic interests/achievement:* 1,247 awards ($13,112,965 total): general academic interests/achievements. *Creative arts/performance:* 236 awards ($2,545,553 total): music, theater/drama. *Special characteristics:* 135 awards ($847,552 total): children of faculty/staff, siblings of current students. ***Tuition waivers:*** Full or partial for employees or children of employees. ***ROTC:*** Army cooperative.

LOANS ***Student loans:*** $12,940,362 (74% need-based, 26% non-need-based). 56% of past graduating class borrowed through all loan programs. *Average indebtedness per student:* $34,326. ***Average need-based loan:*** Freshmen: $4028. Undergraduates: $4616. ***Parent loans:*** $2,549,474 (95% need-based, 5% non-need-based). ***Programs:*** FFEL (Subsidized and Unsubsidized Stafford, PLUS), Perkins, Federal Nursing.

WORK-STUDY ***Federal work-study:*** Total amount: $759,905; 523 jobs averaging $1500.

ATHLETIC AWARDS Total amount: $5,256,852 (45% need-based, 55% non-need-based).

APPLYING FOR FINANCIAL AID ***Required financial aid forms:*** FAFSA, institution's own form, state aid form. ***Financial aid deadline (priority):*** 2/15. ***Notification date:*** 3/1. Students must reply within 3 weeks of notification.

CONTACT Mr. Angelo Araimo, Vice President for Enrollment and Planning, Wagner College, One Campus Road, Staten Island, NY 10301, 718-390-3411 or toll-free 800-221-1010 (out-of-state). *Fax:* 718-390-3105.

WAKE FOREST UNIVERSITY

Winston-Salem, NC

Tuition & fees: $38,622 **Average undergraduate aid package: $29,245**

ABOUT THE INSTITUTION Independent, coed. ***Awards:*** bachelor's, master's, doctoral, and first professional degrees. 39 undergraduate majors. ***Total enrollment:*** 6,862. Undergraduates: 4,476. Freshmen: 1,201. Institutional methodology is used as a basis for awarding need-based institutional aid.

UNDERGRADUATE EXPENSES for 2009–10 ***Application fee:*** $50. ***Comprehensive fee:*** $49,032 includes full-time tuition ($38,206), mandatory fees ($416), and room and board ($10,410). ***College room only:*** $6550.

FRESHMAN FINANCIAL AID (Fall 2008, est.) 430 applied for aid; of those 80% were deemed to have need. 98% of freshmen with need received aid; of those 87% had need fully met. ***Average percent of need met:*** 99% (excluding resources awarded to replace EFC). ***Average financial aid package:*** $28,753 (excluding resources awarded to replace EFC). 7% of all full-time freshmen had no need and received non-need-based gift aid.

UNDERGRADUATE FINANCIAL AID (Fall 2008, est.) 1,802 applied for aid; of those 87% were deemed to have need. 99% of undergraduates with need received aid; of those 62% had need fully met. ***Average percent of need met:*** 98% (excluding resources awarded to replace EFC). ***Average financial aid package:*** $29,245 (excluding resources awarded to replace EFC). 9% of all full-time undergraduates had no need and received non-need-based gift aid.

GIFT AID (NEED-BASED) ***Total amount:*** $29,219,749 (7% federal, 10% state, 78% institutional, 5% external sources). ***Receiving aid:*** Freshmen: 27% (320); all full-time undergraduates: 33% (1,443). ***Average award:*** Freshmen: $23,682; Undergraduates: $24,375. ***Scholarships, grants, and awards:*** Federal Pell, FSEOG, state, private, college/university gift aid from institutional funds.

GIFT AID (NON-NEED-BASED) ***Total amount:*** $8,013,862 (16% federal, 12% state, 56% institutional, 16% external sources). ***Receiving aid:*** Freshmen: 19% (226). Undergraduates: 22% (988). ***Average award:*** Freshmen: $14,742. Undergraduates: $12,784. ***ROTC:*** Army.

LOANS ***Student loans:*** $17,716,431 (73% need-based, 27% non-need-based). 38% of past graduating class borrowed through all loan programs. *Average indebtedness per student:* $24,827. ***Average need-based loan:*** Freshmen: $6536. Undergraduates: $9204. ***Parent loans:*** $7,764,560 (90% need-based, 10% non-need-based). ***Programs:*** FFEL (Subsidized and Unsubsidized Stafford, PLUS), Perkins, state, college/university.

WORK-STUDY ***Federal work-study:*** Total amount: $2,070,320; jobs available. ***State or other work-study/employment:*** Part-time jobs available.

ATHLETIC AWARDS Total amount: $9,492,738 (29% need-based, 71% non-need-based).

APPLYING FOR FINANCIAL AID ***Required financial aid forms:*** FAFSA, CSS Financial Aid PROFILE, state aid form, noncustodial (divorced/separated) parent's statement. ***Financial aid deadline:*** 3/1 (priority: 2/1). ***Notification date:*** Continuous beginning 4/1. Students must reply by 5/1 or within 4 weeks of notification.

CONTACT Adam Holyfield, Assistant Director, Wake Forest University, PO Box 7246, Reynolda Station, Winston-Salem, NC 27109-7246, 336-758-5154. *Fax:* 336-758-4924. *E-mail:* financial-aid@wfu.edu.

WALDEN UNIVERSITY

Minneapolis, MN

CONTACT Financial Aid Office, Walden University, 155 Fifth Avenue South, Minneapolis, MN 55401, 800-444-6795 or toll-free 866-492-5336 (out-of-state). *Fax:* 410-843-6211. *E-mail:* finaid@waldenu.edu.

WALDORF COLLEGE

Forest City, IA

ABOUT THE INSTITUTION Independent Lutheran, coed. ***Awards:*** bachelor's degrees. 31 undergraduate majors. ***Total enrollment:*** 582. Undergraduates: 582. Freshmen: 118.

GIFT AID (NEED-BASED) ***Scholarships, grants, and awards:*** Federal Pell, FSEOG, state, private, college/university gift aid from institutional funds.

GIFT AID (NON-NEED-BASED) ***Scholarships, grants, and awards by category:*** *Academic interests/achievement:* communication, general academic interests/achievements. *Creative arts/performance:* music, theater/drama. *Special achievements/activities:* cheerleading/drum major, junior miss, leadership. *Special characteristics:* children of faculty/staff, religious affiliation.

LOANS ***Programs:*** Federal Direct (Subsidized and Unsubsidized Stafford, PLUS), Perkins, state, alternative loans.

APPLYING FOR FINANCIAL AID ***Required financial aid form:*** FAFSA.

CONTACT Duane Polsdofer, Director of Financial Aid, Waldorf College, 106 South 6th Street, Forest City, IA 50436, 641-585-8120 or toll-free 800-292-1903. *Fax:* 641-585-8125.

WALLA WALLA UNIVERSITY

College Place, WA

Tuition & fees: $21,936 **Average undergraduate aid package: $20,564**

ABOUT THE INSTITUTION Independent Seventh-day Adventist, coed. ***Awards:*** associate, bachelor's, and master's degrees. 85 undergraduate majors. ***Total enrollment:*** 1,800. Undergraduates: 1,563. Freshmen: 315. Both federal and institutional methodology are used as a basis for awarding need-based institutional aid.

UNDERGRADUATE EXPENSES for 2008–09 ***Application fee:*** $40. ***Comprehensive fee:*** $26,256 includes full-time tuition ($21,726), mandatory fees ($210), and room and board ($4320). ***College room only:*** $2665. Full-time tuition and fees vary according to course load and degree level. Room and board charges vary according to housing facility and location. ***Part-time tuition:*** $568 per credit. Part-time tuition and fees vary according to degree level. ***Payment plans:*** Installment, deferred payment.

FRESHMAN FINANCIAL AID (Fall 2007) 328 applied for aid; of those 73% were deemed to have need. 100% of freshmen with need received aid; of those 29% had need fully met. ***Average percent of need met:*** 90% (excluding resources awarded to replace EFC). ***Average financial aid package:*** $18,338 (excluding resources awarded to replace EFC). 26% of all full-time freshmen had no need and received non-need-based gift aid.

UNDERGRADUATE FINANCIAL AID (Fall 2007) 1,330 applied for aid; of those 77% were deemed to have need. 100% of undergraduates with need received aid; of those 20% had need fully met. ***Average percent of need met:*** 88% (excluding resources awarded to replace EFC). ***Average financial aid package:*** $20,564 (excluding resources awarded to replace EFC). 16% of all full-time undergraduates had no need and received non-need-based gift aid.

GIFT AID (NEED-BASED) ***Total amount:*** $11,092,616 (19% federal, 7% state, 52% institutional, 22% external sources). ***Receiving aid:*** Freshmen: 58% (191); all full-time undergraduates: 53% (779). ***Average award:*** Freshmen: $6219; Undergraduates: $7619. ***Scholarships, grants, and awards:*** Federal Pell, FSEOG, state, private, college/university gift aid from institutional funds, Federal Nursing.

GIFT AID (NON-NEED-BASED) ***Total amount:*** $2,363,452 (46% institutional, 54% external sources). ***Receiving aid:*** Freshmen: 68% (225). Undergraduates: 52% (769). ***Average award:*** Freshmen: $5002. Undergraduates: $3843. ***Scholarships, grants, and awards by category:*** *Academic interests/achievement:* biological sciences, business, communication, education, engineering/technologies, English, foreign languages, general academic interests/achievements, humanities, mathematics, religion/biblical studies. *Creative arts/performance:* general creative arts/performance, music, theater/drama. *Special achievements/activities:* leadership. *Special characteristics:* children of faculty/staff, veterans.

LOANS ***Student loans:*** $9,307,245 (89% need-based, 11% non-need-based). 79% of past graduating class borrowed through all loan programs. *Average indebtedness per student:* $28,287. ***Average need-based loan:*** Freshmen: $5950. Undergraduates: $6509. ***Parent loans:*** $1,461,134 (59% need-based, 41% non-need-based). ***Programs:*** FFEL (Subsidized and Unsubsidized Stafford, PLUS), Perkins, Federal Nursing, college/university.

WORK-STUDY ***Federal work-study:*** Total amount: $1,683,712; 653 jobs averaging $2680. ***State or other work-study/employment:*** Total amount: $130,920 (100% need-based). 71 part-time jobs averaging $3111.

APPLYING FOR FINANCIAL AID ***Required financial aid forms:*** FAFSA, institution's own form. ***Financial aid deadline (priority):*** 4/30. ***Notification date:*** Continuous.

CONTACT Ms. Nancy Caldera, Associate Director of Financial Aid, Walla Walla University, 204 South College Avenue, College Place, WA 99324-1198, 509-527-2315 or toll-free 800-541-8900. *Fax:* 509-527-2556. *E-mail:* nancy.caldera@wallawalla.edu.

WALSH COLLEGE OF ACCOUNTANCY AND BUSINESS ADMINISTRATION

Troy, MI

ABOUT THE INSTITUTION Independent, coed. ***Awards:*** bachelor's and master's degrees. 5 undergraduate majors. ***Total enrollment:*** 3,106. Undergraduates: 1,025.

GIFT AID (NEED-BASED) ***Scholarships, grants, and awards:*** Federal Pell, FSEOG, state, private, college/university gift aid from institutional funds.

GIFT AID (NON-NEED-BASED) ***Scholarships, grants, and awards by category:*** *Academic interests/achievement:* business, computer science. *Special characteristics:* previous college experience.

LOANS ***Programs:*** FFEL (Subsidized and Unsubsidized Stafford, PLUS), alternative loans.

APPLYING FOR FINANCIAL AID ***Required financial aid forms:*** FAFSA, institution's own form.

CONTACT Howard Thomas, Director of Student Financial Resources, Walsh College of Accountancy and Business Administration, 3838 Livernois Road, PO Box 7006, Troy, MI 48007-7006, 248-823-1285 or toll-free 800-925-7401 (in-state). *Fax:* 248-524-2520. *E-mail:* hthomas@walshcollege.edu.

WALSH UNIVERSITY

North Canton, OH

CONTACT Holly Van Gilder, Director of Financial Aid, Walsh University, 2020 East Maple NW, North Canton, OH 44720-3396, 330-490-7147 or toll-free 800-362-9846 (in-state), 800-362-8846 (out-of-state). *Fax:* 330-490-7372. *E-mail:* hvangilder@walsh.edu.

WARNER PACIFIC COLLEGE

Portland, OR

Tuition & fees: $16,630 **Average undergraduate aid package: $14,740**

ABOUT THE INSTITUTION Independent religious, coed. ***Awards:*** associate, bachelor's, and master's degrees and post-bachelor's certificates. 29 undergraduate majors. ***Total enrollment:*** 973. Undergraduates: 874. Freshmen: 98. Federal methodology is used as a basis for awarding need-based institutional aid.

UNDERGRADUATE EXPENSES for 2008–09 ***Application fee:*** $50. ***Comprehensive fee:*** $22,958 includes full-time tuition ($16,630) and room and board ($6328). Full-time tuition and fees vary according to course load, location, and reciprocity agreements. Room and board charges vary according to board plan and housing facility. ***Part-time tuition:*** $945 per credit. ***Part-time fees:*** $315 per term. Part-time tuition and fees vary according to course load, location, and reciprocity agreements.

FRESHMAN FINANCIAL AID (Fall 2008, est.) 80 applied for aid; of those 81% were deemed to have need. 100% of freshmen with need received aid; of those 9% had need fully met. ***Average percent of need met:*** 70% (excluding resources awarded to replace EFC). ***Average financial aid package:*** $12,257 (excluding resources awarded to replace EFC). 17% of all full-time freshmen had no need and received non-need-based gift aid.

UNDERGRADUATE FINANCIAL AID (Fall 2008, est.) 366 applied for aid; of those 89% were deemed to have need. 100% of undergraduates with need received aid; of those 11% had need fully met. ***Average percent of need met:*** 72% (excluding resources awarded to replace EFC). ***Average financial aid package:*** $14,740 (excluding resources awarded to replace EFC). 9% of all full-time undergraduates had no need and received non-need-based gift aid.

GIFT AID (NEED-BASED) ***Total amount:*** $2,090,433 (24% federal, 10% state, 60% institutional, 6% external sources). ***Receiving aid:*** Freshmen: 71% (58); all full-time undergraduates: 73% (284). ***Average award:*** Freshmen: $5494; Undergraduates: $5610. ***Scholarships, grants, and awards:*** Federal Pell, FSEOG, state, private, college/university gift aid from institutional funds.

GIFT AID (NON-NEED-BASED) ***Total amount:*** $207,413 (95% institutional, 5% external sources). ***Receiving aid:*** Freshmen: 74% (61). Undergraduates: 76% (294). ***Average award:*** Freshmen: $2421. Undergraduates: $4547. ***Scholarships, grants, and awards by category:*** *Academic interests/achievement:* 302 awards ($990,188 total): biological sciences, general academic interests/achievements, humanities, mathematics, physical sciences, religion/biblical studies, social sciences. *Creative arts/performance:* 27 awards ($65,269 total): music, theater/drama. *Special achievements/activities:* 27 awards ($46,836 total): leadership. *Special characteristics:* 128 awards ($181,794 total): children and siblings of alumni, members of minority groups, religious affiliation. ***ROTC:*** Army cooperative, Air Force cooperative.

LOANS ***Student loans:*** $2,835,893 (75% need-based, 25% non-need-based). 72% of past graduating class borrowed through all loan programs. *Average indebtedness per student:* $26,890. ***Average need-based loan:*** Freshmen: $2780. Undergraduates: $4055. ***Parent loans:*** $620,898 (39% need-based, 61% non-need-based). ***Programs:*** FFEL (Subsidized and Unsubsidized Stafford, PLUS), Perkins.

WORK-STUDY ***Federal work-study:*** Total amount: $315,460; 219 jobs averaging $1440.

ATHLETIC AWARDS Total amount: $577,960 (80% need-based, 20% non-need-based).

APPLYING FOR FINANCIAL AID ***Required financial aid form:*** FAFSA. ***Financial aid deadline:*** Continuous. ***Notification date:*** Continuous beginning 3/1. Students must reply within 2 weeks of notification.

CONTACT Cynthia Pollard, Director of Student Financial Services, Warner Pacific College, 2219 Southeast 68th Avenue, Portland, OR 97215-4099, 503-517-1018 or toll-free 800-582-7885 (in-state), 800-804-1510 (out-of-state). *Fax:* 503-517-1352. *E-mail:* cpollard@warnerpacific.edu.

WARNER UNIVERSITY

Lake Wales, FL

CONTACT Student Financial Services, Warner University, 13895 Highway 27, Lake Wales, FL 33859, 863-638-7202 or toll-free 800-949-7248 (in-state). *Fax:* 863-638-7603. *E-mail:* financialaid@warner.edu.

WARREN WILSON COLLEGE

Swannanoa, NC

Tuition & fees: $24,196 **Average undergraduate aid package: $16,378**

ABOUT THE INSTITUTION Independent religious, coed. ***Awards:*** bachelor's and master's degrees. 27 undergraduate majors. ***Total enrollment:*** 1,002. Undergraduates: 927. Freshmen: 249. Both federal and institutional methodology are used as a basis for awarding need-based institutional aid.

UNDERGRADUATE EXPENSES for 2009–10 ***Comprehensive fee:*** $31,966 includes full-time tuition ($23,896), mandatory fees ($300), and room and board ($7770). ***Part-time tuition:*** $996 per credit.

FRESHMAN FINANCIAL AID (Fall 2008, est.) 205 applied for aid; of those 69% were deemed to have need. 100% of freshmen with need received aid; of those 11% had need fully met. ***Average percent of need met:*** 73% (excluding resources awarded to replace EFC). ***Average financial aid package:*** $16,460 (excluding resources awarded to replace EFC). 13% of all full-time freshmen had no need and received non-need-based gift aid.

UNDERGRADUATE FINANCIAL AID (Fall 2008, est.) 656 applied for aid; of those 84% were deemed to have need. 100% of undergraduates with need received aid; of those 14% had need fully met. ***Average percent of need met:*** 72% (excluding resources awarded to replace EFC). ***Average financial aid package:*** $16,378 (excluding resources awarded to replace EFC). 13% of all full-time undergraduates had no need and received non-need-based gift aid.

GIFT AID (NEED-BASED) ***Total amount:*** $5,884,702 (15% federal, 8% state, 72% institutional, 5% external sources). ***Receiving aid:*** Freshmen: 52% (129); all full-time undergraduates: 54% (499). ***Average award:*** Freshmen: $12,507; Undergraduates: $11,793. ***Scholarships, grants, and awards:*** Federal Pell, FSEOG, state, college/university gift aid from institutional funds, Academic Competitiveness Grant, National Smart Grant.

GIFT AID (NON-NEED-BASED) ***Total amount:*** $955,735 (10% state, 61% institutional, 29% external sources). ***Receiving aid:*** Freshmen: 14% (34). Undergraduates: 10% (95). ***Average award:*** Freshmen: $5489. Undergraduates: $4450. ***Scholarships, grants, and awards by category:*** *Academic interests/achievement:* 166 awards ($423,927 total): general academic interests/achievements. *Creative arts/performance:* 28 awards ($19,500 total): art/fine arts, creative writing. *Special achievements/activities:* 37 awards ($60,029 total): community service, leadership. *Special characteristics:* 121 awards ($311,675 total): children of faculty/staff, general special characteristics, local/state students, previous college experience, religious affiliation.

LOANS ***Student loans:*** $3,413,949 (85% need-based, 15% non-need-based). 44% of past graduating class borrowed through all loan programs. *Average indebtedness per student:* $17,533. ***Average need-based loan:*** Freshmen: $3128. Undergraduates: $3949. ***Parent loans:*** $1,241,670 (72% need-based, 28% non-need-based). ***Programs:*** Federal Direct (Subsidized and Unsubsidized Stafford, PLUS), Perkins, college/university.

WORK-STUDY ***Federal work-study:*** Total amount: $900,000; 488 jobs averaging $2710. ***State or other work-study/employment:*** Total amount: $950,000 (42% need-based, 58% non-need-based). 400 part-time jobs averaging $2600.

APPLYING FOR FINANCIAL AID ***Required financial aid forms:*** FAFSA, institution's own form, state aid form. ***Financial aid deadline (priority):*** 4/1. ***Notification date:*** Continuous. Students must reply by 5/1 or within 3 weeks of notification.

CONTACT Admissions Office, Warren Wilson College, PO Box 9000, Asheville, NC 28815-9000, 800-934-3536. *Fax:* 828-298-1440.

WARTBURG COLLEGE

Waverly, IA

Tuition & fees: $26,160 **Average undergraduate aid package: $20,435**

ABOUT THE INSTITUTION Independent Lutheran, coed. ***Awards:*** bachelor's degrees. 52 undergraduate majors. ***Total enrollment:*** 1,799. Undergraduates: 1,799. Freshmen: 514. Federal methodology is used as a basis for awarding need-based institutional aid.

UNDERGRADUATE EXPENSES for 2008–09 ***Comprehensive fee:*** $33,415 includes full-time tuition ($25,360), mandatory fees ($800), and room and board ($7255). ***College room only:*** $3435. Room and board charges vary according to board plan and housing facility. ***Part-time tuition:*** $910 per course. ***Part-time fees:*** $75 per term. Part-time tuition and fees vary according to course load. ***Payment plan:*** Installment.

FRESHMAN FINANCIAL AID (Fall 2007) 504 applied for aid; of those 83% were deemed to have need. 100% of freshmen with need received aid; of those 36% had need fully met. ***Average percent of need met:*** 90% (excluding resources awarded to replace EFC). ***Average financial aid package:*** $20,779 (excluding resources awarded to replace EFC). 23% of all full-time freshmen had no need and received non-need-based gift aid.

UNDERGRADUATE FINANCIAL AID (Fall 2007) 1,559 applied for aid; of those 86% were deemed to have need. 100% of undergraduates with need received aid; of those 39% had need fully met. ***Average percent of need met:*** 89% (excluding resources awarded to replace EFC). ***Average financial aid package:*** $20,435 (excluding resources awarded to replace EFC). 23% of all full-time undergraduates had no need and received non-need-based gift aid.

GIFT AID (NEED-BASED) ***Total amount:*** $19,669,732 (8% federal, 14% state, 68% institutional, 10% external sources). ***Receiving aid:*** Freshmen: 77% (418); all full-time undergraduates: 77% (1,336). ***Average award:*** Freshmen: $15,882; Undergraduates: $14,669. ***Scholarships, grants, and awards:*** Federal Pell, FSEOG, state, private, college/university gift aid from institutional funds.

GIFT AID (NON-NEED-BASED) ***Total amount:*** $5,569,669 (86% institutional, 14% external sources). ***Receiving aid:*** Freshmen: 10% (57). Undergraduates: 10% (179). ***Average award:*** Freshmen: $15,074. Undergraduates: $14,958. ***Scholarships, grants, and awards by category:*** *Academic interests/achievement:* biological sciences, business, communication, computer science, education, English, general academic interests/achievements, international studies, mathematics, physical sciences, religion/biblical studies. *Creative arts/performance:* art/fine arts, journalism/publications, music. *Special characteristics:* children and siblings of alumni, children of faculty/staff, ethnic background, international students, members of minority groups, out-of-state students, religious affiliation, siblings of current students. ***Tuition waivers:*** Full or partial for employees or children of employees, senior citizens.

LOANS ***Student loans:*** $13,873,076 (57% need-based, 43% non-need-based). 89% of past graduating class borrowed through all loan programs. *Average indebtedness per student:* $31,063. ***Average need-based loan:*** Freshmen: $5324. Undergraduates: $6342. ***Parent loans:*** $1,385,569 (52% need-based, 48% non-need-based). ***Programs:*** FFEL (Subsidized and Unsubsidized Stafford, PLUS), Perkins, alternative loans.

WORK-STUDY ***Federal work-study:*** Total amount: $427,742; jobs available. ***State or other work-study/employment:*** Total amount: $3713 (100% need-based). Part-time jobs available (averaging $2000).

APPLYING FOR FINANCIAL AID ***Required financial aid form:*** FAFSA. ***Financial aid deadline (priority):*** 3/1. ***Notification date:*** Continuous beginning 3/21. Students must reply within 2 weeks of notification.

CONTACT Ms. Jennifer Sassman, Director of Financial Aid, Wartburg College, 100 Wartburg Boulevard, PO Box 1003, Waverly, IA 50677-0903, 319-352-8262 or toll-free 800-772-2085. *Fax:* 319-352-8514. *E-mail:* jennifer.sassman@wartburg.edu.

WASHBURN UNIVERSITY

Topeka, KS

CONTACT Annita Huff, Director of Financial Aid, Washburn University, 1700 SW College Avenue, Topeka, KS 66621, 785-231-1151 or toll-free 800-332-0291 (in-state). *E-mail:* zzahuff@washburn.edu.

WASHINGTON & JEFFERSON COLLEGE

Washington, PA

Tuition & fees: $31,496 **Average undergraduate aid package: $22,221**

ABOUT THE INSTITUTION Independent, coed. ***Awards:*** bachelor's degrees. 31 undergraduate majors. ***Total enrollment:*** 1,519. Undergraduates: 1,519. Freshmen: 399. Both federal and institutional methodology are used as a basis for awarding need-based institutional aid.

UNDERGRADUATE EXPENSES for 2008–09 ***Application fee:*** $25. ***Comprehensive fee:*** $39,984 includes full-time tuition ($31,096), mandatory fees ($400), and room and board ($8488). ***College room only:*** $4994. Room and board charges vary according to board plan and housing facility. ***Part-time tuition:*** $780 per credit hour. Part-time tuition and fees vary according to course load. ***Payment plans:*** Installment, deferred payment.

FRESHMAN FINANCIAL AID (Fall 2008, est.) 348 applied for aid; of those 86% were deemed to have need. 100% of freshmen with need received aid; of those 15% had need fully met. ***Average percent of need met:*** 80% (excluding resources awarded to replace EFC). ***Average financial aid package:*** $23,554 (excluding resources awarded to replace EFC). 24% of all full-time freshmen had no need and received non-need-based gift aid.

UNDERGRADUATE FINANCIAL AID (Fall 2008, est.) 1,240 applied for aid; of those 89% were deemed to have need. 100% of undergraduates with need received aid; of those 19% had need fully met. ***Average percent of need met:*** 77% (excluding resources awarded to replace EFC). ***Average financial aid package:*** $22,221 (excluding resources awarded to replace EFC). 22% of all full-time undergraduates had no need and received non-need-based gift aid.

GIFT AID (NEED-BASED) ***Total amount:*** $17,981,858 (8% federal, 8% state, 82% institutional, 2% external sources). ***Receiving aid:*** Freshmen: 70% (278); all full-time undergraduates: 57% (855). ***Average award:*** Freshmen: $16,433; Undergraduates: $14,747. ***Scholarships, grants, and awards:*** Federal Pell, FSEOG, state, private, college/university gift aid from institutional funds, Academic Competitiveness Grant, National Smart Grant.

GIFT AID (NON-NEED-BASED) ***Total amount:*** $3,869,277 (98% institutional, 2% external sources). ***Receiving aid:*** Freshmen: 70% (278). Undergraduates: 62% (927). ***Average award:*** Freshmen: $11,090. Undergraduates: $9979. ***Scholarships, grants, and awards by category:*** *Academic interests/achievement:* 1,230 awards ($12,930,789 total): business, general academic interests/achievements. *Special characteristics:* 28 awards ($816,542 total): children and siblings of alumni, children of faculty/staff. ***Tuition waivers:*** Full or partial for employees or children of employees. ***ROTC:*** Army cooperative, Air Force cooperative.

LOANS ***Student loans:*** $13,775,193 (60% need-based, 40% non-need-based). 75% of past graduating class borrowed through all loan programs. *Average indebtedness per student:* $20,000. ***Average need-based loan:*** Freshmen: $3934. Undergraduates: $4043. ***Parent loans:*** $2,780,723 (54% need-based, 46% non-need-based). ***Programs:*** FFEL (Subsidized and Unsubsidized Stafford, PLUS), Perkins, college/university.

WORK-STUDY ***Federal work-study:*** Total amount: $1,100,147; 647 jobs averaging $1700. ***State or other work-study/employment:*** Total amount: $201,409 (100% non-need-based). 246 part-time jobs averaging $650.

APPLYING FOR FINANCIAL AID ***Required financial aid form:*** FAFSA. ***Financial aid deadline (priority):*** 2/15. ***Notification date:*** Continuous beginning 3/1. Students must reply by 5/1.

CONTACT Michelle Vettorel, Director of Financial Aid, Washington & Jefferson College, 60 South Lincoln Street, Washington, PA 15301-4801, 724-503-1001 Ext. 6019 or toll-free 888-WANDJAY. *Fax:* 724-250-3340. *E-mail:* mvettorel@washjeff.edu.

WASHINGTON AND LEE UNIVERSITY

Lexington, VA

Tuition & fees: $37,412 **Average undergraduate aid package: $32,977**

ABOUT THE INSTITUTION Independent, coed. ***Awards:*** bachelor's, master's, and first professional degrees. 39 undergraduate majors. ***Total enrollment:*** 2,155. Undergraduates: 1,752. Freshmen: 454. Both federal and institutional methodology are used as a basis for awarding need-based institutional aid.

UNDERGRADUATE EXPENSES for 2008–09 ***Application fee:*** $50. ***Comprehensive fee:*** $45,840 includes full-time tuition ($36,525), mandatory fees ($887), and room and board ($8428). ***College room only:*** $3498. Room and board charges vary according to board plan and housing facility. ***Part-time tuition:*** $1218 per credit hour.

FRESHMAN FINANCIAL AID (Fall 2008, est.) 244 applied for aid; of those 73% were deemed to have need. 100% of freshmen with need received aid; of those 90% had need fully met. ***Average percent of need met:*** 99% (excluding resources awarded to replace EFC). ***Average financial aid package:*** $33,561 (excluding resources awarded to replace EFC). 8% of all full-time freshmen had no need and received non-need-based gift aid.

UNDERGRADUATE FINANCIAL AID (Fall 2008, est.) 797 applied for aid; of those 82% were deemed to have need. 100% of undergraduates with need received aid; of those 86% had need fully met. ***Average percent of need met:*** 99% (excluding resources awarded to replace EFC). ***Average financial aid package:*** $32,977 (excluding resources awarded to replace EFC). 9% of all full-time undergraduates had no need and received non-need-based gift aid.

GIFT AID (NEED-BASED) ***Total amount:*** $16,454,730 (3% federal, 2% state, 93% institutional, 2% external sources). ***Receiving aid:*** Freshmen: 34% (156); all full-time undergraduates: 32% (559). ***Average award:*** Freshmen: $27,989; Undergraduates: $28,384. ***Scholarships, grants, and awards:*** Federal Pell, FSEOG, state, private, college/university gift aid from institutional funds.

GIFT AID (NON-NEED-BASED) ***Total amount:*** $8,340,190 (6% state, 89% institutional, 5% external sources). ***Receiving aid:*** Freshmen: 27% (122). Undergraduates: 33% (577). ***Average award:*** Freshmen: $35,562. Undergraduates: $25,316. ***Scholarships, grants, and awards by category:*** *Academic interests/achievement:* 368 awards ($6,729,096 total): general academic interests/achievements. ***Tuition waivers:*** Full or partial for employees or children of employees. ***ROTC:*** Army cooperative.

LOANS ***Student loans:*** $4,419,589 (40% need-based, 60% non-need-based). 33% of past graduating class borrowed through all loan programs. *Average indebtedness per student:* $23,616. ***Average need-based loan:*** Freshmen: $3101. Undergraduates: $4262. ***Parent loans:*** $3,821,614 (100% non-need-based). ***Programs:*** Federal Direct (Subsidized and Unsubsidized Stafford, PLUS), FFEL (Subsidized and Unsubsidized Stafford, PLUS), Perkins, college/university.

WORK-STUDY ***Federal work-study:*** Total amount: $201,965; 136 jobs averaging $1485. ***State or other work-study/employment:*** Total amount: $450,600 (100% non-need-based). 457 part-time jobs averaging $1374.

APPLYING FOR FINANCIAL AID ***Required financial aid forms:*** FAFSA, CSS Financial Aid PROFILE, noncustodial (divorced/separated) parent's statement, business/farm supplement, federal tax returns. ***Financial aid deadline:*** 3/1. ***Notification date:*** 4/1. Students must reply by 5/1.

CONTACT John DeCourcy, Director, Financial Aid, Washington and Lee University, Gilliam House, 204 West Washington Street, Lexington, VA 24450, 540-458-8717. *Fax:* 540-458-8614. *E-mail:* financialaid@wlu.edu.

WASHINGTON BIBLE COLLEGE

Lanham, MD

Tuition & fees: $10,200 **Average undergraduate aid package: $6656**

ABOUT THE INSTITUTION Independent nondenominational, coed. ***Awards:*** associate, bachelor's, master's, and first professional degrees and post-bachelor's certificates. 7 undergraduate majors. ***Total enrollment:*** 616. Undergraduates: 254. Freshmen: 29. Both federal and institutional methodology are used as a basis for awarding need-based institutional aid.

UNDERGRADUATE EXPENSES for 2008–09 ***Application fee:*** $25. ***One-time required fee:*** $450. ***Comprehensive fee:*** $16,970 includes full-time tuition ($9600), mandatory fees ($600), and room and board ($6770). ***College room only:*** $2730. Full-time tuition and fees vary according to course load and location. Room and board charges vary according to board plan. ***Part-time tuition:*** $400 per credit hour. Part-time tuition and fees vary according to course load and location. ***Payment plan:*** Installment.

FRESHMAN FINANCIAL AID (Fall 2007) 19 applied for aid; of those 79% were deemed to have need. 100% of freshmen with need received aid; of those 13% had need fully met. ***Average percent of need met:*** 53% (excluding resources awarded to replace EFC). ***Average financial aid package:*** $6248 (excluding resources awarded to replace EFC). 15% of all full-time freshmen had no need and received non-need-based gift aid.

UNDERGRADUATE FINANCIAL AID (Fall 2007) 106 applied for aid; of those 90% were deemed to have need. 99% of undergraduates with need received aid; of those 10% had need fully met. ***Average percent of need met:*** 44% (excluding resources awarded to replace EFC). ***Average financial aid package:*** $6656 (excluding resources awarded to replace EFC). 17% of all full-time undergraduates had no need and received non-need-based gift aid.

GIFT AID (NEED-BASED) ***Total amount:*** $327,883 (69% federal, 16% state, 7% institutional, 8% external sources). ***Receiving aid:*** Freshmen: 70% (14); all full-time undergraduates: 60% (75). ***Average award:*** Freshmen: $740; Undergraduates: $2090. ***Scholarships, grants, and awards:*** Federal Pell, FSEOG, state, private, college/university gift aid from institutional funds.

GIFT AID (NON-NEED-BASED) ***Total amount:*** $246,937 (100% institutional). ***Receiving aid:*** Freshmen: 75% (15). Undergraduates: 71% (89). ***Average award:*** Freshmen: $1063. Undergraduates: $1282. ***Scholarships, grants, and awards by category:*** *Academic interests/achievement:* 70 awards ($25,100 total): general academic interests/achievements. *Creative arts/performance:* 16 awards ($42,500 total): music. *Special achievements/activities:* 18 awards ($12,900 total): general special achievements/activities, leadership, religious involvement. *Special characteristics:* 31 awards ($105,974 total): children of faculty/staff, international students, relatives of clergy, siblings of current students, spouses of current students. ***Tuition waivers:*** Full or partial for employees or children of employees.

LOANS ***Student loans:*** $792,245 (43% need-based, 57% non-need-based). 66% of past graduating class borrowed through all loan programs. *Average indebtedness per student:* $19,723. ***Average need-based loan:*** Freshmen: $1943. Undergraduates: $3534. ***Parent loans:*** $75,058 (100% non-need-based). ***Programs:*** FFEL (Subsidized and Unsubsidized Stafford, PLUS).

WORK-STUDY ***Federal work-study:*** Total amount: $54,631; 25 jobs averaging $2185.

APPLYING FOR FINANCIAL AID ***Required financial aid forms:*** FAFSA, institution's own form, CSS Financial Aid PROFILE. ***Financial aid deadline (priority):*** 7/1. ***Notification date:*** Continuous beginning 7/1. Students must reply within 2 weeks of notification.

CONTACT Nichole Sefiane, Financial Aid Director, Washington Bible College, 6511 Princess Garden Parkway, Lanham, MD 20706-3599, 301-552-1400 Ext. 1222 or toll-free 877-793-7227 Ext. 1212. *Fax:* 240-387-1351. *E-mail:* nsefiane@bible.edu.

WASHINGTON COLLEGE

Chestertown, MD

Tuition & fees: $34,005 **Average undergraduate aid package: $22,219**

ABOUT THE INSTITUTION Independent, coed. ***Awards:*** bachelor's and master's degrees. 34 undergraduate majors. ***Total enrollment:*** 1,402. Undergraduates: 1,304. Freshmen: 415. Both federal and institutional methodology are used as a basis for awarding need-based institutional aid.

UNDERGRADUATE EXPENSES for 2008–09 ***Application fee:*** $50. ***One-time required fee:*** $275. ***Comprehensive fee:*** $41,185 includes full-time tuition ($33,385), mandatory fees ($620), and room and board ($7180). ***College room only:*** $3650. Room and board charges vary according to board plan and housing facility. ***Part-time tuition:*** $5565 per course. Part-time tuition and fees vary according to course load. ***Payment plan:*** Installment.

FRESHMAN FINANCIAL AID (Fall 2008, est.) 297 applied for aid; of those 70% were deemed to have need. 100% of freshmen with need received aid; of those 50% had need fully met. ***Average percent of need met:*** 82% (excluding resources awarded to replace EFC). ***Average financial aid package:*** $22,987 (excluding resources awarded to replace EFC). 28% of all full-time freshmen had no need and received non-need-based gift aid.

UNDERGRADUATE FINANCIAL AID (Fall 2008, est.) 785 applied for aid; of those 81% were deemed to have need. 100% of undergraduates with need received aid; of those 48% had need fully met. ***Average percent of need met:*** 82% (excluding resources awarded to replace EFC). ***Average financial aid package:*** $22,219 (excluding resources awarded to replace EFC). 30% of all full-time undergraduates had no need and received non-need-based gift aid.

GIFT AID (NEED-BASED) ***Total amount:*** $9,167,758 (6% federal, 7% state, 85% institutional, 2% external sources). ***Receiving aid:*** Freshmen: 50% (209); all full-time undergraduates: 52% (637). ***Average award:*** Freshmen: $19,757; Undergraduates: $17,417. ***Scholarships, grants, and awards:*** Federal Pell, FSEOG, state, private, college/university gift aid from institutional funds.

GIFT AID (NON-NEED-BASED) ***Total amount:*** $5,427,033 (1% state, 92% institutional, 7% external sources). ***Receiving aid:*** Freshmen: 6% (24). Undergraduates: 7% (86). ***Average award:*** Freshmen: $11,541. Undergraduates: $12,437. ***Scholarships, grants, and awards by category:*** *Academic interests/achievement:* 563 awards ($6,227,761 total): general academic interests/achievements. *Special characteristics:* 45 awards ($781,278 total): children of faculty/staff. ***Tuition waivers:*** Full or partial for employees or children of employees.

LOANS ***Student loans:*** $8,140,594 (29% need-based, 71% non-need-based). 61% of past graduating class borrowed through all loan programs. *Average indebtedness per student:* $20,611. ***Average need-based loan:*** Freshmen: $2380. Undergraduates: $3650. ***Parent loans:*** $3,848,518 (100% non-need-based). ***Programs:*** FFEL (Subsidized and Unsubsidized Stafford, PLUS), Perkins.

WORK-STUDY ***Federal work-study:*** Total amount: $582,913; 290 jobs averaging $2000.

APPLYING FOR FINANCIAL AID ***Required financial aid forms:*** FAFSA, institution's own form. ***Financial aid deadline (priority):*** 2/15. ***Notification date:*** Continuous beginning 2/15. Students must reply by 5/1.

CONTACT Ms. Jean M. Narcum, Director of Financial Aid, Washington College, 300 Washington Avenue, Chestertown, MD 21620-1197, 410-778-7214 or toll-free 800-422-1782. *Fax:* 410-778-7287. *E-mail:* jnarcum2@washcoll.edu.

WASHINGTON STATE UNIVERSITY

Pullman, WA

Tuition & fees (WA res): $7565 **Average undergraduate aid package: $10,366**

ABOUT THE INSTITUTION State-supported, coed. ***Awards:*** bachelor's, master's, doctoral, and first professional degrees and post-bachelor's and post-master's certificates. 127 undergraduate majors. ***Total enrollment:*** 25,352. Undergraduates: 21,149. Freshmen: 3,710. Federal methodology is used as a basis for awarding need-based institutional aid.

UNDERGRADUATE EXPENSES for 2008–09 ***Application fee:*** $50. ***Tuition, state resident:*** full-time $6218; part-time $336 per credit hour. ***Tuition, nonresident:*** full-time $17,254; part-time $888 per credit hour. ***Required fees:*** full-time $1347. Full-time tuition and fees vary according to location and reciprocity agreements. Part-time tuition and fees vary according to course load and reciprocity agreements. ***College room and board:*** $8054; ***Room only:*** $4134. Room and board charges vary according to board plan, housing facility, and location.

FRESHMAN FINANCIAL AID (Fall 2007) 2,404 applied for aid; of those 61% were deemed to have need. 100% of freshmen with need received aid; of those 37% had need fully met. ***Average percent of need met:*** 84% (excluding resources awarded to replace EFC). ***Average financial aid package:*** $9254 (excluding resources awarded to replace EFC). 19% of all full-time freshmen had no need and received non-need-based gift aid.

UNDERGRADUATE FINANCIAL AID (Fall 2007) 11,340 applied for aid; of those 74% were deemed to have need. 98% of undergraduates with need received aid; of those 37% had need fully met. ***Average percent of need met:*** 87% (excluding resources awarded to replace EFC). ***Average financial aid package:*** $10,366 (excluding resources awarded to replace EFC). 7% of all full-time undergraduates had no need and received non-need-based gift aid.

GIFT AID (NEED-BASED) ***Total amount:*** $41,068,751 (39% federal, 52% state, 9% institutional). ***Receiving aid:*** Freshmen: 24% (839); all full-time undergraduates: 33% (5,704). ***Average award:*** Freshmen: $6334; Undergraduates: $6872. ***Scholarships, grants, and awards:*** Federal Pell, FSEOG, state, private, college/university gift aid from institutional funds, United Negro College Fund, Federal Nursing.

GIFT AID (NON-NEED-BASED) ***Total amount:*** $12,618,334 (4% state, 45% institutional, 51% external sources). ***Receiving aid:*** Freshmen: 29% (1,006). Undergraduates: 17% (3,013). ***Average award:*** Freshmen: $3763. Undergraduates: $3519. ***Scholarships, grants, and awards by category:*** *Academic interests/achievement:* agriculture, architecture, area/ethnic studies, biological sciences, business, communication, computer science, education, engineering/technologies, English, foreign languages, general academic interests/achievements, health fields, home economics, humanities, international studies, mathematics, military science, physical sciences, premedicine, social sciences. *Creative arts/performance:* applied art and design, art/fine arts, cinema/film/broadcasting, creative writing, general creative arts/performance, journalism/publications, music, performing arts, theater/drama. *Special achievements/activities:* community service, general special achievements/activities, junior miss, leadership, memberships, religious involvement, rodeo. *Special characteristics:* children and siblings of alumni, children of faculty/staff, children of public servants, children with a deceased or disabled parent, first-generation college students, handicapped students, international students, out-of-state students, public servants, religious affiliation, veterans. ***Tuition waivers:*** Full or partial for employees or children of employees, senior citizens. ***ROTC:*** Army, Naval cooperative, Air Force.

LOANS ***Student loans:*** $62,552,495 (53% need-based, 47% non-need-based). ***Average need-based loan:*** Freshmen: $3528. Undergraduates: $4650. ***Parent loans:*** $22,513,914 (100% non-need-based). ***Programs:*** FFEL (Subsidized and Unsubsidized Stafford, PLUS), Perkins, Federal Nursing, college/university, alternative loans.

WORK-STUDY ***Federal work-study:*** Total amount: $565,479; 401 jobs averaging $3000. ***State or other work-study/employment:*** Total amount: $1,591,461 (100% need-based). 1,161 part-time jobs averaging $3000.

ATHLETIC AWARDS Total amount: $5,519,584 (100% non-need-based).

APPLYING FOR FINANCIAL AID ***Required financial aid form:*** FAFSA. ***Financial aid deadline (priority):*** 2/15. ***Notification date:*** Continuous beginning 4/15.

CONTACT Financial Aid Office, Washington State University, Office of Student Financial Aid, Pullman, WA 99164-1068, 509-335-9711 or toll-free 888-468-6978. *E-mail:* finaid@wsu.edu.

WASHINGTON UNIVERSITY IN ST. LOUIS

St. Louis, MO

Tuition & fees: $38,864 **Average undergraduate aid package: $31,093**

ABOUT THE INSTITUTION Independent, coed. ***Awards:*** bachelor's, master's, doctoral, and first professional degrees and post-bachelor's and post-master's certificates. 163 undergraduate majors. ***Total enrollment:*** 13,339. Undergraduates: 6,985. Freshmen: 1,426. Institutional methodology is used as a basis for awarding need-based institutional aid.

UNDERGRADUATE EXPENSES for 2009–10 ***Application fee:*** $55. ***Comprehensive fee:*** $51,329 includes full-time tuition ($37,800), mandatory fees ($1064), and room and board ($12,465). ***College room only:*** $8061.

FRESHMAN FINANCIAL AID (Fall 2008, est.) 935 applied for aid; of those 58% were deemed to have need. 99% of freshmen with need received aid; of those 100% had need fully met. ***Average percent of need met:*** 100% (excluding resources awarded to replace EFC). ***Average financial aid package:*** $31,564 (excluding resources awarded to replace EFC). 18% of all full-time freshmen had no need and received non-need-based gift aid.

UNDERGRADUATE FINANCIAL AID (Fall 2008, est.) 4,090 applied for aid; of those 59% were deemed to have need. 99% of undergraduates with need received aid; of those 100% had need fully met. ***Average percent of need met:*** 100% (excluding resources awarded to replace EFC). ***Average financial aid package:*** $31,093 (excluding resources awarded to replace EFC). 15% of all full-time undergraduates had no need and received non-need-based gift aid.

GIFT AID (NEED-BASED) ***Total amount:*** $64,976,388 (4% federal, 2% state, 89% institutional, 5% external sources). ***Receiving aid:*** Freshmen: 36% (515);

all full-time undergraduates: 39% (2,365). ***Average award:*** Freshmen: $28,345; Undergraduates: $27,474. ***Scholarships, grants, and awards:*** Federal Pell, FSEOG, state, private, college/university gift aid from institutional funds, United Negro College Fund.

GIFT AID (NON-NEED-BASED) ***Total amount:*** $6,861,814 (3% federal, 5% state, 77% institutional, 15% external sources). ***Receiving aid:*** Freshmen: 4% (59). Undergraduates: 3% (178). ***Average award:*** Freshmen: $8459. Undergraduates: $7386. ***Scholarships, grants, and awards by category:*** *Academic interests/achievement:* architecture, biological sciences, business, communication, computer science, education, engineering/technologies, English, foreign languages, general academic interests/achievements, health fields, humanities, international studies, mathematics, military science, physical sciences, premedicine, religion/biblical studies, social sciences. *Creative arts/performance:* applied art and design, art/fine arts, cinema/film/broadcasting, creative writing, dance, music, performing arts, theater/drama. ***ROTC:*** Army, Air Force cooperative.

LOANS ***Student loans:*** $11,008,890 (90% need-based, 10% non-need-based). 40% of past graduating class borrowed through all loan programs. ***Average need-based loan:*** Freshmen: $4996. Undergraduates: $5872. ***Parent loans:*** $1,134,302 (63% need-based, 37% non-need-based). ***Programs:*** FFEL (Subsidized and Unsubsidized Stafford, PLUS), Perkins, state, college/university.

WORK-STUDY ***Federal work-study:*** Total amount: $1,987,356; 1,041 jobs averaging $1909.

APPLYING FOR FINANCIAL AID ***Required financial aid forms:*** FAFSA, CSS Financial Aid PROFILE, noncustodial (divorced/separated) parent's statement, student and parent 1040 tax return or signed waiver if there is no tax return. ***Financial aid deadline:*** 2/15. ***Notification date:*** 4/1. Students must reply by 5/1 or within 2 weeks of notification.

CONTACT Mr. William Witbrodt, Director of Financial Aid, Washington University in St. Louis, Campus Box 1041, St. Louis, MO 63130-4899, 314-935-5900 or toll-free 800-638-0700. *Fax:* 314-935-4037. *E-mail:* financial@wustl.edu.

WATKINS COLLEGE OF ART, DESIGN, & FILM

Nashville, TN

Tuition & fees: $17,700 **Average undergraduate aid package: $12,350**

ABOUT THE INSTITUTION Independent, coed. ***Awards:*** bachelor's degrees and post-bachelor's certificates. 6 undergraduate majors. ***Total enrollment:*** 393. Undergraduates: 375. Freshmen: 40. Federal methodology is used as a basis for awarding need-based institutional aid.

UNDERGRADUATE EXPENSES for 2008–09 ***Application fee:*** $50. ***One-time required fee:*** $50. ***Tuition:*** full-time $16,500; part-time $550 per hour. ***Required fees:*** full-time $1200; $40 per hour. ***Payment plan:*** Installment.

FRESHMAN FINANCIAL AID (Fall 2007) 37 applied for aid; of those 100% were deemed to have need. 100% of freshmen with need received aid; of those 3% had need fully met. ***Average percent of need met:*** 60% (excluding resources awarded to replace EFC). ***Average financial aid package:*** $8633 (excluding resources awarded to replace EFC). 11% of all full-time freshmen had no need and received non-need-based gift aid.

UNDERGRADUATE FINANCIAL AID (Fall 2007) 162 applied for aid; of those 99% were deemed to have need. 85% of undergraduates with need received aid; of those 1% had need fully met. ***Average percent of need met:*** 60% (excluding resources awarded to replace EFC). ***Average financial aid package:*** $12,350 (excluding resources awarded to replace EFC). 2% of all full-time undergraduates had no need and received non-need-based gift aid.

GIFT AID (NEED-BASED) ***Total amount:*** $420,276 (71% federal, 13% state, 16% institutional). ***Receiving aid:*** Freshmen: 40% (26); all full-time undergraduates: 17% (68). ***Average award:*** Freshmen: $1500; Undergraduates: $1500. ***Scholarships, grants, and awards:*** Federal Pell, FSEOG, state, college/university gift aid from institutional funds, Academic Competitiveness Grant.

GIFT AID (NON-NEED-BASED) ***Total amount:*** $547,238 (52% state, 46% institutional, 2% external sources). ***Receiving aid:*** Freshmen: 32% (21). Undergraduates: 7% (26). ***Average award:*** Freshmen: $1500. Undergraduates: $1500. ***Scholarships, grants, and awards by category:*** *Academic interests/achievement:* 68 awards ($116,626 total): general academic interests/achievements. *Creative arts/performance:* 25 awards ($30,000 total): applied art and design, art/fine arts, cinema/film/broadcasting. *Special achievements/activities:* 7 awards ($19,500 total): general special achievements/activities. *Special characteristics:* 24 awards ($34,625 total). ***Tuition waivers:*** Full or partial for employees or children of employees.

LOANS ***Student loans:*** $1,560,047 (58% need-based, 42% non-need-based). 50% of past graduating class borrowed through all loan programs. *Average indebtedness per student:* $20,000. ***Average need-based loan:*** Freshmen: $3500. Undergraduates: $4000. ***Parent loans:*** $724,894 (100% non-need-based). ***Programs:*** FFEL (Subsidized and Unsubsidized Stafford, PLUS), private alternative loans.

WORK-STUDY ***Federal work-study:*** Total amount: $20,208; 17 jobs averaging $1200. ***State or other work-study/employment:*** Total amount: $20,000 (100% non-need-based). 25 part-time jobs averaging $2000.

APPLYING FOR FINANCIAL AID ***Required financial aid forms:*** FAFSA, institution's own form. ***Financial aid deadline (priority):*** 4/1. ***Notification date:*** Continuous beginning 5/1. Students must reply within 2 weeks of notification.

CONTACT Lyle Jones, Financial Aid Coordinator, Watkins College of Art, Design, & Film, 2298 Rosa L. Parks Boulevard, Nashville, TN 37228, 615-383-4848 Ext. 7421. *Fax:* 615-383-4849. *E-mail:* financialaid@watkins.edu.

WAYLAND BAPTIST UNIVERSITY

Plainview, TX

Tuition & fees: $12,020 **Average undergraduate aid package: $9027**

ABOUT THE INSTITUTION Independent Baptist, coed. ***Awards:*** associate, bachelor's, and master's degrees (branch locations in Anchorage, AK; Amarillo, TX; Luke Airforce Base, AZ; Glorieta, NM; Aiea, HI; Lubbock, TX; San Antonio, TX; Wichita Falls, TX). 27 undergraduate majors. ***Total enrollment:*** 1,234. Undergraduates: 992. Freshmen: 205. Federal methodology is used as a basis for awarding need-based institutional aid.

UNDERGRADUATE EXPENSES for 2008–09 ***Application fee:*** $35. ***One-time required fee:*** $270. ***Comprehensive fee:*** $15,711 includes full-time tuition ($11,400), mandatory fees ($620), and room and board ($3691). ***College room only:*** $1276. Full-time tuition and fees vary according to course load and location. Room and board charges vary according to board plan and housing facility. ***Part-time tuition:*** $380 per semester hour. ***Part-time fees:*** $60 per term. Part-time tuition and fees vary according to course load and location. ***Payment plan:*** Installment.

FRESHMAN FINANCIAL AID (Fall 2008, est.) 161 applied for aid; of those 97% were deemed to have need. 96% of freshmen with need received aid; of those 19% had need fully met. ***Average percent of need met:*** 68% (excluding resources awarded to replace EFC). ***Average financial aid package:*** $7770 (excluding resources awarded to replace EFC). 22% of all full-time freshmen had no need and received non-need-based gift aid.

UNDERGRADUATE FINANCIAL AID (Fall 2008, est.) 662 applied for aid; of those 94% were deemed to have need. 97% of undergraduates with need received aid; of those 18% had need fully met. ***Average percent of need met:*** 68% (excluding resources awarded to replace EFC). ***Average financial aid package:*** $9027 (excluding resources awarded to replace EFC). 19% of all full-time undergraduates had no need and received non-need-based gift aid.

GIFT AID (NEED-BASED) ***Total amount:*** $2,541,193 (10% federal, 39% state, 43% institutional, 8% external sources). ***Receiving aid:*** Freshmen: 69% (138); all full-time undergraduates: 76% (586). ***Average award:*** Freshmen: $6286; Undergraduates: $6753. ***Scholarships, grants, and awards:*** Federal Pell, FSEOG, state, private, college/university gift aid from institutional funds.

GIFT AID (NON-NEED-BASED) ***Total amount:*** $1,437,424 (93% institutional, 7% external sources). ***Receiving aid:*** Freshmen: 8% (15). Undergraduates: 7% (56). ***Average award:*** Freshmen: $9395. Undergraduates: $9900. ***Scholarships, grants, and awards by category:*** *Academic interests/achievement:* 448 awards ($1,095,959 total): biological sciences, business, communication, education, English, general academic interests/achievements, mathematics, physical sciences, religion/biblical studies, social sciences. *Creative arts/performance:* 160 awards ($189,885 total): art/fine arts, journalism/publications, music, theater/drama. *Special achievements/activities:* 123 awards ($74,001 total): cheerleading/drum major, leadership, memberships, religious involvement. *Special characteristics:* 351 awards ($683,053 total): children and siblings of alumni, children of faculty/staff, ethnic background, general special characteristics, international students, local/state students, members of minority groups, relatives of clergy, religious affiliation. ***Tuition waivers:*** Full or partial for employees or children of employees. ***ROTC:*** Army cooperative, Air Force cooperative.

LOANS ***Student loans:*** $3,559,532 (65% need-based, 35% non-need-based). 63% of past graduating class borrowed through all loan programs. *Average indebtedness per student:* $21,575. ***Average need-based loan:*** Freshmen: $2846. Undergraduates: $3414. ***Parent loans:*** $392,523 (100% non-need-based). ***Programs:*** FFEL (Subsidized and Unsubsidized Stafford, PLUS), Perkins, state.

WORK-STUDY ***Federal work-study:*** Total amount: $217,277; 169 jobs averaging $1532. ***State or other work-study/employment:*** Total amount: $119,499 (100% non-need-based). 228 part-time jobs averaging $2583.

ATHLETIC AWARDS Total amount: $1,335,246 (100% non-need-based).

APPLYING FOR FINANCIAL AID ***Required financial aid forms:*** FAFSA, institution's own form. ***Financial aid deadline (priority):*** 5/1. ***Notification date:*** Continuous. Students must reply within 3 weeks of notification.

CONTACT Karen LaQuey, Director of Financial Aid, Wayland Baptist University, 1900 West 7th Street, Plainview, TX 79072-6998, 806-291-3520 or toll-free 800-588-1928. *Fax:* 806-291-1956. *E-mail:* laquey@wbu.edu.

WAYNESBURG UNIVERSITY

Waynesburg, PA

Tuition & fees: $17,080 **Average undergraduate aid package: $12,381**

ABOUT THE INSTITUTION Independent religious, coed. ***Awards:*** associate, bachelor's, master's, and doctoral degrees. 50 undergraduate majors. ***Total enrollment:*** 2,549. Undergraduates: 1,828. Freshmen: 380. Federal methodology is used as a basis for awarding need-based institutional aid.

UNDERGRADUATE EXPENSES for 2008–09 ***Application fee:*** $20. ***Comprehensive fee:*** $24,130 includes full-time tuition ($16,730), mandatory fees ($350), and room and board ($7050). ***College room only:*** $3600. Full-time tuition and fees vary according to class time. Room and board charges vary according to board plan. ***Part-time tuition:*** $700 per credit. Part-time tuition and fees vary according to class time, course load, and location. ***Payment plan:*** Installment.

FRESHMAN FINANCIAL AID (Fall 2008, est.) 388 applied for aid; of those 90% were deemed to have need. 100% of freshmen with need received aid; of those 25% had need fully met. ***Average percent of need met:*** 80% (excluding resources awarded to replace EFC). ***Average financial aid package:*** $13,435 (excluding resources awarded to replace EFC). 6% of all full-time freshmen had no need and received non-need-based gift aid.

UNDERGRADUATE FINANCIAL AID (Fall 2008, est.) 1,538 applied for aid; of those 87% were deemed to have need. 100% of undergraduates with need received aid; of those 24% had need fully met. ***Average percent of need met:*** 77% (excluding resources awarded to replace EFC). ***Average financial aid package:*** $12,381 (excluding resources awarded to replace EFC). 8% of all full-time undergraduates had no need and received non-need-based gift aid.

GIFT AID (NEED-BASED) ***Total amount:*** $11,639,721 (17% federal, 21% state, 58% institutional, 4% external sources). ***Receiving aid:*** Freshmen: 39% (347); all full-time undergraduates: 59% (1,214). ***Average award:*** Freshmen: $10,340; Undergraduates: $9475. ***Scholarships, grants, and awards:*** Federal Pell, FSEOG, state, private, college/university gift aid from institutional funds.

GIFT AID (NON-NEED-BASED) ***Total amount:*** $1,638,091 (2% state, 92% institutional, 6% external sources). ***Receiving aid:*** Freshmen: 5% (43). Undergraduates: 4% (90). ***Average award:*** Freshmen: $7497. Undergraduates: $6914. ***Scholarships, grants, and awards by category:*** *Academic interests/achievement:* 60 awards: biological sciences, business, communication, computer science, education, English, general academic interests/achievements, international studies, mathematics, religion/biblical studies. *Creative arts/performance:* 4 awards ($2000 total): music. *Special achievements/activities:* 65 awards: community service. *Special characteristics:* 50 awards ($500,000 total): children of faculty/staff. ***Tuition waivers:*** Full or partial for employees or children of employees. ***ROTC:*** Army cooperative.

LOANS ***Student loans:*** $12,024,133 (63% need-based, 37% non-need-based). 87% of past graduating class borrowed through all loan programs. *Average indebtedness per student:* $21,500. ***Average need-based loan:*** Freshmen: $3543. Undergraduates: $4024. ***Parent loans:*** $1,946,151 (20% need-based, 80% non-need-based). ***Programs:*** FFEL (Subsidized and Unsubsidized Stafford, PLUS), Perkins, Federal Nursing.

WORK-STUDY ***Federal work-study:*** Total amount: $170,000; 275 jobs averaging $1300.

APPLYING FOR FINANCIAL AID ***Required financial aid form:*** FAFSA. ***Financial aid deadline:*** Continuous. ***Notification date:*** Continuous beginning 2/15. Students must reply within 2 weeks of notification.

CONTACT Matthew C. Stokan, Director of Financial Aid, Waynesburg University, 51 West College Street, Waynesburg, PA 15370-1222, 724-852-3208 or toll-free 800-225-7393. *Fax:* 724-627-6416. *E-mail:* mstokan@waynesburg.edu.

WAYNE STATE COLLEGE

Wayne, NE

CONTACT Mrs. Kyle M. Rose, Director of Financial Aid, Wayne State College, 1111 Main Street, Wayne, NE 68787, 402-375-7230 or toll-free 800-228-9972 (in-state). *Fax:* 402-375-7067. *E-mail:* kyrose1@wsc.edu.

WAYNE STATE UNIVERSITY

Detroit, MI

Tuition & fees (MI res): $8109 **Average undergraduate aid package: $12,357**

ABOUT THE INSTITUTION State-supported, coed. ***Awards:*** bachelor's, master's, doctoral, and first professional degrees and post-bachelor's and post-master's certificates. 85 undergraduate majors. ***Total enrollment:*** 31,016. Undergraduates: 20,122. Freshmen: 2,917. Federal methodology is used as a basis for awarding need-based institutional aid.

UNDERGRADUATE EXPENSES for 2008–09 ***Application fee:*** $30. ***Tuition, state resident:*** full-time $7182; part-time $239.40 per credit hour. ***Tuition, nonresident:*** full-time $16,452; part-time $548.40 per credit hour. ***Required fees:*** full-time $927; $19.40 per credit hour or $172.50 per term. Full-time tuition and fees vary according to course load and student level. Part-time tuition and fees vary according to course load and student level. ***College room and board:*** $6932. Room and board charges vary according to board plan and housing facility. ***Payment plan:*** Installment.

FRESHMAN FINANCIAL AID (Fall 2007) 2,291 applied for aid; of those 83% were deemed to have need. 99% of freshmen with need received aid; of those 11% had need fully met. ***Average percent of need met:*** 68% (excluding resources awarded to replace EFC). ***Average financial aid package:*** $11,827 (excluding resources awarded to replace EFC). 10% of all full-time freshmen had no need and received non-need-based gift aid.

UNDERGRADUATE FINANCIAL AID (Fall 2007) 8,803 applied for aid; of those 88% were deemed to have need. 99% of undergraduates with need received aid; of those 24% had need fully met. ***Average percent of need met:*** 65% (excluding resources awarded to replace EFC). ***Average financial aid package:*** $12,357 (excluding resources awarded to replace EFC). 9% of all full-time undergraduates had no need and received non-need-based gift aid.

GIFT AID (NEED-BASED) ***Total amount:*** $32,757,917 (79% federal, 4% state, 17% institutional). ***Receiving aid:*** Freshmen: 52% (1,466); all full-time undergraduates: 45% (5,663). ***Average award:*** Freshmen: $4473; Undergraduates: $4302. ***Scholarships, grants, and awards:*** Federal Pell, FSEOG, state, private, college/university gift aid from institutional funds, United Negro College Fund.

GIFT AID (NON-NEED-BASED) ***Total amount:*** $18,341,751 (18% state, 59% institutional, 23% external sources). ***Receiving aid:*** Freshmen: 35% (990). Undergraduates: 21% (2,653). ***Average award:*** Freshmen: $5422. Undergraduates: $4748. ***Scholarships, grants, and awards by category:*** *Academic interests/achievement:* 958 awards ($2,449,326 total): area/ethnic studies, biological sciences, business, communication, computer science, education, engineering/technologies, English, foreign languages, general academic interests/achievements, health fields, humanities, international studies, library science, mathematics, military science, physical sciences, premedicine, social sciences. *Creative arts/performance:* 337 awards ($813,149 total): art/fine arts, dance, debating, journalism/publications, music, theater/drama. *Special achievements/activities:* 18 awards ($10,400 total): leadership. *Special characteristics:* 159 awards ($572,477 total): children of faculty/staff. ***Tuition waivers:*** Full or partial for employees or children of employees, senior citizens. ***ROTC:*** Air Force cooperative.

LOANS ***Student loans:*** $78,908,120 (91% need-based, 9% non-need-based). 50% of past graduating class borrowed through all loan programs. *Average indebtedness per student:* $19,618. ***Average need-based loan:*** Freshmen: $3404. Undergraduates: $4379. ***Parent loans:*** $21,466,401 (100% non-need-based). ***Programs:*** Federal Direct (Subsidized and Unsubsidized Stafford, PLUS), Perkins, Federal Nursing, college/university.

WORK-STUDY ***Federal work-study:*** Total amount: $573,406; 391 jobs averaging $2481. ***State or other work-study/employment:*** Total amount: $195,286 (100% need-based). 135 part-time jobs averaging $2578.

ATHLETIC AWARDS Total amount: $2,668,474 (100% non-need-based).

APPLYING FOR FINANCIAL AID ***Required financial aid forms:*** FAFSA, income tax forms, W-2 forms. ***Financial aid deadline:*** 4/30 (priority: 2/15). ***Notification date:*** Continuous beginning 3/1. Students must reply within 2 weeks of notification.

CONTACT Albert Hermsen, Director of Scholarships and Financial Aid, Wayne State University, 3W HNJ Student Services Building, Detroit, MI 48202, 313-577-3378 or toll-free 877-978-4636 (in-state), 877-WSU-INFO (out-of-state). *Fax:* 313-577-6648.

WEBBER INTERNATIONAL UNIVERSITY

Babson Park, FL

Tuition & fees: $17,000 **Average undergraduate aid package: $18,291**

ABOUT THE INSTITUTION Independent, coed. ***Awards:*** associate, bachelor's, and master's degrees. 11 undergraduate majors. ***Total enrollment:*** 601. Undergraduates: 547. Freshmen: 166. Federal methodology is used as a basis for awarding need-based institutional aid.

UNDERGRADUATE EXPENSES for 2008–09 ***Application fee:*** $35. ***Comprehensive fee:*** $23,354 includes full-time tuition ($17,000) and room and board ($6354). ***College room only:*** $4000. Full-time tuition and fees vary according to class time and course load. Room and board charges vary according to board plan. ***Part-time tuition:*** $235 per credit hour. Part-time tuition and fees vary according to course load. ***Payment plan:*** Installment.

FRESHMAN FINANCIAL AID (Fall 2008, est.) 126 applied for aid; of those 79% were deemed to have need. 100% of freshmen with need received aid; of those 7% had need fully met. ***Average percent of need met:*** 51% (excluding resources awarded to replace EFC). ***Average financial aid package:*** $16,247 (excluding resources awarded to replace EFC). 28% of all full-time freshmen had no need and received non-need-based gift aid.

UNDERGRADUATE FINANCIAL AID (Fall 2008, est.) 327 applied for aid; of those 93% were deemed to have need. 100% of undergraduates with need received aid; of those 4% had need fully met. ***Average percent of need met:*** 50% (excluding resources awarded to replace EFC). ***Average financial aid package:*** $18,291 (excluding resources awarded to replace EFC). 25% of all full-time undergraduates had no need and received non-need-based gift aid.

GIFT AID (NEED-BASED) ***Total amount:*** $2,552,377 (33% federal, 44% state, 20% institutional, 3% external sources). ***Receiving aid:*** Freshmen: 60% (100); all full-time undergraduates: 62% (305). ***Average award:*** Freshmen: $12,672; Undergraduates: $12,595. ***Scholarships, grants, and awards:*** Federal Pell, FSEOG, state, private, college/university gift aid from institutional funds.

GIFT AID (NON-NEED-BASED) ***Total amount:*** $1,216,856 (38% state, 60% institutional, 2% external sources). ***Receiving aid:*** Freshmen: 60% (100). Undergraduates: 62% (305). ***Average award:*** Freshmen: $8950. Undergraduates: $5933. ***Scholarships, grants, and awards by category:*** *Academic interests/achievement:* 316 awards ($679,827 total): business, general academic interests/achievements. *Creative arts/performance:* 25 awards ($22,100 total): general creative arts/performance, journalism/publications. *Special achievements/activities:* 432 awards ($2,168,523 total): cheerleading/drum major, community service, general special achievements/activities, leadership, memberships. *Special characteristics:* 133 awards ($557,543 total): children and siblings of alumni, children of faculty/staff, first-generation college students, general special characteristics, international students, local/state students, out-of-state students, siblings of current students. ***Tuition waivers:*** Full or partial for children of alumni, employees or children of employees, adult students, senior citizens.

LOANS ***Student loans:*** $2,293,627 (85% need-based, 15% non-need-based). 66% of past graduating class borrowed through all loan programs. *Average indebtedness per student:* $23,902. ***Average need-based loan:*** Freshmen: $3357. Undergraduates: $4196. ***Parent loans:*** $391,154 (83% need-based, 17% non-need-based). ***Programs:*** FFEL (Subsidized and Unsubsidized Stafford, PLUS), Perkins, alternative loans.

WORK-STUDY ***Federal work-study:*** Total amount: $36,652; 24 jobs averaging $1527. ***State or other work-study/employment:*** Total amount: $66,978 (16% need-based, 84% non-need-based). 41 part-time jobs averaging $1024.

ATHLETIC AWARDS Total amount: $2,166,828 (63% need-based, 37% non-need-based).

APPLYING FOR FINANCIAL AID ***Required financial aid forms:*** FAFSA, state aid form. ***Financial aid deadline:*** 8/1 (priority: 5/1). ***Notification date:*** Continuous. Students must reply within 4 weeks of notification.

CONTACT Ms. Kathleen Wilson, Director of Financial Aid, Webber International University, PO Box 96, Babson Park, FL 33827-0096, 863-638-2930 or toll-free 800-741-1844. *Fax:* 863-638-1317. *E-mail:* wilsonka@webber.edu.

WEBB INSTITUTE

Glen Cove, NY

CONTACT Stephen P Ostendorff, Director of Financial Aid, Webb Institute, Crescent Beach Road, Glen Cove, NY 11542-1398, 516-671-2213 Ext. 104. *Fax:* 516-674-9838. *E-mail:* sostendo@webb-institute.edu.

WEBER STATE UNIVERSITY

Ogden, UT

Tuition & fees (UT res): $3850 **Average undergraduate aid package: $5878**

ABOUT THE INSTITUTION State-supported, coed. ***Awards:*** associate, bachelor's, and master's degrees and post-bachelor's certificates. 85 undergraduate majors. ***Total enrollment:*** 21,388. Undergraduates: 20,870. Freshmen: 2,439. Both federal and institutional methodology are used as a basis for awarding need-based institutional aid.

UNDERGRADUATE EXPENSES for 2008–09 ***Application fee:*** $30. ***Tuition, state resident:*** full-time $3153; part-time $129 per credit hour. ***Tuition, nonresident:*** full-time $10,459; part-time $429 per credit hour. ***Required fees:*** full-time $697. Part-time tuition and fees vary according to course load. Room and board charges vary according to board plan and housing facility. ***Payment plans:*** Installment, deferred payment.

FRESHMAN FINANCIAL AID (Fall 2007) 648 applied for aid; of those 83% were deemed to have need. 88% of freshmen with need received aid; of those 3% had need fully met. ***Average percent of need met:*** 41% (excluding resources awarded to replace EFC). ***Average financial aid package:*** $4567 (excluding resources awarded to replace EFC). 27% of all full-time freshmen had no need and received non-need-based gift aid.

UNDERGRADUATE FINANCIAL AID (Fall 2007) 4,981 applied for aid; of those 91% were deemed to have need. 91% of undergraduates with need received aid; of those 4% had need fully met. ***Average percent of need met:*** 50% (excluding resources awarded to replace EFC). ***Average financial aid package:*** $5878 (excluding resources awarded to replace EFC). 17% of all full-time undergraduates had no need and received non-need-based gift aid.

GIFT AID (NEED-BASED) ***Total amount:*** $13,718,337 (86% federal, 8% state, 6% institutional). ***Receiving aid:*** Freshmen: 20% (307); all full-time undergraduates: 30% (2,807). ***Average award:*** Freshmen: $3121; Undergraduates: $3622. ***Scholarships, grants, and awards:*** Federal Pell, FSEOG, state, private, college/university gift aid from institutional funds.

GIFT AID (NON-NEED-BASED) ***Total amount:*** $2,075,021 (41% institutional, 59% external sources). ***Average award:*** Freshmen: $2083. Undergraduates: $2033. ***Tuition waivers:*** Full or partial for employees or children of employees, senior citizens. ***ROTC:*** Army, Naval, Air Force.

LOANS ***Student loans:*** $22,511,666 (75% need-based, 25% non-need-based). ***Average need-based loan:*** Freshmen: $2906. Undergraduates: $4079. ***Parent loans:*** $155,168 (100% non-need-based). ***Programs:*** FFEL (Subsidized and Unsubsidized Stafford, PLUS), Perkins, college/university, short term tuition loan.

WORK-STUDY ***Federal work-study:*** Total amount: $556,945; jobs available.

ATHLETIC AWARDS Total amount: $2,081,236 (100% non-need-based).

APPLYING FOR FINANCIAL AID ***Required financial aid forms:*** FAFSA, institution's own form. ***Financial aid deadline (priority):*** 3/1. ***Notification date:*** Continuous beginning 3/15. Students must reply within 2 weeks of notification.

CONTACT Mr. Richard O. Effiong, Financial Aid Director, Weber State University, 120 Student Service Center, 1136 University Circle, Ogden, UT 84408-1136, 801-626-7569 or toll-free 800-634-6568 (in-state), 800-848-7770 (out-of-state). *E-mail:* finaid@weber.edu.

WEBSTER UNIVERSITY

St. Louis, MO

Tuition & fees: $20,440 **Average undergraduate aid package: N/A**

ABOUT THE INSTITUTION Independent, coed. ***Awards:*** bachelor's, master's, and doctoral degrees and post-bachelor's and post-master's certificates. 50

undergraduate majors. ***Total enrollment:*** 8,010. Undergraduates: 3,584. Freshmen: 419. Federal methodology is used as a basis for awarding need-based institutional aid.

UNDERGRADUATE EXPENSES for 2008–09 ***Application fee:*** $35. ***Comprehensive fee:*** $29,440 includes full-time tuition ($20,440) and room and board ($9000). ***College room only:*** $4760. Full-time tuition and fees vary according to program. Room and board charges vary according to board plan and housing facility. ***Part-time tuition:*** $525 per credit hour. Part-time tuition and fees vary according to location. ***Payment plan:*** Installment.

FRESHMAN FINANCIAL AID (Fall 2008, est.) 367 applied for aid; of those 80% were deemed to have need. 100% of freshmen with need received aid. 25% of all full-time freshmen had no need and received non-need-based gift aid.

UNDERGRADUATE FINANCIAL AID (Fall 2008, est.) 2,105 applied for aid; of those 85% were deemed to have need. 100% of undergraduates with need received aid. 19% of all full-time undergraduates had no need and received non-need-based gift aid.

GIFT AID (NEED-BASED) ***Total amount:*** $24,010,755 (14% federal, 14% state, 48% institutional, 24% external sources). ***Receiving aid:*** Freshmen: 58% (245); all full-time undergraduates: 57% (1,483). ***Average award:*** Freshmen: $6810; Undergraduates: $6715. ***Scholarships, grants, and awards:*** Federal Pell, FSEOG, state, private, college/university gift aid from institutional funds.

GIFT AID (NON-NEED-BASED) ***Total amount:*** $4,668,505 (1% state, 73% institutional, 26% external sources). ***Receiving aid:*** Freshmen: 52% (219). Undergraduates: 42% (1,096). ***Average award:*** Freshmen: $8065. Undergraduates: $7708. ***Scholarships, grants, and awards by category:*** *Academic interests/achievement:* 1,659 awards ($9,336,501 total): biological sciences, business, communication, education, English, foreign languages, general academic interests/achievements, humanities, international studies. *Creative arts/performance:* 51 awards ($73,750 total): art/fine arts, creative writing, debating, music, theater/drama. *Special achievements/activities:* 9 awards ($18,000 total): leadership. *Special characteristics:* 102 awards ($350,277 total): children and siblings of alumni, children of faculty/staff, ethnic background, international students, members of minority groups, out-of-state students. ***Tuition waivers:*** Full or partial for employees or children of employees. ***ROTC:*** Army cooperative, Air Force cooperative.

LOANS ***Student loans:*** $23,864,741 (91% need-based, 9% non-need-based). 55% of past graduating class borrowed through all loan programs. *Average indebtedness per student:* $24,224. ***Average need-based loan:*** Freshmen: $3837. Undergraduates: $4850. ***Parent loans:*** $2,595,242 (75% need-based, 25% non-need-based). ***Programs:*** FFEL (Subsidized and Unsubsidized Stafford, PLUS), Perkins.

WORK-STUDY ***Federal work-study:*** Total amount: $1,249,410; 588 jobs averaging $2125. ***State or other work-study/employment:*** Total amount: $1,932,486 (74% need-based, 26% non-need-based). 1,080 part-time jobs averaging $1789.

APPLYING FOR FINANCIAL AID ***Required financial aid forms:*** FAFSA, institution's own form. ***Financial aid deadline (priority):*** 4/1. ***Notification date:*** Continuous.

CONTACT Marilynn Shelton, Financial Aid Counselor, Webster University, Financial Aid Office, 470 East Lockwood Avenue, St. Louis, MO 63119, 314-968-6992 Ext. 7671 or toll-free 800-75-ENROL. *Fax:* 314-968-7125. *E-mail:* sheltoma@webster.edu.

WELLESLEY COLLEGE

Wellesley, MA

Tuition & fees: $36,640 **Average undergraduate aid package: $33,843**

ABOUT THE INSTITUTION Independent, women only. ***Awards:*** bachelor's degrees (double bachelor's degree with Massachusetts Institute of Technology). 59 undergraduate majors. ***Total enrollment:*** 2,344. Undergraduates: 2,344. Freshmen: 596. Both federal and institutional methodology are used as a basis for awarding need-based institutional aid.

UNDERGRADUATE EXPENSES for 2008–09 ***Application fee:*** $50. ***Comprehensive fee:*** $47,976 includes full-time tuition ($36,404), mandatory fees ($236), and room and board ($11,336).

FRESHMAN FINANCIAL AID (Fall 2008, est.) 423 applied for aid; of those 81% were deemed to have need. 100% of freshmen with need received aid; of those 100% had need fully met. ***Average percent of need met:*** 100% (excluding resources awarded to replace EFC). ***Average financial aid package:*** $35,289 (excluding resources awarded to replace EFC).

UNDERGRADUATE FINANCIAL AID (Fall 2008, est.) 1,500 applied for aid; of those 88% were deemed to have need. 100% of undergraduates with need received aid; of those 100% had need fully met. ***Average percent of need met:*** 100% (excluding resources awarded to replace EFC). ***Average financial aid package:*** $33,843 (excluding resources awarded to replace EFC).

GIFT AID (NEED-BASED) ***Total amount:*** $41,068,785 (5% federal, 93% institutional, 2% external sources). ***Receiving aid:*** Freshmen: 56% (331); all full-time undergraduates: 58% (1,267). ***Average award:*** Freshmen: $34,528; Undergraduates: $32,375. ***Scholarships, grants, and awards:*** Federal Pell, FSEOG, state, college/university gift aid from institutional funds.

GIFT AID (NON-NEED-BASED) ***Total amount:*** $483,401 (100% external sources). ***ROTC:*** Army cooperative, Air Force cooperative.

LOANS ***Student loans:*** $3,253,424 (74% need-based, 26% non-need-based). 53% of past graduating class borrowed through all loan programs. *Average indebtedness per student:* $12,639. ***Average need-based loan:*** Freshmen: $2417. Undergraduates: $3069. ***Parent loans:*** $3,406,889 (100% non-need-based). ***Programs:*** FFEL (Subsidized and Unsubsidized Stafford, PLUS), Perkins, state, college/university.

WORK-STUDY ***Federal work-study:*** Total amount: $889,575; 736 jobs averaging $1209. ***State or other work-study/employment:*** Total amount: $437,309 (100% need-based). 347 part-time jobs averaging $1260.

APPLYING FOR FINANCIAL AID ***Required financial aid forms:*** FAFSA, institution's own form, CSS Financial Aid PROFILE, business/farm supplement, parents' federal income tax form(s) & W-2 forms, CSS Noncustodial Parent's Statement. ***Financial aid deadline (priority):*** 1/15. ***Notification date:*** 4/1. Students must reply by 5/1.

CONTACT Ms. Kathryn Osmond, Director of Financial Aid, Wellesley College, 106 Central Street, Wellesley, MA 02481-8203, 781-283-2360. *Fax:* 781-283-3946. *E-mail:* finaid@wellesley.edu.

WELLS COLLEGE

Aurora, NY

Tuition & fees: $29,680 **Average undergraduate aid package: $19,260**

ABOUT THE INSTITUTION Independent, coed, primarily women. ***Awards:*** bachelor's degrees. 40 undergraduate majors. ***Total enrollment:*** 579. Undergraduates: 579. Freshmen: 155. Federal methodology is used as a basis for awarding need-based institutional aid.

UNDERGRADUATE EXPENSES for 2009–10 ***Application fee:*** $40. ***Comprehensive fee:*** $38,680 includes full-time tuition ($28,180), mandatory fees ($1500), and room and board ($9000). ***Part-time tuition:*** $790 per credit hour.

FRESHMAN FINANCIAL AID (Fall 2008, est.) 135 applied for aid; of those 84% were deemed to have need. 100% of freshmen with need received aid; of those 27% had need fully met. ***Average percent of need met:*** 87% (excluding resources awarded to replace EFC). ***Average financial aid package:*** $18,810 (excluding resources awarded to replace EFC). 21% of all full-time freshmen had no need and received non-need-based gift aid.

UNDERGRADUATE FINANCIAL AID (Fall 2008, est.) 461 applied for aid; of those 93% were deemed to have need. 100% of undergraduates with need received aid; of those 23% had need fully met. ***Average percent of need met:*** 86% (excluding resources awarded to replace EFC). ***Average financial aid package:*** $19,260 (excluding resources awarded to replace EFC). 15% of all full-time undergraduates had no need and received non-need-based gift aid.

GIFT AID (NEED-BASED) ***Total amount:*** $5,872,159 (15% federal, 12% state, 69% institutional, 4% external sources). ***Receiving aid:*** Freshmen: 73% (113); all full-time undergraduates: 77% (429). ***Average award:*** Freshmen: $14,486; Undergraduates: $13,688. ***Scholarships, grants, and awards:*** Federal Pell, FSEOG, state, private, college/university gift aid from institutional funds.

GIFT AID (NON-NEED-BASED) ***Total amount:*** $553,719 (2% state, 93% institutional, 5% external sources). ***Receiving aid:*** Freshmen: 43% (67). Undergraduates: 39% (218). ***Average award:*** Freshmen: $6622. Undergraduates: $6195. ***Scholarships, grants, and awards by category:*** *Academic interests/achievement:* 92 awards ($461,000 total): general academic interests/achievements. *Special achievements/activities:* 164 awards ($1,030,000 total): leadership. *Special characteristics:* 34 awards ($88,500 total): children and siblings of alumni, international students. ***ROTC:*** Army cooperative, Air Force cooperative.

LOANS ***Student loans:*** $3,644,845 (47% need-based, 53% non-need-based). 80% of past graduating class borrowed through all loan programs. *Average indebtedness per student:* $18,277. ***Average need-based loan:*** Freshmen: $2865. Undergraduates: $4050. ***Parent loans:*** $528,800 (100% non-need-based). ***Programs:*** FFEL (Subsidized and Unsubsidized Stafford, PLUS), Perkins, state.

WORK-STUDY ***Federal work-study:*** Total amount: $110,000; 69 jobs averaging $1600. ***State or other work-study/employment:*** Total amount: $631,287 (89% need-based, 11% non-need-based). 380 part-time jobs averaging $1600.

APPLYING FOR FINANCIAL AID ***Required financial aid form:*** FAFSA. ***Financial aid deadline (priority):*** 2/15. ***Notification date:*** 3/1. Students must reply by 5/1.

CONTACT Ms. Cathleen A. Patella, Director of Financial Aid, Wells College, Route 90, Aurora, NY 13026, 315-364-3289 or toll-free 800-952-9355. *Fax:* 315-364-3227. *E-mail:* cpatella@wells.edu.

WENTWORTH INSTITUTE OF TECHNOLOGY

Boston, MA

ABOUT THE INSTITUTION Independent, coed. ***Awards:*** associate and bachelor's degrees. 14 undergraduate majors. ***Total enrollment:*** 3,816. Undergraduates: 3,816. Freshmen: 851.

GIFT AID (NEED-BASED) ***Scholarships, grants, and awards:*** Federal Pell, FSEOG, state, private, college/university gift aid from institutional funds.

LOANS ***Programs:*** FFEL (Subsidized and Unsubsidized Stafford, PLUS), Perkins, state.

WORK-STUDY ***Federal work-study:*** Total amount: $2,422,590; 1,752 jobs averaging $1600.

APPLYING FOR FINANCIAL AID ***Required financial aid form:*** FAFSA.

CONTACT Anne-marie Caruso, Director of Financial Aid, Wentworth Institute of Technology, 550 Huntington Avenue, Boston, MA 02115-5998, 617-989-4174 or toll-free 800-556-0610. *Fax:* 617-989-4201. *E-mail:* carusoa@wit.edu.

WESLEYAN COLLEGE

Macon, GA

ABOUT THE INSTITUTION Independent United Methodist, undergraduate: women only; graduate: coed. ***Awards:*** bachelor's and master's degrees. 31 undergraduate majors. ***Total enrollment:*** 739. Undergraduates: 624. Freshmen: 90.

GIFT AID (NEED-BASED) ***Scholarships, grants, and awards:*** Federal Pell, FSEOG, state, private, college/university gift aid from institutional funds.

GIFT AID (NON-NEED-BASED) ***Scholarships, grants, and awards by category:*** *Academic interests/achievement:* biological sciences, business, communication, education, English, foreign languages, general academic interests/achievements, humanities, mathematics, premedicine, religion/biblical studies, social sciences. *Creative arts/performance:* art/fine arts, music, theater/drama. *Special achievements/activities:* community service, general special achievements/activities, leadership, religious involvement. *Special characteristics:* adult students, children and siblings of alumni, children of current students, children of faculty/staff, ethnic background, first-generation college students, general special characteristics, handicapped students, international students, out-of-state students, parents of current students, relatives of clergy, religious affiliation, siblings of current students, spouses of current students.

LOANS ***Programs:*** FFEL (Subsidized and Unsubsidized Stafford, PLUS), Perkins, college/university, various alternative or private loans.

APPLYING FOR FINANCIAL AID ***Required financial aid forms:*** FAFSA, institution's own form, state aid form.

CONTACT Kizzy K. Holmes, Associate Director of Financial Aid, Wesleyan College, 4760 Forsyth Road, Macon, GA 31210-4462, 478-757-5205 or toll-free 800-447-6610. *Fax:* 478-757-4030. *E-mail:* financialaid@wesleyancollege.edu.

WESLEYAN UNIVERSITY

Middletown, CT

Tuition & fees: $38,634 **Average undergraduate aid package: $32,002**

ABOUT THE INSTITUTION Independent, coed. ***Awards:*** bachelor's, master's, and doctoral degrees and post-master's certificates. 47 undergraduate majors. ***Total enrollment:*** 3,149. Undergraduates: 2,772. Freshmen: 715. Institutional methodology is used as a basis for awarding need-based institutional aid.

UNDERGRADUATE EXPENSES for 2008–09 ***Application fee:*** $55. ***One-time required fee:*** $300. ***Comprehensive fee:*** $49,270 includes full-time tuition ($38,364), mandatory fees ($270), and room and board ($10,636). Room and board charges vary according to board plan and housing facility. ***Payment plan:*** Installment.

FRESHMAN FINANCIAL AID (Fall 2007) 390 applied for aid; of those 84% were deemed to have need. 100% of freshmen with need received aid; of those 100% had need fully met. ***Average percent of need met:*** 100% (excluding resources awarded to replace EFC). ***Average financial aid package:*** $30,755 (excluding resources awarded to replace EFC). 2% of all full-time freshmen had no need and received non-need-based gift aid.

UNDERGRADUATE FINANCIAL AID (Fall 2007) 1,431 applied for aid; of those 91% were deemed to have need. 100% of undergraduates with need received aid; of those 100% had need fully met. ***Average percent of need met:*** 100% (excluding resources awarded to replace EFC). ***Average financial aid package:*** $32,002 (excluding resources awarded to replace EFC). 3% of all full-time undergraduates had no need and received non-need-based gift aid.

GIFT AID (NEED-BASED) ***Total amount:*** $32,895,772 (6% federal, 1% state, 90% institutional, 3% external sources). ***Receiving aid:*** Freshmen: 40% (294); all full-time undergraduates: 43% (1,186). ***Average award:*** Freshmen: $26,348; Undergraduates: $27,758. ***Scholarships, grants, and awards:*** Federal Pell, FSEOG, state, private, college/university gift aid from institutional funds.

GIFT AID (NON-NEED-BASED) ***Total amount:*** $3,615,525 (100% institutional). ***Receiving aid:*** Freshmen: 1% (6). ***Average award:*** Freshmen: $36,805. Undergraduates: $46,955. ***ROTC:*** Air Force cooperative.

LOANS ***Student loans:*** $6,500,917 (100% need-based). 43% of past graduating class borrowed through all loan programs. *Average indebtedness per student:* $27,402. ***Average need-based loan:*** Freshmen: $3217. Undergraduates: $4741. ***Parent loans:*** $3,577,586 (100% non-need-based). ***Programs:*** Federal Direct (Subsidized and Unsubsidized Stafford, PLUS), Perkins, college/university.

WORK-STUDY ***Federal work-study:*** Total amount: $2,529,652; 1,058 jobs averaging $2190. ***State or other work-study/employment:*** Total amount: $357,687 (100% need-based). 139 part-time jobs averaging $1991.

APPLYING FOR FINANCIAL AID ***Required financial aid forms:*** FAFSA, CSS Financial Aid PROFILE, business/farm supplement. ***Financial aid deadline:*** 2/15. ***Notification date:*** 4/1. Students must reply by 5/1.

CONTACT Jennifer Garratt Lawton, Director of Financial Aid, Wesleyan University, 237 High Street, Middletown, CT 06459-0260, 860-685-2800. *Fax:* 860-685-2801. *E-mail:* finaid@wesleyan.edu.

WESLEY COLLEGE

Dover, DE

ABOUT THE INSTITUTION Independent United Methodist, coed. ***Awards:*** associate, bachelor's, and master's degrees and post-bachelor's and post-master's certificates. 18 undergraduate majors. ***Total enrollment:*** 1,871. Undergraduates: 1,767. Freshmen: 484.

GIFT AID (NEED-BASED) ***Scholarships, grants, and awards:*** Federal Pell, FSEOG, state, private, college/university gift aid from institutional funds.

GIFT AID (NON-NEED-BASED) ***Scholarships, grants, and awards by category:*** *Academic interests/achievement:* general academic interests/achievements. *Special achievements/activities:* community service, general special achievements/activities, leadership, religious involvement.

LOANS ***Programs:*** Federal Direct (Subsidized and Unsubsidized Stafford, PLUS), FFEL (Subsidized and Unsubsidized Stafford, PLUS), Perkins, state, college/university.

APPLYING FOR FINANCIAL AID ***Required financial aid forms:*** FAFSA, institution's own form.

CONTACT James Marks, Director of Student Financial Planning, Wesley College, 120 North State Street, Dover, DE 19901-3875, 302-736-2334 or toll-free 800-937-5398 Ext. 2400 (out-of-state). *Fax:* 302-736-2594. *E-mail:* marksja@wesley.edu.

WESLEY COLLEGE

Florence, MS

ABOUT THE INSTITUTION Independent Congregational Methodist, coed. 2 undergraduate majors.

GIFT AID (NEED-BASED) ***Scholarships, grants, and awards:*** Federal Pell, FSEOG, state, college/university gift aid from institutional funds.

GIFT AID (NON-NEED-BASED) ***Scholarships, grants, and awards by category:*** *Academic interests/achievement:* general academic interests/achievements. *Creative arts/performance:* music. *Special achievements/activities:* leadership, religious involvement.

LOANS ***Programs:*** Federal Direct (Subsidized and Unsubsidized Stafford, PLUS), FFEL (Subsidized and Unsubsidized Stafford, PLUS), Perkins, alternative loans.

WORK-STUDY ***Federal work-study:*** Total amount: $25,296; 16 jobs averaging $1581.

APPLYING FOR FINANCIAL AID ***Required financial aid form:*** FAFSA.

CONTACT William Devore Jr., Director of Financial Aid, Wesley College, PO Box 1070, Florence, MS 39073-1070, 601-845-4086 or toll-free 800-748-9972. *Fax:* 601-845-2266. *E-mail:* wdevore@wesleycollege.edu.

WEST CHESTER UNIVERSITY OF PENNSYLVANIA

West Chester, PA

Tuition & fees (PA res): $6737 **Average undergraduate aid package: $7228**

ABOUT THE INSTITUTION State-supported, coed. ***Awards:*** bachelor's and master's degrees and post-bachelor's and post-master's certificates. 57 undergraduate majors. ***Total enrollment:*** 13,619. Undergraduates: 11,482. Freshmen: 2,002. Federal methodology is used as a basis for awarding need-based institutional aid.

UNDERGRADUATE EXPENSES for 2008–09 ***Application fee:*** $35. ***One-time required fee:*** $1379. ***Tuition, state resident:*** full-time $5358; part-time $223 per credit. ***Tuition, nonresident:*** full-time $13,396; part-time $558 per credit. ***Required fees:*** full-time $1379; $50 per credit. Full-time tuition and fees vary according to course load. Part-time tuition and fees vary according to course load. ***College room and board:*** $6874; ***Room only:*** $4476. Room and board charges vary according to board plan and housing facility. ***Payment plan:*** Installment.

FRESHMAN FINANCIAL AID (Fall 2007) 1,650 applied for aid; of those 63% were deemed to have need. 94% of freshmen with need received aid; of those 39% had need fully met. ***Average percent of need met:*** 61% (excluding resources awarded to replace EFC). ***Average financial aid package:*** $7084 (excluding resources awarded to replace EFC). 6% of all full-time freshmen had no need and received non-need-based gift aid.

UNDERGRADUATE FINANCIAL AID (Fall 2007) 7,478 applied for aid; of those 69% were deemed to have need. 95% of undergraduates with need received aid; of those 41% had need fully met. ***Average percent of need met:*** 64% (excluding resources awarded to replace EFC). ***Average financial aid package:*** $7228 (excluding resources awarded to replace EFC). 3% of all full-time undergraduates had no need and received non-need-based gift aid.

GIFT AID (NEED-BASED) ***Total amount:*** $16,275,323 (37% federal, 42% state, 11% institutional, 10% external sources). ***Receiving aid:*** Freshmen: 35% (679); all full-time undergraduates: 31% (3,244). ***Average award:*** Freshmen: $5251; Undergraduates: $4729. ***Scholarships, grants, and awards:*** Federal Pell, FSEOG, state, college/university gift aid from institutional funds.

GIFT AID (NON-NEED-BASED) ***Total amount:*** $730,261 (7% state, 66% institutional, 27% external sources). ***Receiving aid:*** Freshmen: 8. Undergraduates: 43. ***Average award:*** Freshmen: $2383. Undergraduates: $5224. ***Scholarships, grants, and awards by category:*** *Academic interests/achievement:* business, general academic interests/achievements, mathematics, social sciences. *Creative arts/performance:* music, theater/drama. *Special characteristics:* children of faculty/staff. ***Tuition waivers:*** Full or partial for employees or children of employees, senior citizens. ***ROTC:*** Army cooperative, Air Force cooperative.

LOANS ***Student loans:*** $44,791,831 (74% need-based, 26% non-need-based). 65% of past graduating class borrowed through all loan programs. *Average indebtedness per student:* $25,179. ***Average need-based loan:*** Freshmen: $3523. Undergraduates: $4318. ***Parent loans:*** $3,141,782 (100% non-need-based). ***Programs:*** FFEL (Subsidized and Unsubsidized Stafford, PLUS), Perkins, Federal Nursing.

WORK-STUDY ***Federal work-study:*** Total amount: $669,411; jobs available. ***State or other work-study/employment:*** Part-time jobs available.

ATHLETIC AWARDS Total amount: $655,696 (81% need-based, 19% non-need-based).

APPLYING FOR FINANCIAL AID ***Required financial aid form:*** FAFSA. ***Financial aid deadline (priority):*** 3/1. ***Notification date:*** Students must reply within 4 weeks of notification.

CONTACT Financial Aid Office, West Chester University of Pennsylvania, 138 E.O. Bull Center, West Chester, PA 19383, 610-436-2627 or toll-free 877-315-2165 (in-state). *Fax:* 610-436-2574. *E-mail:* finaid@wcupa.edu.

WESTERN CAROLINA UNIVERSITY

Cullowhee, NC

Tuition & fees (NC res): $4325 **Average undergraduate aid package: $8154**

ABOUT THE INSTITUTION State-supported, coed. ***Awards:*** bachelor's, master's, and doctoral degrees and post-bachelor's and post-master's certificates. 71 undergraduate majors. ***Total enrollment:*** 9,050. Undergraduates: 7,130. Freshmen: 1,224. Federal methodology is used as a basis for awarding need-based institutional aid.

UNDERGRADUATE EXPENSES for 2008–09 ***Application fee:*** $40. ***Tuition, state resident:*** full-time $2078. ***Tuition, nonresident:*** full-time $11,661. ***Required fees:*** full-time $2247. Part-time tuition and fees vary according to course load. ***College room and board:*** $5462; ***Room only:*** $2832. Room and board charges vary according to board plan and housing facility. ***Payment plan:*** Installment.

FRESHMAN FINANCIAL AID (Fall 2008, est.) 979 applied for aid; of those 69% were deemed to have need. 99% of freshmen with need received aid; of those 57% had need fully met. ***Average percent of need met:*** 85% (excluding resources awarded to replace EFC). ***Average financial aid package:*** $8766 (excluding resources awarded to replace EFC). 8% of all full-time freshmen had no need and received non-need-based gift aid.

UNDERGRADUATE FINANCIAL AID (Fall 2008, est.) 4,180 applied for aid; of those 73% were deemed to have need. 98% of undergraduates with need received aid; of those 51% had need fully met. ***Average percent of need met:*** 83% (excluding resources awarded to replace EFC). ***Average financial aid package:*** $8154 (excluding resources awarded to replace EFC). 8% of all full-time undergraduates had no need and received non-need-based gift aid.

GIFT AID (NEED-BASED) ***Total amount:*** $17,700,531 (35% federal, 50% state, 10% institutional, 5% external sources). ***Receiving aid:*** Freshmen: 54% (659); all full-time undergraduates: 50% (2,889). ***Average award:*** Freshmen: $7698; Undergraduates: $6189. ***Scholarships, grants, and awards:*** Federal Pell, FSEOG, state, private, college/university gift aid from institutional funds.

GIFT AID (NON-NEED-BASED) ***Total amount:*** $3,151,027 (1% federal, 51% state, 25% institutional, 23% external sources). ***Receiving aid:*** Freshmen: 9% (113). Undergraduates: 7% (384). ***Average award:*** Freshmen: $2048. Undergraduates: $1564. ***Scholarships, grants, and awards by category:*** *Academic interests/achievement:* 499 awards ($735,072 total): biological sciences, business, communication, education, English, general academic interests/achievements, mathematics. *Creative arts/performance:* 256 awards ($58,850 total): art/fine arts, music, theater/drama. *Special characteristics:* 82 awards ($98,232 total): ethnic background, handicapped students, local/state students, members of minority groups. ***Tuition waivers:*** Full or partial for employees or children of employees, senior citizens.

LOANS ***Student loans:*** $18,241,810 (61% need-based, 39% non-need-based). 33% of past graduating class borrowed through all loan programs. *Average indebtedness per student:* $11,705. ***Average need-based loan:*** Freshmen: $3536. Undergraduates: $4075. ***Parent loans:*** $4,266,461 (29% need-based, 71% non-need-based). ***Programs:*** Federal Direct (Subsidized and Unsubsidized Stafford, PLUS), FFEL (Subsidized and Unsubsidized Stafford, PLUS), Perkins.

WORK-STUDY ***Federal work-study:*** Total amount: $627,952; 408 jobs averaging $1562.

ATHLETIC AWARDS Total amount: $1,689,962 (47% need-based, 53% non-need-based).

APPLYING FOR FINANCIAL AID ***Required financial aid forms:*** FAFSA, institution's own form. ***Financial aid deadline (priority):*** 3/31. ***Notification date:*** Continuous beginning 4/1.

CONTACT Ms. Trina F. Orr, Director of Financial Aid, Western Carolina University, 123 Killian Annex, Cullowhee, NC 28723, 828-227-7292 or toll-free 877-WCU4YOU. *Fax:* 828-227-7042. *E-mail:* torr@email.wcu.edu.

WESTERN CONNECTICUT STATE UNIVERSITY

Danbury, CT

Tuition & fees (CT res): $7088 **Average undergraduate aid package: $10,946**

ABOUT THE INSTITUTION State-supported, coed. ***Awards:*** associate, bachelor's, master's, and doctoral degrees and post-bachelor's certificates. 37 undergraduate majors. ***Total enrollment:*** 6,462. Undergraduates: 5,769. Freshmen: 944. Federal methodology is used as a basis for awarding need-based institutional aid.

UNDERGRADUATE EXPENSES for 2008–09 ***Application fee:*** $50. ***Tuition, state resident:*** full-time $3514; part-time $319 per credit hour. ***Tuition, nonresident:*** full-time $11,373; part-time $319 per credit hour. ***Required fees:*** full-time $3574. Full-time tuition and fees vary according to reciprocity agreements. ***College room and board:*** $9158; ***Room only:*** $5384. Room and board charges vary according to housing facility. ***Payment plan:*** Installment.

FRESHMAN FINANCIAL AID (Fall 2008, est.) 755 applied for aid; of those 89% were deemed to have need. 75% of freshmen with need received aid; of those 93% had need fully met. ***Average percent of need met:*** 78% (excluding resources awarded to replace EFC). ***Average financial aid package:*** $10,628 (excluding resources awarded to replace EFC). 2% of all full-time freshmen had no need and received non-need-based gift aid.

UNDERGRADUATE FINANCIAL AID (Fall 2008, est.) 3,235 applied for aid; of those 91% were deemed to have need. 77% of undergraduates with need received aid; of those 96% had need fully met. ***Average percent of need met:*** 76% (excluding resources awarded to replace EFC). ***Average financial aid package:*** $10,946 (excluding resources awarded to replace EFC). 1% of all full-time undergraduates had no need and received non-need-based gift aid.

GIFT AID (NEED-BASED) ***Total amount:*** $8,290,573 (38% federal, 52% state, 5% institutional, 5% external sources). ***Receiving aid:*** Freshmen: 44% (411); all full-time undergraduates: 38% (1,732). ***Average award:*** Freshmen: $4965; Undergraduates: $4222. ***Scholarships, grants, and awards:*** Federal Pell, FSEOG, state, private, college/university gift aid from institutional funds.

GIFT AID (NON-NEED-BASED) ***Total amount:*** $384,770 (22% federal, 10% state, 55% institutional, 13% external sources). ***Receiving aid:*** Freshmen: 2% (22). Undergraduates: 3% (159). ***Average award:*** Freshmen: $1097. Undergraduates: $1455. ***Scholarships, grants, and awards by category:*** *Academic interests/achievement:* 75 awards ($206,273 total): general academic interests/achievements. ***Tuition waivers:*** Full or partial for employees or children of employees, senior citizens. ***ROTC:*** Army cooperative, Air Force cooperative.

LOANS ***Student loans:*** $11,610,302 (98% need-based, 2% non-need-based). 63% of past graduating class borrowed through all loan programs. *Average indebtedness per student:* $23,970. ***Average need-based loan:*** Freshmen: $7627. Undergraduates: $8544. ***Parent loans:*** $2,459,733 (73% need-based, 27% non-need-based). ***Programs:*** Federal Direct (Subsidized and Unsubsidized Stafford, PLUS), FFEL (Subsidized and Unsubsidized Stafford, PLUS), Perkins.

WORK-STUDY ***Federal work-study:*** Total amount: $81,400; 27 jobs averaging $3015. ***State or other work-study/employment:*** Total amount: $81,400 (100% need-based). 27 part-time jobs averaging $3015.

APPLYING FOR FINANCIAL AID ***Required financial aid forms:*** FAFSA, institution's own form. ***Financial aid deadline:*** 3/30 (priority: 3/1). ***Notification date:*** Continuous beginning 4/15. Students must reply by 5/1 or within 2 weeks of notification.

CONTACT Nancy Barton, Director of Financial Aid, Western Connecticut State University, 181 White Street, Danbury, CT 06810-6860, 203-837-8588 or toll-free 877-837-WCSU. *Fax:* 203-837-8528. *E-mail:* bartonn@wcsu.edu.

WESTERN GOVERNORS UNIVERSITY

Salt Lake City, UT

Tuition & fees: N/R **Average undergraduate aid package: $3966**

ABOUT THE INSTITUTION Independent, coed. ***Awards:*** bachelor's and master's degrees and post-bachelor's certificates. 7 undergraduate majors. ***Total enrollment:*** 9,022. Undergraduates: 6,491. Federal methodology is used as a basis for awarding need-based institutional aid.

FRESHMAN FINANCIAL AID (Fall 2007) ***Average percent of need met:*** 100% (excluding resources awarded to replace EFC). ***Average financial aid package:*** $5013 (excluding resources awarded to replace EFC).

UNDERGRADUATE FINANCIAL AID (Fall 2007) 8,141 applied for aid; of those 68% were deemed to have need. 100% of undergraduates with need received aid. ***Average percent of need met:*** 100% (excluding resources awarded to replace EFC). ***Average financial aid package:*** $3966 (excluding resources awarded to replace EFC).

GIFT AID (NEED-BASED) ***Total amount:*** $5,271,934 (89% federal, 11% institutional). ***Receiving aid:*** Freshmen: 64% (2,246); all full-time undergraduates: 68% (5,572). ***Average award:*** Freshmen: $1784; Undergraduates: $1784. ***Scholarships, grants, and awards:*** Federal Pell, private, college/university gift aid from institutional funds.

GIFT AID (NON-NEED-BASED) ***Receiving aid:*** Undergraduates: 65% (5,280).

LOANS ***Student loans:*** $40,114,645 (45% need-based, 55% non-need-based). 80% of past graduating class borrowed through all loan programs. *Average indebtedness per student:* $18,000. ***Average need-based loan:*** Freshmen: $480. Undergraduates: $480. ***Parent loans:*** $27,035 (100% non-need-based). ***Programs:*** FFEL (Subsidized and Unsubsidized Stafford, PLUS).

APPLYING FOR FINANCIAL AID ***Required financial aid forms:*** FAFSA, institution's own form. ***Financial aid deadline:*** Continuous. ***Notification date:*** Continuous.

CONTACT Stacey Ludwig-Hardman, Director of Academic Services, Western Governors University, 4001 South 700 East Suite 700, Salt Lake City, UT 84107, 801-274-3280 or toll-free 877-435-7948. *Fax:* 801-274-3305. *E-mail:* sludwig@wgu.edu.

WESTERN ILLINOIS UNIVERSITY

Macomb, IL

Tuition & fees (IL res): $8272 **Average undergraduate aid package: $9423**

ABOUT THE INSTITUTION State-supported, coed. ***Awards:*** bachelor's, master's, and doctoral degrees and post-bachelor's certificates. 60 undergraduate majors. ***Total enrollment:*** 13,175. Undergraduates: 10,735. Freshmen: 1,816. Federal methodology is used as a basis for awarding need-based institutional aid.

UNDERGRADUATE EXPENSES for 2008–09 ***Application fee:*** $30. ***Tuition, state resident:*** full-time $6456; part-time $215.20 per semester hour. ***Tuition, nonresident:*** full-time $9684; part-time $322.80 per semester hour. ***Required fees:*** full-time $1816; $60.55 per semester hour. Full-time tuition and fees vary according to course load, location, and student level. Part-time tuition and fees vary according to course load, location, and student level. ***College room and board:*** $7210; ***Room only:*** $4350. Room and board charges vary according to board plan, housing facility, and student level. ***Payment plan:*** Guaranteed tuition.

FRESHMAN FINANCIAL AID (Fall 2008, est.) 1,488 applied for aid; of those 74% were deemed to have need. 98% of freshmen with need received aid; of those 38% had need fully met. ***Average percent of need met:*** 62% (excluding resources awarded to replace EFC). ***Average financial aid package:*** $8626 (excluding resources awarded to replace EFC). 6% of all full-time freshmen had no need and received non-need-based gift aid.

UNDERGRADUATE FINANCIAL AID (Fall 2008, est.) 7,088 applied for aid; of those 79% were deemed to have need. 98% of undergraduates with need received aid; of those 39% had need fully met. ***Average percent of need met:*** 65% (excluding resources awarded to replace EFC). ***Average financial aid package:*** $9423 (excluding resources awarded to replace EFC). 5% of all full-time undergraduates had no need and received non-need-based gift aid.

GIFT AID (NEED-BASED) ***Total amount:*** $29,651,342 (47% federal, 43% state, 7% institutional, 3% external sources). ***Receiving aid:*** Freshmen: 42% (753); all full-time undergraduates: 39% (3,830). ***Average award:*** Freshmen: $8090; Undergraduates: $7825. ***Scholarships, grants, and awards:*** Federal Pell, FSEOG, state, private, college/university gift aid from institutional funds.

GIFT AID (NON-NEED-BASED) ***Total amount:*** $4,361,266 (33% federal, 24% state, 33% institutional, 10% external sources). ***Average award:*** Freshmen: $3993. Undergraduates: $2898. ***Scholarships, grants, and awards by category:*** *Academic interests/achievement:* 3,789 awards ($3,349,809 total): agriculture, biological sciences, business, education, foreign languages, general academic interests/achievements, home economics, mathematics, physical sciences, social sciences. *Creative arts/performance:* 574 awards ($710,672 total): applied art and design, cinema/film/broadcasting, dance, debating, journalism/publications, music, performing arts, theater/drama. *Special achievements/activities:* 304 awards ($225,847 total): community service, leadership. *Special characteristics:* 1,213 awards ($2,208,890 total): children of faculty/staff, general special characteristics, international students, members of minority groups, veterans' children. ***Tuition waivers:*** Full or partial for employees or children of employees, senior citizens. ***ROTC:*** Army.

LOANS ***Student loans:*** $48,740,591 (53% need-based, 47% non-need-based). 60% of past graduating class borrowed through all loan programs. *Average indebtedness per student:* $17,567. ***Average need-based loan:*** Freshmen: $3274. Undergraduates: $4192. ***Parent loans:*** $9,471,292 (66% need-based, 34% non-need-based). ***Programs:*** FFEL (Subsidized and Unsubsidized Stafford, PLUS), Perkins, college/university.

WORK-STUDY ***Federal work-study:*** Total amount: $328,747; 209 jobs averaging $1770. ***State or other work-study/employment:*** Total amount: $1,976,896 (68% need-based, 32% non-need-based). 1,815 part-time jobs averaging $1455.

ATHLETIC AWARDS Total amount: $2,459,474 (42% need-based, 58% non-need-based).

APPLYING FOR FINANCIAL AID ***Required financial aid form:*** FAFSA. ***Financial aid deadline (priority):*** 2/15. ***Notification date:*** Continuous.

CONTACT Financial Aid Office, Western Illinois University, 1 University Circle, Macomb, IL 61455-1390, 309-298-2446 or toll-free 877-742-5948. *Fax:* 309-298-2353. *E-mail:* financial_aid@wiu.edu.

WESTERN INTERNATIONAL UNIVERSITY

Phoenix, AZ

CONTACT Ms. Doris Johnson, Director of Financial Aid, Western International University, 9215 North Black Canyon Highway, Phoenix, AZ 85021-2718, 602-943-2311.

WESTERN KENTUCKY UNIVERSITY

Bowling Green, KY

Tuition & fees (KY res): $6930 **Average undergraduate aid package: $10,360**

ABOUT THE INSTITUTION State-supported, coed. ***Awards:*** associate, bachelor's, master's, and doctoral degrees and post-bachelor's and post-master's certificates. 86 undergraduate majors. ***Total enrollment:*** 19,742. Undergraduates: 16,947. Freshmen: 3,307. Federal methodology is used as a basis for awarding need-based institutional aid.

UNDERGRADUATE EXPENSES for 2008–09 ***Application fee:*** $35. ***Tuition, state resident:*** full-time $6930; part-time $289 per hour. ***Tuition, nonresident:*** full-time $17,088; part-time $712 per hour. Full-time tuition and fees vary according to course load, location, program, and reciprocity agreements. Part-time tuition and fees vary according to course load, location, program, and reciprocity agreements. ***College room and board:*** $5914; ***Room only:*** $3450. Room and board charges vary according to board plan and housing facility. ***Payment plan:*** Installment.

FRESHMAN FINANCIAL AID (Fall 2007) 2,433 applied for aid; of those 75% were deemed to have need. 99% of freshmen with need received aid; of those 35% had need fully met. ***Average percent of need met:*** 35% (excluding resources awarded to replace EFC). ***Average financial aid package:*** $9846 (excluding resources awarded to replace EFC). 21% of all full-time freshmen had no need and received non-need-based gift aid.

UNDERGRADUATE FINANCIAL AID (Fall 2007) 9,857 applied for aid; of those 77% were deemed to have need. 98% of undergraduates with need received aid; of those 33% had need fully met. ***Average percent of need met:*** 33% (excluding resources awarded to replace EFC). ***Average financial aid package:*** $10,360 (excluding resources awarded to replace EFC). 19% of all full-time undergraduates had no need and received non-need-based gift aid.

GIFT AID (NEED-BASED) ***Total amount:*** $23,832,093 (71% federal, 29% state). ***Receiving aid:*** Freshmen: 37% (1,106); all full-time undergraduates: 36% (4,658). ***Average award:*** Freshmen: $4730; Undergraduates: $4535. ***Scholarships, grants, and awards:*** Federal Pell, FSEOG, state, private, college/university gift aid from institutional funds, United Negro College Fund.

GIFT AID (NON-NEED-BASED) ***Total amount:*** $25,601,206 (10% federal, 39% state, 40% institutional, 11% external sources). ***Receiving aid:*** Freshmen: 52% (1,567). Undergraduates: 33% (4,275). ***Average award:*** Freshmen: $4550. Undergraduates: $4275. ***Scholarships, grants, and awards by category:*** *Academic interests/achievement:* 2,059 awards ($7,170,297 total): agriculture, biological sciences, business, communication, education, engineering/technologies, English, foreign languages, general academic interests/achievements, health fields, home economics, mathematics, military science, physical sciences, premedicine, social sciences. *Creative arts/performance:* 354 awards ($1,128,039 total): art/fine arts, cinema/film/broadcasting, dance, debating, general creative arts/performance, journalism/publications, music, theater/drama. *Special achievements/activities:* 201 awards ($233,395 total): general special achievements/activities, leadership, memberships. *Special characteristics:* 1,303 awards ($1,871,298 total): adult students, children of union members/company employees, ethnic background, general special characteristics, handicapped students, international students, local/state students, members of minority groups, out-of-state students, religious affiliation, veterans. ***Tuition waivers:*** Full or partial for children of alumni, employees or children of employees, senior citizens. ***ROTC:*** Army, Air Force cooperative.

LOANS ***Student loans:*** $48,773,327 (51% need-based, 49% non-need-based). 57% of past graduating class borrowed through all loan programs. *Average indebtedness per student:* $15,042. ***Average need-based loan:*** Freshmen: $2962. Undergraduates: $3851. ***Parent loans:*** $7,587,820 (100% non-need-based). ***Programs:*** FFEL (Subsidized and Unsubsidized Stafford, PLUS), Perkins, alternative loans.

WORK-STUDY ***Federal work-study:*** Total amount: $1,374,318; 805 jobs averaging $1366. ***State or other work-study/employment:*** Total amount: $3,464,779 (100% non-need-based). 1,383 part-time jobs averaging $1350.

ATHLETIC AWARDS Total amount: $4,111,482 (100% non-need-based).

APPLYING FOR FINANCIAL AID ***Required financial aid form:*** FAFSA. ***Financial aid deadline (priority):*** 3/15. ***Notification date:*** Continuous.

CONTACT Cindy Burnette, Student Financial Assistance Director, Western Kentucky University, Potter Hall, Room 317, Bowling Green, KY 42101-1018, 270-745-2758 or toll-free 800-495-8463 (in-state). *Fax:* 270-745-6586. *E-mail:* cindy.burnette@wku.edu.

WESTERN MICHIGAN UNIVERSITY

Kalamazoo, MI

Tuition & fees (MI res): $7928 **Average undergraduate aid package: $13,000**

ABOUT THE INSTITUTION State-supported, coed. ***Awards:*** bachelor's, master's, and doctoral degrees and post-bachelor's and post-master's certificates (specialist). 109 undergraduate majors. ***Total enrollment:*** 24,818. Undergraduates: 19,854. Freshmen: 3,828. Federal methodology is used as a basis for awarding need-based institutional aid.

UNDERGRADUATE EXPENSES for 2008–09 ***Application fee:*** $35. ***One-time required fee:*** $300. ***Tuition, state resident:*** full-time $7220; part time $245.06 per credit. ***Tuition, nonresident:*** full-time $17,712; part-time $601.15 per credit. ***Required fees:*** full-time $708; $190.25 per term. Full-time tuition and fees vary according to course load, location, and student level. Part-time tuition and fees vary according to course load, location, and student level. ***College room and board:*** $7377; ***Room only:*** $3689. Room and board charges vary according to board plan. ***Payment plan:*** Installment.

FRESHMAN FINANCIAL AID (Fall 2007) 4,000 applied for aid; of those 85% were deemed to have need. 100% of freshmen with need received aid; of those 35% had need fully met. ***Average percent of need met:*** 85% (excluding resources awarded to replace EFC). ***Average financial aid package:*** $13,000 (excluding resources awarded to replace EFC). 6% of all full-time freshmen had no need and received non-need-based gift aid.

UNDERGRADUATE FINANCIAL AID (Fall 2007) 11,000 applied for aid; of those 82% were deemed to have need. 100% of undergraduates with need received aid; of those 44% had need fully met. ***Average percent of need met:*** 85% (excluding resources awarded to replace EFC). ***Average financial aid package:*** $13,000 (excluding resources awarded to replace EFC). 9% of all full-time undergraduates had no need and received non-need-based gift aid.

GIFT AID (NEED-BASED) ***Total amount:*** $25,448,046 (55% federal, 7% state, 33% institutional, 5% external sources). ***Receiving aid:*** Freshmen: 53% (2,400); all full-time undergraduates: 34% (6,100). ***Average award:*** Freshmen: $5000; Undergraduates: $5000. ***Scholarships, grants, and awards:*** Federal Pell, FSEOG, state, private, college/university gift aid from institutional funds.

GIFT AID (NON-NEED-BASED) ***Total amount:*** $15,305,911 (31% state, 56% institutional, 13% external sources). ***Receiving aid:*** Freshmen: 29% (1,300). Undergraduates: 25% (4,500). ***Average award:*** Freshmen: $2600. Undergraduates: $2900. ***Tuition waivers:*** Full or partial for employees or children of employees, senior citizens. ***ROTC:*** Army.

LOANS ***Student loans:*** $85,233,602 (42% need-based, 58% non-need-based). 55% of past graduating class borrowed through all loan programs. *Average indebtedness per student:* $18,900. ***Average need-based loan:*** Freshmen: $3000. Undergraduates: $4300. ***Parent loans:*** $24,718,859 (51% need-based, 49% non-need-based). ***Programs:*** Federal Direct (Subsidized and Unsubsidized Stafford, PLUS), Perkins, alternative loans.

WORK-STUDY ***Federal work-study:*** Total amount: $1,063,009; jobs available. ***State or other work-study/employment:*** Total amount: $6,280,683 (4% need-based, 96% non-need-based). Part-time jobs available.

ATHLETIC AWARDS Total amount: $4,520,524 (100% non-need-based).

APPLYING FOR FINANCIAL AID ***Required financial aid form:*** FAFSA. ***Financial aid deadline (priority):*** 3/15. ***Notification date:*** Continuous beginning 3/15.

CONTACT Mr. David Ladd, Associate Director of Student Financial Aid, Western Michigan University, 1903 West Michigan Avenue, Faunce Student Services Building, Room 3306, Kalamazoo, MI 49008-5337, 269-387-6000. *E-mail:* david.ladd@wmich.edu.

WESTERN NEW ENGLAND COLLEGE

Springfield, MA

Tuition & fees: $27,470 **Average undergraduate aid package: $17,604**

ABOUT THE INSTITUTION Independent, coed. ***Awards:*** associate, bachelor's, master's, doctoral, and first professional degrees. 39 undergraduate majors. ***Total enrollment:*** 3,722. Undergraduates: 2,796. Freshmen: 739. Federal methodology is used as a basis for awarding need-based institutional aid.

UNDERGRADUATE EXPENSES for 2008–09 ***Application fee:*** $50. ***Comprehensive fee:*** $38,024 includes full-time tuition ($25,556), mandatory fees ($1914), and room and board ($10,554). Full-time tuition and fees vary according to program. Room and board charges vary according to board plan and housing facility. ***Part-time tuition:*** $481 per credit. Part-time tuition and fees vary according to location and program. ***Payment plans:*** Tuition prepayment, installment.

FRESHMAN FINANCIAL AID (Fall 2008, est.) 687 applied for aid; of those 81% were deemed to have need. 100% of freshmen with need received aid; of those 14% had need fully met. ***Average percent of need met:*** 74% (excluding resources awarded to replace EFC). ***Average financial aid package:*** $19,273 (excluding resources awarded to replace EFC). 13% of all full-time freshmen had no need and received non-need-based gift aid.

UNDERGRADUATE FINANCIAL AID (Fall 2008, est.) 2,264 applied for aid; of those 80% were deemed to have need. 99% of undergraduates with need received aid; of those 13% had need fully met. ***Average percent of need met:*** 70% (excluding resources awarded to replace EFC). ***Average financial aid package:*** $17,604 (excluding resources awarded to replace EFC). 11% of all full-time undergraduates had no need and received non-need-based gift aid.

GIFT AID (NEED-BASED) ***Total amount:*** $20,737,824 (8% federal, 3% state, 86% institutional, 3% external sources). ***Receiving aid:*** Freshmen: 76% (557); all full-time undergraduates: 71% (1,781). ***Average award:*** Freshmen: $15,099; Undergraduates: $12,994. ***Scholarships, grants, and awards:*** Federal Pell, FSEOG, state, private, college/university gift aid from institutional funds.

GIFT AID (NON-NEED-BASED) ***Total amount:*** $3,426,944 (26% federal, 74% institutional). ***Receiving aid:*** Freshmen: 6% (42). Undergraduates: 4% (105). ***Average award:*** Freshmen: $10,245. Undergraduates: $9170. ***Scholarships, grants, and awards by category:*** *Academic interests/achievement:* business, engineering/technologies, general academic interests/achievements. *Creative arts/performance:* 1 award ($500 total): music. *Special achievements/activities:* community service, leadership. *Special characteristics:* children of faculty/staff, children of union members/company employees, international students, local/state students, members of minority groups, out-of-state students, siblings of current students. ***Tuition waivers:*** Full or partial for employees or children of employees, senior citizens. ***ROTC:*** Army, Air Force cooperative.

LOANS ***Student loans:*** $22,657,253 (36% need-based, 64% non-need-based). ***Average need-based loan:*** Freshmen: $4027. Undergraduates: $4454. ***Parent loans:*** $7,136,450 (100% non-need-based). ***Programs:*** Federal Direct (Subsidized and Unsubsidized Stafford, PLUS), FFEL (PLUS), Perkins, state.

WORK-STUDY ***Federal work-study:*** Total amount: $1,737,700; 896 jobs averaging $1940. ***State or other work-study/employment:*** Total amount: $660,000 (100% non-need-based). Part-time jobs available.

APPLYING FOR FINANCIAL AID ***Required financial aid forms:*** FAFSA, federal income tax form(s), W-2 forms. ***Financial aid deadline (priority):*** 4/15. ***Notification date:*** Continuous. Students must reply by 5/1 or within 2 weeks of notification.

CONTACT Mrs. Kathy M. Chambers, Associate Director of Student Administrative Services, Western New England College, 1215 Wilbraham Road, Springfield, MA 01110-2684, 413-796-2000 or toll-free 800-325-1122 Ext. 1321. Fax: 413-796-2081. *E-mail:* finaid@wnec.edu.

WESTERN NEW MEXICO UNIVERSITY

Silver City, NM

CONTACT Debra Reyes, Grant Counselor, Western New Mexico University, PO Box 680, Silver City, NM 88062, 575-538-6173 or toll-free 800-872-WNMU (in-state).

WESTERN OREGON UNIVERSITY

Monmouth, OR

Tuition & fees (OR res): $5868 **Average undergraduate aid package: $8323**

ABOUT THE INSTITUTION State-supported, coed. ***Awards:*** bachelor's and master's degrees and post-bachelor's certificates. 35 undergraduate majors. ***Total enrollment:*** 5,371. Undergraduates: 4,703. Freshmen: 911. Federal methodology is used as a basis for awarding need-based institutional aid.

UNDERGRADUATE EXPENSES for 2008–09 ***Application fee:*** $50. ***One-time required fee:*** $136. ***Tuition, state resident:*** full-time $4725; part-time $105 per credit. ***Tuition, nonresident:*** full-time $15,750; part-time $350 per credit. ***Required fees:*** full-time $1143; $91 per credit. Full-time tuition and fees vary according to course level, course load, degree level, and reciprocity agreements. Part-time tuition and fees vary according to course level, course load, degree level, and reciprocity agreements. ***College room and board:*** $7600. Room and board charges vary according to board plan and housing facility. ***Payment plans:*** Guaranteed tuition, deferred payment.

FRESHMAN FINANCIAL AID (Fall 2008, est.) 679 applied for aid; of those 77% were deemed to have need. 100% of freshmen with need received aid; of those 20% had need fully met. ***Average percent of need met:*** 71% (excluding resources awarded to replace EFC). ***Average financial aid package:*** $8352 (excluding resources awarded to replace EFC). 7% of all full-time freshmen had no need and received non-need-based gift aid.

UNDERGRADUATE FINANCIAL AID (Fall 2008, est.) 3,037 applied for aid; of those 80% were deemed to have need. 100% of undergraduates with need received aid; of those 18% had need fully met. ***Average percent of need met:*** 68% (excluding resources awarded to replace EFC). ***Average financial aid package:*** $8323 (excluding resources awarded to replace EFC). 5% of all full-time undergraduates had no need and received non-need-based gift aid.

GIFT AID (NEED-BASED) ***Total amount:*** $10,349,836 (49% federal, 26% state, 5% institutional, 20% external sources). ***Receiving aid:*** Freshmen: 61% (441); all full-time undergraduates: 57% (1,883). ***Average award:*** Freshmen: $6408; Undergraduates: $5944. ***Scholarships, grants, and awards:*** Federal Pell, FSEOG, state, private, college/university gift aid from institutional funds, Academic Competitiveness Grant, National Smart Grant, Federal TEACH Grant.

GIFT AID (NON-NEED-BASED) ***Total amount:*** $1,247,525 (1% federal, 2% state, 32% institutional, 65% external sources). ***Receiving aid:*** Freshmen: 5% (37). Undergraduates: 3% (110). ***Average award:*** Freshmen: $1483. Undergraduates: $2280. ***Scholarships, grants, and awards by category:*** *Academic interests/achievement:* 956 awards ($1,685,567 total): biological sciences, business, computer science, education, English, foreign languages, general academic interests/achievements, humanities, mathematics, physical sciences, premedicine, social sciences. *Creative arts/performance:* 232 awards ($253,364 total): art/fine arts, dance, music, performing arts, theater/drama. *Special achievements/activities:* 375 awards ($814,592 total): community service, general special achievements/activities, leadership. *Special characteristics:* 28 awards ($218,702 total): international students, veterans. ***Tuition waivers:*** Full or partial for employees or children of employees. ***ROTC:*** Army, Air Force cooperative.

LOANS ***Student loans:*** $20,948,901 (67% need-based, 33% non-need-based). 56% of past graduating class borrowed through all loan programs. *Average indebtedness per student:* $22,037. ***Average need-based loan:*** Freshmen: $3190. Undergraduates: $3945. ***Parent loans:*** $5,655,756 (20% need-based, 80% non-need-based). ***Programs:*** Federal Direct (Subsidized and Unsubsidized Stafford, PLUS), Perkins, college/university.

WORK-STUDY ***Federal work-study:*** Total amount: $299,045; 272 jobs averaging $833.

ATHLETIC AWARDS Total amount: $539,661 (57% need-based, 43% non-need-based).

APPLYING FOR FINANCIAL AID ***Required financial aid form:*** FAFSA. ***Financial aid deadline (priority):*** 3/1. ***Notification date:*** Continuous beginning 3/1. Students must reply within 3 weeks of notification.

CONTACT Ms. Donna Fossum, Director of Financial Aid, Western Oregon University, 345 North Monmouth Avenue, Monmouth, OR 97361, 503-838-8475 or toll-free 877-877-1593. *Fax:* 503-838-8200. *E-mail:* finaid@wou.edu.

WESTERN STATE COLLEGE OF COLORADO

Gunnison, CO

ABOUT THE INSTITUTION State-supported, coed. ***Awards:*** bachelor's degrees. 70 undergraduate majors. ***Total enrollment:*** 1,990. Undergraduates: 1,990. Freshmen: 530.

GIFT AID (NEED-BASED) ***Scholarships, grants, and awards:*** Federal Pell, FSEOG, state, private, college/university gift aid from institutional funds.

GIFT AID (NON-NEED-BASED) ***Scholarships, grants, and awards by category:*** *Academic interests/achievement:* general academic interests/achievements. *Creative arts/performance:* art/fine arts, music. *Special achievements/activities:* leadership. *Special characteristics:* children and siblings of alumni.

LOANS ***Programs:*** FFEL (Subsidized and Unsubsidized Stafford, PLUS), Perkins.

WORK-STUDY ***Federal work-study:*** Total amount: $210,000; 121 jobs averaging $953. ***State or other work-study/employment:*** Total amount: $811,000 (25% need-based; 75% non-need-based). 120 part-time jobs averaging $950.

APPLYING FOR FINANCIAL AID ***Required financial aid form:*** FAFSA.

CONTACT Marty Somero, Director, Financial Aid, Western State College of Colorado, Room 207, Taylor Hall, Gunnison, CO 81231, 970-943-3026 or toll-free 800-876-5309. *Fax:* 970-943-3086. *E-mail:* msomero@western.edu.

WESTERN WASHINGTON UNIVERSITY

Bellingham, WA

Tuition & fees (WA res): $5535 **Average undergraduate aid package: $10,032**

ABOUT THE INSTITUTION State-supported, coed. ***Awards:*** bachelor's and master's degrees and post-bachelor's and post-master's certificates. 112 undergraduate majors. ***Total enrollment:*** 14,620. Undergraduates: 13,406. Freshmen: 2,697. Federal methodology is used as a basis for awarding need-based institutional aid.

UNDERGRADUATE EXPENSES for 2008–09 ***Application fee:*** $50. ***Tuition, state resident:*** full-time $4788; part-time $160 per credit hour. ***Tuition, nonresident:*** full-time $16,419; part-time $547 per credit hour. ***Required fees:*** full-time $747. Full-time tuition and fees vary according to course load and location. Part-time tuition and fees vary according to course load and location. ***College room and board:*** $7712. Room and board charges vary according to board plan and housing facility. ***Payment plan:*** Installment.

FRESHMAN FINANCIAL AID (Fall 2008, est.) 1,908 applied for aid; of those 52% were deemed to have need. 95% of freshmen with need received aid; of those 37% had need fully met. ***Average percent of need met:*** 89% (excluding resources awarded to replace EFC). ***Average financial aid package:*** $9925 (excluding resources awarded to replace EFC). 2% of all full-time freshmen had no need and received non-need-based gift aid.

UNDERGRADUATE FINANCIAL AID (Fall 2008, est.) 7,139 applied for aid; of those 65% were deemed to have need. 97% of undergraduates with need received aid; of those 35% had need fully met. ***Average percent of need met:*** 89% (excluding resources awarded to replace EFC). ***Average financial aid package:*** $10,032 (excluding resources awarded to replace EFC). 2% of all full-time undergraduates had no need and received non-need-based gift aid.

GIFT AID (NEED-BASED) ***Total amount:*** $22,807,813 (38% federal, 42% state, 13% institutional, 7% external sources). ***Receiving aid:*** Freshmen: 29% (779); all full-time undergraduates: 29% (3,606). ***Average award:*** Freshmen: $7159; Undergraduates: $7144. ***Scholarships, grants, and awards:*** Federal Pell, FSEOG, state, private, college/university gift aid from institutional funds.

GIFT AID (NON-NEED-BASED) ***Total amount:*** $2,006,616 (6% federal, 7% state, 29% institutional, 58% external sources). ***Receiving aid:*** Freshmen: 2% (48). Undergraduates: 1% (121). ***Average award:*** Freshmen: $1169. Undergraduates: $1622. ***Scholarships, grants, and awards by category:*** *Academic interests/achievement:* biological sciences, business, communication, computer science, education, engineering/technologies, English, foreign languages, general academic interests/achievements, health fields, humanities, library science, mathematics, physical sciences, premedicine, social sciences. *Creative arts/performance:* applied art and design, art/fine arts, cinema/film/broadcasting, creative writing, dance, general creative arts/performance, journalism/publications, music, performing arts, theater/drama. *Special achievements/activities:* community service, leadership, memberships. *Special characteristics:* children of public servants, children of union members/company employees, ethnic background, general special characteristics, international students, local/state students, members of minority groups, previous college experience, veterans. ***Tuition waivers:*** Full or partial for employees or children of employees.

LOANS ***Student loans:*** $34,411,411 (51% need-based, 49% non-need-based). 50% of past graduating class borrowed through all loan programs. *Average indebtedness per student:* $15,560. ***Average need-based loan:*** Freshmen: $3197. Undergraduates: $4092. ***Parent loans:*** $16,685,792 (8% need-based, 92% non-need-based). ***Programs:*** Federal Direct (Subsidized and Unsubsidized Stafford, PLUS), FFEL (PLUS), Perkins, college/university, alternative loans.

WORK-STUDY ***Federal work-study:*** Total amount: $618,229; 196 jobs averaging $3154. ***State or other work-study/employment:*** Total amount: $1,387,347 (100% need-based). 409 part-time jobs averaging $3392.

ATHLETIC AWARDS Total amount: $1,113,011 (28% need-based, 72% non-need-based).

APPLYING FOR FINANCIAL AID ***Required financial aid form:*** FAFSA. ***Financial aid deadline (priority):*** 2/15. ***Notification date:*** Continuous beginning 3/15. Students must reply within 3 weeks of notification.

CONTACT Ms. Fidele Dent, Office Support Supervisor II, Financial Aid, Western Washington University, OM 255 MS 9006, Bellingham, WA 98225-9006, 360-650-3470. *E-mail:* financialaid@wwu.edu.

WESTFIELD STATE COLLEGE

Westfield, MA

Tuition & fees (MA res): $6515 **Average undergraduate aid package: $7294**

ABOUT THE INSTITUTION State-supported, coed. ***Awards:*** bachelor's and master's degrees and post-bachelor's and post-master's certificates. 27 undergraduate majors. ***Total enrollment:*** 5,548. Undergraduates: 4,867. Freshmen: 1,126. Federal methodology is used as a basis for awarding need-based institutional aid.

UNDERGRADUATE EXPENSES for 2008–09 ***Application fee:*** $35. ***Tuition, state resident:*** full-time $970; part-time $85 per credit. ***Tuition, nonresident:*** full-time $7050; part-time $95 per credit. ***Required fees:*** full-time $5545; $100 per credit or $145 per term. ***College room and board:*** $7204. Room and board charges vary according to board plan, housing facility, and location. ***Payment plan:*** Installment.

FRESHMAN FINANCIAL AID (Fall 2007) 821 applied for aid; of those 57% were deemed to have need. 98% of freshmen with need received aid; of those 16% had need fully met. ***Average percent of need met:*** 80% (excluding resources awarded to replace EFC). ***Average financial aid package:*** $7285 (excluding resources awarded to replace EFC). 1% of all full-time freshmen had no need and received non-need-based gift aid.

UNDERGRADUATE FINANCIAL AID (Fall 2007) 3,095 applied for aid; of those 63% were deemed to have need. 97% of undergraduates with need received aid; of those 23% had need fully met. ***Average percent of need met:*** 78% (excluding resources awarded to replace EFC). ***Average financial aid package:*** $7294 (excluding resources awarded to replace EFC). 1% of all full-time undergraduates had no need and received non-need-based gift aid.

GIFT AID (NEED-BASED) ***Total amount:*** $6,997,804 (44% federal, 34% state, 17% institutional, 5% external sources). ***Receiving aid:*** Freshmen: 33% (312); all full-time undergraduates: 31% (1,277). ***Average award:*** Freshmen: $5121; Undergraduates: $4473. ***Scholarships, grants, and awards:*** Federal Pell, FSEOG, state, private, college/university gift aid from institutional funds.

GIFT AID (NON-NEED-BASED) ***Total amount:*** $663,515 (27% state, 34% institutional, 39% external sources). ***Receiving aid:*** Freshmen: 14% (126). Undergraduates: 7% (289). ***Average award:*** Freshmen: $2041. Undergraduates: $3877. ***Scholarships, grants, and awards by category:*** *Academic interests/achievement:* 146 awards ($586,941 total): general academic interests/achievements. *Special characteristics:* 146 awards ($586,941 total). ***Tuition waivers:*** Full or partial for employees or children of employees, senior citizens. ***ROTC:*** Army cooperative, Air Force cooperative.

LOANS ***Student loans:*** $16,315,736 (51% need-based, 49% non-need-based). 72% of past graduating class borrowed through all loan programs. *Average indebtedness per student:* $17,059. ***Average need-based loan:*** Freshmen: $3318. Undergraduates: $3980. ***Parent loans:*** $3,101,469 (11% need-based, 89% non-need-based). ***Programs:*** FFEL (Subsidized and Unsubsidized Stafford, PLUS), Perkins.

WORK-STUDY ***Federal work-study:*** Total amount: $452,727; 343 jobs averaging $1220.

APPLYING FOR FINANCIAL AID ***Required financial aid form:*** FAFSA. ***Financial aid deadline (priority):*** 3/1. ***Notification date:*** 4/15.

CONTACT Catherine Ryan, Financial Aid Director, Westfield State College, 333 Western Avenue, Westfield, MA 01086, 413-572-5218 or toll-free 800-322-8401 (in-state).

WEST LIBERTY STATE UNIVERSITY

West Liberty, WV

Tuition & fees (WV res): $4464 **Average undergraduate aid package: $7067**

ABOUT THE INSTITUTION State-supported, coed. ***Awards:*** associate, bachelor's, and master's degrees. 35 undergraduate majors. ***Total enrollment:*** 2,511. Undergraduates: 2,493. Freshmen: 552. Federal methodology is used as a basis for awarding need-based institutional aid.

UNDERGRADUATE EXPENSES for 2008–09 ***Tuition, state resident:*** full-time $4464; part-time $186 per credit hour. ***Tuition, nonresident:*** full-time $10,896; part-time $454 per credit hour. ***College room and board:*** $6282. Room and board charges vary according to board plan and housing facility. ***Payment plans:*** Installment, deferred payment.

FRESHMAN FINANCIAL AID (Fall 2008, est.) 507 applied for aid; of those 78% were deemed to have need. ***Average financial aid package:*** $5807 (excluding resources awarded to replace EFC).

UNDERGRADUATE FINANCIAL AID (Fall 2008, est.) 2,097 applied for aid; of those 75% were deemed to have need. ***Average financial aid package:*** $7067 (excluding resources awarded to replace EFC).

GIFT AID (NEED-BASED) ***Total amount:*** $4,682,120 (71% federal, 29% state). ***Receiving aid:*** Freshmen: 48% (259); all full-time undergraduates: 51% (1,104). ***Average award:*** Freshmen: $4308; Undergraduates: $4241. ***Scholarships, grants, and awards:*** Federal Pell, FSEOG, state, private, college/university gift aid from institutional funds.

GIFT AID (NON-NEED-BASED) ***Total amount:*** $2,033,484 (53% state, 34% institutional, 13% external sources). ***Receiving aid:*** Freshmen: 27% (147). Undergraduates: 26% (563). ***Scholarships, grants, and awards by category:*** *Academic interests/achievement:* 273 awards ($604,597 total): business, communication, education, English, general academic interests/achievements, health fields, mathematics, physical sciences. *Creative arts/performance:* 69 awards ($155,061 total): art/fine arts, music, theater/drama. *Special achievements/activities:* cheerleading/drum major. *Special characteristics:* 7 awards ($5954 total): children and siblings of alumni, children of faculty/staff. ***Tuition waivers:*** Full or partial for employees or children of employees, senior citizens.

LOANS ***Student loans:*** $11,557,213 (41% need-based, 59% non-need-based). 81% of past graduating class borrowed through all loan programs. *Average indebtedness per student:* $21,097. ***Average need-based loan:*** Freshmen: $3374. Undergraduates: $3696. ***Parent loans:*** $1,274,294 (100% non-need-based). ***Programs:*** Federal Direct (Subsidized and Unsubsidized Stafford, PLUS), Perkins, Federal Nursing, alternative loans.

WORK-STUDY ***Federal work-study:*** Total amount: $133,700; 139 jobs averaging $952. ***State or other work-study/employment:*** Total amount: $319,505 (100% non-need-based). 55 part-time jobs averaging $3993.

ATHLETIC AWARDS Total amount: $518,228 (100% non-need-based).

APPLYING FOR FINANCIAL AID ***Required financial aid form:*** FAFSA. ***Financial aid deadline (priority):*** 3/1. ***Notification date:*** Continuous. Students must reply within 2 weeks of notification.

CONTACT Mr. Scott A. Cook, Executive Director of Enrollment Services and Director of Financial Aid, West Liberty State University, PO Box 295, West Liberty, WV 26074-0295, 304-336-8016 or toll-free 800-732-6204 Ext. 8076. *Fax:* 304-336-8088. *E-mail:* cookscot@westliberty.edu.

WESTMINSTER COLLEGE

Fulton, MO

Tuition & fees: $17,990 **Average undergraduate aid package: $16,188**

ABOUT THE INSTITUTION Independent religious, coed. ***Awards:*** bachelor's degrees. 29 undergraduate majors. ***Total enrollment:*** 1,000. Undergraduates: 1,000. Freshmen: 244. Federal methodology is used as a basis for awarding need-based institutional aid.

UNDERGRADUATE EXPENSES for 2009–10 ***Comprehensive fee:*** $25,110 includes full-time tuition ($17,990) and room and board ($7120). ***College room only:*** $3700. ***Part-time tuition:*** $750 per credit hour.

FRESHMAN FINANCIAL AID (Fall 2008, est.) 198 applied for aid; of those 72% were deemed to have need. 100% of freshmen with need received aid; of those 70% had need fully met. ***Average percent of need met:*** 70% (excluding resources awarded to replace EFC). ***Average financial aid package:*** $16,862 (excluding resources awarded to replace EFC). 40% of all full-time freshmen had no need and received non-need-based gift aid.

UNDERGRADUATE FINANCIAL AID (Fall 2008, est.) 651 applied for aid; of those 81% were deemed to have need. 100% of undergraduates with need received aid; of those 71% had need fully met. ***Average percent of need met:*** 71% (excluding resources awarded to replace EFC). ***Average financial aid package:*** $16,188 (excluding resources awarded to replace EFC). 43% of all full-time undergraduates had no need and received non-need-based gift aid.

GIFT AID (NEED-BASED) ***Total amount:*** $11,546,308 (6% federal, 10% state, 71% institutional, 13% external sources). ***Receiving aid:*** Freshmen: 58% (142); all full-time undergraduates: 54% (524). ***Average award:*** Freshmen: $13,397; Undergraduates: $12,271. ***Scholarships, grants, and awards:*** Federal Pell, FSEOG, state, private, college/university gift aid from institutional funds.

GIFT AID (NON-NEED-BASED) ***Average award:*** Freshmen: $8571. Undergraduates: $9219. ***Scholarships, grants, and awards by category:*** *Academic interests/achievement:* 513 awards ($3,746,903 total): general academic interests/achievements. *Creative arts/performance:* 8 awards ($7500 total): music. *Special achievements/activities:* 143 awards ($149,684 total): general special achievements/activities, leadership. *Special characteristics:* 284 awards ($2,021,418 total): children and siblings of alumni, children of faculty/staff, ethnic background, international students, local/state students, relatives of clergy, religious affiliation, siblings of current students, twins. ***ROTC:*** Army cooperative, Air Force cooperative.

LOANS ***Student loans:*** $3,534,606 (42% need-based, 58% non-need-based). 55% of past graduating class borrowed through all loan programs. *Average indebtedness per student:* $19,845. ***Average need-based loan:*** Freshmen: $3154. Undergraduates: $3704. ***Parent loans:*** $964,308 (100% non-need-based). ***Programs:*** FFEL (Subsidized and Unsubsidized Stafford, PLUS), Perkins.

WORK-STUDY ***Federal work-study:*** Total amount: $90,000; 150 jobs averaging $648. ***State or other work-study/employment:*** Total amount: $250,000 (100% non-need-based). 162 part-time jobs averaging $1664.

APPLYING FOR FINANCIAL AID ***Required financial aid form:*** FAFSA. ***Financial aid deadline (priority):*** 2/15. ***Notification date:*** Continuous beginning 3/15. Students must reply within 3 weeks of notification.

CONTACT Ms. Aimee Bristow, Director of Financial Aid, Westminster College, 501 Westminster Avenue, Fulton, MO 65251-1299, 800-475-3361. *Fax:* 573-592-5255. *E-mail:* aimee.bristow@westminster-mo.edu.

WESTMINSTER COLLEGE

New Wilmington, PA

Tuition & fees: $26,600 **Average undergraduate aid package: $22,230**

ABOUT THE INSTITUTION Independent religious, coed. 52 undergraduate majors. Federal methodology is used as a basis for awarding need-based institutional aid.

UNDERGRADUATE EXPENSES for 2008–09 ***Comprehensive fee:*** $34,710 includes full-time tuition ($25,900), mandatory fees ($700), and room and board ($8110). Room and board charges vary according to board plan. ***Payment plan:*** Installment.

FRESHMAN FINANCIAL AID (Fall 2008, est.) 414 applied for aid; of those 90% were deemed to have need. 100% of freshmen with need received aid; of those 24% had need fully met. ***Average percent of need met:*** 90% (excluding resources awarded to replace EFC). ***Average financial aid package:*** $24,435 (excluding resources awarded to replace EFC). 15% of all full-time freshmen had no need and received non-need-based gift aid.

UNDERGRADUATE FINANCIAL AID (Fall 2008, est.) 1,231 applied for aid; of those 90% were deemed to have need. 100% of undergraduates with need received aid; of those 27% had need fully met. ***Average percent of need met:*** 87% (excluding resources awarded to replace EFC). ***Average financial aid package:*** $22,230 (excluding resources awarded to replace EFC). 17% of all full-time undergraduates had no need and received non-need-based gift aid.

GIFT AID (NEED-BASED) ***Total amount:*** $19,318,255 (7% federal, 9% state, 78% institutional, 6% external sources). ***Receiving aid:*** Freshmen: 83% (371);

all full-time undergraduates: 81% (1,098). ***Average award:*** Freshmen: $20,076; Undergraduates: $17,549. ***Scholarships, grants, and awards:*** Federal Pell, FSEOG, state, private, college/university gift aid from institutional funds.

GIFT AID (NON-NEED-BASED) ***Total amount:*** $3,010,992 (97% institutional, 3% external sources). ***Receiving aid:*** Freshmen: 83% (370). Undergraduates: 79% (1,073). ***Average award:*** Freshmen: $14,863. Undergraduates: $12,168. ***Scholarships, grants, and awards by category:*** *Academic interests/achievement:* 1,281 awards ($13,394,207 total): general academic interests/achievements. *Creative arts/performance:* 168 awards ($143,310 total): cinema/film/broadcasting, general creative arts/performance, music, theater/drama. *Special characteristics:* 463 awards ($1,651,960 total): children and siblings of alumni, general special characteristics, international students, religious affiliation.

LOANS ***Student loans:*** $9,444,156 (94% need-based, 6% non-need-based). 76% of past graduating class borrowed through all loan programs. *Average indebtedness per student:* $25,296. ***Average need-based loan:*** Freshmen: $3996. Undergraduates: $4415. ***Parent loans:*** $2,132,263 (91% need-based, 9% non-need-based). ***Programs:*** FFEL (Subsidized and Unsubsidized Stafford, PLUS), Perkins, Resource Loans.

WORK-STUDY ***Federal work-study:*** Total amount: $845,688; 471 jobs averaging $1805. ***State or other work-study/employment:*** Total amount: $269,401 (71% need-based, 29% non-need-based). 144 part-time jobs averaging $1905.

APPLYING FOR FINANCIAL AID ***Required financial aid forms:*** FAFSA, institution's own form. ***Financial aid deadline (priority):*** 5/1. ***Notification date:*** Continuous. Students must reply within 3 weeks of notification.

CONTACT Mrs. Cheryl A. Gerber, Director of Financial Aid, Westminster College, South Market Street, New Wilmington, PA 16172-0001, 724-946-7102 or toll-free 800-942-8033 (in-state). *Fax:* 724-946-6171. *E-mail:* gerberca@westminster.edu.

WESTMINSTER COLLEGE

Salt Lake City, UT

Tuition & fees: $24,996 **Average undergraduate aid package: $18,693**

ABOUT THE INSTITUTION Independent, coed. ***Awards:*** bachelor's and master's degrees and post-bachelor's certificates. 35 undergraduate majors. ***Total enrollment:*** 2,863. Undergraduates: 2,131. Freshmen: 449. Federal methodology is used as a basis for awarding need-based institutional aid.

UNDERGRADUATE EXPENSES for 2009–10 ***Application fee:*** $40. ***Comprehensive fee:*** $32,002 includes full-time tuition ($24,576), mandatory fees ($420), and room and board ($7006). ***Part-time tuition:*** $1024 per credit hour. ***Part-time fees:*** $122 per term.

FRESHMAN FINANCIAL AID (Fall 2008, est.) 316 applied for aid; of those 77% were deemed to have need. 100% of freshmen with need received aid; of those 54% had need fully met. ***Average percent of need met:*** 91% (excluding resources awarded to replace EFC). ***Average financial aid package:*** $17,205 (excluding resources awarded to replace EFC). 42% of all full-time freshmen had no need and received non-need-based gift aid.

UNDERGRADUATE FINANCIAL AID (Fall 2008, est.) 1,290 applied for aid; of those 85% were deemed to have need. 100% of undergraduates with need received aid; of those 47% had need fully met. ***Average percent of need met:*** 89% (excluding resources awarded to replace EFC). ***Average financial aid package:*** $18,693 (excluding resources awarded to replace EFC). 35% of all full-time undergraduates had no need and received non-need-based gift aid.

GIFT AID (NEED-BASED) ***Total amount:*** $12,404,934 (16% federal, 1% state, 75% institutional, 8% external sources). ***Receiving aid:*** Freshmen: 54% (241); all full-time undergraduates: 56% (1,080). ***Average award:*** Freshmen: $14,306; Undergraduates: $12,759. ***Scholarships, grants, and awards:*** Federal Pell, FSEOG, state, private, college/university gift aid from institutional funds, United Negro College Fund.

GIFT AID (NON-NEED-BASED) ***Total amount:*** $6,111,126 (1% state, 80% institutional, 19% external sources). ***Receiving aid:*** Freshmen: 9% (42). Undergraduates: 6% (107). ***Average award:*** Freshmen: $10,202. Undergraduates: $9530. ***Scholarships, grants, and awards by category:*** *Academic interests/achievement:* 1,752 awards ($12,244,318 total): biological sciences, business, communication, computer science, education, English, general academic interests/achievements, health fields, humanities, international studies, mathematics, military science, physical sciences, premedicine, social sciences. *Creative arts/performance:* 32 awards ($78,000 total): art/fine arts, journalism/publications, music, theater/drama. *Special characteristics:* 121 awards ($296,000 total): adult students, children and siblings of alumni, children of faculty/staff, children of public servants, ethnic background, first-generation college students, handicapped students, international students, local/state students, members of minority groups, public servants, relatives of clergy, religious affiliation, siblings of current students, spouses of current students, veterans, veterans' children. ***ROTC:*** Army cooperative, Naval cooperative, Air Force cooperative.

LOANS ***Student loans:*** $12,426,310 (78% need-based, 22% non-need-based). 66% of past graduating class borrowed through all loan programs. *Average indebtedness per student:* $18,548. ***Average need-based loan:*** Freshmen: $4077. Undergraduates: $5106. ***Parent loans:*** $725,641 (79% need-based, 21% non-need-based). ***Programs:*** FFEL (Subsidized and Unsubsidized Stafford, PLUS), Perkins.

WORK-STUDY ***Federal work-study:*** Total amount: $660,000; 337 jobs averaging $2381. ***State or other work-study/employment:*** Total amount: $514,000 (100% non-need-based). Part-time jobs available.

ATHLETIC AWARDS Total amount: $306,190 (67% need-based, 33% non-need-based).

APPLYING FOR FINANCIAL AID ***Required financial aid form:*** FAFSA. ***Financial aid deadline (priority):*** 4/15. ***Notification date:*** Continuous. Students must reply within 3 weeks of notification.

CONTACT Elizabeth Key, Director of Financial Aid, Westminster College, 1840 South 1300 East, Salt Lake City, UT 84105, 801-832-2500 or toll-free 800-748-4753 (out-of-state). *Fax:* 801-832-2501. *E-mail:* ekey@westminstercollege.edu.

WESTMONT COLLEGE

Santa Barbara, CA

Tuition & fees: $33,170 **Average undergraduate aid package: $22,277**

ABOUT THE INSTITUTION Independent nondenominational, coed. ***Awards:*** bachelor's degrees and post-bachelor's certificates. 43 undergraduate majors. ***Total enrollment:*** 1,336. Undergraduates: 1,336. Freshmen: 389. Federal methodology is used as a basis for awarding need-based institutional aid.

UNDERGRADUATE EXPENSES for 2008–09 ***Application fee:*** $50. ***Comprehensive fee:*** $43,250 includes full-time tuition ($32,150), mandatory fees ($1020), and room and board ($10,080). ***College room only:*** $6260. Room and board charges vary according to board plan. ***Payment plan:*** Installment.

FRESHMAN FINANCIAL AID (Fall 2008, est.) 273 applied for aid; of those 82% were deemed to have need. 100% of freshmen with need received aid; of those 9% had need fully met. ***Average percent of need met:*** 72% (excluding resources awarded to replace EFC). ***Average financial aid package:*** $23,855 (excluding resources awarded to replace EFC). 31% of all full-time freshmen had no need and received non-need-based gift aid.

UNDERGRADUATE FINANCIAL AID (Fall 2008, est.) 899 applied for aid; of those 87% were deemed to have need. 99% of undergraduates with need received aid; of those 8% had need fully met. ***Average percent of need met:*** 67% (excluding resources awarded to replace EFC). ***Average financial aid package:*** $22,277 (excluding resources awarded to replace EFC). 30% of all full-time undergraduates had no need and received non-need-based gift aid.

GIFT AID (NEED-BASED) ***Total amount:*** $12,574,874 (7% federal, 14% state, 77% institutional, 2% external sources). ***Receiving aid:*** Freshmen: 61% (223); all full-time undergraduates: 58% (770). ***Average award:*** Freshmen: $19,597; Undergraduates: $17,287. ***Scholarships, grants, and awards:*** Federal Pell, FSEOG, state, private, college/university gift aid from institutional funds.

GIFT AID (NON-NEED-BASED) ***Total amount:*** $3,898,710 (97% institutional, 3% external sources). ***Receiving aid:*** Freshmen: 5% (18). Undergraduates: 4% (60). ***Average award:*** Freshmen: $12,073. Undergraduates: $11,584. ***Scholarships, grants, and awards by category:*** *Academic interests/achievement:* 856 awards ($6,628,215 total): general academic interests/achievements. *Creative arts/performance:* 81 awards ($156,315 total): art/fine arts, music, theater/drama. *Special achievements/activities:* 58 awards ($148,500 total): general special achievements/activities, leadership. *Special characteristics:* 305 awards ($1,460,163 total): children of faculty/staff, ethnic background, international students. ***Tuition waivers:*** Full or partial for employees or children of employees. ***ROTC:*** Army cooperative, Air Force cooperative.

LOANS ***Student loans:*** $7,152,695 (74% need-based, 26% non-need-based). 59% of past graduating class borrowed through all loan programs. *Average indebtedness per student:* $26,032. ***Average need-based loan:*** Freshmen: $4440. Undergraduates: $5575. ***Parent loans:*** $2,492,831 (45% need-based, 55% non-need-based). ***Programs:*** FFEL (Subsidized and Unsubsidized Stafford, PLUS), Perkins, college/university, alternative loans.

WORK-STUDY ***Federal work-study:*** Total amount: $170,453; 183 jobs averaging $1789.

ATHLETIC AWARDS Total amount: $936,018 (59% need-based, 41% non-need-based).

APPLYING FOR FINANCIAL AID ***Required financial aid form:*** FAFSA. ***Financial aid deadline (priority):*** 3/1. ***Notification date:*** 3/1. Students must reply by 5/1 or within 2 weeks of notification.

CONTACT Mrs. Diane L. Horvath, Director of Financial Aid, Westmont College, 955 La Paz Road, Santa Barbara, CA 93108, 805-565-6061 or toll-free 800-777-9011. *Fax:* 805-565-7157. *E-mail:* dhorvath@westmont.edu.

WEST SUBURBAN COLLEGE OF NURSING

Oak Park, IL

CONTACT Ms. Ruth Rehwadt, Director of Financial Aid, West Suburban College of Nursing, 3 Erie Court, Oak Park, IL 60302, 708-287-8100.

WEST TEXAS A&M UNIVERSITY

Canyon, TX

CONTACT Mr. Jim Reed, Director of Financial Aid, West Texas A&M University, WTAMU Box 60939, Canyon, TX 79016-0001, 806-651-2055 or toll-free 800-99-WTAMU. *Fax:* 806-651-2924. *E-mail:* jreed@mail.wtamu.edu.

WEST VIRGINIA STATE UNIVERSITY

Institute, WV

CONTACT Mrs. Mary Blizzard, Director, Office of Student Financial Assistance, West Virginia State University, PO Box 1000, Ferrell Hall 324, Institute, WV 25112-1000, 304-766-3131 or toll-free 800-987-2112.

WEST VIRGINIA UNIVERSITY

Morgantown, WV

Tuition & fees (WV res): $5100 **Average undergraduate aid package: $6938**

ABOUT THE INSTITUTION State-supported, coed. ***Awards:*** bachelor's, master's, doctoral, and first professional degrees. 79 undergraduate majors. ***Total enrollment:*** 28,840. Undergraduates: 21,930. Freshmen: 5,135. Federal methodology is used as a basis for awarding need-based institutional aid.

UNDERGRADUATE EXPENSES for 2008–09 ***Application fee:*** $25. ***Tuition, state resident:*** full-time $5100; part-time $212 per credit hour. ***Tuition, nonresident:*** full-time $15,770; part-time $657 per credit hour. Full-time tuition and fees vary according to location, program, and reciprocity agreements. Part-time tuition and fees vary according to course load, location, program, and reciprocity agreements. ***College room and board:*** $7434. Room and board charges vary according to board plan, housing facility, and location. ***Payment plan:*** Installment.

FRESHMAN FINANCIAL AID (Fall 2008, est.) 4,033 applied for aid; of those 79% were deemed to have need. 66% of freshmen with need received aid; of those 45% had need fully met. ***Average percent of need met:*** 72% (excluding resources awarded to replace EFC). ***Average financial aid package:*** $6466 (excluding resources awarded to replace EFC). 24% of all full-time freshmen had no need and received non-need-based gift aid.

UNDERGRADUATE FINANCIAL AID (Fall 2008, est.) 14,790 applied for aid; of those 79% were deemed to have need. 76% of undergraduates with need received aid; of those 30% had need fully met. ***Average percent of need met:*** 75% (excluding resources awarded to replace EFC). ***Average financial aid package:*** $6938 (excluding resources awarded to replace EFC). 15% of all full-time undergraduates had no need and received non-need-based gift aid.

GIFT AID (NEED-BASED) ***Total amount:*** $27,937,746 (60% federal, 27% state, 13% institutional). ***Receiving aid:*** Freshmen: 35% (1,787); all full-time undergraduates: 33% (6,697). ***Average award:*** Freshmen: $4082; Undergraduates: $4239. ***Scholarships, grants, and awards:*** Federal Pell, FSEOG, state, private, college/university gift aid from institutional funds.

GIFT AID (NON-NEED-BASED) ***Total amount:*** $30,723,734 (71% state, 21% institutional, 8% external sources). ***Receiving aid:*** Freshmen: 25% (1,282). Undergraduates: 19% (3,977). ***Average award:*** Freshmen: $1676. Undergraduates: $2009. ***Scholarships, grants, and awards by category:*** *Academic interests/achievement:* 3,000 awards ($5,000,000 total): agriculture, architecture, area/ethnic studies, biological sciences, business, communication, computer science, education, engineering/technologies, English, foreign languages, general academic interests/achievements, health fields, home economics, humanities, international studies, library science, mathematics, military science, physical sciences, premedicine, religion/biblical studies, social sciences. *Creative arts/performance:* 100 awards ($965,000 total): art/fine arts, debating, music, theater/drama. *Special achievements/activities:* 12 awards ($91,000 total): general special achievements/activities, leadership. *Special characteristics:* 500 awards ($1,500,000 total): children of faculty/staff, children of union members/company employees, children of workers in trades, ethnic background, general special characteristics, international students, local/state students, members of minority groups. ***Tuition waivers:*** Full or partial for employees or children of employees, senior citizens. ***ROTC:*** Army, Air Force.

LOANS ***Student loans:*** $104,011,002 (32% need-based, 68% non-need-based). ***Average need-based loan:*** Freshmen: $3738. Undergraduates: $4274. ***Parent loans:*** $44,846,696 (100% non-need-based). ***Programs:*** Federal Direct (Subsidized and Unsubsidized Stafford, PLUS), Perkins, college/university.

WORK-STUDY ***Federal work-study:*** Total amount: $1,042,206; 2,100 jobs averaging $2185. ***State or other work-study/employment:*** Total amount: $1,668,833 (100% non-need-based). Part-time jobs available.

ATHLETIC AWARDS Total amount: $4,556,438 (100% non-need-based).

APPLYING FOR FINANCIAL AID ***Required financial aid forms:*** FAFSA, state aid form. ***Financial aid deadline:*** 3/1. ***Notification date:*** Continuous beginning 3/15. Students must reply within 4 weeks of notification.

CONTACT Kaye Widney, Director of Financial Aid, West Virginia University, PO Box 6004, Morgantown, WV 26506-6004, 304-293-5242 or toll-free 800-344-9881. *Fax:* 304-293-4890. *E-mail:* kaye.widney@mail.wvu.edu.

WEST VIRGINIA UNIVERSITY INSTITUTE OF TECHNOLOGY

Montgomery, WV

CONTACT Nina M. Morton, Director of Financial Aid, West Virginia University Institute of Technology, 405 Fayette Pike, Montgomery, WV 25136, 304-442-3032 or toll-free 888-554-8324.

WEST VIRGINIA WESLEYAN COLLEGE

Buckhannon, WV

Tuition & fees: $22,880 **Average undergraduate aid package: $21,756**

ABOUT THE INSTITUTION Independent religious, coed. ***Awards:*** bachelor's and master's degrees. 64 undergraduate majors. ***Total enrollment:*** 1,317. Undergraduates: 1,274. Freshmen: 383. Federal methodology is used as a basis for awarding need-based institutional aid.

UNDERGRADUATE EXPENSES for 2009–10 ***Application fee:*** $35. ***Comprehensive fee:*** $29,680 includes full-time tuition ($22,030), mandatory fees ($850), and room and board ($6800).

FRESHMAN FINANCIAL AID (Fall 2008, est.) 353 applied for aid; of those 88% were deemed to have need. 100% of freshmen with need received aid; of those 26% had need fully met. ***Average percent of need met:*** 85% (excluding resources awarded to replace EFC). ***Average financial aid package:*** $20,820 (excluding resources awarded to replace EFC). 19% of all full-time freshmen had no need and received non-need-based gift aid.

UNDERGRADUATE FINANCIAL AID (Fall 2008, est.) 1,034 applied for aid; of those 89% were deemed to have need. 100% of undergraduates with need received aid; of those 24% had need fully met. ***Average percent of need met:*** 84% (excluding resources awarded to replace EFC). ***Average financial aid package:*** $21,756 (excluding resources awarded to replace EFC). 26% of all full-time undergraduates had no need and received non-need-based gift aid.

GIFT AID (NEED-BASED) ***Total amount:*** $15,530,534 (11% federal, 13% state, 71% institutional, 5% external sources). ***Receiving aid:*** Freshmen: 81% (310); all full-time undergraduates: 74% (917). ***Average award:*** Freshmen: $18,351; Undergraduates: $17,900. ***Scholarships, grants, and awards:*** Federal Pell, FSEOG, state, private, college/university gift aid from institutional funds, Federal Nursing.

GIFT AID (NON-NEED-BASED) ***Total amount:*** $3,312,011 (7% state, 90% institutional, 3% external sources). ***Receiving aid:*** Freshmen: 20% (77). Undergraduates: 16% (202). ***Average award:*** Freshmen: $12,861. Undergraduates: $12,001. ***Scholarships, grants, and awards by category:*** *Academic interests/achievement:* English, general academic interests/achievements, physical sciences. *Creative arts/performance:* art/fine arts, music, performing arts, theater/drama. *Special achievements/activities:* community service, leadership, religious involvement. *Special characteristics:* children and siblings of alumni, children of faculty/staff, general special characteristics, international students, relatives of clergy, religious affiliation.

LOANS ***Student loans:*** $5,960,069 (46% need-based, 54% non-need-based). 73% of past graduating class borrowed through all loan programs. *Average indebtedness per student:* $19,796. ***Average need-based loan:*** Freshmen: $3791. Undergraduates: $4399. ***Parent loans:*** $745,868 (100% non-need-based). ***Programs:*** FFEL (Subsidized and Unsubsidized Stafford, PLUS), Perkins, Federal Nursing, college/university.

WORK-STUDY ***Federal work-study:*** Total amount: $652,639; jobs available. ***State or other work-study/employment:*** Total amount: $183,563 (92% need-based, 8% non-need-based). Part-time jobs available.

ATHLETIC AWARDS Total amount: $3,501,185 (64% need-based, 36% non-need-based).

APPLYING FOR FINANCIAL AID ***Required financial aid form:*** FAFSA. ***Financial aid deadline (priority):*** 2/15. ***Notification date:*** Continuous beginning 3/1. Students must reply within 4 weeks of notification.

CONTACT Susan George, Director of Financial Aid, West Virginia Wesleyan College, 59 College Avenue, Buckhannon, WV 26201, 304-473-8080 or toll-free 800-722-9933 (out-of-state). *E-mail:* george_s@wvwc.edu.

WESTWOOD COLLEGE–ANNANDALE CAMPUS

Annandale, VA

CONTACT Financial Aid Office, Westwood College–Annandale Campus, 7611 Little River Turnpike, 3rd Floor, Annandale, VA 22003, 706-642-3770 or toll-free 800-281-2978.

WESTWOOD COLLEGE–ARLINGTON BALLSTON CAMPUS

Arlington, VA

CONTACT Financial Aid Office, Westwood College–Arlington Ballston Campus, 1901 North Ft. Myer Drive, Arlington, VA 22209, 800-281-2978.

WESTWOOD COLLEGE–ATLANTA NORTHLAKE

Atlanta, GA

CONTACT Financial Aid Office, Westwood College–Atlanta Northlake, 2220 Parklake Drive, Suite 175, Atlanta, GA 30345, 404-962-2999.

WESTWOOD COLLEGE–CHICAGO DU PAGE

Woodridge, IL

CONTACT Financial Aid Office, Westwood College–Chicago Du Page, 7155 Janes Avenue, Woodridge, IL 60517, 630-434-8244 or toll-free 888-721-7646 (in-state).

WHEATON COLLEGE

Wheaton, IL

Tuition & fees: $25,500 **Average undergraduate aid package: $21,185**

ABOUT THE INSTITUTION Independent nondenominational, coed. ***Awards:*** bachelor's, master's, and doctoral degrees and post-bachelor's certificates. 39 undergraduate majors. ***Total enrollment:*** 2,915. Undergraduates: 2,366. Freshmen: 581. Both federal and institutional methodology are used as a basis for awarding need-based institutional aid.

UNDERGRADUATE EXPENSES for 2008–09 ***Application fee:*** $50. ***Comprehensive fee:*** $33,118 includes full-time tuition ($25,500) and room and board ($7618). ***College room only:*** $4524. Full-time tuition and fees vary according to degree level. Room and board charges vary according to board plan and housing facility. ***Part-time tuition:*** $1063 per credit hour. Part-time tuition and fees vary according to course load and degree level. ***Payment plans:*** Installment, deferred payment.

FRESHMAN FINANCIAL AID (Fall 2008, est.) 466 applied for aid; of those 65% were deemed to have need. 99% of freshmen with need received aid; of those 32% had need fully met. ***Average percent of need met:*** 85% (excluding resources awarded to replace EFC). ***Average financial aid package:*** $21,472 (excluding resources awarded to replace EFC). 20% of all full-time freshmen had no need and received non-need-based gift aid.

UNDERGRADUATE FINANCIAL AID (Fall 2008, est.) 1,684 applied for aid; of those 68% were deemed to have need. 98% of undergraduates with need received aid; of those 32% had need fully met. ***Average percent of need met:*** 84% (excluding resources awarded to replace EFC). ***Average financial aid package:*** $21,185 (excluding resources awarded to replace EFC). 19% of all full-time undergraduates had no need and received non-need-based gift aid.

GIFT AID (NEED-BASED) ***Total amount:*** $17,834,247 (8% federal, 2% state, 84% institutional, 6% external sources). ***Receiving aid:*** Freshmen: 48% (277); all full-time undergraduates: 46% (1,045). ***Average award:*** Freshmen: $14,776; Undergraduates: $14,490. ***Scholarships, grants, and awards:*** Federal Pell, FSEOG, state, college/university gift aid from institutional funds.

GIFT AID (NON-NEED-BASED) ***Total amount:*** $1,498,216 (2% federal, 76% institutional, 22% external sources). ***Receiving aid:*** Freshmen: 15% (89). Undergraduates: 17% (390). ***Average award:*** Freshmen: $4375. Undergraduates: $5038. ***Scholarships, grants, and awards by category:*** *Academic interests/achievement:* 600 awards ($599,952 total): biological sciences, business, education, engineering/technologies, foreign languages, general academic interests/achievements, mathematics, premedicine, religion/biblical studies. *Creative arts/performance:* 90 awards ($215,221 total): art/fine arts, music. *Special achievements/activities:* 3 awards ($11,419 total): general special achievements/activities. ***Tuition waivers:*** Full or partial for employees or children of employees. ***ROTC:*** Army.

LOANS ***Student loans:*** $7,824,754 (85% need-based, 15% non-need-based). 57% of past graduating class borrowed through all loan programs. *Average indebtedness per student:* $21,549. ***Average need-based loan:*** Freshmen: $4423. Undergraduates: $4775. ***Parent loans:*** $4,220,179 (56% need-based, 44% non-need-based). ***Programs:*** FFEL (Subsidized and Unsubsidized Stafford, PLUS), Perkins.

WORK-STUDY ***Federal work-study:*** Total amount: $394,933; 280 jobs averaging $1065.

APPLYING FOR FINANCIAL AID ***Required financial aid forms:*** FAFSA, institution's own form. ***Financial aid deadline (priority):*** 2/15. ***Notification date:*** Continuous beginning 3/1.

CONTACT Mrs. Donna Peltz, Director of Financial Aid, Wheaton College, 501 College Avenue, Wheaton, IL 60187-5593, 630-752-5021 or toll-free 800-222-2419 (out-of-state). *E-mail:* finaid@wheaton.edu.

WHEATON COLLEGE

Norton, MA

Tuition & fees: $38,860 **Average undergraduate aid package: $30,159**

ABOUT THE INSTITUTION Independent, coed. ***Awards:*** bachelor's degrees. 43 undergraduate majors. ***Total enrollment:*** 1,655. Undergraduates: 1,655. Freshmen: 420. Institutional methodology is used as a basis for awarding need-based institutional aid.

UNDERGRADUATE EXPENSES for 2008–09 ***Application fee:*** $55. ***One-time required fee:*** $50. ***Comprehensive fee:*** $48,010 includes full-time tuition ($38,585), mandatory fees ($275), and room and board ($9150). ***College room only:*** $4830. ***Payment plans:*** Tuition prepayment, installment.

FRESHMAN FINANCIAL AID (Fall 2008, est.) 279 applied for aid; of those 85% were deemed to have need. 100% of freshmen with need received aid; of those 57% had need fully met. ***Average percent of need met:*** 97% (excluding resources awarded to replace EFC). ***Average financial aid package:*** $29,872 (excluding resources awarded to replace EFC). 13% of all full-time freshmen had no need and received non-need-based gift aid.

UNDERGRADUATE FINANCIAL AID (Fall 2008, est.) 993 applied for aid; of those 86% were deemed to have need. 100% of undergraduates with need received aid; of those 67% had need fully met. ***Average percent of need met:*** 98% (excluding resources awarded to replace EFC). ***Average financial aid package:*** $30,159 (excluding resources awarded to replace EFC). 13% of all full-time undergraduates had no need and received non-need-based gift aid.

GIFT AID (NEED-BASED) ***Total amount:*** $20,735,705 (7% federal, 2% state, 88% institutional, 3% external sources). ***Receiving aid:*** Freshmen: 51% (215); all full-time undergraduates: 47% (781). ***Average award:*** Freshmen: $26,139; Undergraduates: $25,522. ***Scholarships, grants, and awards:*** Federal Pell, FSEOG, state, private, college/university gift aid from institutional funds.

GIFT AID (NON-NEED-BASED) ***Total amount:*** $3,233,511 (89% institutional, 11% external sources). ***Receiving aid:*** Freshmen: 1% (5). Undergraduates: 1% (20). ***Average award:*** Freshmen: $11,915. Undergraduates: $13,222. ***Scholarships, grants, and awards by category:*** *Academic interests/achievement:* 463 awards ($4,553,325 total): general academic interests/achievements. ***Tuition waivers:*** Full or partial for employees or children of employees. ***ROTC:*** Army cooperative.

LOANS ***Student loans:*** $6,376,908 (61% need-based, 39% non-need-based). 53% of past graduating class borrowed through all loan programs. *Average indebtedness per student:* $24,428. ***Average need-based loan:*** Freshmen: $4224. Undergraduates: $4922. ***Parent loans:*** $4,692,985 (100% non-need-based). ***Programs:*** Federal Direct (Subsidized and Unsubsidized Stafford, PLUS), Perkins, MEFA, private educational loans.

WORK-STUDY ***Federal work-study:*** Total amount: $1,416,649; 736 jobs averaging $1814. ***State or other work-study/employment:*** Total amount: $650,336 (31% need-based, 69% non-need-based). 249 part-time jobs averaging $1847.

APPLYING FOR FINANCIAL AID ***Required financial aid forms:*** FAFSA, CSS Financial Aid PROFILE, business/farm supplement, federal income tax form(s). ***Financial aid deadline:*** 2/1. ***Notification date:*** 4/1. Students must reply by 5/1.

CONTACT Ms. Susan Beard, Director of Financial Aid Programs, Wheaton College, 26 East Main Street, Norton, MA 02766, 508-286-8232 or toll-free 800-394-6003. *Fax:* 508-286-3787. *E-mail:* sfs@wheatonma.edu.

WHEELING JESUIT UNIVERSITY

Wheeling, WV

Tuition & fees: $24,390 **Average undergraduate aid package: $21,523**

ABOUT THE INSTITUTION Independent Roman Catholic (Jesuit), coed. ***Awards:*** bachelor's, master's, and doctoral degrees. 55 undergraduate majors. ***Total enrollment:*** 1,303. Undergraduates: 1,061. Freshmen: 182. Federal methodology is used as a basis for awarding need-based institutional aid.

UNDERGRADUATE EXPENSES for 2009–10 ***Application fee:*** $25. ***Tuition:*** full-time $23,590; part-time $655 per hour.

FRESHMAN FINANCIAL AID (Fall 2008, est.) 172 applied for aid; of those 82% were deemed to have need. 100% of freshmen with need received aid; of those 41% had need fully met. ***Average percent of need met:*** 96% (excluding resources awarded to replace EFC). ***Average financial aid package:*** $23,303 (excluding resources awarded to replace EFC). 23% of all full-time freshmen had no need and received non-need-based gift aid.

UNDERGRADUATE FINANCIAL AID (Fall 2008, est.) 766 applied for aid; of those 89% were deemed to have need. 100% of undergraduates with need received aid; of those 36% had need fully met. ***Average percent of need met:*** 92% (excluding resources awarded to replace EFC). ***Average financial aid package:*** $21,523 (excluding resources awarded to replace EFC). 16% of all full-time undergraduates had no need and received non-need-based gift aid.

GIFT AID (NEED-BASED) ***Total amount:*** $2,889,941 (33% federal, 10% state, 57% institutional). ***Receiving aid:*** Freshmen: 59% (108); all full-time undergraduates: 58% (493). ***Average award:*** Freshmen: $6660; Undergraduates: $5743. ***Scholarships, grants, and awards:*** Federal Pell, FSEOG, state, private, college/university gift aid from institutional funds, Federal Nursing.

GIFT AID (NON-NEED-BASED) ***Total amount:*** $8,738,258 (5% state, 91% institutional, 4% external sources). ***Receiving aid:*** Freshmen: 74% (135). Undergraduates: 72% (613). ***Average award:*** Freshmen: $10,406. Undergraduates: $9859. ***Scholarships, grants, and awards by category:*** *Academic interests/achievement:* 642 awards ($6,242,844 total): general academic interests/achievements, premedicine. *Creative arts/performance:* 31 awards ($44,500 total): music. *Special achievements/activities:* 91 awards ($305,376 total): community service, general special achievements/activities. *Special characteristics:* 389 awards ($2,004,409 total): children and siblings of alumni, children of faculty/staff, general special characteristics, religious affiliation.

LOANS ***Student loans:*** $6,507,668 (40% need-based, 60% non-need-based). 88% of past graduating class borrowed through all loan programs. *Average indebtedness per student:* $21,383. ***Average need-based loan:*** Freshmen: $3900. Undergraduates: $4659. ***Parent loans:*** $637,417 (100% non-need-based). ***Programs:*** FFEL (Subsidized and Unsubsidized Stafford, PLUS), Perkins, Federal Nursing, alternative loans.

WORK-STUDY ***Federal work-study:*** Total amount: $268,704; 186 jobs averaging $1445. ***State or other work-study/employment:*** Total amount: $252,918 (100% non-need-based). 169 part-time jobs averaging $1497.

ATHLETIC AWARDS Total amount: $799,160 (100% non-need-based).

APPLYING FOR FINANCIAL AID ***Required financial aid forms:*** FAFSA, institution's own form. ***Financial aid deadline (priority):*** 3/1. ***Notification date:*** Continuous beginning 3/15. Students must reply within 2 weeks of notification.

CONTACT Christie Tomczyk, Director of Financial Aid, Wheeling Jesuit University, 316 Washington Avenue, Wheeling, WV 26003-6295, 304-243-2304 or toll-free 800-624-6992 Ext. 2359. *Fax:* 304-243-4397. *E-mail:* finaid@wju.edu.

WHEELOCK COLLEGE

Boston, MA

Tuition & fees: $28,160 **Average undergraduate aid package: $18,541**

ABOUT THE INSTITUTION Independent, coed, primarily women. ***Awards:*** bachelor's and master's degrees and post-bachelor's and post-master's certificates. 8 undergraduate majors. ***Total enrollment:*** 1,109. Undergraduates: 824. Freshmen: 238. Federal methodology is used as a basis for awarding need-based institutional aid.

UNDERGRADUATE EXPENSES for 2009–10 ***Application fee:*** $35. ***Comprehensive fee:*** $29,280 includes full-time tuition ($27,150), mandatory fees ($1010), and room and board ($1120). ***Part-time tuition:*** $850 per credit.

FRESHMAN FINANCIAL AID (Fall 2008, est.) 209 applied for aid; of those 85% were deemed to have need. 100% of freshmen with need received aid; of those 20% had need fully met. ***Average percent of need met:*** 74% (excluding resources awarded to replace EFC). ***Average financial aid package:*** $19,739 (excluding resources awarded to replace EFC). 21% of all full-time freshmen had no need and received non-need-based gift aid.

UNDERGRADUATE FINANCIAL AID (Fall 2008, est.) 683 applied for aid; of those 88% were deemed to have need. 100% of undergraduates with need received aid; of those 13% had need fully met. ***Average percent of need met:*** 66% (excluding resources awarded to replace EFC). ***Average financial aid package:*** $18,541 (excluding resources awarded to replace EFC). 15% of all full-time undergraduates had no need and received non-need-based gift aid.

GIFT AID (NEED-BASED) ***Total amount:*** $8,552,191 (12% federal, 5% state, 80% institutional, 3% external sources). ***Receiving aid:*** Freshmen: 77% (177); all full-time undergraduates: 75% (583). ***Average award:*** Freshmen: $15,734; Undergraduates: $14,324. ***Scholarships, grants, and awards:*** Federal Pell, FSEOG, state, private, college/university gift aid from institutional funds.

GIFT AID (NON-NEED-BASED) ***Total amount:*** $1,462,235 (1% state, 95% institutional, 4% external sources). ***Receiving aid:*** Freshmen: 14% (32). Undergraduates: 7% (58). ***Average award:*** Freshmen: $10,685. Undergraduates: $9590. ***Scholarships, grants, and awards by category:*** *Academic interests/achievement:* 168 awards ($1,661,465 total): general academic interests/achievements.

LOANS ***Student loans:*** $7,383,678 (70% need-based, 30% non-need-based). 96% of past graduating class borrowed through all loan programs. *Average indebtedness per student:* $35,726. ***Average need-based loan:*** Freshmen: $3916. Undergraduates: $4575. ***Parent loans:*** $1,700,269 (34% need-based, 66% non-need-based). ***Programs:*** FFEL (Subsidized and Unsubsidized Stafford, PLUS), Perkins, state, college/university.

WORK-STUDY ***Federal work-study:*** Total amount: $282,366; 233 jobs averaging $1800.

APPLYING FOR FINANCIAL AID ***Required financial aid form:*** FAFSA. ***Financial aid deadline (priority):*** 2/15. ***Notification date:*** Continuous beginning 3/1. Students must reply by 5/1.

CONTACT Roxanne Dumas, Director of Financial Aid, Wheelock College, 200 The Riverway, Boston, MA 02215-4176, 617-879-2208 or toll-free 800-734-5212 (out-of-state). *Fax:* 617-879-2470. *E-mail:* rdumas@wheelock.edu.

WHITMAN COLLEGE

Walla Walla, WA

Tuition & fees: $35,192 **Average undergraduate aid package: $28,773**

ABOUT THE INSTITUTION Independent, coed. ***Awards:*** bachelor's degrees. 41 undergraduate majors. ***Total enrollment:*** 1,489. Undergraduates: 1,489. Freshmen: 400. Institutional methodology is used as a basis for awarding need-based institutional aid.

UNDERGRADUATE EXPENSES for 2008–09 ***Application fee:*** $45. ***Comprehensive fee:*** $44,004 includes full-time tuition ($34,880), mandatory fees ($312), and room and board ($8812). ***College room only:*** $4060. Room and board charges vary according to board plan and housing facility. ***Part-time tuition:*** $1462 per credit hour. ***Payment plan:*** Deferred payment.

FRESHMAN FINANCIAL AID (Fall 2008, est.) 267 applied for aid; of those 72% were deemed to have need. 100% of freshmen with need received aid; of those 92% had need fully met. ***Average percent of need met:*** 96% (excluding resources awarded to replace EFC). ***Average financial aid package:*** $27,930 (excluding resources awarded to replace EFC). 28% of all full-time freshmen had no need and received non-need-based gift aid.

UNDERGRADUATE FINANCIAL AID (Fall 2008, est.) 808 applied for aid; of those 85% were deemed to have need. 100% of undergraduates with need received aid; of those 92% had need fully met. ***Average percent of need met:*** 98% (excluding resources awarded to replace EFC). ***Average financial aid package:*** $28,773 (excluding resources awarded to replace EFC). 25% of all full-time undergraduates had no need and received non-need-based gift aid.

GIFT AID (NEED-BASED) ***Total amount:*** $16,449,273 (5% federal, 3% state, 92% institutional). ***Receiving aid:*** Freshmen: 48% (192); all full-time undergraduates: 45% (689). ***Average award:*** Freshmen: $23,309; Undergraduates: $23,463. ***Scholarships, grants, and awards:*** Federal Pell, FSEOG, state, private, college/university gift aid from institutional funds.

GIFT AID (NON-NEED-BASED) ***Total amount:*** $4,059,044 (4% state, 75% institutional, 21% external sources). ***Receiving aid:*** Freshmen: 21% (86). Undergraduates: 12% (185). ***Average award:*** Freshmen: $9479. Undergraduates: $7953. ***Scholarships, grants, and awards by category:*** *Academic interests/achievement:* 613 awards ($4,841,943 total): general academic interests/achievements. *Creative arts/performance:* 234 awards ($457,178 total): art/fine arts, debating, music, theater/drama. *Special characteristics:* 202 awards ($5,318,312 total): ethnic background, first-generation college students, international students. ***Tuition waivers:*** Full or partial for employees or children of employees.

LOANS ***Student loans:*** $3,400,935 (77% need-based, 23% non-need-based). 49% of past graduating class borrowed through all loan programs. *Average indebtedness per student:* $16,684. ***Average need-based loan:*** Freshmen: $4088. Undergraduates: $4500. ***Parent loans:*** $1,729,485 (100% non-need-based). ***Programs:*** FFEL (Subsidized and Unsubsidized Stafford, PLUS), Perkins, alternative loans.

WORK-STUDY ***Federal work-study:*** Total amount: $1,084,156; 540 jobs averaging $2145. ***State or other work-study/employment:*** Total amount: $493,945 (44% need-based, 56% non-need-based). 179 part-time jobs averaging $1991.

APPLYING FOR FINANCIAL AID ***Required financial aid forms:*** FAFSA, CSS Financial Aid PROFILE. ***Financial aid deadline:*** 2/1 (priority: 11/15). ***Notification date:*** Continuous beginning 12/20. Students must reply within 2 weeks of notification.

CONTACT Tyson Harlow, Financial Aid Assistant, Whitman College, 345 Boyer Avenue, Walla Walla, WA 99362-2046, 509-527-5178 or toll-free 877-462-9448. *Fax:* 509-527-4967.

WHITTIER COLLEGE

Whittier, CA

Tuition & fees: $32,470 **Average undergraduate aid package: $31,869**

ABOUT THE INSTITUTION Independent, coed. ***Awards:*** bachelor's, master's, and first professional degrees. 25 undergraduate majors. ***Total enrollment:*** 1,962. Undergraduates: 1,259. Freshmen: 310. Both federal and institutional methodology are used as a basis for awarding need-based institutional aid.

UNDERGRADUATE EXPENSES for 2008–09 ***Application fee:*** $50. ***Comprehensive fee:*** $41,520 includes full-time tuition ($31,950), mandatory fees ($520), and room and board ($9050). Room and board charges vary according to board plan. ***Part-time tuition:*** $1340 per unit.

FRESHMAN FINANCIAL AID (Fall 2008, est.) 394 applied for aid; of those 68% were deemed to have need. 100% of freshmen with need received aid; of those 25% had need fully met. ***Average percent of need met:*** 90% (excluding resources awarded to replace EFC). ***Average financial aid package:*** $31,833 (excluding resources awarded to replace EFC). 27% of all full-time freshmen had no need and received non-need-based gift aid.

UNDERGRADUATE FINANCIAL AID (Fall 2008, est.) 1,211 applied for aid; of those 67% were deemed to have need. 100% of undergraduates with need received aid; of those 28% had need fully met. ***Average percent of need met:*** 91% (excluding resources awarded to replace EFC). ***Average financial aid package:*** $31,869 (excluding resources awarded to replace EFC). 25% of all full-time undergraduates had no need and received non-need-based gift aid.

GIFT AID (NEED-BASED) ***Total amount:*** $26,156,719 (6% federal, 85% state, 9% institutional). ***Receiving aid:*** Freshmen: 55% (218); all full-time undergraduates: 54% (650). ***Average award:*** Freshmen: $12,240; Undergraduates: $12,320. ***Scholarships, grants, and awards:*** Federal Pell, FSEOG, state, private, college/university gift aid from institutional funds.

GIFT AID (NON-NEED-BASED) ***Total amount:*** $13,677,581 (96% institutional, 4% external sources). ***Receiving aid:*** Freshmen: 55% (217). Undergraduates: 55% (664). ***Average award:*** Freshmen: $14,133. Undergraduates: $12,670. ***Scholarships, grants, and awards by category:*** *Academic interests/achievement:* general academic interests/achievements. *Creative arts/performance:* art/fine arts, music, theater/drama. *Special characteristics:* children and siblings of alumni, children of faculty/staff, international students. ***Tuition waivers:*** Full or partial for children of alumni, employees or children of employees. ***ROTC:*** Army cooperative, Air Force cooperative.

LOANS ***Student loans:*** $8,498,467 (58% need-based, 42% non-need-based). 73% of past graduating class borrowed through all loan programs. *Average indebtedness per student:* $40,862. ***Average need-based loan:*** Freshmen: $8182. Undergraduates: $10,021. ***Parent loans:*** $2,369,051 (100% need-based). ***Programs:*** Federal Direct (PLUS), FFEL (Subsidized and Unsubsidized Stafford, PLUS), Perkins, alternative financing loans.

WORK-STUDY ***Federal work-study:*** Total amount: $1,818,989; jobs available. ***State or other work-study/employment:*** Total amount: $740,724 (100% non-need-based). Part-time jobs available.

APPLYING FOR FINANCIAL AID ***Required financial aid forms:*** FAFSA, CSS Financial Aid PROFILE. ***Financial aid deadline:*** 6/30 (priority: 3/1). ***Notification date:*** Continuous. Students must reply within 2 weeks of notification.

CONTACT Mr. David Carnevale, Director of Student Financing, Whittier College, 13406 East Philadelphia Street, Whittier, CA 90608-0634, 562-907-4285. *Fax:* 562-464-4560. *E-mail:* dcarneva@whittier.edu.

WHITWORTH UNIVERSITY

Spokane, WA

Tuition & fees: $27,420 **Average undergraduate aid package: $20,881**

ABOUT THE INSTITUTION Independent Presbyterian, coed. ***Awards:*** bachelor's and master's degrees. 43 undergraduate majors. ***Total enrollment:*** 2,607. Undergraduates: 2,331. Freshmen: 533. Federal methodology is used as a basis for awarding need-based institutional aid.

UNDERGRADUATE EXPENSES for 2008–09 ***Comprehensive fee:*** $35,120 includes full-time tuition ($27,100), mandatory fees ($320), and room and board ($7700). Room and board charges vary according to board plan and housing facility. Part-time tuition and fees vary according to class time. ***Payment plan:*** Installment.

FRESHMAN FINANCIAL AID (Fall 2008, est.) 442 applied for aid; of those 80% were deemed to have need. 100% of freshmen with need received aid; of those 22% had need fully met. ***Average percent of need met:*** 86% (excluding resources awarded to replace EFC). ***Average financial aid package:*** $23,147 (excluding resources awarded to replace EFC). 32% of all full-time freshmen had no need and received non-need-based gift aid.

UNDERGRADUATE FINANCIAL AID (Fall 2008, est.) 1,532 applied for aid; of those 86% were deemed to have need. 100% of undergraduates with need received aid; of those 22% had need fully met. ***Average percent of need met:*** 83% (excluding resources awarded to replace EFC). ***Average financial aid package:*** $20,881 (excluding resources awarded to replace EFC). 29% of all full-time undergraduates had no need and received non-need-based gift aid.

GIFT AID (NEED-BASED) ***Total amount:*** $20,926,509 (10% federal, 10% state, 75% institutional, 5% external sources). ***Receiving aid:*** Freshmen: 64% (350); all full-time undergraduates: 62% (1,292). ***Average award:*** Freshmen: $17,899; Undergraduates: $15,277. ***Scholarships, grants, and awards:*** Federal Pell, FSEOG, state, private, college/university gift aid from institutional funds.

GIFT AID (NON-NEED-BASED) ***Total amount:*** $7,466,004 (5% federal, 2% state, 88% institutional, 5% external sources). ***Receiving aid:*** Freshmen: 7% (37). Undergraduates: 7% (153). ***Average award:*** Freshmen: $9880. Undergraduates: $9800. ***Scholarships, grants, and awards by category:*** *Academic interests/achievement:* 1,579 awards ($13,598,162 total): biological sciences, computer science, general academic interests/achievements, military science, physical sciences, premedicine. *Creative arts/performance:* 174 awards ($306,895 total): art/fine arts, journalism/publications, music, theater/drama. *Special achievements/activities:* 36 awards ($26,600 total): religious involvement. *Special characteristics:* 618 awards ($2,866,368 total): children and siblings of alumni, ethnic background, international students, members of minority groups, relatives of clergy, siblings of current students. ***Tuition waivers:*** Full or partial for employees or children of employees. ***ROTC:*** Army cooperative.

LOANS ***Student loans:*** $11,346,511 (76% need-based, 24% non-need-based). 68% of past graduating class borrowed through all loan programs. *Average indebtedness per student:* $19,305. ***Average need-based loan:*** Freshmen: $4173. Undergraduates: $4768. ***Parent loans:*** $3,053,120 (31% need-based, 69% non-need-based). ***Programs:*** Federal Direct (Subsidized and Unsubsidized Stafford, PLUS), FFEL (PLUS), Perkins, college/university.

WORK-STUDY ***Federal work-study:*** Total amount: $1,470,971; 573 jobs averaging $2282. ***State or other work-study/employment:*** Total amount: $819,266 (96% need-based, 4% non-need-based). 215 part-time jobs averaging $3281.

APPLYING FOR FINANCIAL AID ***Required financial aid form:*** FAFSA. ***Financial aid deadline (priority):*** 3/1. ***Notification date:*** Continuous beginning 3/1.

CONTACT Ms. Wendy Z. Olson, Director of Financial Aid, Whitworth University, 300 West Hawthorne Road, Spokane, WA 99251-0001, 509-777-4306 or toll-free 800-533-4668 (out-of-state). *Fax:* 509-777-4601. *E-mail:* wolson@whitworth.edu.

WICHITA STATE UNIVERSITY

Wichita, KS

Tuition & fees (KS res): $5084 **Average undergraduate aid package: $8788**

ABOUT THE INSTITUTION State-supported, coed. ***Awards:*** associate, bachelor's, master's, and doctoral degrees and post-bachelor's and post-master's certificates. 57 undergraduate majors. ***Total enrollment:*** 14,612. Undergraduates: 11,600. Freshmen: 1,420. Federal methodology is used as a basis for awarding need-based institutional aid.

UNDERGRADUATE EXPENSES for 2008–09 ***Application fee:*** $30. ***Tuition, state resident:*** full-time $4144; part-time $138.15 per credit hour. ***Tuition, nonresident:*** full-time $11,821; part-time $394.05 per credit hour. ***Required fees:*** full-time $940; $30.20 per credit hour or $17 per term. Full-time tuition and fees vary according to course load and degree level. Part-time tuition and fees vary according to course load and degree level. ***College room and board:*** $5860. Room and board charges vary according to board plan and housing facility. ***Payment plan:*** Installment.

FRESHMAN FINANCIAL AID (Fall 2007) 1,157 applied for aid; of those 50% were deemed to have need. 98% of freshmen with need received aid; of those 20% had need fully met. ***Average percent of need met:*** 48% (excluding resources awarded to replace EFC). ***Average financial aid package:*** $7257 (excluding resources awarded to replace EFC). 29% of all full-time freshmen had no need and received non-need-based gift aid.

UNDERGRADUATE FINANCIAL AID (Fall 2007) 6,282 applied for aid; of those 58% were deemed to have need. 98% of undergraduates with need received aid; of those 75% had need fully met. ***Average percent of need met:*** 49% (excluding resources awarded to replace EFC). ***Average financial aid package:*** $8788 (excluding resources awarded to replace EFC). 16% of all full-time undergraduates had no need and received non-need-based gift aid.

GIFT AID (NEED-BASED) ***Total amount:*** $10,720,638 (83% federal, 16% state, 1% external sources). ***Receiving aid:*** Freshmen: 26% (353); all full-time undergraduates: 29% (2,171). ***Average award:*** Freshmen: $3661; Undergraduates: $3795. ***Scholarships, grants, and awards:*** Federal Pell, FSEOG, state, private, college/university gift aid from institutional funds, Academic Competitiveness Grant, National Smart Grant.

GIFT AID (NON-NEED-BASED) ***Total amount:*** $5,741,642 (81% institutional, 19% external sources). ***Receiving aid:*** Freshmen: 24% (320). Undergraduates: 11% (854). ***Average award:*** Freshmen: $3756. Undergraduates: $2879. ***Scholarships, grants, and awards by category:*** *Academic interests/achievement:* area/ethnic studies, biological sciences, business, communication, computer science, education, engineering/technologies, English, foreign languages, general academic interests/achievements, health fields, humanities, international studies, mathematics, physical sciences, premedicine, social sciences. *Creative arts/performance:* applied art and design, art/fine arts, creative writing, dance, debating, journalism/publications, music, performing arts, theater/drama. *Special achievements/activities:* cheerleading/drum major, general special achievements/activities, leadership, memberships. *Special characteristics:* adult students, first-generation college students, international students, members of minority groups. ***Tuition waivers:*** Full or partial for employees or children of employees, senior citizens.

LOANS ***Student loans:*** $43,924,155 (55% need-based, 45% non-need-based). 59% of past graduating class borrowed through all loan programs. *Average indebtedness per student:* $22,116. ***Average need-based loan:*** Freshmen: $2933. Undergraduates: $4205. ***Parent loans:*** $1,027,808 (100% non-need-based). ***Programs:*** FFEL (Subsidized and Unsubsidized Stafford, PLUS), Perkins.

WORK-STUDY ***Federal work-study:*** Total amount: $297,258; 94 jobs averaging $9329. ***State or other work-study/employment:*** Total amount: $93,914 (100% need-based). Part-time jobs available.

ATHLETIC AWARDS Total amount: $1,572,726 (100% non-need-based).

APPLYING FOR FINANCIAL AID ***Required financial aid forms:*** FAFSA, institution's own form, state aid form. ***Financial aid deadline (priority):*** 3/1. ***Notification date:*** Continuous beginning 3/1. Students must reply within 2 weeks of notification.

CONTACT Deborah D. Byers, Director of Financial Aid, Wichita State University, 1845 Fairmount, Wichita, KS 67260-0024, 316-978-3430 or toll-free 800-362-2594. *Fax:* 316-978-3396. *E-mail:* deb.byers@wichita.edu.

WIDENER UNIVERSITY

Chester, PA

Tuition & fees: $30,450 **Average undergraduate aid package: $22,870**

ABOUT THE INSTITUTION Independent, coed. ***Awards:*** associate, bachelor's, master's, doctoral, and first professional degrees. 73 undergraduate majors. ***Total enrollment:*** 6,601. Undergraduates: 3,428. Freshmen: 730. Both federal and institutional methodology are used as a basis for awarding need-based institutional aid.

UNDERGRADUATE EXPENSES for 2008–09 ***Application fee:*** $35. ***Comprehensive fee:*** $41,290 includes full-time tuition ($29,990), mandatory fees ($460), and room and board ($10,840). ***College room only:*** $5600. Full-time tuition and fees vary according to class time, course load, and program. Room and board charges vary according to board plan and housing facility. ***Part-time tuition:*** $1000 per credit. ***Payment plan:*** Installment.

FRESHMAN FINANCIAL AID (Fall 2008, est.) 648 applied for aid; of those 91% were deemed to have need. 100% of freshmen with need received aid; of those 16% had need fully met. ***Average percent of need met:*** 80% (excluding resources awarded to replace EFC). ***Average financial aid package:*** $25,555 (excluding resources awarded to replace EFC). 14% of all full-time freshmen had no need and received non-need-based gift aid.

UNDERGRADUATE FINANCIAL AID (Fall 2008, est.) 2,258 applied for aid; of those 91% were deemed to have need. 100% of undergraduates with need received aid; of those 17% had need fully met. ***Average percent of need met:*** 75% (excluding resources awarded to replace EFC). ***Average financial aid package:*** $22,870 (excluding resources awarded to replace EFC). 15% of all full-time undergraduates had no need and received non-need-based gift aid.

GIFT AID (NEED-BASED) ***Total amount:*** $32,891,253 (14% federal, 7% state, 75% institutional, 4% external sources). ***Receiving aid:*** Freshmen: 81% (579); all full-time undergraduates: 74% (1,971). ***Average award:*** Freshmen: $10,523; Undergraduates: $9120. ***Scholarships, grants, and awards:*** Federal Pell, FSEOG, state, private, college/university gift aid from institutional funds, Federal Nursing.

GIFT AID (NON-NEED-BASED) ***Total amount:*** $4,543,133 (5% federal, 88% institutional, 7% external sources). ***Receiving aid:*** Freshmen: 67% (482). Undergraduates: 59% (1,571). ***Average award:*** Freshmen: $12,043. Undergraduates: $10,296. ***Scholarships, grants, and awards by category:*** *Academic interests/achievement:* 2,150 awards ($18,521,742 total): biological sciences, business, communication, computer science, education, engineering/technologies, English, foreign languages, general academic interests/achievements, health fields, humanities, international studies, mathematics, military science, physical sciences, premedicine, social sciences. *Creative arts/performance:* 45 awards ($82,000 total): music. *Special achievements/activities:* 53 awards ($223,345 total): community service, general special achievements/activities, leadership. *Special characteristics:* 192 awards ($2,420,873 total): adult students, children of faculty/staff, ethnic background, international students. ***Tuition waivers:*** Full or partial for employees or children of employees, senior citizens. ***ROTC:*** Army, Naval cooperative, Air Force cooperative.

LOANS ***Student loans:*** $28,973,983 (90% need-based, 10% non-need-based). 93% of past graduating class borrowed through all loan programs. *Average indebtedness per student:* $36,398. ***Average need-based loan:*** Freshmen: $4370. Undergraduates: $5527. ***Parent loans:*** $5,203,033 (83% need-based, 17% non-need-based). ***Programs:*** FFEL (Subsidized and Unsubsidized Stafford, PLUS), Perkins.

WORK-STUDY ***Federal work-study:*** Total amount: $2,360,528; 1,704 jobs averaging $1402. ***State or other work-study/employment:*** Total amount: $170,397 (77% need-based, 23% non-need-based). 350 part-time jobs averaging $1200.

APPLYING FOR FINANCIAL AID ***Required financial aid form:*** FAFSA. ***Financial aid deadline (priority):*** 2/15. ***Notification date:*** Continuous beginning 3/15. Students must reply within 4 weeks of notification.

CONTACT Thomas K. Malloy, Director of Student Financial Services, Widener University, One University Place, Chester, PA 19013-5792, 610-499-4161 or toll-free 888-WIDENER. *Fax:* 610-499-4687. *E-mail:* finaidmc@mail.widener.edu.

WILBERFORCE UNIVERSITY

Wilberforce, OH

CONTACT Director of Financial Aid, Wilberforce University, 1055 North Bickett Road, Wilberforce, OH 45384, 937-708-5727 or toll-free 800-367-8568. *Fax:* 937-376-4752.

WILEY COLLEGE

Marshall, TX

CONTACT Cecelia Jones, Interim Director of Financial Aid, Wiley College, 711 Wiley Avenue, Marshall, TX 75670-5199, 903-927-3210 or toll-free 800-658-6889. *Fax:* 903-927-3366.

WILKES UNIVERSITY

Wilkes-Barre, PA

Tuition & fees: $25,170 **Average undergraduate aid package: $19,642**

ABOUT THE INSTITUTION Independent, coed. ***Awards:*** bachelor's, master's, doctoral, and first professional degrees. 35 undergraduate majors. ***Total enrollment:*** 5,901. Undergraduates: 2,309. Freshmen: 565. Federal methodology is used as a basis for awarding need-based institutional aid.

UNDERGRADUATE EXPENSES for 2008–09 ***Application fee:*** $40. ***Comprehensive fee:*** $35,950 includes full-time tuition ($23,850), mandatory fees ($1320), and room and board ($10,780). ***College room only:*** $6490. Room and board charges vary according to board plan and housing facility. ***Part-time tuition:*** $660 per credit. ***Part-time fees:*** $60 per credit. ***Payment plans:*** Installment, deferred payment.

FRESHMAN FINANCIAL AID (Fall 2008, est.) 534 applied for aid; of those 89% were deemed to have need. 99% of freshmen with need received aid; of those 17% had need fully met. ***Average percent of need met:*** 78% (excluding resources awarded to replace EFC). ***Average financial aid package:*** $20,731 (excluding resources awarded to replace EFC). 11% of all full-time freshmen had no need and received non-need-based gift aid.

UNDERGRADUATE FINANCIAL AID (Fall 2008, est.) 1,977 applied for aid; of those 90% were deemed to have need. 98% of undergraduates with need received aid; of those 16% had need fully met. ***Average percent of need met:*** 75% (excluding resources awarded to replace EFC). ***Average financial aid package:*** $19,642 (excluding resources awarded to replace EFC). 14% of all full-time undergraduates had no need and received non-need-based gift aid.

GIFT AID (NEED-BASED) ***Total amount:*** $23,990,380 (10% federal, 11% state, 77% institutional, 2% external sources). ***Receiving aid:*** Freshmen: 69% (385); all full-time undergraduates: 62% (1,370). ***Average award:*** Freshmen: $9136; Undergraduates: $8398. ***Scholarships, grants, and awards:*** Federal Pell, FSEOG, state, private, college/university gift aid from institutional funds.

GIFT AID (NON-NEED-BASED) ***Total amount:*** $3,155,118 (1% state, 98% institutional, 1% external sources). ***Receiving aid:*** Freshmen: 72% (403). Undergraduates: 62% (1,372). ***Average award:*** Freshmen: $11,397. Undergraduates: $10,474. ***Scholarships, grants, and awards by category:*** *Academic interests/achievement:* general academic interests/achievements. *Creative arts/performance:* performing arts, theater/drama. *Special achievements/activities:* general special achievements/activities, leadership. *Special characteristics:* children of faculty/staff. ***Tuition waivers:*** Full or partial for employees or children of employees. ***ROTC:*** Army cooperative, Air Force.

LOANS ***Student loans:*** $18,160,206 (91% need-based, 9% non-need-based). 88% of past graduating class borrowed through all loan programs. *Average indebtedness per student:* $31,935. ***Average need-based loan:*** Freshmen: $2835. Undergraduates: $3726. ***Parent loans:*** $3,335,892 (89% need-based, 11% non-need-based). ***Programs:*** FFEL (Subsidized and Unsubsidized Stafford, PLUS), Perkins, Federal Nursing, state, college/university, Gulf Oil Loan Fund, Rulison Evans Loan Fund.

WORK-STUDY ***Federal work-study:*** Total amount: $2,568,770; jobs available. ***State or other work-study/employment:*** Part-time jobs available.

APPLYING FOR FINANCIAL AID ***Required financial aid form:*** FAFSA. ***Financial aid deadline (priority):*** 3/1. ***Notification date:*** Continuous.

CONTACT Melanie Mickelson, Interim Vice President Enrollment Services, Wilkes University, 84 W South Street, Wilkes-Barre, PA 18766, 570-408-4000 or toll-free 800-945-5378 Ext. 4400. *Fax:* 570-408-3000. *E-mail:* melanie.mickelson@wilkes.edu.

WILLAMETTE UNIVERSITY

Salem, OR

Tuition & fees: $33,960 **Average undergraduate aid package: $27,974**

ABOUT THE INSTITUTION Independent United Methodist, coed. ***Awards:*** bachelor's, master's, and first professional degrees and post-bachelor's and first professional certificates. 40 undergraduate majors. ***Total enrollment:*** 2,716. Undergraduates: 1,864. Freshmen: 482. Federal methodology is used as a basis for awarding need-based institutional aid.

UNDERGRADUATE EXPENSES for 2008–09 ***Application fee:*** $50. ***Comprehensive fee:*** $41,910 includes full-time tuition ($33,750), mandatory fees ($210), and room and board ($7950). Full-time tuition and fees vary according to course load. Room and board charges vary according to board plan and housing facility. ***Part-time tuition:*** $4220 per course. Part-time tuition and fees vary according to course load. ***Payment plans:*** Tuition prepayment, installment.

FRESHMAN FINANCIAL AID (Fall 2008, est.) 371 applied for aid; of those 75% were deemed to have need. 100% of freshmen with need received aid; of those 25% had need fully met. ***Average percent of need met:*** 93% (excluding resources awarded to replace EFC). ***Average financial aid package:*** $27,374 (excluding resources awarded to replace EFC). 39% of all full-time freshmen had no need and received non-need-based gift aid.

UNDERGRADUATE FINANCIAL AID (Fall 2008, est.) 1,248 applied for aid; of those 86% were deemed to have need. 100% of undergraduates with need received aid; of those 21% had need fully met. ***Average percent of need met:*** 90% (excluding resources awarded to replace EFC). ***Average financial aid package:*** $27,974 (excluding resources awarded to replace EFC). 34% of all full-time undergraduates had no need and received non-need-based gift aid.

GIFT AID (NEED-BASED) ***Total amount:*** $23,564,675 (8% federal, 2% state, 86% institutional, 4% external sources). ***Receiving aid:*** Freshmen: 57% (274); all full-time undergraduates: 60% (1,050). ***Average award:*** Freshmen: $21,412; Undergraduates: $21,304. ***Scholarships, grants, and awards:*** Federal Pell, FSEOG, state, private, college/university gift aid from institutional funds.

GIFT AID (NON-NEED-BASED) ***Total amount:*** $6,336,661 (98% institutional, 2% external sources). ***Receiving aid:*** Freshmen: 22% (107). Undergraduates: 15% (255). ***Average award:*** Freshmen: $11,728. Undergraduates: $10,448. ***Scholarships, grants, and awards by category:*** *Academic interests/achievement:* general academic interests/achievements. *Creative arts/performance:* debating, music, theater/drama. *Special achievements/activities:* community service, leadership. *Special characteristics:* international students, members of minority groups. ***Tuition waivers:*** Full or partial for employees or children of employees. ***ROTC:*** Air Force cooperative.

LOANS ***Student loans:*** $7,775,314 (91% need-based, 9% non-need-based). 63% of past graduating class borrowed through all loan programs. *Average indebtedness per student:* $24,465. ***Average need-based loan:*** Freshmen: $4430. Undergraduates: $5086. ***Parent loans:*** $3,528,902 (67% need-based, 33% non-need-based). ***Programs:*** FFEL (Subsidized and Unsubsidized Stafford, PLUS), Perkins, state.

WORK-STUDY ***Federal work-study:*** Total amount: $1,443,479; 698 jobs averaging $2096. ***State or other work-study/employment:*** 579 part-time jobs averaging $1021.

APPLYING FOR FINANCIAL AID ***Required financial aid form:*** FAFSA. ***Financial aid deadline (priority):*** 2/1. ***Notification date:*** Continuous beginning 4/1. Students must reply by 5/1 or within 2 weeks of notification.

CONTACT Patty Hoban, Director of Financial Aid, Willamette University, 900 State Street, Salem, OR 97301-3931, 503-370-6273 or toll-free 877-542-2787. *Fax:* 503-370-6588. *E-mail:* phoban@willamette.edu.

WILLIAM CAREY UNIVERSITY

Hattiesburg, MS

Tuition & fees: N/R **Average undergraduate aid package: $15,000**

ABOUT THE INSTITUTION Independent Southern Baptist, coed. 32 undergraduate majors. Federal methodology is used as a basis for awarding need-based institutional aid.

UNDERGRADUATE FINANCIAL AID (Fall 2008, est.) 1,720 applied for aid; of those 100% were deemed to have need. 100% of undergraduates with need received aid; of those 93% had need fully met. ***Average percent of need met:*** 90% (excluding resources awarded to replace EFC). ***Average financial aid package:*** $15,000 (excluding resources awarded to replace EFC). 10% of all full-time undergraduates had no need and received non-need-based gift aid.

GIFT AID (NEED-BASED) ***Total amount:*** $6,150,000 (64% federal, 28% state, 8% external sources). ***Receiving aid:*** All full-time undergraduates: 90% (1,715). ***Average award:*** Undergraduates: $7000. ***Scholarships, grants, and awards:*** Federal Pell, FSEOG, state, private, college/university gift aid from institutional funds.

GIFT AID (NON-NEED-BASED) ***Total amount:*** $5,200,000 (100% institutional). ***Receiving aid:*** Undergraduates: 42% (800). ***Average award:*** Undergraduates: $7300. ***Scholarships, grants, and awards by category:*** *Academic interests/achievement:* 900 awards ($5,200,000 total): general academic interests/achievements. *Creative arts/performance:* 75 awards ($350,000 total): art/fine arts, debating, journalism/publications, music, theater/drama. *Special achievements/activities:* 200 awards ($200,000 total): cheerleading/drum major, junior miss, leadership, religious involvement. *Special characteristics:* 225 awards ($350,000 total): children and siblings of alumni, children of educators, children of faculty/staff, first-generation college students, international students, relatives of clergy, religious affiliation, veterans. ***Tuition waivers:*** Full or partial for employees or children of employees.

LOANS ***Student loans:*** $23,000,000 (100% need-based). 85% of past graduating class borrowed through all loan programs. *Average indebtedness per student:* $17,500. ***Average need-based loan:*** Undergraduates: $6500. ***Parent loans:*** $200,000 (100% need-based). ***Programs:*** FFEL (Subsidized and Unsubsidized Stafford, PLUS), Perkins, Federal Nursing, college/university.

WORK-STUDY ***Federal work-study:*** Total amount: $370,000; 300 jobs averaging $1700. ***State or other work-study/employment:*** Total amount: $100,000 (100% non-need-based). 100 part-time jobs averaging $1700.

ATHLETIC AWARDS Total amount: $825,000 (100% non-need-based).

APPLYING FOR FINANCIAL AID ***Required financial aid forms:*** FAFSA, institution's own form, state aid form. ***Financial aid deadline (priority):*** 4/1. ***Notification date:*** Continuous beginning 5/1. Students must reply within 2 weeks of notification.

CONTACT Ms. Brenda Pittman, Associate Director of Financial Aid, William Carey University, 498 Tuscan Avenue, Hattiesburg, MS 39401-5499, 601-318-6153 or toll-free 800-962-5991 (in-state).

WILLIAM JESSUP UNIVERSITY

Rocklin, CA

Tuition & fees: $20,480 **Average undergraduate aid package: $14,956**

ABOUT THE INSTITUTION Independent nondenominational, coed. ***Awards:*** associate and bachelor's degrees and post-bachelor's certificates. 6 undergraduate majors. ***Total enrollment:*** 463. Undergraduates: 460. Freshmen: 57. Federal methodology is used as a basis for awarding need-based institutional aid.

UNDERGRADUATE EXPENSES for 2008–09 ***Application fee:*** $35. ***Comprehensive fee:*** $27,950 includes full-time tuition ($20,480) and room and board ($7470). Full-time tuition and fees vary according to course load. ***Part-time tuition:*** $867 per semester hour. Part-time tuition and fees vary according to course load. ***Payment plan:*** Deferred payment.

FRESHMAN FINANCIAL AID (Fall 2008, est.) 54 applied for aid; of those 76% were deemed to have need. 100% of freshmen with need received aid; of those 20% had need fully met. ***Average percent of need met:*** 74% (excluding resources awarded to replace EFC). ***Average financial aid package:*** $16,789 (excluding resources awarded to replace EFC). 18% of all full-time freshmen had no need and received non-need-based gift aid.

UNDERGRADUATE FINANCIAL AID (Fall 2008, est.) 305 applied for aid; of those 84% were deemed to have need. 99% of undergraduates with need received aid; of those 15% had need fully met. ***Average percent of need met:*** 63% (excluding resources awarded to replace EFC). ***Average financial aid package:*** $14,956 (excluding resources awarded to replace EFC). 13% of all full-time undergraduates had no need and received non-need-based gift aid.

GIFT AID (NEED-BASED) ***Total amount:*** $2,476,701 (18% federal, 32% state, 47% institutional, 3% external sources). ***Receiving aid:*** Freshmen: 30% (17); all full-time undergraduates: 34% (123). ***Average award:*** Freshmen: $10,033; Undergraduates: $9290. ***Scholarships, grants, and awards:*** Federal Pell, FSEOG, state, private, college/university gift aid from institutional funds.

GIFT AID (NON-NEED-BASED) ***Total amount:*** $448,731 (90% institutional, 10% external sources). ***Receiving aid:*** Freshmen: 70% (40). Undergraduates: 58% (208). ***Average award:*** Freshmen: $6900. Undergraduates: $6591. ***Scholarships, grants, and awards by category:*** *Academic interests/achievement:* education, general academic interests/achievements, international studies, religion/biblical studies. *Creative arts/performance:* music. *Special achievements/activities:* leadership, religious involvement. *Special characteristics:* adult students, children of faculty/staff, international students, previous college experience, relatives of clergy, veterans, veterans' children. ***Tuition waivers:*** Full or partial for employees or children of employees.

LOANS ***Student loans:*** $2,127,524 (48% need-based, 52% non-need-based). 65% of past graduating class borrowed through all loan programs. *Average indebtedness per student:* $15,802. ***Average need-based loan:*** Freshmen: $3257. Undergraduates: $4403. ***Parent loans:*** $390,567 (41% need-based, 59% non-need-based). ***Programs:*** FFEL (Subsidized and Unsubsidized Stafford, PLUS).

WORK-STUDY ***Federal work-study:*** Total amount: $50,000; 18 jobs averaging $1792. ***State or other work-study/employment:*** Total amount: $150,000 (33% need-based, 67% non-need-based). Part-time jobs available.

ATHLETIC AWARDS Total amount: $609,778 (67% need-based, 33% non-need-based).

APPLYING FOR FINANCIAL AID ***Required financial aid form:*** FAFSA. ***Financial aid deadline (priority):*** 3/2. ***Notification date:*** Continuous beginning 3/2. Students must reply within 3 weeks of notification.

CONTACT Kristi Kindberg, Financial Aid Administrator, William Jessup University, 790 South 12th Street, San Jose, CA 95112-2381, 408-278-4328 or toll-free 800-355-7522. *Fax:* 408-293-9299. *E-mail:* finaid@sjchristian.edu.

WILLIAM JEWELL COLLEGE

Liberty, MO

ABOUT THE INSTITUTION Independent Baptist, coed. ***Awards:*** bachelor's degrees (also offers evening program with significant enrollment not reflected in profile). 50 undergraduate majors. ***Total enrollment:*** 1,210. Undergraduates: 1,210. Freshmen: 265.

GIFT AID (NEED-BASED) ***Scholarships, grants, and awards:*** Federal Pell, FSEOG, state, college/university gift aid from institutional funds.

GIFT AID (NON-NEED-BASED) ***Scholarships, grants, and awards by category:*** *Academic interests/achievement:* general academic interests/achievements. *Creative arts/performance:* art/fine arts, debating, journalism/publications, music, theater/drama. *Special achievements/activities:* cheerleading/drum major, religious involvement. *Special characteristics:* children and siblings of alumni, children of faculty/staff, siblings of current students.

LOANS ***Programs:*** FFEL (Subsidized and Unsubsidized Stafford, PLUS), Perkins, Federal Nursing, non-Federal alternative loans (non-college).

WORK-STUDY ***Federal work-study:*** Total amount: $526,195; 337 jobs averaging $1485. ***State or other work-study/employment:*** Total amount: $166,446 (100% non-need-based). 163 part-time jobs averaging $800.

APPLYING FOR FINANCIAL AID ***Required financial aid form:*** FAFSA.

CONTACT Sue Armstrong, Director of Financial Aid, William Jewell College, 500 College Hill, Box 1014, T37, Brown Hall, Liberty, MO 64068, 816-415-5973 or toll-free 888-2JEWELL. *Fax:* 816-415-5006. *E-mail:* armstrongs@william.jewell.edu.

WILLIAM PATERSON UNIVERSITY OF NEW JERSEY

Wayne, NJ

Tuition & fees (NJ res): $10,492 Average undergraduate aid package: $13,667

ABOUT THE INSTITUTION State-supported, coed. ***Awards:*** bachelor's and master's degrees and post-bachelor's and post-master's certificates. 53 undergraduate majors. ***Total enrollment:*** 10,256. Undergraduates: 8,741. Freshmen: 1,345. Federal methodology is used as a basis for awarding need-based institutional aid.

UNDERGRADUATE EXPENSES for 2008–09 ***Application fee:*** $50. ***Tuition, state resident:*** full-time $6375; part-time $204.44 per credit. ***Tuition, nonresident:*** full-time $12,933; part-time $418.44 per credit. ***Required fees:*** full-time $4117; $132.56 per credit. Full-time tuition and fees vary according to course load and degree level. Part-time tuition and fees vary according to course load and degree level. ***College room and board:*** $9990; ***Room only:*** $6640. Room and board charges vary according to board plan and housing facility. ***Payment plan:*** Installment.

FRESHMAN FINANCIAL AID (Fall 2008, est.) 1,052 applied for aid; of those 75% were deemed to have need. 97% of freshmen with need received aid; of those 45% had need fully met. ***Average financial aid package:*** $13,834 (excluding resources awarded to replace EFC). 9% of all full-time freshmen had no need and received non-need-based gift aid.

UNDERGRADUATE FINANCIAL AID (Fall 2008, est.) 5,185 applied for aid; of those 80% were deemed to have need. 98% of undergraduates with need received aid; of those 38% had need fully met. ***Average financial aid package:*** $13,667 (excluding resources awarded to replace EFC). 6% of all full-time undergraduates had no need and received non-need-based gift aid.

GIFT AID (NEED-BASED) ***Total amount:*** $17,856,000 (48% federal, 48% state, 4% institutional). ***Receiving aid:*** Freshmen: 34% (412); all full-time undergraduates: 30% (2,154). ***Average award:*** Freshmen: $8540; Undergraduates: $7947. ***Scholarships, grants, and awards:*** Federal Pell, FSEOG, state, college/university gift aid from institutional funds.

GIFT AID (NON-NEED-BASED) ***Total amount:*** $6,630,000 (4% state, 91% institutional, 5% external sources). ***Receiving aid:*** Freshmen: 11% (132). Undergraduates: 8% (586). ***Average award:*** Freshmen: $4509. Undergraduates: $7181. ***Tuition waivers:*** Full or partial for employees or children of employees, senior citizens. ***ROTC:*** Air Force cooperative.

LOANS ***Student loans:*** $51,850,000 (37% need-based, 63% non-need-based). 64% of past graduating class borrowed through all loan programs. *Average indebtedness per student:* $21,459. ***Average need-based loan:*** Freshmen: $3593. Undergraduates: $4521. ***Parent loans:*** $3,400,000 (100% non-need-based). ***Programs:*** Federal Direct (Subsidized and Unsubsidized Stafford, PLUS), FFEL (Subsidized and Unsubsidized Stafford, PLUS), Perkins, state.

WORK-STUDY ***Federal work-study:*** Total amount: $233,000; jobs available. ***State or other work-study/employment:*** Total amount: $275,000 (100% need-based). 229 part-time jobs averaging $3480.

APPLYING FOR FINANCIAL AID ***Required financial aid form:*** FAFSA. ***Financial aid deadline (priority):*** 4/1. ***Notification date:*** Continuous beginning 4/1.

CONTACT Elizabeth Riquez, Director of Financial Aid, William Paterson University of New Jersey, 300 Pompton Road, Wayne, NJ 07470, 973-720-2928 or toll-free 877-WPU-EXCEL (in-state). *Fax:* 973-720-3133. *E-mail:* riqueze@wpunj.edu.

WILLIAM PENN UNIVERSITY

Oskaloosa, IA

CONTACT Cyndi Peiffer, Director of Financial Aid, William Penn University, 201 Trueblood Avenue, Oskaloosa, IA 52577-1799, 641-673-1060 or toll-free 800-779-7366. *Fax:* 641-673-1115. *E-mail:* peifferc@wmpenn.edu.

WILLIAMS BAPTIST COLLEGE

Walnut Ridge, AR

Tuition & fees: $10,950 Average undergraduate aid package: $6081

ABOUT THE INSTITUTION Independent Southern Baptist, coed. 26 undergraduate majors. Federal methodology is used as a basis for awarding need-based institutional aid.

UNDERGRADUATE EXPENSES for 2008–09 ***Comprehensive fee:*** $15,950 includes full-time tuition ($10,200), mandatory fees ($750), and room and board ($5000).

FRESHMAN FINANCIAL AID (Fall 2007) 122 applied for aid; of those 77% were deemed to have need. 100% of freshmen with need received aid. ***Average financial aid package:*** $5008 (excluding resources awarded to replace EFC).

UNDERGRADUATE FINANCIAL AID (Fall 2007) 454 applied for aid; of those 80% were deemed to have need. 100% of undergraduates with need received aid. ***Average financial aid package:*** $6081 (excluding resources awarded to replace EFC).

GIFT AID (NEED-BASED) ***Total amount:*** $1,177,079 (73% federal, 27% state). ***Receiving aid:*** Freshmen: 48% (64); all full-time undergraduates: 53% (260). ***Average award:*** Freshmen: $3347; Undergraduates: $3255. ***Scholarships, grants, and awards:*** Federal Pell, FSEOG, state, private, college/university gift aid from institutional funds.

GIFT AID (NON-NEED-BASED) ***Total amount:*** $1,626,602 (7% state, 74% institutional, 19% external sources). ***Receiving aid:*** Freshmen: 67% (90). Undergraduates: 64% (314). ***Scholarships, grants, and awards by category:*** *Academic interests/achievement:* 428 awards ($1,097,357 total): biological sciences, business, education, general academic interests/achievements, humanities, religion/biblical studies. *Creative arts/performance:* 38 awards ($39,150 total): art/fine arts, music. *Special achievements/activities:* 7 awards ($2233 total): cheerleading/drum major. *Special characteristics:* 173 awards ($194,687 total): children of faculty/staff, international students, members of minority groups, relatives of clergy, religious affiliation.

LOANS ***Student loans:*** $1,894,296 (60% need-based, 40% non-need-based). 65% of past graduating class borrowed through all loan programs. *Average indebtedness per student:* $15,878. ***Average need-based loan:*** Freshmen: $2494. Undergraduates: $3571. ***Parent loans:*** $192,127 (100% non-need-based). ***Programs:*** Federal Direct (Subsidized and Unsubsidized Stafford, PLUS).

WORK-STUDY ***Federal work-study:*** Total amount: $261,634; 207 jobs averaging $1258. ***State or other work-study/employment:*** Total amount: $32,200 (100% non-need-based). 35 part-time jobs averaging $940.

ATHLETIC AWARDS Total amount: $535,441 (100% non-need-based).

APPLYING FOR FINANCIAL AID ***Required financial aid form:*** FAFSA. ***Financial aid deadline:*** Continuous. ***Notification date:*** Continuous beginning 4/1. Students must reply within 2 weeks of notification.

CONTACT Barbara Turner, Director of Financial Aid, Williams Baptist College, 60 West Fulbright Avenue, Walnut Ridge, AR 72476, 870-759-4112 or toll-free 800-722-4434. *Fax:* 870-759-4209. *E-mail:* bturner@wbcoll.edu.

WILLIAMS COLLEGE

Williamstown, MA

Tuition & fees: $37,640 Average undergraduate aid package: $37,857

ABOUT THE INSTITUTION Independent, coed. ***Awards:*** bachelor's and master's degrees. 33 undergraduate majors. ***Total enrollment:*** 2,045. Undergraduates: 1,997. Freshmen: 540. Institutional methodology is used as a basis for awarding need-based institutional aid.

UNDERGRADUATE EXPENSES for 2008–09 ***Application fee:*** $60. ***Comprehensive fee:*** $47,530 includes full-time tuition ($37,400), mandatory fees ($240), and room and board ($9890). ***College room only:*** $5030. Room and board charges vary according to board plan. ***Payment plan:*** Installment.

FRESHMAN FINANCIAL AID (Fall 2008, est.) 334 applied for aid; of those 81% were deemed to have need. 100% of freshmen with need received aid; of those 100% had need fully met. ***Average percent of need met:*** 100% (excluding resources awarded to replace EFC). ***Average financial aid package:*** $39,641 (excluding resources awarded to replace EFC).

UNDERGRADUATE FINANCIAL AID (Fall 2008, est.) 1,111 applied for aid; of those 87% were deemed to have need. 100% of undergraduates with need received aid; of those 100% had need fully met. ***Average percent of need met:***

100% (excluding resources awarded to replace EFC). ***Average financial aid package:*** $37,857 (excluding resources awarded to replace EFC).

GIFT AID (NEED-BASED) ***Total amount:*** $35,061,723 (4% federal, 1% state, 92% institutional, 3% external sources). ***Receiving aid:*** Freshmen: 50% (268); all full-time undergraduates: 49% (960). ***Average award:*** Freshmen: $38,410; Undergraduates: $36,375. ***Scholarships, grants, and awards:*** Federal Pell, FSEOG, state, private, college/university gift aid from institutional funds.

GIFT AID (NON-NEED-BASED) ***Total amount:*** $1,249,195 (100% external sources).

LOANS ***Student loans:*** $1,141,059 (100% non-need-based). 46% of past graduating class borrowed through all loan programs. *Average indebtedness per student:* $9214. ***Parent loans:*** $3,051,936 (100% non-need-based). ***Programs:*** Federal Direct (Subsidized and Unsubsidized Stafford, PLUS), Perkins, college/university.

WORK-STUDY ***Federal work-study:*** Total amount: $604,541; jobs available. ***State or other work-study/employment:*** Total amount: $1,842,640 (45% need-based, 55% non-need-based). Part-time jobs available.

APPLYING FOR FINANCIAL AID ***Required financial aid forms:*** FAFSA, CSS Financial Aid PROFILE, noncustodial (divorced/separated) parent's statement, business/farm supplement, parents' and student's most recent federal tax returns and W-2 forms. ***Financial aid deadline:*** 2/1. ***Notification date:*** 4/1. Students must reply by 5/1.

CONTACT Paul J. Boyer, Director of Financial Aid, Williams College, PO Box 37, Williamstown, MA 01267, 413-597-4181. *Fax:* 413-597-2999. *E-mail:* paul.j.boyer@williams.edu.

WILLIAMSON CHRISTIAN COLLEGE

Franklin, TN

CONTACT Jeanie Maguire, Director of Financial Aid, Williamson Christian College, 200 Seaboard Lane, Franklin, TN 37067, 615-771-7821. *Fax:* 615-771-7810. *E-mail:* info@williamsoncc.edu.

WILLIAM WOODS UNIVERSITY

Fulton, MO

CONTACT Deana Ready, Director of Student Financial Services, William Woods University, One University Avenue, Fulton, MO 65251, 573-592-4232 or toll-free 800-995-3159 Ext. 4221. *Fax:* 573-592-1180.

WILMINGTON COLLEGE

Wilmington, OH

ABOUT THE INSTITUTION Independent Friends, coed. ***Awards:*** bachelor's and master's degrees. 42 undergraduate majors. ***Total enrollment:*** 1,501. Undergraduates: 1,455. Freshmen: 351.

GIFT AID (NON-NEED-BASED) ***Scholarships, grants, and awards by category:*** *Academic interests/achievement:* agriculture, biological sciences, business, communication, education, general academic interests/achievements, international studies, mathematics, physical sciences, premedicine, religion/biblical studies. *Creative arts/performance:* theater/drama. *Special achievements/activities:* leadership. *Special characteristics:* children and siblings of alumni, members of minority groups, religious affiliation, siblings of current students.

WORK-STUDY Federal work-study jobs available.

CONTACT Donna Barton, Coordinator of Financial Aid, Wilmington College, Pyle Center Box 1184, Wilmington, OH 45177, 937-382-6661 Ext. 466 or toll-free 800-341-9318. *Fax:* 937-383-8564.

WILMINGTON UNIVERSITY

New Castle, DE

CONTACT J. Lynn Iocono, Director of Financial Aid, Wilmington University, 320 DuPont Highway, New Castle, DE 19720, 302-328-9437 or toll-free 877-967-5464. *Fax:* 302-328-5902.

WILSON COLLEGE

Chambersburg, PA

Tuition & fees: $25,900 **Average undergraduate aid package: $19,037**

ABOUT THE INSTITUTION Independent religious, women only. ***Awards:*** associate, bachelor's, and master's degrees. 26 undergraduate majors. ***Total enrollment:*** 710. Undergraduates: 692. Freshmen: 87. Federal methodology is used as a basis for awarding need-based institutional aid.

UNDERGRADUATE EXPENSES for 2008–09 ***Application fee:*** $35. ***Comprehensive fee:*** $34,530 includes full-time tuition ($25,350), mandatory fees ($550), and room and board ($8630). ***College room only:*** $4470. ***Part-time tuition:*** $2540 per course. ***Part-time fees:*** $40 per course; $40 per term.

FRESHMAN FINANCIAL AID (Fall 2008, est.) 83 applied for aid; of those 89% were deemed to have need. 100% of freshmen with need received aid; of those 15% had need fully met. ***Average percent of need met:*** 83% (excluding resources awarded to replace EFC). ***Average financial aid package:*** $22,040 (excluding resources awarded to replace EFC). 13% of all full-time freshmen had no need and received non-need-based gift aid.

UNDERGRADUATE FINANCIAL AID (Fall 2008, est.) 285 applied for aid; of those 91% were deemed to have need. 100% of undergraduates with need received aid; of those 13% had need fully met. ***Average percent of need met:*** 76% (excluding resources awarded to replace EFC). ***Average financial aid package:*** $19,037 (excluding resources awarded to replace EFC). 19% of all full-time undergraduates had no need and received non-need-based gift aid.

GIFT AID (NEED-BASED) ***Total amount:*** $4,049,333 (15% federal, 12% state, 69% institutional, 4% external sources). ***Receiving aid:*** Freshmen: 87% (74); all full-time undergraduates: 74% (244). ***Average award:*** Freshmen: $18,101; Undergraduates: $15,240. ***Scholarships, grants, and awards:*** Federal Pell, FSEOG, state, private, college/university gift aid from institutional funds.

GIFT AID (NON-NEED-BASED) ***Total amount:*** $1,053,586 (5% federal, 1% state, 86% institutional, 8% external sources). ***Receiving aid:*** Freshmen: 8% (7). Undergraduates: 8% (26). ***Average award:*** Freshmen: $8818. Undergraduates: $11,330. ***Scholarships, grants, and awards by category:*** *Academic interests/achievement:* 162 awards ($1,112,211 total): biological sciences, business, communication, computer science, education, English, foreign languages, general academic interests/achievements, humanities, international studies, mathematics, physical sciences, premedicine, religion/biblical studies, social sciences. *Creative arts/performance:* 1 award ($1800 total): music. *Special achievements/activities:* 141 awards ($477,896 total): community service, general special achievements/activities, leadership. *Special characteristics:* 51 awards ($392,456 total): adult students, children and siblings of alumni, children of current students, children of faculty/staff, international students, local/state students, relatives of clergy, religious affiliation, veterans. ***ROTC:*** Army cooperative.

LOANS ***Student loans:*** $3,731,602 (67% need-based, 33% non-need-based). 74% of past graduating class borrowed through all loan programs. *Average indebtedness per student:* $29,721. ***Average need-based loan:*** Freshmen: $4414. Undergraduates: $5089. ***Parent loans:*** $1,076,337 (24% need-based, 76% non-need-based). ***Programs:*** FFEL (Subsidized and Unsubsidized Stafford, PLUS), Perkins, college/university.

WORK-STUDY ***Federal work-study:*** Total amount: $31,761; 60 jobs averaging $1500. ***State or other work-study/employment:*** Total amount: $135,000 (32% need-based, 68% non-need-based). 101 part-time jobs averaging $1500.

APPLYING FOR FINANCIAL AID ***Required financial aid forms:*** FAFSA, institution's own form. ***Financial aid deadline (priority):*** 4/30. ***Notification date:*** Continuous.

CONTACT Linda Brittain, Dean of Financial Aid/Senior Enrollment Associate, Wilson College, 1015 Philadelphia Avenue, Chambersburg, PA 17201-1285, 717-262-2002 or toll-free 800-421-8402. *Fax:* 717-262-2546. *E-mail:* finaid@wilson.edu.

WINGATE UNIVERSITY

Wingate, NC

Tuition & fees: $20,140 **Average undergraduate aid package: $17,769**

ABOUT THE INSTITUTION Independent Baptist, coed. ***Awards:*** bachelor's, master's, doctoral, and first professional degrees and post-master's certificates. 41 undergraduate majors. ***Total enrollment:*** 2,129. Undergraduates: 1,446. Federal methodology is used as a basis for awarding need-based institutional aid.

UNDERGRADUATE EXPENSES for 2009–10 ***Application fee:*** $30. ***Comprehensive fee:*** $28,190 includes full-time tuition ($18,990), mandatory fees ($1150), and room and board ($8050). ***Part-time tuition:*** $633 per semester hour. ***Part-time fees:*** $190 per term.

FRESHMAN FINANCIAL AID (Fall 2008, est.) 384 applied for aid; of those 82% were deemed to have need. 100% of freshmen with need received aid; of those 23% had need fully met. ***Average percent of need met:*** 76% (excluding resources awarded to replace EFC). ***Average financial aid package:*** $19,420 (excluding resources awarded to replace EFC). 16% of all full-time freshmen had no need and received non-need-based gift aid.

UNDERGRADUATE FINANCIAL AID (Fall 2008, est.) 1,131 applied for aid; of those 82% were deemed to have need. 95% of undergraduates with need received aid; of those 32% had need fully met. ***Average percent of need met:*** 85% (excluding resources awarded to replace EFC). ***Average financial aid package:*** $17,769 (excluding resources awarded to replace EFC). 14% of all full-time undergraduates had no need and received non-need-based gift aid.

GIFT AID (NEED-BASED) ***Total amount:*** $5,955,973 (25% federal, 28% state, 47% institutional). ***Receiving aid:*** Freshmen: 57% (245); all full-time undergraduates: 51% (716). ***Average award:*** Freshmen: $8510; Undergraduates: $6952. ***Scholarships, grants, and awards:*** state, college/university gift aid from institutional funds.

GIFT AID (NON-NEED-BASED) ***Total amount:*** $9,273,679 (19% state, 75% institutional, 6% external sources). ***Receiving aid:*** Freshmen: 57% (245). ***Average award:*** Freshmen: $8726. Undergraduates: $7313. ***Scholarships, grants, and awards by category:*** *Academic interests/achievement:* general academic interests/achievements. *Creative arts/performance:* music. *Special achievements/activities:* religious involvement. *Special characteristics:* children and siblings of alumni, relatives of clergy, religious affiliation. ***ROTC:*** Army cooperative, Air Force cooperative.

LOANS ***Student loans:*** $14,112,254 (36% need-based, 64% non-need-based). 55% of past graduating class borrowed through all loan programs. *Average indebtedness per student:* $23,279. ***Average need-based loan:*** Freshmen: $3165. Undergraduates: $4165. ***Parent loans:*** $1,996,701 (100% non-need-based).

WORK-STUDY ***Federal work-study:*** Total amount: $104,477; jobs available. ***State or other work-study/employment:*** Total amount: $340,000 (100% non-need-based). Part-time jobs available.

ATHLETIC AWARDS Total amount: $2,251,311 (100% non-need-based).

APPLYING FOR FINANCIAL AID ***Required financial aid form:*** FAFSA. ***Notification date:*** Continuous. Students must reply within 4 weeks of notification.

CONTACT Teresa G. Williams, Director of Financial Planning, Wingate University, Campus Box 3001, Wingate, NC 28174, 704-233-8209 or toll-free 800-755-5550. *Fax:* 704-233-9396. *E-mail:* tgwilliam@wingate.edu.

WINONA STATE UNIVERSITY

Winona, MN

Tuition & fees (MN res): $7627 Average undergraduate aid package: $6020

ABOUT THE INSTITUTION State-supported, coed. ***Awards:*** associate, bachelor's, and master's degrees and post-master's certificates. 104 undergraduate majors. ***Total enrollment:*** 8,220. Undergraduates: 7,608. Freshmen: 1,727. Federal methodology is used as a basis for awarding need-based institutional aid.

UNDERGRADUATE EXPENSES for 2008–09 ***Application fee:*** $20. ***Tuition, state resident:*** full-time $5768. ***Tuition, nonresident:*** full-time $10,372. ***Required fees:*** full-time $1859. ***College room and board:*** $6430; ***Room only:*** $4674. ***Payment plan:*** Installment.

FRESHMAN FINANCIAL AID (Fall 2007) 1,393 applied for aid; of those 68% were deemed to have need. 97% of freshmen with need received aid; of those 8% had need fully met. ***Average percent of need met:*** 32% (excluding resources awarded to replace EFC). ***Average financial aid package:*** $5266 (excluding resources awarded to replace EFC). 16% of all full-time freshmen had no need and received non-need-based gift aid.

UNDERGRADUATE FINANCIAL AID (Fall 2007) 5,058 applied for aid; of those 73% were deemed to have need. 98% of undergraduates with need received aid; of those 10% had need fully met. ***Average percent of need met:*** 38% (excluding resources awarded to replace EFC). ***Average financial aid package:*** $6020 (excluding resources awarded to replace EFC). 9% of all full-time undergraduates had no need and received non-need-based gift aid.

GIFT AID (NEED-BASED) ***Total amount:*** $9,028,595 (52% federal, 36% state, 2% institutional, 10% external sources). ***Receiving aid:*** Freshmen: 31% (542); all full-time undergraduates: 30% (2,088). ***Average award:*** Freshmen: $3863; Undergraduates: $3782. ***Scholarships, grants, and awards:*** Federal Pell, FSEOG, state, private, college/university gift aid from institutional funds.

GIFT AID (NON-NEED-BASED) ***Total amount:*** $5,329,934 (1% state, 68% institutional, 31% external sources). ***Receiving aid:*** Freshmen: 23% (394). Undergraduates: 13% (913). ***Average award:*** Freshmen: $1525. Undergraduates: $2652. ***Scholarships, grants, and awards by category:*** *Academic interests/achievement:* 1,415 awards ($2,491,446 total): general academic interests/achievements. *Creative arts/performance:* 7 awards ($4388 total): art/fine arts, debating, music, theater/drama. *Special characteristics:* 1,204 awards ($2,520,794 total): children and siblings of alumni, children of faculty/staff, local/state students, members of minority groups, out-of-state students. ***Tuition waivers:*** Full or partial for employees or children of employees. ***ROTC:*** Army cooperative.

LOANS ***Student loans:*** $38,697,821 (38% need-based, 62% non-need-based). 73% of past graduating class borrowed through all loan programs. *Average indebtedness per student:* $26,236. ***Average need-based loan:*** Freshmen: $3241. Undergraduates: $4011. ***Parent loans:*** $3,908,360 (100% non-need-based). ***Programs:*** FFEL (Subsidized and Unsubsidized Stafford, PLUS), Perkins, state, college/university.

WORK-STUDY ***Federal work-study:*** Total amount: $422,935; 204 jobs averaging $1891. ***State or other work-study/employment:*** Total amount: $3,657,233 (19% need-based, 81% non-need-based). 384 part-time jobs averaging $1933.

ATHLETIC AWARDS Total amount: $655,210 (100% non-need-based).

APPLYING FOR FINANCIAL AID ***Required financial aid form:*** FAFSA. ***Financial aid deadline:*** Continuous. ***Notification date:*** 5/1. Students must reply within 3 weeks of notification.

CONTACT Cindy Groth, Counselor, Winona State University, PO Box 5838, Winona, MN 55987-5838, 507-457-5090 Ext. 5561 or toll-free 800-DIAL WSU.

WINSTON-SALEM STATE UNIVERSITY

Winston-Salem, NC

ABOUT THE INSTITUTION State-supported, coed. ***Awards:*** bachelor's and master's degrees and post-bachelor's certificates. 48 undergraduate majors. ***Total enrollment:*** 6,422. Undergraduates: 5,975.

GIFT AID (NEED-BASED) ***Scholarships, grants, and awards:*** Federal Pell, FSEOG, state, private, college/university gift aid from institutional funds, United Negro College Fund.

GIFT AID (NON-NEED-BASED) ***Scholarships, grants, and awards by category:*** *Academic interests/achievement:* business, computer science, education, general academic interests/achievements, health fields, mathematics. *Creative arts/performance:* music. *Special achievements/activities:* cheerleading/drum major. *Special characteristics:* adult students, first-generation college students.

LOANS ***Programs:*** FFEL (Subsidized and Unsubsidized Stafford, PLUS), Perkins, state, college/university.

APPLYING FOR FINANCIAL AID ***Required financial aid form:*** FAFSA.

CONTACT Raymond Solomon, Director of Financial Aid Office, Winston-Salem State University, 601 Martin Luther King Jr. Drive, PO Box 19524, Winston-Salem, NC 27110-0003, 336-750-3299 or toll-free 800-257-4052. *Fax:* 336-750-3297.

WINTHROP UNIVERSITY

Rock Hill, SC

Tuition & fees (SC res): $11,060 Average undergraduate aid package: $9550

ABOUT THE INSTITUTION State-supported, coed. ***Awards:*** bachelor's and master's degrees. 33 undergraduate majors. ***Total enrollment:*** 6,249. Undergraduates: 5,068. Freshmen: 1,075. Federal methodology is used as a basis for awarding need-based institutional aid.

UNDERGRADUATE EXPENSES for 2008–09 ***Application fee:*** $40. ***Tuition, state resident:*** full-time $11,060; part-time $460 per semester hour. ***Tuition, nonresident:*** full-time $20,610; part-time $858 per semester hour. Full-time tuition and fees vary according to degree level. Part-time tuition and fees vary according to degree level. ***College room and board:*** $10,040; ***Room only:*** $7800. Room and board charges vary according to board plan and housing facility. ***Payment plan:*** Installment.

FRESHMAN FINANCIAL AID (Fall 2008, est.) 897 applied for aid; of those 76% were deemed to have need. 100% of freshmen with need received aid; of those 27% had need fully met. ***Average percent of need met:*** 72% (excluding resources awarded to replace EFC). ***Average financial aid package:*** $10,796 (excluding resources awarded to replace EFC). 6% of all full-time freshmen had no need and received non-need-based gift aid.

UNDERGRADUATE FINANCIAL AID (Fall 2008, est.) 3,427 applied for aid; of those 80% were deemed to have need. 99% of undergraduates with need received aid; of those 20% had need fully met. ***Average percent of need met:*** 61% (excluding resources awarded to replace EFC). ***Average financial aid package:*** $9550 (excluding resources awarded to replace EFC). 5% of all full-time undergraduates had no need and received non-need-based gift aid.

GIFT AID (NEED-BASED) ***Total amount:*** $16,412,638 (33% federal, 46% state, 18% institutional, 3% external sources). ***Receiving aid:*** Freshmen: 62% (669); all full-time undergraduates: 50% (2,266). ***Average award:*** Freshmen: $8347; Undergraduates: $7243. ***Scholarships, grants, and awards:*** Federal Pell, FSEOG, state, private, college/university gift aid from institutional funds, Federal TEACH Grant.

GIFT AID (NON-NEED-BASED) ***Total amount:*** $9,213,721 (3% federal, 44% state, 43% institutional, 10% external sources). ***Receiving aid:*** Freshmen: 11% (115). Undergraduates: 6% (274). ***Average award:*** Freshmen: $5460. Undergraduates: $4520. ***Scholarships, grants, and awards by category:*** *Academic interests/achievement:* 452 awards ($2,263,654 total): general academic interests/achievements. *Creative arts/performance:* 146 awards ($166,000 total): art/fine arts, dance, music, performing arts, theater/drama. *Special characteristics:* 6 awards ($5850 total): children of faculty/staff. ***Tuition waivers:*** Full or partial for employees or children of employees, senior citizens. ***ROTC:*** Army cooperative.

LOANS ***Student loans:*** $28,393,043 (35% need-based, 65% non-need-based). 70% of past graduating class borrowed through all loan programs. *Average indebtedness per student:* $21,600. ***Average need-based loan:*** Freshmen: $3391. Undergraduates: $4167. ***Parent loans:*** $2,419,622 (100% non-need-based). ***Programs:*** Federal Direct (Subsidized and Unsubsidized Stafford, PLUS), FFEL (PLUS), Perkins.

WORK-STUDY ***Federal work-study:*** Total amount: $240,000; 266 jobs averaging $902. ***State or other work-study/employment:*** Total amount: $2,121,943 (100% non-need-based). Part-time jobs available (averaging $1000).

ATHLETIC AWARDS Total amount: $1,757,548 (30% need-based, 70% non-need-based).

APPLYING FOR FINANCIAL AID ***Required financial aid form:*** FAFSA. ***Financial aid deadline (priority):*** 3/1. ***Notification date:*** Continuous beginning 3/15. Students must reply within 4 weeks of notification.

CONTACT Ms. Leah Sturgis, Assistant Director, Office of Financial Aid, Winthrop University, 119 Tillman Hall, Rock Hill, SC 29733, 803-323-2189 or toll-free 800-763-0230. *Fax:* 803-323-2557. *E-mail:* finaid@winthrop.edu.

WISCONSIN LUTHERAN COLLEGE

Milwaukee, WI

Tuition & fees: $20,560 **Average undergraduate aid package: $16,792**

ABOUT THE INSTITUTION Independent religious, coed. ***Awards:*** bachelor's degrees. 25 undergraduate majors. ***Total enrollment:*** 720. Undergraduates: 720. Freshmen: 181. Federal methodology is used as a basis for awarding need-based institutional aid.

UNDERGRADUATE EXPENSES for 2008–09 ***Application fee:*** $20. ***Comprehensive fee:*** $27,550 includes full-time tuition ($20,420), mandatory fees ($140), and room and board ($6990). ***College room only:*** $3630. Room and board charges vary according to board plan and housing facility. ***Part-time tuition:*** $600 per credit. ***Payment plan:*** Installment.

FRESHMAN FINANCIAL AID (Fall 2008, est.) 199 applied for aid; of those 89% were deemed to have need. 100% of freshmen with need received aid; of those 20% had need fully met. ***Average percent of need met:*** 84% (excluding resources awarded to replace EFC). ***Average financial aid package:*** $17,272 (excluding resources awarded to replace EFC). 17% of all full-time freshmen had no need and received non-need-based gift aid.

UNDERGRADUATE FINANCIAL AID (Fall 2008, est.) 580 applied for aid; of those 91% were deemed to have need. 100% of undergraduates with need received aid; of those 24% had need fully met. ***Average percent of need met:*** 85% (excluding resources awarded to replace EFC). ***Average financial aid package:*** $16,792 (excluding resources awarded to replace EFC). 22% of all full-time undergraduates had no need and received non-need-based gift aid.

GIFT AID (NEED-BASED) ***Total amount:*** $6,359,670 (10% federal, 10% state, 78% institutional, 2% external sources). ***Receiving aid:*** Freshmen: 70% (178); all full-time undergraduates: 75% (524). ***Average award:*** Freshmen: $13,234; Undergraduates: $12,294. ***Scholarships, grants, and awards:*** Federal Pell, FSEOG, state, private, college/university gift aid from institutional funds.

GIFT AID (NON-NEED-BASED) ***Total amount:*** $1,473,800 (1% state, 96% institutional, 3% external sources). ***Receiving aid:*** Freshmen: 7% (19). Undergraduates: 7% (51). ***Average award:*** Freshmen: $8628. Undergraduates: $8484. ***Scholarships, grants, and awards by category:*** *Academic interests/achievement:* 624 awards ($4,295,265 total): biological sciences, business, communication, education, general academic interests/achievements, health fields, international studies, mathematics, religion/biblical studies, social sciences. *Creative arts/performance:* 82 awards ($98,000 total): art/fine arts, music, theater/drama. *Special achievements/activities:* 18 awards ($34,733 total): general special achievements/activities, leadership. *Special characteristics:* 76 awards ($549,052 total): children of faculty/staff, ethnic background, first-generation college students, international students, members of minority groups. ***Tuition waivers:*** Full or partial for employees or children of employees. ***ROTC:*** Army cooperative, Naval cooperative, Air Force cooperative.

LOANS ***Student loans:*** $3,716,763 (69% need-based, 31% non-need-based). 71% of past graduating class borrowed through all loan programs. *Average indebtedness per student:* $17,596. ***Average need-based loan:*** Freshmen: $3251. Undergraduates: $3969. ***Parent loans:*** $1,626,903 (20% need-based, 80% non-need-based). ***Programs:*** FFEL (Subsidized and Unsubsidized Stafford, PLUS), private loans.

WORK-STUDY ***Federal work-study:*** Total amount: $420,472; 242 jobs averaging $1721. ***State or other work-study/employment:*** Total amount: $202,395 (34% need-based, 66% non-need-based). 54 part-time jobs averaging $4027.

APPLYING FOR FINANCIAL AID ***Required financial aid forms:*** FAFSA, institution's own form. ***Financial aid deadline (priority):*** 3/1. ***Notification date:*** Continuous beginning 3/15. Students must reply within 2 weeks of notification.

CONTACT Mrs. Linda Loeffel, Director of Financial Aid, Wisconsin Lutheran College, 8800 West Bluemound Road, Milwaukee, WI 53226-4699, 414-443-8856 or toll-free 888-WIS LUTH. *Fax:* 414-443-8514. *E-mail:* linda.loeffel@wlc.edu.

WITTENBERG UNIVERSITY

Springfield, OH

Tuition & fees: $33,890 **Average undergraduate aid package: $26,618**

ABOUT THE INSTITUTION Independent religious, coed. ***Awards:*** bachelor's and master's degrees. 30 undergraduate majors. ***Total enrollment:*** 1,976. Undergraduates: 1,967. Freshmen: 510. Federal methodology is used as a basis for awarding need-based institutional aid.

UNDERGRADUATE EXPENSES for 2009–10 ***Application fee:*** $40. ***Comprehensive fee:*** $42,662 includes full-time tuition ($33,890) and room and board ($8772). ***College room only:*** $4554. ***Part-time tuition:*** $1130 per credit hour.

FRESHMAN FINANCIAL AID (Fall 2007) 447 applied for aid; of those 83% were deemed to have need. 100% of freshmen with need received aid; of those 44% had need fully met. ***Average percent of need met:*** 91% (excluding resources awarded to replace EFC). ***Average financial aid package:*** $27,461 (excluding resources awarded to replace EFC). 31% of all full-time freshmen had no need and received non-need-based gift aid.

UNDERGRADUATE FINANCIAL AID (Fall 2007) 1,613 applied for aid; of those 86% were deemed to have need. 100% of undergraduates with need received aid; of those 41% had need fully met. ***Average percent of need met:*** 88% (excluding resources awarded to replace EFC). ***Average financial aid package:*** $26,618 (excluding resources awarded to replace EFC). 28% of all full-time undergraduates had no need and received non-need-based gift aid.

GIFT AID (NEED-BASED) ***Total amount:*** $26,547,430 (6% federal, 5% state, 86% institutional, 3% external sources). ***Receiving aid:*** Freshmen: 68% (371); all full-time undergraduates: 71% (1,382). ***Average award:*** Freshmen: $21,917; Undergraduates: $21,261. ***Scholarships, grants, and awards:*** Federal Pell, FSEOG, state, private, college/university gift aid from institutional funds.

GIFT AID (NON-NEED-BASED) ***Total amount:*** $6,653,317 (4% state, 94% institutional, 2% external sources). ***Average award:*** Freshmen: $12,886. Undergraduates: $12,657. ***Scholarships, grants, and awards by category:*** *Academic interests/achievement:* general academic interests/achievements. *Creative arts/performance:* art/fine arts, dance, music, theater/drama. *Special achievements/activities:* community service, general special achievements/activities, leadership. *Special characteristics:* adult students, children and siblings of alumni, children of faculty/staff, ethnic background, international students, local/state students, members of minority groups, relatives of clergy, religious affiliation. ***ROTC:*** Army cooperative, Air Force cooperative.

LOANS ***Student loans:*** $10,548,897 (92% need-based, 8% non-need-based). 75% of past graduating class borrowed through all loan programs. *Average indebtedness per student:* $24,699. ***Average need-based loan:*** Freshmen: $4147. Undergraduates: $4792. ***Parent loans:*** $5,825,425 (85% need-based, 15% non-need-based). ***Programs:*** FFEL (Subsidized and Unsubsidized Stafford, PLUS), Perkins, college/university, alternative loans.

WORK-STUDY ***Federal work-study:*** Total amount: $928,107; 487 jobs averaging $1812. ***State or other work-study/employment:*** Total amount: $1,486,130 (69% need-based, 31% non-need-based). 823 part-time jobs averaging $1853.

APPLYING FOR FINANCIAL AID ***Required financial aid form:*** FAFSA. ***Financial aid deadline (priority):*** 3/1. ***Notification date:*** Continuous beginning 3/1. Students must reply within 2 weeks of notification.

CONTACT Mr. J. Randy Green, Director of Financial Aid, Wittenberg University, PO Box 720, Springfield, OH 45501-0720, 937-327-7321 or toll-free 800-677-7558 Ext. 6314. *Fax:* 937-327-6379. *E-mail:* jgreen@wittenberg.edu.

WOFFORD COLLEGE

Spartanburg, SC

Tuition & fees: $29,465 **Average undergraduate aid package: $27,417**

ABOUT THE INSTITUTION Independent religious, coed. ***Awards:*** bachelor's degrees. 31 undergraduate majors. ***Total enrollment:*** 1,389. Undergraduates: 1,389. Freshmen: 415. Federal methodology is used as a basis for awarding need-based institutional aid.

UNDERGRADUATE EXPENSES for 2008–09 ***Application fee:*** $35. ***Comprehensive fee:*** $37,655 includes full-time tuition ($29,465) and room and board ($8190). ***Part-time tuition:*** $1085 per hour. ***Payment plan:*** Installment.

FRESHMAN FINANCIAL AID (Fall 2008, est.) 293 applied for aid; of those 74% were deemed to have need. 100% of freshmen with need received aid; of those 54% had need fully met. ***Average percent of need met:*** 88% (excluding resources awarded to replace EFC). ***Average financial aid package:*** $27,894 (excluding resources awarded to replace EFC). 23% of all full-time freshmen had no need and received non-need-based gift aid.

UNDERGRADUATE FINANCIAL AID (Fall 2008, est.) 881 applied for aid; of those 81% were deemed to have need. 99% of undergraduates with need received aid; of those 53% had need fully met. ***Average percent of need met:*** 86% (excluding resources awarded to replace EFC). ***Average financial aid package:*** $27,417 (excluding resources awarded to replace EFC). 22% of all full-time undergraduates had no need and received non-need-based gift aid.

GIFT AID (NEED-BASED) ***Total amount:*** $13,212,518 (7% federal, 25% state, 65% institutional, 3% external sources). ***Receiving aid:*** Freshmen: 45% (186); all full-time undergraduates: 48% (649). ***Average award:*** Freshmen: $25,295; Undergraduates: $23,956. ***Scholarships, grants, and awards:*** Federal Pell, FSEOG, state, college/university gift aid from institutional funds.

GIFT AID (NON-NEED-BASED) ***Total amount:*** $8,597,287 (28% state, 64% institutional, 8% external sources). ***Receiving aid:*** Freshmen: 19% (77). Undergraduates: 19% (264). ***Average award:*** Freshmen: $13,011. Undergraduates: $12,836. ***Scholarships, grants, and awards by category:*** *Academic interests/achievement:* general academic interests/achievements. *Creative arts/performance:* music. *Special achievements/activities:* cheerleading/drum major, community service, general special achievements/activities, leadership, religious involvement. *Special characteristics:* children of faculty/staff, general special characteristics, relatives of clergy. ***Tuition waivers:*** Full or partial for employees or children of employees. ***ROTC:*** Army.

LOANS ***Student loans:*** $4,220,339 (60% need-based, 40% non-need-based). 50% of past graduating class borrowed through all loan programs. *Average indebtedness per student:* $17,831. ***Average need-based loan:*** Freshmen: $3655. Undergraduates: $4624. ***Parent loans:*** $1,144,653 (31% need-based, 69% non-need-based). ***Programs:*** FFEL (Subsidized and Unsubsidized Stafford, PLUS), Perkins.

WORK-STUDY ***Federal work-study:*** Total amount: $274,561; jobs available.

ATHLETIC AWARDS Total amount: $3,940,329 (35% need-based, 65% non-need-based).

APPLYING FOR FINANCIAL AID ***Required financial aid form:*** FAFSA. ***Financial aid deadline (priority):*** 3/15. ***Notification date:*** Continuous beginning 3/31. Students must reply by 5/1.

CONTACT Kay C. Walton, Director of Financial Aid, Wofford College, 429 North Church Street, Spartanburg, SC 29303-3663, 864-597-4160. *Fax:* 864-597-4149. *E-mail:* finaid@wofford.edu.

WOODBURY UNIVERSITY

Burbank, CA

Tuition & fees: $26,978 **Average undergraduate aid package: $18,917**

ABOUT THE INSTITUTION Independent, coed. ***Awards:*** bachelor's and master's degrees. 17 undergraduate majors. ***Total enrollment:*** 1,539. Undergraduates: 1,296. Freshmen: 159. Federal methodology is used as a basis for awarding need-based institutional aid.

UNDERGRADUATE EXPENSES for 2008–09 ***Application fee:*** $35. ***Comprehensive fee:*** $35,746 includes full-time tuition ($26,598), mandatory fees ($380), and room and board ($8768). ***College room only:*** $5382. Full-time tuition and fees vary according to course load, degree level, and program. Room and board charges vary according to board plan and housing facility. ***Part-time tuition:*** $867 per unit. Part-time tuition and fees vary according to course load, degree level, and program. ***Payment plans:*** Installment, deferred payment.

FRESHMAN FINANCIAL AID (Fall 2008, est.) 112 applied for aid; of those 95% were deemed to have need. 99% of freshmen with need received aid; of those 4% had need fully met. ***Average percent of need met:*** 58% (excluding resources awarded to replace EFC). ***Average financial aid package:*** $19,273 (excluding resources awarded to replace EFC). 16% of all full-time freshmen had no need and received non-need-based gift aid.

UNDERGRADUATE FINANCIAL AID (Fall 2008, est.) 852 applied for aid; of those 96% were deemed to have need. 99% of undergraduates with need received aid; of those 4% had need fully met. ***Average percent of need met:*** 55% (excluding resources awarded to replace EFC). ***Average financial aid package:*** $18,917 (excluding resources awarded to replace EFC). 12% of all full-time undergraduates had no need and received non-need-based gift aid.

GIFT AID (NEED-BASED) ***Total amount:*** $12,187,631 (18% federal, 27% state, 54% institutional, 1% external sources). ***Receiving aid:*** Freshmen: 73% (105); all full-time undergraduates: 75% (777). ***Average award:*** Freshmen: $15,861; Undergraduates: $14,844. ***Scholarships, grants, and awards:*** Federal Pell, FSEOG, state, private, college/university gift aid from institutional funds.

GIFT AID (NON-NEED-BASED) ***Total amount:*** $968,728 (98% institutional, 2% external sources). ***Receiving aid:*** Freshmen: 2% (3). Undergraduates: 2% (24). ***Average award:*** Freshmen: $14,998. Undergraduates: $12,297. ***Scholarships, grants, and awards by category:*** *Academic interests/achievement:* 725 awards ($3,507,412 total): architecture, general academic interests/achievements. ***Tuition waivers:*** Full or partial for employees or children of employees.

LOANS ***Student loans:*** $9,953,638 (87% need-based, 13% non-need-based). 85% of past graduating class borrowed through all loan programs. *Average indebtedness per student:* $43,854. ***Average need-based loan:*** Freshmen: $3609. Undergraduates: $4879. ***Parent loans:*** $3,725,385 (58% need-based, 42% non-need-based). ***Programs:*** FFEL (Subsidized and Unsubsidized Stafford, PLUS), Perkins, alternative loans.

WORK-STUDY ***Federal work-study:*** Total amount: $128,345; 101 jobs averaging $1757.

APPLYING FOR FINANCIAL AID ***Required financial aid forms:*** FAFSA, institution's own form. ***Financial aid deadline:*** Continuous. ***Notification date:*** Continuous beginning 3/15. Students must reply within 2 weeks of notification.

CONTACT Celeastia Williams, Director of Enrollment Services, Woodbury University, 7500 Glenoaks Boulevard, Burbank, CA 91510, 818-767-0888 Ext. 273 or toll-free 800-784-WOOD. *Fax:* 818-767-4816.

WORCESTER POLYTECHNIC INSTITUTE

Worcester, MA

Tuition & fees: $36,930 **Average undergraduate aid package: $25,876**

ABOUT THE INSTITUTION Independent, coed. ***Awards:*** bachelor's, master's, and doctoral degrees and post-bachelor's and post-master's certificates. 50 undergraduate majors. ***Total enrollment:*** 4,561. Undergraduates: 3,252. Freshmen: 907. Both federal and institutional methodology are used as a basis for awarding need-based institutional aid.

UNDERGRADUATE EXPENSES for 2008–09 ***Application fee:*** $60. ***One-time required fee:*** $200. ***Comprehensive fee:*** $47,810 includes full-time tuition ($36,390), mandatory fees ($540), and room and board ($10,880). ***College room only:*** $6635. Room and board charges vary according to board plan and housing facility. ***Part-time tuition:*** $1011 per credit hour. Part-time tuition and fees vary according to course load. ***Payment plans:*** Installment, deferred payment.

FRESHMAN FINANCIAL AID (Fall 2008, est.) 778 applied for aid; of those 84% were deemed to have need. 99% of freshmen with need received aid; of those 39% had need fully met. ***Average percent of need met:*** 66% (excluding resources awarded to replace EFC). ***Average financial aid package:*** $25,312 (excluding resources awarded to replace EFC). 24% of all full-time freshmen had no need and received non-need-based gift aid.

UNDERGRADUATE FINANCIAL AID (Fall 2008, est.) 2,410 applied for aid; of those 89% were deemed to have need. 98% of undergraduates with need received aid; of those 34% had need fully met. ***Average percent of need met:*** 67% (excluding resources awarded to replace EFC). ***Average financial aid package:*** $25,876 (excluding resources awarded to replace EFC). 26% of all full-time undergraduates had no need and received non-need-based gift aid.

GIFT AID (NEED-BASED) ***Total amount:*** $36,784,390 (6% federal, 2% state, 86% institutional, 6% external sources). ***Receiving aid:*** Freshmen: 70% (636); all full-time undergraduates: 66% (2,029). ***Average award:*** Freshmen: $18,687; Undergraduates: $16,896. ***Scholarships, grants, and awards:*** Federal Pell, FSEOG, state, private, college/university gift aid from institutional funds.

GIFT AID (NON-NEED-BASED) ***Total amount:*** $12,951,675 (81% institutional, 19% external sources). ***Receiving aid:*** Freshmen: 27% (241). Undergraduates: 18% (546). ***Average award:*** Freshmen: $13,887. Undergraduates: $14,155. ***Scholarships, grants, and awards by category:*** *Academic interests/achievement:* 2,199 awards ($25,246,420 total): general academic interests/achievements, premedicine. *Special characteristics:* 53 awards ($194,950 total): children of workers in trades. ***Tuition waivers:*** Full or partial for employees or children of employees. ***ROTC:*** Army, Naval cooperative, Air Force.

LOANS ***Student loans:*** $29,602,073 (37% need-based, 63% non-need-based). 76% of past graduating class borrowed through all loan programs. *Average indebtedness per student:* $37,175. ***Average need-based loan:*** Freshmen: $5784. Undergraduates: $6944. ***Parent loans:*** $6,370,635 (100% non-need-based). ***Programs:*** FFEL (Subsidized and Unsubsidized Stafford, PLUS), Perkins, state, college/university.

WORK-STUDY ***Federal work-study:*** Total amount: $695,719; 583 jobs averaging $1193.

APPLYING FOR FINANCIAL AID ***Required financial aid forms:*** FAFSA, CSS Financial Aid PROFILE, federal income tax form(s), W-2 forms. ***Financial aid deadline:*** 2/1 (priority: 2/1). ***Notification date:*** 4/1. Students must reply by 5/1.

CONTACT Office of Financial Aid, Worcester Polytechnic Institute, 100 Institute Road, Worcester, MA 01609-2280, 508-831-5469. *Fax:* 508-831-5039. *E-mail:* finaid@wpi.edu.

WORCESTER STATE COLLEGE

Worcester, MA

Tuition & fees (MA res): $6170 Average undergraduate aid package: $9086

ABOUT THE INSTITUTION State-supported, coed. ***Awards:*** bachelor's and master's degrees and post-bachelor's and post-master's certificates. 27 undergraduate majors. ***Total enrollment:*** 5,378. Undergraduates: 4,643. Freshmen: 682. Federal methodology is used as a basis for awarding need-based institutional aid.

UNDERGRADUATE EXPENSES for 2008–09 ***Application fee:*** $20. ***Tuition, state resident:*** full-time $970; part-time $40.42 per credit. ***Tuition, nonresident:*** full-time $7050; part-time $293.75 per credit. ***Required fees:*** full-time $5200; $206.25 per credit. Full-time tuition and fees vary according to class time, course load, degree level, and reciprocity agreements. Part-time tuition and fees vary according to class time, course load, degree level, and reciprocity agreements. ***College room and board:*** $8527; ***Room only:*** $5877. Room and board charges vary according to board plan and housing facility. ***Payment plan:*** Installment.

FRESHMAN FINANCIAL AID (Fall 2007) 601 applied for aid; of those 64% were deemed to have need. 97% of freshmen with need received aid; of those 40% had need fully met. ***Average percent of need met:*** 81% (excluding resources awarded to replace EFC). ***Average financial aid package:*** $8704 (excluding resources awarded to replace EFC).

UNDERGRADUATE FINANCIAL AID (Fall 2007) 2,501 applied for aid; of those 67% were deemed to have need. 98% of undergraduates with need received aid; of those 49% had need fully met. ***Average percent of need met:*** 84% (excluding resources awarded to replace EFC). ***Average financial aid package:*** $9086 (excluding resources awarded to replace EFC).

GIFT AID (NEED-BASED) ***Total amount:*** $6,254,163 (44% federal, 28% state, 21% institutional, 7% external sources). ***Receiving aid:*** Freshmen: 47% (322); all full-time undergraduates: 38% (1,262). ***Average award:*** Freshmen: $4252; Undergraduates: $4252. ***Scholarships, grants, and awards:*** Federal Pell, FSEOG, state, private, college/university gift aid from institutional funds.

GIFT AID (NON-NEED-BASED) ***Total amount:*** $330,363 (73% federal, 27% state). ***Receiving aid:*** Freshmen: 24% (162). Undergraduates: 15% (499). ***Tuition waivers:*** Full or partial for employees or children of employees, senior citizens. ***ROTC:*** Army cooperative, Naval cooperative, Air Force cooperative.

LOANS ***Student loans:*** $11,719,187 (35% need-based, 65% non-need-based). 43% of past graduating class borrowed through all loan programs. *Average indebtedness per student:* $16,063. ***Average need-based loan:*** Freshmen: $2059. Undergraduates: $2497. ***Parent loans:*** $1,072,357 (100% non-need-based). ***Programs:*** FFEL (Subsidized and Unsubsidized Stafford, PLUS), Perkins, state.

WORK-STUDY ***Federal work-study:*** Total amount: $214,162; 244 jobs averaging $1500.

APPLYING FOR FINANCIAL AID ***Required financial aid form:*** FAFSA. ***Financial aid deadline:*** 5/1 (priority: 3/1). ***Notification date:*** Continuous. Students must reply within 2 weeks of notification.

CONTACT Jayne McGinn, Director of Financial Aid, Worcester State College, 486 Chandler Street, Worcester, MA 01602, 508-929-8058 or toll-free 866-WSC-CALL. *Fax:* 508-929-8194. *E-mail:* jmcginn@worcester.edu.

WRIGHT STATE UNIVERSITY

Dayton, OH

Tuition & fees (OH res): $7278 Average undergraduate aid package: $9040

ABOUT THE INSTITUTION State-supported, coed. ***Awards:*** associate, bachelor's, master's, doctoral, and first professional degrees and post-master's certificates. 163 undergraduate majors. ***Total enrollment:*** 16,672. Undergraduates: 12,772. Freshmen: 2,616. Federal methodology is used as a basis for awarding need-based institutional aid.

UNDERGRADUATE EXPENSES for 2008–09 ***Application fee:*** $30. ***Tuition, state resident:*** full-time $7278; part-time $219 per credit hour. ***Tuition, nonresident:*** full-time $14,004; part-time $425 per credit hour. Full-time tuition and fees vary according to course load. Part-time tuition and fees vary according to course load. ***College room and board:*** $7180. Room and board charges vary according to board plan and housing facility. ***Payment plan:*** Installment.

FRESHMAN FINANCIAL AID (Fall 2008, est.) 2,228 applied for aid; of those 81% were deemed to have need. 99% of freshmen with need received aid; of those 12% had need fully met. ***Average percent of need met:*** 61% (excluding resources awarded to replace EFC). ***Average financial aid package:*** $8663 (excluding resources awarded to replace EFC). 13% of all full-time freshmen had no need and received non-need-based gift aid.

UNDERGRADUATE FINANCIAL AID (Fall 2008, est.) 8,265 applied for aid; of those 84% were deemed to have need. 99% of undergraduates with need received aid; of those 9% had need fully met. ***Average percent of need met:*** 57% (excluding resources awarded to replace EFC). ***Average financial aid package:*** $9040 (excluding resources awarded to replace EFC). 9% of all full-time undergraduates had no need and received non-need-based gift aid.

GIFT AID (NEED-BASED) ***Total amount:*** $26,780,435 (55% federal, 20% state, 20% institutional, 5% external sources). ***Receiving aid:*** Freshmen: 53% (1,368); all full-time undergraduates: 44% (4,768). ***Average award:*** Freshmen: $5619; Undergraduates: $5248. ***Scholarships, grants, and awards:*** Federal Pell, FSEOG, state, private, college/university gift aid from institutional funds, United Negro College Fund, Federal Nursing, Choose Ohio First Scholarship.

GIFT AID (NON-NEED-BASED) ***Total amount:*** $5,754,489 (17% state, 71% institutional, 12% external sources). ***Receiving aid:*** Freshmen: 7% (176). Undergraduates: 4% (420). ***Average award:*** Freshmen: $3088. Undergraduates: $3613. ***Scholarships, grants, and awards by category:*** *Academic interests/achievement:* 2,130 awards ($5,745,053 total): area/ethnic studies, biological sciences, business, communication, computer science, education, engineering/technologies, English, foreign languages, general academic interests/achievements, health fields, humanities, international studies, mathematics, military science, physical sciences, premedicine, religion/biblical studies, social sciences. *Creative arts/performance:* 273 awards ($645,910 total): applied art and design, art/fine arts, cinema/film/broadcasting, creative writing, dance, general creative arts/performance, music, performing arts, theater/drama. *Special achievements/activities:* 466 awards ($3,343,352 total): cheerleading/drum major, community service, general special achievements/activities, leadership, memberships. *Special characteristics:* 577 awards ($1,635,891 total): adult students, children and siblings of alumni, children of educators, children of faculty/staff, ethnic background, first-generation college students, handicapped students, international students, out-of-state students. ***Tuition waivers:*** Full or partial for employees or children of employees, senior citizens. ***ROTC:*** Army, Air Force.

LOANS ***Student loans:*** $82,477,502 (76% need-based, 24% non-need-based). 71% of past graduating class borrowed through all loan programs. *Average indebtedness per student:* $22,829. ***Average need-based loan:*** Freshmen: $3505. Undergraduates: $4552. ***Parent loans:*** $49,462,132 (28% need-based, 72% non-need-based). ***Programs:*** FFEL (Subsidized and Unsubsidized Stafford, PLUS), Perkins, Federal Nursing, state, college/university, private loans.

WORK-STUDY ***Federal work-study:*** Total amount: $4,877,789; 1,286 jobs averaging $3158.

ATHLETIC AWARDS Total amount: $2,778,417 (31% need-based, 69% non-need-based).

APPLYING FOR FINANCIAL AID ***Required financial aid form:*** FAFSA. ***Financial aid deadline (priority):*** 2/15. ***Notification date:*** Continuous beginning 3/15.

CONTACT Mr. Willie A. Boyd, Director of Financial Aid, Wright State University, 3640 Colonel Glenn Highway, Dayton, OH 45435, 937-775-5721 or toll-free 800-247-1770. *Fax:* 937-775-5795. *E-mail:* willie.boyd@wright.edu.

XAVIER UNIVERSITY

Cincinnati, OH

Tuition & fees: $28,570 **Average undergraduate aid package: $16,838**

ABOUT THE INSTITUTION Independent Roman Catholic, coed. ***Awards:*** associate, bachelor's, master's, and doctoral degrees and post-bachelor's and post-master's certificates. 56 undergraduate majors. ***Total enrollment:*** 6,584. Undergraduates: 3,923. Freshmen: 860. Federal methodology is used as a basis for awarding need-based institutional aid.

UNDERGRADUATE EXPENSES for 2009–10 ***Application fee:*** $35. ***One-time required fee:*** $190. ***Comprehensive fee:*** $38,100 includes full-time tuition ($27,900), mandatory fees ($670), and room and board ($9530). ***College room only:*** $5250. ***Part-time tuition:*** $550 per credit hour.

FRESHMAN FINANCIAL AID (Fall 2008, est.) 676 applied for aid; of those 79% were deemed to have need. 100% of freshmen with need received aid; of those 28% had need fully met. ***Average percent of need met:*** 78% (excluding resources awarded to replace EFC). ***Average financial aid package:*** $16,676 (excluding resources awarded to replace EFC). 31% of all full-time freshmen had no need and received non-need-based gift aid.

UNDERGRADUATE FINANCIAL AID (Fall 2008, est.) 2,210 applied for aid; of those 83% were deemed to have need. 100% of undergraduates with need received aid; of those 24% had need fully met. ***Average percent of need met:*** 73% (excluding resources awarded to replace EFC). ***Average financial aid package:*** $16,838 (excluding resources awarded to replace EFC). 32% of all full-time undergraduates had no need and received non-need-based gift aid.

GIFT AID (NEED-BASED) ***Total amount:*** $20,673,693 (11% federal, 7% state, 79% institutional, 3% external sources). ***Receiving aid:*** Freshmen: 60% (514); all full-time undergraduates: 51% (1,726). ***Average award:*** Freshmen: $11,289; Undergraduates: $11,503. ***Scholarships, grants, and awards:*** Federal Pell, FSEOG, state, private, college/university gift aid from institutional funds.

GIFT AID (NON-NEED-BASED) ***Total amount:*** $14,982,302 (3% state, 83% institutional, 14% external sources). ***Receiving aid:*** Freshmen: 13% (110). Undergraduates: 8% (272). ***Average award:*** Freshmen: $9922. Undergraduates: $10,198. ***Scholarships, grants, and awards by category:*** *Academic interests/achievement:* 1,720 awards ($14,895,171 total): foreign languages, general academic interests/achievements, mathematics, military science, physical sciences, social sciences. *Creative arts/performance:* 108 awards ($484,687 total): art/fine arts, music, performing arts, theater/drama. *Special characteristics:* 293 awards ($1,154,073 total): children and siblings of alumni, international students, members of minority groups, siblings of current students. ***ROTC:*** Army, Air Force cooperative.

LOANS ***Student loans:*** $18,932,050 (67% need-based, 33% non-need-based). 68% of past graduating class borrowed through all loan programs. *Average indebtedness per student:* $22,879. ***Average need-based loan:*** Freshmen: $4470. Undergraduates: $4901. ***Parent loans:*** $4,297,892 (29% need-based, 71% non-need-based). ***Programs:*** FFEL (Subsidized and Unsubsidized Stafford, PLUS), Perkins.

WORK-STUDY ***Federal work-study:*** Total amount: $1,184,083; 560 jobs averaging $2144. ***State or other work-study/employment:*** 51 part-time jobs averaging $1784.

ATHLETIC AWARDS Total amount: $3,569,696 (40% need-based, 60% non-need-based).

APPLYING FOR FINANCIAL AID ***Required financial aid form:*** FAFSA. ***Financial aid deadline (priority):*** 2/15. ***Notification date:*** Continuous beginning 2/15. Students must reply by 5/1.

CONTACT Office of Financial Aid, Xavier University, 3800 Victory Parkway, Cincinnati, OH 45207-5411, 513-745-3142 or toll-free 800-344-4698. *Fax:* 513-745-2806.

XAVIER UNIVERSITY OF LOUISIANA

New Orleans, LA

Tuition & fees: $15,500 **Average undergraduate aid package: $17,684**

ABOUT THE INSTITUTION Independent Roman Catholic, coed. ***Awards:*** bachelor's, master's, and first professional degrees and post-bachelor's certificates. 54 undergraduate majors. ***Total enrollment:*** 3,236. Undergraduates: 2,454. Freshmen: 778. Federal methodology is used as a basis for awarding need-based institutional aid.

UNDERGRADUATE EXPENSES for 2008–09 ***Application fee:*** $25. ***One-time required fee:*** $150. ***Comprehensive fee:*** $22,300 includes full-time tuition ($14,500), mandatory fees ($1000), and room and board ($6800). Room and board charges vary according to housing facility. ***Part-time tuition:*** $650 per semester hour. ***Part-time fees:*** $155 per term. Part-time tuition and fees vary according to course load. ***Payment plan:*** Installment.

FRESHMAN FINANCIAL AID (Fall 2007) 639 applied for aid; of those 91% were deemed to have need. 99% of freshmen with need received aid; of those 28% had need fully met. ***Average percent of need met:*** 86% (excluding resources awarded to replace EFC). ***Average financial aid package:*** $17,348 (excluding resources awarded to replace EFC). 4% of all full-time freshmen had no need and received non-need-based gift aid.

UNDERGRADUATE FINANCIAL AID (Fall 2007) 2,330 applied for aid; of those 90% were deemed to have need. 99% of undergraduates with need received aid; of those 29% had need fully met. ***Average percent of need met:*** 24% (excluding resources awarded to replace EFC). ***Average financial aid package:*** $17,684 (excluding resources awarded to replace EFC). 3% of all full-time undergraduates had no need and received non-need-based gift aid.

GIFT AID (NEED-BASED) ***Total amount:*** $7,661,741 (83% federal, 1% state, 16% external sources). ***Receiving aid:*** Freshmen: 67% (441); all full-time undergraduates: 55% (1,435). ***Average award:*** Freshmen: $5578; Undergraduates: $5255. ***Scholarships, grants, and awards:*** Federal Pell, FSEOG, state, private, college/university gift aid from institutional funds, United Negro College Fund.

GIFT AID (NON-NEED-BASED) ***Total amount:*** $6,815,129 (2% federal, 32% state, 66% institutional). ***Receiving aid:*** Freshmen: 62% (414). Undergraduates: 43% (1,116). ***Average award:*** Freshmen: $7546. Undergraduates: $7975. ***Tuition waivers:*** Full or partial for employees or children of employees. ***ROTC:*** Army cooperative, Naval cooperative, Air Force cooperative.

LOANS ***Student loans:*** $22,360,513 (37% need-based, 63% non-need-based). 70% of past graduating class borrowed through all loan programs. *Average indebtedness per student:* $25,227. ***Average need-based loan:*** Freshmen: $3645. Undergraduates: $4822. ***Parent loans:*** $4,427,571 (100% non-need-based). ***Programs:*** Federal Direct (Subsidized and Unsubsidized Stafford, PLUS), FFEL (Subsidized and Unsubsidized Stafford, PLUS), Perkins.

WORK-STUDY ***Federal work-study:*** Total amount: $260,794; jobs available.

ATHLETIC AWARDS Total amount: $1,021,829 (100% non-need-based).

APPLYING FOR FINANCIAL AID ***Required financial aid form:*** FAFSA. ***Financial aid deadline (priority):*** 1/1. ***Notification date:*** Continuous beginning 4/1. Students must reply within 2 weeks of notification.

CONTACT Mrs. Mildred Higgins, Financial Aid Director, Xavier University of Louisiana, One Drexel Drive, New Orleans, LA 70125-1098, 504-520-7517 or toll-free 877-XAVIERU.

YALE UNIVERSITY

New Haven, CT

Tuition & fees: $35,300 **Average undergraduate aid package: $37,223**

ABOUT THE INSTITUTION Independent, coed. ***Awards:*** bachelor's, master's, doctoral, and first professional degrees and post-master's certificates. 67 undergraduate majors. ***Total enrollment:*** 11,445. Undergraduates: 5,277. Freshmen: 1,318. Both federal and institutional methodology are used as a basis for awarding need-based institutional aid.

UNDERGRADUATE EXPENSES for 2008–09 ***Application fee:*** $75. ***Comprehensive fee:*** $46,000 includes full-time tuition ($35,300) and room and board ($10,700). ***Payment plan:*** Installment.

FRESHMAN FINANCIAL AID (Fall 2008, est.) 892 applied for aid; of those 86% were deemed to have need. 100% of freshmen with need received aid; of those 100% had need fully met. ***Average percent of need met:*** 100% (excluding resources awarded to replace EFC). ***Average financial aid package:*** $38,067 (excluding resources awarded to replace EFC).

UNDERGRADUATE FINANCIAL AID (Fall 2008, est.) 3,013 applied for aid; of those 90% were deemed to have need. 100% of undergraduates with need received aid; of those 100% had need fully met. ***Average percent of need met:*** 100% (excluding resources awarded to replace EFC). ***Average financial aid package:*** $37,223 (excluding resources awarded to replace EFC).

GIFT AID (NEED-BASED) ***Total amount:*** $96,648,942 (4% federal, 91% institutional, 5% external sources). ***Receiving aid:*** Freshmen: 58% (762); all full-time undergraduates: 51% (2,707). ***Average award:*** Freshmen: $36,668; Undergraduates: $35,703. ***Scholarships, grants, and awards:*** Federal Pell, FSEOG, state, private, college/university gift aid from institutional funds, United Negro College Fund.

GIFT AID (NON-NEED-BASED) ***Total amount:*** $637,383 (100% external sources). ***ROTC:*** Army cooperative, Air Force cooperative.

LOANS ***Student loans:*** $2,427,972 (29% need-based, 71% non-need-based). 33% of past graduating class borrowed through all loan programs. *Average indebtedness per student:* $12,297. ***Average need-based loan:*** Freshmen: $2215. Undergraduates: $2486. ***Parent loans:*** $5,366,240 (100% non-need-based). ***Programs:*** FFEL (Subsidized and Unsubsidized Stafford, PLUS), Perkins, state, college/university.

WORK-STUDY ***Federal work-study:*** Total amount: $798,400; 481 jobs averaging $1957. ***State or other work-study/employment:*** Total amount: $2,910,835 (100% need-based). 1,414 part-time jobs averaging $2059.

APPLYING FOR FINANCIAL AID ***Required financial aid forms:*** FAFSA, CSS Financial Aid PROFILE, noncustodial (divorced/separated) parent's statement, business/farm supplement, parent tax returns. ***Financial aid deadline:*** 3/1 (priority: 3/1). ***Notification date:*** 4/1. Students must reply by 5/1 or within 1 week of notification.

CONTACT Student Financial Services, Yale University, PO Box 208288, New Haven, CT 06520-8288, 203-432-0371. *Fax:* 203-777-6100. *E-mail:* sfs@yale.edu.

YESHIVA AND KOLEL BAIS MEDRASH ELYON

Monsey, NY

CONTACT Financial Aid Office, Yeshiva and Kolel Bais Medrash Elyon, 73 Main Street, Monsey, NY 10952, 845-356-7064.

YESHIVA AND KOLLEL HARBOTZAS TORAH

Brooklyn, NY

CONTACT Financial Aid Office, Yeshiva and Kollel Harbotzas Torah, 1049 East 15th Street, Brooklyn, NY 11230, 718-692-0208.

YESHIVA BETH MOSHE

Scranton, PA

CONTACT Financial Aid Office, Yeshiva Beth Moshe, 930 Hickory Street, Scranton, PA 18505-2124, 717-346-1747.

YESHIVA COLLEGE OF THE NATION'S CAPITAL

Silver Spring, MD

CONTACT Financial Aid Office, Yeshiva College of the Nation's Capital, 1216 Arcola Avenue, Silver Spring, MD 20902, 301-593-2534.

YESHIVA DERECH CHAIM

Brooklyn, NY

CONTACT Financial Aid Office, Yeshiva Derech Chaim, 1573 39th Street, Brooklyn, NY 11218, 718-438-5426.

YESHIVA D'MONSEY RABBINICAL COLLEGE

Monsey, NY

CONTACT Financial Aid Office, Yeshiva D'Monsey Rabbinical College, 2 Roman Boulevard, Monsey, NY 10952, 914-352-5852.

YESHIVA GEDOLAH IMREI YOSEF D'SPINKA

Brooklyn, NY

CONTACT Financial Aid Office, Yeshiva Gedolah Imrei Yosef D'Spinka, 1466 56th Street, Brooklyn, NY 11219, 718-851-8721.

YESHIVA GEDOLAH OF GREATER DETROIT

Oak Park, MI

CONTACT Rabbi P. Rushnawitz, Executive Administrator, Yeshiva Gedolah of Greater Detroit, 24600 Greenfield Road, Oak Park, MI 48237-1544, 810-968-3360. *Fax:* 810-968-8613.

YESHIVA GEDOLAH RABBINICAL COLLEGE

Miami Beach, FL

CONTACT Financial Aid Office, Yeshiva Gedolah Rabbinical College, 1140 Alton Road, Miami Beach, FL 33139, 305-673-5664.

YESHIVA KARLIN STOLIN RABBINICAL INSTITUTE

Brooklyn, NY

CONTACT Mr. Daniel Ross, Financial Aid Administrator, Yeshiva Karlin Stolin Rabbinical Institute, 1818 Fifty-fourth Street, Brooklyn, NY 11204, 718-232-7800 Ext. 116. *Fax:* 718-331-4833.

YESHIVA OF NITRA RABBINICAL COLLEGE

Mount Kisco, NY

CONTACT Mr. Yosef Rosen, Financial Aid Administrator, Yeshiva of Nitra Rabbinical College, 194 Division Avenue, Mount Kisco, NY 10549, 718-384-5460. *Fax:* 718-387-9400.

YESHIVA OF THE TELSHE ALUMNI

Riverdale, NY

CONTACT Financial Aid Office, Yeshiva of the Telshe Alumni, 4904 Independence Avenue, Riverdale, NY 10471, 718-601-3523.

YESHIVA OHR ELCHONON CHABAD/WEST COAST TALMUDICAL SEMINARY

Los Angeles, CA

CONTACT Ms. Hendy Tauber, Director of Financial Aid, Yeshiva Ohr Elchonon Chabad/West Coast Talmudical Seminary, 7215 Waring Avenue, Los Angeles, CA 90046-7660, 213-937-3763. *Fax:* 213-937-9456.

YESHIVA SHAAREI TORAH OF ROCKLAND

Suffern, NY

CONTACT Financial Aid Office, Yeshiva Shaarei Torah of Rockland, 91 West Carlton Road, Suffern, NY 10901, 845-352-3431.

YESHIVA SHAAR HATORAH TALMUDIC RESEARCH INSTITUTE

Kew Gardens, NY

CONTACT Mr. Yoel Yankelewitz, Executive Director, Financial Aid, Yeshiva Shaar Hatorah Talmudic Research Institute, 117-06 84th Avenue, Kew Gardens, NY 11418-1469, 718-846-1940.

YESHIVAS NOVOMINSK

Brooklyn, NY

CONTACT Financial Aid Office, Yeshivas Novominsk, 1569 47th Street, Brooklyn, NY 11219, 718-438-2727.

YESHIVATH VIZNITZ

Monsey, NY

CONTACT Financial Aid Office, Yeshivath Viznitz, Phyllis Terrace, PO Box 446, Monsey, NY 10952, 914-356-1010.

YESHIVATH ZICHRON MOSHE

South Fallsburg, NY

CONTACT Ms. Miryom R. Miller, Director of Financial Aid, Yeshivath Zichron Moshe, Laurel Park Road, South Fallsburg, NY 12779, 914-434-5240. *Fax:* 914-434-1009. *E-mail:* lehus@aol.com.

YESHIVAT MIKDASH MELECH

Brooklyn, NY

CONTACT Financial Aid Office, Yeshivat Mikdash Melech, 1326 Ocean Parkway, Brooklyn, NY 11230-5601, 718-339-1090.

YESHIVA TORAS CHAIM TALMUDICAL SEMINARY

Denver, CO

CONTACT Office of Financial Aid, Yeshiva Toras Chaim Talmudical Seminary, 1400 Quitman Street, Denver, CO 80204-1415, 303-629-8200.

YESHIVA UNIVERSITY

New York, NY

CONTACT Jean Belmont, Director of Student Finances, Yeshiva University, 500 West 185th Street, Room 121, New York, NY 10033-3201, 212-960-5269. *Fax:* 212-960-0037. *E-mail:* jbelmont@ymail.yu.edu.

YORK COLLEGE

York, NE

Tuition & fees: $14,000 **Average undergraduate aid package: $11,754**

ABOUT THE INSTITUTION Independent religious, coed. ***Awards:*** associate and bachelor's degrees. 40 undergraduate majors. ***Total enrollment:*** 396. Undergraduates: 396. Freshmen: 110. Institutional methodology is used as a basis for awarding need-based institutional aid.

UNDERGRADUATE EXPENSES for 2008–09 ***Application fee:*** $20. ***Comprehensive fee:*** $18,500 includes full-time tuition ($12,500), mandatory fees ($1500), and room and board ($4500). Full-time tuition and fees vary according to course load. Room and board charges vary according to board plan and housing facility. ***Part-time tuition:*** $390 per credit hour. ***Part-time fees:*** $220 per credit hour. Part-time tuition and fees vary according to course load. ***Payment plan:*** Installment.

FRESHMAN FINANCIAL AID (Fall 2008, est.) 118 applied for aid; of those 80% were deemed to have need. 100% of freshmen with need received aid; of those 26% had need fully met. ***Average percent of need met:*** 76% (excluding resources awarded to replace EFC). ***Average financial aid package:*** $14,102 (excluding resources awarded to replace EFC). 14% of all full-time freshmen had no need and received non-need-based gift aid.

UNDERGRADUATE FINANCIAL AID (Fall 2008, est.) 354 applied for aid; of those 90% were deemed to have need. 100% of undergraduates with need received aid; of those 23% had need fully met. ***Average percent of need met:*** 75% (excluding resources awarded to replace EFC). ***Average financial aid package:*** $11,754 (excluding resources awarded to replace EFC). 12% of all full-time undergraduates had no need and received non-need-based gift aid.

GIFT AID (NEED-BASED) ***Total amount:*** $1,827,205 (33% federal, 2% state, 60% institutional, 5% external sources). ***Receiving aid:*** Freshmen: 76% (94); all full-time undergraduates: 82% (319). ***Average award:*** Freshmen: $7385; Undergraduates: $8203. ***Scholarships, grants, and awards:*** Federal Pell, FSEOG, state, private, college/university gift aid from institutional funds.

GIFT AID (NON-NEED-BASED) ***Total amount:*** $326,387 (97% institutional, 3% external sources). ***Receiving aid:*** Freshmen: 57% (71). Undergraduates: 12% (47). ***Average award:*** Freshmen: $2500. Undergraduates: $7039. ***Scholarships, grants, and awards by category:*** *Academic interests/achievement:* 276 awards ($575,917 total): biological sciences, business, communication, computer science, education, English, general academic interests/achievements, mathematics, premedicine, religion/biblical studies. *Creative arts/performance:* 78 awards ($165,441 total): music, theater/drama. *Special achievements/activities:* 141 awards ($108,142 total): leadership. *Special characteristics:* 84 awards ($325,617 total): children and siblings of alumni, children of faculty/staff, previous college experience, siblings of current students. ***Tuition waivers:*** Full or partial for children of alumni, employees or children of employees, adult students. ***ROTC:*** Army cooperative, Naval cooperative, Air Force cooperative.

LOANS ***Student loans:*** $2,096,980 (43% need-based, 57% non-need-based). 75% of past graduating class borrowed through all loan programs. *Average indebtedness per student:* $22,094. ***Average need-based loan:*** Freshmen: $2957. Undergraduates: $3823. ***Parent loans:*** $309,097 (100% non-need-based). ***Programs:*** FFEL (Subsidized and Unsubsidized Stafford, PLUS), Perkins, alternative loans.

WORK-STUDY ***Federal work-study:*** Total amount: $84,829; 105 jobs averaging $807. ***State or other work-study/employment:*** Total amount: $45,194 (100% non-need-based). 59 part-time jobs averaging $766.

ATHLETIC AWARDS Total amount: $984,120 (85% need-based, 15% non-need-based).

APPLYING FOR FINANCIAL AID ***Required financial aid form:*** FAFSA. ***Financial aid deadline (priority):*** 6/15. ***Notification date:*** Continuous. Students must reply within 4 weeks of notification.

CONTACT Brien Alley, Director of Financial Aid, York College, 1125 East 8th Street, York, NE 68467, 402-363-5624 or toll-free 800-950-9675. *Fax:* 402-363-5623. *E-mail:* balley@york.edu.

YORK COLLEGE OF PENNSYLVANIA

York, PA

Tuition & fees: $13,680 **Average undergraduate aid package: $10,204**

ABOUT THE INSTITUTION Independent, coed. ***Awards:*** associate, bachelor's, and master's degrees. 52 undergraduate majors. ***Total enrollment:*** 5,627. Undergraduates: 5,329. Freshmen: 1,104. Federal methodology is used as a basis for awarding need-based institutional aid.

UNDERGRADUATE EXPENSES for 2008–09 ***Application fee:*** $30. ***Comprehensive fee:*** $21,480 includes full-time tuition ($12,320), mandatory fees ($1360), and room and board ($7800). ***College room only:*** $4400. Room and board charges vary according to housing facility. ***Part-time tuition:*** $385 per credit hour. ***Part-time fees:*** $298 per term. ***Payment plans:*** Tuition prepayment, installment.

FRESHMAN FINANCIAL AID (Fall 2008, est.) 950 applied for aid; of those 66% were deemed to have need. 98% of freshmen with need received aid; of those 28% had need fully met. ***Average percent of need met:*** 73% (excluding resources awarded to replace EFC). ***Average financial aid package:*** $10,323 (excluding resources awarded to replace EFC). 20% of all full-time freshmen had no need and received non-need-based gift aid.

UNDERGRADUATE FINANCIAL AID (Fall 2008, est.) 3,605 applied for aid; of those 71% were deemed to have need. 99% of undergraduates with need received aid; of those 28% had need fully met. ***Average percent of need met:*** 70% (excluding resources awarded to replace EFC). ***Average financial aid package:*** $10,204 (excluding resources awarded to replace EFC). 12% of all full-time undergraduates had no need and received non-need-based gift aid.

GIFT AID (NEED-BASED) ***Total amount:*** $11,155,689 (26% federal, 23% state, 46% institutional, 5% external sources). ***Receiving aid:*** Freshmen: 42% (460); all full-time undergraduates: 38% (1,743). ***Average award:*** Freshmen: $5103; Undergraduates: $4647. ***Scholarships, grants, and awards:*** Federal Pell, FSEOG, state, private, college/university gift aid from institutional funds.

GIFT AID (NON-NEED-BASED) ***Total amount:*** $1,822,861 (85% institutional, 15% external sources). ***Receiving aid:*** Freshmen: 29% (317). Undergraduates: 17% (789). ***Average award:*** Freshmen: $2988. Undergraduates: $3167. ***Scholarships, grants, and awards by category:*** *Academic interests/achievement:* 607 awards ($2,663,549 total): general academic interests/achievements. *Creative arts/performance:* 18 awards ($20,407 total): music. *Special achievements/activities:* 5 awards ($20,535 total): community service, memberships. *Special characteristics:* 35 awards ($56,246 total): children and siblings of alumni, children of union members/company employees, international students, members of minority groups. ***Tuition waivers:*** Full or partial for employees or children of employees. ***ROTC:*** Army cooperative.

LOANS ***Student loans:*** $23,050,440 (44% need-based, 56% non-need-based). 69% of past graduating class borrowed through all loan programs. *Average indebtedness per student:* $20,625. ***Average need-based loan:*** Freshmen: $5248. Undergraduates: $6252. ***Parent loans:*** $3,767,661 (64% need-based, 36% non-need-based). ***Programs:*** Federal Direct (Subsidized and Unsubsidized Stafford, PLUS), FFEL (Subsidized and Unsubsidized Stafford, PLUS), Perkins, Federal Nursing, college/university.

WORK-STUDY ***Federal work-study:*** Total amount: $533,210; 287 jobs averaging $1906. ***State or other work-study/employment:*** Total amount: $26,600 (100% non-need-based). 14 part-time jobs averaging $1921.

APPLYING FOR FINANCIAL AID ***Required financial aid form:*** FAFSA. ***Financial aid deadline (priority):*** 3/1. ***Notification date:*** Continuous beginning 3/1. Students must reply within 4 weeks of notification.

CONTACT Calvin Williams, Director of Financial Aid, York College of Pennsylvania, Country Club Road, York, PA 17405-7199, 717-849-1682 or toll-free 800-455-8018. *Fax:* 717-849-1607. *E-mail:* financialaid@ycp.edu.

YORK COLLEGE OF THE CITY UNIVERSITY OF NEW YORK

Jamaica, NY

Tuition & fees (NY res): $4262 **Average undergraduate aid package: $3795**

ABOUT THE INSTITUTION State and locally supported, coed. ***Awards:*** bachelor's and master's degrees. 36 undergraduate majors. ***Total enrollment:*** 7,157. Undergraduates: 7,111. Freshmen: 1,057. Federal methodology is used as a basis for awarding need-based institutional aid.

UNDERGRADUATE EXPENSES for 2008–09 ***Application fee:*** $65. ***Tuition, state resident:*** full-time $4000; part-time $170 per credit hour. ***Tuition, nonresident:*** full-time $8640; part-time $360 per credit hour. ***Required fees:*** full-time $262. ***Payment plans:*** Guaranteed tuition, installment.

FRESHMAN FINANCIAL AID (Fall 2008, est.) 838 applied for aid; of those 88% were deemed to have need. 98% of freshmen with need received aid. ***Average percent of need met:*** 23% (excluding resources awarded to replace EFC). ***Average financial aid package:*** $3586 (excluding resources awarded to replace EFC).

UNDERGRADUATE FINANCIAL AID (Fall 2008, est.) 3,376 applied for aid; of those 92% were deemed to have need. 99% of undergraduates with need received aid; of those 10% had need fully met. ***Average percent of need met:*** 24% (excluding resources awarded to replace EFC). ***Average financial aid package:*** $3795 (excluding resources awarded to replace EFC). 1% of all full-time undergraduates had no need and received non-need-based gift aid.

GIFT AID (NEED-BASED) ***Total amount:*** $23,491,659 (51% federal, 47% state, 2% institutional). ***Receiving aid:*** Freshmen: 71% (723); all full-time undergraduates: 69% (3,063). ***Average award:*** Freshmen: $1638; Undergraduates: $1608. ***Scholarships, grants, and awards:*** Federal Pell, FSEOG, state, college/university gift aid from institutional funds.

GIFT AID (NON-NEED-BASED) ***Receiving aid:*** Freshmen: 8% (78). Undergraduates: 2% (108). ***Average award:*** Undergraduates: $635. ***Tuition waivers:*** Full or partial for employees or children of employees, senior citizens. ***ROTC:*** Army cooperative, Air Force cooperative.

LOANS ***Student loans:*** $2,415,308 (100% need-based). 9% of past graduating class borrowed through all loan programs. *Average indebtedness per student:* $9351. ***Average need-based loan:*** Freshmen: $1329. Undergraduates: $2078. ***Parent loans:*** $2438 (100% need-based). ***Programs:*** Federal Direct (Subsidized and Unsubsidized Stafford, PLUS), Perkins.

WORK-STUDY ***Federal work-study:*** Total amount: $1,555,344; 1,022 jobs averaging $1517.

APPLYING FOR FINANCIAL AID ***Required financial aid form:*** FAFSA. ***Financial aid deadline:*** Continuous. ***Notification date:*** Continuous beginning 3/1.

CONTACT Ms. Cathy Tsiapanos, Director of Student Financial Services, York College of the City University of New York, 94-20 Guy R. Brewer Boulevard, Jamaica, NY 11451-0001, 718-262-2238. *E-mail:* ctsia@york.cuny.edu.

YOUNGSTOWN STATE UNIVERSITY

Youngstown, OH

Tuition & fees (OH res): $6721 **Average undergraduate aid package: N/A**

ABOUT THE INSTITUTION State-supported, coed. ***Awards:*** associate, bachelor's, master's, doctoral, and first professional degrees and post-bachelor's certificates. 123 undergraduate majors. ***Total enrollment:*** 13,704. Undergraduates: 12,405. Freshmen: 2,181. Federal methodology is used as a basis for awarding need-based institutional aid.

UNDERGRADUATE EXPENSES for 2008–09 ***Application fee:*** $30. ***Tuition, state resident:*** full-time $6492; part-time $280 per credit. ***Tuition, nonresident:*** full-time $12,165; part-time $516 per credit. ***Required fees:*** full-time $229; $10 per credit. Full-time tuition and fees vary according to course load and degree level. Part-time tuition and fees vary according to degree level. ***College room and board:*** $7090. Room and board charges vary according to board plan and housing facility. ***Payment plan:*** Installment.

GIFT AID (NEED-BASED) ***Total amount:*** $27,130,473 (60% federal, 17% state, 7% institutional, 16% external sources). ***Scholarships, grants, and awards:*** Federal Pell, FSEOG, state, private, college/university gift aid from institutional funds.

GIFT AID (NON-NEED-BASED) ***Total amount:*** $7,576,119 (2% federal, 31% state, 67% institutional). ***Scholarships, grants, and awards by category:*** *Academic interests/achievement:* business, computer science, education, engineering/technologies, English, general academic interests/achievements, health fields, humanities, military science. *Creative arts/performance:* music, theater/drama. *Special achievements/activities:* cheerleading/drum major, leadership. *Special characteristics:* adult students, children and siblings of alumni, children of faculty/staff, children of union members/company employees, children of workers in trades, children with a deceased or disabled parent, handicapped students, members of minority groups, spouses of deceased or disabled public servants, veterans, veterans' children. ***Tuition waivers:*** Full or partial for employees or children of employees, senior citizens. ***ROTC:*** Army, Air Force cooperative.

LOANS ***Student loans:*** $62,471,545 (50% need-based, 50% non-need-based). ***Parent loans:*** $3,940,829 (100% non-need-based). ***Programs:*** FFEL (Subsidized and Unsubsidized Stafford, PLUS), Perkins, state, Charles E. Schell, George Wright, Rogers Student Loan, Tri State Area Citizens.

WORK-STUDY ***Federal work-study:*** Total amount: $677,119; 289 jobs averaging $2343. ***State or other work-study/employment:*** Total amount: $4,196,794 (100% non-need-based). Part-time jobs available.

ATHLETIC AWARDS Total amount: $3,253,365 (100% non-need-based).

APPLYING FOR FINANCIAL AID ***Required financial aid forms:*** FAFSA, institution's own form. ***Financial aid deadline (priority):*** 2/15. ***Notification date:*** 5/1.

CONTACT Ms. Beth Bartlett, Administrative Assistant, Youngstown State University, One University Plaza, Youngstown, OH 44555, 330-941-3504 or toll-free 877-468-6978. *Fax:* 330-941-1659. *E-mail:* babartlett@ysu.edu.

ZION BIBLE COLLEGE

Haverhill, MA

CONTACT Financial Aid Office, Zion Bible College, 320 S. Main Street, Haverhill, MA 01835, 978-478-3400 or toll-free 800-356-4014.

Appendix

State Scholarship and Grant Programs

Each state government has established one or more state-administered financial aid programs for qualified students. In many instances, these state programs are restricted to legal residents of the state. However, they often are available to out-of-state students who will be or are attending colleges or universities within the state. In addition to residential status, other qualifications frequently exist.

Gift aid and forgivable loan programs open to undergraduate students for all states and the District of Columbia are described on the following pages. They are arranged in alphabetical order, first by state name, then by program name. The annotation for each program provides information about the program, eligibility, and the contact addresses for applications or further information. Unless otherwise stated, this information refers to awards for 2009–10. Information is provided by the state-sponsoring agency in response to *Peterson's Annual Survey of Non-institutional Aid*, which was conducted between January 2009 and April 2009. Information is accurate when Peterson's receives it. However, it is always advisable to check with the sponsor to ascertain that the information remains correct.

You should write to the address given for each program to request that award details for 2010–11 be sent to you as soon as they are available. Descriptive information, brochures, and application forms for state scholarship programs are usually available from the financial aid offices of public colleges or universities within the specific state. High school guidance offices often have information and relevant forms for awards for which high school seniors may be eligible. Increasingly, state government agencies are putting state scholarship information on state government agency Web sites. In searching state government Web sites, however, you should be aware that the higher education agency in many states is separate from the state's general education office, which is often responsible only for elementary and secondary education. Also, the page at public university Web sites that provides information about student financial aid frequently has a list of state-sponsored scholarships and financial aid programs. College and university Web sites can be easily accessed through www.petersons.com.

Names of scholarship programs are frequently used inconsistently or become abbreviated in popular usage. Many programs have variant names by which they are known. The program's sponsor has approved the title of the program that Peterson's uses in this guide, yet this name may differ from the program's official name or from its most commonly used name.

In addition to the grant aid and forgivable loan programs listed on the following pages, states may also offer internship or work-study programs, graduate fellowships and grants, or low-interest loans. If you are interested in learning more about these other kinds of programs, the state education office that supplies information or applications for the undergraduate scholarship programs listed here should be able to provide information about other kinds of higher education financial aid programs that are sponsored by the state.

ALABAMA

Air Force ROTC College Scholarship. Scholarship program provides three- and four-year scholarships in three different types to high school seniors. All scholarship cadets receive a nontaxable monthly allowance (stipend) during the academic year. For more details refer to Web Site: http://www.afrotc.com/scholarships/hsschol/types.php. *Award:* Scholarship for use in freshman, sophomore, junior, or senior year; renewable. *Award amount:* $9000–$15,000. *Number of awards:* 2000–4000. *Eligibility Requirements:* Applicant must be age 17-30 and enrolled or expecting to enroll full-time at a two-year or four-year institution or university. Applicant must have 3.0 GPA or higher. Available to U.S. citizens. Applicant or parent must meet one or more of the following requirements: Air Force experience; retired from active duty; disabled or killed as a result of military service; prisoner of war; or missing in action. *Application Requirements:* Application, interview, test scores, transcript. *Deadline:* December 1.

Contact Ty Christian, Chief Air Force ROTC Advertising Manager, Air Force Reserve Officer Training Corps, 551 East Maxwell Boulevard, Maxwell Air Force Base, AL 36112-6106. *E-mail:* ty.christian@maxwell.af.mil. *Phone:* 334-953-2278. *Fax:* 334-953-4384. *Web site:* www.afrotc.com.

Alabama G.I. Dependents Scholarship Program. Full scholarship for dependents of Alabama disabled, prisoner of war, or missing-in-action veterans. Child or stepchild must initiate training before 26th birthday; age 30 deadline may apply in certain situations. No age deadline for spouses or widows. *Award:* Scholarship for use in freshman, sophomore, junior, or senior year; renewable. *Award amount:* varies. *Number of awards:* varies. *Eligibility Requirements:* Applicant must be age 30 or under; enrolled or expecting to enroll full- or part-time at a four-year institution or university; resident of Alabama and studying in Alabama. Available to U.S. and non-U.S. citizens. Applicant or parent must meet one or more of the following requirements: general military experience; retired from active duty; disabled or killed as a result of military service; prisoner of war; or missing in action. *Application Requirements:* Application. *Deadline:* varies.

Contact Willie E. Moore, Scholarship Administrator, Alabama Department of Veterans Affairs, PO Box 1509, Montgomery, AL 36102-1509. *E-mail:* wmoore@va.state.al.us. *Phone:* 334-242-5077. *Fax:* 334-242-5102. *Web site:* www.va.alabama.gov.

Alabama National Guard Educational Assistance Program. Renewable award aids Alabama residents who are members of the Alabama National Guard and are enrolled in an accredited college in Alabama. Forms must be signed by a representative of the Alabama Military Department and financial aid officer. Recipient must be in a degree-seeking program. *Award:* Scholarship for use in freshman, sophomore, junior, or senior year; renewable. *Award amount:* $25–$1000. *Number of awards:* up to 575. *Eligibility Requirements:* Applicant must be age 17 and over; enrolled or expecting to enroll full- or part-time at a two-year, four-year, or technical institution or university; resident of Alabama and studying in Alabama. Available to U.S. citizens. Applicant must have served in the Air Force National Guard or Army National Guard. *Application Requirements:* Application. *Deadline:* continuous.

Contact Alabama Commission on Higher Education. *E-mail:* wwall@ache.state.al.us. *Web site:* www.ache.alabama.gov.

Alabama Student Assistance Program. Scholarship award of $300 to $5000 per academic year given to undergraduate students residing in the state of Alabama and attending a college or university in Alabama. *Award:* Grant for use in freshman, sophomore, junior, or senior year; not renewable. *Award amount:* $300–$5000. *Number of awards:* varies. *Eligibility Requirements:* Applicant must be enrolled or expecting to enroll full- or part-time at a two-year, four-year, or technical institution or university; resident of Alabama and studying in Alabama. Available to U.S. citizens. *Application Requirements:* Application. *Deadline:* continuous.

Contact Alabama Commission on Higher Education. *Web site:* www.ache.alabama.gov.

Alabama Student Grant Program. Nonrenewable awards available to Alabama residents for undergraduate study at certain independent colleges within the state. Both full and half-time students are eligible. Deadlines: September 15, January 15, and February 15. *Award:* Grant for use in freshman, sophomore, junior, or senior year; not renewable. *Award amount:* up to $1200. *Number of awards:* up to 1200. *Eligibility Requirements:* Applicant must be enrolled or expecting to enroll full- or part-time at a four-year institution or university; resident of Alabama and studying in Alabama. Available to U.S. citizens. *Application Requirements:* Application. *Deadline:* varies.

Contact Alabama Commission on Higher Education 36130-2000. *Web site:* www.ache.alabama.gov.

Police Officers and Firefighters Survivors Education Assistance Program-Alabama. Provides tuition, fees, books, and supplies to dependents of full-time police officers and firefighters killed in the line of duty. Must attend any Alabama public college as an undergraduate. Must be Alabama resident. *Award:* Scholarship for use in freshman, sophomore, junior, or senior year; renewable. *Award amount:* $2000–$5000. *Number of awards:* 15–30. *Eligibility Requirements:* Applicant must be age 21 or under; enrolled or expecting to enroll full- or part-time at a two-year, four-year, or technical institution or university; single; resident of Alabama and studying in Alabama. Applicant or parent of applicant must have employment or volunteer experience in police/firefighting. Available to U.S. citizens. *Application Requirements:* Application, transcript, birth certificate, marriage license, death certificate, letter from medical doctor. *Deadline:* continuous.

Contact Alabama Commission on Higher Education. *Web site:* www.ache.alabama.gov.

ALASKA

GEAR UP Alaska Scholarship. Scholarship provides up to $7000 each year for up to four years of undergraduate study (up to $3500 each year for half-time study) for students who participated in the GEAR UP Programs in 6th, 7th, and 8th grade and have met the academic milestones established by their district. Must reapply each year and application must be signed by GEAR UP program director. Must be an Alaska high school senior or have an Alaska diploma or GED. Must submit FAFSA and have financial need. Must be under age 22. *Award:* Scholarship for use in freshman, sophomore, junior, or senior year; not renewable. *Award amount:* $3500–$7000. *Number of awards:* varies. *Eligibility Requirements:* Applicant must be age 22 or under; enrolled or expecting to enroll full- or part-time at a two-year or four-year institution or university and resident of Alaska. Available to U.S. citizens. *Application Requirements:* Application, financial need analysis, references, transcript, FAFSA, SAR. *Deadline:* May 31.

Contact Adam Weed, Special Projects Coordinator, Alaska State Department of Education, 801 West 10th Street, Suite 200, PO Box 110500, Juneau, AK 99811-0500. *E-mail:* adam.weed@alaska.gov. *Phone:* 907-465-6685. *Web site:* www.eed.state.ak.us.

ARIZONA

Arizona Private Postsecondary Education Student Financial Assistance Program. Provides grants to financially needy Arizona Community College graduates, to attend a private postsecondary baccalaureate degree-granting institution. *Award:* Forgivable loan for use in junior or senior year; renewable. *Award amount:* $1000–$2000. *Number of awards:* varies. *Eligibility Requirements:* Applicant must be enrolled or expecting to enroll full-time at a four-year institution or university; resident of Arizona and studying in Arizona. Applicant must have 2.5 GPA or higher. Available to U.S. citizens. *Application Requirements:* Application, financial need analysis, transcript, promissory note. *Deadline:* June 30.

Contact Mila Zaporteza, Business Manager, Arizona Commission for Postsecondary Education, 2020 North Central Avenue, Suite 650, Phoenix, AZ 85004-4503. *E-mail:* mila@azhighered.gov. *Phone:* 602-258-2435 Ext. 102. *Fax:* 602-258-2483. *Web site:* www.azhighered.gov.

Leveraging Educational Assistance Partnership. Grants to financially needy students, who enroll in and attend postsecondary education or training in Arizona schools. Program was formerly known as the State Student Incentive Grant or SSIG Program. *Award:* Grant for use in freshman, sophomore, junior, senior, or graduate year; not renewable. *Award amount:* $100–$2500. *Number of awards:* varies. *Eligibility Requirements:* Applicant must be enrolled or expecting to enroll full- or part-time at a two-year, four-year, or technical institution or university; resident of Arizona and studying in Arizona. Available to U.S. citizens. *Application Requirements:* Application, financial need analysis, transcript. *Deadline:* April 30.

Contact Mila A. Zaporteza, Business Manager and LEAP Financial Aid Manager, Arizona Commission for Postsecondary Education, 2020 North Central Avenue, Suite 650, Phoenix, AZ 85004-4503. *E-mail:* mila@azhighered.gov. *Phone:* 602-258-2435 Ext. 102. *Fax:* 602-258-2483. *Web site:* www.azhighered.gov.

Postsecondary Education Grant Program. Awards of up to $2000 to Arizona residents studying in Arizona. May be renewed annually for a maximum of four calendar years. Minimum 2.5 GPA required. Deadline June 30. *Award:* Forgivable loan for use in freshman, sophomore, junior, or senior year; renewable. *Award amount:* $1000–$2000. *Number of awards:* varies. *Eligibility Requirements:* Applicant must be enrolled or expecting to enroll full- or part-time at a four-year institution or university; resident of Arizona and studying in Arizona. Applicant must have 2.5 GPA or higher. Available to U.S. citizens. *Application Requirements:* Application, driver's license, transcript, promissory note. *Deadline:* June 30.

Contact Dr. April L. Osborn, Executive Director, Arizona Commission for Postsecondary Education, 2020 North Central Avenue, Suite 650, Phoenix, AZ 85004-4503. *E-mail:* aosborn@azhighered.gov. *Phone:* 602-258-2435. *Fax:* 602-258-2483. *Web site:* www.azhighered.gov.

ARKANSAS

Arkansas Academic Challenge Scholarship Program. Awards for Arkansas residents who are graduating high school seniors to study at an Arkansas institution. Must have at least a 2.75 GPA, meet minimum ACT composite score standards, and have financial need. Renewable up to three additional years. *Award:* Scholarship for use in freshman, sophomore, junior, or senior year; renewable. *Award amount:* $2500–$3500. *Number of awards:* 7000–10,000. *Eligibility Requirements:* Applicant must be enrolled or expecting to enroll full-time at a two-year or four-year institution or university; resident of Arkansas and studying in Arkansas. Applicant must have 2.5 GPA or higher. Available to U.S. citizens. *Application Requirements:* Application, financial need analysis, test scores, transcript. *Deadline:* June 1.

Contact Tara Smith, Director of Financial Aid, Arkansas Department of Higher Education, 114 East Capitol Avenue, Little Rock, AR 72201-3818. *E-mail:* finaid@adhe.arknet.edu. *Phone:* 501-371-2000. *Fax:* 501-371-2001. *Web site:* www.adhe.edu.

Arkansas Health Education Grant Program (ARHEG). Award provides assistance to Arkansas residents pursuing professional degrees in dentistry, optometry, veterinary medicine, podiatry, chiropractic medicine, or osteopathic medicine at out-of-state, accredited institutions (programs that are unavailable in Arkansas). *Academic Fields/Career Goals:* Animal/Veterinary Sciences; Dental Health/Services; Health and Medical Sciences; Osteopathy. *Award:* Grant for use in freshman, sophomore, junior, senior, or graduate year; renewable. *Award amount:* $5000–$14,600. *Number of awards:* 258–288. *Eligibility Requirements:* Applicant must be enrolled or expecting to enroll full-time at a four-year institution or university and resident of Arkansas. Available to U.S. citizens. *Application Requirements:* Application, affidavit of Arkansas residency. *Deadline:* continuous.

Contact Tara Smith, Director of Financial Aid, Arkansas Department of Higher Education, 114 East Capitol Avenue, Little Rock, AR 72201-3818. *E-mail:* taras@adhe.edu. *Phone:* 501-371-2000. *Fax:* 501-371-2002. *Web site:* www.adhe.edu.

Arkansas Single Parent Scholarship. Scholarships are awarded to economically disadvantaged single parents who reside in Arkansas who have custodial care of at least one minor child and have not already received a baccalaureate degree. Award values, application deadlines, and other criteria vary by county. Visit www.aspsf.org for more information. *Award:* Scholarship for use in freshman, sophomore, junior, or senior year; not renewable. *Award amount:* $200–$1800. *Number of awards:* up to 1600. *Eligibility Requirements:* Applicant must be enrolled or expecting to enroll full- or part-time at a two-year, four-year, or technical institution or university; single; resident of Arkansas and must have an interest in designated field specified by sponsor. Available to U.S. citizens. *Application Requirements:* Application, financial need analysis, interview, references, transcript, statement of goals, FAFSA SAR. *Deadline:* varies.

Contact varies by county, Arkansas Single Parent Scholarship Fund. *Web site:* www.aspsf.org.

Governor's Scholars-Arkansas. Awards for outstanding Arkansas high school seniors. Must be an Arkansas resident and have a high school GPA of at least 3.5 or have scored at least 27 on the ACT. Award is $4000 per year for four years of full-time undergraduate study. Applicants who attain 32 or above on ACT, 1410 or above on SAT and have an academic 3.5 GPA, or are selected as National Merit or National Achievement finalists may receive an award equal to tuition, mandatory fees, room, and board up to $10,000 per year at any Arkansas institution. *Award:* Scholarship for use in freshman, sophomore, junior, or senior year; renewable. *Award amount:* $4000–$10,000. *Number of awards:* up to 375. *Eligibility Requirements:* Applicant must be enrolled or expecting to enroll full-time at a two-year or four-year institution or university; resident of Arkansas and studying in Arkansas. Applicant must have 3.5 GPA or higher. Available to U.S. citizens. *Application Requirements:* Application, test scores, transcript. *Deadline:* February 1.

Contact Tara Smith, Director of Financial Aid, Arkansas Department of Higher Education, 114 East Capitol Avenue, Little Rock, AR 72201-3818. *E-mail:* taras@adhe.edu. *Phone:* 501-371-2000. *Fax:* 501-371-2001. *Web site:* www.adhe.edu.

Law Enforcement Officers' Dependents Scholarship-Arkansas. Scholarship for dependents, under 23 years old, of Arkansas law-enforcement officers killed or permanently disabled in the line of duty. Renewable award is a waiver of tuition, fees, and room at two or four-year Arkansas institution. Submit birth certificate, death certificate, and claims commission report of findings of fact. Proof of disability from State Claims Commission may also be submitted. *Award:* Scholarship for use in freshman, sophomore, junior, or senior year; renewable. *Award amount:* $2000–$2500. *Number of awards:* 27–32. *Eligibility Requirements:* Applicant must be age 23 or under; enrolled or expecting to enroll full- or part-time at a two-year, four-year, or technical institution or university; resident of Arkansas and studying in Arkansas. Applicant or parent of applicant must have employment or volunteer experience in police/firefighting. Available to U.S. citizens. *Application Requirements:* Application. *Deadline:* continuous.

Contact Tara Smith, Director of Financial Aid, Arkansas Department of Higher Education, 114 East Capitol Avenue, Little Rock, AR 72201-3818. *E-mail:* taras@adhe.edu. *Phone:* 501-371-2000. *Fax:* 501-371-2001. *Web site:* www.adhe.edu.

Military Dependent's Scholarship Program-Arkansas. Renewable waiver of tuition, fees, room and board undergraduate students seeking a bachelor's degree or certificate of completion at any public college, university or technical school in Arkansas who qualify as a spouse or dependent child of an Arkansas resident who has been declared to be missing in action, killed in action, a POW, or killed on ordnance delivery, or a veteran who has been declared to be 100 percent totally and permanently disabled during, or as a result of, active military service. *Award:* Scholarship for use in freshman, sophomore, junior, or senior year; renewable. *Award amount:* up to $2500. *Number of awards:* 1. *Eligibility Requirements:* Applicant must be enrolled or expecting to enroll full-time at a two-year, four-year, or technical institution or university; resident of Arkansas and studying in Arkansas. Available to U.S. citizens. Applicant or parent must meet one or more of the following requirements: general military experience; retired from active duty; disabled or killed as a result of military service; prisoner of war; or missing in action. *Application Requirements:* Application, references, report of casualty. *Deadline:* continuous.

Contact Tara Smith, Director of Financial Aid, Arkansas Department of Higher Education, 114 East Capitol Avenue, Little Rock, AR 72201-3818. *E-mail:* taras@adhe.edu. *Phone:* 501-371-2000. *Fax:* 501-371-2001. *Web site:* www.adhe.edu.

Robert C. Byrd Honors Scholarship-Arkansas. Applicant must be a graduate of a public or private school or receive a recognized equivalent of a high school diploma. Must be a resident of Arkansas. Must be admitted to an institution of higher education, demonstrate outstanding academic achievement and show promise of continued academic achievement. Award is $1500 for each academic year for a maximum of four years. *Award:* Scholarship for use in freshman year; renewable. *Award amount:* $1500. *Number of awards:* 62. *Eligibility Requirements:* Applicant must be high school student; planning to enroll or expecting to enroll full-time at a two-year, four-year, or technical institution or university and resident of Arkansas. Available to U.S. citizens. *Application Requirements:* Application, transcript. *Deadline:* February 16.

Contact Margaret Amps, Program Coordinator, Arkansas State Department of Education, Four Capitol Mall, Little Rock, AR 72201. *E-mail:* margaret.amps@arkansas.gov. *Phone:* 501-682-4396. *Web site:* arkansased.org.

Second Effort Scholarship. Awarded to those scholars who achieved one of the 10 highest scores on the Arkansas High School Diploma Test (GED). Must be at least age 18 and not have graduated from high school. Students do not apply for this award, they are contacted by the Arkansas Department of Higher Education. *Award:* Scholarship for use in freshman year; renewable. *Award amount:* up to $1000. *Number of awards:* 10. *Eligibility Requirements:* Applicant must be high school student; age 18 and over; planning to enroll or expecting to enroll full- or part-time at a four-year institution or university; resident of Arkansas and studying in Arkansas. Applicant must have 2.5 GPA or higher. Available to U.S. citizens. *Application Requirements:* Application. *Deadline:* varies.

Contact Tara Smith, Director of Financial Aid, Arkansas Department of Higher Education, 114 East Capitol Avenue, Little Rock, AR 72201-3818. *E-mail:* taras@adhe.edu. *Phone:* 501-371-2000. *Fax:* 501-371-2001. *Web site:* www.adhe.edu.

CALIFORNIA

Cal Grant C. Award for California residents who are enrolled in a short-term vocational training program. Program must lead to a recognized degree or certificate. Course length must be a minimum of 4 months and no longer than 24 months. Students must be attending an approved California institution and show financial need. *Award:* Grant for use in freshman or sophomore year; renewable. *Award amount:* $576–$3168. *Number of awards:* up to 7761. *Eligibility Requirements:* Applicant must be enrolled or expecting to enroll full- or part-time at a two-year or technical institution; resident of California and studying in California. Available to U.S. citizens. *Application Requirements:* Application, financial need analysis, GPA verification. *Deadline:* March 2.

Contact Catalina Mistler, Chief, Program Administration & Services Division, California Student Aid Commission, PO Box 419026, Rancho Cordova, CA 95741-9026. *E-mail:* studentsupport@csac.ca.gov. *Phone:* 916-526-7268. *Fax:* 916-526-8002. *Web site:* www.csac.ca.gov.

Child Development Teacher and Supervisor Grant Program. Award is for those students pursuing an approved course of study leading to a Child Development Permit issued by the California Commission on Teacher Credentialing. In exchange for each year funding is received, recipients agree to provide one year of service in a licensed childcare center. *Academic Fields/Career Goals:* Child and Family Studies; Education. *Award:* Grant for use in freshman, sophomore, junior, senior, or graduate year; renewable. *Award amount:* $1000–$2000. *Number of awards:* up to 300. *Eligibility Requirements:* Applicant must be enrolled or expecting to enroll full- or part-time at a two-year or four-year institution or university; resident of California and studying in California. Applicant or parent of applicant must have employment or volunteer experience in teaching/education. Available to U.S. citizens. *Application Requirements:* Application, financial need analysis, references, GPA verification. *Deadline:* April 16.

Contact Catalina Mistler, Chief, Program Administration & Services Division, California Student Aid Commission, PO Box 419026, Rancho Cordova, CA 95741-9026. *E-mail:* studentsupport@csac.ca.gov. *Phone:* 916-526-7268. *Fax:* 916-526-8002. *Web site:* www.csac.ca.gov.

Competitive Cal Grant A. Award for California residents who are not recent high school graduates attending an approved college or university within the state. Must show financial need and meet minimum 3.0 GPA requirement. *Award:* Grant for use in freshman, sophomore, junior, or senior year; renewable. *Award amount:* $2772–$6636. *Number of awards:* 22,500. *Eligibility Requirements:* Applicant must be enrolled or expecting to enroll full- or part-time at a two-year or four-year institution or university; resident of California and studying in California. Applicant must have 3.0 GPA or higher. Available to U.S. citizens. *Application Requirements:* Application, financial need analysis, GPA verification. *Deadline:* March 2.

Contact Catalina Mistler, Chief, Program Administration & Services Division, California Student Aid Commission, PO Box 419026, Rancho Cordova, CA 95741-9026. *E-mail:* studentsupport@csac.ca.gov. *Phone:* 916-526-7268. *Fax:* 916-526-8002. *Web site:* www.csac.ca.gov.

Cooperative Agencies Resources for Education Program. Renewable award available to California resident enrolled as a full-time student at a two-year California community college. Must currently receive CalWORKs/TANF and have at least one child under fourteen years of age at time of acceptance into CARE program. Must be in EOPS, a single head of household, and age 18 or older. Contact local college EOPS-CARE office for application and more information. To locate nearest campus, see http://www.icanaffordcollege.com/applications/homepage2.cfm. *Award:* Grant for use in freshman or sophomore year; renewable. *Award amount:* varies. *Number of awards:* 10,000–11,000. *Eligibility Requirements:* Applicant must be age 18 and over; enrolled or expecting to enroll full-time at a two-year institution; single; resident of California and studying in California. Available to U.S. citizens. *Application Requirements:* Application, financial need analysis, test scores, transcript. *Deadline:* continuous.

Contact Contact local community college EOPS/CARE program, California Community Colleges. *Web site:* www.cccco.edu.

Entitlement Cal Grant B. Provide grant funds for access costs for low-income students in an amount not to exceed $1551. Must be California residents and enroll in an undergraduate academic program of not less than one academic year at a qualifying postsecondary institution. Must show financial need and meet the minimum 2.0 GPA requirement. *Award:* Grant for use in freshman, sophomore, junior, or senior year; renewable. *Award amount:* $700–$1551. *Number of awards:* varies. *Eligibility Requirements:* Applicant must be age 23 or under; enrolled or expecting to enroll full- or part-time at a two-year, four-year, or technical institution or university; resident of California and studying in California. Available to U.S. citizens. *Application Requirements:* Application, financial need analysis. *Deadline:* March 2.

Contact Catalina Mistler, Chief, Program Administration & Services Division, California Student Aid Commission, PO Box 419026, Rancho Cordova, CA 95741-9026. *E-mail:* studentsupport@csac.ca.gov. *Phone:* 916-526-7268. *Fax:* 916-526-8002. *Web site:* www.csac.ca.gov.

Law Enforcement Personnel Dependents Scholarship. Provides college grants to needy dependents of California law enforcement officers, officers and employees of the Department of Corrections and Department of Youth Authority, and firefighters killed or disabled in the line of duty. *Award:* Grant for use in freshman, sophomore, junior, or senior year; renewable. *Award amount:* $100–$11,259. *Number of awards:* varies. *Eligibility Requirements:* Applicant must be enrolled or expecting to enroll full- or part-time at a two-year or four-year institution or university; resident of California and studying in California. Applicant or parent of applicant must have employment or volunteer experience in police/firefighting. Available to U.S. citizens. *Application Requirements:* Application, financial need analysis, transcript, birth certificate, death certificate of parents or spouse, police report. *Deadline:* continuous.

Contact Catalina Mistler, Chief, Program Administration & Services Division, California Student Aid Commission, PO Box 419026, Rancho Cordova, CA 95741-9026. *E-mail:* studentsupport@csac.ca.gov. *Phone:* 916-526-7268. *Fax:* 916-526-8002. *Web site:* www.csac.ca.gov.

COLORADO

American Legion Auxiliary Department of Colorado Department President's Scholarship for Junior Member. Open to children, spouses, grandchildren, and great-grandchildren of veterans, and veterans who served in the Armed Forces during eligibility dates for membership in the American Legion. Applicants must be Colorado residents who have been accepted by an accredited school in Colorado. *Award:* Scholarship for use in freshman year; not renewable. *Award amount:* up to $500. *Number of awards:* 1–2. *Eligibility Requirements:* Applicant must be high school student; planning to enroll or expecting to enroll full- or part-time at a four-year institution or university; resident of Colorado and studying in Colorado. Available to U.S. citizens. Applicant or parent must meet one or more of the following requirements: general military experience; retired from active duty; disabled or killed as a result of military service; prisoner of war; or missing in action. *Application Requirements:* Application, essay, references, transcript. *Deadline:* April 15.

Contact Jean Lennie, Department Secretary and Treasurer, American Legion Auxiliary Department of Colorado, 7465 East First Avenue, Suite D, Denver, CO 80230. *E-mail:* ala@coloradolegion.org. *Phone:* 303-367-5388. *Fax:* 303-367-0688. *Web site:* www.coloradolegion.org.

American Legion Auxiliary Department of Colorado Past Presidents' Parley Nurses Scholarship. Open to children, spouses, grandchildren, and great-grandchildren of American Legion veterans, and veterans who served in the armed forces during eligibility dates for membership in the American Legion. Must be Colorado residents who have been accepted by an accredited school of nursing in Colorado. *Academic Fields/Career Goals:* Nursing. *Award:* Scholarship for use in freshman, sophomore, junior, senior, or graduate year; not renewable. *Award amount:* up to $500. *Number of awards:* 3–5. *Eligibility Requirements:* Applicant must be enrolled or expecting to enroll full- or part-time at a four-year institution or university; resident of Colorado and studying in Colorado. Applicant or parent of applicant must be member of American Legion or Auxiliary. Available to U.S. citizens. Applicant or parent must meet one or more of the following requirements: general military experience; retired from active duty; disabled or killed as a result of military service; prisoner of war; or missing in action. *Application Requirements:* Application, essay, financial need analysis, references. *Deadline:* April 1.

Contact American Legion Auxiliary Department of Colorado, 7465 East First Avenue, Suite D, Denver, CO 80230. *E-mail:* ala@coloradolegion.org. *Phone:* 303-367-5388. *Web site:* www.coloradolegion.org.

Colorado Leveraging Educational Assistance Partnership (CLEAP). Scholarship of up to $5000 awarded for an undergraduate student enrolled at least half time. Applicant must be a U.S citizen and Colorado resident. *Award:* Scholarship for use in freshman, sophomore, junior, or senior year; not renewable. *Award amount:* up to $5000. *Number of awards:* varies. *Eligibility Requirements:* Applicant must be enrolled or expecting to enroll full- or part-time at a two-year, four-year, or technical institution or university and resident of Colorado. Available to U.S. citizens. *Application Requirements:* Application. *Deadline:* varies.

Contact Colorado Commission on Higher Education. *Web site:* highered.colorado.gov/dhedefault.html.

Colorado Student Grant. Grants for Colorado residents attending eligible public, private, or vocational institutions within the state. Application deadlines vary by institution. Renewable award for undergraduates. Contact the financial aid office at the college/institution for application and more information. *Award:* Grant for use in freshman, sophomore, junior, or senior year; renewable. *Award amount:* $700–$5000. *Number of awards:* varies. *Eligibility Requirements:* Applicant must be enrolled or expecting to enroll full- or part-time at a two-year, four-year, or technical institution or university; resident of Colorado and studying in Colorado. Available to U.S. citizens. *Application Requirements:* Application, financial need analysis, student must have an active FAFSA on file at the institution. *Deadline:* varies.

Contact Colorado Commission on Higher Education. *Web site:* highered.colorado.gov/dhedefault.html.

Colorado Undergraduate Merit Scholarships. Renewable awards for students who are Colorado residents attending Colorado state-supported institutions at the undergraduate level. Must demonstrate superior scholarship or talent. Contact college financial aid office for complete information and deadlines. *Award:* Scholarship for use in freshman, sophomore, junior, or senior year; renewable. *Award amount:* $1294. *Number of awards:* 1158. *Eligibility Requirements:* Applicant must be enrolled or expecting to enroll full- or part-time at a two-year, four-year, or technical institution or university; resident of Colorado and studying in Colorado. Applicant must have 3.5 GPA or higher. Available to U.S. citizens. *Application Requirements:* Application, test scores, transcript. *Deadline:* varies.

Contact Colorado Commission on Higher Education. *Web site:* highered.colorado.gov/dhedefault.html.

Governor's Opportunity Scholarship. Scholarship available for the most needy first-time freshman whose parents' adjusted gross income is less than $26,000. Must be U.S. citizen or permanent legal resident. Work-study is part of the program. This program is in phase out and will sunset in 2012. *Award:* Scholarship for use in freshman year; renewable. *Award amount:* up to $10,700. *Number of awards:* 720. *Eligibility Requirements:* Applicant must be high school student; planning to enroll or expecting to enroll full-time at a two-year, four-year, or technical institution or university; resident of Colorado and studying in Colorado. Available to U.S. citizens. *Application Requirements:* Application, financial need analysis, test scores, transcript. *Deadline:* continuous.

Contact Colorado Commission on Higher Education. *Web site:* highered.colorado.gov/dhedefault.html.

Western Undergraduate Exchange (WUE). Students in designated states can enroll in two- and four-year undergraduate programs at 140 public institutions in participating states and pay 150 percent of resident tuition. Applicants apply directly to the admissions office at participating institution. Applicants must indicate that they want to be considered for the "WUE tuition discount". Participating institutions and the programs of study offered at the WUE rate are listed at http://wiche.edu/sep/wue. *Award:* Scholarship for use in freshman, sophomore, junior, or senior year; renewable. *Award amount:* varies. *Number of awards:* varies. *Eligibility Requirements:* Applicant must be enrolled or expecting to enroll full-time at a two-year or four-year institution; resident of Alaska, Arizona, California, Colorado, Hawaii, Idaho, Montana, Nevada, New Mexico, North Dakota, Oregon, South Dakota, Utah, Washington, or Wyoming and studying in Alaska, Arizona, California, Colorado, Hawaii, Idaho, Montana, Nevada, New Mexico, North Dakota, Oregon, or South Dakota. Available to U.S. citizens. *Application Requirements:* Application, test scores, transcript, varies by institution. *Deadline:* varies.

Contact Ms. Laura Ewing, Administrative Assistant, Student Exchange, Western Interstate Commission for Higher Education, 3035 Center Green Drive, Boulder, CO 80301. *E-mail:* info-sep@wiche.edu. *Phone:* 303-541-0270. *Web site:* www.wiche.edu/sep.

CONNECTICUT

AIFS-HACU Scholarships. Scholarships to outstanding Hispanic students to study abroad with AIFS. Available to students attending HACU member schools. Students will receive scholarships of up to 50 percent of the full program fee. Students must meet all standard AIFS eligibility requirements. Deadlines: April 15 for fall, October 1 for spring, and March 15 for summer. *Award:* Scholarship for use in freshman, sophomore, junior, or senior year; not renewable. *Award amount:* $6000–$8000. *Number of awards:* varies. *Eligibility Requirements:* Applicant must be Hispanic; age 17 and over; enrolled or expecting to enroll full-time at a two-year or four-year institution or university and must have an interest in international exchange. Applicant must have 3.0 GPA or higher. Available to U.S. and non-U.S. citizens. *Application Requirements:* Application, essay, photo, references, transcript. *Fee:* $95. *Deadline:* varies.

Contact David Mauro, Admissions Counselor, American Institute for Foreign Study, River Plaza, 9 West Broad Street, Stamford, CT 06902-3788. *E-mail:* dmauro@aifs.com. *Phone:* 800-727-2437 Ext. 5163. *Fax:* 203-399-5463. *Web site:* www.aifsabroad.com.

Capitol Scholarship Program. Award for Connecticut residents attending eligible institutions in Connecticut or in a state with reciprocity with Connecticut (Massachusetts, Maine, New Hampshire, Pennsylvania, Rhode Island, Vermont, or Washington, D.C). Must be U.S. citizen or permanent resident alien who is a high school senior or graduate. Must rank in top 20% of class or score at least 1800 on SAT. Must show financial need. *Award:* Scholarship for use in freshman, sophomore, junior, or senior year; renewable. *Award amount:* $500–$3000. *Number of awards:* 4500–5500. *Eligibility Requirements:* Applicant must be enrolled or expecting to enroll full- or part-time at a two-year, four-year, or technical institution or university; resident of Connecticut and studying in Connecticut, District of Columbia, Maine, Massachusetts, New Hampshire, Pennsylvania, Rhode Island, or Vermont. Applicant must have 2.5 GPA or higher. Available to U.S. citizens. *Application Requirements:* Application, financial need analysis, test scores, FAFSA. *Deadline:* February 15.

Contact Mrs. Linda Diamond, Senior Associate, Connecticut Department of Higher Education, 61 Woodland Street, Hartford, CT 06105. *E-mail:* csp@ctdhe.org. *Phone:* 860-947-1855. *Fax:* 860-947-1313. *Web site:* www.ctdhe.org.

Connecticut Aid to Public College Students Grant. Award for Connecticut residents attending public colleges or universities within the state. Renewable awards based on financial need. Application deadline varies by institution. Apply at college financial aid office. *Award:* Grant for use in freshman, sophomore, junior, or senior year; renewable. *Award amount:* varies. *Number of awards:* varies. *Eligibility Requirements:* Applicant must be enrolled or expecting to enroll full- or part-time at a two-year or four-year institution or university; resident of Connecticut and studying in Connecticut. Available to U.S. citizens. *Application Requirements:* Financial need analysis, FAFSA. *Deadline:* varies.

Contact Mrs. Omerine Marino, Senior Associate, Connecticut Department of Higher Education, 61 Woodland Street, Hartford, CT 06105. *E-mail:* caps@ctdhe.org. *Phone:* 860-947-1855. *Fax:* 860-947-1838. *Web site:* www.ctdhe.org.

Connecticut Army National Guard 100% Tuition Waiver. Program is for any active member of the Connecticut Army National Guard in good standing. Must be a resident of Connecticut attending any Connecticut state (public) university, community-technical college or regional vocational-technical school. The total number of available awards is unlimited. *Award:* Scholarship for use in freshman, sophomore, junior, or senior year; not renewable. *Award amount:* $16,000. *Number of awards:* varies. *Eligibility Requirements:* Applicant must be age 17-65; enrolled or expecting to enroll full- or part-time at a two-year, four-year, or technical institution or university; resident of Connecticut and studying in Connecticut. Available to U.S. and non-U.S. citizens. Applicant or parent must meet one or more of the following requirements: Army National Guard experience; retired from active duty; disabled or killed as a result of military service; prisoner of war; or missing in action. *Application Requirements:* Application. *Deadline:* July 1.

Contact Capt. Jeremy Lingenfelser, Education Services Officer, Connecticut Army National Guard, 360 Broad Street, Hartford, CT 06105-3795. *E-mail:* education@ct.ngb.army.mil. *Phone:* 860-524-4816. *Fax:* 860-524-4904. *Web site:* www.ct.ngb.army.mil.

Connecticut Independent College Student Grants. Award for Connecticut residents attending an independent college or university within the state on at least a half-time basis. Renewable awards based on financial need. Application deadline varies by institution. Apply at college financial aid office. *Award:* Grant for use in freshman, sophomore, junior, or senior year; renewable. *Award amount:* $250–$8500. *Number of awards:* varies. *Eligibility Requirements:* Applicant must be enrolled or expecting to enroll full- or part-time at a two-year or four-year institution or university; resident of Connecticut and studying in Connecticut. Available to U.S. citizens. *Application Requirements:* Application, financial need analysis, FAFSA. *Deadline:* varies.

Contact Mrs. Omerine Marino, Senior Associate, Connecticut Department of Higher Education, 61 Woodland Street, Hartford, CT 06105. *E-mail:* cics@ctdhe.org. *Phone:* 860-947-1855. *Fax:* 860-947-1838. *Web site:* www.ctdhe.org.

Minority Teacher Incentive Grant Program. Program provides up to $5,000 a year for two years of full-time study in a teacher preparation program for the junior or senior year at a Connecticut college or university. Applicant must be African-American, Hispanic/Latino, Asian American or Native American heritage and be nominated by the Education Dean. Program graduates who teach in Connecticut public schools may be eligible for loan reimbursement stipends up to $2,500 per year for up to four years. *Academic Fields/Career Goals:* Education. *Award:* Grant for use in junior or senior year; renewable. *Award amount:* up to $5000. *Number of awards:* 1–75. *Eligibility Requirements:* Applicant must be American Indian/Alaska Native, Asian/Pacific Islander, Black (non-Hispanic), or Hispanic; enrolled or expecting to enroll full-time at a four-year institution or university and studying in Connecticut. Available to U.S. citizens. *Application Requirements:* Application. *Deadline:* October 1.

Contact Mrs. Omerine Marino, Senior Associate, Connecticut Department of Higher Education, 61 Woodland Street, Hartford, CT 06105. *E-mail:* mtip@ctdhe.org. *Phone:* 860-947-1855. *Fax:* 860-947-1838. *Web site:* www.ctdhe.org.

DELAWARE

Christa McAuliffe Teacher Scholarship Loan-Delaware. Award for legal residents of Delaware who are U.S. citizens or eligible non-citizens. Must be full-time student enrolled at a Delaware college in an undergraduate program leading to teacher certification. High school seniors must rank in upper half of class and have a combined score of 1570 on the SAT. Undergraduates must have at least a 2.75 cumulative GPA. For details visit Web site: http://www.doe.k12.de.us. *Academic Fields/Career Goals:* Education. *Award:* Forgivable loan for use in freshman, sophomore, junior, or senior year; renewable. *Award amount:* $1000–$5000. *Number of awards:* 1–60. *Eligibility Requirements:* Applicant must be enrolled or expecting to enroll full-time at a four-year institution or university; resident of Delaware and studying in Delaware. Available to U.S. citizens. *Application Requirements:* Application, essay, test scores, transcript. *Deadline:* March 28.

Contact Carylin Brinkley, Program Administrator, Delaware Higher Education Commission, Carvel State Office Building, 820 North French Street, Fifth Floor, Wilmington, DE 19801-3509. *E-mail:* cbrinkley@doe.k12.de.us. *Phone:* 302-577-5240. *Fax:* 302-577-6765. *Web site:* www.doe.k12.de.us.

Delaware Nursing Incentive Scholarship Loan. Award for legal residents of Delaware who are U.S. citizens or eligible non-citizens. Must be full-time student enrolled in an accredited program leading to certification as an RN or LPN. High school seniors must rank in upper half of class with at least a 2.5 cumulative GPA. *Academic Fields/Career Goals:* Nursing. *Award:* Forgivable loan for use in freshman, sophomore, junior, or senior year; renewable. *Award amount:* $1000–$5000. *Number of awards:* 1–40. *Eligibility Requirements:* Applicant must be enrolled or expecting to enroll full- or part-time at a two-year or four-year institution and resident of Delaware. Applicant must have 2.5 GPA or higher. Available to U.S. citizens. *Application Requirements:* Application, essay, test scores, transcript. *Deadline:* March 28.

Contact Carylin Brinkley, Program Administrator, Delaware Higher Education Commission, Carvel State Office Building, 820 North French Street, Fifth Floor, Wilmington, DE 19801-3509. *E-mail:* cbrinkley@doe.k12.de.us. *Phone:* 302-577-5240. *Fax:* 302-577-6765. *Web site:* www.doe.k12.de.us.

Delaware Solid Waste Authority John P. "Pat" Healy Scholarship. Award for legal residents of Delaware who are U.S. citizens or eligible non-citizens. Must be high school seniors or full-time college students in their freshman or sophomore years. Must major in either environmental engineering or environmental sciences at a Delaware college. Selection based on financial need, academic performance, community and school involvement, and leadership ability. *Academic Fields/Career Goals:* Engineering-Related Technologies; Environmental Science. *Award:* Scholarship for use in freshman or sophomore year; renewable. *Award amount:* $2000. *Number of awards:* 1. *Eligibility Requirements:* Applicant must be enrolled or expecting to enroll full-time at a two-year or four-year institution or university; resident of Delaware; studying in Delaware and must have an interest in leadership. Applicant or parent of applicant must have employment or volunteer experience in community service. Applicant must have 3.0 GPA or higher. Available to U.S. citizens. *Application Requirements:* Application, financial need analysis, FAFSA, Student Aid Report (SAR). *Deadline:* March 14.

Contact Carylin Brinkley, Program Administrator, Delaware Higher Education Commission, Carvel State Office Building, 820 North French Street, Fifth Floor, Wilmington, DE 19801-3509. *E-mail:* cbrinkley@doe.k12.de.us. *Phone:* 302-577-5240. *Fax:* 302-577-6765. *Web site:* www.doe.k12.de.us.

Diamond State Scholarship. Award for legal residents of Delaware who are U.S. citizens or eligible non-citizens. Must be enrolled as a full-time student in a degree program at a nonprofit, regionally accredited institution. Minimum 3.0 GPA required. High school seniors should rank in upper quarter of class and have a combined score of at least 1800 on the SAT. *Award:* Scholarship for use in freshman year; renewable. *Award amount:* $1250. *Number of awards:* 50. *Eligibility Requirements:* Applicant must be high school student; planning to enroll or expecting to enroll full-time at a four-year institution or university and resident of Delaware. Applicant must have 3.0 GPA or higher. Available to U.S. citizens. *Application Requirements:* Application, essay, test scores, transcript. *Deadline:* March 28.

Contact Carylin Brinkley, Program Administrator, Delaware Higher Education Commission, Carvel State Office Building, 820 North French Street, Fifth Floor, Wilmington, DE 19801-3509. *E-mail:* cbrinkley@doe.k12.de.us. *Phone:* 302-577-5240. *Fax:* 302-577-6765. *Web site:* www.doe.k12.de.us.

Educational Benefits for Children of Deceased Veterans and Others Award. Award for children between the ages of 16 and 24 of deceased/MIA/POW veterans or state police officers. Must have been a resident of Delaware for 3 or more years prior to the date of application. If the applicant's parent is a member of the armed forces, the parent must have been a resident of Delaware at the time of death or declaration of missing in action or prisoner of war status. Award will not exceed tuition and fees at a Delaware public college. *Award:* Grant for use in freshman, sophomore, junior, or senior year; renewable. *Award amount:* varies. *Number of awards:* varies. *Eligibility Requirements:* Applicant must be age 16-24; enrolled or expecting to enroll full-time at a two-year or four-year institution or university and resident of Delaware. Applicant or parent of applicant must have employment or volunteer experience in police/firefighting. Available to U.S. citizens. Applicant or parent must meet one or more of the following requirements: general military experience; retired from active duty; disabled or killed as a result of military service; prisoner of war; or missing in action. *Application Requirements:* Application, verification of service-related death. *Deadline:* continuous.

Contact Delaware Higher Education Commission. *Phone:* 302-577-5240. *Fax:* 302-577-6765. *Web site:* www.doe.k12.de.us.

Governor's Workforce Development Grant. Grants for part-time undergraduate students attending Delaware College of Art and Design, Delaware State University, Delaware Technical and Community College, Goldey-Beacom College, University of Delaware, Wesley College, Widener University (Delaware Campus), or Wilmington College. Must be at least 18 years old, a resident of Delaware, and employed by a company in Delaware that contributes to the Blue Collar Training Fund Program. *Award:* Grant for use in freshman, sophomore, junior, or senior year; renewable. *Award amount:* $2000. *Number of awards:* 40. *Eligibility Requirements:* Applicant must be age 18 and over; enrolled or expecting to enroll full- or part-time at a two-year or four-year institution or university; resident of Delaware and studying in Delaware. Available to U.S. and non-U.S. citizens. *Application Requirements:* Application. *Deadline:* varies.

Contact Carylin Brinkley, Program Administrator, Delaware Higher Education Commission, Carvel State Office Building, 820 North French Street, Fifth Floor, Wilmington, DE 19801-3509. *E-mail:* cbrinkley@doe.k12.de.us. *Phone:* 302-577-5240. *Fax:* 302-577-6765. *Web site:* www.doe.k12.de.us.

Legislative Essay Scholarship. Award for legal residents of Delaware who are U.S. citizens or eligible non-citizens. Must be high school seniors in public or private schools or in home school programs who plans to enroll full-time at a nonprofit, regionally accredited college. Must submit an essay on topic: "Pluribus Unum: Is this motto adopted in 1782 relevant to our country today?". *Award:* Prize for use in freshman year; not renewable. *Award amount:* $1000–$10,000. *Number of awards:* up to 62. *Eligibility Requirements:* Applicant must be high school student; planning to enroll or expecting to enroll full- or part-time at a two-year, four-year, or technical institution or university and resident of Delaware. Available to U.S. citizens. *Application Requirements:* Application, applicant must enter a contest, essay. *Deadline:* November 30.

Contact Carylin Brinkley, Program Administrator, Delaware Higher Education Commission, Carvel State Office Building, 820 North French Street, Fifth Floor, Wilmington, DE 19801-3509. *E-mail:* cbrinkley@doe.k12.de.us. *Phone:* 302-577-5240. *Fax:* 302-577-6765. *Web site:* www.doe.k12.de.us.

Robert C. Byrd Honors Scholarship-Delaware. Award for legal residents of Delaware who are U.S. citizens or eligible non-citizens. For high school seniors who rank in upper quarter of class or GED recipients with a minimum score of 300 and a combined score of at least 1800 on the SAT. Minimum 3.5 GPA required. Must be enrolled at least half-time at a nonprofit, regionally accredited institution. *Award:* Scholarship for use in freshman year; renewable. *Award amount:* $1500. *Number of awards:* 20. *Eligibility Requirements:* Applicant must be high school student; planning to enroll or expecting to enroll full-time at a two-year or four-year institution or university and resident of Delaware. Applicant must have 3.5 GPA or higher. Available to U.S. citizens. *Application Requirements:* Application, essay, test scores, transcript. *Deadline:* March 28.

Contact Carylin Brinkley, Program Administrator, Delaware Higher Education Commission, Carvel State Office Building, 820 North French Street, Fifth Floor, Wilmington, DE 19801-3509. *E-mail:* cbrinkley@doe.k12.de.us. *Phone:* 302-577-5240. *Fax:* 302-577-6765. *Web site:* www.doe.k12.de.us.

Scholarship Incentive Program-Delaware. Award for legal residents of Delaware who are U.S. citizens or eligible non-citizens. Must demonstrate substantial financial need and enroll full-time in an undergraduate degree program at a nonprofit, regionally accredited institution in Delaware or Pennsylvania. Minimum 2.5 GPA required. *Award:* Grant for use in freshman, sophomore, junior, senior, or graduate year; not renewable. *Award amount:* $700–$2200. *Number of awards:* 1000–1300. *Eligibility Requirements:* Applicant must be enrolled or expecting to enroll full-time at a two-year or four-year institution or university; resident of Delaware and studying in Delaware or Pennsylvania. Applicant must have 2.5 GPA or higher. Available to U.S. citizens. *Application Requirements:* Application, financial need analysis, transcript, FAFSA. *Deadline:* April 15.

Contact Carylin Brinkley, Program Administrator, Delaware Higher Education Commission, Carvel State Office Building, 820 North French Street, Fifth Floor, Wilmington, DE 19801-3509. *E-mail:* cbrinkley@doe.k12.de.us. *Phone:* 302-577-5240. *Fax:* 302-577-6765. *Web site:* www.doe.k12.de.us.

State Tuition Assistance. You must enlist in the Delaware National Guard to be eligible for this scholarship award. Award providing tuition assistance for any member of the Air or Army National Guard attending a Delaware two-year or four-year college. Awards are renewable. Applicant's minimum GPA must be 2.0. *Award:* Scholarship for use in freshman, sophomore, junior, or senior year; renewable. *Award amount:* up to $10,000. *Number of awards:* 1–300. *Eligibility Requirements:* Applicant must be enrolled or expecting to enroll full- or part-time at a two-year or four-year institution or university and studying in Delaware. Available to U.S. citizens. Applicant or parent must meet one or more of the following requirements: Air Force National Guard or Army National Guard experience; retired from active duty; disabled or killed as a result of military service; prisoner of war; or missing in action. *Application Requirements:* Application, transcript. *Deadline:* varies.

Contact M.Sgt. Robert Csizmadia, State Tuition Assistance Manager, Delaware National Guard, 1st Regiment Road, Wilmington, DE 19808-2191. *E-mail:* robert.csizmadi@de.ngb.army.mil. *Phone:* 302-326-7012. *Fax:* 302-326-7029. *Web site:* www.delawarenationalguard.com.

DISTRICT OF COLUMBIA

American Council of the Blind Scholarships. Merit-based award available to undergraduate students who are legally blind in both eyes. Submit certificate of legal blindness and proof of acceptance at an accredited postsecondary institution. *Award:* Scholarship for use in freshman, sophomore, junior, or senior year; renewable. *Award amount:* $1000–$2500. *Number of awards:* 16–20. *Eligibility Requirements:* Applicant must be enrolled or expecting to enroll full- or part-time at a four-year institution or university. Applicant must be visually impaired. Applicant must have 3.5 GPA or higher. Available to U.S. citizens. *Application Requirements:* Application, autobiography, essay, references, transcript, evidence of legal blindness, proof of post-secondary school acceptance. *Deadline:* March 1.

Contact Tatricia Castillo, Scholarship Coordinator, American Council of the Blind, 1155 15th Street, NW, Suite 1004, Washington, DC 20005. *E-mail:* tcastillo@acp.org. *Phone:* 202-467-5081. *Fax:* 202-467-5085. *Web site:* www.acb.org.

Bureau of Indian Education Grant Program. Grants are provided to supplement financial assistance to eligible American Indian/Alaska Native students entering college seeking a baccalaureate degree. A student must be a member of, or at least one-quarter degree Indian blood descendent of a member of an American Indian tribe who are eligible for the special programs and services provided by the United States through the Bureau of Indian Affairs to Indians because of their status as Indians. *Award:* Grant for use in freshman year; not renewable. *Award amount:* varies. *Number of awards:* varies. *Eligibility Requirements:* Applicant must be American Indian/Alaska Native; high school student and planning to enroll or expecting to enroll full-time at a two-year or four-year institution or university. Available to U.S. citizens. *Application Requirements:* Application, references, test scores, transcript. *Deadline:* varies.

Contact Paulina Bell, Office Automation Assistant, Bureau of Indian Affairs Office of Indian Education Programs, 1849 C Street, NW, MS 3609-MIB, Washington, DC 20240-0001. *Phone:* 202-208-6123. *Fax:* 202-208-3312. *Web site:* www.oiep.bia.edu.

Central Intelligence Agency Undergraduate Scholarship Program. Need and merit-based award for students with minimum 3.0 GPA, who are interested in working for the Central Intelligence Agency upon graduation. Renewable for four years of undergraduate study. Must apply in senior year of high school or sophomore year in college. For further information refer to Web site: http://www.cia.gov. *Academic Fields/Career Goals:* Accounting; Business/Consumer Services; Computer Science/Data Processing; Economics; Electrical Engineering/Electronics; Foreign Language; Geography; Graphics/Graphic Arts/Printing; International Studies; Political Science; Surveying; Surveying Technology, Cartography, or Geographic Information Science. *Award:* Scholarship for use in freshman, sophomore, junior, or senior year; renewable. *Award amount:* up to $18,000. *Number of awards:* varies. *Eligibility Requirements:* Applicant must be age 18 and over and enrolled or expecting to enroll full-time at a four-year institution or university. Applicant must have 3.0 GPA or higher. Available to U.S. citizens. *Application Requirements:* Application, financial need analysis, resume, references, test scores, transcript. *Deadline:* November 1.

Contact Van Patrick, Chief, College Relations, Central Intelligence Agency, Recruitment Center, L 100 LF7, Washington, DC 20505. *E-mail:* ivanilp0@ucia.gov. *Phone:* 703-613-8388. *Fax:* 703-613-7676. *Web site:* www.cia.gov.

Costas G. Lemonopoulos Scholarship. Scholarships to children of NALC members attending public, four-year colleges or universities supported by the state of Florida or St. Petersburg Junior College. Scholarships are renewable one time. *Award:* Scholarship for use in freshman, sophomore, junior, or senior year; renewable. *Award amount:* varies. *Number of awards:* 1–20. *Eligibility Requirements:* Applicant must be enrolled or expecting to enroll full-time at a two-year or four-year institution or university and studying in Florida. Applicant or parent of applicant must be member of National Association of Letter Carriers. Available to U.S. citizens. *Application Requirements:* Application, references, transcript. *Deadline:* June 1.

Contact National Association of Letter Carriers. *Web site:* www.nalc.org.

DC Leveraging Educational Assistance Partnership Program (LEAP). $250 to $1500 grants available to District of Columbia residents, who qualify for federal need-based aid and are enrolled in undergraduate programs, and pursuing a first baccalaureate degree. Must attend a Title IV eligible college or university at least half-time. *Award:* Grant for use in freshman, sophomore, junior, or senior year; renewable. *Award amount:* $250–$1500. *Number of awards:* up to 3200. *Eligibility Requirements:* Applicant must be enrolled or expecting to enroll full- or part-time at a two-year or four-year institution or university and resident of District of Columbia. Available to U.S. citizens. *Application Requirements:* Application, financial need analysis, transcript, Student Aid Report (SAR), FAFSA. *Deadline:* June 30.

Contact Ms. Rehva D. Jones, Director, Higher Education Financial Services and Preparatory Programs, District of Columbia Office of the State Superintendent, 51 N Street, NE, Lower Level, Washington, DC 20002. *E-mail:* rehva.jones@dc.gov. *Phone:* 202-481-3948. *Fax:* 202-741-6491. *Web site:* www.osse.dc.gov.

Federal Cyber Service: Scholarship For Service (SFS) Program. This program provides scholarships that generally fund books, tuition, room and board, and a stipend while attending a participating institution in an Information Assurance program. Participants must apply directly to participating institutions. *Award:* Scholarship for use in junior or senior year; renewable. *Number of awards:* 1. *Eligibility Requirements:* Applicant must be enrolled or expecting to enroll full-time at a four-year institution or university. Available to U.S. citizens. *Application Requirements:* Application. *Deadline:* varies.

Contact Office of Personnel Management. *Web site:* www.sfs.opm.gov.

Harry S. Truman Scholarship. Scholarships for U.S. citizens or U.S. nationals who are college or university students with junior-level academic standing and who wish to attend professional or graduate school to prepare for careers in government or the nonprofit and advocacy sectors. Candidates must be nominated by their institution. Public service and leadership record considered. Visit Web site: http://www.truman.gov for further information and application. *Academic Fields/Career Goals:* Political Science; Public Policy and Administration. *Award:* Scholarship for use in junior year; renewable. *Award amount:* $30,000. *Number of awards:* 65. *Eligibility Requirements:* Applicant must be enrolled or expecting to enroll full-time at a four-year institution or university and must have an interest in leadership. Available to U.S. citizens. *Application Requirements:* Application, interview, references, policy proposal. *Deadline:* February 5.

Contact Tonji Wade, Program Officer, Harry S. Truman Scholarship Foundation, 712 Jackson Place, NW, Washington, DC 20006. *E-mail:* office@truman.gov. *Phone:* 202-395-4831. *Fax:* 202-395-6995. *Web site:* www.truman.gov.

Montgomery GI Bill (Active Duty) Chapter 30. Award provides up to thirty-six months of education benefits to eligible veterans for college, business school, technical courses, vocational courses, correspondence courses, apprenticeships/job training, or flight training. Must be an eligible veteran with an Honorable Discharge and have high school diploma or GED before applying for benefits. *Award:* Scholarship for use in freshman, sophomore, junior, senior, or graduate year; renewable. *Award amount:* $1101–$37,224. *Number of awards:* varies. *Eligibility Requirements:* Applicant must be enrolled or expecting to enroll full- or part-time at a two-year, four-year, or technical institution or university. Available to U.S. citizens. Applicant or parent must meet one or more of the following requirements: general military experience; retired from active duty; disabled or killed as a result of military service; prisoner of war; or missing in action. *Application Requirements:* Application, proof of active military service of at least 2 years. *Deadline:* continuous.

Contact Keith M. Wilson, Director, Education Service, Department of Veterans Affairs (VA), 810 Vermont Avenue, NW, Washington, DC 20420. *E-mail:* co225a@vba.va.gov. *Phone:* 202-273-7132. *Web site:* www.gibill.va.gov.

Montgomery GI Bill (Selected Reserve). Educational assistance program for members of the selected reserve of the Army, Navy, Air Force, Marine Corps and Coast Guard, as well as the Army and Air National Guard. Available to all reservists and National Guard personnel who commit to a six-year obligation, and remain in the Reserve or Guard during the six years. Award is renewable. Monthly benefit is $309 for up to thirty-six months for full-time. *Award:* Scholarship for use in freshman, sophomore, junior, senior, or postgraduate years; renewable. *Award amount:* up to $3708. *Number of awards:* varies. *Eligibility Requirements:* Applicant must be enrolled or expecting to enroll full- or part-time at a two-year, four-year, or technical institution or university. Available to U.S. citizens. Applicant or parent must meet one or more of the following requirements: general military experience; retired from active duty; disabled or killed as a result of military service; prisoner of war; or missing in action. *Application Requirements:* Application, proof of military service of six years in the reserve or guard. *Deadline:* continuous.

Contact Keith M. Wilson, Director, Education Service, Department of Veterans Affairs (VA), 810 Vermont Avenue, NW, Washington, DC 20420. *E-mail:* co225a@vba.va.gov. *Phone:* 202-273-7132. *Web site:* www.gibill.va.gov.

Reserve Education Assistance Program. The program provides educational assistance to members of National Guard and reserve components. Selected Reserve and Individual Ready Reserve (IRR) who are called or ordered to active duty service in response to a war or national emergency as declared by the president or Congress are eligible. For further information see Web site: http://www.GIBILL.va.gov. *Award:* Scholarship for use in freshman, sophomore, junior, senior, graduate, or postgraduate years; renewable. *Award amount:* $215–$860. *Number of awards:* 1. *Eligibility Requirements:* Applicant must be enrolled or expecting to enroll full- or part-time at a two-year, four-year, or technical institution or university. Available to U.S. citizens. Applicant or parent must meet one or more of the following requirements: general military experience; retired from active duty; disabled or killed as a result of military service; prisoner of war; or missing in action. *Application Requirements:* Application. *Deadline:* continuous.

Contact Keith M. Wilson, Director, Education Service, Department of Veterans Affairs (VA), 810 Vermont Avenue, NW, Washington, DC 20420. *E-mail:* co225a@vba.va.gov. *Phone:* 202-273-7132. *Web site:* www.gibill.va.gov.

Robert C. Byrd Honors Scholarship-District of Columbia. Federally funded, state administered program to recognize exceptionally able high school seniors who show promise of continued excellence in postsecondary education. Must be a U.S. citizen and permanent resident of District of Columbia and be accepted at an accredited institution of higher education in the United States. Minimum 3.2 GPA required. Must be school's nominee. Renewable based on maintenance of satisfactory academic standing. *Award:* Scholarship for use in freshman year;

renewable. *Award amount:* $1500. *Number of awards:* 10. *Eligibility Requirements:* Applicant must be high school student; planning to enroll or expecting to enroll full-time at a four-year institution or university and resident of District of Columbia. Available to U.S. citizens. *Application Requirements:* Application, interview, test scores, transcript, 250-word essay on life goals, nominee form. **Deadline:** March 30.

Contact Claudia Nichols, Director of Student Affairs, District of Columbia Public Schools, 825 North Capitol Street, NE, Sixth Floor, Washington, DC 20002. *E-mail:* claudia.nichols@dc.gov. *Phone:* 202-442-5110. *Fax:* 202-442-5094. *Web site:* www.k12.dc.us.

Survivors and Dependents Educational Assistance (Chapter 35)-VA. Monthly $860 benefits for up to 45 months. Must be spouses or children under age 26 of current veterans missing in action or of deceased or totally and permanently disabled (service-related) service persons. For more information visit the following Web site: http://www.gibill.va.gov. *Award:* Scholarship for use in freshman, sophomore, junior, or senior year; renewable. *Award amount:* up to $10,320. *Number of awards:* 10,733. *Eligibility Requirements:* Applicant must be age 25 or under and enrolled or expecting to enroll full- or part-time at a two-year, four-year, or technical institution or university. Available to U.S. and non-U.S. citizens. Applicant or parent must meet one or more of the following requirements: general military experience; retired from active duty; disabled or killed as a result of military service; prisoner of war; or missing in action. *Application Requirements:* Application, proof of parent or spouse's qualifying service. **Deadline:** continuous.

Contact Keith M. Wilson, Director, Education Service, Department of Veterans Affairs (VA), 810 Vermont Avenue, NW, Washington, DC 20420. *E-mail:* co225a@vba.va.gov. *Phone:* 202-273-7132. *Web site:* www.gibill.va.gov.

Teaching Assistantship in France. Grants support American students as they teach English for 6-9 months in the French school system. Monthly stipend of about 780 euros (net) supports recipient in the life-style of a typical French student. Must be U.S. citizen or a permanent resident (not a French citizen). Proficiency in French is required. and may not have received a similar grant from the French government for the last three years. For additional information and application, visit Web site: http://www.frenchculture.org. *Academic Fields/Career Goals:* Education; Foreign Language. *Award:* Grant for use in junior or senior year; not renewable. *Award amount:* $1013. *Number of awards:* up to 1500. *Eligibility Requirements:* Applicant must be age 20-29; enrolled or expecting to enroll full- or part-time at a four-year institution or university and must have an interest in French language. Available to U.S. citizens. *Application Requirements:* Application, photo, references, self-addressed stamped envelope, transcript. *Fee:* $35.

Contact Cultural Services of the French Embassy. *Web site:* www.frenchculture.org.

United Health Foundation Latino Health Scholars Program. Scholarship for students of Hispanic background who plan to pursue a degree leading to a career in the health field. Must be high school seniors or graduates who plan to enroll in a full-time undergraduate or graduate course. Must maintain a 3.0 GPA and demonstrate commitment to working in underserved communities. *Award:* Scholarship for use in freshman, sophomore, junior, or senior year. *Award amount:* $2500–$5000. *Eligibility Requirements:* Applicant must be Hispanic and enrolled or expecting to enroll full-time at a two-year, four-year, or technical institution or university. Applicant must have 3.0 GPA or higher. Available to U.S. citizens. *Application Requirements:* Application, essay, financial need analysis, resume, references, transcript, proof of family income. **Deadline:** March 15.

Contact Hispanic College Fund. *Web site:* www.hispanicfund.org.

FLORIDA

Access to Better Learning and Education Grant. Grant program provides tuition assistance to Florida undergraduate students enrolled in degree programs at eligible private Florida colleges or universities. Must be a U.S. citizen or eligible non-citizen and must meet Florida residency requirements. The participating institution determines application procedures, deadlines, and student eligibility. *Award:* Grant for use in freshman, sophomore, junior, or senior year; renewable. *Award amount:* up to $1182. *Number of awards:* varies. *Eligibility Requirements:* Applicant must be enrolled or expecting to enroll full-time at a four-year institution or university; resident of Florida and studying in Florida. Available to U.S. citizens. *Application Requirements:* Application. **Deadline:** varies.

Contact Office of Student Financial Assistance, State Scholarship & Grant Programs, Florida State Department of Education, 1940 North Monroe Street, Suite 70, Talllahassee, FL 32303. *Phone:* 888-827-2007. *Web site:* www.floridastudentfinancialaid.org.

Critical Teacher Shortage Student Loan Forgiveness Program-Florida. Award program provides financial assistance to eligible Florida teachers who hold a valid Florida teachers certificate or Florida department of health license, by assisting them in the repayment of undergraduate and graduate educational loans that led to certification in a critical teacher shortage subject area. Must teach full-time at a publicly-funded school. *Academic Fields/Career Goals:* Education. *Award:* Forgivable loan for use in freshman, sophomore, junior, or senior year; renewable. *Award amount:* up to $10,000. *Number of awards:* varies. *Eligibility Requirements:* Applicant must be enrolled or expecting to enroll full- or part-time at a two-year or four-year institution or university and resident of Florida. Applicant or parent of applicant must have employment or volunteer experience in teaching/education. Available to U.S. citizens. *Application Requirements:* Application, transcript. **Deadline:** July 15.

Contact Office of Student Financial Assistance, State Scholarship & Grant Program, Florida State Department of Education, 1940 North Monroe Street, Suite 70, Tallahassee, FL 32303. *E-mail:* osfa@fldoe.org. *Phone:* 888-827-2004. *Web site:* www.floridastudentfinancialaid.org.

Ethics in Business Scholarship. Scholarship program provides assistance to undergraduate college students, who enroll at community colleges and eligible independent postsecondary educational institutions. Scholarships are funded by private and state contributions. Awards are dependent on private, matching funds. *Award:* Scholarship for use in freshman, sophomore, junior, or senior year; not renewable. *Award amount:* varies. *Number of awards:* varies. *Eligibility Requirements:* Applicant must be enrolled or expecting to enroll full-time at a two-year or four-year institution or university; resident of Florida and studying in Florida. Available to U.S. citizens. *Application Requirements:* Application. **Deadline:** varies.

Contact Office of Student Financial Assistance, State Scholarship & Grant Programs, Florida State Department of Education, 1940 North Monroe Street, Suite 70, Tallahassee, FL 32303. *E-mail:* osfa@fldoe.org. *Phone:* 888-827-2004. *Web site:* www.floridastudentfinancialaid.org.

First Generation Matching Grant Program. Need-based grants to Florida resident undergraduate students who are enrolled in state universities in Florida and whose parents have not earned baccalaureate degrees. Available state funds are contingent upon matching contributions from private sources on a dollar-for-dollar basis. *Award:* Grant for use in freshman, sophomore, junior, or senior year; renewable. *Award amount:* varies. *Number of awards:* varies. *Eligibility Requirements:* Applicant must be enrolled or expecting to enroll full- or part-time at an institution or university; resident of Florida and studying in Florida. Available to U.S. citizens. *Application Requirements:* Application, financial need analysis. **Deadline:** varies.

Contact Office of Student Financial Assistance, State Scholarship & Grant

Programs, Florida State Department of Education, 1940 North Monroe Street, Suite 70, Tallahassee, FL 32303. *E-mail:* osfa@fldoe.org. *Phone:* 888-828-2004. *Web site:* www.floridastudentfinancialaid.org.

Florida Bright Futures Scholarship Program. Three lottery-funded scholarships reward Florida high school graduates for high academic achievement. Program is comprised of the following three awards: Florida Academic Scholars Award, Florida Medallion Scholars Award and Florida Gold Seal Vocational Scholars Award. *Award:* Scholarship for use in freshman, sophomore, junior, or senior year; renewable. *Eligibility Requirements:* Applicant must be high school student; planning to enroll or expecting to enroll full- or part-time at a two-year, four-year, or technical institution or university; resident of Florida and studying in Florida. Applicant must have 3.0 GPA or higher. Available to U.S. citizens. *Application Requirements:* Application, test scores.

Contact Office of Student Financial Assistance, State Scholarship & Grant Programs, Florida State Department of Education, 1940 North Monroe Street, Suite 70, Tallahassee, FL 32303. *E-mail:* osfa@fldoe.org. *Phone:* 888-827-2004. *Web site:* www.floridastudentfinancialaid.org.

Florida Postsecondary Student Assistance Grant. Scholarships to degree-seeking, resident, undergraduate students who demonstrate substantial financial need and are enrolled in eligible degree-granting private colleges and universities not eligible under the Florida Private Student Assistance Grant. FSAG is a decentralized program, and each participating institution determines application procedures, deadlines and student eligibility. Number of awards varies. *Award:* Grant for use in freshman, sophomore, junior, or senior year; renewable. *Award amount:* \$200–\$1916. *Number of awards:* varies. *Eligibility Requirements:* Applicant must be enrolled or expecting to enroll full-time at a two-year or four-year institution or university; resident of Florida and studying in Florida. Available to U.S. citizens. *Application Requirements:* Application, financial need analysis. *Deadline:* varies.

Contact Office of Student Financial Assistance, State Scholarship & Grant Programs, Florida State Department of Education, 1940 North Monroe Street, Suite 70, Tallahassee, FL 32303. *E-mail:* osfa@fldoe.org. *Phone:* 888-827-2004. *Web site:* www.floridastudentfinancialaid.org.

Florida Private Student Assistance Grant. Grants for Florida residents who are U.S. citizens or eligible non-citizens attending eligible private, nonprofit, four-year colleges and universities in Florida. Must be a full-time student and demonstrate substantial financial need. For renewal, must have earned a minimum cumulative GPA of 2.0 at the last institution attended. *Award:* Grant for use in freshman, sophomore, junior, or senior year; renewable. *Award amount:* \$200–\$1916. *Number of awards:* varies. *Eligibility Requirements:* Applicant must be enrolled or expecting to enroll full-time at a four-year institution or university; resident of Florida and studying in Florida. Available to U.S. citizens. *Application Requirements:* Application, financial need analysis. *Deadline:* varies.

Contact Office of Student Financial Assistance, State Scholarship & Grant Programs, Florida State Department of Education, 1940 North Monroe Street, Suite 70, Tallahassee, FL 32303. *E-mail:* osfa@fldoe.org. *Phone:* 888-827-2004. *Web site:* www.floridastudentfinancialaid.org.

Florida Public Student Assistance Grant. Grants for Florida residents, U.S. citizens or eligible non-citizens who attend state universities and public community colleges. For renewal, must have earned a minimum cumulative GPA of 2.0 at the last institution attended. Students with documented disabilities are able to qualify for part-time status. *Award:* Grant for use in freshman, sophomore, junior, or senior year; renewable. *Award amount:* \$200–\$1916. *Number of awards:* varies. *Eligibility Requirements:* Applicant must be enrolled or expecting to enroll full- or part-time at a two-year or four-year institution or university; resident of Florida and studying in Florida. Available to U.S. citizens. *Application Requirements:* Application, financial need analysis. *Deadline:* varies.

Contact Office of Student Financial Assistance, State Scholarship & Grant Programs, Florida State Department of Education, 1940 North Monroe Street, Suite 70, Tallahassee, FL 32303. *E-mail:* osfa@fldoe.org. *Phone:* 888-827-2004. *Web site:* www.floridastudentfinancialaid.org.

Florida Student Assistance Grant-Career Education. Need-based grant program available to Florida residents enrolled in certificate programs of 450 or more clock hours at participating community colleges or career centers operated by district school boards. FSAG-CE is a decentralized state of Florida program, which means that each participating institution determines application procedures, deadlines, student eligibility, and award amounts. *Award:* Grant for use in freshman, sophomore, junior, or senior year; renewable. *Award amount:* \$200–\$1916. *Eligibility Requirements:* Applicant must be enrolled or expecting to enroll full- or part-time at a two-year or technical institution; resident of Florida and studying in Florida. Available to U.S. citizens. *Application Requirements:* Application, financial need analysis.

Contact Office of Student Financial Assistance, State Scholarship & Grant Programs, Florida State Department of Education, 1940 North Monroe Street, Suite 70, Tallahassee, FL 32303. *E-mail:* osfa@fldoe.org. *Phone:* 888-847-2004. *Web site:* www.floridastudentfinancialaid.org.

Florida Work Experience Program. Need-based program providing eligible Florida students work experiences that will complement and reinforce their educational and career goals. Must maintain GPA of 2.0. Postsecondary institution will determine applicant's eligibility, number of hours to be worked per week, and the award amount. *Award:* Grant for use in freshman, sophomore, junior, or senior year; renewable. *Award amount:* varies. *Number of awards:* varies. *Eligibility Requirements:* Applicant must be enrolled or expecting to enroll full- or part-time at a two-year or four-year institution or university; resident of Florida and studying in Florida. Available to U.S. citizens. *Application Requirements:* Application, financial need analysis. *Deadline:* varies.

Contact Office of Student Financial Assistance, State Scholarship & Grant Programs, Florida State Department of Education, 1940 North Monroe Street, Suite 70, Tallahassee, FL 32303. *E-mail:* osfa@fldoe.com. *Phone:* 888-827-2004. *Web site:* www.floridastudentfinancialaid.org.

Jose Marti Scholarship Challenge Grant Fund. Award available to Hispanic-American students who were born in, or whose parent was born in a Hispanic country. Must have lived in Florida for one year, be enrolled full-time in Florida at an eligible school, and have a GPA of 3.0 or above. Must be U.S. citizen or eligible non-citizen. FAFSA must be processed by May 15. For more information, visit Web site: www.floridastudentfinancialaid.org/ssfad/home/applyhere.htm. *Award:* Scholarship for use in freshman, sophomore, junior, or senior year; renewable. *Award amount:* \$2000. *Number of awards:* varies. *Eligibility Requirements:* Applicant must be of Hispanic heritage; enrolled or expecting to enroll full-time at a two-year, four-year, or technical institution or university; resident of Florida and studying in Florida. Applicant must have 3.0 GPA or higher. Available to U.S. citizens. *Application Requirements:* Application, financial need analysis. *Deadline:* April 1.

Contact Office of Student Financial Assistance, State Scholarship & Grant Programs, Florida State Department of Education, 1940 North Monroe Street, Suite 70, Tallahassee, FL 32303. *E-mail:* osfa@fldoe.org. *Phone:* 888-827-2004. *Web site:* www.floridastudentfinancialaid.org.

Mary McLeod Bethune Scholarship. Renewable award to Florida students with a GPA of 3.0 or above, who will attend Bethune-Cookman College, Edward Waters College, Florida A&M University, or Florida Memorial University. Must not have previously received a baccalaureate degree. Must demonstrate financial need as specified by the institution. *Award:* Scholarship for use in freshman, sophomore, junior, or senior year; renewable. *Award amount:* $3000. *Number of awards:* varies. *Eligibility Requirements:* Applicant must be enrolled or expecting to enroll full-time at a two-year or four-year institution or university; resident of Florida and studying in Florida. Applicant must have 3.0 GPA or higher. Available to U.S. citizens. *Application Requirements:* Application, financial need analysis.

Contact Office of Student Financial Assistance, State Scholarship & Grant Programs, Florida State Department of Education, 1940 North Monroe Street, Suite 70, Tallahassee, FL 32303. *E-mail:* osfa@fldoe.org. *Phone:* 888-827-2004. *Web site:* www.floridastudentfinancialaid.org.

Robert C. Byrd Honors Scholarship-Florida. One applicant per Florida high school may be nominated by the high school principal or designee by May 15. Must be U.S. citizen or eligible non-citizen and Florida resident. Application must be submitted in the same year as graduation. Must meet selective service system registration requirements. May attend any postsecondary accredited institution. *Award:* Scholarship for use in freshman, sophomore, junior, or senior year; renewable. *Award amount:* $1500. *Eligibility Requirements:* Applicant must be high school student; planning to enroll or expecting to enroll full-time at a technical institution and resident of Florida. Available to U.S. citizens. *Application Requirements:* Application, references, test scores, transcript. *Deadline:* April 15.

Contact Office of Student Financial Assistance, State Scholarship & Grant Programs, Florida State Department of Education, 1940 North Monroe Street, Suite 70, Tallahassee, FL 32303. *E-mail:* osfa@fldoe.org. *Phone:* 888-827-2004. *Web site:* www.floridastudentfinancialaid.org.

Rosewood Family Scholarship Fund. Renewable award for eligible minority students to enable them to attend a Florida public postsecondary institution on a full-time basis. Preference given to direct descendants of African-American Rosewood families affected by the incidents of January 1923. Must be Black, Hispanic, Asian, Pacific Islander, American Indian, or Alaska Native. Must not have previously received a baccalaureate degree. *Award:* Scholarship for use in freshman, sophomore, junior, or senior year; renewable. *Award amount:* up to $4000. *Number of awards:* up to 25. *Eligibility Requirements:* Applicant must be American Indian/Alaska Native, Asian/Pacific Islander, Black (non-Hispanic), or Hispanic; enrolled or expecting to enroll full-time at a two-year, four-year, or technical institution or university and studying in Florida. Available to U.S. citizens. *Application Requirements:* Application, financial need analysis. *Deadline:* April 1.

Contact Office of Student Financial Assistance, State Scholarship & Grant Programs, Florida State Department of Education, 1940 North Monroe Street, Suite 70, Tallahassee, FL 32303. *E-mail:* osfa@fldoe.org. *Phone:* 888-827-2004. *Web site:* www.floridastudentfinancialaid.org.

Scholarships for Children & Spouses of Deceased or Disabled Veterans or Servicemembers. Renewable scholarships for children and spouses of deceased or disabled veterans and service members. Children must be between the ages of 16 and 22, and attend an eligible Florida public, nonpublic postsecondary institution or enrolled part-time. Must ensure that the Florida Department of Veterans Affairs certifies the applicants eligibility. Must maintain GPA of 2.0. *Award:* Scholarship for use in freshman, sophomore, junior, or senior year; renewable. *Award amount:* varies. *Number of awards:* varies. *Eligibility Requirements:* Applicant must be age 16-22; enrolled or expecting to enroll full- or part-time at a two-year, four-year, or technical institution or university; resident of Florida and studying in Florida. Available to U.S. citizens. Applicant or parent must meet one or more of the following requirements: general military experience; retired from active duty; disabled or killed as a result of military service; prisoner of war; or missing in action. *Application Requirements:* Application. *Deadline:* April 1.

Contact Office of Student Financial Assistance, State Scholarship & Grant Programs, Florida State Department of Education, 1940 North Monroe Street, Suite 70, Tallahassee, FL 32303-4759. *Phone:* 888-827-2004. *Web site:* www.floridastudentfinancialaid.org.

William L. Boyd IV Florida Resident Access Grant. Renewable awards to Florida undergraduate students attending an eligible private, nonprofit Florida college or university. Postsecondary institution will determine applicant's eligibility. Renewal applicant must have earned a minimum institutional GPA of 2.0. *Award:* Grant for use in freshman, sophomore, junior, or senior year; renewable. *Award amount:* up to $2837. *Number of awards:* varies. *Eligibility Requirements:* Applicant must be enrolled or expecting to enroll full-time at a four-year institution or university; resident of Florida and studying in Florida. Available to U.S. citizens. *Application Requirements:* Application. *Deadline:* varies.

Contact Office of Student Financial Assistance, State Scholarship & Grant Programs, Florida State Department of Education, 1940 North Monroe Street, Suite 70, Tallahassee, FL 32303. *E-mail:* osfa@fldoe.org. *Phone:* 888-827-2004. *Web site:* www.floridastudentfinancialaid.org.

GEORGIA

American Indian Nurse Scholarship Awards. Renewable award of $500 to $1000. Currently able to fund between 10 and 15 students. Intended originally to benefit females only, the program has expanded to include males and the career goals now include not only nursing careers, but jobs in health care and health education, as well. *Academic Fields/Career Goals:* Health Administration; Nursing. *Award:* Scholarship for use in freshman, sophomore, junior, senior, graduate, or postgraduate years; renewable. *Award amount:* $500–$1000. *Number of awards:* 10–15. *Eligibility Requirements:* Applicant must be American Indian/Alaska Native and enrolled or expecting to enroll full-time at a two-year, four-year, or technical institution or university. Applicant must have 2.5 GPA or higher. Available to U.S. citizens. *Application Requirements:* Application, autobiography, financial need analysis, photo, references, transcript. *Deadline:* continuous.

Contact Mrs. Joe Calvin, Scholarship Awards Consultant, National Society of The Colonial Dames of America, Nine Cross Creek Drive, Birmingham, AL 35213. *E-mail:* info@nscda.org. *Phone:* 205-871-4072. *Web site:* www.nscda.org.

Georgia Leveraging Educational Assistance Partnership Grant Program. Awards based on financial need. Recipients must be eligible for the Federal Pell Grant. Renewable award for Georgia residents enrolled in a state postsecondary institution. Must be U.S. citizen. *Award:* Grant for use in freshman, sophomore, junior, or senior year; renewable. *Award amount:* $300–$2000. *Number of awards:* 2500–3000. *Eligibility Requirements:* Applicant must be enrolled or expecting to enroll full- or part-time at a two-year, four-year, or technical institution or university; resident of Georgia and studying in Georgia. Available to U.S. citizens. *Application Requirements:* Application, financial need analysis. *Deadline:* continuous.

Contact Georgia Student Finance Commission. *Web site:* www.gacollege411.org.

Georgia National Guard Service Cancelable Loan Program. Forgivable loans will be awarded to residents of Georgia maintaining good military standing as an eligible member of the Georgia National Guard who are enrolled at least half-time in an undergraduate degree program at an eligible college, university or technical school within the state of Georgia. *Award:* Forgivable loan for use in freshman, sophomore, junior, or senior year; not renewable. *Award amount:* $150–$1821. *Number of awards:* 200–250. *Eligibility Requirements:* Applicant must be enrolled or expecting to enroll full- or part-time at a two-year, four-year, or technical institution or university; resident of Georgia and studying in Georgia. Available to U.S. citizens. Applicant or parent must meet one or more of the following requirements: Air Force National Guard or Army National Guard experience; retired from active duty; disabled or killed as a result of military service; prisoner of war; or missing in action. *Application Requirements:* Application, financial need analysis. *Deadline:* June 4.

Contact State of Georgia. *Web site:* www.gsfc.org.

Georgia PROMISE Teacher Scholarship Program. Renewable, forgivable loans for junior undergraduates at Georgia colleges who have been accepted for enrollment into a teacher education program leading to initial certification. Minimum cumulative 3.0 GPA required. Recipient must teach at a Georgia public school for one year for each $1500 awarded. Available to seniors for renewal only. Write for deadlines. *Academic Fields/Career Goals:* Education. *Award:* Forgivable loan for use in junior or senior year; not renewable. *Award amount:* $3000–$6000. *Number of awards:* 700–1500. *Eligibility Requirements:* Applicant must be enrolled or expecting to enroll full- or part-time at a four-year institution or university; resident of Georgia and studying in Georgia. Applicant must have 3.0 GPA or higher. Available to U.S. citizens. *Application Requirements:* Application, transcript, selective service registration, official certification of admittance into an approved teacher education program in Georgia. *Deadline:* continuous.

Contact Stan DeWitt, Manager of Teacher Scholarships, Georgia Student Finance Commission, 2082 East Exchange Place, Suite 100, Tucker, GA 30084. *E-mail:* stand@gsfc.org. *Phone:* 770-724-9060. *Fax:* 770-724-9031. *Web site:* www.gacollege411.org.

Georgia Public Safety Memorial Grant/Law Enforcement Personnel Department Grant. Award for children of Georgia law enforcement officers, prison guards, or fire fighters killed or permanently disabled in the line of duty. Must attend an accredited postsecondary Georgia school. Complete the Law Enforcement Personnel Dependents application. *Award:* Grant for use in freshman, sophomore, junior, or senior year; not renewable. *Award amount:* $2000. *Number of awards:* 20–40. *Eligibility Requirements:* Applicant must be enrolled or expecting to enroll full-time at a two-year, four-year, or technical institution or university; resident of Georgia and studying in Georgia. Applicant or parent of applicant must have employment or volunteer experience in police/firefighting. Available to U.S. citizens. *Application Requirements:* Application, selective service registration. *Deadline:* continuous.

Contact Tracy Irleand, Vice President, Georgia Student Finance Commission, 2082 East Exchange Place, Suite 100, Tucker, GA 30084. *E-mail:* tracyi@gsfc.org. *Phone:* 770-724-9000. *Web site:* www.gacollege411.org.

Georgia Tuition Equalization Grant (GTEG). Award for Georgia residents pursuing undergraduate study at an accredited two- or four-year Georgia private institution. Also available to residents of Georgia who live near the State borders to attend certain four-year public colleges out-of-state. *Award:* Grant for use in freshman, sophomore, junior, or senior year; renewable. *Award amount:* $1100. *Number of awards:* 1–35,000. *Eligibility Requirements:* Applicant must be enrolled or expecting to enroll full-time at a two-year or four-year institution or university; resident of Georgia and studying in Alabama, Florida, Georgia, South Carolina, or Tennessee. Available to U.S. citizens. *Application Requirements:* Application, social security number. *Deadline:* continuous.

Contact Tracy Ireland, Vice President, Georgia Student Finance Commission, 2082 East Exchange Place, Suite 100, Tucker, GA 30084. *E-mail:* tracyi@gsfc.org. *Phone:* 770-724-9000. *Web site:* www.gacollege411.org.

Governor's Scholarship-Georgia. Award to assist students selected as Georgia STAR students, or valedictorians. For use at two- and four-year colleges and universities in Georgia. Recipients are selected as entering freshmen. Renewable award of up to $900. Minimum 3.0 GPA required. For information, see Web: www.gacollege411.org. *Award:* Scholarship for use in freshman year; renewable. *Award amount:* up to $900. *Number of awards:* 1000–2000. *Eligibility Requirements:* Applicant must be high school student; planning to enroll or expecting to enroll full-time at a two-year or four-year institution or university; resident of Georgia and studying in Georgia. Applicant must have 3.0 GPA or higher. Available to U.S. citizens. *Application Requirements:* Application, transcript. *Deadline:* continuous.

Contact Tracy Ireland, Vice President, Georgia Student Finance Commission, 2082 East Exchange Place, Suite 100, Tucker, GA 30084. *E-mail:* tracyi@gsfc.org. *Phone:* 770-724-9000. *Web site:* www.gacollege411.org.

HOPE—Helping Outstanding Pupils Educationally. Scholarship and Grant program for Georgia residents who are college undergraduates to attend an accredited two or four-year Georgia institution. Amount up to $3500 for full-time study or $1750 for part-time. Minimum 3.0 GPA required. Renewable if student maintains grades. Write for deadlines. *Award:* Scholarship for use in freshman, sophomore, junior, or senior year; renewable. *Award amount:* $1750–$3500. *Number of awards:* 200,000–210,000. *Eligibility Requirements:* Applicant must be enrolled or expecting to enroll full- or part-time at a two-year or four-year institution or university; resident of Georgia and studying in Georgia. Applicant must have 3.0 GPA or higher. Available to U.S. citizens. *Application Requirements:* Application, high schools must report transcripts to GSFC. *Deadline:* continuous.

Contact Tracy Ireland, Vice President, Georgia Student Finance Commission, 2082 East Exchange Place, Suite 100, Tucker, GA 30084. *E-mail:* tracyi@gsfc.org. *Phone:* 770-724-9000. *Web site:* www.gacollege411.org.

Service-Cancelable Stafford Loan-Georgia. Scholarship assists Georgia students enrolled in critical fields of study in allied health. For use at GSFA-approved schools. Awards $4500 forgivable loan for dentistry students only. Contact school financial aid officer for more details. *Academic Fields/Career Goals:* Dental Health/Services; Health and Medical Sciences; Nursing; Therapy/Rehabilitation. *Award:* Forgivable loan for use in freshman, sophomore, junior, or senior year; not renewable. *Award amount:* $2000–$4500. *Number of awards:* 500–1200. *Eligibility Requirements:* Applicant must be enrolled or expecting to enroll full- or part-time at a two-year, four-year, or technical institution or university; resident of Georgia and studying in Georgia. Available to U.S. citizens. *Application Requirements:* Application, financial need analysis. *Deadline:* continuous.

Contact State of Georgia. *Web site:* www.gsfc.org.

HAWAII

Hawaii State Student Incentive Grant. Grants are given to residents of Hawaii who are enrolled in a participating Hawaiian state school. Funds are for undergraduate tuition only. Applicants must submit a financial need analysis. *Award:* Grant for use in freshman, sophomore, junior, or senior year; renewable. *Award amount:* $200–$2000. *Number of awards:* 470. *Eligibility Requirements:* Applicant must be enrolled or expecting to enroll full- or part-time at a two-year, four-year, or technical institution or university; resident of Hawaii and studying in Hawaii. Available to U.S. citizens. *Application Requirements:* Application, financial need analysis. *Deadline:* continuous.

Contact Janine Oyama, Financial Aid Specialist, Hawaii State Postsecondary Education Commission, University of Hawaii, Honolulu, HI 96822. *Phone:* 808-956-6066.

IDAHO

Freedom Scholarship. Full tuition, room and board scholarship and up to $500 for books per semester for children of Idaho citizens determined by the federal government to have been prisoners of war, missing in action, or killed in action or died of injuries or wounds sustained in action in southeast Asia, including Korea, or who shall become so hereafter, in any area of armed conflicts. Applicant must attend an Idaho public college or university and meet all requirements for regular admission. The award value and the number of awards granted varies. For additional information, see Web site: http://www.boardofed.idaho.gov/scholarships/. *Award:* Scholarship for use in freshman, sophomore, junior, or senior year; not renewable. *Award amount:* varies. *Number of awards:* varies. *Eligibility Requirements:* Applicant must be enrolled or expecting to enroll full- or part-time at a two-year, four-year, or technical institution or university; resident of Idaho and studying in Idaho. Available to U.S. citizens. Applicant or parent must meet one or more of the following requirements: general military experience; retired from active duty; disabled or killed as a result of military service; prisoner of war; or missing in action. *Application Requirements:* Application. *Deadline:* January 15.

Contact Dana Kelly, Program Manager, Idaho State Board of Education, PO Box 83720, Boise, ID 83720-0037. *E-mail:* dana.kelly@osbe.idaho.gov. *Phone:* 208-332-1574. *Web site:* www.boardofed.idaho.gov.

Idaho Minority and "At Risk"; Student Scholarship. Renewable award for Idaho residents who are disabled or members of a minority group and have financial need. Must attend one of eight postsecondary institutions in the state for undergraduate study. Deadlines vary by institution. Must be a U.S. citizen and be a graduate of an Idaho high school. Contact college financial aid office. The awards range up to $3000 a year for a maximum of four years. For additional information, go to Web site: http://www.boardofed.idaho.gov/scholarships/. *Award:* Scholarship for use in freshman, sophomore, junior, or senior year; renewable. *Award amount:* up to $3000. *Number of awards:* 35–40. *Eligibility Requirements:* Applicant must be American Indian/Alaska Native, Black (non-Hispanic), or Hispanic; enrolled or expecting to enroll full-time at a two-year, four-year, or technical institution or university; resident of Idaho and studying in Idaho. Applicant must be hearing impaired, physically disabled, or visually impaired. Available to U.S. citizens. *Application Requirements:* Application, financial need analysis, transcript. *Deadline:* varies.

Contact Dana Kelly, Program Manager, Idaho State Board of Education, PO Box 83720, Boise, ID 83720-0037. *E-mail:* dana.kelly@osbe.idaho.gov. *Phone:* 208-332-1574. *Web site:* www.boardofed.idaho.gov.

Idaho Promise Category A Scholarship Program. Renewable award available to Idaho residents who are graduating high school seniors. Must attend an approved Idaho institution of higher education on full-time basis and be enrolled in an eligible program. Must have a minimum GPA of 3.5 and an ACT score of 28 or above if enrolling in an academic program, and a GPA of 2.8 and must take the COMPASS test if enrolling in a professional-technical program. For additional information, list of eligible programs, and application, go to Web site: http://www.boardofed.idaho.gov/scholarships/. *Award:* Scholarship for use in freshman year; renewable. *Award amount:* $3000. *Number of awards:* 25. *Eligibility Requirements:* Applicant must be high school student; planning to enroll or expecting to enroll full-time at a two-year, four-year, or technical institution or university; resident of Idaho and studying in Idaho. Available to U.S. citizens. *Application Requirements:* Application, applicant must enter a contest, test scores. *Deadline:* January 15.

Contact Idaho State Board of Education. *Web site:* www.boardofed.idaho.gov.

Idaho Promise Category B Scholarship Program. Available to Idaho residents entering college for the first time prior to the age of 22. Must have completed high school or its equivalent in Idaho and have a minimum GPA of 3.0 or an ACT score of 20 or higher. Scholarship limited to four semesters. Please go to Web site for complete information: http://www.boardofed.idaho.gov/scholarships/. *Award:* Scholarship for use in freshman year; renewable. *Award amount:* up to $600. *Number of awards:* varies. *Eligibility Requirements:* Applicant must be high school student; age 22 or under; planning to enroll or expecting to enroll full-time at a two-year, four-year, or technical institution or university; resident of Idaho and studying in Idaho. Applicant must have 3.0 GPA or higher. Available to U.S. citizens. *Application Requirements:* Application, transcript. *Deadline:* continuous.

Contact Dana Kelly, Program Manager, Idaho State Board of Education, PO Box 83720, Boise, ID 83720-0037. *E-mail:* dana.kelly@osbe.idaho.gov. *Phone:* 208-332-1574. *Fax:* 208-334-2632. *Web site:* www.boardofed.idaho.gov.

Leveraging Educational Assistance State Partnership Program (LEAP). One-time award assists students from any state, attending participating Idaho trade schools, colleges, and universities, and majoring in any field except theology or divinity. Must be enrolled for at least six credits and show financial need. Must be U.S. citizen or permanent resident. Deadlines vary by institution. For a list of eligible institutions, go to Web site: http://www.boardofed.idaho.gov/scholarships/. *Award:* Grant for use in freshman, sophomore, junior, or senior year; not renewable. *Award amount:* $400–$5000. *Number of awards:* varies. *Eligibility Requirements:* Applicant must be enrolled or expecting to enroll full- or part-time at a two-year, four-year, or technical institution or university and studying in Idaho. Available to U.S. citizens. *Application Requirements:* Application, financial need analysis, self-addressed stamped envelope. *Deadline:* varies.

Contact Dana Kelly, Student Affairs, Idaho State Board of Education, PO Box 83720, Boise, ID 83720-0037. *Phone:* 208-332-1574. *Fax:* 208-334-2632. *Web site:* www.boardofed.idaho.gov.

Public Safety Officer Dependent Scholarship. Scholarship for dependents of full-time Idaho public safety officers who were killed or disabled in the line of duty. Recipients will attend an Idaho postsecondary institution with a full waiver of fees, including tuition, on-campus housing and campus meal plan, and up to $500 per semester for books and supplies. For complete information, see Web site: http://www.boardofed.idaho.gov/scholarships/. *Award:* Scholarship for use in freshman year; renewable. *Number of awards:* varies. *Eligibility Requirements:* Applicant must be enrolled or expecting to enroll full- or part-time at a two-year or four-year institution or university; resident of Idaho and studying in Idaho. Applicant or parent of applicant must have employment or volunteer experience in police/firefighting. Available to U.S. citizens. *Application Requirements:* Application. *Deadline:* January 15.

Contact Dana Kelly, Program Manager, Idaho State Board of Education, PO Box 83720, Boise, ID 83720-0037. *E-mail:* dana.kelly@osbe.idaho.gov. *Phone:* 208-332-1574. *Web site:* www.boardofed.idaho.gov.

ILLINOIS

Golden Apple Scholars of Illinois. Applicants must be between the ages of 16 and 21 and maintain a GPA of 2.5. Eligible applicants must be residents of Illinois studying in Illinois. Recipients must agree to teach in high-need Illinois schools. *Academic Fields/Career Goals:* Education. *Award:* Scholarship for use in freshman, sophomore, junior, or senior year; renewable. *Award amount:* $4500. *Number of awards:* 125. *Eligibility Requirements:* Applicant must be age 16-21; enrolled or expecting to enroll full-time at a four-year institution or university; resident of Illinois and studying in Illinois. Applicant must have 2.5 GPA or higher. Available to U.S. citizens. *Application Requirements:* Application, autobiography, essay, interview, photo, references, test scores, transcript. *Deadline:* December 1.

Contact Ms. Patricia Kilduff, Director of Recruitment and Placement, Golden Apple Foundation, 8 South Michigan Avenue, Suite 700, Chicago, IL 60603-3318. *E-mail:* kilduff@goldenapple.org. *Phone:* 312-407-0006 Ext. 105. *Fax:* 312-407-0344. *Web site:* www.goldenapple.org.

Grant Program for Dependents of Police, Fire, or Correctional Officers. Awards available to Illinois residents who are dependents of police, fire, and correctional officers killed or disabled in line of duty. Provides for tuition and fees at approved Illinois institutions. Number of grants and individual dollar amount awarded vary. *Award:* Grant for use in freshman, sophomore, junior, senior, graduate, or postgraduate years; renewable. *Award amount:* varies. *Number of awards:* varies. *Eligibility Requirements:* Applicant must be enrolled or expecting to enroll full- or part-time at a two-year, four-year, or technical institution or university; resident of Illinois and studying in Illinois. Applicant or parent of applicant must have employment or volunteer experience in police/firefighting. Available to U.S. citizens. *Application Requirements:* Application, proof of status. *Deadline:* varies.

Contact College Zone Counselor, Illinois Student Assistance Commission (ISAC), 1755 Lake Cook Road, Deerfield, IL 60015-5209. *E-mail:* collegezone@isac.org. *Phone:* 800-899-4722. *Web site:* www.collegezone.org.

Higher Education License Plate Program-HELP. Need-based grants for students who are Illinois residents and attend approved Illinois colleges. May be eligible to receive the grant for the equivalent of 10 semesters of full-time enrollment. Number of grants made through this program and the individual dollar amount awarded varies. *Award:* Grant for use in freshman, sophomore, junior, or senior year; not renewable. *Award amount:* varies. *Number of awards:* varies. *Eligibility Requirements:* Applicant must be enrolled or expecting to enroll full- or part-time at a two-year or four-year institution or university; resident of Illinois and studying in Illinois. Available to U.S. citizens. *Application Requirements:* Application, financial need analysis, FAFSA. *Deadline:* varies.

Contact College Zone Counselor, Illinois Student Assistance Commission (ISAC), 1755 Lake Cook Road, Deerfield, IL 60015-5209. *E-mail:* collegezone@isac.org. *Phone:* 800-899-4722. *Web site:* www.collegezone.org.

Illinois College Savings Bond Bonus Incentive Grant Program. Program offers Illinois college savings bond holders a grant for each year of bond maturity payable upon bond redemption if at least 70 percent of proceeds are used to attend college in Illinois. The amount of grant will depend on the amount of the bond, ranging from a $40 to $440 grant per $5000 of the bond. Applications are accepted between August 1 and May 30 of the academic year in which the bonds matured, or in the academic year immediately following maturity. *Award:* Grant for use in freshman, sophomore, junior, senior, graduate, or postgraduate years; not renewable. *Number of awards:* varies. *Eligibility Requirements:* Applicant must be enrolled or expecting to enroll full- or part-time at a two-year, four-year, or technical institution or university and studying in Illinois. Available to U.S. citizens. *Application Requirements:* Application. *Deadline:* varies.

Contact College Zone Counselor, Illinois Student Assistance Commission (ISAC), 1755 Lake Cook Road, Deerfield, IL 60015-5209. *E-mail:* collegezone@isac.org. *Phone:* 800-899-4722. *Web site:* www.collegezone.org.

Illinois Future Teachers Corps Program. Scholarships are available for students planning to become teachers in Illinois. Students must be Illinois residents, enrolled or accepted as a junior or above in a Teacher Education Program at an Illinois college or university. By receiving the award, students agree to teach for five years at either a public, private, or parochial Illinois preschool, or at a public elementary or secondary school. *Academic Fields/Career Goals:* Education. *Award:* Forgivable loan for use in junior, senior, or graduate year; renewable. *Award amount:* $5000–$15,000. *Number of awards:* 1150. *Eligibility Requirements:* Applicant must be enrolled or expecting to enroll full- or part-time at a four-year institution or university; resident of Illinois and studying in Illinois. Applicant must have 2.5 GPA or higher. Available to U.S. citizens. *Application Requirements:* Application, financial need analysis, FAFSA. *Deadline:* March 1.

Contact College Zone Counselor, Illinois Student Assistance Commission (ISAC), 1755 Lake Cook Road, Deerfield, IL 60015-5209. *E-mail:* collegezone@isac.org. *Phone:* 800-899-4722. *Web site:* www.collegezone.org.

Illinois General Assembly Scholarship. Scholarships available for Illinois students enrolled at an Illinois four-year state-supported college. Must contact the general assembly member for eligibility criteria. Deadline varies. *Award:* Scholarship for use in freshman, sophomore, junior, or senior year; not renewable. *Award amount:* varies. *Number of awards:* varies. *Eligibility Requirements:* Applicant must be enrolled or expecting to enroll full- or part-time at a four-year institution or university; resident of Illinois and studying in Illinois. Available to U.S. citizens. *Application Requirements:* Application. *Deadline:* varies.

Contact College Zone Counselor, Illinois Student Assistance Commission (ISAC), 1755 Lake Cook Road, Deerfield, IL 60015-5209. *E-mail:* collegezone@isac.org. *Phone:* 800-899-4722. *Web site:* www.collegezone.org.

Illinois Monetary Award Program. Awards to Illinois residents enrolled in a minimum of 3 hours per term in a degree program at an approved Illinois institution. See Web site for complete list of participating schools. Must demonstrate financial need, based on the information provided on the Free Application for Federal Student Aid. Number of grants and the individual dollar amount awarded vary. Deadlines: August 15 and September 30. *Award:* Grant for use in freshman, sophomore, junior, or senior year; renewable. *Award amount:* $2365. *Number of awards:* 146,853. *Eligibility Requirements:* Applicant must be enrolled or expecting to enroll full- or part-time at a two-year, four-year, or technical institution or university; resident of Illinois and studying in Illinois. Available to U.S. citizens. *Application Requirements:* Financial need analysis, FAFSA online. *Deadline:* varies.

Contact College Zone Counselor, Illinois Student Assistance Commission (ISAC), 1755 Lake Cook Road, Deerfield, IL 60015-5209. *E-mail:* collegezone@isac.org. *Phone:* 800-899-4722. *Web site:* www.collegezone.org.

Illinois National Guard Grant Program. Active duty members of the Illinois National Guard, or who are within 12 months of discharge, and who have completed one full year of service are eligible. May be used for study at Illinois two- or four-year public colleges for a maximum of the equivalent of four academic years of full-time enrollment. Deadlines: October 1 of the academic year for full year, March 1 for second/third term, or June 15 for the summer term. *Award:* Grant for use in freshman, sophomore, junior, senior, or graduate year; renewable. *Award amount:* varies. *Number of awards:* varies. *Eligibility Requirements:* Applicant must be enrolled or expecting to enroll full- or part-time at a two-year or four-year institution or university; resident of Illinois and studying in Illinois. Available to U.S. citizens. Applicant or parent must meet one or more of the following requirements: Air Force National Guard or Army National Guard experience; retired from active duty; disabled or killed as a result of military service; prisoner of war; or missing in action. *Application Requirements:* Application, documentation of service. *Deadline:* varies.

Contact College Zone Counselor, Illinois Student Assistance Commission (ISAC), 1755 Lake Cook Road, Deerfield, IL 60015-5209. *E-mail:* collegezone@isac.org. *Phone:* 800-899-4722. *Web site:* www.collegezone.org.

Illinois Special Education Teacher Tuition Waiver. Teachers or students who are pursuing a career in special education as public, private or parochial preschool, elementary or secondary school teachers in Illinois may be eligible for this program. This program will exempt such individuals from paying tuition and mandatory fees at an eligible institution, for up to four years. The individual dollar amount awarded are subject to sufficient annual appropriations by the Illinois General Assembly. *Academic Fields/Career Goals:* Special Education. *Award:* Forgivable loan for use in freshman, sophomore, junior, senior, or graduate year; renewable. *Award amount:* varies. *Number of awards:* up to 250. *Eligibility Requirements:* Applicant must be enrolled or expecting to enroll full- or part-time at a four-year institution or university; resident of Illinois and studying in Illinois. Available to U.S. citizens. *Application Requirements:* Application. *Deadline:* March 1.

Contact College Zone Counselor, Illinois Student Assistance Commission (ISAC), 1755 Lake Cook Road, Deerfield, IL 60015-5209. *E-mail:* collegezone@isac.org. *Phone:* 800-899-4722. *Web site:* www.collegezone.org.

Illinois Student-to-Student Program of Matching Grants. Grant is available to undergraduates at participating state-supported colleges. Number of grants and the individual dollar amount awarded vary. Contact financial aid office at the institution. *Award:* Grant for use in freshman, sophomore, junior, or senior year; not renewable. *Award amount:* $300–$1000. *Number of awards:* varies. *Eligibility Requirements:* Applicant must be enrolled or expecting to enroll full- or part-time at a two-year or four-year institution or university; resident of Illinois and studying in Illinois. Available to U.S. citizens. *Application Requirements:* Application, financial need analysis. *Deadline:* varies.

Contact College Zone Counselor, Illinois Student Assistance Commission (ISAC), 1755 Lake Cook Road, Deerfield, IL 60015-5209. *E-mail:* collegezone@isac.org. *Phone:* 800-899-4722. *Web site:* www.collegezone.org.

Illinois Veteran Grant Program-IVG. Awards qualified veterans and pays eligible tuition and fees for study in Illinois public universities or community colleges. Program eligibility units are based on the enrolled hours for a particular term, not the dollar amount of the benefits paid. Applications are available at college financial aid office and can be submitted any time during the academic year for which assistance is being requested. *Award:* Grant for use in freshman, sophomore, junior, senior, or graduate year; renewable. *Award amount:* $1400–$1600. *Number of awards:* 11,000–13,000. *Eligibility Requirements:* Applicant must be enrolled or expecting to enroll full- or part-time at a two-year or four-year institution or university; resident of Illinois and studying in Illinois. Available to U.S. citizens. Applicant or parent must meet one or more of the following requirements: general military experience; retired from active duty; disabled or killed as a result of military service; prisoner of war; or missing in action. *Application Requirements:* Application. *Deadline:* continuous.

Contact College Zone Counselor, Illinois Student Assistance Commission (ISAC), 1755 Lake Cook Road, Deerfield, IL 60015-5209. *E-mail:* collegezone@isac.org. *Phone:* 800-899-4722. *Web site:* www.collegezone.org.

Merit Recognition Scholarship (MRS) Program. One-time awards available to Illinois residents for use at Illinois institutions. Must be ranked in the top 5 percent of high school class or have scored among the top 5 percent on the ACT, SAT, or Prairie State Achievement Exam. Number of scholarships granted varies. *Award:* Scholarship for use in freshman year; not renewable. *Award amount:* up to $1000. *Number of awards:* varies. *Eligibility Requirements:* Applicant must be high school student; planning to enroll or expecting to enroll full- or part-time at a two-year or four-year institution or university; resident of Illinois and studying in Illinois. Applicant must have 3.5 GPA or higher. Available to U.S. citizens. *Application Requirements:* Application, transcript. *Deadline:* June 15.

Contact College Zone Counselor, Illinois Student Assistance Commission (ISAC), 1755 Lake Cook Road, Deerfield, IL 60015-5209. *E-mail:* collegezone@isac.org. *Phone:* 800-899-4722. *Web site:* www.collegezone.org.

MIA/POW Scholarships. One-time award for spouse, child, or step-child of veterans who are missing in action or were a prisoner of war. Must be enrolled at a state-supported school in Illinois. Candidate must be U.S. citizen. Must apply and be accepted before beginning of school. Also for children and spouses of veterans who are determined to be 100 percent disabled as established by the Veterans Administration. Scholarship value and the number of awards granted varies. *Award:* Scholarship for use in freshman, sophomore, junior, or senior year; renewable. *Award amount:* varies. *Number of awards:* varies. *Eligibility Requirements:* Applicant must be enrolled or expecting to enroll full- or part-time at a two-year or four-year institution or university; resident of Illinois and studying in Illinois. Available to U.S. citizens. Applicant or parent must meet one or more of the following requirements: general military experience; retired from active duty; disabled or killed as a result of military service; prisoner of war; or missing in action. *Application Requirements:* Application. *Deadline:* continuous.

Contact Ms. Tracy Smith, Grants Section, Illinois Department of Veterans' Affairs, 833 South Spring Street, Springfield, IL 62794-9432. *Phone:* 217-782-3564. *Fax:* 217-782-4161. *Web site:* www.state.il.us/agency/dva.

Minority Teachers of Illinois Scholarship Program. Award for minority students intending to become school teachers. Number of scholarships and the individual dollar amount awarded vary. *Academic Fields/Career Goals:* Education; Special Education. *Award:* Scholarship for use in freshman, sophomore, junior, senior, graduate, or postgraduate years; renewable. *Award amount:* up to $5000. *Number of awards:* 450–550. *Eligibility Requirements:* Applicant must be American Indian/Alaska Native, Asian/Pacific Islander, Black (non-Hispanic), or Hispanic; enrolled or expecting to enroll full- or part-time at a two-year or four-year institution or university; resident of Illinois and studying in Illinois. Applicant must have 2.5 GPA or higher. Available to U.S. citizens. *Application Requirements:* Application, transcript. *Deadline:* March 1.

Contact College Zone Counselor, Illinois Student Assistance Commission (ISAC), 1755 Lake Cook Road, Deerfield, IL 60015-5209. *E-mail:* collegezone@isac.org. *Phone:* 800-899-4722. *Web site:* www.collegezone.org.

Robert C. Byrd Honors Scholarship-Illinois. Scholarship for Illinois residents and graduating high school seniors accepted on a full-time basis as an undergraduate student at an Illinois college or university. The award is up to $1500 per year, for a maximum of four years. Minimum 3.5 GPA required. Students are automatically considered for this scholarship if they meet the eligibility requirements. High school counselors submit information to selection process. *Award:* Scholarship for use in freshman year; renewable. *Award amount:* up to $1500. *Number of awards:* varies. *Eligibility Requirements:* Applicant must be high school student; planning to enroll or expecting to enroll full-time at a two-year or four-year institution or university; resident of Illinois and studying in Illinois. Applicant must have 3.5 GPA or higher. Available to U.S. citizens. *Application Requirements:* Application, test scores, transcript. *Deadline:* July 15.

Contact College Zone Counselor, Illinois Student Assistance Commission (ISAC), 1755 Lake Cook Road, Deerfield, IL 60015-5209. *E-mail:* collegezone@isac.org. *Phone:* 800-899-4722. *Fax:* 847-831-8549. *Web site:* www.collegezone.org.

Silas Purnell Illinois Incentive for Access Program. Students whose information provided on the FAFSA results in a calculated zero expected family contribution when they are college freshmen may be eligible to receive a grant of up to $500. Must be a U.S. citizen and an Illinois resident studying at a participating Illinois institution. See Web site for complete list of schools and additional requirements. *Award:* Grant for use in freshman year; not renewable. *Award amount:* up to $500. *Number of awards:* varies. *Eligibility Requirements:* Applicant must be high school student; planning to enroll or expecting to enroll full- or part-time at a two-year, four-year, or technical institution or university; resident of Illinois and studying in Illinois. Available to U.S. citizens. *Application Requirements:* Financial need analysis, FAFSA. *Deadline:* July 1.

Contact College Zone Counselor, Illinois Student Assistance Commission (ISAC), 1755 Lake Cook Road, Deerfield, IL 60015-5209. *E-mail:* collegezone@isac.org. *Phone:* 800-899-4722. *Web site:* www.collegezone.org.

Veterans' Children Educational Opportunities. $250 award for each child aged 10 to 18 of a veteran who died or became totally disabled as a result of service during World War I, World War II, Korean, or Vietnam War. Must be Illinois resident studying in Illinois. Death must be service-connected. Disability must be rated 100 percent for two or more years. *Award:* Grant for use in freshman year; not renewable. *Award amount:* $250. *Number of awards:* varies. *Eligibility Requirements:* Applicant must be age 10-18; enrolled or expecting to enroll full- or part-time at a two-year or four-year institution or university; resident of Illinois and studying in Illinois. Available to U.S. citizens. Applicant or parent must meet one or more of the following requirements: general military experience; retired from active duty; disabled or killed as a result of military service; prisoner of war; or missing in action. *Application Requirements:* Application. *Deadline:* June 30.

Contact Tracy Smith, Grants Section, Illinois Department of Veterans' Affairs, 833 South Spring Street, Springfield, IL 62794-9432. *Phone:* 217-782-3564. *Fax:* 217-782-4161. *Web site:* www.state.il.us/agency/dva.

INDIANA

Child of Disabled Veteran Grant or Purple Heart Recipient Grant. Free tuition at Indiana state-supported colleges or universities for children of disabled veterans or Purple Heart recipients. Must submit form DD214 or service record. Covers tuition and mandatory fees. *Award:* Grant for use in freshman, sophomore, junior, senior, graduate, or postgraduate years; renewable. *Award amount:* varies. *Number of awards:* varies. *Eligibility Requirements:* Applicant must be enrolled or expecting to enroll full- or part-time at a two-year or four-year institution or university; resident of Indiana and studying in Indiana. Available to U.S. citizens. Applicant or parent must meet one or more of the following requirements: general military experience; retired from active duty; disabled or killed as a result of military service; prisoner of war; or missing in action. *Application Requirements:* Application, FAFSA. *Deadline:* continuous.

Contact Jon Brinkley, State Service Officer, Indiana Department of Veterans Affairs, 302 West Washington Street, Room E-120, Indianapolis, IN 46204-2738. *E-mail:* jbrinkley@dva.in.gov. *Phone:* 317-232-3910. *Fax:* 317-232-7721. *Web site:* www.in.gov/dva.

Department of Veterans Affairs Free Tuition for Children of POW/MIA's in Vietnam. Renewable award for residents of Indiana who are the children of veterans declared missing in action or prisoner-of-war after January 1, 1960. Provides tuition at Indiana state-supported institutions for undergraduate study. *Award:* Grant for use in freshman, sophomore, junior, senior, graduate, or postgraduate years; renewable. *Award amount:* varies. *Number of awards:* varies. *Eligibility Requirements:* Applicant must be age 24 or under; enrolled or expecting to enroll full- or part-time at a two-year or four-year institution or university; resident of Indiana and studying in Indiana. Available to U.S. citizens. Applicant or parent must meet one or more of the following requirements: general military experience; retired from active duty; disabled or killed as a result of military service; prisoner of war; or missing in action. *Application Requirements:* Application. *Deadline:* continuous.

Contact Jon Brinkley, State Service Officer, Indiana Department of Veterans Affairs, 302 West Washington Street, Room E-120, Indianapolis, IN 46204-2738. *E-mail:* jbrinkley@dva.in.gov. *Phone:* 317-232-3910. *Fax:* 317-232-7721. *Web site:* www.in.gov/dva.

Frank O'Bannon Grant Program. A need-based, tuition-restricted program for students attending Indiana public, private, or proprietary institutions seeking a first undergraduate degree. Students (and parents of dependent students) who are U.S. citizens and Indiana residents must file the FAFSA yearly by the March 10 deadline. *Award:* Grant for use in freshman, sophomore, junior, or senior year; not renewable. *Award amount:* $200–$10,992. *Number of awards:* 48,408–70,239. *Eligibility Requirements:* Applicant must be enrolled or expecting to enroll full-time at a two-year, four-year, or technical institution or university; resident of Indiana and studying in Indiana. Available to U.S. citizens. *Application Requirements:* Application, financial need analysis, FAFSA. *Deadline:* March 10.

Contact Grants Counselor, State Student Assistance Commission of Indiana (SSACI), 150 West Market Street, Suite 500, Indianapolis, IN 46204-2805. *E-mail:* grants@ssaci.state.in.us. *Phone:* 317-232-2350. *Fax:* 317-232-3260. *Web site:* www.in.gov/ssaci.

Hoosier Scholar Award. A $500 nonrenewable award. Based on the size of the senior class, one to three scholars are selected by the guidance counselor's) of each accredited high school in Indiana. The award is based on academic merit and may be used for any educational expense at an eligible Indiana institution of higher education. *Award:* Scholarship for use in freshman year; not renewable. *Award amount:* $500. *Number of awards:* 666–840. *Eligibility Requirements:* Applicant must be high school student; planning to enroll or expecting to enroll full-time at a two-year or four-year institution or university; resident of Indiana and studying in Indiana. Applicant must have 3.5 GPA or higher. Available to U.S. citizens. *Application Requirements:* Application, references. *Deadline:* March 10.

Contact Ada Sparkman, Program Coordinator, State Student Assistance Commission of Indiana (SSACI), 150 West Market Street, Suite 500, Indianapolis, IN 46204-2805. *Phone:* 317-232-2350. *Fax:* 317-232-3260. *Web site:* www.in.gov/ssaci.

Indiana National Guard Supplemental Grant. The award is a supplement to the Indiana Higher Education Grant program. Applicants must be members of the Indiana National Guard. All Guard paperwork must be completed prior to the start of each semester. The FAFSA must be received by March 10. Award covers certain tuition and fees at select public colleges. *Award:* Grant for use in freshman, sophomore, junior, or senior year; not renewable. *Award amount:* $20–$7110. *Number of awards:* 503–925. *Eligibility Requirements:* Applicant must be enrolled or expecting to enroll full- or part-time at a two-year or four-year institution or university; resident of Indiana and studying in Indiana. Available to U.S. citizens. Applicant or parent must meet one or more of the following requirements: Air Force National Guard or Army National Guard experience; retired from active duty; disabled or killed as a result of military service; prisoner of war; or missing in action. *Application Requirements:* Application. *Deadline:* March 10.

Contact Kathryn Moore, Grants Counselor, State Student Assistance Commission of Indiana (SSACI), 150 West Market Street, Suite 500, Indianapolis, IN 46204-2805. *E-mail:* kmoore@ssaci.in.gov. *Phone:* 317-232-2350. *Fax:* 317-232-2360. *Web site:* www.in.gov/ssaci.

Indiana Nursing Scholarship Fund. Need-based tuition funding for nursing students enrolled full- or part-time at an eligible Indiana institution. Must be a U.S. citizen and an Indiana resident and have a minimum 2.0 GPA or meet the minimum requirements for the nursing program. Upon graduation, recipients must practice as a nurse in an Indiana health care setting for two years. *Academic Fields/Career Goals:* Nursing. *Award:* Scholarship for use in freshman, sophomore, junior, or senior year; not renewable. *Award amount:* $200–$5000. *Number of awards:* 490–690. *Eligibility Requirements:* Applicant must be enrolled or expecting to enroll full- or part-time at a two-year or four-year institution or university; resident of Indiana and studying in Indiana. Available to U.S. citizens. *Application Requirements:* Application, financial need analysis, FAFSA. *Deadline:* continuous.

Contact Yvonne Heflin, Director, Special Programs, State Student Assistance Commission of Indiana (SSACI), 150 West Market Street, Suite 500, Indianapolis, IN 46204-

2805. *Phone:* 317-232-2350. *Fax:* 317-232-3260. *Web site:* www.in.gov/ssaci.

National Guard Scholarship Extension Program. A scholarship extension applicant is eligible for a tuition scholarship under Indiana Code 21-13-5-4 for a period not to exceed the period of scholarship extension the applicant served on active duty as a member of the National Guard (mobilized and deployed). Must apply not later than one year after the applicant ceases to be a member of the Indiana National Guard. Applicant should apply through the education officer of their last unit of assignment. *Award:* Grant for use in freshman, sophomore, junior, or senior year; renewable. *Award amount:* varies. *Number of awards:* varies. *Eligibility Requirements:* Applicant must be enrolled or expecting to enroll full- or part-time at a two-year, four-year, or technical institution or university and studying in Indiana. Available to U.S. citizens. Applicant must have served in the Air Force National Guard or Army National Guard. *Application Requirements:* Application. **Deadline:** continuous.

Contact Pamela Moody, National Guard Education Officer, Indiana Department of Veterans Affairs, 302 West Washington Street, Suite E120, Indianapolis, IN 46204. *E-mail:* pamela.moody@in.ngb.army.mil. *Phone:* 317-964-7017. *Fax:* 317-232-7721. *Web site:* www.in.gov/dva.

National Guard Tuition Supplement Program. Applicant must be a member of the Indiana National Guard, in active drilling status, who has not been AWOL during the last 12 months, does not possess a bachelor's degree, possesses the requisite academic qualifications, meets the requirements of the state-supported college or university, and meets all National Guard requirements. *Award:* Grant for use in freshman, sophomore, junior, or senior year; renewable. *Award amount:* varies. *Number of awards:* varies. *Eligibility Requirements:* Applicant must be enrolled or expecting to enroll full- or part-time at a two-year, four-year, or technical institution or university and studying in Indiana. Available to U.S. citizens. Applicant must have served in the Air Force National Guard or Army National Guard. *Application Requirements:* Application, FAFSA. **Deadline:** continuous.

Contact Jon Brinkley, State Service Officer, Indiana Department of Veterans Affairs, 302 West Washington Street, Room E-120, Indianapolis, IN 46204-2738. *E-mail:* jbrinkley@dva.in.gov. *Phone:* 317-232-3910. *Fax:* 317-232-7721. *Web site:* www.in.gov/dva.

Part-Time Grant Program. Program is designed to encourage part-time undergraduates to start and complete their associate or baccalaureate degrees or certificates by subsidizing part-time tuition costs. It is a term-based award that is based on need. State residency requirements must be met and a FAFSA must be filed. Eligibility is determined at the institutional level subject to approval by SSACI. *Award:* Grant for use in freshman, sophomore, junior, or senior year; not renewable. *Award amount:* $20–$4000. *Number of awards:* 4680–6700. *Eligibility Requirements:* Applicant must be enrolled or expecting to enroll part-time at a two-year, four-year, or technical institution or university; resident of Indiana and studying in Indiana. Available to U.S. citizens. *Application Requirements:* Application, financial need analysis. **Deadline:** continuous.

Contact Grants Counselor, State Student Assistance Commission of Indiana (SSACI), 150 West Market Street, Suite 500, Indianapolis, IN 46204-2805. *E-mail:* grants@ssaci.state.in.us. *Phone:* 317-232-2350. *Fax:* 317-232-3260. *Web site:* www.in.gov/ssaci.

Resident Tuition for Active Duty Military Personnel. Applicant must be a nonresident of Indiana serving on active duty and stationed in Indiana and attending any state-supported college or university. Dependents remain eligible for the duration of their enrollment, even if the active duty person is no longer in Indiana. Entitlement is to the resident tuition rate. *Award:* Grant for use in freshman, sophomore, junior, senior, graduate, or postgraduate years; renewable. *Award amount:* varies. *Number of awards:* varies. *Eligibility Requirements:* Applicant must be enrolled or expecting to enroll full- or part-time at a two-year, four-year, or technical institution or university and studying in Indiana. Available to U.S. citizens. Applicant or parent must meet one or more of the following requirements: Air Force, Army, Marine Corps, or Navy experience; retired from active duty; disabled or killed as a result of military service; prisoner of war; or missing in action. *Application Requirements:* Application. **Deadline:** continuous.

Contact Jon Brinkley, State Service Officer, Indiana Department of Veterans Affairs, 302 West Washington Street, Room E-120, Indianapolis, IN 46204-2738. *E-mail:* jbrinkley@dva.in.gov. *Phone:* 317-232-3910. *Fax:* 317-232-7721. *Web site:* www.in.gov/dva.

Tuition and Fee Remission for Children and Spouses of National Guard Members. Award to an individual whose father, mother or spouse was a member of the Indiana National Guard and suffered a service-connected death while serving on state active duty (which includes mobilized and deployed for federal active duty). The student must be eligible to pay the resident tuition rate at the state-supported college or university and must possess the requisite academic qualifications. *Award:* Grant for use in freshman, sophomore, junior, or senior year; renewable. *Award amount:* varies. *Number of awards:* varies. *Eligibility Requirements:* Applicant must be enrolled or expecting to enroll full- or part-time at a two-year, four-year, or technical institution or university and studying in Indiana. Available to U.S. citizens. Applicant or parent must meet one or more of the following requirements: Air Force National Guard or Army National Guard experience; retired from active duty; disabled or killed as a result of military service; prisoner of war; or missing in action. *Application Requirements:* Application, FAFSA. **Deadline:** continuous.

Contact R. Martin Umbarger, Adjutant General, Indiana Department of Veterans Affairs, 2002 South Holt Road, Indianapolis, IN 46241. *E-mail:* r.martin.umbarger@in.ngb.army.mil. *Phone:* 317-247-3559. *Fax:* 317-247-3540. *Web site:* www.in.gov/dva.

Twenty-first Century Scholars Gear Up Summer Scholarship. Grant of up to $3000 that pays for summer school tuition and regularly assessed course fees (does not cover other costs such as textbooks or room and board). *Award:* Scholarship for use in freshman, sophomore, junior, or senior year; not renewable. *Award amount:* up to $3000. *Number of awards:* 1. *Eligibility Requirements:* Applicant must be enrolled or expecting to enroll full-time at a two-year or four-year institution or university; resident of Indiana and studying in Indiana. Available to U.S. citizens. *Application Requirements:* Application, must be in twenty-first century scholars program, high school diploma. **Deadline:** varies.

Contact Coordinator, Office of Twenty-First Century Scholars, State Student Assistance Commission of Indiana (SSACI), 150 West Market Street, Suite 500, Indianapolis, IN 46204. *E-mail:* 21stscholars@ssaci.in.gov. *Phone:* 317-234-1394. *Web site:* www.in.gov/ssaci.

IOWA

All Iowa Opportunity Scholarship. Students attending eligible Iowa colleges and universities may receive awards of up to $6420. Minimum 2.5 GPA. Priority will be given to students who participated in the Federal TRIO Programs, graduated from alternative high schools, and to homeless youth. Applicant must enroll within two academic years of graduating from high school. Maximum individual awards cannot exceed more than the resident tuition rate at Iowa Regent Universities. *Award:* Scholarship for use in freshman or sophomore year; renewable. *Award amount:* up to $6420. *Number of awards:* 179. *Eligibility Requirements:* Applicant must be enrolled or expecting to enroll full- or part-time at a two-year or four-year institution or university; resident of Iowa and studying in Iowa. Applicant must have 3.5 GPA or higher. Available to U.S. citizens. *Application Requirements:* Application, financial need analysis. **Deadline:** May 1.

Contact Todd Brown, Director, Scholarships, Grants, and Loan Forgiveness, Iowa College Student Aid Commission, 200 Tenth Street, Fourth Floor, Des Moines, IA 50309-3609. *E-mail:* todd.brown@iowa.gov. *Phone:* 515-725-3405. *Fax:* 515-725-3401. *Web site:* www.iowacollegeaid.gov.

Governor Terry E. Branstad Iowa State Fair Scholarship. Awards up to four scholarships ranging from $500 to $1000 to students graduating from an Iowa high school. Must actively participate at the Iowa State fair. For more details see Web site: http://www.iowacollegeaid.org. *Award:* Scholarship for use in freshman year; not renewable. *Award amount:* $500–$1000. *Number of awards:* up to 4. *Eligibility Requirements:* Applicant must be high school student; planning to enroll or expecting to enroll full- or part-time at a four-year institution or university; resident of Iowa and studying in Iowa. Available to U.S. citizens. *Application Requirements:* Application, essay, financial need analysis, references, transcript. **Deadline:** May 1.

Contact Misty Burke, Program Planner, Iowa College Student Aid Commission, 200 Tenth Street, Fourth Floor, Des Moines, IA 50309-3609. *E-mail:* misty.burke@iowa.gov. *Phone:* 515-725-3424. *Fax:* 515-725-3401. *Web site:* www.iowacollegeaid.gov.

Iowa Grants. Statewide need-based program to assist high-need Iowa residents. Recipients must demonstrate a high level of financial need to receive awards ranging from $100 to $1000. Awards are prorated for students enrolled for less than full-time. Awards must be used at Iowa postsecondary institutions. *Award:* Grant for use in freshman, sophomore, junior, or senior year; not renewable. *Award amount:* $100–$1000. *Number of awards:* 2100. *Eligibility Requirements:* Applicant must be enrolled or expecting to enroll full- or part-time at a two-year, four-year, or technical institution or university; resident of Iowa and studying in Iowa. Available to U.S. citizens. *Application Requirements:* Application, financial need analysis. **Deadline:** continuous.

Contact Todd Brown, Director, Scholarships, Grants, and Loan Forgiveness, Iowa College Student Aid Commission, 200 Tenth Street, Fourth Floor, Des Moines, IA 50309-3609. *E-mail:* todd.brown@iowa.gov. *Phone:* 515-725-3405. *Fax:* 515-725-3401. *Web site:* www.iowacollegeaid.gov.

Iowa National Guard Education Assistance Program. Program provides postsecondary tuition assistance to members of Iowa National Guard Units. Must study at a postsecondary institution in Iowa. Contact the office for additional information. *Award:* Grant for use in freshman, sophomore, junior, or senior year; not renewable. *Award amount:* $1200–$6420. *Number of awards:* varies. *Eligibility Requirements:* Applicant must be enrolled or expecting to enroll full- or part-time at a two-year, four-year, or technical institution or university; resident of Iowa and studying in Iowa. Available to U.S. citizens. Applicant or parent must meet one or more of the following requirements: Air Force National Guard or Army National Guard experience; retired from active duty; disabled or killed as a result of military service; prisoner of war; or missing in action. *Application Requirements:* Application. **Deadline:** continuous.

Contact Todd Brown, Director, Scholarships, Grants, and Loan Forgiveness, Iowa College Student Aid Commission, 200 Tenth Street, Fourth Floor, Des Moines, IA 50309-3609. *E-mail:* todd.brown@iowa.gov. *Phone:* 515-725-3405. *Fax:* 515-725-3401. *Web site:* www.iowacollegeaid.gov.

Iowa Tuition Grant Program. Program assists students who attend independent postsecondary institutions in Iowa. Iowa residents currently enrolled, or planning to enroll, for at least 3 semester hours at one of the eligible Iowa postsecondary institutions may apply. Awards currently range from $100 to $4000. Grants may not exceed the difference between independent college and university tuition fees and the average tuition fees at the three public Regent universities. *Award:* Grant for use in freshman, sophomore, junior, or senior year; not renewable. *Award amount:* $100–$4000. *Number of awards:* 17,200. *Eligibility Requirements:* Applicant must be enrolled or expecting to enroll full- or part-time at a four-year institution or university; resident of Iowa and studying in Iowa. Available to U.S. citizens. *Application Requirements:* Application, financial need analysis. **Deadline:** July 1.

Contact Todd Brown, Director, Scholarships, Grants, and Loan Forgiveness, Iowa College Student Aid Commission, 200 Tenth Street, Fourth Floor, Des Moines, IA 50309-3609. *E-mail:* todd.brown@iowa.gov. *Phone:* 515-725-3420. *Fax:* 515-725-3401. *Web site:* www.iowacollegeaid.gov.

Iowa Vocational-Technical Tuition Grant Program. Program provides need-based financial assistance to Iowa residents enrolled in career education (vocational-technical), and career option programs at Iowa area community colleges. Grants range from $150 to $1200, depending on the length of the program, financial need, and available funds. *Award:* Grant for use in freshman or sophomore year; not renewable. *Award amount:* $150–$1200. *Number of awards:* 2100. *Eligibility Requirements:* Applicant must be enrolled or expecting to enroll full- or part-time at a technical institution; resident of Iowa and studying in Iowa. Available to U.S. citizens. *Application Requirements:* Application, financial need analysis. **Deadline:** July 1.

Contact Todd Brown, Director, Program Administration, Iowa College Student Aid Commission, 200 Tenth Street, Fourth Floor, Des Moines, IA 50309-3609. *E-mail:* julie.leeper@iowa.gov. *Phone:* 515-725-3405. *Fax:* 515-725-3401. *Web site:* www.iowacollegeaid.gov.

KANSAS

Kansas Educational Benefits for Children of MIA, POW, and Deceased Veterans of the Vietnam War. Scholarship awarded to students who are children of veterans. Must show proof of parent's status as missing in action, prisoner of war, or killed in action in the Vietnam War. Kansas residence required of veteran at time of entry to service. Must attend a state-supported postsecondary school. *Award:* Scholarship for use in freshman, sophomore, junior, or senior year; not renewable. *Award amount:* varies. *Number of awards:* 1. *Eligibility Requirements:* Applicant must be enrolled or expecting to enroll full-time at a two-year, four-year, or technical institution or university and studying in Kansas. Available to U.S. citizens. Applicant or parent must meet one or more of the following requirements: general military experience; retired from active duty; disabled or killed as a result of military service; prisoner of war; or missing in action. *Application Requirements:* Application, birth certificate, school acceptance letter, military discharge of veteran. **Deadline:** varies.

Contact Wayne Bollig, Program Director, Kansas Commission on Veterans Affairs, 700 Jackson, SW, Suite 701, Topeka, KS 66603-3743. *E-mail:* wbollig@kcva.org. *Phone:* 785-296-3976. *Fax:* 785-296-1462. *Web site:* www.kcva.org.

Kansas Ethnic Minority Scholarship. Scholarship program designed to assist financially needy, academically competitive students who are identified as members of any of the following ethnic/racial groups: African American, American Indian or Alaskan Native, Asian or Pacific Islander, or Hispanic. Priority is given to applicants who are freshmen. For more details refer to Web site: http://www.kansasregents.org/financial_aid/minority.html. *Award:* Scholarship for use in freshman, sophomore, junior, or senior year; renewable. *Award amount:* up to $1850. *Number of awards:* varies. *Eligibility Requirements:* Applicant must be American Indian/Alaska Native, Asian/Pacific Islander, Black (non-Hispanic), or Hispanic; enrolled or expecting to enroll full-time at a two-year or four-year institution or university and studying in Kansas. Applicant must have 3.0 GPA or higher. Available to U.S. citizens. *Applica-*

tion Requirements: Application, financial need analysis, test scores. *Fee:* $10. *Deadline:* May 1.

Contact Kansas Board of Regents. *Web site:* www.kansasregents.org.

Kansas Nurse Service Scholarship Program. This is a service scholarship loan program available to students attending two-year or four-year public and private postsecondary institutions as well as vocational technical schools with nursing education programs. Students can be pursuing either LPN or RN licensure. *Academic Fields/Career Goals:* Nursing. *Award:* Scholarship for use in freshman, sophomore, junior, or senior year; renewable. *Award amount:* $3500. *Number of awards:* varies. *Eligibility Requirements:* Applicant must be enrolled or expecting to enroll full-time at a two-year, four-year, or technical institution or university. Available to U.S. citizens. *Application Requirements:* Application, financial need analysis, test scores, transcript. *Fee:* $12. *Deadline:* May 1.

Contact Kansas Board of Regents. *Web site:* www.kansasregents.org.

Kansas Teacher Service Scholarship. Scholarship to encourage talented students to enter the teaching profession and teach in Kansas in specific curriculum areas or in underserved areas of Kansas. For more details, refer to Web site: http://www.kansasregents.org/financial_aid/teacher.html. *Academic Fields/Career Goals:* Education. *Award:* Scholarship for use in junior or senior year; renewable. *Award amount:* $5000. *Number of awards:* varies. *Eligibility Requirements:* Applicant must be enrolled or expecting to enroll full- or part-time at a four-year institution or university. Applicant must have 3.0 GPA or higher. Available to U.S. citizens. *Application Requirements:* Application, essay, financial need analysis, resume, references, test scores, transcript. *Fee:* $12. *Deadline:* May 1.

Contact Kansas Board of Regents. *Web site:* www.kansasregents.org.

Marsha's Angels Scholarship. Scholarship for students who have completed all prerequisites to enter their first year of an accredited nursing program. Applicants living in Sedgwick County, Kansas or one of the surrounding counties may attend an accredited nursing program anywhere in the U.S.; applicants from any other state in the U.S. may use the scholarship to attend a program in Sedgwick County, Kansas, one of the surrounding counties, or St. Luke's College in Missouri. *Academic Fields/Career Goals:* Nursing. *Award:* Scholarship for use in freshman year; not renewable. *Award amount:* $1600–$1800. *Number of awards:* varies. *Eligibility Requirements:* Applicant must be high school student and planning to enroll or expecting to enroll full- or part-time at a four-year institution or university. Available to U.S. citizens. *Application Requirements:* Application, transcript. *Deadline:* June 30.

Contact Scholarship Committee, Marsha's Angels Scholarship Fund, PO Box 401, Valley Center, KS 67147-0401. *E-mail:* marshasangels@gmail.com. *Web site:* www.marshasangels.org.

Ted and Nora Anderson Scholarships. Scholarship of $250 for each semester (one year only) given to the children of American Legion members or Auxiliary members who are holding membership for the past three consecutive years. Children of a deceased member can also apply. Parent of the applicant must be a veteran. Must be high school seniors or college freshmen or sophomores in a Kansas institution. Scholarship for use at an approved college, university, or trade school in Kansas. Must maintain a C average in college. *Award:* Scholarship for use in freshman or sophomore year; not renewable. *Award amount:* $250–$500. *Number of awards:* 4. *Eligibility Requirements:* Applicant must be enrolled or expecting to enroll full-time at a two-year, four-year, or technical institution or university; resident of Kansas and studying in Kansas. Applicant or parent of applicant must be member of American Legion or Auxiliary. Available to U.S. citizens. Applicant or parent must meet one or more of the following requirements: general military experience; retired from active duty; disabled or killed as a result of military service; prisoner of war; or missing in action. *Application Requirements:* Application, essay, financial need analysis, photo, references, transcript. *Deadline:* February 15.

Contact Jim Gravenstein, Chairman, Scholarship Committee, American Legion Department of Kansas, 1314 Topeka Boulevard, SW, Topeka, KS 66612. *Phone:* 785-232-9315. *Fax:* 785-232-1399. *Web site:* www.ksamlegion.org.

KENTUCKY

College Access Program (CAP) Grant. Award for U.S. citizens and Kentucky residents seeking their first undergraduate degree. Applicants enrolled in sectarian institutions are not eligible. Must demonstrate financial need and submit Free Application for Federal Student Aid. Funding is limited. Awards are made on a first-come, first-serve basis. *Award:* Grant for use in freshman, sophomore, junior, or senior year; not renewable. *Award amount:* up to $1900. *Number of awards:* 35,000–40,000. *Eligibility Requirements:* Applicant must be enrolled or expecting to enroll full- or part-time at a two-year, four-year, or technical institution or university; resident of Kentucky and studying in Kentucky. Available to U.S. citizens. *Application Requirements:* Application, financial need analysis, FAFSA. *Deadline:* March 15.

Contact Sheila Roe, Program Coordinator, Kentucky Higher Education Assistance Authority (KHEAA), PO Box 798, Frankfort, KY 40602-0798. *E-mail:* sroe@kheaa.com. *Phone:* 800-928-8926 Ext. 67393. *Fax:* 502-696-7373. *Web site:* www.kheaa.com.

Department of Veterans Affairs Tuition Waiver-KY KRS 164-507. Scholarship available to college students who are residents of Kentucky under the age of 26. *Award:* Scholarship for use in freshman, sophomore, junior, or senior year; not renewable. *Award amount:* varies. *Number of awards:* 400. *Eligibility Requirements:* Applicant must be age 26 or under; enrolled or expecting to enroll full- or part-time at a two-year or four-year institution or university and resident of Kentucky. Available to U.S. citizens. *Application Requirements:* Application. *Deadline:* varies.

Contact Kentucky Department of Veterans Affairs. *Web site:* www.veterans.ky.gov.

Early Childhood Development Scholarship. Awards scholarship with conditional service commitment for part-time students currently employed by participating ECD facility or providing training in ECD for an approved organization. For more information, visit Web site: www.kheaa.com. *Academic Fields/Career Goals:* Child and Family Studies; Education. *Award:* Scholarship for use in freshman, sophomore, junior, or senior year; not renewable. *Award amount:* up to $1800. *Number of awards:* 1000–1100. *Eligibility Requirements:* Applicant must be enrolled or expecting to enroll part-time at a two-year or four-year institution or university; resident of Kentucky and studying in Kentucky. Available to U.S. citizens. *Application Requirements:* Application, financial need analysis. *Deadline:* continuous.

Contact David Lawhorn, Program Coordinator, Kentucky Higher Education Assistance Authority (KHEAA), PO Box 798, Frankfort, KY 40602-0798. *E-mail:* dlawhorn@kheaa.com. *Web site:* www.kheaa.com.

Environmental Protection Scholarship. Renewable awards for college juniors, seniors, and graduate students for tuition, fees, and room and board and a book allowance at a Kentucky public university. Minimum 3.0 GPA required. Must agree to work full-time for the Kentucky Natural Resources and Environmental Protection Cabinet upon graduation. Interview is required. *Academic Fields/Career Goals:* Biology; Civil Engineering; Earth Science; Environmental Science; Hydrology; Mechanical Engineering; Natural Resources; Natural Sciences. *Award:* Scholarship for use in junior or senior year; renewable. *Award amount:* $15,500–$31,000. *Number of awards:* 1–4. *Eligibility Requirements:* Applicant must be enrolled or expecting to enroll full-time at a four-year institution or university and studying in Kentucky. Applicant must have 3.0 GPA or higher. Available to U.S. and non-U.S. citizens. *Application Requirements:* Application, essay, interview, references, transcript, valid work permit for noncitizens. *Deadline:* February 15.

Contact James Kipp, Scholarship Program Coordinator, Kentucky Natural Resources and Environmental Protection Cabinet, 233 Mining/Mineral Resources Building, Lexington, KY 40506-0107. *E-mail:* kipp@uky.edu. *Phone:* 859-257-1299. *Fax:* 859-323-1049. *Web site:* www.dep.ky.gov.

Go Higher Grant. Need-based grant for adult students pursuing their first undergraduate degree. Completion of the FAFSA is required. *Award:* Grant for use in freshman, sophomore, junior, or senior year; not renewable. *Award amount:* $1000. *Number of awards:* 50–200. *Eligibility Requirements:* Applicant must be age 24 and over; enrolled or expecting to enroll full- or part-time at a two-year, four-year, or technical institution or university; resident of Kentucky and studying in Kentucky. Available to U.S. citizens. *Application Requirements:* Application, FAFSA. *Deadline:* continuous.

Contact Becky Gilpatrick, Student Aid Branch Manager, Kentucky Higher Education Assistance Authority (KHEAA), PO Box 798, Frankfort, KY 40206-0798. *E-mail:* rgilpatrick@kheaa.com. *Phone:* 800-928-8926 Ext. 67394. *Web site:* www.kheaa.com.

Kentucky Educational Excellence Scholarship (KEES). Annual award based on yearly high school GPA and highest ACT or SAT score received by high school graduation. Awards are renewable, if required cumulative GPA is maintained at a Kentucky postsecondary school. Must be a Kentucky resident, and a graduate of a Kentucky high school. *Award:* Scholarship for use in freshman, sophomore, junior, or senior year; renewable. *Award amount:* up to $2500. *Number of awards:* 60,000–65,000. *Eligibility Requirements:* Applicant must be high school student; planning to enroll or expecting to enroll full- or part-time at a two-year, four-year, or technical institution or university; resident of Kentucky and studying in Kentucky. Applicant must have 3.5 GPA or higher. Available to U.S. citizens. *Application Requirements:* Application, test scores, transcript. *Deadline:* continuous.

Contact Kentucky Higher Education Assistance Authority (KHEAA). *Web site:* www.kheaa.com.

Kentucky Minority Educator Recruitment and Retention (KMERR) Scholarship. Scholarship for minority teacher candidates who rank in the upper half of their class or have a minimum 2.5 GPA. Must be a U.S. citizen and Kentucky resident enrolled in one of Kentucky's eight public institutions. Must teach one semester in Kentucky for each semester the scholarship is received. *Academic Fields/Career Goals:* Education. *Award:* Forgivable loan for use in freshman, sophomore, junior, or senior year; renewable. *Award amount:* $2500–$5000. *Number of awards:* 400. *Eligibility Requirements:* Applicant must be American Indian/Alaska Native, Asian/Pacific Islander, Black (non-Hispanic), or Hispanic; enrolled or expecting to enroll full-time at a two-year or four-year institution or university; resident of Kentucky and studying in Kentucky. Applicant must have 3.5 GPA or higher. Available to U.S. citizens. *Application Requirements:* Application, references, test scores, transcript. *Deadline:* continuous.

Contact Natasha Murray, State Program Coordinator, Kentucky Department of Education, 500 Mero Street, 17th Floor, Frankfort, KY 40601. *E-mail:* michael.dailey@education.ky.gov. *Phone:* 502-564-1479. *Fax:* 502-564-6952. *Web site:* www.education.ky.gov.

Kentucky Office of Vocational Rehabilitation. Grant provides services necessary to secure employment. Eligible individual must possess physical or mental impairment that results in a substantial impediment to employment; benefit from vocational rehabilitation services in terms of an employment outcome; and require vocational rehabilitation services to prepare for, enter, or retain employment. *Award:* Grant for use in freshman, sophomore, junior, or senior year; renewable. *Award amount:* varies. *Number of awards:* varies. *Eligibility Requirements:* Applicant must be enrolled or expecting to enroll full- or part-time at a two-year, four-year, or technical institution or university. Applicant must be learning disabled or physically disabled. Available to U.S. citizens. *Application Requirements:* Application, financial need analysis, interview, transcript, proof of disability. *Deadline:* continuous.

Contact Charles Puckett, Program Administrator, Kentucky Department of Vocational Rehabilitation, 600 West Cedar Street, Suite 2E, Louisville, KY 40202. *E-mail:* marianu.spencer@mail.state.ky.us. *Phone:* 502-595-4173. *Fax:* 502-564-2358. *Web site:* www.ovr.ky.gov.

Kentucky Teacher Scholarship Program. Awards Kentucky residents attending Kentucky institutions and pursuing initial teacher certification programs. Must teach one semester for each semester of award received. In critical shortage areas, must teach one semester for every two semesters of award received. If teaching service is not rendered, the scholarship converts to a loan that must be repaid with interest. For more information, see Web: www.kheaa.com. *Academic Fields/Career Goals:* Education. *Award:* Forgivable loan for use in freshman, sophomore, junior, or senior year; renewable. *Award amount:* $325–$5000. *Number of awards:* 600–700. *Eligibility Requirements:* Applicant must be enrolled or expecting to enroll full-time at a two-year or four-year institution or university; resident of Kentucky and studying in Kentucky. Available to U.S. citizens. *Application Requirements:* Application, financial need analysis. *Deadline:* May 1.

Contact Becky Gilpatrick, Student Aid Branch Manager, Kentucky Higher Education Assistance Authority (KHEAA), PO Box 798, Frankfort, KY 40602. *E-mail:* tphelps@kheaa.com. *Phone:* 800-928-8926 Ext. 67394. *Fax:* 502-696-7496. *Web site:* www.kheaa.com.

Kentucky Transportation Cabinet Civil Engineering Scholarship Program. Scholarships awarded to qualified Kentucky residents who wish to study civil engineering at University of Kentucky, Western Kentucky University, University of Louisville or Kentucky State University. Applicant should be a graduate of an accredited Kentucky high school or a Kentucky resident. Scholarship recipients are given opportunities to work for the Cabinet during summers and job opportunities upon graduation within the state of KY. *Academic Fields/Career Goals:* Civil Engineering. *Award:* Scholarship for use in freshman, sophomore, junior, or senior year; renewable. *Award amount:* $10,400–$40,000. *Number of awards:* 15–25. *Eligibility Requirements:* Applicant must be enrolled or expecting to enroll full-time at a four-year institution or university; resident of Kentucky and studying in Kentucky. Applicant must have 3.0 GPA or higher. Available to U.S. and non-U.S. citizens. *Application Requirements:* Application, essay, interview, references, test scores, transcript. *Deadline:* March 1.

Contact Jamie Bewley Byrd, Scholarship Program Administrator, Kentucky Transportation Cabinet, 200 Mero Street, Frankfort, KY 40622. *E-mail:* jamie.bewleybyrd@ky.gov. *Web site:* www.transportation.ky.gov.

Kentucky Tuition Grant (KTG). Grants available to Kentucky residents who are full-time undergraduates at an independent college within the state. Based on financial need. Must submit FAFSA. *Award:* Grant for use in freshman, sophomore, junior, or senior year; not renewable. *Award amount:* $200–$3000. *Number of awards:* 12,000–13,000. *Eligibility Requirements:* Applicant must be enrolled or expecting to enroll full-time at a two-year or four-year institution or university; resident of Kentucky and studying in Kentucky. Available to U.S. citizens. *Application Requirements:* Application, financial need analysis, FAFSA. *Deadline:* March 15.

Contact Becky Gilpatrick, Student Aid Branch Manager, Kentucky Higher Education Assistance Authority (KHEAA), PO Box 798, Frankfort, KY 40602-0798. *E-mail:* rgilpatrick@kheaa.com. *Phone:* 800-928-8926 Ext. 67394. *Fax:* 502-696-7496. *Web site:* www.kheaa.com.

Minority Educator Recruitment and Retention Scholarship. Conversion loan or scholarship for Kentucky residents. Provides up to $5000 per academic year to minority students majoring in teacher education and pursuing initial teacher certification. Must be repaid with interest if scholarship requirements are not met. *Academic Fields/Career Goals:* Education; Special Education. *Award:* Forgivable loan for use in freshman, sophomore, junior, or senior year; not renewable. *Award amount:* up to $5000. *Number of awards:* 200–300. *Eligibility Requirements:* Applicant must be American Indian/Alaska Native, Asian/Pacific Islander, Black (non-Hispanic), or Hispanic; enrolled or expecting to enroll full-time at a two-year or four-year institution or university; resident of Kentucky and studying in Kentucky. Applicant must have 3.5 GPA or higher. Available to U.S. citizens. *Application Requirements:* Application. *Deadline:* continuous.

Contact Natasha Murray, Program Director, Kentucky Higher Education Assistance Authority (KHEAA), 500 Metro Street, Frankfort, KY 40601. *E-mail:* natasha.murray@education.ky.gov. *Phone:* 502-564-1479. *Web site:* www.kheaa.com.

Robert C. Byrd Honors Scholarship-Kentucky. Scholarship available to high school seniors who show past high achievement and potential for continued academic success. Must have applied for admission or have been accepted for enrollment at a public or private nonprofit postsecondary school. Must be a Kentucky resident. *Award:* Scholarship for use in freshman, sophomore, junior, or senior year; renewable. *Award amount:* up to $1500. *Number of awards:* varies. *Eligibility Requirements:* Applicant must be high school student; planning to enroll or expecting to enroll full-time at a two-year or four-year institution or university and resident of Kentucky. Applicant must have 3.5 GPA or higher. Available to U.S. citizens. *Application Requirements:* Application, test scores. *Deadline:* March 14.

Contact Donna Melton, Scholarship Committee, Kentucky Department of Education, 500 Mero Street, 17th Floor, Frankfort, KY 40601. *E-mail:* dmelton@kde.state.ky.us. *Phone:* 502-564-1479. *Web site:* www.education.ky.gov.

Touchstone Energy All "A" Classic Scholarship. Award of $1000 for senior student in good standing at a Kentucky high school which is a member of the All Classic. Applicant must be a U.S. citizen and must plan to attend a postsecondary institution in Kentucky in the upcoming year as a full-time student and be drug free. *Award:* Scholarship for use in freshman year; not renewable. *Award amount:* $1000. *Number of awards:* 12. *Eligibility Requirements:* Applicant must be high school student; planning to enroll or expecting to enroll full-time at a two-year, four-year, or technical institution or university; resident of Kentucky and studying in Kentucky. Available to U.S. citizens. *Application Requirements:* Application, essay, photo, references, transcript. *Deadline:* December 3.

Contact David Cowden, Chairperson, Scholarship Committee, Kentucky Touchstone Energy Cooperatives, 1320 Lincoln Road, Lewisport, KY 42351. *E-mail:* allaclassic@alltel.net. *Phone:* 859-744-4812. *Web site:* www.ekpc.coop.

WIRE Scholarships. Scholarship available to Kentucky students who are juniors or seniors in a Kentucky college or university and have 60 credit hours by fall semester. Immediate family of student must be served by one of the state's 24 rural electric distribution cooperatives. Awards based on academic achievement, extracurricular activities, career goals, recommendations. *Award:* Scholarship for use in junior or senior year; not renewable. *Award amount:* $1000. *Number of awards:* 3. *Eligibility Requirements:* Applicant must be enrolled or expecting to enroll full-time at a four-year, or technical institution or university; resident of Kentucky and studying in Kentucky. Available to U.S. citizens. *Application Requirements:* Application, transcript, a letter explaining how this scholarship would enhance your academic goals. *Deadline:* June 19.

Contact Ellie Hobgood, Scholarship Coordinator, Kentucky Association of Electric Cooperatives, Inc., PO Box 32170, Louisville, KY 40232. *E-mail:* ehobgood@kentuckyliving.com. *Phone:* 800-595-4846. *Web site:* www.kaec.com.

LOUISIANA

Hemophilia Federation of America Educational Scholarship. One-time scholarship for persons with hemophilia, attending either full-time or part-time in any accredited two- or four-year college, university, or vocation/technical school in the United States. *Award:* Scholarship for use in freshman, sophomore, junior, or senior year; not renewable. *Award amount:* $1500. *Number of awards:* 1–3. *Eligibility Requirements:* Applicant must be enrolled or expecting to enroll full- or part-time at a two-year, four-year, or technical institution or university. Applicant must be physically disabled. Available to U.S. citizens. *Application Requirements:* Application, essay, financial need analysis, references. *Deadline:* April 30.

Contact Scholarship Committee, Hemophilia Federation of America, 1405 West Pinhook Road, Suite 101, Lafayette, LA 70503. *E-mail:* info@hemophiliafed.org. *Phone:* 337-261-9787. *Web site:* www.hemophiliaed.org.

Leveraging Educational Assistance Program (LEAP)/Special Leveraging Educational Assistance Program (SLEAP). Apply by completing the FAFSA each year. Must be a resident of Louisiana and must be attending an institution in Louisiana. Institution the student plans to attend must recommend student for award. When you submit the FAFSA, you have automatically applied for all four levels of TOPS, for the LA LEAP/SLEAP Grant, for Louisiana Guaranteed Loans, and for Federal Pell Grants and Go Grants. Please do not send separate letters to application to the TOPS office. *Award:* Grant for use in freshman, sophomore, junior, or senior year; renewable. *Award amount:* $200–$2000. *Eligibility Requirements:* Applicant must be enrolled or expecting to enroll full- or part-time at a two-year, four-year, or technical institution or university; resident of Louisiana and studying in Louisiana. Available to U.S. citizens. *Application Requirements:* Application, financial need analysis, FAFSA. *Deadline:* July 1.

Contact Public Information, Louisiana Office of Student Financial Assistance, PO Box 91202, Baton Rouge, LA 70821-9202. *E-mail:* custserv@osfa.state.la.us. *Phone:* 800-259-5626 Ext. 1012. *Fax:* 225-922-0790. *Web site:* www.osfa.state.la.us.

Louisiana Department of Veterans Affairs State Aid Program. Tuition exemption at any state-supported college, university, or technical institute in Louisiana for children (dependents between the ages of 18-25) of veterans that are rated 90 percent or above service connected disabled by the U.S. Department of Veterans Affairs. Tuition exemption also available for the surviving spouse and children (dependents between the ages of 18-25) of veterans who died on active duty, in line of duty, or where death was the result of a disability incurred in or aggravated by military service. For residents of Louisiana. *Award:* Scholarship for use in freshman, sophomore, junior, or senior year; not renewable. *Award amount:* varies. *Number of awards:* varies. *Eligibility Requirements:* Applicant must be age 18-25; enrolled or expecting to enroll full-time at a two-year, four-year, or technical institution or university; resident of Louisiana and studying in Louisiana. Available to U.S. citizens. Applicant or parent must meet one or more of the following requirements: general military experience; retired from active duty; disabled or killed as a result of military service; prisoner of war; or missing in action. *Application Requirements:* Application. *Deadline:* continuous.

Contact Louisiana Department of Veteran Affairs. *Web site:* www.vetaffairs.com.

Louisiana National Guard State Tuition Exemption Program. Renewable award for college undergraduates to receive tuition exemption upon satisfactory performance in the Louisiana National Guard. Applicant must attend a state-funded institution in Louisiana, be a resident and registered voter in Louisiana, meet the academic and residency requirements of the university attended, and provide documentation of Louisiana National Guard enlistment. The exemption can be used for up to 15 semesters. Minimum 2.5 GPA required. *Award:* Scholarship for use in freshman, sophomore, junior, or senior year; renewable. *Award amount:* varies. *Number of awards:* varies. *Eligibility Requirements:* Applicant must be enrolled or expecting to enroll full- or part-time at a two-year, four-year, or technical institution or university; resident of Louisiana and studying in Louisiana. Applicant must have 2.5 GPA or higher. Available to U.S. citizens. Applicant or parent must meet one or more of the following requirements: Air Force National Guard or Army National Guard experience; retired from active duty; disabled or killed as a result of military service; prisoner of war; or missing in action. *Application Requirements:* Application, test scores, transcript. *Deadline:* continuous.

Contact Jona M. Hughes, Education Services Officer, Louisiana National Guard-State of Louisiana, Joint Task Force LA, Building 35, Jackson Barracks, JI-PD, New Orleans, LA 70146-0330. *E-mail:* hughesj@la-arng.ngb.army.mil. *Phone:* 504-278-8531 Ext. 8304. *Fax:* 504-278-8025. *Web site:* www.la.ngb.army.mil.

Robert C. Byrd Honors Scholarship-Louisiana. Applicant must have earned a high school diploma or equivalent (GED) in Louisiana in the same academic year in which the scholarship is to be awarded. Minimum 3.5 GPA required. Must be a U.S. citizen and legal resident of Louisiana. Total number of awards vary each year. *Award:* Scholarship for use in freshman, sophomore, junior, or senior year; renewable. *Award amount:* up to $6000. *Number of awards:* 110. *Eligibility Requirements:* Applicant must be enrolled or expecting to enroll full-time at a four-year institution or university and resident of Louisiana. Applicant must have 2.5 GPA or higher. Available to U.S. citizens. *Application Requirements:* Application, essay, test scores, transcript, selective service form. *Deadline:* March 10.

Contact Melissa Hollins, Scholarship Coordinator, Louisiana State Department of Education, PO Box 94064, Baton Rouge, LA 70804. *E-mail:* melissa.hollins@la.gov. *Phone:* 225-342-2098. *Fax:* 225-342-7316. *Web site:* www.doe.state.la.us.

Rockefeller State Wildlife Scholarship. For high school graduates, college undergraduates, and college graduate students majoring in forestry, wildlife, or marine science. High school graduates and college undergraduates with fewer than 24 hours, must have at least a 2.5 grade point average and have scored at least a 20 on the ACT or a 940 on the SAT. College graduate students must have a grade point average of at least 3.0 in order to apply. Renewable up to five years as an undergraduate and two years as a graduate student. *Academic Fields/Career Goals:* Biology; Marine Biology; Marine/Ocean Engineering; Natural Resources; Oceanography. *Award:* Scholarship for use in freshman, sophomore, junior, or senior year; renewable. *Award amount:* $1000. *Number of awards:* 60. *Eligibility Requirements:* Applicant must be enrolled or expecting to enroll full-time at a four-year institution or university; resident of Louisiana and studying in Louisiana. Applicant must have 2.5 GPA or higher. Available to U.S. citizens. *Application Requirements:* Application, test scores, transcript, FAFSA. *Deadline:* July 1.

Contact Public Information, Louisiana Office of Student Financial Assistance, PO Box 91202, Baton Rouge, LA 70821-9202. *E-mail:* custserv@osfa.state.la.us. *Phone:* 800-259-5626 Ext. 1012. *Fax:* 225-922-0790. *Web site:* www.osfa.state.la.us.

Taylor Opportunity Program for Students. Program awards 8 semesters of tuition to any Louisiana State postsecondary institution. Program awards 8 semesters of an amount equal to the weighted average public tuition fee, to students attending a LAICU private institution. When you submit the FAFSA, you have automatically applied for all four levels of TOPS, for the LA LEAP/SLEAP Grant, for Louisiana Guaranteed Loans, and for Federal Pell Grants and Go Grants. Please do not send separate letters to application to the TOPS office. *Award:* Scholarship for use in freshman, sophomore, junior, or senior year; renewable. *Award amount:* $729–$1747. *Number of awards:* varies. *Eligibility Requirements:* Applicant must be enrolled or expecting to enroll full-time at a two-year, four-year, or technical institution or university; resident of Louisiana and studying in Louisiana. Applicant must have 2.5 GPA or higher. Available to U.S. citizens. *Application Requirements:* Application, test scores, transcript. *Deadline:* July 1.

Contact Public Information, Louisiana Office of Student Financial Assistance, PO Box 91202, Baton Rouge, LA 70821-9202. *E-mail:* custserv@osfa.state.la.us. *Phone:* 800-259-5626 Ext. 1012. *Fax:* 225-922-0790. *Web site:* www.osfa.state.la.us.

Taylor Opportunity Program for Students Award—Performance Level. Program awards 8 semesters of tuition to any Louisiana State postsecondary institution. Program awards an amount equal to the weighted average public tuition fee, to students attending a LAICU private institution. When you submit the FAFSA, you have automatically applied for all four levels of TOPS, for the LA LEAP/SLEAP Grant, for Louisiana Guaranteed Loans, and for Federal Pell Grants and Go Grants. Please do not send separate letters to application to the TOPS office. *Award:* Scholarship for use in freshman, sophomore, junior, or senior year; renewable. *Award amount:* $1129–$1947. *Number of awards:* varies. *Eligibility Requirements:* Applicant must be enrolled or expecting to enroll full-time at a two-year, four-year, or technical institution or university; resident of Louisiana and studying in Louisiana. Applicant must have 3.0 GPA or higher. Available to U.S. citizens. *Application Requirements:* Application, test scores, transcript. *Deadline:* July 1.

Contact Public Information, Louisiana Office of Student Financial Assistance, PO Box 91202, Baton Rouge, LA 70821-9202. *E-mail:* custserv@osfa.state.la.us. *Phone:* 800-259-5626 Ext. 1012. *Fax:* 225-922-0790. *Web site:* www.osfa.state.la.us.

Taylor Opportunity Program for Students—Honors Level. Program awards 8 semesters of tuition to any Louisiana State postsecondary institution. Program awards an amount equal to the weighted average public tuition fee, to students attending a LAICU private institution. In addition $400 per semester is provided. When you submit the FAFSA, you have automatically applied for all four levels of TOPS, for the LA LEAP/SLEAP Grant, for Louisiana Guaranteed Loans, and for Federal Pell Grants and Go Grants. Please do not send separate letters to application to the TOPS office. For more information, see Web: www.fafsa.ed.gov. *Award:* Scholarship for use in freshman, sophomore, junior, or senior year; renewable. *Award amount:* $1129–$2147. *Number of awards:* varies. *Eligibility Requirements:* Applicant must be enrolled or expecting to enroll full-time at a two-year, four-year, or technical institution or university; resident of Louisiana and studying in Louisiana. Applicant must have 3.0 GPA or higher. Available to U.S. citizens. *Application Requirements:* Application, test scores, transcript. *Deadline:* July 1.

Contact Public Information, Louisiana Office of Student Financial Assistance, PO Box 91202, Baton Rouge, LA 70821-9202. *E-mail:* custserv@osfa.state.la.us. *Phone:* 800-259-5626 Ext. 1012. *Fax:* 225-922-0790. *Web site:* www.osfa.state.la.us.

Taylor Opportunity Program for Students Tech Award. Program awards an amount equal to tuition for up to two years of technical training at a Louisiana postsecondary institution that offers a vocational or technical education certificate or diploma program, or a non-academic degree program. Must have completed the TOPS Opportunity core curriculum or the TOPS Tech core curriculum, must have achieved a 2.50 grade point average over the core curriculum only, and must have achieved an ACT score of 17. Program awards an amount equal to the weighted average public tuition fee for technical programs to students attending a LAICU private institution for technical training. When you submit the FAFSA, you have automatically applied for all four levels of TOPS, for the LA LEAP/SLEAP Grant, for Louisiana Guaranteed Loans, and for Federal Pell Grants and Go Grants. Please do not send separate letters to application to the TOPS office. *Award:* Scholarship for use in freshman or sophomore year; renewable. *Award amount:* $308–$880. *Number of awards:* varies. *Eligibility Requirements:* Applicant must be enrolled or expecting to enroll full-time at a technical institution; resident of Louisiana and studying in Louisiana. Applicant must have 2.5 GPA or higher. Available to U.S. citizens. *Application Requirements:* Application, test scores, transcript, ACT of 17 OR SAT of 810. *Deadline:* July 1.

Contact Public Information, Louisiana Office of Student Financial Assistance, PO Box 91202, Baton Rouge, LA 70821-9202. *E-mail:* custserv@osfa.state.la.us. *Phone:* 800-259-5626 Ext. 1012. *Fax:* 225-922-0790. *Web site:* www.osfa.state.la.us.

MAINE

American Legion Auxiliary Department of Maine Daniel E. Lambert Memorial Scholarship. Scholarships to assist young men and women in continuing their education beyond high school. Must demonstrate financial need, must be a resident of the State of Maine, U.S. citizen, and parent must be a veteran. *Award:* Scholarship for use in freshman year; not renewable. *Award amount:* $1000. *Number of awards:* up to 2. *Eligibility Requirements:* Applicant must be high school student; planning to enroll or expecting to enroll full-time at a four-year institution or university and resident of Maine. Available to U.S. citizens. Applicant or parent must meet one or more of the following requirements: general military experience; retired from active duty; disabled or killed as a result of military service; prisoner of war; or missing in action. *Application Requirements:* Application, financial need analysis. *Deadline:* May 1.

Contact American Legion Auxiliary, Department of Maine. *Web site:* www.mainelegion.org.

American Legion Auxiliary Department of Maine National President's Scholarship. Scholarships to children of veterans who served in the Armed Forces during the eligibility dates for The American Legion. One $2500, one $2000, and one $1000 scholarship will be awarded. Applicant must complete 50 hours of community service during his/her high school years. *Award:* Scholarship for use in freshman year; not renewable. *Award amount:* $1000–$2500. *Number of awards:* 3. *Eligibility Requirements:* Applicant must be high school student; planning to enroll or expecting to enroll full-time at a four-year institution or university and resident of Maine. Applicant or parent of applicant must have employment or volunteer experience in community service. Available to U.S. citizens. Applicant or parent must meet one or more of the following requirements: general military experience; retired from active duty; disabled or killed as a result of military service; prisoner of war; or missing in action. *Application Requirements:* Application, essay, references, test scores, transcript. *Deadline:* March 1.

Contact American Legion Auxiliary, Department of Maine. *Web site:* www.mainelegion.org.

American Legion Auxiliary Department of Maine Past Presidents' Parley Nurses Scholarship. One-time award for child, grandchild, sister, or brother of veteran. Must be resident of Maine and wishing to continue education at accredited school in medical field. Must submit photo, doctor's statement, and evidence of civic activity. Minimum 3.5 GPA required. *Academic Fields/Career Goals:* Health and Medical Sciences; Nursing. *Award:* Scholarship for use in freshman, sophomore, junior, or senior year; not renewable. *Award amount:* $300. *Number of awards:* 1. *Eligibility Requirements:* Applicant must be age 18 and over; enrolled or expecting to enroll full-time at a two-year, four-year, or technical institution or university and resident of Maine. Applicant or parent of applicant must have employment or volunteer experience in community service. Applicant must have 2.5 GPA or higher. Available to U.S. citizens. Applicant or parent must meet one or more of the following requirements: general military experience; retired from active duty; disabled or killed as a result of military service; prisoner of war; or missing in action. *Application Requirements:* Application, photo, references, transcript, doctor's statement. *Deadline:* March 31.

Contact American Legion Auxiliary, Department of Maine. *Web site:* www.mainelegion.org.

Early College For ME. Scholarship for high school students who have not made plans for college but are academically capable of success in college. Recipients are selected by their school principal or director. Students must be entering a Maine Community College. Refer to Web site: http://www.mccs.me.edu/scholarships.html. *Award:* Scholarship for use in freshman year; renewable. *Award amount:* $2000. *Number of awards:* 200. *Eligibility Requirements:* Applicant must be high school student; planning to enroll or expecting to enroll full-time at a two-year or four-year institution or university; resident of Maine and studying in Maine. Available to U.S. citizens. *Application Requirements:* Application, financial need analysis, references, transcript. *Deadline:* varies.

Contact Charles P. Collins, State Director, Center for Career Development, Maine Community College System, 323 State Street, Augusta, ME 04330. *E-mail:* ccollins@mccs.me.edu. *Phone:* 207-767-5210 Ext. 4115. *Fax:* 207-629-4048. *Web site:* www.mccs.me.edu.

Educators for Maine Forgivable Loan Program. Forgivable loan for residents of Maine who are high school seniors, college students, or college graduates with a minimum 3.0 GPA, studying or preparing to study teacher education. Must teach in Maine upon graduation. Award based on merit. For application information see Web site: http://www.famemaine.com. *Academic Fields/Career Goals:* Education. *Award:* Forgivable loan for use in freshman, sophomore, junior, or senior year; renewable. *Award amount:* $2000–$3000. *Number of awards:* up to 500. *Eligibility Requirements:* Applicant must be enrolled or expecting to enroll full-time at a two-year or four-year institution or university and resident of Maine. Applicant must have 3.0 GPA or higher. Available to U.S. citizens. *Application Requirements:* Application, essay, test scores, transcript. *Deadline:* May 15.

Contact Finance Authority of Maine. *Web site:* www.famemaine.com.

Maine Rural Rehabilitation Fund Scholarship Program. One-time scholarship open to Maine residents enrolled in or accepted by any school, college, or university. Must be full time and demonstrate financial need. Those opting for a Maine institution given preference. Major must lead to an agricultural career. Minimum 3.0 GPA required. *Academic Fields/Career Goals:* Agribusiness; Agriculture; Animal/Veterinary Sciences. *Award:* Scholarship for use in freshman, sophomore, junior, senior, graduate, or postgraduate years; not renewable. *Award amount:* $800–$2000. *Number of awards:* 10–20. *Eligibility Requirements:* Applicant must be enrolled or expecting to enroll full-time at a two-year, four-year, or technical institution or university and resident of Maine. Applicant must have 3.0 GPA or higher. Available to U.S. citizens. *Application Requirements:* Application, autobiography, financial need analysis, transcript. *Deadline:* June 15.

Contact Jane Aiudi, Director of Marketing, Maine Department of Agriculture, Food and Rural Resources, 28 State House Station, Augusta, ME 04333-0028. *E-mail:* jane.aiudi@maine.gov. *Phone:* 207-287-7628. *Fax:* 207-287-5576. *Web site:* www.maine.gov/agriculture.

Robert C. Byrd Honors Scholarship-Maine. Merit-based, renewable scholarship of up to $1500 annually for graduating high school seniors. Must have a minimum of 3.0 GPA. Must be a resident of Maine. Superior academic performance is the primary criterion. For application, see Web site: http://www.famemaine.com. *Award:* Scholarship for use in freshman year; renewable. *Award amount:* up to $1500. *Number of awards:* up to 30. *Eligibility Requirements:* Applicant must be high school student; planning to enroll or expecting to enroll full-time at a two-year, four-year, or technical institution or university and resident of Maine. Applicant must have 3.0 GPA or higher. Available to U.S. citizens. *Application Requirements:* Application, essay, transcript, high school profile. **Deadline:** May 1.

Contact Finance Authority of Maine. *Web site:* www.famemaine.com.

State of Maine Grant Program. Scholarship for residents of Maine, attending an eligible school in Connecticut, Maine, Massachusetts, New Hampshire, Pennsylvania, Rhode Island, Washington, D.C., or Vermont. Award based on need. Must apply annually. Complete free application for Federal Student Aid to apply. One-time award for undergraduate study. For further information see Web site: http://www.famemaine.com. *Award:* Grant for use in freshman, sophomore, junior, or senior year; not renewable. *Award amount:* \$500–\$1250. *Number of awards:* up to 13,000. *Eligibility Requirements:* Applicant must be enrolled or expecting to enroll full- or part-time at a two-year, four-year, or technical institution or university; resident of Maine and studying in Connecticut, District of Columbia, Maine, Massachusetts, New Hampshire, Pennsylvania, Rhode Island, or Vermont. Available to U.S. citizens. *Application Requirements:* Application, financial need analysis, FAFSA. **Deadline:** May 1.

Contact Finance Authority of Maine. *Web site:* www.famemaine.com.

Tuition Waiver Programs. Provides tuition waivers for children and spouses of EMS personnel, firefighters, and law enforcement officers who have been killed in the line of duty and for students who were foster children under the custody of the Department of Human Services when they graduated from high school. Waivers valid at the University of Maine System, the Maine Technical College System, and Maine Maritime Academy. Applicant must reside and study in Maine. *Award:* Grant for use in freshman, sophomore, junior, or senior year; renewable. *Award amount:* varies. *Number of awards:* up to 30. *Eligibility Requirements:* Applicant must be enrolled or expecting to enroll full- or part-time at a four-year institution or university; resident of Maine and studying in Maine. Applicant or parent of applicant must have employment or volunteer experience in police/firefighting. Available to U.S. citizens. *Application Requirements:* Application, letter from the Department of Human Services documenting that applicant is in their custody and residing in foster care at the time of graduation from high school or its equivalent. **Deadline:** continuous.

Contact Finance Authority of Maine. *Web site:* www.famemaine.com.

U.S. Department of Education Fulbright-Hays Project Abroad Scholarship for Programs in China. Scholarships offered to students who are participating in a CIEE Chinese language programs in China or Taiwan. Must be a U.S. citizen enrolled in a CIEE program. Students must have completed the equivalent of two years study in Chinese language (documented). Deadlines: April 1 and November 1. There is also a return requirement for scholarship awardees to submit a program report and evaluation. *Academic Fields/Career Goals:* Asian Studies; Education. *Award:* Scholarship for use in junior or senior year; not renewable. *Award amount:* \$1000–\$12,000. *Number of awards:* 1–20. *Eligibility Requirements:* Applicant must be enrolled or expecting to enroll full-time at a four-year institution or university and must have an interest in foreign language. Applicant must have 3.0 GPA or higher. Available to U.S. citizens. *Application Requirements:* Application, essay, financial need analysis, references, transcript, copy of passport or birth certificate. **Deadline:** varies.

Contact CIEE: Council on International Educational Exchange. *Web site:* www.ciee.org.

Veterans Dependents Educational Benefits-Maine. Tuition waiver award for dependent children or spouses of veterans permanently and totally disabled resulting from service-connected disability; died from a service-connected disability; at time of death was totally and permanently disabled due to service-connected disability, but whose death was not related to the service-connected disability; or member of the Armed Forces on active duty who has been listed for more than 90 days as missing in action, captured or forcibly detained or interned in the line of duty. Benefits apply only to the University of Maine System, Maine community colleges and Maine Maritime Academy. Must be high school graduate. Must submit with application proof of veteran's VA disability along with dependent verification paperwork such as birth, marriage, or adoption certificate and proof of enrollment in degree program. *Award:* Scholarship for use in freshman, sophomore, junior, or senior year; not renewable. *Award amount:* varies. *Number of awards:* varies. *Eligibility Requirements:* Applicant must be enrolled or expecting to enroll full- or part-time at a two-year or four-year institution or university; resident of Maine and studying in Maine. Available to U.S. citizens. Applicant must have general military experience. *Application Requirements:* Application, see Web site for complete application instructions.

Contact Mrs. Paula Gagnon, Office Associate II, Maine Division of Veterans Services, State House, Station 117, Augusta, ME 04333-0117. *E-mail:* mainebvs@maine.gov. *Phone:* 207-626-4464. *Fax:* 207-626-4471. *Web site:* www.maine.gov/dvem/bvs.

MARYLAND

Charles W. Riley Fire and Emergency Medical Services Tuition Reimbursement Program. Award intended to reimburse members of rescue organizations serving Maryland communities for tuition costs of course work towards a degree or certificate in fire service or medical technology. Must attend a two- or four-year school in Maryland. Minimum 2.0 GPA. The scholarship is worth up to \$6500. *Academic Fields/Career Goals:* Fire Sciences; Health and Medical Sciences; Trade/Technical Specialties. *Award:* Scholarship for use in freshman, sophomore, junior, or senior year; not renewable. *Award amount:* up to \$6500. *Number of awards:* up to 150. *Eligibility Requirements:* Applicant must be enrolled or expecting to enroll full- or part-time at a two-year or four-year institution or university; resident of Maryland and studying in Maryland. Applicant or parent of applicant must have employment or volunteer experience in police/firefighting. Available to U.S. citizens. *Application Requirements:* Application, transcript, tuition receipt, proof of enrollment. **Deadline:** July 1.

Contact Maura Sappington, Office of Student Financial Assistance, Maryland State Higher Education Commission, 839 Bestgate Road, Suite 400, Annapolis, MD 21401-3013. *E-mail:* msapping@mhec.state.md.us. *Phone:* 410-260-4569. *Fax:* 410-260-3203. *Web site:* www.mhec.state.md.us.

Delegate Scholarship Program-Maryland. Delegate scholarships help Maryland residents attending Maryland degree-granting institutions, certain career schools, or nursing diploma schools. May attend out-of-state institution if Maryland Higher Education Commission deems major to be unique and not offered at a Maryland institution. Free Application for Federal Student Aid may be required. Students interested in this program should apply by contacting their legislative district delegate. *Award:* Scholarship for use in freshman, sophomore, junior, or senior year; not renewable. *Award amount:* \$200–\$8650. *Number of awards:* up to 3500. *Eligibility Requirements:* Applicant must be enrolled or expecting to enroll full- or part-time at a two-year, four-year, or technical institution or university; resident of Maryland and studying in Maryland. Available to U.S. citizens. *Application Requirements:* Application, FAFSA. **Deadline:** continuous.

Contact Monica Wheatley, Office of Student Financial Assistance, Maryland State Higher Education Commission, 839 Bestgate Road, Suite 400, Annapolis, MD 21401-3013. *E-mail:* osfamail@mhec.state.md.us. *Phone:* 800-974-1024. *Fax:* 410-260-3200. *Web site:* www.mhec.state.md.us.

Distinguished Scholar Award-Maryland. Renewable award for Maryland students enrolled full-time at Maryland institutions.

National Merit Scholar Finalists automatically offered award. Others may qualify for the award in satisfying criteria of a minimum 3.7 GPA or in combination with high test scores, or for Talent in Arts competition in categories of music, drama, dance, or visual arts. Must maintain annual 3.0 GPA in college for award to be renewed. *Award:* Scholarship for use in freshman, sophomore, junior, or senior year; renewable. *Award amount:* up to $3000. *Number of awards:* up to 1400. *Eligibility Requirements:* Applicant must be high school student; planning to enroll or expecting to enroll full-time at a two-year or four-year institution or university; resident of Maryland and studying in Maryland. Available to U.S. citizens. *Application Requirements:* Application, test scores, transcript. *Deadline:* varies.

Contact Tamika McKelvin, Program Administrator, Maryland State Higher Education Commission, 839 Bestgate Road, Suite 400, Annapolis, MD 21401-3013. *E-mail:* tmckelvi@mhec.state.md.us. *Phone:* 410-260-4546. *Fax:* 410-260-3200. *Web site:* www.mhec.state.md.us.

Distinguished Scholar Community College Transfer Program. Scholarship available for Maryland residents who have completed 60 credit hours or an associate degree at a Maryland community college and are transferring to a Maryland four-year institution. *Award:* Scholarship for use in freshman or sophomore year; renewable. *Award amount:* $3000. *Number of awards:* 127. *Eligibility Requirements:* Applicant must be enrolled or expecting to enroll full-time at a two-year institution; resident of Maryland and studying in Maryland. Available to U.S. citizens. *Application Requirements:* Application, transcript. *Deadline:* March 1.

Contact Maura Sappington, Program Manager, Maryland State Higher Education Commission, 839 Bestgate Road, Suite 400, Annapolis, MD 21401-3013. *E-mail:* msapping@mhec.state.md.us. *Phone:* 410-260-4569. *Fax:* 410-260-3203. *Web site:* www.mhec.state.md.us.

Edward T. Conroy Memorial Scholarship Program. Scholarship for dependents of deceased or 100 percent disabled U.S. Armed Forces personnel; the son, daughter, or surviving spouse of a victim of the September 11, 2001 terrorist attacks who died as a result of the attacks on the World Trade Center in New York City, the attack on the Pentagon in Virginia, or the crash of United Airlines Flight 93 in Pennsylvania; a POW/MIA of the Vietnam Conflict or his/her son or daughter; the son, daughter or surviving spouse (who has not remarried) of a state or local public safety employee or volunteer who died in the line of duty; or a state or local public safety employee or volunteer who was 100 percent disabled in the line of duty. Must be Maryland resident at time of disability. Submit applicable VA certification. Must be at least 16 years of age and attend Maryland institution. *Award:* Scholarship for use in freshman, sophomore, junior, or senior year; renewable. *Award amount:* $7200–$9000. *Number of awards:* up to 121. *Eligibility Requirements:* Applicant must be age 16-24; enrolled or expecting to enroll full- or part-time at a two-year or four-year institution or university; resident of Maryland and studying in Maryland. Applicant or parent of applicant must have employment or volunteer experience in police/firefighting. Available to U.S. citizens. Applicant or parent must meet one or more of the following requirements: general military experience; retired from active duty; disabled or killed as a result of military service; prisoner of war; or missing in action. *Application Requirements:* Application, birth and death certificate, disability papers. *Deadline:* July 15.

Contact Linda Asplin, Office of Student Financial Assistance, Maryland State Higher Education Commission, 839 Bestgate Road, Suite 400, Annapolis, MD 21401-3013. *E-mail:* lasplin@mhec.state.md.us. *Phone:* 410-260-4563. *Fax:* 410-260-3203. *Web site:* www.mhec.state.md.us.

Graduate and Professional Scholarship Program-Maryland. Graduate and professional scholarships provide need-based financial assistance to students attending a Maryland school of medicine, dentistry, law, pharmacy, social work, or nursing. Funds are provided to specific Maryland colleges and universities. Students must demonstrate financial need and be Maryland residents. Contact institution financial aid office for more information. *Academic Fields/Career Goals:* Dental Health/Services; Health and Medical Sciences; Law/Legal Services; Nursing; Social Services. *Award:* Scholarship for use in freshman, sophomore, junior, or senior year; renewable. *Award amount:* $1000–$5000. *Number of awards:* up to 584. *Eligibility Requirements:* Applicant must be enrolled or expecting to enroll full- or part-time at a four-year institution or university; resident of Maryland and studying in Maryland. Available to U.S. citizens. *Application Requirements:* Application, financial need analysis, contact institution financial aid office. *Deadline:* March 1.

Contact Monica Wheatley, Program Manager, Maryland State Higher Education Commission, 839 Bestgate Road, Suite 400, Annapolis, MD 21401. *E-mail:* mwheatle@mhec.state.md.us. *Phone:* 410-260-4560. *Fax:* 410-260-3202. *Web site:* www.mhec.state.md.us.

Howard P. Rawlings Educational Excellence Awards Educational Assistance Grant. Award for Maryland residents accepted or enrolled in a full-time undergraduate degree or certificate program at a Maryland institution or hospital nursing school. Must submit financial aid form by March 1. Must earn 2.0 GPA in college to maintain award. *Award:* Grant for use in freshman, sophomore, junior, or senior year; renewable. *Award amount:* $400–$2700. *Number of awards:* 15,000–30,000. *Eligibility Requirements:* Applicant must be enrolled or expecting to enroll full-time at a two-year or four-year institution or university; resident of Maryland and studying in Maryland. Available to U.S. citizens. *Application Requirements:* Application, financial need analysis. *Deadline:* March 1.

Contact Office of Student Financial Assistance, Maryland State Higher Education Commission, 839 Bestgate Road, Suite 400, Annapolis, MD 21401-3013. *E-mail:* osfamail@mhec.state.md.us. *Phone:* 800-974-1024. *Fax:* 410-260-3200. *Web site:* www.mhec.state.md.us.

Howard P. Rawlings Educational Excellence Awards Guaranteed Access Grant. Award for Maryland resident enrolling full-time in an undergraduate program at a Maryland institution. Must be under 21 at time of first award and begin college within one year of completing high school in Maryland with a minimum 2.5 GPA. Must have an annual family income less than 130 percent of the federal poverty level guideline. *Award:* Grant for use in freshman, sophomore, junior, or senior year; renewable. *Award amount:* $400–$14,800. *Number of awards:* up to 1000. *Eligibility Requirements:* Applicant must be age 21 or under; enrolled or expecting to enroll full-time at a two-year or four-year institution or university; resident of Maryland and studying in Maryland. Applicant must have 3.5 GPA or higher. Available to U.S. citizens. *Application Requirements:* Application, financial need analysis, transcript. *Deadline:* March 1.

Contact Theresa Lowe, Office of Student Financial Assistance, Maryland State Higher Education Commission, 839 Bestgate Road, Suite 400, Annapolis, MD 21401-3013. *E-mail:* osfamail@mhec.state.md.us. *Phone:* 410-260-4555. *Fax:* 410-260-3200. *Web site:* www.mhec.state.md.us.

Janet L. Hoffmann Loan Assistance Repayment Program. Provides assistance for repayment of loan debt to Maryland residents working full-time in nonprofit organizations and state or local governments. Must submit Employment Verification Form and Lender Verification Form. *Academic Fields/Career Goals:* Education; Law/Legal Services; Nursing; Social Services; Therapy/Rehabilitation. *Award:* Grant for use in freshman, sophomore, junior, or senior year; not renewable. *Award amount:* $1500–$10,000. *Number of awards:* up to 700. *Eligibility Requirements:* Applicant must be enrolled or expecting to enroll full-time at a four-year institution or university; resident of Maryland and studying in Maryland. Applicant or parent of applicant must have employment or volunteer experience in government/politics. Available to U.S. citizens. *Application Requirements:* Application, transcript, IRS 1040 form. *Deadline:* September 30.

Contact Tamika McKelvin, Office of Student Financial Assistance, Maryland State Higher Education Commission, 839 Bestgate Road, Suite 400, Annapolis, MD 21401. *E-mail:* tmckelvil@mhec.state.md.us. *Phone:* 410-260-4546. *Fax:* 410-260-3203. *Web site:* www.mhec.state.md.us.

J.F. Tolbert Memorial Student Grant Program. Awards of $500 granted to Maryland residents attending a private career school in Maryland. The scholarship deadline continues. *Award:* Grant for use in freshman or sophomore year; not renewable. *Award amount:* $500. *Number of awards:* 522. *Eligibility Requirements:* Applicant must be enrolled or expecting to enroll full-time at a technical institution; resident of Maryland and studying in Maryland. Available to U.S. citizens. *Application Requirements:* Application, financial need analysis. *Deadline:* continuous.

Contact Glenda Hamlet, Office of Student Financial Assistance, Maryland State Higher Education Commission, 839 Bestgate Road, Suite 400, Annapolis, MD 21401-3013. *E-mail:* osfamail@mhec.state.md.us. *Phone:* 800-974-1024. *Fax:* 410-260-3200. *Web site:* www.mhec.state.md.us.

Part-Time Grant Program-Maryland. Funds provided to Maryland colleges and universities. Eligible students must be enrolled on a part-time basis (6 to 11 credits) in an undergraduate degree program. Must demonstrate financial need and also be Maryland resident. Contact financial aid office at institution for more information. *Award:* Grant for use in freshman, sophomore, junior, or senior year; renewable. *Award amount:* $200–$1500. *Number of awards:* 1800–9000. *Eligibility Requirements:* Applicant must be enrolled or expecting to enroll part-time at a two-year or four-year institution or university; resident of Maryland and studying in Maryland. Available to U.S. citizens. *Application Requirements:* Application, financial need analysis. *Deadline:* March 1.

Contact Monica Wheatley, Program Manager, Maryland State Higher Education Commission, 839 Bestgate Road, Suite 400, Annapolis, MD 21401. *E-mail:* mwheatle@mhec.state.md.us. *Phone:* 410-260-4560. *Fax:* 410-260-3202. *Web site:* www.mhec.state.md.us.

Senatorial Scholarships-Maryland. Renewable award for Maryland residents attending a Maryland degree-granting institution, nursing diploma school, or certain private career schools. May be used out-of-state only if Maryland Higher Education Commission deems major to be unique and not offered at Maryland institution. The scholarship value is $400 to $7000. *Award:* Scholarship for use in freshman, sophomore, junior, or senior year; renewable. *Award amount:* $400–$7000. *Number of awards:* up to 7000. *Eligibility Requirements:* Applicant must be enrolled or expecting to enroll full- or part-time at a two-year, four-year, or technical institution or university; resident of Maryland and studying in Maryland. Available to U.S. citizens. *Application Requirements:* Application, financial need analysis, test scores. *Deadline:* March 1.

Contact Monica Wheatley, Office of Student Financial Assistance, Maryland State Higher Education Commission, 839 Bestgate Road, Suite 400, Annapolis, MD 21401-3013. *E-mail:* osfamail@mhec.state.md.us. *Phone:* 800-974-1024. *Fax:* 410-260-3200. *Web site:* www.mhec.state.md.us.

Tuition Reduction for Non-Resident Nursing Students. Available to nonresidents of Maryland who attend a two-year or four-year public institution in Maryland. It is renewable provided student maintains academic requirements designated by institution attended. Recipient must agree to serve as a full-time nurse in a hospital or related institution for two to four years. *Academic Fields/Career Goals:* Nursing. *Award:* Scholarship for use in freshman, sophomore, junior, or senior year; renewable. *Award amount:* varies. *Number of awards:* varies. *Eligibility Requirements:* Applicant must be enrolled or expecting to enroll full- or part-time at a two-year or four-year institution and studying in Maryland. Available to U.S. citizens. *Application Requirements:* Application. *Deadline:* varies.

Contact Robert Parker, Director, Maryland State Higher Education Commission, 839 Bestgate Road, Suite 400, Annapolis, MD 21401-3013 USA. *E-mail:* rparker@mhec.state.md.us. *Phone:* 410-260-4558. *Fax:* 410-260-3202. *Web site:* www.mhec.state.md.us.

Tuition Waiver for Foster Care Recipients. Applicant must be a high school graduate or GED recipient and under the age of 21. Must either have resided in a foster care home in Maryland at the time of high school graduation or GED reception, or until 14th birthday, and been adopted after 14th birthday. Applicant, if status approved, will be exempt from paying tuition and mandatory fees at a public college in Maryland. *Award:* Grant for use in freshman, sophomore, junior, senior, or graduate year; renewable. *Award amount:* varies. *Number of awards:* varies. *Eligibility Requirements:* Applicant must be age 21 or under; enrolled or expecting to enroll full- or part-time at a two-year or four-year institution or university; resident of Maryland and studying in Maryland. Available to U.S. citizens. *Application Requirements:* Application, financial need analysis, must inquire at financial aid office of schools. *Deadline:* March 1.

Contact Robert Parker, Director, Maryland State Higher Education Commission, 839 Bestgate Road, Suite 400, Annapolis, MD 21401-3013 USA. *E-mail:* rparker@mhec.state.md.us. *Phone:* 410-260-4558. *Fax:* 410-260-3202. *Web site:* www.mhec.state.md.us.

Veterans of the Afghanistan and Iraq Conflicts Scholarship Program. Provides financial assistance to Maryland resident U.S. Armed Forces personnel who served in Afghanistan or Iraq Conflicts and their children or spouses who are attending Maryland institutions. *Award:* Scholarship for use in freshman, sophomore, junior, or senior year; renewable. *Award amount:* $8850. *Number of awards:* 123. *Eligibility Requirements:* Applicant must be enrolled or expecting to enroll full- or part-time at a two-year or four-year institution or university; resident of Maryland and studying in Maryland. Available to U.S. citizens. Applicant or parent must meet one or more of the following requirements: general military experience; retired from active duty; disabled or killed as a result of military service; prisoner of war; or missing in action. *Application Requirements:* Application, financial need analysis, birth certificate/marriage certificate, documentation of military order. *Deadline:* March 1.

Contact Linda Asplin, Program Administrator, Maryland State Higher Education Commission, 839 Bestgate Road, Suite 400, Annapolis, MD 21401-3013. *E-mail:* lasplin@mhec.state.md.us. *Phone:* 410-260-4563. *Fax:* 410-260-3203. *Web site:* www.mhec.state.md.us.

Workforce Shortage Student Assistance Grant Program. Scholarship of $4000 available to students who will be required to major in specific areas and will be obligated to serve in the state of Maryland after completion of degree. *Award:* Scholarship for use in freshman, sophomore, junior, or senior year; renewable. *Award amount:* $4000. *Number of awards:* 1300. *Eligibility Requirements:* Applicant must be enrolled or expecting to enroll full- or part-time at a two-year or four-year institution or university; resident of Maryland and studying in Maryland. Available to U.S. citizens. *Application Requirements:* Application, essay, financial need analysis, resume, references, transcript, certain majors require additional documentation. *Deadline:* July 1.

Contact Maura Sappington, Program Manager, Maryland State Higher Education Commission, 839 Bestgate Road, Suite 400, Annapolis, MD 21401-3013. *E-mail:* msapping@mhec.state.md.us. *Phone:* 410-260-4569. *Fax:* 410-260-3203. *Web site:* www.mhec.state.md.us.

MASSACHUSETTS

Agnes M. Lindsay Scholarship. Scholarships for students with demonstrated financial need who are from rural areas of Massachusetts and attend public institutions of higher education in Massachusetts. Deadline varies. *Award:* Scholarship for use in freshman, sophomore, junior, or senior year; not renewable. *Award amount:* varies. *Number of awards:* varies. *Eligibility Requirements:* Applicant must be enrolled or expecting to enroll full-time at a two-year or four-year institution or university; resident of Massachusetts and studying in Massachusetts. Available to U.S. citizens. *Application Requirements:* Application, financial need analysis. *Deadline:* varies.

Contact Robert Brun, Director of Scholarships and Grants, Massachusetts Office of Student Financial Assistance, 454 Broadway, Suite 200, Revere, MA 02151. *E-mail:* osfa@osfa.mass.edu. *Phone:* 617-727-9420. *Fax:* 617-727-0667. *Web site:* www.osfa.mass.edu.

Christian A. Herter Memorial Scholarship. Renewable award for Massachusetts residents who are in the tenth and eleventh grades, and whose socio-economic backgrounds and environment may inhibit their ability to attain educational goals. Must exhibit severe personal or family-related difficulties, medical problems, or have overcome a personal obstacle. Provides up to 50 percent of the student's calculated need, as determined by federal methodology, at the college of their choice within the continental United States. *Award:* Scholarship for use in freshman year; renewable. *Award amount:* up to $15,000. *Number of awards:* 25. *Eligibility Requirements:* Applicant must be high school student; planning to enroll or expecting to enroll full-time at a two-year, four-year, or technical institution or university and resident of Massachusetts. Applicant must have 2.5 GPA or higher. Available to U.S. citizens. *Application Requirements:* Application, autobiography, financial need analysis, interview, references. *Deadline:* March 14.

Contact Robert Brun, Director of Scholarships and Grants, Massachusetts Office of Student Financial Assistance, 454 Broadway, Suite 200, Revere, MA 02151. *E-mail:* osfa@osfa.mass.edu. *Phone:* 617-727-9420. *Fax:* 617-727-0667. *Web site:* www.osfa.mass.edu.

DSS Adopted Children Tuition Waiver. Need-based tuition waiver for Massachusetts residents who are full-time undergraduate students. Must attend a Massachusetts public institution of higher education and be under 24 years of age. File the FAFSA after January 1. Contact school financial aid office for more information. *Award:* Scholarship for use in freshman, sophomore, junior, or senior year; renewable. *Award amount:* varies. *Number of awards:* varies. *Eligibility Requirements:* Applicant must be age 24 or under; enrolled or expecting to enroll full-time at a two-year or four-year institution and resident of Massachusetts. Available to U.S. and non-Canadian citizens. *Application Requirements:* Application, financial need analysis, FAFSA. *Deadline:* varies.

Contact Robert Brun, Director of Scholarships and Grants, Massachusetts Office of Student Financial Assistance, 454 Broadway, Suite 200, Revere, MA 02151. *E-mail:* osfa@osfa.mass.edu. *Phone:* 617-727-9420. *Fax:* 617-727-0667. *Web site:* www.osfa.mass.edu.

Early Childhood Educators Scholarship Program. Scholarship to provide financial assistance for currently employed early childhood educators and providers who enroll in an associate or bachelor degree program in Early Childhood Education or related programs. Awards are not based on financial need. Individuals taking their first college-level ECE course are eligible for 100 percent tuition, while subsequent ECE courses are awarded at 50 percent tuition. Can be used for one class each semester. *Academic Fields/Career Goals:* Education. *Award:* Scholarship for use in freshman, sophomore, junior, or senior year; not renewable. *Award amount:* $150–$3600. *Number of awards:* varies. *Eligibility Requirements:* Applicant must be enrolled or expecting to enroll full- or part-time at a four-year institution or university. Available to U.S. citizens. *Application Requirements:* Application. *Deadline:* July 1.

Contact Robert Brun, Director of Scholarships and Grants, Massachusetts Office of Student Financial Assistance, 454 Broadway, Suite 200, Revere, MA 02151. *E-mail:* osfa@osfa.mass.edu. *Phone:* 617-727-9420. *Fax:* 617-727-0667. *Web site:* www.osfa.mass.edu.

John and Abigail Adams Scholarship. Scholarship to reward and inspire student achievement, attract more high-performing students to Massachusetts public higher education, and provide families of college-bound students with financial assistance. Must be a U.S. citizen or an eligible non-citizen. There is no application process for the scholarship. Students who are eligible will be notified in the fall of their senior year in high school. *Award:* Scholarship for use in freshman year; not renewable. *Award amount:* varies. *Number of awards:* varies. *Eligibility Requirements:* Applicant must be high school student; planning to enroll or expecting to enroll full-time at a two-year or four-year institution or university; resident of Massachusetts and studying in Massachusetts. Applicant must have 3.0 GPA or higher. Available to U.S. citizens. *Application Requirements: Deadline:* varies.

Contact Robert Brun, Director of Scholarships and Grants, Massachusetts Office of Student Financial Assistance, 454 Broadway, Suite 200, Revere, MA 02151. *E-mail:* osfa@osfa.mass.edu. *Phone:* 617-727-9420. *Fax:* 617-727-0667. *Web site:* www.osfa.mass.edu.

Massachusetts Assistance for Student Success Program. Provides need-based financial assistance to Massachusetts residents to attend undergraduate postsecondary institutions in Connecticut, Maine, Massachusetts, New Hampshire, Pennsylvania, Rhode Island, Vermont, and District of Columbia. High school seniors may apply. Expected Family Contribution (EFC) should be $3850. Timely filing of FAFSA required. *Award:* Grant for use in freshman, sophomore, junior, or senior year; not renewable. *Award amount:* $300–$2400. *Number of awards:* 25,000–30,000. *Eligibility Requirements:* Applicant must be enrolled or expecting to enroll full-time at a two-year, four-year, or technical institution or university; resident of Massachusetts and studying in Connecticut, District of Columbia, Maine, Massachusetts, New Hampshire, Pennsylvania, Rhode Island, or Vermont. Available to U.S. citizens. *Application Requirements:* Financial need analysis, FAFSA. *Deadline:* May 1.

Contact Robert Brun, Director of Scholarships and Grants, Massachusetts Office of Student Financial Assistance, 454 Broadway, Suite 200, Revere, MA 02151. *E-mail:* osfa@osfa.mass.edu. *Phone:* 617-727-9420. *Fax:* 617-727-0667. *Web site:* www.osfa.mass.edu.

Massachusetts Cash Grant Program. A need-based grant to assist with mandatory fees and non-state supported tuition. This supplemental award is available to Massachusetts residents, who are undergraduates at public two-year, four-year colleges and universities in Massachusetts. Must file FAFSA before May 1. Contact college financial aid office for information. *Award:* Grant for use in freshman, sophomore, junior, or senior year; not renewable. *Award amount:* varies. *Number of awards:* varies. *Eligibility Requirements:* Applicant must be enrolled or expecting to enroll full-time at a two-year or four-year institution or university and resident of Massachusetts. Available to U.S. citizens. *Application Requirements:* Application, financial need analysis, FAFSA. *Deadline:* continuous.

Contact Robert Brun, Director of Scholarships and Grants, Massachusetts Office of Student Financial Assistance, 454 Broadway, Suite 200, Revere, MA 02151. *E-mail:* osfa@osfa.mass.edu. *Phone:* 617-727-9420. *Fax:* 617-727-0667. *Web site:* www.osfa.mass.edu.

Massachusetts Gilbert Matching Student Grant Program. Grants for permanent Massachusetts residents attending an independent, regionally accredited Massachusetts school or school of nursing full time. Must be U.S. citizen and permanent legal resident of Massachusetts. File the Free Application for Federal Student Aid after January 1. Contact college financial aid office for complete details and deadlines. *Award:* Grant for use in freshman, sophomore, junior, or senior year; not renewable. *Award amount:* $200–$2500. *Number of awards:* varies. *Eligibility Requirements:* Applicant must be enrolled or expecting to enroll full-time at a four-year institution or university; resident of Massachusetts and studying in Massachusetts. Available to

U.S. citizens. *Application Requirements:* Financial need analysis, FAFSA. *Deadline:* varies.

Contact Robert Brun, Director of Scholarships and Grants, Massachusetts Office of Student Financial Assistance, 454 Broadway, Suite 200, Revere, MA 02151. *E-mail:* rbrun@osfa.mass.edu. *Phone:* 617-727-9420. *Fax:* 617-727-0667. *Web site:* www.osfa.mass.edu.

Massachusetts Part-Time Grant Program. Award for permanent Massachusetts residents who have enrolled part-time for at least one year in a state-approved postsecondary school. The recipient must not have a bachelor's degree. FAFSA must be filed before May 1. Contact college financial aid office for further information. *Award:* Grant for use in freshman, sophomore, junior, or senior year; not renewable. *Award amount:* $200–$1150. *Number of awards:* 200. *Eligibility Requirements:* Applicant must be enrolled or expecting to enroll part-time at a two-year, four-year, or technical institution or university and resident of Massachusetts. Available to U.S. citizens. *Application Requirements:* Application, financial need analysis, FAFSA. *Deadline:* varies.

Contact Robert Brun, Director of Scholarships and Grants, Massachusetts Office of Student Financial Assistance, 454 Broadway, Suite 200, Revere, MA 02151. *E-mail:* osfa@osfa.mass.edu. *Phone:* 617-727-9420. *Fax:* 617-727-0667. *Web site:* www.osfa.mass.edu.

Massachusetts Public Service Grant Program. Scholarships for children and/or spouses of deceased members of fire, police, and corrections departments, who were killed in the line of duty. Awards Massachusetts residents attending Massachusetts institutions. Applicant should have not received a prior bachelor's degree or its equivalent. *Award:* Grant for use in freshman, sophomore, junior, or senior year; not renewable. *Award amount:* varies. *Number of awards:* varies. *Eligibility Requirements:* Applicant must be enrolled or expecting to enroll full-time at a four-year institution or university and resident of Massachusetts. Applicant or parent of applicant must have employment or volunteer experience in police/firefighting. Available to U.S. and non-U.S. citizens. Applicant or parent must meet one or more of the following requirements: general military experience; retired from active duty; disabled or killed as a result of military service; prisoner of war; or missing in action. *Application Requirements:* Application, financial need analysis, copy of birth certificate, copy of veteran's death certificate. *Deadline:* May 1.

Contact Alison Leary, Director of Scholarships and Grants, Massachusetts Office of Student Financial Assistance, 454 Broadway, Suite 200, Revere, MA 02151. *E-mail:* osfa@osfa.mass.edu. *Phone:* 617-727-9420. *Fax:* 617-727-0667. *Web site:* www.osfa.mass.edu.

New England Regional Student Program. Scholarship for residents of New England. Students pay reduced out-of-state tuition at public colleges or universities in other New England states when enrolling in certain majors not offered at public institutions in home state. *Award:* Scholarship for use in freshman, sophomore, junior, or senior year; renewable. *Award amount:* varies. *Number of awards:* 8000. *Eligibility Requirements:* Applicant must be enrolled or expecting to enroll full- or part-time at a two-year or four-year institution or university; resident of Connecticut, Maine, Massachusetts, New Hampshire, Rhode Island, or Vermont and studying in Connecticut, Maine, Massachusetts, New Hampshire, Quebec, or Vermont. Available to U.S. citizens. *Application Requirements:* College application. *Deadline:* continuous.

Contact Wendy Lindsay, Senior Director of Regional Student Program, New England Board of Higher Education, 45 Temple Place, Boston, MA 02111. *E-mail:* tuitionbreak@nebhe.org. *Phone:* 617-357-9620 Ext. 111. *Fax:* 617-338-1577. *Web site:* www.nebhe.org.

Paraprofessional Teacher Preparation Grant. Grant providing financial aid assistance to Massachusetts residents, who are currently employed as paraprofessionals in Massachusetts public schools and wish to obtain higher education and become certified as full-time teachers. *Academic Fields/Career Goals:* Education. *Award:* Grant for use in freshman, sophomore, junior, or senior year; not renewable. *Award amount:* $250–$7500. *Number of awards:* varies. *Eligibility Requirements:* Applicant must be enrolled or expecting to enroll full- or part-time at a two-year or four-year institution or university and resident of Massachusetts. Available to U.S. citizens. *Application Requirements:* Application, FAFSA. *Deadline:* August 1.

Contact Robert Brun, Director of Scholarships and Grants, Massachusetts Office of Student Financial Assistance, 454 Broadway, Suite 200, Revere, MA 02151. *E-mail:* osfa@osfa.mass.edu. *Phone:* 617-727-9420. *Fax:* 617-727-0667. *Web site:* www.osfa.mass.edu.

Robert C. Byrd Honors Scholarship-Massachusetts. Scholarship for high school senior who is a resident of Massachusetts for at least one year prior to the beginning of the academic year he/she will enter college. Must have applied or been accepted to an accredited institution of higher education and be a U.S. citizen, national or permanent resident. *Award:* Scholarship for use in freshman year; renewable. *Award amount:* $1500. *Number of awards:* varies. *Eligibility Requirements:* Applicant must be high school student; planning to enroll or expecting to enroll full-time at a four-year institution or university and resident of Massachusetts. Applicant must have 3.5 GPA or higher. Available to U.S. citizens. *Application Requirements:* Application, transcript. *Deadline:* June 1.

Contact Sally Teixeira, Scholarship Coordinator, Massachusetts Department of Education, 350 Main Street, Malden, MA 02148-5023. *E-mail:* steixeira@doe.mass.edu. *Phone:* 781-338-6304. *Web site:* www.doe.mass.edu.

MICHIGAN

Children of Veterans Tuition Grant. Awards available for students who are children of a disabled or deceased Michigan veteran. Must be enrolled at least half time in a degree-granting Michigan public or private nonprofit institution. Must be a U.S. citizen or permanent resident and must be residing in Michigan. *Award:* Grant for use in freshman, sophomore, junior, or senior year; renewable. *Award amount:* up to $2800. *Number of awards:* varies. *Eligibility Requirements:* Applicant must be age 17-25; enrolled or expecting to enroll full- or part-time at a two-year or four-year institution or university; resident of Michigan and studying in Michigan. Available to U.S. citizens. Applicant or parent must meet one or more of the following requirements: general military experience; retired from active duty; disabled or killed as a result of military service; prisoner of war; or missing in action. *Application Requirements:* Application. *Deadline:* varies.

Contact Scholarship and Grant Director, Michigan Higher Education Assistance Authority, PO Box 30462, Lansing, MI 48909-7962. *E-mail:* osg@michigan.gov. *Phone:* 888-447-2687. *Web site:* www.michigan.gov/studentaid.

Children of Veterans Tuition Grant Program. Undergraduate tuition assistance to certain children older than 16 and less than 26 years of age who have been Michigan residents for the 12 months prior to application. To be eligible a student must be the natural or adopted child of a Michigan veteran. The veteran must have been a legal resident of Michigan immediately before entering military service and did not later reside outside of Michigan for more than two years; or the veteran must have established legal residency in Michigan after entering military service. *Award:* Grant for use in freshman, sophomore, junior, or senior year; renewable. *Award amount:* up to $2800. *Number of awards:* varies. *Eligibility Requirements:* Applicant must be age 16-26; enrolled or expecting to enroll full- or part-time at a two-year or four-year institution or university; resident of Michigan and studying in Michigan. Available to U.S. citizens. Applicant or parent must meet one or more of the following requirements: general military experience; retired from active duty; disabled or killed as a result of military service; prisoner of war; or missing in action. *Application Requirements:* Application. *Deadline:* continuous.

Contact Office of Scholarships and Grants. *Web site:* www.michigan.gov/osg.

Michigan Adult Part-Time Grant. Grant is intended for financially needy, independent undergraduates who have been out of high school for at least two years. Must be enrolled on a part-time basis. Must be Michigan resident. *Award:* Grant for use in freshman, sophomore, junior, or senior year; renewable. *Award amount:* up to $600. *Number of awards:* varies. *Eligibility Requirements:* Applicant must be enrolled or expecting to enroll part-time at a two-year or four-year institution or university; resident of Michigan and studying in Michigan. Available to U.S. citizens. *Application Requirements:*. Financial need analysis. *Deadline:* March 1.

Contact Scholarship and Grant Director, Michigan Higher Education Assistance Authority, PO Box 30462, Lansing, MI 48909-7962. *E-mail:* osg@michigan.gov. *Phone:* 888-447-2687. *Web site:* www.michigan.gov/studentaid.

Michigan Competitive Scholarship. Renewable award of $1300 for Michigan resident to pursue undergraduate study at a Michigan institution. Awards limited to tuition. Must maintain at least a 2.0 grade point average and meet the college's academic progress requirements. Must file Free Application for Federal Student Aid. *Award:* Scholarship for use in freshman, sophomore, junior, or senior year; renewable. *Award amount:* $100–$1300. *Number of awards:* varies. *Eligibility Requirements:* Applicant must be enrolled or expecting to enroll full- or part-time at a two-year or four-year institution or university; resident of Michigan and studying in Michigan. Available to U.S. citizens. *Application Requirements:* Application, financial need analysis, test scores. *Deadline:* March 1.

Contact Scholarship and Grant Director, Michigan Higher Education Assistance Authority, PO Box 30466, Lansing, MI 48909-7962. *E-mail:* osg@michigan.gov. *Phone:* 888-447-2687. *Web site:* www.michigan.gov/studentaid.

Michigan Educational Opportunity Grant. Need-based program for Michigan residents who are at least half-time undergraduates attending public Michigan college or university. Must maintain good academic standing. Award of up to $1000. *Award:* Grant for use in freshman, sophomore, junior, or senior year; renewable. *Award amount:* up to $1000. *Number of awards:* varies. *Eligibility Requirements:* Applicant must be enrolled or expecting to enroll full- or part-time at a two-year or four-year institution or university; resident of Michigan and studying in Michigan. Available to U.S. citizens. *Application Requirements:* Financial need analysis. *Deadline:* March 1.

Contact Scholarship and Grant Director, Michigan Higher Education Assistance Authority, PO Box 30462, Lansing, MI 48909-7962. *E-mail:* osg@michigan.gov. *Phone:* 888-447-2687. *Web site:* www.michigan.gov/studentaid.

Michigan Indian Tuition Waiver. Renewable award provides free tuition for Native-American of 1/4 or more blood degree who attend a Michigan public college or university. Must be a Michigan resident for at least one year. The tuition waiver program covers full-time, part-time or summer school student attending a public, state, community, junior college, public college, or public university. Deadline: continuous. *Award:* Scholarship for use in freshman, sophomore, junior, senior, graduate, or postgraduate years; renewable. *Award amount:* varies. *Number of awards:* varies. *Eligibility Requirements:* Applicant must be American Indian/Alaska Native; enrolled or expecting to enroll full- or part-time at a two-year, four-year, or technical institution or university; resident of Michigan and studying in Michigan. Available to U.S. citizens. *Application Requirements:* Application, driver's license, transcript, tribal certification, proof of residency. *Deadline:* continuous.

Contact Christin McKerchie, Executive Assistant to Programs, Inter-Tribal Council of Michigan Inc., 2956 Ashmun Street, Suite A, Sault Ste. Marie, MI 49783. *Phone:* 906-632-6896 Ext. 136. *Fax:* 906-632 6878. *Web site:* www.itcmi.org.

Michigan Nursing Scholarship. Scholarship for students enrolled in an LPN, associate degree in nursing, bachelor of science in nursing, or master of science in nursing programs. Colleges determine application procedure and select recipients. Recipients must fulfill in-state work commitment or repay scholarship. *Academic Fields/Career Goals:* Nursing. *Award:* Scholarship for use in freshman, sophomore, junior, or senior year; renewable. *Award amount:* up to $4000. *Number of awards:* varies. *Eligibility Requirements:* Applicant must be enrolled or expecting to enroll full- or part-time at a two-year or four-year institution or university; resident of Michigan and studying in Michigan. Available to U.S. citizens. *Application Requirements:* Recipients are selected by their college. *Deadline:* varies.

Contact Scholarship and Grant Director, Michigan Higher Education Assistance Authority, PO Box 30462, Lansing, MI 48909-7962. *E-mail:* osg@michigan.gov. *Phone:* 888-447-2687. *Web site:* www.michigan.gov/studentaid.

Michigan Promise Scholarship. Scholarship available for students who have taken the state's assessment test. Students who meet or exceed test standards may receive $1000 during each of their first two years of college and another $2000 after completing two years with at least a 2.5 GPA. Students who do not meet or exceed state standards may receive $4000 after completing two years of postsecondary study with at least a 2.5 GPA. Must be a Michigan resident enrolled at an approved Michigan postsecondary institution. *Award:* Scholarship for use in freshman, sophomore, or junior year; not renewable. *Award amount:* up to $4000. *Number of awards:* varies. *Eligibility Requirements:* Applicant must be enrolled or expecting to enroll full- or part-time at a two-year, four-year, or technical institution or university; resident of Michigan and studying in Michigan. Available to U.S. citizens. *Application Requirements:* Test scores. *Deadline:* continuous.

Contact Scholarship and Grant Director, Michigan Higher Education Assistance Authority, PO Box 30462, Lansing, MI 48909-7962. *E-mail:* osg@michigan.gov. *Phone:* 888-447-2687. *Web site:* www.michigan.gov/studentaid.

Michigan Tuition Grant. Need-based program. Students must be Michigan residents and attend a Michigan private, nonprofit, degree-granting college. Must file the Free Application for Federal Student Aid and meet the college's academic progress requirements. *Award:* Grant for use in freshman, sophomore, junior, or senior year; renewable. *Award amount:* $100–$2100. *Number of awards:* varies. *Eligibility Requirements:* Applicant must be enrolled or expecting to enroll full- or part-time at a four-year institution or university; resident of Michigan and studying in Michigan. Available to U.S. citizens. *Application Requirements:* Financial need analysis. *Deadline:* July 1.

Contact Scholarship and Grant Director, Michigan Higher Education Assistance Authority, PO Box 30462, Lansing, MI 48909-7962. *E-mail:* osg@michigan.gov. *Phone:* 888-447-2687. *Web site:* www.michigan.gov/studentaid.

Tuition Incentive Program. Award for Michigan residents who receive or have received Medicaid for required period of time through the Department of Human Services. Scholarship provides two years tuition towards an associate degree at a Michigan college or university and $2000 total assistance for third and fourth years. Must apply before graduating from high school or earning a general education development diploma. *Award:* Grant for use in freshman, sophomore, junior, or senior year; renewable. *Award amount:* varies. *Number of awards:* varies. *Eligibility Requirements:* Applicant must be high school student; planning to enroll or expecting to enroll full- or part-time at a two-year or four-year institution or university; resident of Michigan and studying in Michigan. Available to U.S. citizens. *Application Requirements:* Application, Medicaid eligibility for specified period of time. *Deadline:* continuous.

Contact Scholarship and Grant Director, Michigan Higher Education Assistance Authority, PO Box 30462, Lansing, MI 48909-7962. *E-mail:* osg@michigan.gov. *Phone:* 888-447-2687. *Web site:* www.michigan.gov/studentaid.

MINNESOTA

Leadership, Excellence and Dedicated Service Scholarship. Scholarship provides a maximum of thirty $1000 to selected high school seniors who become a member of the Minnesota National Guard and complete the application process. The award recognizes demonstrated leadership, community services and potential for success in the Minnesota National Guard. *Award:* Scholarship for use in freshman year; not renewable. *Award amount:* $1000. *Number of awards:* up to 30. *Eligibility Requirements:* Applicant must be high school student; planning to enroll or expecting to enroll full- or part-time at a two-year, four-year, or technical institution or university; resident of Minnesota and must have an interest in leadership. Applicant or parent of applicant must have employment or volunteer experience in community service. Available to U.S. citizens. Applicant or parent must meet one or more of the following requirements: Air Force National Guard or Army National Guard experience; retired from active duty; disabled or killed as a result of military service; prisoner of war; or missing in action. *Application Requirements:* Essay, resume, references, transcript. *Deadline:* March 15.

Contact Barbara O'Reilly, Education Services Officer, Minnesota Department of Military Affairs, 20 West 12th Street, Veterans Services Building, St. Paul, MN 55155-2098. *E-mail:* barbara.oreilly@mn.ngb.army.mil. *Phone:* 651-282-4508. *Web site:* www.minnesotanationalguard.org.

Minnesota Achieve Scholarship. Minnesota residents who complete one of four sets of rigorous programs of study while in high school or in a home-school setting may be eligible to receive a one-time scholarship of $1200. Student must have graduated from a Minnesota high school after January 1 and completed, with a grade of C or above, all of the required courses. Must have a household adjusted gross income of less than $75,000. Scholarships are available to eligible students up to 4 years after high school graduation. *Award:* Scholarship for use in freshman, sophomore, junior, or senior year; not renewable. *Award amount:* up to $1200. *Number of awards:* varies. *Eligibility Requirements:* Applicant must be enrolled or expecting to enroll full- or part-time at a two-year, four-year, or technical institution or university; resident of Minnesota and studying in Minnesota. Available to U.S. citizens. *Application Requirements:* Application, financial need analysis, test scores, transcript. *Deadline:* varies.

Contact Scholarship Staff, Minnesota Office of Higher Education, 1450 Energy Park Drive, St. Paul, MN 55108. *Phone:* 651-642-0567. *Fax:* 651-642-0675. *Web site:* www.getreadyforcollege.org.

Minnesota GI Bill Program. Provides financial assistance to eligible Minnesota veterans and non-veterans who have served 5 or more years cumulatively as a member of the National Guard or Reserves, and served on or after September 11, 2001. Surviving spouses and children of service members who have died or have a total and permanent disability and who served on or after September 11, 2001, may also be eligible. Full-time students may receive up to $1000 per term, and part-time students up to $500 per term. Maximum lifetime benefit is $10,000. *Award:* Scholarship for use in freshman, sophomore, junior, or senior year; renewable. *Award amount:* up to $3000. *Number of awards:* varies. *Eligibility Requirements:* Applicant must be enrolled or expecting to enroll full- or part-time at a two-year, four-year, or technical institution or university; resident of Minnesota and studying in Minnesota. Available to U.S. citizens. Applicant or parent must meet one or more of the following requirements: general military experience; retired from active duty; disabled or killed as a result of military service; prisoner of war; or missing in action. *Application Requirements:* Application, financial need analysis, military records. *Deadline:* continuous.

Contact Scholarship Staff, Minnesota Office of Higher Education, 1450 Energy Park Drive, St. Paul, MN 55108. *Phone:* 651-642-0567. *Fax:* 651-642-0675. *Web site:* www.getreadyforcollege.org.

Minnesota Indian Scholarship. Scholarship for Minnesota residents who are one-fourth or more American Indian ancestry and attending an eligible Minnesota postsecondary institution. Maximum award is $4000 for undergraduate students and $6000 for graduate students. Scholarships are limited to 3 years for certificate or AA/AS programs, 5 years for bachelor's degree programs, and 5 years for graduate programs. Applicants must maintain satisfactory academic progress, not be in default on student loans, and be eligible to receive Pell or State Grant and have remaining need. *Award:* Scholarship for use in freshman, sophomore, junior, or senior year; renewable. *Award amount:* up to $6000. *Number of awards:* 500–600. *Eligibility Requirements:* Applicant must be American Indian/Alaska Native; enrolled or expecting to enroll full- or part-time at a two-year, four-year, or technical institution or university; resident of Minnesota and studying in Minnesota. Available to U.S. citizens. *Application Requirements:* Application, American Indian ancestry documentation. *Deadline:* varies.

Contact Scholarship Staff, Minnesota Office of Higher Education, 1450 Energy Park Drive, Suite 350, St. Paul, MN 55108. *E-mail:* sandy.bowes@state.mn.us. *Phone:* 651-642-0567 Ext. 1. *Fax:* 651-642-0675. *Web site:* www.getreadyforcollege.org.

Minnesota Nurses Loan Forgiveness Program. Program offering loan repayment to registered nurse and licensed practical nurse students who agree to practice in a Minnesota nursing home or an Intermediate Care Facility for persons with mental retardation for a minimum three-year/four-year service obligation after completion of training. Candidates must apply while still in school. *Academic Fields/Career Goals:* Health and Medical Sciences; Nursing. *Award:* Forgivable loan for use in freshman or sophomore year; not renewable. *Award amount:* $3750. *Eligibility Requirements:* Applicant must be enrolled or expecting to enroll full- or part-time at a two-year or four-year institution or university. Available to U.S. and non-U.S. citizens. *Application Requirements:* Application, essay, resume, references. *Deadline:* December 1.

Contact Minnesota Department of Health. *Web site:* www.health.state.mn.us.

Minnesota Reciprocal Agreement. Renewable tuition waiver for Minnesota residents. Waives all or part of non-resident tuition surcharge at public institutions in Iowa, Kansas, Michigan, Missouri, Nebraska, North Dakota, South Dakota, Wisconsin and Manitoba. Deadline: last day of academic term. *Award:* Scholarship for use in freshman, sophomore, junior, or senior year; renewable. *Award amount:* varies. *Number of awards:* varies. *Eligibility Requirements:* Applicant must be enrolled or expecting to enroll full- or part-time at a two-year, four-year, or technical institution or university; resident of Minnesota and studying in Iowa, Kansas, Manitoba, Michigan, Missouri, Nebraska, North Dakota, South Dakota, or Wisconsin. Available to U.S. citizens. *Application Requirements:* Application. *Deadline:* varies.

Contact Jodi Rouland, Program Assistant, Minnesota Office of Higher Education. *E-mail:* jodi.rouland@state.mn.us. *Phone:* 651-355-0614. *Fax:* 651-642-0675. *Web site:* www.getreadyforcollege.org.

Minnesota State Grant Program. Need-based grant program available for Minnesota residents attending Minnesota colleges. Student covers 46% of cost with remainder covered by Pell Grant, parent contribution and state grant. Students apply with FAFSA and college administers the program on campus. *Award:* Grant for use in freshman, sophomore, junior, or senior year; renewable. *Award amount:* $100–$8661. *Number of awards:* 71,000–81,000. *Eligibility Requirements:* Applicant must be age 17 and over; enrolled or expecting to enroll full- or part-time at a two-year, four-year, or technical institution or university; resident of Minnesota and studying in Minnesota. Available to U.S. citizens. *Application Requirements:* Application, financial need analysis. *Deadline:* varies.

Contact Grant Staff, Minnesota Office of Higher Education, 1450 Energy Park Drive, Suite 350, St. Paul, MN 55108. *Phone:* 651-642-0567 Ext. 1. *Web site:* www.getreadyforcollege.org.

Minnesota State Veterans' Dependents Assistance Program. Tuition assistance to dependents of persons considered to be prisoner-of-war or missing in action after August 1, 1958. Must be Minnesota resident attending Minnesota two- or four-year school. *Award:* Scholarship for use in freshman, sophomore, junior, or senior year; renewable. *Award amount:* varies. *Number of awards:* varies. *Eligibility Requirements:* Applicant must be enrolled or expecting to enroll full- or part-time at a two-year or four-year institution; resident of Minnesota and studying in Minnesota. Available to U.S. citizens. Applicant or parent must meet one or more of the following requirements: general military experience; retired from active duty; disabled or killed as a result of military service; prisoner of war; or missing in action. *Application Requirements:* Application. *Deadline:* continuous.

Contact Minnesota Office of Higher Education. *Web site:* www.getreadyforcollege.org.

Paul and Fern Yocum Scholarship. Scholarship to dependent children of full-time Yocum Oil employees. *Award:* Scholarship for use in freshman, sophomore, junior, senior, or graduate year; not renewable. *Award amount:* $1000. *Number of awards:* 3. *Eligibility Requirements:* Applicant must be enrolled or expecting to enroll full- or part-time at a four-year institution or university. Applicant or parent of applicant must be affiliated with Yocum Oil Company. Available to U.S. and non-Canadian citizens. *Application Requirements:* Application. *Deadline:* April 15.

Contact Donna Paulson, Administrative Assistant, Minnesota Community Foundation, 55 Fifth Street East, Suite 600, St. Paul, MN 55101-1797. *E-mail:* dkp@mncommunityfoundation.org. *Phone:* 651-325-4212. *Web site:* www.mncommunityfoundation.org.

Postsecondary Child Care Grant Program-Minnesota. Grant available for students not receiving MFIP. Based on financial need. Cannot exceed actual child care costs or maximum award chart (based on income). Must be Minnesota resident. For use at Minnesota two- or four-year school, including public technical colleges. *Award:* Grant for use in freshman, sophomore, junior, or senior year; renewable. *Award amount:* $100–$2600. *Number of awards:* varies. *Eligibility Requirements:* Applicant must be enrolled or expecting to enroll full- or part-time at a two-year, four-year, or technical institution or university; resident of Minnesota and studying in Minnesota. Available to U.S. citizens. *Application Requirements:* Application, financial need analysis. *Deadline:* continuous.

Contact Brenda Larter, Program Administrator, Minnesota Office of Higher Education, 1450 Energy Park Drive, Suite 350, St. Paul, MN 55108-5227. *E-mail:* brenda.larter@state.mn.us. *Phone:* 651-355-0612. *Fax:* 651-642-0675. *Web site:* www.getreadyforcollege.org.

Safety Officers' Survivor Grant Program. Grant for eligible survivors of Minnesota public safety officers killed in the line of duty. Safety officers who have been permanently or totally disabled in the line of duty are also eligible. Must be used at a Minnesota institution participating in State Grant Program. Write for details. Must submit proof of death or disability and Public Safety Officers Benefit Fund Certificate. Must apply for renewal each year for four years. *Award:* Grant for use in freshman, sophomore, junior, or senior year; not renewable. *Award amount:* up to $9438. *Number of awards:* 1. *Eligibility Requirements:* Applicant must be age 23 or under; enrolled or expecting to enroll full- or part-time at a two-year, four-year, or technical institution or university; resident of Minnesota and studying in Minnesota. Applicant or parent of applicant must have employment or volunteer experience in police/firefighting. Available to U.S. citizens. *Application Requirements:* Application, proof of death or disability. *Deadline:* continuous.

Contact Brenda Larter, Program Administrator, Minnesota Office of Higher Education. *E-mail:* brenda.larter@state.mn.us. *Phone:* 651-355-0612. *Fax:* 651-642-0675. *Web site:* www.getreadyforcollege.org.

MISSISSIPPI

Critical Needs Teacher Loan/Scholarship. Eligible applicants will agree to employment immediately upon degree completion as a full-time classroom teacher in a public school located in a critical teacher shortage area in the state of Mississippi. Must verify the intention to pursue a first bachelor's degree in teacher education. Award covers tuition and required fees, average cost of room and meals plus allowance for books. Must be enrolled at a Mississippi college or university. *Academic Fields/Career Goals:* Education; Psychology; Therapy/Rehabilitation. *Award:* Forgivable loan for use in junior or senior year; not renewable. *Award amount:* varies. *Number of awards:* varies. *Eligibility Requirements:* Applicant must be enrolled or expecting to enroll full- or part-time at a four-year institution or university; resident of Mississippi and studying in Mississippi. Applicant must have 2.5 GPA or higher. Available to U.S. and non-U.S. citizens. *Application Requirements:* Application, test scores, transcript. *Deadline:* March 31.

Contact Mary J. Covington, Assistant Director, Mississippi State Student Financial Aid, 3825 Ridgewood Road, Jackson, MS 39211-6453. *E-mail:* sfa@ihl.state.ms.us. *Phone:* 800-327-2980. *Web site:* www.ihl.state.ms.us.

Higher Education Legislative Plan (HELP). Eligible applicant must be resident of Mississippi and be freshman and/or sophomore student who graduated from high school within the immediate past two years. Must demonstrate need as determined by the results of the FAFSA: documenting an average family adjusted gross income of $36,500 or less over the prior two years. Must be enrolled full-time at a Mississippi college or university, have a GPA of 2.5 and have scored 20 on the ACT. *Award:* Scholarship for use in freshman or sophomore year; renewable. *Award amount:* varies. *Number of awards:* varies. *Eligibility Requirements:* Applicant must be enrolled or expecting to enroll full-time at a four-year institution or university; resident of Mississippi and studying in Mississippi. Applicant must have 2.5 GPA or higher. Available to U.S. citizens. *Application Requirements:* Application, financial need analysis, test scores, transcript, FAFSA. *Deadline:* March 31.

Contact Mary J. Covington, Assistant Director, Mississippi State Student Financial Aid, 3825 Ridgewood Road, Jackson, MS 39211-6453. *E-mail:* sfa@ihl.state.ms.us. *Phone:* 800-327-2980. *Web site:* www.ihl.state.ms.us.

Mississippi Eminent Scholars Grant. Award for an entering freshmen or as a renewal for sophomore, junior or senior. who are residents of Mississippi. Applicants must achieve a GPA of 3.5 and must have scored 29 on the ACT. Must enroll full-time at an eligible Mississippi college or university. *Award:* Grant for use in freshman, sophomore, junior, or senior year; renewable. *Award amount:* up to $2500. *Number of awards:* varies. *Eligibility Requirements:* Applicant must be enrolled or expecting to enroll full-time at a two-year or four-year institution or university; resident of Mississippi and studying in Mississippi. Applicant must have 3.5 GPA or higher. Available to U.S. citizens. *Application Requirements:* Application, test scores, transcript. *Deadline:* September 15.

Contact Mary J. Covington, Assistant Director, Mississippi State Student Financial Aid, 3825 Ridgewood Road, Jackson, MS 39211-6453. *E-mail:* sfa@ihl.state.ms.us. *Phone:* 800-327-2980. *Web site:* www.ihl.state.ms.us.

Mississippi Health Care Professions Loan/Scholarship Program. Renewable award for junior and senior undergraduates studying psychology or speech pathology, and graduate students studying physical therapy or occupational therapy. Must be Mississippi residents attending four-year colleges or universities in Mississippi. Must fulfill work obligation in Mississippi on the basis of one year's service for one year's loan received, or pay back as loan. *Academic Fields/Career Goals:* Health and Medical Sciences; Psychology; Therapy/Rehabilitation. *Award:* Forgivable loan for use in junior, senior, or graduate year; renewable. *Award amount:* $1500–$6000. *Number of awards:* varies. *Eligibility Requirements:* Applicant must be enrolled or expecting to enroll full-time at a four-year institution or university; resident of Mississippi and studying in Mississippi. Available to U.S. citizens. *Application Requirements:* Application, driver's license, references, transcript. *Deadline:* March 31.

Contact Susan Eckels, Program Administrator, Mississippi State Student Financial Aid, 3825 Ridgewood Road, Jackson, MS 39211-6453. *E-mail:* sme@ihl.state.ms.us. *Phone:* 601-432-6997. *Web site:* www.ihl.state.ms.us.

Mississippi Leveraging Educational Assistance Partnership (LEAP). Award for Mississippi residents enrolled for full-time study at a Mississippi college or university. Based on financial need. Contact college financial aid office. Award value and deadline varies. *Award:* Grant for use in freshman, sophomore, junior, or senior year; renewable. *Award amount:* varies. *Number of awards:* varies. *Eligibility Requirements:* Applicant must be enrolled or expecting to enroll full-time at a two-year or four-year institution or university; resident of Mississippi and studying in Mississippi. Available to U.S. citizens. *Application Requirements:* Application, financial need analysis, FAFSA. *Deadline:* varies.

Contact Mary J. Covington, Assistant Director, Mississippi State Student Financial Aid, 3825 Ridgewood Road, Jackson, MS 39211-6453. *E-mail:* sfa@ihl.state.ms.us. *Phone:* 800-327-2980. *Web site:* www.ihl.state.ms.us.

Mississippi Resident Tuition Assistance Grant. Must be a resident of Mississippi enrolled full-time at an eligible Mississippi college or university. Must maintain a minimum 2.5 GPA each semester. MTAG awards may be up to $500 per academic year for freshman and sophomores and $1000 per academic year for juniors and seniors. *Award:* Grant for use in freshman, sophomore, junior, or senior year; renewable. *Award amount:* $500–$1000. *Number of awards:* varies. *Eligibility Requirements:* Applicant must be enrolled or expecting to enroll full-time at a two-year or four-year institution or university; resident of Mississippi and studying in Mississippi. Applicant must have 2.5 GPA or higher. Available to U.S. citizens. *Application Requirements:* Application, test scores, transcript. *Deadline:* September 15.

Contact Mary J. Covington, Assistant Director, Mississippi State Student Financial Aid, 3825 Ridgewood Road, Jackson, MS 39211-6453. *E-mail:* sfa@ihl.state.ms.us. *Phone:* 800-327-2980. *Web site:* www.ihl.state.ms.us.

Nursing Education Loan/Scholarship-BSN. Award available to junior and senior students pursuing a baccalaureate degree in nursing as well as to the licensed registered nurse who wishes to continue education to the baccalaureate degree. Include transcript and references with application. Minimum 2.5 GPA required. Must be a Mississippi resident and agree to employment in professional nursing (patient care) in Mississippi. *Academic Fields/Career Goals:* Nursing. *Award:* Forgivable loan for use in junior or senior year; renewable. *Award amount:* $4000–$8000. *Number of awards:* varies. *Eligibility Requirements:* Applicant must be enrolled or expecting to enroll full- or part-time at a four-year institution or university; resident of Mississippi and studying in Mississippi. Applicant must have 2.5 GPA or higher. Available to U.S. citizens. *Application Requirements:* Application, driver's license, financial need analysis, references, transcript. *Deadline:* March 31.

Contact Mary J. Covington, Assistant Director, Mississippi State Student Financial Aid, 3825 Ridgewood Road, Jackson, MS 39211-6453. *E-mail:* sfa@ihl.state.ms.us. *Phone:* 800-327-2980. *Web site:* www.ihl.state.ms.us.

William Winter Teacher Scholar Loan. Scholarship available to a junior or senior student at a four-year Mississippi college or university. Applicants must enroll in a program of study leading to a Class "A" teacher educator license. *Academic Fields/Career Goals:* Education. *Award:* Scholarship for use in junior or senior year; renewable. *Award amount:* up to $4000. *Number of awards:* varies. *Eligibility Requirements:* Applicant must be enrolled or expecting to enroll full-time at a four-year institution or university; resident of Mississippi and studying in Mississippi. Applicant must have 2.5 GPA or higher. Available to U.S. citizens. *Application Requirements:* Application. *Deadline:* March 31.

Contact Mary J. Covington, Assistant Director, Mississippi State Student Financial Aid, 3825 Ridgewood Road, Jackson, MS 39211-6453. *E-mail:* sfa@ihl.state.ms.us. *Phone:* 800-327-2980. *Web site:* www.ihl.state.ms.us.

MISSOURI

Access Missouri Financial Assistance Program. Need-based program that provides awards to students who are enrolled full time and have an expected family contribution (EFC) of $12,000 or less based on their Free Application for Federal Student Aid (FAFSA). Awards vary depending on EFC and the type of postsecondary school. *Award:* Grant for use in freshman, sophomore, junior, or senior year; not renewable. *Eligibility Requirements:* Applicant must be enrolled or expecting to enroll full-time at a two-year, four-year, or technical institution or university; resident of Missouri and studying in Missouri. Applicant must have 2.5 GPA or higher. Available to U.S. citizens. *Application Requirements:* FAFSA on file by April 1.

Contact Missouri Coordinating Board for Higher Education. *Web site:* www.dhe.mo.gov.

ACES/PRIMO Program. Program of the Missouri Area Health Education Centers (MAHEC) and the Primary Care Resource Initiative for Missouri students interested in Primary Care. Applicant should have a minimum GPA of 3.0. *Academic Fields/Career Goals:* Health and Medical Sciences. *Award:* Forgivable loan for use in freshman, sophomore, junior, or senior year; not renewable. *Award amount:* $3000–$5000. *Number of awards:* 100. *Eligibility Requirements:* Applicant must be enrolled or expecting to enroll full- or part-time at a four-year institution or university. Applicant must have 3.0 GPA or higher. Available to U.S. and non-U.S. citizens. *Application Requirements:* Application, proof of Missouri residency. *Deadline:* June 30.

Contact Cheryl Thomas, Management Analyst Specialist II, Missouri Department of Health, PO Box 570, Jefferson City, MO 65401-0570. *E-mail:* cheryl.thomas@dhss.mo.gov. *Phone:* 800-891-7415. *Fax:* 573-522-8146. *Web site:* www.dhss.mo.gov.

Environmental Education Scholarship Program (EESP). Scholarship to minority and other underrepresented students pursuing a bachelor's or master's degree in an environmental course of study. Must be a Missouri resident having a cumulative high school GPA of 3.0 or if enrolled in college, must have cumulative GPA of 2.5. *Academic Fields/Career Goals:* Environmental Science. *Award:* Scholarship for use in freshman, sophomore, junior, senior, or graduate year; renewable. *Award amount:* $2000. *Number of awards:* 16. *Eligibility Requirements:* Applicant must be American Indian/Alaska Native, Asian/Pacific Islander, Black (non-Hispanic), or Hispanic; enrolled or expecting to enroll full-time at a four-year institution or university and resident of Missouri. Applicant must have 3.0 GPA or higher. Available to U.S. citizens. *Application Requirements:* Application, essay, references, transcript. *Deadline:* June 1.

Contact Dana Muessig, Executive, Missouri Department of Natural Resources, PO Box 176, Jefferson City, MO 65102. *E-mail:* danamuessig@dnr.mo.gov. *Phone:* 800-361-4827. *Fax:* 573-526-3878. *Web site:* www.dnr.mo.gov.

Lillie Lois Ford Scholarship Fund. Two awards of $1000 each are given each year to one boy and one girl. Applicant must have attended a full session of Missouri Boys/Girls State or Missouri Cadet Patrol Academy. Must be a Missouri resident below age 21, attending an accredited college/university as a full-time student. Must be an unmarried descendant of a veteran having served at least 90 days on active duty in the Army, Air Force, Navy, Marine Corps or Coast Guard of the United States. *Award:* Scholarship for use in freshman year; not renewable. *Award amount:* $1000. *Number of awards:* 2. *Eligibility Requirements:* Applicant must be high school student; age 21 or under; planning to enroll or expecting to enroll full-time at a two-year or four-year institution or university; single and resident of Missouri. Available to U.S. citizens. Applicant or parent must meet one or more of the following requirements: general military experience; retired from active duty; disabled or killed as a result of military service; prisoner of war; or missing in action. *Application Requirements:* Application, financial need analysis, test scores, copy of the veteran's discharge certificate. *Deadline:* April 20.

Contact John Doane, Chairman, Education and Scholarship Committee, American Legion Department of Missouri, PO Box 179, Jefferson City, MO 65102-0179. *Phone:* 417-924-8186. *Web site:* www.missourilegion.org.

Marguerite Ross Barnett Memorial Scholarship. Scholarship was established for students who are employed while attending school part-time. Must be enrolled at least half-time but less than full-time at a participating Missouri postsecondary school, be employed and compensated for at least 20 hours per week, be 18 years of age, be a Missouri resident and a U.S. citizen or a permanent resident. *Award:* Scholarship for use in freshman, sophomore, junior, or senior year; renewable. *Award amount:* varies. *Number of awards:* varies. *Eligibility Requirements:* Applicant must be age 18 and over; enrolled or expecting to enroll part-time at a two-year, four-year, or technical institution or university; resident of Missouri and studying in Missouri. Applicant must have 2.5 GPA or higher. Available to U.S. citizens. *Application Requirements:* FAFSA on file by August 1. *Deadline:* August 1.

Contact Missouri Coordinating Board for Higher Education. *Web site:* www.dhe.mo.gov.

Missouri Higher Education Academic Scholarship (Bright Flight). Program encourages top-ranked high school seniors to attend approved Missouri postsecondary schools. Must be a Missouri resident and a U.S. citizen. Must have a composite score on the ACT or the SAT in the top three percent of all Missouri students taking those tests. Annual scholarship of $2000 is awarded in two payments of $1000 each semester. *Award:* Scholarship for use in freshman, sophomore, junior, or senior year; renewable. *Award amount:* $2000. *Number of awards:* varies. *Eligibility Requirements:* Applicant must be enrolled or expecting to enroll full-time at a two-year, four-year, or technical institution or university; resident of Missouri and studying in Missouri. Applicant must have 2.5 GPA or higher. Available to U.S. citizens. *Application Requirements:* Test scores.

Contact Missouri Coordinating Board for Higher Education. *Web site:* www.dhe.mo.gov.

Missouri Teacher Education Scholarship (General). Nonrenewable award for Missouri high school seniors or Missouri resident college students. Must attend approved teacher training program at a participating Missouri institution and rank in top 15 percent of high school class on ACT/SAT. Merit-based award. Recipients must commit to teach in Missouri for five years at a public elementary or secondary school or award must be repaid. *Academic Fields/Career Goals:* Education. *Award:* Scholarship for use in freshman, sophomore, junior, or senior year; not renewable. *Award amount:* up to $2000. *Number of awards:* 200–240. *Eligibility Requirements:* Applicant must be enrolled or expecting to enroll full-time at a two-year or four-year institution or university; resident of Missouri and studying in Missouri. Available to U.S. citizens. *Application Requirements:* Application, essay, resume, references, test scores, transcript. *Deadline:* February 15.

Contact Laura Harrison, Administrative Assistant II, Missouri Department of Elementary and Secondary Education, PO Box 480, Jefferson City, MO 65102-0480. *E-mail:* laura.harrison@dese.mo.gov. *Phone:* 573-751-1668. *Fax:* 573-526-3580. *Web site:* www.dese.mo.gov.

Primary Care Resource Initiative for Missouri Loan Program. Forgivable loans for Missouri residents attending Missouri institutions pursuing a degree as a primary care physician or dentist, dental hygienist, psychiatrist, psychologist, licensed professional counselor, licensed clinical social worker or dietitian . To be forgiven participant must work in a Missouri health professional shortage area. *Academic Fields/Career Goals:* Dental Health/Services; Health and Medical Sciences; Nursing. *Award:* Forgivable loan for use in freshman, sophomore, junior, senior, or graduate year; not renewable. *Award amount:* $5000–$20,000. *Number of awards:* 100. *Eligibility Requirements:* Applicant must be enrolled or expecting to enroll full- or part-time at a four-year institution or university; resident of Missouri and studying in Missouri. Applicant must have 3.5 GPA or higher. Available to U.S. and non-U.S. citizens. *Application Requirements:* Application, proof of Missouri residency. *Deadline:* June 30.

Contact Cheryl Thomas, Management Analyst Specialist II, Missouri Department of Health, PO Box 570, Jefferson City, MO 65102-0570. *E-mail:* cheryl.thomas@dhss.mo.gov. *Phone:* 800-891-7415. *Fax:* 573-522-8146. *Web site:* www.dhss.mo.gov.

Robert C. Byrd Honors Scholarship-Missouri. Award for high school seniors who are residents of Missouri. Amount of the award each year depends on the amount the state is allotted by the U.S. Department of Education. Maximum amount awarded per student is $1500. Students must rank in top 10 percent of high school class and score in top 10 percent on ACT. *Award:* Scholarship for use in freshman year; renewable. *Award amount:* up to $1500. *Number of awards:* 100–150. *Eligibility Requirements:* Applicant must be high school student; planning to enroll or expecting to enroll full-time at a four-year institution or university and resident of Missouri. Available to U.S. citizens. *Application Requirements:* Application, test scores, transcript. *Deadline:* April 15.

Contact Laura Harrison, Administrative Assistant II, Missouri Department of Elementary and Secondary Education, PO Box 480, Jefferson City, MO 65102-0480. *E-mail:* laura.harrison@dese.mo.gov. *Phone:* 573-751-1668. *Fax:* 573-526-3580. *Web site:* www.dese.mo.gov.

Teacher Education Scholarship. The scholarship is a competitive, one-time, nonrenewable award of $2000 to be used in one academic year. Applicants must be a Missouri resident and a high school senior or student enrolled full-time at a community or four-year college or university in Missouri. *Award:* Scholarship for use in freshman, sophomore, junior, or senior year; not renewable. *Award amount:* up to $2000. *Number of awards:* up to 240. *Eligibility Requirements:* Applicant must be enrolled or expecting to enroll full-time at a two-year or four-year institution or university; resident of Missouri and studying in Missouri. Available to U.S. citizens. *Application Requirements:* Application, applicant must enter a contest, essay, resume, references, test scores, transcript. *Deadline:* February 15.

Contact Ms. Laura Harrison, Administrative Assistant, Missouri State Department of Elementary/Secondary Education, PO Box 480, Jefferson City, MO 65102-0480. *E-mail:* laura.harrison@dese.mo.gov. *Phone:* 573-751-1668. *Fax:* 573-526-3580. *Web site:* www.dese.mo.gov.

MONTANA

Montana Higher Education Opportunity Grant. This grant is awarded based on need to undergraduate students attending either part-time or full-time who are residents of Montana and attending participating Montana schools. Awards are limited to the most needy students.

A specific major or program of study is not required. This grant does not need to be repaid, and students may apply each year. Apply by filing FAFSA by March 1 and contacting the financial aid office at the admitting college. *Award:* Grant for use in freshman, sophomore, junior, or senior year; not renewable. *Award amount:* $400–$600. *Number of awards:* up to 800. *Eligibility Requirements:* Applicant must be enrolled or expecting to enroll full- or part-time at a two-year or four-year institution or university; resident of Montana and studying in Montana. Available to U.S. citizens. *Application Requirements:* Application, financial need analysis, resume, FAFSA. *Deadline:* March 1.

Contact Jamie Dushin, Budget Analyst, Montana Guaranteed Student Loan Program, Office of Commissioner of Higher Education, PO Box 203101, Helena, MT 59620-3101. *E-mail:* jdushin@mgslp.state.mt.us. *Phone:* 406-444-0638. *Fax:* 406-444-1869. *Web site:* www.mgslp.state.mt.us.

Montana Tuition Assistance Program-Baker Grant. Need-based grant for Montana residents attending participating Montana schools who have earned at least $2575 during the previous calendar year. Must be enrolled full time. Grant does not need to be repaid. Award covers the first undergraduate degree or certificate. Apply by filing FAFSA by March 1 and contacting the financial aid office at the admitting college. *Award:* Grant for use in freshman, sophomore, junior, or senior year; not renewable. *Award amount:* $100–$1000. *Number of awards:* 1000–3000. *Eligibility Requirements:* Applicant must be enrolled or expecting to enroll full-time at a two-year or four-year institution or university; resident of Montana and studying in Montana. Available to U.S. citizens. *Application Requirements:* Application, financial need analysis, resume, FAFSA. *Deadline:* March 1.

Contact Jamie Dushin, Budget Analyst, Montana Guaranteed Student Loan Program, Office of Commissioner of Higher Education, PO Box 203101, Helena, MT 59620-3101. *E-mail:* jdushin@mgslp.state.mt.us. *Phone:* 406-444-0638. *Fax:* 406-444-1869. *Web site:* www.mgslp.state.mt.us.

Montana University System Honor Scholarship. Scholarship will be awarded annually to high school seniors graduating from accredited Montana high schools. The MUS Honor Scholarship is a four year renewable scholarship that waives the tuition and registration fee at one of the Montana University System campuses or one of the three community colleges (Flathead Valley in Kalispell, Miles in Miles City or Dawson in Glendive). The scholarship must be used within 9 months after high school graduation. Applicant should have a GPA of 3.4. *Award:* Scholarship for use in freshman year; renewable. *Award amount:* up to $4020. *Number of awards:* up to 200. *Eligibility Requirements:* Applicant must be high school student; planning to enroll or expecting to enroll full-time at a two-year or four-year institution or university; resident of Montana and studying in Montana. Applicant must have 3.5 GPA or higher. Available to U.S. citizens. *Application Requirements:* Application, test scores, transcript, college acceptance letter. *Deadline:* February 15.

Contact Janice Kirkpatrick, Grant and Scholarship Coordinator, Montana Guaranteed Student Loan Program, Office of Commissioner of Higher Education, PO Box 203101, Helena, MT 59620-3101. *E-mail:* jkirkpatrick@mgslp.state.mt.us. *Phone:* 406-444-0638. *Fax:* 406-444-1869. *Web site:* www.mgslp.state.mt.us.

NEBRASKA

Nebraska State Grant. Available to undergraduates attending a participating postsecondary institution in Nebraska. Available to Pell Grant recipients only. Nebraska residency required. Awards determined by each participating institution. Contact financial aid office at institution for application and additional information. *Award:* Grant for use in freshman, sophomore, junior, or senior year; not renewable. *Award amount:* $100–$1600. *Number of awards:* varies. *Eligibility Requirements:* Applicant must be enrolled or expecting to enroll full- or part-time at a two-year, four-year, or technical institution or university; resident of Nebraska and studying in Nebraska. Available to U.S. citizens. *Application Requirements:* Application, financial need analysis. *Deadline:* continuous.

Contact Mr. J. Ritchie Morrow, Financial Aid Coordinator, State of Nebraska, 140 North Eighth Street, Suite 300, PO Box 95005, Lincoln, NE 68509-5005. *E-mail:* rmorrow@ccpe.st.ne.us. *Phone:* 402-471-2847. *Fax:* 402-471-2886. *Web site:* www.ccpe.state.ne.us.

NEVADA

Governor Guinn Millennium Scholarship. Scholarship for high school graduates with a diploma from a Nevada public or private high school in the graduating class of the year 2000 or later. Must complete high school with at least 3.25 GPA. *Award:* Scholarship for use in freshman, sophomore, junior, or senior year; not renewable. *Award amount:* $10,000. *Number of awards:* 1. *Eligibility Requirements:* Applicant must be enrolled or expecting to enroll full-time at a two-year or four-year institution or university and resident of Nevada. Available to U.S. citizens. *Application Requirements:* Application. *Deadline:* varies.

Contact Reba Coombs, Executive Director, Nevada Office of the State Treasurer, 555 East Washington Avenue, Suite 4600, Las Vegas, NV 89101. *E-mail:* info@nevadatreasurer.gov. *Phone:* 702-486-3383. *Fax:* 702-486-3246. *Web site:* www.nevadatreasurer.gov.

Nevada Student Incentive Grant. Grants awarded to undergraduate and graduate students who are Nevada residents pursuing their first degree. Recipients must be enrolled at least halftime and have financial need. Awards may range from $200 to $4000. High school students may not apply. *Award:* Grant for use in freshman, sophomore, junior, senior, or graduate year; not renewable. *Award amount:* $200–$4000. *Number of awards:* 400–800. *Eligibility Requirements:* Applicant must be enrolled or expecting to enroll full- or part-time at a two-year, four-year, or technical institution or university; resident of Nevada and studying in Nevada. Available to U.S. citizens. *Application Requirements:* Application, financial need analysis. *Deadline:* continuous.

Contact Bill Arensdorf, Director, Nevada Department of Education, 700 East Fifth Street, Carson City, NV 89701. *E-mail:* warensdorf@doe.nv.gov. *Phone:* 775-687-9200. *Fax:* 775-687-9113. *Web site:* www.doe.nv.gov.

University and Community College System of Nevada NASA Space Grant and Fellowship Program. The grant provides graduate fellowships and undergraduate scholarship to qualified student majoring in aerospace science, technology and related fields. Must be Nevada resident studying at a Nevada college/university. Minimum 2.5 GPA required. *Academic Fields/Career Goals:* Aviation/Aerospace; Chemical Engineering; Computer Science/Data Processing; Engineering/Technology; Physical Sciences. *Award:* Scholarship for use in freshman, sophomore, junior, senior, or graduate year; not renewable. *Award amount:* $2500–$30,000. *Number of awards:* 1–20. *Eligibility Requirements:* Applicant must be enrolled or expecting to enroll full-time at a two-year or four-year institution or university; resident of Nevada and studying in Nevada. Applicant must have 3.0 GPA or higher. Available to U.S. citizens. *Application Requirements:* Application, autobiography, essay, resume, references, transcript, project proposal, budget. *Deadline:* April 13.

Contact Cindy Routh, Program Coordinator, NASA Nevada Space Grant Consortium, 2215 Raggio Parkway, Reno, NV 89512. *E-mail:* nvsg@dri.edu. *Phone:* 775-673-7674. *Fax:* 775-673-7485. *Web site:* www.unr.edu/spacegrant.

NEW HAMPSHIRE

Leveraged Incentive Grant Program. Grants to provide assistance on the basis of merit and need to full-time undergraduate New Hampshire students at New Hampshire accredited institutions. Must be a New Hampshire resident, and demonstrate financial need as determined by the federal formula and by merit as determined by the institution. Must be a sophomore, junior or senior undergraduate student. *Award:* Grant for use in sophomore, junior, or senior year; not renewable. *Award amount:* \$250–\$7500. *Number of awards:* varies. *Eligibility Requirements:* Applicant must be enrolled or expecting to enroll full-time at a two-year, four-year, or technical institution or university; resident of New Hampshire and studying in New Hampshire. Available to U.S. citizens. *Application Requirements:* Application, financial need analysis. *Deadline:* varies.

Contact Judith A. Knapp, Coordinator of Financial Aid Programs, New Hampshire Postsecondary Education Commission, Three Barrell Court, Suite 300, Concord, NH 03301-8543. *E-mail:* jknapp@pec.state.nh.us. *Phone:* 603-271-2555 Ext. 352. *Fax:* 603-271-2696. *Web site:* www.nh.gov/postsecondary.

New Hampshire Incentive Program (NHIP). Grants to provide financial assistance to New Hampshire students attending eligible institutions in New England. Must demonstrate financial need. May be a part- or full-time undergraduate student with no previous bachelor's degree. *Award:* Grant for use in freshman, sophomore, junior, or senior year; renewable. *Award amount:* \$125–\$1000. *Number of awards:* 4300–4500. *Eligibility Requirements:* Applicant must be enrolled or expecting to enroll full- or part-time at a four-year institution or university; resident of New Hampshire and studying in Connecticut, Maine, Massachusetts, New Hampshire, Rhode Island, or Vermont. Available to U.S. citizens. *Application Requirements:* Application, financial need analysis, FAFSA. *Deadline:* May 1.

Contact Judith A. Knapp, Coordinator of Financial Aid Programs, New Hampshire Postsecondary Education Commission, Three Barrell Court, Suite 300, Concord, NH 03301-8543. *E-mail:* jknapp@pec.state.nh.us. *Phone:* 603-271-2555 Ext. 352. *Fax:* 603-271-2696. *Web site:* www.nh.gov/postsecondary.

Scholarships for Orphans of Veterans-New Hampshire. Scholarship to provide financial assistance (room, board, books and supplies) to children of parents) who served in World War II, Korean Conflict, Vietnam (Southeast Asian Conflict) or the Gulf Wars, or any other operation for which the armed forces expeditionary medal or theater of operations service medal was awarded to the veteran. *Award:* Scholarship for use in freshman, sophomore, junior, or senior year; renewable. *Award amount:* up to \$2500. *Number of awards:* 1–10. *Eligibility Requirements:* Applicant must be age 16-25; enrolled or expecting to enroll full-time at a two-year or four-year institution or university; resident of New Hampshire and studying in New Hampshire. Available to U.S. citizens. Applicant or parent must meet one or more of the following requirements: general military experience; retired from active duty; disabled or killed as a result of military service; prisoner of war; or missing in action. *Application Requirements:* Application. *Deadline:* varies.

Contact Judith A. Knapp, Coordinator of Financial Aid Programs, New Hampshire Postsecondary Education Commission, Three Barrell Court, Suite 300, Concord, NH 03301-8543. *E-mail:* jknapp@pec.state.nh.us. *Phone:* 603-271-2555 Ext. 352. *Fax:* 603-271-2696. *Web site:* www.nh.gov/postsecondary.

Workforce Incentive Program. The program provides incentive for students to pursue careers in critical workforce shortage areas at appropriate New Hampshire institutions and to encourage students to then seek employment in New Hampshire after completion of their career program. May be a part- or full-time student in an approved program, and should demonstrate financial need as determined by the institution. *Academic Fields/Career Goals:* Education; Foreign Language; Nursing; Special Education. *Award:* Forgivable loan for use in freshman, sophomore, junior, senior, graduate, or postgraduate years; not renewable. *Award amount:* varies. *Number of awards:* varies. *Eligibility Requirements:* Applicant must be enrolled or expecting to enroll full- or part-time at a four-year institution or university; resident of New Hampshire and studying in New Hampshire. Available to U.S. citizens. *Application Requirements:* Application. *Deadline:* varies.

Contact Judith A. Knapp, Coordinator of Financial Aid Programs, New Hampshire Postsecondary Education Commission, Three Barrell Court, Suite 300, Concord, NH 03301-8543. *E-mail:* jknapp@pec.state.nh.us. *Phone:* 603-271-2555 Ext. 352. *Fax:* 603-271-2696. *Web site:* www.nh.gov/postsecondary.

NEW JERSEY

American Legion Department of New Jersey High School Oratorical Contest. Award to promote and coordinate the Oratorical Contest Program at the Department, District, County and Post Levels. High School Oratorical Contest is to develop a deeper knowledge and understanding of the constitution of the United States. *Award:* Prize for use in freshman year; not renewable. *Award amount:* \$1000–\$4000. *Number of awards:* 5. *Eligibility Requirements:* Applicant must be high school student; planning to enroll or expecting to enroll full-time at a four-year institution or university and must have an interest in public speaking. Available to U.S. citizens. *Application Requirements:* Application, applicant must enter a contest. *Deadline:* March 8.

Contact Raymond L. Zawacki, Department Adjutant, American Legion Department of New Jersey, 135 West Hanover Street, Trenton, NJ 08618. *E-mail:* ray@njamericanlegion.org. *Phone:* 609-695-5418. *Fax:* 609-394-1532. *Web site:* www.njamericanlegion.org.

ANNA Alcavis International, Inc. Career Mobility Scholarship. Scholarship to students accepted or enrolled in a baccalaureate or higher degree program in nursing. Applicant must hold a current credential as a Certified Nephrology Nurse (CNN) or Certified Dialysis Nurse (CDN) administered by the Nephrology Nursing Certification Commission (NNCC). *Academic Fields/Career Goals:* Nursing. *Award:* Forgivable loan for use in freshman, sophomore, junior, senior, or graduate year; renewable. *Award amount:* \$2000. *Number of awards:* 5. *Eligibility Requirements:* Applicant must be enrolled or expecting to enroll full-time at a four-year institution or university. Applicant or parent of applicant must be member of American Nephrology Nurses' Association. Applicant or parent of applicant must have employment or volunteer experience in nursing. Available to U.S. and non-Canadian citizens. *Application Requirements:* Application, essay, financial need analysis, transcript. *Deadline:* October 15.

Contact Sharon Longton, Awards, Scholarships, and Grants Chairperson, American Nephrology Nurses' Association, East Holly Avenue, PO Box 56, Pitman, NJ 08071-0056. *E-mail:* slongton@dmc.org. *Phone:* 313-966-2674. *Web site:* www.annanurse.org.

Dana Christmas Scholarship for Heroism. Honors young New Jersey residents for acts of heroism. Scholarship is a nonrenewable award of up to \$10,000 for 5 students. This scholarship may be used for undergraduate or graduate study. Deadline varies. *Award:* Scholarship for use in freshman, sophomore, junior, senior, or graduate year; not renewable. *Award amount:* up to \$10,000. *Number of awards:* up to 5. *Eligibility Requirements:* Applicant must be age 21 or under; enrolled or expecting to enroll full- or part-time at a two-year, four-year, or technical institution or university and resident of New Jersey. Available to U.S. citizens. *Application Requirements:* Application. *Deadline:* varies.

Contact Gisele Joachim, Director, Financial Aid Services, New Jersey Higher Education Student Assistance Authority, 4 Quakerbridge Plaza, PO Box 540, Trenton, NJ 08625. *E-mail:* gjoachim@hesaa.org. *Phone:* 800-792-8670 Ext. 2349. *Fax:* 609-588-7389. *Web site:* www.hesaa.org.

Edward J. Bloustein Distinguished Scholars. Renewable scholarship for students who are placed in top 10 percent of their classes and have a minimum combined SAT score of 1260, or ranked first, second or third in their classes as of end of junior year. Must be New Jersey resident and must attend a New Jersey two-year college, four-year college or university, or approved programs at proprietary institutions. Secondary schools must forward to HESAA, the names and class standings for all nominees. Award value up to $1000 and deadline varies. *Award:* Scholarship for use in freshman, sophomore, junior, senior, or graduate year; renewable. *Award amount:* up to $1000. *Number of awards:* varies. *Eligibility Requirements:* Applicant must be enrolled or expecting to enroll full-time at a two-year or four-year institution or university; resident of New Jersey and studying in New Jersey. Available to U.S. citizens. *Application Requirements:* Application, test scores, nomination by high school. *Deadline:* varies.

Contact Carol Muka, Assistant Director of Grants and Scholarships, New Jersey Higher Education Student Assistance Authority, PO Box 540, Trenton, NJ 08625. *E-mail:* cmuka@hesaa.org. *Phone:* 800-792-8670 Ext. 3266. *Fax:* 609-588-2228. *Web site:* www.hesaa.org.

Law Enforcement Officer Memorial Scholarship. Scholarships for full-time undergraduate study at approved New Jersey institutions for the dependent children of New Jersey law enforcement officers killed in the line of duty. Value of scholarship will be established annually. Deadline varies. *Award:* Scholarship for use in freshman, sophomore, junior, or senior year; renewable. *Award amount:* varies. *Number of awards:* varies. *Eligibility Requirements:* Applicant must be enrolled or expecting to enroll full-time at a four-year institution or university; resident of New Jersey and studying in New Jersey. Applicant or parent of applicant must have employment or volunteer experience in police/firefighting. Available to U.S. citizens. *Application Requirements:* Application. *Deadline:* varies.

Contact Carol Muka, Assistant Director of Grants and Scholarships, New Jersey Higher Education Student Assistance Authority, PO Box 540, Trenton, NJ 08625. *E-mail:* cmuka@hesaa.org. *Phone:* 800-792-8670 Ext. 3266. *Fax:* 609-588-2228. *Web site:* www.hesaa.org.

Luterman Scholarship. Applicant must be a natural or adopted descendant of a member of American Legion, Department of New Jersey. Applicant must be a member of the graduating class of high school including Vo-tech. *Award:* Scholarship for use in freshman year; not renewable. *Award amount:* $1000–$4000. *Number of awards:* 7. *Eligibility Requirements:* Applicant must be high school student and planning to enroll or expecting to enroll full-time at a two-year, four-year, or technical institution or university. Applicant or parent of applicant must be member of American Legion or Auxiliary. Available to U.S. citizens. Applicant or parent must meet one or more of the following requirements: Army experience; retired from active duty; disabled or killed as a result of military service; prisoner of war; or missing in action. *Application Requirements:* Application. *Deadline:* February 15.

Contact Raymond L. Zawacki, Department Adjutant, American Legion Department of New Jersey, 135 West Hanover Street, Trenton, NJ 08618. *E-mail:* ray@njamericanlegion.org. *Phone:* 609-695-5418. *Fax:* 609-394-1532. *Web site:* www.njamericanlegion.org.

New Jersey Student Tuition Assistance Reward Scholarship II. Scholarship for high school graduates who plan to pursue a baccalaureate degree at a New Jersey four-year public institution. Scholarship will cover the cost of tuition and approved fees for up to 18 credits per semester when combined with other state, federal and institutional aid. Deadline varies. *Award:* Scholarship for use in freshman year; renewable. *Award amount:* $2000. *Number of awards:* varies. *Eligibility Requirements:* Applicant must be enrolled or expecting to enroll full-time at a four-year institution or university; resident of New Jersey and studying in New Jersey. Applicant must have 3.0 GPA or higher. Available to U.S. citizens. *Application Requirements:* Application, FAFSA. *Deadline:* varies.

Contact Cathleen Lewis, Assistant Director, Client Services, New Jersey Higher Education Student Assistance Authority, 4 Quaker Bridge Plaza, PO Box 540, Trenton, NJ 08625-0540. *E-mail:* clewis@hesaa.org. *Phone:* 609-588-3280. *Fax:* 609-588-2228. *Web site:* www.hesaa.org.

New Jersey War Orphans Tuition Assistance. $500 scholarship to children of those service personnel who died while in the military or due to service-connected disabilities, or who are officially listed as missing in action by the U.S. Department of Defense. Must be a resident of New Jersey for at least one year immediately preceding the filing of the application and be between the ages of 16 and 21 at the time of application. *Award:* Scholarship for use in freshman, sophomore, junior, or senior year; renewable. *Award amount:* $500. *Number of awards:* varies. *Eligibility Requirements:* Applicant must be age 16-21; enrolled or expecting to enroll full-time at a four-year institution or university and resident of New Jersey. Available to U.S. citizens. Applicant or parent must meet one or more of the following requirements: general military experience; retired from active duty; disabled or killed as a result of military service; prisoner of war; or missing in action. *Application Requirements:* Application, transcript. *Deadline:* varies.

Contact Patricia Richter, Grants Manager, New Jersey Department of Military and Veterans Affairs, PO Box 340, Trenton, NJ 08625-0340. *E-mail:* patricia.richter@njdmava.state.nj.us. *Phone:* 609-530-6854. *Fax:* 609-530-6970. *Web site:* www.state.nj.us/military.

New Jersey World Trade Center Scholarship. Scholarship was established by the legislature to aid the dependent children and surviving spouses of New Jersey residents who were killed in the terrorist attacks, or who are missing and officially presumed dead as a direct result of the attacks; applies to instate and out-of-state institutions for students seeking undergraduate degrees. Deadlines: March 1 for fall, October 1 for spring. *Award:* Scholarship for use in freshman, sophomore, junior, or senior year; renewable. *Award amount:* up to $6500. *Number of awards:* varies. *Eligibility Requirements:* Applicant must be enrolled or expecting to enroll full-time at a four-year institution or university and resident of New Jersey. Available to U.S. citizens. *Application Requirements:* Application. *Deadline:* varies.

Contact Giselle Joachim, Director of Financial Aid Services, New Jersey Higher Education Student Assistance Authority, PO Box 540, Trenton, NJ 08625. *E-mail:* gjoachim@hesaa.org. *Phone:* 800-792-8670 Ext. 2349. *Fax:* 609-588-7389. *Web site:* www.hesaa.org.

NJ Student Tuition Assistance Reward Scholarship. Scholarship for students who graduate in the top 20 percent of their high school class. Recipients may be awarded up to five semesters of tuition (up to 15 credits per term) and approved fees at one of New Jersey's nineteen county colleges. *Award:* Scholarship for use in freshman, sophomore, junior, or senior year; renewable. *Award amount:* $2500–$7500. *Number of awards:* varies. *Eligibility Requirements:* Applicant must be enrolled or expecting to enroll full-time at a two-year or four-year institution or university; resident of New Jersey and studying in New Jersey. Applicant must have 3.0 GPA or higher. Available to U.S. citizens. *Application Requirements:* Application, transcript. *Deadline:* varies.

Contact Carol Muka, Assistant Director of Grants and Scholarships, New Jersey Higher Education Student Assistance Authority, PO Box 540, Trenton, NJ 08625. *E-mail:* cmuka@hessa.org. *Phone:* 800-792-8670 Ext. 3266. *Fax:* 609-588-2228. *Web site:* www.hesaa.org.

Outstanding Scholar Recruitment Program. Awards students who meet the eligibility criteria and who are enrolled as first-time freshmen at participating New Jersey institutions receive annual scholarship awards of up to $7500. *Award:* Scholarship for use in freshman, sophomore, junior, or senior year; renewable. *Award amount:* $2500–$7500. *Number of awards:* varies. *Eligibility Requirements:* Applicant must be enrolled or expecting to enroll full-time at a four-year institution or university; resident of New Jersey and studying in New Jersey. Available to U.S. citizens. *Application Requirements:* Application. *Deadline:* varies.

Contact Carol Muka, Assistant Director of Grants and Scholarships, New Jersey Higher Education Student Assistance Authority, PO Box 540, Trenton, NJ 08625. *E-mail:* cmuka@hesaa.org. *Phone:* 800-792-8670 Ext. 3266. *Fax:* 609-588-2228. *Web site:* www.hesaa.org.

Part-Time Tuition Aid Grant (TAG) for County Colleges. Provides financial aid to eligible part-time undergraduate students enrolled for 9 to 11 credits at participating New Jersey community colleges. Deadlines: March 1 for spring and October 1 for fall. *Award:* Grant for use in freshman, sophomore, junior, or senior year; not renewable. *Award amount:* \$419–\$628. *Number of awards:* varies. *Eligibility Requirements:* Applicant must be enrolled or expecting to enroll part-time at a two-year or four-year institution or university; resident of New Jersey and studying in New Jersey. Available to U.S. citizens. *Application Requirements:* Application, financial need analysis. *Deadline:* varies.

Contact Sherri Fox, Acting Director of Grants and Scholarships, New Jersey Higher Education Student Assistance Authority, PO Box 540, Trenton, NJ 08625. *Phone:* 800-792-8670. *Fax:* 609-588-2228. *Web site:* www.hesaa.org.

POW-MIA Tuition Benefit Program. Free undergraduate college tuition provided to any child born or adopted before or during the period of time his or her parent was officially declared a prisoner of war or person missing in action after January 1, 1960. The POW-MIA must have been a New Jersey resident at the time he or she entered the service. Child of veteran must attend either a public or private institution in New Jersey. A copy of DD 1300 must be furnished with the application. Minimum 2.5 GPA required. *Award:* Scholarship for use in freshman, sophomore, junior, or senior year; renewable. *Award amount:* varies. *Number of awards:* varies. *Eligibility Requirements:* Applicant must be enrolled or expecting to enroll full-time at a two-year, four-year, or technical institution or university; resident of New Jersey and studying in New Jersey. Applicant must have 2.5 GPA or higher. Available to U.S. citizens. Applicant or parent must meet one or more of the following requirements: general military experience; retired from active duty; disabled or killed as a result of military service; prisoner of war; or missing in action. *Application Requirements:* Application, transcript, copy of DD 1300. *Deadline:* varies.

Contact Patricia Richter, Grants Manager, New Jersey Department of Military and Veterans Affairs, PO Box 340, Trenton, NJ 08625-0340. *E-mail:* patricia.richter@njdmava.state.nj.us. *Phone:* 609-530-6854. *Fax:* 609-530-6970. *Web site:* www.state.nj.us/military.

Stutz Scholarship. Award to natural or adopted son or daughter of a member of The American Legion, Department of New Jersey. Applicant must be a member of the graduating class of high school including Vo-tech. *Award:* Scholarship for use in freshman year; not renewable. *Award amount:* \$4000. *Number of awards:* 1. *Eligibility Requirements:* Applicant must be high school student and planning to enroll or expecting to enroll full-time at a two-year, four-year, or technical institution or university. Applicant or parent of applicant must be member of American Legion or Auxiliary. Available to U.S. citizens. Applicant or parent must meet one or more of the following requirements: Army experience; retired from active duty; disabled or killed as a result of military service; prisoner of war; or missing in action. *Application Requirements:* Application. *Deadline:* February 15.

Contact Raymond L. Zawacki, Department Adjutant, American Legion Department of New Jersey, 135 West Hanover Street, Trenton, NJ 08618. *E-mail:* ray@njamericanlegion.org. *Phone:* 609-695-5418. *Fax:* 609-394-1532. *Web site:* www.njamericanlegion.org.

Survivor Tuition Benefits Program. The scholarship provides tuition fees for spouses and dependents of law enforcement officers, fire, or emergency services personnel killed in the line of duty. Eligible recipients may attend any independent institution in the state; however, the annual value of the grant cannot exceed the highest tuition charged at a New Jersey public institution. *Award:* Scholarship for use in freshman, sophomore, junior, or senior year; renewable. *Award amount:* varies. *Number of awards:* varies. *Eligibility Requirements:* Applicant must be enrolled or expecting to enroll full- or part-time at a two-year or four-year institution or university; resident of New Jersey and studying in New Jersey. Applicant or parent of applicant must have employment or volunteer experience in police/firefighting. Available to U.S. citizens. *Application Requirements:* Application. *Deadline:* varies.

Contact Carol Muka, Scholarship Coordinator, New Jersey Higher Education Student Assistance Authority, PO Box 540, Trenton, NJ 08625. *E-mail:* cmuka@hesaa.org. *Phone:* 800-792-8670 Ext. 3266. *Fax:* 609-588-2228. *Web site:* www.hesaa.org.

Tuition Aid Grant. The program provides tuition fees to eligible undergraduate students attending participating in-state institutions. Deadlines: March 1 for fall, October 1 for spring. *Award:* Grant for use in freshman, sophomore, junior, or senior year; not renewable. *Award amount:* \$868–\$7272. *Number of awards:* varies. *Eligibility Requirements:* Applicant must be enrolled or expecting to enroll full-time at a two-year or four-year institution or university; resident of New Jersey and studying in New Jersey. Available to U.S. citizens. *Application Requirements:* Application, financial need analysis. *Deadline:* varies.

Contact Sherri Fox, Acting Director of Grants and Scholarships, New Jersey Higher Education Student Assistance Authority, PO Box 540, Trenton, NJ 08625. *Phone:* 800-792-8670. *Fax:* 609-588-2228. *Web site:* www.hesaa.org.

Urban Scholars. Renewable scholarship to high achieving students attending public secondary schools in the urban and economically distressed areas of New Jersey. Students must rank in the top 10 percent of their class and have a GPA of at least 3.0 at the end of their junior year. Must be New Jersey resident and attend a New Jersey two-year college, four-year college or university, or approved programs at proprietary institutions. Students do not apply directly for scholarship consideration. Deadline varies. *Award:* Scholarship for use in freshman, sophomore, junior, or senior year; renewable. *Award amount:* up to \$1000. *Number of awards:* varies. *Eligibility Requirements:* Applicant must be enrolled or expecting to enroll full-time at a two-year or four-year institution or university; resident of New Jersey and studying in New Jersey. Applicant must have 3.0 GPA or higher. Available to U.S. citizens. *Application Requirements:* Application, test scores, nomination by school. *Deadline:* varies.

Contact Carol Muka, Assistant Director of Grants and Scholarships, New Jersey Higher Education Student Assistance Authority, PO Box 540, Trenton, NJ 08625. *E-mail:* cmuka@hesaa.org. *Phone:* 800-792-8670 Ext. 3266. *Fax:* 609-588-2228. *Web site:* www.hesaa.org.

Veterans Tuition Credit Program-New Jersey. Award for New Jersey resident veterans who served in the armed forces between December 31, 1960, and May 7, 1975. Must have been a New Jersey resident at time of induction or discharge or for two years immediately prior to application. *Award:* Scholarship for use in freshman, sophomore, junior, or senior year; renewable. *Award amount:* \$200–\$400. *Number of awards:* varies. *Eligibility Requirements:* Applicant must be enrolled or expecting to enroll full- or part-time at a two-year, four-year, or technical institution or university and resident of New Jersey. Available to U.S. citizens. Applicant or parent must meet one or more of the following requirements: general military experience; retired from active duty; disabled or killed as a result of military service; prisoner of war; or missing in action. *Application Requirements:* Application. *Deadline:* varies.

Contact Patricia Richter, Grants Manager, New Jersey Department of Military and Veterans Affairs, PO Box 340, Trenton, NJ 08625-0340. *E-mail:* patricia.richter@njdmava.state.nj.us. *Phone:* 609-530-6854. *Fax:* 609-530-6970. *Web site:* www.state.nj.us/military.

NEW MEXICO

Allied Health Student Loan Program-New Mexico. Award to New Mexico residents studying in New Mexico to increase the number of physician assistants in areas of the state which have experienced shortages of health practitioners. Provides educational loans to students seeking certification/licensers in an eligible health field. As a condition of each loan, the student must declare intent to practice as a health professional in a designated shortage area. For every year of service, a portion of the loan will be forgiven. *Academic Fields/Career Goals:* Dental Health/Services; Health and Medical Sciences; Nursing; Therapy/Rehabilitation. *Award:* Forgivable loan for use in freshman, sophomore, junior, or senior year; renewable. *Award amount:* up to $12,000. *Number of awards:* 1–40. *Eligibility Requirements:* Applicant must be enrolled or expecting to enroll full- or part-time at a four-year institution or university; resident of New Mexico and studying in New Mexico. Available to U.S. citizens. *Application Requirements:* Application, financial need analysis, transcript, FAFSA. *Deadline:* July 1.

Contact Theresa Acker, Financial Aid Division, New Mexico Commission on Higher Education, 1068 Cerrillos Road, Santa Fe, NM 87505-1650. *E-mail:* theresa.acker@state.nm.us. *Phone:* 505-476-6506. *Fax:* 505-476-6511. *Web site:* www.hed.state.nm.us.

Children of Deceased Veterans Scholarship-New Mexico. Award for New Mexico residents who are children of veterans killed or disabled as a result of service, prisoner of war, or veterans missing in action. Must be between ages 16 and 26. For use at New Mexico schools for undergraduate study. Must submit parent's death certificate and DD form 214. *Award:* Scholarship for use in freshman, sophomore, junior, or senior year; renewable. *Award amount:* $300. *Number of awards:* varies. *Eligibility Requirements:* Applicant must be age 16-26; enrolled or expecting to enroll full- or part-time at a two-year or four-year institution or university; resident of New Mexico and studying in New Mexico. Available to U.S. citizens. Applicant or parent must meet one or more of the following requirements: general military experience; retired from active duty; disabled or killed as a result of military service; prisoner of war; or missing in action. *Application Requirements:* Application, transcript, death certificate or notice of casualty, DD form 214. *Deadline:* continuous.

Contact Alan Martinez, Director, State Benefits Division, New Mexico Veterans Service Commission, Bataan Memorial Building, 407 Galisteo, Room 142, Santa Fe, NM 87504. *E-mail:* alan.martinez@state.nm.us. *Phone:* 505-827-6300. *Fax:* 505-827-6372. *Web site:* www.dvs.state.nm.us.

College Affordability Grant. Grant available to New Mexico students with financial need who do not qualify for other state grants and scholarships to attend and complete educational programs at a New Mexico public college or university. Student must have unmet need after all other financial aid has been awarded. Student may not be receiving any other state grants or scholarships. Renewable upon satisfactory academic progress. *Award:* Grant for use in freshman, sophomore, junior, or senior year; renewable. *Award amount:* up to $1000. *Number of awards:* 1. *Eligibility Requirements:* Applicant must be enrolled or expecting to enroll full- or part-time at a two-year or four-year institution or university; resident of New Mexico and studying in New Mexico. Available to U.S. citizens. *Application Requirements:* Application, financial need analysis, FAFSA. *Deadline:* continuous.

Contact Tashina Banks Acker, Director of Financial Aid, New Mexico Commission on Higher Education, 1068 Cerrillos Road, Santa Fe, NM 87505-1650. *E-mail:* tashina.banks-moore@state.nm.us. *Phone:* 505-476-6549. *Fax:* 505-476-6511. *Web site:* www.hed.state.nm.us.

Legislative Endowment Scholarships. Renewable scholarships to provide aid for undergraduate students with substantial financial need who are attending public postsecondary institutions in New Mexico. Four-year schools may award up to $2500 per academic year, two-year schools may award up to $1000 per academic year. Deadlines varies. *Award:* Scholarship for use in freshman, sophomore, junior, or senior year; renewable. *Award amount:* $1000–$2500. *Number of awards:* 1. *Eligibility Requirements:* Applicant must be enrolled or expecting to enroll full- or part-time at a two-year or four-year institution or university; resident of New Mexico and studying in New Mexico. Available to U.S. citizens. *Application Requirements:* Application, financial need analysis, FAFSA. *Deadline:* varies.

Contact Tashina Banks Moore, Director of Financial Aid, New Mexico Commission on Higher Education, 1068 Cerrillos Road, Santa Fe, NM 87505-1650. *E-mail:* tashina.banks-moore@state.nm.us. *Phone:* 505-475-6549. *Fax:* 505-476-6511. *Web site:* www.hed.state.nm.us.

Legislative Lottery Scholarship. Renewable Scholarship for New Mexico high school graduates or GED recipients who plan to attend an eligible New Mexico public college or university. Must be enrolled full-time and maintain 2.5 GPA. *Award:* Scholarship for use in freshman year; renewable. *Award amount:* varies. *Number of awards:* 1. *Eligibility Requirements:* Applicant must be high school student; planning to enroll or expecting to enroll full-time at a four-year institution or university; resident of New Mexico and studying in New Mexico. Applicant must have 3.5 GPA or higher. Available to U.S. citizens. *Application Requirements:* Application, FAFSA. *Deadline:* varies.

Contact Tashina Banks Moore, Director of Financial Aid, New Mexico Commission on Higher Education, 1068 Cerrillos Road, Santa Fe, NM 87505. *E-mail:* tashina.banks-moore@state.nm.us. *Phone:* 505-476-6549. *Fax:* 505-476-6511. *Web site:* www.hed.state.nm.us.

Minority Doctoral Assistance Loan-For-Service Program. Award program enacted to increase the number of ethnic minorities and women available to teach engineering, physical or life sciences, mathematics, and other academic disciplines in which ethnic minorities or women are demonstrably underrepresented in New Mexico colleges and universities. Award may be renewable for up to four years. *Academic Fields/Career Goals:* Chemical Engineering; Engineering/Technology; Mathematics; Mechanical Engineering; Natural Sciences; Physical Sciences. *Award:* Forgivable loan for use in freshman, sophomore, junior, senior, or graduate year; renewable. *Award amount:* $15,000. *Number of awards:* varies. *Eligibility Requirements:* Applicant must be American Indian/Alaska Native, Asian/Pacific Islander, Black (non-Hispanic), or Hispanic; enrolled or expecting to enroll full-time at a four-year institution or university; resident of New Mexico and studying in New Mexico. Available to U.S. citizens. *Application Requirements:* Application, essay, references, transcript. *Deadline:* March 15.

Contact Theresa Acker, Financial Aid Division, New Mexico Commission on Higher Education, 1068 Cerrillos Road, Santa Fe, NM 87505-1650. *E-mail:* tashina.banks-moore@state.nm.us. *Phone:* 505-476-6506. *Fax:* 505-476-6511. *Web site:* www.hed.state.nm.us.

New Mexico Competitive Scholarship. Scholarships for non-residents or non-citizens of the United States to encourage out-of-state students who have demonstrated high academic achievement in high school to enroll in public four-year universities in New Mexico. Renewable for up to four years. For details visit: http://fin.hed.state.nm.us. *Award:* Scholarship for use in freshman year; renewable. *Award amount:* varies. *Number of awards:* varies. *Eligibility Requirements:* Applicant must be high school student; planning to enroll or expecting to enroll full-time at a four-year institution or university and studying in New Mexico. Available to Canadian and non-U.S.

citizens. *Application Requirements:* Application, essay, references, test scores. *Deadline:* varies.

Contact Tashina Banks Moore, Director of Financial Aid, New Mexico Commission on Higher Education, 1068 Cerrillos Road, Santa Fe, NM 87505. *E-mail:* tashina.banks-moore@state.nm.us. *Phone:* 505-476-6549. *Fax:* 505-476-6511. *Web site:* www.hed.state.nm.us.

New Mexico Scholars' Program. Renewable award program created to encourage New Mexico high school students to attend public postsecondary institutions or the following private colleges in New Mexico: College of Santa Fe, St. John's College, College of the Southwest. For details visit: http://fin.hed.state.nm.us. *Award:* Scholarship for use in freshman year; renewable. *Award amount:* varies. *Number of awards:* 1. *Eligibility Requirements:* Applicant must be high school student; age 21 or under; planning to enroll or expecting to enroll full-time at a two-year or four-year institution; resident of New Mexico and studying in New Mexico. Available to U.S. citizens. *Application Requirements:* Application, financial need analysis, test scores, FAFSA. *Deadline:* varies.

Contact Tashina Banks Moore, Director of Financial Aid, New Mexico Commission on Higher Education, 1068 Cerrillos Road, Santa Fe, NM 87505-1650. *E-mail:* tashina.banks-moore@state.nm.us. *Phone:* 505-476-6549. *Fax:* 505-476-6511. *Web site:* www.hed.state.nm.us.

New Mexico Student Incentive Grant. Grant created to provide aid for undergraduate students with substantial financial need who are attending public colleges or universities or the following eligible colleges in New Mexico: College of Santa Fe, St. John's College, College of the Southwest, Institute of American Indian Art, Crownpoint Institute of Technology, Dine College and Southwestern Indian Polytechnic Institute. Part-time students are eligible for pro-rated awards. *Award:* Grant for use in freshman, sophomore, junior, or senior year; not renewable. *Award amount:* $200–$2500. *Number of awards:* 1. *Eligibility Requirements:* Applicant must be enrolled or expecting to enroll full- or part-time at a two-year, four-year, or technical institution or university; resident of New Mexico and studying in New Mexico. Available to U.S. citizens. *Application Requirements:* Application, financial need analysis, FAFSA. *Deadline:* varies.

Contact Tashina Banks Moore, Director of Financial Aid, New Mexico Commission on Higher Education, 1068 Cerrillos Road, Santa Fe, NM 87505-1650. *E-mail:* tashina.banks-moore@state.nm.us. *Phone:* 505-476-6549. *Fax:* 505-476-6511. *Web site:* www.hed.state.nm.us.

New Mexico Vietnam Veteran Scholarship. Award for Vietnam veterans who have been New Mexico residents for a minimum of ten years and are attending state-funded postsecondary schools. Must have been awarded the Vietnam Campaign medal. Must submit DD 214 and discharge papers. *Award:* Scholarship for use in freshman, sophomore, junior, or senior year; renewable. *Award amount:* $3500–$4000. *Number of awards:* 115. *Eligibility Requirements:* Applicant must be enrolled or expecting to enroll full- or part-time at a two-year, four-year, or technical institution or university; resident of New Mexico and studying in New Mexico. Available to U.S. citizens. Applicant or parent must meet one or more of the following requirements: general military experience; retired from active duty; disabled or killed as a result of military service; prisoner of war; or missing in action. *Application Requirements:* Application, copy of DD Form 214. *Deadline:* continuous.

Contact Alan Martinez, Director, State Benefits Division, New Mexico Veterans Service Commission, Bataan Memorial Building, 407 Galisteo, Room 142, Santa Fe, NM 87504. *E-mail:* alan.martinez@state.nm.us. *Phone:* 505-827-6300. *Fax:* 505-827-6372. *Web site:* www.dvs.state.nm.us.

Nurse Educator Loan-for-Service. Forgivable loan of up to $5000 for New Mexico nursing majors to obtain an undergraduate, graduate, or post graduate degree in the state of New Mexico. Each loan has a service agreement wherein the student declares his/her intent to serve in a nurse faculty position in a New Mexico public, post-secondary institution. For every academic year of service, a portion of the loan is forgiven and if the entire service agreement is fulfilled, the entire loan is eligible for forgiveness. Must be a U.S. citizen. *Academic Fields/Career Goals:* Nursing. *Award:* Forgivable loan for use in senior year; renewable. *Award amount:* up to $5000. *Number of awards:* 1. *Eligibility Requirements:* Applicant must be enrolled or expecting to enroll full- or part-time at a four-year institution or university; resident of New Mexico and studying in New Mexico. Available to U.S. citizens. *Application Requirements:* Application, essay, transcript. *Deadline:* July 1.

Contact Theresa Acker, Financial Aid Division, New Mexico Commission on Higher Education, 1068 Cerrillos Road, Santa Fe, NM 85705-1650. *E-mail:* theresa.acker@state.nm.us. *Phone:* 505-476-6506. *Fax:* 505-476-6511. *Web site:* www.hed.state.nm.us.

Nursing Student Loan-For-Service Program. Award to increase the number of nurses in areas of New Mexico which have experienced shortages by making educational loans to students entering nursing programs. As a condition of each loan, the student shall declare his/her intent to practice as a health professional in a designated shortage area. For every year of service, a portion of the loan will be forgiven. *Academic Fields/Career Goals:* Nursing. *Award:* Forgivable loan for use in freshman, sophomore, junior, or senior year; renewable. *Award amount:* up to $12,000. *Number of awards:* 1. *Eligibility Requirements:* Applicant must be enrolled or expecting to enroll full- or part-time at a four-year institution or university; resident of New Mexico and studying in New Mexico. Available to U.S. citizens. *Application Requirements:* Application, financial need analysis, transcript, FAFSA. *Deadline:* July 1.

Contact Theresa Acker, Financial Aid Division, New Mexico Commission on Higher Education, 1068 Cerrillos Road, Santa Fe, NM 87505-1650. *E-mail:* theresa.acker@state.nm.us. *Phone:* 505-476-6506. *Fax:* 505-476-6511. *Web site:* www.hed.state.nm.us.

Public Service Law Loan Repayment Assistance Program. Program to provide legal educational loan repayment assistance to individuals providing public service in state or local government or the nonprofit sector in New Mexico to low income or underserved residents. *Academic Fields/Career Goals:* Law/Legal Services. *Award:* Forgivable loan for use in freshman, sophomore, junior, or senior year; renewable. *Award amount:* up to $7200. *Number of awards:* 1–16. *Eligibility Requirements:* Applicant must be enrolled or expecting to enroll full-time at a four-year institution or university; resident of New Mexico and studying in New Mexico. Available to U.S. citizens. *Application Requirements:* Application. *Deadline:* February 28.

Contact Theresa Acker, Financial Aid Division, New Mexico Commission on Higher Education, 1068 Cerrillos Road, Santa Fe, NM 87505. *E-mail:* theresa.acker@state.nm.us. *Phone:* 505-476-6506. *Fax:* 505-475-6511. *Web site:* www.hed.state.nm.us.

Teacher Loan-For-Service. Purpose is to proactively address New Mexico's teacher shortage by providing students with the financial resources to complete or enhance their post-secondary teacher preparation education. *Academic Fields/Career Goals:* Education. *Award:* Forgivable loan for use in freshman, sophomore, junior, or senior year; renewable. *Award amount:* up to $4000. *Number of awards:* 1. *Eligibility Requirements:* Applicant must be enrolled or expecting to enroll full- or part-time at a four-year institution or university; resident of New Mexico and studying in New Mexico. Available to U.S. citizens. *Application Requirements:* Application, financial need analysis, FAFSA. *Deadline:* July 1.

Contact Theresa Acker, Financial Aid Division, New Mexico Commission on Higher Education, 1068 Cerrillos Road, Santa Fe, NM 87505-1650. *E-mail:* theresa.acker@state.

nm.us. *Phone:* 505-476-6506. *Fax:* 505-476-6511. *Web site:* www.hed.state.nm.us.

Vietnam Veterans' Scholarship Program. Renewable scholarship program created to provide aid for Vietnam veterans who are undergraduate and graduate students attending public postsecondary institutions or select private colleges in New Mexico. Private colleges include: College of Santa Fe, St. John's College and College of the Southwest. *Award:* Scholarship for use in freshman, sophomore, junior, or senior year; renewable. *Award amount:* varies. *Number of awards:* 1. *Eligibility Requirements:* Applicant must be enrolled or expecting to enroll full-time at a two-year or four-year institution; resident of New Mexico and studying in New Mexico. Available to U.S. citizens. Applicant or parent must meet one or more of the following requirements: general military experience; retired from active duty; disabled or killed as a result of military service; prisoner of war; or missing in action. *Application Requirements:* Application, certification by the NM Veteran's commission. *Deadline:* varies.

Contact Tashina Banks Moore, Director of Financial Aid, New Mexico Commission on Higher Education, 1068 Cerrillos Road, Santa Fe, NM 87505-1650. *E-mail:* tashina.banks-moore@state.nm.us. *Phone:* 505-476-6549. *Fax:* 505-476-6511. *Web site:* www.hed.state.nm.us.

NEW YORK

DAAD University Summer Course Grant. Scholarship for summer language study at Germany's universities. Intermediate level classes; open to students of all fields. *Academic Fields/Career Goals:* Foreign Language. *Award:* Grant for use in sophomore, junior, senior, or graduate year; not renewable. *Award amount:* varies. *Number of awards:* varies. *Eligibility Requirements:* Applicant must be enrolled or expecting to enroll full-time at a four-year institution or university and must have an interest in German language/culture. Available to U.S. and non-U.S. citizens. *Application Requirements:* Application, applicant must enter a contest, essay, resume, references, transcript. *Deadline:* January 31.

Contact Jane Fu, Information Officer, German Academic Exchange Service (DAAD), 871 United Nations Plaza, New York, NY 10017. *E-mail:* daadny@daad.org. *Phone:* 212-758-3223. *Fax:* 212-755-5780. *Web site:* www.daad.org.

Japan-U.S. Friendship Commission Prize for the Translation of Japanese Literature. Annual prize for the best translation into English of a modern work of literature or for the best classical literary translation, or the prize is divided between a classical and a modern work. To qualify, works must be book-length translations of Japanese literary works: novels, collections of short stories, literary essays, memoirs, drama or poetry. *Academic Fields/Career Goals:* Foreign Language. *Award:* Prize for use in freshman, sophomore, junior, or senior year; not renewable. *Award amount:* $3000. *Number of awards:* 2. *Eligibility Requirements:* Applicant must be enrolled or expecting to enroll full- or part-time at a two-year, four-year, or technical institution or university. Available to U.S. citizens. *Application Requirements:* Application, applicant must enter a contest, resume, unpublished manuscripts. *Deadline:* February 29.

Contact Donald Keene Center of Japanese Culture. *Web site:* www.donaldkeenecenter.org.

New York Aid for Part-Time Study (APTS). Renewable scholarship provides tuition assistance to part-time undergraduate students who are New York residents, meet income eligibility requirements and are attending New York accredited institutions. Deadline varies. Must be U.S. citizen. *Award:* Grant for use in freshman, sophomore, junior, or senior year; renewable. *Award amount:* up to $2000. *Number of awards:* varies. *Eligibility Requirements:* Applicant must be enrolled or expecting to enroll part-time at a two-year or four-year institution or university; resident of New York and studying in New York. Available to U.S. citizens. *Application Requirements:* Application, financial need analysis. *Deadline:* varies.

Contact Student Information, New York State Higher Education Services Corporation, 99 Washington Avenue, Room 1320, Albany, NY 12255. *Phone:* 518-473-3887. *Fax:* 518-474-2839. *Web site:* www.hesc.com.

New York Lottery Leaders of Tomorrow (Lot) Scholarship. Scholarship to one eligible graduating senior from every participating public and private high school in New York State is awarded a $1250, four-year college scholarship. Scholarships can only be used toward the cost of tuition. *Award:* Scholarship for use in freshman year; renewable. *Award amount:* $1250. *Number of awards:* varies. *Eligibility Requirements:* Applicant must be high school student; planning to enroll or expecting to enroll full-time at a four-year institution; resident of New York and studying in New York. Applicant must have 3.0 GPA or higher. Available to U.S. citizens. *Application Requirements:* Application, essay, transcript. *Deadline:* March 26.

Contact Scholarship Coordinator, New York Lottery, One Broadway Center, PO Box 7540, Schenectady, NY 12301-7540. *E-mail:* lotscholar@lottery.state.ny.us. *Phone:* 518-525-2686. *Fax:* 518-525-2689. *Web site:* www.nylottery.org.

New York Memorial Scholarships for Families of Deceased Police Officers, Fire Fighters and Peace Officers. Renewable scholarship for families of New York police officers, peace officers, emergency medical service workers or firefighters who died in the line of duty. Provides up to the cost of SUNY educational expenses. *Award:* Scholarship for use in freshman, sophomore, junior, or senior year; renewable. *Award amount:* varies. *Number of awards:* varies. *Eligibility Requirements:* Applicant must be enrolled or expecting to enroll full-time at a four-year institution or university; resident of New York and studying in New York. Applicant or parent of applicant must have employment or volunteer experience in police/firefighting. Available to U.S. citizens. *Application Requirements:* Application, financial need analysis, transcript. *Deadline:* May 1.

Contact Adrienne Day, Associate HESC Information Representative, New York State Higher Education Services Corporation, 99 Washington Avenue, Room 1320, Albany, NY 12255. *E-mail:* aday@hesc.com. *Phone:* 518-474-2991. *Fax:* 518-474-2839. *Web site:* www.hesc.com.

New York State Aid to Native Americans. Award for enrolled members of a New York State tribe and their children who are attending or planning to attend a New York State college and who are New York State residents. Deadlines: July 15 for the fall semester, December 31 for the spring semester, and May 20 for summer session. *Award:* Scholarship for use in freshman, sophomore, junior, or senior year; renewable. *Award amount:* $85–$2000. *Number of awards:* varies. *Eligibility Requirements:* Applicant must be American Indian/Alaska Native; enrolled or expecting to enroll full- or part-time at a two-year, four-year, or technical institution or university; resident of New York and studying in New York. Available to U.S. citizens. *Application Requirements:* Application, financial need analysis, references, transcript. *Deadline:* varies.

Contact Native American Education Unit, New York State Higher Education Services Corporation, EBA Room 475, Albany, NY 12234. *Phone:* 518-474-0537. *Web site:* www.hesc.com.

New York State Tuition Assistance Program. Award for New York state residents attending a New York postsecondary institution. Must be full-time student in approved program with tuition over $200 per year. Must show financial need and not be in default in any other state program. Renewable award of $500 to $5000 dependent on family income and tuition charged. *Award:* Grant for use in freshman, sophomore, junior, or senior year; renewable. *Award amount:* $500–$5000. *Number of awards:* 350,000–360,000. *Eligibility Requirements:* Applicant must be enrolled or expecting to enroll full-time at a two-year or four-year institution or university; resident of New York and studying in New York. Available to U.S. citizens. *Application Requirements:* Application, financial need analysis. *Deadline:* May 1.

Contact Student Information, New York State Higher Education Services Corporation, 99 Washington Avenue, Room 1320, Albany, NY 12255. *Web site:* www.hesc.com.

New York Vietnam/Persian Gulf/Afghanistan Veterans Tuition Awards. Scholarship for veterans who served in Vietnam, the Persian Gulf, or Afghanistan. Must be a New York resident attending a New York institution. Must establish eligibility by September 1. *Award:* Scholarship for use in freshman, sophomore, junior, or senior year; renewable. *Award amount:* \$500–\$1000. *Number of awards:* varies. *Eligibility Requirements:* Applicant must be enrolled or expecting to enroll full- or part-time at a two-year, four-year, or technical institution or university; resident of New York and studying in New York. Available to U.S. citizens. Applicant or parent must meet one or more of the following requirements: general military experience; retired from active duty; disabled or killed as a result of military service; prisoner of war; or missing in action. *Application Requirements:* Application, financial need analysis, transcript. *Deadline:* May 1.

Contact Adrienne Day, Associate HESC Information Representative, New York State Higher Education Services Corporation, 99 Washington Avenue, Room 1320, Albany, NY 12255. *E-mail:* aday@hesc.com. *Phone:* 518-474-2991. *Fax:* 518-474-2839. *Web site:* www.hesc.com.

Regents Award for Child of Veteran. Award for students whose parent, as a result of service in U.S. Armed Forces during war or national emergency, died; suffered a 40 percent or more disability; or is classified as missing in action or a prisoner of war. Veteran must be current New York State resident or have been so at time of death. Student must be a New York resident, attending, or planning to attend, college in New York State. Must establish eligibility before applying for payment. *Award:* Scholarship for use in freshman, sophomore, junior, or senior year; not renewable. *Award amount:* \$450. *Number of awards:* varies. *Eligibility Requirements:* Applicant must be enrolled or expecting to enroll full-time at a two-year or four-year institution or university; resident of New York and studying in New York. Available to U.S. citizens. Applicant or parent must meet one or more of the following requirements: general military experience; retired from active duty; disabled or killed as a result of military service; prisoner of war; or missing in action. *Application Requirements:* Application, proof of eligibility. *Deadline:* May 1.

Contact Rita McGivern, Student Information, New York State Higher Education Services Corporation, 99 Washington Avenue, Room 1320, Albany, NY 12255. *E-mail:* rmcgivern@hesc.com. *Web site:* www.hesc.com.

Regents Professional Opportunity Scholarship. Scholarship for New York residents beginning or already enrolled in an approved degree-granting program of study in New York that leads to licensure in a particular profession. See the Web site for the list of eligible professions. Must be U.S. citizen or permanent resident. Award recipients must agree to practice upon licensure in their profession in New York for 12 months for each annual payment received. Priority given to economically disadvantaged members of minority groups underrepresented in the professions. *Academic Fields/Career Goals:* Accounting; Architecture; Dental Health/Services; Engineering/Technology; Health and Medical Sciences; Interior Design; Landscape Architecture; Law/Legal Services; Nursing; Pharmacy; Psychology; Social Services. *Award:* Scholarship for use in freshman, sophomore, junior, senior, or graduate year; renewable. *Award amount:* up to \$5000. *Number of awards:* 220. *Eligibility Requirements:* Applicant must be enrolled or expecting to enroll full-time at a two-year or four-year institution or university; resident of New York and studying in New York. Available to U.S. citizens. *Application Requirements:* Application. *Deadline:* May 31.

Contact Lewis J. Hall, Supervisor, New York State Education Department, 89 Washington Avenue, Room 1078 EBA, Albany, NY 12234. *E-mail:* scholar@mail.nysed.gov. *Phone:* 518-486-1319. *Fax:* 518-486-5346. *Web site:* www.highered.nysed.gov.

Regents Professional Opportunity Scholarships. Award for New York State residents pursuing career in certain licensed professions. Must attend New York State college. Priority given to economically disadvantaged members of minority group underrepresented in chosen profession and graduates of SEEK, College Discovery, EOP, and HEOP. Must work in New York State in chosen profession one year for each annual payment. Scholarships are awarded to undergraduate or graduate students, depending on the program. *Award:* Scholarship for use in freshman, sophomore, junior, senior, graduate, or postgraduate years; not renewable. *Award amount:* \$1000–\$5000. *Number of awards:* 220. *Eligibility Requirements:* Applicant must be enrolled or expecting to enroll full-time at a two-year or four-year institution or university; resident of New York and studying in New York. Available to U.S. citizens. *Application Requirements:* Application. *Deadline:* May 3.

Contact Scholarship Coordinator, New York State Higher Education Services Corporation, Education Building Addition Room 1071, Albany, NY 12234. *Phone:* 518-486-1319. *Web site:* www.hesc.com.

Robert C. Byrd Honors Scholarship-New York. Award for outstanding high school seniors accepted to U.S. college or university. Based on SAT score and high school average. Minimum 1875 combined SAT score from one sitting. Must be legal resident of New York and a U.S. citizen. Renewable for up to four years. *Award:* Scholarship for use in freshman year; renewable. *Award amount:* \$1500. *Number of awards:* 400. *Eligibility Requirements:* Applicant must be high school student; planning to enroll or expecting to enroll full-time at a two-year or four-year institution or university and resident of New York. Available to U.S. citizens. *Application Requirements:* Application. *Deadline:* March 1.

Contact Lewis J. Hall, Supervisor, New York State Education Department, 89 Washington Avenue, Room 1078 EBA, Albany, NY 12234. *E-mail:* scholar@mail.nysed.gov. *Phone:* 518-486-1319. *Fax:* 518-486-5346. *Web site:* www.highered.nysed.gov.

Scholarship for Academic Excellence. Renewable award for New York residents. Scholarship winners must attend a college or university in New York. 2000 scholarships are for \$1500 and 6000 are for \$500. The selection criteria used are based on Regents test scores or rank in class or local exam. Must be U.S. citizen or permanent resident. *Award:* Scholarship for use in freshman year; renewable. *Award amount:* \$500–\$1500. *Number of awards:* up to 8000. *Eligibility Requirements:* Applicant must be high school student; planning to enroll or expecting to enroll full-time at a two-year or four-year institution or university; resident of New York and studying in New York. Available to U.S. citizens. *Application Requirements:* Application. *Deadline:* December 19.

Contact Lewis J. Hall, Supervisor, New York State Education Department, 89 Washington Avenue, Room 1078 EBA, Albany, NY 12234. *E-mail:* scholar@mail.nysed.gov. *Phone:* 518-486-1319. *Fax:* 518-486-5346. *Web site:* www.highered.nysed.gov.

Scholarships for Academic Excellence. Renewable awards of up to \$1500 for academically outstanding New York State high school graduates planning to attend an approved postsecondary institution in New York State. For full-time study only. Contact high school guidance counselor to apply. *Award:* Scholarship for use in freshman, sophomore, junior, or senior year; renewable. *Award amount:* \$500–\$1500. *Number of awards:* 8000. *Eligibility Requirements:* Applicant must be high school student; planning to enroll or expecting to enroll full-time at a four-year institution or university; resident of New York and studying in New York. Available to U.S. citizens. *Application Requirements:* Application. *Deadline:* varies.

Contact Rita McGivern, Student Information, New York State Higher Education Services Corporation, 99 Washington Avenue, Room 1320, Albany, NY 12255. *E-mail:* rmcgivern@hesc.com. *Web site:* www.hesc.com.

World Trade Center Memorial Scholarship. Renewable awards of up to the cost of educational expenses at a State University of New York four-year college. Available to the children, spouses and financial dependents of victims who died or were severely disabled as a result of the September 11, 2001 terrorist attacks on the U.S. and the rescue and recovery efforts. *Award:* Scholarship for use in freshman, sophomore, junior, or senior year; renewable. *Award amount:* varies. *Number of awards:* varies. *Eligibility Requirements:* Applicant must be enrolled or expecting to enroll full-time at a four-year institution or university; resident of New York and studying in New York. Available to U.S. citizens. *Application Requirements:* Application, financial need analysis, references, transcript. *Deadline:* May 1.

Contact Scholarship Unit, New York State Higher Education Services Corporation, 99 Washington Avenue, Room 1320, Albany, NY 12255. *Phone:* 518-402-6494. *Web site:* www.hesc.com.

NORTH CAROLINA

Federal Supplemental Educational Opportunity Grant Program. Applicant must have exceptional financial need to qualify for this award. Amount of financial need is determined by the educational institution the student attends. Available only to undergraduate students. Recipient must be a U.S. citizen or permanent resident. Priority is given to a students who receive Federal Pell Grants. *Award:* Grant for use in freshman, sophomore, junior, or senior year; not renewable. *Award amount:* $100–$4400. *Number of awards:* varies. *Eligibility Requirements:* Applicant must be enrolled or expecting to enroll full-time at a four-year institution or university and resident of North Carolina. Available to U.S. citizens. *Application Requirements:* Application, financial need analysis, transcript. *Deadline:* continuous.

Contact Federal Student Aid Information Center, College Foundation of North Carolina Inc., PO Box 84, Washington, DC 20044. *Phone:* 800-433-3243. *Web site:* www.cfnc.org.

North Carolina Community College Grant Program. Annual award for North Carolina residents enrolled at least part-time in a North Carolina community college curriculum program. Priority given to those enrolled in college transferable curriculum programs, persons seeking new job skills, women in non-traditional curricula, and those participating in an ABE, GED, or high school diploma program. Contact financial aid office of institution the student attends for information and deadline. Must complete Free Application for Federal Student Aid. *Award:* Grant for use in freshman or sophomore year; renewable. *Award amount:* $683. *Number of awards:* varies. *Eligibility Requirements:* Applicant must be enrolled or expecting to enroll full- or part-time at a two-year or technical institution; resident of North Carolina and studying in North Carolina. Available to U.S. citizens. *Application Requirements:* Application, financial need analysis, FAFSA. *Deadline:* varies.

Contact Bill Carswell, Manager, Scholarship and Grants Division, North Carolina State Education Assistance Authority, PO Box 14103, Research Triangle Park, NC 27709. *E-mail:* carswellb@ncseaa.edu. *Phone:* 919-549-8614. *Fax:* 919-248-4687. *Web site:* www.ncseaa.edu.

North Carolina Division of Services for the Blind Rehabilitation Services. Financial assistance is available for North Carolina residents who are blind or visually impaired and who require vocational rehabilitation to help find employment. Tuition and other assistance provided based on need. Open to U.S. citizens and legal residents of United States. Applicants goal must be to work after receiving vocational services. To apply, contact the local DSB office and apply for vocational rehabilitation services. *Award:* Scholarship for use in freshman, sophomore, junior, or senior year; renewable. *Award amount:* varies. *Number of awards:* varies. *Eligibility Requirements:* Applicant must be enrolled or expecting to enroll full-time at a two-year, four-year, or technical institution or university and resident of North Carolina. Applicant must be visually impaired. Available to U.S. citizens. *Application Requirements:* Application, financial need analysis, interview, proof of eligibility. *Deadline:* continuous.

Contact JoAnn Strader, Chief of Rehabilitation Field Services, North Carolina Division of Services for the Blind, 2601 Mail Service Center, Raleigh, NC 27699-2601. *E-mail:* joann.strader@ncmail.net. *Phone:* 919-733-9700. *Fax:* 919-715-8771. *Web site:* www.ncdhhs.gov.

North Carolina Legislative Tuition Grant Program (NCLTG). Renewable aid for North Carolina residents attending approved private colleges or universities within the state. Must be enrolled full or part-time in an undergraduate program not leading to a religious vocation. Contact college financial aid office for deadlines. *Award:* Grant for use in freshman, sophomore, junior, or senior year; renewable. *Award amount:* $1950. *Number of awards:* varies. *Eligibility Requirements:* Applicant must be enrolled or expecting to enroll full- or part-time at a two-year or four-year institution or university; resident of North Carolina and studying in North Carolina. Available to U.S. citizens. *Application Requirements:* Application. *Deadline:* varies.

Contact Bill Carswell, Manager of Scholarship and Grant Division, North Carolina State Education Assistance Authority, PO Box 13663, Research Triangle Park, NC 27709. *E-mail:* carswellb@ncseaa.edu. *Phone:* 919-549-8614. *Fax:* 919-248-4687. *Web site:* www.ncseaa.edu.

North Carolina National Guard Tuition Assistance Program. Scholarship for members of the North Carolina Air and Army National Guard who will remain in the service for two years following the period for which assistance is provided. Must reapply for each academic period. For use at approved North Carolina institutions. *Award:* Grant for use in freshman, sophomore, junior, senior, or graduate year; not renewable. *Award amount:* up to $2000. *Number of awards:* varies. *Eligibility Requirements:* Applicant must be enrolled or expecting to enroll full- or part-time at a two-year, four-year, or technical institution or university; resident of North Carolina and studying in North Carolina. Available to U.S. citizens. Applicant or parent must meet one or more of the following requirements: Air Force National Guard or Army National Guard experience; retired from active duty; disabled or killed as a result of military service; prisoner of war; or missing in action. *Application Requirements:* Application. *Deadline:* varies.

Contact Anne Gildhouse, Education Services Officer, North Carolina National Guard, Claude T. Bowers Military Center, 4105 Reedy Creek Road, Raleigh, NC 27607-6410. *E-mail:* anne.gildhouse@nc.ngb.army.mil. *Phone:* 919-664-6000. *Fax:* 919-664-6520. *Web site:* www.nc.ngb.army.mil.

North Carolina Sheriffs' Association Undergraduate Criminal Justice Scholarships. One-time award for full-time North Carolina resident undergraduate students majoring in criminal justice at a University of North Carolina school. Priority given to child of any North Carolina law enforcement officer. Letter of recommendation from county sheriff required. *Academic Fields/Career Goals:* Criminal Justice/Criminology; Law Enforcement/Police Administration. *Award:* Scholarship for use in freshman, sophomore, junior, or senior year; not renewable. *Award amount:* $1000–$2000. *Number of awards:* up to 10. *Eligibility Requirements:* Applicant must be enrolled or expecting to enroll full-time at a four-year institution or university; resident of North Carolina and studying in North Carolina. Applicant or parent of applicant must have employment or volunteer experience in police/firefighting. Available to U.S.

citizens. *Application Requirements:* Application, financial need analysis, references, transcript, statement of career goals. *Deadline:* continuous.

Contact Nolita Goldston, Assistant, Scholarship and Grant Division, North Carolina State Education Assistance Authority, PO Box 13663, Research Triangle Park, NC 27709. *E-mail:* ngoldston@ncseaa.edu. *Phone:* 919-549-8614. *Fax:* 919-248-4687. *Web site:* www.ncseaa.edu.

North Carolina Student Loan Program for Health, Science, and Mathematics. Renewable award for North Carolina residents studying health-related fields, or science or math education. Based on merit, need, and promise of service as a health professional or educator in an under-served area of North Carolina. Need two co-signers. Submit surety statement. *Academic Fields/Career Goals:* Dental Health/Services; Health Administration; Health and Medical Sciences; Nursing; Physical Sciences; Therapy/Rehabilitation. *Award:* Forgivable loan for use in freshman, sophomore, junior, senior, or graduate year; renewable. *Award amount:* $3000–$8500. *Number of awards:* 1. *Eligibility Requirements:* Applicant must be enrolled or expecting to enroll full-time at a two-year or four-year institution or university and resident of North Carolina. Available to U.S. citizens. *Application Requirements:* Application, financial need analysis, transcript. *Deadline:* June 1.

Contact Edna Williams, Manager, Selection and Origination, North Carolina State Education Assistance Authority, PO Box 14223, Research Triangle Park, NC 27709. *E-mail:* eew@ncseaa.edu. *Phone:* 800-700-1775 Ext. 4658. *Web site:* www.ncseaa.edu.

North Carolina Teaching Fellows Scholarship Program. Award for North Carolina high school seniors planning to pursue teacher training studies. Must agree to teach in a North Carolina public or government school for four years or repay award. For more details visit Web site: http://www.teachingfellows.org. *Academic Fields/Career Goals:* Education. *Award:* Forgivable loan for use in freshman year; renewable. *Award amount:* $6500. *Number of awards:* 500. *Eligibility Requirements:* Applicant must be high school student; planning to enroll or expecting to enroll full-time at a four-year institution or university; resident of North Carolina and studying in North Carolina. Applicant must have 3.5 GPA or higher. Available to U.S. citizens. *Application Requirements:* Application, essay, interview, references, test scores, transcript. *Deadline:* varies.

Contact Lynne Stewart, Program Officer, North Carolina Teaching Fellows Commission, 3739 National Drive, Suite 100, Raleigh, NC 27612. *E-mail:* tfellows@ncforum.org. *Phone:* 919-781-6833 Ext. 103. *Fax:* 919-781-6527. *Web site:* www.teachingfellows.org.

North Carolina Veterans Scholarships Class I-A. Scholarships for children of certain deceased, disabled or POW/MIA veterans. Award value is $4500 per nine-month academic year in private colleges and junior colleges. No limit on number awarded each year. *Award:* Scholarship for use in freshman, sophomore, junior, or senior year; renewable. *Award amount:* $4500. *Number of awards:* varies. *Eligibility Requirements:* Applicant must be enrolled or expecting to enroll full-time at a two-year, four-year, or technical institution or university; resident of North Carolina and studying in North Carolina. Available to U.S. citizens. Applicant or parent must meet one or more of the following requirements: general military experience; retired from active duty; disabled or killed as a result of military service; prisoner of war; or missing in action. *Application Requirements:* Application, financial need analysis, interview, transcript. *Deadline:* continuous.

Contact Charles Smith, Assistant Secretary, North Carolina Division of Veterans Affairs, 325 North Salisbury Street, Raleigh, NC 27603. *E-mail:* charlie.smith@ncmail.net. *Phone:* 919-733-3851. *Fax:* 919-733-2834. *Web site:* www.doa.state.nc.us/vets/va.htm.

North Carolina Veterans Scholarships Class I-B. Awards for children of veterans rated by USDVA as 100 percent disabled due to wartime service as defined in the law, and currently or at time of death drawing compensation for such disability. Parent must have been a North Carolina resident at time of entry into service. Duration of the scholarship is four academic years (8 semesters) if used within 8 years. No limit on number awarded each year. *Award:* Scholarship for use in freshman, sophomore, junior, or senior year; renewable. *Award amount:* $1500. *Number of awards:* varies. *Eligibility Requirements:* Applicant must be enrolled or expecting to enroll full- or part-time at a two-year, four-year, or technical institution or university; resident of North Carolina and studying in North Carolina. Available to U.S. citizens. Applicant or parent must meet one or more of the following requirements: general military experience; retired from active duty; disabled or killed as a result of military service; prisoner of war; or missing in action. *Application Requirements:* Application, financial need analysis, interview, transcript. *Deadline:* continuous.

Contact Charles Smith, Assistant Secretary, North Carolina Division of Veterans Affairs, 325 North Salisbury Street, Raleigh, NC 27603. *E-mail:* charlie.smith@ncmail.net. *Phone:* 919-733-3851. *Fax:* 919-733-2834. *Web site:* www.doa.state.nc.us/vets/va.htm.

North Carolina Veterans Scholarships Class II. Awards for children of veterans rated by USDVA as much as 20 percent but less than 100 percent disabled due to wartime service as defined in the law, or awarded Purple Heart Medal for wounds received. Parent must have been a North Carolina resident at time of entry into service. Duration of the scholarship is four academic years (8 semesters) if used within 8 years. Free tuition and exemption from certain mandatory fees as set forth in the law in Public, Community and Technical Colleges. *Award:* Scholarship for use in freshman, sophomore, junior, or senior year; renewable. *Award amount:* $4500. *Number of awards:* up to 100. *Eligibility Requirements:* Applicant must be enrolled or expecting to enroll full- or part-time at a two-year, four-year, or technical institution or university; resident of North Carolina and studying in North Carolina. Available to U.S. citizens. Applicant or parent must meet one or more of the following requirements: general military experience; retired from active duty; disabled or killed as a result of military service; prisoner of war; or missing in action. *Application Requirements:* Application, financial need analysis, interview, transcript. *Deadline:* March 1.

Contact Charles Smith, Assistant Secretary, North Carolina Division of Veterans Affairs, 325 North Salisbury Street, Raleigh, NC 27603. *E-mail:* charlie.smith@ncmail.net. *Phone:* 919-733-3851. *Fax:* 919-733-2834. *Web site:* www.doa.state.nc.us/vets/va.htm.

North Carolina Veterans Scholarships Class III. Awards for children of a deceased war veteran, who was honorably discharged and who does not qualify under any other provision within this synopsis or veteran who served in a combat zone or waters adjacent to a combat zone and received a campaign badge or medal and who does not qualify under any other provision within this synopsis. Duration of the scholarship is four academic years (8 semesters) if used within 8 years. *Award:* Scholarship for use in freshman, sophomore, junior, or senior year; renewable. *Award amount:* $4500. *Number of awards:* up to 100. *Eligibility Requirements:* Applicant must be enrolled or expecting to enroll full- or part-time at a two-year, four-year, or technical institution or university; resident of North Carolina and studying in North Carolina. Available to U.S. citizens. Applicant or parent must meet one or more of the following requirements: general military experience; retired from active duty; disabled or killed as a result of military service; prisoner of war; or missing in action. *Application Requirements:* Application, financial need analysis, interview, transcript. *Deadline:* March 1.

Contact Charles Smith, Assistant Secretary, North Carolina Division of Veterans Affairs, 325 North Salisbury Street, Raleigh, NC 27603. *E-mail:* charlie.smith@ncmail.net.

Phone: 919-733-3851. *Fax:* 919-733-2834. *Web site:* www.doa.state.nc.us/vets/va.htm.

North Carolina Veterans Scholarships Class IV. Awards for children of veterans, who were prisoner of war or missing in action. Duration of the scholarship is four academic years (8 semesters) if used within 8 years. No limit on number awarded each year. Award value is $4500 per nine-month academic year in private colleges and junior colleges. *Award:* Scholarship for use in freshman, sophomore, junior, or senior year; renewable. *Award amount:* $4500. *Number of awards:* varies. *Eligibility Requirements:* Applicant must be enrolled or expecting to enroll full- or part-time at a two-year, four-year, or technical institution or university; resident of North Carolina and studying in North Carolina. Available to U.S. citizens. Applicant or parent must meet one or more of the following requirements: general military experience; retired from active duty; disabled or killed as a result of military service; prisoner of war; or missing in action. *Application Requirements:* Application, financial need analysis, interview, transcript. **Deadline:** continuous.

Contact Charles Smith, Assistant Secretary, North Carolina Division of Veterans Affairs, 325 North Salisbury Street, Raleigh, NC 27603. *E-mail:* charlie.smith@ncmail.net. *Phone:* 919-733-3851. *Fax:* 919-733-2834. *Web site:* www.doa.state.nc.us/vets/va.htm.

Nurse Education Scholarship Loan Program (NESLP). Must be U.S. citizen and North Carolina resident. Award available through financial aid offices of North Carolina colleges and universities that offer programs to prepare students for licensure in the state as LPN or RN. Recipients enter contract with the State of North Carolina to work full time as a licensed nurse. Loans not repaid through service must be repaid in cash. Award based upon financial need. Maximum award for students enrolled in Associate Degree Nursing and Practical Nurse Education programs is $5000. Maximum award for students enrolled in a baccalaureate program is $400. *Academic Fields/Career Goals:* Nursing. *Award:* Forgivable loan for use in freshman, sophomore, junior, or senior year; renewable. *Award amount:* $400–$5000. *Number of awards:* varies. *Eligibility Requirements:* Applicant must be enrolled or expecting to enroll full- or part-time at a four-year institution or university; resident of North Carolina and studying in North Carolina. Available to U.S. citizens. *Application Requirements:* Application, financial need analysis. **Deadline:** continuous.

Contact Bill Carswell, Manager of Scholarship and Grant Division, North Carolina State Education Assistance Authority, PO Box 14103, Research Triangle Park, NC 27709. *E-mail:* carswellb@ncseaa.edu. *Phone:* 919-549-8614. *Fax:* 919-248-4687. *Web site:* www.ncseaa.edu.

State Contractual Scholarship Fund Program-North Carolina. Renewable award for North Carolina residents already attending an approved private college or university in the state and pursuing an undergraduate degree. Must have financial need. Contact college financial aid office for deadline and information. May not be enrolled in a program leading to a religious vocation. *Award:* Scholarship for use in freshman, sophomore, junior, or senior year; renewable. *Award amount:* up to $1350. *Number of awards:* varies. *Eligibility Requirements:* Applicant must be enrolled or expecting to enroll full- or part-time at a four-year institution or university; resident of North Carolina and studying in North Carolina. Available to U.S. citizens. *Application Requirements:* Application, financial need analysis. **Deadline:** varies.

Contact Bill Carswell, Manager of Scholarship and Grant Division, North Carolina State Education Assistance Authority, PO Box 13663, Research Triangle Park, NC 27709. *E-mail:* carswellb@ncseaa.edu. *Phone:* 919-549-8614. *Fax:* 919-248-4687. *Web site:* www.ncseaa.edu.

Teacher Assistant Scholarship Fund. Funding to attend a public or private four-year college or university in North Carolina with an approved teacher education program. Applicant must be employed full-time as a teacher assistant in an instructional area while pursuing licensure and maintain employment to remain eligible. Must have at least 3.0 cumulative GPA. Refer to Web site for further details: http://www.ncseaa.edu/tasf.htm. *Academic Fields/Career Goals:* Education. *Award:* Scholarship for use in freshman, sophomore, junior, or senior year; renewable. *Award amount:* $600–$3600. *Number of awards:* varies. *Eligibility Requirements:* Applicant must be enrolled or expecting to enroll full- or part-time at a four-year institution or university; resident of North Carolina and studying in North Carolina. Applicant or parent of applicant must have employment or volunteer experience in teaching/education. Applicant must have 3.0 GPA or higher. Available to U.S. citizens. *Application Requirements:* Application, financial need analysis, transcript, FAFSA. **Deadline:** March 31.

Contact Rashonn Albritton, Processing Assistant, North Carolina State Education Assistance Authority, PO Box 13663, Research Triangle Park, NC 27709. *E-mail:* ralbritton@ncseaa.edu. *Phone:* 919-549-8614. *Fax:* 919-248-4687. *Web site:* www.ncseaa.edu.

University of North Carolina Need-Based Grant. Applicants must be enrolled in at least 6 credit hours at one of sixteen UNC system universities. Eligibility based on need; award varies, consideration for grant automatic when FAFSA is filed. Late applications may be denied due to insufficient funds. *Award:* Grant for use in freshman, sophomore, junior, or senior year; renewable. *Award amount:* varies. *Number of awards:* varies. *Eligibility Requirements:* Applicant must be enrolled or expecting to enroll full- or part-time at an institution or university; resident of North Carolina and studying in North Carolina. Available to U.S. citizens. *Application Requirements:* Application, financial need analysis, FAFSA. **Deadline:** varies.

Contact Bill Carswell, Manager of Scholarship and Grant Division, North Carolina State Education Assistance Authority, PO Box 13663, Research Triangle Park, NC 27709. *E-mail:* carswellb@ncseaa.edu. *Phone:* 919-549-8614. *Fax:* 919-248-4687. *Web site:* www.ncseaa.edu.

University of North Carolina Need Based Grant. Grants available for eligible students attending one of the 16 campuses of the University of North Carolina. Students must be enrolled in at least 6 credit hours at one of the 16 constituent institutions of The University of North Carolina. Award amounts vary based on legislative appropriations. *Award:* Grant for use in freshman, sophomore, junior, or senior year; not renewable. *Award amount:* varies. *Number of awards:* varies. *Eligibility Requirements:* Applicant must be enrolled or expecting to enroll full- or part-time at a four-year institution or university; resident of North Carolina and studying in North Carolina. Available to U.S. citizens. *Application Requirements:* Financial need analysis. **Deadline:** continuous.

Contact College Foundation of North Carolina Inc. *Web site:* www.cfnc.org.

NORTH DAKOTA

North Dakota Indian Scholarship Program. Award of $500 to $2000 per year to assist American Indian students who are North Dakota residents in obtaining a college education. Must have been accepted for admission at an institution of higher learning or state vocational education program within North Dakota. For full-time study only. Based upon scholastic ability and unmet financial need. Minimum 2.0 GPA required. *Award:* Scholarship for use in freshman, sophomore, junior, or senior year; renewable. *Award amount:* $800–$2000. *Number of awards:* 175–230. *Eligibility Requirements:* Applicant must be American Indian/Alaska Native; enrolled or expecting to enroll full-time at a two-year, four-year, or technical institution or university; resident of North Dakota and studying in North Dakota. Available to U.S. citizens. *Application Requirements:* Application, financial need analysis, transcript, proof of tribal enrollment, budget. **Deadline:** July 15.

Contact Rhonda Schauer, Coordinator of American Indian Higher Education, State of

North Dakota, 919 South Seventh Street, Suite 300, Bismarck, ND 58504-5881. *E-mail:* rhonda.schauer@ndus.nodak.edu. *Phone:* 701-328-9661. *Web site:* www.ndus.edu.

North Dakota Scholars Program. Provides scholarships equal to cost of tuition at the public colleges in North Dakota for North Dakota residents. Must score at or above the 95th percentile on ACT and rank in top twenty percent of high school graduation class. Must take ACT in fall. For high school seniors with a minimum 3.5 GPA. Deadline: October or June ACT test date. *Award:* Scholarship for use in freshman year; renewable. *Award amount:* $5000. *Number of awards:* 45–50. *Eligibility Requirements:* Applicant must be high school student; planning to enroll or expecting to enroll full-time at a two-year or four-year institution or university; resident of North Dakota and studying in North Dakota. Available to U.S. citizens. *Application Requirements:* References, test scores. *Deadline:* varies.

Contact Peggy Wipf, Director of Financial Aid, State of North Dakota, 600 East Boulevard Avenue, Department 215, Bismarck, ND 58505-0230. *E-mail:* peggy.wipf@ndus.nodak.edu. *Phone:* 701-328-4114. *Web site:* www.ndus.edu.

North Dakota State Student Incentive Grant Program. Aids North Dakota residents attending an approved college or university in North Dakota. Must be enrolled in a program of at least nine months in length. Must be a U.S. citizen. *Award:* Grant for use in freshman, sophomore, junior, or senior year; renewable. *Award amount:* $800. *Number of awards:* 3500–3700. *Eligibility Requirements:* Applicant must be enrolled or expecting to enroll full-time at a two-year or four-year institution or university; resident of North Dakota and studying in North Dakota. Available to U.S. citizens. *Application Requirements:* Financial need analysis. *Deadline:* March 15.

Contact Peggy Wipf, Director of Financial Aid, State of North Dakota, 600 East Boulevard Avenue, Department 215, Bismarck, ND 58505-0230. *Phone:* 701-328-4114. *Web site:* www.ndus.edu.

OHIO

Ohio Environmental Science & Engineering Scholarships. Merit-based, non-renewable, tuition-only scholarships awarded to undergraduate students admitted to Ohio state or private colleges and universities. Must be able to demonstrate knowledge of, and commitment to, careers in environmental sciences or environmental engineering. *Academic Fields/Career Goals:* Environmental Science. *Award:* Scholarship for use in senior year; not renewable. *Award amount:* $1250–$2500. *Number of awards:* 18. *Eligibility Requirements:* Applicant must be enrolled or expecting to enroll full- or part-time at a two-year or four-year institution or university and studying in Ohio. Applicant must have 3.0 GPA or higher. Available to U.S. citizens. *Application Requirements:* Application, essay, resume, references, self-addressed stamped envelope, transcript. *Deadline:* June 1.

Contact Mr. Lynn E. Elfner, Chief Executive Officer, Ohio Academy of Science/Ohio Environmental Education Fund, 1500 West Third Avenue, Suite 228, Columbus, OH 43212-2817. *E-mail:* oas@iwaynet.net. *Phone:* 614-488-2228. *Fax:* 614-488-7629. *Web site:* www.ohiosci.org.

Ohio Instructional Grant. Award for low- and middle-income Ohio residents attending an approved college or school in Ohio or Pennsylvania. Must be enrolled full-time and have financial need. May be used for any course of study except theology. *Award:* Grant for use in freshman, sophomore, junior, or senior year; renewable. *Award amount:* $78–$5466. *Number of awards:* varies. *Eligibility Requirements:* Applicant must be enrolled or expecting to enroll full-time at a two-year or four-year institution or university; resident of Ohio and studying in Ohio or Pennsylvania. Available to U.S. citizens. *Application Requirements:* Application, financial need analysis. *Deadline:* October 1.

Contact Tamika Braswell, Program Administrator, Ohio Board of Regents, 30 East Broad Street, 36th Floor, Columbus, OH 43215-3414. *E-mail:* tbraswell@regents.state.oh.us. *Phone:* 614-728-8862. *Fax:* 614-752-5903. *Web site:* www.regents.ohio.gov.

Ohio Missing in Action and Prisoners of War Orphans Scholarship. Renewable award aids children of Vietnam conflict servicemen who have been classified as missing in action or prisoner of war. Applicants must be under the age of 25 and be enrolled full-time at an Ohio college. A percentage of tuition is awarded. Dollar value of each award varies. *Award:* Scholarship for use in freshman, sophomore, junior, or senior year; renewable. *Award amount:* varies. *Number of awards:* 1–5. *Eligibility Requirements:* Applicant must be age 25 or under; enrolled or expecting to enroll full-time at a four-year institution or university; resident of Ohio and studying in Ohio. Available to U.S. citizens. Applicant or parent must meet one or more of the following requirements: general military experience; retired from active duty; disabled or killed as a result of military service; prisoner of war; or missing in action. *Application Requirements:* Application. *Deadline:* July 1.

Contact Jathiya Abdullah-Simmons, Program Administrator, Ohio Board of Regents, 30 East Broad Street, 36th Floor, Columbus, OH 43215-3414. *E-mail:* jabdullah-simmons@regents.state.oh.us. *Phone:* 614-752-9528. *Fax:* 614-752-5903. *Web site:* www.regents.ohio.gov.

Ohio National Guard Scholarship Program. Scholarships are for undergraduate studies at an approved Ohio post-secondary institution. Applicants must enlist for six years of Selective Service Reserve Duty in the Ohio National Guard. Scholarship pays 100% instructional and general fees for public institutions and an average of cost of public schools is available for private schools. May reapply up to four years. Deadlines: July 1, November 1, February 1, April 1. *Award:* Scholarship for use in freshman, sophomore, junior, or senior year; not renewable. *Award amount:* up to $3911. *Number of awards:* up to 3500. *Eligibility Requirements:* Applicant must be enrolled or expecting to enroll full- or part-time at a two-year, four-year, or technical institution or university; resident of Ohio and studying in Ohio. Available to U.S. citizens. Applicant or parent must meet one or more of the following requirements: Air Force National Guard or Army National Guard experience; retired from active duty; disabled or killed as a result of military service; prisoner of war; or missing in action. *Application Requirements:* Application. *Deadline:* varies.

Contact Toni Davis, Grants Administrator, Ohio National Guard, 2825 West Dublin Granville Road, Columbus, OH 43235-2789. *E-mail:* toni.davis@tagoh.gov. *Phone:* 614-336-7143. *Fax:* 614-336-7318. *Web site:* www.ongsp.org.

Ohio Safety Officers College Memorial Fund. Renewable award covering up to full tuition is available to children and surviving spouses of peace officers, other safety officers and fire fighters killed in the line of duty in any state. Children must be under 26 years of age. Dollar value of each award varies. Must be an Ohio resident and enroll full-time or part-time at an Ohio college or university. Any spouse/child of a member of the armed services of the U.S., who has been killed in the line duty during Operation Enduring Freedom, Operation Iraqi Freedom or a combat zone designated by the President of the United States. Dollar value of each award varies. *Award:* Scholarship for use in freshman, sophomore, junior, or senior year; renewable. *Award amount:* varies. *Number of awards:* 50–65. *Eligibility Requirements:* Applicant must be age 26 or under; enrolled or expecting to enroll full- or part-time at a two-year or four-year institution or university; resident of Ohio and studying in Ohio. Applicant or parent of applicant must have employment or volunteer experience in police/firefighting. Available to U.S. citizens. *Application Requirements: Deadline:* continuous.

Contact Barbara Thoma, Program Administrator, Ohio Board of Regents, 30 East Broad Street, 36th Floor, Columbus, OH 43215-3414. *E-mail:* bthoma@regents.state.oh.us. *Phone:* 614-752-9535. *Fax:* 614-752-5903. *Web site:* www.regents.ohio.gov.

Ohio War Orphans Scholarship. Aids Ohio residents attending an eligible college in Ohio. Must be between the ages of 16 and 25, the child of a disabled or deceased veteran, and enrolled full-time. Renewable up to five years. Amount of award varies. Must include Form DD214. *Award:* Scholarship for use in freshman, sophomore, junior, or senior year; renewable. *Award amount:* varies. *Number of awards:* 300–450. *Eligibility Requirements:* Applicant must be age 16-25; enrolled or expecting to enroll full-time at a two-year or four-year institution or university; resident of Ohio and studying in Ohio. Available to U.S. citizens. Applicant or parent must meet one or more of the following requirements: general military experience; retired from active duty; disabled or killed as a result of military service; prisoner of war; or missing in action. *Application Requirements:* Application. **Deadline:** July 1.

Contact Jathiya Abdullah-Simmons, Program Administrator, Ohio Board of Regents, 30 East Broad Street, 36th Floor, Columbus, OH 43215-3414. *E-mail:* jabdullah-simmons@regents.state.oh.us. *Phone:* 614-752-9528. *Fax:* 614-752-5903. *Web site:* www.regents.ohio.gov.

OKLAHOMA

Academic Scholars Program. Awards for students of high academic ability to attend institutions in Oklahoma. Renewable up to four years. ACT or SAT scores must fall between 99.5 and 100th percentiles, or applicant must be designated as a National Merit scholar or finalist. Oklahoma public institutions can also select institutional nominees. *Award:* Scholarship for use in freshman year; renewable. *Award amount:* $1800–$5500. *Number of awards:* varies. *Eligibility Requirements:* Applicant must be high school student; planning to enroll or expecting to enroll full-time at a two-year or four-year institution or university and studying in Oklahoma. Available to U.S. citizens. *Application Requirements:* Application, test scores, transcript. **Deadline:** continuous.

Contact Scholarship Programs Coordinator, Oklahoma State Regents for Higher Education, PO Box 108850, Oklahoma City, OK 73101-8850. *E-mail:* studentinfo@osrhe.edu. *Phone:* 800-858-1840. *Fax:* 405-225-9230. *Web site:* www.okhighered.org.

Future Teacher Scholarship-Oklahoma. Open to outstanding Oklahoma high school graduates who agree to teach in shortage areas. Must rank in top 15 percent of graduating class or score above 85th percentile on ACT or similar test, or be accepted in an educational program. Students nominated by institution. Reapply to renew. Must attend college/university in Oklahoma. *Academic Fields/Career Goals:* Education. *Award:* Scholarship for use in freshman, sophomore, junior, senior, or graduate year; renewable. *Award amount:* $500–$1500. *Number of awards:* 85. *Eligibility Requirements:* Applicant must be enrolled or expecting to enroll full- or part-time at a two-year or four-year institution or university; resident of Oklahoma and studying in Oklahoma. Available to U.S. citizens. *Application Requirements:* Application, essay, test scores, transcript. **Deadline:** varies.

Contact Scholarship Programs Coordinator, Oklahoma State Regents for Higher Education, PO Box 108850, Oklahoma City, OK 73101-8850. *E-mail:* studentinfo@osrhe.edu. *Phone:* 800-858-1840. *Fax:* 405-225-9230. *Web site:* www.okhighered.org.

Oklahoma Tuition Aid Grant. Award for Oklahoma residents enrolled at an Oklahoma institution at least part time each semester in a degree program. May be enrolled in two- or four-year or approved vocational-technical institution. Award for students attending public institutions or private colleges. Application is made through FAFSA. *Award:* Grant for use in freshman, sophomore, junior, or senior year; renewable. *Award amount:* $1000–$1300. *Number of awards:* varies. *Eligibility Requirements:* Applicant must be enrolled or expecting to enroll full- or part-time at a two-year, four-year, or technical institution or university; resident of Oklahoma and studying in Oklahoma. Available to U.S. citizens. *Application Requirements:* Application, financial need analysis, FAFSA. **Deadline:** varies.

Contact Alicia Harris, Scholarship Programs Coordinator, Oklahoma State Regents for Higher Education, PO Box 3020, Oklahoma City, OK 73101-3020. *E-mail:* aharris@osrhe.edu. *Phone:* 405-225-9131. *Fax:* 405-225-9230. *Web site:* www.okhighered.org.

Regional University Baccalaureate Scholarship. Renewable award for Oklahoma residents attending one of 11 participating Oklahoma public universities. Must have an ACT composite score of at least 30 or be a National Merit semifinalist or commended student. In addition to the award amount, each recipient will receive a resident tuition waiver from the institution. Must maintain a 3.25 GPA. Deadlines vary depending upon the institution attended. *Award:* Scholarship for use in freshman, sophomore, junior, or senior year; renewable. *Award amount:* $3000. *Number of awards:* varies. *Eligibility Requirements:* Applicant must be enrolled or expecting to enroll full-time at an institution or university; resident of Oklahoma and studying in Oklahoma. Available to U.S. citizens. *Application Requirements:* Application. **Deadline:** varies.

Contact Alicia Harris, Scholarship Programs Coordinator, Oklahoma State Regents for Higher Education, PO Box 108850, Oklahoma City, OK 73101-8850. *E-mail:* aharris@osrhe.edu. *Phone:* 405-225-9131. *Fax:* 405-225-9230. *Web site:* www.okhighered.org.

Robert C. Byrd Honors Scholarship-Oklahoma. Scholarships available to high school seniors. Applicants must be U.S. citizens or national, or be permanent residents of the United States. Must be legal residents of Oklahoma. Must have a minimum ACT composite score of 32 and/or a minimum SAT combined score of 1420 and/or 2130 or a minimum GED score of 700. Application URL: http://www.sde.state.ok.us/Finance/Scholarships/Byrd/Application.pdf. *Award:* Scholarship for use in freshman year; not renewable. *Award amount:* $1500. *Number of awards:* 10. *Eligibility Requirements:* Applicant must be high school student; planning to enroll or expecting to enroll full-time at a four-year institution or university and resident of Oklahoma. Available to U.S. citizens. *Application Requirements:* Application, essay, references, transcript. **Deadline:** April 11.

Contact Certification Specialist, Oklahoma State Department of Education, 2500 North Lincoln Boulevard, Suite 212, Oklahoma City, OK 73105-4599. *Phone:* 405-521-2808. *Web site:* www.sde.state.ok.us.

OREGON

American Ex-Prisoner of War Scholarships: Peter Connacher Memorial Scholarship. Renewable award for American prisoners-of-war and their descendants. Written proof of prisoner-of-war status and discharge papers from the U.S. Armed Forces must accompany application. Statement of relationship between applicant and former prisoner-of-war is required. See Web site at http://www.osac.state.or.us for details. *Award:* Scholarship for use in freshman, sophomore, junior, or senior year; renewable. *Award amount:* varies. *Number of awards:* varies. *Eligibility Requirements:* Applicant must be enrolled or expecting to enroll full-time at a two-year or four-year institution and resident of Oregon. Available to U.S. citizens. Applicant or parent must meet one or more of the following requirements: general military experience; retired from active duty; disabled or killed as a result of military service; prisoner of war; or missing in action. *Application Requirements:* Application, essay, financial need analysis, transcript, military discharge papers, documentation of POW status. **Deadline:** March 1.

Contact Director of Grant Programs, Oregon Student Assistance Commission, 1500 Valley River Drive, Suite 100, Eugene, OR 97401-7020. *Phone:* 800-452-8807 Ext. 7395. *Web site:* www.osac.state.or.us.

American Legion Auxiliary Department of Oregon Department Grants. One-time award for educational use in the state of Oregon. Must be a resident of Oregon who is the child or widow of a veteran or the wife of a disabled veteran. *Award:* Grant for use in freshman, sophomore, junior, or senior year; not renewable. *Award amount:* $1000. *Number of awards:* 2. *Eligibility Requirements:* Applicant must be enrolled or expecting to enroll full- or part-time at a two-year, four-year, or technical institution or university; resident of Oregon and studying in Oregon. Available to U.S. citizens. Applicant or parent must meet one or more of the following requirements: general military experience; retired from active duty; disabled or killed as a result of military service; prisoner of war; or missing in action. *Application Requirements:* Application, essay, financial need analysis, interview, references, test scores, transcript. **Deadline:** March 10.

Contact Virginia Biddle, Secretary/Treasurer, American Legion Auxiliary, Department of Oregon, PO Box 1730, Wilsonville, OR 97070. *E-mail:* alaor@pcez.com. *Phone:* 503-682-3162. *Fax:* 503-685-5008.

American Legion Auxiliary Department of Oregon National President's Scholarship. One-time award for children of veterans who served in the Armed Forces during eligibility dates for American Legion membership. Must be high school senior and Oregon resident. Must be entered by a local American Legion auxiliary unit. Three scholarships of varying amounts. *Award:* Scholarship for use in freshman year; not renewable. *Award amount:* $1000–$2500. *Number of awards:* 3. *Eligibility Requirements:* Applicant must be high school student; planning to enroll or expecting to enroll full- or part-time at a four-year institution or university and resident of Oregon. Available to U.S. citizens. Applicant or parent must meet one or more of the following requirements: general military experience; retired from active duty; disabled or killed as a result of military service; prisoner of war; or missing in action. *Application Requirements:* Application, essay, financial need analysis, interview, references, transcript. **Deadline:** March 1.

Contact Virginia Biddle, Secretary, American Legion Auxiliary, Department of Oregon, PO Box 1730, Wilsonville, OR 97070. *E-mail:* alaor@pcez.com. *Phone:* 503-682-3162. *Fax:* 503-685-5008.

American Legion Auxiliary Department of Oregon Nurses Scholarship. One-time award for Oregon residents who are in their senior year of High School, who are the children of veterans who served during eligibility dates for American Legion membership. Must enroll in a nursing program. Contact local units for application. *Academic Fields/Career Goals:* Nursing. *Award:* Scholarship for use in freshman year; not renewable. *Award amount:* $1500. *Number of awards:* 1. *Eligibility Requirements:* Applicant must be high school student; planning to enroll or expecting to enroll full- or part-time at a four-year institution or university and resident of Oregon. Available to U.S. citizens. Applicant or parent must meet one or more of the following requirements: general military experience; retired from active duty; disabled or killed as a result of military service; prisoner of war; or missing in action. *Application Requirements:* Application, essay, financial need analysis, interview, transcript. **Deadline:** May 15.

Contact Virginia Biddle, Secretary/Treasurer, American Legion Auxiliary, Department of Oregon, PO Box 1730, Wilsonville, OR 97070. *E-mail:* alaor@pcez.com. *Phone:* 503-682-3162. *Fax:* 503-685-5008.

American Legion Auxiliary Department of Oregon Spirit of Youth Scholarship. One-time award available to Oregon high school seniors. Must be a current female junior member of the American Legion Auxiliary with a three-year membership history. Apply through local units. *Award:* Scholarship for use in freshman year; not renewable. *Award amount:* $1000. *Number of awards:* 1. *Eligibility Requirements:* Applicant must be high school student; planning to enroll or expecting to enroll full- or part-time at a four-year institution or university; female and resident of Oregon. Applicant or parent of applicant must be member of American Legion or Auxiliary. Applicant must have 3.0 GPA or higher. Available to U.S. citizens. Applicant or parent must meet one or more of the following requirements: general military experience; retired from active duty; disabled or killed as a result of military service; prisoner of war; or missing in action. *Application Requirements:* Application, essay, financial need analysis, interview, references, transcript. **Deadline:** March 1.

Contact Virginia Biddle, Secretary/Treasurer, American Legion Auxiliary, Department of Oregon, PO Box 1730, Wilsonville, OR 97070. *E-mail:* alaor@pcez.com. *Phone:* 503-682-3162. *Fax:* 503-685-5008.

Dorothy Campbell Memorial Scholarship. Renewable award for female Oregon high school graduates with a minimum 2.75 GPA. Must submit essay describing strong, continuing interest in golf and the contribution that sport has made to applicant's development. For more information, see Web: www.getcollegefunds.org. *Award:* Scholarship for use in freshman, sophomore, junior, or senior year; renewable. *Award amount:* varies. *Number of awards:* varies. *Eligibility Requirements:* Applicant must be enrolled or expecting to enroll full-time at a four-year institution; female; resident of Oregon; studying in Oregon and must have an interest in golf. Applicant must have 2.5 GPA or higher. Available to U.S. citizens. *Application Requirements:* Application, essay, financial need analysis, transcript. **Deadline:** March 1.

Contact Alan Baas, Scholarship Coordinator, Oregon Student Assistance Commission, 1500 Valley River Drive, Suite 100, Eugene, OR 97401-7020. *Phone:* 800-452-8807. *Web site:* www.osac.state.or.us.

Glenn Jackson Scholars Scholarships (OCF). Renewable award for Oregon graduating high school seniors who are dependents of employees or retirees of Oregon Department of Transportation or Parks and Recreation Department. Employees must have worked in their department at least three years as of the March 1 scholarship deadline. Must submit essays on topics announced on Web site: http://www.osac.state.or.us. *Award:* Scholarship for use in freshman, sophomore, junior, or senior year; renewable. *Award amount:* varies. *Number of awards:* varies. *Eligibility Requirements:* Applicant must be high school student; planning to enroll or expecting to enroll full- or part-time at a two-year or four-year institution or university and resident of Oregon. Applicant or parent of applicant must be affiliated with Oregon Department of Transportation Parks and Recreation. Available to U.S. citizens. *Application Requirements:* Application, essay, financial need analysis, references, transcript, activity chart. **Deadline:** March 1.

Contact Director of Grant Programs, Oregon Student Assistance Commission, 1500 Valley River Drive, Suite 100, Eugene, OR 97401-7020. *Phone:* 800-452-8807 Ext. 7395. *Web site:* www.osac.state.or.us.

Laurence R. Foster Memorial Scholarship. One-time award to students enrolled or planning to enroll in a public health degree program. First preference given to those working in the public health field and those pursuing a graduate degree in public health. Undergraduates entering junior or senior year health programs may apply if seeking a public health career, and not private practice. Prefer applicants from diverse cultures. Must provide three references. Additional essay required. Must be resident of Oregon. *Academic Fields/Career Goals:* Public Health. *Award:* Scholarship for use in freshman, sophomore, junior, or senior year; renewable. *Award amount:* varies. *Number of awards:* varies. *Eligibility Requirements:* Applicant must be enrolled or expecting to enroll full- or part-time at a four-year institution and resident of Oregon. Available to U.S. citizens. *Application Requirements:* Application, essay, financial need analysis, references, transcript, activity chart. **Deadline:** March 1.

Contact Rachel Cummings, Scholarship Coordinator, Oregon Student Assistance Commission, 1500 Valley River Drive, Suite 100, Eugene, OR 97401-7020. *Phone:* 800-452-8807 Ext. 7395. *Web site:* www.osac.state.or.us.

Oregon Opportunity Grant. Available to Oregon residents who are undergraduate students enrolled at least half-time in a participating Oregon institution. Must establish financial need, have completed the FAFSA and be eligible for a Federal Pell Grant. Award amounts vary but for full-time students can range from about $1400 per semester for community college students to $2100 to 5000 at a 4-year private college or university. For additional information, and to apply online visit Web site: www.getcollegefunds.org. *Award:* Scholarship for use in freshman, sophomore, junior, or senior year; renewable. *Award amount:* varies. *Number of awards:* up to 24,000. *Eligibility Requirements:* Applicant must be enrolled or expecting to enroll full- or part-time at a two-year or four-year institution or university; resident of Oregon and studying in Oregon. Available to U.S. citizens. *Application Requirements:* Application, financial need analysis, transcript, FAFSA. **Deadline:** March 2.

Contact Director of Grant Programs, Oregon Student Assistance Commission, 1500 Valley River Drive, Suite 100, Eugene, OR 97401-7020. *Phone:* 800-452-8807 Ext. 7395. *Web site:* www.osac.state.or.us.

Oregon Scholarship Fund Community College Student Award. Scholarship open to Oregon residents enrolled or planning to enroll in Oregon community college programs. Recipients may reapply for one additional year. Apply at www.getcollegefunds.org. *Award:* Scholarship for use in freshman or sophomore year; not renewable. *Award amount:* varies. *Number of awards:* varies. *Eligibility Requirements:* Applicant must be enrolled or expecting to enroll full-time at a two-year institution; resident of Oregon and studying in Oregon. Available to U.S. citizens. *Application Requirements:* Application, essay, financial need analysis, transcript, activity chart. **Deadline:** March 1.

Contact Director of Grant Programs, Oregon Student Assistance Commission, 1500 Valley River Drive, Suite 100, Eugene, OR 97401-7020. *Phone:* 800-452-8807 Ext. 7395. *Web site:* www.osac.state.or.us.

Oregon Scholarship Fund Transfer Student Award. Award open to Oregon residents who are currently enrolled in their second year at an Oregon community college and are planning to transfer to a four-year college in Oregon. Prior recipients may apply for one additional year. Apply at www.getcollegefunds.org. *Award:* Scholarship for use in junior or senior year; not renewable. *Award amount:* varies. *Number of awards:* varies. *Eligibility Requirements:* Applicant must be enrolled or expecting to enroll full-time at a two-year or four-year institution; resident of Oregon and studying in Oregon. Available to U.S. citizens. *Application Requirements:* Application, essay, financial need analysis, transcript, activity chart. **Deadline:** March 1.

Contact Director of Grant Programs, Oregon Student Assistance Commission, 1500 Valley River Drive, Suite 100, Eugene, OR 97401-7020. *Phone:* 800-452-8807 Ext. 7395. *Web site:* www.osac.state.or.us.

Oregon Trucking Association Safety Council Scholarship. One-time award available to a child of an Oregon Trucking Association member, or child of employee of member. Applicants must be graduating high school seniors from an Oregon high school, Oregon residency not required . For additional information, see Web site: http://www.osac.state.or.us. *Award:* Scholarship for use in freshman year; not renewable. *Award amount:* varies. *Number of awards:* 4. *Eligibility Requirements:* Applicant must be high school student and planning to enroll or expecting to enroll full-time at a four-year institution. Applicant or parent of applicant must be affiliated with Oregon Trucking Association. Available to U.S. citizens. *Application Requirements:* Application, essay, financial need analysis, references, transcript, activity chart. **Deadline:** March 1.

Contact Director of Grant Programs, Oregon Student Assistance Commission, 1500 Valley River Drive, Suite 100, Eugene, OR 97401-7020. *Phone:* 800-452-8807 Ext. 7395. *Web site:* www.osac.state.or.us.

Oregon Veterans' Education Aid. To be eligible, veteran must have actively served in U.S. armed forces 90 days and been discharged under honorable conditions. Must be U.S. citizen and Oregon resident. Korean War veteran or received campaign or expeditionary medal or ribbon awarded by U.S. armed forces for services after June 30, 1958. Full-time students receive up to $150 per month, and part-time students receive up to $100 per month. *Award:* Grant for use in freshman, sophomore, junior, or senior year; not renewable. *Award amount:* varies. *Number of awards:* up to 100. *Eligibility Requirements:* Applicant must be enrolled or expecting to enroll full- or part-time at a two-year, four-year, or technical institution or university; resident of Oregon and studying in Oregon. Available to U.S. citizens. Applicant must have general military experience. *Application Requirements:* Application, certified copy of DD Form 214. **Deadline:** continuous.

Contact Loriann Sheridan, Educational Aid Coordinator, Oregon Department of Veterans' Affairs, 700 Summer Street, NE, Salem, OR 97301-1289. *E-mail:* sheridl@odva.state.or.us. *Phone:* 503-373-2264. *Fax:* 503-373-2393. *Web site:* www.oregon.gov/odva.

PENNSYLVANIA

Armed Forces Loan Forgiveness Program. Loan forgiveness for non-residents of Pennsylvania who served in Armed Forces in an active duty status after September 11, 2001. Must be a student who either left a PA approved institution of postsecondary education due to call to active duty, or was living in PA at time of enlistment, or enlisted in military immediately after attending a PA approved institution of postsecondary education. Number of loans forgiven varies. *Award:* Forgivable loan for use in freshman, sophomore, junior, or senior year; not renewable. *Award amount:* up to $2500. *Number of awards:* varies. *Eligibility Requirements:* Applicant must be enrolled or expecting to enroll full- or part-time at a two-year, four-year, or technical institution or university. Available to U.S. citizens. Applicant or parent must meet one or more of the following requirements: general military experience; retired from active duty; disabled or killed as a result of military service; prisoner of war; or missing in action. *Application Requirements:* Application. **Deadline:** December 31.

Contact Keith R. New, Vice President, Public Relations, Pennsylvania Higher Education Assistance Agency, 1200 North Seventh Street, Harrisburg, PA 17102-1444. *E-mail:* knew@pheaa.org. *Phone:* 717-720-2509. *Fax:* 717-720-3903. *Web site:* www.pheaa.org.

New Economy Technology and SciTech Scholarships. Renewable award for Pennsylvania residents pursuing a degree in science or technology at a PHEAA-approved two- or four-year Pennsylvania college or university. Must maintain minimum GPA of 3.0. Must commence employment in Pennsylvania in a field related to degree within one year after graduation, and work one year for each year the scholarship was awarded. *Academic Fields/Career Goals:* Engineering/Technology; Engineering-Related Technologies; Natural Sciences; Physical Sciences. *Award:* Scholarship for use in freshman, sophomore, junior, or senior year; renewable. *Award amount:* varies. *Number of awards:* varies. *Eligibility Requirements:* Applicant must be age 18 and over; enrolled or expecting to enroll full-time at a two-year, four-year, or technical institution or university; resident of Pennsylvania and studying in Pennsylvania. Applicant must have 3.0 GPA or higher. Available to U.S. citizens. *Application Requirements:* Application, FAFSA. **Deadline:** December 31.

Contact State Grant and Special Programs Division, Pennsylvania Higher Education Assistance Agency, 1200 North Seventh Street, Harrisburg, PA 17102-1444. *Phone:* 800-692-7392. *Web site:* www.pheaa.org.

Pennsylvania State Grants. Award for Pennsylvania residents attending an approved postsecondary institution as undergraduates in a program of at least two years duration. Renewable for up to eight semesters if applicants show continued need and academic progress. Must submit FAFSA. Number of awards granted varies annually. Scholarship value is $3500 to $4500. Deadlines: May 1 and August 1. *Award:* Grant for use in freshman, sophomore, junior, or senior year; renewable. *Award amount:* $3500–$4500.

Number of awards: varies. *Eligibility Requirements:* Applicant must be enrolled or expecting to enroll full- or part-time at a two-year, four-year, or technical institution or university and resident of Pennsylvania. Available to U.S. citizens. *Application Requirements:* Financial need analysis, FAFSA. *Deadline:* varies.

Contact Keith New, Director of Communications and Press Office, Pennsylvania Higher Education Assistance Agency, 1200 North Seventh Street, Harrisburg, PA 17102-1444. *Phone:* 717-720-2509. *Fax:* 717-720-3903. *Web site:* www.pheaa.org.

Postsecondary Education Gratuity Program. The program offers waiver of tuition and fees for children of Pennsylvania police officers, firefighters, rescue or ambulance squad members, corrections facility employees, or National Guard members who died in line of duty after January 1, 1976. *Award:* Grant for use in freshman, sophomore, junior, or senior year; renewable. *Award amount:* varies. *Number of awards:* varies. *Eligibility Requirements:* Applicant must be age 25 or under; enrolled or expecting to enroll full-time at a two-year or four-year institution or university; resident of Pennsylvania and studying in Pennsylvania. Applicant or parent of applicant must have employment or volunteer experience in police/firefighting. Available to U.S. citizens. Applicant or parent must meet one or more of the following requirements: Air Force National Guard or Army National Guard experience; retired from active duty; disabled or killed as a result of military service; prisoner of war; or missing in action. *Application Requirements:* Application. *Deadline:* August 1.

Contact Keith R. New, Vice President, Public Relations, Pennsylvania Higher Education Assistance Agency, 1200 North Seventh Street, Harrisburg, PA 17102-1444. *E-mail:* knew@pheaa.org. *Phone:* 717-720-2509. *Fax:* 717-720-3903. *Web site:* www.pheaa.org.

Robert C. Byrd Honors Scholarship-Pennsylvania. Awards Pennsylvania residents who are graduating high school seniors. Must rank in the top 5 percent of graduating class, have at least a 3.5 GPA and score 1150 or above on the SAT, 25 or above on the ACT, or 355 or above on the GED. Renewable award and the amount granted varies. Applicants are expected to be a full-time freshman student enrolled at an eligible institution of higher education, following high school graduation. *Award:* Scholarship for use in freshman year; renewable. *Award amount:* $1500. *Number of awards:* varies. *Eligibility Requirements:* Applicant must be high school student; planning to enroll or expecting to enroll full-time at a four-year institution or university and resident of Pennsylvania. Applicant must have 3.5 GPA or higher. Available to U.S. citizens. *Application Requirements:* Application, references, test scores, transcript, letter of acceptance. *Deadline:* May 1.

Contact Keith R. New, Director of Communications and Press Office, Pennsylvania Higher Education Assistance Agency, 1200 North Seventh Street, Harrisburg, PA 17102. *Phone:* 717-720-2509. *Fax:* 717-720-3903. *Web site:* www.pheaa.org.

RHODE ISLAND

Rhode Island State Grant Program. Grants for residents of Rhode Island attending an approved school in United States. Based on need. Renewable for up to four years if in good academic standing and meet financial need requirements. *Award:* Grant for use in freshman, sophomore, junior, or senior year; renewable. *Award amount:* $300–$900. *Number of awards:* 10,000–12,900. *Eligibility Requirements:* Applicant must be enrolled or expecting to enroll full- or part-time at a two-year, four-year, or technical institution or university and resident of Rhode Island. Available to U.S. citizens. *Application Requirements:* Application, financial need analysis. *Deadline:* March 1.

Contact Mr. Michael Joyce, Director of Program Administration, Rhode Island Higher Education Assistance Authority, 560 Jefferson Boulevard, Suite 100, Warwick, RI 02886. *E-mail:* mjoyce@riheaa.org. *Phone:* 401-736-1172. *Fax:* 401-736-1178. *Web site:* www.riheaa.org.

SOUTH CAROLINA

Educational Assistance for Certain War Veterans Dependents Scholarship-South Carolina. Free tuition for South Carolina residents whose parent is a resident, wartime veteran, and meets one of these criteria; awarded Purple Heart or Congressional Medal of Honor; permanently and totally disabled or killed as a result of military service; prisoner of war; or missing in action. Must be age 18-26 and enrolled or expecting to enroll full or part-time at a two-year or four-year technical institution or university in South Carolina. Complete information and qualifications for this award are on Web site: http://www.govoepp.state.sc.us. *Award:* Scholarship for use in freshman, sophomore, junior, or senior year; not renewable. *Award amount:* varies. *Number of awards:* varies. *Eligibility Requirements:* Applicant must be age 18-26; enrolled or expecting to enroll full- or part-time at a two-year, four-year, or technical institution or university; resident of South Carolina and studying in South Carolina. Available to U.S. citizens. Applicant or parent must meet one or more of the following requirements: general military experience; retired from active duty; disabled or killed as a result of military service; prisoner of war; or missing in action. *Application Requirements:* Application, transcript, proof of qualification of veteran. *Deadline:* continuous.

Contact South Carolina Division of Veterans Affairs. *Web site:* www.govoepp.state.sc.us/vetaff.htm.

Palmetto Fellows Scholarship Program. Renewable award for qualified high school seniors in South Carolina to attend a four-year South Carolina institution. The scholarship must be applied directly towards the cost of attendance, less any other gift aid received. *Award:* Scholarship for use in freshman year; renewable. *Award amount:* $6700–$7500. *Number of awards:* 4846. *Eligibility Requirements:* Applicant must be high school student; planning to enroll or expecting to enroll full-time at a four-year institution or university; resident of South Carolina and studying in South Carolina. Applicant must have 3.5 GPA or higher. Available to U.S. citizens. *Application Requirements:* Application, test scores, transcript. *Deadline:* December 15.

Contact Dr. Karen Woodfaulk, Director of Student Services, South Carolina Commission on Higher Education, 1333 Main Street, Suite 200, Columbia, SC 29201. *E-mail:* kwoodfaulk@che.sc.gov. *Phone:* 803-737-2244. *Fax:* 803-737-3610. *Web site:* www.che.sc.gov.

Robert C. Byrd Honors Scholarship-South Carolina. Renewable award for a graduating high school senior from South Carolina, who will be attending a two- or four-year institution. Applicants should be superior students who demonstrate academic achievement and show promise of continued success at a postsecondary institution. Interested applicants should contact their high school counselors after the first week of December for an application. *Award:* Scholarship for use in freshman year; renewable. *Award amount:* varies. *Number of awards:* varies. *Eligibility Requirements:* Applicant must be high school student; planning to enroll or expecting to enroll full-time at a two-year or four-year institution or university and resident of South Carolina. Applicant must have 3.5 GPA or higher. Available to U.S. citizens. *Application Requirements:* Application, test scores, ACT or SAT scores. *Deadline:* varies.

Contact Beth Cope, Program Coordinator, South Carolina Department of Education, 1424 Senate Street, Columbia, SC 29201. *E-mail:* bcope@sde.state.sc.us. *Phone:* 803-734-8116. *Fax:* 803-734-4387. *Web site:* www.ed.sc.gov.

South Carolina HOPE Scholarship. A merit-based scholarship for eligible first-time entering freshman attending a four-year South Carolina institution. Minimum GPA of 3.0 required. Must be a resident of South Carolina. *Award:* Scholarship for use in freshman year; not renewable. *Award amount:* $2800. *Number of awards:* 2605. *Eligibility Requirements:*

Applicant must be high school student; planning to enroll or expecting to enroll full-time at a four-year institution or university; resident of South Carolina and studying in South Carolina. Applicant must have 3.0 GPA or higher. Available to U.S. citizens. *Application Requirements:* Transcript. *Deadline:* continuous.

Contact Gerrick Hampton, Scholarship Coordinator, South Carolina Commission on Higher Education, 1333 Main Street, Suite 200, Columbia, SC 29201. *E-mail:* ghampton@che.sc.gov. *Phone:* 803-737-4544. *Fax:* 803-737-3610. *Web site:* www.che.sc.gov.

South Carolina Need-Based Grants Program. Award based on FAFSA. A student may receive up to $2500 annually for full-time and up to $1250 annually for part-time study. The grant must be applied directly towards the cost of college attendance for a maximum of eight full-time equivalent terms. *Award:* Grant for use in freshman, sophomore, junior, senior, or graduate year; renewable. *Award amount:* $1250–$2500. *Number of awards:* 1–26,730. *Eligibility Requirements:* Applicant must be enrolled or expecting to enroll full- or part-time at a two-year, four-year, or technical institution or university; resident of South Carolina and studying in South Carolina. Available to U.S. citizens. *Application Requirements:* Application, financial need analysis. *Deadline:* continuous.

Contact Dr. Karen Woodfaulk, Director of Student Service, South Carolina Commission on Higher Education, 1333 Main Street, Suite 200, Columbia, SC 29201. *E-mail:* kwoodfaulk@che.sc.gov. *Phone:* 803-737-2244. *Fax:* 803-737-2297. *Web site:* www.che.sc.gov.

South Carolina Teacher Loan Program. One-time awards for South Carolina residents attending four-year postsecondary institutions in South Carolina. Recipients must teach in the South Carolina public school system in a critical-need area after graduation. Twenty percent of loan forgiven for each year of service. Write for additional requirements. *Academic Fields/Career Goals:* Education; Special Education. *Award:* Forgivable loan for use in freshman, sophomore, junior, senior, or graduate year; not renewable. *Award amount:* $2500–$5000. *Number of awards:* up to 1121. *Eligibility Requirements:* Applicant must be enrolled or expecting to enroll full- or part-time at a four-year institution or university; resident of South Carolina and studying in South Carolina. Applicant must have 3.0 GPA or higher. Available to U.S. citizens. *Application Requirements:* Application, references, test scores, promissory note. *Deadline:* June 1.

Contact Jennifer Jones-Gaddy, Vice President, South Carolina Student Loan Corporation, PO Box 21487, Columbia, SC 29221. *E-mail:* jgaddy@slc.sc.edu. *Phone:* 803-798-0916. *Fax:* 803-772-9410. *Web site:* www.scstudentloan.org.

South Carolina Tuition Grants Program. Award assists South Carolina residents attending one of twenty-one approved South Carolina independent colleges. Freshmen must be in upper 3/4 of high school class or have SAT score of at least 900 or ACT of 19 or 2.0 final GAP on SC uniform grading scale. Upper-class students must complete 24 semester hours per year to be eligible. Must complete FAFSA to apply. *Award:* Grant for use in freshman, sophomore, junior, or senior year; renewable. *Award amount:* $100–$3150. *Number of awards:* up to 12,000. *Eligibility Requirements:* Applicant must be enrolled or expecting to enroll full-time at a two-year or four-year institution or university; resident of South Carolina and studying in South Carolina. Available to U.S. citizens. *Application Requirements:* Application, FAFSA. *Deadline:* June 30.

Contact Toni Cave, Financial Aid Counselor, South Carolina Tuition Grants Commission, 800 Dutch Square Boulevard, Suite A 260, Columbia, SC 29210. *E-mail:* toni@sctuitiongrants.org. *Phone:* 803-896-1120. *Fax:* 803-896-1126. *Web site:* www.sctuitiongrants.com.

SOUTH DAKOTA

Haines Memorial Scholarship. One-time scholarship for South Dakota public university students who are sophomores, juniors, or seniors having at least a 2.5 GPA and majoring in a teacher education program. Must include resume with application. Must be South Dakota resident. *Academic Fields/Career Goals:* Education. *Award:* Scholarship for use in sophomore, junior, or senior year; not renewable. *Award amount:* $2150. *Number of awards:* 1. *Eligibility Requirements:* Applicant must be enrolled or expecting to enroll full-time at an institution or university; resident of South Dakota and studying in South Dakota. Applicant must have 3.5 GPA or higher. Available to U.S. citizens. *Application Requirements:* Application, driver's license, essay, resume, typed statement describing personal philosophy and philosophy of education. *Deadline:* February 8.

Contact South Dakota Board of Regents. *Web site:* www.sdbor.edu.

South Dakota Opportunity Scholarship. Renewable scholarship may be worth up to $5000 over four years to students who take a rigorous college-prep curriculum while in high school and stay in the state for their postsecondary education. *Award:* Scholarship for use in freshman year; renewable. *Award amount:* $1000. *Number of awards:* 1000. *Eligibility Requirements:* Applicant must be high school student; planning to enroll or expecting to enroll full-time at a two-year, four-year, or technical institution or university; resident of South Dakota and studying in South Dakota. Applicant must have 3.0 GPA or higher. Available to U.S. citizens. *Application Requirements:* Application, test scores, transcript. *Deadline:* September 1.

Contact Janelle Toman, Scholarship Committee, South Dakota Board of Regents, 306 East Capitol, Suite 200, Pierre, SD 57501-2545. *E-mail:* info@sdbor.edu. *Phone:* 605-773-3455. *Fax:* 605-773-2422. *Web site:* www.sdbor.edu.

TENNESSEE

ASPIRE Award. $1500 supplement to the Tennessee HOPE scholarship. Must meet Tennessee HOPE Scholarship requirements and student's parents must have an Adjusted Gross Income on their federal tax return of $36000 or less. *Award:* Scholarship for use in freshman, sophomore, junior, or senior year; renewable. *Award amount:* up to $1500. *Number of awards:* varies. *Eligibility Requirements:* Applicant must be enrolled or expecting to enroll full- or part-time at a two-year or four-year institution or university; resident of Tennessee and studying in Tennessee. Applicant must have 3.0 GPA or higher. Available to U.S. citizens. *Application Requirements:* Application, financial need analysis. *Deadline:* September 1.

Contact Robert Biggers, Director of Lottery Scholarship Programs, Tennessee Student Assistance Corporation, Parkway Towers, 404 James Robertson Parkway, Suite 1510, Nashville, TN 37243-0820. *E-mail:* robert.biggers@tn.gov. *Phone:* 866-291-2675 Ext. 106. *Fax:* 615-741-6101. *Web site:* www.tn.gov/collegepays.

Christa McAuliffe Scholarship Program. Scholarship to assist and support Tennessee students who have demonstrated a commitment to a career in educating the youth of Tennessee. Offered to college seniors for a period of one academic year. Must have a minimum college GPA of 3.5. Must have attained scores on either the ACT or SAT which meet or exceed the national norms. *Academic Fields/Career Goals:* Education. *Award:* Scholarship for use in senior year; not renewable. *Award amount:* up to $500. *Number of awards:* up to 1. *Eligibility Requirements:* Applicant must be enrolled or expecting to enroll full-time at a four-year institution or university; resident of Tennessee and studying in Tennessee. Applicant must have 2.5 GPA or higher. Available to U.S. citizens. *Application Requirements:* Application, essay. *Deadline:* April 1.

Contact Ms. Kathy Stripling, Scholarship Administrator, Tennessee Student Assistance Corporation, Parkway Towers, 404 James Robertson Parkway, Suite 1510, Nashville, TN 37243-0820. *Phone:* 866-291-2675 Ext. 155. *Fax:* 615-741-6101. *Web site:* www.tn.gov/collegepays.

Dependent Children Scholarship Program. Scholarship aid for Tennessee residents who are dependent children of a Tennessee law enforcement officer, fireman, or an emergency medical service technician who has been killed or totally and permanently disabled while performing duties within the scope of such employment. The scholarship is awarded to full-time undergraduate students for a maximum of four academic years or the period required for the completion of the program of study. *Award:* Scholarship for use in freshman, sophomore, junior, or senior year; renewable. *Award amount:* varies. *Number of awards:* up to 31. *Eligibility Requirements:* Applicant must be enrolled or expecting to enroll full-time at a two-year or four-year institution or university; resident of Tennessee and studying in Tennessee. Applicant or parent of applicant must have employment or volunteer experience in police/firefighting. Available to U.S. citizens. *Application Requirements:* Application, FAFSA. *Deadline:* July 15.

Contact Ms. Naomi Derryberry, Director of Grants, Tennessee Student Assistance Corporation, Parkway Towers, 404 James Robertson Parkway, Suite 1510, Nashville, TN 37243-0820. *E-mail:* naomi.derryberry@tn.gov. *Phone:* 866-291-2675 Ext. 125. *Fax:* 615-741-6101. *Web site:* www.tn.gov/collegepays.

Minority Teaching Fellows Program/Tennessee. Forgivable loan for minority Tennessee residents pursuing teaching careers. Minimum 2.75 GPA required for high school applicant, minimum 2.5 GPA required for college applicant. Must be in the top quarter of the class or score an 18 on ACT. Must teach one year for each year the award is received, or repay loan. *Academic Fields/Career Goals:* Education; Special Education. *Award:* Forgivable loan for use in freshman, sophomore, junior, or senior year; renewable. *Award amount:* up to $5000. *Number of awards:* 19–116. *Eligibility Requirements:* Applicant must be American Indian/Alaska Native, Asian/Pacific Islander, Black (non-Hispanic), or Hispanic; enrolled or expecting to enroll full-time at a two-year or four-year institution or university; resident of Tennessee and studying in Tennessee. Available to U.S. citizens. *Application Requirements:* Application, essay, references, test scores, transcript, statement of intent. *Deadline:* April 15.

Contact Mike McCormack, Scholarship Administrator, Tennessee Student Assistance Corporation, Parkway Towers, 404 James Robertson Parkway, Suite 1510, Nashville, TN 37243-0820. *E-mail:* mike.mccormack@state.tn.us. *Phone:* 866-291-2675 Ext. 140. *Fax:* 615-741-6101. *Web site:* www.tn.gov/collegepays.

Ned McWherter Scholars Program. Award for Tennessee high school seniors with high academic ability. Must have minimum high school GPA of 3.5 and a score of 29 on the ACT or SAT equivalent. Must attend a college or university in Tennessee and be a permanent U.S. citizen. For more information, visit Web site: http://tn.gov/collegepays. *Award:* Scholarship for use in freshman, sophomore, junior, or senior year; renewable. *Award amount:* up to $3000. *Number of awards:* up to 180. *Eligibility Requirements:* Applicant must be enrolled or expecting to enroll full-time at a two-year, four-year, or technical institution or university; resident of Tennessee and studying in Tennessee. Applicant must have 2.5 GPA or higher. Available to U.S. citizens. *Application Requirements:* Application, test scores, transcript. *Deadline:* February 15.

Contact Kathy Stripling, Scholarship Administrator, Tennessee Student Assistance Corporation, 404 James Robertson Parkway, Suite 1510, Parkway Towers, Nashville, TN 37243-0820. *E-mail:* kathy.stripling@state.tn.us. *Phone:* 866-291-2675 Ext. 155. *Fax:* 615-741-6101. *Web site:* www.tn.gov/collegepays.

Tennessee Dual Enrollment Grant. Grant for study at an eligible Tennessee postsecondary institution awarded to juniors and seniors in a Tennessee high school who have been admitted to undergraduate study while still pursuing a high school diploma. For more information, visit Web site: www.tn.gov/collegepays. *Award:* Grant for use in freshman year; renewable. *Eligibility Requirements:* Applicant must be high school student; planning to enroll or expecting to enroll full- or part-time at a two-year or four-year institution or university; resident of Tennessee and studying in Tennessee. Available to U.S. citizens. *Application Requirements:* Application. *Deadline:* September 1.

Contact Robert Biggers, Director of Lottery Scholarship Program, Tennessee Student Assistance Corporation, Parkway Towers, 404 James Robertson Parkway, Suite 1510, Nashville, TN 37243-0820. *E-mail:* robert.biggers@tn.gov. *Phone:* 866-291-2675. *Fax:* 615-741-1601. *Web site:* www.tn.gov/collegepays.

Tennessee Education Lottery Scholarship Program General Assembly Merit Scholarship. Supplemental award of $1,000 to the Tennessee HOPE Scholarship. Entering freshmen must have 3.75 GPA and 29 ACT (1280 SAT). Must be a U.S. citizen and a resident of Tennessee. *Award:* Scholarship for use in freshman, sophomore, junior, or senior year; renewable. *Award amount:* up to $1000. *Number of awards:* varies. *Eligibility Requirements:* Applicant must be enrolled or expecting to enroll full- or part-time at a two-year or four-year institution or university; resident of Tennessee and studying in Tennessee. Available to U.S. citizens. *Application Requirements:* Application. *Deadline:* September 1.

Contact Robert Biggers, Director of Lottery Scholarship Programs, Tennessee Student Assistance Corporation, Parkway Towers, 404 James Robertson Parkway, Suite 1510, Nashville, TN 37243-0820. *E-mail:* tsac.aidinfo@state.tn.us. *Phone:* 866-291-2675 Ext. 106. *Fax:* 615-741-6101. *Web site:* www.tn.gov/collegepays.

Tennessee Education Lottery Scholarship Program Tennessee HOPE Access Grant. Non-renewable award of $2,750 for students at four-year colleges or $1,750 for students at two-year colleges. Entering freshmen must have a minimum GPA of 2.75, ACT score of 18-20 (or SAT equivalent), and parents' adjusted gross income must be $36,000 or less. Recipients will become eligible for Tennessee HOPE Scholarship by meeting HOPE Scholarship renewal criteria. *Award:* Scholarship for use in freshman, sophomore, junior, or senior year; not renewable. *Award amount:* $1750–$2750. *Number of awards:* varies. *Eligibility Requirements:* Applicant must be enrolled or expecting to enroll full- or part-time at a two-year or four-year institution or university; resident of Tennessee and studying in Tennessee. Available to U.S. citizens. *Application Requirements:* Application, financial need analysis. *Deadline:* September 1.

Contact Robert Biggers, Director of Lottery Scholarship Programs, Tennessee Student Assistance Corporation, Parkway Towers, 404 James Robertson Parkway, Suite 1510, Nashville, TN 37243-0820. *E-mail:* robert.biggers@tn.gov. *Phone:* 866-291-2675 Ext. 106. *Fax:* 615-741-6101. *Web site:* www.tn.gov/collegepays.

Tennessee Education Lottery Scholarship Program Tennessee HOPE Scholarship. Award amount is $4,000 for 4-year institutions and $2,000 for 2-year institutions. Must be a Tennessee resident attending an eligible postsecondary institution in Tennessee. For more information, see Web: www.fafsa.ed.gov. *Award:* Scholarship for use in freshman, sophomore, junior, or senior year; renewable. *Award amount:* $2000–$4000. *Number of awards:* varies. *Eligibility Requirements:* Applicant must be enrolled or expecting to enroll full- or part-time at a two-year or four-year institution or university; resident of Tennessee and studying in Tennessee. Applicant must have 3.0 GPA or higher. Available to U.S. citizens. *Application Requirements:* Application. *Deadline:* September 1.

Contact Robert Biggers, Director of Lottery Scholarship Programs, Tennessee Student Assistance Corporation, Parkway Towers, 404 James Robertson Parkway, Suite 1510, Nashville, TN 37243-0820. *E-mail:* robert.biggers@tn.gov. *Phone:* 866-291-2675 Ext. 106. *Fax:* 615-741-6101. *Web site:* www.tn.gov/collegepays.

Tennessee Education Lottery Scholarship Program Wilder-Naifeh Technical Skills

Grant. Award up to $2,000 for students enrolled in a certificate or diploma program at a Tennessee Technology Center. Cannot be prior recipient of Tennessee HOPE Scholarship. For more information, see Web: www.fafsa.ed.gov. *Award:* Grant for use in freshman or sophomore year; renewable. *Award amount:* up to $2000. *Number of awards:* varies. *Eligibility Requirements:* Applicant must be enrolled or expecting to enroll full- or part-time at a technical institution; resident of Tennessee and studying in Tennessee. Available to U.S. citizens. *Application Requirements:* Application. *Deadline:* varies.

Contact Robert Biggers, Director of Lottery Scholarship Programs, Tennessee Student Assistance Corporation, Parkway Towers, 404 James Robertson Parkway, Suite 1510, Nashville, TN 37243-0820. *E-mail:* robert.biggers@tn.gov. *Phone:* 866-291-2675 Ext. 106. *Fax:* 615-741-6101. *Web site:* www.tn.gov/collegepays.

Tennessee HOPE Foster Child Tuition Grant. Renewable tuition award available for recipients of the HOPE Scholarship or HOPE Access Grant. Student must have been in Tennessee state custody as a foster child for at least one year after reaching age 14. Award amount varies and shall not exceed the tuition and mandatory fees at an eligible Tennessee public postsecondary institution. For additional information, visit Web site: www.tn.gov/collegepays. *Award:* Scholarship for use in freshman, sophomore, junior, or senior year; renewable. *Eligibility Requirements:* Applicant must be enrolled or expecting to enroll full- or part-time at a two-year or four-year institution or university; resident of Tennessee and studying in Tennessee. Applicant must have 3.0 GPA or higher. Available to U.S. citizens. *Application Requirements:* Application. *Deadline:* September 1.

Contact Robert Biggers, Directory of Lottery Scholarship Programs, Tennessee Student Assistance Corporation, Parkway Towers, 404 James Robertson Parkway, Suite 1510, Nashville, TN 37243-0820. *E-mail:* robert.biggers@tn.gov. *Phone:* 866-291-2675. *Fax:* 615-741-6101. *Web site:* www.tn.gov/collegepays.

Tennessee Student Assistance Award Program. Award to assist Tennessee residents attending an approved college or university within the state. Complete a Free Application for Federal Student Aid form. FAFSA must be processed by February 15 for priority consideration. For more information, see Web: www.fafsa.ed.gov. *Award:* Grant for use in freshman, sophomore, junior, or senior year; renewable. *Award amount:* $100–$4644. *Number of awards:* 25,000–28,000. *Eligibility Requirements:* Applicant must be enrolled or expecting to enroll full- or part-time at a two-year, four-year, or technical institution or university; resident of Tennessee and studying in Tennessee. Available to U.S. citizens. *Application Requirements:* Application, financial need analysis. *Deadline:* February 15.

Contact Naomi Derryberry, Director of Grants, Tennessee Student Assistance Corporation, Parkway Towers, 404 James Robertson Parkway, Suite 1510, Nashville, TN 37243-0820. *E-mail:* naomi.derryberry@state.tn.us. *Phone:* 866-291-2675 Ext. 125. *Fax:* 615-741-6101. *Web site:* www.tn.gov/collegepays.

Tennessee Teaching Scholars Program. Forgivable loan for college juniors, seniors, and college graduates admitted to an education program in Tennessee with a minimum GPA of 2.75. Students must commit to teach in a Tennessee public school one year for each year of the award. Must be a U.S. citizen and resident of Tennessee. *Academic Fields/Career Goals:* Education. *Award:* Forgivable loan for use in junior or senior year; renewable. *Award amount:* up to $4500. *Number of awards:* up to 160. *Eligibility Requirements:* Applicant must be enrolled or expecting to enroll full- or part-time at a four-year institution or university; resident of Tennessee and studying in Tennessee. Applicant must have 2.5 GPA or higher. Available to U.S. citizens. *Application Requirements:* Application, references, test scores, transcript. *Deadline:* April 15.

Contact Mike McCormack, Scholarship Administrator, Tennessee Student Assistance Corporation, 404 James Robertson Parkway, Suite 1510, Parkway Towers, Nashville, TN 37243-0820. *E-mail:* mike.mccormack@state.tn.us. *Phone:* 615-741-1346. *Fax:* 615-741-6101. *Web site:* www.tn.gov/collegepays.

TEXAS

Conditional Grant Program. Renewable award to students who are considered economically disadvantaged based on federal guidelines. The maximum amount awarded per semester is $3,000 not to exceed $6000 per academic year. Students already enrolled in an undergraduate program should have minimum GPA 2.5 and students newly enrolling should have minimum GPA 3.0. *Academic Fields/Career Goals:* Civil Engineering; Computer Science/Data Processing; Occupational Safety and Health. *Award:* Grant for use in freshman, sophomore, junior, or senior year; renewable. *Award amount:* up to $6000. *Number of awards:* varies. *Eligibility Requirements:* Applicant must be enrolled or expecting to enroll full-time at a four-year institution or university; resident of Texas and studying in Texas. Available to U.S. citizens. *Application Requirements:* Application, essay, interview, references, test scores, transcript. *Deadline:* March 1.

Contact Minnie Brown, Program Coordinator, Texas Department of Transportation, 125 East 11th Street, Austin, TX 78701-2483. *E-mail:* mbrown2@dot.state.tx.us. *Phone:* 512-416-4979. *Fax:* 512-416-4980. *Web site:* www.txdot.gov.

Texas National Guard Tuition Assistance Program. Provides exemption from the payment of tuition to certain members of the Texas National Guard, Texas Air Guard or the State Guard. Must be Texas resident and attend school in Texas. Deadline varies. *Award:* Scholarship for use in freshman, sophomore, junior, or senior year; renewable. *Award amount:* varies. *Number of awards:* varies. *Eligibility Requirements:* Applicant must be enrolled or expecting to enroll full- or part-time at a four-year institution or university; resident of Texas and studying in Texas. Available to U.S. citizens. Applicant or parent must meet one or more of the following requirements: Air Force National Guard or Army National Guard experience; retired from active duty; disabled or killed as a result of military service; prisoner of war; or missing in action. *Application Requirements:* Application. *Deadline:* varies.

Contact State Adjutant General's Office, Texas Higher Education Coordinating Board, PO Box 5218, Austin, TX 78763-5218. *E-mail:* education.office@tx.ngb.army.mil. *Phone:* 512-465-5515. *Web site:* www.collegefortexans.com.

Toward EXcellence Access and Success (TEXAS Grant). Renewable aid for students enrolled in public colleges or universities in Texas. Must be a resident of Texas and have completed the Recommended High School Curriculum or Distinguished Achievement Curriculum in high school. For renewal awards, must maintain a minimum GPA of 2.5. Based on need. Amount of award is determined by the financial aid office of each school. Deadlines vary. Contact the college/university financial aid office for application information. *Award:* Grant for use in freshman, sophomore, junior, or senior year; renewable. *Award amount:* $1730–$5280. *Number of awards:* 50,000–55,000. *Eligibility Requirements:* Applicant must be enrolled or expecting to enroll full- or part-time at a two-year, four-year, or technical institution or university; resident of Texas and studying in Texas. Available to U.S. citizens. *Application Requirements:* Financial need analysis, transcript. *Deadline:* varies.

Contact Financial Aid Office of relevant school, Texas Higher Education Coordinating Board. *Web site:* www.collegefortexans.com.

Tuition Equalization Grant (TEG) Program. Renewable award for Texas residents enrolled full-time at an independent college or university within the state. Based on financial need. Renewal awards require the student to maintain an overall college GPA of at least 2.5. Deadlines vary by institution. Must not be receiving athletic scholarship.

Contact college/university financial aid office for application information. Nonresidents who are National Merit Finalists may also receive awards. *Award:* Grant for use in freshman, sophomore, junior, or senior year; renewable. *Award amount:* $2900–$3334. *Number of awards:* 30,000–31,000. *Eligibility Requirements:* Applicant must be enrolled or expecting to enroll full-time at a two-year or four-year institution or university; resident of Texas and studying in Texas. Available to U.S. citizens. *Application Requirements:* Financial need analysis, FAFSA. *Deadline:* varies.

Contact Financial Aid Office of Relevant Institution, Texas Higher Education Coordinating Board. *Web site:* www.collegefortexans.com.

Vanessa Rudloff Scholarship Program. Scholarships of $1000 awarded to qualified TWLE members and their dependents who are entering or continuing students at an accredited college or university. For details refer to Web Site: http://www.twle.net/ *Award:* Scholarship for use in freshman, sophomore, junior, senior, graduate, or postgraduate years; not renewable. *Award amount:* $1000. *Number of awards:* 4. *Eligibility Requirements:* Applicant must be enrolled or expecting to enroll full- or part-time at a two-year, four-year, or technical institution or university. Applicant or parent of applicant must be member of Texas Women in Law Enforcement. Applicant must have 3.0 GPA or higher. Available to U.S. and non-U.S. citizens. *Application Requirements:* Application, essay, references. *Deadline:* April 15.

Contact Glenda Baker, Scholarship Awards Chairperson, Texas Women in Law Enforcement, 12605 Rhea Court, Austin, TX 78727. *E-mail:* gbakerab@aol.com. *Web site:* www.twle.com.

UTAH

New Century Scholarship. Scholarship for qualified high school graduates of Utah. Must attend Utah state-operated college. Award depends on number of hours student enrolled. Please contact for further eligibility requirements. Eligible recipients receive an award equal to 75 percent of tuition for 60 credit hours toward the completion of a bachelor's degree. For more details see Web site. *Award:* Scholarship for use in freshman, sophomore, junior, or senior year; renewable. *Award amount:* $921–$2199. *Number of awards:* 1. *Eligibility Requirements:* Applicant must be enrolled or expecting to enroll full- or part-time at a four-year institution or university; resident of Utah and studying in Utah. Available to U.S. citizens. *Application Requirements:* Application, transcript, GPA/copy of enrollment verification from an eligible Utah 4-year institution, verification from registrar of completion of requirements for associate's degree. *Deadline:* continuous.

Contact State of Utah. *Web site:* www.utahsbr.edu.

Terrel H. Bell Teaching Incentive Loan. Designed to provide financial assistance to outstanding Utah students pursuing a degree in education. The incentive loan funds full-time tuition and general fees for eight semesters. After graduation/certification the loan may be forgiven if the recipient teaches in a Utah public school or accredited private school (K-12). Dollar value varies. Loan forgiveness is done on a year-for-year basis. For more details see Web site: http://www.utahsbr.edu. *Academic Fields/Career Goals:* Education. *Award:* Forgivable loan for use in freshman, sophomore, junior, or senior year; renewable. *Award amount:* $4400. *Number of awards:* 374. *Eligibility Requirements:* Applicant must be enrolled or expecting to enroll full-time at a two-year or four-year institution or university; resident of Utah and studying in Utah. Available to U.S. citizens. *Application Requirements:* Application, essay, references, test scores, transcript. *Deadline:* varies.

Contact State of Utah. *Web site:* www.utahsbr.edu.

T.H. Bell Teaching Incentive Loan-Utah. Renewable awards for Utah residents who are high school seniors wishing to pursue teaching careers. The award value varies depending upon tuition and fees at a Utah institution. Must agree to teach in a Utah public school or pay back loan through monthly installments. Must be a U.S. citizen. *Academic Fields/Career Goals:* Education. *Award:* Forgivable loan for use in freshman year; renewable. *Award amount:* varies. *Number of awards:* 25–50. *Eligibility Requirements:* Applicant must be high school student; planning to enroll or expecting to enroll full-time at a four-year institution or university; resident of Utah and studying in Utah. Available to U.S. citizens. *Application Requirements:* Application, essay, test scores, transcript. *Deadline:* March 27.

Contact Diane DeMan, Executive Secretary, Utah State Office of Education, 250 East 500 South, PO Box 144200, Salt Lake City, UT 84114. *Phone:* 801-538-7741. *Fax:* 801-538-7973. *Web site:* www.schools.utah.gov/cert.

Utah Centennial Opportunity Program for Education. Award available to students with substantial financial need for use at any of the participating Utah institutions. The student must be a Utah resident. Contact the financial aid office of the participating institution for requirements and deadlines. *Award:* Grant for use in freshman, sophomore, junior, or senior year; not renewable. *Award amount:* $300–$5000. *Number of awards:* up to 7375. *Eligibility Requirements:* Applicant must be enrolled or expecting to enroll full- or part-time at a two-year, four-year, or technical institution or university; resident of Utah and studying in Utah. Available to U.S. citizens. *Application Requirements:* Financial need analysis, FAFSA. *Deadline:* continuous.

Contact Utah State Board of Regents. *Web site:* www.uheaa.org.

Utah Leveraging Educational Assistance Partnership. Award available to Utah resident students with substantial financial need for use at any of the participating Utah institutions. Contact the financial aid office of the participating institution for requirements and deadlines. *Award:* Grant for use in freshman, sophomore, junior, or senior year; not renewable. *Award amount:* $300–$2500. *Number of awards:* up to 3985. *Eligibility Requirements:* Applicant must be enrolled or expecting to enroll full- or part-time at a two-year, four-year, or technical institution or university; resident of Utah and studying in Utah. Available to U.S. citizens. *Application Requirements:* Financial need analysis, FAFSA. *Deadline:* continuous.

Contact Utah State Board of Regents. *Web site:* www.uheaa.org.

VERMONT

Vermont Incentive Grants. Renewable grants for Vermont residents based on financial need. Must meet needs test. Must be college undergraduate or graduate student enrolled full-time at an approved post secondary institution. Only available to U.S. citizens or permanent residents. *Award:* Grant for use in freshman, sophomore, junior, or senior year; renewable. *Award amount:* $500–$10,800. *Number of awards:* varies. *Eligibility Requirements:* Applicant must be enrolled or expecting to enroll full-time at a two-year, four-year, or technical institution or university and resident of Vermont. Available to U.S. citizens. *Application Requirements:* Application, financial need analysis, FAFSA. *Deadline:* continuous.

Contact Grant Program, Vermont Student Assistance Corporation, PO Box 2000, Winooski, VT 05404-2000. *Phone:* 802-655-9602. *Fax:* 802-654-3765. *Web site:* www.vsac.org.

Vermont Non-Degree Student Grant Program. Need-based, renewable grants for Vermont residents enrolled in non-degree programs in a college, vocational school, or high school adult program, that will improve employability or encourage further study. Award amounts vary. *Award:* Grant for use in freshman, sophomore, junior, or senior year; renewable. *Award amount:* varies. *Number of awards:* varies. *Eligibility Requirements:* Applicant must be enrolled or expecting to enroll full- or part-time at a two-year, four-year, or technical institution or university and resident of Vermont. Available to U.S. citizens. *Application Requirements:* Application, financial need analysis. *Deadline:* continuous.

Contact Vermont Student Assistance Corporation. *Web site:* www.vsac.org.

Vermont Part-Time Student Grants. For undergraduates carrying less than twelve credits per semester who have not received a bachelor's degree. Must be Vermont resident. Based on financial need. Complete Vermont Financial Aid Packet to apply. May be used at any approved post-secondary institution. *Award:* Grant for use in freshman, sophomore, junior, or senior year; renewable. *Award amount:* $250–$8100. *Number of awards:* varies. *Eligibility Requirements:* Applicant must be enrolled or expecting to enroll part-time at a four-year institution or university and resident of Vermont. Available to U.S. citizens. *Application Requirements:* Application, financial need analysis. **Deadline:** continuous.

Contact Grant Program, Vermont Student Assistance Corporation, PO Box 2000, Winooski, VT 05404-2000. *Phone:* 802-655-9602. *Fax:* 802-654-3765. *Web site:* www.vsac.org.

Vermont Teacher Diversity Scholarship Program. Loan forgiveness program for students from diverse racial and ethnic backgrounds who attend college in Vermont with a goal of becoming public school teachers. Preference will be given to residents of Vermont. *Academic Fields/Career Goals:* Education. *Award:* Forgivable loan for use in freshman, sophomore, junior, senior, or graduate year; not renewable. *Award amount:* $4000. *Number of awards:* 4. *Eligibility Requirements:* Applicant must be American Indian/Alaska Native, Asian/Pacific Islander, Black (non-Hispanic), or Hispanic; enrolled or expecting to enroll full- or part-time at a four-year institution or university; resident of Vermont and studying in Vermont. Available to U.S. citizens. *Application Requirements:* Application, resume, references, transcript. **Deadline:** April 5.

Contact Ms. Phyl Newbeck, Director, Vermont Teacher Diversity Scholarship Program, PO Box 359, Waterbury, VT 05676-0359. *Phone:* 802-241-3379. *Fax:* 802-241-3369. *Web site:* www.vsc.edu/teacherdiversity/.

VIRGINIA

College Scholarship Assistance Program. Need-based scholarship for undergraduate study by a Virginia resident at a participating Virginia two- or four-year college, or university. Contact financial aid office at the participating Virginia public or nonprofit private institution. The program does not have its own application; institutions use results from the federal FAFSA form. *Award:* Grant for use in freshman, sophomore, junior, or senior year; not renewable. *Award amount:* $400–$5000. *Number of awards:* varies. *Eligibility Requirements:* Applicant must be enrolled or expecting to enroll full- or part-time at a two-year or four-year institution or university; resident of Virginia and studying in Virginia. Available to U.S. citizens. *Application Requirements:* Financial need analysis. **Deadline:** varies.

Contact Contact the financial aid office of participating Virginia college. For additional details, visit www.schev.edu and click on Financial Aid., Virginia State Council of Higher Education. *Web site:* www.schev.edu.

Gheens Foundation Scholarship. Scholarship supports African American students from greater Louisville, KY. For use in one of the following universities: Clark Atlanta University, Morehouse College, Morris Brown College, Spelman College, Tuskegee University, Howard University, Florida A&M, Southern University, Tennessee State or Prairie View University. Apply online at http://www.uncf.org. *Award:* Scholarship for use in freshman, sophomore, junior, or senior year; not renewable. *Award amount:* up to $2000. *Number of awards:* varies. *Eligibility Requirements:* Applicant must be Black (non-Hispanic); enrolled or expecting to enroll full- or part-time at a four-year institution or university; resident of Kentucky and studying in Alabama, District of Columbia, Florida, Georgia, Louisiana, Tennessee, or Texas. Applicant must have 2.5 GPA or higher. Available to U.S. citizens. *Application Requirements:* Application, financial need analysis, transcript. **Deadline:** varies.

Contact United Negro College Fund. *Web site:* www.uncf.org.

Mary Marshall Practical Nursing Scholarships. Award for practical nursing students who are Virginia residents. Must attend a nursing program in Virginia. Recipient must agree to work in Virginia after graduation. Minimum 3.0 GPA required. Scholarship value and the number of scholarships granted varies annually. *Academic Fields/Career Goals:* Nursing. *Award:* Scholarship for use in freshman, sophomore, junior, or senior year; not renewable. *Award amount:* varies. *Number of awards:* varies. *Eligibility Requirements:* Applicant must be enrolled or expecting to enroll full- or part-time at a four-year institution or university; resident of Virginia and studying in Virginia. Applicant must have 3.0 GPA or higher. Available to U.S. citizens. *Application Requirements:* Application, financial need analysis, references, transcript. **Deadline:** June 30.

Contact Mrs. Aileen Harris, Healthcare Workforce Manager, Virginia Department of Health, Office of Minority Health and Public Health Policy, PO Box 2448, 109 Governor Street, Suite 1016-E, Richmond, VA 23218-2448. *E-mail:* aileen.harris@vdh.virginia.gov. *Phone:* 804-864-7435. *Fax:* 804-864-7440. *Web site:* www.vdh.state.va.us/healthpolicy/.

NRA Youth Educational Summit (YES) Scholarships. Awards for Youth Educational Summit participants based on the initial application, on-site debate, and degree of participation during the week-long event. Must be graduating high school seniors enrolled in undergraduate program. Must have a minimum GPA of 3.0. *Award:* Scholarship for use in freshman year; not renewable. *Award amount:* $1000–$10,000. *Number of awards:* 1–6. *Eligibility Requirements:* Applicant must be high school student and planning to enroll or expecting to enroll full- or part-time at a two-year, four-year, or technical institution or university. Applicant must have 3.0 GPA or higher. Available to U.S. citizens. *Application Requirements:* Application, applicant must enter a contest, essay, references, transcript. **Deadline:** March 1.

Contact Event Services Manager, National Rifle Association, 11250 Waples Mill Road, Fairfax, VA 22030. *E-mail:* fnra@nrahq.org. *Phone:* 703-267-1354. *Web site:* www.nrafoundation.org.

Nurse Practitioners/Nurse Midwife Program Scholarships. One-time award for nurse practitioner/nurse midwife students who have been residents of Virginia for at least one year. Must attend a nursing program in Virginia. Recipient must agree to work in an under-served community in Virginia following graduation. The amount of each scholarship award is dependent upon the amount of funds appropriated by the Virginia General Assembly. Minimum 3.0 GPA required. *Academic Fields/Career Goals:* Nursing. *Award:* Scholarship for use in freshman, sophomore, junior, or senior year; not renewable. *Award amount:* $450. *Number of awards:* 5. *Eligibility Requirements:* Applicant must be enrolled or expecting to enroll full- or part-time at a four-year institution or university; resident of Virginia and studying in Virginia. Applicant must have 3.0 GPA or higher. Available to U.S. citizens. *Application Requirements:* Application, financial need analysis, references, transcript. **Deadline:** June 30.

Contact Mrs. Aileen Harris, Healthcare Workforce Manager, Virginia Department of Health, Office of Minority Health and Public Health Policy, PO Box 2448, 109 Governor Street, Suite 1016-E, Richmond, VA 23218-2448. *E-mail:* aileen.harris@vdh.virginia.gov. *Phone:* 804-864-7435. *Fax:* 804-864-7440. *Web site:* www.vdh.state.va.us/healthpolicy/.

Pennsylvania State Employees Scholarship Fund. Scholarships for UNCF students from Pennsylvania. Funds may be used for tuition, room and board, books, or to repay federal student loans. Minimum 2.5 GPA required. Prospective applicants should complete the Student Profile found at Web site: http://www.uncf.org. *Award:* Scholarship for use in freshman, sophomore, junior, or senior year; not renewable. *Award amount:* up to $4000. *Number of awards:* 20. *Eligibility Requirements:* Applicant must be Black (non-Hispanic); enrolled or expecting to enroll full-time at a four-year institution or university and resident of Pennsylvania. Applicant must have 2.5 GPA or higher. Available to U.S. citizens. *Application Requirements:* Application, financial need analysis, student profile. **Deadline:** July 14.

Contact United Negro College Fund. *Web site:* www.uncf.org.

Southside Tobacco Loan Forgiveness Program. Need-based scholarship for Southside Virginia natives to pursue a degree in K-12 teacher education in any four-year U.S. institution and then return to the Southside region to live and work. Must teach in Southside Virginia public school for scholarship/loan forgiveness. *Award:* Forgivable loan for use in freshman, sophomore, junior, or senior year; not renewable. *Award amount:* up to $3750. *Number of awards:* varies. *Eligibility Requirements:* Applicant must be enrolled or expecting to enroll full- or part-time at a two-year or four-year institution or university; resident of Virginia and studying in Virginia. Available to U.S. citizens. *Application Requirements:* Application, financial need analysis. **Deadline:** varies.

Contact Ms. Nancy Breeding, Tobacco Scholarships Administrator, Virginia State Council of Higher Education, SWVA Higher Education Center, PO Box 1987, One Partnership Circle, Abingdon, VA 24212. *E-mail:* nbreeding@swcenter.edu. *Phone:* 276-619-4376. *Fax:* 276-619-4309. *Web site:* www.schev.edu.

State Department Federal Credit Union Annual Scholarship Program. Scholarships available to members who are currently enrolled in a degree program and have completed 12 credit hours of coursework at an accredited college or university. Must have own account in good standing with SDFCU, have a minimum 2.5 GPA, submit official cumulative transcripts, and describe need for financial assistance to continue their education. Scholarship only open to members of State Department Federal Credit Union. *Award:* Scholarship for use in sophomore, junior, or senior year; not renewable. *Award amount:* varies. *Number of awards:* varies. *Eligibility Requirements:* Applicant must be enrolled or expecting to enroll full-time at a four-year institution or university. Applicant must have 2.5 GPA or higher. Available to U.S. and non-U.S. citizens. *Application Requirements:* Application, applicant must enter a contest, financial need analysis, transcript, personal statement. **Deadline:** April 10.

Contact Scholarship Coordinator, State Department Federal Credit Union Annual Scholarship Program, 1630 King Street, Alexandria, VA 22314. *E-mail:* sdfcu@sdfcu.org. *Phone:* 703-706-5187. *Web site:* www.sdfcu.org.

Two-, Three-, Four-Year Army ROTC Green to Gold Scholarship Program. One-time award for selected active duty enlisted members of the Army entering college for the first time, and those who have completed 1 or 2 years of college. Must join school's ROTC program, pass physical, and APFT. U.S. citizens only. Must be at least 17 years of age by college enrollment and under 31 years of age at time of graduation. *Award:* Scholarship for use in freshman, sophomore, or junior year; not renewable. *Award amount:* $10,000–$27,000. *Number of awards:* 190–200. *Eligibility Requirements:* Applicant must be age 17-31 and enrolled or expecting to enroll full-time at a four-year institution or university. Applicant must have 2.5 GPA or higher. Available to U.S. citizens. Applicant must have served in the Army. *Application Requirements:* Application, financial need analysis, interview, photo, references, test scores, transcript. **Deadline:** April 1.

Contact Joycelyn Bryant, Military Personnel Technician Green to Gold Coordinator, Department of the Army, U.S. Army Cadet Command, 55 Patch Road, Building 56, Fort Monroe, VA 23651-1052. *E-mail:* joycelyn.bryant@usacc.army.mil. *Phone:* 757-788-3341. *Fax:* 757-788-4643. *Web site:* www.goarmy.com/rotc.

Virginia Commonwealth Award. Need-based award for undergraduate or graduate study at a Virginia public two- or four-year college, or university. Undergraduates must be Virginia residents. The application and awards process are administered by the financial aid office at the Virginia public institution where student is enrolled. Dollar value of each award varies. Contact financial aid office for application and deadlines. *Award:* Grant for use in freshman, sophomore, junior, or senior year; not renewable. *Award amount:* varies. *Number of awards:* varies. *Eligibility Requirements:* Applicant must be enrolled or expecting to enroll full- or part-time at a two-year or four-year institution or university; resident of Virginia and studying in Virginia. Available to U.S. citizens. *Application Requirements:* Financial need analysis. **Deadline:** varies.

Contact Contact the financial aid office of participating Virginia college. For additional details, visit www.schev.edu and click on Financial Aid., Virginia State Council of Higher Education. *Web site:* www.schev.edu.

Virginia Guaranteed Assistance Program. Awards to undergraduate students proportional to their need, up to full tuition, fees and book allowance. Must be a graduate of a Virginia high school, not home-schooled. High school GPA of 2.5 required. Must be enrolled full-time in a Virginia two- or four-year institution and demonstrate financial need. Must maintain minimum college GPA of 2.0 for renewal awards. *Award:* Scholarship for use in freshman, sophomore, junior, or senior year; not renewable. *Award amount:* varies. *Number of awards:* varies. *Eligibility Requirements:* Applicant must be enrolled or expecting to enroll full-time at a two-year or four-year institution or university; resident of Virginia and studying in Virginia. Applicant must have 2.5 GPA or higher. Available to U.S. citizens. *Application Requirements:* Financial need analysis, transcript. **Deadline:** varies.

Contact Contact the financial aid office of participating Virginia college. For additional details, visit www.schev.edu and click on Financial Aid., Virginia State Council of Higher Education, Contact the financial aid office of participating Virginia college. For additional details, visit www.schev.edu and click on Financial Aid. *Web site:* www.schev.edu.

Virginia Military Survivors and Dependents Education Program. Scholarships for post-secondary students between ages 16 and 19 to attend Virginia state-supported institutions. Must be child or surviving child of veteran who has either been permanently or totally disabled due to war or other armed conflict; died as a result of war or other armed conflict; or been listed as a POW or MIA. Parent must also meet Virginia residency requirements. *Award:* Scholarship for use in freshman, sophomore, junior, senior, or graduate year; renewable. *Award amount:* varies. *Number of awards:* varies. *Eligibility Requirements:* Applicant must be age 16-19; enrolled or expecting to enroll full-time at a two-year, four-year, or technical institution or university; resident of Virginia and studying in Virginia. Available to U.S. citizens. Applicant or parent must meet one or more of the following requirements: general military experience; retired from active duty; disabled or killed as a result of military service; prisoner of war; or missing in action. *Application Requirements:* Application, references. **Deadline:** varies.

Contact Doris Sullivan, Coordinator, Virginia Department of Veterans Services, Poff Federal Building, 270 Franklin Road, SW, Room 503, Roanoke, VA 24011-2215. *Phone:* 540-857-7101 Ext. 213. *Fax:* 540-857-7573. *Web site:* www.dvs.virginia.gov.

Virginia Teaching Scholarship Loan Program. Forgivable loan for Virginia resident students enrolled full- or part-time in a Virginia institution pursuing a teaching degree. The loan is forgiven if the student teaches for specified period of time. Must maintain a minimum GPA of 2.7. Must be nominated by the education department of the eligible institution. *Academic Fields/Career Goals:* Education. *Award:* Forgivable loan for use in sophomore, junior, or senior year; not renewable. *Award amount:* up to $3720. *Number of awards:* varies. *Eligibility Requirements:* Applicant must be enrolled or expecting to enroll full- or part-time at a four-year institution or university and studying in

Virginia. Available to U.S. citizens. *Application Requirements:* Application, references. **Deadline:** varies.

Contact Ms. Pat Burgess Amann, Special Education Human Resources Specialist, Virginia State Council of Higher Education, Virginia Department of Education, P.O. Box 2120, Richmond, VA 23218. *E-mail:* pat.amann@doe.virginia.gov. *Phone:* 804-225-2047. *Fax:* 804-786-6759. *Web site:* www.schev.edu.

Virginia Tuition Assistance Grant Program (Private Institutions). Renewable awards of approximately $3200 annually each for undergraduate and $1900 for graduate and first professional degree students attending an approved private, nonprofit college within Virginia. Must be a Virginia resident and be enrolled full-time. Not to be used for religious study. Information and application available from participating Virginia colleges financial aid office. *Award:* Grant for use in freshman, sophomore, junior, or senior year; renewable. *Award amount:* $1900–$3200. *Number of awards:* 22,000. *Eligibility Requirements:* Applicant must be enrolled or expecting to enroll full-time at a four-year institution or university; resident of Virginia and studying in Virginia. Available to U.S. citizens. *Application Requirements:* Application. **Deadline:** July 31.

Contact Contact the financial aid office of participating private, nonprofit Virginia, college. For additional details, visit www.schev.edu, Virginia State Council of Higher Education. *Web site:* www.schev.edu.

Walter Reed Smith Scholarship. Award for full-time female undergraduate students who are descendant of a Confederate soldier, studying nutrition, home economics, nursing, business administration, or computer science in accredited college or university. Minimum 3.0 GPA required. Submit application and letter of endorsement from sponsoring chapter of the United Daughters of the Confederacy. *Academic Fields/Career Goals:* Business/Consumer Services; Computer Science/Data Processing; Food Science/Nutrition; Home Economics; Nursing. *Award:* Scholarship for use in freshman, sophomore, junior, or senior year; renewable. *Award amount:* $800–$1000. *Number of awards:* 1–2. *Eligibility Requirements:* Applicant must be enrolled or expecting to enroll full-time at a four-year institution or university and female. Applicant or parent of applicant must be member of United Daughters of the Confederacy. Applicant must have 3.0 GPA or higher. Available to U.S. citizens. *Application Requirements:* Application, essay, financial need analysis, photo, references, self-addressed stamped envelope, transcript, copy of applicant's birth certificate, copy of confederate ancestor's proof of service. **Deadline:** March 15.

Contact United Daughters of the Confederacy. *Web site:* www.hqudc.org.

WASHINGTON

American Indian Endowed Scholarship. Awarded to financially needy undergraduate and graduate students with close social and cultural ties with a Native-American community. Must be Washington resident and enrolled full-time at Washington public or private school. Must be committed to use education to return service to the state's American Indian community. *Award:* Scholarship for use in freshman, sophomore, junior, or senior year; renewable. *Award amount:* $500–$2000. *Number of awards:* 10–20. *Eligibility Requirements:* Applicant must be American Indian/Alaska Native; enrolled or expecting to enroll full-time at a two-year, four-year, or technical institution or university; resident of Washington and studying in Washington. Available to U.S. citizens. *Application Requirements:* Application, essay, references, transcript. **Deadline:** February 1.

Contact Ann Voyles, Program Manager, Washington Council for Postsecondary Education, 917 Lakeridge Way, PO Box 43430, Olympia, WA 98504-3430. *E-mail:* annv@hecb.wa.gov. *Phone:* 360-755-7843. *Fax:* 360-704-6243. *Web site:* www.hecb.wa.gov.

Educational Opportunity Grant. Annual grants of $2500 to encourage financially needy, place-bound students to complete bachelor's degree. Must be unable to continue education due to family or work commitments, health concerns, financial needs or other similar factors. Must be Washington residents, and have completed two years of college. Grants can only be used at eligible colleges in Washington. Applications are accepted from the beginning of January through the following months until funds are depleted. *Award:* Grant for use in junior or senior year; renewable. *Award amount:* $2500. *Number of awards:* varies. *Eligibility Requirements:* Applicant must be enrolled or expecting to enroll full-time at a four-year institution; resident of Washington and studying in Washington. Available to U.S. citizens. *Application Requirements:* Application, financial need analysis. **Deadline:** continuous.

Contact Educational Opportunity Grant, Washington Council for Postsecondary Education, 917 Lakeridge Way, PO Box 43430, Olympia, WA 98504-3430. *E-mail:* eog@hecb.wa.gov. *Phone:* 888-535-0747 Ext. 6. *Fax:* 360-753-7861. *Web site:* www.hecb.wa.gov.

Future Teachers Conditional Scholarship and Loan Repayment Program. Participants must agree to teach in Washington K-12 schools in return for conditional scholarships or loan repayments. Applicants must be Washington residents, attend an eligible institution in Washington, and pursue a teaching certificate or specific additional endorsements. Select priority may or may not be available when applying. *Academic Fields/Career Goals:* Education. *Award:* Forgivable loan for use in freshman, sophomore, junior, or senior year; renewable. *Award amount:* $2675–$6200. *Number of awards:* 50. *Eligibility Requirements:* Applicant must be enrolled or expecting to enroll full- or part-time at a two-year or four-year institution or university; resident of Washington and studying in Washington. Available to U.S. citizens. *Application Requirements:* Application, essay, references, transcript, bilingual verification (if applicable). **Deadline:** October 17.

Contact Mary Knutson, Program Manager, Washington Council for Postsecondary Education, 917 Lakeridge Way, PO Box 43430, Olympia, WA 98504-3430. *E-mail:* futureteachers@hecb.wa.gov. *Phone:* 360-753-7845. *Fax:* 360-704-6245. *Web site:* www.hecb.wa.gov.

Health Professionals Scholarship Program. Program was created to attract and retain licensed primary care health professionals, to serve in critical shortage areas in Washington state. Must sign a promissory note agreeing to serve for a minimum of three years in a designated shortage area in Washington state or pay back funds at double penalty with the interest. *Academic Fields/Career Goals:* Health and Medical Sciences. *Award:* Scholarship for use in sophomore, junior, or senior year; renewable. *Award amount:* varies. *Number of awards:* 10–50. *Eligibility Requirements:* Applicant must be enrolled or expecting to enroll full- or part-time at a two-year, four-year, or technical institution or university. Available to U.S. citizens. *Application Requirements:* Application, essay, references, transcript. **Deadline:** April 30.

Contact Rochelle Wambach, Program Administrator, Washington Council for Postsecondary Education, PO Box 43430, Olympia, WA 98504-3430. *E-mail:* kathy.mcvay@doh.wa.gov. *Phone:* 360-753-7847. *Web site:* www.hecb.wa.gov.

Passport to College Promise Scholarship. Scholarship to encourage Washington residents who are former foster care youth to prepare for and succeed in college. Recipients must have spent at least one year in foster care after their 16th birthday. *Award:* Scholarship for use in freshman, sophomore, junior, or senior year; renewable. *Award amount:* $1–$6700. *Number of awards:* 1–150. *Eligibility Requirements:* Applicant must be age 18-26; enrolled or expecting to enroll full- or part-time at a two-year, four-year, or technical institution or university; resident of Washington and studying in Washington. Available to U.S. citizens. *Application Requirements:* Application, financial need analysis, consent form. **Deadline:** continuous.

Contact Ms. Dawn Cypriano-McAferty, Program Manager, Washington Council for Postsecondary Education, 917 Lakeridge Way, SW, PO Box 43430, Olympia, WA 98504-

3430. *E-mail:* passporttocollege@hecb.wa.gov. *Phone:* 888-535-0747 Ext. 5. *Fax:* 360-704-6246. *Web site:* www.hecb.wa.gov.

Washington Award for Vocational Excellence (WAVE). Award to honor vocational students from the legislative districts of Washington. Grants for up to two years of undergraduate resident tuition. Must be enrolled in Washington high school, skills center, or technical college at time of application. To be eligible to apply student must complete 360 hours in single vocational program in high school or one year at technical college. Contact principal or guidance counselor for more information. *Award:* Scholarship for use in freshman, sophomore, junior, or senior year; renewable. *Award amount:* $1–$6720. *Number of awards:* 147. *Eligibility Requirements:* Applicant must be enrolled or expecting to enroll full- or part-time at a two-year, four-year, or technical institution or university; resident of Washington and studying in Washington. Available to U.S. citizens. *Application Requirements:* Application. **Deadline:** February 16.

Contact Terri Colbert, Program Specialist, Washington Council for Postsecondary Education, Workforce Training and Education Coordinating Board, PO Box 43105, Olympia, WA 98504-3105. *E-mail:* tcolbert@wtb.wa.gov or janderson @wtb.wa.gov. *Phone:* 360-753-5680. *Fax:* 360-586-5862. *Web site:* www.hecb.wa.gov.

Washington Scholars Program. Awards high school students from the legislative districts of Washington. Must enroll in college or university in Washington. Scholarships up to four years of full-time resident undergraduate tuition and fees. Student must not be pursuing a degree in theology. Contact principal or guidance counselor for more information. Requires nomination by high school principal and be in the top 1 percent of his or her graduating senior class. *Award:* Scholarship for use in freshman, sophomore, junior, or senior year; renewable. *Award amount:* $1–$6720. *Number of awards:* 147. *Eligibility Requirements:* Applicant must be high school student; planning to enroll or expecting to enroll full- or part-time at a two-year or four-year institution or university; resident of Washington and studying in Washington. Available to U.S. citizens. *Application Requirements:* Application. **Deadline:** January 1.

Contact Ann Voyles, Program Manager, Washington Council for Postsecondary Education, 917 Lakeridge Way, PO Box 43430, Olympia, WA 98504-3430. *E-mail:* annv@hecb.wa.gov. *Phone:* 360-753-7843. *Fax:* 360-704-6243. *Web site:* www.hecb.wa.gov.

Washington State Need Grant Program. The program helps Washington's lowest-income undergraduate students to pursue degrees, hone skills, or retrain for new careers. Students with family incomes equal to or less than 50 percent of the state median are eligible for up to 100 percent of the maximum grant. Students with family incomes between 51 percent and 65 percent of the state median are eligible for up to 75 percent of the maximum grant. Students with family incomes up to 70 percent are eligible for 50 percent of the maximum grant. *Award:* Grant for use in freshman, sophomore, junior, or senior year; not renewable. *Award amount:* $106–$6234. *Number of awards:* 71,233. *Eligibility Requirements:* Applicant must be enrolled or expecting to enroll full- or part-time at a two-year, four-year, or technical institution or university; resident of Washington and studying in Washington. Available to U.S. citizens. *Application Requirements:* Application, financial need analysis, FAFSA. **Deadline:** continuous.

Contact Program Manager, Washington Council for Postsecondary Education. *E-mail:* finaid@hecb.wa.gov. *Web site:* www.hecb.wa.gov.

WEST VIRGINIA

Robert C. Byrd Honors Scholarship-West Virginia. Award for West Virginia residents who have demonstrated outstanding academic achievement. Must be a graduating high school senior. May apply for renewal consideration for a total of four years of assistance. For full-time study only. *Award:* Scholarship for use in freshman year; renewable. *Award amount:* $1500. *Number of awards:* 36. *Eligibility Requirements:* Applicant must be high school student; planning to enroll or expecting to enroll full-time at a two-year, four-year, or technical institution or university and resident of West Virginia. Applicant must have 3.0 GPA or higher. Available to U.S. citizens. *Application Requirements:* Application, test scores, transcript, letter of acceptance from a college/university. **Deadline:** March 1.

Contact Darlene Elmore, Scholarship Coordinator, West Virginia Higher Education Policy Commission-Student Services, 1018 Kanawha Boulevard, East, Suite 700, Charleston, WV 25301. *E-mail:* elmore@hepc.wvnet.edu. *Phone:* 304-558-4618 Ext. 278. *Fax:* 304-558-4622. *Web site:* wvhepcnew.wvnet.edu/.

Underwood-Smith Teacher Scholarship Program. Award for West Virginia residents at West Virginia institutions pursuing teaching careers. Must have a 3.5 GPA after completion of two years of course work. Must teach two years in West Virginia public schools for each year the award is received. Recipients will be required to sign an agreement acknowledging an understanding of the program's requirements and their willingness to repay the award if appropriate teaching service is not rendered. *Academic Fields/Career Goals:* Education. *Award:* Scholarship for use in junior or senior year; renewable. *Award amount:* $1620–$5000. *Number of awards:* 53–60. *Eligibility Requirements:* Applicant must be enrolled or expecting to enroll full-time at a four-year institution or university; resident of West Virginia and studying in West Virginia. Applicant must have 3.0 GPA or higher. Available to U.S. citizens. *Application Requirements:* Application, essay, references. **Deadline:** March 1.

Contact Darlene Elmore, Scholarship Coordinator, West Virginia Higher Education Policy Commission-Student Services, 1018 Kanawha Boulevard, East, Suite 700, Charleston, WV 25301. *E-mail:* elmore@hepc.wvnet.edu. *Phone:* 304-558-4618 Ext. 278. *Fax:* 304-558-4622. *Web site:* wvhepcnew.wvnet.edu/.

West Virginia Engineering, Science and Technology Scholarship Program. Award for full-time students attending West Virginia institutions, pursuing a degree in engineering, science, or technology. Must be a resident of West Virginia. Must have a 3.0 GPA, and after graduation, must work in the fields of engineering, science, or technology in West Virginia one year for each year the award was received. *Academic Fields/Career Goals:* Electrical Engineering/Electronics; Engineering/Technology; Engineering-Related Technologies; Science, Technology, and Society. *Award:* Scholarship for use in freshman, sophomore, junior, or senior year; renewable. *Award amount:* $1500–$3000. *Number of awards:* 200–300. *Eligibility Requirements:* Applicant must be enrolled or expecting to enroll full-time at a two-year, four-year, or technical institution or university; resident of West Virginia and studying in West Virginia. Applicant must have 3.0 GPA or higher. Available to U.S. citizens. *Application Requirements:* Application, essay, test scores, transcript. **Deadline:** March 1.

Contact West Virginia Higher Education Policy Commission-Student Services. *Web site:* wvhepcnew.wvnet.edu/.

West Virginia Higher Education Grant Program. Award available for West Virginia resident for one year immediately preceding the date of application, high school graduate or the equivalent, demonstrate financial need, and enroll as a full-time undergraduate at an approved university or college located in West Virginia or Pennsylvania. *Award:* Grant for use in freshman year; not renewable. *Award amount:* $375–$3542. *Number of awards:* 10,755–11,000. *Eligibility Requirements:* Applicant must be high school student; planning to enroll or expecting to enroll full-time at a four-year institution or university; resident of West Virginia and studying in Pennsylvania or West Virginia. Available to U.S. citizens. *Application Requirements:* Application, financial need analysis, references, test scores, transcript. **Deadline:** March 1.

Contact Judy Smith, Senior Project Coordinator, West Virginia Higher Education

Policy Commission-Student Services, 1018 Kanawha Boulevard East, Suite 700, Charleston, WV 25301-2827. *E-mail:* kee@hepc.wvnet.edu. *Phone:* 304-558-4618. *Fax:* 304-558-4622. *Web site:* wvhepcnew.wvnet.edu/.

WISCONSIN

Handicapped Student Grant-Wisconsin. One-time award available to residents of Wisconsin who have severe or profound hearing or visual impairment. Must be enrolled at least half-time at a nonprofit institution. If the handicap prevents the student from attending a Wisconsin school, the award may be used out-of-state in a specialized college. Refer to Web site for further details: http://www.heab.state.wi.us. *Award:* Grant for use in freshman, sophomore, junior, or senior year; not renewable. *Award amount:* $250–$1800. *Number of awards:* varies. *Eligibility Requirements:* Applicant must be enrolled or expecting to enroll full- or part-time at a four-year institution or university and resident of Wisconsin. Applicant must be hearing impaired or visually impaired. Available to U.S. citizens. *Application Requirements:* Application, financial need analysis. **Deadline:** continuous.

Contact Sandy Thomas, Program Coordinator, Wisconsin Higher Educational Aid Board, PO Box 7885, Madison, WI 53707-7885. *E-mail:* sandy.thomas@wi.gov. *Phone:* 608-266-0888. *Fax:* 608-267-2808. *Web site:* www.heab.wi.gov.

Menominee Indian Tribe Adult Vocational Training Program. Renewable award for enrolled Menominee tribal members to use at vocational or technical schools. Must be at least 1/4 Menominee and show proof of Indian blood. Must complete financial aid form. Deadlines: March 1 and November 1. *Award:* Grant for use in freshman or sophomore year; renewable. *Award amount:* $100–$2200. *Number of awards:* 50–70. *Eligibility Requirements:* Applicant must be American Indian/Alaska Native and enrolled or expecting to enroll full- or part-time at a technical institution. Available to U.S. citizens. *Application Requirements:* Application, financial need analysis, proof of Indian blood. **Deadline:** varies.

Contact Virginia Nuske, Education Director, Menominee Indian Tribe of Wisconsin, PO Box 910, Keshena, WI 54135. *E-mail:* vnuske@mitw.org. *Phone:* 715-799-5110. *Fax:* 715-799-5102. *Web site:* www.menominee-nsn.gov.

Menominee Indian Tribe of Wisconsin Higher Education Grants. Renewable award for enrolled Menominee tribal member to use at a two- or four-year college or university. Must be at least 1/4 Menominee and show proof of Indian blood. Must complete financial aid form. *Award:* Grant for use in freshman, sophomore, junior, or senior year; renewable. *Award amount:* $100–$2200. *Number of awards:* 136. *Eligibility Requirements:* Applicant must be American Indian/Alaska Native and enrolled or expecting to enroll full- or part-time at a two-year or four-year institution or university. Available to U.S. citizens. *Application Requirements:* Application, financial need analysis, proof of Indian blood. **Deadline:** continuous.

Contact Virginia Nuske, Education Director, Menominee Indian Tribe of Wisconsin, PO Box 910, Keshena, WI 54135. *E-mail:* vnuske@mitw.org. *Phone:* 715-799-5110. *Fax:* 715-799-5102. *Web site:* www.menominee-nsn.gov.

Minority Undergraduate Retention Grant-Wisconsin. The grant provides financial assistance to African-American, Native-American, Hispanic, and former citizens of Laos, Vietnam, and Cambodia, for study in Wisconsin. Must be Wisconsin resident, enrolled at least half-time in Wisconsin Technical College System schools, non-profit independent colleges and universities, and tribal colleges. Refer to Web site for further details: http://www.heab.state.wi.us. *Award:* Grant for use in sophomore, junior, or senior year; not renewable. *Award amount:* $250–$2500. *Number of awards:* varies. *Eligibility Requirements:* Applicant must be American Indian/Alaska Native, Asian/Pacific Islander, Black (non-Hispanic), or Hispanic; enrolled or expecting to enroll full- or part-time at a two-year, four-year, or technical institution or university; resident of Wisconsin and studying in Wisconsin. Available to U.S. and non-U.S. citizens. *Application Requirements:* Application, financial need analysis. **Deadline:** continuous.

Contact Mary Lou Kuzdas, Program Coordinator, Wisconsin Higher Educational Aid Board, PO Box 7885, Madison, WI 53707-7885. *E-mail:* mary.kuzdas@wi.gov. *Phone:* 608-267-2212. *Fax:* 608-267-2808. *Web site:* www.heab.wi.gov.

Talent Incentive Program Grant. Grant assists residents of Wisconsin who are attending a nonprofit institution in Wisconsin, and who have substantial financial need. Must meet income criteria, be considered economically and educationally disadvantaged, and be enrolled at least half-time. Refer to Web site for further details: http://www.heab.state.wi.us. *Award:* Grant for use in freshman, sophomore, junior, or senior year; renewable. *Award amount:* $250–$1800. *Number of awards:* varies. *Eligibility Requirements:* Applicant must be enrolled or expecting to enroll full- or part-time at a two-year, four-year, or technical institution or university; resident of Wisconsin and studying in Wisconsin. Available to U.S. citizens. *Application Requirements:* Application, financial need analysis, nomination by financial aid office. **Deadline:** continuous.

Contact Colette Brown, Program Coordinator, Wisconsin Higher Educational Aid Board, PO Box 7885, Madison, WI 53707-7885. *E-mail:* colette.brown@wi.gov. *Phone:* 608-266-1665. *Fax:* 608-267-2808. *Web site:* www.heab.wi.gov.

Veterans Education (VetEd) Reimbursement Grant. Open only to Wisconsin veterans enrolled at approved schools for undergraduate study. Benefit is based on length of time serving on active duty in the armed forces (active duty for training does not apply). Pre-application due no later than 180 days after the start of semester. Application deadline no later than 60 days after the course completion. Veterans may be reimbursed up to 100 percent of tuition and fees at UW—Madison rate for the same number of credits. *Award:* Grant for use in freshman, sophomore, junior, or senior year; renewable. *Award amount:* up to $3594. *Number of awards:* varies. *Eligibility Requirements:* Applicant must be enrolled or expecting to enroll full- or part-time at a two-year, four-year, or technical institution or university; resident of Wisconsin and studying in Minnesota or Wisconsin. Available to U.S. citizens. Applicant or parent must meet one or more of the following requirements: Air Force, Army, Coast Guard, Marine Corps, or Navy experience; retired from active duty; disabled or killed as a result of military service; prisoner of war; or missing in action. *Application Requirements:* Application, pre-application. **Deadline:** varies.

Contact Ms. Leslie Busby-Amegashie, Analyst, Wisconsin Department of Veterans Affairs, PO Box 7843, Madison, WI 53707-7843. *E-mail:* leslie.busby-amegashie@dva.state.wi.us. *Phone:* 800-947-8387. *Web site:* www.dva.state.wi.us.

Wisconsin Academic Excellence Scholarship. Renewable award for high school seniors with the highest GPA in graduating class. Must be a Wisconsin resident attending a nonprofit Wisconsin institution full-time. Scholarship value is $2250 toward tuition each year for up to four years. Must maintain 3.0 GPA for renewal. Refer to your high school counselor for more details. *Award:* Scholarship for use in freshman year; renewable. *Award amount:* up to $2250. *Number of awards:* varies. *Eligibility Requirements:* Applicant must be high school student; planning to enroll or expecting to enroll full-time at a two-year, four-year, or technical institution or university; resident of Wisconsin and studying in Wisconsin. Applicant must have 3.0 GPA or higher. Available to U.S. citizens. *Application Requirements:* Application, test scores, transcript. **Deadline:** continuous.

Contact Nancy Wilkison, Program Coordinator, Wisconsin Higher Educational Aid Board, PO Box 7885, Madison, WI 53707-7885. *E-mail:* nancy.wilkison@wi.gov. *Phone:* 608-267-2213. *Fax:* 608-267-2808. *Web site:* www.heab.wi.gov.

Wisconsin Higher Education Grants (WHEG). Grants for residents of Wisconsin enrolled at least half-time in degree or certificate programs at a University of Wisconsin Institution, Wisconsin Technical College or an approved Tribal College . Must show financial need. Refer to Web site for further details: http://www.heab.wi.gov. *Award:* Grant for use in freshman, sophomore, junior, or senior year; not renewable. *Award amount:* $250–$3000. *Number of awards:* varies. *Eligibility Requirements:* Applicant must be enrolled or expecting to enroll full- or part-time at a two-year, four-year, or technical institution or university; resident of Wisconsin and studying in Wisconsin. Available to U.S. citizens. *Application Requirements:* Application, financial need analysis. **Deadline:** continuous.

Contact Sandra Thomas, Program Coordinator, Wisconsin Higher Educational Aid Board, PO Box 7885, Madison, WI 53707-7885. *E-mail:* sandy.thomas@heab.state.wi.us. *Phone:* 608-266-0888. *Fax:* 608-267-2808. *Web site:* www.heab.wi.gov.

Wisconsin League for Nursing Inc., Scholarship. One-time award for Wisconsin residents who have completed half of an accredited Wisconsin school of nursing program. Financial need of student must be demonstrated. Scholarship applications are mailed by WLN office ONLY to Wisconsin nursing schools in January for distribution to students. Students interested in obtaining an application must contact their nursing school and submit completed applications to their school. Applications sent directly to WLN office will be returned to applicant. For further information visit Web site: http://www.wisconsinwln.org/Scholarships.htm. *Academic Fields/Career Goals:* Nursing. *Award:* Scholarship for use in junior or senior year; not renewable. *Award amount:* $500–$1000. *Number of awards:* 11–35. *Eligibility Requirements:* Applicant must be enrolled or expecting to enroll full-time at a two-year, four-year, or technical institution or university; resident of Wisconsin and studying in Wisconsin. Available to U.S. citizens. *Application Requirements:* Application, essay, financial need analysis. **Deadline:** March 1.

Contact Wisconsin League for Nursing, Inc. *Web site:* www.wisconsinwln.org.

Wisconsin Native American/Indian Student Assistance Grant. Grants for Wisconsin residents who are at least one-quarter American Indian. Must be attending a college or university within the state. Refer to Web site for further details: http://www.heab.state.wi.us. *Award:* Grant for use in freshman, sophomore, junior, or senior year; not renewable. *Award amount:* $250–$1100. *Number of awards:* varies. *Eligibility Requirements:* Applicant must be American Indian/Alaska Native; enrolled or expecting to enroll full- or part-time at a two-year, four-year, or technical institution or university; resident of Wisconsin and studying in Wisconsin. Available to U.S. citizens. *Application Requirements:* Application, financial need analysis. **Deadline:** continuous.

Contact Sandra Thomas, Program Coordinator, Wisconsin Higher Educational Aid Board, PO Box 7885, Madison, WI 53707-7885. *E-mail:* sandy.thomas@wi.gov. *Phone:* 608-266-0888. *Fax:* 608-267-2808. *Web site:* www.heab.wi.gov.

WYOMING

Douvas Memorial Scholarship. Available to Wyoming residents who are first-generation Americans. Must be between 18 and 22 years old. Must be used at any Wyoming public institution of higher education for study in freshman year. *Award:* Scholarship for use in freshman year; not renewable. *Award amount:* $500. *Number of awards:* 1. *Eligibility Requirements:* Applicant must be age 18-22; enrolled or expecting to enroll full- or part-time at a two-year or four-year institution or university; resident of Wyoming and studying in Wyoming. Available to U.S. citizens. *Application Requirements:* Application. **Deadline:** March 24.

Contact Gerry Maas, Director, Health and Safety, Wyoming Department of Education, 2300 Capitol Avenue, Hathaway Building, 2nd Floor, Cheyenne, WY 82002-0050. *E-mail:* gmaas@educ.state.wy.us. *Phone:* 307-777-6282. *Fax:* 307-777-6234.

Hathaway Scholarship. Scholarship for Wyoming students to pursue postsecondary education within the state. Award ranges from $1000 to $1600. Deadline varies. *Award:* Scholarship for use in freshman, sophomore, junior, or senior year; not renewable. *Award amount:* $1000–$1600. *Number of awards:* 1. *Eligibility Requirements:* Applicant must be enrolled or expecting to enroll full-time at a two-year or four-year institution or university; resident of Wyoming and studying in Wyoming. Available to U.S. citizens. *Application Requirements:* Application. **Deadline:** varies.

Contact Kay Post, Director, Wyoming Department of Education, 2020 Grand Avenue, Suite 500, Laramie, WY 82070. *E-mail:* kpost@educ.state.wy.us. *Phone:* 307-777-5599.

Superior Student in Education Scholarship-Wyoming. Scholarship available each year to sixteen new Wyoming high school graduates who plan to teach in Wyoming. The award covers costs of undergraduate tuition at the University of Wyoming or any Wyoming community college. *Academic Fields/Career Goals:* Education. *Award:* Scholarship for use in freshman year; renewable. *Award amount:* varies. *Number of awards:* 16. *Eligibility Requirements:* Applicant must be high school student; planning to enroll or expecting to enroll full-time at a four-year institution or university; resident of Wyoming and studying in Wyoming. Applicant must have 3.0 GPA or higher. Available to U.S. citizens. *Application Requirements:* Application, references, test scores, transcript. **Deadline:** October 31.

Contact Tammy Mack, Assistant Director, Scholarships, State of Wyoming, Administered by University of Wyoming, Student Financial Aid Department 3335, 1000 East University Avenue, Laramie, WY 82071-3335. *E-mail:* finaid@uwyo.edu. *Phone:* 307-766-2117. *Fax:* 307-766-3800. *Web site:* www.uwyo.edu/scholarships.

Vietnam Veterans Award-Wyoming. Scholarship available to Wyoming residents who served in the armed forces between August 5, 1964 and May 7, 1975, and received a Vietnam service medal. *Award:* Scholarship for use in freshman, sophomore, junior, or senior year; renewable. *Award amount:* varies. *Number of awards:* varies. *Eligibility Requirements:* Applicant must be enrolled or expecting to enroll full- or part-time at a two-year or four-year institution or university and resident of Wyoming. Available to U.S. citizens. Applicant or parent must meet one or more of the following requirements: general military experience; retired from active duty; disabled or killed as a result of military service; prisoner of war; or missing in action. *Application Requirements:* Application. **Deadline:** continuous.

Contact Tammy Mack, Assistant Director, Scholarships, State of Wyoming, Administered by University of Wyoming, Student Financial Aid Department 3335, 1000 East University Avenue, Laramie, WY 82071-3335. *E-mail:* finaid@uwyo.edu. *Phone:* 307-766-2117. *Fax:* 307-766-3800. *Web site:* www.uwyo.edu/scholarships.

Indexes

Non-Need Scholarships for Undergraduates

Academic Interests/ Achievements

Agriculture

Abilene Christian University, TX
Angelo State University, TX
Arkansas State University, AR
Auburn University, AL
Austin Peay State University, TN
Berry College, GA
California Polytechnic State University, San Luis Obispo, CA
California State Polytechnic University, Pomona, CA
California State University, Bakersfield, CA
California State University, Chico, CA
California State University, Fresno, CA
California State University, Stanislaus, CA
Clemson University, SC
Dordt College, IA
Eastern Michigan University, MI
Ferris State University, MI
Fort Lewis College, CO
Fort Valley State University, GA
Illinois State University, IL
Iowa State University of Science and Technology, IA
Langston University, OK
Lincoln University, MO
Louisiana State University and Agricultural and Mechanical College, LA
Louisiana Tech University, LA
Lubbock Christian University, TX
Michigan State University, MI
Midway College, KY
Mississippi State University, MS
Montana State University, MT
Murray State University, KY
New Mexico State University, NM
North Carolina State University, NC
North Dakota State University, ND
Northwestern Oklahoma State University, OK
Northwest Missouri State University, MO
The Ohio State University, OH
Oklahoma Panhandle State University, OK
Oklahoma State University, OK
Post University, CT
Purdue University, IN
Sam Houston State University, TX
South Dakota State University, SD
Southeast Missouri State University, MO
Southern Arkansas University–Magnolia, AR
Southern Illinois University Carbondale, IL
Southwest Minnesota State University, MN
State University of New York College of Environmental Science and Forestry, NY
Stephen F. Austin State University, TX
Tennessee Technological University, TN
Texas A&M University, TX
Texas A&M University–Commerce, TX
Texas Christian University, TX
Texas State University–San Marcos, TX
Texas Tech University, TX
The University of Arizona, AZ
University of California, Davis, CA
University of California, Riverside, CA
University of Central Missouri, MO
University of Connecticut, CT
University of Delaware, DE
University of Florida, FL
University of Georgia, GA
University of Guam, GU
University of Idaho, ID
University of Illinois at Urbana–Champaign, IL
University of Kentucky, KY
University of Louisiana at Monroe, LA
University of Maryland, College Park, MD
University of Maryland Eastern Shore, MD
University of Massachusetts Amherst, MA
University of Minnesota, Twin Cities Campus, MN
University of Missouri–Columbia, MO
University of Nebraska–Lincoln, NE
University of New Hampshire, NH
The University of Tennessee, TN
The University of Tennessee at Martin, TN
The University of Texas at San Antonio, TX
University of Vermont, VT
The University of Virginia's College at Wise, VA
University of Wisconsin–Stevens Point, WI
University of Wyoming, WY
Utah State University, UT
Vermont Technical College, VT
Washington State University, WA
Western Illinois University, IL
Western Kentucky University, KY
West Virginia University, WV

Architecture

Arizona State University, AZ
Auburn University, AL
Ball State University, IN
Boston Architectural College, MA
California College of the Arts, CA
California Polytechnic State University, San Luis Obispo, CA
California State Polytechnic University, Pomona, CA
California State University, Bakersfield, CA
City College of the City University of New York, NY
Clemson University, SC
Cooper Union for the Advancement of Science and Art, NY
Drury University, MO
Eastern Michigan University, MI
Ferris State University, MI
Georgia Institute of Technology, GA
Illinois Institute of Technology, IL
Iowa State University of Science and Technology, IA
James Madison University, VA
Kent State University, OH
Lawrence Technological University, MI
Louisiana State University and Agricultural and Mechanical College, LA
Louisiana Tech University, LA
Miami University, OH
Michigan State University, MI
Mississippi State University, MS
Montana State University, MT
New Jersey Institute of Technology, NJ
North Dakota State University, ND
The Ohio State University, OH
Oklahoma State University, OK
Portland State University, OR
Robert Morris College, IL
Savannah College of Art and Design, GA
Southern Illinois University Carbondale, IL
State University of New York College of Environmental Science and Forestry, NY
Texas A&M University, TX
Texas Tech University, TX
The University of Arizona, AZ
University of Colorado at Boulder, CO
University of Florida, FL
University of Idaho, ID
University of Illinois at Chicago, IL
University of Illinois at Urbana–Champaign, IL
The University of Kansas, KS
University of Kentucky, KY
University of Maryland, College Park, MD
University of Massachusetts Amherst, MA
University of Miami, FL
University of Michigan, MI
University of Minnesota, Twin Cities Campus, MN
University of Nebraska–Lincoln, NE
University of Nevada, Las Vegas, NV
University of Oklahoma, OK
University of Oregon, OR
University of South Florida, FL
The University of Tennessee, TN
The University of Texas at Arlington, TX
The University of Texas at San Antonio, TX
University of Utah, UT
University of Washington, WA
University of Wisconsin–Stevens Point, WI

Utah State University, UT
Washington State University, WA
Washington University in St. Louis, MO
West Virginia University, WV
Woodbury University, CA

Area/Ethnic Studies

Arizona State University, AZ
Arkansas State University, AR
Birmingham-Southern College, AL
California State University, Chico, CA
California State University, Fresno, CA
California State University, Stanislaus, CA
City College of the City University of New York, NY
The College of New Rochelle, NY
Eastern Washington University, WA
Fort Lewis College, CO
Furman University, SC
Hope International University, CA
Indiana University of Pennsylvania, PA
Iowa State University of Science and Technology, IA
Kent State University, OH
Marian College, IN
Mississippi State University, MS
Montana State University, MT
Northern Arizona University, AZ
Oakland University, MI
The Ohio State University, OH
Ohio University, OH
Ohio University–Chillicothe, OH
Ohio University–Eastern, OH
Ohio University–Lancaster, OH
Ohio University–Southern Campus, OH
Ohio University–Zanesville, OH
Oklahoma State University, OK
Ouachita Baptist University, AR
Portland State University, OR
Purchase College, State University of New York, NY
The Richard Stockton College of New Jersey, NJ
Saint Louis University, MO
San Diego State University, CA
Sonoma State University, CA
South Dakota State University, SD
Southern Illinois University Carbondale, IL
State University of New York at Binghamton, NY
State University of New York at Oswego, NY
State University of New York at Plattsburgh, NY
State University of New York College at Geneseo, NY
Stetson University, FL
Stony Brook University, State University of New York, NY
The University of Alabama, AL
University of California, Davis, CA
University of California, Riverside, CA
University of Central Missouri, MO
University of Colorado at Boulder, CO
University of Illinois at Urbana–Champaign, IL
The University of Kansas, KS
University of Kentucky, KY
University of Miami, FL
University of Michigan, MI
University of Minnesota, Twin Cities Campus, MN
University of Oklahoma, OK
University of South Carolina, SC
The University of Texas at San Antonio, TX
University of Utah, UT
University of Vermont, VT
University of Wisconsin–Green Bay, WI
University of Wisconsin–La Crosse, WI
Washington State University, WA
Wayne State University, MI
West Virginia University, WV
Wichita State University, KS
Wright State University, OH

Biological Sciences

Abilene Christian University, TX
Alaska Pacific University, AK
Albertus Magnus College, CT
Alderson-Broaddus College, WV
Alfred University, NY
Angelo State University, TX
Arizona State University, AZ
Arkansas State University, AR
Auburn University, AL
Augsburg College, MN
Augustana College, IL
Augustana College, SD
Augusta State University, GA
Austin College, TX
Austin Peay State University, TN
Averett University, VA
Avila University, MO
Bard College, NY
Barton College, NC
Belhaven College, MS
Bellarmine University, KY
Bethel College, IN
Biola University, CA
Birmingham-Southern College, AL
Black Hills State University, SD
Bloomfield College, NJ
Bloomsburg University of Pennsylvania, PA
Boise State University, ID
Bowling Green State University, OH
Brenau University, GA
Brevard College, NC
Bryan College, TN
Buena Vista University, IA
Butler University, IN
California Polytechnic State University, San Luis Obispo, CA
California State Polytechnic University, Pomona, CA
California State University, Bakersfield, CA
California State University, Chico, CA
California State University, Fresno, CA
California State University, Los Angeles, CA
California State University, San Bernardino, CA
California State University, Stanislaus, CA
Calvin College, MI
Campbellsville University, KY
Carroll University, WI
Carson-Newman College, TN
Case Western Reserve University, OH
Centenary College of Louisiana, LA
Central College, IA
Central Methodist University, MO
Central Michigan University, MI
Chapman University, CA
Chatham University, PA
Christopher Newport University, VA
City College of the City University of New York, NY
Clarkson University, NY
Clemson University, SC
Coastal Carolina University, SC
Coe College, IA
The College at Brockport, State University of New York, NY
College of Charleston, SC
The College of Idaho, ID
The College of New Rochelle, NY
College of Saint Mary, NE
College of Staten Island of the City University of New York, NY
The Colorado College, CO
Colorado State University–Pueblo, CO
Columbia College, MO
Columbus State University, GA
Concordia University Chicago, IL
Concordia University, Nebraska, NE
Concordia University Texas, TX
Dalton State College, GA
Dana College, NE
Davidson College, NC
Defiance College, OH
Delta State University, MS
DePauw University, IN
DeSales University, PA
Dordt College, IA
Drury University, MO
D'Youville College, NY
Eastern Michigan University, MI
Eastern Washington University, WA
East Tennessee State University, TN
East Texas Baptist University, TX
Edinboro University of Pennsylvania, PA
Elizabethtown College, PA
Elmhurst College, IL
Elon University, NC
Emporia State University, KS
Fairfield University, CT
Ferris State University, MI
Florida Gulf Coast University, FL
Florida International University, FL
Fordham University, NY
Fort Lewis College, CO
Francis Marion University, SC
Frostburg State University, MD
Furman University, SC
Gannon University, PA
Gardner-Webb University, NC
George Fox University, OR
Georgia Institute of Technology, GA
Georgian Court University, NJ
Georgia Southern University, GA
Glenville State College, WV
Green Mountain College, VT
Grove City College, PA
Guilford College, NC
Hamline University, MN
Hardin-Simmons University, TX
Hawai'i Pacific University, HI
Henderson State University, AR
Howard Payne University, TX
Huntingdon College, AL
Huntington University, IN
Idaho State University, ID
Illinois State University, IL
Indiana University of Pennsylvania, PA
Iowa State University of Science and Technology, IA
Jacksonville State University, AL
James Madison University, VA
John Carroll University, OH
Judson College, AL
Juniata College, PA
Kennesaw State University, GA

Non-Need Scholarships for Undergraduates
Academic Interests/Achievements

Kent State University, OH
King's College, PA
Kutztown University of Pennsylvania, PA
LaGrange College, GA
Lake Forest College, IL
Lebanon Valley College, PA
Lees-McRae College, NC
Lee University, TN
Lewis-Clark State College, ID
Limestone College, SC
Lincoln University, PA
Lindenwood University, MO
Lindsey Wilson College, KY
Lipscomb University, TN
Lock Haven University of Pennsylvania, PA
Long Island University, C.W. Post Campus, NY
Longwood University, VA
Louisiana State University and Agricultural and Mechanical College, LA
Louisiana Tech University, LA
Lycoming College, PA
MacMurray College, IL
Maine Maritime Academy, ME
Malone University, OH
Manhattan College, NY
Marquette University, WI
Marymount University, VA
Maryville University of Saint Louis, MO
Massachusetts College of Liberal Arts, MA
The Master's College and Seminary, CA
Mayville State University, ND
McKendree University, IL
McMurry University, TX
Mercer University, GA
Mesa State College, CO
Michigan State University, MI
Midland Lutheran College, NE
Millersville University of Pennsylvania, PA
Millikin University, IL
Mills College, CA
Mississippi State University, MS
Mississippi University for Women, MS
Missouri University of Science and Technology, MO
Missouri Valley College, MO
Missouri Western State University, MO
Molloy College, NY
Montana State University, MT
Montana State University–Billings, MT
Montclair State University, NJ
Murray State University, KY
Muskingum College, OH
Newberry College, SC
New England College, NH
New Jersey Institute of Technology, NJ
New Mexico State University, NM
North Carolina State University, NC
North Central College, IL
North Dakota State University, ND
Northeastern State University, OK
Northern Arizona University, AZ
Northern Illinois University, IL
Northern Michigan University, MI
Northern State University, SD
North Greenville University, SC
Northwestern Oklahoma State University, OK
Northwestern State University of Louisiana, LA
Northwest Missouri State University, MO
Oakland University, MI
Ohio Northern University, OH
The Ohio State University, OH
Ohio University, OH
Ohio University–Chillicothe, OH
Ohio University–Eastern, OH
Ohio University–Lancaster, OH
Ohio University–Southern Campus, OH
Ohio University–Zanesville, OH
Oklahoma Panhandle State University, OK
Oklahoma State University, OK
Oklahoma Wesleyan University, OK
Old Dominion University, VA
Oral Roberts University, OK
Ouachita Baptist University, AR
Pace University, NY
Pacific University, OR
Piedmont College, GA
Pittsburg State University, KS
Point Loma Nazarene University, CA
Post University, CT
Purchase College, State University of New York, NY
Randolph College, VA
The Richard Stockton College of New Jersey, NJ
Ripon College, WI
Rivier College, NH
Rochester Institute of Technology, NY
Rockford College, IL
Rockhurst University, MO
Sacred Heart University, CT
Saginaw Valley State University, MI
St. Cloud State University, MN
St. Edward's University, TX
St. John Fisher College, NY
St. John's University, NY
Saint Louis University, MO
Salisbury University, MD
Sam Houston State University, TX
San Diego State University, CA
Schreiner University, TX
Seton Hill University, PA
Shepherd University, WV
Shippensburg University of Pennsylvania, PA
Skidmore College, NY
Slippery Rock University of Pennsylvania, PA
Sonoma State University, CA
South Dakota State University, SD
Southeastern Louisiana University, LA
Southeastern Oklahoma State University, OK
Southeast Missouri State University, MO
Southern Illinois University Carbondale, IL
Southern Nazarene University, OK
Southern Oregon University, OR
Southwestern College, KS
Southwestern Oklahoma State University, OK
Southwest Minnesota State University, MN
State University of New York at Binghamton, NY
State University of New York at Fredonia, NY
State University of New York at New Paltz, NY
State University of New York at Oswego, NY
State University of New York at Plattsburgh, NY
State University of New York College at Geneseo, NY
State University of New York College at Old Westbury, NY
State University of New York College at Oneonta, NY
State University of New York College at Potsdam, NY
State University of New York College of Environmental Science and Forestry, NY
Stephen F. Austin State University, TX
Stetson University, FL
Stony Brook University, State University of New York, NY
Tabor College, KS
Tennessee Technological University, TN
Texas A&M University, TX
Texas Christian University, TX
Texas Lutheran University, TX
Texas Tech University, TX
Thiel College, PA
Towson University, MD
Trevecca Nazarene University, TN
Truman State University, MO
The University of Akron, OH
The University of Alabama, AL
University of Alaska Fairbanks, AK
The University of Arizona, AZ
University of California, Davis, CA
University of California, Irvine, CA
University of California, Riverside, CA
University of California, San Diego, CA
University of Central Missouri, MO
University of Central Oklahoma, OK
University of Colorado at Boulder, CO
University of Colorado at Colorado Springs, CO
University of Connecticut, CT
University of Delaware, DE
University of Evansville, IN
University of Houston–Clear Lake, TX
University of Houston–Victoria, TX
University of Idaho, ID
University of Illinois at Urbana–Champaign, IL
The University of Kansas, KS
University of Kentucky, KY
University of Louisiana at Monroe, LA
The University of Maine at Augusta, ME
University of Maine at Fort Kent, ME
University of Mary Hardin-Baylor, TX
University of Maryland, Baltimore County, MD
University of Maryland, College Park, MD
University of Massachusetts Amherst, MA
University of Memphis, TN
University of Miami, FL
University of Michigan, MI
University of Michigan–Dearborn, MI
University of Michigan–Flint, MI
University of Minnesota, Twin Cities Campus, MN
University of Mississippi, MS
University of Missouri–Columbia, MO
University of Missouri–St. Louis, MO
The University of Montana, MT
The University of Montana Western, MT
University of Montevallo, AL
University of Nebraska at Omaha, NE
University of Nebraska–Lincoln, NE
University of Nevada, Las Vegas, NV
University of New England, ME
The University of North Carolina at Asheville, NC
The University of North Carolina at Greensboro, NC
The University of North Carolina Wilmington, NC
University of North Dakota, ND
University of Northern Colorado, CO
University of Northern Iowa, IA
University of Oklahoma, OK
University of Oregon, OR

University of Pittsburgh at Bradford, PA
University of Pittsburgh at Johnstown, PA
University of Portland, OR
University of Puget Sound, WA
University of Richmond, VA
University of St. Thomas, MN
University of South Carolina, SC
University of South Carolina Aiken, SC
The University of South Dakota, SD
University of Southern Indiana, IN
University of South Florida, FL
The University of Tampa, FL
The University of Tennessee at Martin, TN
The University of Texas at Arlington, TX
The University of Texas at Brownsville, TX
The University of Texas at Dallas, TX
The University of Texas at El Paso, TX
The University of Texas at San Antonio, TX
The University of Texas–Pan American, TX
University of the Ozarks, AR
University of the Southwest, NM
University of Tulsa, OK
University of Utah, UT
The University of Virginia's College at Wise, VA
University of West Florida, FL
University of West Georgia, GA
University of Wisconsin–Eau Claire, WI
University of Wisconsin–Green Bay, WI
University of Wisconsin–La Crosse, WI
University of Wisconsin–Parkside, WI
University of Wisconsin–Stevens Point, WI
University of Wisconsin–Superior, WI
University of Wisconsin–Whitewater, WI
Utah State University, UT
Valdosta State University, GA
Valley City State University, ND
Virginia Commonwealth University, VA
Virginia Military Institute, VA
Walla Walla University, WA
Warner Pacific College, OR
Wartburg College, IA
Washington State University, WA
Washington University in St. Louis, MO
Wayland Baptist University, TX
Waynesburg University, PA
Wayne State University, MI
Webster University, MO
Western Carolina University, NC
Western Illinois University, IL
Western Kentucky University, KY
Western Oregon University, OR
Western Washington University, WA
Westminster College, UT
West Virginia University, WV
Wheaton College, IL
Whitworth University, WA
Wichita State University, KS
Widener University, PA
Williams Baptist College, AR
Wilson College, PA
Wisconsin Lutheran College, WI
Wright State University, OH
York College, NE

Business

Abilene Christian University, TX
Adrian College, MI
Alaska Pacific University, AK
Albertus Magnus College, CT
Albion College, MI
Alderson-Broaddus College, WV
Alfred University, NY
Alliant International University, CA
Angelo State University, TX
Aquinas College, TN
Arizona State University, AZ
Arkansas State University, AR
Auburn University, AL
Augsburg College, MN
Augustana College, IL
Augustana College, SD
Augusta State University, GA
Austin College, TX
Austin Peay State University, TN
Averett University, VA
Ball State University, IN
Barton College, NC
Baylor University, TX
Belhaven College, MS
Bellarmine University, KY
Bethel College, IN
Birmingham-Southern College, AL
Black Hills State University, SD
Bloomfield College, NJ
Bloomsburg University of Pennsylvania, PA
Boise State University, ID
Bowling Green State University, OH
Brenau University, GA
Brevard College, NC
Bryan College, TN
Bucknell University, PA
Buena Vista University, IA
Butler University, IN
California Polytechnic State University, San Luis Obispo, CA
California State Polytechnic University, Pomona, CA
California State University, Bakersfield, CA
California State University, Chico, CA
California State University, Fresno, CA
California State University, Fullerton, CA
California State University, Los Angeles, CA
California State University, Northridge, CA
California State University, San Bernardino, CA
California State University, Stanislaus, CA
Calvin College, MI
Campbellsville University, KY
Carroll University, WI
Carson-Newman College, TN
Case Western Reserve University, OH
Centenary College of Louisiana, LA
Central College, IA
Central Methodist University, MO
Central Michigan University, MI
Chatham University, PA
Christopher Newport University, VA
Clarkson University, NY
Clearwater Christian College, FL
Cleary University, MI
Clemson University, SC
Cleveland State University, OH
Coastal Carolina University, SC
Coe College, IA
The College at Brockport, State University of New York, NY
College of Charleston, SC
The College of Idaho, ID
The College of New Rochelle, NY
College of Staten Island of the City University of New York, NY
Colorado School of Mines, CO
Colorado State University–Pueblo, CO
Colorado Technical University Colorado Springs, CO
Colorado Technical University Denver, CO
Columbia College, MO
Columbia College Chicago, IL
Columbia International University, SC
Columbus State University, GA
Concordia College, AL
Concordia University Chicago, IL
Concordia University, Nebraska, NE
Concordia University Texas, TX
Concord University, WV
Creighton University, NE
Dakota State University, SD
Dallas Baptist University, TX
Dalton State College, GA
Dana College, NE
Defiance College, OH
DePauw University, IN
DeSales University, PA
Dordt College, IA
Dowling College, NY
Drury University, MO
D'Youville College, NY
Eastern Michigan University, MI
Eastern Washington University, WA
East Tennessee State University, TN
East Texas Baptist University, TX
Edinboro University of Pennsylvania, PA
Elizabethtown College, PA
Elmhurst College, IL
Elon University, NC
Emmanuel College, GA
Emporia State University, KS
Endicott College, MA
Evangel University, MO
Everest University, FL
Fairfield University, CT
Felician College, NJ
Ferris State University, MI
Five Towns College, NY
Flagler College, FL
Florida Atlantic University, FL
Florida Gulf Coast University, FL
Florida International University, FL
Fordham University, NY
Fort Lewis College, CO
Fort Valley State University, GA
Francis Marion University, SC
Fresno Pacific University, CA
Frostburg State University, MD
Furman University, SC
Gannon University, PA
Gardner-Webb University, NC
Georgia College & State University, GA
Georgian Court University, NJ
Georgia Southern University, GA
Glenville State College, WV
Golden Gate University, CA
Goldey-Beacom College, DE
Gonzaga University, WA
Grace College, IN
Grace University, NE
Grand Valley State University, MI
Green Mountain College, VT
Grove City College, PA
Hardin-Simmons University, TX
Hawai'i Pacific University, HI
Hillsdale Free Will Baptist College, OK
Hope International University, CA
Howard Payne University, TX
Husson University, ME
Idaho State University, ID
Illinois Institute of Technology, IL
Illinois State University, IL

Indiana University of Pennsylvania, PA
Iowa State University of Science and Technology, IA
Jacksonville State University, AL
Jacksonville University, FL
James Madison University, VA
John Carroll University, OH
Juniata College, PA
Kean University, NJ
Kendall College, IL
Kennesaw State University, GA
Kent State University, OH
Kentucky Christian University, KY
Kettering University, MI
King's College, PA
Kutztown University of Pennsylvania, PA
Langston University, OK
Lawrence Technological University, MI
Lee University, TN
Lehigh University, PA
Lewis-Clark State College, ID
Limestone College, SC
Lincoln University, PA
Lindenwood University, MO
Lindsey Wilson College, KY
Lipscomb University, TN
Long Island University, C.W. Post Campus, NY
Longwood University, VA
Louisiana State University and Agricultural and Mechanical College, LA
Louisiana Tech University, LA
Lubbock Christian University, TX
Lycoming College, PA
Lynn University, FL
Lyon College, AR
Maine Maritime Academy, ME
Malone University, OH
Manchester College, IN
Manhattan College, NY
Maranatha Baptist Bible College, WI
Marquette University, WI
Maryville University of Saint Louis, MO
Marywood University, PA
Massachusetts College of Liberal Arts, MA
The Master's College and Seminary, CA
Mayville State University, ND
McKendree University, IL
McMurry University, TX
Mercer University, GA
Mesa State College, CO
Michigan State University, MI
Midland Lutheran College, NE
Midway College, KY
Millersville University of Pennsylvania, PA
Millikin University, IL
Millsaps College, MS
Milwaukee School of Engineering, WI
Minot State University, ND
Misericordia University, PA
Mississippi State University, MS
Mississippi University for Women, MS
Missouri University of Science and Technology, MO
Missouri Valley College, MO
Missouri Western State University, MO
Molloy College, NY
Monmouth University, NJ
Montana State University, MT
Montana State University–Billings, MT
Montana Tech of The University of Montana, MT
Montclair State University, NJ
Mount Mary College, WI
Murray State University, KY
Newberry College, SC
New England College, NH
New Jersey Institute of Technology, NJ
New Mexico State University, NM
North Carolina State University, NC
North Central College, IL
North Dakota State University, ND
Northeastern State University, OK
Northern Arizona University, AZ
Northern Illinois University, IL
Northern Michigan University, MI
Northern State University, SD
Northwestern Oklahoma State University, OK
Northwest Missouri State University, MO
Northwood University, MI
Northwood University, Florida Campus, FL
Northwood University, Texas Campus, TX
Oakland University, MI
Ohio Christian University, OH
Ohio Northern University, OH
The Ohio State University, OH
Ohio University, OH
Ohio University–Chillicothe, OH
Ohio University–Eastern, OH
Ohio University–Lancaster, OH
Ohio University–Southern Campus, OH
Ohio University–Zanesville, OH
Oklahoma City University, OK
Oklahoma Panhandle State University, OK
Oklahoma State University, OK
Old Dominion University, VA
Olivet College, MI
Oral Roberts University, OK
Ouachita Baptist University, AR
Pace University, NY
Pacific University, OR
Peirce College, PA
Piedmont College, GA
Pittsburg State University, KS
Plymouth State University, NH
Point Loma Nazarene University, CA
Portland State University, OR
Post University, CT
Providence College, RI
Purdue University North Central, IN
The Richard Stockton College of New Jersey, NJ
Ripon College, WI
Rivier College, NH
Robert Morris College, IL
Rochester Institute of Technology, NY
Rockford College, IL
Rockhurst University, MO
Sacred Heart University, CT
Saginaw Valley State University, MI
St. Catherine University, MN
St. Cloud State University, MN
St. Edward's University, TX
St. John Fisher College, NY
St. John's University, NY
Saint Louis University, MO
Salisbury University, MD
Sam Houston State University, TX
San Diego State University, CA
Santa Clara University, CA
Schreiner University, TX
Seton Hill University, PA
Shepherd University, WV
Shippensburg University of Pennsylvania, PA
Slippery Rock University of Pennsylvania, PA
Sonoma State University, CA
South Dakota State University, SD
Southeastern Louisiana University, LA
Southeastern Oklahoma State University, OK
Southeast Missouri State University, MO
Southern Adventist University, TN
Southern Arkansas University–Magnolia, AR
Southern Illinois University Carbondale, IL
Southern Illinois University Edwardsville, IL
Southern Nazarene University, OK
Southern Oregon University, OR
Southwestern Christian University, OK
Southwestern College, KS
Southwestern Oklahoma State University, OK
Southwestern University, TX
Southwest Minnesota State University, MN
State University of New York at Binghamton, NY
State University of New York at Fredonia, NY
State University of New York at New Paltz, NY
State University of New York at Oswego, NY
State University of New York at Plattsburgh, NY
State University of New York College at Geneseo, NY
State University of New York College at Oneonta, NY
State University of New York College at Potsdam, NY
Stephen F. Austin State University, TX
Stetson University, FL
Stony Brook University, State University of New York, NY
Susquehanna University, PA
Tennessee Technological University, TN
Texas A&M University, TX
Texas A&M University–Texarkana, TX
Texas Christian University, TX
Texas Lutheran University, TX
Texas State University–San Marcos, TX
Texas Tech University, TX
Thiel College, PA
Towson University, MD
Trevecca Nazarene University, TN
Trinity Christian College, IL
Trinity Lutheran College, WA
Truman State University, MO
Union University, TN
The University of Akron, OH
The University of Alabama, AL
The University of Alabama at Birmingham, AL
The University of Alabama in Huntsville, AL
The University of Arizona, AZ
University of California, Davis, CA
University of California, Riverside, CA
University of California, San Diego, CA
University of Central Missouri, MO
University of Central Oklahoma, OK
University of Colorado at Boulder, CO
University of Colorado at Colorado Springs, CO
University of Connecticut, CT
University of Dallas, TX
University of Dayton, OH
University of Delaware, DE
University of Denver, CO
University of Evansville, IN
University of Florida, FL
University of Georgia, GA
University of Guam, GU
University of Hawaii at Hilo, HI
University of Houston–Clear Lake, TX

University of Houston–Victoria, TX
University of Idaho, ID
University of Illinois at Chicago, IL
University of Illinois at Urbana–Champaign, IL
The University of Iowa, IA
The University of Kansas, KS
University of Kentucky, KY
University of Louisiana at Monroe, LA
The University of Maine at Augusta, ME
University of Maine at Fort Kent, ME
University of Mary Hardin-Baylor, TX
University of Maryland, College Park, MD
University of Maryland Eastern Shore, MD
University of Mary Washington, VA
University of Massachusetts Amherst, MA
University of Memphis, TN
University of Miami, FL
University of Michigan, MI
University of Michigan–Dearborn, MI
University of Michigan–Flint, MI
University of Minnesota, Twin Cities Campus, MN
University of Mississippi, MS
University of Missouri–Columbia, MO
University of Missouri–St. Louis, MO
The University of Montana, MT
The University of Montana Western, MT
University of Nebraska at Omaha, NE
University of Nebraska–Lincoln, NE
University of Nevada, Las Vegas, NV
University of New England, ME
University of New Hampshire, NH
The University of North Carolina at Asheville, NC
The University of North Carolina at Chapel Hill, NC
The University of North Carolina at Greensboro, NC
The University of North Carolina at Pembroke, NC
The University of North Carolina Wilmington, NC
University of North Dakota, ND
University of Northern Colorado, CO
University of Northern Iowa, IA
University of North Florida, FL
University of Oklahoma, OK
University of Oregon, OR
University of Pittsburgh at Bradford, PA
University of Pittsburgh at Johnstown, PA
University of Portland, OR
University of Puget Sound, WA
University of St. Thomas, MN
University of South Alabama, AL
University of South Carolina, SC
University of South Carolina Aiken, SC
The University of South Dakota, SD
University of Southern Indiana, IN
University of South Florida, FL
The University of Tampa, FL
The University of Tennessee, TN
The University of Tennessee at Martin, TN
The University of Texas at Arlington, TX
The University of Texas at Dallas, TX
The University of Texas at El Paso, TX
The University of Texas at San Antonio, TX
The University of Texas–Pan American, TX
University of the Ozarks, AR
University of the Southwest, NM
University of Tulsa, OK
University of Utah, UT
University of Vermont, VT
The University of Virginia's College at Wise, VA
University of Washington, WA
The University of West Alabama, AL
University of West Florida, FL
University of West Georgia, GA
University of Wisconsin–Eau Claire, WI
University of Wisconsin–Green Bay, WI
University of Wisconsin–La Crosse, WI
University of Wisconsin–Parkside, WI
University of Wisconsin–Stevens Point, WI
University of Wisconsin–Stout, WI
University of Wisconsin–Superior, WI
University of Wisconsin–Whitewater, WI
University of Wyoming, WY
Utah State University, UT
Valdosta State University, GA
Valley City State University, ND
Valparaiso University, IN
Virginia Commonwealth University, VA
Virginia Military Institute, VA
Walla Walla University, WA
Wartburg College, IA
Washington & Jefferson College, PA
Washington State University, WA
Washington University in St. Louis, MO
Wayland Baptist University, TX
Waynesburg University, PA
Wayne State University, MI
Webber International University, FL
Webster University, MO
West Chester University of Pennsylvania, PA
Western Carolina University, NC
Western Illinois University, IL
Western Kentucky University, KY
Western New England College, MA
Western Oregon University, OR
Western Washington University, WA
West Liberty State University, WV
Westminster College, UT
West Virginia University, WV
Wheaton College, IL
Wichita State University, KS
Widener University, PA
Williams Baptist College, AR
Wilson College, PA
Wisconsin Lutheran College, WI
Wright State University, OH
York College, NE
Youngstown State University, OH

Communication

Abilene Christian University, TX
Adelphi University, NY
Albertus Magnus College, CT
Albion College, MI
Alderson-Broaddus College, WV
Alfred University, NY
Alliant International University, CA
Angelo State University, TX
Arizona State University, AZ
Arkansas State University, AR
Auburn University, AL
Augsburg College, MN
Augustana College, IL
Augustana College, SD
Augusta State University, GA
Austin College, TX
Austin Peay State University, TN
Avila University, MO
Ball State University, IN
Barton College, NC
Baylor University, TX
Belhaven College, MS
Bethel College, IN
Biola University, CA
Birmingham-Southern College, AL
Black Hills State University, SD
Bloomsburg University of Pennsylvania, PA
Boise State University, ID
Bowling Green State University, OH
Brenau University, GA
Bryan College, TN
Butler University, IN
California Polytechnic State University, San Luis Obispo, CA
California State University, Bakersfield, CA
California State University, Chico, CA
California State University, Fresno, CA
California State University, Fullerton, CA
California State University, Los Angeles, CA
California State University, Northridge, CA
California State University, Stanislaus, CA
Calvin College, MI
Campbellsville University, KY
Case Western Reserve University, OH
Centenary College of Louisiana, LA
Central College, IA
Central Methodist University, MO
Central Michigan University, MI
Chatham University, PA
Christopher Newport University, VA
City College of the City University of New York, NY
Clarkson University, NY
Clemson University, SC
Cleveland State University, OH
The College at Brockport, State University of New York, NY
College of Charleston, SC
The College of New Rochelle, NY
Colorado State University–Pueblo, CO
Columbia College Chicago, IL
Columbia International University, SC
Columbus State University, GA
Concordia University Chicago, IL
Concordia University, Nebraska, NE
Concordia University, St. Paul, MN
Concord University, WV
Dakota State University, SD
Dallas Baptist University, TX
Dana College, NE
Defiance College, OH
DePauw University, IN
DeSales University, PA
Dordt College, IA
Drury University, MO
Eastern Michigan University, MI
East Texas Baptist University, TX
Edinboro University of Pennsylvania, PA
Elizabethtown College, PA
Elmhurst College, IL
Elon University, NC
Emmanuel College, GA
Emporia State University, KS
Evangel University, MO
Ferris State University, MI
Flagler College, FL
Florida International University, FL
Fordham University, NY
Fort Lewis College, CO
Franklin Pierce University, NH
Frostburg State University, MD
Furman University, SC
Gardner-Webb University, NC
Georgia Southern University, GA

Grand Valley State University, MI
Grove City College, PA
Hamline University, MN
Harding University, AR
Hardin-Simmons University, TX
Hastings College, NE
Hawai'i Pacific University, HI
Hofstra University, NY
Hope International University, CA
Howard Payne University, TX
Huntington University, IN
Idaho State University, ID
Illinois State University, IL
Indiana University of Pennsylvania, PA
Iowa State University of Science and Technology, IA
Ithaca College, NY
Jacksonville State University, AL
John Carroll University, OH
Johnson Bible College, TN
Juniata College, PA
Kennesaw State University, GA
Kent State University, OH
King's College, PA
Kutztown University of Pennsylvania, PA
Lee University, TN
Lehigh University, PA
Limestone College, SC
Lincoln University, PA
Lindenwood University, MO
Lipscomb University, TN
Lock Haven University of Pennsylvania, PA
Long Island University, Brooklyn Campus, NY
Louisiana State University and Agricultural and Mechanical College, LA
Lubbock Christian University, TX
Lycoming College, PA
Lynn University, FL
Malone University, OH
Marquette University, WI
Marywood University, PA
Massachusetts College of Liberal Arts, MA
McMurry University, TX
Mesa State College, CO
Michigan State University, MI
Midland Lutheran College, NE
Millersville University of Pennsylvania, PA
Millikin University, IL
Milwaukee School of Engineering, WI
Minot State University, ND
Mississippi State University, MS
Mississippi University for Women, MS
Missouri Valley College, MO
Missouri Western State University, MO
Molloy College, NY
Monmouth University, NJ
Montana State University, MT
Montana State University–Billings, MT
Montclair State University, NJ
Mount Mary College, WI
Murray State University, KY
Newberry College, SC
New England College, NH
New England School of Communications, ME
New Jersey Institute of Technology, NJ
New Mexico State University, NM
North Central College, IL
North Dakota State University, ND
Northeastern State University, OK
Northern Arizona University, AZ
Northern Illinois University, IL
Northern Michigan University, MI
Northern State University, SD
North Greenville University, SC
Northwestern Oklahoma State University, OK
Northwest Missouri State University, MO
Ohio Northern University, OH
The Ohio State University, OH
Ohio University, OH
Ohio University–Chillicothe, OH
Ohio University–Eastern, OH
Ohio University–Lancaster, OH
Ohio University–Southern Campus, OH
Ohio University–Zanesville, OH
Oklahoma City University, OK
Oklahoma State University, OK
Olivet College, MI
Oral Roberts University, OK
Ouachita Baptist University, AR
Pace University, NY
Pittsburg State University, KS
Plymouth State University, NH
Point Loma Nazarene University, CA
Post University, CT
Rivier College, NH
Rochester Institute of Technology, NY
Rockhurst University, MO
St. Cloud State University, MN
St. Edward's University, TX
St. John's University, NY
Saint Louis University, MO
Salisbury University, MD
Sam Houston State University, TX
San Diego State University, CA
Seton Hill University, PA
Shepherd University, WV
Shippensburg University of Pennsylvania, PA
Slippery Rock University of Pennsylvania, PA
Sonoma State University, CA
South Dakota State University, SD
Southeastern Louisiana University, LA
Southeast Missouri State University, MO
Southern Adventist University, TN
Southern Illinois University Carbondale, IL
Southern Nazarene University, OK
Southwestern Oklahoma State University, OK
Southwest Minnesota State University, MN
State University of New York at Fredonia, NY
State University of New York at New Paltz, NY
State University of New York at Oswego, NY
State University of New York at Plattsburgh, NY
State University of New York College at Geneseo, NY
State University of New York College at Potsdam, NY
Stephen F. Austin State University, TX
Stetson University, FL
Tabor College, KS
Tennessee Technological University, TN
Texas Christian University, TX
Texas Tech University, TX
Towson University, MD
Trevecca Nazarene University, TN
Truman State University, MO
Union University, TN
The University of Akron, OH
The University of Alabama, AL
The University of Alabama at Birmingham, AL
University of California, Davis, CA
University of California, San Diego, CA
University of Central Missouri, MO
University of Colorado at Boulder, CO
University of Delaware, DE
University of Evansville, IN
University of Florida, FL
University of Guam, GU
University of Houston–Victoria, TX
University of Idaho, ID
University of Illinois at Urbana–Champaign, IL
The University of Kansas, KS
University of Kentucky, KY
University of Louisiana at Monroe, LA
University of Maine at Fort Kent, ME
University of Mary Hardin-Baylor, TX
University of Maryland, College Park, MD
University of Massachusetts Amherst, MA
University of Memphis, TN
University of Miami, FL
University of Michigan, MI
University of Michigan–Dearborn, MI
University of Michigan–Flint, MI
University of Minnesota, Twin Cities Campus, MN
University of Mississippi, MS
University of Missouri–Columbia, MO
University of Missouri–St. Louis, MO
University of Nebraska at Kearney, NE
University of Nebraska at Omaha, NE
University of Nevada, Las Vegas, NV
University of New England, ME
University of New Orleans, LA
The University of North Carolina at Asheville, NC
The University of North Carolina at Chapel Hill, NC
The University of North Carolina at Greensboro, NC
The University of North Carolina at Pembroke, NC
The University of North Carolina Wilmington, NC
University of North Dakota, ND
University of Northern Colorado, CO
University of Oklahoma, OK
University of Pittsburgh at Bradford, PA
University of Pittsburgh at Johnstown, PA
University of Portland, OR
University of Puget Sound, WA
University of South Carolina, SC
University of South Carolina Aiken, SC
The University of South Dakota, SD
University of South Florida, FL
The University of Tampa, FL
The University of Tennessee, TN
The University of Tennessee at Martin, TN
The University of Texas at Arlington, TX
The University of Texas at El Paso, TX
The University of Texas at San Antonio, TX
The University of Texas at Tyler, TX
The University of Texas–Pan American, TX
University of the Ozarks, AR
University of Tulsa, OK
University of Utah, UT
University of West Georgia, GA
University of Wisconsin–Eau Claire, WI
University of Wisconsin–Green Bay, WI
University of Wisconsin–La Crosse, WI
University of Wisconsin–Parkside, WI
University of Wisconsin–Stevens Point, WI
University of Wisconsin–Superior, WI
University of Wisconsin–Whitewater, WI
University of Wyoming, WY
Utah State University, UT
Valdosta State University, GA

Valley City State University, ND
Walla Walla University, WA
Wartburg College, IA
Washington State University, WA
Washington University in St. Louis, MO
Wayland Baptist University, TX
Waynesburg University, PA
Wayne State University, MI
Webster University, MO
Western Carolina University, NC
Western Kentucky University, KY
Western Washington University, WA
West Liberty State University, WV
Westminster College, UT
West Virginia University, WV
Wichita State University, KS
Widener University, PA
Wilson College, PA
Wisconsin Lutheran College, WI
Wright State University, OH
York College, NE

Computer Science

Albertus Magnus College, CT
Alderson-Broaddus College, WV
Alliant International University, CA
Angelo State University, TX
Arizona State University, AZ
Arkansas State University, AR
Auburn University, AL
Augsburg College, MN
Augustana College, IL
Augustana College, SD
Augusta State University, GA
Austin Peay State University, TN
Bard College, NY
Barton College, NC
Baylor University, TX
Belhaven College, MS
Bethel College, IN
Birmingham-Southern College, AL
Black Hills State University, SD
Bloomfield College, NJ
Bloomsburg University of Pennsylvania, PA
Boise State University, ID
Bowling Green State University, OH
Bryan College, TN
Buena Vista University, IA
Butler University, IN
California Polytechnic State University, San Luis Obispo, CA
California State Polytechnic University, Pomona, CA
California State University, Chico, CA
California State University, Los Angeles, CA
California State University, Northridge, CA
California State University, San Bernardino, CA
California State University, Stanislaus, CA
Calvin College, MI
Campbellsville University, KY
Carroll University, WI
Case Western Reserve University, OH
Central College, IA
Central Methodist University, MO
Central Michigan University, MI
Christopher Newport University, VA
City College of the City University of New York, NY
Clarke College, IA
Clarkson University, NY
Cleary University, MI
Clemson University, SC
The College at Brockport, State University of New York, NY
College of Charleston, SC
College of Staten Island of the City University of New York, NY
Colorado School of Mines, CO
Colorado State University–Pueblo, CO
Colorado Technical University Colorado Springs, CO
Colorado Technical University Denver, CO
Columbus State University, GA
Concordia College, AL
Concordia University Chicago, IL
Concordia University, Nebraska, NE
Dakota State University, SD
Dallas Baptist University, TX
Dalton State College, GA
Defiance College, OH
DePauw University, IN
DeSales University, PA
Dordt College, IA
Drury University, MO
Eastern Michigan University, MI
Eastern Washington University, WA
East Tennessee State University, TN
Edinboro University of Pennsylvania, PA
Elizabethtown College, PA
Elmhurst College, IL
Elon University, NC
Emporia State University, KS
Evangel University, MO
Everest University, FL
Ferris State University, MI
Florida International University, FL
Fort Lewis College, CO
Frostburg State University, MD
Furman University, SC
Gardner-Webb University, NC
George Fox University, OR
Georgia College & State University, GA
Georgia Institute of Technology, GA
Golden Gate University, CA
Graceland University, IA
Grand Valley State University, MI
Harding University, AR
Huntingdon College, AL
Huntington University, IN
Husson University, ME
Idaho State University, ID
Illinois State University, IL
Indiana University of Pennsylvania, PA
Iowa State University of Science and Technology, IA
Jacksonville State University, AL
James Madison University, VA
John Carroll University, OH
Johnson C. Smith University, NC
Juniata College, PA
Kennesaw State University, GA
Kent State University, OH
Kettering University, MI
King's College, PA
Kutztown University of Pennsylvania, PA
Lake Forest College, IL
Lawrence Technological University, MI
Limestone College, SC
Lincoln University, PA
Lindenwood University, MO
Long Island University, C.W. Post Campus, NY
Longwood University, VA
Louisiana State University and Agricultural and Mechanical College, LA
Louisiana Tech University, LA
Lubbock Christian University, TX
Lycoming College, PA
Malone University, OH
Manhattan College, NY
Marymount University, VA
Massachusetts College of Liberal Arts, MA
Mayville State University, ND
McMurry University, TX
Mesa State College, CO
Michigan State University, MI
Millersville University of Pennsylvania, PA
Mills College, CA
Milwaukee School of Engineering, WI
Minot State University, ND
Misericordia University, PA
Mississippi State University, MS
Mississippi University for Women, MS
Missouri University of Science and Technology, MO
Missouri Valley College, MO
Missouri Western State University, MO
Monmouth University, NJ
Montana State University, MT
Montana State University–Billings, MT
Montana Tech of The University of Montana, MT
Murray State University, KY
Muskingum College, OH
New England College, NH
New Jersey Institute of Technology, NJ
New Mexico State University, NM
North Central College, IL
North Dakota State University, ND
Northeastern State University, OK
Northern Arizona University, AZ
Northern Illinois University, IL
Northern Michigan University, MI
Northern State University, SD
Northwestern Oklahoma State University, OK
Northwest Missouri State University, MO
Ohio Northern University, OH
The Ohio State University, OH
Ohio University, OH
Ohio University–Chillicothe, OH
Ohio University–Eastern, OH
Ohio University–Lancaster, OH
Ohio University–Southern Campus, OH
Ohio University–Zanesville, OH
Oklahoma Panhandle State University, OK
Oklahoma State University, OK
Oklahoma Wesleyan University, OK
Ouachita Baptist University, AR
Pace University, NY
Pittsburg State University, KS
Polytechnic Institute of NYU, NY
Portland State University, OR
Post University, CT
Purchase College, State University of New York, NY
Purdue University, IN
The Richard Stockton College of New Jersey, NJ
Ripon College, WI
Rivier College, NH
Robert Morris College, IL
Rochester Institute of Technology, NY
Rockford College, IL
Rollins College, FL
Sacred Heart University, CT
Saginaw Valley State University, MI
St. Cloud State University, MN
St. Edward's University, TX

St. John's University, NY
Saint Louis University, MO
Salisbury University, MD
Sam Houston State University, TX
San Diego State University, CA
Seton Hill University, PA
Shepherd University, WV
Shippensburg University of Pennsylvania, PA
Skidmore College, NY
Slippery Rock University of Pennsylvania, PA
Sonoma State University, CA
South Dakota School of Mines and Technology, SD
South Dakota State University, SD
Southeastern Louisiana University, LA
Southeastern Oklahoma State University, OK
Southeast Missouri State University, MO
Southern Arkansas University–Magnolia, AR
Southern Illinois University Carbondale, IL
Southern Nazarene University, OK
Southwestern College, KS
Southwestern Oklahoma State University, OK
Southwest Minnesota State University, MN
State University of New York at Binghamton, NY
State University of New York at Fredonia, NY
State University of New York at Oswego, NY
State University of New York at Plattsburgh, NY
State University of New York College at Geneseo, NY
State University of New York College at Oneonta, NY
State University of New York College at Potsdam, NY
State University of New York Institute of Technology, NY
Stephen F. Austin State University, TX
Stetson University, FL
Stony Brook University, State University of New York, NY
Tennessee Technological University, TN
Texas A&M University, TX
Texas Tech University, TX
Thiel College, PA
Towson University, MD
Transylvania University, KY
University of Advancing Technology, AZ
The University of Akron, OH
The University of Alabama, AL
The University of Alabama at Birmingham, AL
The University of Alabama in Huntsville, AL
University of California, Davis, CA
University of California, Irvine, CA
University of California, San Diego, CA
University of Central Missouri, MO
University of Central Oklahoma, OK
University of Colorado at Boulder, CO
University of Colorado at Colorado Springs, CO
University of Connecticut, CT
University of Delaware, DE
University of Evansville, IN
University of Florida, FL
University of Guam, GU
University of Hawaii at Hilo, HI
University of Houston–Clear Lake, TX
University of Houston–Victoria, TX
University of Idaho, ID
University of Illinois at Urbana–Champaign, IL
The University of Kansas, KS
University of Kentucky, KY
University of Louisiana at Monroe, LA
University of Maine at Fort Kent, ME
University of Mary Hardin-Baylor, TX
University of Maryland, Baltimore County, MD
University of Maryland, College Park, MD
University of Maryland Eastern Shore, MD
University of Mary Washington, VA
University of Massachusetts Amherst, MA
University of Massachusetts Lowell, MA
University of Miami, FL
University of Michigan, MI
University of Michigan–Dearborn, MI
University of Michigan–Flint, MI
University of Minnesota, Twin Cities Campus, MN
University of Mississippi, MS
University of Missouri–Columbia, MO
University of Missouri–St. Louis, MO
The University of Montana, MT
University of Nebraska at Omaha, NE
University of Nebraska–Lincoln, NE
University of Nevada, Las Vegas, NV
University of New Orleans, LA
The University of North Carolina at Asheville, NC
The University of North Carolina Wilmington, NC
University of North Dakota, ND
University of North Florida, FL
University of Oklahoma, OK
University of Pittsburgh at Bradford, PA
University of Pittsburgh at Johnstown, PA
University of Portland, OR
University of Puget Sound, WA
University of Richmond, VA
University of South Alabama, AL
University of South Carolina, SC
University of South Carolina Aiken, SC
The University of South Dakota, SD
University of South Florida, FL
The University of Tennessee, TN
The University of Tennessee at Martin, TN
The University of Texas at Arlington, TX
The University of Texas at Dallas, TX
The University of Texas at El Paso, TX
The University of Texas at San Antonio, TX
The University of Texas–Pan American, TX
University of Tulsa, OK
University of Utah, UT
University of Vermont, VT
The University of Virginia's College at Wise, VA
University of Washington, WA
The University of West Alabama, AL
University of West Georgia, GA
University of Wisconsin–Eau Claire, WI
University of Wisconsin–La Crosse, WI
University of Wisconsin–Stevens Point, WI
University of Wisconsin–Stout, WI
University of Wisconsin–Superior, WI
University of Wisconsin–Whitewater, WI
University of Wyoming, WY
Utah State University, UT
Valdosta State University, GA
Valley City State University, ND
Virginia Commonwealth University, VA
Virginia Military Institute, VA
Wartburg College, IA
Washington State University, WA
Washington University in St. Louis, MO
Waynesburg University, PA
Wayne State University, MI
Western Oregon University, OR
Western Washington University, WA
Westminster College, UT
West Virginia University, WV
Whitworth University, WA
Wichita State University, KS
Widener University, PA
Wilson College, PA
Wright State University, OH
York College, NE
Youngstown State University, OH

Education

Abilene Christian University, TX
Alaska Pacific University, AK
Albertus Magnus College, CT
Alderson-Broaddus College, WV
Alfred University, NY
Alliant International University, CA
Angelo State University, TX
Aquinas College, TN
Arizona State University, AZ
Arkansas State University, AR
Auburn University, AL
Augsburg College, MN
Augustana College, IL
Augustana College, SD
Augusta State University, GA
Austin College, TX
Austin Peay State University, TN
Averett University, VA
Ball State University, IN
Baptist Bible College of Pennsylvania, PA
The Baptist College of Florida, FL
Barton College, NC
Baylor University, TX
Belhaven College, MS
Bellarmine University, KY
Berklee College of Music, MA
Berry College, GA
Bethel College, IN
Birmingham-Southern College, AL
Black Hills State University, SD
Bloomfield College, NJ
Bloomsburg University of Pennsylvania, PA
Boise State University, ID
Boston University, MA
Bowling Green State University, OH
Brenau University, GA
Brevard College, NC
Bryan College, TN
Buena Vista University, IA
Butler University, IN
California Polytechnic State University, San Luis Obispo, CA
California State Polytechnic University, Pomona, CA
California State University, Bakersfield, CA
California State University, Chico, CA
California State University, Fresno, CA
California State University, Los Angeles, CA
California State University, Northridge, CA
California State University, San Bernardino, CA
California State University, Stanislaus, CA
Calvin College, MI
Campbellsville University, KY
Carroll University, WI
Carson-Newman College, TN
Case Western Reserve University, OH
Catawba College, NC
Centenary College of Louisiana, LA

Central College, IA
Central Methodist University, MO
Central Michigan University, MI
Chatham University, PA
Christopher Newport University, VA
City College of the City University of New York, NY
Clearwater Christian College, FL
Clemson University, SC
Cleveland State University, OH
Coastal Carolina University, SC
The College at Brockport, State University of New York, NY
College of Charleston, SC
The College of Idaho, ID
The College of New Rochelle, NY
College of Saint Mary, NE
College of Staten Island of the City University of New York, NY
Colorado State University–Pueblo, CO
Columbia College, MO
Columbia College Chicago, IL
Columbia International University, SC
Columbus State University, GA
Concordia College, AL
Concordia College–New York, NY
Concordia University Chicago, IL
Concordia University, Nebraska, NE
Concordia University Texas, TX
Concord University, WV
Creighton University, NE
Dakota State University, SD
Dallas Baptist University, TX
Dalton State College, GA
Dana College, NE
Davidson College, NC
Defiance College, OH
DeSales University, PA
Dominican College, NY
Dordt College, IA
Dowling College, NY
Drury University, MO
D'Youville College, NY
Eastern Michigan University, MI
Eastern Washington University, WA
East Tennessee State University, TN
East Texas Baptist University, TX
Edinboro University of Pennsylvania, PA
Elizabethtown College, PA
Elmhurst College, IL
Elon University, NC
Emmanuel College, GA
Emporia State University, KS
Endicott College, MA
Evangel University, MO
Fairfield University, CT
Felician College, NJ
Ferris State University, MI
Five Towns College, NY
Flagler College, FL
Florida Gulf Coast University, FL
Florida International University, FL
Fort Lewis College, CO
Francis Marion University, SC
Frostburg State University, MD
Furman University, SC
Gannon University, PA
Gardner-Webb University, NC
George Fox University, OR
Georgia College & State University, GA
Georgia Southern University, GA
Glenville State College, WV
Grace University, NE
Grand Valley State University, MI
Green Mountain College, VT
Grove City College, PA
Hardin-Simmons University, TX
Henderson State University, AR
Hillsdale Free Will Baptist College, OK
Hope International University, CA
Howard Payne University, TX
Husson University, ME
Idaho State University, ID
Illinois State University, IL
Indiana University of Pennsylvania, PA
Iowa State University of Science and Technology, IA
Jacksonville State University, AL
James Madison University, VA
Jarvis Christian College, TX
John Carroll University, OH
Johnson Bible College, TN
Juniata College, PA
Kean University, NJ
Kendall College, IL
Kennesaw State University, GA
Kent State University, OH
Kentucky Christian University, KY
King's College, PA
Kutztown University of Pennsylvania, PA
LaGrange College, GA
Langston University, OK
Lawrence Technological University, MI
Lees-McRae College, NC
Lee University, TN
Lewis-Clark State College, ID
Limestone College, SC
Lincoln University, MO
Lincoln University, PA
Lindenwood University, MO
Lindsey Wilson College, KY
Lipscomb University, TN
Lock Haven University of Pennsylvania, PA
Long Island University, Brooklyn Campus, NY
Long Island University, C.W. Post Campus, NY
Longwood University, VA
Louisiana State University and Agricultural and Mechanical College, LA
Louisiana Tech University, LA
Lubbock Christian University, TX
Lycoming College, PA
Malone University, OH
Maryville University of Saint Louis, MO
Marywood University, PA
Massachusetts College of Liberal Arts, MA
The Master's College and Seminary, CA
Mayville State University, ND
McMurry University, TX
Mercer University, GA
Mesa State College, CO
Miami University, OH
Michigan State University, MI
Mid-Continent University, KY
Midland Lutheran College, NE
Millersville University of Pennsylvania, PA
Millikin University, IL
Minot State University, ND
Misericordia University, PA
Mississippi State University, MS
Mississippi University for Women, MS
Missouri University of Science and Technology, MO
Missouri Valley College, MO
Missouri Western State University, MO
Molloy College, NY
Monmouth University, NJ
Montana State University, MT
Montana State University–Billings, MT
Montclair State University, NJ
Mount Mary College, WI
Murray State University, KY
Newberry College, SC
New England College, NH
New Mexico State University, NM
North Carolina State University, NC
North Central College, IL
North Dakota State University, ND
Northeastern State University, OK
Northern Arizona University, AZ
Northern Illinois University, IL
Northern Michigan University, MI
Northern State University, SD
North Greenville University, SC
Northwestern Oklahoma State University, OK
Northwestern State University of Louisiana, LA
Northwest Missouri State University, MO
Oakland University, MI
Ohio Christian University, OH
Ohio Northern University, OH
The Ohio State University, OH
Ohio University, OH
Ohio University–Chillicothe, OH
Ohio University–Eastern, OH
Ohio University–Lancaster, OH
Ohio University–Southern Campus, OH
Ohio University–Zanesville, OH
Ohio Valley University, WV
Oklahoma City University, OK
Oklahoma Panhandle State University, OK
Oklahoma State University, OK
Oklahoma Wesleyan University, OK
Olivet College, MI
Oral Roberts University, OK
Ouachita Baptist University, AR
Pace University, NY
Pacific Union College, CA
Pacific University, OR
Piedmont College, GA
Pittsburg State University, KS
Plymouth State University, NH
Point Loma Nazarene University, CA
Portland State University, OR
Post University, CT
Purdue University, IN
Purdue University North Central, IN
Randolph College, VA
The Richard Stockton College of New Jersey, NJ
Ripon College, WI
Rivier College, NH
Rockford College, IL
Sacred Heart University, CT
Saginaw Valley State University, MI
St. Catherine University, MN
St. Cloud State University, MN
St. Edward's University, TX
St. John's University, NY
Saint Louis University, MO
Salisbury University, MD
Sam Houston State University, TX
San Diego State University, CA
Savannah College of Art and Design, GA
Schreiner University, TX
Seton Hill University, PA
Shasta Bible College, CA
Shepherd University, WV

Shippensburg University of Pennsylvania, PA
Slippery Rock University of Pennsylvania, PA
Sonoma State University, CA
South Dakota State University, SD
Southeastern Louisiana University, LA
Southeastern Oklahoma State University, OK
Southeast Missouri State University, MO
Southern Adventist University, TN
Southern Arkansas University–Magnolia, AR
Southern Illinois University Carbondale, IL
Southern Illinois University Edwardsville, IL
Southern Nazarene University, OK
Southern Oregon University, OR
Southwestern Christian University, OK
Southwestern Oklahoma State University, OK
Southwest Minnesota State University, MN
State University of New York at Binghamton, NY
State University of New York at Fredonia, NY
State University of New York at New Paltz, NY
State University of New York at Oswego, NY
State University of New York at Plattsburgh, NY
State University of New York College at Cortland, NY
State University of New York College at Geneseo, NY
State University of New York College at Oneonta, NY
State University of New York College at Potsdam, NY
Stephen F. Austin State University, TX
Stetson University, FL
Stillman College, AL
Tennessee Technological University, TN
Texas A&M University, TX
Texas A&M University–Texarkana, TX
Texas Christian University, TX
Texas Lutheran University, TX
Texas State University–San Marcos, TX
Texas Tech University, TX
Thiel College, PA
Towson University, MD
Trevecca Nazarene University, TN
Truman State University, MO
Union University, TN
The University of Akron, OH
The University of Alabama, AL
The University of Alabama in Huntsville, AL
The University of Arizona, AZ
University of California, Irvine, CA
University of California, Riverside, CA
University of Central Missouri, MO
University of Central Oklahoma, OK
University of Colorado at Boulder, CO
University of Colorado at Colorado Springs, CO
University of Connecticut, CT
University of Dallas, TX
University of Dayton, OH
University of Delaware, DE
University of Evansville, IN
University of Florida, FL
University of Georgia, GA
University of Guam, GU
University of Houston–Clear Lake, TX
University of Houston–Victoria, TX
University of Idaho, ID
University of Illinois at Urbana–Champaign, IL
The University of Kansas, KS
University of Kentucky, KY
University of Louisiana at Monroe, LA
University of Maine at Fort Kent, ME
University of Mary Hardin-Baylor, TX
University of Maryland, Baltimore County, MD
University of Maryland, College Park, MD
University of Maryland Eastern Shore, MD
University of Mary Washington, VA
University of Massachusetts Amherst, MA
University of Memphis, TN
University of Miami, FL
University of Michigan, MI
University of Michigan–Dearborn, MI
University of Michigan–Flint, MI
University of Minnesota, Twin Cities Campus, MN
University of Mississippi, MS
University of Missouri–Columbia, MO
University of Missouri–St. Louis, MO
The University of Montana, MT
The University of Montana Western, MT
University of Montevallo, AL
University of Nebraska at Omaha, NE
University of Nebraska–Lincoln, NE
University of Nevada, Las Vegas, NV
University of New England, ME
University of New Hampshire, NH
University of New Orleans, LA
The University of North Carolina at Asheville, NC
The University of North Carolina at Chapel Hill, NC
The University of North Carolina at Greensboro, NC
The University of North Carolina at Pembroke, NC
The University of North Carolina Wilmington, NC
University of North Dakota, ND
University of Northern Colorado, CO
University of Northern Iowa, IA
University of North Florida, FL
University of Oklahoma, OK
University of Oregon, OR
University of Pittsburgh at Bradford, PA
University of Pittsburgh at Johnstown, PA
University of Portland, OR
University of St. Thomas, MN
University of South Carolina, SC
University of South Carolina Aiken, SC
The University of South Dakota, SD
University of Southern Indiana, IN
University of South Florida, FL
The University of Tampa, FL
The University of Tennessee, TN
The University of Tennessee at Martin, TN
The University of Texas at Arlington, TX
The University of Texas at Brownsville, TX
The University of Texas at El Paso, TX
The University of Texas at San Antonio, TX
The University of Texas–Pan American, TX
University of the Ozarks, AR
University of the Southwest, NM
University of Tulsa, OK
University of Utah, UT
University of Vermont, VT
The University of Virginia's College at Wise, VA
University of Washington, WA
The University of West Alabama, AL
University of West Georgia, GA
University of Wisconsin–Eau Claire, WI
University of Wisconsin–Green Bay, WI
University of Wisconsin–La Crosse, WI
University of Wisconsin–Parkside, WI
University of Wisconsin–Stevens Point, WI
University of Wisconsin–Stout, WI
University of Wisconsin–Superior, WI
University of Wisconsin–Whitewater, WI
University of Wyoming, WY
Utah State University, UT
Valdosta State University, GA
Valley City State University, ND
Virginia Commonwealth University, VA
Walla Walla University, WA
Wartburg College, IA
Washington State University, WA
Washington University in St. Louis, MO
Wayland Baptist University, TX
Waynesburg University, PA
Wayne State University, MI
Webster University, MO
Western Carolina University, NC
Western Illinois University, IL
Western Kentucky University, KY
Western Oregon University, OR
Western Washington University, WA
West Liberty State University, WV
Westminster College, UT
West Virginia University, WV
Wheaton College, IL
Wichita State University, KS
Widener University, PA
William Jessup University, CA
Williams Baptist College, AR
Wilson College, PA
Wisconsin Lutheran College, WI
Wright State University, OH
York College, NE
Youngstown State University, OH

Engineering/Technologies

Alfred University, NY
Arizona State University, AZ
Arkansas State University, AR
Auburn University, AL
Austin College, TX
Averett University, VA
Ball State University, IN
Baylor University, TX
Berklee College of Music, MA
Birmingham-Southern College, AL
Bluefield State College, WV
Boise State University, ID
Boston University, MA
Bowling Green State University, OH
Bryant University, RI
Bucknell University, PA
Butler University, IN
California Polytechnic State University, San Luis Obispo, CA
California State Polytechnic University, Pomona, CA
California State University, Chico, CA
California State University, Fresno, CA
California State University, Fullerton, CA
California State University, Los Angeles, CA
California State University, Northridge, CA
Calvin College, MI
Case Western Reserve University, OH
Centenary College of Louisiana, LA
Central Michigan University, MI
Christian Brothers University, TN
Christopher Newport University, VA
City College of the City University of New York, NY

Clarkson University, NY
Clemson University, SC
Cleveland State University, OH
College of Charleston, SC
The College of New Jersey, NJ
College of Staten Island of the City University of New York, NY
Colorado School of Mines, CO
Colorado State University–Pueblo, CO
Colorado Technical University Colorado Springs, CO
Colorado Technical University Denver, CO
Cooper Union for the Advancement of Science and Art, NY
Dalton State College, GA
Dordt College, IA
Eastern Michigan University, MI
Eastern Washington University, WA
East Tennessee State University, TN
Edinboro University of Pennsylvania, PA
Elizabethtown College, PA
Elon University, NC
Emporia State University, KS
Evangel University, MO
Fairfield University, CT
Ferris State University, MI
Florida Atlantic University, FL
Florida Gulf Coast University, FL
Florida International University, FL
Frostburg State University, MD
Furman University, SC
Gannon University, PA
Geneva College, PA
George Fox University, OR
Georgia Institute of Technology, GA
Georgia Southern University, GA
Gonzaga University, WA
Graceland University, IA
Grand Valley State University, MI
Grove City College, PA
Harding University, AR
Idaho State University, ID
Illinois Institute of Technology, IL
Illinois State University, IL
Indiana University of Pennsylvania, PA
Iowa State University of Science and Technology, IA
James Madison University, VA
The Johns Hopkins University, MD
Kent State University, OH
Kettering University, MI
Langston University, OK
Lawrence Technological University, MI
Lehigh University, PA
Lindenwood University, MO
Lipscomb University, TN
Loras College, IA
Louisiana State University and Agricultural and Mechanical College, LA
Louisiana Tech University, LA
Maine Maritime Academy, ME
Marquette University, WI
Mercer University, GA
Mesa State College, CO
Miami University, OH
Michigan State University, MI
Milwaukee School of Engineering, WI
Mississippi State University, MS
Missouri University of Science and Technology, MO
Missouri Western State University, MO
Montana State University, MT
Montana State University–Billings, MT
Montana Tech of The University of Montana, MT
Murray State University, KY
Muskingum College, OH
New England College, NH
New Jersey Institute of Technology, NJ
New Mexico State University, NM
North Carolina State University, NC
North Dakota State University, ND
Northern Arizona University, AZ
Northern Illinois University, IL
Northern Michigan University, MI
Northwestern State University of Louisiana, LA
Oakland University, MI
Ohio Northern University, OH
The Ohio State University, OH
Ohio University, OH
Ohio University–Chillicothe, OH
Ohio University–Eastern, OH
Ohio University–Lancaster, OH
Ohio University–Southern Campus, OH
Ohio University–Zanesville, OH
Oklahoma Christian University, OK
Oklahoma State University, OK
Old Dominion University, VA
Oral Roberts University, OK
Ouachita Baptist University, AR
Philadelphia University, PA
Pittsburg State University, KS
Point Loma Nazarene University, CA
Polytechnic Institute of NYU, NY
Portland State University, OR
Purdue University, IN
Rice University, TX
Rochester Institute of Technology, NY
Rollins College, FL
Saginaw Valley State University, MI
St. Cloud State University, MN
Saint Louis University, MO
Sam Houston State University, TX
San Diego State University, CA
Santa Clara University, CA
Seattle Pacific University, WA
Shepherd University, WV
Sonoma State University, CA
South Dakota School of Mines and Technology, SD
South Dakota State University, SD
Southeastern Louisiana University, LA
Southeastern Oklahoma State University, OK
Southern Illinois University Carbondale, IL
Southwestern Oklahoma State University, OK
State University of New York at Binghamton, NY
State University of New York at Plattsburgh, NY
State University of New York College at Potsdam, NY
State University of New York College of Environmental Science and Forestry, NY
State University of New York Institute of Technology, NY
Stony Brook University, State University of New York, NY
Tennessee Technological University, TN
Texas A&M University, TX
Texas A&M University–Texarkana, TX
Texas Christian University, TX
Texas Tech University, TX
Union University, TN
The University of Akron, OH
The University of Alabama, AL
The University of Alabama at Birmingham, AL
The University of Alabama in Huntsville, AL
The University of Arizona, AZ
University of California, Davis, CA
University of California, Irvine, CA
University of California, Riverside, CA
University of California, San Diego, CA
University of Central Missouri, MO
University of Colorado at Boulder, CO
University of Colorado at Colorado Springs, CO
University of Connecticut, CT
University of Dayton, OH
University of Delaware, DE
University of Evansville, IN
University of Florida, FL
University of Hartford, CT
University of Idaho, ID
University of Illinois at Urbana–Champaign, IL
The University of Iowa, IA
The University of Kansas, KS
University of Kentucky, KY
University of Maryland, Baltimore County, MD
University of Maryland, College Park, MD
University of Maryland Eastern Shore, MD
University of Massachusetts Amherst, MA
University of Massachusetts Lowell, MA
University of Memphis, TN
University of Miami, FL
University of Michigan, MI
University of Michigan–Dearborn, MI
University of Michigan–Flint, MI
University of Minnesota, Twin Cities Campus, MN
University of Mississippi, MS
University of Missouri–Columbia, MO
University of Missouri–St. Louis, MO
University of Nebraska at Omaha, NE
University of Nebraska–Lincoln, NE
University of Nevada, Las Vegas, NV
University of New Hampshire, NH
The University of North Carolina at Asheville, NC
The University of North Carolina Wilmington, NC
University of North Dakota, ND
University of North Florida, FL
University of Oklahoma, OK
University of Pittsburgh at Bradford, PA
University of Pittsburgh at Johnstown, PA
University of Portland, OR
University of Rochester, NY
University of South Carolina, SC
University of South Carolina Aiken, SC
University of Southern Indiana, IN
University of South Florida, FL
The University of Tennessee, TN
The University of Tennessee at Martin, TN
The University of Texas at Arlington, TX
The University of Texas at Brownsville, TX
The University of Texas at Dallas, TX
The University of Texas at El Paso, TX
The University of Texas at San Antonio, TX
The University of Texas at Tyler, TX
The University of Texas–Pan American, TX
University of Tulsa, OK
University of Utah, UT
University of Vermont, VT
University of Washington, WA
University of Wisconsin–Green Bay, WI

University of Wisconsin–Parkside, WI
University of Wisconsin–Stevens Point, WI
University of Wisconsin–Stout, WI
University of Wyoming, WY
Utah State University, UT
Valdosta State University, GA
Valparaiso University, IN
Virginia Commonwealth University, VA
Virginia Military Institute, VA
Walla Walla University, WA
Washington State University, WA
Washington University in St. Louis, MO
Wayne State University, MI
Western Kentucky University, KY
Western New England College, MA
Western Washington University, WA
West Virginia University, WV
Wheaton College, IL
Wichita State University, KS
Widener University, PA
Wright State University, OH
Youngstown State University, OH

English

Abilene Christian University, TX
Albertus Magnus College, CT
Alfred University, NY
Alliant International University, CA
Angelo State University, TX
Arizona State University, AZ
Arkansas State University, AR
Auburn University, AL
Augsburg College, MN
Augustana College, IL
Augustana College, SD
Augusta State University, GA
Austin College, TX
Austin Peay State University, TN
Averett University, VA
Ball State University, IN
Barton College, NC
Baylor University, TX
Belhaven College, MS
Berry College, GA
Bethel College, IN
Birmingham-Southern College, AL
Black Hills State University, SD
Bloomfield College, NJ
Bloomsburg University of Pennsylvania, PA
Boise State University, ID
Bowling Green State University, OH
Brevard College, NC
Bryan College, TN
Butler University, IN
California Polytechnic State University, San Luis Obispo, CA
California State University, Chico, CA
California State University, Fresno, CA
California State University, Los Angeles, CA
California State University, Northridge, CA
California State University, Stanislaus, CA
Calvin College, MI
Campbellsville University, KY
Case Western Reserve University, OH
Centenary College of Louisiana, LA
Central Methodist University, MO
Central Michigan University, MI
Chatham University, PA
Christopher Newport University, VA
City College of the City University of New York, NY
Clemson University, SC
Cleveland State University, OH
The College at Brockport, State University of New York, NY
College of Charleston, SC
The College of Idaho, ID
The College of New Rochelle, NY
Colorado State University–Pueblo, CO
Columbia College, MO
Columbia International University, SC
Columbus State University, GA
Concordia University Chicago, IL
Concordia University, Nebraska, NE
Concordia University, St. Paul, MN
Concord University, WV
Dakota State University, SD
Dalton State College, GA
Dana College, NE
Defiance College, OH
DePauw University, IN
DeSales University, PA
Dordt College, IA
Drury University, MO
D'Youville College, NY
Eastern Michigan University, MI
Eastern Washington University, WA
East Tennessee State University, TN
East Texas Baptist University, TX
Edinboro University of Pennsylvania, PA
Elizabethtown College, PA
Elmhurst College, IL
Emmanuel College, GA
Emporia State University, KS
Evangel University, MO
Felician College, NJ
Flagler College, FL
Florida International University, FL
Fort Lewis College, CO
Francis Marion University, SC
Frostburg State University, MD
Furman University, SC
Gannon University, PA
Gardner-Webb University, NC
Georgia College & State University, GA
Georgian Court University, NJ
Georgia Southern University, GA
Glenville State College, WV
Graceland University, IA
Grand Valley State University, MI
Green Mountain College, VT
Grove City College, PA
Hamline University, MN
Harding University, AR
Hardin-Simmons University, TX
Hillsdale Free Will Baptist College, OK
Hope International University, CA
Howard Payne University, TX
Idaho State University, ID
Illinois State University, IL
Indiana University of Pennsylvania, PA
Iowa State University of Science and Technology, IA
Jacksonville State University, AL
James Madison University, VA
John Carroll University, OH
Juniata College, PA
Kennesaw State University, GA
Kent State University, OH
King's College, PA
Kutztown University of Pennsylvania, PA
LaGrange College, GA
Lewis-Clark State College, ID
Limestone College, SC
Lincoln University, PA
Lindenwood University, MO
Lindsey Wilson College, KY
Lipscomb University, TN
Lock Haven University of Pennsylvania, PA
Longwood University, VA
Louisiana State University and Agricultural and Mechanical College, LA
Louisiana Tech University, LA
Lubbock Christian University, TX
Lycoming College, PA
MacMurray College, IL
Malone University, OH
Manchester College, IN
Massachusetts College of Liberal Arts, MA
Mayville State University, ND
McMurry University, TX
Mercer University, GA
Mesa State College, CO
Methodist University, NC
Michigan State University, MI
Mid-Continent University, KY
Midland Lutheran College, NE
Millersville University of Pennsylvania, PA
Millikin University, IL
Minot State University, ND
Mississippi State University, MS
Mississippi University for Women, MS
Missouri University of Science and Technology, MO
Missouri Valley College, MO
Missouri Western State University, MO
Molloy College, NY
Montana State University, MT
Montana State University–Billings, MT
Montclair State University, NJ
Mount Mary College, WI
Murray State University, KY
New England College, NH
New Mexico State University, NM
North Central College, IL
North Dakota State University, ND
Northeastern State University, OK
Northern Arizona University, AZ
Northern Illinois University, IL
Northern Michigan University, MI
Northern State University, SD
Northwestern Oklahoma State University, OK
Northwest Missouri State University, MO
Oakland University, MI
Ohio Northern University, OH
The Ohio State University, OH
Ohio University, OH
Ohio University–Chillicothe, OH
Ohio University–Eastern, OH
Ohio University–Lancaster, OH
Ohio University–Southern Campus, OH
Ohio University–Zanesville, OH
Ohio Valley University, WV
Oklahoma Panhandle State University, OK
Oklahoma State University, OK
Old Dominion University, VA
Olivet College, MI
Ouachita Baptist University, AR
Pace University, NY
Pacific University, OR
Piedmont College, GA
Pittsburg State University, KS
Plymouth State University, NH
Post University, CT
Purchase College, State University of New York, NY
Purdue University North Central, IN
Randolph College, VA
Ripon College, WI

Rivier College, NH
Rockford College, IL
Rockhurst University, MO
Sacred Heart University, CT
St. Catherine University, MN
St. Cloud State University, MN
St. Edward's University, TX
St. John Fisher College, NY
Saint Louis University, MO
Salisbury University, MD
Sam Houston State University, TX
San Diego State University, CA
Schreiner University, TX
Seton Hill University, PA
Shepherd University, WV
Shippensburg University of Pennsylvania, PA
Shorter College, GA
Silver Lake College, WI
Slippery Rock University of Pennsylvania, PA
Sonoma State University, CA
South Dakota State University, SD
Southeastern Louisiana University, LA
Southeast Missouri State University, MO
Southern Adventist University, TN
Southern Arkansas University–Magnolia, AR
Southern Illinois University Carbondale, IL
Southern Nazarene University, OK
Southern Oregon University, OR
Southwestern Oklahoma State University, OK
Southwest Minnesota State University, MN
State University of New York at Binghamton, NY
State University of New York at Fredonia, NY
State University of New York at Oswego, NY
State University of New York at Plattsburgh, NY
State University of New York College at Geneseo, NY
State University of New York College at Potsdam, NY
Stetson University, FL
Stony Brook University, State University of New York, NY
Tennessee Technological University, TN
Texas A&M University–Texarkana, TX
Texas Christian University, TX
Texas State University–San Marcos, TX
Texas Tech University, TX
Thiel College, PA
Towson University, MD
Trevecca Nazarene University, TN
Trinity Christian College, IL
Truman State University, MO
The University of Akron, OH
The University of Alabama, AL
The University of Alabama in Huntsville, AL
University of California, Davis, CA
University of California, Riverside, CA
University of Central Missouri, MO
University of Colorado at Boulder, CO
University of Colorado at Colorado Springs, CO
University of Connecticut, CT
University of Delaware, DE
University of Evansville, IN
University of Hawaii at Hilo, HI
University of Idaho, ID
University of Illinois at Urbana–Champaign, IL
The University of Kansas, KS
University of Kentucky, KY
University of Louisiana at Monroe, LA
University of Maine at Fort Kent, ME
University of Mary Hardin-Baylor, TX
University of Maryland, Baltimore County, MD
University of Maryland, College Park, MD
University of Maryland Eastern Shore, MD
University of Mary Washington, VA
University of Massachusetts Amherst, MA
University of Memphis, TN
University of Miami, FL
University of Michigan, MI
University of Michigan–Flint, MI
University of Minnesota, Twin Cities Campus, MN
University of Mississippi, MS
University of Missouri–Columbia, MO
University of Missouri–St. Louis, MO
The University of Montana, MT
The University of Montana Western, MT
University of Nebraska at Omaha, NE
University of Nebraska–Lincoln, NE
University of Nevada, Las Vegas, NV
University of New England, ME
University of New Hampshire, NH
The University of North Carolina at Asheville, NC
The University of North Carolina at Chapel Hill, NC
The University of North Carolina at Greensboro, NC
The University of North Carolina at Pembroke, NC
The University of North Carolina Wilmington, NC
University of North Dakota, ND
University of Northern Colorado, CO
University of Pittsburgh at Bradford, PA
University of Pittsburgh at Johnstown, PA
University of Portland, OR
University of Puget Sound, WA
University of St. Thomas, MN
University of South Carolina, SC
University of South Carolina Aiken, SC
The University of South Dakota, SD
University of South Florida, FL
The University of Tennessee at Martin, TN
The University of Texas at Arlington, TX
The University of Texas at El Paso, TX
The University of Texas at San Antonio, TX
The University of Texas–Pan American, TX
University of the Ozarks, AR
University of the Southwest, NM
University of Tulsa, OK
University of Utah, UT
University of Vermont, VT
The University of Virginia's College at Wise, VA
The University of West Alabama, AL
University of West Georgia, GA
University of Wisconsin–Eau Claire, WI
University of Wisconsin–La Crosse, WI
University of Wisconsin–Parkside, WI
University of Wisconsin–Stevens Point, WI
University of Wisconsin–Superior, WI
University of Wisconsin–Whitewater, WI
University of Wyoming, WY
Utah State University, UT
Valdosta State University, GA
Valley City State University, ND
Virginia Military Institute, VA
Walla Walla University, WA
Wartburg College, IA
Washington State University, WA
Washington University in St. Louis, MO
Wayland Baptist University, TX
Waynesburg University, PA
Wayne State University, MI
Webster University, MO
Western Carolina University, NC
Western Kentucky University, KY
Western Oregon University, OR
Western Washington University, WA
West Liberty State University, WV
Westminster College, UT
West Virginia University, WV
West Virginia Wesleyan College, WV
Wichita State University, KS
Widener University, PA
Wilson College, PA
Wright State University, OH
York College, NE
Youngstown State University, OH

Foreign Languages

Abilene Christian University, TX
Adelphi University, NY
Albertus Magnus College, CT
Alfred University, NY
Alliant International University, CA
Angelo State University, TX
Arizona State University, AZ
Auburn University, AL
Augsburg College, MN
Augustana College, IL
Augustana College, SD
Austin College, TX
Austin Peay State University, TN
Averett University, VA
Ball State University, IN
Baylor University, TX
Belhaven College, MS
Birmingham-Southern College, AL
Black Hills State University, SD
Bloomsburg University of Pennsylvania, PA
Boise State University, ID
Boston University, MA
Bowling Green State University, OH
Bryan College, TN
Butler University, IN
California Polytechnic State University, San Luis Obispo, CA
California State University, Bakersfield, CA
California State University, Chico, CA
California State University, Fresno, CA
California State University, Los Angeles, CA
California State University, San Bernardino, CA
California State University, Stanislaus, CA
Calvin College, MI
Case Western Reserve University, OH
Centenary College of Louisiana, LA
Central College, IA
Central Methodist University, MO
Central Michigan University, MI
Christopher Newport University, VA
City College of the City University of New York, NY
Clarke College, IA
Clemson University, SC
Coe College, IA
The College at Brockport, State University of New York, NY
College of Charleston, SC
The College of Idaho, ID
The College of New Rochelle, NY
Colorado State University–Pueblo, CO
Concordia University Chicago, IL

Concordia University Texas, TX
Dana College, NE
Davidson College, NC
DePauw University, IN
DeSales University, PA
Dordt College, IA
Drury University, MO
Eastern Michigan University, MI
Eastern Washington University, WA
Edgewood College, WI
Edinboro University of Pennsylvania, PA
Elizabethtown College, PA
Elmhurst College, IL
Emporia State University, KS
Evangel University, MO
Fairfield University, CT
Flagler College, FL
Florida International University, FL
Fordham University, NY
Frostburg State University, MD
Furman University, SC
Gannon University, PA
Gardner-Webb University, NC
Georgia College & State University, GA
Georgian Court University, NJ
Georgia Southern University, GA
Grand Valley State University, MI
Grove City College, PA
Hamline University, MN
Hardin-Simmons University, TX
Idaho State University, ID
Illinois Institute of Technology, IL
Illinois State University, IL
Indiana University of Pennsylvania, PA
Iowa State University of Science and Technology, IA
John Carroll University, OH
Juniata College, PA
Kennesaw State University, GA
King's College, PA
Kutztown University of Pennsylvania, PA
Lake Forest College, IL
Lindenwood University, MO
Lock Haven University of Pennsylvania, PA
Louisiana State University and Agricultural and Mechanical College, LA
Louisiana Tech University, LA
Lubbock Christian University, TX
Lycoming College, PA
MacMurray College, IL
Malone University, OH
Manchester College, IN
Manhattan College, NY
Marquette University, WI
Marywood University, PA
Mercer University, GA
Mesa State College, CO
Michigan State University, MI
Millersville University of Pennsylvania, PA
Millikin University, IL
Mississippi State University, MS
Montana State University, MT
Montclair State University, NJ
Murray State University, KY
Newberry College, SC
New Mexico State University, NM
North Central College, IL
Northeastern State University, OK
Northern Arizona University, AZ
Northern Illinois University, IL
Northern Michigan University, MI
Northern State University, SD
Northwestern Oklahoma State University, OK
Northwest Missouri State University, MO
Oakland University, MI
Ohio Northern University, OH
The Ohio State University, OH
Ohio University, OH
Ohio University–Chillicothe, OH
Ohio University–Eastern, OH
Ohio University–Lancaster, OH
Ohio University–Southern Campus, OH
Ohio University–Zanesville, OH
Oklahoma State University, OK
Olivet College, MI
Ouachita Baptist University, AR
Pace University, NY
Pacific University, OR
Piedmont College, GA
Pittsburg State University, KS
Portland State University, OR
Ripon College, WI
Rivier College, NH
Rockford College, IL
Rockhurst University, MO
St. Catherine University, MN
St. Edward's University, TX
St. John Fisher College, NY
Saint Louis University, MO
Salisbury University, MD
Sam Houston State University, TX
San Diego State University, CA
Seton Hill University, PA
Shippensburg University of Pennsylvania, PA
Shorter College, GA
Sonoma State University, CA
South Dakota State University, SD
Southeastern Louisiana University, LA
Southeast Missouri State University, MO
Southern Arkansas University–Magnolia, AR
Southern Illinois University Carbondale, IL
Southern Oregon University, OR
Southwestern Oklahoma State University, OK
State University of New York at Binghamton, NY
State University of New York at Fredonia, NY
State University of New York at Oswego, NY
State University of New York College at Geneseo, NY
State University of New York College at Potsdam, NY
Stetson University, FL
Tennessee Technological University, TN
Texas Tech University, TX
Towson University, MD
Truman State University, MO
The University of Akron, OH
The University of Alabama, AL
University of California, Davis, CA
University of California, Irvine, CA
University of Central Missouri, MO
University of Central Oklahoma, OK
University of Colorado at Boulder, CO
University of Connecticut, CT
University of Dallas, TX
University of Delaware, DE
University of Evansville, IN
University of Idaho, ID
University of Illinois at Urbana–Champaign, IL
The University of Kansas, KS
University of Kentucky, KY
University of Louisiana at Monroe, LA
University of Maine at Fort Kent, ME
University of Mary Hardin-Baylor, TX
University of Maryland, Baltimore County, MD
University of Maryland, College Park, MD
University of Mary Washington, VA
University of Miami, FL
University of Michigan, MI
University of Michigan–Dearborn, MI
University of Michigan–Flint, MI
University of Minnesota, Twin Cities Campus, MN
University of Mississippi, MS
University of Missouri–Columbia, MO
University of Missouri–St. Louis, MO
The University of Montana, MT
University of Nebraska at Omaha, NE
University of Nebraska–Lincoln, NE
University of Nevada, Las Vegas, NV
University of New Orleans, LA
The University of North Carolina at Greensboro, NC
The University of North Carolina Wilmington, NC
University of North Dakota, ND
University of Oklahoma, OK
University of Oregon, OR
University of Portland, OR
University of Puget Sound, WA
University of South Carolina, SC
The University of South Dakota, SD
University of South Florida, FL
The University of Texas at Arlington, TX
The University of Texas at San Antonio, TX
University of Tulsa, OK
University of Utah, UT
University of Vermont, VT
University of West Georgia, GA
University of Wisconsin–Eau Claire, WI
University of Wisconsin–La Crosse, WI
University of Wisconsin–Parkside, WI
University of Wisconsin–Stevens Point, WI
University of Wisconsin–Whitewater, WI
University of Wyoming, WY
Utah State University, UT
Valdosta State University, GA
Valparaiso University, IN
Virginia Commonwealth University, VA
Walla Walla University, WA
Washington State University, WA
Washington University in St. Louis, MO
Wayne State University, MI
Webster University, MO
Western Illinois University, IL
Western Kentucky University, KY
Western Oregon University, OR
Western Washington University, WA
West Virginia University, WV
Wheaton College, IL
Wichita State University, KS
Widener University, PA
Wilson College, PA
Wright State University, OH
Xavier University, OH

Health Fields

Alderson-Broaddus College, WV
Aquinas College, TN
Arizona State University, AZ
Arkansas State University, AR
Auburn University, AL
Augsburg College, MN
Augustana College, SD
Augusta State University, GA
Austin College, TX

Austin Peay State University, TN
Averett University, VA
Ball State University, IN
Barton College, NC
Bastyr University, WA
Baylor University, TX
Bellarmine University, KY
Bethel College, IN
Birmingham-Southern College, AL
Black Hills State University, SD
Bloomfield College, NJ
Bloomsburg University of Pennsylvania, PA
Boise State University, ID
Bowling Green State University, OH
Brenau University, GA
Brevard College, NC
California Polytechnic State University, San Luis Obispo, CA
California State University, Bakersfield, CA
California State University, Chico, CA
California State University, Fresno, CA
California State University, Los Angeles, CA
California State University, San Bernardino, CA
California State University, Stanislaus, CA
Calvin College, MI
Carroll University, WI
Case Western Reserve University, OH
Centenary College of Louisiana, LA
Central College, IA
Central Methodist University, MO
Central Michigan University, MI
Clemson University, SC
The College at Brockport, State University of New York, NY
College of Charleston, SC
The College of New Rochelle, NY
College of Staten Island of the City University of New York, NY
Colorado State University–Pueblo, CO
Columbus State University, GA
Concordia University, Nebraska, NE
Dalton State College, GA
Dana College, NE
Defiance College, OH
DePauw University, IN
DeSales University, PA
Dominican College, NY
Drury University, MO
D'Youville College, NY
Eastern Michigan University, MI
Eastern Washington University, WA
East Tennessee State University, TN
East Texas Baptist University, TX
Edinboro University of Pennsylvania, PA
Elizabethtown College, PA
Elmhurst College, IL
Emmanuel College, GA
Emporia State University, KS
Endicott College, MA
Everest University, FL
Felician College, NJ
Ferris State University, MI
Florida Gulf Coast University, FL
Florida International University, FL
Francis Marion University, SC
Frostburg State University, MD
Furman University, SC
Gardner-Webb University, NC
Georgia College & State University, GA
Georgia Southern University, GA
Grace University, NE
Grand Valley State University, MI
Harding University, AR
Hardin-Simmons University, TX
Hawai'i Pacific University, HI
Houston Baptist University, TX
Husson University, ME
Idaho State University, ID
Illinois Institute of Technology, IL
Illinois State University, IL
Indiana University of Pennsylvania, PA
Iowa State University of Science and Technology, IA
Jacksonville State University, AL
James Madison University, VA
John Carroll University, OH
Juniata College, PA
Kean University, NJ
Kennesaw State University, GA
Kent State University, OH
Kentucky State University, KY
King's College, PA
Kutztown University of Pennsylvania, PA
LaGrange College, GA
Langston University, OK
Lewis-Clark State College, ID
Lindenwood University, MO
Long Island University, Brooklyn Campus, NY
Long Island University, C.W. Post Campus, NY
Louisiana Tech University, LA
Lycoming College, PA
Malone University, OH
Marquette University, WI
Marymount University, VA
Maryville University of Saint Louis, MO
Marywood University, PA
Massachusetts College of Liberal Arts, MA
Mayville State University, ND
Medcenter One College of Nursing, ND
Medical College of Georgia, GA
Medical University of South Carolina, SC
Mercy College of Northwest Ohio, OH
Mesa State College, CO
Michigan State University, MI
Midland Lutheran College, NE
Midway College, KY
Millersville University of Pennsylvania, PA
Millikin University, IL
Milwaukee School of Engineering, WI
Minot State University, ND
Misericordia University, PA
Mississippi State University, MS
Mississippi University for Women, MS
Missouri Western State University, MO
Molloy College, NY
Monmouth University, NJ
Montana State University, MT
Montana State University–Billings, MT
Montana Tech of The University of Montana, MT
Mount Mary College, WI
Murray State University, KY
New England College, NH
New Mexico State University, NM
North Dakota State University, ND
Northeastern State University, OK
Northern Arizona University, AZ
Northern Illinois University, IL
Northern Michigan University, MI
Northwestern Oklahoma State University, OK
Northwestern State University of Louisiana, LA
Northwest Missouri State University, MO
Oakland University, MI
Ohio Christian University, OH
Ohio Northern University, OH
The Ohio State University, OH
Ohio University, OH
Ohio University–Chillicothe, OH
Ohio University–Eastern, OH
Ohio University–Lancaster, OH
Ohio University–Southern Campus, OH
Ohio University–Zanesville, OH
Oklahoma City University, OK
Oklahoma Panhandle State University, OK
Old Dominion University, VA
Oral Roberts University, OK
Oregon Health & Science University, OR
Ouachita Baptist University, AR
Pace University, NY
Pacific University, OR
Piedmont College, GA
Pittsburg State University, KS
Plymouth State University, NH
Point Loma Nazarene University, CA
Purdue University, IN
Purdue University North Central, IN
The Richard Stockton College of New Jersey, NJ
Robert Morris College, IL
Rochester Institute of Technology, NY
Rockhurst University, MO
Sacred Heart University, CT
Saginaw Valley State University, MI
St. Catherine University, MN
St. Cloud State University, MN
Saint Francis Medical Center College of Nursing, IL
St. John's University, NY
Saint Louis University, MO
Salisbury University, MD
San Diego State University, CA
Shepherd University, WV
Slippery Rock University of Pennsylvania, PA
Sonoma State University, CA
South Dakota State University, SD
Southeastern Louisiana University, LA
Southeast Missouri State University, MO
Southern Adventist University, TN
Southern Arkansas University–Magnolia, AR
Southern Illinois University Carbondale, IL
Southern Illinois University Edwardsville, IL
Southern Oregon University, OR
Southwestern College, KS
Southwestern Oklahoma State University, OK
State University of New York at Binghamton, NY
State University of New York at New Paltz, NY
State University of New York at Plattsburgh, NY
State University of New York College at Old Westbury, NY
State University of New York Upstate Medical University, NY
Stephen F. Austin State University, TX
Stony Brook University, State University of New York, NY
Tennessee Technological University, TN
Texas A&M University, TX
Texas Christian University, TX
Thomas Jefferson University, PA
Trinity Christian College, IL
The University of Akron, OH
The University of Alabama at Birmingham, AL

The University of Alabama in Huntsville, AL
University of California, Davis, CA
University of California, Irvine, CA
University of Central Missouri, MO
University of Central Oklahoma, OK
University of Colorado at Boulder, CO
University of Colorado at Colorado Springs, CO
University of Connecticut, CT
University of Delaware, DE
University of Evansville, IN
University of Florida, FL
University of Guam, GU
University of Hartford, CT
University of Hawaii at Hilo, HI
University of Illinois at Urbana–Champaign, IL
The University of Kansas, KS
University of Kentucky, KY
University of Louisiana at Monroe, LA
University of Maine at Fort Kent, ME
University of Mary Hardin-Baylor, TX
University of Maryland, College Park, MD
University of Maryland Eastern Shore, MD
University of Massachusetts Amherst, MA
University of Massachusetts Boston, MA
University of Massachusetts Lowell, MA
University of Memphis, TN
University of Miami, FL
University of Michigan, MI
University of Michigan–Flint, MI
University of Minnesota, Twin Cities Campus, MN
University of Mississippi, MS
University of Missouri–Columbia, MO
University of Missouri–St. Louis, MO
The University of Montana, MT
University of Nebraska–Lincoln, NE
University of Nevada, Las Vegas, NV
University of New England, ME
University of New Hampshire, NH
The University of North Carolina at Asheville, NC
The University of North Carolina at Chapel Hill, NC
The University of North Carolina at Greensboro, NC
The University of North Carolina at Pembroke, NC
The University of North Carolina Wilmington, NC
University of North Dakota, ND
University of Northern Colorado, CO
University of North Florida, FL
University of Pittsburgh at Bradford, PA
University of Portland, OR
University of Saint Francis, IN
University of South Carolina, SC
University of Southern Indiana, IN
University of South Florida, FL
The University of Tampa, FL
The University of Tennessee, TN
The University of Tennessee at Martin, TN
The University of Texas at Arlington, TX
The University of Texas at Brownsville, TX
The University of Texas at El Paso, TX
The University of Texas at Tyler, TX
The University of Texas Health Science Center at Houston, TX
The University of Texas–Pan American, TX
University of Tulsa, OK
University of Utah, UT
University of Vermont, VT
The University of Virginia's College at Wise, VA
University of Washington, WA
University of West Georgia, GA
University of Wisconsin–Eau Claire, WI
University of Wisconsin–Green Bay, WI
University of Wisconsin–La Crosse, WI
University of Wisconsin–Parkside, WI
University of Wisconsin–Stevens Point, WI
University of Wisconsin–Superior, WI
University of Wyoming, WY
Utah State University, UT
Valdosta State University, GA
Valparaiso University, IN
Virginia Commonwealth University, VA
Washington State University, WA
Washington University in St. Louis, MO
Wayne State University, MI
Western Kentucky University, KY
Western Washington University, WA
West Liberty State University, WV
Westminster College, UT
West Virginia University, WV
Wichita State University, KS
Widener University, PA
Wisconsin Lutheran College, WI
Wright State University, OH
Youngstown State University, OH

Home Economics

Arizona State University, AZ
Auburn University, AL
Averett University, VA
Baylor University, TX
Bowling Green State University, OH
California Polytechnic State University, San Luis Obispo, CA
Carson-Newman College, TN
Eastern Michigan University, MI
Fort Valley State University, GA
Idaho State University, ID
Illinois State University, IL
Indiana University of Pennsylvania, PA
Iowa State University of Science and Technology, IA
Jacksonville State University, AL
Lipscomb University, TN
Louisiana State University and Agricultural and Mechanical College, LA
Louisiana Tech University, LA
Mississippi State University, MS
Mississippi University for Women, MS
Montana State University, MT
Montclair State University, NJ
Mount Mary College, WI
New Mexico State University, NM
North Dakota State University, ND
Northeastern State University, OK
Northern Arizona University, AZ
Northwest Missouri State University, MO
The Ohio State University, OH
Ohio University, OH
Ohio University–Chillicothe, OH
Ohio University–Eastern, OH
Ohio University–Lancaster, OH
Ohio University–Southern Campus, OH
Ohio University–Zanesville, OH
Oklahoma State University, OK
Ouachita Baptist University, AR
Pittsburg State University, KS
Point Loma Nazarene University, CA
St. Catherine University, MN
Sam Houston State University, TX
Seton Hill University, PA
Shepherd University, WV
South Dakota State University, SD
Southeastern Louisiana University, LA
Southeast Missouri State University, MO
Southern Illinois University Carbondale, IL
State University of New York at Plattsburgh, NY
State University of New York College at Oneonta, NY
Stephen F. Austin State University, TX
Tennessee Technological University, TN
Texas State University–San Marcos, TX
Texas Tech University, TX
The University of Akron, OH
The University of Alabama, AL
University of California, Davis, CA
University of Central Missouri, MO
University of Central Oklahoma, OK
University of Idaho, ID
University of Illinois at Urbana–Champaign, IL
University of Kentucky, KY
University of Louisiana at Monroe, LA
University of Maryland Eastern Shore, MD
University of Minnesota, Twin Cities Campus, MN
University of Missouri–Columbia, MO
University of Nebraska at Omaha, NE
University of Nebraska–Lincoln, NE
The University of North Carolina at Greensboro, NC
University of Northern Colorado, CO
The University of Tennessee at Martin, TN
University of Vermont, VT
University of Wisconsin–Stevens Point, WI
University of Wisconsin–Stout, WI
University of Wyoming, WY
Utah State University, UT
Washington State University, WA
Western Illinois University, IL
Western Kentucky University, KY
West Virginia University, WV

Humanities

Alaska Pacific University, AK
Albertus Magnus College, CT
Alderson-Broaddus College, WV
Alfred University, NY
Alliant International University, CA
Arizona State University, AZ
Arkansas State University, AR
Auburn University, AL
Augustana College, IL
Augustana College, SD
Austin College, TX
Austin Peay State University, TN
Averett University, VA
Avila University, MO
Ball State University, IN
Barton College, NC
Baylor University, TX
Belhaven College, MS
Berry College, GA
Birmingham-Southern College, AL
Black Hills State University, SD
Bloomfield College, NJ
Bloomsburg University of Pennsylvania, PA
Boise State University, ID
Bowling Green State University, OH
Brenau University, GA
Bryan College, TN
Buena Vista University, IA

Butler University, IN
California Polytechnic State University, San Luis Obispo, CA
California State Polytechnic University, Pomona, CA
California State University, Bakersfield, CA
California State University, Chico, CA
California State University, Fresno, CA
California State University, Fullerton, CA
California State University, Stanislaus, CA
Calvin College, MI
Campbellsville University, KY
Carroll University, WI
Case Western Reserve University, OH
Centenary College of Louisiana, LA
Central College, IA
Central Methodist University, MO
Central Michigan University, MI
Christopher Newport University, VA
City College of the City University of New York, NY
Clarkson University, NY
Clemson University, SC
Coastal Carolina University, SC
The College at Brockport, State University of New York, NY
College of Charleston, SC
The College of Idaho, ID
The College of New Rochelle, NY
College of Staten Island of the City University of New York, NY
College of the Holy Cross, MA
Columbia College, MO
Columbus State University, GA
Concordia University, Nebraska, NE
Dallas Baptist University, TX
Dalton State College, GA
Defiance College, OH
DeSales University, PA
Dordt College, IA
Drury University, MO
D'Youville College, NY
Eastern Michigan University, MI
East Texas Baptist University, TX
Edinboro University of Pennsylvania, PA
Elizabethtown College, PA
Elmhurst College, IL
Emporia State University, KS
Evangel University, MO
Flagler College, FL
Florida Gulf Coast University, FL
Florida International University, FL
Fort Lewis College, CO
Francis Marion University, SC
Fresno Pacific University, CA
Frostburg State University, MD
Furman University, SC
Gannon University, PA
Gardner-Webb University, NC
Georgia College & State University, GA
Georgia Southern University, GA
Grand Valley State University, MI
Hardin-Simmons University, TX
Hope International University, CA
Idaho State University, ID
Illinois State University, IL
Indiana University of Pennsylvania, PA
Iowa State University of Science and Technology, IA
Jacksonville State University, AL
James Madison University, VA
Juniata College, PA
Kean University, NJ
Kennesaw State University, GA
King's College, PA
Kutztown University of Pennsylvania, PA
Lawrence Technological University, MI
Lewis-Clark State College, ID
Limestone College, SC
Lincoln University, PA
Lindenwood University, MO
Longwood University, VA
Louisiana State University and Agricultural and Mechanical College, LA
Lubbock Christian University, TX
Lycoming College, PA
Malone University, OH
Manchester College, IN
Massachusetts College of Liberal Arts, MA
Mesa State College, CO
Mid-Continent University, KY
Midland Lutheran College, NE
Millersville University of Pennsylvania, PA
Millikin University, IL
Minot State University, ND
Mississippi State University, MS
Mississippi University for Women, MS
Missouri University of Science and Technology, MO
Missouri Valley College, MO
Missouri Western State University, MO
Monmouth University, NJ
Montana State University, MT
Montana State University–Billings, MT
Montclair State University, NJ
Mount Mary College, WI
Murray State University, KY
Newberry College, SC
New England College, NH
New Jersey Institute of Technology, NJ
New Mexico State University, NM
North Carolina State University, NC
North Central College, IL
North Dakota State University, ND
Northeastern State University, OK
Northern Arizona University, AZ
Northern Illinois University, IL
Northern State University, SD
Northwestern State University of Louisiana, LA
Northwest Missouri State University, MO
Oakland University, MI
Ohio Northern University, OH
The Ohio State University, OH
Ohio University, OH
Ohio University–Chillicothe, OH
Ohio University–Eastern, OH
Ohio University–Lancaster, OH
Ohio University–Southern Campus, OH
Ohio University–Zanesville, OH
Oklahoma State University, OK
Old Dominion University, VA
Ouachita Baptist University, AR
Pace University, NY
Pacific University, OR
Piedmont College, GA
Point Loma Nazarene University, CA
Portland State University, OR
Post University, CT
Purchase College, State University of New York, NY
Purdue University, IN
Rensselaer Polytechnic Institute, NY
The Richard Stockton College of New Jersey, NJ
Ripon College, WI
Rivier College, NH
Rockhurst University, MO
Sacred Heart University, CT
St. Catherine University, MN
St. Edward's University, TX
St. John Fisher College, NY
Saint Louis University, MO
Salisbury University, MD
Sam Houston State University, TX
Savannah College of Art and Design, GA
Seton Hill University, PA
Shepherd University, WV
Shippensburg University of Pennsylvania, PA
Sonoma State University, CA
South Dakota State University, SD
Southeastern Louisiana University, LA
Southeast Missouri State University, MO
Southern Illinois University Carbondale, IL
Southwestern University, TX
State University of New York at Binghamton, NY
State University of New York at Fredonia, NY
State University of New York at Oswego, NY
State University of New York at Plattsburgh, NY
State University of New York College at Geneseo, NY
State University of New York College at Potsdam, NY
Stetson University, FL
Tabor College, KS
Tennessee Technological University, TN
Texas Tech University, TX
The University of Akron, OH
The University of Alabama in Huntsville, AL
The University of Arizona, AZ
University of California, Davis, CA
University of California, Irvine, CA
University of California, Riverside, CA
University of California, Santa Cruz, CA
University of Central Missouri, MO
University of Colorado at Boulder, CO
University of Connecticut, CT
University of Dayton, OH
University of Delaware, DE
University of Evansville, IN
University of Houston–Clear Lake, TX
University of Houston–Victoria, TX
University of Idaho, ID
University of Illinois at Urbana–Champaign, IL
The University of Kansas, KS
University of Maine at Fort Kent, ME
University of Mary Hardin-Baylor, TX
University of Maryland, Baltimore County, MD
University of Maryland, College Park, MD
University of Mary Washington, VA
University of Massachusetts Amherst, MA
University of Massachusetts Lowell, MA
University of Memphis, TN
University of Miami, FL
University of Michigan, MI
University of Michigan–Flint, MI
University of Minnesota, Twin Cities Campus, MN
University of Mississippi, MS
University of Missouri–St. Louis, MO
The University of Montana, MT
The University of Montana Western, MT
University of Nebraska–Lincoln, NE
University of Nevada, Las Vegas, NV
University of New England, ME

Non-Need Scholarships for Undergraduates
Academic Interests/Achievements

University of New Hampshire, NH
The University of North Carolina at Greensboro, NC
The University of North Carolina Wilmington, NC
University of North Dakota, ND
University of Oklahoma, OK
University of Pittsburgh at Bradford, PA
University of Pittsburgh at Johnstown, PA
University of Portland, OR
University of Puget Sound, WA
University of St. Thomas, MN
University of South Alabama, AL
University of South Carolina, SC
University of South Carolina Aiken, SC
The University of South Dakota, SD
University of Southern Indiana, IN
University of South Florida, FL
The University of Tennessee, TN
The University of Tennessee at Martin, TN
The University of Texas at Arlington, TX
The University of Texas at El Paso, TX
The University of Texas at San Antonio, TX
University of the Ozarks, AR
University of the Southwest, NM
University of Utah, UT
University of Vermont, VT
The University of Virginia's College at Wise, VA
University of West Georgia, GA
University of Wisconsin–Green Bay, WI
University of Wisconsin–Stevens Point, WI
University of Wisconsin–Superior, WI
University of Wisconsin–Whitewater, WI
Utah State University, UT
Valdosta State University, GA
Valley City State University, ND
Virginia Commonwealth University, VA
Walla Walla University, WA
Warner Pacific College, OR
Washington State University, WA
Washington University in St. Louis, MO
Wayne State University, MI
Webster University, MO
Western Oregon University, OR
Western Washington University, WA
Westminster College, UT
West Virginia University, WV
Wichita State University, KS
Widener University, PA
Williams Baptist College, AR
Wilson College, PA
Wright State University, OH
Youngstown State University, OH

International Studies

Albertus Magnus College, CT
Alfred University, NY
Alliant International University, CA
Angelo State University, TX
Augsburg College, MN
Augustana College, SD
Austin College, TX
Austin Peay State University, TN
Ball State University, IN
Barton College, NC
Baylor University, TX
Belhaven College, MS
Birmingham-Southern College, AL
Bloomsburg University of Pennsylvania, PA
Boise State University, ID
Bowling Green State University, OH
Buena Vista University, IA
Butler University, IN
California Polytechnic State University, San Luis Obispo, CA
California State University, Chico, CA
California State University, Stanislaus, CA
Calvin College, MI
Carroll University, WI
Case Western Reserve University, OH
Central College, IA
Central Michigan University, MI
Chatham University, PA
City College of the City University of New York, NY
Clemson University, SC
The College at Brockport, State University of New York, NY
College of Staten Island of the City University of New York, NY
Columbia International University, SC
Columbus State University, GA
Concordia University Texas, TX
Culver-Stockton College, MO
Dana College, NE
Defiance College, OH
DePauw University, IN
D'Youville College, NY
Elizabethtown College, PA
Elmhurst College, IL
Frostburg State University, MD
Furman University, SC
Gannon University, PA
Georgia College & State University, GA
Georgia Southern University, GA
Grace University, NE
Grand Valley State University, MI
Hampshire College, MA
Henderson State University, AR
Hope International University, CA
Idaho State University, ID
Illinois State University, IL
Indiana University of Pennsylvania, PA
Iowa State University of Science and Technology, IA
James Madison University, VA
Juniata College, PA
Kean University, NJ
Kennesaw State University, GA
Kent State University, OH
Keuka College, NY
Kutztown University of Pennsylvania, PA
Lawrence Technological University, MI
Lindenwood University, MO
Lock Haven University of Pennsylvania, PA
Longwood University, VA
Louisiana Tech University, LA
Lycoming College, PA
Malone University, OH
Mercer University, GA
Michigan State University, MI
Millikin University, IL
Mississippi State University, MS
Monmouth University, NJ
Montclair State University, NJ
Murray State University, KY
New England College, NH
North Central College, IL
Northern Arizona University, AZ
Northern Illinois University, IL
Northern Michigan University, MI
Northern State University, SD
Ohio Northern University, OH
The Ohio State University, OH
Ohio University, OH
Ohio University–Chillicothe, OH
Ohio University–Eastern, OH
Ohio University–Lancaster, OH
Ohio University–Southern Campus, OH
Ohio University–Zanesville, OH
Oklahoma State University, OK
Ouachita Baptist University, AR
Portland State University, OR
Post University, CT
Rochester Institute of Technology, NY
St. Cloud State University, MN
St. Edward's University, TX
Saint Louis University, MO
San Diego State University, CA
South Dakota State University, SD
Southeastern Louisiana University, LA
Southeast Missouri State University, MO
Southern Illinois University Carbondale, IL
Southwestern University, TX
State University of New York at Binghamton, NY
State University of New York at Fredonia, NY
State University of New York at Oswego, NY
State University of New York at Plattsburgh, NY
State University of New York College at Cortland, NY
State University of New York College at Geneseo, NY
Tennessee Technological University, TN
Texas Christian University, TX
Texas State University–San Marcos, TX
Texas Tech University, TX
The University of Akron, OH
University of California, Davis, CA
University of California, Irvine, CA
University of Colorado at Boulder, CO
University of Connecticut, CT
University of Delaware, DE
University of Evansville, IN
University of Illinois at Urbana–Champaign, IL
The University of Kansas, KS
University of Kentucky, KY
University of Mary Hardin-Baylor, TX
University of Maryland, College Park, MD
University of Memphis, TN
University of Miami, FL
University of Michigan, MI
University of Michigan–Dearborn, MI
University of Michigan–Flint, MI
University of Minnesota, Twin Cities Campus, MN
University of Mississippi, MS
University of Missouri–St. Louis, MO
The University of Montana, MT
University of Nebraska–Lincoln, NE
University of Nevada, Las Vegas, NV
University of New England, ME
University of New Orleans, LA
The University of North Carolina Wilmington, NC
University of North Dakota, ND
University of North Florida, FL
University of Oklahoma, OK
University of Puget Sound, WA
University of St. Thomas, MN
University of South Alabama, AL
University of South Carolina, SC
University of South Florida, FL
The University of Tennessee, TN
The University of Texas at Arlington, TX
The University of Texas at El Paso, TX

The University of Texas at San Antonio, TX
University of Tulsa, OK
University of Utah, UT
University of Vermont, VT
University of Wisconsin–Eau Claire, WI
University of Wisconsin–Stevens Point, WI
University of Wisconsin–Stout, WI
University of Wyoming, WY
Utah State University, UT
Villanova University, PA
Virginia Military Institute, VA
Wartburg College, IA
Washington State University, WA
Washington University in St. Louis, MO
Waynesburg University, PA
Wayne State University, MI
Webster University, MO
Westminster College, UT
West Virginia University, WV
Wichita State University, KS
Widener University, PA
William Jessup University, CA
Wilson College, PA
Wisconsin Lutheran College, WI
Wright State University, OH

Library Science

Arkansas State University, AR
California Polytechnic State University, San Luis Obispo, CA
Emporia State University, KS
Illinois State University, IL
Iowa State University of Science and Technology, IA
Kent State University, OH
Kutztown University of Pennsylvania, PA
Lindenwood University, MO
Lock Haven University of Pennsylvania, PA
Mayville State University, ND
Mississippi State University, MS
Murray State University, KY
Northeastern State University, OK
Northern Arizona University, AZ
Northwestern Oklahoma State University, OK
Sam Houston State University, TX
The University of Alabama, AL
University of Central Missouri, MO
University of Idaho, ID
University of Illinois at Urbana–Champaign, IL
University of Louisiana at Monroe, LA
University of Maryland, College Park, MD
University of Michigan, MI
University of Minnesota, Twin Cities Campus, MN
The University of North Carolina at Greensboro, NC
University of South Carolina, SC
University of South Florida, FL
The University of Tennessee, TN
Utah State University, UT
Valdosta State University, GA
Valley City State University, ND
Virginia Polytechnic Institute and State University, VA
Wayne State University, MI
Western Washington University, WA
West Virginia University, WV

Mathematics

Abilene Christian University, TX
Albertus Magnus College, CT
Albion College, MI
Alderson-Broaddus College, WV
Alfred University, NY
Angelo State University, TX
Arizona State University, AZ
Arkansas State University, AR
Ashland University, OH
Auburn University, AL
Augsburg College, MN
Augustana College, IL
Augustana College, SD
Augusta State University, GA
Austin Peay State University, TN
Averett University, VA
Ball State University, IN
Bard College, NY
Barton College, NC
Baylor University, TX
Belhaven College, MS
Bethel College, IN
Birmingham-Southern College, AL
Black Hills State University, SD
Bloomfield College, NJ
Bloomsburg University of Pennsylvania, PA
Boise State University, ID
Bowling Green State University, OH
Brevard College, NC
Bryan College, TN
Bucknell University, PA
Buena Vista University, IA
Butler University, IN
California Polytechnic State University, San Luis Obispo, CA
California State Polytechnic University, Pomona, CA
California State University, Bakersfield, CA
California State University, Chico, CA
California State University, Fresno, CA
California State University, Fullerton, CA
California State University, Los Angeles, CA
California State University, Northridge, CA
California State University, San Bernardino, CA
California State University, Stanislaus, CA
Calvin College, MI
Campbellsville University, KY
Carroll University, WI
Carson-Newman College, TN
Case Western Reserve University, OH
Centenary College of Louisiana, LA
Central College, IA
Central Methodist University, MO
Central Michigan University, MI
Chatham University, PA
Christopher Newport University, VA
City College of the City University of New York, NY
Clarkson University, NY
Clemson University, SC
Coastal Carolina University, SC
The College at Brockport, State University of New York, NY
College of Charleston, SC
The College of Idaho, ID
The College of New Rochelle, NY
College of Saint Mary, NE
College of Staten Island of the City University of New York, NY
The Colorado College, CO
Colorado School of Mines, CO
Colorado State University–Pueblo, CO
Columbus State University, GA
Concordia University Chicago, IL
Concordia University, Nebraska, NE
Concordia University, St. Paul, MN
Dakota State University, SD
Dallas Baptist University, TX
Dana College, NE
Davidson College, NC
Defiance College, OH
DePauw University, IN
DeSales University, PA
Dordt College, IA
Drury University, MO
Duke University, NC
Eastern Michigan University, MI
Eastern Washington University, WA
East Tennessee State University, TN
East Texas Baptist University, TX
Edinboro University of Pennsylvania, PA
Elizabethtown College, PA
Elmhurst College, IL
Elon University, NC
Emporia State University, KS
Evangel University, MO
Ferris State University, MI
Florida Gulf Coast University, FL
Florida International University, FL
Fort Lewis College, CO
Francis Marion University, SC
Frostburg State University, MD
Furman University, SC
Gannon University, PA
Gardner-Webb University, NC
George Fox University, OR
Georgia College & State University, GA
Georgian Court University, NJ
Georgia Southern University, GA
Glenville State College, WV
Grand Valley State University, MI
Hardin-Simmons University, TX
Henderson State University, AR
Hillsdale Free Will Baptist College, OK
Howard Payne University, TX
Huntingdon College, AL
Huntington University, IN
Idaho State University, ID
Illinois State University, IL
Indiana University of Pennsylvania, PA
Iowa State University of Science and Technology, IA
Jacksonville State University, AL
James Madison University, VA
John Carroll University, OH
Johnson C. Smith University, NC
Juniata College, PA
Kennesaw State University, GA
Kent State University, OH
Kentucky State University, KY
Kettering University, MI
King's College, PA
Knox College, IL
Kutztown University of Pennsylvania, PA
Lake Forest College, IL
Lawrence Technological University, MI
Lees-McRae College, NC
Lewis-Clark State College, ID
Limestone College, SC
Lincoln University, PA
Lindenwood University, MO
Lindsey Wilson College, KY
Lipscomb University, TN
Lock Haven University of Pennsylvania, PA
Long Island University, C.W. Post Campus, NY
Longwood University, VA

Louisiana State University and Agricultural and Mechanical College, LA
Louisiana Tech University, LA
Lycoming College, PA
Malone University, OH
Manhattan College, NY
Manhattanville College, NY
Marquette University, WI
Marymount University, VA
Marywood University, PA
Massachusetts College of Liberal Arts, MA
The Master's College and Seminary, CA
Mayville State University, ND
McMurry University, TX
Mesa State College, CO
Michigan State University, MI
Millersville University of Pennsylvania, PA
Millikin University, IL
Mills College, CA
Minot State University, ND
Mississippi State University, MS
Mississippi University for Women, MS
Missouri University of Science and Technology, MO
Missouri Valley College, MO
Missouri Western State University, MO
Molloy College, NY
Monmouth University, NJ
Montana State University, MT
Montana State University–Billings, MT
Montana Tech of The University of Montana, MT
Montclair State University, NJ
Mount Mary College, WI
Murray State University, KY
Muskingum College, OH
Newberry College, SC
New England College, NH
New Jersey Institute of Technology, NJ
New Mexico State University, NM
North Carolina State University, NC
North Central College, IL
North Dakota State University, ND
Northeastern State University, OK
Northern Arizona University, AZ
Northern Illinois University, IL
Northern Michigan University, MI
Northern State University, SD
Northwestern Oklahoma State University, OK
Northwestern State University of Louisiana, LA
Northwest Missouri State University, MO
Ohio Northern University, OH
The Ohio State University, OH
Ohio University, OH
Ohio University–Chillicothe, OH
Ohio University–Eastern, OH
Ohio University–Lancaster, OH
Ohio University–Southern Campus, OH
Ohio University–Zanesville, OH
Oklahoma Panhandle State University, OK
Oklahoma State University, OK
Ouachita Baptist University, AR
Pace University, NY
Pacific University, OR
Piedmont College, GA
Pittsburg State University, KS
Plymouth State University, NH
Point Loma Nazarene University, CA
Purchase College, State University of New York, NY
Purdue University, IN
Randolph College, VA
Rensselaer Polytechnic Institute, NY
The Richard Stockton College of New Jersey, NJ
Ripon College, WI
Rivier College, NH
Rochester Institute of Technology, NY
Rockford College, IL
Rockhurst University, MO
Rollins College, FL
Sacred Heart University, CT
Saginaw Valley State University, MI
St. Catherine University, MN
St. Cloud State University, MN
St. Edward's University, TX
St. John Fisher College, NY
St. John's University, NY
Saint Louis University, MO
Salisbury University, MD
Sam Houston State University, TX
San Diego State University, CA
Schreiner University, TX
Seton Hill University, PA
Shepherd University, WV
Shippensburg University of Pennsylvania, PA
Skidmore College, NY
Sonoma State University, CA
South Dakota School of Mines and Technology, SD
South Dakota State University, SD
Southeastern Louisiana University, LA
Southeastern Oklahoma State University, OK
Southeast Missouri State University, MO
Southern Adventist University, TN
Southern Arkansas University–Magnolia, AR
Southern Illinois University Carbondale, IL
Southern Nazarene University, OK
Southern Oregon University, OR
Southwestern Oklahoma State University, OK
Southwestern University, TX
Southwest Minnesota State University, MN
State University of New York at Binghamton, NY
State University of New York at Fredonia, NY
State University of New York at Oswego, NY
State University of New York at Plattsburgh, NY
State University of New York College at Cortland, NY
State University of New York College at Geneseo, NY
State University of New York College at Potsdam, NY
Stephen F. Austin State University, TX
Stetson University, FL
Tennessee Technological University, TN
Texas A&M University–Texarkana, TX
Texas Christian University, TX
Texas Lutheran University, TX
Texas Tech University, TX
Thiel College, PA
Towson University, MD
Trinity Christian College, IL
Truman State University, MO
Union University, TN
The University of Akron, OH
The University of Alabama, AL
The University of Alabama at Birmingham, AL
University of California, Davis, CA
University of California, Riverside, CA
University of California, San Diego, CA
University of Central Missouri, MO
University of Central Oklahoma, OK
University of Colorado at Boulder, CO
University of Colorado at Colorado Springs, CO
University of Connecticut, CT
University of Dallas, TX
University of Delaware, DE
University of Evansville, IN
University of Houston–Clear Lake, TX
University of Houston–Victoria, TX
University of Idaho, ID
University of Illinois at Urbana–Champaign, IL
The University of Kansas, KS
University of Kentucky, KY
University of Louisiana at Monroe, LA
The University of Maine at Augusta, ME
University of Maine at Fort Kent, ME
University of Mary Hardin-Baylor, TX
University of Maryland, Baltimore County, MD
University of Maryland, College Park, MD
University of Maryland Eastern Shore, MD
University of Mary Washington, VA
University of Massachusetts Amherst, MA
University of Memphis, TN
University of Miami, FL
University of Michigan, MI
University of Michigan–Dearborn, MI
University of Michigan–Flint, MI
University of Minnesota, Twin Cities Campus, MN
University of Mississippi, MS
University of Missouri–Columbia, MO
University of Missouri–St. Louis, MO
The University of Montana, MT
The University of Montana Western, MT
University of Nebraska at Omaha, NE
University of Nebraska–Lincoln, NE
University of Nevada, Las Vegas, NV
University of New England, ME
University of New Hampshire, NH
University of New Orleans, LA
The University of North Carolina at Asheville, NC
The University of North Carolina at Chapel Hill, NC
The University of North Carolina at Greensboro, NC
The University of North Carolina Wilmington, NC
University of North Dakota, ND
University of Northern Colorado, CO
University of Northern Iowa, IA
University of Oklahoma, OK
University of Pittsburgh at Bradford, PA
University of Pittsburgh at Johnstown, PA
University of Portland, OR
University of Puget Sound, WA
University of Richmond, VA
University of St. Thomas, MN
University of South Carolina, SC
University of South Carolina Aiken, SC
The University of South Dakota, SD
University of Southern Indiana, IN
University of South Florida, FL
The University of Tennessee at Martin, TN
The University of Texas at Arlington, TX
The University of Texas at Brownsville, TX
The University of Texas at Dallas, TX
The University of Texas at El Paso, TX
The University of Texas at San Antonio, TX
The University of Texas–Pan American, TX
University of the Ozarks, AR

University of the Southwest, NM
University of Tulsa, OK
University of Utah, UT
University of Vermont, VT
The University of Virginia's College at Wise, VA
University of West Georgia, GA
University of Wisconsin–Eau Claire, WI
University of Wisconsin–La Crosse, WI
University of Wisconsin–Parkside, WI
University of Wisconsin–Stevens Point, WI
University of Wisconsin–Stout, WI
University of Wisconsin–Superior, WI
University of Wisconsin–Whitewater, WI
University of Wyoming, WY
Utah State University, UT
Valdosta State University, GA
Valley City State University, ND
Virginia Commonwealth University, VA
Virginia Military Institute, VA
Walla Walla University, WA
Warner Pacific College, OR
Wartburg College, IA
Washington State University, WA
Washington University in St. Louis, MO
Wayland Baptist University, TX
Waynesburg University, PA
Wayne State University, MI
West Chester University of Pennsylvania, PA
Western Carolina University, NC
Western Illinois University, IL
Western Kentucky University, KY
Western Oregon University, OR
Western Washington University, WA
West Liberty State University, WV
Westminster College, UT
West Virginia University, WV
Wheaton College, IL
Wichita State University, KS
Widener University, PA
Wilson College, PA
Wisconsin Lutheran College, WI
Wright State University, OH
Xavier University, OH
York College, NE

Military Science

Alfred University, NY
Angelo State University, TX
Arizona State University, AZ
Arkansas State University, AR
Augusta State University, GA
Austin Peay State University, TN
Ball State University, IN
Baylor University, TX
Black Hills State University, SD
Boise State University, ID
Boston College, MA
Bowling Green State University, OH
California Polytechnic State University, San Luis Obispo, CA
California State University, Fullerton, CA
Carson-Newman College, TN
Central Michigan University, MI
Christopher Newport University, VA
Clarkson University, NY
Clemson University, SC
The College at Brockport, State University of New York, NY
College of Saint Benedict, MN
College of the Holy Cross, MA
Colorado School of Mines, CO
Columbus State University, GA
Creighton University, NE
Dana College, NE
DeSales University, PA
Dickinson College, PA
Eastern Washington University, WA
East Tennessee State University, TN
Edinboro University of Pennsylvania, PA
Elon University, NC
Florida Institute of Technology, FL
Fort Valley State University, GA
Furman University, SC
Georgia Southern University, GA
Gonzaga University, WA
Idaho State University, ID
Illinois State University, IL
Iowa State University of Science and Technology, IA
Jacksonville State University, AL
James Madison University, VA
John Carroll University, OH
Kent State University, OH
Lawrence Technological University, MI
Lehigh University, PA
Lincoln University, MO
Lindenwood University, MO
Longwood University, VA
Louisiana State University and Agricultural and Mechanical College, LA
Louisiana Tech University, LA
Manhattan College, NY
Mercer University, GA
Michigan State University, MI
Mississippi State University, MS
Missouri University of Science and Technology, MO
Missouri Valley College, MO
Missouri Western State University, MO
Montana State University, MT
New Mexico State University, NM
North Carolina Agricultural and Technical State University, NC
North Dakota State University, ND
Northern Arizona University, AZ
Northern Michigan University, MI
North Greenville University, SC
The Ohio State University, OH
Ohio University, OH
Ohio University–Chillicothe, OH
Ohio University–Eastern, OH
Ohio University–Lancaster, OH
Ohio University–Southern Campus, OH
Ohio University–Zanesville, OH
Oklahoma State University, OK
Old Dominion University, VA
Olivet Nazarene University, IL
Pittsburg State University, KS
Providence College, RI
Purdue University, IN
Rensselaer Polytechnic Institute, NY
Ripon College, WI
Rochester Institute of Technology, NY
St. Edward's University, TX
St. John's University, NY
Saint Louis University, MO
St. Mary's University, TX
Sam Houston State University, TX
San Diego State University, CA
Santa Clara University, CA
Shippensburg University of Pennsylvania, PA
South Dakota State University, SD
Southeast Missouri State University, MO
Southern Illinois University Carbondale, IL
Stephen F. Austin State University, TX
Stetson University, FL
Tennessee Technological University, TN
Texas Christian University, TX
Texas State University–San Marcos, TX
Texas Tech University, TX
Truman State University, MO
The University of Akron, OH
The University of Alabama, AL
University of Alaska Fairbanks, AK
The University of Arizona, AZ
University of Central Missouri, MO
University of Central Oklahoma, OK
University of Colorado at Boulder, CO
University of Colorado at Colorado Springs, CO
University of Delaware, DE
University of Florida, FL
University of Idaho, ID
University of Illinois at Urbana–Champaign, IL
The University of Iowa, IA
University of Kentucky, KY
University of Louisiana at Monroe, LA
University of Maryland, College Park, MD
University of Massachusetts Amherst, MA
University of Memphis, TN
University of Michigan, MI
University of Minnesota, Twin Cities Campus, MN
University of Mississippi, MS
The University of Montana, MT
University of New Hampshire, NH
University of New Orleans, LA
University of North Dakota, ND
University of Northern Colorado, CO
University of Portland, OR
University of Puerto Rico, Mayagüez Campus, PR
University of Rochester, NY
The University of Scranton, PA
University of South Alabama, AL
University of South Carolina, SC
The University of South Dakota, SD
University of South Florida, FL
The University of Tampa, FL
The University of Tennessee, TN
The University of Tennessee at Martin, TN
The University of Texas at Arlington, TX
The University of Texas at El Paso, TX
The University of Texas–Pan American, TX
University of Utah, UT
University of Vermont, VT
University of West Florida, FL
University of Wisconsin–La Crosse, WI
University of Wisconsin–Stevens Point, WI
University of Wyoming, WY
Valdosta State University, GA
Villanova University, PA
Virginia Commonwealth University, VA
Virginia Military Institute, VA
Washington State University, WA
Washington University in St. Louis, MO
Wayne State University, MI
Western Kentucky University, KY
Westminster College, UT
West Virginia University, WV
Whitworth University, WA
Widener University, PA
Wright State University, OH
Xavier University, OH
Youngstown State University, OH

Physical Sciences

Abilene Christian University, TX
Alaska Pacific University, AK
Albertus Magnus College, CT
Alderson-Broaddus College, WV
Alfred University, NY
Angelo State University, TX
Arizona State University, AZ
Arkansas State University, AR
Ashland University, OH
Auburn University, AL
Augsburg College, MN
Augustana College, IL
Augustana College, SD
Augusta State University, GA
Austin College, TX
Austin Peay State University, TN
Averett University, VA
Ball State University, IN
Bard College, NY
Barton College, NC
Baylor University, TX
Bethel College, IN
Birmingham-Southern College, AL
Black Hills State University, SD
Bloomfield College, NJ
Bloomsburg University of Pennsylvania, PA
Boise State University, ID
Bowling Green State University, OH
Brevard College, NC
Bryan College, TN
Bucknell University, PA
Butler University, IN
California Polytechnic State University, San Luis Obispo, CA
California State Polytechnic University, Pomona, CA
California State University, Bakersfield, CA
California State University, Chico, CA
California State University, Fresno, CA
California State University, Los Angeles, CA
California State University, San Bernardino, CA
California State University, Stanislaus, CA
Calvin College, MI
Campbellsville University, KY
Carroll University, WI
Case Western Reserve University, OH
Centenary College of Louisiana, LA
Central College, IA
Central Methodist University, MO
Central Michigan University, MI
Chapman University, CA
Chatham University, PA
Clarkson University, NY
Clemson University, SC
Coe College, IA
The College at Brockport, State University of New York, NY
College of Charleston, SC
The College of Idaho, ID
The College of New Jersey, NJ
The College of New Rochelle, NY
College of Staten Island of the City University of New York, NY
The Colorado College, CO
Colorado School of Mines, CO
Colorado State University–Pueblo, CO
Columbia College, MO
Columbus State University, GA
Concordia University, Nebraska, NE
Concordia University, St. Paul, MN
Davidson College, NC
Defiance College, OH
DePauw University, IN
DeSales University, PA
Dominican University, IL
Dordt College, IA
Drury University, MO
Eastern Michigan University, MI
Eastern Washington University, WA
East Texas Baptist University, TX
Edinboro University of Pennsylvania, PA
Elizabethtown College, PA
Elmhurst College, IL
Elon University, NC
Emporia State University, KS
Evangel University, MO
Fairfield University, CT
Florida Atlantic University, FL
Florida Gulf Coast University, FL
Florida International University, FL
Fort Lewis College, CO
Frostburg State University, MD
Furman University, SC
Gardner-Webb University, NC
George Fox University, OR
Georgia College & State University, GA
Georgia Institute of Technology, GA
Georgian Court University, NJ
Graceland University, IA
Grand Valley State University, MI
Grove City College, PA
Hamline University, MN
Hampshire College, MA
Hardin-Simmons University, TX
Howard Payne University, TX
Idaho State University, ID
Illinois State University, IL
Indiana University of Pennsylvania, PA
Iowa State University of Science and Technology, IA
Jacksonville State University, AL
James Madison University, VA
Jamestown College, ND
John Carroll University, OH
Juniata College, PA
Kennesaw State University, GA
Kent State University, OH
Kettering University, MI
King's College, PA
Kutztown University of Pennsylvania, PA
Lake Forest College, IL
Lawrence Technological University, MI
Lewis-Clark State College, ID
Limestone College, SC
Lincoln University, PA
Lindenwood University, MO
Lock Haven University of Pennsylvania, PA
Loras College, IA
Louisiana State University and Agricultural and Mechanical College, LA
Louisiana Tech University, LA
Lubbock Christian University, TX
Lycoming College, PA
Malone University, OH
Massachusetts College of Liberal Arts, MA
The Master's College and Seminary, CA
Mayville State University, ND
McMurry University, TX
Mesa State College, CO
Michigan State University, MI
Midland Lutheran College, NE
Millersville University of Pennsylvania, PA
Millikin University, IL
Mills College, CA
Misericordia University, PA
Mississippi State University, MS
Mississippi University for Women, MS
Missouri University of Science and Technology, MO
Missouri Valley College, MO
Missouri Western State University, MO
Montana State University, MT
Montana State University–Billings, MT
Montana Tech of The University of Montana, MT
Montclair State University, NJ
Mount Mary College, WI
Mount Union College, OH
Muskingum College, OH
Newberry College, SC
New Mexico State University, NM
North Carolina State University, NC
North Central College, IL
North Dakota State University, ND
Northeastern State University, OK
Northern Arizona University, AZ
Northern Illinois University, IL
Northern Michigan University, MI
Northern State University, SD
Northwestern Oklahoma State University, OK
Northwestern State University of Louisiana, LA
Northwest Missouri State University, MO
Oberlin College, OH
Ohio Northern University, OH
The Ohio State University, OH
Ohio University, OH
Ohio University–Chillicothe, OH
Ohio University–Eastern, OH
Ohio University–Lancaster, OH
Ohio University–Southern Campus, OH
Ohio University–Zanesville, OH
Oklahoma Panhandle State University, OK
Oklahoma State University, OK
Old Dominion University, VA
Ouachita Baptist University, AR
Pace University, NY
Pacific University, OR
Pittsburg State University, KS
Plymouth State University, NH
Portland State University, OR
Purdue University, IN
Randolph College, VA
The Richard Stockton College of New Jersey, NJ
Ripon College, WI
Rochester Institute of Technology, NY
Rockford College, IL
Rockhurst University, MO
Rollins College, FL
Sacred Heart University, CT
Saginaw Valley State University, MI
St. Catherine University, MN
St. Cloud State University, MN
St. Edward's University, TX
St. John Fisher College, NY
Saint Louis University, MO
Salisbury University, MD
Sam Houston State University, TX
San Diego State University, CA
Schreiner University, TX
Seton Hill University, PA
Shepherd University, WV
Shippensburg University of Pennsylvania, PA
Skidmore College, NY
Slippery Rock University of Pennsylvania, PA
Sonoma State University, CA

South Dakota State University, SD
Southeastern Louisiana University, LA
Southeastern Oklahoma State University, OK
Southeast Missouri State University, MO
Southern Arkansas University–Magnolia, AR
Southern Illinois University Carbondale, IL
Southern Nazarene University, OK
Southern Oregon University, OR
Southwestern Oklahoma State University, OK
Southwest Minnesota State University, MN
State University of New York at Binghamton, NY
State University of New York at Fredonia, NY
State University of New York at Oswego, NY
State University of New York at Plattsburgh, NY
State University of New York College at Cortland, NY
State University of New York College at Geneseo, NY
State University of New York College at Old Westbury, NY
State University of New York College at Oneonta, NY
State University of New York College at Potsdam, NY
State University of New York College of Environmental Science and Forestry, NY
Stephen F. Austin State University, TX
Stetson University, FL
Stony Brook University, State University of New York, NY
Tennessee Technological University, TN
Texas A&M University, TX
Texas Christian University, TX
Texas Lutheran University, TX
Texas Tech University, TX
Thiel College, PA
Trevecca Nazarene University, TN
Truman State University, MO
The University of Akron, OH
The University of Alabama, AL
The University of Alabama in Huntsville, AL
University of Alaska Fairbanks, AK
The University of Arizona, AZ
University of California, Irvine, CA
University of California, Riverside, CA
University of California, San Diego, CA
University of California, Santa Cruz, CA
University of Central Missouri, MO
University of Central Oklahoma, OK
University of Colorado at Boulder, CO
University of Colorado at Colorado Springs, CO
University of Connecticut, CT
University of Dallas, TX
University of Delaware, DE
University of Evansville, IN
University of Idaho, ID
University of Illinois at Urbana–Champaign, IL
The University of Kansas, KS
University of Kentucky, KY
University of Louisiana at Monroe, LA
University of Mary Hardin-Baylor, TX
University of Maryland, Baltimore County, MD
University of Maryland, College Park, MD
University of Maryland Eastern Shore, MD
University of Mary Washington, VA
University of Massachusetts Amherst, MA
University of Memphis, TN
University of Miami, FL
University of Michigan, MI
University of Michigan–Dearborn, MI
University of Michigan–Flint, MI
University of Minnesota, Twin Cities Campus, MN
University of Mississippi, MS
The University of Montana, MT
The University of Montana Western, MT
University of Montevallo, AL
University of Nebraska at Omaha, NE
University of Nebraska–Lincoln, NE
University of Nevada, Las Vegas, NV
University of New England, ME
University of New Orleans, LA
The University of North Carolina at Asheville, NC
The University of North Carolina at Greensboro, NC
The University of North Carolina at Pembroke, NC
The University of North Carolina Wilmington, NC
University of North Dakota, ND
University of Northern Colorado, CO
University of Northern Iowa, IA
University of Oklahoma, OK
University of Oregon, OR
University of Pittsburgh at Bradford, PA
University of Pittsburgh at Johnstown, PA
University of Portland, OR
University of Puget Sound, WA
University of Richmond, VA
University of St. Thomas, MN
University of South Carolina, SC
University of South Carolina Aiken, SC
University of South Florida, FL
The University of Tennessee at Martin, TN
The University of Texas at Arlington, TX
The University of Texas at Dallas, TX
The University of Texas at El Paso, TX
The University of Texas at San Antonio, TX
University of Tulsa, OK
University of Utah, UT
University of Vermont, VT
The University of Virginia's College at Wise, VA
University of West Georgia, GA
University of Wisconsin–Eau Claire, WI
University of Wisconsin–Green Bay, WI
University of Wisconsin–La Crosse, WI
University of Wisconsin–Parkside, WI
University of Wisconsin–Stevens Point, WI
University of Wisconsin–Stout, WI
University of Wisconsin–Superior, WI
University of Wisconsin–Whitewater, WI
University of Wyoming, WY
Utah State University, UT
Valdosta State University, GA
Valley City State University, ND
Valparaiso University, IN
Virginia Commonwealth University, VA
Warner Pacific College, OR
Wartburg College, IA
Washington State University, WA
Washington University in St. Louis, MO
Wayland Baptist University, TX
Wayne State University, MI
Western Illinois University, IL
Western Kentucky University, KY
Western Oregon University, OR
Western Washington University, WA
West Liberty State University, WV
Westminster College, UT
West Virginia University, WV
West Virginia Wesleyan College, WV
Whitworth University, WA
Wichita State University, KS
Widener University, PA
Wilson College, PA
Wright State University, OH
Xavier University, OH

Premedicine

Albertus Magnus College, CT
Albion College, MI
Alderson-Broaddus College, WV
Alfred University, NY
American Jewish University, CA
Angelo State University, TX
Arizona State University, AZ
Arkansas State University, AR
Auburn University, AL
Augustana College, SD
Austin College, TX
Averett University, VA
Avila University, MO
Baylor University, TX
Belhaven College, MS
Birmingham-Southern College, AL
Boise State University, ID
Brevard College, NC
Bryan College, TN
California State University, Bakersfield, CA
California State University, Stanislaus, CA
Calvin College, MI
Campbellsville University, KY
Carroll University, WI
Case Western Reserve University, OH
Centenary College of Louisiana, LA
Central College, IA
Central Methodist University, MO
Chatham University, PA
City College of the City University of New York, NY
Clearwater Christian College, FL
Clemson University, SC
Coe College, IA
The College at Brockport, State University of New York, NY
College of Charleston, SC
The College of Idaho, ID
The College of New Rochelle, NY
College of Staten Island of the City University of New York, NY
Colorado State University–Pueblo, CO
Concordia University, Nebraska, NE
Dallas Baptist University, TX
Dana College, NE
Davidson College, NC
Defiance College, OH
DeSales University, PA
Dordt College, IA
Drury University, MO
D'Youville College, NY
Edinboro University of Pennsylvania, PA
Elizabethtown College, PA
Elmhurst College, IL
Elon University, NC
Emory & Henry College, VA
Emporia State University, KS
Fort Valley State University, GA
Francis Marion University, SC
Frostburg State University, MD
Furman University, SC
Gannon University, PA
Gardner-Webb University, NC

Grand Valley State University, MI
Hamline University, MN
Hardin-Simmons University, TX
Howard Payne University, TX
Idaho State University, ID
Illinois State University, IL
Indiana State University, IN
Indiana University of Pennsylvania, PA
Iowa State University of Science and Technology, IA
James Madison University, VA
John Carroll University, OH
Judson College, AL
Juniata College, PA
Kennesaw State University, GA
King's College, PA
Lindenwood University, MO
Lindsey Wilson College, KY
Lipscomb University, TN
Louisiana State University and Agricultural and Mechanical College, LA
Lycoming College, PA
Malone University, OH
Mayville State University, ND
McMurry University, TX
Midway College, KY
Millikin University, IL
Mills College, CA
Mississippi State University, MS
Missouri University of Science and Technology, MO
Missouri Valley College, MO
Montana State University–Billings, MT
Muskingum College, OH
North Central College, IL
North Dakota State University, ND
Northeastern State University, OK
Northern Arizona University, AZ
Northern Michigan University, MI
Northwestern Oklahoma State University, OK
Ohio Northern University, OH
The Ohio State University, OH
Ohio University, OH
Ohio University–Chillicothe, OH
Ohio University–Eastern, OH
Ohio University–Lancaster, OH
Ohio University–Southern Campus, OH
Ohio University–Zanesville, OH
Oklahoma State University, OK
Ouachita Baptist University, AR
Piedmont College, GA
Providence College, RI
Randolph College, VA
Ripon College, WI
Rivier College, NH
Rochester Institute of Technology, NY
Rockford College, IL
Rockhurst University, MO
Sacred Heart University, CT
St. Catherine University, MN
Saint Louis University, MO
Salisbury University, MD
Schreiner University, TX
Seton Hill University, PA
Shepherd University, WV
Sonoma State University, CA
South Dakota State University, SD
Southeast Missouri State University, MO
Southern Illinois University Carbondale, IL
Southwestern University, TX
Southwest Minnesota State University, MN
State University of New York at Binghamton, NY
State University of New York at Oswego, NY
State University of New York at Plattsburgh, NY
State University of New York College at Geneseo, NY
State University of New York College at Oneonta, NY
State University of New York College of Environmental Science and Forestry, NY
Stephen F. Austin State University, TX
Stetson University, FL
Sweet Briar College, VA
Tennessee Technological University, TN
Texas Christian University, TX
Texas Lutheran University, TX
Texas Tech University, TX
Truman State University, MO
Union University, TN
The University of Akron, OH
The University of Alabama, AL
University of California, Davis, CA
University of California, Riverside, CA
University of California, San Diego, CA
University of Central Missouri, MO
University of Colorado at Boulder, CO
University of Colorado at Colorado Springs, CO
University of Connecticut, CT
University of Dallas, TX
University of Delaware, DE
University of Evansville, IN
University of Hartford, CT
University of Idaho, ID
University of Illinois at Urbana–Champaign, IL
The University of Kansas, KS
University of Mary Hardin-Baylor, TX
University of Maryland, College Park, MD
University of Massachusetts Amherst, MA
University of Memphis, TN
University of Miami, FL
University of Michigan, MI
University of Michigan–Flint, MI
University of Minnesota, Twin Cities Campus, MN
University of Mississippi, MS
University of Missouri–Columbia, MO
The University of Montana, MT
The University of Montana Western, MT
University of Nebraska at Omaha, NE
University of Nebraska–Lincoln, NE
University of Nevada, Las Vegas, NV
University of New England, ME
The University of North Carolina at Asheville, NC
The University of North Carolina at Greensboro, NC
The University of North Carolina Wilmington, NC
University of North Dakota, ND
University of Pittsburgh at Bradford, PA
University of Pittsburgh at Johnstown, PA
University of Portland, OR
University of Puget Sound, WA
University of South Carolina, SC
The University of South Dakota, SD
University of Southern Indiana, IN
University of South Florida, FL
The University of Tennessee at Martin, TN
The University of Texas–Pan American, TX
University of the Ozarks, AR
University of the Southwest, NM
University of Tulsa, OK
University of Vermont, VT
The University of Virginia's College at Wise, VA
University of West Georgia, GA
University of Wisconsin–Eau Claire, WI
University of Wisconsin–Green Bay, WI
University of Wisconsin–Parkside, WI
University of Wisconsin–Stevens Point, WI
University of Wisconsin–Whitewater, WI
Utah State University, UT
Valdosta State University, GA
Virginia Military Institute, VA
Washington State University, WA
Washington University in St. Louis, MO
Wayne State University, MI
Western Kentucky University, KY
Western Oregon University, OR
Western Washington University, WA
Westminster College, UT
West Virginia University, WV
Wheaton College, IL
Wheeling Jesuit University, WV
Whitworth University, WA
Wichita State University, KS
Widener University, PA
Wilson College, PA
Worcester Polytechnic Institute, MA
Wright State University, OH
York College, NE

Religion/Biblical Studies

Abilene Christian University, TX
Alaska Bible College, AK
Albertus Magnus College, CT
Alderson-Broaddus College, WV
Appalachian Bible College, WV
Augsburg College, MN
Augustana College, IL
Augustana College, SD
Austin College, TX
Averett University, VA
Baptist Bible College of Pennsylvania, PA
The Baptist College of Florida, FL
Barton College, NC
Baylor University, TX
Belhaven College, MS
Belmont University, TN
Berry College, GA
Bethel College, IN
Birmingham-Southern College, AL
Bloomfield College, NJ
Bloomsburg University of Pennsylvania, PA
Brevard College, NC
Bryan College, TN
California Baptist University, CA
California State University, Bakersfield, CA
Calvin College, MI
Campbellsville University, KY
Carson-Newman College, TN
Case Western Reserve University, OH
Centenary College of Louisiana, LA
Central Christian College of the Bible, MO
Central College, IA
Central Methodist University, MO
Christopher Newport University, VA
Clearwater Christian College, FL
The College of Idaho, ID
The College of New Rochelle, NY
Columbia College, MO
Columbia International University, SC
Concordia College, AL
Concordia College–New York, NY
Concordia University, OR

Concordia University Chicago, IL
Concordia University, Nebraska, NE
Concordia University, St. Paul, MN
Dallas Baptist University, TX
Dana College, NE
Defiance College, OH
DeSales University, PA
Dordt College, IA
Eastern Michigan University, MI
East Texas Baptist University, TX
Edinboro University of Pennsylvania, PA
Elizabethtown College, PA
Elmhurst College, IL
Elon University, NC
Emmanuel College, GA
Emory & Henry College, VA
Evangel University, MO
Faulkner University, AL
Felician College, NJ
Flagler College, FL
Florida Gulf Coast University, FL
Furman University, SC
Gannon University, PA
Gardner-Webb University, NC
Geneva College, PA
George Fox University, OR
Grace University, NE
Grove City College, PA
Hardin-Simmons University, TX
Hastings College, NE
Hellenic College, MA
Hillsdale Free Will Baptist College, OK
Hope International University, CA
Houston Baptist University, TX
Howard Payne University, TX
Idaho State University, ID
James Madison University, VA
John Carroll University, OH
Johnson Bible College, TN
Kentucky Christian University, KY
King's College, PA
LaGrange College, GA
Lebanon Valley College, PA
Lee University, TN
Limestone College, SC
Lindsey Wilson College, KY
Lipscomb University, TN
Lubbock Christian University, TX
Lycoming College, PA
MacMurray College, IL
Malone University, OH
Manhattan Christian College, KS
Maranatha Baptist Bible College, WI
Marian College, IN
Marywood University, PA
The Master's College and Seminary, CA
McKendree University, IL
McMurry University, TX
Mercer University, GA
Mid-Continent University, KY
Midland Lutheran College, NE
Milligan College, TN
Mississippi State University, MS
Missouri Baptist University, MO
Montclair State University, NJ
Nazarene Bible College, CO
Newberry College, SC
North Central College, IL
Northern Arizona University, AZ
North Greenville University, SC
Ohio Christian University, OH
Ohio Northern University, OH
Ohio Valley University, WV
Oklahoma Baptist University, OK
Oklahoma Christian University, OK
Oklahoma City University, OK
Oklahoma Wesleyan University, OK
Oral Roberts University, OK
Ouachita Baptist University, AR
Piedmont College, GA
Point Loma Nazarene University, CA
Ripon College, WI
Roanoke Bible College, NC
Rockhurst University, MO
St. Edward's University, TX
Saint Francis University, PA
Saint Louis University, MO
San Diego State University, CA
Schreiner University, TX
Seton Hill University, PA
Shorter College, GA
Southeast Missouri State University, MO
Southern Adventist University, TN
Southern Illinois University Carbondale, IL
Southern Nazarene University, OK
Southwestern Christian University, OK
Southwestern College, KS
Stetson University, FL
Texas Christian University, TX
Thiel College, PA
Trevecca Nazarene University, TN
Trinity College of Florida, FL
Trinity Lutheran College, WA
Union University, TN
The University of Arizona, AZ
University of California, Davis, CA
University of Central Missouri, MO
University of Connecticut, CT
University of Dallas, TX
University of Delaware, DE
University of Evansville, IN
University of Illinois at Urbana–Champaign, IL
The University of Kansas, KS
University of Mary Hardin-Baylor, TX
University of Mary Washington, VA
University of Miami, FL
University of Minnesota, Twin Cities Campus, MN
University of Mississippi, MS
University of Missouri–Columbia, MO
The University of North Carolina at Greensboro, NC
University of Portland, OR
University of St. Thomas, MN
University of South Carolina, SC
University of South Florida, FL
University of the Ozarks, AR
University of the Southwest, NM
University of Tulsa, OK
Valparaiso University, IN
Walla Walla University, WA
Warner Pacific College, OR
Wartburg College, IA
Washington University in St. Louis, MO
Wayland Baptist University, TX
Waynesburg University, PA
West Virginia University, WV
Wheaton College, IL
William Jessup University, CA
Williams Baptist College, AR
Wilson College, PA
Wisconsin Lutheran College, WI
Wright State University, OH
York College, NE

Social Sciences

Abilene Christian University, TX
Alaska Pacific University, AK
Albertus Magnus College, CT
Alderson-Broaddus College, WV
Alfred University, NY
Alliant International University, CA
Angelo State University, TX
Arizona State University, AZ
Arkansas State University, AR
Ashland University, OH
Auburn University, AL
Augsburg College, MN
Augustana College, IL
Augustana College, SD
Augusta State University, GA
Austin College, TX
Austin Peay State University, TN
Ball State University, IN
Barton College, NC
Baylor University, TX
Belhaven College, MS
Bethel College, IN
Birmingham-Southern College, AL
Black Hills State University, SD
Bloomfield College, NJ
Bloomsburg University of Pennsylvania, PA
Boise State University, ID
Bowling Green State University, OH
Brevard College, NC
Bryan College, TN
Butler University, IN
California Polytechnic State University, San Luis Obispo, CA
California State Polytechnic University, Pomona, CA
California State University, Bakersfield, CA
California State University, Chico, CA
California State University, Fresno, CA
California State University, Fullerton, CA
California State University, Los Angeles, CA
California State University, Northridge, CA
California State University, San Bernardino, CA
California State University, Stanislaus, CA
Calvin College, MI
Campbellsville University, KY
Carroll University, WI
Case Western Reserve University, OH
Centenary College of Louisiana, LA
Central College, IA
Central Methodist University, MO
Central Michigan University, MI
Chatham University, PA
City College of the City University of New York, NY
Clarkson University, NY
Clemson University, SC
The College at Brockport, State University of New York, NY
College of Charleston, SC
The College of Idaho, ID
The College of New Rochelle, NY
College of Staten Island of the City University of New York, NY
Colorado State University–Pueblo, CO
Columbia College, MO
Concordia College–New York, NY
Concordia University, Nebraska, NE
Concordia University, St. Paul, MN
Concordia University Texas, TX
Concord University, WV
Dalton State College, GA

Dana College, NE
Defiance College, OH
DeSales University, PA
Dordt College, IA
Drury University, MO
D'Youville College, NY
Eastern Michigan University, MI
Eastern Washington University, WA
East Tennessee State University, TN
East Texas Baptist University, TX
Edinboro University of Pennsylvania, PA
Elizabethtown College, PA
Elmhurst College, IL
Elon University, NC
Emporia State University, KS
Evangel University, MO
Flagler College, FL
Florida Atlantic University, FL
Florida Gulf Coast University, FL
Florida International University, FL
Fort Lewis College, CO
Fort Valley State University, GA
Francis Marion University, SC
Fresno Pacific University, CA
Frostburg State University, MD
Furman University, SC
Gannon University, PA
Gardner-Webb University, NC
Georgia College & State University, GA
Georgia Southern University, GA
Glenville State College, WV
Grand Valley State University, MI
Green Mountain College, VT
Grove City College, PA
Hampshire College, MA
Hardin-Simmons University, TX
Hawai'i Pacific University, HI
Hope International University, CA
Howard Payne University, TX
Idaho State University, ID
Illinois State University, IL
Indiana University of Pennsylvania, PA
Iowa State University of Science and Technology, IA
Jacksonville State University, AL
James Madison University, VA
John Carroll University, OH
Juniata College, PA
Kennesaw State University, GA
Kent State University, OH
King's College, PA
LaGrange College, GA
Lewis-Clark State College, ID
Limestone College, SC
Lincoln University, PA
Lindenwood University, MO
Lock Haven University of Pennsylvania, PA
Longwood University, VA
Louisiana Tech University, LA
Lubbock Christian University, TX
Lycoming College, PA
Malone University, OH
Marymount University, VA
Massachusetts College of Liberal Arts, MA
The Master's College and Seminary, CA
Mayville State University, ND
McMurry University, TX
Mesa State College, CO
Michigan State University, MI
Mid-Continent University, KY
Midland Lutheran College, NE
Millersville University of Pennsylvania, PA
Minot State University, ND
Misericordia University, PA
Mississippi State University, MS
Missouri University of Science and Technology, MO
Missouri Valley College, MO
Missouri Western State University, MO
Monmouth University, NJ
Montana State University, MT
Montana State University–Billings, MT
Montclair State University, NJ
Mount Mary College, WI
Newberry College, SC
New England College, NH
New Mexico State University, NM
North Carolina State University, NC
North Central College, IL
North Dakota State University, ND
Northeastern State University, OK
Northern Arizona University, AZ
Northern Illinois University, IL
Northern Michigan University, MI
Northern State University, SD
Northwestern Oklahoma State University, OK
Northwest Missouri State University, MO
Ohio Northern University, OH
The Ohio State University, OH
Ohio University, OH
Ohio University–Chillicothe, OH
Ohio University–Eastern, OH
Ohio University–Lancaster, OH
Ohio University–Southern Campus, OH
Ohio University–Zanesville, OH
Oklahoma State University, OK
Ouachita Baptist University, AR
Pace University, NY
Pacific University, OR
Piedmont College, GA
Pittsburg State University, KS
Plymouth State University, NH
Point Loma Nazarene University, CA
Portland State University, OR
Post University, CT
Purchase College, State University of New York, NY
Randolph College, VA
The Richard Stockton College of New Jersey, NJ
Ripon College, WI
Rivier College, NH
Rochester Institute of Technology, NY
Rockford College, IL
Rockhurst University, MO
St. Catherine University, MN
St. Cloud State University, MN
St. Edward's University, TX
Saint Francis University, PA
Saint Louis University, MO
Salisbury University, MD
Sam Houston State University, TX
San Diego State University, CA
Schreiner University, TX
Seton Hill University, PA
Shepherd University, WV
Shippensburg University of Pennsylvania, PA
Slippery Rock University of Pennsylvania, PA
Sonoma State University, CA
South Dakota State University, SD
Southeastern Louisiana University, LA
Southeastern Oklahoma State University, OK
Southeast Missouri State University, MO
Southern Arkansas University–Magnolia, AR
Southern Illinois University Carbondale, IL
Southern Oregon University, OR
Southwestern College, KS
Southwestern Oklahoma State University, OK
Southwestern University, TX
Southwest Minnesota State University, MN
State University of New York at Fredonia, NY
State University of New York at Oswego, NY
State University of New York at Plattsburgh, NY
State University of New York College at Geneseo, NY
State University of New York College at Oneonta, NY
State University of New York College at Potsdam, NY
Stetson University, FL
Stony Brook University, State University of New York, NY
Tennessee Technological University, TN
Texas A&M University–Texarkana, TX
Texas Christian University, TX
Texas Tech University, TX
Thomas More College, KY
Trevecca Nazarene University, TN
Truman State University, MO
The University of Akron, OH
The University of Alabama, AL
The University of Alabama in Huntsville, AL
University of California, Davis, CA
University of California, Irvine, CA
University of California, Riverside, CA
University of California, San Diego, CA
University of California, Santa Cruz, CA
University of Central Missouri, MO
University of Central Oklahoma, OK
University of Colorado at Boulder, CO
University of Connecticut, CT
University of Delaware, DE
University of Evansville, IN
University of Hawaii at Hilo, HI
University of Houston–Clear Lake, TX
University of Houston–Victoria, TX
University of Idaho, ID
University of Illinois at Urbana–Champaign, IL
The University of Kansas, KS
University of Louisiana at Monroe, LA
University of Maine at Fort Kent, ME
University of Mary Hardin-Baylor, TX
University of Maryland, Baltimore County, MD
University of Maryland, College Park, MD
University of Maryland Eastern Shore, MD
University of Mary Washington, VA
University of Massachusetts Amherst, MA
University of Memphis, TN
University of Miami, FL
University of Michigan, MI
University of Michigan–Dearborn, MI
University of Michigan–Flint, MI
University of Minnesota, Twin Cities Campus, MN
University of Mississippi, MS
University of Missouri–Columbia, MO
The University of Montana, MT
The University of Montana Western, MT
University of Nebraska at Omaha, NE
University of Nebraska–Lincoln, NE
University of Nevada, Las Vegas, NV
University of New England, ME
The University of North Carolina at Asheville, NC
The University of North Carolina at Greensboro, NC

The University of North Carolina Wilmington, NC
University of North Dakota, ND
University of Northern Colorado, CO
University of Northern Iowa, IA
University of Oklahoma, OK
University of Oregon, OR
University of Pittsburgh at Bradford, PA
University of Pittsburgh at Johnstown, PA
University of Portland, OR
University of Puget Sound, WA
University of St. Thomas, MN
University of South Carolina, SC
University of South Carolina Aiken, SC
The University of South Dakota, SD
University of Southern Indiana, IN
University of South Florida, FL
The University of Tampa, FL
The University of Tennessee, TN
The University of Tennessee at Martin, TN
The University of Texas at Arlington, TX
The University of Texas at San Antonio, TX
The University of Texas–Pan American, TX
University of the Ozarks, AR
University of the Southwest, NM
University of Tulsa, OK
University of Utah, UT
University of Vermont, VT
The University of Virginia's College at Wise, VA
University of West Georgia, GA
University of Wisconsin–Eau Claire, WI
University of Wisconsin–Green Bay, WI
University of Wisconsin–La Crosse, WI
University of Wisconsin–Stevens Point, WI
University of Wisconsin–Superior, WI
University of Wisconsin–Whitewater, WI
University of Wyoming, WY
Utah State University, UT
Valdosta State University, GA
Valley City State University, ND
Valley Forge Christian College, PA
Warner Pacific College, OR
Washington State University, WA
Washington University in St. Louis, MO
Wayland Baptist University, TX
Wayne State University, MI
West Chester University of Pennsylvania, PA
Western Illinois University, IL
Western Kentucky University, KY
Western Oregon University, OR
Western Washington University, WA
Westminster College, UT
West Virginia University, WV
Wichita State University, KS
Widener University, PA
Wilson College, PA
Wisconsin Lutheran College, WI
Wright State University, OH
Xavier University, OH

Creative Arts/Performance

Applied Art and Design

Arcadia University, PA
Arizona State University, AZ
Art Academy of Cincinnati, OH
The Art Institute of Boston at Lesley University, MA
Auburn University, AL
Belhaven College, MS
Bloomfield College, NJ
Brenau University, GA
Brooks Institute, CA
Bucknell University, PA
California College of the Arts, CA
California Institute of the Arts, CA
California Polytechnic State University, San Luis Obispo, CA
California State University, Chico, CA
Central Michigan University, MI
City College of the City University of New York, NY
Clemson University, SC
College for Creative Studies, MI
The College of New Rochelle, NY
Colorado State University–Pueblo, CO
Columbia College Chicago, IL
Converse College, SC
Dana College, NE
Eastern Michigan University, MI
Emmanuel College, GA
The Evergreen State College, WA
Fashion Institute of Technology, NY
Ferris State University, MI
Flagler College, FL
Georgia College & State University, GA
Grace College, IN
Graceland University, IA
Grand Valley State University, MI
Illinois State University, IL
Indiana University of Pennsylvania, PA
Iowa State University of Science and Technology, IA
Kean University, NJ
Kutztown University of Pennsylvania, PA
Lindenwood University, MO
Lindsey Wilson College, KY
Louisiana State University and Agricultural and Mechanical College, LA
Louisiana Tech University, LA
Marian College, IN
Massachusetts College of Liberal Arts, MA
Memphis College of Art, TN
Mercyhurst College, PA
Mississippi College, MS
Mississippi State University, MS
Missouri Valley College, MO
Mount Ida College, MA
Mount Mary College, WI
Murray State University, KY
New England College, NH
New Mexico State University, NM
Northeastern State University, OK
Northern Arizona University, AZ
Northern Illinois University, IL
Northern Michigan University, MI
Ohio Northern University, OH
Ohio University, OH
Ohio University–Chillicothe, OH
Ohio University–Eastern, OH
Ohio University–Lancaster, OH
Ohio University–Southern Campus, OH
Ohio University–Zanesville, OH
Oklahoma Baptist University, OK
Oklahoma Christian University, OK
Oklahoma City University, OK
Oral Roberts University, OK
Otis College of Art and Design, CA
The Richard Stockton College of New Jersey, NJ
Ringling College of Art and Design, FL
Rivier College, NH
Robert Morris College, IL
Rochester Institute of Technology, NY
Rocky Mountain College of Art + Design, CO
Sacred Heart University, CT
St. Cloud State University, MN
Salem State College, MA
Salisbury University, MD
San Diego State University, CA
Seton Hill University, PA
Shepherd University, WV
Silver Lake College, WI
Slippery Rock University of Pennsylvania, PA
Sonoma State University, CA
Southeastern Louisiana University, LA
Southern Illinois University Carbondale, IL
Southwestern Oklahoma State University, OK
State University of New York at Fredonia, NY
State University of New York College at Geneseo, NY
Stephen F. Austin State University, TX
Stetson University, FL
Texas Christian University, TX
Texas State University–San Marcos, TX
Texas Tech University, TX
The University of Akron, OH
University of California, San Diego, CA
University of Central Missouri, MO
University of Central Oklahoma, OK
University of Delaware, DE
University of Idaho, ID
University of Illinois at Chicago, IL
University of Illinois at Urbana–Champaign, IL
The University of Kansas, KS
University of Kentucky, KY
University of Maryland, College Park, MD
University of Nebraska at Kearney, NE
University of Nevada, Las Vegas, NV
The University of North Carolina at Chapel Hill, NC
University of Northern Iowa, IA
University of South Florida, FL
The University of Texas at El Paso, TX
University of West Florida, FL
University of West Georgia, GA
University of Wisconsin–Parkside, WI
University of Wisconsin–Stevens Point, WI
University of Wisconsin–Stout, WI
Utah State University, UT
Valley City State University, ND
Virginia Intermont College, VA
Virginia Polytechnic Institute and State University, VA
Washington State University, WA
Washington University in St. Louis, MO
Watkins College of Art, Design, & Film, TN
Western Illinois University, IL
Western Washington University, WA
Wichita State University, KS
Wright State University, OH

Art/Fine Arts

Abilene Christian University, TX
Adelphi University, NY
Adrian College, MI
Alabama Agricultural and Mechanical University, AL
Albertus Magnus College, CT
Albion College, MI
Albright College, PA
Alderson-Broaddus College, WV
Alfred University, NY
Alma College, MI
Angelo State University, TX
Arcadia University, PA
Arizona State University, AZ

Non-Need Scholarships for Undergraduates
Creative Arts/Performance

Arkansas State University, AR
Art Academy of Cincinnati, OH
The Art Institute of Boston at Lesley University, MA
Ashland University, OH
Auburn University, AL
Augsburg College, MN
Augustana College, IL
Augustana College, SD
Augusta State University, GA
Austin College, TX
Austin Peay State University, TN
Averett University, VA
Avila University, MO
Baker University, KS
Ball State University, IN
Barton College, NC
Baylor University, TX
Belhaven College, MS
Bellarmine University, KY
Berry College, GA
Bethany College, KS
Bethany Lutheran College, MN
Bethel College, IN
Bethel College, KS
Bethel University, MN
Biola University, CA
Birmingham-Southern College, AL
Black Hills State University, SD
Bloomfield College, NJ
Bluefield College, VA
Bluffton University, OH
Boise State University, ID
Boston University, MA
Bowling Green State University, OH
Bradley University, IL
Brenau University, GA
Brevard College, NC
Bryan College, TN
Bucknell University, PA
Buena Vista University, IA
Butler University, IN
California Baptist University, CA
California College of the Arts, CA
California Institute of the Arts, CA
California Polytechnic State University, San Luis Obispo, CA
California State University, Bakersfield, CA
California State University, Chico, CA
California State University, Fresno, CA
California State University, Fullerton, CA
California State University, Los Angeles, CA
California State University, San Bernardino, CA
California State University, Stanislaus, CA
Calvin College, MI
Campbellsville University, KY
Canisius College, NY
Carroll University, WI
Carson-Newman College, TN
Case Western Reserve University, OH
Cedar Crest College, PA
Centenary College of Louisiana, LA
Central College, IA
Central Michigan University, MI
Chapman University, CA
Christopher Newport University, VA
City College of the City University of New York, NY
Clarke College, IA
Clemson University, SC
The Cleveland Institute of Art, OH
Cleveland State University, OH
Coastal Carolina University, SC
Coe College, IA
The College at Brockport, State University of New York, NY
College for Creative Studies, MI
College of Charleston, SC
The College of Idaho, ID
College of Mount St. Joseph, OH
The College of New Jersey, NJ
The College of New Rochelle, NY
College of Notre Dame of Maryland, MD
College of Saint Benedict, MN
College of Saint Mary, NE
College of Staten Island of the City University of New York, NY
College of Visual Arts, MN
Colorado State University, CO
Colorado State University–Pueblo, CO
Columbia College, MO
Columbia College Chicago, IL
Columbus College of Art & Design, OH
Columbus State University, GA
Concordia University Chicago, IL
Concordia University, Nebraska, NE
Concordia University, St. Paul, MN
Concord University, WV
Cooper Union for the Advancement of Science and Art, NY
Cornell College, IA
Cornish College of the Arts, WA
Creighton University, NE
Culver-Stockton College, MO
Daemen College, NY
Dana College, NE
Davidson College, NC
Delta State University, MS
DePaul University, IL
DePauw University, IN
Dillard University, LA
Doane College, NE
Drake University, IA
Drury University, MO
Eastern Michigan University, MI
Eastern Washington University, WA
East Tennessee State University, TN
Edgewood College, WI
Edinboro University of Pennsylvania, PA
Elizabethtown College, PA
Elmhurst College, IL
Elon University, NC
Emmanuel College, GA
Emory & Henry College, VA
Emory University, GA
Emporia State University, KS
Endicott College, MA
Eureka College, IL
Evangel University, MO
The Evergreen State College, WA
Fairfield University, CT
Ferris State University, MI
Finlandia University, MI
Flagler College, FL
Florida Gulf Coast University, FL
Fort Lewis College, CO
Francis Marion University, SC
Franklin College, IN
Frostburg State University, MD
Furman University, SC
George Fox University, OR
Georgetown College, KY
Georgia College & State University, GA
Georgian Court University, NJ
Georgia Southern University, GA
Georgia Southwestern State University, GA
Goucher College, MD
Grace College, IN
Grand Valley State University, MI
Grand View University, IA
Green Mountain College, VT
Greensboro College, NC
Gustavus Adolphus College, MN
Hamline University, MN
Hanover College, IN
Harding University, AR
Hardin-Simmons University, TX
Hastings College, NE
Henderson State University, AR
Hendrix College, AR
Hobart and William Smith Colleges, NY
Hofstra University, NY
Hollins University, VA
Hope College, MI
Houghton College, NY
Houston Baptist University, TX
Howard Payne University, TX
Huntington University, IN
Idaho State University, ID
Illinois College, IL
Illinois State University, IL
Indiana State University, IN
Indiana University of Pennsylvania, PA
Iowa State University of Science and Technology, IA
Jacksonville State University, AL
James Madison University, VA
Jamestown College, ND
Johnson Bible College, TN
Judson College, AL
Juniata College, PA
Kansas City Art Institute, MO
Kean University, NJ
Kent State University, OH
Kentucky State University, KY
Knox College, IL
Kutztown University of Pennsylvania, PA
Lake Forest College, IL
Lewis-Clark State College, ID
Limestone College, SC
Lincoln University, MO
Lindenwood University, MO
Lipscomb University, TN
Lock Haven University of Pennsylvania, PA
Long Island University, Brooklyn Campus, NY
Long Island University, C.W. Post Campus, NY
Longwood University, VA
Louisiana State University and Agricultural and Mechanical College, LA
Louisiana Tech University, LA
Lourdes College, OH
Loyola University Chicago, IL
Lubbock Christian University, TX
Lycoming College, PA
Lyme Academy College of Fine Arts, CT
Lyon College, AR
Maine College of Art, ME
Marian College, IN
Maryville College, TN
Maryville University of Saint Louis, MO
Marywood University, PA
Massachusetts College of Liberal Arts, MA
McMurry University, TX
McPherson College, KS
Memphis College of Art, TN
Mercer University, GA

Mercyhurst College, PA
Mesa State College, CO
Messiah College, PA
Miami University, OH
Midland Lutheran College, NE
Millersville University of Pennsylvania, PA
Milligan College, TN
Millikin University, IL
Millsaps College, MS
Mills College, CA
Minnesota State University Moorhead, MN
Mississippi College, MS
Mississippi State University, MS
Mississippi University for Women, MS
Missouri Southern State University, MO
Missouri Western State University, MO
Molloy College, NY
Monmouth College, IL
Montana State University, MT
Montana State University–Billings, MT
Montclair State University, NJ
Mount Ida College, MA
Mount Mary College, WI
Mount Mercy College, IA
Mount St. Mary's University, MD
Mount Union College, OH
Murray State University, KY
Muskingum College, OH
Nazareth College of Rochester, NY
Nebraska Wesleyan University, NE
New England College, NH
Newman University, KS
New Mexico State University, NM
New York City College of Technology of the City University of New York, NY
North Central College, IL
North Dakota State University, ND
Northeastern State University, OK
Northern Arizona University, AZ
Northern Illinois University, IL
Northern State University, SD
Northland College, WI
North Park University, IL
Northwestern Oklahoma State University, OK
Northwestern State University of Louisiana, LA
Northwest Missouri State University, MO
Ohio Northern University, OH
Ohio University, OH
Ohio University–Chillicothe, OH
Ohio University–Eastern, OH
Ohio University–Lancaster, OH
Ohio University–Southern Campus, OH
Ohio University–Zanesville, OH
Oklahoma Baptist University, OK
Oklahoma City University, OK
Oklahoma Panhandle State University, OK
Oklahoma State University, OK
Old Dominion University, VA
Olivet College, MI
Olivet Nazarene University, IL
Oral Roberts University, OK
Oregon College of Art & Craft, OR
Otis College of Art and Design, CA
Ouachita Baptist University, AR
Our Lady of the Lake University of San Antonio, TX
Pacific Lutheran University, WA
Peace College, NC
Piedmont College, GA
Point Loma Nazarene University, CA
Portland State University, OR
Purchase College, State University of New York, NY
Randolph College, VA
Rhode Island College, RI
The Richard Stockton College of New Jersey, NJ
Ringling College of Art and Design, FL
Ripon College, WI
Rivier College, NH
Roberts Wesleyan College, NY
Rochester Institute of Technology, NY
Rocky Mountain College of Art + Design, CO
Rollins College, FL
Sacred Heart University, CT
Saginaw Valley State University, MI
St. Ambrose University, IA
St. Catherine University, MN
St. Cloud State University, MN
St. Edward's University, TX
Saint Francis University, PA
Saint John's University, MN
St. John's University, NY
Saint Louis University, MO
Saint Mary's University of Minnesota, MN
Saint Michael's College, VT
St. Norbert College, WI
Saint Vincent College, PA
Salem State College, MA
Sam Houston State University, TX
San Diego State University, CA
Savannah College of Art and Design, GA
School of the Art Institute of Chicago, IL
Schreiner University, TX
Seattle Pacific University, WA
Seattle University, WA
Seton Hill University, PA
Shepherd University, WV
Shippensburg University of Pennsylvania, PA
Shorter College, GA
Silver Lake College, WI
Simpson College, IA
Slippery Rock University of Pennsylvania, PA
Sonoma State University, CA
South Dakota State University, SD
Southeastern Louisiana University, LA
Southern Adventist University, TN
Southern Arkansas University–Magnolia, AR
Southern Illinois University Carbondale, IL
Southern Illinois University Edwardsville, IL
Southern Nazarene University, OK
Southern Oregon University, OR
Southwest Baptist University, MO
Southwestern Oklahoma State University, OK
Southwestern University, TX
Southwest Minnesota State University, MN
Spring Arbor University, MI
State University of New York at Binghamton, NY
State University of New York at Fredonia, NY
State University of New York at New Paltz, NY
State University of New York at Plattsburgh, NY
State University of New York College at Cortland, NY
State University of New York College at Geneseo, NY
State University of New York College at Potsdam, NY
Stephen F. Austin State University, TX
Stetson University, FL
Sweet Briar College, VA
Temple University, PA
Tennessee Technological University, TN
Texas A&M University–Commerce, TX
Texas Christian University, TX
Texas Tech University, TX
Thomas More College, KY
Towson University, MD
Transylvania University, KY
Trinity University, TX
Truman State University, MO
Union University, TN
The University of Akron, OH
The University of Alabama, AL
The University of Alabama at Birmingham, AL
The University of Alabama in Huntsville, AL
University of Alaska Fairbanks, AK
The University of Arizona, AZ
University of California, Irvine, CA
University of California, Riverside, CA
University of California, Santa Cruz, CA
University of Central Missouri, MO
University of Central Oklahoma, OK
University of Colorado at Boulder, CO
University of Connecticut, CT
University of Dallas, TX
University of Dayton, OH
University of Delaware, DE
University of Denver, CO
University of Evansville, IN
University of Florida, FL
University of Guam, GU
University of Hartford, CT
University of Hawaii at Hilo, HI
University of Idaho, ID
University of Illinois at Chicago, IL
University of Illinois at Urbana–Champaign, IL
The University of Kansas, KS
University of Kentucky, KY
University of La Verne, CA
University of Louisiana at Monroe, LA
University of Maine at Presque Isle, ME
University of Mary Hardin-Baylor, TX
University of Maryland, Baltimore County, MD
University of Maryland, College Park, MD
University of Maryland Eastern Shore, MD
University of Mary Washington, VA
University of Massachusetts Amherst, MA
University of Memphis, TN
University of Miami, FL
University of Michigan–Dearborn, MI
University of Michigan–Flint, MI
University of Mississippi, MS
University of Missouri–St. Louis, MO
The University of Montana, MT
The University of Montana Western, MT
University of Montevallo, AL
University of Nebraska at Kearney, NE
University of Nebraska at Omaha, NE
University of Nebraska–Lincoln, NE
University of Nevada, Las Vegas, NV
University of New Hampshire, NH
University of North Alabama, AL
The University of North Carolina at Asheville, NC
The University of North Carolina at Chapel Hill, NC
The University of North Carolina at Greensboro, NC
The University of North Carolina Wilmington, NC
University of North Dakota, ND

University of Northern Iowa, IA
University of North Florida, FL
University of Oklahoma, OK
University of Oregon, OR
University of Puget Sound, WA
University of Redlands, CA
University of Richmond, VA
University of Saint Francis, IN
University of Science and Arts of Oklahoma, OK
University of South Alabama, AL
University of South Carolina, SC
University of South Carolina Aiken, SC
The University of South Dakota, SD
University of Southern Indiana, IN
University of Southern Mississippi, MS
University of South Florida, FL
The University of Tampa, FL
The University of Tennessee, TN
The University of Tennessee at Martin, TN
The University of Texas at Brownsville, TX
The University of Texas at El Paso, TX
The University of Texas at San Antonio, TX
The University of Texas at Tyler, TX
The University of Texas of the Permian Basin, TX
The University of Texas–Pan American, TX
University of the Cumberlands, KY
University of the Incarnate Word, TX
University of the Ozarks, AR
University of Tulsa, OK
University of Utah, UT
University of Washington, WA
University of West Florida, FL
University of West Georgia, GA
University of Wisconsin–Green Bay, WI
University of Wisconsin–La Crosse, WI
University of Wisconsin–Parkside, WI
University of Wisconsin–Stout, WI
University of Wisconsin–Whitewater, WI
Utah State University, UT
Valdosta State University, GA
Valley City State University, ND
Valley Forge Christian College, PA
Valparaiso University, IN
Virginia Commonwealth University, VA
Virginia Intermont College, VA
Virginia Polytechnic Institute and State University, VA
Virginia Wesleyan College, VA
Wabash College, IN
Warren Wilson College, NC
Wartburg College, IA
Washington State University, WA
Washington University in St. Louis, MO
Watkins College of Art, Design, & Film, TN
Wayland Baptist University, TX
Wayne State University, MI
Webster University, MO
Western Carolina University, NC
Western Kentucky University, KY
Western Oregon University, OR
Western Washington University, WA
West Liberty State University, WV
Westminster College, UT
Westmont College, CA
West Virginia University, WV
West Virginia Wesleyan College, WV
Wheaton College, IL
Whitman College, WA
Whittier College, CA
Whitworth University, WA
Wichita State University, KS
William Carey University, MS
Williams Baptist College, AR
Winona State University, MN
Winthrop University, SC
Wisconsin Lutheran College, WI
Wittenberg University, OH
Wright State University, OH
Xavier University, OH

Cinema/Film/Broadcasting

Arizona State University, AZ
Arkansas State University, AR
Auburn University, AL
Baker University, KS
Ball State University, IN
Baylor University, TX
Biola University, CA
Bloomfield College, NJ
Bowling Green State University, OH
Brenau University, GA
Butler University, IN
California Institute of the Arts, CA
California Polytechnic State University, San Luis Obispo, CA
California State University, Chico, CA
Central Michigan University, MI
Chapman University, CA
City College of the City University of New York, NY
The College at Brockport, State University of New York, NY
The College of New Rochelle, NY
Colorado State University–Pueblo, CO
Columbia College Chicago, IL
DeSales University, PA
Eastern Michigan University, MI
Eastern Washington University, WA
Edinboro University of Pennsylvania, PA
Five Towns College, NY
Flagler College, FL
Florida State University, FL
Georgia Southern University, GA
Grace University, NE
Grand Valley State University, MI
Harding University, AR
Henderson State University, AR
Illinois State University, IL
Ithaca College, NY
James Madison University, VA
Lindenwood University, MO
Long Island University, Brooklyn Campus, NY
Long Island University, C.W. Post Campus, NY
Marywood University, PA
Massachusetts College of Liberal Arts, MA
Minnesota State University Moorhead, MN
Mississippi State University, MS
Missouri Valley College, MO
Montana State University, MT
Montclair State University, NJ
Mount Union College, OH
North Central College, IL
Northern Arizona University, AZ
Northwestern Oklahoma State University, OK
Northwestern State University of Louisiana, LA
Northwest Missouri State University, MO
Ohio University, OH
Ohio University–Chillicothe, OH
Ohio University–Eastern, OH
Ohio University–Lancaster, OH
Ohio University–Southern Campus, OH
Ohio University–Zanesville, OH
Oral Roberts University, OK
Point Park University, PA
Purchase College, State University of New York, NY
Rhode Island College, RI
Rochester Institute of Technology, NY
St. Cloud State University, MN
St. John's University, NY
Saint Joseph's College, IN
San Diego State University, CA
Sonoma State University, CA
Southern Illinois University Carbondale, IL
Southwestern College, KS
State University of New York at Binghamton, NY
Texas Christian University, TX
Trevecca Nazarene University, TN
Union University, TN
The University of Alabama, AL
University of California, Irvine, CA
University of California, San Diego, CA
University of California, Santa Cruz, CA
University of Central Florida, FL
University of Central Missouri, MO
University of Colorado at Boulder, CO
The University of Kansas, KS
University of Kentucky, KY
University of Maryland, Baltimore County, MD
University of Memphis, TN
University of Miami, FL
University of Michigan–Dearborn, MI
University of Mississippi, MS
University of Nebraska–Lincoln, NE
University of Nevada, Las Vegas, NV
The University of North Carolina at Greensboro, NC
The University of North Carolina Wilmington, NC
University of South Florida, FL
University of Utah, UT
University of Wisconsin–Whitewater, WI
Virginia Polytechnic Institute and State University, VA
Washington State University, WA
Washington University in St. Louis, MO
Watkins College of Art, Design, & Film, TN
Western Illinois University, IL
Western Kentucky University, KY
Western Washington University, WA
Westminster College, PA
Wright State University, OH

Creative Writing

Alderson-Broaddus College, WV
Arizona State University, AZ
Auburn University, AL
Augustana College, IL
Augustana College, SD
Augusta State University, GA
Austin Peay State University, TN
Belhaven College, MS
Bowling Green State University, OH
Brenau University, GA
Bucknell University, PA
California College of the Arts, CA
California Institute of the Arts, CA
California Polytechnic State University, San Luis Obispo, CA
California State University, Chico, CA
Case Western Reserve University, OH
Central College, IA

Central Michigan University, MI
Chapman University, CA
City College of the City University of New York, NY
Cleveland State University, OH
Coe College, IA
The College at Brockport, State University of New York, NY
The College of New Rochelle, NY
Colorado State University, CO
Columbia College Chicago, IL
Creighton University, NE
Davidson College, NC
DeSales University, PA
Drury University, MO
Duke University, NC
Eastern Michigan University, MI
Eastern Washington University, WA
Edgewood College, WI
Emmanuel College, GA
Emporia State University, KS
The Evergreen State College, WA
Frostburg State University, MD
Furman University, SC
Georgia College & State University, GA
Georgian Court University, NJ
Graceland University, IA
Grove City College, PA
Hamline University, MN
Hampshire College, MA
Hardin-Simmons University, TX
Hobart and William Smith Colleges, NY
Hollins University, VA
Hood College, MD
Hope College, MI
Illinois State University, IL
Knox College, IL
Lake Forest College, IL
Lewis-Clark State College, ID
Louisiana Tech University, LA
Lycoming College, PA
Mesa State College, CO
Michigan State University, MI
Minnesota State University Moorhead, MN
Mississippi State University, MS
Murray State University, KY
New England College, NH
Northern Arizona University, AZ
Northern Illinois University, IL
Northwestern State University of Louisiana, LA
Ohio Northern University, OH
The Ohio State University, OH
Oklahoma State University, OK
Pace University, NY
Plymouth State University, NH
Purchase College, State University of New York, NY
Randolph College, VA
The Richard Stockton College of New Jersey, NJ
Rockhurst University, MO
Sacred Heart University, CT
St. Cloud State University, MN
Salem State College, MA
San Diego State University, CA
Seton Hill University, PA
Sonoma State University, CA
Southern Illinois University Carbondale, IL
Southern Oregon University, OR
Southwest Minnesota State University, MN
State University of New York at Binghamton, NY
State University of New York College at Geneseo, NY
Stephens College, MO
Susquehanna University, PA
Texas Christian University, TX
The University of Akron, OH
The University of Alabama, AL
University of Alaska Fairbanks, AK
University of California, Riverside, CA
University of Central Missouri, MO
University of Colorado at Boulder, CO
University of Idaho, ID
The University of Kansas, KS
University of Kentucky, KY
University of Louisiana at Monroe, LA
University of Maryland, Baltimore County, MD
University of Michigan–Dearborn, MI
University of Mississippi, MS
The University of Montana, MT
University of Nebraska at Omaha, NE
University of Nevada, Las Vegas, NV
The University of North Carolina Wilmington, NC
University of Redlands, CA
University of South Carolina Aiken, SC
The University of South Dakota, SD
University of Southern Indiana, IN
University of South Florida, FL
The University of Tampa, FL
The University of Texas at San Antonio, TX
University of Utah, UT
The University of Virginia's College at Wise, VA
The University of West Alabama, AL
University of Wisconsin–Stevens Point, WI
University of Wisconsin–Whitewater, WI
Ursinus College, PA
Virginia Polytechnic Institute and State University, VA
Wabash College, IN
Warren Wilson College, NC
Washington State University, WA
Washington University in St. Louis, MO
Webster University, MO
Western Washington University, WA
Wichita State University, KS
Wright State University, OH

Dance

Adelphi University, NY
Albion College, MI
Alma College, MI
Angelo State University, TX
Arizona State University, AZ
Baker University, KS
Ball State University, IN
Belhaven College, MS
Birmingham-Southern College, AL
Boise State University, ID
The Boston Conservatory, MA
Bowling Green State University, OH
Brenau University, GA
Bucknell University, PA
Butler University, IN
California Institute of the Arts, CA
California Polytechnic State University, San Luis Obispo, CA
California State University, Bakersfield, CA
California State University, Chico, CA
California State University, Fullerton, CA
Case Western Reserve University, OH
Cedar Crest College, PA
Centenary College of Louisiana, LA
Central Michigan University, MI
Chapman University, CA
Cleveland State University, OH
The College at Brockport, State University of New York, NY
The College of New Rochelle, NY
The College of Wooster, OH
Colorado State University, CO
Columbia College Chicago, IL
Columbus State University, GA
Concordia University, Nebraska, NE
Cornish College of the Arts, WA
Creighton University, NE
DeSales University, PA
Duquesne University, PA
Eastern Michigan University, MI
Emmanuel College, GA
Florida International University, FL
Florida State University, FL
Fordham University, NY
Goucher College, MD
Grand Valley State University, MI
Gustavus Adolphus College, MN
Hastings College, NE
Hawai'i Pacific University, HI
Henderson State University, AR
Hendrix College, AR
Hobart and William Smith Colleges, NY
Hofstra University, NY
Hollins University, VA
Hope College, MI
Idaho State University, ID
Indiana University of Pennsylvania, PA
Ithaca College, NY
James Madison University, VA
The Juilliard School, NY
Kent State University, OH
Knox College, IL
Kutztown University of Pennsylvania, PA
Lees-McRae College, NC
Lindenwood University, MO
Long Island University, Brooklyn Campus, NY
Long Island University, C.W. Post Campus, NY
Manhattanville College, NY
Marymount Manhattan College, NY
Mercyhurst College, PA
Mesa State College, CO
Millikin University, IL
Mississippi State University, MS
Missouri Valley College, MO
Missouri Western State University, MO
Montana State University, MT
Montclair State University, NJ
Murray State University, KY
Nicholls State University, LA
Northeastern State University, OK
Northern Illinois University, IL
Northwestern State University of Louisiana, LA
Oakland University, MI
Ohio Northern University, OH
The Ohio State University, OH
Ohio University, OH
Ohio University–Chillicothe, OH
Ohio University–Eastern, OH
Ohio University–Lancaster, OH
Ohio University–Southern Campus, OH
Ohio University–Zanesville, OH
Oklahoma City University, OK
Old Dominion University, VA

Pacific Lutheran University, WA
Palm Beach Atlantic University, FL
Plymouth State University, NH
Point Park University, PA
Purchase College, State University of New York, NY
Rhode Island College, RI
The Richard Stockton College of New Jersey, NJ
Rockford College, IL
St. Ambrose University, IA
St. John's University, NY
Salem State College, MA
Sam Houston State University, TX
San Diego State University, CA
Santa Clara University, CA
Slippery Rock University of Pennsylvania, PA
Sonoma State University, CA
Southeastern Louisiana University, LA
Southern Arkansas University–Magnolia, AR
Southern Illinois University Carbondale, IL
Southern Illinois University Edwardsville, IL
Southwestern College, KS
State University of New York at Binghamton, NY
State University of New York at Fredonia, NY
State University of New York College at Geneseo, NY
State University of New York College at Potsdam, NY
Stephens College, MO
Texas Christian University, TX
Texas Tech University, TX
Towson University, MD
The University of Akron, OH
The University of Alabama, AL
The University of Arizona, AZ
University of California, Irvine, CA
University of California, Riverside, CA
University of California, San Diego, CA
University of Colorado at Boulder, CO
University of Florida, FL
University of Hartford, CT
University of Idaho, ID
University of Illinois at Urbana–Champaign, IL
The University of Kansas, KS
University of Kentucky, KY
University of Maryland, Baltimore County, MD
University of Maryland, College Park, MD
University of Mary Washington, VA
University of Massachusetts Amherst, MA
University of Memphis, TN
The University of Montana, MT
University of Nebraska–Lincoln, NE
University of Nevada, Las Vegas, NV
University of New Hampshire, NH
The University of North Carolina at Greensboro, NC
University of Northern Colorado, CO
University of Oklahoma, OK
University of Oregon, OR
University of Puerto Rico, Mayagüez Campus, PR
University of Richmond, VA
University of Saint Francis, IN
University of South Carolina, SC
University of Southern Mississippi, MS
University of South Florida, FL
The University of Texas of the Permian Basin, TX
The University of Texas-Pan American, TX
University of Utah, UT
The University of West Alabama, AL
University of Wisconsin–Green Bay, WI
University of Wisconsin–Stevens Point, WI
University of Wyoming, WY
Virginia Commonwealth University, VA
Virginia Intermont College, VA
Washington University in St. Louis, MO
Wayne State University, MI
Western Illinois University, IL
Western Kentucky University, KY
Western Oregon University, OR
Western Washington University, WA
Wichita State University, KS
Winthrop University, SC
Wittenberg University, OH
Wright State University, OH

Debating

Abilene Christian University, TX
Alderson-Broaddus College, WV
Arizona State University, AZ
Arkansas State University, AR
Augustana College, IL
Austin Peay State University, TN
Baker University, KS
Ball State University, IN
Baylor University, TX
Berry College, GA
Bethany Lutheran College, MN
Bethel College, KS
Bethel University, MN
Boise State University, ID
Bowling Green State University, OH
California Polytechnic State University, San Luis Obispo, CA
California State University, Chico, CA
Carroll College, MT
Carson-Newman College, TN
Cedarville University, OH
The College of Idaho, ID
The College of New Rochelle, NY
Concordia College, MN
Creighton University, NE
Culver-Stockton College, MO
DePaul University, IL
Doane College, NE
Drury University, MO
Eastern Michigan University, MI
Emporia State University, KS
Ferris State University, MI
Florida College, FL
George Fox University, OR
Gonzaga University, WA
Gustavus Adolphus College, MN
Harding University, AR
Hastings College, NE
Henderson State University, AR
Houston Baptist University, TX
Idaho State University, ID
Illinois State University, IL
Kentucky Christian University, KY
Lewis & Clark College, OR
Lewis-Clark State College, ID
Liberty University, VA
Linfield College, OR
Louisiana Tech University, LA
Loyola University Chicago, IL
Malone University, OH
Mercer University, GA
Methodist University, NC
Michigan State University, MI
Midland Lutheran College, NE
Mississippi State University, MS
Missouri Southern State University, MO
Mount Union College, OH
Murray State University, KY
Muskingum College, OH
North Central College, IL
North Dakota State University, ND
Northeastern State University, OK
Northern Arizona University, AZ
Northern Illinois University, IL
Northwestern Oklahoma State University, OK
Northwest Missouri State University, MO
Northwest University, WA
Ohio University, OH
Ohio University–Chillicothe, OH
Ohio University–Eastern, OH
Ohio University–Lancaster, OH
Ohio University–Southern Campus, OH
Ohio University–Zanesville, OH
Oklahoma Panhandle State University, OK
Pace University, NY
Pacific Lutheran University, WA
Pacific University, OR
Point Loma Nazarene University, CA
Ripon College, WI
St. John's University, NY
Santa Clara University, CA
South Dakota State University, SD
Southern Illinois University Carbondale, IL
Southwest Baptist University, MO
Southwest Minnesota State University, MN
Tennessee Technological University, TN
Towson University, MD
Trinity University, TX
Truman State University, MO
The University of Akron, OH
The University of Alabama, AL
University of Central Missouri, MO
University of Denver, CO
The University of Kansas, KS
University of Kentucky, KY
University of La Verne, CA
University of Louisiana at Monroe, LA
University of Mary, ND
University of Miami, FL
University of Michigan–Dearborn, MI
University of Mississippi, MS
University of Missouri–Kansas City, MO
University of Nebraska at Kearney, NE
University of Nebraska at Omaha, NE
University of Nevada, Las Vegas, NV
University of North Dakota, ND
University of Puget Sound, WA
University of Redlands, CA
University of South Carolina, SC
The University of South Dakota, SD
University of Southern California, CA
University of South Florida, FL
The University of Texas at San Antonio, TX
University of the Cumberlands, KY
University of the Pacific, CA
University of the Southwest, NM
University of Vermont, VT
University of West Georgia, GA
University of Wisconsin–Eau Claire, WI
University of Wyoming, WY
Vanguard University of Southern California, CA
Wayne State University, MI
Webster University, MO
Western Illinois University, IL
Western Kentucky University, KY
West Virginia University, WV

Whitman College, WA
Wichita State University, KS
Willamette University, OR
William Carey University, MS
Winona State University, MN

Journalism/Publications

Abilene Christian University, TX
Albright College, PA
Alderson-Broaddus College, WV
Angelo State University, TX
Arizona State University, AZ
Arkansas State University, AR
Auburn University, AL
Austin Peay State University, TN
Averett University, VA
Baker University, KS
Ball State University, IN
Baylor University, TX
Belhaven College, MS
Berry College, GA
Bethany Lutheran College, MN
Bethel College, IN
Biola University, CA
Boise State University, ID
Bowling Green State University, OH
Brenau University, GA
Brevard College, NC
Bryan College, TN
California Polytechnic State University, San Luis Obispo, CA
California State University, Chico, CA
California State University, Fresno, CA
California State University, Los Angeles, CA
California State University, Northridge, CA
California State University, San Bernardino, CA
Campbellsville University, KY
Carroll University, WI
Carson-Newman College, TN
Central Michigan University, MI
The College at Brockport, State University of New York, NY
The College of New Rochelle, NY
Colorado State University–Pueblo, CO
Columbia College Chicago, IL
Concord University, WV
Creighton University, NE
Delta State University, MS
DePauw University, IN
Dordt College, IA
Eastern Washington University, WA
East Tennessee State University, TN
Edinboro University of Pennsylvania, PA
Elon University, NC
Emory & Henry College, VA
Faulkner University, AL
Ferris State University, MI
Florida College, FL
Florida International University, FL
Fort Valley State University, GA
Franklin College, IN
Frostburg State University, MD
Georgia College & State University, GA
Glenville State College, WV
Grand Valley State University, MI
Harding University, AR
Hardin-Simmons University, TX
Hastings College, NE
Hawai'i Pacific University, HI
Henderson State University, AR
Huntington University, IN
Indiana University of Pennsylvania, PA
Iowa State University of Science and Technology, IA
Ithaca College, NY
Jacksonville State University, AL
James Madison University, VA
John Brown University, AR
Kent State University, OH
Kentucky State University, KY
Lees-McRae College, NC
Liberty University, VA
Lincoln University, MO
Lipscomb University, TN
Lock Haven University of Pennsylvania, PA
Long Island University, C.W. Post Campus, NY
Louisiana State University and Agricultural and Mechanical College, LA
Louisiana Tech University, LA
Loyola University Chicago, IL
Lubbock Christian University, TX
Malone University, OH
Marywood University, PA
Massachusetts College of Liberal Arts, MA
McPherson College, KS
Mesa State College, CO
Michigan State University, MI
Midland Lutheran College, NE
Mississippi State University, MS
Mississippi University for Women, MS
Missouri Southern State University, MO
Missouri Valley College, MO
Mount Union College, OH
Murray State University, KY
Muskingum College, OH
Newman University, KS
New Mexico State University, NM
North Central College, IL
North Dakota State University, ND
Northeastern State University, OK
Northern Arizona University, AZ
Northern Illinois University, IL
North Greenville University, SC
North Park University, IL
Northwestern Oklahoma State University, OK
Northwestern State University of Louisiana, LA
Northwest Missouri State University, MO
Nyack College, NY
Oglethorpe University, GA
Ohio Northern University, OH
The Ohio State University, OH
Ohio University, OH
Ohio University–Chillicothe, OH
Ohio University–Eastern, OH
Ohio University–Lancaster, OH
Ohio University–Southern Campus, OH
Ohio University–Zanesville, OH
Ohio Valley University, WV
Oklahoma Christian University, OK
Oklahoma State University, OK
Olivet College, MI
Oral Roberts University, OK
Ouachita Baptist University, AR
Pacific University, OR
Point Park University, PA
Rhode Island College, RI
The Richard Stockton College of New Jersey, NJ
Rivier College, NH
Robert Morris College, IL
St. Cloud State University, MN
St. John's University, NY
Samford University, AL
San Diego State University, CA
Schreiner University, TX
Seton Hill University, PA
Sonoma State University, CA
South Dakota State University, SD
Southern Adventist University, TN
Southern Illinois University Carbondale, IL
Southern Oregon University, OR
Southwestern College, KS
Southwest Minnesota State University, MN
State University of New York at Binghamton, NY
State University of New York at Plattsburgh, NY
State University of New York College at Geneseo, NY
Stephen F. Austin State University, TX
Stony Brook University, State University of New York, NY
Tabor College, KS
Texas A&M University, TX
Texas A&M University–Commerce, TX
Texas Christian University, TX
Texas Lutheran University, TX
Texas State University–San Marcos, TX
Texas Tech University, TX
Trinity Christian College, IL
Union University, TN
The University of Akron, OH
The University of Alabama, AL
University of California, San Diego, CA
University of Central Missouri, MO
University of Central Oklahoma, OK
University of Colorado at Boulder, CO
University of Florida, FL
University of Guam, GU
University of Idaho, ID
University of Illinois at Urbana–Champaign, IL
The University of Kansas, KS
University of Kentucky, KY
University of La Verne, CA
University of Louisiana at Monroe, LA
University of Mary Washington, VA
University of Massachusetts Amherst, MA
University of Memphis, TN
University of Miami, FL
University of Michigan, MI
University of Michigan–Dearborn, MI
University of Mississippi, MS
University of Missouri–Columbia, MO
The University of Montana, MT
University of Nebraska at Kearney, NE
University of Nebraska at Omaha, NE
University of Nebraska–Lincoln, NE
University of Nevada, Las Vegas, NV
University of North Alabama, AL
The University of North Carolina at Chapel Hill, NC
The University of North Carolina at Pembroke, NC
University of Oklahoma, OK
University of Oregon, OR
University of Pittsburgh at Johnstown, PA
University of St. Thomas, MN
University of South Alabama, AL
University of South Carolina, SC
University of South Carolina Aiken, SC
University of South Florida, FL
The University of Tampa, FL
The University of Tennessee at Martin, TN
The University of Texas at Arlington, TX
The University of Texas at El Paso, TX

The University of Texas–Pan American, TX
University of the Cumberlands, KY
University of Utah, UT
The University of Virginia's College at Wise, VA
The University of West Alabama, AL
University of West Georgia, GA
University of Wisconsin–Green Bay, WI
University of Wisconsin–Whitewater, WI
Utah State University, UT
Valley City State University, ND
Virginia Polytechnic Institute and State University, VA
Wabash College, IN
Wartburg College, IA
Washington State University, WA
Wayland Baptist University, TX
Wayne State University, MI
Webber International University, FL
Western Illinois University, IL
Western Kentucky University, KY
Western Washington University, WA
Westminster College, UT
Whitworth University, WA
Wichita State University, KS
William Carey University, MS

Music

Abilene Christian University, TX
Adelphi University, NY
Adrian College, MI
Agnes Scott College, GA
Alabama Agricultural and Mechanical University, AL
Alaska Bible College, AK
Albion College, MI
Albright College, PA
Alcorn State University, MS
Alderson-Broaddus College, WV
Alma College, MI
Andrews University, MI
Angelo State University, TX
Anna Maria College, MA
Arizona State University, AZ
Arkansas State University, AR
Asbury College, KY
Ashland University, OH
Auburn University, AL
Augsburg College, MN
Augustana College, IL
Augustana College, SD
Augusta State University, GA
Austin College, TX
Austin Peay State University, TN
Averett University, VA
Avila University, MO
Baker University, KS
Baldwin-Wallace College, OH
Ball State University, IN
Baptist Bible College of Pennsylvania, PA
The Baptist College of Florida, FL
Barton College, NC
Baylor University, TX
Belhaven College, MS
Bellarmine University, KY
Belmont University, TN
Beloit College, WI
Benedictine College, KS
Benedictine University, IL
Berklee College of Music, MA
Berry College, GA
Bethany College, KS
Bethany Lutheran College, MN
Bethel College, IN
Bethel College, KS
Bethel University, MN
Biola University, CA
Birmingham-Southern College, AL
Black Hills State University, SD
Bluefield College, VA
Bluffton University, OH
Boise State University, ID
The Boston Conservatory, MA
Boston University, MA
Bowling Green State University, OH
Bradley University, IL
Brenau University, GA
Brevard College, NC
Brewton-Parker College, GA
Bridgewater College, VA
Bryan College, TN
Bucknell University, PA
Buena Vista University, IA
Butler University, IN
California Baptist University, CA
California Institute of the Arts, CA
California Polytechnic State University, San Luis Obispo, CA
California State University, Bakersfield, CA
California State University, Chico, CA
California State University, East Bay, CA
California State University, Fresno, CA
California State University, Fullerton, CA
California State University, Los Angeles, CA
California State University, Northridge, CA
California State University, San Bernardino, CA
California State University, Stanislaus, CA
Calvin College, MI
Campbellsville University, KY
Canisius College, NY
Carleton College, MN
Carroll University, WI
Carson-Newman College, TN
Case Western Reserve University, OH
Catawba College, NC
The Catholic University of America, DC
Cedarville University, OH
Centenary College of Louisiana, LA
Central College, IA
Central Methodist University, MO
Central Michigan University, MI
Centre College, KY
Chapman University, CA
Christopher Newport University, VA
City College of the City University of New York, NY
Clarke College, IA
Clear Creek Baptist Bible College, KY
Clearwater Christian College, FL
Cleveland Institute of Music, OH
Cleveland State University, OH
Coastal Carolina University, SC
Coe College, IA
The College at Brockport, State University of New York, NY
College of Charleston, SC
The College of Idaho, ID
College of Mount St. Joseph, OH
The College of New Jersey, NJ
The College of New Rochelle, NY
College of Saint Benedict, MN
College of Saint Mary, NE
The College of St. Scholastica, MN
College of Staten Island of the City University of New York, NY
College of the Holy Cross, MA
The College of William and Mary, VA
The College of Wooster, OH
Colorado School of Mines, CO
Colorado State University, CO
Colorado State University–Pueblo, CO
Columbia College, MO
Columbia College Chicago, IL
Columbia International University, SC
Columbus State University, GA
Concordia College, AL
Concordia College, MN
Concordia College–New York, NY
Concordia University, OR
Concordia University Chicago, IL
Concordia University, Nebraska, NE
Concordia University, St. Paul, MN
Concordia University Texas, TX
Concord University, WV
Converse College, SC
Corban College, OR
Cornell College, IA
Cornish College of the Arts, WA
Covenant College, GA
Creighton University, NE
Crown College, MN
Culver-Stockton College, MO
Dakota State University, SD
Dallas Baptist University, TX
Dana College, NE
Davidson College, NC
Delta State University, MS
DePaul University, IL
DePauw University, IN
DeSales University, PA
Dillard University, LA
Doane College, NE
Dominican University of California, CA
Dordt College, IA
Drake University, IA
Drury University, MO
Duquesne University, PA
Eastern Kentucky University, KY
Eastern Michigan University, MI
Eastern Washington University, WA
East Tennessee State University, TN
East Texas Baptist University, TX
Edgewood College, WI
Edinboro University of Pennsylvania, PA
Elizabethtown College, PA
Elmhurst College, IL
Elon University, NC
Emmanuel College, GA
Emory & Henry College, VA
Emory University, GA
Emporia State University, KS
Eureka College, IL
Evangel University, MO
Fairfield University, CT
Faulkner University, AL
Ferris State University, MI
Five Towns College, NY
Florida Atlantic University, FL
Florida College, FL
Florida Gulf Coast University, FL
Florida International University, FL
Florida State University, FL
Fordham University, NY
Fort Lewis College, CO
Fort Valley State University, GA
Francis Marion University, SC
Franklin & Marshall College, PA
Franklin College, IN

Fresno Pacific University, CA
Frostburg State University, MD
Furman University, SC
Gannon University, PA
Gardner-Webb University, NC
Geneva College, PA
George Fox University, OR
Georgetown College, KY
Georgia College & State University, GA
Georgian Court University, NJ
Georgia Southern University, GA
Georgia Southwestern State University, GA
Gettysburg College, PA
Glenville State College, WV
Gonzaga University, WA
Gordon College, MA
Goucher College, MD
Grace Bible College, MI
Grace College, IN
Graceland University, IA
Grace University, NE
Grand Valley State University, MI
Grand View University, IA
Green Mountain College, VT
Greensboro College, NC
Grove City College, PA
Guilford College, NC
Gustavus Adolphus College, MN
Hamline University, MN
Hampton University, VA
Hanover College, IN
Harding University, AR
Hardin-Simmons University, TX
Hastings College, NE
Hawai'i Pacific University, HI
Heidelberg University, OH
Henderson State University, AR
Hendrix College, AR
Hillsdale Free Will Baptist College, OK
Hobart and William Smith Colleges, NY
Hofstra University, NY
Hollins University, VA
Hope College, MI
Hope International University, CA
Houghton College, NY
Houston Baptist University, TX
Howard Payne University, TX
Huntingdon College, AL
Huntington University, IN
Idaho State University, ID
Illinois College, IL
Illinois State University, IL
Illinois Wesleyan University, IL
Indiana University of Pennsylvania, PA
Iona College, NY
Iowa State University of Science and Technology, IA
Ithaca College, NY
Jacksonville State University, AL
James Madison University, VA
Jamestown College, ND
John Brown University, AR
Johnson Bible College, TN
Johnson C. Smith University, NC
Judson College, AL
The Juilliard School, NY
Juniata College, PA
Kean University, NJ
Kennesaw State University, GA
Kent State University, OH
Kentucky Christian University, KY
Kentucky State University, KY
Knox College, IL
Kutztown University of Pennsylvania, PA
LaGrange College, GA
Lake Forest College, IL
Lambuth University, TN
Lancaster Bible College, PA
Langston University, OK
Lawrence University, WI
Lebanon Valley College, PA
Lee University, TN
Lehigh University, PA
Lewis & Clark College, OR
Lewis-Clark State College, ID
Liberty University, VA
Limestone College, SC
Lincoln Memorial University, TN
Lincoln University, MO
Lincoln University, PA
Lindenwood University, MO
Lindsey Wilson College, KY
Linfield College, OR
Lipscomb University, TN
Lock Haven University of Pennsylvania, PA
Long Island University, Brooklyn Campus, NY
Long Island University, C.W. Post Campus, NY
Longwood University, VA
Loras College, IA
Louisiana State University and Agricultural and Mechanical College, LA
Louisiana Tech University, LA
Lourdes College, OH
Loyola University Chicago, IL
Lubbock Christian University, TX
Luther College, IA
Lycoming College, PA
Lynn University, FL
Lyon College, AR
Malone University, OH
Manhattan Christian College, KS
Manhattan College, NY
Mannes College The New School for Music, NY
Maranatha Baptist Bible College, WI
Marian College, IN
Marian University, WI
Martin Luther College, MN
Maryville College, TN
Marywood University, PA
Massachusetts College of Liberal Arts, MA
The Master's College and Seminary, CA
Mayville State University, ND
McKendree University, IL
McMurry University, TX
McPherson College, KS
Mercer University, GA
Mercyhurst College, PA
Mesa State College, CO
Messiah College, PA
Methodist University, NC
Miami University, OH
Michigan State University, MI
Midland Lutheran College, NE
Millersville University of Pennsylvania, PA
Milligan College, TN
Millikin University, IL
Millsaps College, MS
Mills College, CA
Minnesota State University Moorhead, MN
Mississippi College, MS
Mississippi State University, MS
Mississippi University for Women, MS
Missouri Baptist University, MO
Missouri Southern State University, MO
Missouri University of Science and Technology, MO
Missouri Valley College, MO
Missouri Western State University, MO
Molloy College, NY
Monmouth College, IL
Montana State University, MT
Montana State University–Billings, MT
Montclair State University, NJ
Montreat College, NC
Mount Aloysius College, PA
Mount Marty College, SD
Mount Mary College, WI
Mount Mercy College, IA
Mount Union College, OH
Mount Vernon Nazarene University, OH
Murray State University, KY
Muskingum College, OH
Nazareth College of Rochester, NY
Neumann University, PA
Newberry College, SC
New England Conservatory of Music, MA
Newman University, KS
New Mexico State University, NM
New York City College of Technology of the City University of New York, NY
Nicholls State University, LA
North Carolina Agricultural and Technical State University, NC
North Carolina State University, NC
North Central College, IL
North Dakota State University, ND
Northeastern State University, OK
Northern Arizona University, AZ
Northern Illinois University, IL
Northern Michigan University, MI
Northern State University, SD
North Greenville University, SC
Northland College, WI
North Park University, IL
Northwest Christian University, OR
Northwestern College, MN
Northwestern Oklahoma State University, OK
Northwestern State University of Louisiana, LA
Northwestern University, IL
Northwest Missouri State University, MO
Northwest University, WA
Notre Dame de Namur University, CA
Nyack College, NY
Oakland University, MI
Oberlin College, OH
Occidental College, CA
Oglethorpe University, GA
Ohio Christian University, OH
Ohio Northern University, OH
The Ohio State University, OH
Ohio University, OH
Ohio University–Chillicothe, OH
Ohio University–Eastern, OH
Ohio University–Lancaster, OH
Ohio University–Southern Campus, OH
Ohio University–Zanesville, OH
Ohio Valley University, WV
Oklahoma Baptist University, OK
Oklahoma Christian University, OK
Oklahoma City University, OK
Oklahoma Panhandle State University, OK
Oklahoma State University, OK
Oklahoma Wesleyan University, OK
Old Dominion University, VA
Olivet College, MI

Olivet Nazarene University, IL
Oral Roberts University, OK
Ouachita Baptist University, AR
Our Lady of the Lake University of San Antonio, TX
Pacific Lutheran University, WA
Pacific University, OR
Palm Beach Atlantic University, FL
Peabody Conservatory of Music of The Johns Hopkins University, MD
Peace College, NC
Philadelphia Biblical University, PA
Piedmont College, GA
Pittsburg State University, KS
Plymouth State University, NH
Point Loma Nazarene University, CA
Portland State University, OR
Presbyterian College, SC
Purchase College, State University of New York, NY
Purdue University, IN
Randolph College, VA
Rhode Island College, RI
Rice University, TX
The Richard Stockton College of New Jersey, NJ
Ripon College, WI
Roberts Wesleyan College, NY
Rockford College, IL
Rockhurst University, MO
Rollins College, FL
Rowan University, NJ
Sacred Heart University, CT
Saginaw Valley State University, MI
St. Ambrose University, IA
St. Catherine University, MN
St. Cloud State University, MN
Saint Francis University, PA
Saint John's University, MN
St. John's University, NY
Saint Joseph's College, IN
Saint Joseph's University, PA
Saint Louis University, MO
St. Mary's University, TX
Saint Mary's University of Minnesota, MN
St. Norbert College, WI
St. Olaf College, MN
Saint Vincent College, PA
Saint Xavier University, IL
Salem College, NC
Salem State College, MA
Salisbury University, MD
Samford University, AL
Sam Houston State University, TX
San Diego State University, CA
San Francisco Conservatory of Music, CA
Santa Clara University, CA
Schreiner University, TX
Seattle University, WA
Seton Hill University, PA
Shasta Bible College, CA
Shepherd University, WV
Shippensburg University of Pennsylvania, PA
Shorter College, GA
Silver Lake College, WI
Simpson College, IA
Simpson University, CA
Skidmore College, NY
Slippery Rock University of Pennsylvania, PA
Sonoma State University, CA
South Carolina State University, SC
South Dakota State University, SD
Southeastern Louisiana University, LA
Southeastern Oklahoma State University, OK
Southeast Missouri State University, MO
Southern Adventist University, TN
Southern Arkansas University–Magnolia, AR
Southern Illinois University Carbondale, IL
Southern Illinois University Edwardsville, IL
Southern Nazarene University, OK
Southern Oregon University, OR
Southern Utah University, UT
Southwest Baptist University, MO
Southwestern Christian University, OK
Southwestern College, KS
Southwestern Oklahoma State University, OK
Southwestern University, TX
Southwest Minnesota State University, MN
Spring Arbor University, MI
State University of New York at Binghamton, NY
State University of New York at Fredonia, NY
State University of New York at New Paltz, NY
State University of New York at Plattsburgh, NY
State University of New York College at Cortland, NY
State University of New York College at Geneseo, NY
State University of New York College at Oneonta, NY
State University of New York College at Potsdam, NY
Stephen F. Austin State University, TX
Stetson University, FL
Stillman College, AL
Stony Brook University, State University of New York, NY
Susquehanna University, PA
Sweet Briar College, VA
Tabor College, KS
Taylor University, IN
Temple University, PA
Tennessee Technological University, TN
Texas A&M University–Commerce, TX
Texas Christian University, TX
Texas Lutheran University, TX
Texas State University–San Marcos, TX
Texas Tech University, TX
Thiel College, PA
Tiffin University, OH
Towson University, MD
Transylvania University, KY
Trevecca Nazarene University, TN
Trinity Christian College, IL
Trinity International University, IL
Trinity Lutheran College, WA
Trinity University, TX
Troy University, AL
Truman State University, MO
Tuskegee University, AL
Union College, KY
Union University, TN
The University of Akron, OH
The University of Alabama, AL
The University of Alabama at Birmingham, AL
The University of Alabama in Huntsville, AL
University of Alaska Fairbanks, AK
The University of Arizona, AZ
University of Arkansas, AR
University of California, Irvine, CA
University of California, Riverside, CA
University of California, Santa Cruz, CA
University of Central Florida, FL
University of Central Missouri, MO
University of Central Oklahoma, OK
University of Colorado at Boulder, CO
University of Connecticut, CT
University of Dallas, TX
University of Dayton, OH
University of Delaware, DE
University of Denver, CO
University of Evansville, IN
The University of Findlay, OH
University of Florida, FL
University of Georgia, GA
University of Guam, GU
University of Hartford, CT
University of Hawaii at Hilo, HI
University of Idaho, ID
University of Illinois at Chicago, IL
University of Illinois at Urbana–Champaign, IL
The University of Iowa, IA
The University of Kansas, KS
University of Kentucky, KY
University of La Verne, CA
University of Louisiana at Monroe, LA
The University of Maine at Augusta, ME
University of Mary, ND
University of Mary Hardin-Baylor, TX
University of Maryland, Baltimore County, MD
University of Maryland, College Park, MD
University of Maryland Eastern Shore, MD
University of Mary Washington, VA
University of Massachusetts Amherst, MA
University of Massachusetts Lowell, MA
University of Memphis, TN
University of Miami, FL
University of Michigan, MI
University of Michigan–Flint, MI
University of Minnesota, Morris, MN
University of Mississippi, MS
University of Missouri–Columbia, MO
University of Missouri–Kansas City, MO
University of Missouri–St. Louis, MO
The University of Montana, MT
University of Montevallo, AL
University of Nebraska at Kearney, NE
University of Nebraska at Omaha, NE
University of Nebraska–Lincoln, NE
University of Nevada, Las Vegas, NV
University of Nevada, Reno, NV
University of New Hampshire, NH
University of New Orleans, LA
University of North Alabama, AL
The University of North Carolina at Asheville, NC
The University of North Carolina at Chapel Hill, NC
The University of North Carolina at Greensboro, NC
The University of North Carolina at Pembroke, NC
The University of North Carolina Wilmington, NC
University of North Dakota, ND
University of Northern Colorado, CO
University of Northern Iowa, IA
University of North Florida, FL
University of Oklahoma, OK
University of Oregon, OR
University of Portland, OR
University of Puerto Rico, Mayagüez Campus, PR
University of Puget Sound, WA

University of Redlands, CA
University of Richmond, VA
University of Saint Francis, IN
University of St. Thomas, MN
University of San Diego, CA
University of Science and Arts of Oklahoma, OK
University of South Alabama, AL
University of South Carolina, SC
University of South Carolina Aiken, SC
The University of South Dakota, SD
University of Southern Maine, ME
University of Southern Mississippi, MS
University of South Florida, FL
The University of Tampa, FL
The University of Tennessee at Martin, TN
The University of Texas at Arlington, TX
The University of Texas at Brownsville, TX
The University of Texas at El Paso, TX
The University of Texas at San Antonio, TX
The University of Texas at Tyler, TX
The University of Texas of the Permian Basin, TX
The University of Texas–Pan American, TX
University of the Cumberlands, KY
University of the Ozarks, AR
University of the Pacific, CA
University of the Southwest, NM
University of Tulsa, OK
University of Utah, UT
University of Vermont, VT
University of Virginia, VA
The University of Virginia's College at Wise, VA
University of Washington, WA
The University of West Alabama, AL
University of West Florida, FL
University of West Georgia, GA
University of Wisconsin–Eau Claire, WI
University of Wisconsin–Green Bay, WI
University of Wisconsin–La Crosse, WI
University of Wisconsin–Parkside, WI
University of Wisconsin–Stevens Point, WI
University of Wisconsin–Stout, WI
University of Wisconsin–Whitewater, WI
University of Wyoming, WY
Utah State University, UT
Valdosta State University, GA
Valley City State University, ND
Valley Forge Christian College, PA
Valparaiso University, IN
Vanguard University of Southern California, CA
Virginia Commonwealth University, VA
Virginia Intermont College, VA
Virginia Military Institute, VA
Virginia Polytechnic Institute and State University, VA
Virginia Wesleyan College, VA
Wabash College, IN
Wagner College, NY
Walla Walla University, WA
Warner Pacific College, OR
Wartburg College, IA
Washington Bible College, MD
Washington State University, WA
Washington University in St. Louis, MO
Wayland Baptist University, TX
Waynesburg University, PA
Wayne State University, MI
Webster University, MO
West Chester University of Pennsylvania, PA
Western Carolina University, NC
Western Illinois University, IL
Western Kentucky University, KY
Western New England College, MA
Western Oregon University, OR
Western Washington University, WA
West Liberty State University, WV
Westminster College, MO
Westminster College, PA
Westminster College, UT
Westmont College, CA
West Virginia University, WV
West Virginia Wesleyan College, WV
Wheaton College, IL
Wheeling Jesuit University, WV
Whitman College, WA
Whittier College, CA
Whitworth University, WA
Wichita State University, KS
Widener University, PA
Willamette University, OR
William Carey University, MS
William Jessup University, CA
Williams Baptist College, AR
Wilson College, PA
Wingate University, NC
Winona State University, MN
Winthrop University, SC
Wisconsin Lutheran College, WI
Wittenberg University, OH
Wofford College, SC
Wright State University, OH
Xavier University, OH
York College, NE
York College of Pennsylvania, PA
Youngstown State University, OH

Performing Arts

Adelphi University, NY
Albertus Magnus College, CT
Albion College, MI
Alderson-Broaddus College, WV
Alfred University, NY
Alma College, MI
Angelo State University, TX
Arizona State University, AZ
Arkansas State University, AR
Auburn University, AL
Augsburg College, MN
Augustana College, SD
Augusta State University, GA
Avila University, MO
Ball State University, IN
Belhaven College, MS
Birmingham-Southern College, AL
Bloomfield College, NJ
Bluefield College, VA
Boise State University, ID
The Boston Conservatory, MA
Bowling Green State University, OH
Brenau University, GA
Bryan College, TN
Bucknell University, PA
California Institute of the Arts, CA
California Polytechnic State University, San Luis Obispo, CA
California State University, Chico, CA
California State University, Fullerton, CA
Calvin College, MI
Carroll University, WI
Case Western Reserve University, OH
Cedar Crest College, PA
Centenary College of Louisiana, LA
Central Michigan University, MI
Chapman University, CA
City College of the City University of New York, NY
Clemson University, SC
Coe College, IA
The College at Brockport, State University of New York, NY
College of Charleston, SC
The College of Idaho, ID
The College of New Rochelle, NY
Columbia College Chicago, IL
Columbia International University, SC
Columbus State University, GA
Corban College, OR
Cornell College, IA
Creighton University, NE
Delta State University, MS
DePaul University, IL
DePauw University, IN
DeSales University, PA
Eastern Michigan University, MI
Edgewood College, WI
Elizabethtown College, PA
Elon University, NC
Emerson College, MA
Emmanuel College, GA
Eureka College, IL
Fairfield University, CT
Flagler College, FL
Florida Atlantic University, FL
Florida International University, FL
Fort Lewis College, CO
Franklin College, IN
Franklin Pierce University, NH
Fresno Pacific University, CA
Frostburg State University, MD
Gannon University, PA
Georgetown College, KY
Georgia College & State University, GA
Goucher College, MD
Green Mountain College, VT
Hastings College, NE
Henderson State University, AR
Hillsdale Free Will Baptist College, OK
Hobart and William Smith Colleges, NY
Idaho State University, ID
Illinois State University, IL
Indiana State University, IN
Indiana University of Pennsylvania, PA
Ithaca College, NY
The Juilliard School, NY
Juniata College, PA
Kennesaw State University, GA
Kent State University, OH
Kentucky Christian University, KY
Kentucky State University, KY
Lees-McRae College, NC
Lehigh University, PA
Liberty University, VA
Limestone College, SC
Lincoln University, MO
Lindenwood University, MO
Louisiana State University and Agricultural and Mechanical College, LA
Louisiana Tech University, LA
Lubbock Christian University, TX
Manhattanville College, NY
Mannes College The New School for Music, NY
Marian College, IN
Marymount Manhattan College, NY
Marywood University, PA
Massachusetts College of Liberal Arts, MA

Mesa State College, CO
Michigan State University, MI
Mississippi State University, MS
Mississippi University for Women, MS
Missouri Valley College, MO
Molloy College, NY
Montclair State University, NJ
Mount Aloysius College, PA
New Mexico State University, NM
Northeastern State University, OK
Northern Arizona University, AZ
Northern Illinois University, IL
Northwestern State University of Louisiana, LA
Northwest University, WA
Nyack College, NY
Oakland University, MI
Oglethorpe University, GA
Ohio Northern University, OH
The Ohio State University, OH
Ohio University, OH
Ohio University–Chillicothe, OH
Ohio University–Eastern, OH
Ohio University–Lancaster, OH
Ohio University–Southern Campus, OH
Ohio University–Zanesville, OH
Ohio Valley University, WV
Oklahoma Baptist University, OK
Oklahoma City University, OK
Oklahoma Panhandle State University, OK
Old Dominion University, VA
Olivet Nazarene University, IL
Ouachita Baptist University, AR
Pace University, NY
Point Park University, PA
Purchase College, State University of New York, NY
The Richard Stockton College of New Jersey, NJ
Rockford College, IL
Rockhurst University, MO
St. Andrews Presbyterian College, NC
St. Cloud State University, MN
Saint Louis University, MO
Salem State College, MA
Samford University, AL
San Diego State University, CA
Seattle Pacific University, WA
Seton Hill University, PA
Shepherd University, WV
Slippery Rock University of Pennsylvania, PA
Sonoma State University, CA
South Dakota State University, SD
Southeastern Louisiana University, LA
Southern Illinois University Carbondale, IL
Southern Nazarene University, OK
Southwestern College, KS
Southwest Minnesota State University, MN
State University of New York at Binghamton, NY
State University of New York at Fredonia, NY
State University of New York at New Paltz, NY
State University of New York College at Geneseo, NY
State University of New York College at Potsdam, NY
Stephens College, MO
Tabor College, KS
Temple University, PA
Texas A&M University, TX
Texas Christian University, TX
Texas Tech University, TX
Tiffin University, OH
The University of Akron, OH
The University of Alabama at Birmingham, AL
The University of Arizona, AZ
University of California, San Diego, CA
University of Central Missouri, MO
University of Colorado at Boulder, CO
University of Florida, FL
University of Guam, GU
University of Hartford, CT
University of Hawaii at Hilo, HI
University of Idaho, ID
University of Illinois at Chicago, IL
University of Illinois at Urbana–Champaign, IL
The University of Kansas, KS
University of Kentucky, KY
University of Louisiana at Monroe, LA
University of Maine at Fort Kent, ME
University of Maryland, Baltimore County, MD
University of Maryland, College Park, MD
University of Maryland Eastern Shore, MD
University of Miami, FL
University of Mississippi, MS
University of Missouri–Kansas City, MO
The University of Montana, MT
University of Nebraska at Omaha, NE
University of Nebraska–Lincoln, NE
University of Nevada, Las Vegas, NV
The University of North Carolina at Greensboro, NC
University of Northern Colorado, CO
University of Oklahoma, OK
University of Oregon, OR
University of Portland, OR
University of Richmond, VA
University of South Florida, FL
The University of Tampa, FL
The University of Texas at El Paso, TX
University of Tulsa, OK
University of Utah, UT
The University of Virginia's College at Wise, VA
University of Washington, WA
University of West Georgia, GA
University of Wisconsin–Stevens Point, WI
Utah State University, UT
Valparaiso University, IN
Virginia Commonwealth University, VA
Virginia Intermont College, VA
Virginia Polytechnic Institute and State University, VA
Washington State University, WA
Washington University in St. Louis, MO
Western Illinois University, IL
Western Oregon University, OR
Western Washington University, WA
West Virginia Wesleyan College, WV
Wichita State University, KS
Wilkes University, PA
Winthrop University, SC
Wright State University, OH
Xavier University, OH

Theater/Drama

Abilene Christian University, TX
Adelphi University, NY
Adrian College, MI
Albertus Magnus College, CT
Albion College, MI
Albright College, PA
Alderson-Broaddus College, WV
Alma College, MI
Angelo State University, TX
Arcadia University, PA
Arizona State University, AZ
Arkansas State University, AR
Ashland University, OH
Auburn University, AL
Augsburg College, MN
Augustana College, IL
Augustana College, SD
Augusta State University, GA
Austin College, TX
Austin Peay State University, TN
Averett University, VA
Avila University, MO
Baker University, KS
Ball State University, IN
Barton College, NC
Baylor University, TX
Belhaven College, MS
Belmont Abbey College, NC
Benedictine College, KS
Berry College, GA
Bethany College, KS
Bethany Lutheran College, MN
Bethel College, IN
Bethel College, KS
Bethel University, MN
Biola University, CA
Birmingham-Southern College, AL
Black Hills State University, SD
Bloomfield College, NJ
Bluefield College, VA
Boise State University, ID
The Boston Conservatory, MA
Boston University, MA
Bowling Green State University, OH
Bradley University, IL
Brenau University, GA
Brevard College, NC
Bryan College, TN
Bucknell University, PA
Buena Vista University, IA
Butler University, IN
California Baptist University, CA
California Institute of the Arts, CA
California Polytechnic State University, San Luis Obispo, CA
California State University, Bakersfield, CA
California State University, Chico, CA
California State University, Fresno, CA
California State University, Fullerton, CA
California State University, Los Angeles, CA
California State University, San Bernardino, CA
Calvin College, MI
Campbellsville University, KY
Carroll College, MT
Carroll University, WI
Case Western Reserve University, OH
Catawba College, NC
The Catholic University of America, DC
Cedar Crest College, PA
Centenary College of Louisiana, LA
Central College, IA
Central Methodist University, MO
Central Michigan University, MI
Centre College, KY
Chapman University, CA
Chatham University, PA
Christopher Newport University, VA
Clarke College, IA

Clemson University, SC
Cleveland State University, OH
Coastal Carolina University, SC
Coe College, IA
The College at Brockport, State University of New York, NY
College of Charleston, SC
The College of Idaho, ID
The College of New Rochelle, NY
College of Saint Benedict, MN
College of Staten Island of the City University of New York, NY
The College of William and Mary, VA
The College of Wooster, OH
Colorado State University, CO
Columbia College Chicago, IL
Columbus State University, GA
Concordia College, MN
Concordia University, Nebraska, NE
Concordia University, St. Paul, MN
Concord University, WV
Converse College, SC
Cornell College, IA
Cornish College of the Arts, WA
Creighton University, NE
Culver-Stockton College, MO
Dana College, NE
Davidson College, NC
DePaul University, IL
DeSales University, PA
Dillard University, LA
Doane College, NE
Dordt College, IA
Drake University, IA
Drury University, MO
Eastern Michigan University, MI
Eastern Washington University, WA
East Tennessee State University, TN
East Texas Baptist University, TX
Edgewood College, WI
Elizabethtown College, PA
Elmhurst College, IL
Elon University, NC
Emmanuel College, GA
Emory University, GA
Emporia State University, KS
Eureka College, IL
Evangel University, MO
Faulkner University, AL
Ferris State University, MI
Five Towns College, NY
Flagler College, FL
Florida College, FL
Florida International University, FL
Florida State University, FL
Fort Lewis College, CO
Francis Marion University, SC
Franklin College, IN
Franklin Pierce University, NH
Fresno Pacific University, CA
Frostburg State University, MD
Furman University, SC
Gannon University, PA
Gardner-Webb University, NC
George Fox University, OR
Georgetown College, KY
Georgia College & State University, GA
Georgia Southern University, GA
Goucher College, MD
Grace College, IN
Graceland University, IA
Grand Valley State University, MI
Grand View University, IA
Green Mountain College, VT
Greensboro College, NC
Guilford College, NC
Gustavus Adolphus College, MN
Hamline University, MN
Hanover College, IN
Hardin-Simmons University, TX
Hastings College, NE
Henderson State University, AR
Hendrix College, AR
Hofstra University, NY
Hope College, MI
Howard Payne University, TX
Huntington University, IN
Idaho State University, ID
Illinois College, IL
Illinois State University, IL
Illinois Wesleyan University, IL
Indiana University of Pennsylvania, PA
Iowa State University of Science and Technology, IA
Ithaca College, NY
Jacksonville State University, AL
James Madison University, VA
Jamestown College, ND
The Juilliard School, NY
Kean University, NJ
Kennesaw State University, GA
Kent State University, OH
Kentucky Christian University, KY
Knox College, IL
LaGrange College, GA
Lake Forest College, IL
Lambuth University, TN
Lees-McRae College, NC
Lee University, TN
Lehigh University, PA
Lewis-Clark State College, ID
Limestone College, SC
Lincoln University, MO
Lindenwood University, MO
Linfield College, OR
Lipscomb University, TN
Long Island University, C.W. Post Campus, NY
Longwood University, VA
Louisiana State University and Agricultural and Mechanical College, LA
Louisiana Tech University, LA
Loyola University Chicago, IL
Lubbock Christian University, TX
Lycoming College, PA
Lyon College, AR
Malone University, OH
Marian College, IN
Marquette University, WI
Marymount Manhattan College, NY
Maryville College, TN
Marywood University, PA
Massachusetts College of Liberal Arts, MA
Mayville State University, ND
McMurry University, TX
McPherson College, KS
Mercer University, GA
Mesa State College, CO
Messiah College, PA
Methodist University, NC
Miami University, OH
Michigan State University, MI
Midland Lutheran College, NE
Millikin University, IL
Millsaps College, MS
Minnesota State University Moorhead, MN
Mississippi State University, MS
Mississippi University for Women, MS
Missouri Baptist University, MO
Missouri Southern State University, MO
Missouri University of Science and Technology, MO
Missouri Valley College, MO
Molloy College, NY
Monmouth College, IL
Montana State University, MT
Montana State University–Billings, MT
Montclair State University, NJ
Mount Marty College, SD
Mount Mercy College, IA
Mount Union College, OH
Murray State University, KY
Muskingum College, OH
Nazareth College of Rochester, NY
Newberry College, SC
New England College, NH
New England Conservatory of Music, MA
Newman University, KS
New Mexico State University, NM
Niagara University, NY
North Carolina Agricultural and Technical State University, NC
North Central College, IL
North Dakota State University, ND
Northeastern State University, OK
Northern Arizona University, AZ
Northern Illinois University, IL
Northern Michigan University, MI
Northern State University, SD
North Greenville University, SC
North Park University, IL
Northwestern College, MN
Northwestern Oklahoma State University, OK
Northwestern State University of Louisiana, LA
Northwest Missouri State University, MO
Northwest University, WA
Nyack College, NY
Oglethorpe University, GA
Ohio Northern University, OH
The Ohio State University, OH
Ohio University, OH
Ohio University–Chillicothe, OH
Ohio University Eastern, OH
Ohio University–Lancaster, OH
Ohio University–Southern Campus, OH
Ohio University–Zanesville, OH
Ohio Valley University, WV
Oklahoma Baptist University, OK
Oklahoma Christian University, OK
Oklahoma City University, OK
Oklahoma Panhandle State University, OK
Oklahoma State University, OK
Old Dominion University, VA
Olivet Nazarene University, IL
Ouachita Baptist University, AR
Pace University, NY
Pacific Lutheran University, WA
Pacific University, OR
Palm Beach Atlantic University, FL
Peace College, NC
Piedmont College, GA
Plymouth State University, NH
Point Loma Nazarene University, CA
Point Park University, PA
Portland State University, OR
Providence College, RI
Purchase College, State University of New York, NY

Randolph College, VA
Rhode Island College, RI
The Richard Stockton College of New Jersey, NJ
Rider University, NJ
Ripon College, WI
Rockford College, IL
Rockhurst University, MO
Rollins College, FL
Saginaw Valley State University, MI
St. Ambrose University, IA
St. Andrews Presbyterian College, NC
St. Cloud State University, MN
St. Edward's University, TX
Saint John's University, MN
Saint Joseph's College, IN
Saint Joseph's University, PA
Saint Louis University, MO
Saint Mary's University of Minnesota, MN
St. Norbert College, WI
Saint Vincent College, PA
Salem State College, MA
San Diego State University, CA
Santa Clara University, CA
Schreiner University, TX
Seattle University, WA
Seton Hill University, PA
Shepherd University, WV
Shippensburg University of Pennsylvania, PA
Shorter College, GA
Simpson College, IA
Slippery Rock University of Pennsylvania, PA
Sonoma State University, CA
South Dakota State University, SD
Southeastern Louisiana University, LA
Southeastern Oklahoma State University, OK
Southeast Missouri State University, MO
Southern Adventist University, TN
Southern Arkansas University–Magnolia, AR
Southern Illinois University Carbondale, IL
Southern Illinois University Edwardsville, IL
Southern Oregon University, OR
Southern Utah University, UT
Southwest Baptist University, MO
Southwestern Christian University, OK
Southwestern College, KS
Southwestern Oklahoma State University, OK
Southwestern University, TX
Southwest Minnesota State University, MN
State University of New York at Binghamton, NY
State University of New York at Fredonia, NY
State University of New York at Plattsburgh, NY
State University of New York College at Geneseo, NY
State University of New York College at Oneonta, NY
State University of New York College at Potsdam, NY
Stephen F. Austin State University, TX
Stephens College, MO
Stetson University, FL
Tabor College, KS
Taylor University, IN
Texas A&M University, TX
Texas A&M University–Commerce, TX
Texas Christian University, TX
Texas Lutheran University, TX
Texas State University–San Marcos, TX
Texas Tech University, TX
Thomas More College, KY
Tiffin University, OH
Towson University, MD
Transylvania University, KY
Trinity Christian College, IL
Trinity University, TX
Troy University, AL
Truman State University, MO
Union University, TN
The University of Akron, OH
The University of Alabama, AL
The University of Alabama at Birmingham, AL
University of Alaska Fairbanks, AK
The University of Arizona, AZ
University of Arkansas, AR
University of California, Irvine, CA
University of California, Riverside, CA
University of California, Santa Cruz, CA
University of Central Florida, FL
University of Central Missouri, MO
University of Central Oklahoma, OK
University of Colorado at Boulder, CO
University of Connecticut, CT
University of Dallas, TX
University of Delaware, DE
University of Denver, CO
University of Evansville, IN
The University of Findlay, OH
University of Florida, FL
University of Hartford, CT
University of Hawaii at Hilo, HI
University of Idaho, ID
University of Illinois at Chicago, IL
University of Illinois at Urbana–Champaign, IL
The University of Kansas, KS
University of Kentucky, KY
University of La Verne, CA
University of Louisiana at Monroe, LA
University of Mary, ND
University of Maryland, Baltimore County, MD
University of Maryland, College Park, MD
University of Maryland Eastern Shore, MD
University of Mary Washington, VA
University of Massachusetts Amherst, MA
University of Miami, FL
University of Michigan, MI
University of Michigan–Flint, MI
University of Mississippi, MS
University of Missouri–Columbia, MO
The University of Montana, MT
University of Nebraska at Omaha, NE
University of Nebraska–Lincoln, NE
University of Nevada, Las Vegas, NV
University of Nevada, Reno, NV
University of New Hampshire, NH
University of New Orleans, LA
The University of North Carolina at Asheville, NC
The University of North Carolina at Chapel Hill, NC
The University of North Carolina at Greensboro, NC
The University of North Carolina Wilmington, NC
University of North Dakota, ND
University of Northern Colorado, CO
University of Northern Iowa, IA
University of Oklahoma, OK
University of Oregon, OR
University of Pittsburgh at Johnstown, PA
University of Portland, OR
University of Puget Sound, WA
University of Richmond, VA
University of Science and Arts of Oklahoma, OK
University of South Alabama, AL
University of South Carolina, SC
The University of South Dakota, SD
University of Southern Indiana, IN
University of Southern Maine, ME
University of Southern Mississippi, MS
University of South Florida, FL
The University of Tennessee at Martin, TN
The University of Texas at Arlington, TX
The University of Texas at El Paso, TX
The University of Texas–Pan American, TX
University of the Cumberlands, KY
University of the Ozarks, AR
University of Tulsa, OK
University of Utah, UT
University of Vermont, VT
The University of Virginia's College at Wise, VA
University of West Florida, FL
University of West Georgia, GA
University of Wisconsin–Eau Claire, WI
University of Wisconsin–Green Bay, WI
University of Wisconsin–La Crosse, WI
University of Wisconsin–Parkside, WI
University of Wisconsin–Stevens Point, WI
University of Wisconsin–Whitewater, WI
University of Wyoming, WY
Utah State University, UT
Valdosta State University, GA
Valley City State University, ND
Valparaiso University, IN
Vanguard University of Southern California, CA
Virginia Commonwealth University, VA
Virginia Intermont College, VA
Virginia Polytechnic Institute and State University, VA
Virginia Wesleyan College, VA
Wabash College, IN
Wagner College, NY
Walla Walla University, WA
Warner Pacific College, OR
Washington State University, WA
Washington University in St. Louis, MO
Wayland Baptist University, TX
Wayne State University, MI
Webster University, MO
West Chester University of Pennsylvania, PA
Western Carolina University, NC
Western Illinois University, IL
Western Kentucky University, KY
Western Oregon University, OR
Western Washington University, WA
West Liberty State University, WV
Westminster College, PA
Westminster College, UT
Westmont College, CA
West Virginia University, WV
West Virginia Wesleyan College, WV
Whitman College, WA
Whittier College, CA
Whitworth University, WA
Wichita State University, KS
Wilkes University, PA
Willamette University, OR
William Carey University, MS
Winona State University, MN
Winthrop University, SC
Wisconsin Lutheran College, WI
Wittenberg University, OH

Wright State University, OH
Xavier University, OH
York College, NE
Youngstown State University, OH

Special Achievements/ Activities

Cheerleading/Drum Major

Abilene Christian University, TX
Angelo State University, TX
Arkansas State University, AR
Ashland University, OH
Auburn University, AL
Avila University, MO
Baker University, KS
Belhaven College, MS
Bellarmine University, KY
Bethany College, KS
Bethel College, IN
Bluefield State College, WV
Boise State University, ID
Brevard College, NC
Brewton-Parker College, GA
California Baptist University, CA
Campbellsville University, KY
Central Methodist University, MO
Cleveland State University, OH
Coastal Carolina University, SC
Columbus State University, GA
Concordia College, AL
Culver-Stockton College, MO
Delta State University, MS
Drury University, MO
Eastern Kentucky University, KY
East Texas Baptist University, TX
Evangel University, MO
Faulkner University, AL
Florida Institute of Technology, FL
Francis Marion University, SC
Gardner-Webb University, NC
Georgia Southern University, GA
Graceland University, IA
Harding University, AR
Hastings College, NE
Hawai'i Pacific University, HI
Henderson State University, AR
Houston Baptist University, TX
Huntingdon College, AL
Huntington University, IN
Idaho State University, ID
James Madison University, VA
John Brown University, AR
Kentucky State University, KY
Langston University, OK
Lees-McRae College, NC
Lee University, TN
Limestone College, SC
Lincoln Memorial University, TN
Lincoln University, MO
Lindenwood University, MO
Lindsey Wilson College, KY
Lipscomb University, TN
Long Island University, Brooklyn Campus, NY
Louisiana Tech University, LA
Lubbock Christian University, TX
Lyon College, AR
McKendree University, IL
McPherson College, KS
Mesa State College, CO
Methodist University, NC
Mid-Continent University, KY
Milligan College, TN
Mississippi State University, MS
Missouri Baptist University, MO
Missouri Valley College, MO
Missouri Western State University, MO
Montana State University–Billings, MT
Mountain State University, WV
Murray State University, KY
Newberry College, SC
Nicholls State University, LA
Northeastern State University, OK
Northern Michigan University, MI
Northwestern Oklahoma State University, OK
Northwestern State University of Louisiana, LA
Northwest Missouri State University, MO
Northwood University, MI
The Ohio State University, OH
Oklahoma Christian University, OK
Oklahoma City University, OK
Oklahoma Panhandle State University, OK
Oklahoma State University, OK
Old Dominion University, VA
Olivet Nazarene University, IL
Oral Roberts University, OK
Ouachita Baptist University, AR
St. Edward's University, TX
Saint Francis University, PA
St. John's University, NY
Saint Joseph's College, IN
Saint Louis University, MO
St. Mary's University, TX
Sam Houston State University, TX
Shorter College, GA
Southeastern Louisiana University, LA
Southeastern Oklahoma State University, OK
Southeast Missouri State University, MO
Southern Arkansas University–Magnolia, AR
Southern Illinois University Carbondale, IL
Southern Nazarene University, OK
Southwestern Christian University, OK
Southwestern College, KS
Southwestern Oklahoma State University, OK
Stephen F. Austin State University, TX
Stetson University, FL
Tabor College, KS
Temple University, PA
Tennessee Technological University, TN
Texas A&M University–Commerce, TX
Texas Christian University, TX
Tiffin University, OH
Union College, KY
Union University, TN
The University of Alabama, AL
The University of Alabama at Birmingham, AL
The University of Alabama in Huntsville, AL
University of Central Missouri, MO
University of Delaware, DE
University of Idaho, ID
University of Kentucky, KY
University of Louisiana at Monroe, LA
University of Mary, ND
University of Mary Hardin-Baylor, TX
University of Maryland, College Park, MD
University of Massachusetts Amherst, MA
University of Memphis, TN
University of Mississippi, MS
The University of Montana, MT
University of Nebraska at Kearney, NE
University of Nebraska–Lincoln, NE
University of Nevada, Las Vegas, NV
University of North Alabama, AL
The University of North Carolina Wilmington, NC
University of Puerto Rico, Mayagüez Campus, PR
University of Saint Francis, IN
University of Science and Arts of Oklahoma, OK
University of South Carolina, SC
University of South Carolina Aiken, SC
University of Southern Mississippi, MS
The University of Tennessee at Martin, TN
The University of Texas at Arlington, TX
The University of Texas at El Paso, TX
The University of Texas at San Antonio, TX
The University of Texas–Pan American, TX
University of the Cumberlands, KY
University of Tulsa, OK
University of Utah, UT
The University of West Alabama, AL
University of Wyoming, WY
Virginia Intermont College, VA
Virginia Polytechnic Institute and State University, VA
Wayland Baptist University, TX
Webber International University, FL
West Liberty State University, WV
Wichita State University, KS
William Carey University, MS
Williams Baptist College, AR
Wofford College, SC
Wright State University, OH
Youngstown State University, OH

Community Service

Adelphi University, NY
Agnes Scott College, GA
Alaska Pacific University, AK
Albertus Magnus College, CT
Alliant International University, CA
Arcadia University, PA
Arkansas State University, AR
The Art Institute of Boston at Lesley University, MA
Augsburg College, MN
Augusta State University, GA
Austin College, TX
Ball State University, IN
Baylor University, TX
Bellarmine University, KY
Beloit College, WI
Bentley University, MA
Berry College, GA
Bethel University, MN
Biola University, CA
Bloomfield College, NJ
Boise State University, ID
Bradley University, IL
Brevard College, NC
Bryan College, TN
California Polytechnic State University, San Luis Obispo, CA
California State University, Bakersfield, CA
California State University, Chico, CA
California State University, Fresno, CA
California State University, Los Angeles, CA
California State University, San Bernardino, CA
California State University, Stanislaus, CA
Calvin College, MI
Cedar Crest College, PA
Centenary College of Louisiana, LA

Non-Need Scholarships for Undergraduates
Special Achievements/Activities

City College of the City University of New York, NY
Clark University, MA
Clemson University, SC
The College at Brockport, State University of New York, NY
College of Mount St. Joseph, OH
The College of New Rochelle, NY
College of Notre Dame of Maryland, MD
College of Saint Mary, NE
College of Staten Island of the City University of New York, NY
The College of Wooster, OH
Colorado State University–Pueblo, CO
Columbus State University, GA
Concordia College–New York, NY
Concord University, WV
Cornell College, IA
Dallas Baptist University, TX
Dalton State College, GA
Davidson College, NC
Defiance College, OH
DePaul University, IL
DePauw University, IN
Dominican University of California, CA
Edgewood College, WI
Elmhurst College, IL
Elon University, NC
Endicott College, MA
The Evergreen State College, WA
Finlandia University, MI
Florida Gulf Coast University, FL
Frostburg State University, MD
Furman University, SC
Gannon University, PA
Georgia College & State University, GA
Georgia Southern University, GA
Green Mountain College, VT
Greensboro College, NC
Hampshire College, MA
Hendrix College, AR
Hillsdale Free Will Baptist College, OK
Hollins University, VA
Houston Baptist University, TX
Howard Payne University, TX
Illinois College, IL
Illinois Institute of Technology, IL
Illinois State University, IL
Indiana University of Pennsylvania, PA
Iowa State University of Science and Technology, IA
John Carroll University, OH
Johnson Bible College, TN
Johnson C. Smith University, NC
Juniata College, PA
Kean University, NJ
Kennesaw State University, GA
Kent State University, OH
Kentucky Christian University, KY
Keuka College, NY
King's College, PA
Knox College, IL
Kutztown University of Pennsylvania, PA
Lewis & Clark College, OR
Lewis-Clark State College, ID
Lincoln Christian College, IL
Lindenwood University, MO
Lipscomb University, TN
Loyola University Chicago, IL
Malone University, OH
Manhattan College, NY
Manhattanville College, NY
Marian College, IN
Marymount University, VA
Maryville College, TN
Maryville University of Saint Louis, MO
Marywood University, PA
McKendree University, IL
McPherson College, KS
Mercer University, GA
Mercyhurst College, PA
Michigan State University, MI
Midland Lutheran College, NE
Millersville University of Pennsylvania, PA
Milligan College, TN
Millikin University, IL
Millsaps College, MS
Minnesota State University Moorhead, MN
Misericordia University, PA
Missouri Valley College, MO
Missouri Western State University, MO
Molloy College, NY
Montclair State University, NJ
Mount Ida College, MA
Muskingum College, OH
New England College, NH
Newman University, KS
Niagara University, NY
Nichols College, MA
North Central College, IL
Northeastern State University, OK
Nyack College, NY
Oglethorpe University, GA
Ohio Northern University, OH
Ohio Valley University, WV
Oklahoma State University, OK
Old Dominion University, VA
Olivet College, MI
Oral Roberts University, OK
Pace University, NY
Pacific Union College, CA
Pacific University, OR
Pitzer College, CA
Point Park University, PA
Portland State University, OR
Presentation College, SD
Providence College, RI
Randolph College, VA
Regis College, MA
The Richard Stockton College of New Jersey, NJ
Robert Morris College, IL
Rochester Institute of Technology, NY
Rockford College, IL
Rockhurst University, MO
Sacred Heart University, CT
Saginaw Valley State University, MI
St. Catherine University, MN
St. Cloud State University, MN
St. Edward's University, TX
St. John Fisher College, NY
St. John's University, NY
St. Lawrence University, NY
St. Louis College of Pharmacy, MO
Saint Louis University, MO
St. Olaf College, MN
Schreiner University, TX
Seton Hill University, PA
Shippensburg University of Pennsylvania, PA
Simmons College, MA
Simpson College, IA
Slippery Rock University of Pennsylvania, PA
Sonoma State University, CA
South Dakota State University, SD
Southern Adventist University, TN
Southern Illinois University Carbondale, IL
Southern Oregon University, OR
Southwestern College, KS
Spring Hill College, AL
State University of New York at Binghamton, NY
State University of New York at Plattsburgh, NY
State University of New York College at Cortland, NY
State University of New York College at Geneseo, NY
State University of New York College at Oneonta, NY
State University of New York College at Potsdam, NY
Stetson University, FL
Suffolk University, MA
Sweet Briar College, VA
Texas A&M University–Texarkana, TX
Texas Tech University, TX
Trinity College of Florida, FL
Unity College, ME
The University of Akron, OH
The University of Alabama, AL
The University of Alabama in Huntsville, AL
University of Alaska Fairbanks, AK
University of Arkansas, AR
University of California, San Diego, CA
University of Colorado at Boulder, CO
University of Colorado at Colorado Springs, CO
University of Connecticut, CT
University of Delaware, DE
University of Denver, CO
University of Florida, FL
University of Hartford, CT
University of Hawaii at Hilo, HI
University of Houston–Clear Lake, TX
University of Houston–Downtown, TX
University of Houston–Victoria, TX
The University of Kansas, KS
University of La Verne, CA
University of Louisiana at Monroe, LA
University of Maine at Presque Isle, ME
University of Mary Hardin-Baylor, TX
University of Massachusetts Dartmouth, MA
University of Massachusetts Lowell, MA
University of Michigan, MI
University of Michigan–Dearborn, MI
University of Michigan–Flint, MI
University of Mississippi, MS
University of Nebraska–Lincoln, NE
University of Nevada, Las Vegas, NV
University of New England, ME
University of New Hampshire, NH
The University of North Carolina at Asheville, NC
The University of North Carolina at Chapel Hill, NC
The University of North Carolina at Greensboro, NC
University of North Florida, FL
University of Richmond, VA
University of South Carolina, SC
University of Southern Maine, ME
The University of Texas at Arlington, TX
The University of Texas–Pan American, TX
The University of Texas Southwestern Medical Center at Dallas, TX
University of the Cumberlands, KY
University of Tulsa, OK
University of Vermont, VT

The University of Virginia's College at Wise, VA
University of West Georgia, GA
University of Wisconsin–Eau Claire, WI
University of Wisconsin–Green Bay, WI
University of Wisconsin–La Crosse, WI
University of Wisconsin–Parkside, WI
University of Wisconsin–Stout, WI
Ursuline College, OH
Valdosta State University, GA
Valley Forge Christian College, PA
Virginia Polytechnic Institute and State University, VA
Virginia Wesleyan College, VA
Wabash College, IN
Warren Wilson College, NC
Washington State University, WA
Waynesburg University, PA
Webber International University, FL
Western Illinois University, IL
Western New England College, MA
Western Oregon University, OR
Western Washington University, WA
West Virginia Wesleyan College, WV
Wheeling Jesuit University, WV
Widener University, PA
Willamette University, OR
Wilson College, PA
Wittenberg University, OH
Wofford College, SC
Wright State University, OH
York College of Pennsylvania, PA

Hobbies/Interests

Albright College, PA
Angelo State University, TX
Augusta State University, GA
Brevard College, NC
California State Polytechnic University, Pomona, CA
California State University, Chico, CA
California State University, San Bernardino, CA
Centenary College of Louisiana, LA
The College at Brockport, State University of New York, NY
The College of New Rochelle, NY
Corban College, OR
Dalton State College, GA
Florida Institute of Technology, FL
Hawai'i Pacific University, HI
Illinois Institute of Technology, IL
Indiana University of Pennsylvania, PA
Mesa State College, CO
Michigan State University, MI
Millsaps College, MS
Missouri Valley College, MO
The Ohio State University, OH
St. John's University, NY
South Dakota State University, SD
Southern Oregon University, OR
Southwest Minnesota State University, MN
State University of New York College at Cortland, NY
Stephen F. Austin State University, TX
The University of Alabama, AL
University of Michigan–Flint, MI
University of Minnesota, Twin Cities Campus, MN
University of South Alabama, AL
University of Wisconsin–Eau Claire, WI
Valdosta State University, GA

Junior Miss

Albright College, PA
Augsburg College, MN
Belhaven College, MS
Bethel University, MN
Birmingham-Southern College, AL
Bluefield State College, WV
Campbellsville University, KY
Carroll University, WI
Cedar Crest College, PA
The College of New Rochelle, NY
College of Saint Benedict, MN
Concordia University Texas, TX
Georgetown College, KY
Georgia Southern University, GA
Grace College, IN
Grand View University, IA
Gustavus Adolphus College, MN
Hardin-Simmons University, TX
Idaho State University, ID
Lebanon Valley College, PA
Lewis-Clark State College, ID
Lindenwood University, MO
Lindsey Wilson College, KY
Louisiana Tech University, LA
McDaniel College, MD
McMurry University, TX
Michigan State University, MI
Midway College, KY
Mississippi State University, MS
Mississippi University for Women, MS
Missouri Valley College, MO
Murray State University, KY
Northeastern State University, OK
Ohio Northern University, OH
Oklahoma City University, OK
Point Park University, PA
South Dakota State University, SD
Spring Arbor University, MI
Texas Lutheran University, TX
The University of Alabama, AL
The University of Alabama at Birmingham, AL
The University of Alabama in Huntsville, AL
University of Idaho, ID
University of Mississippi, MS
University of Montevallo, AL
The University of North Carolina at Asheville, NC
The University of North Carolina at Greensboro, NC
University of South Alabama, AL
University of Wyoming, WY
Washington State University, WA
William Carey University, MS

Leadership

Abilene Christian University, TX
Agnes Scott College, GA
Alaska Pacific University, AK
Albertus Magnus College, CT
Albright College, PA
Alderson-Broaddus College, WV
Alfred University, NY
Alliant International University, CA
American Jewish University, CA
American University, DC
Andrews University, MI
Angelo State University, TX
Aquinas College, TN
Arcadia University, PA
Arkansas State University, AR
Asbury College, KY
Auburn University, AL
Augsburg College, MN
Augustana College, SD
Augusta State University, GA
Austin College, TX
Austin Peay State University, TN
Ave Maria University, FL
Averett University, VA
Babson College, MA
Baker University, KS
Baldwin-Wallace College, OH
Ball State University, IN
Baptist Bible College of Pennsylvania, PA
Bard College, NY
Barton College, NC
Baylor University, TX
Belhaven College, MS
Bellarmine University, KY
Bethel College, IN
Bethel University, MN
Biola University, CA
Bloomfield College, NJ
Bluefield State College, WV
Bluffton University, OH
Boise State University, ID
Boston University, MA
Bowdoin College, ME
Bowling Green State University, OH
Bradley University, IL
Brenau University, GA
Brevard College, NC
Bryan College, TN
Bucknell University, PA
Buena Vista University, IA
California Polytechnic State University, San Luis Obispo, CA
California State Polytechnic University, Pomona, CA
California State University, Chico, CA
California State University, Fresno, CA
California State University, Fullerton, CA
California State University, Northridge, CA
California State University, Stanislaus, CA
Campbellsville University, KY
Carroll University, WI
Carson-Newman College, TN
Case Western Reserve University, OH
Cedar Crest College, PA
Cedarville University, OH
Centenary College, NJ
Centenary College of Louisiana, LA
Central Methodist University, MO
Central Michigan University, MI
Christian Brothers University, TN
Christopher Newport University, VA
City College of the City University of New York, NY
Claremont McKenna College, CA
Clarke College, IA
Clarkson University, NY
Clearwater Christian College, FL
Clemson University, SC
The College at Brockport, State University of New York, NY
The College of Idaho, ID
College of Mount St. Joseph, OH
The College of New Rochelle, NY
College of Notre Dame of Maryland, MD
College of St. Joseph, VT
College of Saint Mary, NE
Colorado State University–Pueblo, CO
Columbia College, MO
Columbia College Chicago, IL

Columbia International University, SC
Columbus State University, GA
Concordia University, OR
Concordia University Texas, TX
Concord University, WV
Converse College, SC
Corban College, OR
Cornell College, IA
Covenant College, GA
Creighton University, NE
Crown College, MN
Dallas Baptist University, TX
Dalton State College, GA
Dana College, NE
Davidson College, NC
Defiance College, OH
Delta State University, MS
DePaul University, IL
DePauw University, IN
DeSales University, PA
Dickinson College, PA
Dominican University, IL
Dordt College, IA
Drury University, MO
Duke University, NC
Eastern Michigan University, MI
East Tennessee State University, TN
East Texas Baptist University, TX
Elmira College, NY
Elon University, NC
Embry-Riddle Aeronautical University, AZ
Embry-Riddle Aeronautical University, FL
Embry-Riddle Aeronautical University Worldwide, FL
Emmanuel College, GA
Emory University, GA
Endicott College, MA
Eureka College, IL
Evangel University, MO
Faulkner University, AL
Finlandia University, MI
Flagler College, FL
Florida Gulf Coast University, FL
Fort Lewis College, CO
Franklin Pierce University, NH
Frostburg State University, MD
Furman University, SC
Gannon University, PA
George Fox University, OR
Georgetown College, KY
Georgia College & State University, GA
Georgia Institute of Technology, GA
Georgia Southern University, GA
Georgia Southwestern State University, GA
Golden Gate University, CA
Gonzaga University, WA
Gordon College, MA
Graceland University, IA
Grace University, NE
Green Mountain College, VT
Greensboro College, NC
Grove City College, PA
Hampshire College, MA
Harding University, AR
Hardin-Simmons University, TX
Hawai'i Pacific University, HI
Henderson State University, AR
Hendrix College, AR
Hobart and William Smith Colleges, NY
Hofstra University, NY
Hollins University, VA
Hope International University, CA
Howard Payne University, TX
Husson University, ME
Idaho State University, ID
Illinois College, IL
Illinois Institute of Technology, IL
Illinois State University, IL
Indiana University of Pennsylvania, PA
Iowa State University of Science and Technology, IA
Ithaca College, NY
James Madison University, VA
Jamestown College, ND
John Brown University, AR
John Carroll University, OH
Johnson Bible College, TN
Johnson C. Smith University, NC
Juniata College, PA
Kean University, NJ
Kennesaw State University, GA
Kent State University, OH
Kentucky Christian University, KY
Keuka College, NY
King's College, PA
Kutztown University of Pennsylvania, PA
Kuyper College, MI
LaGrange College, GA
Lake Forest College, IL
Lancaster Bible College, PA
Langston University, OK
Lees-McRae College, NC
Lee University, TN
Le Moyne College, NY
Lewis & Clark College, OR
Lewis-Clark State College, ID
Limestone College, SC
Lincoln Christian College, IL
Lindenwood University, MO
Lindsey Wilson College, KY
Linfield College, OR
Lipscomb University, TN
Lock Haven University of Pennsylvania, PA
Long Island University, Brooklyn Campus, NY
Louisiana State University and Agricultural and Mechanical College, LA
Loyola University Chicago, IL
Lubbock Christian University, TX
Lycoming College, PA
Lynn University, FL
Malone University, OH
Manhattan Christian College, KS
Manhattan College, NY
Manhattanville College, NY
Mary Baldwin College, VA
Marymount University, VA
Maryville College, TN
Maryville University of Saint Louis, MO
Marywood University, PA
Massachusetts College of Liberal Arts, MA
The Master's College and Seminary, CA
McDaniel College, MD
McKendree University, IL
Mercyhurst College, PA
Mesa State College, CO
Messiah College, PA
Methodist University, NC
Miami University, OH
Michigan State University, MI
Midland Lutheran College, NE
Midway College, KY
Millsaps College, MS
Misericordia University, PA
Mississippi College, MS
Mississippi State University, MS
Mississippi University for Women, MS
Missouri Southern State University, MO
Missouri Valley College, MO
Missouri Western State University, MO
Molloy College, NY
Monmouth University, NJ
Montclair State University, NJ
Montreat College, NC
Mount Aloysius College, PA
Mount Ida College, MA
Mount Mary College, WI
Mount Mercy College, IA
Murray State University, KY
Muskingum College, OH
National University, CA
New England College, NH
Newman University, KS
New Mexico State University, NM
Nichols College, MA
North Carolina State University, NC
Northeastern State University, OK
Northern Illinois University, IL
Northern Michigan University, MI
Northern State University, SD
Northland College, WI
Northwest Christian University, OR
Northwestern College, MN
Northwestern Oklahoma State University, OK
Northwestern State University of Louisiana, LA
Northwest Missouri State University, MO
Northwest University, WA
Northwood University, MI
Nyack College, NY
Occidental College, CA
Ohio Christian University, OH
Ohio Northern University, OH
The Ohio State University, OH
Ohio Valley University, WV
Oklahoma Baptist University, OK
Oklahoma Christian University, OK
Oklahoma City University, OK
Oklahoma State University, OK
Old Dominion University, VA
Olivet College, MI
Oral Roberts University, OK
Pace University, NY
Pacific Lutheran University, WA
Pacific Union College, CA
Peirce College, PA
Piedmont College, GA
Pitzer College, CA
Portland State University, OR
Presbyterian College, SC
Presentation College, SD
Purdue University, IN
Purdue University North Central, IN
Randolph College, VA
Regis College, MA
Rice University, TX
The Richard Stockton College of New Jersey, NJ
Ripon College, WI
Roberts Wesleyan College, NY
Rochester Institute of Technology, NY
Rockford College, IL
Rockhurst University, MO
Sacred Heart University, CT
Saginaw Valley State University, MI
St. Andrews Presbyterian College, NC
St. Catherine University, MN
St. Edward's University, TX
St. John's University, NY

Saint Joseph's University, PA
St. Louis College of Pharmacy, MO
Saint Louis University, MO
Saint Mary's College of California, CA
Saint Mary's University of Minnesota, MN
Saint Vincent College, PA
Saint Xavier University, IL
Salem College, NC
Samford University, AL
Sam Houston State University, TX
San Diego State University, CA
Schreiner University, TX
Scripps College, CA
Seattle University, WA
Seton Hill University, PA
Shepherd University, WV
Shippensburg University of Pennsylvania, PA
Simpson College, IA
Simpson University, CA
Slippery Rock University of Pennsylvania, PA
Sonoma State University, CA
South Dakota State University, SD
Southeastern Louisiana University, LA
Southeast Missouri State University, MO
Southern Adventist University, TN
Southern Arkansas University–Magnolia, AR
Southern Illinois University Carbondale, IL
Southern Oregon University, OR
Southern Utah University, UT
Southwestern College, KS
Southwestern University, TX
Southwest Minnesota State University, MN
State University of New York at Binghamton, NY
State University of New York at Fredonia, NY
State University of New York at Plattsburgh, NY
State University of New York College at Cortland, NY
State University of New York College at Geneseo, NY
State University of New York College at Oneonta, NY
State University of New York College at Potsdam, NY
State University of New York College of Environmental Science and Forestry, NY
Stephen F. Austin State University, TX
Stephens College, MO
Stetson University, FL
Taylor University, IN
Texas A&M University, TX
Texas A&M University–Commerce, TX
Texas A&M University–Texarkana, TX
Texas Christian University, TX
Texas College, TX
Texas Lutheran University, TX
Thiel College, PA
Thomas More College, KY
Trinity Christian College, IL
Trinity College, CT
Trinity College of Florida, FL
Trinity International University, IL
Trinity Lutheran College, WA
Troy University, AL
Truman State University, MO
Union University, TN
Unity College, ME
The University of Akron, OH
The University of Alabama at Birmingham, AL
The University of Alabama in Huntsville, AL
University of Alaska Fairbanks, AK
The University of Arizona, AZ
University of Arkansas, AR
University of California, San Diego, CA
University of California, Santa Cruz, CA
University of Central Florida, FL
University of Central Missouri, MO
University of Central Oklahoma, OK
University of Colorado at Boulder, CO
University of Colorado at Colorado Springs, CO
University of Connecticut, CT
University of Dallas, TX
University of Delaware, DE
University of Denver, CO
University of Evansville, IN
University of Florida, FL
University of Hawaii at Hilo, HI
University of Houston–Clear Lake, TX
University of Houston–Downtown, TX
University of Houston–Victoria, TX
University of Idaho, ID
University of Illinois at Urbana–Champaign, IL
The University of Kansas, KS
University of Kentucky, KY
University of La Verne, CA
University of Louisiana at Monroe, LA
The University of Maine at Augusta, ME
University of Mary, ND
University of Mary Hardin-Baylor, TX
University of Mary Washington, VA
University of Massachusetts Amherst, MA
University of Massachusetts Boston, MA
University of Memphis, TN
University of Michigan, MI
University of Michigan–Dearborn, MI
University of Michigan–Flint, MI
University of Minnesota, Twin Cities Campus, MN
University of Mississippi, MS
The University of Montana, MT
University of Nebraska at Omaha, NE
University of Nebraska–Lincoln, NE
University of Nevada, Las Vegas, NV
University of New England, ME
University of New Orleans, LA
University of North Alabama, AL
The University of North Carolina at Asheville, NC
The University of North Carolina at Chapel Hill, NC
The University of North Carolina at Greensboro, NC
The University of North Carolina Wilmington, NC
University of North Dakota, ND
University of Northern Iowa, IA
University of North Florida, FL
University of Oklahoma, OK
University of Pittsburgh at Greensburg, PA
University of Pittsburgh at Johnstown, PA
University of Puget Sound, WA
University of South Alabama, AL
University of South Carolina, SC
University of Southern California, CA
University of Southern Indiana, IN
University of Southern Mississippi, MS
The University of Tampa, FL
The University of Tennessee at Martin, TN
The University of Texas at Arlington, TX
The University of Texas at Dallas, TX
The University of Texas at El Paso, TX
The University of Texas–Pan American, TX
University of the Cumberlands, KY
University of the Ozarks, AR
University of the Southwest, NM
University of Tulsa, OK
University of Utah, UT
University of Vermont, VT
University of Washington, WA
University of West Georgia, GA
University of Wisconsin–Eau Claire, WI
University of Wisconsin–Green Bay, WI
University of Wisconsin–La Crosse, WI
University of Wisconsin–Parkside, WI
University of Wisconsin–Stevens Point, WI
University of Wisconsin–Stout, WI
University of Wisconsin–Whitewater, WI
University of Wyoming, WY
Ursinus College, PA
Ursuline College, OH
Valley Forge Christian College, PA
Virginia Military Institute, VA
Virginia Polytechnic Institute and State University, VA
Virginia Wesleyan College, VA
Wabash College, IN
Walla Walla University, WA
Warner Pacific College, OR
Warren Wilson College, NC
Washington Bible College, MD
Washington State University, WA
Wayland Baptist University, TX
Wayne State University, MI
Webber International University, FL
Webster University, MO
Wells College, NY
Western Illinois University, IL
Western Kentucky University, KY
Western New England College, MA
Western Oregon University, OR
Western Washington University, WA
Westminster College, MO
Westmont College, CA
West Virginia University, WV
West Virginia Wesleyan College, WV
Wichita State University, KS
Widener University, PA
Wilkes University, PA
Willamette University, OR
William Carey University, MS
William Jessup University, CA
Wilson College, PA
Wisconsin Lutheran College, WI
Wittenberg University, OH
Wofford College, SC
Wright State University, OH
York College, NE
Youngstown State University, OH

Memberships

Adelphi University, NY
Albright College, PA
American University, DC
Angelo State University, TX
Arcadia University, PA
The Art Institute of Boston at Lesley University, MA
Auburn University, AL
Averett University, VA
Birmingham-Southern College, AL
Boston University, MA
California State University, Chico, CA
California State University, San Bernardino, CA
California State University, Stanislaus, CA

Carroll University, WI
Carson-Newman College, TN
Cedar Crest College, PA
The College of New Rochelle, NY
College of Notre Dame of Maryland, MD
Concordia University, Nebraska, NE
Corban College, OR
Dallas Baptist University, TX
Dalton State College, GA
Delta State University, MS
Eastern Michigan University, MI
East Tennessee State University, TN
Emmanuel College, GA
Emporia State University, KS
Ferris State University, MI
Flagler College, FL
Georgia Southern University, GA
Gonzaga University, WA
Grove City College, PA
Hamline University, MN
Hawai'i Pacific University, HI
Idaho State University, ID
Illinois Institute of Technology, IL
Johnson & Wales University, CO
Johnson & Wales University, FL
Johnson & Wales University, RI
Johnson & Wales University—Charlotte Campus, NC
Kennesaw State University, GA
Kettering University, MI
Lock Haven University of Pennsylvania, PA
Longwood University, VA
Loyola University Chicago, IL
Marymount University, VA
Massachusetts College of Liberal Arts, MA
Medcenter One College of Nursing, ND
Mercer University, GA
Michigan State University, MI
Mississippi State University, MS
Molloy College, NY
Newman University, KS
North Dakota State University, ND
Northern Michigan University, MI
Northwestern Oklahoma State University, OK
Northwestern State University of Louisiana, LA
Northwest Missouri State University, MO
Northwood University, MI
Northwood University, Florida Campus, FL
Northwood University, Texas Campus, TX
The Ohio State University, OH
Oklahoma State University, OK
Old Dominion University, VA
Olivet College, MI
Oral Roberts University, OK
Pacific University, OR
Peirce College, PA
Portland State University, OR
Ripon College, WI
St. Catherine University, MN
Saint Louis University, MO
Saint Mary's College of California, CA
Salem State College, MA
Schreiner University, TX
Sonoma State University, CA
South Dakota State University, SD
Southeastern Louisiana University, LA
Southern Oregon University, OR
Southwestern College, KS
State University of New York College at Geneseo, NY
Texas A&M University, TX
Texas A&M University–Texarkana, TX
Texas Christian University, TX
Texas Lutheran University, TX
Texas Tech University, TX
Towson University, MD
The University of Akron, OH
The University of Alabama at Birmingham, AL
University of Houston–Victoria, TX
University of Louisville, KY
University of Mary, ND
University of Michigan–Dearborn, MI
University of Mississippi, MS
University of Missouri–St. Louis, MO
University of Nebraska at Omaha, NE
University of North Dakota, ND
University of South Carolina, SC
The University of Texas–Pan American, TX
University of Vermont, VT
University of Washington, WA
University of West Georgia, GA
University of Wisconsin–Eau Claire, WI
University of Wisconsin–La Crosse, WI
University of Wisconsin–Stout, WI
Virginia Polytechnic Institute and State University, VA
Washington State University, WA
Wayland Baptist University, TX
Webber International University, FL
Western Kentucky University, KY
Western Washington University, WA
Wichita State University, KS
Wright State University, OH
York College of Pennsylvania, PA

Religious Involvement

Adrian College, MI
Alaska Bible College, AK
Alaska Pacific University, AK
Albright College, PA
Alma College, MI
Amridge University, AL
Andrews University, MI
Anna Maria College, MA
Appalachian Bible College, WV
Augsburg College, MN
Austin College, TX
Averett University, VA
Avila University, MO
Baker University, KS
Baptist Bible College of Pennsylvania, PA
Barton College, NC
Baylor University, TX
Bellarmine University, KY
Belmont Abbey College, NC
Berry College, GA
Bethel College, IN
Bethel University, MN
Birmingham-Southern College, AL
Brewton-Parker College, GA
Bryan College, TN
Calvin College, MI
Campbellsville University, KY
Canisius College, NY
Carroll College, MT
Carroll University, WI
Cedar Crest College, PA
Centenary College of Louisiana, LA
Central College, IA
Central Methodist University, MO
The College at Brockport, State University of New York, NY
The College of New Rochelle, NY
College of Notre Dame of Maryland, MD
The College of Wooster, OH
Columbia College, MO
Concordia University, OR
Concordia University, Nebraska, NE
Concordia University Texas, TX
Corban College, OR
Cornell College, IA
Dallas Baptist University, TX
Dana College, NE
Davidson College, NC
Defiance College, OH
Drury University, MO
Eastern Michigan University, MI
East Texas Baptist University, TX
Elizabethtown College, PA
Elon University, NC
Emmanuel College, GA
Endicott College, MA
Evangel University, MO
Fairfield University, CT
Faulkner University, AL
Finlandia University, MI
Flagler College, FL
Franciscan University of Steubenville, OH
Furman University, SC
Gardner-Webb University, NC
George Fox University, OR
Georgetown College, KY
Georgia Southern University, GA
Graceland University, IA
Grace University, NE
Green Mountain College, VT
Greensboro College, NC
Grove City College, PA
Guilford College, NC
Harding University, AR
Hawai'i Pacific University, HI
Hellenic College, MA
Hendrix College, AR
Hillsdale Free Will Baptist College, OK
Hope International University, CA
Houghton College, NY
Houston Baptist University, TX
Howard Payne University, TX
Huntington University, IN
John Carroll University, OH
Johnson Bible College, TN
Kentucky Christian University, KY
Kutztown University of Pennsylvania, PA
Kuyper College, MI
Lambuth University, TN
Lancaster Bible College, PA
Lee University, TN
Limestone College, SC
Lindsey Wilson College, KY
Lipscomb University, TN
Lynn University, FL
Malone University, OH
Marian College, IN
McPherson College, KS
Mercyhurst College, PA
Midland Lutheran College, NE
Midway College, KY
Millsaps College, MS
Mississippi College, MS
Missouri Baptist University, MO
Molloy College, NY
Mount Vernon Nazarene University, OH
Newberry College, SC
Newman University, KS
North Central College, IL
North Dakota State University, ND
North Park University, IL

Nyack College, NY
Oglethorpe University, GA
Ohio Valley University, WV
Oklahoma Baptist University, OK
Oklahoma City University, OK
Oklahoma Wesleyan University, OK
Olivet Nazarene University, IL
Oral Roberts University, OK
Pacific Union College, CA
Pacific University, OR
Palm Beach Atlantic University, FL
Presbyterian College, SC
Presentation College, SD
Roanoke Bible College, NC
Sacred Heart University, CT
Saint Francis University, PA
St. John's University, NY
Saint Louis University, MO
St. Olaf College, MN
Schreiner University, TX
Seton Hill University, PA
Shorter College, GA
Silver Lake College, WI
Simpson College, IA
Simpson University, CA
Southern Adventist University, TN
Southwest Baptist University, MO
Southwestern Christian University, OK
Southwestern College, KS
Stetson University, FL
Tabor College, KS
Texas Christian University, TX
Texas Lutheran University, TX
Thomas More College, KY
Transylvania University, KY
Trinity College of Florida, FL
Trinity International University, IL
Trinity Lutheran College, WA
Union University, TN
The University of Alabama at Birmingham, AL
University of Mary Hardin-Baylor, TX
The University of North Carolina at Greensboro, NC
University of Puget Sound, WA
University of Saint Francis, IN
University of South Carolina, SC
University of the Cumberlands, KY
University of the Incarnate Word, TX
University of the Pacific, CA
The University of Virginia's College at Wise, VA
University of West Georgia, GA
University of Wisconsin–Stout, WI
Valley Forge Christian College, PA
Valparaiso University, IN
Virginia Polytechnic Institute and State University, VA
Virginia Wesleyan College, VA
Washington Bible College, MD
Washington State University, WA
Wayland Baptist University, TX
West Virginia Wesleyan College, WV
Whitworth University, WA
William Carey University, MS
William Jessup University, CA
Wingate University, NC
Wofford College, SC

Rodeo

Angelo State University, TX
Boise State University, ID
California Polytechnic State University, San Luis Obispo, CA
Hastings College, NE
Idaho State University, ID
Iowa State University of Science and Technology, IA
Lewis-Clark State College, ID
Michigan State University, MI
Missouri Valley College, MO
Murray State University, KY
New Mexico State University, NM
Northwestern Oklahoma State University, OK
Oklahoma Panhandle State University, OK
Oklahoma State University, OK
Sam Houston State University, TX
South Dakota State University, SD
Southern Arkansas University–Magnolia, AR
Southwestern Oklahoma State University, OK
Stephen F. Austin State University, TX
Texas A&M University, TX
Texas Tech University, TX
University of Idaho, ID
The University of Montana, MT
The University of Montana Western, MT
University of Nevada, Las Vegas, NV
The University of Tennessee at Martin, TN
The University of West Alabama, AL
University of Wyoming, WY
Washington State University, WA

Special Characteristics

Adult Students

Agnes Scott College, GA
Allegheny College, PA
American University, DC
Arkansas State University, AR
Averett University, VA
Ball State University, IN
Barton College, NC
Bellarmine University, KY
Berry College, GA
Bethel College, IN
Biola University, CA
Birmingham-Southern College, AL
Bloomfield College, NJ
California Baptist University, CA
California State University, Chico, CA
Calvin College, MI
Campbellsville University, KY
Carroll University, WI
Cedar Crest College, PA
Coe College, IA
College of Mount St. Joseph, OH
Concordia University Texas, TX
Dalton State College, GA
Dominican University of California, CA
Edinboro University of Pennsylvania, PA
Elon University, NC
Emmanuel College, GA
Evangel University, MO
The Evergreen State College, WA
Faulkner University, AL
Ferris State University, MI
Florida Gulf Coast University, FL
Fordham University, NY
Francis Marion University, SC
Franklin Pierce University, NH
Frostburg State University, MD
Gannon University, PA
Georgia College & State University, GA
Golden Gate University, CA
Grace University, NE
Grand Valley State University, MI
Greensboro College, NC
Hastings College, NE
Hillsdale Free Will Baptist College, OK
Hollins University, VA
Indiana University of Pennsylvania, PA
Iowa State University of Science and Technology, IA
Juniata College, PA
Kent State University, OH
Lancaster Bible College, PA
Lincoln University, MO
Lipscomb University, TN
Long Island University, C.W. Post Campus, NY
Lourdes College, OH
Loyola University Chicago, IL
Marian College, IN
Marywood University, PA
Mercer University, GA
Messiah College, PA
Midway College, KY
Millsaps College, MS
Mississippi State University, MS
Mississippi University for Women, MS
Monmouth University, NJ
Montana State University–Billings, MT
Murray State University, KY
New Mexico State University, NM
North Central College, IL
Northern Illinois University, IL
Northern State University, SD
Northwestern State University of Louisiana, LA
Oakland University, MI
Ohio Christian University, OH
The Ohio State University, OH
Ohio Valley University, WV
Oklahoma State University, OK
Pace University, NY
Piedmont College, GA
Point Park University, PA
Portland State University, OR
Purdue University North Central, IN
Randolph College, VA
Regis College, MA
The Richard Stockton College of New Jersey, NJ
St. Catherine University, MN
St. Edward's University, TX
Saint Francis University, PA
Salem State College, MA
San Diego State University, CA
Seton Hill University, PA
Simpson College, IA
Sonoma State University, CA
South Dakota State University, SD
Southeast Missouri State University, MO
Southern Arkansas University–Magnolia, AR
Southern Oregon University, OR
Spring Arbor University, MI
State University of New York at Binghamton, NY
State University of New York College at Cortland, NY
State University of New York College at Geneseo, NY
State University of New York College at Potsdam, NY
Stephen F. Austin State University, TX
Sweet Briar College, VA
Texas Christian University, TX
Thomas More College, KY

Towson University, MD
The University of Akron, OH
The University of Alabama at Birmingham, AL
University of Central Missouri, MO
University of Connecticut, CT
University of Hartford, CT
The University of Kansas, KS
University of Kentucky, KY
University of Maine at Fort Kent, ME
University of Maryland, College Park, MD
University of Maryland Eastern Shore, MD
University of Mary Washington, VA
University of Massachusetts Boston, MA
University of Massachusetts Dartmouth, MA
University of Memphis, TN
University of Michigan–Flint, MI
University of Mississippi, MS
University of Nebraska at Omaha, NE
University of Nevada, Las Vegas, NV
University of Nevada, Reno, NV
University of New Orleans, LA
The University of North Carolina at Asheville, NC
The University of North Carolina at Greensboro, NC
University of Northern Colorado, CO
University of South Carolina, SC
The University of Tennessee at Martin, TN
The University of Texas at Dallas, TX
University of Vermont, VT
University of West Georgia, GA
University of Wisconsin–Eau Claire, WI
University of Wisconsin–Green Bay, WI
University of Wisconsin–La Crosse, WI
University of Wisconsin–Parkside, WI
University of Wisconsin–Stevens Point, WI
University of Wisconsin–Stout, WI
University of Wisconsin–Whitewater, WI
University of Wyoming, WY
Western Kentucky University, KY
Westminster College, UT
Wichita State University, KS
Widener University, PA
William Jessup University, CA
Wilson College, PA
Wittenberg University, OH
Wright State University, OH
Youngstown State University, OH

Children and Siblings of Alumni

Adelphi University, NY
Adrian College, MI
Alaska Pacific University, AK
Albion College, MI
Albright College, PA
Alliant International University, CA
Alma College, MI
American International College, MA
American University, DC
Anna Maria College, MA
Appalachian Bible College, WV
Arcadia University, PA
Arkansas State University, AR
Asbury College, KY
Ashland University, OH
Auburn University, AL
Augsburg College, MN
Augustana College, IL
Augustana College, SD
Averett University, VA
Avila University, MO
Baker University, KS
Baldwin-Wallace College, OH
Ball State University, IN
Baptist Bible College of Pennsylvania, PA
Barton College, NC
Benedictine University, IL
Bethany College, KS
Bethel College, KS
Bethel University, MN
Biola University, CA
Birmingham-Southern College, AL
Bloomfield College, NJ
Boston University, MA
Bowling Green State University, OH
Bradley University, IL
Bryan College, TN
Bryant University, RI
California Baptist University, CA
California State Polytechnic University, Pomona, CA
Calumet College of Saint Joseph, IN
Calvin College, MI
Canisius College, NY
Carroll University, WI
Carson-Newman College, TN
Cedar Crest College, PA
Cedarville University, OH
Centenary College, NJ
Central College, IA
Central Methodist University, MO
Central Michigan University, MI
Centre College, KY
Chapman University, CA
Chatham University, PA
Chestnut Hill College, PA
Christian Brothers University, TN
Clarke College, IA
Clearwater Christian College, FL
Cleveland State University, OH
Coe College, IA
The College at Brockport, State University of New York, NY
The College of Idaho, ID
College of Mount St. Joseph, OH
The College of St. Scholastica, MN
Colorado School of Mines, CO
Colorado State University–Pueblo, CO
Columbia College, MO
Columbia International University, SC
Concordia University Chicago, IL
Concordia University, Nebraska, NE
Concordia University Texas, TX
Converse College, SC
Corban College, OR
Crown College, MN
Culver-Stockton College, MO
Daemen College, NY
Dakota State University, SD
Dalton State College, GA
Delta State University, MS
DePauw University, IN
Dickinson College, PA
Dominican University, IL
Dominican University of California, CA
Dordt College, IA
Dowling College, NY
Drake University, IA
Drury University, MO
Duke University, NC
Duquesne University, PA
D'Youville College, NY
Eastern Kentucky University, KY
Eastern Michigan University, MI
East Texas Baptist University, TX
Edinboro University of Pennsylvania, PA
Elmhurst College, IL
Embry-Riddle Aeronautical University, AZ
Embry-Riddle Aeronautical University, FL
Emporia State University, KS
Endicott College, MA
Eureka College, IL
Evangel University, MO
Fairfield University, CT
Faulkner University, AL
Ferris State University, MI
Florida Institute of Technology, FL
Florida International University, FL
Fordham University, NY
Fort Lewis College, CO
Francis Marion University, SC
Franklin College, IN
Franklin Pierce University, NH
George Fox University, OR
Georgia Southern University, GA
Gonzaga University, WA
Gordon College, MA
Graceland University, IA
Grace University, NE
Grand Valley State University, MI
Grand View University, IA
Green Mountain College, VT
Greensboro College, NC
Gustavus Adolphus College, MN
Gwynedd-Mercy College, PA
Hanover College, IN
Hartwick College, NY
Henderson State University, AR
Heritage Christian University, AL
Hillsdale Free Will Baptist College, OK
Hofstra University, NY
Hollins University, VA
Hood College, MD
Hope International University, CA
Houghton College, NY
Houston Baptist University, TX
Howard Payne University, TX
Huntingdon College, AL
Huntington University, IN
Idaho State University, ID
Illinois Institute of Technology, IL
Indiana State University, IN
Iona College, NY
Iowa State University of Science and Technology, IA
Ithaca College, NY
James Madison University, VA
John Brown University, AR
Kennesaw State University, GA
Kent State University, OH
Kentucky Christian University, KY
Kettering University, MI
Keuka College, NY
Lake Forest College, IL
Lambuth University, TN
Lancaster Bible College, PA
Lawrence University, WI
Lebanon Valley College, PA
Le Moyne College, NY
Lewis-Clark State College, ID
Limestone College, SC
Lincoln University, PA
Lindsey Wilson College, KY
Lipscomb University, TN
Long Island University, Brooklyn Campus, NY
Long Island University, C.W. Post Campus, NY

Longwood University, VA
Loras College, IA
Louisiana State University and Agricultural and Mechanical College, LA
Louisiana Tech University, LA
Luther College, IA
MacMurray College, IL
Malone University, OH
Manchester College, IN
Maranatha Baptist Bible College, WI
Marian College, IN
Marymount University, VA
Maryville College, TN
Maryville University of Saint Louis, MO
Marywood University, PA
The Master's College and Seminary, CA
Medcenter One College of Nursing, ND
Mercyhurst College, PA
Merrimack College, MA
Messiah College, PA
Methodist University, NC
Michigan State University, MI
Mid-Continent University, KY
Midland Lutheran College, NE
Midway College, KY
Millikin University, IL
Misericordia University, PA
Mississippi College, MS
Mississippi State University, MS
Mississippi University for Women, MS
Missouri Baptist University, MO
Missouri Southern State University, MO
Missouri University of Science and Technology, MO
Missouri Valley College, MO
Molloy College, NY
Monmouth University, NJ
Montana State University–Billings, MT
Montclair State University, NJ
Mount Union College, OH
Murray State University, KY
Muskingum College, OH
Nazareth College of Rochester, NY
Nebraska Wesleyan University, NE
Newberry College, SC
New England College, NH
Newman University, KS
New Mexico State University, NM
Nichols College, MA
Northeastern State University, OK
Northern Arizona University, AZ
Northwest Missouri State University, MO
Northwood University, MI
Northwood University, Florida Campus, FL
Northwood University, Texas Campus, TX
Notre Dame de Namur University, CA
Nyack College, NY
The Ohio State University, OH
Oklahoma Baptist University, OK
Oklahoma State University, OK
Oklahoma Wesleyan University, OK
Olivet College, MI
Oral Roberts University, OK
Ouachita Baptist University, AR
Pacific Lutheran University, WA
Pacific University, OR
Palm Beach Atlantic University, FL
Peirce College, PA
Pittsburg State University, KS
Point Park University, PA
Post University, CT
Principia College, IL
Randolph-Macon College, VA
Rensselaer Polytechnic Institute, NY
Rhode Island College, RI
Ripon College, WI
Rivier College, NH
Roanoke Bible College, NC
Roberts Wesleyan College, NY
Rockford College, IL
Rockhurst University, MO
St. Catherine University, MN
St. John Fisher College, NY
Saint Joseph's College, IN
Saint Joseph's University, PA
St. Lawrence University, NY
Saint Martin's University, WA
Saint Mary's College of California, CA
St. Mary's College of Maryland, MD
Saint Mary's University of Minnesota, MN
Salem State College, MA
Salisbury University, MD
San Diego State University, CA
Santa Clara University, CA
Seattle Pacific University, WA
Seattle University, WA
Seton Hill University, PA
Shimer College, IL
Shippensburg University of Pennsylvania, PA
Silver Lake College, WI
Simmons College, MA
Simpson College, IA
Slippery Rock University of Pennsylvania, PA
Sonoma State University, CA
Southeastern Oklahoma State University, OK
Southern Adventist University, TN
Southern Arkansas University–Magnolia, AR
Southern Illinois University Carbondale, IL
Southern Nazarene University, OK
Southern Utah University, UT
Southwestern Christian University, OK
Southwestern Oklahoma State University, OK
Southwest Minnesota State University, MN
State University of New York at Fredonia, NY
State University of New York College at Cortland, NY
State University of New York College at Potsdam, NY
Stephens College, MO
Stetson University, FL
Stony Brook University, State University of New York, NY
Suffolk University, MA
Susquehanna University, PA
Tabor College, KS
Taylor University, IN
Tennessee Technological University, TN
Texas Lutheran University, TX
Texas State University–San Marcos, TX
Thiel College, PA
Thomas More College, KY
Trine University, IN
Trinity Christian College, IL
Trinity International University, IL
Truman State University, MO
Union College, KY
Union University, TN
The University of Alabama at Birmingham, AL
University of Arkansas, AR
University of Central Missouri, MO
University of Colorado at Colorado Springs, CO
University of Delaware, DE
University of Evansville, IN
University of Guam, GU
University of Houston–Clear Lake, TX
University of Idaho, ID
University of Illinois at Urbana–Champaign, IL
University of Kentucky, KY
University of La Verne, CA
University of Mary Hardin-Baylor, TX
University of Mary Washington, VA
University of Massachusetts Amherst, MA
University of Michigan–Dearborn, MI
University of Michigan–Flint, MI
University of Mississippi, MS
University of Missouri–Columbia, MO
The University of Montana, MT
University of Nebraska at Omaha, NE
University of Nebraska–Lincoln, NE
University of Nevada, Las Vegas, NV
University of Nevada, Reno, NV
University of New England, ME
University of New Hampshire, NH
University of New Orleans, LA
The University of North Carolina at Asheville, NC
The University of North Carolina at Pembroke, NC
University of Northern Colorado, CO
University of Oklahoma, OK
University of Rochester, NY
University of South Alabama, AL
University of South Carolina, SC
University of Southern California, CA
University of Southern Mississippi, MS
The University of Tampa, FL
The University of Tennessee, TN
University of the Cumberlands, KY
University of the Incarnate Word, TX
University of the Ozarks, AR
University of Tulsa, OK
University of West Florida, FL
University of West Georgia, GA
University of Wisconsin–Green Bay, WI
University of Wisconsin–La Crosse, WI
University of Wyoming, WY
Ursinus College, PA
Ursuline College, OH
Utah State University, UT
Valparaiso University, IN
Virginia Military Institute, VA
Warner Pacific College, OR
Wartburg College, IA
Washington & Jefferson College, PA
Washington State University, WA
Wayland Baptist University, TX
Webber International University, FL
Webster University, MO
Wells College, NY
West Liberty State University, WV
Westminster College, MO
Westminster College, PA
Westminster College, UT
West Virginia Wesleyan College, WV
Wheeling Jesuit University, WV
Whittier College, CA
Whitworth University, WA
William Carey University, MS
Wilson College, PA
Wingate University, NC
Winona State University, MN
Wittenberg University, OH
Wright State University, OH
Xavier University, OH
York College, NE
York College of Pennsylvania, PA

Youngstown State University, OH

Children of Current Students

Alliant International University, CA
Alma College, MI
Augustana College, SD
Avila University, MO
Bethel College, KS
Bryan College, TN
California State Polytechnic University, Pomona, CA
Carroll University, WI
Central College, IA
The College of New Rochelle, NY
Columbia College, MO
Elmhurst College, IL
Emmanuel College, GA
Finlandia University, MI
Franklin Pierce University, NH
Grace University, NE
Green Mountain College, VT
Huntington University, IN
Johnson Bible College, TN
Lancaster Bible College, PA
Marymount University, VA
Maryville University of Saint Louis, MO
Marywood University, PA
Midland Lutheran College, NE
Misericordia University, PA
Missouri Baptist University, MO
Mount Aloysius College, PA
Mount Marty College, SD
Northwest University, WA
Palm Beach Atlantic University, FL
Rivier College, NH
Rockford College, IL
Sacred Heart University, CT
St. Catherine University, MN
Union University, TN
The University of Alabama at Birmingham, AL
University of Hartford, CT
University of Michigan–Dearborn, MI
Valley Forge Christian College, PA
Wilson College, PA

Children of Educators

Agnes Scott College, GA
Alfred University, NY
Allegheny College, PA
Appalachian Bible College, WV
Austin Peay State University, TN
Bard College, NY
Benedictine College, KS
Bennington College, VT
Bryan College, TN
Campbellsville University, KY
Canisius College, NY
Centenary College of Louisiana, LA
The College of Idaho, ID
Columbia College, MO
Columbus College of Art & Design, OH
Concordia University, Nebraska, NE
Cornell College, IA
DeSales University, PA
Dowling College, NY
East Texas Baptist University, TX
Emory & Henry College, VA
Endicott College, MA
Evangel University, MO
Flagler College, FL
Florida College, FL
Franklin Pierce University, NH
Grand View University, IA
Hastings College, NE
Hendrix College, AR
Heritage Christian University, AL
Jacksonville University, FL
John Brown University, AR
John Carroll University, OH
Johnson Bible College, TN
Judson College, AL
King's College, PA
Lees-McRae College, NC
Lipscomb University, TN
Lycoming College, PA
Maranatha Baptist Bible College, WI
Mary Baldwin College, VA
Mississippi State University, MS
Mount St. Mary's University, MD
Nebraska Wesleyan University, NE
New England College, NH
Northern Arizona University, AZ
Occidental College, CA
Oklahoma Wesleyan University, OK
Palm Beach Atlantic University, FL
Rockford College, IL
Saint Anselm College, NH
St. Catherine University, MN
Saint Francis University, PA
Saint Mary's College of California, CA
Salem College, NC
Seattle University, WA
Simpson College, IA
Sonoma State University, CA
Southern Illinois University Carbondale, IL
Southwestern College, KS
Susquehanna University, PA
Tennessee Technological University, TN
Texas Christian University, TX
Union University, TN
Unity College, ME
The University of Alabama at Birmingham, AL
University of Kentucky, KY
University of Memphis, TN
University of St. Thomas, MN
The University of Scranton, PA
The University of Tennessee at Martin, TN
Villanova University, PA
William Carey University, MS
Wright State University, OH

Children of Faculty/Staff

Abilene Christian University, TX
Adelphi University, NY
Adrian College, MI
Agnes Scott College, GA
Alaska Bible College, AK
Alaska Pacific University, AK
Alcorn State University, MS
Alderson-Broaddus College, WV
Alfred University, NY
Allegheny College, PA
Alliant International University, CA
American International College, MA
American University, DC
Amridge University, AL
Andrews University, MI
Anna Maria College, MA
Appalachian Bible College, WV
Arkansas State University, AR
Asbury College, KY
Ashland University, OH
Auburn University, AL
Augustana College, IL
Augustana College, SD
Austin College, TX
Austin Peay State University, TN
Avila University, MO
Baker University, KS
Ball State University, IN
Baptist Bible College of Pennsylvania, PA
Bard College, NY
Barton College, NC
Baylor University, TX
Belhaven College, MS
Bellarmine University, KY
Belmont Abbey College, NC
Belmont University, TN
Bennington College, VT
Berklee College of Music, MA
Berry College, GA
Bethany Lutheran College, MN
Bethel College, IN
Bethel College, KS
Bethel University, MN
Biola University, CA
Birmingham-Southern College, AL
Bloomsburg University of Pennsylvania, PA
Bluefield College, VA
Bluffton University, OH
Bowdoin College, ME
Bowling Green State University, OH
Bradley University, IL
Brenau University, GA
Brevard College, NC
Brewton-Parker College, GA
Bryan College, TN
Buena Vista University, IA
California Baptist University, CA
California State University, Bakersfield, CA
California State University, Chico, CA
California State University, Stanislaus, CA
Calvin College, MI
Campbellsville University, KY
Canisius College, NY
Carroll College, MT
Carroll University, WI
Case Western Reserve University, OH
Cedarville University, OH
Centenary College, NJ
Centenary College of Louisiana, LA
Central College, IA
Central Methodist University, MO
Central Michigan University, MI
Centre College, KY
Chatham University, PA
Chestnut Hill College, PA
Clarke College, IA
Clarkson University, NY
Cleary University, MI
Clemson University, SC
Coe College, IA
The College of Idaho, ID
College of Mount St. Joseph, OH
The College of New Rochelle, NY
The College of St. Scholastica, MN
College of the Holy Cross, MA
College of Visual Arts, MN
Colorado State University, CO
Colorado State University–Pueblo, CO
Columbia College, MO
Columbia College Chicago, IL
Columbus College of Art & Design, OH
Concordia College–New York, NY
Concordia University, OR
Concordia University Chicago, IL
Concordia University, Nebraska, NE

Concordia University, St. Paul, MN
Concordia University Texas, TX
Converse College, SC
Corban College, OR
Cornell College, IA
Covenant College, GA
Creighton University, NE
Crown College, MN
Culver-Stockton College, MO
Daemen College, NY
Dallas Baptist University, TX
Dalton State College, GA
Defiance College, OH
Delta State University, MS
DePaul University, IL
DePauw University, IN
DeSales University, PA
Dickinson College, PA
Dillard University, LA
Dominican College, NY
Dominican University of California, CA
Dordt College, IA
Dowling College, NY
Drury University, MO
Duquesne University, PA
D'Youville College, NY
Eastern Kentucky University, KY
East Texas Baptist University, TX
Edgewood College, WI
Edinboro University of Pennsylvania, PA
Elizabethtown College, PA
Elmira College, NY
Elon University, NC
Embry-Riddle Aeronautical University, AZ
Embry-Riddle Aeronautical University, FL
Embry-Riddle Aeronautical University Worldwide, FL
Emmanuel College, GA
Emory & Henry College, VA
Emporia State University, KS
Eureka College, IL
Evangel University, MO
Faulkner University, AL
Felician College, NJ
Finlandia University, MI
Fisk University, TN
Flagler College, FL
Florida College, FL
Florida Institute of Technology, FL
Fordham University, NY
Fort Lewis College, CO
Franciscan University of Steubenville, OH
Francis Marion University, SC
Franklin & Marshall College, PA
Franklin College, IN
Franklin Pierce University, NH
Free Will Baptist Bible College, TN
Fresno Pacific University, CA
Furman University, SC
Gardner-Webb University, NC
Geneva College, PA
George Fox University, OR
Georgetown College, KY
Georgetown University, DC
Georgia College & State University, GA
Georgian Court University, NJ
Gonzaga University, WA
Grace Bible College, MI
Grace College, IN
Graceland University, IA
Grace University, NE
Grand Valley State University, MI
Grand View University, IA
Greensboro College, NC
Guilford College, NC
Hampshire College, MA
Hanover College, IN
Harding University, AR
Hardin-Simmons University, TX
Hartwick College, NY
Hastings College, NE
Heidelberg University, OH
Henderson State University, AR
Hendrix College, AR
Heritage Christian University, AL
Hollins University, VA
Hood College, MD
Hope International University, CA
Houghton College, NY
Houston Baptist University, TX
Howard Payne University, TX
Huntingdon College, AL
Huntington University, IN
Idaho State University, ID
Illinois College, IL
Illinois Institute of Technology, IL
Illinois State University, IL
Illinois Wesleyan University, IL
Indiana State University, IN
Indiana University of Pennsylvania, PA
Iona College, NY
Ithaca College, NY
Jacksonville University, FL
James Madison University, VA
Jamestown College, ND
John Brown University, AR
John Carroll University, OH
The Johns Hopkins University, MD
Johnson & Wales University, CO
Johnson & Wales University, FL
Johnson & Wales University, RI
Johnson & Wales University—Charlotte Campus, NC
Johnson Bible College, TN
Johnson C. Smith University, NC
Judson College, AL
Juniata College, PA
Kendall College, IL
Kent State University, OH
Kentucky Christian University, KY
Kettering University, MI
Keuka College, NY
King's College, PA
Kutztown University of Pennsylvania, PA
Kuyper College, MI
LaGrange College, GA
Lambuth University, TN
Lancaster Bible College, PA
Lawrence Technological University, MI
Lebanon Valley College, PA
Lees-McRae College, NC
Lee University, TN
Lehigh University, PA
Lewis & Clark College, OR
Liberty University, VA
Limestone College, SC
Lincoln Christian College, IL
Lincoln Memorial University, TN
Lincoln University, MO
Lincoln University, PA
Lindsey Wilson College, KY
Linfield College, OR
Lipscomb University, TN
Long Island University, Brooklyn Campus, NY
Long Island University, C.W. Post Campus, NY
Louisiana Tech University, LA
Loyola University New Orleans, LA
Lubbock Christian University, TX
Lycoming College, PA
Lynn University, FL
Lyon College, AR
MacMurray College, IL
Maine College of Art, ME
Maine Maritime Academy, ME
Malone University, OH
Manhattan Christian College, KS
Manhattan College, NY
Maranatha Baptist Bible College, WI
Marian College, IN
Marian University, WI
Marquette University, WI
Mary Baldwin College, VA
Marymount University, VA
Maryville College, TN
Maryville University of Saint Louis, MO
Marywood University, PA
Massachusetts College of Art and Design, MA
Massachusetts College of Pharmacy and Health Sciences, MA
The Master's College and Seminary, CA
McKendree University, IL
McMurry University, TX
Memphis College of Art, TN
Mercer University, GA
Mercyhurst College, PA
Merrimack College, MA
Messiah College, PA
Methodist University, NC
Miami University, OH
Michigan State University, MI
Mid-Continent University, KY
Midland Lutheran College, NE
Midway College, KY
Milligan College, TN
Millsaps College, MS
Mills College, CA
Milwaukee School of Engineering, WI
Minnesota State University Moorhead, MN
Misericordia University, PA
Mississippi College, MS
Mississippi State University, MS
Mississippi University for Women, MS
Missouri Baptist University, MO
Missouri Southern State University, MO
Missouri Valley College, MO
Missouri Western State University, MO
Molloy College, NY
Monmouth University, NJ
Montana State University–Billings, MT
Montreat College, NC
Mount Marty College, SD
Mount Mary College, WI
Mount Saint Mary College, NY
Mount St. Mary's University, MD
Mount Union College, OH
Mount Vernon Nazarene University, OH
Murray State University, KY
Nazareth College of Rochester, NY
Nebraska Christian College, NE
Nebraska Wesleyan University, NE
Neumann University, PA
Newberry College, SC
New England College, NH
Newman University, KS
New Mexico State University, NM
Niagara University, NY

Nicholls State University, LA
Nichols College, MA
North Central College, IL
North Dakota State University, ND
Northeastern State University, OK
Northern Arizona University, AZ
Northern Illinois University, IL
Northern Michigan University, MI
North Greenville University, SC
Northwest Christian University, OR
Northwestern College, MN
Northwestern Oklahoma State University, OK
Northwestern State University of Louisiana, LA
Northwest University, WA
Northwood University, MI
Northwood University, Florida Campus, FL
Northwood University, Texas Campus, TX
Notre Dame de Namur University, CA
Nyack College, NY
Occidental College, CA
Oglethorpe University, GA
Ohio Christian University, OH
Ohio Northern University, OH
The Ohio State University, OH
Ohio University, OH
Ohio University–Chillicothe, OH
Ohio University–Eastern, OH
Ohio University–Lancaster, OH
Ohio University–Southern Campus, OH
Ohio University–Zanesville, OH
Ohio Valley University, WV
Oklahoma Baptist University, OK
Oklahoma Christian University, OK
Oklahoma City University, OK
Oklahoma Panhandle State University, OK
Oklahoma Wesleyan University, OK
Old Dominion University, VA
Olivet College, MI
Olivet Nazarene University, IL
Oral Roberts University, OK
Ouachita Baptist University, AR
Our Lady of Holy Cross College, LA
Our Lady of the Lake University of San Antonio, TX
Pace University, NY
Pacific University, OR
Palm Beach Atlantic University, FL
Peace College, NC
Philadelphia Biblical University, PA
Piedmont College, GA
Plymouth State University, NH
Point Park University, PA
Presbyterian College, SC
Presentation College, SD
Principia College, IL
Purdue University, IN
Purdue University North Central, IN
Quinnipiac University, CT
Ramapo College of New Jersey, NJ
Randolph College, VA
Randolph-Macon College, VA
Regis College, MA
Rensselaer Polytechnic Institute, NY
The Richard Stockton College of New Jersey, NJ
Ripon College, WI
Roanoke Bible College, NC
Robert Morris College, IL
Roberts Wesleyan College, NY
Rochester Institute of Technology, NY
Rockford College, IL
Rockhurst University, MO
Rocky Mountain College of Art + Design, CO
Sacred Heart University, CT
St. Ambrose University, IA
Saint Anselm College, NH
St. Catherine University, MN
St. Cloud State University, MN
St. Edward's University, TX
Saint Francis University, PA
St. John's College, NM
St. John's University, NY
Saint Joseph's College, IN
Saint Joseph's College of Maine, ME
St. Louis Christian College, MO
St. Louis College of Pharmacy, MO
Saint Louis University, MO
Saint Martin's University, WA
Saint Mary's College of California, CA
St. Mary's College of Maryland, MD
Saint Mary's University of Minnesota, MN
St. Norbert College, WI
Saint Paul's College, VA
Saint Xavier University, IL
Salem College, NC
Salem State College, MA
Samford University, AL
San Diego State University, CA
Santa Clara University, CA
Schreiner University, TX
Seattle Pacific University, WA
Seattle University, WA
Seton Hill University, PA
Sewanee: The University of the South, TN
Shorter College, GA
Simpson College, IA
Simpson University, CA
Skidmore College, NY
Slippery Rock University of Pennsylvania, PA
Sonoma State University, CA
South Dakota State University, SD
Southeastern Louisiana University, LA
Southeast Missouri State University, MO
Southern Arkansas University–Magnolia, AR
Southern Connecticut State University, CT
Southern Illinois University Carbondale, IL
Southern Illinois University Edwardsville, IL
Southern Nazarene University, OK
Southwestern Christian University, OK
Southwestern College, KS
Southwestern University, TX
Spring Arbor University, MI
Spring Hill College, AL
State University of New York at Binghamton, NY
State University of New York College at Potsdam, NY
Stephen F. Austin State University, TX
Stephens College, MO
Stetson University, FL
Stillman College, AL
Stonehill College, MA
Suffolk University, MA
Susquehanna University, PA
Tabor College, KS
Taylor University, IN
Temple University, PA
Tennessee Technological University, TN
Texas A&M University, TX
Texas Christian University, TX
Texas Lutheran University, TX
Texas Tech University, TX
Thiel College, PA
Thomas More College, KY
Tiffin University, OH
Towson University, MD
Transylvania University, KY
Trevecca Nazarene University, TN
Trine University, IN
Trinity Christian College, IL
Trinity College of Florida, FL
Trinity Lutheran College, WA
Truman State University, MO
Tuskegee University, AL
Union College, NY
Union University, TN
University of Advancing Technology, AZ
The University of Alabama at Birmingham, AL
The University of Arizona, AZ
University of Arkansas, AR
University of Bridgeport, CT
University of Central Missouri, MO
University of Connecticut, CT
University of Dallas, TX
University of Dayton, OH
University of Delaware, DE
University of Denver, CO
University of Evansville, IN
The University of Findlay, OH
University of Florida, FL
University of Guam, GU
University of Hartford, CT
University of Idaho, ID
University of Illinois at Urbana–Champaign, IL
The University of Kansas, KS
University of Kentucky, KY
University of La Verne, CA
University of Louisiana at Monroe, LA
The University of Maine at Augusta, ME
University of Maine at Fort Kent, ME
University of Maine at Presque Isle, ME
University of Mary, ND
University of Mary Hardin-Baylor, TX
University of Maryland Eastern Shore, MD
University of Mary Washington, VA
University of Massachusetts Amherst, MA
University of Massachusetts Boston, MA
University of Massachusetts Dartmouth, MA
University of Memphis, TN
University of Miami, FL
University of Michigan, MI
University of Michigan–Dearborn, MI
University of Mississippi, MS
The University of Montana Western, MT
University of Nebraska at Kearney, NE
University of Nebraska at Omaha, NE
University of Nevada, Las Vegas, NV
University of New Hampshire, NH
University of New Hampshire at Manchester, NH
University of North Alabama, AL
The University of North Carolina at Asheville, NC
The University of North Carolina at Chapel Hill, NC
The University of North Carolina at Greensboro, NC
The University of North Carolina Wilmington, NC
University of North Dakota, ND
University of Northern Colorado, CO
University of Notre Dame, IN
University of Pittsburgh at Johnstown, PA
University of Portland, OR
University of Puerto Rico, Mayagüez Campus, PR

University of Puget Sound, WA
University of Rochester, NY
University of Saint Francis, IN
University of St. Thomas, MN
University of San Diego, CA
University of Science and Arts of Oklahoma, OK
The University of Scranton, PA
University of South Alabama, AL
University of South Carolina, SC
University of Southern California, CA
University of Southern Indiana, IN
University of Southern Maine, ME
University of Southern Mississippi, MS
The University of Tampa, FL
The University of Tennessee at Martin, TN
The University of Texas at Tyler, TX
University of the Cumberlands, KY
University of the Incarnate Word, TX
University of the Ozarks, AR
University of the Southwest, NM
University of the Virgin Islands, VI
University of Tulsa, OK
University of Utah, UT
The University of West Alabama, AL
Ursinus College, PA
Ursuline College, OH
Utah State University, UT
Valley City State University, ND
Valley Forge Christian College, PA
Valparaiso University, IN
Vanguard University of Southern California, CA
Villanova University, PA
Virginia Intermont College, VA
Virginia Military Institute, VA
Virginia Polytechnic Institute and State University, VA
Virginia Wesleyan College, VA
Wabash College, IN
Wagner College, NY
Walla Walla University, WA
Warren Wilson College, NC
Wartburg College, IA
Washington & Jefferson College, PA
Washington Bible College, MD
Washington College, MD
Washington State University, WA
Wayland Baptist University, TX
Waynesburg University, PA
Wayne State University, MI
Webber International University, FL
Webster University, MO
West Chester University of Pennsylvania, PA
Western Illinois University, IL
Western New England College, MA
West Liberty State University, WV
Westminster College, MO
Westminster College, UT
Westmont College, CA
West Virginia University, WV
West Virginia Wesleyan College, WV
Wheeling Jesuit University, WV
Whittier College, CA
Widener University, PA
Wilkes University, PA
William Carey University, MS
William Jessup University, CA
Williams Baptist College, AR
Wilson College, PA
Winona State University, MN
Winthrop University, SC
Wisconsin Lutheran College, WI
Wittenberg University, OH
Wofford College, SC
Wright State University, OH
York College, NE
Youngstown State University, OH

Children of Public Servants

American International College, MA
California State University, San Bernardino, CA
College of Staten Island of the City University of New York, NY
Dowling College, NY
Georgia Southern University, GA
Graceland University, IA
Louisiana Tech University, LA
Mercer University, GA
Mississippi State University, MS
Monmouth University, NJ
New Mexico State University, NM
Northern Arizona University, AZ
Northwestern State University of Louisiana, LA
The Ohio State University, OH
Peirce College, PA
Salem State College, MA
Sonoma State University, CA
Southeastern Louisiana University, LA
Southern Illinois University Carbondale, IL
Tennessee Technological University, TN
The University of Alabama at Birmingham, AL
University of Delaware, DE
University of Kentucky, KY
University of Memphis, TN
University of Nevada, Las Vegas, NV
University of New Orleans, LA
The University of Texas at Dallas, TX
University of Utah, UT
University of Wisconsin–Green Bay, WI
Valdosta State University, GA
Washington State University, WA
Western Washington University, WA
Westminster College, UT

Children of Union Members/Company Employees

Adrian College, MI
Auburn University, AL
Averett University, VA
California State University, Bakersfield, CA
Calvin College, MI
Carroll College, MT
Central Michigan University, MI
Dowling College, NY
Eastern Washington University, WA
East Tennessee State University, TN
Edinboro University of Pennsylvania, PA
Emporia State University, KS
Frostburg State University, MD
Grand Valley State University, MI
Hofstra University, NY
Husson University, ME
Illinois State University, IL
Kennesaw State University, GA
Kent State University, OH
Kutztown University of Pennsylvania, PA
Massachusetts College of Art and Design, MA
Mercer University, GA
Michigan State University, MI
Mid-Continent University, KY
Millersville University of Pennsylvania, PA
Millikin University, IL
Montana State University–Billings, MT
New Mexico State University, NM
Northern Michigan University, MI
The Ohio State University, OH
The Richard Stockton College of New Jersey, NJ
St. Cloud State University, MN
Saint Paul's College, VA
Salem State College, MA
Shorter College, GA
Slippery Rock University of Pennsylvania, PA
Sonoma State University, CA
Southwest Minnesota State University, MN
Stephen F. Austin State University, TX
Stonehill College, MA
Texas Christian University, TX
The University of Alabama, AL
The University of Alabama at Birmingham, AL
University of Connecticut, CT
University of Guam, GU
University of Hartford, CT
University of Kentucky, KY
University of Massachusetts Boston, MA
University of Michigan–Flint, MI
University of Nevada, Las Vegas, NV
University of Northern Colorado, CO
University of South Carolina, SC
University of Wisconsin–La Crosse, WI
University of Wisconsin–Parkside, WI
Western Kentucky University, KY
Western New England College, MA
Western Washington University, WA
West Virginia University, WV
York College of Pennsylvania, PA
Youngstown State University, OH

Children of Workers in Trades

Dowling College, NY
Grand Valley State University, MI
Kennesaw State University, GA
Marywood University, PA
New Mexico State University, NM
The Ohio State University, OH
San Diego State University, CA
Sonoma State University, CA
South Dakota State University, SD
Texas Christian University, TX
The University of Alabama at Birmingham, AL
University of Kentucky, KY
University of Michigan, MI
University of Michigan–Dearborn, MI
University of South Carolina, SC
University of Wisconsin–Parkside, WI
West Virginia University, WV
Worcester Polytechnic Institute, MA
Youngstown State University, OH

Children with a Deceased or Disabled Parent

Anna Maria College, MA
The Baptist College of Florida, FL
California State University, San Bernardino, CA
Clarke College, IA
The College of New Jersey, NJ
College of Staten Island of the City University of New York, NY
Edinboro University of Pennsylvania, PA
Fordham University, NY
Georgia College & State University, GA
Harding University, AR

Illinois State University, IL
Kent State University, OH
Kentucky State University, KY
Lees-McRae College, NC
Lipscomb University, TN
Louisiana State University and Agricultural and Mechanical College, LA
Marian University, WI
Millikin University, IL
New Mexico State University, NM
Northeastern State University, OK
Pace University, NY
Santa Clara University, CA
Seton Hill University, PA
Southern Illinois University Carbondale, IL
The University of Alabama at Birmingham, AL
University of Hartford, CT
University of Kentucky, KY
University of Louisiana at Monroe, LA
University of Massachusetts Dartmouth, MA
The University of Montana, MT
University of Nevada, Las Vegas, NV
University of New Orleans, LA
University of South Carolina, SC
The University of Texas at Arlington, TX
University of Utah, UT
The University of Virginia's College at Wise, VA
Washington State University, WA
Youngstown State University, OH

Ethnic Background

Abilene Christian University, TX
Alaska Pacific University, AK
Albright College, PA
Alderson-Broaddus College, WV
Alliant International University, CA
American University, DC
Arkansas State University, AR
The Art Institute of Boston at Lesley University, MA
Asbury College, KY
Auburn University, AL
Augustana College, SD
Austin College, TX
Austin Peay State University, TN
Baker University, KS
Bellarmine University, KY
Benedictine College, KS
Berry College, GA
Bethel College, KS
Bethel University, MN
Biola University, CA
Birmingham-Southern College, AL
Bluefield College, VA
Boise State University, ID
Buena Vista University, IA
California State University, Bakersfield, CA
California State University, Chico, CA
California State University, Stanislaus, CA
Calvin College, MI
Cedarville University, OH
Centenary College, NJ
Centenary College of Louisiana, LA
Centre College, KY
Clearwater Christian College, FL
Clemson University, SC
The College at Brockport, State University of New York, NY
College of Saint Benedict, MN
The College of St. Scholastica, MN
Colorado State University–Pueblo, CO
Columbia International University, SC
Cornell College, IA
Dakota State University, SD
Dana College, NE
Dominican University of California, CA
Drew University, NJ
Duke University, NC
Eastern Michigan University, MI
Eastern Washington University, WA
Elmhurst College, IL
Elon University, NC
Fairfield University, CT
Ferris State University, MI
Flagler College, FL
Florida Gulf Coast University, FL
Fort Lewis College, CO
Franklin College, IN
Furman University, SC
Gannon University, PA
George Fox University, OR
Grace College, IN
Grace University, NE
Grove City College, PA
Gustavus Adolphus College, MN
Hamline University, MN
Hardin-Simmons University, TX
Hawai'i Pacific University, HI
Hood College, MD
Hope College, MI
Idaho State University, ID
Illinois College, IL
Illinois Institute of Technology, IL
Indiana University of Pennsylvania, PA
Iowa State University of Science and Technology, IA
John Brown University, AR
John Carroll University, OH
Johnson Bible College, TN
Johnson C. Smith University, NC
Juniata College, PA
Kennesaw State University, GA
Kent State University, OH
Kentucky State University, KY
Kenyon College, OH
LaGrange College, GA
Langston University, OK
Lawrence University, WI
Lebanon Valley College, PA
Lewis-Clark State College, ID
Long Island University, Brooklyn Campus, NY
Lourdes College, OH
Lyon College, AR
Macalester College, MN
Manchester College, IN
Maryville University of Saint Louis, MO
Marywood University, PA
McMurry University, TX
Medical University of South Carolina, SC
Michigan State University, MI
Millsaps College, MS
Minot State University, ND
Mississippi University for Women, MS
Missouri Southern State University, MO
Molloy College, NY
Montana State University–Billings, MT
Mount Union College, OH
Muskingum College, OH
New England College, NH
New Mexico State University, NM
North Carolina Agricultural and Technical State University, NC
North Dakota State University, ND
Northern Illinois University, IL
Northern State University, SD
Northland College, WI
Northwestern College, MN
Oakland University, MI
The Ohio State University, OH
Ohio Valley University, WV
Oklahoma State University, OK
Ouachita Baptist University, AR
Pacific University, OR
Portland State University, OR
Randolph-Macon College, VA
Rensselaer Polytechnic Institute, NY
The Richard Stockton College of New Jersey, NJ
Sacred Heart University, CT
St. Catherine University, MN
St. John Fisher College, NY
Saint Luke's College, MO
Sewanee: The University of the South, TN
Shepherd University, WV
Simpson College, IA
Slippery Rock University of Pennsylvania, PA
Sonoma State University, CA
South Dakota State University, SD
Southwestern College, KS
Southwest Minnesota State University, MN
State University of New York at Binghamton, NY
State University of New York at Fredonia, NY
State University of New York at New Paltz, NY
State University of New York College at Geneseo, NY
State University of New York College at Potsdam, NY
Stetson University, FL
Taylor University, IN
Tennessee Technological University, TN
Texas Christian University, TX
Union University, TN
The University of Alabama at Birmingham, AL
The University of Arizona, AZ
University of Arkansas, AR
University of California, San Diego, CA
University of Central Missouri, MO
University of Central Oklahoma, OK
University of Delaware, DE
University of Hartford, CT
University of Idaho, ID
The University of Kansas, KS
University of Kentucky, KY
University of La Verne, CA
The University of Maine at Augusta, ME
University of Maine at Presque Isle, ME
University of Mary Hardin-Baylor, TX
University of Michigan–Dearborn, MI
University of Minnesota, Morris, MN
University of Mississippi, MS
University of Missouri–Kansas City, MO
University of Missouri–St. Louis, MO
University of Nebraska at Kearney, NE
University of Nebraska at Omaha, NE
University of Nebraska–Lincoln, NE
University of Nevada, Las Vegas, NV
University of Nevada, Reno, NV
University of New England, ME
The University of North Carolina at Asheville, NC
The University of North Carolina at Greensboro, NC
University of North Dakota, ND

University of Northern Colorado, CO
University of South Carolina, SC
University of Southern Mississippi, MS
The University of Tennessee at Martin, TN
The University of Texas at El Paso, TX
The University of Texas at San Antonio, TX
The University of Texas–Pan American, TX
University of the Ozarks, AR
University of Utah, UT
University of Vermont, VT
The University of Virginia's College at Wise, VA
University of Wisconsin–Eau Claire, WI
University of Wisconsin–Green Bay, WI
University of Wisconsin–La Crosse, WI
University of Wisconsin–Parkside, WI
University of Wisconsin–Stevens Point, WI
University of Wisconsin–Whitewater, WI
University of Wyoming, WY
Valley City State University, ND
Wartburg College, IA
Wayland Baptist University, TX
Webster University, MO
Western Carolina University, NC
Western Kentucky University, KY
Western Washington University, WA
Westminster College, MO
Westminster College, UT
Westmont College, CA
West Virginia University, WV
Whitman College, WA
Whitworth University, WA
Widener University, PA
Wisconsin Lutheran College, WI
Wittenberg University, OH
Wright State University, OH

First-Generation College Students

Abilene Christian University, TX
American International College, MA
American University, DC
Angelo State University, TX
Appalachian State University, NC
Arkansas State University, AR
Austin College, TX
Averett University, VA
Birmingham-Southern College, AL
Bluefield College, VA
Boise State University, ID
Brenau University, GA
Cabarrus College of Health Sciences, NC
California State University, Bakersfield, CA
California State University, Chico, CA
California State University, San Bernardino, CA
California State University, Stanislaus, CA
Calvin College, MI
Central Michigan University, MI
Centre College, KY
The College at Brockport, State University of New York, NY
The College of Idaho, ID
Colorado State University, CO
Colorado State University–Pueblo, CO
Columbia College, MO
Creighton University, NE
DePauw University, IN
Dominican University of California, CA
Dowling College, NY
Edinboro University of Pennsylvania, PA
Elon University, NC
Emmanuel College, GA
The Evergreen State College, WA
Fairfield University, CT
Finlandia University, MI
Flagler College, FL
Fort Lewis College, CO
Georgia Southern University, GA
Glenville State College, WV
Graceland University, IA
Guilford College, NC
Gustavus Adolphus College, MN
Idaho State University, ID
Illinois State University, IL
Iowa State University of Science and Technology, IA
John Carroll University, OH
Kent State University, OH
Kenyon College, OH
Kutztown University of Pennsylvania, PA
LaGrange College, GA
Lewis-Clark State College, ID
Limestone College, SC
Long Island University, Brooklyn Campus, NY
Lyon College, AR
Massachusetts College of Liberal Arts, MA
Mesa State College, CO
Michigan State University, MI
Millsaps College, MS
Minnesota State University Moorhead, MN
Mississippi State University, MS
Monmouth University, NJ
Montana State University–Billings, MT
Montreat College, NC
Newman University, KS
Northern Arizona University, AZ
Oklahoma State University, OK
Ouachita Baptist University, AR
Pacific Lutheran University, WA
Pacific University, OR
The Richard Stockton College of New Jersey, NJ
St. John Fisher College, NY
Saint Louis University, MO
Salem State College, MA
Salisbury University, MD
San Diego State University, CA
Sonoma State University, CA
South Dakota State University, SD
Southeast Missouri State University, MO
Southern Nazarene University, OK
Southwest Minnesota State University, MN
State University of New York at New Paltz, NY
Stephen F. Austin State University, TX
Tennessee Technological University, TN
Texas A&M University, TX
Texas Lutheran University, TX
Texas State University–San Marcos, TX
Texas Tech University, TX
The University of Alabama at Birmingham, AL
University of California, San Diego, CA
University of Central Florida, FL
University of Colorado at Boulder, CO
University of Colorado at Colorado Springs, CO
University of Delaware, DE
University of Hartford, CT
University of Idaho, ID
University of Illinois at Urbana–Champaign, IL
The University of Kansas, KS
University of Kentucky, KY
University of La Verne, CA
University of Maryland Eastern Shore, MD
University of Massachusetts Boston, MA
University of Massachusetts Dartmouth, MA
University of Michigan–Flint, MI
University of Mississippi, MS
The University of Montana Western, MT
University of Nebraska at Kearney, NE
University of Nebraska at Omaha, NE
University of Nevada, Las Vegas, NV
University of Nevada, Reno, NV
University of North Alabama, AL
The University of North Carolina at Asheville, NC
University of North Florida, FL
University of South Carolina, SC
University of South Carolina Upstate, SC
The University of Texas at Arlington, TX
The University of Texas at San Antonio, TX
University of Utah, UT
University of Vermont, VT
The University of West Alabama, AL
University of West Florida, FL
University of Wisconsin–Eau Claire, WI
University of Wisconsin–La Crosse, WI
University of Wisconsin–Stout, WI
University of Wyoming, WY
Virginia Intermont College, VA
Virginia Polytechnic Institute and State University, VA
Washington State University, WA
Webber International University, FL
Westminster College, UT
Whitman College, WA
Wichita State University, KS
William Carey University, MS
Wisconsin Lutheran College, WI
Wright State University, OH

Handicapped Students

Appalachian State University, NC
Arkansas State University, AR
Augusta State University, GA
Austin College, TX
Boise State University, ID
Bryan College, TN
California State University, Chico, CA
California State University, Fresno, CA
California State University, San Bernardino, CA
Calvin College, MI
Central College, IA
Clear Creek Baptist Bible College, KY
The College of St. Scholastica, MN
College of Staten Island of the City University of New York, NY
Colorado State University–Pueblo, CO
Columbia College Chicago, IL
Creighton University, NE
Dordt College, IA
Eastern Washington University, WA
Edinboro University of Pennsylvania, PA
Emporia State University, KS
Florida Gulf Coast University, FL
Fordham University, NY
Fort Lewis College, CO
Fort Valley State University, GA
Francis Marion University, SC
Gardner-Webb University, NC
Georgia College & State University, GA
Georgia Southern University, GA
Grand Valley State University, MI
Hofstra University, NY
Idaho State University, ID

James Madison University, VA
Kennesaw State University, GA
Kent State University, OH
Kutztown University of Pennsylvania, PA
Lock Haven University of Pennsylvania, PA
Louisiana Tech University, LA
Massachusetts College of Liberal Arts, MA
Michigan State University, MI
Midland Lutheran College, NE
Mississippi State University, MS
Murray State University, KY
New Mexico State University, NM
North Carolina Agricultural and Technical State University, NC
Northern Arizona University, AZ
Northern State University, SD
The Ohio State University, OH
Oklahoma State University, OK
Old Dominion University, VA
Ouachita Baptist University, AR
Portland State University, OR
Roanoke Bible College, NC
Sacred Heart University, CT
Sam Houston State University, TX
San Diego State University, CA
Santa Clara University, CA
Shepherd University, WV
Shippensburg University of Pennsylvania, PA
Sonoma State University, CA
South Dakota State University, SD
Southeastern Louisiana University, LA
Southern Illinois University Carbondale, IL
Southwest Minnesota State University, MN
State University of New York at Binghamton, NY
State University of New York at New Paltz, NY
State University of New York College at Potsdam, NY
Texas Christian University, TX
Texas State University–San Marcos, TX
Texas Tech University, TX
Towson University, MD
The University of Akron, OH
The University of Alabama at Birmingham, AL
University of California, San Diego, CA
University of Colorado at Colorado Springs, CO
University of Hartford, CT
University of Idaho, ID
University of Kentucky, KY
University of Mary Hardin-Baylor, TX
University of Massachusetts Amherst, MA
University of Memphis, TN
University of Michigan, MI
University of Michigan–Dearborn, MI
University of Michigan–Flint, MI
University of Mississippi, MS
University of Nebraska at Omaha, NE
University of Nebraska–Lincoln, NE
University of Nevada, Las Vegas, NV
University of New Hampshire, NH
The University of North Carolina at Asheville, NC
The University of North Carolina at Greensboro, NC
University of North Dakota, ND
University of Northern Colorado, CO
University of South Carolina, SC
The University of Tennessee at Martin, TN
The University of Texas at Arlington, TX
The University of Texas at Dallas, TX
The University of Texas at San Antonio, TX
University of Utah, UT
University of West Florida, FL
University of West Georgia, GA
University of Wisconsin–Green Bay, WI
University of Wisconsin–Stout, WI
University of Wisconsin–Whitewater, WI
University of Wyoming, WY
Washington State University, WA
Western Carolina University, NC
Western Kentucky University, KY
Westminster College, UT
Wright State University, OH
Youngstown State University, OH

International Students

Adrian College, MI
Agnes Scott College, GA
Alaska Pacific University, AK
Alderson-Broaddus College, WV
Alfred University, NY
Allegheny College, PA
Alliant International University, CA
Andrews University, MI
Appalachian Bible College, WV
Asbury College, KY
Ashland University, OH
Augsburg College, MN
Augustana College, IL
Augustana College, SD
Austin College, TX
Averett University, VA
Baker University, KS
Ball State University, IN
Barton College, NC
Belhaven College, MS
Bellarmine University, KY
Benedictine College, KS
Bentley University, MA
Bethany College, KS
Bethel College, IN
Bethel College, KS
Bethel University, MN
Biola University, CA
Bloomsburg University of Pennsylvania, PA
Bluffton University, OH
Boise State University, ID
Bowling Green State University, OH
Brenau University, GA
Brevard College, NC
Brewton-Parker College, GA
Bridgewater College, VA
Bryan College, TN
Buena Vista University, IA
California State University, Chico, CA
Calvin College, MI
Campbellsville University, KY
Canisius College, NY
Carroll College, MT
Carroll University, WI
Centenary College of Louisiana, LA
Central College, IA
Central Methodist University, MO
Central Michigan University, MI
Clarke College, IA
Clarkson University, NY
Clear Creek Baptist Bible College, KY
Coastal Carolina University, SC
Coe College, IA
The College at Brockport, State University of New York, NY
The College of Idaho, ID
College of Notre Dame of Maryland, MD
College of Saint Benedict, MN
The College of St. Scholastica, MN
College of Staten Island of the City University of New York, NY
Colorado State University–Pueblo, CO
Columbia College, MO
Columbia International University, SC
Concordia College, MN
Concordia University Chicago, IL
Concordia University, Nebraska, NE
Corban College, OR
Cornell College, IA
Covenant College, GA
Crown College, MN
Culver-Stockton College, MO
Dana College, NE
Defiance College, OH
DePauw University, IN
Dickinson College, PA
Dominican University, IL
Dominican University of California, CA
Dordt College, IA
Drake University, IA
Duquesne University, PA
Eastern Michigan University, MI
East Texas Baptist University, TX
Edinboro University of Pennsylvania, PA
Elizabethtown College, PA
Elmira College, NY
Elon University, NC
Emmanuel College, GA
Emporia State University, KS
Endicott College, MA
Ferris State University, MI
Finlandia University, MI
Florida Gulf Coast University, FL
Fort Lewis College, CO
Fort Valley State University, GA
Franciscan University of Steubenville, OH
Francis Marion University, SC
Franklin Pierce University, NH
Free Will Baptist Bible College, TN
Frostburg State University, MD
Furman University, SC
Gannon University, PA
George Fox University, OR
Georgia College & State University, GA
Gonzaga University, WA
Graceland University, IA
Grace University, NE
Grand Valley State University, MI
Green Mountain College, VT
Greensboro College, NC
Gustavus Adolphus College, MN
Hamline University, MN
Hampton University, VA
Hanover College, IN
Harding University, AR
Hartwick College, NY
Harvey Mudd College, CA
Hawai'i Pacific University, HI
Henderson State University, AR
Hendrix College, AR
Hollins University, VA
Hood College, MD
Hope International University, CA
Houghton College, NY
Huntingdon College, AL
Huntington University, IN
Idaho State University, ID
Illinois College, IL
Illinois Institute of Technology, IL
Illinois Wesleyan University, IL

Indiana University of Pennsylvania, PA
Iowa State University of Science and Technology, IA
Jacksonville University, FL
James Madison University, VA
Jamestown College, ND
John Brown University, AR
Johnson Bible College, TN
Juniata College, PA
Kendall College, IL
Kennesaw State University, GA
Kent State University, OH
Kentucky Christian University, KY
Keuka College, NY
King's College, PA
Kuyper College, MI
Lancaster Bible College, PA
Lebanon Valley College, PA
Lees-McRae College, NC
Liberty University, VA
Life University, GA
Lincoln University, PA
Lipscomb University, TN
Long Island University, Brooklyn Campus, NY
Long Island University, C.W. Post Campus, NY
Louisiana Tech University, LA
MacMurray College, IL
Malone University, OH
Manchester College, IN
Mannes College The New School for Music, NY
Marian College, IN
Marymount University, VA
Marywood University, PA
The Master's College and Seminary, CA
Mayville State University, ND
McMurry University, TX
Mercer University, GA
Merrimack College, MA
Mesa State College, CO
Michigan State University, MI
Midland Lutheran College, NE
Millersville University of Pennsylvania, PA
Millikin University, IL
Minot State University, ND
Mississippi University for Women, MS
Monmouth College, IL
Monmouth University, NJ
Montclair State University, NJ
Montreat College, NC
Mount Marty College, SD
Mount Mary College, WI
Mount Union College, OH
Mount Vernon Nazarene University, OH
Murray State University, KY
Nebraska Christian College, NE
Nebraska Wesleyan University, NE
Newberry College, SC
New England College, NH
Newman University, KS
New Mexico State University, NM
North Central College, IL
Northern Arizona University, AZ
Northern Illinois University, IL
Northern Michigan University, MI
Northern State University, SD
Northwestern College, MN
Northwestern State University of Louisiana, LA
Northwestern University, IL
Northwest University, WA
Nyack College, NY
Ohio Christian University, OH
Ohio Northern University, OH
Ohio Valley University, WV
Oklahoma Christian University, OK
Oklahoma Wesleyan University, OK
Old Dominion University, VA
Olivet College, MI
Oral Roberts University, OK
Ouachita Baptist University, AR
Pace University, NY
Pacific Lutheran University, WA
Pacific University, OR
Peirce College, PA
Piedmont College, GA
Plymouth State University, NH
Point Park University, PA
Portland State University, OR
Quinnipiac University, CT
Ramapo College of New Jersey, NJ
Randolph College, VA
Regis College, MA
The Richard Stockton College of New Jersey, NJ
Ripon College, WI
Rivier College, NH
Roanoke Bible College, NC
Roberts Wesleyan College, NY
Rochester Institute of Technology, NY
Rockford College, IL
St. Ambrose University, IA
St. Catherine University, MN
Saint Francis University, PA
Saint John's University, MN
Saint Louis University, MO
St. Norbert College, WI
St. Olaf College, MN
Schreiner University, TX
Seattle Pacific University, WA
Seton Hill University, PA
Silver Lake College, WI
Simpson College, IA
Sonoma State University, CA
South Dakota State University, SD
Southeastern Louisiana University, LA
Southeast Missouri State University, MO
Southern Adventist University, TN
Southern Illinois University Carbondale, IL
Southern Oregon University, OR
Southwestern College, KS
Southwest Minnesota State University, MN
Spring Arbor University, MI
State University of New York at Fredonia, NY
State University of New York at Plattsburgh, NY
State University of New York College at Oneonta, NY
Stetson University, FL
Sweet Briar College, VA
Tabor College, KS
Taylor University, IN
Texas Christian University, TX
Towson University, MD
Trinity Lutheran College, WA
Truman State University, MO
Union University, TN
The University of Akron, OH
The University of Alabama, AL
The University of Arizona, AZ
University of Arkansas, AR
University of Bridgeport, CT
University of Evansville, IN
University of Guam, GU
University of Hartford, CT
University of Idaho, ID
The University of Kansas, KS
University of Kentucky, KY
University of La Verne, CA
University of Louisiana at Monroe, LA
The University of Maine at Augusta, ME
University of Maine at Fort Kent, ME
University of Maine at Presque Isle, ME
University of Mary, ND
University of Mary Hardin-Baylor, TX
University of Miami, FL
University of Michigan, MI
University of Michigan–Dearborn, MI
University of Michigan–Flint, MI
University of Minnesota, Morris, MN
University of Mississippi, MS
University of Missouri–Columbia, MO
The University of Montana, MT
The University of Montana Western, MT
University of Montevallo, AL
University of Nebraska at Kearney, NE
University of Nebraska at Omaha, NE
University of Nebraska–Lincoln, NE
University of Nevada, Las Vegas, NV
University of New Hampshire, NH
University of New Orleans, LA
The University of North Carolina at Asheville, NC
The University of North Carolina at Chapel Hill, NC
The University of North Carolina at Greensboro, NC
University of North Dakota, ND
University of Northern Colorado, CO
University of North Florida, FL
University of Oregon, OR
University of Puget Sound, WA
University of Redlands, CA
University of Rochester, NY
University of Science and Arts of Oklahoma, OK
University of South Carolina, SC
University of Southern California, CA
The University of Tampa, FL
The University of Texas at Dallas, TX
The University of Texas at El Paso, TX
The University of Texas–Pan American, TX
University of the Ozarks, AR
University of West Georgia, GA
University of Wisconsin–Eau Claire, WI
University of Wisconsin–La Crosse, WI
University of Wisconsin–Parkside, WI
University of Wisconsin–Stevens Point, WI
University of Wisconsin–Stout, WI
University of Wisconsin–Whitewater, WI
University of Wyoming, WY
Ursinus College, PA
Utah State University, UT
Valdosta State University, GA
Valley City State University, ND
Valparaiso University, IN
Wabash College, IN
Wartburg College, IA
Washington Bible College, MD
Washington State University, WA
Wayland Baptist University, TX
Webber International University, FL
Webster University, MO
Wells College, NY
Western Illinois University, IL
Western Kentucky University, KY
Western New England College, MA

Western Oregon University, OR
Western Washington University, WA
Westminster College, MO
Westminster College, PA
Westminster College, UT
Westmont College, CA
West Virginia University, WV
West Virginia Wesleyan College, WV
Whitman College, WA
Whittier College, CA
Whitworth University, WA
Wichita State University, KS
Widener University, PA
Willamette University, OR
William Carey University, MS
William Jessup University, CA
Williams Baptist College, AR
Wilson College, PA
Wisconsin Lutheran College, WI
Wittenberg University, OH
Wright State University, OH
Xavier University, OH
York College of Pennsylvania, PA

Local/State Students

Abilene Christian University, TX
Alaska Bible College, AK
Alaska Pacific University, AK
Albertus Magnus College, CT
Alcorn State University, MS
Alliant International University, CA
American University, DC
Anna Maria College, MA
Arkansas State University, AR
The Art Institute of Boston at Lesley University, MA
Auburn University, AL
Augustana College, SD
Augusta State University, GA
Austin College, TX
Averett University, VA
Ball State University, IN
Barton College, NC
Belhaven College, MS
Bellarmine University, KY
Benedictine College, KS
Berry College, GA
Bethel College, KS
Boise State University, ID
Boston University, MA
Brevard College, NC
Bryan College, TN
Bryant University, RI
California State University, Chico, CA
California State University, Fresno, CA
California State University, Stanislaus, CA
Centenary College, NJ
Centenary College of Louisiana, LA
Central Michigan University, MI
Clarke College, IA
Clarkson University, NY
Clemson University, SC
Coastal Carolina University, SC
The College at Brockport, State University of New York, NY
College of St. Joseph, VT
Columbia College, MO
Columbus College of Art & Design, OH
Concordia University, Nebraska, NE
Cornell College, IA
Creighton University, NE
Culver-Stockton College, MO
Dakota State University, SD
Dana College, NE
DePauw University, IN
Dominican University of California, CA
Dordt College, IA
Dowling College, NY
Duke University, NC
Eastern Washington University, WA
East Texas Baptist University, TX
Edgewood College, WI
Edinboro University of Pennsylvania, PA
Elizabethtown College, PA
Elmira College, NY
Endicott College, MA
Faulkner University, AL
Ferris State University, MI
Flagler College, FL
Florida Gulf Coast University, FL
Florida State University, FL
Fort Lewis College, CO
Fort Valley State University, GA
Franciscan University of Steubenville, OH
Franklin Pierce University, NH
Frostburg State University, MD
Furman University, SC
Gardner-Webb University, NC
Georgetown College, KY
Georgia College & State University, GA
Graceland University, IA
Grace University, NE
Guilford College, NC
Hamline University, MN
Hardin-Simmons University, TX
Hawai'i Pacific University, HI
Hollins University, VA
Hope International University, CA
Houghton College, NY
Howard Payne University, TX
Huntingdon College, AL
Idaho State University, ID
Iowa State University of Science and Technology, IA
The Johns Hopkins University, MD
Juniata College, PA
Kennesaw State University, GA
Kentucky State University, KY
Kutztown University of Pennsylvania, PA
Lees-McRae College, NC
Lee University, TN
Lewis-Clark State College, ID
Liberty University, VA
Limestone College, SC
Lock Haven University of Pennsylvania, PA
Longwood University, VA
Lourdes College, OH
Loyola University Maryland, MD
Lyon College, AR
Marywood University, PA
Massachusetts College of Liberal Arts, MA
Mayville State University, ND
McDaniel College, MD
McMurry University, TX
McPherson College, KS
Medcenter One College of Nursing, ND
Medical University of South Carolina, SC
Mercer University, GA
Mesa State College, CO
Miami University, OH
Michigan State University, MI
Minot State University, ND
Mississippi State University, MS
Missouri Southern State University, MO
Monmouth University, NJ
Montana State University–Billings, MT
Montreat College, NC
Murray State University, KY
Muskingum College, OH
Newberry College, SC
New England College, NH
New Mexico State University, NM
New York City College of Technology of the City University of New York, NY
Northern Arizona University, AZ
Northern State University, SD
Nyack College, NY
Ohio Valley University, WV
Oklahoma Baptist University, OK
Oklahoma Panhandle State University, OK
Old Dominion University, VA
Ouachita Baptist University, AR
Pacific University, OR
Post University, CT
Randolph College, VA
The Richard Stockton College of New Jersey, NJ
Ripon College, WI
Saginaw Valley State University, MI
St. Catherine University, MN
St. Cloud State University, MN
St. John Fisher College, NY
St. John's University, NY
St. Louis College of Pharmacy, MO
Saint Michael's College, VT
San Diego State University, CA
Schreiner University, TX
Shepherd University, WV
Shippensburg University of Pennsylvania, PA
Shorter College, GA
Silver Lake College, WI
Slippery Rock University of Pennsylvania, PA
Sonoma State University, CA
Southern Adventist University, TN
Southern Nazarene University, OK
Southwest Baptist University, MO
Southwestern Oklahoma State University, OK
Southwest Minnesota State University, MN
State University of New York at Binghamton, NY
State University of New York at Fredonia, NY
State University of New York College at Cortland, NY
State University of New York College at Geneseo, NY
State University of New York College at Oneonta, NY
State University of New York College at Potsdam, NY
State University of New York Institute of Technology, NY
Stephen F. Austin State University, TX
Stephens College, MO
Stetson University, FL
Sweet Briar College, VA
Tabor College, KS
Tennessee Technological University, TN
Texas A&M University, TX
Texas Christian University, TX
Trinity Christian College, IL
Tuskegee University, AL
Unity College, ME
University of Advancing Technology, AZ
The University of Akron, OH
The University of Alabama at Birmingham, AL
The University of Alabama in Huntsville, AL
University of Alaska Fairbanks, AK
University of Bridgeport, CT

University of Colorado at Boulder, CO
University of Colorado at Colorado Springs, CO
University of Connecticut, CT
University of Delaware, DE
University of Denver, CO
University of Georgia, GA
University of Hartford, CT
University of Hawaii at Hilo, HI
University of Idaho, ID
University of Illinois at Urbana–Champaign, IL
The University of Kansas, KS
The University of Maine at Augusta, ME
University of Mary, ND
University of Mary Hardin-Baylor, TX
University of Mary Washington, VA
University of Michigan, MI
University of Michigan–Flint, MI
University of Mississippi, MS
University of Missouri–St. Louis, MO
University of Nevada, Las Vegas, NV
University of Nevada, Reno, NV
University of New Hampshire, NH
University of New Orleans, LA
The University of North Carolina at Asheville, NC
The University of North Carolina Wilmington, NC
University of Northern Colorado, CO
University of Oregon, OR
University of South Carolina, SC
University of Southern Maine, ME
University of Southern Mississippi, MS
The University of Texas at Dallas, TX
The University of Texas at El Paso, TX
The University of Texas at San Antonio, TX
The University of Texas–Pan American, TX
The University of Virginia's College at Wise, VA
University of West Georgia, GA
University of Wisconsin–Eau Claire, WI
University of Wisconsin–Green Bay, WI
University of Wisconsin–La Crosse, WI
University of Wisconsin–Parkside, WI
University of Wisconsin–Stout, WI
University of Wisconsin–Whitewater, WI
University of Wyoming, WY
Valley Forge Christian College, PA
Virginia Military Institute, VA
Virginia Polytechnic Institute and State University, VA
Warren Wilson College, NC
Wayland Baptist University, TX
Webber International University, FL
Western Carolina University, NC
Western Kentucky University, KY
Western New England College, MA
Western Washington University, WA
Westminster College, MO
Westminster College, UT
West Virginia University, WV
Wilson College, PA
Winona State University, MN
Wittenberg University, OH

Married Students

Appalachian Bible College, WV
Auburn University, AL
Baptist Bible College of Pennsylvania, PA
California State University, Chico, CA
The College at Brockport, State University of New York, NY
Columbia International University, SC
Emmanuel College, GA
Franklin Pierce University, NH
Free Will Baptist Bible College, TN
Georgia Southern University, GA
Grace University, NE
Johnson Bible College, TN
Lancaster Bible College, PA
Mid-Continent University, KY
New Mexico State University, NM
Northwest University, WA
Ouachita Baptist University, AR
Roanoke Bible College, NC
Sonoma State University, CA
State University of New York at Binghamton, NY
The University of Alabama at Birmingham, AL
The University of Kansas, KS
University of Nevada, Reno, NV
The University of North Carolina Wilmington, NC
Valley Forge Christian College, PA

Members of Minority Groups

Abilene Christian University, TX
Alaska Pacific University, AK
Alcorn State University, MS
Alice Lloyd College, KY
Alliant International University, CA
American University, DC
Appalachian State University, NC
Arkansas State University, AR
The Art Institute of Boston at Lesley University, MA
Assumption College, MA
Augsburg College, MN
Augustana College, IL
Augustana College, SD
Austin Peay State University, TN
Baker University, KS
Baldwin-Wallace College, OH
Ball State University, IN
Beloit College, WI
Benedictine College, KS
Bentley University, MA
Berry College, GA
Bethel College, IN
Bethel University, MN
Bluefield College, VA
Bluffton University, OH
Boise State University, ID
Bowling Green State University, OH
Bradley University, IL
Bryant University, RI
California State Polytechnic University, Pomona, CA
California State University, Chico, CA
California State University, Stanislaus, CA
Calvin College, MI
Carson-Newman College, TN
Centenary College of Louisiana, LA
Central College, IA
Central Connecticut State University, CT
Central Michigan University, MI
Clarke College, IA
Clarkson University, NY
Clemson University, SC
Coe College, IA
The College at Brockport, State University of New York, NY
The College of Idaho, ID
The College of New Jersey, NJ
The College of St. Scholastica, MN
College of Staten Island of the City University of New York, NY
The College of Wooster, OH
Concordia University, Nebraska, NE
Cornell College, IA
Covenant College, GA
Creighton University, NE
Crown College, MN
Dakota State University, SD
Dana College, NE
Defiance College, OH
Dominican University of California, CA
Dordt College, IA
Duquesne University, PA
Eastern Kentucky University, KY
Eastern Michigan University, MI
East Tennessee State University, TN
Edinboro University of Pennsylvania, PA
Elizabethtown College, PA
Elmhurst College, IL
Elon University, NC
Emporia State University, KS
The Evergreen State College, WA
Fairfield University, CT
Ferris State University, MI
Flagler College, FL
Florida Gulf Coast University, FL
Florida International University, FL
Fort Valley State University, GA
Franklin & Marshall College, PA
Franklin College, IN
Fresno Pacific University, CA
Gannon University, PA
Gardner-Webb University, NC
George Fox University, OR
Georgia College & State University, GA
Georgia Southern University, GA
Golden Gate University, CA
Gonzaga University, WA
Graceland University, IA
Grace University, NE
Grove City College, PA
Gustavus Adolphus College, MN
Hamline University, MN
Hampton University, VA
Hanover College, IN
Idaho State University, ID
Illinois College, IL
Illinois State University, IL
Indiana State University, IN
Iowa State University of Science and Technology, IA
Ithaca College, NY
John Brown University, AR
Johnson Bible College, TN
Kendall College, IL
Kennesaw State University, GA
Kent State University, OH
Kentucky Christian University, KY
Kettering University, MI
King's College, PA
Kuyper College, MI
Lawrence Technological University, MI
Lehigh University, PA
Le Moyne College, NY
Lewis-Clark State College, ID
Lipscomb University, TN
Lock Haven University of Pennsylvania, PA
Louisiana Tech University, LA
Lourdes College, OH
Loyola University Maryland, MD
Luther College, IA

Non-Need Scholarships for Undergraduates
Special Characteristics

Lyon College, AR
Manchester College, IN
Marian College, IN
Maryville College, TN
Maryville University of Saint Louis, MO
Massachusetts College of Liberal Arts, MA
Mayville State University, ND
Medical University of South Carolina, SC
Mercer University, GA
Mesa State College, CO
Miami University, OH
Michigan State University, MI
Midland Lutheran College, NE
Midway College, KY
Millsaps College, MS
Minnesota State University Moorhead, MN
Minot State University, ND
Misericordia University, PA
Mississippi University for Women, MS
Missouri University of Science and Technology, MO
Missouri Western State University, MO
Monmouth University, NJ
Montana State University–Billings, MT
Mount St. Mary's University, MD
Mount Union College, OH
Mount Vernon Nazarene University, OH
Murray State University, KY
Muskingum College, OH
New Mexico State University, NM
New York City College of Technology of the City University of New York, NY
Nicholls State University, LA
North Carolina Agricultural and Technical State University, NC
Northern Illinois University, IL
Northern Michigan University, MI
Northern State University, SD
Northwest Missouri State University, MO
The Ohio State University, OH
Ohio University, OH
Ohio University–Chillicothe, OH
Ohio University–Eastern, OH
Ohio University–Lancaster, OH
Ohio University–Southern Campus, OH
Ohio University–Zanesville, OH
Old Dominion University, VA
Ouachita Baptist University, AR
Pacific Union College, CA
Point Park University, PA
Polytechnic Institute of NYU, NY
Portland State University, OR
Rensselaer Polytechnic Institute, NY
The Richard Stockton College of New Jersey, NJ
Rider University, NJ
Ripon College, WI
Rochester Institute of Technology, NY
Rowan University, NJ
Sacred Heart University, CT
Saginaw Valley State University, MI
St. Ambrose University, IA
St. Cloud State University, MN
St. John Fisher College, NY
Saint Joseph's University, PA
Saint Louis University, MO
Saint Mary's University of Minnesota, MN
Saint Michael's College, VT
Saint Vincent College, PA
Salem State College, MA
Seattle University, WA
Sewanee: The University of the South, TN
Shepherd University, WV
Simpson College, IA
Simpson University, CA
Slippery Rock University of Pennsylvania, PA
Sonoma State University, CA
South Dakota State University, SD
Southeastern Louisiana University, LA
Southeast Missouri State University, MO
Southern Adventist University, TN
Southern Arkansas University–Magnolia, AR
Southern Oregon University, OR
Southern Polytechnic State University, GA
Southern Utah University, UT
Southwestern College, KS
Southwest Minnesota State University, MN
Spring Arbor University, MI
State University of New York at Binghamton, NY
State University of New York at Fredonia, NY
State University of New York at New Paltz, NY
State University of New York College at Cortland, NY
State University of New York College at Geneseo, NY
State University of New York College at Potsdam, NY
State University of New York College of Environmental Science and Forestry, NY
State University of New York Institute of Technology, NY
Stetson University, FL
Stonehill College, MA
Susquehanna University, PA
Tennessee Technological University, TN
Texas Christian University, TX
Thomas Jefferson University, PA
Thomas More College, KY
Transylvania University, KY
Trine University, IN
Trinity Christian College, IL
Trinity International University, IL
Union University, TN
Unity College, ME
The University of Akron, OH
The University of Alabama at Birmingham, AL
The University of Alabama in Huntsville, AL
University of Alaska Fairbanks, AK
University of California, San Diego, CA
University of Central Missouri, MO
University of Central Oklahoma, OK
University of Delaware, DE
University of Evansville, IN
University of Florida, FL
University of Hartford, CT
University of Idaho, ID
The University of Kansas, KS
University of Kentucky, KY
University of Maine at Fort Kent, ME
University of Mary Hardin-Baylor, TX
University of Massachusetts Dartmouth, MA
University of Memphis, TN
University of Michigan, MI
University of Michigan–Dearborn, MI
University of Michigan–Flint, MI
University of Minnesota, Morris, MN
University of Mississippi, MS
University of Missouri–Columbia, MO
University of Missouri–Kansas City, MO
University of Missouri–St. Louis, MO
The University of Montana, MT
The University of Montana Western, MT
University of Nebraska at Omaha, NE
University of Nebraska–Lincoln, NE
University of Nevada, Las Vegas, NV
University of Nevada, Reno, NV
University of New England, ME
University of New Orleans, LA
The University of North Carolina at Asheville, NC
The University of North Carolina at Greensboro, NC
University of North Dakota, ND
University of Northern Colorado, CO
University of Northern Iowa, IA
University of North Florida, FL
University of Oklahoma, OK
The University of Scranton, PA
University of South Alabama, AL
University of South Carolina, SC
University of Southern California, CA
University of Southern Indiana, IN
The University of Tennessee at Martin, TN
The University of Texas at Dallas, TX
The University of Texas at El Paso, TX
The University of Texas at San Antonio, TX
University of the Ozarks, AR
University of West Florida, FL
University of West Georgia, GA
University of Wisconsin–Eau Claire, WI
University of Wisconsin–Green Bay, WI
University of Wisconsin–La Crosse, WI
University of Wisconsin–Parkside, WI
University of Wisconsin–Stevens Point, WI
University of Wisconsin–Stout, WI
University of Wisconsin–Whitewater, WI
Valdosta State University, GA
Valley City State University, ND
Villanova University, PA
Virginia Intermont College, VA
Virginia Polytechnic Institute and State University, VA
Warner Pacific College, OR
Wartburg College, IA
Wayland Baptist University, TX
Webster University, MO
Western Carolina University, NC
Western Illinois University, IL
Western Kentucky University, KY
Western New England College, MA
Western Washington University, WA
Westminster College, UT
West Virginia University, WV
Whitworth University, WA
Wichita State University, KS
Willamette University, OR
Williams Baptist College, AR
Winona State University, MN
Wisconsin Lutheran College, WI
Wittenberg University, OH
Xavier University, OH
York College of Pennsylvania, PA
Youngstown State University, OH

Out-of-State Students

Abilene Christian University, TX
Alaska Pacific University, AK
Appalachian State University, NC
Arkansas State University, AR
Auburn University, AL
Averett University, VA
Baker University, KS
Bellarmine University, KY
Benedictine College, KS
Benedictine University, IL
Bethel University, MN

Bluffton University, OH
Boise State University, ID
Brewton-Parker College, GA
Buena Vista University, IA
California State University, Chico, CA
Centenary College, NJ
Centenary College of Louisiana, LA
Central College, IA
Central Michigan University, MI
Coastal Carolina University, SC
The College at Brockport, State University of New York, NY
The College of New Rochelle, NY
Colorado State University–Pueblo, CO
Dalton State College, GA
Dana College, NE
Defiance College, OH
Delta State University, MS
Dordt College, IA
Eastern Michigan University, MI
Edinboro University of Pennsylvania, PA
Flagler College, FL
Florida Gulf Coast University, FL
Fort Lewis College, CO
Fort Valley State University, GA
Francis Marion University, SC
Franklin College, IN
Frostburg State University, MD
Gardner-Webb University, NC
George Fox University, OR
Georgetown College, KY
Georgia College & State University, GA
Grace University, NE
Grand Valley State University, MI
Gustavus Adolphus College, MN
Hanover College, IN
Hardin-Simmons University, TX
Hawai'i Pacific University, HI
Heidelberg University, OH
Henderson State University, AR
Hollins University, VA
Idaho State University, ID
Illinois College, IL
Iowa State University of Science and Technology, IA
James Madison University, VA
Kendall College, IL
Kent State University, OH
Lewis-Clark State College, ID
Limestone College, SC
Lincoln University, MO
Louisiana Tech University, LA
Lourdes College, OH
Massachusetts College of Liberal Arts, MA
Mayville State University, ND
McKendree University, IL
McMurry University, TX
Mesa State College, CO
Miami University, OH
Michigan State University, MI
Minot State University, ND
Misericordia University, PA
Mississippi State University, MS
Mississippi University for Women, MS
Missouri University of Science and Technology, MO
Missouri Western State University, MO
Monmouth College, IL
Monmouth University, NJ
Montana State University–Billings, MT
Murray State University, KY
New College of Florida, FL
New Jersey Institute of Technology, NJ
New Mexico State University, NM
Nicholls State University, LA
Northeastern State University, OK
Northern Arizona University, AZ
Northern Michigan University, MI
Northwestern State University of Louisiana, LA
Northwest Missouri State University, MO
Nyack College, NY
Oakland University, MI
Ohio Christian University, OH
The Ohio State University, OH
Oklahoma Baptist University, OK
Oklahoma Panhandle State University, OK
Oklahoma State University, OK
Ouachita Baptist University, AR
Pacific Lutheran University, WA
Piedmont College, GA
Portland State University, OR
Ramapo College of New Jersey, NJ
Randolph-Macon College, VA
Ripon College, WI
Robert Morris College, IL
Roberts Wesleyan College, NY
Rockford College, IL
St. Catherine University, MN
St. Cloud State University, MN
Saint Michael's College, VT
Shepherd University, WV
Shorter College, GA
Simpson University, CA
Slippery Rock University of Pennsylvania, PA
Sonoma State University, CA
Southeastern Louisiana University, LA
Southeastern Oklahoma State University, OK
Southeast Missouri State University, MO
Southern Adventist University, TN
Southern Arkansas University–Magnolia, AR
Southwestern Oklahoma State University, OK
State University of New York at Binghamton, NY
State University of New York at Fredonia, NY
State University of New York at Plattsburgh, NY
Stephens College, MO
Tabor College, KS
Tennessee Technological University, TN
Texas Christian University, TX
Texas Tech University, TX
Transylvania University, KY
Trinity Christian College, IL
The University of Akron, OH
The University of Alabama, AL
The University of Alabama at Birmingham, AL
University of Arkansas, AR
University of Central Missouri, MO
University of Colorado at Colorado Springs, CO
University of Connecticut, CT
University of Florida, FL
University of Idaho, ID
The University of Kansas, KS
University of Louisiana at Monroe, LA
University of Mary Hardin-Baylor, TX
University of Maryland, College Park, MD
University of Michigan, MI
University of Michigan–Dearborn, MI
University of Mississippi, MS
University of Missouri–Columbia, MO
University of Missouri–Kansas City, MO
The University of Montana, MT
University of Montevallo, AL
University of Nebraska at Kearney, NE
University of Nebraska at Omaha, NE
University of Nebraska–Lincoln, NE
University of Nevada, Las Vegas, NV
University of New Orleans, LA
University of North Alabama, AL
The University of North Carolina at Chapel Hill, NC
The University of North Carolina at Greensboro, NC
University of Northern Colorado, CO
University of North Florida, FL
University of Science and Arts of Oklahoma, OK
University of South Carolina, SC
University of Southern Indiana, IN
University of Southern Maine, ME
University of Southern Mississippi, MS
The University of Tennessee at Martin, TN
The University of Texas at Dallas, TX
The University of Texas at El Paso, TX
The University of Texas at San Antonio, TX
The University of Texas–Pan American, TX
University of Utah, UT
University of Wisconsin–La Crosse, WI
University of Wisconsin–Stevens Point, WI
University of Wisconsin–Stout, WI
University of Wisconsin–Whitewater, WI
University of Wyoming, WY
Virginia Military Institute, VA
Virginia Polytechnic Institute and State University, VA
Wartburg College, IA
Washington State University, WA
Webber International University, FL
Webster University, MO
Western Kentucky University, KY
Western New England College, MA
Winona State University, MN
Wright State University, OH

Parents of Current Students

Alabama Agricultural and Mechanical University, AL
The College of New Rochelle, NY
Columbia College, MO
Emmanuel College, GA
Fairfield University, CT
Franklin Pierce University, NH
Green Mountain College, VT
Huntington University, IN
Johnson Bible College, TN
Malone University, OH
Marymount University, VA
Maryville University of Saint Louis, MO
Midland Lutheran College, NE
Millikin University, IL
Mississippi University for Women, MS
Missouri Baptist University, MO
Mount Aloysius College, PA
Mount Marty College, SD
Mount Mary College, WI
New England College, NH
Northwest University, WA
Pace University, NY
Rockford College, IL
Seton Hill University, PA
State University of New York at Fredonia, NY
Stephens College, MO
The University of Alabama at Birmingham, AL
University of Hartford, CT
University of the Incarnate Word, TX

Previous College Experience

Abilene Christian University, TX
American International College, MA
American University, DC
Anna Maria College, MA
Bellarmine University, KY
Benedictine University, IL
Bethel College, KS
Birmingham-Southern College, AL
Boise State University, ID
Brevard College, NC
Cedar Crest College, PA
Centenary College, NJ
Central College, IA
The College at Brockport, State University of New York, NY
The College of New Rochelle, NY
College of St. Joseph, VT
The College of St. Scholastica, MN
Columbia College, MO
Defiance College, OH
Eastern Michigan University, MI
East Texas Baptist University, TX
Elmira College, NY
Ferris State University, MI
Florida Institute of Technology, FL
Gardner-Webb University, NC
Golden Gate University, CA
Hawai'i Pacific University, HI
Hendrix College, AR
Hollins University, VA
Idaho State University, ID
Illinois College, IL
Illinois Institute of Technology, IL
Illinois State University, IL
Indiana State University, IN
Lake Forest College, IL
Lancaster Bible College, PA
Lees-McRae College, NC
Lewis-Clark State College, ID
Lock Haven University of Pennsylvania, PA
Lourdes College, OH
Manchester College, IN
Manhattanville College, NY
McDaniel College, MD
McMurry University, TX
Memphis College of Art, TN
Midland Lutheran College, NE
Midway College, KY
Misericordia University, PA
Mississippi State University, MS
Monmouth University, NJ
Mount Mercy College, IA
New Mexico State University, NM
Nicholls State University, LA
Northwest Missouri State University, MO
The Ohio State University, OH
Oklahoma State University, OK
Old Dominion University, VA
Ouachita Baptist University, AR
Pace University, NY
Palm Beach Atlantic University, FL
Point Park University, PA
The Richard Stockton College of New Jersey, NJ
Ripon College, WI
Saint Francis University, PA
Saint Louis University, MO
Shepherd University, WV
Slippery Rock University of Pennsylvania, PA
Sonoma State University, CA
Southeast Missouri State University, MO
Southwest Minnesota State University, MN
State University of New York at Fredonia, NY
State University of New York College at Potsdam, NY
State University of New York Institute of Technology, NY
Stephen F. Austin State University, TX
Texas Christian University, TX
The University of Alabama at Birmingham, AL
University of Arkansas, AR
University of Bridgeport, CT
University of Central Missouri, MO
University of Hartford, CT
The University of Kansas, KS
University of Michigan–Dearborn, MI
University of Mississippi, MS
University of Nevada, Las Vegas, NV
University of New Orleans, LA
The University of North Carolina Wilmington, NC
University of Oklahoma, OK
University of Science and Arts of Oklahoma, OK
University of Wisconsin–Eau Claire, WI
University of Wisconsin–Stout, WI
Warren Wilson College, NC
Western Washington University, WA
William Jessup University, CA
York College, NE

Public Servants

College of Staten Island of the City University of New York, NY
Dowling College, NY
Grand Valley State University, MI
Hardin-Simmons University, TX
Hofstra University, NY
Kentucky State University, KY
Liberty University, VA
Michigan State University, MI
Missouri Baptist University, MO
Nicholls State University, LA
Northwestern State University of Louisiana, LA
Salem State College, MA
Southern Illinois University Carbondale, IL
Tennessee Technological University, TN
The University of Alabama at Birmingham, AL
University of Kentucky, KY
University of Memphis, TN
University of New Orleans, LA
The University of Texas at Arlington, TX
The University of Texas at Dallas, TX
Washington State University, WA
Westminster College, UT

Relatives of Clergy

Abilene Christian University, TX
Albion College, MI
American University, DC
Appalachian Bible College, WV
Arcadia University, PA
Ashland University, OH
Augsburg College, MN
Austin College, TX
Averett University, VA
Avila University, MO
Baker University, KS
Baptist Bible College of Pennsylvania, PA
Barton College, NC
Bethany College, KS
Bethel College, IN
Bethel College, KS
Bethel University, MN
Biola University, CA
Birmingham-Southern College, AL
Bluffton University, OH
Boston University, MA
Brevard College, NC
Brewton-Parker College, GA
Bryan College, TN
California Baptist University, CA
Campbellsville University, KY
Carson-Newman College, TN
Cedar Crest College, PA
Centenary College of Louisiana, LA
Central Methodist University, MO
Chestnut Hill College, PA
Clarke College, IA
Columbia International University, SC
Concordia College–New York, NY
Concordia University, OR
Corban College, OR
Cornell College, IA
Crown College, MN
Dallas Baptist University, TX
Davidson College, NC
DePauw University, IN
DeSales University, PA
Dominican College, NY
Drury University, MO
Duquesne University, PA
Elon University, NC
Emmanuel College, GA
Evangel University, MO
Faulkner University, AL
Free Will Baptist Bible College, TN
Fresno Pacific University, CA
Furman University, SC
Gardner-Webb University, NC
George Fox University, OR
Georgetown College, KY
Gordon College, MA
Grace Bible College, MI
Grace College, IN
Grace University, NE
Green Mountain College, VT
Greensboro College, NC
Harding University, AR
Hardin-Simmons University, TX
Hastings College, NE
Hawai'i Pacific University, HI
Heidelberg University, OH
Hendrix College, AR
Hillsdale Free Will Baptist College, OK
Hope International University, CA
Houghton College, NY
Houston Baptist University, TX
Howard Payne University, TX
Huntington University, IN
Jamestown College, ND
John Brown University, AR
Johnson Bible College, TN
Judson College, AL
King's College, PA
LaGrange College, GA
Lambuth University, TN
Lancaster Bible College, PA
Lees-McRae College, NC
Lindsey Wilson College, KY
Lipscomb University, TN
Lycoming College, PA
Malone University, OH
Maranatha Baptist Bible College, WI
The Master's College and Seminary, CA

McMurry University, TX
Mercer University, GA
Merrimack College, MA
Messiah College, PA
Methodist University, NC
Mid-Continent University, KY
Midway College, KY
Millikin University, IL
Millsaps College, MS
Misericordia University, PA
Mississippi College, MS
Missouri Baptist University, MO
Montreat College, NC
Mount Union College, OH
Mount Vernon Nazarene University, OH
Muskingum College, OH
Nebraska Christian College, NE
Nebraska Wesleyan University, NE
Newberry College, SC
Niagara University, NY
North Central College, IL
North Park University, IL
Northwest Christian University, OR
Northwestern College, MN
Northwest University, WA
Nyack College, NY
Ohio Christian University, OH
Ohio Northern University, OH
Ohio Valley University, WV
Oklahoma Baptist University, OK
Oklahoma City University, OK
Oklahoma Wesleyan University, OK
Olivet Nazarene University, IL
Oral Roberts University, OK
Ouachita Baptist University, AR
Our Lady of Holy Cross College, LA
Pacific Lutheran University, WA
Pacific University, OR
Peace College, NC
Philadelphia Biblical University, PA
Presbyterian College, SC
Randolph College, VA
Randolph-Macon College, VA
Regis College, MA
Roberts Wesleyan College, NY
St. John's University, NY
Saint Mary's College of California, CA
Salem College, NC
Samford University, AL
Schreiner University, TX
Seattle Pacific University, WA
Sewanee: The University of the South, TN
Shasta Bible College, CA
Simpson College, IA
Simpson University, CA
Southwest Baptist University, MO
Southwestern Christian University, OK
Southwestern University, TX
Spring Arbor University, MI
Stonehill College, MA
Susquehanna University, PA
Texas Christian University, TX
Thiel College, PA
Transylvania University, KY
Trevecca Nazarene University, TN
Trinity College of Florida, FL
Union University, TN
The University of Alabama at Birmingham, AL
University of Mary Hardin-Baylor, TX
The University of North Carolina at Chapel Hill, NC
University of Portland, OR
University of South Carolina, SC
University of the Cumberlands, KY
University of the Ozarks, AR
University of Tulsa, OK
Ursuline College, OH
Valley Forge Christian College, PA
Valparaiso University, IN
Virginia Wesleyan College, VA
Washington Bible College, MD
Wayland Baptist University, TX
Westminster College, MO
Westminster College, UT
West Virginia Wesleyan College, WV
Whitworth University, WA
William Carey University, MS
William Jessup University, CA
Williams Baptist College, AR
Wilson College, PA
Wingate University, NC
Wittenberg University, OH
Wofford College, SC

Religious Affiliation

Abilene Christian University, TX
Adrian College, MI
Agnes Scott College, GA
Alaska Bible College, AK
Alaska Pacific University, AK
Albertus Magnus College, CT
Alderson-Broaddus College, WV
Appalachian Bible College, WV
Arcadia University, PA
Ashland University, OH
Augustana College, IL
Augustana College, SD
Averett University, VA
Avila University, MO
Baker University, KS
Baldwin-Wallace College, OH
The Baptist College of Florida, FL
Barton College, NC
Benedictine College, KS
Bethany College, KS
Bethel College, IN
Bethel College, KS
Bethel University, MN
Birmingham-Southern College, AL
Bluefield College, VA
Bluffton University, OH
Boston University, MA
Brevard College, NC
Brewton-Parker College, GA
Bridgewater College, VA
Bryan College, TN
Buena Vista University, IA
Calvin College, MI
Campbellsville University, KY
Canisius College, NY
Cedar Crest College, PA
Cedarville University, OH
Centenary College, NJ
Centenary College of Louisiana, LA
Central College, IA
Central Methodist University, MO
Christian Brothers University, TN
Clarke College, IA
Clearwater Christian College, FL
The College at Brockport, State University of New York, NY
College of St. Joseph, VT
The College of St. Scholastica, MN
Columbia College, MO
Columbia International University, SC
Concordia College–New York, NY
Concordia University, OR
Concordia University Chicago, IL
Concordia University, St. Paul, MN
Concordia University Texas, TX
Cornell College, IA
Covenant College, GA
Creighton University, NE
Culver-Stockton College, MO
Dallas Baptist University, TX
Dana College, NE
Defiance College, OH
DePauw University, IN
DeSales University, PA
Dillard University, LA
Doane College, NE
Dominican University, IL
Dordt College, IA
Drury University, MO
Duquesne University, PA
Eastern Michigan University, MI
East Texas Baptist University, TX
Edinboro University of Pennsylvania, PA
Elizabethtown College, PA
Elmhurst College, IL
Emmanuel College, GA
Emory & Henry College, VA
Emory University, GA
Emporia State University, KS
Endicott College, MA
Eureka College, IL
Evangel University, MO
Fairfield University, CT
Faulkner University, AL
Finlandia University, MI
Franklin College, IN
Fresno Pacific University, CA
Furman University, SC
Gannon University, PA
Geneva College, PA
George Fox University, OR
Georgetown College, KY
Georgia College & State University, GA
Georgian Court University, NJ
Grace College, IN
Graceland University, IA
Green Mountain College, VT
Greensboro College, NC
Hanover College, IN
Hardin-Simmons University, TX
Hastings College, NE
Hawai'i Pacific University, HI
Heidelberg University, OH
Hillsdale Free Will Baptist College, OK
Houghton College, NY
Howard Payne University, TX
Huntingdon College, AL
Huntington University, IN
Illinois College, IL
Illinois Wesleyan University, IL
Iona College, NY
Iowa State University of Science and Technology, IA
Jamestown College, ND
Jarvis Christian College, TX
Johnson Bible College, TN
Judson College, AL
Kennesaw State University, GA
Kentucky Christian University, KY
LaGrange College, GA
Lambuth University, TN
Lancaster Bible College, PA
Lees-McRae College, NC

Liberty University, VA
Lindsey Wilson College, KY
Loyola University Chicago, IL
Luther College, IA
Lyon College, AR
MacMurray College, IL
Malone University, OH
Manchester College, IN
Marian College, IN
Maryville College, TN
Marywood University, PA
McKendree University, IL
McMurry University, TX
McPherson College, KS
Medical College of Georgia, GA
Mercer University, GA
Messiah College, PA
Methodist University, NC
Michigan State University, MI
Midland Lutheran College, NE
Midway College, KY
Millsaps College, MS
Misericordia University, PA
Missouri Baptist University, MO
Molloy College, NY
Montreat College, NC
Mount Aloysius College, PA
Mount Marty College, SD
Mount Vernon Nazarene University, OH
Muskingum College, OH
Newberry College, SC
Northwest Christian University, OR
Northwest University, WA
Nyack College, NY
Ohio Christian University, OH
Ohio Northern University, OH
Ohio Valley University, WV
Oklahoma Baptist University, OK
Oklahoma Wesleyan University, OK
Olivet College, MI
Olivet Nazarene University, IL
Ouachita Baptist University, AR
Our Lady of Holy Cross College, LA
Pacific Lutheran University, WA
Pacific Union College, CA
Presbyterian College, SC
Randolph College, VA
Regis College, MA
Ripon College, WI
Roberts Wesleyan College, NY
Sacred Heart University, CT
St. Catherine University, MN
St. Edward's University, TX
St. John's University, NY
Saint Louis University, MO
Saint Michael's College, VT
Saint Vincent College, PA
Schreiner University, TX
Seattle Pacific University, WA
Seattle University, WA
Shorter College, GA
Simpson College, IA
Simpson University, CA
Southeastern Louisiana University, LA
Southern Nazarene University, OK
Southwestern Christian University, OK
Southwestern College, KS
Southwestern University, TX
Spring Arbor University, MI
Stephen F. Austin State University, TX
Tabor College, KS
Taylor University, IN
Texas Christian University, TX
Texas Lutheran University, TX
Thiel College, PA
Thomas More College, KY
Transylvania University, KY
Trevecca Nazarene University, TN
Trinity International University, IL
Trinity Lutheran College, WA
Union College, KY
Union University, TN
The University of Alabama at Birmingham, AL
University of Dallas, TX
University of Dayton, OH
University of Evansville, IN
University of Hartford, CT
University of La Verne, CA
University of Mary Hardin-Baylor, TX
The University of North Carolina at Chapel Hill, NC
The University of North Carolina at Greensboro, NC
University of South Carolina, SC
University of the Cumberlands, KY
University of the Ozarks, AR
University of Tulsa, OK
Ursuline College, OH
Valparaiso University, IN
Villanova University, PA
Virginia Intermont College, VA
Virginia Wesleyan College, VA
Warner Pacific College, OR
Warren Wilson College, NC
Wartburg College, IA
Washington State University, WA
Wayland Baptist University, TX
Western Kentucky University, KY
Westminster College, MO
Westminster College, PA
Westminster College, UT
West Virginia Wesleyan College, WV
Wheeling Jesuit University, WV
William Carey University, MS
Williams Baptist College, AR
Wilson College, PA
Wingate University, NC
Wittenberg University, OH

Siblings of Current Students

Albright College, PA
Anna Maria College, MA
Asbury College, KY
Augsburg College, MN
Augustana College, IL
Augustana College, SD
Avila University, MO
Baldwin-Wallace College, OH
Baptist Bible College of Pennsylvania, PA
Barton College, NC
Beloit College, WI
Benedictine University, IL
Bethel College, IN
Bethel College, KS
Brevard College, NC
Bridgewater College, VA
Bryant University, RI
Buena Vista University, IA
California Baptist University, CA
Carroll College, MT
Carroll University, WI
Carson-Newman College, TN
Cedar Crest College, PA
Centenary College, NJ
Central College, IA
Central Methodist University, MO
Chatham University, PA
Clarke College, IA
Clearwater Christian College, FL
Coe College, IA
The College of New Rochelle, NY
The College of St. Scholastica, MN
Columbia College, MO
Corban College, OR
Creighton University, NE
Crown College, MN
Daemen College, NY
DeSales University, PA
Doane College, NE
Dominican University, IL
East Texas Baptist University, TX
Elizabethtown College, PA
Elmhurst College, IL
Elmira College, NY
Embry-Riddle Aeronautical University, FL
Emmanuel College, GA
Eureka College, IL
Faulkner University, AL
Felician College, NJ
Finlandia University, MI
Florida Institute of Technology, FL
Franciscan University of Steubenville, OH
Franklin College, IN
Franklin Pierce University, NH
Gonzaga University, WA
Grace University, NE
Green Mountain College, VT
Greensboro College, NC
Gustavus Adolphus College, MN
Gwynedd-Mercy College, PA
Hanover College, IN
Harding University, AR
Hardin-Simmons University, TX
Hartwick College, NY
Hastings College, NE
Hillsdale Free Will Baptist College, OK
Hood College, MD
Hope International University, CA
Houghton College, NY
Houston Baptist University, TX
Huntington University, IN
Iona College, NY
Ithaca College, NY
James Madison University, VA
Jamestown College, ND
John Brown University, AR
Johnson Bible College, TN
Johnson C. Smith University, NC
Kettering University, MI
Keuka College, NY
King's College, PA
Lancaster Bible College, PA
Lee University, TN
Limestone College, SC
Long Island University, C.W. Post Campus, NY
Loras College, IA
Lynn University, FL
MacMurray College, IL
Malone University, OH
Marian College, IN
Marian University, WI
Marymount University, VA
Maryville University of Saint Louis, MO
Marywood University, PA
McDaniel College, MD
Mercer University, GA
Merrimack College, MA

Messiah College, PA
Midland Lutheran College, NE
Misericordia University, PA
Missouri Baptist University, MO
Molloy College, NY
Monmouth College, IL
Mount Aloysius College, PA
Mount Marty College, SD
Mount Mary College, WI
Mount St. Mary's University, MD
Mount Vernon Nazarene University, OH
Muskingum College, OH
Nazareth College of Rochester, NY
Nebraska Wesleyan University, NE
Newberry College, SC
New England College, NH
Newman University, KS
Nichols College, MA
Northwest Christian University, OR
Northwestern College, MN
Northwest University, WA
Northwood University, MI
Northwood University, Florida Campus, FL
Northwood University, Texas Campus, TX
Oglethorpe University, GA
Ohio Christian University, OH
Ohio Northern University, OH
Olivet College, MI
Oral Roberts University, OK
Pacific Union College, CA
Palm Beach Atlantic University, FL
Peace College, NC
Point Park University, PA
Post University, CT
Quinnipiac University, CT
Randolph-Macon College, VA
Regis College, MA
Ripon College, WI
Rivier College, NH
Roberts Wesleyan College, NY
Rockford College, IL
Rockhurst University, MO
Sacred Heart University, CT
Saint Anselm College, NH
St. Catherine University, MN
Saint Francis University, PA
Saint Joseph's College, IN
Saint Joseph's College of Maine, ME
St. Lawrence University, NY
Saint Louis University, MO
Saint Martin's University, WA
Saint Michael's College, VT
Schreiner University, TX
Seton Hill University, PA
Shorter College, GA
Simpson College, IA
Simpson University, CA
Southern Adventist University, TN
Spring Hill College, AL
Stephens College, MO
Stonehill College, MA
Suffolk University, MA
Thiel College, PA
Union University, TN
The University of Alabama at Birmingham, AL
University of Dallas, TX
University of Evansville, IN
University of Hartford, CT
University of Mary, ND
University of New England, ME
The University of Scranton, PA
University of the Cumberlands, KY
University of the Ozarks, AR
University of Tulsa, OK
Ursinus College, PA
Ursuline College, OH
Valley Forge Christian College, PA
Wagner College, NY
Wartburg College, IA
Washington Bible College, MD
Webber International University, FL
Western New England College, MA
Westminster College, MO
Westminster College, UT
Whitworth University, WA
Xavier University, OH
York College, NE

Spouses of Current Students

Alaska Bible College, AK
American University, DC
Appalachian Bible College, WV
Augustana College, SD
Avila University, MO
The Baptist College of Florida, FL
Bethel College, IN
Bethel College, KS
Boise State University, ID
Bryan College, TN
Carroll College, MT
Carroll University, WI
Central Methodist University, MO
The College of New Rochelle, NY
Columbia College, MO
Columbia International University, SC
Elmhurst College, IL
Emmanuel College, GA
Finlandia University, MI
Franklin Pierce University, NH
Fresno Pacific University, CA
Georgian Court University, NJ
Grace University, NE
Heritage Christian University, AL
Hillsdale Free Will Baptist College, OK
Hope International University, CA
Huntington University, IN
Jamestown College, ND
Johnson Bible College, TN
Lancaster Bible College, PA
Lee University, TN
Malone University, OH
Maranatha Baptist Bible College, WI
Marian College, IN
Maryville University of Saint Louis, MO
Marywood University, PA
Messiah College, PA
Midland Lutheran College, NE
Mount Aloysius College, PA
Mount Marty College, SD
Mount Vernon Nazarene University, OH
New Mexico State University, NM
Northwest University, WA
Nyack College, NY
Pacific Union College, CA
Palm Beach Atlantic University, FL
Roanoke Bible College, NC
St. Catherine University, MN
Saint Joseph's College of Maine, ME
Simpson University, CA
Southern Adventist University, TN
Trinity College of Florida, FL
Union University, TN
The University of Alabama at Birmingham, AL
University of Mississippi, MS
University of Southern Indiana, IN
Valley Forge Christian College, PA
Washington Bible College, MD
Westminster College, UT

Spouses of Deceased or Disabled Public Servants

College of Staten Island of the City University of New York, NY
Francis Marion University, SC
Grand Valley State University, MI
Michigan State University, MI
Mississippi State University, MS
Northeastern State University, OK
Northern Arizona University, AZ
Pace University, NY
Southern Illinois University Carbondale, IL
The University of Alabama, AL
The University of Alabama at Birmingham, AL
University of Connecticut, CT
University of Kentucky, KY
University of South Carolina, SC
University of Utah, UT
Youngstown State University, OH

Twins

Calvin College, MI
Central College, IA
Dominican University, IL
East Texas Baptist University, TX
Emmanuel College, GA
Finlandia University, MI
Maryville University of Saint Louis, MO
Millikin University, IL
Mount Aloysius College, PA
Ouachita Baptist University, AR
Randolph College, VA
Sacred Heart University, CT
Simpson College, IA
Union University, TN
The University of Alabama at Birmingham, AL
University of Hartford, CT
Virginia Polytechnic Institute and State University, VA
Westminster College, MO

Veterans

Alliant International University, CA
Amridge University, AL
Appalachian Bible College, WV
Appalachian State University, NC
Arkansas State University, AR
Augustana College, SD
Austin Peay State University, TN
Ball State University, IN
Barton College, NC
Bluefield College, VA
Boise State University, ID
California State University, Bakersfield, CA
Campbellsville University, KY
Carroll College, MT
Cedarville University, OH
Central Michigan University, MI
Cleary University, MI
The College at Brockport, State University of New York, NY
Columbia College, MO
Columbia International University, SC
Concordia University Texas, TX
Edinboro University of Pennsylvania, PA
EDP College of Puerto Rico, Inc., PR

Emporia State University, KS
The Evergreen State College, WA
Ferris State University, MI
Francis Marion University, SC
Free Will Baptist Bible College, TN
Frostburg State University, MD
Furman University, SC
Georgian Court University, NJ
Grand Valley State University, MI
Greensboro College, NC
Hollins University, VA
Hope International University, CA
Indiana State University, IN
John Carroll University, OH
Kendall College, IL
Kentucky State University, KY
Lees-McRae College, NC
Liberty University, VA
Louisiana Tech University, LA
Massachusetts College of Art and Design, MA
McMurry University, TX
Michigan State University, MI
Midway College, KY
Minot State University, ND
Monmouth College, IL
Monmouth University, NJ
Montana State University–Billings, MT
Montreat College, NC
New Mexico State University, NM
Nicholls State University, LA
Northern Arizona University, AZ
Northern Illinois University, IL
Northwestern State University of Louisiana, LA
Ohio Christian University, OH
Oklahoma Panhandle State University, OK
Pace University, NY
Robert Morris College, IL
Rochester Institute of Technology, NY
Salem State College, MA
San Diego State University, CA
Shasta Bible College, CA
Sonoma State University, CA
South Dakota State University, SD
Southern Connecticut State University, CT
Southern Illinois University Carbondale, IL
Southwest Minnesota State University, MN
Susquehanna University, PA
Texas A&M University, TX
Texas Christian University, TX
Texas Tech University, TX
Thomas Jefferson University, PA
Towson University, MD
University of Advancing Technology, AZ
The University of Alabama at Birmingham, AL
University of Connecticut, CT
University of Illinois at Urbana–Champaign, IL
University of Kentucky, KY
University of Mary, ND
University of Maryland Eastern Shore, MD
University of Massachusetts Amherst, MA
University of Massachusetts Boston, MA
University of Massachusetts Dartmouth, MA
University of Michigan–Dearborn, MI
University of Minnesota, Morris, MN
The University of Montana, MT
The University of Montana Western, MT
University of Montevallo, AL
University of Nebraska at Kearney, NE
University of Nevada, Las Vegas, NV
The University of North Carolina at Asheville, NC
The University of North Carolina at Greensboro, NC
University of Northern Colorado, CO
University of Rochester, NY
University of Southern Mississippi, MS
The University of Texas at Dallas, TX
The University of Texas–Pan American, TX
University of the Virgin Islands, VI
The University of Virginia's College at Wise, VA
University of Wisconsin–Green Bay, WI
University of Wisconsin–Stevens Point, WI
University of Wisconsin–Stout, WI
University of Wyoming, WY
Walla Walla University, WA
Washington State University, WA
Western Kentucky University, KY
Western Oregon University, OR
Western Washington University, WA
Westminster College, UT
William Carey University, MS
William Jessup University, CA
Wilson College, PA
Youngstown State University, OH

Veterans' Children

Appalachian State University, NC
Arkansas State University, AR
Benedictine College, KS
Boise State University, ID
Brevard College, NC
Central Michigan University, MI
Coastal Carolina University, SC
College of Staten Island of the City University of New York, NY
Columbia International University, SC
Concordia University Texas, TX
Edinboro University of Pennsylvania, PA
EDP College of Puerto Rico, Inc., PR
Emporia State University, KS
The Evergreen State College, WA
Fort Lewis College, CO
Francis Marion University, SC
Free Will Baptist Bible College, TN
Frostburg State University, MD
Glenville State College, WV
Grand Valley State University, MI
Hope International University, CA
Illinois Institute of Technology, IL
John Carroll University, OH
Kendall College, IL
Kennesaw State University, GA
Louisiana Tech University, LA
Michigan State University, MI
Minot State University, ND
Montreat College, NC
New Mexico State University, NM
Northern Arizona University, AZ
Northwestern State University of Louisiana, LA
Ohio Christian University, OH
Oklahoma Panhandle State University, OK
Old Dominion University, VA
Purdue University North Central, IN
Salem State College, MA
South Dakota State University, SD
Southeastern Louisiana University, LA
Southwest Minnesota State University, MN
Texas A&M University, TX
Texas Christian University, TX
Texas Tech University, TX
University of Advancing Technology, AZ
The University of Alabama at Birmingham, AL
University of California, San Diego, CA
University of Kentucky, KY
The University of Maine at Augusta, ME
University of Maine at Presque Isle, ME
University of Michigan–Dearborn, MI
University of Minnesota, Morris, MN
University of Montevallo, AL
University of Nebraska at Kearney, NE
University of Nebraska at Omaha, NE
University of Nebraska–Lincoln, NE
University of Nevada, Las Vegas, NV
University of New Orleans, LA
The University of North Carolina at Asheville, NC
The University of North Carolina at Greensboro, NC
University of North Dakota, ND
University of Puerto Rico, Mayagüez Campus, PR
University of Southern Indiana, IN
The University of Texas at Dallas, TX
The University of Virginia's College at Wise, VA
University of Wisconsin–La Crosse, WI
University of Wisconsin–Stout, WI
Virginia Commonwealth University, VA
Virginia Polytechnic Institute and State University, VA
Western Illinois University, IL
Westminster College, UT
William Jessup University, CA
Youngstown State University, OH

Athletic Grants for Undergraduates

Archery

Texas A&M University, TX	W

Baseball

Abilene Christian University, TX	M
Academy of Art University, CA	M
Adelphi University, NY	M
Alabama Agricultural and Mechanical University, AL	M
Alcorn State University, MS	M
Alderson-Broaddus College, WV	M
Alice Lloyd College, KY	M
Angelo State University, TX	M
Appalachian State University, NC	M
Arizona State University, AZ	M
Arkansas State University, AR	M
Arkansas Tech University, AR	M
Asbury College, KY	M
Ashland University, OH	M
Auburn University, AL	M
Auburn University Montgomery, AL	M
Augustana College, SD	M
Austin Peay State University, TN	M
Avila University, MO	M
Azusa Pacific University, CA	M
Baker University, KS	M
Ball State University, IN	M
Barton College, NC	M
Baylor University, TX	M
Belhaven College, MS	M
Bellarmine University, KY	M
Belmont Abbey College, NC	M
Belmont University, TN	M
Benedictine College, KS	M
Bentley University, MA	M
Bethany College, KS	M
Bethel College, IN	M
Biola University, CA	M
Blessing-Rieman College of Nursing, IL	M,W
Bloomfield College, NJ	M
Bloomsburg University of Pennsylvania, PA	M
Bluefield College, VA	M
Bluefield State College, WV	M
Bowling Green State University, OH	M
Bradley University, IL	M
Brevard College, NC	M
Brewton-Parker College, GA	M
Brigham Young University, UT	M
Bryan College, TN	M
Butler University, IN	M
California Baptist University, CA	M
California Polytechnic State University, San Luis Obispo, CA	M
California State Polytechnic University, Pomona, CA	M
California State University, Chico, CA	M
California State University, Fresno, CA	M
California State University, Fullerton, CA	M
California State University, Los Angeles, CA	M
California State University, Northridge, CA	M
California State University, Sacramento, CA	M
California State University, San Bernardino, CA	M
Campbellsville University, KY	M
Canisius College, NY	M
Carson-Newman College, TN	M
Catawba College, NC	M
Cedarville University, OH	M
Central Connecticut State University, CT	M
Central Methodist University, MO	M
Central Michigan University, MI	M
Chestnut Hill College, PA	M
Christian Brothers University, TN	M
Clarion University of Pennsylvania, PA	M
Clarke College, IA	M
Cleveland State University, OH	M
Coastal Carolina University, SC	M
College of Charleston, SC	M
The College of Idaho, ID	M
College of the Ozarks, MO	M
The College of William and Mary, VA	M
Colorado School of Mines, CO	M
Columbus State University, GA	M
Concordia University, OR	M
Concordia University, Nebraska, NE	M
Concordia University, St. Paul, MN	M
Concord University, WV	M
Coppin State University, MD	M
Corban College, OR	M
Covenant College, GA	M
Creighton University, NE	M
Culver-Stockton College, MO	M
Dakota State University, SD	M
Dallas Baptist University, TX	M
Dana College, NE	M
Davidson College, NC	M
Delta State University, MS	M
Dixie State College of Utah, UT	M
Doane College, NE	M
Dominican College, NY	M
Dordt College, IA	M
Dowling College, NY	M
Drury University, MO	M
Duke University, NC	M
Duquesne University, PA	M
Eastern Illinois University, IL	M
Eastern Michigan University, MI	M
East Tennessee State University, TN	M
Elon University, NC	M
Embry-Riddle Aeronautical University, FL	M
Emmanuel College, GA	M
Emporia State University, KS	M
Evangel University, MO	M
Fairfield University, CT	M
Fairleigh Dickinson University, Metropolitan Campus, NJ	M
Faulkner University, AL	M
Felician College, NJ	M
Flagler College, FL	M
Florida Atlantic University, FL	M
Florida Gulf Coast University, FL	M
Florida Institute of Technology, FL	M
Florida International University, FL	M
Florida State University, FL	M
Fort Hays State University, KS	M
Francis Marion University, SC	M
Franklin Pierce University, NH	M
Freed-Hardeman University, TN	M
Furman University, SC	M
Gannon University, PA	M
Gardner-Webb University, NC	M
George Mason University, VA	M
Georgetown College, KY	M
Georgetown University, DC	M
The George Washington University, DC	M
Georgia College & State University, GA	M
Georgia Institute of Technology, GA	M
Georgia Southern University, GA	M
Georgia Southwestern State University, GA	M
Georgia State University, GA	M
Gonzaga University, WA	M
Grace College, IN	M
Graceland University, IA	M
Grand Valley State University, MI	M
Grand View University, IA	M
Harding University, AR	M
Hawai'i Pacific University, HI	M
Henderson State University, AR	M
Hofstra University, NY	M
Houston Baptist University, TX	M

Athletic Grants for Undergraduates

Baseball

Huntington University, IN	M
Illinois Institute of Technology, IL	M
Illinois State University, IL	M
Indiana State University, IN	M
Indiana University Bloomington, IN	M
Indiana University of Pennsylvania, PA	M
Indiana University–Purdue University Fort Wayne, IN	M
Inter American University of Puerto Rico, Arecibo Campus, PR	M
Iona College, NY	M
Jacksonville University, FL	M
James Madison University, VA	M
Jamestown College, ND	M
Kansas State University, KS	M
Kennesaw State University, GA	M
Kent State University, OH	M
Kentucky State University, KY	M
Kentucky Wesleyan College, KY	M
Kutztown University of Pennsylvania, PA	M
Lamar University, TX	M
Lambuth University, TN	M
Lane College, TN	M
Lee University, TN	M
Le Moyne College, NY	M
Lewis-Clark State College, ID	M
Liberty University, VA	M
Limestone College, SC	M
Lincoln Memorial University, TN	M
Lindenwood University, MO	M
Lindsey Wilson College, KY	M
Lipscomb University, TN	M
Lock Haven University of Pennsylvania, PA	M
Long Island University, Brooklyn Campus, NY	M
Long Island University, C.W. Post Campus, NY	M
Longwood University, VA	M
Louisiana State University and Agricultural and Mechanical College, LA	M
Lubbock Christian University, TX	M
Lyon College, AR	M
Malone University, OH	M
Marian College, IN	M
The Master's College and Seminary, CA	M
Mayville State University, ND	M
McKendree University, IL	M
Mercer University, GA	M
Mercyhurst College, PA	M
Mesa State College, CO	M
Metropolitan State College of Denver, CO	M
Miami University, OH	M
Michigan State University, MI	M
MidAmerica Nazarene University, KS	M
Mid-Continent University, KY	M
Millersville University of Pennsylvania, PA	M
Milligan College, TN	M
Minnesota State University Mankato, MN	M
Minot State University, ND	M
Mississippi State University, MS	M
Missouri Baptist University, MO	M
Missouri Southern State University, MO	M
Missouri State University, MO	M
Missouri University of Science and Technology, MO	M
Missouri Western State University, MO	M
Molloy College, NY	M
Monmouth University, NJ	M
Mount Marty College, SD	M
Mount Mercy College, IA	M
Mount Olive College, NC	M
Mount St. Mary's University, MD	M
Mount Vernon Nazarene University, OH	M
Murray State University, KY	M
Newberry College, SC	M
New Jersey Institute of Technology, NJ	M
Newman University, KS	M
New Mexico State University, NM	M
Niagara University, NY	M
Nicholls State University, LA	M
North Carolina State University, NC	M
North Dakota State University, ND	M
Northeastern State University, OK	M
Northeastern University, MA	M
Northern Kentucky University, KY	M
North Greenville University, SC	M
Northwestern State University of Louisiana, LA	M
Northwestern University, IL	M
Northwest Missouri State University, MO	M
Northwood University, MI	M
Northwood University, Florida Campus, FL	M
Northwood University, Texas Campus, TX	M
Nova Southeastern University, FL	M
Oakland University, MI	M
The Ohio State University, OH	M
Ohio University, OH	M
Ohio Valley University, WV	M
Oklahoma Baptist University, OK	M
Oklahoma Christian University, OK	M
Oklahoma City University, OK	M
Oklahoma Panhandle State University, OK	M
Oklahoma State University, OK	M
Old Dominion University, VA	M
Olivet Nazarene University, IL	M
Oral Roberts University, OK	M
Oregon State University, OR	M
Ouachita Baptist University, AR	M
Pace University, NY	M
Palm Beach Atlantic University, FL	M
Penn State University Park, PA	M
Pepperdine University, CA	M
Philadelphia University, PA	M
Pittsburg State University, KS	M
Point Loma Nazarene University, CA	M
Point Park University, PA	M
Portland State University, OR	M
Presbyterian College, SC	M
Purdue University, IN	M
Purdue University North Central, IN	M
Quinnipiac University, CT	M
Radford University, VA	M
Rider University, NJ	M
Robert Morris College, IL	M
Rockhurst University, MO	M
Rollins College, FL	M
Sacred Heart University, CT	M
Saginaw Valley State University, MI	M
St. Ambrose University, IA	M
St. Andrews Presbyterian College, NC	M
St. Cloud State University, MN	M
St. Edward's University, TX	M
St. John's University, NY	M
Saint Joseph's College, IN	M
Saint Joseph's University, PA	M
Saint Leo University, FL	M
Saint Louis University, MO	M
Saint Martin's University, WA	M
Saint Mary's College of California, CA	M
St. Mary's University, TX	M
St. Thomas University, FL	M
Saint Xavier University, IL	M
Samford University, AL	M
Sam Houston State University, TX	M
San Diego State University, CA	M
San Francisco State University, CA	M
San Jose State University, CA	M
Santa Clara University, CA	M
Savannah College of Art and Design, GA	M
Seton Hill University, PA	M
Shepherd University, WV	M
Shippensburg University of Pennsylvania, PA	M
Shorter College, GA	M
Simpson University, CA	M
Slippery Rock University of Pennsylvania, PA	M
Sonoma State University, CA	M
South Dakota State University, SD	M
Southeastern Louisiana University, LA	M
Southeastern Oklahoma State University, OK	M
Southeast Missouri State University, MO	M
Southern Arkansas University–Magnolia, AR	M
Southern Connecticut State University, CT	M
Southern Illinois University Carbondale, IL	M
Southern Illinois University Edwardsville, IL	M
Southern Nazarene University, OK	M
Southern New Hampshire University, NH	M
Southern Polytechnic State University, GA	M
Southern Utah University, UT	M
Southwest Baptist University, MO	M
Southwestern Oklahoma State University, OK	M
Southwest Minnesota State University, MN	M
Spring Arbor University, MI	M
Spring Hill College, AL	M
Stanford University, CA	M
State University of New York at Binghamton, NY	M
Stetson University, FL	M

Stonehill College, MA M
Stony Brook University, State University of New York, NY M
Tarleton State University, TX M
Taylor University, IN M
Temple University, PA M
Tennessee Technological University, TN M
Texas A&M University, TX M
Texas Christian University, TX M
Texas State University–San Marcos, TX M
Texas Tech University, TX M
Tiffin University, OH M
Towson University, MD M
Trevecca Nazarene University, TN M
Trinity Christian College, IL M
Trinity International University, IL M
Troy University, AL M
Truman State University, MO M
Tuskegee University, AL M
Union College, KY M
Union University, TN M
University at Albany, State University of New York, NY M
University at Buffalo, the State University of New York, NY M
The University of Akron, OH M
The University of Alabama, AL M
The University of Alabama at Birmingham, AL M
The University of Alabama in Huntsville, AL M
The University of Arizona, AZ M
University of Arkansas, AR M
University of Bridgeport, CT M
University of California, Davis, CA M
University of California, Irvine, CA M
University of California, Los Angeles, CA M
University of California, Riverside, CA M
University of Central Florida, FL M
University of Central Missouri, MO M
University of Central Oklahoma, OK M
University of Connecticut, CT M
University of Dayton, OH M
University of Delaware, DE M
University of Evansville, IN M
The University of Findlay, OH M
University of Florida, FL M
University of Georgia, GA M
University of Hartford, CT M
University of Hawaii at Manoa, HI M
University of Houston, TX M
University of Illinois at Chicago, IL M
The University of Iowa, IA M
The University of Kansas, KS M
University of Kentucky, KY M
University of Louisiana at Monroe, LA M
University of Louisville, KY M
University of Maine, ME M
University of Mary, ND M
University of Maryland, Baltimore County, MD M
University of Maryland, College Park, MD M
University of Maryland Eastern Shore, MD M
University of Massachusetts Amherst, MA M
University of Massachusetts Lowell, MA M
University of Memphis, TN M
University of Miami, FL M
University of Michigan, MI M
University of Minnesota, Crookston, MN M
University of Minnesota, Duluth, MN M
University of Minnesota, Twin Cities Campus, MN M
University of Mississippi, MS M
University of Missouri–Columbia, MO M
University of Missouri–St. Louis, MO M
University of Mobile, AL M
University of Montevallo, AL M
University of Nebraska at Kearney, NE M
University of Nebraska at Omaha, NE M
University of Nebraska–Lincoln, NE M
University of Nevada, Las Vegas, NV M
University of Nevada, Reno, NV M
University of New Haven, CT M
University of New Orleans, LA M
University of North Alabama, AL M
The University of North Carolina at Asheville, NC M
The University of North Carolina at Chapel Hill, NC M
The University of North Carolina at Greensboro, NC M
The University of North Carolina at Pembroke, NC M
The University of North Carolina Wilmington, NC M
University of North Dakota, ND M
University of Northern Colorado, CO M
University of Northern Iowa, IA M
University of North Florida, FL M
University of Notre Dame, IN M
University of Oklahoma, OK M
University of Oregon, OR M
University of Pittsburgh, PA M
University of Portland, OR M
University of Rhode Island, RI M
University of Richmond, VA M
University of Saint Francis, IN M
University of San Diego, CA M
University of Science and Arts of Oklahoma, OK M
University of South Alabama, AL M
University of South Carolina, SC M
University of South Carolina Aiken, SC M
University of South Carolina Upstate, SC M
University of Southern California, CA M
University of Southern Indiana, IN M
University of Southern Mississippi, MS M
University of South Florida, FL M
The University of Tampa, FL M
The University of Tennessee, TN M
The University of Tennessee at Martin, TN M
The University of Texas at Arlington, TX M
The University of Texas at Brownsville, TX M
The University of Texas at San Antonio, TX M
The University of Texas of the Permian Basin, TX M
The University of Texas–Pan American, TX M
University of the Cumberlands, KY M
University of the Incarnate Word, TX M
University of the Pacific, CA M
University of the Southwest, NM M
University of Utah, UT M
University of Virginia, VA M
The University of Virginia's College at Wise, VA M
University of West Florida, FL M
University of West Georgia, GA M
University of Wisconsin–Parkside, WI M
Utah Valley University, UT M
Valdosta State University, GA M
Valley City State University, ND M
Valparaiso University, IN M
Vanderbilt University, TN M
Vanguard University of Southern California, CA M
Villanova University, PA M
Virginia Commonwealth University, VA M
Virginia Intermont College, VA M
Virginia Military Institute, VA M
Wagner College, NY M
Wake Forest University, NC M
Washington State University, WA M
Wayland Baptist University, TX M
Wayne State University, MI M
Webber International University, FL M
West Chester University of Pennsylvania, PA M
Western Carolina University, NC M
Western Illinois University, IL M
Western Kentucky University, KY M
Western Michigan University, MI M
Western Oregon University, OR M
West Liberty State University, WV M
West Virginia University, WV M
West Virginia Wesleyan College, WV M
Wheeling Jesuit University, WV M
Wichita State University, KS M
Wingate University, NC M
Winona State University, MN M
Winthrop University, SC M
Wofford College, SC M
Wright State University, OH M
Xavier University, OH M
York College, NE M
Youngstown State University, OH M

Basketball

Abilene Christian University, TX M,W
Academy of Art University, CA M,W
Adams State College, CO M,W
Adelphi University, NY M,W
Alabama Agricultural and Mechanical University, AL M,W
Alcorn State University, MS M,W
Alderson-Broaddus College, WV M,W
Alice Lloyd College, KY M,W

Basketball

American University, DC M,W
Angelo State University, TX M,W
Appalachian State University, NC M,W
Arizona State University, AZ M,W
Arkansas State University, AR M,W
Arkansas Tech University, AR M,W
Asbury College, KY M,W
Ashland University, OH M,W
Assumption College, MA M,W
Auburn University, AL M,W
Auburn University Montgomery, AL M,W
Augustana College, SD M,W
Augusta State University, GA M,W
Austin Peay State University, TN M,W
Avila University, MO M,W
Azusa Pacific University, CA M,W
Baker University, KS M,W
Ball State University, IN M,W
Barton College, NC M,W
Baylor University, TX M,W
Belhaven College, MS M,W
Bellarmine University, KY M,W
Belmont Abbey College, NC M,W
Belmont University, TN M,W
Benedictine College, KS M,W
Bentley University, MA M,W
Bethany College, KS M,W
Bethel College, IN M,W
Bethel College, KS M,W
Biola University, CA M,W
Black Hills State University, SD M,W
Blessing-Rieman College of Nursing, IL M,W
Bloomfield College, NJ M,W
Bloomsburg University of Pennsylvania, PA M,W
Bluefield College, VA M,W
Bluefield State College, WV M,W
Boise State University, ID M,W
Boston College, MA M,W
Bowling Green State University, OH M,W
Bradley University, IL M,W
Brenau University, GA W
Brevard College, NC M,W
Brewton-Parker College, GA M,W
Brigham Young University, UT M,W
Bryan College, TN M,W
Bryant University, RI M,W
Bucknell University, PA M,W
Butler University, IN M,W
California Baptist University, CA M,W
California Polytechnic State University, San Luis Obispo, CA M,W
California State Polytechnic University, Pomona, CA M,W
California State University, Bakersfield, CA M
California State University, Chico, CA M,W
California State University, Fresno, CA M,W
California State University, Fullerton, CA M,W
California State University, Long Beach, CA M,W
California State University, Los Angeles, CA M,W
California State University, Northridge, CA M,W
California State University, Sacramento, CA M,W
California State University, San Bernardino, CA M,W
Campbellsville University, KY M,W
Canisius College, NY M,W
Carroll College, MT M,W
Carson-Newman College, TN M,W
Catawba College, NC M,W
Cedarville University, OH M,W
Central Connecticut State University, CT M,W
Central Methodist University, MO M,W
Central Michigan University, MI M,W
Chaminade University of Honolulu, HI M
Chestnut Hill College, PA M,W
Christian Brothers University, TN M,W
Clarion University of Pennsylvania, PA M,W
Clarke College, IA M,W
Clayton State University, GA M,W
Clemson University, SC M,W
Cleveland State University, OH M,W
Coastal Carolina University, SC M,W
Colgate University, NY M,W
College of Charleston, SC M,W
The College of Idaho, ID M,W
College of Saint Mary, NE W
College of the Holy Cross, MA M,W
College of the Ozarks, MO M,W
The College of William and Mary, VA M,W
Colorado School of Mines, CO M,W
Colorado State University, CO M,W
Colorado State University–Pueblo, CO M,W
Columbia College, MO M,W
Columbus State University, GA M,W
Concordia University, OR M,W
Concordia University, Nebraska, NE M,W
Concordia University, St. Paul, MN M,W
Concord University, WV M,W
Coppin State University, MD M,W
Corban College, OR M,W
Covenant College, GA M,W
Creighton University, NE M,W
Culver-Stockton College, MO M,W
Daemen College, NY M,W
Dakota State University, SD M,W
Dallas Baptist University, TX M
Dana College, NE M,W
Davenport University, MI M,W
Davidson College, NC M,W
Delta State University, MS M,W
DePaul University, IL M,W
Dillard University, LA M,W
Dixie State College of Utah, UT M,W
Doane College, NE M,W
Dominican College, NY M,W
Dominican University of California, CA M,W
Dordt College, IA M,W
Dowling College, NY M,W
Drake University, IA M,W
Drury University, MO M,W
Duke University, NC M,W
Duquesne University, PA M,W
Eastern Illinois University, IL M,W
Eastern Michigan University, MI M,W
Eastern Washington University, WA M,W
East Tennessee State University, TN M,W
Edinboro University of Pennsylvania, PA M,W
Elon University, NC M,W
Embry-Riddle Aeronautical University, FL M
Emmanuel College, GA M,W
Emporia State University, KS M,W
Evangel University, MO M,W
The Evergreen State College, WA M,W
Fairfield University, CT M,W
Fairleigh Dickinson University, Metropolitan Campus, NJ M,W
Fairmont State University, WV M,W
Faulkner University, AL M
Felician College, NJ M,W
Ferris State University, MI M,W
Flagler College, FL M,W
Florida Atlantic University, FL M,W
Florida College, FL M
Florida Gulf Coast University, FL M,W
Florida Institute of Technology, FL M,W
Florida International University, FL M,W
Florida State University, FL M,W
Fort Hays State University, KS M,W
Fort Lewis College, CO M,W
Fort Valley State University, GA M,W
Francis Marion University, SC M,W
Franklin Pierce University, NH M,W
Freed-Hardeman University, TN M,W
Furman University, SC M,W
Gannon University, PA M,W
Gardner-Webb University, NC M,W
George Mason University, VA M,W
Georgetown College, KY M,W
Georgetown University, DC M,W
The George Washington University, DC M,W
Georgia College & State University, GA M,W
Georgia Institute of Technology, GA M,W
Georgian Court University, NJ W
Georgia Southern University, GA M,W
Georgia Southwestern State University, GA M,W
Georgia State University, GA M,W
Glenville State College, WV M,W
Gonzaga University, WA M,W
Grace College, IN M,W
Graceland University, IA M,W
Grand Valley State University, MI M,W
Grand View University, IA M,W
Hampton University, VA M,W
Harding University, AR M,W
Hawai'i Pacific University, HI M,W
Henderson State University, AR M,W
Hofstra University, NY M,W
Holy Family University, PA M,W
Hope International University, CA M,W
Houghton College, NY M,W
Houston Baptist University, TX M,W
Humboldt State University, CA M,W
Huntington University, IN M,W
Idaho State University, ID M,W
Illinois Institute of Technology, IL M,W
Illinois State University, IL M,W
Indiana State University, IN M,W
Indiana University Bloomington, IN M,W

Indiana University of Pennsylvania, PA	M,W
Indiana University–Purdue University Fort Wayne, IN	M,W
Indiana University–Purdue University Indianapolis, IN	M,W
Indiana University South Bend, IN	M,W
Indiana University Southeast, IN	M,W
Inter American University of Puerto Rico, Arecibo Campus, PR	M
Inter American University of Puerto Rico, Guayama Campus, PR	M,W
Iona College, NY	M,W
Iowa State University of Science and Technology, IA	M,W
Jacksonville University, FL	M,W
James Madison University, VA	M,W
Jamestown College, ND	M,W
John Brown University, AR	M,W
Johnson C. Smith University, NC	M,W
Judson College, AL	W
Kansas State University, KS	M,W
Kennesaw State University, GA	M,W
Kent State University, OH	M,W
Kentucky State University, KY	M,W
Kentucky Wesleyan College, KY	M,W
Kutztown University of Pennsylvania, PA	M,W
Lamar University, TX	M,W
Lambuth University, TN	M,W
Lane College, TN	M,W
Lee University, TN	M,W
Lehigh University, PA	M,W
Le Moyne College, NY	M,W
Lewis-Clark State College, ID	M,W
Liberty University, VA	M,W
Limestone College, SC	M,W
Lincoln Memorial University, TN	M,W
Lindenwood University, MO	M,W
Lindsey Wilson College, KY	M,W
Lipscomb University, TN	M,W
Lock Haven University of Pennsylvania, PA	M,W
Long Island University, Brooklyn Campus, NY	M,W
Long Island University, C.W. Post Campus, NY	M,W
Longwood University, VA	M,W
Louisiana State University and Agricultural and Mechanical College, LA	M,W
Loyola University Chicago, IL	M,W
Loyola University Maryland, MD	M,W
Loyola University New Orleans, LA	M,W
Lubbock Christian University, TX	M,W
Lyon College, AR	M,W
Malone University, OH	M,W
Marian College, IN	M,W
Marquette University, WI	M,W
The Master's College and Seminary, CA	M,W
Mayville State University, ND	M,W
McKendree University, IL	M,W
Mercer University, GA	M,W
Mercyhurst College, PA	M,W
Merrimack College, MA	M,W
Mesa State College, CO	M,W
Metropolitan State College of Denver, CO	M,W
Miami University, OH	M,W
Michigan State University, MI	M,W
Michigan Technological University, MI	M,W
MidAmerica Nazarene University, KS	M,W
Midway College, KY	W
Millersville University of Pennsylvania, PA	M,W
Milligan College, TN	M,W
Minnesota State University Mankato, MN	M,W
Minot State University, ND	M,W
Mississippi State University, MS	M,W
Missouri Baptist University, MO	M,W
Missouri Southern State University, MO	M,W
Missouri State University, MO	M,W
Missouri University of Science and Technology, MO	M,W
Missouri Western State University, MO	M,W
Molloy College, NY	M,W
Monmouth University, NJ	M,W
Montana State University, MT	M,W
Montana State University–Billings, MT	M,W
Montana Tech of The University of Montana, MT	M,W
Mountain State University, WV	M
Mount Marty College, SD	M,W
Mount Mercy College, IA	M,W
Mount Olive College, NC	M,W
Mount St. Mary's University, MD	M,W
Mount Vernon Nazarene University, OH	M,W
Murray State University, KY	M,W
Newberry College, SC	M,W
New Jersey Institute of Technology, NJ	M,W
Newman University, KS	M,W
New Mexico State University, NM	M,W
Niagara University, NY	M,W
Nicholls State University, LA	M,W
North Carolina State University, NC	M,W
North Dakota State University, ND	M,W
Northeastern State University, OK	M,W
Northeastern University, MA	M,W
Northern Arizona University, AZ	M,W
Northern Kentucky University, KY	M,W
Northern Michigan University, MI	M,W
Northern State University, SD	M,W
North Greenville University, SC	M,W
Northwestern State University of Louisiana, LA	M,W
Northwestern University, IL	M,W
Northwest Missouri State University, MO	M,W
Northwest University, WA	M,W
Northwood University, MI	M,W
Notre Dame de Namur University, CA	M,W
Nova Southeastern University, FL	M,W
Oakland University, MI	M,W
The Ohio State University, OH	M,W
Ohio University, OH	M,W
Ohio Valley University, WV	M,W
Oklahoma Baptist University, OK	M,W
Oklahoma Christian University, OK	M,W
Oklahoma City University, OK	M,W
Oklahoma Panhandle State University, OK	M,W
Oklahoma State University, OK	M,W
Old Dominion University, VA	M,W
Olivet Nazarene University, IL	M,W
Oral Roberts University, OK	M,W
Oregon Institute of Technology, OR	M
Oregon State University, OR	M,W
Ouachita Baptist University, AR	M,W
Pace University, NY	M,W
Palm Beach Atlantic University, FL	M,W
Penn State University Park, PA	M,W
Pepperdine University, CA	M,W
Philadelphia University, PA	M,W
Pittsburg State University, KS	M,W
Point Loma Nazarene University, CA	M,W
Point Park University, PA	M,W
Portland State University, OR	M,W
Presbyterian College, SC	M,W
Providence College, RI	M,W
Purdue University, IN	M,W
Purdue University Calumet, IN	M,W
Purdue University North Central, IN	M
Quinnipiac University, CT	M,W
Radford University, VA	M,W
Reinhardt College, GA	M,W
Rider University, NJ	M,W
Robert Morris College, IL	M,W
Robert Morris University, PA	M,W
Roberts Wesleyan College, NY	M,W
Rockhurst University, MO	M,W
Rollins College, FL	M,W
Sacred Heart University, CT	M,W
Saginaw Valley State University, MI	M,W
St. Ambrose University, IA	M,W
St. Andrews Presbyterian College, NC	M,W
St. Cloud State University, MN	M,W
St. Edward's University, TX	M,W
Saint Francis University, PA	M,W
St. John's University, NY	M,W
Saint Joseph's College, IN	M,W
Saint Joseph's University, PA	M,W
Saint Leo University, FL	M,W
Saint Louis University, MO	M,W
Saint Martin's University, WA	M,W
Saint Mary's College of California, CA	M,W
St. Mary's University, TX	M,W
Saint Michael's College, VT	M,W
Saint Xavier University, IL	M
Samford University, AL	M,W
Sam Houston State University, TX	M,W
San Diego State University, CA	M,W
San Francisco State University, CA	M,W
San Jose State University, CA	M,W
Santa Clara University, CA	M,W
Savannah College of Art and Design, GA	M,W
Seattle Pacific University, WA	M,W
Seton Hill University, PA	M,W
Shepherd University, WV	M,W
Shippensburg University of Pennsylvania, PA	M,W
Shorter College, GA	M,W
Silver Lake College, WI	M,W
Simpson University, CA	M,W
Slippery Rock University of Pennsylvania, PA	M,W
Sonoma State University, CA	M,W

South Carolina State University, SC M,W
South Dakota School of Mines and Technology, SD M,W
South Dakota State University, SD M,W
Southeastern Louisiana University, LA M,W
Southeastern Oklahoma State University, OK M,W
Southeast Missouri State University, MO M,W
Southern Arkansas University–Magnolia, AR M,W
Southern Connecticut State University, CT M,W
Southern Illinois University Carbondale, IL M,W
Southern Illinois University Edwardsville, IL M,W
Southern Methodist University, TX M,W
Southern Nazarene University, OK M,W
Southern New Hampshire University, NH M,W
Southern Oregon University, OR M,W
Southern Polytechnic State University, GA M,W
Southern Utah University, UT M,W
Southwest Baptist University, MO M,W
Southwestern College, KS M,W
Southwestern Oklahoma State University, OK M,W
Southwest Minnesota State University, MN M,W
Spring Arbor University, MI M,W
Spring Hill College, AL M,W
Stanford University, CA M,W
State University of New York at Binghamton, NY M,W
Stephen F. Austin State University, TX M,W
Stephens College, MO W
Stetson University, FL M,W
Stonehill College, MA M,W
Stony Brook University, State University of New York, NY M,W
Tarleton State University, TX M,W
Taylor University, IN M,W
Temple University, PA M,W
Tennessee Technological University, TN M,W
Texas A&M University, TX M,W
Texas Christian University, TX M,W
Texas State University–San Marcos, TX M,W
Texas Tech University, TX M,W
Tiffin University, OH M,W
Towson University, MD M,W
Trevecca Nazarene University, TN M,W
Trinity Christian College, IL M,W
Trinity International University, IL M,W
Troy University, AL M,W
Truman State University, MO M,W
Tuskegee University, AL M,W
Union College, KY M,W
Union University, TN M,W
University at Albany, State University of New York, NY M,W
University at Buffalo, the State University of New York, NY M,W
The University of Akron, OH M,W
The University of Alabama, AL M,W
The University of Alabama at Birmingham, AL M,W
The University of Alabama in Huntsville, AL M,W
University of Alaska Fairbanks, AK M,W
The University of Arizona, AZ M,W
University of Arkansas, AR M,W
University of Bridgeport, CT M,W
University of California, Davis, CA M,W
University of California, Irvine, CA M,W
University of California, Los Angeles, CA M,W
University of California, Riverside, CA M,W
University of Central Florida, FL M,W
University of Central Missouri, MO M,W
University of Central Oklahoma, OK M,W
University of Cincinnati, OH M,W
University of Colorado at Boulder, CO M,W
University of Colorado at Colorado Springs, CO M,W
University of Connecticut, CT M,W
University of Dayton, OH M,W
University of Delaware, DE M,W
University of Denver, CO M,W
University of Evansville, IN M,W
The University of Findlay, OH M,W
University of Florida, FL M,W
University of Georgia, GA M,W
University of Hartford, CT M,W
University of Hawaii at Manoa, HI M,W
University of Houston, TX M,W
University of Idaho, ID M,W
University of Illinois at Chicago, IL M,W
University of Illinois at Springfield, IL M,W
The University of Iowa, IA M,W
The University of Kansas, KS M,W
University of Kentucky, KY M,W
University of Louisiana at Monroe, LA M,W
University of Louisville, KY M,W
University of Maine, ME M,W
The University of Maine at Augusta, ME M,W
University of Mary, ND M,W
University of Maryland, Baltimore County, MD M,W
University of Maryland, College Park, MD M,W
University of Maryland Eastern Shore, MD M,W
University of Massachusetts Amherst, MA M,W
University of Massachusetts Lowell, MA M,W
University of Memphis, TN M,W
University of Miami, FL M,W
University of Michigan, MI M,W
University of Michigan–Dearborn, MI M,W
University of Minnesota, Crookston, MN M,W
University of Minnesota, Duluth, MN M,W
University of Minnesota, Twin Cities Campus, MN M,W
University of Mississippi, MS M,W
University of Missouri–Columbia, MO M,W
University of Missouri–Kansas City, MO M,W
University of Missouri–St. Louis, MO M,W
University of Mobile, AL M,W
The University of Montana, MT M,W
The University of Montana Western, MT M,W
University of Montevallo, AL M,W
University of Nebraska at Kearney, NE M,W
University of Nebraska at Omaha, NE M,W
University of Nebraska–Lincoln, NE M,W
University of Nevada, Las Vegas, NV M,W
University of Nevada, Reno, NV M,W
University of New Hampshire, NH M,W
University of New Haven, CT M,W
University of New Orleans, LA M,W
University of North Alabama, AL M,W
The University of North Carolina at Asheville, NC M,W
The University of North Carolina at Chapel Hill, NC M,W
The University of North Carolina at Greensboro, NC M,W
The University of North Carolina at Pembroke, NC M,W
The University of North Carolina Wilmington, NC M,W
University of North Dakota, ND M,W
University of Northern Colorado, CO M,W
University of Northern Iowa, IA M,W
University of North Florida, FL M,W
University of North Texas, TX M,W
University of Notre Dame, IN M,W
University of Oklahoma, OK M,W
University of Oregon, OR M,W
University of Pittsburgh, PA M,W
University of Pittsburgh at Johnstown, PA M,W
University of Portland, OR M,W
University of Puerto Rico, Río Piedras, PR M,W
University of Rhode Island, RI M,W
University of Richmond, VA M,W
University of Saint Francis, IN M,W
University of San Diego, CA M,W
University of Science and Arts of Oklahoma, OK M,W
University of South Alabama, AL M,W
University of South Carolina, SC M,W
University of South Carolina Aiken, SC M,W
University of South Carolina Upstate, SC M,W
The University of South Dakota, SD M,W
University of Southern California, CA M,W
University of Southern Indiana, IN M,W
University of Southern Mississippi, MS M,W
University of South Florida, FL M,W
The University of Tampa, FL M,W
The University of Tennessee, TN M,W
The University of Tennessee at Chattanooga, TN M,W
The University of Tennessee at Martin, TN M,W
The University of Texas at Arlington, TX M,W
The University of Texas at El Paso, TX M,W
The University of Texas at San Antonio, TX M,W

The University of Texas of the Permian Basin, TX M,W
The University of Texas–Pan American, TX M,W
University of the Cumberlands, KY M,W
University of the Incarnate Word, TX M,W
University of the Pacific, CA M,W
University of the Southwest, NM M,W
University of Tulsa, OK M,W
University of Utah, UT M,W
University of Vermont, VT M,W
University of Virginia, VA M,W
The University of Virginia's College at Wise, VA M,W
University of West Florida, FL M,W
University of West Georgia, GA M,W
University of Wisconsin–Green Bay, WI M,W
University of Wisconsin–Madison, WI M,W
University of Wisconsin–Milwaukee, WI M,W
University of Wisconsin–Parkside, WI M,W
University of Wyoming, WY M,W
Ursuline College, OH W
Utah State University, UT M,W
Utah Valley University, UT M,W
Valdosta State University, GA M,W
Valley City State University, ND M,W
Valparaiso University, IN M,W
Vanderbilt University, TN M,W
Vanguard University of Southern California, CA M,W
Villanova University, PA M,W
Virginia Commonwealth University, VA M,W
Virginia Intermont College, VA M,W
Virginia Military Institute, VA M
Wagner College, NY M,W
Wake Forest University, NC M,W
Warner Pacific College, OR M,W
Washington State University, WA M,W
Wayland Baptist University, TX M,W
Wayne State University, MI M,W
Webber International University, FL M,W
Weber State University, UT M,W
West Chester University of Pennsylvania, PA M,W
Western Carolina University, NC M,W
Western Illinois University, IL M,W
Western Kentucky University, KY M,W
Western Michigan University, MI M,W
Western Oregon University, OR M,W
Western Washington University, WA M,W
West Liberty State University, WV M,W
Westminster College, UT M,W
West Virginia University, WV M,W
West Virginia Wesleyan College, WV M,W
Wheeling Jesuit University, WV M,W
Wichita State University, KS M,W
Wingate University, NC M,W
Winona State University, MN M,W
Winthrop University, SC M,W
Wofford College, SC M,W
Wright State University, OH M,W
Xavier University, OH M,W
Xavier University of Louisiana, LA M,W
York College, NE M,W
Youngstown State University, OH M,W

Bowling

Adelphi University, NY W
Arkansas State University, AR W
Baker University, KS W
Bellarmine University, KY W
Fairleigh Dickinson University, Metropolitan Campus, NJ W
Hampton University, VA W
Johnson C. Smith University, NC W
Kutztown University of Pennsylvania, PA W
Lindenwood University, MO M,W
Lindsey Wilson College, KY M,W
McKendree University, IL M,W
Missouri Baptist University, MO M
Newman University, KS M,W
Robert Morris College, IL M,W
Sacred Heart University, CT W
Saginaw Valley State University, MI M
St. Ambrose University, IA M,W
South Carolina State University, SC W
University of Nebraska–Lincoln, NE W
Webber International University, FL M,W

Cheerleading

Adelphi University, NY W
Arkansas Tech University, AR M,W
Auburn University Montgomery, AL M,W
Austin Peay State University, TN M,W
Avila University, MO W
Baker University, KS M,W
Benedictine College, KS M,W
Bethel College, IN M,W
Brevard College, NC W
Brewton-Parker College, GA M,W
Brigham Young University, UT M,W
California Baptist University, CA M,W
Campbellsville University, KY M,W
Clayton State University, GA W
College of Charleston, SC M,W
Culver-Stockton College, MO M,W
Delta State University, MS M,W
Dixie State College of Utah, UT M,W
Drake University, IA M,W
Drury University, MO M,W
Emporia State University, KS M,W
Freed-Hardeman University, TN W
Gardner-Webb University, NC M,W
George Mason University, VA M,W
Georgetown College, KY W
Georgia Institute of Technology, GA M,W
Grace College, IN M,W
Hawai'i Pacific University, HI M,W
Hofstra University, NY M,W
Hope International University, CA M,W
Houston Baptist University, TX M,W
Kennesaw State University, GA W
Liberty University, VA M,W
Lindenwood University, MO M,W
Lindsey Wilson College, KY M,W
Marian College, IN M,W
McKendree University, IL M,W
Metropolitan State College of Denver, CO M,W
MidAmerica Nazarene University, KS M,W
Mississippi State University, MS M,W
Montana State University, MT M,W
Newberry College, SC W
Northern Arizona University, AZ M,W
Northern Kentucky University, KY M,W
North Greenville University, SC M,W
Northwest Missouri State University, MO M,W
Northwood University, MI M,W
Oklahoma City University, OK M,W
Oklahoma Panhandle State University, OK W
Old Dominion University, VA M,W
Olivet Nazarene University, IL M,W
Presbyterian College, SC M,W
Robert Morris College, IL W
St. Ambrose University, IA M,W
Saint Joseph's College, IN M,W
Southeastern Louisiana University, LA M,W
Southeast Missouri State University, MO M,W
Southern Methodist University, TX M,W
Southern Nazarene University, OK M,W
Southwestern College, KS M,W
Tarleton State University, TX M,W
Temple University, PA M,W
Tennessee Technological University, TN M,W
Tiffin University, OH M,W
Union College, KY M,W
Union University, TN W
The University of Alabama, AL M,W
The University of Alabama in Huntsville, AL M,W
University of Central Florida, FL M,W
University of Delaware, DE M,W
University of Hawaii at Manoa, HI M,W
University of Louisiana at Monroe, LA M,W
University of Louisville, KY M,W
University of Maryland, College Park, MD W
University of Memphis, TN M,W
University of Michigan, MI M,W
University of Mississippi, MS M,W
University of Mobile, AL W
University of Nevada, Las Vegas, NV M,W
The University of North Carolina Wilmington, NC W
University of Oklahoma, OK M,W
University of Oregon, OR W
University of Saint Francis, IN M,W
University of Science and Arts of Oklahoma, OK M,W
University of South Carolina Aiken, SC M,W
The University of Tennessee, TN M,W
The University of Texas of the Permian Basin, TX W
University of the Cumberlands, KY M,W
University of the Incarnate Word, TX W
University of Utah, UT M,W
University of West Georgia, GA M,W
University of Wyoming, WY M,W
Wayland Baptist University, TX M,W
Weber State University, UT M,W
West Chester University of Pennsylvania, PA W
West Virginia University, WV M,W

Crew

Boston College, MA W
California State University, Sacramento, CA M,W
Clemson University, SC W

Athletic Grants for Undergraduates

Crew

Creighton University, NE W
Dowling College, NY M,W
Duke University, NC W
Duquesne University, PA W
Eastern Michigan University, MI W
Fairfield University, CT M,W
Florida Institute of Technology, FL M,W
George Mason University, VA W
The George Washington University, DC M,W
Indiana University Bloomington, IN W
Jacksonville University, FL M,W
Kansas State University, KS W
Loyola University Maryland, MD M,W
Mercyhurst College, PA M,W
Michigan State University, MI W
Murray State University, KY M,W
Northeastern University, MA M,W
Nova Southeastern University, FL W
Old Dominion University, VA W
Robert Morris University, PA W
Sacred Heart University, CT W
Saint Joseph's University, PA M,W
Southern Methodist University, TX W
Stanford University, CA M,W
Stetson University, FL M,W
Temple University, PA M,W
University at Buffalo, the State University of New York, NY W
The University of Alabama, AL W
University of California, Davis, CA W
University of California, Irvine, CA M,W
University of Delaware, DE W
The University of Iowa, IA W
The University of Kansas, KS W
University of Louisville, KY W
University of Massachusetts Amherst, MA W
University of Michigan, MI M,W
The University of North Carolina at Chapel Hill, NC W
University of Notre Dame, IN W
University of Oklahoma, OK W
University of Rhode Island, RI W
University of San Diego, CA M,W
University of Southern California, CA W
The University of Tampa, FL W
The University of Tennessee, TN W
University of Tulsa, OK W
University of Virginia, VA W
Villanova University, PA W
Washington State University, WA W
Western Washington University, WA M,W
West Virginia University, WV W

Cross-Country Running

Abilene Christian University, TX M,W
Academy of Art University, CA M,W
Adams State College, CO M,W
Adelphi University, NY M,W
Alabama Agricultural and Mechanical University, AL M,W
Alcorn State University, MS M,W
Alderson-Broaddus College, WV M,W
American University, DC M,W
Angelo State University, TX M,W
Appalachian State University, NC M,W
Arizona State University, AZ M,W
Arkansas State University, AR M,W
Arkansas Tech University, AR W
Asbury College, KY M,W
Ashland University, OH M,W
Auburn University, AL M,W
Augustana College, SD M,W
Augusta State University, GA M,W
Austin Peay State University, TN M,W
Azusa Pacific University, CA M,W
Baker University, KS M,W
Ball State University, IN M,W
Barton College, NC M,W
Baylor University, TX M,W
Belhaven College, MS M,W
Bellarmine University, KY M,W
Belmont Abbey College, NC M,W
Belmont University, TN M,W
Benedictine College, KS M,W
Bentley University, MA M,W
Bethany College, KS M,W
Bethel College, IN M,W
Bethel College, KS M,W
Biola University, CA M,W
Black Hills State University, SD M,W
Bloomfield College, NJ M,W
Bloomsburg University of Pennsylvania, PA M,W
Bluefield College, VA M,W
Bluefield State College, WV M,W
Boise State University, ID M,W
Boston College, MA M,W
Bowling Green State University, OH M,W
Bradley University, IL M,W
Brenau University, GA W
Brevard College, NC M,W
Brigham Young University, UT M,W
Bryan College, TN M,W
Bucknell University, PA W
Butler University, IN M,W
California Baptist University, CA M,W
California Polytechnic State University, San Luis Obispo, CA M,W
California State Polytechnic University, Pomona, CA M,W
California State University, Chico, CA M,W
California State University, Fresno, CA M,W
California State University, Fullerton, CA M,W
California State University, Long Beach, CA M,W
California State University, Los Angeles, CA W
California State University, Northridge, CA M,W
California State University, Sacramento, CA M,W
Campbellsville University, KY M,W
Canisius College, NY M,W
Carroll College, MT M,W
Carson-Newman College, TN M,W
Catawba College, NC M,W
Cedarville University, OH M,W
Central Connecticut State University, CT M,W
Central Methodist University, MO M,W
Central Michigan University, MI M,W
Chaminade University of Honolulu, HI M,W
Chestnut Hill College, PA M,W
Christian Brothers University, TN M,W
Clarion University of Pennsylvania, PA W
Clarke College, IA M,W
Clayton State University, GA M,W
Clemson University, SC M,W
Cleveland State University, OH W
Coastal Carolina University, SC M,W
College of Charleston, SC M,W
The College of Idaho, ID M,W
College of Saint Mary, NE W
The College of William and Mary, VA M,W
Colorado School of Mines, CO M,W
Colorado State University, CO M,W
Colorado State University–Pueblo, CO W
Columbus State University, GA M,W
Concordia University, OR M,W
Concordia University, Nebraska, NE M,W
Concordia University, St. Paul, MN M,W
Concord University, WV M,W
Coppin State University, MD M,W
Corban College, OR M,W
Covenant College, GA M,W
Creighton University, NE M,W
Culver-Stockton College, MO M,W
Daemen College, NY M,W
Dakota State University, SD M,W
Dallas Baptist University, TX W
Dana College, NE M,W
Davenport University, MI M,W
Davidson College, NC M,W
Delta State University, MS W
DePaul University, IL M,W
Dixie State College of Utah, UT M,W
Doane College, NE M,W
Dominican College, NY M,W
Dordt College, IA M,W
Dowling College, NY M,W
Drake University, IA M,W
Drury University, MO M,W
Duquesne University, PA M,W
Eastern Illinois University, IL M,W
Eastern Michigan University, MI M,W
Eastern Washington University, WA M,W
East Tennessee State University, TN M,W
Edinboro University of Pennsylvania, PA M,W
Elon University, NC M,W
Embry-Riddle Aeronautical University, FL M,W
Emporia State University, KS M,W
Evangel University, MO M,W
The Evergreen State College, WA M,W
Fairfield University, CT M,W
Fairleigh Dickinson University, Metropolitan Campus, NJ M,W
Felician College, NJ M,W
Ferris State University, MI M,W
Flagler College, FL M,W
Florida Gulf Coast University, FL M,W
Florida Institute of Technology, FL M,W
Florida International University, FL M,W
Florida State University, FL M,W
Fort Hays State University, KS M,W
Fort Lewis College, CO M,W
Francis Marion University, SC M,W
Furman University, SC M,W
Gannon University, PA M,W
Gardner-Webb University, NC M,W
George Mason University, VA M,W

Georgetown College, KY	M,W
Georgetown University, DC	M,W
The George Washington University, DC	M,W
Georgia College & State University, GA	M,W
Georgia Institute of Technology, GA	M,W
Georgian Court University, NJ	W
Georgia Southern University, GA	W
Georgia State University, GA	M,W
Glenville State College, WV	M,W
Grace College, IN	M,W
Graceland University, IA	M,W
Grand Valley State University, MI	M,W
Grand View University, IA	M,W
Hampton University, VA	M,W
Harding University, AR	M,W
Hawai'i Pacific University, HI	M,W
Henderson State University, AR	W
Hofstra University, NY	M,W
Holy Family University, PA	M,W
Houghton College, NY	M,W
Houston Baptist University, TX	M,W
Humboldt State University, CA	M,W
Huntington University, IN	M,W
Idaho State University, ID	M,W
Illinois Institute of Technology, IL	M,W
Illinois State University, IL	M,W
Indiana State University, IN	M,W
Indiana University Bloomington, IN	M,W
Indiana University of Pennsylvania, PA	M,W
Indiana University–Purdue University Fort Wayne, IN	M,W
Indiana University–Purdue University Indianapolis, IN	M,W
Inter American University of Puerto Rico, Guayama Campus, PR	M,W
Iona College, NY	M,W
Iowa State University of Science and Technology, IA	M,W
Jacksonville University, FL	W
James Madison University, VA	W
Jamestown College, ND	M,W
Johnson C. Smith University, NC	M,W
Kansas State University, KS	M,W
Kennesaw State University, GA	M,W
Kent State University, OH	M,W
Kentucky State University, KY	M,W
Kentucky Wesleyan College, KY	M,W
Kutztown University of Pennsylvania, PA	M,W
Lamar University, TX	M,W
Lee University, TN	M,W
Le Moyne College, NY	M,W
Lewis-Clark State College, ID	M,W
Liberty University, VA	M,W
Limestone College, SC	M,W
Lincoln Memorial University, TN	M,W
Lindenwood University, MO	M,W
Lindsey Wilson College, KY	M,W
Lipscomb University, TN	M,W
Lock Haven University of Pennsylvania, PA	M,W
Long Island University, Brooklyn Campus, NY	M,W
Long Island University, C.W. Post Campus, NY	M,W
Longwood University, VA	M,W
Louisiana State University and Agricultural and Mechanical College, LA	M,W
Loyola University Chicago, IL	M,W
Loyola University Maryland, MD	M,W
Lyon College, AR	M,W
Malone University, OH	M,W
Marian College, IN	M,W
Marquette University, WI	M,W
The Master's College and Seminary, CA	M,W
McKendree University, IL	M,W
Mercer University, GA	M,W
Mercyhurst College, PA	M,W
Merrimack College, MA	W
Mesa State College, CO	W
Miami University, OH	M,W
Michigan State University, MI	M,W
MidAmerica Nazarene University, KS	M,W
Millersville University of Pennsylvania, PA	M,W
Milligan College, TN	M,W
Minnesota State University Mankato, MN	M,W
Minot State University, ND	M,W
Mississippi State University, MS	M,W
Missouri Baptist University, MO	M,W
Missouri Southern State University, MO	M,W
Missouri State University, MO	W
Missouri University of Science and Technology, MO	M,W
Molloy College, NY	M,W
Monmouth University, NJ	M,W
Montana State University, MT	M,W
Montana State University–Billings, MT	M,W
Mount Marty College, SD	M,W
Mount Mercy College, IA	M,W
Mount Olive College, NC	M,W
Mount St. Mary's University, MD	M,W
Mount Vernon Nazarene University, OH	M,W
Murray State University, KY	M,W
Newberry College, SC	M,W
New Jersey Institute of Technology, NJ	M,W
Newman University, KS	M,W
New Mexico State University, NM	M,W
Niagara University, NY	M,W
Nicholls State University, LA	M,W
North Carolina State University, NC	M,W
North Dakota State University, ND	M,W
Northeastern University, MA	M,W
Northern Arizona University, AZ	M,W
Northern Kentucky University, KY	M,W
Northern Michigan University, MI	W
Northern State University, SD	M,W
North Greenville University, SC	M,W
Northwestern State University of Louisiana, LA	M,W
Northwestern University, IL	W
Northwest Missouri State University, MO	M,W
Northwest University, WA	M,W
Northwood University, MI	M,W
Northwood University, Texas Campus, TX	M,W
Notre Dame de Namur University, CA	M,W
Nova Southeastern University, FL	M,W
Oakland University, MI	M,W
The Ohio State University, OH	M,W
Ohio University, OH	M,W
Ohio Valley University, WV	M,W
Oklahoma Baptist University, OK	M,W
Oklahoma Christian University, OK	M,W
Oklahoma Panhandle State University, OK	M,W
Oklahoma State University, OK	M,W
Olivet Nazarene University, IL	M,W
Oral Roberts University, OK	M,W
Oregon Institute of Technology, OR	M,W
Ouachita Baptist University, AR	W
Pace University, NY	M,W
Palm Beach Atlantic University, FL	M,W
Penn State University Park, PA	M,W
Pepperdine University, CA	M,W
Pittsburg State University, KS	M,W
Point Loma Nazarene University, CA	M,W
Point Park University, PA	M,W
Portland State University, OR	M,W
Presbyterian College, SC	M,W
Providence College, RI	M,W
Purdue University, IN	M,W
Quinnipiac University, CT	M,W
Radford University, VA	M,W
Rider University, NJ	M,W
Robert Morris College, IL	M,W
Roberts Wesleyan College, NY	M,W
Sacred Heart University, CT	M,W
Saginaw Valley State University, MI	M,W
St. Ambrose University, IA	M,W
St. Andrews Presbyterian College, NC	M,W
St. Cloud State University, MN	M
St. Edward's University, TX	M,W
Saint Francis University, PA	M,W
St. John's University, NY	W
Saint Joseph's College, IN	M,W
Saint Joseph's University, PA	M,W
Saint Leo University, FL	M,W
Saint Louis University, MO	M,W
Saint Martin's University, WA	M,W
Saint Mary's College of California, CA	M,W
St. Thomas University, FL	M,W
Saint Xavier University, IL	W
Samford University, AL	M,W
Sam Houston State University, TX	M,W
San Diego State University, CA	W
San Francisco State University, CA	M,W
San Jose State University, CA	M,W
Santa Clara University, CA	M,W
Savannah College of Art and Design, GA	M,W
Seattle Pacific University, WA	M,W
Seton Hill University, PA	M,W
Shippensburg University of Pennsylvania, PA	M,W
Shorter College, GA	M,W
Silver Lake College, WI	M,W
Simpson University, CA	M,W
Slippery Rock University of Pennsylvania, PA	M,W
Sonoma State University, CA	M
South Carolina State University, SC	M,W
South Dakota School of Mines and Technology, SD	M,W
South Dakota State University, SD	M,W

Southeastern Louisiana University, LA M,W
Southeastern Oklahoma State University, OK W
Southeast Missouri State University, MO M,W
Southern Arkansas University–Magnolia, AR W
Southern Connecticut State University, CT M,W
Southern Illinois University Carbondale, IL M,W
Southern Illinois University Edwardsville, IL M,W
Southern Methodist University, TX W
Southern Nazarene University, OK M,W
Southern New Hampshire University, NH M,W
Southern Oregon University, OR M,W
Southwest Baptist University, MO M,W
Southwestern College, KS M,W
Southwestern Oklahoma State University, OK W
Spring Arbor University, MI M,W
Spring Hill College, AL M,W
Stanford University, CA M,W
State University of New York at Binghamton, NY M,W
Stephen F. Austin State University, TX M,W
Stephens College, MO W
Stetson University, FL M,W
Stonehill College, MA M,W
Stony Brook University, State University of New York, NY M,W
Tarleton State University, TX M,W
Taylor University, IN M,W
Tennessee Technological University, TN M,W
Texas A&M University, TX M,W
Texas Christian University, TX M,W
Texas State University–San Marcos, TX M,W
Texas Tech University, TX M,W
Tiffin University, OH M,W
Towson University, MD M,W
Trinity Christian College, IL M,W
Troy University, AL M,W
Truman State University, MO M,W
Union College, KY M,W
Union University, TN W
University at Albany, State University of New York, NY M,W
University at Buffalo, the State University of New York, NY M,W
The University of Akron, OH M,W
The University of Alabama, AL M,W
The University of Alabama at Birmingham, AL W
The University of Alabama in Huntsville, AL M,W
University of Alaska Fairbanks, AK M,W
The University of Arizona, AZ M,W
University of Arkansas, AR M,W
University of California, Davis, CA M,W
University of California, Irvine, CA M,W
University of California, Los Angeles, CA M,W
University of California, Riverside, CA M,W
University of Central Florida, FL M,W
University of Central Missouri, MO M,W
University of Central Oklahoma, OK M,W
University of Cincinnati, OH M,W
University of Colorado at Boulder, CO M,W
University of Colorado at Colorado Springs, CO M,W
University of Connecticut, CT M,W
University of Dayton, OH M,W
University of Evansville, IN M,W
The University of Findlay, OH M,W
University of Florida, FL M,W
University of Georgia, GA M,W
University of Hartford, CT M,W
University of Hawaii at Manoa, HI W
University of Houston, TX M,W
University of Idaho, ID M,W
University of Illinois at Chicago, IL M,W
The University of Iowa, IA M,W
The University of Kansas, KS M,W
University of Kentucky, KY M,W
University of Louisiana at Monroe, LA M,W
University of Louisville, KY M,W
University of Maine, ME M,W
University of Mary, ND M,W
University of Maryland, Baltimore County, MD M,W
University of Maryland, College Park, MD M,W
University of Massachusetts Amherst, MA M,W
University of Massachusetts Lowell, MA M,W
University of Memphis, TN M,W
University of Miami, FL M,W
University of Michigan, MI M,W
University of Minnesota, Duluth, MN M,W
University of Minnesota, Twin Cities Campus, MN M,W
University of Mississippi, MS M,W
University of Missouri–Columbia, MO M,W
University of Missouri–Kansas City, MO M,W
University of Mobile, AL M,W
The University of Montana, MT M,W
University of Nebraska at Kearney, NE M,W
University of Nebraska at Omaha, NE W
University of Nebraska–Lincoln, NE M,W
University of Nevada, Las Vegas, NV W
University of Nevada, Reno, NV W
University of New Hampshire, NH M,W
University of New Haven, CT M,W
University of North Alabama, AL M,W
The University of North Carolina at Asheville, NC M,W
The University of North Carolina at Chapel Hill, NC M,W
The University of North Carolina at Greensboro, NC M,W
The University of North Carolina at Pembroke, NC M,W
The University of North Carolina Wilmington, NC M,W
University of Northern Colorado, CO W
University of Northern Iowa, IA M,W
University of North Florida, FL M,W
University of North Texas, TX M,W
University of Notre Dame, IN M,W
University of Oklahoma, OK M,W
University of Oregon, OR M,W
University of Pittsburgh, PA M,W
University of Portland, OR M,W
University of Puerto Rico, Río Piedras, PR M,W
University of Rhode Island, RI M,W
University of Richmond, VA W
University of Saint Francis, IN M,W
University of San Diego, CA M,W
University of South Alabama, AL M,W
University of South Carolina, SC W
University of South Carolina Aiken, SC W
University of South Carolina Upstate, SC M,W
The University of South Dakota, SD M,W
University of Southern California, CA M,W
University of Southern Indiana, IN M,W
University of Southern Mississippi, MS W
University of South Florida, FL M,W
The University of Tampa, FL M,W
The University of Tennessee, TN M,W
The University of Tennessee at Chattanooga, TN M,W
The University of Tennessee at Martin, TN M,W
The University of Texas at Arlington, TX M,W
The University of Texas at El Paso, TX M,W
The University of Texas at San Antonio, TX M,W
The University of Texas of the Permian Basin, TX M,W
The University of Texas–Pan American, TX M,W
University of the Cumberlands, KY M,W
University of the Incarnate Word, TX M,W
University of the Pacific, CA W
University of the Southwest, NM M,W
University of Tulsa, OK M,W
University of Utah, UT W
University of Vermont, VT M,W
University of Virginia, VA M,W
The University of Virginia's College at Wise, VA M,W
University of West Florida, FL M,W
University of West Georgia, GA M,W
University of Wisconsin–Green Bay, WI M,W
University of Wisconsin–Madison, WI M,W
University of Wisconsin–Milwaukee, WI M,W
University of Wisconsin–Parkside, WI M,W
University of Wyoming, WY M,W
Ursuline College, OH W
Utah State University, UT M,W
Utah Valley University, UT M,W
Valdosta State University, GA M,W
Valparaiso University, IN M,W
Vanderbilt University, TN M,W
Vanguard University of Southern California, CA M,W
Villanova University, PA M,W
Virginia Commonwealth University, VA M,W
Virginia Military Institute, VA M,W

Wagner College, NY M,W
Wake Forest University, NC M,W
Warner Pacific College, OR M,W
Washington State University, WA M,W
Wayland Baptist University, TX M,W
Wayne State University, MI M,W
Webber International University, FL M,W
Weber State University, UT M,W
West Chester University of Pennsylvania, PA M,W
Western Carolina University, NC M,W
Western Illinois University, IL M,W
Western Kentucky University, KY M,W
Western Michigan University, MI W
Western Oregon University, OR M,W
Western Washington University, WA M,W
West Liberty State University, WV M,W
West Virginia University, WV W
West Virginia Wesleyan College, WV M,W
Wheeling Jesuit University, WV M,W
Wichita State University, KS M,W
Wingate University, NC M
Winona State University, MN W
Winthrop University, SC M,W
Wofford College, SC M,W
Wright State University, OH M,W
Xavier University, OH M,W
Youngstown State University, OH M,W

Equestrian Sports

Auburn University, AL W
Baylor University, TX W
California State University, Fresno, CA W
Midway College, KY W
Murray State University, KY M,W
Oklahoma Panhandle State University, OK W
Oklahoma State University, OK W
Sacred Heart University, CT W
St. Andrews Presbyterian College, NC M,W
Savannah College of Art and Design, GA M,W
Seton Hill University, PA M,W
Southern Methodist University, TX W
Southwestern Oklahoma State University, OK M,W
Stonehill College, MA W
Texas A&M University, TX W
Texas Christian University, TX W
Tiffin University, OH M,W
University of Georgia, GA W
University of South Carolina, SC W
The University of Tennessee at Martin, TN W
Virginia Intermont College, VA M,W

Fencing

California State University, Fullerton, CA M,W
Cleveland State University, OH M,W
Fairleigh Dickinson University, Metropolitan Campus, NJ W
New Jersey Institute of Technology, NJ M,W
Northwestern University, IL W
The Ohio State University, OH M,W
Penn State University Park, PA M,W
Sacred Heart University, CT W
St. John's University, NY M,W
Stanford University, CA M,W
Temple University, PA W
University of Notre Dame, IN M,W
Wayne State University, MI M,W

Field Hockey

American University, DC W
Appalachian State University, NC W
Ball State University, IN W
Bellarmine University, KY W
Bentley University, MA W
Bloomsburg University of Pennsylvania, PA W
Boston College, MA W
Catawba College, NC W
Central Michigan University, MI W
Colgate University, NY W
College of the Holy Cross, MA M
The College of William and Mary, VA W
Davidson College, NC W
Duke University, NC W
Fairfield University, CT W
Franklin Pierce University, NH W
Hofstra University, NY W
Houghton College, NY W
Indiana University of Pennsylvania, PA W
James Madison University, VA W
Kent State University, OH W
Kutztown University of Pennsylvania, PA W
Lindenwood University, MO W
Lock Haven University of Pennsylvania, PA W
Long Island University, C.W. Post Campus, NY W
Longwood University, VA W
Mercyhurst College, PA W
Merrimack College, MA W
Miami University, OH W
Michigan State University, MI W
Millersville University of Pennsylvania, PA W
Missouri State University, MO W
Monmouth University, NJ W
Northeastern University, MA W
Northwestern University, IL W
The Ohio State University, OH W
Ohio University, OH W
Old Dominion University, VA W
Penn State University Park, PA W
Philadelphia University, PA W
Providence College, RI W
Quinnipiac University, CT W
Radford University, VA W
Rider University, NJ W
Robert Morris University, PA W
Sacred Heart University, CT W
Saint Francis University, PA W
Saint Joseph's University, PA W
Saint Louis University, MO W
Seton Hill University, PA W
Shippensburg University of Pennsylvania, PA W
Slippery Rock University of Pennsylvania, PA W
Southern Connecticut State University, CT W
Stanford University, CA W
Stonehill College, MA W
Temple University, PA W
Towson University, MD W
University at Albany, State University of New York, NY W
University of Connecticut, CT W
University of Delaware, DE W
The University of Iowa, IA W
University of Louisville, KY W
University of Maine, ME W
University of Maryland, College Park, MD W
University of Massachusetts Amherst, MA W
University of Massachusetts Lowell, MA W
University of Michigan, MI W
University of New Hampshire, NH W
The University of North Carolina at Chapel Hill, NC W
University of Richmond, VA W
University of the Pacific, CA W
University of Vermont, VT W
University of Virginia, VA W
Villanova University, PA W
Virginia Commonwealth University, VA W
Wake Forest University, NC W
West Chester University of Pennsylvania, PA W

Football

Abilene Christian University, TX M
Adams State College, CO M
Alabama Agricultural and Mechanical University, AL M
Alcorn State University, MS M
Angelo State University, TX M
Appalachian State University, NC M
Arizona State University, AZ M
Arkansas State University, AR M
Arkansas Tech University, AR M
Ashland University, OH M
Auburn University, AL M
Augustana College, SD M
Austin Peay State University, TN M
Avila University, MO M
Azusa Pacific University, CA M
Baker University, KS M
Ball State University, IN M
Baylor University, TX M
Belhaven College, MS M
Benedictine College, KS M
Bentley University, MA M
Bethany College, KS M
Bethel College, KS M
Black Hills State University, SD M
Blessing-Rieman College of Nursing, IL M
Bloomsburg University of Pennsylvania, PA M
Boise State University, ID M
Boston College, MA M
Bowling Green State University, OH M
Brevard College, NC M
Brigham Young University, UT M
California Polytechnic State University, San Luis Obispo, CA M
California State University, Fresno, CA M

California State University, Northridge, CA M
California State University, Sacramento, CA M
Campbellsville University, KY M
Carroll College, MT M
Carson-Newman College, TN M
Catawba College, NC M
Central Methodist University, MO M
Central Michigan University, MI M
Clarion University of Pennsylvania, PA M
Clemson University, SC M
Coastal Carolina University, SC M
The College of William and Mary, VA M
Colorado School of Mines, CO M
Colorado State University, CO M
Colorado State University–Pueblo, CO M
Concordia University, Nebraska, NE M
Concordia University, St. Paul, MN M
Concord University, WV M
Culver-Stockton College, MO M
Dakota State University, SD M
Dallas Baptist University, TX W
Dana College, NE M
Davidson College, NC M
Delta State University, MS M
Dixie State College of Utah, UT M
Doane College, NE M
Dordt College, IA M
Duke University, NC M
Duquesne University, PA M
Eastern Illinois University, IL M
Eastern Michigan University, MI M
Eastern Washington University, WA M
Edinboro University of Pennsylvania, PA M
Elon University, NC M
Emporia State University, KS M
Evangel University, MO M
Fairmont State University, WV M
Faulkner University, AL M
Ferris State University, MI M
Florida Atlantic University, FL M
Florida International University, FL M
Florida State University, FL M
Fort Hays State University, KS M
Fort Lewis College, CO M
Fort Valley State University, GA M
Furman University, SC M
Gardner-Webb University, NC M
Georgetown College, KY M
Georgetown University, DC M
Georgia Institute of Technology, GA M
Georgia Southern University, GA M
Glenville State College, WV M
Graceland University, IA M
Grand Valley State University, MI M
Grand View University, IA M
Hampton University, VA M
Harding University, AR M
Henderson State University, AR M
Hofstra University, NY M
Humboldt State University, CA M
Idaho State University, ID M
Illinois State University, IL M
Indiana State University, IN M
Indiana University Bloomington, IN M
Indiana University of Pennsylvania, PA M
Iowa State University of Science and Technology, IA M
James Madison University, VA M
Jamestown College, ND M
Johnson C. Smith University, NC M
Kansas State University, KS M
Kent State University, OH M
Kentucky State University, KY M
Kentucky Wesleyan College, KY M
Kutztown University of Pennsylvania, PA M
Lamar University, TX M
Lambuth University, TN M
Lane College, TN M
Liberty University, VA M
Lindenwood University, MO M
Lock Haven University of Pennsylvania, PA M
Louisiana State University and Agricultural and Mechanical College, LA M
Malone University, OH M
Marian College, IN M
Mayville State University, ND M
McKendree University, IL M
Mercyhurst College, PA M
Mesa State College, CO M
Miami University, OH M
Michigan State University, MI M
Michigan Technological University, MI M
MidAmerica Nazarene University, KS M
Millersville University of Pennsylvania, PA M
Minnesota State University Mankato, MN M
Minot State University, ND M
Mississippi State University, MS M
Missouri Southern State University, MO M
Missouri State University, MO M
Missouri University of Science and Technology, MO M
Missouri Western State University, MO M
Monmouth University, NJ M
Montana State University, MT M
Montana Tech of The University of Montana, MT M
Murray State University, KY M
Newberry College, SC M
New Mexico State University, NM M
Nicholls State University, LA M
North Carolina State University, NC M
North Dakota State University, ND M
Northeastern State University, OK M
Northeastern University, MA M
Northern Arizona University, AZ M
Northern Michigan University, MI M
Northern State University, SD M
North Greenville University, SC M
Northwestern State University of Louisiana, LA M
Northwestern University, IL M
Northwest Missouri State University, MO M
Northwood University, MI M
The Ohio State University, OH M
Ohio University, OH M
Oklahoma Panhandle State University, OK M
Oklahoma State University, OK M
Old Dominion University, VA M
Olivet Nazarene University, IL M
Oregon State University, OR M
Ouachita Baptist University, AR M
Penn State University Park, PA M
Pittsburg State University, KS M
Portland State University, OR M
Presbyterian College, SC M
Purdue University, IN M
Robert Morris University, PA M
Sacred Heart University, CT M
Saginaw Valley State University, MI M
St. Ambrose University, IA M
St. Cloud State University, MN M
Saint Joseph's College, IN M
Saint Xavier University, IL M
Samford University, AL M
Sam Houston State University, TX M
San Diego State University, CA M
San Jose State University, CA M
Seton Hill University, PA M
Shepherd University, WV M
Shippensburg University of Pennsylvania, PA M
Slippery Rock University of Pennsylvania, PA M
South Carolina State University, SC M
South Dakota School of Mines and Technology, SD M
South Dakota State University, SD M
Southeastern Louisiana University, LA M
Southeastern Oklahoma State University, OK M
Southeast Missouri State University, MO M
Southern Arkansas University–Magnolia, AR M
Southern Connecticut State University, CT M
Southern Illinois University Carbondale, IL M
Southern Methodist University, TX M
Southern Nazarene University, OK M
Southern Oregon University, OR M
Southern Utah University, UT M
Southwest Baptist University, MO M
Southwestern College, KS M
Southwestern Oklahoma State University, OK M
Southwest Minnesota State University, MN M
Stanford University, CA M
Stephen F. Austin State University, TX M
Stonehill College, MA M
Stony Brook University, State University of New York, NY M
Tarleton State University, TX M
Taylor University, IN M
Temple University, PA M
Tennessee Technological University, TN M
Texas A&M University, TX M
Texas Christian University, TX M

Texas State University–San Marcos, TX M
Texas Tech University, TX M
Tiffin University, OH M
Towson University, MD M
Trinity International University, IL M
Troy University, AL M
Truman State University, MO M
Tuskegee University, AL M
Union College, KY M
University at Albany, State University of New York, NY M
University at Buffalo, the State University of New York, NY M
The University of Akron, OH M
The University of Alabama, AL M
The University of Alabama at Birmingham, AL M
The University of Arizona, AZ M
University of Arkansas, AR M
University of California, Los Angeles, CA M
University of Central Florida, FL M
University of Central Missouri, MO M
University of Central Oklahoma, OK M
University of Cincinnati, OH M
University of Colorado at Boulder, CO M
University of Connecticut, CT M
University of Delaware, DE M
The University of Findlay, OH M
University of Florida, FL M
University of Georgia, GA M
University of Hawaii at Manoa, HI M
University of Houston, TX M
University of Idaho, ID M
The University of Iowa, IA M
The University of Kansas, KS M
University of Kentucky, KY M
University of Louisiana at Monroe, LA M
University of Louisville, KY M
University of Maine, ME M
University of Mary, ND M
University of Maryland, College Park, MD M
University of Massachusetts Amherst, MA M
University of Memphis, TN M
University of Miami, FL M
University of Michigan, MI M
University of Minnesota, Crookston, MN M
University of Minnesota, Duluth, MN M
University of Minnesota, Twin Cities Campus, MN M
University of Mississippi, MS M
University of Missouri–Columbia, MO M
The University of Montana, MT M
The University of Montana Western, MT M
University of Nebraska at Kearney, NE M
University of Nebraska at Omaha, NE M
University of Nebraska–Lincoln, NE M,W
University of Nevada, Las Vegas, NV M
University of Nevada, Reno, NV M
University of New Hampshire, NH M
University of New Haven, CT M
University of North Alabama, AL M
The University of North Carolina at Chapel Hill, NC M
The University of North Carolina at Pembroke, NC M
University of North Dakota, ND M
University of Northern Colorado, CO M
University of Northern Iowa, IA M
University of North Texas, TX M
University of Notre Dame, IN M
University of Oklahoma, OK M
University of Oregon, OR M
University of Pittsburgh, PA M
University of Rhode Island, RI M
University of Richmond, VA M
University of Saint Francis, IN M
University of South Carolina, SC M
The University of South Dakota, SD M
University of Southern California, CA M
University of Southern Mississippi, MS M,W
University of South Florida, FL M
The University of Tennessee, TN M
The University of Tennessee at Chattanooga, TN M
The University of Tennessee at Martin, TN M
The University of Texas at El Paso, TX M
University of the Cumberlands, KY M
University of Tulsa, OK M
University of Utah, UT M
University of Virginia, VA M
The University of Virginia's College at Wise, VA M
University of West Georgia, GA M
University of Wisconsin–Madison, WI M
University of Wyoming, WY M
Utah State University, UT M
Valdosta State University, GA M
Valley City State University, ND M
Vanderbilt University, TN M
Villanova University, PA M
Virginia Military Institute, VA M
Virginia Polytechnic Institute and State University, VA M
Wagner College, NY M
Wake Forest University, NC M
Washington State University, WA M
Wayne State University, MI M
Webber International University, FL M
Weber State University, UT M
West Chester University of Pennsylvania, PA M
Western Carolina University, NC M
Western Illinois University, IL M
Western Kentucky University, KY M
Western Michigan University, MI M
Western Oregon University, OR M
Western Washington University, WA M
West Liberty State University, WV M
West Virginia University, WV M
West Virginia Wesleyan College, WV M
Wingate University, NC M
Winona State University, MN M
Wofford College, SC M
Youngstown State University, OH M

Golf

Abilene Christian University, TX M
Academy of Art University, CA M
Adams State College, CO M,W
Adelphi University, NY M
Alabama Agricultural and Mechanical University, AL M
Alcorn State University, MS M,W
Appalachian State University, NC M,W
Arizona State University, AZ M,W
Arkansas State University, AR M,W
Arkansas Tech University, AR M
Ashland University, OH M,W
Auburn University, AL M,W
Augustana College, SD W
Austin Peay State University, TN M,W
Avila University, MO W
Azusa Pacific University, CA M
Baker University, KS M,W
Ball State University, IN M
Barton College, NC M
Baylor University, TX M,W
Belhaven College, MS M,W
Bellarmine University, KY M,W
Belmont Abbey College, NC M,W
Belmont University, TN M,W
Benedictine College, KS M,W
Bethany College, KS M
Bethel College, IN M,W
Bethel College, KS M,W
Biola University, CA M,W
Bluefield College, VA M
Bluefield State College, WV M
Boise State University, ID M,W
Boston College, MA M,W
Bowling Green State University, OH M,W
Bradley University, IL M,W
Brevard College, NC M,W
Brigham Young University, UT M,W
Butler University, IN M,W
California Baptist University, CA M,W
California Polytechnic State University, San Luis Obispo, CA M,W
California State University, Bakersfield, CA M
California State University, Chico, CA M,W
California State University, Fresno, CA M,W
California State University, Northridge, CA M
California State University, Sacramento, CA M
California State University, San Bernardino, CA M
Campbellsville University, KY M,W
Canisius College, NY M
Carroll College, MT M,W
Carson-Newman College, TN M
Catawba College, NC M,W
Cedarville University, OH M
Central Connecticut State University, CT M,W
Chestnut Hill College, PA M,W
Christian Brothers University, TN M,W
Clarion University of Pennsylvania, PA M
Clarke College, IA M,W
Clayton State University, GA M
Clemson University, SC M
Cleveland State University, OH M
Coastal Carolina University, SC M,W
College of Charleston, SC M,W

The College of Idaho, ID M,W
Colorado State University, CO M,W
Colorado State University–Pueblo, CO M,W
Columbus State University, GA M
Concordia University, OR M,W
Concordia University, Nebraska, NE M,W
Concordia University, St. Paul, MN M,W
Concord University, WV M
Covenant College, GA M,W
Creighton University, NE M,W
Culver-Stockton College, MO M,W
Daemen College, NY M
Dallas Baptist University, TX W
Dana College, NE W
Davenport University, MI M,W
Davidson College, NC M
Delta State University, MS M
DePaul University, IL M
Dixie State College of Utah, UT M
Doane College, NE M,W
Dominican College, NY M
Dominican University of California, CA M,W
Dordt College, IA M
Dowling College, NY M
Drake University, IA M
Drury University, MO M,W
Duke University, NC M,W
Duquesne University, PA M
Eastern Illinois University, IL M,W
Eastern Michigan University, MI M,W
Eastern Washington University, WA W
East Tennessee State University, TN M,W
Elon University, NC M,W
Embry-Riddle Aeronautical University, FL M,W
Evangel University, MO M,W
Fairfield University, CT M,W
Fairleigh Dickinson University, Metropolitan Campus, NJ M,W
Fairmont State University, WV M
Faulkner University, AL M
Ferris State University, MI M,W
Flagler College, FL M,W
Florida Gulf Coast University, FL M,W
Florida Institute of Technology, FL M,W
Florida International University, FL W
Florida State University, FL M,W
Fort Hays State University, KS M
Fort Lewis College, CO M
Fort Valley State University, GA M
Francis Marion University, SC M
Furman University, SC M,W
Gannon University, PA M,W
Gardner-Webb University, NC M,W
George Mason University, VA M
Georgetown College, KY M,W
Georgetown University, DC M
The George Washington University, DC M
Georgia College & State University, GA M
Georgia Institute of Technology, GA M
Georgia Southern University, GA M
Georgia Southwestern State University, GA M
Georgia State University, GA M,W
Glenville State College, WV M,W
Grace College, IN M
Graceland University, IA M,W
Grand Valley State University, MI M,W
Grand View University, IA M,W
Hampton University, VA M,W
Harding University, AR M,W
Hawai'i Pacific University, HI M
Henderson State University, AR M,W
Hofstra University, NY M,W
Holy Family University, PA M
Houston Baptist University, TX M,W
Huntington University, IN M
Idaho State University, ID M,W
Illinois State University, IL M,W
Indiana State University, IN W
Indiana University Bloomington, IN M,W
Indiana University of Pennsylvania, PA M
Indiana University–Purdue University Fort Wayne, IN M,W
Indiana University–Purdue University Indianapolis, IN M
Iona College, NY M
Iowa State University of Science and Technology, IA M,W
Jacksonville University, FL M,W
James Madison University, VA M,W
Jamestown College, ND M,W
John Brown University, AR M
Johnson C. Smith University, NC M,W
Kansas State University, KS M,W
Kennesaw State University, GA M,W
Kent State University, OH M,W
Kentucky State University, KY M
Kentucky Wesleyan College, KY M,W
Kutztown University of Pennsylvania, PA W
Lamar University, TX M,W
Lambuth University, TN M
Lee University, TN M
Le Moyne College, NY M
Lewis-Clark State College, ID M,W
Liberty University, VA M
Limestone College, SC M,W
Lincoln Memorial University, TN M,W
Lindenwood University, MO M,W
Lindsey Wilson College, KY M,W
Lipscomb University, TN M,W
Long Island University, Brooklyn Campus, NY M,W
Longwood University, VA M,W
Louisiana State University and Agricultural and Mechanical College, LA M,W
Loyola University Chicago, IL M,W
Loyola University Maryland, MD M
Lyon College, AR M,W
Malone University, OH M,W
Marian College, IN M,W
Marquette University, WI M
The Master's College and Seminary, CA M
McKendree University, IL M,W
Mercer University, GA M,W
Mercyhurst College, PA M,W
Mesa State College, CO W
Miami University, OH M
Michigan State University, MI M,W
Millersville University of Pennsylvania, PA M
Milligan College, TN M
Minnesota State University Mankato, MN M,W
Mississippi State University, MS M,W
Missouri Baptist University, MO M
Missouri Southern State University, MO M
Missouri State University, MO M,W
Missouri Western State University, MO M
Monmouth University, NJ M,W
Montana State University, MT W
Montana Tech of The University of Montana, MT M,W
Mount Mercy College, IA M,W
Mount Olive College, NC M
Mount St. Mary's University, MD M,W
Mount Vernon Nazarene University, OH M
Murray State University, KY M,W
Newberry College, SC M,W
Newman University, KS M,W
New Mexico State University, NM M,W
Niagara University, NY M,W
Nicholls State University, LA M,W
North Carolina State University, NC M
North Dakota State University, ND W
Northeastern State University, OK M,W
Northern Arizona University, AZ W
Northern Kentucky University, KY M,W
Northern Michigan University, MI M
Northern State University, SD W
North Greenville University, SC M
Northwestern University, IL M,W
Northwest Missouri State University, MO W
Northwood University, MI M,W
Northwood University, Florida Campus, FL M,W
Northwood University, Texas Campus, TX M,W
Notre Dame de Namur University, CA M
Nova Southeastern University, FL M,W
Oakland University, MI M,W
The Ohio State University, OH M,W
Ohio University, OH M,W
Ohio Valley University, WV M,W
Oklahoma Baptist University, OK M,W
Oklahoma Christian University, OK M
Oklahoma City University, OK M,W
Oklahoma Panhandle State University, OK M,W
Oklahoma State University, OK M,W
Old Dominion University, VA M,W
Olivet Nazarene University, IL M
Oral Roberts University, OK M,W
Oregon State University, OR M,W
Ouachita Baptist University, AR M
Our Lady of the Lake University of San Antonio, TX M,W
Pace University, NY M,W
Penn State University Park, PA M,W
Pepperdine University, CA M,W
Philadelphia University, PA M
Pittsburg State University, KS M
Point Loma Nazarene University, CA M
Portland State University, OR M,W
Presbyterian College, SC M,W
Purdue University, IN M,W

Quinnipiac University, CT M
Radford University, VA M,W
Reinhardt College, GA M,W
Rider University, NJ M
Robert Morris College, IL M,W
Robert Morris University, PA M,W
Roberts Wesleyan College, NY M,W
Rockhurst University, MO M,W
Rollins College, FL M,W
Sacred Heart University, CT M,W
Saginaw Valley State University, MI M
St. Ambrose University, IA M,W
St. Andrews Presbyterian College, NC M,W
St. Cloud State University, MN W
St. Edward's University, TX M,W
Saint Francis University, PA M,W
St. John's University, NY M,W
Saint Joseph's College, IN M,W
Saint Joseph's University, PA M
Saint Leo University, FL M,W
Saint Martin's University, WA M,W
Saint Mary's College of California, CA M
St. Mary's University, TX M
St. Thomas University, FL M,W
Saint Xavier University, IL M
Samford University, AL M,W
Sam Houston State University, TX M,W
San Diego State University, CA M,W
San Jose State University, CA M,W
Santa Clara University, CA M,W
Savannah College of Art and Design, GA M,W
Seton Hill University, PA M,W
Shorter College, GA M,W
Silver Lake College, WI M,W
Simpson University, CA M,W
South Carolina State University, SC M,W
South Dakota State University, SD M,W
Southeastern Louisiana University, LA M
Southern Illinois University Carbondale, IL M,W
Southern Illinois University Edwardsville, IL M,W
Southern Methodist University, TX M,W
Southern Nazarene University, OK M,W
Southern Utah University, UT M
Southwest Baptist University, MO M
Southwestern College, KS M,W
Southwestern Oklahoma State University, OK M,W
Southwest Minnesota State University, MN W
Spring Arbor University, MI M
Spring Hill College, AL M,W
Stanford University, CA M,W
State University of New York at Binghamton, NY M
Stephen F. Austin State University, TX M
Stetson University, FL M,W
Tarleton State University, TX W
Taylor University, IN M
Temple University, PA M
Tennessee Technological University, TN M,W
Texas A&M University, TX M,W
Texas Christian University, TX M,W
Texas State University–San Marcos, TX M,W
Texas Tech University, TX M,W
Tiffin University, OH M,W
Towson University, MD M,W
Trevecca Nazarene University, TN M,W
Troy University, AL M,W
Truman State University, MO M,W
Tuskegee University, AL M
Union College, KY M,W
Union University, TN M
University at Albany, State University of New York, NY W
The University of Akron, OH M,W
The University of Alabama, AL M,W
The University of Alabama at Birmingham, AL M,W
The University of Arizona, AZ M,W
University of Arkansas, AR M,W
University of California, Davis, CA M,W
University of California, Irvine, CA M,W
University of California, Los Angeles, CA M,W
University of California, Riverside, CA M,W
University of Central Florida, FL M,W
University of Central Missouri, MO M
University of Central Oklahoma, OK M,W
University of Cincinnati, OH M
University of Colorado at Boulder, CO M,W
University of Colorado at Colorado Springs, CO M
University of Connecticut, CT M
University of Dayton, OH M,W
University of Denver, CO M,W
University of Evansville, IN M,W
The University of Findlay, OH M,W
University of Florida, FL M,W
University of Georgia, GA M,W
University of Hartford, CT M,W
University of Hawaii at Manoa, HI M,W
University of Houston, TX M
University of Idaho, ID M,W
University of Illinois at Springfield, IL M,W
The University of Iowa, IA M,W
The University of Kansas, KS M,W
University of Kentucky, KY M,W
University of Louisiana at Monroe, LA M
University of Louisville, KY M,W
University of Mary, ND M,W
University of Maryland, College Park, MD M,W
University of Memphis, TN M,W
University of Miami, FL W
University of Michigan, MI M,W
University of Minnesota, Twin Cities Campus, MN M,W
University of Mississippi, MS M,W
University of Missouri–Columbia, MO M,W
University of Missouri–Kansas City, MO M,W
University of Missouri–St. Louis, MO M,W
University of Mobile, AL M,W
The University of Montana, MT W
The University of Montana Western, MT M,W
University of Montevallo, AL M,W
University of Nebraska at Kearney, NE M,W
University of Nebraska–Lincoln, NE M,W
University of Nevada, Las Vegas, NV M
University of Nevada, Reno, NV M,W
University of New Haven, CT M
University of New Orleans, LA M
University of North Alabama, AL M
The University of North Carolina at Chapel Hill, NC M,W
The University of North Carolina at Greensboro, NC M,W
The University of North Carolina at Pembroke, NC M,W
The University of North Carolina Wilmington, NC M,W
University of Northern Colorado, CO M,W
University of Northern Iowa, IA M,W
University of North Florida, FL M
University of North Texas, TX M,W
University of Notre Dame, IN M,W
University of Oklahoma, OK M,W
University of Oregon, OR M,W
University of Portland, OR M,W
University of Rhode Island, RI M
University of Richmond, VA M,W
University of Saint Francis, IN M
University of San Diego, CA M
University of South Carolina, SC M,W
University of South Carolina Aiken, SC M
University of South Carolina Upstate, SC M,W
The University of South Dakota, SD M,W
University of Southern California, CA M,W
University of Southern Indiana, IN M,W
University of Southern Mississippi, MS M,W
University of South Florida, FL M,W
The University of Tampa, FL M
The University of Tennessee, TN M,W
The University of Tennessee at Chattanooga, TN M
The University of Tennessee at Martin, TN M
The University of Texas at Arlington, TX M
The University of Texas at Brownsville, TX M,W
The University of Texas at El Paso, TX M
The University of Texas at San Antonio, TX M
The University of Texas–Pan American, TX M,W
University of the Cumberlands, KY M,W
University of the Incarnate Word, TX M,W
University of the Pacific, CA M
University of the Southwest, NM M,W
University of Tulsa, OK M,W
University of Utah, UT M
University of Virginia, VA M,W
University of West Florida, FL M
University of West Georgia, GA M,W
University of Wisconsin–Green Bay, WI M,W
University of Wisconsin–Madison, WI M,W
University of Wisconsin–Parkside, WI M
University of Wyoming, WY M,W
Ursuline College, OH W
Utah State University, UT M
Utah Valley University, UT M,W

Valdosta State University, GA M
Vanderbilt University, TN M,W
Virginia Commonwealth University, VA M
Virginia Intermont College, VA M
Virginia Military Institute, VA M
Virginia Polytechnic Institute and State University, VA M
Wagner College, NY M,W
Wake Forest University, NC M,W
Washington State University, WA M,W
Wayland Baptist University, TX M,W
Wayne State University, MI M
Webber International University, FL M,W
Weber State University, UT M,W
West Chester University of Pennsylvania, PA M,W
Western Carolina University, NC M,W
Western Illinois University, IL M
Western Kentucky University, KY M,W
Western Michigan University, MI W
Western Washington University, WA M,W
West Liberty State University, WV M,W
West Virginia Wesleyan College, WV M,W
Wheeling Jesuit University, WV M,W
Wichita State University, KS M,W
Wingate University, NC M,W
Winona State University, MN M,W
Winthrop University, SC M,W
Wofford College, SC M,W
Wright State University, OH M
Xavier University, OH M,W
Youngstown State University, OH M

Gymnastics

Arizona State University, AZ W
Auburn University, AL W
Ball State University, IN W
Boise State University, ID W
Bowling Green State University, OH W
Brigham Young University, UT W
California State University, Fullerton, CA W
California State University, Sacramento, CA W
Central Michigan University, MI W
The College of William and Mary, VA M,W
Eastern Michigan University, MI W
The George Washington University, DC W
Illinois State University, IL W
Iowa State University of Science and Technology, IA W
Kent State University, OH W
Louisiana State University and Agricultural and Mechanical College, LA W
Michigan State University, MI W
North Carolina State University, NC W
The Ohio State University, OH M,W
Oregon State University, OR W
Penn State University Park, PA M,W
San Jose State University, CA W
Seattle Pacific University, WA W
Southeast Missouri State University, MO W
Southern Connecticut State University, CT W
Southern Utah University, UT W
Stanford University, CA M,W
Temple University, PA M,W
Towson University, MD W
The University of Alabama, AL W
The University of Arizona, AZ W
University of Arkansas, AR W
University of Bridgeport, CT W
University of California, Davis, CA W
University of California, Los Angeles, CA W
University of Denver, CO W
University of Florida, FL W
University of Georgia, GA W
University of Illinois at Chicago, IL M,W
The University of Iowa, IA M,W
University of Kentucky, KY W
University of Maryland, College Park, MD W
University of Michigan, MI M,W
University of Minnesota, Twin Cities Campus, MN M,W
University of Missouri–Columbia, MO W
University of Nebraska–Lincoln, NE M,W
University of New Hampshire, NH W
The University of North Carolina at Chapel Hill, NC W
University of Oklahoma, OK M,W
University of Pittsburgh, PA W
University of Utah, UT W
Utah State University, UT W
West Chester University of Pennsylvania, PA W
Western Michigan University, MI W
West Virginia University, WV W
Winona State University, MN W

Ice Hockey

Bentley University, MA M
Boston College, MA M,W
Bowling Green State University, OH M
Canisius College, NY M
Clarkson University, NY M,W
Colgate University, NY M,W
College of the Holy Cross, MA M,W
The Colorado College, CO M
Davenport University, MI M
Dordt College, IA M
Ferris State University, MI M
Mercyhurst College, PA M,W
Merrimack College, MA M
Miami University, OH M
Michigan State University, MI M
Michigan Technological University, MI M
Minnesota State University Mankato, MN M,W
Niagara University, NY M,W
Northeastern University, MA M,W
Northern Michigan University, MI M
The Ohio State University, OH M,W
Providence College, RI M,W
Quinnipiac University, CT M,W
Rensselaer Polytechnic Institute, NY M,W
Robert Morris University, PA M,W
Sacred Heart University, CT M
St. Cloud State University, MN M,W
St. Lawrence University, NY M,W
The University of Alabama in Huntsville, AL M
University of Alaska Fairbanks, AK M
University of Connecticut, CT M,W
University of Denver, CO M
University of Maine, ME M,W
University of Massachusetts Amherst, MA M
University of Massachusetts Lowell, MA M
University of Michigan, MI M
University of Minnesota, Duluth, MN M,W
University of Minnesota, Twin Cities Campus, MN M,W
University of Nebraska at Omaha, NE M
University of New Hampshire, NH M,W
University of North Dakota, ND M,W
University of Notre Dame, IN M
University of Vermont, VT M,W
University of Wisconsin–Madison, WI M,W
Wayne State University, MI W
Western Michigan University, MI M

Lacrosse

Adelphi University, NY M,W
American University, DC W
Bellarmine University, KY M
Belmont Abbey College, NC M,W
Bentley University, MA M,W
Bloomsburg University of Pennsylvania, PA W
Boston College, MA W
Bucknell University, PA M,W
California State University, Fresno, CA W
Canisius College, NY M,W
Catawba College, NC M
Central Connecticut State University, CT W
Chestnut Hill College, PA M,W
Colgate University, NY M,W
The College of William and Mary, VA W
Davenport University, MI M,W
Davidson College, NC W
Dominican College, NY M,W
Dominican University of California, CA M
Dowling College, NY M,W
Duke University, NC M,W
Duquesne University, PA W
Edinboro University of Pennsylvania, PA W
Fairfield University, CT M,W
Fort Lewis College, CO W
Gannon University, PA W
George Mason University, VA W
Georgetown University, DC M,W
Georgian Court University, NJ W
Hofstra University, NY M,W
Holy Family University, PA W
Indiana University of Pennsylvania, PA W
Iona College, NY W
James Madison University, VA W
The Johns Hopkins University, MD M,W
Kutztown University of Pennsylvania, PA W
Lehigh University, PA M,W
Le Moyne College, NY M,W
Limestone College, SC M,W
Lindenwood University, MO M,W
Lock Haven University of Pennsylvania, PA W

Long Island University, Brooklyn Campus, NY	W
Long Island University, C.W. Post Campus, NY	M,W
Longwood University, VA	W
Mercyhurst College, PA	M,W
Merrimack College, MA	W
Millersville University of Pennsylvania, PA	W
Missouri Baptist University, MO	M,W
Molloy College, NY	M,W
Monmouth University, NJ	W
Mount St. Mary's University, MD	M,W
Niagara University, NY	W
Northwestern University, IL	W
Notre Dame de Namur University, CA	M
The Ohio State University, OH	M,W
Old Dominion University, VA	W
Pace University, NY	M
Penn State University Park, PA	M,W
Philadelphia University, PA	W
Presbyterian College, SC	M,W
Providence College, RI	M
Quinnipiac University, CT	M,W
Robert Morris University, PA	M,W
Sacred Heart University, CT	M,W
St. Andrews Presbyterian College, NC	M,W
Saint Francis University, PA	W
St. John's University, NY	M
Saint Joseph's University, PA	M,W
Saint Leo University, FL	M
Savannah College of Art and Design, GA	W
Seton Hill University, PA	M,W
Shepherd University, WV	W
Shippensburg University of Pennsylvania, PA	W
Slippery Rock University of Pennsylvania, PA	W
Southern Connecticut State University, CT	W
Southern New Hampshire University, NH	M,W
Stanford University, CA	W
State University of New York at Binghamton, NY	M,W
Stonehill College, MA	W
Stony Brook University, State University of New York, NY	M,W
Temple University, PA	W
Towson University, MD	M,W
University at Albany, State University of New York, NY	M,W
University of California, Davis, CA	W
University of Cincinnati, OH	W
University of Delaware, DE	M,W
University of Denver, CO	M,W
University of Florida, FL	W
University of Hartford, CT	M
University of Louisville, KY	W
University of Maryland, Baltimore County, MD	M,W
University of Maryland, College Park, MD	M,W
University of Massachusetts Amherst, MA	M,W
University of Minnesota, Duluth, MN	M
University of New Hampshire, NH	W
University of New Haven, CT	W
The University of North Carolina at Chapel Hill, NC	M,W
University of Notre Dame, IN	M,W
University of Oregon, OR	W
University of Richmond, VA	W
University of Vermont, VT	M,W
University of Virginia, VA	M,W
Vanderbilt University, TN	W
Virginia Military Institute, VA	M
Virginia Polytechnic Institute and State University, VA	W
Wagner College, NY	M,W
West Chester University of Pennsylvania, PA	W
Wheeling Jesuit University, WV	M
Wingate University, NC	M

Riflery

Austin Peay State University, TN	W
Lindenwood University, MO	M,W
Mercer University, GA	M
Murray State University, KY	M,W
Tennessee Technological University, TN	M,W
Texas Christian University, TX	W
The University of Akron, OH	W
University of Alaska Fairbanks, AK	M,W
University of Kentucky, KY	M,W
University of Memphis, TN	M,W
University of Mississippi, MS	W
University of Missouri–Kansas City, MO	M,W
University of Nebraska–Lincoln, NE	W
University of Nevada, Reno, NV	M,W
The University of Tennessee at Martin, TN	M,W
Virginia Military Institute, VA	M,W
West Virginia University, WV	M,W

Rugby

Eastern Illinois University, IL	W
West Chester University of Pennsylvania, PA	W

Sailing

Hampton University, VA	M,W

Skiing (Cross-Country)

The College of Idaho, ID	M,W
Montana State University, MT	M,W
Northern Michigan University, MI	M,W
St. Cloud State University, MN	W
University of Alaska Fairbanks, AK	M,W
University of Colorado at Boulder, CO	M,W
University of Denver, CO	M,W
University of Nevada, Reno, NV	M,W
University of New Hampshire, NH	M,W
University of Utah, UT	M,W
University of Vermont, VT	M,W
University of Wisconsin–Green Bay, WI	M,W

Skiing (Downhill)

The College of Idaho, ID	M,W
Montana State University, MT	M,W
University of Colorado at Boulder, CO	M,W
University of Denver, CO	M,W
University of Massachusetts Amherst, MA	M,W
University of Nevada, Reno, NV	M,W
University of New Hampshire, NH	M,W
University of Utah, UT	M,W
University of Vermont, VT	M,W

Soccer

Abilene Christian University, TX	W
Academy of Art University, CA	M,W
Adams State College, CO	M,W
Adelphi University, NY	M,W
Alabama Agricultural and Mechanical University, AL	M
Alcorn State University, MS	W
Alderson-Broaddus College, WV	M,W
American University, DC	M,W
Angelo State University, TX	W
Appalachian State University, NC	M,W
Arizona State University, AZ	W
Arkansas State University, AR	W
Asbury College, KY	M,W
Ashland University, OH	M,W
Auburn University, AL	W
Auburn University Montgomery, AL	M,W
Augustana College, SD	W
Austin Peay State University, TN	W
Avila University, MO	M,W
Azusa Pacific University, CA	M,W
Baker University, KS	M,W
Barton College, NC	M,W
Baylor University, TX	W
Belhaven College, MS	M,W
Bellarmine University, KY	M,W
Belmont Abbey College, NC	M,W
Belmont University, TN	M,W
Benedictine College, KS	M,W
Bentley University, MA	M,W
Bethany College, KS	M,W
Bethel College, IN	M,W
Bethel College, KS	M,W
Biola University, CA	M,W
Blessing-Rieman College of Nursing, IL	M,W
Bloomfield College, NJ	M,W
Bloomsburg University of Pennsylvania, PA	M,W
Bluefield College, VA	M,W
Boston College, MA	M,W
Bowling Green State University, OH	M,W
Bradley University, IL	M
Brenau University, GA	W
Brevard College, NC	M,W
Brewton-Parker College, GA	M,W
Brigham Young University, UT	W
Bryan College, TN	M,W
Bucknell University, PA	M,W
Butler University, IN	M,W
California Baptist University, CA	M,W
California Polytechnic State University, San Luis Obispo, CA	M,W
California State Polytechnic University, Pomona, CA	M,W
California State University, Bakersfield, CA	M
California State University, Chico, CA	M,W
California State University, Fresno, CA	W
California State University, Fullerton, CA	M,W
California State University, Long Beach, CA	W

Soccer

California State University, Los Angeles, CA M,W
California State University, Northridge, CA M
California State University, Sacramento, CA M,W
California State University, San Bernardino, CA M,W
Campbellsville University, KY M,W
Canisius College, NY M,W
Carroll College, MT W
Carson-Newman College, TN M,W
Catawba College, NC M,W
Cedarville University, OH M,W
Central Connecticut State University, CT M,W
Central Methodist University, MO M,W
Central Michigan University, MI W
Chestnut Hill College, PA M,W
Christian Brothers University, TN M,W
Clarke College, IA M,W
Clayton State University, GA M,W
Clemson University, SC M,W
Cleveland State University, OH M
Coastal Carolina University, SC M,W
Colgate University, NY M,W
College of Charleston, SC M,W
The College of Idaho, ID M,W
College of Saint Mary, NE W
College of the Holy Cross, MA M,W
The College of William and Mary, VA M,W
The Colorado College, CO W
Colorado School of Mines, CO M,W
Colorado State University–Pueblo, CO M,W
Columbia College, MO M
Columbus State University, GA W
Concordia University, OR M,W
Concordia University, Nebraska, NE M,W
Concordia University, St. Paul, MN W
Concord University, WV W
Corban College, OR M,W
Covenant College, GA M,W
Creighton University, NE M,W
Culver-Stockton College, MO M,W
Daemen College, NY M,W
Dallas Baptist University, TX W
Dana College, NE M,W
Davenport University, MI M,W
Davidson College, NC M,W
Delta State University, MS M,W
DePaul University, IL M,W
Dixie State College of Utah, UT M,W
Doane College, NE M,W
Dominican College, NY M,W
Dominican University of California, CA M,W
Dordt College, IA M,W
Dowling College, NY M,W
Drake University, IA M,W
Drury University, MO M,W
Duke University, NC M,W
Duquesne University, PA M,W
Eastern Illinois University, IL M,W
Eastern Michigan University, MI W
Eastern Washington University, WA W
East Tennessee State University, TN M,W
Edinboro University of Pennsylvania, PA W
Elon University, NC M,W
Embry-Riddle Aeronautical University, FL M,W
Emmanuel College, GA M,W
Emporia State University, KS W
The Evergreen State College, WA M,W
Fairfield University, CT M,W
Fairleigh Dickinson University, Metropolitan Campus, NJ M,W
Faulkner University, AL M,W
Felician College, NJ M,W
Ferris State University, MI M,W
Flagler College, FL M,W
Florida College, FL M,W
Florida Gulf Coast University, FL M,W
Florida Institute of Technology, FL M,W
Florida International University, FL M,W
Florida State University, FL W
Fort Lewis College, CO M,W
Francis Marion University, SC M,W
Franklin Pierce University, NH M,W
Freed-Hardeman University, TN M,W
Furman University, SC M,W
Gannon University, PA M,W
Gardner-Webb University, NC M,W
George Mason University, VA M,W
Georgetown College, KY M,W
Georgetown University, DC M,W
The George Washington University, DC M,W
Georgia College & State University, GA W
Georgian Court University, NJ W
Georgia Southern University, GA M,W
Georgia Southwestern State University, GA M,W
Georgia State University, GA M,W
Gonzaga University, WA M,W
Grace College, IN M,W
Graceland University, IA M,W
Grand Valley State University, MI W
Grand View University, IA M,W
Harding University, AR M,W
Hartwick College, NY M
Hawai'i Pacific University, HI M,W
Hofstra University, NY M,W
Holy Family University, PA M,W
Hope International University, CA M,W
Houghton College, NY M,W
Houston Baptist University, TX M,W
Humboldt State University, CA M,W
Huntington University, IN M,W
Idaho State University, ID W
Illinois Institute of Technology, IL M,W
Illinois State University, IL W
Indiana State University, IN W
Indiana University Bloomington, IN M,W
Indiana University of Pennsylvania, PA W
Indiana University–Purdue University Fort Wayne, IN M,W
Indiana University–Purdue University Indianapolis, IN M,W
Inter American University of Puerto Rico, Guayama Campus, PR M
Iona College, NY M,W
Iowa State University of Science and Technology, IA W
Jacksonville University, FL M,W
James Madison University, VA M,W
Jamestown College, ND M,W
John Brown University, AR M,W
Judson College, AL W
Kennesaw State University, GA W
Kent State University, OH W
Kentucky Wesleyan College, KY M,W
Kutztown University of Pennsylvania, PA M,W
Lambuth University, TN M,W
Lee University, TN M,W
Lehigh University, PA M,W
Le Moyne College, NY M,W
Liberty University, VA M,W
Limestone College, SC M,W
Lincoln Memorial University, TN M,W
Lindenwood University, MO M,W
Lindsey Wilson College, KY M,W
Lipscomb University, TN M,W
Lock Haven University of Pennsylvania, PA M,W
Long Island University, Brooklyn Campus, NY M,W
Long Island University, C.W. Post Campus, NY M,W
Longwood University, VA M,W
Louisiana State University and Agricultural and Mechanical College, LA W
Loyola University Chicago, IL M,W
Loyola University Maryland, MD M,W
Lyon College, AR M,W
Malone University, OH M,W
Marian College, IN M,W
Marquette University, WI M,W
The Master's College and Seminary, CA M,W
McKendree University, IL M,W
Mercer University, GA M,W
Mercyhurst College, PA M,W
Merrimack College, MA W
Mesa State College, CO M,W
Metropolitan State College of Denver, CO M,W
Miami University, OH W
Michigan State University, MI M,W
MidAmerica Nazarene University, KS M,W
Mid-Continent University, KY M
Midway College, KY W
Millersville University of Pennsylvania, PA M,W
Milligan College, TN M,W
Minnesota State University Mankato, MN W
Mississippi State University, MS W
Missouri Baptist University, MO M,W
Missouri Southern State University, MO M,W
Missouri State University, MO M,W
Missouri University of Science and Technology, MO M,W
Molloy College, NY M,W
Monmouth University, NJ M,W
Montana State University–Billings, MT M,W
Mountain State University, WV M,W
Mount Marty College, SD M,W
Mount Mercy College, IA M,W
Mount Olive College, NC M,W
Mount St. Mary's University, MD M,W

Mount Vernon Nazarene University, OH M,W
Murray State University, KY W
Newberry College, SC M,W
New Jersey Institute of Technology, NJ M,W
Newman University, KS M,W
Niagara University, NY M,W
Nicholls State University, LA W
North Carolina State University, NC M,W
North Dakota State University, ND W
Northeastern State University, OK M,W
Northeastern University, MA M,W
Northern Arizona University, AZ W
Northern Kentucky University, KY M,W
Northern Michigan University, MI W
Northern State University, SD W
North Greenville University, SC M,W
Northwestern State University of Louisiana, LA W
Northwestern University, IL M,W
Northwest Missouri State University, MO W
Northwest University, WA M,W
Northwood University, MI M,W
Northwood University, Florida Campus, FL M,W
Northwood University, Texas Campus, TX M,W
Notre Dame de Namur University, CA M,W
Nova Southeastern University, FL M,W
Oakland University, MI M,W
The Ohio State University, OH M,W
Ohio University, OH W
Ohio Valley University, WV M,W
Oklahoma Christian University, OK M,W
Oklahoma City University, OK M,W
Oklahoma State University, OK W
Old Dominion University, VA M,W
Olivet Nazarene University, IL M,W
Oral Roberts University, OK M,W
Oregon State University, OR M,W
Ouachita Baptist University, AR M,W
Our Lady of the Lake University of San Antonio, TX M,W
Pace University, NY W
Palm Beach Atlantic University, FL M,W
Penn State University Park, PA M,W
Pepperdine University, CA W
Philadelphia University, PA M,W
Point Loma Nazarene University, CA M,W
Point Park University, PA M
Portland State University, OR W
Presbyterian College, SC M,W
Providence College, RI M,W
Purdue University, IN W
Quinnipiac University, CT M,W
Radford University, VA M,W
Reinhardt College, GA M,W
Rider University, NJ M,W
Robert Morris College, IL M,W
Robert Morris University, PA M,W
Roberts Wesleyan College, NY M,W
Rockhurst University, MO M,W
Rollins College, FL M,W
Sacred Heart University, CT M,W
Saginaw Valley State University, MI M,W
St. Ambrose University, IA M,W
St. Andrews Presbyterian College, NC M,W
St. Cloud State University, MN W
St. Edward's University, TX M,W
Saint Francis University, PA M,W
St. John's University, NY M,W
Saint Joseph's College, IN M,W
Saint Joseph's University, PA M,W
Saint Leo University, FL M,W
Saint Louis University, MO M,W
Saint Mary's College of California, CA M,W
St. Mary's University, TX M
St. Thomas University, FL M,W
Saint Xavier University, IL M,W
Samford University, AL W
Sam Houston State University, TX W
San Diego State University, CA M,W
San Francisco State University, CA M,W
San Jose State University, CA M,W
Santa Clara University, CA M,W
Savannah College of Art and Design, GA M,W
Seattle Pacific University, WA M
Seton Hill University, PA M,W
Shepherd University, WV M,W
Shippensburg University of Pennsylvania, PA M,W
Shorter College, GA M,W
Simpson University, CA M,W
Slippery Rock University of Pennsylvania, PA M,W
Sonoma State University, CA M,W
South Carolina State University, SC W
South Dakota State University, SD W
Southeastern Louisiana University, LA W
Southeast Missouri State University, MO W
Southern Connecticut State University, CT M,W
Southern Illinois University Edwardsville, IL M,W
Southern Methodist University, TX M,W
Southern Nazarene University, OK M,W
Southern New Hampshire University, NH M,W
Southern Oregon University, OR W
Southern Polytechnic State University, GA M
Southwest Baptist University, MO W
Southwestern College, KS M,W
Southwestern Oklahoma State University, OK W
Southwest Minnesota State University, MN W
Spring Arbor University, MI M,W
Spring Hill College, AL M,W
Stanford University, CA M,W
State University of New York at Binghamton, NY M,W
Stephen F. Austin State University, TX W
Stetson University, FL M,W
Stonehill College, MA M,W
Stony Brook University, State University of New York, NY M,W
Taylor University, IN M,W
Temple University, PA M,W
Tennessee Technological University, TN W
Texas A&M University, TX W
Texas Christian University, TX W
Texas State University–San Marcos, TX W
Texas Tech University, TX W
Tiffin University, OH M,W
Towson University, MD M,W
Trevecca Nazarene University, TN M,W
Trinity Christian College, IL M,W
Trinity International University, IL M,W
Troy University, AL W
Truman State University, MO M,W
Union College, KY M,W
Union University, TN M,W
University at Albany, State University of New York, NY M,W
University at Buffalo, the State University of New York, NY M,W
The University of Akron, OH M,W
The University of Alabama, AL W
The University of Alabama at Birmingham, AL M,W
The University of Alabama in Huntsville, AL M,W
The University of Arizona, AZ W
University of Arkansas, AR W
University of Bridgeport, CT M,W
University of California, Davis, CA M,W
University of California, Irvine, CA M,W
University of California, Los Angeles, CA M,W
University of Central Florida, FL M,W
University of Central Missouri, MO W
University of Central Oklahoma, OK W
University of Cincinnati, OH M,W
University of Colorado at Boulder, CO W
University of Colorado at Colorado Springs, CO M
University of Connecticut, CT M,W
University of Dayton, OH M,W
University of Delaware, DE M,W
University of Denver, CO M,W
University of Evansville, IN M,W
The University of Findlay, OH M,W
University of Florida, FL W
University of Georgia, GA W
University of Hartford, CT M,W
University of Hawaii at Manoa, HI W
University of Houston, TX W
University of Idaho, ID W
University of Illinois at Chicago, IL M
University of Illinois at Springfield, IL M,W
The University of Iowa, IA W
The University of Kansas, KS W
University of Kentucky, KY M,W
University of Louisiana at Monroe, LA W
University of Louisville, KY M,W
University of Maine, ME M,W
The University of Maine at Augusta, ME W
University of Mary, ND M,W
University of Maryland, Baltimore County, MD M,W
University of Maryland, College Park, MD M,W
University of Massachusetts Amherst, MA M,W
University of Memphis, TN M,W
University of Miami, FL W
University of Michigan, MI M,W

University of Minnesota, Crookston, MN W
University of Minnesota, Duluth, MN W
University of Minnesota, Twin Cities Campus, MN W
University of Mississippi, MS W
University of Missouri–Columbia, MO W
University of Missouri–Kansas City, MO M
University of Missouri–St. Louis, MO M,W
University of Mobile, AL M,W
University of Montevallo, AL M,W
University of Nebraska–Lincoln, NE W
University of Nevada, Las Vegas, NV M,W
University of Nevada, Reno, NV W
University of New Hampshire, NH M,W
University of New Haven, CT M,W
University of North Alabama, AL W
The University of North Carolina at Asheville, NC M,W
The University of North Carolina at Chapel Hill, NC M,W
The University of North Carolina at Greensboro, NC M,W
The University of North Carolina at Pembroke, NC M,W
The University of North Carolina Wilmington, NC M,W
University of Northern Colorado, CO W
University of Northern Iowa, IA W
University of North Florida, FL M,W
University of North Texas, TX W
University of Notre Dame, IN M,W
University of Oklahoma, OK W
University of Oregon, OR W
University of Pittsburgh, PA M,W
University of Portland, OR M,W
University of Puerto Rico, Río Piedras, PR M
University of Rhode Island, RI M,W
University of Richmond, VA M,W
University of Saint Francis, IN M,W
University of San Diego, CA M,W
University of Science and Arts of Oklahoma, OK M,W
University of South Alabama, AL W
University of South Carolina, SC M,W
University of South Carolina Aiken, SC M,W
University of South Carolina Upstate, SC M,W
The University of South Dakota, SD W
University of Southern California, CA W
University of Southern Indiana, IN M,W
University of Southern Mississippi, MS W
University of South Florida, FL M,W
The University of Tampa, FL M,W
The University of Tennessee, TN W
The University of Tennessee at Chattanooga, TN M,W
The University of Tennessee at Martin, TN W
The University of Texas at Brownsville, TX M,W
The University of Texas of the Permian Basin, TX M,W
University of the Cumberlands, KY M,W
University of the Incarnate Word, TX M,W
University of the Pacific, CA W
University of the Southwest, NM M,W
University of Tulsa, OK M,W
University of Utah, UT W
University of Vermont, VT M,W
University of Virginia, VA M,W
University of West Florida, FL M,W
University of West Georgia, GA W
University of Wisconsin–Green Bay, WI M,W
University of Wisconsin–Madison, WI M,W
University of Wisconsin–Milwaukee, WI M,W
University of Wisconsin–Parkside, WI M,W
University of Wyoming, WY W
Ursuline College, OH W
Utah State University, UT W
Utah Valley University, UT W
Valparaiso University, IN M,W
Vanderbilt University, TN M,W
Vanguard University of Southern California, CA M,W
Villanova University, PA M,W
Virginia Commonwealth University, VA M,W
Virginia Military Institute, VA M
Virginia Polytechnic Institute and State University, VA M,W
Wagner College, NY W
Wake Forest University, NC M,W
Washington State University, WA W
Wayland Baptist University, TX M,W
Webber International University, FL M,W
Weber State University, UT W
West Chester University of Pennsylvania, PA M,W
Western Carolina University, NC W
Western Illinois University, IL M,W
Western Michigan University, MI M,W
Western Oregon University, OR W
Western Washington University, WA M,W
Westminster College, UT M,W
West Virginia University, WV M,W
West Virginia Wesleyan College, WV M,W
Wheeling Jesuit University, WV M,W
Wingate University, NC M
Winona State University, MN W
Winthrop University, SC M
Wofford College, SC M,W
Wright State University, OH M,W
Xavier University, OH M,W
York College, NE M,W

Softball

Abilene Christian University, TX W
Academy of Art University, CA W
Adams State College, CO W
Adelphi University, NY W
Alcorn State University, MS W
Alderson-Broaddus College, WV W
Angelo State University, TX W
Appalachian State University, NC W
Arizona State University, AZ W
Asbury College, KY W
Ashland University, OH W
Auburn University, AL W
Auburn University Montgomery, AL W
Augustana College, SD W
Austin Peay State University, TN W
Avila University, MO W
Azusa Pacific University, CA W
Baker University, KS W
Ball State University, IN W
Barton College, NC W
Baylor University, TX W
Belhaven College, MS W
Bellarmine University, KY W
Belmont Abbey College, NC W
Belmont University, TN W
Benedictine College, KS W
Bentley University, MA W
Bethany College, KS W
Bethel College, IN W
Biola University, CA W
Bloomfield College, NJ W
Bloomsburg University of Pennsylvania, PA W
Bluefield College, VA W
Bluefield State College, WV W
Boston College, MA W
Bowling Green State University, OH W
Bradley University, IL W
Brenau University, GA W
Brevard College, NC W
Brewton-Parker College, GA W
Brigham Young University, UT W
Butler University, IN W
California Baptist University, CA W
California Polytechnic State University, San Luis Obispo, CA W
California State University, Bakersfield, CA W
California State University, Chico, CA W
California State University, Fresno, CA W
California State University, Fullerton, CA W
California State University, Long Beach, CA W
California State University, Northridge, CA W
California State University, Sacramento, CA W
California State University, San Bernardino, CA W
Campbellsville University, KY W
Canisius College, NY W
Carson-Newman College, TN W
Catawba College, NC W
Cedarville University, OH W
Central Connecticut State University, CT W
Central Methodist University, MO W
Central Michigan University, MI W
Chaminade University of Honolulu, HI W
Chestnut Hill College, PA W
Christian Brothers University, TN W
Clarion University of Pennsylvania, PA W
Clarke College, IA W
Cleveland State University, OH W
Coastal Carolina University, SC W
Colgate University, NY W
College of Charleston, SC W
The College of Idaho, ID W
College of Saint Mary, NE W
Colorado School of Mines, CO W
Colorado State University, CO W

Colorado State University–Pueblo, CO W
Columbia College, MO W
Columbus State University, GA W
Concordia University, OR W
Concordia University, Nebraska, NE W
Concordia University, St. Paul, MN W
Corban College, OR W
Covenant College, GA W
Creighton University, NE W
Culver-Stockton College, MO W
Dakota State University, SD W
Dana College, NE W
Delta State University, MS W
DePaul University, IL W
Dixie State College of Utah, UT W
Doane College, NE W
Dominican College, NY W
Dominican University of California, CA W
Dordt College, IA W
Dowling College, NY W
Drake University, IA W
Drury University, MO W
Eastern Illinois University, IL W
Eastern Michigan University, MI W
East Tennessee State University, TN W
Edinboro University of Pennsylvania, PA W
Elon University, NC W
Emmanuel College, GA W
Emporia State University, KS W
Evangel University, MO W
Fairfield University, CT W
Fairleigh Dickinson University, Metropolitan Campus, NJ W
Faulkner University, AL W
Felician College, NJ W
Ferris State University, MI W
Flagler College, FL W
Florida Atlantic University, FL W
Florida Gulf Coast University, FL W
Florida Institute of Technology, FL W
Florida International University, FL W
Florida State University, FL W
Fort Lewis College, CO W
Francis Marion University, SC W
Franklin Pierce University, NH W
Freed-Hardeman University, TN W
Furman University, SC W
Gannon University, PA W
Gardner-Webb University, NC W
George Mason University, VA W
Georgetown College, KY W
Georgia College & State University, GA W
Georgia Institute of Technology, GA W
Georgian Court University, NJ W
Georgia Southern University, GA W
Georgia Southwestern State University, GA W
Georgia State University, GA W
Glenville State College, WV W
Grace College, IN W
Graceland University, IA W
Grand Valley State University, MI W
Grand View University, IA W
Hampton University, VA W
Hawai'i Pacific University, HI W
Henderson State University, AR W
Hofstra University, NY W
Holy Family University, PA W
Hope International University, CA W
Houston Baptist University, TX W
Humboldt State University, CA W
Huntington University, IN W
Illinois State University, IL W
Indiana State University, IN W
Indiana University Bloomington, IN W
Indiana University of Pennsylvania, PA W
Indiana University–Purdue University Fort Wayne, IN W
Indiana University–Purdue University Indianapolis, IN W
Inter American University of Puerto Rico, Arecibo Campus, PR W
Inter American University of Puerto Rico, Guayama Campus, PR M,W
Iona College, NY W
Iowa State University of Science and Technology, IA W
Jacksonville University, FL W
James Madison University, VA W
Jamestown College, ND W
Johnson C. Smith University, NC W
Judson College, AL W
Kennesaw State University, GA W
Kent State University, OH W
Kentucky State University, KY W
Kentucky Wesleyan College, KY W
Kutztown University of Pennsylvania, PA W
Lambuth University, TN W
Lee University, TN W
Lehigh University, PA W
Le Moyne College, NY W
Liberty University, VA W
Limestone College, SC M,W
Lincoln Memorial University, TN W
Lindenwood University, MO W
Lindsey Wilson College, KY W
Lipscomb University, TN W
Lock Haven University of Pennsylvania, PA W
Long Island University, Brooklyn Campus, NY W
Long Island University, C.W. Post Campus, NY W
Longwood University, VA W
Louisiana State University and Agricultural and Mechanical College, LA W
Lubbock Christian University, TX W
Lyon College, AR W
Malone University, OH W
Marian College, IN W
Mayville State University, ND W
McKendree University, IL W
Mercer University, GA W
Mercyhurst College, PA W
Merrimack College, MA W
Mesa State College, CO W
Metropolitan State College of Denver, CO W
Miami University, OH W
MidAmerica Nazarene University, KS W
Mid-Continent University, KY W
Midway College, KY W
Millersville University of Pennsylvania, PA W
Milligan College, TN W
Minnesota State University Mankato, MN W
Minot State University, ND W
Mississippi State University, MS W
Missouri Baptist University, MO W
Missouri Southern State University, MO W
Missouri State University, MO W
Missouri University of Science and Technology, MO W
Missouri Western State University, MO W
Molloy College, NY W
Monmouth University, NJ W
Mountain State University, WV W
Mount Marty College, SD W
Mount Mercy College, IA W
Mount Olive College, NC W
Mount St. Mary's University, MD W
Mount Vernon Nazarene University, OH W
Murray State University, KY W
Newberry College, SC W
Newman University, KS W
New Mexico State University, NM W
Niagara University, NY W
Nicholls State University, LA W
North Carolina State University, NC W
North Dakota State University, ND W
Northeastern State University, OK W
Northern Kentucky University, KY W
Northern State University, SD W
North Greenville University, SC W
Northwestern State University of Louisiana, LA W
Northwestern University, IL W
Northwest Missouri State University, MO W
Northwood University, MI W
Northwood University, Florida Campus, FL W
Northwood University, Texas Campus, TX W
Notre Dame de Namur University, CA W
Nova Southeastern University, FL W
Oakland University, MI W
The Ohio State University, OH W
Ohio University, OH W
Ohio Valley University, WV W
Oklahoma Baptist University, OK W
Oklahoma Christian University, OK W
Oklahoma City University, OK W
Oklahoma Panhandle State University, OK W
Oklahoma State University, OK W
Olivet Nazarene University, IL W
Oregon Institute of Technology, OR W
Oregon State University, OR W
Ouachita Baptist University, AR W
Pace University, NY W
Palm Beach Atlantic University, FL W
Philadelphia University, PA W
Pittsburg State University, KS W
Point Loma Nazarene University, CA W
Point Park University, PA W
Portland State University, OR W

Presbyterian College, SC W
Providence College, RI W
Purdue University, IN W
Purdue University North Central, IN W
Quinnipiac University, CT W
Radford University, VA W
Reinhardt College, GA W
Rider University, NJ W
Robert Morris College, IL W
Robert Morris University, PA W
Rockhurst University, MO W
Rollins College, FL W
Sacred Heart University, CT W
Saginaw Valley State University, MI W
St. Ambrose University, IA W
St. Andrews Presbyterian College, NC W
St. Cloud State University, MN W
St. Edward's University, TX W
Saint Francis University, PA W
St. John's University, NY W
Saint Joseph's College, IN W
Saint Joseph's University, PA W
Saint Leo University, FL W
Saint Louis University, MO W
Saint Martin's University, WA W
Saint Mary's College of California, CA W
St. Thomas University, FL W
Saint Xavier University, IL W
Samford University, AL W
Sam Houston State University, TX M,W
San Diego State University, CA W
San Francisco State University, CA W
Savannah College of Art and Design, GA W
Seton Hill University, PA W
Shepherd University, WV W
Shippensburg University of Pennsylvania, PA W
Shorter College, GA W
Simpson University, CA W
Slippery Rock University of Pennsylvania, PA W
Sonoma State University, CA W
South Carolina State University, SC W
South Dakota State University, SD W
Southeastern Louisiana University, LA W
Southeastern Oklahoma State University, OK W
Southeast Missouri State University, MO W
Southern Arkansas University–Magnolia, AR W
Southern Connecticut State University, CT W
Southern Illinois University Carbondale, IL W
Southern Illinois University Edwardsville, IL W
Southern Nazarene University, OK W
Southern New Hampshire University, NH W
Southern Oregon University, OR W
Southern Utah University, UT W
Southwest Baptist University, MO W
Southwestern College, KS W
Southwestern Oklahoma State University, OK W
Southwest Minnesota State University, MN W
Spring Arbor University, MI W
Spring Hill College, AL W
Stanford University, CA W
State University of New York at Binghamton, NY W
Stephen F. Austin State University, TX W
Stephens College, MO W
Stetson University, FL W
Stonehill College, MA W
Stony Brook University, State University of New York, NY W
Tarleton State University, TX W
Taylor University, IN W
Temple University, PA W
Tennessee Technological University, TN W
Texas A&M University, TX W
Texas State University–San Marcos, TX W
Texas Tech University, TX W
Tiffin University, OH W
Towson University, MD W
Trevecca Nazarene University, TN W
Trinity Christian College, IL W
Trinity International University, IL W
Troy University, AL W
Truman State University, MO W
Union College, KY W
Union University, TN W
University at Albany, State University of New York, NY W
University at Buffalo, the State University of New York, NY W
The University of Akron, OH W
The University of Alabama, AL W
The University of Alabama at Birmingham, AL W
The University of Alabama in Huntsville, AL W
The University of Arizona, AZ W
University of Arkansas, AR W
University of Bridgeport, CT W
University of California, Davis, CA W
University of California, Los Angeles, CA W
University of California, Riverside, CA W
University of Central Missouri, MO W
University of Central Oklahoma, OK W
University of Colorado at Colorado Springs, CO W
University of Connecticut, CT W
University of Dayton, OH W
University of Delaware, DE W
University of Evansville, IN W
The University of Findlay, OH W
University of Florida, FL W
University of Georgia, GA W
University of Hartford, CT W
University of Hawaii at Manoa, HI W
University of Houston, TX W
University of Illinois at Chicago, IL W
University of Illinois at Springfield, IL W
The University of Iowa, IA W
The University of Kansas, KS W
University of Kentucky, KY W
University of Louisiana at Monroe, LA W
University of Louisville, KY W
University of Maine, ME W
University of Mary, ND W
University of Maryland, Baltimore County, MD W
University of Maryland, College Park, MD W
University of Massachusetts Amherst, MA W
University of Michigan, MI W
University of Michigan–Dearborn, MI M
University of Minnesota, Crookston, MN W
University of Minnesota, Duluth, MN W
University of Minnesota, Twin Cities Campus, MN W
University of Mississippi, MS W
University of Missouri–Columbia, MO W
University of Missouri–Kansas City, MO W
University of Missouri–St. Louis, MO W
University of Mobile, AL W
University of Nebraska at Kearney, NE W
University of Nebraska at Omaha, NE W
University of Nebraska–Lincoln, NE W
University of Nevada, Las Vegas, NV W
University of Nevada, Reno, NV W
University of New Haven, CT W
University of North Alabama, AL W
The University of North Carolina at Chapel Hill, NC W
The University of North Carolina at Greensboro, NC W
The University of North Carolina at Pembroke, NC W
The University of North Carolina Wilmington, NC W
University of North Dakota, ND W
University of Northern Colorado, CO W
University of Northern Iowa, IA W
University of North Florida, FL W
University of North Texas, TX M
University of Notre Dame, IN W
University of Oklahoma, OK W
University of Oregon, OR W
University of Pittsburgh, PA W
University of Puerto Rico, Río Piedras, PR M,W
University of Rhode Island, RI W
University of Saint Francis, IN W
University of San Diego, CA W
University of Science and Arts of Oklahoma, OK W
University of South Carolina, SC W
University of South Carolina Aiken, SC W
University of South Carolina Upstate, SC W
The University of South Dakota, SD W
University of Southern Indiana, IN W
University of Southern Mississippi, MS W
University of South Florida, FL W
The University of Tampa, FL W
The University of Tennessee, TN W

The University of Tennessee at Chattanooga, TN W
The University of Tennessee at Martin, TN W
The University of Texas at Arlington, TX M
The University of Texas at San Antonio, TX W
The University of Texas of the Permian Basin, TX W
University of the Cumberlands, KY W
University of the Incarnate Word, TX W
University of the Pacific, CA W
University of the Southwest, NM W
University of Tulsa, OK W
University of Utah, UT W
University of Virginia, VA W
The University of Virginia's College at Wise, VA W
University of West Florida, FL W
University of West Georgia, GA W
University of Wisconsin–Green Bay, WI W
University of Wisconsin–Madison, WI W
University of Wisconsin–Parkside, WI W
Ursuline College, OH W
Utah State University, UT W
Utah Valley University, UT W
Valdosta State University, GA W
Valley City State University, ND W
Valparaiso University, IN W
Vanguard University of Southern California, CA W
Villanova University, PA W
Virginia Intermont College, VA W
Wagner College, NY W
Wayne State University, MI W
Webber International University, FL W
West Chester University of Pennsylvania, PA W
Western Carolina University, NC W
Western Illinois University, IL W
Western Kentucky University, KY W
Western Michigan University, MI W
Western Oregon University, OR W
Western Washington University, WA W
West Liberty State University, WV W
West Virginia Wesleyan College, WV W
Wheeling Jesuit University, WV W
Wichita State University, KS W
Wingate University, NC W
Winona State University, MN W
Winthrop University, SC W
Wright State University, OH W
York College, NE W
Youngstown State University, OH W

Swimming and Diving

Adams State College, CO W
Adelphi University, NY M,W
American University, DC M,W
Arizona State University, AZ M,W
Asbury College, KY M,W
Ashland University, OH M,W
Auburn University, AL M,W
Ball State University, IN M,W
Bentley University, MA M,W
Biola University, CA M,W
Bloomsburg University of Pennsylvania, PA M,W
Boston College, MA M,W
Bowling Green State University, OH W
Brenau University, GA W
Brigham Young University, UT M,W
Bucknell University, PA M,W
California Baptist University, CA M,W
California Polytechnic State University, San Luis Obispo, CA M,W
California State University, Bakersfield, CA M,W
California State University, Fresno, CA W
California State University, Northridge, CA M,W
California State University, San Bernardino, CA M,W
Campbellsville University, KY W
Canisius College, NY M,W
Catawba College, NC M,W
Central Connecticut State University, CT W
Clarion University of Pennsylvania, PA M,W
Clemson University, SC M,W
Cleveland State University, OH M,W
College of Charleston, SC M,W
The College of Idaho, ID M,W
College of Saint Mary, NE W
The College of William and Mary, VA M
Colorado State University, CO W
Davidson College, NC M,W
Delta State University, MS M,W
Drury University, MO M,W
Duquesne University, PA M,W
Eastern Illinois University, IL M,W
Eastern Michigan University, MI M,W
Edinboro University of Pennsylvania, PA M,W
Fairfield University, CT M,W
Fairmont State University, WV M,W
Florida Gulf Coast University, FL W
Florida State University, FL M,W
Gannon University, PA M,W
Gardner-Webb University, NC M,W
George Mason University, VA M,W
The George Washington University, DC M,W
Georgia Institute of Technology, GA M,W
Georgia Southern University, GA W
Grand Valley State University, MI M,W
Henderson State University, AR M,W
Illinois Institute of Technology, IL M,W
Illinois State University, IL W
Indiana University Bloomington, IN M,W
Indiana University of Pennsylvania, PA W
Indiana University–Purdue University Indianapolis, IN M,W
Iona College, NY M,W
Iowa State University of Science and Technology, IA M,W
James Madison University, VA W
Kutztown University of Pennsylvania, PA M,W
Limestone College, SC M,W
Lindenwood University, MO M,W
Lock Haven University of Pennsylvania, PA W
Long Island University, C.W. Post Campus, NY W
Louisiana State University and Agricultural and Mechanical College, LA M,W
Loyola University Maryland, MD M,W
Malone University, OH M,W
Mesa State College, CO W
Metropolitan State College of Denver, CO M,W
Miami University, OH M,W
Michigan State University, MI M,W
Millersville University of Pennsylvania, PA W
Minnesota State University Mankato, MN M,W
Missouri State University, MO M,W
Missouri University of Science and Technology, MO M
Mount St. Mary's University, MD W
New Jersey Institute of Technology, NJ M,W
New Mexico State University, NM W
Niagara University, NY M,W
North Carolina State University, NC M,W
Northeastern University, MA W
Northern Arizona University, AZ W
Northern Michigan University, MI W
Northern State University, SD W
Northwestern University, IL M,W
Oakland University, MI M,W
The Ohio State University, OH M,W
Ohio University, OH W
Old Dominion University, VA M,W
Oregon State University, OR W
Ouachita Baptist University, AR M,W
Penn State University Park, PA M,W
Pepperdine University, CA W
Providence College, RI M,W
Purdue University, IN M,W
Radford University, VA W
Rider University, NJ M,W
Robert Morris College, IL W
Sacred Heart University, CT W
St. Cloud State University, MN M,W
Saint Francis University, PA M,W
Saint Leo University, FL M,W
Saint Louis University, MO M,W
San Diego State University, CA W
San Jose State University, CA W
Savannah College of Art and Design, GA M,W
Shippensburg University of Pennsylvania, PA M,W
South Dakota State University, SD M,W
Southern Connecticut State University, CT M,W
Southern Illinois University Carbondale, IL M,W
Southern Methodist University, TX M,W
Stanford University, CA M,W
State University of New York at Binghamton, NY M,W
Stephens College, MO W
Stony Brook University, State University of New York, NY M,W
Texas A&M University, TX M,W
Texas Christian University, TX M,W
Towson University, MD M,W

Truman State University, MO M,W
Union College, KY M,W
University at Buffalo, the State University of New York, NY M,W
The University of Akron, OH W
The University of Alabama, AL M,W
University of Alaska Fairbanks, AK W
The University of Arizona, AZ M,W
University of Arkansas, AR W
University of Bridgeport, CT W
University of California, Davis, CA M,W
University of California, Irvine, CA M,W
University of California, Los Angeles, CA W
University of Cincinnati, OH M,W
University of Connecticut, CT M,W
University of Delaware, DE W
University of Denver, CO M,W
University of Evansville, IN M,W
The University of Findlay, OH M,W
University of Florida, FL M,W
University of Georgia, GA M,W
University of Hawaii at Manoa, HI M,W
University of Houston, TX W
University of Illinois at Chicago, IL M,W
The University of Iowa, IA M,W
The University of Kansas, KS W
University of Kentucky, KY M,W
University of Louisiana at Monroe, LA M,W
University of Louisville, KY M,W
University of Maine, ME W
University of Maryland, Baltimore County, MD M,W
University of Maryland, College Park, MD M,W
University of Massachusetts Amherst, MA M,W
University of Massachusetts Lowell, MA M
University of Miami, FL W
University of Michigan, MI M,W
University of Minnesota, Twin Cities Campus, MN M,W
University of Missouri–Columbia, MO M,W
University of Nebraska at Kearney, NE W
University of Nebraska–Lincoln, NE W
University of Nevada, Las Vegas, NV M,W
University of Nevada, Reno, NV W
University of New Hampshire, NH W
University of New Orleans, LA M,W
The University of North Carolina at Chapel Hill, NC M,W
The University of North Carolina Wilmington, NC M,W
University of North Dakota, ND W
University of Northern Colorado, CO W
University of Northern Iowa, IA W
University of North Florida, FL W
University of North Texas, TX W
University of Notre Dame, IN M,W
University of Pittsburgh, PA M,W
University of Puerto Rico, Río Piedras, PR M,W
University of Rhode Island, RI W
University of Richmond, VA W
University of San Diego, CA W
University of South Carolina, SC M,W
The University of South Dakota, SD M,W
University of Southern California, CA M,W
The University of Tampa, FL M,W
The University of Tennessee, TN M,W
The University of Texas of the Permian Basin, TX M,W
University of the Cumberlands, KY M,W
University of the Incarnate Word, TX M,W
University of the Pacific, CA M,W
University of Utah, UT M,W
University of Vermont, VT W
University of Virginia, VA M,W
University of Wisconsin–Green Bay, WI M,W
University of Wisconsin–Madison, WI M,W
University of Wisconsin–Milwaukee, WI M,W
University of Wyoming, WY M,W
Valparaiso University, IN M,W
Villanova University, PA W
Virginia Military Institute, VA M
Virginia Polytechnic Institute and State University, VA M,W
Wagner College, NY W
Washington State University, WA W
Wayne State University, MI M,W
West Chester University of Pennsylvania, PA M,W
Western Illinois University, IL M,W
Western Kentucky University, KY M,W
West Virginia University, WV M,W
West Virginia Wesleyan College, WV M,W
Wheeling Jesuit University, WV M,W
Wingate University, NC M,W
Wright State University, OH M,W
Xavier University, OH M,W

Table Tennis

Lindenwood University, MO M,W
University of Puerto Rico, Río Piedras, PR M,W

Tennis

Abilene Christian University, TX M,W
Academy of Art University, CA W
Adelphi University, NY M,W
Alcorn State University, MS M,W
American University, DC M,W
Appalachian State University, NC M,W
Arizona State University, AZ W
Arkansas State University, AR W
Arkansas Tech University, AR W
Asbury College, KY M,W
Auburn University, AL M,W
Auburn University Montgomery, AL M,W
Augustana College, SD W
Augusta State University, GA M,W
Austin Peay State University, TN M,W
Azusa Pacific University, CA M
Baker University, KS M,W
Ball State University, IN M,W
Barton College, NC M,W
Baylor University, TX M,W
Belhaven College, MS M,W
Bellarmine University, KY M,W
Belmont Abbey College, NC M,W
Belmont University, TN M,W
Bentley University, MA M,W
Bethany College, KS M,W
Bethel College, IN M,W
Bethel College, KS M,W
Biola University, CA M,W
Bloomfield College, NJ M
Bloomsburg University of Pennsylvania, PA M,W
Bluefield College, VA M,W
Bluefield State College, WV M,W
Boise State University, ID M,W
Boston College, MA M,W
Bowling Green State University, OH W
Bradley University, IL M,W
Brenau University, GA W
Brevard College, NC M,W
Brigham Young University, UT M,W
Butler University, IN M,W
California Baptist University, CA M,W
California Polytechnic State University, San Luis Obispo, CA M,W
California State Polytechnic University, Pomona, CA M,W
California State University, Bakersfield, CA W
California State University, Fresno, CA M,W
California State University, Fullerton, CA W
California State University, Long Beach, CA W
California State University, Los Angeles, CA W
California State University, Northridge, CA W
California State University, Sacramento, CA M,W
Campbellsville University, KY M,W
Carson-Newman College, TN M,W
Catawba College, NC M,W
Cedarville University, OH M,W
Chaminade University of Honolulu, HI M,W
Chestnut Hill College, PA M,W
Christian Brothers University, TN M,W
Clarion University of Pennsylvania, PA W
Clarke College, IA W
Clayton State University, GA W
Clemson University, SC M,W
Cleveland State University, OH W
Coastal Carolina University, SC M,W
College of Charleston, SC M,W
The College of Idaho, ID W
The College of William and Mary, VA M,W
Colorado State University, CO W
Colorado State University–Pueblo, CO M,W
Columbus State University, GA M,W
Concordia University, Nebraska, NE M,W
Concord University, WV M,W
Coppin State University, MD M,W
Covenant College, GA W
Creighton University, NE M,W
Dallas Baptist University, TX W
Davidson College, NC M,W
Delta State University, MS M,W
DePaul University, IL M,W
Dixie State College of Utah, UT W
Dominican University of California, CA M,W
Dordt College, IA M,W
Dowling College, NY M,W

Drake University, IA M,W
Drury University, MO M,W
Duke University, NC M,W
Duquesne University, PA M,W
Eastern Illinois University, IL M,W
Eastern Michigan University, MI W
Eastern Washington University, WA M,W
East Tennessee State University, TN M,W
Elon University, NC M,W
Embry-Riddle Aeronautical University, FL M,W
Emmanuel College, GA M,W
Emporia State University, KS M,W
Evangel University, MO M,W
Fairfield University, CT M,W
Fairleigh Dickinson University, Metropolitan Campus, NJ M,W
Fairmont State University, WV M,W
Ferris State University, MI M,W
Flagler College, FL M,W
Florida Gulf Coast University, FL M,W
Florida Institute of Technology, FL M,W
Florida International University, FL W
Florida State University, FL M,W
Fort Hays State University, KS W
Fort Valley State University, GA M,W
Francis Marion University, SC M,W
Franklin Pierce University, NH M,W
Furman University, SC M,W
Gardner-Webb University, NC M,W
George Mason University, VA M,W
Georgetown College, KY M,W
Georgetown University, DC W
The George Washington University, DC M,W
Georgia College & State University, GA M,W
Georgia Institute of Technology, GA M,W
Georgian Court University, NJ W
Georgia Southern University, GA M,W
Georgia Southwestern State University, GA M,W
Georgia State University, GA M,W
Gonzaga University, WA M,W
Grace College, IN M,W
Graceland University, IA M,W
Grand Valley State University, MI M,W
Hampton University, VA M,W
Harding University, AR M,W
Hawai'i Pacific University, HI M,W
Henderson State University, AR M,W
Hofstra University, NY M,W
Holy Family University, PA W
Hope International University, CA M,W
Huntington University, IN M,W
Idaho State University, ID M,W
Illinois State University, IL M,W
Indiana State University, IN M,W
Indiana University Bloomington, IN M,W
Indiana University of Pennsylvania, PA W
Indiana University–Purdue University Fort Wayne, IN M,W
Indiana University–Purdue University Indianapolis, IN M,W
Iowa State University of Science and Technology, IA W
Jacksonville University, FL M,W
James Madison University, VA M,W
John Brown University, AR M,W
Johnson C. Smith University, NC M,W
Judson College, AL W
Kansas State University, KS W
Kennesaw State University, GA W
Kutztown University of Pennsylvania, PA M,W
Lamar University, TX M,W
Lambuth University, TN M,W
Lee University, TN M,W
Le Moyne College, NY M,W
Lewis-Clark State College, ID M,W
Liberty University, VA M,W
Limestone College, SC M,W
Lincoln Memorial University, TN M,W
Lindenwood University, MO M,W
Lindsey Wilson College, KY M,W
Lipscomb University, TN M,W
Long Island University, Brooklyn Campus, NY W
Long Island University, C.W. Post Campus, NY W
Longwood University, VA M,W
Louisiana State University and Agricultural and Mechanical College, LA M,W
Loyola University Maryland, MD M,W
Malone University, OH M,W
Marian College, IN M,W
Marquette University, WI M,W
The Master's College and Seminary, CA W
McKendree University, IL M,W
Mercer University, GA M,W
Mercyhurst College, PA M,W
Merrimack College, MA W
Mesa State College, CO M,W
Metropolitan State College of Denver, CO M,W
Miami University, OH W
Michigan State University, MI M,W
Michigan Technological University, MI W
Midway College, KY W
Millersville University of Pennsylvania, PA M,W
Milligan College, TN M,W
Minnesota State University Mankato, MN M,W
Mississippi State University, MS M,W
Missouri Baptist University, MO M,W
Missouri Southern State University, MO W
Missouri Western State University, MO W
Molloy College, NY W
Monmouth University, NJ M,W
Montana State University, MT M,W
Montana State University–Billings, MT M,W
Mount Olive College, NC M,W
Mount St. Mary's University, MD M,W
Murray State University, KY M,W
Newberry College, SC M,W
New Jersey Institute of Technology, NJ M,W
Newman University, KS M,W
New Mexico State University, NM M,W
Niagara University, NY M,W
Nicholls State University, LA W
North Carolina State University, NC M,W
Northeastern State University, OK W
Northeastern University, MA M
Northern Arizona University, AZ M,W
Northern Kentucky University, KY M,W
Northern State University, SD W
North Greenville University, SC M,W
Northwestern State University of Louisiana, LA W
Northwestern University, IL M,W
Northwest Missouri State University, MO M,W
Northwood University, MI M,W
Northwood University, Florida Campus, FL M,W
Notre Dame de Namur University, CA W
Oakland University, MI W
The Ohio State University, OH M,W
Oklahoma Baptist University, OK M,W
Oklahoma Christian University, OK M,W
Oklahoma State University, OK M,W
Old Dominion University, VA M,W
Olivet Nazarene University, IL M,W
Oral Roberts University, OK M,W
Ouachita Baptist University, AR M,W
Our Lady of the Lake University of San Antonio, TX M,W
Pace University, NY M,W
Palm Beach Atlantic University, FL M,W
Penn State University Park, PA M,W
Pepperdine University, CA M,W
Philadelphia University, PA M,W
Point Loma Nazarene University, CA M,W
Portland State University, OR M,W
Presbyterian College, SC M,W
Providence College, RI W
Purdue University, IN M,W
Quinnipiac University, CT M,W
Radford University, VA M,W
Reinhardt College, GA M,W
Rider University, NJ M,W
Robert Morris College, IL W
Robert Morris University, PA M,W
Roberts Wesleyan College, NY M,W
Rockhurst University, MO M,W
Rollins College, FL M,W
Sacred Heart University, CT M,W
Saginaw Valley State University, MI W
St. Ambrose University, IA M,W
St. Andrews Presbyterian College, NC M,W
St. Cloud State University, MN M,W
St. Edward's University, TX M,W
Saint Francis University, PA M,W
St. John's University, NY M,W
Saint Joseph's College, IN M,W
Saint Joseph's University, PA M,W
Saint Leo University, FL M,W
Saint Louis University, MO M,W
Saint Mary's College of California, CA M,W
St. Mary's University, TX M,W
St. Thomas University, FL M,W
Samford University, AL M,W
Sam Houston State University, TX M,W
San Diego State University, CA M,W
San Jose State University, CA W
Santa Clara University, CA M,W

Savannah College of Art and Design, GA M,W
Seton Hill University, PA M,W
Shepherd University, WV M,W
Shippensburg University of Pennsylvania, PA W
Shorter College, GA M,W
Slippery Rock University of Pennsylvania, PA W
Sonoma State University, CA M,W
South Carolina State University, SC M,W
South Dakota State University, SD M,W
Southeastern Louisiana University, LA M,W
Southeastern Oklahoma State University, OK M,W
Southeast Missouri State University, MO W
Southern Arkansas University–Magnolia, AR W
Southern Illinois University Carbondale, IL M,W
Southern Illinois University Edwardsville, IL M,W
Southern Methodist University, TX M,W
Southern Nazarene University, OK M,W
Southern New Hampshire University, NH M,W
Southern Oregon University, OR W
Southern Utah University, UT W
Southwest Baptist University, MO M,W
Southwestern College, KS M,W
Southwest Minnesota State University, MN W
Spring Arbor University, MI M,W
Spring Hill College, AL M,W
Stanford University, CA M,W
State University of New York at Binghamton, NY M,W
Stephen F. Austin State University, TX W
Stephens College, MO W
Stetson University, FL M,W
Stonehill College, MA M,W
Stony Brook University, State University of New York, NY M,W
Tarleton State University, TX W
Taylor University, IN M,W
Temple University, PA M,W
Tennessee Technological University, TN M,W
Texas A&M University, TX M,W
Texas Christian University, TX M,W
Texas State University–San Marcos, TX W
Texas Tech University, TX M,W
Tiffin University, OH M,W
Towson University, MD M,W
Troy University, AL M,W
Truman State University, MO M,W
Tuskegee University, AL M,W
Union College, KY M,W
University at Albany, State University of New York, NY W
University at Buffalo, the State University of New York, NY M,W
The University of Akron, OH W
The University of Alabama, AL M,W
The University of Alabama at Birmingham, AL M,W
The University of Alabama in Huntsville, AL M,W
The University of Arizona, AZ M,W
University of Arkansas, AR M,W
University of California, Davis, CA M,W
University of California, Irvine, CA M,W
University of California, Los Angeles, CA M,W
University of California, Riverside, CA M,W
University of Central Florida, FL M,W
University of Central Oklahoma, OK M,W
University of Cincinnati, OH M,W
University of Colorado at Boulder, CO W
University of Colorado at Colorado Springs, CO M,W
University of Connecticut, CT M,W
University of Dayton, OH M,W
University of Denver, CO M,W
University of Evansville, IN W
The University of Findlay, OH M,W
University of Florida, FL M,W
University of Georgia, GA M,W
University of Hartford, CT M,W
University of Hawaii at Manoa, HI M,W
University of Houston, TX W
University of Idaho, ID M,W
University of Illinois at Chicago, IL M,W
University of Illinois at Springfield, IL M,W
The University of Iowa, IA M,W
The University of Kansas, KS W
University of Kentucky, KY M,W
University of Louisville, KY M,W
University of Mary, ND M,W
University of Maryland, Baltimore County, MD M,W
University of Maryland, College Park, MD M,W
University of Maryland Eastern Shore, MD M
University of Massachusetts Amherst, MA W
University of Massachusetts Lowell, MA M,W
University of Memphis, TN M,W
University of Miami, FL M,W
University of Michigan, MI M,W
University of Minnesota, Crookston, MN W
University of Minnesota, Duluth, MN W
University of Minnesota, Twin Cities Campus, MN M,W
University of Mississippi, MS M,W
University of Missouri–Columbia, MO W
University of Missouri–Kansas City, MO M,W
University of Missouri–St. Louis, MO M,W
University of Mobile, AL M,W
The University of Montana, MT M,W
University of Montevallo, AL W
University of Nebraska at Kearney, NE M,W
University of Nebraska–Lincoln, NE M,W
University of Nevada, Las Vegas, NV M,W
University of Nevada, Reno, NV M,W
University of New Hampshire, NH W
University of New Haven, CT W
University of New Orleans, LA M,W
University of North Alabama, AL M,W
The University of North Carolina at Asheville, NC M,W
The University of North Carolina at Chapel Hill, NC M,W
The University of North Carolina at Greensboro, NC M,W
The University of North Carolina at Pembroke, NC W
The University of North Carolina Wilmington, NC M,W
University of Northern Colorado, CO M,W
University of Northern Iowa, IA W
University of North Florida, FL M,W
University of Notre Dame, IN M,W
University of Oklahoma, OK M,W
University of Oregon, OR M,W
University of Pittsburgh, PA W
University of Portland, OR M,W
University of Puerto Rico, Río Piedras, PR M,W
University of Rhode Island, RI W
University of Richmond, VA M,W
University of Saint Francis, IN W
University of San Diego, CA M,W
University of South Alabama, AL M,W
University of South Carolina, SC M,W
University of South Carolina Aiken, SC M,W
University of South Carolina Upstate, SC M,W
The University of South Dakota, SD W
University of Southern California, CA M,W
University of Southern Indiana, IN M,W
University of Southern Mississippi, MS M,W
University of South Florida, FL M,W
The University of Tampa, FL W
The University of Tennessee, TN M,W
The University of Tennessee at Chattanooga, TN M,W
The University of Tennessee at Martin, TN M,W
The University of Texas at Arlington, TX M,W
The University of Texas at El Paso, TX W
The University of Texas at San Antonio, TX M,W
The University of Texas–Pan American, TX M,W
University of the Cumberlands, KY M,W
University of the Incarnate Word, TX M,W
University of the Pacific, CA M,W
University of Tulsa, OK M,W
University of Utah, UT M,W
University of Virginia, VA M,W
The University of Virginia's College at Wise, VA M,W
University of West Florida, FL M,W
University of Wisconsin–Green Bay, WI M,W
University of Wisconsin–Madison, WI M,W
University of Wisconsin–Milwaukee, WI M,W
University of Wyoming, WY W
Ursuline College, OH W
Utah State University, UT M,W
Valdosta State University, GA M,W
Valparaiso University, IN M,W

Vanderbilt University, TN	M,W
Vanguard University of Southern California, CA	M,W
Virginia Commonwealth University, VA	M,W
Virginia Military Institute, VA	M
Virginia Polytechnic Institute and State University, VA	M,W
Wagner College, NY	M,W
Wake Forest University, NC	M,W
Washington State University, WA	W
Wayne State University, MI	M,W
Webber International University, FL	M,W
Weber State University, UT	M,W
West Chester University of Pennsylvania, PA	M,W
Western Carolina University, NC	W
Western Illinois University, IL	M,W
Western Kentucky University, KY	M,W
Western Michigan University, MI	M,W
West Liberty State University, WV	M,W
West Virginia University, WV	W
West Virginia Wesleyan College, WV	M,W
Wichita State University, KS	M,W
Wingate University, NC	M,W
Winona State University, MN	M,W
Winthrop University, SC	M,W
Wofford College, SC	M,W
Wright State University, OH	M,W
Xavier University, OH	M,W
Xavier University of Louisiana, LA	M,W
Youngstown State University, OH	M,W

Track and Field

Abilene Christian University, TX	M,W
Academy of Art University, CA	M,W
Adams State College, CO	M,W
Adelphi University, NY	M,W
Alabama Agricultural and Mechanical University, AL	M,W
Alcorn State University, MS	M,W
Alderson-Broaddus College, WV	M,W
American University, DC	M,W
Angelo State University, TX	M,W
Appalachian State University, NC	M,W
Arizona State University, AZ	M,W
Arkansas State University, AR	M,W
Ashland University, OH	M,W
Auburn University, AL	M,W
Augustana College, SD	M,W
Austin Peay State University, TN	W
Azusa Pacific University, CA	M,W
Baker University, KS	M,W
Ball State University, IN	M,W
Baylor University, TX	M,W
Bellarmine University, KY	M,W
Belmont University, TN	M,W
Benedictine College, KS	M,W
Bentley University, MA	M,W
Bethany College, KS	M,W
Bethel College, IN	M,W
Bethel College, KS	M,W
Biola University, CA	M,W
Black Hills State University, SD	M,W
Bloomsburg University of Pennsylvania, PA	M,W
Boise State University, ID	M,W
Boston College, MA	M,W
Bowling Green State University, OH	W
Bradley University, IL	W
Brevard College, NC	M,W
Brigham Young University, UT	M,W
California Polytechnic State University, San Luis Obispo, CA	M,W
California State Polytechnic University, Pomona, CA	M,W
California State University, Bakersfield, CA	M,W
California State University, Chico, CA	M,W
California State University, Fresno, CA	M,W
California State University, Fullerton, CA	M,W
California State University, Long Beach, CA	M,W
California State University, Los Angeles, CA	M,W
California State University, Northridge, CA	M,W
California State University, Sacramento, CA	M,W
Campbellsville University, KY	M,W
Carson-Newman College, TN	M,W
Cedarville University, OH	M,W
Central Connecticut State University, CT	M,W
Central Methodist University, MO	M,W
Central Michigan University, MI	M,W
Clarion University of Pennsylvania, PA	W
Clarke College, IA	M,W
Clayton State University, GA	M,W
Clemson University, SC	M,W
Cleveland State University, OH	W
Coastal Carolina University, SC	M,W
College of Charleston, SC	W
The College of Idaho, ID	M,W
The College of William and Mary, VA	M,W
Colorado School of Mines, CO	M,W
Colorado State University, CO	M,W
Colorado State University–Pueblo, CO	W
Concordia University, OR	M,W
Concordia University, Nebraska, NE	M,W
Concordia University, St. Paul, MN	M,W
Concord University, WV	M,W
Coppin State University, MD	M,W
Culver-Stockton College, MO	M,W
Dakota State University, SD	M,W
Dallas Baptist University, TX	W
Dana College, NE	M,W
Davenport University, MI	M,W
Davidson College, NC	M,W
DePaul University, IL	M,W
Doane College, NE	M,W
Dordt College, IA	M,W
Drake University, IA	M,W
Duquesne University, PA	M,W
Eastern Illinois University, IL	M,W
Eastern Michigan University, MI	M,W
Eastern Washington University, WA	M,W
East Tennessee State University, TN	M,W
Edinboro University of Pennsylvania, PA	M,W
Elon University, NC	W
Embry-Riddle Aeronautical University, FL	M,W
Emporia State University, KS	M,W
Evangel University, MO	M,W
Fairleigh Dickinson University, Metropolitan Campus, NJ	M,W
Felician College, NJ	M,W
Ferris State University, MI	M,W
Florida International University, FL	M,W
Florida State University, FL	M,W
Fort Hays State University, KS	M,W
Fort Valley State University, GA	M,W
Furman University, SC	M,W
Gardner-Webb University, NC	M,W
George Mason University, VA	M,W
Georgetown College, KY	M,W
Georgetown University, DC	M,W
Georgia Institute of Technology, GA	M,W
Georgian Court University, NJ	W
Georgia Southern University, GA	W
Georgia State University, GA	M,W
Glenville State College, WV	M,W
Grace College, IN	M,W
Graceland University, IA	M,W
Grand Valley State University, MI	M,W
Grand View University, IA	M,W
Hampton University, VA	M,W
Harding University, AR	M,W
Holy Family University, PA	M,W
Houghton College, NY	M,W
Houston Baptist University, TX	M,W
Humboldt State University, CA	M,W
Huntington University, IN	M,W
Idaho State University, ID	M,W
Illinois State University, IL	M,W
Indiana State University, IN	M,W
Indiana University Bloomington, IN	M,W
Indiana University of Pennsylvania, PA	M,W
Indiana University–Purdue University Fort Wayne, IN	W
Inter American University of Puerto Rico, Guayama Campus, PR	M,W
Iona College, NY	M,W
Iowa State University of Science and Technology, IA	M,W
Jacksonville University, FL	W
James Madison University, VA	W
Jamestown College, ND	M,W
Johnson C. Smith University, NC	M,W
Kansas State University, KS	M,W
Kennesaw State University, GA	M,W
Kent State University, OH	M,W
Kentucky State University, KY	M,W
Kutztown University of Pennsylvania, PA	M,W
Lamar University, TX	M,W
Liberty University, VA	M,W
Limestone College, SC	W
Lindenwood University, MO	M,W
Lindsey Wilson College, KY	M,W
Lock Haven University of Pennsylvania, PA	M,W
Long Island University, Brooklyn Campus, NY	M,W
Louisiana State University and Agricultural and Mechanical College, LA	M,W
Loyola University Chicago, IL	M,W
Loyola University Maryland, MD	M,W
Malone University, OH	M,W
Marian College, IN	M,W
Marquette University, WI	M,W

The Master's College and Seminary, CA M,W
McKendree University, IL M,W
Mesa State College, CO W
Miami University, OH M,W
Michigan State University, MI M,W
MidAmerica Nazarene University, KS M,W
Midway College, KY W
Millersville University of Pennsylvania, PA M,W
Minnesota State University Mankato, MN M,W
Minot State University, ND M,W
Mississippi State University, MS M,W
Missouri Baptist University, MO M,W
Missouri Southern State University, MO M,W
Missouri State University, MO W
Missouri University of Science and Technology, MO M,W
Monmouth University, NJ M,W
Montana State University, MT M,W
Mount Marty College, SD M,W
Mount Mercy College, IA M,W
Mount St. Mary's University, MD M,W
Murray State University, KY M,W
New Mexico State University, NM W
Nicholls State University, LA M,W
North Carolina State University, NC M,W
North Dakota State University, ND M,W
Northeastern University, MA M,W
Northern Arizona University, AZ M,W
Northern Michigan University, MI W
Northern State University, SD M,W
Northwestern State University of Louisiana, LA M,W
Northwest Missouri State University, MO M,W
Northwest University, WA M,W
Northwood University, MI M,W
Northwood University, Texas Campus, TX M,W
The Ohio State University, OH M,W
Ohio University, OH W
Oklahoma Baptist University, OK M,W
Oklahoma Christian University, OK M,W
Oklahoma City University, OK M,W
Oklahoma State University, OK M,W
Olivet Nazarene University, IL M,W
Oral Roberts University, OK M,W
Oregon Institute of Technology, OR M,W
Pace University, NY M,W
Penn State University Park, PA M,W
Pittsburg State University, KS M,W
Point Loma Nazarene University, CA M,W
Portland State University, OR M,W
Providence College, RI M,W
Purdue University, IN M,W
Quinnipiac University, CT M,W
Radford University, VA M,W
Rider University, NJ M,W
Robert Morris College, IL W
Robert Morris University, PA M,W
Roberts Wesleyan College, NY M,W
Sacred Heart University, CT M,W
Saginaw Valley State University, MI M,W
St. Ambrose University, IA M,W
St. Cloud State University, MN M,W
Saint Francis University, PA M,W
St. John's University, NY W
Saint Joseph's College, IN M,W
Saint Joseph's University, PA M,W
Saint Louis University, MO M,W
Saint Martin's University, WA M,W
Samford University, AL M,W
Sam Houston State University, TX M,W
San Diego State University, CA W
San Francisco State University, CA W
Santa Clara University, CA M,W
Seattle Pacific University, WA M,W
Seton Hill University, PA M,W
Shippensburg University of Pennsylvania, PA M,W
Shorter College, GA M,W
Slippery Rock University of Pennsylvania, PA M,W
South Carolina State University, SC M,W
South Dakota School of Mines and Technology, SD M,W
South Dakota State University, SD M,W
Southeastern Louisiana University, LA M,W
Southeast Missouri State University, MO M,W
Southern Connecticut State University, CT M,W
Southern Illinois University Carbondale, IL M,W
Southern Illinois University Edwardsville, IL M,W
Southern Nazarene University, OK M,W
Southern Oregon University, OR M,W
Southern Utah University, UT M,W
Southwest Baptist University, MO M,W
Southwestern College, KS M,W
Spring Arbor University, MI M,W
Stanford University, CA M,W
State University of New York at Binghamton, NY M,W
Stephen F. Austin State University, TX M,W
Stonehill College, MA M,W
Stony Brook University, State University of New York, NY M,W
Tarleton State University, TX M,W
Taylor University, IN M,W
Temple University, PA M,W
Tennessee Technological University, TN W
Texas A&M University, TX M,W
Texas Christian University, TX M,W
Texas State University–San Marcos, TX M,W
Texas Tech University, TX M,W
Tiffin University, OH M,W
Towson University, MD M,W
Trinity Christian College, IL M,W
Troy University, AL M,W
Truman State University, MO M,W
Tuskegee University, AL M,W
Union College, KY M,W
University at Albany, State University of New York, NY M,W
University at Buffalo, the State University of New York, NY M,W
The University of Akron, OH M,W
The University of Alabama, AL M,W
The University of Alabama at Birmingham, AL W
The University of Alabama in Huntsville, AL M,W
The University of Arizona, AZ M,W
University of Arkansas, AR M,W
University of California, Davis, CA M,W
University of California, Irvine, CA M,W
University of California, Los Angeles, CA M,W
University of California, Riverside, CA M,W
University of Central Florida, FL W
University of Central Missouri, MO M,W
University of Cincinnati, OH M
University of Colorado at Boulder, CO M,W
University of Connecticut, CT M,W
University of Dayton, OH W
University of Delaware, DE W
The University of Findlay, OH M,W
University of Florida, FL M,W
University of Georgia, GA M,W
University of Hawaii at Manoa, HI W
University of Houston, TX M,W
University of Idaho, ID M,W
University of Illinois at Chicago, IL M,W
The University of Iowa, IA M,W
The University of Kansas, KS M,W
University of Kentucky, KY M,W
University of Louisiana at Monroe, LA M,W
University of Louisville, KY M,W
University of Maine, ME M,W
University of Mary, ND M,W
University of Maryland, Baltimore County, MD M,W
University of Maryland, College Park, MD M,W
University of Massachusetts Amherst, MA M,W
University of Massachusetts Lowell, MA M,W
University of Memphis, TN M,W
University of Miami, FL M,W
University of Michigan, MI M,W
University of Minnesota, Duluth, MN M,W
University of Minnesota, Twin Cities Campus, MN M,W
University of Mississippi, MS M,W
University of Missouri–Columbia, MO M,W
University of Missouri–Kansas City, MO M,W
University of Mobile, AL M,W
The University of Montana, MT M,W
University of Nebraska at Kearney, NE M,W
University of Nebraska–Lincoln, NE M,W
University of Nevada, Las Vegas, NV W
University of Nevada, Reno, NV W
University of New Hampshire, NH M,W
University of New Haven, CT M,W
The University of North Carolina at Asheville, NC M,W
The University of North Carolina at Chapel Hill, NC M,W
The University of North Carolina at Pembroke, NC M,W
The University of North Carolina Wilmington, NC M,W
University of North Dakota, ND M,W
University of Northern Colorado, CO M,W

University of Northern Iowa, IA M,W
University of North Florida, FL M,W
University of North Texas, TX M,W
University of Notre Dame, IN M,W
University of Oklahoma, OK M,W
University of Oregon, OR M,W
University of Pittsburgh, PA M,W
University of Portland, OR M,W
University of Puerto Rico, Río Piedras, PR M,W
University of Rhode Island, RI M,W
University of Richmond, VA W
University of Saint Francis, IN M,W
University of San Diego, CA W
University of South Alabama, AL M,W
University of South Carolina, SC M,W
University of South Carolina Upstate, SC M,W
The University of South Dakota, SD M,W
University of Southern California, CA M,W
University of Southern Mississippi, MS M,W
University of South Florida, FL M,W
The University of Tennessee, TN M,W
The University of Texas at Arlington, TX M,W
The University of Texas at El Paso, TX M,W
The University of Texas at San Antonio, TX M,W
The University of Texas–Pan American, TX M,W
University of the Cumberlands, KY M,W
University of the Incarnate Word, TX M,W
University of the Southwest, NM M,W
University of Tulsa, OK M,W
University of Utah, UT W
University of Vermont, VT M,W
University of Virginia, VA M,W
University of Wisconsin–Madison, WI M,W
University of Wisconsin–Milwaukee, WI M,W
University of Wisconsin–Parkside, WI M,W
University of Wyoming, WY M,W
Ursuline College, OH W
Utah State University, UT M,W
Utah Valley University, UT M,W
Valparaiso University, IN M,W
Vanderbilt University, TN W
Vanguard University of Southern California, CA M,W
Villanova University, PA M,W
Virginia Commonwealth University, VA M,W
Virginia Military Institute, VA M,W
Virginia Polytechnic Institute and State University, VA M,W
Wagner College, NY M,W
Wake Forest University, NC M,W
Washington State University, WA M,W
Wayland Baptist University, TX M,W
Webber International University, FL M,W
Weber State University, UT M,W
West Chester University of Pennsylvania, PA M,W
Western Carolina University, NC M,W
Western Illinois University, IL M,W
Western Kentucky University, KY M,W
Western Michigan University, MI W
Western Oregon University, OR M,W
Western Washington University, WA M,W
West Liberty State University, WV M,W
West Virginia University, WV W
West Virginia Wesleyan College, WV M,W
Wheeling Jesuit University, WV M,W
Wichita State University, KS M,W
Winona State University, MN W
Winthrop University, SC M,W
Wofford College, SC M,W
Wright State University, OH W
Xavier University, OH M,W
Youngstown State University, OH M,W

Ultimate Frisbee

Ohio University–Zanesville, OH M,W
St. Louis Christian College, MO M,W
University of Rhode Island, RI M,W

Volleyball

Abilene Christian University, TX W
Academy of Art University, CA W
Adams State College, CO W
Adelphi University, NY W
Alabama Agricultural and Mechanical University, AL W
Alcorn State University, MS W
Alderson-Broaddus College, WV W
American University, DC W
Angelo State University, TX W
Appalachian State University, NC W
Arizona State University, AZ W
Arkansas State University, AR W
Arkansas Tech University, AR W
Asbury College, KY W
Ashland University, OH W
Auburn University, AL W
Augustana College, SD W
Austin Peay State University, TN W
Avila University, MO W
Azusa Pacific University, CA W
Baker University, KS W
Ball State University, IN M,W
Barton College, NC W
Baylor University, TX W
Belhaven College, MS W
Bellarmine University, KY W
Belmont University, TN W
Benedictine College, KS W
Bentley University, MA W
Bethany College, KS W
Bethel College, IN W
Bethel College, KS W
Biola University, CA W
Black Hills State University, SD W
Blessing-Rieman College of Nursing, IL M,W
Bloomfield College, NJ W
Bluefield College, VA W
Boise State University, ID W
Boston College, MA W
Bowling Green State University, OH W
Bradley University, IL W
Brenau University, GA W
Brevard College, NC W
Brewton-Parker College, GA W
Brigham Young University, UT M,W
Bryan College, TN W
Butler University, IN W
California Baptist University, CA M,W
California Polytechnic State University, San Luis Obispo, CA W
California State Polytechnic University, Pomona, CA W
California State University, Bakersfield, CA W
California State University, Fresno, CA W
California State University, Fullerton, CA W
California State University, Long Beach, CA M,W
California State University, Los Angeles, CA W
California State University, Northridge, CA M,W
California State University, Sacramento, CA W
California State University, San Bernardino, CA W
Campbellsville University, KY W
Canisius College, NY W
Carroll College, MT W
Carson-Newman College, TN W
Catawba College, NC W
Cedarville University, OH W
Central Connecticut State University, CT W
Central Methodist University, MO W
Central Michigan University, MI W
Chaminade University of Honolulu, HI W
Chestnut Hill College, PA W
Christian Brothers University, TN W
Clarion University of Pennsylvania, PA W
Clarke College, IA M,W
Clemson University, SC W
Cleveland State University, OH W
Coastal Carolina University, SC W
Colgate University, NY W
College of Charleston, SC W
The College of Idaho, ID W
College of Saint Mary, NE W
College of the Ozarks, MO W
The College of William and Mary, VA W
Colorado School of Mines, CO W
Colorado State University, CO W
Colorado State University–Pueblo, CO W
Columbia College, MO W
Concordia University, OR W
Concordia University, Nebraska, NE W
Concordia University, St. Paul, MN W
Concord University, WV W
Coppin State University, MD W
Corban College, OR W
Covenant College, GA W
Creighton University, NE W
Culver-Stockton College, MO W
Daemen College, NY W
Dakota State University, SD W
Dallas Baptist University, TX W
Dana College, NE W
Davenport University, MI W
Davidson College, NC W
DePaul University, IL W
Dillard University, LA W
Dixie State College of Utah, UT W
Doane College, NE W

Athletic Grants for Undergraduates
Volleyball

Dominican College, NY W
Dominican University of California, CA W
Dordt College, IA W
Dowling College, NY W
Drake University, IA W
Drury University, MO W
Duke University, NC W
Duquesne University, PA W
Eastern Illinois University, IL W
Eastern Michigan University, MI W
Eastern Washington University, WA W
East Tennessee State University, TN W
Edinboro University of Pennsylvania, PA W
Elon University, NC W
Embry-Riddle Aeronautical University, AZ W
Embry-Riddle Aeronautical University, FL W
Emporia State University, KS W
Evangel University, MO W
The Evergreen State College, WA W
Fairfield University, CT W
Fairleigh Dickinson University, Metropolitan Campus, NJ W
Faulkner University, AL W
Ferris State University, MI W
Flagler College, FL W
Florida Atlantic University, FL W
Florida College, FL W
Florida Gulf Coast University, FL W
Florida Institute of Technology, FL W
Florida International University, FL W
Florida State University, FL W
Fort Hays State University, KS W
Fort Lewis College, CO W
Fort Valley State University, GA W
Francis Marion University, SC W
Franklin Pierce University, NH W
Freed-Hardeman University, TN W
Furman University, SC W
Gannon University, PA W
Gardner-Webb University, NC W
George Mason University, VA M,W
Georgetown College, KY W
Georgetown University, DC W
The George Washington University, DC W
Georgia Institute of Technology, GA W
Georgian Court University, NJ W
Georgia Southern University, GA W
Georgia State University, GA W
Glenville State College, WV W
Gonzaga University, WA W
Grace College, IN W
Graceland University, IA M,W
Grand Valley State University, MI W
Grand View University, IA W
Hampton University, VA W
Harding University, AR W
Hawai'i Pacific University, HI W
Henderson State University, AR W
Hofstra University, NY W
Holy Family University, PA W
Hope International University, CA W
Houghton College, NY W
Houston Baptist University, TX W
Humboldt State University, CA W
Huntington University, IN W
Idaho State University, ID W
Illinois Institute of Technology, IL W
Illinois State University, IL W
Indiana State University, IN W
Indiana University Bloomington, IN W
Indiana University of Pennsylvania, PA W
Indiana University–Purdue University Fort Wayne, IN M,W
Indiana University–Purdue University Indianapolis, IN W
Indiana University Southeast, IN W
Iona College, NY W
Iowa State University of Science and Technology, IA W
Jacksonville University, FL W
James Madison University, VA W
Jamestown College, ND W
John Brown University, AR W
Johnson C. Smith University, NC W
Judson College, AL W
Kansas State University, KS W
Kennesaw State University, GA W
Kent State University, OH W
Kentucky State University, KY W
Kentucky Wesleyan College, KY W
Kutztown University of Pennsylvania, PA W
Lamar University, TX W
Lee University, TN W
Lehigh University, PA W
Le Moyne College, NY W
Lewis-Clark State College, ID W
Liberty University, VA W
Limestone College, SC M,W
Lincoln Memorial University, TN W
Lindenwood University, MO M,W
Lindsey Wilson College, KY W
Lipscomb University, TN W
Lock Haven University of Pennsylvania, PA W
Long Island University, Brooklyn Campus, NY W
Long Island University, C.W. Post Campus, NY W
Louisiana State University and Agricultural and Mechanical College, LA W
Loyola University Chicago, IL M,W
Loyola University Maryland, MD W
Lubbock Christian University, TX W
Lyon College, AR W
Malone University, OH W
Marian College, IN W
Marquette University, WI W
The Master's College and Seminary, CA W
Mayville State University, ND W
McKendree University, IL W
Mercer University, GA W
Mercyhurst College, PA M,W
Merrimack College, MA W
Mesa State College, CO W
Metropolitan State College of Denver, CO W
Miami University, OH W
Michigan State University, MI W
Michigan Technological University, MI W
MidAmerica Nazarene University, KS W
Mid-Continent University, KY W
Midway College, KY W
Millersville University of Pennsylvania, PA W
Milligan College, TN W
Minnesota State University Mankato, MN W
Minot State University, ND W
Mississippi State University, MS W
Missouri Baptist University, MO M,W
Missouri Southern State University, MO W
Missouri State University, MO W
Missouri University of Science and Technology, MO W
Missouri Western State University, MO W
Molloy College, NY W
Montana State University, MT W
Montana State University–Billings, MT W
Montana Tech of The University of Montana, MT W
Mountain State University, WV W
Mount Marty College, SD W
Mount Mercy College, IA W
Mount Olive College, NC M,W
Mount Vernon Nazarene University, OH W
Murray State University, KY W
Newberry College, SC W
New Jersey Institute of Technology, NJ M,W
Newman University, KS W
New Mexico State University, NM W
Niagara University, NY W
Nicholls State University, LA W
North Carolina State University, NC W
North Dakota State University, ND W
Northeastern University, MA W
Northern Arizona University, AZ W
Northern Kentucky University, KY W
Northern Michigan University, MI W
Northern State University, SD W
North Greenville University, SC W
Northwestern State University of Louisiana, LA W
Northwestern University, IL W
Northwest Missouri State University, MO W
Northwest University, WA W
Northwood University, MI W
Northwood University, Florida Campus, FL W
Notre Dame de Namur University, CA W
Nova Southeastern University, FL W
Oakland University, MI W
The Ohio State University, OH M,W
Ohio University, OH W
Ohio University–Zanesville, OH M,W
Ohio Valley University, WV W
Oklahoma Panhandle State University, OK W
Olivet Nazarene University, IL W
Oral Roberts University, OK W
Oregon Institute of Technology, OR W

Oregon State University, OR W
Ouachita Baptist University, AR W
Pace University, NY W
Palm Beach Atlantic University, FL W
Penn State University Park, PA M,W
Pepperdine University, CA M,W
Philadelphia University, PA W
Pittsburg State University, KS W
Point Loma Nazarene University, CA W
Point Park University, PA W
Portland State University, OR W
Presbyterian College, SC W
Providence College, RI W
Purdue University, IN W
Purdue University North Central, IN M
Quinnipiac University, CT W
Radford University, VA W
Rider University, NJ W
Robert Morris College, IL W
Robert Morris University, PA W
Roberts Wesleyan College, NY W
Rockhurst University, MO W
Rollins College, FL W
Sacred Heart University, CT M,W
Saginaw Valley State University, MI W
St. Ambrose University, IA M,W
St. Andrews Presbyterian College, NC W
St. Cloud State University, MN W
St. Edward's University, TX W
Saint Francis University, PA M,W
St. John's University, NY W
Saint Joseph's College, IN W
Saint Leo University, FL W
St. Louis Christian College, MO M,W
Saint Louis University, MO W
Saint Martin's University, WA W
Saint Mary's College of California, CA W
St. Mary's University, TX W
St. Thomas University, FL W
Saint Xavier University, IL W
Samford University, AL W
Sam Houston State University, TX W
San Diego State University, CA W
San Francisco State University, CA W
San Jose State University, CA W
Santa Clara University, CA W
Savannah College of Art and Design, GA W
Seattle Pacific University, WA W
Seton Hill University, PA W
Shepherd University, WV W
Shippensburg University of Pennsylvania, PA W
Shorter College, GA W
Simpson University, CA W
Slippery Rock University of Pennsylvania, PA W
Sonoma State University, CA W
South Carolina State University, SC W
South Dakota School of Mines and Technology, SD W
South Dakota State University, SD W
Southeastern Louisiana University, LA W
Southeastern Oklahoma State University, OK W
Southeast Missouri State University, MO W
Southern Arkansas University–Magnolia, AR W
Southern Connecticut State University, CT W
Southern Illinois University Carbondale, IL W
Southern Illinois University Edwardsville, IL W
Southern Methodist University, TX W
Southern Nazarene University, OK W
Southern New Hampshire University, NH W
Southern Oregon University, OR W
Southwest Baptist University, MO W
Southwestern College, KS W
Southwest Minnesota State University, MN W
Spring Arbor University, MI W
Spring Hill College, AL W
Stanford University, CA M,W
State University of New York at Binghamton, NY W
Stephen F. Austin State University, TX W
Stephens College, MO W
Stetson University, FL W
Stonehill College, MA W
Stony Brook University, State University of New York, NY W
Tarleton State University, TX W
Taylor University, IN W
Temple University, PA W
Tennessee Technological University, TN W
Texas A&M University, TX W
Texas Christian University, TX W
Texas State University–San Marcos, TX W
Texas Tech University, TX W
Tiffin University, OH W
Towson University, MD W
Trevecca Nazarene University, TN W
Trinity Christian College, IL W
Trinity International University, IL W
Troy University, AL W
Truman State University, MO W
Tuskegee University, AL W
Union College, KY W
Union University, TN W
University at Albany, State University of New York, NY W
University at Buffalo, the State University of New York, NY W
The University of Akron, OH W
The University of Alabama, AL W
The University of Alabama at Birmingham, AL W
The University of Alabama in Huntsville, AL W
University of Alaska Fairbanks, AK W
The University of Arizona, AZ W
University of Arkansas, AR W
University of Bridgeport, CT W
University of California, Davis, CA W
University of California, Irvine, CA M,W
University of California, Los Angeles, CA M,W
University of California, Riverside, CA W
University of Central Florida, FL W
University of Central Missouri, MO W
University of Central Oklahoma, OK W
University of Cincinnati, OH W
University of Colorado at Boulder, CO W
University of Colorado at Colorado Springs, CO W
University of Connecticut, CT W
University of Dayton, OH W
University of Delaware, DE W
University of Denver, CO W
University of Evansville, IN W
The University of Findlay, OH W
University of Florida, FL W
University of Georgia, GA W
University of Hartford, CT W
University of Hawaii at Manoa, HI M,W
University of Houston, TX W
University of Idaho, ID W
University of Illinois at Chicago, IL W
University of Illinois at Springfield, IL W
The University of Iowa, IA W
The University of Kansas, KS W
University of Kentucky, KY W
University of Louisiana at Monroe, LA W
University of Louisville, KY W
University of Maine, ME W
University of Mary, ND W
University of Maryland, Baltimore County, MD W
University of Maryland, College Park, MD W
University of Massachusetts Lowell, MA W
University of Memphis, TN W
University of Miami, FL W
University of Michigan, MI W
University of Michigan–Dearborn, MI W
University of Minnesota, Crookston, MN W
University of Minnesota, Duluth, MN W
University of Minnesota, Twin Cities Campus, MN W
University of Mississippi, MS W
University of Missouri–Columbia, MO W
University of Missouri–Kansas City, MO W
University of Missouri–St. Louis, MO W
University of Mobile, AL W
The University of Montana, MT W
The University of Montana Western, MT W
University of Montevallo, AL W
University of Nebraska at Kearney, NE W
University of Nebraska at Omaha, NE W
University of Nebraska–Lincoln, NE W
University of Nevada, Las Vegas, NV W
University of Nevada, Reno, NV W
University of New Hampshire, NH W
University of New Haven, CT M,W
University of New Orleans, LA W
University of North Alabama, AL W
The University of North Carolina at Asheville, NC W
The University of North Carolina at Chapel Hill, NC W
The University of North Carolina at Greensboro, NC W

The University of North Carolina at Pembroke, NC W
The University of North Carolina Wilmington, NC W
University of North Dakota, ND W
University of Northern Colorado, CO W
University of Northern Iowa, IA W
University of North Florida, FL W
University of North Texas, TX W
University of Notre Dame, IN W
University of Oklahoma, OK W
University of Oregon, OR W
University of Pittsburgh, PA W
University of Portland, OR W
University of Puerto Rico, Río Piedras, PR M,W
University of Rhode Island, RI W
University of Saint Francis, IN W
University of San Diego, CA W
University of South Alabama, AL W
University of South Carolina, SC W
University of South Carolina Aiken, SC W
University of South Carolina Upstate, SC W
The University of South Dakota, SD W
University of Southern California, CA M,W
University of Southern Indiana, IN W
University of Southern Mississippi, MS W
University of South Florida, FL W
The University of Tampa, FL W
The University of Tennessee, TN W
The University of Tennessee at Chattanooga, TN W
The University of Tennessee at Martin, TN W
The University of Texas at Arlington, TX W
The University of Texas at Brownsville, TX W
The University of Texas at El Paso, TX W
The University of Texas at San Antonio, TX W
The University of Texas of the Permian Basin, TX W
The University of Texas–Pan American, TX W
University of the Cumberlands, KY W
University of the Incarnate Word, TX W
University of the Pacific, CA M,W
University of Tulsa, OK W
University of Utah, UT W
University of Virginia, VA W
The University of Virginia's College at Wise, VA W
University of West Georgia, GA W
University of Wisconsin–Green Bay, WI W
University of Wisconsin–Madison, WI W
University of Wisconsin–Milwaukee, WI W
University of Wisconsin–Parkside, WI W
University of Wyoming, WY W
Ursuline College, OH W
Utah State University, UT W
Utah Valley University, UT W
Valdosta State University, GA W
Valley City State University, ND W
Valparaiso University, IN W
Vanguard University of Southern California, CA W
Villanova University, PA W
Virginia Commonwealth University, VA W
Virginia Intermont College, VA W
Wake Forest University, NC W
Warner Pacific College, OR W
Washington State University, WA W
Wayland Baptist University, TX W
Wayne State University, MI W
Weber State University, UT W
West Chester University of Pennsylvania, PA W
Western Carolina University, NC W
Western Illinois University, IL W
Western Kentucky University, KY W
Western Michigan University, MI W
Western Oregon University, OR W
Western Washington University, WA W
West Liberty State University, WV W
Westminster College, UT W
West Virginia University, WV W
West Virginia Wesleyan College, WV W
Wheeling Jesuit University, WV W
Wichita State University, KS W
Wingate University, NC W
Winona State University, MN W
Winthrop University, SC W
Wofford College, SC W
Wright State University, OH W
Xavier University, OH W
Youngstown State University, OH W

Water Polo

Arizona State University, AZ W
California Baptist University, CA M,W
California State University, Bakersfield, CA W
California State University, Long Beach, CA M,W
Chaminade University of Honolulu, HI M
Colorado State University, CO W
The George Washington University, DC M
Hartwick College, NY W
Indiana University Bloomington, IN W
Iona College, NY W
Lindenwood University, MO M,W
Mercyhurst College, PA M,W
Pepperdine University, CA M
San Diego State University, CA W
San Jose State University, CA W
Santa Clara University, CA M,W
Stanford University, CA M,W
University of California, Davis, CA M,W
University of California, Irvine, CA M
University of California, Los Angeles, CA M,W
University of Hawaii at Manoa, HI W
University of Maryland, College Park, MD W
University of Michigan, MI M,W
University of Puerto Rico, Río Piedras, PR M,W
University of Southern California, CA M,W
University of the Pacific, CA M,W
Wagner College, NY W

Weight Lifting

University of Puerto Rico, Río Piedras, PR M,W

Wrestling

Adams State College, CO M
American University, DC M
Appalachian State University, NC M
Arizona State University, AZ M
Ashland University, OH M
Augustana College, SD M
Baker University, KS M
Bethel College, IN M
Bloomsburg University of Pennsylvania, PA M
Boise State University, ID M
Bucknell University, PA M
California Baptist University, CA M
California Polytechnic State University, San Luis Obispo, CA M
California State University, Bakersfield, CA M
California State University, Fullerton, CA M
Campbellsville University, KY M
Carson-Newman College, TN M
Central Michigan University, MI M
Clarion University of Pennsylvania, PA M
Cleveland State University, OH M
Colorado School of Mines, CO M
Colorado State University–Pueblo, CO M
Concordia University, Nebraska, NE M
Dana College, NE M
Davidson College, NC M
Duquesne University, PA M
Eastern Michigan University, MI M
Edinboro University of Pennsylvania, PA M
Embry-Riddle Aeronautical University, AZ M
Fort Hays State University, KS M
Gannon University, PA M
Gardner-Webb University, NC M
George Mason University, VA M
Hofstra University, NY M
Indiana University Bloomington, IN M
Iowa State University of Science and Technology, IA M
Jamestown College, ND M,W
Kent State University, OH M
Kutztown University of Pennsylvania, PA M
Lehigh University, PA M
Liberty University, VA M
Limestone College, SC M
Lindenwood University, MO M
Lock Haven University of Pennsylvania, PA M
McKendree University, IL M
Mercyhurst College, PA M
Mesa State College, CO M
Michigan State University, MI M
Millersville University of Pennsylvania, PA M
Minnesota State University Mankato, MN M

Missouri Baptist University, MO M
Murray State University, KY M
Newberry College, SC M
Newman University, KS M
North Carolina State University, NC M
North Dakota State University, ND M
Northern State University, SD M
Northwestern University, IL M
The Ohio State University, OH M
Ohio University, OH M
Oklahoma City University, OK M,W
Oklahoma State University, OK M
Old Dominion University, VA M
Oregon State University, OR M
Penn State University Park, PA M
Portland State University, OR M
Purdue University, IN M
Rider University, NJ M
Sacred Heart University, CT M
St. Cloud State University, MN M
San Francisco State University, CA M
Shippensburg University of Pennsylvania, PA M
South Dakota State University, SD M
Southern Illinois University Edwardsville, IL M
Southern Oregon University, OR M
Southwest Minnesota State University, MN M
Stanford University, CA M
State University of New York at Binghamton, NY M
Truman State University, MO M
University at Buffalo, the State University of New York, NY M
University of California, Davis, CA M
University of Central Missouri, MO M
University of Central Oklahoma, OK M
The University of Findlay, OH M
The University of Iowa, IA M
University of Mary, ND M
University of Maryland, College Park, MD M
University of Michigan, MI M
University of Minnesota, Twin Cities Campus, MN M
University of Missouri–Columbia, MO M
University of Nebraska at Kearney, NE M
University of Nebraska at Omaha, NE M
University of Nebraska–Lincoln, NE M
The University of North Carolina at Chapel Hill, NC M
The University of North Carolina at Greensboro, NC M
The University of North Carolina at Pembroke, NC M
University of Northern Colorado, CO M
University of Northern Iowa, IA M
University of Oklahoma, OK M
University of Pittsburgh, PA M
University of Pittsburgh at Johnstown, PA M
University of Puerto Rico, Río Piedras, PR M,W
The University of Tennessee at Chattanooga, TN M
University of the Cumberlands, KY M,W
University of Virginia, VA M
University of Wisconsin–Madison, WI M
University of Wisconsin–Parkside, WI M
University of Wyoming, WY M
Utah Valley University, UT M
Virginia Military Institute, VA M
West Liberty State University, WV M
West Virginia University, WV M

Co-op Programs

Alabama Agricultural and Mechanical University, AL
Alcorn State University, MS
Alfred University, NY
American Jewish University, CA
American University, DC
Andrews University, MI
Anna Maria College, MA
Antioch University McGregor, OH
Aquinas College, TN
Arcadia University, PA
Arizona State University, AZ
Art Academy of Cincinnati, OH
Athens State University, AL
Auburn University, AL
Auburn University Montgomery, AL
Augsburg College, MN
Augustana College, SD
Augusta State University, GA
Austin Peay State University, TN
Averett University, VA
Avila University, MO
Azusa Pacific University, CA
Ball State University, IN
Barton College, NC
Bastyr University, WA
Bates College, ME
Belmont Abbey College, NC
Belmont University, TN
Benedictine College, KS
Berry College, GA
Biola University, CA
Black Hills State University, SD
Bloomsburg University of Pennsylvania, PA
Boise State University, ID
The Boston Conservatory, MA
Bowling Green State University, OH
Bradley University, IL
Brewton-Parker College, GA
Brigham Young University, UT
Bryn Athyn College of the New Church, PA
Buffalo State College, State University of New York, NY
Butler University, IN
California Christian College, CA
California College of the Arts, CA
California Institute of Technology, CA
California Institute of the Arts, CA
California Polytechnic State University, San Luis Obispo, CA
California State Polytechnic University, Pomona, CA
California State University, Bakersfield, CA
California State University, Chico, CA
California State University, East Bay, CA
California State University, Fresno, CA
California State University, Fullerton, CA
California State University, Los Angeles, CA
California State University, Sacramento, CA
California State University, San Bernardino, CA
California State University, Stanislaus, CA
Calumet College of Saint Joseph, IN
Canisius College, NY
Carnegie Mellon University, PA
Carroll College, MT
Case Western Reserve University, OH
The Catholic University of America, DC
Central Connecticut State University, CT
Chatham University, PA
Chestnut Hill College, PA
Christendom College, VA
Christian Brothers University, TN
Christopher Newport University, VA
City College of the City University of New York, NY
Clarion University of Pennsylvania, PA
Clarke College, IA
Clarkson University, NY
Clayton State University, GA
Cleary University, MI
Clemson University, SC
Cleveland State University, OH
Coastal Carolina University, SC
The College at Brockport, State University of New York, NY
College for Creative Studies, MI
College of Charleston, SC
The College of Idaho, ID
College of Mount St. Joseph, OH
The College of New Rochelle, NY
College of Staten Island of the City University of New York, NY
College of the Atlantic, ME
College of the Ozarks, MO
The College of Wooster, OH
Colorado School of Mines, CO
Colorado State University, CO
Colorado State University–Pueblo, CO
Colorado Technical University Colorado Springs, CO
Colorado Technical University Denver, CO
Colorado Technical University Sioux Falls, SD
Columbia International University, SC
Columbus State University, GA
Concordia College, MN
Coppin State University, MD
Corban College, OR
Cornell University, NY
Cornish College of the Arts, WA
Dakota State University, SD
Davenport University, MI
Defiance College, OH
Delaware Valley College, PA
Delta State University, MS
Denison University, OH
DePaul University, IL
Dillard University, LA
Dixie State College of Utah, UT
Doane College, NE
Dominican College, NY
Dowling College, NY
Drake University, IA
Drury University, MO
Eastern Michigan University, MI
Eastern Washington University, WA
East Tennessee State University, TN
East-West University, IL
Elmhurst College, IL
Embry-Riddle Aeronautical University, AZ
Embry-Riddle Aeronautical University, FL
Embry-Riddle Aeronautical University Worldwide, FL
Emory & Henry College, VA
Emory University, GA
Eureka College, IL
Everest University, FL
The Evergreen State College, WA
Fairleigh Dickinson University, College at Florham, NJ
Fairleigh Dickinson University, Metropolitan Campus, NJ
Fairmont State University, WV
Felician College, NJ
Ferris State University, MI
Fisk University, TN
Five Towns College, NY
Florida Atlantic University, FL
Florida Gulf Coast University, FL
Florida Institute of Technology, FL
Florida International University, FL
Florida State University, FL
Fort Lewis College, CO
Fort Valley State University, GA
Franklin College, IN
Freed-Hardeman University, TN
Gannon University, PA
Gardner-Webb University, NC
Geneva College, PA
George Mason University, VA
Georgetown College, KY
The George Washington University, DC
Georgia Institute of Technology, GA
Georgia Southern University, GA
Georgia State University, GA
Glenville State College, WV
Gordon College, MA
Grace College, IN
Graceland University, IA
Grace University, NE
Grand Valley State University, MI
Grand View University, IA
Green Mountain College, VT
Guilford College, NC
Gustavus Adolphus College, MN
Gwynedd-Mercy College, PA
Hampton University, VA
Harding University, AR
Hawai'i Pacific University, HI
Hendrix College, AR
Hodges University, FL
Holy Family University, PA
Humboldt State University, CA
Huntingdon College, AL
Husson University, ME
Illinois Institute of Technology, IL

Illinois State University, IL
Indiana State University, IN
Indiana University Bloomington, IN
Indiana University East, IN
Indiana University Northwest, IN
Indiana University of Pennsylvania, PA
Indiana University–Purdue University Fort Wayne, IN
Indiana University–Purdue University Indianapolis, IN
Iowa State University of Science and Technology, IA
Jacksonville University, FL
Jamestown College, ND
Jarvis Christian College, TX
John Carroll University, OH
John Jay College of Criminal Justice of the City University of New York, NY
Johnson Bible College, TN
Johnson C. Smith University, NC
Kansas City Art Institute, MO
Kansas State University, KS
Kean University, NJ
Keene State College, NH
Kendall College, IL
Kennesaw State University, GA
Kent State University, OH
Kentucky State University, KY
Kettering University, MI
Keuka College, NY
Kuyper College, MI
Lamar University, TX
Lane College, TN
Lawrence Technological University, MI
Lee University, TN
Lehigh University, PA
LeTourneau University, TX
Lewis-Clark State College, ID
Lexington College, IL
Liberty University, VA
Lincoln University, PA
Lindenwood University, MO
Lindsey Wilson College, KY
Lock Haven University of Pennsylvania, PA
Long Island University, Brooklyn Campus, NY
Long Island University, C.W. Post Campus, NY
Loras College, IA
Louisiana State University and Agricultural and Mechanical College, LA
Lourdes College, OH
Luther Rice University, GA
Lynn University, FL
MacMurray College, IL
Maine Maritime Academy, ME
Marian College, IN
Marian University, WI
Marquette University, WI
Maryville University of Saint Louis, MO
Massachusetts Institute of Technology, MA
The Master's College and Seminary, CA
Mayville State University, ND
Medgar Evers College of the City University of New York, NY
Menlo College, CA
Mercer University, GA
Mercyhurst College, PA
Merrimack College, MA
Mesa State College, CO
Methodist University, NC
Metropolitan State College of Denver, CO
Miami University, OH
Michigan State University, MI
Michigan Technological University, MI
Millersville University of Pennsylvania, PA
Milligan College, TN
Millikin University, IL
Minnesota State University Mankato, MN
Minot State University, ND
Misericordia University, PA
Mississippi College, MS
Mississippi State University, MS
Missouri Southern State University, MO
Missouri State University, MO
Missouri University of Science and Technology, MO
Molloy College, NY
Monmouth University, NJ
Monroe College, NY
Monroe College, NY
Montana State University–Billings, MT
Montana Tech of The University of Montana, MT
Montclair State University, NJ
Mountain State University, WV
Mount Holyoke College, MA
Mount Ida College, MA
Mount Marty College, SD
Mount Olive College, NC
Mount Saint Mary College, NY
Mount Union College, OH
Murray State University, KY
Nazareth College of Rochester, NY
Neumann University, PA
Newberry College, SC
New Jersey City University, NJ
New Jersey Institute of Technology, NJ
Newman University, KS
New Mexico State University, NM
Niagara University, NY
Nicholls State University, LA
Nichols College, MA
North Carolina State University, NC
North Dakota State University, ND
Northeastern State University, OK
Northeastern University, MA
Northern Arizona University, AZ
Northern Kentucky University, KY
Northern State University, SD
Northland College, WI
Northwestern State University of Louisiana, LA
Northwestern University, IL
Northwest University, WA
Northwood University, MI
Notre Dame de Namur University, CA
Oakland University, MI
Oglethorpe University, GA
Ohio Northern University, OH
The Ohio State University, OH
Ohio University, OH
Oklahoma Baptist University, OK
Oklahoma City University, OK
Old Dominion University, VA
Olivet College, MI
Oregon Institute of Technology, OR
Oregon State University, OR
Otis College of Art and Design, CA
Ouachita Baptist University, AR
Our Lady of Holy Cross College, LA
Pace University, NY
Pacific Lutheran University, WA
Pacific Union College, CA
Pacific University, OR
Parsons The New School for Design, NY
Peace College, NC
Peirce College, PA
Penn State Abington, PA
Penn State Altoona, PA
Penn State Berks, PA
Penn State Erie, The Behrend College, PA
Penn State Harrisburg, PA
Penn State University Park, PA
Pennsylvania College of Technology, PA
Piedmont College, GA
Pittsburg State University, KS
Pitzer College, CA
Polytechnic Institute of NYU, NY
Portland State University, OR
Presentation College, SD
Providence College, RI
Purdue University, IN
Purdue University Calumet, IN
Purdue University North Central, IN
Ramapo College of New Jersey, NJ
Reed College, OR
Reinhardt College, GA
Rensselaer Polytechnic Institute, NY
Rider University, NJ
Robert Morris College, IL
Robert Morris University, PA
Roberts Wesleyan College, NY
Rochester Institute of Technology, NY
Rockhurst University, MO
Rocky Mountain College of Art + Design, CO
Roger Williams University, RI
Rose-Hulman Institute of Technology, IN
Rutgers, The State University of New Jersey, Camden, NJ
Rutgers, The State University of New Jersey, Newark, NJ
Rutgers, The State University of New Jersey, New Brunswick, NJ
Sacred Heart University, CT
Saginaw Valley State University, MI
St. Ambrose University, IA
Saint Joseph's University, PA
Saint Louis University, MO
Saint Martin's University, WA
Saint Mary's College, IN
St. Mary's College of Maryland, MD
St. Mary's University, TX
Saint Mary's University of Minnesota, MN
Saint Vincent College, PA
Saint Xavier University, IL
Samford University, AL
Samuel Merritt University, CA
San Francisco State University, CA
San Jose State University, CA
Santa Clara University, CA
Schreiner University, TX
Shepherd University, WV
Shimer College, IL
Shippensburg University of Pennsylvania, PA
Silver Lake College, WI
Simmons College, MA
Simpson College, IA
Sonoma State University, CA
South Carolina State University, SC
South Dakota School of Mines and Technology, SD
South Dakota State University, SD
Southern Connecticut State University, CT
Southern Illinois University Carbondale, IL
Southern Illinois University Edwardsville, IL
Southern Methodist University, TX
Southern New Hampshire University, NH
Southern Oregon University, OR

Southern Polytechnic State University, GA
Southern Utah University, UT
Southwest Baptist University, MO
State University of New York at New Paltz, NY
State University of New York at Oswego, NY
State University of New York at Plattsburgh, NY
State University of New York College at Cortland, NY
State University of New York College of Agriculture and Technology at Cobleskill, NY
State University of New York College of Environmental Science and Forestry, NY
Stephens College, MO
Stevenson University, MD
Stillman College, AL
Suffolk University, MA
Tarleton State University, TX
Taylor University, IN
Temple University, PA
Tennessee Technological University, TN
Texas A&M University, TX
Texas Tech University, TX
Thiel College, PA
Thomas Aquinas College, CA
Thomas More College, KY
Towson University, MD
Trine University, IN
Trinity Christian College, IL
Trinity College of Florida, FL
Tuskegee University, AL
Union College, KY
Union University, TN
University at Buffalo, the State University of New York, NY
University of Advancing Technology, AZ
The University of Akron, OH
The University of Alabama, AL
The University of Alabama at Birmingham, AL
The University of Alabama in Huntsville, AL
University of Alaska Fairbanks, AK
University of Arkansas, AR
University of Bridgeport, CT
University of California, Riverside, CA
University of California, San Diego, CA
University of California, Santa Cruz, CA
University of Central Florida, FL
University of Central Missouri, MO
University of Cincinnati, OH
University of Colorado at Boulder, CO
University of Colorado at Colorado Springs, CO
University of Colorado Denver, CO
University of Connecticut, CT
University of Dayton, OH
University of Delaware, DE
University of Denver, CO
University of Evansville, IN
The University of Findlay, OH
University of Florida, FL
University of Georgia, GA
University of Hartford, CT
University of Hawaii at Manoa, HI
University of Houston, TX
University of Houston–Clear Lake, TX
University of Idaho, ID
University of Illinois at Chicago, IL
University of Illinois at Springfield, IL
The University of Iowa, IA
The University of Kansas, KS
University of Kentucky, KY
University of Louisiana at Monroe, LA
University of Louisville, KY
University of Maine, ME
University of Maine at Fort Kent, ME
University of Maine at Presque Isle, ME
University of Mary, ND
University of Maryland, Baltimore County, MD
University of Maryland, College Park, MD
University of Maryland Eastern Shore, MD
University of Maryland University College, MD
University of Mary Washington, VA
University of Massachusetts Amherst, MA
University of Massachusetts Boston, MA
University of Massachusetts Dartmouth, MA
University of Massachusetts Lowell, MA
University of Memphis, TN
University of Michigan, MI
University of Michigan–Dearborn, MI
University of Michigan–Flint, MI
University of Minnesota, Twin Cities Campus, MN
University of Missouri–Columbia, MO
University of Missouri–Kansas City, MO
University of Missouri–St. Louis, MO
The University of Montana, MT
The University of Montana Western, MT
University of Nebraska at Kearney, NE
University of Nebraska at Omaha, NE
University of Nebraska–Lincoln, NE
University of Nevada, Las Vegas, NV
University of New England, ME
University of New Hampshire, NH
University of New Haven, CT
University of New Orleans, LA
University of North Alabama, AL
The University of North Carolina at Pembroke, NC
The University of North Carolina Wilmington, NC
University of North Dakota, ND
University of Northern Colorado, CO
University of Northern Iowa, IA
University of North Florida, FL
University of North Texas, TX
University of Oklahoma, OK
University of Oregon, OR
University of Pittsburgh, PA
University of Pittsburgh at Johnstown, PA
University of Puget Sound, WA
University of Rhode Island, RI
University of Richmond, VA
University of Saint Francis, IN
University of South Alabama, AL
University of South Carolina, SC
University of South Carolina Aiken, SC
University of South Carolina Upstate, SC
University of Southern California, CA
University of Southern Indiana, IN
University of Southern Maine, ME
University of Southern Mississippi, MS
University of South Florida, FL
The University of Tampa, FL
The University of Tennessee, TN
The University of Tennessee at Chattanooga, TN
The University of Tennessee at Martin, TN
The University of Texas at Arlington, TX
The University of Texas at Brownsville, TX
The University of Texas at Dallas, TX
The University of Texas at El Paso, TX
The University of Texas at San Antonio, TX
The University of Texas at Tyler, TX
The University of Texas–Pan American, TX
University of the Cumberlands, KY
University of the Incarnate Word, TX
University of the Ozarks, AR
University of the Pacific, CA
University of Utah, UT
University of Vermont, VT
University of Virginia, VA
The University of Virginia's College at Wise, VA
University of West Florida, FL
University of West Georgia, GA
University of Wisconsin–Eau Claire, WI
University of Wisconsin–La Crosse, WI
University of Wisconsin–Madison, WI
University of Wisconsin–Milwaukee, WI
University of Wisconsin–Oshkosh, WI
University of Wisconsin–Stout, WI
University of Wisconsin–Superior, WI
University of Wisconsin–Whitewater, WI
Ursuline College, OH
Utah State University, UT
Utah Valley University, UT
Utica College, NY
Valdosta State University, GA
Valley City State University, ND
Valparaiso University, IN
Vanderbilt University, TN
Vassar College, NY
Vermont Technical College, VT
Villanova University, PA
Virginia Commonwealth University, VA
Virginia Polytechnic Institute and State University, VA
Walla Walla University, WA
Warner Pacific College, OR
Warren Wilson College, NC
Washington Bible College, MD
Washington University in St. Louis, MO
Watkins College of Art, Design, & Film, TN
Wayne State University, MI
Webber International University, FL
Weber State University, UT
Webster University, MO
Western Carolina University, NC
Western Connecticut State University, CT
Western Kentucky University, KY
Western Washington University, WA
Westfield State College, MA
Westminster College, MO
Westminster College, UT
Whitman College, WA
Wichita State University, KS
Widener University, PA
Wilkes University, PA
Willamette University, OR
Wilson College, PA
Winthrop University, SC
Wittenberg University, OH
Worcester Polytechnic Institute, MA
Wright State University, OH
Xavier University, OH
Xavier University of Louisiana, LA
York College, NE
York College of Pennsylvania, PA
York College of the City University of New York, NY
Youngstown State University, OH

ROTC Programs

Air Force

Adelphi University, NY*
Agnes Scott College, GA*
Alaska Pacific University, AK*
American University, DC*
Angelo State University, TX
Anna Maria College, MA*
Aquinas College, TN*
Arizona State University, AZ
Asbury College, KY*
Assumption College, MA*
Auburn University, AL
Auburn University Montgomery, AL*
Augsburg College, MN*
Austin Peay State University, TN*
Babson College, MA*
Baker University, KS*
Baldwin-Wallace College, OH*
Baylor University, TX
Belhaven College, MS*
Bellarmine University, KY*
Belmont Abbey College, NC*
Bentley University, MA*
Bethel College, IN*
Bethel University, MN*
Biola University, CA*
Birmingham-Southern College, AL*
Bloomsburg University of Pennsylvania, PA*
Boston College, MA*
Bowling Green State University, OH
Brandeis University, MA*
Bridgewater State College, MA*
Brigham Young University, UT
Bryn Mawr College, PA*
Butler University, IN*
California Baptist University, CA*
California Institute of Technology, CA*
California State Polytechnic University, Pomona, CA*
California State University, Fresno, CA
California State University, Los Angeles, CA*
California State University, Northridge, CA*
California State University, Sacramento, CA
California State University, San Bernardino, CA
Carnegie Mellon University, PA
Carroll University, WI*
Carson-Newman College, TN*
Case Western Reserve University, OH*
The Catholic University of America, DC*
Cazenovia College, NY*
Cedarville University, OH*
Central Connecticut State University, CT*
Central Methodist University, MO*
Centre College, KY*
Chaminade University of Honolulu, HI*
Chapman University, CA*
Chatham University, PA*
Christian Brothers University, TN*
City College of the City University of New York, NY*
Claremont McKenna College, CA*
Clarkson University, NY
Clark University, MA*
Clayton State University, GA*
Clearwater Christian College, FL*
Clemson University, SC
Cleveland State University, OH*
Coe College, IA*
The College at Brockport, State University of New York, NY*
College of Charleston, SC*
College of Mount St. Joseph, OH*
The College of New Jersey, NJ*
College of Saint Mary, NE*
The College of St. Scholastica, MN*
College of the Holy Cross, MA*
Colorado State University, CO
Columbia College, MO*
Columbia University, School of General Studies, NY*
Concordia College, MN*
Concordia University, OR*
Concordia University, Nebraska, NE*
Concordia University, St. Paul, MN*
Concordia University Texas, TX*
Corban College, OR*
Cornell University, NY
Creighton University, NE*
Dakota State University, SD*
Dallas Baptist University, TX*
Dana College, NE*
Davidson College, NC*
DePauw University, IN*
DeVry University, AZ
Dillard University, LA*
Doane College, NE*
Dowling College, NY*
Drake University, IA*
Duke University, NC
Duquesne University, PA*
Eastern Michigan University, MI*
Elmhurst College, IL*
Elmira College, NY*
Elon University, NC*
Embry-Riddle Aeronautical University, AZ
Embry-Riddle Aeronautical University, FL
Emory University, GA*
Endicott College, MA*
Fairfield University, CT*
Fairleigh Dickinson University, College at Florham, NJ*
Fairleigh Dickinson University, Metropolitan Campus, NJ*
Faulkner University, AL*
Florida Atlantic University, FL*
Florida College, FL*
Florida Hospital College of Health Sciences, FL*
Florida International University, FL
Florida State University, FL
Franklin Pierce University, NH*
Free Will Baptist Bible College, TN*
George Fox University, OR*
George Mason University, VA*
Georgetown College, KY*
Georgetown University, DC*
The George Washington University, DC*
Georgia Institute of Technology, GA
Georgia State University, GA*
Gordon College, MA*
Grace University, NE*
Grand View University, IA*
Greensboro College, NC*
Guilford College, NC*
Hamilton College, NY*
Hamline University, MN*
Harvard University, MA*
Harvey Mudd College, CA
Hawai'i Pacific University, HI*
Heidelberg University, OH*
Huntingdon College, AL*
Illinois Institute of Technology, IL
Indiana State University, IN
Indiana University Bloomington, IN
Indiana University–Purdue University Indianapolis, IN*
Indiana University South Bend, IN*
Iona College, NY*
Iowa State University of Science and Technology, IA
Ithaca College, NY*
James Madison University, VA*
John Brown University, AR*
John Jay College of Criminal Justice of the City University of New York, NY*
The Johns Hopkins University, MD*
Johnson C. Smith University, NC*
Kansas State University, KS
Kean University, NJ*
Keene State College, NH*
Kennesaw State University, GA
Kent State University, OH
Kentucky State University, KY*
La Roche College, PA*
Lawrence Technological University, MI*
Le Moyne College, NY*
Lewis-Clark State College, ID*
Liberty University, VA*
Lincoln University, PA*
Lindenwood University, MO*
Linfield College, OR*
Lipscomb University, TN*
Long Island University, C.W. Post Campus, NY*
Louisiana State University and Agricultural and Mechanical College, LA
Lourdes College, OH*
Loyola University Chicago, IL*
Loyola University Maryland, MD*
Loyola University New Orleans, LA*
Lubbock Christian University, TX*
Lynn University, FL*
Macalester College, MN*
Malone University, OH*
Manhattan Christian College, KS*

*program is offered at another college's campus

Marquette University, WI
Mary Baldwin College, VA*
Marywood University, PA*
Massachusetts Institute of Technology, MA
Mayville State University, ND*
McKendree University, IL*
McMurry University, TX*
Mercyhurst College, PA*
Merrimack College, MA*
Methodist University, NC*
Metropolitan State College of Denver, CO*
Miami University, OH
Michigan State University, MI
Michigan Technological University, MI
MidAmerica Nazarene University, KS*
Milwaukee School of Engineering, WI*
Misericordia University, PA*
Mississippi State University, MS
Mississippi University for Women, MS*
Missouri University of Science and Technology, MO
Molloy College, NY*
Monmouth University, NJ*
Montana State University, MT
Montclair State University, NJ*
Mount Holyoke College, MA*
Mount Union College, OH*
National University, CA*
Nazareth College of Rochester, NY*
Nebraska Methodist College, NE*
Nebraska Wesleyan University, NE*
New England College, NH*
New Jersey Institute of Technology, NJ
New Mexico State University, NM
New York City College of Technology of the City University of New York, NY*
North Carolina State University, NC
North Central College, IL*
North Dakota State University, ND
Northeastern University, MA*
Northern Arizona University, AZ
Northern Kentucky University, KY*
Northwestern College, MN*
Northwestern University, IL*
Oakland University, MI*
Occidental College, CA*
Ohio Northern University, OH*
The Ohio State University, OH
Ohio University, OH
Ohio University–Chillicothe, OH*
Ohio University–Lancaster, OH*
Ohio Valley University, WV*
Ohio Wesleyan University, OH*
Oklahoma Baptist University, OK*
Oklahoma Christian University, OK*
Oklahoma City University, OK*
Oklahoma State University, OK
Oral Roberts University, OK*
Oregon State University, OR
Our Lady of Holy Cross College, LA*
Our Lady of the Lake College, LA*
Our Lady of the Lake University of San Antonio, TX*
Pace University, NY*
Pacific University, OR*
Peace College, NC*
Penn State Abington, PA*
Penn State Altoona, PA
Penn State University Park, PA
Pepperdine University, CA*
Philadelphia Biblical University, PA*
Pitzer College, CA*
Plymouth State University, NH*
Point Loma Nazarene University, CA*
Point Park University, PA*
Polytechnic Institute of NYU, NY*
Pomona College, CA*
Portland State University, OR*
Princeton University, NJ*
Purdue University, IN
Quinnipiac University, CT*
Ramapo College of New Jersey, NJ*
Rensselaer Polytechnic Institute, NY
Rhodes College, TN*
Rivier College, NH*
Robert Morris University, PA*
Roberts Wesleyan College, NY*
Rochester Institute of Technology, NY
Rose-Hulman Institute of Technology, IN
Rutgers, The State University of New Jersey, Camden, NJ*
Rutgers, The State University of New Jersey, Newark, NJ
Rutgers, The State University of New Jersey, New Brunswick, NJ
St. Catherine University, MN*
St. Edward's University, TX*
St. John Fisher College, NY*
Saint Joseph's University, PA
St. Lawrence University, NY*
Saint Leo University, FL*
St. Louis College of Pharmacy, MO*
Saint Louis University, MO
Saint Mary's College, IN*
Saint Mary's College of California, CA*
St. Mary's University, TX*
Saint Michael's College, VT*
St. Thomas University, FL*
Saint Vincent College, PA*
Saint Xavier University, IL*
Salem State College, MA*
Samford University, AL
Samuel Merritt University, CA*
San Diego State University, CA
San Francisco State University, CA*
San Jose State University, CA
Santa Clara University, CA*
Scripps College, CA*
Seattle Pacific University, WA*
Seton Hill University, PA*
Shepherd University, WV*
Skidmore College, NY*
Smith College, MA*
Sonoma State University, CA*
South Carolina State University, SC*
South Dakota State University, SD
Southeast Missouri State University, MO
Southern Connecticut State University, CT*
Southern Illinois University Carbondale, IL
Southern Illinois University Edwardsville, IL
Southern Methodist University, TX*
Southern Nazarene University, OK*
Southern New Hampshire University, NH*
Southern Polytechnic State University, GA*
Spelman College, GA*
Spring Arbor University, MI*
Spring Hill College, AL*
Stanford University, CA*
State University of New York at Binghamton, NY*
State University of New York College at Cortland, NY*
State University of New York College at Geneseo, NY*
State University of New York College at Old Westbury, NY*
State University of New York College at Potsdam, NY*
State University of New York College of Environmental Science and Forestry, NY*
Stephens College, MO*
Stony Brook University, State University of New York, NY*
Swarthmore College, PA*
Temple University, PA*
Tennessee Technological University, TN*
Texas A&M University, TX
Texas Christian University, TX
Texas Lutheran University, TX*
Texas State University–San Marcos, TX
Texas Tech University, TX
Thomas More College, KY*
Tiffin University, OH*
Towson University, MD*
Transylvania University, KY*
Trinity University, TX*
Troy University, AL
Tufts University, MA*
Tuskegee University, AL
Union College, NY*
University at Albany, State University of New York, NY*
The University of Akron, OH*
The University of Alabama, AL
The University of Alabama at Birmingham, AL*
The University of Arizona, AZ
University of Arkansas, AR
University of California, Berkeley, CA
University of California, Davis, CA*
University of California, Irvine, CA*
University of California, Los Angeles, CA
University of California, Riverside, CA*
University of California, Santa Cruz, CA*
University of Central Florida, FL
University of Central Missouri, MO*
University of Cincinnati, OH
University of Colorado at Boulder, CO
University of Colorado Denver, CO*
University of Connecticut, CT
University of Dallas, TX*
University of Dayton, OH*
University of Delaware, DE
University of Denver, CO*
The University of Findlay, OH*
University of Florida, FL
University of Georgia, GA
University of Hartford, CT*
University of Hawaii at Manoa, HI
University of Idaho, ID*
University of Illinois at Chicago, IL*
The University of Iowa, IA
The University of Kansas, KS
University of Kentucky, KY
University of Louisville, KY
The University of Maine at Augusta, ME*
University of Mary Hardin-Baylor, TX*
University of Maryland, College Park, MD
University of Massachusetts Amherst, MA
University of Massachusetts Lowell, MA
University of Memphis, TN
University of Miami, FL
University of Michigan, MI
University of Michigan–Dearborn, MI*
University of Minnesota, Crookston, MN*
University of Minnesota, Duluth, MN
University of Minnesota, Twin Cities Campus, MN
University of Mississippi, MS

ROTC Programs

Air Force

University of Missouri–Columbia, MO
University of Missouri–Kansas City, MO*
University of Missouri–St. Louis, MO*
University of Mobile, AL*
University of Montevallo, AL*
University of Nebraska at Omaha, NE
University of Nebraska–Lincoln, NE
University of New Hampshire, NH
University of New Hampshire at Manchester, NH*
University of New Orleans, LA*
The University of North Carolina at Chapel Hill, NC
The University of North Carolina at Greensboro, NC*
The University of North Carolina at Pembroke, NC
University of North Dakota, ND
University of Northern Colorado, CO
University of North Texas, TX
University of Notre Dame, IN
University of Oklahoma, OK
University of Oregon, OR*
University of Pennsylvania, PA*
University of Pittsburgh, PA
University of Pittsburgh at Greensburg, PA*
University of Portland, OR
University of Puerto Rico, Río Piedras, PR
University of Redlands, CA*
University of Rochester, NY*
University of San Diego, CA*
The University of Scranton, PA*
University of South Alabama, AL
University of South Carolina, SC
University of Southern California, CA
University of Southern Maine, ME*
University of Southern Mississippi, MS
University of South Florida, FL
The University of Tampa, FL*
The University of Tennessee, TN
The University of Texas at Arlington, TX*
The University of Texas at Dallas, TX*
The University of Texas at El Paso, TX
The University of Texas at San Antonio, TX
University of the Incarnate Word, TX*
University of the Pacific, CA*
University of Tulsa, OK*
University of Utah, UT
University of Virginia, VA
University of West Florida, FL
University of Wisconsin–Madison, WI
University of Wisconsin–Milwaukee, WI*
University of Wisconsin–Superior, WI*
University of Wisconsin–Whitewater, WI
University of Wyoming, WY
Utah State University, UT
Utah Valley University, UT*
Utica College, NY*
Valdosta State University, GA
Valparaiso University, IN*
Vanderbilt University, TN*
Vanguard University of Southern California, CA*
Villanova University, PA*
Virginia Military Institute, VA
Virginia Polytechnic Institute and State University, VA
Warner Pacific College, OR*
Washington & Jefferson College, PA*
Washington State University, WA
Washington University in St. Louis, MO*
Wayland Baptist University, TX*
Wayne State University, MI*
Weber State University, UT
Webster University, MO*
Wellesley College, MA*
Wells College, NY*
Wesleyan University, CT*
West Chester University of Pennsylvania, PA*
Western Connecticut State University, CT*
Western Kentucky University, KY*
Western New England College, MA*
Western Oregon University, OR*
Westfield State College, MA*
Westminster College, MO*
Westminster College, UT*
West Virginia University, WV
Widener University, PA*
Wilkes University, PA
Willamette University, OR*
William Paterson University of New Jersey, NJ*
Wingate University, NC*
Wittenberg University, OH*
Worcester Polytechnic Institute, MA
Worcester State College, MA*
Wright State University, OH
Xavier University, OH*
Xavier University of Louisiana, LA*
Yale University, CT*
York College, NE*
York College of the City University of New York, NY*
Youngstown State University, OH*

Army

Allen College, IA*
Alvernia University, PA*
Anderson University, SC*
Armstrong Atlantic State University, GA
Aurora University, IL*
Barry University, FL*
Becker College, MA*
California Lutheran University, CA*
California State University, Dominguez Hills, CA*
California State University, San Marcos, CA*
Calvary Bible College and Theological Seminary, MO*
Capitol College, MD*
Castleton State College, VT*
Central State University, OH
Central Washington University, WA
Champlain College, VT*
The Citadel, The Military College of South Carolina, SC
Concordia University, MI*
Cornerstone University, MI*
East Carolina University, NC
Eastern Connecticut State University, CT*
Eastern Oregon University, OR
Eckerd College, FL*
Emmanuel College, MA*
Grambling State University, LA
Hampden-Sydney College, VA*
High Point University, NC*
Howard University, DC
The Jewish Theological Seminary, NY*
Lehman College of the City University of New York, NY*
Lenoir-Rhyne University, NC*
Lewis University, IL*
Loyola Marymount University, CA*
Marist College, NY
Marshall University, WV
Middle Tennessee State University, TN
Morehead State University, KY
Morningside College, IA*
New York Institute of Technology, NY
Northeastern Illinois University, IL*
Park University, MO
Rosemont College, PA*
Russell Sage College, NY*
San Diego Christian College, CA*
Southern University and Agricultural and Mechanical College, LA
Southern Wesleyan University, SC*
State University of New York College of Technology at Canton, NY*
Syracuse University, NY
Tennessee State University, TN*
Texas A&M University–Corpus Christi, TX
Tulane University, LA
University of Arkansas at Monticello, AR
University of Central Arkansas, AR
University of Charleston, WV
University of Hawaii–West Oahu, HI*
University of Nebraska Medical Center, NE*
The University of North Carolina at Charlotte, NC
The University of Texas at Austin, TX
University of the District of Columbia, DC*
University of the Sciences in Philadelphia, PA*
Wentworth Institute of Technology, MA*
Winston-Salem State University, NC

Naval

Armstrong Atlantic State University, GA*
Becker College, MA*
California State University, San Marcos, CA*
The Citadel, The Military College of South Carolina, SC
The Jewish Theological Seminary, NY*
Miami University Hamilton, OH*
Southern University and Agricultural and Mechanical College, LA
Tennessee State University, TN*
Texas A&M University at Galveston, TX
Tulane University, LA
The University of Texas at Austin, TX

program is offered at another college's campus

Tuition Waivers

Adult Students

Alaska Pacific University, AK
Albright College, PA
Augustana College, SD
Barton College, NC
Bethel College, IN
Bluefield State College, WV
California State University, Stanislaus, CA
Clarke College, IA
The College of Idaho, ID
College of the Atlantic, ME
Concord University, WV
Creighton University, NE
DeSales University, PA
Dowling College, NY
Emmanuel College, GA
Goucher College, MD
Hastings College, NE
Hood College, MD
John Brown University, AR
Juniata College, PA
Lane College, TN
Mercyhurst College, PA
Messiah College, PA
Mount Union College, OH
Nebraska Wesleyan University, NE
New England College, NH
North Park University, IL
Randolph College, VA
St. Ambrose University, IA
St. Andrews Presbyterian College, NC
Shimer College, IL
Southern Adventist University, TN
Trinity College, CT
University of North Dakota, ND
Utah State University, UT
Webber International University, FL
Wittenberg University, OH
York College, NE

Children of Alumni

Adrian College, MI
Albright College, PA
Arcadia University, PA
Augsburg College, MN
Avila University, MO
Baldwin-Wallace College, OH
Barton College, NC
Bethel College, KS
Cedar Crest College, PA
Central Michigan University, MI
Christian Brothers University, TN
Clarke College, IA
The College of Idaho, ID
Columbia College, MO
Concordia University Chicago, IL
Dana College, NE
Delta State University, MS
Dominican University, IL
Dowling College, NY
Drake University, IA
Drury University, MO
D'Youville College, NY
Faulkner University, AL
Georgetown College, KY
Hellenic College, MA
Hillsdale Free Will Baptist College, OK
Hood College, MD
Huntingdon College, AL
John Brown University, AR
Kentucky Wesleyan College, KY
Louisiana State University and Agricultural and Mechanical College, LA
Louisiana Tech University, LA
MacMurray College, IL
Marian College, IN
Marymount University, VA
Messiah College, PA
Michigan Technological University, MI
Midland Lutheran College, NE
Minot State University, ND
Mississippi State University, MS
Missouri Baptist University, MO
Missouri State University, MO
Mount Union College, OH
Murray State University, KY
Nazareth College of Rochester, NY
New England College, NH
North Dakota State University, ND
Northwestern College, MN
Nyack College, NY
Ohio Wesleyan University, OH
Oklahoma State University, OK
Oral Roberts University, OK
Peirce College, PA
Point Park University, PA
Roanoke Bible College, NC
St. Ambrose University, IA
Saint Joseph's College, IN
Saint Martin's University, WA
St. Thomas University, FL
Silver Lake College, WI
South Dakota State University, SD
Southeastern Oklahoma State University, OK
Southern Arkansas University–Magnolia, AR
Texas Lutheran University, TX
Thomas More College, KY
Union University, TN
University of Central Missouri, MO
University of Evansville, IN
The University of Findlay, OH
University of Idaho, ID
University of Louisiana at Lafayette, LA
University of Louisiana at Monroe, LA
University of Minnesota, Duluth, MN
University of Mississippi, MS
University of Nebraska at Omaha, NE
University of Nevada, Las Vegas, NV
University of Nevada, Reno, NV
University of New England, ME
University of Oklahoma, OK
The University of South Dakota, SD
University of Southern Mississippi, MS
University of the Ozarks, AR
University of Wisconsin–Stevens Point, WI
University of Wisconsin–Whitewater, WI
University of Wyoming, WY
Utah State University, UT
Valley City State University, ND
Webber International University, FL
Western Kentucky University, KY
Westminster College, MO
Whittier College, CA
Wittenberg University, OH
York College, NE

Minority Students

Bloomsburg University of Pennsylvania, PA
Concordia University Chicago, IL
Dowling College, NY
Edinboro University of Pennsylvania, PA
Fort Lewis College, CO
Geneva College, PA
Illinois Institute of Technology, IL
Illinois State University, IL
John Brown University, AR
Lock Haven University of Pennsylvania, PA
MacMurray College, IL
Mayville State University, ND
Messiah College, PA
Minot State University, ND
Montana State University, MT
Montana State University–Billings, MT
Nazareth College of Rochester, NY
North Dakota State University, ND
Northern Illinois University, IL
Portland State University, OR
St. Ambrose University, IA
Saint Joseph's College, IN
St. Thomas University, FL
Shepherd University, WV
Slippery Rock University of Pennsylvania, PA
Southeastern Oklahoma State University, OK
State University of New York College at Potsdam, NY
University at Buffalo, the State University of New York, NY
University of Evansville, IN
University of Hawaii at Manoa, HI
University of Idaho, ID
University of Maine at Fort Kent, ME
University of Maine at Presque Isle, ME
University of Michigan–Flint, MI
University of Minnesota, Morris, MN
The University of Montana, MT
University of North Dakota, ND
University of Rhode Island, RI
University of Southern Maine, ME
University of Wisconsin–Eau Claire, WI
University of Wisconsin–La Crosse, WI
Utah State University, UT
Wittenberg University, OH

Senior Citizens

Adams State College, CO
Alaska Pacific University, AK
Albertus Magnus College, CT
Albright College, PA
American International College, MA
Angelo State University, TX
Anna Maria College, MA
Appalachian Bible College, WV
Appalachian State University, NC
Arkansas State University, AR
Arkansas Tech University, AR
Athens State University, AL
Augsburg College, MN
Augustana College, SD
Augusta State University, GA
Austin Peay State University, TN
Avila University, MO
Baker University, KS
Barton College, NC
Bellarmine University, KY
Belmont Abbey College, NC
Belmont University, TN
Benedictine College, KS
Berry College, GA
Bethel College, KS
Black Hills State University, SD
Bloomfield College, NJ
Bloomsburg University of Pennsylvania, PA
Bluefield State College, WV
Boise State University, ID
Boston University, MA
Bowling Green State University, OH
Bradley University, IL
Brevard College, NC
Brewton-Parker College, GA
Bridgewater College, VA
Bryn Athyn College of the New Church, PA
Burlington College, VT
California State University, Chico, CA
California State University, Fresno, CA
California State University, Fullerton, CA
California State University, Long Beach, CA
California State University, Northridge, CA
California State University, Sacramento, CA
California State University, Stanislaus, CA
Calumet College of Saint Joseph, IN
Campbellsville University, KY
Carson-Newman College, TN
Cedarville University, OH
Central Connecticut State University, CT
Central Michigan University, MI
Chestnut Hill College, PA
Christopher Newport University, VA
City College of the City University of New York, NY
Clarion University of Pennsylvania, PA
Clarke College, IA
Clayton State University, GA
Cleary University, MI
Clemson University, SC
Cleveland State University, OH
Coastal Carolina University, SC
The College at Brockport, State University of New York, NY
College of Charleston, SC
The College of Idaho, ID
The College of New Jersey, NJ
The College of New Rochelle, NY
College of St. Joseph, VT
College of Saint Mary, NE
The College of St. Scholastica, MN
College of the Atlantic, ME
The College of William and Mary, VA
Columbus State University, GA
Concordia College–New York, NY
Concordia University Chicago, IL
Concord University, WV
Connecticut College, CT
Covenant College, GA
Culver-Stockton College, MO
Daemen College, NY
Dakota State University, SD
Dalton State College, GA
Delta State University, MS
DeSales University, PA
Dixie State College of Utah, UT
Doane College, NE
Dominican College, NY
Dominican University of California, CA
Dordt College, IA
Dowling College, NY
Drake University, IA
Duquesne University, PA
D'Youville College, NY
Eastern Kentucky University, KY
East Tennessee State University, TN
Elmhurst College, IL
Emmanuel College, GA
Emporia State University, KS
Fairleigh Dickinson University, Metropolitan Campus, NJ
Florida Atlantic University, FL
Florida Gulf Coast University, FL
Florida Institute of Technology, FL
Florida International University, FL
Florida State University, FL
Fort Hays State University, KS
Fort Valley State University, GA
Francis Marion University, SC
Franklin College, IN
Fresno Pacific University, CA
Frostburg State University, MD
Gannon University, PA
Gardner-Webb University, NC
George Fox University, OR
George Mason University, VA
Georgia College & State University, GA
Georgia Southern University, GA
Georgia State University, GA
Glenville State College, WV
Goucher College, MD
Grace College, IN
Graceland University, IA
Grand View University, IA
Hanover College, IN
Harding University, AR
Hillsdale Free Will Baptist College, OK
Hofstra University, NY
Holy Family University, PA
Houghton College, NY
Huntington University, IN
Husson University, ME
Idaho State University, ID
Illinois State University, IL
Indiana State University, IN
Indiana University–Purdue University Fort Wayne, IN
Iona College, NY
James Madison University, VA
John Brown University, AR
John Jay College of Criminal Justice of the City University of New York, NY
Kean University, NJ
Keene State College, NH
Kennesaw State University, GA
Kent State University, OH
Kentucky State University, KY
Kentucky Wesleyan College, KY
King's College, PA
Kutztown University of Pennsylvania, PA
Lamar University, TX
La Roche College, PA
Lebanon Valley College, PA
Lehigh University, PA
Lewis-Clark State College, ID
Lincoln Memorial University, TN
Lincoln University, MO
Lindenwood University, MO
Lindsey Wilson College, KY
Linfield College, OR
Lock Haven University of Pennsylvania, PA
Longwood University, VA
Loras College, IA
Louisiana Tech University, LA
Lourdes College, OH
Loyola University New Orleans, LA
Lynchburg College, VA
MacMurray College, IL
Malone University, OH
Manhattanville College, NY
Marian College, IN
Marian University, WI
Marymount University, VA
Maryville University of Saint Louis, MO
Marywood University, PA
Massachusetts College of Liberal Arts, MA
Mayville State University, ND
Medical University of South Carolina, SC
Merrimack College, MA
Messiah College, PA
Michigan Technological University, MI
MidAmerica Nazarene University, KS
Midland Lutheran College, NE
Midway College, KY
Millersville University of Pennsylvania, PA
Minnesota State University Mankato, MN
Minnesota State University Moorhead, MN
Mississippi State University, MS
Missouri Baptist University, MO
Missouri Southern State University, MO
Missouri State University, MO
Missouri Western State University, MO
Monmouth University, NJ
Montana State University, MT
Montana State University–Billings, MT
Montclair State University, NJ
Mountain State University, WV
Mount Mary College, WI
Mount Vernon Nazarene University, OH
Murray State University, KY
Nebraska Wesleyan University, NE
New England College, NH
New Jersey City University, NJ
New Mexico Institute of Mining and Technology, NM
New Mexico State University, NM
Niagara University, NY
Nichols College, MA
North Carolina Agricultural and Technical State University, NC
North Carolina State University, NC
North Central College, IL

North Dakota State University, ND
Northeastern State University, OK
Northeastern University, MA
Northern Illinois University, IL
Northern Kentucky University, KY
Northern Michigan University, MI
Northwestern Oklahoma State University, OK
Northwestern State University of Louisiana, LA
Northwest Missouri State University, MO
The Ohio State University, OH
Ohio University–Eastern, OH
Ohio Valley University, WV
Oklahoma Panhandle State University, OK
Oklahoma Wesleyan University, OK
Old Dominion University, VA
Pace University, NY
Pacific Union College, CA
Peace College, NC
Pikeville College, KY
Plymouth State University, NH
Portland State University, OR
Post University, CT
Providence College, RI
Purdue University, IN
Purdue University Calumet, IN
Radford University, VA
Ramapo College of New Jersey, NJ
Reinhardt College, GA
The Richard Stockton College of New Jersey, NJ
Rivier College, NH
Roanoke College, VA
St. Ambrose University, IA
St. Andrews Presbyterian College, NC
St. Catherine University, MN
St. Cloud State University, MN
St. John's University, NY
St. Mary's College of Maryland, MD
St. Olaf College, MN
Saint Vincent College, PA
Saint Xavier University, IL
Salem State College, MA
Salisbury University, MD
San Francisco State University, CA
Seattle Pacific University, WA
Shasta Bible College, CA
Shepherd University, WV
Shimer College, IL
Shippensburg University of Pennsylvania, PA
Shorter College, GA
Silver Lake College, WI
Skidmore College, NY
Slippery Rock University of Pennsylvania, PA
South Carolina State University, SC
South Dakota School of Mines and Technology, SD
South Dakota State University, SD
Southeastern Louisiana University, LA
Southeastern Oklahoma State University, OK
Southeast Missouri State University, MO
Southern Adventist University, TN
Southern Arkansas University–Magnolia, AR
Southern Connecticut State University, CT
Southern Illinois University Carbondale, IL
Southern Oregon University, OR
Southern Polytechnic State University, GA
Southwestern College, KS
Southwestern Oklahoma State University, OK
Southwest Minnesota State University, MN
State University of New York College at Old Westbury, NY
State University of New York College of Agriculture and Technology at Cobleskill, NY
Stephen F. Austin State University, TX
Suffolk University, MA
Tarleton State University, TX
Taylor University, IN
Texas A&M University–Commerce, TX
Texas Tech University, TX
Thiel College, PA
Tiffin University, OH
Towson University, MD
Trevecca Nazarene University, TN
Trinity Christian College, IL
Trinity College of Florida, FL
Trinity Lutheran College, WA
Truman State University, MO
Union College, KY
Union College, NY
University at Albany, State University of New York, NY
The University of Akron, OH
University of Arkansas, AR
University of Bridgeport, CT
University of Central Florida, FL
University of Central Missouri, MO
University of Colorado at Boulder, CO
University of Connecticut, CT
University of Dayton, OH
University of Delaware, DE
University of Evansville, IN
The University of Findlay, OH
University of Florida, FL
University of Georgia, GA
University of Hartford, CT
University of Houston–Clear Lake, TX
University of Houston–Downtown, TX
University of Houston–Victoria, TX
University of Idaho, ID
University of Illinois at Chicago, IL
University of Illinois at Springfield, IL
University of Illinois at Urbana–Champaign, IL
University of Kentucky, KY
University of Louisiana at Lafayette, LA
The University of Maine at Augusta, ME
University of Maine at Fort Kent, ME
University of Maine at Presque Isle, ME
University of Mary, ND
University of Maryland, Baltimore County, MD
University of Maryland Eastern Shore, MD
University of Maryland University College, MD
University of Mary Washington, VA
University of Massachusetts Amherst, MA
University of Massachusetts Boston, MA
University of Massachusetts Dartmouth, MA
University of Massachusetts Lowell, MA
University of Memphis, TN
University of Michigan, MI
University of Michigan–Dearborn, MI
University of Michigan–Flint, MI
University of Minnesota, Crookston, MN
University of Minnesota, Morris, MN
University of Minnesota, Twin Cities Campus, MN
University of Mississippi, MS
University of Missouri–Columbia, MO
University of Missouri–St. Louis, MO
The University of Montana, MT
The University of Montana Western, MT
University of Nevada, Las Vegas, NV
University of Nevada, Reno, NV
University of New Hampshire at Manchester, NH
University of New Orleans, LA
University of North Alabama, AL
The University of North Carolina at Asheville, NC
The University of North Carolina at Chapel Hill, NC
The University of North Carolina at Pembroke, NC
The University of North Carolina Wilmington, NC
University of North Dakota, ND
University of North Florida, FL
University of North Texas, TX
University of Oklahoma, OK
University of Rhode Island, RI
University of St. Thomas, TX
University of Science and Arts of Oklahoma, OK
The University of Scranton, PA
University of South Carolina, SC
University of South Carolina Aiken, SC
University of South Carolina Beaufort, SC
University of South Carolina Upstate, SC
The University of South Dakota, SD
University of Southern Mississippi, MS
University of South Florida, FL
The University of Tennessee, TN
The University of Tennessee at Chattanooga, TN
The University of Tennessee at Martin, TN
The University of Texas at Brownsville, TX
The University of Texas at Dallas, TX
The University of Texas at Tyler, TX
The University of Texas–Pan American, TX
University of the Incarnate Word, TX
University of the Virgin Islands, VI
University of Utah, UT
University of Vermont, VT
University of Virginia, VA
University of Washington, WA
University of West Florida, FL
University of West Georgia, GA
University of Wisconsin–Green Bay, WI
University of Wisconsin–Milwaukee, WI
University of Wisconsin–Parkside, WI
University of Wisconsin–Stevens Point, WI
University of Wisconsin–Whitewater, WI
University of Wyoming, WY
Ursinus College, PA
Utah State University, UT
Utica College, NY
Villanova University, PA
Virginia Commonwealth University, VA
Virginia Intermont College, VA
Virginia Polytechnic Institute and State University, VA
Virginia Wesleyan College, VA
Wartburg College, IA
Washington State University, WA
Wayne State University, MI
Webber International University, FL
Weber State University, UT
Wells College, NY
West Chester University of Pennsylvania, PA

Western Carolina University, NC
Western Connecticut State University, CT
Western Illinois University, IL
Western Kentucky University, KY
Western Michigan University, MI
Western New England College, MA
Westfield State College, MA
West Liberty State University, WV
West Virginia University, WV
Wichita State University, KS
Widener University, PA
William Paterson University of New Jersey, NJ
Winthrop University, SC
Wittenberg University, OH
Worcester State College, MA
Wright State University, OH
Xavier University, OH
York College of the City University of New York, NY
Youngstown State University, OH

Tuition Payment Alternatives

Abilene Christian University, TX I,P
Adams State College, CO D,I
Adelphi University, NY D,I
Adrian College, MI I
Agnes Scott College, GA I
Alabama Agricultural and Mechanical University, AL I
Alaska Pacific University, AK D,G,I
Albertus Magnus College, CT I
Albion College, MI D,I
Albright College, PA I
Alderson-Broaddus College, WV I
Allegheny College, PA I,P
Alma College, MI D,I
American Indian College of the Assemblies of God, Inc., AZ I
American International College, MA I,P
American Jewish University, CA I
American University, DC I
Amherst College, MA D,I
Angelo State University, TX I
Anna Maria College, MA I
Appalachian Bible College, WV I
Appalachian State University, NC I
Aquinas College, TN I
Arcadia University, PA D,I
Arizona State University, AZ I
Arkansas State University, AR I
Arkansas Tech University, AR D,I
Art Academy of Cincinnati, OH I
Auburn University, AL P
Auburn University Montgomery, AL I
Augsburg College, MN I
Augustana College, IL I,P
Augustana College, SD I
Augusta State University, GA G
Austin College, TX I
Austin Peay State University, TN I
Avila University, MO D,G,I
Azusa Pacific University, CA I
Babson College, MA I
Baker University, KS I
Baldwin-Wallace College, OH D,I
Ball State University, IN I
Baptist Bible College of Pennsylvania, PA I
The Baptist College of Florida, FL I
Bard College, NY I,P
Barnard College, NY D,I,P
Barton College, NC I
Bates College, ME I,P
Baylor University, TX I
Bellarmine University, KY I
Belmont Abbey College, NC D,I
Belmont University, TN D,I
Beloit College, WI I
Benedictine College, KS I
Benedictine University, IL D,I
Bennington College, VT I
Bentley University, MA I
Berry College, GA I
Bethany College, KS I
Bethany Lutheran College, MN I
Bethel College, IN I
Bethel College, KS D,I
Biola University, CA I
Black Hills State University, SD D,I
Blessing-Rieman College of Nursing, IL I
Bloomfield College, NJ D,I
Bloomsburg University of Pennsylvania, PA I
Bluefield State College, WV I
Bluffton University, OH I
Boise State University, ID I
Boston Architectural College, MA I
Boston College, MA I
The Boston Conservatory, MA I
Boston University, MA I,P
Bowdoin College, ME D,I
Bowling Green State University, OH I
Bradley University, IL I
Brandeis University, MA I
Brenau University, GA I
Brevard College, NC I
Brewton-Parker College, GA I
Bridgewater College, VA I
Bridgewater State College, MA I
Brown University, RI G,I,P
Bryant University, RI I
Bryn Athyn College of the New Church, PA I
Bryn Mawr College, PA I,P
Bucknell University, PA I,P
Buena Vista University, IA I
Buffalo State College, State University of New York, NY I
Burlington College, VT I
Butler University, IN I
Cabarrus College of Health Sciences, NC I
California Baptist University, CA I
California Christian College, CA I
California College of the Arts, CA D,I
California Institute of Technology, CA D,I
California Institute of the Arts, CA I
California Polytechnic State University, San Luis Obispo, CA I
California State Polytechnic University, Pomona, CA D,I
California State University, Chico, CA D,I
California State University, East Bay, CA I
California State University, Fresno, CA I
California State University, Fullerton, CA D,I
California State University, Long Beach, CA I
California State University, Los Angeles, CA I
California State University, Northridge, CA I
California State University, Sacramento, CA I
California State University, Stanislaus, CA D,I
Calumet College of Saint Joseph, IN I
Calvin College, MI I,P
Campbellsville University, KY I
Canisius College, NY D,I,P
Carnegie Mellon University, PA I
Carroll University, WI I
Carson-Newman College, TN D,I
Case Western Reserve University, OH I
Catawba College, NC I
The Catholic University of America, DC I,P
Cazenovia College, NY I
Cedar Crest College, PA D,I
Cedarville University, OH I
Centenary College, NJ I
Central Connecticut State University, CT I
Central Methodist University, MO I
Central Michigan University, MI G,I
Centre College, KY I
Chaminade University of Honolulu, HI I
Chapman University, CA D,I,P
Chatham University, PA I
Chestnut Hill College, PA D,I
Christian Brothers University, TN D,I
Christopher Newport University, VA I
City College of the City University of New York, NY D
Claremont McKenna College, CA I,P
Clarion University of Pennsylvania, PA I
Clarke College, IA D,I
Clarkson University, NY I,P
Clayton State University, GA G
Clearwater Christian College, FL I
Cleary University, MI D,G,I
Clemson University, SC I
Cleveland State University, OH I
Coastal Carolina University, SC I
Colgate University, NY D,I,P
The College at Brockport, State University of New York, NY D,I
College for Creative Studies, MI I
College of Charleston, SC I
The College of New Jersey, NJ I
The College of New Rochelle, NY I
College of Saint Benedict, MN I,P
College of St. Joseph, VT I

D = deferred payment system; *G* = guaranteed tuition rate; *I* = installment payments; *P* = prepayment locks in tuition rate

College of Saint Mary, NE D,I
The College of St. Scholastica, MN I
College of the Atlantic, ME I
College of the Holy Cross, MA I,P
College of the Ozarks, MO I
College of Visual Arts, MN I
The College of William and Mary, VA I
The College of Wooster, OH I
The Colorado College, CO I
Colorado School of Mines, CO I
Colorado State University, CO I
Columbia College, MO D
Columbia University, School of General Studies, NY I,P
Columbus State University, GA G
Concordia College, AL D,I
Concordia College–New York, NY I
Concordia University Chicago, IL I
Concordia University, Nebraska, NE I
Concordia University, St. Paul, MN I
Concordia University Wisconsin, WI D,G,I
Concord University, WV I
Connecticut College, CT I
Corban College, OR I
Cornell College, IA D
Cornell University, NY I
Covenant College, GA I
Creighton University, NE I
Culver-Stockton College, MO I
Curry College, MA I
Daemen College, NY D,I
Dakota State University, SD D,I
Dallas Baptist University, TX D,I
Dana College, NE D,I
Davenport University, MI I
Delta State University, MS I
Denison University, OH I
DePauw University, IN D,I,P
DeSales University, PA D,I
Dickinson College, PA I
Dixie State College of Utah, UT I
Doane College, NE I
Dominican College, NY D,I
Dominican University, IL I
Dominican University of California, CA I
Dordt College, IA I
Dowling College, NY D,I
Drake University, IA I
Drury University, MO D,I,P
Duke University, NC D,I,P
Duquesne University, PA I
D'Youville College, NY D,I,P
Earlham College, IN D,I,P
Eastern Illinois University, IL I
Eastern Kentucky University, KY D
Eastern Michigan University, MI I
Eastern Washington University, WA I
East Tennessee State University, TN D,I
East Texas Baptist University, TX G,I
Edgewood College, WI I
Edinboro University of Pennsylvania, PA I
EDP College of Puerto Rico, Inc., PR I
Elizabethtown College, PA I
Elmhurst College, IL I
Elmira College, NY P
Elon University, NC I
Embry-Riddle Aeronautical University, AZ D,I
Embry-Riddle Aeronautical University, FL D,I
Embry-Riddle Aeronautical University Worldwide, FL D
Emerson College, MA I
Emmanuel College, GA I
Emory & Henry College, VA I
Emporia State University, KS D,I
Endicott College, MA I
Eugene Lang College The New School for Liberal Arts, NY I
Evangel University, MO I
The Evergreen State College, WA I
Excelsior College, NY I
Fairfield University, CT I
Fairleigh Dickinson University, College at Florham, NJ D,I
Fairleigh Dickinson University, Metropolitan Campus, NJ D,I
Fairmont State University, WV I
Faulkner University, AL D,I
Ferris State University, MI D,I
Finlandia University, MI I
Fisk University, TN I
Florida Atlantic University, FL D,I,P
Florida College, FL I
Florida Hospital College of Health Sciences, FL D,I
Florida Institute of Technology, FL I
Florida State University, FL I,P
Fordham University, NY I
Fort Hays State University, KS I
Fort Lewis College, CO I
Fort Valley State University, GA G
Franciscan University of Steubenville, OH I
Francis Marion University, SC I
Franklin & Marshall College, PA D,I
Franklin College, IN I
Franklin Pierce University, NH I
Free Will Baptist Bible College, TN D,I
Fresno Pacific University, CA I
Frostburg State University, MD D
Furman University, SC I
Gannon University, PA D,I
Gardner-Webb University, NC I
Geneva College, PA I
George Fox University, OR I
George Mason University, VA D,I
Georgetown College, KY D
Georgia College & State University, GA G,I
Georgia Institute of Technology, GA G
Georgian Court University, NJ I
Georgia Southern University, GA G
Georgia State University, GA G
Gettysburg College, PA I,P
Glenville State College, WV I
Golden Gate University, CA D,I
Goldey-Beacom College, DE D,I
Goucher College, MD I,P
Grace Bible College, MI I
Grace College, IN I
Graceland University, IA I
Grand Valley State University, MI D,I
Grand View University, IA I
Green Mountain College, VT I
Greensboro College, NC I
Grinnell College, IA I,P
Grove City College, PA I
Guilford College, NC I
Gwynedd-Mercy College, PA I
Hamilton College, NY I
Hamline University, MN I
Hampshire College, MA I
Hampton University, VA D
Hanover College, IN I
Harding University, AR I,P
Hardin-Simmons University, TX D,G,I,P
Harrisburg University of Science and Technology, PA I
Hartwick College, NY I
Harvard University, MA I,P
Harvey Mudd College, CA I
Hastings College, NE D,I
Haverford College, PA I
Hawai'i Pacific University, HI I
Heidelberg University, OH I
Hellenic College, MA D,I
Hendrix College, AR I
Heritage Christian University, AL D,I
Hillsdale Free Will Baptist College, OK I
Hobart and William Smith Colleges, NY I,P
Hodges University, FL I
Hofstra University, NY D,I
Hollins University, VA I
Holy Family University, PA D,I
Hood College, MD D,I,P
Hope College, MI I
Hope International University, CA I
Houghton College, NY I
Houston Baptist University, TX I
Howard Payne University, TX G,I
Humboldt State University, CA I
Hunter College of the City University of New York, NY I
Huntingdon College, AL D,G
Huntington University, IN I
Husson University, ME I,P
Idaho State University, ID D
Illinois College, IL D,I
Illinois Institute of Technology, IL D,I
Illinois State University, IL G,I
Illinois Wesleyan University, IL I
Indiana State University, IN D,I
Indiana University Bloomington, IN D
Indiana University East, IN D
Indiana University Kokomo, IN D
Indiana University Northwest, IN D,I
Indiana University of Pennsylvania, PA D,I
Indiana University–Purdue University Fort Wayne, IN D,I
Indiana University–Purdue University Indianapolis, IN D,I
Indiana University South Bend, IN D
Indiana University Southeast, IN D
Iona College, NY D,I
Ithaca College, NY I
James Madison University, VA I
Jamestown College, ND I
John Brown University, AR I
John Carroll University, OH I

D = deferred payment system; *G* = guaranteed tuition rate; *I* = installment payments; *P* = prepayment locks in tuition rate

Institution	Alternatives
John Jay College of Criminal Justice of the City University of New York, NY	I
The Johns Hopkins University, MD	I
Johnson Bible College, TN	I
Johnson C. Smith University, NC	I
Judson College, AL	I
The Juilliard School, NY	I
Juniata College, PA	I
Kansas State University, KS	D,I
Kean University, NJ	D,I
Keene State College, NH	I
Kennesaw State University, GA	D
Kent State University, OH	D,I,P
Kentucky Christian University, KY	I
Kentucky State University, KY	D,I
Kentucky Wesleyan College, KY	D,I
Kenyon College, OH	I
Kettering University, MI	I
Keuka College, NY	I
King's College, PA	D,I
Knox College, IL	I
Kutztown University of Pennsylvania, PA	D,I
LaGrange College, GA	I
Lake Forest College, IL	I
Lamar University, TX	I
Lambuth University, TN	I
Lane College, TN	D,I
La Roche College, PA	I
Lawrence Technological University, MI	I
Lawrence University, WI	I,P
Lebanon Valley College, PA	I,P
Lees-McRae College, NC	I
Lee University, TN	D
Lehigh University, PA	I,P
Le Moyne College, NY	D,I
LeTourneau University, TX	I
Lewis & Clark College, OR	I
Lewis-Clark State College, ID	D
Lexington College, IL	G,I
Liberty University, VA	I
Life University, GA	I
Limestone College, SC	I
Lincoln Christian College, IL	D,I
Lincoln Memorial University, TN	D,I
Lincoln University, MO	I
Lincoln University, PA	D,I
Lindenwood University, MO	D,I
Lindsey Wilson College, KY	I
Linfield College, OR	I
Lipscomb University, TN	D,I
Lock Haven University of Pennsylvania, PA	D,I
Long Island University, Brooklyn Campus, NY	D,I
Long Island University, C.W. Post Campus, NY	D,I
Longwood University, VA	I
Loras College, IA	I
Louisiana State University and Agricultural and Mechanical College, LA	D
Louisiana Tech University, LA	D,I
Lourdes College, OH	D,I
Loyola University New Orleans, LA	I
Lubbock Christian University, TX	I
Luther College, IA	I
Lycoming College, PA	I
Lyme Academy College of Fine Arts, CT	I
Lynchburg College, VA	I,P
Lyon College, AR	I
Macalester College, MN	I
MacMurray College, IL	I
Maine College of Art, ME	I
Maine Maritime Academy, ME	I
Malone University, OH	I
Manchester College, IN	I
Manhattanville College, NY	D,I
Maranatha Baptist Bible College, WI	I
Marian College, IN	I
Marian University, WI	I
Mary Baldwin College, VA	I
Marylhurst University, OR	I
Marymount Manhattan College, NY	I
Marymount University, VA	I
Maryville College, TN	I
Maryville University of Saint Louis, MO	D,I
Marywood University, PA	D,I
Massachusetts College of Art and Design, MA	I
Massachusetts College of Pharmacy and Health Sciences, MA	I
Massachusetts Institute of Technology, MA	I
The Master's College and Seminary, CA	I
Mayville State University, ND	I
McDaniel College, MD	I,P
McKendree University, IL	I
McMurry University, TX	I
McPherson College, KS	I
Medgar Evers College of the City University of New York, NY	D,I
Medical University of South Carolina, SC	I
Memphis College of Art, TN	I
Menlo College, CA	I
Mercer University, GA	I
Mercy College of Northwest Ohio, OH	D,I
Mercyhurst College, PA	I
Merrimack College, MA	G,I
Mesa State College, CO	I
Messiah College, PA	I
Miami University, OH	I
Michigan State University, MI	D
Michigan Technological University, MI	D,I
MidAmerica Nazarene University, KS	I
Middlebury College, VT	P
Midland Lutheran College, NE	I
Midway College, KY	D
Millersville University of Pennsylvania, PA	I
Milligan College, TN	I
Millikin University, IL	I
Mills College, CA	I
Milwaukee School of Engineering, WI	I
Minnesota State University Mankato, MN	I
Minnesota State University Moorhead, MN	I
Minot State University, ND	I
Misericordia University, PA	D,I
Mississippi College, MS	D,I
Mississippi State University, MS	I
Mississippi University for Women, MS	D,I
Missouri Baptist University, MO	I
Missouri State University, MO	D,P
Missouri University of Science and Technology, MO	I
Missouri Western State University, MO	D,I
Molloy College, NY	I
Monmouth University, NJ	I
Monroe College, NY	I
Montana State University, MT	D,I
Montana State University–Billings, MT	I
Montana Tech of The University of Montana, MT	D,I
Montclair State University, NJ	I
Montreat College, NC	I
Mountain State University, WV	I
Mount Ida College, MA	I
Mount Marty College, SD	I
Mount Mary College, WI	I
Mount Mercy College, IA	I
Mount Saint Mary College, NY	I
Mount St. Mary's University, MD	I
Mount Union College, OH	I,P
Mount Vernon Nazarene University, OH	I
Muhlenberg College, PA	I
Murray State University, KY	I
Naropa University, CO	I
Nazarene Bible College, CO	I
Nazareth College of Rochester, NY	D
Nebraska Wesleyan University, NE	D,I
Neumann University, PA	I
New College of Florida, FL	D,I
New England College, NH	I
New Jersey City University, NJ	D
New Jersey Institute of Technology, NJ	I
Newman University, KS	I
New Mexico Institute of Mining and Technology, NM	D
New Mexico State University, NM	D,I
New York City College of Technology of the City University of New York, NY	D
New York University, NY	D,I
Niagara University, NY	D,I
Nicholls State University, LA	D,I
Nichols College, MA	I
North Carolina Agricultural and Technical State University, NC	I
North Carolina State University, NC	I
North Carolina Wesleyan College, NC	I
North Central College, IL	I
North Dakota State University, ND	I
Northeastern State University, OK	P
Northeastern University, MA	I
Northern Arizona University, AZ	G,I
Northern Illinois University, IL	G,I
Northern Kentucky University, KY	I
Northern Michigan University, MI	D,I
Northern State University, SD	I
North Greenville University, SC	I
Northland College, WI	I
North Park University, IL	I

Northwest Christian University, OR D,I
Northwestern College, MN I
Northwestern Oklahoma State University, OK I
Northwestern State University of Louisiana, LA I
Northwest Missouri State University, MO D,I
Northwest University, WA I
Nova Southeastern University, FL D,I
Nyack College, NY I
Oakland University, MI D,I
Oberlin College, OH I
Oglethorpe University, GA I,P
The Ohio State University, OH I
Ohio University, OH I
Ohio University–Eastern, OH I
Ohio Valley University, WV I
Ohio Wesleyan University, OH I
Oklahoma Christian University, OK I
Oklahoma City University, OK D,I
Oklahoma Panhandle State University, OK G,I
Oklahoma State University, OK I
Oklahoma Wesleyan University, OK D,I
Old Dominion University, VA D,I
Olivet College, MI I
Olivet Nazarene University, IL I
Oral Roberts University, OK I
Oregon College of Art & Craft, OR I
Oregon Health & Science University, OR I
Oregon State University, OR D
Otis College of Art and Design, CA I
Ouachita Baptist University, AR D,I
Our Lady of the Lake University of San Antonio, TX D,I
Pace University, NY I
Pacific Lutheran University, WA I
Pacific Union College, CA G,I
Palm Beach Atlantic University, FL I
Peabody Conservatory of Music of The Johns Hopkins University, MD I
Peace College, NC I
Peirce College, PA I
Pennsylvania College of Technology, PA D
Pepperdine University, CA I
Philadelphia Biblical University, PA I
Philadelphia University, PA D,I
Piedmont College, GA I
Pikeville College, KY I
Pittsburg State University, KS I
Pitzer College, CA D,I
Plymouth State University, NH I
Point Park University, PA D,I
Polytechnic Institute of NYU, NY D,G,I
Pomona College, CA I
Portland State University, OR I
Post University, CT I
Pratt Institute, NY D,I
Prescott College, AZ D,I
Princeton University, NJ D,I
Principia College, IL I
Providence College, RI I
Purchase College, State University of New York, NY I
Purdue University, IN I
Purdue University Calumet, IN D
Purdue University North Central, IN I
Radford University, VA I
Ramapo College of New Jersey, NJ I
Randolph College, VA I
Reed College, OR I
Regis College, MA I
Reinhardt College, GA I
Rensselaer Polytechnic Institute, NY I
Rhode Island College, RI I
Rhodes College, TN I
The Richard Stockton College of New Jersey, NJ D,I
Rider University, NJ I
Ringling College of Art and Design, FL I
Ripon College, WI I
Rivier College, NH D,I
Roanoke Bible College, NC D
Roanoke College, VA I
Robert Morris College, IL I
Robert Morris University, PA D,I
Roberts Wesleyan College, NY I
Rochester Institute of Technology, NY D,I,P
Rockford College, IL I
Roger Williams University, RI D,I
Rollins College, FL I
Rose-Hulman Institute of Technology, IN I,P
Rowan University, NJ D
Rutgers, The State University of New Jersey, Camden, NJ I
Rutgers, The State University of New Jersey, Newark, NJ I
Rutgers, The State University of New Jersey, New Brunswick, NJ I
Sacred Heart University, CT I
Saginaw Valley State University, MI I
St. Ambrose University, IA I
St. Andrews Presbyterian College, NC I
Saint Anthony College of Nursing, IL D,I
St. Cloud State University, MN I
St. Edward's University, TX D,I
Saint Francis Medical Center College of Nursing, IL I
Saint Francis University, PA I
St. John Fisher College, NY D,I
Saint John's University, MN I,P
St. John's University, NY D,G,I
Saint Joseph's College, IN I
Saint Joseph's College of Maine, ME I
Saint Joseph's University, PA D,I
St. Lawrence University, NY I
St. Louis College of Pharmacy, MO I
Saint Louis University, MO I
Saint Martin's University, WA I
Saint Mary's College, IN I
Saint Mary's College of California, CA I
St. Mary's College of Maryland, MD I
St. Mary's University, TX I,P
Saint Mary's University of Minnesota, MN I
Saint Michael's College, VT I
St. Norbert College, WI D,I
St. Olaf College, MN I
St. Thomas University, FL I
Saint Vincent College, PA I
Saint Xavier University, IL I
Salem College, NC I
Salem State College, MA I
Salisbury University, MD I
Salve Regina University, RI I
Sam Houston State University, TX I
Samuel Merritt University, CA I
San Diego State University, CA I
San Francisco Conservatory of Music, CA I
San Francisco State University, CA I
San Jose State University, CA I
Santa Clara University, CA I
Sarah Lawrence College, NY I
Savannah College of Art and Design, GA I
Schreiner University, TX I
Scripps College, CA I
Seattle Pacific University, WA I
Seton Hill University, PA D,I
Sewanee: The University of the South, TN D,I
Shasta Bible College, CA I
Shepherd University, WV I
Shimer College, IL I
Shippensburg University of Pennsylvania, PA I
Shorter College, GA I
Silver Lake College, WI D,I
Simmons College, MA I
Simpson College, IA I
Simpson University, CA D
Skidmore College, NY I,P
Slippery Rock University of Pennsylvania, PA I
South Carolina State University, SC D,I
South Dakota School of Mines and Technology, SD I
South Dakota State University, SD D,I
Southeastern Louisiana University, LA D,I
Southeast Missouri State University, MO D,I
Southern Adventist University, TN D,I,P
Southern Arkansas University–Magnolia, AR I
Southern Connecticut State University, CT D,I
Southern Illinois University Carbondale, IL G,I
Southern Methodist University, TX I,P
Southern New Hampshire University, NH I
Southern Oregon University, OR D
Southern Polytechnic State University, GA G
Southern Utah University, UT I
Southwest Baptist University, MO I
Southwestern College, KS I
Southwestern Oklahoma State University, OK I
Southwestern University, TX I
Southwest Minnesota State University, MN I
Spring Arbor University, MI I
Spring Hill College, AL I
State University of New York at Fredonia, NY I
State University of New York at New Paltz, NY I
State University of New York at Oswego, NY I

D = deferred payment system; *G* = guaranteed tuition rate; *I* = installment payments; *P* = prepayment locks in tuition rate

Institution	Code
State University of New York at Plattsburgh, NY	D,I
State University of New York College at Geneseo, NY	D,I
State University of New York College at Old Westbury, NY	I
State University of New York College at Oneonta, NY	I
State University of New York College at Potsdam, NY	I
State University of New York College of Agriculture and Technology at Cobleskill, NY	I
State University of New York College of Environmental Science and Forestry, NY	D,I
State University of New York Institute of Technology, NY	D,I
State University of New York Upstate Medical University, NY	I
Stephen F. Austin State University, TX	I
Stephens College, MO	I
Stetson University, FL	I
Stevenson University, MD	D,I
Stillman College, AL	D
Stonehill College, MA	I,P
Stony Brook University, State University of New York, NY	I
Suffolk University, MA	D,I
Tarleton State University, TX	I
Taylor University, IN	I
Temple University, PA	I
Tennessee Technological University, TN	I
Texas A&M University, TX	I
Texas A&M University–Commerce, TX	I
Texas A&M University–Texarkana, TX	I
Texas Christian University, TX	I
Texas Lutheran University, TX	I
Texas State University–San Marcos, TX	I
Texas Tech University, TX	I
Thiel College, PA	I
Thomas Aquinas College, CA	I
Thomas More College, KY	D,I
Thomas More College of Liberal Arts, NH	I
Tiffin University, OH	I
Towson University, MD	G,I,P
Trevecca Nazarene University, TN	I
Trine University, IN	I
Trinity Christian College, IL	I
Trinity College, CT	I
Trinity College of Florida, FL	I
Trinity International University, IL	I
Trinity Lutheran College, WA	I
Troy University, AL	I
Truman State University, MO	I
Tufts University, MA	I,P
Tuskegee University, AL	I
Union College, KY	I
Union College, NY	I
Union University, TN	D,I
University at Albany, State University of New York, NY	I
University at Buffalo, the State University of New York, NY	I
University of Advancing Technology, AZ	I
The University of Akron, OH	I
The University of Alabama, AL	D,I
The University of Alabama in Huntsville, AL	D
University of Arkansas, AR	I
University of Bridgeport, CT	D,I
University of California, Berkeley, CA	I
University of California, Irvine, CA	I
University of California, Riverside, CA	D
University of California, Santa Cruz, CA	D,I
University of Central Florida, FL	D,P
University of Central Missouri, MO	D,I
University of Central Oklahoma, OK	D,G,I
University of Cincinnati, OH	I
University of Colorado at Boulder, CO	D
University of Colorado at Colorado Springs, CO	I
University of Colorado Denver, CO	D,I
University of Connecticut, CT	D,I
University of Dallas, TX	I
University of Dayton, OH	D
University of Delaware, DE	I
University of Denver, CO	D
University of Evansville, IN	I
The University of Findlay, OH	I
University of Florida, FL	D,P
University of Georgia, GA	G
University of Hartford, CT	I,P
University of Hawaii at Manoa, HI	I
University of Houston, TX	I
University of Houston–Clear Lake, TX	D,I
University of Houston–Downtown, TX	I
University of Houston–Victoria, TX	I
University of Idaho, ID	D,I
University of Illinois at Chicago, IL	G,I
University of Illinois at Springfield, IL	G,I
University of Illinois at Urbana–Champaign, IL	G
The University of Iowa, IA	I
The University of Kansas, KS	G,I
University of Kentucky, KY	I
University of La Verne, CA	D,I
University of Louisiana at Lafayette, LA	D
University of Louisiana at Monroe, LA	D
University of Maine, ME	I
The University of Maine at Augusta, ME	I
University of Maine at Fort Kent, ME	I
University of Maine at Presque Isle, ME	D,I
University of Mary, ND	I
University of Mary Hardin-Baylor, TX	I
University of Maryland, Baltimore County, MD	I
University of Maryland, College Park, MD	D,I
University of Maryland Eastern Shore, MD	D,I
University of Maryland University College, MD	I
University of Mary Washington, VA	I
University of Massachusetts Amherst, MA	I
University of Massachusetts Boston, MA	I
University of Massachusetts Dartmouth, MA	I
University of Massachusetts Lowell, MA	I
University of Memphis, TN	I
University of Miami, FL	D,I,P
University of Michigan, MI	I
University of Michigan–Dearborn, MI	I
University of Michigan–Flint, MI	I
University of Minnesota, Crookston, MN	G,I
University of Minnesota, Duluth, MN	I
University of Minnesota, Morris, MN	I
University of Minnesota, Twin Cities Campus, MN	I
University of Mississippi, MS	P
University of Missouri–Columbia, MO	I
University of Missouri–Kansas City, MO	I
University of Missouri–St. Louis, MO	I
University of Mobile, AL	I
The University of Montana, MT	D,I
The University of Montana Western, MT	D
University of Montevallo, AL	I
University of Nebraska at Kearney, NE	I
University of Nebraska at Omaha, NE	D,I
University of Nebraska–Lincoln, NE	I
University of Nevada, Las Vegas, NV	D
University of Nevada, Reno, NV	D
University of New England, ME	I
University of New Hampshire, NH	I
University of New Haven, CT	I
University of New Orleans, LA	D,I
University of North Alabama, AL	I
The University of North Carolina at Chapel Hill, NC	D,I
The University of North Carolina at Greensboro, NC	I
The University of North Carolina at Pembroke, NC	I
The University of North Carolina Wilmington, NC	I
University of North Dakota, ND	D
University of Northern Colorado, CO	D
University of Northern Iowa, IA	I
University of North Florida, FL	D
University of North Texas, TX	I
University of Notre Dame, IN	I
University of Oklahoma, OK	G,I
University of Oregon, OR	I
University of Pennsylvania, PA	I,P
University of Pittsburgh, PA	D,I
University of Pittsburgh at Bradford, PA	I
University of Puerto Rico, Río Piedras, PR	D
University of Puget Sound, WA	D,I
University of Redlands, CA	I
University of Rhode Island, RI	I
University of Richmond, VA	D,I
University of Rochester, NY	I
University of St. Thomas, TX	D,I

University of Science and Arts of Oklahoma, OK I
The University of Scranton, PA I
University of South Alabama, AL I
University of South Carolina, SC D,I
University of South Carolina Aiken, SC D
University of South Carolina Upstate, SC D
The University of South Dakota, SD D
University of Southern California, CA D,I,P
University of Southern Indiana, IN I
University of Southern Maine, ME I
University of Southern Mississippi, MS I
University of South Florida, FL I
The University of Tampa, FL I
The University of Tennessee, TN I
The University of Tennessee at Chattanooga, TN D
The University of Tennessee at Martin, TN D
The University of Texas at Arlington, TX I
The University of Texas at Brownsville, TX I
The University of Texas at Dallas, TX G,I
The University of Texas at El Paso, TX G,I
The University of Texas at San Antonio, TX D,I
The University of Texas at Tyler, TX I
The University of Texas–Pan American, TX I
The University of Texas Southwestern Medical Center at Dallas, TX I
University of the Cumberlands, KY I
University of the Incarnate Word, TX I
University of the Ozarks, AR I
University of the Pacific, CA D
University of the Southwest, NM D
University of the Virgin Islands, VI D,I
University of Tulsa, OK I,P
University of Utah, UT I
University of Vermont, VT D,I
University of Virginia, VA I
The University of West Alabama, AL D
University of West Florida, FL D,P
University of West Georgia, GA G
University of Wisconsin–Eau Claire, WI I
University of Wisconsin–Green Bay, WI I
University of Wisconsin–La Crosse, WI I
University of Wisconsin–Milwaukee, WI I
University of Wisconsin–Oshkosh, WI I
University of Wisconsin–Parkside, WI I
University of Wisconsin–Stevens Point, WI I
University of Wisconsin–Stout, WI I
University of Wisconsin–Superior, WI I
University of Wisconsin–Whitewater, WI I
University of Wyoming, WY D,I
Ursinus College, PA I
Ursuline College, OH I
Utah State University, UT D
Utah Valley University, UT D,I
Utica College, NY D,I
Valley Forge Christian College, PA I
Valparaiso University, IN D,I
Vanderbilt University, TN I,P
Vassar College, NY I
Villanova University, PA I
Virginia Commonwealth University, VA I
Virginia Intermont College, VA I
Virginia Military Institute, VA I
Virginia Polytechnic Institute and State University, VA I
Virginia Wesleyan College, VA D,I
Wabash College, IN I,P
Walla Walla University, WA D,I
Warren Wilson College, NC I
Wartburg College, IA I
Washington & Jefferson College, PA D,I
Washington Bible College, MD I
Washington College, MD I
Washington University in St. Louis, MO I,P
Watkins College of Art, Design, & Film, TN I
Wayland Baptist University, TX I
Waynesburg University, PA I
Wayne State University, MI I
Webber International University, FL I
Weber State University, UT D,I
Webster University, MO I
Wells College, NY I
Wesleyan University, CT I
West Chester University of Pennsylvania, PA I
Western Carolina University, NC I
Western Connecticut State University, CT I
Western Illinois University, IL G
Western Kentucky University, KY I
Western Michigan University, MI I
Western New England College, MA I,P
Western Oregon University, OR D,G
Western Washington University, WA I
Westfield State College, MA I
West Liberty State University, WV D,I
Westminster College, MO I
Westminster College, PA I
Westminster College, UT D,I
Westmont College, CA I
West Virginia University, WV I
Wheaton College, IL D,I
Wheaton College, MA I,P
Wheelock College, MA I,P
Whitman College, WA D
Whitworth University, WA I
Wichita State University, KS I
Widener University, PA I
Wilkes University, PA D,I
Willamette University, OR I,P
William Jessup University, CA D
William Paterson University of New Jersey, NJ I
Williams College, MA I
Wingate University, NC I
Winona State University, MN I
Winthrop University, SC I
Wisconsin Lutheran College, WI I
Wittenberg University, OH I
Wofford College, SC I
Woodbury University, CA D,I
Worcester Polytechnic Institute, MA D,I
Worcester State College, MA I
Wright State University, OH I
Xavier University, OH D,I
Xavier University of Louisiana, LA I
Yale University, CT I
York College, NE I
York College of Pennsylvania, PA I,P
York College of the City University of New York, NY G,I
Youngstown State University, OH I

D = deferred payment system; *G* = guaranteed tuition rate; *I* = installment payments; *P* = prepayment locks in tuition rate

Notes

Notes

Notes

Notes